CHILDREN'S CATALOG

SIXTEENTH EDITION

STANDARD CATALOG SERIES

JULIETTE YAAKOV, GENERAL EDITOR

CHILDREN'S CATALOG
FICTION CATALOG
JUNIOR HIGH SCHOOL LIBRARY CATALOG
PUBLIC LIBRARY CATALOG
SENIOR HIGH SCHOOL LIBRARY CATALOG

CHILDREN'S CATALOG

SIXTEENTH EDITION

EDITED BY
JULIETTE YAAKOV
WITH THE ASSISTANCE OF
ANNE PRICE

NEW YORK
THE H. W. WILSON COMPANY
1991

Printed in the United States of America

Library of Congress Cataloging-in-Publication Data

Children's catalog. — 16th ed. / edited by Juliette Yaakov with the assistance of Anne Price.

p. cm. — (Standard catalog series)

Includes index.

ISBN 0-8242-0805-6 (lib. bdg. : alk. paper)

1. Children's literature—Bibliography. 2. Cataloging of children's literature—Specimens. 3. Libraries, Children's—Book lists. 4. School libraries—Book lists. I. Yaakov, Juliette. II. Price, Anne, 1946- . III. H.W. Wilson Company. IV. Series.

Z1037.C54443 1991
[PN1009.A1]
011.62—dc20 **91-27841**
CIP

PREFACE

This new sixteenth edition of *Children's Catalog* carries on the intent of the first edition, published in 1909: to include the best books for children in the fields of fiction and nonfiction. At a time when libraries and media centers are pressed to make the most of scarce resources, this endeavor takes on added import. The Catalog continues to serve as a practical tool for locating books on a particular subject, as a buying guide, as a cataloging aid, and as an aid in checking a library's holdings in order to uncover strengths and weaknesses in the collection. Teachers and administrators involved in implementing a literature-based curriculum will find it a support.

In addition to the bound volume of the sixteenth edition itself, the service unit includes four annual supplements to be published in 1992, 1993, 1994, and 1995. Purchasers of the sixteenth edition will receive the supplements without further charge.

Preparation. In preparing this edition The H.W. Wilson Company has benefited from the work of two groups of experts in library service to children. An advisory committee of distinguished librarians reevaluated the titles listed in the previous edition of the Catalog and its supplements, and also proposed new titles. Among its concerns were interest; relevance; accuracy; currency, especially for nonfiction in social studies and the sciences; coverage of minorities and non-Western cultures; avoidance of stereotyping; and authenticity in retellings of folk literature. It considered quality of illustration as well as text. The list resulting from the committee's deliberations was then submitted to a group of consultants—experienced children's librarians and school media specialists from dispersed geographical areas—who actually elected the titles. Their vote often represents the composite judgment of a number of their colleagues.

Scope and Purpose. The Catalog includes books and magazines for children from preschool through sixth grade. In addition, it provides the following sources for the children's librarian or media specialist: titles on the history and development of children's literature, including criticism; bibliographies; aids for book selection; guides to the operation of media centers; and periodicals relating to library science, reviewing, and education. Awards and prizes, such as Newbery and Caldecott medal winners and honor books, are also noted.

The sixteenth edition includes 6,061 titles and 7,189 analytical entries. Although it can be considered a basic collection, the list will undoubtedly have to be supplemented by those libraries serving large systems and those that must satisfy users with special needs. To accommodate the precocious child, this edition should be used with the sixth edition of *Junior High School Library Catalog,* published in 1990.

The general features of the last edition have been retained. An editorial practice inaugurated with the fourteenth edition is again followed: only the first book in a fiction series is cited in full; the others in the sequence are listed briefly, without annotation. Paperbacks are included in instances where no hardcover is available; they are also mentioned when they are available in addition to the hardcover edition, whether from the same publisher or a different publisher. The advisory committee encourages those who object to acquiring paperback editions to consider the services of a commercial rebinder. Bilingual editions are listed. Non-English language versions obtainable from the publisher of the English-language edition are noted, as are large-print editions. Books listed are published in the United States, or published in Canada or the United Kingdom and distributed in the United States.

The following are excluded: textbooks, other than history and criticism of children's literature; most novelty books; nonprint materials (nonprint versions of many of the works listed may be found in standard directories); and titles that are out of print, with the exception of a few children's classics, notable anthologies, and standard reference tools recommended for retention by the advisory committee.

Organization. The Catalog is divided into three parts for effective use.

Part 1, the Classified Catalog, is arranged according to the Abridged Dewey Decimal Classification. Fiction, story collections, and easy books follow the nonfiction classes. Within classes, arrangement is by main entry, with complete bibliographical information given for each book. Prices have been obtained from the publishers and are as up to date as possible. They are always subject to change, however, and should be verified as time passes. Grade level designation, suggested subject headings based on *Sears List of Subject Headings,* a descriptive annotation, and an evaluation, frequently from a quoted source, are included.

Part 2 is an author, title, subject, and analytical index that serves as a comprehensive key to Part 1. Analytical entries provide indexing for parts of works and are an important feature of the Catalog. Subject analytics give access to those parts of books not covered by the subject headings for the whole, while author and title analytics provide an approach to collections, especially of stories and tales.

Part 3 is a directory of the publishers and distributors found in Part 1.

To gain the greatest benefit from the Catalog it is advisable to consult the next section: How to Use Children's Catalog.

Acknowledgments. This Catalog could not have been published without the cooperative efforts of publishers and the library community. The H.W. Wilson Company expresses its appreciation to those publishers who generously supplied copies of their books, as well as information on editions and prices. The Company also wishes to acknowledge its debt to the two groups of librarians who gave so liberally of their time and knowledge: the advisory committee and the consultants. Their names appear below.

The advisory committee comprised:

Ellen M. Stepanian, Chair
Director of Library Media
Shaker Heights City School District
Shaker Heights, Ohio

Therese Bigelow, Director
Wayne County Public Library System
Goldsboro, N.C.

Patricia Cianciolo, Professor of Education
Michigan State University
East Lansing, Mich.

Judith F. Davie, Director
Educational Media Services
Greensboro City Schools
Greensboro, N.C.

Joyce Gunn-Bradley, Senior Branch Librarian
San Ramon Library
San Ramon, Calif.

Elizabeth F. Howard, Professor of Library Science
West Virginia University
Morgantown, W. Va.

The following consultants participated in the voting:

Christine A. Behrmann, Children's Materials Specialist
The New York Public Library
New York, N.Y.

Jane Botham, Coordinator of Children's Services
Milwaukee Public Library
Milwaukee, Wis.

Elizabeth Breting, Director
Children's Services
Kansas City Public Library
Kansas City, Mo.

Priscilla Drach, Children's Service Manager
Cuyahoga County Public Library
Cleveland, Ohio

Eileen Dunne, Coordinator of
Library Services
Abilene Independent School District
Abilene, Tex.

Barbara Howell, Librarian
Increase Miller Elementary School
Goldens Bridge, N.Y.

Mary D. Lankford, Director
Library Media Services
Irving Independent School District
Irving, Tex.

Linda Perkins, Librarian
Berkeley Public Library
Berkeley, Calif.

Maria B. Salvadore, Coordinator
Children's Services
District of Columbia Public Library
Washington, D.C.

Frances V. Sedney, Coordinator
Children's Services
Harford County Library
Belcamp, Md.

Amy Spaulding, Associate Professor
Division of Library and Information
Science
St. John's University
Jamaica, N.Y.

Jane Walsh, Chairperson
Evaluation Committee
Newton Public Schools
Newtonville, Mass.

HOW TO USE CHILDREN'S CATALOG

Children's Catalog is arranged in three parts: Part 1. Classified Catalog; Part 2. Author, Title, Subject, and Analytical Index; Part 3. Directory of Publishers and Distributors.

USES OF THE CATALOG

Children's Catalog is designed to serve several purposes:

As an aid in purchasing. The Catalog is designed to assist in the selection and ordering of titles. Annotations are provided for each title and information is given concerning publisher, ISBN, and price for the editions that are available. Since Part 1 is arranged by the Dewey Decimal Classification, the Catalog may also be used as a checklist to identify those parts of the library collection that are weak or outdated. It would not be advisable, of course, for a library to depend upon a single aid in book selection. Each library will want to take into account the special character of the school and community it serves.

As a cataloging aid. For this purpose full bibliographical information is provided in Part 1, including recommended subject headings based upon *Sears List of Subject Headings* and a suggested classification derived from the *Abridged Dewey Decimal Classification.* The analytic entries in Part 2 augment the library's catalog by providing access to parts of composite works.

As a reference aid. Reference work is facilitated both through the annotations in Part 1 and by the subject and analytical approach in Part 2. In addition, Part 2 provides access under names of illustrators, lists award winners under Caldecott Medal books and Newbery Medal books, and collects entries for folk and fairy tales under uniform titles based on the *Index to Fairy Tales, Myths and Legends* by Mary Huse Eastman and the later volumes by Norma Olin Ireland.

As an aid for curriculum support. The classified approach, subject indexing, annotations, and grade level designations all help teachers implementing a literature-based curriculum to choose books appropriate for classroom use.

As an aid in rebinding, discarding, and replacing. It is possible to see what other titles on a subject are available, a factor that often influences the decision whether to discard, rebind, or replace a book.

As an instructional aid in library schools. The Catalog is of use in courses that deal with book selection, particularly on the preschool and elementary levels.

DESCRIPTION OF THE CATALOG

Part 1. Classified Catalog

The Classified Catalog is arranged with the nonfiction books first, classified by the Dewey Decimal Classification in numerical order from 000 to 999. Individual biographies are classed at 92 and follow the 920's (collective biography). Following the nonfiction are the fiction books, designated by the symbol "Fic"; the short story collections, denoted by "S C"; and finally the easy books, consisting mostly of picturebooks and fiction for children in preschool through grade three, which are marked "E." An Outline of Classification, which serves as a table of contents to the Classified Catalog, is reproduced on page 2. It is important to mention that many books may be correctly classified in more than one area. If a particular title is not found where it might be expected in the Classification, the Index in Part 2 should be checked to determine if the title is classified elsewhere in the schedules.

Each book is listed under its main entry, which will usually be the author. The following is a typical entry:

> **Ekey, Robert**
> Fire! in Yellowstone; story by Robert Ekey. Gareth Stevens Children's Bks. 1990 32p il map lib bdg $10.95 (2-4) **574.5**
> 1. Forest fires 2. Yellowstone National Park 3. Forest ecology
> ISBN 0-8368-0226-8 LC 89-43156
> "A True adventure"
> Adapted from an adult book: Yellowstone on fire, published 1989 by The Billings Gazette
> Discusses the fire that ravaged nearly one million acres of Yellowstone National Park during several months in 1988, and explains the two sides to the controversy over letting nature take its course
> A "Well-written and excellently photographed book. . . . Good thought-provoking questions stimulate class discussions." Sci Child
> Includes glossary and bibliography

In this entry the name of the author is given in conformity with *Anglo-American Cataloguing Rules,* 2nd edition, 1988 revision. It is inverted and is printed in dark or bold face type. References are made in Part 2 from variant forms of names.

The first element of the body of the entry is the title of the book, *Fire! in Yellowstone.* The phrase that follows gives the names of those responsible for the creation of the book.

The information that the book is published by Gareth Stevens Children's Bks. follows. Reference to Part 3 will show that this publisher is located at 1555 N. River Center Dr., River Center Bldg., Suite 201, Milwaukee, Wis. 53212. This information, with the price, is useful in ordering books. 1990 is the date when this book was published. It contains 32 pages, illustrations, and a map. It currently sells in a library binding edition for $10.95. As time passes, however, prices should be rechecked with the publisher for possible changes. The designation (2-4) indicates that this book is useful for children in the second to fourth grades. It is difficult to make generalizations as to the reading ability of children and for this reason the grading given is rather flexible. Most listings are graded; exceptions are easy books, professional tools for the librarian, and some reference books.

At the end of the last line in the body of the entry is the figure 574.5 in bold face type. This is the classification number according to the *Abridged Dewey Decimal Classification.* 574.5 is the classification for ecology.

The numbered terms "1. Forest fires 2. Yellowstone National Park 3. Forest ecology" are the recommended subject headings for this book. Sometimes the subjects assigned to the entire book will not show that there are portions of the book dealing with more specific topics. In such cases, subject analytic entries are made in Part 2. All subject headings are based upon *Sears List of Subject Headings.*

The ISBN (International Standard Book Number) is included to facilitate ordering. The Library of Congress control number is provided when available.

Following are five notes supplying additional information about the book. The first pertains to the publisher's series. The second relates the publishing history of the book. The third is a brief description of the book's content while the fourth is an evaluation of the book, here excerpted from the periodical *Science and Children.* The final note records the presence of special features, in this case a glossary and a bibliography. Such descriptive and critical notes are useful in selecting books for acquisition and in determining which of several books on a subject are best suited to an individual reader.

Part 2. Author, Title, Subject, and Analytical Index

This is an alphabetical index of all the books entered in the Catalog. Each book is entered under author, title if distinctive, subject, and under joint author and illustrator if any. Also included are the subject, author and title analytics for the books analyzed. References are made from variant forms of names, from terms not used as subject headings to the preferred term, and from terms used as subject headings to related or more specific headings. The classification number is the key to the main entry of the book in Part 1.

The following are examples of index entries for the sample provided:

Author	**Ekey, Robert** Fire! in Yellowstone (2-4)	**574.5**
Title	**Fire!** in Yellowstone. Ekey, R.	**574.5**
Subject	**Forest fires** Ekey, R. Fire! in Yellowstone (2-4)	**574.5**

Examples of other types of entries:

Joint Author	**Eisenberg, Lisa, 1949-** (jt. auth) McMullan, K. Snakey riddles	**793.73**
Illustrator	**Miller, Ron, 1947-** (il) Adler, I. Mathematics	**510**
Author Analytic	**Milne, A. A. (Alan Alexander), 1882-1956** The house at Pooh Corner (1-4) **Fic** *also in* Milne, A. A. The world of Pooh p153-314	**Fic**
Title Analytic	The **house** at Pooh Corner. Milne, A. A. **Fic** *also in* Milne, A. A. The world of Pooh p153-314	**Fic**
Subject Analytic	**Chavez, Cesar, 1927-** *See/See also pages in the following book(s):* Jacobs, W. J. Great lives: human rights p238-44 (5 and up)	**920**
Uniform Title	**Cinderella** Climo, S. The Egyptian Cinderella **398.2** Ehrlich, A. Cinderella *In* Ehrlich, A. The Random House book of fairy tales p138-49 **398.2** Farjeon, E. The glass slipper **Fic** Galdone, P. Cinderella **398.2** Grimm, J. Ashtenputtel *In* Best-loved folktales of the world p68-75 **398.2** Grimm, J. Cinderella *In* Grimm, J. The complete Grimm's fairy tales p121-28	**398.2**

Part 3. Directory of Publishers and Distributors

This Directory provides the full name, address, and related information for the publisher or distributor of the books listed in Part 1.

TABLE OF CONTENTS

Preface v

How to Use Children's Catalog ix

Part 1. Classified Catalog 1

Outline of Classification 2

Part 2. Author, Title, Subject, and Analytical Index 747

Part 3. Directory of Publishers and Distributors 1335

PART 1

CLASSIFIED CATALOG

Outline of Classification

Reproduced below is the Second Summary of the Dewey Decimal Classification.* Part 1 of the Catalog is arranged according to the Dewey schedules, and the outline thus serves as a table of contents. Fiction (Fic), Story collections (S C), and Easy books (E) have been added at the end of the summary, since these sections are included in the Catalog.

000 Generalities
010 Bibliography
020 Library & information sciences
030 General encyclopedic works
040
050 General serials & their indexes
060 General organizations & museology
070 News media, journalism, publishing
080 General collections
090 Manuscripts & rare books

100 Philosophy & psychology
110 Metaphysics
120 Epistemology, causation, humankind
130 Paranormal phenomena
140 Specific philosophical schools
150 Psychology
160 Logic
170 Ethics (Moral philosophy)
180 Ancient, medieval, Oriental philosophy
190 Modern Western philosophy

200 Religion
210 Natural theology
220 Bible
230 Christian theology
240 Christian moral & devotional theology
250 Christian orders & local church
260 Christian social theology
270 Christian church history
280 Christian denominations & sects
290 Other & comparative religions

300 Social sciences
310 General statistics
320 Political science
330 Economics
340 Law
350 Public administration
360 Social services; association
370 Education
380 Commerce, communications, transport
390 Customs, etiquette, folklore

400 Language
410 Linguistics
420 English & Old English
430 Germanic languages German
440 Romance languages French
450 Italian, Romanian, Rhaeto-Romanic
460 Spanish & Portuguese languages
470 Italic languages Latin
480 Hellenic languages Classical Greek
490 Other languages

500 Natural sciences & mathematics
510 Mathematics
520 Astronomy & allied sciences
530 Physics
540 Chemistry & allied sciences
550 Earth sciences
560 Paleontology Paleozoology
570 Life sciences
580 Botanical sciences
590 Zoological sciences

600 Technology (Applied sciences)
610 Medical sciences Medicine
620 Engineering & allied operations
630 Agriculture
640 Home economics & family living
650 Management & auxiliary services
660 Chemical engineering
670 Manufacturing
680 Manufacture for specific uses
690 Buildings

700 The arts
710 Civic & landscape art
720 Architecture
730 Plastic arts Sculpture
740 Drawing & decorative arts
750 Painting & paintings
760 Graphic arts Printmaking & prints
770 Photography & photographs
780 Music
790 Recreational & performing arts

800 Literature & rhetoric
810 American literature in English
820 English & Old English literatures
830 Literatures of Germanic languages
840 Literatures of Romance languages
850 Italian, Romanian, Rhaeto-Romanic
860 Spanish & Portuguese literatures
870 Italic literatures Latin
880 Hellenic literatures Classical Greek
890 Literatures of other languages

900 Geography & history
910 Geography & travel
920 Biography, genealogy, insignia
930 History of ancient world
940 General history of Europe
950 General history of Asia Far East
960 General history of Africa
970 General history of North America
980 General history of South America
990 General history of other areas

Fic Fiction
S C Story collections
E Easy books

* Reproduced from the Dewey Decimal Classification Abridged Edition 12, published in 1990, by permission of Forest Press, a division of OCLC Online Computer Library Center, owner of copyright.

CHILDREN'S CATALOG

SIXTEENTH EDITION

CLASSIFIED CATALOG

000 GENERALITIES

001.9 Controversial knowledge

Berger, Melvin, 1927-

UFOs, ETs & visitors from space. Putnam 1988 79p il lib bdg $11.95 (5 and up) **001.9**

1. Unidentified flying objects
ISBN 0-399-61218-1 LC 87-29094

Discusses the possibility of life on other planets, describes some of the best known sightings of unidentified flying objects in recent times, and speculates about possible visits to Earth made by extraterrestrials

"Berger takes the role of debunker here, at least in most of the cases he discusses. He admits that while 90 percent of UFO sightings and encounters with ET-like beings are false, there are some incidents that have never been reasonably explained. . . . There is much here to pique the curiosity of young readers who seem to have a natural interest in this topic." Booklist

Cohen, Daniel, 1936-

The world of UFOs. Lippincott 1978 160p il $13.95 (6 and up) **001.9**

1. Unidentified flying objects
ISBN 0-397-31780-8 LC 77-11659

A history of unidentified flying objects including accounts of several famous sightings and results of federal investigations

"The author seems to have written a balanced as well as entertaining book on the history of the UFO social phenomenon. It is not a definitive work, but it is complete enough to give the reader a solidly based and reasonable opinion of what has gone on." Horn Book

Includes bibliography

004 Data processing. Computer science

Simon, Seymour, 1931-

Bits and bytes: a computer dictionary for beginners; illustrated by Barbara and Ed Emberley. Crowell 1985 32p il (Let's-read-and-find-out science bks) lib bdg $12.89; pa $4.50 (k-3) **004**

1. Computers—Dictionaries 2. Electronic data processing—Dictionaries
ISBN 0-690-04475-5 (lib bdg); 0-06-445014-7 (pa) LC 85-47533

"A Computer book 3"

This "is a computer dictionary for beginners. It defines all the typical computer words and phrases like 'RAM,' 'ROM,' 'bit,' 'byte' and 'word processing.' Each term is clearly and accurately defined and has colorful illustrations which add to the meaning of each definition. Although meant for the juvenile reader, this book would be helpful to anyone interested in understanding . . . computer jargon." Appraisal

Meet the computer; illustrated by Barbara and Ed Emberley. Harper & Row 1985 32p il (Let's-read-and-find-out science bks) $12.95; pa $4.50 (k-3) **004**

1. Computers
ISBN 0-690-04447-X; 0-06-445011-2 (pa) LC 84-45338

"A Computer book 1"

The book "shows what a computer can do. Large diagrams coupled with simple description provide an overview of a computer's innards and workings. The Emberleys' brightly colored cartoon robots, astronaut mice, computer parts and children—many highlighted by a black background—flow across the pages. The final two-page illustration showing children at work on several types of programs ties the whole together. Information is summarized on the last two pages." SLJ

005 Computer programming, programs, data

Simon, Seymour, 1931-

How to talk to your computer; illustrated by Barbara and Ed Emberley. Harper & Row 1985 32p il (Let's-read-and-find-out science bks) $12.95; lib bdg $12.89; pa $4.50 (k-3) **005**

1. Programming (Computers) 2. LOGO (Computer program language) 3. BASIC (Computer program language)
ISBN 0-690-04449-6; 0-690-04450-X (lib bdg); 0-06-445010-4 (pa) LC 84-45337

"A Computer book 2"

This volume "explains how a computer knows what to do. Sequential thinking and the BASIC and LOGO languages are briefly introduced in text and illustrations. . . . The eye-catching format and instructive illustrations are sure to please many a prospective young programmer." SLJ

011.6 General bibliographies of works for specific kinds of users

Association for Library Service to Children (U.S.). International Relations Committee

Children's books of international interest; Barbara Elleman, editor; International Relations Committee, Association for Library Service to Children, American Library Association. 3rd ed. American Lib. Assn. 1984 101p pa $7.50 **011.6**

1. Children's literature—Bibliography
ISBN 0-8389-3314-9 LC 84-20336

First published 1972 under the editorship of Virginia Haviland

An annotated list of some 300 children's books produced in the United States that are recommended for translation throughout the world

"Although the titles selected are specifically geared to reveal aspects of life in the U.S., the list also stands as a sound representation of first-rate, high-appeal children's books. . . . Each book is assigned an age range and neatly described in a brief annotation. A directory of publishers and an index top off this useful, attractively designed resource." Booklist

Association for Library Service to Children (U.S.). Notable Children's Books, 1976-1980, Reevaluation Committee

Notable children's books, 1976-1980; prepared by the Notable Children's Books, 1976-1980, Reevaluation Committee, Association for Library Service to Children, American Library Association. American Lib. Assn. 1986 70p pa $6.95 **011.6**

1. Children's literature—Bibliography 2. Books and reading—Best books
ISBN 0-8389-3333-5 LC 86-3039

Also available for $4 each are volumes covering 1940-1970 (ISBN 0-8389-3182-0) and 1971-1975 (ISBN 0-8389-3252-5)

"Each entry provides basic bibliographic information and is briefly, but clearly, annotated. The general arrangement is by age group . . . and the books are listed alphabetically by author within each subdivision. . . . Materials are indexed by author, title, illustrator, editor/compiler/translator/adaptor, and genre." Am Ref Books Annu, 1987

Barstow, Barbara

Beyond picture books; a guide to first readers; [by] Barbara Barstow, Judith Riggle. Bowker 1989 336p $39.95 **011.6**

1. Children's literature—Bibliography 2. Books and reading—Best books
ISBN 0-8352-2515-1 LC 89-30798

"First readers are defined here as books intended for children at a first or second grade level (occasionally third) that have a recognizable format and generally belong to a series. . . . In order to be included in this bibliography the following criteria were used. The book had to be well-written, contain accurate information, have stories or subjects of interest to children in the primary grades, and have illustrations that complement the text and are attractive to children. Both in- and out-of-print books are included here." Preface

For a fuller review see: Booklist, Oct 1, 1989

Baskin, Barbara Holland, 1929-

Books for the gifted child; by Barbara H. Baskin and Karen H. Harris. Bowker 1980-1988 2v (Serving special needs ser) v1 $34.95; v2 $39.95 **011.6**

1. Children's literature—Bibliography 2. Books and reading—Best books 3. Gifted children
ISBN 0-8352-1161-4 (v1); 0-8352-2467-8 (v2)
LC 79-27431

Volume two published under the authorship of Paula Hauser and Gail A. Nelson

The main section of each volume is an annotated list of nearly 200 books considered to be appropriate for gifted children from preschool to adolescence. The entries are arranged alphabetically by author and contain full bibliographic information. Reading levels are also indicated

Best books for children, preschool through grade 6; John T. Gillespie and Corinne J. Naden, editors. 4th ed. Bowker 1990 1002p $44.95 **011.6**

1. Children's literature—Bibliography 2. Books and reading—Best books
ISBN 0-8352-2668-9 LC 89-29625

First published 1978

"Entries, arranged under eight major headings (Literature, Biography, the Arts and Language, History and Geography, Social Institutions and Issues, Personal Development, Physical and Applied Sciences, and Recreation), include author, title, grade level, illustrator (if applicable), publisher, date, price, ISBN, and a brief annotation. . . . A welcome tool for collection development and preparing bibliographies." J Youth Serv Libr

For a fuller review see: Booklist, Dec. 15, 1990

Books for children. Library of Congress; distributed by Superintendent of Docs. pa $1 **011.6**

1. Children's literature—Bibliography 2. Books and reading—Best books
ISSN 0882-5343

Annual. First published 1964 with title: Children's books

Compiled by the Children's Literature Center of the Library of Congress under the supervision of Margaret N. Coughlan. Earlier editions compiled under the supervision of Virginia Haviland

This annotated list of recommended books for preschool through junior high school age children is arranged by categories such as: picture books and picture stories; stories for the middle group; fiction for older readers; folklore; poetry, rhymes, songs and plays; art and hobbies; biography; history, people, and places; nature and science. Reading levels are indicated

Carroll, Frances Laverne

Exciting, funny, scary, short, different, and sad books kids like about animals, science, sports, families, songs, and other things; [by] Frances Laverne Carroll and Mary Meacham. American Lib. Assn. 1984 192p pa $10 **011.6**

1. Children's literature—Bibliography 2. Books and reading—Best books
ISBN 0-8389-0423-8 LC 84-20469

"A reader's advisor for elementary school-age children . . . lists titles to answer children's book requests. Compilers Frances Laverne Carroll and Mary Meacham describe popular titles selected through a survey of children's librarians, arranged by categories that include scary books, sad stories, and exciting stories, and by in-demand subjects ranging from pets to computers." Am Libr

Cianciolo, Patricia J.

Picture books for children. 3rd ed. American Lib. Assn. 1990 230p il pa $25 **011.6**

1. Picture books for children—Bibliography 2. Books and reading—Best books
ISBN 0-8389-0527-7 LC 89-29718

First edition by the Picture Book Committee of the National Council of Teachers of English, edited by Patricia Jean Cianciolo, published 1973 by the National Council of Teachers of English

"Annotated entries for the 464 books are divided into four broad categories: 'Me and My Family,' 'Other People,' 'The World I Live In,' and 'The Imaginative World.' Within each category, titles are arranged alphabetically by author. Information for each book includes title, illustrator, translator or adapter if applicable, publisher and publication date, and intended age group." Booklist

Cuddigan, Maureen

Growing pains; helping children deal with everyday problems through reading; [by] Maureen Cuddigan and Mary Beth Hanson. American Lib. Assn. 1988 165p pa $17.50 **011.6**

1. Children's literature—Bibliography
ISBN 0-8389-0469-6 LC 88-3451

"Focusing on books for children aged 2 to 8, Cuddigan and Hanson use subcategories to narrow their 13 topics into useful areas for librarians and other adults looking for books on subjects that concern children today. Common problems dealt with are going to school, moving, death of a pet, divorce, child abuse, hearing problems, love, loneliness, foster care, and lying. An introduction to each portion sets the tone. Throughout, concise annotations, grade ranges, and related titles are provided. Worthwhile and timely." Booklist

Dreyer, Sharon Spredemann

The bookfinder; a guide to children's literature about the needs and problems of youth aged 2-15. American Guidance Service 1977-1989 4v v1-3 o.p.; v4 $75, pa $40 **011.6**

1. Children's literature—Bibliography LC 78-105919

Volume 5 in preparation

Contents: [v1 Annotations of books published through 1974]; v2 Annotations of books published 1975-1978; v3 Annotations of books published 1979 through 1982; v4 Annotations of books published 1983 through 1986 (ISBN 0-913476-50-1; 0-913476-51-X)

"The guides describe and categorize current children's books according to 450 psychological, behavioral, and developmental topics. . . . 'The Bookfinder' is superior to other guides to books dealing with emotions and human problems because of its full and analytical reviews, scope of topics indexed, ease of access, and frequency of publication. Recommended as first choice for elementary and middle school collections." Wynar. Guide to Ref Books for Sch Media Cent. 3d edition

The **Elementary** school library collection; a guide to books and other media, phases 1-2-3. Brodart $99.95 **011.6**

1. Catalogs, Classified 2. Children's literature—Bibliography 3. Audiovisual materials—Catalogs 4. School libraries—Catalogs

First published 1965. Revised biennially

This is "a core collection of currently available books, nonprint media, magazines, and professional reference materials for elementary schools (K-6). The classified (DDC plus fiction and easy) arrangement, fully cataloged entries, and indexes make ESLC a media catalog as well as a selection tool. . . . Entries give full cataloging data, prices, Fry readability level and interest level codes, acquisition phase, concise annotations, and subject headings. Author, title, and subject indexes are appended. Highly recommended." Wynar. Guide to Ref Books for Sch Media Cent. 3d edition

Ettlinger, John R. T.

Choosing books for young people; a guide to criticism and bibliography; [by] John R.T. Ettlinger and Diana Spirt. v2: 1976-1984. Oryx Press 1987 152p $43.50 **011.6**

1. Children's literature—Bibliography
2. Bibliography—Bibliography
3. Books—Reviews—Bibliography
ISBN 0-89774-247-8

Volume one covering the years 1945-1975 published 1982 by the American Library Association o.p.

This volume includes book selection sources "published in the United States, Great Britain and Canada from 1976 to 1984. French-Canadian materials are also included. . . . The 415 alphabetically arranged critical and descriptive annotations present information in terms used by the book's author either by direct quotation or by paraphrase and indicate the usefulness of each tool." Voice Youth Advocates

Fiction, folklore, fantasy & poetry for children, 1876-1985. Bowker 1986 2v $499.95 **011.6**

1. Children's literature—Bibliography
ISBN 0-8352-1831-7 LC 84-20474

Contents: v 1 Authors; illustrators; v2 Titles; awards

This "is a comprehensive listing of children's literature published over the last century. The 133,000 entries, taken from the *Publisher's Trade List Annual* and verified in other sources, are listed by author, title, and illustrator. A fourth section lists the year-by-year winners of 20 major children's-book awards. Entries, in a format similar to Bowker's *Books in Print*, give the title, author or editor, illustrator, their birth and death dates, series, pagination, publication date, LC card number, ISBN, publisher, and other information when available." Am Libr

For younger readers: braille and talking books. Library of Congress. Natl. Lib. Service for the Blind & Physically Handicapped pa gratis **011.6**

1. Blind—Books and reading—Bibliography 2. Talking books—Bibliography 3. Children's literature—Bibliography
ISSN 0093-2825

Biennial. First published 1964

This bibliography lists braille, disc, and cassette books which are available on loan from the National Library Service for the Blind and Physically Handicapped. The annotated entries, which include grading, are arranged in non-fiction and fiction categories. There are separate sections listing materials for very young readers and Spanish-language books. Author and title indexes are included

Freeman, Judy

Books kids will sit still for; the complete read-aloud guide; Judy Freeman. 2nd ed. Bowker 1990 660p il $29.95 **011.6**

1. Children's literature—Bibliography 2. Books and reading—Best books
ISBN 0-8352-3010-4 LC 90-2373

First published 1984 by Alleyside Press

The author "discusses the hows and whys of reading aloud and suggests 2,117 tested titles . . . for preschool to grade six." J Youth Serv Libr

For a fuller review see: Booklist, Feb. 15, 1991

A **Guide** to non-sexist children's books; Denise Wilms and Ilene Cooper, editors. v2: 1976-1985. Academy Chicago 1987 250p $17.95; pa $8.95 **011.6**

1. Sex role—Bibliography 2. Children's literature—Bibliography
ISBN 0-89733-161-3; 0-89733-162-1 (pa)
LC 86-32262

Also available: Volume 1 compiled by Judith Adell and Hilary Dole Klein published 1976, $14.95, pa $5.95 (ISBN 0-915864-01-0; 0-915864-02-9)

Divided by age groups, "each section is further divided into fiction and nonfiction. The nonfiction subjects are heavy on female biographies, and listed fiction titles emphasize strong female characters. The more than 600 titles included here give a hefty number of examples of role-free characters, both real and imaginary, male and female. . . . Both this title and its still-available prequel will be helpful to children's and school librarians as a collection management tool and a program and book discussion resource for role-free units." J Youth Serv Libr

Junior high school library catalog; edited by Juliette Yaakov. 6th ed. Wilson, H.W. 1990 802p lib bdg $105 **011.6**

1. Catalogs, Classified 2. School libraries (High school)—Catalogs
ISBN 0-8242-0799-8 LC 90-44498

"Standard catalog series"

First published 1965

Kept up to date by annual supplements which are included in price of main volume

This collection of recommended materials includes 3,219 titles and some 3,600 analytical entries of books for grades seven through nine. Entries contain full bibliographic information, Dewey Decimal classification number, subject headings, descriptive, and when possible, critical annotations

"This series belongs on every school and public library shelf as a valuable reference tool." Booklist

Lima, Carolyn W.

A to zoo: subject access to children's picture books; [by] Carolyn W. Lima, John A. Lima. 3rd ed. Bowker 1989 xxiv, 939p $44.95 **011.6**

1. Picture books for children—Bibliography
ISBN 0-8352-2599-2 LC 89-15916

First published 1982

"This picture book index contains 700 subjects and 12,000 fiction and nonfiction picture book titles. . . . [There are] three section guides: a list of subject headings based on library terms and questions, including cross references; a subject guide—the 700 subjects with picture books listed alphabetically by author; a bibliographic guide—including ISBN numbers only for titles added in this edition. A title and illustrator index conclude the reference tool." J Youth Serv Libr

For a fuller review see: Booklist, Feb. 1, 1990

Magazines for school libraries; for elementary, junior high school, and high school libraries; [edited by] Bill Katz. Bowker 1987 238p $49.95 **011.6**

1. Periodicals—Bibliography
ISSN 0000-0957
ISBN 0-8352-2316-7

New edition in preparation

"From his *Magazines for Libraries* [5th ed.], Katz has selected about one fifth of the titles and their annotations. Many of the parent work's more specialized categories such as accounting, physics, and urban studies are absent from the seventy-three subject categories used to organize the 1,300 annotations. For the most part, the annotations are reprinted verbatim. . . . An indication of age level—elementary/junior high, high school, or professional—has been added to the brief reviews." Wilson Libr Bull

This reference work "should be considered as a selection tool in all school libraries." Booklist

National Council of Teachers of English. Committee on the Elementary School Booklist

Adventuring with books; a booklist for pre-K-grade 6; [by] Mary Jett-Simpson, editor, and the Committee on the Elementary School Booklist of the National Council of Teachers of English. 9th ed. National Council of Teachers of English 1989 549p pa $16.50 **011.6**

1. Children's literature—Bibliography 2. Books and reading—Best books

ISBN 0-8141-0078-3 LC 89-12906

First published 1950. Editors vary

"Describing the selected 1,800 children's books, published between 1985 and 1988, the book is designed to supplement earlier editions, even though some additional lists of notable titles published before 1985 are included. A well-designed table of contents allows users to access numerous topics that match the elementary curriculum. Entries provide suggested grade levels, and annotations are succinct yet properly informative. . . . This relatively inexpensive treasure trove belongs in each teacher's desk and on every library's shelves." Booklist

National Council of Teachers of English. Committee on the Junior High and Middle School Booklist

Your reading: a booklist for junior high and middle school students; James E. Davis and Hazel K. Davis, editors, and the Committee on the Junior High and Middle School Booklist of the National Council of Teachers of English. 7th ed. National Council of Teachers of English 1988 494p pa $13.95 **011.6**

1. Children's literature—Bibliography 2. Young adults' literature—Bibliography 3. Books and reading—Best books

ISBN 0-8141-5939-7 LC 88-25148

First published 1954

"Organized in numerous categories of fiction and nonfiction, this annotated booklist for junior high and middle school students, which includes nearly 2,000 books will be useful to YA librarians and teachers." Booklist

Olexer, Marycile E., 1941-

Poetry anthologies for children and young people. American Lib. Assn. 1985 xxii, 285p $40 **011.6**

1. Poetry—Bibliography 2. Books and reading—Best books

ISBN 0-8389-0430-0 LC 85-6033

"This index explores more than 300 different volumes. In a detailed and lengthy analysis of each of the included collections (works of one author) and anthologies (works by various poets), Olexer describes the work, justifies its inclusion, discusses possible uses, and suggests an age level best served by the selection. An example of a poem is included. There are short annotations for other high-quality offerings, though not as critically examined, listed at the conclusion. Sources for evaluation of poetry . . . are appended. A specialized bibliography, this can best be used when developing poetry units where Olexer's clear joy of verse can be extended." Booklist

Pilla, Marianne Laino, 1955-

The best: high/low books for reluctant readers. Libraries Unlimited 1990 100p pa $11.50 **011.6**

1. High interest-low vocabulary books—Bibliography 2. Slow learning children—Books and reading

ISBN 0-87287-532-6 LC 90-5756

"A Libraries Unlimited data book"

This "bibliography is aimed at librarians, teachers, and other adults who hope to introduce the pleasures of recreational reading to reluctant readers in grades 3-12. . . . The 374 entries were chosen on the basis of quality, reading level, and general appeal. Both fiction and nonfiction titles are included, as well as some out-of-print titles that are noted as such. Entries are numbered and listed in alphabetical order by author, with titles in boldface type. Annotations are brief. . . . The books are indexed by title, subject, grade level, and reading level. . . . Well-organized information, 'user-friendly' print, and convenient format and size combine to make this a useful reference tool." J Youth Serv Libr

Reference books for young readers; authoritative evaluations of encyclopedias, atlases, and dictionaries; Marion Sader, editor; Brent Allison, Shirley A. Fitzgibbons, Rebecca L. Thomas, consultants. Bowker 1988 615p il (Bowker buying guide ser) lib bdg $49.95 **011.6**

1. Reference books—Bibliography

ISBN 0-8352-2366-3 LC 87-38234

"Presented here are 200 very extensive reviews of three types of books—encyclopedias, dictionaries and other word books, and atlases. . . . All reviews are written by professional librarians and subject matter specialists. . . . Especially useful are the glossary of terms in the chapters and the facsimile pages which give you a chance to actually see what the book looks like without having it in your hand." Voice Youth Advocates

For a fuller review see: Booklist, Sept. 1, 1988

Includes bibliography

Richardson, Selma K.

Magazines for children; a guide for parents, teachers, and librarians; Selma K. Richardson. 2nd ed. American Lib. Assn. 1991 xxxv, 139p pa $19.95 **011.6**

1. Periodicals—Bibliography

ISBN 0-8389-0552-8 LC 90-45152

First published 1983

Organized by magazine name this "guide offers subscription information, as well as a detailed discussion of the magazine's editorial content: regular features; columns; audience age." SLJ

Schon, Isabel
Basic collection of children's books in Spanish. Scarecrow Press 1986 230p $20 **011.6**

1. Latin American literature—Bibliography 2. Spanish literature—Bibliography 3. Children's literature—Bibliography
ISBN 0-8108-1904-X LC 86-13911

This bibliography "recommends some 500 titles that can be used to develop an existing collection or to create a new library serving Hispanic children from pre-school through sixth grade. To aid non-Spanish-speaking selectors, author Isabel Schon has translated each title into English, supplied an annotation, and given grade level and price. The entries are grouped by reference works, nonfiction (arranged by Dewey classification), publishers' series, fiction, easy books, and professional books. The 240-page bibliography is indexed by author, title, and subject and includes a listing of dealers of Spanish-language books." Am Libr

Books in Spanish for children and young adults: an annotated guide [series I-V] Scarecrow Press 1978-1989 5v v1 $16.50; v2, 3, 5 ea $20; v4 $29.50 **011.6**

1. Latin American literature—Bibliography 2. Spanish literature—Bibliography 3. Children's literature—Bibliography
ISBN 0-8108-1176-6 (v1); 0-8108-1620-2 (v2); 0-8108-1807-8 (v3); 0-8108-2004-8 (v4); 0-8108-2238-5 (v5)

Series VI in preparation

A selection guide for books in Spanish written by Hispanic authors for children of preschool through high school age originating mostly from Latin American countries and Spain. Each volume covers roughly a three-year period. Arranged by country and by topic

"The author's no-nonsense annotations of books not recommended add credibility to those she recommends highly." Booklist

Wilson, George, 1920-
Books for children to read alone; a guide for parents and librarians; [by] George Wilson, Joyce Moss. Bowker 1988 184p $39.95 **011.6**

1. Children's literature—Bibliography 2. Books and reading—Best books
ISBN 0-8352-2346-9 LC 88-10430

This is an annotated bibliography of over 350 fiction and non-fiction titles recommended for readers ages 5-8. The book is divided into seven chapters according to half-year readability levels, starting with books for beginning readers through books for the second half of grade three. There are separate subject, readability, author, and title indexes

Wynar, Christine Gehrt, 1933-
Guide to reference books for school media centers. 3rd ed. Libraries Unlimited 1986 407p $36 **011.6**

1. Reference books—Bibliography
ISBN 0-87287-545-8 LC 86-20156

First published 1973

"This outstanding guide contains over 2,000 entries organized by subject. . . . Materials include titles for school media centers serving students from kindergarten through 12th grade." Sci Books Films

015.73 Bibliographies and catalogs of works issued or printed in the United States

Children's books in print. Bowker $110 **015.73**

1. Children's literature—Bibliography
ISSN 0069-3480 LC 70-101705

Annual. First published 1969

"Gives current publisher's information for juvenile titles listed in their catalogs as 'in print.' Useful, but not complete." N Y Public Libr. Ref Books for Child Collect

Subject guide to Children's books in print. Bowker $110 **015.73**

1. Children's literature—Bibliography 2. Catalogs, Subject
ISSN 0000-0167 LC 70-101705

Annual. First published 1970

This publication provides a subject approach to its companion work: Children's books in print. The headings used are based on the Sears list of subject headings supplemented by headings from LC. Entries include author, title, publisher, year of publication, binding, price, ISBN, and, in some cases, grade level. A directory of publishers and distributors is included

016 Bibliographies and catalogs of works on specific subjects or in specific disciplines

Friedberg, Joan Brest, 1927-
Accept me as I am: best books of juvenile nonfiction on impairments and disabilities; [by] Joan Brest Friedberg, June B. Mullins, Adelaide Weir Sukiennik. Bowker 1985 363p il (Serving special needs ser) $34.95 **016**

1. Physically handicapped—Bibliography 2. Mentally handicapped—Bibliography 3. Children's literature—Bibliography
ISBN 0-8352-1974-7 LC 85-3778

"A selective guide to 350 nonfiction books, mostly biographies/autobiographies and informational titles for school-aged children and young adults published to 1984. Arranged by type of disability/impairment, it includes full bibliographic information, grade level and lengthy, critical annotations. Valuable essays on stereotyping and the role of non-fiction in this subject area." N Y Public Libr. Ref Books for Child Collect

Kister, Kenneth F., 1935-
Best encyclopedias: a guide to general and specialized encyclopedias. Oryx Press 1986 356p $39.50 **016**

1. Encyclopedias and dictionaries—Bibliography
ISBN 0-89774-171-4

Also available: Kister's Concise guide to best encyclopedias pa $16.50 (ISBN 0-89774-484-5)

Successor to: Encyclopedia buying guide, published by Bowker

"This comparative, critical guide includes 52 general encyclopedias, adult and juvenile. Strengths and weaknesses are illustrated with specific examples. In addition '450 recommended specialized encyclopedias' are covered with short quotes from other reviews. Valuable introductory chapter with background information on secondhand encyclopedias, selection criteria, etc. Good collection development tool for librarians and selection tool for parents, etc." N Y Public Libr. Ref Books for Child Collect

016.3 Bibliographies of the social sciences

Notable children's trade books in the field of social studies. Children's Bk. Council pa gratis **016.3**

1. Social sciences—Bibliography 2. Books and reading—Best books

An annual annotated list, reprinted from an issue of the periodical Social Education, of the preceding year's best trade books in the field of social studies of interest to children in grades K-8. Prepared by the Book Review Subcommittee of the National Council for the Social Studies—Children's Book Council Joint Committee. Titles are selected for emphasis on human relations, originality, readability and, when appropriate, illustrations. General reading levels (primary, intermediate, advanced) are indicated

016.3058 Bibliographies of racial, ethnic, national groups

The **Black** experience in children's books; selected by the New York Public Library, Black Experience in Children's Books Committee. New York Public Lib. pa $5 **016.3058**

1. Blacks—Bibliography

First published 1957. Periodically revised

"Annotated list of folklore, fiction and non-fiction portraying Black life for children from preschool to age 12. Arranged geographically; appendix lists Black authors and illustrators whose works appear on this list." N Y Public Libr. Ref Books for Child Collect

016.3627 Bibliographies of problems of and services to young people

Bernstein, Joanne E.
Books to help children cope with separation and loss; an annotated bibliography; [by] Joanne E. Bernstein and Masha Kabakow Rudman. v3. Bowker 1989 xxi, 532p $39.95 **016.3627**

1. Children's literature—Bibliography
2. Bereavement—Bibliography
ISBN 0-8352-2510-0 LC 88-7591

The second edition, covering the years 1955 to 1982, is available for $39.95 (ISBN 0-8352-1484-2)

First published 1977

This volume provides "annotations for more than 600 books useful in bibliotherapy. It supplements the second edition. . . . The titles included are written for children ages 3 to 16 . . . with 90 percent of them published between 1983 and 1988. . . . Titles are arranged in categories by the primary loss experience dealt with in the work. . . . Each entry includes full bibliographic citation, availability in hardcover or paperback, interest level or intended ages, reading level based on the Fry Readability Graph, and a lengthy annotation." Booklist

016.3713 Bibliographies of instructional materials

Notable children's films and videos, filmstrips, and recordings, 1973-1986; prepared by Notable Films, Filmstrips, and Recordings, 1973-1986 Retrospective Task Force, Association for Library Service to Children, American Library Association. American Lib. Assn. 1987 118p pa $8.95 **016.3713**

1. Audiovisual materials—Bibliography
ISBN 0-8389-3342-4 LC 87-14395

An annotated listing of 159 films, 80 filmstrips, and 180 records for children through age 14, each entry having been designated as "notable" by respective ALSC committees. Arranged alphabetically by title, each entry provides producer, performer, distributor, copyright, format, purchase price, rental price, length, and grade level information. Indexed by subject, author, performer, and illustrator

016.3726 Bibliographies of language arts

Greene, Ellin, 1927-
Storytelling: a selected annotated bibliography; [by] Ellin Greene, George Shannon. Garland 1986 xxvi, 183p (Garland reference lib. of social science) $25 **016.3726**

1. Storytelling—Bibliography 2. Books and reading
ISBN 0-8240-8749-6 LC 84-48877

"An introductory essay presents a historical overview of storytelling in U.S. libraries, and the major influences on organized storytelling for children. . . . The book's purpose is to call attention to readings that deepen the storyteller's understanding of the function of storytelling in human development, give a historical sense of organized storytelling in libraries, and offer practical aids in the selection, preparation, and presentation of stories." Publisher's note

016.5 Bibliographies of science

Appraisal; science books for young people. Children's Science Bk. Review Com. $24 per year **016.5**

1. Science—Bibliography—Periodicals 2. Books—Reviews
ISSN 0003-7052

Quarterly. First published 1967

This periodical reviews science books for elementary and secondary school students. "Each review has a critical annotation by a children's librarian and a specialist in the field. Their dual evaluations give a sharply defined, enhanced perspective to the educational merits of the book in question. Works are rated according to five assessments from 'excellent' to 'unsatisfactory'. . . . *Appraisal* focuses on important subject matter for acquisition in school library collections." Katz. Mag for Sch Libr

The **Best** science books & A-V materials for children; compiled and edited by Susan M. O'Connell, Valerie J. Montenegro, Kathryn Wolff. American Assn. for the Advancement of Science 1988 335p $20 **016.5**

1. Science—Bibliography 2. Audiovisual materials—Bibliography 3. Books and reading—Best books
ISBN 0-87168-316-4 LC 88-10575

First published 1983 with title: The Best science books for children

"An annotated list of science and mathematics books, films, filmstrips, and videocassettes for children ages five through twelve selected from the pages of *Science Books and Films* magazine." Title page

"This must-purchase bibliography covers twelve hundred books and audiovisual materials. . . . The bibliography is arranged in classified order by science topic and contains complete bibliographic information and the original review. Indexes to authors, title, subjects, and series are provided, plus a distributors' index." Am Ref Books Annu, 1989

Kennedy, DayAnn M.
Science & technology in fact and fiction: a guide to children's books; [by] DayAnn M. Kennedy, Stella S. Spangler, Mary Ann Vanderwerf. Bowker 1990 319p $35 **016.5**

1. Science—Bibliography 2. Technology—Bibliography 3. Children's literature—Bibliography 4. Books and reading—Best books
ISBN 0-8352-2708-1 LC 89-27374

This guide contains "more than 350 entries, a list of suggested readings (for adults), and indexes by author, title, illustator, subject *and* Fry readability level. . . . Each title is accompanied by bibliographic information, grade and/or reading level, and series notation (if needed). This is followed by a plot summary, and an evaluation." J Youth Serv Libr

"Unique in that it includes fiction, emphasizes books for the lower grades, and has lengthy annotations. This easy-to-use reference should prove helpful to librarians, teachers, and parents." Booklist

Outstanding science trade books for children. Children's Bk. Council pa gratis **016.5**

1. Science—Bibliography 2. Books and reading—Best books

An annual annotated list, reprinted from an issue of the periodical Science and Children, of the preceding year's best trade books in the field of science of interest to children in grades K-8. Prepared by a Book Review Committee appointed by the National Science Teachers Association in cooperation with the Children's Book Council. Titles are selected for accuracy, readability and pleasing format. Grade levels are indicated

Science Books & Films. American Assn. for the Advancement of Science $35 per year **016.5**

1. Science—Bibliography—Periodicals 2. Books—Reviews 3. Audiovisual materials—Reviews
ISSN 0098-342X

Five issues a year. First published 1965 with title: Science Books, a quarterly review

"This review service assists in the selection of scientific and technical books and nonprint media. Titles are reviewed for designated readers in elementary school through college and for general audiences. Trade books, textbooks (except those for grades K through 12), 16mm films, video programs, and educational filmstrips are covered. . . . Reviewers' comments are no-nonsense, highlighted appraisals of content and quality. Materials deficient in technical accuracy are soundly criticized. 'Science Books and Films' readily serves curriculum and collection development needs for classrooms and school libraries." Katz. Mag for Libr. 5th edition

016.510 Bibliographies of mathematics

Roberts, Patricia, 1936-

Counting books are more than numbers: an annotated action bibliography; [by] Patricia L. Roberts. Library Professional Publs. 1990 270p $32.50 **016.510**

1. Counting—Bibliography 2. Picture books for children—Bibliography

ISBN 0-208-02216-3 LC 89-19936

"Includes annotations for 350 children's books that could be used to stimulate thinking about concepts such as counting, number sequence, one-to-one correspondence, place value, sets, addition, subtraction, multiplication, division, money, measurement, temperature, and time. This book is most useful for teachers of Grades K-2." Read Teach

For a fuller review see: Booklist, March 15, 1990

016.79143 Bibliographies of motion pictures

Parent's choice guide to videocassettes for children; edited by Diana Huss Green [et al.] and the editors of Consumer Reports Books. Consumers Union of U.S. 1989 270p pa $14.95 **016.79143**

1. Videotapes—Catalogs 2. Motion pictures—Catalogs

ISBN 0-89043-240-6 LC 88-71035

"The suggestions are a mix of educational programming, cartoons, and feature films for preschoolers through teens, including some unusual choices of adult movies for young adult audiences. Reviews (of about 200 words) are written by TV and film critics and arranged by topic (sports, drama, coming-of-age, fantasy/science fiction, etc.). Pertinent books that complement the video selections are also listed, chosen by public and school librarians." Booklist

016.8 Bibliographies of literature

Adamson, Lynda G.

A reference guide to historical fiction for children and young adults. Greenwood Press 1987 401p lib bdg $59.95 **016.8**

1. Historical fiction—Bibliography 2. Books and reading—Best books

ISBN 0-313-25002-2 LC 87-7533

"This volume describes 80 award-winning authors of historical fiction and their works written since 1940. Included as part of each entry for the authors are a bibliography of their works, very brief biographical information, plot summaries for most works, the author's honors, and a summary of usual themes and style." Booklist

Anderson, Vicki, 1928-

Fiction sequels for readers age 10-16; an annotated bibliography of books in succession. McFarland & Co. 1990 150p pa $19.95 **016.8**

1. Children's literature—Bibliography 2. Young adults' literature—Bibliography

ISBN 0-89950-519-8 LC 89-43686

"The author has compiled a list of 1500 titles by about 350 authors. . . . Information is arranged alphabetically by author and provides the title, placement in the sequence, publisher, publication date, and a brief annotation of the content." Voice Youth Advocates

For a fuller review see: Booklist, Aug. 1990

Baskin, Barbara Holland, 1929-

More notes from a different drummer; a guide to juvenile fiction portraying the disabled; by Barbara H. Baskin and Karen H. Harris. Bowker 1984 495p (Serving special populations ser) $39.95 **016.8**

1. Handicapped—Fiction—Bibliography 2. Children's literature—Bibliography

ISBN 0-8352-1871-6 LC 84-12283

"This extends the author's earlier edition [entered below] to include 450 new fiction titles published between 1976 and 1981 concerning the disabled. Lengthy annotations remain thoughtful and informative. Earlier work should be retained." N Y Public Libr. Ref Books for Child Collect

Notes from a different drummer; a guide to juvenile fiction portraying the handicapped; by Barbara H. Baskin and Karen H. Harris. Bowker 1978 c1977 375p il $34.95 **016.8**

1. Handicapped—Fiction—Bibliography 2. Children's literature—Bibliography

ISBN 0-8352-0978-4 LC 77-15067

"Comprehensive guide to juvenile fiction written between 1940 and 1975 that depicts mentally and physically disabled characters. Critical and descriptive annotations, reading level and analysis of depiction of the disabled are included." N Y Public Libr. Ref Books for Child Collect

Hall, Susan, 1940-

Using picture storybooks to teach literary devices; recommended books for children and young adults. Oryx Press 1990 168p il $24.95 **016.8**

1. Children's literature—Bibliography 2. Picture books for children—Bibliography 3. Literature—Study and teaching

ISBN 0-89774-582-5 LC 89-8574

The author "advocates the use of high-quality picture storybooks—partly because of their accessible format—to teach children and young adults about complex literary elements. After five brief introductory chapters, a source list arranged alphabetically by literary device (e.g., alliteration, allusion, ambiguity) comprises the balance of the book. Each literary device is defined and followed by an annotated list of representative picture storybooks,

Hall, Susan, 1940-—*Continued*
including an example of how the device is used in each book." Booklist

"This is a well conceived and functional bibliography. . . . It will encourage one to take a longer look at the picture storybook genre and its application to older youth. An excellent addition to the reference collection of any school or public library." Voice Youth Advocates

Lynn, Ruth Nadelman, 1948-
Fantasy literature for children and young adults; an annotated bibliography. 3rd ed. Bowker 1989 xlvii, 771p $39.95 **016.8**

1. Fantastic fiction—Bibliography 2. Fairy tales—Bibliography
ISBN 0-8352-2347-7 LC 88-8162

First published 1979 with title: Fantasy for children

This volume "annotates 3,300 fantasy novels and collections for youth in grades three through 12. Part one contains annotated bibliographies by subject. . . . Part Two is a research guide with sections on references, and authors studies." Voice Youth Advocates

For a fuller review see: Booklist, May 1, 1989

016.973 Bibliographies of United States history

VanMeter, Vandelia
American history for children and young adults: an annotated bibliographic index. Libraries Unlimited 1990 324p $26.50 **016.973**

1. United States—History—Bibliography
ISBN 0-87287-731-0 LC 90-5815

"A Libraries Unlimited data book"

This work "begins with General History followed by divisions chronologically arranged by various time periods in American history. . . . There are subject headings within each time period division which coordinate with Sears headings and are arranged alphabetically. The annotations are brief and to the point, containing author, title, publisher, copyright date, and number of pages. Price and review sources are also given. . . . There are 2,901 titles listed, including fiction, nonfiction, and biography." Voice Youth Advocates

For a fuller review see: Booklist, Sept. 1, 1990

020.5 Library and information sciences—Serial publications

Wilson Library Bulletin. Wilson, H.W. $46 per year **020.5**

1. Library science—Periodicals 2. Libraries—Periodicals 3. Books and reading—Periodicals
ISSN 0043-5651

Monthly except July and August. First published 1914 with title: The Wilson Bulletin

"The only privately published general-interest library periodical other than *Library Journal, Wilson Library Bulletin* is a polished monthly that provides as excellent view of the current U.S. library scene. Articles frequently focus on user services and new technology. . . . Reviews—of children's picture books, young adult books, murder mysteries, films, records, professional reading, library software, reference books and general book reviews—are selective and well written. This is a basic purchase for most professional collections." Katz. Mag for Sch Libr

021.7 Promotion of libraries, information centers

Matthews, Judy Gay
ClipArt & dynamic designs for libraries & media centers; [by] Judy Gay Matthews, Michael Mancarella, Shirley Lambert. Libraries Unlimited 1988-1989 2v il v1 pa $28; v2 pa $26.50 **021.7**

1. Graphic arts—Handbooks, manuals, etc. 2. Instructional materials centers—Handbooks, manuals, etc. 3. Libraries—Handbooks, manuals, etc.
ISBN 0-87287-636-5 (v1); 0-87287-750-7 (v2)
LC 87-33877

Contents: v1 Books & basics; v2 Computers and audiovisual

"Basics on lettering, layout, and working with a printer are succeeded by some simple projects for posters, fliers, and bookmarks. Pages and pages of clip art follow, organized into broad categories. . . . Paper is thick and glossy for sharp copies and easy scoring. Useful in classroom or media center/library." Booklist

Includes glossary and bibliography

025.3 Bibliographic analysis and control

ALA filing rules; [prepared by the] Filing Committee, Resources and Technical Services Division, American Library Association. American Lib. Assn. 1980 50p pa $8 **025.3**

1. Files and filing 2. Library catalogs
ISBN 0-8389-3255-X LC 80-22186

Successor to: ALA Rules for filing catalog cards, second edition

"This edition of ALA's library catalog 'Filing Rules' was issued to correspond with requirements of the 'Anglo-American Cataloguing Rules' 2d ed. [entered below] and machine filing applications. The rules represent a major change and simplification from the 1968 edition. Major features are the adoption of the 'file-as-is' principle, non-hierarchical structure (no distinction among person, place, thing, and title in identical headings) and two categories of rules, general and special." Wynar. Guide to Ref Books for Sch Media Cent. 3d edition

According to a 1981 announcement of the American Library Association, this may be considered as an alternative to, rather than a definite replacement for, the 1968 edition of ALA Rules for filing catalog cards. Libraries may choose to continue using the earlier publication

Cataloging correctly for kids; an introduction to the tools; edited by Sharon Zuiderveld. rev ed. American Lib. Assn. 1991 78p il pa $12.50 **025.3**

1. Cataloging
ISBN 0-8389-3395-5 LC 91-8675

First edition by the Cataloging of Children's Materials Committee published 1989

A collection of articles which discuss the various tools which can be used to establish and maintain cataloging standards in children's collections. Among the topics presented are the Library of Congress' annotated cards program, selecting a cataloging vendor, and cataloging nonbook materials. A set of guidelines developed by the Cataloging of Children's Materials Committee is also given

Includes bibliographic references

Frost, Carolyn O., 1940-

Media access and organization; a cataloging and reference sources guide for nonbook materials. Libraries Unlimited 1989 xxi, 265p lib bdg $29.50 **025.3**

1. Cataloging—Audiovisual materials
ISBN 0-87287-583-0 LC 88-27302

This volume "begins by discussing the organization of AACR2 and focuses on the rules that apply to nonbook materials. Frost continues by examining in detail various types of nonprint items from cartographic materials to microforms. She begins each section with a discussion and commentary on problem areas in bibliographic control, organization and description of each type of media, and cites key rules from AACR2 and AACR2, 1988 rev. . . . A really comprehensive, up-to-date, and helpful look at the cataloging of nonbook material." Voice Youth Advocates

Includes bibliographic references

Gorman, Michael, 1941-

The concise AACR2, 1988 revision. American Lib. Assn. 1989 161p pa $15 **025.3**

1. Anglo-American cataloguing rules 2. Cataloging
ISBN 0-8389-3362-9 LC 89-15110

Based on Anglo-American cataloguing rules, 2nd edition, 1988 revision, available for $35 (ISBN 0-8389-3346-7); pa $25 (ISBN 0-8389-3360-2)

"Many smaller libraries will find this volume more helpful than the complete *AACR2*, although some may eventually progress to the full set of rules. Part 1 provides rules for the description of library materials; part 2, rules for choice of access points, headings for persons, geographic names, headings for corporate bodies, uniform titles, and references. Capitalization rules, glossary and comparative table of *AACR2* and *Concise AACR2* rules appended." Booklist

Miller, Rosalind E.

Commonsense cataloging; a cataloger's manual; [by] Rosalind E. Miller & Jane C. Terwillegar. 4th ed rev. Wilson, H.W. 1990 180p pa $23 **025.3**

1. Cataloging
ISBN 0-8242-0789-0 LC 89-70716

First edition by Esther J. Piercy published 1965; this is a revision of the fourth edition published 1989

This practical manual for the beginning cataloger discusses such topics as: applications of AACR2; subject organization; Dewey classification; subject access; cataloging with copy; mechanical preparation and maintenance; special problems posed by serials, maps, kits and electronic software; computers and cataloging

Includes glossary and bibliography

025.4 Subject analysis and control

Dewey, Melvil, 1851-1931

Abridged Dewey decimal classification and relative index; devised by Melvil Dewey. ed 12, edited by John P. Comaromi [et al.]. Forest Press 1990 857p $75 **025.4**

1. Classification, Dewey Decimal
ISBN 0-910608-42-3 LC 90-31428

First abridged edition published 1894

The 12th Abridged Edition is an abridgement of the four-volume 20th Edition. Adapted to the needs of small and growing libraries, the 12th Abridged Edition is designed primarily for school and public libraries with collections of up to 20,000 titles

Sears list of subject headings. 14th ed, edited by Martha T. Mooney. Wilson, H.W. 1991 731p $42 **025.4**

1. Subject headings
ISBN 0-8242-0803-X LC 91-10290

Also available: Canadian companion to 13th edition $15 (ISBN 0-8242-0754-8) with new edition in preparation; Spanish version of 12th edition with title: Sears Lista de encabezamientos de materia $45 (ISBN 0-8242-0704-1)

First published 1923 with title: List of subject headings for small libraries, by Minnie Earl Sears

This list of headings follows the Library of Congress form of headings with appropriate adaptations to meet the needs of smaller libraries. This edition features suggested classification numbers for the subject headings. The numbers are based upon the Twelfth Edition of the Abridged Dewey Classification and relative index

025.7 Physical preparation for storage of library materials

Greenfield, Jane

Books: their care and repair. Wilson, H.W. 1984 204p il $34 **025.7**

1. Books—Conservation and restoration
ISBN 0-8242-0695-9 LC 83-25926

Greenfield, Jane—*Continued*

"Geared to librarians, this useful handbook explains in clear, precise language how major and minor book repairs can be performed in-house without costly materials. Greenfield, a conservator of rare books, has compiled information on paper mending, pamphlet binding, tip-ins, hinge and joint repairs, and protective wrappings. She also furnishes basic background material on the structure of books and how proper care prevents deterioration. Simple line drawings supplement the text." Booklist

Includes glossary and bibliography

027 General libraries, information centers

Gibbons, Gail

Check it out! the book about libraries. Harcourt Brace Jovanovich 1985 unp il lib bdg $12.95; pa $3.95 (k-3) **027**

1. Libraries
ISBN 0-15-216400-6; 0-15-216401-4 (pa) LC 85-5414

The author explains what is found in a library and how different libraries serve their communities

"Gibbons provides a solid base for spinoff discussions, making the book useful as an introduction to library skills and for discussion in story hours." SLJ

027.4 Public libraries

Rockwell, Anne F., 1934-

I like the library; by Anne Rockwell. Dutton 1977 unp il $11.95 (k-1) **027.4**

1. Public libraries
ISBN 0-525-32528-X LC 77-6365

"In a brief text printed beneath explicit pictures, a small boy tells of his weekly visit to the public library." Horn Book

"The element most often missing in children's books about libraries is delight. It's here in abundance. Pictures [by the author] and story line blend to relate the experiences of a preschool child." Booklist

027.62 Libraries for children and young adults

MacDonald, Margaret Read

Booksharing: 101 programs to use with preschoolers; with illustrations by Julie Liana MacDonald. Library Professional Publs. 1988 236p il $32.50 **027.62**

1. Children's libraries 2. Library services 3. Books and reading
ISBN 0-208-02159-0 LC 87-35777

The author "provides 101 complete, 45-minute programs to use with children ages 2½ to 6; each of the thematic sessions lists several books, followed by songs, films, poems, creative dramatics, science experiments, and art and craft experiences. . . . A complete alphabetical bibliography, an index of films, and musical notations are appended." Booklist

Nichols, Judy

Storytimes for two-year-olds; illustrations by Lora Sears. American Lib. Assn. 1987 141p il pa $20 **027.62**

1. Storytelling 2. Children's libraries
ISBN 0-8389-0451-3 LC 86-32151

The opening chapters discuss the benefits of introducing toddlers to the library and a step-by-step description of a typical story program complete with books, fingerplays, music, and active dramatics. What follows are 33 program themes popular with two-year-olds

This volume "is a wealth of complete bibliographies and ready-made programs. . . . Children's librarians can enthusiastically and confidently approach toddler story times with this book in hand." J Youth Serv Libr

Rollock, Barbara T.

Public library services for children; with a foreword by Augusta Baker. Library Professional Publs. 1988 228p $32.50 **027.62**

1. Children's libraries 2. Children—Books and reading
ISBN 0-208-02016-0 LC 88-12863

"This book will focus from a practitioner's point of view on the state of the art in children's public library services in the mid-1980s, and on at least some of the social forces in this century which have combined to alter the perspectives and potentials of library services to children." Introduction

Includes bibliography

027.6205 Libraries for children and young adults—Serial publications

Emergency Librarian. Dyad Services $45 per year **027.6205**

1. Children's libraries—Periodicals 2. School libraries—Periodicals 3. Books—Reviews
ISSN 0315-8888

Five issues a year. First published 1973

"A Canadian publication aimed at teachers and librarians working with children and young adults in public and school libraries. Each issue includes four or five articles, as well as reviews of professional reading, children's recordings, magazines for young people and paperbacks for children and young adults. . . . The writing is imaginative, and the coverage of children's and young adult librarianship broad enough that librarians anywhere will find this worthwhile." Katz. Mag for Sch Libr

Journal of Youth Services in Libraries. American Lib. Assn. $30 per year **027.6205**

1. Young adults' library services—Periodicals 2. Children's libraries—Periodicals 3. Books—Reviews
ISSN 0894-2498

Quarterly. Formerly Top of the News

"As a source for ideas and critical thinking on issues of concern to librarians serving children and young adults, this journal is excellent. . . . The articles are

Journal of Youth Services in Libraries—*Continued*
written for the most part by practicing librarians and reflect the reality of library work with young people." Katz. Mag for Sch Libr

027.8 School libraries

American Association of School Librarians
Information power; guidelines for school library media programs; prepared by the American Association of School Librarians and Association for Educational Communications and Technology. American Lib. Assn.; Association for Educ. Communications & Technology 1988 171p il pa $12.95 **027.8**

1. School libraries 2. Instructional materials centers
ISBN 0-8389-3352-1 LC 88-3480

Replaces Media programs: district and school, published 1975

"The book begins with the mission statement—to ensure that students and staff are effective users of ideas and information—and lists five challenges that library media specialists face. Following are individual chapters, complete with helpful bibliographies, that discuss programs; roles and responsibilities; leadership, planning, and management; personnel; resources and equipment; facilities; and district, regional and state leadership." Booklist

Includes bibliography

Anderson, Pauline, 1918-
Planning school library media facilities; [by] Pauline H. Anderson. Library Professional Publs. 1990 260p $32.50; pa $22 **027.8**

1. School libraries 2. Instructional materials centers
ISBN 0-208-02253-8; 0-208-02254-6 (pa) LC 89-13801

The author begins "with political planning, moves on to needs assessment, and then covers the specifics of developing a plan, working with an architect, contracting, moving, and having a grand opening. Her entire discussion is grounded in (applause!) the curricular framework of *Information Power* [entered above]." Booklist

Includes bibliographic references

Jay, Hilda L., 1921-
Developing library-museum partnerships to serve young people; [by] Hilda L. Jay and M. Ellen Jay. Library Professional Publs. 1984 180p $25; pa $19.50 **027.8**

1. Libraries and schools 2. Museums and schools
ISBN 0-208-01941-3; 0-208-01921-9 (pa) LC 84-9682

This "handbook suggests ways to coordinate library-museum partnerships, highlight museum resources in the card catalog, and take advantage of existing museum programs. The bulk of the book offers more than 100 models of curricular tie-ins using museum resources on a wide range of topics, from 'scrimshaw' to 'solar energy.' . . . The authors' broad definition of museums . . . will help interested librarians to recognize exciting resources available in their own communities. A helpful bibliography is appended." Booklist

Smith, Jane Bandy
Library media center programs for middle schools: a curriculum-based approach. American Lib. Assn. 1988 150p pa $24.95 **027.8**

1. School libraries 2. Instructional materials centers
ISBN 0-8389-0500-5 LC 88-7762

"This is a no-nonsense handbook for implementing the library media center professional guidelines covered in *Information Power: Guidelines for School Library Media Programs* [entered above]. . . . Leaning heavily upon the principle of instructional design, the author gives practical, objective instructions for planning, implementing, and evaluating multifaceted school library media services for middle schools." Booklist

Van Orden, Phyllis J.
The collection program in schools; concepts, practices, and information sources. Libraries Unlimited 1988 xxi, 347p $27.50 **027.8**

1. School libraries
ISBN 0-87287-572-5 LC 87-33892

"The book is divided into three major parts, the first concerned with the library facility, the second with the selection of materials for the collection, and the third with administrative details." Voice Youth Advocates

Includes bibliographies

027.805 School libraries—Serial publications

Library Talk; the magazine for elementary school libraries. Linworth Pub. $35 per year **027.805**

1. School libraries—Periodicals

Bimonthly. First published 1988

Provides articles, tips and ideas for day-to-day school library management. Each issue highlights a particular concern of the school librarian

School Library Journal; the magazine of children's, young adult, and school libraries. Bowker $59 per year **027.805**

1. School libraries—Periodicals 2. Books—Reviews
ISSN 0362-8930

Monthly. First published 1954 with title: Junior Libraries

"This is the leading magazine for childrens' and young adult public librarians and school librarians. The articles are timely, well edited, and full of information. Besides the feature articles, the journal includes a calendar, news, notes on people, a checklist of inexpensive pamphlets, posters, and the like, and lots of reviews, concisely written and evaluative. . . . Besides reviews of books, SLJ provides reviews of micro software and audiovisuals. This is an absolutely essential purchase for all libraries

School Library Journal—*Continued*
serving children and/or young adults." Katz. Mag for Libr. 6th edition

School Library Media Annual. Libraries Unlimited lib bdg $29.50 **027.805**

1. School libraries—Yearbooks 2. Instructional materials centers—Yearbooks
ISSN 0739-7712

Annual. First published 1983

Provides "background information for media specialists at all levels, teachers, reference librarians, and other individuals or groups needing professional resources and covers important events, issues, concepts, and trends." Am Ref Books Annu, 1984

School Library Media Quarterly. American Lib. Assn. $35 per year **027.805**

1. School libraries—Periodicals 2. Instructional materials centers—Periodicals
ISSN 0278-4823

Quarterly. First published 1972 with title: School Media Quarterly, as a successor to School Libraries

"Journal of the American Association of School Librarians"

"This is an attractive and well-edited publication. Each issue of 75 or more pages includes five or six articles as well as numerous regular departments including news and notes on people and publications, readers' queries, an idea exchange, reviews of professional books, and software reviews. The articles are well written and range from the practical . . . to theoretical. . . . Although not as comprehensive as *School Library Journal* in news coverage and reviews, this journal . . . is an essential for school library collections." Katz. Mag for Sch Libr

028 Reading and use of other information media

Bodart-Talbot, Joni

Booktalk! 2-3; booktalking for all ages and audiences. Wilson, H.W. 1985-1988 2v ea pa $30 **028**

1. Books and reading
ISBN 0-8242-0716-5 (v2); 0-8242-0764-5 (v3)

First published 1980 with title: Booktalk! booktalking and school visiting for young adult audiences

Volume three has subtitle: More booktalks for all ages and audiences, and contains a combined index to talks in both Booktalk! 2 and 3

The author "explains what booktalking is, and how and why to do it. The information and advice are presented clearly and with much enthusiasm. The information ranges from how to make contacts with the schools to suggestions concerning what to wear while booktalking. At the end of the book are lists of the booktalks by age level and by subject as well as a list of short films that can be used in programs. Bodart does an excellent job of presenting her ideas as well as those of other librarians from around the country." Voice Youth Advocates

Rochman, Hazel

Tales of love and terror; booktalking the classics, old and new. American Lib. Assn. 1987 120p pa $15.95 **028**

1. Books and reading 2. Literature—Stories, plots, etc.
ISBN 0-8389-0463-7 LC 86-32285

The author "demonstrates how booktalks can be used to reach a wide variety of students, and to interest individual students in many different types of books. . . . Rochman's booktalks begin with themes of nearly universal interest, such as love and terror, to provide a framework for brief descriptions of a dozen or more titles. . . . Later chapters in 'Tales of Love and Terror' demonstrate how a single book may relate to many different themes, and describe the range of books which might be used. . . . Special attention is devoted to overcoming students' usual dread of 'the classics' by showing how the classics speak to contemporary problems and ideas." Publisher's note

Thomas, Rebecca L.

Primaryplots; a book talk guide for use with readers ages 4-8. Bowker 1989 392p $39.95 **028**

1. Children's literature—Bibliography 2. Books and reading 3. Literature—Stories, plots, etc.
ISBN 0-8352-2514-3 LC 88-34054

This is "essentially a book talk guide for use with children in grades K-3. It includes brief summaries of the books featured, information on the authors, materials and activities for book talks, lists of similar and/or related titles, audiovisuals and thematic materials." Libr J

For a fuller review see: Booklist, July, 1989

028.1 Reviews of books and other media

The **Best** in children's books; the University of Chicago guide to children's literature, 1966-1972—1979-1984; written and edited by Zena Sutherland. University of Chicago Press 1973-1986 3v **028.1**

1. Children's literature—Bibliography 2. Books and reading—Best books 3. Books—Reviews
LC 85-31820

Successor to: Good books for children; a selection of outstanding children's books published 1950-65, compiled by Mary K. Eakin, available for $25 (ISBN 0-226-17916-8)

Volumes available are: 1966-1972 $25 (ISBN 0-226-78057-0); 1973-1978 $25 (ISBN 0-226-78059-7); 1979-1984 $35 (ISBN 0-226-78060-0)

Each volume covers 1400 titles "taken from 'The Bulletin of the Center for Children's Books.' Each listing denotes plot, type of illustration, reading level and/or special interest reader, and identifies titles of special distinction." Am Ref Books Annu, 1987

Booklist. American Lib. Assn. $56 per year **028.1**

1. Books—Reviews 2. Books and reading—Best books
ISSN 0006-7385

Booklist—*Continued*

Semimonthly September through June; monthly July and August. First published 1905 with title: A.L.A. Booklist. Merged with Subscription Books Bulletin in 1956

"*Booklist's* clear organizational format facilitates selective scanning. Only recommended titles are reviewed, allowing the reader a quick, high-quality overview of the best in new books. . . . Regular sections review new books for young adults and children and survey the latest films, videos, classroom filmstrips, and selected, educational microcomputer software. . . . An inserted section, 'Reference Books Bulletin,' appearing in each issue [and available in an annual cumulation for $22.50] constitutes a separate publication with longer profiles of major reference works and more abbreviated entries on continuations, supplements, and serials. *Booklist* is an essential and increasingly valuable selection tool for public and school libraries." Katz. Mag for Libr. 6th edition

Bulletin of the Center for Children's Books. University of Chicago Press $29 per year **028.1**

1. Books—Reviews 2. Children's literature—Reviews—Periodicals
ISSN 0008-9036

Monthly except August. First published 1945 for the University of Chicago, Graduate Library School

Each issue "reviews about 70 fiction and nonfiction works in brief and primarily descriptive terms, reserving criticism for the designated rating, which ranges from 'recommended' to 'unusual appeal.' . . . The quality of this tool is consistently satisfactory in its choice of titles for both school and leisure reading requirements." Katz. Mag for Sch Libr

Children's book review index. Gale Res. $95 **028.1**

1. Books—Reviews—Indexes 2. Children's literature—Reviews—Indexes LC 75-27408

A five volume master cumulation, 1965-1984 (ISBN 0-8103-2046-0) is available for $375

Annual. First published 1975

Based on Book Review Index, "each annual volume of 'CBRI' consists of all entries and review citations for juvenile books in the 'BRI' database for that year. Each entry lists author, title, and review citations from over 100 periodicals. Includes a list of periodicals indexed and a title index." Wynar. Guide to Ref Books for Sch Media Cent. 3rd edition

Gillespie, John Thomas, 1928-

Juniorplots 3: a book talk guide for use with readers ages 12-16; by John T. Gillespie with Corinne J. Naden. Bowker 1987 352p $29.95 **028.1**

1. Books—Reviews 2. Literature—Stories, plots, etc. 3. Books and reading
ISBN 0-8352-2367-1 LC 87-27305

Presents summaries of eighty fiction and nonfiction titles divided by eight basic behavioral themes

Juniorplots: a book talk manual for teachers and librarians; by John Gillespie and Diana Lembo. Bowker 1967 222p $29.95 **028.1**

1. Books—Reviews 2. Literature—Stories, plots, etc. 3. Books and reading
ISBN 0-3352-0063-9 LC 67-18146

Contains plot summaries of eighty books to be used in book talk with young people

More juniorplots: a guide for teachers and librarians; by John T. Gillespie. Bowker 1977 xxv, 253p $29.95 **028.1**

1. Books—Reviews 2. Literature—Stories, plots, etc. 3. Books and reading
ISBN 0-8352-1002-2 LC 77-8786

This volume analyzes seventy-two titles organized under nine developmental goals associated with adolescence

Parents' Choice: a review of children's media. Parents' Choice Foundation $15 per year **028.1**

1. Children's literature—Reviews—Periodicals 2. Audiovisual materials—Reviews

Quarterly. First published 1979

This most important feature of *Parent's Choice* is the well-balanced reviews of children's media. Selection guidance is provided for parents and librarians on books, TV programs, movies, videos, computer software, music, toys, and games. . . . Annotated bibliographies provide an opportunity for further research. Articles are entertaining and often provide helpful hints on how to contribute informally to a child's education. The advisory board is comprised of eminent professors, authors, poets, and publishers." Katz. Mag for Sch Libr

Spirt, Diana L.

Introducing bookplots 3; a book talk guide for use with readers ages 8-12. Bowker 1988 xxi, 352p $39.95 **028.1**

1. Books—Reviews 2. Literature—Stories, plots, etc. 3. Books and reading
ISBN 0-8352-2345-0 LC 87-37513

"This is a sequel to the author's *Introducing Books* (1970) and *Introducing More Books* (1978) and includes books published from 1979 to 1986. . . . Each of the entries for the 81 featured titles includes paragraphs on plot summary, thematic analysis, discussion materials, and related materials." Booklist

The **Web**; edited and distributed by Charlotte Huck & Janet Hickman. Ohio State Univ. $6 per year **028.1**

1. Books—Reviews 2. Children's literature—Reviews—Periodicals

Quarterly. First published 1976

This publication sponsored by Ohio State University's education department "is outstanding for two reasons. First and foremost, the book reviews are excellent. Here is not only the opinion of the reviewer, but more often than not comments by students who read the works. Second, each issue is tied to a theme, or a web, which suggests books suitable for the theme and for related

The Web—*Continued*
curriculum. Normally the focus is on a topical item, from the weather to national holidays. All of this is offered in a modest, yet attractive package." Katz. Mag for Sch Libr

028.5 Reading and use of other information media by children and young adults

Anderson, Celia Catlett, 1936-
Nonsense literature for children; Aesop to Seuss; [by] Celia Catlett Anderson and Marilyn Fain Apseloff; foreword by William Cole; afterword by Nancy Willard. Library Professional Publs. 1989 273p il $32.50 **028.5**

1. Children's literature—History and criticism
ISBN 0-208-02161-2 LC 88-27108

"After defining nonsense as 'not the absence of sense but a clever subversion of it that heightens rather than destroys meaning,' the authors trace the history of verse and prose nonsense literature from the Greek dramatists down to such twentieth practitioners as Charles Addams and Nancy Willard. Other chapters discuss the benefits of nonsense, the philosophy and appeal of nonsense, nonsense creatures, didacticism and nonsense illustrations. Contributors discuss the psychological aspects of nonsense, Sesame Street and the theater of the absurd. An important book for all who work with children." Child Book Rev Serv

Includes bibliographies

The **Arbuthnot** lectures, 1970-1979/1980-1989; [by] Association for Library Service to Children, American Library Association. American Lib. Assn. 1980-1990 2v **028.5**

1. Children's literature—History and criticism

Analyzed in Essay and general literature index

Volumes available are: 1970-1979 $15 (ISBN 0-8389-3240-1); 1980-1989 pa $25 (ISBN 0-8389-3388-2)

These volumes contain lectures presented in honor of May Hill Arbuthnot by twenty distinguished international authorities on children's literature. Among the lecturers are John Rowe Townsend, Jean Fritz, Sheila Egoff, Virginia Betancourt, Fritz Eichenberg, and Aidan Chambers

Ashe, Rosalind
Children's literary houses; famous dwellings in children's fiction; [by] Rosalind Ashe and Lisa Tuttle; researched by Talia Rodgers. Facts on File 1984 unp il $17.95 (3-5) **028.5**

1. Houses in literature 2. Children's literature—History and criticism
ISBN 0-87196-971-8 LC 84-10143

Describes and provides illustrations, maps, and plans of eight famous fictional houses featured in David Copperfield, Little Women, Robinson Crusoe, Alice in Wonderland, Charlotte's Web and other classic stories

Bauer, Caroline Feller, 1935-
This way to books; drawings by Lynn Gates. Wilson, H.W. 1983 363p il $40 **028.5**

1. Books and reading 2. Children's literature
ISBN 0-8242-0678-9 LC 82-19985

"Designed to involve children in books, this compendium is chock-full of ideas for programs, booktalks, games, crafts, and exhibits. Bauer's upbeat tone lends enthusiasm, and her numerous suggestions, which include easy-to-implement activities, short poems, directions for crafts, recipes, and unusual but effective bibliographies, will inspire readers with new ideas. . . . Teachers, librarians, and other adults working with children will find the collection worthwhile and helpful as a springboard to their own variations." Booklist

Caldecott Medal books, 1938-1957; with the artist's acceptance papers & related material chiefly from The Horn Book Magazine; edited by Bertha Mahony Miller and Elinor Whitney Field. Horn Bk. 1957 329p il $22.95 **028.5**

1. Children's literature—History and criticism 2. Illustrators
ISBN 0-87675-001-3 LC 57-11582

"Horn Book papers"

"A companion volume to the editors' 'Newbery Medal books: 1922-1955' [entered below]. A short study of Randolph Caldecott, for whom the award is named, prefaces the chronological listing of the award books. With this listing are given the acceptance speech of each artist and a biographical sketch of each." Booklist

Followed by: Newbery and Caldecott Medal books: 1956-1965—1966-1975, entered below

Carpenter, Humphrey
The Oxford companion to children's literature; [by] Humphrey Carpenter and Mari Prichard. Oxford Univ. Press 1984 586p il $45 **028.5**

1. Children's literature—Dictionaries
ISBN 0-19-211582-0 LC 83-15130

"One volume work with brief critiques of authors illustrators, books, characters, and radio and television programs. Largely British in coverage of materials but does include most Newbery winners as well as well-known American, Australian and Canadian authors. Contemporary and historical subjects related to children's literature are examined." N Y Public Libr. Ref Books for Child Collect

Chambers, Aidan, 1934-
Booktalk: occasional writing on literature and children. Harper & Row 1985 183p $13.95 **028.5**

1. Children's literature—History and criticism
ISBN 0-06-021249-7 LC 85-45389

"A Charlotte Zolotow book"

"Selected from the author's work of the past decade is a challenging collection of lectures, articles, and essays centered on the human significance of Story—its indispensability and its vital connection with language as

Chambers, Aidan, 1934-—*Continued*
well as the ways of telling it and the process of reading it." J Youth Serv Libr

This "book works on two levels: as a critical commentary on children's books and writers and as a model for book discussion." Horn Book

Introducing books to children. 2nd ed, completely rev and expanded. Horn Bk. 1983 223p $16.95 **028.5**

1. Books and reading 2. Reading 3. Children's literature—History and criticism
ISBN 0-87675-284-9 LC 82-21357

First published 1973 by Heinemann Educational Books

"In a series of essays, the British author, critic, and contributor to 'Horn Book' suggests ideas, methods, and useful approaches to linking books and children." Booklist

Includes bibliographies

Children's literature review; excerpts from reviews, criticism, and commentary on books for children. Gale Res. il ea $92 **028.5**

1. Children's literature—History and criticism 2. Books—Reviews

First published 1976. Frequency varies

"Each volume includes from 14 to 20 authors, arranged alphabetically, giving for each: a biographical-critical introduction, the author's commentary; general commentary excerpted from articles; titles, arranged chronologically; and citations for original sources. A cumulative index to authors, titles, and critics is in each volume." Wynar. Guide to Ref Books for Sch Media Cent. 3d edition

Cook, Elizabeth

The ordinary and the fabulous; an introduction to myths, legends and fairy tales. 2nd ed. Cambridge Univ. Press 1976 xx, 182p $27.95; pa $13.95 **028.5**

1. Children's literature—History and criticism 2. Books and reading 3. Storytelling
ISBN 0-521-20825-4; 0-521-09961-7 (pa) LC 75-7213

First published 1962

The author's "discussions include the significance and values found in myths and fairy tales; suggest various myths for different age groups with comments on children's responses; deal with practical problems of the storyteller, and reproduce and dissect parallel passages from children's book versions and their original sources. The annotated selective bibliography, though excellent, is British oriented." Booklist

Crosscurrents of criticism; Horn book essays, 1968-1977; selected and edited by Paul Heins. Horn Bk. 1977 359p $14.95 **028.5**

1. Children's literature—History and criticism
ISBN 0-87675-034-X LC 77-24256

Analyzed in Essay and general literature index

Companion volume to: A Horn Book Sampler on children's books and reading and Horn Book Reflections on children's books and reading, both entered below

A collection of 45 essays selected from The Horn Book Magazine. "Articles grouped around topics such as status of children's literature, classification, standards, current trends, fantasy, humor, the historical scene, internationalism, translation concerns, and books and authors offer a wide diversification of thought and opinion in the field of criticism. Index to authors and titles appended." Booklist

Egoff, Sheila A.

Worlds within; children's fantasy from the Middle Ages to today. American Lib. Assn. 1988 339p $35 **028.5**

1. Children's literature—History and criticism 2. Fantastic fiction—History and criticism
ISBN 0-8389-0494-7 LC 88-10058

"Following an opening chapter on the roots, substance, types, and value of fantasy for children [Egoff] examines the genre chronologically. The fluid text, for the most part, is divided by decade, starting with the Middle Ages and continuing into the 1980s. In her discussion, Egoff reflects on more than 375 novels, often comparing and contrasting them with other books of merit and commenting on the book's contribution, uniqueness, and role as trendsetter." Booklist

England, Claire

ChildView: evaluating and reviewing materials for children; [by] Claire England, Adele M. Fasick. Libraries Unlimited 1987 207p il $24.50 **028.5**

1. Books and reading 2. Books—Reviews 3. Children's literature—History and criticism
ISBN 0-87287-519-9 LC 87-2635

This is a "textbook on the theory and practice of evaluating and reviewing material for children. The first part of [the] book, which deals with establishing the environment, discusses in individual chapters: aspects of children's development, issues in reviewing materials for children, the context of reviewing, and the craft of reviewing. . . . The second half of the book is then devoted to dealing with a variety of formats such as: materials for early childhood; traditional materials; fiction; poetry; biography and history; informational materials; dictionaries and encyclopedias; and nonprint materials." Wilson Libr Bull

"A well-written, thoughtfully constructed presentation that will be helpful in children's literature courses, for in-service training, and as a self-help guide for would-be and current reviewers and selectors of children's books." Booklist

Includes bibliographies

Field, Carolyn W., 1916-

Values in selected children's books of fiction and fantasy; [by] Carolyn W. Field, Jaqueline Shachter Weiss. Library Professional Publs. 1987 298p $27.50 **028.5**

1. Children's literature—History and criticism
ISBN 0-208-02100-0 LC 87-3874

Field, Carolyn W., 1916—*Continued*

This "selection tool identifies more than 700 books of fiction and fantasy that have positive values inherent to their story lines. . . . The 10 referenced areas are cooperation, courage, friendship and love of animals, friendship and love of people, humaneness, ingenuity, loyalty, maturing, responsibility, and self-respect. Each section categorizes books into age ranges . . . and concludes with a short summary and bibliographic references. Plots are lucidly described with attention to the emphasized value for which each book has been listed. Child appeal has also been considered. . . . Librarians as well as parents and other adults looking for reading materials that support positive values but are not didactic will want to add this excellent title to their collections." Booklist

Hazard, Paul, 1878-1944

Books, children, and men; translated by Marguerite Mitchell, with an introduction by Sheila A. Egoff. 5th ed. Horn Bk. 1983 196p pa $11.95 **028.5**

1. Children's literature—History and criticism 2. Books and reading
ISBN 0-87675-059-5 LC 82-25851

Original French edition, 1932. First United States edition, 1944

A series of essays in which the author discusses children's books in terms of the cultures of various peoples

Includes bibliography

Hearne, Betsy Gould

Choosing books for children; a commonsense guide; [by] Betsy Hearne. rev, expanded, and updated. Delacorte Press 1990 228p il $16.95; pa $9.95 **028.5**

1. Books and reading 2. Children's literature—History and criticism 3. Children's literature—Bibliography
ISBN 0-385-30084-0; 0-385-30108-1 (pa)
LC 89-71459

First published 1981

This "conversational guide includes an excellent chapter on censorship and thoughtful recommendations for selecting books for young people at different developmental stages. A treat for librarians as well as for its intended audience of parents, grandparents, etc." Booklist

Includes bibliographic references

Horn Book reflections on children's books and reading; selected from eighteen years of The Horn Book Magazine, 1949-1966; edited by Elinor Whitney Field. Horn Bk. 1969 367p pa $6.95 **028.5**

1. Children's literature—History and criticism
ISBN 0-87675-033-1 LC 75-89793

Companion volume to: A Horn Book sampler on children's books and reading, entered below, and Cross-currents of criticism: Horn Book essays, 1968-1977, entered above

This collection of "articles and essays relating to various aspects of children's reading and literature includes material by authors, illustrators, parents, teachers, and librarians." Booklist

A **Horn** Book sampler on children's books and reading; selected from twenty-five years of The Horn Book Magazine, 1924-1948; edited by Norma R. Fryatt; introduction by Bertha Mahony Miller. Horn Bk. 1959 261p $9.50; pa $6.95 **028.5**

1. Children's literature—History and criticism
ISBN 0-87675-030-7; 0-87675-031-5 (pa)
LC 59-15028

Analyzed in Essay and general literature index

"Articles, editorials, book reviews, and a few poems reprinted from the 'Horn Book' from its founding in 1924 to 1948. The sampler includes essays by authors on how certain of their stories came to be written, evaluations of the work of such illustrators as Kate Greenaway, Arthur Rackham, and Leslie Brooke, criticisms of single books and of trends in children's literature, discussions of fairy tales and books for small children, and a group of papers addressed to parents." Booklist

Huck, Charlotte S.

Children's literature in the elementary school; [by] Charlotte S. Huck, Susan Hepler, Janet Hickman. 4th ed. Holt, Rinehart & Winston 1987 753p il $29.95 **028.5**

1. Children's literature—History and criticism
ISBN 0-03-041770-8 LC 86-29467

First published 1961

"Standard text covering the use of children's literature in the classroom. Various chapters cover highlights of basic genres; includes good bibliographies." N Y Public Libr. Ref Books for Child Collect

Jordan, Alice Mabel

From Rollo to Tom Sawyer, and other papers; [by] Alice M. Jordan; decorations by Nora S. Unwin. Horn Bk. 1948 160p pa $6.95 **028.5**

1. Children's literature—History and criticism
ISBN 0-87675-058-7 LC 48-9996

Analyzed in Essay and general literature index

"Three essays in the book concern children's magazines of the Nineteenth Century, one is a lecture given by Miss Jordan in 1940, and five essays are about important [19th century] authors and editors of children's books." SLJ

Kimmel, Margaret Mary
For reading out loud! a guide to sharing books with children; [by] Margaret Mary Kimmel & Elizabeth Segel; drawings by Michael Hays; foreword by Fred M. Rogers. rev & expanded ed. Delacorte Press 1988 266p il $16.95; Dell pa $6.95 **028.5**

1. Books and reading 2. Children's literature—Bibliography 3. Books—Reviews
ISBN 0-385-29660-6; 0-440-52670-1 (pa)
LC 87-30515

First published 1983

"Practical tips couple with descriptions of more than 300 child-tested titles to help librarians, teachers, parents, and other adults wanting to find quality read-aloud titles to bring children and books together. . . . An invaluable offering from two top-notch professionals." Booklist

Kobrin, Beverly
Eyeopeners! how to choose and use children's books about real people, places, and things; photographs by Richard Steinheimer and Shirley Burman. Viking 1988 317p il o.p.; Penguin Bks. paperback available $7.95 **028.5**

1. Children's literature—History and criticism 2. Books and reading
ISBN 0-14-046830-7 (pa) LC 88-40115

"Following an introduction by Jim Trelease and several short chapters on promoting, using and choosing good books, a bibliography of more than 500 titles appears. Arranged by subject, the selections include complete imprint information and meaningful annotations, as well as tips for linking the books to other offerings. Kobrin's enthusiasm is contagious, and her knowledge of nonfiction is stimulating and far reaching. Her book provides a quick reference source for librarians, teachers, parents, and other adults working with children." Booklist

National Council of Teachers of English. Committee on Literature in the Elementary Language Arts
Raising readers; a guide to sharing literature with young children; [by] Linda Leonard Lamme [et al.] Walker & Co. 1980 xxiii, 200p $11.95 **028.5**

1. Books and reading
ISBN 0-8027-0654-1 LC 80-80454

"The text, divided into four main chapters (sharing literature with your infant, your toddler, your prereader, and your beginning reader), discusses various aspects of the age level, offers practical advice and ways to motivate readers, and presents a selected bibliography of home libraries, characteristics of good literature, and storytelling activities are some of the other topics covered in this worthwhile book." Booklist

Newbery and Caldecott Medal books, 1966-1975; with acceptance papers, biographies, and related material chiefly from The Horn Book magazine; edited by Lee Kingman. Horn Bk. 1975 xx, 321p il $22.95 **028.5**

1. Newbery Medal books 2. Caldecott Medal books 3. Children's literature—History and criticism 4. Authors 5. Illustrators
ISBN 0-87675-003-X LC 75-20167

Volume for 1956-1965 o.p.

"Brings up to date the volumes, 'Newbery Medal books: 1922-1955 [entered below], Caldecott Medal books: 1938-1957,' and Newbery and Caldecott Medal books: 1956-1965 [entered above].' Gives for each Newbery or Caldecott award winner his acceptance speech, a biographical note, and a book note. An excerpt from each Newbery book gives an example of the writer's style; a sample illustration from each Caldecott book is supplemented by notes on size, medium, printing process, number of illustrations and type used." Choice

Newbery and Caldecott Medal books, 1976-1985; with acceptance papers, biographies, and related material chiefly from The Horn Book magazine; edited by Lee Kingman. Horn Bk. 1986 358p il $24.95 **028.5**

1. Newbery Medal books 2. Caldecott Medal books 3. Children's literature—History and criticism 4. Authors 5. Illustrators
ISBN 0-87675-004-8 LC 86-15223

This volume "compiles the winning speeches, biographies and book notes for the 1976 through 1985 awards. It includes essays by Barbara Bader, Ethel Heins and Zena Sutherland." Bookbird

Newbery Medal books, 1922-1955; with their authors' acceptance papers & related material chiefly from The Horn Book magazine; edited by Bertha Mahony Miller and Elinor Whitney Field. Horn Bk. 1955 458p il $22.95 **028.5**

1. Newbery Medal books 2. Children's literature—History and criticism 3. Authors
ISBN 0-87675-000-5 LC 55-13968

Companion volume to: Caldecott Medal books, 1938-1957, entered above

"Largely biographical notes about award recipients and the acceptance papers." A L A. Ref Sources for Small & Medium-sized Libr. 4th edition

Followed by: Newbery and Caldecott Medal books, 1956-1965/1976-1985 entered above

Once upon a time—: celebrating the magic of children's books in honor of the twentieth anniversary of Reading is Fundamental. Putnam 1986 64p il $14.95; pa $6.95 **028.5**

1. Books and reading 2. Children's literature 3. Authors, American 4. Illustrators
ISBN 0-399-21369-4; 0-399-21370-8 (pa)
LC 86-18715

Once upon a time—: celebrating the magic of children's books in honor of the twentieth anniversary of Reading is Fundamental—*Continued*

An illustrated collection of true and fictional anecdotes, stories, and reminiscences by well-known children's authors and illustrators about books and the experience of reading

"A distinguished group of authors, including Katherine Paterson, Judy Blume, Dr. Seuss and Virginia Hamilton, and illustrators, including Maurice Sendak, Tomie dePaola, James Marshall, Ed Young and Edward Gorey, have contributed short essays and original art to a delightful, contemplative volume about reading." N Y Times Book Rev

Only connect: readings on children's literature; edited by Sheila Egoff, G.T. Stubbs, and L.F. Ashley. 2nd ed. Oxford Univ. Press 1980 457p pa $14.95 **028.5**

1. Children's literature—History and criticism
ISBN 0-19-540309-6 LC 81-452868

First published 1969 and analyzed in Essay and general literature index

Among the contributors to this collection of 38 essays on children's literature are: J. R. R. Tolkien, Graham Greene, Maurice Sendak, Sylvia Engdahl and John Goldthwaite

Paterson, Katherine

The spying heart; more thoughts on reading and writing books for children. Lodestar Bks. 1989 196p $15.95; pa $8.95 **028.5**

1. Children's literature 2. Children—Books and reading
ISBN 0-525-67267-2; 0-525-67269-9 (pa) LC 88-17686

Companion volume to: Gates of excellence: on reading and writing books for children (1981)

In speeches, essays, and book reviews, the novelist Katherine Paterson discusses why she writes children's books, where her ideas come from, how she develops her characters and realistic plots, and her experiences growing up in China

"Other writers will appreciate 'Why,' in which Paterson explains why she writes for children; critics should value the keen insights she shows in her own book reviews; and her concerns about book banning are sure to be of interest to librarians. The purity of writing and clarity of thought evidenced in Paterson's children's books are equally apparent here." Booklist

Sendak, Maurice

Caldecott & Co.: notes on books and pictures. Farrar, Straus & Giroux 1988 216p il $18.95; pa $8.95 **028.5**

1. Children's literature—History and criticism 2. Illustrators
ISBN 0-374-22598-2; 0-374-52218-9 (pa) LC 87-19772

"Michael di Capua books"

A collection of 32 essays, speeches and reviews culled from the author/illustrator's critical work of the past 33 years

The author offers a "remarkably clear and consistent vision of excellence in both children's picture books and popular culture." N Y Times Book Rev

Sutherland, Zena, 1915-

Children and books; [by] Zena Sutherland, May Hill Arbuthnot; chapters contributed by Dianne L. Monson. Scott, Foresman il $28.95 **028.5**

1. Children's literature—History and criticism

First edition by May Hill Arbuthnot published 1947. Periodically revised

This work, considered "the reigning textbook in the field, also serves as a handbook for anyone who needs an overview of the subject or facts about that much-studied relationship between children and books or a list of some of the best titles in particular genres. . . . Interspersed throughout the text are 'Viewpoint' columns that give background information on specific issues. An abundance of bibliographies is provided." Wynar. Guide to Ref Books for Sch Media Cent. 3d edition

Townsend, John Rowe

A sense of story; essays on contemporary writers for children. Horn Bk. 1973 c1971 215p pa $6.95 **028.5**

1. Children's literature—History and criticism
ISBN 0-87675-276-8

First published 1971 by Lippincott and analyzed in Essay and general literature index

This introduction to the work of nineteen English-language writers for children consists of essays on L. M. Boston, John Christopher, Eleanor Estes, Leon Garfield, Madeleine L'Engle, and others. It includes brief biographical details of the writers, notes by the authors on themselves and lists of their books

A sounding of storytellers; new and revised essays on contemporary writers for children. Lippincott 1979 218p $15.25 **028.5**

1. Children's literature—History and criticism
ISBN 0-397-31882-0 LC 79-2418

Analyzed in Essay and general literature index

The author has taken seven of the nineteen essays from his earlier book: A sense of story (entered above), and combined them with seven new essays. The new essays included deal with the work of Nina Bawden, Vera and Bill Cleaver, Peter Dickinson, Virginia Hamilton, E. L. Konigsburg, Penelope Lively and Jill Paton Walsh

Written for children; an outline of English-language children's literature. 3rd rev ed. Lippincott 1988 384p il $18.95 **028.5**

1. Children's literature—History and criticism
ISBN 0-397-32298-4

First published 1965 in the United Kingdom; first United States edition published 1967 by Lothrop, Lee & Shepard Books

Townsend, John Rowe—*Continued*

A survey of the development of children's books in England, the United States, Australia, and other parts of the English-speaking world. The author covers fiction as well as poetry and picture books

Includes bibliography

Trelease, Jim

The new read-aloud handbook. 2nd rev ed. Penguin Bks. 1989 xxvi, 290p il pa $9.95 **028.5**

1. Books and reading 2. Children's literature—Bibliography

ISBN 0-14-046881-1 LC 89-31925

First published 1982 with title: The read-aloud handbook

"Trelease shares his firm belief in books. A pep talk, with new research on the value of reading aloud and new methods for its encouragement, is followed by the 'Treasury of Read-Alouds,' featuring 300 children's books . . . all nicely annotated and with notes leading to even more titles. An essential library book, of value to parents and professionals." Booklist

Yolen, Jane

Touch magic; fantasy, faerie and folklore in the literature of childhood; Jane Yolen. Philomel Bks. 1981 96p il $12.95 **028.5**

1. Children's literature—History and criticism 2. Folklore

ISBN 0-399-20830-5 LC 81-10578

Contents: How basic is shazam?; The lively fossil; Once upon a time; The eye and the ear; Touch magic; The mask on the lapel; Tough magic; Here there be dragons; The gift of tongues; An inlet for apple pie

"This should be required reading for teachers, librarians, and parents especially. The historical background of folk literature is absorbing reading." Child Book Rev Serv

Includes bibliography

028.505 Children's reading—Serial publications

Bookbird. ARNIS $14 per year **028.505**

1. Children's literature—Periodicals 2. Books—Reviews 3. Books and reading—Best books

ISSN 0006-7377

Quarterly. First published 1962. Publisher varies

Issued by the International Board on Books for Young People and the International Institute for Children's Literature and Reading Research

"This English-language journal provides news and literary essays on the most pertinent activities of the 16 countries that contribute to this worldwide effort. Articles, criticism, and occasional brief book reviews survey the best of children's literature." Katz. Mag for Sch Libr

Five Owls; a publication for readers personally and professionally involved in children's literature. 2004 Sheridan Ave. S., Minneapolis, MN 55405 $18 per year **028.505**

1. Children's literature—Periodicals 2. Books—Reviews

ISSN 0892-6735

Bimonthly. First published 1986

Contains articles on children's literature, bibliographies, and reviews of recent books

The **Horn** Book Guide to Children's and Young Adult Books. Horn Bk. $50 per year **028.505**

1. Children's literature—Periodicals 2. Books—Reviews

ISSN 1044-405X

Biannual. First published 1990

A review "of all hardcover trade children's books published in the U.S. during the previous six months. Each issue . . . contain[s] brief critical evaluations of about 1500 books, along with ordering information and numerical ratings. . . . Fiction is organized by age categories; nonfiction is grouped by subject under general Dewey Decimal System headings. Author, illustrator, title and subject indices are included." Publ Wkly

"Due to the brevity of the annotations, this guide should not serve as a sole source for selecting books. . . . However, for libraries that order at a slower pace, or wish an overview for additional purchasing, the guide could supplement other review sources and offer useful information for ordering." J Youth Serv Libr

The **Horn** Book Magazine. Horn Bk. $36 per year **028.505**

1. Children's literature—Periodicals 2. Books and reading—Best books 3. Books—Reviews

ISSN 0018-5078

Bimonthly. First published 1924 with title: The Horn Book

"One of the oldest, most reputable review journals for children's literature and educational materials. Every issue contains highly readable articles. . . . However, the reviews are the 'meat' of this magazine, covering new editions and reissues, suggested paperback purchases, books in Spanish, and even occasional recommendations for storytelling or exhibition-viewing purposes. . . . *Horn Book* is an authoritative tool for professionals who work with preschool to junior high school readers." Katz. Mag for Libr. 6th edition

The **Kobrin** Letter; concerning children's books about real people, places and things. 732 Greer Rd., Palo Alto, CA 94303 $12 per year **028.505**

1. Children's literature—Periodicals 2. Books—Reviews

ISSN 0271-1990

Seven issues a year. First published 1980

Each four-page issue contains reviews of approximately fifteen recommended titles on a particular topic. Full bibliographic information and age level are given

031 American general encyclopedic works

Compton's encyclopedia and fact-index. Compton's Learning 26v il maps apply to publisher for price **031**

1. Encyclopedias and dictionaries

Also available CD-ROM version, Compton's MultiMedia encyclopedia

First published 1922 with title: Compton's pictured encyclopedia. Frequently revised

Supplemented by: Compton yearbook

"An encyclopedia for young adults, ages nine through eighteen, for home and school use, with emphasis on practical and curriculum-related information. Among the . . . contributors are scholars, writers, and notable librarians. Arrangement is letter by letter and each volume . . . is divided into two parts. The illustrated 'Fact Index' at the back refers the readers to text and illustrations in the volume at hand and to information contained elsewhere in the set." A L A. Ref Sources for Small & Medium-sized Libr. 4th edition

For a fuller review see: Booklist, Oct. 15, 1989

Merit students encyclopedia. Macmillan Educ. Co. 20v il maps apply to publisher for price **031**

1. Encyclopedias and dictionaries

First published 1967 by Crowell-Collier Educational Corporation. Frequently revised

This work "is intended to serve the student from grades 5 through high school. The scope and content of the set is based on analysis of published curriculum material; good subject balance is maintained. Individual articles are written for grade levels at which they are expected to be taught, without controlled vocabulary. . . . Articles are accurate, objective, and clearly written. . . . *Merit* has been commended for its balanced treatment of controversial subjects." Wynar. Guide to Ref Books for Sch Media Cent. 3d edition

For a fuller review see: Booklist, Oct. 1, 1990

The **New** book of knowledge; the children's encyclopedia. Grolier 21v il maps apply to publisher for price **031**

1. Encyclopedias and dictionaries

First published 1966 as successor to: The Book of knowledge. Frequently revised

Supplemented by: The New book of knowledge annual

"Curriculum-oriented, it is designed and organized to be especially useful in meeting children's curriculum and out-of-school needs for information. Its broad coverage of well-illustrated general information is presented in language easily comprehended by elementary school children. Superbly illustrated, highly reliable, current encyclopedia that provides coverage of general information for beginning users. Dictionary Index with encapsulated fact entries." N Y Public Libr. Ref Books for Child Collect

For a fuller review see: Booklist, Oct. 1, 1990

The **World** Book encyclopedia. World Bk. 22v il maps apply to publisher for price **031**

1. Encyclopedias and dictionaries

Also available CD-ROM Information finder

First published 1917-1918 by Field Enterprises. Frequently revised

Supplemented by: The World Book year book

"Curriculum-oriented, this superior encyclopedia is well-edited and produced to meet the reference and informational needs of students from grade four through high school. Long standing tradition of excellence for readability, accuracy, authoritativeness, objectivity, judicious and extensive use of outstanding graphics and timeliness." N Y Public Libr. Ref Books for Child Collect

For a fuller review see: Booklist, Oct. 1, 1990

031.02 American books of miscellaneous facts

Information please almanac, atlas & yearbook. Houghton Mifflin $12.95; pa $6.95 **031.02**

1. Almanacs 2. Statistics—Yearbooks 3. United States—Statistics LC 47-845

Annual. First published 1947 by Doubleday. Publisher varies

"An almanac of miscellaneous information, with a general topical arrangement and a subject index. Includes extensive statistical and historical information on the United States; chronology of the year's events; statistical and historical descriptions of the various countries of the world; sports records; motion picture, theatrical, and literary awards, etc., and many kinds of general information. Sources for many of the tables and special articles are noted. A 'People' section lists many celebrated persons, giving profession, place and date of birth, and death date if deceased." Sheehy. Guide to Ref Books. 10th edition

Kane, Joseph Nathan, 1899-

Famous first facts: a record of first happenings, discoveries, and inventions in American history. 4th ed expanded & rev. Wilson, H.W. 1981 1350p $78 **031.02**

1. Encyclopedias and dictionaries 2. United States—History—Dictionaries

ISBN 0-8242-0661-4 LC 81-3395

First published 1933

"A classic in the ever-popular area of 'firsts' and curiosities. Kane identifies over 9,000 inventions, discoveries, and first happenings, both natural and man-made, that took place on the American continent from A.D. 1007 to the present. The main section lists each event alphabetically by subject and gives concise explanations of its significance. Source citations are provided for some, but not all entries. Location of specific information is facilitated by cross-references and four indexes: by year, month and day, names of people, and state and municipality where the event took place." Wynar. Guide to Ref Books for Sch Media Cent. 3d edition

The World almanac and book of facts. Newspaper Enterprise Assn. il maps $14.95; pa $6.95 **031.02**

1. Almanacs 2. Statistics—Yearbooks 3. United States—Statistics LC 4-3781

Also available from St. Martin's Press

Annual. First published 1868. Publisher varies

"Almanac of choice. Basic almanac format. Concentrates on year covered, giving statistical information, chronological survey. Information is in brief form. Excellent index." N Y Public Libr. Ref Books for Child Collect

032.02 English books of miscellaneous facts

The Guinness book of answers; the complete reference handbook. Guinness Bks. distributed by Facts on File il $17.95 **032.02**

1. Encyclopedias and dictionaries

First published 1978. Periodically revised

"Arranged in typical almanac style by general topics, this handbook presents information that will fulfill many reference needs. Most of the thirty sections contain a generous glossary of terms as well as useful tables, charts, and figures. . . . A generous . . . index allows easy access to the extensive information in this source. Even though it is a British publication . . . this does not detract from the value of the book, which will be used by researchers and browsers alike." SLJ [review of 1989 edition]

Guinness book of records. Facts on File il $17.95; lib bdg $21.49 **032.02**

1. Curiosities and wonders

Also available Bantam Books paperback edition $5.95

Annual. First published 1955 in the United Kingdom; in the United States 1962. Variant title: Guinness book of world records

Editors vary

"Ready reference for current record holders in all fields, some esoteric. Index provides access to information arranged in broad subject categories. Must be replaced annually." N Y Public Libr. Ref Books for Child Collect

051 American general serial publications and their indexes

Abridged Readers' guide to periodical literature. Wilson, H.W. $80 per year **051**

1. Periodicals—Indexes

ISSN 0001-334X LC 38-34737

Also available on CD-ROM

First published July 1935. Monthly except June, July, and August (The indexing for these months is included in the September issue). Permanent bound annual cumulations

An index to 68 periodicals of general interest which have been chosen by the subscribers to the index from the approximately 190 periodicals covered by the unabridged Readers' Guide to Periodical Literature. The form of indexing is the same as that used in the unabridged Readers' Guide

"Designed especially for school and small public libraries unable to afford the regular Readers' guide." Sheehy. Guide to Ref Books. 10th edition

Children's Magazine Guide; subject index to children's magazines. Bowker $33 per year **051**

1. Periodicals—Indexes

ISSN 0743-9873

Nine issues a year. First published 1949 with title: Subject index to Children's Magazines. Publisher and frequency vary

A "subject guide to selected magazines published specifically for students in elementary and junior high school grades. . . . The guide . . . indexes 36 periodicals for children and nine additional magazines for use by teachers and librarians. The ninth issue, published in August, is an annual cumulation." SLJ

Cricket; the magazine for children. Carus Corp. $29.97 **051**

1. Children's literature—Periodicals

ISSN 0090-6034

Monthly. First published 1973 by Open Court Publishing

"Children's literature, poems, stories, articles, songs, crafts, and jokes are the focus of Cricket. . . . A high-quality, tasteful publication. Contributors are internationally known authors (e.g., Eleanor Estes, Lloyd Alexander, Jean Fritz) and illustrators (David McPhail, Tomie dePaola, Steven Gammell). Each issue is done in black and white and one other color. Cricket exposes children to a large variety of writing styles and artwork in children's books." Katz. Mag for Libr. 6th edition

Highlights for Children. P.O. Box 269, Columbus, OH 43272 $19.95 per year **051**

1. Children's literature—Periodicals

ISSN 0018-165X

Eleven issues a year. First published 1946

This magazine "is intended for children of all ages . . . and carries stories, articles, and regular items appropriate to various reading and interest levels. The diversity of subject matter places this magazine among the few general-interest ones available for children. . . . [Included in each issue are] crafts and projects; puzzles, hidden pictures, and word games; and contributions from children." Richardson. Mag for Child. 2d edition

060.4 General rules of order (Parliamentary procedure)

Powers, David Guy

How to run a meeting; drawings by Anne Canevari Green. rev ed, by Mary K. Harmon. Watts 1985 61p il lib bdg $10.40 (4 and up) **060.4**

1. Parliamentary practice
ISBN 0-531-04641-9 LC 84-23441

"A First book"

First published 1967 with title: The first book of how to run a meeting

Describes how and why democratic meetings work and gives instructions on the procedures for conducting a meeting, voting, and making and amending motions

"This excellent simplified version of Robert's Rules of Order [entered below] will be of interest to any person who needs help in following correct parliamentary procedure. . . . Its straightforward presentation [is] touched with humorous cartoon illustrations. . . . Recommended as both introductory and reference material." Voice Youth Advocates

Robert, Henry Martyn, 1837-1923

The Scott, Foresman Robert's Rules of order newly revised. A new and enl ed, by Sarah Corbin Robert, with the assistance of Henry M. Robert III, William J. Evans. Scott, Foresman $18.95; pa $9.95 **060.4**

1. Parliamentary practice

A simplified paperback version with title: The new Robert's Rules of order, by Mary A. De Vries, is available from New Am. Lib. for $4.95 (ISBN 0-451-16378-8)

First published 1876 as: Pocket manual of rules of order for deliberate assemblies. Later editions have title: Robert's Rules of order

"A compendium of parliamentary law, explaining methods of organizing and conducting the business of societies, conventions, and other assemblies." A L A. Ref Sources for Small & Medium-sized Libr. 4th edition

070 News media, journalism, publishing

Gibbons, Gail

Deadline! from news to newspaper. Crowell 1987 unp il lib bdg $13.89 (1-3) **070**

1. Newspapers
ISBN 0-690-04602-2 LC 86-47654

Examines the diverse behind-the-scenes activities of a typical working day at a small daily newspaper, from morning preparations for meeting the deadline to the moment the afternoon papers leave the presses

This book "presents a clear picture of both the contents of the newspaper and technical process of printing it. . . . The people depicted are multiethnic, with both men and women filling vital positions on the paper; one employee works from a wheelchair. . . . Gibbons's thorough research is evident again. Such a base of knowledge is necessary to enable a writer to distill information in both text and illustration, presenting just the right details to illuminate the subject for younger readers." Horn Book

Leedy, Loreen, 1959-

The furry news; how to make a newspaper; written and illustrated by Loreen Leedy. Holiday House 1990 unp il lib bdg $13.95 (k-3) **070**

1. Newspapers
ISBN 0-8234-0793-4 LC 89-20094

Big Bear, Rabbit, and the other animals work hard to write, edit, and print their newspaper, "The Furry News." Includes tips for making your own newspaper and defines a number of newspaper terms

"Framing basic information about newspaper creation within a context of animals being funny, this is a light and sensible introduction to news gathering and dissemination. . . . The large full-color cartoons and silly business reinforce, rather than detract from, the engaging instruction." Bull Cent Child Books

Includes glossary

070.5 Publishing

Greenfeld, Howard

Books: from writer to reader. rev ed. Crown 1989 197p il $19.95; pa $12.95 (6 and up) **070.5**

1. Books 2. Book industries and trade 3. Printing
ISBN 0-517-56840-3; 0-517-56841-1 (pa)
LC 88-11876

First published 1976

Providing "information on every phase (editing, designing, layout, printing, binding, selling) of book production, from writer to reader, Greenfeld calls on his background as author, publisher, editor, and 'seller of books' to provide accuracy and know-how. Particular attention is paid to technological advances in the industry and today's heavy use of and dependency on computers." Booklist

Includes glossary and bibliography

070.5025 Publishing—Directories

Children's media market place; Dolores Blythe Jones, consulting editor. 3d ed. Neal-Schuman 1988 397p pa $45 **070.5025**

1. Publishers and publishing—Directories
2. Audiovisual materials—Directories
ISBN 1-55570-007-1 LC 88-60792

First edition edited by Deirdre Boyle and Stephen Calvert published 1978 by Gaylord Professional Publications

"This helpful reference tool provides information about publishers, audio-visual producers and distributors, periodicals, reviewers, wholesalers, agents, bookstores, book clubs, television programming, federal grants, awards, and other pertinent resources. Public librarians in particular will find that it answers many questions

Children's media market place—*Continued*
from parents and other adults interested in the expanding field of children's services." Booklist

070.505 Publishing—Serial publications

Publisher's Weekly; the international news magazine of book publishing. Bowker $97 per year **070.505**

1. Publishers and publishing—Periodicals 2. Books—Reviews

ISSN 0000-0019

Weekly. First published 1872

"PW is the trade journal for America's publishing and bookselling industry. Consequently, this is a major source that offers advance news about new titles; critical notes on important publications; and a useful series of forecasts, editorials, author profiles, interviews, and best-sellers lists. . . . Large announcement issues, which appear in the spring and fall, pinpoint current publishing trends. . . . The magazine provides a remarkably balanced overview, . . . of the state-of-the national (U.S.) publishing situation. Although Publishers Weekly reviews are fairly brief and often directed toward the bookseller, libraries will be missing basic information on acquisitions if they do not subscribe to this title." Katz. Mag for Libr. 6th edition

071 Journalism and newspapers—North America

Fleming, Thomas J., 1927-

Behind the headlines; the story of American newspapers. Walker & Co. 1989 154p (Walker's American history ser. for young people) $14.95; lib bdg $15.85 (5 and up) **071**

1. American newspapers 2. Reporters and reporting

ISBN 0-8027-6890-3; 0-8027-6891-1 (lib bdg)

LC 89-5690

Surveys the history of American newspapers and how reporting techniques and perceptions have changed over the years

"There are no slow news days in this view of the fourth estate, but along with all the fireworks, Fleming provides solid information on how the American newspaper industry flourished in the nineteenth century, illustrating in the process how a high literacy rate can actually change the course of history." Booklist

Includes bibliography

100 PHILOSOPHY, PARAPSYCHOLOGY AND OCCULTISM, PSYCHOLOGY

133.1 Apparitions

Cohen, Daniel, 1936-

Phone call from a ghost; strange tales from modern America; illustrated with photographs and drawings by David Linn. Dodd, Mead 1988 110p il $10.95; Pocket Bks. pa $2.75 (4-6) **133.1**

1. Ghosts

ISBN 0-396-09266-7; 0-671-68242-3 (pa)

LC 87-36513

A collection of ghostly encounters, all concerning American ghosts reported in such places as suburban homes, city apartments, at a state college, and on airplanes

"Bizzare, funny, and fascinating, these contemporary ghost stories are sure to find plenty of fans." Booklist

133.3 Divinatory arts

Schwartz, Alvin, 1927-

Telling fortunes; love magic, dream signs, and other ways to learn the future; illustrations by Tracey Cameron. Lippincott 1987 128p il $12.95; lib bdg $12.89; Harper & Row pa $4.95 (4-6) **133.3**

1. Divination 2. Fortune telling 3. Astrology

ISBN 0-397-32132-5; 0-397-32133-3 (lib bdg); 0-06-446094-0 (pa)

LC 85-45174

This is a "compilation of fortune-telling beliefs, traditions, and folklore which emphasizes the fun to be had in trying each method. With his customary thoroughness, Schwartz has amassed an amusing catalog of both familiar and little-known methods of fortune-telling. . . . Procedures and step-by-step directions are included when necessary, enabling readers of all ages to become amateur fortune-tellers. The simple pen-and-ink drawings are competent yet fail to match the often light-hearted text. As with his other works, Schwartz' thorough notes, list of sources used, and related bibliography are indispensible for both readers and librarians." SLJ

133.4 Demonology and witchcraft

Jackson, Shirley, 1919-1965

The witchcraft of Salem Village. Random House 1987 c1956 146p lib bdg $8.99; pa $2.95 (4 and up) **133.4**

1. Witchcraft 2. Salem (Mass.)—History

ISBN 0-394-90369-2 (lib bdg); 0-394-89176-7 (pa)

LC 87-4543

"Landmark books"

A reissue of the title first published 1956. Copyright renewed 1984

Jackson, Shirley, 1919-1965—*Continued*

"A simple, chilling account of the witchcraft trials of 1692 and '93 when, because of testimony given by a group of little girls, twenty persons were executed as witches and others died in jail. There is good introductory background and though the story's subject is by nature horrifying the book does not play on the emotions. . . . It presents a difficult theme lucidly and without condescension." Horn Book

Krensky, Stephen, 1953-

Witch hunt; it happened in Salem Village; illustrated by James Watling. Random House 1989 48p il lib bdg $6.99; pa $2.95 (2-4) **133.4**

1. Witchcraft 2. Salem (Mass.)—History

ISBN 0-394-91923-8 (lib bdg); 0-394-81923-3 (pa)

LC 88-42865

"Step into reading. A step 4 book"

A retelling of the madness that overtook Salem Village, Massachusetts, when several young girls accused a number of adults in the community of being witches

This account possesses a "smooth, storytelling style that admits the dramatic without spilling into the sensational. . . . While some of the watercolor illustrations seem content to evoke a generic colonialism, many, including the cover, have the requisite dark drama." Bull Cent Child Books

McHargue, Georgess

Meet the witches. Lippincott 1984 119p il (Eerie ser) lib bdg $11.89 (4 and up) **133.4**

1. Witchcraft

ISBN 0-397-32072-8 LC 83-48446

An analysis of the various elements of witchcraft: primitive, classical, fairy-tale, pagan, historical, and modern. "Witches from Oriental, African, and Pacific cultures are portrayed along with those of Western civilization and certain witch characteristics are linked with classical mythologies, fertility cults, and legends about vampires and zombies. . . . The concluding chapter outlines tenets shared by the four schools of modern-day witchcraft, which is distinct from Satanism. An eclectic selection of engravings, art reproductions, and photographs provides illustration." Booklist

152.1 Sensory perception

Cobb, Vicki

How to really fool yourself; illusions for all your senses; illustrated by Leslie Morrill. Lippincott 1981 145p il $12.95; lib bdg $13.89 (5 and up) **152.1**

1. Senses and sensation 2. Perception 3. Optical illusions

ISBN 0-397-31906-1; 0-397-31907-X (lib bdg)

LC 79-9620

"The book begins with an explanation of perception and explores many different sensory aspects of it through experiments, definitions of important terms (italicized), background information and how illusions affect us in everyday life. It concludes with how some great misconceptions such as the earth being flat were disproved. . . . All the senses are covered here, even the 'sense' of imagination. The book is easy to read, and directions are clear and accurate, viewing illusions from a scientific viewpoint. . . . Interesting, informative, and fun both for kids to use on their own and for science classes." SLJ

152.14 Visual perception

O'Neill, Catherine, 1950-

You won't believe your eyes! National Geographic Soc. 1987 104p il $6.95; lib bdg $8.50 (4 and up) **152.14**

1. Optical illusions 2. Perception

ISBN 0-87044-611-8; 0-87044-616-9 (lib bdg)

LC 87-7637

"Books for world explorers"

"Introduces the world of visual illusion, describing the workings of the eye-brain system and how different types of illusions in nature, in art, and in architecture occur." Publisher's note

This book "is filled with exciting full-color photographs and drawings. The captions are excellent, and the five chapters of prose are well-crafted. . . . As is appropriate for the intended audience, primary attention is given to demonstrating clearly many familiar illusions. This book is not an introduction to brain function, projective geometry, or laser optics. Nevertheless, it should stimulate many young people to do further reading into the mathematics and science of visual perception and illusions." Appraisal

Includes bibliography

Simon, Seymour, 1931-

The optical illusion book; drawings by Constance Ftera. Morrow 1984 78p il lib bdg $12.88; pa $6.95 (4 and up) **152.14**

1. Optical illusions

ISBN 0-688-03255-9 (lib bdg); 0-688-03254-0 (pa)

LC 83-43222

First published 1976 by Four Winds Press

The author "discusses how what we think we see may be affected by past experience, familiarity with perspective, how light or color can effect illusion, and how much of our visual impression may be determined by the brain rather than the eye. There is also an interesting chapter on optical illusion in art, and several suggestions for readers' experiments." Bull Cent Child Books

152.4 Emotions and feelings

Aliki

Feelings. Greenwillow Bks. 1984 32p il $13.95; lib bdg $13.88; Morrow pa $3.95 (k-3) **152.4**

1. Emotions

ISBN 0-688-03831-X; 0-688-03832-8 (lib bdg); 0-688-06518-X (pa) LC 84-4098

"Small pen-and-ink cartoons with vivid coloring depict boys and girls interacting and experiencing the full range of feelings which evolve in everyday settings. This creative, unique book would be ideal for parent/child inter-

Aliki—*Continued*
action or use by elementary teachers in language arts classes. Children will enjoy the comic book 'frame' format." Child Book Rev Serv

153 Conscious mental processes and intelligence

Yepsen, Roger B.
Smarten up! how to increase your brain power; [by] Roger Yepsen; illustrations by the author. Little, Brown 1990 117p il $13.95 (5 and up) **153**

1. Intellect 2. Brain
ISBN 0-316-96864-1 LC 89-39448

This book discusses "various influences on the brain, from exercise to drugs, to food, and how to use the brain more effectively, as in the areas of memory, creativity and right brain/left brain interaction." BAYA Book Rev

"Filled with anecdotes, tips, experiments, and various odd bits, this is an engagingly chatty survey of the powers of the human brain. Much of the information is useful—how to remember facts for tests, how to sleep well, what to eat for alertness—and much more of it is fun: how thunderstorms clear the head, what colors encourage certain moods, why 'more lefties wear sweaters to their birthday parties.' . . . This has a let's-take-a-look spirit that's infectious." Bull Cent Child Books

153.1 Memory and learning

Meltzer, Milton, 1915-
The landscape of memory. Viking Kestrel 1987 133p $12.95 (6 and up) **153.1**

1. Memory
ISBN 0-670-80821-0 LC 86-32406

"Memory is explored from various angles, including types of memory, fact knowledge and skill memory, memory capacity, loss of memory, and methods of increasing memory. Both current research and historical data are cited. The intentional distortion or repression of memory for political reasons is discussed, as is the use of memories to keep alive historical wrongs so that they will not be committed again." Horn Book

"While the material might present something of a challenge for the less scientific reader, Meltzer's writing style is breezy and makes dry information into a thoroughly compelling read." Publ Wkly

Includes glossary and bibliography

153.4 Knowledge (Cognition)

Burns, Marilyn
The book of think; or, How to solve a problem twice your size; written by Marilyn Burns; illustrated by Martha Weston. Little, Brown 1976 125p il $14.95; pa $8.95 (4 and up) **153.4**

1. Thought and thinking 2. Problem solving
ISBN 0-316-11742-0; 0-316-11743-9 (pa) LC 76-17848

"A Brown paper school book"

"A provocative text invites the reader to solve problems by looking for alternatives, sharpening the senses, studying people, and expressing ideas in words. Brain-teasers, riddles, and suggested projects are interpolated and represented by black-and-white line drawings." LC. Child Books, 1976

Nozaki, Akihiro
Anno's hat tricks; text by Akihiro Nozaki; pictures by Mitsumasa Anno. Philomel Bks. 1985 41p il $13.95 (1-4) **153.4**

1. Problem solving 2. Logic 3. Mathematics
ISBN 0-399-21212-4 LC 84-18900

Three children, Tom, Hannah, and Shadowchild, who represents the reader, are made to guess, using the concept of binary logic, the color of the hats on their heads. An introduction to logical thinking and mathematical problem-solving

"An introduction to 'if . . . , then . . . ' thinking for those who enjoy intellectual puzzles, enlivened by Anno's charming illustrations. The early puzzles are fairly easy; succeeding ones grow in difficulty. Along the way, the author helps the reader cultivate a method for attacking logical puzzles. There is a note for parents and older readers to help them use the book with children." Sci Child

154.6 Sleep phenomena

Silverstein, Alvin
The mystery of sleep; by Alvin and Virginia Silverstein; illustrated by Nelle Davis. Little, Brown 1987 43p il lib bdg $12.95 (4-6) **154.6**

1. Sleep 2. Dreams
ISBN 0-316-79117-2 LC 86-20104

Discusses the subject of sleep, including animal sleep, dreams, nightmares, and sleep problems

"Satisfyingly information packed, the book links research findings with readers' experiences while being neither oversimplified nor patronizing. . . . Davis' upbeat drawings are a great addition and set a cozy mood. This is a fine book for readers curious about an aspect of themselves that they can't observe directly." SLJ

155.4 Child psychology

Harris, Robie H.
Before you were three; how you began to walk, talk, explore, and have feelings; by Robie H. Harris & Elizabeth Levy; with photographs by Henry E. F. Gordillo. Delacorte Press 1977 142p il hardcover o.p. paperback available $7.95 **155.4**

1. Child development
ISBN 0-440-00471-3 (pa) LC 76-5587

Follows the physical and mental development of a boy and a girl from their birth to age three

Rogers, Fred
Making friends; photographs by Jim Judkis. Putnam 1987 unp il $12.95; pa $5.95 (k-1) **155.4**

1. Friendship
ISBN 0-399-21382-1; 0-399-21385-6 (pa)
LC 86-12353

"From its opening lines ('When people like each other and like to do things together, they're friends. Can you think of someone who's your friend?'), Rogers's inimitable voice reaches out to his small readers with understanding and reassurance. He describes the pleasures of friendship as well as potential problem areas. . . . Judkis's large color photos capture the range of emotions Rogers writes about." Publ Wkly

Moving; photographs by Jim Judkis. Putnam 1987 unp il $12.95; pa $5.95 (k-1) **155.4**

1. Moving, Household
ISBN 0-399-21383-X; 0-399-21384-8 (pa) LC 86-9426

"Following a little boy and his parents from their old house to their new one, full-color photographs and simple text express both the adventure and travail of a family's relocation. . . . If Mr. Rogers 'levels' with children rather than writing down to them, Judkis provides comparable illustrations by taking most of the photographs from a child's-eye view rather than shooting down from an adult's perspective. Using people who look like neighbors rather than actors or models gives the clear, colorful photos an appealing visual counterpoint to the carefully worded but informal text." Booklist

Rosenberg, Maxine B., 1939-
Being a twin, having a twin; photographs by George Ancona. Lothrop, Lee & Shepard Bks. 1985 unp il $11.95; lib bdg $11.88 (2-4) **155.4**

1. Twins
ISBN 0-688-04328-3; 0-688-04329-1 (lib bdg)
LC 84-17159

Describes the experiences of several different sets of twins, both identical and fraternal

"The author presents a warm and very personal look at twins. . . . Ancona's photographs . . . show a variety of action and subjects. Common situations that any child can relate to form the background for the photographs, and the text points out what would be special about the situation for a twin. The title subtly reinforces the message that there is a difference about individuality if one is a twin: one is somehow an inextricable part of someone else. A fascinating study, the book is the answer to a long unfulfilled need in material for children." Horn Book

155.9 Environmental psychology

Bernstein, Joanne E.
Loss and how to cope with it. Seabury Press 1977 151p il o.p.; Houghton Mifflin paperback available $4.95 (5 and up) **155.9**

1. Death 2. Bereavement
ISBN 0-395-30012-6 (pa) LC 76-50027

"A Clarion book"

"The author relates death to losses of other kinds, from the infant's temporary loss as a parent leaves the room to the adult's permanent loss of a favorite necklace or a job. She explains that, from childhood, experiencing inevitable losses helps prepare us to handle death. She then alerts the reader to the succession of feelings that accompanies mourning and provides sound advice about coping." Kobrin Letter

Includes bibliography

Hyde, Margaret Oldroyd, 1917-
Meeting death; [by] Margaret O. Hyde and Lawrence E. Hyde. Walker & Co. 1989 129p il $14.95; lib bdg $15.85 (5 and up) **155.9**

1. Death 2. Bereavement
ISBN 0-8027-6873-3; 0-8027-6874-1 (lib bdg)
LC 88-27933

Provides information to promote the acceptance of the concept of death, discussing such aspects as the terminally ill, suicide, grief and mourning, and the treatment of death in various cultures

"The format is staid, and the inclusion of individual experiences with various forms of death do not always ring true. But, in general, this offers thought-provoking material that will be useful to students or those simply interested in a topic that's often tough to talk about." Booklist

Includes bibliography

The **Kids'** book about death and dying; by and for kids; [by] the Unit at Fayerweather Street School; edited and coordinated by Eric E. Rofes. Little, Brown 1985 119p $14.95 (5 and up) **155.9**

1. Death
ISBN 0-316-75390-4 LC 85-180

"This book is the thoughts, perceptions and feelings of 14 students, ages 11-14, who spent a year studying and sharing various aspects of death. . . . Chapter topics include funeral customs; death of pets; death of family members; violent death; and life after death." Voice Youth Advocates

"The best aspects of student authorship, case histories, handbooks, cultural anthropology, bibliographies, advice books and almanacs are all blended together. Although it is written in a readable and almost casual manner, the content is far from casual. . . . Quotes, footnotes and specific references to data sources are sprinkled liberally within and around lists, charts, etc. . . . A unique and valuable book." SLJ

Krementz, Jill
How it feels when a parent dies. Knopf 1981 110p il hardcover o.p. paperback available $7.95 (4 and up) **155.9**

1. Death 2. Bereavement
ISBN 0-394-75854-4 (pa) LC 80-8808

This book is "a hopeful tribute to the healing power sustained by young survivors, who are competently interviewed and photographed in their widely varied reactions and situations. The subjects range in age from 7 to 16

Krementz, Jill—*Continued*

and cope with a variety of deaths by suicide, accident, and illness. Adults helping children through a hard time will better understand their charges' problems through the honest opinions expressed here, and young readers might feel less alone." Booklist

LeShan, Eda J.

Learning to say good-by; when a parent dies; illustrated by Paul Giovanopoulos. Macmillan 1976 85p il $12.95; Avon Bks. pa $6.95 (4 and up) **155.9**

1. Death 2. Bereavement
ISBN 0-02-756360-X; 0-380-40105-3 (pa)
LC 76-15155

The author "puts the bereaved children in touch with their grief. She then proceeds to explain the universality and validity of these feelings and how to cope with them healthfully. Actual examples illustrate many of her points." SLJ

Includes bibliography

When a parent is very sick; by Eda LeShan; illustrated by Jacqueline Rogers. Atlantic Monthly Press 1986 132p il $14.95 (4 and up) **155.9**

1. Sick 2. Parent and child
ISBN 0-87113-095-5 LC 86-3523

The author "provides a self-help guide for children whose parents are temporarily, chronically, or terminally ill. Through a combination of discussion and numerous anecdotes, the author explains how young people can deal with such situations, what fears they might have and how they can cope with those fears, what support systems are available, and how they can communicate usefully with family, friends, and medical professionals to get the information and help they need. The practical realism of LeShan's approach is reassuring in itself. . . . A useful book on a subject seldom discussed." Booklist

Rogers, Fred

When a pet dies; photographs by Jim Judkis. Putnam 1988 unp il lib bdg $12.95; pa $5.95 (k-1) **155.9**

1. Death 2. Bereavement 3. Pets
ISBN 0-399-21504-2 (lib bdg); 0-399-21529-8 (pa)
LC 87-18207

Explores the feelings of frustration, sadness, and loneliness that a youngster may feel when a pet dies

"The format and typography are clear and attractive, the language and concepts simple but sound psychologically, and the material geared either for an adult to share or for children to read alone." SLJ

Stein, Sara Bonnett

About dying; an open family book for parents and children together; by Sara Bonnett Stein, in cooperation with Gilbert W. Kliman [and others]; photography by Dick Frank; graphic design, Michel Goldberg. Walker & Co. 1977 47p il $10.95; pa $7.95 (k-3) **155.9**

1. Death
ISBN 0-8027-6170-0; 0-8027-7223-4 (pa)
LC 73-15268

"A book with two running texts, one addressed to parents and the other to be read aloud to small children, is illustrated with photographs. The text for adults discusses children's needs and fears, the ways in which a parent can describe death, help a child grow in understanding, and the behavior patterns that can show a child's fears or confusion in reacting to the death of a pet or a person. The attitude stressed is that of being open and natural." Bull Cent Child Books

179 Other ethical norms

Pringle, Laurence P.

The animal rights controversy; [by] Laurence Pringle. Harcourt Brace Jovanovich 1989 103p $16.95 (6 and up) **179**

1. Animal abuse
ISBN 0-15-203559-1 LC 89-11095

Presents viewpoints of both scientists and animal rights advocates on the use of animals for scientific research, for food, and for human enjoyment

"Whether describing the procedures of 'factory farming' or Draize testing, Pringle is never sensational, making this book both a sensible witness and an effective counterpoint to overheated propaganda. . . . Black-and-white photographs illustrate the points without sensationalizing them." Bull Cent Child Books

Includes bibliography

200 RELIGION

220.5 Bible—Modern versions

Bible

The Holy Bible; containing the Old and New Testaments; translated out of the original tongues; and with the former translations diligently compared and revised by King James's special command, 1611. Oxford Univ. Press prices vary **220.5**

Available in various bindings and editions

The authorized or King James Version originally published 1611

The Holy Bible: revised standard version. 2nd ed, containing the Old and New Testaments. . . . Reference ed. Nelson, T. maps prices vary **220.5**

Bible—*Continued*

Available in various bindings in regular and large print editions

"Translated from the original languages; being the version set forth A.D. 1611, revised A.D. 1881-1885 and A.D. 1901, compared with the most ancient authorities and revised A.D. 1946-1952. Second edition of the New Testament A.D. 1971." Title page

220.8 Nonreligious subjects treated in Bible

Bible. Selections

Animals of the Bible; a picture book by Dorothy P. Lathrop; with text selected by Helen Dean Fish from the King James Bible. Harper & Row 1987 65p il $13.95; pa $13.89 (1-4) **220.8**

1. Bible—Natural history
ISBN 0-397-31536-8; 0-397-30047-6 (pa)

Awarded the Caldecott Medal, 1938

A reissue of the title first published 1937 by Lippincott

"Dorothy Lathrop's love and understanding of animals, the sensitiveness and joy with which she draws them, make her the ideal artist for such a volume. It is more than a beautiful picture book, for she has studied the fauna and flora of Bible lands until each animal and bird, each flower and tree, is true to natural history." N Y Times Book Rev

Paterson, John (John Barstow)

Consider the lilies; plants of the Bible; [by] John and Katherine Paterson; paintings by Anne Ophelia Dowden. Crowell 1986 96p il $13.95; lib bdg $13.89 (5 and up) **220.8**

1. Bible—Natural history 2. Plants
ISBN 0-690-04461-5; 0-690-04463-1 (lib bdg) LC 85-43603

This book gives information "on forty-five shrubs, crops, trees, weeds, fruits and flowers mentioned in the Old and New Testaments with emphassis on the . . . symbolic values of each. Divided into three groups—plants of Revelation, Necessity, and Celebration—each plant is cited in a Bible story or passage (quoted from the King James, New English, or Revised Standard versions of the Bible or paraphrased)." SLJ

"The quality of the art and intelligent explanations coupled with carefully selected examples from both Old and New Testaments will make the book prime read-aloud material for family sharing, Sunday School classes, and religious reports." Bull Cent Child Books

220.9 Bible—Geography, history, biography, stories

Bible. Selections

Tomie dePaola's book of Bible stories. Putnam 1989 127p il $18.95 **220.9**

1. Bible stories
ISBN 0-399-21690-1 LC 88-26468

"A collection of 17 stories from the Old Testament, 15 from the New Testament, and 4 psalms. The text is from the New International Version. . . . De Paola uses the text as written with some abridgement to make the stories an appropriate length. Done in his typical style, the illustrations feature stylized people and objects. . . . There are several illustrations for each story, many of which are full page, and most make dramatic use of color. The large format enhances the impact of the pictures." SLJ

Hofman, Ya'ir

The world of the Bible for young readers; [by] Yair Hoffman; edited by Ilana Shamir. Viking Kestrel 1989 96p il $15.95 (5 and up) **220.9**

1. Bible—Biography 2. Bible stories
ISBN 0-670-81739-2 LC 88-20832

This "oversize volume is jam-packed with information about the history of the Jewish people as well as their neighbors from around 2000 B.C. to the third century A.D. The information is parceled out in text, boxed insets, and captions to handsome color photographs, maps, charts, and drawings—more than 300 of them. Each chapter covers a particular period of biblical history with an accent on those leaders who shaped their eras. A time line and glossary are appended." Booklist

Stoddard, Sandol, 1927-

The Doubleday illustrated children's Bible; paintings by Tony Chen. Doubleday 1983 384p il $25; pa $14.95 (4-6) **220.9**

1. Bible stories
ISBN 0-385-18541-3; 0-385-18521-9 LC 82-45340

An illustrated retelling of more than 100 stories from the Old and New Testaments

"There are many pluses here: inviting format, easy reading, plentiful illustrations, large clear type and an appealing cover featuring Noah's ark. This is an excellent selection, particularly for libraries lacking a basic collection of Bible stories." SLJ

221.9 Bible. Old Testament—Geography, history, biography, stories

Fisher, Leonard Everett, 1924-

The Wailing Wall. Macmillan 1989 unp il map $14.95 (4 and up) **221.9**

1. Jews—History 2. Western Wall (Jerusalem) 3. Bible stories
ISBN 0-02-735310-9 LC 88-27192

Fisher, Leonard Everett, 1924-—*Continued*

"Fisher recounts the history of the Western (Wailing) Wall of the Second Temple in Jerusalem. Briefly, beginning in Abraham's time, he chronicles the building and destruction of the First and Second Temples, Palestine's occupation by various cultures, and the history of the Jewish people in the Holy Land to the present. A chronology and a well-defined map of the area further clarify the information. Dramatic, two-page paintings in black-and-white acrylics showing architecture, costumes, and weapons of various periods enliven the text." SLJ

Gellman, Marc

Does God have a big toe? stories about stories in the Bible; paintings by Oscar de Mejo. Harper & Row 1989 88p il $15.95; lib bdg $15.89 (4-6) **221.9**

1. Bible stories
ISBN 0-06-022432-0; 0-06-022433-9 (lib bdg)
LC 89-1893

"A *midrash*, in Jewish tradition, is a story about a story in the Bible. Rabbi Gellman provides modern *midrashim* for young readers as he looks at some familiar tales through new eyes. In one, the animals in the garden of Eden are unhappy with Adam because he's always giving them lists of things to do. So God invents the Sabbath when there are no lists and no work. In another, Gellman explains that God picked Moses to lead the children of Israel out of Egypt because he needed a Jew who knew about freedom, and Moses was the only Jew who was not a slave." Booklist

"Oscar de Mejo's primitive-style paintings suit the text exactly. Adam and Eve, for example, pop up behind the bushes in the Garden of Eden, just as a child might imagine them. These tales have the ring of genuine folk-fables and the wit of a single, affectionate heart." N Y Times Book Rev

222 Historical books of Old Testament

Bach, Alice

Moses' ark: stories from the Bible; [retold by] Alice Bach & J. Cheryl Exum; illustrated by Leo and Diane Dillon. Delacorte Press 1989 183p il $14.95 (4-6) **222**

1. Bible stories
ISBN 0-385-29778-5 LC 89-1069

"These 13 tales are based on new translations from the Hebrew, and the book's highly readable introduction explains how the authors chose and retold their material, often using modern archaeological finds to extend details of life in biblical times. Favorite stories are here—the creation of Adam and Eve, Noah's ark—but the authors have also included more obscure tales, for instance, the meetings between Saul and the medium at Endor and between Solomon and the Queen of Sheba. Each story is followed by notes, which add texture and nuance. The Dillons' dramatic gray-and black-toned artwork, bordered in vivid green, completes this evocative and useful work." Booklist

Chaikin, Miriam, 1928-

Exodus; adapted from the Bible by Miriam Chaikin; illustrated by Charles Mikolaycak. Holiday House 1987 unp il $14.95 (2-4) **222**

1. Moses (Biblical figure) 2. Bible stories
ISBN 0-8234-0607-5 LC 85-27361

"Oversize pages, lavishly illustrated, provide a visual interpretation of the Biblical story of the plagues in Egypt that led to a pharaoh's reluctant permission for the departure of the Hebrew slaves and of their journey to the promised land. Chaikin has done a good job of adapting the story so that it is simplified and coherent yet preserves the flow of Biblical language. Mikolaycak's paintings, in his distinctively bold and flowing style, are carefully integrated with textual references; they extend the story and add excitement to its inherent drama." Bull Cent Child Books

Joshua in the Promised Land; woodcuts by David Frampton. Clarion Bks. 1982 83p il $12.95 (4 and up) **222**

1. Joshua (Biblical figure) 2. Bible stories
ISBN 0-89919-120-7 LC 82-4131

"Except for a bit of condensing, dialogue, and some extra characters (Mrs. Joshua and household), Chaikin sticks to the biblical story in which Joshua, successor to Moses, is commanded by God to lead the Israelites into Canaan and capture the Promised Land. Those familiar with more sanitized versions of Bible stories may be surprised at the jealous and vengeful God of the Old Testament. . . . This is written at a level children can understand, and it would certainly make a good starting point for a discussion of the Bible and biblical times." Booklist

The seventh day: the story of the Jewish Sabbath; woodcuts by David Frampton. Doubleday 1980 47p il o.p.; Schocken Bks. paperback available $4.95 (4 and up) **222**

1. Sabbath 2. Bible stories
ISBN 0-8052-0743-0 (pa) LC 78-22789

A narrative version of the Old Testament passages describing how the Jewish Sabbath came to be

"This goes beyond the story of the Jewish Sabbath to become a simplified, gracefully narrated account of the main events in Genesis and Exodus, well-suited to reading aloud for family sharing, classroom study of various religions, or Hebrew school instruction. . . . Frampton's black-and-white woodcuts match the dignity of the text and at the same time assert their own originality of concept." Booklist

De Paola, Tomie, 1934-

David and Goliath; retold and illustrated by Tomie dePaola. Winston Press 1984 unp il $12.95; pa $5.95 (k-3) **222**

1. David, King of Israel 2. Goliath (Biblical figure) 3. Bible stories
ISBN 0-86683-820-1; 0-86683-700-0 (pa)
LC 84-254400

Paperback edition includes cutouts

De Paola, Tomie, 1934-—*Continued*

A picture book retelling of the Biblical story of the shepherd boy David whose faith in God enabled him to defeat the Philistine giant Goliath and save the Israelites

Noah and the ark; retold and illustrated by Tomie DePaola. Winston Press 1983 unp il $12.95 (k-2) 222

1. Noah's ark 2. Bible stories
ISBN 0-86683-819-8 LC 84-149424

"In an unadorned retelling of the Noah story, de Paola provides an ark and set of animals that resemble a carefully carved wooden-toy set and places them in a stylized small-format setting. Colors are mostly earth tones, relieved by the red tile of the ark's roof and the deep blue-green of the water. . . . A simple version that makes smooth reading aloud for the very young." Booklist

Fisher, Leonard Everett, 1924-

The seven days of creation; adapted from the Bible and illustrated by Leonard Everett Fisher. Holiday House 1981 unp il lib bdg $14.95; pa $5.95 (k-3) 222

1. Creation 2. Bible stories
ISBN 0-8234-0398-X (lib bdg); 0-8234-0757-8 (pa) LC 81-2952

The author "remains true to the creation account found in Genesis while simplifying the language for his intended audience. Despite the fact that he condenses the account, he maintains the essential story. Rich full-color illustrations reinforce the majestic quality of Fisher's adaptation. . . . The book's large pictures and sparse text make it ideal for reading aloud to a group." SLJ

Geisert, Arthur

The ark. Houghton Mifflin 1988 48p il lib bdg $15.95 (k-3) 222

1. Noah's ark 2. Bible stories
ISBN 0-395-43078-X LC 88-15889

"Beginning with God's decision to destroy his creation—except for Noah and his family—Geisert details the story on buff-colored pages. The illustrator employs intricate cross hatching and unusual perspectives to show Noah building the ark and housing all the creatures of the earth. . . . As a result of its astonishing illustrations, as well as its compact text, this book can be used with a wide range of audiences, all of whom will no doubt want to look closely at the meticulous detail that abounds on every spread." Booklist

Hogrogian, Nonny

Noah's ark; illustrated by Nonny Hogrogian. Knopf 1986 unp il $12.95; lib bdg $12.99 (k-3) 222

1. Noah's ark 2. Bible stories
ISBN 0-394-88191-5; 0-394-98191-X (lib bdg) LC 86-97

"A reverent version of the Biblical story, with a sonorous paraphrased text and illustrations full of Hogrogian's gently romanticized animals. . . . The animals steal this show: they fly, swim, crawl, or pace everywhere, their natural postures and expressive faces in sharp contrast to the subdued, stylized human figures." SLJ

Hutton, Warwick

Adam and Eve; the Bible story; adapted and illustrated by Warwick Hutton. Margaret K. McElderry Bks. 1987 unp il $13.95 (k-3) 222

1. Adam (Biblical figure) 2. Eve (Biblical figure) 3. Creation 4. Bible stories
ISBN 0-689-50433-0 LC 86-27690

"Using the first three chapters of Genesis in the King James version, Hutton retells the familiar story from the first day of Creation to Adam and Eve's expulsion from the garden of Eden." Horn Book

"Until they share the fruit of knowledge, Adam and Eve are sketched in matter-of-fact nudity amid Eden's floral profusion. After eating the apple, they either cover themselves or are observed from discreet distances or in rear views. Hutton's streaks of light pierce the shadowy garden overgrowth like knowledge penetrating innocence in this evocative interpretation." Booklist

Noah and the ark; illustrated by Pauline Baynes; text from the revised standard version of the Bible. Holt & Co. 1988 unp il $14.95 (1-3) 222

1. Noah's ark 2. Bible stories
ISBN 0-8050-0886-1 LC 87-46412

A "visual interpretation of the story of Noah." SLJ

"The paintings are variously and cleverly framed: waves leap out of trompe l'oeil edges, animals crawl onto the facing page, a volcano erupts into the margin. There is plenty here to hold the eye, and the ear will be caught as well." Bull Cent Child Books

Segal, Lore Groszmann

The book of Adam to Moses; [by] Lore Segal and Leonard Baskin. Knopf 1987 115p il lib bdg $14.99; Schocken Bks. pa $11.95 (4-6) 222

1. Bible stories
ISBN 0-394-96757-7 (lib bdg); 0-8052-0961-1 (pa) LC 87-2581

A modern English version of the stories of the five books of Moses

"What Segal has done is simplify the language and give cohesion to the narrative without sacrificing sonority, sequence, or flow. The tone is reverent, the language comprehensible. Baskin's black-and-white illustrations are handsome in their dramatic sweep and strength." Bull Cent Child Books

Singer, Isaac Bashevis, 1904-1991

The wicked city; pictures by Leonard Everett Fisher; translated by the author and Elizabeth Shub. Farrar, Straus & Giroux 1972 unp il $8.95 (3-6) **222**

1. Lot (Biblical figure) 2. Sodom (Ancient city) 3. Bible stories

ISBN 0-374-38426-6 LC 72-175144

"From the Old Testament, this is a retelling of the destruction of Sodom and the Story of Abraham, Lot, and his wicked wife and daughters." SLJ

"The drama of the story is heightened by the deep-red monotone of the full-page illustrations. With details supplied only by a skillful use of white lines and cross-hatching, the illustrations are particularly effective in character portrayal, and together with the somber story, form a remarkable unified whole." Horn Book

224 Prophetic books of Old Testament

Hutton, Warwick

Jonah and the great fish; retold and illustrated by Warwick Hutton. Atheneum Pubs. 1984 unp il $13.95 (k-3) **224**

1. Jonah (Biblical figure) 2. Bible stories

ISBN 0-689-50283-4 LC 83-15477

"A Margaret K. McElderry Book"

"Hewing faithfully to the Old Testament account but rounding it out without the extended parable at the end, [the author] retells the story in simple prose that echoes the dignity of the Biblical narrative. . . . Luminescent panoramic watercolors depict both the human emotions and the epic events, highlighting the drama of the familiar tale and making a beautiful book." Horn Book

Spier, Peter, 1927-

The Book of Jonah; retold and illustrated by Peter Spier. Doubleday 1985 unp il maps $12.99; lib bdg $11.95 (k-3) **224**

1. Jonah (Biblical figure) 2. Bible stories

ISBN 0-385-19334-3; 0-385-19335-1 (lib bdg)

LC 85-1676

This "story of disobedient Jonah retains the drama of the original, and the full-color pictures are wonderful, enhanced by details that mark them distinctively Spier's. Older boys and girls and adults will find the author's afterword additionally absorbing. . . . There is a history of Nineveh illustrated by maps showing ancient and modern areas, the latter pinpointing the city's ruins today." Publ Wkly

232.9 Family and life of Jesus

Bible. N.T. Selections

The Christ child; as told by Matthew and Luke; made by Maud and Miska Petersham. Doubleday 1931 unp il $12.95; pa $4.95 (k-3) **232.9**

1. Jesus Christ—Nativity

ISBN 0-385-07260-0; 0-385-15841-6 (pa)

LC 31-28341

The artists "have interpreted through pictures the spirit of the Holy Land which was the background of the childhood of Jesus. With the exception of the prophecy from the book of Isaiah, the text is from the gospels of Matthew and Luke. A picture book of unusual beauty." Cleveland Public Libr

The Christmas story; from the King James version; illuminated by Isabelle Brent. Dial Bks. for Young Readers 1989 unp il $13.95 (k-3) **232.9**

1. Jesus Christ—Nativity

ISBN 0-8037-0730-4 LC 89-1149

"The text, extracted from the King James Version of the Bible, is a seamless interweaving of selections from the Gospels of Luke and Matthew. The exquisite illustrations are rendered in the style of medieval manuscript and glow with a lovely light." Horn Book Guide

Christmas, the King James Version; with pictures by Jan Pieńkowski. Knopf 1984 unp il hardcover o.p. paperback available $6.95 **232.9**

1. Jesus Christ—Nativity

ISBN 0-394-82609-4 (pa) LC 84-5719

Uses the words of the Gospels of Luke and Matthew to present the story of the birth of Jesus

"Jan Pienowski's illustrations, with their black silhouette cutouts against brilliant color, are worth the price of the book, and should encourage parents to go to the Bible and read the entire story to the children." N Y Times Book Rev

Easter, the King James Version; with pictures by Jan Pieńkowski. Knopf 1989 unp il $18.95 (4 and up) **232.9**

1. Jesus Christ

ISBN 0-394-82455-5 LC 88-13183

This is an illustrated version of an account of the crucifixion and resurrection of Jesus. The text comprises selections from the King James version of the Bible, with passages from each of the four gospels

"Dazzling beauty and poignant emotion suffuse these illustrations, which give an intensely personal interpretation of the King James version of the Easter gospels." SLJ

Branley, Franklyn Mansfield, 1915-
The Christmas sky; by Franklyn M. Branley; illustrated by Stephen Fieser. rev ed. Crowell 1990 47p il $14.95; lib bdg $14.89 (3-6) 232.9

1. Jesus Christ—Nativity 2. Magi 3. Stars
ISBN 0-690-04770-3; 0-690-04772-X (lib bdg) LC 89-71210

A revised and newly illustrated edition of the title first published 1966

"Branley asks what might have caused the star the Wise Men followed to appear in the heavens. He discusses theories and rules out by evidence shooting stars, (too short a duration) comets, and novas (none visible around the time of Jesus' birth). Branley then deduces the year and season of Jesus' birth through a series of old tax records, facts of Herod's rule and death, and the times when desert people grazed sheep." SLJ

"Fieser's illustrations have transformed Branley's work, highlighting the narrative elements, heightening the drama, and involving readers to an extent unusual in a nonfiction book." Booklist

Brown, Margaret Wise, 1910-1952
Christmas in the barn; pictures by Barbara Cooney. Crowell 1952 unp il $12.95; HarperCollins Pubs. pa $4.95 (k-2) 232.9

1. Jesus Christ—Nativity 2. Bible stories
ISBN 0-690-19272-X; 0-06-443082-0 (pa) LC 52-7858

A retelling of the Nativity story in simple rhyme. The illustrations are large and detailed

There is "use of modern dress in the pictures instead of the traditional Biblical costume, but this does not detract from the spirit of Barbara Cooney's illustrations. They are lovely." Libr J

De Paola, Tomie, 1934-
The miracles of Jesus; retold from the Bible and illustrated by Tomie dePaola. Holiday House 1987 unp il $14.95 (1-3) 232.9

1. Jesus Christ 2. Bible stories
ISBN 0-8234-0635-0 LC 86-18297

"Thirteen miracles, with the Biblical texts only slightly shortened and simplified, are retold with the beauty and dignity of the original. The artist's typical stylized, flat, highly decorative illustrations of sturdy, pensive figures, their faces often expressing awe, in soft, warm tones, have a still, timeless quality particularly appropriate to the spirituality and eternity of the subject." SLJ

Kurelek, William, 1927-1977
A northern nativity; Christmas dreams of a prairie boy. Tundra Bks. 1976 unp il $14.95 (4 and up) 232.9

1. Jesus Christ—Nativity 2. Canada—Social life and customs
ISBN 0-88776-071-6 LC 76-23274

Each of "20 anecdotal accounts is accompanied by a painting and recalls [the author/artist's] personal dreams of watching the Holy Family as they seek shelter and succor from farmers, fishermen, lumbermen, truckers, skiers and rod riders; from Eskimos, blacks, Indians and Mennonites." N Y Times Book Rev

"The familiar events are revitalized and given added dimension when relocated in Canada during the Depression years. . . . The magnificent representational paintings, in combination with a nonsentimental but moving text, place religious experience in the context of daily life." Horn Book

Laird, Elizabeth
The road to Bethlehem; an Ethiopian nativity; foreword by Terry Waite. Holt & Co. 1987 32p il $12.95 (4-6) 232.9

1. Jesus Christ—Nativity 2. Bible stories
ISBN 0-8050-0539-0 LC 87-45112

The author "collects a variety of Ethiopian tales about the birth of Christ and the life of the Holy Family and unites them . . . [with] illustrations taken from 18th-century illuminated manuscripts created for Ethiopian kings and now housed in the British Library." N Y Times Book Rev

"Informative explanations of symbolic content and historical detail accompany vellum paintings. . . . These interpretations help the reader understand an exotic culture and its ways. There is much to digest: a foreword by Terry Waite; a summation of Christianity's origins in northern Africa; and the modern translation itself. This book will best suit readers whose curiosity will be aroused by such an intriguing subject, or those mature enough to appreciate the intricacies of the effort." Publ Wkly

Lindgren, Astrid, 1907-
Christmas in the stable; pictures by Harald Wiberg. Coward-McCann 1962 unp il lib bdg $6.99; pa $4.95 (k-2) 232.9

1. Jesus Christ—Nativity
ISBN 0-698-30042-4 (lib bdg); 0-698-20489-1 (pa) LC 62-14449

A "tender telling of the Christmas story by a Swedish mother to her small child, who visualizes the birth of Jesus as happening now on a farm like their own." Wis Libr Bull

"Beautiful paintings of the Swedish countryside interpret the . . . story." N Y Public Libr

Winthrop, Elizabeth
A child is born: the Christmas story; adapted from the New Testament by Elizabeth Winthrop; illustrated by Charles Mikolaycak. Holiday House 1983 unp il lib bdg $14.95 (k-3) 232.9

1. Jesus Christ—Nativity 2. Bible stories
ISBN 0-8234-0472-2 LC 82-11728

"A deftly simplified story of the Nativity is based on the Books of St. Luke and St. Matthew, King James version. There are some omissions, but none of import, and Winthrop has kept the beauty of the Biblical languge, deleting only for the sake of easy comprehension. Mikolaycak's paintings are stunning; they are bold in composition but reverent in mood, colorful, and dramatic." Bull Cent Child Books

Winthrop, Elizabeth—*Continued*

He is risen: the Easter story; adapted from the New Testament by Elizabeth Winthrop; illustrated by Charles Mikolaycak. Holiday House 1985 unp il lib bdg $14.95 (2-5) **232.9**

1. Jesus Christ 2. Easter 3. Bible stories
ISBN 0-8234-0547-8 LC 84-15869

"The Easter story, adapted from the King James Version of the Gospels of John and Matthew, has been slightly altered and some of the obscure passages omitted for the benefit of young readers." Child Book Rev Serv

"Mikolaycak's potent, yet emotionally controlled compositions are enclosed along with the text in narrow, rust-colored borders that echo the earthy tones of the pictures themselves. Sensuous lines and superbly modeled figures possess a serene elegance, while occasional stylized images, such as the blood on Christ's torso, allow sensitive little ones a margin of distance from a potentially disturbing chain of events. The text is lengthy, and adults may want to paraphrase the story in parts to hold youngsters' attention, but older listeners will be moved by the timelessness of the language and the reverent beauty of Mikolaycak's spellbinding interpretation." Booklist

242 Devotional literature

Field, Rachel, 1894-1942

Prayer for a child; pictures by Elizabeth Orton Jones. Macmillan 1944 unp il $10.95; pa $3.95 (k-3) **242**

1. Prayers
ISBN 0-02-735190-4; 0-02-043070-1 (pa)
LC 44-47191

Awarded the Caldecott Medal, 1945

One of Rachel Field's "greatest legacies to [children] has been this [brief] prayer. It was written for her own daughter, but now belongs to all boys and girls everywhere. It is a prayer, beautifully written and . . . bespeaking the faith, love, hopes, and the trust of little children." Libr J

"The pictures have a freshness and childlikeness which match the text perfectly." Boston Globe

First prayers; illustrated by Tasha Tudor. Random House 1989 c1982 48p il $6.95 (k-3) **242**

1. Prayers
ISBN 0-394-84429-7 LC 88-30672

First published 1952 by Oxford University Press in both Catholic and Protestant editions

Protestant edition

"Athough its small size makes it more suitable for home purchase, many libraries will want this tiny gem of a book. There are prayers for morning, evening, and meals, some less familiar, but all within the understanding of a child. Delicately and tenderly illustrated." Booklist [review of 1959 edition]

Tambourines! Tambourines to glory! prayers and poems; selected by Nancy Larrick; illustrated by Geri Greinke. Westminster Press 1982 117p il $8.95 (3-6) **242**

1. Prayers 2. Religious poetry
ISBN 0-664-32689-7 LC 81-23158

The editor "brings together seventy-six selections and groups them around such concepts as thankfulness for the beauty of the world, petitions for others, blessings for animals, and personal perceptions and problems. The supplications and the invocations are drawn from various sources, Christian and non-Christian—from individual poets and from traditional material. . . . Avoiding any sectarian or theological considerations, the anthology is ecumenical in the most generous sense of the word. The line drawings accompanying each selection are decorative or illustrative but occasionally irrelevant. With indexes of poems, poets, and first lines." Horn Book

Thanks be to God; prayers from around the world; selected and illustrated by Pauline Baynes. Macmillan 1990 unp il $9.95 **242**

1. Prayers
ISBN 0-02-708541-4 LC 89-28622

An illustrated collection of prayers from England, Japan, India, and other nations

"This is a thoughtful collection of prayers, most brief and many rhyming, that appeal without dogmatic distractions to a child's sense of the Infinite. Delicate ornamentations are scattered throughout the spaciously set text, with the bottom third of each page given over to precise, small-scaled illustrations that unify the prayers/poems on each spread." Bull Cent Child Books

289.7 Mennonite churches

Ammon, Richard

Growing up Amish; illustrated with photographs, maps, and drawings. Atheneum Pubs. 1989 102p il maps $12.95 (5 and up) **289.7**

1. Amish 2. Pennsylvania Dutch
ISBN 0-689-31387-X LC 88-27493

Ammon attempts to explore "the traditional rural lifestyle of the Amish by focusing on a child named Anna and describing the activities that occupy her and her family throughout the year. School, chores, farm work, church, and play—all have their place in a life that centers on religion and family." Booklist

"Though the story form occasionally seems young and contrived, the text flows well and provides a warm, interesting view of the durable Amish culture. . . . The attractive format includes rather wide pages, photographs that are good but dark in tone, occasional insets of added information, verses and music, . . . and a good bibliography." Horn Book

291 Comparative religion and religious mythology

Bulfinch, Thomas, 1796-1867
Bulfinch's mythology (6 and up) **291**
1. Mythology 2. Folklore—Europe 3. Chivalry
Some editions are:
Crowell $17.95 (ISBN 0-690-57260-3)
Modern Lib. (Modern Lib. giants) $13.95 (ISBN 0-394-60437-7)
New Am. Lib. 2v pa v1 $3.95, v2 $4.95 (ISBN 0-451-62444-0; 0-451-62252-9)
First combined edition published 1913 by Crowell. First published in three separate volumes 1855, 1858 and 1862 respectively
Contents: The age of fable; The age of chivalry; Legends of Charlemagne
"The basic work on classical mythology. Includes information on Greek, Roman, Norse, Egyptian, Asian, Germanic myths, as well as the Arthurian cycle and other heroic epics." N Y Public Libr. Ref Books for Child Collect

Hamilton, Virginia, 1936-
In the beginning; creation stories from around the world; told by Virginia Hamilton; illustrated by Barry Moser. Harcourt Brace Jovanovich 1988 161p il lib bdg $18.95 (5 and up) **291**
1. Creation 2. Mythology
ISBN 0-15-238740-4 LC 88-6211
A Newbery Medal honor book, 1989
"Hamilton has gathered 25 creation myths from various cultures and retold them in language true to the original. Images from the tales are captured in Moser's 42 full-page illustrations, tantalizing oil paintings that are rich with somber colors and striking compositions. Included in the collection are the familiar stories (biblical creation stories, Greek and Roman myths), and some that are not so familiar (tales from the Australian aborigines, various African and native American tribes, as well as from countries like Russia, China, and Iceland). At the end of each tale, Hamilton provides a brief commentary on the story's origin and originators." Booklist
Includes bibliography

291.4 Religious experience, life, practice

Baylor, Byrd
The way to start a day; by Byrd Baylor; illustrated by Peter Parnall. Scribner 1978 unp il lib bdg $12.95; Macmillan pa $3.95 (1-3) **291.4**
1. Worship 2. Sun worship
ISBN 0-684-15651-2 (lib bdg); 0-689-71054-2 (pa) LC 78-113
A Caldecott Medal honor book, 1979
Text and illustrations describe how people all over the world celebrate the sunrise
"While the format is that of a picture book, the concepts in the poetic text of this handsome volume are more appropriate for independent readers who can grasp the historic and ritual values of Baylor's thoughts." Bull Cent Child Books

292 Classical religion and religious mythology

Asimov, Isaac, 1920-
Words from the myths; decorations by William Barss. Houghton Mifflin 1961 225p il $14.95; New Am. Lib. pa $2.50 (6 and up) **292**
1. Mythology, Classical 2. English language—Etymology
ISBN 0-395-06568-2; 0-451-14097-4 (pa) LC 61-5137
The author's "informal retelling and discussion of the myths to point out the scores of words rooted in mythology and to explain their usage in the English language provide a fresh look at the myths and a better understanding of the words and expressions derived from them." Booklist

Benson, Sally, 1900-1972
Stories of the gods and heroes; illustrations by Steele Savage. Dial Bks. for Young Readers 1940 256p il $15.95 (5 and up) **292**
1. Mythology, Classical
ISBN 0-8037-8291-8 LC 40-33522
This is "a fine collection of Greek myths based on Bulfinch's 'Age of Fable,' some edited and others entirely rewritten." Adventuring with Books. 2d edition

Colum, Padraic, 1881-1972
The Golden Fleece and the heroes who lived before Achilles; illustrated by Willy Pogany. Macmillan 1962 c1921 316p il $14.95; pa $7.95 (5 and up) **292**
1. Argonauts (Greek mythology) 2. Mythology, Classical
ISBN 0-02-723620-X; 0-02-042260-1 (pa) LC 62-16104
A reissue of the title first published 1921
Contents: The voyage to Colchis; The return to Greece; The heroes of the quest
"Mr. Colum preserves the spirit of the Greek tales and weaves them into a magic whole. In this he is aided by the spirited drawings." Booklist

Evslin, Bernard, 1922-
Hercules; illustrated by Jos. A. Smith. Morrow 1984 144p il lib bdg $14.95 (5 and up) **292**
1. Hercules (Legendary character)
ISBN 0-688-02748-2 LC 83-23834
Retells the adventures of the demi-god Hercules as he struggles to accomplish seemingly impossible tasks
"Evslin mixes Greek names of gods and goddesses with the more common Roman variant of the hero's

Evslin, Bernard, 1922-—*Continued*
name, rather than the Greek 'Heracles.' The tale is softened to some extent and certain of the 12 labors are omitted entirely. . . . Evslin invests the story with easy dialogue and razor-sharp wit. . . . A zesty recounting that can stand alone or lead readers to fuller tellings of the Hercules story." Booklist

Jason and the Argonauts; illustrated by Bert Dodson. Morrow 1986 165p il lib bdg $13 (6 and up) **292**

1. Jason (Greek mythology) 2. Argonauts (Greek mythology)
ISBN 0-688-06245-8 LC 85-32114

Ekion, the son of Hermes, relates how he came to be one of Jason's Argonauts and the adventures they shared in search of the Golden Fleece

The author "has sifted through the multitude of legends that make up the Argosy and has written a unique version of Jason's adventures. . . . Evslin uses contemporary language and a generous amount of dialogue but never loses the grandeur of the Greek epic. Bert Dodson's creative illustrations enhance the tale. I highly recommend this book as a masterful introduction to Greek mythology." Best Sellers

Fisher, Leonard Everett, 1924-

Jason and the golden fleece; written and illustrated by Leonard Everett Fisher. Holiday House 1990 unp il map $14.95 (3-6) **292**

1. Jason (Greek mythology) 2. Argonauts (Greek mythology)
ISBN 0-8234-0794-2 LC 89-20074

This is a retelling of the Greek legend. . . . "Jason sails forth to capture the Golden Fleece from distant Colchis. Four impossible tasks prescribed by the King of Colchis are accomplished with the help of Medea, the king's daughter, and the two escape with the Golden Fleece. Jason, Medea, and their two sons are happy, until Jason falls in love with Glauce." SLJ

"The book is well-paced, all of the story's major elements are included and readers will certainly be carried along by the episodic flow. Fisher's vivid art makes masterful use of each spread to advance the narrative and expand the text." Publ Wkly

Includes bibliography

The Olympians; great gods and goddesses of ancient Greece. Holiday House 1984 unp il $14.95; pa $5.95 **292**

1. Mythology, Classical
ISBN 0-8234-0522-2; 0-8234-0740-3 (pa) LC 84-516

Offers brief biographical sketches of the twelve gods and goddesses that reside on Mount Olympus including such information as their Roman names, their parents, and the symbols that represent them

"Each portrait has a massive, almost sculptured look despite the fact that the paintings are in full color. . . . This is a handsome book, and it's an excellent introduction to the Greek/Roman pantheon." Bull Cent Child Books

Includes bibliography

Theseus and the Minotaur; written and illustrated by Leonard Everett Fisher. Holiday House 1988 unp il map lib bdg $14.95 (1-3) **292**

1. Theseus (Greek mythology) 2. Minotaur (Greek mythology)
ISBN 0-8234-0703-9 LC 88-1970

Retells the Greek myth of the hero Theseus and his battle with the bull-headed monster called the Minotaur

"Fisher's paintings, styled in monumental proportions, somber colors, and simple compositions, are well suited to a Greek tale of heroic deeds and death. . . . Fisher has also done a careful job of selecting and consolidating various versions, for which he cites sources in the beginning. An impressive meeting of myth and picture book." Bull Cent Child Books

Gates, Doris, 1901-

A fair wind for Troy; drawings by Charles Mikolaycak. Viking 1976 84p il o.p.; Penguin Bks. paperback available $4.95 (4 and up) **292**

1. Mythology, Classical
ISBN 0-14-031718-X (pa) LC 76-27738

The author "recounts the events that led up to the Trojan War: the wooing of Helen, the oaths of the suitors, the judgment of Paris, the abduction of Helen, the madness of Odysseus, and the conscripting of Achilles." Horn Book

"The complicated gods' hierarchy falls easily into place, tension is high, and small parts played by Achilles, Odysseus, and other humans may well motivate additional reading. Mikolaycak's gray-shaded drawings add tremendous power." Booklist

Includes glossary

The golden god: Apollo; illustrated by Constantinos CoConis. Viking 1973 110p il o.p.; Penguin Bks. paperback available $4.95 (4 and up) **292**

1. Apollo (Greek deity)
ISBN 0-14-031647-7 (pa) LC 72-91397

"Sixteen stories involving Apollo which treat his birth, his victory over the serpent, Python, his fruitless pursuit of Daphne, the loss of his son Phaethon, and his relationship with his twin sister Artemis." SLJ

"The illustrations emerge as the most significant accomplishment for they sometimes capture the horror and the strength of the myths, which the text often fails to convey." Horn Book

Includes glossary

Lord of the sky: Zeus; illustrated by Robert Handville. Viking 1972 126p il o.p.; Penguin Bks. paperback available $4.95 (4 and up) **292**

1. Zeus (Greek deity)
ISBN 0-14-031532-2 (pa) LC 72-80514

A retelling of myths in which Zeus plays a part. Included are stories about Io, Deucalion, Baucis and Philemon, Europa, Cadmus, Theseus, Ariadne, Minos and Dionysus

"Although the myths related to Zeus are many, complicated, and often erotic, Gates has managed to distill readable stories without distorting the spirit of the

Gates, Doris, 1901-—*Continued*
original too much." Booklist
Includes glossary

Mightiest of the mortals: Heracles; illustrated by Richard Cuffari. Viking 1975 94p il o.p.; Penguin Bks. paperback available $4.95 (4 and up) **292**

1. Hercules (Legendary character)
ISBN 0-14-031531-4 (pa) LC 75-16374

A retelling of the Greek myths in which the demi-god Heracles plays a part, including the tales of the twelve labors imposed upon him by Hera

"The narrative provides an admirable preparation for many classical allusions which children will encounter in subsequent readings. A glossary is thoughtfully provided, and Cuffari's stylized 'Grecian urn' drawings of action and heroism are most appropriate." SLJ

Two queens of heaven: Aphrodite [and] Demeter; illustrated by Trina Schart Hyman. Viking 1974 94p il o.p.; Penguin Bks. paperback available $4.95 (4 and up) **292**

1. Aphrodite (Greek deity) 2. Demeter (Greek deity)
ISBN 0-14-031646-9 (pa) LC 73-17423

A retelling of some Greek myths in which the goddesses of love and fertility play a major role. Included are the stories of Adonis, Anchises and Aphrodite, Pygmalion, Atalanta, Cupid and Psyche, Hero and Leander, Pyramus and Thisbe, Demeter and Persephone, and Aphrodite's birth from the sea foam

"Trina Hyman's artistic conception of the deities is classical, and her fine-boned, bared figures, executed in flowing pencil drawings, actively project the emotional pitch of the text." Booklist

Includes glossary

The warrior goddess: Athena; illustrated by Don Bolognese. Viking 1972 121p il o.p.; Penguin Bks. paperback available $4.95 (4 and up) **292**

1. Athena (Greek deity)
ISBN 0-14-031530-6 (pa) LC 72-80515

A retelling of the story of Athena's birth along with other myths in which the Greek goddess plays a part. Included are stories about Aglauros, Perseus, Medusa, Andromeda, Bellerophon, Jason, Heracles, Medea, and Arachne

"A simplified, highly readable version of Greek myths. . . . Strong, black-and-white pictures accompany the text." Publ Wkly

Includes glossary

Hamilton, Edith, 1867-1963

Mythology; illustrated by Steele Savage. Little, Brown 1942 497p il $17.95; New Am. Lib. pa $4.95 (6 and up) **292**

1. Mythology, Classical 2. Mythology, Norse
ISBN 0-316-34114-2; 0-451-62702-4 (pa)
LC 42-12948

Contents: The gods, the creation and the earliest heroes; Stories of love and adventure; Great heroes before the Trojan War; Heroes of the Trojan War; Great families of mythology; Less important myths; Mythology of the Norsemen; Genealogical tables

Hawthorne, Nathaniel, 1804-1864

A wonder-book, and Tanglewood tales; illustrated by Gustaf Tenggren. Houghton Mifflin 1951 421p il o.p.; Ohio State Univ. Press reprint available $35 (5 and up) **292**

1. Mythology, Classical
ISBN 0-8142-0158-X

A combined edition of two titles first published 1852 and 1853 respectively

"Greek myths retold as fairy tales for nineteenth-century children, lighter in tone and with moral implications, suitable as an introduction to classical mythology for younger children." Hodges. Books for Elem Sch Libr

Hodges, Margaret

The arrow and the lamp; the story of Psyche; retold by Margaret Hodges; illustrated by Donna Diamond. Little, Brown 1989 unp il $14.95 **292**

1. Psyche (Greek deity) 2. Eros (Greek deity) 3. Aphrodite (Greek deity) 4. Mythology, Classical
ISBN 0-316-36790-7 LC 86-2728

Based on an original story by Lucius Apuleius

Relates how Psyche married the god of love, Eros, how she lost him, and had to overcome many obstacles before she became an immortal and could join him on Mount Olympus

Hutton, Warwick

Theseus and the Minotaur; retold and illustrated by Warwick Hutton. Margaret K. McElderry Bks. 1989 unp il $13.95 (3-5) **292**

1. Theseus (Greek mythology) 2. Minotaur (Greek mythology)
ISBN 0-689-50473-X LC 88-26875

Recounts how Theseus killed the monster, Minotaur, with the help of Ariadne

Hutton "makes specific use of patterns and designs of Minoan artifacts, architecture, and costume. And whether he depicts action viewed from daring perspectives or in broad panoramas or whether he reveals character in close-ups, his narrative paintings carry emotional intensity and are imbued with personal as well as with universal meanings." Horn Book

Low, Alice, 1926-

The Macmillan book of Greek gods and heroes; illustrated by Arvis Stewart. Macmillan 1985 184p il $15.95 (3-6) **292**

1. Mythology, Classical
ISBN 0-02-761390-9 LC 85-7170

This collection "tells of the Olympians and of the grand drama, both tragic and comic, that they played out in the heavens and on the earth. It tells, too, of the many mortals with whom they became entangled, both simple people like Pandora and Pygmalion and great heroes like Heracles and Perseus. Included are the popular myths and the legend of Odysseus." Publisher's note

"The tales are clearly told, without embroidery. A

Low, Alice, 1926-—*Continued*

useful index not only refers the reader to a page or pages, but briefly identifies the character or subject as well. Watercolors in glowing earth tones with touches of blue and decorative pen-and-ink drawings enhance the book's appeal." Booklist

McDermott, Gerald

Daughter of Earth; a Roman myth; retold and illustrated by Gerald McDermott. Delacorte Press 1984 unp il $15 (2-4) **292**

1. Demeter (Greek deity) 2. Persephone (Greek deity) 3. Mythology, Classical

ISBN 0-385-29294-5 LC 82-23585

"McDermott has used opaque gouache on a prepared surface to mimic the effect of ancient frescos. The story is Ovid's version of how Proserpina is carried off to the Underworld by Pluto—a classical mythological explanation for the origin of the seasons." SLJ

"Scholars will appreciate the studied plenitude of historical, literary, and artistic detail, but youngsters will be impressed mainly by the size and showiness of the book's illustrations, making this an effective choice for sharing with large read-aloud groups." Booklist

Osborne, Mary Pope, 1949-

Favorite Greek myths; retold by Mary Pope Osborne; illustrated by Troy Howell. Scholastic 1989 81p il lib bdg $14.95 (3-6) **292**

1. Mythology, Classical

ISBN 0-590-41338-4 LC 87-32332

Retells twelve tales from Greek mythology, including the stories of King Midas, Echo and Narcissus, the Golden Apples, and Cupid and Psyche

"Osborne's retellings are both lively and descriptive, while Howell's full-color, often iridescent illustrations set the scene and mood at the start of each tale." Publ Wkly

Includes glossary and bibliography

Usher, Kerry

Heroes, gods & emperors from Roman mythology; text by Kerry Usher; illustrations by John Sibbick. Schocken Bks. 1984 c1983 132p il map (World mythologies ser) $16.95 (5 and up) **292**

1. Mythology, Classical

ISBN 0-8052-3880-8 LC 83-11085

First published 1983 in the United Kingdom

"Opening chapters provide an overview of Roman history and explain the origins of Roman myths and religious beliefs and the influence of the Near East, as well as Greece, upon Roman mythology. Common practices of worship and celebration in families and communities are also described. . . . The book is clearly written and well organized. The style is accessible and unpretentious but does not always convey the beauty and power of these myths." SLJ

293 Germanic religion and religious mythology

Barth, Edna

Balder and the mistletoe; a story for the winter holidays; retold by Edna Barth; pictures by Richard Cuffari. Houghton Mifflin 1979 64 p il $10.95 (3-5) **293**

1. Balder (Norse deity) 2. Loki (Norse deity) 3. Mythology, Norse

ISBN 0-395-28956-4 LC 78-4523

"A Clarion book"

First published by Seabury Press

A retelling of the Norse legend of how Balder, god of light and joy, was brought down by the evil Loki with an arrow made of mistletoe

"The narrative style is clear and lively, and the characterization of Balder has both grace and sharpness; he is presented as 'fairest of all the gods . . . free of any arrogance' and one who 'radiated peace and well-being.' The atmosphere of the story has an almost palpable quality of contrasting darkness and light. The drawings, among the artist's last work, have a notable strength and beauty appropriate to the otherworldliness of the ancient tale." Horn Book

Colum, Padraic, 1881-1972

The children of Odin; the book of northern myths; illustrated by Willy Pogány. Macmillan 1984 c1920 271p il $12.95; pa $7.95 (5 and up) **293**

1. Mythology, Norse

ISBN 0-02-722890-8; 0-02-042100-1 (pa) LC 83-20367

A reissue of the title first published 1920

Contents: Dwellers in Asgard; Odin the wanderer; Witch's heart; Sword of the Volsungs and Twilight of the gods

"The stories of the Norse sagas, from the Twilight of the gods to the destruction of Asgard, are told in a connected narrative that flows in a simple rhythmic prose sometimes poetic." Booklist

296.4 Judaism—Traditions, rites, public services

Adler, David A., 1947-

A picture book of Hanukkah; illustrated by Linda Heller. Holiday House 1982 32p il $13.95; pa $5.95 (1-3) **296.4**

1. Hanukkah

ISBN 0-8234-0458-7; 0-8234-0574-5 (pa) LC 82-2942

"The author explains the origin of Hanukkah, 2000 years ago in Judea, when the Maccabees rebelled against the oppressive Greek ruler Antiochus. Under the Jewish leader Judah, the Maccabees won their battle and restored their temple in Jerusalem, destroyed by the Greek army. The victory is still celebrated in a way described in the book's finale." Publ Wkly

"Heller's stippled, stylized artwork is particularly effective here, her use of gold tones giving a glow to the whole work." Booklist

Adler, David A., 1947-—*Continued*

A picture book of Passover; illustrated by Linda Heller. Holiday House 1982 32p il $13.95; pa $5.95 (1-3) **296.4**

1. Passover
ISBN 0-8234-0439-0; 0-8234-0609-1 (pa) LC 81-6983

"Divided into two parts, this tells first the story of the Israelites' settlement in Egypt, their eventual enslavement, the 10 plagues, and the Exodus. A second section briefly lays out what 'we' do to celebrate the holiday of Passover, from the search for 'hamez' to the seder wine." Booklist

"Illustrations with a distinctly Egyptian style decorate this outstanding book, making it an excellent choice for sharing with all children." Child Book Rev Serv

Burns, Marilyn

The Hanukkah book; illustrated by Martha Weston. Four Winds Press 1981 120p il $13.95 (4 and up) **296.4**

1. Hanukkah
ISBN 0-02-716140-4 LC 80-27935

Beginning with the historical background, "this book offers a thoughtful, sensitive, broad approach to the Jewish holiday. It explores the past, and gives a number of new ways to enrich Hanukkah, plus recipes, craft projects, and games. Included is a section on how Jewish children might feel about celebrating Hanukkah instead of Christmas and lots of advice on creative living as a minority." Child Book Rev Serv

Chaikin, Miriam, 1928-

Ask another question; the story & meaning of Passover; illustrated by Marvin Friedman. Clarion Bks. 1985 89p il lib bdg $13.95 (4 and up) **296.4**

1. Passover
ISBN 0-89919-281-5 LC 84-12744

Discusses the history and importance of Passover, a celebration of freedom commemorating the exodus of Moses and the Israelites from Egypt, where they had long been slaves

"Two elements make this treatment unique. . . . First is the portrayal of Passover as it is currently celebrated in other countries. Discussion of the importance of the holiday to modern Soviet Jews, Israelis and the Falasha Jews of Ethiopia makes this book a timely piece. The emphasis on women's roles in the development and presentation of the holiday is a second aspect that makes this text notable." SLJ

Includes glossary and bibliography

Esther; illustrated by Vera Rosenberry. Jewish Publ. Soc. 1987 unp il $9.95 (1-3) **296.4**

1. Esther, Queen of Persia 2. Purim
ISBN 0-8276-0272-3 LC 86-20183

Chaikin "retells the biblical story of Esther and how she saved her people from the evil Haman. The smooth text ends with a brief inclusion about the holiday of Purim and how each year Jews celebrate it by reading aloud Esther's story, sending presents to one another, and making merry. The book is handsomely illustrated by Rosenberry's full-page pencil illustrations, one facing each page of text. . . . Although this story is not a substitute for the megillah (the biblical version of Esther's story read at Purim), it makes a fine introduction for younger children and will acquaint them with the historical reasons for the holiday." Booklist

Hanukkah; illustrated by Ellen Weiss. Holiday House 1990 unp il lib bdg $14.95 (k-2) **296.4**

1. Hanukkah
ISBN 0-8234-0816-7 LC 89-77512

"The first three-quarters of this informational book is a synopsis in simple prose of the wicked acts of King Antiochus, the uprising of the Jews under Mattathias, and the miracle of the holy oil. The last quarter shows families celebrating Hanukkah today." SLJ

"Pen-and-ink drawings accompany a simple yet graceful text. . . . Weiss' brightly colored drawings effectively reinforce the story's message. A useful introduction to Hanukkah and its traditions." Booklist

Light another candle; the story and meaning of Hanukkah; illustrated by Demi. Clarion Bks. 1981 80p il $10.50 (3-6) **296.4**

1. Hanukkah
ISBN 0-395-31026-1 LC 80-28137

"Delicate pen-and-ink drawings accented in bright red add a festive note to the study of the Hanukkah festival. Emphasis is placed throughout not only on the relationship between holiday traditions and historical events but also on the religious aspects of the celebration. . . . Chapters on Jewish law; the types and significance of Hanukkah foods, games, and gifts; local variations on the festival theme; and anecdotes from the Holocaust era documenting the holiday's role in Jewish life round out the presentation." Horn Book

Includes glossary and bibliography

Make noise, make merry; the story and meaning of Purim; illustrated by Demi. Clarion Bks. 1983 90p il $11.95; pa $4.95 (3-6) **296.4**

1. Purim
ISBN 0-89919-140-1; 0-89919-424-9 (pa) LC 82-12926

"Providing a first section on the historical background for the period in which the Persian king Ahasweros (Xerxes) reigned, Chaikin then tells—in a smooth fictionalization—the story of his queen, Esther, who saved the lives of her people, the Persian Jews. The last sections of the book focus on how the holiday grew in importance and on how it is celebrated. . . . The format is handsome, with wide margins and with deep purple illustrations, delicate in detail and strong in composition, often incorporating traditional designs or motifs of Mid-Eastern art." Bull Cent Child Books

Includes glossary and bibliography

Menorahs, mezuzas, and other Jewish symbols; illustrated by Erika Weihs. Clarion Bks. 1990 102p il $14.95 (5 and up) **296.4**

1. Jewish art and symbolism 2. Judaism—Customs and practices
ISBN 0-89919-856-2 LC 89-77719

Chaikin, Miriam, 1928-—*Continued*

Explains the history and significance of many Jewish symbols, such as the Shield of David, the menorah, and the mezuza, and discusses holiday symbols and rituals

"Embellished with bibliographical references as well as Weihs' simple yet elegant and wonderfully dramatic scratchboard illustrations, this smoothly woven patchwork of history and culture is a fine introduction that will attract browsers and be useful for children investigating the subject of symbolism in school." Booklist

Shake a palm branch; the story and meaning of Sukkot; illustrated by Marvin Friedman. Clarion Bks. 1984 88p il lib bdg $12.95; pa $4.95 (3-6) **296.4**

1. Sukkoth

ISBN 0-89919-254-8 (lib bdg); 0-89919-428-1 (pa) LC 84-5022

"This introduction of the Jewish harvest festival of Sukkot begins with an account of its observance at the time of Abraham, then goes on to present the milestones of Jewish history as turning points in the development of the holiday. . . . The latter sections of the book provide a . . . description of Sukkot as it is practiced today. . . . [The author] gives a variety of alternate explanations for the meanings of the holiday's central symbols. . . . Where appropriate, she also mentions recent antisexist changes in Jewish observance. She lists holiday foods and songs, and provides two glossaries, a reading list and an index which is admirably thorough for such a thin volume. Attractive black-and-gold drawings enliven the clear, engaging text." SLJ

Sound the shofar; the story and meaning of Rosh Hashanah and Yom Kippur; illustrated by Erika Weihs. Clarion Bks. 1986 90p il $13.95; pa $4.95 (3-6) **296.4**

1. Rosh ha-Shanah 2. Yom Kippur

ISBN 0-89919-373-0; 0-89919-427-3 (pa) LC 86-2651

Discusses the origin and development of Rosh Hashanah and Yom Kippur, their major symbols, and ways of observing them in the world today and in different times in history

"The author tackles complex themes—creation, divine judgement and forgiveness—and provides familiar legends, interesting derivations for varying customs and food, and some thought-provoking explanations of the earliest celebrations." Publ Wkly

Includes bibliography

Drucker, Malka, 1945-

Celebrating life: Jewish rites of passage. Holiday House 1984 96p il lib bdg $11.95 (4 and up) **296.4**

1. Judaism—Customs and practices

ISBN 0-8234-0539-7 LC 84-4684

This book "examines the traditional Jewish ceremonies associated with birth, adolescence, marriage and death. An informative and clearly written text provides readers with an interesting introduction to four of the most fundamental aspects of Jewish life. . . . From traditional to contemporary times, the rites of Brit Milah (circumcision), Bar/Bat Mitzvah (puberty), Kiddushin (betrothal) and Shivah (mourning) are presented. . . . Suitable for both Jewish and non-Jewish readers." SLJ

Includes glossary

Hanukkah; eight nights, eight lights; drawings by Brom Hoban. Holiday House 1980 95p il lib bdg $14.95 (4 and up) **296.4**

1. Hanukkah

ISBN 0-8234-0377-7 LC 80-15852

Introduces the history, customs, rituals, foods, games, and gifts associated with the Festival of Lights and includes recipes, crafts, and puzzles for celebrating the Jewish holiday

"This is a well-written, informative book. . . . What makes it outstanding, however, is its thoroughness. . . . A bibliography, glossary, and index make this handy as a reference tool too." Child Book Rev Serv

Ehrlich, Amy, 1942-

The story of Hanukkah; told by Amy Ehrlich; paintings by Ori Sherman. Dial Bks. 1989 unp il $14.95; lib bdg $14.89 (1-3) **296.4**

1. Hanukkah

ISBN 0-8037-0615-4; 0-8037-0616-2 (lib bdg) LC 88-31109

"The story of how the single lamp kept burning is told in straightforward text and set off by stunning, folkloric illustrations." N Y Times Book Rev

Greenfeld, Howard

Bar mitzvah; illustrated by Elaine Grove. Holt & Co. 1981 unp il $7.95 (5 and up) **296.4**

1. Bar mitzvah

ISBN 0-03-053861-0 LC 81-5104

"In clear, simple terms, the author discusses the ancient tradition of the Bar Mitzvah, when 13-year-old boys are considered old enough to join the company of men in religious ceremonies. The text describes the differences observed by Orthodox, Conservative and Reformed Jews and each step in the rites marking the youth's coming of age. In a concluding chapter, Greenfeld adds information about girls who are Bat Mitzvah at age 12 (since females are believed to mature earlier), and mentions strides affording women equality with males in the Jewish community." Publ Wkly

"This is an expert blend of scholarship and style. An impressive background of Jewish law and lore is well integrated with the main theme. The writing is intelligent, yet never obscure—a style appealing to a wide age range. The scratchboard illustrations by Elaine Grove are attractive and complement the text." SLJ

Hirsh, Marilyn, 1944-1988

I love Hanukkah; written and illustrated by Marilyn Hirsh. Holiday House 1984 unp il $12.95; pa $5.95 (k-3) **296.4**

1. Hanukkah

ISBN 0-8234-0525-7; 0-8234-0622-9 (pa) LC 84-497

"At Hanukkah, a small boy, who remembers only the candles from the previous year, is told the Hanukkah story by his grandfather, and then describes the eight-day celebration." SLJ

"The color artwork features large, sturdy drawings of the family, while the scenes of the ancient Hanukkah

Hirsh, Marilyn, 1944-1988—*Continued*
story are drawn on a smaller scale. A welcome picture-book edition that will prove handy to have on the shelves during the Holiday season." Booklist

Koralek, Jenny
Hanukkah, the festival of lights; written by Jenny Koralek; illustrated by Juan Wijngaard. Lothrop, Lee & Shepard Bks. 1990 29p il $13.95; lib bdg $13.88 (k-3) **296.4**

1. Hanukkah
ISBN 0-688-09329-9; 0-688-09330-2 (lib bdg) LC 89-8064

This book relates the events commemorated by the Jewish festival of Hanukkah, including the desecration of the Temple by Antiochus, the revolt of the Maccabees against foreign domination, and the rededication of the Temple

"The tone of this simplified text is almost folklore. . . . Facing each page of text is a formal, full-page illustration (framed, ironically, between marbled Corinthian columns) depicting a scene from the story with distant elegance." Bull Cent Child Books

Metter, Bert
Bar mitzvah, bat mitzvah; how Jewish boys & girls come of age; illustrated by Marvin Friedman. Clarion Bks. 1984 55p il hardcover o.p. paperback available $4.95 (4 and up) **296.4**

1. Bar mitzvah 2. Bat mitzvah
ISBN 0-89919-292-0 (pa) LC 83-23230

"The author gives the historical background for the celebration of induction into the adult religious community in the Jewish religion. He describes the preparation of boys (bar mitzvah) and girls (bat mitzvah) for the event, the ceremonies (with some variations in different countries) and the meaning of the occasion for the celebrant." Bull Cent Child Books

"Friedman's arresting illustrations emphasize the informational points in this lucid, concise coverage of a special day for Jewish adolescents." Publ Wkly

Schwartz, Lynne Sharon
The four questions; text by Lynne Sharon Schwartz; paintings by Ori Sherman. Dial Bks. 1989 unp il $15.95; lib bdg $15.89 (k-3) **296.4**

1. Passover
ISBN 0-8037-0600-6; 0-8037-0601-4 (lib bdg) LC 88-18881

This book explores the meaning of Passover by explicating the symbolism of the seder and the four questions

"Framed by the rituals of a Seder, an excellent text gives brief background on the celebration of Passover. . . . The stunningly stylized illustrations facing each page of text are a sophisticated carnival of animals that reflect a kind of Chagallian surrealism grounded by strongly outlined shapes, deep colors, and dense compositions." Bull Cent Child Books

Silverman, Maida
Festival of freedom; the story of Passover; retold by Maida Silverman; illustrated by Carolyn S. Ewing. Simon & Schuster 1988 unp il $7.95; pa $2.95 (1-3) **296.4**

1. Passover
ISBN 0-671-64567-6; 0-671-66340-2 (pa) LC 87-30388

"A Little Simon book"

"A retelling of the Passover story of Moses leading the enslaved Israelites out of Egypt. The full-color illustrations, although somewhat idealized, help to make the story vivid. The style is simple, direct, and clear. Special sections illustrate and describe the Seder. Included are two recipes for haroset, one of the symbolic foods on the seder plate. Also included are words and music for the traditional song 'Dayenu.'" SLJ

300 SOCIAL SCIENCES

302.2 Communication

Adkins, Jan
Symbols, a silent language; written, designed, and illustrated by Jan Adkins. Walker & Co. 1978 31p il hardcover o.p. paperback available $4.95 (4-6) **302.2**

1. Signs and symbols
ISBN 0-8027-7216-1 (pa) LC 78-2977

Text and illustrations explore the uses and meaning of the various families of symbols including traffic signs, map symbols, trademarks, and many others

Fisher, Leonard Everett, 1924-
Symbol art; thirteen [square]s, [circle]s, [triangle]s from around the world; written and illustrated by Leonard Everett Fisher. Four Winds Press 1985 61p il $12.95 (4 and up) **302.2**

1. Signs and symbols
ISBN 0-387-15203-2 LC 85-42805

In this volume the author "covers the meanings of symbols and their importance in business, religion, music, astrology, magic, and sciences. Each of the descriptive sections examines the history of the symbols and their uses." SLJ

Fisher "provides, on a large, double-page spread, easily discernible, key symbols connected with that field. Juxtaposed with the text are evocative, scratchboard drawings done in deep rustic browns against a stark white field. Language and history students will profit from this intriguing look at universal, nonverbal communication devices." Booklist

Silverstein, Alvin
Wonders of speech; [by] Alvin and Virginia Silverstein; illustrated by Gordon Tomei. Morrow Junior Bks. 1988 154p il $12.95 (6 and up) **302.2**

1. Communication 2. Speech
ISBN 0-688-06534-1 LC 87-31370

"Beginning with the physiology of speech, the concise text discusses how we learn to talk, subtleties of meaning, using speech effectively, and speech abnormalities. A brief examination of talking machines and speculation about speech capabilities of other animals round out a fascinating exploration of oral communication." Sci Child

Includes bibliography

304.6 Population

Ashabranner, Melissa
Counting America; the story of the United States census; [by] Melissa Ashabranner, Brent Ashabranner. Putnam 1989 101p il $14.95 (5 and up) **304.6**

1. United States—Census
ISBN 0-399-21747-9 LC 88-37572

Traces the history of the population census and describes how and why information about the number and characteristics of the people living in the United States is gathered every ten years

"What might seem to be a dry subject is brought to life in a readable text that includes humorous anecdotes reported by various enumerators. The photographs, sketches, and other graphics are of excellent quality and are well chosen and placed to clarify and extend the text." Horn Book

Includes glossary and bibliography

305.23 Young people

Burns, Marilyn
I am not a short adult! getting good at being a kid; illustrated by Martha Weston. Little, Brown 1977 125 p il $14.95; pa $7.95 (3-6) **305.23**

1. Children 2. Human behavior
ISBN 0-316-11745-5; 0-316-11746-3 (pa) LC 77-24486

"A Brown paper school book"

"A scatter gun approach, but nonetheless one of the few available, to discussing the state of childhood with children. There are some opening nudges to help find out 'what kind of kid you are' with lists and games; a brief social history of children's treatment by adults; an examination of children's legal status; a look at the influences and institutions that most affect children (the family, school, television); facts about work, finances and protection from child abuse; and suggestions about communication with adults." Booklist

305.4 Women

Ash, Maureen
The story of the women's movement. Childrens Press 1989 30p il (Cornerstones of freedom) lib bdg $13.27; pa $3.95 (3-6) **305.4**

1. Feminism 2. Women's movement
ISBN 0-516-04724-8 (lib bdg); 0-516-44724-6 (pa) LC 89-17325

This title discusses the history of the women's movement in England and the United States

This "book gives a broad treatment of historical events and [is] illustrated with numerous photographs, reproductions, and drawings." SLJ

305.8 Racial, ethnic, national groups

The **Black** Americans: a history in their own words, 1619-1983; edited by Milton Meltzer. Crowell 1984 306p il $14.95; lib bdg $14.89; pa $5.95 (6 and up) **305.8**

1. Blacks—History—Sources
ISBN 0-690-04419-4; 0-690-04418-6 (lib bdg); 0-06-446055-X (pa) LC 83-46160

This is a revised and updated edition of In their own words: a history of the American Negro, edited by Milton Meltzer and published in three volumes, 1964-1967

A history of black people in the United States, as told through letters, speeches, articles, eyewitness accounts, and other documents

Hamanaka, Sheila
The journey; Japanese Americans, racism and renewal; painting and text by Sheila Hamanaka; book design by Steve Frederick. Orchard Bks. 1990 39p il $18.95; lib bdg $18.99 (5 and up) **305.8**

1. Japanese Americans 2. World War, 1939-1945—United States 3. Japanese Americans—Evacuation and relocation, 1942-1945
ISBN 0-531-05849-2; 0-531-08449-3 (lib bdg) LC 89-22877

"A Richard Jackson book"

"Using details from a five-panel mural depicting the experience of Japanese-Americans during World War II, Hamanaka combines a portrait of their terror and dignity with a well-researched and uncompromising text." Horn Book Guide

Hewett, Joan
Hector lives in the United States now; the story of a Mexican-American child; photographs by Richard Hewett. Lippincott 1990 44p il $13.95; lib bdg $13.89 (3-5) **305.8**

1. Mexican Americans
ISBN 0-397-32295-X; 0-397-32278-X (lib bdg) LC 89-36572

Hewett, Joan—*Continued*

Text and photographs document the day-to-day happenings and milestones in the life of Hector, a young Mexican boy whose family seeks amnesty in the United States under the Immigration Reform and Control Act

"The flavor of Hispanic culture emerges throughout, and it's clear that Hector is at home with himself and his bicultural heritage. An attractive portrait, this may be particularly welcome in areas with large Hispanic populations." Booklist

Includes bibliography

The **In** America series. Lerner Publs. 1980-1991 16v ea lib bdg $9.95 (5 and up) **305.8**

1. Ethnic groups 2. Minorities

Some newly revised and recently published titles in this series are: The American Indian in America, by J. C. Jones v2 (revised edition of v1 in preparation); The Blacks in America, by E. Spangler; The Danes in America, by P. L. Petersen; The Filipinos in America, by F. H. Winter; The Finns in America, by E. Engle; The French in America, by V. B. Kunz; The Greeks in America, by J. C. Jones; The Irish in America, by J. E. Johnson; The Japanese in America, by N. L. Leathers; The Jews in America, by F. Butwin; The Koreans in America, by W. Patterson and H. Kim; The Lebanese in America, by E. M. Harik; The Mexicans in America, by J. Pinchot; The Puerto Ricans in America, by R. J. Larsen; The Scots and Scotch-Irish in America, by J. E. Johnson; The Vietnamese in America, by P. Rutledge

This series of books deals with the background, social life, problems and achievements of various ethnic and minority groups in the United States, including their immigrant experiences and subsequent life in America. Illustrated with photographs

The **Jewish** Americans: a history in their own words, 1650-1950; edited by Milton Meltzer. Crowell 1982 174p il lib bdg $14.89 (6 and up) **305.8**

1. Jews—United States—History—Sources
ISBN 0-690-04228-0 LC 81-43886

"Excerpts from letters, journals, books, documents, and assorted other sources provide a varied, firsthand look at Jewish experience in America from colonial times to 1950 when Holocaust survivors made their way to the U.S. . . . [The author] offers commentary before each [selection] helping to clarify context or define perspective by illuminating the times contemporary to the writing." Booklist

"The book has multiple curriculum uses and will be a welcome addition to any library. Interesting historical photographs and a comprehensive index add to [its] usefulness." SLJ

Includes bibliography

Meltzer, Milton, 1915-

The Chinese Americans. Crowell 1980 181p il map $13.95; lib bdg $13.89 (6 and up) **305.8**

1. Chinese Americans
ISBN 0-690-04039-3; 0-690-04038-5 (lib bdg) LC 79-3419

"Summary of the history of Chinese Americans: their cultural and agricultural contributions; their problems of prejudice, discrimination, and stereotyping; their underappreciated engineering achievement in helping to build the transcontinental railroad. The book establishes facts and corrects false ideas." Horn Book

"Based on intensive and extensive research, carefully organized, written in a serious tone that forsakes objectivity only when the author protests injustice, this is a beautifully knit and comprehensive book." Bull Cent Child Books

Includes bibliography

The Hispanic Americans; illustrated with photographs by Morrie Camhi & Catherine Noren. Crowell 1982 149p il maps $14.95; lib bdg $14.89 (6 and up) **305.8**

1. Hispanic Americans
ISBN 0-690-04110-1; 0-690-04111-X (lib bdg) LC 81-43314

"By interviewing and profiling various Hispanics who came to the U.S. to live, Meltzer delves into the social and economic problems they encountered. For younger readers who want information about immigrants from Cuba, Puerto Rico, and Mexico." Booklist

World of our fathers: the Jews of Eastern Europe. Farrar, Straus & Giroux 1974 274p il maps $13.95 (6 and up) **305.8**

1. Jews—Eastern Europe
ISBN 0-374-38530-0 LC 74-14755

This book describes "Jewish life in Eastern Europe up to the time millions of Jews emigrated to the United States. . . . The author uses diaries, letters, documents, newspaper accounts, songs, maps, poems, memoirs, weaving them into a historical narrative that details what led Jews to abandon their old world and venture to the new." Publisher's note

Includes glossary and bibliography

Wolf, Bernard, 1930-

In this proud land; the story of a Mexican American family. Lippincott 1978 95p il lib bdg $12.89 (4 and up) **305.8**

1. Mexican Americans 2. Migrant labor
ISBN 0-397-32268-2 LC 78-9680

"Photojournalist Bernard Wolf tells the story of David and Maria Hernandez and their seven children as they live and work together. The Hernandezes are one of many such Mexican-American families who live in South Texas and migrate north every summer to supplement their small incomes by doing farm labor. Wolf captures, through black-and-white photographs and a strong, simple text, the essence of the family's everyday lives—the difficulties as well as the warmth they share in working together." Child Book Rev Serv

306.05 Culture and institutions—Serial publications

Faces; the magazine about people. Cobblestone Pub. $21.95 per year **306.05**

1. Anthropology—Periodicals
ISSN 0749-1387

Faces—*Continued*
Nine issues a year.

Published with the cooperation of the American Museum of Natural History

A magazine for young people designed to introduce them "to the fascination of natural history and anthropology. There are some 8 to 10 articles in each well-illustrated number. Some issues concentrate on a particular subject. . . . Numerous projects for children are scattered throughout the magazine." Katz. Mag for Sch Libr

306.8 Marriage and family

Cole, Joanna

The new baby at your house; photographs by Hella Hammid. Morrow 1985 48p il $11.95; lib bdg $11.88; pa $4.95 (k-3) **306.8**

1. Infants 2. Brothers and sisters
ISBN 0-688-05806-X; 0-688-05807-8 (lib bdg); 0-688-07418-9 (pa) LC 85-10653

Describes the activities and changes involved in having a new baby in the house and the feelings experienced by the older brothers and sisters

"The large black-white photos of several families of different races are pleasing, if a little dark. A five-page 'Note To Parents' with a further reading list gives practical tips on minimizing sibling rivalry. Cole puts in a lot of warm and realistic comments about older children's probable feelings, addressing the main body of text to 'you.' This is a fine addition to the field." SLJ

Hodder, Elizabeth

Stepfamilies. Gloucester Press 1990 62p il (Understanding social issues) lib bdg $11.90 (5 and up) **306.8**

1. Stepfamilies
ISBN 0-531-17226-0 LC 89-81611

The author discusses stepfamilies and ways in which they differ from nuclear families

"The use of individual case histories and recorded conversations effectively extend the sensible and unbiased conclusions about a subject increasingly important in view of rapid changes in social patterns. The photographs too are well chosen to exemplify the types and ages of children who will be inevitably affected by the artificial construction of extended families." Grow Point

Includes glossary

Jenness, Aylette

Families; a celebration of diversity, commitment, and love; photographs by the author. Houghton Mifflin 1989 47p il $13.95 (4 and up) **306.8**

1. Family
ISBN 0-395-47038-2 LC 89-7507

Photographs and text depict the lives of seventeen families from around the country, some with step relationships, divorce, gay parents, foster siblings, and other diverse components. The material was originally a traveling exhibition, begun at the Children's Museum in Boston

"Individual and familial black-and-white photos accompany each single-page textual family portrait; they are relayed with candid sensitivity that will elicit thoughtful and emotional responses from readers and will encourage comparisons to their own family units. A diverse bibliography offers titles ranging from poetry to fiction and nonfictional representations of families. An accessible, attractive work with broad appeal that will provide good fodder for discussion and serve as a genesis for similar class projects." SLJ

LeShan, Eda J.

Grandparents: a special kind of love; illustrated by Tricia Taggart. Macmillan 1984 119p il $11.95 (4 and up) **306.8**

1. Grandparents 2. Conflict of generations
ISBN 0-02-756380-4 LC 84-5673

The author "presents matter-of-factly such issues as why grandparents and parents sometimes differ in attitudes; multigenerational living situations; learning about getting old (Alzheimer's disease and strokes); and multiple sets of grandparents. . . . The soft black-and-white illustrations add to the feeling of affection which permeates the work. . . Invaluable for parents and children to share." Horn Book

When grownups drive you crazy. Macmillan 1988 121p $12.95 (4 and up) **306.8**

1. Parent and child 2. Conflict of generations
ISBN 0-02-756340-5 LC 87-22005

Explores the conflicts and misunderstandings that occur between adults and children and offers advice to youngsters on understanding and dealing with the things adults do that distress them

"Understanding is the key here; LeShan's warm, supportive world will go a long way toward bringing her young readers to a more mature view of themselves and the grown-ups in their lives." Booklist

Rosenberg, Maxine B., 1939-

Living in two worlds; illustrated with photographs by George Ancona; afterword by Philip Spivey. Lothrop, Lee & Shepard Bks. 1986 46p il $11.95; lib bdg $11.88 (2-4) **306.8**

1. Children of intermarriage 2. Parent and child
ISBN 0-688-06278-4; 0-688-06279-2 (lib bdg) LC 85-23990

"The focus of this photodocumentary is on children of biracial parents, the features they inherit from their respective genetic pools, the sometimes awkward position this puts them in socially, the strengths represented by the diversity of their worlds. Several families are spotlighted, including racial mixes of white, black, Chinese, and Asian Indian, along with Jewish and Christian heritages." Bull Cent Child Books

"In all cases, the children are well aware they are different, but also appreciative of their dual racial backgrounds. . . . Rosenberg's message—that 'race is the least important part of people' and that 'it is possible to respect differences and live comfortably together'—becomes clear. Well photographed and smoothly written, this book will be a useful tool for classroom discussion and lessons in racial tolerance." Booklist

306.89 Separation and divorce

Brown, Laurene Krasny

Dinosaurs divorce; a guide for changing families; [by] Laurene Krasny Brown and Marc Brown. Atlantic Monthly Press 1986 31p il lib bdg $13.95 (k-4) **306.89**

1. Divorce
ISBN 0-87113-089-0 LC 86-1079

"After a table of contents and glossary of relevant terms (readers are challenged to find the starred ones in the book) come 11 sections on some reasons why parents divorce, on likely repercussions and reactions, and on ways to deal with visitations, living in two homes, dealing with holidays, and adjusting to new developments such as parent dating, remarriage, and step-siblings." Bull Cent Child Books

"The picture-book, almost comic-book, format, the touches of humor, and the distancing effect of the dinosaurs as surrogate humans may make the book accessible to young or extremely anxious children. A thoughtful, useful book." Horn Book

Includes glossary

Krementz, Jill

How it feels when parents divorce. Knopf 1984 115p il $12.95; pa $7.95 (4 and up) **306.89**

1. Divorce
ISBN 0-394-54079-4; 0-394-75855-2 (pa)
LC 83-48856

In a personal interview format "19 boys and girls, ranging in age from 7 to 16 years, tell of their parents' divorces and of the effects the divorce has had on them and their families." SLJ

"The full-page portraits that precede each piece are exceptionally expressive. While the accounts have many similarities, experiences and personalities are unique; Krementz' ear for language ensures that the children project their own individuality." Horn Book

Stein, Sara Bonnett

On divorce; an open family book for parents and children together; Thomas R. Holman, consultant; photographs by Erika Stone. Walker & Co. 1979 47p il o.p. paperback available $4.95 (k-3) **306.89**

1. Divorce
ISBN 0-8027-7226-9 (pa) LC 78-19687

Two separate texts appear on each page. One, in large type, is written on a child's level. The other, intended for adults, presents psychological explanations of the family's behavior

"The scope of 'On Divorce,' makes it a perceptive book to share with children whose own families are intact." SLJ

307.7 Specific kinds of communities

Provensen, Alice, 1918-

Town & country; [by] Alice and Martin Provensen. Crown 1985 c1984 unp il $9.95 (k-2) **307.7**

1. City life 2. Farm life 3. Villages
ISBN 0-517-55594-8 LC 84-12693

First published 1984 in the United Kingdom

Describes life in a big city and on a farm near a village

"Oversize pages filled with colorful drawings, details that fill but do not seem to crowd the pages, interesting urban perspectives and rural landscapes are combined in a book that should make children feel that both city and country are nice places to live. The authors point out differences, but their accent is always positive. So much to do, so much to enjoy, wherever you live." Bull Cent Child Books

Von Tscharner, Renata

New Providence; a changing cityscape; conceived by Renata von Tscharner and Ronald Lee Fleming (the Townscape Institute); illustrations by Denis Orloff. Harcourt Brace Jovanovich 1987 unp il $10.95 (3-6) **307.7**

1. Cities and towns—Pictorial works 2. Urban renewal—Pictorial works
ISBN 0-15-200540-4 LC 86-46225

"Gulliver books"

"The changing view over the years of the main street in the fictional town of New Providence is the focus of this . . . study of cityscapes in picture-book format. . . . Alternating pages contain commentary, pointing out specific happenings and briefly explaining socioeconomic effects on New Providence. The pages containing text have partial reproductions in black and white of the large illustrations, which zero in on specific points." Booklist

"A thoughtful and imaginative visualization. . . . All details . . . are accounted for and help make readers more fully understand the changes in the buildings and streets. Seasonal changes also add visual texture." SLJ

322.4 Political action groups

Meltzer, Milton, 1915-

The truth about the Ku Klux Klan. Watts 1982 120p il lib bdg $12.90 (6 and up) **322.4**

1. Ku Klux Klan
ISBN 0-531-04498-X LC 82-8532

The book discusses the emergence of the Ku Klux Klan during Reconstruction, its rebirth during the 1920's and 1960's, Klan activity today, who joins it and why, and what can be done about it

"Meltzer is one of the best social historians writing for children, and he somehow manages to maintain an admirable objectivity while listing in detail the atrocities done in the name of white supremacy." SLJ

Includes bibliography

323.4 Specific civil rights; limitation and suspension of civil rights

McKissack, Patricia C., 1944-
The Civil Rights Movement in America from 1865 to the present; by Patricia and Fredrick McKissack. Childrens Press 1987 320p il $38.60 (5 and up) 323.4

1. Blacks—Civil rights 2. Blacks—History
ISBN 0-516-00580-4 LC 86-9636

This "history of the civil-rights struggle in America . . . begins with the aftermath of the Civil War, describing the social conditions and political climate that resulted in the first rights for blacks. . . . As the McKissacks move into the twentieth century, issues of child labor, women's suffrage, and the great immigration movements receive coverage. And through each twentieth-century presidency, the gains, setbacks, and major social and political currents are described . . . plentifully illustrated with photographs. . . . This should find heavy use in school and public libraries; it offers a well-defined overview." Booklist

323.44 Freedom of action (Liberty)

Evans, J. Edward
Freedom of the press. Lerner Publs. 1990 72p il (American politics) lib bdg $9.95 (5 and up) 323.44

1. Freedom of the press
ISBN 0-8225-1752-3 LC 89-13297

This book explains what freedom of the press is, its history in colonial times, its meaning in the Constitution, and current controversial issues challenging the boundaries of this freedom

"The coverage is logical and systematic and gives a good overview of the subject, including a brief but interesting discussion of the student press. Well-chosen illustrations add to the informative quality of the text." SLJ

Includes bibliography

Intellectual freedom manual; compiled by the Office for Intellectual Freedom of the American Library Association. 3rd ed. American Lib. Assn. 1989 xxxiii, 230p pa $17.50 323.44

1. Intellectual freedom 2. Libraries—Censorship
ISBN 0-8389-3368-8 LC 88-39674

First published 1974

Contents: Library Bill of Rights; Freedom to read; Intellectual freedom; Intellectual freedom and the law; Before the censor comes: essential preparations; Assistance from ALA; Working for intellectual freedom

"This manual is designed to answer the many practical questions that confront librarians in applying the principles of intellectual freedom to library service." Preface

Includes bibliography

Newsletter on Intellectual Freedom. American Lib. Assn. $25 per year 323.44

1. Intellectual freedom—Periodicals 2. Censorship—Periodicals
ISSN 0028-9485

Bimonthly. First published 1952

This "newsletter reports on challenges to intellectual freedom across the United States. Also provided are details on court rulings affecting intellectual freedom, book reviews and Intellectual Freedom Committee reports. A particularly noteworthy feature is the continuing bibliography of journal articles on intellectual freedom. This newsletter is a basic source for this crucial information and should be in every library collection." Katz. Mag for Sch Libr

Weiss, Ann E., 1943-
Who's to know? information, the media, and public awareness. Houghton Mifflin 1990 182p $14.95 (5 and up) 323.44

1. Freedom of information 2. Freedom of the press 3. Privacy, Right of
ISBN 0-395-49702-7 LC 89-26901

Does the public have a right to know? Discusses factors that may interfere with that right and limit public knowledge, using examples from current events which dramatize the complex issues of media censorship

The author's "extensive use of both historical and current events (from William Randolph Hearst's involvement in the Spanish-American war to CNN's coverage of Tiananmen Square) adds depth to her analysis. Weiss marshalls her facts and figures with authority. She provides balanced coverage of such complex issues as personal privacy vs. the right to know." Bull Cent Child Books

Includes bibliographic references

323.6 Citizenship and related topics

Swanson, June
I pledge allegiance; pictures by Rick Hanson. Carolrhoda Bks. 1990 39p il lib bdg $9.95 (2-4) 323.6

1. Bellamy, Francis 2. Pledge of Allegiance 3. Citizenship
ISBN 0-87614-393-1 LC 89-35414

"A Carolrhoda on my own book"

Describes how and why the Pledge of Allegiance was written, how it has changed in wording over the years, and precisely what it means

"The illustrations, in oils, enhance the text by giving an appropriate sense of time and place throughout. While other flag books may mention the pledge, this book fills a gap by making it the entire focus. . . . Social studies and ESL curricula will be enriched by this book." SLJ

324 The political process

Hewett, Joan

Getting elected; the diary of a campaign; photographs by Richard Hewett. Lodestar Bks. 1989 48p il $13.95 (4 and up) **324**

1. Molina, Gloria 2. Elections
ISBN 0-525-67259-1 LC 88-11109

Follows the political campaign of Gloria Molina as she seeks election to the Los Angeles City Council

"The present-tense narrative allows tension to build nicely as the election draws closer. . . . All elements of grassroots action are carefully documented—stuffing envelopes, canvassing door-to-door, carefully acquiring data on each voter. . . . The book will both inspire and instruct prospective office seekers in the art of running a successful campaign." Horn Book

Includes bibliography

325 International migration and colonization

Kurelek, William, 1927-1977

They sought a new world; the story of European immigration to North America; paintings and comments by William Kurelek; additional text by Margaret S. Engelhart. Tundra Bks. 1985 48p il map $14.95 (4 and up) **325**

1. Canada—Immigration and emigration 2. United States—Immigration and emigration
ISBN 0-88776-172-0

Engelhart "pieces together an empathetic look at the experience of being a European immigrant in North America from about 1850 to 1950. Incorporated into her text are quotations from several of Kurelek's earlier books (he died in 1977), providing vivid glimpses of his family's experiences as Ukrainian immigrants in Canada." Booklist

This "work records the courage of immigrants to North America as well as the work they did and the settings in which they labored. . . . Engelhart's writing is direct and informative; comments by Kurelek are shown in italics. The paintings are vivid and varied, some showing detail of people working or of interior scenes, but the most impressive are those outdoor scenes that reflect the wide skies, the changing colors of the seasons, the vastness of the land." Bull Cent Child Books

325.73 Immigration to the United States

Fisher, Leonard Everett, 1924-

Ellis Island; gateway to the New World. Holiday House 1986 64p il map $13.95 (4 and up) **325.73**

1. Ellis Island Immigration Station 2. United States—Immigration and emigration
ISBN 0-8234-0612-1 LC 86-2286

Companion volume to: The Statue of Liberty, entered in class 974.7

"This is a detailed history of the island in Upper New York Bay that eventually came to be called Ellis Island. It served for many years as the entry point for immigrants, and it is this aspect that Fisher stresses, describing the laws that affected immigrants and the procedures that were used to screen and process them." Bull Cent Child Books

"Fisher relates the experiences of the immigrants in a straightforward manner, but his . . . [illustrations] often show the callousness with which these people were treated. . . . The black-and-white reproductions and Fisher's scratchboard drawings are excellent and enhance understanding of the clear, descriptive text." SLJ

Freedman, Russell

Immigrant kids. Dutton 1980 72p il lib bdg $13.95 (4 and up) **325.73**

1. Children of immigrants 2. United States—Immigration and emigration 3. City life
ISBN 0-525-32538-7 LC 79-20060

The author has "assembled an interesting collection of old photographs for a book that gives a broad view of the experiences of immigrant children in an urban environment. The text is divided into such areas as the journey to America, schools, play, work (much of it illegal), and home life. Photographs are carefully placed in relation to textual references, and the text itself is enlivened by quotations from the reminiscences of several people about their first days in the United States as child immigrants. Large, clear print and an index add to the book's usefulness." Horn Book

Jacobs, William Jay

Ellis Island; new hope in a new land. Scribner 1990 34p il lib bdg $13.95 (3-5) **325.73**

1. Ellis Island Immigration Station 2. United States—Immigration and emigration
ISBN 0-684-19171-7 LC 89-38075

Traces the history of Ellis Island and immigration to America and describes the experiences of immigrants arriving in 1907

"A book that is lavishly illustrated with photographs. . . . It will give children a realistic look at how children like themselves came to this country, the hardships they underwent during their voyages, and the anxieties and uncertainties they faced in their new country." SLJ

Rosenberg, Maxine B., 1939-

Making a new home in America; illustrated with photographs by George Ancona. Lothrop, Lee & Shepard Bks. 1986 unp il $11.95; lib bdg $11.88 (4-6) **325.73**

1. United States—Immigration and emigration
ISBN 0-688-05824-8; 0-688-05825-6 (lib bdg)
LC 85-11642

"This is a photo essay . . . about contemporary immigration, looking at the lives of children who have recently come from Japan, Guyana, India, Cuba and Vietnam in a wide range of social circumstances." N Y Times Book Rev

"The simple text describes the anticipation of new lives, the homesickness, and the difficulties with new language and customs as well as the sharing of native

Rosenberg, Maxine B., 1939-—*Continued*
foods and traditions with American classmates and neighbors. Handsome in appearance and thoughtfully constructed as a vehicle to promote personal understanding, the book comes at a time of great need to develop multicultural awareness among children." Horn Book

Siegel, Beatrice
Sam Ellis's island; illustrated by DyAnne DiSalvo-Ryan. Four Winds Press 1985 86p il $11.95 (3-6) **325.73**
1. Ellis Island Immigration Station 2. United States—Immigration and emigration
ISBN 0-02-782720-8 LC 85-42799
Seigel "tells about the island in New York Harbor that the colonial merchant Sam Ellis bought, which became the landing point for the great flood of immigrants." N Y Times Book Rev
The author "does an excellent job of making a narrative out of a mass of carefully researched historical information; her style is direct and neither too dry nor too casual, and her text gives many interesting facts about the Revolutionary War and New York City history as well as about Ellis and the small piece of land that was to become internationally known." Bull Cent Child Books
Includes bibliography

326 Slavery and emancipation

Lester, Julius
To be a slave; illustrated by Tom Feelings. Dial Bks. for Young Readers 1968 160p il $13.95; Scholastic pa $2.50 (6 and up) **326**
1. Slavery—United States
ISBN 0-8032-8955-6; 0-590-40682-5 (pa)
LC 68-28738
"Through the words of the slave, interwoven with strongly sympathetic commentary, the reader learns what it is to be another man's property; how the slave feels about himself; and how he feels about others. Every aspect of slavery, regardless of how grim, has been painfully and unrelentingly described." Read Ladders for Hum Relat. 6th edition
Includes bibliography

Meltzer, Milton, 1915-
All times, all peoples: a world history of slavery; illustrated by Leonard Everett Fisher. Harper & Row 1980 65p il lib bdg $13.89 (4 and up) **326**
1. Slavery—History
ISBN 0-06-024187-X LC 79-2810
The author "discusses slavery as a part of world history, showing how it developed from economic situations and desire for power. Using examples from Egypt, Rome, China, and other cultures, as well as the United States, he explains how slavery affected society and the life of the individual slave." SLJ
Meltzer "has dipped into his deep knowledge of the subject to write a brief, but not superficial, account in clear, trenchant terms." Horn Book

331.4 Women workers

Merriam, Eve, 1916-
Mommies at work; illustrated by Eugenie Fernandes. Simon & Schuster Bks. for Young Readers 1989 unp il lib bdg $5.95 (k-3) **331.4**
1. Women—Employment 2. Occupations
ISBN 0-671-64386-X LC 88-19796
Examines many different jobs performed by working mothers, including counting money in banks and building bridges

331.7 Labor by industry and occupation

Aaseng, Nathan, 1956-
Midstream changes; people who started over and made it work. Lerner Publs. 1990 80p il lib bdg $10.95 (5 and up) **331.7**
1. Career changes 2. Vocational guidance
ISBN 0-8225-0681-5 LC 89-37220
Presents the stories of famous people who achieved great success after changing careers in mid-life
"Throughout, Aaseng provides a compelling account as he shows how an unlikely chain of events turned fortuitous for men like Milton Bradley, Levi Strauss, and William Coleman; period photographs and definitions of business terms expand this fascinating work." Booklist
Includes bibliographic references

Johnson, Neil
All in a day's work; twelve Americans talk about their jobs. Little, Brown 1989 89p il lib bdg $14.95 (4 and up) **331.7**
1. Occupations 2. Work
ISBN 0-316-46957-2 LC 89-32624
"Joy Street books"
Photographs accompany a text which examines the following occupations: musician, detective, farmer, television journalist, judge, computer programmer, restaurateur, social worker, Air Force pilot, nurse, assembly-line worker, and teacher

331.8 Labor unions, labor-management bargaining and disputes

Flagler, John J.
The labor movement in the United States; series editor: M. Barbara Killen. Lerner Publs. 1990 112p il (Economics for today) lib bdg $14.95 (5 and up) **331.8**
1. Labor unions
ISBN 0-8225-1778-7 LC 89-36242
The author tells "about the bitter struggle to establish labor unions in the U.S., their rise to power, and their current decline. With some archival photographs, he reveals the grim facts (including child labor and

Flagler, John J.—*Continued*

dangerous working conditions) behind the 'good-old-days' stereotypes. Other fine sections deal with the role of immigrant workers, the New Deal, women in the work force during World War II, and the present growth of relatively unskilled, low-paying jobs." Booklist

Includes glossary

McKissack, Patricia C., 1944-

A long hard journey; the story of the Pullman porter; by Patricia and Frederick McKissack. Walker & Co. 1989 144p il (Walker's American history ser. for young people) $17.95; lib bdg $18.85 (5 and up) **331.8**

1. Brotherhood of Sleeping Car Porters 2. Railroads—Employees

ISBN 0-8027-6884-9; 0-8027-6885-7 (lib bdg) LC 89-9139

Coretta Scott King Award for text, 1990

"Covering a 150-year period, this sympathetic account successfully focuses on the efforts of a small group who sought to gain recognition for the Brotherhood of Sleeping Car Porters, the first black American-controlled union. Led by Asa Philip Randolph, better known to recent generations as the organizer of the 1963 march on Washington, this revolt is profiled in an approach that emphasizes the men's commitment and sacrifices during their intensive 12-year stuggle." Booklist

Includes bibliography

332.024 Personal finance

Kyte, Kathleen Sharar, 1946-

The kids' complete guide to money; drawings by Richard Brown. Knopf 1984 89p il lib bdg $10.99; pa $4.95 (4 and up) **332.024**

1. Finance, Personal 2. Consumer education

ISBN 0-394-96672-4 (lib bdg); 0-394-86672-X (pa) LC 84-3962

"This outline of personal finance for children includes some creative money-saving ideas. . . . Starting with a caricature of an imaginery advertising campaign, Kyte gives sensible advice on resisting the blandishments of advertising and peer pressure and briefly covers budgeting, money making and wise shopping. She also includes ideas on bartering, swapping, sharing, borrowing and other money-saving techniques and an especially valuable chapter on discount and free entertainment." SLJ

Includes bibliography

Wilkinson, Elizabeth, 1926-

Making cents; every kid's guide to money, how to make it, what to do with it; drawings by Martha Weston. Little, Brown 1989 128p il $14.95; pa $8.95 (4 and up) **332.024**

1. Moneymaking projects for children 2. Finance, Personal

ISBN 0-316-94101-8; 0-316-94102-6 (pa) LC 88-34634

"A Brown paper school book"

The author presents advice on making money through a variety of activities such as garage sales, dog walking, making Halloween costumes and beach sitting. This is an adaptation of Good Cents, by the Amazing Life Games Company

"Ideas are accompanied by a wealth of whimsical pencil drawings, most of which offer detailed instructions . . . or suggest creative activities." SLJ

332.1 Banks and banking

Adler, David A., 1947-

Banks: where the money is; illustrated by Tom Huffman. Watts 1985 32p il (Money power bk) lib bdg $9.90 (2-4) **332.1**

1. Banks and banking

ISBN 0-531-04878-0 LC 85-8848

Explains how a bank works through its functions of saving, lending, the use of checks, and other aspects of banking

"Adler clearly presents the business of banking in this book. His explanations are simple and easy to understand. The history of banking is included. The black-and-white illustrations are cartoon-like and lighten the text. New vocabulary, such as *currency* and *interest*, is printed in bold type and explained in context. Few books on banks and banking are available, and this one, whose content is up-to-date, is a good one." SLJ

332.4 Money

Cribb, Joe

Money. Knopf 1990 63p il (Eyewitness bks) $13.95; lib bdg $14.99 (4 and up) **332.4**

1. Money

ISBN 0-679-80438-2; 0-679-90438-7 (lib bdg) LC 89-15589

Examines, in text and photographs, the symbolic and material meaning of money, from shekels, shells, and beads to gold, silver, checks, and credit cards. Also discusses how coins and banknotes are made, the value of money during wartime, and how to collect coins

333.79 Energy

Gardiner, Brian

Energy demands. Gloucester Press 1990 36p il maps (Green issues) lib bdg $11.90 (5 and up) **333.79**

1. Energy conservation
ISBN 0-531-17197-3 LC 89-81597

This book "surveys how we presently supply our energy needs (oil, natural gas, coal, and nuclear power) and tells why alternative methods must be developed. Citing dwindling resources and the excess carbon dioxide produced from fossil fuels, Gardiner pushes for development of renewable sources including solar energy, wind power, and biofuels." Booklist

Includes glossary

333.91 Water

Ancona, George, 1929-

Riverkeeper; photographs and text by George Ancona. Macmillan 1990 unp il $13.95 (3-6) **333.91**

1. Cronin, John 2. Hudson River (N.Y. and N.J.) 3. Water—Pollution 4. Nature conservation
ISBN 0-02-700911-4 LC 89-36777

"A photo-essay about the environmentalist, hired by the Hudson River Fishermen's Association as caretaker of one of New York's most important waterways, describes his work as a boatman, wildlife monitor, pollution detective, political activist, and public speaker." Sci Child

"A balanced, rational presentation, the book speaks directly to our times in a manner as informative as it is appealing." Horn Book

Miller, Christina G.

Coastal rescue: preserving our seashores; by Christina G. Miller and Louise A. Berry. Atheneum Pubs. 1989 120p il $13.95 (5 and up) **333.91**

1. Seashore ecology 2. Marine pollution
ISBN 0-689-31288-1 LC 88-27520

"This examination of a threatened U.S. ecosystem describes the way beaches build and shift naturally, then goes on to show how artificial breakwaters, coastal construction, and pollution have destroyed both wildlife and the terrain that supports them. The text is well written and organized, with black-and-white photographs and drawings adequately extending the information." Bull Cent Child Books

Includes glossary and bibliography

338.1 Agriculture. Food supply

Fine, John Christopher

The hunger road. Atheneum Pubs. 1988 148p il $12.95 (5 and up) **338.1**

1. Food supply 2. Famines
ISBN 0-689-31361-6 LC 87-27794

The author "gives the historical, political and statistical details of famines and malnutrition in Cambodia, Ethiopia, Asia, the Middle East, Latin America, the Sahel, the Congo and right here in the U.S." Publ Wkly

"Fine's explanations of extremely complicated situations are clear and direct. . . . All in all, this is an adequate book on a difficult and timely subject. Includes an excellent bibliography." Voice Youth Advocates

341 International law

Rocha, Ruth

The Universal Declaration of Human Rights; an adaptation for children by Ruth Rocha and Otavio Roth. United Nations 1989 unp il $9.95 (k-2) **341**

1. Civil rights
ISBN 92-1-100424-1

This simplified version of the Universal Declaration of Human Rights includes background information and illustrations by Otavio Roth

342 Constitutional and administrative law

Commager, Henry Steele, 1902-

The great Constitution; a book for young Americans. Macmillan 1961 128p il $7.50 (5 and up) **342**

1. United States—Constitutional history
ISBN 0-672-50299-2 LC 61-7914

First published by Bobbs-Merrill

This description of the Constitution tells of the work and ideals of George Washington, James Madison, Alexander Hamilton, and the others who were a part of its creation. It describes the many difficulties of preparing a document that would provide a better government than the Articles of Confederation had, and indicates the attitudes of the states to the new Constitution

Fritz, Jean

Shhh! we're writing the Constitution; illustrated by Tomie dePaola. Putnam 1987 64p il $13.95; pa $5.95 (3-5) **342**

1. United States—Constitutional history
ISBN 0-399-21403-8; 0-399-21404-6 (pa)
LC 86-22528

This book "describing the writing and ratification of the Constitution, is both informative and entertaining. In her own unique, enlightening style, filled with honesty and detailed accuracy, Jean Fritz gives a vivid, vibrant picture of the 1787 Constitutional Convention. The wonderful, full-color illustrations are a perfect match for the captivating text. An added bonus is the inclusion of the complete text of the historic document." Child Book Rev Serv

Hauptly, Denis J., 1945-
"A convention of delegates"; the creation of the Constitution. Atheneum Pubs. 1987 148p il $12.95 (5 and up) **342**

1. United States—Constitutional history
ISBN 0-689-31148-6 LC 86-17260

The author "presents the background, personalities, and events of the Constitutional Convention of 1787, where the American form of government was hammered out. His straightforward approach to the facts will be useful to students researching the topic, and he brings the historical tableaux to life through excellent portrayals of key figures such as George Washington, James Madison, Edmund Randolph, William Peterson, Roger Sherman, Benjamin Franklin, Alexander Hamilton, and John Jay. . . . A list of delegates, the text of the Constitution with the amendments, and a bibliography are appended. An intriguing introduction to a potentially dry subject." Booklist

Mabie, Margot C. J.
The Constitution; reflection of a changing nation. Holt & Co. 1987 148p il $12.95 (6 and up) **342**

1. United States—Constitutional history
ISBN 0-8050-0335-5 LC 86-33502

"Beginning with the confederation, this book shows the development of a need for the Constitution. The personalities of the framers and their state's interests are portrayed, giving a lively picture of the compromises involved in the final document. The ratification process, the Bill of Rights, and the later amendments are covered and there is a chapter on the judiciary's role in interpreting the constitution. The full text of the Constitution and its amendments is included." Child Book Rev Serv
Includes glossary and bibliography

Maestro, Betsy, 1944-
A more perfect union; the story of our Constitution; illustrated by Giulio Maestro. Lothrop, Lee & Shepard Bks. 1987 48p il $15.95; lib bdg $15.88; pa $5.95 (2-4) **342**

1. United States—Constitutional history
ISBN 0-688-06839-1; 0-688-06840-5 (lib bdg); 0-688-10192-5 (pa) LC 87-4083

The Maestros "cover the birth of the Constitution from the initial decision to hold the convention, through the summer meetings in Philadelphia, the ratification struggle, the first election, and the adoption of the Bill of Rights." SLJ

"A simple, straightforward account using an oversize format with full-color illustration throughout. There is an excellent, fact-filled addenda that also includes the Preamble, chronologies and summaries of the Articles of the Constitution, the Bill of Rights, the Amendments and the Connecticut Compromise. This fine book places important events in historical context." Publ Wkly

Sgroi, Peter P.
The living Constitution: landmark Supreme Court decisions; [by] Peter Sgroi. Messner 1987 129p il $9.59 (5 and up) **342**

1. United States. Supreme Court 2. United States—Constitutional history
ISBN 0-671-61972-1 LC 86-23521

Explores the function and adaptability of the Constitution through a description and analysis of three major decisions—Marbury vs. Madison, Dred Scott, and United States vs. Nixon

"Tautly constructed and thoroughly researched." SLJ
Includes bibliography

Spier, Peter, 1927-
We the people; the Constitution of the United States of America. Doubleday 1987 unp il $13.95; lib bdg $14.99 (2-4) **342**

1. United States—Constitutional history
ISBN 0-385-23589-5; 0-385-23789-5 (lib bdg) LC 86-24205

This "book opens with a basic textbook background describing the historical facts that resulted in the Constitution. The opening Preamble is richly illustrated to convey the wonderful diversity of America. The basic rights which the Constitution guarantees are expressed in cartoon-like drawings which can be easily comprehended by the reader. The complete text of the Constitution and its amendments are provided in the back. A good resource for Social Studies classes." Child Book Rev Serv

347 Civil procedure and courts

Greene, Carol
The Supreme Court. Childrens Press 1985 44p il $13.27 (1-3) **347**

1. United States. Supreme Court
ISBN 0-516-01943-0 LC 84-23230

"A New true book"

Describes the function and structure of the Supreme Court and gives a brief overview of some important cases and well-known justices

Stein, R. Conrad, 1937-
The story of the powers of the Supreme Court. Childrens Press 1989 31p il $12.60 (4-6) **347**

1. United States. Supreme Court 2. Constitutional law
ISBN 0-516-04721-3 LC 89-15885

A brief overview explaining how the Supreme Court is the ultimate interpreter of our Constitution

"The information is interestingly presented, with enough material to satisfy report writers. . . . Illustrated with color photographs and historical drawings." Booklist

353.04 The cabinet

Parker, Nancy Winslow

The president's cabinet and how it grew; with an introduction by Dean Rusk. new ed. HarperCollins Pubs. 1991 40p il maps $14.95; lib bdg $14.89 (3-5) **353.04**

1. Cabinet officers
ISBN 0-06-021617-4; 0-06-021618-2 (lib bdg)
LC 89-70851

First published 1978 by Parents Magazine Press

Outlines the purpose and historical development of the President's cabinet, and explains the functions of each cabinet post

355.3 Organization and personnel of military forces

Cosner, Shaaron, 1940-

War nurses. Walker & Co. 1988 106p il $16.95; lib bdg $17.85 (6 and up) **355.3**

1. Nurses 2. Hospitals, Military
ISBN 0-8027-6826-1; 0-8027-6828-8 (lib bdg)
LC 88-14245

Traces the history of organized military nursing during wartime, from its beginnings during the Civil War to the conflict in Vietnam

"The text is factual but not dry; the black-and-white photographs, many historical, are revealing. Background information is livened by quotes from letters (no sources cited) and occasionally fictionalized stories about individuals who pioneered the field, from Clara Barton and Florence Nightingale to contemporary women who have crusaded for recognition of nurses' status as veterans." Bull Cent Child Books

355.8 Military equipment and supplies

Byam, Michèle

Arms & armor. Knopf 1988 63p il (Eyewitness bks) $13.95; lib bdg $14.99 (4 and up) **355.8**

1. Arms and armor
ISBN 0-394-89622-X; 0-394-99622-4 (lib bdg)
LC 87-26449

A photo essay examining the design, construction, and uses of hand weapons and armor from a Stone Age axe to the revolvers and rifles of the Wild West

"The brilliantly colored photos have a luminous sheen, imparting an almost three-dimensional quality." Booklist

362.1 Physical illness. Medical care

Krementz, Jill

How it feels to fight for your life. Little, Brown 1989 131p il $15.95 (4 and up) **362.1**

1. Diseases
ISBN 0-316-50364-9
LC 89-7960
"Joy Street books"

Twelve children tell how they battle pain, uncertainty, and the changes brought about in their lives by serious illness such as cancer, severe burns, asthma, and kidney failure

"The children who look out at us from the photographs and speak about themselves and their illnesses, their families, doctors and schoolmates, display an extraordinary awareness and acceptance of the reality of their situations. . . . However, they are not passively resigned; they have not given up hope for themselves or their futures. But neither are they practicing denial or magical thinking. They are remarkably well informed and articulate about their illnesses, and they are determined to do what they must to extend and enhance their lives." N Y Times Book Rev

Lee, Sally

Donor banks: saving lives with organ and tissue transplants. Watts 1988 95p il lib bdg $10.40 (5 and up) **362.1**

1. Transplantation of organs, tissues, etc.
2. Preservation of organs, tissues, etc.
ISBN 0-531-10475-3
LC 87-27304
"A First book"

This book explains "how organs are removed, stored, matched, and delivered. Blood, eye, organ, skin, and bone banks are detailed, followed by a plea for more donors. Each chapter begins with a scenario describing an actual transplant case, followed by information on the organs themselves and the transplant procedure. Finally, storage methods and banks are explained." SLJ

"Lee's writing style is smooth throughout, and the scientific information is peppered with real incidents. . . . Well-chosen black-and-white photographs appear on almost every page." Booklist

Includes glossary

Rockwell, Anne F., 1934-

The emergency room; [by] Anne & Harlow Rockwell. Macmillan 1985 unp il $13.95 (k-2) **362.1**

1. Hospitals 2. Medical care
ISBN 0-02-777300-0
LC 84-20161

This book explores the equipment and procedures of a hospital emergency room by describing what one patient sees while being treated for a sprained ankle

"Large, rounded letters and short lines of print encourage the child to read the book. Although the hospital personnel are depicted, the clean-lined illustrations emphasize the sophisticated emergency room apparatus. The drawings show enough detail to interest reluctant older readers. Light, bright color imparts a reassuring warmth to the surroundings." Horn Book

Rogers, Fred

Going to the hospital; photographs by Jim Judkis. Putnam 1988 unp il lib bdg $12.95; pa $5.95 (k-2) **362.1**

1. Hospitals 2. Medical care
ISBN 0-399-21503-4 (lib bdg); 0-399-21530-1 (pa) LC 87-19170

Describes what happens during a stay in the hospital, including some of the common forms of medical treatment

"The author's style is just right for this level of information book: reassuring yet candid, matter-of-fact about those aspects of hospitalization that may be frightening or painful, yet not in itself alarming." Bull Cent Child Books

362.2 Mental and emotional illnesses and disturbances

Dinner, Sherry H.

Nothing to be ashamed of: growing up with mental illness in your family. Lothrop, Lee & Shepard Bks. 1989 212p lib bdg $13; pa $8 (5 and up) **362.2**

1. Mental illness
ISBN 0-688-08482-6 (lib bdg); 0-688-08493-1 (pa) LC 88-13244

"The intent of this book is to inform family members, particularly adolescents, about the nature, causes, and treatments of selected emotional and mental disorders, such as schizophrenia, mood, anxiety, eating disorders, and Alzheimer's disease. The author's approach is to follow the traditional disease model, then to trace the course of these above-mentioned categories of behavior disorder from symptoms through treatment to adaptation within the family system." Sci Books Films

"One of the valuable points in this book is that young adults do not have to feel alone in their emotions towards this family crisis, and can cope sucessfully as well as advance their own lives. A glossary and list of support organizations with addresses are included in the book." Voice Youth Advocates

362.29 Substance abuse

O'Neill, Catherine, 1950-

Focus on alcohol; illustrated by David Neuhaus. 21st Cent. Bks. (Frederick) 1990 56p col il (Drug-alert bk) $14.95 (3-6) **362.29**

1. Alcohol 2. Alcoholism
ISBN 0-941477-96-7 LC 89-20410

The author discusses the history, use, and dangers of alcohol, the problems of alcoholism, and coping with the pressures to drink

"This book does not presuppose any other introduction to the subject, and the detail and reading level make it very suitable for the intended age group." Sci Child

Rosenberg, Maxine B., 1939-

Not my family: sharing the truth about alcoholism. Bradbury Press 1988 97p $12.95 (4 and up) **362.29**

1. Alcoholics 2. Parent and child
ISBN 0-02-777911-4 LC 88-10468

The author of this book "interviewed eight youngsters referred to her through treatment centers and six adult children of alcoholics about their family experiences. The bibliography is addressed to adults as well as children, and there is also a list of seven national organizations that can be contacted for help." N Y Times Book Rev

Shulman, Jeffrey, 1951-

Focus on cocaine and crack; illustrated by David Neuhaus. 21st Cent. Bks. (Frederick) 1990 56p il (Drug-alert bk) $14.95 (3-6) **362.29**

1. Cocaine 2. Crack (Drug) 3. Drug abuse
ISBN 0-941477-98-3 LC 89-20446

Discusses how cocaine and crack affect the mind and body and presents a brief history of cocaine use

"A truthful, factual . . . book about drugs for elementary school children. . . . The facts are all here, simplified, but complete enough to relay the message—drugs are dangerous. The information is sufficient for reports, even on a middle-school level. Analogies are in the realm of children's experience without making the activity appear desirable." SLJ

Includes glossary and bibliographic references

Turck, Mary

Crack & cocaine; edited by Laurie Beckelman; consultant, Elaine Wynne. Crestwood House 1990 48p il (Facts about) $10.95 (4-6) **362.29**

1. Cocaine 2. Crack (Drug)
ISBN 0-89686-491-X LC 89-25409

"The author explains the addictive nature of these popular drugs and offers supportive advice on how to avoid them, helping kids to 'just say no' a little more easily. Some may be bothered by the photographs, several of which picture the drugs and their accompanying paraphernalia." Booklist

Includes glossary and bibliography

Zeller, Paula Klevan

Focus on marijuana; illustrated by David Neuhaus. 21st Cent. Bks. (Frederick) 1990 56p il (Drug-alert bk) $14.95 (3-6) **362.29**

1. Marijuana
ISBN 0-941477-97-5 LC 89-20430

Describes the history, effects, social aspects, and physical dangers of using marihuana

The book points "out new findings on the dangers of this drug and includes a good section on using dogs to detect this substance. . . . [The volume] includes an index and glossary, and is illustrated with pastel-shaded black-line drawings." Booklist

362.3 Mental retardation

Bergman, Thomas

We laugh, we love, we cry; children living with mental retardation. Gareth Stevens Children's Bks. 1989 48p il (Don't turn away) lib bdg $9.95 (1-3) **362.3**

1. Mentally handicapped children
ISBN 1-55532-914-4 LC 88-42971

Original Swedish edition, 1977

Describes the home life, physiotherapy, and schooling of two mentally retarded sisters

Includes glossary and bibliography

362.4 Problems of and services to people with physical disabilities

Alexander, Sally Hobart

Mom can't see me; photograhs by George Ancona. Macmillan 1990 unp il $14.95 (3-5) **362.4**

1. Blind 2. Mothers and daughters
ISBN 0-02-700401-5 LC 89-13241

Blind author Alexander gives "readers a picture of her life, told from the vantage point of her nine-year-old daughter. . . . Alexander participates in all the family activities: cooking, cleaning, taking the children to lessons, and volunteering at school. She includes some of the frustrations of blindness as well, such as the fear children express of 'catching' blindness and the sadness that Alexander feels in not seeing what her children are seeing. Ancona's clear black-and-white photographs greatly amplify the text, showing the family at work and play. This is one of the best books available on blindness." SLJ

Bergman, Thomas

Finding a common language; children living with deafness. Gareth Stevens Children's Bks. 1989 48p il (Don't turn away) lib bdg $9.95 (1-3) **362.4**

1. Deaf
ISBN 1-55532-916-0 LC 88-42969

Original Swedish edition, 1987

Follows the activities of a six-year-old Swedish girl as she attends a nursery school for the deaf

Includes glossary and bibliography

On our own terms; children living with physical disabilities. Gareth Stevens Children's Bks. 1989 48p il (Don't turn away) lib bdg $9.95 (1-3) **362.4**

1. Physically handicapped children
ISBN 1-55532-942-X LC 88-42973

Original Swedish edition, 1981

Describes the activities at the Caroline Hospital in Stockholm where children with congenital handicaps receive training and physiotherapy

Includes glossary and bibliography

Seeing in special ways; children living with blindness. Gareth Stevens Children's Bks. 1989 54p il (Don't turn away) lib bdg $9.95 (1-3) **362.4**

1. Blind
ISBN 1-55532-915-2 LC 88-42970

Original Swedish edition, 1976

Interviews with a group of blind and partially sighted children in Sweden reveal their feelings about their disability and the ways they use their other senses to help them see

Includes glossary and bibliography

Butler, Beverly, 1932-

Maggie by my side. Dodd, Mead 1987 96p il $12.95 (4 and up) **362.4**

1. Guide dogs 2. Blind
ISBN 0-396-08862-7 LC 86-32883

"Butler, who lost her sight at 14, is forced to find a new dog when her latest dog dies. At a guide dog school in Ohio she is introduced to a German shepherd, Maggie. In this concisely written book, Butler explains about guide dogs and the training that both they and their owners receive. . . . Numerous black-and-white photographs add to the text and are well placed to supplement it." SLJ

Butler, Dorothy, 1925-

Cushla and her books. Horn Bk. 1980 c1979 128p il o.p. paperback available $12.95 **362.4**

1. Yeoman, Cushla, 1971- 2. Handicapped children 3. Books and reading
ISBN 0-87675-283-0 (pa) LC 79-25695

First published 1979 in the United Kingdom

"Cushla was born with multiple birth defects . . . and almost died at least twice before her first birthday. Her development lagged behind that of normal peers except in the area of speech and cognition, and her poor coordination and motor skills narrowed her ability to experience the world around her. Yet she also had an astounding grasps of concepts and an insatiable appetite for learning. The most successful therapeutic medium for Cushla turned out to be books, which her family began reading aloud to her when she was only four months old. . . . Butler, who originally wrote this work as a Ph.D. thesis, includes plenty of back-up material to document Cushla's problems and treatment. Invaluable for libraries serving parents of handicapped children, and primary education teachers, and children's and school librarians." Libr J

Emmert, Michelle

I'm the big sister now; pictures by Gail Owens. Whitman, A. 1989 unp il lib bdg $12.95 (3-5) **362.4**

1. Emmert, Amy 2. Cerebral palsy 3. Sisters
ISBN 0-8075-3458-7 LC 89-5584

"A loving account of life with a child severely handicapped by cerebral palsy is related by her younger sister. Candid details of her care, including feeding through a

Emmert, Michelle—*Continued*
gastrostomy tube and changing diapers, are presented. Afterword on cerebral palsy." Horn Book Guide

Kuklin, Susan
Thinking big; the story of a young dwarf; text and photographs by Susan Kuklin. Lothrop, Lee & Shepard Bks. 1986 unp il $12.95; lib bdg $12.88 (2-5) **362.4**

1. Osborn, Jaime 2. Dwarfs
ISBN 0-688-05826-4; 0-688-05827-2 (lib bdg) LC 85-10425

Text and photographs depict the life of an eight-year-old dwarf who lives in an average-sized family and attends a regular school

"The text and photographs are well integrated and clearly show Jaime in some situations where, because of her short stature, she needs help and in other situations where she is able to adapt. The author writes in a straightforward, unemotional tone while effectively creating a positive and reassuring mood. . . . An epilogue gives further information on dwarfism for teachers and parents." Horn Book

Peterson, Jeanne Whitehouse
I have a sister—my sister is deaf; pictures by Deborah Ray. Harper & Row 1977 unp il $13.95; lib bdg $13.89; pa $4.95 (k-3) **362.4**

1. Deaf 2. Sisters
ISBN 0-06-024701-0; 0-06-024702-9 (lib bdg); 0-06-443059-6 (pa) LC 76-24306

"Being deaf has some assets as well as liabilities. This book helps to point out some ways a deaf child compensates and some ways that other senses are developed more fully. It has an appreciation for accomplishments and strengths. It gives a picture of a warm relationship between a girl and her younger deaf sister." Child Book Rev Serv

"A lovely, tender story, with a sense of poetry that is quite captivating. The pencil sketch illustrations by Deborah Ray aptly evoke the mood of the text." Babbling Bookworm

Rosenberg, Maxine B., 1939-
Finding a way; living with exceptional brothers and sisters; photographs by George Ancona. Lothrop, Lee & Shepard Bks. 1988 48p il $12.95; lib bdg $12.88 (2-4) **362.4**

1. Physically handicapped children 2. Brothers and sisters
ISBN 0-688-06873-1; 0-688-06874-X (lib bdg) LC 88-6776

"Rosenberg writes about what it is like to be the brother or sister of a child who has a special physical problem; covered here are diabetes, asthma, and spina bifida. What is most valuable in her writing is the objectivity with which she approaches the fact that the sibling who is not disabled also has problems of acceptance and adjustment; a second strength is the recurrent emphasis on the positive, both in the coverage of sibling relationships and in the demonstration of the fact that, disabled or not, children have similar needs and interests." Bull Cent Child Books

My friend Leslie; the story of a handicapped child; photographs by George Ancona. Lothrop, Lee & Shepard Bks. 1983 48p il $13; lib bdg $13.88 (1-3) **362.4**

1. Physically handicapped children
ISBN 0-688-01690-1; 0-688-01691-X (lib bdg) LC 82-12734

"In a photodocumentary about a child with multiple handicaps, the text is narrated by Leslie's best friend and kindergarten classmate Karin. Leslie is legally blind, has some hearing loss, a cleft palate, muscular disability, and ptosis of the eyelids. She's needed surgery several times, and she's a merry, friendly child whose classmates help her when help is needed, accept her as she is, and enjoy her company." Bull Cent Child Books

"This title shows a positive, practical approach to having handicapped children in an ordinary classroom setting. It is a good, realistic explanation that children will be able to comprehend." Child Book Rev Serv

"The black-and-white photographs by Ancona go well with the text and enhace the message of the book." SLJ

Roy, Ron, 1940-
Move over, wheelchairs coming through! seven young people in wheelchairs talk about their lives; photographs by Rosmarie Hausherr. Clarion Bks. 1985 83p il $13.95 (3 and up) **362.4**

1. Physically handicapped children
ISBN 0-89919-249-1 LC 84-14314

"Brief studies of seven disabled children, aged 8 to 19. Each short chapter describes the handicap and how the young person copes with it from a wheelchair. The text stresses what the children can do and how they face barriers in the world as they go to school, to restaurants and around their home towns. Both text and well-placed, high-quality photographs emphasize the daily activities of these children, showing that they like to do the things their friends and family do. The children all take part in sports and other physical activities." SLJ

Includes bibliography

Smith, Elizabeth Simpson
A guide dog goes to school; the story of a dog trained to lead the blind; illustrated by Bert Dodson. Morrow 1987 51p il $12.95; lib bdg $12.88 (3-5) **362.4**

1. Guide dogs
ISBN 0-688-06844-8; 0-688-06846-4 (lib bdg) LC 87-11056

"The author describes the life, selection, and training of a golden retriever puppy from birth until it graduates with its master and begins a new life as a guide dog. Sixteen full-page drawings complement the text. A brief introduction describes the history of guide dog use and a postscript cautions against disturbing a guide dog when it is working. This book accurately and sensitively portrays the concern, effort, and nurturing that are required to select and train any guide dog." Sci Child

Wolf, Bernard, 1930-
Anna's silent world. Lippincott 1977 48p il $12.95 (2-4) **362.4**

1. Deaf
ISBN 0-397-31739-5 LC 76-52943

"Anna, born deaf, leads for all intents and purposes a normal life. This has been possible because of family support, special training, and sound-amplifying technology that maximizes what little hearing she does possess. Wolf's photographs and running text take us into Anna's life, showing her in a round of activities with family, friends, teachers, and pets. Information on deafness and the kinds of therapy that work to overcome it twine through the text." Booklist

Don't feel sorry for Paul; written and photographed by Bernard Wolf. Lippincott 1974 94p il lib bdg $13.89 (3-6) **362.4**

1. Physically handicapped children
ISBN 0-397-32269-0

"Written in the form of a documentary, [this book] presents the highlights of several weeks in the life of Paul Jockimo, a child born without a right hand and foot, and with a deformed left hand and left foot. In stark pictures with accompanying text, we see Paul's deformities and watch as he puts on the three prosthetic devices. We follow him bicycling, playing, going to school, celebrating his seventh birthday, and, finally, winning second prize in a horse show. We also follow him through a session at the Institute for Rehabilitative Medicine after he has broken two of his prostheses, and we learn how artificial devices that substitute for feet are made." N Y Times Book Rev

"Photographs of superb quality illustrate a text written with candor and dignity." Bull Cent Child Books

362.7 Problems of and services to young people

Krementz, Jill
How it feels to be adopted. Knopf 1982 107p il $15.95; pa $7.95 (4 and up) **362.7**

1. Adoption
ISBN 0-394-52851-4; 0-394-75853-6 (pa) LC 82-48011

"Nineteen youngsters ranging in age from 8 to 16 voice their feelings about being adopted. All are glad to be part of their families; more at odds are their thoughts on their biological mothers. There is universal curiosity about their roots, and many of the kids display an interest in either searching for their birth mothers or being sought out by them—not to set aside their real families, but simply to know more about who they are. . . . Several of the accounts are by youngsters who 'have' found their birth mothers and are in the process of getting to know them. Single-parent adoptees are included, too." Booklist

Includes bibliography

Rosenberg, Maxine B., 1939-
Being adopted; photographs by George Ancona. Lothrop, Lee & Shepard Bks. 1984 unp il $13.95; lib bdg $13.88 (2-4) **362.7**

1. Interracial adoption
ISBN 0-688-02672-9; 0-688-02673-7 (lib bdg) LC 83-17522

"The author stresses the problems adoptive children—especially those from other countries or those who look markedly different from other members of their families—have in ajusting to their new homes." Bull Cent Child Books

"Although most of the crisp black-and-white photographs appearing on every page are purposely posed to go along with the narrative, they are relaxed and informal in style, successfully capturing the warmth of these special family relationships. This exceptional photo-documentary look at an increasingly common type of adoption will be reassuring for children who are adopted and enlightening for those who aren't." Booklist

Sobol, Harriet Langsam, 1936-
We don't look like our Mom and Dad; photographs by Patricia Agre. Coward-McCann 1984 32p il $11.95 (2-5) **362.7**

1. Interracial adoption 2. Korean Americans
ISBN 0-698-20608-8 LC 83-24040

"Through photographs and narrative, the concerns of two Korean boys adopted by a childless American couple are explored. Their curiosity about their biological parents and their occasional discomfort in American society are described in a realistic way." Child Book Rev Serv

"Patricia Agre's photographs reflect the warm and loving family life in which Mr. and Mrs. Levin help their sons grow up as Levins—with a Korean heritage." Kobrin Letter

Terkel, Susan Neiburg, 1948-
Feeling safe, feeling strong; how to avoid sexual abuse and what to do if it happens to you; [by] Susan N. Terkel & Janice E. Rench. Lerner Publs. 1984 68p il lib bdg $9.95 (4 and up) **362.7**

1. Child molesting
ISBN 0-8225-0021-3 LC 84-9664

This book presents "six stories, each about a young person faced with a particular type of abuse, from obscene phone calls to incest. In every case the young person either gets control of the situation alone or goes to an adult who helps. All six stories are followed by facts about the type of abuse and information on how to avoid or seek help." Child Book Rev Serv

"This polished, professional presentation offers a wealth of sound information and advice. The tone is supportive and straight-forward; it's useful for both the independent reader and the teacher or parent who wishes to educate young audiences on the topic." Booklist

Wachter, Oralee

No more secrets for me; illustrated by Jane Aaron. Little, Brown 1983 46p il $14.95; pa $4.95 (2-5) **362.7**

1. Child molesting
ISBN 0-316-91490-8; 0-316-91491-6 (pa) LC 83-12077

This book "is adapted from Wachter's award-winning film, animated by Aaron, whose colored sketches illustrate the text. There are stories about children preyed upon sexually by adults: a stepfather, babysitter, camp counselor. . . . Boys and girls of all ages learn that bodily assaults must be reported, no matter who makes them, regardless of threats or orders to keep 'the game our little secret.'" Booklist

362.84 Problems of and services to members of racial, ethnic, national groups

Ashabranner, Brent K., 1921-

Into a strange land: unaccompanied refugee youth in America; [by] Brent Ashabranner and Melissa Ashabranner; illustrated with photographs. Dodd, Mead 1987 120p il $12.95 (5 and up) **362.84**

1. Refugees
ISBN 0-396-08841-4 LC 86-24357

"This book explores the plight of unaccompanied refugee children as they struggle to make a new home in the U.S. These children come from a variety of circumstances: some are orphaned; some have been smuggled out by parents who hope that their futures will be brighter in the U.S.; and some are Amerasian children who are outcasts in their own cultures. . . . The Ashabranners have conducted extensive interviews with the children, with their foster parents, and with the social workers and other personnel who engineer the fates of these youngsters." Booklist

Includes bibliography

363 Other social problems and services

Pringle, Laurence P.

Living in a risky world; [by] Laurence Pringle. Morrow Junior Bks. 1989 105p il $12.95 (6 and up) **363**

1. Environmental health 2. Safety education
ISBN 0-688-04326-7 LC 88-31686

In this study the author attempts to explore "the scientific and social factors in risk assessment and risk management. The problems associated with acid rain, carcinogens, and other hazardous results of human activity and counter-measures, such as animal testing and the science of toxicology, are cited, and the study of risk as a distinct field of specialization is [considered]." Horn Book

Includes glossary and bibliography

363.1 Public safety programs

Hjelmeland, Andy

Drinking & driving; edited by Laurie Beckelman; consultant, Elaine Wynne. Crestwood House 1990 48p il (Facts about) $10.95 (4-6) **363.1**

1. Youth—Alcohol use 2. Drunk driving
ISBN 0-89686-496-0 LC 89-25406

Discusses the consequences of drinking and then driving, with a step-by-step scenario of what happens to a driver who is arrested for drunk driving. Includes addresses to write to for more information

Includes glossary

363.3 Other aspects of public safety

Gibbons, Gail

Fire! Fire! Crowell 1984 unp il $13.95; lib bdg $13.89; pa $4.95 (1-3) **363.3**

1. Fire fighting
ISBN 0-690-04417-8; 0-690-04416-X (lib bdg); 0-06-446058-4 (pa) LC 83-46162

This book "depicts fire fighting in the city, country, forest, and on the water, and integrates some points on fire safety." Child Book Rev Serv

The author/illustrator "uses bright colors and simplified diagrams to convey the excitement and teamwork necessary in firefighting. There are details for children to pore over and the equipment in the illustrations is clearly labeled." SLJ

Our violent earth. National Geographic Soc. 1982 103p il $6.95; lib bdg $8.50 (4 and up) **363.3**

1. Natural disasters
ISBN 0-87044-383-6; 0-87044-388-7 (lib bdg) LC 80-8797

"Books for world explorers"

Describes the causes and effects of such geologic and atmospheric phenomena as earthquakes, volcanoes, storms, drought, fire, and flood

Includes bibliography

Wolf, Bernard, 1930-

Firehouse. Morrow 1983 80p il $11.95; lib bdg $11.88 (3-6) **363.3**

1. Fire departments 2. Fire fighters 3. Fire prevention
ISBN 0-688-01734-7; 0-688-01735-5 (lib bdg) LC 83-1174

A "look at life behind-the-scenes in a big-city firehouse, in this case Manhattan's Engine Company 33 of the Lower East Side. Wolf shows the fire fighters at 'home' and on the streets in an . . . array of photographs (some photographed under difficult circumstances) that capture not only the danger and drama of a hot call but also the lighter moments of in-station daily life." Booklist

"Action-filled photographs portray with remarkable immediacy the daily drama of a fire fighter's work." Horn Book

363.4 Controversies related to public morals and customs

Hyde, Margaret Oldroyd, 1917-
Drug wars. Walker & Co. 1990 103p $11.95; lib bdg $12.85 (6 and up) **363.4**
1. Drug abuse
ISBN 0-8027-6900-4; 0-8027-6901-2 (lib bdg)
LC 89-37548
"Covering cocaine, heroin, marijuana, alcohol, and tobacco in separate chapters, Hyde makes important distinctions about the nature of each drug; places its use in historical, political, and cultural context; and suggests strategies for controlling the drug's use or abuse. She discusses preventive education, early intervention, medical advances in understanding and treating addictions, legalization, interdiction, legal sanctions, and increased health awareness among consumers." Voice Youth Advocates
Includes bibliography

363.5 Housing

Shachtman, Tom, 1942-
The president builds a house; photographs by Margaret Miller; introduction by Jimmy Carter. Simon & Schuster Bks. for Young Readers 1989 unp il $14.95 (3-5) **363.5**
1. Habitat for Humanity Inc. 2. Housing
ISBN 0-671-67705-5 LC 88-33267
"A well-organized photo essay shows how volunteers from the Habitat for Humanity organization, including former President Jimmy Carter and his wife, built 20 houses in Atlanta in one week during the summer of 1988. The short text gives the history of the group and its goals." N Y Times Book Rev

363.7 Environmental problems and services

Baines, John D. (John David), 1943-
Acid rain; [by] John Baines. Steck-Vaughn 1990 48p il (Conserving our world) $15.95 (5 and up) **363.7**
1. Acid rain
ISBN 0-8114-2385-9 LC 89-21656
Discusses the vast contamination of forests and lakes throughout the world by the acidity in the rainfall
"The book concludes by reviewing previously presented information and evaluating suggested tentative solutions. In addition, there are a glossary of terms, suggestions for further study, a directory of conservation organizations, and an index. Acid Rain is highly recommended for supplementary reading and study in a classroom situation. It is also an excellent introductory resource text in summary form." Sci Books Films

Hadingham, Evan
Garbage! where it comes from, where it goes; [by] Evan & Janet Hadingham. Simon & Schuster Bks. for Young Readers 1990 48p il maps $14.95; pa $5.95 (5 and up) **363.7**
1. Refuse and refuse disposal
ISBN 0-671-69424-3; 0-671-69426-X (pa)
LC 89-26205
"A Novabook"
Published in association with WGBH, Boston
Documents the ever-increasing problem of what can be done to dispose of our garbage
"A realistic presentation of the enormity of a current problem, emphasizing the difficulties of finding answers, but encouraging personal and political alternatives. Each page is lavishly illustrated with high-quality color photographs; inserts enhance the basic text with 'Amazing Garbage Facts' and similar material." SLJ

Hare, Tony
Acid rain. Gloucester Press 1990 32p il map (Save our Earth) lib bdg $11.90 (5 and up) **363.7**
1. Acid rain 2. Pollution
ISBN 0-531-17247-3 LC 90-3228
Examines the cause and effects of acid rain, and shows how it can be prevented
Includes glossary

Johnson, Rebecca L.
The greenhouse effect; life on a warmer planet. Lerner Publs. 1990 112p il (Discovery!) lib bdg $15.95 (5 and up) **363.7**
1. Greenhouse effect
ISBN 0-8225-1591-1 LC 89-49760
Discusses what the greenhouse effect is, research into its causes, and its possible impact on our planet
"The tone throughout is balanced and emphasizes the role of data in building models and making predictions. The book is well designed, and the color photographs are attractive and appropriate. The information and illustrations in this book would be quite useful to elementary teacher introducing environmental concepts." Sci Books Films
Includes glossary

Maurer, R. (Richard)
Junk in space. Simon & Schuster Bks. for Young Readers 1989 48p il maps $14.95; pa $5.95 (4-6) **363.7**
1. Space environment 2. Refuse and refuse disposal
ISBN 0-671-67768-3; 0-671-67767-5 (pa)
LC 89-30060
"A Novabook"
Published in association with WGBH Boston
"Tons of space litter orbit the Earth. The moon and several planets are dotted with technological trash and garbage left behind during exploration. An interesting text, supplemented by fine, full-color photographs and

Maurer, R. (Richard)—*Continued*
clear diagrams, marks locations and orbits, and explains how the junk got there and the problems it may cause in the future." Sci Child

Pringle, Laurence P.

Global warming; [by] Laurence Pringle. Arcade Pub. 1990 46p il maps $14.95 (3-5) **363.7**

1. Greenhouse effect
ISBN 1-55970-012-2 LC 89-82204

"An assessment of the greenhouse threat in an appealing format with thorough, up-to-date information on the causes and effects of temperature changes around the world. Includes a discussion of reducing greenhouse gases." Sci Child

Includes glossary

Throwing things away; from middens to resource recovery; by Laurence Pringle. Crowell 1986 90p il $12.95; lib bdg $12.89 (6 and up) **363.7**

1. Refuse and refuse disposal
ISBN 0-690-04420-8; 0-690-04421-6 (lib bdg) LC 83-46165

"Taking a sobering look at the problems of landfill sites and garbage dumps, Pringle describes the problems (increasing) of health hazards, pollution by seepage and toxic wastes, and environmental disturbance. He looks at the solutions that have been tried . . . and at some of the legal and ethical issues raised by such aspects of our wasteful society as the impact on animal predators, the effects of their changed behavior, the assignment of responsibility when there is environmental or personal damage, or the individual's role in conservation, disposal, and recycling programs." Bull Cent Child Books

"Accessible without being condescending, the work (complete with bibliography) will serve student and teacher well." Voice Youth Advocates

Woods, Geraldine, 1948-

Pollution; [by] Geraldine and Harold Woods. Watts 1985 64p il lib bdg $9.40 (6 and up) **363.7**

1. Pollution
ISBN 0-531-04916-7 LC 84-20982

"A First book"

This book describes the causes of pollution, air and water pollution, pesticide pollution, garbage and toxic wastes, and the dangers of nuclear pollution

"This slim book is packed with statistics and information. It is grim and thought provoking." Voice Youth Advocates

Includes glossary and bibliography

369.463 Girl Scouts and Girl Guides

World Association of Girl Guides and Girl Scouts

Trefoil round the world; girl guiding and girl scouting in many lands. World Assn. of Girl Guides & Girl Scouts il pa $7 **369.463**

1. Girl Scouts

First published 1958. Periodically revised

This history of girl scouting tells how the World Association of Girl Guides and Girl Scouts began, and includes words of promise and law, mottos, and programs of the member countries

370.9 Education—Historical and geographic treatment

Loeper, John J.

Going to school in 1776. Atheneum Pubs. 1973 79p il $13.95 (4 and up) **370.9**

1. Education—United States—History 2. Schools—United States—History 3. United States—Social life and customs—1600-1775, Colonial period
ISBN 0-689-30089-1 LC 72-86940

The author tells what it was like to be a child and to go to school in America in 1776. He describes children's dress, schools, teachers, school books, lessons, discipline and after-school recreation

Includes bibliography

Going to school in 1876. Atheneum Pubs. 1984 83p il $11.95 (4 and up) **370.9**

1. Education—United States—History 2. Schools—United States—History 3. United States—Social life and customs
ISBN 0-689-31015-3 LC 83-15669

Describes the life of school children in 1876: their dress, teachers, schoolhouses, books, lessons, discipline, and pastimes

"Punctuated with excerpts from diaries, correspondence, newspaper advertisements and contemporary textbooks, as well as black-and-white prints highlighting various aspects of the society in 1876, the book breathes life into history." SLJ

Includes bibliography

371.3 Methods of instruction and study

James, Elizabeth
How to be school smart; secrets of successful schoolwork; [by] Elizabeth James & Carol Barkin; pictures by Roy Doty; with an introduction by M. Jean Greenlaw. Lothrop, Lee & Shepard Bks. 1988 94p il lib bdg $12.88; pa $6.95 (5 and up) 371.3

1. Study, Method of
ISBN 0-688-06799-9 (lib bdg); 0-688-06798-0 (pa) LC 87-2899

"The authors discuss home study areas, time management, learning styles, homework, test taking, and attitude. . . . The book is full of practical hints such as using a tape recorder for note taking and studying, making flash cards, etc. The chapter on test taking includes many helpful strategies. This positive book will help students interested in improving their schoolwork." Voice Youth Advocates

371.3025 Audio and visual materials—Directories

Audio video market place; the complete A/V business directory. Bowker il pa $75 371.3025

1. Audiovisual materials—Directories
ISSN 0067-0553

Annual. First published 1969 with title: Audiovisual market place

At head of title: AVMP

"A guide to firms and individuals that produce, supply, or service audiovisual materials. Covers both software and hardware. Supplementary lists include reference books and directories, periodicals and trade journals, and associations." A L A. Ref Sources for Small & Medium-sized Libr. 4th edition

371.9 Special education

Fisher, Gary L.
The survival guide for kids with LD (learning differences); by Gary L. Fisher and Rhoda Woods Cummings; edited by Nancy J. Nielsen; illustrated by Jackie Urbanovic. Free Spirit 1990 97p il pa $9.95 (5 and up) 371.9

1. Learning disabilities
ISBN 0-915793-18-0 LC 89-37084

This book discusses different types of disorders, programs at school, coping with negative feelings, and making friends

"Format and organization, of critical importance to the readers, is excellent. The text is interspersed with black and white cartoon drawings, quotes from kids age eight to 12, and material boxed for emphasis. A final section for parents and teachers offers a short bibliography of books and other materials of interest to LD students, a list of LD organizations, and a note to parents from the authors stressing their belief that home is a haven and homework should be kept to a minimum since a school day is frustration enough." Voice Youth Advocates

372.05 Elementary education—Serial publications

Childhood Education. Association for Childhood Educ. Int. $65 per year 372.05

1. Education, Elementary—Periodicals
ISSN 0009-4056

Five issues a year. First published 1924. Subtitle and frequency of publication vary

"A journal for teachers, teachers-in-training, teacher educators, parents, day care workers, librarians, pediatricians and other child caregivers."

This journal "is written in a popular style understandable by layperson and professional and is suitable for parents and for professionals involved in the education of children and young adults. The articles stress the practical approach to child development. . . . Regular departments include book reviews of books for children and professionals, reviews of films and pamphlets, summaries of current research in magazine articles and ERIC documents, software reviews, information from the field, and comments from readers and the editor. It is recommended that this magazine be considered by all libraries for purchase." Katz. Mag for Sch Libr

Instructor. Scholastic $14.95 per year 372.05

1. Education, Elementary—Periodicals
ISSN 1049-5851

Nine issues a year. First published 1891. Title and publisher vary

"Directed to the elementary school teacher, this magazine is a gold mine of activities, ideas, and resources to make classroom teaching and learning an active, fun experience. The emphasis is on the practical. Brief articles, usually written by experienced grade school teachers, share successful learning activities and ideas for zippy lessons. There is an abundance of illustrations, material on curriculum, trends in education, and arts and crafts suggestions." Katz. Mag for Sch Libr

372.1 Organization and management of elementary schools; curriculum

Cole, Ann
I saw a purple cow, and 100 other recipes for learning; [by] Ann Cole [et al.]; illustrated by True Kelley. Little, Brown 1972 96p il $14.95; pa $8.95 372.1

1. Education, Preschool 2. Amusements
ISBN 0-316-15174-2; 0-316-15175-0 (pa) LC 72-404

"Based on research done in Project Headstart, this book serves as a guide to the effective use of throw-away objects found in the house and environs as creative learning devices for young children. It is geared to the

Cole, Ann—*Continued*
important first six years of children's lives and attempts to help the untrained mother during this period." Libr J

Purple cow to the rescue; by Ann Cole, Carolyn Haas, Betty Weinberger; illustrated by True Kelley. Little, Brown 1982 160p il $14.95; pa $8.95 **372.1**

1. Education, Preschool 2. Education, Elementary 3. Amusements
ISBN 0-316-15104-1; 0-316-15106-8 (pa)
LC 81-17156

A collection of activities grouped into six general areas: "'Getting to Know and Like Yourself' (ways to build a positive self-image); 'Learning to Be Independent' (doing things for and by yourself); 'Learning the Basics' (skill-building by working with scissors, crayons, paint, and clay); 'Traveling' . . . 'Moving' . . . and 'Winding Down' (quiet breaks in a busy day). . . . While the original Purple Cow book [entered above] provided a preschool 'curriculum' for the younger set, this . . . focuses on a broader age range." Introduction

372.4 Reading

Kaye, Peggy, 1948-
Games for reading; playful ways to help your child read; written by Peggy Kaye; with illustrations by the author. Pantheon Bks. 1984 213p il $15.95; pa $10.95 **372.4**

1. Reading 2. Games
ISBN 0-394-52785-2; 0-394-72149-7 (pa)
LC 83-19403

"This guide suggests a whole new way for parents and teachers to encourage reading as a delightful activity. Besides the reading-aloud concept, suggestions include 70 clear-cut games and activities that contribute to reading development. The author suggests a bingo game to learn vocabulary. A rhyming game helps children hear letter sounds more accurately. There are mazes and puzzles, games that train the ear so a child can sound out words, games that awaken a child's imagination and creativity, and games that encourage motivation for reading." Read Teach

Includes bibliography

The **RIF** guide to encouraging young readers; a fun-filled sourcebook of over 200 favorite reading activities of kids and parents from across the country, plus an annotated list of books and resources; by Reading is Fundamental; edited by Ruth Graves. Doubleday 1987 324p hardcover o.p. paperback available $9.95 **372.4**

1. Reading 2. Games
ISBN 0-385-24110-0 (pa) LC 86-24055

"Gathered from Reading Is Fundamental (RIF) volunteers across the country, the more than 200 activities described here are designed to engage children in the fun of words and reading. Usually one idea per page is presented with ages and needed materials noted at the top. The easy-to-carry-out projects revolve around food, the backyard, television tie-ins, shopping, and family car trips. . . . Appended: bibliographies for children and resources for parents, including magazine and book clubs for kids." Booklist

372.405 Reading—Serial publications

The **Reading** Teacher. International Reading Assn. $30 per year **372.405**

1. Reading—Periodicals
ISSN 0034-0561

Nine issues a year, from October to May. First published 1947

"The basic journal for teachers of elementary and middle school reading. . . . Articles are brief, topical, and usually clearly written. This is a clearinghouse for all kinds of reading information—from software evaluations to conference and association news to a brief section where teachers can present good teaching ideas and activities. This title should be scanned by every reading teacher." Katz. Mag for Sch Libr

372.6 Language arts (Communication skills). Storytelling

Baker, Augusta, 1911-
Storytelling: art and technique; by Augusta Baker and Ellin Greene. 2nd ed. Bowker 1987 182p il $29.95 **372.6**

1. Storytelling
ISBN 0-8352-2336-1 LC 87-26539
First published 1977

This book examines the history, purpose, and value of storytelling as practiced in the United States. The preparation, presentation, and administration of story hour programs is discussed and an overview of currently available materials is provided

Includes bibliography

Bauer, Caroline Feller, 1935-
Handbook for storytellers. American Lib. Assn. 1977 381p il music pa $22.50 **372.6**

1. Storytelling
ISBN 0-8389-0225-1 LC 76-56385

"Design by Vladimir Reichl. Pen-and-ink drawings by Kevin Royt"

"Bauer presents multitudinous simple but ingenious ideas for the storyteller—magnetic boards, puppets, paper cut-outs, videotapes, picture posters, costumes, favors, music, and much more. Divided into four parts, the book covers (1) planning, preparation, and promotion; (2) sources for storytelling; (3) multimedia storytelling; and (4) programs for specific age and interest groups. This volume complements other works in the field, such as Ruth Sawyer's 'The way of the storyteller,' Marie Shedlock's 'The art of the storyteller,' and Sylvia Ziskind's 'Telling stories to children,' [all entered below]. It expands upon these basic works by adding multimedia storytelling techniques and a great variety of mechanical aids, as well as illustrations and examples of appropriate

Bauer, Caroline Feller, 1935-—*Continued*
materials." Choice
Includes bibliographies

Carlson, Bernice Wells
Listen! and help tell the story; illustrated by Burmah Burris. Abingdon Press 1965 176p il $9.95 **372.6**
1. Storytelling 2. Literature—Collected works
ISBN 0-687-22096-3 LC 65-14090
"Pre-schoolers learn first to listen and then to participate in these finger-plays, action verses and poems with sound effects and choruses which may be used with either a single child or any sized group." Ont Libr Rev
"Though Miss Carlson states that the book is for the child's own use, its basic value will be to teachers and parents. . . . The art work is uneven in quality but has the merit of showing racial integration." SLJ

Champlin, Connie (Constance J.)
Storytelling with puppets; [by] Connie Champlin and Nancy Renfro. American Lib. Assn. 1985 293p il pa $19.95 **372.6**
1. Storytelling 2. Puppets and puppet plays
ISBN 0-8389-0421-1 LC 84-18406
"The book deals with adapting stories for puppetry, building a puppet collection, roles for the puppets, paticipatory storytelling, and presentation formats. The practical hints, drawings, and patterns are especially useful to beginning librarians and storytellers and, at the same time, the numerous, innovative ideas will spark renewed interest in more experienced professionals. The appendix includes puppetry and storytelling organizations as well as bibliographies of puppetry and storytelling books." Booklist

DeWit, Dorothy, 1916-1980
Children's faces looking up; program building for the storyteller. American Lib. Assn. 1979 156p $15 **372.6**
1. Storytelling
ISBN 0-8389-0272-3 LC 78-10702
"Discussion of storytelling's evolution, a definition of the tellable tale, and recognition of quality material precede the six sample programs. These center on motifs such as magic, holidays, animals, and feasting. An extensive bibliography of sources is appended." Booklist

Hopkins, Lee Bennett, 1938-
Pass the poetry, please! rev enl & updated ed. Harper & Row 1987 262p $18.95; pa $10.95 **372.6**
1. Poetry—Study and teaching
ISBN 0-06-022602-1; 0-06-446062-2 (pa)
LC 86-45758
First published 1972
"Following his introductory comments on what poetry is and the reasons for exposing children to it, Hopkins introduces 20 contemporary poets . . . and suggests specific works from their repertoires. In a third section, the author gives ways to rouse children's interest in writing poetry and then rounds out his presentation with ideas to help children appreciate verse in the home, library, and classroom. Hopkins' excitement about his topic overflows the pages and will be an inspirational source for the novice and the experienced adult working at bringing children and poetry together." Booklist
Includes bibliographies

Juba this and Juba that; story hour stretches for large and small groups; selected by Virginia A. Tashjian; with illustrations by Victoria de Larrea. Little, Brown 1969 116p il $14.95 **372.6**
1. Storytelling 2. Literature—Collected works
ISBN 0-316-83230-8 LC 69-10666
Companion volume to: With a deep sea smile, entered below
"A useful source of chants, poetry and rhyme, stories, finger plays, riddles, songs, tongue twisters, and jokes. The selections accompanied by lively orange and black illustrations, are all suitably silly. They require and inspire audience participation." SLJ

MacDonald, Margaret Read
Twenty tellable tales; audience participation folktales for the beginning storyteller; drawings by Roxane Murphy. Wilson, H.W. 1986 220p il $32 **372.6**
1. Storytelling 2. Folklore 3. Fairy tales
ISBN 0-8242-0719-X LC 85-26565
"Dividing her book into three sections—tales, notes, and sources—MacDonald gives instructions for selecting, shaping, learning, and telling each tale and includes notes on their origin as well as comments on audience participation and performance style in other cultures. All the tales are short and include repetitive verses, making them highly suitable for telling aloud." Booklist
Includes bibliography

When the lights go out; twenty scary tales to tell; illustrations by Roxane Murphy. Wilson, H.W. 1988 176p il $30 **372.6**
1. Storytelling 2. Horror—Fiction 3. Folklore
ISBN 0-8242-0770-X LC 88-14197
"Divided into six sections—Not Too Scary, Scary in the Dark, Gross Stuff, Jump Tales, Tales to Act Out, and Tales to Draw or Stir Up—the selections will be especially useful around Halloween, although, as the author points out, the book can be used year round. Following each inclusion are helpful notes on telling the stories and a section that gives sources on origins and variants. Murphy's decorative drawings introduce chapters and are scattered throughout the text. Several concluding chapters list bibliographies and provide other helpful information." Booklist

Pellowski, Anne

The family storytelling handbook; how to use stories, anecdotes, rhymes, handkerchiefs, paper, and other objects to enrich your family traditions; illustrated by Lynn Sweat. Macmillan 1987 150p il $15.95 **372.6**

1. Storytelling
ISBN 0-02-770610-9 LC 87-7981

"In brief chapters divided into the why, when, what, and how of telling stories, this renowned storyteller gives all the basics along with amusing anecdotes. She also includes stories to tell using a variety of methods." Child Book Rev Serv

"The author's encouraging, easy style will motivate parents and other adults, but this will also serve beginning librarians who need support as well as the simple storytelling basics. A bibliography, compilation of sources, and a list of storytelling events around the world are appended." Booklist

The story vine; a source book of unusual and easy-to-tell stories from around the world; illustrated by Lynn Sweat. Macmillan 1984 116p il 14.95; pa $7.95 **372.6**

1. Storytelling 2. Folklore
ISBN 0-02-770590-0; 0-02-044690-X (pa)
LC 83-27307

"The two dozen folk stories in this book use aids; string or braided yarn, picture-drawing, dolls, a traditional musical instrument, or the storyteller's fingers. Step-by-step directions with drawings make this a practical book for the storyteller, and there's a bibliography at the end of each section, helpful in building an extensive aided-story collection. Ingenious are the 'sand stories' from Australia. These and others can inspire children to tell aided stories of their own." Read Teach

The world of storytelling. expanded and rev ed. Wilson, H.W. 1990 xxi, 311p il $32 **372.6**

1. Storytelling
ISBN 0-8242-0788-2 LC 90-31151

First published 1977

This guide "reviews the oral traditions from which literature for children grew, addresses the controversy between storytellers and folklorists, and offers a modern-day definition for storytelling. *The world of storytelling* also includes chapters on: types of storytelling—bardic, folk, religious, theatrical, library and institutional, campground and playground, hygienic and therapeutic storytelling; format and style of storytelling—opening and closing of a story session; language, voice, and audience response; musical accompaniment; pictures and objects used; training of storytellers—history and survey of training methods; visuality, orality, and literacy; storytelling festivals." Publisher's note

"This is an important work for collections serving adult students of storytelling and the oral tradition." J Youth Serv Libr

Includes bibliography

Sawyer, Ruth, 1880-1970

The way of the storyteller. Viking 1962 360p il o.p.; Penguin Bks. paperback available $8.95 **372.6**

1. Storytelling 2. Literature—Collected works
ISBN 0-14-004436-1 (pa) LC 62-15697

First published 1942

"This is not primarily a book on how to tell stories; it is rather the whole philosophy of story telling as a creative art. From her own rich experience the author writes inspiringly of the background, experience, creative imagination, technique and selection essential to this art. A part of the book is devoted to a few well-loved stories with suggestions and comments." Booklist

Includes bibliography

Shedlock, Marie L., 1854-1935

The art of the story-teller; foreword by Anne Carroll Moore. 3d ed rev, with a new bibliography by Eulalie Steinmetz. Dover Publs. 1951 xxi, 290p pa $5.95 **372.6**

1. Storytelling 2. Literature—Collected works
ISBN 0-486-20635-1 LC 52-9976

First published 1915

"This has long been considered one of the . . . standard books on storytelling. . . . Suggestions for selecting and for telling stories are included as well as eighteen of Miss Shedlock's own favorites. Miss Steinmetz' bibliography . . . seems to me a particularly good one, covering a wide variety of stories." Horn Book

With a deep sea smile; story hour stretches for large or small groups; selected by Virginia A. Tashjian; illustrated by Rosemary Wells. Little, Brown 1974 132p il music $16.95 **372.6**

1. Storytelling 2. Literature—Collected works
ISBN 0-316-83216-2 LC 72-8874

Companion volume to: Juba this and Juba that, entered above

This is a collection of chants, poetry, rhymes, stories, finger plays, riddles, songs, tongue twisters and jokes planned for use as story hour activities. They are taken from a wide variety of sources

"Hints are offered on using the material. Prefacing each selection, and of even greater value, are specific suggestions for stimulating participation. Lively illustrations capture the fun of the contents, making the book attractive to children as well as to adults." Horn Book

Ziskind, Sylvia, 1906-

Telling stories to children. Wilson, H.W. 1976 162p $25 **372.6**

1. Storytelling
ISBN 0-8242-0588-X LC 75-42003

"Guidelines on selecting stories stress the importance of being comfortable with the tale; carefully kept file cards are suggested as a key to fastening the story firmly in mind. There's advice on presenting poetry and using creative dramatics: and a chapter on planning the story hour provides sample introductions and run-throughs for several age groups and audience types. Throughout, there are numerous examples of stories and poems that have

Ziskind, Sylvia, 1906-—*Continued*
worked well for Ziskind, and her extensive bibliography includes source collections of both poetry and stories plus lists of personal favorites. Professional materials on voice and speech, creative dramatics, and puppetry, as well as foreign-language story books, are also listed." Booklist

372.605 Language arts—Serial publications

Language Arts. National Council of Teachers of English $40 per year **372.605**

1. English language—Study and teaching—Periodicals
ISSN 0360-9170

Eight issues a year. First published 1924 with title: Elementary English Review. Also published previously with title: Elementary English

This journal "is a potpourri of articles, debates, interviews, poetry, letters, program descriptions, and position papers. The material is well written, topical, and very practical. Often articles present views from other disciplines such as psychology and linguistics that have implications for language arts teaching. An extremely well put together title." Katz. Mag for Sch Libr

381 Internal commerce (Domestic trade)

Gibbons, Gail

Department store. Crowell 1984 unp il lib bdg $13.89; pa $4.95 (k-3) **381**

1. Department stores
ISBN 0-690-04367-8 (lib bdg); 0-06-446028-2 (pa)
LC 83-45053

"Illustrations with clean lines, almost garish colors, and tidy composition show the many departments, the store layout, and some of the special services of a department store. The text is direct and simple; some of the pictures use balloon captions to give additional information. For most children, the variety and bustle of a large store is interesting; this will give them some background to help them understand the complexity and diversity of a department store." Bull Cent Child Books

Horwitz, Joshua

Night markets; bringing food to a city. Crowell 1984 89p il $12.95; lib bdg $12.89; pa $6.95 (3-6) **381**

1. Markets 2. New York (N.Y.)—Commerce 3. Food supply
ISBN 0-690-04378-3; 0-690-04379-1 (lib bdg); 0-06-446046-0 (pa) LC 83-45242

This book shows "how millions of people in a big city get meat, fish, vegetables and fruit to eat and flowers to satisfy other needs. . . . Text and . . . black-and-white photos reveal the work of teams who are busy from evening through dawn, transporting food via air and in trucks to central points in [New York City]." Publ Wkly

"The brief text accompanies large black-and-white photographs which are, with a few exceptions, clear and well executed. This is an attractive book that encompasses many subjects: careers, city life, transportation, community helpers and food supply." SLJ

383 Postal communication

DiCerto, J. J.

The pony express; hoofbeats in the wilderness; [by] Joseph J. DiCerto. Watts 1989 64p il map lib bdg $11.90 (4 and up) **383**

1. Pony express
ISBN 0-531-10751-5 LC 88-34548

"A First book"

Describes the circumstances under which the Pony Express was founded, how it was organized, the rough territory and general hardships faced by the riders, and the technological innovation that ended it

"The most impressive feature of [this volume] is the full-color, informatively subtitled illustrations, which are well designed with adequate white space for easy readability." SLJ

Includes bibliography

Gibbons, Gail

The post office book; mail and how it moves. Crowell 1982 unp il $13.95; lib bdg $13.89 (k-3) **383**

1. Postal service
ISBN 0-690-04198-5; 0-690-04199-3 (lib bdg)
LC 81-43888

In this book the author "touches briefly on the history of mail delivery and traces the route of a letter from posting to delivery." Booklist

"The red, white, and blue associated with the United States postal system have been used to enliven the meticulous pen-and-ink drawings that trace the many processes involved in transferring mail from sender to recipient. Because the illustrations are carefully designed to explain concepts, much information is conveyed with a minimum of text. . . . The narrative's forthright tone complements the style of the pictures." Horn Book

385 Railroad transportation

Sattler, Helen Roney

Train whistles; a language in code; with pictures by Giulio Maestro. rev ed. Lothrop, Lee & Shepard Bks. 1985 unp il $13; lib bdg $12.88 (k-2) **385**

1. Railroads—Signaling 2. Locomotives
ISBN 0-688-03978-2; 0-688-03980-4 (lib bdg)
LC 84-11279

A revised and newly illustrated edition of the title first published 1977

Describes the use of train whistles as signals and what some of these signals mean

"Well-designed double-page spreads feature close-ups of railroad cars, views of station yards, and panoramic landscapes showing trains traveling through the richly varied countryside. . . . Sattler's text flows well, imparting information about the language of train whistles in a lightly fictionalized mode wholly appropriate for this age level. Young train buffs can actually learn the code, while

Sattler, Helen Roney—*Continued*
others will enjoy the trip without feeling overloaded with technical details. A beautiful picture book on an ever-popular subject." Booklist

386 Inland waterway and ferry transportation

Scarry, Huck, 1953-
Life on a barge; a sketchbook. Prentice-Hall 1982 69p il $10.95 (3-6) **386**
1. Canals 2. Boats and boating
ISBN 0-13-535831-0 LC 81-20976
Discusses the canals found around the world, the barges which use them, and the people who operate these boats
"The text, written in an easy, almost conversational tone, accompanies pages of fine pencil sketches. . . . Scarry has packed in a lot of information regarding shipping via barges and touches topics ranging from Archimedes' principle of water displacement to the history and uses of sugar beets." SLJ

387.1 Ports. Lighthouses

Gibbons, Gail
Beacons of light: lighthouses. Morrow Junior Bks. 1990 unp il $12.95; lib bdg $12.88 (1-3) **387.1**
1. Lighthouses
ISBN 0-688-07379-4; 0-688-07380-8 (lib bdg)
LC 89-33884
The author traces the development of lighthouses "from hilltop bonfires to the electronically controlled beacons that flash warnings to today's passing ships. Drawings of specific lighthouses grace every page. . . . Readers are told of lighthouse keepers' duties, the changing technology of lighthouses, and their status today as high-tech markers." Booklist
"The history of lighthouses is told in a picture book format for independent readers. Although the narrative is simple, the vocabulary and some of the concepts are more difficult than is typical in picture books. . . . However, each difficult concept is clarified with supplementary illustrations or text." Bull Cent Child Books

387.2 Ships

Barton, Byron
Boats. Crowell 1986 unp il $6.95; lib bdg $11.89 (k-1) **387.2**
1. Boats and boating 2. Ships
ISBN 0-694-00059-0; 0-690-04536-0 (lib bdg)
LC 85-47900
Depicts a variety of boats and a cruise ship docking and unloading passengers
"Thick black outlines contain vivid colors . . . clean lines, bright hues, and undemanding text." Booklist

Gibbons, Gail
Boat book. Holiday House 1983 unp il lib bdg $13.95; pa $5.95 (k-2) **387.2**
1. Boats and boating 2. Ships
ISBN 0-8234-0478-1 (lib bdg); 0-8234-0709-8 (pa)
LC 82-15851
An introduction to "all sorts of seafaring craft . . . [including] speedboats, sailboats, canoes, cruise ships, police and fire boats, and commercial and military vessels. Various means of propulsion (wind, oars and paddles, engine power) are explained, as are the uses of each type of boat." Publ Wkly
"The text, though stilted, is logically presented in a non-condescending manner. Bright color illustrations throughout show an array of boats moving through the water. . . . Most of the illustrations are full page, and all of them are playfully bordered with a scalloped edge that resembles an ocean wave." SLJ

Rockwell, Anne F., 1934-
Boats; by Anne Rockwell. Dutton 1982 unp il $11.95; pa $3.95 (k-1) **387.2**
1. Boats and boating 2. Ships
ISBN 0-525-44004-6; 0-525-44219-7 (pa) LC 82-2420
The author describes "boats that float on quiet ponds, rivers 'and the wide, blue sea.' The craft, ranging from tiny sailboats that children maneuver in a park pool to great liners, are all manned by bears who will gain the affection of tykes and also introduce them to boats that are for work, for play; boats that go fast or slow, that float, are pushed and/or pulled by motors, etc." Publ Wkly
"The cheerful line drawings filled with rich, limpid watercolors show the boats on water of varied shades of blue. Of certain appeal to the young, unsophisticated viewer, the book is an outstanding example of an informational picture book." Horn Book

387.7 Air transportation

Barton, Byron
Airplanes. Crowell 1986 unp il $6.95; lib bdg $11.89 (k-1) **387.7**
1. Airplanes
ISBN 0-694-00060-4; 0-690-04532-8 (lib bdg)
LC 85-47899
Brief text and illustrations present a variety of airplanes and what they do, "as well as some of the usual scenes surrounding each (e.g., workers checking a passenger plane). Brightly colored illustrations outlined in heavy black convey a bold and simple first impression, yet they portray a good number of accurate details that preschoolers find so fascinating." SLJ

Airport. Crowell 1982 unp il $12.95; lib bdg $12.89; pa $3.95 (k-1) **387.7**
1. Airports 2. Airplanes
ISBN 0-690-04168-3; 0-690-04169-1 (lib bdg); 0-06-443145-2 (pa) LC 79-7816
"In a brightly illustrated book, the author/artist captures the hustle and bustle of passenger traffic from arrival at the terminal to take off." Kobrin Letter

Rogers, Fred
Going on an airplane; photographs by Jim Judkis. Putnam 1989 unp il $12.95; pa $5.95 (k-2) **387.7**
1. Airports 2. Airplanes
ISBN 0-399-21635-9; 0-399-21633-2 (pa)
LC 88-30736
Details an airplane trip from packing and arriving at the airport to the moment the plane comes down to land in a new city
The text is "accompanied by excellent photographs featuring two young passengers, one traveling with her parents and one traveling by himself, well tended by crew members. Good preparation for a first flight." Horn Book

388.1 Roads and highways

Gibbons, Gail
From path to highway: the story of the Boston Post Road. Crowell 1986 32p il $12.95; lib bdg $13.89 (1-3) **388.1**
1. Roads—History 2. New England—Description and travel
ISBN 0-690-04513-1; 0-690-04514-X (lib bdg)
LC 85-47897
"The author goes back 500 years to trace the development of the Boston Post Road (connecting Boston and New York City), as it changed from a narrow path into a modern, four-lane highway. In doing so, Gibbons touches upon important stages of the nation's history." Publ Wkly
"The clear, factual, and deliberate text is matched by completely charming illustrations. . . . A wonderful introduction to roads, transportation, history, progress." Bull Cent Child Books

388.3 Vehicular transportation

Tunis, Edwin, 1897-1973
Wheels: a pictorial history; written and illustrated by Edwin Tunis. Crowell 1977 c1955 96p il $24.95 (5 and up) **388.3**
1. Carriages and carts 2. Transportation—History
ISBN 0-690-01282-9 LC 76-25809
A reissue of the title first published 1955 by World Publishing Company
Beginning with the first primitive roller this history of land transportation, exclusive of railroads, progresses to the earliest known wheeled vehicle, the Elamite chariot, through Egyptian, Greek, Roman, Oriental chariots, and carts, through the development of the road coaches of Europe and on to automobiles and buses

391 Costume and personal appearance

Barkin, Carol, 1944-
The scary Halloween costume book; by Carol Barkin and Elizabeth James; illustrated by Katherine Coville. Lothrop, Lee & Shepard Bks. 1983 94p il $11.95; lib bdg $11.88 (3-6) **391**
1. Costume 2. Halloween
ISBN 0-688-00956-5; 0-688-00957-3 (lib bdg)
LC 81-14249
A book of instructions for making a variety of easy and scary outfits and creating ghoulish faces for Halloween
"The directions for each costume and facial design are clear; charcoal illustrations show the delightfully creepy finished products. A thorough index provides an easy way to discover how to blacken teeth, act like a witch and more." SLJ

Chernoff, Goldie Taub
Easy costumes you don't have to sew; costumes designed and illustrated by Margaret A. Hartelius. Four Winds Press 1975 41p il $11.95 (3-5) **391**
1. Costume 2. Paper crafts
ISBN 0-02-718230-4 LC 76-46428
"Garbage bags, cartons, cardboard, paper bags, and old white sheets provide the basis for a variety of easy-to-make costumes. At-hand materials (newspaper, milk cartons, string) and clear directions result in simply constructed snowmen, mice, shaggy dogs, turtles, ladybugs, bats, skeletons, robots, totem poles, and even a group dragon. Each two-page spread is devoted to one costume, with careful diagrams, lists of necessary materials, precise instructions for each part, and guidelines for putting on the costume." Booklist

Cummings, Richard, 1931-
101 costumes for all ages, all occasions; illustrated by Opal Jackson. Plays 1987 194p il pa $10 **391**
1. Costume
ISBN 0-8238-0286-8 LC 87-20298
A reissue of the title first published 1970 by D. McKay
"Numbered 1 through 101, costumes vary from those that can be made instantly (caveman, Frankenstein, ghost) to those fashioned from items found around the house. . . . The black-and-white drawings that accompany each description lack detail, but they do give a general idea of the finished product. With costumes from 24 countries and numerous historical periods, this will be of help for both drama groups and party goers." Booklist

Hofsinde, Robert, 1902-1973
Indian costumes; written and illustrated by Robert Hofsinde (Gray-Wolf). Morrow 1968 94p il lib bdg $11.88 (3-6) **391**
1. Indians of North America—Costume and adornment
ISBN 0-688-31614-X LC 68-11895
"The distinctive costumes of ten different North American Indian tribal groups are here illustrated, showing their ceremonial, warring or everyday apparel. Black and white drawings help in explaining how they were made." Bruno. Books for Sch Libr, 1968
The tribes represented are the Apache, Blackfoot, Crow, Iroquois, Navaho, Northwest Coast Indians, Ojibwa, Pueblo, Seminole and Sioux Indians

Hunt, Kari
Masks and mask makers; [by] Kari Hunt and Bernice Wells Carlson. Abingdon Press 1961 67p il $8.75 (5 and up) **391**
1. Masks (Facial) 2. Masks (Sculpture)
ISBN 0-687-23705-X LC 61-5097
A "survey of different types of masks worn by man since primitive times. The authors tell what peoples have used the various masks, and what social and symbolic functions masks have served. Legends and ceremonies associated with their use are described, and instructions are given for homemade masks." AAAS Sci Book List for Child
Includes bibliography

Morris, Ann
Hats, hats, hats; photographs by Ken Heyman. Lothrop, Lee & Shepard Bks. 1989 unp il $12.95; lib bdg $12.88 (k-3) **391**
1. Hats
ISBN 0-688-06338-1; 0-688-06339-X (lib bdg)
LC 88-26676
This book introduces a variety of hats worn around the world
"The vivid color photographs, one or two per page, show people engaged in lively activities while . . . wearing their hats. Each picture offers a strong ethnic identity or a thought-provoking human interaction, with captions of only a few words in large print. An unusual index . . . gives background information about the pictures, citing the countries of origin and a few facts about each . . . kind of hat." SLJ

Roy, Ron, 1940-
Whose shoes are these? photographs by Rosmarie Hausherr. Clarion Bks. 1988 40p il lib bdg $12.95 (k-2) **391**
1. Shoes
ISBN 0-318-35963-4 LC 87-24279
Text and photographs describe the appearance and function of almost twenty types of shoes, including work boots, snowshoes, and basketball sneakers
"Roy tickles viewers' imaginations with a question and then provides a longer-than-you-would-expect answer. Crisp black-and-white photographs capture shoes and feet in action; an enjoyable, informative choice for preschoolers and even those slightly older." Booklist

392 Customs of life cycle and domestic life

Lasker, Joe
Merry ever after; the story of two medieval weddings; written and illustrated by Joe Lasker. Viking 1976 unp il o.p.; Penguin Bks. paperback available $4.95 (3-5) **392**
1. Marriage customs and rites 2. Weddings 3. Civilization, Medieval
ISBN 0-14-050280-7 (pa) LC 75-22017
"Set in medieval Europe, the story tells of the arranged marriage of Anne and Gilbert and, coincidentally, of the marriage of the rather coarser-looking Martha and Simon. The first couple were very rich; the second, peasants." Saturday Rev
"Basing his richly colored and detailed pictures on medieval paintings, Lasker has illustrated his text in a way that can help readers visualize the costumes, architecture, and customs of aristocrats and peasants of medieval Europe. . . . The text, like the illustrations, gives many facts about medieval life styles; the writing is direct and informal; the pictures are handsome." Bull Cent Child Books

Perl, Lila
Candles, cakes, and donkey tails; birthday symbols and celebrations; illustrations by Victoria de Larrea. Clarion Bks. 1984 71p il $13.95; pa $4.95 (3-6) **392**
1. Birthdays
ISBN 0-89919-250-5; 0-89919-315-3 (pa) LC 84-5803
Discusses the significance of birthday symbols and customs, such as candles, cakes, and spanks, and includes information on birthday horoscopes, birthstones, and celebrations in other countries
"Line drawings highlighted with light blue illustrate the clear, informal text and capture the diversity of cultures and the mood of festive celebration that the book conveys." SLJ

393 Death customs

Berrill, Margaret
Mummies, masks, & mourners; illustrated by Chris Molan and with photographs. Lodestar Bks. 1990 c1989 48p il (Time detectives) $14.95 (4-6) **393**
1. Funeral rites and ceremonies 2. Mummies
ISBN 0-525-67282-6 LC 89-31822
First published 1989 in the United Kingdom
"This book examines funeral rites and burial customs discovered by archeology and discusses what the excavations of ancient graves can teach scientists about the lives and belief systems of past societies. Among the peoples covered are the Stone Age inhabitants of Çatal Hüyük (Turkey), the ancient Egyptians, the Sumerians, the Siberians, the Celts of Lindow (England), and the Basket Makers of the American Southwest." SLJ
"The topic is far-reaching, but manageable, the writing is consistently lively, the graphics and layout are

Berrill, Margaret—*Continued*
pleasing." Child Book Rev Serv

Includes glossary

Perl, Lila

Mummies, tombs, and treasure; secrets of ancient Egypt; drawings by Erika Weihs. Clarion Bks. 1987 120p il lib bdg $14.95; pa $5.95 (4 and up) **393**

1. Mummies 2. Funeral rites and ceremonies 3. Egypt—Antiquities

ISBN 0-89919-407-9 (lib bdg); 0-395-54796-2 (pa) LC 86-17646

The author incorporates "information on burial customs, religious beliefs, and historical background along with specifics of the mummification process and the archeological finds that have kept the study of the dead a dynamic one. Without getting too wordy, Perl has included specifics: examination of bone development by X-rays, for instance, . . . [and] the discovery of Tutankhamen's tomb." Bull Cent Child Books

This "book is attractive, readable, plentifully illustrated with drawings and black-and-white photographs. There are sufficient grisly details to keep the pages turning, and readers will come away with a healthy understanding of Egyptian religion, scientific accomplishments, and architectural skills. Phonetic pronunciations throughout make this easily accessible." Appraisal

Includes bibliography

394 General customs

Lasker, Joe

A tournament of knights; written and illustrated by Joe Lasker. Crowell 1986 unp il $12.95; lib bdg $12.89; pa $4.95 (1-3) **394**

1. Knights and knighthood—Fiction 2. Civilization, Medieval

ISBN 0-690-04541-7; 0-690-04542-5 (lib bdg); 0-06-443192-4 (pa) LC 85-48075

The author "describes a medieval tournament, from the pronouncement and tent raisings, to the gathering of knights and testing of noble-born in melee and joust. Lasker makes it clear that these duels were violent and costly—often the loser became a prisoner who had to ransom his horse, arms, and armor, perhaps even land. The story here is of a young lord who must defend his father's barony against an experienced knight errant." Bull Cent Child Books

"We are lucky to have Mr. Lasker's beautifully illustrated account of how a tournament took place, how the horses were prepared, how the knights were armored. A glossary defines the terms; a picture on the back cover identifies the equipment of a knight and the parts of his armor. This is exactly the kind of specific information that young readers treasure." N Y Times Book Rev

394.1 Customs—Eating, drinking

Aliki

A medieval feast; written and illustrated by Aliki. Crowell 1983 unp il $13.95; lib bdg $13.89; pa $5.95 (2-5) **394.1**

1. Dinners and dining—History 2. Courts and courtiers 3. Civilization, Medieval 4. Festivals—History

ISBN 0-690-04245-0; 0-690-04246-9 (lib bdg); 0-06-446050-9 (pa) LC 82-45923

"In pictures of minute, charming detail and vibrant, translucent colors, Aliki takes us through the ritual of preparation and the enthusiastic consumption of a medieval feast served to a king and his retinue when they stop for a few days at Camdenton Manor. Not to be outdone by the art, the text has its own various facets. There is the fictional story set in type outside the art and there is within the paintings a collection of delightful historical, gastronomical, agricultural, and zoological facts printed by hand. And throughout the spendid whole are border decorations worthy of the great illuminated manuscripts." Child Book Rev Serv

Cobb, Vicki

Feeding yourself; pictures by Marylin Hafner. Lippincott 1989 32p il $11.95; lib bdg $11.89 (1-3) **394.1**

1. Tableware

ISBN 0-397-32324-7; 0-397-32325-5 (lib bdg) LC 88-14192

Describes how knives, forks, spoons, and chopsticks came to be invented and how they are used today in eating

The utensils' "origins and uses in many cultures are interpreted through Hafner's lively watercolor ilustrations, which are true to the text, yet humorous. Detailed instructions using chopsticks will intrigue readers of all ages." SLJ

Giblin, James, 1933-

From hand to mouth; or, How we invented knives, forks, spoons, and chopsticks & the table manners to go with them; [by] James Cross Giblin. Crowell 1987 86p il $12.95; lib bdg $12.89 (4 and up) **394.1**

1. Tableware 2. Table etiquette

ISBN 0-690-04660-X; 0-690-04662-6 (lib bdg) LC 86-29341

The author "traces the history of eating utensils and customs from the ancient world to the present. Beginning with the use of small spears to pick meat out of the fire and spoons made of curved goat horns, he follows the development to the controversial introduction of forks, the invention of stainless steel, and the return to casual eating practices with the popularity of fast foods. Readers will be especially interested in the information on eating customs and table manners in different eras and cultures." SLJ

Includes bibliography

394.2 Customs—Special occasions

The **American** book of days; compiled and edited by Jane M. Hatch. 3d ed. Wilson, H.W. 1978 xxvi, 1214p $80 **394.2**

1. Holidays 2. Fasts and feasts 3. Festivals—United States

ISBN 0-8242-0593-6 LC 78-16239

First edition, by George W. Douglas, published 1937

"Emphasis is on historical events relating to the founding and development of the U.S. and major religious and public holidays; descriptive articles; chronological order with detailed index by topic, key people and events." N Y Public Libr. Ref Books for Child Collect

Barkin, Carol, 1944-

Happy Thanksgiving! by Carol Barkin & Elizabeth James; pictures by Giora Carmi. Lothrop, Lee & Shepard Bks. 1987 80p il $12.95; lib bdg $12.88 (4-6) **394.2**

1. Thanksgiving Day

ISBN 0-688-06800-6; 0-688-06801-4 (lib bdg) LC 86-33734

The authors "have compiled a variety of suggestions for projects and activities, recipes, jokes, and decorations. The meaning and history of Thanksgiving are expounded and made relevant for today's children." Child Book Rev Serv

"Teachers will certainly find this worthwhile for class projects, and children who locate the book on their own will be enthusiastic about the many ideas." Booklist

Happy Valentine's Day! by Carol Barkin & Elizabeth James; pictures by Martha Weston. Lothrop, Lee & Shepard Bks. 1988 96p il $12.95; lib bdg $12.88 (4-6) **394.2**

1. Valentine's Day 2. Handicraft 3. Cookery

ISBN 0-688-06796-4; 0-688-06797-2 (lib bdg) LC 87-35812

Presents a short history of Valentine's Day and includes recipes for appropriate foods and desserts and instructions for making Valentines and other decorations

Barth, Edna

Hearts, cupids, and red roses; the story of the Valentine symbols; illustrations by Ursula Arndt. Clarion Bks. 1974 64p il $13.95; pa $5.95 (3-6) **394.2**

1. Valentine's Day 2. Signs and symbols

ISBN 0-395-28841-X; 0-89919-036-7 (pa) LC 73-7128

First published by Seabury Press

The author explores the "symbols and legends associated with Valentine's Day in various countries." Publisher's note

Includes an annotated list of children's Valentine's Day stories and poems, and a list of sources

Includes bibliography

Holly, reindeer, and colored lights; the story of the Christmas symbols; illustrated by Ursula Arndt. Clarion Bks. 1971 96p il $13.95; pa $4.95 (3-6) **394.2**

1. Christmas 2. Signs and symbols

ISBN 0-395-28842-8; 0-89919-037-5 (pa) LC 71-157731

First published by Seabury Press

The author tells the story behind such Christmas symbols as the star, the tree, the Yule log, Santa Claus, Christmas colors, etc. She stresses the similarities between Christmas and earlier pagan festivals that celebrated the winter solstice and describes some of the varying practices in different countries

"The well-written text is concise and interesting and the two-colored marginal drawings are festive. A selected list of books containing Christmas stories and poems is appended." Booklist

Lilies, rabbits, and painted eggs; the story of the Easter symbols; illustrations by Ursula Arndt. Clarion Bks. 1970 63p il $12.95; pa $4.95 (3-6) **394.2**

1. Easter 2. Signs and symbols

ISBN 0-395-28844-4; 0-395-30550-0 (pa) LC 74-97033

First published by Seabury Press

Traces the history of Easter symbols from their Christian and pagan origins to such present-day additions as rabbits and new clothes

"The small pen drawings which illustrate the symbols and the celebrations will please the children, and an index and a bibliography of other Easter books will please the librarian." Horn Book

Shamrocks, harps, and shillelaghs; the story of the St. Patrick's Day symbols; illustrations by Ursula Arndt. Clarion Bks. 1977 95p il $14.95; pa $4.95 (3-6) **394.2**

1. Saint Patrick's Day 2. Signs and symbols

ISBN 0-395-28845-2; 0-89919-038-3 (pa) LC 77-369

First published by Seabury Press

"Irish history, lore, and legend are part of a wealth of information provided about Patrick the real missionary, St. Patrick's Day, and its celebration. Includes lists of stories for St. Patrick's Day and sources." LC. Child Books, 1977

Turkeys, Pilgrims, and Indian corn; the story of the Thanksgiving symbols; illustrations by Ursula Arndt. Clarion Bks. 1975 96p il $13.95; pa $4.95 (3-6) **394.2**

1. Thanksgiving Day 2. Pilgrims (New England colonists) 3. Signs and symbols

ISBN 0-395-28846-0; 0-89919-039-1 (pa) LC 75-4703

First published by Seabury Press

This book provides "information about the Pilgrims' voyage to and life in America and their dealings with the Indians. (The point is made, but not belabored, that the settled land was taken from the Indians.) Interesting sidelights are included about prominent men and women, myths such as Plymouth Rock, and harvest feasts in cultures around the world." SLJ

Barth, Edna—*Continued*

Witches, pumpkins, and grinning ghosts; the story of the Halloween symbols; illustrations by Ursula Arndt. Clarion Bks. 1972 95p il $12.95; pa $4.95 (3-6) **394.2**

1. Halloween 2. Signs and symbols
ISBN 0-395-28847-9; 0-89919-040-5 (pa) LC 72-75705

First published by Seabury Press

"This discusses the origins of Halloween and the way it is celebrated today in different countries. Witches (male and female), bats, toads, ghosts, traditional foods, and other customs and symbols related to All Saint's Day are covered. Barth also touches on the incorporation of pagan beliefs into Christianity." SLJ

"A diverting as well as useful account appropriately illustrated with drawings in black and orange." Booklist

Bartlett, Robert Merrill, 1898-

Thanksgiving Day; illustrations by W. T. Mars. Crowell 1965 unp il (Crowell holiday bk) lib bdg $12.89 (1-3) **394.2**

1. Thanksgiving Day 2. Pilgrims (New England colonists)
ISBN 0-690-81045-8 LC 65-16178

Here is "a simple, brief history of the custom of giving thanks at harvest time from the days of ancient Greece to the present with emphasis on the Pilgrims and their thanksgiving celebrations of 1621 and 1623." Booklist

Borten, Helen

Halloween; written and illustrated by Helen Borten. Crowell 1965 unp il (Crowell holiday bk) lib bdg $12.89 (1-3) **394.2**

1. Halloween
ISBN 0-690-36314-1 LC 65-16184

"Tells how modern Halloween customs and activities derived from ancient pagan and Christian autumn festivals and the witches' sabbaths held in various European countries. Appropriate colored or black-and-white illustrations on almost every page supplement the brief, lucid text." Booklist

Brown, Tricia

Chinese New Year; photographs by Fran Ortiz. Holt & Co. 1987 unp il $12.95 (2-4) **394.2**

1. Chinese New Year 2. Chinese Americans—Social life and customs
ISBN 0-8050-0497-1 LC 87-8532

Text and photographs depict the celebration of Chinese New Year by Chinese Americans living in San Francisco's Chinatown

"The photographs are excellent and well-matched to the text. Intimate and charming scenes of family life are contrasted with public shopping and parade shots." SLJ

Bulla, Clyde Robert, 1914-

St. Valentine's Day; illustrations by Valenti Angelo. Crowell 1965 unp il (Crowell holiday bk) lib bdg $12.89 (1-3) **394.2**

1. Valentine's Day
ISBN 0-690-71744-X LC 65-11643

"A brief and simple text about the origins of the legends and celebration of St. Valentine's Day and about the way the holiday is observed." Bull Cent Child Books

Chase's annual events; special days, weeks & months. Contemporary Bks. $29.95 **394.2**

1. Calendars 2. Almanacs 3. Holidays
ISSN 0740-5286

Annual. First published 1958 with title: Chase's calendar of annual events

Edited by William D. and Helen M. Chase

Arranged chronologically this reference work "includes significant historical events the editor chose from the past five decades and special days of other countries. The inclusion of presidential proclamations shows its national focus, but many local events are listed as well. Many unusual sponsored events are listed with the name and address of the sponsor. *Chases's* has an excellent index, which includes the names of events, locations, and broad subject areas." Booklist

Cooney, Barbara, 1917-

Christmas; written and illustrated by Barbara Cooney. Crowell 1967 unp il (Crowell holiday bk) lib bdg $12.89 (1-3) **394.2**

1. Christmas
ISBN 0-690-19201-0 LC 67-18510

Beginning with the story of the birth of Jesus, this book describes the customs and legends woven into the celebration of Christmas in different parts of the world

De Paola, Tomie, 1934-

The family Christmas tree book; written and illustrated by Tomie de Paola. Holiday House 1980 unp il lib bdg $13.95; pa $5.95 (k-3) **394.2**

1. Christmas
ISBN 0-8234-0416-1 (lib bdg); 0-8234-0535-4 (pa) LC 80-12081

"A family discusses the history and folklore of Christmas trees and ornaments as they cut, haul, stand, and decorate their own tree." Child Book Rev Serv

Dunkling, Leslie, 1935-

A dictionary of days. Facts on File 1988 156p il $19.95; pa $10.95 **394.2**

1. Holidays 2. Festivals
ISBN 0-8160-1916-9; 0-8160-2138-4 (pa) LC 88-3703

This "book is divided into two parts: the dictionary of over 800 entries; then a calendar of named days. It is intended to fill the need for a reader's guide to named days, with entries drawn from 27 categories: political,

Dunkling, Leslie, 1935-—*Continued*
folkloric, ethnic, literary, etc., with a substantial number from religious feasts and holy days. The unusual and curious, such as Pig Face Sunday and Dipping Day, will attract the browser, yet the dictionary also serves general readers and students who need to identify Boxing Day, Yom Kippur, or a reference from Shakespeare." Libr J

Festivals; compiled by Ruth Manning-Sanders; illustrations by Raymond Briggs. Dutton 1973 c1972 188p il $8.95 (3-6) **394.2**

1. Festivals 2. Holidays
ISBN 0-525-29675-1 LC 72-78084

First published 1972 in the United Kingdom

An anthology of stories, poems and reminiscences describing customs and celebrations from many countries of the world. Each special day is preceded by background material on the origin of the holiday

Fisher, Aileen Lucia, 1906-

Easter; [by] Aileen Fisher; illustrations by Ati Forberg. Crowell 1968 unp il (Crowell holiday bk) lib bdg $12.89 (1-3) **394.2**

1. Jesus Christ 2. Easter
ISBN 0-690-25236-6 LC 67-23666

The author describes the world-wide celebration of springtime through the ages, and retells the story of Jesus of Nazareth

Gibbons, Gail

Easter. Holiday House 1989 unp il lib bdg $13.95 (k-2) **394.2**

1. Easter
ISBN 0-8234-0737-3 LC 88-23292

Examines the background, significance, symbols, and traditions of Easter

Gibbons "simplifies complex beliefs and traditions in a straightforward way, though transitions are occasionally abrupt. Pleasing watercolors outlined in black ink illustrate the text." Booklist

Halloween. Holiday House 1984 unp il lib bdg $13.95; pa $5.95 (k-2) **394.2**

1. Halloween
ISBN 0-8234-0524-9 (lib bdg); 0-8234-0577-X (pa) LC 84-519

The author "describes the origins of Halloween beliefs and observances, and discusses the many ways it is celebrated today: the costumes, parties, carved pumpkins, trick-or-treat visiting, games, visits to 'haunted' houses, and costume contests. The text is terse, the subject one in which most children will be interested. . . . The illustrations are bright and bold, with filled pages but no fussy details." Bull Cent Child Books

Happy birthday! Holiday House 1986 unp il $13.95 (k-2) **394.2**

1. Birthdays
ISBN 0-8234-0614-8 LC 86-297

Examines the historical beliefs, traditions, and celebrations associated with birthdays

"Simple text explains that everybody has one and tells why the traditional cake is round, why there's a candle for each year, why the candles are blown out and other historical birthday customs. . . . The story is accompanied by brightly colored artwork, complete with ribbons, confetti, party hats and decorations, making this book as festive and fun as the day it describes." Publ Wkly

Thanksgiving Day. Holiday House 1983 unp il lib bdg $13.95; pa $5.95 (k-2) **394.2**

1. Thanksgiving Day
ISBN 0-8234-0489-7 (lib bdg); 0-8234-0576-1 (pa) LC 83-175

This book presents information about the first Thanksgiving and the way that holiday is celebrated today

Valentine's Day. Holiday House 1986 unp il $13.95; pa $5.95 (k-2) **394.2**

1. Valentine's Day
ISBN 0-8234-0572-9; 0-8234-0764-0 (pa) LC 85-916

The author "briefly describes the history, meaning, and customs of Valentine's Day in picture-book format. Simple line drawings are brightened with the bright, crisp colors that are the artist's hallmark. . . . On the last two pages she shows how to make valentines and a valentine box. A useful addition to a holiday collection for young children and a serviceable read-aloud choice for classrooms where Valentine's Day is celebrated." Booklist

Giblin, James, 1933-

Fireworks, picnics, and flags; [by] James Cross Giblin; illustrated by Ursula Arndt. Clarion Bks. 1983 90p il $13.95; pa $4.95 (3-6) **394.2**

1. Fourth of July
ISBN 0-89919-146-0; 0-89919-174-6 (pa) LC 82-9612

Traces the social history behind America's celebration of Independence Day and explains the background of such national symbols as the flag, the bald eagle, the Liberty Bell, and Uncle Sam

"Giblin was the editor of Edna Barth's books on holiday symbols; according to his author's note, he knew that Barth intended to write about the Fourth of July and took on the project himself after her death. The result is consistent in both format and spirit with the well-known Barth series, complete with Arndt's unpretentious two-color drawings." Booklist

The truth about Santa Claus. Crowell 1985 86p il $12.95; lib bdg $12.89 (4 and up) **394.2**

1. Santa Claus 2. Christmas
ISBN 0-690-04483-6; 0-690-04484-4 (lib bdg) LC 85-47541

"Historical discussion of the religious, mythological, folk and commercial traditions that have become the contemporary image of Santa Claus." Soc Educ

"Reproductions of paintings and cartoons, as well as photographs, illustrate the diverse European legends and the contemporary Santa Claus figure. . . . An interesting picture of the ways in which customs arise, fuse, change, are diffused only to change again." Bull Cent Child Books

Includes bibliography

Gregory, Ruth W. (Ruth Wilhelme), 1910-
Anniversaries and holidays. 4th ed. American Lib. Assn. 1983 262p $25 **394.2**
1. Holidays 2. Calendars 3. Birthdays
ISBN 0-8389-0389-4 LC 83-3784
First edition by Mary Emogene Hazeltine published 1928
"Covers, in calendar form, the names of important people, holidays, religious festivals and special events for nearly 200 countries. Annotated bibliographies about holidays, etc." N Y Public Libr. Ref Books for Child Collect

Grigoli, Valorie
Patriotic holidays and celebrations. Watts 1985 66p il lib bdg $9.40 (4 and up) **394.2**
1. Holidays 2. Patriotism
ISBN 0-531-10044-8 LC 85-7270
"A First book"
"Each holiday is described, beginning with its history, various types of celebrations, concluding with when and where it is observed. Each chapter closes with suggestions for holiday activities. . . . Holidays are listed in chronological order in the back of the book. Black-and-white photographs enhance the text." SLJ

Henderson, Kathy
Christmas trees. Childrens Press 1989 45p il $13.27; pa $4.95 (2-4) **394.2**
1. Christmas
ISBN 0-516-01162-6; 0-516-41162-4 (pa) LC 89-859
"New true book"
This book provides background lore on Christmas trees and a discussion of how they are grown for decorating our homes at Christmas
"Captioned, mostly full-color photographs on nearly every page provide visual interest, while short sentences and a simple writing style allows easy access for beginning readers without sacrificing substance." Booklist

Laird, Elizabeth
Happy birthday! a book of birthday celebrations; [illustrated by] Satomi Ichikawa; text by Elizabeth Laird. Philomel Bks. 1988 c1987 60p il $13.95 (1-3) **394.2**
1. Birthdays
ISBN 0-399-21421-6 LC 87-11110
First published 1987 in the United Kingdom
"The book gives ideas and instructions with clear illustrations on how to make birthday cards, gifts, and wrapping paper; how to wrap presents; how to make paper decorations; and how to bake a cake and create different shaped cakes. Laird suggests foods and gives ideas for costumes, masks, and games. Also included are each month's birthstones and flowers and birthday customs in other countries. The color illustrations in watercolor and felt-tip pens are realistic and lend to the attractiveness of the book." SLJ

Lubin, Leonard B., 1943-
Christmas gift-bringers. Lothrop, Lee & Shepard Bks. 1989 unp il $12.95; lib bdg $12.88 **394.2**
1. Christmas 2. Santa Claus
ISBN 0-688-07019-1; 0-688-07020-5 (lib bdg) LC 89-2292
"When young Sidney announces to his mouse family that there is no Santa, his horrified father takes them all to the attic to read about Saint Nicholas, Father Christmas, Christkindl, Befana, the Julnisse, and all the other familiar Christmas figures. Sidney is converted. Pleasantly presented Christmas information, with decorative, detailed illustrations." Horn Book
Includes bibliography

Munro, Roxie, 1945-
Christmastime in New York City. Dodd, Mead 1987 unp il $13.95 (2-4) **394.2**
1. Christmas—Pictorial works 2. New York (N.Y.)—Social life and customs—Pictorial works
ISBN 0-396-08909-7 LC 86-32914
The author/illustrator "has chosen locations and scenes that capture the essence of New York: the Macy's Thanksgiving Day parade, Park Avenue lights, Christmas icons like the Medieval Court Christmas Tree in the Metropolitan Museum of Art, Lord & Taylor's windows and the wreathed lions at the entrance to the public library. From a panoramic cover view of Rockefeller Center's famous Christmas tree, to a behind-the-scenes glimpse of the lighted Times Square apple, ready to usher in the New Year for the crowds below, Munro's paintings are magic and memorable." Publ Wkly

Penner, Lucille Recht
The Thanksgiving book. Hastings House 1986 160p il $14.95; lib bdg $14.89 (5 and up) **394.2**
1. Thanksgiving Day
ISBN 0-8038-7228-3; 0-8038-9291-8 (lib bdg) LC 84-518
"The book traces the history of the thanksgiving ritual, including ancient celebrations—such as those of the Greeks and Romans—and the South American Indian harvest festivals. While the author does devote a substantial section to that famous meal in Plymouth, Massachusetts, and the subsequent events that resulted in the American holiday, she also sheds light on many contemporary international harvest festivals." Horn Book
"This well-researched book is a treasury of information about our least-commercialized but most heartfelt celebration." Publ Wkly
Includes bibliography

Perl, Lila
Piñatas and paper flowers; holidays of the Americas in English and Spanish; illustrated by Victoria de Larrea. Clarion Bks. 1983 91p il $12.95; pa $5.95 (4 and up) **394.2**
1. Holidays 2. Folklore—Latin America 3. Bilingual books—Spanish-English
ISBN 0-89919-112-6; 0-89919-155-X (pa) LC 82-1211

Perl, Lila—*Continued*

Text and title page in English and Spanish; Spanish version by Alma Flor Ada

A brief overview of eight holidays and their customs as celebrated in the Americas. Holidays covered include: The New Year, Three Kings' Day; Carnival and Easter; St. John the Baptist Day; Columbus Day; Halloween; The Festival of the Sun; and Christmas

Phelan, Mary Kay

The Fourth of July; illustrated by Symeon Shimin. Crowell 1966 unp il (Crowell holiday bk) lib bdg $12.89 (1-3) **394.2**

1. Fourth of July

ISBN 0-690-31415-9 LC 65-25909

"This account begins with a brief history of the events leading up to the Declaration of Independence and mention of some of the key leaders in the Continental Congress. How news of the Declaration was spread throughout the colonies and celebrations by the people are described. There is also mention of many events that have taken place on the anniversary of Independence Day." SLJ

"Symeon Shimin's light wash illustrations are soberly, historically patriotic." N Y Times Book Rev

Sandak, Cass R., 1950-

Columbus Day. Crestwood House 1990 48p il (Holidays) lib bdg $10.95 (4-6) **394.2**

1. Columbus, Christopher 2. Columbus Day 3. America—Exploration

ISBN 0-89686-498-7 LC 89-25399

Discusses why and how Columbus Day is celebrated and highlights the life and voyages of the famous explorer

Includes bibliography

Take joy! The Tasha Tudor Christmas book; selected, edited and illustrated by Tasha Tudor. Philomel Bks. 1980 c1966 157p il music $16.95 **394.2**

1. Christmas

ISBN 0-399-20766-X

First published 1966 by World Publishing Company

"A collection of Christmas stories, poems, customs, and carols and their music, celebrating both the religious and the secular aspects of the holiday. Included are the particular traditions and recipes of the Tudor family." Adventuring with Books. 2d edition

"Generously illustrated with tenderness and reverence in full-color and black-and-white pictures." Booklist

Tudor, Tasha

A time to keep: the Tasha Tudor book of holidays; written and illustrated by Tasha Tudor. Rand McNally 1977 unp il $12.95 (k-3) **394.2**

1. Holidays

ISBN 0-528-80219-2 LC 77-9067

"Nostalgic memories of days long ago shimmer across the pages, as Tasha Tudor reminisces about her family's early New England festivities. Twelfth Night charades, Valentine's Day cards, maple sugaring, Easter eggs, maypoles, Fourth of July picnics, Halloween pumpkins, Thanksgiving turkeys, and Christmas créches are remembered in brief narrative and depicted in soft delicate watercolors. Twinings of pines, grasses, and herbs border the pictures, which are filled with the Corgis, cats, looms, marionettes, wheelbarrows, cider presses, lanterns, and fascinating minutiae found in the artist's own home." Booklist

Van Straalen, Alice

The book of holidays around the world. Dutton 1986 192p il $14.95 (4 and up) **394.2**

1. Holidays

ISBN 0-525-44270-7 LC 86-11674

"Using the calendar as a basis, van Straalen presents a chronological listing of events to celebrate each day of the year. Succinct descriptions define the usually one festivity per date, giving the country of origin and brief comments about the holiday. While most of the inclusions are national or religious holidays, some regional festivals and birthdays of famous people are also included. . . . The book is a browser's delight, with pleasing page design, heavy paper, and well-produced graphics that illustrate one celebration on nearly every double-page spread." Booklist

Waters, Kate

Lion dancer: Ernie Wan's Chinese New Year; by Kate Waters and Madeline Slovenz-Low; photographs by Martha Cooper. Scholastic 1990 unp il $12.95 (k-3) **394.2**

1. Chinese New Year 2. Chinese Americans

ISBN 0-590-43046-7 LC 89-6423

Describes six-year-old Ernie Wan's preparations, at home and in school, for the Chinese New Year celebrations and his first public performance of the lion dance

"While some of the pictures look posed, the marvelously colorful photographs successfully capture Ernie's pride and anticipation as he is dressed in his gorgeous costume and the excitement and swirling movement of the subsequent parade. Illustrations of a Chinese lunar calendar and a Chinese horoscope are extra dividends in a useful and appealing book." Horn Book

395 Etiquette (Manners)

Joslin, Sesyle

What do you do, dear? pictures by Maurice Sendak. Harper & Row 1985 c1961 unp il $13.95; lib bdg $13.89; pa $4.50 (k-2) **395**

1. Etiquette

ISBN 0-201-09387-1; 0-06-023075-4 (lib bdg); 0-06-443113-4 (pa) LC 84-43139

First published 1961 by Addison-Wesley

Joslin, Sesyle—*Continued*

A "handbook of etiquette for young ladies and gentlemen to be used as a guide for everyday social behavior." The Author

"The propriety of what the well-mannered child will do is related to extraordinary situations, as for example: The Sheriff of Nottingham interrupts you while you are reading, to take you to jail; you will, naturally, 'Find a bookmark to save your place.' Sendak's pictures account for a great share of the fun." Horn Book

A "wonderful spoof on manners in a hilarious picture-book made for laughing aloud." Child Study Assoc of Am

What do you say, dear? pictures by Maurice Sendak. Harper & Row 1986 c1958 unp il $13.95; lib bdg $13.89; pa $3.50 (k-2) **395**

1. Etiquette
ISBN 0-210-09391-X; 0-06-023074-6 (lib bdg); 0-06-443112-6 (pa) LC 84-43140

A Caldecott Medal honor book, 1959

First published 1958 by Addison-Wesley

A "handbook of etiquette for young ladies and gentlemen to be used as a guide for everyday social behavior." The Author

"A rollicking introduction to manners for the very young. A series of delightfully absurd situations—being introduced to a baby elephant, bumping into a crocodile, being rescued from a dragon—are posed and appropriately answered. The illustrations are among Sendak's best—and funniest." Bull Cent Child Books

This "funny and imaginative picture book . . . may stimulate children to invent situations of their own." Booklist

398 Folklore

Borland, Hal, 1900-1978

Plants of Christmas; paintings by Anne Ophelia Dowden. rev ed. Crowell 1987 c1969 21p il $14.95; lib bdg $14.89 (5 and up) **398**

1. Plants—Folklore 2. Christmas
ISBN 0-690-04649-9; 0-690-04650-2 (lib bdg) LC 87-552

First published 1969 by Golden Press

This book explores the legends and symbols of the traditional plants of Christmas, such as English holly, ivy, mistletoe, and poinsettia. Botanical paintings illustrate the text

Lurie, Alison

Fabulous beasts; tales by Alison Lurie; pictures by Monika Beisner. Farrar, Straus & Giroux 1981 unp il $12.95 (4 and up) **398**

1. Animals, Mythical
ISBN 0-374-32242-2 LC 81-12546

Describes the habits and characteristics of strange beasts and birds, including the unicorn, griffin, phoenix, and basilisk, once thought to live in wild and distant parts of the world

"Beisner's fabulous paintings in glorious colors illustrate Lurie's splendid tales of mythical animals. . . . The Gryphon, Phoenix, Dragon and other strange beings captivate the reader, even if they don't win one's heart." Publ Wkly

MacDonald, Margaret Read

The storyteller's sourcebook; a subject, title, and motif index to folklore collections for children. Neal-Schuman; Gale Res. 1982 818p $95 **398**

1. Folklore—Indexes
ISBN 0-8103-0471-6 LC 82-954

"Locates tales by subject, ethnic or geographical area; includes variants and specific titles in collections and gives tale synopsis. Also indexes picture books. Confined to folktales. Epics, romances, tall tales and literary fairy tales are omitted. Current through 1980. Does not supplant Ireland's 'Index to Fairy Tales' [entered in class 398.2]." N Y Public Libr. Ref Books for Child Collect

McHargue, Georgess

The beasts of never; a history natural & unnatural of monsters mythical & magical; illustrated by Frank Bozzo. rev and expanded ed. Delacorte Press 1988 118p il $14.95; Aladdin Bks. (NY) pa $5.95 (4 and up) **398**

1. Animals, Mythical
ISBN 0-385-29573-1; 0-672-50217-8 (pa) LC 86-29374

First published 1968 by Bobbs-Merrill

The author "describes a host of land, air, and sea creatures of literature and legend and explains their possible origins. . . . Bozzo's attractive illustrations are reproduced in a dusty rose wash." Booklist

Includes bibliography

Meet the werewolf; drawings by Stephen Gammell. Lippincott 1976 79p il $11.95 (4 and up) **398**

1. Werewolves 2. Animals, Mythical
ISBN 0-397-31662-3 LC 75-34046

In addition to werewolves, "other protean creatures of folk literature such as swans, selchies or seal folk, the badgers and foxes of Japan, Scandinavia's berserkers, and the were-jaguars of South America are described. Readers are then regaled with stories as well as some real people who were believed to be werewolves and sentenced as such. There is also a discussion of the 'reality' of werewolves and the historical conditions which gave rise to beliefs in them. . . . For young readers who love to be terrified and are old enough to handle the gore, this is choice. The illustrations are excellent as well." SLJ

Opie, Iona Archibald

The lore and language of schoolchildren; by Iona and Peter Opie. Oxford Univ. Press 1960 c1959 417p il maps $39.95; pa $9.95 **398**

1. Folklore—Great Britain
ISBN 0-19-827206-5; 0-19-282059-1 (pa) LC 60-905

A collection of the "rhymes, riddles, incantations, jeers, torments, parodies, nicknames, holiday customs, and other types of lore that is . . . transmitted orally, some of it over a period of hundreds of years. The basic study was made in Great Britain and detailed analysis of geographic usage is made for Great Britain but some usage in other countries is also noted. Chiefly of interest to folklorists, teachers, librarians, and others who work with children but nostalgic appeal for the general reader." Booklist

Pellowski, Anne

Hidden stories in plants; unusual and easy-to-tell stories from around the world together with creative things to do while telling them; illustrated by Lynn Sweat. Macmillan 1990 93p il $14.95 (4 and up) **398**

1. Plants—Folklore 2. Handicraft
ISBN 0-02-770611-7 LC 89-37166

Presents myths, legends, tales, and folklore about plants and describes how to use plants to make ornaments, toys, disguises, dolls, and musical instruments

"What makes this book so outstanding is that it can be used for a wide variety of purposes. The book would be quite effective as part of a whole language unit about plants, other cultures, or storytelling." Sci Books Films

Includes bibliographic references

Perl, Lila

Blue Monday and Friday the Thirteenth; illustrations by Erika Weihs. Clarion Bks. 1986 96p il lib bdg $12.95 (4-6) **398**

1. Folklore 2. Calendars 3. Holidays
ISBN 0-89919-327-7 LC 85-13051

"Perl's purpose here is to explain how each of the days of the week received its name and how the different catch phrases, customs and superstitions associated with each came into being. She draws heavily on both the mythology and folk customs of many lands. . . . Additionally, children learn why certain holidays became associated with specific days." SLJ

"Sprinkled with anecdotes, laced with folklore, Perl's book entices readers into thinking about familiar territory in a new way. . . . Weihs's pictures, which resemble woodcuts, help to make this an accessible, lively book." Publ Wkly

Includes bibliography

Don't sing before breakfast, don't sleep in the moonlight; everyday superstitions and how they began; illustrated by Erika Weihs. Clarion Bks. 1988 90p il $13.95 (4-6) **398**

1. Superstition
ISBN 0-89919-504-0 LC 87-24295

Examines common superstitions associated with the events of a typical day, how these superstitions developed, and how they influence our behavior today

"Writing conversationally and informatively, Perl considers the meaning of well-known expressions, such as 'not worth his salt,' as she weaves ancient rhymes into her fascinating analyses of individual superstitions. Adding to the mystery are Weihs' finely executed woodcuts, which provide appropriate flavor." Booklist

Includes bibliography

Schwartz, Alvin, 1927-

Cross your fingers, spit in your hat: superstitions and other beliefs; collected by Alvin Schwartz; illustrated by Glen Rounds. Lippincott 1974 161p il lib bdg $12.89 (4 and up) **398**

1. Superstition
ISBN 0-397-32436-7 LC 73-21912

This is a compilation of superstitions about such subjects as love and marriage, food and drink, witches, travel, the human body, ailments and curses, plants and animals, and death

"This delightful book reveals the sometimes humorous but always interesting ideas people have about what's happening. . . . Comically illustrated by Glen Rounds, this book will give hours of fun and fascinating information about people and their beliefs." Child Book Rev Serv

Includes bibliography

Flapdoodle: pure nonsense from American folklore; collected by Alvin Schwartz; illustrated by John O'Brien. Lippincott 1980 125p il $12.95; lib bdg $12.89 (4 and up) **398**

1. Folklore—United States 2. American wit and humor
ISBN 0-397-31919-3; 0-397-31920-7 (lib bdg) LC 79-9618

"Included are samples of spoonerisms, double-talk, visual jokes, tricks, silly rhymes, and shaggy dog stories. The introduction states that some of the folklore is old, and some of it new; children may be surprised to find several of the jokes and rhymes currently very much alive in the schoolyard. Nearly every page of the entertaining book is decorated with a suitably absurd line drawing. Notes, sources, and bibliography." Horn Book

Kickle snifters and other fearsome critters; collected from American folklore by Alvin Schwartz; illustrated by Glen Rounds. Lippincott 1976 63p il lib bdg $12.89 (2-5) **398**

1. Folklore—United States 2. Animals, Mythical
ISBN 0-397-32161-9 LC 75-29048

The compiler and illustrator "have collaborated on an imaginary bestiary, a collection of grotesque creatures—some of them illusions of fear and terror, others the pure, tall-tale inventions of 'frontiersmen, woodsmen, cowboys, and carnival sharps to prank the tenderfoot and pass the time.'" Horn Book

"The scratchy, vigorous illustrations by Rounds extend the text and often add a humorous note." Bull Cent

Schwartz, Alvin, 1927-—*Continued*
Child Books
Includes bibliography

Tomfoolery: trickery and foolery with words; collected from American folklore by Alvin Schwartz; illustrated by Glen Rounds. Lippincott 1973 127p il $12.95; lib bdg $12.89 (4 and up) **398**

1. Folklore—United States 2. American wit and humor 3. Riddles
ISBN 0-397-31466-3; 0-397-32437-5 (lib bdg) LC 72-12900

"This is a sampling of verbal trickery garnered not only from folklore archives, publications, and folklorists but also from Schwartz's childhood, his children, and other children. Rounds' amusing line drawings add visual interest to the collection which includes wisecracks, riddles, practical jokes, double talk, endless tales, and anecdotes with trick endings. Appended are notes, sources, and a bibliography." Booklist

Witcracks: jokes and jests from American folklore; illustrated by Glen Rounds. Lippincott 1973 128p il $12.89 (4 and up) **398**

1. Folklore—United States 2. American wit and humor 3. Jokes
ISBN 0-397-31475-2 LC 73-7630

A collection of American humor including "riddles, shaggy dog stories, Tom Swifties, hate jokes, noodle-head humor, ethnic humor, and knock-knock jokes." Bull Cent Child Books

"Short explanations about when and why such jokes are told precede each section; copious notes give the origins of jokes and stories; and black-and-white line drawings add to the humor. It is unfortunate, however, that hate or ethnic jokes as well as sick jokes popular in the '50's have been included." SLJ

Includes bibliography

398.03 Folklore—Encyclopedias and dictionaries

Briggs, Katharine Mary

An encyclopedia of fairies; hobgoblins, brownies, bogies, and other supernatural creatures; [by] Katherine Briggs. Pantheon Bks. 1977 c1976 481p il $12.95; pa $11.95 **398.03**

1. Fairies—Dictionaries 2. Folklore—Great Britain—Dictionaries
ISBN 0-394-40918-3; 0-394-73467-X (pa) LC 76-12939

First published 1976 in the United Kingdom with title: A dictionary of fairies

"This eclectic encyclopedia covers British fairy lore, broadly constituted as 'that whole area of the supernatural which is not claimed by angels, devils or ghosts.' Entries are alphabetically arranged and terms are capitalized in the text to indicate that they have separate entries. . . . Supplementary material includes a selected reading list and indexes of tale types and motifs mentioned in the text." Libr J

398.2 Folk literature

Sagas, romances, legends, ballads, and fables in prose form, and fairy tales, folk tales, and tall tales are included here, instead of with the literature of the country of origin, to keep the traditional material together and to make it more readily accessible. Modern fairy tales are classified with Fiction, Story collections (SC), or Easy books (E)

Aardema, Verna

Bimwili & the Zimwi; a tale from Zanzibar; retold by Verna Aardema; pictures by Susan Meddaugh. Dial Bks. for Young Readers 1985 unp il $12.95; lib bdg $12.89; pa $3.95 (k-2) **398.2**

1. Folklore—Zanzibar
ISBN 0-8037-0212-4; 0-8037-0213-2 (lib bdg); 0-8037-0553-0 (pa) LC 85-4449

Text adapted from Little sister and the Zimwi, published 1969 in Tales for the third ear. Another version: The children and the Zimwi, published 1896 in Swahili stories

A Swahili girl is abducted by Zimwi, an ugly ogre, and told to be the voice inside his singing drum

"Making the most of each dramatic situation, the bright watercolor and pencil illustrations are well suited to sharing with a group of children. . . . A tightly written, slightly scary story with a heroine who uses her wits and courage to overcome a powerful enemy, this could become a favorite for reading aloud to children in the primary grades." Booklist

Bringing the rain to Kapiti Plain; a Nandi tale; retold by Verna Aardema; pictures by Beatriz Vidal. Dial Bks. for Young Readers 1981 unp il $13.95; lib bdg $13.89; pa $3.95 (k-2) **398.2**

1. Folklore—Africa 2. Stories in rhyme 3. Droughts—Fiction
ISBN 0-8037-0809-2; 0-8037-0807-6 (lib bdg); 0-8037-0904-8 (pa) LC 80-25886

"Retold from an African folk tale, this is a cumulative rhyming tale with the rhythm and repetition of 'The House that Jack Built.' It tells of how Ki-pat, the herdsman, works out a clever method to save the plain from a long drought." SLJ

"Effective both in the rhythm of its metered storytelling and in the brilliance of its stylized paintings, the panoramic picture book quickly engages both eye and ear." Horn Book

Oh, Kojo! How could you! an Ashanti tale; retold by Verna Aardema; pictures by Marc Brown. Dial Bks. for Young Readers 1984 unp il $12.95; lib bdg $12.89; pa $3.95 (k-3) **398.2**

1. Ashanti (African people)—Folklore
ISBN 0-8037-0006-7; 0-8037-0007-5 (lib bdg); 0-8037-0449-6 (pa) LC 84-1710

"An adaptation of the author's earlier book, 'The Na of Wa' [1960]." Horn Book

"An Ananse story that explains why cats are favored over dogs in Ashantiland. The text and full-color illustra-

Aardema, Verna—*Continued*
tions combine to make a fun book that is sure to be enjoyed by many." Child Book Rev Serv

Princess Gorilla and a new kind of water; a Mpongwe tale; retold by Verna Aardema; pictures by Victoria Chess. Dial Bks. for Young Readers 1988 unp il $10.95; lib bdg $10.89 (k-2) **398.2**

1. Folklore—Africa, West
ISBN 0-8037-0412-7; 0-8037-0413-5 (lib bdg) LC 86-32888

"King Gorilla is intent on selecting a strong, brave husband for his daughter. Whoever can quaff a barrel of vinegar, he declares, shall be the one. . . . Aardema has created a high-spirited, infectiously funny story, and the language of the tale is jaunty, playful and sure—perfect for reading aloud. Chess's illustrations are an inspired choice. Her animals scheme, boast, swagger, spit and, in the case of the princess, chortle with glee—each expression hilariously rendered in her lush pen-and-watercolor scenes." Publ Wkly

Rabbit makes a monkey of lion; a Swahili tale; retold by Verna Aardema; pictures by Jerry Pinkney. Dial Bks. for Young Readers 1989 unp il $11.95; lib bdg $11.89 (k-2) **398.2**

1. Folklore—Zanzibar 2. Animals—Fiction
ISBN 0-8037-0297-3; 0-8037-0298-1 (lib bdg) LC 86-11523

Text adapted from The hare and the lion, published 1901 in Zanzibar tales

With the help of his friends Bush-rat and Turtle, smart and nimble Rabbit makes a fool of the mighty but slow-witted king of the forest

"Aardema's version of the tale reinforces the amusing trickster qualities of rascally Rabbit, making it a sure-fire choice for sharing with groups of children, who will instantly root for her success. Pinkney's lovely watercolor and pencil paintings in hues of green, brown, and gold fill the pages with lush scenes which evoke the East African setting." Horn Book

The Vingananee and the tree toad; a Liberian tale; retold by Verna Aardema; with illustrations by Ellen Weiss. Warne 1983 unp il $12.95; Penguin Bks. pa $4.95 (k-3) **398.2**

1. Folklore—Liberia 2. Animals—Fiction
ISBN 0-7232-6217-9; 0-14-050890-2 (pa) LC 82-13473

A strange animal called the Vingananee beats up all the other animals and eats their stew until the tiny Tree Toad offers to fight him

"Aardema has admirably retold this finely crafted story by replicating in her text the vitality and nuance of the oral tradition as well as the strong moral backbone of folk humor. . . . Weiss' illustrations, pen-and-ink and watercolors in shades of gentle earthtones, with a blue sky, deepen and detail the text." SLJ

What's so funny, Ketu? a Nuer tale; retold by Verna Aardema; pictures by Marc Brown. Dial Bks. for Young Readers 1982 unp il $9.95; lib bdg $12.89; pa $3.95 (k-2) **398.2**

1. Folklore—Sudan
ISBN 0-8037-9364-2; 0-8037-9370-7 (lib bdg); 0-8037-0646-4 (pa) LC 81-68776

Earlier version of this story by the author published 1960 by Coward-McCann with title: Otwe

"Retelling of 'The man and the snake' in Neur customs and folklore, by Ray Huffman." Verso of title page

For saving the life of a snake, Ketu is rewarded by being allowed to hear animals think

"Brown's full-page pencil and ink drawings with black, brown, yellow and red halftones are often composed to contrast Ketu's delight with the anger and disruption around him. The large figures, with their exaggerated expressions and gestures, reinforce and enhance this funny story which demands reading aloud." SLJ

Who's in Rabbit's house? a Masai tale; retold by Verna Aardema; pictures by Leo and Diane Dillon. Dial Bks. for Young Readers 1977 unp il $14.95; lib bdg $14.89; pa $4.95 (k-3) **398.2**

1. Masai (African people)—Folklore 2. Animals—Fiction 3. Folklore—Africa, East
ISBN 0-8037-9550-5; 0-8037-9551-3 (lib bdg); 0-8037-9549-1 (pa) LC 77-71514

This "tale relates the attempts of Rabbit to regain possession of her house after it is taken over by an intruder. Rabbit's friends offer suggestions on how to solve the problem, but the solution comes from 'an unexpected source.' The story, adapted from the Masai tale 'The Long One,' uses repetition of key phrases to produce a rhythmic read-aloud text. The Dillons skillfully present their artistry in a vivid, colorful and impressive manner which contributes to the story and sets the tone." Child Book Rev Serv

Why mosquitoes buzz in people's ears; a West African tale retold; pictures by Leo and Diane Dillon. Dial Bks. for Young Readers 1975 unp il $14.95; lib bdg $14.89; pa $4.95 (k-3) **398.2**

1. Folklore—Africa, West 2. Mosquitoes—Fiction 3. Animals—Fiction
ISBN 0-8037-6089-2; 0-8037-6087-6 (lib bdg); 0-8037-6088-4 (pa) LC 74-2886

Awarded the Caldecott Medal, 1976

This tale relates "how a mosquito's silly lie to an iguana sets in motion a cumulative series of events that finally causes Mother Owl not to call up the sun. The resulting hardship ends only after King Lion traces the problem back to its source." Booklist

"Stunning full-color illustrations—watercolor sprayed with air gun, overlayed with pastel, cut out and repasted—give an eye-catching abstract effect and tell the story with humor and power." SLJ

Aesop

Aesop's fables; illustrated by Heidi Holder. Viking 1981 25p il $13.95 **398.2**

1. Fables
ISBN 0-670-10643-7 LC 80-26265

Contents: The dove and the snake; The country mouse and the city mouse; The bat, the bramblebush, and the cormorant; A laden ass and a horse; The fox and the grapes; The marriage of the sun; The cock and the jewel; The hare and the tortoise; The stag and the hounds

"It would be difficult to imagine an 'Aesop's Fables' more beautifully illustrated or lovingly designed than this edition. The pictures, first drawn in pencil, then traced in pen and ink, were finished in watercolor. The results are Rackham-style illustrations filled with intricate detail. . . . The fables and their morals are retold in clear but sophisticated language, so despite the picture-book format, this is not appropriate for young children; others will be captivated." Booklist

Aesop's fables; illustrated by Lisbeth Zwerger. Picture Bk. Studio 1989 unp il $15.95 (1-3) **398.2**

1. Fables
ISBN 0-88708-108-8 LC 89-31370

"A Michael Neugebauer book"

Contents: Town mouse & country mouse; The milkmaid & her pail; The man & the satyr; The shepherd's boy & the wolf; The hares & the frogs; The monkey & the camel; The fox & the grapes; The hare & the tortoise; The fox & the crow; The dog & the sow; The moon & her mother; The ass & the lap dog

"The characters—both animal and human—are executed in a fairly realistic manner which accommodates Zwerger's impish sense of humor. The balance between each page of text and its accompanying illustration is pleasing, with the book's overall effect being one of a leisurely journey through the reasons for human behavior." SLJ

Afanas'ev, A. N. (Aleksandr Nikolaevich), 1826-1871

Russian fairy tales; translated by Norbert Guterman from the collections of Aleksandr Afanas'ev; illustrated by Alexander Alexeieff; folkloristic commentary by Roman Jakobson. Pantheon Bks. 1975 c1945 661p il o.p. paperback available $13.95 (4 and up) **398.2**

1. Folklore—Soviet Union 2. Fairy tales
ISBN 0-394-73090-9 (pa) LC 75-327368

A reprint of the title first published 1945

Afanas'ev's "tales carry the reader to faraway Russian villages, long winter nights, deep snow, thatched huts, forests teeming with wild animals and muzhiks (peasants), who have never progressed beyond the very beginnings of human civilization. . . . [This is a] beautiful book. I recommend it to all readers, young and old who are interested in the folktale and its unique qualities." N Y Times Book Rev

Includes bibliographic references

Russian folk tales; illustrated by Ivan I. Bilibin; translated [from the Russian] by Robert Chandler. Random House 1980 77p il $14.95 (4 and up) **398.2**

1. Folklore—Soviet Union 2. Fairy tales
ISBN 0-394-51353-3 LC 80-50746

"Seven of the more romantic, complex, and haunting traditional stories collected by a great nineteenth-century Russian folklorist are displayed here. . . . Ivan Bilibin, a Russian illustrator of the late nineteenth and early twentieth centuries, relied heavily on decorative folk arts for his opulent color illustrations and border designs. Rich, dark tones are used to create pictures with depth and drama. . . . Memorable characters, from Baba-Yaga and Koshchev the Deathless to Vasilisa the Beautiful and Marya Morevna, people the stories." Booklist

Alexander, Ellen

Llama and the great flood; a folktale from Peru. Crowell 1989 39p il $13.95; lib bdg $13.89 (1-3) **398.2**

1. Folklore—Peru
ISBN 0-690-04727-4; 0-690-04729-0 (lib bdg) LC 88-1194

In this Peruvian myth about the great flood, a llama warns his master of the coming destruction and suggests taking refuge on a high peak in the Andes

"A note explains the background of the story and some of the artist's graphic motifs, which she attributes to 'several pre-Inca cultures such as the Wari and the Moche.' The full-color wash drawings are vivid even if the human figures are somewhat stiffly drafted, and the rocky landscapes are expressive—literally, when parts of the terrain take on the aspect of faces." Bull Cent Child Books

Anno, Mitsumasa, 1926-

Anno's Aesop; a book of fables by Aesop and Mr. Fox; retold and illustrated by Mitsumasa Anno. Orchard Bks. 1989 63p il $18.95; lib bdg $18.99 (2-4) **398.2**

1. Fables
ISBN 0-531-05774-7; 0-531-08374-8 (lib bdg) LC 88-60087

This book presents an illustrated collection of Aesop's fables interwoven with Father Fox's own interpretations of the stories

"Distinguishing the illustrations is a diversity of color and style; yet the slightly ironic humor and the verbal and visual cross-references interlinking texts and pictures all work to create a fluent, unified book." Horn Book

The **Arabian** nights entertainments; selected and edited by Andrew Lang; with numerous illustrations by H. J. Ford. Dover Publs. 1969 424p il pa $6.95 (5 and up) **398.2**

1. Arabs—Folklore 2. Fairy tales
ISBN 0-486-22289-6 LC 69-17098

Also available in hardcover from Smith, P. $16.50 (ISBN 0-8446-0752-5)

First published 1898 in England

The Arabian nights entertainments — *Continued*

"A collection of popular tales assembled over many centuries, and well known in Europe from the 18th cent. It contains the stories of 'Aladdin, Alibaba, and Sindbad the sailor'. . . . The framing story in which the tales are set concerns Scheherazade, who is determined to delay her royal husband's plan of killing her—he has taken to murdering his wives because the first was unfaithful to him—by telling him a story every evening. She leaves each evening's tale incomplete until the next day, so that he has to spare her life in order to hear its conclusion. He is so entertained that he finally abandons his murderous plan." Oxford Companion to Child Lit

Asbjørnsen, Peter Christen, 1812-1885

East of the sun and west of the moon: old tales from the North; illustrated by Kay Nielsen. Doubleday 1977 c1976 108p il o.p. (3-6) **398.2**

1. Folklore—Norway 2. Fairy tales LC 77-74791

First published 1976 in the United Kingdom

"Six of the 15 Norwegian stories in this famous collection, first published in 1914, are reprinted here with Nielsen's black-and-white drawings and 13 of his paintings." Booklist

The **Baby's** story book; [compiled and illustrated by] Kay Chorao. Dutton 1985 64p il $13.95 (k-1) **398.2**

1. Fables 2. Folklore
ISBN 0-525-44200-6 LC 84-26005

"This collection of traditional, familiar childhood tales, briefly told, is well suited to younger listeners and illustrated with rich, full-color scenes. Among the stories are 'Goldilocks and the Three Bears,' 'The Three Billy Goats Gruff,' and 'Little Red Riding Hood.' There are three fables, 'The Dog and the Bone,' 'The Wind and the Sun,' and 'The Lion and the Mouse'. . . . Accompanying the 15 inclusions are Chorao's well-realized scenes, which project an appealing innocence and display more than a little humor." Booklist

Bang, Molly

Wiley and the Hairy Man; adapted from an American folk tale. Macmillan 1976 64p il $9.95; pa $3.95 (1-4) **398.2**

1. Blacks—Folklore 2. Folklore—Southern States
ISBN 0-02-708370-5; 0-689-71162-X (pa)
LC 75-38581

"A Ready-to-read book"

In this adaptation of an Alabama folk yarn "the swamp-dwelling Hairy Man must be tricked three times before a person is safe from being caught and carried off by him. Wiley, a Black boy, twice meets the Hairy Man in the swamp, and both times quick thinking and his hound dogs save him. On the critical third time, Wiley's mother traps the conjure man into taking a piglet instead of her son." SLJ

Barth, Edna

Jack-o'-lantern; pictures by Paul Galdone. Clarion Bks. 1974 unp il $12.95; pa $4.95 (2-4) **398.2**

1. Folklore 2. Halloween—Fiction
ISBN 0-395-28763-4; 0-89919-123-1 (pa)
LC 73-20194

First published by Seabury Press

Retells the story of the first jack o'lantern, made to light the way of Mean Jack who, unwanted in heaven and hell, had to wander the earth for eternity

"Although this is presented in a picture book format, the tale is enjoyed by children of all ages and by adults and is an excellent choice for storytelling. Paul Galdone's pictures in orange and brown add humor and atmosphere to this Halloween-oriented version." Read Teach

Baylor, Byrd

Moon song; illustrations by Ronald Himler. Scribner 1982 unp il $10.95 (1-3) **398.2**

1. Pima Indians—Legends 2. Coyote (Legendary character) 3. Moon—Fiction
ISBN 0-684-17463-4 LC 81-18427

After giving birth to Coyote "the Moon has work to do; she can't stay with her child. But when Coyote sees her; he rushes to the top of a hill, howling for his mother. . . . That is how the Pimas tell about nights when Coyote and his descendants gather on the hills and sing their longing song to the Moon, and she fills them with mysterious power." Publ Wkly

This book "pairs Baylor's graceful language with heavily shaded black-and-white illustrations by Ronald Himler. Many of these are impressively stark and dramatic." SLJ

Bennett, Jill, 1947-

Teeny tiny; retold by Jill Bennett; pictures by Tomie dePaola. Putnam 1986 c1985 unp il lib bdg $8.95 (k-1) **398.2**

1. Folklore—Great Britain 2. Ghosts—Fiction
ISBN 0-399-21293-0 LC 85-12347

First published 1985 in the United Kingdom

Retells the tale of the teeny-tiny woman who finds a teeny-tiny bone in a churchyard and puts it away in her cupboard before she goes to sleep

"This vintage tale gets a glowing refurbishing in dePaola's warm scenes that show . . . while the woman is going about her business, a trio of ghosts peers over her shoulder; it is these prowling figures who make the deliciously scary demand—'Give me my bone'—and bring about the story's surprise finish. Cream-colored pages back a colorful palette that seems especially rich." Booklist

Berger, Terry

Black fairy tales; drawings by David Omar White. Atheneum Pubs. 1969 137p il hardcover o.p. paperback available $3.95 (4 and up) **398.2**

1. Folklore—Africa, Southern 2. Fairy tales
ISBN 0-689-70402-X (pa) LC 70-75517

Berger, Terry—*Continued*

Adapted from "Fairy tales from South Africa" by E. J. Bourhill, published 1908 in England

These ten folk and fairy tales from the Swazi, Shangani, Msuto and other Black peoples of South Africa "are filled with ogres, enchanted beasts, and giants. A glossary explains unfamiliar words. These stories would be of particular interest to those preparing Black Heritage curricula." Keating. Build Bridges of Understanding Between Cultures

Berry, James

Spiderman Anancy; written by James Berry; illustrated by Joseph Olubo. Holt & Co. 1989 c1988 119p il $13.95 (5 and up) **398.2**

1. Folklore—West Indies
ISBN 0-8050-1207-9 LC 89-33418

First published 1988 in the United Kingdom with title: Anancy-Spiderman

"This collection of 20 Anancy stories springs from Africa by way of the West Indies. . . . Just as in the African tales, the clever trickster uses cunning and spunk, but the colloquial speech patterns used in Berry's stories add distinctive spice. Olubo's evocative black-and-white ink drawings successfully combine the human/animal facets of the characters. A lively resource." Booklist

Best-loved folktales of the world; selected and with an introduction by Joanna Cole; illustrated by Jill Karla Schwarz. Doubleday 1983 xxiv, 792p il pa $14.95 **398.2**

1. Folklore 2. Fairy tales
ISBN 0-385-18949-4 LC 81-43288

"200 tales from widely ranging countries of the world make up this diversified collection that should be a useful resource for the teller as well as the reader of tales. Familiar classics and lesser known stories are arranged geographically by region, but access can also be obtained through an index of categories, which is appended. Here, users can find tales through motifs, such as trickster heroes, giants and ogres, fables with a moral, quests, and magical helpers." Booklist

Bierhorst, John

Doctor Coyote; a native American Aesop's fables; retold by John Bierhorst; pictures by Wendy Watson. Macmillan 1987 unp il $15.95 (1-4) **398.2**

1. Aztecs—Legends 2. Coyote (Legendary character) 3. Fables
ISBN 0-02-709780-3 LC 86-8669

"These stories, printed for the first time in English, are taken from an early copy of Aesop found in Mexico where the fables were translated into Aztec by a 16th century scribe. Coyote, a perpetual trickster who appears in various North American Indian tales, becomes the main character in the fables." Child Book Rev Serv

"Elaborate cartoons . . . take such vast liberties with lore (a modern gas station, a chicken in a sleeping bag, everyone decked out in squash blossom necklaces) that you're back in a secret garden of delight. Don't miss this unique, perfectly turned-out book." Read Teach

Birdseye, Tom

A song of stars; an Asian legend; adapted by Tom Birdseye; illustrated by Ju-hong Chen. Holiday House 1990 unp il $14.95 (3-5) **398.2**

1. Folklore—China 2. Milky Way—Fiction
ISBN 0-8234-0790-X LC 89-20066

"When Princess Chauchau, who weaves the shimmering threads of the firmament, and Newlang, the herdsman, fall in love, they neglect their important duties. As punishment, the Emperor of the Heavens banishes them to opposite sides of the Milky Way and decrees that they will be allowed to meet only once a year. When the seventh night of the seventh month finally comes, Newlang attempts to reach his wife but is forced back by the turbulent river of stars. The merciful emperor then sends the magpies to create a bridge that enables Chauchau to join her husband." Booklist

"The lush illustrations, which at times are reminiscent of Brian Wildsmith's early work, complement the romantic quality of the retelling." Horn Book

Bishop, Claire Huchet

The five Chinese brothers; by Claire Huchet Bishop and Kurt Wiese. Coward-McCann 1938 unp il $7.95; pa $5.95 (1-3) **398.2**

1. Folklore—China
ISBN 0-698-20044-6; 0-698-20642-8 (pa) LC 38-27908

A "tale about five brothers who looked exactly alike. Each one had a special attribute—one had a neck of iron, another could hold his breath indefinitely—and they all come to the aid of the first when he is sentenced to die." Booklist

"A picture-story book which has the flavor of a folk tale, and the repetition and rhythm that appeal to little children. Kurt Wiese's gaily exaggerated illustrations in black and yellow capture the blithe quality of the story. Excellent for storytelling." N Y Libr

The **Blue** fairy book; edited by Andrew Lang; with numerous illustrations by H. J. Ford and G. P. Jacomb Hood. Dover Publs. 1965 390p il pa $6.95 (4-6) **398.2**

1. Folklore 2. Fairy tales
ISBN 0-486-21437-0 LC 65-25707

Also available in hardcover from Smith, P. $17.50 (ISBN 0-8446-5495-7)

Companion volume to: The Green fairy book, The Red fairy book, and The Yellow fairy book, each entered separately; also available: The Pink fairy book pa $6.95 (ISBN 0-486-21792-2) and in hardcover from Smith, P. for $17.50 (ISBN 0-8446-0755-X)

A reprint of the title first published 1889 by Longmans

A collection of thirty-seven fairy tales from various countries, consisting largely of old favorites from such sources as Perrault, the Brothers Grimm, Madame D'Aulnoy, Asbjörnsen and Möe, the Arabian Nights and Swift's Gulliver's travels

Bolliger, Max

Tales of a long afternoon; five fables and one other; retold by Max Bolliger; paintings by Jindra Čapek; translated by Joel Agee. Dutton 1989 c1988 unp il $13.95 (k-3) **398.2**

1. Fables
ISBN 0-525-44546-3 LC 89-34536
First published 1988 in Switzerland

"On a beautiful afternoon, eight animals gather together to have a party. When evening comes, the animals decide to entertain themselves. Fox tells [the Aesop fable] 'The Fox and the Raven,' . . . angering Raven because of the story's ending. Then Turtle tells 'The Turtle and the Hare,' much to Hare's disgust, etc. The animals begin to fight, but resolve to be friends after an old lion tells 'The Mouse and the lion.'" SLJ

"Perfect for readers who are . . . just beginning to comprehend other people's feelings and the give-and-take of friendship, this book features Capek's exquisitely dramatic illustrations. The rich color tones (the iridescent blue of the peacock's neck) and evocative facial expressions (the angry dog's crazed eyes) are reminiscent of antique pictures." Booklist

Bowden, Joan Chase, 1925-

Why the tides ebb and flow; illustrated by Marc Brown. Houghton Mifflin 1979 unp il $14.95; pa $4.95 (k-2) **398.2**

1. Folklore 2. Tides—Fiction
ISBN 0-395-28378-7; 0-395-54952-3 (pa) LC 79-12359

In this folktale explaining why the sea has tides, an old woman threatens to pull the rock from the hole in the ocean floor if Sky Spirit does not honor his promise to give her shelter

"The lyrical text, perfect for reading aloud, is touched with humor and lightly seasoned with onomatopoeic expressions. The elegant illustrations sweep in broad strokes across buff-colored pages, suggesting the strength of the elemental forces against which the defiant old woman wages her battle. The figures have a sculptured appearance, underscoring the story's mythic quality; their faces are marvelously responsive." Horn Book

Brett, Jan, 1949-

Beauty and the beast; retold and illustrated by Jan Brett. Clarion Bks. 1989 unp il lib bdg $14.95 (1-3) **398.2**

1. Folklore—France 2. Fairy tales
ISBN 0-89919-497-4 LC 88-16965

Through her great capacity to love, a kind and beautiful maid releases a handsome prince from the spell which has made him an ugly beast

"A Beauty of distinguished appearance, a delightful set of animal servants, and a suitably hideous Beast are presented in Jan Brett's distinctive, decorative style. Small details, such as tapestries mirroring the action of the tale, add to the effect of the simply written story." Horn Book Guide

Goldilocks and the three bears; retold and illustrated by Jan Brett. Dodd, Mead 1987 unp il $13.95; pa $5.95 (k-2) **398.2**

1. Folklore 2. Bears—Fiction
ISBN 0-396-08925-9; 0-399-22004-6 (pa) LC 87-565

"Sharp-eyed children will be delighted with this new edition of an old favorite, faithfully and smoothly adapted from Andrew Lang's *Green Fairy Book*. . . . Brett has included wonderful details in her drawings; children will look for the mice scampering about the pages and will be attracted to the Scandinavian-style costumes of Goldilocks and the three bears. . . . Large enough to share with groups but with enough detail to withstand repeated individual readings, the book infuses the old nursery tale with new life." Horn Book

The mitten; a Ukrainian folktale; adapted and illustrated by Jan Brett. Putnam 1989 unp il $14.95 (k-2) **398.2**

1. Folklore—Ukraine 2. Animals—Fiction
ISBN 0-399-21920-X LC 88-32198

"Grandmother knits snow-white mittens that Nikki takes on an adventure. Readers will enjoy the charm and humor in the portrayal of the animals as they make room for each newcomer in the mitten and sprawl in the snow after the big sneeze." Horn Book Guide

Brown, Marcia, 1918-

Backbone of the king; the story of Paka'a and his son Ku. University of Hawaii Press 1984 c1966 180p il $12.95 (5 and up) **398.2**

1. Legends—Hawaii
ISBN 0-8248-0963-7 LC 66-18180
"A Kolowalu book"

A reprint of the title first published 1966 by Scribner

"Based on The Hawaiian story of Pakaa and Kuapakaa, the personal attendants of Keawenuiaumi . . . collected, assembled, selected, and edited by Moses K. Nakuina. Honolulu, n.d. Translation from the Hawaiian by Dorothy M. Kahanaui." Verso of title page

"This story of a courageous Hawaiian boy who helped to restore his father to his rightful place in the King's court is told in distinguished style and illustrated with stunning linoleum prints by the author. Suggested for reading aloud at story time, or as background reading in the study of the fiftieth state." Hodges. Books for Elem Sch Libr

Includes glossary

Dick Whittington and his cat; told and cut in linoleum by Marcia Brown. Scribner 1950 unp il lib bdg $13.95 (k-3) **398.2**

1. Whittington, Richard, d. 1423—Fiction 2. Legends—Great Britain
ISBN 0-684-18998-4 LC 50-9157

A Caldecott Medal honor book, 1951

This retelling of the English legend about the merchant Dick Whittington who became Lord Mayor of London tells how young Dick achieved fame and fortune by selling his cat to a king who was plagued by rats

"The print, black and clear, balances the bold lines of the linoleum blocks; the pictures combine strength of line, and a sense of design with vigorous action. The version is complete in the thread of the story but sim-

Brown, Marcia, 1918-—*Continued*
pler and less wordy in places than in some of those given in the fairy tale collections." Ont Libr Rev

Once upon a mouse; a fable cut in wood. Atheneum Pubs. 1961 unp il $13.95; pa $3.95 (k-3) **398.2**

1. Folklore—India 2. Fables
ISBN 0-684-12662-1; 0-689-71343-6 (pa)
LC 61-14769

Awarded the Caldecott Medal, 1962
At head of title: From ancient India
A "fable from the Indian 'Hitopadesa.' There is lively action in spreads showing how a hermit 'thinking about big and little' suddenly saves a mouse from a crow and then from larger enemies by turning the little creature into the forms of bigger and bigger animals—until as a royal tiger it has to be humbled." Horn Book
"The illustrations are remarkably beautiful. The emotional elements of the story . . . are conveyed with just as much intensity as the purely visual ones." New Yorker

Stone soup; an old tale; told and pictured by Marcia Brown. Scribner 1947 unp il $12.95; pa $5.95 (k-3) **398.2**

1. Folklore—France
ISBN 0-684-92296-7; 0-684-16217-2 (pa)
LC 47-11630

A Caldecott Medal honor book, 1948
"When the people in a French village heard that three soldiers were coming, they hid all their food for they knew what soldiers are. However, when the soldiers began to make soup with water and stones the pot gradually filled with all the vegetables which had been hidden away. The simple language and quiet humour of this folktale are amplified and enriched by gay and witty drawings of clever light-hearted soldiers, and the gullible 'light-witted' peasants." Ont Libr Rev

Bryan, Ashley, 1923-

Beat the story-drum, pum-pum; retold and illustrated by Ashley Bryan. Atheneum Pubs. 1980 68p il $13.95; pa $6.95 (1-4) **398.2**

1. Folklore—Nigeria
ISBN 0-689-31356-X; 0-689-71107-7 (pa)
LC 80-12045

Coretta Scott King Award for illustration, 1981
"Five African folk tales for storytelling, humorous, informal and direct, with the rhythm and idiom of the African oral tradition. Integrated into the text are the appropriate actions, beats and chants and changing voices (even animal noises) for each character. . . . Beautifully illustrated with bold stylized woodcuts, some in black and white, some also with brick red and mustard yellow." SLJ

The cat's purr; written & illustrated by Ashley Bryan. Atheneum Pubs. 1985 42p il lib bdg $10.95 (k-2) **398.2**

1. Folklore—West Indies 2. Cats—Fiction
ISBN 0-689-31086-2 LC 84-21534

Cat and Rat are friends, but when Rat tricks Cat and plays the cat drum, which only cats may play, Cat ends up swallowing the drum, and that is how he got his purr
"Sketchy reddish-brown drawings follow the action but lack the excitement and subtle humor of the text. However, this is a story that begs to be learned and told aloud rather than read, and it should not be negated because of the bland illustrations. The complete text of a version of the tale published in 1936 appears at the conclusion." SLJ

The dancing granny; retold and illustrated by Ashley Bryan. Atheneum Pubs. 1977 unp il o.p.; Aladdin Bks. (NY) paperback available $6.95 (1-4) **398.2**

1. Folklore—West Indies
ISBN 0-689-71149-2 (pa) LC 76-25847

Spider Ananse gets Granny started dancing so he can raid her garden—but his own trick does him in
"A touch of rhyming talk and the visual portrayal of Ananse as a slouch-hatted dude spice Bryan's exuberant, musical retelling of a trickster story from the Antilles. Both Granny Anika . . . and Ananse himself are heartily evoked in visual and verbal terms. . . . The overall text with its song chants and snatches of dialogue is rich for reading aloud." Booklist

Lion and the ostrich chicks, and other African tales; retold and illustrated by Ashley Bryan. Atheneum Pubs. 1986 87p il $13.95 (4-6) **398.2**

1. Folklore—Africa
ISBN 0-689-31311-X LC 86-3349

The author "presents four stories representing various cultures of Africa, while his dynamic, somewhat stylized black-and-white drawings, augmented by five illustrations in red, black, and gold, add not only decorative designs but a handsome choreography of animated creatures. . . . Playing with the sounds as well as with the meanings of words, Ashley Bryan invites oral interpretation of the tales by his liberal use of onomatopoeic language, alliteration, interior rhymes, and repeated rhythmic chants. He indicates the source of each tale, although by his own admission he is more interested in approaching 'the spirit of the Black oral tradition' than he is in 'literal authenticity.'" Horn Book
Includes bibliography

Turtle knows your name; retold and illustrated by Ashley Bryan. Atheneum Pubs. 1989 unp il $12.95 (1-3) **398.2**

1. Folklore—West Indies
ISBN 0-689-31578-3 LC 89-2

"A Jean Karl book"
"In a story about a boy with a long name, verbal images are as important as visual ones, for the storytelling is filled with repetition, rhythm, and rhyme, while the watercolor paintings are bursting with vitality." Horn Book Guide

Carpenter, Frances

Tales of a Chinese grandmother; illustrated by Malthé Hasselriis. Tuttle 1973 261p pa $8.95 (4 and up) **398.2**

1. Folklore—China 2. Fairy tales
ISBN 0-8048-1042-7 LC 72-77514

"Tut books"

Carpenter, Frances—*Continued*

First published 1937 by Doubleday

"Thirty Chinese folk stories and legends from various sources are retold with the full flavor of the Orient. . . . They are told to a boy and girl by their grandmother on occasions in their daily life which suggest a story. Useful for storytelling." Booklist

"Phrased with grace and charm, the stories are revelatory of Chinese beliefs in years past, and of customs and home life. Drawings in color and black and white." N Y Libr

Carrick, Carol

Aladdin and the wonderful lamp; illustrated by Donald Carrick. Scholastic 1990 unp il $12.95 (2-4) **398.2**

1. Fairy tales 2. Arabs—Folklore

ISBN 0-590-41679-0 LC 87-32322

Recounts the tale of a poor tailor's son who becomes a wealthy prince with the help of a magic lamp he finds in an enchanted cave

"This Aladdin, though no angel, isn't quite the irresponsible ne'er-do-well found in the longer version. Donald Carrick's elaborate, well-controlled watercolor paintings are full of patterns and details. Drama is there too, in the faces and the sweep of scenes where pivotal events occur. A single edition well worth having." Booklist

Cauley, Lorinda Bryan, 1951-

The town mouse and the country mouse; retold and illustrated by Lorinda Bryan Cauley. Putnam 1984 unp il $11.95; pa $5.95 (k-3) **398.2**

1. Mice—Fiction 2. Fables

ISBN 0-399-21123-3; 0-399-21126-8 (pa) LC 84-11532

A retelling of the Aesop fable in which a town mouse and a country mouse exchange visits and discover each is suited to his own home

"Renewing the spirit of old-time tales is a Cauley speciality, and she does wonders for the fable about differing notions on the good life. . . . Enchanting paintings of each locale in full color emphasize the Victorian setting in the Country Mouse's simple abode and the Town Mouse's veritable mansion." Publ Wkly

The **Classic** fairy tales; [edited by] Iona and Peter Opie. Oxford Univ. Press 1974 336p il hardcover o.p. paperback available $10.95 **398.2**

1. Fairy tales

ISBN 0-19-520219-8 (pa) LC 73-90332

This book "contains the earliest published English texts of the tales selected, together with notes on the history and analogues of the stories." Oxford Companion to Child Lit

"Helpful indexing, bibliography, list of sources of illustrations." Choice

Cleaver, Elizabeth, 1939-1985

The enchanted caribou. Atheneum Pubs. 1985 30p il $11.95 (2-4) **398.2**

1. Indians of North America—Legends

ISBN 0-689-31170-2 LC 85-7465

An Inuit tale about shamans and transformation. Three brave young hunters befriend a maiden who is mysteriously changed into a white caribou

"The book has been illustrated with photographs of shadow puppet figures, and the illustrator provides information on how to create a shadow puppet theater to tell the tale and includes puppet figures that can be xeroxed and used for productions. But the book is not merely utilitarian, for the illustrations, bold, black shapes set against spare white space, stand on their own as artistic creations which give a wonderful feeling for the tundra." Horn Book

Climo, Shirley, 1928-

The Egyptian Cinderella; illustrated by Ruth Heller. Crowell 1989 unp il $14.95; lib bdg $14.89 (k-2) **398.2**

1. Folklore—Egypt 2. Fairy tales

ISBN 0-690-04822-X; 0-690-04824-6 (lib bdg) LC 88-37547

In this version of Cinderella set in Egypt in the sixth century B.C., Rhodopes, a slave girl, eventually comes to be chosen by the Pharaoh to be his queen

"The drafting in the full-page spreads is dutifully reminiscent of the two-dimensional style of Egyptian art, and the compositions are well-designed to incorporate the print, but the pinks, purples, and greens seem artificially bright, oddly out of keeping with their setting. For the many children who study Egypt in grade school, this will be valuable if for nothing else but to let them know that the tale stretches back at least 2,500 years." Bull Cent Child Books

Someone saw a spider; spider facts and folktales; illustrated by Dirk Zimmer. Crowell 1985 133p il $12.95; lib bdg $12.89 (4 and up) **398.2**

1. Spiders—Fiction 2. Folklore

ISBN 0-690-04435-6; 0-690-04436-4 (lib bdg) LC 84-45340

"Climo retells tales from Japan, Africa, America, Scotland, and Russia, showing the spider's wise, crafty, and magical sides. There are facts about spiders—body parts, web spinning, and mating practices—as well as spider folklore. . . . Zimmer's black-and-white line drawings are humorous and, in places, as delicate as a spider's web." Booklist

Includes bibliographic references

Cohen, Barbara, 1932-

Yussel's prayer; a Yom Kippur story; retold by Barbara Cohen; illustrated by Michael J. Deraney. Lothrop, Lee & Shepard Bks. 1981 unp il lib bdg $12.88 (3-5) **398.2**

1. Jews—Folklore 2. Prayers—Fiction 3. Yom Kippur—Fiction

ISBN 0-688-00461-X LC 80-25377

Cohen, Barbara, 1932-—*Continued*

A cowherd's simple but sincere Yom Kippur prayer is instrumental in ending the day's fast

"The legend is masterfully interpreted in soft-focus sepia drawings full of fine textures, careful shadowing, and understated detail. They're deep and rich, with a slightly mystical aura that suits the story's religious core." Booklist

Cole, Joanna

Bony-Legs; pictures by Dirk Zimmer. Four Winds Press 1983 unp il $10.95; Scholastic pa $2.95 (k-3) **398.2**

1. Folklore—Soviet Union 2. Fairy tales
ISBN 0-02-722970-X; 0-590-33222-8 (pa) LC 82-7424

"Based on the tale 'Baba-Yaga' in Russian fairy tales by Aleksandr Afanas'ev." Verso of title page

When a terrible witch vows to eat her for supper, a little girl escapes with the help of a mirror and comb given to her by the witch's cat and dog

"The rich text leaves out some of the grisly details of the original without castrating the story, and it is matched by clear yet densely lined drawings that borrow some from Ivan Bilibin's earlier illustrations, yet add amusing detail and fine design and layout of their own." SLJ

Conover, Chris, 1950-

Mother Goose and the sly fox; retold and with pictures by Chris Conover. Farrar, Straus & Giroux 1989 unp il $13.95 (k-2) **398.2**

1. Folklore
ISBN 0-374-35072-8 LC 89-45502

"Mother Goose, who watches over her seven goslings and one do-nothing mouse, goes to market one day. The goslings innocently open the door to a hungry fox, who needs food for his own young cubs. Six of the goslings are bagged and carted off, but Mother Goose saves her children when the lazy fox takes a nap." Publ Wkly

"Conover's glowing watercolors outlined in ink are full of charming detail; the fully realized animals, dressed in seventeenth-century garb, star in evocative double- and single-page spreads." Booklist

Cooney, Barbara, 1917-

The little juggler; adapted from an old French legend and illustrated by Barbara Cooney. Hastings House 1982 46p il $10.95 (3-6) **398.2**

1. Legends—France 2. Christmas—Fiction 3. Miracles—Fiction
ISBN 0-8038-4239-2 LC 61-10576

A reissue with new illustrations of the title first published 1961

The story of a little juggler's search for a special Christmas gift for the Christ child

This tale "bears some resemblance to the Italian legend beautifully portrayed in Tomie de Paola's 'Clown of God' [entered below]. Black line work alternates with illustrations brightened by piercing greens, reds, and blues, making this a worthwhile addition to the Christmas book shelf." Booklist

Cooper, Susan, 1935-

The selkie girl; retold by Susan Cooper; illustrated by Warwick Hutton. Margaret K. McElderry Bks. 1986 unp il $13.95; pa $4.95 (2-4) **398.2**

1. Folklore—Great Britain 2. Seals (Animals)—Fiction
ISBN 0-689-50390-3; 0-689-71467-4 (pa)
LC 86-70147

A retelling of the legend from British coasts and islands in which a man falls in love with a beautiful seal girl and forces her to live on land and be his bride

"The prose is rhythmic, the pictures cool and blue-hued, with loose shapes and pages bled to give a sense of boundlessness. The selkie appears naked with her sisters in the first spread, but discreetly so, all the better to contrast with her primly confined form as she stares longingly to sea with her first child. The seascapes and shore scenes are light-filled, vintage Hutton." Bull Cent Child Books

The silver cow: a Welsh tale; retold by Susan Cooper; illustrated by Warwick Hutton. Atheneum Pubs. 1983 unp il lib bdg $13.95 (1-3) **398.2**

1. Folklore—Wales 2. Cattle—Fiction
ISBN 0-689-50236-2 LC 82-13928

"A Margaret K. McElderry book"

A young Welsh boy is rewarded for his beautiful harp playing with a silver cow, the gift of the magic people living in the lake. The cow makes his family rich but when his father becomes greedy the magic people take their revenge

"A lilting text, complemented by luminous watercolor illustrations, captures the enchantment inherent in a traditional tale explaining the genesis of the water lilies fringing Llyn Barfog, 'the bearded lake,' set high in the Welsh hills." Horn Book

Courlander, Harold, 1908-

The cow-tail switch, and other West African stories; by Harold Courlander and George Herzog; drawings by Madye Lee Chastain. Holt & Co. 1987 143p il $12.95; pa $4.95 (4-6) **398.2**

1. Folklore—Africa, West 2. Ashanti (African people)—Folklore
ISBN 0-8050-0288-X; 0-8050-0298-7 (pa)
LC 86-46267

A Newbery Medal honor book, 1948

A reissue of the title first published 1947

"The seventeen stories mostly gathered in the Ashanti country, are fresh to collections and are told with humor and originality. Their themes, chosen with discrimination, are frequently primitive explanations of the origin of folk sayings and customs, or show examples of animal trickery and ingenuity." Horn Book

Includes glossary and bibliography

The **Crest** and the hide, and other African stories of heroes, chiefs, bards, hunters, sorcerers, and common people; [compiled by] Harold Courlander; illustrations by Monica Vachula. Coward, McCann & Geoghegan 1982 137p il $11.95 (5 and up) **398.2**

1. Folklore—Africa
ISBN 0-698-20536-7 LC 81-9739

A "collection of 20 African tales marked by wit and verbal economy. The majority are brief (only a few stretch beyond the two-to-three-page average length) and make salient comment on matters of friendship, goodness rewarded, the merits of wisdom, or the price of indulgence. Humans rather than animals figure in the actions, and the stories' messages speak transculturally with no problem. Notes and commentary are appended; information here includes a story's origins, its teller, and data that sketches the story's cultural context. With intermittent pen-and-ink sketches." Booklist

Creswick, Paul, 1866-1947

Robin Hood; illustrated by N.C. Wyeth. Scribner 1984 362p il $22.50 (5 and up) **398.2**

1. Robin Hood (Legendary character)
ISBN 0-684-18162-2 LC 84-10662

A reissue of a title first published 1917 by McKay

Recounts the life and adventures of Robin Hood, who, with his band of followers, lived as an outlaw in Sherwood Forest dedicated to fight against tyranny

Croll, Carolyn, 1945-

The little snowgirl: an old Russian tale; adapted and illustrated by Carolyn Croll. Putnam 1989 unp il $13.95 (k-2) **398.2**

1. Folklore—Soviet Union 2. Fairy tales 3. Christmas—Fiction
ISBN 0-399-21691-X LC 88-30667

"A Whitebird book"

Based on Ransome's version of the Russian fairy tale. Caterina and Pavel's wish for a child is fulfilled when the snowgirl Pavel makes in the yard comes alive

"The colorless snowgirl contrasts well with the bright village backgrounds. While adult readers will see similarities to Tomie dePaola's style, children will relate to Croll's own use of color and contour. Russian vocabulary and an easy narrative voice make this a highly appealing book." Booklist

Crossley-Holland, Kevin

British folk tales; new versions. Orchard Bks. 1987 383p $22.95 (4 and up) **398.2**

1. Folklore—Great Britain
ISBN 0-531-05733-X LC 87-9918

This collection includes "ghost stories, hero tales, tales of trials and conflict, brave princes, tricksters, fairies, and goblins. . . . Familiar old favorites such as 'Jack and the Beanstalk' and 'The Three Bears' rub elbows with lesser known versions of old favorites such as 'Mossycoat,' a version of Cinderella, and 'Hughbo,' a version of 'The Shoemaker and the Elves.' . . . A pronunciation guide (although it is not comprehensive) and an appendix giving scholarly sources and author's comments adds to the value of this highly recommended collection." SLJ

Curry, Jane Louise, 1932-

Back in the beforetime; tales of the California Indians; retold by Jane Louise Curry; illustrated by James Watts. Margaret K. McElderry Bks. 1987 134p il $13.95 (4-6) **398.2**

1. Indians of North America—Legends 2. Coyote (Legendary character)
ISBN 0-689-50410-1 LC 86-21339

A retelling of twenty-two legends about the creation of the world from a variety of California Indian tribes

"The predominantly humorous tone of the stories is highlighted by the black-and-white illustrations, each with its geometrically patterned border. Curry's rhythmic prose lends itself well to storytelling or reading aloud." SLJ

Curtis, Edward S., 1868-1952

The girl who married a ghost, and other tales from The North American Indian; collected, and with photographs by Edward S. Curtis; edited by John Bierhorst. Four Winds Press 1978 115p il $11.95 (4 and up) **398.2**

1. Indians of North America—Legends
ISBN 0-02-709740-4 LC 77-21515

"These nine haunting stories and the marvelous photos are taken from the 'The North American Indian' (a twenty-volume series begun in 1907). . . . The editor, John Bierhorst, has grouped these stories by nine geographical and tribal sources with a summary for each of the nine sections. The stories are stark and fearful, unlike many young people's books about Indians which dilute and soften reality in the legends. . . . Beautiful authentic photographs and excellent book design all contribute to this highly recommended book." Babbling Bookworm

Includes bibliography

De la Mare, Walter, 1873-1956

Molly Whuppie; retold by Walter de la Mare; illustrated by Errol Le Cain. Farrar, Straus & Giroux 1983 unp il $11.95 (k-3) **398.2**

1. Folklore—Great Britain 2. Fairy tales 3. Giants—Fiction
ISBN 0-374-35000-0 LC 82-83099

"The story of the clever girl who three times escapes from the giant and wins a prince apiece for herself and her sisters is told with good cadence and pace, and the romantic illustrations, richly colored, often humorous in detail, are handsome in composition, each full-page painting facing a page of text with a deft silhouette picture tucked into a corner of the broad margin." Bull Cent Child Books

De Paola, Tomie, 1934-

The clown of God; an old story; told and illustrated by Tomie de Paola. Harcourt Brace Jovanovich 1978 unp il $13.95; pa $4.95 (k-3) **398.2**

1. Legends 2. Miracles—Fiction 3. Christmas—Fiction
ISBN 0-15-219175-5; 0-15-618192-4 (pa) LC 78-3845

This legend is retold, as in Barbara Cooney's The little juggler (entered above), as a Christmas tale of simple reverence, but is here given an Italian setting. An orphan whose juggling skill led him to a career as a traveling entertainer has grown old and clumsy and returns as a hungry beggar to his birthplace. On Christmas Eve in the monastery church a miracle occurs as he summons his last strength to make his only possible offering

"Mr. de Paola has written the tale with love, tenderness, and joy. He has executed authentic Renaissance illustrations that are magnificent in design and beauty." Child Book Rev Serv

The legend of Old Befana; an Italian Christmas story; retold and illustrated by Tomie de Paola. Harcourt Brace Jovanovich 1980 unp il lib bdg $14.95; pa $3.95 (k-3) **398.2**

1. Befana (Legendary character) 2. Folklore—Italy 3. Christmas—Fiction
ISBN 0-15-243816-5 (lib bdg); 0-15-243817-3 (pa) LC 80-12293

Because Befana's household chores kept her from finding the Baby King, she searches to this day, leaving gifts for children on the Feast of the Three Kings

This version of the Italian legend "is attractively designed with rich colors and decorative detail. The tale is told in simple but effective language." SLJ

The legend of the Indian paintbrush; retold and illustrated by Tomie dePaola. Putnam 1988 unp il lib bdg $13.95; pa $5.95 (k-3) **398.2**

1. Indians of North America—Legends
ISBN 0-399-21534-4 (lib bdg); 0-399-21777-0 (pa) LC 87-20160

A "folktale of the Plains Indians that reveals how the Indian Paintbrush, the state flower of Wyoming, first bloomed. An Indian boy's dream to recreate the colors of the sunset comes true when he discovers paintbrushes filled with the colors he needs. A voice in the night had promised him this because he had shared his artistic talent with his people." Child Book Rev Serv

"The native American motifs are rendered simply and authentically; the night sky and glorious sunset spreads are truly beautiful with line, color, and form perfectly balanced to capture the text." Horn Book

Tony's bread: an Italian folktale. Putnam 1989 unp il $13.95 (k-2) **398.2**

1. Folklore—Italy
ISBN 0-399-21693-6 LC 88-7687

"A Whitebird book"

"This tale captures the flavor of an Italian folk tale with both textual and visual humor. The story of Angelo—a rich, young nobleman from Milan who attempts to win the hand of his true love, the beautiful daughter of Tony the baker—explains the origin of *panettone,* the delicious Milanese Christmas bread made with eggs, raisins, and candied fruit. . . . The pictures and story combine to make a delectable Christmas treat." Horn Book

De Regniers, Beatrice Schenk

Everyone is good for something; pictures by Margot Tomes. Clarion Bks. 1980 unp il $13.95 (k-3) **398.2**

1. Folklore—Soviet Union
ISBN 0-395-28967-X LC 79-12223

"Inept Jack is the despair of his poor, widowed mother. He makes a shambles of every chore, every attempt to get work. One day, Jack earns a penny by agreeing to drown a cat that, like himself, is good for nothing. Instead, he spends the penny to buy the poor cat a fish. The two outcasts become buddies and sail to a far-off island, where the cat shows what he's good for and Jack goes home, richly rewarded, to prove that he's like every other person in the world: good for something." Publ Wkly

"Vignetted pictures of varied sizes and shapes, limited earth colors, lots of white spaces, excellent design and understated humor all make for appealing illustrations, well matched to the text." SLJ

Jack the giant killer; Jack's first & finest adventure retold in verse as well as other useful information about giants including How to shake hands with a giant; pictures by Anne Wilsdorf. Atheneum Pubs. 1987 unp il $12.95 (k-3) **398.2**

1. Folklore—Great Britain 2. Fairy tales 3. Giants—Fiction
ISBN 0-689-31218-0 LC 86-3606

"De Regniers retells in verse the first episode of a classic folktale. . . . In a companionable gathering of legend and lore, the author appends seven old sayings or beliefs, such as 'A cave is the hollow bone of a giant's leg.' Each is colorfully illustrated in a double-page spread. The last section consists of advice on shaking a giant's hand. . . . Wilsdorf's spirited full-color illustrations depict the hero as a cocky, saucy lad and the giant as fearsome, greedy, and not too bright." Booklist

Little Sister and the Month Brothers; retold by Beatrice Schenk de Regniers; pictures by Margot Tomes. Clarion Bks. 1976 unp il $8.95 (k-3) **398.2**

1. Slavs—Folklore 2. Fairy tales
ISBN 0-8164-3147-7 LC 75-4594

First published by Seabury Press

"A story that has Cinderella elements and the familiar folk theme of virtue rewarded. Orphaned, Little Sister is overworked and abused by her stepmother and stepsister. Sent to find violets in midwinter, she appeals to the Month brothers, who bring a quick and magical springtime flowering." Bull Cent Child Books

"The author's retelling of a traditional Slavic tale is a bit effusive and self-conscious but it is redeemed by her sense of humor and the inherent qualities of the story. And Margot Tomes's brilliant pictures add immensely to the adventures of Little Sister." Publ Wkly

DeFelice, Cynthia C.

The dancing skeleton; illustrated by Robert Andrew Parker. Macmillan 1989 unp il $13.95 (k-3) **398.2**

1. Folklore—United States
ISBN 0-02-726452-1 LC 88-30245

"Aaron Kelly got up out of his grave, went home and sat down in his chair by the fire. Here's the story of how the fiddler who wanted to court Aaron's widow got rid of the skeleton. The elegant watercolor illustrations capture the way the skeleton dances himself to bits, as well as the mood of night in the graveyard." N Y Times Book Rev

Demi, 1942-

A Chinese zoo: fables and proverbs; adapted and illustrated by Demi. Harcourt Brace Jovanovich 1987 unp il $14.95 (3-5) **398.2**

1. Folklore—China 2. Fables
ISBN 0-15-217510-5 LC 86-33562

"Demi has adapted 13 fables and proverbs from the Chinese tradition and illustrated them with breathtaking grace and style. . . . Demi's exquisite watercolors of the hedgehogs, pandas, deer, and unicorns which populate the fables appear on an open fan on each spread. Adding to the book's aura of authenticity are the beautifully-wrought Chinese characters that accompany each proverb. A perfect blending of excellent writing and beautifully stylized illustrations." SLJ

The empty pot. Holt & Co. 1990 unp il $15.95 (k-3) **398.2**

1. Folklore—China
ISBN 0-8050-1217-6 LC 89-39062

"Ping is a Chinese boy with an emerald green thumb; he can make anything grow 'as if by magic.' One day the Emperor announces that he needs a successor. . . . He gives each child one seed, and the one who grows the best flower will take over after him. . . . On the day of the competition, [Ping] is the only child with an empty pot; all the others bring lush plants. But the Emperor has tricked everyone by distributing cooked seeds, unable to grow; and Ping, with his empty pot, is the only honest gardener—and the winner." Publ Wkly

"This simple story with its clear moral is illustrated with beautiful paintings. . . . A beautifully crafted book that will be enjoyed as much for the richness of its illustrations as for the simplicity of its story." SLJ

The magic boat. Holt & Co. 1990 unp il $15.95 (k-3) **398.2**

1. Folklore—China
ISBN 0-8050-1141-2 LC 90-4425

"Young Chang selflessly rescues a drowning old man and is rewarded with two gifts. When an evil stranger steals the magic boat, Chang needs his second gift—the magical power of the old man—to help retrieve it. Demi's retelling of this traditional tale is illustrated with graceful detailed, Chinese-inspired art, liberally garnished with gold." Horn Book Guide

Deuchar, Ian

The prince and the mermaid. Dial Bks. for Young Readers 1989 unp $12.95 (2-5) **398.2**

1. Folklore—France 2. Fairy tales
ISBN 0-8037-0638-3 LC 88-33395

The Prince and the mermaid's happy marriage is threatened when a wicked witch casts an evil spell

"The story moves swiftly from beginning to end, with an equitable balance of action and description. . . . Older fairy-tale fans will love this romantic and tragic tale, which is suitable for reading aloud or for individual use." SLJ

The **Diane** Goode book of American folk tales and songs; collected by Ann Durell. Dutton 1989 63p il music lib bdg $14.95 (2-5) **398.2**

1. Folklore—United States 2. Folk songs—United States
ISBN 0-525-44458-0 LC 89-1097

"Ann Durell has selected nine stories and seven songs from various regions and ethnic groups, and Diane Goode's wonderfully expressive illustrations grace every page. . . . The folk songs . . . will be familiar to most schoolchildren, and because the simple melodic lines are included, they will be accessible for singing and playing." Horn Book

Edwards, Roberta

Five silly fishermen; illustrated by Sylvie Wickstrom. Random House 1989 32p il lib bdg $6.99; pa $2.95 (k-2) **398.2**

1. Folklore
ISBN 0-679-80092-6 (lib bdg); 0-679-80092-1 (pa)
LC 89-42508

"Step into reading. A step 1 book"

In this "variation of the old tale, five fishermen spend the day fishing, and before going home, decide to count to make sure one of them has not drowned during the day. Each fisherman counts and comes up with only four fishermen, forgetting himself as he counts. They cry and bemoan the loss of their friend until a little girl comes along and 'finds' their missing friend in exchange for a fish." SLJ

"The simple text works well with the softly colored, neatly executed drawings. This traditional tale is sure to amuse beginning readers, who will get a lesson in logic as well." Booklist

Ehrlich, Amy, 1942-

The Random House book of fairy tales; adapted by Amy Ehrlich; illustrated by Diane Goode; with an introduction by Bruno Bettelheim. Random House 1985 208p il $16.95; lib bdg $14.99 (k-3) **398.2**

1. Folklore 2. Fairy tales
ISBN 0-394-85693-7; 0-394-95693-1 (lib bdg)
LC 83-13833

"Ehrlich has chosen nineteen tales, primarily from the Grimm, Perrault, and Andersen collections, capably retelling some of the most familiar fairy tales in a direct and simple style. The book is profusely illustrated, with

Ehrlich, Amy, 1942-—*Continued*
full color and black and white alternating in double-page spreads. The color is soft, usually pastel, and blends comic and romantic details deftly; the black and white pictures are even softer, with an almost hazy look, gray-toned and never sharp in line." Bull Cent Child Books

Includes bibliography

Rapunzel; re-told by Amy Ehrlich; pictures by Kris Waldherr. Dial Bks. 1989 unp il $11.95; lib bdg $11.89 (1-3) **398.2**

1. Folklore—Germany 2. Fairy tales
ISBN 0-8037-0654-5; 0-8037-0655-3 (lib bdg)
LC 88-25918

A retelling of the Grimm fairy tale about the beautiful girl imprisoned in a lonely tower by a witch

"Events are somewhat telescoped . . . but what is lost in suspense is gained in pace. In Waldherr's clear, soft, colored-pencil drawings, blues and greens set off Rapunzel's red-gold tresses. The witch is such a slender and attractive senior that her traditionally evil behavior is rather a shock. The layout is notable: each vignette is edged by either a landscape or a floral design linked to the story." SLJ

Esbensen, Barbara Juster

Ladder to the sky; how the gift of healing came to the Ojibway nation: a legend; retold by Barbara Juster Esbensen; illustrated by Helen K. Davie. Little, Brown 1989 unp il $14.95 (k-3) **398.2**

1. Chippewa Indians—Legends
ISBN 0-316-24952-1 LC 87-22729

"A retelling of the Ojibway or Chippewa legend that explains why healing powers were given to Indian medicine men. Elegant, luminous illustrations are set within borders or entwined leaves and herbs. A substantial addition to folklore collections about native Americans." Horn Book Guide

The star maiden: an Ojibway tale; retold by Barbara Juster Esbensen; illustrated by Helen K. Davie. Little, Brown 1988 unp il lib bdg $14.95 (k-3) **398.2**

1. Chippewa Indians—Legends
ISBN 0-316-24951-3 LC 87-3247

"Based on an Ojibway or Chippewa Native American legend, this tells why there are water lilies. It is a lovely retelling which keeps the dignity and wonder associated with Native American attitudes towards nature. The watercolor illustrations are remarkable for their authentic details and the borders which are based on Ojibway pattern. This is a must for units on American Indians." Child Book Rev Serv

Evans, C. S. (Charles Seddon), 1883-1944

The sleeping beauty; told by C. S. Evans and illustrated by Arthur Rackham. Heinemann, W. 1972 110p il $14.95 (3-5) **398.2**

1. Fairy tales
ISBN 0-434-95860-3

A reprint of the title first published 1920 by Lippincott

This is an expanded, novel-length version of the popular fairy tale about the beautiful princess who is put into an enchanted sleep for one hundred years, until the kiss of a prince awakens her

This edition contains "the black-and-white (mostly) illustrations which Rackham prepared in silhouette fashion for the edition he originally illustrated. It . . . is charming." Best Sellers

Forest, Heather

The baker's dozen; a colonial American tale; retold by Heather Forest; illustrated by Susan Gaber. Harcourt Brace Jovanovich 1988 unp il lib bdg $13.95 (k-3) **398.2**

1. Folklore—United States
ISBN 0-15-200412-2 LC 87-17103

"Gulliver books"

"A seventeenth-century legend describes the rise and fall of a prosperous baker whose famous St. Nicholas cookies bring him a booming business until he begins to cheat his customers. Even then his reputation draws crowds, but a mysterious old woman curses him for his greed, and thereafter everything goes wrong. Only on her return visit, when he adds an extra cookie to her dozen, does good fortune return—thus the custom of giving thirteen to a dozen." Bull Cent Child Books

"Gaber's elegant watercolors are vivid and stylized, showing a dusted palette of burgundies with charcoal and burnished oranges. This is a fine explanation of a long-standing custom, and Forest backs it up with an author's note on the facts." Publ Wkly

The woman who flummoxed the fairies; an old tale from Scotland; retold by Heather Forest; illustrated by Susan Gaber. Harcourt Brace Jovanovich 1990 unp il $14.95 (k-2) **398.2**

1. Folklore—Scotland 2. Cake—Fiction
ISBN 0-15-200648-6 LC 88-28448

"Gulliver books"

Asked to make a cake for the fairies, a clever baker-woman must figure out a way to prevent the fairies from wanting to keep her with them always to bake her delicious cakes

"While depicting a strong, resourceful heroine, Forest's graceful retelling perfectly captures the story's fairy-tale flavor. Using deep tones of violet, blue and green, Gaber's haunting paintings range from the wonderfully eerie to the comfortably reassuring." Publ Wkly

Freedman, Florence B. (Florence Bernstein)

Brothers: a Hebrew legend; retold by Florence B. Freedman; with illustrations by Robert Andrew Parker. Harper & Row 1985 unp il $11.95; lib bdg $11.89 (k-2) **398.2**

1. Jews—Folklore 2. Brothers—Fiction
ISBN 0-06-021871-1; 0-06-021872-X (lib bdg)
LC 85-42616

"Simple retelling of an ancient Hebrew legend about the loving relationship between Dan and Joel. When hard times strike, each brother displays his concern for the other's well-being" Soc Educ

Freedman, Florence B. (Florence Bernstein) —*Continued*

"Parker echoes the simplicity in his striking full-page watercolor illustrations with pen-and-ink detail. The use of shadows and subtle shadings gives a feeling of warmth to the golden-toned afternoons and the brilliant blueness of night. The religious aspect of this Hebrew legend has been played down here, giving it universal appeal." SLJ

Fritz, Jean

Brendan the Navigator; a history mystery about the discovery of America; illustrated by Enrico Arno. Coward, McCann & Geoghegan 1979 31p il $7.95 (3-5) **398.2**

1. Brendan, Saint, the Voyager, ca. 483-577 2. America—Exploration
ISBN 0-698-20473-5 LC 78-13247

Recounts St. Brendan's life and voyage to North America long before the Vikings arrived

"Jean Fritz's narrative is beautifully cadenced, lively and wry. Her historical postscript is all right, too, and the two-color illustrations are appropriately convoluted and Celtic." N Y Times Book Rev

The good giants and the bad pukwudgies; illustrated by Tomie de Paola. Putnam 1982 unp il hardcover o.p. paperback available $5.95 (k-3) **398.2**

1. Wampanoag Indians—Legends 2. Cape Cod (Mass.)—Fiction
ISBN 0-399-21732-0 (pa) LC 81-17921

The author "retells a legend of the Wampanoag Indians of Massachusetts, combining several tales to form a 'why' story that explains how Buzzard's Bay, Nantucket, and Martha's Vineyard as well as some smaller islands were formed. . . . There's some crowding of plot, but it's compensated for by the style, the humor (especially in the terse New England speech pattern in dialogues between Maushop and his wife) and in the illustrations, which are, like all de Paola's work, stylized and rather stiff, but excellent in color and composition." Bull Cent Child Books

Gág, Wanda, 1893-1946

Gone is gone; or, The story of a man who wanted to do housework; retold and illustrated by Wanda Gág. Coward-McCann 1935 unp il lib bdg $5.99 (k-3) **398.2**

1. Folklore—Bohemia (Czechoslovakia)
ISBN 0-698-30179-X LC 35-27311

The author retells a humorous folk tale which she heard as a child in Bohemia. "Told in informal conversational style, it follows one catastrophe after another as they happen in the brief space of a morning when a peasant farmer takes over what he calls the 'puttering and pottering' of housework in order that his wife might toil in the fields and learn how hard 'his' work is. The full flavor of the tale is conveyed in the numerous small drawings by the author. Excellent version for use in story-telling." N Y Libr

Wanda Gág's The sorcerer's apprentice; illustrated by Margot Tomes. Coward, McCann & Geoghegan 1979 c1947 unp il lib bdg $6.95 (k-3) **398.2**

1. Folklore—Germany 2. Fairy tales
ISBN 0-698-20481-6 LC 78-23990

"The text was adapted by W. Gág from several sources, and originally appeared in the collection More tales from Grimm [entered under Grimm]." Verso of title page

"A boy, pretending he cannot read or write, is accepted as the apprentice of a wicked sorcerer; and studying his master's books in secret, he not only outwits the magician but saves his own life." Horn Book

"This small book has a macabre note that is nicely echoed by the pictures (alternately in color and in black and white) which combine eerie details with a sort of peasant scruffiness. While the vocabulary is fairly sophisticated, the story . . . can be read with descretion to younger children." Bull Cent Child Books

Galdone, Joanna

The tailypo; a ghost story; told by Joanna Galdone; illustrated by Paul Galdone. Clarion Bks. 1984 unp il $13.95; pa $4.95 (k-3) **398.2**

1. Folklore—United States
ISBN 0-395-28809-6; 0-395-30084-3 (pa) LC 77-23289

First published by Seabury Press

"An old man lives in the Tennessee backwoods with his three hunting dogs, Uno, Ino and Cumptico-Calico. . . . The old man sees an odd animal squeezing through a crack in his cabin and grabs it. All he gets is its tail but he makes a snack of that and gets into bed with a satisfied appetite. But the dismembered [creature] wants its tail back. When he haunts the old man with his keening, 'Tailypo, tailypo, all I want is my tailypo' in vain, he settles for vengeance instead." Publ Wkly

"The energetic postures of the old man and his dogs form a strong accompaniment to the clean, vigorous storytelling, and the subtly underplayed color in the paintings not only suggests the ghostliness of the story but is pleasing in itself." Horn Book

"The violent ending of the story (in which the farmer is 'scratched . . . to pieces' and his cabin destroyed) may bother some young children." SLJ

Galdone, Paul, 1914-1986

Cinderella. McGraw-Hill 1978 unp il $14.95 (k-2) **398.2**

1. Folklore—France 2. Fairy tales
ISBN 0-07-022684-9 LC 78-7614

Based on Perrault's French version of the fairy tale about the mistreated kitchen maid who attends the royal ball with the aid of her fairy godmother

"This is an eminently robust version of the story. . . . Moreover, the ambitious spreads reflect Galdone's essential lightheartedness of style; comedy seeps through in the pompous, snobby faces of the stepmother and sisters. Dialogue gives the text an informal feeling but does adhere to folktale conventions. . . . Visually, this has surefire child appeal; it's a good working interpretation." Booklist

Galdone, Paul, 1914-1986—*Continued*

The elves and the shoemaker; retold and illustrated by Paul Galdone. Clarion Bks. 1984 unp il $13.95; pa $4.95 (k-2) **398.2**

1. Folklore—Germany 2. Fairy tales
ISBN 0-89919-226-2; 0-89919-422-2 (pa)

LC 83-14979

"Based on Lucy Crane's translation from the German of the Brothers Grimm." Title page

A pair of elves help a poor shoemaker become successful, and the shoemaker and his wife reward them with elegant outfits

"The pictures in flashing hues emphasize the secret helpers' impishness; they seem to be performing the service more for a lark than in the name of sweet charity." Publ Wkly

The gingerbread boy. Clarion Bks. 1975 unp il $13.95; pa $4.95 (k-2) **398.2**

1. Folklore 2. Fairy tales
ISBN 0-395-28799-5; 0-89919-163-0 (pa)

LC 74-11461

First published by Seabury Press

"A lively version of the tale of the gingerbread boy who sprang into action as soon as he was baked and gleefully eluded all would-be captors until he was finally outwitted by a fox. The artist's gingerbread boy is a strong-legged, cocky individual, who sets out on a merry race through the countryside. The action of the tale is well-paced; large, humorous illustrations with stone fences, a covered bridge, and hearty rural folk suggest a New England background, while the triumphant fox is the epitome of all slyness." Horn Book

Henny Penny; retold and illustrated by Paul Galdone. Clarion Bks. 1968 unp il $13.95; pa $4.95 (k-2) **398.2**

1. Folklore 2. Animals—Fiction
ISBN 0-395-28800-2; 0-89919-225-4 (pa)

LC 68-24735

First published by Seabury Press

A folktale also popularly known as Chicken Little. "The simple retelling has a different ending which makes the fox seem somewhat less villainous—when Henny Penny and her credulous friends follow Foxy Loxy into the cave they are never seen again and the king is never told that the sky is falling, but Foxy Loxy, his wife, and seven little foxes (appealingly portrayed in a picture as a family group) still remember the fine feast they had that day." Booklist

King of the Cats; a ghost story; by Joseph Jacobs retold and illustrated by Paul Galdone. Clarion Bks. 1980 unp il $13.95; pa $4.95 (k-2) **398.2**

1. Folklore—Great Britain 2. Fairy tales 3. Cats—Fiction
ISBN 0-395-29030-9; 0-89919-400-1 (pa)

LC 79-16659

"In this retelling of a century-old English tale, a woman and her cat wait long into the evening for the return of the gravedigger husband. Finally he bursts into the cottage wild-eyed and demands, 'Who is Tom Tildrum?' As he goes on to recount a funeral procession of black cats that he witnessed, his own cat, Old Tom, is much affected by the description." SLJ

"Galdone follows closely, in his adaptation, the version by Joseph Jacobs on which this tale is based . . . but has simplified the exposition and removed the dialect from the dialogue. A smooth retelling, the story is handsomely illustrated by large-scale pictures that fill, but do not crowd, the pages; Galdone's draughtsmanship is at its best here. . . . A good choice for telling to young children or for reading aloud." Bull Cent Child Books

The little red hen. Clarion Bks. 1973 unp il $13.95; pa $4.95 (k-2) **398.2**

1. Folklore 2. Chickens—Fiction
ISBN 0-395-28803-7; 0-89919-349-8 (pa)

LC 72-97770

First published by Seabury Press

"In a light-hearted interpretation of the old tale, a domesticated little hen, complete with mobcap and apron, busies herself in a picturesquely shabby cottage while her three house mates—a cat, a dog, and a mouse—doze blissfully. The industry of the little hen produces a cake; and only when 'a delicious smell filled the cozy little house,' do her lazy companions come to life." Horn Book

"The large, clear, colorful pictures perfectly suit the book for pre-school story hours; the simple text, with one or two lines per page, will make it a success with beginning readers." SLJ

Little Red Riding Hood; adapted from the retelling by the Brothers Grimm [by] Paul Galdone. McGraw-Hill 1974 unp il lib bdg $14.95 (k-2) **398.2**

1. Folklore—Germany 2. Wolves—Fiction
ISBN 0-07-022732-2 LC 74-6426

The folktale about the innocent little girl's encounter with a villainous wolf is illustrated by the adapter "in a retelling that adheres to the Grimm version with both Grandmother and Red Riding Hood eaten up and later rescued by a passing huntsman." Booklist

"The appealing format—comfortable size, attractive (though sometimes slapdash) full-color illustrations—and a traditional happy ending will make this version a favorite with small children. . . . Galdone's larger, bright illustrations make this better for showing to groups." SLJ

The monkey and the crocodile; a Jataka tale from India. Clarion Bks. 1969 unp il $13.95; pa $4.95 (k-2) **398.2**

1. Folklore—India 2. Fables 3. Animals—Fiction 4. Jataka stories
ISBN 0-395-28806-1; 0-89919-524-5 (pa)

LC 78-79939

First published by Seabury Press

Illustrated by Galdone, this is a retelling of one of the Jataka fables about Buddha in his animal incarnations. "The crocodile wants a meal of monkey, but the intended prey is far wilier than his antagonist." SLJ

The story "has the humor, plot, and movement to make it a good book for any young child, even one unused to stories: the brilliant colors, clear pictures, and brief text should make it very successful for sharing with groups of children." Horn Book

Galdone, Paul, 1914-1986—*Continued*

Puss in boots. Clarion Bks. 1976 unp il $13.95; pa $4.95 (k-2) **398.2**

1. Folklore—France 2. Fairy tales
ISBN 0-395-28808-8; 0-89919-192-4 (pa)
LC 75-25505

First published by Seabury Press

"Galdone follows Perrault's story line faithfully, as Puss works mischief to obtain a fortune for his master. The writing, fluid and readable, makes even this familiar tale sound fresh—no mean feat. Galdone's large, humorous caricatures—easily seen for story hour—have great gusto, and Puss is the embodiment of cleverness and knavery." SLJ

The teeny-tiny woman; a ghost story. Clarion Bks. 1984 unp il $13.95; pa $4.95 (k-2) **398.2**

1. Folklore—Great Britain 2. Ghosts—Fiction
ISBN 0-89919-270-X; 0-89919-463-X (pa)
LC 84-4311

Retold and illustrated by Galdone, this is an English folk tale about a "teeny-tiny woman who lives in a teeny-tiny house in a teeny-tiny village goes for a teeny-tiny walk, etc. Opening the gates to a churchyard, she finds a bone that will add flavor to the soup she plans for supper. Back home, she goes to bed but is alarmed by a voice . . . demanding, 'Give me back my bone!'" Publ Wkly

"Quarter-inch type will attract reticent readers, and the comfortable, cozy country and cottage scenes defuse whatever scariness young readers might conjure up. Fences, trees, balustrades and cupboards in murky, inky tones are designed to suggest watchful faces and add to the atmospheric tension of the narrative." SLJ

Three Aesop fox fables. Clarion Bks. 1971 unp il $13.95 (k-3) **398.2**

1. Fables 2. Foxes—Fiction
ISBN 0-395-28810-X LC 79-133061

First published by Seabury Press

A retelling of The fox and the grapes, The fox and the stork, and The fox and the crow

"Paul Galdone's bright-eyed fox is the quintessence of merry cunning. . . . The pictures, full of movement and humor, are especially good for showing to a group because of the large animal figures and simple composition." Saturday Rev

The three bears. Clarion Bks. 1972 unp il $12.95; pa $4.95 (k-2) **398.2**

1. Folklore 2. Bears—Fiction
ISBN 0-395-28811-8; 0-590-11820-X (pa)
LC 78-158833

First published by Seabury Press

In Galdone's illustrations for his retelling of the tale of Goldilocks, "his three bears are beautifully groomed, civilized creatures, living a life of rustic contentment in an astonishingly verdant forest, while his Goldilocks is a horrid, be-ringletted, overdressed child who rampages wantonly through the bears' tidy home." Times Lit Suppl

The three Billy Goats Gruff. Clarion Bks. 1973 unp il $13.95; pa $4.95 (k-2) **398.2**

1. Folklore—Norway 2. Goats—Fiction
ISBN 0-395-28812-6; 0-89919-035-9 (pa)
LC 72-85338

First published by Seabury Press

In this retelling of the old Norwegian folk tale, "the goats flummox the wicked troll and send him over the rickety bridge to a watery grave." Publ Wkly

"Galdone's illustrations are in his usual bold, clear style. The three Billy Goats Gruff are expressively drawn, and the troll looks appropriately ferocious and ugly. The large, lively, double-page spreads are sure to win a responsive audience at story hour." SLJ

The three little pigs. Clarion Bks. 1970 unp il $13.95; pa $4.95 (k-2) **398.2**

1. Folklore—Great Britain 2. Pigs—Fiction 3. Wolves—Fiction
ISBN 0-395-28813-4; 0-89919-275-0 (pa)
LC 75-115780

First published by Seabury Press

A retelling of the classic English folktale about two little pigs whose poorly built houses are inadequate to protect them from a hungry wolf and their brother whose sturdily constructed brick house enables him to survive and triumph over the wolf

"The illustrator has adapted Joseph Jacobs' well-loved version of the tale and brought it to life in vibrant line-and-watercolor drawings. . . . A balanced, sunnily attractive picture book." Horn Book

The three sillies; by Joseph Jacobs; retold and illustrated by Paul Galdone. Clarion Bks. 1981 unp il $9.95 (k-3) **398.2**

1. Folklore—Great Britain
ISBN 0-395-30172-6 LC 80-22197

A young man believes his sweetheart and her family are the three silliest people in the world until he meets three others who are even sillier

"Galdone's sketchy cartoon-style drawings, enlivened with tomato-soup red and lemon yellow, are in keeping with the ridiculous tenor of this 'fool's tale.'" SLJ

The turtle and the monkey; a Philippine tale. Clarion Bks. 1983 unp il $13.95; pa $4.95 (k-2) **398.2**

1. Folklore—Philippines 2. Turtles—Fiction 3. Monkeys—Fiction
ISBN 0-89919-145-2; 0-395-54425-4 (pa) LC 82-9596

In order to get her share of the banana tree she has found floating in the river, Turtle must outwit the very greedy Monkey

"Bright, animated pictures, deft in line and use of color, are drawn with a high comic sense on oversize pages; there is good integration of pictures and text in a story that is based on the briar patch version of the trickster being tricked. . . . A strong appeal to the read-aloud audience in the cheerful pictures and the story's humor should be augmented by their response to the meting out of justice." Bull Cent Child Books

What's in fox's sack? an old English tale; retold and illustrated by Paul Galdone. Clarion Bks. 1982 unp il $9.95; pa $4.95 (k-2) **398.2**

1. Folklore—Great Britain 2. Foxes—Fiction
ISBN 0-89919-062-6; 0-89919-491-5 (pa)
LC 81-10251

"This is the story of a trickster who is tricked, a sly fox who leaves his sack at a series of homes, each time warning the occupant not to peek; each time she does,

Galdone, Paul, 1914-1986—*Continued*

and he takes better booty for his sack. From a bumblebee to a rooster to a pig to a boy (with improving prospects for the fox's dinner) until the last woman, suspicious, substitutes a large ferocious dog for the boy. The fox runs for his life, the released boy and the large dog share a treat of gingerbread fresh out of the oven." Bull Cent Child Books

"Galdone's version of an old English tale rolls onward as it discloses ever more absurdities, repeating the key phrases, the kind of story little ones like best. The full-color pictures are dazzlingly dressy and very funny." Publ Wkly

Ginsburg, Mirra

The Chinese mirror; adapted from a Korean folktale by Mirra Ginsburg; illustrated by Margot Zemach. Harcourt Brace Jovanovich 1988 unp il lib bdg $14.95 (k-3) **398.2**

1. Folklore—Korea

ISBN 0-15-200420-3 LC 86-22940

"Gulliver books"

"A man brings a mirror—an object unknown to his fellow villagers—home from a trip to China. He secretes it in a chest, but when his curious family each indulge in a peek and see a different image (his or her own face, of course), each has a different reaction." Booklist

"This elegantly simple little story is a seamless blend of folk-tale adaptation with illustrations that were inspired by Korean genre paintings of the eighteenth century." Horn Book

The magic stove; illustrated by Linda Heller. Coward, McCann & Geoghegan 1983 unp il $11.95 (k-2) **398.2**

1. Folklore—Soviet Union

ISBN 0-698-20566-9 LC 82-12523

This adaptation of a Russian folk tale tells "the story of a rooster who produces a magic stove (it makes any kind of pie one requests) and then retrieves it from the avaricious king who has stolen it from the peasant couple who had kindly shared their home and their bounty." Bull Cent Child Books

"Lovely, stylized provincial drawings accompany the text in muted vibrant color." Child Book Rev Serv

Goble, Paul

Buffalo woman; story and illustrations by Paul Goble. Bradbury Press 1984 unp il $13.95; Aladdin Bks. (NY) pa $3.95 (1-3) **398.2**

1. Indians of North America—Legends 2. Bison—Fiction

ISBN 0-02-737720-2; 0-689-71109-3 (pa)

LC 83-15704

A young hunter marries a female buffalo in the form of a beautiful maiden, but when his people reject her he must pass several tests before being allowed to join the buffalo nation

"Each page sparkles with the lupins and yuccas of the Southwest and teems with native birds, butterflies, and small animals, the richness of detail never detracting from the overall design of the handsome illustrations. The author-artist successfully combines a compellng version of an old legend with his own imaginative and striking visual interpretation." Horn Book

Includes bibliography

The gift of the sacred dog; story and illustrations by Paul Goble. Bradbury Press 1980 unp il $13.95; pa $4.95 (2-4) **398.2**

1. Indians of North America—Legends 2. Horses—Fiction

ISBN 0-02-736560-3; 0-02-043280-1 (pa)

LC 80-15843

The author "presents one of the common myths of how the Plains Indians got horses. In this case, a boy from a tribe whose members are starving because they cannot find buffalo goes to a high mountain to talk to the Great Spirit. From heaven the boy gets sacred dogs (horses) for hunting the buffalo." Child Book Rev Serv

"Goble's handsome paintings, vigorous in composition and often delicate in style, often stylized, always reflect his identification with the Native American way of life and his empathy with their respect for natural things. . . . The text, which can be read aloud to younger children, ends with Sioux songs about horses and buffalo." Bull Cent Child Books

The great race of the birds and animals; story and illustrations by Paul Goble. Bradbury Press 1985 unp il $12.95; Aladdin Bks. (NY) pa $4.95 (1-3) **398.2**

1. Indians of North America—Legends

ISBN 0-02-736950-1; 0-689-71452-1 (pa) LC 85-4202

A retelling of the Cheyenne and Sioux myth about the Great Race, a contest called by the Creator to settle the question whether man or buffalo should have supremacy and thus become the guardians of Creation

"Inspired by his long-standing preoccupation with American Indian history and mythology, the author-artist has created another in a series of handsome picture books. . . . With variety in color, pattern, and page design, the brilliant illustrations strengthen the drama and powerfully depict the animals—their massed effects and their individual characteristics." Horn Book

Her seven brothers; story and illustrations by Paul Goble. Bradbury Press 1988 unp il $13.95 (k-3) **398.2**

1. Cheyenne Indians—Legends 2. Stars—Fiction

ISBN 0-02-737960-4 LC 86-31776

Retells the Cheyenne legend in which a girl and her seven chosen brothers become the Big Dipper

"The story is lovely: the retelling echoes its delicate and gentle charm. The illustrations, although executed in Goble's distinctive style, emphasize the flora and fauna associated with hope and spring. The pages are filled with detail, yet they do not seem busy but rather representative of nature's magnificent bounty—a romanticist's view of the world. The author's note not only gives the sources for his art and for his retelling but also describes the particular techniques employed for the illustrations." Horn Book

Goble, Paul—*Continued*

Iktomi and the berries; a Plains Indian story; retold and illustrated by Paul Goble. Orchard Bks. 1989 unp il $14.95; lib bdg $14.99 (k-3) **398.2**

1. Dakota Indians—Legends
ISBN 0-531-05819-0; 0-531-08419-1 (lib bdg)
LC 88-23353

"A Richard Jackson book"

"Iktomi's coyote-skin disguise may make him feel wily, but it also keeps him from seeing what's right under his nose: the very prairie dogs he's hunting. With typical Iktomi illogic, the great hunter switches prey and nearly drowns while trying to pick berries from a reflection in the river." Publisher's note

"Vibrant watercolor and ink illustrations grace the pages of this attractive and useful story." Horn Book

Iktomi and the boulder; a Plains Indian story; retold and illustrated by Paul Goble. Orchard Bks. 1988 unp il $13.95; lib bdg $13.99 (k-3) **398.2**

1. Dakota Indians—Legends
ISBN 0-531-05760-7; 0-531-08360-8 (lib bdg)
LC 87-35789

"A Richard Jackson book"

Iktomi, a Plains Indian trickster, attempts to defeat a boulder with the assistance of some bats, in this story which explains why the Great Plains are covered with small stones

"Goble has adapted his usually formal narrative style to suit this boisterous trickster tale. The type is large, the narrative voice is informal, offering numerous asides from Iktomi and the storyteller. Goble's signature ink and vivid watercolor illustrations contain more movement than usual, and fewer stylized symbols are in evidence. . . . A deft blending of text and illustration which will appeal to a wide audience." SLJ

Iktomi and the ducks; a Plains Indian story; retold and illustrated by Paul Goble. Orchard Bks. 1990 unp il $14.95; lib bdg $14.99 (k-3) **398.2**

1. Dakota Indians—Legends
ISBN 0-531-05883-2; 0-531-08483-3 (lib bdg)
LC 89-71025

"A Richard Jackson book"

"Iktomi tricks a flock of ducks into dancing with their eyes closed while he beats the dance rhythm with a big stick. Actually, he keeps time by whacking the unsuspecting birds on their heads until one opens his eyes and gives the alarm. While his birds roast over the campfire, Iktomi gets stuck between two trees, loses his duck dinner to Coyote, and burns his mouth on the coals: the trickster, tricked." Booklist

"As with the other Iktomi stories, the printed story is creatively designed on the page: bold-face lettering for the story line, gray italics for asides that can be read to the audience, and small type for droll comments to be read optionally to a large group. The effect in words and pictures is lively." SLJ

Star Boy; retold and illustrated by Paul Goble. Bradbury Press 1983 unp il $13.95 (2-4) **398.2**

1. Siksika Indians—Legends
ISBN 0-02-722660-3 LC 82-20599

This is a retelling of the Blackfeet Indian "legend of Star Child, called Scarface by his people after the Sun marks him as a reminder of his mother's disobedience. Ugly and poor, Star Boy loses hopes of wedding the girl he loves, daughter of a chief. She gives him the courage, however, to persevere in finding the torturous way to Sky World where Sun rewards the youth with beauty and riches. The Sun also gives Star Boy the secret of the Sun Dance, the gift he brings to the Blackfeet, and it is this benison that the tribe celebrates each year." Publ Wkly

"This strong sense of design, the restrained and effective use of color, and the stylized use of Native American motifs in bold composition contribute to the distinctive work that won Goble the Caldecott Medal." Bull Cent Child Books

Godden, Rumer, 1907-

The valiant chatti-maker; illustrated by Jeroo Roy. Viking 1983 61p il $9.95 (3-6) **398.2**

1. Folklore—India
ISBN 0-670-74236-8 LC 83-7000

When he inadvertently captures the tiger that has been terrorizing the neighborhood, a poor potter not only gains fame and fortune but the unwanted honor of leading the Raja's army against an invading enemy

"This retelling of an Indian dumb-luck tale gives a vivid picture of the customs, dress and rigid social structure of traditional India. The style and language is farcial yet crisp. . . . The tongue-in-cheek humor is very effective." SLJ

Goodall, John S., 1908-

Little Red Riding Hood. Margaret K. McElderry Bks. 1988 unp il $14.95 (k-2) **398.2**

1. Folklore—Germany 2. Stories without words 3. Wolves—Fiction
ISBN 0-689-50457-8 LC 87-34245

"In this wordless version of the oft-illustrated tale, the young heroine is depicted as a maiden mouse. Goodall's traditional half-page format achieves a pleasing sense of balance and perspective as the main action takes place in the center of the book, with smaller incidents and detail flowing out from this focal point. A judicious use of color heightens the drama. . . . In true folkloric fashion the violence here is graphic and the fear real, but the relief at the rescue is deeply felt." SLJ

Puss in boots. Margaret K. McElderry Bks. 1990 56p il $14.95 (k-3) **398.2**

1. Folklore—France 2. Fairy tales 3. Stories without words
ISBN 0-689-50521-3

In this wordless version of the popular tale Goodall "follows the familiar antics of the flamboyant, jaunty Puss as he helps a poor miller's son gain favor with the king to win the princess' hand in marriage. The only text is a brief summary at the beginning of each double-

Goodall, John S., 1908-—*Continued*
page spread. . . . Goodall's use of half-page paintings inserted between every double-page spread adds a clever element to plot development. . . . Goodall offers a shiny new look at an age-old tale, providing ample opportunity for oral and written interpretations." Booklist

Grandfather tales; American-English folk tales; selected and edited by Richard Chase; illustrated by Berkeley Williams, Jr. Houghton Mifflin 1948 239p il $13.95 (4 and up) **398.2**

1. Folklore—Southern States
ISBN 0-395-06692-1 LC 48-7912

Folklore gathered in Alabama, "North Carolina, Virginia and Kentucky. Written down only after many tellings, these [twenty-four] humorous tales are told in the vernacular of the region with added touches of local color provided by the storytellers as they meet together to keep Old-Christmas Eve. . . . Of special interest to storytellers." Booklist

The **Green** fairy book; edited by Andrew Lang; with numerous illustrations by H. J. Ford. Dover Publs. 1965 366p il pa $6.95 (4-6) **398.2**

1. Folklore 2. Fairy tales
ISBN 0-486-21439-7 LC 65-25709

Also available in hardcover from Smith, P. $16.75 (ISBN 0-8446-5056-0)

A reprint of the title first published 1892 by Longmans

This collection of forty-two fairy tales from various countries includes many from the Brothers Grimm and several by the Comte de Caylus. Other sources include Madame D'Aulnoy, Paul Sebillot, Charles Deulin, Fénelon, and traditional tales from Spain and China

Greene, Ellin, 1927-

The legend of the Christmas rose; [by] Selma Lagerlöf; retold by Ellin Greene; with illustrations by Charles Mikolaycak. Holiday House 1990 unp il lib bdg $15.95 (2-4) **398.2**

1. Folklore—Sweden 2. Christmas—Fiction
ISBN 0-8234-0821-3 LC 89-77511

In hope of getting her husband pardoned, an exiled outlaw's wife agrees to reveal to an old monk the miracle in Goïnge Forest, where every Christmas Eve a beautiful garden blooms in remembrance of the birth of the Christ Child

"Greene's prose is crisp and elegant, and Mikolaycak's lightly brooding illustrations—in somber browns and greys—tie in well with the story's myth-like elements." Publ Wkly

Grifalconi, Ann

The village of round and square houses. Little, Brown 1986 unp il lib bdg $14.95 (k-3) **398.2**

1. Folklore—Africa
ISBN 0-316-32862-6 LC 85-24150

A Caldecott Medal honor book, 1987

A grandmother explains to her listeners why in their village on the side of a volcano the men live in square houses and the women in round ones

The author "illustrates her own tale, told to her by a young girl who grew up in Tos. The resting purple volcano, suddenly erupting into orange; the eerie orange sun; the villagers covered with ash; the fiery colored skies; the dense, lush jungles—all are captured beautifully by Grifalconi's art." Publ Wkly

Grimm, Jacob, 1785-1863

About wise men and simpletons; twelve tales from Grimm; translated by Elizabeth Shub; etchings by Nonny Hogrogian. Macmillan 1986 c1971 118p il $13.95 (3-6) **398.2**

1. Folklore—Germany 2. Fairy tales
ISBN 0-02-737450-5 LC 85-15330

A reissue of the title first published 1971

"This collection includes such favorites as 'Hansel and Gretel,' 'The Bremen Town Musicians,' and 'Rumpelstiltskin.' The versions are brief, less ornamented than they are in familiar versions, and chosen because, Elizabeth Shub says in her preface, 'here, even more than in later editions, the storyteller's voice is omnipresent.'" Sutherland. The Best in Child Books

"Nonny Hogrogian's etchings, spare and deft, are beautifully appropriate for the ingenuous simplicity of the writing." Saturday Rev

The bear and the kingbird; a tale from the Brothers Grimm; translated by Lore Segal; pictures by Chris Conover. Farrar, Straus & Giroux 1979 unp il $12.95 (k-3) **398.2**

1. Folklore—Germany 2. Fairy tales
ISBN 0-374-30618-4 LC 79-118605

When the bear insults the kingbird's chicks, a humorous battle ensues between the land animals and the flying creatures of the world

"This is one of the more curious and lesser known Grimm tales and has not a human character in it. Conover has not so much illustrated the tale as made an illuminated edition of it. Her paintings are rich in color, detail, and quiet humor. . . . The book's old world design makes it best for one-to-one sharing or individual reading rather than group presentation." SLJ

The complete Grimm's fairy tales; introduction by Padraic Colum; folkloristic commentary by Joseph Campbell; 212 illustrations by Josef Scharl. Pantheon Bks. 1974 c1972 836p il $17.50; pa $11.95 (4 and up) **398.2**

1. Folklore—Germany 2. Fairy tales
ISBN 0-394-49415-6; 0-395-70930-6 (pa)

A reissue of the edition first published 1944 with title: Grimm's fairy tales. Copyright renewed 1972

"The text of this edition is based on the translation of Margaret Hunt. It has been thoroughly revised, corrected and completed by James Stern." Verso of title page

"A standard edition of the collected household tales. A discussion of folk literature, with examples from the Grimm's stories, adds to the value of the book." Bull Cent Child Books

Grimm, Jacob, 1785-1863—*Continued*

The fisherman and his wife; a tale from the brothers Grimm; translated by Randall Jarrell; pictures by Margot Zemach. Farrar, Straus & Giroux 1980 unp il $13.95; pa $4.95 (k-3) **398.2**

1. Folklore—Germany 2. Fairy tales
ISBN 0-374-32340-2; 0-374-42326-1 (pa) LC 79-3248

The fisherman's greedy wife is never satisfied with the wishes granted to them by an enchanted fish

"The hilarious tale of greed and retribution is handsomely illustrated in an oversize format that is used to full advantage by Zemach, whose paintings are imaginative, comic, and effective in composition and color. Jarrell's translation of the story is flowing and colloquial, as nice to use for storytelling as it is to read aloud." Bull Cent Child Books

Hansel and Gretel; [by] the Brothers Grimm; pictures by Susan Jeffers. Dial Bks. 1980 unp il $14.95; lib bdg $14.89; pa $4.95 (k-3) **398.2**

1. Folklore—Germany 2. Fairy tales
ISBN 0-8037-3492-1; 0-8037-3491-3 (lib bdg); 0-8037-0318-X (pa) LC 80-15079

"A simple, crisply stated translation tells this timeless story of innocence pitted against evil. . . . Jeffers's stunning full-color illustrations expand both the children's purity and the malevolence of the stepmother/witch in an atmosphere that is flawlessly and beautifully executed." Booklist

Hansel and Gretel; by the Brothers Grimm; illustrated by Lisbeth Zwerger; translated by Elizabeth D. Crawford. Picture Bk. Studio 1988 unp il $14.95 (k-3) **398.2**

1. Folklore—Germany 2. Fairy tales
ISBN 0-88708-068-5 LC 87-32833

"A Michael Neugebauer book"

First published 1979 by Morrow

When they are left in the woods by their parents, two children find their way home despite an encounter with a wicked witch

"Working from a faithful translation of the original text, Zwerger has created rosy-cheeked, appealing children who look as if they have just descended the Alps. The witch, by contrast, is a shapeless, fiery-eyed ghoul with real scare potential." Publ Wkly

The juniper tree, and other tales from Grimm; selected by Lore Segal and Maurice Sendak; translated by Lore Segal; with four tales translated by Randall Jarrell; pictures by Maurice Sendak. Farrar, Straus & Giroux 1973 2v (332p) il boxed set $24.50 (4 and up) **398.2**

1. Folklore—Germany 2. Fairy tales
ISBN 0-374-18057-1 LC 73-82698

"Through 27 selections, Segal and Sendak brilliantly expose the underside of Grimms' fairy tale world. The happily-ever-after tinkering re-tellers will gasp at some of the grizzly goings-on. . . . However, the collection, which contains many unfamiliar tales, is not monotonously morbid. . . . The translations, smooth and chatty, echo the tales' oral origins, but it is the artwork which is unforgettable. The superbly detailed pen-and-ink drawings are reminiscent of German woodcuts. . . . Although not for the timid, this is a truly towering achievement in good book-making for children." SLJ

Little Red Cap; by the Brothers Grimm; illustrated by Lisbeth Zwerger; translated from the German by Elizabeth D. Crawford. Morrow 1983 unp il $11.95; lib bdg $11.88 (k-2) **398.2**

1. Folklore—Germany 2. Wolves—Fiction
ISBN 0-688-01715-0; 0-688-01716-9 (lib bdg) LC 82-14211

In this translation of Little Red Riding Hood "Little Red Cap strays from the path while taking wine and cake to grandmother. The wolf then gobbles up grandmother and Red Cap. Justice ultimately prevails when the hunter cuts open the wolf, frees the child and grandmother and finishes off the wolf." SLJ

This translation "gives the text a smooth pace and natural-sounding dialogue. Simple in format, the book alternates a page of text with a full-page illustration. Washes in muted earth tones provide suggestions of backgrounds against which expressively drawn figures play out their familiar roles." Horn Book

More tales from Grimm; freely translated and illustrated by Wanda Gág. Coward, McCann & Geoghegan 1981 c1947 257p il pa $5.95 (4-6) **398.2**

1. Folklore—Germany 2. Fairy tales
ISBN 0-698-20534-0 LC 81-66879

Companion volume to: Tales from Grimm, entered below

First published 1947. Copyright renewed 1974

A collection of 32 tales from Grimm including many lesser-known tales "freely translated yet retaining the essence of the original tales. This is the book which Wanda Gág was working on at the time of her death. Although the translation of the text was ready for the press, the drawings were in varying stages of completeness." Booklist

The pictures are "drawn with humor and charm. Finely made, the book is a pleasure to hold in the hand and a joy to read." Horn Book

The seven ravens; [by] the Brothers Grimm; illustrated by Lisbeth Zwerger; translation from the German by Elizabeth D. Crawford. Picture Bk. Studio 1989 unp il $14.95 (k-3) **398.2**

1. Folklore—Germany 2. Fairy tales
ISBN 0-88708-092-8 LC 83-61777

First published 1981 by Morrow

"Here seven brothers are changed into 'seven coal-black ravens' after they fail to return from fetching water for their sister's christening quickly enough to satisfy their father. Their sister, feeling herself responsible, sets out to undo the terrible magic. . . . Miss Zwerger is a lyrically witty artist; there is smooth movement in her warmly hued pictures, as well as visual sophistication. . . . The translation, by Elizabeth D. Crawford, is felicitous and true to the original." N Y Times Book Rev

Grimm, Jacob, 1785-1863—*Continued*

Tales from Grimm; freely translated and illustrated by Wanda Gàg. Coward, McCann & Geoghegan 1981 c1936 237p il pa $5.95 (4-6) **398.2**

1. Folklore—Germany 2. Fairy tales
ISBN 0-698-20533-2 LC 81-66878

First published 1936

"Sixteen of the Grimm fairy and household tales ranging from the familiar Cinderella, Rapunzel, and The fisherman and his wife, to the less known Six servants . . . and Lean Liesl and Lanky Lenz." N Y Libr

"Miss Gág has made a thoroughly satisfying book, and one that children will at once feel belongs to them. In her translations and in her drawings Miss Gág has caught the essence of the folktale, its drama, its wonder, its humor, its joy, and with a fine freshness and zest she is bringing these qualities to boys and girls." N Y Times Book Rev

Includes glossary

The twelve dancing princesses; retold from a story by the Brothers Grimm; illustrated by Errol Le Cain. Viking 1978 unp il o.p.; Puffin Bks. paperback available $3.95 (k-3) **398.2**

1. Folklore—Germany 2. Fairy tales
ISBN 0-14-050322-6 (pa) LC 78-8578

A retelling of the tale of 12 princesses who dance secretly all night long, and the soldier who follows them and discovers where they dance

"With cleverly concealed touches of fantasy and humor and resplendent with rich, subdued colors, each full-page illustration faces a page of text framed by a border." Horn Book

Wanda Gág's Jorinda and Joringel; illustrated by Margot Tomes. Coward, McCann & Geoghegan 1978 unp il $6.95 (k-3) **398.2**

1. Folklore—Germany 2. Fairy tales
ISBN 0-698-20440-9 LC 77-26680

In this version of the Grimm Brothers' tale, a witch changes Jorinda into a nightingale. Her sweetheart Joringel discovers through a dream how to save her. This translation appeared previously in Gág's More Tales from Grimm

"Wanda Gág's flowing translation . . . is the inspiration for a small, beautifully crafted book in which full-color illustrations alternating with detailed pen-and-ink drawings complement the ingeniousness of the narrative." Horn Book

Wanda Gág's The earth gnome; illustrated by Margot Tomes. Coward-McCann 1985 unp il $8.95 (k-2) **398.2**

1. Folklore—Germany 2. Fairy tales
ISBN 0-698-20618-5 LC 84-23804

In this translation from the Grimm story, an earth gnome helps a hunter boy rescue three princesses who are trapped underground by many-headed dragons

"Gág's smoothly cadenced translation flows effortlessly, and Tomes' drawings, whether they be pen-and-ink or color, are full of character. Her hero has an earnest innocence that pointedly contrasts with his shiftier brothers, and background tableaus display a flavorful medieval aura. The book's design is impeccable; its small scale is no drawback for showcasing Tomes' atmospheric pictures." Booklist

Wanda Gag's The six swans; illustrations by Margot Tomes. Coward, McCann & Geoghegan 1982 unp il $8.95 (1-3) **398.2**

1. Folklore—Germany 2. Fairy tales
ISBN 0-698-20552-9 LC 82-1566

This volume contains "Gág's translation of the Grimm story about a young princess who toils in silence for six years to free her six brothers from a stepmother's spell of turning them into swans." Booklist

"A favorite Grimm story is smoothly translated and effectively illustrated in a small book for which the picture are nicely scaled. Double-page spreads are alternately in black and white and in quiet earth colors, with a delicate line and economical draughtsmanship." Bull Cent Child Books

Guy, Rosa

Mother Crocodile; Maman-Caïman; by Birago Diop; translated and adapted by Rosa Guy; illustrated by John Steptoe. Delacorte Press 1981 unp il $8.89; lib bdg $8.95 (k-3) **398.2**

1. Folklore—Senegal 2. Crocodiles—Fiction
ISBN 0-385-28455-1; 0-385-28454-3 (lib bdg) LC 80-393

Coretta Scott King Award for illustration, 1982

In this folk tale from Senegal, the old storyteller Uncle Amadou says that "Mother Crocodile probably had the best memory on earth. . . . But her children . . . ignored her when she warned that they should learn from past experience. Then, warring men returned to the land, and the conquerors sought crocodile skins from which to make purses for their wives. Only through recalling Mother Crocodile's stories were the young ones able—literally—to save their skins." Horn Book

"Artist Steptoe's characteristic style is softened here by lighter colors, spatter-brush effects, and stencilike patterning for his framed scenes of the crocodiles' world." Booklist

Hague, Kathleen, 1949-

East of the sun and west of the moon; retold by Kathleen and Michael Hague; illustrated by Michael Hague. Harcourt Brace Jovanovich 1980 31p il hardcover o.p. paperback available $3.95 (4-6) **398.2**

1. Folklore—Norway 2. Fairy tales
ISBN 0-15-224703-3 (pa) LC 80-13499

This Scandinavian tale, adapted from the Asbjornsen and Moe collection, tells of a girl who travels east of the sun and west of the moon to free her beloved prince from a magic spell

"Hague's pictures add depth to the story . . . and his line and color work are done with vigor and care." Booklist

Hague, Kathleen, 1949-—*Continued*

The man who kept house; retold by Kathleen and Michael Hague; illustrated by Michael Hague. Harcourt Brace Jovanovich 1981 32p il $12.95; pa $3.95 (k-3) **398.2**

1. Folklore—Norway

ISBN 0-15-251698-0; 0-15-251699-9 (pa) LC 80-26258

Convinced his work in the fields is harder than his wife's work at home, a farmer trades places with her for the day

The authors "fashion a robust story full of descriptive phrases and lively action. Except for a resplendent two-page spread where details and intense color cover the entire area . . . Michael Hague has pleasingly varied his style, confining the illustrations to simple scenes effectively set against white space." Booklist

Haley, Gail E.

A story, a story; an African tale retold and illustrated by Gail E. Haley. Atheneum Pubs. 1970 unp il lib bdg $14.95; pa $4.95 (k-3) **398.2**

1. Folklore—Africa 2. Spiders—Fiction

ISBN 0-689-20511-2 (lib bdg); 0-689-71201-4 (pa) LC 69-18961

Awarded the Caldecott Medal, 1971

"The story explains the origin of that favorite African folk material, the spider tale. Here Ananse, the old spider man, wanting to buy the Sky God's stories, completes by his cleverness three seemingly impossible tasks set as the price for the golden box of stories which he takes back to earth." Sutherland. The Best in Child Books

Hamilton, Virginia, 1936-

The people could fly: American black folktales; told by Virginia Hamilton; illustrated by Leo and Diane Dillon. Knopf 1985 178p il $15.95; lib bdg $14.99 (4 and up) **398.2**

1. Blacks—Folklore

ISBN 0-394-86925-7; 0-394-96925-1 (lib bdg) LC 84-25020

Coretta Scott King Award for text, 1986

"Hamilton retells 24 representative black folktales. . . . The stories are organized into four sections: tales of animals; the supernatural; the real, extravagant, and fanciful; and freedom tales." Booklist

The author "has been successful in her efforts to write these tales in the Black English of the slave storytellers. Her scholarship is unobtrusive and intelligible. She has provided a glossary and notes concerning the origins of the tales and the different versions in other cultures. Handsomely illustrated." N Y Times Book Rev

Hancock, Sibyl

Esteban and the ghost; adapted by Sibyl Hancock; pictures by Dirk Zimmer. Dial Bks. for Young Readers 1983 unp il $10.95; lib bdg $10.89; pa $3.95 (k-3) **398.2**

1. Folklore—Spain 2. Ghosts—Fiction 3. Halloween—Fiction

ISBN 0-8037-2443-8; 0-8037-2411-X (lib bdg); 0-8037-0230-2 (pa) LC 82-22125

Esteban, a merry Spanish tinker, spends All Hallows' Eve in a haunted castle and helps a ghost win his way into heaven

"This adaptation of a Spanish folktale . . . is well told, with a rich vocabulary and some wonderful sound effects for story hours. The black line drawings with full color washes are dusty but not dull, and complement the story." Child Book Rev Serv

The **Hare** and the tortoise; pictures by Paul Galdone. McGraw-Hill 1962 unp il lib bdg $12.94 (k-3) **398.2**

1. Fables 2. Rabbits—Fiction 3. Turtles—Fiction

ISBN 0-07-022713-6 LC 62-9988

"Whittlesey House publications"

A fable about the boastful, swift hare who, because he is overconfident and stops to take a nap, loses a race to the slow but steady tortoise

"An ingratiating picture-book treatment of Aesop's fable. The drawings mingle lively forest animals with flowers and grasses done in green, brown, and yellow. Although a little undisciplined in composition, the double-page spreads provide plenty of visual entertainment. Text, in large print, is from Joseph Jacobs." SLJ

Harper, Wilhelmina

The Gunniwolf; retold by Wilhelmina Harper; illustrated by William Wiesner. Dutton 1967 unp il $11.95 (k-1) **398.2**

1. Folklore—Southern States

ISBN 0-525-31139-4 LC 67-22387

Text, adapted from a Southern nonsense tale, first published 1918 in the author's collection: Story hour favorites

A retelling of the folktale about Little Girl who ignores her mother's warnings, wanders into the jungle searching for pretty flowers, and encounters the fierce Gunniwolf

"Pictures are green and orange with numerous black lines." Bruno. Books for Sch Libr, 1968

Hastings, Selina

Sir Gawain and the Green Knight; words by Selina Hastings; illustrations by Juan Wijngaard. Lothrop, Lee & Shepard Bks. 1981 unp il $12.95 (3 and up) **398.2**

1. Arthurian romances 2. Gawain (Legendary character)

ISBN 0-688-00592-6 LC 80-85379

An Arthurian "tale of young Gawain's proving at the hands of the Green Knight. His adventures during a winter's search for the Green Chapel and his tests of purity in Sir Bercilak's castle serve as an archetypal example of Round Table fare." Booklist

"Hastings reduces the poem's 2530 long lines to 23

Hastings, Selina—*Continued*

pages of simple prose, losing much of the powerful detail and the deep resonances of Celtic folklore, Western Christianity and English custom and ideals. But the author does tell the essential story well, if rather humorlessly. The colored paintings illustrating the text are simply ravishing, capturing the awestruck court, the wild landscape and the forceful characters. A handsome book worth the price for the pictures alone." SLJ

Sir Gawain and the loathly lady; retold by Selina Hastings; illustrated by Juan Wijngaard. Lothrop, Lee & Shepard Bks. 1985 unp il $13 (3 and up) **398.2**

1. Arthurian romances 2. Gawain (Legendary character)

ISBN 0-688-05823-X LC 85-63

After a horrible hag saves King Arthur's life by answering a riddle, Sir Gawain agrees to marry her to save the King's honor and thus releases her from an evil enchantment

"This version of the old romance . . . is charmingly retold and gloriously illustrated. . . . Wijngaard combines the illuminator's precision with a modern miniaturist's detailed perspective; each page of text is framed with manuscript-inspired designs of lacy leaves in scarlet, blue and gold, inset with wonderful, naturalistic paintings. These are full of details for readers to discover." SLJ

Hirsh, Marilyn, 1944-1988

Could anything be worse? A Yiddish tale; retold and illustrated by Marilyn Hirsh. Holiday House 1974 unp il hardcover o.p. paperback available $5.95 (k-3) **398.2**

1. Jews—Folklore

ISBN 0-8234-0655-5 (pa) LC 73-17364

Convinced nothing could be worse than the noise and confusion of his home, a man consults his rabbi who has some very wise advice

"A tale found in many cultures, here adapted from the Yiddish version, is nicely told and illustrated. . . . One of the most durable of the count-your-blessings tales . . . pleasant to read alone or aloud, although the format indicates wider read-aloud use." Bull Cent Child Books

Hodges, Margaret

If you had a horse; steeds of myth and legend; illustrated by D. Benjamin van Steenburgh. Scribner 1984 130p il $12.95 (4 and up) **398.2**

1. Folklore 2. Horses—Fiction

ISBN 0-684-18220-3 LC 84-14024

"A collection of nine folk tales with a common theme, horses. Different cultures and time periods are represented: Celtic, Arabian and Greek folktales, as well as a more modern American Pecos Bill tale. All these tales have broad appeal, action and drama; some have ironic endings. Mature readers will read them on their own, but these stories will make excellent read-alouds." SLJ

Saint George and the dragon; a golden legend; adapted by Margaret Hodges from Edmund Spenser's Faerie Queene; illustrated by Trina Schart Hyman. Little, Brown 1984 32p il hardcover o.p. paperback available $5.95 (2-5) **398.2**

1. George, Saint, d. 303 2. Knights and knighthood—Fiction 3. Dragons—Fiction

ISBN 0-316-36795-8 (pa) LC 83-19980

Awarded the Caldecott Medal, 1985

Retells the segment from Spenser's The Faerie Queene, in which George, the Red Cross Knight, slays the dreadful dragon that has been terrorizing the countryside for years and brings peace and joy to the land

"Hyman's illustrations are uniquely suited to this outrageously romantic and appealing legend. . . . The paintings are richly colored, lush, detailed and dramatic. . . . This is a beautifully crafted book, a fine combination of author and illustrator." SLJ

The voice of the great bell; by Lafcadio Hearn; retold by Margaret Hodges; illustrated by Ed Young. Little, Brown 1989 unp il lib bdg $14.95 (k-3) **398.2**

1. Folklore—China

ISBN 0-316-36791-5 LC 88-15389

Retold from the story: The soul of the great bell, by Lafcadio Hearn, first published 1887 in the collection Some Chinese ghosts. The text of this edition first appeared 1963 in: Tell it again: great tales from around the world

A Chinese bell-maker's daughter makes a noble sacrifice so that the casting of the Great Bell for the emperor will be flawless

Hogrogian, Nonny

The contest; adapted and illustrated by Nonny Hogrogian. Greenwillow Bks. 1976 unp il lib bdg $12.88 (1-3) **398.2**

1. Folklore—Armenia

ISBN 0-688-84042-6 LC 75-40389

A Caldecott Medal honor book, 1977

A "gently humorous retelling of an Armenian folk tale about two robbers who not only share the same occupation but are engaged to the same girl." SLJ

"The symmetrical elements of the tale, which create arabesques of humor, are well-served by the full-color, full-page illustrations and by the pencil drawings scattered through the text. Some of the colored illustrations are bordered by oriental rug patterns, and all of the paintings and drawings are strong in their depiction of Armenian physiognomy." Horn Book

The devil with the three golden hairs; a tale from the Brothers Grimm; retold and illustrated by Nonny Hogrogian. Knopf 1983 unp il $10.95; lib bdg $10.99 (k-3) **398.2**

1. Folklore—Germany 2. Fairy tales

ISBN 0-394-85560-4; 0-394-95560-9 (lib bdg) LC 82-12735

This adaptation of the German folk tale relates "the trials of a youth destined to marry a princess. Because the young man is poor, the king sends him on missions that would kill an ordinary mortal, if they could be

Hogrogian, Nonny—*Continued*

accomplished. One is to snatch three golden hairs from the devil's head. Every step of the brave lad's perilous journey, leading to his triumph, comes alive in this saga of good and evil." Publ Wkly

"The accompanying pictures are accomplished and absorbing. Hogrogian's soft touch and her preference for rich, mellow color that shines against drab backgrounds make the art glow from within." Booklist

The Glass Mountain; retold from the tale by the Brothers Grimm (originally entitled "The raven") and illustrated by Nonny Hogrogian. Knopf 1985 unp il $11.95; lib bdg $12.99 (k-3) **398.2**

1. Folklore—Germany 2. Fairy tales
ISBN 0-394-86724-6; 0-394-96724-0 (lib bdg)
LC 84-7848

A man wins the hand of a princess after releasing her from the enchantment that has changed her into a raven

"Using both frames and borders for paintings in soft, bright colors, Hogrogian surrounds her illustrations with backgrounds that are like a pastel rainbow of book linings, veined and swirling. The page layout is both dignified and colorful, the mood restrainedly romantic." Bull Cent Child Books

"The strength of the story, the simplicity and grace of the writing, and the physical beauty of the book make it a good choice for reading aloud to older children." Booklist

One fine day. Macmillan 1971 unp il $12.95; pa $3.95 (k-3) **398.2**

1. Folklore—Armenia 2. Foxes—Fiction
ISBN 0-02-744000-1; 0-02-043620-3 (pa)
LC 75-119834

Awarded the Caldecott Medal, 1972

When a fox drinks the milk in an old woman's jug, she chops off his tail and refuses to sew it back on unless he gives her milk back. The author-illustrator's cumulative tale, based on an Armenian folktale, tells of the many transactions the fox must go through before his tail is restored

"A charming picture book that is just right for reading aloud to small children, the scale of the pictures also appropriate for group use." Sutherland. The Best in Child Books

Hooks, William H.

Moss gown; illustrations by Donald Carrick. Clarion Bks. 1987 48p il $13.95 (k-3) **398.2**

1. Fairy tales
ISBN 0-89919-460-5 LC 86-17199

After failing to flatter her father as much as her two evil sisters, Candace is banished from his plantation and only after much time and meeting her Prince Charming, is her father able to appreciate her love

"Many children and most adults will recognize in 'Moss Gown' the Cinderella story, while the most astute may note its resemblance to 'King Lear.' But everyone will enjoy this beautifully told North Carolina tale from the oral tradition. Carrick, a master of the dark and mysterious, has created haunting illustrations that are a wonderful complement to the story." Child Book Rev Serv

The three little pigs and the fox; illustrated by S.D. Schindler. Macmillan 1989 unp il $13.95 (k-3) **398.2**

1. Folklore—United States 2. Pigs—Folklore
ISBN 0-02-744431-7 LC 88-29296

In this Appalachian version of the classic tale, Hamlet, the youngest pig, rescues her two greedy brothers from the clutches of the mean, tricky old drooly-mouth fox

"With an ear for colloquial wit and an eye on the family dynamic that sends these characters on their journey of maturation, Hooks has found a perfect fit in Schindler's watercolor scenes. Drafted with ease of proportion, colored with rural blends, and elegantly underplayed in expression, the animals are fresh and funny without being self-conscious." Bull Cent Child Books

Huck, Charlotte S.

Princess Furball; retold by Charlotte Huck; illustrated by Anita Lobel. Greenwillow Bks. 1989 unp il $13.95; lib bdg $13.88 (1-3) **398.2**

1. Fairy tales
ISBN 0-688-07837-0; 0-688-07838-9 (lib bdg)
LC 88-18780

This book is about a "princess who rebels against her tyrannical father and makes the most of her gifts to survive in another kingdom and win the hand of the king. This narrative focuses on the ingenuity of a girl who plots her own destiny." N Y Times Book Rev

"The paintings glimmer with intense colors—Lobel's flair for both historical and humorous detail has never been more apparent, nor more luxuriously bold." SLJ

Hutton, Warwick

Beauty and the beast; retold and illustrated by Warwick Hutton. Atheneum Pubs. 1985 unp il $12.95 (1-4) **398.2**

1. Folklore—France 2. Fairy tales
ISBN 0-689-50316-4 LC 84-48441

"A Margaret K. McElderry book"

"Hutton retells the story of the beast whose true form (a young and handsome prince) reappears when Beauty declares her love, engendered by his kindness and patience and love. The watercolor illustrations are rich and imaginative, with settings that have a Moorish influence and a beast who is like a giant cat, ugly of face, walking like a man. Hutton is particularly good at using light and shadow to establish mood." Bull Cent Child Books

Hyman, Trina Schart, 1939-

Little Red Riding Hood; by the Brothers Grimm retold and illustrated by Trina Schart Hyman. Holiday House 1983 unp il lib bdg $14.95; pa $5.95 (k-2) **398.2**

1. Folklore—Germany 2. Wolves—Fiction
ISBN 0-8234-0470-6 (lib bdg); 0-8234-0653-9 (pa)
LC 82-7700

Hyman, Trina Schart, 1939-—*Continued*

This retelling "basically follows the Grimm story, although the text has been fleshed out with some extraneous details (for instance, the little girl is called Elisabeth). . . . The illustrations seem to be a labor of love; richly colored paintings of the forest teem with exquisitely detailed plant and animal life, and the interior scenes, awash with atmospheric light, are beautifully composed and executed." Horn Book

Index to fairy tales, 1949-1972; including folklore, legends & myths, in collections; [compiled] by Norma Olin Ireland. Faxon 1973 xxxviii, 741p o.p.; Scarecrow Press reprint available $45 **398.2**

1. Folklore—Indexes 2. Fairy tales—Indexes 3. Legends—Indexes 4. Mythology—Indexes
ISBN 0-8108-2011-0 LC 73-173454

"Useful reference series"

This and the following volumes are continuations of Index to fairy tales, myths and legends, and its two supplements, compiled by Mary Huse Eastman, published 1926-1952 by Faxon and now o.p.

A title and subject index to stories in 406 collections

Index to fairy tales, 1973-1977; including folklore, legends and myths in collections; fourth supplement compiled by Norma Olin Ireland. Faxon 1979 259p o.p.; Scarecrow Press reprint available $29.50 **398.2**

1. Folklore—Indexes 2. Fairy tales—Indexes 3. Legends—Indexes 4. Mythology—Indexes
ISBN 0-8108-1855-8 LC 79-16150

"Useful reference series"

A title and subject index to tales in 130 collections

Index to fairy tales, 1978-1986; including folklore, legends, and myths in collections; fifth supplement compiled by Norma Olin Ireland and Joseph W. Sprug. Scarecrow Press 1989 575p $49.50 **398.2**

1. Folklore—Indexes 2. Fairy tales—Indexes 3. Legends—Indexes 4. Mythology—Indexes
ISBN 0-8108-2194-X LC 89-6042

This supplement indexes "262 collections published between 1978 and 1986. Subject headings have been added to reflect the changing interests of children and their mentors. . . . This supplement continues the basic arrangement of its predecessors. It begins with a list of collections analyzed with their source codes. Following is the combined subject-title index, with references to the source codes and pagination given under the titles of the stories." Booklist

Isadora, Rachel

The princess and the frog; adapted from the Frog King and Iron Heinrich by the Brothers Grimm. Greenwillow Bks. 1989 unp il $12.95; lib bdg $12.88 (k-2) **398.2**

1. Folklore—Germany 2. Fairy tales
ISBN 0-688-06373-X; 0-688-06374-8 (lib bdg) LC 88-61

As payment for retrieving the princess's ball, the frog exacts a promise which the princess is reluctant to fulfill

"Isadora freely adapts—and illustrates with lush paintings—the Grimm tale. . . . Isadora provides a smooth retelling and rich watercolor art that fills the pages. Her impressionist portraits, whether of a princess or a frog, catch the eye and hold attention. Verdant backgrounds and shafts of sunlight illuminate the scenes and extend the book's luxuriant feel, while silhouetted characters on the ribbon-bordered pages of text add a piquant note." Booklist

Ishii, Momoko, 1907-

The tongue-cut sparrow; retold by Momoko Ishii; illustrated by Suekichi Akaba; translated from the Japanese by Katherine Paterson. Lodestar Bks. 1987 unp il $13.95 (k-3) **398.2**

1. Folklore—Japan
ISBN 0-525-67199-4 LC 86-29314

A "traditional Japanese folk tale about a kind old man who befriends a sparrow and is richly rewarded, and his greedy wife who is taught her lesson." N Y Times Book Rev

"The free-flowing, graceful yet lively translation retains several Japanese onomatopoeic words, which are explained at the end of the book. . . . Traditional black brush drawings in a free and animated style mirror the spirited tale and establish—despite the occasional addition of color—a connection with classic Japanese scroll work." Horn Book

The **Jack** tales; with an appendix compiled by Herbert Halpert; and illustrations by Berkeley Williams, Jr. Houghton Mifflin 1943 201p il $13.95 (4-6) **398.2**

1. Folklore—Southern States
ISBN 0-395-06694-8 LC 43-12028

"Told by R. M. Ward and his kindred in the Beech Mountain section of Western North Carolina and by other descendants of Council Harmon (1803-1896) elsewhere in the Southern mountains; with three tales from Wise County, Virginia. Set down from these sources and edited by Richard Chase." Title page

"Humor, freshness, colorful American background, and the use of one character as a central figure in the cycle mark these 18 folk tales, told here in the dialect of the mountain country of North Carolina. A scholarly appendix by Herbert Halpert, giving sources and parallels, increases the book's value as a contribution to American folklore. Black-and-white illustrations in the spirit of the text." Booklist

Jacobs, Joseph, 1854-1916

English fairy tales; collected by Joseph Jacobs; illustrated by John D. Batten. [3rd ed]. Dover Publs. 1967 261p il pa $5.95 (4-6) **398.2**

1. Folklore—Great Britain 2. Fairy tales
ISBN 0-486-21818-X LC 67-19703

Also available in hardcover from Smith, P. $15.50 (ISBN 0-8446-2303-2)

Jacobs, Joseph, 1854-1916—*Continued*

First published 1890 in the United Kingdom. First American edition published 1891 by Putnam. Variant title: English folk and fairy tales

"As outstanding as the best collections of fairy tales of any country, are those of the folk-lore of the British Isles made by Joseph Jacobs. In his re-writing of the [forty-one] stories, he has preserved their humour and dramatic power, and while simplifying dialect, has retained its full flavor. He intends his stories to be read aloud, and while children enjoy them for their own reading, this makes them invaluable for the story-teller who appreciates a colloquial, conversational style." Toronto Public Libr

Includes notes and references

The fables of Aesop; selected, told anew, and their history traced by Joseph Jacobs; done into pictures by Richard Heighway. Schocken Bks. 1966 xxv, 181p il hardcover o.p. paperback available $8.95 (4 and up) **398.2**

1. Fables
ISBN 0-8052-0138-6 (pa) LC 66-24908

First published 1894 by Macmillan

A collection of 82 fables considered by Jacobs to be among the most effective and familiar of the hundreds attributed to Aesop

Tattercoats; collected and edited by Joseph Jacobs; illustrated by Margot Tomes. Putnam 1989 unp il $14.95 (k-2) **398.2**

1. Folklore—Great Britain 2. Fairy tales
ISBN 0-399-21584-0 LC 88-2357

Retells the traditional English tale of how poor, neglected Tattercoats comes to marry the Prince

"Margot Tomes's unpretentious and charming illustrations draw out the melodrama of the story. She works adroitly with shades of brown, gray and black, with Tattercoats portrayed in a simple yellow dress with yellow hair." N Y Times Book Rev

Johnston, Tony

The badger and the magic fan; a Japanese folktale; adapted by Tony Johnston; illustrated by Tomie dePaola. Putnam 1990 unp il $13.95 (k-3) **398.2**

1. Folklore—Japan
ISBN 0-399-21945-5 LC 89-4027

"A Whitehead book"

"The *tengu*, goblins of Japan, relish the magic fan that allows them to make their long noses even longer and short again. A greedy badger, after changing himself into a girl, steals the fan, elongates the nose of a beautiful princess, and then agrees to reduce the ugly appendage for half her father's kingdom." Booklist

"Bright oranges, purples, peaches, pinks, and reds flamboyantly illustrate a funny Japanese folk tale. . . . The combined humor of the illustrations and fast-paced narrative guarantee a wide appeal for kids." Bull Cent Child Books

Karlin, Barbara

Cinderella; retold by Barbara Karlin; illustrated by James Marshall. Little, Brown 1989 unp il lib bdg $12.95 (k-2) **398.2**

1. Fairy tales
ISBN 0-316-54654-2 LC 88-25913

"Those seeking a condensed version of the classic fairy tale will find just what they want in Karlin's brief retelling; without compromising the original, she has pared the story down to the essential action by eliminating much of the descriptive material. . . . James Marshall's witty, warts-and-all illustrations add the sparkle that brings out the best in Karlin's straightforward retelling." Horn Book

Keats, Ezra Jack, 1916-1983

John Henry; an American legend; story and pictures by Ezra Jack Keats. Knopf 1987 unp il lib bdg $11.99; pa $3.95 (k-3) **398.2**

1. John Henry (Legendary character)
ISBN 0-394-99052-8 (lib bdg); 0-394-89052-3 (pa) LC 86-27453

First published 1965 by Pantheon

This is a picture book retelling of the legend of the Black American folk hero who drove spikes for the railroads

"The dynamic power with which John Henry wields his hammer is matched by the strong illustrations: brilliant oranges and reds contrast with grays and blacks that are often silhouettes; unusual backgrounds produce startling effects. A good picture-story to show to a group." Horn Book

Kellogg, Steven, 1941-

Chicken Little; retold & illustrated by Steven Kellogg. Morrow 1985 unp il $13; lib bdg $12.88 (k-3) **398.2**

1. Folklore 2. Animals—Fiction
ISBN 0-688-05690-3; 0-688-05691-1 (lib bdg) LC 84-25519

Chicken Little and his feathered friends, alarmed that the sky seems to be falling, are easy prey to hungry Foxy Loxy when he poses as a police officer in hopes of tricking them into his truck

"Kellogg has enlivened the text [by] giving it some modern touches (Turkey Lurkey carries golf clubs, Foxy Loxy is caught when a 'hippoliceman' tumbles out of a patrol helicopter to land him). Children have always enjoyed the repetition and cumulation of the story, as well as the silliness of the fowls who believe the sky is falling; here there's added fun." Bull Cent Child Books

Paul Bunyan; a tall tale; retold and illustrated by Steven Kellogg. Morrow 1984 unp il $15.95; lib bdg $15.88; pa $5.95 (k-3) **398.2**

1. Bunyan, Paul (Legendary character) 2. Tall tales
ISBN 0-688-03849-2; 0-688-03850-6 (lib bdg); 0-688-05800-0 (pa) LC 83-26684

"Numerous events from the legendary north woodsman's life have been linked together as Bunyan and Babe, his big blue ox, traverse the U.S." Booklist

"Kellogg uses oversize pages for busy, detail-crowded

Kellogg, Steven, 1941-—*Continued*
illustrations that have vitality and humor, echoing the exaggeration and ebullience of the story." Bull Cent Child Books

Pecos Bill; a tall tale; retold and illustrated by Steven Kellogg. Morrow 1986 unp il $14.95; lib bdg $14.88 (k-3) **398.2**

1. Pecos Bill (Legendary character) 2. Tall tales
ISBN 0-688-05871-X; 0-688-05872-8 (lib bdg)
LC 86-784

Incidents from the life of Pecos Bill, from his childhood among the coyotes to his unusual wedding day

"Although there's a lot going on in these pictures, they're not cluttered; both the gradations of color and the page design smooth the lines of continuous action and tumult of humorous detail. Kellogg's portrayal of Pecos Bill as a perpetual boy will appeal to children. The retelling is a smooth adaptation for introducing young listeners to longer versions or to accompany storytelling sessions centered around tall-tale heroes." Bull Cent Child Books

Kendall, Carol

Sweet and sour; tales from China; retold by Carol Kendall and Yao-wen Li; drawings by Shirley Felts. Clarion Bks. 1979 c1978 111p il $13.95 (4-6) **398.2**

1. Folklore—China
ISBN 0-395-28958-0 LC 78-24349

First published 1978 in the United Kingdom; first United States edition published by Seabury Press

This is a "collection of twenty-four Chinese tales of every kind and from many eras." Horn Book

"The style of the retellings is brisk and readable. . . . The black-and-white illustrations . . . are well drawn and have a delicacy of their own produced with fine line and stipple." SLJ

Kismaric, Carole, 1942-

The rumor of Pavel and Paali; a Ukrainian folktale; adapted by Carole Kismaric; illustrated by Charles Mikolaycak. Harper & Row 1988 unp il $13.95; lib bdg $13.89 (1-3) **398.2**

1. Folklore—Ukraine 2. Fairy tales
ISBN 0-06-023277-3; 0-06-023278-1 (lib bdg)
LC 87-19958

When cruel Pavel wins a wager against his kind twin brother Paali, he exacts a terrible price, but greed soon leads Pavel to his downfall

This "is a powerful blend of traditional folklore, compelling images, and masterful storytelling. . . . The literate text possesses a flowing lyricism which purposely understates the drama of the story. The glorious, richly detailed illustrations . . . glow with vigor and life. . . . Equally suitable for storytelling or independent reading, this book achieves a perfect union of text and illustrations." SLJ

Knutson, Barbara

How the guinea fowl got her spots; a Swahili tale of friendship; retold and illustrated by Barbara Knutson. Carolrhoda Bks. 1990 unp il lib bdg $12.95 (k-3) **398.2**

1. Folklore—Africa 2. Guinea fowl—Fiction
ISBN 0-87614-416-4 LC 89-25191

"In this traditional Swahili folktale, Guinea Fowl twice saves her friend Cow from Lion. In return, Cow sprinkles milk over the formerly all-black guinea fowl, disguising her from the lion and allowing her to easily hide in the grasses. . . . Knutson's scratchboard illustrations . . . perfectly match the content and tone of the story. . . . The placement of the drawings and the exquisite design create a harmony that makes this a strikingly handsome addition to folktale collections." SLJ

Lang, Andrew, 1844-1912

Aladdin and the wonderful lamp; retold by Andrew Lang; illustrated by Errol Le Cain. Viking 1981 31p il o.p.; Puffin Bks. paperback available $4.95 (2-4) **398.2**

1. Fairy tales 2. Arabs—Folklore
ISBN 0-14-050389-7 (pa) LC 81-4861

Recounts the tale of a poor tailor's son who becomes a wealthy prince with the help of a magic lamp he finds in an enchanted cave

"Lots of deep, brooding color and extensive rococo ornamentation fit both the story's Middle Eastern setting and its undertones of evil and foreboding. . . . The story's text has strength, too, being measured in tone and medievally flavored, with sprinkles of archaic phrasing." Booklist

Langton, Jane

The hedgehog boy; a Latvian folktale; retold by Jane Langton; illustrated by Ilse Plume. Harper & Row 1985 40p il $12.95; lib bdg $13.89 (k-3) **398.2**

1. Folklore—Latvia
ISBN 0-06-023696-5; 0-06-023697-3 (lib bdg)
LC 83-47698

A princess is forced to marry a prickly hedgehog boy and is astounded when remorse over a thoughtless act of hers transforms him into a handsome young man

"Set in Latvia in the medieval days of field and castle, the story line unfolds along an unwavering course, emphasizing that quality which underlies all virtues—fidelity. . . . In part it is simply a romantic story of the love between an impulsive princess and a prickly 'pincushion' of a boy. But it is also an intricate tale—a tapestry of virtues and values." Christ Sci Monit

Lattimore, Deborah Nourse

Why there is no arguing in heaven; a Mayan myth. Harper & Row 1989 unp il $13.95; lib bdg $13.89 (3-6) **398.2**

1. Mayas—Legends
ISBN 0-06-023717-1; 0-06-023718-X (lib bdg)
LC 87-35045

Lattimore, Deborah Nourse—*Continued*

Hunab Ku, the first Creator God of the Mayas, challenges the Moon Goddess and Lizard House to create a being to worship him, but the Maize God succeeds where the others fail

"Based on research into ancient documents . . . this lively retelling of the Mayan creation myth combines several versions into a straightforward plot line with a smoothly flowing text suitable for independent reading or oral interpretation. . . . The accompanying illustrations . . . depict the setting as a lush, tropical paradise; the characters are suggestive of reliefs and statues from the pre-Columbian period. Bold and dynamic, the paintings capture the earthy humor of the tale, enhancing its impact." Horn Book

Le Prince de Beaumont, Madame, 1711-1780

Beauty and the beast; a fairy tale; translated by Richard Howard; illustrated by Hilary Knight; with an afterword by Jean Cocteau. Simon & Schuster Bks. for Young Readers 1990 35p il $14.95 (1-4) **398.2**

1. Folklore—France 2. Fairy tales
ISBN 0-671-70720-5 LC 90-31556

"In Howard's lengthy but smooth and coherent text, the greed and jealousy of Beauty's sisters, the consequences of the family's misfortunes, and the splendors of the Beast's palace are faithfully described in complex, stately language. . . . While the text is nicely modulated and suited to the story, Knight's illustrations are quite another matter, featuring vapid faces, awkward figures, and uninspired composition." SLJ

Leach, Maria, 1892-1977

Whistle in the graveyard; folktales to chill your bones; illustrated by Ken Rinciari. Viking 1974 128p il o.p.; Penguin Bks. paperback available $3.95 (4-6) **398.2**

1. Folklore 2. Ghosts—Fiction
ISBN 0-14-031529-2 (pa) LC 73-22255

These "stories, drawn from many cultures and far distant lands, deal with bogeys and bugaboos, ghosts, witch lore, supernatural manifestations, and haunted places from the White House to the Tower of London." Horn Book

The author "has authenticated each tale, and Rinciari's pen-and-ink sketches add a spine-tingling touch." SLJ

Includes bibliography

Lee, Jeanne M.

Legend of the Li River; an ancient Chinese tale; retold and illustrated by Jeanne M. Lee. Holt & Co. 1983 unp il $11.95 (k-3) **398.2**

1. Folklore—China 2. Great Wall of China—Fiction
ISBN 0-03-063523-3 LC 83-79

A sea princess who wishes to lessen the hardships of the poor laborers employed in building the Great Wall of China seeks help from the Goddess of Mercy

"A lyrically retold legend. . . . Combining abstract backgrounds of flat color with figures of almost naïve simplicity, the illustrations have tranquility befitting the poignancy of the story." Horn Book

Legend of the Milky Way; retold and illustrated by Jeanne M. Lee. Holt & Co. 1982 unp il $11.50; pa $5.95 (k-3) **398.2**

1. Folklore—China 2. Milky Way—Fiction
ISBN 0-8050-0217-0; 0-8050-1361-X (pa) LC 81-6906

Retells the Chinese legend of the Weaver Princess who came down from heaven to marry a mortal, a love story represented in the stars of the Milky Way

"The cool colors and serene lines of Lee's artwork capture the subtle emotions in this retelling." Booklist

Toad is the uncle of heaven; a Vietnamese folk tale; retold and illustrated by Jeanne M. Lee. Holt & Co. 1985 unp il $13.95; pa $4.95 (k-3) **398.2**

1. Folklore—Vietnam 2. Toads—Fiction
ISBN 0-03-004652-1; 0-8050-1147-1 (pa) LC 85-5639

Toad leads a group of animals to ask the King of Heaven to send rain to the parched earth

"The story is simple and reminiscent of motifs common to many cultures. . . . The author's simple prose and beautiful page design, far from being static or stilted, are fluid and convey movement and earthy humor. Her tale of courage born of common sense and perseverance will satisfy a wide audience." Horn Book

Lent, Blair, 1930-

Baba Yaga; by Ernest Small; illustrated by Blair Lent. Houghton Mifflin 1966 48p il $13.95 (k-3) **398.2**

1. Folklore—Soviet Union
ISBN 0-395-16975-5

"Little Marusia searching for turnips in the forest comes on the house of a wicked witch. . . . Baba Yaga takes little Marusia captive, but Marusia shows herself more than a match for the witch's evil . . . ways. The story is a composite of many of the Baba Yaga stories told to Russian children." Christ Sci Monit

"While rather cursory this tale is redeemed by illustrations that sweep, tumble and soar through the environs of Baba Yaga's haunted forest." N Y Times Book Rev

Lesser, Rika

Hansel and Gretel; retold by Rika Lesser; illustrated by Paul O. Zelinsky. Putnam 1989 c1984 unp il $14.95; pa $5.95 (1-3) **398.2**

1. Folklore—Germany 2. Fairy tales
ISBN 0-399-21733-9; 0-399-21725-8 (pa) LC 88-30615

A Caldecott Medal honor book, 1985

First published 1984 by Dodd, Mead

"Lesser's telling reflects the earliest, clean-lined versions and leaves out the psychological embellishments frequently included in other settings. . . . Zelinsky has chosen a painterly style that suggests the naturalistic genre works of the 17th-Century Dutch or German. The paintings are rich in detail of forest and architecture and consistent in the costuming." SLJ

Lester, Julius

Further tales of Uncle Remus; the misadventures of Brer Rabbit, Brer Fox, Brer Wolf, the Doodang, and other creatures; as told by Julius Lester; illustrated by Jerry Pinkney. Dial Bks. 1990 148p il $15; lib bdg $14.89 (4-6) **398.2**

1. Blacks—Folklore 2. Animals—Fiction
ISBN 0-8037-0610-3; 0-8037-0611-1 (lib bdg)
LC 88-20223

"This collection focuses primarily on the misadventures of Brer Fox, Brer Wolf, and Brer Bear, with Brer Rabbit's role somewhat reduced. The double-page spreads in full color and the plentiful black-and-white sketches are consistently excellent. Storytellers will be especially pleased to find 'Taily-po' included." Horn Book

How many spots does a leopard have? and other tales; illustrated by David Shannon. Scholastic 1989 72p il $13.95 (2-5) **398.2**

1. Folklore—Africa
ISBN 0-590-41973-0 LC 88-33647

An illustrated collection of twelve folk tales, ten African and two Jewish

"The combination of the two cultures works well; each story in this eclectic collection begs to be read aloud. . . . Lester's retellings are beguiling and graceful, his language attuned to each story's nuances. Shannon's striking paintings, in rich browns and greens, are as full of depth as the stories themselves." Publ Wkly

The knee-high man, and other tales; pictures by Ralph Pinto. Dial Bks. 1972 28p il $11.95; pa $3.95 (k-3) **398.2**

1. Blacks—Folklore 2. Folklore—United States 3. Animals—Fiction
ISBN 0-8037-4593-1; 0-8037-0234-5 (pa)
LC 72-181785

The author retells six animal stories from black folklore

"These are excellent for story telling and should be so presented for the greatest impact." N Y Times Book Rev

More tales of Uncle Remus; further adventures of Brer Rabbit, his friends, enemies, and others; as told by Julius Lester; illustrated by Jerry Pinkney. Dial Bks. 1988 143p il $15; lib bdg $14.89 (4-6) **398.2**

1. Blacks—Folklore 2. Animals—Fiction
ISBN 0-8037-0419-4; 0-8037-0420-8 (lib bdg)
LC 86-32890

A retelling of thirty-seven additional classic Afro-American tales

Includes bibliography

The tales of Uncle Remus; the adventures of Brer Rabbit; as told by Julius Lester; illustrated by Jerry Pinkney. Dial Bks. 1987 151p il $16.95; lib bdg $14.89 (4-6) **398.2**

1. Blacks—Folklore 2. Animals—Fiction
ISBN 0-8037-0271-X; 0-8037-0272-8 (lib bdg)
LC 85-20449

This adaptation of 48 Brer Rabbit stories "is the work of a writer familiar with the methodology of folkloristic and historical research but also with the techniques of flavoring fiction. Lester himself makes wry narrative asides that punctuate but don't intrude on the stories the way the 'Uncle Remus' framework did. . . . Pinkney's illustrations—black-and-white drawings with occasional double-page spreads in full color—are well drafted, fresh, and funny." Bull Cent Child Books

Lister, Robin

The legend of King Arthur; retold by Robin Lister; illustrated by Alan Baker. Doubleday 1990 c1988 93p il $15.95 (4 and up) **398.2**

1. Arthur, King 2. Arthurian romances
ISBN 0-385-26369-4 LC 88-36262

First published 1988 in the United Kingdom

A retelling of fourteen tales from the legend of King Arthur, beginning with the wizard Merlin and ending with the departure of Arthur for the magical isle of Avalon

"A wonderful, personal sense of mystery and magic infuse the text, making [Merlin's] role in the legends everywhere apparent. The full-color illustrations on almost every page (and one double-page spread) adorn an unintimidating and worthy collection of the essential moments in Arthurian lore." Booklist

Littledale, Freya, 1929-

The elves and the shoemaker; retold by Freya Littledale; pictures by Brinton Turkle. Four Winds Press 1975 unp il o.p.; Scholastic paperback available $3.95 (k-3) **398.2**

1. Folklore—Germany 2. Fairy tales
ISBN 0-590-33305-4 (pa) LC 75-12500

This is "a picture-book version of the famous tale about the destitute shoemaker who is rescued from poverty by the aid of two energetic elves, who appear at midnight to make shoes." SLJ

"Few illustrators could infuse the familiar fairy-tale with so much charm as Brinton Turkle has. His pictures dance with life and color in an authentic 19th century setting. And Ms. Littledale's retelling is equally compelling." Publ Wkly

Lottridge, Celia B. (Celia Barker)

The name of the tree; a Bantu folktale; retold by Celia Barker Lottridge; and illustrated by Ian Wallace. Margaret K. McElderry Bks. 1989 unp il $14.95 (k-3) **398.2**

1. Folklore—Africa
ISBN 0-689-50490-X LC 89-2430

Lottridge, Celia B. (Celia Barker) — *Continued*

"When in time of drought the animals leave the land of the short grass in search of food, they find a tree that will give up its fruit only to someone who knows its name. The story moves quickly in an easy, conversational style, and the grainy illustrations capture the parched, cracked countryside." Horn Book Guide

Louie, Ai-Ling, 1949-

Yeh-Shen; a Cinderella story from China; retold by Ai-Ling Louie; illustrated by Ed Young. Philomel Bks. 1982 unp il $13.95 (2-4) **398.2**

1. Folklore—China 2. Fairy tales
ISBN 0-399-20900-X LC 80-11745

This version of the Cinderella story, in which a young girl overcomes the wickedness of her stepsister and stepmother to become the bride of a prince, is based on ancient Chinese manuscripts written 1000 years before the earliest European version

"The reteller has cast the tale in well-cadenced prose, fleshing out the spare account with elegance and grace. In a manner reminiscent of Chinese scrolls and of decorated folding screens, the text is chiefly set within vertical panels, while the luminescent illustrations—less narrative than emotional—often increase their impact by overspreading the narrow framework or appearing on pages of their own." Horn Book

Lurie, Alison

The heavenly zoo; legends and tales of the stars; retold by Alison Lurie; with pictures by Monika Beisner. Farrar, Straus & Giroux 1980 c1979 61p il $12.95 (4 and up) **398.2**

1. Stars—Fiction 2. Legends 3. Mythology
ISBN 0-374-32910-9 LC 79-21263

Sixteen legends of the constellations and how they got their names, taken from such varied sources as ancient Greece, Babylon, Egypt, Sumeria, the Bible, Norway, the Balkans, Indonesia, and the American Indians

The retellings "are brief and smoothly written and nicely varied in sources if not in style. . . . Each tale has one handsome color painting with the creature shown in the firmament, stars superimposed. A nice collection, this should be useful as an adjunct to curricular units on mythology or astronomy." Bull Cent Child Books

The **Magic** orange tree, and other Haitian folktales; collected by Diane Wolkstein; drawings by Elsa Henriquez. Knopf 1978 212p il music o.p.; Schocken Bks. paperback available $9.95 (5 and up) **398.2**

1. Folklore—Haiti
ISBN 0-8052-0650-7 (pa) LC 77-15003

"A rare collection of folktales and songs is presented in this volume. Miss Wolkstein travelled throughout Haiti listening to the many storytellers in all areas. Each of the twenty-eight tales is preceded by an introduction which details the circumstances surrounding the collection of each story. The blend of cultures found in Haiti is well-depicted in her selections. The introduction in itself is as spellbinding as are the stories. . . . An added delight is the inclusion of music and words in both English and Creole." Bibliophile

Mahy, Margaret

The seven Chinese brothers; illustrated by Jean and Mou-Sien Tseng. Scholastic 1990 unp $12.95 (1-3) **398.2**

1. Folklore—China 2. Fairy tales
ISBN 0-590-42055-0 LC 88-33668

A story about "seven brothers, each of whom was blessed with an extraordinary power. Together, they use their amazing talents to avoid death at the hands of Emperor Ch'in Shih Huang, while trying to help the exhausted conscripted laborers working on the Great Wall." Child Book Rev Serv

"Based on the same Chinese folk tale as Bishop's classic *Five Chinese Brothers* [entered above], this longer story has a different plot, but shares the motif of brother succeeding brother, their unique magical powers making various means of execution impossible. . . . The handsome watercolor illustrations show a sensitivity to landscape and character portrayal (avoiding the controversy of the Bishop illustrations), a hint of humor, and a flair for the dramatic. Written with Mahy's accustomed storytelling skill, this book will find an eager audience as a read-aloud for elementary school children." Booklist

Marriott, Alice Lee, 1910-

American Indian mythology; Alice Marriott and Carol K. Rachlin. Crowell 1968 211p il hardcover o.p. paperback available $4.95 **398.2**

1. Indians of North America—Legends
ISBN 0-8152-0335-7 (pa) LC 68-21613

"A fascinating collection of myths, legends and contemporary folklore which the authors have obtained in most cases directly from Indians. . . . With each tale there is a brief introduction to the tribe. Subjects include myths of creation; the world and the hereafter; 'how-and-why' stories told to children; historic legends and witchcraft. Among the tribes represented are Cheyenne, Modoc, Ponca, Hopi, Kiowa, Comanche and Zuni." Publ Wkly

Includes bibliography

Marshak, S. (Samuil), 1887-1964

The Month-Brothers; a Slavic tale; retold by Samuil Marshak; translation from the Russian by Thomas P. Whitney; illustrated by Diane Stanley. Morrow 1983 unp il lib bdg $12.88 (1-3) **398.2**

1. Slavs—Folklore 2. Fairy tales
ISBN 0-688-01510-7 LC 82-7927

A retelling of the Slavic folktale in which a young girl outwits her greedy stepmother and stepsister with the help of the Month Brothers who use their magic to enable her to fulfill seemingly impossible tasks

"Here is a beautiful book sure to delight a wide audience. . . . The language of the translation is readable, idiomatic English, neither archaic nor too informal. Stan-

Marshak, S. (Samuil), 1887-1964 — *Continued*

ley's watercolors are beautifully executed with intricate details of pattern and full color." Child Book Rev Serv

Marshall, James, 1942-

Goldilocks and the three bears; retold and illustrated by James Marshall. Dial Bks. for Young Readers 1988 unp il $11.95; lib bdg $11.89 (k-2) **398.2**

1. Folklore 2. Bears—Fiction
ISBN 0-8037-0542-5; 0-8037-0543-3 (lib bdg)
LC 87-32983

A Caldecott Medal honor book, 1989

"Marshall's Goldilocks, the naughty little girl who disrupts a placid bear household, is no adorable blond moppet led more by curiosity than by mischievous intent. Instead, she is a sturdy, brazen, mini-hussy who stomps over the doorsill with a determined set to her mouth and a confident bounce in her step. . . . The big cartoonlike pictures depict a cozy modern setting for the respectable, suburban bears with snug rooms cluttered with books, bulbous upholstered furniture and a messy little bear's room. . . . The story contains a genuine enjoyment of Goldilock's adventures as they are reflected in Marshall's usual slapdash and rollicking illustrations." Horn Book

Little Red Riding Hood; retold and illustrated by James Marshall. Dial Bks. for Young Readers 1987 unp il $10.95; lib bdg $10.89 (k-2) **398.2**

1. Folklore—Germany 2. Wolves—Fiction
ISBN 0-8037-0344-9; 0-8037-0345-7 (lib bdg)
LC 86-16722

A "retelling of the familiar tale . . . maintaining the integrity of the Grimm Brothers' version, with both Grandma and Red Riding Hood eaten and later rescued by a hunter." SLJ

This version "will have both children and their parents gripped with the drama and amused by the up-to-date dialogue. . . . The humorous, slightly sinister illustrations display Marshall's wacky style to its best advantage. Funny and wonderful for reading aloud." Horn Book

The three little pigs; retold and illustrated by James Marshall. Dial Bks. for Young Readers 1989 unp il $11.95; lib bdg $11.95 (k-2) **398.2**

1. Folklore—Great Britain 2. Pigs—Fiction 3. Wolves—Fiction
ISBN 0-8037-0591-3; 0-8037-0594-8 (lib bdg)
LC 88-33411

"In his spiffed-up version of the story, the three porkers follow the traditional course of straw, sticks, and bricks with the traditional results, but the players and accoutrements have a bit more zip than those in other versions. . . . The large, exuberant, cartoonlike illustrations provide much additional entertainment, jouncing readers along delightfully from one amusing scene to the next." Horn Book

Martin, Eva

Tales of the Far North; pictures by László Gál. Dial Bks. for Young Readers 1987 c1984 123p il $12.95 (2-5) **398.2**

1. Folklore—Canada 2. Fairy tales
ISBN 0-8037-0319-8
LC 85-46068

First published 1984 in Canada with title: Canadian fairy tales

"Adapted from the French and English folklore of Canada, this collection of twelve fairy tales shows the values of the culture, magic and the supernatural, the rewards of courage and hard work, and the success of the simpleton and younger brother." Child Book Rev Serv

The "full-page illustrations create a mythic mini-world for each story, preserving the sense of time past with full-color scenes framed by narrow black-and-white drawings. A lively source for both children and storytellers." Bull Cent Child Books

Includes bibliographic references

Mayer, Marianna, 1945-

Beauty and the beast; retold by Marianna Mayer; illustrated by Mercer Mayer. Four Winds Press 1978 unp il $15.95; pa $5.95 (1-4) **398.2**

1. Folklore—France 2. Fairy tales
ISBN 0-02-765270-X; 0-689-71151-4 (pa)
LC 78-54679

Through her great capacity to love, a kind and beautiful maid releases a handsome prince from the spell which has made him an ugly beast

"This fresh, new version of the classic French tale is a valid condensation of its lengthier ancestors. Ms. Mayer's clear, crisp style perfectly complements the book's visual qualities. Mercer Mayer's illustrations are, quite simply, superb. They are dramatic and evocative, rich in warm, earth tones and exotic detail." Child Book Rev Serv

Mayo, Gretchen

Star tales; North American Indian stories about the stars; retold [and] illustrated by Gretchen Will Mayo. Walker & Co. 1987 96p il maps $11.95; lib bdg $12.85 (4 and up) **398.2**

1. Indians of North America—Legends 2. Stars—Fiction
ISBN 0-8027-6672-2; 0-8027-6673-0 (lib bdg)
LC 86-23360

A collection of legends from different North American tribes about the stars, moon and the night sky

"This is a handsome book, with large clear type, plenty of white space, a handsome black-and-white illustration at the head of each story, and stylized Indian symbols heading the page of introductory material that precedes each story." SLJ

Includes glossary

McDermott, Gerald

Anansi the spider; a tale from the Ashanti; adapted and illustrated by Gerald McDermott. Holt & Co. 1972 unp il $11.95; pa $5.95 (k-3) **398.2**

1. Folklore—Ghana 2. Ashanti (African people)—Folklore 3. Spiders—Fiction
ISBN 0-8050-0310-X; 0-8050-0311-8 (pa)
LC 76-150028

A Caldecott Medal honor book, 1973

The adaptation of this traditional tale of Ghana is based on an animated film by McDermott. It tells of Anansi, a spider, who is saved from terrible fates by his six sons and is unable to decide which of them to reward. The solution to his predicament is also an explanation for how the moon was put into the sky

"This folk tale is illustrated with strikingly stylized, boldly colored designs based on the traditional geometrical forms of Ashanti art." Saturday Rev

"The simplicity of the writing style makes this a good adaptation for reading aloud to young children or as a source for storytelling." Bull Cent Child Books

Arrow to the sun; a Pueblo Indian tale; adapted and illustrated by Gerald McDermott. Viking 1974 unp il $14.95; Penguin Bks. pa $4.95 (k-3) **398.2**

1. Pueblo Indians—Legends
ISBN 0-670-13369-8; 0-14-050211-4 (pa)
LC 73-16172

Awarded the Caldecott Medal, 1975

This myth tells how Boy searches for his immortal father, the Lord of the Sun, in order to substantiate his paternal heritage. Shot as an arrow to the sun, Boy passes through the four chambers of ceremony to prove himself. Accepted by his father, he returns to earth to bring the Lord of the Sun's spirit to the world of men

"The simple, brief text—which suggests similar stories in religion and folklore—is amply illustrated in full-page and doublespread pictures. . . . The strong colors and the bold angular forms powerfully accompany the text." Horn Book

The stonecutter; a Japanese folk tale; adapted and illustrated by Gerald McDermott. Viking 1975 unp il o.p.; Penguin Bks. paperback available $4.95 (k-3) **398.2**

1. Folklore—Japan
ISBN 0-14-050289-0 (pa) LC 74-26823

A Japanese stonecutter "is blinded by greed as he longs to be transformed first into a prince and then subsequently into the sun, a cloud, and finally the mighty mountain where he had once labored. In documenting his downfall, a restrained text, suggesting the subtle brevity of haiku, is combined with brilliant, four-color illustrations." Horn Book

McFarland, John B., 1943-

The exploding frog and other fables from Aesop; retold by John McFarland; illustrated by James Marshall. Little, Brown 1981 52p il hardcover o.p. paperback available $8.70 (k-3) **398.2**

1. Fables
ISBN 0-316-55577-0 (pa) LC 80-20841

"Thirty-nine fables are retold one to a page with large animal illustrations. . . . The morals that usually accompany Aesop's tales are missing, and some stories seem to hang at the end." Child Book Rev Serv

"Seen as never before and as only Marshall could portray them in improbable colors, the goofy characters of Aesop's morals are irresistible." Publ Wkly

McGovern, Ann

Too much noise; illustrated by Simms Taback. Houghton Mifflin 1967 44p il $14.95; Scholastic pa $2.25 (k-3) **398.2**

1. Folklore
ISBN 0-395-18110-0; 0-317-69684-X (pa) LC 67-4450

"The too crowded house of a familiar old tale becomes a too noisy house in this entertaining picture-book story. Bothered by the noises in his house, an old man follows the advice of the village wise man by first acquiring and then getting rid of a cow, donkey, sheep, hen, dog, and cat. Only then can he appreciate how quiet his house is. The simplicity and straightforwardness of the folktale are evident in both the telling of the cumulative story and in the amusing colored illustrations." Booklist

McKinley, Robin

The outlaws of Sherwood. Greenwillow Bks. 1988 282p $11.95; Ace Bks. pa $3.95 (6 and up) **398.2**

1. Robin Hood (Legendary character)
ISBN 0-688-07178-3; 0-441-64451-1 (pa)
LC 88-45227

"McKinley takes a fresh look at a classic, changing some of the events or deviating from standard characterization to gain new dimensions. Her afterword explains her artistic compromise with myth and history, her wish to write a version that is 'historically unembarrassing.' With a few exceptions, she has done that admirably, creating a story that has pace and substance and style, and that is given nuance and depth by the characterization." Bull Cent Child Books

McVitty, Walter

Ali Baba and the forty thieves; retold by Walter McVitty and illustrated by Margaret Early. Abrams 1990 c1989 unp il $14.95 (1-3) **398.2**

1. Arabs—Folklore 2. Fairy tales
ISBN 0-8109-1888-9 LC 88-31341

First published 1989 in Australia

"Lovely paintings in the style of Persian miniatures and a rich use of gold in the decorative borders framing text and pictures make a sumptuous presentation of the old tale of the brothers Cassim and Ali Baba. Walter

McVitty, Walter—*Continued*
McVitty's rendering retains most of the story elements with a slight variation in the origins of the servant Morgiana, whose cleverness saves Ali Baba's life and fortune." Horn Book

Mikolaycak, Charles, 1937-
Babushka; an old Russian folktale; retold and illustrated by Charles Mikolaycak. Holiday House 1984 unp il lib bdg $14.95; pa $5.95 (k-3) **398.2**

1. Folklore—Soviet Union
ISBN 0-8234-0520-6 (lib bdg); 0-8234-0712-8 (pa) LC 84-500

Retells the traditional tale of the old lady who, having missed her chance to take gifts to the newborn Christ Child, still wanders leaving gifts for all children in hopes that, one day, she will come upon Him

"Exquisitely detailed pencil drawings are richly hued by shading of watercolors and pencils. . . . A fine book, one that will serve children well." SLJ

The **Monkey's** haircut, and other stories told by the Maya; edited by John Bierhorst; illustrated by Robert Andrew Parker. Morrow 1986 152p il $13 (5 and up) **398.2**

1. Mayas—Legends
ISBN 0-688-04269-4 LC 85-28471

"A collection of 22 stories told by the Maya people of Mexico, some of which are from ancient traditions and some of which reflect the influence of Western European traditions on Mexican folk tales. Bierhorst has included a lengthy introduction to help teachers and librarians to see the connections between these tales and those of the West and to point out how the tales reflect the life style and beliefs of the Maya people. . . . Each story is illustrated by a simple black-and-white drawing which highlights a special moment in the tale. . . . Bierhorst's book provides a valuable addition to folklore collections." SLJ

Includes bibliography

Monroe, Jean Guard
They dance in the sky: native American star myths; [by] Jean Guard Monroe and Ray A. Williamson; illustrations by Edgar Stewart. Houghton Mifflin 1987 130p il $13.95 (4 and up) **398.2**

1. Indians of North America—Legends
2. Stars—Fiction
ISBN 0-395-39970-X LC 86-27547

"The first two groups of stories deal with the Pleiades and the Big Dipper; thereafter, they are organized by geographic area. Each group has introductory notes about the tribes of the area and their general beliefs, providing a context for the legends which follow." SLJ

"The brevity of each selection provides easy entry for reluctant readers, while the content of the complete collection is worthy of the most advanced readers." ALAN

Includes glossary and bibliography

Morgan, Pierr
The turnip; an old Russian folktale; retold and illustrated by Pierr Morgan. Philomel Bks. 1990 unp il lib bdg $13.95 (k-2) **398.2**

1. Folklore—Soviet Union
ISBN 0-399-22229-4 LC 89-34023

One of Dedoushka's turnips grows to such an enormous size that the whole family, including the dog, cat, and mouse, is needed to pull it up

This "picture book version of a popular Russian folktale . . . uses the lively retelling found in Katherine Milhous and Alice Dalgliesh's *Once on a Time* (1938). . . . The paintings, done in the Slavic tradition, make use of bold colors and rough textures and are complemented by a crisp, pleasing design." Booklist

Morimoto, Junko
The inch boy; illustrated by Junko Morimoto. Viking Kestrel 1986 unp il o.p.; Penguin Bks. paperback available $3.95 (k-3) **398.2**

1. Folklore—Japan
ISBN 0-14-050677-2 (pa) LC 85-40592

In this Japanese folktale, an inch-high boy proves himself a warrior by vanquishing the dreaded giant red demon with his cunning and bravery

"Morimoto's illustrations are large and bold. Striking colors splash across the pages, and a full-page Buddha appears dramatically luminescent. The perspective—often from the view of a small figure looking up—will delight young sensibilities. The action and humor of the harmonious pictures and text make this an excellent choice for group presentation." SLJ

Moroney, Lynn
Baby rattlesnake; told by Te Ata; adapted by Lynn Moroney; illustrated by Veg Reisberg. Children's Bk. Press 1989 30p il $12.95 (k-2) **398.2**

1. Chickasaw Indians—Legends
2. Rattlesnakes—Fiction
ISBN 0-89239-049-2 LC 89-9892

"Baby Rattlesnake wants a rattle that's just like his big brother and sister's in this native American cautionary tale. The young snake makes such a ruckus that the elders decide to give in to him, even though he is still too young to use his rattle wisely. As the elders predict, Baby Rattlesnake creates mischief with his new power. He meets his match, however, when he tries to scare the chief's daughter." SLJ

"The short sentences, onomatopoeia, and repetition will hold the attention of the youngest listeners as will the boldly colored, stylized gouache and cut-paper illustrations that depict the endearing Rattlesnake family." Booklist

Mosel, Arlene

The funny little woman; retold by Arlene Mosel; pictures by Blair Lent. Dutton 1972 unp il $15.95; pa $4.95 (k-2) **398.2**

1. Folklore—Japan

ISBN 0-525-30265-4; 0-525-45036-X (pa) LC 75-179046

Awarded the Caldecott Medal, 1973

Based on Lafcadio Hearn's The old woman and her dumpling

While chasing a dumpling, a little lady is captured by wicked creatures from whom she escapes with the means of becoming the richest woman in Japan

"The tale unfolds in a simple tellable style. . . . Using elements of traditional Japanese art, the illustrator has made marvelously imaginative pictures. . . . All the inherent drama and humor of the story are manifest in the illustrations." Horn Book

Tikki Tikki Tembo; retold by Arlene Mosel; illustrated by Blair Lent. Holt & Co. 1968 unp il $14.95; pa $5.95 (k-2) **398.2**

1. Folklore—China 2. Names, Personal—Fiction

ISBN 0-8050-0662-1; 0-8050-1166-8 (pa) LC 68-11839

A "Chinese folk tale about a first son with a very long name. When Tikki Tikki Tembo-No Sa Rembo-Chari Bari Ruchi-Pip Peri Pembo fell into the well, it took his little brother so long to say his name and get help that Tikki almost drowned." Hodges. Books for Elem Sch Libr

"In this polished version of a story hour favorite, beautifully stylized wash drawings of serene Oriental landscapes are in comic contrast to amusingly visualized folk and the active disasters accruing to the possessor of a 21-syllable, irresistibly chantable name." Best Books of the Year, 1968

Mwalimu

Awful aardvark; by Mwalimu and Adrienne Kennaway. Little, Brown 1989 unp il $14.95 (k-2) **398.2**

1. Folklore—Africa 2. Aardvark—Fiction

ISBN 0-316-59218-8 LC 89-80028

Published in the United Kingdom with title: Awkward aardvark

"In folktale style, Mongoose conspires with other jungle animals to stop Aardvark's loud snoring, but the monkeys, lion, and rhinoceros only manage to rouse him briefly. It is the lowly termites that topple his tree." Bull Cent Child Books

"The double-page spreads seem to linger on the rounded shapes and rough textures of the animals as they move across the pages amid the hot greens, yellows, and browns of the background. The well-paced story reads aloud well, and Kennaway's illustrations make even swarming nests of crawling termites into splendidly decorative and eye-catching arrangements." Horn Book

The **Naked** bear; folktales of the Iroquois; edited by John Bierhorst; illustrated by Dirk Zimmer. Morrow 1987 xx, 123p il $14.95 (4 and up) **398.2**

1. Iroquois Indians—Legends 2. Indians of North America—Legends

ISBN 0-688-06422-1 LC 86-21836

"Following a brief introduction on the storytelling and culture of the Six Nations of the Iroquois are sixteen folktales with some haunting themes and images. Consistently woven through them all is the close relationship of human and animal, as well as ubiquitous magic powers upon which mortals often call to combat extraordinary forces. . . . These tales are easy to read and taut enough to tell, each sustained with the suspense of life and death situations." Bull Cent Child Books

Includes bibliography

Nesbit, E. (Edith), 1858-1924

Melisande; written by E. Nesbit; illustrated by P.J. Lynch; with an introduction by Naomi Lewis. Harcourt Brace Jovanovich 1989 unp il $13.95 (k-2) **398.2**

1. Fairy tales

ISBN 0-15-253164-5 LC 88-37190

Originally appeared in the author's Nine unlikely tales for children (1901)

Cursed by an evil fairy at her christening, Princess Melisande grows up bald but finds herself facing another set of problems when her wish for golden hair is fulfilled

"E. Nesbit's offhand treatment of fairy tale traditions and the final clever solution make a most satisfactory story. The fantastic, medieval illustrations show the influence of Rackham but reflect the humorous, quizzical quality of the tale." Horn Book

Norman, Howard

How Glooskap outwits the Ice Giants, and other tales of the Maritime Indians; retold by Howard Norman; wood engravings by Michael McCurdy. Little, Brown 1989 60p il lib bdg $14.95 (3-6) **398.2**

1. Indians of North America—Legends

ISBN 0-316-61181-6 LC 89-2379

"Joy Street books"

Six tales featuring the mythical giant who roamed the coast to New England and Canada, created the Indian peoples to keep him company, and fought battles to protect them ever after

These tales "are witty, fresh, and stylish. . . . Executed with technical virtuosity, the handsome black-and-white wood engravings engage the eye with dramatic perspectives, expressive characterizations, and intricate detailing. A field-tested delight for reading aloud and storytelling." Booklist

Nunes, Susan, 1937-

Tiddalick the frog; illustrated by Ju-Hong Chen. Atheneum Pubs. 1989 unp il $13.95 (k-2) **398.2**

1. Australian aborigines—Folklore 2. Frogs—Fiction

ISBN 0-689-31502-3 LC 89-1

Nunes, Susan, 1937-—*Continued*

"This adaptation of an aboriginal story (the source is not provided) concerns an enormous, bad-tempered frog who drinks up all the fresh water in the world. Although the other animals relate their tales of suffering to him . . . the monster fails to release his load. Next, they take turns trying to make him laugh, and in the fairy-tale tradition, it is the last and smallest creature, the eel Noyang, who succeeds when he accidentally dances himself into knots." Booklist

"Chen's watercolors are gracefully patterned in dancing rhythms that reflect the tale itself. The dominant hues of blue and green are punctuated by parched yellows, burnt orange, and scorched red. Told and illustrated without pretension, this is a choice representation of Australian lore." Bull Cent Child Books

Ormerod, Jan

The frog prince; retold by Jan Ormerod and David Lloyd; illustrated by Jan Ormerod. Lothrop, Lee & Shepard Bks. 1990 unp il $12.95; lib bdg $12.88 (k-3) **398.2**

1. Folklore—Germany 2. Fairy tales
ISBN 0-688-09568-2; 0-688-09569-0 (lib bdg) LC 89-12977

In this version of the fairy tale, "it is the princess' growing fondness for the frog and the fact that she allows him to sleep on her pillow three times that breaks the enchantment, transforming him into a handsome prince." SLJ

"Although textually straightforward, this is a visually sophisticated treatment of Grimm's tale. . . . Ormerod paints a somber world dominated by grays and greens, with only an occasional splash of gold or orange for relief. Not until the final spread, when the princess and her prince are married, does a fuller, lighter palette emerge." Publ Wkly

The story of Chicken Licken. Lothrop, Lee & Shepard Bks. 1986 c1985 unp il $13 (k-2) **398.2**

1. Folklore
ISBN 0-688-06058-7 LC 85-7911

First published 1985 in the United Kingdom

"Here the story of the gullible chicken is being acted out by a group of schoolchildren in an auditorium. One by one, the actors appear—everyone from Henny Penny to Drake Lake—much to the appreciation of the silhouetted parental audience that sits in the foreground. But the action is not only on stage. Careful observers will notice a baby in the audience who climbs out of his carryall basket and unobtrusively, page by page, makes his way up a short flight of steps until he is center stage. The contrast of shiny bright colors and the black silhouettes gives an interesting effect resulting in a warm and personal book that extends the appeal of the original story. Great fun for a read-aloud." Booklist

Oxenbury, Helen, 1938-

The Helen Oxenbury nursery story book. Knopf 1985 72p il $12.95; lib bdg $12.99 (k-1) **398.2**

1. Folklore 2. Fairy tales
ISBN 0-394-87519-2; 0-394-97519-7 (lib bdg) LC 84-28887

Includes ten familiar folk tales, such as "Goldilocks and the Three Bears," "The Elves and the Shoemaker," and "Little Red Riding Hood"

"Emphasizing the universality and the timelessness of the stories, the artist has given some of the human characters a vaguely contemporary appearance. Her line is firm; her instinct for color superb; and from the smaller pictures to the full-page ones the artwork exudes vigor, movement, and an ebullient humor that manages to be both naive and sly." Horn Book

Parks, Van Dyke

Jump! the adventures of Brer Rabbit; by Joel Chandler Harris; adapted by Van Dyke Parks and Malcolm Jones; illustrated by Barry Moser. Harcourt Brace Jovanovich 1986 40p il $15.95 (1-4) **398.2**

1. Blacks—Folklore 2. Animals—Fiction
ISBN 0-15-241350-2 LC 86-7654

A retelling of five folktales in which crafty Brer Rabbit tries to outsmart all the other creatures in the animal community

"Moser's watercolors restore much of the humor to the five stories, which will probably have a robust appeal for some." Publ Wkly

Jump again! more adventures of Brer Rabbit; by Joel Chandler Harris; adapted by Van Dyke Parks; illustrated by Barry Moser. Harcourt Brace Jovanovich 1987 39p il $16.95 (1-4) **398.2**

1. Blacks—Folklore 2. Animals—Fiction
ISBN 0-15-241352-9 LC 86-33622

"This second volume of Brer Rabbit tales, wittily retold by a contemporary songwriter (one song is included) and beautifully illustrated with watercolor portraits of the characters by a distinguished artist, is as accomplished and appealing as the first." N Y Times Book Rev

Jump on over! the adventures of Brer Rabbit and his family; by Joel Chandler Harris; adapted by Van Dyke Parks; illustrated by Barry Moser. Harcourt Brace Jovanovich 1989 39p il $15.95 (1-4) **398.2**

1. Blacks—Folklore 2. Animals—Folklore
ISBN 0-15-241354-5 LC 89-7417

A collection of five tales in which Brer Rabbit outwits Brer Fox, Brer Wolf, and Brer Bear in order to ensure his family's survival during a drought

"No child can resist such a trickster, and no adult can resist Moser's sly portraits, with their varied perspectives, uncanny draftsmanship, and sparely detailed southern settings. Parks' adaptations are looser and more comfortably idiomatic this time around; music to his song 'Home' is appended." Bull Cent Child Books

Paterson, Katherine
The tale of the mandarin ducks; illustrated by Leo & Diane Dillon. Lodestar Bks. 1989 unp il $14.95 (1-3) **398.2**

1. Folklore—Japan 2. Ducks—Fiction
ISBN 0-525-67283-4 LC 88-30484

"A Japanese fairy tale, in picture-book format, about a Mandarin duck caught and caged at the whim of a wealthy Japanese lord. Separated from his mate, the bird languishes in captivity until a compassionate servant girl sets him free. The lord sentences the girl and her beloved to death, but they in turn are freed and rewarded with happiness." Booklist

"Paterson's story is rich with magic, compassion and love. The Dillons' elegantly detailed watercolor and pastel drawings, in the style of 18th-century Japanese woodcuts, are exquisite." Publ Wkly

Perrault, Charles, 1628-1703
Cinderella; or, The little glass slipper; a free translation from the French of Charles Perrault; with pictures by Marcia Brown. Scribner 1954 unp il $13.95; Atheneum Pubs. pa $4.95 (k-3) **398.2**

1. Folklore—France 2. Fairy tales
ISBN 0-684-12676-1; 0-689-70484-4 (pa)
LC 54-12897

Awarded the Caldecott Medal, 1955

This is the classic story of the poor, good-natured girl who works for her selfish step-sisters until a fairy godmother transforms her into a beautiful 'princess' for just one night

"A distinguished picture book. . . . The story can be used for telling, but it is perfect for the picture-book hour. With soft, delicate colors and lines that subtly suggest, Miss Brown creates a thoroughly fairyland atmosphere, at the same time recreating the sophistication of the French Court with its golden coach, canopied bed, dazzling chandeliers, liveried footmen, curled and pompadoured ladies, and peruked (bewigged) courtiers." Libr J

Puss in boots; illustrated by Fred Marcellino; translated by Malcolm Arthur. Farrar, Straus & Giroux 1990 unp il $14.95 (k-3) **398.2**

1. Folklore—France 2. Fairy tales
ISBN 0-374-36160-6 LC 90-82136

A Caldecott Medal honor book, 1991

"Opulently designed and handsomely illustrated, this picture book provides a fitting showcase for Perrault's artful tale of deceit and resourcefulness. Unsullied by type, the striking front of the book features a close-up portrait of the cat's face. Befitting a fairy tale, the artwork inside is suffused with a golden light that proclaims the story to be from a sunnier, more dreamlike world." Booklist

Plume, Ilse
The Bremen town musicians; retold and illustrated by Ilse Plume. Doubleday 1980 unp il o.p.; HarperCollins Pubs. paperback available $5.95 (k-3) **398.2**

1. Folklore—Germany 2. Animals—Fiction
ISBN 0-06-443141-X (pa) LC 79-6622

A Caldecott Medal honor book, 1981

A retelling of an old Grimm's tale in which "a donkey, cat, dog, and rooster find that their usefulness to their masters has gone, and they set out to make new lives for themselves. When their 'music' frightens away some robbers, they find a quiet, peaceful world and live happily ever after." Child Book Rev Serv

The author/illustrator's "realistic illustrations have . . . mild and unpretentious charm; the animal principals are too conventionally bland, but the human bit players individualized and appealing. The style of the crayon-like paintings is pleasantly naive." SLJ

The story of Befana; an Italian Christmas tale; illustrated and retold by Ilse Plume. Godine 1981 27p il $12.95 (1-3) **398.2**

1. Befana (Legendary character) 2. Folklore—Italy 3. Christmas—Fiction
ISBN 0-87923-420-2 LC 81-81811

Retells the traditional tale of the poor peasant woman who set out to find the Christ Child and wanders to this day, carrying a sack of gifts for good children

"The retelling lacks the terseness associated with simple folk tales; starting with an explanatory introduction, the artist presents a somewhat elaborated narrative. . . . Occupying every right-hand page in the elegantly produced book, the paintings with their Italianate architecture and stylized Tuscan landscapes are given individuality by a striking use of luminous full color." Horn Book

The **Prince** who knew his fate; an ancient Egyptian tale; translated from hieroglyphs and illustrated by Lise Manniche. Metropolitan Mus. of Art; Philomel Bks. 1982 c1981 unp il $10.95 (1-3) **398.2**

1. Folklore—Egypt 2. Fairy tales
ISBN 0-399-20850-X LC 81-10740

Retells the 3,000 year-old Egyptian tale of the prince whose fate, to die by a crocodile, a snake, or a dog, is decreed at his birth. Includes additional information about the background of the story and the civilization of ancient Egypt

"The story line is tight enough for picture-book audiences; slightly older children will be intrigued by the information in Manniche's extensive afterword. Here she explains how the papyrus story was incomplete and how she evolved her own happy conclusion. . . . It's ideal for classroom units on Egypt or can stand alone for those looking for simple entertainment." Booklist

Pyle, Howard, 1853-1911
King Stork; illustrated by Trina Schart Hyman. Little, Brown 1973 48p il hardcover o.p. paperback available $6.95 (k-3) **398.2**

1. Fairy tales
ISBN 0-316-72441-6 (pa) LC 78-182249

Pyle, Howard, 1853-1911—*Continued*

Text first published 1888 in the author's collection: The wonder clock, entered below

Pyle's story of a poor drummer youth who wins a beautiful but wicked princess "with the help of King Stork's magic and 'tames' her . . . is fluidly illustrated with medieval scenes. . . . [It is] a story in the devious-female, dominating-male tradition." Booklist

"The illustrations fit the various moods of the story. . . . The princess is scantily-clad yet certainly beautiful. Children will enjoy the detailed illustrations and the simplicity and magical qualities of the story." SLJ

The merry adventures of Robin Hood of great renown in Nottinghamshire; as written and illustrated by Howard Pyle. Scribner 1976 288p il $35; Dover Publs. pa $5.95 (5 and up) **398.2**

1. Robin Hood (Legendary character)
ISBN 0-684-14838-2; 0-486-22043-5 (pa)

First published 1883

Twenty-two stories of Robin Hood and his adventures with the King's foresters in Sherwood Forest

"Of all the books of Robin Hood this is best for literary style, adherence to the spirit and events of the old ballads and wealth of historical background." Toronto Public Libr

"The author illustrates in a most appropriately picturesque style for young people." Baker. Guide to the Best Fic

The story of King Arthur and his knights; written and illustrated by Howard Pyle. Scribner 1984 312p il $17.95; New Am. Lib. pa $3.95 (6 and up) **398.2**

1. Arthur, King 2. Arthurian romances
ISBN 0-684-14814-5; 0-451-52488-8 (pa) LC 84-50167

A reissue of the title first published 1903

The first of a four-volume series retelling the Arthurian legends

"An introduction to the loftiest of medieval romances, worthy in style and illustrations of its noble theme." Hodges. Books for Elem Sch Libr

The story of Sir Launcelot and his companions. Scribner 1985 340p il $17.95 (6 and up) **398.2**

1. Lancelot (Legendary character) 2. Arthurian romances
ISBN 0-684-18313-7

A reissue of the title first published 1907

This third book of the series follows "Sir Launcelot's adventures as he rescues Queen Guinevere from the clutches of Sir Mellegrans, does battle with the Worm of Corbin, wanders as a madman in the forest and is finally returned to health by the Lady Elaine." Best Sellers

The story of the champions of the Round Table; written and illustrated by Howard Pyle. Scribner 1984 328p il $17.95; Dover Publs. pa $7.95 (6 and up) **398.2**

1. Arthurian romances
ISBN 0-684-18171-1; 0-486-21883-X (pa)

A reissue of the title first published 1905

Contents: The story of Launcelot; the book of Sir Tristram; The book of Sir Percival

"Pyle's second volume of Arthurian legends will be of interest to motivated students of literature and history, as well as useful in professional collections for comparisons and source work. In spite of the archaic language . . . the narrative depth and graphic force . . . will draw in readers." Booklist

The story of the Grail and the passing of Arthur. Scribner 1985 258p il $17.95 (6 and up) **398.2**

1. Arthur, King 2. Arthurian romances 3. Grail—Fiction
ISBN 0-684-18483-4 LC 85-40302

A reissue of the title first published 1910

This volume follows the adventures of Sir Geraint, Galahad's quest for the holy Grail, the battle between Launcelot and Gawaine, and the slaying of Mordred

The wonder clock; or, Four & twenty marvelous tales, being one for each hour of the day; written & illustrated by Howard Pyle; embellished with verses by Katharine Pyle. Dover Publs. 1965 318p il pa $5.95 (4-6) **398.2**

1. Folklore 2. Fairy tales
ISBN 0-486-21446-X (pa)

Also available in hardcover from Smith, P. $17.25 (ISBN 0-8446-2767-4)

A reprint of the title first published 1887 by Harper

"Tales told by the puppet figures of an old clock found in Time's garret." Hodges. Books for Elem Sch Libr

"Pyle adapted tales from Grimm and other legends in his own lively and humorous way." Adventuring with Books. 2d edition

Quayle, Eric

The shining princess, and other Japanese legends; illustrated by Michael Foreman. Arcade Pub. 1989 111p il $15.95 (5 and up) **398.2**

1. Folklore—Japan
ISBN 1-55970-039-4 LC 89-84076

A "collection of Japanese legends drawn from the two earliest-known English translations." Publisher's note

This "collection of ten exciting tales is surely destined to become a standard source of Japanese folktales. . . . Each tale is sure to enthrall read-aloud audiences as well as independent readers. Foreman's remarkable watercolors, perfectly suited to each text, complete the package." SLJ

Ransome, Arthur, 1884-1967

The Fool of the World and the flying ship; a Russian tale retold by Arthur Ransome; pictures by Uri Shulevitz. Farrar, Straus & Giroux 1968 unp il $15.95; pa $4.95 (k-3) **398.2**

1. Folklore—Soviet Union
ISBN 0-374-32442-5; 0-374-42438-1 (pa)

LC 68-54105

Awarded the Caldecott Medal, 1969

"An Ariel book"

Text first published 1916 in Ransome's Old Peter's Russian tales

The Fool of the World, was the third and youngest son whose parents thought little of him. When the Czar announced that his daughter would marry the hero who could bring him a flying ship, Fool of the World went looking and found one. Aided in surprising ways by eight peasants with magical powers, he then had to outwit the treacherous Czar

This "is a fascinating tale, told with humor and grace and brought vividly to life by Uri Shulevitz's illustrations." N Y Times Book Rev

Rayevsky, Inna

The talking tree; an old Italian tale; retold by Inna Rayevsky; illustrated by Robert Rayevsky. Putnam 1989 unp il $14.95 (k-3) **398.2**

1. Folklore—Italy 2. Fairy tales
ISBN 0-399-21631-6 LC 88-32105

"Adapted from the title story of Augusta Baker's collection *The Talking Tree* [1955], this Italian folktale presents a king who searches for a magical tree and finds a witch-imprisoned princess instead." Bull Cent Child Books

"The text is crisp and well paced, without resorting to contrived archaisms or modern slang. Illustrations and text achieve a comfortable relationship, and the overall design of the book is pleasing. The story is not commonly known, but it contains enough familiar elements to strike an immediate chord with readers." SLJ

The **Red** fairy book; edited by Andrew Lang; with numerous illustrations by H. J. Ford and Lancelot Speed. Dover Publs. 1966 367p il pa $6.95 (4-6) **398.2**

1. Folklore 2. Fairy tales
ISBN 0-486-21673-X LC 66-24134

Also available in hardcover from Smith, P. $16 (ISBN 0-8446-0756-8)

A reprint of the title first published 1890 by Longmans

"This book includes a wide assortment of fairy tales from French, Scandinavian, German, and Rumanian folklore sources, including tales of the Brothers Grimm and Madame d'Aulnoy. Accompanying the 37 stories are 100 line drawings." Adventuring with Books. 2d edition

Reeves, James, 1909-1978

English fables and fairy stories; retold by James Reeves; illustrated by Joan Kiddell-Monroe. Oxford Univ. Press 1954 234p il (Oxford myths and legends) $14.95; pa $7.95 (4-6) **398.2**

1. Folklore—Great Britain 2. Fairy tales
ISBN 0-19-274101-2; 0-19-274137-3 (pa)

LC 54-39522

A "collection of nineteen English tales, told in language beautiful for either reading or telling. Several familiar tales are included with old favorites such as 'Molly Whipple,' 'Dick Whittington', and 'Jack and the Beanstalk.'" Second Educ Board

Reyher, Rebecca Hourwich, 1897-1987

My mother is the most beautiful woman in the world; a Russian folktale retold by Becky Reyher; pictures by Ruth Gannett. Lothrop, Lee & Shepard Bks. 1962 c1945 39p il lib bdg $12.88 (1-4) **398.2**

1. Folklore—Soviet Union
ISBN 0-688-51251-8

A Caldecott Medal honor book, 1946

First published 1945 by Howell, Soskin

A Russian folktale about a little peasant girl, lost in the wheat fields, who tried to describe her mother as the "most beautiful woman in the world." When an exceptionally ugly woman claimed the little girl, they remembered the proverb: "We do not love people because they are beautiful, but they seem beautiful to us because we love them"

"Though its people are Russian peasants a long time ago and though Ruth Gannett has brought them to us in brilliant, convincing pictures, there is not a little listening child to whom it is read that will not claim it for his own. These are just the right pictures for a story told in just the right way." N Y Her Trib Books

Riordan, James, 1936-

The woman in the moon, and other tales of forgotten heroines; illustrated by Angela Barrett. Dial Bks. for Young Readers 1985 c1984 86p il $11.95; lib bdg $11.89 (4 and up) **398.2**

1. Folklore 2. Fairy tales
ISBN 0-8037-0194-2; 0-8037-0196-9 (lib bdg)

LC 84-20050

First published 1984 in England

This anthology of thirteen folktales focuses on heroines from various cultures

"The stories are written in a flowing narrative style ideally suited for storytelling or reading aloud. The engravings which accompany each tale are realistic, intricately detailed and perfect for the tales." SLJ

Includes bibliography

Robbins, Ruth

Baboushka and the three kings; illustrated by Nicolas Sidjakov; adapted from a Russian folk tale. Houghton Mifflin 1960 unp il $13.95; pa $3.95 (1-4) **398.2**

1. Folklore—Soviet Union 2. Christmas—Fiction
ISBN 0-395-27673-X; 0-395-42647-2 (pa) LC 60-15036

Awarded the Caldecott Medal, 1961

First published by Parnassus Press

A retelling of the Christmas legend about the old woman who declined to accompany the three kings on their search for the Christ Child and has ever since then searched for the Child on her own. Each year as she renews her search she leaves gifts at the homes she visits, acting, in this respect, as a Russian equivalent to Santa Claus

"Mystery and dignity are in the retelling. . . . At the end of the book is the story in verse set to original music." Horn Book

Rockwell, Anne F., 1934-

Puss in boots, and other stories; told and illustrated by Anne Rockwell. Macmillan 1988 88p il $15.95 (2-4) **398.2**

1. Folklore 2. Fairy tales
ISBN 0-02-777781-2 LC 87-14976

"Rockwell retells 12 fairy tales and fables remembered from her childhood. Although some elements of these stories differ from most familiar versions, their timelessness will cast a spell once more. Among the book's pleasing physical features are its fine, heavy pages; its wide margins; and the full-color illustrations on each double-page spread. The simple line drawings with their bright, clear colors have a childlike innocence and charm." Booklist

The three bears & 15 other stories; selected [retold] and illustrated by Anne Rockwell. Crowell 1975 116p il $13.95; lib bdg $13.89; HarperCollins Pubs. pa $7.95 (k-3) **398.2**

1. Folklore 2. Fairy tales
ISBN 0-690-00597-0; 0-690-00598-9 (lib bdg); 0-06-440142-1 (pa) LC 74-5381

A collection of sixteen famous children's stories including Lazy Jack, The three little pigs, The gingerbread man, and The shoemaker and the elves

This is "a square, solid volume that is inviting to look at and comfortable to hold. . . . Since the sources, though well-known, are not indicated in the book, the stories take on a certain anonymity; and no feeling of period or nationality can be observed in the bright and cheerful, firmly limned, full-color paintings that are scattered generously through the book." Horn Book

Rogasky, Barbara

Rapunzel; from the Brothers Grimm; retold by Barbara Rogasky; with illustrations by Trina Schart Hyman. Holiday House 1982 unp il lib bdg $14.95; pa $5.95 (1-3) **398.2**

1. Folklore—Germany 2. Fairy tales
ISBN 0-8234-0454-4 (lib bdg); 0-8234-0652-0 (pa) LC 81-6419

A retelling of the folktale "about the beautiful girl whose lover climbs her rope of golden hair and whose cruel treatment by a possessive witch ends when Rapunzel, her prince, and their infant twins are united." Bull Cent Child Books

"Some of Hyman's familiar specialities . . . appear again to advantage. . . . Most engaging of all are the lovely borders and vignettes on every page, filled with fruits, flowers, small landscapes and decorative patterns. The highly organized layout and borders, attractive in themselves, enhance Hyman's art by imposing a kind of discipline on her romantic style." SLJ

The water of life; a tale from the Brothers Grimm; retold by Barbara Rogasky; illustrated by Trina Schart Hyman. Holiday House 1986 unp il $14.95 (1-3) **398.2**

1. Folklore—Germany 2. Fairy tales
ISBN 0-8234-0552-4 LC 84-19226

A prince searching for the Water of Life to cure his dying father finds an enchanted castle, a lovely princess, and treachery from his older brothers

"This traditional tale with all the trappings of magical elements, romance, and underlying psychological truth, is brought to life by Rogasky's spirited telling and Hyman's lush illustrations." SLJ

Rohmer, Harriet

Brother Anansi and the cattle ranch; told by James de Sauza; adapted by Harriet Rohmer; illustrations by Stephen Von Mason; version in Spanish, Rosalma Zubizarretta. Children's Bk. Press 1989 32p il $12.95 (3-6) **398.2**

1. Folklore 2. Bilingual books—Spanish-English
ISBN 0-89239-044-1 LC 88-37091

"Anansi, the traditional West African trickster, also made his way into Caribbean, Central American, and North American folklore. In this modern bilingual version Brother Anansi is a man living on the Nicaraguan coast. When Brother Tiger wins the lottery, Anansi devises a way to acquire all of Tiger's money." Horn Book

This tale is "recently collected, imaginatively illustrated, and solidly translated. . . . [It is] retold in simple, colloquial language. . . . The full-page artwork . . . is represented in a primitive and naturalistic style; the Central American tale [has] bold, flat, stylized figures that are intensely colored with acrylics." Booklist

Ross, Tony, 1938-

Hansel and Gretel. Andersen Press; distributed by David & Charles 1990 c1989 unp il $13.95 (k-3) **398.2**

1. Folklore—Germany 2. Fairy tales
ISBN 0-86264-210-8

First published 1989 in the United Kingdom

"Ross preserves the bare bones of the story line but embellishes it with imaginative details. . . . The language makes this a delightful read-aloud, particularly for children who already know the traditional story. The rosy-cheeked, snub-nosed children and sharp-featured gray villains, will be familiar to Ross' fans. Here he also uses line to create texture and a sense of grim darkness. . . . The book is a good contrast to other less traditional versions." SLJ

Mrs. Goat and her seven little kids. Atheneum Pubs. 1990 unp il $13.95 (k-2) **398.2**

1. Folklore—Germany 2. Fairy tales
ISBN 0-689-31624-0 LC 89-17933

Mother Goat rescues six of her kids after they are swallowed by a wicked wolf

"Ross has retold and retained the essence of the Grimms' 'The Wolf and the Seven Young Kids.' . . . Using contemporary language and references, Ross adds humor to the story through slapdash, colorful watercolor illustrations that appear on each double-page spread. The traditional ending has been softened, although the feisty youngest kid bites and hammers the wolf as he attempts to get into the house. Children should enjoy this slapstick, action-packed tale." SLJ

Rounds, Glen, 1906-

Ol' Paul, the mighty logger. Holiday House 1976 93p il $14.95; pa $4.95 (3-6) **398.2**

1. Bunyan, Paul (Legendary character)
ISBN 0-8234-0269-X; 0-8234-0713-6 (pa) LC 75-22163

First published 1936

"Being a true account of the seemingly incredible exploits and inventions of the great Paul Bunyan, profusely illustrated by drawings made at the scene by the author, Glen Rounds, and now republished in this special fortieth anniversary edition." Subtitle

San Souci, Robert, 1946-

The boy and the ghost; by Robert D. San Souci; illustrated by J. Brian Pinkney. Simon & Schuster Bks. for Young Readers 1989 unp il $13.95 (k-3) **398.2**

1. Blacks—Folklore 2. Ghosts—Fiction
ISBN 0-671-67176-6 LC 89-4185

A poor boy hopes to win a fortune for himself and his family by spending the night in a haunted house and bravely standing up to a frightening ghost

"Many librarians will recognize in this southern black tale a variant of 'The Tinker and the Ghost.' . . . San Souci has a full note on his own sources and has adapted turn-of-the-century story fragments . . . with a natural ease that sits well in a picture-book medium, including the low-key dialect. J. Brian Pinkney's watercolors have a style of wash over sketch-work not unlike that of his father, the notable Jerry Pinkney, to whom he will inevitably be compared. However, Brian's human figures and faces have a distinctive grace and versatility. His subtly hued scenes maintain a spacious simplicity of composition that makes his first book a choice one for group read-alouds." Bull Cent Child Books

The enchanted tapestry; a Chinese folktale; retold by Robert D. San Souci; pictures by László Gál. Dial Bks. for Young Readers 1987 unp il $11.95; lib bdg $11.89; pa $3.95 (k-3) **398.2**

1. Folklore—China
ISBN 0-8037-0304-X; 0-8037-0306-6 (lib bdg); 0-8037-0862-9 (pa) LC 85-29283

"This story, based on a Chinese legend, is a variation on the testing of a faithful child. A widow weaves exquisite silk tapestries to support her three sons. One day the wind tears her masterwork out of its frame. The two older sons, both greedy cowards, search for it. They encounter a sorceress and fail to meet her challenges. The youngest son succeeds." N Y Times Book Rev

"The soft-hued, delicately detailed illustrations capture the beauty of the tapestry. The suspense builds, and young listeners caught up in the story are rewarded with a happy ending." Child Book Rev Serv

The legend of Scarface; a Blackfeet Indian tale; adapted by Robert San Souci; illustrated by Daniel San Souci. Doubleday 1978 unp il hardcover o.p. paperback available $5.95 (2-4) **398.2**

1. Siksika Indians—Legends
ISBN 0-385-15874-2 (pa) LC 77-15170

A retelling of a Blackfeet Indian legend in which a young brave travels to the land of the Sun to ask for the hand of his beloved

"A greatly abbreviated retelling of the classic hero tales so well set down by George Grinnell in his 'Blackfoot Lodge Tales.' . . . The twelve large full-color paintings have a dramatic strength, realistically interpreting the action, the Indian characters, and the animals." Horn Book

Robert D. San Souci's The six swans; illustrated by Daniel San Souci. Simon & Schuster Bks. for Young Readers 1989 unp il lib bdg $14.95 (2-4) **398.2**

1. Folklore—Germany 2. Fairy tales
ISBN 0-671-65848-4 LC 88-11375

"In this Brothers Grimm story, a young princess works diligently to save her six brothers from an evil stepmother who has turned the boys into swans." Booklist

"The retelling is smooth. . . . San Souci's somewhat formal watercolor illustrations provide a well-focused medieval setting and add drama to the story." SLJ

Short & shivery; thirty chilling tales; retold by Robert D. San Souci; illustrated by Katherine Coville. Doubleday 1987 175p il $10.95; pa $5.95 (4 and up) **398.2**

1. Folklore 2. Ghosts—Fiction
ISBN 0-385-23886-X; 0-385-26426-7 (pa) LC 86-29067

San Souci, Robert, 1946-—*Continued*

"A collection of spooky stories, competently adapted and retold (sometimes quite freely) from world folklore, including Japan, Africa, and Latin America, as well as Europe and the U.S. . . . The stories drawn from collections of regional American folklore are not only the freshest, but often the scariest. Sources are fully documented at the back of the book. . . . Many of the stories will be effective as read-alouds. There are some delicious shivers here, with plenty of fodder for an active imagination, as well as excitement." SLJ

Song of Sedna; adapted by Robert D. San Souci; illustrated by Daniel San Souci. Doubleday 1981 unp il hardcover o.p. paperback available $5.95 (2-4) **398.2**

1. Inuit—Folklore
ISBN 0-385-24823-7 (pa) LC 80-627

An adaptation of an Eskimo legend. "Discovering that her mate is a bird-spirit who had appeared to her in human form, the beautiful Sedna flees with her father. Her husband follows in vengeful pursuit, and her father is so frightened that he hurls his daughter into the sea; she is carried by a whale to a watery throne on the peak of an underwater mountain. There she is proclaimed goddess of the sea." Bull Cent Child Books

"This hauntingly beautiful story is spectacularly illustrated. It should capture the attention of young and old alike." Child Book Rev Serv

The talking eggs; a folktale from the American South; retold by Robert D. San Souci; pictures by Jerry Pinkney. Dial Bks. for Young Readers 1989 unp il $12.95; lib bdg $12.89 (k-3) **398.2**

1. Folklore—Southern States
ISBN 0-8037-0619-7; 0-8037-0620-0 (lib bdg) LC 88-33469

A Caldecott Medal honor book, 1990

A Southern folktale in which kind Blanche, following the instructions of an old witch, gains riches, while her greedy sister makes fun of the old woman and is duly rewarded

"Adapted from a Creole folk tale originally included in a collection of Louisiana stories by folklorist Alcee Fortier, this tale captures the flavor of the nineteenth-century South in its language and story line. . . . Jerry Pinkney's watercolors are chiefly responsible for the excellence of the book; his characters convey their moods with vivid facial expressions. A wonderful book to read aloud." Horn Book

The white cat; an Old French fairy tale; retold by Robert D. San Souci; illustrated by Gennady Spirin. Orchard Bks. 1989 unp il $15.95; lib bdg $15.99 (2-4) **398.2**

1. Folklore—France 2. Fairy tales
ISBN 0-531-05809-3; 0-531-08409-4 (lib bdg) LC 88-19698

"Based on Madame D'Aulnoy's 1698 literary tale, which in turn draws on a folktale in which a king sends his three sons on three tests to decide their inheritance. The youngest son produces, at the end of the first year, the tiniest dog and, at the end of the second year, the finest linen—both with the help of a magical white cat who becomes his human bride when he breaks a spell bewitching her." Bull Cent Child Books

"San Souci's retelling is suitably magical and mysterious, and his words flow like music. Spirin's sumptuous paintings, each abounding with meticulous detail from foreground to furthest distance, glow with light and expression." Publ Wkly

Young Merlin; illustrated by Daniel Horne. Doubleday 1990 unp il $13.95; lib bdg $14.99 (2-5) **398.2**

1. Merlin (Legendary character) 2. Folklore—Great Britain
ISBN 0-385-24800-8; 0-385-24801-6 (lib bdg) LC 88-30916

Presents the life of Merlin the magician from his miraculous birth through the age of seventeen, before he met King Arthur

This book "is handsomely designed, offering intriguing perspectives, subtle lines, and warm, deep colors. . . . Text and pictures are well balanced. . . . A good choice for reading aloud or for individual enjoyment." SLJ

Sanderson, Ruth, 1951-

The twelve dancing princesses; retold and illustrated by Ruth Sanderson. Little, Brown 1990 unp il lib bdg $14.95 (k-3) **398.2**

1. Folklore—Germany 2. Fairy tales
ISBN 0-316-77017-5 LC 88-28637

This is a retelling of the Grimm fairy tale. A king's daughters dance their slippers to shreds every night until the castle gardener discovers their secret and breaks the spell through his love for the youngest princess

"The text reads smoothly, with a straightforward formality that is complemented by the classic nature of the illustrations. Painted in oil, in a realistic yet romantic style, the pictures have the dark, rich texture of old velvet. . . . A fine addition to any fairy-tale collection." SLJ

Sanfield, Steve

The adventures of High John the Conqueror; illustrated by John Ward. Orchard Bks. 1988 113p il $12.95; lib bdg $12.99 (4 and up) **398.2**

1. Blacks—Folklore
ISBN 0-531-05807-7; 0-531-08407-8 (lib bdg) LC 88-17946

"A Richard Jackson book"

"A competent retelling of 16 African-American folktales about the black trickster hero who always manages to outwit others, particularly his white master. Simply told in language comprehensible to very young readers, these tales are short, funny, and entertaining. . . . Fourteen full-page black-and-white pencil drawings illustrate some of the more dramatic moments in the stories." SLJ

Includes bibliography

Sawyer, Ruth, 1880-1970

Journey cake, ho! illustrated by Robert McCloskey. Viking 1953 45p il o.p.; Puffin Bks. paperback available $3.95 (k-2) **398.2**

1. Folklore
ISBN 0-14-050275-0 (pa) LC 53-3366

A Caldecott Medal honor book, 1954

Sawyer, Ruth, 1880-1970—*Continued*

Johnny is leaving the farm because of hard times when his Journey Cake leads him on a merry chase that results in a farm yard full of animals and the family all together again

Johnny is "drawn with that rollicking bold humor that has made Mr. McCloskey popular. The story is rather odd, but probably good fun for small children who will laugh at a cake that rolls and sings a repeated verse." N Y Her Trib Books

Schwartz, Alvin, 1927-

All of our noses are here, and other noodle tales; retold by Alvin Schwartz; pictures by Karen Ann Weinhaus. Harper & Row 1985 64p il lib bdg $11.89; pa $3.50 (1-3) **398.2**

1. Folklore 2. Wit and humor

ISBN 0-06-025288-X (lib bdg); 0-06-444108-3 (pa) LC 84-48330

"An I can read book"

This companion volume to: There is a carrot in my ear, and other noodle tales, entered below, contains additional stories about members of the Brown family

"The illustrations show them looking very much like mice and always smiling and cheerful. Cousins, no doubt, to the Stupids, the family is bound to be as appealing to young readers. With a list of sources." Horn Book

I saw you in the bathtub, and other folk rhymes; collected by Alvin Schwartz; pictures by Syd Hoff. Harper & Row 1989 64p il $10.95; lib bdg $10.89 (1-3) **398.2**

1. Folklore

ISBN 0-06-025298-7; 0-06-025299-5 (lib bdg) LC 88-16111

"An I can read book"

Presents an illustrated collection of traditional folk rhymes, some composed by children

"Kids may be surprised to see their recess yells on the printed page but will relish the confirmation of significance. Hoff's full-color cartoons interpret the rhymes literally, an approach that leads to some pretty surreal results." Bull Cent Child Books

In a dark, dark room, and other scary stories; retold by Alvin Schwartz; illustrated by Dirk Zimmer. Harper & Row 1984 63p il $10.95; lib bdg $10.81 (k-3) **398.2**

1. Folklore 2. Ghosts—Fiction 3. Horror—Fiction

ISBN 0-06-025271-5; 0-06-025274-X (lib bdg) LC 83-47699

"An I can read book"

This is a collection of "seven traditional tales from around the world retold in simple yet effective language. . . . The chill here springs from suspense, an eerie setting or a ghostly surprise, rather than from blood and gore. Though pared down somewhat from longer versions, the stories retain their genuine creepiness. . . . The colorfully dark illustrations are sinister without being gruesome and add a comic touch." SLJ

More scary stories to tell in the dark; collected & retold from folklore by Alvin Schwartz; drawings by Stephen Gammell. Lippincott 1984 100p il $12.95; lib bdg $12.89; HarperCollins Pubs. pa $3.50 (4 and up) **398.2**

1. Folklore—United States 2. Ghosts—Fiction 3. Horror—Fiction

ISBN 0-397-32081-7; 0-397-32082-5 (lib bdg); 0-06-440177-4 (pa) LC 83-49494

This companion volume to the title entered below contains additional stories of ghosts, murders, graveyards and other horrors

"The stories are all short and lively, very tellable, and greatly enhanced by the gray, ghoulish, horrifying illustrations of dismembered bodies, hideous creatures, and mysterious lights. A fine compendium by a well-known collector, easily accessible to young readers." Horn Book

Includes bibliography

Scary stories to tell in the dark; collected from American folklore by Alvin Schwartz; with drawings by Stephen Gammell. Lippincott 1981 111p il $12.95; lib bdg $12.89; HarperCollins Pubs. pa $3.95 (4 and up) **398.2**

1. Folklore—United States 2. Ghosts—Fiction

ISBN 0-397-31926-6; 0-397-31927-4 (lib bdg); 0-06-440170-7 (pa) LC 80-8728

"A collection of scary, semi-scary, and humorous stories about ghosts and witches collected from American folklore. Most of the stories (poems and songs also) are very short and range from the traditional to the modern. The author includes suggestions on how to tell scary stories effectively." Bull Cent Child Books

"The scholarship in the source notes and bibliography will be useful to serious literature students." SLJ

There is a carrot in my ear, and other noodle tales; retold by Alvin Schwartz; pictures by Karen Ann Weinhaus. Harper & Row 1982 64p il $10.95; lib bdg $10.89; pa $3.50 (1-3) **398.2**

1. Folklore 2. Wit and humor

ISBN 0-06-025233-2; 0-06-025234-0 (lib bdg); 0-06-444103-2 (pa) LC 80-8442

"An I can read book"

This "is a collection of six stories from sources . . . as diverse as American 'Little Moron' stories, ancient Greek tales and vaudeville pieces. Explaining in his foreword that a 'noodle is a silly person,' reteller Alvin Schwartz goes on to introduce the noodly Brown family and reveal their various foibles. . . . Most of the stories don't appear in other beginning noodle collections and will provide laughs for readers who catch the puns and absurdities the stories hinge on. The drawings by Karen Ann Weinhaus . . . show funny, pointy-proboscised folk blissfully unaware of their own goofiness." SLJ

Schwartz, Alvin, 1927-—*Continued*

Whoppers; tall tales and other lies; collected from American folklore by Alvin Schwartz; illustrated by Glen Rounds. Lippincott 1975 127p il $11.25; HarperCollins Pubs. pa $3.95 (4 and up) **398.2**

1. Folklore—United States 2. Tall tales
ISBN 0-397-31575-9; 0-06-446091-6 (pa)

LC 74-32024

Excerpted and adapted from a variety of sources, this is an "assemblage of tall tales and whoppers from American folklore. They range from brief one-liners, some of which are strung into tall stories, to rambling discourses on preposterous turns of events." Booklist

"Fans of Pecos Bill, Paul Bunyan, and other heroes of tall tales should appreciate this sampling . . . and Rounds' scribbly sketches add a quiet folksy humor of their own." SLJ

Scieszka, Jon

The true story of the three little pigs; pictures by Lane Smith. Viking Kestrel 1989 unp il $13.95 (k-3) **398.2**

1. Folklore—Great Britain 2. Pigs—Fiction 3. Wolves—Fiction
ISBN 0-670-82759-2 LC 89-8953

The wolf gives his own outlandish version of what really happened when he tangled with the three little pigs

"The 'excited and funky' illustrations match the hilarious revisionist text to a standard story." N Y Times Book Rev

Seeger, Pete

Abiyoyo; based on a South African lullaby and folk story; text by Pete Seeger; illustrations by Michael Hays. Macmillan 1986 unp il $15.95 (k-2) **398.2**

1. Folklore—South Africa 2. Magicians—Fiction 3. Giants—Fiction
ISBN 0-02-781490-4 LC 85-15341

Banished from the town for making mischief, a little boy and his father are welcomed back when they find a way to make the dreaded giant Abiyoyo disappear

"Told in the familiar Seeger style, with brief musical phrases of the one-word song incorporated in the text and printed complete at the end, and with illustrations full of light and color, this rendering of a South African tale is a pleasure. The giant is imposing but not too scary for the youngest listener leaning over the book while a parent tells the story." N Y Times Book Rev

Seuling, Barbara

The teeny tiny woman; an old English ghost tale; retold and illustrated by Barbara Seuling. Viking 1976 unp il o.p.; Puffin Bks. paperback available $3.95 (k-2) **398.2**

1. Folklore—Great Britain 2. Ghosts—Fiction
ISBN 0-14-050266-1 (pa) LC 75-22160

"A retelling of the old story about a teeny tiny woman who finds a bone, takes it home for soup, and is finally driven to give it up by a ghostly voice in the night. Circular drawings pencilled in soft grey and lavender humorously interpret the story with details of the teeny tiny house and the teeny tiny woman's companionable duck. A simple but engaging contribution to the picture-folklore shelf." Booklist

Shannon, George, 1952-

Stories to solve; folktales from around the world told by George Shannon; illustrated by Peter Sis. Greenwillow Bks. 1985 55p il $11.95; lib bdg $11.88 (3 and up) **398.2**

1. Folklore 2. Riddles
ISBN 0-688-04303-8; 0-688-04304-6 (lib bdg)

LC 84-18656

"Each of these 14 delightful folktales is a short puzzle to be solved through cleverness, common sense or careful observations of details in the text. . . . Storytellers, scout leaders, teachers and librarians will welcome this collection of short folktales. It will attract readers because of its brevity and humor and because of the intrigue of solving the puzzles. Sis' pointillistic pen-and-ink drawings illustrate each puzzle, and sometimes clarify the solutions." SLJ

Includes bibliographic references

Sherlock, Sir Philip Manderson, 1902-

Anansi, the spider man; Jamaican folk tales; told by Philip M. Sherlock; illustrated by Marcia Brown. Crowell 1954 112p il $14.95 (4-6) **398.2**

1. Folklore—Jamaica
ISBN 0-690-08905-8 LC 54-5619

Fifteen West Indian stories about the Caribbean folk hero Anansi "who was a man when things went well, but who became a spider when he was in great danger. . . . The author tells the stories simply and directly, with respect of their 'folk' quality. Line illustrations by Marcia Brown are excellent, and have caught the gaiety of the tales." Ont Libr Rev

West Indian folk-tales; retold by Philip Sherlock; illustrated by Joan Kiddell-Monroe. Oxford Univ. Press 1966 151p il (Oxford myths and legends) $14.95; pa $6.95 (4-6) **398.2**

1. Folklore—West Indies
ISBN 0-19-274116-0; 0-19-274127-6 (pa)

LC 66-701268

"Twenty-one tales of the ancient peoples, the Caribs and the Arawaks, are intertwined here with the folklore of the African slaves. Simply structured and ably retold, the collection includes the familiar 'pourquoi' (why) stories, several tales of Anansi, the spiderman, and other legends that recount the trials and successes of the West Indian birds and animals." SLJ

Sherman, Josepha

Vassilisa the wise; a tale of medieval Russia; retold by Josepha Sherman; illustrated by Daniel San Souci. Harcourt Brace Jovanovich 1988 unp il lib bdg $14.95 (2-4) **398.2**

1. Folklore—Soviet Union
ISBN 0-15-293240-2 LC 87-8563

A clever and beautiful woman uses her wits to get her husband out of Prince Vladimir's prison

"San Souci's handsome watercolor illustrations are elegant and dynamic, large and authoritative, and reflect the drama and the setting." Horn Book

Shetterly, Susan Hand, 1942-

The dwarf-wizard of Uxmal; told by Susan Hand Shetterly; illustrated by Robert Shetterly. Atheneum Pubs. 1990 unp il $13.95 (3-5) **398.2**

1. Mayas—Legends 2. Folklore—Mexico
ISBN 0-689-31455-8 LC 89-32864

This is a Mayan legend from the Mexican Yucatan. With the magical aid of the old woman who hatched him from an egg, the diminutive Tol proves himself greater than the ruler of the city of Uxmal and takes his place as leader of the people

"The expressiveness of the writing is matched by the boldly colored paintings, which boast a good mix of realistic and exaggerated details. The artist captures the lush atmosphere of the Mayan landscape, using the tortoise and snake motifs (found on Uxmal buildings today) and depicting the Temple of the Dwarf with great acumen." Booklist

Shub, Elizabeth

Clever Kate; adapted from a story by the Brothers Grimm; pictures by Anita Lobel. Macmillan 1973 62p il hardcover o.p. paperback available $3.95 (1-3) **398.2**

1. Folklore—Germany
ISBN 0-689-710771 (pa) LC 72-81063

"Ready-to-read"

Because of her naîveté Kate both loses her husband's treasure and gains it back again

"A credit to the easy-to-read genre, this retains the absurdity of the original folklore in a new framework of simple but uncondescending short sentences. . . . Every page has either a floral-framed drawing on it or a full-page illustration opposite, providing plenty of visual action in tones of blue, green, and yellow." Booklist

Shulevitz, Uri, 1935-

The treasure. Farrar, Straus & Giroux 1978 unp il $13.95; pa $3.95 (k-3) **398.2**

1. Folklore
ISBN 0-374-37740-5; 0-374-47955-0 (pa) LC 78-12952

A Caldecott Medal honor book, 1980

This is the "tale of a poor man, here named Isaac, who three times dreams of a voice telling him to go to the capital and look for a treasure under the bridge by the palace. When he gets to the capital, the captain of the guard tells him of his dream: a treasure is buried under the stove of a man named Isaac back in Isaac's home city. So Isaac returns home, finds the treasure under his own stove, and lives happily ever after." SLJ

"Although the story is known in many cultures the retelling suggests the Hassidic tradition. . . . The eastern European influence is extended in the illustrations." Horn Book

Siberell, Anne

Whale in the sky. Dutton 1982 unp il $12.95; pa $3.95 (k-3) **398.2**

1. Indians of North America—Legends 2. Totems and totemism—Fiction 3. Animals—Fiction
ISBN 0-525-44021-6; 0-525-44197-2 (pa) LC 82-2483

"A Unicorn book"

"The author-artist's block prints (and the story she tells) are based on the carvings of totem poles of the Northwest Coast Indians. . . . Thunderbird punishes Whale because he is chasing salmon in the river, and elicits a promise the Whale will stay in the sea." Bull Cent Child Books

"The artist has made pictures of considerable beauty and strength, adding atmosphere and dramatic emphasis to the brief story told in lean narrative prose." Horn Book

Simon, Solomon, 1895-1970

More wise men of Helm and their merry tales; edited by Hannah Grad Goodman; illustrated by Stephen Kraft. Behrman House 1965 119p il pa $6.50 (4 and up) **398.2**

1. Jews—Folklore 2. Folklore—Poland
ISBN 0-87441-126-2 (pa) LC 65-14594

Companion volume: Wise men of Helm available in paperback for $6.50 (ISBN 0-87441-125-4)

"This second collection of tales about the mythical Jewish community in Poland is great fun to read." Libr J

Singer, Isaac Bashevis, 1904-1991

The golem; illustrations by Uri Shulevitz. Farrar, Straus & Giroux 1982 83p il $12.95 (5 and up) **398.2**

1. Legends, Jewish
ISBN 0-374-32741-6 LC 82-12028

"A masterful retelling of the legend of the golem, the huge clay man created by a rabbi of Prague to help one of his people unjustly accused of a crime. Singer invests the dramatic story with color and compassion. . . . The grave, dramatic Shulevitz pictures, soft in execution and strong in composition, and admirably suited to the stark strength of the legend so vividly retold by the author." Bull Cent Child Books

Mazel and Shlimazel; or, The milk of a lioness; pictures by Margot Zemach; translated from the Yiddish by the author and Elizabeth Shub. Farrar, Straus & Giroux 1967 42p il $14.95 (2-5) **398.2**

1. Jews—Folklore
ISBN 0-374-34884-7 LC 67-19887

Singer, Isaac Bashevis, 1904-1991 — *Continued*

"An Ariel book"

The happiness of Tam, a poor peasant lad, and lovely Crown Princess Nesika depends upon the outcome of a battle of wits between Mazel, the spirit of good luck, and Shlimazel, the spirit of bad luck

This story "is based on a Jewish folk tale. . . . The way Shlimazel contrives to win the wager is a witty surprise, and how, moreover, the story-teller arranges to have the story end happily after all is also ingenious and satisfying. The colored illustrations . . . have the flavor of folk art but, like the text, are anything but artless." New Yorker

When Shlemiel went to Warsaw & other stories; pictures by Margot Zemach; translated by the author and Elizabeth Shub. Farrar, Straus & Giroux 1968 115p il $13.95; pa $3.45 (4 and up) **398.2**

1. Jews—Folklore
ISBN 0-374-38316-2; 0-374-48365-5 (pa) LC 68-30932

A Newbery Award honor book, 1969

"An Ariel book"

"A fine collection of five retold traditional Yiddish folk tales and three original stories. . . . The original stories—'Tsirtsur and Peziza,' 'Rabbi Leib and the Witch Cunegunde,' and 'Menaseh's Dream'—blend well with the reworked tales, and Margot Zemach's delightful black-and-white illustrations fittingly capture moods and protagonists." SLJ

Zlateh the goat, and other stories; pictures by Maurice Sendak; translated from the Yiddish by the author and Elizabeth Shub. Harper & Row 1966 90p il $15.95; lib bdg $15.89; pa $4.95 (4 and up) **398.2**

1. Jews—Folklore
ISBN 0-06-025698-2; 0-06-025699-0 (lib bdg); 0-06-440147-2 (pa) LC 66-8114

A Newbery Award honor book, 1967

"Seven tales drawn from middle-European Jewish village life, with illustrations which extend the humor and subtlety of the situations." Hodges. Books for Elem Sch Libr

Sleeping beauty & other favourite fairy tales; chosen and translated by Angela Carter; illustrated by Michael Foreman. Schocken Bks. 1984 c1982 128p il $12.95 (3 and up) **398.2**

1. Folklore—France 2. Fairy tales
ISBN 0-8052-3921-9 LC 84-1451

First published 1982 in the United Kingdom

"Ten Perrault tales, complete with morals, and two by Madame LePrince de Beaumont ('Beauty and the Beast' and 'Sweetheart') constitute this . . . collection of French fairy tales." Booklist

"Carter's untangled English couple with Foreman's dark illuminations help readers to pierce to the hearts of these tales. . . . Foreman's full-color illustrations enchance the tales' energy." SLJ

Snyder, Dianne

The boy of the three-year nap; illustrated by Allen Say. Houghton Mifflin 1988 32p il $14.95 (1-3) **398.2**

1. Folklore—Japan
ISBN 0-395-44090-4 LC 87-30674

A Caldecott Medal honor book, 1989

"Japan's contribution to the trickster folktale, in which a lazy son cons a rich man, only to be outsmarted by his own, even trickier mother. Lilting prose and shimmering illustrations combine in perfect harmony." SLJ

Spagnoli, Cathy

Nine-in-one, Grr! Grr! a folktale from the Hmong people of Laos; told by Blia Xiong; adapted by Cathy Spagnoli; illustrated by Nancy Hom. Children's Bk. Press 1989 30p il $12.95 (k-2) **398.2**

1. Folklore—Laos 2. Tigers—Fiction
ISBN 0-89239-048-4 LC 89-9891

When the great god Shao promises Tiger nine cubs each year, Bird comes up with a clever trick to prevent the land from being overrun by tigers

"Simply and eloquently told, this *pourquoi* tale from a minority Laotian culture is boldly illustrated in a style adapted from the multi-imaged embroidered story cloths of the Hmong people. Its rhythmic text and appealing, brightly colored pictures make it a good choice for preschool story hours." Booklist

Stamm, Claus

Three strong women; a tall tale from Japan; pictures by Jean and Mou-sien Tseng. Viking 1990 unp il $12.95 (k-3) **398.2**

1. Folklore—Japan 2. Tall tales
ISBN 0-670-83323-1 LC 89-48758

A newly illustrated edition of the title first published 1962

"Forever-Mountain is a famous wrestler, smug and rather conceited—until he meets Maru-me. Along with her mother and grandmother, she shows him what real strength is. Under their tutelage, he gains not only physical prowess, but the humility of the truly strong. This version of the Japanese tall tale is filled with sly humor and witty exaggeration. The Tsengs' illustrations match the text perfectly; the glowing watercolors evoke a rural Japan of long ago. . . . With its unconventional approach to issues of gender, size, strength, and power, this is a robust addition to any folktale collection." SLJ

Stephens, James, 1882-1950

Irish fairy tales; illustrated by Arthur Rackham. Macmillan 1968 c1920 318p il $12.95 (6 and up) **398.2**

1. Folklore—Ireland 2. Legends—Ireland 3. Fairy tales
ISBN 0-02-788000-1

First published 1920

The collection includes ten hero tales and legends from Ireland. Among them are tales of Fionn and Fianna, The Carl of the Drab Coat, and Becuma

"There is much good narrative, much humour, and,

Stephens, James, 1882-1950—*Continued*
usually, unstrained simplicity in the book, but above all there are passages of enchanting beauty." Times Lit Suppl

Steptoe, John, 1950-1989

Mufaro's beautiful daughters; an African tale. Lothrop, Lee & Shepard Bks. 1987 unp il $13.95; lib bdg $13.88 (k-3) **398.2**

1. Folklore—Africa
ISBN 0-688-04045-4; 0-688-04046-2 (lib bdg) LC 84-7158

A Caldecott Medal honor book, 1988; Coretta Scott King award for illustration, 1988

Mufaro's two beautiful daughters, one bad-tempered, one kind and sweet, go before the king, who is choosing a wife

"The pace of the text matches the rhythm of the illustrations—both move in dramatic unity to the climax. By changing perspective the artist not only captures the lush, rich background but also the personalities of the characters with revealing studies of their faces." Horn Book

The story of Jumping Mouse; a native American legend; retold and illustrated by John Steptoe. Lothrop, Lee & Shepard Bks. 1984 unp il $12.50; lib bdg $12.88; pa $4.95 (1-3) **398.2**

1. Indians of North America—Legends
ISBN 0-688-01902-1; 0-688-01903-X (lib bdg); 0-688-08740-X (pa) LC 82-14848

A Caldecott Medal honor book, 1985

"By keeping hope alive within himself, a mouse is successful in his quest for the far-off land. Steptoe's retelling of an unattributed tribal legend is exquisite in its use of language and in its expansive drawings which employ dazzling subtleties of light and shadow." SLJ

Stevens, Janet

How the Manx cat lost its tail; retold and illustrated by Janet Stevens. Harcourt Brace Jovanovich 1989 unp il $14.95 (k-2) **398.2**

1. Folklore 2. Cats—Fiction
ISBN 0-15-236765-9 LC 88-37952

A retelling of how the Manx cat lost its tail in the door of Noah's ark

"Stephens' expansive watercolors create dramatic tension by juxtaposing the growing storm with the anxious and skittish expressions of the animals. A different angle on an old familiar story." SLJ

The town mouse and the country mouse; an Aesop fable; adapted and illustrated by Janet Stevens. Holiday House 1987 unp il $13.95; pa $5.95 (k-2) **398.2**

1. Mice—Fiction 2. Fables
ISBN 0-8234-0633-4; 0-8234-0733-0 (pa) LC 86-14276

A town mouse and a country mouse exchange visits and discover each is suited to his or her own home

"In her usual sassy fashion, Stevens takes a classic tale . . . and turns it into a comic romp. . . . The cheerful watercolors showcase not only Stevens' humor, but also her strong sense of color and composition. . . . Text and graphics are in harmony, and the large-scale drawings will make this tale a welcome read-aloud in story hours." Booklist

Sutcliff, Rosemary, 1920-

The light beyond the forest; the quest for the Holy Grail; decorations by Shirley Felts. Dutton 1980 143p $13.95 (4 and up) **398.2**

1. Arthur, King 2. Grail—Fiction 3. Arthurian romances
ISBN 0-525-33665-6 LC 79-23396

First published 1979 in the United Kingdom

This is a retelling of the adventures of King Arthur's knights as they search for the Holy Grail. "After a vision of the Cup from the Last Supper appears, Sir Lancelot, Sir Galahad, Sir Bors, and Sir Percival quit Camelot to look for the Grail, knowing that only the world's most perfect knight will succeed. The individual adventures, which take on a loftier meaning as the journeys also become the knights' personal searches for God, will be most appreciated by special readers interested in King Arthur and his time." Booklist

Followed by: The sword and the circle, entered below

The road to Camlann; decorations by Shirley Felts. Dutton 1982 142p $14.95 (4 and up) **398.2**

1. Arthur, King 2. Arthurian romances
ISBN 0-525-44018-6 LC 82-9481

First published 1981 in the United Kingdom

"This book completes Rosemary Sutcliff's Arthurian trilogy, begun with 'The Light Beyond the Forest' [entered above] and 'The Sword and the Circle' [entered below]. Here Sutcliff describes the events from the coming of Mordred to the death of Lancelot. The title refers to The Last Battle, in which Arthur and his civilization perish. Sutcliff writes with her usual economy and rich prose, with a touch of archaic diction in the speeches. . . . Other than Malory, I can think of no better introduction to the whole sweep of Arthurian stories and values." SLJ

The sword and the circle; King Arthur and the Knights of the Round Table. Dutton 1981 260p $13.95 (4 and up) **398.2**

1. Arthur, King 2. Arthurian romances
ISBN 0-525-40585-2 LC 81-9759

The second volume in the author's Arthurian trilogy, begun with: The light beyond the forest, entered above. The events in this volume precede those in the earlier volume

"The author has brought together thirteen stories associated with the Arthurian cycle, beginning with 'The Coming of Arthur' and concluding not with the passing of Arthur but with 'The Coming of Perceval.' Although she has relied on Malory's 'Morte d'Arthur' for most of her material, she has drawn upon other medieval sources for some of her best storytelling: For example 'Sir Gawain and the Green Knight' comes from a Middle English poem, and the twenty-nine-page 'Tristan and

Sutcliff, Rosemary, 1920-—*Continued*
Iseult' is indebted to Godfrey of Strasburg's version." Horn Book

Followed by: The road to Camlann, entered above

Tadjo, Véronique, 1955-
Lord of the dance; an African retelling by Véronique Tadjo. Lippincott 1989 unp il $12.95; lib bdg $12.89 (1-3) **398.2**

1. Folklore—Ivory Coast
ISBN 0-397-32351-4; 0-397-32352-2 (lib bdg) LC 89-2785

Poetically retells the story of the Senufo people of Ivory Coast

"The narrative is poetically rhythmic without becoming singsong or forced, the art leaps with color and strikingly balanced shapes. The concept itself is lyrical: the Mask leaves the spirit world and comes among men and women to lead their songs of joy and sadness. Even when traditions are buried in concrete and steel, the voice survives. Folk art motifs border many of the pictures, and a note on the cultural life of the Senufo people, as well as on Tadjo's collection and adaptation of the song, provide valuable context." Bull Cent Child Books

The **Tall** book of nursery tales; pictures by Feodor Rojankovsky. Artists & Writers Guild 1944 120p il $9.95 (k-2) **398.2**

1. Folklore 2. Fairy tales
ISBN 0-06-025065-8 LC 44-3881

A collection of 24 well-known traditional tales such as Little Red Riding Hood, The three bears, The gingerbread boy, The ugly duckling, etc.

"Its long, narrow shape not only makes library shelving difficult but some kindergarten teachers feel it also makes handling itself a problem as far as small children are concerned. However, the many, many illustrations—both colored and black and white—are delightful and the stories themselves are the best-known versions with only here and there a milder rendering." Libr J

Te Kanawa, Kiri
Land of the long white cloud; Maori myths, tales and legends; illustrated by Michael Foreman. Arcade Pub. 1990 118p il $16.95 (3-6) **398.2**

1. Maoris—Folklore
ISBN 1-55970-046-7 LC 89-45534

"Opera singer Dame Kiri Te Kanawa retells the Maori folktales she remembers from her childhood in New Zealand." Booklist

"Lively and full of action, adventure, and magic, the collection is well balanced with myths, hero legends, fairy tales, and *pourquoi* stories. . . . Jewel-toned watercolor illustrations capture the vibrant quality of the stories and convey the changing moods of sea and sky. This book is a rich source of Pacific island material." SLJ

Terada, Alice M.
Under the starfruit tree; folktales from Vietnam; told by Alice M. Terada; illustrations by Janet Larsen; introduction and notes by Mary C. Austin. University of Hawaii Press 1989 136p il $15.95 (4-6) **398.2**

1. Folklore—Vietnam
ISBN 0-8248-1252-2 LC 89-5123

"A Kolowalu book"

"Twenty-seven tales culled from North and South Vietnam and translated by native speakers are grouped in four sections: foibles and quirks; tales from the lowlands and the highlands; the spirit world; and food, love and laughter. . . . Each narration is followed by an afterword that . . . reveals customs, beliefs and values." Publ Wkly

"Although the book's format is not particularly attractive, these 27 stories from Vietnam will certainly find a place on library shelves. . . . Occasional black-and-white drawings add some visual interest." Booklist

Includes bibliography

Timpanelli, Gioia
Tales from the roof of the world; folktales of Tibet; retold by Gioia Timpanelli; illustrated by Elizabeth Kelly Lockwood. Viking 1984 53p il $11.95 (4-6) **398.2**

1. Folklore—Tibet (China)
ISBN 0-670-71249-3 LC 83-19826

"Four folktales from Tibetan storytellers make up this slender . . . volume. In three stories, passive central characters experience misfortune but ultimately enjoy honor and wealth; the narrative that will most appeal to children relates how a merchant employs a combination of wits and good luck to establish his reputation as a clairvoyant and marry a princess. Crisply stylized, decorative pen-and-ink borders surround each page of text, incorporating images from the stories along with eight Buddhist symbols that are interpreted in an appendix." Booklist

Tomie dePaola's Favorite nursery tales. Putnam 1986 127p il $17.95 (k-3) **398.2**

1. Folklore 2. Fables
ISBN 0-399-21319-8 LC 85-28302

"The book begins, appropriately enough, with a verse about reading picture books from Stevenson's *Child's Garden of Verses*, followed by Longfellow's 'Children's Hour.' The story selections—'Johnny Cake,' 'The Little Red Hen,' Rumpelstiltskin, 'The Princess and the Pea,' 'The Tortoise and the Hare,' 'The House on the Hill,' and 22 more." Booklist

"DePaola's droll, witty, and very funny illustrations capture the essence of each story from a child's point of view. It's unlikely that any adult will get away with reading just one of these selections for a bedtime story. . . . The beautiful layout of these pages, in which the print and pictures are perfectly at ease with one another, invites confident new readers as well as adults for reading aloud." SLJ

Torre, Betty L.

The luminous pearl; a Chinese folktale; retold by Betty L. Torre; illustrated by Carol Inouye. Orchard Bks. 1990 unp il $14.95; lib bdg $14.99 (k-3) **398.2**

1. Folklore—China
ISBN 0-531-05890-5; 0-531-08490-6 (lib bdg) LC 89-70999

"Adapted from 'The pearl that shone by night' from Favorite folktales of China, translated by John Minford." Verso of title page

Two brothers go on a quest for a luminous pearl in order to win the Dragon King's beautiful daughter for a wife

"In straightforward prose, the writer has made the folktale live. Each of the detailed and vibrant illustrations is spread over a double page and effectively evokes the Chinese folktale world." Child Book Rev Serv

Tresselt, Alvin R.

The mitten; an old Ukrainian folktale; retold by Alvin Tresselt; illustrated by Yaroslava; adapted from the version by E. Rachev. Lothrop, Lee & Shepard Bks. 1964 unp il lib bdg $12.88; Mulberry Bks. pa $4.95 (k-2) **398.2**

1. Folklore—Ukraine 2. Animals—Fiction
ISBN 0-688-51053-1 (lib bdg); 0-688-09238-1 (pa) LC 64-14436

"On the coldest day of the year a little Ukrainian boy loses his fur-lined mitten, which becomes so overcrowded with animals seeking a snug shelter that it finally bursts. Brightly colored pictures show the animals dressed in typical Ukrainian costumes." Hodges. Books for Elem Sch Libr

Uchida, Yoshiko

The magic listening cap; more folk tales from Japan; retold and illustrated by Yoshiko Uchida. Harcourt Brace Jovanovich 1955 146p il o.p.; Creative Arts paperback available $7.95 (3-6) **398.2**

1. Folklore—Japan 2. Fairy tales
ISBN 0-88739-016-1 (pa) LC 55-5240

These fourteen Japanese folk tales are retold "with charm and humor and display those universal elements of the folk lore that will give them wide appeal. Several of the stories have counterparts in other folk lore. The stories are suitable for reading aloud, or for telling, and will also be of interest to students of comparative folk lore." Bull Cent Child Books

Includes glossary

The two foolish cats; suggested by a Japanese folktale; illustrated by Margot Zemach. Margaret K. McElderry Bks. 1987 unp il $13.95 (k-3) **398.2**

1. Folklore—Japan 2. Cats—Fiction
ISBN 0-689-50397-0 LC 86-12660

"Big Daizo and Little Suki are cats who live at the edge of a pine forest in Japan. One day, having had no luck hunting or fishing for food, they come upon two rice cakes in the tall reeds. Their foolish quarrel over the larger rice cake brings them to the wise monkey, who solves their problem in an unexpected way." Publisher's note

"Zemach's drawings, which have so expertly evoked Eastern Europe, here have a striking Oriental feel as delicate watercolors and bold black brush strokes flow over two-page spreads. A deft combination of story and pictures." Booklist

Vuong, Lynette Dyer, 1938-

The brocaded slipper, and other Vietnamese tales; illustrations by Vo-Dinh Mai. HarperCollins Pubs. 1982 111p il $13.95 (3-6) **398.2**

1. Folklore—Vietnam 2. Fairy tales
ISBN 0-201-08088-5 LC 81-19139

First published by Addison-Wesley

"These five Vietnamese fairy tales have motifs that will be familiar to Western readers. The title story is a 'Cinderella' variant. 'Little Finger of the Watermelon Patch' is similar to 'Thumbelina.' 'The Fairy Grotto,' in which a man enters fairyland and then comes back to a world that is 300 years older, has a protagonist not unlike Rip van Winkle. In 'Master Frog' the frog heroine must survive in cruel and humble circumstances before she is reunited with her true love." Booklist

"The stories . . . are often more satisfyingly complex than their Western counterparts. . . . The simple, fluid ink-wash illustrations are captioned in both English and Vietnamese. An excellent and unusual addition to folklore collections." SLJ

Walker, Barbara K.

A treasury of Turkish folktales for children; retold by Barbara K. Walker. Linnet Bks. 1988 155p $17.50 (4 and up) **398.2**

1. Folklore—Turkey
ISBN 0-208-02206-6 LC 88-6859

"The 34 stories are organized into sections on animals, fables, Keloglan tales, Nasreddin Hoca tales, witch/giant/jinn/dragon tales, trickster tales, tales of fate, and stories of wish fulfillment. The tonal range offers great variety for storytelling, reading aloud, or just plain entertainment among children fond of folktales, though the format is formidable for young readers." Bull Cent Child Books

Includes glossary

Watson, Richard Jesse, 1951-

Tom Thumb; retold and illustrated by Richard Jesse Watson. Harcourt Brace Jovanovich 1989 unp il $12.95 (k-3) **398.2**

1. Folklore 2. Fairy tales
ISBN 0-15-289280-X LC 87-12045

After many adventures, a tiny boy, no bigger than his father's thumb, earns a place as the smallest Knight of the Round Table

"Although it is not stated, this is a loose adaptation of an English variant of the tale. . . . However, Watson's heroic ending, in which Tom Thumb replaces the giant's beloved broken shell, is not mentioned in other variants available. The writing borders on the flowery, but is

Watson, Richard Jesse, 1951-—*Continued*
quite readable. The realistic, microscopically detailed tempera and watercolor illustrations are particularly suitable for this tale. . . . The subject and these illustrations will ensure this book's popularity with young readers and their parents." SLJ

The **Whistling** skeleton; American Indian tales of the supernatural; collected by George Bird Grinnell; edited by John Bierhorst; illustrated by Robert Andrew Parker. Four Winds Press 1982 110p il $12.95 (3-6) **398.2**

1. Indians of North America—Legends
ISBN 0-590-07801-1 LC 81-69517

A collection of nine legends from "the three tribes Grinnell knew best: The Pawnee, the Blackfeet, and the Cheyenne—nomadic, warlike peoples. The tales deal with ghosts, talking animals, magic, prophecy, transformation, and resurrection." Horn Book

"The editorial preface is lengthy and informative, giving good background information about the Plains Indians, including information on the tellers whose stories Grinnell collected in the late nineteenth century. The stories are told in a rather flat, straightforward style; each incorporates some aspect of the supernatural." Bull Cent Child Books

Includes glossary and bibliography

Wildsmith, Brian, 1930-

The hare and the tortoise; based on the fable by La Fontaine. Oxford Univ. Press 1966 unp il $12.95; pa $4.95 (k-2) **398.2**

1. Fables 2. Rabbits—Fiction 3. Turtles—Fiction
ISBN 0-19-279625-9; 0-19-272126-7 (pa)

"Wildsmith tells, simply and eloquently, his version of the La Fontaine fable about the slow and steady tortoise who wins the race from the quick and careless hare. The paintings are astonishing creations in all the colors of the spectrum. The vistas of a countryside bursting with blooms, birds soring overhead as interested observers like the animals gathered along the route; every one of the scenes is a wonder." Publ Wkly

The miller, the boy and the donkey. Oxford Univ. Press 1969 unp il $12.95; pa $5.95 (k-2) **398.2**

1. Fables
ISBN 0-19-279652-6; 0-19-272114-3 (pa)

Adapted and illustrated by Brian Wildsmith

The miller and his son take their donkey to market to sell him. To keep him clean they decide to carry him, but a passing farmer laughs at them and they ride the donkey instead. Thus begins a series of suggestions from other people they meet as to who should ride the donkey. The poor miller is utterly confused trying to please everyone and in the end decides that next time he will only please himself

"A spirited and attractive picture book." Child Books, 1970

The rich man and the shoe-maker; a fable by La Fontaine; illustrated by Brian Wildsmith. Oxford Univ. Press 1965 unp il o.p. paperback available $5.95 (k-2) **398.2**

1. Fables
ISBN 0-19-272104-6 (pa)

This "fable—the tale of the poor but carefree shoemaker to whom sudden wealth brought only anxiety and distress—has been freely adapted into simple prose. Amplifying the story with an imaginative life of their own, the pictures are full of shapes, angles, and rhythmic patterns, while the sheer glory of dynamic color carries its own emotional impact." Horn Book

Williams-Ellis, Amabel, 1894-1984

Tales from the enchanted world; illustrated by Moira Kemp. Little, Brown 1988 c1987 195p il $17.95 (4 and up) **398.2**

1. Folklore 2. Fairy tales
ISBN 0-316-94133-6 LC 87-82561

First published 1987 in the United Kingdom with title: The enchanted world

"This collection of tales includes folk tales and legends gathered on Williams-Ellis' travels to many countries. . . . The 22 tales are told in a fashion clearly derived from the oral tradition. . . . Each tale is followed by a short statement as to origin, including, in some instances, references to further sources. The stories themselves make this a valuable work; the accompanying illustrations make it outstanding. . . . With the rich color illustrations and the humor and joy of the black-and-white sketches, each tale becomes a small picture book." SLJ

Wolkstein, Diane

The banza; a Haitian story; pictures by Marc Brown. Dial Bks. for Young Readers 1981 unp il $12.95; lib bdg $12.89; pa $4.95 (k-3) **398.2**

1. Folklore—Haiti
ISBN 0-8037-0428-3; 0-8037-0429-1 (lib bdg); 0-8037-0058-X (pa) LC 81-65845

"Cabree the goat becomes friends with a young tiger named Teegra. . . . Teegra gives Cabree a 'banza' (an old African instrument something like a banjo), which belonged to his uncle, for protection. When Cabree is surrounded by ten hungry tigers, she plays the banza, mobilizing her own resources to frighten the tigers away." Interracial Books Child Bull

"Told with rich economy, this brief tale is laced with action and humor; . . . Brown's solid, textured drawings in bright Caribbean colors are a fine extension of the text, and their size and clarity make the book excellent for sharing with groups." SLJ

The magic wings; a tale from China; illustrated by Robert Andrew Parker. Dutton 1983 unp il $10.95; pa $4.95 (2-4) **398.2**

1. Folklore—China
ISBN 0-525-44062-3 (lib bdg); 0-525-44275-8 (pa) LC 83-1611

"A Unicorn book"

Wolkstein, Diane—*Continued*

A strange event occurs across the land when a little Chinese goose girl sprinkles her shoulders with water and begins to wave her arms, believing that she will sprout wings, fly, and enjoy all the beautiful flowers of spring

"Parker's distinctive line work is so appropriate for this tale. . . . The use of color matches the use of line. The different hues have a life of their own, overlapping the object lines and building a gentle movement of color that often suggests light and shadow and at other times just animates the surface. Parker includes rich architectural detail to draw attention to the Chinese locale." Wilson Libr Bull

The Red Lion; a tale of ancient Persia; retold by Diane Wolkstein; illustrated by Ed Young. Crowell 1977 unp il lib bdg $8.61 (3-5) **398.2**

1. Folklore—Iran
ISBN 0-690-01346-9 LC 77-3963

Before he can be crowned King of Persia, Azgid must prove his courage by fighting the Red Lion

"Told in a flowing, rhythmic style, the tale is a superb addition to the storyteller's repertoire. The detailed, handsomely designed illustrations, suggestive of Persian miniatures, complement the tone and mood, but they are not smoothly integrated with the text." Horn Book

Womenfolk and fairy tales; edited by Rosemary Minard; illustrated by Suzanna Klein. Houghton Mifflin 1975 163p il $13.95 (3-6) **398.2**

1. Folklore 2. Fairy tales 3. Women—Fiction
ISBN 0-395-20276-0 LC 74-26555

This collection features stories by the Brothers Grimm, Lafcadio Hearn, Andrew Lang, Joseph Jacobs, and others

"Although the tales are available in a multitude of collections, this handsomely illustrated volume brings them together in a convenient form for those searching for feminist folklore." Horn Book

Yagawa, Sumiko

The crane wife; retold by Sumiko Yagawa; translation from the Japanese by Katherine Paterson; illustrated by Suekichi Akaba. Morrow 1981 unp il $12.95; pa $3.95 (1-3) **398.2**

1. Folklore—Japan
ISBN 0-688-00496-2; 0-688-07048-5 (pa)
LC 80-29278

Original Japanese edition, 1979

After Yohei tends a wounded crane, a beautiful young woman begs to become his wife and three times weaves for him an exquisite silken fabric on her loom

"One of Japan's best-loved folktales is given a treatment worthy of its popularity. . . . Katherine Paterson has done a fine job of translation, keeping in a few Japanese words to good effect. But it is Suekichi Akaba's illustrations that will be remembered. The muted line-and-wash drawings done on textured paper make use of traditional Japanese techniques." Booklist

The **Yellow** fairy book; edited by Andrew Lang; with numerous illustrations by H. J. Ford. Dover Publs. 1966 321p il pa $6.95 (4-6) **398.2**

1. Folklore 2. Fairy tales
ISBN 0-486-21674-8 LC 66-24132

Also available in hardcover from Smith, P. $17 (ISBN 0-8446-0758-4)

A reprint of the title first published 1894 by Longmans

A collection of more than 40 tales, including many by Andersen and the Brothers Grimm, and others from the folklore of Hungary, Russia, Poland, Iceland, Germany, France, England, and the American Indians

Yep, Laurence

The rainbow people; [retold by] Lawrence Yep; illustrated by David Wiesner. Harper & Row 1989 194p il $13.95; lib bdg $13.89 (4 and up) **398.2**

1. Folklore—China
ISBN 0-06-026760-7; 0-06-026761-5 (lib bdg)
LC 88-21203

"Twenty Chinese folktales, selected and retold by Yep from those collected in the 1930s in the Oakland Chinatown as part of a WPA project. . . . The tales, while drawn from and depicting Chinese culture, present a variety of familiar motifs and types: wizards and saints, shape changing and magical objects, pourquoi tales and lessons. An 'Afterword' provides suggestions for further reading on Chinese folktales. This is an excellent introduction to Chinese and Chinese-American folklore." SLJ

Yolen, Jane

The sleeping beauty; retold by Jane Yolen; illustrated by Ruth Sanderson. Knopf 1986 unp il $12.95 (k-2) **398.2**

1. Fairy tales
ISBN 0-394-55433-7 LC 86-45374

"An Ariel book"

Enraged at not being invited to the princess's christening, the wicked fairy casts a spell that dooms the princess to sleep for 100 years

"Yolen's graceful retelling of the Sleeping Beauty story suits the painterly yet lifelike feel of the illustrations. . . . The pictures are solemn and formal, with a brooding quality that suits the story's magical happenings. . . . This ambitious, meticulous presentation invites close inspection." Booklist

Tam Lin; an old ballad; retold by Jane Yolen and illustrated by Charles Mikolaycak. Harcourt Brace Jovanovich 1990 unp $14.95 (3-6) **398.2**

1. Folklore—Scotland 2. Fairy tales
ISBN 0-15-284261-6 LC 88-2280

In this retelling of an old Scottish ballad, a Scottish lass, on the Halloween after her sixteenth birthday, reclaims her family home which has been held for years by the fairies and at the same time effects the release of Tam Lin, a human held captive by the Queen of the Fey

Yolen, Jane—*Continued*

"Yolen's prose is both vivid and economical—it reads aloud very well, and Mikolaycak's brooding pictures swirl with motion, drama, and a compelling play of pattern and color." Booklist

Young, Ed

Lon Po Po; a Red-Riding Hood story from China; translated and illustrated by Ed Young. Philomel Bks. 1989 unp il $14.95 (1-3) **398.2**

1. Folklore—China 2. Wolves—Fiction
ISBN 0-399-21619-7 LC 88-15222

Awarded the Caldecott Medal, 1990

Three sisters staying home alone are endangered by a hungry wolf who is disguised as their grandmother

"The text possesses that matter-of-fact veracity that characterizes the best fairy tales. The watercolor and pastel pictures are remarkable: mystically beautiful in their depiction of the Chinese countryside, menacing in the exchanges with the wolf, and positively chilling in the scenes inside the house. Overall, this is an outstanding achievement that will be pored over again and again." SLJ

Zelinsky, Paul O.

Rumpelstiltskin; from the German of the Brothers Grimm; retold & illustrated by Paul O. Zelinsky. Dutton 1986 unp il lib bdg $13.95 (k-4) **398.2**

1. Folklore—Germany 2. Fairy tales
ISBN 0-525-44265-0 LC 86-4482

A Caldecott Medal honor book, 1987

"The paintings feature a realistic miller's daughter who gets unexpected help in turning her bunches of hay into shimmering gold thread from a gnomelike little man outfitted in medieval garb. Zelinsky makes thoughtful use of composition and provides strong interplay between light and shadow. His jeweled tones and precise renderings give his pictures a museum-quality look. . . . Zelinsky's story uses an . . . ending in which the little man runs off rather than tearing himself in half when his name is discovered. The tale also has subtle feminist overtones—it is the miller's daughter and a female servant who outwit Rumpelstiltskin. A lush and substantial offering." Booklist

Zemach, Harve

A penny a look; an old story retold by Harve Zemach; pictures by Margot Zemach. Farrar, Straus & Giroux 1971 unp il $14.95; pa $4.95 (k-3) **398.2**

1. Folklore
ISBN 0-374-35793-5; 0-374-45758-1 (pa)
LC 71-161373

"A redheaded rascal persuades his reluctant brother, a lazy good-for-nothing, to go with him to capture a one-eyed man to exhibit in the marketplace for a penny a look. The scheme backfires: the brothers are captured and the redheaded rascal is put in a cage while the lazy good-for-nothing is made to collect the pennies paid to see a two-eyed man with red hair." Booklist

"Delightfully droll, fancifully detailed pen-and-ink and watercolor illustrations add enormously to the wry, sly proceedings." SLJ

Zemach, Margot

The little red hen; an old story. Farrar, Straus & Giroux 1983 unp il $11.95; Penguin Bks. pa $3.50 (k-2) **398.2**

1. Folklore 2. Chickens—Fiction
ISBN 0-374-34621-6; 0-14-050567-9 (pa)
LC 83-14159

A retelling of the traditional tale about the little red hen whose lazy friends are unwilling to help her plant, harvest, or grind the wheat into flour, but all are willing to help her eat the bread that she makes from it

"The pleasingly retold, rhythmical text is appropriately extended by scrappy, cartoonish, softly glowing color illustrations. The animals are anthropomorphized just enough, and their characters perfectly caught." Child Book Rev Serv

The three little pigs; an old story. Farrar, Straus & Giroux 1989 unp il $12.95; pa $3.95 (k-2) **398.2**

1. Folklore—Great Britain 2. Pigs—Fiction 3. Wolves—Fiction
ISBN 0-374-37527-5; 0-374-47717-5 (pa)
LC 87-73488

"Michael di Capua books"

Zemach "has brought a familiar, often-told tale to life with marvelous ink-and-watercolor illustrations. Her wolf, wearing a dapper green hat and radiating slyness with every inch of his furry self, cuts a spendidly sinister figure as he attempts to wile his way to three pork chop dinners. With simple, lively sentences Zemach has related the complete story, including the apple-picking and country fair episodes." Horn Book

The three wishes; an old story. Farrar, Straus & Giroux 1986 unp il $13.95 (k-2) **398.2**

1. Folklore 2. Wishes—Fiction
ISBN 0-374-37529-1 LC 86-80956

In this "version of the familiar folk tale, a woodcutter and his wife rescue an imp in the forest. He gives them three wishes, which they foolishly manage to squander on a long chain of sausages." N Y Times Book Rev

This "is a natural for the picture-book format, and Zemach has taken full advantage of the humor with her watercolor illustrations. . . . The characters are homely and affectionate, their dog an amusing echo of their own lively expressions. This has always been a successful storytelling choice; now it will serve as a popular book to share aloud." Bull Cent Child Books

Zhang Xiu Shi
Monkey and the White Bone Demon; adapted by Zhang Xiu Shi from the novel, The pilgrimage to the West, by Wu Cheng En; illustrated by Lin Zheng [et al]; translated by Ye Ping Kuei and revised by Jill Morris. Viking 1984 unp il $10.95 (3-6) **398.2**

1. Folklore—China
ISBN 0-670-48574-8 LC 83-17670

Published in association with Liaoning Fine Arts Publishing House

"Drawn from a . . . sixteenth-century Chinese tale, this is the story of the monk Hsuan Tsang's quest for the ancient Buddhist scriptures. Monkey, his loyal disciple, leads the way, using his amazing power to defend Hsuan Tsang." Publisher's note

Zimmerman, H. Werner
Henny Penny. Scholastic 1989 28p il $8.95 (k-2) **398.2**

1. Folklore 2. Animals—Fiction
ISBN 0-590-42390-8 LC 88-22796

Henny Penny and her friends are on their way to tell the king that the sky is falling when they meet a hungry fox

"An old favorite tale is given an enthusiastic retelling in this engaging picture book. Matching the familiar story with intensely hued watercolors, Zimmermann infuses his visuals with humor. . . . The large-scale illustrations, which cover most of each page, offer eye-catching perspectives, sometimes even aerial points of view, that let readers in on the joke. The large typeface will encourage beginning readers to attempt this one solo, while younger children will relish this appealing book read aloud." Booklist

398.6 Riddles

Schwartz, Alvin, 1927-
Ten copycats in a boat, and other riddles; by Alvin Schwartz; pictures by Marc Simont. Harper & Row 1980 63p il lib bdg $9.89; pa $3.50 (1-3) **398.6**

1. Riddles 2. Folklore
ISBN 0-06-025238-3 (lib bdg); 0-06-444076-1 (pa) LC 79-2811

"An I can read book"

A collection of riddles selected from folklore around the world

"Most of Alvin Schwartz' old puzzles and jokes will be painfully familiar . . . but readers coming to [this book] for the first time will chuckle rather than groan at the wordplay and sense of the ridiculous. Marc Simont's line drawings, in curiously '50s-ish muted golds, pinks and grays, do a good job of explaining answers." SLJ

Unriddling: all sorts of riddles to puzzle your guessery; collected from American folklore by Alvin Schwartz; drawings by Sue Truesdell. Lippincott 1983 118p il lib bdg $12.89; HarperCollins Pubs. pa $4.95 (4 and up) **398.6**

1. American wit and humor 2. Riddles
ISBN 0-397-32030-2; 0-06-446057-6 (pa) LC 82-48778

"Schwartz has made this volume useful as well as entertaining by dividing his puzzles into categories, some of which depend on visual interpretation, many of which are based on traditional American humor. The quality is high, and the compiler provides answers to the riddle jokes, punctuation riddles, rebus riddles, etc., as well as information about sources, notes on the puzzles, and a fairly extensive divided bibliography." Bull Cent Child Books

Swann, Brian
A basket full of white eggs; riddle-poems; pictures by Ponder Goembel. Orchard Bks. 1988 31p il $14.95; lib bdg $14.99 (k-3) **398.6**

1. Riddles 2. Folklore
ISBN 0-531-05734-8; 0-531-08334-9 (lib bdg) LC 87-11220

"These 15 riddles are poetry and puzzle rolled into one. Nine far-flung cultural regions (Yucatan, Mexico, Alaska, Italy, Lithuania, Turkey, the Philippines, Africa, and Arabia) inspired these new rewrites of old formulas. Most reflect the natural world, especially animal life and sky events." SLJ

"This captivating collaboration teams Swann's poetically phrased riddles culled from various world cultures with Goembel's exquisite watercolor-and-color-pencil interpretations of their answers. The results are double-page spreads gloriously visualizing the terrain, climate, costume, and inhabitants indigenous to the lands of the riddles' origins while simultaneously suggesting the appropriate response to the riddles." Booklist

398.8 Rhymes and rhyming games

Anna Banana: 101 jump-rope rhymes; compiled by Joanna Cole; illustrated by Alan Tiegreen. Morrow Junior Bks. 1989 64p il $11.95; pa $6.95 (2-4) **398.8**

1. Jump rope rhymes 2. Games
ISBN 0-688-07788-9; 0-688-08809-0 (pa) LC 88-29108

An illustrated collection of jump rope rhymes arranged according to the type of jumping they are meant to accompany

"Heavily inked drawings provide cartoon-style humor; sources for jump-rope rhymes and an index of first lines are appended." Booklist

The **Annotated** Mother Goose; nursery rhymes old and new; arranged and explained by William S. Baring-Gould & Ceil Baring-Gould; illustrated by Walter Crane [et al.] with chapter decorations by E. M. Simon. Potter 1962 350p il o.p.; New Am. Lib. paperback available $10.95 **398.8**

1. Nursery rhymes
ISBN 0-452-00971-5 (pa) LC 62-21606

A fully annotated edition containing more than 1,000 rhymes—originals, variations, allusions and sources. Includes over 200 illustrations by various artists

Includes bibliography

Aylesworth, Jim, 1943-

The completed hickory dickory dock; illustrated by Eileen Christelow. Atheneum Pubs. 1990 unp il $12.95 (k-2) **398.8**

1. Nursery rhymes
ISBN 0-689-31606-2 LC 89-38484

"This extended version of the familiar nursery rhyme successfully combines simple counting concepts, the numbers one through 12 and a gentle introduction to telling time. Laced with phonetic harmonies, the additional verses have a nonsensical, bouncing quality that offer a fun-filled challenge for little ones to master. . . . The endearingly chubby mouse and his family are humorously portrayed in Christelow's colorful, frantic cartoons." Publ Wkly

The **Baby's** lap book; [compiled and illustrated by] Kay Chorao. rev ed. Dutton 1990 58p il lib bdg $13.95 (k-1) **398.8**

1. Nursery rhymes
ISBN 0-525-44604-4 LC 89-23273

First published 1977

A collection of more than fifty traditional nursery rhymes accompanied by "Chorao's soft, eminently careful pencil drawings of the characters and their situations. Innocence is all pervasive, in the alternating pastel pink and yellow pages that nicely counter the light grays of the framed drawings; in the young faces, both animal and human; and in the fullness of cozy interiors and bucolic outdoor field and forest scenes. The artist's light hand is right for her interpretation, unabashedly, uncloyingly sweet, and admirably suited to its purpose." Booklist [review of 1977 edition]

Bodecker, N. M., d. 1988

It's raining, said John Twaining; Danish nursery rhymes; translated and illustrated by N. M. Bodecker. Atheneum Pubs. 1973 unp il $6.95; pa $1.95 (k-2) **398.8**

1. Nursery rhymes
ISBN 0-689-30316-5; 0-689-70437-2 (pa) LC 72-85912

"A Margaret K. McElderry book"

These "nursery rhymes are quite different from what we are used to, but they read easily and well. Almost immediately they begin to seem familiar to us in their warmth and simplicity. . . . [The] full-color pictures set different moods to evoke the particular feelings of a rhyme, and which are always rather unexpected. . . . Here are tender, simple, silly nursery rhymes that Danish men and women have grown up with, each specially interpreted for us in an enormously varied and well-constructed picture book. They give us another slant and great pleasure." N Y Times Book Rev

The **Comic** adventures of Old Mother Hubbard and her dog; illustrated by Tomie de Paola. Harcourt Brace Jovanovich 1981 unp il $13.95; pa $3.95 (k-3) **398.8**

1. Nursery rhymes
ISBN 0-15-219541-6; 0-15-219542-4 (pa) LC 80-19270

This "version of the popular, early-nineteenth-century nursery rhyme places two familiar and beloved characters in a theatrical setting lavish with magnificent costumes and props. Spectators in box seats attending to the trials of the solicitous, beribboned dame and her mischievous poodle include Humpty Dumpty, the King and Queen of Hearts, and Little Bo Peep, while the stage curtains are decorated with scenes from the stories of still other well-known Mother Goose characters. The fun and action of the story are captured perfectly in a series of large, framed illustrations." Child Book Rev Serv

Demi, 1942-

Dragon kites and dragonflies; a collection of Chinese nursery rhymes; adapted and illustrated by Demi. Harcourt Brace Jovanovich 1986 unp il lib bdg $14.95 (k-2) **398.8**

1. Nursery rhymes
ISBN 0-15-224199-X LC 86-7637

An illustrated collection of twenty-two traditional Chinese nursery rhymes

"Sumptuously handsome illustrations in the vivid, jewel-bright colors of Chinese folk art are the setting for [these verses]. . . . Most of the poems are characterized by humor, energy, and strong rhythms. . . . With a wealth of visual details and a seamless blend of words and art, Demi has created a book to be enjoyed and treasured." Horn Book

Emberley, Barbara

Drummer Hoff; adapted by Barbara Emberley; illustrated by Ed Emberley. Simon & Schuster 1987 c1967 unp il lib bdg $12.95; pa $5.95 (k-3) **398.8**

1. Nursery rhymes
ISBN 0-671-66682-7 (lib bdg); 0-671-66745-9 (pa) LC 87-35755

Awarded the Caldecott Medal, 1968

First published 1967 by Prentice-Hall

"A cumulative folk rhyme is adapted in spirited style and illustrated with arresting black woodcuts accented with brilliant color. The characters who participate in the building and firing of a cannon—'Sergeant Crowder brought the powder, Corporal Farrell brought the barrel,' etc.—are hilariously rugged characters, while 'Drummer Hoff who fired it off stands by, deadpan, waiting to

Emberley, Barbara—*Continued*
touch off the marvelously satisfying explosion." Hodges. Books for Elem Sch Libr

Galdone, Paul, 1914-1986

The cat goes fiddle-i-fee; adapted and illustrated by Paul Galdone. Clarion Bks. 1985 unp il lib bdg $12.95 (k-1) **398.8**

1. Nursery rhymes
ISBN 0-89919-336-6 LC 85-2686

An old English rhyme names all the animals a farm boy feeds on his daily rounds

"Galdone's line-and-watercolor illustrations have all the verve and accessible good humor associated with his work, and the varied and irresistible rhythm of the verses carries the nonsense along at a good pace, enhancing its appeal to the very young. Whether told or sung, this is a diverting selection for preschool story times." Booklist

Three little kittens. Clarion Bks. 1986 unp il $13.95; pa $4.95 (k-1) **398.8**

1. Nursery rhymes 2. Cats—Poetry
ISBN 0-89919-426-5; 0-89919-796-5 (pa) LC 86-2655

Three little kittens lose, find, soil, and wash their mittens

"Galdone's characteristically exuberant pen-and-wash drawings fill these pages with feline faces, first rueful then joyful, then repentant, and finally excited about the prospects of catching 'a rat close by.' This is one of those sustained nursery rhymes that initiates youngest listeners into the concentration required for stories, and there's enough dramatic movement and color contrast in the art to hold toddlers' attention." Bull Cent Child Books

The **Glorious** Mother Goose; selected by Cooper Edens; with illustrations by the best artists from the past. Atheneum Pubs. 1988 88p il $15.95 (k-2) **398.8**

1. Nursery rhymes
ISBN 0-689-31434-5 LC 87-35491

"The 42 rhymes collected here are the tried and true; what distinguishes this compilation are the wisely chosen, diverse graphics that grace the pages. For the most part, two illustrations—varying between full color and black and white—by artists working in the late-nineteenth and early-twentieth centuries have been chosen for each rhyme, usually with the intention of depicting different interpretations. . . . The work of artists such as Randolph Caldecott, Walter Crane, Arthur Rackham, L. Leslie Brooke, E. Boyd Smith, Margaret Tarrant, William Donahey, Charles Robinson, and Fern Bisel Peat contribute to the overall fine effect." Booklist

Granfa' Grig had a pig, and other rhymes without reason from Mother Goose; compiled and illustrated by Wallace Tripp. Little, Brown 1976 96p il $17.95; pa $10.95 (k-3) **398.8**

1. Nursery rhymes
ISBN 0-316-85282-1; 0-316-85284-8 (pa) LC 76-25234

"Children of all ages and their parents will have fun exploring the jolly scrap-bag of nursery rhymes. The illustrations are full of detail; there are caricatures of famous people (Toscanini as the conductor of Old King Cole's band); contemporary allusions (the picture with 'The fox gives warning,/It's a cold frosty morning' shows the fox as a TV weatherman); and surprising interpretations (the grand old Duke of York's ten thousand men are depicted as toy soldiers). . . . The characters are frequently charming and expressive animals, and the action is portrayed vigorously. A lively, colorful book, sometimes far from traditional but always exuding an air of high good humor." Horn Book

The **Helen** Oxenbury nursery rhyme book; rhymes chosen by Brian Alderson. Morrow 1986 66p il $15 (k-2) **398.8**

1. Nursery rhymes 2. Poetry—Collected works
ISBN 0-688-06899-5 LC 86-12779

Companion volume to: The Helen Oxenbury nursery story book, entered under Oxenbury in class 398.2

An illustrated collection of approximately sixty nursery rhymes, including a mixture of popular and lesser known rhymes. Chosen from Oxenbury and Alderson's earlier collection: Cakes and custard (1975)

"Oxenbury's liking for comedy shows up clearly in her illustrations. . . . Textured, colored-pencil drawings with a soft edge to their mostly cheeky lines—are placed about the page as breaks in the text; only a few are full-page portraits or scenarios. Handsome and fun, this is a nice change of pace from more traditional samplings of Mother Goose." Booklist

If all the seas were one sea; etchings by Janina Domanska. Macmillan 1987 c1971 unp il $12.95 (k-2) **398.8**

1. Nursery rhymes
ISBN 0-02-732540-7 LC 73-146621

A Caldecott Medal honor book, 1972

A reissue of the title first published 1971

"The familiar nursery rhyme about a tree made of all the trees in the world falling into a sea made of all the seas in the world . . . is illustrated with the intricate but not too-busy geometric figures that are distinctively Domanska's style. The designs are stunning and sophisticated and color is used with enough restraint so that the two do not compete." Sutherland. The Best in Child Books

James Marshall's Mother Goose. Farrar, Straus & Giroux 1979 unp il $12.95; pa $3.95 (k-3) **398.8**

1. Nursery rhymes
ISBN 0-374-33653-9; 0-374-43723-8 (pa) LC 79-2574

"Clean, translucent pastel colors and jolly cartoon figures give this limited collection [of thirty-five rhymes] a cheerful countenance. . . . Several of the old favorites are here, plus a number of lesser known rhymes such as little Poll Parrot and Little Tommy Tittlemouse. The illustrations depict the action in a literal way, with a breezy, occasionally offbeat humor." Booklist

Jeffers, Susan
Three jovial huntsmen; adapted and illustrated by Susan Jeffers. Bradbury Press 1973 unp il o.p.; Aladdin Bks. (NY) paperback available $3.95 (k-2) **398.8**
ISBN 0-689-71309-6 (pa) LC 70-122739
A Caldecott Medal honor book, 1974
Title on cover: Mother Goose—Three jovial huntsmen
"The story involves three dimwits who hunt through a forest full of game without ever seeing any. However, viewers will have the pleasure of spotting all the nearly hidden animals the huntsmen either fail to see or mistake for something else." SLJ

The **Little** dog laughed; [illustrated by] Lucy Cousins. Dutton 1990 c1989 64p il lib bdg $14.95 (k-2) **398.8**
1. Nursery rhymes
ISBN 0-525-44573-0 LC 89-34517
First published 1989 in the United Kingdom
A collection of sixty-four nursery rhymes
"This vibrant, joyous collection of familiar and beloved nursery rhymes is certain to be solid competition for the many fine books of this genre. . . . The childlike tempra artwork is irresistible in its bright boldness and immediately captures attention. Each cleanly formatted page contains at least one rhyme. . . . The end product is creativeness at its best." SLJ

Marguerite de Angeli's book of nursery and Mother Goose rhymes. Doubleday 1954 192p il $19.95 (k-2) **398.8**
1. Nursery rhymes
ISBN 0-385-07232-5 LC 54-9838
A Caldecott Medal honor book, 1955
Marguerite de Angeli "has compiled and illustrated a beautiful edition that offers nearly 400 rhymes, all the old favorites and the less familiar, and over 250 lovely, imaginative pictures, both in full color and in black and white." Wis Libr Bull

Mother Goose; a collection of classic nursery rhymes; selected and illustrated by Michael Hague. Holt & Co. 1984 61p il $14.95 (k-2) **398.8**
1. Nursery rhymes
ISBN 0-8050-0214-6 LC 83-22559
A collection of 47 rhymes. "The selection of rhymes ranges from the familiar ('Humpty Dumpty,' 'Little Miss Muffet') to the more obscure ('Bobby Shafto's Gone to Sea')." Booklist
This is "a fine book—vibrant and alive and inviting, and it ranks right along with the greats. There are stylistic allusions to Brooke, Crane, Parrish, Rackham . . . even Hague's Cowardly Lion is here. Each image is so inviting that children and adults will want to learn the verse and hold fast to that wonderful picture." SLJ

Mother Goose; seventy-seven verses with pictures by Tasha Tudor. McKay, D. 1944 87p il $9.95 (k-2) **398.8**
1. Nursery rhymes
ISBN 0-8098-1901-5
A Caldecott Medal honor book, 1945
First published by H. Z. Walck
A lovely "Mother Goose, fresh in its interpretation both as to selection and illustration. . . . The book is smaller than usual for Mother Goose; the pictures in soft colors and in black and white are quaint and charming." Booklist

Mother Goose; nursery rhymes; illustrated by Brian Wildsmith. Oxford Univ. Press 1964 80p il $12.95; pa $7.95 (k-2) **398.8**
1. Nursery rhymes
ISBN 0-19-279611-9; 0-19-272180-1 (pa)
Has also been published with title: Brian Wildsmith's Mother Goose
These eighty-six verses "are well selected and include many quaint and lesser-known verses." Book Week
"The artist's wholly original, sophisticated yet childlike interpretation of long-familiar material is revealed in his clever composition, unconventional humor, and characteristic watercolor technique with its use of geometric patterns and brilliant chromatic modulations." Horn Book

The **Mother** Goose treasury; [illustrated by] Raymond Briggs. Coward-McCann 1966 217p il o.p.; Dell paperback available $8.95 (k-3) **398.8**
1. Nursery rhymes
ISBN 0-440-46408-0 (pa)
The versions of these 408 verses were taken from rhymes included in The Oxford Nursery rhyme book, by Iona and Peter Opie, entered below
"What is special about this edition is that it has been illustrated by Raymond Briggs, who made some 890 drawings and paintings that are a delight, especially in color." Best Sellers

Nicola Bayley's book of nursery rhymes. Knopf 1977 c1975 unp il hardcover o.p. paperback available $3.95 (k-1) **398.8**
1. Nursery rhymes
ISBN 0-679-80204-5 (pa) LC 76-57923
First published 1976 in the United Kingdom
"Nicola Bayley has created illustrations for 22 familiar nursery rhymes." West Coast Rev Books

A **Nursery** companion; provided by Iona and Peter Opie. Oxford Univ. Press 1980 128p il $25 **398.8**
1. Nursery rhymes 2. Picture books for children 3. English literature—Collected works
ISBN 0-19-212213-4 LC 82-460507
"Reproduced with their original pictures and with slightly edited texts are about two dozen 'pretty books,' publications that were extremely popular with children and adults in the early nineteenth century. Included are alphabet books like 'The History of an apple pie,' old favorites like 'The House that Jack built,' such less familiar comic adventures as 'The History of the sixteen wonderful old women,' and the cumulative rhyme 'The Gaping, wide-mouthed, waddling frog.' These booklets are so scarce today the Opies were over thirty years assembling the ones for this volume." Child Book Rev Serv
Includes bibliographic references

The **Oxford** dictionary of nursery rhymes; edited by Iona and Peter Opie. Oxford Univ. Press 1951 xxvii, 1467p il $47.50 **398.8**

1. Nursery rhymes—Dictionaries
ISBN 0-19-869111-4 LC 51-14126

"A collection of 550 rhymes, songs and riddles which, through the years, have come to be associated with childhood. While some are printed here with variations, notes on all of them list approximate age, first appearance in print, literary and historical associations, and parallels in other languages. . . . Arrangement is alphabetical according to the most important word. Nearly 100 reproductions scattered through the text show the changes in illustration of nursery literature during the past two centuries. An index of notable figures and an index of first lines make for easy reference. A comprehensive and authoritative study of the subject, this is an essential tool for all who are engaged in the study or teaching of children's literature." Wilson Libr Bull

The **Oxford** Nursery rhyme book; assembled by Iona and Peter Opie; with additional illustrations by Joan Hassall. Oxford Univ. Press 1955 223p il $29.95 **398.8**

1. Nursery rhymes
ISBN 0-19-869112-2 LC 55-12050

This collection "begins with the simplest ditties and progresses to more mature riddles, songs, and ballads. Almost every verse has a picture—small and black only, but amazingly effective. Many of the illustrations are taken from the old chapbooks and toy books. The work of Thomas and John Bewick is well represented, and the distinguished drawings of contemporary artist Joan Hassall are in keeping with their style." Sutherland. Child & Books. 6th edition

Patz, Nancy

Moses supposes his toeses are roses and 7 other silly old rhymes; retold and illustrated by Nancy Patz. Harcourt Brace Jovanovich 1983 unp il $12.95; pa $3.95 (k-2) **398.8**

1. Nursery rhymes
ISBN 0-15-255690-7; 0-15-255691-5 (pa) LC 82-3099

"Eight English and American nonsense rhymes have lilt, nonsense, and humor. On each page, the ebullient paintings erupt from their tidy frames with vigorous and at times grotesque people and animals painted in the style of eighteenth and nineteenth century Pennsylvania Dutch pictures." Bull Cent Child Books

Potter, Beatrix, 1866-1943

Cecily Parsley's nursery rhymes. Warne 34p il $4.95; pa $2.25 (k-3) **398.8**

1. Nursery rhymes
ISBN 0-7232-3482-5; 0-7232-3507-4 (pa)

First published 1922

Illustrated by the author, this book consists of rhymes about Cecily Parsley, a rabbit who "brewed good ale for gentlemen" until she ran away; Goosey, goosey, gander; A little pig who couldn't find his way home; Mistress Pussy; Three blind mice; Little Tom Tinker's dog, etc.

The **Random** House book of Mother Goose; selected and illustrated by Arnold Lobel. Random House 1986 176p il $14.95; lib bdg $14.99 (k-2) **398.8**

1. Nursery rhymes
ISBN 0-394-86799-8; 0-394-96799-2 (lib bdg)
LC 86-47532

"Arnold Lobel has included over 300 nursery rhymes in this Mother Goose collection. Some are known, while others are less familiar. Lobel's colorful, bright, lively illustrations will, for the most part, delight young children. However, the pictures are overpowering at times and, in contrast, the print is quite small. A helpful addition is an index of first lines. A worthwhile addition to every library's Mother Goose section." Child Book Rev Serv

The **Real** Mother Goose; illustrated by Blanche Fisher Wright. Checkerboard Press 1987 c1944 128p il $9.95 (k-2) **398.8**

1. Nursery rhymes
ISBN 0-02-689038-0 LC 87-13778

First published 1916 by Rand McNally

A comprehensive collection of over three-hundred traditional nursery rhymes

The **Rooster** crows; a book of American rhymes and jingles; [compiled and illustrated by] Maud and Miska Petersham. Macmillan 1945 unp il $13.95 (k-2) **398.8**

1. Nursery rhymes 2. Folklore—United States
ISBN 0-02-773100-6 LC 46-446

Awarded the Caldecott Medal, 1946

A "collection of the familiar rhymes and jingles known to succeeding generations of children and chanted in their play, such as game rhymes, counting-out rhymes, rope-skipping rhymes." Wis Libr Bull

"The Petershams have made delightful pictures in soft harmonious colors, with plenty of humor. . . . They have made a beautiful book and the publishers have given it clear large type for young readers." Horn Book

Sendak, Maurice

Hector Protector, and As I went over the water; two nursery rhymes with pictures. Harper & Row 1965 unp il $14.95; lib bdg $14.89; pa $5.95 (k-1) **398.8**

1. Nursery rhymes
ISBN 0-06-025485-8; 0-06-025486-6 (lib bdg); 0-06-443237-8 (pa) LC 65-8256

"The fun the artist must have had in illustrating these two nursery rhymes will surely carry over to the reader and viewer of this diverting picture book. With originality and imaginativeness . . . Sendak not only interprets but extends the rhymes in his delightful pictures." Booklist

Sing a song of sixpence; pictures by Tracey Campbell Pearson. Dial Bks. for Young Readers 1985 unp il $10.95; lib bdg $10.89; pa $3.95 (k-2) **398.8**

1. Nursery rhymes
ISBN 0-8037-0151-9; 0-8037-0152-7 (lib bdg); 0-8037-0492-5 (pa) LC 84-14206

"The traditional rhyme provides a skeleton for a riotous picture-story that fleshes out the spare images of the text. . . . Fluid pen-and-ink drawings suffused with sunny color are full of motion: the flight of the birds and the children's romp. The rounded figures in old-fashioned dress project their appreciation of a good joke. Pearson's visual interpretation provides further storytelling beyond the rhyme. Words and music are appended." Horn Book

Tail feathers from Mother Goose; the Opie rhyme book. Little, Brown 1988 124p il $15.95 (k-2) **398.8**

1. Nursery rhymes
ISBN 0-316-65081-1 LC 88-45307

An illustrated collection of traditional verses, most of which have never been published before

"The book is filled with glorious illustrations by sixty-two children's book illustrators from around the globe, including Maurice Sendak, Quentin Blake, Ron Maris, Shirley Hughes, Jan Ormerod, Helen Oxenbury, and Anthony Browne. A double-page spread for each illustrator provides a panoply of styles and a broad sweep of technique in a riot of color." Horn Book

Ten potatoes in a pot, and other counting rhymes; selected by Michael Jay Katz; pictures by June Otani. Harper & Row 1990 unp il $12.95; lib bdg $12.89 (k-2) **398.8**

1. Nursery rhymes 2. Counting
ISBN 0-06-023106-8; 0-06-023107-6 (lib bdg) LC 89-15583

A collection of traditional counting rhymes, including both popular and little-known verses

"There is a definite sense of fun to the collection as a whole, and Otani's illustrations have an antique flavor—they deliberately echo Greenaway, Pyle, and other nineteenth-century figures in their interpretations of the rhymes' actions. Good for reading aloud with groups as well as with individuals." Booklist

This little pig-a-wig, and other rhymes about pigs; chosen by Lenore Blegvad; illustrated by Erik Blegvad. Atheneum Pubs. 1978 unp il $11.95 (k-2) **398.8**

1. Nursery rhymes 2. Pigs—Poetry
ISBN 0-689-50110-2 LC 78-7015

"A Margaret K. McElderry book"

"Lenore's selections of verses from English and American lore show that porkers have always enjoyed a place in the poetic imagination. 'To Market, to Market,' 'Tom, Tom the Piper's Son,' 'This Little Piggy Went to Market' and other familiar rhymes appear along with . . . chants not so well known." Publ Wkly

"The rhymes are tantalizingly silly . . . and hop along with sounds children will enjoy repeating out loud. . . . The artist's full-color illustrations alternating with black and white have a satisfying rural charm." Booklist

To market! To market! illustrated by Peter Spier. Doubleday 1967 unp il $8.95; pa $5.95 (k-2) **398.8**

1. Nursery rhymes
ISBN 0-385-08755-1; 0-385-05352-5 (pa) LC 67-18664

"Nineteen traditional rhymes and proverbs have been woven into a charming tapestry of 19th century American rural life. . . . Most of the rhymes date back to English sources, but they seem quite at home in the New England setting." SLJ

Tomie dePaola's Mother Goose. Putnam 1985 127p il $17.95 (k-2) **398.8**

1. Nursery rhymes
ISBN 0-399-21258-2 LC 84-26314

This "is a large, ample, unfussy edition of every child's first staple of literature. . . . The neat, flat illustrations are darkly outlined and colored generally in the illustrator's favorite palette of clear pinks, blues, and violets and surrounded with a lot of white space. Each verse is pictured in a simple and unmistakable interpretation. . . . The rhymes are the familiar ones, 'Humpty Dumpty,' 'Simple Simon,' 'Old Mother Hubbard.' . . . Roughly similar rhymes are grouped together—rhymes about going to bed, love, birds, animals, weather, the sea. The very last selections are children's prayers. . . . A perfectly basic and lovely Mother Goose, lavish yet simple, and a splendid beginning for the youngest listener." Horn Book

Tortillitas para mamá and other nursery rhymes; Spanish and English; selected and translated by Margot C. Griego [et al.]; illustrated by Barbara Cooney. Holt & Co. 1981 unp il $14.95; pa $5.95 (k-2) **398.8**

1. Nursery rhymes 2. Folklore—Latin America 3. Bilingual books—Spanish-English
ISBN 0-8050-0285-5; 0-8050-0317-7 (pa) LC 81-4823

A bilingual collection of 13 popular Latin American nursery rhymes

The purpose of this book "is to preserve a unique aspect of Hispanic culture which deserves to be passed down to all children. . . . However, it can be recommended only with hesitation. . . . [Some of the rhymes are] the most sexist kind of nursery rhyme in our culture. . . . The translations present another problem. In almost every case, they are literal, stilted, graceless and just plain silly. . . . The illustrations are strikingly beautiful, capturing the rich color and texture of some parts of South America. . . . [But their] homogenized view of Latin Americans can easily lead to the perpetuation of some familiar stereotypes." Interracial Books Child Bull

Trot, trot to Boston: play rhymes for baby; compiled by Carol F. Ra; pictures by Catherine Stock. Lothrop, Lee & Shepard Bks. 1987 unp il $12.95; lib bdg $12.88 (k-1) **398.8**

1. Nursery rhymes 2. Finger play
ISBN 0-688-06190-7; 0-688-06191-5 (lib bdg) LC 86-7354

Trot, trot to Boston: play rhymes for baby—*Continued*

"This book presents twenty-two traditional nursery rhymes with illustrations and instructions for accompanying finger plays." Bull Cent Child Books

"Stock's watercolors seem to shimmer with a light of their own, defined by free-flowing lines. An exuberant abundance of color and pattern alternately excites and overwhelms the eye. . . . A sparkling collection to charm children and parents." Booklist

Wendy Watson's Mother Goose. Lothrop, Lee & Shepard Bks. 1989 160p il $19.95 (k-2) **398.8**

1. Nursery rhymes
ISBN 0-688-05708-X LC 88-37913

This book "will appeal to many for its lively but gentle illustrations with their combination of child-like simplicity and often intricate details. Soft blue-grays and greens with touches of orange, pink, and gold predominate in these delicately robust pictures of round-faced human characters and humorous, if not always identifiable, animals." SLJ

398.9 Proverbs

Fraser, Betty, 1928-
First things first; an illustrated collection of sayings useful and familiar for children. Harper & Row 1990 unp il $12.95; lib bdg $12.89 (k-2) **398.9**

1. Proverbs
ISBN 0-06-021854-1; 0-06-021855-X (lib bdg)
LC 86-42993

"Fraser explains and illustrates 30 familiar adages in an engaging presentation that is sustained by fresh, involving pictures. . . . To make these maxims meaningful, Fraser uses pencil-and wash illustrations that busily play out the minidramas. . . . A smooth blending of instruction and entertainment." Booklist

400 LANGUAGE

410 Linguistics

Chermayeff, Ivan, 1932-
First words; premiers mots; by Ivan and Jane Clark Chermayeff. Abrams 1990 27p il $16.95 (k-3) **410**

1. Language and languages 2. Polyglot dictionaries 3. Art appreciation
ISBN 0-8109-3300-4 LC 89-18166

Thirteen simple words, including "house," "cat," and "boat," appear in English, French, German, Spanish, and Italian, illustrated by masterworks from five Paris museums

"The selection of pictures and objects is diverse; furniture, porcelain, antique dolls, a weathervane, and tapestry and other textiles from many countries and periods are part of the inviting assortment of museum pieces, which are all identified on a concluding page. A final pronunciation guide is also included. . . . The Chermayeffs' compendium, ingenious in its simplicity, offers images to savor and a spark to inspire viewing, creative expression, and discussion." Horn Book

Kaye, Cathryn Berger
Word works; why the alphabet is a kid's best friend; illustrated by Martha Weston. Little, Brown 1985 128p il $14.95; pa $7.95 (4 and up) **410**

1. Language arts 2. Vocabulary
ISBN 0-316-48376-1; 0-316-48375-3 (pa)
LC 84-17154

"A Brown paper school book"

Explores the ways words are used in everyday life, in talking, writing, communicating, and thinking, as well as in creating stories and poems, printing books, playing games, and programming computers

The author uses a "fresh, original and nondidactic approach to information-sharing with children. . . . Energetic, resourceful, inquisitive children are going to love *Word Works.*" SLJ

411 Writing systems

Ogg, Oscar
The 26 letters. rev ed. Crowell 1971 294p il $13.45 **411**

1. Alphabet 2. Writing—History 3. Printing—History
ISBN 0-690-84115-9 LC 70-140646

First published 1948

"Beginning with the earliest man (35,000-15,000 B.C.), his implements and his culture, this . . . book traces through the centuries the development of writing from the earliest cave drawings in northern Spain to the modern linotype." Libr J

419 Structured verbal language other than spoken and written

Ancona, George, 1929-
Handtalk zoo; [by] George Ancona & Mary Beth. Four Winds Press 1989 unp il $15.95 (k-3) **419**

1. Sign language 2. Animals
ISBN 0-02-700801-0 LC 88-36861

"Readers learn to sign the names of animals as they tour the zoo with five special children. Full-color photographs and minimal text chronicle a day of visiting animals, eating lunch, and going home tired. Signs are repeated, and numbers and the finger alphabet appear in black-and-white boxes." Sci Child

"George Ancona's brilliantly colored photographs with close-ups of the children and the animals will be appealing to readers. Although some of the signed words are blurs of motion that might be confusing to children trying to imitate them, other photos of signs capture very clearly the essence of the animal, like the elephant's trunk or the zebra's stripes." Horn Book

Baker, Pamela J., 1947-

My first book of sign; illustrations by Patricia Bellan Gillen. Gallaudet Univ. Press 1986 76p il $12.95 (k-3) **419**

1. Sign language

ISBN 0-930323-20-3 LC 86-14937

"A Kendall Green publication"

Pictures of children demonstrate the forming in sign language of 150 basic alphabetically arranged words, accompanied by illustrations of the words themselves. Includes a discussion of fingerspelling and general rules for signing

"Looking like an ABC book, this is both appealing and useful. . . . Illustrations are brightly colored and have an even mixture of boys and girls of various racial backgrounds, some with hearing aids, some without. Some are a bit confusing because the chubby fingers are not always clearly distinguished from the thumb, but the descriptions in back help with clarification. Printed on glossy paper in a large format, this book is a good addition to most sign language collections for children." SLJ

Charlip, Remy

Handtalk: an ABC of finger spelling & sign language; [by] Remy Charlip, Mary Beth [and] George Ancona. Four Winds Press 1980 unp il lib bdg $15.95; Aladdin Bks. (NY) pa $4.95 (k-3) **419**

1. Sign language

ISBN 0-02-718130-8; 0-689-71108-5 (pa)

First published 1974 by Parents Magazine Press

This book provides an "introduction to the two modes of manual communication used primarily by the deaf: signs (gestures which represent words) and fingerspelling (the process by which words are spelled using the letters of the manual alphabet). . . . The format includes full-page scenes of persons making various signs, with insets at the bottom of each page which illustrate the fingerspelling of the word represented by the sign." Sci Books

Handtalk birthday; a number & story book in sign language; [by] Remy Charlip, Mary Beth [and] George Ancona. Four Winds Press 1987 unp il $14.95 (k-3) **419**

1. Sign language 2. Birthdays

ISBN 0-02-718080-8 LC 86-22755

This picture book "finds Mary Beth celebrating a birthday. Guessing what's in her birthday packages provides a perfect opportunity to introduce sign language vocabulary. . . . Fingerspelling and signing combine with the action of the double-page spread photographs [by George Ancona] to tell the story." SLJ

"While the book can be used in picture-book story hours for the hearing impaired, it is not restricted to a particular group. . . . The photographs are as dynamic as the concept. Brilliantly composed, they range in perspective from close-up shots of Mary Beth's expressive face to joyous group portraits and from full-page spreads to sequences of small candids." Horn Book

Fronval, George

Indian signs and signals; by George Fronval and Daniel DuBois. Sterling 1979 c1978 80p il o.p.; Bonanza Bks. reprint available $8.98 (4 and up) **419**

1. Indians of North America—Sign language

ISBN 0-517-46612-0 LC 78-57792

Original French edition, 1976

"Translated by E. W. Egan; photographs by George C. Hight; illustrations by Jean Marcellin; period paintings by George Catlin." Verso of title page

This is a "book in large format on American Indian sign language, much of which is still used today by native Americans. The signs are clearly illustrated by photographs of members of a contemporary Kiowa family demonstrating their use. At the end of the book is a small section covering smoke signals, trail signs, the language of feathers, the language of blankets, and the use of body paint. This book belongs in the library of everyone interested in Indians." Child Book Rev Serv

Greene, Laura, 1935-

Sign language talk; by Laura Greene and Eva Barash Dicker. Watts 1989 95p il lib bdg $11.90 (5 and up) **419**

1. Sign language

ISBN 0-531-10597-0 LC 88-5617

"A First book"

The authors "discuss how to formulate grammatically correct sentences in American Sign Language. Also known as Ameslan or ASL, this sign-language system is different from Signed English and is used mainly by deaf adults. While providing background in such areas as the parts of signs, the book includes, in the margins, clear line drawings of specific signs correlating to the main ideas of the paragraphs. Rules for word order, negation, and tense are carefully described and are followed by three illustrated dialogues to be used for practice. For further enjoyment, there are chapters devoted to games, poetry, and music." Booklist

Includes bibliography

Hofsinde, Robert, 1902-1973

Indian sign language; written and illustrated by Robert Hofsinde (Gray-Wolf). Morrow 1956 96p il lib bdg $12.88 (3-6) **419**

1. Indians of North America—Sign language

ISBN 0-688-31610-7 LC 56-5178

"This book shows how to form the gestures representing about five hundred words [in Indian sign language] ranging from familiar terms, such as 'man,' 'beaver,' and 'rapids,' to modern additions like 'motion picture' and 'coffee.' The key words are printed in heavy type, and are accompanied by concise directions and explanatory sketches. Words related in meaning are arranged in groups, and there is an alphabetical index." Ont Libr Rev

422 Etymology of standard English

McMillan, Bruce
Super, super, superwords. Lothrop, Lee & Shepard Bks. 1989 unp il $11.95; lib bdg $11.88 (k-2) **422**
1. Vocabulary 2. English language—Comparison
ISBN 0-688-08098-7; 0-688-08099-5 (lib bdg) LC 88-9342

Adjectives are used visually and grammatically to demonstrate the three degrees of comparison: positive, comparative, and superlative

"Each trio of words is accompanied by a double-page spread of three cheerful photographs of kids at play. Probably most envied will be the child who was allowed to sharpen her pencil down to a stub to illustrate short, shorter, shortest. Page layout is consistent (small, bigger, biggest, photographs running from left to right) which may reinforce the concept but gives the book a static design. Because the words are confined to -er and-est comparatives (a limitation the afterword acknowledges) be prepared for a rash of good, gooder, goodest, but for what it does, this is one of the bestest language concept books around." Bull Cent Child Books

Sarnoff, Jane
Words: a book about the origins of everyday words and phrases; by Jane Sarnoff and Reynold Ruffins. Scribner 1981 64p il $11.95 (4 and up) **422**
1. English language—Etymology
ISBN 0-684-16958-4 LC 81-8943

"Following a discussion of the language sources that have contributed to contemporary English, the authors describe the origins of individual words (occasionally groups of words or variants of words) within certain categories. . . . A section that discusses (very briefly) suffixes, prefixes, word roots, etc. is appended." Bull Cent Child Books

Terban, Marvin
Guppies in tuxedos: funny eponyms; illustrated by Giulio Maestro. Clarion Bks. 1988 64p il $12.95; pa $4.95 (3-5) **422**
1. English language—Etymology
ISBN 0-89919-509-1; 0-89919-770-1 (pa) LC 87-32630

Traces the origins of more than 100 eponymous words—words derived from the names of people or places

"Terban's writing style is lively and informal, but he packs in a lot of information and makes all the information easily accessible and interesting for young readers. Maestro's black-and-white pen-and-pencil cartoons are highlighted with orange. They contain little jokes about the words portrayed. This is a book that is sure to help students to better understand the intricacies of the English language." SLJ

Includes bibliography

423 English language—Dictionaries

12,000 words; a supplement to Webster's third new international dictionary. Merriam-Webster 1986 212p $10.95 **423**
1. English language—Dictionaries 2. Words, New—Dictionaries
ISBN 0-87779-207-0 LC 86-12598

Supplement to Webster's third new international dictionary of the English language, entered below

Replaces 6,000 words and 9,000 words

"Records many of the new words and meanings established since 'Webster's Third' was compiled and also includes older words that were left out of the original work." Booklist

The **American** Heritage children's dictionary. Houghton Mifflin 1986 848p il $13.95 (3-6) **423**
1. English language—Dictionaries
ISBN 0-395-42529-8 LC 86-7349

"The 36,000 word entries are based 'on a computerized study of the words that children need and use.' The entries, arranged in double columns, contain clear meanings, full-sentence examples, pronunciation guides, and are accompanied by more than 800 color photographs and drawings." Booklist

"Excellent reference book for this age group. Its word definitions are easy to understand, and it has many features that would make it appealing to children." Am Ref Books Annu, 1988

The **American** Heritage first dictionary. Houghton Mifflin 1986 340p il $11.95 (1-3) **423**
1. English language—Dictionaries
ISBN 0-395-42530-1 LC 86-7363

Revised edition of: My first dictionary, published 1980

"Definitions, Stephen Krensky; illustrator, George Ulrich." Introduction

"Nearly 1,700 main entry words are included, 500 of which are found most frequently in children's first readers. The remainder is a 'broad selection of other words children see and use every day.' Definitions are clear and adequate. The illustrations are in bright primary colors; the print is large, strong, and easily read." Booklist

Bellamy, John, 1948-
The Doubleday children's thesaurus; illustrated by Peter Stevenson. Doubleday 1987 198p il $12.95 (4-6) **423**
1. English language—Synonyms and antonyms
ISBN 0-385-23833-9 LC 86-16217

An illustrated thesaurus presenting over 6,000 word entries accompanied by synonyms, antonyms, and homonyms

The **Cat** in the Hat beginner book dictionary; by the Cat himself and P. D. Eastman. Beginner Bks. 1964 133p il $8.95; lib bdg $8.99 (k-3) **423**

1. English language—Dictionaries
ISBN 0-394-81009-0; 0-394-91009-5 (lib bdg)

Also available French-English edition (0-394-81063-5) and Spanish-English edition (0-394-81542-4) each $14.95

"This alphabetically arranged dictionary, illustrated with rollicking funny drawings by the popular author-illustrator, explains word meanings with sentences and pictures. It intends to help pre-schoolers 'recognize, remember, and really enjoy a basic vocabulary of 1,350 words.'" Peterson. Ref Books for Child

Corbeil, Jean-Claude

The Facts on File junior visual dictionary; [by] Jean-Claude Corbeil, Ariane Archambault. Facts on File 1989 159p il $18.95 (3-6) **423**

1. Picture dictionaries
ISBN 0-8160-2222-4

"The concept of using clearly-drawn illustrations of everyday objects to name their parts is immediately attractive. This is especially true for young adults who like to know what to call things and feel more worldly when they can. The best feature of this dictionary is that all the illustrations are in vivid color. . . . Every means of enhancing a reference work is used here. Each page has a color border to focus attention on the object in the center. The illustrations are large and lifelike, and they have been selected to appeal to young people with developing interests." Am Ref Books Annu, 1990

Grisewood, John

The Doubleday children's dictionary. Doubleday 1989 319p il $14.95 (4 and up) **423**

1. English language—Dictionaries
ISBN 0-385-26356-2 LC 89-30106

This dictionary "offers definitions for more than 8,000 words. . . . The word is emphasized in boldface print, followed by an abbreviation for part of speech and one or more definitions. Sample phrases and sentences printed in italics put the words in context. Pronunciation is given for a minority of words, often in terms of 'rhymes with.' While compiled in Great Britain, American spelling is used. . . . Colorful illustrations appear on almost every page. An italicized sentence is placed next to the picture so the reader can easily relate the picture with the appropriate word." Booklist

Hillerich, Robert L., 1927-

The American Heritage picture dictionary; illustrations by Maggie Swanson. Houghton Mifflin 1986 138p il $9.95 (k-1) **423**

1. English language—Dictionaries 2. Picture dictionaries
ISBN 0-395-42531-X LC 86-15279

A dictionary for preschool and early elementary grades, with each of the approximately 900 words defined by a sentence using the word to describe the object or activity portrayed in the accompanying illustration

"The almost 650 illustrations are in bright, clear colors. There are several family groupings of different races whose members and pets appear frequently in the illustrations and example sentences. The illustrations are nonsexist." Booklist

The **Lincoln** writing dictionary for children. Harcourt Brace Jovanovich 1988 901p il $17.95 (4 and up) **423**

1. English language—Dictionaries
ISBN 0-15-152394-0 LC 88-11167

A dictionary which includes quotations from famous writers and articles on writing and editing. There are 35,000 entry terms and over 750 illustrations

Macmillan dictionary for children; Judith S. Levey, editor-in-chief. Macmillan il $14.95 (3 and up) **423**

1. English language—Dictionaries

First published 1975. Periodically revised

"Bright, colorful, easy-to-use design, with simple, clear definitions make this an inviting choice for beginning readers through middle grades. Current, one of the finest." N Y Public Libr. Ref Books for Child Collect

Macmillan dictionary for students; edited by William D. Halsey. Macmillan $16.95 (4 and up) **423**

1. English language—Dictionaries

First published 1973 with title: Macmillan dictionary. Variant title: Macmillan contemporary dictionary. Periodically revised

"The word stock was selected from 'the language of everyday speech and conversation' and from subjects studied in school. Illustrations, many in two colors, clarify definitions but are used sparingly. Precision, clarity, and conciseness characterize the definitions. Appendixes include a simple style manual, brief chronology of United States history, and a glossary of computer terms. The dictionary will satisfy . . . students' need for pronunciations, meanings, and spellings of familiar and unfamiliar words." Wilson Libr Bull

Macmillan very first dictionary; a magic world of words. Macmillan 1983 264p il $10.95 (1-3) **423**

1. English language—Dictionaries
ISBN 0-02-761730-0 LC 82-22901

First published 1977 with title: The Magic world of words

Edited by Christopher G. Morris

"This alphabetical guide is designed to be used by children who are beyond picture wordbooks but have not yet grown into full-fledged dictionaries. In addition to the 1,500 words, illustrated with more than 500 illustrations, front and back matter contains explanatory remarks on how words and writing came to be, and introductory comments on world geography." Booklist

The **Random** House school dictionary; the Random House dictionary of the English language; Stuart Berg Flexner, editor in chief. Eugene P. Shewmaker, managing editor. school edition. Random House $23.96 (4 and up) **423**

First published 1970 with title: The Random House dictionary of the English language, school edition. Frequently reprinted with minor revisions

Based on the Random House unabridged and college dictionaries "the *School Dictionary* makes full use of the parent volumes' 'word frequency studies, citation files, and other scholarly resources.' The word list is based on the occurrence of words in U.S. school textbooks, works of children's literature, popular magazines, and newspapers recommended for students, as well as on conversational English that students are likely to encounter. This is a relatively brief dictionary, but, as such, it is just comprehensive enough to meet most of its objectives in satisfying its intended readers." Ref Books for Young Readers

The **Random** House thesaurus; edited by Jess Stein and Stuart Berg Flexner. college ed. Random House 1984 812p thumb-indexed $14.95; McKay, D. pa $10.95 **423**

1. English language—Synonyms and antonyms

ISBN 0-394-52949-9 (thumb-indexed); 0-679-72710-8 (pa) LC 84-4914

"Based upon the Reader's Digest family word finder, c1975." Verso of title page

An alphabetical listing of over 11,000 main-entry word lists which group together more than 200,000 synonyms and antonyms by meaning. Also included are sample sentences for every main entry (and for each meaning)

Schiller, Andrew, 1919-

Roget's children's thesaurus; [by] Andrew Schiller, William A. Jenkins. HarperCollins Pubs. 1991 240p il $12.95 (3-5) **423**

1. English language—Synonyms and antonyms

ISBN 0-06-275004-6 LC 90-40962

Replaces the authors' In other words: a beginning Thesaurus

Under alphabetically arranged entries are more than a thousand words with illustrative sentences to help the middle grader in choosing the exact word from several synonyms

Roget's student thesaurus; [by] Andrew Schiller, William A. Jenkins. HarperCollins Pubs. 1991 447p il $11.95 (5 and up) **423**

1. English language—Synonyms and antonyms

ISBN 0-06-275005-4 LC 90-5094

Replaces the authors' Junior thesaurus: In other words II

An illustrated alphabetical list of words, their synonyms, antonyms, and the shades of meaning between them

Scott, Foresman intermediate dictionary; by E. L. Thorndike, Clarence J. Barnhart. HarperCollins Pubs. il $17.95 (5 and up) **423**

1. English language—Dictionaries

First published 1971 with title: Thorndike-Barnhart intermediate dictionary. Frequently revised

This dictionary "is the middle volume in the publisher's . . . series of dictionaries for young readers. . . . The work is intended for both home study and school use by students in middle and junior high schools. . . . The major strength of this dictionary lies in its comprehensiveness. Entries thoroughly reflect not only the textbook language that students of this level will encounter but also the vocabulary to which they will be exposed in oral classroom instruction and in their private reading." Ref Books for Young Readers

Thorndike-Barnhart children's dictionary; by E. L. Thorndike, Clarence L. Barnhart. Scott, Foresman il $14.95 (3-5) **423**

1. English language—Dictionaries

Same as: Scott, Foresman beginning dictionary. First published 1945 by Scott, Foresman with title: Thorndike century beginning dictionary. Title and publishers vary. Frequently revised

A beginning dictionary which includes illustrations, examples of usage in most definitions, and self-teaching lessons for developing skills in using the dictionary

Webster's elementary dictionary. Merriam-Webster 1986 18, 582p il $11.95 (4-6) **423**

1. English language—Dictionaries

ISBN 0-87779-475-8 LC 86-5268

Replaces: Webster's Beginning dictionary, published 1980

This beginning dictionary contains over 32,000 entries and over 600 full color illustrations

"If it is possible to put together a 'scholarly' children's dictionary, then Merriam-Webster has succeeded with the *Webster's Elementary Dictionary.* Admirably, the publisher has attempted not to compromise quality for the sake of simplicity. The problem is that this is not an easy dictionary for children to use without assistance. The guide to the dictionary's use may be especially difficult to understand because of its large amount of explanatory (although excellent) text." Ref Books for Young Readers

Webster's intermediate dictionary. Merriam-Webster 1986 14a, 943p il $10.95 (5 and up) **423**

1. English language—Dictionaries

ISBN 0-87779-379-4 LC 86-5428

First published 1972

This dictionary includes "more than 65,000 vocabulary entries, including new terms from medicine and health, computers, world and national politics, media and communications." Publisher's note

Webster's school dictionary. brand new ed. Merriam-Webster 1986 16a, 1167p il $12.95 (6 and up) **423**

1. English language—Dictionaries

ISBN 0-87779-280-1 LC 86-5269

First published 1980

This dictionary "includes more than 85,000 entries, over 91,000 definitions that reflect today's language, plus a special section on abbreviations and symbols for chemical elements." Publisher's note

Webster's third new international dictionary of the English language; unabridged. Merriam-Webster il **423**

1. English language—Dictionaries

Prices vary according to binding

First published 1828 with title: An American dictionary of the English language, by Noah Webster. Also appeared with titles: Webster's Unabridged dictionary, Webster's International dictionary of the English language, and Webster's New International dictionary of the English language. This edition first published 1961. Frequently reprinted with additions and changes to keep it up to date

"The largest and most prestigious dictionary published in the United States, 'Webster's third' . . . [covers] English language in use since 1755. . . . Outstanding for its numerous illustrative quotations, impeccable authority, and etymologies. The clear, accurate definitions are given in historical order. The most reliable, comprehensive, and up-to-date general unabridged dictionary." A L A. Ref Sources for Small & Medium-sized Libr. 4th edition [review of 1981 edition]

Webster's II Riverside children's dictionary. Riverside 1984 20, 778p il pa $8.95 (3-6) **423**

1. English language—Dictionaries

ISBN 0-395-37884-2

This dictionary contains some 40,000 entries, 1200 drawings, over 250 word history paragraphs and some synonym paragraphs. Appended material includes measurement tables, chronology of U.S. history events, U.S. Presidents, abbreviations, manual and Braille alphabets, Morse code chart, geographic lists, maps of the U.S., North America and the world, and a chart of the solar system

Words for new readers. Scott, Foresman 1990 312p il $10.95 (k-1) **423**

1. Picture dictionaries 2. English language—Dictionaries

ISBN 0-673-28496-4 LC 90-5073

Also available from HarperCollins Pubs. is another picture dictionary for preschool through first grade: Good morning, words! for $8.95 (ISBN 0-06-017902-3)

Also published with title: My first picture dictionary

"Fifteen hundred words, chosen from textbooks and everyday life, are included. Most entries have a definition, an example sentence, and a picture. . . . Illustrations are in varied media: photographs, drawings, and cartoons; each is labeled with the entry word. . . *Words for New Readers* is an attractive book that combines an understanding of young children with dictionary conventions." Booklist

The **World** Book dictionary; edited by Clarence L. Barnhart, Robert K. Barnhart. World Bk. 2v il apply to publisher for price (5 and up) **423**

1. English language—Dictionaries

"A Thorndike-Barnhart dictionary"

First published 1963 with title: The World Book Encyclopedia dictionary. Revised annually

"Easy to use, carefully edited unabridged dictionary suitable for use in children's rooms. Definitions, usage notes and word histories; accurate and up-to-date." NY Public Libr. Ref Books for Child Collect

The **World** Book student dictionary. World Bk. 1989 900p il apply to publisher for price (3-5) **423**

1. English language—Dictionaries

"This dictionary is a reprint of the *Childcraft Dictionary* sold by World Book, Inc. with its *Childcraft Encyclopedia*; the only change is the addition of 16 pages of student exercises. . . . A 20-page introduction gives detailed instructions for interpreting the entries. A 62-page 'Reference Section' at the end includes word study exercises and a series of word games along with dictionary-style lists of presidents, states, and so forth. . . . Elementary school students will be comfortable using this commendable source." SLJ

427 Nonstandard English

Juster, Norton, 1929-

As: a surfeit of similes; pictures by David Small. Morrow Junior Bks. 1989 unp il $9.95; lib bdg $9.88 (3-5) **427**

1. English language—Terms and phrases

ISBN 0-688-08139-8; 0-688-08140-1 (lib bdg) LC 88-8449

"Clever drawings that are scratchy, often cross-hatched, animated and amusing, illustrate a series of similes-in-verse that are interrupted a few times by dialogue. . . . The repetitive form produces deja vu reading, but the book should indelibly imprint the simile in readers' minds; it is more often funny than forced, and the appeals of rhyme and metric lilt make it easy to remember verses and likely that they will be quoted." Bull Cent Child Books

Terban, Marvin

Mad as a wet hen! and other funny idioms; illustrated by Giulio Maestro. Clarion Bks. 1987 64p il $13.95; pa $4.95 (3-5) **427**

1. English language—Idioms 2. English language—Terms and phrases

ISBN 0-89919-478-8; 0-89919-479-6 (pa) LC 86-17575

Illustrates and explains over 100 common English idioms, in categories including animals, body parts, and colors

"Maestro's two-color cartoonlike illustrations are amusing and informative themselves, providing visual clues that support the textual explanations. . . . Although some of the expressions included are dated, the al-

Terban, Marvin—*Continued*
phabetical index enables teachers and librarians to pick and choose. This book might be particularly beneficial in schools having a large ESL program, especially for older, more advanced students." SLJ

Punching the clock: funny action idioms; illustrated by Tom Huffman. Clarion Bks. 1990 63p il $13.95; pa $4.95 (3-6) **427**

1. English language—Idioms
ISBN 0-89919-864-3; 0-89919-865-1 (pa)
LC 89-38087

The author "explains nearly 100 different expressions that add spirit to our language. Arranged in groupings, the idioms are used in sentences ('Don't believe him. He's just *playing possum*') and explained in context, often with delineation of its origin. . . . Not only will children enjoy browsing through this humorously illustrated book, but language arts teachers will find it a boon for units on writing." Booklist

Includes bibliographic references

Superdupers! really funny real words; illustrated by Giulio Maestro. Clarion Bks. 1989 63p il $13.95; pa $4.95 (3-5) **427**

1. Vocabulary 2. English language—Etymology
ISBN 0-89919-804-X; 0-395-51123-2 (pa)
LC 88-38325

Explains the meaning and origins of over 100 nonsense words that make the English language more colorful including such examples as "flip-flop," "fuzzy-wuzzy," "cancan," and "tutti frutti"

Includes bibliography

428 Standard English usage

Heller, Ruth

A cache of jewels and other collective nouns; written and illustrated by Ruth Heller. Grosset & Dunlap 1987 unp il $10.95 (k-2) **428**

1. English language—Terms and phrases
ISBN 0-448-19211-X LC 87-80254

"In light verse and brightly colored pictures, Heller provides an introduction to a specialized part of speech, the collective noun. She lists and depicts more than 25, including such familiar terms as 'batch of bread' and 'bunch of bananas,' as well as more unusual phrases. . . . The concept will stimulate the curiosity and imaginations of children with an ear for language. The illustrations, containing large, bold objects in simple yet striking compositions, ensure a visually inspiring exploration as well." Publ Wkly

Kites sail high: a book about verbs; written and illustrated by Ruth Heller. Grosset & Dunlap 1988 unp il $10.95 (k-2) **428**

1. English language—Grammar
ISBN 0-448-10480-6 LC 87-82718

This "book explicates and celebrates verbs of all kinds, in ebullient verses which themselves sail and soar. . . . The verses are accompanied by bold, gaily colored graphics that are especially striking for their skillful use of pattern and design." Publ Wkly

Many luscious lollipops: a book about adjectives; written and illustrated by Ruth Heller. Grosset & Dunlap 1989 unp il lib bdg $13.95 (k-2) **428**

1. English language—Grammar
ISBN 0-448-03151-5 LC 88-83045

"The text begins: 'An adjective's terrific/when you want to be specific/It easily identifies/by number, color or by size/TWELVE LARGE, BLUE, GORGEOUS butterflies.' And there they are, blue and yellow, filling a double-page spread. . . . There is great diversity and technical brilliance in the art work, and the text has rhyme, rhythm, humor, and a very clear presentation of the concepts of different kinds of adjectives and what they do." Bull Cent Child Books

McMillan, Bruce

Becca backward, Becca frontward; a book of concept pairs. Lothrop, Lee & Shepard Bks. 1986 unp il $12.95; lib bdg $12.88 (k-2) **428**

1. English language—Synonyms and antonyms
ISBN 0-688-06282-2; 0-688-06283-0 (lib bdg)
LC 86-7221

"A dozen pairs of opposites illustrated with full color photographs of a young girl. This is a well-designed book, with large, clear photographs to illustrate each of the pairs printed on facing pages and with the concept word printed in bold letters below each photograph. Becca is charming, the photographs are beautiful, and, in most instances, the concepts are very clear." SLJ

Here a chick, there a chick. Lothrop, Lee & Shepard Bks. 1983 unp il $13.95; lib bdg $13.88 (k-2) **428**

1. English language—Synonyms and antonyms
ISBN 0-688-02000-3; 0-688-02001-1 (lib bdg)
LC 82-20348

"Bright, bold photographs in color of a little yellow chick following a trail of feed illustrate various concepts in a book for the very young. Beginning on the title page with an egg near a bag of feed, the book proceeds to explain visually such concepts and actions as inside and outside, straight and crooked, stand and sit. Some of the concepts—for example, left and right—may be more challenging than others. At the bottom of each page a word is placed in bold letters beneath a full-page picture. . . . The photographs are clear and simple, and children should enjoy following the perky chick from the beginning to the end of its trail." Horn Book

438 Standard German usage

Cooper, Lee Pelham

Fun with German; [by] Lee Cooper; illustrated by Elizabeth M. Githens. Little, Brown 1965 119p il lib bdg $15.95 (4 and up) **438**

1. German language
ISBN 0-316-15588-8 LC 65-18362

Cooper, Lee Pelham—*Continued*
"Using a circus motif [the author] begins with phrases and sentence sequences to introduce vowel and consonant sounds and a few essentials of grammar, and then presents stories, games, songs, and ideas and activities for a German club. Includes a guide to pronunciation symbols and a German-English vocabulary." Booklist
"A delightful introduction to the German language. . . . The phonetic symbols are excellent, especially for those sounds which do not have exact English equivalents. Elizabeth Githens has contributed lively and amusing illustrations." SLJ

463 Spanish language—Dictionaries

Emberley, Rebecca
My house/mi casa: a book in two languages. Little, Brown 1990 unp il lib bdg $14.95 (k-3) **463**
1. Picture dictionaries 2. Bilingual books—Spanish-English 3. Spanish language
ISBN 0-316-23637-3 LC 89-12893
"Lively, brilliantly colored collages are used to illustrate various objects in English and Spanish. Young readers will find it little trouble to learn the words for such an appealing house and its furnishings, pets, toys, and surroundings." Horn Book Guide

Taking a walk/caminando: a book in two languages. Little, Brown 1990 unp il lib bdg $14.95 (k-3) **463**
1. Picture dictionaries 2. Bilingual books—Spanish-English 3. Spanish language
ISBN 0-316-23640-3 LC 89-12923
Labeled illustrations and Spanish and English text introduce the things a child sees while on a walk
The "book uses brightly patterned collages to illustrate the sights a child would see in a walk around his neighborhood. The definitions in Spanish and English are clear, and the subjects, such as blue jeans and swings, are interesting to a child. A fine example of a bilingual book." Horn Book Guide

468 Standard Spanish usage

Cooper, Lee Pelham
More fun with Spanish; [by] Lee Cooper; illustrated by Ann Atene. Little, Brown 1967 120p il lib bdg $14.95 (4 and up) **468**
1. Spanish language
ISBN 0-316-15616-7 LC 67-17287
Companion volume to: Fun with Spanish (1960)
This volume "contains 11 entertaining stories each of which introduces a new point of grammar, but without the reader's awareness until the end of the story when the grammar point is summarized for emphasis. The text is entirely in Spanish, the only English appearing in the pronunciation guide and 24-page vocabulary. Copiously illustrated with lively two-color drawings." Booklist

493 Non-Semitic Afro-Asiatic languages

Katan, Norma Jean
Hieroglyphs, the writing of ancient Egypt; by Norma Jean Katan with Barbara Mintz. Atheneum Pubs. 1981 96p il map $12.95 **493**
1. Egyptian language 2. Hieroglyphics
ISBN 0-689-50176-5 LC 80-13576
"A Margaret K. McElderry book"
Explains the origins of hieroglyphics and what they mean, tells how this ancient form of writing was decoded, and describes the training and importance of scribes
"A clear, concise, and animated text has been handsomely designed and illustrated. . . . An excellent appetite arouser for more books on ancient Egypt." Child Book Rev Serv

500 NATURAL SCIENCES AND MATHEMATICS

Grillone, Lisa
Small worlds close up; [by] Lisa Grillone & Joseph Gennaro. Crown 1978 unp il $12.95 (5 and up) **500**
1. Science—Pictorial works 2. Electron microscope and microscopy 3. Photography—Scientific applications
ISBN 0-517-53289-1 LC 77-15860
Photographs taken with a powerful scanning electron microscope reveal the composition of numerous common objects including hair, salt crystals, and a pin
"The authors have produced spectacular photographs (mineral, vegetable and animal) of such things as the opening where venom shoots out through a snake fang, a small lizard's toes that enable it to cling to a pane of glass, what it is that makes a cork buoyant, and an opal sparkle. The large photographs are clear and accompanied by short appropriate captions." Appraisal

Hidden worlds. National Geographic Soc. 1981 104p il $6.95; lib bdg $8.50 (5 and up) **500**
1. Nature study 2. Vision 3. Microscope and microscopy 4. Telescope
ISBN 0-87044-336-4; 0-87044-341-0 (lib bdg)
LC 79-3244
"Books for world explorers"
This book presents information "about the use of cameras and light to view objects normally unseen by the human eye. Six chapters by assorted authors explore aspects of microscopy, x-rays, telescopes, satellites, animal and human vision, light, and photography." Appraisal
"The illustrations are designed to spur the reader's imagination. . . . Although third graders might enjoy looking at the photographs, the book would be more appreciated by older students." Sci Books Films
Includes glossary and bibliography

Simon, Seymour, 1931-
The dinosaur is the biggest animal that ever lived, and other wrong ideas you thought were true; illustrated by Giulio Maestro. Lippincott 1984 64p il $12.95; lib bdg $12.89; pa $3.95 (3-6) **500**

1. Science—Miscellanea
ISBN 0-397-32075-2; 0-397-32076-0 (lib bdg); 0-06-446053-3 (pa) LC 83-48960

Explains why many commonly accepted scientific "facts"—lightning never strikes twice, the sky is blue, snakes are slimy, etc.—are untrue

"If you think that dinosaurs were the biggest animals that ever lived, or that the sun is farthest from the earth in winter, or that a compass needle points to the North Pole—you're wrong. Simon debunks these and 26 other myths in a breezy, eclectic science lesson that sets the facts straight. Many of the mistaken notions are familiar ones; each merits a double-page explanation bolstered with humorous cartoons and occasional diagrams. This should have lots of popular appeal." Booklist

Hidden worlds; pictures of the invisible. Morrow 1983 48p il $13.95; lib bdg $13.88 (5 and up) **500**

1. Science—Pictorial works 2. Photography—Scientific applications 3. Microscope and microscopy
ISBN 0-688-02464-5; 0-688-02465-3 (lib bdg)
LC 83-5407

This book "introduces young readers to worlds which are too small, too far away or too fast to see. Large, outstanding photographs convey the incredible variety in these unseen worlds. Included in the book are photographs of the eye of an ant, a bullet slicing a playing card and the surface of a star. Accompanying the photographs are careful explanations of the methodologies that were used to produce the pictures. . . . Simon's explanations of these techniques are concise and easy to understand. The book is divided into five sections: those dealing with hidden worlds in general, in the body, of time, of the earth and of space." SLJ

Why in the world? National Geographic Soc. 1985 104p il $6.95; lib bdg $8.50 (4 and up) **500**

1. Science
ISBN 0-87044-573-1; 0-87044-578-2 (lib bdg)
LC 85-18862

"Books for world explorers"

"Arranged by subject in a question-answer format, a variety of scientific topics are discussed. Each page is illustrated by a photograph, diagram or cartoon, with explanatory text of a half-page or less." SLJ

"While the book will have appeal for the scientifically curious, it is mainly intended as a supplementary classroom tool. An enclosed Teacher's Guide suggests an experiment to accompany each section of the book, and a large folded chart features on one side an astronaut floating in space along with an explanation of how he does it; on the other, is a trivia-type science game. Access to specific information is available through the well cross-referenced index." Booklist

Why on earth? National Geographic Soc. 1988 96p il $7.95; lib bdg $9.50 (4 and up) **500**

1. Science
ISBN 0-87044-701-7; 0-87044-706-8 (lib bdg)
LC 88-25486

"Books for world explorers"

Questions and answers present information on science topics, including human physiology, animal behavior, earth science, and natural science

"The question-and-answer format, appealing color photographs, clearly-written text, and interesting topics are sure to appeal to browsers. A good index helps to locate specific information. Although the answers are relatively short, they provide basic information about a variety of topics. A quality selection." SLJ

502.8 Science—auxiliary techniques and procedures; apparatus, equipment, materials

Bleifeld, Maurice
Experimenting with a microscope; illustrations by Anne Canevari Green. Watts 1988 110p il lib bdg $12.40 (5 and up) **502.8**

1. Microscope and microscopy
ISBN 0-531-10580-6 LC 88-14043

"A Venture book"

Provides a brief history of the microscope and discusses how the microscope works, its parts, the preparation of slides, and how the microscope is used to view various specimens

"The writing is clear and interesting; there are plenty of very helpful illustrations and photographs. This is a fine introduction to microscopy for young people." Appraisal

Selsam, Millicent Ellis, 1912-
Greg's microscope; pictures by Arnold Lobel. Harper & Row 1963 64p il lib bdg $10.89; pa $3.50 (1-3) **502.8**

1. Microscope and microscopy
ISBN 0-06-025296-0 (lib bdg); 0-06-444144-X (pa)
LC 63-8002

"A Harper I can read book"

"The acquisition of a microscope entices Greg into looking at anything tiny, so he prepares his own slides of salt and sugar, water and flour, and bits of many other household things. Eventually he isolates some amoebae from his fish tank, but finds himself third in the microscope line—Mother and Dad are in front." NY Times Book Rev

503 Science—Encyclopedias and dictionaries

The New book of popular science. Grolier 6v il maps apply to publisher for price **503**

1. Science—Dictionaries 2. Technology—Dictionaries 3. Natural history—Dictionaries

First published 1924 with title: The Book of popular science. Changed to present title 1978. Annually revised

The information in this set is classified under such broad categories as astronomy & space science, computers & mathematics, earth sciences, energy, environmental sciences, physical sciences, general biology, plant life, animal life, mammals, human sciences and technology

505 Science—Serial publications

3-2-1 Contact. Children's Television Workshop $15.97 per year **505**

1. Science—Periodicals 2. Technology—Periodicals
ISSN 0195-4105

Monthly except February and August. First published 1979

This magazine "specializes in science and technology and is intended for the 8-14 age group. Printed on glossy paper, issues are filled with informative articles, puzzles, projects, experiments, questions and answers, and a serialized science mystery. . . . The layout is inviting and the many excellent full-color illustrations and photographs supplement a thoughtfully conceived magazine." Katz. Mag for Sch Libr

Chickadee: the Canadian magazine for young children. Young Naturalist Foundation $14.95 per year **505**

1. Natural history—Periodicals
ISSN 0707-4611

Monthly except July and August. First published 1979

Similar in format to Owl, entered below, but designed for younger children. Includes stories about wildlife and outdoor life, fiction, games, puzzles and things to do or make

Owl; the discovery magazine for children. Young Naturalist Foundation $14.95 per year **505**

1. Natural history—Periodicals
ISSN 0382-6627

Monthly except July and August. First published 1976 as successor to The Young Naturalist

"Intended for children ages 7-14, [this magazine] includes a wide range of material, mostly nonfiction. Articles are about animals, science, technology, natural phenomena, experiments, and people. The activities, puzzles, games, and a cartoon story are creative and challenging. The layout is varied and aesthetically pleasing. Printed on glossy paper and with stunning color photographs, including an animal centerfold each month, the magazine reflects high editorial and artistic standards." Katz. Mag for Sch Libr

Ranger Rick. National Wildlife Federation $14 per year **505**

1. Natural history—Periodicals
ISSN 0738-6656

Monthly. First published 1967 with title: Ranger Rick's Nature Magazine

This magazine "is designed to give children ages 6-12 a program of activities and information that will help them learn about wildlife and about the environment. More than half of the pages is given to pictorial matter. Stunning full-color photographs and illustration . . . supplement the lucidly written material—stories about other children, science features, and projects; and clever word games, jokes, mazes, and puzzles." Katz. Mag for Sch Libr

Your Big Backyard. National Wildlife Federation $10 per year **505**

1. Natural history—Periodicals

Monthly. First published 1979

"Developed to help preschool children ages 3-5 to learn about the world of nature, the pages are highlighted by splendid color photographs of animals and wildlife, superb in detail. . . . The text is printed in large type and carefully place on each page. The 'Read to Me' story, then poems, puzzles, games, and projects can easily be completed with help from adults. . . . Highly recommended." Katz. Mag for Sch Libr

507 Science—Education and related topics

Adams, Richard Craig

Science with computers; [by] Richard C. Adams. Watts 1987 128p il (Experimental science ser) lib bdg $12.90 (6 and up) **507**

1. Science—Experiments 2. Computers
ISBN 0-531-10324-2 LC 86-26725

The author "provides a series of utility programs written for the Apple computer. . . . Following a brief introduction to using computers in science, chapters on number crunching and statistics are provided. The information presented on statistics is practical and understandable. Adams also discusses computer simulations and database uses in science, the use of the computer as a lab tool, and ideas on using a computer to help interpret data. Each chapter ends with suggestions for science fair projects." SLJ

Includes bibliography

Allison, Linda, 1948-

Gee, Wiz! how to mix art and science or the art of thinking scientifically; illustrated by Linda Allison. Little, Brown 1983 128p il lib bdg $13.95; pa $7.95 (4 and up) **507**

1. Science—Experiments
ISBN 0-316-03444-4 (lib bdg); 0-316-03445-2 (pa) LC 83-9834

"A Brown paper school book"

Allison, Linda, 1948-—*Continued*

"There are activites with color, soap bubbles, capillarity, surface tension, immiscible liquids, vision, magnification, symmetry, center of mass, and falling bodies. All are safe to do, and the required materials are easily available." Appraisal

"The authors have endeavored to make science fun by presenting a cartoon strip format in addition to chapter introductions and a clear scientific method of approach." Child Book Rev Serv

Ardley, Neil, 1937-

Working with water. Watts 1983 32p il (Action science) lib bdg $11.90 (4 and up) **507**

1. Water—Experiments 2. Science—Experiments
ISBN 0-531-04519-6 LC 82-51008

An "illustrated collection of 23 experiments and scientific explanations. Emulsion, water pressure, surface tension, density, evaporation and condensation are all demonstrated. Students will find the experiments fun. The readily available equipment and lucid directions make the experiments appropriate for classroom and/or home use. Some students may need further discussion for the concepts to transfer." SLJ

Includes glossary

Cobb, Vicki

More science experiments you can eat; illustrated by Giulio Maestro. Lippincott 1979 126p il $12.95; lib bdg $13.89; pa $4.95 (5 and up) **507**

1. Science—Experiments 2. Cookery
ISBN 0-397-31828-6; 0-397-31878-2 (lib bdg); 0-06-446003-7 (pa) LC 78-12732

This book utilizes some basic principles of science and applies them to typical foodstuffs so that the reader might learn about the nature of these foods. Among the simple scientific processes introduced are: heating, cooling, freezing, thawing, dehydration, distillation, mixing, infusing, and of course, tasting

Science experiments you can eat; illustrated by Peter Lippman. Lippincott 1972 127p il lib bdg $12.89; pa $4.95 (5 and up) **507**

1. Science—Experiments 2. Cookery
ISBN 0-397-31179-6 (lib bdg); 0-06-446002-9 (pa) LC 71-151474

Experiments with food demonstrates various scientific principles and produce an eatable result. Includes fruit drinks, grape jelly, muffins, chop suey, yogurt, and other foods

"All in all, the book is a delightful combination of learning by doing, and of relating common activities to basic scientific principles." Sci Books

Herbert, Don

Mr. Wizard's supermarket science; illustrated by Roy McKie. Random House 1980 96p il lib bdg $8.99; pa $7.95 (4 and up) **507**

1. Science—Experiments
ISBN 0-394-93800-3 (lib bdg); 0-394-83800-9 (pa) LC 79-27217

Gives directions for about 100 simple experiments using items available in the supermarket. Includes explanations of the scientific principles demonstrated

This book is "high on safety and always cautions the young reader to seek help from an adult when using heat or unfamiliar materials. This fascinating book forces the reader out of the mold of 'functional fixedness' and into a pattern of 'functional freedom' by learning to use common items in uncommon ways." Appraisal

Kramer, Stephen

How to think like a scientist; answering questions by the scientific method; [by] Stephen P. Kramer; illustrated by Felicia Bond. Crowell 1987 44p il $11.95; lib bdg $11.89 (3-5) **507**

1. Science—Methodology
ISBN 0-690-04563-8; 0-690-04565-4 (lib bdg) LC 85-43604

An "exploration of the ways questions are asked and how scientists try to make sure that the questions are answered correctly. Relying on concrete story examples, Kramer shows how observed information can result in different or incorrect conclusions. Examples are also used to explain the principles of the scientific method." Booklist

"This is a pleasant book with an open format; an amusing halftone cartoon on almost every page illustrates the child oriented experiments and supports the light tone of the book." SLJ

Saul, Wendy, 1946-

Science fare: an illustrated guide and catalog of toys, books, and activities for kids; [by] Wendy Saul, with Alan R. Newman; introduction by Isaac Asimov. Harper & Row 1986 295p il hardcover o.p. paperback available $14.95 **507**

1. Science—Study and teaching
ISBN 0-06-091218-9 (pa) LC 85-45657

This resource guide includes "lists of recommended books on particular topics and for particular age groups; lists of scientific supply houses; suggestions on science equipment such as microscopes, telescopes and scientific toys; lists of appropriate magazines, science catalogs, and science organizations for juniors and adults. There are also some wonderful short essays on developing inquiry skills, asking and answering questions, and science and children's literature. The style is clear, breezy, and colloquial. This book is an indispensable reference tool." Appraisal

Walker, Ormiston H.

Experimenting with air and flight; illustrated by Anne Canevari Green. Watts 1989 96p il lib bdg $12.40 (6 and up) **507**

1. Flight—Experiments 2. Science—Experiments
ISBN 0-531-10670-5 LC 88-38063

"A Venture book"

This volume presents experiments which seek to demonstrate "the forces of lift, thrust, drag, and gravity as they apply to birds, airplanes, helicopters, balloons, and kites." Booklist

"The experiments use common materials and household appliances. Those that require adult supervision are indicated, and any hazards are noted at the beginning of the experiment, even if its result is revealed by so doing. Illustration are black-and-white photographs and pen-and-ink line drawings, with good diagrams to clarify the instructions. An excellent addition to the engineering (and science) section of any library serving young people." SLJ

Includes bibliography

Willow, Diane

Science sensations; [by] Diane Willow and Emily Curran; illustrated by Lady McCrady. Addison-Wesley 1989 95p il pa $16.95; $8.95 (3-5) **507**

1. Science—Experiments
ISBN 0-201-51747-7 (pa); 0-201-07189-4 LC 88-27226

Activities/experiments to give a new awareness of the world around us. Treats such areas as light, color, shadows, reflections, motion pictures, illusion, and patterns

"The 43 activities are grouped into 10 categories, thus covering a broad range of topics. It is evident that each of these investigations has been extensively tested with children. Directions are carefully worded for middle and upper elementary school students so that they can do all of these activities with little or no help from adults. . . . This activity book is highly recommended." Sci Books Films

Wyler, Rose

Science fun with mud and dirt; pictures by Pat Stewart. Messner 1987 c1986 48p il lib bdg $11.38; pa $4.95 (2-4) **507**

1. Science—Experiments 2. Soils
ISBN 0-671-55569-3 (lib bdg); 0-671-62904-2 (pa) LC 86-8388

"Explanations of different types of soil, where they come from, insects and animals that live underground, and how plants grow in it are followed by easy-to-follow experiments, including Wyler's recipes for mud pies. The materials needed can be found around the home (or outside), and experiments can be done alone or by groups." SLJ

"Most, if not all, of the experiments seem appropriate for the age level. Rose Wyler has written an interesting and easily understood book. The illustrations are appealing and complement the prose very well." Appraisal

Science fun with peanuts and popcorn; pictures by Pat Stewart. Messner 1986 48p il lib bdg $11.38; pa $4.95 (2-4) **507**

1. Science—Experiments 2. Plants 3. Popcorn
ISBN 0-671-55572-3 (lib bdg); 0-671-62452-0 (pa) LC 85-8892

Experiments for home or the classroom with seeds and plants, showing what is inside seeds, how roots form, and how plants grow

"Many black-and-white drawings highlighted in yellow show children busy with science activities . . . aimed at explaining scientific principles and methods. . . . Scientifically inclined children will enjoy the challenges offered for experimentation at home as well as at school." Booklist

Science fun with toy boats and planes; pictures by Pat Stewart. Messner 1986 46p il lib bdg $11.38; pa $4.95 (2-4) **507**

1. Science—Experiments 2. Boats and boating 3. Airplanes
ISBN 0-671-55573-1 (lib bdg); 0-671-62453-9 (pa) LC 85-8842

Easy experiments to do at home or school with home equipment, showing basic principles of how boats float and move and how planes fly

"The clear text is brief and is supplemented by clarifying illustrations and step-by-step diagrams in gray and yellow. For each concept, simple experiments are outlined, along with questions that will pique interest and help to direct readers. The materials can be easily found at home or at school. Young experimenters can do many of the experiments alone, but some require adult supervision for cutting. The book could be used by individuals, small groups, or by teacher and class in science study." SLJ

Science fun with toy cars and trucks; pictures by Pat Stewart. Messner 1988 48p il $11.38; pa $4.95 (2-4) **507**

1. Science—Experiments
ISBN 0-671-63784-3; 0-671-65854-9 (pa) LC 87-20326

Wyler "uses toy cars and trucks to present some basic scientific principles. Concepts of force, friction, and inertia are demostrated: using a roller skate, children are shown how to build their own toy car and are then asked to observe how the car and other toy vehicles move under various conditions. . . . A toy garage generates discussion of lubrication and the work-reducing capability of ramps and pulleys. There's meaty science here, all in the guise of fun." Booklist

Zubrowski, Bernie, 1939-

Balloons; building and experimenting with inflatable toys; illustrated by Roy Doty. Morrow Junior Bks. 1990 79p il lib bdg $12.95; pa $6.95 (3-6) **507**

1. Science—Experiments 2. Balloons
ISBN 0-688-08325-0 (lib bdg); 0-688-08324-2 (pa) LC 89-37265

"A Boston Children's Museum activity book"

The author seeks to "demonstrate the scientific principles of force and pressure through projects and experiments using . . . [objects such as] balloons, rubber

Zubrowski, Bernie, 1939-—*Continued*
bands, and paper milk cartons." SLJ

"The scientific content is accurately presented in a manner that is appealing to a young reader. Safety is stressed throughout the book, but this is the type of book that does not require adult supervision. The experiments are fun, safe, and challenging." Sci Books Films

507.05 Science—Education and related topics—Serial publications

Science and Children. National Science Teachers Assn. $43 per year **507.05**

1. Science—Study and teaching—Periodicals
ISSN 0036-8148

Eight issues a year, September through May. First published 1963 as successor to: Elementary School Science Bulletin

"A carefully edited, well-illustrated magazine for use by the science teacher in the elementary grades, including junior high school. Articles, usually by teachers, cover various methods of making science a living subject for students. . . . Concentration is on astronomy, biology, chemistry, earth sciences, and physics. . . . The regular features include reviews not only of new books but also of audiovisual materials and scientific kits. This is the basic magazine of its type, and it should be found in all teacher collections in elementry and junior high school libraries." Katz. Mag for Sch Libr

The **Science** Teacher. National Science Teachers Assn. $43 per year **507.05**

1. Science—Study and teaching—Periodicals
ISSN 0036-8555

Monthly September through May. First published 1934

"Articles are on methods of teaching science . . . and for the most part are written by high school teachers. Other columns and features concentrate on the activities of individuals and the association. Reviews of software, audiovisual materials, and teaching aids are an important feature." Katz. Mag for Sch Libr

507.8 Science—Use of apparatus and equipment in study and teaching

Markle, Sandra, 1946-

The young scientist's guide to successful science projects; illustrations by Marti Shohet. Lothrop, Lee & Shepard Bks. 1990 112p il lib bdg $12.88; pa $6.95 (5 and up) **507.8**

1. Science—Experiments
ISBN 0-688-07217-8 (lib bdg); 0-688-09137-7 (pa) LC 89-45290

"Markle offers a step-by-step explanation of what an experiment is and how to design, perform, interpret, and display the finished product. She covers issues from choosing the topic to controlling variables to answering a science fair judge's questions, as she gradually nudges readers into understanding the how and why of the scientific method. . . . Effectively illustrated with line drawings, this book is pleasingly simple and direct in both design and writing." Booklist

Science experiments on file: experiments, demonstrations, and projects for school and home. Facts on File 1988 1 v various paging il loose-leaf $145 (6 and up) **507.8**

1. Science—Experiments
ISBN 0-8160-1888-X LC 88-3883

"Eighty-four inexpensive, innovative, reproductible experiments in the categories of earth science, biology, physical science/chemistry, and physics are included. . . . Each experiment includes introductions, time and materials needed, safety precautions, procedures, and analysis. . . . Experiments are aimed at students in grades six through twelve and were prepared by a group of science teachers who have received awards from the National Science Foundation." Am Libr

For a fuller review see: Booklist, June 1, 1989

508 Natural history

Björk, Christina

Linnea's almanac; text [by] Christina Björk; drawings [by] Lena Anderson. R & S Bks. 1989 61p il $11.95 (2-5) **508**

1. Nature study
ISBN 91-29-59176-7 LC 89-83540

Original Swedish edition, 1982

Linnea, featured in Linnea in Monet's garden and Linnea's windowsill garden (entered in Fiction section and class 635 respectively), "is inspired by the *Old Farmer's Almanac* to track the growing things in her city world. Month by month, the round-faced girl with stick-straight hair never lacks for activities, whether making flower garlands, identifying birds or creating a Christmas-present collage out of beach debris." Publ Wkly

"The book is unusually fresh and charming in its approach; the many facts are presented agreeably and lightened by the child's pleasure in activities which young readers could copy." Grow Point

Hirschi, Ron

Spring; photographs by Thomas D. Mangelsen. Cobblehill Bks. 1990 unp il $13.95 (k-2) **508**

1. Spring
ISBN 0-525-65037-7 LC 89-49039

"A Wildlife seasons book"

"Focusing on spring as a time of birth and renewal for animals, this features large, high-quality color photographs showing awakening bears and marmots, birds in their nests, and many animal babies. The simple text is set in bold, large type with plenty of white space. . . . The book includes a detailed afterword that extends the information." Booklist

Winter; photographs by Thomas D. Mangelsen. Cobblehill Bks. 1990 unp il $13.95 (k-2) **508**

1. Winter
ISBN 0-525-65026-1 LC 89-23935

Hirschi, Ron—*Continued*

"A Wildlife seasons book"

"Readers explore winter scenes in the wilderness as spare, poetic text and crisp, closeup photographs bring groups of animals to life." Sci Child

MacFarlane, Ruth B. Alford

Making your own nature museum; illustrated by Jean Lynn Alred. Watts 1989 128p il lib bdg $11.90 (5 and up) **508**

1. Nature study
ISBN 0-531-10809-0 LC 89-31826

"A Venture book"

"Extremely detailed advice on collecting, preparing, preserving, and displaying natural history items such as plants, insects, bones, minerals, and fossils. Aspects of safety and legality are covered." Horn Book Guide

"While few students may actually set up a nature museum, many can benefit from MacFarlane's experience as a biologist and science-museum curator, particularly when it's time to fulfill scouting merit badge requirements, complete biology projects, or prepare science fair exhibits. Teachers and camp leaders will also find good ideas and sound expertise here." Booklist

Includes bibliography

Markle, Sandra, 1946-

Exploring spring; a season of science activities, puzzles and games. Atheneum Pubs. 1990 122p il $13.95 (4 and up) **508**

1. Spring 2. Science—Miscellanea
ISBN 0-689-31341-1 LC 89-394

A collection of springtime activities which include stories, observations of nature, handicraft, games and puzzles

"Most units have line drawings to illustrate the topic; there are no photographs. This is an enjoyable activity book for the imaginative child." Sci Books Films

Exploring summer; illustrated with drawings and computer graphics by the author. Atheneum Pubs. 1987 170p il $14.95 (4 and up) **508**

1. Summer 2. Science—Miscellanea
ISBN 0-689-31212-1 LC 86-17322

"Activities cover such topics as animal behavior, insects, plant growth and behavior, heat, bird houses, deserts, summer weather, the changing of seasons, and summer recreation." Sci Child

The author "writes with clarity and a slight breeziness. Her six multifaceted chapters are illustrated sparingly with small, sketchy drawings, and the pages are attractively designed with eye-catching subheadings in bold print. . . . An appealing and useful presentation, the book truly has something for every interest and will also extend the enjoyment of summer across the other seasons." Horn Book

Exploring winter; written and illustrated by Sandra Markle. Atheneum Pubs. 1984 154p il $12.95 (4 and up) **508**

1. Winter 2. Science—Miscellanea
ISBN 0-689-31065-X LC 84-3049

"A compendium of science, history, crafts, games, riddles and lore related to winter. A few of the topics included are the causes of winter, animals and plants in winter, Eskimos, ways to build an igloo, the story of Ursa Major and Ursa Minor, Arctic and Antarctic explorers, visible pollutants in snow, an instant cocoa recipe, and a wind chill factor chart. Scattered throughout the book are riddles, with answers provided in code." Booklist

"Remarkable in its variety, this collection of winter lore is both entertaining and informative." SLJ

Rights, Mollie

Beastly neighbors; all about wild things in the city, or why earwigs make good mothers; written by Mollie Rights; illustrations by Kim Solga. Little, Brown 1981 125p il $14.95; pa $7.95 (4 and up) **508**

1. Nature study
ISBN 0-316-74576-6; 0-316-74577-4 (pa) LC 80-21556

"A Brown paper school book"

Describes some of the animals that live in the soil, under leaves, bricks, or boards, and around the roots of plants and suggests ways the reader may study their characteristics and behavior more closely

"The author provides clear and often deep explanations of scientific questions; in addition, she poses some provocative questions of her own. . . . The monchromatic drawings are instructive and often whimsical. There is no index, but a comprehensive table of contents makes individual topics easy to locate." SLJ

Thomson, Peggy, 1922-

Auks, rocks and the odd dinosaur; inside stories from the Smithsonian's Museum of Natural History. Crowell 1985 120p il $13.95; lib bdg $14.89 (5 and up) **508**

1. National Museum of Natural History (U.S.)
ISBN 0-690-04491-7; 0-690-04492-5 (lib bdg) LC 85-47744

The author describes "the fascinating oddities assembled in the Smithsonian's Museum of Natural History. Revealed are the difficulties in reconstructing life forms and the remarkable ingenuity employed to create exhibits in a believable and realistic format. Black-and-white photos include several rare finds from the 1880s. . . . Illustrations and text complement the overall format." SLJ

Whitfield, Philip J.

Why do the seasons change? questions on nature's rhythms and cycles answered by the Natural History Museum; [by] Philip Whitfield & Joyce Pope. Viking 1987 96p il maps lib bdg $16.95 (4 and up) **508**

1. Natural history
ISBN 0-670-81860-7 LC 87-40133

In question-and-answer format, the authors discuss topics "from ice ages and climatology to reproduction and migration, from human physiology and epidemics

Whitfield, Philip J.—*Continued*
to the life cycle of certain animals." Grow Point

"Questions are grouped together by topic with each page having one or two questions with a direct answer followed by a brief but easily understood explanation. . . . While not useful for reports, this visually appealing and well-organized book should be popular with curious youngsters." SLJ

Wilkes, Angela
My first nature book. Knopf 1990 48p il $9.95; lib bdg $10.99 (1-4) **508**

1. Nature study
ISBN 0-394-86610-X; 0-394-96610-4 (lib bdg) LC 89-8019

Provides an introduction to nature through a variety of simple indoor and outdoor activities including collecting seeds, feeding birds, watching a butterfly grow, and others

This "is an attractive and appealing activity book. It is quite a large book, and this format allows the illustrations to be life size. This results in a work that has dramatic visual impact. The design of each page is well planned, relying on photographs as well as text." Appraisal

509 Science—Historical and geographic treatment

Beshore, George W.
Science in ancient China; [by] George Beshore. Watts 1988 95p il map lib bdg $10.40 (5 and up) **509**

1. Science—China—History 2. Science and civilization
ISBN 0-531-10485-0 LC 87-23748

"A First book"

Surveys the achievements of the ancient Chinese in science, medicine, astronomy, and cosmology, and describes such innovations as rockets, wells, the compass, water wheels, and movable type

"Attractive black-and-white photographs and historical illustrations appear on almost every page." Booklist

Includes glossary and bibliography

Gay, Kathlyn
Science in ancient Greece. Watts 1988 95p il map lib bdg $10.40 (5 and up) **509**

1. Science—Greece—History 2. Science and civilization
ISBN 0-531-10487-7 LC 87-23747

"A First book"

Discusses the theories of ancient Greek philosopher-scientists such as Ptolemy, Pythagoras, Hippocrates, and Aristotle, and describes scientific discoveries and their applications in ancient Greece

Includes glossary and bibliography

Harris, Jacqueline L., 1929-
Science in ancient Rome. Watts 1988 72p il map lib bdg $10.40 (5 and up) **509**

1. Science—Rome—History 2. Science and civilization
ISBN 0-531-10595-4 LC 88-2649

"A First book"

This book describes the role of science in Roman agriculture, medicine, metallurgy, and architecture

"Each chapter concetrates on a specific aspect of Roman technology, including engineering, architecture, mining, farming, public health, medicine, the development of cartography, and the implementation of the Julian calendar. A final chapter attempts to succinctly summarize the Roman technological and architectural legacy. . . . The information, although carefully edited and brief, is accurate and well presented. Illustrations throughout complement the text in a pleasing format." Sci Books Films

Includes glossary and bibliography

510 Mathematics

Adler, Irving
Mathematics; illustrated by Ron Miller. Doubleday 1990 45p il $11.95; lib bdg $12.99 (4 and up) **510**

1. Mathematics
ISBN 0-385-26142-X; 0-385-26143-8 (lib bdg) LC 89-32712

An introduction to the science of numbers and space, discussing basic concepts, and including an introduction to computer programming, mathematical games, and activities

"An excellent book in every way. The mathematical principles are enrichment-level concepts, clearly explained with text and illustration. . . . It's a simple book, and that's its beauty. Younger children will enjoy the large format, and those who have access to computers will find their knowledge of them extended with instruction in a little Basic programming while conveying fascinating number facts." SLJ

510.7 Mathematics—Education and related topics

Arithmetic Teacher. National Council of Teachers of Mathematics $45 per year **510.7**

1. Arithmetic—Study and teaching—Periodicals
ISSN 0004-136X

Monthly September through May. First published 1954

"The basic periodical for the teaching of mathematics in an elementary school, this offers specific ideas about how to improve teaching methods. The emphasis is on new approaches to pedagogical techniques. There are contributors from both teachers and those who teach the teachers, and from professional mathematicians. Reports on research are included. A useful feature offers reviews not only of books, but of related materials, including computer software. . . . A basic title for elementary school collections." Katz. Mag for Sch Libr

511 Mathematics—General topics

Anno, Mitsumasa, 1926-

Socrates and the three little pigs; pictures by Mitsumasa Anno; text by Tuyosi Mori. Philomel Bks. 1986 44p il $13.95 (4-6) **511**

1. Probabilities 2. Mathematics
ISBN 0-399-21310-4 LC 85-21564

"In this entertaining book that combines learning with fun, Socrates is the name of the wolf in the story of the three little pigs. He is trying to determine in which of five houses he is most likely to find one or more of the pigs. The outstanding illustrations show all the possibilities, and Socrates and the reader discover the basic ideas that underlie combinations, permutations, probabilities, odds, and making choices." Sci Books Films

512 Algebra and number theory

Anno, Masaichiro

Anno's mysterious multiplying jar; [by] Masaichiro and Mitsumasa Anno; illustrated by Mitsumasa Anno. Philomel Bks. 1983 unp il $14.95 (2-5) **512**

1. Factorials 2. Mathematics
ISBN 0-399-20951-4 LC 82-22413

Simple text and pictures introduce the mathematical concept of factorials

This book "begins with a painting of a handsome blue and white lidded jar, moves into fantasy with pictures of the water in the jar becoming a sea on which an old sailing ship is moving, transfers to an island on the sea, and goes on to describe the rooms in the houses in the kingdoms on the mountains in the countries on the island. Each time the number grows: one island, two countries, three mountains, etc. How many jars, then, were in the boxes that were in the cupboards in the rooms? . . . The explanation is in itself clear, and is expanded by other examples of factorials. The weakness of the book is that the first set of pages seems designed, in appearance and concept, for very young children, whereas the final pages are more appropriate for older ones." Bull Cent Child Books

513 Arithmetic

Adler, David A., 1947-

Roman numerals; illustrated by Byron Barton. Crowell 1977 33p il (Young math bks) lib bdg $12.89 (2-4) **513**

1. Numerals
ISBN 0-690-01302-7 LC 77-2270

"Adler provides exercises on how to write Roman numerals and handle the subscription principle involved in writing the symbols representing four and nine. He also explains the historical origins of the symbols for five and ten plus the uses and development of Roman numerals—information difficult to obtain for this age level." SLJ

"A simple demonstration with labeled cards clearly explains how the symbols are ordered; another practice lesson tests readers' comprehension of when to use subtraction symbols. . . . A jaunty cartoon figure acts out textual descriptions against an orange-and-brown backdrop. It's a light, lucid, good-humored lesson." Booklist

Anno, Mitsumasa, 1926-

Anno's math games. Philomel Bks. 1987 104p il $18.95 (k-3) **513**

1. Mathematics
ISBN 0-399-21151-9 LC 86-30513

"From extremely simple 'what is different?' pictures, Anno quickly builds in complexity to tables, mapping, bar graphs, and visual presentations of proportions." SLJ

Anno leads "the reader into an enchanting world full of interesting observations of things that are different and the same, that combine and come apart, and turn out to be an introduction to mathematics so sophisticated it is absolutely simple and clear. The watercolor illustrations are cheery." N Y Times Book Rev

Anno's math games II. Philomel Bks. 1989 103p il $19.95 (k-3) **513**

1. Mathematics
ISBN 0-399-21615-4 LC 86-30513

"The book presents mathematics and a great deal more with many pictures and very little to read. There are sections on counting, numeration, and measurement as well as left-right orientation, conservation, block building, comparing and contrasting, and other types of picture puzzles." Sci Child

Burns, Marilyn

The I hate mathematics! book; illustrated by Martha Hairston. Little, Brown 1975 127p il $14.95; pa $8.95 (5 and up) **513**

1. Mathematics
ISBN 0-316-11740-4; 0-316-11741-2 (pa) LC 75-6707

"A Brown paper school book"

"This lively collection of puzzles, riddles, magic tricks, and brain teasers provides a painless introduction to mathematical concepts and terms through the process of experimentation and discovery. The cartoon-like illustration and breezy titles . . . should appeal to the not-so-mathematically inclined as well as to puzzle devotees. Required materials are readily available and inexpensive; the techniques described are educationally sound and exciting. An excellent resource for parents, teachers, and children." Horn Book

Math for smarty pants; illustrated by Martha Weston. Little, Brown 1982 128p il $13.95; pa $7.95 (5 and up) **513**

1. Mathematics
ISBN 0-316-11738-2; 0-316-11739-0 (pa)
LC 81-19314

"A Brown paper school book"

Text, illustrations, and suggested activities offer a common-sense approach to mathematic fundamentals for those who are slightly terrified of numbers

This book "is a step up for those readers who have mastered the concepts in the author's 'I Hate Mathematics! Book' [entered above]." Booklist

Fisher, Leonard Everett, 1924-

Number art: thirteen 1 2 3s from around the world; written and illustrated by Leonard Everett Fisher. Four Winds Press 1982 61p il $12.95 (4 and up) **513**

1. Numerals

ISBN 0-02-735240-4 LC 82-5050

"Traces the history and design of 13 systems of numerical notation—Arabic, Armenian, Brahmi, Chinese, Egyptian, Gothic, Greek, Mayan, Roman, Runes, Sanskrit, Thai and Tibetan. Beautifully designed, this book will be useful as an introduction to the different number systems." N Y Public Libr. Ref Books for Child Collect

Froman, Robert

The greatest guessing game; a book about dividing; illustrated by Gioia Fiammenghi. Crowell 1978 33p il (Young math bks) lib bdg $12.89 (2-4) **513**

1. Arithmetic

ISBN 0-690-01376-0 LC 77-5463

This introduction to division compares the operation to a guessing game by showing how objects may be divided among several friends

Sitomer, Mindel, 1903-

How did numbers begin? [by] Mindel and Harry Sitomer; illustrated by Richard Cuffari. Crowell 1976 33p il (Young math bks) lib bdg $12.89 (2-4) **513**

1. Numeration

ISBN 0-690-00794-9 LC 75-11756

Briefly explains the matching and comparison of quantities, the naming and ordering of numbers, and counting—all steps in the history of numbers

Watson, Clyde

Binary numbers; illustrated by Wendy Watson. Crowell 1977 33p il (Young math bks) lib bdg $12.89 (2-4) **513**

1. Binary system (Mathematics)

ISBN 0-690-00993-3 LC 75-29161

"An excellent way to teach the concept of binary numbers by using manipulatives. Contains information on how to write binary numerals, an interesting story about doubling, and a secret binary number code." Sci Child

513.028 Arithmetic—Techniques, procedures, apparatus, equipment, materials

Dilson, Jesse

The abacus: a pocket computer; drawings by Angela Pozzi. St. Martin's Press 1975 c1968 143p il pa $6.95 (5 and up) **513.028**

1. Abacus

ISBN 0-312-00140-1

First published 1968

This book describes the development of the abacus, its colorul history, and its use in the Orient. Instructions for making and using an abacus are included

516 Geometry

Froman, Robert

Angles are easy as pie; illustrated by Byron Barton. Crowell 1976 c1975 33p il (Young math bks) lib bdg $12.89 (2-4) **516**

1. Geometry

ISBN 0-690-00916-X LC 75-6608

"Angles are invitingly defined as delicious pieces of pie which are divided among Barton's hungry-looking and Hester-like alligators. Other everyday angles are pointed out and are used to build triangles, quadrangles, and various polygons. Instructions for cutting out angles and making figures are clearly incorporated into the text." Appraisal

Hoban, Tana

Shapes, shapes, shapes. Greenwillow Bks. 1986 unp il $11.75; lib bdg $11.88 (k-2) **516**

1. Geometry

ISBN 0-688-05832-9; 0-688-05833-7 (lib bdg) LC 85-17569

Photographs of familiar objects such as chair, barrettes, and manhole cover present a study of rounded and angular shapes

"Tana Hoban has created an excellent concept book that will encourage children to look for specific shapes in everyday urban scenes. There are triangles, circles, trapezoids, and so on, in photographs of such varied subjects as buildings, laundries and street vendor's wares. The photographs not only serve to teach shapes and colors but are works of art themselves. . . . This book not only succeeds in helping children learn shapes, but helps to instill in them observational instincts that are such an important, integral part of many disciplines, especially science." Appraisal

Rogers, Paul, 1950-
The shapes game; pictures by Sian Tucker; verse by Paul Rogers. Holt & Co. 1990 unp il $12.95 (k-2) **516**

1. Geometry
ISBN 0-8050-1280-X LC 89-19957

"Designed to encourage children's visual acuity in distinguishing shapes, this book introduces circles, sqares, triangles, crescents, rectangles, spirals, ovals, diamonds, and stars. A page that has a rhyming text and the appropriate shapes faces a page on which the shapes are combined in a montage." Bull Cent Child Books

"The rhyming verse offers children a delightful excursion into the world of shapes. Colorful collage illustrations add zest to the 'I spy' game. A lively and enjoyable experience." Child Book Rev Serv

Testa, Fulvio, 1947-
If you look around you. Dial Bks. for Young Readers 1983 unp il $10.95; pa $3.95 (k-3) **516**

1. Geometry
ISBN 0-8037-0003-2; 0-8037-0432-1 (pa) LC 83-5310

Geometric shapes are depicted in scenes of children in- and out-of-doors

"The deeply hued pictures adroitly juggle a clean format with cleverly detained content, making them easy to take in at a glance, yet worth a second look. This fine introduction to shapes will work equally well with individuals and groups." Booklist

520 Astronomy and allied sciences

Hirst, Robin
My place in space; by Robin and Sally Hirst; illustrated by Roland Harvey with Joe Levine. Orchard Bks. 1990 unp il $13.95; lib bdg $13.99 (2-4) **520**

1. Astronomy
ISBN 0-531-05859-X; 0-531-08459-0 (lib bdg) LC 89-37893

First published 1988 in Australia

"Little drawings of a small Australian town serve as foreground for dramatic paintings of the universe—all illustrating exactly where Henry Wilson and his sister Rosie live. The science is sound, presented in enough detail to be interesting but with enough simplicity to be recalled and repeated aloud." Bull Cent Child Books

Wyler, Rose
The starry sky; pictures by Steven James Petruccio. Messner 1989 32p il (Outdoor science bk) lib bdg $10.98; pa $3.95 (k-4) **520**

1. Astronomy
ISBN 0-671-66345-3 (lib bdg); 0-671-66349-6 (pa) LC 88-31192

The author discusses night and day, the rotation of the earth, the phases of the moon, the stars, and the planets

"In this wonderful book . . . beautiful and scientifically correct illustrations masterfully capture the child's imagination. Simple experiments reinforce concepts that help children to understand day and night, stars, and the Earth's movement." Sci Child

520.5 Astronomy—Serial publications

Odyssey: space exploration and astronomy for young people. Kalmbach $21 **520.5**

1. Astronomy—Periodicals
ISSN 0163-0946

Monthly. First published 1979 by AstroMedia Corp.

"Brilliantly colored from cover to cover, *Odyssey* is a fun-filled educational children's magazine for the 8-12 age group. Each issue contains five to seven excellently written and illustrated articles and regular sections describing basic concepts of astronomy. . . . In addition, the magazine is jam-packed with word games, puzzles, cutout projects, card games, and a continuous space adventure comic strip." Katz. Mag for Sch Libr

522 Techniques, procedures, apparatus, equipment, materials of astronomy

Lampton, Christopher
The space telescope. Watts 1987 70p il lib bdg $10.40 (5 and up) **522**

1. Hubble Space Telescope 2. Astronomy
ISBN 0-531-10221-1 LC 86-23351

"A First book"

"Following a brief history of astronomy from the ancient naked eye astronomers, Lampton describes the Hubble Space Telescope (HST) [developed] for the 1988 shuttle launch. As background, he explains many modern astronomical terms and scientific theories, such as galaxies, quasars, black holes, and Hubbard's 'big bang' theory of the creation of the universe." SLJ

Includes bibliography

523 Specific celestial bodies and phenomena

Atkinson, Stuart
Journey into space; illustrated by Jonathan Duval. Viking 1988 80p il lib bdg $14.95 (4-6) **523**

1. Astronomy 2. Universe
ISBN 0-670-82306-6 LC 87-51436

"Science fact and fiction mingle in a whirlwind tour of the solar system and beyond. Written as the travel diary of an enthusiastic young contest-winner from the next century, Atkinson's book takes readers from Mercury . . . to Pluto, and thence to the small research colony orbiting Proxima Centauri, where the tourist group receives lectures on the stars, galaxies, and the Big Bang." SLJ

"Up-to-the-minute knowledge is discussed and wonderful vivid photographs and drawings are on every page.

Atkinson, Stuart—*Continued*
What an excellent and practical way to review our newly acquired facts on astronomy." Child Book Rev Serv

Berger, Melvin, 1927-
Star gazing, comet tracking, and sky mapping; illustrated by William Negron. Putnam 1985 80p il lib bdg $10.99 (5 and up) **523**

1. Astronomy 2. Stars
ISBN 0-399-61211-4 LC 84-8302

"Approximately half of this book is packed with information about thirty constellations, including locations, names of their major stars, and relevant legends. The remainder of the book catalogs and describes major comets and gives brief instructions for amateur astronomical activities. The volume might serve as a reference book, but it is unlikely that any child (or adult) would read through all the masses of data from beginning to end." Child Book Rev Serv

Includes bibliography

Branley, Franklyn Mansfield, 1915-
Sun dogs and shooting stars; a skywatcher's calendar; by Franklyn M. Branley; illustrated by True Kelley. Houghton Mifflin 1980 115p il $14.95 (5 and up) **523**

1. Astronomy 2. Meteorology
ISBN 0-395-29520-3 LC 80-17430

"After an introduction to the calendar is a brief summary of the seasonal night skies and information on solstices or equinoxes, etc.; then, in a month-by-month arrangement within each season, there is information on the names of the months, what sky events occur that month and anecdotal material on important events or persons connected to the month. . . . The style is chatty and encouraging; the solid information clearly presented." SLJ

Includes bibliography

Cole, Joanna
The magic school bus, lost in the solar system; illustrated by Bruce Degen. Scholastic 1990 unp il $13.95 (2-4) **523**

1. Astronomy 2. Outer space—Exploration 3. Planets
ISBN 0-590-41428-3 LC 89-10185

"The planetarium is closed for repairs, so the Magic School Bus blasts off on a real tour of the solar system. After their previous field trips, the children in Ms. Frizzle's class are all blasé about such things; as they land on the Moon, Venus, and Mars, and fly by the other planets and the Sun, they comment on what they see, generate a blizzard of one- or two-sentence reports on special topics and—even while Ms. Frizzle is temporarily left behind in the asteroid belt—crack terrible jokes." SLJ

Dickinson, Terence
Exploring the night sky; the equinox astronomy guide for beginners; illustrated by John Bianchi. Camden House (Charlotte) 1987 72p il $15.95; pa $9.95 (5 and up) **523**

1. Astronomy
ISBN 0-920656-64-1; 0-920656-66-8 (pa)

This book takes readers "from the Moon (1.3 light-seconds) to the galactic field in general (300 million light-years)—with a quick spin about the solar system, adding season-by-season charts of the salient planets, stars, and constellations visible from North America." SLJ

"A good introduction to astronomy for young readers. . . . The author wisely offers only a little unsupported speculation about the unknowns of our universe, and he makes a significant effort to point out our inability to understand the physical nature of many of these celestial objects due to our lack of firsthand observation and the incomprehensible vastness of the subject." Best Sci Books & A-V Materials for Child

Includes glossary and bibliography

Jobb, Jamie
The night sky book; an everyday guide to every night; illustrated by Linda Bennett. Little, Brown 1977 127p il $14.95 (4 and up) **523**

1. Astronomy
ISBN 0-316-46551-8 LC 77-24602

"A Brown paper school book"

An introductory stargazing manual including information and projects on the zodiac, moon, time, solar system, and finding directions and location using the stars

Krupp, E. C. (Edwin C.)
The Big Dipper and you; illustrated by Robin Rector Krupp. Morrow Junior Bks. 1989 48p il $13.95; lib bdg $13.88 (3-5) **523**

1. Stars 2. Ursa Major
ISBN 0-688-07191-0; 0-688-07192-9 (lib bdg) LC 88-1501

"An easy-to-understand, informative description of our most easily recognizable constellation and how the movement of the Earth and stars change the picture of our night sky. Includes information on the North Star, distances in space, and how to locate other constellations using the Big Dipper as a guide." Sci Child

Lampton, Christopher
Stars & planets; illustrated by Ron Miller. Doubleday 1988 41p il $10.95; lib bdg $11.99 (3-6) **523**

1. Stars 2. Planets 3. Astronomy 4. Outer space—Exploration
ISBN 0-385-23785-5; 0-385-23786-3 (lib bdg) LC 87-13628

"In addition to the *Stars and Planets* of the title, Lampton covers 12 other topics, including asteroids, comets, meteors, exploring the universe, and extra-terrestrial beings. Novice astronomers will find enough

Lampton, Christopher—*Continued*
here to whet their appetites, especially considering the oversized color illustrations. Indeed, the illustrations are one of the nicest features of the book, their size making them excellent for class display." SLJ

Simon, Seymour, 1931-
Look to the night sky: an introduction to star watching. Viking 1977 87p il o.p.; Penguin Bks. paperback available $5.95 (4 and up) **523**
1. Astronomy
ISBN 0-14-049185-6 (pa) LC 77-24181
"An experienced stargazer gives practical advice to beginnners of an enjoyable hobby. Various schemes are explained for finding constellations. Also discussed are the moon, planets, comets, meteorites, eclipses, and other heavenly phenomena." Child Book Rev Serv
Includes bibliography

Weiss, Malcolm E.
Sky watchers of ages past; illustrated by Eliza McFadden. Houghton Mifflin 1982 84p il $7.95 (5 and up) **523**
1. Astronomy 2. Archeology
ISBN 0-395-29525-4 LC 81-20142
"Using techniques of the Pueblos, the Mayans, and the early people of Stonehenge as examples, Weiss discusses the methods that various ancient people used to record the passing of seasons. Although they had none of today's technology, these and other early astronomers developed accurate ways to study the heavens. The text not only describes how they made their calculations, but also carefully probes why." Booklist
Includes bibliography

523.1 The universe; space, galaxies, quasars

Apfel, Necia H., 1930-
Nebulae; the birth and death of stars. Lothrop, Lee & Shepard Bks. 1988 48p il $13.95; lib bdg $13.88 (4 and up) **523.1**
1. Galaxies 2. Stars
ISBN 0-688-07228-3; 0-688-07229-1 (lib bdg) LC 86-33765
Describes how nebulae or clouds of dust particles and gases in space form from the residue of dying stars and how some nebulae contain matter from which stars are born
"The photographs of nebulae and other formations are stunning. Apfel's text is straightforward and informative without overwhelming readers; each paragraph is a small, comprehensible essay beautifully matched with a clear, captioned, full-color photograph. This picture book is a delightful, accessible introduction to an appealing topic." Publ Wkly
Includes bibliography

Asimov, Isaac, 1920-
Mythology and the universe. Stevens, G. 1990 32p il (Isaac Asimov's library of the universe) lib bdg $9.95 (3-5) **523.1**
1. Astronomy 2. Universe
ISBN 1-55532-403-7 LC 89-11360
This illustrated book "covers astrology, constellations, superstitious responses to comets and eclipses, the zodiac, pole stars, and people in the moon." SLJ
Includes glossary and bibliography

Branley, Franklyn Mansfield, 1915-
Mysteries of the universe; by Franklyn M. Branley; diagrams by Sally J. Bensusen. Lodestar Bks. 1984 71p il (Mysteries of the universe ser) $10.95 (6 and up) **523.1**
1. Universe
ISBN 0-525-66914-0 LC 83-25302
Discusses the various theories concerning the creation, expansion, and possible end of the universe. Also defines such phenomena as black holes, neutrons, pulsars, red shifts, and other discoveries that further enhance our knowledge of the world beyond our planet
"The book's strength is in Branley's explanations, which both clarify the substance of the question and trace the scientific logic that suggests certain solutions. He defines many concepts and procedures along the way so that readers get a good dose of background information." Booklist

Simon, Seymour, 1931-
Galaxies. Morrow Junior Bks. 1988 unp il $12.95; lib bdg $12.88 (2-5) **523.1**
1. Galaxies
ISBN 0-688-08002-2; 0-688-08004-9 (lib bdg) LC 87-23967
"This is a step-by-step introduction to and description of the many galaxies in the universe. . . . He includes discussions of the ways in which astronomers classify galaxies, black holes, smaller satellite galaxies such as the Magellanic Clouds and supernovas. The terms are explained within the text." Publ Wkly
"This fine introduction to an awe-inspiring subject will surely stimulate interest in stargazing, further reading, and investigation." Horn Book

523.2 Solar system

Rathbun, Elizabeth
Exploring your solar system. National Geographic Soc. 1989 96p il $7.95; lib bdg $9.50 (4 and up) **523.2**
1. Solar system 2. Outer space—Exploration
ISBN 0-87044-703-3; 0-87044-708-4 (lib bdg) LC 89-3138
"Books for world explorers"
Presents a guided tour of the nine planets within the solar system. Also discusses the Milky Way Galaxy, comets, and the search for extraterrestrial intelligence
Includes bibliography

523.3 Moon

Branley, Franklyn Mansfield, 1915-

The moon seems to change; by Franklyn M. Branley; illustrations by Barbara and Ed Emberley. rev ed. Crowell 1987 29p il (Let's-read-and-find-out science bks) $12.95; lib bdg $12.89; pa $4.50 (k-3) **523.3**

1. Moon
ISBN 0-690-04583-2; 0-690-04585-9 (lib bdg); 0-06-445065-1 (pa) LC 86-47747

A revised and newly illustrated edition of the title first published 1960

The author "explains the waxing and waning of the moon and compares the length of a day on earth and on the moon. Each page has colorful explanatory illustrations. . . . Branley's brief-easy-to-read text and the Emberleys' diagrams make this book a welcome addition to science collections for young children or the picture book section." SLJ

What the moon is like; [by] Franklyn M. Branley; illustrated by True Kelley. rev ed. Crowell 1986 31p il (Let's-read-and-find-out science bks) lib bdg $12.89; pa $3.95 (k-3) **523.3**

1. Moon
ISBN 0-690-04512-3 (lib bdg); 0-06-445052-X (pa) LC 85-45400

A revised and newly illustrated edition of the title first published 1963

"NASA photographs and information gathered by the Apollo space missions are incorporated into [this book] along with a comparative description of how the moon's composition, terrain, and atmosphere differ from the earth's." Booklist

"This is a good first introduction to the subject, neither too technical nor diluted to blandness. The illustrations combine a few unimpressive photos . . . with a new set of simple, clear, uncluttered drawings, including a map showing the Apollo landing sites." SLJ

Couper, Heather

The moon; [by] Heather Couper and Nigel Henbest. Watts 1987 c1986 32p il (Space scientist) lib bdg $10.90 (4 and up) **523.3**

1. Moon
ISBN 0-531-10266-1 LC 86-50350

First published 1986 in the United Kingdom

"The text progresses in logical fashion from the most obvious aspects of the Moon, such as phases and tides, to its origin, geology and geography. There is an abundance of excellent photographs, illustrations and diagrams, that readily support a clear and succinct text." Appraisal

Includes glossary

Davis, Don

The moon; [by] Don Davis and David Hughes. Facts on File 1989 45p il (Planetary exploration) $13.95 (4-6) **523.3**

1. Moon
ISBN 0-8160-2046-9 LC 89-31688

Discusses the latest data available about our moon, including a review of conditions there which could support life

Simon, Seymour, 1931-

The moon. Four Winds Press 1984 unp il $12.95 (1-4) **523.3**

1. Moon
ISBN 0-02-782840-9 LC 83-11707

"This book provides [an] . . . introduction to the Moon's composition, the lunar environment, and the information gathered by the 'Apollo' space expeditions." Sci Child

"A large, square book with large, clear print and a text that is lucid, continuous, accurate, and clearly written." Bull Cent Child Books

523.4 Planets

Asimov, Isaac, 1920-

How did we find out about Neptune? illustrated by Erika Kors. Walker & Co. 1990 59p il $12.95; lib bdg $13.85 (5 and up) **523.4**

1. Neptune (Planet)
ISBN 0-8027-6981-0; 0-8027-6982-9 (lib bdg) LC 90-38771

An account of astronomers' observations over the years leading to the discovery of Neptune's existence

"An excellent resource for learning about the solar system and discovering how observation and prediction can lead to new scientific knowledge." Sci Child

Pluto: a double planet? Stevens, G. 1990 32p il (Isaac Asimov's library of the universe) lib bdg $9.95 (3-5) **523.4**

1. Pluto (Planet)
ISBN 1-55532-373-1 LC 89-11290

Introduces this small, distant, and mysterious planet, surveying its discovery sixty years ago, peculiar orbit, and recently discovered satellite

Includes glossary and bibliography

Branley, Franklyn Mansfield, 1915-

Saturn; the spectacular planet; illustrated by Leonard Kessler. Crowell 1983 57p il 12.95; lib bdg $12.89; pa $4.95 (4 and up) **523.4**

1. Saturn (Planet)
ISBN 0-690-04213-2; 0-690-04214-0 (lib bdg); 0-06-446056-4 (pa) LC 81-43890

Describes the physical features and characteristics of Saturn and its satellites, and presents theories about its rings

"Color photographs from 'Voyager I' and 'Voyager II' convey Saturn's beauty. Black-and-white drawings com-

Branley, Franklyn Mansfield, 1915-—*Continued*

pare Earth and Saturn. This book will be a welcome addition to elementary libraries." Sci Child

Uranus; the seventh planet; [by] Franklyn M. Branley; illustrations by Yvonne Buchanan. Crowell 1988 53p il (Voyage into space bk) $11.95; lib bdg $11.89 (3-6) **523.4**

1. Project Voyager 2. Uranus (Planet)
ISBN 0-690-04685-5; 0-690-04687-1 (lib bdg)
LC 87-35046

Describes the physical characteristics, movements, satellites, and other features of Uranus, with an emphasis on recent discoveries from Project Voyager

"Black-and-white Voyager II photographs show details of the surfaces of Uranus and her satellites. Black-and-white line drawings are used to illustrate explanations, and a color photo insert is also included." SLJ

Includes bibliography

Halliday, Ian

Saturn; [by] Don Davies and Ian Halliday. Facts on File 1989 45p il (Planetary exploration) $13.95 (4-6) **523.4**

1. Saturn (Planet)
ISBN 0-8160-2049-3 LC 89-31685

This book uses the latest data available from recent Pioneer and Voyager missions to present what is known about the planet Saturn

Harris, Alan, 1944-

The great Voyager adventure; a guided tour through the solar system; [by] Alan Harris and Paul Weissman. Messner 1990 79p il $10.95; lib bdg $12.98 (5 and up) **523.4**

1. Project Voyager 2. Planets 3. Outer space—Exploration
ISBN 0-671-72539-4; 0-671-72538-6 (lib bdg)
LC 90-6423

Discusses the Voyager space probes and the information they have brought back about Jupiter, Saturn, Uranus, and Neptune

"The authors write with clarity and enthusiasm, imparting plenty of information without bogging down in technical detail. Their tale of discovery is enhanced by arrays of sharp, well-chosen photographs, mostly in color, plus a running timeline and plenty of tables and diagrams." SLJ

Includes glossary

Lauber, Patricia, 1924-

Journey to the planets. 3rd ed. Crown 1990 90p il $16.95; lib bdg $16.99 (4 and up) **523.4**

1. Planets
ISBN 0-517-58121-3; 0-517-58125-6 (lib bdg)
LC 90-33102

First published 1982

Explores the planets of our solar system, highlighting the prominent features of each. Includes new photos and information gathered by the Voyager explorations

Simon, Seymour, 1931-

Jupiter. Morrow 1985 unp il $14.95; lib bdg $14.88 (1-4) **523.4**

1. Jupiter (Planet)
ISBN 0-688-05796-9; 0-688-05797-7 (lib bdg)
LC 85-2922

Describes the characteristics of the planet Jupiter and its moons as revealed by photographs sent back by two unmanned Voyager spaceships which took one-and-one half years to reach this distant giant

"Large color (and black-and-white) photographs taken by the two Voyager spacecraft are the primary focus and will attract even resolute non-science readers." Appraisal

Mars. Morrow 1987 unp il $13; lib bdg $12.88; pa $5.95 (1-4) **523.4**

1. Mars (Planet)
ISBN 0-688-06584-8; 0-688-06585-6 (lib bdg); 0-688-09928-9 (pa) LC 86-31106

"There is no life on Mars. And there are no 'canals' on its surface. Scientists have ascertained this information from the Viking spacecraft landing in 1975. Astonishing pictures of the red planet are some of the highlights of this book that illuminate the way we think about Mars and about space. Simon has combined these vivid resources, with his characteristic spare, smooth prose." Publ Wkly

Saturn. Morrow 1985 unp il $13; lib bdg $12.88; pa $4.95 (1-4) **523.4**

1. Saturn (Planet)
ISBN 0-688-05798-5; 0-688-05799-3 (lib bdg); 0-688-08404-4 (pa) LC 85-2995

Describes the sixth planet from the sun, its rings, and its moons, and includes photographs taken in outer space

"The only flaw is a poor explanation of the orbits of the particles that make up Saturn's rings: explaining that Saturn's gravity keeps the rings from flying off into space, Simon says that gravity pulls them toward the center of the planet but fails to explain that their motion prevents their actually falling to the planet's surface. This quibble does not significantly detract from [the book's] overall quality. . . . It is the color photos that steal the show." SLJ

Uranus. Morrow 1987 unp il $13; lib bdg $12.88; pa $5.95 (1-4) **523.4**

1. Uranus (Planet)
ISBN 0-688-06582-1; 0-688-06583-X (lib bdg); 0-688-09929-7 (pa) LC 86-31223

This introduction to the seventh planet in the solar system incorporates data results from a 1986 pass by Voyager 2

"The photographs are mostly from those sent back by the spacecraft and show amazing detail which is clearly explained in the text." Horn Book

Yeomans, Donald K.
The distant planets; [by] Don Davis and Donald K. Yeomans. Facts on File 1989 45p il (Planetary exploration) $13.95 (4-6) **523.4**

1. Uranus (Planet) 2. Neptune (Planet) 3. Pluto (Planet)
ISBN 0-8160-2050-7 LC 89-31684

Discusses what is known of the occupants of the "deep freeze regions" of the solar system, Uranus, Neptune, and Pluto, based on current NASA data

523.5 Meteoroids, solar wind, zodiacal light

Lauber, Patricia, 1924-
Voyagers from space; meteors and meteorites; illustrated with photographs, and with drawings by Mike Eagle. Crowell 1989 74p il $14.95; lib bdg $14.89 (4 and up) **523.5**

1. Meteors 2. Asteroids 3. Comets
ISBN 0-690-04632-4; 0-690-04634-0 (lib bdg) LC 86-47745

Discusses asteroids, comets, and meteorites, explaining where they come from, how they were formed, and what effect these voyagers from space have when they streak past the Earth or plummet to its surface

"The design of the book is crisp and clean, with excellent photographs and drawings well chosen to illustrate the various phases of meteorites." Horn Book

Includes bibliography

523.6 Comets

Asimov, Isaac, 1920-
Comets and meteors. Stevens, G. 1990 32p il (Isaac Asimov's library of the universe) lib bdg $9.95 (3-5) **523.6**

1. Comets 2. Meteors
ISBN 1-55532-400-2 LC 89-4632

Discusses the characteristics of comets and meteors and cites both famous appearances and unexplained mysteries connected with them

Includes glossary and bibliography

Branley, Franklyn Mansfield, 1915-
Shooting stars; by Franklyn M. Branley; illustrated by Holly Keller. Crowell 1989 32p il (Let's-read-and-find-out science bks) $12.95; lib bdg $12.89 (k-3) **523.6**

1. Meteors
ISBN 0-690-04701-0; 0-690-04703-7 (lib bdg) LC 88-14190

Explains what shooting stars are, what they are made of, and what happens to them when they land on Earth

"At times, the text is almost lyrical, while brightly colored, cartoon-style graphics (plus a few photos) catch the eye." Booklist

523.7 Sun

Asimov, Isaac, 1920-
How did we find out about sunshine? illustrated by David Wool. Walker & Co. 1987 63p il $10.95; lib bdg $12.85 (5 and up) **523.7**

1. Force and energy 2. Sun
ISBN 0-8027-6697-8; 0-8027-6698-6 (lib bdg) LC 86-32581

"A historical overview of the importance of the Sun and humans' attempts to understand it. Discoveries by Galileo, Copernicus, Cassini, Newton, and Helmholtz, among others, and the discovery of nuclear energy are explained in a clear, easy-to-follow text. Readers readily understand how one discovery leads to new questions and that the process continues today." Sci Child

Branley, Franklyn Mansfield, 1915-
Eclipse: darkness in daytime; by Franklyn M. Branley; illustrated by Donald Crews. rev ed. Crowell 1988 32p il (Let's-read-and-find-out science bks) $12.95; lib bdg $12.89; Harper & Row pa $4.50 (k-3) **523.7**

1. Eclipses, Solar
ISBN 0-690-04617-0; 0-690-04619-7 (lib bdg); 0-06-445081-3 (pa) LC 87-45276

A reissue with new illustrations of the title first published 1973

This "book describes a total solar eclipse and how living things react to this daytime darkness. Mentioned also are myths of old. Partial eclipse and annular eclipse are also described." Sci Books Films

"Crews' illustrations offer a rich tapestry of pastels. The images are often impressionistic and soft, but sometimes Crews will call attention to some detail by the use of color or placing an object at an unusual angle. The results are striking and make an effective complement to this wonderful book that eclipses all others on the subject for this grade level." SLJ

The sun; our nearest star; [by] Franklyn M. Branley; illustrated by Don Madden. rev ed. Crowell 1988 31p il (Let's-read-and-find-out science bks) $12.95; lib bdg $12.89; Harper & Row pa $4.50 (k-3) **523.7**

1. Sun
ISBN 0-690-04680-4; 0-690-04678-2 (lib bdg); 0-06-445073-2 (pa) LC 87-45678

A revised and newly illustrated edition of the title first published 1961

Describes the sun and how it provides the light and energy which allow plant and animal life to exist on the earth

Gibbons, Gail

Sun up, sun down; written and illustrated by Gail Gibbons. Harcourt Brace Jovanovich 1983 unp il $13.95; pa $3.95 (1-3) **523.7**

1. Sun
ISBN 0-15-282781-1; 0-15-282782-X (pa) LC 82-23420

The author explains "the sun and its effect on the earth. Narrated by a little girl who notices the sun shining when she wakes up one morning, this . . . [book covers] what the sun does, what makes shadows, how the sun helps form rain clouds, and how it keeps the planet warm." Booklist

"Most of the information provided is explained by the child, who has an understanding of seasons, the concept of east and west and a firm grasp of distance and other concepts related to facts about the sun. The significance of some statements may elude younger children but the basic ideas, i.e., the sun's warmth and its power to help plants grow, will come through. The illustrations clarify the text with bold, clear drawings in full color." SLJ

Lampton, Christopher

The sun. Watts 1982 71p il lib bdg $10.40 (4 and up) **523.7**

1. Sun
ISBN 0-531-04390-8 LC 81-21991
"A First book"

Discusses changing ideas about the nature of the sun from ancient to modern times, what is presently believed about its formation, composition and activity, and its effects on the earth. Includes black and white and color photographs and other black and white illustrations

"The book is highly recommended as supplementary reading on astronomy for upper-elementary and junior-high students." Sci Books Films

Includes glossary and bibliography

Levasseur-Regourd, Anny-Chantal

Our sun and the inner planets; [by] Don Davis and Anny Chantal Levasseur-Regourd. Facts on File 1989 45p il (Planetary exploration) $13.95 (4-6) **523.7**

1. Sun 2. Solar system
ISBN 0-8160-2045-0 LC 89-31689

Text and illustrations present what astronomers now know about the "nuclear powerhouse" that dominates our solar system

Simon, Seymour, 1931-

The sun. Morrow 1986 unp il $14.95; lib bdg $14.88; pa $5.95 (1-4) **523.7**

1. Sun
ISBN 0-688-05857-4; 0-688-05858-2 (lib bdg); 0-688-09236-5 (pa) LC 85-32018

Describes the nature of the sun, its origin, source of energy, layers, atmosphere, sunspots, and activity

"Stunning full-color photographs show the turbulent surface of the sun, and clear illustrations clarify the cause and effect of such phenomena as gigantic prominences (geysers of flaming gas) and flares (fiery explosions with the power of ten million hydrogen bombs that last but a few minutes)." Publ Wkly

523.8 Stars

Berger, Melvin, 1927-

Bright stars, red giants, and white dwarfs. Putnam 1983 64p il $12.99 (5 and up) **523.8**

1. Stars
ISBN 0-399-61209-2 LC 82-23052

The author "follows a protostar to its maturity as a bright star, and then to its old age as a red giant. The star proceeds even further to a number of possibilities: white dwarf, supernova, pulsar and even to the enigmatic black hole in space." Child Book Rev Serv

"Key terminology is explained in context, and there is a glossary for backup. Black-and-white space photographs provide illustration." Booklist

Branley, Franklyn Mansfield, 1915-

The Big Dipper; by Franklyn M. Branley; illustrated by Molly Coxe. rev ed. HarperCollins Pubs. 1991 32p il (Let's-read-and-find-out science bks) $13.95; lib bdg $13.88 (k-3) **523.8**

1. Ursa Major
ISBN 0-06-020511-3; 0-06-020512-1 (lib bdg) LC 90-31199

A revised and newly illustrated edition of the title first published 1962

Explains basic facts about the Big Dipper, including which stars make up the constellation, how its position changes in the sky, and how it points to the North Star

Journey into a black hole; by Franklyn M. Branley; illustrated by Marc Simont. Crowell 1986 32p il (Let's-read-and-find-out science bks) lib bdg $12.89; pa $4.50 (k-3) **523.8**

1. Black holes (Astronomy)
ISBN 0-690-04544-1 (lib bdg); 0-690-445075-9 (pa) LC 85-48249

The author attempts "to explain how a black hole arises, what happens in its vicinity, and how astronomers might recognize one." Sci Books Films

"Simont's paintings effectively convey the mystery and magnitude of the unimaginable, the space and distance and density of a black hole. They are deft in interpreting Branley's lucid text, which skillfully streamlines the explanation of a complicated astronomical phenomenon so that it will be comprehensible to primary grades readers." Bull Cent Child Books

The sky is full of stars; illustrated by Felicia Bond. Crowell 1981 34p il (Let's-read-and-find-out science bks) lib bdg $12.89; pa $4.50 (k-3) **523.8**

1. Stars
ISBN 0-690-04123-3 (lib bdg); 0-06-445002-3 (pa) LC 81-43037

Branley, Franklyn Mansfield, 1915- —*Continued*

"This picture-book introduction to stargazing explains what constellations are and helps youngsters find them in seasonal skies. Brief background information calls attention to star colors and differing brightness; it also notes star movement. . . . A unique feature is the use of real photographs to picture some of the constellations. These appear twice, once unmarked, as you would really see them, and again with the constellation outlined. This gives youngsters a realistic idea of how obscure some figures can seem, yet how simple they are once one knows where to look. With cheery cartoon drawings in black and white or blue and yellow." Booklist

Star guide; [by] Franklyn M. Branley; illustrated by Ellen Eagle. Crowell 1987 51p il (Voyage into space bk) $11.95; lib bdg $12.89 (3-6) **523.8**

1. Stars
ISBN 0-690-04350-3; 0-690-04351-1 (lib bdg)
LC 82-45928

Describes the composition and behavior of stars and notes which ones can be seen at different times of the year

"Illustrated with a mix of soft charcoal drawings, astronomy photographs, and clear diagrams." Booklist

Superstar; the Supernova of 1987; [by] Franklyn M. Branley; illustrations by True Kelley. Crowell 1990 58p il (Voyage into space bk) $13.95; lib bdg $13.89 (3-6) **523.8**

1. Supernovae
ISBN 0-690-04839-4; 0-690-04841-6 (lib bdg)
LC 89-71164

Describes the nature and origin of supernovas, how they provide information on the formation of stars and planets, and what was learned from study of Supernova 1987A

"Illustrating the book are drawings, black-and-white photographs, and colorplates, the latter providing strikingly beautiful photos, including views of the 1987 supernova, the Chilean observatory from which it was first reported, and a neutrino detector. . . . Readers of any age seeking a basic summary of up-to-date knowledge on supernovas will be well served by Branley's book." Booklist

Includes bibliography

Rey, H. A. (Hans Augusto), 1898-1977

Find the constellations. rev ed. Houghton Mifflin 1976 72p il $14.95; pa $7.95 **523.8**

1. Stars
ISBN 0-395-24509-5; 0-395-24418-8 (pa)
LC 76-370489

First published 1954

"Constellation diagrams are presented with and without connecting lines and are drawn for 40° N. Latitude to cover the continental United States. The use of color in these diagrams is a refreshing change from the black-and-white usually used. Key words in the text are also highlighted in color, and the text includes at critical points several self-tests with inverted answer keys. Scientific accuracy is stressed, stellar magnitudes are indicated on the diagrams, and the concept of light year is discussed. Some of the myths surrounding the names of the constellations are given." Sci Books Films

"This is unquestionably a readable, enjoyable, and informative guide." SLJ

Simon, Seymour, 1931-

Stars. Morrow 1986 unp il $14.95; lib bdg $14.88 (1-4) **523.8**

1. Stars
ISBN 0-688-05855-8; 0-688-05856-6 (lib bdg)
LC 85-32012

"The brief text and dazzling illustrations serve as a sort of picture glossary introducing the terminology of stellar objects. *Stars* presents constellations; the distance to, size, and temperature of the stars; the nuclear power source of stellar energy; binary systems, clusters, galaxies, and quasars; the possibility of other solar systems; and stellar evolution, novae, black holes, neutron stars, and pulsars." SLJ

523.9 Satellites and rings; eclipses, transits, occultations

Kelch, Joseph W., 1958-

Small worlds: exploring the 60 moons of our solar system. Messner 1990 157p il $13.95; lib bdg $16.98 (6 and up) **523.9**

1. Satellites 2. Solar system
ISBN 0-671-70014-6; 0-671-70013-8 (lib bdg)
LC 87-2424

Discusses the origin and characteristics of each of the moons circling the planets of the solar system and presents information on both manned and unmanned space exploration

"An exciting book that clearly differentiates fact from theory. . . . A 20-page 'Checklist of Moons,' a tabular summary of each satellite's characteristics, is a valuable feature. The index is inclusive and accurate. The illustrations are mostly black-and-white photographs scattered throughout the book and color photographs grouped in the center. All are cited in the text and are well-chosen to illustrate Kelch's verbal descriptions. A must purchase because it brings together so much information." SLJ

525 Earth (Astronomical geography)

Asimov, Isaac, 1920-

How did we find out the Earth is round? illustrated by Matthew Kalmenoff. Walker & Co. 1972 59p il lib bdg $10.85 (5 and up) **525**

1. Earth
ISBN 0-8027-6122-4 LC 72-81378

"Early theories of the shape and structure of the earth are discussed, ending with the proof supplied by the explorations of Columbus and Magellan." Best Books for Child

"Well written, authentic, readily understood. This book

Asimov, Isaac, 1920-—*Continued*
should appeal to a wide range of readers." Adventuring with Books

Branley, Franklyn Mansfield, 1915-
Mysteries of planet earth; diagrams by Sally J. Bensusen. Lodestar Bks. 1989 70p il (Mysteries of the universe ser) $12.95 (6 and up) **525**

1. Astronomy 2. Earth
ISBN 0-525-67278-8 LC 88-31076

Among the topics discussed are: radioactive dating, the origin of life, magnetism, rotation, movements of continents, and motions of the air and sea

Includes bibliography

Sunshine makes the seasons; by Franklyn M. Branley; illustrated by Giulio Maestro. rev ed. Crowell 1986 32p il (Let's-read-and-find-out science bks) lib bdg $12.89; pa $3.95 (k-3) **525**

1. Seasons
ISBN 0-690-04482-8 (lib bdg); 0-06-445019-8 (pa) LC 85-42750

First published 1974

"The narrative and illustrations describe the real and apparent motions of the sun and the earth relative to one another and their relationships to changes of season. . . . Although there is nothing earth-shaking about the quality of the illustrations, it is appropriate for the topics covered, and it should be attractive to those for whom the book seems designed." Sci Books Films

What makes day and night; [by] Franklyn M. Branley; illustrated by Arthur Dorros. rev ed. Crowell 1986 32p il (Let's-read-and-find-out science bks) lib bdg $11.89; pa $4.50 (k-3) **525**

1. Earth 2. Day 3. Night
ISBN 0-690-04524-7 (lib bdg); 0-06-445050-3 (pa) LC 85-47903

A revised and newly illustrated edition of the title first published 1961

A simple explanation of how the rotation of the earth causes night and day

The illustrations feature "clear, colorful and sometimes mildly silly scenes that add some playfulness." SLJ

Fradin, Dennis B.
Earth. Childrens Press 1989 45p il lib bdg $13.27; pa $4.95 (2-4) **525**

1. Earth
ISBN 0-516-01172-3 (lib bdg); 0-516-41172-1 (pa) LC 89-9982

"New true book"

Discusses the Earth as a planet and describes its temperatures, movements in space, and other characteristics

"Illustrated with helpful full-color photographs and diagrams. Glossaries and brief fact lists appended." Booklist

Lauber, Patricia, 1924-
Seeing Earth from space. Orchard Bks. 1990 80p il maps $19.95; lib bdg $19.99 (4 and up) **525**

1. Earth sciences 2. Earth
ISBN 0-531-05902-2; 0-531-08502-3 (lib bdg) LC 89-77523

"This book uses photographs taken in space by astronauts and man-made satellites to describe Earth. It also discusses remote sensors and how they are used to study our planet." Voice Youth Advocates

"Well researched, clearly written, and beautifully made, this eye-opening book represents non-fiction at its best." Booklist

Includes bibliography

Simon, Seymour, 1931-
Earth, our planet in space. Four Winds Press 1984 unp il $12.95 (1-4) **525**

1. Earth
ISBN 0-02-782830-1 LC 83-11706

"The author discusses our world's unique position in space and how our days, seasons, and topography are affected by our position there." Booklist

"Black and white photographs of good quality are carefully combined with textual references to achieve a maximum level of conveyance of information. . . . This . . . title should be welcome because of the clean layout of pages, the careful and accurate marshalling of facts, the directness of style, and the combination of good coverage and controlled scope." Bull Cent Child Books

526 Mathematical geography

Mango, Karin N., 1936-
Mapmaking; illustrated with maps and drawings by Judith Hoffman Corwin, and photographs. Messner 1984 106p il maps lib bdg $9.29 (4 and up) **526**

1. Map drawing
ISBN 0-671-45518-4 LC 83-25084

The author "describes the history and techniques of mapmaking, the different kinds of maps and their purposes and the various symbols used. The scope is large, ranging from a child's hand-drawn neighborhood map to maps of the world, undersea and space." SLJ

"Clearly written and well organized, this is a creditable introduction to the subject. Corwin's attractive maps and drawings aptly illustrate the text." Booklist

Includes bibliography

529 Chronology

Anno, Mitsumasa, 1926-
Anno's sundial. Philomel Bks. 1987 28p il map $16.95 (4 and up) **529**

1. Sundials 2. Time
ISBN 0-399-21374-0 LC 86-91447

The author explains how the earth's movements around the sun and the resulting movement of shadows have been used to tell time, using illustrations that pop up or fold out to demonstrate how sundials work

"The pop-up features of the book, like the text, re-

Anno, Mitsumasa, 1926-—*Continued*

quire attentive study of the diagrams and the explanations of principles involved. . . . Anno's treatment of this very basic set of scientific principles is informative and demanding; his multidimensional figures invite reader involvement and seem very likely to stimulate further exploration of the ideas by older children and adolescents with a penchant for science." Horn Book

Burns, Marilyn

This book is about time; illustrated by Martha Weston. Little, Brown 1978 127p il $14.95; pa $7.95 (5 and up) **529**

1. Time

ISBN 0-316-11752-8; 0-316-11750-1 (pa) LC 78-6614

"A Brown paper school book"

Burns describes when, why, and how people started to measure time and discusses such topics as time zones, biorhythms, and jet lag. Also includes instructions for a variety of related projects

Fisher, Leonard Everett, 1924-

Calendar art; thirteen days, weeks, months, and years from around the world; written and illustrated by Leonard Everett Fisher. Four Winds Press 1987 61p il $14.95 (4 and up) **529**

1. Calendars

ISBN 0-02-735350-8 LC 86-25835

"Fisher explains the origins of the calendar and the human need to divide the solar year into months, weeks, and days. He describes 13 such calendars, ranging through history from the Aztecs, Babylonians, and Egyptians to . . . those in more recent history, including the one formed during the French Revolution and the 1930 World Calendar." SLJ

"The information is clear, concise, and fascinating. . . . Whether used for browsing, curriculum enhancement, reference, or study of graphics, the book illuminates the subject instead of merely conveying information." Horn Book

McMillan, Bruce

Time to—. Lothrop, Lee & Shepard Bks. 1989 unp il $13.95; lib bdg $13.88 (k-2) **529**

1. Time 2. Clocks and watches

ISBN 0-688-08855-4; 0-688-08856-2 (lib bdg) LC 89-2325

"Two aspects are taught: through an engaging child's sequenced activities (waking up, eating, going to school, etc.), the passage of time is demonstrated, and the hour-by-hour changes on a clock face, and the accompanying digital display at page bottom, show how time is measured. . . . The vigor and clarity of the overall presentation, and the naturalness of the children and the setting, add up to a 'timely' purchase for librarians." Booklist

530 Physics

Cobb, Vicki

Why can't you unscramble an egg? and other not such dumb questions about matter; with illustrations by Ted Enik. Lodestar Bks. 1990 40p il $12.95 (3-5) **530**

1. Matter

ISBN 0-525-67293-1 LC 89-33465

Answers nine questions about matter, such as why does an ice cube float?, how much does air weigh?, how does wood burn? and other concepts about the nature of matter

"Cobb uses these questions as starting points for further discussion of various scientific principles. Included are a few activities that children can perform on their own. The book is illustrated with black-and-white cartoon line drawings, which add to the author's lighthearted tone." SLJ

530.1 Physics—Theories and mathematical physics

Apfel, Necia H., 1930-

It's all relative; Einstein's theory of relativity; diagrams by Yukio Kondo. Lothrop, Lee & Shepard Bks. 1981 141p il hardcover o.p. paperback available $7.25 (6 and up) **530.1**

1. Relativity (Physics)

ISBN 0-688-04301-1 (pa) LC 80-28188

Besides discussing the principles of relativity, the author explains such concepts as the relationship between time and space, gravitation and acceleration, the bending of light rays and the curvature of space

530.8 Testing and measurement

Bendick, Jeanne, 1919-

How much & how many? the story of weights and measures. rev ed. Watts 1989 144p il lib bdg $13.90 (5 and up) **530.8**

1. Weights and measures

ISBN 0-531-10679-9 LC 88-38065

First published 1947

Compares and explains weights and measures throughout the world as well as the history of many current standards

"The book provides solid information on weights and measures in clear, accessible language. [Illustrated with] photographs, charts, maps, and reproductions of artwork." Booklist

531 Mechanics. Solid mechanics

Branley, Franklyn Mansfield, 1915-

Gravity is a mystery; by Franklyn M. Branley; illustrated by Don Madden. rev ed. Crowell 1986 32p il (Let's-read-and-find-out science bks) $12.95; lib bdg $12.89; pa $4.50 (k-3) **531**

1. Gravitation
ISBN 0-690-04526-3; 0-690-04527-1 (lib bdg); 0-06-445057-0 (pa) LC 85-48247

First published 1970

"Branley talks about the gravitational forces exerted by the earth, moon, sun, and planets on objects in or on them." Booklist

"Madden's cartoon-like illustrations are specifically wedded to the scientific information presented by Branley." Libr J

Weight and weightlessness; illustrated by Graham Booth. Crowell 1972 c1971 33p il (Let's-read-and-find-out science bks) lib bdg $12.89 (k-3) **531**

1. Gravitation 2. Weightlessness
ISBN 0-690-87329-8 LC 70-132292

The author provides a simple explanation of the subjects of gravity and weightlessness, drawing examples from both everyday life and the world of space. The principles behind how a spaceship is sent into orbit are also discussed

Cobb, Vicki

Why doesn't the earth fall up? and other not such dumb questions about motion; illustrated by Ted Enik. Lodestar Bks. 1988 40p il $12.95 (3-5) **531**

1. Motion
ISBN 0-525-67253-2 LC 88-11108

"Four cartoon kids and an omniscient narrator explore nine questions about motion: motions which children can cause and watch, how they can detect motions that they cannot feel, Newton's laws, center of gravity, orbits, and pendula. Along the way, there are simple experiments and brief mention of Newton, Galileo, and Copernicus. It's all very short and simple, in an open, appealing format, and for the most part the science does not suffer from the simplification." SLJ

Horvatic, Anne

Simple machines; photographs by Stephen Bruner. Dutton 1989 unp il $13.95 (1-3) **531**

1. Mechanics 2. Machinery
ISBN 0-525-44492-0 LC 88-29997

Describes five simple machines--lever, wheel, inclined plane, screw, and wedge--and explains how they work

"Uncluttered pages with well-composed photographs and large but unobtrusive print result in an appealing beginning book on the subject. The text unfolds in a clear, logical way. . . . Teachers will find the volume helpful in supplementing a third- or fourth-grade science unit on energy, while children will enjoy the book for its immediate visual appeal." Horn Book

White, Jack R.

The hidden world of forces. Dodd, Mead 1987 143p il lib bdg $11.95 (5 and up) **531**

1. Force and energy
ISBN 0-396-08947-X LC 87-17910

Discusses some of the forces at work in the universe, such as electromagnetism, gravitation, surface tension, and friction, with illustrative experiments

"The text is accurate throughout, with none of the science errors that can occur when a topic is simplified. The photographic illustrations all make relevant points, and the writing style is compelling in its clarity, though at a fairly sophisticated reading level." Sci Books Films

534 Sound and related vibrations

Branley, Franklyn Mansfield, 1915-

High sounds, low sounds; [by] Franklyn M. Branley; illustrated by Paul Galdone. Crowell 1967 unp il (Let's-read-and-find-out science bks) lib bdg $12.89 (k-3) **534**

1. Sound
ISBN 0-690-38018-6 LC 67-23662

"This book describing sounds and how they are made also contains several experiments that illustrate the basic concepts of physics involved." Chicago Public Libr

"Humorous illustrations reinforce the ideas expressed in a very simple text." Booklist

Broekel, Ray, 1923-

Sound experiments. Childrens Press 1983 45p il lib bdg $13.27; pa $4.95 (2-4) **534**

1. Sound—Experiments
ISBN 0-516-01686-5 (lib bdg); 0-516-41686-3 (pa) LC 82-17869

"A New true book"

Briefly discusses sound, pitch, sound travel, sound waves, vibration, frequency, length, and thickness, with simple experiments to demonstrate each concept

Includes glossary

Kettelkamp, Larry, 1933-

The magic of sound; illustrated with drawings by Anthony Kramer and photographs. Newly rev ed. Morrow 1982 80p il lib bdg $12.88 (4-6) **534**

1. Sound
ISBN 0-688-01493-3 LC 82-6510

"The concepts of sound, its propagation through a material, its production, and its uses in industry and medicine are clearly and simply described. The book's four chapters are well organized and are filled with simple yet good experiments to illustrate the various aspects of sound. All of the suggested experiments can be done by a child without adult supervision or assistance except the one device that is meant to imitate gunshots. . . . The techniques of sound reproduction of records or

Kettelkamp, Larry, 1933-—*Continued*
tape cassettes are clearly presented through illustrations. Similarly, explanations of how some of the common means of communications work, such as telephones and radios, will also interest young readers." Sci Books Films

535 Light and related radiations

Dorros, Arthur
Me and my shadow. Scholastic 1990 unp il lib bdg $12.95 (k-3) **535**

1. Shades and shadows
ISBN 0-590-42772-5 LC 89-10100

The author "discusses how the position of a light source affects the length of an object's umbra and explains how shading in art can help define the shape of an object. Day and night, the phases of the moon, and eclipses are detailed, and shadow puppets, X rays and sonograms are mentioned as well." Booklist

"The text is clear, specific, and to the point. Brightly hued watercolor and pencil illustrations have a breezy style. . . . This book should be well received by teachers looking for useful material for science activities as well as by parents." SLJ

Goor, Ron, 1940-
Shadows; here, there, and everywhere; [by] Ron & Nancy Goor. Crowell 1981 47p il lib bdg $12.89 (k-3) **535**

1. Shades and shadows
ISBN 0-690-04133-0 LC 81-43036

Presents information about shadows, including how they are formed, why they can be of various lengths, and how they reveal the shape and texture of things

"The well-placed, striking photographs effectively illustrate the strange and often beautiful shapes of shadows." Horn Book

Gore, Sheila
My shadow; photographs by Fiona Pragoff. Doubleday 1990 25p il (Simple science) $6.95; lib bdg $7.99 (k-2) **535**

1. Shades and shadows
ISBN 0-385-41130-8; 0-385-41198-7 (lib bdg) LC 89-35955

This book uses simple activities to introduce basic concepts about shadows

This book has "clear photographs, presented in an appealing, easy-to-hold size. . . . Appended . . . are additional activities, along with further explantory notes for parents and teachers. Sure to stimulate children's critical thinking abilities." SLJ

Simon, Seymour, 1931-
Shadow magic; illustrated by Stella Ormai. Lothrop, Lee & Shepard Bks. 1985 48p il $12.95; lib bdg $12.89 (k-3) **535**

1. Shades and shadows
ISBN 0-688-02681-8; 0-688-02682-6 (lib bdg) LC 84-4433

"A look at shadows: what they are, how they are created, how they can be used. Simon's clear, direct text explains, among other things, that night is caused by the Earth's shadow. A consideration of sundials includes directions for making one from readily available materials, and suggestions are given for a hand-shadow show." SLJ

"Illustrated with pencil-and-wash drawings that are uneven but largely effective in backing up the text." Booklist

Taylor, Barbara, 1954-
Bouncing and bending light; photographs by Peter Millard. Watts 1990 32p il (Science starters) lib bdg $11.40 (3-5) **535**

1. Light 2. Mirrors 3. Lenses 4. Science—Experiments
ISBN 0-531-14014-8 LC 89-36213

Presents projects and experiments demonstrating the effects of mirrors and lenses on rays of light

"The material is scientifically correct and quite comprehensive. The experiments require only readily available materials to carry them out." Sci Books Films

Includes glossary

Color and light; photographs by Peter Millard. Watts 1990 32p il (Science starters) lib bdg $11.40 (3-5) **535**

1. Color 2. Light 3. Science—Experiments
ISBN 0-531-14015-6 LC 89-16686

Explains the properties of light which make variation in color possible and suggests projects and experiments to demonstrate such principles

"The presentation is creative and thorough, giving young scientists intriguing ideas for use in class and home projects." Booklist

Includes glossary

White, Jack R.
The invisible world of the infrared; illustrated with photographs and drawings. Dodd, Mead 1984 124p il $11.95 (5 and up) **535**

1. Infrared radiation
ISBN 0-396-08319-6 LC 83-25441

"Among the subjects covered are the nature of infrared radiation, its discovery and measurement, and its uses in physics, geology, astronomy, cartography, energy conservation, meteorology, medicine, weaponry, and other fields. Terms that might be unfamiliar to the reader are defined parenthetically in the text. Diagrams, drawings, and photographs illustrate and clarify discussions of concepts and applications." Booklist

"Numerous black-and-white photographs and drawings are an excellent complement to the text. A technical subject excellently handled." SLJ

535.6 Color

Branley, Franklyn Mansfield, 1915-
Color, from rainbows to lasers; [by] Franklyn M. Branley; illustrated by Henry Roth. Crowell 1978 87p il lib bdg $13.89 (6 and up) **535.6**

1. Color
ISBN 0-690-03847-X LC 76-46304

The author begins this explanation of color "by discussing the nature of light waves and light energy. The origin of the color spectrum is treated next, followed by discussions of the physiology of color, some physical phenomena which produce color effects, the basic colors, and the measurement of color." Sci Books Films

Includes bibliography

Emberley, Ed
Green says go. Little, Brown 1968 32p il $14.95 (k-3) **535.6**

1. Color
ISBN 0-316-23599-7 LC 68-21165

The author "first shows primary, secondary and complementary colors and then demonstrates how the addition of black or white can darken or lighten colors. The second part of the book plays with some of the color-associated terms in common use . . . and points out various ways in which color is used for communication." Saturday Rev

"An instructive and provocative exploration of color, presented in a picture book with bold designs, strong colors, and a touch of humor." Booklist

Hoban, Tana
Of colors and things. Greenwillow Bks. 1989 unp il $13.95; lib bdg $13.88 (k-2) **535.6**

1. Color
ISBN 0-688-07534-7; 0-688-07535-5 (lib bdg) LC 88-11101

Photographs of toys, food, and other common objects are grouped on each page according to color

"Hoban hits on a simple device to heighten a child's awareness, but what lifts this above the average concept book is the quality of its design and illustration." Booklist

536 Heat

Maestro, Betsy, 1944-
Temperature and you; by Betsy and Giulio Maestro. Lodestar Bks. 1989 unp il $13.95 (1-3) **536**

1. Temperature 2. Thermometers and thermometry
ISBN 0-525-67271-0 LC 88-12934

The authors discuss what temperature is and how it is measured

"A little biology is provided as well in portions that describe body temperature, fever, and steps taken to keep a body warm or cool. Friendly pictures in perky colors show specifically what the authors are talking about; the book's open, cheerful appearance makes this suitable as a nonfiction read-aloud." Booklist

537 Electricity and electronics

Berger, Melvin, 1927-
Switch on, switch off; illustrated by Carolyn Croll. Crowell 1989 32p il (Let's-read-and-find-out science bks) $12.95; lib bdg $13.89; pa $4.50 (k-3) **537**

1. Electricity
ISBN 0-690-04784-3; 0-690-04786-X (lib bdg); 0-06-445097-X (pa) LC 88-17638

"This book presents rudimentary exploration of electricity and how electrical current flows to the light switch in a child's room. Follow the current from the generator to a power plant to the switch on the wall. Includes instructions for a simple generator. A good, first look at a topic that mystifies young scientists." Sci Child

Markle, Sandra, 1946-
Power up; experiments, puzzles, and games exploring electricity. Atheneum Pubs. 1989 40p il $13.95 (3-5) **537**

1. Electricity—Experiments
ISBN 0-689-31442-6 LC 88-7772

The author "focuses principally on circuits, conductors, and bulbs as conveyors of electricity in an informative, extended science lesson that is a model of clarity and simplicity. At the outset she lists easily obtained supplies for demonstrating the principles discussed." Horn Book

Math, Irwin, 1940-
More wires and watts: understanding and using electricity; illustrations by Hal Keith. Scribner 1988 82p il $13.95 (6 and up) **537**

1. Electricity—Experiments
ISBN 0-684-18914-3 LC 88-15767

Companion volume: Wires and watts available $14.95, pa $4.95 (ISBN 0-684-16854-5; 0-689-71298-7)

This volume "resembles its predecessor in format and approach but provides a new, more modern set of projects for experimenters and hobbyists. . . . These projects emphasize solid state devices and include directions for building sensors for light, temperature, and moisture; a fire alarm; weather instruments; photographic equipment; and games." SLJ

537.6 Electric currents (Electrodynamics) and thermoelectricity

Asimov, Isaac, 1920-
How did we find out about superconductivity? illustrated by Erika Kors. Walker & Co. 1988 64p il $10.95; lib bdg $11.85 (5 and up) **537.6**

1. Electricity 2. Superconductors and superconductivity
ISBN 0-8027-6776-1; 0-8027-6778-8 (lib bdg) LC 87-24142

"Asimov traces the advances that led to current work on high temperature superconductivity from the early work on temperature through the liquefaction of gases and startling discovery of zero electrical resistance at very low temperatures. The text is brief, coherent, and very readable." Sci Child

539 Modern physics

Berger, Melvin, 1927-
Atoms, molecules, and quarks; illustrations by Greg Wenzel. Putnam 1986 79p il $11.99 (6 and up) **539**

1. Atoms 2. Molecules 3. Quarks
ISBN 0-399-61213-0 LC 86-636

An explanation of the composition, behavior, and uses of atoms, molecules, and quarks, the building blocks of the universe

"Beginning physics students who ask 'What is the world made of?' will find this introduction . . . lucid and thorough. Chapters discuss each of the elements individually and include helpful diagrams and drawings. Background information and recent scientific advances in the subject are related, and some at-home experiments (building a cloud chamber, observing how molecules behave) are suggested." Booklist

Includes glossary

Bronowski, Jacob, 1908-1974
Biography of an atom; by J. Bronowski and Millicent E. Selsam; illustrated with pictures by Weimer Pursell and with photographs. Harper & Row 1965 43p il lib bdg $12.89 (4 and up) **539**

1. Atoms 2. Carbon
ISBN 0-06-020641-1 LC 64-19708

"The history of a carbon atom is traced beginning with its formation in a star, from which it escapes in a stellar explosion, to its assimilation in our solar system, and its present participation in the natural cycles of mineral, vegetable and animal matter on earth." Sci Books Films

"The very best kind of science writing: simple, lucid, dignified, well-organized and stripped of nonessentials." Bull Cent Child Books

539.7 Atomic and nuclear physics

Asimov, Isaac, 1920-
How did we find out about nuclear power? illustrated by David Wool. Walker & Co. 1976 64p il lib bdg $12.85 (5 and up) **539.7**

1. Nuclear energy
ISBN 0-8027-6266-2 LC 76-12057

"Asimov describes the accrued knowledge that, over a century, made it possible for scientists to perfect techniques of nuclear fusion and fission. The material is chronologically arranged, so that the reader can understand how each new discovery about atomic structure contributed to the body of nuclear knowledge, and can appreciate how discoveries in science may be based on the work of predecessors. The author concludes with a discussion of controlled nuclear fusion that could give new resources to an energy-starved world." Bull Cent Child Books

Berger, Melvin, 1927-
Our atomic world. Watts 1989 64p il lib bdg $10.90 (4 and up) **539.7**

1. Atoms 2. Nuclear physics
ISBN 0-531-10690-X LC 88-31339

"A First book"

Introduces basic theories about the nature and behavior of the atom and the field of nuclear physics

"Although his topic is complicated, Berger successfully uses a straightforward writing style to explain basic theories of nuclear physics. . . . After final chapters on subatomic particles and quarks, a glossary consolidates all the text's boldfaced words. A fine enrichment resource." Booklist

McGowen, Tom
Radioactivity: from the Curies to the atomic age. Watts 1986 59p il (History of science) lib bdg $10.40 (6 and up) **539.7**

1. Curie, Marie, 1867-1934 2. Curie, Pierre, 1859-1906 3. Radioactivity
ISBN 0-531-10132-0 LC 85-24684

Discusses discoveries, developments, and scientists in the field of radioactivity, which has revolutionized physics and medicine, with particular emphasis on the work done by the Curies

In this "short history of the discovery of radiation, McGowen does a beautiful job of linking separate events into a cohesive narrative of scientific inquiry." Sci Books Films

Includes bibliography

540.7 Chemistry—Education and related topics

Cobb, Vicki

Chemically active!: experiments you can do at home; illustrated by Theo Cobb. Lippincott 1985 154p il $13.95; lib bdg $13.89; pa $4.95 (5 and up) **540.7**

1. Chemistry—Experiments
ISBN 0-397-32079-5; 0-397-32080-9 (lib bdg); 0-06-446101-7 (pa) LC 83-49490

Gives instructions for performing a variety of experiments, using easily available materials, that illustrate some basic principles of chemistry

"This is a fun chemistry book. It introduces the subject in a way that will catch interest and not intimidate. The experiments are designed to be performed in a home kitchen and many use ingenious set-ups." Appraisal

Gardner, Robert, 1929-

Kitchen chemistry: science experiments to do at home. [rev ed]. Messner 1989 128p il lib bdg $11.98; pa $4.95 (4 and up) **540.7**

1. Chemistry—Experiments
ISBN 0-671-67776-4 (lib bdg); 0-671-67576-1 (pa) LC 88-23128

First published 1982

This book contains instructions for conducting sixty-one chemical experiments using the stove, refrigerator, counter, sink, and materials commonly found in the kitchen

"Safety is the key word in this easy-to-use book. . . . The experiments are well-designed, leading young scientists logically through basic chemical principles without a heavy dose of discussion." Appraisal

Kramer, Alan

How to make a chemical volcano and other mysterious experiments. Watts 1989 111p il lib bdg $11.90 (4-6) **540.7**

1. Chemistry—Experiments
ISBN 0-531-10771-X LC 89-8994

The author presents various experiments, using household chemicals or materials, in order to demonstrate chemical principles

"Kids will enjoy identifying with 13-year-old Alan Kramer, who has been dabbling in chemistry since fourth grade. . . . [The] hands-on approach is hard to resist. All but one of the experiments can be done using common household materials, and the several that we tested worked as promised. The easy-to-follow, clearly illustrated instructions include 'Caution' warnings for steps which suggest adult supervision. . . . Kramer's low-key enthusiasm makes this ideal for the reluctant scientist." Bull Cent Child Books

Includes bibliography

Zubrowski, Bernie, 1939-

Messing around with baking chemistry; by Bernie Zubrowski; illustrated by Signe Hanson. Little, Brown 1981 63p il hardcover o.p. paperback available $6.95 (5 and up) **540.7**

1. Baking 2. Chemistry—Experiments
ISBN 0-316-9887-4 (pa) LC 81-4291

"A Children's Museum activity book"

Presents experiments and projects to explore what happens when batter and dough turn into cake and bread. Emphasizes the properties of baking powder, baking soda, and yeast

"Directions throughout are clear and simple. . . . Hanson's black-and-white illustrations are clear and helpful with no attempt to be cute or funny." Sci Books Films

547 Organic chemistry

Cobb, Vicki

Gobs of goo; illustrated by Brian Schatell. Lippincott 1983 38p il $12.95; lib bdg $12.89 (2-4) **547**

1. Chemistry 2. Science—Experiments
ISBN 0-397-32021-3; 0-397-32022-1 (lib bdg) LC 82-48457

This book describes various types of sticky substances and shows how they are made and used in everyday life

"This book is excellent for stimulating curiosity in youngsters. The materials are common household items, and the experiments are short and diverse. The scientific explanations are well integrated and will be highly informative." Sci Books Films

548 Crystallography

Stangl, Jean

Crystals and crystal gardens you can grow. Watts 1990 64p il lib bdg $10.90 (4 and up) **548**

1. Crystallography 2. Science—Experiments
ISBN 0-531-10889-9 LC 89-38999

"A First book"

The author discusses the nature and structure of crystals and presents experiments in crystal formation

With "clear explanatory background on crystal formations, and easy directions for experiments, this will meet a real need in every classroom and public library collection." Bull Cent Child Books

Includes bibliography

549 Mineralogy

McGowen, Tom

Album of rocks and minerals; illustrated by Rod Ruth. Rand McNally 1981 61p il $8.95; Checkerboard Press pa $4.95 (4 and up) **549**

1. Mineralogy 2. Rocks
ISBN 0-528-82400-7; 0-02-688504-2 (pa) LC 81-8558

The text opens with a general discussion and is followed by more detailed information on where various rocks and minerals are found, what the properties of individual specimens are, what they look like and how they are used. More than 75 specimens are illustrated in full color to facilitate identification

Podendorf, Illa, 1903-1983

Rocks and minerals. Childrens Press 1982 45p il lib bdg $13.27; pa $4.95 (1-4) **549**

1. Rocks 2. Mineralogy
ISBN 0-516-01648-2 (lib bdg); 0-516-41648-0 (pa) LC 81-38494

"A New true book"

First published 1958 with title: The true book of rocks and minerals

Simple introduction to formation and identification of a variety of rocks and minerals. Illustrated with photographs including some in full color

Includes glossary

Symes, R. F.

Rocks & minerals; written by R.F. Symes and the staff of the Natural History Museum, London. Knopf 1988 63p il (Eyewitness bks) $12.95; lib bdg $13.99 (4 and up) **549**

1. Mineralogy 2. Rocks
ISBN 0-394-89621-1; 0-394-99621-6 (lib bdg) LC 87-26514

Text and photographs examine the creation, importance, erosion, mining, and uses of rocks and minerals

"The material presented is technically sound and well and appropriately condensed. This book is not a textbook, nor is it a field manual. As a general reference for the lay person, it provides, through the use of visual aids and associated text, useful information for individuals with no formal training in geology." Sci Books Films

Zim, Herbert S.

Rocks and minerals; a guide to familiar minerals, gems, ores and rocks; by Herbert S. Zim and Paul R. Shaffer; illustrated by Raymond Perlman. Golden Press Bks. 1957 160p il maps (Golden nature guide) lib bdg $11.54 (4 and up) **549**

1. Mineralogy 2. Rocks
ISBN 0-307-63502-3 LC 57-3710

"Introductory material on the earth and its rocks gives basic geological information, and activities for amateurs are suggested in identifying, collecting and studying rocks and minerals. Colored diagrams and pictures of specimens aid in identification. Descriptions [of over 400 specimens] include information on formation, structure, use and importance." Bull Cent Child Books

550 Earth sciences

Gallant, Roy A.

Our restless earth; illustrations by Anne Canevari Green. Watts 1986 96p il lib bdg $10.40 (4 and up) **550**

1. Geology
ISBN 0-531-10205-X LC 86-11176

"A First book"

This volume "focuses on the earth's formation, continental drift, and the forces that effect geologic and climatic changes, describing what happens both above sea level and on the ocean floor." Booklist

"This should be a hit with young geologists. Interesting reading that will also be useful for reports because of the easy accessibility of facts through the index and chapter headings." SLJ

Includes glossary

551.1 Gross structure and properties of the earth

Aylesworth, Thomas G.

Moving continents; our changing earth. Enslow Pubs. 1990 64p il maps (Earth processes bk) $15.95 (6 and up) **551.1**

1. Plate tectonics 2. Continental drift 3. Geology
ISBN 0-89490-273-3 LC 89-33549

The author "relates how the theory of plate tectonics developed into a coherent explanation of the planet's structure, accounting for such phenomena as earthquakes, volcanoes, and continental drift. The text is clear and well organized, but more and better quality graphics are needed. . . . On the plus side, Aylesworth carefully includes in a final chapter respected scientific opinion that dissents with the continental drift (but not plate tectonic) theory. A glossary and a list of further reading are appended." Booklist

Cole, Joanna

The magic school bus inside the Earth; illustrated by Bruce Degen. Scholastic 1987 40p il $13.95; pa $3.95 (2-4) **551.1**

1. Earth—Internal structure 2. Geology
ISBN 0-590-40759-7; 0-590-40760-0 (pa) LC 87-4563

In this book Ms. Frizzle teaches "geology via a field trip through the center of the earth. As her class learns about fossils, rocks, and volcanoes, so will readers, absorbing information painlessly as they vicariously travel through the caves, tunnels, and up through the cone of a volcanic island shortly before it erupts. . . . Degen's bright, colorful artwork includes many witty details to delight observant children. Carried in cartoonlike balloons, the schoolmates' thoughts, banter, and asides add spice to the geology lesson. Bright, sassy, and savvy, the magic school bus books rate high in child appeal." Booklist

McNulty, Faith
How to dig a hole to the other side of the world; pictures by Marc Simont. Harper & Row 1979 32p il lib bdg $12.89; pa $3.95 (2-4) **551.1**

1. Earth—Internal structure 2. Geology
ISBN 0-06-024148-9 (lib bdg); 0-06-443218-1 (pa)
LC 78-22479

A child takes an imaginary 8,000-mile journey through the earth and discovers what's inside

"The material will be useful collateral reading for students studying the internal structure of our planet." Sci Books Films

551.2 Volcanoes, earthquakes, thermal waters and gases

Branley, Franklyn Mansfield, 1915-
Earthquakes; by Franklyn M. Branley; illustrated by Richard Rosenblum. Crowell 1990 32p il (Let's-read-and-find-out science bks) $12.95; lib bdg $12.89 (k-3) **551.2**

1. Earthquakes
ISBN 0-690-04661-8; 0-690-04663-4 (lib bdg)
LC 89-35424

The author "explains what earthquakes are, where they occur, and how they change the earth. He also describes some famous quakes of the past and the efforts of scientists to predict and measure earthquakes today. On every page, line drawings, bright with watercolor washes, illustrate scenes such as shaking cityscapes, concepts such as waves emanating from the epicenter of a quake, and practical advice on what to do when the house begins to jiggle." Booklist

Volcanoes; by Franklyn M. Branley; illustrated by Marc Simont. Crowell 1985 32p il (Let's-read-and-find-out science bks) $12.95; lib bdg $12.89; pa $4.50 (k-3) **551.2**

1. Volcanoes
ISBN 0-690-04451-8; 0-690-04431-3 (lib bdg); 0-06-445059-7 (pa) LC 84-45344

Explains how volcanoes are formed and how they affect the earth when they erupt

"Incorporating details sparingly, the book provides clear, easily understandable descriptions of technical points. . . . Effective also are the illustrations, for not only do they beautifully portray in vivid color the geological phenomena, but they also depict an assortment of human figures—including a plump, bespectacled geologist—with a bit more humor than might ordinarily be found in a book on this subject." Horn Book

Lauber, Patricia, 1924-
Volcano: the eruption and healing of Mount St. Helens. Bradbury Press 1986 60p il $14.95 (4 and up) **551.2**

1. Mount Saint Helens (Wash.) 2. Volcanoes
ISBN 0-02-754500-8 LC 85-22442

A Newbery Medal honor book, 1987

"A clearly written account of the volcano's 1980 eruption in Washington State, with handsome color photographs of every phase of the eruption and its aftermath. Perhaps most interesting is the detailed description of the healing process—what flora and fauna survived and how." N Y Times Book Rev

Place, Marian T. (Marian Templeton), 1910-
Mount St. Helens; a sleeping volcano awakes. Dodd, Mead 1981 158p il lib bdg $10.95 (5 and up) **551.2**

1. Mount Saint Helens (Wash.) 2. Volcanoes
ISBN 0-396-07976-8 LC 81-43222

"Readers are offered an insider's view of the events surrounding the May 18, 1980, eruption of Mount St Helens. Using eyewitness and survivor accounts, Place covers the havoc the volcano wreaked in both human and financial terms." Booklist

"One of the most thrilling accounts available of the 1980 eruption that excited the entire country. . . . Unbelievable photographs enhance this well-written and amazing story." Child Book Rev Serv

Simon, Seymour, 1931-
Volcanoes. Morrow Junior Bks. 1988 unp il $12.95; lib bdg $12.88 (2-5) **551.2**

1. Volcanoes
ISBN 0-688-07411-1; 0-688-07412-X (lib bdg)
LC 87-33316

"Using examples like St. Helens and the volcanoes of Iceland and Hawaii, the author is able to address all aspects of his subject: the history, nature and causes of volcanoes." Publ Wkly

"The photographs are large, informative, and spectacular, reproduced in brilliant color. Aside from one confusing map of the earth's tectonic plates, this is a solid introduction." Bull Cent Child Books

551.3 Surface and exogenous processes and their agents

Bannan, Jan Gumprecht
Sand dunes. Carolrhoda Bks. 1989 47p il (Carolrhoda earth watch bk) lib bdg $12.95; pa $6.95 (3-6) **551.3**

1. Sand dunes
ISBN 0-87614-321-4 (lib bdg); 0-87614-513-6 (pa)
LC 87-27978

"A look at the birth, formation, and movement of sand dunes along the Oregon cost line. Beautiful, full-color photographs and lucid text explain how the forces of sand, wind, water, and plant life determine the life cycles of sand dunes. A well-organized text assures reader understanding of the more difficult concepts." Sci Child

Includes glossary

Gans, Roma, 1894-
Danger—icebergs! illustrated by Richard Rosenblum. rev ed. Crowell 1987 32p il (Let's-read-and-find-out science bks) $12.95; lib bdg $12.89; pa $4.50 (k-3) **551.3**

1. Icebergs
ISBN 0-690-04627-8; 0-690-04629-4 (lib bdg); 0-06-445066-X (pa) LC 87-531

A revised and newly illustrated edition of the title first published 1964

Explains how icebergs are formed from glaciers, move into the ocean, create hazards to ships, and sometimes melt away

Simon, Seymour, 1931-
Icebergs and glaciers. Morrow 1987 unp il $13; lib bdg $12.88 (3-5) **551.3**

1. Glaciers 2. Icebergs
ISBN 0-688-06186-9; 0-688-06187-7 (lib bdg) LC 86-18142

"After an explanation of the consistency of snowflakes, packed snow, and ice fields, the text describes the movement of glaciers by sliding or creeping, various processes of measurement, landscape alteration, geological effects of glacial movement, and the formation of icebergs." Bull Cent Child Books

The author "chronicles the development of glaciers and icebergs with a wonderfully clear, almost Spartan text that receives all of the support necessary from the magnificent color photographs which accompany it. . . . This book would be an excellent addition to any elementary school library or any personal juvenile collection." Appraisal

Walker, Sally M.
Glaciers; ice on the move. Carolrhoda Bks. 1990 47p il (Carolrhoda earth watch bk) lib bdg $12.95 (4-6) **551.3**

1. Glaciers
ISBN 0-87614-373-7 LC 89-22102

This volume examines "how glaciers are formed, how they move, how they terminate, and how they have changed the surface and shape of the terrain over which they have moved. Walker discusses the possibilites of tapping glaciers as possible sources of clean water and of energy." Bull Cent Child Books

"The author manages to pack a significant amount of information into a slim volume. . . . The prose is clear, and, with minor exceptions, the illustrations are extraordinarily good." Sci Books Films

551.4 Geomorphology and hydrosphere

Gans, Roma, 1894-
Caves; illustrated by Giulio Maestro. Crowell 1976 32p il (Let's-read-and-find-out science bks) lib bdg $12.89 (k-3) **551.4**

1. Caves
ISBN 0-690-01070-2 LC 76-4881

The author describes "the ways in which caves are formed, the range of size from a small animal's lair to an enormous cavern, and the lure of cave exploration to amateurs (spelunkers) and scientists (speleologists) alike. . . . Gauged in extent and difficulty for a young independent reader, the book describes stalactites and stalagmites, cave tunnels, and the blind fish that inhabit the water in some caves." Bull Cent Child Books

"The book is illustrated with water color drawings in blue, gray, and black which help suggest the damp darkness of the cave's interior." Appraisal

Henderson, Kathy
The Great Lakes. Childrens Press 1989 45p il lib bdg $13.27 (2-4) **551.4**

1. Great Lakes
ISBN 0-516-01163-4 LC 88-34670

"A New true book"

An introduction to the five fresh-water lakes that contain one-fifth of the earth's standing fresh water

"Captioned, mostly full-color photographs on nearly every page provide visual interest, while short sentences and a simple writing style allows easy access for beginning readers without sacrificing substance." Booklist

Peters, Lisa Westberg
The sun, the wind and the rain; illustrated by Ted Rand. Holt & Co. 1988 unp il $13.95; pa $4.95 (k-2) **551.4**

1. Mountains 2. Nature
ISBN 0-8050-0699-0; 0-8050-1481-0 (pa) LC 87-23808

"This colorfully illustrated book presents geology concepts to young children. Pictures of a young girl making a mountain of sand and of a regular mountain are paired to introduce children to the ideas of mountain building, weathering, and erosion. . . . This book is a good addition to a classroom library for children who can read or for younger nonreaders who can follow the pictures." Sci Child

551.46 Hydrosphere. Oceanography

Bramwell, Martyn
The oceans. Watts 1987 32p il maps (Earth science lib) lib bdg $9.90 (4-6) **551.46**

1. Ocean
ISBN 0-531-10356-0 LC 86-51410

This book contains 13 colorfully illustrated two-page chapters on such topics as: ocean currents; explorers and traders; the surging tides; and life in the oceans

Includes glossary

Cook, Jan Leslie
The mysterious undersea world. National Geographic Soc. 1980 104p il $6.95; lib bdg $8.50 (4 and up) **551.46**
1. Ocean 2. Marine biology 3. Underwater exploration
ISBN 0-87044-317-8; 0-87044-322-4 (lib bdg)
LC 79-1791
"Books for world explorers"
Introduces the ocean and its movements, marine animals and plants, sunken treasure, submersibles, aquariums, and oceanariums
"The book is enhanced by a folder of classroom activities of skill-building puzzles and games with duplicating masters and library catalog cards for the teacher." Sci Books Films

Johnson, Rebecca L.
Diving into darkness: a submersible explores the sea. Lerner Publs. 1989 72p il lib bdg $15.95 (4 and up) **551.46**
1. Submersibles 2. Underwater exploration
ISBN 0-8225-1587-3 LC 88-27154
"A brief, straightforward history of undersea explorations, followed by a discussion of the work of Edwin Link. The equipment used during the course of a dive is effectively described. Photographs are vivid and well chosen; the environmental aspect is mentioned." Horn Book
Includes glossary

Simon, Seymour, 1931-
How to be an ocean scientist in your own home; illustrated by David A. Carter. Lippincott 1988 136p il $12.95; lib bdg $12.89 (4 and up) **551.46**
1. Oceanography—Experiments
ISBN 0-397-32291-7; 0-397-32292-5 (lib bdg)
LC 87-45988
"Twenty-four easy-to-understand experiments with readily available materials that can be done safely at home are described clearly and provocatively. Labeled line drawings illustrate activities that range from investigating seawater to making waves to hatching and studying brine shrimp. Includes suppliers for aquarium materials." Sci Child
Includes bibliography

Oceans. Morrow Junior Bks. 1990 unp il $13.95; lib bdg $13.88 (3-5) **551.46**
1. Ocean
ISBN 0-688-09453-8; 0-688-09454-6 (lib bdg)
LC 89-28452
This book "covers the geography of the ocean floor, major currents, and El Nino (a shift in the prevailing currents that causes severe climactic changes). Tides, tsunami, waves, coastal erosion, and marine life are also touched upon." Booklist
"Simon presents clear, simplified explanations of natural phenomena with well-chosen full-color photographs that go beyond decoration. He includes good black-and-white diagrams of how tides work and how waves form and transfer energy. The endpapers are maps of the world showing how and where the major currents flow." SLJ

551.48 Hydrology

Bramwell, Martyn
Rivers and lakes. Watts 1987 c1986 31p il (Earth science lib) lib bdg $9.90 (4-6) **551.48**
1. Rivers 2. Lakes
ISBN 0-531-10262-9 LC 86-50354
First published 1986 in the United Kingdom
This book "explains the origins of these water sources and their development. Specific habitats and wildlife associated with each water body are described. The remarkable properties of water and its function as 'nature's bloodstream' are apprised. Bramwell details drought, underground rivers, water at work, and pollution. . . . Could be used for both research and teacher-guided explorations." SLJ
Includes glossary

Cole, Joanna
The magic school bus at the waterworks; illustrated by Bruce Degen. Scholastic 1986 39p il $12.95; pa $3.95 (2-4) **551.48**
1. Water 2. Water supply
ISBN 0-590-40361-3; 0-590-40360-5 (pa) LC 86-6672
The author presents "specific facts about water and a memorable image of the water cycle process. The story involves a 'strange' teacher who takes her class on a magical trip: up to the clouds—down to earth in raindrops—down a stream into a reservoir where the water is purified—finally into the underground pipes leading back to school. The illustrations both enhance the humor and provide visual presentation of the water cycle." Appraisal

551.5 Meteorology

Bramwell, Martyn
Weather. Watts 1988 c1987 32p il maps (Earth science lib) lib bdg $9.90 (4-6) **551.5**
1. Weather
ISBN 0-531-10357-9 LC 86-51411
First published 1987 in the United Kingdom
An "overview of the science of meteorology, with explanations of the atmosphere and forces that cause clouds, winds, and weather. Discussion of weather observing and forecasting includes mention of how technology may change the weather." SLJ
Includes glossary

Branley, Franklyn Mansfield, 1915-

Air is all around you; by Franklyn M. Branley; illustrated by Holly Keller. rev ed. Crowell 1986 31p il (Let's-read-and-find-out science bks) $12.95; lib bdg $12.88; pa $4.50 (k-3) **551.5**

1. Air
ISBN 0-690-04502-6; 0-690-04503-4 (lib bdg); 0-06-445048-1 (pa) LC 85-45405

A revised and newly illustrated edition of the title first published 1962

Describes the various properties of air and shows how to prove that air takes up space and that there is air dissolved in water

"Illustrations in both bold and pastel colors are coordinated with the easy-to-read text and make this an eye-pleasing and informative book." SLJ

Flash, crash, rumble, and roll; by Franklyn M. Branley; pictures by Barbara and Ed Emberley. rev ed. Crowell 1985 31p il (Let's-read-and-find-out science bks) lib bdg $12.89; pa $4.50 (k-3) **551.5**

1. Thunderstorms 2. Lightning 3. Rain and rainfall
ISBN 0-690-04425-9 (lib bdg); 0-06-445012-0 (pa) LC 84-45333

First published 1964

The author "explains how thunderclouds form, why lightning occurs, and why thunder sometimes sounds so loud. He discusses the dangers of lightning and describes the best ways to stay safe." Publisher's note

It's raining cats and dogs; all kinds of weather, and why we have it; by Franklyn M. Branley; illustrated by True Kelley. Houghton Mifflin 1987 112p il $12.95 (3-6) **551.5**

1. Rain and rainfall 2. Weather
ISBN 0-395-33070-X LC 86-27546

"Human hailstones, pink and green snow, St. Elmo's Fire, dancing devils, horse latitudes, and contrails and distrails are among the curiosities explained in this anecdotal . . . discussion of weather phenomena. . . . There are . . . lists of precautions to follow during lightning and tornadoes as well as . . . instructions for measuring rainfall, wind velocity, and air pollution." Horn Book

The author "intersperses factual information about clouds, precipitation, and winds with interesting anecdotes and easy experiments. The amusing black-and-gray wash illustrations are helpful in setting up the experiments." SLJ

Includes bibliography

Dorros, Arthur

Feel the wind; written and illustrated by Arthur Dorros. Crowell 1989 32p il (Let's-read-and-find-out science bks) $12.95; lib bdg $12.89; pa $4.50 (k-3) **551.5**

1. Winds
ISBN 0-690-04739-8; 0-690-04741-X (lib bdg); 0-06-445095-3 (pa) LC 88-18961

"The motion of air in the form of wind is discernible in many ways. Simple text accompanied by bright illustrations explains the causes, power, effects, and uses of wind. Encourages outdoor experimentation." Sci Child

Gallant, Roy A.

Rainbows, mirages and sundogs; the sky as a source of wonder. Macmillan 1987 94p il $12.95 (4 and up) **551.5**

1. Meteorology 2. Optics
ISBN 0-02-737010-0 LC 86-23728

Discusses and explains visual phenomena seen in the sky, primarily interactions of light and atmosphere such as rainbows, mirages, the twinkling of stars, the blue color of the sky, and the Northern Lights

"The lucid, thorough text raises questions, provides considerable scientific detail, and includes instructions for conducting intriguing and relatively simple demonstrations. . . . There are captioned diagrams to illustrate many of the explanations, and several of the photographs have an almost surreal look as they capture instances of light that are indeed unearthly." Horn Book

Simon, Seymour, 1931-

Storms. Morrow Junior Bks. 1989 unp il $12.95; lib bdg $12.88 (2-4) **551.5**

1. Storms
ISBN 0-688-07413-8; 0-688-07414-6 (lib bdg) LC 88-22045

This book describes the atmospheric conditions which create thunderstorms, hailstorms, lightning, tornadoes, and hurricanes and how violent weather affects the environment and people

"The half- to full-page glossy color photographs are sure to attract young readers as will the subject. *Storms* is an excellent way to introduce the science of meteorology to children." Sci Books Films

Smith, Howard Everett, 1927-

Weather; by Howard E. Smith; illustrated by Jeffrey Bedrick. Doubleday 1990 45p il $10.95; lib bdg $11.99 (4-6) **551.5**

1. Weather
ISBN 0-385-26085-7; 0-385-26086-5 (lib bdg) LC 89-1111

"The drama initiated by the weather is clearly communicated in Bedrick's colorful illustrations and Smith's vivid prose. Seemingly all weather conditions are discussed, with the focus on the causes and effects of each. A well-written explanation of the greenhouse effect and its ramifications for the future ends the volume. Information is plentiful, explanations are good, and record statistics abound." SLJ

551.55 Atmospheric disturbances and formations

Armbruster, Ann
Tornadoes; [by] Ann Armbruster and Elizabeth A. Taylor. Watts 1989 64p il lib bdg $11.40 (4-6) **551.55**

1. Tornadoes
ISBN 0-531-10755-8 LC 89-31827

"A First book"

Describes the causes, different parts, and movements of tornadoes, discusses how they are tracked and studied by scientists, and suggests science projects and related activities

Includes bibliography

Branley, Franklyn Mansfield, 1915-
Hurricane watch; by Franklyn M. Branley; illustrated by Giulio Maestro. Crowell 1985 32p il (Let's-read-and-find-out science bks) $12.95; lib bdg $12.89; pa $4.50 (k-3) **551.55**

1. Hurricanes
ISBN 0-690-04470-4; 0-690-04471-2 (lib bdg); 0-06-445062-7 (pa) LC 85-47534

The author describes the origin and nature of hurricanes and ways of staying safe when threatened by one of these dangerous storms

"A readable and practical introduction to the origins and behavior of hurricanes, the destructive results of these storms, the methods of tracking them, and safety precautions for protecting property and people. Line drawings crayoned with generally muted tones of blue, green, red, and yellow diagram the storms and picture home scenes and storm-ridden towns; gray wash lends an effectively somber air to views of the hurricane and its effects." Horn Book

551.57 Hydrometeorology

Branley, Franklyn Mansfield, 1915-
Rain & hail; illustrated by Harriett Barton. rev ed. Crowell 1983 39p il (Let's-read-and-find-out science bks) lib bdg $12.89 (k-3) **551.57**

1. Rain and rainfall 2. Hail
ISBN 0-690-04353-8 LC 83-45058

A newly illustrated edition of the title first published 1963

A "clear, simple explanation of where rain and hail come from, tracing the cycle from water vapor to raindrops and hail. . . . Whereas the original illustrations were merely decorative and are now dated, Barton's new watercolors are good-humored pictures that add extra information as well as diagrams that simply detail the text." SLJ

Snow is falling; by Franklyn M. Branley; illustrated by Holly Keller. rev ed. Crowell 1986 32p il (Let's-read-and-find-out science bks) $12.95; lib bdg $12.89; pa $4.50 (k-3) **551.57**

1. Snow
ISBN 0-690-04547-6; 0-690-04548-4 (lib bdg); 0-06-445058-9 (pa) LC 85-48256

A newly illustrated edition of the title first published 1963

Describes the characteristics of snow, its usefulness to plants and animals, and the hazards it can cause

"The vocabulary level allows beginning readers to manage the material with little help, with the advantage of the child having the chance to experience firsthand the idea that books don't always have to have a story; books filled with facts also can be interesting. The illustrations are colorful and childlike. They provide not only visual satisfaction but visual information." Sci Books Films

De Paola, Tomie, 1934-
The cloud book; words and pictures by Tomie de Paola. Holiday House 1975 30p il lib bdg $13.95; pa $5.95 (k-3) **551.57**

1. Clouds
ISBN 0-8234-0259-2 (lib bdg); 0-8234-0531-1 (pa) LC 74-34493

The author instructs "young readers about the ten most common types of clouds, how they were named, and what they mean in terms of changing weather. Actually a very good text to use for early science instruction. Includes a scattering of traditional myths that have clouds as a basis." Adventuring With Books

Sugarman, Joan, 1917-
Snowflakes; illustrated by Jennifer Dewey. Little, Brown 1985 53p il $13.95 (4-6) **551.57**

1. Snow
ISBN 0-316-82112-8 LC 85-15948

"Snowflakes shapes—stars, needles, feathers, pyramids—are discussed and illustrated with pen-and-ink drawings. Clear explanations of how crystals are formed and a succinct summary of the study of snowflakes throughout history are presented. Readers also learn how to catch a snowflake." Sci Child

551.6 Climatology and weather

Gibbons, Gail
Weather forecasting. Four Winds Press 1987 unp il $13.95 (1-3) **551.6**

1. Weather forecasting
ISBN 0-02-737250-2 LC 86-7602

"The book is divided into four sections, one per season, which treat different kinds of weather as they're observed, recorded, and reported at a weather station." Bull Cent Child Books

"Any child can learn the basic concepts from the text at the bottom of each page, while the precocious can garner an impressive weather vocabulary by absorbing

Gibbons, Gail—*Continued*
the terms labeled and defined within the artwork. Brightly illustrated with the artist's usual bold, flat colors, this book will serve as an appealing introduction to weather forecasting for young children." Booklist

Weather words and what they mean. Holiday House 1990 unp il $13.95 (1-3) **551.6**

1. Weather
ISBN 0-8234-0805-1 LC 89-39515

The author discusses the meaning of meteorological terms such as temperature, air pressure, thunderstorm and moisture

"Gibbons' easily identifiable artistic style works well with her explanations of sometimes misunderstood weather-related terms. Drawings are appealing, attractively arranged, and closely matched to the textual information. . . . An attractive introduction for weather units in the primary grades." SLJ

Lambert, David, 1932-
Weather and its work; [by] David Lambert & Ralph Hardy. Facts on File 1984 64p il (World of science) $15.95 (5 and up) **551.6**

1. Weather 2. Climate
ISBN 0-87196-987-4

Partial contents: Clouds; Rain; Thunderstorms; Freezing; The wind; Cyclones and anticyclones; Hurricanes and tornadoes; Droughts and floods; Weather forecasting; Altering the weather; Seasons; Tropical rainy climates; Deserts; Temperate climates; Polar climates; Mountain climates; Glossary

The authors' "treatment is substantive, comprehensive and clearly understandable even in its detailed sections. . . . The chapter outlining the effects of water, ice and wind on land forms is especially well done." SLJ

Tannenbaum, Beulah
Making and using your own weather station; by Beulah Tannenbaum and Harold E. Tannenbaum; illustrations by Anne Canevari Green. Watts 1989 111p il maps lib bdg $11.90 (5 and up) **551.6**

1. Weather forecasting 2. Meteorology—Experiments
ISBN 0-531-10675-6 LC 88-31374

"A Venture book"

This book contains "instructions for constructing barometers, thermometers, sling psychrometers, rain gauges, wind vanes, and anemometers; each project is accompanied with a discussion of how and why it works and suggested experiments." Bull Cent Child Books

"Some experiments may require adult direction in material collection and assembly. For those really inspired, some adult guidance may also be required to refer the reader to related texts with more in-depth explanations. But for most, this book stands alone as an excellent guide to the elements which affect us everyday." Voice Youth Advocates

Includes glossary and bibliography

552 Petrology

De Paola, Tomie, 1934-
The quicksand book. Holiday House 1977 unp il lib bdg $13.95; pa $5.95 (k-3) **552**

1. Quicksand
ISBN 0-8234-0291-6 (lib bdg); 0-8234-0532-X (pa) LC 76-28762

"Jungle Girl, swinging on a vine from her treehouse, falls into a patch of . . . [quicksand] but, fortunately, is observed by Jungle Boy. As she slowly sinks, her scholarly bespectacled young Tarzan delivers a long but interesting lecture on the properties of and useful means of rescue from quicksand." Horn Book

"A deft blend of fact and fiction is illustrated with ebullient paintings framed in enormous leaves that remind the lap audience of the jungle setting and that provide a corner for silent action that gives a third dimension. . . . And the information about quicksand is accurate, too. Very nice." Bull Cent Child Books

Gans, Roma, 1894-
Rock collecting; illustrated by Holly Keller. Crowell 1984 28p il (Let's-read-and-find-out science bks) hardcover o.p. paperback available $4.50 (k-3) **552**

1. Rocks—Collectors and collecting
ISBN 0-06-445063-5 (pa) LC 83-46170

The author includes some "hints on how to start and organize a rock collection, but the major emphasis of the book is on the history, types and uses of rocks. She refers to the use of concrete for sidewalks and chalk for blackboards, and also some historical applications, such as the pyramids in Egypt. The three main kinds of rocks—igneous, metamorphic and sedimentary—are also explained with examples." SLJ

"The text is considerably enlivened by Keller's three-color, cartoon-style pictures and clearly labeled diagrams. Actual small photographs of rocks are also inserted into the art." Booklist

Selsam, Millicent Ellis, 1912-
A first look at rocks; by Millicent E. Selsam and Joyce Hunt; illustrated by Harriett Springer. Walker & Co. 1984 32p il lib bdg $12.85 (1-3) **552**

1. Rocks 2. Petrology
ISBN 0-8027-6531-9 (lib bdg) LC 83-40394

This book describes the three main types of rocks: sedimentary, metamorphic, and igneous

"There are frequent references in the text to the large, carefully-detailed black-and-white drawings which clearly show distinguishing characteristics." SLJ

553.7 Water

Seixas, Judith S.

Water: what it is, what it does; illustrated by Tom Huffman. Greenwillow Bks. 1987 56p il $10.25; lib bdg $10.85 (1-3) **553.7**

1. Water

ISBN 0-688-06607-0; 0-688-06608-9 (lib bdg)

LC 86-14926

"A Greenwillow read-alone book"

A simple introduction to water, describing its properties, uses, and interaction with people and the environment. Includes five basic experiments

"Readers should gain from *Water* a scientific understanding and appreciation of water's importance to all life forms and the need to protect and conserve it as a natural resource. The format is clear, the illustrations add to the text, and the sequence is logical." SLJ

557 Earth sciences—North America

O'Neill, Catherine, 1950-

Natural wonders of North America. National Geographic Soc. 1984 103p il maps $6.95; lib bdg $8.50 (5 and up) **557**

1. Geology—North America

ISBN 0-87044-514-6; 0-87044-519-7 (lib bdg)

LC 84-16614

"Books for world explorers"

This title discusses "formations of nature in all areas of the continent, and explains how they came to be." Publisher's note

"Spectacular full-color photographs make this useful volume a pleasure for browsing. Though not all-inclusive, the book shows a great variety of 'wonders,' from the Canadian tundra to a volcano in Mexico, from the Bay of Fundy to the Bonneville Salt Flats, from Greenland's glaciers to the Badlands of South Dakota. . . . Many clear maps and diagrams are provided." Booklist

Includes bibliography

560 Paleontology. Paleozoology

Aliki

Fossils tell of long ago. rev ed. Crowell 1990 32p il (Let's-read-and-find-out science bks) $13.95; lib bdg $13.89 (k-3) **560**

1. Fossils

ISBN 0-690-04844-0; 0-690-31379-9 (lib bdg)

LC 89-17247

First published 1972

"Information about how fossils are formed and discovered is presented in simple text and an appealing variety of colorful illustrations. Includes directions for creating a fossil." Sci Child

Arnold, Caroline, 1944-

Trapped in tar; fossils from the Ice Age; photographs by Richard Hewett. Clarion Bks. 1987 57p il $12.95 (3-5) **560**

1. Fossils 2. Mammals, Fossil

ISBN 0-89919-415-X LC 86-17614

"California's Rancho La Brea tar pits are the subject of this photo essay, which explains what the tar pits are and why they are important for scientists studying Ice Age life. . . . Arnold describes how the remains are excavated and briefly surveys the kinds of large and small animals that have been discovered." Booklist

"In addition to the inherent child appeal of the subject and the clear explanations, the book has a lively format, with pictures dramatically featuring young museum visitors in involved inspection or even hands-on experience of the displays." Bull Cent Child Books

Baylor, Byrd

If you are a hunter of fossils; [illustrated by] Peter Parnall. Scribner 1980 unp il $13.95; pa $4.95 (3-5) **560**

1. Fossils

ISBN 0-684-16419-1; 0-689-70773-8 (pa)

LC 79-17926

A fossil hunter looking for signs of an ancient sea in the rocks of a western Texas mountain describes how the area must have looked millions of years ago

"Handsomely designed and illustrated, this book is not a guide to the collection or identification of fossils but rather is a poetic look at fossil collecting. Attractive pastel illustrations juxtapose images of rock outcrops with reconstructions of prehistoric animals. While the artistry in the illustrations is good, the accuracy is very poor. . . . The information conveyed in the text, however, is generally good and clearly written." Sci Books Films

Cohen, Daniel, 1936-

Prehistoric animals; illustrated by Pamela Ford Johnson. Doubleday 1988 41p il $9.95; lib bdg $11.99 (4-6) **560**

1. Prehistoric animals 2. Fossils

ISBN 0-385-23416-3; 0-385-23417-1 (lib bdg)

LC 86-19666

Discusses more than twenty prehistoric animals, how they were discovered, their modern counterparts, and theories on their extinction

"Cohen offers a bright, oversize album of prehistoric mammals and birds. Visuals are important; each spread features a box of text surrounded by a page-filling illustration. The text is smooth and economical, first describing the ascendancy of birds and mammals after dinosaurs died out and then looking at an array of other beasts that walk the earth no more." Booklist

Eldredge, Niles

The fossil factory; a kid's guide to digging up dinosaurs, exploring evolution, and finding fossils; [by] Niles, Douglas, and Gregory Eldredge; illustrations by True Kelley and Steve Lindblom. Addison-Wesley 1989 111p il pa $8.95 (4-6) **560**

1. Fossils 2. Dinosaurs
ISBN 0-201-18599-7 LC 89-6548

The authors discuss evolution, paleontology, fossils, and fossil collecting

"The lively text hops and skips from place to place, intermingling facts and funny tidbits that cover a wide range of topics. . . . The dinosaur facts reflect up-to-date information, as do the theories presented on their extinction. . . . In general, the cartoon drawings work well with the playfulness of the text." SLJ

Elting, Mary, 1909-

The Macmillan book of dinosaurs and other prehistoric creatures; illustrated by John Hamberger. Macmillan 1984 80p il $14.95; pa $8.95 (4 and up) **560**

1. Fossils 2. Dinosaurs
ISBN 0-02-733430-9; 0-02-043000-0 (pa) LC 84-4372

"Watercolor scenes on nearly every page [present] the 12 major time periods of life on Earth. A one-page table listing the periods by name includes their beginning times figured back from today plus a one-or two-sentence summary of the types of life forms common to each period. These periods are described chronologically in individual chapters. Circumstances surrounding significant fossil finds are included with descriptions of typical life forms prevalent during each period." SLJ

"The text is smooth and careful to point out areas of uncertainty or speculation as well as opposing theories." Booklist

Includes glossary

Gibbons, Gail

Prehistoric animals. Holiday House 1988 unp il lib bdg $13.95 (k-2) **560**

1. Prehistoric animals 2. Fossils
ISBN 0-8234-0707-1 LC 88-4661

Introduces, in text and illustrations, a variety of prehistoric animals whose fossilized remains have provided scientists with clues about their physical characteristics and the environment in which they lived

"A prehistoric animal 'timeline,' covering a period from 65 million to 10 thousand years ago, is helpful. Color illustrations of the animals set against simple stylized backgrounds offer a suggestion of scale." Booklist

Lauber, Patricia, 1924-

Dinosaurs walked here, and other stories fossils tell. Bradbury Press 1987 56p il $15.95 (3-5) **560**

1. Fossils 2. Geology 3. Dinosaurs
ISBN 0-02-754510-5 LC 86-8239

Discusses how fossilized remains of plants and animals reveal the characteristics of the prehistoric world

"A marvelous introduction to fossils, those fascinating windows to ancient landscapes and seascapes of Earth's prehistoric past. The polished, lucid text is accompanied by superb, full-color photographs, paintings, and maps in an appealing volume." Sci Child

Taylor, Paul D. (Paul Durnford), 1952-

Fossil. Knopf 1990 63p il (Eyewitness bks) $13.95; lib bdg $14.99 (4 and up) **560**

1. Fossils
ISBN 0-679-80440-4; 0-679-90440-9 (lib bdg)
LC 89-36444

This book "details how fossils are formed and what man has learned about life on Earth from discovering them. The sections on early paleontology, fossil folklore, and the tools of paleontology are particularly well done." SLJ

567.9 Fossil reptiles. Dinosaurs

Aliki

Digging up dinosaurs. rev ed. Crowell 1988 32p il (Let's-read-and-find-out science bks) $12.70; lib bdg $12.95; pa $4.50; Harper & Row pa $3.95 (k-3) **567.9**

1. Dinosaurs
ISBN 0-690-04714-2; 0-690-04716-9 (lib bdg); 0-06-445078-3 (pa); 0-06-445078-3 (pa) LC 87-29949

A revised and newly illustrated edition of the title first published 1981

Briefly introduces various types of dinosaurs, explaining how scientist find, preserve, and reassemble the giant dinosaur skeletons seen in museums

Dinosaur bones. Crowell 1988 32p il (Let's-read-and-find-out science bks) $12.95; lib bdg $12.89; pa $4.50 (k-3) **567.9**

1. Dinosaurs 2. Fossils
ISBN 0-690-04549-2; 0-690-04550-6 (lib bdg); 0-06-445077-5 (pa) LC 85-48246

"An easy-to-read look at the development of dinosaur paleontology from first finds and early skeptics to the study of the fossilization process and a quick overview of the dinosaur age. Informative text is paired with clever drawings that include fascinating insights and witty asides. Includes an indexed glossary of dinosaurs mentioned in the book." Sci Child

Dinosaurs are different. Crowell 1985 32p il (Let's-read-and-find-out science bks) $12.95; lib bdg $12.89; pa $4.50 (k-3) **567.9**

1. Dinosaurs
ISBN 0-690-04456-9; 0-690-04458-5 (lib bdg); 0-06-445056-2 (pa) LC 84-45332

This work discusses how the various orders and suborders of dinosaurs were similar and different in structure and appearance

"This book is excellent in its organization and treatment of the material. The illustrations are fairly good and do a reasonable job of supplementing the text." Sci Books Films

Aliki—*Continued*

My visit to the dinosaurs; by Aliki. rev ed. Crowell 1985 32p il (Let's-read-and-find-out science bks) $12.95; lib bdg $12.89; pa $4.50 (k-3) **567.9**

1. Dinosaurs
ISBN 0-690-04422-4; 0-690-04423-2 (lib bdg); 0-06-445020-1 (pa) LC 85-47538

First published 1969

"This book introduces young children to dinosaurs through a visit to a natural history museum. The simple text explains how paleontologists discovered dinosaur bones and reconstructed the reptiles' skeletons from their fossilized remains. Also included are brief descriptions of the more well-known dinosaurs, accompanied by full-color illustrations of the creatures as they once appeared." SLJ

Arnold, Caroline, 1944-

Dinosaur mountain; graveyard of the past; photographs by Richard Hewett. Clarion Bks. 1989 48p il lib bdg $14.95 (4 and up) **567.9**

1. Dinosaurs 2. Dinosaur National Monument (Colo. and Utah)
ISBN 0-89919-693-4 LC 88-30218

This book describes the work of paleontologists in learning about dinosaurs, especially the discoveries made at Dinosaur National Monument

"Arnold seamlessly blends general information about paleontology with facts about specific finds near the Monument and additionally offers intriguing descriptions of ongoing work. . . . Lively writing, a dramtic subject, and a sure-fire hit with young readers." Horn Book

Dinosaurs down under and other fossils from Australia; photographs by Richard Hewett. Clarion Bks. 1990 48p il maps lib bdg $14.95 (4 and up) **567.9**

1. Dinosaurs 2. Fossils 3. Museums—Technique
ISBN 0-89919-814-7 LC 89-32783

"Describes how a museum mounts an exhibit and gives specifics about fossils unique to Australia, with focus on the exhibit 'Kadimakara: Fossils of the Australian Dreamtime,' Los Angeles, 1988. Excellent photographs give readers a you-are-there feeling for a museum. Maps illustrate plate tectonics." Sci Child

Barton, Byron

Dinosaurs, dinosaurs. Crowell 1989 unp il $7.95; lib bdg $13.89 (k-2) **567.9**

1. Dinosaurs
ISBN 0-694-00269-0; 0-690-04768-1 (lib bdg) LC 88-22938

Also available HarperCollins Big book edition $19.95 (ISBN 0-06-020410-9)

This book examines the many different kinds of dinosaurs, big and small, those with spikes and those with long, sharp teeth

"Barton conveys the primordial sense of excitement that draws children to these beasts. Despite the illustrations' simplicity, Barton's dinosaurs' expressions are not mammalian smiles; they have a saurian quality all their own. The endpapers identify the creatures by scientific name and pronunciation. Barton wisely keeps his text simple, describing dinosaurs only by size and physical features." SLJ

Booth, Jerry

The big beast book; dinosaurs and how they got that way; drawings by Martha Weston. Little, Brown 1988 128p il $14.95; pa $7.95 (3-6) **567.9**

1. Dinosaurs
ISBN 0-316-10263-6; 0-316-10266-0 (pa) LC 87-36206

"A Brown paper school book"

An introduction to dinosaurs with instructions for related projects

"Teachers, parents, and students looking for science and other school or personal projects will find this book a marvelous resource. The line drawings are detailed, and, at times, humorous." Appraisal

Includes glossary and bibliography

Branley, Franklyn Mansfield, 1915-

What happened to the dinosaurs? [by] Franklyn M. Branley; illustrated by Marc Simont. Crowell 1989 30p il (Let's-read-and-find-out science bks) $12.95; lib bdg $12.89 (k-3) **567.9**

1. Dinosaurs
ISBN 0-690-04747-9; 0-690-04749-5 (lib bdg) LC 88-37626

Describes various scientific theories which explore the extinction of the dinosaurs

"This book couches complex ideas and some difficult vocabulary in a pleasant picture book format, implying a younger audience than would usually be comfortable with this material. Marc Simont's softly colored scenes, broadly sketched in watercolor, flow well and include attractive pictures of both the dinosaur era and the contemporary world. A tantalizing and fresh approach." Horn Book

Carrick, Carol

The crocodiles still wait; pictures by Donald Carrick. Houghton Mifflin 1980 unp il lib bdg $13.95 (1-3) **567.9**

1. Crocodiles 2. Reptiles, Fossil 3. Dinosaurs
ISBN 0-395-29102-X LC 79-23519

"A Clarian book"

In prehistoric times, a 50-foot-long mother crocodile defends her eggs and newly hatched young from attacks by bird eating dinosaurs and Tyrannosaurus Rex

"A provocative easy-to-read science book. . . . Animated and dramatic color-washed drawings show open-mouthed crocodiles as well as the duck-billed dinosaur and the Tyrannosaurus Rex." Horn Book

Cobb, Vicki

The monsters who died; a mystery about dinosaurs; illustrated by Greg Wenzel. Coward-McCann 1983 63p il $10.95 (3-5) **567.9**

1. Dinosaurs 2. Fossils
ISBN 0-698-20571-5 LC 82-14252

This "book presents seven sets of fossil drawings as clues to the shapes, sizes and functions of specific dinosaurs and their relatives. Seven other dinosaurs are given one paragraph treatments." SLJ

Cohen, Daniel, 1936-

Dinosaurs; illustrated by Jean Zallinger. Doubleday 1987 41p il $9.95; lib bdg $9.95 (1-3) **567.9**

1. Dinosaurs
ISBN 0-385-23414-7; 0-385-23415-5 (lib bdg) LC 85-29306

Explores the world of dinosaurs, describing their fossil remains, major types, probable appearance and behavior, and current theories about their extinction and relationship with modern reptiles and birds

This book "is just what most kids want when they ask for a book about dinosaurs. It's big (but not thick), and has plenty of colorful illustrations and just enough text to cover the dinosaur basics. Clear charts of dinosaurs' lifespans and locations of dinosaur fossil finds decorate the endpapers, and an index makes the text (if not the charts) more accessible." SLJ

Monster dinosaur. Lippincott 1983 179p il $11.95 (5 and up) **567.9**

1. Dinosaurs
ISBN 0-397-31953-3 LC 82-48460

An informal potpourri of facts, theories, and lore about dinosaurs and the people who study them

"A lively, challenging discussion of changing beliefs, theories, and lore about dinosaurs presented in readable journalistic style." Sci Child

Includes bibliography

Gibbons, Gail

Dinosaurs. Holiday House 1987 unp il lib bdg $13.95; pa $5.95 (k-2) **567.9**

1. Dinosaurs
ISBN 0-8234-0657-1 (lib bdg); 0-8234-0708-X (pa) LC 87-364

"Two-page spreads illustrate and highlight well-known dinosaurs and give an idea of each one's size, habitat, eating habits and behavior—as well as a phonetic pronunciation of its name. In closing, Gibbons describes the two leading theories on the decline of the dinosaurs: either the planet grew too hot or meteoritic dust in the atmosphere caused it to cool down. An appendix describes the information gained from fossilized dinosaur footprints. Pleasant and informative." Publ Wkly

Jacobs, Francine, 1935-

Supersaurus; pictures by D.D. Tyler. Putnam 1982 45p il lib bdg $6.99 (1-3) **567.9**

1. Dinosaurs
ISBN 0-399-61150-9 LC 81-7375

"A See & read book"

Details a paleontologist's 1972 discovery in western Colorado of the biggest dinosaur bones yet

"The subject is appealing, the narrative framework restrained, the text useful in establishing the ways in which scientists compare and classify materials." Bull Cent Child Books

Lasky, Kathryn

Dinosaur dig; photographs by Christopher G. Knight. Morrow Junior Bks. 1990 unp il $13.95; lib bdg $13.88 (3 and up) **567.9**

1. Dinosaurs 2. Reptiles, Fossil
ISBN 0-688-08574-1; 0-688-08575-X (lib bdg) LC 89-13212

"An infomative text combines geological history, field methodology, and human emotions in a colorful photo-essay that features families participating in an expedition to discover dinosaur fossils. Young and old sift dirt and risk blisters unearthing finds under a paleontologist's guidance in the Montana Badlands." Sci Child

Lauber, Patricia, 1924-

The news about dinosaurs. Bradbury Press 1989 48p il $14.95 (4-6) **567.9**

1. Dinosaurs
ISBN 0-02-754520-2 LC 88-24140

The author "describes current ideas about dinosaurs' herding instincts, their coloration, and the way in which they raised their young. She also explains why dinosaurs are now thought to be related to birds and some of the conflicting opinions of dinosaur extinction." SLJ

"This is one of the most attractively illustrated children's books on dinosaurs ever produced. The colorful artwork, drawn from a number of contemporary sources, is dynamic, dramatic, and set in naturalistic backgrounds but executed with a high degree of attention to scientific detail." Sci Books Films

McGowen, Tom

Album of dinosaurs; illustrated by Rod Ruth. rev and updated ed. Checkerboard Press 1987 60p il pa $4.95 (4 and up) **567.9**

1. Dinosaurs
ISBN 0-02-688500-X LC 86-31711

First published 1972 by Rand McNally

A brief introduction to the history and characteristics of dinosaurs in general, with specific details of twelve different kinds

Most, Bernard, 1937-

The littlest dinosaurs. Harcourt Brace Jovanovich 1989 unp il $12.95 (k-2) **567.9**

1. Dinosaurs
ISBN 0-15-248125-7 LC 88-30063

Describes some of the smaller dinosaurs, all measuring fourteen feet or under, in terms of fact and fancy

This book is "a bright, fresh addition to the shelves and shelves of children's titles about those prehistoric beasts that fascinate the very young. . . . The illustrations are imaginative and the dinosaurs themselves eminently traceable, another passion of young dinosaur lovers." N Y Times Book Rev

Norman, David

Dinosaur; written by David Norman and Angela Milner. Knopf 1989 unp il (Eyewitness bks) $13.95; lib bdg $14.99 (4 and up) **567.9**

1. Dinosaurs
ISBN 0-394-82253-6; 0-394-92253-0 (lib bdg) LC 88-27167

Text and photographs explore the world of the dinosaurs, focusing on such aspects as their teeth, feet, eggs, and fossils

"*Dinosaur* is complete, authoritative, exact, and imaginative. It is sure to survive when many other dinosaur books become extinct." Sci Books Films

Peters, David, 1954-

A gallery of dinosaurs & other early reptiles; written and illustrated by David Peters. Knopf 1989 64p il $14.95; lib bdg $14.99 (4-6) **567.9**

1. Dinosaurs 2. Reptiles, Fossil
ISBN 0-394-89982-2; 0-394-99982-7 (lib bdg) LC 88-36400

A "large-format compendium of dinosaurs and other early reptiles. Full-color paintings include humans to depict scale. Four gatefold pages demonstrate extreme size. Includes brief, informative text on each creature and an introductory overview." Sci Child

Sattler, Helen Roney

Baby dinosaurs; illustrated by Jean Zallinger. Lothrop, Lee & Shepard Bks. 1984 32p il $12.95; lib bdg $12.88 (1-4) **567.9**

1. Dinosaurs
ISBN 0-688-03817-4; 0-688-03818-2 (lib bdg) LC 83-25631

"This book presents theories about the early life of dinosaurs based on the discoveries of fossilized baby dinosaurs." Sci Child

"Zallinger's color pictures recreate the great creatures and their world of 225 million years ago with convincing realism. Closing the book, a time chart and pronunciation guide describe the periods in the Mesozoic Era and list the dinosaurs alive in each." Publ Wkly

Dinosaurs of North America; illustrated by Anthony Rao; with an introduction by John H. Ostrom. Lothrop, Lee & Shepard Bks. 1981 151p il $14.95 (5 and up) **567.9**

1. Dinosaurs
ISBN 0-688-51952-0 LC 80-27411

"Arranged by broad geologic time periods (Triassic, Jurassic, Cretaceous), this carefully researched book features more than 80 different types of dinosaurs native to North America. Each category, introduced with descriptions of the period, explains the creatures' various physical characteristics, eating habits, habitats, and other pertinent details. A final chapter explores the mystery of dinosaur extinction." Booklist

Includes bibliography

The new illustrated dinosaur dictionary; with a foreword by John H. Ostrom; illustrated by Joyce Powzyk. rev ed. Lothrop, Lee & Shepard Bks. 1990 363p il maps $24.95; pa $14.95 (5 and up) **567.9**

1. Dinosaurs—Dictionaries
ISBN 0-688-08462-1; 0-688-10043-0 (pa) LC 90-3313

First published 1983 with title: The illustrated dinosaur dictionary

Sattler "has assembled brief descriptions of more than 350 dinosaurs . . . plus general information under such headings as Food, Size, Teeth, and Parental Care. Each entry includes the Greek or Latin derivation of the dinosaur's name, scientific classification, physical characteristics, and the geologic period and geographic area in which the dinosaur lived. . . . Black-and-white line drawings are scattered throughout the text, and there is a 12-page color gallery." Booklist

Includes bibliography

Pterosaurs, the flying reptiles; illustrations by Christopher Santoro. Lothrop, Lee & Shepard Bks. 1985 43p il $13; lib bdg 12.88 (1-4) **567.9**

1. Reptiles, Fossil 2. Prehistoric animals
ISBN 0-688-03995-2; 0-688-03996-0 (lib bdg) LC 84-4428

Introduces the various species of flying reptiles, probably covered with fur or long hair, possibly warm-blooded, and known only from fossil evidence, which inhabited the earth in the age of dinosaurs

"The author has distilled extensive information and explanation into a cogent, clearly stated narrative which provides children with new material on a very appealing subject." Horn Book

Tyrannosaurus rex and its kin: the Mesozoic monsters; illustrated by Joyce Powzyk. Lothrop, Lee & Shepard Bks. 1989 48p il $14.95; lib bdg $13.88 (4-6) **567.9**

1. Dinosaurs
ISBN 0-688-07747-1; 0-688-07748-X (lib bdg) LC 88-1577

Discusses the fossil remains, probable appearance, and possible behavior of the gigantic flesh-eating dinosaurs of the Mesozoic, including Tyrannosaurus rex, Allosaurus, and such lesser known relatives as Acrocanthosaurus and Baryonyx walkeri

"Generously scaled, labelled watercolor illustrations will

Sattler, Helen Roney—*Continued*
attract young browsers. . . . A helpful map and a time chart augment the catalogue-style text." Bull Cent Child Books

Includes bibliography

Simon, Seymour, 1931-

The largest dinosaurs; illustrated by Pamela Carroll. Macmillan 1986 32p il $12.95 (1-3) **567.9**

1. Dinosaurs
ISBN 0-02-782910-3 LC 85-24088

Surveys findings on Brachiosaurus, Diplodocus, and four other examples of the largest dinosaurs, including the locations of the discoveries and explanations of their names

"Against an imposing array of black-and-white line-and-wash drawings, Simon explores the latest theories on what these animals looked like, how and where they lived, and what they ate. . . . Illustrations include both overall views of the species as well as conceptions of what physical details such as heads, feet, or tails may have looked like. An explanation of mystery surrounding dinosaurs' extinction rounds out the presentation. Useful for students and browsers, this may also be read aloud to children unable to read it on their own." Booklist

Includes glossary

New questions and answers about dinosaurs; illustrated by Jennifer Dewey. Morrow Junior Bks. 1990 45p col il $13.95; lib bdg $13.88 (3-6) **567.9**

1. Dinosaurs
ISBN 0-688-08195-9; 0-688-08196-7 (lib bdg) LC 88-36226

"The book answers twenty-two questions, including 'which was the biggest dinosaur,' 'which dinosaur had the most teeth,' and 'what color were the dinosaurs.' One paragraph of text is used per double-page spread with illustrations filling the remaining space. The subjects are portrayed in soft crayon drawings." Horn Book

The smallest dinosaurs; illustrated by Anthony Rao. Crown 1982 47p il lib bdg $12.95; pa $4.95 (1-3) **567.9**

1. Dinosaurs
ISBN 0-517-54425-3; 0-517-56550-1 (pa) LC 81-3247

Discusses seven dinosaurs, all about the size of a dog or chicken, which are believed to be the bird's prehistoric cousin

"Both text and illustrations are flowing and substantial in detail. This book also provides . . . frequent indications of what scientists do not yet know about dinosaurs and might discover in the future." SLJ

569 Fossil mammals

Aliki

Wild and woolly mammoths; written and illustrated by Aliki. Crowell 1977 unp il (Let's-read-and-find-out science bks) lib. bdg $12.89; pa $4.50 (k-3) **569**

1. Mammoths
ISBN 0-690-01276-4 (lib bdg); 0-06-445005-9 (pa) LC 76-18082

An easy-to-read account of the woolly mammoth, a giant land mammal which has been extinct for over 11,000 years

This is "an engaging introduction to archeology and prehistoric times for young scientists." SLJ

Giants from the past: the age of mammals; photographs by Joseph H. Bailey. National Geographic Soc. 1983 104p il $6.95; lib bdg $8.50 (5 and up) **569**

1. Mammals, Fossil 2. Extinct animals
ISBN 0-87044-424-7; 0-87044-429-8 (lib bdg) LC 81-47893

"Books for world explorers"

"Traces the development of the first mammals, many of which grew to giant proportions in order to survive the violent changes of the Ice Age. Many superb photos—all in color—and drawings. Informative and clearly-written text. Photographs of digging for and preserving fossils and building a mastodon." Sci Child

Includes glossary and bibliography

573.2 Evolution and genetics of humankind

Cole, Joanna

The human body: how we evolved; illustrated by Walter Gaffney-Kessell and Juan Carlos Barberis. Morrow 1987 63p il $12.95; lib bdg $12.88 (4 and up) **573.2**

1. Man—Origin 2. Man, Prehistoric
ISBN 0-688-06719-0; 0-688-06720-4 (lib bdg) LC 86-23679

"The interesting story of human evolution is punctuated by fascinating explanations of the development of specific parts of the human body. Not only are descriptions of development of the brain, foot, hair, eyes, hands, opposable thumb, skull and jaw clear and simple, but the reasons behind the development of these body parts are rivetingly imparted. Ideas are also portrayed through many beautiful sketches. . . . This is a must-read book that will not only inform but encourage the reader's creative thinking process." Sci Books Films

Lasky, Kathryn

Traces of life; the origins of humankind; illustrated by Whitney Powell. Morrow Junior Bks. 1989 144p il maps $16.95 (5 and up) **573.2**

1. Man—Origin 2. Man, Prehistoric
ISBN 0-688-07237-2 LC 89-12092

Lasky, Kathryn—*Continued*

"The history of hominid research and the work of scientists involved are accurately and pleasantly described in an easy-to-read chronology. A comprehensible guide to how various finds and reconstructions explain the evolution of *Homo sapiens.*" Sci Child

Includes bibliography

573.3 Prehistoric humankind

Sattler, Helen Roney

Hominids: a look back at our ancestors; illustrated by Christopher Santoro. Lothrop, Lee & Shepard Bks. 1988 125p il lib bdg $15.95 (5 and up) **573.3**

1. Man, Prehistoric
ISBN 0-688-06061-7 LC 86-10624

A "chronological examination of the ancestry of the human family in which the fossil record is the link that helps describe changes in human form and behavior through the millennia. Special emphasis is given to the changes in brain size, tooth size and function, the onset of bipedalism, and the importance of toolmaking." Sci Child

"The text provides a sensible summary of the generally accepted knowledge in this area as well as the lack of knowledge about many details and the abundance of controversial knowledge, though, happily, it avoids creation science and evolutionary biology. This book is a significant accomplishment." Sci Books Films

Includes bibliography

574.1 Physiology

Branley, Franklyn Mansfield, 1915-

Oxygen keeps you alive; by Franklyn M. Branley; illustrated by Don Madden. Crowell 1971 33p il (Let's read-and-find-out science bks) hardcover o.p. paperback available $4.50 (k-3) **574.1**

1. Respiration 2. Oxygen
ISBN 0-06-445021-X (pa) LC 73-139093

"The importance of oxygen to man, animals, and plants is emphasized in an easy-to-read account which gives brief, elementary descriptions of human respiration and of photosynthesis in plants, an explanation of how fish breathe, and a simple experiment to show the presence of dissolved oxygen in water. The picture book is enhanced by cheerful drawings in color and in black and white." Booklist

Silverstein, Alvin

Nature's living lights; fireflies and other bioluminescent creatures; [by] Alvin and Virginia Silverstein; illustrated by Pamela and Walter Carroll. Little, Brown 1988 42p il $12.95 (5 and up) **574.1**

1. Bioluminescence
ISBN 0-316-79119-9 LC 87-2727

"The chemical reaction that causes some insects, fish, plants, and fungi to light up in the dark is explained. Uses of bioluminescence for the creatures' interaction with their own species, other species, and the environment are described and wonderfully illustrated with white drawings on navy blue pages. Applications in commerce and medicine are included." Sci Child

Includes glossary

574.5 Ecology

Baylor, Byrd

The desert is theirs; illustrated by Peter Parnall. Scribner 1975 unp il lib bdg $13.95; pa $3.95 (1-4) **574.5**

1. Desert ecology 2. Papago Indians
ISBN 0-684-14266-X (lib bdg); 0-689-71105-X (pa) LC 74-24417

"Poetic interpretations of Papago Indians' ecological and spiritual relationships with desert resources. . . . Illustrations add to the usefulness of this mood piece for sensitizing children to respect for nature, reading aloud, studying Indian cultures and techniques of using line, space and color." Read Teach

Bender, Lionel

Desert. Watts 1989 32p col il (Story of the earth) lib bdg $11.90 (3-5) **574.5**

1. Desert ecology
ISBN 0-531-10707-8 LC 87-51612

"This book describes the animals and plants that inhabit deserts around the world. It illustrates various ways that deserts are formed and how they change through time." Sci Child

Includes glossary

Catchpole, Clive

Deserts; pictures by Brian McIntyre. Dial Bks. for Young Readers 1984 unp il maps (Living world) $10.95; pa $4.95 (2-4) **574.5**

1. Desert ecology
ISBN 0-8037-0035-0; 0-8037-0037-7 (pa) LC 83-7757

First published 1983 in the United Kingdom

Text and illustrations describe the unique characteristics and conditions of the desert including the climate and rich and varied plant and animal life

"Deserts differ greatly, and this point is well made here. Selections of flora and fauna from different kinds of deserts are well chosen, accurately presented, and colorfully illustrated." Sci Books Films

Grasslands; pictures by Peter Snowball. Dial Bks. for Young Readers 1984 unp il (Living world) $10.95; pa $4.95 (2-4) **574.5**

1. Grassland ecology
ISBN 0-8037-0082-2; 0-8037-0083-0 (pa) LC 83-27123

This volume "briefly describes the wildlife of the world's plains, prairies, pampas and savannas—the grazing animals, scavengers, predators and birds that inhabit them. The majority of the book is filled with vivid, realistic illustrations that depict animals of the

Catchpole, Clive—*Continued*
area—the wildebeest, gazelle, cheeta, vulture, kangaroo, rhea and bison, among others." SLJ

Jungles; pictures by Denise Finney. Dial Bks. for Young Readers 1984 unp il (Living world) $10.95; pa $4.95 (2-4) **574.5**

1. Jungle ecology
ISBN 0-8037-0034-2; 0-8037-0036-9 (pa) LC 83-7796
First published 1983 in the United Kingdom

Text and pictures present the many beautiful and unusual forms of life that thrive in the jungle

"This book effectively communicates the spirit of the ecosystem, the interaction between animals and plants and some salient facts. A fine introduction to natural science." SLJ

Mountains; pictures by Brian McIntyre. Dial Bks. for Young Readers 1984 unp il map (Living world) $10.95; pa $4.95 (2-4) **574.5**

1. Mountain ecology
ISBN 0-8037-0086-5; 0-8037-0087-3 (pa) LC 83-25273

This book "includes limited examples of alpine flowers, insects, and birds and describes how they exist in their inhospitable surroundings. The main focus is on mammals such as marmots, mountain goats, and grizzly bears. Brief, crisply written descriptions comment on the animals' most interesting characteristics and adaptations and serve to whet curiosity rather than provide textlike information." Horn Book

Cobb, Vicki
This place is wet; illustrated by Barbara Lavallee. Walker & Co. 1989 unp il (Imagine living here) $12.95; lib bdg $13.85 (2-4) **574.5**

1. Rain forest ecology 2. Amazon River valley
ISBN 0-8027-6880-6; 0-8027-6881-4 (lib bdg) LC 89-32445

Focuses on the land, ecology, people, and animals of the Amazon rain forest in Brazil, presenting it as an example of a place where there is so much water that some houses need to be built on stilts

Ekey, Robert
Fire! in Yellowstone; story by Robert Ekey. Gareth Stevens Children's Bks. 1990 32p il map lib bdg $10.95 (2-4) **574.5**

1. Forest fires 2. Yellowstone National Park 3. Forest ecology
ISBN 0-8368-0226-8 LC 89-43156
"A True adventure"

Adapted from an adult book: Yellowstone on fire, published 1989 by The Billings Gazette

Discusses the fire that ravaged nearly one million acres of Yellowstone National Park during several months in 1988, and explains the two sides to the controversy over letting nature take its course

A "Well-written and excellently photographed book. . . . Good thought-provoking questions stimulate class discussions." Sci Child

Includes glossary and bibliography

Forsyth, Adrian
Journey through a tropical jungle; with an afterword by HRH Prince Philip, the Duke of Edinburgh. Simon & Schuster Bks. for Young Readers 1988 80p il map lib bdg $14.95 (4 and up) **574.5**

1. Rain forest ecology 2. Natural history—Costa Rica
ISBN 0-671-66262-7 LC 88-14683

In this photo essay, the author, a Canadian naturalist, describes the climate, plants, animals and people he encountered in a trek through the Monteverde Cloud Forest Reserve in Costa Rica

"The book emphasizes the diversity of animal and plant life encountered and includes a gentle treatment of human encroachment. While the book may fail in its larger intent to plead the case for tropical forest conservation, readers of all ages may well develop a strong desire to emulate the author and totally immerse themselves in a natural environment. The balance between text and photographs is good, and the index is helpful." Sci Books Films

George, Jean Craighead, 1919-
One day in the alpine tundra; illustrations by Walter Gaffney-Kessell. Crowell 1984 44p il $13.95; lib bdg $13.89 (4-6) **574.5**

1. Mountain ecology 2. Tundra ecology
ISBN 0-690-04325-2; 0-690-04326-0 (lib bdg) LC 82-45590

"What's life like above the tree line? This is the story—partly fictional—of how plants and animals have adapted to the harsh conditions of the tops of mountains." Sci Child

Includes bibliography

One day in the desert; illustrated by Fred Brenner. Crowell 1983 48p il lib bdg $13.89 (4-6) **574.5**

1. Desert ecology 2. Sonoran Desert 3. Papago Indians
ISBN 0-690-04341-4 LC 82-45924

Explains how the animal and human inhabitants of the Sonoran Desert of Arizona, including a mountain lion, a roadrunner, a coyote, a tortoise, and members of the Papago Indian tribe, adapt to and survive the desert's merciless heat

"With a measured, yet vivid, style, this simplified introduction to desert ecology makes a memorable impact that goes beyond ready reference facts. Delicate black-and-white sketches, well placed on each page, break up the text and illustrate the plants and animals discussed." SLJ

Includes bibliography

One day in the prairie; illustrated by Bob Marstall. Crowell 1986 42p il $12.95; lib bdg $11.89 (4-6) **574.5**

1. Prairie ecology 2. Tornadoes
ISBN 0-690-04564-6; 0-690-04566-2 (lib bdg) LC 85-48254

George, Jean Craighead, 1919-—*Continued*

The animals on a prairie wildlife refuge sense an approaching tornado and seek protection before it touches down and destroys everything in its path

"Black-and-white pencil drawings expand the text and bring out the threat of the coming tornado. There is a bibliography of titles on more specific aspects of the prairie ecosystem, and a short index. George provides a brief but intense and detailed look at the North American prairie, equally suitable for a homework assignment or for browsing." SLJ

One day in the tropical rain forest; illustrated by Gary Allen. Crowell 1990 56p il $11.95; lib bdg $11.89 (4-6) **574.5**

1. Rain forest ecology 2. Natural history—Venezuela
ISBN 0-690-04767-3; 0-690-04769-X (lib bdg)
LC 89-36583

"The final day of a struggle between developers and conservationists over the Tropical Rain Forest of the Macaw as seen by a young Indian boy. A beautifully written story details the complexity, majesty, and interdependence of flora and fauna and teaches about indigenous people and scientists who inhabit a small part of Venezuela's rain forest." Sci Child

Includes bibliography

One day in the woods; illustrated by Gary Allen. Crowell 1988 42p il $11.95; lib bdg $11.89 (4-6) **574.5**

1. Forest ecology 2. Birds
ISBN 0-690-04722-3; 0-690-04724-X (lib bdg)
LC 87-21712

Rebecca discovers many things about plant and animal life when she spends the day in Teatown Woods in the Hudson Highlands of New York looking for the ovenbird

"Through naturalist George's precise descriptions, readers follow Rebecca's progress through the day discovering the secrets of the spring foliage and learning much about the temperate forest and its inhabitants. Allen's refined pencil drawings of the skunk, wood ducks, flying squirrel, gypsy moth caterpillar, and other creatures that Rebecca encounters on her quest beautifully transcribe George's textual details." Booklist

Includes bibliography

Jaspersohn, William

How the forest grew; illustrated by Chuck Eckart. Greenwillow Bks. 1989 55p il $12.95 (2-4) **574.5**

1. Forest ecology
ISBN 0-688-80232-X
LC 79-16286

"A Greewillow read-alone book"

A reissue of the title first published 1980

This "book traces the growth of a Massachusetts hardwood forest. . . . The book recounts each stage of the forest's growth and explains the reasons for the succession of diffrent types of plant and animal life." Horn Book

"Many beautifully detailed black-and-white sketches thoroughly capture the atmosphere of the developing forest." Appraisal

Landau, Elaine

Tropical rain forests around the world. Watts 1990 64p il maps lib bdg $10.90 (4 and up) **574.5**

1. Rain forest ecology
ISBN 0-531-10896-1
LC 89-24810

"A First book"

Discusses where rain forests are located, what conditions are necessary for their growth, the enormous variety of plant life found in rain forests, and the various animals and millions of insects that live there. Important, timely chapters discuss why rain forests are important (including a discussion of what products we derive from the rain forests) and what's happening to them today." SLJ

Includes glossary and bibliography

Lerner, Carol, 1927-

A forest year. Morrow 1987 48p il $12.95; lib bdg $12.88 (3-5) **574.5**

1. Forest ecology 2. Seasons
ISBN 0-688-06413-2; 0-688-06414-0 (lib bdg)
LC 86-9741

"Arranged by season, this book provides 16 glimpses of the plants and animals that might live in a typical forest in the eastern half of the United States. For every season there are four full-page water-color illustrations, each facing a page of descriptive text and each highlighting a set of wildlife: mammals, birds, reptiles and amphibians, or insects." Booklist

"The pictures fill whole pages and some double-spread half-pages with beautifully composed detail; circled insets showing selected magnified items are included for closer viewing in some scenes." Horn Book

Newton, James R.

A forest is reborn; illustrated by Susan Bonners. Crowell 1982 28p il $12.95; lib bdg $12.89 (2-4) **574.5**

1. Forest ecology 2. Forest fires
ISBN 0-690-04231-0; 0-690-04232-9 (lib bdg)
LC 82-1399

Describes how a forest renews itself through a process called plant succession after a destructive fire

"Readers will gain a sense of the interrelatedness of all living things, and the continual process of change that occurs in the forest environment." SLJ

Rain shadow; illustrated by Susan Bonners. Crowell 1983 32p il $12.95; lib bdg $12.89 (2-5) **574.5**

1. Rain and rainfall 2. Weather 3. Ecology
ISBN 0-690-04344-9; 0-690-04345-7 (lib bdg)
LC 82-45927

Explains how the "rain shadow," or dry environment, develops on the leeward side of many high mountain ranges, and contrasts it with the rain forest, or wetter environment, on the windward side

"A 'rain-shadow' environment is not a simple concept for young readers to comprehend. James Newton has explained the concept in a clear, straightforward manner which is not condescending. . . . Susan Bonners's sensitive black and white drawings provide the reader with the visual impact of the text." Appraisal

Norsgaard, E. Jaediker (Ernestine Jaediker)
Nature's great balancing act; in our own backyard; photographs by Campbell Norsgaard. Cobblehill Bks. 1990 63p il $14.95 (4-6) **574.5**

1. Ecology
ISBN 0-525-65028-8 LC 89-38589

"Cobblehill books"

"The interrelationships of plants, animals, insects, and birds are explored in a semi-wild New England backyard. Excellent photographs complement a lively text." Sci Child

Includes glossary

Patent, Dorothy Hinshaw
Yellowstone fires; flames and rebirth; photos by William Muñoz and others. Holiday House 1990 40p il $14.95 (2-4) **574.5**

1. Forest fires 2. Yellowstone National Park 3. Forest ecology
ISBN 0-8234-0807-8 LC 89-24544

An account of the 1988 forest fire in Yellowstone National Park

"This is the only book which covers some financial issues, the media depiction of the fire, and the animals and birds disturbed or killed by firefighters. . . . Clear, colorful photos illustrate points covered in the text." SLJ

Podendorf, Illa, 1903-1983
Jungles. Childrens Press 1982 45p il maps lib bdg $13.27 (2-4) **574.5**

1. Jungle ecology
ISBN 0-516-01631-8 LC 82-4454

"A New true book"

First published 1959 with title: The true book of jungles

Discusses the climate and locations of jungles and describes the plants of which jungles are made and the animals and people that live in jungles

This book "would be useful in a primary-grade study of ecosystems. . . . [A] good feature of this book is inclusion of photographs of children who live in jungles and their homes." Sci Books Films

Includes glossary

Schwartz, David M., 1951-
The hidden life of the forest; photographs by Dwight Kuhn; text by David M. Schwartz. Crown 1988 unp il lib bdg $12.95 (3-5) **574.5**

1. Forest ecology
ISBN 0-517-57058-0 LC 88-11865

Photographs and text introduce the animals, insects, and plants in a forest

"This exceptionally attractive children's book is distinguished by color photographs that range from excellent to breathtaking. The text is competently written but seldom sparkles. . . . Some basic concepts of natural history, such as change of seasons, flowers leading to fruit development, and adaptations of predators, are inserted skillfully enough for the young reader to learn without feeling taught." Sci Books Films

The hidden life of the meadow; photographs by Dwight Kuhn; text by David M. Schwartz. Crown 1988 unp il lib bdg $12.95 (3-5) **574.5**

1. Grassland ecology
ISBN 0-517-57059-9 LC 88-14934

Examines the animals, plants, snd ecology of a typical American meadow

"The closeups are remarkable for their color reproduction, composition, and clarity, whether the subject is an owl in flight or a microscopic amoeba. The effect is one of walking, invisibly cloaked, through the environment for a look at the shyest and smallest of creatures." Bull Cent Child Books

Simon, Seymour, 1931-
Deserts. Morrow Junior Bks. 1990 unp il maps $13.95; lib bdg $13.88 (3-5) **574.5**

1. Desert ecology
ISBN 0-688-07415-4; 0-688-07416-2 (lib bdg) LC 89-39738

Describes the nature and characteristics of deserts, where they are located, and how they are formed

"Spectacular photos of the deserts of the American southwest are used to show the various features from rippling sand, to wind-eroded rock formations, to the sparse vegetation characteristic of the area. There is a little information on how both plant and animal life have adapted to the harsh climate, and on the wonderful public lands such as Monument Valley, The Grand Canyon, etc." SLJ

Vogel, Carole Garbuny
The great Yellowstone fire; [by] Carole Garbuny Vogel and Kathryn Allen Goldner. Sierra Club Bks.; Little, Brown 1990 30p il $14.95 (3-6) **574.5**

1. Forest fires 2. Yellowstone National Park 3. Forest ecology
ISBN 0-316-90522-4 LC 89-29318

Describes the 1988 Yellowstone National Park forest fires and their effects on the ecology

"Well-chosen photographs . . . include many full-page scenes and are particularly effective in conveying the power of the fires, the human involvement, and the park as a habitiat for animals. The descriptive prose in this book clearly and vividly conveys events and their significance as history." Horn Book

Watts, Barrie
24 hours in a forest; text and photography by Barrie Watts. Watts 1990 44p il lib bdg $11.90 (5 and up) **574.5**

1. Forest ecology
ISBN 0-531-14036-9 LC 89-38986

"An informative visual study of a forest during a summer day. An array of animals and plants emerge in early morning, daytime, evening, and at nights as readers follow the rhythms of forest life." Sci Child

Includes glossary

Weiwandt, Thomas

The hidden life of the desert; photographs and text by Thomas Wiewandt. Crown 1990 unp il $12.95; lib bdg $13.99 (3-5) **574.5**

1. Desert ecology
ISBN 0-517-57355-5; 0-517-57356-3 (lib bdg) LC 89-22263

"Unusual desert plants and animals are described in straightforward text and beautiful illustrations that diminish the stereotypical view of a barren desert environment. A spectacular, complex view of a desert ecosystem in the American Southwest." Sci Child

Whitfield, Philip J.

Can the whales be saved? Questions about the natural world and threats to it's survival answered by the Natural History Museum; [by] Philip Whitfield. Viking Kestrel 1989 96p il maps $16.95 (4 and up) **574.5**

1. Natural history 2. Nature conservation
ISBN 0-670-82753-3

"Question-and-answer format about not only whales but all aspects of the wonderful, varied plant and animal life of our Earth trying to survive the menace of global pollution of air, land, and water." Soc Educ

Includes glossary

574.87 Cytology (Cell biology)

Asimov, Isaac, 1920-

How did we find out about DNA? illustrated by David Wool. Walker & Co. 1985 61p il $10.85; lib bdg $9.95 (5 and up) **574.87**

1. DNA
ISBN 0-8027-6596-3; 0-8027-6604-8 (lib bdg) LC 85-15589

This book describes the discovery of deoxyribonucleic acid, a complex molecule found in all cells and which plays a vital part in heredity

574.92 Aquatic biology. Marine biology

Arnold, Caroline, 1944-

A walk on the Great Barrier Reef; photographs by Arthur Arnold; with additional photographs by Marty Snyderman [et al.] Carolrhoda Bks. 1988 47p il (Carolrhoda nature watch bk) lib bdg $12.95; pa $6.95 (3-6) **574.92**

1. Coral reefs and islands 2. Marine animals 3. Great Barrier Reef (Australia)
ISBN 0-87614-285-4 (lib bdg); 0-87614-501-2 (pa) LC 87-27746

The author leads "the reader on a tour of discovery that explores the structure of the reef and the life cycles and habits of its various inhabitants. Following a discussion of how the reef was formed, the book includes diagrams of the three types of coral reef formations (fringing, barrier, and atoll)." Sci Child

"The fascinating plants and animals of Australia's Great Barrier Reef are described in a straightforward way and illustrated with stunning, clear full-color photographs." SLJ

Includes glossary

Bellamy, David J.

The rock pool; with illustrations by Jill Dow. Potter 1988 unp il (Our changing world) $9.95 (1-4) **574.92**

1. Marine ecology
ISBN 0-517-56977-9 LC 88-4167

"The author begins his tour of the pool with the small creatures and seaweeds then moves to the larger fish. Everything seems to be ideal and in balance in this habitat. A storm occurs that causes an ocean tanker to spill oil thus the tidal pool is damaged so severely it seems its inhabitants will be unable to survive. As time passes the tides do cleanse the pool, and within a year the pool has begun to be a community again." Appraisal

Johnson, Sylvia A.

Coral reefs; photographs by Shohei Shirai. Lerner Publs. 1984 55p il (Lerner natural science bk) lib bdg $12.95; pa $5.95 (4 and up) **574.92**

1. Coral reefs and islands 2. Marine animals
ISBN 0-8225-1451-6 (lib bdg); 0-8225-1451-6 (pa) LC 84-816

Adapted from a work by Shohei Shirai published 1975 in Japan

"Beginning with a description of a coral polyp itself, through some of the varied members of that unusual group, to the types of coral reefs and a brief look at some of the fish, crabs, starfish and other animals that call the reef home, this is a colorful introduction to the strange and beautiful world of the coral reef. Unusual terms that are defined in the glossary are in bold type; a two-page note on scientific classification is also included." SLJ

Lavies, Bianca

Lily pad pond; text and photographs by Bianca Lavies. Dutton 1989 unp il $13.95 (k-2) **574.92**

1. Pond ecology
ISBN 0-525-44483-1 LC 88-31697

"Details of life in a woodland pond, with particular emphasis on a tadpole turned bullfrog. Different animals in the food chain are brilliantly photographed as they search for food in a competitive world." Sci Child

McCauley, Jane R., 1947-

Let's explore a river; photographs by Joseph H. Bailey. National Geographic Soc. 1988 32p il (k-3) **574.92**

1. Freshwater animals 2. Freshwater plants 3. Rivers
ISBN 0-87044-741-6; 0-87044-746-7 LC 88-25349

McCauley, Jane R., 1947-—*Continued*

Available only as part of a 4v set for 11.95, lib bdg $13.95. Other titles in the set are: Animals at play, by K. M. Kostyal, class 591.5; Animals in summer, by Jane K. McCauley, class 591.5; and Busy beavers, by M. Barbara Brownell

"Books for young explorers"

Three children accompany their father in a canoe and explore the plant and animal life along a river near their home

Includes bibliography

McGovern, Ann

Down under, down under; diving adventures on the Great Barrier Reef; photographs by Jim and Martin Scheiner and the author. Macmillan 1989 48p il $14.95 (3-6) **574.92**

1. Marine biology 2. Scuba diving 3. Great Barrier Reef (Australia)
ISBN 0-02-765770-1 LC 88-30530

A twelve-year-old girl recounts her experiences on the Great Barrier Reef, encountering sharks, sea snakes, and giant clams, exploring the wreck of a ghost ship, observing shore life, and exploring the reef from a dive boat as well as a helicopter

"The first person narrative is a wonderful way for young people to learn about underwater life. This experience is enhanced by the outstanding color photographs. Technically reliable, competently photographed, and engagingly written, here is one of the best books of its kind." Appraisal

Parker, Steve

Pond & river; written by Steve Parker. Knopf 1988 63p il (Eyewitness bks) $13.95; lib bdg $14.99 (4 and up) **574.92**

1. Pond ecology 2. River ecology
ISBN 0-394-89615-7; 0-394-99615-1 (lib bdg)
LC 88-1575

An "introduction to the plants and animals found in various aquatic habitats. . . . This is first and foremost a picture book; each section consists of an introductory paragraph and several pages full of labeled and captioned photographs and illustrations of plants and animals. The photographs are excellent and are a first-rate way for youngsters to identify the more common organisms found in aquatic habitats." Sci Books Films

Seashore; written by Steve Parker. Knopf 1989 63p il (Eyewitness bks) $13.95; lib bdg $14.99 (4 and up) **574.92**

1. Seashore 2. Marine animals 3. Marine plants
ISBN 0-394-82254-4; 0-394-92254-9 (lib bdg)
LC 88-27173

A photo essay introduces the animal inhabitants of the seashore, including fish, crustaceans, snails, and shorebirds

This book "contains . . . exquisite, three dimensional photographs and a myriad of easily digested facts about life where land and sea meet. . . . Better for browsing than in-depth research." BAYA Book Rev

Reid, George K.

Pond life; a guide to common plants and animals of North America ponds and lakes; by George K. Reid, under the editorship of Herbert S. Zim and George S. Fichter; illustrated by Sally D. Kaicher and Tom Dolan. Golden Press Bks. 1967 160p il (Golden nature guide) pa $4 (4 and up) **574.92**

1. Pond ecology
ISBN 0-307-24017-7 LC 67-16477

The book "explains the dynamics of a pond or lake, shows some of the plants, animals, insects, and fishes likely to be found in or near it, and tells how to collect specimens." Publ Wkly

Includes bibliography

Schwartz, David M., 1951-

The hidden life of the pond; photographs by Dwight Kuhn. Crown 1988 unp il lib bdg $12.95 (3-5) **574.92**

1. Pond ecology
ISBN 0-517-57060-2 LC 88-11863

This book "presents the wide and complex variety of life in an American pond. . . . Plant, insect, bird, and mammal life are described, accompanied by excellent clear, crisp color photographs." SLJ

Silverstein, Alvin

Life in a tidal pool; [by] Alvin and Virginia Silverstein; illustrated by Pamela and Walter Carroll. Little, Brown 1990 60p il $14.95 (4-6) **574.92**

1. Marine ecology
ISBN 0-316-79120-2 LC 89-12676

Describes the varied forms of shore life found in and around tidal pools and discusses their struggle for survival

Information is "presented in a lively style to interest both landlocked readers and coastal inhabitants." SLJ

Includes glossary

Stolz, Mary, 1920-

Night of ghosts and hermits; nocturnal life on the seashore; illustrated by Susan Gallagher. Harcourt Brace Jovanovich 1985 47p il $12.95 (3-5) **574.92**

1. Marine animals 2. Seashore
ISBN 0-15-257333-X LC 84-15665

"A blending of fiction and science. On a beach on the Gulf of Mexico, three brothers reluctantly leave their sandcastle. That night the seemingly peaceful shore comes to life as a ghost crab escapes a heron's notice, a whelk and a horse conch battle, a loggerhead turtle lays her eggs, and a hermit crab finds a new home. Soft, luminous illustrations capture the drama and beauty of the seashore after dark." Sci Child

Includes glossary and bibliography

Zim, Herbert S.

Seashores; a guide to animals and plants along the beaches; by Herbert S. Zim and Lester Ingle; illustrated by Dorothea and Sy Barlowe; sponsored by the Wildlife Management Institute. Golden Press Bks. 1955 160p il pa $4.95 (4 and up) **574.92**

1. Marine biology
ISBN 0-307-24496-2 LC 55-2608

"A Golden nature guide"

"A comprehensive pocket guide for identifying 'plant and animal life found in North American tidal waters.' Algae, sponges, corals, shellfish, birds, flowering plants, etc. are included with brief descriptive text and illustrations in full color. Index." Horn Book

574.999 Astrobiology

Branley, Franklyn Mansfield, 1915-

Is there life in outer space? Franklyn M. Branley; illustrated by Don Madden. Crowell 1984 32p il (Let's-read-and-find-out science bks) $12.95; lib bdg $12.89 (k-3) **574.999**

1. Life on other planets 2. Outer space—Exploration
ISBN 0-690-04374-0; 0-690-04375-9 (lib bdg)
LC 83-45057

This book describes what "investigations have shown about the moon and Mars, what is known about other planets in the solar system that makes it unlikely that they sustain life, and what probably exists of life on planets in other galaxies. . . . Branley makes it clear that his opinions on the last topic are conjectural." Bull Cent Child Books

Mysteries of life on earth and beyond; [by] Franklyn M. Branley; diagrams by Sally J. Bensusen. Lodestar Bks. 1987 66p il (Mysteries of the universe ser) $12.95 (6 and up) **574.999**

1. Life on other planets 2. Outer space—Exploration
ISBN 0-525-67195-1 LC 86-19929

The author "compares Earth with other planets, writes about the origins of life on Earth, explores the possibility of life on other planets, describes the methods of searching for extra-terrestrial life and discusses the kinds of signals Earth sends to the stars. . . . For the reader who wants an overview or a review and is not interested in in-depth coverage, Branley's book is a good choice. It is well organized and written in a readable style. The illustrations and graphics add to the understanding of ideas presented in the text. It is a good addition and should be well used by space buffs." Appraisal

Includes bibliography

Poynter, Margaret

Cosmic quest; searching for intelligent life among the stars; by Margaret Poynter and Michael J. Klein. Atheneum Pubs. 1984 124p il $11.95 (5 and up) **574.999**

1. Life on other planets 2. Interstellar communication
ISBN 0-689-31068-4 LC 84-6191

This "account, which includes the use of computers, describes the search for intelligent life in the universe, from theories about the origin of the universe and of life to the use of radio telescopes and the collection of wave data. Also included is the International SETI Petition signed by 73 internationally renowned scientists." Sci Child

Includes glossary and bibliography

575 Evolution and genetics

Cole, Joanna

Evolution; illustrated by Aliki. Crowell 1987 31p il (Let's-read-and-find-out science bks) $12.95; lib bdg $12.89; pa $4.50 (k-3) **575**

1. Evolution 2. Fossils
ISBN 0-690-04596-4; 0-690-04598-0 (lib bdg); 0-06-445086-4 (pa) LC 87-638

Describes, using evidence found in fossil layers, how one-cell organisms evolved into complex plants and animals

"The text is lucid, simple, and sequential; the drawings are carefully labelled and are nicely integrated with the text, and the format is spacious, with broad margins and good-sized print." Bull Cent Child Books

Gallant, Roy A.

Before the sun dies; the story of evolution. Macmillan 1989 190p il $15.95 (6 and up) **575**

1. Evolution
ISBN 0-02-735771-6 LC 88-8284

"An outline of the history of evolution, relying heavily on fossil evidence for the depictions of life in earlier ages. Beginning with a . . . description of the scientific definition of living processes, Gallant proceeds to cover the formation and evolution of the universe, the galaxies, and the physical Earth, and presents early and current ideas of how life began here." SLJ

"The book has an exceptionally nice format; the slightly wide page size is pleasant as is the design of the chapter headings. The captioned pictures and diagrams are useful adjuncts rather than dominant features of the book, and there is a good bibliography including both children's books and more advanced sources." Horn Book

Includes glossary

575.1 Genetics

Bornstein, Sandy

What makes you what you are; a first look at genetics. Messner 1989 115p il lib bdg $11.98; pa $6.95 (5 and up) **575.1**

1. Genetics
ISBN 0-671-63711-8 (lib bdg); 0-671-68650-X (pa)
LC 89-9440

The author addresses "cell structure and division, discusses dominant and recessive traits, and . . . examines DNA." SLJ

"The book tries to explain the scientific aspects of cell division in a manner comprehensible to the young

Bornstein, Sandy—*Continued*
reader. The attempt, although forced, is good. Mendel's experiments are explained simply. . . . The readable and informative book is highly recommended because it can be used with so many different audiences." Sci Books Films

Includes bibliography

Patent, Dorothy Hinshaw

Grandfather's nose; why we look alike or different; illustrations by Diane Palmisciano. Watts 1989 32p il (Discovering science bk) lib bdg $12.90 (k-2) **575.1**

1. Genetics
ISBN 0-531-10716-7 LC 89-9140

Discusses basic genetics, explaining how the combination of genes passed on from our parents makes each of us a unique individual

This is "an excellent book on genetics. . . . The words and pictures make this topic, which could be complicated, accessible to young children in an informative, interesting, and scientifically accurate fashion." Appraisal

"This book is a must for every media center." Sci Child

Showers, Paul

Me and my family tree; illustrated by Don Madden. Crowell 1978 33p il (Let's-read-and-find-out science bks) lib bdg $13.89 (k-3) **575.1**

1. Heredity
ISBN 0-690-03887-9 LC 77-26595

"Showers has written a delightful book about heredity. Don Madden's black-and-white and color illustrations add to the book's attraction. The story is of a red-haired boy who talks about his parents, grandparents, and great-grandparents. Traits are defined, and the work of Gregor Mendel is reviewed simply. This book could be read to or by children." Sci Child

581 Botany

Black, David

Plants; [by] David Black & Anthony Huxley. Facts on File 1985 64p il (World of science) $15.95 (5 and up) **581**

1. Plants
ISBN 0-8160-1065-X LC 84-1654

This book presents a survey of plant life illustrated with color photographs and diagrams. A glossary is included

Burnie, David

Plant; written by David Burnie. Knopf 1989 63p il (Eyewitness bks) $13.95; lib bdg $14.99 (4 and up) **581**

1. Plants
ISBN 0-394-82252-8; 0-394-92252-2 (lib bdg) LC 88-27172

A photo essay introduces the world of plants, including the germination of seeds, plant defenses, and uses of plants

"Probably the most impressive feature of this book is the quality of the carefully composed images, such as the parts of a plant, the time-lapse aging of a blossom, and the photographs shot through a microscope. Each superbly designed two-page spread contains a complete topic. . . . Everything from the history of botany to plant lore gets its due." Sci Books Films

Cross, Diana Harding

Some plants have funny names; illustrated by Jan Brett. Crown 1983 47p il lib bdg $8.95 (k-3) **581**

1. Plant names, Popular 2. Plants
ISBN 0-517-54840-2 LC 82-23438

This book "covers some unusually named plants that grow in North America. . . . The information is brief, a few pages on each, perhaps just enough to encourage observation. There are facts on what the plant looks like, its uses, where it can be found. Included are jack-in-the-pulpit, lady's slippers, Indian pipe and marshmallow. . . . The drawings with just a touch of color are appealing and the style of writing is clear and simple." Appraisal

Facklam, Howard

Plants: extinction or survival? [by] Howard and Margery Facklam. Enslow Pubs. 1990 96p il maps lib bdg $16.95 (6 and up) **581**

1. Plant conservation 2. Seeds
ISBN 0-89490-248-2 LC 89-17038

Describes the importance of germplasm and how storage banks around the world are preserving plant seeds so that plant species will not be lost through disease and environmental conditions

"The book's strength lies in its thoughtful approach and coverage of modern plant-gene engineering. A well-illustrated and clearly explicated chapter on protoplasm fusion and recombinant DNA points the direction for future food and medicinal plants." SLJ

Includes bibliography

Selsam, Millicent Ellis, 1912-

A first look at the world of plants; by Millicent E. Selsam and Joyce Hunt; illustrated by Harriett Springer. Walker & Co. 1978 32p il lib bdg $9.85 (1-3) **581**

1. Plants
ISBN 0-8027-6299-9 LC 77-78088

This introduction to plant study includes illustrated pages on bacteria, algae, bryophytes, fungi, ferns, gymnosperms, and angiosperms. The author shows how each class differs from the others, and provides games where the reader is invited to match names and pictures

"Just enough material, just enough classification in the plant world is included in an excellent book for the primary-grades reader. . . . The text and illustrations are nicely coordinated." Bull Cent Child Books

581.1 Physiology of plants

Asimov, Isaac, 1920-

How did we find out about photosynthesis? illustrated by Erika Kors. Walker & Co. 1989 64p il $11.95; lib bdg $12.85 (5 and up) **581.1**

1. Photosynthesis
ISBN 0-8027-6899-7; 0-8027-6886-5 (lib bdg)
LC 89-5832

Traces the scientific discoveries that led to our understanding of photosynthesis and how this process relates to the food supply, changing ecological balance, and threats to the Earth's atmosphere

"A complicated book, but certainly a worthwhile purchase for school libraries." Appraisal

581.5 Botany—Ecology

Cole, Joanna

Plants in winter; illustrated by Kazue Mizumura. Crowell 1973 33p il (Let's-read-and-find-out science bks) lib bdg $12.89 (k-3) **581.5**

1. Plants 2. Trees 3. Botany—Ecology
ISBN 0-690-62886-2 LC 73-1771

This book describes how various plants survive during the winter. Leafy and evergreen trees and plants with underground stems, bulbs, shoots and seeds are differentiated

"The text is clear and simple and is accompanied by wash drawings. Considering how slight a volume this is, it covers a wide range of plants. . . . This is an attractive and informative introduction to plant life." Appraisal

581.6 Economic botany

Lerner, Carol, 1927-

Dumb cane and daffodils; poisonous plants in the house and garden. Morrow Junior Bks. 1990 32p il $13.95; lib bdg $13.88 (4-6) **581.6**

1. Poisonous plants
ISBN 0-688-08791-4; 0-688-08796-5 (lib bdg)
LC 89-33622

Describes the physical characteristics, natural habitats, and harmful effects of several varieties of plants grown in North America

"Lerner's detailed botanical drawings and paintings are the real highlight of the book, though descriptions of the plants and explanations of their effects on humans, especially children and house pets, are capably written." Bull Cent Child Books

Moonseed and mistletoe; a book of poisonous wild plants. Morrow Junior Bks. 1988 32p il $12.95; lib bdg $12.88 (4-6) **581.6**

1. Poisonous plants
ISBN 0-688-07307-7; 0-688-07308-5 (lib bdg)
LC 87-13989

Beginning with "poison ivy and poison oak and other species that irritate the skin, five groups of plants are considered. . . . Varieties of berries, wildflowers, bushes, and trees that are poisonous if eaten are discussed, and the final chapter, 'Deck the Halls,' is devoted to holly, mistletoe, and bittersweet. One full-page color painting in each chapter groups the plants discussed, and small sketches of some leaves, fruit, or roots are set into the text." Horn Book

"An accessible beginning book on an eternally popular topic." SLJ

582 Seed-bearing plants

Dowden, Anne Ophelia Todd, 1907-

The clover and the bee; a book of pollination; [by] Anne Ophelia Dowden; illustrated by the author. Crowell 1989 90p il $17.95; lib bdg $17.89 (5 and up) **582**

1. Flowers 2. Fertilization of plants
ISBN 0-690-04677-4; 0-690-04679-0 (lib bdg)
LC 87-30116

Explains the process of pollination, describing the reproductive parts of a flower and the role that insects, birds, mammals, wind, and water play in the process

"Impeccable detail in both text and illustrations makes this the most beautiful as well as the most comprehensive work on pollination available to children." Horn Book

From flower to fruit; illustrated by the author. Crowell 1984 56p il $14.95 (5 and up) **582**

1. Flowers 2. Fruit 3. Seeds 4. Fertilization of plants
ISBN 0-690-04402-X LC 83-46163

Text and drawings explain how flowers mature into seed-bearing fruit

"The text is deceptively brief but information packed, and though scientific terms are defined as they are introduced, their proliferation is likely to daunt readers new to the subject. . . . This is an elegantly embellished, albeit demanding, biology lesson, particularly recommended as exciting corollary material for classroom studies." Booklist

Jordan, Helene J.

How a seed grows; illustrated by Joseph Low. Crowell 1960 unp il (Let's-read-and-find-out science bks) lib bdg $12.89 (k-3) **582**

1. Seeds
ISBN 0-690-40645-2 LC 60-11541

"Begins by explaining that the seeds of different plants are different and grow differently. Then suggests that the student plant and care for some bean seeds in order to observe how they develop; thus it effectively teaches the beginner how a seed grows into a plant." AAAS Sci Book List for Child

Lauber, Patricia, 1924-
From flower to flower; animals and pollination; photographs by Jerome Wexler. Crown 1986 57p il $13.95 (2-4) **582**

1. Flowers 2. Fertilization of plants 3. Bees
ISBN 0-517-55539-5 LC 86-4566

The author discusses "the pollination of flowers by insects and other small animals. General statements of how pollination occurs are closely followed by examples of how the principles are carried out with ingenious individuality by specific plants and animals." Booklist

"Emphasis is on the remarkable work of bees in this excellent book on how flowers are pollinated. The many large and clear black-and-white photographs by master cameraman Jerome Wexler complement and enhance Patricia Lauber's carefully crafted text." Child Book Rev Serv

Seeds pop, stick, glide; text by Patricia Lauber; photographs by Jerome Wexler. Crown 1991 c1981 57p il lib bdg $14.99 (2-4) **582**

1. Seeds
ISBN 0-517-58554-5 LC 80-14553

First published 1981

Text and photographs describe the many different ways that seeds travel and disperse

"Well-balanced, this book includes all the important aspects needed for a general understanding of the methods of seed dispersal. The simple language is clear, flowing, and at the same time, scientifically precise. The black-and-white photographs are superb. .. . Even more outstanding is the coordination between text and illustrations." Sci Books Films

Lerner, Carol, 1927-
Plant families. Morrow Junior Bks. 1989 32p il $12.95; lib bdg $12.88 (4 and up) **582**

1. Plants 2. Botany
ISBN 0-688-07881-8; 0-688-07882-6 (lib bdg) LC 88-26653

This book "provides a concise introduction to taxonomic principles of plant identification through examination of 12 of the largest and most common plant families: buttercup, mustard, pink, mint, pea, rose, parsley, composite, lily, arum, grass, and orchid. Each group is discussed in simplified, accurate terms, complete with pronunciation keys within the text and a brief, appended glossary." Sci Books Films

Overbeck, Cynthia
How seeds travel; photographs by Shabo Hani. Lerner Publs. 1982 48p il (Lerner natural science bk) lib bdg $12.95; pa $5.95 (4 and up) **582**

1. Seeds
ISBN 0-8225-1474-5 (lib bdg); 0-8225-9569-9 (pa) LC 81-17217

Adapted from a work by Shabo Hani published 1978 in Japan

This book "explores the ways seeds leave their parent plants to establish themselves in appropriate terrain." Booklist

"New and difficult concept words are listed in bold type as they appear in the text. All color graphics are excellent; the close-up photographs are stunning." SLJ

Wexler, Jerome
Flowers, fruits, seeds. Prentice-Hall Bks. for Young Readers 1987 unp il lib bdg $12.95 (k-2) **582**

1. Flowers 2. Fruit 3. Seeds
ISBN 0-13-322397-3 LC 86-30616

"Photographs of plants and trees present an array of flowers, fruits and finally seeds; the text makes the point that the function of flowers is to produce fruit and that of fruit, to protect seeds, from which plants grow." Publ Wkly

"Coupling the sparest of texts with his stunning full-color photographs, Wexler presents a simple, effective botany lesson." Booklist

582.1 Herbaceous and woody plants

Petrides, George A.
A field guide to trees and shrubs; illustrated by George A. Petrides, Roger Tory Peterson. 2nd. Houghton Mifflin 1972 xxxii, 428p il hardcover o.p. paperback available $13.95 **582.1**

1. Trees—North America 2. Shrubs 3. Climbing plants
ISBN 0-395-17579-8 (pa) LC 76-157132

"The Peterson field guide series"

First published 1958

"Field marks of all trees, shrubs, and woody vines that grow wild in the northeastern and north-central United States and in southeastern and south-central Canada." Title page

"Descriptions and clear drawings compare similar species. Includes silhouettes showing typical branching of many of the trees." AAAS Sci Book List. 3d edition

582.13 Herbaceous flowering plants

Dowden, Anne Ophelia Todd, 1907-
State flowers; illustrated by the author. Crowell 1978 86p il lib bdg $13.89 (5 and up) **582.13**

1. State flowers
ISBN 0-690-03884-4 LC 78-51927

The author/illustrator has "etched the leaves, stems, petals, and stamens, capturing the intricate individuality of each flower in its natural shades and colors. Statutes enacting the state flower laws are given verbatim along with historical and other background information appearing in the brief text juxtaposed with the paintings. Except in a few cases where two states have the same

Dowden, Anne Ophelia Todd, 1907-—*Continued*
flower and thus are placed together, an alphabetical order by state is observed." Booklist

Robbins, Ken
A flower grows. Dial Bks. for Young Readers 1990 unp il $12.95; lib bdg $12.89 (2-4) **582.13**
1. Flowers
ISBN 0-8037-0764-9; 0-8037-0765-7 (lib bdg) LC 89-12016
"The life cycle of an amaryllis plant, from its beginning as an unattractive bulb to its gorgeous blossoming and subsequent rest, is beautifully illustrated and described in interesting text. Includes helpful hints on growing an amaryllis indoors." Sci Child

Selsam, Millicent Ellis, 1912-
A first look at flowers; by Millicent E. Selsam and Joyce Hunt; illustrated by Harriett Springer. Walker & Co. 1976 c1977 31p il lib bdg $9.85 (1-3) **582.13**
1. Flowers
ISBN 0-8027-6282-4 LC 76-57063
"Text and corresponding black-and-white illustrations direct children's attention to flower shape, arrangement on the stalk, petal formation, location and number of stamens and pistils, etc. Nine flowers pictured in the text appear again on the last pages for a recognition test." SLJ
"Meticulously drawn pictures . . . of flowers and flower parts add to the usefulness of a succinctly written introduction to the subject, and the authors incorporate into the text such basic scientific principles as observation, identification, and comparison. The writing is direct and simple." Bull Cent Child Books

Zim, Herbert S.
Flowers; a guide to familiar American wildflowers; by Herbert S. Zim and Alexander C. Martin; illustrated by Rudolf Freund; 134 paintings in full color; sponsored by the Wildlife Management Institute. Golden Press Bks. 1950 157p il maps pa $3.95 (4 and up) **582.13**
1. Wild flowers
ISBN 0-307-24491-1 LC 50-8172
First published by Simon & Schuster
"To facilitate identification the flowers are arranged in four groups according to color. Each flower is pictured in color with a range map. . . . Brief descriptive text gives characteristics, habitat, growing season and family." Booklist

582.16 Trees

Burnie, David
Tree; written by David Burnie. Knopf 1988 63p il (Eyewitness bks) $13.95; lib bdg $14.99 (4 and up) **582.16**
1. Trees
ISBN 0-394-89617-3; 0-394-99617-8 (lib bdg) LC 88-1572
"Every imaginable aspect of the life of a tree is examined in a series of 2-page poster-format chapters, from 'The Birth of a Tree' to 'The Death of a Tree.' Anatomy, physiology, reproduction, growth and development are described using the best photographs I have seen in botanical literature and succinct, lively captions. Each page is a delight to the eye. . . . Of particular note is the coverage of tree diseases and pollution including acid rain, and the practical, amateur study of trees." Sci Books Films

Dowden, Anne Ophelia Todd, 1907-
The blossom on the bough; a book of trees; illustrated by the author. Crowell 1975 71p il $14.89 (5 and up) **582.16**
1. Trees 2. Forests and forestry
ISBN 0-690-00384-6 LC 74-6192
In this volume the "importance of forests and forest regions in the United States, the parts and cycles of trees, and the functions of flowers and fruits are described in words and pencil drawings by a well-known botanical artist." LC. Child Books, 1975

Hindley, Judy
The tree; written by Judy Hindley; illustrated by Alison Wisenfeld. Potter 1990 unp il lib bdg $14.99 (3-5) **582.16**
1. Trees
ISBN 0-517-57630-9 LC 89-16105
"An introduction to 12 trees includes botany background, a poem, folklore, and uses associated with each tree. Hawthorn, ash, sycamore, horse-chestnut, willow, fir, beech, birch, plane, elm, apple, and oak trees are described in double-page spreads that feature detailed folk-art illustrations." Sci Child
"The striking beauty of this book sets it apart from the many scientifically oriented volumes in print; the elaborate calligraphy and delicate drawings make it pleasing to the eye. Twelve familiar trees are each lovingly described with a single page of spare but well-chosen words." SLJ

Romanova, N. (Natal'iâ)
Once there was a tree; by Natalia Romanova; pictures by Gennady Spirin. Dial Bks. for Young Readers 1985 unp il $11.95; pa $4.95 (2-4) **582.16**
1. Trees 2. Forest ecology
ISBN 0-8037-0235-3; 0-8037-0705-3 (pa) LC 85-6730
Original Russian edition, 1983
An old stump attracts many living creatures, even man, and when it is gone, a new tree attracts the same creatures, who need it for a variety of reasons

Romanova, N. (Natal'īā)—*Continued*

"The illustrations make up for what may be translation errors, and the writing is more poetic than didactic. The paintings, too, are lyrical both in landscape vistas and in close botanical detail." Bull Cent Child Books

Selsam, Millicent Ellis, 1912-

Tree flowers; illustrated by Carol Lerner. Morrow 1984 31p il lib bdg $12.88 (4 and up) **582.16**

1. Trees
ISBN 0-688-02769-5 LC 83-17353

"Twelve flowering trees, including some unlikely ones like pussy willow, are described by type and pollination method. Excellent general information about tree reproduction in the introduction is followed by a two-page spread on each tree. Lovely watercolor drawings, with attention to cutaway details, complement the text, which explains the growth cycle and appropriate uses of the trees. This is an exceptional botany book for young readers." Sci Child

Zim, Herbert S.

Trees; a guide to familiar American trees; by Herbert S. Zim and Alexander C. Martin; illustrated by Dorothea and Sy Barlowe. rev ed. Golden Press Bks. 1956 160p il maps (Golden nature guide) pa $2.95 (4 and up) **582.16**

1. Trees—United States
ISBN 0-307-24494-6 LC 57-3009

First published 1952 by Simon & Schuster

"A beginner's pocket-size guidebook . . . illustrates in color and describes . . . American trees, pointing up the features important in identification—form and height of tree, leaves, bark, fruit, flowers, buds—and including, in most cases, a range map." Booklist

583 Dicotyledons

Bash, Barbara

Desert giant; the world of the saguaro cactus. Sierra Club Bks.; Little, Brown 1989 unp il $14.95 (3-5) **583**

1. Cactus
ISBN 0-316-08301-1 LC 88-4706

"Animals find food and shelter in the towering plant of the Sonoran desert, and the local Tohono O'odom Indians have multiple uses for it. The cactus's 200-year life cycle is depicted as part of the ecosystem with colorful illustrations and clear text." Sci Child

Tree of life: the world of the African baobab. Sierra Club Bks. 1990 c1989 unp il (Tree tales) $14.95 (3-5) **583**

1. Baobab
ISBN 0-316-08305-4 LC 89-6028

Text and pictures document the life cycle of this amazing tree of the African savannah, and portrays the animals and people it helps to support

"Beautiful watercolors in an oversize format enhance the easy-to-read text which tells about the interdependence of living things." Child Book Rev Serv

Overbeck, Cynthia

Cactus; photographs by Shabo Hani. Lerner Publs. 1982 48p il (Lerner natural science bk) lib bdg $12.95; pa $5.95 (4 and up) **583**

1. Cactus
ISBN 0-8225-1469-9 (lib bdg); 0-8225-9556-7 (pa) LC 82-211

Adapted from a work by Shabo Hani published 1975 in Japan

Describes the special parts of the cactus plant and how they work together to enable the plant to survive in the desert by storing water

Includes glossary

Carnivorous plants; photographs by Kiyoshi Shimizu. Lerner Publs. 1982 48p il (Lerner natural science bk) lib bdg $12.95; pa $5.95 (4 and up) **583**

1. Insectivorous plants
ISBN 0-8225-1470-2 (lib bdg); 0-8225-9535-4 (pa) LC 81-17234

Adapted from a work by Kiyoshi Shimizu published 1975 in Japan

Describes the Venus fly trap, sundew, pitcher plant, and bladderwort, and explains how active and passive traps work in these meat-eating plants

Includes glossary

585 Gymnosperms (Naked-seed plants)

Adler, David A., 1947-

Redwoods are the tallest trees in the world; illustrated by Kazue Mizumura. Crowell 1978 32p il (Let's-read-and-find-out science bks) lib bdg $12.89 (k-3) **585**

1. Redwood
ISBN 0-690-01368-X LC 77-4713

"A young boy tells what he knows about the redwood trees he saw in a California national park. There a ranger explained about them and the kind of habitat they require. . . . Informative and admiring in an understated way." Booklist

588 Bryophytes

Johnson, Sylvia A.

Mosses; photographs by Masana Izawa. Lerner Publs. 1983 48p il (Lerner natural science bk) lib bdg $12.95; pa $5.95 (4 and up) **588**

1. Mosses
ISBN 0-8225-1482-6 (lib bdg); 0-8225-9563-X (pa) LC 83-17488

Adapted from a work by Masana Izawa published 1981 in Japan

Johnson, Sylvia A.—*Continued*

A description of mosses, in which the text "pays close attention to botanical detail, describing where mosses fit in the plant kingdom and examining their two-stage reproductive system. There are a number of difficult terms defined in context, with pronunciation guides found in the glossary." Booklist

"The photographs and diagrams work with the text making the concepts easy to understand." SLJ

589.2 Fungi

Froman, Robert

Mushrooms and molds; illustrated by Grambs Miller. Crowell 1972 33p il lib bdg $12.89 (1-3) **589.2**

1. Mushrooms 2. Molds (Botany)

ISBN 0-690-56603-4 LC 71-187936

The book gives "information on fungi covering their growth from mycelium, their manufacture of soil for green plants, and their reproduction by spores. Suggestions for growing bread molds and making mushroom spore patterns are intriguing and practical for small children." Booklist

"The definitions included within the text are scientifically accurate, yet very simple. The drawings on each page clearly show what the author is explaining." SLJ

Johnson, Sylvia A.

Mushrooms; photographs by Masana Izawa. Lerner Publs. 1982 48p il (Lerner natural science bk) lib bdg $12.95 (4 and up) **589.2**

1. Mushrooms

ISBN 0-8225-1473-7 LC 82-212

Adapted from a work by Masana Izawa published 1977 in Japan

Discusses how mushrooms and other fungi get their food, grow and produce more of their own kind

"The writing is competent, but it is the artistic color photographs on every page that make this a standout." Booklist

Includes glossary

Selsam, Millicent Ellis, 1912-

Mushrooms; [by] Millicent E. Selsam; photographs by Jerome Wexler. Morrow 1986 48p il $12.95; lib bdg $12.89 (2-4) **589.2**

1. Mushrooms

ISBN 0-688-06248-2; 0-688-06249-0 (lib bdg) LC 85-18953

"Concentrating on a variety of mushroom commonly sold in grocery stores, the book provides a historical overview of the plant, details the process of commercially growing mushrooms in compost, and—with the use of some fine close-up photography—describes the physical components of the plant itself." Horn Book

589.3 Algae

Kavaler, Lucy

Green magic: algae rediscovered; illustrated with photographs and with drawings by Jean Helmer. Crowell 1983 120p il $12.95 (5 and up) **589.3**

1. Algae

ISBN 0-690-04221-3 LC 81-43872

The author "describes the structure and variety of algae, the fossil findings, established phenomena, old and new uses of algae for food, fertilizer, and sewage purification, and discusses some of the ways in which algae may be used to alleviate food shortages in the future or serve myriad purposes on space flights." Bull Cent Child Books

"Illustrated with a mixture of photographs and graceful, soft-pencil scientific drawings, this is smoothly written and nicely designed—an attractive, readable introduction to the subject." Booklist

589.4 Specific types of algae

Daegling, Mary

Monster seaweeds; the story of the giant kelps. Dillon Press 1986 119p il maps (Ocean world lib) lib bdg $11.95 (4 and up) **589.4**

1. Algae 2. Ecology

ISBN 0-87518-350-6 LC 86-13591

"An extremely valuable natural resource or an important part of the ocean food chain, kelp (or seaweed) is a part of ocean life that most of us think of only when it gets in our way at the beach. This book clearly details the life cycle of kelp, its relationship to ocean life in general, its value to us, particularly the algin derived from it, and the . . . way in which it is harvested and processed. Useful mainly as a source of information for reports, this book is very clearly written with a helpful use of sub-headings in chapters. It is enhanced by wonderful pictures and clear drawings." Appraisal

Includes glossary and bibliography

590.74 Zoological museums, collections, exhibits

Brennan, John, 1952-

Zoo day; by John Brennan and Leonie Keaney. Carolrhoda Bks. 1989 c1987 unp il lib bdg $9.95 (k-3) **590.74**

1. Zoos

ISBN 0-87614-358-3 LC 88-20344

First published 1987 in Australia

"Brennan and Keaney take readers through a typical day at an Australian zoo. From 6:00 in the morning to 6:30 in the evening, exhibits are visited when something of note is occurring: a baby gorilla playing with his keeper, a wombat in the nursery being fed a bottle, or Syrian bears engaging in a playful wrestling match. To help young readers keep track of the changing time, a clock is pictured on each page. . . . Not a ground-breaking title but handy for its clear photographs and brief, to-the-point descriptions." Horn Book

Gibbons, Gail
Zoo. Crowell 1987 unp il $13.95; lib bdg $12.89; pa $4.95 (k-2) **590.74**

1. Zoos
ISBN 0-690-04631-6; 0-690-04633-2 (lib bdg); 0-06-446096-7 (pa) LC 87-582

Provides a behind-the-scenes look at a working day at the zoo, from the moment the workers arrive until the night guard locks the gate

"The writing is crisp, clear, and informative. This interesting and authoritative look behind the zoo scenes is illustrated in Gibbons' usual flat, simple, clearly-defined style in the very bright colors so appealing to young children." SLJ

Grosvenor, Donna K.
Zoo babies; with photographs by the author. National Geographic Soc. 1978 31p il (k-3) **590.74**

1. Zoos 2. Animals—Infancy
ISBN 0-87044-265-1; 0-87044-270-8 LC 77-95413

Available only as part of 4v set for $10.95, lib bdg $12.95. Other titles in set are: Animals that live at sea, by J. A. Straker; Explore a spooky swamp, by W. W. Cortesi; and Animals in danger, by Peggy D. Winston

"Books for young explorers"

Through color photographs 17 varieties of baby animals are introduced. The text explains how the zoo personnel meet their special needs

Johnston, Ginny, 1946-
Windows on wildlife; [by] Ginny Johnston and Judy Cutchins. Morrow Junior Bks. 1990 48p il $13.95; lib bdg $13.88 (3-6) **590.74**

1. Zoos 2. Aquariums
ISBN 0-688-07872-9; 0-688-07873-7 (lib bdg) LC 89-34487

"From gavials lazing in a jungle river to kelp swaying in a sunlit sea, two bright photo-essays provide an enticing glimpse of six natural habitat exhibits around the country—Zoo Atlanta in Georgia; Sea World's Penguin Encounter in Orlando, Florida; the Bronx Zoo's Jungle World in New York; the Hippoquarium in the Toledo Zoo in Ohio; the Zoological Park's Forest Aviary in North Carolina; and the Monterey Bay Aquarium in California." Sci Child

Includes glossary

Machotka, Hana
What do you do at a petting zoo? Morrow Junior Bks. 1990 unp il $13.95; lib bdg $13.88 (k-2) **590.74**

1. Zoos 2. Animals
ISBN 0-688-08737-X; 0-688-08738-8 (lib bdg) LC 89-34478

"Seven animals—a goat, hen, donkey, pig, duck, sheep, and llama—are individually introduced in photographs that picture only part of the animal, encouraging children to join a game to guess its identity. A large photograph of each animal follows, accompanied by a page describing habits and characteristics that a child would be likely to observe at close range. The text is brief, including just enough information to pique interest and spark discussion. A unique and engaging subject presented in an eye-catching format seemingly designed with large groups of listeners in mind." Horn Book

Rinard, Judith E., 1947-
Zoos without cages; by Judith E. Rinard. National Geographic Soc. 1981 104p il $6.95; lib bdg $8.50 (5 and up) **590.74**

1. Zoos
ISBN 0-87044-335-6; 0-87044-340-2 (lib bdg) LC 79-3243

"Books for world explorers"

Discusses the concept of open zoos, introduces some zoo workers, and describes some activities happening in zoos today

Thomson, Peggy, 1922-
Keepers and creatures at the National Zoo; photographs by Paul S. Conklin. Crowell 1988 198p il $13.95; lib bdg $13.89 (5 and up) **590.74**

1. National Zoological Park (U.S.)
ISBN 0-690-04710-X; 0-690-04712-6 (lib bdg) LC 87-47697

Describes, in text and illustrations, the many different tasks performed by keepers at the National Zoo and the interrelationship between them and the animals they care for

"Plenty of photographs with informative, often witty captions enliven the text and tone. A realistic, yet optimistic book for young people interested in a career working with animals, this gives insight into numerous species as well as the humans responsible for preserving them." Bull Cent Child Books

591 Zoology

Animal families of the wild; animal stories by Roger Caras [et al.]; edited by William F. Russell; with art by John Butler. Crown 1990 82p il $12.95; lib bdg $13.99 (5 and up) **591**

1. Animals
ISBN 0-517-57358-X; 0-517-57359-8 (lib bdg) LC 89-22226

"Each of five excerpts (drawn from *The Endless Migrations* by Roger Caras, *The Whispering Land* by Gerald Durrell, *The Last Eagle* by Dan Mannix, *Centennial* by James Michener, and *Never Cry Wolf* by Farley Mowat) focuses on a specific animal behavior that illustrates the extremes to which animals will go to perpetuate a healthy species. This excellent collection has realistic full-color paintings and black-and-white sketches. . . . An engrossing book for the study of nature, families, or literature." Booklist

Includes bibliography

Cole, Joanna

Large as life daytime animals; life size paintings by Kenneth Lilly; text by Joanna Cole. Knopf 1985 unp il $9.95; lib bdg $12.99 (k-3) **591**

1. Animals

ISBN 0-394-87188-X; 0-394-97188-4 (lib bdg)

LC 85-4301

Brief text and life-size illustrations present the characteristics of a variety of small animals. Includes the ermine, squirrel monkey, bee hummingbird, birdwing butterfly, and others

"The recurrent problem of information books on animals, the difficulty of relative scale, has been solved here. . . . Certain animals are seen, in actual size, close to some object which makes the scale easy to appreciate." Grow Point

Large as life nighttime animals; life size paintings by Kenneth Lilly; text by Joanna Cole. Knopf 1985 30p il $9.95; lib bdg $12.99 (k-3) **591**

1. Animals

ISBN 0-394-87189-8; 0-394-97189-2 (lib bdg)

LC 85-7593

This work introduces various small nocturnal animals, including the elf owl, fennec fox, chinchilla, royal antelope, and giant toad

"The pictures are faithfully realistic in detail . . . and they have a strong textural quality. . . . The page-size has to some extent influenced choice of subjects, and not many subjects are covered—but the high quality of the pictures and the accuracy of the simple text give the book minor reference use in addition to browsing pleasure." Bull Cent Child Books

Heberman, Ethan

The city kid's field guide. Simon & Schuster Bks. for Young Readers 1989 48p il $14.95; pa $5.95 (4 and up) **591**

1. Animals

ISBN 0-671-67749-7; 0-671-67746-2 (pa)

LC 89-30062

"A Novabook"

Published in association with WGBH Boston

"Clear, full-color photographs, interesting diagrams, and an engaging text describe a wide array of plants and animals available for observation in urban neighborhoods. Readers find that vacant lots are never vacant, parks are always populated, and a city home harbors more denizens than just the family." Sci Child

Hoban, Tana

A children's zoo. Greenwillow Bks. 1985 unp il $13.95; lib bdg $13.88 (k-2) **591**

1. Animals

ISBN 0-688-05202-9; 0-688-05204-5 (lib bdg)

LC 84-25318

This is a photographic "portfolio of zoo denizens. . . . Each species is matted with a narrow white line, framed in black, and placed opposite a black page against which . . . white sans serif letters list three of that species' characteristics as well as its name." Horn Book

"For the most part, the photographs are standard zoo fare, but a few are truly different and amusing." SLJ

Includes glossary

McGrath, Susan, 1955-

Saving our animal friends. National Geographic Soc. 1986 32p il (k-3) **591**

1. Wildlife conservation

ISBN 0-87044-635-5; 0-87044-640-1 LC 86-5177

Available only as part of 4v set for $10.95, lib bdg $12.95. Other titles in set are: Animals and their hiding places, by Jane R. McCauley, class 591.5; Animals that live in trees, by Jane R. McCauley, class 591.5; and Baby bears and how they grow, by Jane Heath Buxton, class 599.74

"Books for young explorers"

"The 5 wonderful animals who highlight *Saving Our Animal Friends* are manatees, alligators, great whales, sea turtles, and whooping cranes. Wonderful photos and text show how we can assist in hatching whooping crane eggs and sea turtle eggs so that the young are protected from their natural enemies. Readers learn that litter such as metal flip tops and plastic six-pack holders can injure wildlife. . . . Respect for wildlife, a reverence for nature, is the theme of a book such as this." Read Teach

Pope, Joyce

Do animals dream? children's questions about animals most often asked of the Natural History Museum; answered by Joyce Pope. Viking Kestrel 1986 96p il $16.95 (4 and up) **591**

1. Animals

ISBN 0-670-81233-1 LC 86-40029

Questions and answers present information on animals under a variety of topics, such as Why do some animals hibernate? Do animals talk to each other? and Why do fleas jump?

"Numerous black-and-white (and some color) illustrations and diagrams not only clarify the answers and examples, but are also a major contribution to the great visual appeal of this book." SLJ

Rinard, Judith E., 1947-

Wildlife, making a comeback; how humans are helping. National Geographic Soc. 1987 104p il $6.95; lib bdg $8.50 (4 and up) **591**

1. Wildlife conservation

ISBN 0-87044-656-8; 0-87044-661-4 (lib bdg)

LC 87-22078

"Books for world explorers"

"The author identifies four ways to conserve wildlife: passing laws to stop the killing or collecting of endangered species; setting aside areas of wild habitat as parks and wildlife reserves; studying species of plants and animals in their natural habitats to learn how to better protect them; and, when the species can no longer survive in their habitats, keeping captive individual animals and trying to breed them. . . . The book concludes with a list of organizations that will provide information about various kinds of wildlife." Sci Child

Includes bibliography

Simon, Seymour, 1931-
Animal fact/animal fable; illustrated by Diane de Groat. Crown 1979 unp il lib bdg $11.95; pa $4.95 (1-4) **591**

1. Animals
ISBN 0-517-53474-6 (lib bdg); 0-517-53794-X (pa) LC 78-14866

"After a brief explanation of the terms 'fact' and 'fable,' the author proceeds to either verify or dispel many common beliefs about animals. Each fable is accompanied by a full-color illustration, a comical exaggeration of the belief. Following the factual statement is another picture and a short explanation of the actual behavior of the animal." Child Book Rev Serv

"Done in watercolors of muted tones, the pictures are admirable and the text is informative. A very fine collaboration." SLJ

591.05 Zoology—Serial publications

International Wildlife. National Wildlife Federation $15 per year **591.05**

1. Wildlife conservation—Periodicals
ISSN 0020-9112

Bimonthly. First published 1971

"This publication's 50-plus pages are chock-full of color photographs and interesting tidbits on the aspects of nature that exist all around us but are seldom noticed. As the title indicates, it is international in scope. It has excellent photography, and the text is easy to read and informative. Excellent for browsing; the photography alone makes the magazine worth acquiring." Katz. Mag for Sch Libr

Zoonooz. Zoological Soc. of San Diego $10 per year **591.05**

1. Zoos—Periodicals
ISSN 0044-5282

Monthly. First published 1926

This magazine describes the activities and exhibits of the San Diego Zoo. It includes illustrated articles written by members of the Zoo's staff

591.1 Physiology of animals

Heller, Ruth
Chickens aren't the only ones. Grosset & Dunlap 1981 unp il $8.95 (k-1) **591.1**

1. Reproduction 2. Animals—Infancy
ISBN 0-448-01872-1 LC 80-85257

A pictorial introduction to the animals that lay eggs, including chickens as well as other birds, reptiles, amphibians, fishes, insects, and even a few mammals

The animals "are displayed in buoyant but realistic full-color drawings that sing out from the page. It's unusual to see a science lesson so festively done for such a young audience; in fact this has the fun of pure fiction, though it is straight fact." Booklist

Lauber, Patricia, 1924-
What's hatching out of that egg? Crown 1991 c1979 unp il lib bdg $14.99 (k-3) **591.1**

1. Animals—Infancy 2. Reproduction
ISBN 0-517-58553-7 LC 79-12054

First published 1979

Lauber's book "opens with the photograph of an egg in its natural setting, and the reader is invited to guess its identity. Sequential pictures show the hatchings and the animals at progressively older stages until the adult appears. . . . The process is repeated for ten more animals—including an ostrich, an alligator, a frog, a snake, and a platypus." Horn Book

"This book will make an excellent nature study lesson for story hour by a teacher or librarian." Sci Books Films

McClung, Robert M.
The amazing egg. Dutton 1980 116p il $15.95 (4 and up) **591.1**

1. Eggs 2. Reproduction
ISBN 0-525-25480-3 LC 79-23461

"A Unicorn book"

The author's "introduction to the many processes of embryology begins traditionally with the chicken and its eggs and moves on to jellyfish and worms, mollusks, arthropods, insects, fish, amphibians, reptiles and birds. The concluding chapter on mammals includes those that lay eggs, those that deposit the embryo into pouches and those with placental embryos. The text surveys representative species, explaining in brief chapter sections a wide range of ideas and physiological patterns." SLJ

"McClung writes in a straightforward, lucid style, with good organization of material and good integration of text and illustrations; the latter are soft, accurately detailed, pencil drawings." Bull Cent Child Books

591.4 Anatomy and morphology of animals

Goor, Ron, 1940-
All kinds of feet; Ron and Nancy Goor. Crowell 1984 48p il (Let's-read-and-find-out science bks) lib bdg $12.89 (k-3) **591.4**

1. Foot
ISBN 0-690-04385-6 (lib bdg) LC 83-45239

"This book presents the types of feet found in the animal kingdom and describes how each type is suited to the needs of different animals. The straightforward text is supported by many well-chosen photographs. The uniqueness of human beings is emphasized, too." Sci Child

Heads; [by] Ron and Nancy Goor. Atheneum Pubs. 1988 64p il $13.95 (2-4) **591.4**

1. Senses and sensation 2. Head
ISBN 0-689-31400-0 LC 87-30262

Compares and contrasts the characteristics of the eyes, ears, nose, and mouth of a variety of animals

"Not only are the fascinating ways in which animals utilize their senses considered, but different adaptations of the same animals, such as the mouths of the white

Goor, Ron, 1940-—*Continued*
and the black rhinos, are shown to underline the influence of the environment. . . . Clearly written and usable." Booklist

591.5 Ecology of animals

Animal architects. National Geographic Soc. 1987 104p il $6.95; lib bdg $8.50 (4 and up) **591.5**

1. Animals—Habitations
ISBN 0-87044-612-6; 0-87044-617-7 (lib bdg) LC 87-12198

"Books for world explorers"

"Readers are introduced to the many different animals that build nests. Among this group are the mallee fowl of Australia with its three-foot deep pits and the ant lion with its tiny sand traps, the marmots with their burrows and the beavers in their mounds, the mud dauber wasp with its mud nest and the spittlebug's bubble nest. The photographs are enhanced by the clearly written text which explains the animal behavior involved in nest building." SLJ

Arnosky, Jim

Crinkleroot's book of animal tracking. Bradbury Press 1989 48p il $13.95 (3-5) **591.5**

1. Animal tracks
ISBN 0-02-705851-4 LC 88-15353

First published 1979 by Putnam with title: Crinkleroot's book of animal tracks and wildlife signs

"Crinkleroot—a curious old codger with a long white beard and hiking stick—provides young readers with clear, accurate information on some habits of wildlife common to the northeastern United States. His short discourses are accompanied by precisely-drawn illustrations showing the tracks of each animal or bird. Each creature's habitats and unusual habits are included, as well." SLJ

Secrets of a wildlife watcher; written and illustrated by Jim Arnosky. Lothrop, Lee & Shepard Bks. 1983 64p il $13.95; lib bdg $11.88 (4 and up) **591.5**

1. Nature study 2. Animals—Habits and behavior
ISBN 0-688-02079-8; 0-688-02081-X (lib bdg) LC 82-24920

"Explains techniques for finding, stalking, and watching such wildlife as owls, deer, squirrels, and rabbits. Over 100 full-color and black-and-white drawings depicting animal tracks, signs, feeding habits, and the like." Sci Child

"Arnosky's delight in wildlife, and the effectiveness with which he conveys it, conspire to lure the young naturalist, book in hand, out into the wild. The book's attention to detail and straightforward manner make it a fine choice for a beginner watcher of any age." Appraisal

Dewey, Jennifer

Can you find me? a book about animal camouflage. Scholastic 1989 unp il $13.95 (2-4) **591.5**

1. Camouflage (Biology)
ISBN 0-590-41552-2 LC 88-18346

"Luminous, colorful illustrations highlight an easy-to-read text that describes a variety of creatures and the natural camouflage that allows them to blend into their environments. A surprise ending includes the human animal." Sci Child

Epstein, Sam, 1909-

Bugs for dinner? the eating habits of neighborhood creatures; by Sam and Beryl Epstein; illustrated by Walter Gaffney-Kessell. Macmillan 1989 48p il $12.95 (4-6) **591.5**

1. Animals—Food
ISBN 0-02-733501-1 LC 88-26654

Recounts how squirrels, robins, grasshoppers, and other creatures in an urban environment find their food and avoid being eaten themselves

"This readable overview of the food-finding methods of familiar animals will enrich all future encounters with them. Detailed, scientific pen-and-ink illustrations add to the book's usefulness." Horn Book

Facklam, Margery

And then there was one; the mysteries of extinction; illustrations by Pamela Johnson. Little, Brown 1990 56p il lib bdg $14.95 (4-6) **591.5**

1. Extinct animals 2. Rare animals 3. Wildlife conservation
ISBN 0-316-25984-5 LC 89-70133

"A Lucas-Evans book"

Examines the many reasons for the extinction and near-extinction of animal species. Discusses how some near-extinctions have been reversed through special breeding programs and legislation to save endangered species

"The book is a tour de force in arguing for ecological balance. The fine-honed pencil drawings, spacious format, and creamy paper contribute to a handsomely designed volume." Bull Cent Child Books

Do not disturb; the mysteries of animal hibernation and sleep; illustrations by Pamela Johnson. Sierra Club Bks.; Little, Brown 1989 47p il lib bdg $12.95 (3-6) **591.5**

1. Animals—Hibernation 2. Sleep
ISBN 0-316-27379-1 LC 88-10921

"A Lucas-Evans book"

This book discusses "hibernation; estivation (summertime hibernation); and sleep in mammals, birds, and fish." SLJ

"Exquisite pencil drawings of animals in their assorted habitats support the text. A handsomely designed, informative book." Booklist

Facklam, Margery—*Continued*

Partners for life; the mysteries of animal symbiosis; illustrations by Pamela Johnson. Sierra Club Bks. 1989 48p il lib bdg $13.95 (3-6) **591.5**

1. Animals—Habits and behavior 2. Ecology
ISBN 0-316-25983-7 LC 88-35929

"A Lucas-Evans book"

"Ants, cleaner fish, hungry mosquitoes, and cowbirds have their symbiotic relationships with other creatures in common. Delicate, black-and-white drawings and a clear text explain the unique pairings in an especially pleasing format." Sci Child

Freedman, Russell

When winter comes; pictures by Pamela Johnson. Dutton 1981 48p il $10.95 (k-3) **591.5**

1. Animals—Habits and behavior 2. Winter
ISBN 0-525-42583-7 LC 80-22831

"A Smart cat book"

This book describes how various animals prepare for and survive the winter season

"A fine example of an animal science book written for nearly new readers. Short chapters are sequentially developed by season with separate sections on hibernation and migration as well as winter survival techniques. The index facilitates access to the relatively detailed content. Lots of white space, large, easy-to-read print taking up an average of one-half of each page and close-up, realistic pencil sketches of animals on almost every page demonstrate an awareness of and concern for, the intended audience." SLJ

Harrar, George

Signs of the apes, songs of the whales; adventures in human-animal communication; [by] George & Linda Harrar. Simon & Schuster Bks. for Young Readers 1989 48p il maps $14.95; pa $5.95 (4 and up) **591.5**

1. Animal intelligence
ISBN 0-671-67748-9; 0-671-67745-4 (pa) LC 89-30061

"A Novabook"

Published in association with WGBH Boston

"An engaging report of what researchers have been able to discover about the capacity for intelligence in gorillas, chimpanzees, humpback whales, and dolphins. The pleasing format describes what scientists have learned about animal communication and experiments in teaching animals human communication." Sci Child

Hess, Lilo

Secrets in the meadow. Scribner 1986 64p il $13.95 (4 and up) **591.5**

1. Animals—Habits and behavior 2. Ecology
ISBN 0-684-18525-3 LC 85-43350

Describes the many animals to be found in a meadow, seemingly a serene place, yet teeming with life in the form of deer, rabbits, ants, spiders, raccoons, bats, and others creatures

"Black-and-white photographs are clear and involving. After one's submergence in the text, the conclusion comes as a shock when surveyors invade the area for work on a housing development. Hess' last page of questions ('Where will all the animals go?') gives readers pause for serious environmental thought. A glossary and index are appended." Bull Cent Child Books

Hirschi, Ron

Who lives in—the forest? photographs by Galen Burrell. Dodd, Mead 1987 unp il (Where animals live) $9.95; pa $3.95 (k-2) **591.5**

1. Forest animals
ISBN 0-396-09121-0; 0-396-09122-9 (pa) LC 87-8879

"Superb, close-up, full-color photographs support simple, bold text that enables young readers to take a close look at a forest and discover its many inhabitants. Includes an informative afterword." Sci Child

Who lives in—the mountains? photographs by Galen Burrell. Putnam 1989 unp il (Where animals live) lib bdg $9.95 (k-2) **591.5**

1. Alpine animals
ISBN 0-399-21900-5 LC 87-25160

A tiny bird in each photograph leads the reader through the mountain forests and streams to view the mountain goats, pikas, bluebirds, and other animals that live in the high country

"The pages are handsomely composed, with the spare text balancing the stunning photographs. An afterword . . . provides additional information on the species mentioned, along with a plea for conservation awareness." Booklist

Who lives on—the prairie? photographs by Galen Burrell. Putnam 1989 unp il (Where animals live) lib bdg $9.95 (k-2) **591.5**

1. Prairie animals
ISBN 0-399-21901-3 LC 87-25159

Text and photographs introduce the sights and sounds of life on the prairie, including the prairie dog, dancing birds, and long-tailed weasel

"The color photographs are beautiful, capturing both the vast space and the small, intricate loveliness of a prairie. The text is simple, providing names and interesting information about the creatures who live there. The book ends with an invitation to readers to think about what it was like when 'the land thundered beneath the feet of so many bison that you could never count them all,' and an afterword for older readers about the plight of the prairie." Read Teach

Hirschland, Roger B.

How animals care for their babies. National Geographic Soc. 1987 28p il (k-3) **591.5**

1. Animals—Habits and behavior 2. Animals—Infancy
ISBN 0-87044-678-9; 0-87044-683-5 LC 87-12411

Available only as part of 4v set for $10.95, lib bdg $12.95. Other titles in set are: Africa's animal giants, by Jane McCauley, How animals talk, by Susan McGrath, entered below; and Raccoons, by K. M. Kostya

Hirschland, Roger B.—*Continued*
"Books for young explorers"

This illustrated text "covers nesting, feeding, educating, protecting, and playing behaviors. Examples used vary from insects like the wolf spiders carrying their young on their backs to salamanders protecting their eggs." Sci Child

Includes bibliography

Hornblow, Leonora, 1920-

Animals do the strangest things; by Leonora and Arthur Hornblow; illustrated by Keith Kohler. Random House 1990 61p il (Step-up nature bks) lib bdg $6.99; pa $3.95 (1-3) **591.5**

1. Animals—Habits and behavior
ISBN 0-394-94308-2 (lib bdg); 0-394-84308-8 (pa) LC 88-37710

A newly illustrated edition of the title first published 1964

Describes nineteen animals that have peculiar and strange characteristics, including the platypus which has poison spurs on its legs, the opossum which fools its enemies by pretending to be dead, and the bat which navigates by built-in sonar

How animals behave: a new look at wildlife. National Geographic Soc. 1984 104p il $6.95; lib bdg $8.50 (5 and up) **591.5**

1. Animals—Habits and behavior
ISBN 0-87044-500-6; 0-87044-505-7 (lib bdg) LC 84-989

"Books for world explorers"

Explains how different animals obtain their food, protect themselves, court a mate, care for their eggs and their young, and live together. Includes profiles of animal behaviorists and research methods they have used

"The writing is clear and easy to read, but it is not stilted or boring. The abundant color photographs, many full page, are of excellent quality and well labeled." SLJ

Hughey, Patricia

Scavengers and decomposers: the cleanup crew; illustrated by Bruce Hiscock. Atheneum Pubs. 1984 56p il $13.95 (5 and up) **591.5**

1. Animals—Habits and behavior 2. Ecology
ISBN 0-689-31032-3 LC 83-17474

Describes the characteristics and habits of various insects, birds, and other animals that clean up waste materials in the environment

"The author writes clearly and includes some tips on observing small scavengers. . . . Well-placed pen-and-ink drawings augment the text." Horn Book

Includes glossary and bibliography

Johnson, Rebecca L.

The secret language: pheromones in the animal world. Lerner Publs. 1989 64p il lib bdg $14.95 (5 and up) **591.5**

1. Animal communication
ISBN 0-8225-1586-5 LC 88-19175

"After describing how pheromones are used to bring about behavioral changes, the author focuses on the honey bee, a species which uses pheromones to regulate almost all activities. . . . The author concludes with ways in which knowledge of pheromones can benefit humans: attracting helpful insects, fighting insect pests, and learning more about animal and human behavior. A useful and attractive title." Appraisal

"Forty excellent photographs (38 in color and 2 in black and white) and 4 excellent line drawings (all from the one bee chapter) are included, as well as a useful glossary and index." Sci Books Films

Kohl, Judith

Pack, band, and colony; the world of social animals; [by] Judith & Herbert Kohl; pictures by Margaret La Farge. Farrar, Straus & Giroux 1983 114p il $13.95 (5 and up) **591.5**

1. Animals—Habits and behavior
ISBN 0-374-35694-7 LC 82-20951

The authors compare "the socially dominant, tightly controlled carnivorous wolf family with the loosely associated lemur band and with the physiologically and environmentally fixed caste system of the termite city." Sci Books Films

"This finely etched examination of animal life and observation techniques will appeal to animal lovers and should inspire future natural scientists." SLJ

Includes bibliographies

The view from the oak; the private worlds of other creatures; by Judith and Herbert Kohl; illustrated by Roger Bayless. Sierra Club Bks.; Little, Brown 1988 c1977 110p il $13.95 (6 and up) **591.5**

1. Animals—Habits and behavior 2. Senses and sensation
ISBN 0-316-50137-9 LC 88-2069

A reissue of the title first published 1977

"An oak tree may be home to a fox, a nest to a beetle, and a source of food for a woodpecker. How a bee senses a flavor differs from the way an ant or person sees, touches, or smells it. With simple, clearly phrased examples, the Kohls describe an animal's world of experience or its 'unwelt.' Sprinkling in scientific, literary, and philosophical references . . . the authors gracefully introduce the subject of ethology." SLJ

"An excellent treatment of an abstract topic." Child Book Rev Serv

Includes bibliography

Kostyal, K. M., 1951-

Animals at play. National Geographic Soc. 1988 32p il (k-3) **591.5**

1. Animals—Habits and behavior
ISBN 0-87044-739-4; 0-87044-744-0 LC 88-15209

Available only as part of a 4v set for $10.95, lib bdg $12.95. Other titles in the set are: Animals in summer, by Jane R. McCauley, entered below; Busy beavers, by M. Barbara Brownell; and Let's explore a river, by Jane R. McCauley, class 574.92

"Books for young explorers"

Kostyal, K. M., 1951-—*Continued*

Discusses the way in which a variety of animals play, including the baboon, brown bear, and fox

Includes bibliography

Lavies, Bianca

Tree trunk traffic; text and photographs by Bianca Lavies. Dutton 1989 unp il $13.95 (k-2) **591.5**

1. Animals 2. Ecology 3. Trees
ISBN 0-525-44495-5 LC 88-30001

This book "gives young readers a glimpse of the wildlife activities on and around a 70-year-old maple tree. Color photographs by the author provide close-up views of squirrels, a cicada, baby crab spiders, a skipper, and assassin bugs, among other animals." Sci Books Films

"While the full-color photos are superior to the text, which is a tinge anthropomorphic, Lavies' facility with a lens presents readers with valuable visual insights for their nature studies." Booklist

McCauley, Jane R., 1947-

Animals and their hiding places. National Geographic Soc. 1986 31p il (k-3) **591.5**

1. Animals—Habitations 2. Camouflage (Biology)
ISBN 0-87044-637-1; 0-87044-642-8 (lib bdg)
LC 86-12848

Available only as part of 4v set for $10.95, lib bdg $12.95. Other titles in set are: Animals that live in trees, entered below; Baby bears and how they grow, by Jane Heath Buxton, class 599.74; and Saving our animal friends, by Susan McGrath, class 591

"Books for young explorers"

Describes the various places in which animals seek safety and shelter for themselves, for their young, and for their food

Animals in summer. National Geographic Soc. 1988 30p il (k-3) **591.5**

1. Animals—Habits and behavior
ISBN 0-87044-738-6; 0-87044-743-2 LC 88-19678

Available only as part of a 4v set for 10.95, lib bdg $12.95. Other titles in the set are: Animals at play, by K. M. Kostyal, entered above; Busy beavers, by M. Barbara Brownell; and Let's explore a river, by Jane R. McCauley, class 574.92

"Books for young explorers"

This book observes and explains the summer behavior of several animals living in meadow and woodland habitats

Includes bibliography

Animals that live in trees. National Geographic Soc. 1986 32p il (k-3) **591.5**

1. Animals—Habitations 2. Trees
ISBN 0-87044-636-3; 0-87044-641-X (lib bdg)
LC 86-12593

Available only as part of 4v set for $10.95, lib bdg $12.95. Other titles in set are: Animals and their hiding places, entered above; Baby bears and how they grow, by Jane Heath Buxton, class 599.74; and Saving our animal friends, by Susan McGrath, class 591

"Books for young explorers"

Introduces a variety of animals, such as koala, fruit bat, walkingstick, snail, and howler monkey, that seek safety, food, and shelter in trees

Ways animals sleep; by Jane R. McCauley. National Geographic Soc. 1983 32p il (k-3) **591.5**

1. Sleep 2. Animals—Habits and behavior
ISBN 0-87044-489-1; 0-87044-494-8 (lib bdg)
LC 83-13189

Available only as part of 4v set for $10.95, lib bdg $12.95. Other titles in set are: Animals helping people, by Suzanne Venino, class 636.088; Baby birds and how they grow, by Jane R. McCauley, class 598; and Creatures small and furry, by Donald J Crump, class 599

"Books for young explorers"

This title "features 25 animals, birds and insects organized according to sleep habits and location. There are tree sleepers; sleepers in crowds, such as walruses, who, in turning over, disturb one another with a ripple effect; water sleepers and cat-nappers." SLJ

McClung, Robert M.

Animals that build their homes. National Geographic Soc. 1976 26p il (k-3) **591.5**

1. Animals—Habitations
ISBN 0-87044-200-7; 0-87044-205-8 (lib bdg)
LC 76-2117

Available only as part of a 4v set for $10.95, lib bdg $12.95. Other titles in set are: Camping adventure, by William R. Gray; The playful dolphins, by Linda McCarter Bridge, class 599.5; and Wonders of the desert world, by Judith E. Rinard

"Books for young explorers"

Examines "the habitats of creatures such as the badger, crayfish, woodpecker, weaverbird, wasp, termite, and honeybee." Booklist

"The excellent color photographs are visually instructive and closely correlated with the text. . . . The writing is simple, clear, and down-to-earth. Both the non-reader and beginning reader should enjoy this scientifically accurate book." Appraisal

McGrath, Susan, 1955-

The amazing things animals do. National Geographic Soc. 1989 96p il $7.95; lib bdg $9.50 (4 and up) **591.5**

1. Animals—Habits and behavior
ISBN 0-87044-704-1; 0-87044-709-2 (lib bdg)
LC 89-9428

"Books for world explorers"

Examines how different animals move, communicate, raise their young, take in nourishment, and defend themselves

Includes bibliography

How animals talk. National Geographic Soc. 1987 32p il (k-3) **591.5**

1. Animal communication
ISBN 0-87044-679-7; 0-87044-684-3 LC 87-14173

Available only as part of 4v set for $10.95, lib bdg $12.95. Other titles in set are: Africa's animal giants, by Jane McCauley; How animals care for their babies, by

McGrath, Susan, 1955-—*Continued*
Roger Hirschland, entered above; and Raccoons, by K. M. Kostya

"Books for young explorers"

This book "shows the body posture, smells, sounds, and touches used by animals to communicate. Described and beautifully pictured are manatees 'kissing' in greeting and monkeys grooming each other." Sci Child

Includes bibliography

Neuman, Pearl

When winter comes; illustrated by Richard Roe. Raintree Pubs. 1989 30p il (Real readers) $12.33 (1-3) **591.5**

1. Animals—Habits and behavior 2. Winter
ISBN 0-8172-3519-1 LC 89-3595

Explains how the woodchuck, black bear, red fox, and Canadian goose cope with winter in the northern parts of North America

"The text, together with attractive four-color drawings, both informs and entertains and does both quite well. A section at the end of the book offers suggestions to adults for extending the child's reading experience. In sum, this good book will be useful both in the elementary classroom and at home." Sci Books Films

Parnall, Peter

Woodpile; written and illustrated by Peter Parnall. Macmillan 1990 unp il $14.95 (1-4) **591.5**

1. Animals—Habits and behavior
ISBN 0-02-770155-7 LC 89-29322

"A lyrical portrait of a habitat depicts how a variety of woodland creatures live, hide, store food, and stalk prey in the nooks and crannies in and around a common woodpile. Encourages readers to look beyond the obvious when observing nature." Sci Child

"Ink, pencil, and watercolor drawings in pale shades of yellow, green, and brown provide close-up views of animal life within the woodpile, as quiet and gentle as the lyrical text." SLJ

Patent, Dorothy Hinshaw

Singing birds and flashing fireflies; illustrations by Mary Morgan. Watts 1989 32p il (Discovering science bk) lib bdg $12.90 (k-2) **591.5**

1. Animal communication
ISBN 0-531-10717-5 LC 89-9081

This book illustrates how animals use a variety of signals to communicate with each other

"Patent offers a simple lesson on animal communication. . . . Accompanying pictures depict phenomena described in the text; the drawings are clean and crisp, though the humans (and an occasional animal) look a little too precious. Useful for science units." Booklist

Podendorf, Illa, 1903-1983

Animal homes; by Illa Podendorf. Childrens Press 1982 45p il lib bdg $13.27 (2-4) **591.5**

1. Animals—Habitations
ISBN 0-516-01666-0 (lib bdg) LC 82-4466

"A New true book"

First published 1960 with title: The true book of animal homes

This book describes a variety of animal homes, shelters constructed by man for domesticated and zoo animals, and explains that some animals do not build homes

Powzyk, Joyce Ann

Animal camouflage; a closer look. Bradbury Press 1990 40p il $15.95 (3-6) **591.5**

1. Camouflage (Biology)
ISBN 0-02-774980-0 LC 89-9848

"Concealing coloration, disruptive coloration, disguise, mimicry, and masking are methods of animal camouflage exemplified in 13 double-page-spread case studies. Additional information about featured animals and further examples of animals that hide their presence are included." Sci Child

Includes glossary and bibliography

Pringle, Laurence P.

Animals at play; [by] Laurence Pringle. Harcourt Brace Jovanovich 1985 70p il $12.95 (5 and up) **591.5**

1. Animals—Habits and behavior
ISBN 0-15-203554-0 LC 85-901

"A fascinating look at the importance of animal play shown in such species as the cat, dog, wolf, bear, bat, and monkey. The text draws on studies by several ethologists. Excellent black-and-white photographs provide examples of familiar animals engaging in various kinds of play." Sci Child

Includes bibliography

Feral: tame animals gone wild. Macmillan 1983 110p il lib bdg $11.95 (5 and up) **591.5**

1. Animals—Habits and behavior
ISBN 0-02-775420-0 LC 82-60741

"A fascinating study of common animals that were formerly domesticated and have gone wild. Dogs, cats, pigs, horses, and burros are among the animals included. Examines their natural habitats, behavior, our means of controling them, and the impact of these animals on the environment." Sci Child

Includes bibliography

Home; how animals find comfort and safety; [by] Laurence Pringle. Scribner 1987 71p il $12.95 (4 and up) **591.5**

1. Animals—Habitations
ISBN 0-684-18526-1 LC 87-13119

The author examines the characteristics of the many different types of places in which animals make their home, and what these choices reveal about their relation-

Pringle, Laurence P.—*Continued*
ships with other things in the environment
Includes bibliography

Rinard, Judith E., 1947-
Creatures of the night; by Judith E. Rinard. National Geographic Soc. 1977 31p il (k-3) **591.5**
1. Animals—Habits and behavior
ISBN 0-87044-245-7; 0-87044-250-3 LC 77-76968
Available only as part of 4v set for $10.95, lib bdg $12.95. Other titles in set are: The blue whale, by Donna K. Grosvenor, class 599.5; Let's go to the moon, by Janis Knudsen Wheat; and, What happens in the spring, by Kathleen Costello Beer
"Books for young explorers"
This book describes the after-dark activities of a number of nocturnal animals in simple text and color photographs

San Souci, Daniel
North country night. Doubleday 1990 unp il $14.95; lib bdg $15.99 (2-4) **591.5**
1. Animals—Habits and behavior
ISBN 0-385-41319-X; 0-385-41320-3 (lib bdg) LC 89-39930
"One night in a moonlit winter wood reveals, with striking illustrations, the activities of nocturnal animals and several relationships between predator and prey." Sci Child

Sattler, Helen Roney
Fish facts & bird brains: animal intelligence; illustrated by Giulio Maestro. Lodestar Bks. 1984 127p il $13.95 (5 and up) **591.5**
1. Animal intelligence
ISBN 0-525-66915-9 LC 83-20805
"Sattler's serious book in a silly cover reveals fascinating facts about a variety of animals—from flatworms to elephants. . . . The chapter on techniques for testing a pet's IQ is an especially appealing bonus, but the cartoon-style illustrations are both inappropriate and distracting. A substantial further readings section is included." Sci Child

The **Secret** world of animals. National Geographic Soc. 1986 104p il $6.95; lib bdg $8.50 (4 and up) **591.5**
1. Animals—Habitations
ISBN 0-87044-575-8; 0-87044-580-4 (lib bdg) LC 86-5141
"Books for world explorers"
Text and pictures take the reader inside animal homes—used for resting, sheltering from weather, escaping enemies, and raising young
"Preparation and upkeep of quarters, secrets of hibernation, tactics for surviving the seasons, and sharing living areas are also addressed. The photographs are well captioned, adding to the text. The wildlife described ranges from the familiar bee, wasp, snake, and fish to the less well known such as the ghost crab and the warthog." Booklist
Includes bibliography

Venino, Suzanne
Amazing animal groups. National Geographic Soc. 1981 32p il lib bdg (k-3) **591.5**
1. Animals—Habits and behavior
ISBN 0-87044-402-6; 0-87044-407-7 LC 81-47743
Available only as part of a 4v set for $10.95, lib bdg $12.95 Other titles in set are: Wild cats, by Peggy D. Winston; Life in ponds and streams, by William H. Amos, class 591.92; and Strange animals of Australia: koalas and kangaroos, by Toni Eugene
"Books for young explorers"
Illustrated with photographs, this book describes the behavior of animals that live in large social groups, including elephants, zebras, gorillas, wolves, prairie dogs, fishes, ants and penguins

591.9 Geographic treatment of animals

Amazing animals of Australia. National Geographic Soc. 1985 c1984 104p il $6.95; lib bdg $8.50 (4 and up) **591.9**
1. Animals—Australia
ISBN 0-87044-515-4; 0-87044-520-0 (lib bdg) LC 84-29558
"Books for world explorers"
Describes the kangaroo, platypus, and other animals native to Australia and discusses their origin and adaptation to their environment
"Suitable for both browsing and extended reading, this volume will be a colorful addition to nature collections. Reading list appended. Poster and activity kit included." Booklist

Powzyk, Joyce Ann
Wallaby Creek; [by] Joyce Powzyk. Lothrop, Lee & Shepard Bks. 1985 unp il map $12.95; lib bdg $12.88 (3-6) **591.9**
1. Animals—Australia
ISBN 0-688-05692-X; 0-688-05693-8 (lib bdg) LC 84-29757
The author describes the unique and varied assortment of animals she observed during a stay at Wallaby Creek, Australia. Her own watercolor paintings of goannas, cockatoos, kookaburras, platypuses, wallabies, kangaroos, koalas, dingoes, and other animals accompany her descriptions
"Physical characteristics, eating habits, and distinctive traits get casual but accurate mention in a first-person narrative that aligns science with wild-life adventure." Bull Cent Child Books

Rinard, Judith E., 1947-
The world beneath your feet. National Geographic Soc. 1985 32p il (k-3) **591.9**
1. Animals
ISBN 0-87044-561-8; 0-87044-566-9 (lib bdg)
LC 85-13642
Available only as part of 4v set for $10.95, lib bdg $12.95. Other titles in set are: Creatures of the woods, by Toni Eugene; Helping our animal friends, by Judith E. Rinard, class 636.088; and Penguins and polar bears, by Sandra Lee Crow
"Books for young explorers"
Describes briefly the characteristics of the various animals that live underneath the soil

591.92 Aquatic zoology. Marine zoology

Amos, William Hopkins
Life in ponds and streams; by William H. Amos. National Geographic Soc. 1981 30p il (k-3) **591.92**
1. Freshwater animals 2. Pond ecology
ISBN 0-87044-404-2; 0-87044-409-2 (lib bdg)
LC 81-47745
Available only as part of a 4v set for $10.95, lib bdg $12.95 Other titles in set are: Wild cats, by Peggy D. Winston; Amazing animal groups, by Suzanne Venino, class 591.5; and Strange animals of Australia: koalas and kangeroos, by Toni Eugene
"Books for young explorers"
An introductory look at animals that live in ponds and streams
This book "which gives viewers close-up looks and simple, clear descriptions of pond life, would be ideal pre-field trip material." Booklist

593.7 Hydrozoa and scyphozoa

Coldrey, Jennifer
The world of a jellyfish; text by Jennifer Coldrey and David Shale; photographs by Oxford Scientific Films. Stevens, G. 1987 32p il (Where animals live) lib bdg $9.95 (k-2) **593.7**
1. Jellyfish
ISBN 1-55532-073-2 LC 86-5704
Text and illustrations describe the physical characteristics, habits, and natural environment of the jellyfish, focusing on the Portuguese man-of-war

593.9 Echinodermata

Hurd, Edith Thacher, 1910-
Starfish; illustrated by Lucienne Bloch. Crowell 1962 unp il (Let's-read-and-find-out science bks) lib bdg $12.89 (k-3) **593.9**
1. Starfishes
ISBN 0-690-77069-3 LC 62-7742
"An easy introduction to the world of starfishes. Touches on the feeding habits, life cycle, structure and power of regeneration of these interesting creatures." AAAS Sci Book List for Child

594 Mollusks and mollusk-like animals

Abbott, R. Tucker (Robert Tucker), 1919-
Seashells of the world; a guide to the better-known species; under the editorship of Herbert S. Zim; illustrated by George and Marita Sandström. rev ed. Golden Press Bks. 1985 160p il maps pa $3.95 (5 and up) **594**
1. Shells
ISBN 0-307-24410-5 LC 86-162343
"A Golden guide"
First published 1962
This guide identifies over 500 sea shells of the world. Locations of shell regions and tips on collecting are included. Illustrated with colored drawings

Arthur, Alex
Shell; written by Alex Arthur. Knopf 1989 62p il (Eyewitness bks) $12.95; lib bdg $13.99 (4 and up) **594**
1. Shells
ISBN 0-394-82256-0; 0-394-92256-5 (lib bdg)
LC 88-13449
"Arthur showcases varieties of shelled mollusks, echinoderms, crustaceans, turtles, tortoises, and terrapins, illustrating how shells and pearls form and comparing species that inhabit such different environments as fresh-water bodies and coral reefs." Booklist

Buholzer, Theres
Life of the snail. Carolrhoda Bks. 1987 c1985 47p il (Carolrhoda nature watch bk) lib bdg $12.95 (3-6) **594**
1. Snails
ISBN 0-87614-246-3 LC 86-21544
Original German edition published 1984 in Switzerland; this translation first published 1985 in the United Kingdom
Describes the physical characteristics, habits, and natural environment of the snail
This "is a detailed, informative and very attractive work. . . . The colored photographs are outstanding. They show in detail exactly what the text is describing, and they also provide a source of information that supplements the text. There is a useful glossary and index. This book is a winner." Appraisal

Carrick, Carol
Octopus; illustrated by Donald Carrick. Clarion Bks. 1978 unp il $14.95 (2-4) **594**
1. Octopus
ISBN 0-395-28777-4 LC 77-12769
First published by Seabury Press

Carrick, Carol—*Continued*

"Carrick follows a female octopus as she skims along the ocean floor, finding meals of lobster and crab and encountering her enemy, the moray eel. A male octopus comes to her, they mate, and she moves away to find and prepare a place tp lay her eggs. As she waits for her young to hatch, she rarely stirs, slowing starving to death. The thoughtfully written text is complemented by expressive pen-and-wash drawings in cool sea colors." SLJ

Florian, Douglas, 1950-

Discovering seashells. Scribner 1986 unp il $10.95 (1-3) **594**

1. Shells
ISBN 0-684-18740-X LC 86-11903

"In addition to some really beautiful illustrations of shells, *Discovering Seashells* includes information on the two types of mollusks—univalve and bivalve—and describes the various habitats of mollusks whose shells are commonly found on both the East and West coasts of the United States, plus a few from foreign waters. Suggestions are given for starting a shell collection." Horn Book

Selsam, Millicent Ellis, 1912-

A first look at seashells; by Millicent E. Selsam and Joyce Hunt; illustrated by Harriett Springer. Walker & Co. 1983 32p il lib bdg $9.85 (1-3) **594**

1. Shells 2. Mollusks
ISBN 0-8027-6503-3 LC 83-5876

The authors teach "that shellfish are divided into two main groups, univalves and bivalves, and then proceed to illustrate both. The real effectiveness of the book lies in its direct question and answer approach; the text poses questions that readers answer with the help of the illustrations. The black-and-white drawings are skillfully done and in each case precisely illustrate the authors' points." SLJ

595.3 Crustaceans and chelicerates

Holling, Holling C., 1900-1973

Pagoo; illustrated by the author and Lucille Webster Holling. Houghton Mifflin 1957 86p il lib bdg $15.95; pa $7.95 (4 and up) **595.3**

1. Crabs 2. Marine animals
ISBN 0-395-06826-6 (lib bdg); 0-395-53964-1 (pa) LC 56-5551

"The life cycle of the hermit crab and a close-up of the teeming life of the tide pool are presented . . . in an animated narrative, scientifically detailed marginal drawings, and handsome full page colored pictures." Booklist

Johnson, Sylvia A.

Hermit crabs; photographs by Kazunari Kawashima. Lerner Publs. 1989 47p il (Lerner natural science bk) lib bdg $12.95 (4 and up) **595.3**

1. Crabs
ISBN 0-8225-1488-5 LC 89-8221

This adaptation of Kazunari Kawashima's Hermit Crabs discusses "physical and behavior characteristics common to all crabs, the special characteristics of hermit crabs, and the way they differ from true crabs." SLJ

"Any classroom that contains a hermit crab, any person who owns one as a pet, or any science teachers who include marine education in their curricula should have a copy of this book. It is lavishly illustrated with color photographs and drawings. The text is clearly written, with new terms printed in bold face type when they are first introduced. The book also contains a glossary and index so readers should be able to easily locate information." Sci Teach

McDonald, Megan

Is this a house for Hermit Crab? pictures by S.D. Schindler. Orchard Bks. 1990 unp il $14.95; lib bdg $14.99 (k-2) **595.3**

1. Crabs
ISBN 0-531-05855-7; 0-531-08455-8 (lib bdg) LC 89-35653

"A Richard Jackson book"

"Hermit Crab has outgrown his house once again and prowls the beach looking for the right new domicile. Along the way he tries out a tin can, a bucket and a log, before he finds the right fit. The text has a read-aloud cadence and the illustrations are spacious and charming." N Y Times Book Rev

595.4 Arachnids

Hawes, Judy

My daddy longlegs; illustrated by Walter Lorraine. Crowell 1972 31p il (Let's-read-and-find-out science bks) lib bdg $12.89 (k-3) **595.4**

1. Spiders
ISBN 0-690-56656-5 LC 74-175107

"Big print, engaging style, lively illustrations and fascinating information combine to make this an altogether charming book. The reader is urged to catch a few Daddy Longlegs and is told how, when, and where to do this, how to observe them, what to look for and how to build a home for them while the study is in progress. Youngsters may well find this an embarkation point for an enthusiastic study of nature." Appraisal

Hopf, Alice Lightner, 1904-1988

Spiders; [by] Alice L. Hopf; photographs by Ann Moreton. Cobblehill Bks. 1990 64p il $13.95 (4 and up) **595.4**

1. Spiders
ISBN 0-525-65017-2 LC 89-9716

Hopf, Alice Lightner, 1904-1988 — *Continued*

Describes, in text and photographs, the physical characteristics, habits, and natural environment of a variety of spiders

"The lively text discusses web weavers, hunters, mating and motherhood, and those spiders whose large size and poisonous nature attract attention. The close-up color photography is excellent. . . . This splendid addition to science shelves will instruct, enchant, and astonish." Booklist

Lane, Margaret, 1907-

The spider; by Margaret Lane; pictures by Barbara Firth. Dial Bks. for Young Readers 1982 unp il $9.95; pa $3.50 (1-3) **595.4**

1. Spiders

ISBN 0-8037-8303-5; 0-8037-8308-6 (pa)

LC 82-71354

An introduction to various types of spiders, their living and mating habits, and techniques for survival

"The page-filling illustrations show common spider habitats and pictures some of the species described in the text." Booklist

Patent, Dorothy Hinshaw

The lives of spiders. Holiday House 1980 128p il $13.95 (5 and up) **595.4**

1. Spiders

ISBN 0-8234-0418-8 LC 80-14801

The author "delves into the social and anti-social habits of spiders. . . . Web-spinning, hunting and trapping, mating and egg-laying, and relation to other animal life are all covered in a well-researched and organized text that is abundantly illustrated." Booklist

Includes glossary and bibliography

Spider magic. Holiday House 1982 40p il lib bdg $12.95 (2-4) **595.4**

1. Spiders

ISBN 0-8234-0438-2 LC 81-85088

"Short explanations of physiology, use of silk, eating habits, family behavior and growth are followed by a single page of text opposite a full-page picture on each of several species. The choice of title isn't paticularly apt—the author is objective, knowledgeable and straightforward; there is no mention or implication of anything 'magic' about spiders. Though the amount of information is limited, it has been thoughtfully prepared and attractively presented, and the book will serve well as a precursor to more difficult titles." SLJ

Schnieper, Claudia

Amazing spiders; photographs by Max Meier. Carolrhoda Bks. 1989 48p il (Carolrhoda nature watch bk) lib bdg $12.95; pa $6.95 (3-6) **595.4**

1. Spiders

ISBN 0-87614-342-7 (lib bdg); 0-87614-518-7 (pa)

LC 88-39199

Introduces the varieties, appearance, behavior, and life cycles of spiders

"The text is clearly written, well organized, and lavishly illustrated; the excellent photographs reveal careful composition." SLJ

Includes glossary

595.7 Insects

Cole, Joanna

An insect's body; photographs by Jerome Wexler and Raymond A. Mendez. Morrow 1984 48p il $13.95; lib bdg $13.88 **595.7**

1. Crickets

ISBN 0-688-02771-7; 0-688-02772-5 (lib bdg)

LC 83-22027

The author "explains the anatomy of the cricket, its compound eyes, efficient digestive system, and unique mating habits, to name but a few of the areas. The lucid text is dramatized by stunning black-and-white photos that give children a very special look at how these insects live, reproduce, and function, while clearly labeled diagrams provide additional information. While this is particularly suitable for middle-graders, anyone whose curiosity is intact cannot help but be captivated by this fascinating work." Booklist

Dorros, Arthur

Ant cities; written and illustrated by Arthur Dorros. Crowell 1987 28p il (Let's-read-and-find-out science bks) $12.95; lib bdg $12.89; pa $3.95 (k-3) **595.7**

1. Ants

ISBN 0-690-04568-9; 0-690-04570-0 (lib bdg); 0-06-445079-1 (pa) LC 85-48244

"Using harvester ants as a basic example, Dorros shows how the insects build tunnels with rooms for different functions and how workers, queens, and males have distinct roles in the ant hill. Along the way, she works in details of food and reproduction, ending with descriptions of other kinds of ants and suggestions for ways to observe them (including instructions for making an ant farm). The text is simple without becoming choppy, the full-color illustrations are inviting as well as informative." Bull Cent Child Books

Fischer-Nagel, Heiderose, 1956-

An ant colony; by Heiderose and Andreas Fischer-Nagel. Carolrhoda Bks. 1989 47p il (Carolrhoda nature watch bk) lib bdg $12.95; pa $6.95 (3-6) **595.7**

1. Ants

ISBN 0-87614-333-8 (lib bdg); 0-87614-519-5 (pa)

LC 88-31564

Original German edition published 1985 in Switzerland

Describes the life cycle and community life of ants

"The reading level is appropriate for the elementary age group, and several features, such as highlighted vocabulary terms, will aid students and teachers. Although the text is not divided into chapters, it flows well and contains a good index." Sci Child

Includes glossary

Fischer-Nagel, Heiderose, 1956-—*Continued*

The housefly; by Heiderose and Andreas Fischer-Nagel. Carolrhoda Bks. 1990 48p il (Carolrhoda nature watch bk) lib bdg $12.95 (3-6) **595.7**

1. Flies
ISBN 0-87614-374-5 LC 89-32365

Original German edition published 1988 in Switzerland

Describes, in text and illustrations, the physical characteristics, habits, natural environment, and relationship with humans of the housefly

"Large, closeup and magnified color pictures match with paragraphs which are like lengthened captions. They are sure to motivate young readers without much emphasis on terminology. . . . The text is easy to read and interesting." Appraisal

Includes glossary

Life of the butterfly; by Heiderose and Andreas Fischer-Nagel. Carolrhoda Bks. 1987 47p il (Carolrhoda nature watch bk) lib bdg $12.95; pa $6.95 (3-6) **595.7**

1. Butterflies
ISBN 0-87614-244-7 (lib bdg); 0-87614-484-9 (pa) LC 86-23217

Original German edition published 1983 in Switzerland

"The authors describe the insect's mating and egg-laying activities; the physical and behavioral characteristics of each of the four stages of development; diet; habitat; protective coloration; natural enemies; and function in the pollination of flowers." SLJ

"The reader is drawn in by the magnificent photographs; close-up shots of butterflies on brilliantly colored blossoms highlight the beauty of these creatures. The text is well organized and, in clear language, explains the metamorphosis and other aspects of the butterfly's existence." Sci Books Films

Life of the honeybee; by Heiderose and Andreas Fischer-Nagel. Carolrhoda Bks. 1986 48p il (Carolrhoda nature watch bk) lib bdg $12.95; pa $6.95 (3-6) **595.7**

1. Bees
ISBN 0-87614-241-2 (lib bdg); 0-87614-470-9 (pa) LC 85-13960

Original German edition published 1983 in Switzerland

"Greatly magnified pictures . . . depict the tasks of the three kinds of bees and help explain metamorphosis, pollination, and hive formation." Booklist

Includes glossary

Life of the ladybug; by Heiderose and Andreas Fischer-Nagel. Carolrhoda Bks. 1986 48p il (Carolrhoda nature watch bk) lib bdg $12.95 (3-6) **595.7**

1. Ladybirds
ISBN 0-87614-240-4 LC 85-25467

Original German edition published 1981 in Switzerland

The text "describes the insects' physical and behavioral characteristics, metamorphosis and diet; it also explains their benefits to humankind. The book concentrates on the seven-spot variety, but a few other species of ladybugs are also mentioned and illustrated." SLJ

Includes glossary

Gibbons, Gail

Monarch butterfly. Holiday House 1989 unp il $13.95 (1-3) **595.7**

1. Butterflies
ISBN 0-8234-0773-X LC 89-1880

"Large-scale paintings, clearly detailed, and a simply written, sequential text describe the life cycle of the monarch butterfly and its migratory patterns. This is Gibbons at her best, providing information in a text that is cohesive and comprehensible." Bull Cent Child Books

Goor, Ron, 1940-

Insect metamorphosis; from egg to adult; [by] Ron and Nancy Goor. Atheneum Pubs. 1990 26p il $13.95 (2-6) **595.7**

1. Insects
ISBN 0-689-31445-0 LC 89-15144

Explains how insects grow, describing the various stages of incomplete and complete metamorphosis

"Outstanding, closeup photography and intriguing text carefully illustrate each stage of insect development. Numerous examples of interesting species help readers become skillful observers of insects in their natural habitats." Sci Child

Harrison, Virginia, 1966-

The world of honeybees; words by Virginia Harrison; photography by Oxford Scientific Films. Stevens, G. 1990 32p il (Where animals live) lib bdg (k-2) **595.7**

1. Bees
ISBN 0-8368-0142-3 LC 89-33936

Adapted from Christopher O'Toole's The honeybee in the meadow

Describes the appearance, life cycle, social order, and activities of honeybees that live in the meadow

Includes glossary

Herberman, Ethan

The great butterfly hunt; the mystery of the migrating monarchs. Simon & Schuster Bks. for Young Readers 1990 48p il maps $14.95; pa $5.95 (4-6) **595.7**

1. Butterflies
ISBN 0-671-69427-8; 0-671-69428-6 (pa) LC 90-31571

"A Novabook"

Published in association with WGBH Boston

Examines the migration patterns of the monarch butterfly, describes the study and discoveries that yielded knowledge of these movements, and speculates on the origin of the insect and why it travels such long distances

"Herberman's stirring account of the hunt, the people involved, and the latest discoveries about monarch behavior is embellished and enriched by excellent full-color photographs and diagrams." Kobrin Letter

Johnson, Sylvia A.

Beetles; photographs by Isao Kishida. Lerner Publs. 1982 48p il (Lerner natural science bk) $12.95 (4 and up) **595.7**

1. Beetles
ISBN 0-8225-1476-1 LC 82-7230

Adapted from a work by Isao Kishida published 1971 in Japan

"Remarkable color photographs . . . allow readers to see the insects in various stages of development. [The book] features the scarab beetle, but other species are pictured and discussed. . . . The well-considered details . . . include nicely textured paper, the inclusion of Latin names, and the important words in bold type, which later appear in a glossary." Booklist

Chirping insects; photographs by Yuko Sato. Lerner Publs. 1986 47p il (Lerner natural science bk) lib bdg $12.95; pa $5.95 (4 and up) **595.7**

1. Insects
ISBN 0-8225-1486-9 (lib bdg); 0-8225-1486-9 (pa) LC 86-15380

Adapted from: The world of chirping insects by Hidetomo Oda, published 1976 in Japan

This book "highlights the biology and taxonomy of the sound-making insects and how they produce their distinctive 'chirps'; it addresses primarily the order Orthoptera—'straight-winged' insects—which includes the short- and long-horned grasshoppers and the crickets, but it also considers the order Homoptera, which includes the cicadas." Sci Books Films

"Scientific names and proper terminology for body parts and processes are adhered to, and crystal-clear, captioned color photographs support the explanations." Booklist

Includes glossary

Fireflies; photographs by Satoshi Kuribayashi. Lerner Publs. 1986 47p il (Lerner natural science bk) lib bdg $12.95 (4 and up) **595.7**

1. Fireflies
ISBN 0-8225-1485-0 LC 86-26

Describes the physical characteristics, habits, and natural environment of the soft-bodied member of the beetle family that uses its light to attract a mate

The text is accompanied by "striking full-color photographs with concise, well-stated captions." Booklist

Includes glossary

Ladybugs; photographs by Yuko Sato. Lerner Publs. 1983 48p il (Lerner natural science bk) lib bdg $12.95 (4 and up) **595.7**

1. Ladybirds
ISBN 0-8225-1481-8 LC 83-18777

Adapted from a work by Yuko Sato published 1978 in Japan

"Examines the metamorphosis of the ladybug, its behavior, and its usefulness in controlling harmful insects in fields and gardens." Sci Child

This is "a prodigious pictorial book. . . . The sharp illustrations will hold the young readers' interest and at the same time expose them to explicit entomological educational material." Appraisal

Includes glossary

Wasps; photographs by Hiroshi Ogawa. Lerner Publs. 1984 48p il (Lerner natural science bk) lib bdg $12.95 (4 and up) **595.7**

1. Wasps
ISBN 0-8225-1460-5 LC 83-23847

Adapted from a work by Hiroshi Ogawa published 1975 in Japan

This book "tells the detailed life story of the wasp, beginning with the foundress of the colony who emerges from hibernation in the spring to the reproductive wasps who emerge and mate in late summer to the death of the males and the hibernation of the females over the winter." Sci Books Films

"The diagrams and outstanding color photos detailing the life stages and behavior of wasps clarify many concepts that might be difficult to visualize." Booklist

Includes glossary

Water insects; photographs by Modoki Masuda. Lerner Publs. 1989 48p il (Lerner natural science bk) lib bdg $12.95 (4 and up) **595.7**

1. Insects
ISBN 0-8225-1489-3 LC 89-12372

Adapted from a work by Modoki Masuda published 1987 in Japan

Describes the physical characteristics, behavior, and life cycles of some insects that spend most of their lives in the water

"Colorful, informative, and interesting, this will fascinate children looking for report materials as well as casual browsers. . . . Habitats, reproduction, and hibernation are all discussed in detail and clarified with many fine, full-color, captioned photographs. Difficult words are defined, although not always when they first appear. A glossary, scientific classification chart, and index complete the well-organized volume." SLJ

Kerby, Mona

Cockroaches; [illustrations by Anne Canevari Green] Watts 1989 64p il lib bdg $11.40 (4-6) **595.7**

1. Cockroaches
ISBN 0-531-10689-6 LC 88-37857

"A First book"

Examines the body parts, behavior, and likes and dislikes of one of the oldest creatures in the world

"Diagrams, drawings, full-color photographs, and a well-organized text describe the structure and behavior of various species of cockroaches. Includes suggestions for experimentation and observation, and a list of cockroach suppliers." Sci Child

Includes glossary

Lavies, Bianca
Backyard hunter: the praying mantis; text and photographs by Bianca Lavies. Dutton 1990 unp il $13.95 (2-4) **595.7**

1. Praying mantis
ISBN 0-525-44547-1 LC 89-37485

"Outstanding photographs document a thorough discussion of the behavior, life cycle, and development of an impressive insect that eats other insects alive. Insect observers will find the account stimulating and informative." Sci Child

McLaughlin, Molly
Dragonflies. Walker & Co. 1989 28p il $14.95; lib bdg $15.85 (3-5) **595.7**

1. Dragonflies
ISBN 0-8027-6846-6; 0-8027-6847-4 (lib bdg) LC 88-20632

The "text introduces a variety of types [of dragonflies] and describes the life cycle of the jewel-like insect." Sci Child

"Excellent color photographs (with varying degrees of magnification) are well-placed in relation to the text and are adequately provided with full captions, adding to the visual appeal and the accessibility of a fine science book." Bull Cent Child Books

Milne, Lorus Johnson, 1912-
Nature's clean-up crew: the burying beetles; [by] Lorus J. Milne and Margery Milne; with photographs by the authors. Dodd, Mead 1982 62p il $8.95 (4 and up) **595.7**

1. Beetles
ISBN 0-396-08038-3 LC 81-15127

Describes the physical characteristics, reproductive life cycle, and behavior patterns of the burying beetles

Mitchell, Robert T.
Butterflies and moths; a guide to the more common American species; by Robert T. Mitchell and Herbert S. Zim; illustrated by Andre Durenceau. rev ed. Golden Press Bks. 1987 160p il pa $3.95 (4 and up) **595.7**

1. Butterflies 2. Moths
ISBN 0-307-24052-5 LC 87-171378

First published 1964

Text and photographs provide information and description of butterflies and moths commonly found in the United States

Mound, L. A. (Laurence Alfred), 1934-
Insect; written by Laurence Mound. Knopf 1990 63p il (Eyewitness bks) $13.95; lib bdg $14.99 (4 and up) **595.7**

1. Insects
ISBN 0-679-80441-2; 0-679-90441-7 (lib bdg) LC 89-15603

"Insect anatomy, particular insect species, and how insects survive and relate to other living things in an appealing, thorough presentation suitable for browsing or close study." Sci Child

O'Toole, Christopher
Discovering flies; illustrations by Wendy Meadway. Bookwright Press 1987 c1986 46p il (Discovering nature) lib bdg $11.40 (3-6) **595.7**

1. Flies
ISBN 0-531-18097-2 LC 86-71272

First published 1986 in the United Kingdom

This volume discusses many types of flies, their body details, life cycles, habits and useful ecological activities

Includes bibliography

Overbeck, Cynthia
Ants; by Cynthia Overbeck; photographs by Satoshi Kuribayashi. Lerner Publs. 1982 48p il (Lerner natural science bk) lib bdg $12.95; pa $5.95 (4 and up) **595.7**

1. Ants
ISBN 0-8225-1468-0 (lib bdg); 0-8225-9525-7 (pa) LC 81-17216

Adapted from a work by Satoshi Kuribayashi published 1971 in Japan

Text and color photographs depict the characteristics and behavior of ants

"New and difficult concept words are listed in bold type as they appear in the text. All color graphics are excellent; the close-up photographs are stunning." SLJ

Dragonflies; photographs by Yuko Sato. Lerner Publs. 1982 48p il (Lerner natural science bk) lib bdg $12.95 (4 and up) **595.7**

1. Dragonflies
ISBN 0-8225-1477-X LC 82-7221

Adapted from a Japanese work by Yuko Sato

This book describes the "habits, behavior, and life history of one of the oldest and most beneficial insects, the dragonfly. . . . Numerous, elegant, lusted-finish color illustrations . . . complement the text. . . . Simple technical terms that are commonly used in entomology texts are introduced. This lucidly written book will attract and hold the attention of young readers." Sci Books Films

Parker, Nancy Winslow
Bugs; [by] Nancy Winslow Parker and Joan Richards Wright; illustrations by Nancy Winslow Parker. Greenwillow Bks. 1987 40p il $11.95; lib bdg $11.88; pa $3.95 (1-3) **595.7**

1. Insects
ISBN 0-688-06623-2; 0-688-06624-0 (lib bdg); 0-688-08296-3 (pa) LC 86-29387

Insects are depicted in drawings accompanied by short alliterative verses identifying them. The animal's common and scientific names, physical or behavioral characteristics, and habitat and geographical range are provided

Parker, Nancy Winslow—*Continued*

"The authors use the word *bug* as children use it and present insects that children may know, such as flies, ants, fleas, cicadas, roaches, head lice, and fireflies. The text may not answer all their questions, but it's an excellent starting place. The thoughtfully planned layout and Parker's appealing, full-color illustrations of the children, pets, and bugs lend this book a certain charm that might be unexpected, given its subject matter." Booklist

Includes bibliography

Patent, Dorothy Hinshaw

Looking at ants. Holiday House 1989 48p il $12.95 (3-5) **595.7**

1. Ants

ISBN 0-8234-0771-3 LC 89-1943

"Working with her usual thoroughness, Patent offers students brief chapters on ants' physical characteristics, hierarchical social structure, work roles within colonies, communication capabilities, and mutually beneficial host-tenant relationship with plants (for example, the whistling thorn acacia of Africa). She also stresses the worldwide ecological significance of these creatures." Booklist

Mosquitoes. Holiday House 1986 40p il $12.95 (4 and up) **595.7**

1. Mosquitoes

ISBN 0-8234-0627-X LC 86-45387

Discusses the mosquito's habits, development, and diseases it carries, as well as ways to control these creatures

"The layout is clean, and the first-class text is made even stronger by the pictures, some of which are scanning electron micrographs—their clarity will surely intrigue readers." Booklist

Pringle, Laurence P.

Killer bees. rev ed. Morrow Junior Bks. 1990 56p il maps $12.95; lib bdg $12.88; pa $6.95 (4 and up) **595.7**

1. Bees

ISBN 0-688-09617-4; 0-688-09524-0 (lib bdg); 0-688-09618-2 (pa) LC 90-34658

First published 1986 with title: Here come the killer bees

Describes the characteristics and behavior of Africanized bees and discusses how they came to Brazil, how they have now spread northward as far as the United States, and their potentially disruptive influence on the native honeybee population, crop yields, and the honey and beeswax industry

Includes glossary and bibliography

Ryder, Joanne

Where butterflies grow; pictures by Lynne Cherry. Lodestar Bks. 1989 unp il lib bdg $13.95 (k-2) **595.7**

1. Butterflies

ISBN 0-525-67284-2 LC 88-37989

Describes what it feels like to change from a caterpillar into a butterfly. Includes gardening tips to attract butterflies

"The book is packed with good information presented in an imaginative way. Cherry's illustrations span the full page, using boxes in sequence to magnify details or follow action. Another special feature of her lush watercolors is the many small creatures hidden among the plant life, inviting readers to sharpen their powers of observation." SLJ

Saintsing, David

The world of butterflies; text by David Saintsing; photographs by Oxford Scientific Films. Stevens, G. 1987 32p il (Where animals live) lib bdg $9.95 (k-2) **595.7**

1. Butterflies

ISBN 1-55532-072-4 LC 86-5706

Simple text and photographs depict butterflies feeding, breeding, and defending themselves in their natural habitats

Selsam, Millicent Ellis, 1912-

Backyard insects; [by] Millicent E. Selsam and Ronald Goor; photographs by Ronald Goor. Four Winds Press 1981 40p il o.p.; Scholastic paperback available $2.95 (k-3) **595.7**

1. Insects 2. Camouflage (Biology)

ISBN 0-590-42256-1 (pa) LC 82-18390

Text and photographs discuss common garden insects and their protective appearance which includes camouflage, warning colors, and copycat characteristics

A first look at caterpillars; by Millicent E. Selsam and Joyce Hunt; illustrated by Harriett Springer. Walker & Co. 1987 34p il $10.95; lib bdg $11.85 (1-3) **595.7**

1. Caterpillars

ISBN 0-8027-6700-1; 0-8027-6702-8 (lib bdg) LC 87-18999

This book focuses "on distinguishing characteristics of caterpillars. Using puzzles, the child searches for differences, thereby learning the basis of scientific classification. . . . The book has four sections: 'Caterpillars in General,' 'Caterpillars That Become Moths,' 'Caterpillars That Become Butterflies,' and 'Telling Caterpillars Apart.' Information is also included on raising caterpillars." Sci Child

A "very informative and enjoyable introduction to the precise and detailed operation of scientific classification for young readers." Sci Books Films

A first look at insects; by Millicent E. Selsam and Joyce Hunt; illustrated by Harriett Springer. Walker & Co. 1975 31p il lib bdg $12.85 (1-3) **595.7**

1. Insects

ISBN 0-8027-6182-8 LC 73-92451

The authors "introduce and explain basic distinguishing characteristics of insects such as shapes, antennae, wings, and mouth parts. The book concludes with a few suggestions for simple ways to collect insects. The text is easy to read and well spaced. Harriett Springer's black-and-white drawings are exceptional." Sci Child

Selsam, Millicent Ellis, 1912-—*Continued*
Terry and the caterpillars; pictures by Arnold Lobel. Harper & Row 1962 64p il (Science I can read bk) lib bdg $11.89 (k-3) **595.7**

1. Caterpillars
ISBN 0-06-025406-8 LC 62-13309

"A little girl finds three caterpillars, puts them into a jar, and watches all the stages of their life: caterpillar to cocoon to moth to egg and back to caterpillar again." Hodges. Books for Elem Sch Libr

Van Woerkom, Dorothy
Hidden messages; by Dorothy Van Woerkom; illustrated by Lynne Cherry. Crown 1979 unp il lib bdg $6.95 (2-4) **595.7**

1. Ants 2. Animal communication
ISBN 0-517-53520-3 LC 78-10705

Describes Ben Franklin's experiments with ant communication, Jean Henri Fabre's with moths, and the subsequent discovery by scientists of pheromones by which animals do indeed convey messages

Watts, Barrie
Honeybee. Silver Burdett Press 1990 c1989 24p il $6.95; lib bdg $9.98 (k-3) **595.7**

1. Bees
ISBN 0-382-24013-8; 0-382-24011-1 (lib bdg) LC 89-38981

"A Stopwatch book"

First published 1989 in the United Kingdom

Describes the life cycle and behavior of the honeybee

"Immaculately reproduced photographic enlargements transport readers into a hive to observe the life cycle of these small creatures. The striking camerawork focuses on newly laid eggs in their honeycomb, reveals pupae developing in their cells; and shows a queen and her workers leaving for a new home." Booklist

Whalley, Paul Ernest Sutton
Butterfly & moth; written by Paul Whalley. Knopf 1988 63p il (Eyewitness bks) $13.95; lib bdg $14.99 (4 and up) **595.7**

1. Butterflies 2. Moths
ISBN 0-394-89618-1; 0-394-99618-6 (lib bdg) LC 88-1574

This book "explores the changes that occur at each stage of the life cycles of these insects. Temperate, mountain, and exotic species are described as are shapes, camouflage, and mimicry." Sci Teach

"This is an impressive, informative, and high-quality book, yet is quite inexpensive. I highly recommend it to schools and general readers." Sci Books Films

Zim, Herbert S.
Insects; a guide to familiar American insects; by Herbert S. Zim and Clarence Cottam; illustrated by James Gordon Irving. Golden Press Bks. il pa $4.95 (4 and up) **595.7**

1. Insects

"Golden guide"

First published 1951 by Simon & Schuster. Periodically revised

This guide to familiar American insects describes their life cycles, feeding, habits and ranges, with color illustrations

Includes bibliography

596 Vertebrates

Parker, Steve
Skeleton; written by Steve Parker. Knopf 1988 63p il (Eyewitness bks) $13.95; lib bdg $14.99 (4 and up) **596**

1. Skeleton 2. Bones
ISBN 0-394-89620-3; 0-394-99620-8 (lib bdg) LC 87-26314

"An introduction to the structure and evolution of human and animal skeletal systems. Photographs of actual bones are used with some drawings to illustrate the book. There is a brief text, but the bulk of the book is the illustrations and their captions." BAYA Book Rev

Selsam, Millicent Ellis, 1912-
A first look at animals with backbones; by Millicent E. Selsam and Joyce Hunt; illustrated by Harriet[t] Springer. Walker & Co. 1978 32p il lib bdg $9.85 (1-3) **596**

1. Vertebrates
ISBN 0-8027-6339-1 LC 78-4321

An introduction to the characteristics of the major groups of vertebrates: fish, amphibians, reptiles, birds, and mammals

"This serves as a good introduction to scientific classification as well as to the subject of vertebrates. The text has large print, good spacing, good placement of illustrations in relation to text, and good sequence of material, moving from the general to the specific." Bull Cent Child Books

597 Cold-blooded vertebrates. Fishes

The **Audubon** Society field guide to North American fishes, whales, and dolphins; [by] Herbert T. Boschung, Jr. [et al.]; visual key by Carol Nehring and Jordan Verner. Knopf 1983 848p il maps $15.95 (5 and up) **597**

1. Fishes—North America 2. Whales 3. Dolphins
ISBN 0-394-53405-0 LC 83-47962

"A Chanticleer Press edition. The Audubon Society field guide series"

The Audubon Society field guide to North American fishes, whales, and dolphins — *Continued*

This guide has "a first section containing excellent photographs of 529 marine and freshwater fishes and 45 cetacean species found in or near North America north of Mexico, and a second section giving brief descriptions of each species. . . . The well-organized and well-written text includes descriptions of physical features, habitat, range (generally with a small map), and related or similar species." Choice

Includes glossary

Berger, Gilda

Sharks; illustrated by Christopher Santoro. Doubleday 1987 41p il $10.95; lib bdg $11.99 (2-4) **597**

1. Sharks
ISBN 0-385-23418-X; 0-385-23419-8 (lib bdg) LC 85-29327

Explores the world of sharks, including historical data, current information on shark research and sightings, and descriptions of the behavior and physical characteristics of twenty major types

Facts are "presented in a clearly written and easy-to-understand text. . . . The color illustrations appear on every page of this large format book to amplify the text." SLJ

Blassingame, Wyatt

Wonders of sharks. Dodd, Mead 1984 96p il $10.95 (4 and up) **597**

1. Sharks
ISBN 0-396-08463-X LC 84-10097

"Dodd, Mead wonders books"

An "account of the physical characteristics and behavior of various types of sharks. . . . In addition to explaining the life cycle, body systems, and behavior of several species, Blassingame includes material on shark fishing for pleasure and for profit, experiments with shark repellents, and the need for further research on sharks. Many black-and-white photographs illustrate the text." Booklist

Blumberg, Rhoda, 1917-

Sharks. Watts 1976 77p il lib bdg $10.40 (4 and up) **597**

1. Sharks
ISBN 0-531-00846-0 LC 75-45120

"A First book"

A "straightforward presentation of the various types of sharks, their physical characteristics, habitats, feeding habits, reproduction, and communication abilities. Blumberg talks about the shark's sea companions—pilot fish and suckerfish—as well as its enemies. . . . Material covering individual species . . . is interspersed with interesting stories." Booklist

Includes glossary and bibliography

Coupe, Sheena

Sharks; [written by Sheena and Robert Coupe] Facts on File 1990 68p il maps (Great creatures of the world) $17.95 (5 and up) **597**

1. Sharks
ISBN 0-8160-2270-4 LC 89-34671

Describes the physical; characteristics, habits, and natural environment of sharks and discusses their evolution and relationship with human beings

"The many orders of sharks and their unique physiology are described, including an excellent section on reproduction. A series of incredible photographs shows the birth of shark pups. Much of the text is devoted to the issue of shark attacks with interesting observations and statistics. . . . Illustrated with a stunning collection of color photographs, charts, tables, and maps." SLJ

Freedman, Russell

Killer fish. Holiday House 1982 40p il lib bdg $12.95 (3-5) **597**

1. Marine animals 2. Fishes
ISBN 0-8234-0449-8 LC 81-85089

"Large, usually clear photographs illustrate a text that . . . describes some varieties of sharks, stingrays and jellyfish, barracudas and piranhas, the electric rays and eels, and species of octopuses, all creatures whose bite, sting, shock, or stranglehold are dangerous and at times fatal." Bull Cent Child Books

"Though it is mentioned that some of these animals seldom if ever kill human beings, the book focuses on the dramatic in the choice of title, pictures, and some phrasing . . . Children, however, will find the subject matter and format very inviting. On the whole it is a responsible, informative and attractive presentation." SLJ

Sharks. Holiday House 1985 40p il lib bdg $12.95 (3-5) **597**

1. Sharks
ISBN 0-8234-0582-6 LC 85-42881

A physical description of sharks and a discussion of their methods of hunting, details of birth, and their usefulness to humans

"The numerous black-and-white photographs are well coordinated with the text. The writing is lucid and succinct; most unfamiliar terms are explained. Freedman uses some interesting analogies to better illustrate facts about sharks. . . . Although nothing new is offered, 'Sharks' will make a useful, entertaining addition to an already large array of shark books." SLJ

Lane, Margaret, 1907-

The fish; the story of the stickleback; by Margaret Lane; pictures by John Butler. Dial Bks. for Young Readers 1982 c1981 unp il $8.95; pa $3.50 (1-3) **597**

1. Sticklebacks
ISBN 0-8037-2580-9; 0-8037-2603-1 (pa) LC 81-5545

First published 1981 in the United Kingdom with title: The stickleback

This book "exclusively covers the three-spined stickleback, but Lane uses this fresh and saltwater fish as a microcosm of fishes in general." Booklist

McGowen, Tom

Album of sharks; illustrated by Rod Ruth. Rand McNally 1977 60p il $8.95; pa $4.95 (4 and up) **597**

1. Sharks

ISBN 0-528-82023-0; 0-02-688513-1 (pa) LC 77-5172

This general introduction discusses the food, habitat, and size of twelve different types of sharks

Parker, Steve

Fish; written by Steve Parker. Knopf 1990 63p il (Eyewitness bks) $13.95; lib bdg $14.99 (4 and up) **597**

1. Fishes

ISBN 0-679-80439-0; 0-679-80439-5 (lib bdg) LC 89-36445

This illustrated guide to fish life discusses "color as camouflage, types of early fishes, oddities in the fish world, and fish physiology (feeding, breathing, reproducing, and defending themselves)." Booklist

Sattler, Helen Roney

Sharks, the super fish; illustrated by Jean Zallinger. Lothrop, Lee & Shepard Bks. 1986 96p il $15.95 (4 and up) **597**

1. Sharks

ISBN 0-688-03993-6 LC 84-4381

"The first five chapters of the book give general information about sharks—their body structure, their feeding habits, their life cycles, their enemies and their interactions with humans." Appraisal

"Although the title and some chapter headings tend to be a bit dramatic, the book does not otherwise sensationalize the subject. The copious shaded drawings include numerous detailed diagrams and some pleasant full-page scenes; occasionally the small pictures accompanying the entries run into problems of perspective, as with the bonnethead shark, but the illustrations are both attractive and informative. An excellent choice for libraries, the book would also be a wonderful gift for young shark fans. List of sources, bibliography, and index." Horn Book

Selsam, Millicent Ellis, 1912-

A first look at sharks; by Millicent E. Selsam and Joyce Hunt; illustrated by Harriett Springer. Walker & Co. 1979 32p il lib bdg $12.85 (1-3) **597**

1. Sharks

ISBN 0-8027-6373-1 LC 79-2200

"Physical characteristics such as gills, fins, shape of head, and markings are named and described, while carefully drawn black line and gray-shaded drawings, appropriately large and clear, allow easy identification." Booklist

Zim, Herbert S.

Fishes; a guide to fresh- and salt-water species; by Herbert S. Zim and Hurst H. Shoemaker; illustrated by James Gordon Irving. Golden Press Bks. il pa $4.95 (4 and up) **597**

1. Fishes

"Golden guide"

First published 1956 by Simon & Schuster. Periodically revised

"A pocket identification guide with suggestions for collecting, classifying, and photographing fishes." Hodges. Books for Elem Sch Libr

Includes bibliography

597.6 Amphibians

Parker, Nancy Winslow

Frogs, toads, lizards, and salamanders; [by] Nancy Winslow Parker and Joan Richards Wright; illustrations by Nancy Winslow Parker. Greenwillow Bks. 1990 48p il maps $13.95; lib bdg $13.88 (k-3) **597.6**

1. Frogs 2. Toads 3. Lizards 4. Salamanders

ISBN 0-688-08680-2; 0-688-08681-0 (lib bdg) LC 89-11686

The authors "introduce 16 species of amphibian and reptile via a deft balance of comic rhyming couplet and illustration on each left-hand page and carefully labeled scientific drawing on the right. The collaborators indicate each animal's maximum size, genus, species and subspecies, whether it is diurnal or nocturnal, and describe the anatomy of each in the picture glossary that precedes a glossary of terms." Kobrin Letter

Stebbins, Robert C. (Robert Cyril), 1915-

A field guide to western reptiles and amphibians; text and illustrations by Robert C. Stebbins. 2nd ed rev. Houghton Mifflin 1985 336p il $17.95; pa $12.95 **597.6**

1. Reptiles 2. Amphibians

ISBN 0-395-38254-8; 0-395-38253-X (pa) LC 84-25125

"The Peterson field guide series"

First published 1966

Sponsored by the National Audubon Society and National Wildlife Federation

"Field marks of all species in western North America, including Baja California." Title page

This field guide features over 240 species, most accompanied by illustration and distribution map. Coverage includes Baja California and information on reptile reproduction

Includes bibliography

597.8 Anura (Salientia)

Cole, Joanna

A frog's body; with photographs by Jerome Wexler. Morrow 1980 47p il $12.95; lib bdg $12.88 **597.8**

1. Frogs

ISBN 0-688-22228-5; 0-688-32228-X (lib bdg)

LC 80-10705

"Cole and Wexler have constructed a superb introduction to the life processes and anatomy of the adult bullfrog. The author is exceptionally skillful at selecting interesting bits of information . . . and deftly combining explanations of fact and concepts in a simple, lucid text. Wexler's photographs, in color and black-and-white, include almost uncanny shots of the frog in motion. . . . The photographs are complemented by clear drawings of the frog's internal organs. This will stand among the best of many fine books available on a subject popular with children." SLJ

Florian, Douglas, 1950-

Discovering frogs. Scribner 1986 unp il $10.95 (1-3) **597.8**

1. Frogs

ISBN 0-684-18688-8

LC 86-6731

This book "includes information on the life cycle of the frog, various kinds of frogs and toads, and a simple message about conservation. Just enough information is provided to satisfy initial curiosity about the subject and whet the appetite for the truly interested." Horn Book

"A short, clear text accompanies delightful watercolor illustrations of 28 different frogs." N Y Times Book Rev

Lacey, Elizabeth A.

The complete frog; a guide for the very young naturalist; illustrated by Christopher Santoro. Lothrop, Lee & Shepard Bks. 1989 72p il $12.95; lib bdg $12.88 (4-6) **597.8**

1. Frogs

ISBN 0-688-08017-0; 0-688-08018-9 (lib bdg)

LC 88-9343

The author examines "the differences between frogs and toads, describes why frogs are well adapted to their particular habitats, and looks at reproductive cycles, feeding habits, and the transformation from tadpole to frog. An album of some [unusual] species (illustrated in color) follows, and the book ends with a look at frogs in the lore and literature of assorted cultures." Booklist

Santoro's "illustrations in color featured in the chapter 'The Odd Fellows' steal the show as they detail the truly startling and uncommon members of the frog family. Without resorting to overstatement or attention-getting exclamation points, Lacey conveys her awe and admiration for the successful survival of these small creatures." Horn Book

Includes bibliography

597.9 Reptiles

Ancona, George, 1929-

Turtle watch; photographs and text by George Ancona. Macmillan 1987 unp il $13.95 (2-4) **597.9**

1. Sea turtles 2. Endangered species 3. Wildlife conservation

ISBN 0-02-700910-6

LC 87-9316

An illustrated look at a project in Brazil designed to save sea turtles on the verge of extinction

"The details of the turtles' egg-laying, of the project's operation, and of two local children's participation are vividly projected in both pictures and text. The ending seems abrupt—one wishes for more information on the habits and characteristics of the sea turtle, but the book is successful within its defined focus; it will serve as a springboard to further exploration." Bull Cent Child Books

Includes bibliography

Bare, Colleen Stanley

Never kiss an alligator! photographs by the author. Cobblehill Bks. 1989 unp il $12.95 (k-2) **597.9**

1. Alligators

ISBN 0-525-65003-2

LC 88-32659

This book discusses the characteristics and habits of alligators

"A rhythmic but informative text makes firm grounding for vivid color photographs of alligators, including a labelled skull, eggs and babies, comparisons with crocodiles, and numerous shots of alligators in their habitats. The layout is varied without sacrifice of clarity and the selection of detail is discriminating." Bull Cent Child Books

Brenner, Barbara

A snake-lover's diary. Addison-Wesley 1970 90p il $12.95; lib bdg $12.89 (5 and up) **597.9**

1. Snakes

ISBN 0-201-09349-9; 0-06-020697-7 (lib bdg)

LC 79-98113

A young boy keeps a diary recording the physical characteristics and habits of the reptiles he catches during a spring and summer

Broekel, Ray, 1923-

Snakes. Childrens Press 1982 45p il $13.27; pa $4.95 (2-4) **597.9**

1. Snakes

ISBN 0-516-01649-0; 0-516-41649-9 (pa)

LC 81-38487

"A New true book"

Describes the physiology, habits, and behavior of snakes

Cole, Joanna

A snake's body; photographs by Jerome Wexler. Morrow 1981 48p il $12.95; lib bdg $12.88 **597.9**

1. Snakes 2. Pythons
ISBN 0-688-00702-3; 0-688-00703-1 (lib bdg) LC 81-9443

Examines the unique anatomical features of an Indian python that enable it and other snakes to survive without legs

"Wexler's photographs, stills or action shots, are of the high quality his fans have come to expect: clean, sharp lines, good closeups, clear magnification. Like other books in the author's anatomical series, this has a well-organized continuous text, careful integration of illustrative and textual material, and a direct style for the accurate information provided." Bull Cent Child Books

Cutchins, Judy

Scoots, the bog turtle; by Judy Cutchins and Ginny Johnston; illustrated by Frances Smith. Atheneum Pubs. 1989 32p il $12.95 (1-3) **597.9**

1. Turtles
ISBN 0-689-31440-X LC 88-19262

"The story of one year in the life of an imaginary bog turtle details the trials and tribulations of finding food and avoiding becoming food for other bog inhabitants. The fictionalized depiction of a wildlife habitat in the North Carolina mountains is illustrated with vibrant, full-color paintings." Sci Child

Freedman, Russell

Killer snakes. Holiday House 1982 40p il $12.95 (2-5) **597.9**

1. Snakes
ISBN 0-8234-0460-9 LC 82-80821

The author describes "over thirty of the world's deadliest snakes, discussing their habits and habitats, why and how they kill." Bull Cent Child Books

"Several pages of clear, concise text are devoted to each snake group while excellent black-and-white photos of the particular species will capture the reader's attention immediately. A well-thought-out book in every respect, this lives up to its rather sensational title." Booklist

Rattlesnakes. Holiday House 1984 40p il lib bdg $12.95 (3-5) **597.9**

1. Rattlesnakes
ISBN 0-8234-0536-2 LC 84-4602

Describes the characteristics, habits, and behavior of the rattlesnake, a type of pit viper found only in the Americas, but especially in the United States and Mexico

"A wide selection of black-and-white photographs include some fascinating pictures of males performing their 'combat dance' during mating season and of a sattler drinking during the mating season and of a rattler striking. . . . The writing is clear and never stilted, and the photographs are well-coordinated with the text." SLJ

Gross, Ruth Belov, 1929-

Snakes. rev ed. Four Winds Press 1990 63p il $13.95 (3-5) **597.9**

1. Snakes
ISBN 0-02-737022-4 LC 89-38254

First published 1973

This book "covers basic information about all snakes: baby snakes, shedding, . . . food, methods of getting food, enemies and methods of movement. This section of the book is illustrated with black and white photographs. . . . The second section of the book contains information about specific poisonous and non-poisonous snakes in the United States, as well as the boa, python, anaconda and cobra." Appraisal

Harrison, Virginia, 1966-

The world of snakes; words by Virginia Harrison; photographs by Oxford Scientific Films. Stevens, G. 1990 32p il (Where animals live) lib bdg $10.95 (k-2) **597.9**

1. Snakes
ISBN 0-8368-0143-1 LC 89-4634

Adapted from Mike Linley's The snake in the grass, entered below

Text and photographs depict the lives of snakes in their natural settings, showing how they feed, defend themselves, and breed

Includes glossary

Hess, Lilo

That snake in the grass. Scribner 1987 48p il $12.95 (3-5) **597.9**

1. Snakes
ISBN 0-684-18591-1 LC 86-24826

In this book about snakes, the author "begins with a brief discussion of myths, superstitions, and the practices of Indian fakirs and moves on to aspects of physiology, family groupings, killing and feeding, laying and hatching of eggs, and birth of live young. The final pages discuss capturing and caring for pet snakes. Hess's text is deftly constructed and accompanied by an attractive selection of photographs depicting many species. The names of the species generally accompany the uncaptioned pictures. An informative and interesting presentation, the introductory survey stands with the best books available at this level." Horn Book

Johnston, Ginny, 1946-

Scaly babies; reptiles growing up; [by] Ginny Johnston and Judy Cutchins. Morrow Junior Bks. 1988 40p il $13.95; lib bdg $13.88; pa $4.95 (3-5) **597.9**

1. Reptiles
ISBN 0-688-07305-0; 0-688-07306-9 (lib bdg); 0-688-09998-X (pa) LC 87-18559

This book offers a look at young snakes, lizards, crocodilians, and turtles during their first year of life

"In this outstanding book, text, design, graphics, and photographs work beautifully to provide basic information. . . . The quality and choice of photographs are particularly noteworthy." Horn Book

Includes glossary

Lauber, Patricia, 1924-

Snakes are hunters; illustrated by Holly Keller. Crowell 1988 32p il (Let's-read-and-find-out science bks) $12.95; lib bdg $12.89; pa $4.50 (k-3) **597.9**

1. Snakes

ISBN 0-690-04628-6; 0-690-04630-8 (lib bdg); 0-06-445091-0 (pa) LC 87-47695

Describes the physical characteristics of a variety of snakes and how they hunt, catch, and eat their prey

"Holly Keller's bright and cheerful drawings make a potentially frightening subject more approachable and add just enough detail to enhance the brief text. An upbeat, simple, and readable presentation of an inherently interesting subject." Horn Book

Lavies, Bianca

The secretive timber rattlesnake; text and photographs by Bianca Lavies. Dutton Children's Bks. 1990 unp il $13.95 (3-6) **597.9**

1. Rattlesnakes

ISBN 0-525-44572-2 LC 90-31964

"An informative, handsome photo-essay documents the behaviors of the timber rattlesnake and demonstrates how the impressive reptile contributes to the balance of nature." Sci Child

Linley, Mike

The snake in the grass; text by Mike Linley; photographs by Oxford Scientific Films. Stevens, G. 1990 32p il (Animal habitats) lib bdg $10.95 (3-6) **597.9**

1. Snakes

ISBN 0-8368-0118-0 LC 89-4621

Text and photographs depict snakes feeding, breeding, and defending themselves in their natural habitats

Includes glossary

Ryder, Joanne

Lizard in the sun; illustrated by Michael Rothman. Morrow Junior Bks. 1990 unp il $13.95; lib bdg $13.88 (k-2) **597.9**

1. Lizards

ISBN 0-688-07172-4; 0-688-07173-2 (lib bdg) LC 89-33886

"A Just for a day book"

A child is transformed into an anole for a day and discovers what it is like to be a tiny lizard changing colors in a sunny, leafy world

"The essence of the anole is caught through a subtle blending of clear, lyrical text and vibrant illustrations. . . . Although the text is relatively sparse, much information is imparted about the behavior of the anole." SLJ

Schnieper, Claudia

Chameleons; photographs by Max Meier. Carolrhoda Bks. 1989 47p il (Carolrhoda nature watch bk) lib bdg $12.95; pa $6.95 (3-6) **597.9**

1. Chameleons

ISBN 0-87614-341-9 (lib bdg); 0-87614-520-9 (pa) LC 88-37646

Original German edition published 1986 in Switzerland

Discusses the physical characteristics, behavior, and life cycle of the lizard known for its ability to change its color

"The book has many outstanding features—good quality paper and typography, excellent photography, a fine index, and much current information on the subject. Students, with the help of the teacher, will find this book an important supplement in reptile study." Sci Child

Lizards; photographs by Max Meier. Carolrhoda Bks. 1990 47p il (Carolrhoda nature watch bk) lib bdg $12.95 (3-6) **597.9**

1. Lizards

ISBN 0-87614-405-9 LC 89-22158

Original German edition published 1988 in Switzerland

"Schnieper handily describes the unique features of the lizard's body, its breeding habits, and its broad distribution across the globe. Meier's vivid, full-color, captioned photographs clarify and extend the information presented." SLJ

Includes glossary

Scott, Jack Denton, 1915-

Alligator; words by Jack Denton Scott; photographs by Ozzie Sweet. Putnam 1984 64p il $12.95 (4 and up) **597.9**

1. Alligators

ISBN 0-399-21011-3 LC 84-9927

This "volume chronicles the alligator's time on Earth from the Mesozoic era to its present resurgence because of the protection of the Endangered Species Act. All facets of alligator life are covered: physical appearance, habitat, breeding and reproduction." SLJ

"This handsome book is amply illustrated with remarkable black-and-white photographs of alligators in their natural habitats. The text is well written and scientifically accurate." Sci Child

Selsam, Millicent Ellis, 1912-

A first look at poisonous snakes; by Millicent E. Selsam and Joyce Hunt; illustrated by Harriett Springer. Walker & Co. 1987 32p il $10.95; lib bdg $12.85 (1-3) **597.9**

1. Snakes

ISBN 0-8027-6681-1; 0-8027-6683-8 (lib bdg) LC 86-33979

The authors discuss "categorizing and identifying poisonous snakes, including the cobra family, vipers, pit vipers, and sea snakes. The snake's ecological importance is mentioned, along with warnings on respecting and avoiding poisonous types." Bull Cent Child Books

Selsam, Millicent Ellis, 1912-—*Continued*

"A clear, concise writing style makes the book an excellent choice for reports. Springer's naturalistic, gray-shaded drawings have a degree of sophistication that gives the book wider appeal and use than the title implies." Booklist

Simon, Seymour, 1931-

Poisonous snakes; illustrated by William R. Downey. Four Winds Press 1981 74p il $13.95 (4 and up) **597.9**

1. Snakes
ISBN 0-02-782850-6 LC 80-23938

Describes the behavior and characteristics of different kinds of poisonous snakes, including cobras, rattlesnakes, and water moccasins

Includes bibliography

Stone, Lynn M.

Alligators and crocodiles. Childrens Press 1989 45p il lib bdg $13.27; pa $4.95 (2-4) **597.9**

1. Alligators 2. Crocodiles
ISBN 0-516-01170-7 (lib bdg); 0-516-41170-5 (pa) LC 89-9985

"A New true book"

Describes the physical characteristics, behavior, habitats, and different species of alligators and crocodiles

"Captioned, mostly full-color photographs on nearly every page provide visual interest, while short sentences and a simple writing style allows easy access for beginning readers without sacrificing substance." Booklist

Includes glossary

598 Birds

Arnold, Caroline, 1944-

Ostriches and other flightless birds; photographs by Richard R. Hewett. Carolrhoda Bks. 1990 47p il map (Carolrhoda nature watch bk) lib bdg $12.95 (3-6) **598**

1. Ostriches 2. Birds
ISBN 0-87614-377-X LC 89-820

An introduction to the physical characteristics, habits, and natural environment of ostriches and a variety of other birds that do not fly including the rhea, emu, cassowary, kiwi, and tinamou

"The photographs dramatically enhance the text. Feathers of ostriches and other birds are compared. An egg is held in a hand, effectively demonstrating its size. Bones of these flightless birds are different. Photographs and text combine to make these concepts clear, as well as others related to their speed, eye size, and preening." Appraisal

Includes glossary

Penguin; photographs by Richard Hewett. Morrow Junior Bks. 1988 48p il $12.95; lib bdg $12.88 (3-6) **598**

1. Penguins
ISBN 0-688-07706-4; 0-688-07707-2 (lib bdg) LC 87-31458

Discusses the physical characteristics, habits, and life cycle of the Magellanic penguin, a native of South America. Focuses on the lives of Humberto and Domino, a pair of Magellanics at the San Francisco Zoo, as they prepare a nest and care for their baby chick, Uno

"The author and photographer provide an interesting account. . . . Excellent nonfiction for both students and browsers." Booklist

Saving the peregrine falcon; photographs by Richard R. Hewett. Carolrhoda Bks. 1985 48p il (Carolrhoda nature watch bk) lib bdg $12.95; pa $6.95 (3-6) **598**

1. Falcons 2. Birds—Protection
ISBN 0-87614-225-0; 0-87614-523-3 (pa) LC 84-15576

Describes the efforts of scientists who are trying to save the peregrine falcon from extinction by taking the fragile eggs that would not survive in the wild, hatching them, raising the chicks, and then releasing the birds back into the wild

"An outstanding account of scientists' ingenious efforts to increase the population of the endangered peregrine falcon. The peregrine falcon's strength and beauty are conveyed through striking color photographs and clearly written text." Sci Child

Includes glossary

Bash, Barbara

Urban roosts: where birds nest in the city. Sierra Club Bks.; Little, Brown 1990 unp il $14.95 (1-4) **598**

1. Birds—Eggs and nests
ISBN 0-316-08306-2 LC 89-70187

"Excellent treatment of an unusual subject reveals that human-made places of steel, stone, and concrete are home to a variety of birds. Includes information on sparrows, finches, barn and snowy owls, swallows, swifts, nighthawks, killdeers, pigeons, wrens, crows, starlings, and falcons that have successfully adapted to city life." Sci Child

Blassingame, Wyatt

Wonders of crows. Dodd, Mead 1979 96p il $9.95 (5 and up) **598**

1. Crows
ISBN 0-396-07649-1 LC 78-21633

"Dodd, Mead wonders books"

Discusses the origin, characteristics, habits, and enemies of the crow. Also briefly describes the care of the pet crow

"Mr. Blassingame's very readable, highly interesting and amusing presentation of the crow family in general is enlivened by revealing stories about special corvine characters. . . . The book is illustrated by super black and white photographs." Appraisal

Blassingame, Wyatt—*Continued*
Wonders of egrets, bitterns, and herons. Dodd, Mead 1982 80p il $9.95 (5 and up) **598**
1. Herons
ISBN 0-396-08033-2 LC 81-17258
"Dodd, Mead wonders books"
Describes thirteen North American species of long-legged and long-necked migratory wading birds, including the great egret, American bittern, and Louisiana heron
"A very useful chart shows the comparative size and markings of six of the birds that in the field appear almost identical. This is a well-researched book, intelligently organized and illustrated and useful for its delineation among this family of high-profile waders." SLJ

Bonners, Susan, 1947-
A penguin year; written and illustrated by Susan Bonners. Delacorte Press 1981 unp il $11.95; lib bdg $12.95 (k-3) **598**
1. Penguins
ISBN 0-385-28021-1; 0-385-28022-X (lib bdg) LC 79-53595
A book about the "life cycle, habitat, and characteristics of the Adelie penguins of the Antarctic. . . . Two specific penguins are named to help us follow their activities." Child Book Rev Serv
The author-artist "supplements a simple text with attractive watercolor illustrations in black and a wide range of blues to produce a handsome informative volume." Horn Book

Burnie, David
Bird; written by David Burnie. Knopf 1988 63p il (Eyewitness bks) $13.95; lib bdg $14.99 (4 and up) **598**
1. Birds
ISBN 0-394-89619-X; 0-394-99619-4 (lib bdg) LC 87-26441
A photo essay on the world of birds examining such topics as body construction, feathers and flight, the adaptation of beaks and feet, feeding habits, courtship, nests and eggs, and bird watching
"From first impression to final reading, this photographic encyclopedia on the world of birds is an inviting pleasure. . . . *Bird* has a distinctly British tone, and many of the illustrative species are not native to the United States, but since they are each selected as examples of various adaptations, this should cause no problems." Sci Books Films

Burton, Maurice, 1898-
Birds. Facts on File 1985 64p il (World of science) $15.95 (5 and up) **598**
1. Birds
ISBN 0-8160-1063-3
This book "begins with definitions and general characteristics, including special sections on feathers, evolution, flight, sense organs, feeding, songs, and nest-building. . . . Many different species are discussed, each in a one- or two-page spread, emphasizing special adaptations, physical features, and behavior." Booklist
Includes glossary

Cole, Joanna
A bird's body; photographs by Jerome Wexler. Morrow 1982 48p il $12.95; lib bdg $12.88 **598**
1. Birds
ISBN 0-688-01470-4; 0-688-01471-2 (lib bdg) LC 82-6446
"A bird's body is designed primarily for flight, and expectedly, Cole spends a significant part of her examination explaining both how a bird flies and how its anatomy makes that possible. A parakeet and a cockatiel are her subjects, and Wexler's able photographs include numerous close-ups of body parts, flight, and some behavior traits. There are also descriptions of birds' digestive systems, vision, breathing, and hearing." Booklist

Dewey, Jennifer
The Adélie penguin. Little, Brown 1989 48p il lib bdg $15.95 (2-4) **598**
1. Penguins
ISBN 0-316-18207-9 LC 88-13010
At head of title: Birds of Antarctica
This book follows several months in the life cycle of the Adélie penguin. Mating, egg laying, migration and care of the young are discussed
"Pastel drawings in a simple color scheme of blue, green, yellow, and black lend warmth and luminosity to the inevitably white world." Horn Book

DeWitt, Lynda
Eagles, hawks, and other birds of prey. Watts 1989 63p il lib bdg $11.90 (4 and up) **598**
1. Birds of prey
ISBN 0-531-19570-9 LC 88-31371
"A First book"
"Illustrated with superb color photographs, the text discusses the characteristics and ecology of vultures, eagles, kites, hawks, falcons, and owls. . . . A good index and a glossary add to the overall superior quality of the book." Sci Books Films

Esbensen, Barbara Juster
Great northern diver: the loon; illustrated by Mary Barrett Brown. Little, Brown 1990 unp il lib bdg $14.95 (1-4) **598**
1. Loons
ISBN 0-316-24954-8 LC 89-31571
"An informative narrative and handsome, detailed illustrations portray the beguiling loon, one of the most primitive bird species in the United States, in its warm-weather habitat." Sci Child

Fischer-Nagel, Heiderose, 1956-
Season of the white stork; by Heiderose and Andreas Fischer-Nagel; translated from the German by Elise H. Scherer. Carolrhoda Bks. 1986 48p il (Carolrhoda nature watch bk) lib bdg $12.95 (3-6) **598**

1. Storks
ISBN 0-87614-242-0 LC 85-13274

Original German edition published 1984 in Switzerland

"In a clear and straightforward way, the authors tell the reader how storks eat, nest, mate and rear their young. Stunning color photographs fill every page and add even more to an already fine job." Appraisal

Includes glossary

Goldin, Augusta R.
Ducks don't get wet; illustrated by Leonard Kessler. rev ed. Crowell 1989 29p il (Let's-read-and-find-out science bks) $12.95; lib bdg $12.89 (k-3) **598**

1. Ducks
ISBN 0-690-04780-0; 0-690-04782-7 (lib bdg) LC 88-18073

First published 1965

Describes the habits and behavior of ducks, emphasizing the physical characteristics which prevent their getting wet

Harrison, Virginia, 1966-
The world of a falcon; words by Virginia Harrison; photographs by Mike Birkhead, Oxford Scientific Films. Stevens, G. 1988 32p il (Where animals live) lib bdg $10.95 (k-2) **598**

1. Falcons
ISBN 1-55532-308-1 LC 87-42611

Adapted from Mike Birkhead's The falcon over the town

"The book describes kestrels, members of the family of falcons. It includes sections on their habitats, body, head, flying, food and feeding, hunting, reproduction, home life, and relations with other animals and humans." Sci Books Films

Includes glossary

Heinrich, Bernd, 1940-
An owl in the house; a naturalist's diary; adapted by Alice Calaprice; with drawings and photographs by the author. Little, Brown 1990 119p il $14.95 (4 and up) **598**

1. Owls
ISBN 0-316-35456-2 LC 89-12473

"Joy Street books"

"When the author found a great horned owlet half-frozen in the snow near his house in Vermont, he took the tiny bird home and raised him to maturity. Adapted from the adult book *One Man's Owl* by science book editor Alice Calaprice, this first-person diary details the first two years of Bubo's life. Heinrich describes the owl's changing behavior and development as well as the bond that evolved between himself and the owl." Booklist

Hirschi, Ron
City geese; color photographs by Galen Burrell. Dodd, Mead 1987 45p il $12.95 (3-5) **598**

1. Geese
ISBN 0-396-08819-8 LC 86-19676

The author documents "the life cycle of Canada geese living year-round on the city pond at Fort Collins, Colorado. . . . A final section [discusses] the role of city sanctuaries in preserving seriously depleted bird species." Appraisal

"Burrell's full-color shots of the geese and their surroundings are clear and effective; some are illustrative of behavior mentioned in the text while others are purely aesthetic, almost romantic studies of these birds." Booklist

Hunt, Patricia, 1929-
Snowy owls; illustrated with photographs. Dodd, Mead 1982 62p il $8.95 (3-5) **598**

1. Owls
ISBN 0-396-08073-1 LC 82-7361

"A Skylight book"

Describes the physical characteristics, natural habitat, and life cycle of the snowy owl, a bird of prey of the far north

"Smoothly written and to the point, this is an efficient introduction. With crisp, well-chosen black-and-white photographs." Booklist

Johnson, Sylvia A.
Inside an egg; photographs by Kiyoshi Shimizu. Lerner Publs. 1982 48p il (Lerner natural science bk) lib bdg $12.95; pa $4.95 (4 and up) **598**

1. Eggs 2. Chickens
ISBN 0-8225-1472-9 (lib bdg); 0-8225-9522-2 (pa) LC 81-17235

Adapted from a work by Kiyoshi Shimizu published 1975 in Japan

Text and photographs trace the development of a chicken egg from the time it is laid until it is hatched

"New and difficult concept words are listed in bold type as they appear in the text. All color graphics are excellent; the close-up photographs are stunning. The format and general layout of text to photograph is without confusion and the [book is] loaded with facts." SLJ

Includes glossary

Kaufmann, John
Birds are flying; written and illustrated by John Kaufmann. Crowell 1979 34p il (Let's-read-and-find-out science bks) $12.95 (k-3) **598**

1. Birds—Flight
ISBN 0-690-03941-7 LC 78-22510

Kaufmann, John—*Continued*

"This simple text offers a good deal of accurate information about the different ways in which birds fly. The anatomical and skeletal features that give them this ability and the various flying practices of specific types of birds are demonstrated in elementary terms. The drawings strike a balance between scientific and decorative, with some effective use of gold on black and white." Booklist

Lang, Aubrey

Eagles; photographs by Wayne Lynch; general editor, R.D. Lawrence. Sierra Club Bks. 1990 62p il maps (Sierra Club wildlife lib) $14.95 (3-6) **598**

1. Eagles
ISBN 0-316-51387-3 LC 90-8729

"Discussion of physical characteristics focuses on body features crucial to the eagle's life as a hunter: eyes, feet, beak, ears, and wings. . . . Hunting, eating, nest building, and rearing of the young are described in other short segments. . . . Along with the numerous handsome photographs there are pen drawings in framed insets which feature body parts, comparative silhouettes, sky dancing, use of air currents, distribution maps, and the progression of pesticides through the food chain. The inherent appeal of the eagles is beautifully conveyed." Horn Book

Lavine, Sigmund A.

Wonders of turkeys; [by] Sigmund A. Lavine & Vincent Scuro. Dodd, Mead 1984 64p il $10.95 (5 and up) **598**

1. Turkeys
ISBN 0-396-08333-1 LC 84-1638

"Dodd, Mead wonders books"

This "introduction to the native American bird contains a wealth of information about both wild and domestic turkeys. Historical background and folklore are presented along with a discussion of the origin of the word 'turkey.' Various breeds are described and some are illustrated with black-and-white photographs." SLJ

McCauley, Jane R., 1947-

Baby birds and how they grow. National Geographic Soc. 1983 31p il lib bdg (k-3) **598**

1. Birds
ISBN 0-87044-487-5; 0-87044-492-1 (lib bdg) LC 83-13150

Available only as part of 4v set for $10.95, lib bdg $12.95. Other titles in set are: Animals helping people, by Suzanne Venino, class 636.088; Creatures small and furry, by Donald J. Crump, class 599; and Ways animals sleep, by Jane R. McCauley, class 591.5

"Books for young explorers"

"A brief, continuous text is adequately organized and simply written, describing the ways in which parent birds house, feed, teach, and care for their young. Handsome color photographs (with labels) fill the oversize pages. This isn't comprehensive, but it's a good introduction to the topic." Bull Cent Child Books

McGowen, Tom

Album of birds; illustrated by Rod Ruth. Rand McNally 1982 61p il $8.95; lib bdg $8.97 (4 and up) **598**

1. Birds
ISBN 0-528-82413-9; 0-528-80076-0 (lib bdg) LC 82-9128

Discusses the evolution of birds from reptiles, the way of life of different types of birds, the adaptation of species to their niches, the care of baby birds, and migration

"The book concludes with a random presentation of 48 bird portraits and commentary, a pronunciation guide, and an index. Full-page color plates and dozens of black-and-white and color drawings, which are appealing and for the most part well done, are provided. The text is clearly written, relatively accurate, and free from anthropomorphisms." Sci Books Films

Patent, Dorothy Hinshaw

Where the bald eagles gather; photographs by William Muñoz. Clarion Bks. 1984 56p il map $14.95; Houghton Mifflin pa $5.95 (4 and up) **598**

1. Bald eagle 2. Glacier National Park (Mont.)
ISBN 0-89919-230-0; 0-395-52598-5 (pa) LC 83-20852

Describes the annual autumn gathering of bald eagles in Glacier National Park and examines the work of the wildlife research project that bands the birds for later tracking that will provide information on the habits and life cycle of our national bird

"Exceptional photographs set the mood for this informative book. . . . The text contains interesting well-organized information as well as a fine description of how scientists work." Appraisal

Wild turkey, tame turkey; photographs by William Muñoz. Clarion Bks. 1989 57p il $14.95 (3-6) **598**

1. Turkeys
ISBN 0-89919-704-3 LC 89-613

"A well-written text enhanced by full-color photographs explains the similarities and differences between the native American wild turkey and the domesticated variety. Discusses the importance of maintaining the wild turkey population. Raises concern for the welfare of domesticated turkeys and other farm animals." Sci Child

Peterson, Roger Tory, 1908-

A field guide to the birds; a completely new guide to all the birds of eastern and central North America; text and illustrations by Roger Tory Peterson; maps by Virginia Marie Peterson. 4th ed, completely rev and enl. Houghton Mifflin 1980 384p il maps $17.95; pa $13.95 **598**

1. Birds—North America
ISBN 0-395-26621-1; 0-395-26619-X (pa) LC 80-14304

Also available in abridged form with title: Peterson first guide to birds of North America, by Roger Tory Peterson pa $4.95 (ISBN 0-395-40684-6)

Peterson, Roger Tory, 1908-—*Continued*
"The Peterson field guide series"
First published 1934
Sponsored by the National Audubon Society and National Wildlife Federation
This guide to birds found east of the Rocky Mountains contains colored illustrations painted by the author, with description of each species on the facing page. Views of young birds and seasonal variations in plumage are included. Birds are arranged in eight major groups of body shape. There are also 390 colored maps showing summer and winter range

A field guide to western birds; text and illustrations by Roger Tory Peterson; maps by Virginia Marie Peterson. 3rd ed, completely rev and enl. Houghton Mifflin 1989 432p il maps $17.95; pa $12.95 **598**
1. Birds—West (U.S.)
ISBN 0-395-08085-1; 0-395-51424-X (pa)
LC 89-31517

"The Peterson field guide series"
First published 1941
"A completely new guide to field marks of all species found in North America west of the 100th meridian and north of Mexico." Title page
Sponsored by the National Audubon Society, the National Wildlife Federation, and the Roger Tory Peterson Institute
This guide illustrates over 1,000 birds (700 species) on 165 color plates. In addition, over 400 distribution maps are included

Robbins, Chandler S.
Birds of North America; a guide to field identification; by Chandler S. Robbins, Bertel Bruun, and Herbert S. Zim; illustrated by Arthur Singer. expanded rev ed. Golden Press Bks. 1983 360p il maps $12.95; pa $9.95 (4 and up) **598**
1. Birds—North America
ISBN 0-307-37002-X; 0-307-33656-5 (pa)
LC 83-60422
"Golden field guide"
First published 1966
"Water birds are presented first, followed by land birds; within each of these two main divisions, arrangement is by related groups of species. Featured are carefully made, full-color illustrations, clear textual descriptions, and detailed range maps." Booklist

Ryden, Hope
America's bald eagle; written and photographed by Hope Ryden. Putnam 1985 63p il $11.95 (4 and up) **598**
1. Bald eagle
ISBN 0-399-21181-0
LC 84-18234
The author "observes the habits of the bald eagle, discusses conservation programs such as 'hacking' and raptor rehabilitation centers, and stresses the importance of the 1973 Endangered Species Act. A comprehensive study with excellent black-and-white photographs." Sci Child

Sattler, Helen Roney
The book of eagles; illustrated by Jean Day Zallinger. Lothrop, Lee & Shepard Bks. 1989 64p il maps $14.95; lib bdg $14.88 (4 and up) **598**
1. Eagles
ISBN 0-688-07021-3; 0-688-07022-1 (lib bdg)
LC 88-38806
"Comprehensive treatment of different species of eagles found in many parts of the world. Numerous full-color paintings on almost every page illustrate various eagle behaviors." Sci Child
Includes glossary and bibliography

Schlein, Miriam
Pigeons; photographs by Margaret Miller. Crowell 1989 43p il $12.95; lib bdg $12.89 (4-6) **598**
1. Pigeons
ISBN 0-690-04808-4; 0-690-04810-6 (lib bdg)
LC 88-35286
Explains how pigeons, descendants of wild rock doves, live their lives, raise their young, and have been useful throughout history to people
"Miller's black-and-white photography is of top quality, as are the historical photos and other illustrations that accompany accounts of homing pigeon's heroic flights, passenger pigeon's extinction, and other information. A must for urban nature study." Bull Cent Child Books

Scott, Jack Denton, 1915-
Swans; photographs by Ozzie Sweet. Putnam 1987 64p il $13.95 (4 and up) **598**
1. Swans
ISBN 0-399-21406-2
LC 87-20447
Text and photographs depict the physical characteristics, behavior, and life cycle of swans in their natural habitat
"Accomplished wildlife photographer Sweet's dramatic black-and-white shots augment the text's enlightening description of physical characteristics and behavior. . . . The author terms swans as 'birds of character,' and he and Sweet succeed in portraying them as such; straightforward for reports, engrossing for browsing." Booklist

Selsam, Millicent Ellis, 1912-
A first look at bird nests; by Millicent E. Selsam and Joyce Hunt; illustrated by Harriett Springer. Walker & Co. 1984 32p il lib bdg $9.85 (1-3) **598**
1. Birds—Eggs and nests
ISBN 0-8027-6565-3
LC 84-15238
An introduction to the many places birds make their nests, such as chimneys, cliffs, bushes, traffic lights, and window ledges, and the unusual things that might be built into the nests
"A text geared to spur careful observation and critical thinking is paired with black-and-white pencil drawings of various birds and their nests." Booklist

Selsam, Millicent Ellis, 1912-—*Continued*

A first look at birds; by Millicent E. Selsam and Joyce Hunt; illustrated by Harriett Springer. Walker & Co. 1974 c1973 35p il lib bdg $12.85 (1-3) **598**

1. Birds

ISBN 0-8027-6164-X LC 73-81404

This book "invites the young child to use his powers of observation and learn to identify birds. Simple questions and matching games encourage the child to notice color, size, shape, feet, and feathers—important factors in bird identification. The illustrations are large, clear and well-labeled. Red and blue are used in the section on colors, but all other illustrations are black and white." Appraisal

A first look at owls, eagles, and other hunters of the sky; by Millicent E. Selsam and Joyce Hunt; illustrated by Harriett Springer. Walker & Co. 1986 32p il $10.95; lib bdg $10.85 (1-3) **598**

1. Birds of prey

ISBN 0-8027-6625-0; 0-8027-6642-0 (lib bdg) LC 86-7738

The authors "introduce birds of prey—owls, hawks, eagles, falcons, and vultures—to young children, encouraging them to notice differences in shapes and sizes and to identify some of the species. Springer's precise black-and-white drawings serve the text well; the distinctions the authors address are clear, and youngsters should have no trouble observing them. They point out which creatures hunt by day and which by night and draw attention to the physical characteristics that enable each bird to better capture its prey. Not a field guide but a useful overview that will effectively acquaint young children with these handsome birds." Booklist

Van Wormer, Joe, 1913-

Eagles. Lodestar Bks. 1985 56p il $14.95 (4 and up) **598**

1. Eagles

ISBN 0-525-67154-4 LC 84-13684

"The biology, behavior, and history of the American bald eagle and the golden eagle are presented in an informative and interesting text that should encourage a much-needed feeling of respect for this endangered animal. Wonderful black-and-white photographs." Sci Child

Zim, Herbert S.

Birds; a guide to the most familiar American birds; by Herbert S. Zim and Ira N. Gabrielson; revised and updated by Chandler S. Robbins; illustrated by James Gordon Irving. rev ed. Golden Press Bks. il maps pa $3.95 (4 and up) **598**

1. Birds

"Golden guide"

First published 1949 by Simon & Schuster. Periodically revised

This book contains full color pictures of the most familiar American birds. The text describes additional related and similar species

Includes bibliography

599 Mammals

Bramwell, Martyn

Mammals: the small plant-eaters; [by] Martyn Bramwell and Steve Parker, with contributions by Jill Bailey and Linda Losito. Facts on File 1988 96p il (Encyclopedia of the animal world) $17.95 (4 and up) **599**

1. Herbivores

ISBN 0-8160-1958-4 LC 88-16934

Examines those mammals which are herbivores, including koalas, marmots, hamsters, and squirrels

"Outstanding action photographs and drawings of animals at work and play in their habitats complement an easy-to-read text." SLJ

Includes bibliography

Burton, Maurice, 1898-

Warm-blooded animals. Facts on File 1985 64p il $15.95 (5 and up) **599**

1. Mammals

ISBN 0-8160-1059-5

"An informative and highly readable book about the classification of warm-blooded animals. The first few pages describe the general characteristics of a mammal, its hair and fur, and the structure of its skeleton. The rest of the book deals with the classifications of mammals, such as insectivores, wild dogs, and pandas. Each group is clearly described in two full pages, which include photographs. There is an index and a glossary." Sci Child

Crump, Donald J.

Creatures small and furry. National Geographic Soc. 1983 26p il (k-3) **599**

1. Mammals

ISBN 0-87044-486-7; 0-87044-491-3 LC 83-13456

Available only as part of 4v set for $10.95, lib bdg $12.95. Other titles in set are: Animals helping people, by Suzanne Venino, class 636.088; Baby birds and how they grow, by Jane R. McCauley, class 598; and Ways animals sleep, by Jane R. McCauley, class 591.5

"Books for young explorers"

This volume "introduces 22 small mammals, including voles, squirrels and anteaters. Endpaper drawings indicate size comparisons." SLJ

Kerrod, Robin, 1938-

Mammals: primates, insect eaters, and baleen whales. Facts on File 1988 96p il (Encyclopedia of the animal world) $17.95 (4 and up) **599**

1. Mammals

ISBN 0-8160-1961-4 LC 88-16931

Kerrod, Robin, 1938-—*Continued*

Introduces a number of mammals, including the bat, baboon, and gray whale

"This is not a treatise on taxonomy but an informative survey of the life styles of animals. Young nature lovers will be fascinated by the brief essays that highlight the characteristics unique to each animal group. . . . The strongest point of this book is the spectacular photography, which includes sensitive close-up portraits of animals in natural positions." Sci Books Films

Includes bibliography

Lilly, Kenneth

Kenneth Lilly's animals; text by Joyce Pope. Lothrop, Lee & Shepard Bks. 1988 93p il maps lib bdg $16.95 (3 and up) **599**

1. Animals
ISBN 0-688-07696-3 LC 87-31147

"Each beautiful, full-color illustration is accompanied by one page of descriptive text which provides valuable information on how a variety of animals are adapted to their particular habitats. Animals are grouped according to habitat: hot forests, cool forests, seas and rivers, grasslands, deserts, and mountains." Sci Child

O'Toole, Christopher

Mammals: the hunters; [by] Christopher O'Toole and John Stidworthy. Facts on File 1988 96p il (Encyclopedia of the animal world) $17.95 (4 and up) **599**

1. Mammals
ISBN 0-8160-1959-2 LC 88-16933

"This book introduces mammals who are carnivores. A chapter on each mammal includes habitat, physical features, and lifestyles. A fact panel with color-coded symbols shows distribution of the mammal on a world map, diet, habitat, size, color, and lifespan. There are outstanding full-color photographs. A glossary and index are also included. An excellent resource for any age reader." Okla State Dept of Educ

Includes bibliography

Parker, Steve

Mammal; written by Steve Parker. Knopf 1989 63p il (Eyewitness bks) $13.95; lib bdg $14.99 (4 and up) **599**

1. Mammals
ISBN 0-394-82258-7; 0-394-92258-1 (lib bdg) LC 88-22656

Photographs and text examine the world of mammals, depicting their development, feeding habits, courtship rituals, protective behavior, and physical adaptation to their various ways of life

This book takes a "comprehensive yet detailed look at members of the class that includes humans. Filled with color photographs keyed to the text, the book provides ample illustrations of a variety of mammals and their unique traits." Sci Books Films

Selsam, Millicent Ellis, 1912-

Keep looking! by Millicent Selsam and Joyce Hunt; illustrated by Normand Chartier. Macmillan 1989 32p il $13.95 (k-2) **599**

1. Animals
ISBN 0-02-781840-3 LC 88-1416

"After inviting readers into a country landscape, the authors explore the common and often overlooked animal life abundant there. Children are encouraged to look for signs of wild creatures." SLJ

"Simple yet well-crafted descriptions highlight the animal activities depicted in Chartier's handsome double-page watercolors. Using unusual perspectives, the artist heightens the immediacy of the drawings." Booklist

Stidworthy, John

Mammals: the large plant-eaters. Facts on File 1988 96p il (Encyclopedia of the animal world) $17.95 (4 and up) **599**

1. Herbivores
ISBN 0-8160-1960-6 LC 88-16935

Introduces mammals which live and feed on the plains and savannahs, such as gazelles, tapirs, and kangaroos

Includes bibliography

Zim, Herbert S.

Mammals; a guide to familiar American species; 218 animals in full color; by Herbert S. Zim and Donald F. Hoffmeister; illustrated by James Gordon Irving. rev ed. Golden Press Bks. il pa $3.95 (4 and up) **599**

1. Mammals

"Golden guide"

First published 1955 by Simon & Schuster. Periodically revised

This guide presents general and specific information about mammals commonly found in North America

Includes bibliography

599.2 Marsupials

Arnold, Caroline, 1944-

Kangaroo; photographs by Richard Hewett. Morrow 1987 48p il $12.95; lib bdg $12.88 (3-5) **599.2**

1. Kangaroos
ISBN 0-688-06480-9; 0-688-06481-7 (lib bdg) LC 86-18103

Discusses the kangaroo family, their characteristics and behavior, and, in particular, the experiences of an Australian couple with an orphaned baby kangaroo during his first year in which they prepared him to be on his own

"Vivid descriptions . . . enhance the writing, as do the copious photographs. They range from action shots of leaping kangaroos to an impressive close-up of a tiny, glistening joey newly arrived in its mother's pouch." Horn Book

Arnold, Caroline, 1944-—*Continued*
Koala; photographs by Richard Hewett. Morrow 1987 48p il $12.95; lib bdg $12.88 (3-5) **599.2**

1. Koalas
ISBN 0-688-06478-7; 0-688-06479-5 (lib bdg)
LC 86-18092

This "account provides standard information on physical characteristics, behavior, care of the young, related species, and efforts at conservation. . . . Interwoven into *Koalas* is the rearing of one youngster until in early maturity she is selected, along with three other young females, for shipment to the San Francisco Zoo." SLJ

Rue, Leonard Lee
Meet the opossum; Leonard Lee Rue III with William Owen; illustrated with photographs by Leonard Lee Rue III. Dodd, Mead 1983 62p lib bdg $8.95 (4 and up) **599.2**

1. Opossums
ISBN 0-396-08221-1
LC 83-14033

"Seven chapters cover topics such as physical features, range and spread, reproduction, life of the young in the pouch, behavior, foods, home and habitat, and human relations." Sci Books Films

"Any vocabulary which might be new to the reader is carefully defined. . . . This is a skillfully written book that could only be enhanced with the addition of colored photographs instead of the black and white ones that are included." Appraisal

Selsam, Millicent Ellis, 1912-
A first look at kangaroos, koalas, and other animals with pouches; by Millicent E. Selsam and Joyce Hunt; illustrated by Harriett Springer. Walker & Co. 1985 32p il $9.95; lib bdg $9.85 (1-3) **599.2**

1. Marsupials
ISBN 0-8027-6600-5; 0-8027-6579-3 (lib bdg)
LC 85-3126

Describes the kangaroo and other pouched animals and discusses why most of them are isolated in Australia

This book "aims to develop young readers' powers of observation by helping them distinguish among the characteristics of various species. The text is well recommended. . . . Important scientific terminology is presented with easily understood definitions and pronunciation guides. All species are illustrated, and their names appear in bold type. The black-and-white illustrations would have been more appealing in color, but this is a minor criticism of a highly recommended book." Sci Books Films

599.3 Unguiculata

Blassingame, Wyatt
The strange armadillo. Dodd, Mead 1983 64p il lib bdg $8.95 (4 and up) **599.3**

1. Armadillos
ISBN 0-396-08180-0
LC 83-9073

"A Skylight book"

"Describes the characteristics and habits of our nine-banded armadillo and the possible use of the animal in leprosy research. Includes other armadillos as well as their relatives the anteaters and sloths. An interesting and clearly written text. Unusually clear and fascinating photographs." Sci Child

Lavies, Bianca
It's an armadillo; text and photographs by Bianca Lavies. Dutton 1989 unp il $13.95 (1-3) **599.3**

1. Armadillos
ISBN 0-525-44523-4
LC 89-31821

Text and photographs describe the physical characteristics, eating habits, reproduction, and infancy of the nine-banded armadillo

"The text correlates perfectly with the full-color photographs and offers a mix of basic life-cycle information and interesting behavioral sidelights. Moreover, the text flows well; here is a nonfiction title that will be right at home in a story hour." Booklist

599.32 Lagomorphs and rodents

Arnosky, Jim
Come out, muskrats. Lothrop, Lee & Shepard Bks. 1989 unp il $12.95; lib bdg $12.88 (k-2) **599.32**

1. Muskrats
ISBN 0-688-05457-9; 0-688-05458-7 (lib bdg)
LC 88-26611

"Clearly emphasizing the crepuscular and nocturnal nature of muskrats, the text's colorful two-page drawings captivate the senses. One experiences the behavior of the animals as well as the water, air, scenery, and sounds around them. This is an excellent 'read-to' book, and the large-print format is ideal for the novice reader." Sci Child

Casey, Denise
The friendly prairie dog; illustrated with color photographs by Tim W. Clark and others. Dodd, Mead 1987 40p il lib bdg $11.95 (k-3) **599.32**

1. Prairie dogs
ISBN 0-396-08901-1
LC 86-23932

Text and illustrations portray prairie dogs' lives, from feeding and raising the young, to coexisting with other wildlife

"Casey has combined a spare, accurate text with some excellent color photos to produce a good introduction to the black-tailed prairie dog." SLJ

Fischer-Nagel, Heiderose, 1956-
A look through the mouse hole; by Heiderose and Andreas Fischer-Nagel. Carolrhoda Bks. 1989 47p il (Carolrhoda nature watch bk) $12.95 (3-6) **599.32**

1. Mice
ISBN 0-87614-326-5
LC 88-39639

Fischer-Nagel, Heiderose, 1956-—*Continued*

Original German edition published 1986 in Switzerland

Photographs and text observe the behavior of a family of mice living in a basement, comparing their habits to those of outdoor mice. Includes information on the care of pet mice

"The narrative is clearly written and flows smoothly except for rare occasions in which it is interrupted by personal observations. Large print, an open format, and striking photographs will hold readers' attention." SLJ

Includes glossary

Lane, Margaret, 1907-

The beaver; pictures by David Nockels. Dial Bks. for Young Readers 1982 c1981 unp il $8.95; pa $3.50 (1-3) **599.32**

1. Beavers

ISBN 0-8037-0624-3; 0-8037-0637-5 (pa) LC 81-67074

First published 1981 in the United Kingdom

The author "covers the animal's habits and habitat with a special nod to the animal's dam-building abilities." Booklist

"The soft, full-color illustrations are attractive, although sometimes fuzzy. . . . 'The Beaver' has [no] index, table of contents or page numbers which makes for limited use as a reference source even in the primary grades. But the [book] is visually attractive, simple to read and will find an audience in young readers interested in nature." SLJ

McNulty, Faith

Woodchuck; pictures by Joan Sandin. Harper & Row 1974 64p il (Science I can read bk) lib bdg $10.89 (k-3) **599.32**

1. Marmots

ISBN 0-06-024167-5 LC 74-3585

"A year in the life of a small creature of fields and meadows is presented with clarity, simplicity, and effectiveness. . . . Accompanied by realistic illustrations containing just enough detail to supplement the text, the activities of a female woodchuck are followed from the end of one hibernation period to the beginning of the next." Horn Book

Rue, Leonard Lee

Meet the beaver; [by] Leonard Lee Rue III, with William Owen; illustrated with photographs by Leonard Lee Rue III. Dodd, Mead 1986 80p il lib bdg $11.99 (4 and up) **599.32**

1. Beavers

ISBN 0-399-61236-X LC 86-13456

Discusses the physical characteristics, behavior, range, food habits, and enemies of one of the few animals that purposely alters an environment to fit its needs

"This is an accurate, detailed introduction to *castor canadensis*: his life and his work. . . . Crisp black-and-white photos complement the text, and give readers a clear visual image of this shy, elusive animal whose fur was an important factor in the economy of a developing nation." SLJ

Ryden, Hope

The beaver. Putnam 1986 62p il $12.95 (3-5) **599.32**

1. Beavers

ISBN 0-399-21364-3 LC 86-9425

Text and photographs describe the physical characteristics and habits of the beaver and illustrate the beneficial effects of his work on the environment that he inhabits

Silverstein, Alvin

Mice: all about them; by Alvin Silverstein and Virginia B. Silverstein; with photographs by Robert A. Silverstein. Lippincott 1980 152p il lib bdg $12.89 (5 and up) **599.32**

1. Mice

ISBN 0-397-31923-1 LC 79-9621

"The authors discuss the order, suborders, families, and varieties of rodents that include rats and mice before moving to such topics as adaptability, place in the food chain, habits and habitats, and physical characteristics. They describe mice as pets and as predators who contribute to human welfare by destroying insects, and discuss at length the usefulness of mice as laboratory animals and their appeal as pets, giving advice on the latter." Bull Cent Child Books

"Many black and white photographs enrich a readable text." Appraisal

Includes bibliography

599.4 Bats

Hopf, Alice Lightner, 1904-1988

Bats; [by] Alice L. Hopf; illustrated with photographs by Merlin D. Tuttle. Dodd, Mead 1985 64p il lib bdg $9.95 (3-6) **599.4**

1. Bats

ISBN 0-396-08502-4 LC 84-28712

"A Skylight book"

Describes the characteristics, habits, and natural environment of a variety of common and unusual bats

"A strong conservation message is presented in the final chapter which discusses, among other problems, the uses of pesticides, tourists upsetting normal bat behavior and the loss of natural habitats. The black-and-white photographs are clear, unusual and truly distinguished." SLJ

Schlein, Miriam

The billions of bats; illustrated by Walter Kessell. Lippincott 1982 56p il lib bdg $12.89 (3-5) **599.4**

1. Bats

ISBN 0-397-31985-1 LC 81-47752

Discusses several unusual varieties of the more than 800 different kinds of bats, such as the vampire bat, the flying fox, the tomb bat, and the sword-nosed bat

"Finely developed drawings provide excellent visualizations of several truly unusual animals." SLJ

Shebar, Sharon Sigmond, 1945-
Bats; [by] Sharon Sigmond Shebar and Susan E. Shebar. Watts 1990 64p il lib bdg $11.90 (5 and up) **599.4**
1. Bats
ISBN 0-531-10863-5 LC 90-31329
"A First book"
"A well written account of a much maligned animal dispels widely held myths about a mammal that antedated human appearance on Earth by millions of year. Bat species, use of echolocation, migration, hibernation, reproduction, and place in the ecosystem are included." Sci Child
Includes glossary and bibliographic references

599.5 Cetaceans and sirenians

Amazing animals of the sea; marine mammals. National Geographic Soc. 1981 104p il $6.95; lib bdg $8.50 (5 and up) **599.5**
1. Mammals, Marine
ISBN 0-87044-382-8; 0-87044-387-9 (lib bdg) LC 80-8796
"Books for world explorers"
Illustrated with photographs, this book presents the characteristics and habits of the whale, dolphin, manatee, sea otter, sea lion, seal, and other marine mammals
Includes bibliography

Behrens, June
Dolphins! Childrens Press 1989 47p il lib bdg $14.60; pa $5.95 (2-4) **599.5**
1. Dolphins
ISBN 0-516-00517-0 (lib bdg); 0-516-40517-9 (pa) LC 89-33846
The author discusses the physical characteristics, intelligence, and behavior of the dolphin
"Behrens' approach is both instructive and appealing as she combines a conversational narrative with crisp color photos of many members of this cetacean group of sea mammals. Though subject headers are not used, youngsters will have no difficulty gleaning the information . . . needed for reports. A glossary with pronunciation guide adds further clarity to this treatment." Booklist

Berger, Gilda
Whales; illustrated by Lisa Bonforte. Doubleday 1987 41p il $9.95 (2-4) **599.5**
1. Whales
ISBN 0-385-23420-1 LC 86-16500
Describes the biological makeup and behavior of some twenty whale species, including killer whales, blue whales, dolphins, and porpoises, and discusses their relationship to man and their threat of extinction
"Bonforte's full-color illustrations adequately convey the distinctions between whales; author and artist give readers much to pore over, consider and enjoy." Publ Wkly

Bridge, Linda McCarter
The playful dolphins; photographs by Lowell Georgia. National Geographic Soc. 1976 32p il (k-3) **599.5**
1. Dolphins
ISBN 0-87044-200-7; 0-87044-205-8 LC 76-2118
Available only as part of a 4v set for $10.95, lib bdg $12.95. Other titles in set are: Animals that build their homes, by Robert M. McClung, class 591.5; Camping adventures, by William R. Gray; and Wonders of the desert world, by Judith E. Rinard
"Books for young explorers"
These "animals seem to leap from the pages as they perform their pranks from oceanarium stages; information on their care and living habits is also included." Booklist
"The text seems to be of secondary importance to the excellent and large color photographs." Appraisal

Clark, Margaret Goff
The vanishing manatee. Cobblehill Bks. 1990 64p il $13.95 (4 and up) **599.5**
1. Manatees
ISBN 0-525-65024-5 LC 89-38676
"Facts, anecdotes, and details describe the physical characteristics and behaviors of the friendly and curious manatee, Florida's largest mammal. Includes a discussion of research efforts to ensure manatee survival in their aquatic environment and sources for more information. A charming, instructive study." Sci Child

Dow, Lesley
Whales. Facts on File 1990 68p il (Great creatures of the world) $17.95 (5 and up) **599.5**
1. Whales
ISBN 0-8160-2271-2 LC 89-34670
Describes the physical characteristics, habits, and natural environment of whales and discusses their evolution and relationship with human beings
This book is "filled with amazing photographs, some of which actually make me gasp with delight. Graceful and anatomically accurate renderings round out its visual appeal." Appraisal

Grosvenor, Donna K.
The blue whale; paintings by Larry Foster. National Geographic Soc. 1977 29p il (k-3) **599.5**
1. Whales
ISBN 0-87044-243-0; 0-87044-250-3 LC 77-76971
Available only as part of a 4v set for $10.95, lib bdg $12.95. Other titles in set are: Creatures of the night, by Judith E. Rinard, class 591.5; Let's go to the moon, by Janis Knudsen Wheat; and What happens in the spring, by Kathleen Costello Beer
"Books for young explorers"
This book presents a year in the life of a female blue whale and her offspring

Grover, Wayne

Dolphin adventure; a true story; illustrated by Jim Fowler. Greenwillow Bks. 1990 47p il $11.95 (3-5) **599.5**

1. Dolphins
ISBN 0-688-09442-2 LC 89-27226

"While scuba diving off the Florida coast, the author was approached by two adult dolphins and their baby, who had a fishhook in its back. After the dolphins circled and clicked at him, Grover realized that he was being asked for help. He patiently soothed the baby dolphin and removed the embedded hook with his diving knife while the parent dolphins drove off sharks." Booklist

"This a fascinating story, nicely illustrated with drawings in shades of gray, black, and white." SLJ

McNulty, Faith

Whales: their life in the sea; illustrations by John Schoenherr. Harper & Row 1975 88p il lib bdg $12.89 (5 and up) **599.5**

1. Whales
ISBN 0-06-024169-1 LC 74-020395

"Comprehensive coverage of whales, including what they eat, where they live, and how they communicate and care for their young. . . . McNulty describes such aspects of the whales' ocean life as depth and length of dives, echo location, and humanlike sociability. Beginning with a chapter on evolution of whales, the author highlights the outstanding differences between the various species and concludes with a plea to save these creatures of the sea." Booklist

Includes bibliography

Milton, Joyce

Whales; the gentle giants; illustrated by Alton Langford. Random House 1989 48p il lib bdg $6.99; pa $2.95 (1-3) **599.5**

1. Whales
ISBN 0-394-99809-X (lib bdg); 0-394-89809-5 (pa) LC 88-15616

"Step into reading. A step 2 book"

This book discusses different types of whales and "how they care for their young and defend each other against predators, how they migrate, how they sleep in the water, and how and what they eat." SLJ

"Illustrated with appropriately scaled dramatic portraits that dive across double-page spreads, this easy-reader treatment of a popular subject leaps with appeal. Milton understands what kids like about whales . . . and packs a considerable amount of information into the constraints of the format." Bull Cent Child Books

Morris, Robert A.

Dolphin; pictures by Mamoru Funai. Harper & Row 1975 62p il (Science I can read bk) lib bdg $10.89; pa $3.50 (k-3) **599.5**

1. Dolphins
ISBN 0-06-024342-2 (lib bdg); 0-06-444043-5 (pa) LC 75-6292

"The book is meant to be read aloud by a young child, and despite necessary vocabulary constraints, the text contains much information about dolphins, including how they are born, how they breathe, what they eat, their natural enemies and how they communicate with one another." Sci Books Films

Patent, Dorothy Hinshaw

All about whales. Holiday House 1987 48p il $12.95 (2-4) **599.5**

1. Whales
ISBN 0-8234-0644-X LC 86-27126

An "introduction to many aspects of whale physiology and behavior. Brief segments of text and a handsome selection of photographs describe the general physical characteristics of whales and then move on to the best known species of toothed and baleen whales. The discussion covers the growth of whales, care of the young, feeding, use of the senses, communication, and interaction with humans." SLJ

"Clear, concise prose is accompanied by a superb selection of nicely captioned photographs, each of which illustrates a particular anatomical feature or behavior of these amazing marine mammals." Appraisal

Dolphins and porpoises. Holiday House 1987 89p il $14.95 (5 and up) **599.5**

1. Dolphins 2. Porpoises
ISBN 0-8234-0663-6 LC 87-45332

"A fascinating book about dolphins and porpoises that holds the reader spellbound as the anatomy, feeding habits, complex sonar system, social organization, and reproduction of these friendly mammals are discussed. Beautiful, black-and-white photographs enhance the text. Includes cetacean classifications." Sci Child

Humpback whales; photographs by Deborah A. Glockner-Ferrari and Mark J. Ferrari. Holiday House 1989 32p il $14.95 (1-3) **599.5**

1. Whales
ISBN 0-8234-0779-9 LC 89-2026

Describes the physical characteristics, habitat, and behavior of the humpback whale

Looking at dolphins and porpoises. Holiday House 1989 48p il lib bdg $12.95 (3-5) **599.5**

1. Dolphins 2. Porpoises
ISBN 0-8234-0748-9 LC 88-39985

Discusses the characteristics and habits, the family life and intelligence of dolphins and porpoises

"A good introduction to a topic most children find interesting, this has a combination of spacious format, good black and white photographs, clear writing, accuracy, and capable organization of material (logical, sequential) that should appeal to readers in the middle grades or to younger children to whom the text may be read aloud." Bull Cent Child Books

Whales, giants of the deep. Holiday House 1984 90p il map lib bdg $14.95 (5 and up) **599.5**

1. Whales
ISBN 0-8234-0530-3 LC 84-729

Patent, Dorothy Hinshaw—*Continued*

"This study of whales is distinguished in content, illustration, and format. It contains . . . scientific data on bearing and rearing the young, migratory patterns, feeding habits, and the whale's complex sonar system. A brief history of whaling and a discussion of [the] save-the-whale movement are also included." Sci Child

Reeves, Randall R.

The Sea World book of dolphins; [by] Randall R. Reeves and Stephen Leatherwood. Harcourt Brace Jovanovich 1987 111p il pa $9.95 (4 and up) **599.5**

1. Dolphins

ISBN 0-15-271957-1 LC 86-32004

"A comprehensive book about dolphins that discusses the evolution and adaptations that permit these beautiful, large-brained, sociable mammals to feed, play, bear young, and nurse in the water. Captive dolphins, conservation efforts, and species indigenous to rivers, coasts, the continental shelf, and oceans are described. Includes listings of scientific names and relative sizes." Sci Child

Includes bibliography

Rinard, Judith E., 1947-

Dolphins: our friends in the sea; dolphins and other toothed whales. National Geographic Soc. 1986 104p il $6.95; lib bdg $8.50 (4 and up) **599.5**

1. Dolphins

ISBN 0-87044-609-6; 0-87044-614-2 (lib bdg)

"Books for world explorers"

A "look at killer whales and other dolphins in the wild and in captivity and at the scientists who study them. Special feature pages focus on stories of particularly friendly dolphins from around the world as well as from mythology." Booklist

Includes bibliography

Sattler, Helen Roney

Whales, the nomads of the sea; illustrated by Jean Day Zallinger. Lothrop, Lee & Shepard Bks. 1987 126p il lib bdg $14 (4 and up) **599.5**

1. Whales 2. Dolphins

ISBN 0-688-05587-7 LC 86-10397

The author discusses "the perennially fascinating whale, porpoise, and dolphin. Seven introductory chapters . . . investigate the behavior and general characteristics of these intelligent mammals. The text is packed with accurate and intriguing information and is enlivened with accounts of Sattler's experiences while watching whales. . . . A glossary of the known whale species offers straightforward information on each, including common and scientific names, geographical range, and physical descriptions." Horn Book

Includes bibliography

Sibbald, Jean H.

The manatee. Dillon Press 1990 59p il (Dillon remarkable animals bk) $12.95 (3-5) **599.5**

1. Manatees

ISBN 0-87518-429-4 LC 89-26048

"A general introduction to the manatee (or sea cow) and its relatives around the world. The primary emphasis is on the Florida manatee—where it lives, what it eats, and how the increasing development of its habitat is endangering its chances for survival. A slightly fictionalized account of one manatee's life dramatizes the manmade dangers the animals face." SLJ

"The writing style is clear and direct. . . . The photographs . . . are excellent. They are plentiful, colorful and well labeled." Appraisal

Includes glossary

Simon, Seymour, 1931-

Whales. Crowell 1989 unp il $15.95; lib bdg $15.89 (3-5) **599.5**

1. Whales

ISBN 0-690-04756-8; 0-690-04758-4 (lib bdg) LC 87-45285

"Whales in their natural habitat, the sea and the sky, are lavishly illustrated in this introduction to their physical characteristics and biology. The full-color photographs are lush, the text is succinct, and the oversized format sets off the large scale of these huge, magnificent creatures. Unusual close-ups show body angles not often seen. . . . A beautiful and factual addition for all collections." SLJ

599.6 Paenungulata

Schlein, Miriam

Elephants; scientific consultant: Cynthia Moss; photographs by Leonard Lee Rue III and Len Rue Jr. Atheneum Pubs. 1990 31p il (Jane Goodall's animal world) $11.95; pa $3.95 (4-6) **599.6**

1. Elephants

ISBN 0-689-31468-X; 0-689-71395-9 (pa) LC 89-38551

"A Byron Preiss book"

The author "covers information about the adult animal and the baby, discusses the elephant's need for protection, and gives other helpful material about these creatures as well. Full-color photographs are used exclusively." Booklist

Yoshida, Toshi, 1911-

Elephant crossing; written and illustrated by Toshi Yoshida. Philomel Bks. 1989 unp il $14.95 (1-3) **599.6**

1. Elephants

ISBN 0-399-21745-2 LC 88-34877

"In this companion to *Young Lions* [entered in class 599.74], an elephant herd successfully fends off predatory lions before being faced with an even greater hazard: a giant cloud of desert grasshoppers. The insects quickly strip the plain of grass and leaves and provoke the

Yoshida, Toshi, 1911-—*Continued*
elephants and giraffes to stampede." Bull Cent Child Books

"Sometimes crayoned or chalked on textured paper, at other times evincing the smoother consistency of oils and watercolors, Yoshida's art evokes the African plain with authenticity and style. A masterful addiction to elementary nature collections." Booklist

599.72 Odd-toed ungulates

Arnold, Caroline, 1944-
Zebra; photographs by Richard Hewett. Morrow 1987 48p il $13.95; lib bdg $13.88 (3-5) **599.72**

1. Zebras
ISBN 0-688-07067-1; 0-688-07068-X (lib bdg)
LC 87-1503

The author gives basic information on the behavior patterns, physical characteristics, reproduction, species and subspecies of zebras, using as a focal point a newborn zebra living at New Jersey's wildlife park

"Excellent full-color photographs demonstrate [the] creature's unique appearance and habits. Often capturing the animals in striking poses, the pictures illustrate well the information offered in text. Page layout is spacious and attractive, giving the book an inviting, unintimidating look." Booklist

599.73 Even-toed ungulates

Arnold, Caroline, 1944-
Giraffe; photographs by Richard Hewett. Morrow 1987 48p il $12.95; lib bdg $12.88 (3-5) **599.73**

1. Giraffes
ISBN 0-688-07069-8; 0-688-07070-1 (lib bdg)
LC 87-1502

The author describes the characteristics and habitats of giraffes and discusses life for these animals at a large open-air wildlife park in New Jersey

"Hewett has a good eye for detail and composition and provides a fine variety of shots of individual animals and groups resting, eating, moving, and occasionally interacting with humans. . . . The care given to both the writing and photography is also demonstrated in the attractive layout of the pages." Horn Book

Hippo; photographs by Richard Hewett. Morrow Junior Bks. 1989 48p il $12.95; lib bdg $12.88 (3-5) **599.73**

1. Hippopotamus
ISBN 0-688-08145-2; 0-688-08146-0 (lib bdg)
LC 88-39794

Presents the characteristics and habits of hippopotamuses in the wild and of a family at the San Francisco Zoo

"Hewett's charming full-color photographs succeed in making this admittedly odd-looking animal . . . engaging. . . . A well-rounded look at the hippopotamus for unsophisticated readers." SLJ

Llama; photographs by Richard Hewett. Morrow Junior Bks. 1988 48p il $12.95; lib bdg $12.88 (3-5) **599.73**

1. Llamas
ISBN 0-688-07540-1; 0-688-07541-X (lib bdg)
LC 87-27130

Describes the characteristics and behavior of llamas and their usefulness to man, discusses other members of the lamoid family, and reports on the growing number of llamas now being bred in the United States

Tule elk; photographs by Richard R. Hewett. Carolrhoda Bks. 1989 47p il (Carolrhoda nature watch bk) lib bdg $12.95 (3-6) **599.73**

1. Elk
ISBN 0-87614-343-5
LC 88-31565

"Tule elk—a smaller California subspecies, less familiar than the Rocky Mountain variety—were practically extinct in the early twentieth century. Efforts to restore the species are reported along with characteristics of the breed." Horn Book

Hirschi, Ron
Headgear; photographs by Galen Burrell. Dodd, Mead 1986 63p il lib bdg $12.95 (4 and up) **599.73**

1. Horns 2. Mammals
ISBN 0-396-08673-X
LC 85-20407

Discusses the characteristics and habitats of horned and antlered North American animals, such as elk, bighorn, pronghorn, moose, caribou, deer, and mountain goat, and presents some of the folklore associated with these animals' headgear

"Forty superb color photographs closely follow the text. There are no tables, charts, maps, artwork, or diagrams—just interesting reading and beautiful pictures. . . . A one-page glossary and two-page index complete the book." Sci Books Films

Lepthien, Emilie U. (Emilie Utteg)
Buffalo. Childrens Press 1989 45p il lib bdg $13.27; pa $4.95 (2-4) **599.73**

1. Bison
ISBN 0-516-01161-8 (lib bdg); 0-516-41161-6 (pa)
LC 89-457

This book presents a "chronology and natural history of the near demise and eventual rise of North American bison. The heaviest emphasis is on the necessary exploitation of them by American Indians and the wanton destruction by early Western settlers and sport hunters. Conservation laws, advocate groups, and programs to restore sizeable, natural herds are recounted. The eventual success from hundreds of the animals in the late 1800's to nearly 100,000 today is strong support for educating youngsters to value natural resources." Appraisal

Leslie-Melville, Betty

Daisy Rothschild. Doubleday 1987 42p il $12.95; lib bdg $13.99 (1-3) **599.73**

1. Giraffes

ISBN 0-385-23895-9; 0-385-23896-7 (lib bdg) LC 86-29070

The author describes her relationship with a Rothschild giraffe, a nearly extinct species, in Kenya

Leslie-Melville "provides an unusual look into the world of the giraffe, an animal that at first appears aloof and indifferent, but in reality is quite loving. More importantly, *Daisy Rothschild* eloquently points out the difference that just two people can make in the fight to protect endangered animals." Publ Wkly

Nicholson, Darrel

Wild boars; photographs by Craig Blacklock. Carolrhoda Bks. 1987 47p il (Carolrhoda nature watch bk) lib bdg $12.95 (3-6) **599.73**

1. Boars

ISBN 0-87614-308-7 LC 87-677

"Straightforward, informative text and fine, full-color photographs introduce the Eurasian wild boar, brought to North America for hunting and studied at a Minnesota farm. An excellent book about a hardy, adaptable animal." Sci Child

Patent, Dorothy Hinshaw

Buffalo; the American bison today; photographs by William Muñoz. Clarion Bks. 1986 73p il $12.95 (4 and up) **599.73**

1. Bison

ISBN 0-89919-345-5 LC 85-25483

"As the buffalo is followed through the seasons in Yellowstone National Park and the National Bison Range in Montana, Patent discusses both the habits and behavior of this historically important animal and the careful management needed to maintain it in its current artificial environment." SLJ

This "is a captivating account of the contemporary bison. The author's portrayal of this imposing creature is forthright, realistic and creative. William Munoz' marvelous photos add greatly to describing the rutting rituals of summer, the population management in the fall, the bison's struggles for food in the winter and the birth and care of its newborn in the spring. This little book is action-packed, informative, and titillating." Appraisal

Rue, Leonard Lee

Meet the moose; [by] Leonard Lee Rue III, with William Owen; illustrated with photographs by Leonard Lee Rue III. Dodd, Mead 1985 78p il lib bdg $9.95 (4 and up) **599.73**

1. Moose

ISBN 0-396-08605-5 LC 84-26058

This work discusses the physical characteristics, range, and habits of the moose

The author's "vast experience photographing moose in the wild has given this excellent text a vital and alive tone. Informative descriptions of antler growth, care and growth of the young, life style of the moose and their few enemies are all a part of this lively well photographed book." Appraisal

Sattler, Helen Roney

Giraffes; the sentinels of the Savannas; illustrated by Christopher Santoro. Lothrop, Lee & Shepard Bks. 1990 80p il $14.95; lib bdg $14.88 (5 and up) **599.73**

1. Giraffes

ISBN 0-688-08284-X; 0-688-08285-8 (lib bdg) LC 89-2287

"A comprehensive examination of Giraffidae, from fossil remains to the benign giants of today, in an elegant format enhanced by rich sepia illustrations and cream-colored paper. Includes a glossary, geological timeline, and scientific classifications. Bibliography." Sci Child

Schlein, Miriam

Hippos; photographs by Leonard Lee Rue III and Len Rue, Jr. Atheneum Pubs. 1989 30p il (Jane Goodall's animal world) $11.95; pa $3.95 (4-6) **599.73**

1. Hippopotamus

ISBN 0-689-31469-8; 0-689-71321-5 (pa) LC 89-6464

"A Byron Preiss book"

Introduces the physical characteristics, behavior, habitat, reproduction, and life cycle of the hippo

Waters, John F.

Camels: ships of the desert; illustrated by Reynold Ruffins. Crowell 1974 33p il (Let's-read-and-find-out science bks) lib bdg $12.89 (k-3) **599.73**

1. Camels

ISBN 0-690-00395-1 LC 73-14514

Comparing the camel's physical characteristics to man's, this book explains how camels withstand the desert sand, heat, and lack of water and food

599.74 Carnivores

Arnold, Caroline, 1944-

Cheetah; photographs by Richard Hewett. Morrow Junior Bks. 1989 48p il $12.95; lib bdg $12.88 (3-5) **599.74**

1. Cheetahs

ISBN 0-688-08143-6; 0-688-08144-4 (lib bdg) LC 88-39940

"A full-color photo essay about the daily activities of cheetahs in the wild and in captivity. Includes information about the scientific community's efforts to save cheetahs from extinction and a portrait of Damara, a tame cheetah from the Wildlife Safari in Winston, Oregon." Sci Child

Arnosky, Jim

Watching foxes. Lothrop, Lee & Shepard Bks. 1985 unp il $12.95; lib bdg $12.88 (k-2) **599.74**

1. Foxes
ISBN 0-688-04259-7; 0-688-04260-0 (lib bdg) LC 84-20157

"Arnosky shares his observations of four fox pups at play while mother fox is hunting. Their antics unfold in a series of double-page spreads. One or two brief sentences in large type accompany each pair of pages. . . . The illustrations, in color pencil and watercolor wash, are clear and attractive; they will be readily interpreted by the very young audience for whom they are intended." SLJ

Ashby, Ruth

Sea otters. Atheneum Pubs. 1990 30p il map (Jane Goodall's animal world) $11.95 (4-6) **599.74**

1. Otters
ISBN 0-689-31472-8 LC 89-38552
"A Byron Preiss book"

An introduction to sea otters, aquatic mammals that live in the north Pacific and rarely come to land

Tigers. Atheneum Pubs. 1990 30p il map (Jane Goodall's animal world) $11.95 (4-6) **599.74**

1. Tigers
ISBN 0-689-31474-4 LC 89-38549
"A Byron Preiss book"

This introduction to tigers includes "information on the animal's habitat and geographical location, ancestors, the species' community life, physical characteristics, birth and growing up, daily routines, and protection of the species." Appraisal

Bare, Colleen Stanley

Elephants on the beach; photographs by the author. Cobblehill Bks. 1990 31p il $12.95 (1-3) **599.74**

1. Seals (Animals)
ISBN 0-525-65018-0 LC 89-32267

"Elephants on the beach are elephant seals from Antarctica and the Pacific coast. The large animals of the sea with the unusual looking proboscis is shown in its daily routine and compared to other pinnipeds." Sci Child

"The author's crisp color camera shots sport a narrow blue band, and it is this discreet framing that allows them to be arranged on the page in a seemingly casual mix of angles and sizes. . . . The text has a clarity that is almost terse; yet it is this directness that will satisfy children's curiosity about one of nature's more unusual looking animals." Booklist

Sea lions; illustrated with photographs by the author. Dodd, Mead 1986 64p il lib bdg $9.95 (3-5) **599.74**

1. Seals (Animals)
ISBN 0-396-08719-1 LC 85-16276
"A Skylight book"

"The book covers behavior, birth, growth, and enemies—both animal and human. It also talks about some of the diseases to which the animals are susceptible and the effects of the disastrous warming of the seas called El Nino." Appraisal

"This is another outstanding animal book by the author-photographer. The world of the sea lion is presented in beautifully colored photographs and an easy, readable text. The author has done thorough research, added photographs, color and black and white and put together a very interesting and exciting book to look at and to read." Okla State Dept of Educ

Brenner, Barbara

Two orphan cubs; [by] Barbara Brenner and May Garelick; illustrated by Erika Kors. Walker & Co. 1989 unp il $12.95; lib bdg $13.85 (k-3) **599.74**

1. Bears
ISBN 0-8027-6868-7; 0-8027-6869-5 (lib bdg) LC 88-23245

After their mother is killed by poachers, two bear cubs are rescued by a wildlife scientist who transfers them to another cave where he hopes they'll be adopted by a new mother

"This pleasant story is accompanied by gentle and simple pencil drawings highlighted in green. Although it is designated as nonfiction, it would probably circulate better as a picture book. It should also work nicely in a story hour setting." SLJ

Brownell, M. Barbara

Amazing otters. National Geographic Soc. 1989 32p il (k-3) **599.74**

1. Otters
ISBN 0-87044-770-X; 0-87044-775-0 LC 89-3278

Available only as part of a 4v set for $15.95, lib bdg $18.95. Other titles in the set are: Animal clowns, by Jane R. McGoldrick; Cottontails: little rabbits of field and forest, by Ron Fisher; and Animals of the high mountains, by Judith E. Rinard

"Books for young explorers"

Introduces in text and illustrations, the physical characteristics, habits, and natural environment of the otter

Includes bibliography

Buxton, Jane Heath, 1948-

Baby bears and how they grow. National Geographic Soc. 1986 32p il (k-3) **599.74**

1. Bears
ISBN 0-87044-634-7; 0-87044-639-8 LC 86-2481

Available only as part of 4v set for $10.95, lib bdg $12.95. Other titles in set are: Animals and their hiding places, by Jane R. McCauley, class 591.5; Animals that live in trees, by Jane R. McCauley, class 591.5; and Saving our animal friends, by Susan McGrath, class 591

"Books for young explorers"

Describes the daily life of various baby bears, including black bears, polar bears, and brown bears

Calabro, Marian

Operation grizzly bear. Four Winds Press 1989 118p il $12.95 (5 and up) **599.74**

1. Grizzly bear 2. Yellowstone National Park

ISBN 0-02-716241-9 LC 88-37497

"This is a study of the research carried out by naturalists Frank and John Craighead in Yellowstone National Park between 1959 and 1971. They examined grizzly feeding, mating, and hibernating patterns, tracked their territorial ranges, and observed cub-rearing practices." Bull Cent Child Books

"This book deals sensitively with the issue of human/wildlife relationships without belittling the danger involved. 'Operation Grizzly Bear' is illustrated with numerous black and white photographs, and is well indexed." Voice Youth Advocates

Includes bibliography

Hurd, Edith Thacher, 1910-

Song of the sea otter; pictures by Jennifer Dewey. Sierra Club Bks. 1983 unp il lib bdg $9.95; pa $5.95 (2-4) **599.74**

1. Otters

ISBN 0-394-96191-9 (lib bdg); 0-316-38323-6 (pa) LC 83-4675

Illustrated with pencil drawings, this book covers the life of a young sea otter, from his birth to his first steps to independence, describing his relationship to his mother and to the world around him

"Although a lyrical evocation more than an objective discussion, the text provides specific information about a large number of sea creatures in the ecosystem. . . . Soft black-and-white drawings carry the listener along with the sea otter's adventures and are sufficiently detailed to identify the flora and fauna mentioned in the text." Horn Book

Jin Xuqi

The giant panda; [by] Jin Xuqi and Markus Kappeler; translated by Noel Simon. Putnam 1986 46p il $14.95 (5 and up) **599.74**

1. Giant panda

ISBN 0-399-21389-9 LC 86-9480

Original German edition published in Switzerland

"In addition to facts about habits and habitat, the authors describe the successful efforts being made to protect and foster the animal that is so appealing in this book, as it is in zoos in or outside of China." Bull Cent Child Books

Johnson, Sylvia A.

Elephant seals; photographs by Frans Lanting. Lerner Publs. 1989 48p il (Lerner natural science bk) lib bdg $12.95 (4 and up) **599.74**

1. Seals (Animals)

ISBN 0-8225-1487-7 LC 88-12924

"Many full-color photographs supplement a clear text explaining the life cycle, physical characteristics, habits, and natural environment of the unusual looking sea mammal." Sci Child

Includes glossary

Wolf pack; tracking wolves in the wild; [by] Sylvia A. Johnson & Alice Aamodt. Lerner Publs. 1985 96p il map lib bdg $14.95; pa $5.95 (4 and up) **599.74**

1. Wolves

ISBN 0-8225-1577-6 (lib bdg); 0-8225-9526-5 (pa) LC 85-37

"This book traces the development of wolves from pups. Discusses social development and communication within a family group and includes chapters on tracking wolves and myths surrounding wolves. A well-written, interesting, and informative account with excellent photographs and illustrations." Sci Child

Includes glossary

LaBonte, Gail

The arctic fox. Dillon Press 1989 60p il (Dillon remarkable animals bk) $10.95 (3-5) **599.74**

1. Foxes

ISBN 0-87518-390-5 LC 88-18967

This book examines the appearance, habitat, and behavior of the arctic fox, discusses its relationship with humans, and describes a year in the life of an arctic fox

"Young students will enjoy learning about the arctic fox's food-gathering methods, for it is both scavenger and predator. . . . Both the spectacular full-color photographs and the well-written text make this an excellent choice." Sci Child

Lane, Margaret, 1907-

The fox; pictures by Kenneth Lilly. Dial Bks. 1982 unp il $9.95; pa $3.50 (1-3) **599.74**

1. Foxes

ISBN 0-8037-2491-8; 0-8037-2493-4 (pa) LC 82-71355

"This slim volume presents a good deal of information about the life of the fox. This animal's methods of hunting and staking out territory, of mating and raising young, and of adapting to pressures from human encroachment on its habitats are discussed in clear language challenging to but appropriate for the intended audience. . . . The striking [color] drawings on each page enhance the story." Sci Books Films

Lavine, Sigmund A.

Wonders of badgers. Dodd, Mead 1985 64p il lib bdg $10.95 (4 and up) **599.74**

1. Badgers

ISBN 0-396-08581-4 LC 84-25941

"Dodd, Mead wonders books"

Discusses the characteristics of American and European badgers, as well as more exotic species, and includes lore that has grown up around these intelligent and often misunderstood creatures

"Although there are some problems with the book's organization, the information is accurate and very interesting. . . . The book is well illustrated with black-

Lavine, Sigmund A.—*Continued*
and-white photographs and line drawings." Sci Books Films

Wonders of foxes. Dodd, Mead 1986 80p il lib bdg $10.95 (4 and up) **599.74**

1. Foxes
ISBN 0-396-08857-0 LC 86-16717

"Dodd, Mead wonders books"

"Although concentrating on the behavior and physical characteristics of *Vulpes vulpes*, the red fox, Lavine includes chapters on the origins of foxes, folklore and superstition, and man's relationship to this adaptable and often misunderstood creature. Other species are briefly discussed, including the tree-climbing gray fox and more exotic relatives in Africa and South America. The well-organized text is coherent and easily understood. Numerous black-and-white photographs—although of uneven quality—add to the text." SLJ

Wonders of tigers. Dodd, Mead 1987 79p il lib bdg $11.95 (4 and up) **599.74**

1. Tigers
ISBN 0-396-09153-9 LC 87-15721

"Dodd, Mead wonders books"

The first chapter "reviews the tiger's evolutionary history, classification, and habitat requirements. Other chapters deal with mythology, popular uses, superstitions, physical characteristics, behavior, and relationships with humans past and present." Sci Books Films

"Undoubtedly, this is one of the most informative and interesting books on tigers that one could ever hope for. . . . Old prints add to the interest and pleasure while imparting a sense of historical perspective." Appraisal

Lawrence, R. D., 1921-

Wolves. Sierra Club Bks. 1990 62p il maps (Sierra Club wildlife lib) $14.95 (3-6) **599.74**

1. Wolves
ISBN 0-316-51676-7 LC 90-8730

"A sympathetic, up-to-date treatment of wolves with special emphasis on the social nature of wild wolves. Includes a wealth of information about the growth and development of pups from a variety of species." Sci Child

Leighner, Alice Mills

Reynard; the story of a fox returned to the wild; story and photos by Alice Mills Leighner. Atheneum Pubs. 1986 48p il $11.95 (2-4) **599.74**

1. Foxes
ISBN 0-689-31189-3 LC 85-26848

The author describes the habits and rehabilitation of a young red fox found on the highway and brought to a special center, where it was taught how to survive in the wild before being released again

"The simply told story of the young fox' development from a fuzzy little bundle to adulthood and the arrival of a mate will please animal lovers. Enough factual information is deftly brought in to make the book useful for readers in search of fox facts." Booklist

Lewin, Ted

Tiger trek; written and illustrated by Ted Lewin. Macmillan 1990 unp il $14.95 (2-4) **599.74**

1. Tigers
ISBN 0-02-757381-8 LC 89-12710

"A simple story and beautiful watercolors describe a tiger as she hunts to feed herself and her cubs. Includes a visit to wildlife preserves in India, where a variety of indigenous animal and plant life can be seen." Sci Child

Matthews, Downs

Polar bear cubs; photographs by Dan Guravich. Simon & Schuster Bks. for Young Readers 1989 unp il lib bdg $13.95 (2-4) **599.74**

1. Polar bears
ISBN 0-671-66757-2 LC 88-10284

Describes the life of a pair of polar bear cubs as they play, explore, and learn to hunt with their mother

"Guravich's close-ups speak of long, cold vigils and an uncanny command of technology to capture creature habit and characteristics, including some unusually humorous poses. From one frozen Arctic endpaper to the other, this is picture book nonfiction at its best." Bull Cent Child Books

McClung, Robert M.

Lili: a giant panda of Sichuan; illustrated by Irene Brady. Morrow Junior Bks. 1988 85p il $12.95; lib bdg $12.88 (3-6) **599.74**

1. Giant panda
ISBN 0-688-06942-8; 0-688-06943-6 (lib bdg) LC 87-28271

"A well-written story that follows the first several years of a female panda's life in the only remaining natural habitat for the panda, China's Sichuan Province. Text includes a discussion of threats to the survival of the less than one thousand pandas alive today as well as current preservation efforts." Sci Child

Includes bibliography

McGuire, Leslie, 1945-

Lions; photographs by Leonard Lee Rue III and Len Rue, Jr. Atheneum Pubs. 1989 31p il (Jane Goodall's animal world) $11.95; pa $3.95 (4-6) **599.74**

1. Lions
ISBN 0-689-31470-1; 0-689-71322-3 (pa) LC 89-6469

"A Byron Preiss book"

Introduces the physical characteristics, behavior, habitat, reproduction, and life cycle of the lion

"Illustrated with clear, full-color photographs and well organized for young researchers." Booklist

North, Sterling, 1906-1974

Rascal; illustrated by John Schoenherr. Dutton 1984 c1963 189p il $13.95; Avon Bks. pa $2.75 (5 and up) **599.74**

1. Raccoons
ISBN 0-525-18839-8; 0-380-01518-8 (pa) LC 84-10292

A Newbery Award honor book, 1964

First published 1963 with subtitle: A memoir of a better era

A book about Rascal "a young raccoon, Sterling North's pet the year he was eleven, in rural Wisconsin. . . . The book calls up a series of marvelous pictures; boy fishing in peaceful company of raccoon, boy riding on bike with raccoon (a demon for speed) standing up in the bike basket, raccoon with friend, a prize trotting horse, raccoon helping boy to win a pie-eating contest. A central episode is about an idyllic camping trip." Publ Wkly

Patent, Dorothy Hinshaw

Seals, sea lions, and walruses. Holiday House 1990 88p il $14.95 (5 and up) **599.74**

1. Seals (Animals) 2. Walruses
ISBN 0-8234-0834-5 LC 90-55101

"A competent, well-organized look at the lives of three mammals called pinnipeds because of their unique, fin-like feet. Clear photographs enrich informative, accurate text. Includes a list of scientific names." Sci Child

Includes glossary

The way of the grizzly; photographs by William Muñoz. Clarion Bks. 1987 65p il $12.95 (4 and up) **599.74**

1. Grizzly bear
ISBN 0-89919-383-8 LC 86-17562

Describes, in text and illustrations, the physical characteristics, habits, and natural environment of the grizzly bear and discusses the threats that humans pose to their survival

This "is a slim book with an ample number of black-and-white photographs of reasonable quality and easy-to-read, anecdotal text. . . . On the whole, the material appears to be factually correct, serving as a reasonable introduction to the life and times of the North American grizzly." Sci Books Films

Pringle, Laurence P.

Bearman: exploring the world of black bears; photographs by Lynn Rogers. Scribner 1989 42p il $13.95 (3-5) **599.74**

1. Bears
ISBN 0-684-19094-X LC 89-5890

Examines the physical characteristics, habits, and natural environment of the American black bear

"Sharp, full-color photographs taken by Rogers himself (with photographic credits provided for pictures of Rogers) accompany the thoughtful, informative text." Sci Child

Includes bibliography

Ryden, Hope

Bobcat; written and photographed by Hope Ryden. Putnam 1983 62p il $12.95 (5 and up) **599.74**

1. Bobcat
ISBN 0-399-20976-X LC 82-21621

"Describes the habits and characteristics of our native bobcats as well as their place in the animal world. Written by a naturalist. Detailed descriptions and excellent black-and-white photographs." Sci Child

Ryder, Joanne

White bear, ice bear; illustrated by Michael Rothman. Morrow Junior Bks. 1989 unp il $13.95; lib bdg $13.88 (k-2) **599.74**

1. Polar bears
ISBN 0-688-07174-0; 0-688-07175-9 (lib bdg) LC 87-36781

"A Just for a day book"

Describes the awakening, feeding, and wandering of a polar bear, from its own viewpoint

"Neither the polar bear nor the Arctic are named, but the poetic text set within the full double-page illustrations draws the reader into the cold and ice. . . . Although the science content of this book is limited, the younger reader will enjoy it as a poetic evocation of the polar bear in its icy domain." Sci Books Films

Schlein, Miriam

Pandas. Atheneum Pubs. 1989 30p il (Jane Goodall's animal world) $11.95; pa $3.95 (4-6) **599.74**

1. Giant panda
ISBN 0-689-31471-X; 0-689-31319-3 (pa) LC 89-6463

"A Byron Preiss book"

This book "explains the scientific debate about which family pandas belong to (bear or raccoon) and includes some interesting sidelights about the panda's diet (although they mostly eat bamboo, they are really carnivores)." Booklist

Project panda watch; illustrated by Robert Shetterly. Atheneum Pubs. 1984 87p il $11.95 (4 and up) **599.74**

1. Giant panda 2. Wildlife conservation
ISBN 0-689-31071-4 LC 84-2914

This book focuses partly on efforts to save the giant panda from extinction by providing food during shortages in the supply of its usual bamboo diet. It is "an account of the work of Chinese and American scientists studying pandas in the Wolong Nature Preserve in China, with chapters on zoo pandas as well." N Y Times Book Rev

Includes glossary and bibliography

Schnieper, Claudia
On the trail of the fox; photographs by Felix Labhardt. Carolrhoda Bks. 1986 47p il (Carolrhoda nature watch bk) lib bdg $12.95; pa $6.95 (3-6) **599.74**

1. Foxes
ISBN 0-87614-287-0 (lib bdg); 0-87614-480-6 (pa) LC 86-6893

Original German edition published 1985 in Switzerland

This book "was photographed in a very naturally constructed game preserve and provides a remarkable documentary of the daily life and mating of a pair of red foxes and the subsequent care of the new litter by the vixen. The beauty of the foxes with their alert, intelligent-looking faces and the affection between the adults, the mother, and her growing pups are truly irresistable. The foxes are also shown as hunters, sometime thieves, and as fierce defenders of their territory, but the author candidly admires the sharp senses, keen survival instincts, and adaptability of this often mistrusted species." Horn Book

Schwartz, Alvin, 1927-
Fat man in a fur coat, and other bear stories; collected and retold by Alvin Schwartz; pictures by David Christiana. Farrar, Straus & Giroux 1984 167p il $12.95; pa $3.50 (4 and up) **599.74**

1. Bears
ISBN 0-374-32291-0; 0-374-42273-7 (pa) LC 84-4161

A "portrayal of bears as truly extraordinary, intelligent, sometimes humorous animals who have been misunderstood and abused by most yet revered and respected by many. Schwartz includes 50 stories—old and recent, true and tall—and intermingles straight factual material on the animals. . . . The sources, notes and bibliography are comprehensive." SLJ

"Softly textured, dramatically effective pencil drawings illustrates a nicely varied anthology." Bull Cent Child Books

Selsam, Millicent Ellis, 1912-
A first look at seals, sea lions, and walruses; by Millicent E. Selsam and Joyce Hunt; illustrated by Harriett Springer. Walker & Co. 1988 36p il maps $10.95; lib bdg $11.85 (1-3) **599.74**

1. Seals (Animals) 2. Walruses
ISBN 0-8027-6787-7; 0-8027-6788-5 (lib bdg) LC 87-29491

This "introduction teaches scientific classification by high-lighting the physical differences among true seals, eared seals, and walruses: flippers, ears, markings, size, tusks, whiskers, and others. . . . Except for the map, coverage is confined to the animals' physical characteristics, without facts on habitat, food, life cycle, etc." SLJ

Yoshida, Toshi, 1911-
Young lions; written and illustrated by Toshi Yoshida. Philomel Bks. 1989 unp il $14.95 (1-3) **599.74**

1. Lions
ISBN 0-399-21546-8 LC 87-29162

Companion volume to: Elephant crossing, entered in class 599.6

Original Japanese edition, 1982

"Three young lions leave the pride to attempt their first hunt. They encounter a variety of African plains animals depicted in panoramic, full-color pages. The descriptive text details their return home without success and a happy reunion with their mother." Sci Child

599.8 Primates

Selsam, Millicent Ellis, 1912-
A first look at monkeys and apes; by Millicent E. Selsam and Joyce Hunt; illustrated by Harriett Springer. Walker & Co. 1979 32p il maps lib bdg $9.85 (1-3) **599.8**

1. Monkeys 2. Apes
ISBN 0-8027-6359-6 LC 79-4701

"The authors describe characteristics which separate different monkeys by dividing them into two groups, New and Old World monkeys. Further separations and their characteristics follow." Sci Child

599.88 Apes

Goodall, Jane
The chimpanzee family book; with photographs by Michael Neugebauer. Picture Bk. Studio 1989 unp il $17.95 (3-5) **599.88**

1. Chimpanzees
ISBN 0-88708-090-1 LC 88-33359

The primatologist describes a day in the life of a chimpanzee family, noting the animals' "behavior, relationships, and interactions with other animals and with their environment." Booklist

The photographs "are both appropriate and inviting. The writing is informative and comfortable to read. Goodall combines factual events with personal reminiscence and observations." SLJ

Chimps. Atheneum Pubs. 1989 31p il map (Jane Goodall's animal world) $11.95; pa $3.95 (4-6) **599.88**

1. Chimpanzees
ISBN 0-689-31467-1; 0-689-71320-7 (pa) LC 89-6474

"A Byron Preiss book"

Introduces the physical characteristics, behavior, habitat, reproduction, and life cycle of the chimpanzee

Klingsheim, Trygve Bj

Julius; by Trygve Klingsheim; photographs by Arild Jakobsen. Delacorte Press 1987 c1986 unp il $11.95 (1-4) **599.88**

1. Chimpanzees
ISBN 0-385-29611-8 LC 87-6846

Original Norwegian edition, 1983; first English translation published 1986 in the United Kingdom

"Julius, a lovable chimpanzee, is initially rejected by his chimp family and temporarily adopted by two families affiliated with the Kristiansand Zoo in Norway." Sci Child

"The brief text is sometimes anthropomorphic in tone, but this is balanced by a lavish use of rather nice color photos. . . . The book is engaging (as is Julius himself) and empathy-building." SLJ

McClung, Robert M.

Gorilla; illustrated by Irene Brady. Morrow 1984 92p il lib bdg $12.88 (4 and up) **599.88**

1. Gorillas
ISBN 0-688-03876-X LC 84-718

This book "provides an accurate and interesting account of the natural history of gorillas in a fictional format. . . . The story follows a band of gorillas and describes their foods, movements, behaviors, and interactions with other species, especially humans. The human characters include two young scientists who are studying the gorilla band and poachers who ambush the band. . . . The book is an eloquent statement of the gorilla's precarious position in Africa and at the same time conveys a wealth of information about the animal's natural history." Sci Books Films

Includes bibliography

McNulty, Faith

With love from Koko; illustrated by Annie Cannon. Scholastic 1990 unp il $12.95 (1-3) **599.88**

1. Gorillas 2. Animal communication
ISBN 0-590-42774-1 LC 89-6183

The author records her visit with Koko, a young gorilla in California who uses sign language and who experiences many of the same feelings a child feels

"McNulty does an exceptionally find job of capturing the anticipation, fear, and excitement of her visit with Koko, and of conveying her respect for this unique creature. . . . Cannon's watercolor drawings help to capture the gentle side of Koko's personality." SLJ

Patterson, Francine

Koko's kitten; photographs by Ronald H. Cohn. Scholastic 1985 unp il $9.95; pa $3.95 (1-4) **599.88**

1. Gorillas 2. Cats 3. Animal communication
ISBN 0-590-33811-0; 0-590-33812-9 (pa) LC 85-2311

The real life experience of Koko, a gorilla in California who uses sign language, with a young kitten whom she loved and grieved over when it died

"Children will empathize with Koko's feelings of love and later grief when her kitten All Ball is killed. And like Koko, they will experience a sense of well-being when, over the mourning, Koko establishes a new and loving relationship with Lipstick, her new kitten." Read Teach

Koko's story; photographs by Ronald H. Cohn. Scholastic 1987 unp il $10.95; pa $4.95 (1-4) **599.88**

1. Gorillas 2. Animal communication
ISBN 0-590-40272-2; 0-590-41364-3 (pa)
LC 86-17717

"The author begins by describing how she first saw Koko when the gorilla was three months old; a year later, Patterson began teaching Koko sign language. Soon the gorilla was signing requests for food, and gradually her vocabulary expanded to 500 words. Also introduced is Michael, Koko's playmate and potential breeding partner. Patterson describes the gorillas' daily lives, relates amusing anecdotes, and speculates on what the future will hold for Koko and Michael. The oversize volume is profusely illustrated with color photographs." Booklist

Powzyk, Joyce Ann

Tracking wild chimpanzees in Kibira National Park; [by] Joyce Powzyk. Lothrop, Lee & Shepard Bks. 1988 32p il $13.95; lib bdg $13.88 (3-6) **599.88**

1. Chimpanzees 2. Burundi—Description and travel
ISBN 0-688-06733-6; 0-688-06734-4 (lib bdg)
LC 87-16099

The author describes her visit to the The Kibira National Park to see chimpanzees, and shares her observations of people, culture, and wildlife in Burundi as well

"Although the volume's size and appearance suggest a picture book audience, this is in fact research material for older elementary-grade readers, with information that is personalized by experience and objectified by ecological themes." Bull Cent Child Books

Includes glossary

Schlein, Miriam

Gorillas. Atheneum Pubs. 1990 31p il map (Jane Goodall's animal world) $11.95; pa $3.95 (4-6) **599.88**

1. Gorillas
ISBN 0-689-31473-6; 0-689-71396-7 (pa)
LC 89-38550

"A Byron Preiss book"

An illustrated introduction to the environment, evolution, senses, reproduction, family relationships, and ecological position of gorillas

600 TECHNOLOGY (APPLIED SCIENCES)

Cooper, Chris
How everyday things work; [by] Chris Cooper & Tony Osman. Facts on File 1984 64p il (World of science) $15.95 (5 and up) **600**

1. Technology 2. Machinery
ISBN 0-87196-988-2

"The authors present the essentials of the operation of heating/cooling systems, cameras, motion pictures, audio/video equipment, electronics and mechanical devices such as bicycles, gears, elevators, escalators and typewriters. Brief histories of some of these items are incorporated into the descriptions of how they work. Especially useful or well-done are passages on transistors, batteries, AM/FM radios, photo development and compact discs, while a few topics, such as air conditioning, tape recording and video-cassette recorders, are treated quite superficially." SLJ

Includes glossary

Folsom, Michael
The Macmillan book of how things work; by Michael Folsom and Marcia Folsom; illustrations by Brad Hamann. Macmillan 1987 80p il $15.95; pa $8.95 (4 and up) **600**

1. Technology
ISBN 0-02-735360-5; 0-689-71139-5 (pa)
LC 86-23761

An "introduction to the operation of numerous devices used about the home, office, and community. The last category includes devices used in transportation, music, and medicine." Sci Books Films

"The explanations are selectively simplified and clear, as are the labelled color drawings and diagrams in their uncluttered, two-column format." Bull Cent Child Books

Macaulay, David, 1946-
The way things work. Houghton Mifflin 1988 384p il $29.95 (5 and up) **600**

1. Technology 2. Machinery 3. Inventions
ISBN 0-395-42857-2 LC 88-11270

"There are four parts to the book: The Mechanics of Movement, Harnessing the Elements, Working with Waves, and Electricity and Automation with each part broken into subparts based on specific principles. Also included is a guide to the invention of major machines through history." Voice Youth Advocates

The author "takes the pain out of physics (a word he uses sparingly) in a busy, marvelously clever and imaginative tome. . . . His freestyle sketches (sepia-toned with splashes of color) spread lavishly across the pages and work splendidly with the text to clarify the operational principles involved." Booklist

Includes glossary

609 Technology—Historical and geographic treatment

Aaseng, Nathan, 1956-
The inventors: Nobel prizes in chemistry, physics, and medicine. Lerner Publs. 1988 79p il (Nobel Prize winners) lib bdg $11.95 (5 and up) **609**

1. Inventors 2. Inventions 3. Nobel prizes
ISBN 0-8225-0651-3 LC 87-3979

Discusses eight inventions or discoveries (X ray, radio, EKG, phase contrast microscope, transistor, radiocarbon dating, laser, and CT scan) which brought the Nobel prize to their developers

In this "book the narrative style carries the reader into a series of dramatic stories linked by common themes." Booklist

Includes glossary

Murphy, Jim, 1947-
Guess again: more weird & wacky inventions. Bradbury Press 1986 91p il $12.95 (4 and up) **609**

1. Inventions
ISBN 0-02-767720-6 LC 85-24320

Companion volume to: Weird and wacky inventions (1978)

"Murphy presents a number of unusual inventions and invites readers, through the descriptions and drawings, to guess their purpose. . . . Each of the 45 inventions is illustrated with patent drawings or magazine illustrations. Easy-to-understand explanations describe how the inventions worked (or didn't)." Booklist

Includes bibliography

610 Medical sciences. Medicine

Fradin, Dennis B.
Medicine; yesterday, today, and tomorrow; [by] Dennis Brindell Fradin. Childrens Press 1989 222p il $33.27 (6 and up) **610**

1. Medicine
ISBN 0-516-00538-3 (lib bdg) LC 88-15336

"This work surveys the history and current status of the field of medicine and makes projections for the future about such developments as genetic engineering and the conquest of disease." SLJ

The author presents "fascinating links between history, biology, and the medical profession. . . . Liberally augmented by historical art work, full-color photographs, and clear diagrams, this high-quality work also features portraits of contemporary physicians performing trailblazing research. A fine reference source for a wide range of readers." Booklist

Includes glossary and bibliography

610.69 Medical personnel

DeSantis, Kenny

A doctor's tools; photographs by Patricia A. Agre; introduction by Fred Agre. Dodd, Mead 1985 47p il lib bdg $9.95; pa $3.95 (k-2) **610.69**

1. Physicians 2. Medical care
ISBN 0-396-08516-4 (lib bdg); 0-396-08739-6 (pa)
LC 85-7026

Identifies common doctor's tools such as the stethoscope, blood pressure cuff, and thermometer, and describes how they are used and what they feel like

"This straightforward, photographic treatment of common instruments that frequently frighten children in the course of an examination will be enormously helpful to use before visiting the doctor's office. . . . Clear and to the point, from stethoscope to band-aid." Bull Cent Child Books

Kuklin, Susan

When I see my doctor. Bradbury Press 1988 unp il $12.95 (k-2) **610.69**

1. Medical care
ISBN 0-02-751232-0 LC 87-25621

Four-year-old Thomas describes his trip to the doctor for a physical checkup

"No painful procedures are included, although Thomas does have a blood test and an oral vaccination. The outstanding feature of [this book] is the photographs, which are clear, colorful, natural, and unposed." SLJ

Rockwell, Harlow, 1910-1988

My doctor. Macmillan 1973 unp il lib bdg $12.95; Harper & Row pa $3.95 (k-1) **610.69**

1. Physicians 2. Medicine
ISBN 0-02-777480-5 (lib bdg); 0-06-446010-X (pa)
LC 72-92442

The author describes a child's routine examination in a doctor's office, pointing out the familiar instruments and materials used for checkups

"Satisfying and reassuring in its explicit, calm presentation of standard medical office equipment, the book is also noteworthy for avoiding stereotyped roles without blatantly advertising the fact. 'My doctor' is depicted as a woman." Horn Book

611 Human anatomy, cytology (cell biology), histology (tissue biology)

Balestrino, Philip

The skeleton inside you; illustrated by True Kelley. rev ed. Crowell 1989 32p il (Let's-read-and-find-out science bks) $12.95; lib bdg $12.89 (k-3) **611**

1. Skeleton 2. Bones
ISBN 0-690-04731-2; 0-690-04733-9 (lib bdg)
LC 88-23672

A revised and newly illustrated edition of the title first published 1971

Balestrino seeks to "explain the human skeleton: what it is and what it does for us. He tells how the 206 different bones of the skeleton are joined together, how they grow, and how they help make blood for your whole body. He also describes what happens when bones break, and how they mend." Publisher's note

"Colorful, entertaining illustrations provide an excellent supplement to the clearly written text. . . . [This] is highly recommended as an introductory science book for young children." Sci Books Films

612 Human physiology

Aliki

My feet. Crowell 1990 31p il (Let's-read-and-find-out science bks) $12.95; lib bdg $12.89 (k-3) **612**

1. Foot
ISBN 0-690-04813-0; 0-690-04815-7 (lib bdg)
LC 89-49357

"An extensive discussion of feet, through simple text and playful illustration, demonstrates their parts, relative sizes, what they do, and what they wear in different seasons. Includes a handicapped child whose crutches supplement feet." Sci Child

My hands. rev ed. Crowell 1990 32p il (Let's-read-and-find-out science bks) $12.95; lib bdg $12.89 (k-3) **612**

1. Hand
ISBN 0-690-04878-5; 0-690-04880-7 (lib bdg)
LC 89-49158

First published 1962

The author "calls attention to hand structure—fingers, nails, an opposable thumb—and the special ways we use our hands to carry on everyday activities. . . . The jaunty illustrations and simple but efficient text combine for a fresh take on some very basic information." Booklist

Brenner, Barbara

Bodies; with photographs and design by George Ancona. Dutton 1973 unp il $13.95 (k-2) **612**

1. Physiology 2. Anatomy, Human
ISBN 0-525-26770-0 LC 72-89838

This book tells what human bodies are made of, how they differ from other things, how they function, what activities they perform, and how each individual body is unique

"The crisp, skillfully assembled photographs (including two of undressed children and one of a child sitting on a toilet) are matched by the text which is mature in tone and presents factual material without condescension." Libr J

Bruun, Ruth Dowling

The human body; by Ruth Dowling Bruun and Bertel Bruun; illustrated by Patricia J. Wynne. Random House 1982 96p il lib bdg $11.99; pa $10.95 (4 and up) **612**

1. Anatomy, Human 2. Physiology
ISBN 0-394-94424-0 (lib bdg); 0-394-84424-6 (pa)
LC 82-5210

This book "describes the various areas of the body (head, torso, etc.) and follows with descriptions of the body's systems (skeletal, muscular, digestive, reproductive, etc.)." SLJ

"The illustrations are large and well labeled. . . . The book makes good use of analogies. . . . The layout is excellent. Text and related illustrations always appear on the same or facing pages. The reproductive system is handled in the same style as the rest of the book. It answers all the common questions about one's own and the opposite sex without embarrassment, moralizing, or becoming controversial. There is little discussion of disease. The index is good." Voice Youth Advocates

Cole, Joanna

Cuts, breaks, bruises, and burns; how your body heals; illustrated by True Kelley. Crowell 1985 47p il $12.95; lib bdg $12.89 (3-5) **612**

1. Wounds and injuries 2. Blood 3. Physiology
ISBN 0-690-04437-2; 0-690-04438-0 (lib bdg)
LC 84-45335

Explains how specialized cells in the body function to heal simple wounds and injuries

"Cole has taken a complex subject and successfully rendered it in simple language for young readers. The excellent illustrations are fun, informative, self-explanatory, and a useful adjunct to the text. This book will be a useful addition to primary school libraries." Sci Books Films

The magic school bus inside the human body; illustrated by Bruce Degen. Scholastic 1989 unp il lib bdg $13.95; pa $3.95 (2-4) **612**

1. Physiology 2. Anatomy, Human
ISBN 0-590-41426-7 (lib bdg); 0-590-41427-5 (pa)
LC 88-3070

"Ms. Frizzle's class leaves on a trip to the science museum, but stops for a snack along the way. Arnold is left behind when his classmates reboard the bus. Meanwhile, Ms. Frizzle has miniaturized the bus and its riders. Unwittingly, Arnold swallows it. Traveling through Arnold's insides, the class visits his digestive system, arteries, lungs, heart, brain, and muscles, finally departing through his nostrils when he sneezes." Booklist

"This is an enjoyable look at factual material painlessly packaged with the ribbons and balloons of jokes and asides meant to appeal to kids. Degen's zany, busy, full-color drawings fill the pages with action and information far beyond the text." SLJ

Elting, Mary, 1909-

The Macmillan book of the human body; illustrated by Kirk Moldoff. Macmillan 1986 80p il $15.95; pa $8.95 (4 and up) **612**

1. Anatomy, Human 2. Physiology
ISBN 0-02-733440-6; 0-02-043080-9 (pa)
LC 85-24204

Describes the physical characteristics and functions of the various parts of the body

"This book presents, 'the physical characteristics and functions of the various parts of the body.' The text is actually more comprehensive than that because it includes a discussion of biological clocks and how enzymes and the immune system work. The book even closes with a sensitive treatment of human sexuality. The real kudos go to the illustrations, however, which are reproduced in full color. Not only are they delicately contrived, they are attractive and instructive." Sci Books Films

Includes glossary

Miller, Jonathan, 1934-

The human body; with three-dimensional, movable illustrations showing the workings of the human body designed by David Pelham. Viking 1983 unp il $19.95 (4 and up) **612**

1. Anatomy, Human 2. Physiology
ISBN 0-670-38605-7 LC 83-80311

"This book's six 'pop-up' semidiagrammatic representations of the skull and facial muscles, the inner ear, the torso (chest, abdomen, and muscles), the rib cage and lungs, the heart, and the upper torso (including the muscles of the arms in detail) dramatically illustrate how these parts of the body are put together and, in a limited way, how they function. The pop-ups are surrounded by explanatory text." Sci Books Films

Settel, Joanne

Why does my nose run? (and other questions kids ask about their bodies); [by] Joanne Settel, Nancy Baggett; illustrated by Linda Tunney. Atheneum Pubs. 1985 83p il $10.95; Ivy Bks. pa $3.95 (4 and up) **612**

1. Physiology 2. Anatomy, Human
ISBN 0-689-31078-1; 0-8041-0578-2 (pa)
LC 84-21549

Facts about human physiology in question-and-answer format, dealing with such phenomena as blinking, crying, burping, shivering, and sweating, as well as goose bumps, dizziness, pimples, allergies, and flat feet

"The answers are well organized, technically sound, and should satisfy even the most inquisitive child. (Some younger children may need help in interpreting some of the more complex words.) The material and format will serve parents better than science teachers; however, the book would be an excellent addition to a classroom or school library. It is a valuable springboard for discussions of subject matter that is familiar to all children." Sci Books Films

Seuling, Barbara

You can't sneeze with your eyes open & other freaky facts about the human body. Lodestar Bks. 1986 72p il $10.95; Ivy Bks. pa $2.95 (4 and up) **612**

1. Physiology 2. Anatomy, Human
ISBN 0-525-67185-4; 0-8041-0350-X (pa) LC 86-6304

This book "covers a variety of oddities about the human body. Entries are grouped by topic, covering the body in general, body systems and functions, the brain, birth and death, diseases, medical practices, and 'beliefs and curiosities.' In all, a wide range of information is covered. . . . Some of the facts are interesting and may promote a desire for further research on the topic; others are rather ho-hum. Cartoons drawn in fine line break up the text and reinforce the light tone of the book." SLJ

Silverstein, Alvin

The story of your foot; [by] Alvin Silverstein and Virginia B. Silverstein; illustrated by Greg Wenzel. Putnam 1987 80p il lib bdg $9.99 (5 and up) **612**

1. Foot
ISBN 0-399-61216-5 LC 86-12293

This introductory text examines foot anatomy, physiology, growth, and fitness

"The writing is clear and concise, with technical terms italicized and defined within the text. . . . Illustrations are nicely detailed black-and-white drawings that are appropriate and accurately labeled. A three-title bibliography is included." SLJ

The story of your hand; by Alvin Silverstein and Virginia B. Silverstein; illustrated by Greg Wenzel. Putnam 1985 79p il $9.99 (5 and up) **612**

1. Hand 2. Left- and right-handedness
ISBN 0-399-61212-2 LC 85-520

"Text and drawings present the evolution, physiology, and anatomy of the hand and its use as a tool, sense organ, and communicator." Booklist

Whitfield, Philip J.

Why do our bodies stop growing? questions about human anatomy answered by the Natural History Museum; [by] Philip Whitfield & Ruth Whitfield. Viking Kestrel 1988 95p il $16.95 (5 and up) **612**

1. Physiology 2. Anatomy, Human
ISBN 0-670-82331-7 LC 88-80669

"Questions such as Why do we get goose bumps? and How much water is in the body? offer an interesting organizational device and attention-grabber for this anatomy encyclopedia. Arranged loosely by body part—skin, bones, muscles—questions ask not only how the body functions but what hazards cigarette smoke, polluted air, and drugs taken by athletes to enhance their performances have on their athletic prowess. . . . Adroitly executed diagrams and easily scanned charts aid the clearly written paragraphs, creating a lively, enjoyable title." Booklist

612.1 Blood and circulation

Asimov, Isaac, 1920-

How did we find out about blood? illustrated by David Wool. Walker & Co. 1986 63p il $10.95; lib bdg $11.85 (5 and up) **612.1**

1. Blood
ISBN 0-8027-6647-1; 0-8027-6649-8 (lib bdg)
LC 86-15844

Traces the development of scientific knowledge about the functions of blood in the body, from beliefs held by the ancient Greeks to discoveries in more modern times

"This clearly written book, with much information packed into it, is an interesting portrayal of the history of our understanding of the heart, circulation, and the components of blood. A great deal of biology and, in particular immunology, is taught along with the fascinating historical perspective. Excellent line drawings are used for illustration." Appraisal

Parker, Steve

The heart and blood. rev ed. Watts 1989 48p il (Human body) lib bdg $12.90; pa $4.95 (4 and up) **612.1**

1. Heart 2. Blood—Circulation
ISBN 0-531-10711-6 (lib bdg); 0-531-24604-3 (pa)
LC 88-51610

First published 1982 under the authorship of Brian R. Ward

Discusses the heart, arteries, veins, blood, and other parts of the body's circulatory system and the causes and prevention of coronary heart disease

Includes glossary

Showers, Paul

A drop of blood; illustrated by Don Madden. rev ed. Crowell 1989 30p il (Let's-read-and-find-out science bks) $12.95; lib bdg $12.88; Harper & Row pa $4.50 (k-3) **612.1**

1. Blood
ISBN 0-690-04715-0; 0-690-04717-7 (lib bdg); 0-06-445090-2 (pa) LC 88-3623

First published 1967

"A simple, entertaining introduction to blood and its function. The information is basic but lively and highly readable, peppered with rhymes that reinforce the text. Simple activities are included. What really makes this book special are Madden's energetic, full-color illustrations, which are mostly depictions of a young boy and his highly expressive dog engaged in some activity related to the text. A couple of drawings of blood components are included, but the style is fully in keeping with the rest of the illustrations, light and interpretive rather than precisely detailed." SLJ

612.3 Digestion

Parker, Steve

Food and digestion. rev ed. Watts 1990 48p il (Human body) lib bdg $12.90; pa $4.95 (4 and up) **612.3**

1. Digestion
ISBN 0-531-14027-X (lib bdg); 0-531-24603-5 (pa) LC 89-36399

First published 1982 under the authorship of Brian R. Ward

An introduction to the digestive system, discussing each stage of digestion, the organs which aid in the digestive process, and the assimilation of nutrients into the body's structure

Includes glossary

Showers, Paul

What happens to a hamburger; illustrated by Anne Rockwell. rev ed. Crowell 1985 32p il (Let's-read-and-find-out science bks) $12.95; lib bdg $12.89; Harper & Row pa $4.50 (k-3) **612.3**

1. Digestion
ISBN 0-690-04426-7; 0-690-04427-5 (lib bdg); 0-06-445013-9 (pa) LC 84-45343

First published 1970

A "step-by-step explanation of digestion. . . . Pastel illustrations enliven the text. . . . Easy 'kitchen' experiments demonstrate physical and chemical changes in the food which has been eaten, and simple diagrams illustrate what happens to food in each area of the system, emphasizing that food is the source of our bodies' energy and it makes bones and muscles strong." SLJ

612.6 Reproduction, development, maturation

Andry, Andrew C.

How babies are made; by Andrew C. Andry and Steven Schepp; illustrated by Blake Hampton. Time-Life Bks. 1968 unp il o.p.; Little, Brown paperback available $8.95 (k-3) **612.6**

1. Reproduction 2. Sex education
ISBN 0-316-04227-7 (pa) LC 68-55284

"The illustrations give clear physiological information about intercourse, pregnancy and birth, and the text moves from flowers to animals to humans in a brief commentary on each illustration." AAAS Sci Book List for Child

Cole, Joanna

How you were born; by Joanna Cole. Morrow 1984 48p il $12.95; lib bdg $12.88; pa $4.95 (k-2) **612.6**

1. Pregnancy 2. Childbirth 3. Infants
ISBN 0-688-01710-X; 0-688-01709-6 (lib bdg); 0-688-05801-9 (pa) LC 83-17314

This book "about family love and the joy of birth . . . describes the development of the fetus, the birth process, and the newborn baby's first experiences as a family member." Sci Child

"Clarity and immediacy are the earmarks of this outstanding collaboration of text and photography. . . . A sure selection to help parents either answer perennial questions or prepare their children for the arrival of a new baby." Booklist

Includes bibliography

Kitzinger, Sheila, 1929-

Being born; photography by Lennart Nilsson. Grosset & Dunlap 1986 64p il $15.95 (3-5) **612.6**

1. Pregnancy 2. Fetus 3. Childbirth
ISBN 0-448-18990-9 LC 86-80513

Photographs and text describe the baby's nine-month journey from conception to birth

"An astounding photo-essay on fetal development. Microphotography shows sperm entering the ovum, then, via a fiber optic lens, the growth of the fetus from a few weeks until the infant's birth. Tiny white silhouettes of the actual size of the fetus at 30 and 37 days are juxtaposed against the enlarged fetal photographs. Subsequent stages are represented lifesize on the page, brilliant color against the glossy black page. Kitzinger's second-person text matches the pictures in wonder and delight." SLJ

Marzollo, Jean

Getting your period; a book about menstruation; illustrated by Kent Williams; introduction by Marcia Storch. Dial Bks. for Young Readers 1988 99p il $13.95; pa $6.95 (5 and up) **612.6**

1. Menstruation
ISBN 0-8037-0355-4; 0-8037-0356-2 (pa) LC 88-3986

The author "combines information on menstruation with quotations that show a reassuring range of reactions from girls who tell about their own concerns and experiences. . . . Common physical and emotional symptoms are the emphasis here, but there are brief factual references to PMS, toxic shock syndrome, and sexually transmitted diseases (including AIDS)." Bull Cent Child Books

Nourse, Alan Edward, 1928-

Menstruation; by Alan E. Nourse. rev ed. Watts 1987 79p il lib bdg $10.40 (6 and up) **612.6**

1. Menstruation
ISBN 0-531-10308-0 LC 86-24732

"A First book"

First published 1980

Discusses the menstrual cycle, abnormalities and their treatment, and the significance of menstruation in one's life

"Rather homely, simple pencil drawings quite adequately diagram the physiology and include a patient in position for a pelvic examination along with a picture of the speculum." Appraisal

Waxman, Stephanie, 1944-
What is a girl? what is a boy? Crowell 1989 unp il $10.95; lib bdg $10.89 (k-1) **612.6**

1. Sex education
ISBN 0-690-04709-6; 0-690-04711-8 (lib bdg) LC 87-36528

First published 1976 by Peace Press

Simple text and photographs explain the biological differences between males and females and illustrate the similarities between the sexes

"A simple, straightforward, cut-through-the-garbage explanation of what does — and doesn't — make a boy or a girl. The black-and-white photographs of charming children in various states of dress and undress, and the startling but to-the-point pictures of pleasant-looking nude adults, set the record straight with humor, intelligence and earthy candor." N Y Times Book Rev

612.7 Motor functions and skin (integument), hair, nails

Parker, Steve
The skeleton and movement. rev ed. Watts 1989 48p il (Human body) lib bdg $12.90; pa $4.95 (4 and up) **612.7**

1. Skeleton 2. Muscles
ISBN 0-531-10709-4 (lib bdg); 0-531-24606-X (pa) LC 88-51608

First published 1981 under the authorship of Brian R. Ward

This book discusses "the structure of bones and muscles; cartilage, ligaments, and tendons; the skull, the backbone, and the rib cage; and other related topics." Publisher's note

Includes glossary

612.8 Nervous functions. Sensory functions

Aliki
My five senses. rev ed. Crowell 1989 31p il (Let's-read-and-find-out science bks) $12.95; lib bdg $12.89; Harper & Row pa $4.50 (k-3) **612.8**

1. Senses and sensation
ISBN 0-690-04794-0; 0-690-04792-4 (lib bdg); 0-06-445083-X (pa) LC 88-35350

Also available HarperCollins Big book edition $19.95 (ISBN 0-06-020050-2)

First published 1962

The faculties of touch, hearing, sight, smelling and taste are introduced in relation to everyday experiences

"Each sense is used independently to observe common phenomena. Next, the author demonstrates more than one sense being used. . . . The book effectively introduced the five senses to young people." Appraisal

Berger, Melvin, 1927-
Why I cough, sneeze, shiver, hiccup, & yawn; illustrated by Holly Keller. Crowell 1983 34p il (Let's-read-and-find-out science bks) lib bdg $12.89 (k-3) **612.8**

1. Reflexes 2. Nervous system
ISBN 0-690-04254-X (lib bdg) LC 82-45587

An introduction to reflex acts that explains why we cough, sneeze, shiver, hiccup, yawn, and blink

"This book would be an excellent way to introduce children to a study of the human body, since [these] are questions that children really do ask. In finding out the answers . . . they will gain a very basic understanding of the nervous system, and can also have fun trying out such reflexes as the knee jerk or the painter reflex. The alternating black and white and colored drawings are appealing as well as informative." Appraisal

Brenner, Barbara
Faces; photographs by George Ancona. Dutton 1970 unp il lib bdg $13.95 (k-2) **612.8**

1. Senses and sensation
ISBN 0-525-29518-6 LC 70-102737

In this book, the five senses are explored through photographs and text which depict the variations in facial features and explain how ears, eyes, noses, and mouths respond

Bruun, Ruth Dowling
The brain—what it is, what it does; by Ruth Dowling Bruun and Bertel Bruun; illustrated by Peter Bruun. Greenwillow Bks. 1989 63p il $11.95; lib bdg $11.88 (1-3) **612.8**

1. Brain
ISBN 0-688-08453-2; 0-688-08454-0 (lib bdg) LC 88-21182

"A Greenwillow read-alone book"

The authors "cover what the brain is made of, how people think and learn, what constitutes intelligence and feelings, and why people sleep. The authors also warn about the effects of drugs and alcohol on the brain. The subject matter necessitates a number of difficult words, which are explained in context as well as in the glossary; however, there is no pronunciation guide. Simple line drawings dotted with orange break up the text and are surprisingly informative considering their simplicity." Booklist

Facklam, Margery
The brain; magnificent mind machine; [by] Margery and Howard Facklam; illustrated with drawings by Paul Facklam and with photographs. Harcourt Brace Jovanovich 1982 118p il $12.95 (6 and up) **612.8**

1. Brain
ISBN 0-15-211388-6 LC 81-47529

The authors trace the history of brain research and include discussions of biofeedback, memory, sleep, dreams, hypnosis and brainwashing

"Illustrations that range from an eighteenth-century

Facklam, Margery—*Continued*
engraving of scientist Galvani's laboratory to photos of CAT-scan readouts enliven the text. Glossary and bibliography appended." Booklist

Martin, Paul D., 1946-
Messengers to the brain: our fantastic five senses. National Geographic Soc. 1984 104p il $6.95; lib bdg $8.50 (5 and up) **612.8**
1. Senses and sensation 2. Brain
ISBN 0-87044-499-9; 0-87044-504-9 (lib bdg)
LC 82-45636
"Books for world explorers"
This book "describes the ways in which the five human senses function to give the individual information, to furnish esthetic pleasure, to alert the brain to possible danger, to contribute in many ways to the coordinated functions of the human body." Bull Cent Child Books
"The illustrations complement the text and include electron micrographs, biological photographs, computer graphics and diagrams. Throughout, peripheral sensory structures and the corresponding color-coded analytical centers in the brain are depicted; this feature will help students visualize the main theme while focusing on the detailed material in each chapter." Sci Books Films
Includes glossary and bibliography

Parker, Steve
The brain and nervous system. rev ed. Watts 1990 48p il (Human body) lib bdg $12.90 (4 and up) **612.8**
1. Brain 2. Nervous system
ISBN 0-531-14026-1 LC 89-36486
First published 1981 under the authorship of Brian R. Ward
"Parker describes the control system of the body: its structure and function, sleep mechanism, reflexes and autonomic nervous system, and the two brain hemispheres. He also touches on memory, mental health, and aging." SLJ
Includes bibliography

The ear and hearing. rev ed. Watts 1989 40p il (Human body) lib bdg $12.90; pa $4.95 (4 and up) **612.8**
1. Ear 2. Hearing
ISBN 0-531-10712-4 (lib bdg); 0-531-24601-9 (pa)
LC 88-51611
First published 1981 under the authorship of Brain R. Ward
Examines the anatomy of the ear, how the ear receives sounds and transfers them to the brain, how to protect our hearing, and current developments in hearing aids and surgery
Includes glossary

The eye and seeing. rev ed. Watts 1989 48p il (Human body) lib bdg $12.90; pa $4.95 (4 and up) **612.8**
1. Eye 2. Vision
ISBN 0-531-10654-3 (lib bdg); 0-531-24602-7 (pa)
LC 88-51606
First published 1982 under the authorship of Brain R. Ward
The author discusses the structure of the eye and how we see; how the lens provides an image on the retina; the functions of rods and cones; and defects of vision, eyeglasses, contact lens, colorblindness, etc.
Includes glossary

Touch, taste and smell. rev ed. Watts 1989 40p il (Human body) lib bdg $12.90; pa $4.95 (4 and up) **612.8**
1. Touch 2. Taste 3. Smell
ISBN 0-531-10655-1 (lib bdg); 0-531-24607-8 (pa)
LC 88-51607
First published 1982 under the authorship of Brian R. Ward
The book "explains the physiological process at work in each of these sensations, including identification of the organs involved and descriptions of how they transmit their vital information to the brain." Booklist
Includes glossary

Sharp, Pat
Brain power! secrets of a winning team; illustrated by Martha Weston. Lothrop, Lee & Shepard Bks. 1984 56p il $10.25; lib bdg $9.55 (4 and up) **612.8**
1. Brain
ISBN 0-688-02679-6; 0-688-02680-X (lib bdg)
LC 83-14896
A "basic explanation of what the brain does and how it carries on its work. [The author] describes the scope of the brain's control of body functions, enumerates its parts, and explains what their specific jobs are." Booklist
The author "uses a chatty, game-oriented approach and amusing two-color drawings. . . . The book includes all of the basic information one would expect in such a title." Appraisal

Showers, Paul
Ears are for hearing; illustrated by Holly Keller. Crowell 1990 32p il (Let's-read-and-find-out science bks) $12.95; lib bdg $12.89 (k-3) **612.8**
1. Hearing 2. Ear
ISBN 0-690-04718-5; 0-690-04720-7 (lib bdg)
LC 89-17479
This book covers "the anatomy and function of the ear . . . detailing the mechanics of hearing, the role of the inner ear in balance, and cause of hearing loss." SLJ
"The illustrator has supplied good diagrams and peopled the book with perky characters to help the reader understand how sound travels through the ear to send messages to the brain." Horn Book

Silverstein, Alvin
World of the brain; [by] Alvin and Virginia Silverstein; illustrated by Warren Budd. Morrow 1986 197p il lib bdg $12.95 (6 and up) **612.8**
1. Brain 2. Nervous system
ISBN 0-688-05777-2 LC 85-31007

Silverstein, Alvin—*Continued*

Describes the physical structure and functions of the brain and the nervous system. Also discusses various mental disorders, their causes, and their treatment

"This is a fine book covering all of the major areas of basic research regarding the brain. Not only are topics discussed in considerable depth, . . . but many clear, concise examples of processes and behavior are given to further elucidate the text." Appraisal

Stafford, Patricia

Your two brains; illustrated by Linda Tunney. Atheneum Pubs. 1986 75p il $11.95 (5 and up) **612.8**

1. Brain

ISBN 0-689-31142-7 LC 85-28575

A simple explanation of the separate function of each half of the brain describing what each half does, how they work together, and how one can achieve whole brain thinking

"There are discussions of right- and left-handedness and genius, and well-known but accurately presented descriptions of highly creative, famous individuals add to the usefulness of this little gem." Sci Books Films

Includes glossary and bibliography

613 Promotion of health

Brown, Laurene Krasny

Dinosaurs alive and well!: a guide to good health; [by] Laurie Krasny Brown, Marc Brown. Little, Brown 1990 32p il $14.95 (k-3) **613**

1. Health

ISBN 0-316-10998-3 LC 89-37182

The authors present advice on nutrition, hygiene, exercise, first aid, and ways of handling stress

"A liberal mix of humorous dinosaurs and lively text create a unique treatment in health education. . . . Frequent exposure to this book will help children realize the ultimate goal—that of staying healthy and feeling good about themselves. An upbeat mood pervades this nonpatronizing treatment of an otherwise 'doesn't-everybody-know-that' subject. The exuberant watercolor illustrations make the book a complete success." SLJ

Shaw, Diana

Make the most of a good thing: you! Atlantic Monthly Press 1986 209p il $13.95 (5 and up) **613**

1. Adolescence 2. Health 3. Hygiene

ISBN 0-87113-039-4 LC 85-71372

Offers the adolescent girl advice on sexual changes in the body, diet and nourishment, exercise, dealing with stress, and staying healthy

"Sound and practical advice about coping with the bodily changes, confusion, and decisions of early adolescence. Written in a light style, it's a confidence builder for girls aged 10 to 14." Sci Child

Includes bibliography

613.2 Dietetics

Arnold, Caroline, 1944-

Too fat? Too thin? Do you have a choice? foreword by Tony Greenberg. Morrow 1984 100p lib bdg $11.88; pa $5.25 (6 and up) **613.2**

1. Reducing

ISBN 0-688-02780-6 (lib bdg); 0-688-02779-2 (pa) LC 83-23841

"A practical reference explains the principles of nutrition, the factors involved in eating behavior, and the underlying basis for obesity." Booklist

613.6 Promotion of health—Special topics

Brown, Marc Tolon

Dinosaurs, beware! a safety guide; [by] Marc Brown and Stephen Krensky. Little, Brown 1982 30p il $13.95; pa $5.95 (k-2) **613.6**

1. Accidents—Prevention

ISBN 0-316-11228-3; 0-316-11219-4 (pa) LC 82-15207

"An Atlantic Monthly Press book"

Illustrated by Marc Brown

Approximately sixty safety tips are demonstrated by dinosaurs in situations at home, during meals, camping, in the car, and in other familiar places

"Bright colors and the expressive antics of your average, residential dinosaur effectively illustrate a multitude of common-sense safety tips. . . . The text is clear and to the point. The presentation is non-threatening and in a more or less do's-and-don'ts style. All tips are appropriate for the intended age group." SLJ

613.7 Physical fitness

Sullivan, George, 1927-

Better weight training for boys; with photographs by Ann Hagen Griffiths. Dodd, Mead 1983 63p il hardcover o.p. paperback available $3.95 (4 and up) **613.7**

1. Weight lifting

ISBN 0-396-08293-9 (pa) LC 82-19871

The author "introduces readers to the techniques of using light weights to condition and strengthen the body, not to the sport of weight lifting. He covers the equipment which is needed, specific exercises for various parts of the body, how to set up an individual weight training program and competitive weight lifting. Plenty of black-and-white photos and line drawings fill the text. A useful book for young men needing an introduction to a training method which is also good for improving skills in various sports." SLJ

613.9 Birth control and sex hygiene

Cole, Joanna

Asking about sex and growing up; a question-and-answer book for girls and boys; illustrated by Alan Tiegreen. Morrow Junior Bks. 1988 90p il $12.95; pa $4.95 (4-6) **613.9**

1. Sex education
ISBN 0-688-06927-4; 0-688-06928-2 (pa)
LC 87-26140

"After an introduction and list of helpful books for parents and kids, Cole has grouped the questions by subject: growing up, finding out about sex, the different development of girls and boys, masturbation, crushes, intercourse, childbirth, preventing pregnancy, pregnancy, homosexuality, and protection from sexual abuse and disease. The tone of the text is straightforward but reassuring, with an emphasis on the emotional as well as the physical. Cole seems well aware that extensive information may seem too much for kids of this age, and she keeps her answers brief and to the point, a few sentences to a few paragraphs each." Bull Cent Child Books

Johnson, Eric W.

Love and sex and growing up; with illustrations by Vivien Cohen. new ed. Bantam Bks. 1990 95p il $13.99; pa $3.50 (4 and up) **613.9**

1. Sex education
ISBN 0-553-05864-9; 0-553-15800-7 (pa)
LC 89-18255

"A Bantam Skylark book"

First published 1970 by Lippincott

Describes the process of human reproduction from fertilization to birth, explains growth and sexual maturation, and discusses sexually transmitted diseases

"Notable features include an extensive glossary with pronunciations, text-page referrals, and cross-references; a multiple-choice test is provided with permission to reproduce it for class use. Working from his stated principles of individual worth, consideration, and responsibility, Johnson's presentation on the 'complicated and wonderful, but usually not perfect' aspects of love and sex merits priority purchase consideration." Booklist

People, love, sex, and families; answers to questions that preteens ask; illustrations by David Wool. Walker & Co. 1985 122p il lib bdg $14.85 (5 and up) **613.9**

1. Sex education 2. Adolescence
ISBN 0-8027-6605-6 LC 85-15381

"This book is the result of a survey conducted by Johnson, who polled 1,000 young people on what they *really* wanted to know about people, love, sex, and families. . . . Within these categories he presents information on a broad range of subjects: prejudice, sexual abuse, rape, homosexuality, venereal disease, menopause, abortion, divorce, and incest. While sexual matters are clearly important, they are not the sole focus." Booklist

"This is a good resource for those inquisitive not only about their bodies but about all the implications of being sexually active." Sci Books Films

Madaras, Lynda

The what's happening to my body? book for boys: a growing up guide for parents and sons; [by] Lynda Madaras with Dane Saavedra; drawings by Jackie Aher. new ed. Newmarket Press 1987 251p il $16.95; pa $9.95 (6 and up) **613.9**

1. Adolescence 2. Hygiene 3. Sex education
ISBN 1-55704-002-8; 0-937858-99-4 (pa)
LC 87-28116

First published 1984

Discusses the changes that take place in a boy's body during puberty, including information on the body's changing size and shape, the growth spurt, reproductive organs, pubic hair, beards, pimples, voice changes, wet dreams, and puberty in girls

"A good addition to a library's health or sex education collection." Voice Youth Advocates

Includes bibliography

The what's happening to my body? book for girls: a growing up guide for parents and daughters; [by] Lynda Madaras with Area Madaras; drawings by Claudia Ziroli and Jackie Aher. new ed. Newmarket Press 1987 269p il $16.95; pa $9.95 (6 and up) **613.9**

1. Adolescence 2. Hygiene 3. Sex education
ISBN 1-55704-001-X; 0-937858-98-6 (pa)
LC 87-28117

First published 1983 with title: What's happening to my body? A growing up guide for mothers and daughters

This is a "beginning book to help girls going through puberty understand their bodies and how they are changing and realize what they are going through is normal and part of growing up. The book is geared for girls between the ages of nine and 15 and is really one of those books that should be read by both parents and daughters and then discussed. It does give factual information and tries to present both sides of an issue making it a good addition to any school library's sex education collection." Voice Youth Advocates

Includes bibliography

614.4 Incidence of and public measures to prevent disease

Showers, Paul

No measles, no mumps for me; illustrated by Harriett Barton. Crowell 1980 33p il (Let's-read-and-find-out science bks) lib bdg $12.89 (k-3) **614.4**

1. Vaccination 2. Immunity
ISBN 0-690-04018-0 LC 79-7106

"A simple, accurate account of how immunization fights disease, how antibodies form and how they protect against infection. Within a narrative framework, a child tells readers that, unlike his grandmother who had childhood illnesses, he is protected through shots and drops.

Showers, Paul—*Continued*
Though the use of a child narrator is awkward, the text gives good concise information on a complex topic. The full-page drawings (alternating between four color and black and white) give the book a pleasant, upbeat look." SLJ

615 Pharmacology and therapeutics

Jacobs, Francine, 1935-
Breakthrough; the true story of penicillin; illustrated with photographs. Dodd, Mead 1985 128p il lib bdg $10.95 (5 and up) **615**
1. Penicillin
ISBN 0-396-08579-2 LC 84-26037
This work describes the history of penicillin from the discovery of the mold by Fleming through the years of work by such scientists as Chain, Heatley, Florey, and Sheehan who purified, tested, synthesized, and eventually presented the "miracle" drug to the world
"By capitalizing on the human aspects of the events the author lures the reader into the less spicy details of the scientific events leading to the discovery . . . [and] provides an excellent illustration of the effects of the political and economic climate on scientific progress." Appraisal
Includes bibliography

616 Diseases

Arnold, Caroline, 1944-
Pain: what is it? how do we deal with it? illustrated by Frank Schwarz. Morrow 1986 86p il $12.95; lib bdg $12.88 (6 and up) **616**
1. Pain
ISBN 0-688-05710-1; 0-688-05711-X (lib bdg) LC 85-29815
The author "begins with descriptions of different kinds of pains and of the facts that pain thresholds vary and that pain is difficult to measure. The major part of the text focuses on the ways in which pain can be controlled, alleviated, or overcome—including such measures as biofeedback, hypnosis, and surgery or acupuncture in addition to medication." Bull Cent Child Books
"More often than not, the illustrations do not add any new information to the text, but the book is clearly written and covers material not generally available for this age group." SLJ
Includes glossary

616.1 Diseases of the cardiovascular system

Silverstein, Alvin
Heart disease: America's #1 killer; [by] Alvin and Virginia B. Silverstein. New and updated. Lippincott 1985 150p il $12.95; lib bdg $12.89 (6 and up) **616.1**
1. Heart—Diseases
ISBN 0-397-32083-3; 0-397-32084-1 (lib bdg) LC 83-49495
First published 1976 by Follett
This volume includes "chapters on heart disease, heart attacks, the effects of diet and exercise, hazards to the healthy heart (including stress), diagnosing and treating heart disease, and how the chance of heart disease in young people can be lessened. . . . The text is readable. Even when material is necessarily technical, it is presented in an interesting manner. This is a very good sourcebook." Appraisal

616.4 Diabetes

Tiger, Steven
Diabetes; illustrated by Michael Reingold. Messner 1987 63p il (Understanding disease ser) lib bdg $11.98 (5 and up) **616.4**
1. Diabetes
ISBN 0-671-63273-6 LC 86-23498
This book discusses "diabetes, its history, victims, treatment, and current developments in research. Diabetes Types I and II are examined as aberrations of the metabolic process, . . . followed by mention of the lesser types, including diabetes during pregnancy, hyperglycemia, and hypoglycemia. Symptoms and diagnosis, current treatment, and the outlook for the disease conclude the text." SLJ
Includes glossary

616.7 Diseases of the musculoskeletal system

Anderson, Madelyn Klein
Arthritis. Watts 1989 93p il lib bdg $12.40 (5 and up) **616.7**
1. Arthritis
ISBN 0-531-10801-5 LC 89-5745
"A Venture book"
The author discusses the many different types of arthritis, what causes them, how they are treated, and how people learn to cope with them
"Although arthritis is commonly thought of as attacking the aged, Anderson makes it clear that young people are affected as well. By outlining widely varied types of the disease—including degenerative, inflammatory, infective, and metabolic —Anderson presents a serviceable overview of symptoms and treatments." Bull Cent Child Books
Includes glossary

616.8 Diseases of the nervous system and mental disorders

Beckelman, Laurie

Alzheimer's disease; consultant, Elaine Wynne. Crestwood House 1990 48p il (Facts about) $10.95 (4-6) **616.8**

1. Alzheimer's disease
ISBN 0-89686-489-8 LC 89-25251

"A simple, effective presentation of facts and misconceptions about the mysterious brain disease that afflicts a large number of the elderly. Discusses diagnosis, care, and treatment through a first-person narrative detailing the author's experiences with her grandmother. An appropriate starting point for discussion of a difficult family situation. Includes a listing of resource organizations." Sci Child

Includes glossary

Frank, Julia

Alzheimer's disease; the silent epidemic. Lerner Publs. 1985 80p il lib bdg $9.95 (6 and up) **616.8**

1. Alzheimer's disease
ISBN 0-8225-1578-4 LC 84-23320

This book presents "a case study of Sarah, a mother and grandmother who slowly loses her mental capabilities, while describing the pressures this puts on the patient and the family who cares for her. Aided by diagrams, the text explains the physiological processes of Alzheimer's and details how the disease is diagnosed and the steps that are being taken to find a cure. . . . This does not make for pleasant or even hopeful reading, but it is a sound introduction to a problem that will continue to face numerous families." Booklist

Landau, Elaine

Alzheimer's disease. Watts 1987 67p il lib bdg $10.40 (5 and up) **616.8**

1. Alzheimer's disease
ISBN 0-531-10376-5 LC 87-2095

"A First book"

Discusses this degenerative disease of the nervous system, its effect on the patient's family members, and suggestions for coping and care

"Much of the information presented is anecdotal, with family members of Alzheimer's patients relating their own stories. It makes for interesting reading, and much useful information is imparted in the process." SLJ

Includes bibliography

616.86 Substance abuse (Drug abuse)

Friedman, David P.

Focus on drugs and the brain; illustrated by David Neuhaus. 21st Cent. Bks. (Frederick) 1990 64p il (Drug-alert bk) $14.95 (3-6) **616.86**

1. Drugs 2. Drug abuse 3. Psychotropic drugs
ISBN 0-941477-95-9 LC 89-28417

The author begins "by defining psychoactive drugs—those that change the way people think, feel, or behave—and explaining why people use them. He then describes the function of the brain and nervous system and delineates how these drugs affect the body. The author also provides information on addiction and drug treatment." Booklist

This book "provides a fine introduction to the topic of licit and illicit drugs. It explains enough about brain function so that young people will understand why psychoactive drugs are so pleasureable and potentially dangerous." Appraisal

Includes glossary

Hyde, Margaret Oldroyd, 1917-

Alcohol: uses and abuses; [by] Margaret O. Hyde. Enslow Pubs. 1988 96p il lib bdg $14.95 (6 and up) **616.86**

1. Alcohol 2. Alcoholism
ISBN 0-89490-155-9 LC 87-12161

The author "describes the medical and social problems that alcohol causes alcoholics and the community in which they live. . . . Using hypothetical cases and simulated situations, she equips readers with information on how to get help for the alcoholic, how to get help for themselves as children of alcoholics, and how to act in social situations, emphasizing that sometimes there are no right answers and that not all stories have a happy ending." SLJ

"It is factual, yet interesting, due to its many vignettes of young peoples' experiences with alcohol. This book is also non-judgmental and extremely accurate and up-to-date with its information." BAYA Book Rev

Includes glossary and bibliography

Know about drugs; [by] Margaret O. Hyde; illustrated by Susan Greenstein. 3rd ed. Walker & Co. 1990 76p il $12.95; lib bdg $13.85 (4 and up) **616.86**

1. Drug abuse 2. Drugs
ISBN 0-8027-6922-5; 0-8027-6923-3 (lib bdg)
LC 89-71380

First published 1971

"Includes general information on drugs and drug abuse, followed by more specific information on a variety of drugs including alcohol, nicotine, marijuana, and cocaine. The final chapters suggest ways to say no and how to feel good without drugs. The book is well organized, with a lot of concise, useful information packed into each page." Voice Youth Advocates

Hyde, Margaret Oldroyd, 1917-—*Continued*

Know about smoking; [by] Margaret O. Hyde; illustrated by Dennis Kendrick. rev ed. Walker & Co. 1990 80p il $12.95; lib bdg $13.85 (4 and up) **616.86**

1. Smoking
ISBN 0-8027-6924-1; 0-8027-6926-8 (lib bdg) LC 89-25022

First published 1983

"Various aspects of smoking are treated in a straightforward, no-frills style: how not to start; smokers vs. nonsmokers, cigarette advertising, smokeless tobacco (including snuff and chewing tobacco), and the difficulties of quitting. . . . This is a rather simplistic overview . . . useful for a basic introduction." Voice Youth Advocates

Perry, Robert Louis, 1950-

Focus on nicotine and caffeine; [by] Robert Perry; illustrated by David Neuhaus. 21st Cent. Bks. (Frederick) 1990 64p il (Drug-alert bk) $14.95 (3-6) **616.86**

1. Smoking 2. Caffeine
ISBN 0-941477-99-1 LC 89-20409

The author discusses the history, effects, social aspects, and physical dangers of using tobacco and caffeine products

"An excellent resource for teachers in the elementary grades." Sci Books Films

Seixas, Judith S.

Drugs—what they are, what they do; illustrated by Tom Huffman. Greenwillow Bks. 1987 47p il $10.25; lib bdg $10.88 (1-3) **616.86**

1. Drugs 2. Drug abuse
ISBN 0-688-07399-9; 0-688-07400-6 (lib bdg) LC 86-33624

"A Greenwillow read-alone book"

This book "begins with a definition of drugs and [seeks to] explain such topics as drug tolerance, and what factors can influence the effect of a drug on a person. The test focuses on psychoactive drugs like stimulants and hallucinogens." Appraisal

"The book's organization helps take the reader on a journey through readable text and clever illustrations about the different kinds of psychoactive drugs, how they are used, how they make one feel, and what their effects are. There is also an important chapter on 'How to Say No,' giving the reader many appropriate responses if asked to try drugs. It is important that young children be educated through excellent books of this type on the hazards and consequences of drug use." Sci Books Films

Tobacco; what it is, what it does; illustrated by Tom Huffman. Greenwillow Bks. 1981 55p il $12.95 (1-3) **616.86**

1. Smoking
ISBN 0-688-00769-4 LC 81-837

"A Greenwillow read-alone book"

The text begins with "a brief geographical history of tobacco, then concentrates on cigarette smoking in particular; its social history, consequences for health and the psychological factors involved in starting and stopping. The antismoking case, is well-documented with many physiological explanations, and though the cartoonlike line drawings and diagrams are not detailed . . . this emerges as a well-reasoned argument and a useful source of information." SLJ

Stwertka, Eve

Marijuana; by Eve and Albert Stwertka. rev ed. Watts 1986 64p il lib bdg $10.40 (5 and up) **616.86**

1. Marijuana
ISBN 0-531-10122-3 LC 85-22526

"A First book"

First published 1979

"This comprehensive description of marijuana includes a history of its use, its appearance while growing, its effects on body and mind, and a careful discussion about its legalization." Sci Child

Includes glossary and bibliography

Ward, Brian R.

Smoking and health. Watts 1986 48p il (Life guides) lib bdg $12.40 (4 and up) **616.86**

1. Smoking
ISBN 0-531-10180-0 LC 85-52043

The author "describes how tobacco affects different aspects of the body, financial cost to the community because of absenteeism, and the different forms of tobacco that are grown and used worldwide." Booklist

"Each chapter of the book is brief, the print is large, the pictures are bright, and the pages are oversize. The design and style are obviously to entice younger readers. . . . The concluding chapter, stating why the author considers smoking a moral problem, could provide the basis for a thoughful discussion with students of any age." Voice Youth Advocates

Includes glossary

Woods, Geraldine, 1948-

Drug use and drug abuse. rev ed. Watts 1986 64p il lib bdg $10.40 (4 and up) **616.86**

1. Drug abuse 2. Drugs
ISBN 0-531-10114-2 LC 85-22531

"A First book"

First published 1979

"Woods presents a factual introduction to drugs—both legitimate use and illegal abuse. Included are discussions of over-the-counter drugs and prescribed medications, but more completely, problems associated with recreational drug consumption. The nature of addiction in relation to marijuana, cocaine, uppers and downers, narcotics, LSD and other hallucinogens, as well as tobacco and alcohol, are presented." SLJ

"Interesting, and very useful overview of the serious antisocial activity of drug abuse." Sci Books Films

Includes glossary and bibliography

616.9 Other diseases

Berger, Melvin, 1927-
Germs make me sick! illustrated by Marylin Hafner. Crowell 1985 32p il (Let's-read-and-find-out science bks) $12.95; lib bdg $12.89; Harper & Row pa $4.50 (k-3) **616.9**

1. Bacteriology 2. Viruses
ISBN 0-690-04428-3; 0-690-04429-1 (lib bdg); 0-06-445053-8 (pa) LC 84-45334

The text explains "how bacteria and viruses affect human beings, how their presence is detected by doctors, and what can be done to cure or alleviate the damage they cause. The book concludes with a few basic rules for maintaining good health." Bull Cent Child Books

"Sprightly and expressive drawings of contemporary children in familiar scenes . . . emphasize the part germs can play in everyday life." Horn Book

Landau, Elaine
Lyme disease. Watts 1990 63p il lib bdg $10.90 (4 and up) **616.9**

1. Lyme disease
ISBN 0-531-10931-3 LC 89-70514

"A First book"

The author examines topics such as "the tick that causes the disease, its life cycle, and the ways in which it infects and affects human beings and other life forms; she discusses symptoms, progress of Lyme disease, and treatment, and . . . current measures of prevention and of diagnosis." Bull Cent Child Books

This "book provides [a] clear introduction to the disease. . . . Landau keeps to basics. . . . Plentiful photographs support the text and the book's design is handsome." Booklist

Includes glossary and bibliography

Patent, Dorothy Hinshaw
Germs! Holiday House 1983 40p il lib bdg $12.95 (4 and up) **616.9**

1. Communicable diseases 2. Immunity
ISBN 0-8234-0481-1 LC 82-48749

"Explains what germs are, how they attack the body, and how the body protects itself against their onslaught. Includes material on immunization and research in disease control. Clear text supported by an attractive format and many exceptional photographs, including some of very high magnification and a sequence revealing how an anti-biotic kills bacteria. Concludes with a brief discussion of future problems and hopes." Sci Child

Silverstein, Alvin
Lyme disease, the great imitator; how to prevent and cure it; by Alvin Silverstein, Virginia Silverstein & Robert Silverstein; with a foreword by Leonard H. Sigal. AVSTAR Pub. Corp. 1990 126p il lib bdg $12.95; pa $5.95 (6 and up) **616.9**

1. Lyme disease
ISBN 0-9623653-8-6 (lib bdg); 0-9623653-9-4 (pa) LC 90-81250

Discusses the scope and history of this growing health problem, its medical and ecological background, symptoms, diagnosis, treatment, practical methods for avoiding infection, and current research into possible cures

Includes glossary and bibliography

616.97 Diseases of the immune system

Hausherr, Rosmarie
Children and the AIDS virus; a book for children, parents, & teachers. Clarion Bks. 1989 48p il lib bdg $13.95; pa $4.95 (1-3) **616.97**

1. AIDS (Disease)
ISBN 0-89919-834-1 (lib bdg); 0-395-51167-4 (pa) LC 88-39196

In this book the author seeks to explain what a virus is, how the AIDS virus affects the body, and how it is contracted. She examines the lives of two children who have AIDS

"With thoughtfully composed black-and-white photos attractively placed throughout, Hausherr's text forthrightly and nonthreateningly fosters schoolchildren's understanding of AIDS." Booklist

Includes bibliography

Silverstein, Alvin
Learning about AIDS; [by] Alvin and Virginia Silverstein. Enslow Pubs. 1989 64p il lib bdg $13.95 (4-6) **616.97**

1. AIDS (Disease)
ISBN 0-89490-176-1 LC 87-24373

The authors provide an introduction to the causes and treatment of AIDS

"An informative text is marred by dull and useless gray drawings. Wide spacing makes for easy reading, and no knowledge of the body is assumed. Technical terms are explained in the short glossary." SLJ

616.99 Tumors and cancers

Bergman, Thomas
One day at a time; children living with leukemia. Gareth Stevens Children's Bks. 1989 56p il (Don't turn away) lib bdg $9.95 (1-3) **616.99**

1. Leukemia
ISBN 1-55532-913-6 LC 88-42972

Bergman, Thomas—*Continued*

This book records in photographs and text, some of the experiences of leukemia patients Hanna and Frederick, ages 2 and three. Appended are a question and answer section

"Noted Swedish photographer, Bergman . . . looks unflinchingly at children who have had to cope with difficulties most people can only imagine; yet there's not a trace of condescension—only a sense of caring and an affirmation of life. . . . Uniquely informative and will push readers to reexamine their own feelings about seriously disabled individuals." Booklist

Includes glossary and bibliography

Monroe, Judy

Leukemia. Crestwood House 1990 48p il (Facts about) lib bdg $10.95 (4-6) **616.99**

1. Leukemia

ISBN 0-89686-532-0 LC 90-33663

Describes childhood leukemia, its symptoms, characteristics, and the history of its discovery. Examines the progress that has been made in treating the disease

"Concise, well formatted, and [covers] many aspects of the [topic]. . . . Also great introductory material for older readers with no background in the subject." SLJ

Includes glossary

Silverstein, Alvin

Cancer: can it be stopped? [by] Alvin and Virginia B. Silverstein. new rev ed. Lippincott 1987 153p il $12.95; lib bdg $12.89 (6 and up) **616.99**

1. Cancer

ISBN 0-397-32202-X; 0-397-32203-8 (lib bdg)

LC 86-45500

First published 1972 by Day

Explains the various forms of cancer, their symptoms, possible causes, and treatment; and discusses research being conducted to find better means of preventing, detecting, treating, and curing this disease

Includes bibliography

617.6 Dentistry

Betancourt, Jeanne, 1941-

Smile! how to cope with braces; illustrated by Mimi Harrison. Knopf 1982 87p il lib bdg $10.99; pa $5.95 (4 and up) **617.6**

1. Orthodontics

ISBN 0-394-94732-0 (lib bdg); 0-394-84732-6 (pa)

LC 81-11800

General information and practical advice for people who are having their teeth straightened. Discusses the causes of crooked teeth and how to cope with the problems of wearing braces

DeSantis, Kenny

A dentist's tools; photographs by Patricia A. Agre; introduction by Bruce E. Golden. Dodd, Mead 1988 47p il $10.95; pa $4.95 (k-2) **617.6**

1. Dentistry

ISBN 0-396-09043-5; 0-396-09044-3 (pa)

LC 87-36505

Introduces the tools a dentist uses to inspect, clean, polish, and repair teeth

"Here a simply written text, clear photographs that are well-placed in relation to the text and that are adequately labelled, and neat organization . . . keep the information sequential and pertinent. The photographs show men and women as dentists, the patients are racially diverse. At best, reassuring; in any case, useful." Bull Cent Child Books

Kuklin, Susan

When I see my dentist. Bradbury Press 1988 unp il $12.95 (k-2) **617.6**

1. Dentistry

ISBN 0-02-751231-2 LC 87-25695

"Erica's trip to the dentist includes visiting his assistant for teeth cleaning, a brushing lesson, and an explanation of how sugar harms teeth. As Dr. Steve examines and x-rays her teeth, he explains every procedure to Erica." Booklist

"Kuklin has included rather serious-looking pictures with less formal moments; this accounts for her reassuring tone, which neither white-washes the truth nor makes the visit sound too scary." Publ Wkly

Rockwell, Harlow, 1910-1988

My dentist. Greenwillow Bks. 1975 unp il $12.95; lib bdg $12.88 (k-1) **617.6**

1. Dentistry

ISBN 0-688-80011-4; 0-688-84004-3 (lib bdg)

LC 75-6974

This is a "straightforward run-through of a routine trip to the dentist. A young patient describes each of the pieces of standard dental equipment she sees on her visit and explains how her dentist uses them." SLJ

"Because of the simple, restrained format, and because of the precise, detailed illustrations, the author-illustrator has been able to turn what can be a frightening experience for a child into an understandable, necessary event." Horn Book

Rogers, Fred

Going to the dentist; photographs by Jim Judkis. Putnam 1989 unp il $13.95; pa $5.95 (k-2) **617.6**

1. Dentistry

ISBN 0-399-21636-7; 0-399-21634-0 (pa)

LC 88-15045

This work describes a visit to the dentist and the procedures and equipment which will be encountered during a dental examination

"The attractively photographed volume features young patients and dentists in a happy mix of races and genders, and timely inclusion of the now standard gloves

Rogers, Fred—*Continued*
and masks worn by staff sets this book apart." Horn Book

Ward, Brian R.
Dental care. Watts 1986 48p il (Life guides) lib bdg $12.40 (4 and up) **617.6**

1. Teeth
ISBN 0-531-10179-7 LC 85-52044

This book "outlines the makeup and function of each type of tooth, and explains decay and gum disease. Preventive dental care and the effects of sugar and diet are studied and modern dental repair is examined." SLJ

"Information and advice useful for both school reports and personal reading in an attractively illustrated, invitingly designed book. . . . Specialized vocabulary is highlighted in boldface type and defined in a forty-one word glossary. Superior diagrams augment a large-print text." Appraisal

617.7 Ophthalmology

Silverstein, Alvin
Glasses and contact lenses; your guide to glasses, eye wear, and eye care; [by] Alvin & Virginia B. Silverstein. Lippincott 1989 135p il $12.95; lib bdg $12.89 (6 and up) **617.7**

1. Eyeglasses 2. Contact lenses
ISBN 0-397-32184-8; 0-397-32185-6 (lib bdg)
LC 88-13026

"A well-written text explains the structure of the eye, how it works, and how glasses and contact lenses help to correct vision problems. Includes discussion of special lenses and surgery as well as how to properly care for your eyes." Sci Child

Includes bibliography

617.8 Otology and audiology

Levine, Edna Simon, 1910-
Lisa and her soundless world; by Edna S. Levine; illustrated by Gloria Kamen. Human Sciences Press 1974 unp il $16.95; pa $9.95 (1-3) **617.8**

1. Deafness 2. Deaf
ISBN 0-87705-104-6; 0-89885-204-8 (pa)
LC 73-14819

This explanation of deafness and the deaf child's predicament follows the progress of a little girl with impaired hearing who gains some hearing by using a hearing aid and learns to lip read and use speech

"The book accomplishes several things: it makes the deaf child's plight explicit, it makes clear the difficulty a deaf child has in learning to speak, it explains why a child so handicapped may feel angry and unloved, and it stresses the fact that the halting speech of the deaf may be governed by physical limitations, that it is not due to a lack of intelligence." Bull Cent Child Books

Litchfield, Ada Bassett
A button in her ear; by Ada B. Litchfield; pictures by Eleanor Mill. Whitman, A. 1976 unp il lib bdg $12.95 (1-3) **617.8**

1. Hearing aids 2. Deafness
ISBN 0-8075-0987-6 LC 75-28390

"Concept book"

"As the story follows Angela from her handicap-caused confusion through her hearing test and eventually to her adjustment to her new hearing aid, the reader is informed as well as warmed by the inner feelings of the child experiencing the hearing loss. A hearing aid is shown to be as acceptable as eye glasses. This book should be required reading for all children with hearing loss as well as their families, friends and classmates." Sci Books Films

"Although this is a 'problem' book, the problem is treated creatively. There is a lightness and subtle humor about the statements which are misinterpreted by Angela and by her decision to turn down her hearing aid when she chooses 'not' to hear something. This book may help the thousands of deaf and hard of hearing children develop a positive attitude toward their hearing aids." Child Book Rev Serv

617.9 Geriatric, pediatric, military, plastic surgery, transplantation of tissue and organs, anesthesiology

Beckelman, Laurie
Transplants. Crestwood House 1990 48p il (Facts about) lib bdg $10.95 (4-6) **617.9**

1. Transplantation of organs, tissues, etc.
ISBN 0-89686-572-X LC 90-33665

Discusses recent advances in human organ transplantation, describes techniques of transplant surgery, explains how agencies match organ donors and recipients, and profiles the experiences of a teenaged recipient of a new heart

"Well written, explicit, and appropriate to the age level. The full-color photographs are excellent and well captioned." SLJ

620 Engineering and allied operations

Weitzman, David L.
Windmills, bridges & old machines; discovering our industrial past; by David Weitzman. Scribner 1982 114p il $15.95 (5 and up) **620**

1. Windmills—History 2. Bridges—History 3. Machinery—History
ISBN 0-684-17456-1 LC 82-3231

"Early furnaces, engines, bridges, locomotives, canals, and foundries are examined through text, sharp photographs, and clear diagrams, with old relics still in evidence as a focal point. The author discusses their use, importance and disappearance including a lot of fascinating trivia along the way." Booklist

621.31 Generation, modification, storage, transmission of electric power

Cobb, Vicki

More power to you; illustrated by Bill Ogden. Little, Brown 1986 50p il (How the world works) lib bdg $11.95 (4-6) **621.31**

1. Electric power
ISBN 0-316-14899-7 LC 85-23926

Explains electric power and other forms of power, answering such questions as "How does electric power make a light turn on?" Includes experiments and tricks

"As Cobb informs she challenges her audience to think beyond the basic details. This, combined with the experiments at the end . . . makes readers active participants." SLJ

621.381 Electronics

Asimov, Isaac, 1920-

How did we find out about microwaves? illustrated by Erika Kors. Walker & Co. 1989 63p il $10.95; lib bdg $12.85 (5 and up) **621.381**

1. Microwaves
ISBN 0-8027-6837-7; 0-8027-6838-5 (lib bdg) LC 88-20470

Describes the discovery of microwaves and explains how they function and their many uses

"An excellent summary of how scientists gradually made discoveries about microwaves and how this knowledge has been used in many different ways. . . . The information is presented in a concise and fast-paced manner, yet the book is always readable, and gives young people a clear understanding of how scientific discoveries are built upon the discoveries that proceeded them." SLJ

621.44 Geothermal engineering

Jacobs, Linda

Letting off steam; the story of geothermal energy. Carolrhoda Bks. 1989 47p il (Carolrhoda earth watch bk) lib bdg $12.95; pa $6.95 (3-6) **621.44**

1. Geothermal resources 2. Steam
ISBN 0-87614-300-1 (lib bdg); 0-87614-510-1 (pa) LC 88-6147

The author examines how geothermal energy, the force underlying hot springs, geysters, and mudpots, is being used as an alternative energy source in various parts of the world

This "is an extremely interesting book. . . . Linda Jacobs has taken a relatively advanced scientific topic and made it accessible for young readers. Her format combines well-explained vocabulary with excellent photographs, diagrams, and boxed topic highlights." Appraisal

621.48 Nuclear engineering

Pringle, Laurence P.

Nuclear energy: troubled past, uncertain future. Macmillan 1989 124p il $13.95 (5 and up) **621.48**

1. Nuclear energy
ISBN 0-02-775391-3 LC 88-28664

First published 1979 with title: Nuclear power

The author looks "at nuclear energy, examining the history, development, and current status of nuclear technology—from the basic physics of splitting the atom to the search for an ultrasafe reactory—and the many changes in nuclear economics, politics, and safety that have occured in the 1980s." Publisher's note

"The information is current, in depth, and clearly presented. The physics behind nuclear reactors is explained without writing down to readers or losing them in technical jargon. . . . Highly recommended." Voice Youth Advocates

Includes glossary and bibliography

621.8 Machine engineering

Adkins, Jan

Moving heavy things; written and illustrated by Jan Adkins. Houghton Mifflin 1980 47p il lib bdg $13.95 (5 and up) **621.8**

1. Machinery 2. Mechanics
ISBN 0-395-29206-9 LC 80-464

Discusses "the science and art of moving weighty objects. Traditional principles for multiplying strength and reducing friction are cataloged along with descriptions of clever and ingenious techniques. . . . Clear, attractive and often humourous drawings enrich and increase understanding of the text." SLJ

Ancona, George, 1929-

Monster movers; photographs and text by George Ancona. Dutton 1983 48p il lib bdg $15.95 (3-5) **621.8**

1. Conveying machinery 2. Machinery
ISBN 0-525-44063-1 LC 83-5504

Describes the various kinds of huge machines used to move ores and other bulky and heavy materials from one place to another

Ancona mixes "striking photographs, a lucid text and a fascinating subject with winning results. . . . The juxtaposition of photos and text is well done and the captions are an aid to readers." SLJ

Hoban, Tana

Dig, drill, dump, fill. Greenwillow Bks. 1975 unp il $13.88 (k-2) **621.8**

1. Machinery—Pictorial works
ISBN 0-688-84016-7 LC 75-11987

"This all-photographic presentation shows loaders, rollers, dump trucks, and other heavy construction machines at work. What they are and what they do are explained simply and concisely in a three-page picture glossary." Publisher's note

Marston, Hope Irvin, 1935-

Load lifters: derricks, cranes, and helicopters. Dodd, Mead 1988 64p il $13.95 (3-6) **621.8**

1. Hoisting machinery 2. Cranes, derricks, etc.
ISBN 0-396-09226-8 LC 87-27195

Introduces hoists, derricks, cranes, helicopters and other machines that lift heavy loads

"The book moves from labeled drawings of the lifters to clear, mostly full-color photographs of guy derricks, tower cranes, and Super Stallion helicopters. . . . Although chapter divisions might have helped to organize this study of hoisting equipment, the natural high interest of the topic will more than make up for any weakness, especially with reluctant readers thrilled by things mechanical." Booklist

Rockwell, Anne F., 1934-

Machines; by Anne & Harlow Rockwell. Macmillan 1972 unp il lib bdg $12.95; Harper & Row pa $3.95 (k-1) **621.8**

1. Machinery
ISBN 0-02-777520-8 (lib bdg); 0-06-446009-6 (pa)
LC 72-185149

This book describes machines and machine parts: pulley, block and tackle, gear, jackscrew, sprocket

"One of the highlights of the book is the use of full-color watercolor paintings as illustrations of the types of machines. Large primary print is used describing the simple machines such as the wheel or gears." Sci Books

Stephen, R. J.

Cranes. Watts 1986 32p il lib bdg $11.40 (2-4) **621.8**

1. Cranes, derricks, etc.
ISBN 0-531-10183-5 LC 85-42089

"Picture library"

This book explains how cranes lift and move heavy objects and how they are used in such places as construction sites, docks, factories, warehouses, and railroads

Employing "clear color photographs and briskly informative, simple text . . . [the book] will prove irresistible to browsing young machinists." Bull Cent Child Books

Weiss, Harvey

Machines and how they work; written and illustrated by Harvey Weiss. Crowell 1983 80p il lib bdg $12.89 (4 and up) **621.8**

1. Machinery
ISBN 0-690-04300-7 LC 82-45925

"Describes how six simple machines—the lever, inclined plane, screw, wedge, wheel-and-axle, and pulley—serve human needs. Provides well-organized information about each machine in both the text and the informative, frequently humorous drawings. Includes suggestions for simple machines older children can make." Sci Child

Zubrowski, Bernie, 1939-

Wheels at work; building and experimenting with models of machines; illustrated by Roy Doty. Morrow 1986 112p il lib bdg $11.88; pa $6.95 (4-6) **621.8**

1. Machinery 2. Wheels 3. Science—Experiments
ISBN 0-688-06348-9 (lib bdg); 0-688-06349-7 (pa)
LC 86-12500

"A Boston Children's Museum activity book"

Instructions for using readily available materials to make models of machines such as pulleys, windlasses, and water wheels, with suggested experiments to demonstrate their capabilities

"Since most models have more than one easily adjusted variation, this book is great vacation-time fun for mechanically minded young people. An adult might need to help with hammering a hole in one model and puncturing holes (in soft materials) in others, giving parents and children an opportunity to explore simple physics together. An invaluable resource book." SLJ

621.9 Tools and fabricating equipment

Gibbons, Gail

Tool book. Holiday House 1982 unp il lib bdg $13.95; pa $5.95 (k-2) **621.9**

1. Tools
ISBN 0-8234-0444-7 (lib bdg); 0-8234-0694-6 (pa)
LC 81-13386

This book depicts a number of different tools used in building and the kinds of work they are used for

"Gibbons's pictures are clear, colorful, accurate, and detailed. It is simple enough to use with a toddler who has just discovered tools yet sophisticated enough for a first grader to learn about tools and their use." Child Book Rev Serv

Rockwell, Anne F., 1934-

The toolbox; by Anne & Harlow Rockwell. Macmillan 1971 unp il $12.95; Aladdin Bks. (NY) pa $3.95 (k-1) **621.9**

1. Tools
ISBN 0-02-777540-2; 0-689-71382-7 (pa)
LC 72-119836

Illustrated by Harlow Rockwell, this book describes the contents of a toolbox and explains the uses of each tool

"A picture book celebrates with unadorned economy of words and illustrations the simple beauty of useful tools. The brief text is printed in clear, handsome type; very little boys—and undoubtedly some girls as well—will pore over the appreciative portraits of common implements, which make ingenious use of watercolor to show textures and surfaces of wood and metal." Horn Book

623 Military and nautical engineering

Cummings, Richard, 1931-

Make your own model forts & castles; written and illustrated by Richard Cummings. McKay, D. 1977 122p il $8.95 (5 and up) **623**

1. Fortification—Models 2. Castles—Models
ISBN 0-679-20400-8 LC 77-3970

Discusses the construction of small-scale forts, castles, and other fortifications for use with miniature soldiers

Includes bibliography

Giblin, James, 1933-

Walls; defenses throughout history; by James Cross Giblin. Little, Brown 1984 113p il $14.95 (5 and up) **623**

1. Walls—History 2. Fortification—History
ISBN 0-316-30954-0 LC 84-15444

"The text begins with a description of a wall made from mammoth bones by hunters during the Ice Age. The author progresses through the centuries, discussing people and memorable events connected with the Walls of Jericho, Hadrian's Wall, the Maginot Line, the Great Wall of China, Carcassonne (the famous walled French city) and other barricades." Publ Wkly

"Well-placed and adequate labelled drawings and photographs extend and complement the text of a book that is carefully organized, capably written, and nicely varied." Bull Cent Child Books

Includes glossary and bibliography

623.4 Ordnance

Wilkinson, Frederick, 1922-

Arms and armor; [by] F. Wilkinson. Watts 1984 32p il lib bdg $7.99 (3-5) **623.4**

1. Arms and armor 2. Firearms
ISBN 0-531-03772-X LC 83-51438

"Easy-read fact books"

This "is a chronological history of weaponry from the Stone Age to modern times, with close-up examinations of the development of swords, artillery, pistols, and rifles." Booklist

"The book is well illustrated with color photographs, drawings and diagrams. This slight book might serve as a lead-in to the many more extensive books on the subject." SLJ

Includes glossary

623.7 Military vehicles

Graham, Ian, 1953-

Combat aircraft. Gloucester Press 1990 c1989 32p il (How it works) lib bdg $11.90 (4 and up) **623.7**

1. Airplanes, Military
ISBN 0-531-17205-8 LC 89-81600

First published 1989 in the United Kingdom

This book "describes the designs, capabilities, and technology of today's combat aircraft, including bombers, fighter planes, transport planes, and reconnaissance aircraft." Publisher's note

Includes glossary

623.8 Nautical engineering and seamanship

Rutland, Jonathan

See inside a submarine. rev ed. Warwick Press 1988 31p il lib bdg $10.40 (4-6) **623.8**

1. Nuclear submarines
ISBN 0-531-19032-3 LC 87-51053

First published 1980

Illustrated with photographs, drawings, and full-color paintings, this book focuses on nuclear submarines. After a brief history of submarines, it describes the inner workings of a typical nuclear submarine. Besides the military functions of nuclear submarines the book covers other uses, such as scientific research and exploration

Includes glossary

Weiss, Harvey

Submarines and other underwater craft. Crowell 1990 64p il $12.95; lib bdg $12.89 (4 and up) **623.8**

1. Submarines 2. Submersibles
ISBN 0-690-04759-2; 0-690-04761-4 (lib bdg) LC 89-37614

The author examines "the principles on which submersibles work . . . [and their] history. Subsequent discussion covers war uses and antisubmarine tactics, disasters, life aboard submarines, movement underwater, and the design and uses of . . . different machines." Horn Book

624.1 Structural engineering and underground construction

Gibbons, Gail

Tunnels. Holiday House 1984 unp il lib bdg $12.95; pa $5.95 (k-3) **624.1**

1. Tunnels
ISBN 0-8234-0507-9 (lib bdg); 0-8234-0670-9 (pa) LC 83-18589

After "noting the underground passages animals build for homes and food storage, the book emphasizes the tunnels humans build to gain access to raw materials, such as ore and coal, and to gain passage under cities, under water, and through mountains. Tunnel shapes and types are discussed." Horn Book

The author "describes the different kinds of tunnels and illustrates their structures in cutaway diagrams. Most children find the subject appealing, and this introduces it very simply. The flat colors in some pictures combined with a stylized treatment of mass add a static note." Bull Cent Child Books

Macaulay, David, 1946-
Underground. Houghton Mifflin 1976 109p il $15.95; pa $6.95 (4 and up) **624.1**
1. Civil engineering 2. Building 3. Public utilities
ISBN 0-395-24739-X; 0-395-34065-9 (pa)
LC 76-13688

In this "examination of the intricate support systems that lie beneath the street levels of our cities, Macaulay explains the ways in which foundations for buildings are laid or reinforced, and how the various utilities or transportation services are constructed." Bull Cent Child Books

"Introduced by a visual index—a bird's eye view of a busy, hypothetical intersection with colored indicators marking the specific locations analyzed in subsequent pages—detailed illustrations are combined with a clear, precise narrative to make the subject comprehensible and fascinating." Horn Book

Includes glossary

625.1 Railroads

Barton, Byron
Trains. Crowell 1986 unp il $6.95; lib bdg $11.89 (k-1) **625.1**
1. Railroads
ISBN 0-694-00061-2; 0-690-04534-4 (lib bdg)
LC 85-47898

Brief text and illustrations present a variety of trains and what they do

"The concepts are simple and Barton's illustrations are just enough, and no more." Publ Wkly

Gibbons, Gail
Trains. Holiday House 1987 unp il lib bdg $13.95; pa $5.95 (k-2) **625.1**
1. Railroads
ISBN 0-8234-0640-7 (lib bdg); 0-8234-0699-7 (pa)
LC 86-19595

Gibbons illustrates different kinds of trains, past and present, and describes their features and functions

Rockwell, Anne F., 1934-
Trains. Dutton 1988 unp il $10.95 (k-2) **625.1**
1. Railroads
ISBN 0-525-44377-0 LC 87-22180

"A delightful introduction to a variety of trains that includes steam engines, modern diesel and electric locomotives, subways and monorails. Simple text and bright, full-color drawings that include anthropomorphic foxes." Sci Child

625.2 Railroad rolling stock

Scarry, Huck, 1953-
Aboard a steam locomotive; a sketchbook. Prentice-Hall Bks. for Young Readers 1987 unp il $12.95 (4 and up) **625.2**
1. Locomotives 2. Railroads—History
ISBN 0-13-000373-5 LC 86-16957

"How a locomotive works and what parts go together to make up a locomotive are explained. . . . Other sections include an enumeration of the duties of the engineer and fireman; the importance of signals and signalling systems; various aspects of a train journey; steam trains of the past; and a history of the development of the steam locomotive and railroading." SLJ

The text "is relatively brief; far more information is contained in the illustrations, which include not only well-drafted portraits of particular models but also a wealth of diagrams, which visually explain the technical details that Scarry makes reference to in his narrative." Booklist

Includes bibliography

625.7 Roads

Gibbons, Gail
New road! Crowell 1983 unp il $13.95; lib bdg $14.89; Harper & Row pa $4.95 (k-3) **625.7**
1. Roads
ISBN 0-690-04342-2; 0-690-04343-0 (lib bdg); 0-06-446059-2 (pa) LC 82-45917

This "book describes how roads are constructed, focusing on the variety of people with differing skills who participate in the planning and construction of the road and the kinds of equipment used in the actual construction. . . . The final pages of the book consist of a brief pictorial history of roads from Roman times to the concrete and asphalt roads of the present day." SLJ

"The crisp lines and bright poster colors of this road-building exposition are inviting. Gibbons shows the process, scene by scene, from start to finish." Booklist

628.1 Water supply

Cobb, Vicki
The trip of a drip; illustrated by Elliot Kreloff. Little, Brown 1986 50p il (How the world works) lib bdg $11.95 (4-6) **628.1**
1. Water supply 2. Water—Purification
ISBN 0-316-14900-4 LC 85-23960

"This book gives a straightforward account of how drinking water is usually obtained by rural dwellers from aquifers through wells and springs and by urban residents from surface water in rivers, lakes, and reservoirs. Water purification and sewage treatment are explained simply and well through diagrams and text." Sci Books Films

628.9 Fire-fighting technology

Maass, Robert
Fire fighters. Scholastic 1989 unp il $12.95 (2-3) **628.9**
1. Fire fighters
ISBN 0-590-41459-3 LC 88-18340

This describes what it means to be a firefighter, including life at the firehouse, practice drills, service to the community, and fire emergencies

"Many full-color photographs, some of excellent artistic quality, illustrate this behind-the-scenes look at the life of a big-city fire fighter. The brief text is clearly written.

Maass, Robert—*Continued*

. . . Although most young aspiring fire fighters might seek the excitement of danger, Maass' book, in its realistic look at the other activities of fire fighters, provides a reasonable balance." SLJ

Marston, Hope Irvin, 1935-

Fire trucks. Dodd, Mead 1984 55p il $11.95 (2-4) **628.9**

1. Fire engines
ISBN 0-396-08451-6 LC 84-8068

"A comprehensive look at firefighting equipment, including trucks, fireboats, and helicopters. For each kind of fire truck there is a description of the equipment and its functions, accompanied by a large black-and-white photograph. Throughout, the author emphasizes the importance of brave men and women firefighters." Child Book Rev Serv

Rockwell, Anne F., 1934-

Fire engines; by Anne Rockwell. Dutton 1986 unp il $11.95 (k-1) **628.9**

1. Fire engines
ISBN 0-525-44259-6 LC 86-4464

Describes the parts of a fire engine and how fire fighters use them to fight fires

This book provides "crisp, bright illustrations in a spectrum of primary colors; a direct, simple text that is personalized by the use of the first person to heighten the appeal to very young children; and solid information conveyed in a picture book format." SLJ

629.04 Transportation engineering

Goor, Ron, 1940-

In the driver's seat; [by] Ron & Nancy Goor. Crowell 1982 77p il lib bdg $12.89 (2-4) **629.04**

1. Vehicles
ISBN 0-690-04177-2 LC 81-43885

The authors "put young readers into the driver's seat of a range of novel vehicles: a front-end loader, a Goodyear blimp, a Concorde jet, and an M60 tank, to name a few. A large-print, widely spaced text describes how each vehicle moves and points out certain primary controls. Camera-eye views of the actual seat areas are clear, making it easy to see the various dials, levers, or pedals mentioned in the explanations. This will find most use as a browser's item, but one that has built-in appeal—especially for reluctant readers with a mechanical bent." Booklist

Rockwell, Anne F., 1934-

Things that go; [by] Anne Rockwell. Dutton 1986 23p il lib bdg $10.95 (k-1) **629.04**

1. Transportation 2. Vehicles
ISBN 0-525-44266-9 LC 86-6199

Trains, tow trucks, sailboats, buses, sleds, jeeps, bicycles, and other things that go can be seen in the city, in the country, on the water, in the park, and many other places

"Rockwell's familiar animals briskly propel the vehicles, toys and tools; each confetti-colored spread is crammed with action. An amiable compendium of information for young readers." Publ Wkly

629.1 Aerospace engineering

Moxon, Julian

How jet engines are made. Facts on File 1985 32p il (How it is made) lib bdg $12.95 (4 and up) **629.1**

1. Airplanes—Engines
ISBN 0-8160-0037-9 LC 84-21049

This introduction to jet engines covers operating principles, materials used, and assembly procedures

This volume is "lavishly illustrated with several fully captioned color photographs or drawings on every page. . . . In plain, uncondescending style and short sentences, the text conveys a great deal of technical information." Booklist

Includes glossary

629.13 Aeronautics

Berliner, Don, 1930-

Before the Wright brothers. Lerner Publs. 1990 72p il lib bdg $11.95 (5 and up) **629.13**

1. Aeronautics—History 2. Flight—History
ISBN 0-8225-1588-1 LC 89-31837

The author "tracks the evolution of successful human-controlled flight through a series of short vignettes of experimenters, beginning with George Cayley in the early 1800s. Unfamiliar names, such as William Henson and John Stringfellow, are intermixed with more familiar ones, such as Hiram Maxim, Otto Lilienthal, Octave Chanute, and Samuel Langley." Sci Books Films

"Berliner writes clear, declarative sentences filled with the facts needed for reports. Every page has a well-drawn sketch or a clearly reproduced archival photograph, giving a period atmosphere to the book." SLJ

Includes bibliography

Boyne, Walter J., 1929-

The Smithsonian book of flight for young people. Atheneum Pubs. 1988 128p il $16.95; pa $9.95 (4 and up) **629.13**

1. Aeronautics—History 2. Flight—History
ISBN 0-689-31422-1; 0-689-71212-X (pa)
LC 87-35912

The author "uses clear, concise text and nearly one hundred color and black-and-white photographs to present the history of aviation and explore the triumphs and failures of those who dared to soar like a bird." Sci Child

Includes bibliography

Gibbons, Gail

Flying. Holiday House 1986 unp il lib bdg $13.95 (k-2) **629.13**

1. Aeronautics—History 2. Flight—History
ISBN 0-8234-0599-0 LC 85-22027

Presents a brief history of flight, from balloons evolving into more sophisticated means of air transportation such as helicopters, jet planes, and shuttles

"In primary-color gaiety, Gibbons envisions the history of flight. From the first balloon launch of small barnyard animals to a rocket's stunning ascent, a variety of flying machines race across the pages. Both their development and purposes are covered: cameras aboard a blimp peer into athletic stadiums, propeller planes fight fires and dust crops, and helicopters aid in traffic reporting and rescues at sea. Flying into and out of stylized clouds, Gibbons' vehicles lend vigor to her concise, clear text as she briefly tracks aeronautical highlights." Booklist

Maurer, R. (Richard)

Airborne; the search for the secret of flight. Simon & Schuster Bks. for Young Readers 1990 48p il $14.95; pa $5.95 (5 and up) **629.13**

1. Aeronautics—History 2. Flight—History
ISBN 0-671-69422-7; 0-671-69423-5 (pa) LC 90-9710

"A Novabook"

Published in association with WGBH Boston

This book "begins with experiments and designs for airships, hot air balloons, and gliders from the 1600s; and briefly traces each discovery and development that led to the Wright Brothers' flight in 1903. The text is well written and . . . each page includes drawings, photos, or reproductions. . . . Four experiments are included (such as making a hot-air balloon out of tissue paper and a blow dryer), all of which are well illustrated and explained within the capabilities of the intended age group." SLJ

Scarry, Huck, 1953-

Balloon trip; a sketchbook. Prentice-Hall 1983 68p il maps $10.95 (3-6) **629.13**

1. Balloons
ISBN 0-13-055939-3 LC 82-23002

Original French edition, 1982

"Profusely and effectively illustrated with black and white sketches, this oversize book describes in detail the author's journey with a Swiss balloonist, giving facts about how the balloon is constructed and flown. This is followed by a brief history of ballooning, and then by an account of a second flight, this time in a hot-air balloon. . . . The writing is informal, informative, and occasionally humorous, with a good sense of narrative." Bull Cent Child Books

Includes bibliography

Taylor, Richard L., d. 1982

The first flight; the story of the Wright brothers. Watts 1990 63p il lib bdg $10.90 (4 and up) **629.13**

1. Wright, Wilbur, 1867-1912 2. Wright, Orville, 1871-1948 3. Aeronautics—History
ISBN 0-531-10891-0 LC 89-24774

"A First book"

In this account of the "brothers' lives (from 1899 to December 17, 1903) . . . Taylor lays out the aspects of the Wrights' challenge—lift, control, power, and actually learning to fly—and fleshes out the arduous events of their solution." Booklist

"Taylor's lively narrative . . . includes biographical details, a brief description of Wright brothers memorials, and statistics of the first four flights. Black-and-white and color photographs add to the historical detail." SLJ

Includes bibliography

Tessendorf, K. C.

Barnstormers & daredevils. Atheneum Pubs. 1988 88p il $13.95 (4 and up) **629.13**

1. Air pilots 2. Aeronautics—History
ISBN 0-689-31346-2 LC 87-15194

This is an "account of some of the young barnstormers and daredevils who helped to bring aviation to the common people of this country. . . . The list of flyers is by no means exhaustive, but it does include such names as Wiley Post, Charles Lindbergh, Gladys Ingle, and the 13 Black Cats." SLJ

"Aviation history buffs will revel in Tessendorf's intriguing account of death-defying aerial burlesque." Booklist

Includes bibliography

629.133 Aircraft types

Jefferis, David

Helicopters. Warwick Press 1990 c1989 32p il (Read about) lib bdg $10.90 (1-3) **629.133**

1. Helicopters
ISBN 0-531-19069-2 LC 89-22543

First published 1989 in the United Kingdom

Explains how helicopters function and describes the different types and their military and civilian uses

Includes glossary

Helicopters; illustrated by Ron Jobson, Terry Hadler and Michael Roffe. Watts 1989 c1988 32p il (Wings, the conquest of the air) lib bdg $11.90 (4 and up) **629.133**

1. Helicopters
ISBN 0-531-10636-5 LC 88-50379

First published 1988 in the United Kingdom

"The military history of [helicopters] in Korea, Vietnam, and Afghanistan is mentioned as well as the craft's versatility in geological surveys, search-and-rescue flights, Antarctic research, space-capsule pickup, and smuggler and drug-runner patrols." Booklist

Includes glossary

Supersonic flight; illustrated by Terry Hadler, Ron Jobson and Michael Roffe. Watts 1989 c1988 32p il (Wings, the conquest of the air) lib bdg $11.90 (4 and up) **629.133**

1. Supersonic transport planes
ISBN 0-531-10637-3 LC 88-50378

Jefferis, David—*Continued*

First published 1988 in the United Kingdom

This book contains the "trailblazing statistical firsts that aviation enthusiasts love, along with tantalizing prototypes of combat jets, post-Concorde passenger carriers, 'spaceplanes' (shuttles that fly to and from orbit), and airports of the twenty-first century." Booklist

Includes glossary

Munro, Roxie, 1945-

Blimps. Dutton 1988 unp il $12.95 (2-4) **629.133**

1. Airships

ISBN 0-525-44441-6 LC 88-18138

A "description of blimps, their history, manufacture, and historical as well as current use. Munro also delineates the launching and piloting of the large airship. Her watercolor illustrations are attractive in their simplicity, although there are no diagrams to aid understanding. The text, however, is concise and easy to understand." SLJ

Rockwell, Anne F., 1934-

Planes; by Anne Rockwell. Dutton 1985 unp il lib bdg $11.95; pa $3.95 (k-1) **629.133**

1. Airplanes

ISBN 0-525-44159-X (lib bdg); 0-525-44540-4 (pa) LC 84-13732

"With simple text and clear, cheerful watercolors, Rockwell introduces preschoolers to airplanes. Her brightly colored illustrations depict seaplanes and helicopters, jets and model planes as they fly over mountains, seas, cities and farms, propelled by engines, propellers or (in the case of hang gliders) the wind. . . . This is a fine primary presentation of a popular, often requested subject." SLJ

Stoff, Joshua

Dirigible; written and illustrated by Joshua Stoff. Atheneum Pubs. 1985 106p il $12.95 (3-6) **629.133**

1. Airships

ISBN 0-689-31084-6 LC 85-7461

This book describes the building, launching, missions, and final dismantling of a hypothetical rigid airship, based on the careers of three Navy dirigibles

"Authoritatively written, and well illustrated with pen and ink sketches, the book is both aesthetically appealing and technically informative. . . . Although Dirigible is a book about a fictitious dirigible, the composite history and illustrations yield factual information, all of which is surprisingly interesting and absorbing to read." Appraisal

Includes bibliography

629.22 Types of vehicles

Weiss, Harvey

Model cars and trucks and how to build them. Crowell 1974 74p il lib bdg $13.89 (4 and up) **629.22**

1. Automobiles—Models 2. Trucks—Models

ISBN 0-690-04842-4 LC 74-7403

Included here are instructions for making seven basic wooden model cars and trucks, with ideas for modifications and improvisations to create other vehicles such as racing cars, fire trucks, derricks, tractors, and bulldozers

"The clear text is full of practical suggestions and reminders and is reinforced by the simple plans and drawings." Horn Book

629.222 Passenger automobiles

Cole, Joanna

Cars and how they go; illustrated by Gail Gibbons. Crowell 1983 unp il $12.95; lib bdg $12.89; pa $3.95 (2-4) **629.222**

1. Automobiles

ISBN 0-690-04261-2; 0-690-04262-0 (lib bdg); 0-06-446052-5 (pa) LC 82-45575

"The author explains that wheels make cars go, and describes the several procedures that turn the wheels and the moving or stationary parts that are involved." Bull Cent Child Books

"This picture-book explanation of how a car works is an interesting example of how a complicated topic can be rendered in basic terms without sacrificing key concepts. . . . Gibbons' crisp, pure, sunny illustrations do a good deal of explaining." Booklist

Rockwell, Anne F., 1934-

Cars; by Anne Rockwell. Dutton 1984 unp il $11.95; pa $3.95 (k-1) **629.222**

1. Automobiles

ISBN 0-525-44079-8; 0-525-44241-3 (pa) LC 83-14080

"Rockwell's bright watercolor paintings depict a world in which all sorts of cars are driven to a variety of places by a cast of canine characters." Booklist

"Humor and universality are introduced through the canine characters who operate, service, or travel in the engaging vehicles. Despite their generic similarities, each dog is given an expression suited to the occasion." Horn Book

Sutton, Richard

Car; written by Richard Sutton. Knopf 1990 63p il (Eyewitness bks) $13.95; lib bdg $14.99 (4 and up) **629.222**

1. Automobiles

ISBN 0-679-80743-8; 0-679-90743-2 (lib bdg) LC 90-4025

A photo essay about the history, development, and impact of automobiles from horseless carriages and Model T Fords to today's high performance racing cars; detailed cutaway photos show how the moving parts of

Sutton, Richard—*Continued*
a car work

This book's "highly detailed, crisp photographs are a delight. . . . Its dynamic presentation and technical detail will truly entertain and inform anyone interested in automobiles." SLJ

629.223 Light trucks

Sullivan, George, 1927-

Here come the monster trucks. Cobblehill Bks. 1989 64p il $14.95 (3-6) **629.223**

1. Trucks
ISBN 0-525-65005-9 LC 88-38464

Narrates the short history of monster trucks—ordinary pickup trucks on four enormous tires—describing some of the outstanding examples of these unusual vehicles, which can be used to crush cars, race, jump cars, and engage in mud bog competition

"Color photographs show action shots; the material is clearly presented; an index and a glossary of 'Monster Words and Terms' are included. Not every reader's book, this, but for the vehicle-mad boy or girl, appealing." Bull Cent Child Books

629.224 Trucks

Barton, Byron

Trucks. Crowell 1986 unp il $6.95; lib bdg $11.89 (k-1) **629.224**

1. Trucks
ISBN 0-694-00062-0; 0-690-04530-1 (lib bdg)
LC 85-47901

Brief text and illustrations present a variety of trucks from cement trucks to ice-cream trucks, and what they do

"A tightly focused (book) . . . featuring Barton's trademark bright, blocky graphics and spare text." Publ Wkly

Magee, Doug, 1947-

Trucks you can count on. Dodd, Mead 1985 unp il lib bdg $11.95 (k-2) **629.224**

1. Trucks 2. Counting
ISBN 0-396-08507-5 LC 84-21057

"This work introduces the tractor trailer, allowing the reader to count its parts using the numbers from one to ten, and its wheels using the numbers to eighteen." SLJ

"This picture-book introduction to tractor-trailer trucks features well-chosen black-and-white photographs to give youngsters a close-up view of the large vehicles and show the extent of the transportation services they provide. . . . A clean presentation, effectively tailored to younger audiences." Booklist

Rockwell, Anne F., 1934-

Trucks; by Anne Rockwell. Dutton 1984 unp il $11.95; pa $3.95 (k-1) **629.224**

1. Trucks
ISBN 0-525-44147-6; 0-525-44432-7 (pa) LC 84-1556

In this volume "Rockwell introduces the very young to the world of trucks—a world 'peopled' with fully-clothed cats. Illustrated with her usual clear, amusing watercolors, the book begins and ends with toy trucks and in between touches upon such common favorites as ice cream trucks, firetrucks and garbage trucks. The text is simple, sometimes overly so. . . . The appeal to very young children is heightened by the stylistic use of the first person plural." SLJ

629.225 Work vehicles

Rockwell, Anne F., 1934-

Big wheels; by Anne Rockwell. Dutton 1986 unp il $11.95 (k-1) **629.225**

1. Vehicles 2. Machinery
ISBN 0-525-44226-X LC 85-16248

Introduces a variety of working vehicles and their purpose. Includes bulldozers, cement mixers, snow plows, tractor scrapers, and other large-wheeled vehicles

"Although the author-artist has supplied a very brief text, she uses active, vivid verbs, such as *dig, dump,* and *chop up,* effectively conveying a sense of the machinery in the fewest words necessary. Likewise, her illustrations contain exactly the right amount of detail to satisfy but not confuse." Horn Book

629.227 Cycles

Jaspersohn, William

Motorcycle: the making of a Harley-Davidson. Little, Brown 1984 80p il $14.95 (5 and up) **629.227**

1. Harley-Davidson motorcycle
ISBN 0-316-45817-1 LC 84-14355

Text and photographs follow a motorcycle at the Harley Davidson factory from start to finish

"The process is clearly explained and carefully photographed, though sometimes captions are needed to clarify which part of the nearby text they're displaying." Booklist

Rockwell, Anne F., 1934-

Bikes; [by] Anne Rockwell. Dutton 1987 unp il lib bdg $9.95 (k-2) **629.227**

1. Bicycles and bicycling
ISBN 0-525-44287-1 LC 86-19923

This "picture book shows tigers in a wide variety of locales riding an even greater variety of bikes. . . . Unicycles, tandems, high-speed racers and slower, clumsier delivery bikes are all introduced. Even the more unusual types join the collection: the stationary exercise bike, a trick motorcycle, a motor scooter, trail bikes and mopeds." Publ Wkly

This "is vintage Rockwell: bright, amusing watercolors that convey a comforting tone and illustrate a very simple text." SLJ

629.228 Racing cars

Graham, Ian, 1953-

Racing cars. Gloucester Press 1990 c1989 32p il (How it works) lib bdg $11.90 (4 and up) **629.228**

1. Automobile racing 2. Automobiles
ISBN 0-531-17206-6 LC 89-81601

First published 1989 in the United Kingdom

This book "covers the technical side of racing cars—the various mechanical parts, the source of power, the different kinds of cars—as well as the history of the racing car, race tactics, and safety." Booklist

Includes glossary

629.28 Motor land vehicles and cycles—Tests, driving, maintenance, repairs

Gibbons, Gail

Fill it up! all about service stations. Crowell 1985 unp il $13.95; lib bdg $13.89; Harper & Row pa $4.95 (k-3) **629.28**

1. Automobiles—Service stations
ISBN 0-690-04439-9; 0-690-04440-2 (lib bdg); 0-06-446051-7 (pa) LC 84-45345

"Gibbons records an array of typical activities carried on by men and women on the day shift at John and Peggy's Service Station: not only do the attendants pump gas, but the mechanics replace worn parts, adjust brakes, check wheels, fix flat tires, change oil, and so forth." Booklist

"The concise text is well integrated with bright, cheerful illustration in which equipment described in the text is labeled with the correct terminology. A final page features names and pictures of common service station tools. Accurate and appealing." SLJ

629.4 Astronautics

Branley, Franklyn Mansfield, 1915-

Rockets and satellites; by Franklyn M. Branley; illustrated by Giulio Maestro. 2nd rev ed. Crowell 1987 32p il (Let's-read-and-find-out science bks) $13.95; lib bdg $13.89; pa $4.50 (k-3) **629.4**

1. Rockets (Aeronautics) 2. Artificial satellites
ISBN 0-690-04591-3; 0-690-04593-X (lib bdg); 0-06-445061-9 (pa) LC 86-47748

A revised and newly illustrated edition of the title first published 1961

Simple text with illustrations explains rockets and satellites and describes their capabilities and functions; space shuttles are also discussed

This book "makes a valued contribution to science collections for young readers." Booklist

Smith, Howard Everett, 1927-

Daring the unknown: a history of NASA; [by] Howard E. Smith. Harcourt Brace Jovanovich 1987 178p il $14.95 (5 and up) **629.4**

1. United States. National Aeronautics and Space Administration 2. Astronautics—History
ISBN 0-15-200435-1 LC 86-33617

"Gulliver books"

"Lucid text and excellent, black-and-white and color photographs convey the history of the American Space Program from the challenge of Sputnik, to the dramatic Apollo Moon landing, to the shocking Challenger disaster, and plans for future exploration." Sci Child

Includes bibliography

629.44 Auxiliary spacecraft

Branley, Franklyn Mansfield, 1915-

From Sputnik to space shuttles; into the new space age; by Franklyn M. Branley. Crowell 1986 53p il (Voyage into space bk) $12.95; lib bdg $12.89 (3-6) **629.44**

1. Artificial satellites
ISBN 0-690-04531-X; 0-690-04533-6 (lib bdg) LC 85-43186

Traces the history of artificial satellites from the launching of Sputnik and discusses how these satellites have aided advances in communication, weather forecasting, scientific experiments and generally changed the way we live

"Well-placed black-and-white illustrations are supplemented by a small section of bright, clear color photos. This can be used to introduce longer books on communications, space exploration, geography or new technology." SLJ

Includes bibliography

Fichter, George S.

The space shuttle. rev ed. Watts 1990 64p il lib bdg $10.90 (4 and up) **629.44**

1. Space shuttles
ISBN 0-531-10815-5 LC 89-38618

"A First book"

First published 1981

A history of the space shuttle's development, with information on its functions and on the flights of individual spacecraft

"The text is sprinkled with interesting photographs, both color and black and white. The shuttle disaster of 1986 is handled clearly and unemotionally, with emphasis placed on NASA's attempts to revive the space program. . . . This is an easily read and informative overview of the shuttle with an accessible text and colorful format that are appealing for young readers." Appraisal

Kerrod, Robin, 1938-

See inside a space station. rev ed. Warwick Press 1988 31p il lib bdg $11.90 (4-6) **629.44**

1. Space stations
ISBN 0-531-19031-5 LC 87-51052

Kerrod, Robin, 1938-—*Continued*
First published 1978

This "is a large format book containing a series of short chapters, many photographs, and full-color and black-and-white artwork. . . . [It] contains information about the Mir space station launched by the U.S.S.R. in 1986 and the NASA space station planned for the 1990s. . . . The appended time chart, listing staffed and unstaffed flights and their significance, could prove useful." Booklist

Includes glossary

Vogt, Gregory
Space stations. Watts 1990 32p il (Space library) lib bdg $11.90 (4 and up) **629.44**

1. Space stations
ISBN 0-531-10460-5 LC 87-51222

This volume "chronicles the history of Salyut, Skylab, and Mir as well as the multinational plans now underway for additional space stations. The last chapters deal with space colonies." Booklist

Includes glossary

629.45 Manned space flight

Barton, Byron
I want to be an astronaut. Crowell 1988 unp il $7.95; lib bdg $12.89 (k-1) **629.45**

1. Astronautics
ISBN 0-694-00261-5; 0-690-04744-4 (lib bdg) LC 87-24311

"First-person text describes the experiences the speaker might have on a space mission. Simple text and bold, full-color illustrations are a delightful introduction to an astronaut's activities." Sci Child

Long, Kim
The astronaut training book for kids. Lodestar Bks. 1990 116p il $15.95 (5 and up) **629.45**

1. Astronautics—Vocational guidance
ISBN 0-525-67296-6 LC 89-34668

"A practical guide intended to give a head start to those interested in pursuing an aerospace career. The author is clearly excited about the potential for today's child in the space industry and conveys the feeling in a readable and interesting text." Horn Book Guide

Includes glossary and bibliographies

Ride, Sally K.
To space & back; by Sally Ride with Susan Okie. Lothrop, Lee & Shepard Bks. 1986 96p il $16.95; pa $9.95 (4 and up) **629.45**

1. Space flight 2. Space shuttles
ISBN 0-688-06159-1; 0-688-09211-1 (pa) LC 85-23757

This "account of a space journey, from blastoff to landing, gives intimate, you-are-there details of adjusting to weightlessness, preparing and eating meals, going to the bathroom, sleeping, washing, dressing, and working on scientific projects or up-keep technology on board the shuttle. Ride gives plenty of examples from her own experience but keeps the focus generalized enough to be broadly informative." Bull Cent Child Books

Includes glossary

Sullivan, George, 1927-
The day we walked on the moon; a photo history of space exploration. Scholastic 1990 72p il $14.95; pa $4.95 (4 and up) **629.45**

1. Outer space—Exploration
ISBN 0-590-43632-5; 0-590-42760-1 (pa) LC 89-24234

"Sullivan documents the history of U.S. space exploration, providing newspaper clippings and news and NASA photographs. . . . Using the U.S. moon landing to introduce this story of human and technological achievement, Sullivan considers such successes as the first woman in space and the first spacewalk . . . Skylab, and the space shuttles. . . . Sections on astronaut training and future projects round out the treatment." Booklist

"Writing in his usual clear, concise way, this reliable author focuses special attention on the achievements of the *Appollo* and Space Shuttle programs rather than on the personal lives of astronauts." SLJ

Includes bibliography

629.8 Automatic control engineering

Harrar, George
Radical robots; can you be replaced? Simon & Schuster Bks. for Young Readers 1990 48p il $14.95; pa $5.95 (5 and up) **629.8**

1. Robots 2. Robotics
ISBN 0-671-69420-0; 0-671-69421-9 (pa) LC 90-31572

"A Novabook"

Published in association with WGBH Boston

This book examines the design, construction, and applications of robots, discussing what they can and cannot do and the extent to which they can develop their own intelligence

"Bright, full-color photos; blocky fanciful paintings; an easy text; and plenty of brief sidebar essays. . . . This colorful book will certainly attract casual browsers, and if Harrar skips blithely past the difficult political and economic issues of robot glorification, he writes in a vivid, engaging way that compensates for the speed with which he covers the subject." SLJ

Lauber, Patricia, 1924-
Get ready for robots! illustrated by True Kelley. Crowell 1987 32p il (Let's-read-and-find-out science bks) lib bdg $13.89; Harper & Row pa $4.50 (k-3) **629.8**

1. Robots
ISBN 0-690-04578-6 (lib bdg); 0-06-445080-5 (pa) LC 85-48255

Lauber, Patricia, 1924-—*Continued*

"The text opens with a dream sequence of that common misconception of robots as household companions and then sets out to show their actual current capabilities. There's a bit of background on computer signals, sensors, dependence on robots for dangerous or intricate manufacturing jobs, and of course employment of robots in satellites and space probes." Bull Cent Child Books

"This should answer many students' questions, and at the same time draw a clear line between what is factually true and what is speculatively possible. Kelley's simple black outline drawings filled with flat colors brighten every page and clearly illuminate the facts of the text." SLJ

Skurzynski, Gloria

Robots: your high-tech world. Bradbury Press 1990 64p il $15.95 (5 and up) **629.8**

1. Robots 2. Robotics
ISBN 0-02-782917-0 LC 89-70805

The author presents a "comprehensive look at the history, development, and future of robotics in industry, medicine, and space exploration; she explains how robots work and what they can do as she explores the connection between computers and robots. In an inviting format, information is presented both in text and captions. The well-chosen photographs are attractively arranged to add pace, variety, and excitement to the book." Horn Book

630.1 Agriculture—Philosophy and theory. Country and farm life

Allen, Thomas B., 1928-

On Granddaddy's farm. Knopf 1989 unp il $13.95; lib bdg $14.99 (1-3) **630.1**

1. Farm life 2. Grandparents 3. Tennessee—Description
ISBN 0-394-89613-0; 0-394-99613-5 (lib bdg) LC 88-23374

The author relates the events from the 1930s when he and his cousins spent summers on their grandparents's farm in the hills of Tennessee

"Straightforward, unadorned prose and stunning muted colored paintings. Scenes of farmyard creatures, chores, and playtime effectively capture one's interest as they bring to life a less technological era. The book is a gem that should not be missed." Child Book Rev Serv

Ancona, George, 1929-

The American family farm; a photo essay by George Ancona; text by Joan Anderson. Harcourt Brace Jovanovich 1989 unp il $18.95 (5 and up) **630.1**

1. Farm life 2. Agriculture
ISBN 0-15-203025-5 LC 88-30068

"George Ancona and Joan Anderson reflect on both the adversities of farm life and its benefits in this photo essay, which is divided into three segments devoted to a dairy farm in Massachusetts, a poultry farm in Georgia, and a hog, cattle, and grain farm in Iowa. . . . The exceptional collaboration of photographer and author results in both an integrated flow of uncaptioned, black-and-white photographs and text and a discerning view into the lives of real people." Horn Book

Bellville, Cheryl Walsh, 1944-

Farming today yesterday's way. Carolrhoda Bks. 1984 40p il lib bdg $9.95 (2-4) **630.1**

1. Farm life 2. Dairying 3. Horses
ISBN 0-87614-220-X LC 84-3215

"Pictures and text introduce Tom Saunders, who keeps 12 cows and an assortment of other animals, including seven draft horses, which provide the power for the farm's machinery. . . . Photographs show how Saunders uses his horses in the planting and harvesting cycles that rule on the farm." Booklist

"The text is clear and informative; the vocabulary appropriate for the subject and grade level. Unfamiliar terms are printed in boldface type and explained in both the text and the glossary." SLJ

Demuth, Patricia, 1948-

Joel, growing up a farm man; text by Patricia Demuth; photographs by Jack Demuth. Dodd, Mead 1982 143p il lib bdg $12.95 (5 and up) **630.1**

1. Farm life
ISBN 0-396-07997-0 LC 81-43219

This book focuses on a thirteen-year-old boy who works on his family's farm, caring for livestock, harvesting hay, and preparing to manage the farm himself one day

"Photographs of good quality make processes and equipment more comprehensible to readers with no experience of farm life. The text is capably written, carefully detailed, and informative." Bull Cent Child Books

Gibbons, Gail

Farming. Holiday House 1988 unp il lib bdg $13.95; pa $5.95 (k-2) **630.1**

1. Farm life 2. Agriculture
ISBN 0-8234-0682-2; 0-8234-0797-7 (pa) LC 87-21254

"Simple text and full-color illustrations describe the many indoor and outdoor chores that are performed on a family farm each season. Fields are plowed and planted; animals are born, fed and cared for; and crops are harvested. Includes brief explanations of different kinds of specialized farms." Sci Child

Graff, Nancy Price, 1953-

The strength of the hills; a portrait of a family farm; photographs by Richard Howard. Little, Brown 1989 80p il $14.95 (4 and up) **630.1**

1. Farm life
ISBN 0-316-32277-6 LC 89-7950

This "photo-essay follows the daily routines of Bill and Jenny Nelson and their four children on a Vermont dairy farm." Bull Cent Child Books

"With evocative prose and dominant, well-executed,

Graff, Nancy Price, 1953-—*Continued*
black-and-white photographs, the book . . . details the real work of each family member. . . . It is a natural, unglamorous portrayal of a single day, and captures the determination, luck, and labor it takes to keep a farm going." SLJ

633.1 Cereal grains

Aliki
Corn is maize; the gift of the Indians; written and illustrated by Aliki. Crowell 1976 33p il (Let's-read-and-find-out science bks) lib bdg $12.89; Harper & Row pa $4.50 (k-3) **633.1**

1. Corn
ISBN 0-690-00975-5; 0-06-445026-0 (pa) LC 75-6928

In this book, the author provides a history of corn, or maize, and "also the life cycle of the plant itself, its growth and reproductive patterns, and its many uses. Excellent illustrations by the author help convey both cultural aspects and technological uses of corn." Sci Child

Johnson, Sylvia A.
Rice; photographs by Noboru Moriya. Lerner Publs. 1985 46p il (Lerner natural science bk) lib bdg $12.95 (4 and up) **633.1**

1. Rice
ISBN 0-8225-1466-4 LC 85-19754

Adapted from a work by Noboru Moriya published 1973 in Japan

The author "covers the growth and cultivation of this member of the grass family and includes discussion of its importance as a primary food crop for one-half of the world's peoples." Booklist

Includes glossary

Wheat; photographs by Masaharu Suzuki. Lerner Publs. 1990 48p il (Lerner natural science bk) lib bdg $12.95 (4 and up) **633.1**

1. Wheat
ISBN 0-8225-1490-7 LC 89-13237

Explains the life cycle of wheat, its varieties, its cultivation, its harvesting, and its importance in feeding millions of people all over the world

"Scientific terms are used when necessary. Maps are used to show the locations of major grain producting areas of the world. . . . This is a good choice for scientific study of the wheat kernal and how it grows." SLJ

Includes glossary

Patent, Dorothy Hinshaw
Wheat, the golden harvest; photographs by William Muñoz. Dodd, Mead 1987 62p il $12.95 (4-6) **633.1**

1. Wheat
ISBN 0-396-08781-7 LC 86-32801

Text and photographs describe how different varieties of wheat are planted, harvested, and processed into foods

"The text is liberally illustrated with color and black-and-white photos. The captions add to the text's content." SLJ

Includes glossary

633.5 Fiber crops

Selsam, Millicent Ellis, 1912-
Cotton; [by] Millicent E. Selsam; photographs by Jerome Wexler. Morrow 1982 48p il $12.95; lib bdg $12.88 (3-5) **633.5**

1. Cotton
ISBN 0-688-01499-2; 0-688-01500-X (lib bdg) LC 82-6496

Surveys the history, growth cycle, processing, and varied uses of one of the world's most important fiber plants

"The book is well written and can be easily understood by mid- to upper-elementary school children. . . . Wexler's photographs and the diagrams do much to enhance the text." Sci Books Films

633.6 Sugar, syrup, starch crops

Lasky, Kathryn
Sugaring time; photographs by Christopher G. Knight. Macmillan 1983 unp il $11.95; pa $3.95 (5 and up) **633.6**

1. Maple sugar
ISBN 0-02-751680-6; 0-689-71081-X (pa) LC 82-23928

A Newbery Medal honor book, 1984

"The author explains the steps involved in making maple syrup, from 'breaking out' the sugar trails to grading the final product. The book chronicles the activities of the Lacey family during the March sugaring time on their Vermont farm." Horn Book

"Laskey's text is informative and contains a down-home charm. Knight's photos portray not only the sugaring process but also the warmth and love of the Lacey clan." Publ Wkly

634 Orchards, fruit, forestry

Johnson, Sylvia A.
Apple trees; photographs by Hiroo Koike. Lerner Publs. 1983 48p il (Lerner natural science bk) $12.95 (4 and up) **634**

1. Apple
ISBN 0-8225-1479-6 LC 83-16230

Adapted from a work by Hiroo Koike published 1976 in Japan

The book "offers botanical descriptions of how these trees produce their fruits. Seasonal changes in the tree and a thorough explanation of fertilization and seed-formation processes are central. The use of insecticides is mentioned (they 'have to be used carefully, or they can kill helpful insects as well as harmful ones'), and harvesting patterns are briefly described." Booklist

Includes glossary

Parnall, Peter

Apple tree; written and illustrated by Peter Parnall. Macmillan 1988 c1987 unp il lib bdg $13.95 (k-3) **634**

1. Apple 2. Ecology
ISBN 0-02-770160-3 LC 86-23730

Describes the many ways an apple tree interacts with insects, birds, and other animals during a full year of its development

"Charcoal-gray drawings of the tree are embellished with soft bursts of pastel color that draw attention to narrative focal points—spring blossoms, tiny green beetles, a robin's nest. . . . A quiet study that implicitly encourages readers to look closely at the commonplace and note its significance to the natural landscape." Booklist

Patent, Dorothy Hinshaw

An apple a day; from orchard to you; photographs by William Muñoz. Cobblehill Bks. 1990 64p il $13.95 (3-6) **634**

1. Apple
ISBN 0-525-65020-2 LC 89-33504

"A comprehensive account of the six varieties of apples that comprise over 80 percent of the U.S. crop. Includes importation by Europeans, propagation, shaping, blossoms, the role of bees, combatting pests, harvesting, storing, sorting, packing, and selling." Sci Child

Schnieper, Claudia

An apple tree through the year; photographs by Othmar Baumli. Carolrhoda Bks. 1987 48p il (Carolrhoda nature watch bk) lib bdg $12.95; pa $6.95 (3-6) **634**

1. Apple
ISBN 0-87614-248-X; 0-87614-483-0 (pa) LC 87-7997

Original German edition published 1982 in Switzerland

"While tracing the development of an apple tree from bud to fruit, Schnieper also follows the progress of an apple tree through the four seasons. Although the book focuses on a single tree's progress, information about other creatures is also presented, thus providing an overview of life in an orchard. Beautiful full-color photos and black-and-white line drawings highlight and elucidate the text. An excellent explanation of grafting is also included." SLJ

Includes glossary

634.9 Forestry

Kurelek, William, 1927-1977

Lumberjack; paintings and story by William Kurelek. Houghton Mifflin 1974 unp il o.p.; Tundra Bks. reprint available $17.95 (3-5) **634.9**

1. Lumber and lumbering
ISBN 0-88776-052-X LC 74-9377

Twenty-five color paintings portray life in a lumber camp and the lumberjack at work. The accompanying text tells of the author's experiences in Canadian lumber camps just after World War II

635 Garden crops (Horticulture). Vegetables

Björk, Christina

Linnea's windowsill garden; by Christina Björk and Lena Anderson; translated by Joan Sandin. R & S Bks. 1988 59p il $11.95 (3-6) **635**

1. Gardening 2. Plants
ISBN 91-29-59064-7 LC 87-15016

Original Swedish edition, 1978

A "young plant lover gives information about every aspect of indoor gardening: choosing, planting, pruning, fertilizing, spraying, adjusting light and water." Bull Cent Child Books

Linnea's "zeal is infectious; readers will be looking around the house for seeds they can press into soil or coax into germination. Anderson's two-color illustrations explicate the projects cleanly and clearly, giving gardeners an excellent idea of when to look for shoots and when to run for the insecticide." Publ Wkly

Brown, Marc Tolon

Your first garden book; [by] Marc Brown. Little, Brown 1981 48p il $12.45; pa $5.95 (1-3) **635**

1. Gardening
ISBN 0-316-11217-8; 0-316-11215-1 (pa) LC 81-3681

"An Atlantic Monthly Press book"

Suggested projects outline for beginning gardeners how to sprout seeds, turn soil, plant, and care for the results

"Reading this book will be fun. Sound gardening advice shares the pages with jokes, riddles and assorted tidbits of information. Brown's industrious animals make each page attractive and humorous. . . . Brown also shows a variety of easily made birdhouses and feeders and other garden-related crafts." Child Book Rev Serv

Huff, Barbara A.

Greening the city streets; the story of community gardens; photographs by Peter Ziebel. Clarion Bks. 1990 61p il $15.95 **635**

1. Gardening 2. Community life 3. New York (N.Y.)—Description
ISBN 0-89919-741-8 LC 89-22193

"The depiction of successful community gardens organized and maintained by amateurs of all ages demonstrates that urban life need not be colorless. Manhattan's Sixth Street and Avenue B Garden is highlighted. Includes a list of gardening organizations." Sci Child

Includes bibliography

Johnson, Sylvia A.

Potatoes; photographs by Masaharu Suzuki. Lerner Publs. 1984 47p il (Lerner natural science bk) lib bdg $12.95 (4 and up) **635**

1. Potatoes
ISBN 0-8225-1459-1 LC 84-5760

Johnson, Sylvia A.—*Continued*

Adapted from a work by Masaharu Suzuki published 1981 in Japan

"The book describes the growth of the potato from planting through harvesting. It explains the photosynthesis process and the growth of the tubers at the ends of the rhizomes. Insect and disease problems are discussed. Important and unfamiliar terms are printed in bold type in the text and are also listed in a glossary. The text is well written and the color photography is excellent." SLJ

Kuhn, Dwight

More than just a vegetable garden; photos and text by Dwight Kuhn. Silver Press 1990 40p il $12.95; lib bdg $15.98 (2-4) **635**

1. Vegetable gardening 2. Ecology
ISBN 0-671-69645-9; 0-671-69643-3 (lib bdg) LC 89-39504

Companion volume to: More than just a flower garden, entered in class 635.9

"A beautifully photographed look at the changing world of a vegetable garden and the many creatures that inhabit it is enhanced with clear, informative text. Includes simple instructions for starting a garden." Sci Child

Includes glossary

Oechsli, Helen

In my garden; a child's gardening book; [by] Helen & Kelly Oechsli. Macmillan 1985 32p il $12.95 (1-3) **635**

1. Vegetable gardening
ISBN 0-02-768510-1 LC 84-21285

This book "introduces a number of easily grown vegetables and provides some friendly advice on how to get a garden started. Beginners are counseled on how to find a good spot . . . how to prepare the soil, and how to plant. For plants that are growing, there is advice on weeding and, when seedlings are large enough, thinning. For youngsters with no outdoor space, some indoor gardening alternatives are suggested. . . . Perky cartoon illustrations in bright colors depict a variety of plants as well as sunny scenes of kids in the middle of gardening activities." Booklist

Sobol, Harriet Langsam, 1936-

A book of vegetables; [by] Harriet L. Sobol; photographs by Patricia A. Agre. Dodd, Mead 1984 unp il lib bdg $10.95 (1-3) **635**

1. Vegetables
ISBN 0-396-08450-8 LC 84-5991

An "introduction to how 14 vegetables are grown in the field. Highlighted are the vegetables' special characteristics, the ways they grow, and the fact that many emerge from fertilized flowers. (The author also includes interesting historical information on each.) Excellent close-up photographs—many in vivid color—help to clarify the simple text." Sci Child

Turner, Dorothy

Potatoes; illustrations by John Yates. Carolrhoda Bks. 1989 c1988 32p il (Foods we eat) lib bdg $9.95 (1-3) **635**

1. Potatoes
ISBN 0-87614-362-1 LC 88-24156

First published 1988 in the United Kingdom

"The history, methods of cultivation, uses, and nutritional value of potatoes. The well-done, cross-cultural, comprehensive book is generously illustrated with full-color photographs, engravings, and diagrams. Includes art projects and recipes." Sci Child

Includes glossary

Watts, Barrie

Tomato. Silver Burdett Press 1990 c1989 24p il $6.95 (k-3) **635**

1. Tomatoes
ISBN 0-382-24010-3 LC 89-38982

"A Stopwatch book"

First published 1989 in the United Kingdom

Follows, in text and illustrations, the development of a tomato from seedling to full maturity

"The photos, many in close-up, are so clear and well lit that every tiny hair glistens. History, gardening tips, and recipes are not included here: the scope of this book is strictly the growth of a tomato plant, and is presented exceptionally well." SLJ

635.9 Flowers and ornamental plants

Kuhn, Dwight

More than just a flower garden; photos and text by Dwight Kuhn. Silver Press 1990 40p il $12.95; lib bdg $15.98 (2-4) **635.9**

1. Flower gardening 2. Ecology
ISBN 0-671-69644-0; 0-671-69642-4 (lib bdg) LC 89-39511

Companion volume to: More than just a vegetable garden, enter in class 635

Describes the living things in a flower garden, focusing on the dynamic variety of plants and the creatures that depend on them. Includes tips for starting your own flower garden

"The text is not technical in [this] . . . stunningly photographed book. . . . Each enlargement of a part of a plant is the last word in clarity and beauty. In addition to gorgeous flowers . . . pictures are included of birds, worms, insects and other familiar garden visitors." Child Book Rev Serv

Includes glossary

Laird, Elizabeth

Rosy's garden: a child's keepsake of flowers; text by Elizabeth Laird, [illustrations by] Satomi Ichikawa. Philomel Bks. 1990 48p il $16.95 (3-5) **635.9**

1. Flowers
ISBN 0-399-21881-5 LC 89-22955

Laird, Elizabeth—*Continued*

Visiting her grandmother in the country, Rosy learns facts and folklore about flowers as she presses flowers, gathers seeds, and makes potpourri

"One of the things Rosy learns is how to make potpourri, and that word best describes this book. Grandmother's reminiscences, flower poems, some history and legends of individual flowers, the meanings of their names, and a few recipes are scattered randomly throughout, seemingly as a vehicle for Ichikawa's beautiful, botanically correct watercolors." SLJ

Patent, Dorothy Hinshaw

Flowers for everyone; photographs by William Muñoz. Cobblehill Bks. 1990 64p il $13.95 (4 and up) **635.9**

1. Flowers

ISBN 0-525-65025-3 LC 89-23937

The author discusses "the social significance of flowers, . . . how today's varieties are produced and distributed, . . . how flowers produce seeds or bulbs, . . . [and] the companies that make up the flower industry, including seed businesses, whose sole purpose is to provide seed; 'flower farmers,' who cultivate blossoms for florists; and nurseries, which grow starter plants for home gardeners." Booklist

"Profusely illustrated with large, often dazzling, color photographs. . . . Patent discusses the patient gamble of individual gardeners and large nurseries in developing new varieties and gives some interesting facts about plants of special interest to many hobbists—orchids, for example. The writing is crisp and direct; a glossary [is included]." Bull Cent Child Books

636 Animal husbandry

Tafuri, Nancy

Spots, feathers, and curly tails. Greenwillow Bks. 1988 unp il $11.95; lib bdg $11.88 (k-2) **636**

1. Domestic animals

ISBN 0-688-07536-3; 0-688-07537-1 (lib bdg) LC 87-15638

Questions and answers highlight some outstanding characteristics of farm animals, such as a chicken's feathers and a horse's mane

"In the watercolor illustrations with black pen outline, Nancy Tafuri manages in the simplest style to give energy and personality to the animals through the angle of a head or the set of a snout. The story will provide a successful experience for both child and adult reader and is an ideal book for the beginning reader to entertain a younger sibling in a game they'll both enjoy." Horn Book

636.08 Production and maintenance, animals for specific purposes, veterinary sciences

Curtis, Patricia, 1923-

The animal shelter; photographs by David Cupp. Dutton 1984 163 p il $13.95 (5 and up) **636.08**

1. Animal abuse

ISBN 0-525-66783-0 LC 83-8908

"Lodestar books"

This book "begins by describing several cases of people bringing their pets to the animal shelter. The next section describes the history of humane societies and mentions some of the people involved in their founding. Several of the legal aspects of the rights of animals are discussed such as abuse, cruelty, neglect, dogfighting, rights and responsibilities of owners." Voice Youth Advocates

Includes bibliography

Fischer-Nagel, Heiderose, 1956-

Inside the burrow: the life of the golden hamster; by Heiderose and Andreas Fischer-Nagel. Carolrhoda Bks. 1986 47p il (Carolrhoda nature watch bk) $12.95; pa $6.95 (3-6) **636.08**

1. Hamsters

ISBN 0-87614-286-2; 0-87614-478-4 (pa) LC 86-2591

Original German edition published 1984 in Switzerland

Describes the characteristics and behavior of hamsters both in the wild and in captivity, as demonstrated by a pair observed in a burrow built by the authors. Includes information on caring for pet hamsters

The authors combine "brilliantly clear color photography with an impersonal, informational text." Bull Cent Child Books

Hess, Lilo

Time for ferrets. Scribner 1987 48p il $12.95 (3-5) **636.08**

1. Ferrets

ISBN 0-684-18788-4 LC 87-9765

"According to Hess, ferrets—a domesticated member of the weasel family—recently have become popular as pets. Her congenial photo essay follows the care of three young animals abandoned on the farm of an Animal Rescue Shelter worker. The narrative accompanying the attractive photographs describes their physical characteristics and temperament, proper housing and sleeping arrangements, feeding, handling, grooming, and health matters." SLJ

636.088 Animals for specific purposes

Arnold, Caroline, 1944-

Pets without homes; photographs by Richard Hewett. Clarion Bks. 1983 46p il lib bdg $14.95 (k-3) **636.088**

1. Pets 2. Animal abuse

ISBN 0-89919-191-6 LC 83-2106

"The book focuses on one puppy picked up by a police officer whose job includes work for the city's animal shelter, enforcement of municipal laws about animals, and giving talks at schools." Bull Cent Child Books

"Hewett's photographs are engaging, expressive and well composed. The clean, varied, well-chosen layout complements the emotional points of the text. Throughout, the text and illustrations form a harmonious unity of compassion and care beyond the lucid, informative focus of the book." SLJ

Bare, Colleen Stanley

Guinea pigs don't read books; photographs by the author. Dodd, Mead 1985 unp il $11.95 (k-2) **636.088**

1. Guinea pigs

ISBN 0-399-21910-2 LC 84-18707

"Color photographs of good quality illustrate a text that is simply written, an excellent first book on the subject for young children. The text points out what guinea pigs do and what they cannot do; it shows some of the varieties of the species, and it points out that guinea pigs make good pets, being calm and gentle animals that like to be held and cuddled." Bull Cent Child Books

Chrystie, Francis N., 1904-1986

Pets; a complete handbook on the care, understanding, and appreciation of all kinds of animal pets; with illustrations by Gillett Good Griffin. 3d rev ed. Little, Brown 1974 xxi, 269p il $15.95 (4 and up) **636.088**

1. Pets

ISBN 0-316-14051-1 LC 73-21819

First published 1953

Contents: Dogs; Cats; Small caged animals; Caged birds; Aquarium and vivarium pets; Wild animals and birds; Farm animals; Ponies and saddle horses; First aid and common diseases

Hess, Lilo

Making friends with guinea pigs. Scribner 1983 48p il $12.95 (4-6) **636.088**

1. Guinea pigs

ISBN 0-684-17853-2 LC 82-21632

Describes the experiences of three guinea pigs born in the same litter as one becomes a child's pet, another a laboratory animal and later a class mascot, and the third a prize specimen for showing and breeding

"Smoothly written and well photographed in black and white, this is a practical, light introduction to the species." Booklist

Pope, Joyce

Taking care of your gerbils; photographs by: Sally Anne Thompson and R.T. Willbie/animal photography. Watts 1987 32p il lib bdg $10.90; pa $3.95 (3-5) **636.088**

1. Gerbils

ISBN 0-531-10190-8 (lib bdg); 0-531-15168-9 (pa) LC 85-52086

Aimed at the beginning pet owner, this book covers choosing and caring for gerbils, as well as creating a "gerbilarium" for burrowing and tunnelling, and tips on finding wild food

Taking care of your mice and rats; photographs by: Sally Anne Thompson and R.T. Willbie/animal photography. Watts 1988 c1987 32p il lib bdg $10.90; pa $3.95 (3-5) **636.088**

1. Mice 2. Rats

ISBN 0-531-10190-6 (lib bdg); 0-531-15172-7 (pa) LC 85-52087

First published 1987 in the United Kingdom

The author discusses the selection, feeding, exercise and hygiene of pet mice and rats

Taking care of your rabbit; photographs by: Sally Anne Thompson and R.T. Willbie/animal photography. Watts 1987 32p il lib bdg $10.90; pa $3.95 (3-5) **636.088**

1. Rabbits

ISBN 0-531-10189-4 (lib bdg); 0-531-15171-9 (pa) LC 85-52085

Basic information on varieties, selection, care and hygiene is supplemented by hints on building hutches and cages, food preferences and housetraining

Rinard, Judith E., 1947-

Helping our animal friends; photographs by Susan McElhinney. National Geographic Soc. 1985 31p il (k-3) **636.088**

1. Pets 2. Animals

ISBN 0-87044-559-6; 0-87044-564-2 (lib bdg) LC 85-2994

Available only as part of 4v set for $10.95, lib bdg $12.95. Other titles in set are: Creatures of the woods, by Toni Eugene; Penguins and polar bears, by Sandra Lee Crow; and The world beneath your feet, by Judith E. Rinard, entered in class 591.9

"Books for young explorers"

Children demonstrate proper care of pets and of sick or helpless wild animals who may need our help from time to time

Silverstein, Alvin

Hamsters: all about them; [by] Alvin & Virginia Silverstein; with photographs by Frederick Breda. Lothrop, Lee & Shepard Bks. 1974 126p il lib bdg $12.88 (5 and up) **636.088**

1. Hamsters

ISBN 0-688-50056-0 LC 74-8863

This book is a manual for the hamster owner, with information on the care, feeding, housing, and breeding of these pets. Types of hamsters and their use in laboratory research is also discussed

Simon, Norma

Cats do, dogs don't; pictures by Dora Leder. Whitman, A. 1986 unp il lib bdg $12.95 (k-2) **636.088**

1. Dogs 2. Cats

ISBN 0-8075-1102-1 LC 86-5618

This volume describes "the advantages and disadvantages of each kind of pet. . . . The expressive full-color illustrations, some of which are two-page spreads, feature boys and girls of various races, charmingly yet realistically interacting with their dogs and cats. The cool, clear colors Leder uses are easy on the eyes, and she shows off her skill for drawing animals in the diversity of breeds she portrays." Booklist

Sproule, Anna

Guinea pigs; [by] Anna and Michael Sproule. Bookwright Press 1989 46p il (Know your pet) lib bdg $11.90 (4 and up) **636.088**

1. Guinea pigs

ISBN 0-531-18265-7 LC 88-26221

Describes the physical characteristics, habits, and natural environment of guinea pigs and gives instruction on how to care for them as pets

"Neat, thorough instructions on buying and caring, . . . breeding and varieties." Horn Book Guide

Includes glossary and bibliography

Mice and rats; [by] Anna and Michael Sproule. Bookwright Press 1989 46p il (Know your pet) lib bdg $11.90 (4 and up) **636.088**

1. Mice 2. Rats

ISBN 0-531-18266-5 LC 88-26206

Describes the physical characteristics, habits, and natural environment of domesticated mice and rats and gives instructions on how to care for them as pets

Includes glossary and bibliography

Stewart, John, 1920-

Elephant school; written and photographed by John Stewart. Pantheon Bks. 1982 55p il lib bdg $10.99 (4-6) **636.088**

1. Elephants—Training 2. Thailand—Social life and customs

ISBN 0-394-95085-2 LC 81-20796

A "school in Thailand educates its students—young elephants—for a lifetime of work in the country's teak forests. Somchai, a Thai boy, will spend four years at the school training Pang Pon, the elephant assigned to him; he is a mahout, or elephant man. The book describes the boy's routine at the Young Elephant Training Center as he learns to 'break' his new calf and to teach her the various skills for forestry work." Horn Book

Venino, Suzanne

Animals helping people. National Geographic Soc. 1983 31p il (k-3) **636.088**

1. Working animals

ISBN 0-87044-490-5; 0-87044-495-6 (lib bdg) LC 83-13184

Available only as part of 4v set for $10.95, lib bdg $12.95. Other titles in set are: Baby birds and how they grow, by Jane R. McCauley, class 598; Creatures small and furry, by Donald J. Crump, class 599; and Ways animals sleep, by Jane R. McCauley, class 591.5

"Books for young explorers"

Briefly describes some of the many tasks that animals perform and other ways in which they benefit people

The book "includes an international cast of camels from Africa, elephants and water buffalo from Asia, sled dogs from the Arctic, donkeys and horses from Europe and sheep from the American southwest." SLJ

Weber, William J.

Care of uncommon pets; rabbits, guinea pigs, hamsters, mice, rats, gerbils, chickens, ducks, frogs, toads and salamanders, turtles and tortoises, snakes and lizards, and budgerigars; photographs by the author. Holt & Co. 1979 222p il $10.95; pa $5.95 (5 and up) **636.088**

1. Pets

ISBN 0-8050-0294-4; 0-8050-0320-7 (pa) LC 78-14093

"Clear, detailed advice on housing and breeding of each is provided, including step-by-step directions for building cages. The author, a veterinarian, also discusses diseases common to each type of pet and suggests prevention and treatments. . . . Although amphibian aquariums are described, aquariums for fish have been excluded." SLJ

Includes glossary and bibliographies

Wexler, Jerome

Pet mice; text and photos by Jerome Wexler. Whitman, A. 1989 48p il $13.95 (3-6) **636.088**

1. Mice

ISBN 0-8075-6524-5

Text and color photographs describe how to house, feed, and handle a pair of pet mice and the families they produce

"A wealth of information on the selection, care, breeding, and training of pet mice. Attractive color photographs highlight and supplement the text. Wexler's writing is clear and his advice practical. . . . This is

Wexler, Jerome—*Continued*
an excellent resource for both new and experienced pet mice owners." SLJ

636.1 Horses and related animals

Cole, Joanna
A horse's body; photographs by Jerome Wexler. Morrow 1981 45p il $13.95; lib bdg $13.88 **636.1**

1. Horses
ISBN 0-688-00362-1; 0-688-00363-X (lib bdg) LC 80-28147

An introduction to the horse, its habits, anatomy, physiology, and evolution

"A sensible, straightforward, and comprehensive introduction to the anatomy of the horse, neatly packaged in a simple format." Horn Book

"This can be read aloud to younger children and will attract older reluctant readers, too." SLJ

Featherly, Jay
Mustangs: wild horses of the American West. Carolrhoda Bks. 1986 47p il (Carolrhoda nature watch bk) lib bdg $12.95 (3-6) **636.1**

1. Horses
ISBN 0-87614-293-5 LC 86-8314

Describes the habits and behavior of the wild horses which have roamed across the American West for hundreds of years

"A generous supply of full-color photographs anchors this introduction to wild horses of the American West. . . . The writing is smooth, and a glossary is appended; this is an attractive introduction for younger readers." Booklist

Henry, Marguerite, 1902-
Album of horses; illustrated by Wesley Dennis. Rand McNally 1951 112p il $11.95 (4 and up) **636.1**

1. Horses
ISBN 0-528-82050-8 LC 51-15002

"A handsomely illustrated volume describing 20 breeds of horses, from the Shetland pony to the thoroughbred race horse, anecdotal in style and including many little-known facts." Hodges. Books for Elem Sch Libr

Isenbart, Hans-Heinrich, 1923-
Birth of a foal; photographs by Thomas David. Carolrhoda Bks. 1986 48p il (Carolrhoda nature watch bk) lib bdg $12.95 (3-6) **636.1**

1. Horses
ISBN 0-87614-239-0 LC 85-17406

Original German edition published 1983 in Switzerland

This book describes the birth and first few hours of a foal's life

"The text is quite detailed, containing many facts and figures about the developing fetus, how long it takes to be born, size and weight at birth, etc. . . . The illustrations are color photographs, varying somewhat in quality. Although most of the photographs are sharp and clear, a few are fuzzy or grainy. . . . All of the photographs are appropriate for even very young readers." Appraisal

Includes glossary

Jurmain, Suzanne
Once upon a horse; a history of horses—and how they shaped our history. Lothrop, Lee & Shepard Bks. 1989 176p il $15.95 (6 and up) **636.1**

1. Horses
ISBN 0-688-05550-8 LC 88-17522

"To describe the horse's contribution to history, Jurmain includes myths, legends, art, and fact in a readable narrative. The subject is divided by chapters that cover each type of interaction between horses and people (e.g. 'The War-Horse,' 'The Messenger,' 'The Racehorse'). The result is a special-interest book for the combination horse lover/history buff. The photographs of period artwork have been carefully selected." Bull Cent Child Books

Includes bibliography

LaBonte, Gail
The miniature horse. Dillon Press 1990 59p il (Dillon remarkable animals bk) $12.95 (3-5) **636.1**

1. Horses
ISBN 0-87518-424-3 LC 89-26046

The author describes the appearance, behavior, and rearing of the miniature horse and discusses its development, uses, and growing popularity in North America

"Excellent full-color action photographs, including those matching a miniature ear-to-ear with a child and nose-to-nose with a dog to establish its relative size, make the book as appealing as its subject. The glossary of bold-type words, index, and list of places that welcome visits expand the book's information potential." SLJ

Lavine, Sigmund A.
Wonders of draft horses; [by] Sigmund A. Lavine and Brigid Casey. Dodd, Mead 1983 79p il lib bdg $10.95 (4 and up) **636.1**

1. Horses
ISBN 0-396-08138-X LC 82-46002

"Dodd, Mead wonders books"

"This volume surveys the six most popular breeds: Belgian, Clydesdale, Percheron, Shire, Suffolk and American Cream. The draft horse in history and contemporary uses on farms and in cities are discussed." SLJ

"The book makes effective uses of numerous drawings and photographs, although they are all black and white unfortunately, and it will make a good library reference acquisition." Sci Books Films

Patent, Dorothy Hinshaw

Appaloosa horses; photographs by William Muñoz. Holiday House 1988 74p il $14.95 (4 and up) **636.1**

1. Horses

ISBN 0-8234-0706-3 LC 88-4470

"Following a discussion of the Nez Perce and Palouse tribes' development of the horses and the subsequent disbanding of the animals by white settlers are chapters on Appaloosa traits and on organizations sponsoring activities for riders. Black-and-white photographs show common markings, including blankets and spots, roans, and combinations. A natural for browsers in 'the horse stage' or students seeking information for reports." Bull Cent Child Books

Includes glossary and bibliography

Draft horses; photographs by William Muñoz. Holiday House 1986 86p il lib bdg $12.95 (4 and up) **636.1**

1. Horses

ISBN 0-8234-0597-4 LC 85-21998

This book "traces the history of draft horses, distinguishes among the prominent breeds, and describes their contributions to farm work, the competitions testing their strength, and some basic points of care and training. Although color photography would have augmented the careful textual references to various breeds markings, the abundant black-and-white photos are clear, well-composed, and handsomely informative." Bull Cent Child Books

Includes glossary and bibliography

A horse of a different color; photographs by William Muñoz. Dodd, Mead 1988 64p il lib bdg $13.95 (4 and up) **636.1**

1. Horses

ISBN 0-396-08836-8 LC 87-25165

"Excellent full-color photographs and easy-to-read text explain the derivation and variation of common and unusual horse colors and markings. A must for the horse enthusiast and informative for the inquisitive." Sci Child

Includes glossary

Horses of America. Holiday House 1981 80p il lib bdg $14.95 (4 and up) **636.1**

1. Horses

ISBN 0-8234-0399-8 LC 81-4165

Discusses the evolution and characteristics of various breeds of horses and identifies breeds for work, sports, and pleasure, and those that are "all-around" horses

"Striking photographs supplement the concise text, making a volume less detailed than some books on horses but one that is nevertheless a valuable and attractive reference work." Horn Book

Includes glossary and bibliography

Quarter horses; photographs by William Muñoz and others. Holiday House 1985 91p il lib bdg $12.95 (4 and up) **636.1**

1. Horses

ISBN 0-8234-0573-7 LC 85-904

This book describes the "history of the popular American Quarter Horse, its migration across the United States, famous Quarter Horses, the uses of the Quarter Horse on a ranch or farm, Quarter Horse competitions and racing." SLJ

"Captioned black and white photographs abound to illustrate and expand upon the text. Thoroughly researched and well-written, this book will be enjoyed." Appraisal

Includes glossary and bibliography

Sayer, Angela

The young rider's handbook. Arco 1984 c1980 224p il $9.95 (5 and up) **636.1**

1. Ponies 2. Horseback riding

ISBN 0-668-06044-1 LC 83-19734

First published 1980 in the United Kingdom

"Despite its title, this manual for young equestrians is more concerned with selection, everyday care, and health of ponies . . . than with actual riding techniques. . . . British origins of the text surface occasionally, especially in the section dealing with pedigreed ponies, but there is still a plethora of advice and instruction applicable to any pony keeper." Booklist

Includes glossary

636.2 Ruminants. Bovines. Cattle

Kaizuki, Kiyonori

A calf is born; translated from the Japanese by Cathy Hirano. Orchard Bks. 1990 unp il $13.95; lib bdg $13.99 (k-2) **636.2**

1. Cattle 2. Reproduction

ISBN 0-531-05862-X; 0-531-08462-0 (lib bdg) LC 89-23091

Original Japanese edition, 1988

This book describes the birth of a calf one cold winter night and his first day of life as he learns to stand, ventures out of doors, and nuzzles up to his tired mother

"The Japanese farm setting is very much like its American counterpart and brings an added universal touch to the story. Golden browns and tans predominate in the wintry pictures capturing well the ebb and flow of farmyard activity." Booklist

McFarland, Cynthia

Cows in the parlor; a visit to a dairy farm. Atheneum Pubs. 1990 unp il $13.95 (1-3) **636.2**

1. Dairying

ISBN 0-689-31584-8 LC 89-14972

The author discusses the daily routine of Clear Creek Farm and its herd of fifty dairy cows

This book "clearly shows the basic workings of a dairy farm, including haymaking, silaging, feeding, and automatic milking. The color photos are sometimes dark . . . but the commonsensical tone informing both text and pictures is forthrightly informative." Bull Cent Child Books

636.3 Sheep and goats

Paladino, Catherine
Spring fleece; a day of sheepshearing. Little, Brown 1990 48p il lib bdg $14.95 (3-6) **636.3**

1. Sheep 2. Wool
ISBN 0-316-68890-8 LC 89-12820

"Joy Street books"

"A handsome photo-essay describes the work of sheep-shearers as they travel to two New England farms. A comprehensive look at an ancient craft told with warmth and drama." Sci Child

"Silvery black-and-white photographs document the process of wool 'harvesting.' . . . This focuses on the small unmechanized family farm, and the tone is nostalgic. . . . Along with the time-ago atmosphere, however, is plenty of solid, interesting, and well-organized information. This is an engaging addition for the where-does-it-come-from collection." Bull Cent Child Books

636.5 Poultry. Chickens

Cole, Joanna
A chick hatches; photographs by Jerome Wexler. Morrow 1976 46p il lib bdg $12.88 (k-3) **636.5**

1. Chickens 2. Reproduction 3. Eggs
ISBN 0-688-32087-2 LC 76-29017

"A simply written account of the development from egg to embryo to fetus to chick is made more meaningful by the accompanying photographs, some in color and almost all enlarged. The writing is matter-of-fact, but the pictures of the developing fetus make the recurrent miracle of reproduction vividly clear." Bull Cent Child Books

Selsam, Millicent Ellis, 1912-
Egg to chick; by Millicent E. Selsam; pictures by Barbara Wolff. rev ed. Harper & Row 1970 63p il (Science I can read bk) $11.89; pa $3.50 (k-3) **636.5**

1. Chickens 2. Embryology 3. Eggs
ISBN 0-06-025290-1; 0-06-444113-X (pa) LC 74-85034

First published 1946

Easy-to-read science text traces the fertilization of the egg and the growth and hatching out of the chick

636.6 Birds other than poultry

Mowat, Farley
Owls in the family; illustrated by Robert Frankenberg. Little, Brown 1961 103p il $14.95; Bantam Bks. pa $2.75 (4 and up) **636.6**

1. Owls
ISBN 0-316-58641-2; 0-553-15585-7 (pa) LC 62-7169

"An Atlantic Monthly Press book"

"Two owls, Wol and Weeps, who are found as babies at the beginning of this account, were the author's own pets during his boyhood in Saskatoon. The description of the owls' endearing and humorous traits, their intelligence and mischief in upsetting household and neighbors, is continuously absorbing and provocative of hearty laughter. Their personalities are vividly different. . . . Outstanding for reading aloud." Horn Book

636.7 Dogs

American Kennel Club
The complete dog book. Howell Bk. House il $19.95 **636.7**

1. Dogs

First published 1935. Frequently revised

"The official guide to 124 AKC registered breeds and their history, appearance, selection, training, care and feeding, and first aid. Some color plates." N Y Public Libr. Ref Books for Child Collect

Ancona, George, 1929-
Sheep dog; words and photographs by George Ancona. Lothrop, Lee & Shepard Bks. 1985 unp il $12.95; lib bdg $12.88 (4 and up) **636.7**

1. Sheep dogs 2. Working animals
ISBN 0-688-04118-3; 0-688-04119-1 (lib bdg) LC 84-20100

Describes the various breeds of dogs used to guard and herd sheep, explains how they work, and discusses the importance of these dogs to the sheep industry

Black-and-white photographs depict the "natural setting for the dogs at work and play. The text is concise, interesting and highly informative for research for both dogs and the sheep industry. George Ancona is a professional photographer, but it is his special affinity for children that contributes to the appeal of this book. It is a must for the ever popular book section about dogs." Okla State Dept of Educ

Includes bibliography

Cohen, Susan, 1938-
What kind of dog is that? rare & unusual breeds of dogs; [by] Susan and Daniel Cohen. Cobblehill Bks. 1989 131p il $12.95 (4 and up) **636.7**

1. Dogs
ISBN 0-525-65011-3 LC 89-34462

Discusses the history, physical characteristics, and behavior of twenty-five unusual dog breeds including the Fila Brasileiro, the Peruvian Inca Orchid, the Jack Russell Terrier, and the Chinese Crested

Written with "humor and a lively style. . . . A wonderful picture of each breed emerges, reinforced by expressive black-and-white photographs."

Includes bibliography

Cole, Joanna

A dog's body; photographs by Jim and Ann Monteith. Morrow 1986 48p il $12.95; lib bdg $12.88 **636.7**

1. Dogs
ISBN 0-688-04153-1; 0-688-04154-X (lib bdg) LC 85-25885

"Cole discusses dogs' lupine ancestry, how different breeds were developed, why certain senses are more important than others." Bull Cent Child Books

"A clear and simple account of how a dog's body is suited for his lifestyle. . . . Black-and-white photographs and line drawings enhance the text. This book will be helpful to 3rd and 4th graders writing reports and will be enjoyed by younger children and parents who want to know more about their favorite pet." Appraisal

My puppy is born; photographs by Margaret Miller. rev and expanded ed. Morrow Junior Bks. 1991 unp il $13.95; lib bdg $13.88; pa $4.95 (k-3) **636.7**

1. Dogs 2. Reproduction
ISBN 0-688-09770-7; 0-688-09771-5 (lib bdg); 0-688-10198-4 (pa) LC 90-42011

A revised and newly illustrated edition of the title first published 1973

"As a little girl anxiously awaits the birth of puppies by the Norfolk terrier next door, a story unfolds. The puppies' arrival and first few weeks of life and development are shown and described in a simple narrative." SLJ

Exquisitely sharp, well-designed color photos capture the events, stage by stage. . . . As the puppy grows, the reader watches its first halting steps, messy eating habits, and snoozing poses. A gem for preschoolers and a sure bet for older youngsters." Booklist

Curtis, Patricia, 1923-

Cindy, a hearing ear dog; photographs by David Cupp. Dutton 1981 55p il $13.95 (3-5) **636.7**

1. Hearing ear dogs 2. Dogs—Training
ISBN 0-525-27950-4 LC 80-24487

This book tells the story of Cindy's rescue from an animal shelter to train her to be a hearing ear dog. The photo-essay format describes "her weeks of training by a . . . team of college students and with her new owner—a deaf teenager." Horn Book

Greff, the story of a guide dog; photographs by Mary Bloom. Lodestar Bks. 1982 53 p il $9.95 (5 and up) **636.7**

1. Guide dogs
ISBN 0-525-66754-7 LC 81-23623

Traces the life of a Labrador retriever from birth through training at the Guide Dog Foundation, where he is introduced to the blind owner for whom he will be responsible

"A generous open format and abundant pictures of Greff and his people give the book an inviting look. This is a personable, appealing introduction to a subject kids find perennially intriguing." Booklist

Fischer-Nagel, Heiderose, 1956-

A puppy is born; by Heiderose & Andreas Fischer-Nagel; translated by Andrea Mernan. Putnam 1985 unp il $10.95 (1-4) **636.7**

1. Dogs 2. Reproduction
ISBN 0-399-21234-5 LC 85-3505

Photographs and text portray the birth and first few weeks of four wirehaired dachshunds

"This Fischer-Nagels' text reads more like a story than nonfiction, but it is chock-full of information. Puppies make naturally engaging photographic subjects, but these color pictures are exceptional—sharp, action-filled, and fully capturing all the canines' charms. Sure to elicit oohs and aahs from young readers, yet useful as well." Booklist

Hausherr, Rosmarie

My first puppy. Four Winds Press 1986 64p il $12.95 (1-3) **636.7**

1. Dogs
ISBN 0-02-743410-9 LC 86-14979

Photographs and text follow a girl as she selects her first puppy and learns about its feeding, grooming, training, and medical care. A section for parents discusses where and how to acquire a dog, spaying and neutering, various aspects of home care, and suggested rules for children

Kuklin, Susan

Taking my dog to the vet. Bradbury Press 1988 unp il $12.95 (k-2) **636.7**

1. Dogs 2. Veterinary medicine
ISBN 0-02-751234-7 LC 88-5047

"A little girl takes her Cairn Terrier to the veterinarian for his annual check-up. The vet is gentle and explains to Minal what he is doing to her dog and why. . . . Color photographs illustrate the text well and add a warm touch to the story." SLJ

Pinkwater, Jill

Superpuppy: how to choose, raise, and train the best possible dog for you; by Jill and D. Manus Pinkwater; line drawings by Jill Pinkwater. Clarion Bks. 1977 206p il $13.95; pa $7.95 (5 and up) **636.7**

1. Dogs
ISBN 0-395-28878-9; 0-89919-084-7 (pa) LC 76-8825

First published by Seabury Press

"The authors begin by suggesting that you examine your reasons for owning a dog. The rest of the book details all the problems and rewards of caring for a dog." Publ Wkly

Includes bibliography

Pope, Joyce
Taking care of your dog; photographs by: Sally Anne Thompson and R.T. Willbie/animal photography. Watts 1986 32p il lib bdg $10.90; pa $3.95 (3-5) **636.7**

1. Dogs
ISBN 0-531-10160-6 (lib bdg); 0-531-15166-6 (pa)
LC 85-51604

The author describes briefly different types of breeds, food and hygiene, equipment and training, and the dog owner's responsibilities

Siegel, Mary-Ellen
More than a friend: dogs with a purpose; by Mary-Ellen Siegel and Hermine M. Koplin; photographs by Stephanie Bee Koplin. Walker & Co. 1984 133p il $10.95 (5 and up) **636.7**

1. Dogs
ISBN 0-8027-6558-0 LC 84-17253

Describes some of the jobs for which dogs have been trained and their work as hunters, shepherds, guides for the handicapped, guards, detectives, and friends and companions

Includes bibliography

Silverstein, Alvin
Dogs: all about them; by Alvin and Virginia Silverstein; with an introduction by John C. McLoughlin. Lothrop, Lee & Shepard Bks. 1986 256p il lib bdg $11.75 (5 and up) **636.7**

1. Dogs
ISBN 0-688-04805-6 LC 84-29723

Discusses the evolution of dogs and their uses throughout history and includes information on different breeds, training, care as pets, relationship with people, and other relevant topics

"This book is superb; its informative; its readable, and most of all its enjoyable." Appraisal

Includes bibliography

Smith, Elizabeth Simpson
A service dog goes to school; the story of a dog trained to help the disabled; illustrated by Steven Petruccio. Morrow Junior Bks. 1988 65p il $12.95; lib bdg $12.88 (3-5) **636.7**

1. Dogs—Training 2. Animals and the handicapped
ISBN 0-688-07648-3; 0-688-07649-1 (lib bdg)
LC 88-17598

Follows the selection raising, training, and placement with a young disabled boy of a service dog named Licorice. Includes a list of service dog schools and organizations

"A photoessay might have had more immediacy than Smith's fictionalized account, which features many pencil illustrations, but format notwithstanding, this volume has both drama and heartfelt emotion, along with useful information." Booklist

636.8 Cats

Cole, Joanna
A cat's body; photographs by Jerome Wexler. Morrow 1982 48p il $11.95; lib bdg $12.88 **636.8**

1. Cats
ISBN 0-688-01052-0; 0-688-01054-7 (lib bdg)
LC 81-22386

The authors "show how well designed and programmed a cat is to catch small rodents (but not birds) and how its abilities, instincts and ways of socializing with other cats fit into the domestic cat's life with humans. The brief, substantive text, clear, informative photos and open, welcoming layout will attract preschoolers." SLJ

De Paola, Tomie, 1934-
The kids' cat book; written and illustrated by Tomie de Paola. Holiday House 1979 unp il lib bdg $13.95; pa $5.95 (2-4) **636.8**

1. Cats
ISBN 0-8234-0365-3 (lib bdg); 0-8234-0534-6 (pa)
LC 79-2090

Patrick goes to Granny Twinkle's for a free kitten and learns everything there is to know about cats—their different breeds, care, place in art and literature, and history

"The illustrations add great touches of humor and show cats being cats everywhere. All those who have new kittens will find useful information." Child Book Rev Serv

Hausherr, Rosmarie
My first kitten. Four Winds Press 1985 48p il $12.95 (1-3) **636.8**

1. Cats
ISBN 0-02-743420-6 LC 85-42804

Seven-year-old Adam has a summer full of new experiences and responsibilities when he receives a kitten for a pet

"Quite a bit of information on cats works its way into the story, including safety tips, health needs, and feline habits both funny and annoying. A last page addressed to parents summarizes tips on pet care. The black-and-white photographs are large, clear, and well-composed, with no posturing on the part of the people or cutesiness in the presentation of the animal. An attractive introduction to responsible pet ownership." Bull Cent Child Books

Hess, Lilo
A cat's nine lives. Scribner 1984 47p il $12.95 (2-5) **636.8**

1. Cats
ISBN 0-684-18073-1 LC 83-20236

Chronicles the nine lives of Misty, a purebred Persian cat, from her birth in a cattery, through several owners, a stint as a show cat, a stay in an animal shelter, a period of homelessness, and finally a good home with a loving owner

Misty's "experiences will carry built-in appeal for

Hess, Lilo—*Continued*
young children, who will also absorb an important lesson on being responsible for their pets. The author's appealing black-and-white photographs help tell the story." Booklist

Kuklin, Susan
Taking my cat to the vet. Bradbury Press 1988 unp il $12.95 (k-2) **636.8**
1. Cats 2. Veterinary medicine
ISBN 0-02-751233-9 LC 88-5052
"Young Ben tells readers about taking his cat Willa, adopted as a kitten from the A.S.P.C.A., to the veterinarian for a standard checkup. The vet . . . explains her way through the examination, testing Willa's eyes and ears, taking her temperature, trimming her nails, and giving her shots. The dialogue rarely strains to be informative, and the large color photographs are well composed and businesslike." Bull Cent Child Books

Overbeck, Cynthia
Cats; photographs by Shin Yoshino. Lerner Publs. 1983 48p il (Lerner natural science bk) lib bdg $12.95 (4 and up) **636.8**
1. Cats
ISBN 0-8225-1480-X LC 83-17530
Adapted from a work by Shin Yoshino published 1980 in Japan
This book "dwells primarily on domestic felines as it describes appearance, behavior, and reproductive patterns, though wild species make appearances throughout the narrative." Booklist
Books in this series have been translated "into a lucid flowing text for the American public. The superior color photographs do justice to the text." Appraisal
Includes glossary

637 Processing dairy and related products

Carrick, Donald
Milk. Greenwillow Bks. 1985 unp il lib bdg $12.88 (k-1) **637**
1. Milk 2. Dairying
ISBN 0-688-04823-4 LC 84-25879
"This beautifully illustrated book follows milk from the farm to the grocer's shelf. The large, clear print and carefully detailed full-page illustrations make this an excellent read-aloud book for young children. A delightful vicarious experience that can set the stage for a field trip to a dairy farm." Sci Child

Cobb, Vicki
The scoop on ice cream; illustrated by G. Brian Karas. Little, Brown 1985 57p il (How the world works) $11.95 (4-6) **637**
1. Ice cream, ices, etc.
ISBN 0-316-14895-4 LC 85-6881
Outlines the ingredients and making of ice cream and the role played by the manufacturers, retailers, and suppliers of this popular dessert. Includes a taste test and recipe for the homemade variety
"There is scarcely any question children might ask that is not answered in 'The Scoop on Ice Cream.' In fact sections of the text, for example, 'the Ice Cream Factory' and 'Sugar' may come close to telling more than some readers will care to know. . . . The line drawings that illustrate the text leave something to be desired if they are intended to clarify the concepts, but there is a good index." Appraisal

Gibbons, Gail
The milk makers. Macmillan 1985 unp il $13.95; pa $3.95 (k-2) **637**
1. Dairying 2. Dairy cattle
ISBN 0-02-736640-5; 0-689-71116-6 (pa)
LC 84-20081
Explains how cows produce milk and how it is processed before being delivered to stores
"Starting with dairy cows grazing at pasture, nothing is overlooked in the procedure, from the role of the calf to winter feed and shelter, the function of four stomachs, milking, milk handling, and the operation of a dairy. Diagrams of the cow stomachs as well as the machines used at farm and dairy leave no question unanswered, although city children will be unfamiliar with what it means to breed a cow. Finally, there is a pictorial list of the many other dairy products found in most homes." Sci Books Films

Giblin, James, 1933-
Milk: the fight for purity; [by] James Cross Giblin; illustrated with photographs and prints. Crowell 1986 106p il $12.70; lib bdg $12.89 (5 and up) **637**
1. Milk 2. Dairying
ISBN 0-690-04572-7; 0-690-04574-3 (lib bdg)
LC 85-48252
The author "discusses the history of milk as a central source of nutrition, from ancient times to the present, and as a carrier of disease due to ignorance and careless handling. Given high profile here are the people responsible for creating standards—from Louis Pasteur to Nathan Straus, a man who understood the importance of pure milk early on and provided it to poor families and orphans. Also covered are more than recent problems that have plagued the industry, from radiation poisoning . . . to salmonella poisoning." Publ Wkly
"Clearly written and well illustrated . . . this book also contains an index and a bibliography documenting the thorough research that went into its writing." Appraisal

Jaspersohn, William
Ice cream; written and photographed by William Jaspersohn. Macmillan 1988 43p il $13.95 (3-5) **637**
1. Ben & Jerry's Homemade Inc. 2. Ice cream, ices, etc.
ISBN 0-02-747821-1 LC 87-38331

Jaspersohn, William—*Continued*

"Looking at a small Vermont manufacturer, Ben & Jerry's, Jaspersohn describes in text and black-and-white photographs how ice cream is made, from cow to cone. The photos are clear and precise and in most cases add detail to the text rather than just mirroring it. Informative diagrams provide more information. Jaspersohn's text is well written and full of interesting details that will fascinate youngsters." SLJ

639 Hunting, fishing, conservation, related technologies

Simon, Seymour, 1931-

Pets in a jar; collecting and caring for small wild animals; illustrated by Betty Fraser. Viking 1975 95p il o.p.; Penguin Bks. paperback available $5.95 (4 and up) **639**

1. Invertebrates 2. Pets
ISBN 0-14-049186-4 (pa) LC 74-14905

The author "offers valuable information not readily found elsewhere on collecting and maintaining hydras, planaria, several water insects, crickets, ants, saltwater brine shrimp, hermit crabs, and starfish. Moreover, he suggests experiments such as causing a planarian to generate two heads." Horn Book

639.2 Commercial fishing, whaling, sealing

Scarry, Huck, 1953-

Life on a fishing boat; a sketchbook. Prentice-Hall 1983 69p il maps $10.95 (3-6) **639.2**

1. Fisheries 2. Fishing 3. Boats and boating
ISBN 0-13-535856-6 LC 83-9631

The author-illustrator's "personalized look at the fishing industry, mostly as it operates off Frances' Brittany coast and in the North Sea. Scarry went aboard several fishing vessels, and what he saw is deftly recorded on these pages. Besides shipboard scenes, readers also see dockside and port activities, market operations, and canning factories. At the close is a brief look at what's caught where in North American waters." Booklist

639.3 Culture of cold-blooded vertebrates. Of fish

Pope, Joyce

Taking care of your fish; photographs by: Sally Anne Thompson and R. T. Willbie/animal photography. Watts 1988 c1987 32p il lib bdg $10.90; pa $3.95 (3-5) **639.3**

1. Aquariums 2. Fishes
ISBN 0-531-10192-4 (lib bdg); 0-531-15167-0 (pa) LC 85-52088

First published 1987 in the United Kingdom

Provides tips on keeping a fish as a pet, including how to select, house, feed, and care for your new fish

639.9 Conservation of biological resources

Mallory, Ken

Rescue of the stranded whales; [by] Kenneth Mallory and Andrea Conley. Simon & Schuster Bks. for Young Readers 1989 63p il $14.95 (5 and up) **639.9**

1. New England Aquarium Corporation 2. Whales 3. Wildlife conservation
ISBN 0-671-67122-7 LC 88-26408

"A New England Aquarium book"

Published in association with the New England Aquarium

"Three pilot whales saved in a 1986 Cape Cod beaching are restored at the New England Aquarium and returned to the sea. A true ecological drama told in a moving narrative with numerous clear, full-color photographs." Sci Child

McNulty, Faith

Peeping in the shell; a whooping crane is hatched; illustrations by Irene Brady. Harper & Row 1986 58p il $11.95; lib bdg $11.89 (2-5) **639.9**

1. Cranes (Birds) 2. Eggs 3. Birds—Protection
ISBN 0-06-024134-9; 0-06-024135-7 (lib bdg) LC 85-45837

The text describes how a scientist "courts" a whooping crane and how the resulting egg is carefully incubated until it hatches

"Brady's soft pencil drawings, generously distributed throughout an open format, lend grace to the text. A fine read-aloud for primary-grade science units as well as an unusual resource for independent readers." Bull Cent Child Books

Patent, Dorothy Hinshaw

Where the wild horses roam; photographs by William Muñoz. Clarion Bks. 1989 72p il lib bdg $15.95 (4 and up) **639.9**

1. Horses 2. Wildlife conservation
ISBN 0-89919-507-5 LC 88-20360

This book describes the history of wild horses in the United States, protective legislation, the horses' life in the wild, problems caused by overpopulation, and possible solutions, including refuges, the Adopt-A-Horse program; and birth control. A list of wild horse protection associations is appended

"The handsome color photographs, including stunning western landscapes, will hook horse lovers, and the indexed text provides students with smoothly written information for reports." Bull Cent Child Books

Patent, Dorothy Hinshaw—*Continued*

The whooping crane; a comeback story; photographs by William Muñoz. Clarion Bks. 1988 88p il $14.95 (5 and up) **639.9**

1. Cranes (Birds) 2. Birds—Protection 3. Wildlife conservation
ISBN 0-89919-455-9 LC 88-2871

Traces the forty-year-old and ongoing attempt to save the endangered whooping crane from extinction, focusing on efforts at wildlife refuges and the captive breeding program

Pringle, Laurence P.

Saving our wildlife; [by] Laurence Pringle. Enslow Pubs. 1990 64p il lib bdg $13.95 (5 and up) **639.9**

1. Wildlife conservation 2. Endangered species
ISBN 0-89490-204-0 LC 89-32872

The author discusses "factors contributing to species endangerment and extinction, . . . [and] how wildlife refuges and captive breeding and relocation programs have operated to preserve a variety of game and nongame species." Booklist

"A well-rounded, well-organized presentation of the problem of saving wildlife. . . . The science is correct, concise, and (as it should be) a nice springboard for further inquiry." Appraisal

Includes bibliography

Scott, Jack Denton, 1915-

Orphans from the sea; words by Jack Denton Scott; photographs by Ozzie Sweet. Putnam 1982 61p il $10.95 (4 and up) **639.9**

1. Birds—Protection 2. Suncoast Seabird Sanctuary (Fla.)
ISBN 0-399-20858-5 LC 82-409

This book describes the work of the Suncoast Sanctuary, which specializes in the rescue and repair of orphaned and injured seabirds and other wild creatures

"Beautiful well-placed black-and-white photographs—many of them full-page—show the workings of the facility and staff as well as the sometimes comical, proud, or graceful inhabitants. Entertaining, informative, and heart-warming, the book inspires a respect for wild creatures and an admiration for the people working to save them." Horn Book

Smith, Roland, 1951-

Sea otter rescue; the aftermath of an oil spill; photographs by the author. Cobblehill Bks. 1990 64p il $13.95 (5 and up) **639.9**

1. Otters 2. Wildlife conservation 3. Oil spills
ISBN 0-525-65041-5 LC 89-49446

"Focusing on a single species, Smith illustrates the damage the Exxon *Valdez* oil spill caused to all species in Alaska's Prince William Sound in the spring of 1989. . . . Although the writing is sometimes dry, this information-packed book not only introduces the sea otter but also describes what was involved in setting up an animal-rescue operation in a small, remote town. Almost every page has an excellent quality, full-color photograph of a different phase of the rescue." SLJ

White, Sandra Verrill

Sterling; the rescue of a baby harbor seal; by Sandra Verrill White and Michael Filisky. Crown 1989 unp il $14.95 (2-4) **639.9**

1. New England Aquarium Corporation 2. Seals (Animals) 3. Wildlife conservation
ISBN 0-517-57112-9 LC 88-16185

"A New England Aquarium book"

"Abundant, full-color photographs and simple text describe the New England Aquarium's rescue and nurture of an orphaned seal pup. Emphasizes environmental issues as the rehabilitated healthy seal is later returned to the wild." Sci Child

640.73 Consumer education

Schmitt, Lois

Smart spending; a young consumer's guide. Scribner 1989 102p $11.95 (5 and up) **640.73**

1. Consumer education
ISBN 0-684-19035-4 LC 88-29524

The author offers advice on how to recognize and avoid consumer traps. Case studies discuss misleading advertising, consumer fraud, mail order problems, refund policies, product safety, food poisoning, fad diets, money management, and effective complaining

"Schmitt's integration of teen-oriented case studies into his brisk, no-nonsense text is an engaging approach. Money is a mesmerizing topic and youngsters are bound to keep reading. . . . Clearly delineated chapters make this a handy resource for assignments." Booklist

Zillions; a Consumer Reports publication for young people. Consumers Union of U.S. $11.95 per year **640.73**

1. Consumer education—Periodicals
ISSN 0190-1966

Bimonthly. First published 1980 with title: Penny Power

This consumer education magazine for young people ages 8 to 14 includes articles about evaluating products, shopping hints, price comparisons, book reviews, quizzes, recipes, posters, cartoons and letters from readers

641.1 Applied nutrition

Ward, Brian R.

Diet and nutrition. Watts 1987 48p il (Life guides) lib bdg $12.40 (4 and up) **641.1**

1. Nutrition 2. Diet
ISBN 0-531-10259-9 LC 86-50357

This book "provides information on eating for health, including sections on proteins, fat, carbohydrates, vitamins, fiber and minerals. It provides information on obesity, anorexia, bulimia, and diverticulitis. The vegetarian diet is briefly discussed as an eating alternative. Problems with eating excessive saturated fats, salt, additives and processed foods are presented." Appraisal

"I highly recommend this book as a contemporary overview for classroom use." Sci Books Films

641.3 Food

Ancona, George, 1929-
Bananas; from Manolo to Margie. Clarion Bks. 1982 unp il lib bdg $14.95 (3-5) **641.3**

1. Banana
ISBN 0-89919-100-2 LC 82-1247

"From Manolo, who lives on a Honduran banana plantation with his family, to Margie, who shops for fruit with her mother in an American grocery store, the book relates the banana's story. Included are a brief history of the fruit, a description of its growth and harvest, and a travelogue of the two-week journey the banana takes by train, boat, and truck to wholesale markets." Horn Book

"Juxtaposition of photos and text is excellent, as is the design." SLJ

Includes glossary

Cuyler, Margery
The all-around pumpkin book; illustrated by Corbett Jones. Holt & Co. 1980 95p il pa $3.95 (4-6) **641.3**

1. Pumpkin 2. Cookery 3. Handicraft
ISBN 0-03-056818-8 LC 79-3532

"The author offers notes on the history of pumpkins and on their uses by primitive peoples in addition to material on pumpkins in legend, history, and present-day festivals. . . . The text discusses planting and growing the vegetable as well as carving and dressing up jack-o-lanterns. Recipes for cooking and baking with pumpkins, along with crafts projects and party ideas, take up about half the book which ends with a collection of jokes and puns." Horn Book

De Paola, Tomie, 1934-
The popcorn book. Holiday House 1978 unp il lib bdg $13.95; pa $5.95 (k-3) **641.3**

1. Popcorn
ISBN 0-8234-0314-9 (lib bdg); 0-8234-05338 (pa) LC 77-21456

"While one twin prepares the treat, the other stays close-by and reads aloud what popcorn is, how it's cooked, stored, and made, how the Indians of the Americas discovered it, and who eats the most. . . . The best thing about popcorn, the twins decide, is eating it. Two recipes are included." Babbling Bookworm

The author-artist's "amusing soft-color pictures—each bordered with a lavender frame—show action in the past or the present while a few lines of text or balloon speeches describe what is happening." Horn Book

Foodworks; over 100 science activities and fascinating facts that explore the magic of food; from the Ontario Science Centre; illustrated by Linda Hendry. Addison-Wesley 1987 90p il pa $7.95 (4-6) **641.3**

1. Food 2. Nutrition 3. Science—Experiments
ISBN 0-201-11470-4 LC 87-1796

"One- or two-page sections on many aspects of food, nutrition, health, plants, and animals each include facts and statistics . . . plus 'try this' activities and questions." SLJ

"The writing style and drawings are up-beat and lively, making this an appealing book for browsing and science projects alike. Teachers will also appreciate this guide to active learning." Appraisal

Hughes, Meredith Sayles
The great potato book; by Meredith Sayles Hughes and E. Thomas Hughes; illustrations by G. Brian Karas. Macmillan 1986 73p il $11.95 (3-5) **641.3**

1. Potatoes
ISBN 0-02-745300-6 LC 85-24033

Discusses many aspects of the potato; its history, usefulness, and folklore, with games, jokes, and rhymes

"Whatever you wanted to know (and more) about potatoes has been lightly tossed into this collage of information. . . . Needless to say, the text jumps around a bit, from a discussion of potato beetles, for instance, to instructions for planting grass seed on a carved potato. . . . Browsers probably won't mind, however, since the format is open, the black-and-white drawings and photos eye-catching." Bull Cent Child Books

Seixas, Judith S.
Junk food—what it is, what it does; illustrated by Tom Huffman. Greenwillow Bks. 1984 47p il $12.95; lib bdg $12.88 (1-3) **641.3**

1. Food 2. Nutrition
ISBN 0-688-02559-5; 0-688-02560-9 (lib bdg) LC 83-14135

"A Greenwillow read-alone book"

An introduction to facts about junk food—what it is, where it is found, and how it affects the body—with suggestions for snacking more nutritionally

"The text is straightforward, logical, easily understood and mildly admonishing. . . . Though the anti-junk position is clearly stated, it's never a diatribe that would turn kids off. A clearly rational exposition on an increasingly important subject." SLJ

641.5 Cooking

Amari, Suad
Cooking the Lebanese way; photographs by Robert L. & Diane Wolfe. Lerner Publs. 1986 47p il map (Easy menu ethnic cookbooks) lib bdg $9.95 (5 and up) **641.5**

1. Cookery, Lebanese
ISBN 0-8225-0913-X LC 85-18172

An introduction to the cooking of Lebanon featuring such traditional recipes as kabobs, hummus and tahini dip, chard and yogurt soup, and cracked wheat pilaf. Also includes information on the history, geography, customs and people of this Middle Eastern country

Bacon, Josephine, 1942-
Cooking the Israeli way; photographs by Robert L. & Diane Wolfe. Lerner Publs. 1986 51p il map (Easy menu ethnic cookbooks) lib bdg $9.95 (5 and up) **641.5**

1. Cookery, Israeli 2. Cookery, Jewish
ISBN 0-8225-0912-1 LC 85-18059

An introduction to the cooking of Israel including such traditional recipes as cheese blintzes, turkey schnitzel, felafel in pita, and poppyseed cake. Also includes information on the geography, customs, and people of the Middle Eastern country

Better Homes and Gardens step-by-step kids' cook book. Meredith Corp. 1984 96p il $5.95 (4 and up) **641.5**

1. Cookery
ISBN 0-696-01325-8 LC 83-61317

"After some basic cooking tips, the book continues with simple recipes that require no cooking . . . and quickly moves on to more complicated dishes. . . . Most ambitious are the meal-menu recipes, such as crispy oven chicken. Instructions are divided into blocks with appealing color photographs . . . across from each step. . . . Large, clear type and an especially attractive layout are the frosting on the cake." Booklist

Bisignano, Alphonse
Cooking the Italian way. Lerner Publs. 1982 46p il map (Easy menu ethnic cookbooks) lib bdg $9.95 (5 and up) **641.5**

1. Cookery, Italian
ISBN 0-8225-0906-7 LC 82-12641

Introduces the land, people, and regional cooking of Italy and includes recipes for such dishes as Minestrone soup, spaghetti with meat sauce, and chicken cacciatore

Christian, Rebecca
Cooking the Spanish way. Lerner Publs. 1982 46p il map (Easy menu ethnic cookbooks) lib bdg $9.95 (5 and up) **641.5**

1. Cookery, Spanish
ISBN 0-8225-0908-3 LC 82-4709

Following brief introductions to the history, land and food of Spain, the author presents recipes for dishes such as: lentil soup, flan, paella and gazpacho

Chung, Okwha
Cooking the Korean way; [by] Okwha Chung & Judy Monroe; photographs by Robert L. & Diane Wolfe. Lerner Publs. 1988 47p il map (Easy menu ethnic cookbooks) lib bdg $9.95 (5 and up) **641.5**

1. Cookery, Korean
ISBN 0-8225-0921-0 LC 87-4014

The authors introduce the cooking and food habits of Korea and provide brief information on the geography and history of the country

Crocker, Betty
Betty Crocker's cookbook for boys and girls. rev ed. Golden Press Bks. 1984 94p il $6.95 (3-6) **641.5**

1. Cookery
ISBN 0-307-09943-1 LC 83-82255

First published 1957 by Simon & Schuster. First Golden Press edition published in 1965 had title: Betty Crocker's New boys and girls cook book

A picture cookbook with step-by-step recipes for breads, main dishes, vegetables, party treats, and snacks

Hargittai, Magdolna
Cooking the Hungarian way; photographs by Robert L. and Diane Wolfe. Lerner Publs. 1986 47p il map (Easy menu ethnic cookbooks) lib bdg $9.95 (5 and up) **641.5**

1. Cookery, Hungarian
ISBN 0-8225-0916-4 LC 86-10661

An introduction to the cooking of Hungary, including recipes for such dishes as goulash, stuffed peppers, and paprika chicken. Also discusses the geography and history of this central European country

Hautzig, Esther Rudomin
Holiday treats; illustrated by Yaroslava. Macmillan 1983 86p il $12.95 (3 and up) **641.5**

1. Cookery
ISBN 0-02-743350-1 LC 83-9347

A collection of recipes, which can be prepared for the most part without adult help, for sixteen holidays throughout the year, including Purim, Halloween, Mother's Day, and Christmas

Hill, Barbara W., 1941-
Cooking the English way. Lerner Publs. 1982 46p il map (Easy menu ethnic cookbooks) lib bdg $9.95 (5 and up) **641.5**

1. Cookery, British
ISBN 0-8225-0903-2 LC 82-257

The author shares British customs and traditions along with recipes for breakfasts, lunches, tea-times and dinners. Illustrated with color photos and line drawings

Kaufman, Cheryl Davidson
Cooking the Caribbean way; photographs by Robert L. and Diane Wolfe. Lerner Publs. 1988 45p il map (Easy menu ethnic cookbooks) lib bdg $9.95 (5 and up) **641.5**

1. Cookery, Caribbean
ISBN 0-8225-0920-2 LC 87-37850

This introduction to the history and food of the Caribbean includes recipes and a glossary of culinary terms and ingredients

Linde, Polly van der
Around the world in 80 dishes; by Polly and Tasha Van der Linde; pictures by Horst Lemke. Scroll Press 1971 85p il $10.95 (3-6) **641.5**

1. Cookery
ISBN 0-87592-007-1 LC 71-160447

"Easy-to-follow recipes for 53 dishes from many different countries which utilize common or readily obtainable ingredients, are presented in a cookbook written by two sisters, ages ten and eight. The cheerfully illustrated book is divided into sections of side dishes, soups, eggs, fish, meats, vegetables and salad, sauces and dressings, desserts, and drinks." Booklist

Madavan, Vijay
Cooking the Indian way; photographs by Robert L. & Diane Wolfe. Lerner Publs. 1985 50p il map (Easy menu ethnic cookbooks) lib bdg $9.95 (5 and up) **641.5**

1. Cookery, Indic
ISBN 0-8225-0911-3 LC 84-28906

An introduction to the cooking of India featuring such traditional recipes as lamb kebabs, yogurt chicken, pumpkin curry, and apple chutney. Background information on the geography, customs, and people of India is provided

Munsen, Sylvia
Cooking the Norwegian way. Lerner Publs. 1982 46p il map (Easy menu ethnic cookbooks) lib bdg $9.95 (5 and up) **641.5**

1. Cookery, Norwegian
ISBN 0-8225-0901-6 LC 82-259

An introduction to Norway is followed by recipes for such traditional fare as fruit soup, Christmas bread and rice pudding. Illustrated with color photos and line drawings

Nabwire, Constance R.
Cooking the African way; [by] Constance Nabwire & Bertha Vining Montgomery; photographs by Robert L. & Diane Wolfe. Lerner Publs. 1988 46p il map (Easy menu ethnic cookbooks) lib bdg $9.95 (5 and up) **641.5**

1. Cookery, African
ISBN 0-8225-0919-9 LC 88-8877

This introduction to the cookery of East and West Africa features recipes, a glossary of culinary terms, and some information about the land and people

New junior cook book. 5th ed. Meredith Corp. 1989 80p il $7.95 (3-6) **641.5**

1. Cookery
ISBN 0-696-01147-6 LC 89-60202

First published 1955 with title: Better Homes and Gardens junior cook book

Illustrated directions for making simple beverages, desserts, main dishes, salads, and vegetables, for planning menus, and for using kitchen equipment

"An emphasis on nutrition is noted; each of the 61 recipes is nutritionally analyzed. . . . Selections from all the basic food groups are presented in a crisply designed format, which includes microwave directions where applicable and a red-apple symbol for recipes that can be made without adult help. Enticing full-color photos and renamed goodies add flair." Booklist

Nguyen, Chi Thien, 1933-
Cooking the Vietnamese way; [by] Chi Nguyen & Judy Monroe; photographs by Robert L. & Diane Wolfe. Lerner Publs. 1985 47p il map (Easy menu ethnic cookbooks) lib bdg $9.95 (5 and up) **641.5**

1. Cookery, Vietnamese
ISBN 0-8225-0914-8 LC 84-27816

An introduction to the cooking of Vietnam featuring such recipes as spring rolls, sweet and sour soup, and Vietnamese fried rice. Also includes information about the land, history, and holidays of this south-east Asian country

Osborne, Christine
Middle Eastern food and drink. Bookwright Press 1988 48p il (Food and drink) lib bdg $12.40 (4-6) **641.5**

1. Cookery, Middle Eastern 2. Beverages 3. Middle East—Social life and customs
ISBN 0-531-18200-2 LC 87-73161

Describes, in text and illustrations, the food and beverages of the Middle East in relation to the region's history, geography, and culture. Also includes recipes and information about specialties and festive foods from specific Middle Eastern countries

Includes bibliography

Parnell, Helga
Cooking the German way; photographs by Robert L. and Diane Wolfe. Lerner Publs. 1988 45p il map (Easy menu ethnic cookbooks) lib bdg $9.95 (5 and up) **641.5**

1. Cookery, German
ISBN 0-8225-0918-0 LC 87-36642

Introduces the history, land, and food of Germany and includes recipes for such dishes as potato dumplings, noodle salad, and Black Forest torte

Penner, Lucille Recht
The colonial cookbook; illustrated with prints and photographs selected and arranged by Laura Geringer. Hastings House 1976 128p il map $10.95 (5 and up) **641.5**

1. Cookery 2. United States—Social life and customs—1600-1775, Colonial period
ISBN 0-8038-1202-7 LC 76-26550

"Early methods of preparing and preserving are described; instructions for adapting them to use with present-day utensils and ingredients are given. . . . The book offers a view of the daily lives and customs of those with whom the recipes originated as well as the interesting derivations of several commonly used words like 'dessert' and 'ketchup.'" Horn Book

Includes bibliography

Perl, Lila
Hunter's stew and hangtown fry: what pioneer America ate and why; pictures by Richard Cuffari. Clarion Bks. 1977 156p il map $13.95 (4 and up) **641.5**

1. Cookery 2. United States—Social life and customs
ISBN 0-395-28922-X LC 77-5366

First published by Seabury Press

"This is a culinary cultural history of the growing United States during the 19th Century. The author divides the country into five sections and, in a readable style, describes the people, the food, and the ambience of the times. There are 20 choice and representative recipes, a few at the end of each chapter." SLJ

"Illustrated with atmospheric gray wash over black line drawings. Worthwhile for social history studies." Booklist

Includes bibliography

Slumps, grunts, and snickerdoodles: what Colonial America ate and why; drawings by Richard Cuffari. Clarion Bks. 1975 125p il map $13.95 (4 and up) **641.5**

1. Cookery 2. United States—Social life and customs—1600-1775, Colonial period
ISBN 0-395-28923-8 LC 75-4894

First published by Seabury Press

"In three major chapters dividing the pre-Revolutionary colonies into regions—New England, Middle Atlantic, Southern—the author explains ' . . . not only "what" the colonists ate and "why," but . . . the geographical and historical background as well as the intimate domestic surroundings.' . . . Emphasis is on foods grown in different areas and how traditional recipes developed from the materials available, but local manners and mores are also skillfully woven into the narrative." SLJ

Plotkin, Gregory
Cooking the Russian way; [by] Gregory & Rita Plotkin; photographs by Robert L. & Diane Wolfe. Lerner Publs. 1986 47p il map (Easy menu ethnic cookbooks) lib bdg $9.95 (5 and up) **641.5**

1. Cookery, Russian
ISBN 0-8225-0915-6 LC 86-7155

Introduces the cooking and food habits of the Soviet Union, including such recipes as borscht, chicken kiev, and beef stroganoff, and provides brief information on the geography and history of the country

Villios, Lynne W.
Cooking the Greek way; photographs by Robert L. & Diane Wolfe. Lerner Publs. 1984 51p il map (Easy menu ethnic cookbooks) lib bdg $9.95 (5 and up) **641.5**

1. Cookery, Greek
ISBN 0-8225-0910-5 LC 84-12585

This introduction to Greece and its cuisine includes recipes for authentic Greek foods such as dolmades, baklava, and spinach pie, plus several other recipes for main dishes, appetizers, and desserts

Waldee, Lynne Marie
Cooking the French way. Lerner Publs. 1982 47p il map (Easy menu ethnic cookbooks) $9.95 (5 and up) **641.5**

1. Cookery, French
ISBN 0-8225-0904-0 LC 82-258

This introduction to French cookery provides instructions for making basic sauces, entrees, soups, breads and desserts. Illustrated with color photos and line drawings

Walker, Barbara Muhs, 1928-
The Little House cookbook; frontier foods from Laura Ingalls Wilder's classic stories; by Barbara M. Walker; illustrated by Garth Williams. Harper & Row 1979 240p il $13.95; lib bdg $13.89; pa $5.95 (5 and up) **641.5**

1. Wilder, Laura Ingalls, 1867-1957 2. Cookery 3. Frontier and pioneer life
ISBN 0-06-026418-7; 0-06-026419-5 (lib bdg); 0-06-446090-8 (pa) LC 76-58733

Recipes based on the pioneer food written about in the "Little House" books of Laura Ingalls Wilder, along with quotes from the books and descriptions of the food and cooking of pioneer times

"Illustrated by Williams's familiar warm drawings, the adaptations of menus from pioneer days include paragaphs describing the Wilder and Ingalls families working together, preparing holiday meals, individual

Walker, Barbara Muhs, 1928-—*Continued*
foods, special treats and staple fare." Publ Wkly
Includes bibliographical references

Weston, Reiko
Cooking the Japanese way. Lerner Publs. 1983 45p il map (Easy menu ethnic cookbooks) lib bdg $9.95 (5 and up) **641.5**
1. Cookery, Japanese
ISBN 0-8225-0905-9 LC 82-12656
An introduction to the cooking of Japan featuring basic recipes for soups, appetizers, main dishes, side dishes, and desserts. Also describes some special ingredients used in Japanese dishes, how to set a Japanese table, and how to eat with chopsticks

Yu, Ling
Cooking the Chinese way. Lerner Publs. 1982 46p il map (Easy menu ethnic cookbooks) lib bdg $9.95 (5 and up) **641.5**
1. Cookery, Chinese
ISBN 0-8225-0902-4 LC 82-263
Simple instructions for preparing Chinese appetizers, soups, rice, main dishes, vegetables and desserts. Illustrated with color photos and line drawings

Zamojska-Hutchins, Danuta
Cooking the Polish way; photographs by Robert L. and Diane Wolfe. Lerner Publs. 1984 49p il (Easy menu ethnic cookbooks) lib bdg $9.95 (5 and up) **641.5**
1. Cookery, Polish
ISBN 0-8225-0909-1 LC 84-11226
An introduction to the cooking of Poland, featuring traditional recipes for lunch, appetizers, dinner, and desserts. Also includes information on the geography, customs, and people of Poland

641.8 Cooking specific kinds of composite dishes

Better homes and gardens cookies for kids. Meredith Corp. 1983 96p il pa $5.95 **641.8**
1. Cookies
ISBN 0-696-00865-3 LC 82-80528
"Here's a selection that is bound to be popular with family cooks. The entire book is devoted to cookies that children can help prepare and enjoy. Creative ideas abound such as brownie dominoes, rocky-road pizza, and lollipop cookies. Both traditional as well as novel cookie recipes are offered, each presented in a simple, step-by-step style. . . . A unique, fun selection. Fine value. 89 recipes." Booklist

Morris, Ann
Bread, bread, bread; photographs by Ken Heyman. Lothrop, Lee & Shepard Bks. 1989 unp il $12.95; lib bdg $12.88 (k-3) **641.8**
1. Bread
ISBN 0-688-06335-7; 0-688-06334-9 (lib bdg) LC 88-26677
This photo essay shows different kinds of bread around the world from baguettes to challah
"Each picture offers a strong ethnic identity or a thought-provoking human interaction, with captions of only a few words in large print. An unusual index . . . gives background information about the pictures, citing the countries of origin and a few facts about each type of bread." SLJ

Pillar, Marjorie
Pizza man. Crowell 1990 unp il $11.95; lib bdg $11.89 (k-2) **641.8**
1. Pizza
ISBN 0-690-04836-X; 0-690-04838-6 (lib bdg) LC 89-35526
This book describes the steps in making a pizza pie, from the moment the pizza man starts mixing the dough until he serves a slice to a hungry customer
"Photographs of how a pizza man makes his pies and takes care of his pizzeria are both informative and enticing." Read Teach

646 Sewing, clothing and accessories, management of personal and family living

Cobb, Vicki
Getting dressed; pictures by Marylin Hafner. Lippincott 1989 31p il $11.95; lib bdg $11.89 (1-3) **646**
1. Clothing and dress
ISBN 0-397-32142-2; 0-397-32143-0 (lib bdg) LC 87-26097
Presents simple historical background on the things that fasten our clothes, such as elastic, zippers, buttons, and sticky tapes
"Brightly colored illustrations (some showing enlarged details) contribute to a light tone that makes [this] nonfiction book enjoyable as well as informative." Bull Cent Child Books

646.2 Sewing and related operations

Siegel, Beatrice
The sewing machine. Walker & Co. 1984 56p il (Inventions that changed our lives) lib bdg $10.95 (4 and up) **646.2**
1. Sewing machines
ISBN 0-8027-6532-7 LC 83-40397
Text and illustrations present the invention and development of a machine which liberated people from the drudgery of sewing by hand
"A simple, clear history of the men whose individual

Siegel, Beatrice—*Continued*
patents and/or ideas helped create the sewing machine. This is an intriguing topic and one that can only be found as chapters in books of inventions. Photographs, drawings, cartoons and diagrams are fairly well integrated into the text. Useful for research." SLJ

Includes bibliographic references

646.7 Management of personal and family living. Grooming

Cobb, Vicki

Keeping clean; pictures by Marylin Hafner. Lippincott 1989 32p il $11.95; lib bdg $11.89 (1-3) **646.7**

1. Grooming, Personal 2. Hygiene
ISBN 0-397-32312-3; 0-397-32313-1 (lib bdg)
LC 88-2930

This book "discusses the importance of good grooming and . . . [examines] how soap is made and how modern plumbing systems allow us to have hot and cold water from indoor taps." Booklist

"The conversational writing style is concise and straightforward, leavened with touches of light humor. . . . The watercolor-and-ink illustrations add interest, clarification, and/or humor to every page." SLJ

648 Housekeeping

Rockwell, Anne F., 1934-

Nice and clean; [by] Anne and Harlow Rockwell. Macmillan 1984 unp il $12.95 (k-2) **648**

1. House cleaning
ISBN 0-02-777290-X
LC 84-3945

"A preschool child narrates this concept book, carefully explaining how he and his parents clean their home. The clear and direct text is accompanied by the Rockwells' warmly realistic watercolor illustrations." SLJ

649 Child rearing

Cole, Joanna

Your new potty; photographs by Margaret Miller. Morrow Junior Bks. 1989 40p il $10.95; lib bdg $10.88; pa $10.95 **649**

1. Toilet training
ISBN 0-688-06105-2; 0-688-06106-0 (lib bdg); 0-688-08966-6 (pa)
LC 88-39862

This book begins with an "introduction for parents that briefly but thoroughly covers such topics as when to start toilet training, how to prepare your child and switching to underpants. The focus then turns to two children, Steffie and Ben, following them as they master the use of the toilet. The photographs and text explain in toddler-geared language that growing up also includes learning to use the toilet." Publ Wkly

650.1 Personal success in business

Barkin, Carol, 1944-

Jobs for kids; the guide to having fun and making money; [by] Carol Barkin & Elizabeth James; illustrated by Roy Doty. Lothrop, Lee & Shepard Bks. 1990 113p il lib bdg $11.88; pa $7.95 (5 and up) **650.1**

1. Moneymaking projects for children 2. Children—Employment 3. Finance, Personal
ISBN 0-688-09324-8 (lib bdg); 0-688-09323-X (pa)
LC 89-45900

Discusses the advantages of working and offers tips on assessing your talents and abilities, finding a job, acting responsibly, handling disasters, and setting prices

"The friendly tone is appealing, and even kids who aren't looking for work are likely to tuck away some of this counsel for future reference. Occasional cartoon drawings break up the text." Booklist

652 Processes of written communication

Janeczko, Paul B., 1945-

Loads of codes and secret ciphers. Macmillan 1984 108p il $11.95 (5 and up) **652**

1. Cryptography 2. Ciphers
ISBN 0-02-747810-6
LC 84-5791

"Information on breaking codes as well as on building simple coding devices to transmit secret messages is interspersed with historical background notes on the ciphers used, for instance, by the 1920s hobos, cowboys of the Old West, and the U.S. naval navigators. Practice codes are given with handy answers for beginners to check out their expertise." Booklist

Mango, Karin N., 1936-

Codes, ciphers, and other secrets. Watts 1988 93p il lib bdg $10.40 (4 and up) **652**

1. Cryptography 2. Ciphers
ISBN 0-531-10575-X
LC 88-5638

"A First book"

Describes the many ways of hiding the real meaning of what someone is trying to say by using a code or replacing the message with a cipher

"Enciphered and encoded sentences from a Sherlock Holmes story form a thread through the book's numerous examples, which are pleasingly combined with Mango's anecdotal history of the subject. Diagrams illuminate the construction of a St. Cyr's slide, a cipher wheel, and other devices." Booklist

Includes bibliography

Schwartz, Alvin, 1927-
The cat's elbow, and other secret languages; collected by Alvin Schwartz; pictures by Margot Zemach. Farrar, Straus & Giroux 1982 82p il $12.95 (4 and up) **652**

1. Ciphers 2. Cryptography
ISBN 0-374-31224-9 LC 81-5513

Beginning with Pig Latin "Schwartz progresses to more arcane explanations of twisting languages, for fun and sometimes practical purposes. The folklorist gives examples of codes used by kids in Africa, China, Germany and, most notably, by the entire town, adults and children, in Boonville, Calif. From the 1880s onward, the citizens have been frustrating outsiders with their private communications in Boontling." Publ Wkly

"Funny, exuberant Alvin Schwartz is a lucid teacher, clearly describing 13 secret languages and codes . . . and demonstrating them with riddles and jokes. . . . The proverbial children of all ages will find the book irresistible." SLJ

Includes bibliography

659.13 Signs and signboards

Goor, Ron, 1940-
Signs; [by] Ron and Nancy Goor. Crowell 1983 unp il $12.89 (k-2) **659.13**

1. Signs and signboards
ISBN 0-690-04355-4 LC 83-47649

This "selection of black-and-white photographs depicts directional signs which we see everyday. A simple text defines and classifies the signs and asks children to match or find the opposites." Child Book Rev Serv

Hoban, Tana
I read signs. Greenwillow Bks. 1983 unp il $13.95; lib bdg $13.88; pa $3.95 (k-2) **659.13**

1. Signs and signboards
ISBN 0-688-02317-7; 0-688-02318-5 (lib bdg); 0-688-07331-X (pa) LC 83-1482

In this book "30 verbal and 27 symbolic street signs have been caught on location in close-ups with a minimum of background to give just a soupçon of milieu (city, sky or apple tree) or hint of meaning ('Beware of dog' on chain link fence). Design is bold; primary colors are emphasized. The familiar predominates; more unusual signs . . . add interest." SLJ

I read symbols. Greenwillow Bks. 1983 unp il $13.95; lib bdg $13.88 (k-2) **659.13**

1. Signs and signboards 2. Signs and symbols
ISBN 0-688-02331-2; 0-688-02332-0 (lib bdg) LC 83-1481

This picture book "shows sharp, full-color close-up photographs of common signs . . . displaying some 27 road, street, and building symbols that youngsters will find it worthwhile to know." Booklist

"The only words in Hoban's new book appear on the last two pages, explaining what the symbols in her photos say. She has, however, photographed so impressively in color virtually all the instantly informative messages that even little children will not need the postscript except to confirm their findings. . . . The pictures in this book can teach one to really see and comprehend the meanings in everyday things most of us ignore." Publ Wkly

I walk and read. Greenwillow Bks. 1984 unp il $10.25; lib bdg $10.88 (k-2) **659.13**

1. Signs and signboards
ISBN 0-688-02575-7; 0-688-02576-5 (lib bdg) LC 83-14215

"In this book of brightly-colored photographs, Hoban invites children to experience the diversity of signs, including restaurant, traffic and emergency signs. A tool for perceptual learning, this book will help children experience the colors, shapes and textures of signs without leaving their seats. Symbols often accompany or are integrated within the sign itself, and children will be able to interpret meaning without being able to read." SLJ

662 Technology of explosives, fuels, related products

Brenner, Martha
Fireworks tonight! new rev ed. Hastings House 1986 128p il $13.95; lib bdg $13.89 (5 and up) **662**

1. Fireworks
ISBN 0-8038-9288-8; 0-8038-9285-3 (lib bdg)
First published 1984

Following an account of "the use of fireworks throughout history to the present day, the work describes the various families who produce fireworks and then details the kinds of fireworks that are available for both home use and for large displays. The reader is given a tour through a fireworks factory and then accompanies a fireworks team as it puts on a major show." Appraisal

"The many illustrations include some from 1635, 1747, the 1800s, early 1900s, and even the 1986 Liberty Weekend. . . . Teachers could use this book for general awareness and for timely safety reminders for holiday celebrations in which fireworks are used." Sci Books Films

Includes bibliography

665.5 Petroleum

Rutland, Jonathan
See inside an oil rig and tanker. rev ed. Warwick Press 1988 31p il lib bdg $11.90 (4-6) **665.5**

1. Oil well drilling, Submarine 2. Petroleum industry and trade
ISBN 0-531-19046-3 LC 88-50109
First published 1978

This book "provides an overview of the whole crude oil search-and-recovery process, including use of drilling rigs, production platforms, and undersea pipelines; specialized functions of the oil tanker; and operation of the refinery. . . . Illustrations showing labeled cutaway views . . . will enhance readers' comprehension." Booklist

Includes glossary

666 Ceramic and allied technologies

Gibbons, Gail

The pottery place. Harcourt Brace Jovanovich 1987 unp il $12.95 (1-3) **666**

1. Pottery
ISBN 0-15-263265-4 LC 86-32790

"The author-illustrator states in a brief text the steps and the tools involved in making clay pots, from the mixing and kneading of the clay itself, through the shaping of the pots on the wheel, the firing of the greenware, and the glazing. All these details are described to a young child visiting the potter in her studio. . . . The watercolor medium offers a soft, restful ambiance that is a departure from the author-illustrator's usual style." Horn Book

668 Technology of other organic products

Cobb, Vicki

The secret life of cosmetics: a science experiment book; illustrated by Theo Cobb. Lippincott 1985 111p il $13.95; lib bdg $13.89 (5 and up) **668**

1. Cosmetics 2. Science—Experiments
ISBN 0-397-32121-X; 0-397-32122-8 (lib bdg) LC 85-40097

The author "examines cosmetics: soaps, lotions, perfumes, shampoos, conditioners, and makeup. She often provides a brief historical perspective of each substance . . . as well as information on the scientific principles that underlie it. . . . There are some good opportunities here for science experiments or classroom demonstrations, and the subject is sure to interest many who would not otherwise think in scientific terms. Illustrated with pen-and-ink cartoon drawings." Booklist

670 Manufacturing

Cobb, Vicki

The secret life of hardware: a science experiment book; illustrated by Bill Morrison. Lippincott 1982 90p il $13.95; lib bdg $13.89 (5 and up) **670**

1. Manufactures 2. Science—Experiments
ISBN 0-397-31999-1; 0-397-32000-0 (lib bdg) LC 81-48607

Examines the inventory of a hardware store from the tools to glues and suggests experiments which demonstrate the scientific principles and legends behind these items

"The text is both a well-written guide to and source of explanation of the experiments, but in addition the student scientists are given hints to try new things on their own." Appraisal

Tunis, Edwin, 1897-1973

Colonial craftsmen and the beginnings of American industry; written and illustrated by Edwin Tunis. Crowell 1976 c1965 159p il $24.95 (5 and up) **670**

1. Decorative arts 2. United States—Social life and customs—1600-1775, Colonial period 3. Handicraft
ISBN 0-690-01062-1 LC 75-29612

A reprint of the title first published 1965 by World Publishing Company

"Superb illustrations and comprehensive text describe the working methods, products, houses, shops and trades of the New World." N Y Public Libr. Ref Books for Child Collect

676 Pulp and paper technology

Perrins, Lesley, 1953-

How paper is made; design, Arthur Lockwood. Facts on File 1985 32p il (How it is made) $12.95 (4 and up) **676**

1. Paper
ISBN 0-8160-0036-0 LC 84-18638

The author discusses "the history, development of production techniques, varied uses and the environmental effects of the manufacturing process of paper." SLJ

678 Elastomers and elastomer products

Graham, Ada

The big stretch: the complete book of the amazing rubber band; by Ada and Frank Graham; pictures by Richard Rosenblum. Knopf 1985 81p il $9.95; lib bdg $10.99 (3-6) **678**

1. Rubber
ISBN 0-394-85758-5; 0-394-95758-X (lib bdg) LC 83-25615

Explains how rubber bands are made, discusses the rubber band industry, and lists some of the 2000 modern uses for rubber bands. Includes several experiments and amusements using rubber bands

"A little experimental physics, a little history, a little technology and a good deal of humor are extracted here from a commonplace topic for curious youngsters. . . . It is a delight to see so much relevant matter drawn out of a modest topic." Sci Am

681 Precision instruments and other devices

Cobb, Vicki

Writing it down; pictures by Marylin Hafner. Lippincott 1989 32p il $11.95; lib bdg $11.89 (1-3) **681**

1. Writing—Materials and instruments
ISBN 0-397-32326-3; 0-397-32327-1 (lib bdg) LC 88-14191

Cobb, Vicki—*Continued*

Simple descriptions of paper, pencils, pens, and crayons explain how they work and how they were invented

The "behind-the-scenes stories of things children use daily are just right for primary-grade readers who can easily understand the concepts. [This] excellent addition to nonfiction collections will be fun to booktalk, and may be used as [a] model of effective writing and illustration for children." SLJ

681.1 Instruments for measuring time

Gibbons, Gail

Clocks and how they go. Crowell 1979 unp il lib bdg $13.89 (2-4) **681.1**

1. Clocks and watches
ISBN 0-690-03974-3 (lib bdg) LC 78-22498

This book explains "what makes things tick—literally. The mechanisms for time-telling are shown, gear by gear, each in its own color. . . . It describes in detail the weight-clock and the spring-clock and covers time from the sun-dial to the digital readout." Books of the Times

"Bold, straightforward illustrations in clear bright colors accompany simple explanations. . . . An admirable example of the kind of book that explains for the young reader how mechanical things work." Horn Book

Zubrowski, Bernie, 1939-

Clocks; building and experimenting with model timepieces; illustrated by Roy Doty. Morrow 1988 112p il lib bdg $12.88; pa $7.95 (4 and up) **681.1**

1. Clocks and watches
ISBN 0-688-06926-6 (lib bdg); 0-688-06925-8 (pa) LC 87-18467

"A Boston Children's Museum activity book"

"From simple sundials and hourglasses to more complex water and mechanical timepieces, this guide to clock building has clear, step-by-step instructions, includes good diagrams, and requires only easily obtainable materials like pop bottles, sand, and string (and, for the more complicated projects, plastic tubing and pulleys). Occasionally the focus seems to shift from how to tell time to principles of mechanics and physics." Bull Cent Child Books

684 Furnishings and home workshops. Woodworking and metal working

Adkins, Jan

Toolchest; written, designed, and illustrated by Jan Adkins; carpenter in residence, Joseph Karson. Walker & Co. 1973 48p il $6.95; pa $4.95 (5 and up) **684**

1. Carpentry—Tools 2. Woodwork
ISBN 0-8027-6153-4; 0-8027-7218-8 (pa) LC 72-81374

"Meticulously illustrated with drawings that show exact details of tools, hardware, wood grains, and techniques, this is a superb first book for the amateur carpenter. Adkins explains the uses of each tool, the ways in which each variety of saw or chisel is fitted for a particular task, such procedures as dowelling, gluing, or cutting a tenon and mortise, and he describes the uses for each kind of nail and screw. This most useful book concludes with advice on the care of tools." Bull Cent Child Books

Lasson, Robert, 1922-

If I had a hammer: woodworking with seven basic tools; photographs by Jeff Murphy. Dutton 1974 76p il lib bdg $8.95 (4 and up) **684**

1. Carpentry—Tools 2. Woodwork
ISBN 0-525-32532-8 LC 74-6457

Text and photographs introduce seven hand tools and give instructions for six woodworking projects using them

"Large black-and-white photographs clarify each stage of instruction for the six projects which are sound and simple enough for independent completion by a child capable of reading the text." Booklist

Weiss, Harvey

Hammer & saw; an introduction to woodworking. Crowell 1981 79p il lib bdg $12.89 (5 and up) **684**

1. Woodwork
ISBN 0-690-04131-4 LC 81-43032

"Using clearly worded step-by-step directions, the author starts with the basics—sawing wood and how and where to hammer a nail. Later chapters deal with methods of measuring, drilling holes, planing, and finishing. The projects are generally illustrated with cheerful, amusing drawings and enlivened with bits of history and informal comments." Horn Book

685 Leather and fur goods, and related products

Cobb, Vicki

Sneakers meet your feet; illustrated by Theo Cobb. Little, Brown 1985 48p il (How the world works) lib bdg $11.95 (4-6) **685**

1. Shoe industry
ISBN 0-316-14896-2 LC 85-6895

"From the description of the structure of the foot and the way it adapts to pressure and various activities the text goes on to tell how the components of sneakers are produced. Rubber, cloth (canvas made from cotton or nylon made from chemicals), and leather go into the making of the popular sneaker." Appraisal

"In addition to the economics lessons of supply and demand, readers are told that manufacturers try to keep the costs low by manufacturing sneakers in the Orient, where labor costs are lower. The black-and-white drawings and diagrams . . . are effective in showing how machines work and in labeling component parts. Suitable for purchase by all libraries." SLJ

686 Printing and related activities. Book arts

Aliki

How a book is made; written and illustrated by Aliki. Crowell 1986 32p il $13.95; lib bdg $13.89; Harper & Row pa $4.95 (2-5) **686**

1. Books 2. Book industries and trade 3. Publishers and publishing 4. Printing
ISBN 0-690-04496-8; 0-690-04498-4 (lib bdg); 0-06-446085-1 (pa) LC 85-48156

Describes the stages in making a book, starting with the writing of the manuscript and the drawing of the pictures, and explaining all the technical processes leading to printed and bound copies

"With charm and whimsy, and using a cartoon format, Aliki delightfully shares the agonies and ecstasies of being an author/artist. . . . Her fictional characters are all adorable cats, which makes Goodbooks Publishing Company a very caring, helpful, happy 'cat house'." Child Book Rev Serv

690 Buildings

Barton, Byron

Building a house. Greenwillow Bks. 1981 unp il lib bdg $13.88; pa $4.95 (k-1) **690**

1. Building 2. Houses
ISBN 0-688-84291-7 (lib bdg); 0-688-09356-6 (pa) LC 80-22674

"In the simplest possible book on building a house, a step-by-step, one-line description is given of the major factors in construction. Such workers as bricklayers, carpenters, plumbers, electricians, and painters do their own jobs until the small, bright red-and-green house is completed and a family moves in. Flat drawings in brilliant primary colors enable the very young to visualize the methods of housebuilding." Horn Book

Machines at work. Crowell 1987 unp il $7.95; lib bdg $12.89 (k-1) **690**

1. Building
ISBN 0-694-00190-2; 0-690-04573-5 (lib bdg) LC 86-24221

"Double-page illustrations depict a busy day at a construction site as workers (with the positive inclusion of women) knock down a building and start a new one." SLJ

"The short, punchy narrative reinforces the dynamics of the illustrations. . . . This should be a popular read-aloud for preschoolers and satisfying read-alone for beginners." Publ Wkly

Cobb, Vicki

Skyscraper going up! a pop-up book; design and paper engineering by John Strejan. Crowell 1987 unp il $14.95 (1-3) **690**

1. Skyscrapers
ISBN 0-690-04525-5 LC 86-47795

"The book traces the construction of the Equitable Center in New York, and the title page quite properly credits John Strejan just below the author, for Mr. Strejan's design and paper engineering here is a feat nearly as impressive as that of the skyscraper engineers themselves. In the pages of 'Skyscraper Going Up!' paper bulldozers move, paper steel beams and glass sheathing are guided into place, and then, in a spectacular finale, a foot-high version of the Equitable Tower itself pops up, looking far more appealing than the real one on Seventh Avenue. It is all spectacular fun, and the text is rigorous in its accuracy." N Y Times Book Rev

Gibbons, Gail

How a house is built. Holiday House 1990 unp il $13.95 (k-2) **690**

1. Building 2. Houses
ISBN 0-8234-0841-8 LC 90-55107

This book describes how the surveyor, heavy machinery operators, carpenter crew, plumbers, and other workers build a house

"With her customary bright illustrations, Gibbons gives a fine introduction to the construction of a wood-frame house. . . . Construction machines and materials as well as parts of the house are identified, and each stage of construction logically follows the others. Workers are drawn in both sexes and several skin tones." Booklist

Up goes the skyscraper! Four Winds Press 1986 unp il $12.95; Macmillan pa $4.95 (k-2) **690**

1. Skyscrapers 2. Building
ISBN 0-02-736780-0; 0-689-71411-4 (pa) LC 85-16245

"Without oversimplification, the author traces in straightforward text and brightly colored pictures the construction of a skyscraper from the clearing of the site to tenant move-in." SLJ

Giblin, James, 1933-

Let there be light: a book about windows; [by] James Cross Giblin; illustrated with photographs and prints. Crowell 1988 162p il $14.95; lib bdg $14.89 (5 and up) **690**

1. Windows
ISBN 0-690-04693-6; 0-690-04695-2 (lib bdg) LC 87-35052

Surveys the development of windows from prehistory to the modern era. The author discusses shapes, sizes, materials used, as well as social and political influences

"Splendid illustrations abound in this fascinating history of windows. Much information is also included about making stained glass in this highly recommended book." Child Book Rev Serv

Includes bibliography

Macaulay, David, 1946-

Mill. Houghton Mifflin 1983 128p il $15.95; pa $7.95 (4 and up) **690**

1. Mills and millwork 2. Textile industry—History
ISBN 0-395-34830-7; 0-395-52019-3 (pa) LC 83-10652

Macaulay, David, 1946-—*Continued*

This is an "account of the development of four fictional 19th-Century Rhode Island cotton mills. In explaining the construction and operation of a simple water-wheel powered wooden mill, as well as the more complex stone, turbine and steam mills to follow, the author also describes the rise and decline of New England's textile industry." SLJ

Includes glossary

Unbuilding. Houghton Mifflin 1980 78p il $15.95; pa $7.95 (4 and up) **690**

1. Empire State Building (New York, N.Y.) 2. Building 3. Skyscrapers

ISBN 0-395-29457-6; 0-395-45425-5 (pa) LC 80-15491

This fictional account of the dismantling and removal of the Empire State Building describes the structure of a skyscraper and explains how such an edifice would be demolished

"Save for the fact that one particularly stunning double-page spread is marred by tight binding, the book is a joy: accurate, informative, handsome, and eminently readable." Bull Cent Child Books

Robbins, Ken

Building a house. Four Winds Press 1984 unp il $13.95 (3-6) **690**

1. Building 2. Houses

ISBN 0-02-777400-7 LC 83-16513

"A photo essay describing the design and construction of a contemporary, architect-designed wood frame house." N Y Times Book Rev

"Impeccably organized and lucidly written, this is one of the best books on construction that has appeared: the continuous text is broken into logical topics, the development is sequential, and the author has included all major facts without over-explaining any single procedure. The photographs are of good quality and are carefully integrated with the text." Bull Cent Child Books

Walker, Lester

Housebuilding for children; written, photographed, and illustrated by Les Walker; preface by Nonny Hogrogian. Overlook Press 1977 174p il $16.95; pa $11.95 (2 and up) **690**

1. Building 2. Houses

ISBN 0-87951-059-5; 0-87951-332-2 (pa) LC 76-47220

"This book is written for young people who want to build houses just as older people do. I designed six small houses that would educate children in the different 'real-life' ways of building houses." Introduction

"An enthusiastically written and clearly illustrated guide. Preparatory projects are included to help children learn the use of basic tools and methods. The six houses—including a tree house—were all built by children from seven to nine, supervised by an adult. Full-page photographs of the young builders and of houses under construction appear on nearly every other page, adjacent to drawings of materials and the step-by-step procedures." Horn Book

Weiss, Harvey

Model buildings and how to make them; illustrated with photos and drawings by the author. Crowell 1979 95p il lib bdg $13.95 (4 and up) **690**

1. Buildings—Models

ISBN 0-690-04725-8 LC 77-26597

"Divided into two sections, building from cardboard and building from wood, the text . . . leads hobbyists into the proper techniques, complete with tool requirements and procedures for measuring, cutting, bending, scoring, gluing, and planning to scale. Directions for constructing basic houses, elaborate castles, and usable dollhouses include details for finishing porches, chimneys, turrets, windows, and doors." Booklist

"An excellent introduction to an intriguing hobby." Horn Book

694 Wood construction. Carpentry

Walker, Lester

Carpentry for children; preface by David Macaulay. Overlook Press 1982 208p il hardcover o.p. paperback available $11.95 (4 and up) **694**

1. Carpentry 2. Handicraft

ISBN 0-87951-990-8 (pa) LC 82-3469

A step-by-step guide to carrying out such carpentry projects as a birdhouse, candle chandelier, doll cradle, puppet theater, and coaster car

697 Heating, ventilating, air-conditioning engineering

Giblin, James, 1933-

Chimney sweeps: yesterday and today; by James Cross Giblin; illustrated by Margot Tomes. Crowell 1982 56p il $12.95; lib bdg $12.89; Harper & Row pa $4.95 (4-6) **697**

1. Chimneys

ISBN 0-690-04192-6; 0-690-04193-4 (lib bdg); 0-06-446061-4 (pa) LC 81-43878

The author "explores the history, folklore and romance of the chimney sweep in this introduction to an old and colorful profession. Following the sweep from his European beginnings to his present-day operation in America, the author details changes and developments in practice. . . . Giblin's relaxed, affable manner belies the amount of information he offers in this highly accessible, enjoyable history of the chimney sweep. Fine illustrations by Margot Tomes complement the text." SLJ

Includes bibliography

700 THE ARTS

708 Art—Galleries, museums private collections

Brown, Laurene Krasny
Visiting the art museum; [by] Laurene Krasny Brown and Marc Brown. Dutton 1986 32p il lib bdg $12.95; pa $4.95 (k-3) **708**

1. Art—Museums 2. Art appreciation
ISBN 0-525-44233-2; 0-525-44568-4 (pa) LC 85-32552

As a family wanders through an art museum, they see examples of various art styles from primitive through twentieth-century pop art

"A lively, fact-filled introduction to the art museum for the whole family, with animated drawings and full-color reproductions of art from all over the world. . . . All of the paintings are identified, both in the text and in the back, and all possible periods of art—from primitive to modern—are shown." Publ Wkly

709.01 Arts of nonliterate peoples, and earliest times to 499

Baylor, Byrd
Before you came this way; illustrated by Tom Bahti. Dutton 1969 unp il lib bdg $8.95 (1-4) **709.01**

1. Indians of North America—Art 2. Cave drawings
ISBN 0-525-26312-8 LC 74-81709

"A handsome book, thought-provoking and written with lyric simplicity; the illustrations, on handmade bark paper, are in the style of the prehistoric rock pictures on which the book is based. Walking in the quiet of a canyon in the Southwest, you wonder if you are the first to pass this way . . . then you see that some brother, long-dead, has made a record of his people and their lives: the animals they hunted, the battles and the feasts, the masks of the dancers. The writing style is sensitively attuned to the dignity and mystery of the subject." Sutherland. The Best in Child Books

711 Area planning

Macaulay, David, 1946-
City: a story of Roman planning and construction. Houghton Mifflin 1974 112p il $14.95; pa $6.95 (4 and up) **711**

1. City planning—Rome 2. Civil engineering 3. Architecture, Roman
ISBN 0-395-19492-X; 0-395-34922-2 (pa) LC 74-4280

"By following the inception, construction, and development of an imaginary Roman city, the account traces the evolution of Verbonia from the selection of its site under religious auspices in 26 B.C. to its completion in 100 A.D." Horn Book

Includes glossary

720 Architecture

Isaacson, Philip M., 1924-
Round buildings, square buildings, & buildings that wiggle like a fish; with photographs by the author. Knopf 1988 121p il $14.95; lib bdg $16.99; pa $10.95 (4 and up) **720**

1. Architecture
ISBN 0-394-89382-4; 0-394-99382-9 (lib bdg); 0-679-80649-0 (pa) LC 87-16967

This discussion of architecture presents ninety-three buildings and structures from various times and places, including Stonehenge, Chartres, the Taj Mahal, the Great Mosque in Córdoba, the Parthenon, and the Brooklyn Bridge

"Beautifully composed and reproduced color photographs are numbered for reference in the text, which describes almost poetically the effects of contrasting architectural elements, styles, shapes, materials, and functions. . . . The writing is lyrical without abandoning fact, and the photographic perspectives are arresting." Bull Cent Child Books

726 Buildings for religious and related purposes

Macaulay, David, 1946-
Cathedral: the story of its construction. Houghton Mifflin 1973 77p il $14.95; pa $6.95 (4 and up) **726**

1. Cathedrals 2. Architecture, Gothic
ISBN 0-395-17513-5; 0-395-31668-5 (pa) LC 73-6634

A Caldecott Medal honor book, 1974

This is a description, illustrated with black-and-white line drawings, of the construction of an imagined representative Gothic cathedral "in southern France from its conception in 1252 to its completion in 1338. The spirit that motivated the people, the tools and materials they used, the steps and methods of constructions, all receive . . . attention." Booklist

Includes glossary

Pyramid. Houghton Mifflin 1975 80p il $14.95; pa $6.95 (4 and up) **726**

1. Pyramids 2. Egypt—Civilization
ISBN 0-395-21407-6; 0-395-32121-2 (pa) LC 75-9964

The construction of a pyramid in 25th century B.C. Egypt is described "beginnning with the reasons why the ancient Egyptians attached so much importance to the building of permanent, magnificent tombs. Information about selection of the site, drawing of the plans, calculating compass directions, clearing and leveling the ground, and quarrying and hauling the tremendous blocks of granite and limestone is conveyed as much by pictures as by text." Horn Book

Includes glossary

728 Residential and related buildings

Huntington, Lee Pennock

Americans at home; four hundred years of American houses. Coward, McCann & Geoghegan 1981 80p il $9.95 (6 and up) **728**

1. Architecture, Domestic 2. Houses
ISBN 0-698-20530-8 LC 81-4972

The author "describes the different architectural styles popular throughout the country's history and the ways in which fashion, climate, and social and economic conditions tempered these developments." Booklist

"This book was written for a wide audience. The style is simple and straightforward, and while the vocabulary is challenging in specific instances, it can be understood with alacrity by young readers. The many pictures allow comparison with the verbal descriptions." Best Sellers

Weiss, Harvey

Shelters: from tepee to igloo. Crowell 1988 74p il $10.95; lib bdg $10.89 (4 and up) **728**

1. Houses 2. Architecture, Domestic
ISBN 0-690-04553-0; 0-690-04555-7 (lib bdg) LC 87-47698

Describes a number of shelters constructed from different types of materials and suitable for varying climates, including tepees, yurts, log cabins, stone houses, and igloos

"Complementing the text are many humorous, captioned black-and-white wash illustrations that show precisely how each shelter is constructed." SLJ

Yue, Charlotte

The igloo; [by] Charlotte and David Yue. Houghton Mifflin 1988 117p il $13.95 **728**

1. Igloos 2. Inuit
ISBN 0-395-44613-9 LC 88-6154

Describes how an igloo is constructed and the role it plays in the lives of the Eskimo people. Also discusses many other aspects of Eskimo culture that have helped them adapt to life in the Arctic

"This book is a tidy source of reference information, curriculum support, and just plain compelling reading." SLJ

Includes bibliography

Yue, David

The tipi: a center of native American life; by David and Charlotte Yue. Knopf 1984 77p il lib bdg $10.99; pa $10.95 (4 and up) **728**

1. Indians of North America—Housing
ISBN 0-394-96177-3 (lib bdg); 0-394-86177-9 (pa) LC 83-19529

"The tipi of the Plains Indians was a dwelling uniquely adapted to the social patterns of its inventors and to the climactic conditions of the environment. A sequence of five chapters demonstrates the remarkable structural sophistication of the tipi and the aesthetic and spiritual significance of its design and decoration. . . . An abundance of attractive pencil drawings illustrate each step of construction and furnishing." Horn Book

728.8 Large and elaborate private dwellings

Adkins, Jan

The art and industry of sandcastles; being an illustrated guide to basic constructions along with divers information devised by one Jan Adkins, a wily fellow. Walker & Co. 1971 xxixp il maps hardcover o.p. paperback available $4.95 (4 and up) **728.8**

1. Castles
ISBN 0-8027-7205-6 (pa) LC 76-141615

"Designed with an unobtrusive mastery of form and line the text and illustrations together serve both as a sophisticated guide to making sandcastles and as a record of the evolution of castle building in Europe. The explanation of various processes used to make sand structures and to build various kinds of actual castles is given in a pleasing, skillfully presented book for all ages, with information included on the duties of major personnel in the traditional castle." Booklist

Macaulay, David, 1946-

Castle. Houghton Mifflin 1977 74p il $14.95; pa $6.95 (4 and up) **728.8**

1. Castles 2. Fortification
ISBN 0-395-25784-0; 0-395-32920-5 (pa) LC 77-7159

A Caldecott Medal honor book, 1978

Macaulay depicts "the history of an imaginary thirteenth-century castle—built to subdue the Welsh hordes—from the age of construction to the age of neglect, when the town of Aberwyfern no longer needs a fortified stronghold." Economist

"The line drawings are meticulous in detail, lucidly illustrating architectural features described in the text and injected with a refreshing humor. . . . The writing is clear, crisp, and informative, with a smooth narrative flow." Bull Cent Child Books

Includes glossary

Unstead, R. J. (Robert John)

See inside a castle. rev ed. Warwick Press 1986 31p il $10.40; lib bdg $11.90 (5 and up) **728.8**

1. Castles
ISBN 0-531-09119-8; 0-531-09134-1 (lib bdg) LC 85-52284

First published 1977 in the United Kingdom

This book "covers life during medieval times from 950-1291. The evolution of castle life is chronicled with numerous annotated illustrations and succinct text." SLJ

Includes glossary and bibliography

736 Carving and carvings. Paper cutting and folding

Araki, Chiyo

Origami in the classroom. Tuttle 1965-1968 2v il ea $11.95 (4 and up) **736**

1. Origami 2. Paper crafts
ISBN 0-8048-0452-1; 0-8048-0453-2 LC 65-13412

Book I has subtitle: Activities for autumn through Christmas. Book II has subtitle: Activities for winter through summer

Original patterns of graduated difficulty are presented for various holidays, events, seasons, etc. Measurements, length of time, and materials necessary are given for most projects

Irvine, Joan, 1951-

How to make pop-ups; illustrated by Barbara Reid. Morrow Junior Bks. 1988 c1987 93p il lib bdg $12.88; pa $6.95 (3-6) **736**

1. Paper crafts 2. Handicraft
ISBN 0-688-07903-2 (lib bdg); 0-688-07902-4 (pa) LC 87-28306

First published 1987 in Canada

"This how-to book covers an art form that is found rarely in other craft books. The pop-ups described and illustrated range from very simple cards to the complex making of a pop-up book. The directions are concise and easy to follow, while the well-done black-and-white illustrations enhance the instructions by showing exactly how each pop-up fits together. . . . An excellent addition to the crafts section." SLJ

Sarasas, Claude

The ABC's of origami; paper folding for children; illustrated by the author. Tuttle 1964 55p il $9.50 (4-6) **736**

1. Origami 2. Alphabet
ISBN 0-8048-0000-6 LC 64-17160

First published 1951 in Japan

Here are "diagramed directions for folding 26 objects from Albatross to Zebra with each heading [first in English and then] translated into French and transliterated Japanese. Color illustrations show finished object against an oriental background." SLJ

737.4 Coins

Hughes, Roderick P.

Fell's United States coin book. Fell il $14.95; pa $9.95 **737.4**

1. Coins

First edition published 1949 under the authorship of Jacques Del Monte. Some editions under the authorship of Charles J. Andrews. Periodically revised

This guide contains complete tables showing today's value of every coin minted in the United States. Along with illustrations is information on the history of coins, speculation and investment, how to start a collection, how to sell coins and recognize worthless coins

Reinfeld, Fred, 1910-1964

Catalogue of the world's most popular coins; by Fred Reinfeld and Burton Hobson. Sterling pa $19.95 **737.4**

1. Coins

First published 1956. Periodically revised. Publisher varies

Editor: 1983- Robert Obojski

"Modern and ancient coins and their values are arranged by country with historical notes about each. Many illustrations enhance the information about those coins most sought by collectors and most likely to increase in value." A L A. Ref Sources for Small & Medium-sized Libr. 4th edition

741 Drawing and drawings

Raphael, Elaine

Drawing history: Ancient Egypt; [by] Elaine Raphael & Don Bolognese. Watts 1989 32p il lib bdg $12.40 (4 and up) **741**

1. Drawing 2. Egypt—Civilization
ISBN 0-531-10698-5 LC 88-13873

Companion volumes covering Ancient Greece and Ancient Rome are also available

This introduction to ancient Egypt through drawing and painting, provides historical information as well as step-by-step drawing instructions for each topic

"The drawings are accurate and pleasing to the eye. . . . The authors take care in describing how these drawings differ from those actually done by the Egyptians, although these drawings were 'influenced by the art found in the Pharoah's tombs.'" SLJ

Includes glossary

741.2 Drawing—Techniques, procedures, apparatus, equipment, materials

Bolognese, Don

Pen & ink; by Don Bolognese and Elaine Raphael. Watts 1986 64p il (Illustrator's lib) lib bdg $10.90 (4 and up) **741.2**

1. Pen drawing
ISBN 0-531-10133-9 LC 86-1552

A guide for the novice illustrator to using pen and ink, including choosing pens, keeping a sketch book, trying different techniques, and developing a personal style

"Throughout the authors emphasize the components of illustration (calling it a form of storytelling) and encourage experimentation, use of the imagination, and constant practice. A fine introduction for the novice artist." Booklist

Devonshire, Hilary

Drawing; photography: Chris Fairclough. Watts 1990 48p il (Fresh start) lib bdg $11.90 (4 and up) **741.2**

1. Drawing
ISBN 0-531-10855-4 LC 89-36496

An introduction, in text and photographs, to drawing techniques and the range of materials used to produce a variety of textures and effects

"The level of sophistication and end product achieved with simple materials makes [this book an] excellent choice for use with a wide audience." Booklist

Emberley, Ed

Ed Emberley's big green drawing book. Little, Brown 1979 91p il $14.95; pa $7.95 (2-5) **741.2**

1. Drawing
ISBN 0-316-23595-4; 0-316-23596-2 (pa)
LC 79-16247

The author "combines basic shapes (circles, triangles, lines, squiggles) to create a variety of cartoon people and animals. The crisp green-and-black illustrations on a white background are large and well spaced. . . . As in his other drawing books, Emberley's wordless step-by-step method is easy to follow; even very young children can successfully reproduce the simple but appealing figures." SLJ

Ed Emberley's big red drawing book. Little, Brown 1987 unp il $14.95; pa $7.95 (2-5) **741.2**

1. Drawing
ISBN 0-316-23434-6; 0-316-23435-4 (pa) LC 87-3091

The author explains "how to create objects and figures by building up a series of simple lines and squiggles into a more complicated and complete whole. The color red suggests most of the subjects, among them a U.S. flag, a fire engine, and assorted red-and-green Christmas items." Booklist

Ed Emberley's drawing book: make a world. Little, Brown 1972 unp il $13.95 (2-5) **741.2**

1. Drawing
ISBN 0-316-23598-9 LC 70-154962

"Emberley gives directions for drawing, among a myriad of other things, 10 different kinds of cars, 16 varieties of trucks, and animals of all species including anteaters and dinosaurs." Book World

"The final three pages, which supply suggestions for making comic strips, posters, mobiles and games, help make the volume particularly appealing. For all developing artists and even plain scribblers." Horn Book

Ed Emberley's picture pie: a circle drawing book. Little, Brown 1984 unp il $14.95; pa $7.95 (2-5) **741.2**

1. Drawing 2. Paper crafts
ISBN 0-316-23425-7; 0-316-23426-5 (pa) LC 84-9666

"Shows how to make myriad designs based on circle cutouts. Whole circles, halves, quarters, and eights are layered and arranged to form gloriously colorful geometric collages, borders, patterns, and—with the addition of a few dots and lines—processions of birds, flowers, fish, plants, and much more. The array of spectacular sample designs is followed by suggestions for putting the artwork to use and adding further embellishments." Booklist

741.5 Cartoons, caricatures, comics

Ames, Lee J., 1921-

Draw 50 famous cartoons. Doubleday 1979 unp il $12.95; pa $6.95 (4 and up) **741.5**

1. Cartoons and caricatures 2. Drawing
ISBN 0-385-13661-7; 0-385-19521-4 (pa) LC 78-1173

Step-by-step sequential drawings illustrate the techniques needed to draw such cartoon characters as Popeye, Dagwood, Magilla Gorilla and Scooby Doo

Benjamin, Carol Lea

Cartooning for kids. Crowell 1982 71p il lib bdg $12.89; pa $4.95 (4-6) **741.5**

1. Cartoons and caricatures 2. Drawing
ISBN 0-690-04208-6 (lib bdg); 0-06-446063-0 (pa)
LC 81-43876

Outlines how to draw simple cartoons from circles, dots, lines, and curves and how to add professional touches such as shading, decorative detail, or color

"Written in a cheerful, humorous tone and full of line drawings, the book encourages the budding cartoonist to use his imagination to create his own successful cartoon." Horn Book

Hoff, Syd, 1912-

The young cartoonist; the ABC's of cartooning. Stravon Educ. Press 1983 192p il $19.95 (4 and up) **741.5**

1. Cartoons and caricatures
ISBN 0-87396-094-7 LC 82-5980

"A Rainbow book"

This book covers such aspects of cartooning as "how to draw faces, figures, and expressions and how to block out a composition." Horn Book

"This is less a book of useful instructions than a series of examples of the cartoonist's work: pages of figures based on a particular line, pages in which features are added, one by one. . . . There's a chapter on how to make up jokes and choose captions. This could be used for imitation, but ideas that might act as a catalyst for creativity are sparse." Bull Cent Child Books

Weiss, Harvey

Cartoons and cartooning. Houghton Mifflin 1990 64p il $13.95 (4 and up) **741.5**

1. Cartoons and caricatures
ISBN 0-395-49217-3 LC 89-39596

"Weiss describes cartoons from the past as well as what the art of cartooning has become. Comic strips, gag panels, story cartoons, political or editorial cartoons, and the art of caricature, as well as the business of cartooning, comic books, and animated cartoons are all

Weiss, Harvey—*Continued*
included. The chapter gives some hints about doing your own cartoons." SLJ

"This entire book has the instant appeal and immediate impact typical of good comic books: brief but interesting text and well executed, eye-catching illustrations." Voice Youth Advocates

Includes bibliography

741.6 Graphic design, illustration and commercial art

The **Illustrator's** notebook; edited by Lee Kingman. Horn Bk. 1978 153p il $28.95 **741.6**

1. Illustration of books 2. Illustrators 3. Children's literature—History and criticism
ISBN 0-87675-013-7 LC 77-20028

This is a collection of excerpts from articles originally published in "Horn Book Magazine." The artists discuss their feelings about book illustration in terms of its history and its significance as an art form and as a means of communication. They also discuss various illustration techniques, including woodcut, lithography, collage and color separation. The book contains over a hundred illustrations, many in color, that provide examples of the illustrator's craft

Includes bibliography

Illustrators of children's books. Horn Bk. 1947-1978 4v il v 1, 4 ea $35.95; v2, 3 ea $30.95 **741.6**

1. Illustration of books 2. Illustrators 3. Children's literature—History and criticism LC 47-31264

Contents: v 1 1744-1945, compiled by Bertha E. Mahony, Louise Payson Latimer and Beulah Folmsbee (ISBN 0-87675-015-3); v2 1946-1956, compiled by Ruth Hill Viguers, Marcia Dalphin and Bertha Mahony Miller (ISBN 0-87675-016-1); v3 1957-1966, compiled by Lee Kingman, Joanne Foster and Ruth Giles Lontoft (ISBN 0-87675-017-X); v4 1967-1976, compiled by Lee Kingman, Grace Allen Hogarth and Harriet Quimby (ISBN 0-87675-018-8)

"A standard source for information about the history and development of children's book illustration and biographies of illustrators, each volume includes essays, biographies, and bibliographies." Wynar. Guide to Ref Books for Sch Media Cent. 2d edition

Lacy, Lyn Ellen

Art and design in children's picture books; an analysis of Caldecott award-winning illustrations. American Lib. Assn. 1986 229p $25 **741.6**

1. Caldecott Medal books 2. Illustration of books 3. Picture books for children
ISBN 0-8389-0446-7 LC 86-1163

Using thirteen Caldecott-winning picture books as examples for art analysis, the author "attempts to show how picture books can be used to teach the fundamental elements of art: line, color, light and dark, shape and space. After an introductory chapter about art terms, the nature of the picture book, and comments about the picture-book audience, Lacy devotes an entire chapter to each of the five fundamental elements. . . . This book is likely to prove most useful to media specialists and art teachers who would like to combine picture books and art appreciation. Picture-book reviewers and other students of the picture book may glean some help in analyzing illustrations. Access to the Caldecott winners is necessary as sample illustrations are not provided." J Youth Serv Libr

Includes bibliographic references and glossary

Lanes, Selma G.

Art of Maurice Sendak. Abrams 1980 278p il $34.95 **741.6**

1. Sendak, Maurice
ISBN 0-8109-8063-0 LC 80-10796

The author "tells the story of Sendak's career as an illustrator of his own and others' books. . . . Ninety-four full-color illustrations and 165 black and white ones (including many sketches and preliminary drawings) sample the career from 1950 to 1981. The reader will learn a great deal about the planning and execution of children's books along the way." Best Sellers

Potter, Beatrix, 1866-1943

The art of Beatrix Potter; with an appreciation by Anne Carroll Moore and notes to each section by Enid and Leslie Linder. 5th ed. Warne 1972 406p il $30 **741.6**

ISBN 0-7232-1457-3 LC 76-358049

First published 1955

This study of Beatrix Potter's work includes a total of 330 reproductions, 205 of them in color. It traces the development of the artist and includes copies of preliminary drawings, manuscripts, and letters

Includes bibliography

741.9 Collections of drawings

I never saw another butterfly; children's drawings and poems from Terezin Concentration Camp, 1942-1944. 2d ed. Schocken Bks. 1978 80p il pa $6.95 **741.9**

1. Child artists 2. Child authors 3. Terezin (Czechoslovakia: Concentration camp)
ISBN 0-8052-0598-5 LC 78-3542

Original Czech edition, 1959; first United States edition published 1964 by McGraw Hill

Edited by Hana Volavková

"A collection of eloquent, touching poems and drawings created by Jewish children marked for death who passed through Theresienstadt Concentration Camp during World War II. A gift to the children of the world. . . . Epilogue by Jiri Weil." Keating. Build Bridges of Understanding Between Cultures

743 Drawing and drawings by subject

Ames, Lee J., 1921-

Draw 50 beasties and yugglies and turnover uglies and things that go bump in the night. Doubleday 1988 unp il $12.95; lib bdg $13.99; pa $6.95 (4 and up) **743**

1. Drawing 2. Monsters in art
ISBN 0-385-24625-0; 0-385-24626-9 (lib bdg); 0-385-26767-3 (pa) LC 88-16143

Provides step-by-step instructions for drawing monsters, goons, and gruesome beasts

Ames "encourages readers to take plenty of time and suggests very lightly sketching out the step-by-step drawings so that mistakes may be rectified. This one, with its popular subject of imaginative monsters and other nightmare inhabitants, will be a sure-fire circulator." SLJ

Draw 50 boats, ships, trucks & trains. Doubleday 1976 unp il $12.95; pa $5.95 (4 and up) **743**

1. Drawing 2. Vehicles in art
ISBN 0-385-08903-1; 0-385-23630-1 (pa) LC 75-19011

Step-by-step instructions for drawing fifty different ships, boats, trucks, and trains

Draw 50 buildings and other structures. Doubleday 1980 unp il lib bdg $13.99 (4 and up) **743**

1. Drawing 2. Buildings in art
ISBN 0-385-14401-6 LC 79-7483

This is similar in format to the author's other books. Step by step procedures enable the reader to draw houses from the U.S. and Ireland, bridges and even a torii (a Japanese gateway)

Draw 50 cars, trucks, and motorcycles. Doubleday 1986 unp il $12.95; lib bdg $13.99; pa $6.95 (4 and up) **743**

1. Drawing 2. Vehicles in art
ISBN 0-385-19059-X; 0-385-19060-3 (lib bdg); 0-385-24639-0 (pa) LC 85-13157

Ames "demonstrates how to develop a finished drawing of sports cars, classic cars, racers, bicycles, motorcycles, and trucks, using a series of simple lines." SLJ

Draw 50 cats. Doubleday 1986 unp il $12.95; lib bdg $13.99; pa $5.95 (4 and up) **743**

1. Drawing 2. Cats in art 3. Animal painting and illustration
ISBN 0-385-23484-8; 0-385-23485-6 (lib bdg); 0-385-24640-4 (pa) LC 86-8964

Step-by-step instructions on how to draw a variety of cats, including domestic breeds, wild cats, cuddly kittens, and celebrity cats

Draw 50 dinosaurs and other prehistoric animals; with a foreword by George Zappler. Doubleday 1977 unp il $12.95; pa $6.95 (4 and up) **743**

1. Drawing 2. Dinosaurs in art 3. Animal painting and illustration
ISBN 0-385-11134-7; 0-385-19520-6 (pa) LC 76-7285

Step-by-step instructions for drawing a variety of dinosaurs and other prehistoric animals

Draw 50 dogs. Doubleday 1981 unp il $12.95; lib bdg $13.99; pa $6.95 (4 and up) **743**

1. Drawing 2. Animal painting and illustration 3. Dogs in art
ISBN 0-385-15686-3; 0-385-15687-1 (lib bdg); 0-385-23431-7 (pa) LC 79-6853

"Ames' six-step drawings guide youngsters along toward fashioning their own canine figures. Each species starts out with an ultrasimple shape; ovals, circles, or rectangular extensions suggest developing proportions that lead to the completed sketch." Booklist

Draw 50 holiday decorations; [by] Lee J. Ames with Ray Burns. Doubleday 1987 unp il $12.95; lib bdg $13.99; pa $6.95 (4 and up) **743**

1. Drawing 2. Holiday decorations
ISBN 0-385-19057-3; 0-385-19058-1 (lib bdg); 0-385-26770-3 (pa) LC 87-15581

Step-by-step instructions for drawing a variety of holiday subjects such as Baby New Year, Cupid and his arrow, July 4th rockets, turkey, pumpkin, Easter basket, Santa Claus, and a menorah

Draw 50 horses. Doubleday 1984 unp il $12.95; lib bdg $12.95; pa $5.95 (4 and up) **743**

1. Drawing 2. Horses in art 3. Animal painting and illustration
ISBN 0-385-17640-6; 0-385-17641-X (lib bdg); 0-385-17642-2 (pa) LC 81-43646

Step-by-step instructions for drawing different breeds of horses in a variety of poses

Draw 50 sharks, whales, and other sea creatures; [by] Lee J. Ames with Warren Budd. Doubleday 1989 unp il $12.95; lib bdg $13.99 (4 and up) **743**

1. Drawing 2. Marine animals in art 3. Animal painting and illustration
ISBN 0-385-24627-7; 0-385-24628-5 (lib bdg) LC 88-35163

Provides step-by-step instructions for drawing a variety of sharks, whales, and other sea creatures, including the hammerhead shark, humpback whale, and giant sea turtle

Arnosky, Jim

Drawing from nature. Lothrop, Lee & Shepard Bks. 1982 unp il $13.95; pa $8.95 (5 and up) **743**

1. Drawing 2. Animal painting and illustration
ISBN 0-688-01295-7; 0-688-07075-2 (pa)
LC 82-15327

The author "shows how to draw land and water—both above and below the surface—how to draw snow, animal tracks in it and in mud, how to draw animals still and in motion, birds in flight and landing." SLJ

"The text is as graceful as the art, and it is full of advice on sharpening awareness. The casual artist will be inspired by this book, but it will be of most use to those young and old alike who have already exhibited an inclination or definite talent for drawing." Booklist

Drawing life in motion. Lothrop, Lee & Shepard Bks. 1984 unp il $12.95; pa $8.95 (4 and up) **743**

1. Drawing 2. Animal painting and illustration
ISBN 0-688-03803-4; 0-688-07076-0 (pa)
LC 83-25129

The author/artist provides tips on how to illustrate motion in both plants and animals

"Intended for artists with some experience, the book is not a step-by-step manual for beginners but, at all times, encourages young people to rely on their own observations." Horn Book

Sketching outdoors in autumn. Lothrop, Lee & Shepard Bks. 1988 46p il $12.95 (5 and up) **743**

1. Drawing 2. Animal painting and illustration
ISBN 0-688-06288-1 LC 88-1244

Provides drawings of landscapes, plants, and animals the artist observed in autumn

"As a tool in the classroom, it would be a wonderful enhancement to the study of autumn, going beyond the familiar display of colorful leaves." Sci Books Films

Sketching outdoors in spring. Lothrop, Lee & Shepard Bks. 1987 48p il $12.95 (5 and up) **743**

1. Drawing 2. Animal painting and illustration
ISBN 0-688-06284-9 LC 86-21308

Similar in format to the title entered above, this book focuses on nature drawing during the spring

Sketching outdoors in summer. Lothrop, Lee & Shepard Bks. 1988 47p il $12.95; Avon Bks. pa $2.95 (5 and up) **743**

1. Drawing 2. Animal painting and illustration
ISBN 0-688-06286-5; 0-380-71314-4 (pa)
LC 87-29728

Similar in format to the title entered above, this book focuses on nature drawing during the summer months

Sketching outdoors in winter. Lothrop, Lee & Shepard Bks. 1988 48p il $12.95 (5 and up) **743**

1. Drawing 2. Animal painting and illustration
ISBN 0-688-06290-3 LC 88-2202

Similar in format to the titles entered above, this book covers nature drawing during the winter

Emberley, Ed

Ed Emberley's drawing book of faces. Little, Brown 1975 32p il lib bdg $13.95 (2-5) **743**

1. Drawing 2. Face in art
ISBN 0-316-23609-8 LC 74-32033

Provides step-by-step instructions for drawing a wide variety of faces reflecting various emotions and professions

Ed Emberley's great thumbprint drawing book. Little, Brown 1977 37p il lib bdg $12.95 (2-5) **743**

1. Drawing
ISBN 0-316-23613-6 LC 76-57346

"The artist shows how to combine thumbprints and simple lines to create a multitude of animals, people, birds, and flowers." Booklist

"There is little text; most of the book consists of illustrations, step-by-step, of making pictures out of thumbprints. A few Emberley embellishments and a page that suggests other ways of making prints (carrot or potato) are included." Bull Cent Child Books

Frame, Paul, 1913-

Drawing cats and kittens. Watts 1979 71p il (How-to-draw bk) lib bdg $10.90 (4 and up) **743**

1. Drawing 2. Cats in art 3. Animal painting and illustration
ISBN 0-531-02282-X LC 79-11935

"This is for serious beginners, ones willing to put in the practice time Frame stresses is necessary to develop drawing skills. The overall emphasis is on studied observations of form, with exercises that allow work on problems such as perspective changes or distribution of light and shadow. . . . Sketches are plentiful and helpful as practice ideals. The parade of completed cats that finishes the presentation gives readers a standard to aim for." Booklist

745.5 Handicrafts

Haldane, Suzanne

Painting faces. Dutton 1988 32p il lib bdg $13.95 (4-6) **745.5**

1. Decoration and ornament 2. Face
ISBN 0-525-44408-4 LC 88-3706

Text and photographs introduce painted faces from various cultures and countries. The book includes directions that children can follow for painting some of them

"Many young readers will be content to browse through the pictures rather than spend time on the text. Even so, the book will open up connections to other times and societies as well as stimulate a popular activity. Warnings about skin allergies are included." Bull Cent Child Books

Kerina, Jane

African crafts; illustrated by Tom Feelings, with diagrams by Marylyn Katzman. Lion Bks. 1970 64p il lib bdg $11.95 (4 and up) **745.5**

1. Handicraft
ISBN 0-87460-084-1 LC 69-18916

This book includes "directions for making a variety of useful and decorative objects in the tradition of African craftsmen, including pottery, jewelry, wood carvings, calabash kitchen-ware, Akuaba dolls, tie-dyed cloth, a musical instrument, and simple danshiki and other articles of clothing. The objects, which utilize easily obtainable materials, are identified as to their use, history, and region of origin. Clear drawings show the finished objects and some of the steps in their creation. Since the directions are frequently sketchy, children may require adult help in making many of the projects." Books for Child, 1970-1971

Kohn, Bernice

The beachcomber's book; illustrations by Arabelle Wheatley. Viking 1970 96p il o.p.; Puffin Bks. paperback available $5.95 (3-6) **745.5**

1. Handicraft 2. Seashore 3. Marine biology
ISBN 0-14-049158-9 (pa)

"This book includes advice on shell collecting, a home aquarium, collecting and cooking food, drying flowers, and making objects out of sand, driftwood, pebbles, shells, animal skeletons, et cetera. There are several projects for which adult assistance is suggested, but most of them are fairly simple; some supplies are needed, but these tend to be easily obtainable and not expensive." Sutherland. The Best in Child Books

Includes bibliography

Parish, Peggy, 1927-1988

Let's be early settlers with Daniel Boone; drawings by Arnold Lobel. Harper & Row 1967 96p il lib bdg $12.89 (2-5) **745.5**

1. Handicraft 2. Frontier and pioneer life 3. Costume
ISBN 0-06-024648-0 LC 67-14068

"Simple instructions and helpful drawings for making pioneer houses, clothing, weapons, and other objects needed for a project on frontier life or for costumes of the period." Hodges. Books for Elem Sch Libr

Rockwell, Harlow, 1910-1988

I did it. Macmillan 1974 56p il o.p.; Aladdin Bks. (NY) paperback available $3.95 (1-3) **745.5**

1. Handicraft
ISBN 0-684-71126-3 (pa) LC 73-19059

"Ready-to-read"

In this how-to book the "projects are varied; making a paper airplane, writing a message in invisible ink, making a picture out of dried foods, making a papier mâché fish, making a paper bag mask, and baking bread. Good format, clear instructions, and a variety of things to do." Bull Cent Child Books

Sattler, Helen Roney

Recipes for art and craft materials; with new illustrations by Marti Shohet. rev ed. Lothrop, Lee & Shepard Bks. 1987 144p il $11.95; lib bdg $10.88 (4 and up) **745.5**

1. Handicraft—Equipment and supplies 2. Artists' materials
ISBN 0-688-07374-3; 0-688-07375-1 (lib bdg) LC 86-34271

First published 1973

The author explains "how to make pastes and glues, modeling compounds, papier-mâché, casting compounds, paints, inks, flower preservatives, recycled paper, and more. Activities are studies in applied science that invite investigations, encourage careful observation, and celebrate the cleverness of hands as well as brain." Sci Child

Wilkes, Angela

My first activity book; [photographs by Dave King] Knopf 1990 c1989 48p il $11.95; lib bdg $10.99 (1-5) **745.5**

1. Handicraft
ISBN 0-394-86583-9; 0-394-96583-3 (lib bdg) LC 89-2640

First published 1989 in the United Kingdom

Instructions for making masks, jewelry, Christmas tree decorations, and other objects from material readily available in the home

"This large-sized volume contains a treasure trove of inviting and imaginative things to make. Concise directions are amplified by bright, step-by-step photographs." Publ Wkly

745.54 Paper handicrafts

Corwin, Judith Hoffman

Papercrafts; origami, papier-mâché, and collage. Watts 1988 72p il lib bdg $11.90 (3 and up) **745.54**

1. Paper crafts
ISBN 0-531-10465-6 LC 87-21611

This book includes "24 activities involving origami, papier-mâché, and collage. Origami projects include several animals, a mask, and some flowers. The papier-mâché section gives a recipe for paste followed by directions for making beads, a ladybug, and several other items. Collage offerings are the most diverse and plentiful: birds, a cat, bunnies, circus performers, and other amply decorated figures." Booklist

"Illustrations in two colors are plentiful, instructions are clear and specific, and materials lists are complete." SLJ

Lancaster, John, 1930-

Paper sculpture; photography: Chris Fairclough. Watts 1989 48p il (Fresh start) lib bdg $11.90 (4 and up) **745.54**

1. Paper crafts
ISBN 0-531-10758-2 LC 89-8887

Lancaster, John, 1930-—*Continued*
Provides step-by-step instructions on how to make paper and create art objects by tearing, folding, and weaving paper
The book is "clear, concise, and well formatted. The print is fairly large, and the text is easy to read. . . . Provides enough information to complete the projects but not so much that imagination is stifled." SLJ
Includes bibliography

Renfro, Nancy
Bags are big! a paper bag craft book; written and illustrated by Nancy Renfro; photographs by Nancy Scanlan. Nancy Renfro Studios 1986 63p il pa $12.95
745.54
1. Paper crafts 2. Handicraft
ISBN 0-931044-10-3
"This book shows how even the lowly paper bag can be transformed by the wizardry of our imaginations into something marvelous or magical. . . . It features animated and colorful illustrations and photos, and will make a good addition to any classroom, recreational or library how-to corner." Sch Arts

West, Robin
Dinosaur discoveries; how to create your own prehistoric world; photographs by Bob and Diane Wolfe; drawings by Mindy Rabin. Carolrhoda Bks. 1989 71p il lib bdg $14.95 (3-5) **745.54**
1. Paper crafts 2. Dinosaurs
ISBN 0-87614-351-6 LC 88-32513
"This attractive book gives directions for making three-dimensional paper models of nine prehistoric creatures and three prehistoric plants. Included are dinosaurs, a mammoth, and a giant dragonfly. . . . Directions are given in clearly worded, numbered paragraphs supplemented by an informative color photograph of each project and a sequence of illustrative diagrams." SLJ

745.59 Making specific objects

Hautzig, Esther Rudomin
Make it special; cards, decorations, and party favors for holidays and other special occasions; [by] Esther Hautzig; illustrated by Martha Weston. Macmillan 1986 86p il $11.95 (4-6) **745.59**
1. Holiday decorations 2. Gifts
ISBN 0-02-743370-6 LC 86-8616
The author "gives ideas and instructions for designing holiday and greeting cards, decorating the house and table for special events, and making party favors and gifts." Booklist
"Most of the projects suggested in this how-to book require materials that are easily obtainable and that are free or inexpensive. . . . The material is adequately organized. . . . The illustrations are useful for the most part, although on some pages there are step-by-step diagrams that are cluttered." Bull Cent Child Books

Meyer, Carolyn
Christmas crafts; things to make the 24 days before Christmas; pictures by Anita Lobel. Harper & Row 1974 136p il $13.95 (5 and up) **745.59**
1. Christmas decorations 2. Handicraft 3. Cookery
ISBN 0-06-024197-7 LC 74-2608
Here are instructions for making two dozen crafted objects appropriate to the Christmas season, including egg ornaments, gingerbread sculptures, St Lucia buns, piñatas, and pomander balls
"The author has actually collected Advent and Christmas traditions from many cultures; and she describes the religious symbolism, the historical significance, and the folklore associated with each project. Materials used are inexpensive and accessible; instructions are simple and sensible." Horn Book

Parish, Peggy, 1927-1988
December decorations; a holiday how-to book; illustrated by Barbara Wolff. Macmillan 1975 64p il $9.95 (1-3) **745.59**
1. Holiday decorations 2. Handicraft 3. Christmas decorations
ISBN 0-02-769920-X LC 75-14285
"Ready-to-read handbook"
"Each of 30 holiday-season decorations is explained separately and simply for the youngest readers. Primary-grade children can manage the project alone in many cases, and materials are easily obtained. . . . Illustrations in green and black do a good job of explaining steps." Booklist

A **Pumpkin** in a pear tree; creative ideas for twelve months of holiday fun; by Ann Cole [et.al]; illustrated by Debby Young. Little, Brown 1976 112p il lib bdg $14.95; pa $8.95 (1-4) **745.59**
1. Holiday decorations 2. Handicraft 3. Games 4. Cookery
ISBN 0-316-15110-6 (lib bdg); 0-316-15111-4 (pa)
LC 75-17645
Suggestions for simple projects, games, and crafts, using common household materials, for holidays throughout the year

Wright, Lyndie
Masks; photography: Chris Fairclough. Watts 1990 48p il (Fresh start) lib bdg $11.90 (4 and up) **745.59**
1. Masks (Facial) 2. Handicraft
ISBN 0-531-10856-2 LC 89-36533
Provides step-by-step illustrated instructions for making a variety of masks, including painted masks, balloon masks, cardboard robot masks, and shadow masks
"Clear instructions and crisp, full-color photographs create an attractive and logical format." SLJ
Includes bibliography

745.592 Toys, models, miniatures, related objects

Blocksma, Mary

Action contraptions; easy-to-make toys that really move; by Mary Blocksma and Dewey Blocksma; illustrated by Sandra Hulst. Prentice-Hall Bks. for Young Readers 1988 c1987 64p il lib bdg $10.95 (2-5) **745.592**

1. Toys 2. Handicraft
ISBN 0-13-003352-9 LC 87-2295

"This volume features action toys such as tops, wind toys, and cars. The projects are made from recycled objects (plastic soda bottles), simple materials found at home (paper plates and cups), and inexpensive items (ping pong balls)." SLJ

"Hulst's uncluttered diagrams on every page provide the needed visual guidance. Appealing for children working alone or in groups." Booklist

Churchill, E. Richard (Elmer Richard)

Fast & funny paper toys you can make; illustrated by James Michaels. Sterling 1989 128p il $14.95; pa $7.95 (3 and up) **745.592**

1. Toys 2. Handicraft
ISBN 0-8069-5770-0; 0-8069-5771-9 (pa) LC 89-32411

This book provides directions for making paper toys that move from household articles. Includes boats, noisemakers, puppets, mobiles, and more

"Milk cartons, cereal boxes, notebook paper, rubber bands, and tape are among the easily accessible materials used, making this an ideal resource where budgets are tight. Numbered illustrations on every page augment the clear step-by-step instructions." Booklist

Instant paper airplanes; illustrated by James Michaels. Sterling 1988 128p il $14.95; pa $7.95 (3-5) **745.592**

1. Airplanes—Models 2. Paper crafts
ISBN 0-8069-6796-X; 0-8069-6797-8 (pa) LC 88-12325

"Churchill gives directions for no less than 28 different folded paper gliders, divided into six groups ranging from the very easiest to fold and fly to experimental designs. He intersperses the definitions of many aeronautical terms in boxes with the step-by-step directions for each plane. He then incorporates these terms into the directions so that thoughtful readers can gain 'hands-on' knowledge of them. All directions are concise and clear. Diagrams show step-by-step procedures and are well marked and easily referred to in the narrative." SLJ

Paper toys that fly, soar, zoom, & whistle; illustrated by James Michaels. Sterling 1989 128p il $14.95 (4 and up) **745.592**

1. Paper crafts 2. Airplanes—Models
ISBN 0-8069-6840-0 LC 88-30311

"Churchill has assembled directions for over 30 models, from spinners to flying tubes, all of which can be made from notebook paper, empty cereal boxes, paper plates, or newspaper (two of the three kites require dowels). Most take only moments to construct and need no fine adjustments to glide, whirl, or soar spectacularly." SLJ

"Black-and-white line drawings capably abet the step-by-step directions, and animal cartoon figures add a spark of humor." Booklist

Elbert, Virginie

Folk toys around the world and how to make them; by Virginie Fowler; illustrations by the author. Prentice-Hall 1984 172p il $10.95 (5 and up) **745.592**

1. Toys 2. Folk art 3. Handicraft
ISBN 0-13-323148-8 LC 83-21285

This book describes traditional toys from countries around the world and includes illustrated instructions for making over 30 different toys using paint, papier-mâché, salt dough, glue, fabric and other common materials

The "projects are carefully presented through lists of required tools and materials, step-by-step instructions, and precisely detailed line drawings." Horn Book

Pearson, Tracey Campbell

Dollhouse people; a doll family you can make. Viking 1984 74p il $12.95; Penguin Bks. pa $6.95 (3-5) **745.592**

1. Dolls 2. Handicraft
ISBN 0-670-43433-7; 0-14-049175-9 (pa) LC 83-25992

Includes patterns and easy-to-follow instructions for making the various members of the Littlefield doll family. Accompanying text relates the family's history from the first meeting of the grandparents to the arrival of all the Littlefield grandchildren

"The brief story line about the family may stimulate the creation of a complete family saga and the settings to enact the drama. . . . The dolls are not especially difficult to make (although some adult help will be needed) and the sense of accomplishment should encourage a new generation of creative stitchers." SLJ

Roche, P. K. (Patricia K.), 1935-

Dollhouse magic; how to make and find simple dollhouse furniture; photographs by John Knott; drawings by Richard Cuffari. Dial Bks. 1977 58p il hardcover o.p. paperback available $2.95 (2-4) **745.592**

1. Dollhouses 2. Handicraft
ISBN 0-8037-1767-9 (pa) LC 76-42932

"Instructions describe the making of sofas, chairs, beds and other furniture, and small items such as lamps, mirrors, rugs, and curtains. . . . Each photograph of a furnished room shows doll-size teddy bears appearing to be comfortable occupants." Horn Book

"There is good emphasis on the child modifying the directions for his/her own needs and taste. The photographs and illustrations are clear and exact." Child Book Rev Serv

Simon, Seymour, 1931-

The paper airplane book; illustrated by Byron Barton. Viking 1971 48p il lib bdg $11.95 (3-5) **745.592**

1. Airplanes—Models 2. Paper crafts
ISBN 0-670-53797-7 LC 71-162669

Step-by-step instructions for making paper airplanes with suggestions for experimenting with them

Sullivan, St. Clair Adams

Bats, butterflies, and bugs; a book of action toys; [by] S. Adams Sullivan. Little, Brown 1990 79p il $14.95 (3-5) **745.592**

1. Toys 2. Handicraft
ISBN 0-316-82185-3 LC 89-39792

Instructions for making a variety of toys which look like bugs, butterflies, or bats

"Clear line drawings on every page supplement the written directions, while their lighthearted tone raises expectations for fun. A treasure trove for teachers seeking to extend the science curriculum through the arts program, this will appeal directly to kids as well." Booklist

Zubrowski, Bernie, 1939-

Tops; building and experimenting with spinning toys; illustrated by Roy Doty. Morrow Junior Bks. 1989 96p il lib bdg $11.88; pa $6.95 (4-6) **745.592**

1. Toys
ISBN 0-688-08811-2 (lib bdg); 0-688-07561-4 (pa)
LC 88-30463

"A Boston Children's Museum activity book"

"The main purpose of this book is to promote fun—the enjoyment of constructing toys and then experimenting with them. Directions are given for building these toys in such a way that one characteristic of them can be changed, allowing experimenters to compare the behavior of two objects. As well as learning some physics about rotating bodies and optics, students will find ideas for science research investigations. Construction materials may be found in the home or purchased from hardware or craft shops. Directions and diagrams for assembly are clear." SLJ

745.6 Calligraphy, illumination, heraldic design

Adkins, Jan

Letterbox: the art & history of letters. Walker & Co. 1981 48p il $10.95; lib bdg $11.85 (4 and up) **745.6**

1. Lettering 2. Calligraphy
ISBN 0-8027-6385-5; 0-8027-6386-3 (lib bdg)
LC 79-48050

Traces the history of letters and examines the evolution of different styles of calligraphy and printing

"An inspiring guide to perfection of penmanship." Booklist

Includes bibliography

Baron, Nancy

Getting started in calligraphy. Sterling 1979 95p il spiral binding $9.95 (5 and up) **745.6**

1. Calligraphy
ISBN 0-8069-8840-1 LC 78-66311

Introduces the fundamentals of calligraphy with a discussion of the necessary materials and several alphabets

"Helpful specific suggestions on the do's and don'ts of letter formations. . . . Samples, suggestions of ways to effectively use calligraphy, master sheet guidelines, a glossary, and a brief bibliography round out the text." Booklist

Fisher, Leonard Everett, 1924-

Alphabet art: thirteen ABCs from around the world; written and illustrated by Leonard Everett Fisher. Four Winds Press 1985 c1978 61p il lib bdg $14.95 (4 and up) **745.6**

1. Alphabets 2. Lettering
ISBN 0-02-735230-7 LC 84-28752

A reissue of the title first published 1978

"Well written and beautifully designed book. Provides brief information on the people and background for each of the following alphabets in use around the world today—Arabic, Cherokee, Chinese, Cyrillic, Eskimo, Gaelic, German, Greek, Hebrew, Japanese, Sanskrit, Thai and Tibetan." N Y Public Libr. Ref Books for Child Collect

749 Furniture and accessories

Rosenberg, Maxine B., 1939-

Artists of handcrafted furniture at work; with photographs by George Ancona. Lothrop, Lee & Shepard Bks. 1988 61p il lib bdg $14.95 (4 and up) **749**

1. Furniture 2. Occupations
ISBN 0-688-06875-8 LC 87-29342

The author "presents four artists who work in wood. She explores the reasons that they have pursued their craft and their training and education. She compares their approaches to design issues dealing with form and function, and probes the creative process." SLJ

"Ancona's fine photographs skillfully convey the work of this challenging craft and the whimsicality and beauty of the completed furniture." Horn Book

758 Other subjects in painting

Arnosky, Jim

In the forest; a portfolio of paintings. Lothrop, Lee & Shepard Bks. 1989 28p il $13.95; lib bdg $13.88 (4 and up) **758**

1. Forest ecology—Pictorial works
ISBN 0-688-08162-2; 0-688-09138-5 (lib bdg)
LC 89-2341

"Evocative oil paintings are accompanied by intelligent commentary on particular aspects of the forest—from the growth cycle that reclaims abandoned farmlands to the

Arnosky, Jim—*Continued*

various kinds of wildlife one might see. Spanning two seasons, the book's illustrations are alight with the rich colors of autumn and the muted shades of winter." Publ Wkly

Near the sea; a portfolio of paintings. Lothrop, Lee & Shepard Bks. 1990 28p il $13.95; lib bdg $13.88 (4 and up) **758**

1. Seashore in art
ISBN 0-688-08164-9; 0-688-09327-2 (lib bdg)
LC 90-5722

"On textured canvas, Arnosky's oil paintings chronicle his stay on a small island off the rocky coast of Maine. His artist's eye captures the sweep of ocean cliffs and saltwater marshes as well as the details of a tidal pool and of freshly caught bluefish. Accompanying each painting are a few paragraphs of information that form a word picture of his experience." Horn Book

"Arnosky's love of nature and his sharp eye for both natural and artistic details are very clearly displayed here. The paintings are well reproduced, and their serene vistas easily communicate the appeal of the coastal landscape." Booklist

759 Painting—Historical and geographic treatment

Ventura, Piero

Great painters. Putnam 1984 160p il $20.95 (5 and up) **759**

1. Painters 2. Painting—History
ISBN 0-399-21115-2 LC 84-3423

The author "presents a . . . work of art history that begins with the earliest known painters of ancient Greece and carries through to Picasso and the Cubists. Between come all the major names and movements from the Italian, Dutch, German, English, and French schools of painting, fleshed out in a narrative full of anecdote and lively detail. . . . A lengthy appended section defines styles and periods and provides efficient biographies of the great painters." Booklist

Woolf, Felicity

Picture this; a first introduction to paintings. Doubleday 1990 c1989 40p il $14.95; lib bdg $15.99 (4 and up) **759**

1. Painting—History 2. Art appreciation
ISBN 0-385-41135-9; 0-385-41136-7 (lib bdg)
LC 89-30459

First published 1989 in the United Kingdom

An introduction to western painting from 1400 to 1950 using famous works from major movements to illustrate the development of western art and explain basic concepts

"*Picture This* is a solid, up-to-date, and informative introduction to major paintings of the past." SLJ

Includes glossary

759.13 American painting

Raboff, Ernest

Frederic Remington. Lippincott 1988 unp il (Art for children) $11.95; Harper & Row pa $5.95 (4 and up) **759.13**

1. Remington, Frederic, 1861-1909
ISBN 0-397-32220-8; 0-06-446079-7 (pa)
LC 87-16865

First published 1973 by Doubleday

A brief biography of the artist and sculptor accompanies fifteen color reproductions and critical interpretations of his works

759.3 German painting

Raboff, Ernest

Albrecht Dürer. Lippincott 1988 unp il (Art for children) $11.95; Harper & Row pa $5.95 (4 and up) **759.3**

1. Dürer, Albrecht, 1471-1528
ISBN 0-397-32216-X; 0-06-446071-1 (pa)
LC 87-16863

First published 1970 by Doubleday

A brief biography of the German painter and printmaker accompanies fifteen color reproductions and critical interpretations of his works

Paul Klee. Lippincott 1988 unp il (Art for children) $11.95; Harper & Row pa $5.95 (4 and up) **759.3**

1. Klee, Paul, 1879-1940
ISBN 0-397-32226-7; 0-06-446065-7 (pa)
LC 87-16864

First published 1968 by Doubleday

A brief biography of this twentieth-century German artist accompanies reproductions and analyses of several of his works

759.4 French painting

Degas, Edgar, 1834-1917

Meet Edgar Degas; [by the] National Gallery of Canada; [compiled by] Anne Newlands. Lippincott 1989 c1988 unp il $13.95 (3-5) **759.4**

1. Artists, French
ISBN 0-397-32369-7 LC 88-32035

First published 1988 in Canada

Presents the life and paintings of Edgar Degas in a first person narrative drawn from letters, notebooks, and people's stories about the artist

"The conversational tone is immediate and informative without becoming dry, as much art history commentary can be. The fifteen paintings, mostly one to a page on the recto, are center stage, with vivid color reproduction and spacious white frames." Bull Cent Child Books

Munthe, Nelly, 1947-

Meet Matisse; written by Nelly Munthe. Little, Brown 1983 45p il $14.95 (4 and up) **759.4**

1. Matisse, Henri
ISBN 0-316-58960-8 LC 83-9905

An introduction to the cut-outs of Henri Matisse, who concentrated on this technique of artistic expression in his final years. Instructions are included for several of Matisse's artistic techniques

"Art teachers and students will enjoy the fresh approach of this introduction to the ideas, techniques and later works of Henri Matisse. . . . This imaginative study . . . will help readers understand Matisse's work, and the analytic processes should serve them in looking at all art." SLJ

Raboff, Ernest

Henri de Toulouse-Lautrec. Lippincott 1988 unp il (Art for children) $11.95; Harper & Row pa $5.95 (4 and up) **759.4**

1. Toulouse-Lautrec, Henri de, 1864-1901
ISBN 0-397-32229-1; 0-06-446070-3 (pa) LC 87-16861

First published 1970 by Doubleday

A brief biography of the French painter accompanies fifteen color reproductions and critical interpretations of his works

Henri Matisse. Lippincott 1988 unp il (Art for children) $11.95; Harper & Row pa $7.95 (4 and up) **759.4**

1. Matisse, Henri
ISBN 0-397-32238-0; 0-06-446080-0 (pa) LC 87-16866

A brief biography of the modern French artist accompanies reproductions and analyses of several of his works

Henri Rousseau. Lippincott 1988 unp il (Art for children) $11.95; Harper & Row pa $5.95 (4 and up) **759.4**

1. Rousseau, Henri Julien Félix, 1844-1910
ISBN 0-397-32221-6; 0-06-446069-X (pa) LC 87-16862

First published 1970 by Doubleday

A brief biography of Henri Rousseau accompanies fifteen color reproductions and critical interpretations of his works

Paul Gauguin. Lippincott 1988 unp il (Art for children) $11.95; Harper & Row pa $5.95 (4 and up) **759.4**

1. Gauguin, Paul, 1848-1903
ISBN 0-397-32225-9; 0-06-446078-9 (pa) LC 87-16914

Revised edition of: Paul Gauguin by Adeline Peter and Ernest Raboff, published 1974 by Doubleday

A brief biography of the French artist accompanies reproductions and analyses of several of his works

Pierre-Auguste Renoir. Lippincott 1987 unp il (Art for children) $11.95; Harper & Row pa $7.95 (4 and up) **759.4**

1. Renoir, Auguste, 1841-1919
ISBN 0-397-32217-8; 0-06-446068-1 (pa) LC 87-45154

First published 1970 by Doubleday

A brief biography of the artist accompanies color reproductions and analyses of fifteen of his works

759.5 Italian painting

Raboff, Ernest

Leonardo da Vinci. Lippincott 1987 unp il (Art for children) $11.95; Harper & Row pa $7.95 (4 and up) **759.5**

1. Leonardo, da Vinci, 1452-1519
ISBN 0-397-32218-6; 0-06-446076-2 (pa) LC 87-45155

First published 1971 by Doubleday

Explains some basic techniques of Da Vinci by analyzing several of his better-known paintings

Michelangelo Buonarroti. Lippincott 1988 unp il (Art for children) $11.95; Harper & Row pa $7.95 (4 and up) **759.5**

1. Michelangelo Buonarroti, 1475-1564
ISBN 0-397-32223-2; 0-06-446074-6 (pa) LC 87-45313

First published 1971 by Doubleday

A brief biography of this Italian Renaissance painter accompanies 14 full color reproductions and analyses of several of his works

Raphael Sanzio. Lippincott 1988 unp il (Art for children) $11.95; Harper & Row pa $5.95 (4 and up) **759.5**

1. Raphael, 1483-1520
ISBN 0-397-32227-5; 0-06-446075-4 (pa) LC 87-45314

First published 1971 by Doubleday

A brief biography of Raphael accompanies color reproductions and critical interpretations of many of his works

759.6 Spanish painting

Raboff, Ernest

Diego Rodriguez de Silva y Velasquez. Lippincott 1988 unp il (Art for children) $11.95; Harper & Row pa $5.95 (4 and up) **759.6**

1. Velázquez, Diego, 1599-1660
ISBN 0-397-32219-4; 0-06-446073-8 (pa) LC 87-16915

First published 1970 by Doubleday

A brief biography of the seventeenth-century Spanish painter accompanies fifteen color reproductions and critical interpretations of his works

Raboff, Ernest—*Continued*

Pablo Picasso. Lippincott 1987 unp il (Art for children) $11.95; Harper & Row pa $7.95 (4 and up) **759.6**

1. Picasso, Pablo, 1881-1973
ISBN 0-397-32224-0; 0-06-446067-3 (pa) LC 87-45156

First published 1968 by Doubleday

A brief biography of the famous artist accompanies reproductions and analyses of several of his works

759.7 Russian painting

Raboff, Ernest

Marc Chagall. Lippincott 1988 unp il (Art for children) $11.95; Harper & Row pa $5.95 (4 and up) **759.7**

1. Chagall, Marc, 1887-1985
ISBN 0-397-32222-4; 0-06-446066-5 (pa) LC 87-45312

First published 1968 by Doubleday

A simple introduction to the twentieth-century Russian painter and several of his works. Includes 14 full color reproductions of his paintings

759.9492 Dutch painting

Raboff, Ernest

Rembrandt. Lippincott 1987 unp il (Art for children) $11.95; Harper & Row pa $5.95 (4 and up) **759.9492**

1. Rembrandt Harmenszoon van Rijn, 1606-1669
ISBN 0-397-32228-3; 0-06-446072-X (pa) LC 87-45157

First published 1970 by Doubleday

A brief biography of the seventeenth-century Dutch artist accompanies a discussion of thirteen of his works

Vincent van Gogh. Lippincott 1988 unp il (Art for children) $11.95; Harper & Row pa $7.95 (4 and up) **759.9492**

1. Gogh, Vincent van, 1853-1890
ISBN 0-397-32230-5; 0-06-446077-0 (pa) LC 87-45315

Revised edition of: Vincent Van Gogh by Adeline Peter and Ernest Raboff, published 1974 by Doubleday

A brief biography of this nineteenth-century Dutch painter accompanies reproductions and analyses of several of his works

761 Relief processes (Block printing)

Haddad, Helen R.

Potato printing. Crowell 1981 62p il lib bdg $13.89 (4-6) **761**

1. Printing 2. Handicraft
ISBN 0-690-04089-X LC 80-2458

Describes how to use an ordinary potato to print pictures, designs, and messages on paper or fabric

"The step-by-step drawings are so carefully arranged throughout that even reluctant readers should be able to print successfully. This attractively designed book is a promising basis for geometry, art and craft sessions and is also a book children are likely to pick up on their own." SLJ

Pettit, Florence Harvey

The stamp-pad printing book; [by] Florence H. Pettit; illustrated with designs and drawings by the author and with photographs by Robert M. Pettit. Crowell 1979 153p il $12.95 (5 and up) **761**

1. Printing 2. Handicraft
ISBN 0-690-03967-0 LC 78-22504

Directions for using a stamp pad and paper to print bookmarks, note paper, posters, greeting cards, wrapping paper, and many other useful things

"A thorough guide to the craft, the attractive book provides a springboard for the beginner's own imagination." Horn Book

770 Photography and photographs

Freeman, Tony

Photography; written and photographed by Tony Freeman. Childrens Press 1983 45p il lib bdg $13.27 (2-4) **770**

1. Photography
ISBN 0-516-01704-7 LC 83-7359

"A New true book"

Briefly describes the basic principles of photography, how a camera works, the different types of cameras and films, how film is developed, and techniques for taking pictures

Owens-Knudsen, Vick

Photography basics; introduction by Dennis Simonetti; photographs by the students of Glen Rock Junior and Senior High School; diagrams and drawings by Mike Petronella; created and produced by Arvid Knudsen. Prentice-Hall 1983 48p il (High-tech basics bks) lib bdg $9.95 (5 and up) **770**

1. Photography
ISBN 0-13-664995-5 LC 83-9775

An introduction to basic techniques of photography and various types of cameras and their uses

"This is a tightly drawn, concise and welcome addition to the field. . . . Especially helpful is the darkroom chapter, which combines lucid text with excellent illustrations. Accompanying photographs, as one would expect, are appropriate and clear." SLJ

Includes glossary and bibliography

778.9 Photography of specific subjects

Van Wormer, Joe, 1913-

How to be a wildlife photographer. Lodestar Bks. 1982 153p il $10.95 (6 and up) **778.9**

1. Photography of animals
ISBN 0-525-66772-5 LC 82-248

"The author outlines the basics of camera work, then explains the special requirements of animal photography in habitat." Publ Wkly

"Generally, the writing is clear. Van Wormer's photographs are generously supplied throughout the book, with detailed captions containing specifics like f-stops and film type." SLJ

Includes bibliography

779 Photographs

Hoban, Tana

Shadows and reflections. Greenwillow Bks. 1990 unp il $12.95; lib bdg $12.88 **779**

1. Shades and shadows—Pictorial works
2. Photography, Artistic
ISBN 0-688-07089-2; 0-688-07090-6 (lib bdg) LC 89-30461

Photographs without text feature shadows and reflections of various objects, animals, and people

"This imaginative, wordless book of color photographs is a visual treat, offering witty and subtle sets of images for enriching the eyes of children and adults." SLJ

780 Music

McLeish, Kenneth, 1940-

The Oxford first companion to music; [by] Kenneth and Valerie McLeish. Oxford Univ. Press 1982 various paging il $24.95 (5 and up) **780**

1. Music
ISBN 0-19-314303-8 LC 82-223971

Chapter headings: Music round the world, Instruments and orchestras; Singing and dancing; The story of music; Composers and their music; Writing music

"Many excellent recommendations for listening are made throughout the book. As far as it goes, the text is clear and accurate, with many cross-references included in the body of the work. . . . The oversize format and generous use of illustration will appeal to browsers." SLJ

Includes glossary

780.3 Music—Encyclopedias and dictionaries

Hurd, Michael

The Oxford junior companion to music; based on the original publication by Percy Scholes. 2d ed. Oxford Univ. Press 1979 352p il $35 (5 and up) **780.3**

1. Music—Dictionaries
ISBN 0-19-314302-X LC 80-460130
First published 1954

"Basic reference work for elementary and junior high schools; contains brief articles on composers, instruments, musical terms, people and places. Richly illustrated with photographs, drawings and diagrams." N Y Public Libr. Ref Books for Child Collect

780.89 Music with respect to specific racial, ethnic, national groups

Fichter, George S.

American Indian music and musical instruments; with instructions for making the instruments; drawings and diagrams by Marie and Nils Ostberg. McKay, D. 1978 115p il map music $8.95 (5 and up) **780.89**

1. Indians of North America—Songs and music
2. Musical instruments
ISBN 0-679-20443-1 LC 77-14906

This is a "book on the music of the American Indians covering the songs and music of the major events in their lives—birth, death, harvest, the hunt, warfare, etc." Bull Cent Child Books

"An excellent book, including not only descriptions, words, and sometimes music for various types of Indian songs, but also directions, with diagrams, for making and decorating the instruments described. Well written and tastefully illustrated, this is a fine addition to either Native American or Ethnomusicology collections." SLJ

Includes bibliography

780.9 Music—Historical and geographical treatment

Ventura, Piero

Great composers. Putnam 1989 124p il $20.95 (5 and up) **780.9**

1. Composers 2. Music
ISBN 0-399-21746-0 LC 89-32861

Briefly introduces the greatest composers over the centuries and the contributions they made to the development of music. "Early segments are devoted to the Chinese, Indians, Egyptians, and Greeks and Romans, but the majority of the book focuses on individual figures, from Vivaldi, Handel, Beethoven, Chopin, and Debussy, to Gershwin, Louis Armstrong, and Duke Ellington. Ventura stresses their artistic personalities and talks about their talents in the context of the time in which they

Ventura, Piero—*Continued*
lived. . . . A highly pleasurable invitation to the world of music." Booklist

781.62 Folk music

The **Erie** Canal; illustrated by Peter Spier. Doubleday 1970 unp il map music $10.95; pa $5.95 (k-4) **781.62**

1. Folk songs—United States
ISBN 0-385-06777-1; 0-385-05234-0 (pa) LC 70-102055

An American folk song is recreated in full-color scenes. Historical notes, a map of the canal which served as a busy trade route, and the musical arrangement for the song is included

The illustrator "records detail with the meticulous accuracy of the historian and the appreciative eye of the artist." Horn Book

The **Fox** went out on a chilly night; an old song; illustrated by Peter Spier. Doubleday 1961 unp il music $11.95 (k-3) **781.62**

1. Folk songs—United States
ISBN 0-385-07990-7 LC 60-7139

Set in New England, this old song tells about the trip the fox father made to town to get some of the farmer's plump geese for his family's dinner, and how he manages to evade the farmer who tries to shoot him

"A true picture book in the Caldecott-Brooke tradition. Fine drawings, lovely colors, and pictures so full of amusing details that young viewers will make fresh discoveries every time they . . . scrutinize these beautiful, action-filled pages." Horn Book

Hush little baby; pictures by Jeanette Winter. Pantheon Bks. 1984 unp il music lib bdg $11.99 (k-1) **781.62**

1. Lullabies 2. Folk songs
ISBN 0-394-96325-3 (lib bdg) LC 83-12182

In an old lullaby a baby is promised an assortment of presents from its adoring parent

The illustrator's "toned-down rusty, green and gray effects in the pictures here emphasize the soothing spirit of the traditional lullaby. . . . A simple musical arrangement of the verses is appended." Publ Wkly

Langstaff, John M.
Frog went a-courtin'; retold by John Langstaff; with pictures by Feodor Rojankovsky. Harcourt Brace Jovanovich 1955 unp il music $14.95; pa $3.95 (k-3) **781.62**

1. Folk songs
ISBN 0-15-230214-X; 0-15-633900-5 (pa) LC 55-5237

"Retelling of a merry old Scottish ballad with many-colored illustrations about the marriage between Mr. Frog and Miss Mouse. A composite American version set to Appalachian mountain music." Chicago Public Libr

Oh, a-hunting we will go; [by] John Langstaff; pictures by Nancy Winslow Parker. Atheneum Pubs. 1974 unp il music $14.95 (k-2) **781.62**

1. Folk songs
ISBN 0-689-50007-6 LC 74-76274

"A Margaret K. McElderry book"

The nonsense verses of this folk song trace the hunt for such animals as an armadillo, a fox, and a snake, and describe the imagined treatment of each animal once it is caught

"The 12 stanzas are complemented by Parker's droll crayon illustrations (the fox caught in the box is watching TV), and a score for guitar and piano is appended. An amusing addition to 'song' picture books." SLJ

Over in the meadow; with pictures by Feodor Rojankovsky. Harcourt Brace Jovanovich 1957 unp il music $14.95; pa $3.95 (k-2) **781.62**

1. Folk songs 2. Counting
ISBN 0-15-258854-X; 0-15-670500-1 (pa) LC 57-8587

"This old counting rhyme tells of ten meadow families whose mothers advise them to dig, run, sing, play, hum, build, swim, wink, spin and hop. The illustrations, half in full color, show the combination of realism and imagination which little children like best. The tune, arranged simply, is on the last page, and children will have fun acting the whole thing out." Horn Book

Leodhas, Sorche Nic, 1898-1968
Always room for one more; illustrated by Nonny Hogrogian. Holt & Co. 1965 unp il music $9.95; pa $3.95 (k-3) **781.62**

1. Folk songs, Scottish
ISBN 0-8050-0331-2; 0-8050-0330-4 (pa) LC 65-12881

Awarded the Caldecott Medal, 1966

"A picture book based on an old Scottish folk song about hospitable Lachie MacLachlan, who invited in so many guests that his little house finally burst. Rhymed text . . . a glossary of Scottish words, and music for the tune are combined into an effective whole." Hodges. Books for Elem Sch Libr

London Bridge is falling down! illustrated by Peter Spier. Doubleday 1967 unp il music $10.95 (k-2) **781.62**

1. Folk songs, English 2. Nursery rhymes
ISBN 0-385-08717-9 LC 67-17695

This picture book illustrated with scenes of eighteenth-century London presents the traditional verses of the Mother Goose nursery rhyme. The musical score is included, as well as a three-page historical sketch of London Bridge through the centuries

Old MacDonald had a farm (k-2) **781.62**

1. Folk songs—United States

Some editions are:

Dial Bks. for Young Readers $9.95, lib bdg $9.89 Pictures by Tracey Campbell Pearson (ISBN 0-8037-0068-7; 0-8037-0070-9)

Holiday House lib bdg $14.95, pa $5.95 Illustrated by Glen Rounds (ISBN 0-8234-0739-X; 0-8234-0846-9)

Old MacDonald had a farm—*Continued*
Putnam $13.95 Illustrated by Lorinda Bryan Cauley (ISBN 0-399-21628-6)

Pearson's "funny and richly detailed illustrations give a fresh look to an old song. Large format and double spread pages make it excellent for storytime." Child Book Rev Serv

"Rounds drafts portraits of some very expressive and feisty animals. . . . The large type and larger than life-size animals—each displayed on its own page—will keep children turning the pages and singing along." Horn Book

Quackenbush, Robert M., 1929-
She'll be comin' round the mountain; [by] Robert Quackenbush. Lippincott 1973 unp il music $13.89 (k-3) **781.62**

1. Folk songs—United States
ISBN 0-397-32266-6 LC 73-2943

"A picture book in play form, this old railroad song is presented in bold purples and blues, golds and oranges. The animated full-page pictures freely interpret the song: a Wild West show, traveling by train, is coming into Pughtown for a one-night stand. Before the train arrives, Sneaky Pete, Rattlesnake Hank and Crumby Joe attempt to rob it. But, the show's star, Little Annie, snares the robbers with her lasso . . . and the show can go on." Babbling Bookworm

"Quackenbush has amiably included a piano accompaniment and a suitably silly number game to decide Annie's future." Booklist

Seeger, Ruth Crawford, 1901-1953
American folk songs for children in home, school and nursery school; a book for children, parents and teachers; illustrated by Barbara Cooney. Doubleday 1948 190p il music hardcover o.p. paperback available $8.95 **781.62**

1. Folk songs—United States 2. Singing games
ISBN 0-385-15788-6 (pa) LC 48-9384

A big book of 90 folk songs from all parts of the country that may be sung and acted out with many variations. The tunes and piano accompaniments are simple enough for most adults to play. It is a source book for family fun

There's a hole in the bucket; [by] Nadine Bernard Westcott. Harper & Row 1990 unp il music $12.95; lib bdg $12.89 (k-2) **781.62**

1. Folk songs
ISBN 0-06-026422-5; 0-06-026423-3 (lib bdg) LC 89-34538

As Liza instructs Henry how to fix a hole in the bucket, Henry gives her all the reasons why he can't. An illustrated version of a humorous old folk song

"Westcott's characterizations are right on target, and children will enjoy the song's repetition. . . . A musical score is included. Sprightly illustrations accompany this humorous adaptation of the familiar folksong." SLJ

Wendy Watson's Frog went a-courting. Lothrop, Lee & Shepard Bks. 1990 unp il music $13.95; lib bdg $13.88 (k-2) **781.62**

1. Folk songs
ISBN 0-688-06539-2; 0-688-06540-6 (lib bdg) LC 89-63022

"To accompany her favorite verses of this well-known folk song about the courtship and marriage of frog and Miss Mouse, Wendy Watson has chosen to create in gentle watercolors a miniature world full of dramatic and comic detail. Because of the small size of the animals in some of the drawings, the book is best suited for sharing with individual children." Horn Book

782.25 Sacred songs

What a morning! the Christmas story in black spirituals; selected and edited by John Langstaff; illustrated by Ashley Bryan; arrangements for singing and piano by John Andrew Ross. Margaret K. McElderry Bks. 1987 unp il music $13.95 **782.25**

1. Spirituals (Songs) 2. Carols
ISBN 0-689-50422-5 LC 87-750130

This "volume presents five black spirituals that celebrate the Christmas story. Langstaff has chosen 'Mary Had a Baby,' 'My Lord, What a Morning,' 'Go Tell it on the Mountain,' 'Sister Mary Had One Child,' and 'Behold That Star' as songs that chronologically introduce the Nativity as well as exemplify the rhythmic spirit and poetic nuance of this musical genre." Booklist

"Bryan's illustrations tie into the African-American theme, showing a black Holy family and multiracial wise men and shepherds. Bold brush strokes line each landscape and every garment; the star of Bethlehem, through the religious prism, reveals colors of rainbow hues. This collection of songs exhibits an intimacy and compassion that give these spirituals a stunning universality." Publ Wkly

782.28 Carols

The **Friendly** beasts; an old English Christmas carol; illustrated by Tomie de Paola. Putnam 1981 unp il music $13.95; pa $5.95 (k-3) **782.28**

1. Carols
ISBN 0-399-20739-2; 0-399-20777-5 (pa) LC 80-15391

In this old English Christmas carol the friendly stable beasts tell of the gifts they have given to the newborn Jesus

"The words of a familiar English Christmas carol are illustrated in a reverent mood, placid and gentle, and more spacious than the pages of most de Paola books. The soft colors of the ink paintings of scenes from the stable are framed lightly, and the Nativity story is, visually, prefaced and concluded by pages in frieze style with choir boys. The notation—melody line only—for the song about the beasts who pay homage on Christmas Eve is included at the back of the book." Bull Cent Child Books

Mohr, Joseph, 1792-1848
Silent night; verses by Joseph Mohr; illustrated by Susan Jeffers. Dutton 1984 unp il music $12.95; pa $4.95 (k-2) **782.28**

1. Carols
ISBN 0-525-44144-1; 0-8037-4443-9 (pa) LC 84-8113

An illustrated version of the well-known German Christmas hymn celebrating the birth of Christ

"The book has a sumptuous appearance. . . . Elegant and ambitious, this will be a strong visual draw in any Christmas book display." Booklist

Tom Glazer's Christmas songbook; by Tom Glazer; illustrated by Barbara Corrigan. Doubleday 1989 122p il music pa $14.95 **782.28**

1. Carols
ISBN 0-385-24641-2 LC 88-751568

Some "forty traditional carols and holiday songs are each preceded by a short paragraph of historical background or . . . facts about it. . . . Musical accompaniment for both piano or guitar and a first-line index is provided." SLJ

"Corrigan's pictures are bright and crisp, with a folk-art flavor and a definite charm in their depiction of an array of Christmas-inspired scenes." Booklist

Tomie dePaola's book of Christmas carols. Putnam 1987 81p il music $17.95 **782.28**

1. Carols
ISBN 0-399-21432-1 LC 86-755157

This collection contains "more than 30 well-known traditional carols. . . . Music is rendered in singable and playable keys . . . but no chords are given." SLJ

"The carols are lovingly placed among pictures with varied settings: Victorian and biblical, some on gatefold pages. DePaola's intense hues—slate blues, rich burgundies and mossy greens—reflect the way colors show up in a wintry background. His Christmas spirit, here of subdued joy, is infectious." Publ Wkly

We wish you a merry Christmas; a traditional Christmas carol; pictures by Tracey Campbell Pearson. Dial Bks. for Young Readers 1983 unp il music $8.95; lib bdg $8.89; pa $3.95 **782.28**

1. Carols
ISBN 0-8037-9368-5; 0-8037-9400-2 (lib bdg); 0-8037-0310-4 (pa) LC 82-22224

"A group of young carollers, trudging about in the snow, is welcomed indoors by an elderly, hospitable couple." Bull Cent Child Books

"Using as her text nothing more than the four stanzas of the familiar carol, the illustrator has concocted a thoroughly captivating picture book. . . . Washed with clear vibrant color, the lively ink drawings are full of hilarious detail, extrapolating the carol's inherent humor. Words and music are appended." Horn Book

782.42 Songs

Arroz con leche; popular songs and rhymes from Latin America; selected and illustrated by Lulu Delacre; English lyrics by Elena Paz; musical arrangements by Ana-María Rosado. Scholastic 1989 32p il music $12.95 (k-3) **782.42**

1. Folk songs 2. Folklore—Latin America 3. Bilingual books—Spanish-English
ISBN 0-590-41887-4

This is a bilingual collection of twelve folk songs and rhymes from Puerto Rico, Mexico and Argentina. Instructions for fingerplays and games accompany some of the songs. Musical arrangements for nine of the entries are included at the end of the book

"Delacre has selected lilting verses that are pleasing to the ear—ones likely to encourage non-Spanish-speakers to join in the fun. . . . Fresh, springlike colors brighten the pictures, though some faces look more Anglo than expected. An author's note explains that many of the scenes depict real places." Booklist

Bangs, Edward, 1756-1818
Steven Kellogg's Yankee Doodle; written by Edward Bangs. Four Winds Press 1980 c1976 unp il music lib bdg $13.95 (k-3) **782.42**

1. National songs, American
ISBN 0-02-749800-X LC 80-17024

A reprint of the 1976 edition published by Parents' Magazine Press

An illustrated version of the popular Revolutionary War song, originally penned in 1775 by Harvard student Edward Bangs. . . . A commentary about the history of the song and its variations precedes the text; the eight measures of the familiar melody are given at the end of the book." Horn Book

"The color illustrations are zesty and action filled. . . . But Kellogg's rewording of some of the well-known verses are downright silly. In an attempt to please feminists, for instance, he has changed . . . 'and with the girls be handy' (which meant something) to 'with the folks be handy' (which means nothing)." Publ Wkly

Conover, Chris, 1950-
Six little ducks; retold and illustrated by Chris Conover. Crowell 1976 unp il music lib bdg $13.89 (k-2) **782.42**

1. Songs
ISBN 0-690-01037-0 LC 75-22155

"Music [for piano or guitar] and lyrics are provided at the back of the book for an adaptation of a children's song. . . . The ducks go to market, lose their wares, are rejected by a hostile baker when they ask for bread, go home and bake their own bread, and go to a party." Bull Cent Child Books

The **Farmer** in the dell **782.42**

1. Folk songs—United States 2. Singing games

The Farmer in the dell—*Continued*

Some editions are:

Viking Kestrel $12.95 Pictures by Mary Maki Rae (ISBN 0-670-81853-4)

Whitman, A. $12.95 Illustrated by Kathy Parkinson (ISBN 0-8075-2271-6)

"The Parkinson offering is the more traditional of the two. The song's story is told with a line of text below each picture; soft-colored artwork shows the farmer milking his cow, proposing to his love, marrying her, and later, his pregnant wife working in the field. . . . Rae's version of the song features brighter and more innovative graphics. She uses lovely deep-colored hues and eye-catching designs styled in panels to tell the story in a more abstract way. A simple melody for the familiar music leads off the Parkinson edition; Rae provides the music . . . notes the origin of game, and gives directions on how to play it for the uninitiated." Booklist

The **Fireside** book of children's songs; collected & edited by Marie Winn; musical arrangements by Allan Miller; illustrated by John Alcorn. Simon & Schuster 1966 192p il music $12.95 **782.42**

1. Songs 2. Folk songs

ISBN 0-671-25820-6 LC 65-17108

The book is divided into five parts: Good morning and good night, Birds and beasts, Nursery songs, Silly songs, and Singing games and rounds

"Over 100 songs for preschool and elementary age children are contained in this most attractive volume. . . . The accompaniments are simple, and guitar chords are provided. . . . Stylized decorations in mustard, rust, and shocking pink add to the overall appeal of the volume. Highly recommended for homes, schools, and public libraries." SLJ

The **Fireside** book of fun and game songs; collected and edited by Marie Winn; musical arrangements by Allan Miller; illustrated by Whitney Darrow, Jr. Simon & Schuster 1974 222p il music $14.95 **782.42**

1. Songs 2. Singing games

ISBN 0-671-65213-3 LC 74-6957

The songs are divided into ten categories which include cumulative and diminishing songs, echo songs, motion and wordplay songs, question and answer songs, and rounds

"Although many of the individual items could be found in other books, some would be almost impossible to locate elsewhere. Musical arrangements and accompaniments are simple, and spirited drawings add to the innocent merriment." Horn Book

Glazer, Tom

Music for ones and twos; songs and games for the very young child; drawings by Karen Ann Weinhaus. Doubleday 1982 96p il music pa $9.95 **782.42**

1. Songs 2. Singing games

ISBN 0-385-14252-8 LC 82-45199

"This collection includes familiar standards as well as new songs describing children's daily activities. The songs are suitable for use with one child or with small groups. The black-and-white illustrations are fun to look at and make up stories about." Child Book Rev Serv

Tom Glazer's Treasury of songs for children; illustrated by John O'Brien. Doubleday 1988 256p il music spiral binding $14.95 (3-5) **782.42**

1. Songs

ISBN 0-385-23693-X LC 86-753397

A newly illustrated version of: Tom Glazer's Treasury of folk songs, published 1964

"Words and sheet music for 130 of America's favorite songs are presented with pertinent, historical annotations." Soc Educ

Go in and out the window; an illustrated songbook for young people; music arranged and edited by Dan Fox; commentary by Claude Marks. Metropolitan Mus. of Art; Holt & Co. 1987 144p il music $16.95; $19.95 **782.42**

1. Metropolitan Museum of Art (New York, N.Y.) 2. Songs

ISBN 0-87099-500-6; 0-8050-0628-1 (Holt) LC 87-752208

"Sixty-one favorite songs . . . are presented alphabetically and illustrated with treasures from the Metropolitan Museum of Art. . . . The songs . . . are traditional rather than contemporary and come primarily from America and England, while the pictures, jewelry, sculpture, photographs, and so forth span 5,000 years of worldwide art." Booklist

"Imaginative and luxurious, the volume should stimulate and challenge the adult to deepen the awareness and broaden the aesthetic horizons of the young." Horn Book

I know an old lady who swallowed a fly; illustrations by Glen Rounds. Holiday House 1990 unp il lib bdg $14.95 **782.42**

1. Folk songs

ISBN 0-8234-0814-0 LC 89-46244

"On the left side of the page are the creatures that poor old lady swallowed: the fly, spider, bird, cat, dog, goat and horse—each enormous and slightly, well, weird. The text and the fly are on the right side. She died, of course. Perfectly wonderful for singing aloud." N Y Times Book Rev

Key, Francis Scott, 1779-1843

The Star-Spangled Banner; illustrated by Peter Spier. Doubleday 1973 unp il map music $12.95; lib bdg $11.95 **782.42**

1. National songs, American

ISBN 0-385-09458-2; 0-385-07746-7 (lib bdg) LC 73-79712

Key, Francis Scott, 1779-1843—*Continued*

An illustrated version of Francis Scott Key's text for our national anthem. It includes an historical note on the writing of the song, a reproduction of the original manuscript, and a musical arrangement

Kovalski, Maryann, 1951-

The wheels on the bus. Little, Brown 1987 unp il music $11.95; pa $4.95 (k-2) **782.42**

1. Songs

ISBN 0-316-50256-1; 0-316-50259-6 (pa) LC 87-3441

"Joy Street books"

In this adaptation of a traditional children's song, "a long wait at the bus stop precipitates a suggestion from a grandmother that she and her two grandchildren pass the time by singing 'The Wheels on the Bus.' . . . Kovalski expertly conveys the spirit with which people sing this song. . . . The action of the song is followed through in detail, flowing from page to page with a cast of assorted characters depicted in watercolor with pencil illustrations." SLJ

The **Lap-time** song and play book; edited by Jane Yolen; with musical arrangements by Adam Stemple; pictures by Margot Tomes. Harcourt Brace Jovanovich 1989 32p il music $15.95 (k-2) **782.42**

1. Songs 2. Singing games 3. Nursery rhymes 4. Finger play

ISBN 0-15-243588-3 LC 88-752289

"Tomes's dancing mice and well-dressed pigs are beguiling additions to a collection of sixteen familiar nursery games and rhymes for small children. Each game is accompanied by a brief paragraph on its origin and instructions on how it may be played; a simple musical notation is included when appropriate. An author's note about lap songs is appended." Horn Book

The **Laura** Ingalls Wilder songbook; favorite songs from the "Little House" books; compiled and edited by Eugenia Garson; arranged for piano and guitar by Herbert Haufrecht; illustrated by Garth Williams. Harper & Row 1968 160p il music $18.95; lib bdg $18.89 (3 and up) **782.42**

1. Songs, American

ISBN 0-06-021933-5; 0-06-021934-3 (lib bdg) LC 68-24327

"A former children's librarian has researched, compiled, and annotated 62 of the songs that appear in Wilder's 'Little house' books. Brief notes with the music indicate the page of the story on which each song appears and gives, when available, information about the song, composer, or lyricist." Booklist

Lullabies and night songs; [edited by] William Engvick; music by Alec Wilder; pictures by Maurice Sendak. Harper & Row 1965 1965p il music $25.95 (k-3) **782.42**

1. Lullabies 2. Songs

ISBN 0-06-021820-7

"The editor has selected verses, in addition to some of his own, from poets as notable and varied as Eleanor Farjeon, Tennyson, Thurber, Stevenson, Kipling, Walter de la Mare, and William Blake, as well as many anonymous, traditional poems like 'Sleep, Baby, Sleep,' 'Wee Willie Winkie,' 'Now the Day is Over.'" Horn Book

The **Lullaby** songbook; edited by Jane Yolen; with musical arrangements by Adam Stemple; pictures by Charles Mikolaycak. Harcourt Brace Jovanovich 1986 31p il music $13.95 (1-3) **782.42**

1. Lullabies 2. Songs

ISBN 0-15-249903-2 LC 85-752855

"Fifteen mostly familiar lullabies are presented with musical accompaniment in this lusciously designed book. Full-color pictures and frames edge the large white spreads that contain the music and brief notes on the songs' origins. Mikolaycak's rich, full-bodied scenes receive their drama from intense color and vigorous composition. Whether the art is a full-page illustration opposite the music or a mélange of images that gracefully interrupt the stark visual effect around a double spread of music, there is always a satisfying arrangement of hues and smoothly drafted figures and objects." Booklist

The **Mother** Goose songbook; by Tom Glazer; illustrated by David McPhail. Doubleday 1990 95p il music $17.95; pa $12.95 (k-2) **782.42**

1. Songs 2. Nursery rhymes

ISBN 0-385-41474-9; 0-385-24631-5 (pa) LC 88-753151

"A bright, fresh collection of 44 rhymes set to music. . . . Many of the traditional words and music have a new arrangement to them. . . . The arrangements are intelligent and loaded with personality, but they are not difficult to play. McPhail's witty watercolor illustrations complement each song and add new life to the standard characters." SLJ

Nelson, Esther L.

The funny song-book; illustrations by Joyce Behr. Sterling 1984 96p il $14.95 **782.42**

1. Songs

ISBN 0-8069-4682-2 LC 84-89

"This collection of 60 humorous songs offers representatives of many genres, from cumulative songs to parodies to those that tell a story. There are lots of goofy, easy-to-remember lyrics and well-known melodies. . . . The songs are scored simply for piano and guitar, and sprightly illustrations in shades of gray and black are pleasantly lighthearted." Booklist

Peterson, Carolyn Sue, 1938-

Index to children's songs; a title, first line, and subject index; compiled by Carolyn Sue Peterson and Ann D. Fenton. Wilson, H.W. 1979 318p $33 **782.42**

1. Songs—Indexes
ISBN 0-8242-0638-X LC 79-14265

"A numbered indexed list of 298 children's song books published between 1909 and 1977, identifying more than 5000 songs (both American and foreign) and variations, arranged alphabetically by author. There are also a title and first line index and a subject index, using more than 1000 subject headings. The titles are likely to be held in schools." A L A. Ref Sources for Small & Medium-sized Libr. 4th edition

Raffi

The 2nd Raffi songbook; design and illustration by Joyce Yamamoto. Crown 1987 104p il music spiral binding $15.95 (k-2) **782.42**

1. Songs
ISBN 0-517-56637-0

"42 songs from Raffi's albums: Baby Beluga, Rise and shine and One light, one sun; piano arrangements by Catherine Ambrose." Title page

These "songs, including 'Wheels on the Bus,' 'Baby Beluga,' and 'Time to Sing,' . . . are presented with simple, decorative graphics." Horn Book

Baby Beluga; illustrated by Ashley Wolff. Crown 1990 unp il music (Raffi songs to read) $9.95; lib bdg $10.99 (k-2) **782.42**

1. Songs 2. Whales—Songs and music
ISBN 0-517-57839-5; 0-517-57840-9 (lib bdg)
LC 89-49367

Presents the illustrated text to the song about the little white whale who swims wild and free

"Wolff's striking double-page spreads show the young whale among its fellow Arctic Sea inhabitants. Diversifying her views, the illustrator eyes Baby Beluga and mother swimming together underwater; takes an aerial angle, looking down on the whales from a puffin's perspective; and observes the icy yet welcoming formations where seals, polar bears, and an Eskimo find shelter. . . . An inviting approach to reading encouragement." Booklist

Down by the bay; illustrated by Nadine Bernard Westcott. Crown 1987 unp il music (Raffi songs to read) lib bdg $9.95; pa $3.95 (k-2) **782.42**

1. Songs
ISBN 0-517-56644-3 (lib bdg); 0-517-56645-1 (pa)
LC 87-750291

This illustrated version of one of Raffi's songs depicts a variety of unusual sights to be seen "down by the bay"

The "cheerful nonsense verses are illustrated with equal cheer. Westcott's scraggly lines and bright, clear colors humorously portray the busy children, jolly animals, and frantic mothers that populate the song." SLJ

Five little ducks; illustrated by Jose Aruego and Ariane Dewey. Crown 1989 unp il music (Raffi songs to read) $9.95 (k-2) **782.42**

1. Songs
ISBN 0-517-56945-0 LC 88-3752

"In bold colors and uncluttered spreads, Aruego and Dewey present Mother Duck and her five ducklings waddling 'over the hills and far away'. . . . But after each outing, one less duckling returns until all have left the nest. Come spring, however, Mother is greeted by all five youngsters returning with their own quacking broods." Booklist

One light, one sun; illustrated by Eugenie Fernandes. Crown 1988 unp il music (Raffi songs to read) $9.95; pa $3.95 (k-2) **782.42**

1. Songs
ISBN 0-517-56785-7; 0-517-57644-9 (pa)
LC 87-22256

This book "describes how some things are shared by everyone in the world. The illustrations capture this theme by showing three different families engaged in similar daily activities (playing, mealtime, bedtime, etc.). Brightly colored illustrations depict a single parent family, a handicapped child, and an extended family living under one roof. The words of the song are set apart from the pictures, making it easy to read or sing along as the pages are turned." SLJ

The Raffi Christmas treasury; fourteen illustrated songs and musical arrangements; illustrated by Nadine Bernard Westcott. Crown 1988 84p il music lib bdg $17.95 **782.42**

1. Carols 2. Songs
ISBN 0-517-56806-3 LC 88-750620

"The fourteen songs, taken from 'Raffi's Christmas Album,' include both traditional carols and original melodies. . . . Although the buoyant, cheerful spirit of Raffi's collection could easily defy accurate visual interpretation, Nadine Westcott should take a bow. Brimming with cheer, warmth, and humor, her watercolor illustrations play their role to perfection." Horn Book

The Raffi singable songbook; with illustrations by Joyce Yamamoto. Crown 1987 106p il music $15.95 (k-2) **782.42**

1. Songs
ISBN 0-517-56638-9

"A collection of 51 songs from Raffi's first three records for young children." Title page

"Presented in large, easy-to-read type and with spiral bindings that will stay open at the keyboard, these offerings include piano accompaniment and guitar chord charts. [The book] has colorful, childlike drawings scattered throughout." Booklist

Raffi—*Continued*

Shake my sillies out; illustrated by David Allender. Crown 1987 unp il music (Raffi songs to read) lib bdg $9.95; pa $3.95 (k-2) **782.42**

1. Songs
ISBN 0-517-56646-X (lib bdg); 0-517-56647-8 (pa)
LC 87-750478

"Unable to get to sleep, the forest animals burst into song and dance around until they end up at Camp Mariposa where first the campers and then the rescuers join in. The slight text is a simple action song that should make this popular. The exuberant pictures add to the fun." Child Book Rev Serv

Wheels on the bus; illustrated by Sylvie Kantorovitz Wickstrom. Crown 1988 unp il music (Raffi songs to read) lib bdg $9.95; pa $3.95 (k-2) **782.42**

1. Songs
ISBN 0-517-56784-9 (lib bdg); 0-517-57645-7 (pa)
LC 87-30126

"As the bus—or *autobus,* according to its sign—bounces through what appears to be a French town, slightly cartoonlike watercolors portray the humorous cast of players. An impish little girl, a young couple with a baby, a peasant woman with her goose, and others crowd on board to 'go up and down/up and down'—collide might be more accurate—as the bus rolls forward." Horn Book

Singing bee! a collection of favorite children's songs; compiled by Jane Hart; pictures by Anita Lobel. Lothrop, Lee & Shepard Bks. 1989 160p il music $17.95; pa $11.95 (k-3) **782.42**

1. Songs
ISBN 0-699-41975-5; 0-688-09113-X (pa)
LC 82-15296

This is "a fine collection of songs for young children, arranged primarily by origin (English traditional) but partly by form (rounds) or by season (Christmas, Hanukkah) or by function (singing games). Subject and title indexes give access to the selections, and both simple guitar chords and simple piano accompaniments are provided." Bull Cent Child Books

"The glory of the book is its illustrations, which provide an imaginative, lively, often witty visual commentary. Because much of the material is traditional, the artist used historical settings; and her 'interest in all things theatrical' and her 'love of eighteenth-century garb' is visible in the profusion of pictures in black and white and in warm, luminous color." Horn Book

Songs from Mother Goose; with the traditional melody for each; compiled by Nancy Larrick; illustrated by Robin Spowart. Harper & Row 1989 70p il music $16.95; lib bdg $16.89 (k-3) **782.42**

1. Songs 2. Nursery rhymes
ISBN 0-06-023713-9; 0-06-023714-7 (lib bdg)
LC 88-754466

"Larrick has gathered fifty-six traditional and popular Mother Goose rhymes for this logically arranged and welcome collection; each rhyme is accompanied by its traditional eighteenth- or nineteenth-century melody. . . . Intended as a book for adults and children to share, each spacious page is decorated with Spowart's bright yet gentle illustrations, which literally interpret each rhyme." Horn Book

Staines, Bill

All God's critters got a place in the choir; words and music by Bill Staines; pictures by Margot Zemach. Dutton 1989 unp il music $13.95 (k-2) **782.42**

1. Songs 2. Animals
ISBN 0-525-44469-6 LC 88-31696

This is an illustrated version of the children's song about musical animals. The score is included at the end of the volume

"While the noise of the animals' brays, moos, and quacks will be more fun when led and encouraged by a skilled folk singer, the rollicking, good-natured illustrations provide plenty of amusement for those who just want to look." Horn Book

The **Twelve** days of Christmas **782.42**

1. Carols

Some editions are:

HarperCollins Pubs. $16.95; lib bdg $16.89 Illustrated by Ilse Plume (ISBN 0-06-024737-1; 0-06-024738-X)

Putnam $14.95 Illustrated by Jan Brett (ISBN 0-399-22037-2)

Illustrated versions of The Christmas carol in which a young woman's true love sends her extravagant gifts on each of the twelve days of Christmas. Both include music

"Reminiscent of illuminated manuscripts of the Middle Ages, Plume's lyrical paintings incorporate exquisitely rendered flowers, fruits and animals into elaborate Italian Renaissance settings, in which a golden-haired maiden is given the familiar series of Christmas gifts by her generous 'true love.'" Publ Wkly

"Brett provides a beautifully executed visual feast in which each of the Christmas gifts merits a two-page spread. . . . Side borders throughout the book tell the story of an eighteenth-century family's Christmas preparations while top panels feature exquisitely wrought holiday decorations. Christmas greetings in twelve different languages are tucked into the bottom corners of each page. An eye-catching, three-dimensional effect is achieved as the drummers, maids, geese, and others seemingly step over the borders." Booklist

Watson, Clyde

Father Fox's feast of songs; words and music by Clyde Watson; pictures by Wendy Watson. Philomel Bks. 1983 31p il music $10.95; pa $5.95 (k-3) **782.42**

1. Songs
ISBN 0-399-20886-0; 0-399-20928-X (pa)

"From the sisters' previous books, 'Father Fox's Penny-rhymes . . . and 'Catch Me & Kiss Me & Say It Again' [both entered in class 811] the author has selected twenty-one bouncy, rhythmic verses and has set them to simple, singable tunes for young children. And

Watson, Clyde—*Continued*
for the older children or the adults who may be assisting, guitar chords and uncomplicated piano accompaniments are included." Horn Book

Weiss, Nicki, 1951-
If you're happy and you know it; eighteen story songs set to pictures by Nicki Weiss; music arranged by John Krumich. Greenwillow Bks. 1987 40p il music $13 (k-2) **782.42**

1. Songs
ISBN 0-688-06444-2 LC 86-753170

"The lettering and the scores are all hand-done, perfectly clear for humming alone, but not as easy for simple piano accompaniment—some of the bars aren't presented conventionally, as on a sheet of music, and are sometimes even upside down. This whimsical touch doesn't hamper the exuberance of Weiss's characters, who dance, prance, stomp, clap and all but samba to the tunes herein." Publ Wkly

784.19 Musical instruments

Ardley, Neil, 1937-
Music. Knopf 1989 63p il (Eyewitness bks) $12.95; lib bdg $13.99 (4 and up) **784.19**

1. Musical instruments
ISBN 0-394-82259-5; 0-394-92259-X (lib bdg) LC 88-13394

Text and pictures introduce musical instruments from early times to the present—from pipes and flutes to electronic synthesizers

"Interesting historical asides and highlights about famous musicians contrast with the precisely labeled parts of the numerous illustrated instruments." Booklist

Walther, Tom, 1950-
Make mine music! written and illustrated by Tom Walther. Little, Brown 1981 126p il $14.95; pa $7.95 (5 and up) **784.19**

1. Musical instruments 2. Handicraft
ISBN 0-316-92111-4; 0-316-92112-2 (pa) LC 80-23600

"A Brown paper school book"

"The author discusses a variety of musical instruments and includes directions for making and playing them. The instructions for making the instruments are relatively easy for children to understand; however, it should be noted that some jobs require tools such as drills and saws that should be used under adult supervision. The format makes a distinction between the discussion of the instruments . . . and the directions for making them. . . . The book is illustrated with attractive line drawings. A brief list of books about musical instruments has been included." SLJ

Wiseman, Ann Sayre, 1926-
Making musical things; improvised instruments; [by] Ann Wiseman. Scribner 1979 63p il $13.95 (3-6) **784.19**

1. Musical instruments 2. Handicraft
ISBN 0-684-16114-1 LC 79-4474

Wiseman's "clever black-and-white drawings and short, clear directions show how to make over fifty basic but ingenious musical instruments. Many of the supplies needed can be found around the house, particularly in the kitchen." Babbling Bookworm

Includes bibliography

784.2 Symphony orchestra

Prokofiev, Sergey, 1891-1953
Peter and the wolf; adapted from the musical tale by Sergei Prokofiev; illustrated by Erna Voight. Godine 1980 c1979 unp il music $12.95 (1-4) **784.2**

1. Wolves—Fiction
ISBN 0-87923-331-1 LC 79-92902

Original German edition of this version published 1979

A story version of the Russian composer's tale for orchestra and narrator about a boy who captures a wolf. "Voigt's shimmering landscapes and whimsical characters act out the sequence of events related in brisk prose. The full-page, full-color and handsome illustrations alternate with pages of text and with pictures of the individual orchestral instruments. . . . There are also brief selections from the score and a bracingly humorous view of the entire company—wolf included—tuning up their instruments as if they were about to perform the spirited music." Publ Wkly

Picture book versions entered in Easy section

788 Wind instruments and their music

Krementz, Jill
A very young musician; written and photographed by Jill Krementz. Simon & Schuster Bks. for Young Readers 1991 unp il $14.95 (3-6) **788**

1. Music—Study and teaching
ISBN 0-671-72687-0 LC 90-10017

This photo-essay is about "fifth grader Josh Broder, a trumpet player. Josh enjoys playing his instrument, participating in musical activities in and out of school and, in the summer, studying at Interlochen. He's serious about music lessons and practice, but it's clear that he has a sense of humor and enjoys other interests. . . . In addition to describing his musical life, Josh discusses all of the instruments in the school band." Bull Cent Child Books

"Sprinkled throughout Josh's first-person narrative are nuggets of information that aspiring musicians will appreciate." Publ Wkly

790.1 Recreational activities

Caney, Steven
Steven Caney's kids' America. Workman 1978 414p il map hardcover o.p. paperback available $11.95 (4 and up) **790.1**

1. Amusements 2. Handicraft 3. United States—Social life and customs
ISBN 0-911104-80-1 (pa) LC 77-27465

Introduces aspects of American life from the colonial period to the present. Suggests such activities as handicraft projects, genealogy searches, and games

Robinson, Jeri
Activities for anyone, anytime, anywhere; illustrated by Barbara Bruno. Little, Brown 1983 88p il $14.95; pa $10.95 (5 and up) **790.1**

1. Amusements 2. Games
ISBN 0-316-75144-8; 0-316-75145-6 (pa) LC 82-15353

"Children's Museum activity book"

"Aimed at adults and young people working with children, this [is a] compendium of ideas on how to keep kids amused. . . . There are practical tips for managing successful group outings, an array of easy-to-do projects and entertainments." Booklist

791.3 Circuses

Machotka, Hana
The magic ring; a year with the Big Apple Circus; introduction by Paul Binder. Morrow 1988 72p il $13.95; pa $8.95 (3-6) **791.3**

1. Big Apple Circus 2. Circus
ISBN 0-688-07449-9; 0-688-08222-X (pa) LC 87-28230

Briefly surveys the history of circuses and describes the growth, rehearsals, performances, and personnel of the successful one-ring circus known as the Big Apple Circus

"Author/photographer Machotka masterfully captures the personalities, warmth and spirit of this unique non-profit endeavor. . . . Vivid, full-color photos enhance and expand the text. In sum, *The Magic Ring* masterfully communicates the excitement that this small gem of a circus inspires in its audiences." Publ Wkly

791.43 Motion pictures

Gibbons, Gail
Lights! Camera! Action! how a movie is made. Crowell 1985 unp il $13.95; lib bdg $13.89; Macmillan pa $3.95 (1-3) **791.43**

1. Motion pictures—Production and direction
ISBN 0-690-04476-3; 0-690-04477-1 (lib bdg); 0-06-446088-6 (pa) LC 85-47536

A step-by-step description of how a movie is made, including writing the script, casting, rehearsing, creating the scenery and costumes, editing the film, and attending the premiere

"Characteristically graphic writing explains the processes involved in bringing a major movie from idea through its glittering premiere. Boldly colored, detailed cartoons show men and women handling their responsibilities (scriptwriter, producer, art director, casting director, editors: a myriad of specialists). Like all Gibbons's primers on facets of modern life, the movie book stands out as attractive and useful." Publ Wkly

791.45 Television

Scott, Elaine, 1940-
Ramona: behind the scenes of a television show; written by Elaine Scott; photographs by Margaret Miller. Morrow Junior Bks. 1988 88p il $14.95; lib bdg $14.88 (4 and up) **791.45**

1. Ramona (Television program)
2. Television—Production and direction
ISBN 0-688-06818-9; 0-688-06819-7 (lib bdg) LC 87-33313

"This book gives readers an insider's view of a television show from conception to broadcast. . . . Each step is explained as it took place during the filming of *Ramona*, a 10-part television series based on Beverly Cleary's . . . books about Ramona Quimby." Booklist

"The text, liberally illustrated with photographs of people and procedures, is direct, clear, sequential, and informative." Bull Cent Child Books

791.5 Puppetry and toy theaters

Renfro, Nancy
Puppet show made easy! photographs by Nancy Scanlan; illustrated by Ellen Scott Turner and Nany Renfro. Nancy Renfro Studios 1984 80p il (Puppetry in education) pa $12.95 (3-6) **791.5**

1. Puppets and puppet plays
ISBN 0-931044-13-8

Contents: On with the show; A story; From story to script; Building the show; Staging the show; Show time!

The emphasis is on creating one's own scenario, hand puppets of different types, and stagecraft, with how-to directions throughout

792.3 Pantomime

Straub, Cindie
Mime: basics for beginners; [by] Cindie and Matthew Straub; photography by Jeff Blanton. Plays 1984 152p il $12.95 (6 and up) **792.3**

1. Mime
ISBN 0-8238-0263-9 LC 84-11694

Drawings and photographs accompany a discussion of the physical and technical aspects of mime

Includes glossary

792.5 Opera

Price, Leontyne

Aïda; as told by Leontyne Price; illustrated by Leo and Diane Dillon. Harcourt Brace Jovanovich 1990 unp il $15.95 (4 and up) **792.5**

1. Operas—Stories, plots, etc.
ISBN 0-15-200405-X LC 89-36481

Coretta Scott King Award for illustration, 1990

"Gulliver books"

"Based on the opera by Giuseppi Verdi"

Tragedy results when an enslaved Ethiopian princess falls in love with an Egyptian general

"The text appears on the left surmounted by a friezelike series of figures which interpret the action; on the right, a full-page illustration focuses on a particular character or grouping. A worthy introduction to the opera for a varied audience." Horn Book Guide

Rosenberg, Jane, 1949-

Sing me a story; the Metropolitan Opera's book of opera stories for children; introduction by Luciano Pavarotti. Thames & Hudson 1989 158p il $24.95 (4-6) **792.5**

1. Operas—Stories, plots, etc.
ISBN 0-500-01467-1 LC 88-51929

"Alongside the so-called ABC's—*Aida, La Boheme* and *Carmen*—are less often performed works such as *L'Enfant et les Sortileges, Porgy and Bess* and *The Love for Three Oranges.* The author skillfully refers to specific musical passages and uses dialogue drawn from the libretto to link each story to an actual performance. . . . Although brief accounts in general cannot do justice to the deep emotion and psychological insight of *Pagliacci* or *The Magic Flute,* these failings are more than redeemed by Rosenberg's handsomely detailed watercolors, which convey the opulent sensuality of opera at its most sublime." Publ Wkly

792.8 Ballet and modern dance

Elliott, Donald

Frogs and the ballet; illustrated by Clinton Arrowood. Gambit 1979 xxi, 57p il $12.95; pa $8.95 (4 and up) **792.8**

1. Ballet
ISBN 0-87645-099-0; 0-87645-119-9 (pa)
LC 78-19566

Introduces familiar ballet steps, demonstrating what lies behind these seemingly effortless movements and how they are woven into classical ballet

"The carefully executed full-page ink illustrations precisely depict each page of accurate description. So what if the dancers are frogs? . . . For balletomanes it is hysterically funny. As for the majority, who are not and couldn't care less, this zany book draws them in, despite themselves." SLJ

Isadora, Rachel

My ballet class. Greenwillow Bks. 1980 unp il $12.95 (1-3) **792.8**

1. Ballet
ISBN 0-688-80253-2 LC 79-16297

"This is a short look at a young girl's experience in ballet class. The large, close-up line drawings show male and female students changing, doing warm-up exercises, doing the five basic positions, and practicing leaps with their male instructor." Child Book Rev Serv

"The book is excellent: simply written, nicely illustrated, and introducing ballet basics not only in a way that is clear but also in a tone that suggests ballet lessons are enjoyable." Bull Cent Child Books

Klein, Norma, 1938-1989

Baryshnikov's Nutcracker; with photographs by Ken Regan; additional photographs by Christopher Little and Martha Swope; choreography by Mikhail Baryshnikov; music by Peter Ilyich Tchaikovsky. Putnam 1983 unp il $12.95 (3 and up) **792.8**

1. Ballets—Stories, plots, etc. 2. Fairy tales 3. Christmas—Fiction
ISBN 0-399-12887-5 LC 83-11174

"Starring Mikhail Baryshnikov and Gelsey Kirkland with Alexander Mintz. Produced and written for television by Yanna Kroyt Brandt; directed by Tony Charmoli; production designed by Boris Aronson; executive producer: Herman Krawitz." Title page

With the help of a young girl, a nutcracker becomes a handsome prince. Illustrated with photos from a performance by the American Ballet Theatre

Krementz, Jill

A very young dancer. Knopf 1976 unp il o.p.; Dell paperback available $7.95 (3-6) **792.8**

1. Ballet
ISBN 0-440-49212-2 (pa) LC 76-13700

"A black-and-white photo essay, depicting the training, selection, and performance of the leading child ballerina for Balanchine's annual New York City Ballet production of 'The Nutcracker.' The large, clear photos follow ten-year-old Stephanie through her lessons, with glimpses of her and her family at home, to the auditions, rehearsals, costume fittings, make-up and performance. The simple text is kept to a minimum." SLJ

"When an outstanding photographer has an equally remarkable subject, the result is a rare treat." Publ Wkly

Kuklin, Susan

Going to my ballet class. Bradbury Press 1989 unp il $12.95 (4-6) **792.8**

1. Ballet
ISBN 0-02-751235-5 LC 88-37556

"Color photographs show young boys and girls in a ballet class for beginners; the pictures are technically good and visually appealing as well as informative. The text is simply written in first person, so that facts about lessons and positions and steps are always from a child's

Kuklin, Susan—*Continued*
viewpoint. The book concludes with a section (in smaller print) addressed to adults, giving some useful advice on choosing a ballet class and on researching what's available and has a good professional reputation." Bull Cent Child Books

793 Indoor games and amusements

Rockwell, Anne F., 1934-
Things to play with; [by] Anne Rockwell. Dutton 1988 24p il lib bdg $11.95 (k-1) **793**

1. Amusements 2. Play
ISBN 0-525-44409-2 LC 87-33399

Introduces a variety of situations and objects that may be used for play, including things to play with in the yard, at school, on snow and ice, and at a party

"Each category merits a double-page spread of boxed scenes featuring an animal child and toy. The pages are visually full, laid out in comic-book style, with no intervening space between frames. Rockwell's neat line work and cheery colors create a lighthearted mood that perfectly suits the parent-child sharing for which this is designed." Booklist

793.3 Social, folk, national dancing

Ancona, George, 1929-
Dancing is. Elsevier-Dutton 1981 48p il lib bdg $13.95 (3-5) **793.3**

1. Dancing 2. Folk dancing
ISBN 0-525-28490-7 LC 81-3296

Text and photographs introduce some dances of various countries around the world

"The photographs vary in shape and size—some spill from one page onto the page opposite—adding considerably to the liveliness of the book. A minimum of text accompanies the pictures, but each dance is identified. The last pages of the book give brief descriptions of the dance steps and a little historical background." Horn Book

793.73 Puzzles and puzzle games

Adler, David A., 1947-
The carsick zebra and other animal riddles; illustrated by Tomie de Paola. Holiday House 1983 unp il $10.95 (1-3) **793.73**

1. Riddles
ISBN 0-8234-0479-X LC 82-48750

In this collection of riddles "the questions appear at the top of the page, Tomie dePaola's simple yet witty black-and-white drawings fill the middle, and the answer appears at the bottom." Booklist

A teacher on roller skates and other school riddles; illustrated by John Wallner. Holiday House 1989 unp il $10.95 (k-3) **793.73**

1. Riddles
ISBN 0-8234-0775-6 LC 89-1929

A collection of jokes and riddles about school

The twisted witch, and other spooky riddles; illustrated by Victoria Chess. Holiday House 1985 unp il $10.95 (1-3) **793.73**

1. Riddles
ISBN 0-8234-0571-0 LC 85-909

"An irresistible cauldron of 60 riddles for the witching season. On each page, a pithy riddle is paired with a playful black-and-white drawing, and the result is more often hilarious than horrifying. In fact, it is the illustrations, detailed down to witches' warts and monsters' toenails, that revive the deader punch lines." SLJ

Calmenson, Stephanie
What am I? very first riddles; pictures by Karen Gundersheimer. Harper & Row 1989 unp il $11.95; lib bdg $11.89 (k-2) **793.73**

1. Riddles
ISBN 0-06-020997-6; 0-06-020998-4 (lib bdg) LC 87-22959

A collection of easy-to-read riddles in verse about everyday objects

"Never tricky and always toddler-tested (keys, flowers, a swing), the riddles provide the appeal of rhyming as well as pride in the accomplishment of figuring out the answer. And, of course, the fun of shouting it out. Tidy drawings on the riddle page provide visual nudges; illustrations of the mystery of objects are generic enough to be readily identified while maintaining interest through color (a yellow telephone) and detail (a terrific toy train)." Bull Cent Child Books

Cerf, Bennett, 1898-1971
Bennett Cerf's book of animal riddles; illustrated by Roy McKie. Beginner Bks. 1964 62p il lib bdg $7.99 (k-3) **793.73**

1. Riddles
ISBN 0-394-90034-0 LC 64-11246

Title on spine: Animal riddles

A book of easy-reading riddles about animals such as "Why are fish so smart? They always go around in schools"

"The kind of humor that adults find obvious and absurd but most children think hilarious. . . . Roy McKie's boldly madcap illustrations have the same tongue-in-cheek spirit." N Y Times Book Rev

Bennett Cerf's book of riddles; illustrated by Roy McKie. Beginner Bks. 1960 62p il $6.95; lib bdg $7.99 (k-3) **793.73**

1. Riddles
ISBN 0-394-80015-X; 0-394-90015-4 (lib bdg) LC 60-13492

Cerf, Bennett, 1898-1971—*Continued*

These thirty-one riddles are arranged with the riddles being asked on one page and answered on the next, to keep the element of surprise

"Simple cartoonlike drawings use strong colour for their effect." Ont Libr Rev

Cricket's jokes, riddles and other stuff; compiled by Marcia Leonard and the editors of Cricket magazine; designed by John Grandits. Random House 1977 unp il $4.95; lib bdg $3.99 (1-4) **793.73**

1. Riddles 2. Jokes 3. Wit and humor
ISBN 0-394-83545-X; 0-394-93545-4 (lib bdg)
LC 77-3164

"Contents are divided into elephant jokes, limericks, tongue twisters and other nonsense, the kinds youngsters adore." Publ Wkly

De Regniers, Beatrice Schenk

It does not say meow, and other animal riddle rhymes; pictures by Paul Galdone. Clarion Bks. 1972 unp il $14.95 (k-1) **793.73**

1. Riddles 2. Animals—Poetry
ISBN 0-395-28822-3
LC 72-75709

First published by Seabury Press

A "riddle book for the very young in which clues to the identity of each of nine different animals including a cat, elephant, ant, dog, frog, and mice are given in a short rhyming verse and full-page illustration. The correct answer appears in a captioned double-spread picture on the following pages." Booklist

"Young readers will relate to the children in the book who are pictured visiting the zoo, watching birds, playing Indians, etc. The colorful illustrations are appealing." SLJ

Gounaud, Karen Jo

A very mice joke book; illustrated by Lynn Munsinger. Houghton Mifflin 1981 47p il $12.95; pa $4.95 **793.73**

1. Riddles
ISBN 0-395-30445-8; 0-395-30442-3 (pa)
LC 80-25413

This book "probably contains every word play you'll ever want to hear on mouse and mice. The book has been specified 'all ages,' which is no more than fair, since very few kids will be able to identify a historic mouse dictator named Mouseolini or know that squeakiesies is where mice hung out in the 1920's. Still there are some wonderfully wacky riddles like: 'What do you throw at newlywed cats? White mice.' And: 'What is the capital of Miceland? Mousecow.' Nearly every page is enlivened with . . . black-and-white drawings." N Y Times Book Rev

Jensen, Virginia Allen

Red thread riddles; [by] Virginia Allen Jensen and Polly Edman. Putnam 1980 c1979 unp il pa $12.95 **793.73**

1. Riddles 2. Blind—Books and reading
ISBN 0-399-20955-7
LC 79-28168

First published by Collins

Rhymed text in print and braille presents several riddles. The initial letters of each answer spell out the answer to yet another question

"Sighted children can close their eyes and try to follow the thread, imagining what the experience of braille reading must be for a blind person. At the end there is an alphabet. . . . Children are truly fascinated by being able to compare the two forms of words, and may be encouraged in their appreciation of and respect for those who are blind." SLJ

Keller, Charles, 1942-

It's raining cats and dogs; cat and dog jokes; compiled by Charles Keller; illustrated by Robert Quackenbush. Pippin Press 1988 unp il lib bdg $10.95 (2-4) **793.73**

1. Jokes
ISBN 0-945912-01-3
LC 88-12421

"Keller runs the gamut here from clever to just plain silly. Puns . . . and word play . . . account for most of the entries, with a few leaning too hard on adult-sounding aphorisms. . . . Black-and-white cartoons echo the low-down humor in an easy-to-read book that will quickly find its own audience." Bull Cent Child Books

Kessler, Leonard P., 1920-

Old Turtle's riddle and joke book; [by] Leonard Kessler. Greenwillow Bks. 1986 47p il $12.95; lib bdg $12.88 (1-3) **793.73**

1. Riddles
ISBN 0-688-05953-8; 0-688-05954-6 (lib bdg)
LC 85-12565

"A Greenwillow read-alone book"

"Old Turtle is compiling a riddle book, which serves as a convenient excuse for all of his friends to tell him their favorites. . . . The jokes veer from being integrated into the story to appearing as abrupt block sections of riddles from each animal friend. The slight pretext for the joke sessions won't bother young readers; they'll devour the wordplay, enjoy the riddle-followed-by-a-box-with-the-upside-down-answer-and-a-cartoon-illustration format, and snort over the additional cracks made by a pair of birds at the bottom of each page." SLJ

Livingston, Myra Cohn

My head is red and other riddle rhymes; illustrated by Tere LoPrete. Holiday House 1990 unp il $12.95 (k-2) **793.73**

1. Riddles
ISBN 0-8234-0806-X
LC 89-24528

"This book begs to be read aloud, though the level of difficulty varies; some answers are a bit abstract for preschoolers, while others are made for them. . . . The finesse of both artwork and rhymes sets this volume apart from many other riddle books, and it should fit well in a group setting." Booklist

Maestro, Giulio, 1942-

Halloween howls; riddles that are a scream. Dutton 1983 unp il $9.95 (2-4) **793.73**

1. Riddles
ISBN 0-525-44059-3 LC 83-1419

"Maestro's cornucopia of riddles stars ghosts, monsters, skeletons, ghouls and witches all cavorting in funny, violently colored pictures. Since kids dearly love this brand of humor, the book should be very popular among boys and girls planning Halloween festivities." Publ Wkly

A raft of riddles. Dutton 1982 unp il $10.95 (2-4) **793.73**

1. Riddles
ISBN 0-525-44017-8 LC 82-2402

"Although the jokes are nothing special, they are paired with delightful watercolor pictures that make this far superior to run-of-the-mill riddle books with black line illustration. Cartoon-style drawings washed with cheerful colors take almost the whole of each page, with riddle and answer at either the top or bottom. More than 50 riddles in all." Booklist

Riddle romp; written and illustrated by Giulio Maestro. Clarion Bks. 1983 unp il $13.95; pa $4.95 (2-4) **793.73**

1. Riddles
ISBN 0-89919-180-0; 0-89919-207-6 (pa) LC 83-2067

"61 riddles, with a large two-color (black with red or yellow) cartoon separating the question at the top of the page from the answer at the bottom. The pictures work well with the text but do not always serve as adequate clues for solving the riddles. Nevertheless, this is a fun book that will appeal not only to children who will benefit from the wordplay, but also to older children who will enjoy teasing their contemporaries." SLJ

Riddle roundup. Clarion Bks. 1989 64p il $13.95; pa $4.95 (2-4) **793.73**

1. Riddles
ISBN 0-89919-508-3; 0-89919-537-7 (pa) LC 86-33403

A collection of sixty-one riddles based on different kinds of word play such as puns, homonyms, and homographs

What's a frank frank? tasty homograph riddles. Clarion Bks. 1984 64p il $12.95; pa $4.95 (2-4) **793.73**

1. Riddles 2. Word games
ISBN 0-89919-297-1; 0-89919-317-X (pa) LC 84-5021

"Homographs are the inspiration for this collection of riddles that will set youngsters to thinking about the idiosyncrasies of their language. 'What's a spare spare? A skinny extra tire.' Is an example of the sort of wordplay that passes for good, pedantic humor. . . . Maestro's accompanying cartoons are adequate but not especially fresh; still, they do help liven up the atmosphere and give some of the more esoteric jokes a concrete base." Booklist

McMullan, Kate, 1947-

Snakey riddles; by Katy Hall and Lisa Eisenberg; pictures by Simms Taback. Dial Bks. for Young Readers 1990 48p il $9.95; lib bdg $9.89 (k-2) **793.73**

1. Riddles
ISBN 0-8037-0669-3; 0-8037-0670-7 (lib bdg) LC 88-23687

"Dial easy-to-read"

An illustrated collection of riddles about snakes

"Riddle lovers will groan with delight at some of these riddles. . . . The best thing about the book is the cleverly drawn, lively cartoon illustrations. Long, colorful snakes form borders framing the text and picture for each riddle." SLJ

Phillips, Louis

263 brain busters; just how smart are you, anyway? illustrated by James Stevenson. Viking Kestrel 1985 87p il $10.95 (4-6) **793.73**

1. Puzzles 2. Mathematical recreations 3. Literary recreations
ISBN 0-670-80412-6 LC 85-40444

A collection of mathematical and verbal brain-teasing questions interspersed with "brain vacation" jokes

Going ape; jokes from the jungle; illustrated by Bob Shein. Viking Kestrel 1988 58p il lib bdg $10.95 (3-5) **793.73**

1. Jokes 2. Riddles
ISBN 0-670-81520-9 LC 87-28928

A collection of riddles, jokes, and puns about all kinds of animals from aardvarks to zebras

"Phillips has collected some familiar . . . and some not so familiar . . . animal jokes in his new compilation. . . . Phillips has organized the jokes in sections on reptiles; felines; birds; monkeys; and even jumbo jokes, which include elephants and hippos. Comic black-and-white line drawings with a wash enliven most pages." SLJ

Haunted house jokes; illustrated by James Marshall. Viking Kestrel 1987 57p il lib bdg $10.95 (3-5) **793.73**

1. Jokes 2. Riddles
ISBN 0-670-81050-9 LC 87-8336

A "collection of riddles, jokes, knock-knocks, and puns, gathered into chapters by creatures (ghosts, werewolves, skeletons, etc.) and profusely illustrated with Marshall's goofy, unthreatening figures." SLJ

How do you get a horse out of the bathtub? profound answers to preposterous questions; illustrated by James Stevenson. Viking 1983 71p il $10.95; Puffin Bks. pa $4.95 (5 and up) **793.73**

1. American wit and humor 2. Jokes 3. Questions and answers
ISBN 0-670-38119-5; 0-14-031618-3 (pa) LC 82-60080

Phillips, Louis—*Continued*

"Stevenson's ink drawings, comic and animated, add to the entertainment value of a series of questions and (silly) answers that should be enjoyed by young readers, as most riddle/joke books are. These, arranged more or less by subject, range from clever puns to weak nonsense, although there are comparatively few peurile answers. There are, on the other hand, some answers that use words that some middle grades readers may not know." Bull Cent Child Books

Steig, William, 1907-

C D C? Farrar, Straus & Giroux 1984 unp il $7.95 (3-6) **793.73**

1. Word games

ISBN 0-374-31015-7 LC 84-48515

Companion volume: C D B! available from Simon & Schuster pa $3.95 (ISBN 0-671-66689-4)

"Steig has devised letter and number sequences, with a few figures like $ and ¢ thrown in for good measure, which, when pronounced aloud, translate roughly into captions for the accompanying cartoon drawings. The cartoons also contain helpful clues to the words' meanings, as in the title phrase, which is matched with a drawing of a man and boy looking out at sea. Some of these quips contain references that children will have difficulty interpreting. . . . Also the vocabulary is often demanding." Booklist

"Flawlessly executed, purely pleasurable, the book is definitely 'D Q-R' for doldrums at any season." Horn Book

Terban, Marvin

The dove dove; funny homograph riddles; illustrated by Tom Huffman. Clarion Bks. 1988 64p il lib bdg $12.95; pa $4.95 (3-6) **793.73**

1. Riddles 2. Word games

ISBN 0-89919-723-X (lib bdg); 0-89919-810-4 (pa) LC 88-2611

"An introduction to the sometimes confusing world of homographs—words that are spelled alike, but are pronounced differently and have different meanings. Using the general pattern of riddle and accompanying illustration, Terban leads readers through a variety of homographs. . . . The format of the book appears to be designed for readers in grades three and four. However, despite good textual organization and entertaining and helpful illustrations showing animals enacting the homographs as clues, some homographs may prove much too difficult for that age group, and the format seems too young for older students. The book will prove of interest to those students who enjoy the challenge of, and appreciate, word play." SLJ

The **Upside** down riddle book; riddles compiled and edited by Louis Phillips; upside down graphics by Beau Gardner. Lothrop, Lee & Shepard Bks. 1982 unp il $12.95; lib bdg $12.88 (k-2) **793.73**

1. Riddles

ISBN 0-688-00931-X; 0-688-00932-8 (lib bdg) LC 82-73

The book contains "fourteen riddles in verse with the solutions in upside-down graphic design. The appeal is to both verbal and visual imagination and can be enjoyed by individuals or a group." SLJ

"It is the stunning illustrations that give the book its spectacular character." Publ Wkly

793.8 Magic and related activities

Broekel, Ray, 1923-

Hocus pocus: magic you can do; [by] Ray Broekel and Laurence B. White, Jr; illustrated by Mary Thelen. Whitman, A. 1984 48p il $10.95 (3-5) **793.8**

1. Magic 2. Tricks

ISBN 0-8075-3350-5 LC 83-26096

Step-by-step instructions for twenty simple magic tricks, together with tips on patter, timing, slight-of-hand, and misdirection for the beginning magician

"Most children, if they read carefully, will be able to figure out the tricks. The black-and-white illustrations dabbed with purple are clearly marked, and the jokes that accompany them add a spot of humor." Booklist

Now you see it: easy magic for beginners; by Ray Broekel and Laurence B. White, Jr; illustrated by Bill Morrison. Little, Brown 1979 57p il $12.95 (3-5) **793.8**

1. Magic 2. Tricks

ISBN 0-316-93595-6 LC 78-21900

The 40 selections in this book "have been collected with amateur magic shows in mind, many needing simple but preplanned setups. In each case the trick is given, followed by an easy-to-follow explanation of how it is done. Props can be quickly assembled from household items; and when water or confetti is called for, the authors are quick to suggest an outdoors setting." Booklist

Cobb, Vicki

Bet you can! science possibilities to fool you; [by] Vicki Cobb and Kathy Darling; illustrated by Stella Ormai. Lothrop, Lee & Shepard Bks. 1990 112p il $13.95 (4 and up) **793.8**

1. Scientific recreations 2. Tricks

ISBN 0-688-09865-7 LC 90-6690

First published 1983 by Avon Books

Provides instructions for more than sixty tricks based on scientific experiments described in the text

Bet you can't! science impossibilities to fool you; by Vicki Cobb and Kathy Darling; illustrated by Martha Weston. Lothrop, Lee & Shepard Bks. 1980 128p il $12.95; lib bdg $12.88 (4 and up) **793.8**

1. Scientific recreations 2. Tricks

ISBN 0-688-41905-4; 0-688-51905-9 (lib bdg) LC 79-9254

Cobb, Vicki—*Continued*

More than 60 tricks are contained in this book. "Explanations of the scientific principles that make the trick impossible to accomplish are included. Some explanations contain an example from a child's everyday life in which the same scientific principles apply." Sci Books Films

Magic—naturally! science entertainment & amusements; illustrated by Lance R. Miyamoto. Lippincott 1976 159p il $12.95 (4 and up) **793.8**

1. Scientific recreations 2. Magic 3. Tricks
ISBN 0-397-31631-3 LC 76-13179

"Thirty magic tricks with accompanying scientific explanations are arranged according to phenomena of mechanics, fluids, energy, chemistry, and perception. The emphasis is on fun, however, with the information presented to insure a true understanding of the 'magic.' Each stunt describes what happens, explains the setup and act, and gives tips for the performance." Booklist

Friedhoffer, Robert

Magic tricks, science facts; illustrated by Richard Kaufman; photographs by Timothy White. Watts 1990 126p il lib bdg $12.90 (5 and up) **793.8**

1. Scientific recreations 2. Magic 3. Tricks
ISBN 0-531-10902-X LC 89-28487

This "book contains almost two dozen magic tricks. The tricks are based on either math or science principles. . . . Most of the chemistry and physiology tricks are more suitable for older children and should be performed with adult supervision, especially when chemicals must be handled." Sci Books Films

Includes bibliography

Kettelkamp, Larry, 1933-

Magic made easy; drawings by Loring Eutemey; photographs by Donovan Klotzbeacher. Newly rev ed. Morrow 1981 96p il $13.95; lib bdg $13.88 (4 and up) **793.8**

1. Magic 2. Tricks
ISBN 0-688-00458-X; 0-688-00377-X (lib bdg) LC 80-22947

First published 1954

Describes twenty-one tricks illustrated with diagrams, drawings, and photographs and suggests the accompanying line of patter

Severn, Bill

Magic fun for everyone; illustrations by Fred Kraus. Dutton 1986 180p il $16.95; pa $8.95 (6 and up) **793.8**

1. Magic 2. Tricks
ISBN 0-525-24485-9; 0-525-48253-9 (pa) LC 86-11480

This collection features tricks with standard props (playing cards, ropes and paper, coins and bills) as well as comedy tricks and mental miracles. Diagrams and instructions are given for each, plus full details for effective presentations

Sheridan, Jeff

Nothing's impossible! stunts to entertain and amaze; photography by Jim Moore. Lothrop, Lee & Shepard Bks. 1982 64p il $12.95 (5 and up) **793.8**

1. Magic 2. Tricks
ISBN 0-688-01169-1 LC 81-20780

"Using inexpensive or readily available props, the tricks range from optical illusion to cleverly manipulated scientific principles and a little trompe l'oeil; all are clearly explained and well illustrated." Horn Book

Simon, Seymour, 1931-

Soap bubble magic; illustrated by Stella Ormai. Lothrop, Lee & Shepard Bks. 1985 48p il $11.95; lib bdg $11.88 (1-3) **793.8**

1. Scientific recreations
ISBN 0-688-02684-2; 0-688-02685-0 (lib bdg) LC 84-4432

Explains what soap bubbles are, how they are formed, and what can be done with them

"Interracial, nonsexist illustrations accompany a text designed to encourage children to think for themselves. . . . The experiments use simple, inexpensive home or schoolroom materials, some of them made by the child." Sci Books Films

White, Laurence B.

Math-a-magic: number tricks for magicians; [by] Laurence B. White and Ray Broekel; illustrated by Meyer Seltzer. Whitman, A. 1989 unp il $10.95 (3-6) **793.8**

1. Mathematical recreations 2. Magic 3. Tricks
ISBN 0-8075-4994-0 LC 89-35395

"Each of the 21 tricks is presented in three sections: 'The Trick,' 'How to do it,' and 'The Math-A-Magic Secret' of why the trick works. . . . The showmanship and production of the trick as magic is stressed, with the math in the background as the key to making the tricks work." SLJ

"The explanations, accompanied when necessary by drawings of cards, coins, and equations, clearly explain each mystery to readers. . . . Teachers seeking trade books to supplement the workbooks, to enrich the curriculum, or enliven their classes will find good material here." Booklist

Wyler, Rose

Magic secrets; by Rose Wyler and Gerald Ames; pictures by Arthur Dorros. rev ed. Harper & Row 1990 63p il $10.95; lib bdg $10.89 (1-3) **793.8**

1. Tricks 2. Magic
ISBN 0-06-026646-5; 0-06-026647-3 (lib bdg) LC 89-35841

"An I can read book"

Wyler, Rose—*Continued*

A revised and newly illustrated edition of the title first published 1967

Easy magic tricks for the aspiring young magician

Spooky tricks; by Rose Wyler and Gerald Ames; pictures by Talivaldis Stubis. Harper & Row 1968 64p il $10.89 (1-3) **793.8**

1. Magic 2. Tricks
ISBN 0-06-026634-1 LC 68-16822

"An I can read book"

Readers can learn such tricks as making ghosts appear, cats sparkle in the dark, girls disappear, and boys float on air

793.9 Other indoor diversions

Gryski, Camilla, 1948-

Cat's cradle, owl's eyes; a book of string games; illustrated by Tom Sankey. Morrow 1984 c1983 78p il lib bdg $12.88; pa $6.95 (4-6) **793.9**

1. String figures
ISBN 0-688-03940-5 (lib bdg); 0-688-03941-3 (pa) LC 84-9075

First published 1983 in Canada

This "book contains readily grasped directions for tricky, entertaining play. Sankey illustrates cat's cradle and its variations with expert, well-defined drawings of each step in the games. Children should enjoy practising manual dexterity as they master the feats described by themselves or in groups." Publ Wkly

"Brief notes on the ethnic and historical background accompany each figure, adding to the pleasure of achievement." Horn Book

Many stars & more string games; illustrated by Tom Sankey. Morrow 1985 80p il lib bdg $11.88; pa $7.95 (4-6) **793.9**

1. String figures
ISBN 0-688-05793-4 (lib bdg); 0-688-05792-6 (pa) LC 85-4875

A collection of string games culled from various cultures. "The figures proceed in order of difficulty; directions are clear, with blue arrow lines that clarify complicated maneuvers. Several stories to tell with string figures are also included. Straightforward, clearly illustrated, and marked by an infectious enthusiasm, this should be a fine resource for performing storytellers as well as dabbling readers." Booklist

Super string games; illustrated by Tom Sankey. Morrow Junior Bks. 1988 c1987 80p il lib bdg $11.88; pa $6.95 (4-6) **793.9**

1. String figures
ISBN 0-688-07685-8 (lib bdg); 0-688-07684-X (pa) LC 87-18365

First published 1987 in Canada

"This collection of 25 string figures from around the world is for the nimble-fingered of all ages who have mastered simple string figures like cat's cradle and are ready to move on to something more complicated. The directions and illustrations are clear, including a suggestion for how to turn the pages when your hands are all tied up." Child Book Rev Serv

794 Indoor games of skill

Zaslavsky, Claudia, 1917-

Tic tac toe, and other three-in-a row games from ancient Egypt to the modern computer; illustrated by Anthony Kramer. Crowell 1982 90p il map lib bdg $11.89 (4 and up) **794**

1. Games
ISBN 0-690-04317-1 LC 82-45186

Traces the history and development of the three-in-a-row game for two players, popular all over the world, that is similar to games played in ancient Egypt

"The attractive size, good looking drawings and very readable format make this a worthwhile book for any collection." Appraisal

796 Athletic and outdoor sports and games

Allen, Anne

Sports for the handicapped. Walker & Co. 1981 80p il lib bdg $10.85 (5 and up) **796**

1. Sports for the handicapped
ISBN 0-8027-6437-1 LC 81-50738

"Chapters on skiing, wheelchair basketball, swimming, track and field, football and horseback riding feature youngsters who have physical impairments or severe hearing or vision loss, but who have made sports an important part of their lives. The fascinating photographs provide evidence that there are some satisfactions uniquely available through sports." SLJ

Fisher, Leonard Everett, 1924-

The sports; written and illustrated by Leonard Everett Fisher. Holiday House 1980 62p il (Nineteenth century America) $7.95 (4 and up) **796**

1. Sports—History
ISBN 0-8234-0419-6 LC 80-16467

The author "describes the inception of many kinds of sports, the ways in which they were organized or played, and the people (almost entirely men) who were prominent either in the sport itself or in sports promotion." Bull Cent Child Books

"The text is illustrated by the award winner's masterful etchings, depicting horse racing, sailing, gymnastics, Olympic events, etc." Publ Wkly

Gibbons, Gail

Playgrounds. Holiday House 1985 unp il $12.95 (k-1) **796**

1. Playgrounds
ISBN 0-8234-0553-2 LC 84-19285

Gibbons, Gail—*Continued*

Introduces the various types of playground equipment, including swings, slides, and sandboxes, as well as games and toys that may be enjoyed at the playground

"Gibbons' text offers opportunities for children to extend their vocabularies and compare differences in swings, slides, climbing apparatus and sandbox tools. Bold colors and detailed captioned illustrations show children busily engaged in each of the activities while parents watch nearby. The figures and the equipment are placed against a gravelly-textured background, creating an unusual contrast. A colorful treatment of a subject familiar to young children but seldom discussed in picture book format." SLJ

Hammond, Tim

Sports; written by Tim Hammond. Knopf 1988 63p il (Eyewitness bks) $13.95; lib bdg $14.99 (4 and up) **796**

1. Sports

ISBN 0-394-89616-5; 0-394-99616-X (lib bdg) LC 88-1573

Examines the equipment, rules, and background of many different team, target, and court sports, including soccer, rugby, Gaelic football, softball, cricket, ice hockey, table tennis, archery, and pool

Aside from "minor errors, the book is both informative and eye-pleasing. While there isn't a complete explanation of the rules of each sport, readers can garner a basic understanding. The photographs used to show the technological advances in sporting equipment are a story in themselves and form the basis of the book." SLJ

Sports Illustrated for Kids. Time $15.95 per year **796**

1. Sports—Periodicals

ISSN 1042-394X

Monthly. First published 1989

This magazine features articles about young people in sports, biographies of pros, playing tips, stories and puzzles

"The excitement and tension of sports are captured in the action-filled full-color photographs and brisk writing. . . . The focus of the . . . magazine is on fun, but stories 'emphasize the importance of values such as hard work, teamwork, practice, fair play, and a positive attitude.'" Richardson. Mag for Child. 2d edition

Sportworks; more than fifty fun games and activities that explore the science of sports; from the Ontario Science Centre; illustrated by Pat Cupples. Addison-Wesley 1989 96p il $8.95 (4 and up) **796**

1. Games 2. Sports

ISBN 0-201-15296-7 LC 88-34317

The authors outline various experiments and activities with which they seek to illustrate the scientific aspects of sports

"Students interested in trivia and information on the human body, sports, and sports activities will find Sportworks entertaining and informative. . . . The suggested activities permit active involvement and experimentation with the concepts. Each spread has black-and-white sketches that entertain or visually explain the subject. . . . Topics range from checking the heart rate to parachuting and proteins." SLJ

Sullivan, George, 1927-

Any number can play; illustrated by John Caldwell. Crowell 1990 126p il $13.95; lib bdg $13.89 (3-6) **796**

1. Sports—History

ISBN 0-690-04812-2; 0-690-04814-9 (lib bdg) LC 89-35501

This is "an anecdotal book on sports uniform numbers. While its reference value may be limited, this is where readers will find the football jersey numbers of former U.S. presidents, a list of the 15 numbers retired by the Boston Celtics, and the reasons players have chosen, and refused, to wear certain numbers. Cartoon-like drawings keep the tone light, while the short chapters of one to three pages make this an easy book to pick up for a little reading." Booklist

796.03 Sports—Encyclopedias and dictionaries

Berger, Melvin, 1927-

Sports; drawings by Anne Canevari Green. Watts 1983 96p il lib bdg $10.40 (5 and up) **796.03**

1. Sports—Dictionaries 2. Athletes—Dictionaries

ISBN 0-531-04540-4 LC 82-16093

"A Reference first book"

Alphabetically arranged entries include "descriptions of sports, sports terms, outstanding players, trophies, and special sports events." Bull Cent Child Books

The author "has covered broad terms and famous athletes; thus, this title could be used to answer general sports questions when brief answers are acceptable. . . . Photographs add interest and diagrams are helpful." SLJ

Guinness book of sports records. Facts on File il $18.75; pa $12.95 **796.03**

1. Sports

First published 1972. Editors vary. Variant titles: Guinness sports record book; Guinness book of sports records, winners and & champions

Taken in part from the Guinness Book of world records, entered in class 032

This compilation presents records set in over seventy sports and games from archery to yachting, including auto racing, orienteering, pool and fishing. Material is arranged alphabetically by sport

796.1 Miscellaneous games

Bley, Edgar S.

The best singing games for children of all ages; drawings by Patt Willen, piano arrangements by Margaret Chase. Sterling 1957 96p il music hardcover o.p. paperback available $9.95 **796.1**

1. Singing games 2. Songs

ISBN 0-8069-7956-9 (pa) LC 57-13285

"More than 50 musical games, jump-rope jingles, and play party games, with words, musical scores, and directions for action. Arranged by age levels and illustrated with helpful drawings." Hodges. Books for Elem Sch Libr

Brown, Marc Tolon

Finger rhymes; collected and illustrated by Marc Brown. Dutton 1980 32p il $11.95 (k-2) **796.1**

1. Finger play 2. Nursery rhymes
ISBN 0-525-29732-4 LC 80-11492

"A Unicorn book"

Presents 14 rhymes with instructions for accompanying finger plays

Hand rhymes; collected and illustrated by Marc Brown. Dutton 1985 31p il lib bdg $12.95 (k-2) **796.1**

1. Finger play 2. Nursery rhymes
ISBN 0-525-44201-4 LC 84-25918

This collection "contains several adaptations, some new and lively material, and a few old favorites. . . . There are finger-plays about favorite domestic animals, and especially appealing is one about a caterpillar that turns into a butterfly. Each double-page spread contains the rhyme, with small but carefully detailed diagrams of the accompanying finger action and warmly colorful, amusing illustrations of fat kittens, bemused ducks, and happy children. Cozy, useful, and a pleasure to look at, the book is for those who deal with a lap-sitter as well as for the storyteller." Horn Book

Play rhymes; collected and illustrated by Marc Brown. Dutton 1987 32p il lib bdg $12.95 (k-2) **796.1**

1. Finger play 2. Nursery rhymes
ISBN 0-525-44336-3 LC 87-13537

A collection of twelve play rhymes with illustrations to demonstrate the accompanying finger plays or physical activities. Includes music for the six rhymes which are also songs

"While most of the rhymes are well-known and frequently included in other collections, there are several less familiar and delightful rhymes that parents, librarians, and teachers of the very young will want to add to their repertoire. The illustrations are full-color pastels with many small details and humorous elements to appeal to children. This is a good choice for program planning or for a rainy afternoon with a favorite child." SLJ

Clap your hands; finger rhymes; chosen by Sarah Hayes; illustrated by Toni Goffe. Lothrop, Lee & Shepard Bks. 1988 29p il $13; lib bdg $12.88 (k-2) **796.1**

1. Finger play 2. Nursery rhymes
ISBN 0-688-07692-0; 0-688-07693-9 (lib bdg) LC 87-16958

"This bouncy collection of 23 finger games includes old favorites as well as lesser-known selections. The charming cartoon-like ink and watercolor illustrations are well placed, with many single rhymes placed on double-page spreads. Children and animals are shown enacting the finger rhymes instead of using written instructions." SLJ

Eden, Maxwell

Kiteworks: explorations in kite building & flying. Sterling 1989 287p il $19.95 (5 and up) **796.1**

1. Kites
ISBN 0-8069-6712-9 LC 89-11372

"Detailing specific instructions for making a variety of kites and noting the necessary materials, the interesting text explores kite lore, kite inventors, and the philosophy and science of kite flying. Colorfully illustrated, Eden's guide includes practical advice on kite repairs, safety, and clubs and events." Booklist

Includes bibliography

Gibbons, Gail

Catch the wind! all about kites. Little, Brown 1989 unp il $12.95 (1-3) **796.1**

1. Kites
ISBN 0-316-30955-9 LC 88-28820

"Two children visit Ike's Kite Shop, where proprietor Ike is happy to tell the children about his myriad models and how to fly them. The information he dispenses includes brief bits of kite history and a description of such items as box, bowed, and compound kites. The artist's trademark pen lines and bright colors back her text, and instructions for making and flying a simple flat kite are included at the end. (Safety precautions appear here, too)." Booklist

Glazer, Tom

Do your ears hang low?: 50 more musical fingerplays; illustrated by Mila Lazarevich. Doubleday 1980 112p il $12.95 (k-3) **796.1**

1. Singing games 2. Finger play 3. Songs
ISBN 0-385-12602-6 LC 78-20072

The author presents a "set of songs with piano arrangements and guitar songs. The black and white illustrations are humorous. . . . Directions for fingerplay are included with each song. The book has enough range of sophistication to be used with very young children or to be used by older children alone or in groups." Bull Cent Child Books

Eye winker, Tom Tinker, chin chopper; fifty musical fingerplays; illustrated by Ron Himler. Doubleday 1973 91p il hardcover o.p. paperback available $11.95 (k-3) **796.1**

1. Singing games 2. Finger play 3. Songs
ISBN 0-385-08200-2 (pa) LC 72-97497

This collection of 50 songs, with piano arrangements, guitar chords and instructions for finger and body movements, "represent three distinct groups: fingerplay songs, such as 'Eentsy, Weentsy Spider'; familiar action rhymes 'newly set to music,' like 'Here Is the Church' and 'Pat-A-Cake'; and many songs—both new and traditional—set down with totally new fingerplays." Horn Book

Grayson, Marion F., 1906-1976
Let's do fingerplays; illustrated by Nancy Weyl. Luce, R.B. 1962 109p il $12.95 (k-2) **796.1**

1. Finger play
ISBN 0-88331-003-1 LC 62-10217

"Approximately 200 rhymes and songs, with directions for accompanying finger plays, are organized under such headings as Animal Antics, Counting and Counting Out, and Holidays and Special Occasions." Hodges. Books for Elem Sch Libr

Miss Mary Mack and other children's street rhymes; compiled by Joanna Cole and Stephanie Calmenson; illustrated by Alan Tiegreen. Morrow Junior Bks. 1990 64p lib bdg $11.88; pa $6.95 (1-4) **796.1**

1. Games 2. Nursery rhymes
ISBN 0-688-08330-7 (lib bdg); 0-688-09749-9 (pa) LC 89-37266

This is a collection of over 100 traditional childhood hand-clapping and street rhymes

"Tiegreen's lighthearted pen-and-ink illustrations are sure to tickle the fancy of young readers. . . . A book that's sure to produce smiles in any story hour or program." SLJ

Opie, Iona Archibald
Children's games in street and playground; by Iona and Peter Opie. Oxford Univ. Press 1969 xxvi, 371p il maps hardcover o.p. paperback available $10.95 **796.1**

1. Games 2. Folklore
ISBN 0-19-281489-3 (pa) LC 76-437542

"Chasing, catching; seeking; hunting; racing; duelling; exerting; daring; guessing; acting; pretending." Title page

"Illustrated with game diagrams and photographs. . . . This volume concerns the 'games that children, aged about 6-12, play of their own accord when out of doors, and usually out of sight.' Compared and documented both geographically and in relation to earlier lore are hundreds of examples of starting-out or counting-out rhymes, ritualistic folk dialogues, chants of chasing and catching games, and the many other categories named in the subtitle. These are helpfully indexed to make the book a useful reference work as well as fascinating reading." Horn Book

Outdoor fun; by the editors of OWL and Chickadee Magazines; edited by Catherine Ripley. Little, Brown 1990 32p il lib bdg $12.95 (1-4) **796.1**

1. Outdoor recreation
ISBN 0-316-67738-8 LC 89-63185

"Joy Street books"

This book provides "a collection of projects and activities, each presented on a double-page spread including instructions and large full-color photographs or ink-and-watercolor illustrations. . . . The ideas include scarecrow building, juggling, making sandals from newspaper, playing Inuit games, dog washing, and making a Chinese dragon costume." Booklist

"Attractive color photographs and an accessible magazine format invite readers to participate in a variety of outdoor crafts, activities, and challenges." Bull Cent Child Books

Rockwell, Anne F., 1934-
Games (and how to play them); [text and] pictures by Anne Rockwell. Crowell 1973 43p il $13.95 (k-4) **796.1**

1. Games
ISBN 0-690-32159-7 LC 72-10936

"A compendium of 43 noisy, quiet, indoor, outdoor activities." N Y Times Book Rev

"A book that can be used with younger children as well as by independent readers. The explanations are brief but clear; the pictures are often informative and always attractive with animals as characters and with intriguing details." Bull Cent Child Books

Stamp your feet; action rhymes; chosen by Sarah Hayes; illustrated by Toni Goffe. Lothrop, Lee & Shepard Bks. 1988 29p il $13; lib bdg $12.88 (k-2) **796.1**

1. Nursery rhymes 2. Games
ISBN 0-688-07694-7; 0-688-07695-5 (lib bdg) LC 87-29779

"Twenty action rhymes that are suitable for use in preschool storyhours. Pen-and-ink and watercolor drawings demonstrate possible actions to accompany the rhymes. . . . The poems are ebullient." SLJ

What shall we do and Alee galloo! play songs and singing games for young children; collected & edited by Marie Winn; musical arrangements by Allan Miller; pictures by Karla Kuskin. Harper & Row 1970 87p il music lib bdg $13.89 (k-2) **796.1**

1. Singing games 2. Songs
ISBN 0-06-026537-X LC 72-85039

These "forty-seven play games and songs, both familiar and less known, have large-print music and lyrics (piano and guitar accompaniment) and instructions for group participation." Child Books, 1970

796.2 Active games requiring equipment

Kalbfleisch, Susan
Jump! the new jump rope book; illustrations by Laurie McGugan. Morrow 1987 c1985 128p il $12.95; pa $6.95 (3-6) **796.2**

1. Rope skipping
ISBN 0-688-06929-0; 0-688-06930-4 (pa) LC 86-23578

First published 1985 in Canada with title: Skip to it!

An introduction to jumping rope with instructions for easy and advanced tricks

"An easy-to-follow primer for beginners or for practiced skippers who want to get serious about their sport." Booklist

Sullivan, George, 1927-
Better roller skating for boys and girls. Dodd, Mead 1980 64p il $9.95; pa $2.95 (4 and up) **796.2**
1. Roller skating
ISBN 0-396-07784-6; 0-396-08291-2 (pa)
LC 79-22717
The author provides basic information about roller skating, including the sport's history, equipment, techniques, advanced maneuvers and safety. There are also discussions of recreational skating, speed skating, roller skate dancing and roller skate hockey
Includes glossary

796.323 Basketball

Anderson, Dave
The story of basketball; foreword by Julius Erving. Morrow 1988 182p il $12.95; pa $8.95 (5 and up) **796.323**
1. Basketball
ISBN 0-688-06748-4; 0-688-06749-2 (pa) LC 88-6842
"Divided into two sections, the book first views basketball historically. . . . The second part of the discussion gives the important elements of the game: shooting, passing, rebounding, defensive moves, and coaching. Rather than simply explaining these fundamentals, Anderson illustrates them by citing the careers of various athletes." Booklist

Antonacci, Robert Joseph, 1916-
Basketball for young champions; [by] Robert J. Antonacci and Jene Barr; illustrated by Patti Boyd. 2d ed. McGraw-Hill 1979 183p il (Young champion ser) $10.95 (5 and up) **796.323**
1. Basketball
ISBN 0-07-002141-4 LC 78-8029
First published 1960
"Instruction in how to guard, dribble, shoot for the basket, pass and catch the basketball. Within each chapter specific shots, dribbles, passes, etc. are described as well as exercise for both solo and group use that will improve players' skills. A clearly written, detailed, and helpful guide for both boys and girls." SLJ

Boyd, Brendan C.
Hoops: behind the scenes with the Boston Celtics; photographs by Henry Horenstein; text by Brendan Boyd and Robert Garrett. Little, Brown 1989 127p il $15.95; pa $8.95 (5 and up) **796.323**
1. Boston Celtics (Basketball team) 2. Basketball
ISBN 0-316-37319-2; 0-316-37309-5 (pa)
LC 88-82539
The authors "offer readers a behind-the-scenes look at a professional basketball team, the Boston Celtics. Calling the book 'a family album,' the authors spotlight not only well-known players, but also other contributors to the team. . . . Horenstein's expressive black-and-white photographs contribute to the backstage feeling." Booklist

Sullivan, George, 1927-
Better basketball for boys. New and completely updated ed. Dodd, Mead 1980 64p il $9.95 (4 and up) **796.323**
1. Basketball
ISBN 0-396-07857-5 LC 80-1011
First published 1960 under the authorship of David C. Cooke
The author "details ball handling, passing, various shots, rebounding and offensive and defensive skills. . . . Well illustrated with lots of black-and-white photos and diagrams." SLJ
Includes glossary

Better basketball for girls. Dodd, Mead 1978 64p il lib. bdg $9.95 (4 and up) **796.323**
1. Basketball
ISBN 0-396-07580-0 LC 78-7732
"Sullivan gives a brief history of women's basketball in the United States, makes some suggestions for getting in condition and choosing sneakers, and launches into a skill-by-skill explanation of techniques and skills (various passes, various shots, screening, getting free, etc.) and concludes with several chapters on team defense and defensive play." Bull Cent Child Books
Includes glossary

796.332 American football

Anderson, Dave
The story of football; foreword by O.J. Simpson. Morrow 1985 196p il lib bdg $13.95; pa $8.95 (5 and up) **796.332**
1. Football
ISBN 0-688-05634-2 (lib bdg); 0-688-05635-0 (pa)
LC 85-7195
"After a solid historical background centered around the personalities who forwarded the game from the late nineteenth century, this overview proceeds through chapters on each position, its functions and moves, and its best representatives. Here Anderson proves particularly adept at moving from one great name to the next in a telling pattern instead of a hodgepodge. . . . Intelligent coverage for fans and players alike." Bull Cent Child Books

Madden, John
The first book of football. Crown 1988 90p il $10.95 (5 and up) **796.332**
1. Football
ISBN 0-517-56981-7 LC 87-37981
"Combining anecdotes with the nitty-gritty of the discipline, Madden describes how football is played and introduces the offense, defense, and specialty teams. Using diagrams, he explains how to play the game better, and even how to watch a game with an eye toward improving skills. . . . A good mix of down-home wisdom and cagey advice. . . . Illustrated with photographs and diagrams." Booklist

Sullivan, George, 1927-
All about football. Dodd, Mead 1987 128p il $10.95; pa $6.95 (4 and up) **796.332**
1. Football
ISBN 0-396-09095-8; 0-399-21907-2 (pa)
LC 87-17383

The author explains the game of football: "how it is played, the various playing positions, basic offensive and defensive strategy. There is a bit of football history, a close-up look at the field and equipment, and an explanation of competition at the different levels, with various conferences, leagues, and ruling bodies defined. . . . [Players] including Joe Namath, O.J. Simpson, Roger Staubach, and Jim Brown, are profiled." Publisher's note

Includes glossary

Better football for boys. New and completely updated ed. Dodd, Mead 1980 64p il $9.95; pa $2.95 (4 and up) **796.332**
1. Football
ISBN 0-396-07843-5; 0-396-08241-6 (pa)
LC 80-12597

First published 1958 under the authorship of David C. Cooke

The author covers the basics: passing, punting, kicking, blocking, and tackling. Illustrated with black-and-white photos and diagrams

Includes glossary

Quarterback; illustrated with photographs by the author and line drawings by Don Madden. Crowell 1982 50p il $11.95 (4 and up) **796.332**
1. Football
ISBN 0-690-04241-8 LC 81-43889

Discusses what it takes to become a quarterback, how to train with weights, how to pass and handle the ball, and how to improve one's performance

"Beginning quarterbacks will find a host of tips and lots of advice for successful plays in this slim introduction to the position. Sullivan defines just what it is the quarterback does, lists 'what it takes,' and then offers a systematic approach for developing the necessary skills. There's humor in the squiggly cartoon drawings, but it is the generous selection of black-and-white photographs that offer the most constructive illustration." Booklist

796.334 Soccer

Dolan, Edward F., 1924-
Starting soccer; a handbook for boys & girls; photographs by Jameson C. Goldner. Harper & Row 1976 114p il $5.95; Wilshire Publs. pa $5 (5 and up) **796.334**
ISBN 0-06-021682-4; 0-87980-352-5 (pa) LC 76-3838

Divided into three main sections (The Basics, Game Time and Building Your Skills), this book covers such specifics as kicking, rules and the different playing positions, along with practice mini-games and warm-up exercises

The book is "well illustrated with black-and-white photographs." Booklist

Jackson, C. Paul (Caary Paul), 1902-
How to play better soccer; illustrated by Don Madden. Crowell 1978 147p il lib bdg $12.89 (4 and up) **796.334**
1. Soccer
ISBN 0-690-03828-3 LC 76-51450

The author "gives a history of the game, and explains the rules and techniques. . . . Team play and position play are lucidly described and the diagrams illustrating them are well-placed and adequately labelled. A chart of official signals, a glossary, and an index are appended." Bull Cent Child Books

Sullivan, George, 1927-
Better soccer for boys and girls. Dodd, Mead 1978 64p il $10.99 (4 and up) **796.334**
1. Soccer
ISBN 0-399-61232-7 LC 77-16869

The author "describes the way the game is played, explains the rules, includes a quiz to make sure the reader understands them, and gives detailed advice on each aspect of play." Bull Cent Child Books

Includes glossary

796.342 Tennis

Sullivan, George, 1927-
Better tennis for boys and girls. Dodd, Mead 1987 62p il $10.99 (4 and up) **796.342**
1. Tennis
ISBN 0-399-61264-5 LC 86-29123

"An overview of rules, scoring, equipment, strokes, and terms for beginners. The difference between the grip for the forehand and backhand is difficult to see from the photographs, but generally the good quality photographs and diagrams clearly depict aspects of the game. Terms are defined within the text as well as in a glossary of terms at the back. Safety is minimally presented." SLJ

796.357 Baseball

Appel, Martin, 1948-
The first book of baseball. Crown 1988 95p il lib bdg $9.95 (4-6) **796.357**
1. Baseball
ISBN 0-517-56726-1 LC 88-47653

"Basic rules of play and tips on batting and pitching strategies precede a break-down of what goes on during the professional season from the spring-training camps and minor-league farm teams' first exercises through the off-season award announcements and Hall of Fame election. A yearly rundown of significant events digests baseball history, providing readers with an overview of important players and a background of the game's development." Booklist

Arnow, Jan, 1947-
Louisville Slugger; the making of a baseball bat; written and photographed by Jan Arnow. Pantheon Bks. 1984 39p il $11.95; lib bdg $12.99 (4 and up) **796.357**

1. Baseball—Equipment and supplies
ISBN 0-394-86297-X; 0-394-96297-4 (lib bdg)
LC 84-7049

"A step-by-step fascinating account of the making of a professional baseball bat from the search for the right ash tree, to its final shaping by hand, to the specifications of each individual player. Profusely illustrated with full-page black and white photographs, this book makes the process come alive and tells children about an artifact still made with pride." Soc Educ

Grosshandler, Henry
Everyone wins at tee ball; [by] Henry and Janet Grosshandler. Cobblehill Bks. 1990 unp il lib bdg $12.95 (k-3) **796.357**

1. Baseball
ISBN 0-525-65016-4 LC 89-7875

This "book introduces youngsters to the basic rules and skills of a game that is similar to baseball but styled for players too young to hit a pitched ball. . . . The format, with large type and few sentences on each page, will enable some players to read the book independently, but the main audience is a slightly younger child." Booklist

Jaspersohn, William
Bat, ball, glove; the making of major league baseball gear. Little, Brown 1989 93p il $14.95 (3-5) **796.357**

1. Baseball—Equipment and supplies
ISBN 0-316-45820-1 LC 88-27198

"The process that the Rawlings Sporting Goods Company uses to make and deliver gloves, baseballs, uniforms, and bats to major league players is told in this informative and fun-to-read book. The book is loaded with entertaining details and interviews with those who make, market, and use Rawlings gear (including Ozzie Smith, Vince Coleman, and Darryl Strawberry). . . . Crisp black-and-white photographs fill nearly every page and couldn't be better at explaining the text." SLJ

Kalb, Jonah
The easy baseball book; illustrated by Sandy Kossin. Houghton Mifflin 1976 49p il $14.95 (3-5) **796.357**

1. Baseball
ISBN 0-395-24385-8 LC 75-44085

In short simple sentences, the author "gives directions for hitting . . . as well as fielding and pitching. The basic directions for each skill are followed by sections on common mistakes and practice tips." SLJ

Kreutzer, Peter
Little League's official how-to-play baseball book; [by] Peter Kreutzer and Ted Kerley; illustrated by Alexander Verbitsky. Doubleday 1990 210p il $19.95; pa $12.95 (4 and up) **796.357**

1. Little League Baseball, Inc. 2. Baseball
ISBN 0-385-41227-4; 0-385-41278-9 (pa)
LC 89-28097

The "contents include gripping, throwing, and catching the ball; hitting; bunting; base running; sliding; pitching; defensive positioning; fitness; and warm-ups. . . . An added bonus is the inclusion of the Official Little League playing rules." Voice Youth Advocates

This book "provides sound advice on the strategy of playing various positions in the field as well as the basics of hitting. . . . A useful resource for players willing to work at improving their skills." Booklist

Ritter, Lawrence S.
The story of baseball; foreword by Ted Williams. rev ed. Morrow 1990 210p il $13.95; pa $8.95 (5 and up) **796.357**

1. Baseball
ISBN 0-688-09056-7; 0-688-09057-5 (pa)
LC 89-48952

First published 1983

This illustrated history focuses on the stars of the game. Discussions of batting, pitching, fielding, base running, and strategy are included

Sullivan, George, 1927-
The art of base-stealing. Dodd, Mead 1982 126p il $11.95 (5 and up) **796.357**

1. Baseball
ISBN 0-396-08040-5 LC 81-17430

"The rise and decline of stealing bases is traced through baseball history to give the reader a perspective on the careers of those whose skills have made the record books. . . . Sullivan's detailed discussion and statistics focus on techniques used by Ty Cobb, Max Carey, Lou Brock, and others. The numerous black-and-white photographs and drawings, many from early baseball history, complement a text that increases appreciation for the moves required and gives young players tips on how to watch the pitcher and improve their own stealing." Booklist

Baseball kids. Cobblehill Bks. 1990 96p il $13.95 (4 and up) **796.357**

1. Baseball
ISBN 0-525-65023-7 LC 89-29102

"Sullivan presents profiles of individual players on two Little League teams. . . . Following a brief introduction, each of the 12 chapters looks at a particular Little Leaguer, how he developed an interest in playing the game, and the nuances of various playing positions and batting styles." SLJ

"The writing is clear and interesting, and on the theory that kids learn well from their peers, this book may succeed in teaching some fundamentals and finer points of the game." Booklist

Includes glossary

Sullivan, George, 1927-—*Continued*

Better baseball for boys. new and completely updated ed. Dodd, Mead 1981 63p il lib bdg $9.95; pa $2.95 (4 and up) **796.357**

1. Baseball
ISBN 0-396-07912-1 (lib bdg); 0-396-08288-2 (pa) LC 80-22022

First published 1959 under the authorship of David C. Cooke

The author provides "tips on running, hitting, throwing, and fielding in such a way that the reader becomes familiar with the game and not inundated with useless facts and trivia." Voice Youth Advocates

Pitcher; illustrated with photographs by the author and line drawings by Don Madden. Crowell 1986 53p il lib bdg $11.89 (3-6) **796.357**

1. Baseball
ISBN 0-690-04539-5 LC 85-47939

"Aiming at Little League players, Sullivan focuses on the essential skills young pitchers must master to refine and improve their game. He provides practical tips on warming up, delivery, grip, developing control, and pitching strategy with black-and-white sequence photographs of pitchers in action. . . . Sullivan's text is honed to a compact style—one that is informative and accessible to young pitchers needing simple guidance in learning the basics correctly. Madden's line drawings add a humorous, light touch." Booklist

796.4 Weight lifting, track and field, gymnastics

McMane, Fred

Track & field basics; illustrated by Art Seiden; photographs by Jacob Brown; created and produced by Arvid Knudsen. Prentice-Hall 1983 48p il (Sports basics bks) $9.95 (4 and up) **796.4**

1. Track athletics
ISBN 0-13-925966-X LC 82-21458

The author "lays out 'Track & Field Basics' in terms of rules, proper training and a description of various events. The text is supplemented by above-average photos and diagrams. Each event is given only two or three pages of attention but for what it is—an introduction to the basics—this book does an adequate job." SLJ

796.44 Sports gymnastics

Krementz, Jill

A very young gymnast; written and photographed by Jill Krementz. Knopf 1978 unp il hardcover o.p.; Dell paperback available $6.95 (3-6) **796.44**

1. Gymnastics
ISBN 0-440-49213-0 (pa) LC 78-5502

"The author-photographer accompanied ten-year-old Torrance York, aspiring Olympic gymnast, through a year's worth of training and competition. . . . [The book explores] every aspect of the sport, from the endless practices—sometimes fun, sometimes frustrating—to the always exciting competitions." Horn Book

This "is a beautifully photographed, expertly produced study of a young athlete." SLJ

Murdock, Tony

Gymnastics; [by] Tony Murdock and Nik Stuart; foreword by Elena Shoushounova. rev ed. Watts 1989 112p il lib bdg $13.40 (4 and up) **796.44**

1. Gymnastics
ISBN 0-531-10770-1 LC 89-8870

First published 1980

The book provides a step-by-step approach to gymnastics and includes sections on equipment, conditioning, floor exercise techniques, and various routines. A final chapter details the careers of several Olympic medalists

796.47 Acrobatics, tumbling, trampolining, contortion

Schmidt, Diane

I am a Jesse White tumbler; text and photographs by Diane Schmidt. Whitman, A. 1990 unp il lib bdg $13.95 **796.47**

1. Conner, Kenyon 2. Jesse White Tumbling Team 3. Acrobats and acrobatics
ISBN 0-8075-3444-7 LC 89-16590

Kenyon Conner, an eighth-grader from Chicago, tells of his life with the Jesse White Tumbling Team, a program designed to help inner city young people complete school and avoid drugs and crime. Text and photographs describe the team's acrobatic performances

This is "an honest and unaffected narrative. . . . Unlike many glamorous photodocumentaries, this does not gloss over the discipline of performing on the hot streets during a street fair or a freezing field during the intermission of a football game." Bull Cent Child Books

796.48 Olympic games

Glubok, Shirley

Olympic games in ancient Greece; by Shirley Glubok and Alfred Tamarin. Harper & Row 1976 116p il lib bdg $13.89 (5 and up) **796.48**

1. Olympic games 2. Civilization, Greek
ISBN 0-06-022048-1 (lib bdg) LC 75-25408

"The authors take a systematic look at the ancient Greek Olympics around 400 B.C. . . . The subsequent narrative describes the pageantry and the competitions, many of which have come down to us in modern form while others, such as chariot races and the race in armor, have passed out of existence. Bits of Greek history influencing the games, recorded anecdotes, and legends add color to the account." Booklist

796.6 Cycling and related activities

Sullivan, George, 1927-

Better bicycling for boys and girls. New and completely updated ed. Dodd, Mead 1984 64p il hardcover o.p. paperback available $2.95 (4 and up) **796.6**

1. Bicycles and bicycling

ISBN 0-396-08479-6 (pa) LC 84-13650

First published 1974

"Sullivan provides a brief history and background of the popularity of bike riding, touring, and competition. . . . Bike selection, safety, and techniques are discussed as well as mechanical parts, gear ratios, accessories, maintenance, and repair. Sharp, clear black-and-white photographs are well placed within a text that is reliable [and] comprehensive." Booklist

Includes glossary

Better BMX riding and racing for boys and girls; illustrated with photographs and diagrams. Dodd, Mead 1984 64p il $9.95 (4 and up) **796.6**

1. Bicycle racing

ISBN 0-396-08331-5 LC 83-25440

This book is intended "for beginning BMXers. The excitement of a bicycle motocross race is proclaimed in the first chapter. Careful detailing of the history of the sport, basics of selecting BMX machine parts or preassembled bicycles, racing gears and basic racing and freestyle (stunt) techniques assure aspiring racers a good start in the sport. Readers are then led through a meet and provided with simple bicycle maintenance procedures. Throughout, clear and well-captioned black-and-white photographs and diagrams enhance the crisp style of the text." SLJ

796.8 Combat sports

Brimner, Larry Dane

Karate. Watts 1988 71p il lib bdg $10.40 (5 and up) **796.8**

1. Karate

ISBN 0-531-10480-X LC 87-25341

"A First book"

"Briefly surveying the development of karate styles, the author stresses developing disciplined, controlled power by progressive mastery of moves from white- to black-belt level. Mixed quality black-and-white photographs accompany the descriptions of stances, kicks, punches, and combinations, but the text provides a clear, concise survey of the sport and guidance in preparing for formal instruction." Booklist

Includes bibliography

Kozuki, Russell

Junior karate; photographs by the author. Sterling 1971 128p il $11.95; lib bdg $14.49 (5 and up) **796.8**

1. Karate

ISBN 0-8069-4446-3; 0-8069-4447-1 (lib bdg) LC 71-167665

Instructions for basic karate exercises, stances, blocking techniques, strikes, kicks, and contests. Illustrated with photographs

Nardi, Thomas J.

Karate basics; photographs by David J. Garr; drawings by Michael Petronella; created and produced by Arvid Knudsen. Prentice-Hall 1984 48p il (Sports basics bks) $10.95 (4 and up) **796.8**

1. Karate

ISBN 0-13-514548-1 LC 84-6929

"Nardi explains karate clearly, from its philosophical and historical background to the basic physical techniques and training. A full range of information is offered, in fairly small print, with most instructions accompanied by black-and-white photographs." SLJ

Ribner, Susan

The martial arts; by Susan Ribner and Richard Chin; drawings by Melanie Arwin. Harper & Row 1978 181p il lib bdg $12.89; pa $4.95 (5 and up) **796.8**

1. Martial arts

ISBN 0-06-025000-3 (lib bdg); 0-06-440139-1 (pa) LC 76-58713

"A general introduction to the martial arts, this provides information about the lesser known types such as kendo as well as karate, judo, etc. Wisely, the authors have not attempted to write a 'how to' manual. They concentrate on the principles behind each form, its history, and underlying philosophy." SLJ

Sullivan, George, 1927-

Better wrestling for boys. Dodd, Mead 1986 63p il $10.99 (4 and up) **796.8**

1. Wrestling

ISBN 0-399-61237-8 LC 85-20740

Discusses the history, weight classes, equipment, moves, and holds of boys' wrestling and explains how a match is scored and how team competition works

"The author accompanies his clear description of the various holds, maneuvers, and combinations with black-and-white photographic sequences that help clarify the text. A glossary is appended." Booklist

796.91 Ice skating

Krementz, Jill

A very young skater; written and photographed by Jill Krementz. Knopf 1979 unp il hardcover o.p.; Dell paperback available $6.95 (3-6) **796.91**

1. Healy, Katherine 2. Ice skating
ISBN 0-440-49214-9 (pa) LC 79-2209

"Illustrated with photographs in black and white, featuring a confident ten-year-old for whom skating is the hub of existence. Written in the first person, the brief text is an introduction to the various facets of Katherine Healey's life: her home, school, family, friends and, above all, the world of skating—practice sessions, competitions, and ice shows. . . . Although the search for perfection is not minimized, the emphasis is on triumph rather than on trials." Horn Book

MacLean, Norman

Ice skating basics; illustrations by Bill Gow with photographs; created and produced by Arvid Knudsen. Prentice-Hall 1984 47p il (Sports basics bks) $9.95 (4 and up) **796.91**

1. Ice skating
ISBN 0-13-448762-1 LC 84-6933

An introduction to the basic techniques of ice skating with information on equipment, exercises, and training for competitions

"The author's enthusiasm for his subject is evident throughout the book. Maneuvers are clearly explained in conversational tone and the drawings are a great help." SLJ

796.93 Skiing

Krementz, Jill

A very young skier; written and photographed by Jill Krementz. Dial Bks. for Young Readers 1990 unp il $14.95; lib bdg $14.89 (3-6) **796.93**

1. Cimino, Stephanie 2. Skis and skiing
ISBN 0-8037-0821-1; 0-8037-0823-8 (lib bdg) LC 89-28760

"Stephanie Cimino, the attractive nine-year-old subject of this profile, lives in Sun Valley, Idaho, where she competes in both downhill and cross-country ski events. . . . [This book follows] her through scenes at home and on the slopes as she explains the fitting and use of skis and poles, basic procedures in skiing, her various lessons, and assorted recreational and racing experiences." Horn Book

796.962 Ice hockey

Kalb, Jonah

The easy hockey book; illustrated by Bill Morrison. Houghton Mifflin 1977 64p il $13.95 (3-5) **796.962**

1. Ice hockey
ISBN 0-395-25842-1 LC 77-9917

"This is not, the author states firmly, a book intended to teach readers to play hockey, but a compilation of advice on individual aspects of the game (skating forward, skating backward, passing, shooting, and the most common mistakes in all of these) so that the reader can be a better player. . . . It doesn't give game rules, but it does discuss equipment." Bull Cent Child Books

MacLean, Norman

Hockey basics; introduction by Emile Francis; illustrated by Bill Gow; photography by Con Roach; created and produced by Arvid Knudsen. Prentice-Hall 1983 48p il (Sports basics bks) $10.95 (4 and up) **796.962**

1. Ice hockey
ISBN 0-13-392506-4 LC 83-9451

The author "discusses the sport's history, equipment used and fundamentals of play. Offensive and defensive plays, as well as the role of the goal tender, are explained and penalties are listed. . . . Diagrams, drawings and photographs help provide readers with more of an understanding of the text." SLJ

Solomon, Chuck

Playing hockey. Crown 1990 unp il $9.95; lib bdg $10.99 (2-4) **796.962**

1. Ice hockey
ISBN 0-517-57414-4; 0-517-57415-2 (lib bdg) LC 89-1031

Follows, in text and photographs, young ice hockey players as they practice and play on outdoor ponds in city leagues

"Not long on information, the brief text and full-color photographs mainly capture the mood of kids playing hockey." Booklist

797.1 Boating

Moran, Tom, 1943-

Canoeing is for me; photographs by Robert L. Wolfe. Lerner Publs. 1984 47p il (Sports for me bks) lib bdg $8.95 (3-5) **797.1**

1. Canoes and canoeing
ISBN 0-8225-1142-8 LC 83-19957

"Brothers Adam and John Paul describe what happens when they first learn how to use a canoe properly. It's a fairly simple lesson: how to enter a canoe, the terminology of its parts, how to paddle and steer and how to carry a canoe on land (get help). There's also a warning to always use a personal flotation device (formerly

Moran, Tom, 1943-—*Continued*
called a life jacket)." SLJ
Includes glossary

797.2 Swimming and diving

McGovern, Ann
Night dive; photographs by Martin Scheiner and James B. Scheiner. Macmillan 1984 56p il $14.95 (3-5) **797.2**
1. Scuba diving 2. Marine biology
ISBN 0-02-765710-8 LC 84-7163
"This first-person narrative recounts the story of a 12-year-old girl's first night-diving adventures in the Caribbean. Beautiful color photographs illustrate this absorbing science story and document the narrator's underwater experiences with such ocean denizens as the octopus and the shark." Sci Child

Sullivan, George, 1927-
Better swimming for boys and girls; with photographs by Ann Hagen Griffiths. Dodd, Mead 1982 63p il lib bdg $9.95 (4 and up) **797.2**
1. Swimming
ISBN 0-396-08071-5 LC 82-4992
"Essentially what Sullivan offers is efficient description of swimming's basic strokes and turns, explaining how they're properly done and providing photo sequences that demonstrate swimmers performing the strokes from start to finish. Attractively designed and simply written, this is useful as a primer for beginners or as ready review for the more accomplished swimmer who may be interested in competitive swimming." Booklist
Includes glossary

797.5 Air sports

Sullivan, George, 1927-
The Thunderbirds; illustrated with photographs. Dodd, Mead 1986 64p il $12.95 (4 and up) **797.5**
1. United States. Air Force. Thunderbirds 2. Aeronautics, Military
ISBN 0-396-08787-6 LC 86-6259
Describes the operation of the U.S. Air Force's crack aerial demonstration squadron, the Thunderbirds, including the team's history, selection and training of pilots, and planning and executing a show
The book is "nicely organized, with a good index and outstanding color photographs. The text is clear and honest and will have a definite appeal for airplane lovers." SLJ

798.2 Horsemanship

Krementz, Jill
A very young rider; written and photographed by Jill Krementz. Knopf 1977 unp il $8.95 (3-6) **798.2**
1. Malloy, Vivi 2. Horseback riding
ISBN 0-394-41092-0 LC 77-74996
In this photo-essay, "Krementz follows ten-year-old Vivi Malloy who owns her own horse and, with her sister, competes in major regional horse shows. Vivi is seen performing the daily tasks of mucking out stables, grooming and exercising her pony, and taking riding lessons, as well as going through the exacting but exciting routines of horse show competition." SLJ

799.1 Fishing

Arnosky, Jim
Flies in the water, fish in the air: a personal introduction to fly fishing. Lothrop, Lee & Shepard Bks. 1986 96p il $12.95 (5 and up) **799.1**
1. Fly casting
ISBN 0-688-05834-5 LC 84-29684
An anecdotal account of the pleasures of fly fishing, discussing the choice and use of tackle, kinds of flies, walking in water, and watching for fish
"This book is a hybrid. Coupled with a how-to manual on fly fishing is a naturalist's exploration of freshwater streams and ponds and their inhabitants. . . . The author's delightful, intricately detailed black-and-white drawings complement the clear, informative prose." Appraisal

Freshwater fish & fishing; illustrated by the author. Four Winds Press 1982 63p il $10.95 (4 and up) **799.1**
1. Fishing 2. Fishes
ISBN 0-02-705850-6 LC 81-12520
"This beginners' guide focuses on trout, sunfish, perch and pike, catfish and carp—both descriptions of the fish and their habitat and sound, practical fishing advice, including easy step-by-step instructions for making your own flies, cork popping bugs, and rubber tails for spoon lures." SLJ

800 LITERATURE AND RHETORIC

803 Literature—Encyclopedias and dictionaries

Brewer's dictionary of phrase and fable; by Ivor H. Evans. Harper & Row $35 **803**
1. Literature—Dictionaries 2. Allusions
First published 1870
A collection of more than "20,000 terms, phrases, names of real, fictitious and mythical characters from world history, the arts, science and fable; slang supersti-

Brewer's dictionary of phrase and fable— *Continued*
tions, and customs ancient and contemporary; etymological information." N Y Public Libr. Ref Books for Child Collect

808 Rhetoric

Asher, Sandy, 1942-
Where do you get your ideas? helping young writers begin; illustrated by Susan Hellard. Walker & Co. 1987 88p il $12.95; lib bdg $13.85 (5 and up) **808**

1. Authorship
ISBN 0-8027-6690-0; 0-8027-6691-9 (lib bdg)
LC 86-28258

In this manual featuring quotes from well-known children's authors, "Asher makes many of the usual suggestions—keep a journal, listen in on conversations—but she also includes much more: exercises . . . , ideas on ways to structure a written piece, and a bibliography." Booklist

"Amusing black-and-white drawings accompany the light but informative text. . . . Teachers and librarians who wish to promote creative writing will find this a useful tool." SLJ

Wild words! how to train them to tell stories; illustrated by Dennis Kendrick. Walker & Co. 1989 110p il $13.95; lib bdg $14.85 (5 and up) **808**

1. Authorship
ISBN 0-8027-6887-3; 0-8027-6888-1 (lib bdg)
LC 89-5692

Presents advice for budding writers on how to put ideas down on paper in language that is expressive and literate, how to bring characters to life, how to line up a plot, and how to polish the final product

"Pen-and-ink cartoon sketches enliven the book, which will be of most use when introduced by an enthusiastic teacher. A final chapter suggests many other books whose aim is to improve writing." Booklist

Includes bibliography

Benjamin, Carol Lea
Writing for kids. Crowell 1985 102p il lib bdg $12.89; pa $4.95 (4 and up) **808**

1. English language—Composition and exercises 2. Authorship
ISBN 0-690-04490-9 (lib bdg); 0-06-446012-6 (pa)
LC 85-42831

An introduction to writing discussing such aspects as how to get ideas as well as how to work from sentence to paragraph to finished story or essay

"Photos and illustrations are exhibited as food-for-writing or follow-up enhancement. Browsers can pick and choose what appeals to them at the moment, from ways of making and using blank books to getting carried away by the quotes that open up the chapters. Simple without being simplistic, sound without being heavy, orderly without being locked into a sequence, this is a great choice for public and school libraries as well as for homes." SLJ

Brandt, Sue R., 1916-
How to write a report; illustrated by Anne Canevari Green. rev ed. Watts 1986 94p il lib bdg $10.40 (4 and up) **808**

1. Report writing
ISBN 0-531-10216-5 LC 86-9056

"A First book"

Revised edition with new illustrations of a title published in 1968

Step-by-step instructions for writing a report, including choosing and understanding the subject, building a bibliography, taking notes, outlining, and writing the final draft

"On the whole, this worthwhile revision is a well-written, well-organized introduction to a subject that too many students learn by trial and error." Booklist

Cassedy, Sylvia, 1930-1989
In your own words; a beginner's guide to writing. rev ed. Crowell 1990 219p $13.95; lib bdg $13.89; HarperCollins Pubs. pa $7.95 (6 and up) **808**

1. Authorship 2. English language—Composition and exercises 3. Poetics
ISBN 0-690-04821-1; 0-690-04823-8 (lib bdg); 0-06-446102-5 (pa) LC 89-78079

First published 1979 by Doubleday

This guide to creative writing includes the fundamentals of writing myths, science fiction, ghost stories, essays, school reports, and poetry

Includes bibliographic references

Mischel, Florence
How to write a letter; by Florence D. Mischel; illustrated by Anne Canevari Green. rev ed. Watts 1988 90p il lib bdg $10.40 (5 and up) **808**

1. Letter writing
ISBN 0-531-10587-3 LC 88-10263

"A First book"

Revised edition of: The first book of letter writing, by Helen Jacobson and Florence Mischel, published 1957

Discusses the importance of letter writing as a means of prompt and in-depth communication, from sharing experiences with family and friends to expressing opinions to government officials and others. Includes advice on writing business and friendly letters and information on postage, punctuation, and addresses

808.06 Writing children's literature

Hunter, Mollie, 1922-
Talent is not enough; Mollie Hunter on writing for children. Harper & Row 1976 126p hardcover o.p. paperback available $9.95 **808.06**

1. Authorship 2. Children's literature—Technique
ISBN 0-06-446105-X (pa) LC 76-3841

Hunter, Mollie, 1922-—*Continued*

In this book based on a series of lectures delivered in 1975, the author "speaks succinctly and wittily about the demanding, satisfying craft of writing. Her remarks include personal feelings and rich interpretations of historical fiction, fantasy, and folklore." Booklist

Includes bibliography

808.8 Literature—Collections

Bauer, Caroline Feller, 1935-

Celebrations; read-aloud holiday and theme book programs; drawings by Lynn Gates Bredeson. Wilson, H.W. 1985 301p il $40 **808.8**

1. Holidays 2. Literature—Collected works 3. Books and reading 4. Children's libraries

ISBN 0-8242-0708-4 LC 85-714

"Aimed at librarians and other adults who work with middle-grade children, this book offers a potpourri of ideas and suggestions for planning holiday programs. Each chapter focuses on a holiday—some well known, some concocted by Bauer—and includes prose [and poetry] selections, activities, and a booklist." Booklist

The **Family** read-aloud Christmas treasury; selected by Alice Low; illustrated by Marc Brown. Little, Brown 1989 136p il $17.95 **808.8**

1. Christmas 2. Literature—Collected works

ISBN 0-316-53371-8 LC 89-83826

"Joy Street books"

"Over 50 excerpts or abridgments from well-known children's books by such authors as Beverly Cleary, Carolyn Haywood, Russell Hoban, and Jane Thayer; poetry old and new; plus words to a few holiday carols grace this collection with humor and heart. The book is indespensible for librarians and teachers searching for holiday pieces of various lengths and weights to read aloud to a variety of ages. Brown's exuberant watercolors add warmth and good spirits for laptime and story hour listeners." SLJ

Halloween: stories and poems; edited by Caroline Feller Bauer; illustrated by Peter Sis. Lippincott 1989 78p il $11.95; lib bdg $11.89 (2-4) **808.8**

1. Halloween 2. Literature—Collected works

ISBN 0-397-32300-X; 0-397-32301-8 (lib bdg) LC 88-2675

"Most of the stories and poems in [this] . . . anthology concern spooky happenings suitable for reading on Halloween though not directly related to the holiday. . . . While many of the selections are readily available elsewhere, this anthology is a good choice for libraries needing more books of spooky stories and poems." Booklist

Includes bibliography

Herds of thunder, manes of gold; a collection of horse stories and poems; compiled and edited by Bruce Coville; illustrated by Ted Lewin. Doubleday 1989 176p il $15.95 (4 and up) **808.8**

1. Horses—Fiction 2. Literature—Collected works

ISBN 0-385-24642-0 LC 88-34651

A collection of seventeen stories, poems, and excerpts from books about horses, by well-known authors over several centuries

"Although the contents can be found elsewhere, this collection is exceptionally well chosen and illustrated beautifully with paintings in full color that celebrate the horse. A very nice compilation, attractively illustrated and designed." Horn Book

The **Laugh** book; a new treasury of humor for children; compiled by Joanna Cole and Stephanie Calmenson; drawings by Marylin Hafner. Doubleday 1986 302p il $15.95 (4-6) **808.8**

1. Literature—Collected works 2. Wit and humor

ISBN 0-385-18559-6 LC 85-13113

"Jokes, riddles, tongue twisters, knock-knocks, limericks, puzzles, and games. Also included are nonsense poems by . . . Shel Silverstein, Lewis Carroll, Edward Lear, and Ogden Nash." Publisher's note

Rainy day: stories and poems; edited by Caroline Feller Bauer; illustrated by Michele Chessare. Lippincott 1986 74p il $13.95; lib bdg $13.89 (2-4) **808.8**

1. Literature—Collected works

ISBN 0-397-32104-X; 0-397-32105-8 (lib bdg) LC 85-45170

"Three tall tales—'Cloudy with a Chance of Meatballs' (contemporary), 'The Jolly Tailor' (Polish), and 'When the Rain Came Up from China' (Paul Bunyan) are bolstered with 23 short poems, a double-page spread of sayings, one of 'rainy day facts,' and a few suggested activities. Black-and-white wash drawings (sometimes monotonous) illustrate almost every page in a young format suitable for a picture-book audience as well as good primary readers." Bull Cent Child Books

Includes bibliography

The **Read-aloud** treasury; compiled by Joanna Cole and Stephanie Calmenson; illustrated by Ann Schweninger. Doubleday 1988 255p il $17.95 (k-2) **808.8**

1. Literature—Collected works

ISBN 0-385-18560-X LC 86-24138

An illustrated collection of classic and modern nursery rhymes, poems, stories, and activity games

"A lively and surprisingly inclusive treasury. . . . Some of the most valuable items include five stories reprinted with their original illustrations: 'Little Bear Goes to the Moon' from *Little Bear, Sylvester and the Magic Pebble, Angus and the Cat, Corduroy* and 'The Very Tall Mouse and the Very Short Mouse' from *Mouse Tales*. . . . Schweninger's full-color illustrations complement and enhance the positive and inviting tone of this collection." Publ Wkly

The **Scott,** Foresman anthology of children's literature; [collected by] Zena Sutherland, Myra Cohn Livingston. Scott, Foresman 1984 xxi, 1002p il $50 **808.8**

1. Literature—Collected works
ISBN 0-673-15527-7 LC 83-17194

Successor to: The Arbuthnot anthology of children's literature, 4th edition (1976) compiled by May Hill Arbuthnot and others and revised by Zena Sutherland

An anthology of nursery rhymes, poetry, folk literature, fantasy, realistic fiction, historical fiction, biography, and nonfiction. Also includes a list of major books, a list of highlights in the history and development of children's literature, and essays for adults working with children

Snowy day: stories and poems; edited by Caroline Feller Bauer; illustrated by Margot Tomes. Lippincott 1986 68p il lib bdg $12.89 (2-4) **808.8**

1. Literature—Collected works
ISBN 0-397-32177-5 LC 85-45858

This collection "features three short stories—Uchida's Japanese 'New Year's Hats for the Statues,' Singer's Jewish 'The Snow in Chelm,' and Bauer's adaptation of the Russian 'Marika the Snowmaiden.' The 28 poems include selections by X. J. Kennedy, Gwendolyn Brooks, David McCord, Lilian Moore, Dennis Lee, Kaye Starbird, John Ciardi, Myra Cohn Livingston, Karla Kuskin, and others." Bull Cent Child Books

"Margot Tomes's charming, evocative, black-and-white illustrations of snowflakes and leafless trees, sleds, and snowballs add the perfect touch to a wintry treat." Horn Book

Includes bibliography

Windy day: stories and poems; edited by Caroline Feller Bauer; illustrated by Dirk Zimmer. Lippincott 1988 74p il $12.95; lib bdg $12.89 (2-4) **808.8**

1. Literature—Collected works
ISBN 0-397-32207-0; 0-397-32208-9 (lib bdg)
LC 86-42994

"Twenty-nine poems, three stories, two fact pages, and a page of craft ideas pretty much cover the subject. . . . Familiar children's poets such as Jack Prelutsky, Lillian Moore, and Felice Holman are included, as well as poets such as William Carlos Williams, usually only accessible via adult poetry collections. The stories include a Chinese folk tale, an original tale by Christian Garrison, and a rollicking story by Ruth Park. Dirk Zimmer's black-and-white drawings have depth, detail, and humor and add much to the collection." SLJ

Includes bibliography

808.81 Poetry—Collections

The **Baby's** bedtime book; [compiled and illustrated by] Kay Chorao. Dutton 1984 64p il $13.95 (k-1) **808.81**

1. Poetry—Collected works 2. Nursery rhymes 3. Lullabies
ISBN 0-525-44149-2 LC 84-6067

This collection includes traditional rhymes, lullabies and prayers ("Now I lay me down to sleep") and poems by authors including Blake, Kipling, Tennyson, Rossetti and Robert Louis Stevenson

"Luminous cross-hatched illustrations create magic for the 27 poems collected here. Each poem is adorned with Chorao's softly-colored full-page illustrations, bordered in tranquil blue. The poems include a few selections that well deserve a place in childhood, such as 'Hush, Little Baby' and 'Rock-a-bye Baby'; the majority are less familiar, including a few very special selections, such as Naidu's 'Cradle Song.'" SLJ

The **Baby's** good morning book; [compiled and illustrated by] Kay Chorao. Dutton 1986 64p il $13.95 (k-1) **808.81**

1. Poetry—Collected works 2. Nursery rhymes
ISBN 0-525-44257-X LC 86-6415

This volume offers a "group of verses evocative of morning. Some of the poems are presented in full; others are excerpted from longer works. The moods vary from sassy to somnambulant. . . . There are 26 poems in all, set off by Chorao's warm, sunny pictures rich with fresh, morning hues and tender children's faces." Booklist

Carle, Eric

Eric Carle's animals, animals; poems compiled by Laura Whipple. Philomel Bks. 1989 82p il $18.95 (1-3) **808.81**

1. Animals—Poetry 2. Poetry—Collected works
ISBN 0-399-21744-4 LC 88-31646

"Illustrations take center stage in *Eric Carle's Animals Animals* . . . compiled by Laura Whipple. The well-chosen poems are from a variety of sources—the Bible, Shakespeare, Japanese Haiku, Pawnee Indian, weather sayings and contemporary poets like Judith Viorst, Ogden Nash, and Jack Prelutsky. On many pages the poem may be only two or three lines but the pictures are full-page spreads in Mr. Carle's familiar vividly colored, collage style." Kobrin Letter

Cat poems; selected by Myra Cohn Livingston; illustrated by Trina Schart Hyman. Holiday House 1987 32p il lib bdg $13.95 (1-3) **808.81**

1. Cats—Poetry 2. Poetry—Collected works
ISBN 0-8234-0631-8 LC 86-14810

Companion volume to: Dog poems, entered below

"A collection of 19 poems about cats—some old and familiar, some relatively new and surprising—by, among other writers, Eve Merriam, Karla Kuskin, William Jay Smith and X. J. Kennedy." N Y Times Book Rev

"Livingston's eclectic collection of cat-inspired poetry does a nice job of reflecting the many moods and modes of felines, as well as the human fascination with these sometimes inscrutable animal companions. . . . Hyman's drawings top off the offering with some knowing evocations of cat behavior. Pleasingly designed and well chosen, this collection should suit feline fanciers nicely." Booklist

Cats are cats; poems compiled by Nancy Larrick; drawings by Ed Young. Philomel Bks. 1988 80p il lib bdg $17.95 **808.81**

1. Cats—Poetry 2. Poetry—Collected works
ISBN 0-399-21517-4 LC 87-16728

Companion volume to: Mice are nice, entered below

A collection of thirty-six poems about all kinds of cats, from old grumbling cats to proud cats who sit tall, by poets including Eve Merriam, Jane Yolen, John Ciardi, and T. S. Eliot

"This is a solid selection with striking art, the latter especially notable for varied textures and perspectives that catch the reader by surprise as often as do the verbal nuances." Bull Cent Child Books

A **Christmas** feast: poems, sayings, greetings, and wishes; compiled by Edna Barth; etchings by Ursula Arndt. Clarion Bks. 1979 xx, 156p il $12.95 (4 and up) **808.81**

1. Christmas—Poetry 2. Poetry—Collected works
ISBN 0-395-28965-3 LC 79-13282

"Gathered from a span of five centuries, this collection . . . provides a rich sampling for holiday festivities and quiet moments alone. The selections are arranged under broad title categories . . . and include contemporary authors (Aileen Fisher, Elizabeth Coatsworth), classic writers (Tennyson, Longfellow, Shakespeare) and traditional offerings from folk literature." Booklist

Christmas poems; selected by Myra Cohn Livingston; illustrated by Trina Schart Hyman. Holiday House 1984 32p il lib bdg $13.95 (k-3) **808.81**

1. Christmas—Poetry 2. Poetry—Collected works
ISBN 0-8234-0508-7 LC 83-18559

The selections "range from the Nativity to John Ciardi's speculations about how Santa gets down to Key West to a nice limerick applauding Mrs. S. Claus. The collection gets its unity from Trina Schart Hyman's drawings, placing all the figures in the vicinity of a Christmas tree supervised by the family cat." Read Teach

The **Columbia** Granger's index to poetry; indexing anthologies published through June 30, 1989; edited by Edith P. Hazen, Deborah J. Fryer. 9th ed completely rev. Columbia Univ. Press 1990 xxviii, 2082p $175 **808.81**

1. Poetry—Indexes
ISBN 0-231-07104-3 LC 90-1334

First edition, edited by Edith Granger, published 1904 by A. C. McClurg with title: Index to poetry and recitations. Fifth through eighth editions have title: Granger's index to poetry

"A very useful index important in public, college, and school libraries as it indexes a large number of standard and popular collections of poetry. . . . Because of the number of titles indexed in earlier editions, but omitted in later ones, most libraries will find it advantageous to keep all." Sheehy. Guide to Ref Books. 10th edition

Dilly dilly piccalilli; poems for the very young; chosen by Myra Cohn Livingston; illustrated by Eileen Christelow. Margaret K. McElderry Bks. 1989 68p il $12.95 (2-4) **808.81**

1. American poetry—Collected works 2. English poetry—Collected works
ISBN 0-689-50466-7 LC 88-23005

A collection of poems about such topics as bugs, weather, food, and the sea, by poets ranging from Robert Louis Stevenson and Walter de la Mare to Gwendolyn Brooks and Arnold Lobel

"Livingston's ordering and placement of selections is astute; subjects seem to flow effortlessly from one page to the next. . . . Christelow's pleasant pencil drawings are interspersed sparingly throughout; they overwhelm neither the poetry nor a child's imagination by offering an overly literal interpretation." Horn Book

Dog poems; selected by Myra Cohn Livingston; illustrated by Leslie Morrill. Holiday House 1990 32p il lib bdg $12.95 (1-3) **808.81**

1. Dogs—Poetry 2. Poetry—Collected works
ISBN 0-8234-0776-4 LC 89-2061

Companion volume to: Cat poems, entered above

A collection of poems by a variety of authors celebrating the joys of canines, from puppies to old hounds, from Chihuahuas to mongrels

Surprisingly varied in form, mood, and subject, the poems not only portray the idiosyncrasies of individual hounds, but also show many facets of the complex relationships between children and their dogs. . . . Morrill contributes lively pencil drawings, which appear on every double-page spread, with verve and sensitivity. Read individually or to a group, this collection will tap into many children's experiences." Booklist

Easter poems; selected by Myra Cohn Livingston; illustrated by John Wallner. Holiday House 1985 32p il lib bdg $13.95 (3-5) **808.81**

1. Easter—Poetry 2. Poetry—Collected works
ISBN 0-8234-0546-X LC 84-15866

A collection of poems on Easter themes by John Ciardi, William Jay Smith, Joan Aiken, and other authors, including poems translated from Russian and German

"Notable for their composition and textural qualities, Wallner's black and white illustrations are each touched with the purple or green of traditional Easter coloring. Livingston, a distinguished anthologist and poet, uses none of her own work here. . . . [This is a] fresh, verdant, and varied Easter anthology." Bull Cent Child Books

Favorite poems, old and new; selected for boys and girls; by Helen Ferris; illustrated by Leonard Weisgard. Doubleday 1957 598p il $18.95 (4-6) **808.81**

1. Poetry—Collected works
ISBN 0-385-07696-7 LC 57-11418

An anthology of more than seven hundred poems divided into eighteen sections related to children's interests that enable the reader either to browse or to find a special poem for a special occasion

Favorite poems, old and new—*Continued*

"This collection with its Leonard Weisgard illustrations is a treasure for the children's library shelves and for the family to own." Wis Libr Bull

Halloween poems; selected by Myra Cohn Livingston; illustrated by Stephen Gammell. Holiday House 1989 30p il lib bdg $12.95 (k-3) **808.81**

1. Halloween—Poetry 2. Poetry—Collected works
ISBN 0-8234-0762-4 LC 89-1741

Eighteen poems celebrate the holiday of pumpkins, black cats, witches, and ghosts

"This is a wise selection and has considerable variety of mood, style, and form. The selections are interpreted with relish in Gammell's black and white illustrations." Bull Cent Child Books

Index to children's poetry; a title, subject, author, and first line index to poetry in collections for children and youth; compiled by John E. and Sara W. Brewton. Wilson, H.W. 1942-1965 3v **808.81**

1. Poetry—Indexes LC 42-20148

Basic volume published 1942 $48 (ISBN 0-8242-0021-7); first supplement published 1954 $35 (ISBN 0-8242-0022-5); second supplement published 1965 $35 (ISBN 0-8242-0023-3)

The main volume indexes 15,000 poems by 2,500 authors in 130 collections. The two supplements analyze another 15,000 poems by 2700 authors in 151 collections

"This tool is an invaluable reference source." Peterson. Ref Books for Child

Index to poetry for children and young people; a title, subject, author, and first line index to poetry in collections for children and young people. Wilson, H.W. 1972-1989 4v **808.81**

1. Poetry—Indexes

A continuation of: Index to children's poetry, entered above. The volume published 1972 covering 1964-1969 compiled by John E. and Sara W. Brewton and G. Meredith Blackburn III $43 (ISBN 0-8242-0435-2); 1970-1975 published 1978 compiled by John E. Brewton, G. Meredith Blackburn III and Lorraine A. Blackburn $43 (ISBN 0-8242-0621-5); 1976-1981 published 1984 compiled by John E. Brewton, G. Meredith Blackburn III and Lorraine A. Blackburn $43 (ISBN 0-8242-0681-9); 1982-1987 published 1989 compiled by G. Meredith Blackburn III and Lorraine A. Blackburn $48 (ISBN 0-8242-0773-4)

Each volume analyzes approximately 10,000 poems by some 2,000 authors in more than 110 collections. Over 2,000 subject headings are used in each volume

Mice are nice; poems compiled by Nancy Larrick; art by Ed Young. Philomel Bks. 1990 45p il $15.95 **808.81**

1. Mice—Poetry 2. Poetry—Collected works
ISBN 0-399-21495-X LC 87-11159

Companion volume to: Cats are cats, entered above

A collection of poems about mice by David McCord, A. A. Milne, John Ciardi, Ian Serraillier, and others

"For the most part the verses are lighthearted, humorous, and affectionate, with quick, brisk rhythms and sporadic flashes of surprise. Although the individual poems can be found elsewhere, the book is well worth purchasing for the sake of Ed Young's exemplary art. Charcoal and pastel illustrations portray tiny, bright-eyed mice—frequently drawn to scale against full-page renderings of cats or human hands and faces—with their long tails trailing gracefully behind." Horn Book

New Year's poems; selected by Myra Cohn Livingston; illustrated by Margot Tomes. Holiday House 1987 32p il lib bdg $12.95 (1-3) **808.81**

1. New Year—Poetry 2. Poetry—Collected works
ISBN 0-8234-0641-5 LC 86-22885

"Livingston has commissioned 13 New Years poems from contemporary poets for children, added 2 new poems of her own, and 2 others which have been previously published. . . . The poems describe a range of feelings about the new year from hopefulness to merriment and celebration." SLJ

"This diverse and engaging collection of poems for the New Year is . . . annotated with explanations of regional customs. . . . Tomes' three-color illustrations are as spare and elegant as winter itself." Publ Wkly

The **Oxford** book of Christmas poems; edited by Michael Harrison and Christopher Stuart-Clark. Oxford Univ. Press 1983 160p il $12.95; pa $7.95 (4 and up) **808.81**

1. Christmas—Poetry 2. Poetry—Collected works
ISBN 0-19-276051-3; 0-19-276080-7 (pa)
LC 85-120897

This "collection of 120 British and American poems is organized into four sections around the season of winter, the coming of Advent, the Nativity and celebration of Christmas, and the anticipation of a new year. The poets are both well and lesser known, carefully chosen for a balance of old and new." Booklist

Piping down the valleys wild; poetry for the young of all ages; edited with a new introduction by Nancy Larrick; illustrated by Ellen Raskin. Delacorte Press 1985 xxiv, 253p il $14.95; Dell pa $3.50 **808.81**

1. Poetry—Collected works
ISBN 0-385-29429-8; 0-440-46952-X (pa)

A reissue with new introduction of the title first published 1968

Dylan Thomas, Eve Merriam, Carl Sandburg, and Gwendolyn Brooks are among the authors included

"A pleasant, quite comprehensive collection that includes little unfamiliar material; the selections range widely in source, somewhat less widely in mood. . . . An index of first lines and an author-title index [are] appended. The compiler's introduction is addressed to adults and discusses reading aloud to the young." Sutherland. The Best in Child Books

Poems of A. Nonny Mouse; selected by Jack Prelutsky; illustrated by Henrik Drescher. Knopf 1989 unp il $12.95; lib bdg $13.99 (1-3) **808.81**

1. Poetry—Collected works
ISBN 0-394-88711-5; 0-394-98711-X (lib bdg) LC 89-31672

"With tongue firmly in cheek, Prelutsky prefaces this comical collection of traditional and anonymous verses by elucidating the trials and tribulations of A. Nonny Mouse. Ms. Mouse—obviously 'no ordinary rodent'—claims that a typographical error caused all her 'little verses' to be printed under the wrong name, a mistake Prelutsky rectifies with the publication of this book. . . . Children will enjoy spotting Ms. Mouse on every page as she exhorts Drescher's droll characters in their wacky pursuits and smiles serenely at a world where boots have sharp teeth and a dog's tail turns into a snake." Publ Wkly

Room for me and a mountain lion; poetry of open space; selected by Nancy Larrick. Evans & Co. 1974 191p il hardcover o.p. paperback available $6.95 (5 and up) **808.81**

1. Nature in poetry 2. Poetry—Collected works
ISBN 0-87131-569-6 (pa) LC 73-87710

A collection of poems celebrating the beauty of nature and open space. Some of the poets included are: D. H. Lawrence, Eve Merriam, Galway Kinnell, William Stafford, Theodore Roethke, Maxine Kumin, Ted Hughes, and Robert Frost

"The poems are generally short, comprehensible, relevant to the theme and illustrated by good photographs." Child Book Rev Serv

Side by side; poems to read together; collected by Lee Bennett Hopkins; illustrated by Hilary Knight. Simon & Schuster Bks. for Young Readers 1988 80p il lib bdg $14.95 (1-3) **808.81**

1. Poetry—Collected works
ISBN 0-671-63579-4 LC 87-33025

A collection of poems especially chosen to be read aloud, by authors ranging from Lewis Carroll and Robert Louis Stevenson to Gwendolyn Brooks and David McCord

"With the rhythmic, sometimes narrative verses, and the joyful antics of the characters prancing across the pages, this collection offers visual as well as aural treats for children and adults to savor together." Booklist

Sing a song of popcorn; every child's book of poems; illustrated by nine Caldecott Medal artists, Marcia Brown [et al.]; selected by Beatrice Schenk de Regniers [et al.] Scholastic 1988 142p il lib bdg $16.95 **808.81**

1. Poetry—Collected works
ISBN 0-590-40645-0 LC 87-4330

Revised edition of: Poems children will sit still for, published 1969

A collection of 128 poems by a variety of well-known authors with illustrations by nine Caldecott medalists

"A pleasant book, still a useful if conservative anthology, this has title, author, and first line indexes, and brief notes on the illustrators." Bull Cent Child Books

Sprints and distances; sports in poetry and the poetry in sport; [compiled by] Lillian Morrison; illustrated by Clare and John Ross. Crowell 1965 211p il lib bdg $13.89 (5 and up) **808.81**

1. Sports—Poetry 2. Poetry—Collected works
ISBN 0-690-04840-8 LC 65-14906

"The poems included here range from memorable newspaper verse to pieces by Pindar, Virgil, Wordsworth, and Yeats. They vary in form from simple quatrains to intricate modern verse." Prefatory note

Subject index to poetry for children and young people, 1957-1975; compiled by Dorothy B. Frizzell Smith and Eva L. Andrews. American Lib. Assn. 1977 1035p $45 **808.81**

1. Poetry—Indexes
ISBN 0-8389-0242-1 LC 77-3296

"The index provides access by subject to poems for children contained in 263 anthologies. The 2,000 'Sears' (10th ed.) headings are supplemented by headings for scientific, geographic, ethnic, and current topics. Age levels are included in the citations. This volume supplements, but does not supersede, Violet Sell's 'Subject Index to Poetry for Children and Young People.'" Wynar. Guide to Ref Books for Sch Media Cent. 3d edition

Talking to the sun: an illustrated anthology of poems for young people; selected and introduced by Kenneth Koch and Kate Farrell. Metropolitan Mus. of Art; Holt & Co. 1985 112p il $19.95 **808.81**

1. Poetry—Collected works
ISBN 0-8050-0144-1 LC 85-15428

"Poems from a wide variety of times and cultures and reproductions from the Metropolitan Museum of Art are organized by themes that include spring, love, nonsense, animals, and the secrets beneath the ordinary." Booklist

Thanksgiving poems; selected by Myra Cohn Livingston; illustrated by Stephen Gammell. Holiday House 1985 32p il lib bdg $12.95 (k-3) **808.81**

1. Thanksgiving Day—Poetry 2. Poetry—Collected works
ISBN 0-8234-0570-2 LC 85-762

"The two-color illustrations have a soft, melting quality that is given contrast by precision of line on some pages, so that the pictures have a range in technique and mood that matches the poems they illustrate." Bull Cent Child Books

"Shaded pencil drawings tinged with peach and robin's egg blue prove the versatility of the illustrator, who matches the mood of the poetry with stunning Indian portraits, views of the barren November land, and squiggly-line cartoon drawings." Horn Book

These small stones; poems selected by Norma Farber and Myra Cohn Livingston. Harper & Row 1987 84p $12.95; lib bdg $12.89 (3-5) **808.81**

1. Poetry—Collected works
ISBN 0-06-024013-X; 0-06-024014-8 (lib bdg) LC 87-264

"A Charlotte Zolotow book"

An "anthology of 60 poems celebrating 'all sorts of small things.' Farber and Livingston's selections include a fine range of poets, from an anonymous 8th-Century Japanese writer to the familiar Neruda, Kennedy, Holman, Zolotow, and Reeves; haiku and nursery riddles also appear. Less than a third of the poems are available in other standard collections." SLJ

This collection "encourages children of all ages to look around them and cultivate their own thoughtful eye, their own keen vision, their own unique place in the greater scheme of things." Wilson Libr Bull

Tomie dePaola's book of poems. Putnam 1988 96p il $17.95 (2-4) **808.81**

1. Poetry—Collected works
ISBN 0-399-21540-9 LC 87-7325

An illustrated collection of poems by such authors as Dorothy Aldis, Carl Sandburg, Langston Hughes, and Federico Garcia Lorca

"Selections range across ethnic lines to encompass childhood interests—the seasons, playtime, the moon, animals, food, and nonsense verses—and vary in length and theme. DePaola ties the offerings together in a congenial, thoughtful, well-conceived, and at times amusing manner. The visual vignettes amplify as well as decorate the poetry, and his characters sport diverse and intriguing clothes, hairdos, and facial expressions, giving individuality to each of the pages." Booklist

Valentine poems; selected by Myra Cohn Livingston; illustrated by Patience Brewster. Holiday House 1987 32p il lib bdg $13.95 (k-3) **808.81**

1. Valentine's Day—Poetry 2. Poetry—Collected works
ISBN 0-8234-0587-7 LC 85-31723

"A short anthology of poems for Valentine's Day that combines first-rate humorous and romantic verses by both contemporary and traditional poets. Both young listeners and independent readers will find the selections appealing. Brewster's humorous red and blue pencil illustrations of animals suit each poem, such as the two rabbits who show Love's strength for Karla Kuskin's 'To You'. . . . A plus for both school and public libraries needing Valentine's Day material." SLJ

When the dark comes dancing; a bedtime poetry book; compiled by Nancy Larrick; illustrated by John Wallner. Philomel Bks. 1983 79p il $17.95 (k-3) **808.81**

1. Poetry—Collected works 2. Lullabies
ISBN 0-399-20807-0 LC 81-428

An "anthology of poems and lullabies for young children. . . . Among the contributors are Eleanor Farjeon, Aileen Fisher, Arthur Guiterman, Karla Kuskin, Myra Cohn Livingston, Eve Merriam, Christina Rossetti, and Robert Louis Stevenson." Bull Cent Child Books

"Both old and new poets are represented, folk songs range from as far away as Russia and Africa, and kept throughout is a happy balance of the simplest rhymes with those of more complex imagery. The illustrations, most of them in color, are done in soft pastels, and in their decorative detail and slightly surrealistic flavor they complement the serene and dreamlike quality of the book." Horn Book

Includes bibliography

Why am I grown so cold? poems of the unknowable; edited by Myra Cohn Livingston. Atheneum Pubs. 1982 269p $14.95 (5 and up) **808.81**

1. Supernatural—Poetry 2. Poetry—Collected works
ISBN 0-689-50242-7 LC 82-6646

"A Margaret K. McElderry book"

"Shakespeare, Sandburg, Shel Silverstein, Tolkien, Ted Hughes, Goethe, Felice Holman, Joan Aiken, Pablo Neruda are only a few of the poets represented in the selections that deal with sorcery, devils, fairies, portents, mermaids—the gamut of arcana." Publ Wkly

"An inspired anthology, generous in both quantity and quality, will attract poetry lovers with its rich language and non-poetry lovers with the strong expressions of its eerie theme." Booklist

808.82 Drama—Collections

Bauer, Caroline Feller, 1935-

Presenting reader's theater; plays and poems to read aloud; drawings by Lynn Gates Bredeson. Wilson, H.W. 1987 238p il $40 **808.82**

1. Drama—Collected works 2. Drama in education
ISBN 0-8242-0748-3 LC 87-2105

The author has dramatized poems, folktales and excerpts from contemporary books to introduce children to reading

This book "provides a wealth of script material for children to read aloud before an audience or for their own pleasure." SLJ

The **Big** book of Christmas plays; 21 modern and traditional one-act plays for the celebration of Christmas; edited by Sylvia E. Kamerman. Plays 1988 357p $16.95 **808.82**

1. Christmas—Drama 2. One act plays
ISBN 0-8238-0288-4 LC 88-15691

This collection includes "adaptations of scenes from *Little Women, Les Misérables,* and *A Christmas Carol* . . . [as well as] more modern offerings. . . . The table of contents, which seemingly includes something for everyone from lower grades through high school, is arranged by age group. Appended production notes lists characters, playing time, costumes, props, setting, lighting, and sound effects." Booklist

Play index. Wilson, H.W. 1953-1988 7v **808.82**

1. Drama—Indexes
ISSN 0554-3037

Play index—*Continued*

First published 1953, covering the years 1949-1952, and edited by Dorothy Herbert West and Dorothy Margaret Peake $17. Additional volumes: 1953-1960 $22 edited by Estelle A. Fidell and Dorothy Margaret Peake; 1961-1967 $25 edited by Estelle A. Fidell; 1968-1972 $30 edited by Estelle A. Fidell; 1973-1977 $38 edited by Estelle A. Fidell; 1978-1982 $45 edited by Juliette Yaakov; 1983-1987 $55 edited by Juliette Yaakov and John Greenfieldt

Play index indexes plays in collections and single plays; one-act and full-length plays; radio, television, and Broadway plays; plays for amateur production; plays for children, young adults, and adults. It is divided into four parts. Part I is an author, title, and subject index; the author or main entry includes the title of the play, brief synopsis of the plot, number of acts and scenes, size of cast, number of sets, and bibliographic information. Part II is a list of collections indexed, and Part III, a cast analysis, lists plays by the type of cast and number of players required. Part IV is a directory of publishers and distributors

"For all those interested in contemporary drama—casual reader and serious scholar, audience member and performer, producer and director—all seven volumes of the *Play Index* series provide invaluable information." Am Ref Books Annu, 1989

Plays; the drama magazine for young people. Plays $23 per year **808.82**

1. Drama—Periodicals 2. College and school drama—Periodicals

ISSN 0032-1540

Monthly October through May, except January/February combined. First published 1941

A "pocket-sized magazine of 80 pages, which follows a set pattern of publishing nine or ten royalty free plays. The plays are divided in each number by grade level for junior/senior high and middle/lower grades, and these are followed by creative dramatics, skits, puppet plays, dramatized classics, and so on. Each play includes complete production notes." Katz. Mag for Sch Libr

808.87 Satire and humor—Collections

Espy, Willard R.

A children's almanac of words at play; illustrations by Bruce Cayard. Potter 1982 243p il $15.95; pa $10.95 (3-6) **808.87**

1. Wit and humor 2. Word games

ISBN 0-517-54660-4; 0-517-54666-3 (pa) LC 82-7593

William Cole, Leo Rosten, Eleanor Farjeon and Arnold Adoff are among those represented in this assortment of writings, including limericks, riddles, puns puzzles, tongue twisters, poetry, malapropisms, palindromes, Tom Swifties, and Spoonerisms, for each day of the year

Rosenbloom, Joseph

Knock-knock! who's there; drawings by Sandy Hoffman. Sterling 1984 128p il $11.95; lib bdg $14.49 (4 and up) **808.87**

1. Jokes

ISBN 0-8069-4696-2; 0-8069-4697-0 (lib bdg) LC 84-8617

"Some of the jokes have seen the light of day before, but many will be fresh even to jaded readers—or jokesters. The black-and-white cartoon illustrations add zest to the fun. Sure to be appreciated by its intended readers." SLJ

Laughs, hoots & giggles; illustrations by Joyce Behr & Sanford Hoffman. Sterling 1984 480p il hardcover o.p. paperback available $9.95 (4 and up) **808.87**

1. Wit and humor

ISBN 0-8069-6492-8 (pa) LC 84-8911

This volume contains "riddles, knock-knocks (one for every letter of the alphabet), put-downs . . . jokes, verse (including limericks), and a grab bag of small amusements (in some cases very small) that don't fit into any other category. Heavy black scrawls pass for artwork, and while they're not much, they break up the format." Booklist

808.88 Collections of miscellaneous writings

Bartlett, John, 1820-1905

Familiar quotations. Little, Brown $35 **808.88**

1. Quotations

First published 1855. Periodically revised. Editors vary

"A collection of passages, phrases and proverbs traced to their sources in ancient and modern literature." Subtitle [of 15th edition]

"Comprehensive collection of quotations arranged by author in chronological order with author and keyword indexes." N Y Public Libr. Ref Books for Child Collect

Best wishes, amen; a new collection of autograph verses; [compiled by] Lillian Morrison; illustrated by Loretta Lustig. Crowell 1974 195p il o.p.; HarperCollins Pubs. paperback available $4.50 (5 and up) **808.88**

1. Epigrams

ISBN 0-06-446089-4 (pa) LC 74-2456

An "autograph-album sized book with selections culled from actual autograph books of children. Some of the selections are as old as the hills. Atrocious puns, insults, nonsense rhymes—all are here in abundance to tickle the funnybones of the cornball humor crowd. . . . A final selection contains Spanish autograph rhymes, plus translations, again gathered from actual albums of Spanish-speaking children in New York City." SLJ

Brandreth, Gyles Daubeney, 1948-

The biggest tongue twister book in the world; by Gyles Brandreth; illustrations by Alex Chin. 3rd ed. Sterling 1980 c1978 128p il $12.95; lib bdg $15.29; pa $3.95 (4 and up) **808.88**

1. Tongue twisters

ISBN 0-8069-4594-X; 0-8069-4595-8 (lib bdg); 0-8069-8972-6 (pa) LC 81-116246

Brandreth, Gyles Daubeney, 1948- — *Continued*

Text first published 1977 in the United Kingdom with title: Tongue twisters

"Hundreds of linguistic acrobatics test the flexibility of agile tongues in this collection of challenging twisters. Arranged in broad alphabetical order, the selections range from short one-liners ('Shipshape suit shops ship shapely suits') to longer ones of 4, 8, even 20 lines. . . . Cartoon line drawings embellish the pages." Booklist

Keller, Charles, 1942-

Tongue twisters; illustrated by Ron Fritz. Simon & Schuster Bks. for Young Readers 1989 unp il $13.95; pa $7.95 (3-6) **808.88**

1. Tongue twisters
ISBN 0-671-67123-5; 0-671-67975-9 (pa) LC 88-26448

An illustrated collection of tongue twisters and other hard to say rhymes

"With up to three tongue twisters on a page, each individually illustrated in line and watercolor, the double-page spreads sometimes have a busy look. Actually, a certain level of frenzy seems appropriate; the consistency of hue throughout the book and the neat bordering of each page with a thin black line keep the activity in bounds. An appealing romp." Booklist

Schwartz, Alvin, 1927-

Busy buzzing bumblebees and other tongue twisters; illustrated by Kathie Abrams. Harper & Row 1982 63p il $10.95; lib bdg $10.89; pa $3.50 (k-3) **808.88**

1. Tongue twisters
ISBN 0-06-025268-5; 0-06-025269-3 (lib bdg); 0-06-444036-2 (pa) LC 81-48639

"An I can read book"

A collection of forty-six tongue twisters, each "printed one to a page with bright, caricaturelike illustrations that provide a context, extend the meaning, and add touches of broad humor." Horn Book

A twister of twists, a tangler of tongues; tongue twisters; collected by Alvin Schwartz; illustrated by Glen Rounds. Lippincott 1972 125p il $13.95; Harper & Row pa $4.95 (4 and up) **808.88**

1. Tongue twisters
ISBN 0-397-31387-X; 0-06-446004-5 (pa) LC 72-1434

This is a collection of tongue twisters in both prose and verse, including several in other languages

"The selection of well-known and not-so-well-known tongue twisters should provide endless hours of elocutionary diversion for young and old alike. . . . A helpful series of notes, sources, and bibliographic references give added dimension to a light-hearted, yet incisive, compilation, highlighted by the jovial line drawings." Horn Book

810.8 American literature—Collections

Diane Goode's American Christmas. Dutton Children's Bks. 1990 80p il lib bdg $14.95 **810.8**

1. Christmas 2. American literature—Collected works
ISBN 0-525-44620-6 LC 89-25605

"This generous, festively illustrated collection of stories, poems and songs captures the holiday as celebrated by many different Americans." N Y Times Book Rev

Free to be—a family; conceived by Marlo Thomas. Bantam Bks. 1987 176p il music $19.95; pa $12.95 **810.8**

1. American literature—Collected works 2. Family life
ISBN 0-553-05235-7; 0-553-34559-1 (pa) LC 87-47581

"This sequel to *Free to Be . . . You and Me* [entered below] celebrates 'all kinds of belonging' and the extraordinary diversity among families. The theme of this timely anthology is the extension of the concept of 'family' to include adoptive and foster families, step-families, relatives, friends, community, culture, and—ultimately—global humanity. The nearly 50 selections include stories, poems, short plays, essays, comics, and songs." SLJ

Free to be—you and me; conceived by Marlo Thomas; developed and edited by Carole Hart [et. al]; editor Francine Klagsbrun; art director: Samuel N. Antupit. McGraw-Hill 1974 143p il music o.p.; Bantam Bks. paperback available $10.95 **810.8**

1. American literature—Collected works 2. Individuality 3. Social role
ISBN 0-553-34544-3 (pa)

"A project of the Ms. Foundation, Inc." Title page

The theme of this collection of twenty-five songs, stories, poems and a dialogue is that children should develop as individuals and be independent of obsolete sexual and racial role myths. Fifteen of the selections originally were recorded on a 1973 album of the same title

This collection "is a significant step toward filling the need for nonsexist material for children. . . . The total adds up to a qualitatively uneven but still useful endeavor at encouraging children to be themselves." Booklist

Stone Soup; the magazine by children. Children's Art Foundation $22 per year **810.8**

1. Child authors—Periodicals 2. Child artists—Periodicals
ISSN 0094-579X

Five issues a year; bi-monthly except July/August. First published 1973

"The only literary magazine devoted exclusively to children's writing and art. . . . Editors select only the very best from material submitted by children from all over the world. Each issue includes stories, poems, book reviews, and black-and-white drawings done by children

Stone Soup—*Continued*
ages 6-12. The no-nonsense format is conservative and aesthetically pleasing. . . . This magazine offers quality work in a quality format and is highly recommended for school libraries." Katz. Mag for Sch Libr

811 American poetry

Adoff, Arnold, 1935-

All the colors of the race: poems; illustrated by John Steptoe. Lothrop, Lee & Shepard Bks. 1982 56p il $12.95; lib bdg $12.88 (4-6) **811**

1. Family—Poetry 2. Race awareness—Poetry
ISBN 0-688-00879-8; 0-688-00880-1 (lib bdg)
LC 81-11777

This "cycle of poems is written from the viewpoint of a child who has one parent who is black and Protestant, one who is white and Jewish. The poetry is free and flowing, reflecting the facets of the child's feelings. . . . The illustrations, brown and white, are often angular in block print style, speckled and stylized, and they echo the vitality and tenderness of the poems' moods." Bull Cent Child Books

Eats: poems; illustrated by Susan Russo. Lothrop, Lee & Shepard Bks. 1979 unp il $13.95; lib bdg $12.88 (3-5) **811**

1. Food—Poetry
ISBN 0-688-41901-1; 0-688-51901-6 (lib bdg)
LC 79-11300

All of the "smells, tastes, and obsessive cravings—pizzas, burgers, ice cream, etc.—are evoked in poems and verse-recipes that range in tone from dreamy to passionate. . . . Russo's brown-tone illustrations have sufficient precision to depict each topic but retain a smoky, slight blurriness that carries on the reveries of the verses. Readers of all ages will relate to Adoff's blissful musings and fancies and occasional whimsy." Booklist

Sports pages; illustrations by Steve Kuzma. Lippincott 1986 79p il $14.95; lib bdg $14.89; pa $5.95 (4 and up) **811**

1. Sports—Poetry
ISBN 0-397-32102-3; 0-397-32103-1 (lib bdg); 0-06-446098-3 (pa) LC 85-45169

Free verse poems about the experiences and feelings of young athletes involved in various sports, illustrated with pencil sketches

"The poems are in the voices of young athletes of both sexes, and they capture hope or despair, excitement or exhaustion, the bonding in a team sport, the isolation of the single participant. Adoff writes with a control of structure that never impedes the movement of the poem. This is one of his best collections." Bull Cent Child Books

Baylor, Byrd

Desert voices. Scribner 1981 unp il $13.95 (1-4) **811**

1. Desert animals—Poetry
ISBN 0-684-16712-3 LC 80-17061

Ten desert creatures "each speak a poetic (free form) piece about their lives, homes and place in the desert world. The essential nature of each animal, whether patient or playful, alert or ominous, is conveyed with simplicity and energy in the well-phrased text and is further illuminated in Parnall's drawings, which are at once bold and delicate." SLJ

Benét, Rosemary

A book of Americans; by Rosemary and Stephen Vincent Benét; illustrated by Charles Child. Holt & Co. 1986 1933 114p il $12.95; pa $4.95 (4 and up) **811**

1. United States—Biography—Poetry 2. United States—History—Poetry
ISBN 0-8050-0284-7; 0-8050-0297-9 (pa)

A reissue of the title first published 1933 by Farrar and Rinehart; copyright renewed 1961

A collection of poems portraying 56 famous historical figures from Columbus to Woodrow Wilson

Bodecker, N. M., d. 1988

Snowman sniffles, and other verse; illustrated by the author. Atheneum Pubs. 1983 67p il $10.95 (3-5) **811**

1. Humorous poetry
ISBN 0-689-50263-X LC 82-13927

"A Margaret K. McElderry book"

"Line drawings, very small and very animated, illustrate a cheerful collection of deft and usually brief poems that are just as suitable for reading aloud to younger children as for the independent reader in the primary grades. The poems have wit and humor, and—albeit less often—evocative imagery, and they are all child-oriented, many of them about animals or weather. The book has nice integration of text and illustration on pages with plenty of space to set off the poems." Bull Cent Child Books

Brooks, Gwendolyn

Bronzeville boys and girls; pictures by Ronni Solbert. Harper & Row 1956 40p il lib bdg $12.89 (2-5) **811**

1. Blacks—Poetry
ISBN 0-06-020651-9 LC 56-8152

A collection of thirty-six poems about everyday experiences of children. "While the children are black and the place is Chicago, the place might be anywhere and the children, any children." Natl Counc of Teach of Engl. Adventuring with Books. 2d edition

"Ronni Solbert's sensitive and expressive drawings reflect and extend the mode and beauty of the poetry." Chicago Sunday Trib

Brown, Margaret Wise, 1910-1952

Nibble nibble: poems for children; illustrated by Leonard Weisgard. Harper & Row 1986 c1959 unp il lib bdg $13.89 (k-3) **811**

1. Nature in poetry
ISBN 0-201-09291-3 LC 84-43128

Brown, Margaret Wise, 1910-1952 — *Continued*

"A Young Scott book"

First published 1959 by W. R. Scott

Twenty-five poems, about insects, fish, animals, birds, and the seasons

"The pleasingly cadenced verses are fresh and childlike, and the illustrations in black, white, and cool green are lovely; together they make a harmonious, evocative whole which young children will enjoy." Booklist

Cassedy, Sylvia, 1930-1989

Roomrimes: poems; illustrations by Michele Chessare. Crowell 1987 71p il $12.95; lib bdg $12.89 (3-6) **811**

1. Alphabet

ISBN 0-690-04466-6; 0-690-04467-4 (lib bdg) LC 86-4583

In this "collection of 26 poems about rooms or spaces, each letter of the alphabet is represented from attic to loft to zoo via unrhymed, rhymed, and even haiku poetry." SLJ

The author's "range of skill and depth of perception in these poems are stunning. . . . Chessare's witty and versatile black-and-white illustrations keep pace with the rich, remarkable text." Publ Wkly

Caudill, Rebecca, 1899-1985

Wind, sand and sky; illustrated by Donald Carrick. Dutton 1976 unp il $8.95 (1-4) **811**

1. Deserts—Poetry

ISBN 0-525-42899-2 LC 75-34113

"The deserts of our country assume a new meaning after reading this . . . book of haiku. The words and pictures capture an element of beauty unsuspected by most children." Read Teach

Child, Lydia Maria Francis, 1802-1880

Over the river and through the wood (k-2) **811**

1. Thanksgiving Day—Poetry 2. Songs

Some editions are:

Coward, McCann & Geoghegan $8.95 Pictures by Brinton Turkle (ISBN 0-698-20301-1; LC 74-79700)

Little, Brown lib bdg $14.95 Illustrated by Iris Van Rynbach (ISBN 0-316-13873-8; LC 88-4712)

Text originally published in volume 2 of the author's Flowers for children, 1844, under title: A boy's Thanksgiving Day

Illustrated versions of a poem about a family's visit to their grandparents for Thanksgiving. Both editions include music

Turkle's "pictures, realistic in period detail, are evocative and are framed so that each looks as though it were in an album. Pictures of the visiting family are in color and alternate with quiet black and white pictures of the grandparental preparations." Bull Cent Child Books

"Van Rynbach's watercolors celebrate the open country with expansive vistas of chilly fields, busy skating ponds, and cozy-looking houses that beckon visitors." Booklist

Ciardi, John, 1916-1986

The hopeful trout and other limericks; illustrated by Susan Meddaugh. Houghton Mifflin 1989 52p il $13.95 (2-4) **811**

1. Limericks

ISBN 0-395-43606-0 LC 87-23587

"A posthumous gathering of limericks by the well-known poet offers insight into the traditional pyrotechnics of the form—a saucy blending of wit with rhythmic phrases. Some celebrate disasters; some affront; others introduce characters one hopes never to meet. . . . Susan Meddaugh's black-and-white illustrations complement the irreverent tone, nicely opening up the pages so that the volume will appeal to lovers of joke books, those reluctant to tackle long selections, and even those searching for an offbeat comment to write in an autograph book." Horn Book

I met a man; illustrated by Robert Osborn. Houghton Mifflin 1961 74p il hardcover o.p. paperback available $6.95 (1-3) **811**

1. Nonsense verses

ISBN 0-395-17447-3 (pa) LC 60-9094

"These poems were written for a special pleasure: I wanted to write the first book my daughter read herself. To bring them within her first-grade range I based them on the two most elementary word lists in general use. . . . The basic devices of these poems for leading the child to new words are rhyme, riddles, context, and word games." Author's note

Ciardi's "imagination, fluency in rhyme, and delight in plays on words lift the results of his intention above the limitation of the first-grade word lists. . . . The cartoonish drawings admirably suit the moods of his fantastic sequences. . . . An honest and original attempt to make both poetry and learning fun." Horn Book

You read to me, I'll read to you; drawings by Edward Gorey. Lippincott 1962 64p il lib bdg $12.89; pa $5.95 (1-4) **811**

1. Humorous poetry

ISBN 0-397-30646-6 (lib bdg); 0-06-446060-6 (pa) LC 62-16296

Thirty-five "imaginative and humorous poems for an adult and a child to read aloud together. Written in a basic first-grade vocabulary, the poems to be read by the child alternate with poems to be read by the adult." Booklist

Clifton, Lucille, 1936-

Everett Anderson's goodbye; illustrated by Ann Grifalconi. Holt & Co. 1983 unp il $10.95; pa $3.95 (k-3) **811**

1. Death—Poetry 2. Fathers—Poetry 3. Blacks—Poetry

ISBN 0-8050-0235-9; 0-8050-0800-4 (pa) LC 82-23426

Coretta Scott King Award for text, 1984

"Through moving poetry and expressive drawings, children will share Everett Anderson's despair and final acceptance of his father's death. Each of the five poems expresses one of the stages of grief: denial, anger, bargaining, depression and acceptance. These five stages are

Clifton, Lucille, 1936-—*Continued*
listed at the beginning of the book. Charcoal drawings of a young black child and his loving mother have a soft texture, but strong white highlights add drama." SLJ

Other available titles about Everett Anderson are:
Everett Anderson's nine month long (1978)
Some of the days of Everett Anderson (1970)

Cummings, E. E. (Edward Estlin), 1894-1962

Hist whist; illustrated by Deborah Kogan Ray. Crown 1989 unp il $10.95; lib bdg $11.99 (k-2) **811**

1. Halloween—Poetry
ISBN 0-517-57360-1; 0-517-57258-3 (lib bdg) LC 89-596

"On a Halloween night in the country, costumed figures assemble in the dark for a wild, spooky romp, ending with the children gleefully unmasked. Words appear in white superimposed over rich gold-and-orange tones that glow in the deep blues and browns of the torch- and moonlit scenes. The artwork captures the mystery and magic of the poem." Booklist

Hist whist and other poems for children; illustrated by David Calsada; edited by George J. Firmage. Liveright 1983 unp il $12.95 (3-6) **811**

1. Nonsense verses
ISBN 0-87140-640-3 LC 84-121364

"Sixteen of the twenty poems chosen for this collection by the poet appeared in a privately printed edition of 500 copies entitled 16 Poèmes Enfantins in January 1962. The complete selection and the illustrations especially prepared for this new edition are published here for the first time." Editor's note

"This edition is illustrated with one pen-and-ink drawing for each poem, giving fresh interpretation to such well-known poems as 'Just-spring.'" SLJ

De Regniers, Beatrice Schenk

The way I feel—sometimes; illustrated by Susan Meddaugh. Clarion Bks. 1988 48p il lib bdg $13.95 (1-3) **811**

ISBN 0-89919-647-0 LC 87-18245

Presents a collection of poems about feelings, from anger to acceptance

"The tone ranges from outrageous to wistful, with an overriding spunkiness that children will find appealing; use of a pleasantly multicultural neighborhood also underscores the universality of emotions. Meddaugh's drawings perked with brightly colored washes capture the flavor." Booklist

Dickinson, Emily, 1830-1886

I'm nobody! who are you? poems of Emily Dickinson for children; illustrated by Rex Schneider; with an introduction by Richard B. Sewall. Stemmer House 1978 84p il $21.95; pa $14.95 (3-6) **811**

ISBN 0-916144-21-6; 0-916144-22-4 (pa) LC 78-6828

"A Barbara Holdridge book"

This collection of Emily Dickinson's poetry is illustrated with full color drawings depicting life in nineteenth century New England

Includes glossary

Poems for youth; edited by Alfred Leete Hampson; foreword by May Lamberton Becker; illustrations by George and Doris Hauman. Little, Brown 1934 unp il $12.95 (5 and up) **811**

ISBN 0-316-18418-7 LC 34-40845

"Poems written by Emily Dickinson for her young niece and nephews serve as an excellent introduction to the poet. Indexed by first lines." Hodges. Books for Elem Sch Libr

"The illustrations have a grace and delicacy that is most appropriate." N Y Times Book Rev

Eliot, T. S. (Thomas Stearns), 1888-1965

Growltiger's last stand; with The pekes and the pollicles and The song of the Jellicles; with pictures by Errol Le Cain. Farrar, Straus & Giroux; Harcourt Brace Jovanovich 1987 c1986 unp il $12.95; pa $4.95 (2-5) **811**

ISBN 0-374-32809-9; 0-374-42811-5 (pa)

An illustrated presentation of three cat poems taken from the author's Old Possum's book of practical cats, first published 1939. This edition first published 1986 in the United Kingdom

This book is "best suited to readers with enough sophistication to appreciate the poet's wide-ranging vocabulary, frequent syntactical inversions and sly humor. Others may not know how to respond to the outward fierceness of the title poem or to the more clearly playful but still bellicose [second poem]. . . . Le Cain's richly textured illustrations are often droll, occasionally rather fearsome and always striking, particularly in his use of symmetry and pattern." Publ Wkly

Esbensen, Barbara Juster

Cold stars and fireflies; poems of the four seasons; illustrated by Susan Bonners. Crowell 1984 70p il lib bdg $12.89 (4 and up) **811**

1. Nature in poetry 2. Seasons—Poetry
ISBN 0-690-04363-5 LC 83-45051

"Nature and the changing seasons are the subjects of Esbensen's 43 poems, which are arranged according to season and illustrated with evocative, shadowy shapes touched with grays and reds." Booklist

Words with wrinkled knees: animal poems; pictures by John Stadler. Crowell 1986 unp il $11.95; lib bdg $11.89 (2-5) **811**

1. Animals—Poetry
ISBN 0-690-04504-2; 0-690-04505-0 (lib bdg) LC 85-47886

Esbensen, Barbara Juster—*Continued*

A collection of poems about words that express the essence of the animals they identify

"The black-and-white drawings are sometimes as inventive as the poems." Bull Cent Child Books

Farber, Norma

How does it feel to be old? illustrated by Trina Schart Hyman. Dutton 1979 unp il $12.95; pa $3.95 (2-4) **811**

1. Old age—Poetry

ISBN 0-525-32414-3; 0-525-44367-3 (pa) LC 79-11516

"A Unicorn book"

In this poem a grandmother explains to her granddaughter some of the thoughts and feelings, advantages and disadvantages that accompany being old

"The detailed pen-and-ink drawings abound with fascinating clutter—photographs in elaborate frames, twisting candelabras, and ornate china. Poet and artist have achieved a remarkable union of spirit, expressing in verse and evocative illustrations the bittersweet accumulation of a lifetime of memories." Horn Book

Field, Eugene, 1850-1895

Poems of childhood; illustrated by Maxfield Parrish. Scribner 1896 228p il o.p.; Airmont paperback available $1.95 **811**

ISBN 0-8049-0211-9 (pa)

This is a collection of poems both serious and fun, from "Love-songs of childhood" and "With trumpet and drum" which were first published 1894 and 1892 respectively

Fields, Julia

The green lion of Zion Street; illustrated by Jerry Pinkney. Margaret K. McElderry Bks. 1988 unp il $13.95 (k-3) **811**

1. Blacks—Poetry

ISBN 0-689-50414-4 LC 87-15519

The author "uses the voice of a child to reflect the feelings of a group of children towards the majesty and mystery of a sculptured lion. The lines, which use some of the idioms of Black speech, are impressionistic, vividly expressing the children's pleasure in using their imaginations as well as in working up a pleasurable fright in a safe situation. . . . Pinkney's paintings are deft: children huddled against the cold penetration of a foggy morning, the lion looming blank-eyed and massive in the gray day." Bull Cent Child Books

Fleischman, Paul

I am phoenix: poems for two voices; illustrated by Ken Nutt. Harper & Row 1985 51p il $11.95; lib bdg $11.89 (4 and up) **811**

1. Birds—Poetry

ISBN 0-06-021881-9; 0-06-021882-7 (lib bdg) LC 85-42615

Companion volume to: Joyful noise, entered below

"A Charlotte Zolotow book"

A collection of poems about birds to be read aloud by two voices

"Devotés of the almost lost art of choral reading should be among the first to appreciate this collection. . . . Printed in script form, the selections . . . have a cadenced pace and dignified flow; their combination of imaginative imagery and realistic detail is echoed by the combination of stylized fantasy and representational drawings in the black and white pictures, all soft line and strong nuance." Bull Cent Child Books

Joyful noise: poems for two voices; illustrated by Eric Beddows. Harper & Row 1988 44p il $12.95; lib bdg $12.89 (4 and up) **811**

1. Insects—Poetry

ISBN 0-06-021852-5; 0-06-021853-3 (lib bdg) LC 87-45280

Awarded the Newbery Medal, 1989

Companion volume to: I am phoenix

"A Charlotte Zolotow book"

"This collection of poems for two voices explores the lives of insects. Designed to be read aloud, the phrases of the poems are spaced vertically on the page in two columns, one for each reader. The voices sometimes alternate, sometimes speak in chorus, and sometimes echo each other." Booklist

"There are fourteen poems in the handsomely designed volume, with stylish endpapers and wonderfully interpretive black-and-white illustrations. Each selection is a gem, polished perfection." Horn Book

Frost, Robert, 1874-1963

Birches; illustrated by Ed Young. Holt & Co. 1988 unp il $13.95; pa $5.95 (1-3) **811**

1. Trees—Poetry

ISBN 0-8050-0570-6; 0-8050-1316-4 (pa) LC 86-4787

An illustrated version of the well-known poem written in 1916, about birch trees and the pleasures of climbing them

"The freedom called for in the sweep and depth of Frost's words should not be hemmed in by rigidly defined illustrations, and Young allows this license, giving the viewer ample opportunity to absorb and be absorbed by the imagery. The text is set two to three lines to a page, with the poem repeated in its entirety at the end." Booklist

Stopping by woods on a snowy evening; illustrated by Susan Jeffers. Dutton 1978 unp il $11.95 (k-3) **811**

1. Winter—Poetry

ISBN 0-525-40115-6 LC 78-8134

Illustrations of wintry scenes accompany each line of the well-known poem

"There is such delicate strength to this famous poem that stretching it to book size might easily have become a heavy-handed venture. Fortunately the artist has taken great care to love, honor and faithfully follow the words. Her drawing, which tends at times to prettification, is for the most part softly restrained. You can almost hear the silence of the woods in it." N Y Times Book Rev

Giovanni, Nikki

Spin a soft black song: poems for children; illustrated by George Martins. rev ed. Hill & Wang 1985 57p il $9.95; pa $3.50 (3-6) **811**

1. Blacks—Poetry
ISBN 0-8090-8796-0; 0-374-46469-3 (pa)
LC 84-19287

First published 1971

A poetry collection which recounts the feelings of black children about their neighborhoods, American society, and themselves

"A beautifully illustrated book of poems about black children for children of all ages. . . . Simple in theme but a very moving collection nonetheless." Read Ladders for Hum Relat. 5th edition

Greenfield, Eloise, 1929-

Daydreamers; [illustrated by] Tom Feelings. Dial Press 1981 unp il $11.95; lib bdg $11.89; pa $3.95 (3-6) **811**

1. Dreams—Poetry 2. Blacks—Poetry
ISBN 0-8037-2137-4; 0-8037-2134-X (lib bdg); 0-8037-0167-5 (pa) LC 80-27262

This is a "poem about the child who daydreams, and who is changed by the introspective quiet of that dreaming." Bull Cent Child Books

"Expressive, soul-searching portraits of Black young people—ranging from early innocent childhood to adolescence on the brink of maturity—are uncannily echoed by the pellucid sensitive words. Done in sepia or in tones of gray, the portrayals display a quiet, pensive vitality." Horn Book

Honey, I love, and other love poems; pictures by Diane and Leo Dillon. Crowell 1978 unp il $12.95; lib bdg $12.89; pa $3.50 (2-4) **811**

1. Blacks—Poetry 2. Love poetry
ISBN 0-690-01334-5; 0-690-03845-3 (lib bdg); 0-06-443097-9 (pa) LC 77-2845

"These 16 poems explore facets of warm, loving relationships with family, friends and schoolmates as experienced by a young Black girl. Central to the theme of the book is the idea that the child loves herself and is very confident in expressing that love." Interracial Books Child Bull

"The Dillons transform this quiet book into magic with soft, grey charcoal renderings of the young girl and her friends, overlaid with child-like brown scratchboard pictures embodying the images in the poems." SLJ

Nathaniel talking; illustrated by Jan Spivey Gilchrist. Black Butterfly Children's Bks. 1989 c1988 unp il $11.95 (2-4) **811**

1. Blacks—Poetry
ISBN 0-86316-200-2 LC 88-51011

Coretta Scott King Award for illustration, 1990

"The rhythm of Greenfield's text is infectious from a very early line: 'It's Nathaniel talking/and Nathaniel's me/I'm talking about/My philosophy/About the things I do/And the people I see/All told in the words/Of Nathaniel B. Free/That's me.' Her sentiments are equally affecting, but in a more sobering way; Nathaniel wonders when he'll ever be old enough not to have to answer a question 'I don't know,' and he remembers his mother, who has died. . . . His experiences are warmly universal, as are Gilchrist's depictions of his joyful and sorrowful moments." Publ Wkly

Under the Sunday tree; paintings by Amos Ferguson; poems by Eloise Greenfield. Harper & Row 1988 38p il $12.95; lib bdg $12.89; pa $3.50 (2-4) **811**

1. Bahamas—Poetry
ISBN 0-06-022254-9; 0-06-022257-3 (lib bdg); 0-06-443257-2 (pa) LC 87-29373

"This collection of poems and paintings present a vivid picture of life in the Bahamas. The poems cover a variety of subjects and occasionally seem to have been written to go with a painting. The folk-art styled paintings are detailed, vibrant and certainly evoke a picture of island life." Child Book Rev Serv

Grimes, Nikki

Something on my mind; [illustrated by] Tom Feelings; words by Nikki Grimes. Dial Bks. 1978 unp il $8.95; lib bdg $8.44; pa $3.95 **811**

1. Blacks—Poetry
ISBN 0-8037-8229-2; 0-8037-8225-X (lib bdg); 0-8037-0273-6 (pa) LC 77-86266

Coretta Scott King Award for illustrations, 1979

"The black and white drawings of black children by Feelings were used by Grimes as bases for prose poems that interpret the pictures. The drawings are sensitive portraits, some beautifully shaded and soft, others looking like deft, unfinished sketches. The poems vary in depth and treatment, some fragmentary and others imbued with poignant emotion; all are serious, some reflecting the black experience and others—most of the selections—capturing universal longings or reactions of childhood." Bull Cent Child Books

Hale, Sarah Josepha

Mary had a little lamb unp il (k-2) **811**

1. Nursery rhymes 2. Sheep—Poetry

Some editions are:

Holiday House lib bdg $13.95; pa $5.95 illustrations by Tomie de Paola (ISBN 0-8234-0509-5; 0-8234-0519-2) with musical accompaniment

Scholastic lib bdg $12.95 photos by Bruce McMillan (ISBN 0-590-43773-9)

First published 1830 by Marsh, Capen & Lyon with title: Mary's lamb

The famous nineteenth-century nursery rhyme about the school-going lamb

Highwater, Jamake

Moonsong lullaby; photographs by Marcia Keegan. Lothrop, Lee & Shepard Bks. 1981 unp il $12.95 (k-2) **811**

1. Indians of North America—Poetry 2. Night—Poetry
ISBN 0-688-00427-X LC 81-1909

Highwater, Jamake—*Continued*

As the moon moves across the sky, it observes the activities of an Indian camp and the natural phenomena surrounding it

"The tone poem, quiet and reverent, has a warmth that is nicely contrasted with the cool night skies of the handsome color photographs. . . . The moment for this book may have to be chosen, but at the right moment this celebration of the affinity between the Native American and the natural world should reach and touch children." Bull Cent Child Books

Hoban, Russell

Egg thoughts, and other Frances songs; pictures by Lillian Hoban. Harper & Row 1972 31p il $12.95; lib bdg $12.89 (k-2) **811**

ISBN 0-06-022331-6; 0-06-022332-4 (lib bdg) LC 70-183162

In this collection of poems, Frances the badger focuses "on eggs cooked in various ways, a wellworn favorite doll, string, homework, little sister Gloria, and other joys and tribulations of childhood." Booklist

"Frances' thoughts and observations though not always fluidly expressed, are childlike and unselfconsciously amusing, and the verse is complemented by illustrations that are equally down-to-earth and appealing." SLJ

Other available titles about Frances entered in class E

Hooper, Patricia, 1941-

A bundle of beasts; illustrated by Mark Steele. Houghton Mifflin 1987 60p il $12.95 (3-6) **811**

1. Animals—Poetry 2. English language—Terms and phrases

ISBN 0-395-44259-1 LC 86-34413

"A collection of amusingly illustrated poems about different animals described by their correct collective nouns—for example, a knot of toads, a murder of crows, a leap of leopards and a trip of goats as well as the more familiar gaggle of geese and pride of lions." N Y Times Book Rev

"An author's note on the origin of the terms and a list of suggested readings for discovering others conclude this original combination of craft and cunning. Choice verse for a browse, a class-read-aloud, or a language arts program." Bull Cent Child Books

Hughes, Langston, 1902-1967

The dream keeper, and other poems; illustrations by Helen Sewell. Knopf 1986 c1932 77p il lib bdg $10.99 (5 and up) **811**

1. Blacks—Poetry

ISBN 0-394-91096-6 LC 85-19762

A reissue of the title first published 1932

A collection of fifty-nine poems, selected by the author, including lyrical poems, songs, and blues, many exploring the black experience

Kennedy, X. J.

Brats; illustrations by James Watts. Atheneum Pubs. 1986 42p il $11.95 (3-6) **811**

1. Nonsense verses

ISBN 0-689-50392-X LC 85-20018

Companion volume to: Fresh brats, entered below

"A Margaret K. McElderry book"

"Forty-two brief verses, mostly rhymed quatrains, celebrate or denigrate the actions of mischievous children, many of whom meet fearful fates. These are bright, tight, and inventive, with plenty of playground chanting potential. . . . A few of the selections have a slightly grisly ring (specifically, in the case of Louise, who sneaks up on a snoozing bear), but it's all done in high humor, as are the slapstick black-and-white drawings that illustrate the spacious pages. Neatly crafted poetry that will be highly popular as well." Bull Cent Child Books

The forgetful wishing well: poems for young people; with illustrations by Monica Incisa. Atheneum Pubs. 1985 88p $11.95 (4 and up) **811**

ISBN 0-689-50317-2 LC 84-45977

"A Margaret K. McElderry book"

Seventy poems deal with the challenges of growing up, curious beasts and birds, city life, and other subjects both realistic and fanciful

"Characterized by fresh imagery, related to but not restricted by everyday expressions, these are poems to delight the ear and stimulate the imagination. Strategically placed full-page, pen-and-ink drawings add a restrained decorative note to a handsomely designed small volume." Horn Book

Fresh brats; illustrations by James Watts. Margaret K. McElderry Bks. 1990 44p il $13.95 (3-6) **811**

1. Nonsense verses

ISBN 0-689-50499-3 LC 89-38031

Companion volume to: Brats, entered above

This book "contains 44 short comic verses about mischievous children. As in the previous collection, Watts has contributed 16 black-and-white drawings that highlight the actions in the verse." SLJ

"For children who think poetry too sweet and sentimental, Kennedy's acerbic wit is the perfect antidote to their preconceptions." Booklist

Ghastlies, goops & pincushions: nonsense verse; drawings by Ron Barrett. Margaret K. McElderry Bks. 1989 56p il $12.95 (3-6) **811**

1. Nonsense verses

ISBN 0-689-50477-2 LC 88-28663

"A diverse collection of short, amusing poems, Kennedy's . . . book takes imagination in many directions. Children will savor his high-flying nonsense and his deliciously malicious wit. . . . Barrett's black-and-white drawings, appearing on nearly every other page, underscore the humor with their lively, exaggerated interpretation of the poetry. A fine choice for children who like their poetry comical, and their comedy droll." Booklist

Kuskin, Karla

Any me I want to be: poems. Harper & Row 1972 unp il lib bdg $11.89 (1-4) **811**

ISBN 0-06-023616-7 LC 77-105485

Illustrated by the author

These thirty poems "do not describe: instead, the poet has tried—and, with refreshing, edged but gentle humor and not an ounce of condescension, succeeded—'to get inside each subject and briefly be it.' . . . The subjects—and moods and pacing, too—range from a mirror to the moon." Saturday Rev

Dogs & dragons, trees & dreams: a collection of poems. Harper & Row 1980 85p il lib bdg $12.89 (2-4) **811**

ISBN 0-06-023544-6 LC 79-2814

A representative collection of Karla Kuskin's poetry with introductory notes on poetry writing and appreciation

"Karla Kuskin's work has imagination and verve, but her diction is not always impeccable; by her own admission, her poems are 'relaxed.' But she exhorts adults to read poetry to children and to encourage them to read and to write." Horn Book

Near the window tree: poems and notes. Harper & Row 1975 63p il lib bdg $12.89 (2-5) **811**

ISBN 0-06-023540-3 LC 74-20394

"An Ursula Nordstrom book"

In the notes preceding each of her thirty-two verses, Mrs. Kuskin describes how she "felt when she was making her poems. . . . [Some of her poems focus on] words like bug, moustache, worm, cat, and family." Christ Sci Monit

"Not only can one enjoy the poetry, but the drawings and the accompanying notes give a sense of conversing with the author and understanding what goes on before, during, and after a poem. This combination is very useful to a classroom teacher who is interested in stirring children to write." Read Teach

Lessac, Frané

Caribbean canvas. Lippincott 1989 c1987 unp il $14.95; lib bdg $14.89 **811**

1. Poetry—Collected works 2. Caribbean region in art

ISBN 0-397-32367-0; 0-397-32368-9 (lib bdg)

LC 88-36555

First published 1987 in the United Kingdom

"This is a collection of Lessac's paintings of island life in Antigua, Barbados, Grenada, St. Kitts, Nevis, Redonda, and the Grenadines. [It also contains] West Indian proverbs and poems from a dozen poets, including Edward Brathwaite, A.L. Hendricks, and Evan Jones." Publisher's note

"A sampling of poetry and Lessac's idiosyncratic paintings is blended into a flavorful evocation of life in the Caribbean islands. The poems and proverbs included seem almost an afterthought to the striking illustrations, which, through brown faces, neon colors, and assorted scenes of buildings, beaches, and people, suggest both the joy and the harsher realities of tropical life." Booklist

Lewis, J. Patrick

A hippopotamusn't and other animal verses; pictures by Victoria Chess. Dial Bks. for Young Readers 1990 unp il $12.95; lib bdg $12.89 (k-3) **811**

1. Animals—Poetry 2. Humorous poetry

ISBN 0-8037-0518-2; 0-8037-0519-0 (lib bdg)

LC 87-24579

This is a collection of light verse that "concentrates on an intriguing selection of birds and beasts. Varied poetic forms include, among others, lively quatrains, couplets, and limericks as well as a charming haiku. . . . The tone is light; the effect genuinely humorous rather than merely funny—a mood complemented by Victoria Chess's colorful, expressive, and at times oh-so-subtly wicked illustrations. Her delicate, agile use of line underscores the quick wit of the poet to perfection." Horn Book

Lewis, Richard

In the night, still dark; illustrated by Ed Young. Atheneum Pubs. 1988 unp il $13.95 (1-3) **811**

1. Creation—Poetry

ISBN 0-689-31310-1 LC 87-11538

"This poem is an abridgment of *The Kumulipo*, the Hawaiian creation chant. It begins with the 'darkness of the night, nothing but night,' and follows the creation of the world to man and the dawn of the first day. Lewis's adaptation of this tale has retained a richness of language and the rhythm of a chant, but it is also entirely accessible to young children. And Young's illustrations are superb; his use of electric—but somehow muted—pinks, oranges, greens, blues and reds provides an evocative, mythical background for the stark white lettering of the text. Together author and artist have created an outstanding version of a centuries-old story." Publ Wkly

Little, Jean, 1932-

Hey world, here I am! illustrations by Sue Truesdell. Harper & Row 1989 88p il $12.95; lib bdg $12.89; pa $2.95 (4-6) **811**

ISBN 0-06-023989-1; 0-06-024006-7 (lib bdg); 0-06-440384-X (pa) LC 88-10987

Text first published 1986 in Canada

A collection of poems and brief vignettes from the perspective of a girl named Kate Bloomfield, reflecting her views on friendship, school, family life, and the world

"Engaging and often humorous, the vignettes are short enough to capture even the most reluctant reader yet deep enough to make the most sophisticated think. . . . Truesdell's gray line-and-wash illustrations are a fine, funny touch." Booklist

Livingston, Myra Cohn

Birthday poems; illustrated by Margot Tomes. Holiday House 1989 32p il lib bdg $13.95 (k-3) **811**

1. Birthdays—Poetry
ISBN 0-8234-0783-7 LC 89-2114

"In this collection of poems centered around the festive theme of birthdays, there are games, good things to eat, prizes, and lots of presents. But best of all are Margot Tomes's illustrations of the variety of children who enjoy them. Humorous touches, such as the stuffed monsters who leer out at the reader in 'Pinning the Tail on the Donkey.' make this a special treat." Horn Book

Celebrations; Myra Cohn Livingston, poet; Leonard Everett Fisher, painter. Holiday House 1985 unp il lib bdg $14.95; pa $5.95 (1-3) **811**

1. Holidays—Poetry
ISBN 0-8234-0550-8 (lib bdg); 0-8234-0654-7 (pa) LC 84-19216

"Sixteen short, mainly rhymed verses celebrate major holidays beginning with New Year's and ending with Christmas. A final page recalls that special event, 'birthday.' The book exhibits a fine variety of moods; all the poems would work with the intended audience. . . . Visually dramatic, the illustrations pack a punch. All but three of the poems appear on double-page spreads with text on one side, the painting encompassing both. In addition, the large page size, lack of margins, brilliant colors and surprising compositions all add a great sense of excitement." SLJ

A circle of seasons; Myra Cohn Livingston, poet; Leonard Everett Fisher, painter. Holiday House 1982 unp il lib bdg $14.95; pa $5.95 (1-3) **811**

1. Seasons—Poetry
ISBN 0-8234-0452-8 (lib bdg); 0-8234-0696-3 (pa) LC 81-20305

"A cycle of 12 quatrains, each with its own brief refrain, celebrates the four seasons depicted in expressionistic oil paintings." Booklist

"The paintings are stunning, bold and stylized but with delicate details; there is variety in the brushwork and use of color, uniformity in the excellent use of space and shape to achieve effective compositions. Nice to read alone, or aloud, nice to look at." Bull Cent Child Books

Earth songs; Leonard Everett Fisher, painter. Holiday House 1986 unp il lib bdg $14.95 **811**

1. Earth—Poetry
ISBN 0-8234-0615-6 LC 86-341

"The poetry is first-person—the Earth tells her mountains, her forests, her deserts, and her waters, and each page reminds readers of the power and grandeur of our often taken-for-granted surroundings." SLJ

"Fisher's majestic paintings bring drama to such descriptions as the 'red mouth' of a volcano and the round O of earth surrounded by a golden halo of light in a star-flecked sky. This book will challenge the minds and enrich the vision of its young readers." Publ Wkly

Sea songs; Myra Cohn Livingston, poet; Leonard Everett Fisher, painter. Holiday House 1986 unp il lib bdg $14.95 **811**

1. Sea poetry
ISBN 0-8234-0591-5 LC 85-16422

Poetic images of cresting waves, mermaids, sunken ships, and other aspects of the sea

"The language is strong and beautiful ('Galleons, shouldered on scaly arms,' or 'Lost in her midnight witchery moon watches'). The poems are perfectly matched by Fisher's powerful double-page acrylic paintings. For once time and tide do wait—to be savored and enjoyed by readers." SLJ

Sky songs; Myra Cohn Livingston, poet; Leonard Everett Fisher, painter. Holiday House 1984 31p il lib bdg $14.95 **811**

1. Sky—Poetry
ISBN 0-8234-0502-8 LC 83-12955

"Fourteen poems consisting of three cinquains each address the heavenly bodies—the moon, stars, planets, and shooting stars—and the changing moods of the sky from dawn to sunset, through storms and smog." Horn Book

"The author and artist combine their talents to create a book that is a pleasure to see and to read. Livingston's poems . . . are honed and sensitive, while Fisher's paintings combine, in double-page spreads, vibrant colors, and effective use of space, and wonderful variation of mood in handsomely composed paintings." Bull Cent Child Books

A song I sang to you: a selection of poems; illustrated by Margot Tomes; introduction by David McCord. Harcourt Brace Jovanovich 1984 84p il $12.95 (k-3) **811**

ISBN 0-15-277105-0 LC 84-4585

An illustrated collection of more than sixty poems drawn from the author's earlier works

"This collection is geared for the read-aloud audience, logically grouped, and attractively illustrated with black and white drawings. They were fine poems when they first appeared, and are fine poems now especially and wisely selected for younger children." Bull Cent Child Books

Lobel, Arnold

The book of pigericks: pig limericks. Harper & Row 1983 48p il $14.95; lib bdg $14.89; pa $5.95 (1-3) **811**

1. Pigs—Poetry 2. Limericks
ISBN 0-06-023982-4; 0-06-023983-2 (lib bdg); 0-06-443163-0 (pa) LC 82-47730

"The heroes and heroines of these rhymes—pictured in soft, subtle colors with affectionate humor and lyric expressiveness—are for the most part middle class, middle aged lady and gentleman pigs in elaborate 19th-century attire. . . . Limerick lovers expect exuberance, inventiveness, literary lunacy—in short, the unexpected. And it is plentiful here." N Y Times Book Rev

Lobel, Arnold—*Continued*

Whiskers & rhymes; written and illustrated by Arnold Lobel. Greenwillow Bks. 1985 48p il $13; lib bdg $12.88; pa $3.95 (1-3) **811**

1. Humorous poetry 2. Nursery rhymes
ISBN 0-688-03835-2; 0-688-03836-0 (lib bdg); 0-688-08291-2 (pa) LC 83-25424

These poems are "lilting, brief, comic, often nonsensical, occasionally related to a Mother Goose rhyme. . . . They have that fun-to-say/easy-to-memorize quality. . . . There are clever pictures, softly tinted and drawn with panache, on every page, and the layout of illustrations and poems on the pages has been done to make both communications maximally effective." Bull Cent Child Books

Longfellow, Henry Wadsworth, 1807-1882

The children's own Longfellow. Houghton Mifflin 1920 103p il $12.95 (5 and up) **811**

ISBN 0-395-06889-4
First published 1908
Includes 8 colored illustrations by various artists

Contents: The wreck of the Hesperus; The village blacksmith; Evangeline [selection]; The song of Hiawatha [selection]; The building of the ship; The castle-builder; Paul Revere's ride; The building of the Long Serpent

Hiawatha; pictures by Susan Jeffers. Dial Bks. for Young Readers 1983 unp il $13.95; lib bdg $13.89 (k-3) **811**

1. Indians of North America—Poetry 2. Indians of North America—Legends
ISBN 0-8037-0013-X; 0-8037-0014-8 (lib bdg) LC 83-7225

Verses excerpted from the poem first published 1855 with title: Song of Hiawatha

"Jeffers has captured the essence of this brief section from the classic poem. . . . The pale tints of the pictures are in complete harmony with nature and with the text and show in detail how Hiawatha might have seen his world. A fine first exposure to the poem for children and a beautiful artistic experience." SLJ

Hiawatha's childhood; illustrated by Errol Le Cain. Farrar, Straus & Giroux 1984 unp il $14.95; Puffin Bks. pa $3.95 (k-3) **811**

1. Indians of North America—Poetry 2. Indians of North America—Legends
ISBN 0-374-33065-4; 0-14-050562-8 (pa) LC 84-47969

Verses excerpted from the poem first published 1855 with title: Song of Hiawatha

Describes the childhood of the legendary Iroquois Indian, Hiawatha

"Le Cain uses the deep hues of a woodland setting. Dusky greens, tans, blues, and oranges provide brooding, smoky, dense compositions that also carry a strong decorative element. . . . This . . . is rich, almost tapestrylike in its complexities and in its reverential intimations of mood. A careful, ambitious, and largely successful interpretation." Booklist

Paul Revere's ride il (k-3) **811**

1. Revere, Paul, 1735-1818—Poetry 2. Lexington, Battle of, 1775—Poetry

Some editions are:

Dutton $14.95 Illustrated by Ted Rand (ISBN 0-525-44610-9)

Greenwillow Bks. $13.95; lib bdg $11.88 Illustrated by Nancy Winslow Parker (ISBN 0-688-04014-4; 0-688-04015-2)

The famous narrative poem recreating Paul Revere's midnight ride in 1775 to warn the people of the Boston countryside that the British were coming

"Nancy Winslow Parker's rendering . . . both delights and instructs young and older readers alike. In addition to her simple and charming drawings, she includes an informative note on the setting, a clear map of 1775 Boston, and a section defining difficult words and terms." Child Book Rev Serv

"Rand's illustrations . . . are impressionistic in the use of color and light, yet realistic in historical interpretation. . . . The wide double-page spreads have a panoramic vision and a dramatic impetus that make this the version of choice for reading aloud." Booklist

Margolis, Richard J.

Secrets of a small brother; illustrated by Donald Carrick. Macmillan 1984 unp il $11.95 (1-3) **811**

1. Brothers—Poetry
ISBN 0-02-762280-0 LC 84-3878

"A collection of short poems about the thoughts and feelings of a small boy in relation to his older brother. His reactions are sensitively and sometimes humorously voiced as the brothers play, fight, and share happiness and sorrow. The charming free verse poems will be enjoyed by young children, especially those with brothers. The black-and-white illustrations are realistic and appealing." Child Book Rev Serv

Marzollo, Jean

The teddy bear book; pictures by Ann Schweninger. Dial Bks. for Young Readers 1989 unp il $11.95; lib bdg $11.89 (k-2) **811**

1. Teddy bears—Poetry
ISBN 0-8037-0524-7; 0-8037-0633-2 (lib bdg) LC 87-24538

"These poems are adaptations of songs, jump rope rhymes, ball-bouncing chants, cheers, and story poems that are passed from generation to generation and child to child in the oral tradition. Since love of teddy bears is another tradition continually passed on, it seemed natural to connect bears and rhymes." Preface

"Schweninger's bright and cheerful watercolor illustrations complement the text without overwhelming it." SLJ

McCord, David Thompson Watson, 1897-

All day long: fifty rhymes of the never was and always is; by David McCord; drawings by Henry B. Kane. Little, Brown 1966 104p il $12.95 (4-6) **811**

ISBN 0-316-55508-8 LC 66-17688

McCord, David Thompson Watson, 1897- —*Continued*

Poems about the haunting delights, surprises and wit of childhood

"The topics are simple but intriguing, the writing has rhythm, humor, and imaginative zest; the black and white illustrations are attractive, many of them also humorous." Bull Cent Child Books

One at a time; his collected poems for the young; with full subject index as well as an index of first lines; [by] David McCord; with illustrations by Henry B. Kane. Little, Brown 1977 494p il $18.95 (4-6) **811**

ISBN 0-316-55516-9 LC 77-21792

A collection of poems previously published in All day long and Take sky (each entered separately) and in Away and ago (1975); Far and few (1952); and For me to say (1970)

"This one-volume edition, with a short introduction by the poet . . . is likely to be most useful to teachers and school resource persons; children's collections that already hold the five individual titles should find those sufficient for use by young readers." SLJ

Speak up: more rhymes of the never was and always is; by David McCord; illustrated by Marc Simont. Little, Brown 1980 68p il $13.95 (4-6) **811**

ISBN 0-316-55517-7 LC 80-15260

"The 50 poems, about all sorts of things—butterflies, windshield wipers, long words, joggers, worms—are uneven in quality. Some catch McCord's wit, playfulness and disciplined shaping. Others are merely cute or clever; a few are flat and uninspired. Its pleasant, unintimidating format and the humorous sketches make it attractive." SLJ

Take sky: more rhymes of the never was and always is; by David McCord; drawings by Henry B. Kane. Little, Brown 1962 107p il $12.95 (4-6) **811**

ISBN 0-316-55509-6 LC 62-12392

A collection of forty-eight humorous poems on various subjects ranging in form from short verses to longer narrative poetry

"Diversity of imagination and humor makes a volume that bears dipping into again and again for quiet enjoyment and for reading aloud. Henry Kane's pencil drawings, make beautiful pages, with great variety in layout." Horn Book

McGinley, Phyllis, 1905-1978

The year without a Santa Claus; pictures by Kurt Werth. Lippincott 1957 unp il $12.95; lib bdg $14.89 (k-3) **811**

1. Christmas—Poetry

ISBN 0-397-30399-8; 0-397-31969-X (lib bdg) LC 57-10332

The author's verse and "the illustrator's agreeable pictures give new life to an old theme. When Santa Claus announces that he is much too tired for Christmas capers and is going to take his first vacation, the weeping children of the world . . . decide to give Santa a Merry Christmas. What happens when Santa receives his gifts climaxes a story-poem which will be enjoyed by the whole family." Booklist

McMillan, Bruce

One sun: a book of terse verse; written & photo-illustrated by Bruce McMillan. Holiday House 1990 unp il lib bdg $14.95 (k-3) **811**

1. Beaches—Poetry

ISBN 0-8234-0810-8 LC 89-24625

Describes a day at the beach in a series of terse verses (verses made up of two monosyllabic words that rhyme) accompanied by photographs

"There is a strong textural element; readers can practically feel the sand in their shoes. Teachers may enjoy trying out the rhyming game concepts with their students, while everyone else will simply enjoy the pleasure of a perfect sunny day at the seaside." SLJ

Merriam, Eve, 1916-

Blackberry ink; pictures by Hans Wilhelm. Morrow 1985 unp il $12.95; lib bdg $12.88 (k-2) **811**

1. Humorous poetry 2. Nonsense verses

ISBN 0-688-04150-7; 0-688-04151-5 (lib bdg) LC 84-16633

"These 24 simple poems touch everyday objects and occurrences—elusive butterflies, seasonal happenings, favorite foods, bedtime routine, animal antics and more. . . . The smiling teddy on the cover appears throughout the pages in the midst of charming watercolor illustrations featuring delightfully devilish children and whimsical animals. Merriam's poems are great fun to read. . . . Sure to tickle small funnybones everywhere and to provide many moments of pleasure." SLJ

Chortles: new and selected wordplay poems; illustrations by Sheila Hamanaka. Morrow Junior Bks. 1989 53p il $11.95; lib bdg $11.88 (3-6) **811**

ISBN 0-688-08152-5; 0-688-08153-3 (lib bdg) LC 88-29129

"A selection of forty-seven new and previously published verses by a popular writer that promises to delight pun and poetry lovers, young and old. . . . Humorous pencil drawings appropriately reflect the spirit of the collection." Horn Book

Fresh paint; new poems by Eve Merriam; woodcuts by David Frampton. Macmillan 1986 unp il $11.95 (4 and up) **811**

ISBN 0-02-766860-6 LC 85-23742

Forty-five poems on subjects ranging from the squat mushroom to the new moon

"The variety of rhyming patterns, the freshness of vision, and the deceptive ease with which image and idea are summoned up contribute a liveliness, sophistication, and vitality often missing in poetry for the young. The attractive black-and-white woodcuts nicely complement the quirky and playful quality of the poetry itself." Horn Book

Merriam, Eve, 1916-—*Continued*
Halloween A B C; illustrations by Lane Smith. Macmillan 1987 unp il $14.95 (k-2) **811**

1. Halloween—Poetry 2. Alphabet
ISBN 0-02-766870-3 LC 86-23772

"These 26 Halloween poems, one for each letter of the alphabet, are, like most of Merriam's work, imaginative, inventive, and playful. Her unusual rhythms, rhythmic schemes, and twists of word or image are often humorous as well as seasonally spooky. . . . Smith's dark oil paintings on ecru pages match both the mood and the wit of the poems. . . . This is not a book for young children to learn the alphabet, but it is a witty, whimsical, and happily shivery book for Halloween sharing." SLJ

A poem for a pickle: funnybone verses; pictures by Sheila Hamanaka. Morrow Junior Bks. 1989 unp il $12.95; lib bdg $12.88 (k-2) **811**

ISBN 0-688-08137-1; 0-688-08138-X (lib bdg) LC 88-22047

This "collection includes 28 short, witty poems. . . . Using overlapping lines of finely shaded color, Hamanaka creates lively artwork with refreshingly varied composition and points of view. A visually appealing poetry book with lots of classroom potential." Booklist

You be good and I'll be night: jump-on-the-bed poems; pictures by Karen Lee Schmidt. Morrow Junior Bks. 1988 unp il $12.95; lib bdg $12.88 (k-2) **811**

ISBN 0-688-06742-5; 0-688-06743-3 (lib bdg) LC 87-24859

This "collection of twenty-eight poems features mostly jump-rope rhythms and chanting rhymes. . . . Each poem is accompanied with bouncy watercolor scenes, often including comically incongruous animals. . . . A few are too jingly, but on the whole this is nonsense with flair." Bull Cent Child Books

Millay, Edna St. Vincent, 1892-1950
Edna St. Vincent Millay's poems selected for young people; woodcuts by Ronald Keller. new ed. Harper & Row 1979 115p il $13.95 (4 and up) **811**

ISBN 0-06-024218-3 LC 77-25671
First published 1929

"The poems are drawn from Renascence [1917], A few figs from thistles [1921]; Second April [1921], and The Harp-weaver [1923 Pulitzer Prize winner]. . . . The new illustrations—woodcuts in chalk blue and black—are tastefully done and carefully placed within the book. They merely suggest scenes and images, and a number of pages are unillustrated." Horn Book

Mizumura, Kazue
If I were a cricket . . . Crowell 1973 unp il lib bdg $13.89 (k-2) **811**

1. Love poetry 2. Animals—Poetry
ISBN 0-690-00076-6 LC 73-3495

"Small creatures such as a spider, firefly, snail, etc. are used to pronounce tender messages of love. . . . The appealing word images and mosaic-like drawings—pastels alternating with spreads done in black, white, and gray—will provide many opportunities for sharing warm feelings with very young children." SLJ

Moore, Clement Clarke, 1779-1863
The night before Christmas (k-3) **811**

1. Santa Claus—Poetry 2. Christmas—Poetry

Some editions are:

Clarion Bks. $13.95 Illustrated by Wendy Watson (ISBN 0-395-53624-3)
Doubleday $5.95 Illustrated by Elisa Trimby (ISBN 0-385-13615-3)
Holiday House lib bdg $14.95; pa $5.95 Illustrated by Tomie de Paola (ISBN 0-8234-0414-5; 0-8234-0417-X)
Holt & Co. $10.95 Illustrated by Michael Hague (ISBN 0-8050-0900-0)
Houghton Mifflin $13.95 With pictures by Jessie Willcox Smith (ISBN 0-395-06952-1) Has title: 'Twas the night before Christmas
Knopf $10.95 Illustrated by Scott Gustafson (ISBN 0-394-54809-4)
Knopf $9.95; lib bdg $10.99 Illustrated by Anita Lobel (ISBN 0-394-86863-3; 0-394-96863-8)
Macmillan $9.95 Illustrated by Tasha Tudor (ISBN 0-528-82181-4)
Philomel Bks. $15.95 (ISBN 0-399-21614-6) An antique reproduction
Random House $6.95; lib bdg $8.99 Illustrated by Cheryl Harness (ISBN 0-394-82698-1; 0-394-92698-6)
Random House lib bdg $15.99 Illustrated with paintings by Grandma Moses (ISBN 0-679-91526-5)
Simon & Schuster $5.95; pa $2.25 Illustrated by Tien (ISBN 0-671-62209-9; 0-671-68408-6)

Text first published 1823 with title: A visit from St. Nicholas

This popular Christmas poem has been a favorite with American children ever since the author wrote it for his children in 1822. It is from this poem that we get the names for the Christmas reindeer

Moore, Lilian, 1909-
Something new begins: new and selected poems; illustrated by Mary Jane Dunton. Atheneum Pubs. 1982 114p il $11.95 (4 and up) **811**

ISBN 0-689-30818-3 LC 82-1723

"Fifteen new verses, along with selections from previously published books such as 'I Thought I Heard a City,' 'See My Lovely Poison Ivy,' and 'Think of Shadows,' provide a wide range of topics." Booklist

"Dunton's unerring touch contributes illustrations that emphasize the glad, sensitive or funny lyrics that will evoke responses from young readers. Short, authoritative poems express ideas on subjects as big as a whale and as tiny as beach stones and a myriad of things in between." Publ Wkly

Morrison, Bill, 1935-

Squeeze a sneeze. Houghton Mifflin 1977 32p il lib bdg $13.95; pa $3.95 (k-3) **811**

1. Nonsense verses
ISBN 0-395-25151-6 (lib bdg); 0-395-44238-9 (pa) LC 76-62503

Illustrated by the author

The author "uses nonsense rhyming to teach creative word association as well as word enjoyment. Readers are invited to follow the author's examples of word play such as 'share a pear with a hungry bear' or 'make sure it's dark if you bark at a shark." SLJ

"The rhymes are nonsensical, but the illustrations make the word plays work. Young children will delight in hearing, repeating, and seeing this book. It is a book that a child would return to, time and time again." Child Book Rev Serv

Nash, Ogden, 1902-1971

Custard and company: poems; selected and illustrated by Quentin Blake. Little, Brown 1980 128p il $12.95; pa $4.95 (3 and up) **811**

1. Humorous poetry
ISBN 0-316-59834-8; 0-316-59855-0 (pa) LC 79-25742

"The cartoonist-illustrator has assembled this anthology of [84 of] his favorite Nash poems and provided illustrations for each one." SLJ

"The inspired lunacy of Nash's poems is wonderfully echoed by the scratchy, flyaway line drawings." Bull Cent Child Books

O'Neill, Mary Le Duc, 1908-1990

Hailstones and halibut bones; adventures in color; newly illustrated by John Wallner. Doubleday 1989 1961 unp il $12.95; lib bdg $13.99; pa $5.95 (k-3) **811**

1. Color—Poetry
ISBN 0-385-24484-3; 0-385-24485-1 (lib bdg); 0-385-41078-6 (pa) LC 88-484

A newly illustrated edition of the title first published 1961

Twelve poems reflect the author's feelings about various colors

"Wallner has created montages of each poem's images and colored them with various hues of the featured color. The results do complement the moods of the poems." SLJ

A **Peaceable** kingdom; the Shaker abecedarius; illustrated by Alice and Martin Provensen; afterword by Richard Meran Barsam. Viking 1978 unp il $13.95 (k-3) **811**

1. Alphabet 2. Animals—Poetry
ISBN 0-670-54500-7 LC 78-125

Text first published in Shaker Manifesto of July, 1882 under title: Animal rhymes

"Combining familiar home and barnyard creatures with those found only in whimsy, the Shakers taught their children the alphabet through this 26-line rhymed verse, which uses a successive letter at the beginning of each line." Booklist

"Done in muted color, the illustrations are full of straight-faced humor; too skillfully composed and executed to look quite like primitives, they display, nevertheless, a winsome naiveté." Horn Book

Plath, Sylvia

The bed book; pictures by Emily Arnold McCully. Harper & Row 1976 unp il $12.95; pa $4.95 (k-2) **811**

1. Bedtime—Poetry
ISBN 0-06-024746-0; 0-06-443184-3 (pa) LC 76-3825

"Children have special feelings about their own beds and Plath's inventive poem will enhance those feelings. With McCully's humorous illustrations, the child can see beds that are for fishing, beds for cats, and a bed for a troupe of acrobats—to mention only a few. This is a special book, especially beautiful and insightful, in a way that speaks directly to young children." Child Book Rev Serv

Pomerantz, Charlotte

All asleep; illustrated by Nancy Tafuri. Greenwillow Bks. 1984 32p il o.p.; Puffin Bks. paperback available $3.95 (k-2) **811**

1. Sleep—Poetry 2. Lullabies
ISBN 0-14-050548-2 (pa) LC 83-25337

Fifteen poems and lullabies "of varying moods: some soft songs lull listeners while others tease or gently cajole. All are oriented toward young children and their families, their worlds and their concerns." SLJ

"Rich, full-color illustrations back up the poems, each of which is framed against an appropriate spread that flows to the edge of the page. The colors are appealing—lush golds, reds, blues, and pinks—and the line work is crisp and clean. A most attractive book that should get plenty of wear." Booklist

If I had a paka: poems in eleven languages; illustrated by Nancy Tafuri. Greenwillow Bks. 1982 unp il lib bdg $11.88 (1-3) **811**

ISBN 0-688-00837-2 LC 81-6624

This "collection of 12 short poems is in English, but each poem uses a few words from a different language." SLJ

The author "has written some charming poems. . . . The foreign words are melodious and interesting, and they can always be understood in the context of the poems. The illustrations by Nancy Tafuri are exquisite combinations of design, color and feeling." N Y Times Book Rev

Prelutsky, Jack

The baby Uggs are hatching; pictures by James Stevenson. Greenwillow Bks. 1982 32p il $13.95; lib bdg $13.88; pa $3.95 (k-3) **811**

1. Nonsense verses
ISBN 0-688-00922-0; 0-688-00923-9 (lib bdg); 0-688-09239-X (pa) LC 81-7266

Prelutsky, Jack—*Continued*

This volume contains humorous poems about imaginary creatures with names like: Ugg, Quossible, Smasheroo, Flotterzott, and Grebbles

"The catchy rhythms, humorous drawings, and deliciously alarming subjects make a splendid book." Horn Book

Beneath a blue umbrella: rhymes; pictures by Garth Williams. Greenwillow Bks. 1990 64p il lib bdg $15.95 (k-3) **811**

1. Nonsense verses 2. Nursery rhymes
ISBN 0-688-06429-9 LC 86-19406

Companion volume to: Ride a purple pelican, entered below

A collection of illustrated humorous poems in which a hungry hippo raids a melon stand, a butterfly tickles a girl's nose, and children frolic in a Mardi Gras parade

"Prelutsky has an unerring sense of popular appeal; these verses bounce as rhythmically as children do on a bed or jumping rope. They also feature plenty of reassurance and humor, staples for chanting. Garth Williams' homey pen drawing and luminous colors enliven each full-page illustration with a dramatic simplicity set off by spacious book design." Bull Cent Child Books

Circus; pictures by Arnold Lobel. Macmillan 1974 unp il hardcover o.p. paperback available $3.95 (k-3) **811**

1. Circus—Poetry
ISBN 0-689-70806-8 (pa) LC 73-6055

Prelutsky "presents the attractions of the big top in verses and they are made visible in Lobel's witty color pictures. . . . For children who haven't experienced the thrills of the greatest show on earth, this book tells about the performing seals, the acrobats, sword-swallowers, fire eaters, human cannonballs and more." Publ Wkly

The Headless Horseman rides tonight; more poems to trouble your sleep; illustrated by Arnold Lobel. Greenwillow Bks. 1980 38p il $13.95; lib bdg $13.88 (2-5) **811**

1. Monsters—Poetry
ISBN 0-688-80273-7; 0-688-84273-9 (lib bdg) LC 80-10372

"In a companion volume to 'Nightmares: Poems to Trouble Your Sleep' [entered below] poet and artist again collaborate to elicit feelings of . . . terror. . . . In addition to the perambulating mummy, the author deals with, among others, a writhing specter on a misty moor, a zombie, a sorceress, a baleful banshee . . . the abominable snowman and a headless horseman." Horn Book

The author's "rhymes are as lethal, lithe, and literate as ever and Lobel wrings every atmospheric ounce out of them." SLJ

It's Christmas; pictures by Marylin Hafner. Greenwillow Bks. 1981 46p il $12.95; lib bdg $12.88; Scholastic pa $2.50 (1-3) **811**

1. Christmas—Poetry
ISBN 0-688-00439-3; 0-688-00440-7 (lib bdg); 0-590-40584-5 (pa) LC 81-1100

"A Greenwillow read-alone book"

"The poems cover subjects of interest to children—making a Christmas list, performing in the school assembly, cutting a Christmas tree . . . [and dealing] with the disappointments that sometimes occur: being sick on Christmas, getting underwear as a gift and having a new sled but no snow. Marilyn Hafner's cartoonlike drawings add to the fun." SLJ

It's Halloween; pictures by Marylin Hafner. Greenwillow Bks. 1977 56p il $12.95; lib bdg $12.88; Scholastic pa $2.50 (1-3) **811**

1. Halloween—Poetry
ISBN 0-688-80102-1; 0-688-84102-3 (lib bdg); 0-590-41536-0 (pa) LC 77-2141

"A Greenwillow read-alone book"

"A gathering of thirteen light-hearted verses celebrates for beginning readers the deliciously frightening aspects of Halloween. Although a few seem constrained by the format, the majority demonstrate the inventive use of words and agile rhythms characteristic of the poet's style. . . . The illustrations, most of them in four colors, highlight the contrast between the real and the imagined, thus providing an appropriate visual extension for the simple text." Horn Book

It's snowing! It's snowing! pictures by Jeanne Titherington. Greenwillow Bks. 1984 47p il $11.75; lib bdg $11.88 (1-3) **811**

1. Winter—Poetry 2. Snow—Poetry
ISBN 0-688-01512-3; 0-688-01513-1 (lib bdg) LC 83-16583

"Soft gray-and-white drawings washed with blue complement seventeen poems that celebrate a child's delight in snow. From 'One Last Little Leaf' to 'The Snowman's Lament' the course of a season is marked by the natural phenomena and human activities of winter. . . . An easy-to-read format and large print suit the facility of the rhyme and accessibility of the imagery. Where more challenging vocabulary is introduced, contextual clues help the beginning reader." Horn Book

It's Thanksgiving; pictures by Marylin Hafner. Greenwillow Bks. 1982 47p il $12.95; lib bdg $12.88; Scholastic pa $2.50 (1-3) **811**

1. Thanksgiving Day—Poetry
ISBN 0-688-00441-5; 0-688-00442-3 (lib bdg); 0-590-41571-9 (pa) LC 81-1929

"A Greenwillow read-alone book"

This "collection of poems about Thanksgiving has rhyme, rhythm, and humor as well as a variety of topics: helping Grandma with the meal, watching Daddy watch a football game, seeing a Thanksgiving Day parade, working on school projects, not being able to eat any of the holiday treats because of braces, and the Pilgrim Thanksgiving. The poems are illustrated by brisk, often comic drawings, line and wash. This isn't great poetry, but it has a bouncy quality that's appealing." Bull Cent Child Books

Prelutsky, Jack—*Continued*

It's Valentine's Day; pictures by Yossi Abolafia. Greenwillow Bks. 1983 47p il $12.95; lib bdg $12.88; Scholastic pa $2.50 (1-3) **811**

1. Valentine's Day—Poetry
ISBN 0-688-02311-8; 0-688-02312-6 (lib bdg); 0-590-40979-4 (pa) LC 83-1449

"A Greenwillow read-alone book"

"The 14 poems here range from the genuine joy of 'It's Valentine's Day' . . . to the giddy goofiness of 'I love you more than applesauce' or 'Jelly Jill loves Weasel Will'. . . .The rhymes are generally simple but clever and the line drawings in red and blue, with their expressive faces and explanatory vignettes, add tremendously to the enjoyment of the poetry." SLJ

My parents think I'm sleeping: poems; pictures by Yossi Abolafia. Greenwillow Bks. 1985 47p il $13.95; lib bdg $13.88 (2-4) **811**

1. Sleep—Poetry
ISBN 0-688-04018-7; 0-688-04019-5 (lib bdg) LC 84-13640

This is a collection of humorous poems about bedtime

"Sometimes humorous, sometimes thoughtfully quiet, the poems reflect an interesting range of reactions to the night. . . . Illustrations, done for the most part in appropriate shades of gray and blue with occasional glints of yellow light, extend the nuances of the poetry. While some of the selections may seem a bit limper than the poet's usual crisp, fresh fare, the book will probably still find an audience with Prelutsky fans." Horn Book

The new kid on the block: poems; drawings by James Stevenson. Greenwillow Bks. 1984 159p il $14.95; lib bdg $12.88 (3-6) **811**

1. Humorous poetry
ISBN 0-688-02271-5; 0-688-02272-3 (lib bdg) LC 83-20621

Companion volume to: Something big has been here, entered below

"Most of the 100-plus poems here are mini-jokes, wordplay, and character sketches . . . with liberal doses of monsters and meanies as well as common, garden-variety child mischief." Booklist

"The author's rollicking, silly poems bounce and romp with fun; Stevenson's cartoon-like sketches capture the hilarity with equal skill. A book everyone will enjoy dipping into." Child Book Rev Serv

Nightmares: poems to trouble your sleep; illustrated by Arnold Lobel. Greenwillow Bks. 1976 38p il $13.95; lib bdg $13.88 (2-5) **811**

1. Monsters—Poetry
ISBN 0-688-80053-X; 0-688-84053-1 (lib bdg) LC 76-4820

Companion volume to: The Headless Horseman rides tonight, entered above

This "collection of poems is calculated to evoke icy apprehension, and the poems about wizards, bogeymen, ghouls, ogres (well, one poem apiece to each or to others of their ilk) are exaggerated just enough to bring simultaneous grins and shudders. Prelutsky uses words with relish and his rhyme and rhythm are, as usual, deft. Lobel's illustrations are equally adroit, macabre yet elegant." Bull Cent Child Books

The queen of Eene; pictures by Victoria Chess. Greenwillow Bks. 1978 32p il lib bdg $11.88 (k-3) **811**

1. Nonsense verses
ISBN 0-688-84144-9 LC 77-17311

"Fourteen original poems are presented in . . . picturebook format. Humorous, nonsensical, the verses mostly concern foolish characters like 'The Pancake Collector' who explains, 'I have pancakes in most of my pockets,/and concealed in the linings of suits./There are tiny ones stuffed in my mittens/and larger ones packed in my boots.' . . . Most of the poems are given a double-page spread and all are accompanied by detailed, appropriately droll black-and-white illustrations. It's an attractive package, and most children will enjoy the contents whether they are reading or listening." SLJ

Ride a purple pelican; pictures by Garth Williams. Greenwillow Bks. 1986 64p il $14.95 (k-3) **811**

1. Nonsense verses 2. Nursery rhymes
ISBN 0-688-04031-4 LC 84-6024

Companion volume to: Beneath a blue umbrella, entered above

A collection of short nonsense verses and nursery rhymes

"Prelutsky has caught the rhythm and spirit of nursery rhymes in 29 short poems about drum-beating bunnies, bullfrogs on parade, Chicago winds, giant sequoias and other wondrous things. Many of these easy-to-remember poems are filled with delicious sounding American and Canadian place names. Garth Williams' full-color, full-page illustrations are good complements to the poems. Highly recommended." Child Book Rev Serv

Rolling Harvey down the hill; illustrated by Victoria Chess. Greenwillow Bks. 1980 30p il $12.95; lib bdg $12.88 (1-3) **811**

1. Friendship—Poetry 2. Humorous poetry
ISBN 0-688-80258-3; 0-688-84258-5 (lib bdg) LC 79-18236

"Fifteen contemporary poems describe the mischievous antics of five apartment-house buddies." Child Book Rev Serv

"Chess' puckish black-and-white scenes cash in on all the text's mischief. The motley cast is suitably disheveled and just bizarre enough in expression. This is fresh, funny, and quite in tune with scampish concerns." Booklist

The sheriff of Rottenshot: poems; pictures by Victoria Chess. Greenwillow Bks. 1982 32p il $12.95; lib bdg $13.88 (2-5) **811**

1. Nonsense verses
ISBN 0-688-00205-6; 0-688-00198-X (lib bdg) LC 81-6420

"Macabre art with a silver lining, the often-gruesome Chess drawings have robust humor of their own, for almost every lumpish human or lurking beast has either enough exaggeration or enough of a twinkle to be funny. Thus the illustrations are admirably suited to the often-ghoulish and very funny poems that Prelutsky writes with a strong use of meter and some entertaining wordplay." Bull Cent Child Books

Prelutsky, Jack—*Continued*
The snopp on the sidewalk, and other poems; pictures by Byron Barton. Greenwillow Bks. 1977 unp il lib bdg $11.88 (k-4) **811**
1. Nonsense verses
ISBN 0-688-84084-1 LC 76-46323
Twelve poems about snopps, grobbles, flonsters, and other fantastic creatures
"Employing alliteration, metaphor, repetition, and portmanteau words within the framework of traditional rhymed verse forms, the poet has conjured into reality a menagerie of imaginary beings. . . . Despite the pseudomacabre situations, the tone of the twelve poems is gleefully ghoulish without being gruesome, a mood complemented by the modulating grays and curvilinear patterns of the stylized, cartoonlike illustrations. A delectably bizarre gathering of marvelously outrageous nonsense." Horn Book

Something big has been here; drawings by James Stevenson. Greenwillow Bks. 1990 160p il $14.95 (3-5) **811**
1. Humorous poetry
ISBN 0-688-06434-5 LC 89-34773
Companion volume to: The new kid on the block, entered above
An illustrated collection of humorous poems on a variety of topics
"Puns and verbal surprises abound. Clever use of alliteration and abundant variety in the sound and texture of words add to the pleasure. . . . Stevenson's small cartoons of snaggle-toothed animals and deadpan children extend and expand the mad humor of the poems, supporting but never overwhelming their good-natured fun. A fine prescription against the blues at any time of year." Horn Book

Tyrannosaurus was a beast; illustrated by Arnold Lobel. Greenwillow Bks. 1988 31p il $13.95; lib bdg $13.88 (2-5) **811**
ISBN 0-688-06442-6; 0-688-06443-4 (lib bdg)
LC 87-25131
A collection of humorous poems about dinosaurs
"Fourteen dinosaurs meet their match in this outstanding author/illustrator team. While Prelutsky's short, pithy, often witty verses sum up their essential characters, Lobel's line and watercolor portraits bring the beasts to life, enormous yet endearingly vulnerable." Booklist

Riley, James Whitcomb, 1849-1916
The gobble-uns'll git you ef you don't watch out! James Whitcomb Riley's "Little Orphant Annie"; illustrated by Joel Schick. Lippincott 1975 unp il $13.95 (1-4) **811**
1. Monsters—Poetry
ISBN 0-397-31621-6 LC 74-23110
This is the classic story poem of ill-mannered children spirited away by the ferocious Gobble-uns, as told by Little Orphant Annie
"This 1885 poem in Midwest dialect has always given a few chills to those with vivid imaginations. Now the 'Gobble-uns' have been sketched in all their sinister glory—and they look a lot like your average, mean-eyed, snaggle-toothed heavy. . . . The black and white drawings of rotund Annie and the characters in her stories help clarify obscurities in the verse for youngsters." Child Book Rev Serv

Ryder, Joanne
Under your feet; illustrated by Dennis Nolan. Four Winds Press 1990 unp il $13.95 (k-3) **811**
1. Nature—Poetry 2. Seasons—Poetry
ISBN 0-02-777955-6 LC 89-33897
"Following a boy through the seasons, . . . [these poems] tell of the animals beneath his feet: moles race along their tunnels below the ground, fish dart though the lake as he swims, worms huddle together in deep winter burrows, a cricket beneath a stone feels the ground shake as the boy passes." Booklist
"The tone is reverent and hushed, the illustrations splendidly vibrant and accurate. . . . Both language and art offer an intriguing look at the world under children's feet." Publ Wkly

Sandburg, Carl, 1878-1967
Rainbows are made: poems; selected by Lee Bennett Hopkins; wood engravings by Fritz Eichenberg. Harcourt Brace Jovanovich 1982 81p il $15.95; pa $8.95 (5 and up) **811**
ISBN 0-15-265480-1; 0-15-265481-X (pa)
LC 82-47934
This book "offers some 70 short poems by Carl Sandburg and groups them by theme: the seasons, the sea, the imaginative mind, etc. Each theme explores different aspects of poetic creativity as envisioned by Sandburg and illustrated by Fritz Eichenberg's wood engravings. Eichenberg has truly captured the power and vigorousness of Sandburg's verse." SLJ

Service, Robert W. (Robert William), 1874-1958
The cremation of Sam McGee; paintings by Ted Harrison; introduction by Pierre Berton. Greenwillow Bks. 1987 c1986 unp il $14.95; Hancock House pa $5.95 (4 and up) **811**
1. Yukon Territory—Poetry
ISBN 0-688-06903-7; 0-88839-223-0 (pa)
LC 86-14971
Text first published 1907. This newly illustrated edition first published 1986 in Canada
"In the tradition of tall tales, the story of Sam McGee is told here in Service's original rollicking verses. Pledged to cremate his friend Sam, the narrator tells how, after carting the frozen body for miles, he stuffs it into a ship's roaring furnace. To his surprise, when he later opens the door he discovers Sam alive . . . and warm for the first time 'since he left Tennessee.'" Publ Wkly
"A fine example of a 20th-Century regional ballad, one that tells of the profound cold of the Yukon and how it affected the lives of two gold miners." SLJ

Service, Robert W. (Robert William), 1874-1958—*Continued*

The shooting of Dan McGrew; paintings by Ted Harrison. Godine 1988 unp il $14.95; Hancock House pa $5.95 (4 and up) **811**

1. Yukon Territory—Poetry
ISBN 0-87923-748-1; 0-88839-224-9 (pa) LC 88-6124

Text first published 1907

A narrative poem set in the Yukon describing the shoot-out in a saloon between a trapper and the man who stole his girl

"While the action of the poem is intense and demanding, the painterly illustrations by Harrison are overwhelmingly powerful; they seem to take on a life of their own, drawing readers' attentions away from the text and toward the surrealistic interpretation of events. . . . Harrison creates a pulsating world of hate and destruction; it's a fascinating interpretation of a well-known poem." Publ Wkly

Siebert, Diane

Mojave; paintings by Wendell Minor. Crowell 1988 unp il $14.95; lib bdg $13.89 (1-3) **811**

1. Deserts—Poetry
ISBN 0-690-04567-0; 0-690-04569-7 (lib bdg) LC 86-24329

"Paintings of the desert and its creatures illustrate a first-person poem in the voice of the Mojave." Bull Cent Child Books

"Regular rhythms and clever rhymes propel us through space and the vagaries of time. Wendell Minor's artistic vision at times parallels that of Georgia O'Keeffe. . . . [This is] a beautifully orchestrated book of illustrated poems." Christ Sci Monit

Silverstein, Shel

A light in the attic. Harper & Row 1981 167p il $14.95; lib bdg $14.89 (3 and up) **811**

1. Humorous poetry 2. Nonsense verses
ISBN 0-06-025673-7; 0-06-025674-5 (lib bdg) LC 80-8453

This collection of more than one hundred poems "will delight lovers of Silverstein's raucous, rollicking verse and his often tender, whimsical, philosophical advice. . . . The poems are tuned in to kids' most hidden feelings, dark wishes and enjoyment of the silly. . . . The witty line drawings are a full half of the treat of this wholly satisfying anthology by the modern successor to Edward Lear and Hilaire Belloc." SLJ

Where the sidewalk ends; the poems & drawings of Shel Silverstein. Harper & Row 1974 166p il $14.95; lib bdg $14.89 (3 and up) **811**

1. Humorous poetry 2. Nonsense verses
ISBN 0-06-025667-2; 0-06-025668-0 (lib bdg) LC 70-105486

"There are skillful, sometimes grotesque line drawings with each of the 127 poems, which run in length from a few lines to a couple of pages. The poems are tender, funny, sentimental, philosophical, and ridiculous in turn, and they're for all ages." Saturday Rev

Singer, Marilyn, 1948-

Turtle in July; illustrated by Jerry Pinkney. Macmillan 1989 unp il $13.95 (2-4) **811**

1. Animals—Poetry
ISBN 0-02-782881-6 LC 89-2745

"A bullhead catfish lying in the sediment at the bottom of a pond sets down the underlying rhythm of the changing seasons in this symphony of verses that features an animal for each month of the year. The variety of wildlife and the corresponding changes in meter and tone, combined with Jerry Pinkney's lush, full-page illustrations in full color, create a vivid picture book that is visually as well as auditorily pleasing." Horn Book

Thayer, Ernest Lawrence, 1863-1940

Casey at the bat **811**

1. Baseball—Poetry LC 88-45290

Some editions are:

Godine $12.95; pa $8.95 Illustrated by Barry Moser; afterword by Donald Hall (ISBN 0-87923-722-8)

Putnam lib bdg $13.95; pa $1.95 With additional text and illustrations by Patricia Polacco (ISBN 0-399-21585-9; 0-698-20486-7)

Raintree Pubs. lib bdg $27.99 Illustrated by Ken Bachaus (ISBN 0-8172-2243-X) includes cassette

Smith, P. $15 Illustrated by Jim Hull; introduction by Martin Gardner (ISBN 0-8446-5613-5)

Workman pa $5.95 Drawings by Keith Bendis; introduction by Roger Kahn (ISBN 0-89480-303-4) Has title: The illustrated Casey at the bat

First published 1888

A narrative poem about the celebrated baseball player who strikes out at the crucial moment of a game

Van Vorst, Marie Louise, 1867-1936

A Norse lullaby; [by] M. L. van Vorst; illustrated by Margot Tomes. Lothrop, Lee & Shepard Bks. 1988 unp il $12.95; lib bdg $12.88 (k-1) **811**

ISBN 0-688-05812-4; 0-688-05813-2 (lib bdg) LC 87-31058

"Van Vorst's poem was first published in 1897 in *St. Nicholas Magazine*. In simple rhyme it speaks of harsh winter landscapes, the shelter of a cozy, firelit house; and the safety of a parent's arms. . . . The circular-shaped pictures, evoking the original turn-of-the-century setting, fade into the expanse of white pages, which mirror the poem's snowy images. A lilting piece that evokes feelings of love, this seems a soothing choice for rocking a child to sleep." Booklist

Viorst, Judith

If I were in charge of the world and other worries; poems for children and their parents; illustrated by Lynne Cherry. Atheneum Pubs. 1981 56p il lib bdg $13.95; pa $3.95 (3-6) **811**

ISBN 0-689-30863-9 (lib bdg); 0-689-70770-3 (pa)
LC 81-2342

"Forty-one lively, funny poems written from a wry, self-deprecating point of view. Some poems verge on adult feelings—such as a broken heart or a lyrical appreciation of spring—but most of them deal with children's worries, to which the author seems to be specially attuned. . . . There are several sly alternative endings to classic fairy tales and poems of social ineptitude among the young. . . . The black-and-white illustrations, although attractive, do not particularly suit the modern tenor of the poems." Horn Book

Watson, Clyde

Catch me & kiss me & say it again: rhymes; pictures by Wendy Watson. Philomel Bks. 1978 62p il $10.95; pa $5.95 (k-1) **811**

1. Nursery rhymes
ISBN 0-399-20948-4; 0-399-20954-9 (pa)
LC 78-17644

First published by Collins & World

A collection of rhymes "for brushing teeth, learning how to walk, playing finger games, grabbing a diaper, clipping fingernails, dividing things fairly, getting fed, undergoing thunderstorms, bathing, going to bed, and having fun in all kinds of everyday ways." Booklist

"There is warmth and whimsy, immediacy and laughter in the pictured doings of a family of four inhabiting a New England farmhouse; and the pages are filled with gentle tones of primary color." SLJ

Father Fox's pennyrhymes; illustrated by Wendy Watson. Crowell 1971 56p il $13.95; lib bdg $13.89; pa $4.95 (k-3) **811**

1. Nonsense verses 2. Nursery rhymes
ISBN 0-690-29213-9; 0-690-29214-7 (lib bdg); 0-06-443137-1 (pa) LC 71-146291

"A collection of short, original nonsense rhymes, illustrated with a bounty of high-spirited pictures. Some of the verses are impish or boisterous or just plain silly; some are similar to counting-out rhymes and jump-rope jingles; a few are as gentle as lullabies. All are highly rhythmic and reminiscent of the traditional rhymes of folklore. The water-color-and-ink illustrations are somewhat whimsical in their busyness; tiny pictures printed in sequence—like comic strips—as well as single, full-page pictures are brimming with minute detail and activity." Horn Book

Wells, Carolyn, 1869-1942

A Christmas alphabet; from a poem; with illustrations by twenty-seven artists from the past. Putnam 1989 unp il $15.95 (k-3) **811**

1. Christmas—Poetry 2. Alphabet
ISBN 0-399-21683-9 LC 88-31689

A poem in which every letter of the alphabet decribes a different aspect of Christmas and its celebration

"Selections from children's publications at the turn of the century illustrate this holiday alphabet. Historians of children's literature will recognize [the illustrators]. . . . Others will simply enjoy these old-fashioned, sometimes humorous, mostly unsentimental depictions of children and animals celebrating the season's delights in times gone by." SLJ

Whitman, Walt, 1819-1892

Voyages; selected by Lee Bennett Hopkins; with illustrations by Charles Mikolaycak. Harcourt Brace Jovanovich 1988 73p il $15.95 (6 and up) **811**

ISBN 0-15-294495-8 LC 87-33353

A collection of fifty-three poems and selections from poems focusing on the people and places encountered by the nineteenth-century American writer from his mid-thirties through his early seventies

"Mikolaycak's bold black-and-white illustrations depict the strong organic and spiritual bond between man and nature—open and vast horizons form the backgrounds of pictures of young and determined men, throughout which also appear icons of America." Publ Wkly

Willard, Nancy

The ballad of Biddy Early; illustrated by Barry Moser. Knopf 1989 unp il $13.95; lib bdg $14.99 (4 and up) **811**

1. Early, Biddy, 1798-1874—Poetry
ISBN 0-394-88414-0; 0-394-98414-5 (lib bdg)
LC 88-29187

"These 15 poems praise Biddy Early, the wise woman of Ireland's County Clare who lived from 1798 to 1874. Beginning with the ballad of the title, Willard invites listeners in with limericks, songs, and poems. The poems tell of magic and mystery, witchcraft, the supernatural, and murder; how nature and animals revered Biddy Early; how she read the future and cured illness." SLJ

"Moser's paintings, especially of Biddy as a young and, later, an old woman (facing different ways), relate animals and humans with facial expressions that reflect a common spiritual kingdom. The tales of Biddy Early have found two able tellers." Bull Cent Child Books

A visit to William Blake's inn; poems for innocent and experienced travelers; illustrated by Alice and Martin Provensen. Harcourt Brace Jovanovich 1981 44p il $13.95 (2-5) **811**

1. Nonsense verses
ISBN 0-15-293822-2 LC 80-27403

Awarded the Newbery Medal, 1982 and also a Caldecott Medal honor book for the same year

"This entertaining collection of sixteen nonsense verses describes the lively goings-on among several incongruous travelers who put up at an imaginary inn run by the English poet William Blake. Inspired by Blake's poems and catching their rhythms and something of their oblique way of looking at things, the poems are in various forms and move along with a good beat." Child Book Rev Serv

"The illustrations are full of stylized naïveté—a rather

Willard, Nancy—*Continued*
sedate, late-eighteenth-century, middle-class kind of innocence. Done chiefly in glowing tawny colors, the pictures are highly decorative, and the whole book, printed on buff paper speckled to simulate an antique look, presents an elegant appearance." Horn Book

The voyage of the Ludgate Hill; travels with Robert Louis Stevenson; illustrated by Alice and Martin Provensen. Harcourt Brace Jovanovich 1987 unp il $14.95 (2-5) **811**

1. Stevenson, Robert Louis, 1850-1894—Poetry
ISBN 0-15-294464-8 LC 86-19502

"Inspired by Stevenson's letters, Nancy Willard has written a poem, part fact part fantasy, about his stormy ocean voyage from London to New York on a cargo-carrying steamer in 1887. Stevenson and his wife, and a few other adventurous passengers, are joined in this journey by a bevy of assorted animals: apes and baboons, monkeys and stallions, not to mention the ship-master's cat." N Y Times Book Rev

"The Provensens' paintings, brush stroked in buff, brown, and blue, are mannered, with a restrained humor based on a juxtaposition of the mundane with the unreal. A delight to read aloud, this will need some background explanation from adults." Bull Cent Child Books

Worth, Valerie

More small poems; pictures by Natalie Babbitt. Farrar, Straus & Giroux 1976 41p il $8.95 (3-5) **811**

ISBN 0-374-35022-1 LC 76-28323

"The author and the illustrator . . . have created [a] miniature treasury of spontaneous, expressive verse. Homely, everyday items are endowed with unexpected new life. . . . With economy of phrase, deceptive simplicity, and artless skill the poet celebrates, among other things, a pumpkin, a toad, a safety pin, a kitten, weeds, earthworms, and sidewalks." Horn Book

Small poems; pictures by Natalie Babbitt. Farrar, Straus & Giroux 1972 41p il $8.95 (3-5) **811**

ISBN 0-374-37072-9 LC 72-81488

"In twenty-four poems about such topics as raw carrots, cows, jewels, grasses, and crickets, the author gives added dimensions to the object by a suggestive turn of phrase or an unusual perspective. . . . The illustrations, in perfect harmony with the poems, suggest the possibilities of the items but are never so precise as to limit their potential scope." Horn Book

Small poems again; pictures by Natalie Babbitt. Farrar, Straus & Giroux 1986 41p il $8.95 (3-5) **811**

ISBN 0-374-37074-5 LC 85-47513

A "collection of short poems mostly about small things and creatures—jacks, robins, asparagus, coat hangers and even fleas." N Y Times Book Rev

"The variety of poetic forms, including internal rhymes and blank verse, are a welcome change from the more conventional rhyming patterns in much of children's poetry. Natalie Babbitt's drawings are a perfect expression of the poems' images. . . . They are direct and simple enough to be accessible to children, yet the images are so apt and fresh that adults will also find joy in them." Horn Book

Still more small poems; pictures by Natalie Babbitt. Farrar, Straus & Giroux 1978 41p il $8.95 (3-5) **811**

ISBN 0-374-37258-6 LC 78-11739

"Sketches, in free verse, of everyday objects, animals, places, sensations, and situations, from sounds a bell makes . . . to a drowsy turtle's speculations . . . to the miraculous ability of a hen, 'all quirk/And freak and whim' to produce so pure and calm an item as an egg." SLJ

"Small is beautiful. The collaborators always prove that economy can result in images rich as Croesus. . . . Ink drawings as understated yet infused with mystery as the lines . . . amplify mood and meaning." Publ Wkly

Yolen, Jane

Best witches: poems for Halloween; illustrated by Elise Primavera. Putnam 1988 45p il $14.95 (3-5) **811**

1. Witches—Poetry 2. Halloween—Poetry
ISBN 0-399-21539-5 LC 88-5866

The author presents her own poetry on witches, ghosts, magic, and other aspects of Halloween

"There's nice control of form, meter, rhyme, and scansion in this collection; there are moments of spine-chill that middle-grades readers will enjoy; there is, as prime appeal, a humor that has verve and sophistication but is never inaccessible. The ebullience of Yolen's poetry is matched by that of Primavera's paintings, which are colorful but pleasantly gruesome, with a great deal of vitality and antic humor." Bull Cent Child Books

Bird watch: a book of poetry; illustrations by Ted Lewin. Philomel Bks. 1990 unp il $15.95 (3-6) **811**

1. Birds—Poetry
ISBN 0-399-21612-X LC 89-34024

A collection of poems describing a variety of birds and their activities

"Though some of the poems deal with subjects beyond the experience of most children, all are carefully wrought and thoughtful. Lewin's breathtaking watercolors marvelously complement Yolen's graceful language and gentle humor, and a glossary at the end supplies interesting facts about each species of bird included in the volume." Publ Wkly

Dinosaur dances; illustrated by Bruce Degen. Putnam 1990 39p il $14.95 (3-5) **811**

1. Dinosaurs—Poetry 2. Humorous poetry
ISBN 0-399-21629-4 LC 88-11661

Seventeen whimsical poems featuring allosaurus, stegosaurus, tyrannosaurus, and other dancing dinosaurs

"The silly pictures, filled with clever touches and subtle (?) spoof, do more than their share in making the prehistoric party irresistible, especially for dinosaur afficionados." Child Book Rev Serv

Yolen, Jane—*Continued*

Ring of earth: a child's book of seasons; illustrated by John Wallner. Harcourt Brace Jovanovich 1986 unp il $14.95 (3-6) **811**

1. Seasons—Poetry 2. Animals—Poetry

ISBN 0-15-267140-4 LC 86-4800

The author "has written four short poems about the seasons of the year from the viewpoint of the Weasel in Winter, the Spring-Peeper in the Spring, the Dragonfly in Summer, and the Goose in the Fall." Child Book Rev Serv

"The picture book format is a bit deceptive here, for both the poetry and the art have a more sophisticated appeal. . . . Wallner's mottled paintings are gracefully composed across double-page spreads to pick up Yolen's circle motifs with interlocking rings and overlapping round frames connecting the cyclical flora and fauna reflected in the verses. A rewarding selection for classroom poetry groups or family sharing in a quieter context." Bull Cent Child Books

The three bears rhyme book; illustrated by Jane Dyer. Harcourt Brace Jovanovich 1987 32p il lib bdg $14.95 (k-2) **811**

1. Bears—Poetry

ISBN 0-15-286386-9 LC 86-19514

"The 16 poems offered here assume that Goldilocks and the three bears maintain a close friendship in spite of their initial encounter, which is not mentioned. The verses describe familiar activities such as taking a walk, eating porridge, having a birthday party, and going out in the rain." SLJ

"The universality of the events will certainly appeal to young listeners who'll find the words mirroring their own everyday activities. As for the illustrations, there's just one word for them—delightful. Executed in soft watercolors and colored pencils, the pictures are charming without being cloying, the humor is amusing without being broad." Booklist

811.008 American poetry—Collections

Christmas in the stable; poems selected and illustrated by Beverly K. Duncan. Harcourt Brace Jovanovich 1990 32p il $14.95 (2-4) **811.008**

1. Christmas—Poetry 2. Poetry—Collected works

ISBN 0-15-217758-2 LC 88-37953

A collection of poems by Jane Yolen, Elizabeth Coatsworth, Norma Farber, and others, each from the point of view of an animal or about the animals in the stable where the Christ Child lay asleep

"Though suffused with a spirit of peace and wonder, the pieces are refreshingly unsentimental and free of cliche. . . . Each selection and the animal painting that illustrates it are framed together with thin colored borders and centered against a tapestrylike background that is detailed with plants appropriate to the season. The graceful designs were inspired by medieval manuscripts and possess a similar quality of serenity and grace." Booklist

Click, rumble, roar; poems about machines; poems selected by Lee Bennett Hopkins; photographs by Anna Held Audette. Crowell 1987 40p il $11.70; lib bdg $11.89 (2-5) **811.008**

1. Machinery—Poetry 2. American poetry—Collected works

ISBN 0-690-04587-5; 0-690-04589-1 (lib bdg) LC 86-47746

A collection of eighteen poems about machines by Myra Cohn Livingston, Eve Merriam, David McCord, and others

"The eighteen poems in the slim, attractive collection cover the range of the car wash and parking lot, bulldozers, tractors, garbage trucks, escalators, helicopters, and pocket calculators. Some are brief observations; others offer stimulating insights. There is great variety of form and plenty of humor. . . . The often eloquent, full-page photographs accompanying the poems will lure browsers into sampling the poetry." Horn Book

Dinosaurs: poems; selected by Lee Bennett Hopkins; illustrated by Murray Tinkleman. Harcourt Brace Jovanovich 1987 46p il $12.95 (3-5) **811.008**

1. Dinosaurs—Poetry 2. American poetry—Collected works

ISBN 0-15-223495-0 LC 86-14818

"In this volume of 18 poems, Hopkins invites us to 'Reflect upon the dinosaur,/A giant that exists no more.' With poems by Myra Cohn Livingston, Lilian Moore, Valerie Worth and others, the collection explores fossils . . . and the museums that house [them]." Publ Wkly

"The collection will offer a spur to the imagination which more scientific material may lack. Minutely cross-hatched, black-and-white illustrations effectively recreate the nubbly, grainy skins of the mysterious, ponderous creatures and the swamps and savannas of their remote and shadowy world. Index of authors, titles, and first lines." Horn Book

Good books, good times! selected by Lee Bennett Hopkins; pictures by Harvey Stevenson. Harper & Row 1990 31p il $12.95; lib bdg $12.89 (1-3) **811.008**

1. Books and reading—Poetry 2. American poetry—Collected works

ISBN 0-06-022527-0; 0-06-022528-9 (lib bdg) LC 89-49108

"A Charlotte Zolotow book"

An anthology of poems about the joys of books and reading. Includes selections by David McCord, Karla Kuskin, Myra Cohn Livingston, and Jack Prelutsky

"The tone of the poems, the majority of which have not yet appeared in anthologies, ranges from exuberant to meditative. The collection will excite any parent, teacher, or librarian looking for brief, accessible poems on the subject of books and reading. Stevenson's lighthearted watercolors perfectly capture the jubilant mood of the book." Horn Book

I am the darker brother; an anthology of modern poems by Negro Americans; drawings by Benny Andrews; foreword by Charlemae Rollins. Macmillan 1968 128p il hardcover o.p. paperback available $4.95 (5 and up) **811.008**

1. American poetry—Black authors—Collected works
ISBN 0-02-041120-0 (pa) LC 68-12077

Edited by: Arnold Adoff

"Selections by 28 American Negro poets who reflect on the past, the current social scene, and the hope for the future." Libr J

"A most interesting anthology, with many contributions from such well-known poets as Brooks, Dunbar, Hayden, Hughes, and McKay, and a broad representation of selections from the work of some two dozen other modern authors." Bull Cent Child Books

In the witch's kitchen; poems for Halloween; compiled by John E. Brewton, Lorraine A. Blackburn, George M. Blackburn III; illustrated by Harriett Barton. Crowell 1980 88p il lib bdg $12.89 (3-6) **811.008**

1. Halloween—Poetry 2. American poetry—Collected works
ISBN 0-690-04062-8 (lib bdg) LC 79-7822

"Familiar Halloween motifs are to be found in the forty-six poems gathered into a gleefully ghoulish medley for younger audiences. Works by such well-known writers for children as John Ciardi, Aileen Fisher, X. J. Kennedy, David McCord, and Jack Prelutsky are included as well as traditional rhymes and chants. . . . The imaginative, slightly cartoonlike illustrations are appropriately executed in black, gray, and white. An inviting and serviceable collection for a varied audience. With indexes of authors, titles, and first lines." Horn Book

The **Merry-go-round** poetry book; compiled by Nancy Larrick; illustrated by Karen Gundersheimer. Delacorte Press 1989 unp il $14.95 (k-2) **811.008**

1. American poetry—Collected works
ISBN 0-385-29814-5 LC 89-1110

This is a collection of poems by such authors as Ruth Krauss, Wendy Watson, John Ciardi and Jane Yolen

"Though slender in format, this volume contains a well-chosen treasure trove of light, short verse for reading aloud to preschool and early elementary school children. Gundersheimer's captivating line drawings fill the pages with appealing animals and small children." Booklist

More surprises; selected by Lee Bennett Hopkins; illustrated by Megan Lloyd. Harper & Row 1987 64p il $10.95; lib bdg $10.89 (1-3) **811.008**

1. American poetry—Collected works
ISBN 0-06-022604-8; 0-06-022605-6 (lib bdg)
LC 86-45335

Companion volume to: Surprises, entered below

"An I can read book. A Charlotte Zolotow book"

A collection of poems with topics ranging from school to birds to nonsense

"This is the perfect compilation to teach the joys of poetry to very young children. Words and rhyme schemes are simple enough for beginning readers to handle themselves, and the offerings by poets such as Aileen Fisher, William Cole, Karla Kuskin, and Jack Prelutsky are filled with humor and verve." Booklist

My black me: a beginning book of black poetry. Dutton 1974 83p $12.95 (5 and up) **811.008**

1. American poetry—Black authors—Collected works
ISBN 0-525-35460-3 LC 73-16445

Edited by: Arnold Adoff

This collection of fifty poems contains works by Langston Hughes, Don L. Lee, Nikki Giovanni and others. The book's "six sections are untitled and loosely grouped thematically. . . . Topics covered are pride in Blackness, modern heroes and martyrs (e.g., Malcolm X and Dr. King), ghetto life, as well as the struggles and mistreatment of Blacks in this country." SLJ

On city streets; an anthology of poetry; selected by Nancy Larrick; illustrated with photographs by David Sagarin. Evans & Co. 1968 158p il hardcover o.p. paperback available $6.95 (5 and up) **811.008**

1. City life—Poetry 2. American poetry—Collected works
ISBN 0-87131-551-3 (pa) LC 68-30505

"Representing the personal choices of numerous city children, this inviting anthology offers a variety of significant poetic interpretations of the wonders, tragedies, pleasures, and sorrows of urban life. Poems by Carl Sandburg, Walt Whitman, Langston Hughes, E. B. White, Rachel Field, and such fine but lesser-known poets as Gwendolyn Brooks, Charles Reznikoff, James Tate, and Lawrence Ferlinghetti are presented in a pleasing format copiously illustrated with photographs of city scenes." Booklist

The **Oxford** book of children's verse in America; edited by Donald Hall. Oxford Univ. Press 1985 xxxviii, 319p $24.95 **811.008**

1. American poetry—Collected works
ISBN 0-19-503539-9 LC 84-20755

Companion volume to: The Oxford book of children's verse, entered in class 821.008

"Hall's intention, expressed in the introduction, is to create an anthology of American poetry actually written for or adopted by children during a particular historical period. The emphasis is on authenticity rather than personal taste." SLJ

"A fine and carefully winnowed collection of American poetry is gathered in a book that will interest students of children's literature and young people who simply enjoy browsing." Horn Book

A **Paper** zoo; a collection of animal poems by modern American poets; selected by Renée Karol Weiss; pictures by Ellen Raskin. Macmillan 1987 c1968 38p il $11.95 (1-4) **811.008**

1. Animals—Poetry 2. American poetry—Collected works
ISBN 0-02-792750-4 LC 86-21733

A Paper zoo—*Continued*
A reissue of the title first published 1968
"This collection of animal poems by well-known poets such as Robert Frost, Emily Dickinson, T. S. Eliot, and Randall Jarrell is brightly illustrated in green and orange drawings that resemble paper cuts." Booklist

The **Place** my words are looking for; what poets say about and through their work; selected by Paul B. Janeczko. Bradbury Press 1990 150p il $13.95 (4 and up) **811.008**
1. American poetry—Collected works 2. Poetics
ISBN 0-02-747671-5 LC 89-39331
"More than forty contemporary poets are included: Eve Merriam, X. J. Kennedy, Felice Holman, Gary Soto, Mark Vinz, Karla Kuskin, and John Updike, among others. Their contributions vary widely in theme and mood and style, though the preponderance of the pieces are written in modern idiom and unrhymed meter. The accompanying comments frequently are as insightful and eloquent as the poems themselves." Horn Book

Poem stew; poems selected by William Cole; pictures by Karen Ann Weinhaus. Lippincott 1981 84p il o.p.; HarperCollins Pubs. paperback available $4.95 (3-6) **811.008**
1. Food—Poetry 2. Dinners and dining—Poetry 3. American poetry—Collected works
ISBN 0-06-440136-7 (pa) LC 81-47106
"Drawn from anonymous and traditional sources as well as from the works of such poets as Ogden Nash, John Ciardi, Jack Prelutsky, Myra Cohn Livingston, and the selector himself, the poems celebrate the subject of food. But they haven't been chosen for their appeal to gourmet palates; rather they comment on occasions when particular items of food become the impetus for a humorous narrative, lyric, or epigram. . . . With indexes of authors and titles." Horn Book

Poems for Jewish holidays; selected by Myra Cohn Livingston; illustrated by Lloyd Bloom. Holiday House 1986 32p il lib bdg $12.95 (k-3) **811.008**
1. Fasts and feasts—Judaism—Poetry 2. American poetry—Collected works
ISBN 0-8234-0606-7 LC 85-27179
"Sixteen poems celebrate 12 Jewish holidays. The poems vary from the traditional 'Had Gadya' taken from the Passover Haggadah, to the more playful, contemporary 'First Night of Hanukkah' by Ruth Rosten and the more sensitive and moving 'Tisha B'Av,' which commemorates a Jewish day of mourning, by Meyer Hahn. Several of the poems were commissioned for this volume, and therefore do not appear anywhere else. Images effectively convey the moods of different holidays. However, it is Bloom's black-and-white illustrations that make this a truly distinguished book. Each of the ten full-page charcoal paintings captures the different aspects of the Jewish experience while keeping with the spirit of the poem." SLJ

Poems for mothers; selected by Myra Cohn Livingston; illustrated by Deborah Kogan Ray. Holiday House 1988 32p il lib bdg $13.95 (3-5) **811.008**
1. Mothers—Poetry 2. American poetry—Collected works
ISBN 0-8234-0678-4 LC 87-19629
Companion volume: Poems for fathers (1989)
"This collection of 20 poems—12 commissioned especially for this book—celebrate the diversity of motherhood. There are mothers of various ethnic backgrounds, moms who work at home and away from home, stepmothers, and single parents as well as 'traditional' mothers and absent mothers. Each poem is written from a child's point of view, and each captures a mother's special trait." SLJ
"Ray's line-swept drawings with blue and peach tones capture feelings of closeness—and, occasionally, distance—between the figures of mother and child." Bull Cent Child Books

Poetry for holidays; [compiled by] Nancy Larrick; drawings by Kelly Oechsli. Garrard 1966 64p il lib bdg $6.69 (1-4) **811.008**
1. Holidays—Poetry 2. American poetry—Collected works
ISBN 0-8116-4100-7 LC 66-10724
Poems for Halloween, Christmas, Saint Valentine's Day, Easter, and other holidays, by such authors as Harry Behn, Marchette Chute, Aileen Fisher, Langston Hughes, Henry Wadsworth Longfellow, and Ruth Sawyer
"The more than 50 poems covering 10 holidays and special days are tried and true, the drawings are enjoyable, and the collection is of a length to appeal to and be easily handled by children." Booklist

Reflections on a gift of watermelon pickle . . . and other modern verse; [compiled by] Stephen Dunning, Edward Lueders, Hugh Smith. Lothrop, Lee & Shepard Bks. 1967 c1966 139p il $14.95; lib bdg $13.88 (6 and up) **811.008**
1. American poetry—Collected works
ISBN 0-688-41231-9; 0-688-51231-3 (lib bdg) LC 67-29527
First published 1966 by Scott, Foresman in a text edition
"Although some of the [114] selections are by recognized modern writers, many are by minor or unknown poets, and few will be familiar to the reader. Nearly all are fresh in approach and contemporary in expression. . . . Striking photographs complementing or illuminating many of the poems enhance the attractiveness of the volume." Booklist

Surprises; selected by Lee Bennett Hopkins; illustrated by Megan Lloyd. Harper & Row 1984 64p il $10.95; lib bdg $10.89; pa $3.50 (1-3) **811.008**
1. American poetry—Collected works
ISBN 0-06-022584-X; 0-06-022585-8 (lib bdg); 0-06-444105-9 (pa) LC 83-47712
"An I can read book. A Charlotte Zolotow book"

Surprises—*Continued*

Hopkins has put together a "collection of poems from the proverbial star-studded cast: X. J. Kennedy, Myra Cohn Livingston, Nikki Giovanni, Russell Hoban, Eve Merriam, Langston Hughes, Christina Rossetti, Carl Sandburg and on and on. These 38 poems, most previously published elsewhere, employ short words and simple language to tell their tale or paint their picture and often make good read-alouds as well as smart choices for beginning readers." SLJ

Followed by: More surprises, entered above

This delicious day; 65 poems; selected by Paul B. Janeczko. Orchard Bks. 1987 81p $11.95; lib bdg $11.99 (5 and up) **811.008**

1. American poetry—Collected works
ISBN 0-531-05724-0; 0-531-08324-1 (lib bdg)
LC 87-7717

"Sixty-five poems by fifty-five poets are represented, including N. M. Bodecker, Russell Hoban, X. J. Kennedy, Karla Kuskin, David McCord, Theodore Roethke, Carl Sandburg, Judith Thurman, William Carlos Williams, and Valerie Worth; Dennis Lee's hard-to-find 'Alligator Pie' is also included. Nor are the selections tired from constant recycling." Horn Book

A **Week** of lullabies; compiled and edited by Helen Plotz; illustrations by Marisabina Russo. Greenwillow Bks. 1988 31p il $11.95; lib bdg $11.88 (k-2) **811.008**

1. Sleep—Poetry 2. Lullabies 3. American poetry—Collected works
ISBN 0-688-06652-6; 0-688-06653-4 (lib bdg)
LC 86-18458

An illustrated collection of lullabies and bedtime poems by authors including Nikki Giovanni, Tennyson, and Jack Prelutsky, grouped by days of the week

This book is "unified by its clean, colorful contemporary illustrations. . . . The illustrations are both decorative and expressive, for each selection is accompanied by a full-page painting that encapsulates the essence of its text. Simple flat figures dominate each picture, which is brought to fulfillment with unexpected details found in the wide borders." Horn Book

812 American drama

Gotwalt, Helen Louise Miller

Everyday plays for boys and girls; by Helen Louise Miller. Plays 1986 198p pa $12 (4 and up) **812**

1. One act plays
ISBN 0-8238-0274-4
LC 86-8884

Fifteen one-act plays reflecting the interests of boys and girls in the lower and middle grades

Special plays for holidays; by Helen Louise Miller. Plays 1986 187p pa $12 **812**

1. Holidays—Drama 2. One act plays
ISBN 0-8238-0275-2
LC 86-9332

A collection of fifteen one-act plays celebrating holidays throughout the school year, from Halloween to Mother's Day

Rockwell, Thomas, 1933-

How to eat fried worms, and other plays; illustrated by Joel Schick. Delacorte Press 1980 142p il $9.95; lib bdg $9.89 (4-6) **812**

ISBN 0-440-03498-1; 0-440-03499-X (lib bdg)
LC 78-72854

"Though the combination of slapstick humor and ghoulish silliness in these four plays is a winning one, the zaniness often lapses into sheer hysteria. The title play (an adaptation of Rockwell's popular 1973 novel) is also the most successful, as the worm eating episodes reach new and revolting heights. The least successful is 'Myron Mere,' 'a slight effort in which the villainous Mere captures a queen and turns her into a butterfly. In 'Aiiieeeeeeeee' havoc breaks loose as seven demons attack a town and are finally overcome by a princess and humble villager. 'The Heiress, or the Croak of Doom' dramatizes the plight of Helen, being driven insane by two evil paper boys after her inherited fortune." SLJ

Thane, Adele

Plays from famous stories and fairy tales; royalty-free dramatizations of favorite children's stories. Plays 1983 c1967 463p pa $15 (4-6) **812**

1. One act plays 2. Folk drama
ISBN 0-8238-0060-1
LC 83-23039

First published 1967

"Twenty-eight royalty-free, one act plays are included in this collection of adaptations from well-known folktales, fairy tales, children's classics and old favorites. The dramatizations are simple, often compressing into a scene or two several incidents from a book; they are adequately written and some are moderately funny. Because of the appeal of the sources, a useful collection. Brief notes on costumes, props, lights, setting, et cetera, are appended." Bull Cent Child Books

812.008 American drama—Collections

Holiday plays round the year; edited by Sylvia E. Kamerman. Plays 1983 291p pa $13.95 (4 and up) **812.008**

1. One act plays 2. Holidays—Drama
ISBN 0-8238-0261-2
LC 83-13218

"The 27 modern holiday plays in this collection have been taken from various issues of 'Play' magazine; they cover 12 common holidays. Production notes at the end of the book list number of characters (2 to more than 23), playing time, costumes, properties and setting but no age or grade levels." SLJ

"The contemporary plays do not seem as dated as is sometimes the case in these anthologies. . . . [These plays] are royalty free. The staging and costuming are simple, and ample production notes are provided." Booklist

MacDonald, Margaret Read
The skit book; 101 skits from kids; illustrations by Marie-Louise Scull. Linnet Bks. 1990 147p il $25; pa $15 (4 and up) **812.008**

1. Skits 2. Child authors
ISBN 0-208-02258-9; 0-208-02283-X (pa)
LC 89-29654

A collection of skits written by young people with instructions for performance

"A list of characters, an outline of the action, and suggested dialogue or improvisations for each is given rather than the formal scripts, stage directions, and production notes. . . . Props and scenery are kept to a minimum, and in keeping with the oral tradition, flexibility in length and numbers of actors, as well as variations on the action are indicated." SLJ

Includes bibilography

817.008 American satire and humor—Collections

The **Random** House book of humor for children; selected by Pamela Pollack; illustrated by Paul O. Zelinsky. Random House 1988 310p il $15.95; lib bdg $16.99 (4-6) **817.008**

1. Humorous stories
ISBN 0-394-88049-8; 0-394-98049-2 (lib bdg)
LC 86-31478

"The list of authors excerpted here reads like a 'Who's Who' of children's literature: Babbitt, Blume, Byars, Cleary, Dahl, Fitzhugh, McCloskey, Singer, Thurber, and Twain, to name just a few. Most of the 34 selections are chapters from longer novels. . . . Although some chapters work better than others out of context, most of the offerings stand quite well on their own, and the stories chosen are fine examples of humorous prose. The best use for the collection might be a sampler from which readers may choose books they want to enjoy in their entirety." Booklist

818 American miscellany

Brown, Margaret Wise, 1910-1952
The fish with the deep sea smile; stories and poems for reading to young children; illustrated by Roberta Rauch. Linnet Bks. 1988 c1938 128p il lib bdg $18 (1-3) **818**

ISBN 0-208-02193-0
LC 87-26227

A reissue of the title first published 1938 by Dutton

A compilation of the author's stories and poems, illustrated with sketches by her sister

"The author has succeeded in telling stories that young children will find diverting. Some are wildly fantastic, some funny, some a little sad, but all human." Springfield Repub

Sandburg, Carl, 1878-1967
The Sandburg treasury; prose and poetry for young people; introduction by Paula Sandburg; illustrated by Paul Bacon. Harcourt Brace Jovanovich 1970 480p il $24.95 (5 and up) **818**

ISBN 0-15-270180-X
LC 79-120818

"Including, 'Rootabaga stories,' 'Early moon,' 'Wind song,' 'Abe Lincoln grows up,' 'Prairie-town boy.'" Title page

This volume brings together all of Sandburg's books for young people; his whimsical stories, two books of poetry, a version of his biography of Abraham Lincoln, and portions of his autobiography specially edited for children

821 English poetry

Belloc, Hilaire, 1870-1953
The bad child's book of beasts, and More beasts for worse children, and A moral alphabet; with pictures by B. T. B. Dover Publs. 1961 157p il pa $3.50 (1-4) **821**

1. Animals—Poetry 2. Nonsense verses
ISBN 0-486-20749-8
LC 61-2226

The bad child's book of beasts was first published 1896 in the United Kingdom, 1923 in the United States; More beasts for worse children was first published 1897 in the United Kingdom, 1923 in the United States; A moral alphabet was first published 1899 in the United Kingdom

The bad child's book of beasts and More beasts for worse children combine "absurd verses and line drawings presenting the idiosyncracies of such beasts as the Yak, the Dodo and the Camelopard." Toronto Public Libr. Books for Boys & Girls

Carroll, Lewis, 1832-1898
Lewis Carroll's Jabberwocky; illustrated by Jane Breskin Zalben; with annotations by Humpty Dumpty. Warne 1977 unp il $11.95 **821**

1. Nonsense verses
ISBN 0-7232-6145-8
LC 77-75040

"In Zalben's intricate double-page watercolor illustrations interpreting Lewis Carroll's nonsense poem 'Jabberwocky,' Humpty Dumpty takes readers through a fantasy world in which trees grow candy and cakes, a raccoon-like creature has three tails and an eye patch, and green pigs shed green tears. Zalben uses color well and the nonsense is visualized in a style rich in detail without appearing cluttered. An annotation of the poem, in the form of a discussion between Alice and Humpty Dumpty, appears as a natural extension at the end of this book which could be useful as a handsome starting point for teaching creative poetry or language development." SLJ

Carroll, Lewis, 1832-1898—*Continued*

The walrus and the carpenter; illustrations by Jane Breskin Zalben; with annotations by Tweedledee and Tweedledum. Holt & Co. 1986 unp il $13.95; pa $4.95 **821**

1. Nonsense verses

ISBN 0-8050-0071-2; 0-8050-1482-9 (pa) LC 85-7591

A walrus and a carpenter encounter some oysters during their walk on the beach—an unfortunate meeting for the oysters

"The two-page spreads are executed in vibrant colors and include some eye-catching details. . . . Effective page composition and the type, bold and properly placed, work together, giving an overall pleasant design to the book." Booklist

Coleridge, Sara, 1802-1852

January brings the snow; a book of months; paintings by Jenni Oliver. Dial Bks. for Young Readers 1986 unp il $10.95; lib bdg $10.89 (k-2) **821**

1. Months—Poetry

ISBN 0-8037-0313-9; 0-8037-0314-7 (lib bdg) LC 85-23789

Each month brings something new and different in this rhyme about the changing seasons

"The illustrations on the cover and the first two pages are lovely and set expectations for close ties between the essence of each month and its graphic depiction." Child Book Rev Serv

Coltman, Paul, 1917-

Tog the Ribber; or, Granny's tale; poem by Paul Coltman; illustrated by Gillian McClure. Farrar, Straus & Giroux 1985 unp il $12.95 (3-5) **821**

ISBN 0-374-37630-1 LC 84-82555

The book's verse-story describes "the lifelong affect of an incident when, as a child, the narrator saw a skeleton dangling from the branches as she made her way home, and fled from the corpse which, she felt sure, was pursuing her with evil intent. The experience unhinged her—and her language." Grow Point

This work "is reminiscent of Lewis Carroll, but may prove less comprehensive to some readers, since there are both invented words and words that are garbled. However, the story line is clear, the poem has good pace and suspense, and there's humor in the word-play. The illustrations are stunning." Bull Cent Child Books

De la Mare, Walter, 1873-1956

Peacock pie; a book of rhymes; with pictures by Louise Brierley. Holt & Co. 1989 111p il $17.95 (4 and up) **821**

ISBN 0-8050-1124-2 LC 89-1828

De la Mare's collection of poems describing the capers of fairies, princes, beasts, children, witches, farmers, and kings "first appeared in [the United Kingdom in] 1913. . . . [The present] edition contains de la Mare's . . . revised and expanded 1924 text." Publisher's note

"The poems are placed cleanly on the page. Brierley's accompanying sketches and watercolors offer a thoughtful counterpoint to the poems." SLJ

Rhymes and verses; collected poems for children; with drawings by Ellinore [sic] Blaisdell. Holt & Co. 1988 c1947 344p $15.95; pa $7.95 (4 and up) **821**

ISBN 0-8050-0847-0; 0-8050-0848-9 (pa) LC 88-45278

A reissue of the title first published 1947

This volume contains selections from the published works of this English poet. The poems are arranged under such headings as: Green grow the rashes, O; All round about the town; All creatures great and small; Fairies—witches—phantoms, etc.

Fatchen, Max

The country mail is coming; poems from down under; with illustrations by Catharine O'Neill. Little, Brown 1990 62p il $13.95 (3-5) **821**

1. Country life—Poetry

ISBN 0-316-27493-3 LC 89-31654

"Joy Street books"

First published 1987 in Australia

This is a collection of poems based on the author's childhood impressions and his memories of Australian country life

"Fatchen's most intriguing poems are not those that recall the popular verse of Silverstein or Prelutsky, however, but those that provide unusual perspectives. . . . O'Neill's loosely drawn, gray wash sketches emphasize the humorous aspects of the selections but are equally appropriate for the more contemplative verse. A fresh new voice for the poetry shelf." Horn Book

Hughes, Ted, 1930-

Season songs; pictures by Leonard Baskin. Viking 1975 77p il o.p.; Ultramarine reprint available $20 (6 and up) **821**

1. Seasons—Poetry 2. Nature in poetry

ISBN 0-670-62725-9 LC 74-18280

"The poems included here are . . . distilled from the Devon countryside, a region of unique charm and natural beauty. They are more than image, color, sound: they are alive with whatever it is that vibrates on the downs of Devon. Hughes does not describe; he evokes and enchants. . . . Metrically they owe somewhat to Old English verse. There are even echoes of nursery rhymes. The book has delightful illustrations in color and in black and white by the distinguished American artist, Leonard Baskin." Choice

Lawrence, D. H. (David Herbert), 1885-1930

Birds, beasts, and the third thing; poems; selected and illustrated by Alice and Martin Provensen; introduction by Donald Hall. Viking 1982 unp il $13.95 (3-6) **821**

ISBN 0-670-16779-7 LC 81-70405

"Twenty-three poems—most of them fairly short—are accompanied by paintings that attempt not to illustrate the selections but to place them in the context of D.

Lawrence, D. H. (David Herbert), 1885-1930—*Continued*

H. Lawrence's early life in Nottingham. The verses range from the poet's impatience with people . . . through sympathy with living creatures . . . to cosmic mysteries. . . . Predominantly employing tones of umber, burnt sienna, and gray, the artists picture the coal-mining town, the old-fashioned schoolroom, and the touches of nature that could have been the source of the writer's childhood impressions." Horn Book

Lear, Edward, 1812-1888

The complete nonsense of Edward Lear; edited and introduced by Holbrook Jackson. Dover Publs. 1951 288p il pa $5.95 **821**

1. Nonsense verses
ISBN 0-486-20167-8 LC 51-14566

Also available in hardcover from Smith, P. $15.50 (ISBN 0-8446-0722-3)

A reprint of the 1947 Faber edition published in the United Kingdom

"This is a choice contribution to the literature of laughter. Limericks, verses of all kinds, alphabets and botanics are as daft and amusing as the pictures." Adventuring With Books

An Edward Lear alphabet; illustrations by Carol Newsom. Lothrop, Lee & Shepard Bks. 1983 unp il lib bdg $11.88; pa $3.95 (k-2) **821**

1. Alphabet 2. Nonsense verses
ISBN 0-688-00965-4 (lib bdg); 0-688-06523-6 (pa)
LC 82-10037

"Lear's nonsense rhymes, lilting and humorous, are as palatable today as an aid to learning the alphabet as they were when first written, over a century ago. Here the illustrator uses animal characters in large-scale watercolor paintings, richly detailed and textured, set off by ample white space, for a letter and verse per page." Bull Cent Child Books

Edward Lear's The Scroobious Pip; completed by Ogden Nash; illustrated by Nancy Ekholm Burkert. Harper & Row 1968 unp il $14.95; lib bdg $14.89; pa $5.95 **821**

1. Animals—Poetry 2. Nonsense verses
ISBN 0-06-023764-3; 0-06-023765-1 (lib bdg); 0-06-443132-0 (pa) LC 68-10373

The original unfinished text was first published 1953 in the U.S. by the Harvard University Press in the author's: Teapots and quails

"A beautiful book, its large pages filled with pictures of birds, beasts, fish, and insects; handsome in format and design, the book is distinguished by the delicate charm of the illustrations. The Lear verses, left incomplete at his death, have been filled in by Nash; his additions are in brackets." Bull Cent Child Books

How pleasant to know Mr. Lear! Edward Lear's selected works; with an introduction and notes by Myra Cohn Livingston. Holiday House 1982 123p il $13.95 **821**

1. Nonsense verses
ISBN 0-8234-0462-5 LC 82-80822

"Each section begins with a note by the compiler, and notes on sources, as well as a combined title/first line index are appended. While the poetry is easily available elsewhere, it is useful to have the combination of poetry by Lear and information about him, each reinforcing the other." Bull Cent Child Books

The Jumblies (2-6) **821**

1. Nonsense verses

Some editions are:

Adama Bks. $6.95 Drawings by Edward Gorey (ISBN 0-915361-34-5)

Putnam $14.95 Illustrated by Ted Rand (ISBN 0-399-21632-4)

First published 1900

This collection of nonsense verse features the adventures of the Jumblies who go to sea in a sieve

The nonsense verse of Edward Lear; illustrated by John Vernon Lord. Harmony Bks. 1984 234p il $8.95 **821**

1. Nonsense verses
ISBN 0-517-55501-8 LC 84-8967

"The nonsense verse of Edward Lear approaches new levels of wackiness when complemented by Lord's absurd drawings, which are stylistically similar to political cartoons. . . . The drawings are visually complex and faithful to the text; they entertain and illuminate at the same time. His very fine pen strokes produce a variety of patterns that give a kinetic quality to the pictures—they almost leap off the page." SLJ

The owl and the pussycat (k-2) **821**

1. Nonsense verses LC 84-24897

Some editions are:

Clarion Bks. $13.95, pa $4.95 Illustrated by Paul Galdone (ISBN 0-89919-505-9; 0-89919-854-6)

Holiday House $13.95 Illustrated by Janet Stevens (ISBN 0-8234-0474-9)

Putnam $12.95, pa $4.95 Illustrated by Lorinda Bryan Cauley (ISBN 0-399-21254-X; 0-399-21253-1)

Putnam $14.95 Illustrated by Jan Brett (ISBN 0-399-21925-0)

First published 1871

After a courtship voyage of a year and a day, Owl and Pussy finally buy a ring from Piggy and are blissfully wed

Milne, A. A. (Alan Alexander), 1882-1956

Now we are six; with decorations by Ernest H. Shepard. Dutton 1961 c1927 104p il $9.95; Dell pa $3.25 (k-3) **821**

ISBN 0-525-36126-X; 0-440-46485-4 (pa)
LC 61-16258

First published 1927. "Reprinted September 1961 in this completely new format designed by Warren Chappell." Verso of title page

Milne, A. A. (Alan Alexander), 1882-1956
—Continued

"The boy or girl who has liked 'When were were very young' and 'Winnie-the-Pooh' will enjoy reading about Alexander Beetle who was mistaken for a match, the knight whose armor didn't squeak, and the old sailor who had so many things which he wanted to do. There are other entertaining poems, also, and many pictures as delightful as the verses." Pittsburgh

When we were very young; with decorations by Ernest H. Shepard. Dutton 1961 c1924 102p il $9.95; Dell pa $3.25 (k-3) **821**

ISBN 0-525-42580-2; 0-440-49485-0 (pa)
LC 61-16259

First published 1924. "Reprinted September 1961 in this completely new format designed by Warren Chappell." Verso of title page

Verse "written for Milne's small son Christopher Robin, which for its bubbling nonsense, its whimsy, and the unexpected surprises of its rhymes and rhythms, furnishes immeasurable joy to children." Right Book for the Right Child

"Mr. Milne's gay jingles have found a worthy accompaniment in the charming illustrations of Mr. Shepard." Saturday Rev

The world of Christopher Robin; the complete When we were very young and Now we are six; with decorations and new illustrations in full color, by E. H. Shepard. Dutton 1958 234p il $13.95 (k-3) **821**

ISBN 0-525-43292-2 LC 58-9571

Also available as part of a boxed set together with: The world of Pooh, entered in the Fiction section, for $29.95 (ISBN 0-525-43348-1)

In this combined edition of the two titles entered separately "the black-and-white illustrations of the original book have been retained and in addition the artist has created end papers and eight full-page illustrations in color." Booklist

Nichols, Grace

Come on into my tropical garden; poems for children; illustrations by Caroline Binch. Lippincott 1990 c1988 48p il $10.95; lib bdg $10.89 (3-5) **821**

1. Caribbean region—Poetry
ISBN 0-397-32350-6; 0-397-32349-2 (lib bdg)
LC 89-36335

First published 1988 in the United Kingdom

A collection of poems which evoke the Caribbean, its people, and its landscapes

"Idiomatic, rich in rhythms, reflecting the atmosphere of Caribbean leisure and fun, the poems sound out a child's voice—perceptive, shrewd and at times confessional. Vital, smooth grey and black pictures embellish a stirring collection." Grow Point

Noyes, Alfred, 1880-1958

The highwayman (5 and up) **821**

1. Robbers and outlaws—Poetry LC 83-725

Some editions are:

Harcourt Brace Jovanovich $14.95 Illustrated by Neil Waldman (ISBN 0-15-234340-7)
Lothrop, Lee & Shepard Bks. $11.95; lib bdg $11.88 Illustrated by Charles Mikolaycak (ISBN 0-688-02117-4; 0-688-02118-2)

Returning by moonlight to the inn where his true love, the landlord's daughter, awaits him, the highwayman is unaware that the king's soldiers also lie in wait for him, concealed in the girl's bedroom

"Waldman's watercolors, both abstract and realistic, capture the haunting, tragic spirit of the text. His broad palette glows, and his frequent use of shadow and silhouette is magnificent." Publ Wkly

"Mikolaycak's paintings are effectively framed by ample white space, black and greys, with effective touches of pinkish red in strong, stark pictures." Bull Cent Child Books

Stevenson, Robert Louis, 1850-1894

Block city; illustrated by Ashley Wolff. Dutton 1988 unp il $12.95 (k-2) **821**

ISBN 0-525-44399-1 LC 87-33397

"Wolff's colorful paintings, which resemble block prints, cleverly combine with and enrich Stevenson's poem. Large two-page spreads show a young boy at home reading on a rainy day. As he starts to build with his blocks on the floor he creates an elaborate landscape that comes alive. The hard edges of the cut block contrast with muted colors that fade off into the distance to echo the corresponding relationship in the poem whereby the solid building blocks combine with the child's imagination to create a world of palaces and harbors, sailing ships, and kings." SLJ

A child's garden of verses (k-4) **821**

Some editions are:

ABC-CLIO $13.95 Large print edition (ISBN 1-85089-924-X)
Buccaneer Bks. $18.95 (ISBN 0-89966-594-2)
Chronicle Bks. $15.95 A classic illustrated edition conceived & collected by Cooper Edens (ISBN 0-87701-608-9)
Contemporary Bks. $14.95 Illustrated by T. Lewis (ISBN 0-8092-4356-3)
Delacorte Press $14.95 Illustrated by Michael Foreman (ISBN 0-385-29430-1)
Grosset & Dunlap $6.95 Illustrated by Gyo Fujikawa (ISBN 0-448-02878-6)
Oxford Univ. Press $12.95, pa $8.95 Illustrated by Brian Wildsmith (ISBN 0-19-276032-7; 0-19-276065-3)
Scribner $16.95 (Scribner illustrated classics) Illustrated by Jessie Willcox Smith (ISBN 0-684-20949-7)

First published 1885 in the United Kingdom with title: Penny whistles

"Verses known and loved by one generation after another. Among the simpler ones for pre-school children are: Rain; At the Seaside; and Singing." Right Book for the Right Child

My shadow (k-3) **821**

1. Shades and shadows—Poetry

Some editions are:

Godine $14.95 Illustrations by Glenna Lang (ISBN 0-87923-788-0)
Putnam $14.95 Illustrated by Ted Rand (ISBN 0-399-22216-2)

Stevenson, Robert Louis, 1850-1894—*Continued*

Illustrated versions of Stevenson's popular poem in which a child tells about her relationship with her shadow

"Lang's flat acrylic paintings eliminate natural shadows and reduce volumes to shapes—as shadows do." SLJ

"Rather than following one child through the activities suggested in this classic poem, Rand skips about the world for a multi-cultural view of children and their shadowplay. The result is an exuberant version that revitalizes the familiar lines. . . . The scenes, which stretch across double-page spreads, are unified by their impressionistic style, subtle colors, and joyful mood." Booklist

821.008 English poetry—Collections

A **Child's** treasury of poems; edited by Mark Daniel. Dial Bks. for Young Readers 1986 153p il $15.95 (3-5) **821.008**

1. English poetry—Collected works 2. Nursery rhymes
ISBN 0-8037-0330-9 LC 86-2194

A collection of rhymes, verses, songs, lullabies, and jingles from the nineteenth and early twentieth centuries, illustrated with paintings from those eras

"Reproduction of the 51 full-color illustrations is outstanding, bringing a richness of color seldom seen in poetry books. Small silhouettes and engravings decorate those pages without paintings. Many nursery rhymes are included, along with poems by Eugene Field, Emily Dickinson, Rudyard Kipling, George MacDonald, Christina Rossetti, Robert Louis Stevenson, and William Wordsworth, to name a few. . . . Although a few paintings do not match their poems in every detail, this is an unusual and satisfying book." Booklist

Creatures; poems selected by Lee Bennett Hopkins; illustrated by Stella Ormai. Harcourt Brace Jovanovich 1985 32p il lib bdg $14.95 (3-5) **821.008**

1. English poetry—Collected works 2. American poetry—Collected works 3. Monsters—Poetry
ISBN 0-15-220875-5 LC 84-15698

"Ghosties, ghoulies and fantastical beings dance through the 18 poems by Rachel Field, Ted Hughes, Karla Kuskin and others, accompanied by Ormai's green and gray pencil drawings that capture the mood of the poems." SLJ

Ghost poems; edited by Daisy Wallace; illustrated by Tomie de Paola. Holiday House 1979 30p il lib bdg $12.95; pa $4.95 (1-4) **821.008**

1. Ghosts—Poetry 2. English poetry—Collected works 3. American poetry—Collected works
ISBN 0-8234-0344-0 (lib bdg); 0-8234-0849-3 (pa)
LC 78-11028

"Mostly inducing titters rather than terrors—is this collection by rhymsters with an active sense of the absurd. . . . Among the 17 entertainers are the old Scottish prayers ('Ghosties and Ghoulies'), two American Indian songs and contributions from conjurers of the past and present: Nancy Willard, Lilian Moore. X. J. Kennedy, Jack Prelutsky, et al., as well as anonymous selections from legends." Publ Wkly

"Illustrated with a quick and fearsome flourish by Tomie de Paola. . . . Here are wonderful poems to frighten young children with—but not really." N Y Times Book Rev

A **Great** big ugly man came up and tied his horse to me; a book of nonsense verse; [compiled and] illustrated by Wallace Tripp. Little, Brown 1973 46p il lib bdg $14.95; pa $6.95 (k-3) **821.008**

1. Nonsense verses 2. English poetry—Collected works 3. American poetry—Collected works
ISBN 0-316-85280-5 (lib bdg); 0-316-85281-3 (pa)
LC 74-189265

This book is "a case of an imaginative illustrator taking a new look at some old words—nursery rhymes, oral chants, verse and occasional doggerel, and coming up with some zany interpretations. Assorted animals and humans frolic through the pages in a lively series of 41 bits of verse spanning several centuries. . . . About half the verses are nursery rhymes; the rest run to oral verse, some limericks and one parody." N Y Times Book Rev

If there were dreams to sell; compiled by Barbara Lalicki; illustrated by Margot Tomes. Lothrop, Lee & Shepard Bks. 1984 unp il lib bdg $12.88 (k-3) **821.008**

1. Alphabet 2. English poetry—Collected works 3. American poetry—Collected works
ISBN 0-688-03822-0 LC 84-907

In this collection "each letter of the alphabet appears in upper- and lowercase and is represented by a poem, nursery rhyme, phrase, or word. . . . An addendum gives a paragraph's worth of information about each of the textual choices, some of which are by literary lights such as Tennyson, Longfellow, Coleridge, and Pope." Booklist

"Tomes' magical illustrations are glorious, and her scenes of elves, animals and British and Colonial American villages and villagers radiate with energy and activity." SLJ

Knock at a star; a child's introduction to poetry; [compiled by] X.J. Kennedy, Dorothy M. Kennedy; illustrated by Karen Ann Weinhaus. Little, Brown 1982 148p il $14.95 (3-6) **821.008**

1. English poetry—Collected works 2. American poetry—Collected works
ISBN 0-316-48853-4 LC 82-7328

"The anthology is stocked with poems chosen from a myriad of varied poets, ranging from Blake and Herrick to David McCord, Eve Merriam, and Bob Dylan. . . . The commentaries have avoided both pedantry and prettification by stressing the naturalness of the poetic experience." Horn Book

"The abundant illustrations are whimsical and similar to Arnold Lobel's style, and would appeal especially to younger readers. If any book can win young readers to poetry, this one can, for there's not a poem in it that isn't a chuckle, a scare, or an illumination." SLJ

Laughable limericks; compiled by Sara and John E. Brewton; illustrated by Ingrid Fetz. Crowell 1965 147p il music lib bdg $12.89 (4 and up) **821.008**

1. Limericks 2. English poetry—Collected works 3. American poetry—Collected works
ISBN 0-690-04887-4 LC 65-16179

"Humorous verses are cleverly grouped into such engaging categories as 'Animals—Friendly and 'Tame,' 'Behavior—Scroobious and Strange.' Among the more popular authors included are R. L. Stevenson, Lewis Carroll, Rudyard Kipling, Walter de la Mare, David McCord, Ogden Nash, and John Ciardi. . . . The humorous and imaginative drawings are very appropriate." SLJ

Miracles: poems by children of the English-speaking world; collected by Richard Lewis. Simon & Schuster 1966 215p il hardcover o.p. paperback available $5.95 **821.008**

1. English poetry—Collected works 2. Child authors
ISBN 0-671-42797-0 (pa) LC 66-20248

Poems on a variety of subjects by children between the ages if 4 and 13. The authors come from such varied backgrounds as the United States, England, Ireland, New Zealand, Kenya, Uganda, and Australia

"Poems chosen with a keen appreciation of the spontaneity of children's creative expression." Child Books, 1966

Monster poems; edited by Daisy Wallace; illustrated by Kay Chorao. Holiday House 1976 29p il lib bdg $12.95; pa $4.95 (1-4) **821.008**

1. Monsters—Poetry 2. English poetry—Collected works 3. American poetry—Collected works
ISBN 0-8234-0268-1 (lib bdg); 0-8234-0848-5 (pa) LC 75-17680

"These poems, collected from several sources, feature a Griggle who giggles while eating lunch, a nine-foot Ugstabuggle with hairy, grasping hands, a spangled pandemonium who is missing from the zoo, an Ombley-Gombley who sits upon a train track, and a Slithergadee who crawls out of the sea. Chorao's orange-and-blue creatures swarm over and around the rhymes, which are set off in white blocks, and lurk in corners and margins to add humor and eye-catching novelty for the reader." Booklist

My tang's tungled and other ridiculous situations; humorous poems collected by Sara and John E. Brewton and G. Meredith Blackburn III; illustrated by Graham Booth. Crowell 1973 111p il lib bdg $13.89 (3-6) **821.008**

1. Humorous poetry 2. English poetry—Collected works 3. American poetry—Collected works
ISBN 0-690-04778-9 LC 73-254

This collection "includes tongue tanglers, topsy-turvies, poems about the vexations of family life, the peculiarities of animal life, and the contradictions of school life—as well as a liberal sprinkling of just plain nonsense." Horn Book

"The assortment of authors is impressive: T. S. Eliot, Elizabeth Coatsworth, Theodore Roethke, Hilaire Belloc, Shel Silverstein and John Ciardi are a few. . . . Small chuckles and big laughs abound here. The illustrations are ridiculously funny." Publ Wkly

A New treasury of children's poetry; old favorites and new discoveries; selected and introduced by Joanna Cole; illustrated by Judith Gwyn Brown. Doubleday 1984 224p il $17.95 **821.008**

1. English poetry—Collected works 2. American poetry—Collected works
ISBN 0-385-18539-1 LC 83-20821

This "anthology of more than 200 poems is arranged in nine subject-oriented sections which include animals, holidays, silly rhymes and nature. It is a collection of Cole's personal favorites, and there is an emphasis on 19th- and 20th-Century American poets." SLJ

"Animated line drawings, some soberly representational but most comical and/or grotesque, illustrate a book in which the selections are arranged so that they progress from simple poems for very young children and, with increasing complexity, move on to poems for older readers. . . . There's little unusual here, but it's an anthology of solid worth." Bull Cent Child Books

Of quarks, quasars, and other quirks; quizzical poems for the supersonic age; collected by Sara and John E. Brewton and John Brewton Blackburn; illustrated by Quentin Blake. Crowell 1977 114p il $12.95; lib bdg $13.89 (5 and up) **821.008**

1. English poetry—Collected works 2. American poetry—Collected works 3. Civilization, Modern—Poetry
ISBN 0-690-01286-1; 0-690-04885-8 (lib bdg) LC 76-54747

"An anthology of children's poetry spoofing modern life and scientific progress. Credit card overuse, TV mania, computer craziness, transplants, and atomic bombs are parodied in original and outrageous verse with serious undertones. . . . With such contributors as Eve Merriam, Ogden Nash, and John Updike." SLJ

Oh, such foolishness! poems selected by William Cole; pictures by Tomie de Paola. Lippincott 1978 96p il $11.95 (3-6) **821.008**

1. Nonsense verses 2. English poetry—Collected works 3. American poetry—Collected works
ISBN 0-397-31807-3 LC 78-1622

"Cole's witty compendium of nonsense verses could well serve as an introduction to poetry for youngsters not attuned to it. Selections from known and not-so-well-known as well as anonymous authors make it a well rounded collection. Good for reading aloud and a welcome addition to the children's shelf. De Paola's zany pen-and-ink drawings pinpoint such foolishness." Child Book Rev Serv

Oh, that's ridiculous! poems selected by William Cole; drawings by Tomi Ungerer. Viking 1972 80p il o.p.; Puffin Bks. paperback available $3.95 (3-6) **821.008**

1. Nonsense verses 2. English poetry—Collected works 3. American poetry—Collected works

ISBN 0-14-032857-2 (pa) LC 70-183934

"Here are limericks and nonsense rhymes by various authors, including Gelett Burgess, Ogden Nash, Theodore Roethke, A. E. Housman, and others

"There are a few rhymes that have the tinge of children;s doggerel, but most of them are delightfully silly. . . . The illustrations are divinely, fittingly mad." Bull Cent Child Books

The **Oxford** book of children's verse; chosen and edited with notes by Iona and Peter Opie. Oxford Univ. Press 1973 xxxi, 407p il $29.95 **821.008**

1. English poetry—Collected works 2. American poetry—Collected works

ISBN 0-19-812140-7 LC 73-76871

Companion volume to: The Oxford book of children's verse in America, entered in class 811.008

Arranged chronologically, these 332 selections from British and American children's poetry include works by such poets as Chaucer, Charles and Mary Lamb, Kipling, Farjeon, Milne, Eliot and Nash

Poems to read to the very young; selected by Josette Frank; illustrated by Eloise Wilkin. Random House 1982 45p il $7.95 (k-2) **821.008**

1. English poetry—Collected works 2. American poetry—Collected works

ISBN 0-394-85188-9 LC 82-518

A collection of short poems on various subjects, by Robert Louis Stevenson, A.A. Milne, Christina Rossetti, and other authors

"Wilkin's innocent, childlike faces add charm; and though in places the reproduction is fuzzy, the full-color scenes are affectionately appealing within an alluring page design. An early introduction to poetry that parents will find especially enjoyable for one-to-one sharing." Booklist

The **Poetry** troupe; an anthology of poems to read aloud; compiled by Isabel Wilner; decorations by Isabel Wilner. Scribner 1977 223p il lib bdg $13.95 **821.008**

1. English poetry—Collected works 2. American poetry—Collected works

ISBN 0-684-15198-7 LC 77-9439

"During her years as a librarian in an elementary laboratory school on a college campus, the compiler has worked with children in 'poetry troupes' that invite both active participation and passive listening. The groups vary in age, taste, and sophistication; girls and boys help to hunt down the poems to be shared and present them in an assortment of ways to classes of college students as well as of children. The collection represents poetry that has brought great pleasure to readers and to audiences; and while most of the authors are familiar enough, the poems themselves are buoyant and unhackneyed. . . . With indexes of authors, titles, and first lines." Horn Book

Rainbow in the sky; collected and edited by Louis Untermeyer; illustrated by Reginald Birch. Golden anniversary ed. Harcourt Brace Jovanovich 1985 c1935 xxvii, 498p il $19.95 (k-4) **821.008**

1. English poetry—Collected works 2. American poetry—Collected works 3. Nursery rhymes

ISBN 0-15-265479-8 LC 84-19306

A reissue of the title first published 1935. Copyright renewed 1963

"More than five hundred poems from Mother Goose to modern times are included in this anthology for younger children. Mr. Birch's drawings in black and white are lively and . . . amusing." N Y Public Libr

The **Random** House book of poetry for children; selected and introduced by Jack Prelutsky; illustrated by Arnold Lobel. Random House 1983 248p il $15.95; lib bdg $15.99 **821.008**

1. American poetry—Collected works 2. English poetry—Collected works

ISBN 0-394-85010-6; 0-394-95010-0 (lib bdg) LC 83-2990

Opening poems for each section especially written for this anthology by Jack Prelutsky

In this anthology emphasis "is placed on humor and light verse; but serious and thoughtful poems are also included. . . . Approximately two thirds of the selections were written within the past forty years—the splendid contributions of such writers as John Ciardi, Aileen Fisher, Dennis Lee, Myra Cohn Livingston, David McCord, Eve Merriam, and Lilian Moore. [There are] . . . samplings of earlier poets from Shakespeare and Blake to Emily Dickinson and Walter de la Mare." Horn Book

Read-aloud rhymes for the very young; selected by Jack Prelutsky; illustrated by Marc Brown; with an introduction by Jim Trelease. Knopf 1986 98p il $14.95; lib bdg $14.99 (k-2) **821.008**

1. English poetry—Collected works 2. American poetry—Collected works 3. Nursery rhymes

ISBN 0-394-87218-5; 0-394-97218-X (lib bdg) LC 86-7147

"Prelutsky has selected and combined joyous, sensitive poems . . . by such traditional poets as Dorothy Aldis and A. A. Milne, as well as by more contemporary poets such as Karla Kuskin, Dennis Lee, and Prelutsky himself. All are lively, rhythmic poems that young children will enjoy. . . . Brown's bright pastel illustrations effectively use framing, action, and cheerful creatures to echo the light tone of the book. The poems are arranged with others of the same topic and include popular concerns of small children such as animals, bath time, dragons, and play. Teachers and librarians will appreciate poems about seasons, months, holidays, and special events that can be easily incorporated into story hours and classroom life." SLJ

Shrieks at midnight; macabre poems, eerie and humorous; selected by Sara and John E. Brewton; drawings by Ellen Raskin. Crowell 1969 177p il $13.95 (4 and up) **821.008**

1. English poetry—Collected works 2. American poetry—Collected works
ISBN 0-690-73518-9 LC 69-11824

A "collection of spooky, weird, extremely humorous poems, including funny bits of terror by such poets as Lewis Carroll, Ogden Nash, Hilaire Belloc, Langston Hughes, Dorothy Parker, James Reeves, and a few good old 'Author Unknowns.' Puns, epitaphs, and old ballads are represented." SLJ

They've discovered a head in the box for the bread, and other laughable limericks; collected by John E. Brewton and Lorraine A. Blackburn; illustrated by Fernando Krahn. Crowell 1978 129p il lib bdg $13.89 (4 and up) **821.008**

1. Limericks
ISBN 0-690-03883-6 LC 77-26598

"A grab bag of more than 200 limericks. . . . Loosely grouped by topic—animals, music, love, silly mistakes . . . etc.—the verses vary in their level of sophistication but strike a mean of easy, literal humor. Krahn's doughy cartoons are on hand to generate additional amusement; useful as a broad sampler, with indexes of authors, titles, and first lines appended." Booklist

Tripp, Wallace, 1940-
Marguerite, go wash your feet. Houghton Mifflin 1985 48p il lib bdg $15.95; pa $5.95 (1-3) **821.008**

1. Humorous poetry 2. English poetry—Collected works 3. American poetry—Collected works
ISBN 0-395-35392-0 (lib bdg); 0-395-39894-0 (pa)
LC 85-7616

A collection of amusing verses by a variety of poets, including Emily Dickinson, Spike Milligan, Shakespeare, and others less well known

"Tripp's taste in irreverent nonsense is impeccable; his talent for illustrating it is remarkable. . . . There is something here for everyone: young children will enjoy the language rhythms and cartoon drawings, older ones will pick up on the forthright jokes, while adults will enjoy the artistic allusions and sassier poems that require some background for full appreciation." Booklist

Wider than the sky: poems to grow up with; collected and edited by Scott Elledge. Harper & Row 1990 358p $19.95; lib bdg $19.89 (5 and up) **821.008**

1. English poetry—Collected works 2. American poetry—Collected works
ISBN 0-06-021786-3; 0-06-021787-1 (lib bdg)
LC 90-4135

"This substantial, eclectic gathering of diverse forms includes classic and contemporary selections on a variety of subjects, ranging from love to nature, from the sublime to the ridiculous. . . . It is essentially a browsing collection, yet the arrangement is not quite as random as a first glance might indicate. Several poems with similar themes or which benefit from close juxtaposition are sequentially placed." Horn Book

Includes bibliographic references

Witch poems; edited by Daisy Wallace; illustrated by Trina Schart Hyman. Holiday House 1976 30p il lib bdg $12.95; pa $4.95 (1-4) **821.008**

1. Witches—Poetry 2. English poetry—Collected works 3. American poetry—Collected works
ISBN 0-8234-0281-9 (lib bdg); 0-8234-0850-7 (pa)
LC 76-9036

"A collection of 20 short witch poems, most by contemporary authors (X. J. Kennedy, Karla Kuskin, and company) but also including four traditional chants." SLJ

"All the poems are rich in the rhymes, refrains and wordplay of which good incantations are made." N Y Times Book Rev

822 English drama

George, Richard R.
Roald Dahl's James and the giant peach; a play; adapted by Richard R. George; introduction by Roald Dahl. Puffin Bks. 1983 91p il pa $3.50 (3-5) **822**

ISBN 0-14-031464-4 LC 83-206783

Adapted from the story by Roald Dahl entered in the Fiction section

"Dahl's popular story about James, who has fantastic adventures once he leaves his terrible home, has been well dramatized, but condensed considerably, by George. In addition to the script, George provides suggestions for staging, directions for easily-made costumes and scenery, with diagrams and lighting procedures. The cast of 18 characters can be expanded with 'Cloud-Men,' 'onlookers' and 'passengers' or it can be reduced by having children double-up on parts." SLJ

822.3 William Shakespeare

Lamb, Charles, 1775-1834
Tales from Shakespeare; by Charles & Mary Lamb **822.3**

1. Shakespeare, William, 1564-1616—Adaptations

Some editions are:

Crown $12.99 With sundry pictures and illuminations both in color and in line by Elizabeth Shippen Green Elliott (ISBN 0-517-62156-8)
Dent [distributed by Biblio Distr. Centre] $13.95; pa $3.95 (Everyman's library) With illustrations by Elizabeth Blaisdell (ISBN 0-460-00008-X; 0-460-01008-5)
New Am. Lib. pa $3.95 (ISBN 0-451-52391-1)
Puffin Bks. pa $2.25 (ISBN 0-14-035088-8)

First published 1807

"The *Tales* were the first version of 'Shakespeare' to be published specifically for children. They are written in a clear, vigorous style, not often encumbered by the attempt to make the language resemble that of the original. A lot is left out. . . . But the literary quality of the *Tales* makes them outshine almost every other English children's book of this period, and they proved

Lamb, Charles, 1775-1834—*Continued*
an immediate and lasting success." Oxford Companion to Child Lit

828 English miscellany

Carroll, Lewis, 1832-1898
The complete works of Lewis Carroll; with an introduction by Alexander Woollcott; and the illustrations by John Tenniel. Nonesuch Press; distributed by Viking 1990 c1989 1165p il $35 **828**

ISBN 1-871061-14-8 LC 89-60108

Also available Random House edition $15.95 (ISBN 0-394-60485-7)

This edition first published 1939 in the United Kingdom

In addition to Alice's adventures in Wonderland, Through the looking glass, Sylvie and Bruno, Sylvie and Bruno concluded, The hunting of the snark, Phantasmagoria and other poems, and Three sunsets and other poems, this volume collects Carroll's shorter prose, verse, stories, games, puzzles, problems, acrostics and a selection from Symbolic logic

Mahy, Margaret
Nonstop nonsense; illustrated by Quentin Blake. Margaret K. McElderry Bks. 1989 c1977 120p il $12.95 (4-6) **828**

ISBN 0-689-50483-7 LC 88-8401

First published 1977 in the United Kingdom

A collection of whimsical stories and poems about such creatures as a word wizard, a poetical cat, and a very small ghost who lives inside a book

"Author and artist join forces in a kind of perfect, if unholy, matrimony; Quentin Blake's delightfully mad drawings gambol blithely over the pages." Horn Book

Milne, A. A. (Alan Alexander), 1882-1956
The Christopher Robin story book; decorations by Ernest H. Shepard. Dutton 1966 c1929 171p il $7.95 (k-3) **828**

ISBN 0-525-27933-4 LC 66-12251

A reissue in new format of the title first published 1929; copyright renewed 1957

"Introduced and selected by the author from When we were very young; Now we are six; Winnie-the-Pooh; The house at Pooh Corner." Title page

"You will find here a collection of verses and stories, mostly about a little boy called Christopher Robin." Author's note

Descriptions of the titles listed above can be found entered separately. Winnie-the-Pooh and The house at Pooh Corner are entered separately in the Fiction section, and the other two titles are in class 821

Pooh's bedtime book; illustrated by Ernest H. Shepard; colored by Gail Owens. Dutton 1980 40p il $9.95 (1-3) **828**

ISBN 0-525-37373-X LC 80-65523

"This is simply a collection of excerpts from Milne's 'When We Were Very Young, 'Winnie-the-Pooh,' 'Now We Are Six' and 'The House at Pooh Corner' (all Dutton). The poems 'Us Two' and 'Vespers' frame the collection; the remaining poems are 'Sneezles, 'Furry Bear' and 'Rice Pudding.' The stories are 'Winnie-the-Pooh and Some Bees'; 'An Expotition to the North Pole,' which has the wonderful 'Sing Ho! for the life of a Bear!' and Roo's learning to swim; and 'Tigger Comes to the Forest.' The illustrations are from the original Ernest Shepard designs." SLJ

Thomas, Dylan, 1914-1953
A child's Christmas in Wales. il (5 and up) **828**

1. Christmas—Wales

Some editions are:

Godine $13.95; pa $7.95 Illustrated by Edward Ardizzone (ISBN 0-87923-339-7; 0-87923-529-2)

Holiday House lib bdg $14.95 Illustrated by Trina Schart Hyman (ISBN 0-8234-0565-6)

New Directions $14.95; pa $4.95 Illustrated by Fritz Eichenberg (ISBN 0-8112-1154-1; 0-8112-0203-8)

First published 1954 by New Directions

A portrait of Christmas Day in a small Welsh town and of the author's childhood there

For any season of the year "the language is enchanting and the poetry shines with an unearthly radiance." N Y Times Book Rev

829 Old English (Anglo-Saxon)

Crossley-Holland, Kevin
Beowulf; [illustrated by] Charles Keeping; [retold by] Kevin Crossley-Holland. Oxford Univ. Press 1984 c1982 46p il $14.95; pa $6.95 (5 and up) **829**

ISBN 0-19-279770-0; 0-19-272184-4 (pa)

First published 1982 in the United Kingdom

"When he hears of the havoc being wrought upon the Danes by Grendel, Beowulf volunteers to travel to Denmark to rid his father's friends of this enemy. Although the monster has defeated all others, Beowulf slays both him and his mother and returns to his homeland a gift-laden hero. The story of his death over 50 years later while slaying yet another dragon is told in the final chapter. This retelling of the classic epic maintains much of the ancient storytelling tradition in its richly tapestried prose. It is told in a high, formal style worthy of an epic, yet the picture book format makes it accessible to today's youth. Keeping's harsh, stark etchings enhance the somber majesty of the tale." SLJ

841 French poetry

Cendrars, Blaise, 1887-1961
Shadow; translated and illustrated by Marcia Brown from the French of Blaise Cendrars. Scribner 1982 unp il $13.95 (1-3) **841**

ISBN 0-684-17226-7 LC 81-9424

Awarded the Caldecott Medal, 1983

Cendrars, Blaise, 1887-1961—*Continued*

Original text first published in France

This is the French poet's "version of a West African folk tale about a spirit that is at once elusive and multiform." N Y Times Book Rev

"Inspired by the exotic atmosphere and the dramatic possibilities of the text, Brown has choreographed a sequence of almost theatrical illustrations, placing human and animal figures—and their shadows—against brilliant, contrasting, always changing settings. Resplendent—yet controlled—in color, texture, and form, the work is an impressive, sophisticated example of the art of the picture book." Horn Book

883 Classical Greek epic poetry and fiction

Colum, Padraic, 1881-1972

The children's Homer: The adventures of Odysseus and The tale of Troy; illustrated by Willy Pogany. Collier Bks. 1982 c1946 247p il pa $7.95 (4 and up) **883**

1. Homer—Adaptations 2. Odysseus (Greek mythology) 3. Trojan War

ISBN 0-02-042520-1 LC 82-12643

First published 1918 by Macmillan with title: The adventures of Odysseus and The tale of Troy

A retelling of the events of the Trojan War and the wanderings of Odysseus based on Homer's Iliad and Odyssey

"Padraic Colum has given the ever absorbing romance in a manner which is equally enthralling to the adult or the boy or girl, carrying anyone who possesses imagination into the Greece of long ago. The spirit of both text and illustrations is the spirit of Homer." Wis Libr Bull

Picard, Barbara Leonie

The Iliad of Homer; retold by Barbara Leonie Picard; illustrated by Joan Kiddell-Monroe. Oxford Univ. Press 1960 208p il $16.95 (6 and up) **883**

1. Homer—Adaptations 2. Trojan War

ISBN 0-19-274517-4

"Rounding out the course of the Trojan War in the ninth year, as given by Homer, Miss Picard provides a Prologue explaining how the war with Troy began, and an Epilogue recounting how the war ended. Finally, she includes a . . . glossary identifying the long cast of humans and gods taking part in the conduct of the war." Horn Book

891 East-Indo European literatures

Beach, Milo Cleveland

The adventures of Rama; with illustrations from a sixteenth-century Mughal manuscript. Freer Gallery of Art 1983 62p il $15 (4 and up) **891**

1. Rāma (Hindu deity) 2. Illumination of books and manuscripts

ISBN 0-934686-51-3 LC 83-1473

"Reproductions from a late-sixteenth-century manuscript illuminated in the Mogul style are a fitting complement to this retelling of tales from the 'Ramayana,' epic of Hindu India. . . . In a style that conveys the ancient eloquence of the legend's oral tradition, Beach smoothly relates an abridged version of the story of King Dasaratha's long-awaited heir, Rama, who is actually the incarnation of the divine Vishnu. . . . A stunning introduction in picture-book format to a classic of Indian literature." Booklist

891.7 East Slavic literatures. Russian literature

A **Harvest** of Russian children's literature; edited with introduction and commentary by Miriam Morton; foreword by Ruth Hill Viguers. University of Calif. Press 1967 474p il $45 **891.7**

1. Russian literature—Collected works

ISBN 0-520-00886-3 LC 67-21384

This is "a superb anthology for any collection, useful for a number of diverse purposes and, better still, a source of pleasure in its variety, scope, and quality. . . . The selections range from classic writers like Tolstoy and Gorky to contemporary authors, some of whose work has already been published in English—Chukovsky and Sholokhov, for example. The book's contents are divided both by age groups and by genre or type of literature; the illustrations are also from Russian children's books. Many of the selections are preceded by notes about the authors. The editor has provided a long, thoughtful, and informative introduction. Separate author and title indexes are appended." Sutherland. The Best in Child Books

895.6 Japanese literature

In a spring garden; edited by Richard Lewis; pictures by Ezra Jack Keats. Dial Bks. for Young Readers 1989 c1965 unp il $13.95; pa $4.95 (k-3) **895.6**

1. Haiku 2. Japanese poetry—Collected works 3. Nature in poetry

ISBN 0-8037-4024-7; 0-8037-4033-6 (pa) LC 65-23965

First published 1965

"Translations of haiku by such Japanese poets as Issa and Buson." Horn Book

These brief verses "follow a day in spring from a red

In a spring garden—*Continued*
morning sky to the passing of a giant firefly." Child Books Too Good to Miss

897 Literatures of North American native languages

Dancing teepees: poems of American Indian youth; selected by Virginia Driving Hawk Sneve, with art by Stephen Gammell. Holiday House 1989 32p il $14.95; pa $5.95 (3-5) **897**

1. Indians of North America—Poetry
ISBN 0-8234-0724-1; 0-8234-0879-5 (pa) LC 88-11075

An illustrated collection of poems from the oral tradition of Native Americans

This is an "eclectic collection, drawn from a variety of tribal traditions. Printed on heavy paper, the book is illustrated with a catalogue of marvelously rendered designs and motifs, ranging from those of the Northwest Coast to the intricate beadwork patterns of the Great Lakes and the zigzag geometric borders of Southwestern pottery." N Y Times Book Rev

In the trail of the wind: American Indian poems and ritual orations; edited by John Bierhorst. Farrar, Straus & Giroux 1971 201p il $6.95 (5 and up) **897**

1. Indians—Poetry
ISBN 0-374-33640-7 LC 71-144822

This "collection of poetry, taken from the oral literature of more than 30 tribes of Indians of North, Central, and South America and the Eskimos, is arranged topically under such headings as The beginning, Of rain and birth, The words of war, and Death. . . . Background information on certain aspects of Indian thought and the problems of translation are discussed in the introduction. Appended are notes on each poem including translator and source; a glossary of tribes, cultures, and languages; and suggestions for further reading." Booklist

"A fascinating book to read, and to reread. . . . Its illustrations, selected from period engravings, makes it a distinguished book to look at as well." Publ Wkly

The **Sacred** path; spells, prayers & power songs of the American Indians; edited by John Bierhorst. Morrow 1983 191p il $15.95; pa $7.95 (5 and up) **897**

1. Indians—Poetry
ISBN 0-688-01699-5; 0-688-02647-8 (pa) LC 82-14118

"Containing both traditional and contemporary material, this is a compilation of American Indian poetry that is arranged by stages of the life cycle, beginning with poems and chants of birth and infancy, and progressing through stages and activities of life to prayers and songs for the dying and the dead. . . . The tribal source for each selection is printed below the poem; appended are editorial notes, a bibliography of sources, and a glossary of tribes, cultures and languages." Bull Cent Child Books

900 GEOGRAPHY AND HISTORY

909 World history. Civilization

Arnold, Guy

Datelines of world history. Warwick Press 1983 93p il maps lib bdg $13.90 (5 and up) **909**

1. World history 2. Chronology, Historical
ISBN 0-531-09212-7 LC 83-1085

"The date coverage ranges from 40,000 B.C. to 1983. This reference book . . . includes a biographical index, a political glossary and a brief 'Who's Who in History' section. Time-lines are used to point out what events were taking place simultaneously in different parts of the world. . . . Brief essays and excellent illustrations are included in every section." SLJ

Haskins, James, 1941-

Count your way through the Arab world; by Jim Haskins; illustrations by Dana Gustafson. Carolrhoda Bks. 1987 unp il lib bdg $11.95 (2-4) **909**

1. Arab countries
ISBN 0-87614-304-4 LC 87-6391

Uses Arabic numerals from one to ten to introduce concepts about Arab countries and Arab culture

Rahn, Joan Elma, 1929-

More plants that changed history; illustrated by the author. Atheneum Pubs. 1985 126p il maps $11.95 (5 and up) **909**

1. Civilization 2. Botany, Economic
ISBN 0-689-31099-4 LC 84-21563

Companion volume to: Plants that changed history (1982)

"The author describes how writing evolved through the discovery of papyrus and paper, the development of and increasing uses for rubber, and the introduction of tea and opium. Rahn provides much more than a general detailing of each plant's history. . . . [She] writes expressively, and the information should prove an invaluable curriculum supplement." Booklist

Includes bibliography

Ventura, Piero

There once was a time. Putnam 1987 158p il $19.95 (5 and up) **909**

1. World history
ISBN 0-399-21356-2 LC 86-25237

This is a "social history of Western civilization, beginning in Ancient Egypt and Greece, and ending at the turn of the 20th Century. Ventura takes a cross section of important civilizations at key times in history. . . . Each time period is broken down into nine sections that examine society and government, housing, agriculture, arts and trade, economy, fashion, transportation, inventions and technology, and warfare. . . . A page and

Ventura, Piero—*Continued*
a half of well-drawn, appropriately colored, richly detailed illustrations accompany the half page of text. . . . The broad scope prevents much detail about any given society, and there is no index, making this an unlikely choice for assignments, but it is well-conceived, accurate, and excellent for browsing or recreational reading." SLJ

909.07 World history—ca. 500-1450/1500

Anno, Mitsumasa, 1926-
Anno's medieval world; adapted from the translation by Ursula Synge. Philomel Bks. 1980 unp il $16.95; lib bdg $12.99 (3-6) **909.07**

1. Civilization, Medieval 2. Universe 3. Science and civilization
ISBN 0-399-20742-2; 0-399-61153-3 (lib bdg) LC 79-28367

Original Japanese edition, 1979

The author describes scientific beliefs concerning the universe in the Middle Ages up to the Age of Reason. Through text and paintings Anno looks at the culture, "fears and superstitions, as well as the growing advances in scientific thought and inquiry." Publisher's note

"The detailed scientific explanation, along with a chronology and notes that are appended, will need adult interpretation. For an older audience than the picture-book format implies, but nonetheless fascinating." Booklist

Hunt, Jonathan
Illuminations; written and illustrated by Jonathan Hunt. Bradbury Press 1989 unp il $16.95 (2-4) **909.07**

1. Alphabet 2. Civilization, Medieval 3. Illumination of books and manuscripts
ISBN 0-02-745770-2 LC 88-38967

"An oversized, elaborately illustrated, eclectic alphabetic view of the Middle Ages from Alchemist to Zither, with illuminated initials based on a twelfth-century alphabet, this book is for browsing rather than reference, and useful for introducing or complementing history units." Horn Book Guide

Includes bibliography

909.82 World history—20th century, 1900-1999

Tames, Richard
The 1950s. Watts 1990 48p il (Picture history of the 20th century) lib bdg $12.90 (6 and up) **909.82**

1. History, Modern—1900-1999 (20th century)
ISBN 0-531-14034-2 LC 88-50367

This book "highlights principal events of the 1950's. . . . Organized by topic (2 pages of mostly photos on each topic, whether film and theatre, growing up, the United States in the 50's, Europe, or the Communist World), the text is supplemented by 2 tables (33 Personalities of the 50's and a chronological listing of events) and an index." BAYA Book Rev

Wood, Tim
The 1940s; [by] Tim Wood and R.J. Unstead. Watts 1990 48p il (Picture history of the 20th century) lib bdg $12.90 (6 and up) **909.82**

1. History, Modern—1900-1999 (20th century) 2. World War, 1939-1945
ISBN 0-531-14035-0 LC 88-50368

Text and pictures cover issues and events of the 1940s, including World War II, the post-war United States, India and Israel, science and technology, fashion, popular pastimes, and the arts. Also included are a biographical reference section and a year by year chronology

910 Geography and travel

Bell, Neill, 1946-
The book of where; or, How to be naturally geographic; illustrated by Richard Wilson. Little, Brown 1982 119p il maps $14.95; pa $8.95 (5 and up) **910**

1. Geography
ISBN 0-316-08830-7; 0-316-08831-5 (pa) LC 81-19315

"A Brown paper school book"

This geography book contains "a series of exercises that are designed to teach children directions, map reading, a . . . spectrum of concepts that concern U.S. and world geography and geology and continental drift." Sci Books Films

"The tone is personable and supportive, and the book's considerable length is tempered by lots of jocular cartoon illustrations, diagrams, and relevant asides. . . . Ideal for independent study or as a classroom activity source book, this gets some key lessons across in a refreshingly unpedantic fashion." Booklist

Brown, Laurene Krasny
Dinosaurs travel; a guide for families on the go; [by] Laurie Krasny Brown and Marc Brown. Little, Brown 1988 32p il lib bdg $13.95; pa $5.95 (k-3) **910**

1. Travel
ISBN 0-316-11076-0 (lib bdg); 0-316-11253-4 (pa) LC 87-36637

Text and illustrations of dinosaur characters discuss the practicalities and pleasures of travel, from packing up and taking off to returning home again

"The advice is practical and straightforward, and the three or four illustrations on each page are delightfully silly. . . . A perfect introduction to armchair traveling, as well as a soaring success as an opener for primary grade units on transportation." SLJ

Heinrichs, Susan

The Pacific Ocean. Childrens Press 1986 45p il lib bdg $13.27; pa $4.95 (2-4) **910**

1. Pacific Ocean
ISBN 0-516-01295-9 (lib bdg); 0-516-41295-7 (pa)
LC 86-9653

"A New true book"

Provides basic information about the Pacific Ocean, including wave formation, currents, tides, marine biology, and the landscape of the ocean floor

Includes glossary

910.3 Geography—Dictionaries, encyclopedias, gazetteers

Exploring your world: the adventure of geography. National Geographic Soc. 1989 608p il maps $29.95; lib bdg $34.95 **910.3**

1. Geography—Dictionaries
ISBN 0-87044-726-2; 0-87044-727-0 (lib bdg)
LC 89-13099

"Arranged in dictionary form, the 334 encyclopedic entries cover a wide array of geographical topics and range in size from a paragraph (i.e., lagoon) to as many as fifteen pages (i.e., agriculture). Individual countries, states, mountains, and rivers are not included except as examples within the topical entries. Virtually every entry is followed by a large number of cross-references which provide students with valuable paths to more information. . . . More than one thousand photographs, diagrams, and charts delight the eye and provide a valuable additional learning modality." SLJ

Lands and peoples. Grolier 6v il maps lib bdg set $184.50 **910.3**

1. Geography—Dictionaries 2. World history—Dictionaries 3. Civilization—Dictionaries

Originally published 1929-30. Periodically revised

Contents: v 1 Africa; v2 Asia, Australia, New Zealand, Oceania; v3-4 Europe; v5 North America; v6 South and Central America, Antarctica, Facts and figures, Selected readings, Index

"The uniform format for each country provides basic data, color maps and photos, and an article about the people, land, economy, and history. . . . The editors state that 'the basic principle' of their editorial policy 'is presentation of fact, not opinion.' Articles are generally objective; however, controversial issues are often avoided." Wynar. Guide to Ref Books for Sch Media Cent. 3d edition

Webster's new geographical dictionary. Merriam-Webster il maps $19.95 **910.3**

1. Geography—Dictionaries 2. Gazetteers

First published 1949 with title: Webster's geographical dictionary. Periodically revised

"Concise and easy-to-read gazetteer, listing both ancient and modern place names. Most entries include pronunciation, brief description, population and brief history. Includes numerous charts and lists, some maps and a list of geographical terms from other languages." NY Public Libr. Ref Books for Child Collect

Worldmark encyclopedia of the nations. Worldmark Press; distributed by Wiley 5v il maps set $315 **910.3**

1. Geography—Dictionaries 2. World history—Dictionaries 3. World politics—Dictionaries

First published 1960 in one volume, arranged in one alphabet. Periodically revised

"Condensed factual information on 176 countries. Fifty different subjects are examined for each country—climate, religion, transportation, economy, banking, government, resources, education, etc. The volume on the United Nations treats its organization and operation. Supplements encyclopedias." N Y Public Libr. Ref Books for Child Collect

910.4 Accounts of travel. Seafaring life. Buried treasure

Ballard, Robert D.

Exploring the Titanic; edited by Patrick Crean; illustrations by Ken Marschall. Scholastic 1988 64p il $14.95 (4 and up) **910.4**

1. Titanic (Steamship) 2. Shipwrecks 3. Underwater exploration
ISBN 0-590-41953-6 LC 88-6478

"A Scholastic/Madison Press book"

"In straightforward prose, complemented by excellent illustrations, the story of the Titanic's first and final voyage as well as that of her rediscovery and exploration is told. The text captures the drama of both the night of the sinking as well as that of the discovery of the great ship on the ocean floor. The technically accurate and lucid explanations are greatly enhanced by Marshall's stunning paintings, as well as by diagrams and current and period photographs." SLJ

The lost wreck of the Isis; by Robert D. Ballard with Rick Archbold. Scholastic 1990 63p il maps (Time quest bk) $15.95 (4 and up) **910.4**

1. Shipwrecks 2. Underwater exploration 3. Romans
ISBN 0-590-43852-2 LC 89-70280

"A Scholastic/Madison Press book"

"The JASON Project's Mediterranean expedition to study the remains of an ancient Roman shipwreck is recounted in an entertaining, skillful blend of scientific exploration, archaeology, and history. Includes flashbacks to the fourth century." Sci Child

Includes glossary and bibliography

Fine, John Christopher

Sunken ships & treasure; written & illustrated with photographs by John Christopher Fine. Atheneum Pubs. 1986 119p il $16.95 (5 and up) **910.4**

1. Shipwrecks 2. Buried treasure
ISBN 0-689-31280-6 LC 86-3652

"An International Oceanographic Foundation selection"

The author "describes the investigations of various treasure seekers and ocean explorers and also relates the historical, technical, and environmental information that

Fine, John Christopher—*Continued*
shipwrecks have provided over the years. Included are comments on ancient Mediterranean wrecks, sunken World War II submarines, as well as the *Titanic* and *Andrea Doria* disasters." Booklist

"The book is short, easily read, and well illustrated with attractive color photographs." SLJ

Includes bibliography

Gibbons, Gail
Sunken treasure. Crowell 1988 32p il $13.95; lib bdg $13.89; HarperCollins Pubs. pa $4.95 (2-4) **910.4**

1. Nuestra Señora de Atocha (Ship) 2. Buried treasure 3. Shipwrecks

ISBN 0-690-04734-7; 0-690-04736-3 (lib bdg); 0-06-446097-5 (pa) LC 87-30114

"Gibbons concentrates on the ancient Spanish galleon, the *Atocha*, which sank off the coast of Florida in 1662, describing under labeled headings the sinking, the search, the find, recording, salvage, restoration and preservation, cataloguing, and eventual distribution of the treasure. . . . The reader learns of the great variety of experts employed on these projects, from the work of marine archaeologists to the contributions of historians, cataloguers, and artists as well. A handsomely designed book, well organized, and easily accessible to younger readers." Horn Book

Hackwell, W. John
Diving to the past: recovering ancient wrecks. Scribner 1988 54p il $13.95 (4 and up) **910.4**

1. Underwater exploration 2. Shipwrecks 3. Archeology

ISBN 0-684-18918-6 LC 87-233529

"Straightforward, well-honed text, complemented by softly colored pencil sketches, describes how ancient wrecks are excavated by marine archaeologists who, armed with high-tech equipment and scientific expertise, seek clues to our human past." Sci Child

Hidden treasures of the sea. National Geographic Soc. 1988 104p il $6.95; lib bdg $8.50 (4 and up) **910.4**

1. Buried treasure 2. Shipwrecks

ISBN 0-87044-658-4; 0-87044-663-0 (lib bdg) LC 88-5142

"Books for world explorers"

An introduction to nautical archeology, focusing on social, cultural, and political history as exposed by shipwrecks from ancient times to the present

Includes bibliography

Humble, Richard, 1945-
The travels of Marco Polo; illustrated by Richard Hook. Watts 1990 32p il maps (Exploration through the ages) lib bdg $11.90 (4-6) **910.4**

1. Polo, Marco, 1254-1323? 2. Voyages and travels 3. Explorers 4. China—Description and travel

ISBN 0-531-14022-9 LC 89-36214

Discusses the journey of Marco Polo to the court of the Mongol emperor, Kublai Khan, in the thirteenth century and includes his lesser-known journeys as well

"The format, with full-page, well-drawn color illustrations extended by historical reproductions, will draw readers in; the large print makes the text easily accessible. But most importantly, the book employs a lively writing style that should attract those outside the report-seekers realm." Booklist

Includes glossary

Schwartz, Alvin, 1927-
Gold & silver, silver & gold; tales of hidden treasure; collected and retold by Alvin Schwartz; pictures by David Christiana. Farrar, Straus & Giroux 1988 128p il maps $13.95 (5 and up) **910.4**

1. Buried treasure

ISBN 0-374-32690-8 LC 88-45326

"Legend, folklore, fact, and fiction combine in this compilation of 25 brief works having to do with buried treasure." Soc Educ

"The inclusion of an unsolved cipher giving directions to buried gold and silver should keep young code fanatics busy for some time. Christiana's fine-textured pencil drawings lend an air of mystery and drama that heightens the book's appeal. An excellent work on a high-interest subject, this will be a natural for booktalks." Booklist

Includes bibliographic references

910.5 Geography—Serial publications

National Geographic World. National Geographic Soc. $10.95 per year (3-6) **910.5**

1. Geography—Periodicals

ISSN 0361-5499

Monthly. First published 1975

This "publication for children 8 to 13 aims to combine information and entertainment in factual stories and colorful pictures about people and places, science, sports, adventure, and animals. . . . The full-color pictures on glossy-coated paper are in keeping with the well-known parent publication; however, page size is larger here, 8¼ by 10¾ inches. . . . The subject matter of this splendid and enlightening pictorial magazine is in keeping with the many interests of children. . . . Puzzles and things to make add to the fun of an issue. Occasionally, 'super-size pullout pages' that can be opened and posted appear as a supplement. . . . The aim to bring a *world* of interesting information to children is well met." Richardson. Mag for Child. 2d edition

912 Atlases. Maps

Goode's world atlas. Rand McNally il maps $24.95 **912**

1. Atlases

All editions, from the first in 1922 to 1949, published with title: Goode's school atlas. Through the eighth edition compiled by John Paul Goode, thereafter edited by

Goode's world atlas—*Continued*
Edward B. Espenshade, Jr. Periodically revised

"Physical, political and economic atlas arranged by continent and region. Includes metropolitan area maps and much statistical data. Number of thematic maps has been increased. Standard atlas for elementary school children." N Y Public Libr. Ref Books for Child Collect

"An excellent student atlas, a first choice for k-12." Wynar. Guide to Ref Books for Sch Media Cent. 3d edition

Hammond ambassador world atlas. Hammond il maps $49.95 **912**

1. Atlases

First published 1954. Frequently revised

"Comprehensive with clear usable format. Supplemental material includes gazetteer-index, zip codes, geographical terms, etc. 40% devoted to U.S. and the states." N Y Public Libr. Ref Books for Child Collect

Hammond citation world atlas. Hammond il maps $29.95 **912**

1. Atlases

First published 1966. Periodically revised

Each section concerning a state or country has an index that lists the cities in that area, the population, the map coordinates, and for the United States ZIP code numbers are given. Topographic maps which indicate valleys and mountains of each section are given along with resource area maps indicating dominant land use, minerals and manufacturing assets of the area. Inset maps of major cities are included plus the national flags for foreign countries

Lambert, David, 1932-
Maps and globes. Bookwright Press 1987 c1986 32p il maps (Topics) lib bdg $8.99 (3-5) **912**

1. Maps 2. Globes

ISBN 0-531-18112-X LC 86-70974

First published 1986 in England

This volume "explains how these helpful tools are made, what they are used for, and how to work with them, touching on the latest way of drawing maps—with a computer." Booklist

Includes glossary and bibliography

National Geographic atlas of the world. 6th ed. National Geographic Soc. 1990 136p il maps $82.95; flexible bdg $66.95 **912**

1. Atlases

ISBN 0-87044-399-2; 0-87044-398-4 (flexible bdg) LC 90-675129

First published 1963

This atlas features "satellite images of all the continents, in addition to detailed regional reference maps. A new foldout world map . . . uses the Robinson projection. . . . [Also included are] full-color political maps, urban and regional maps, and ocean floor maps, as well as illustrations, charts, tables, and a 150,000 place-name index." Publisher's note

National Geographic picture atlas of our world. National Geographic Soc. 1990 256p il maps $29.95 **912**

1. Atlases

ISBN 0-87044-812-2

First published 1979

This atlas focuses on over 170 countries, plus the oceans and the polar regions. More than 120 maps place each country in its continental setting, and text and pictures provide information on its people, history, language, economy, etc.

Includes glossary

Rand McNally children's atlas of the United States. Rand McNally 1989 109p il maps $12.95 (4-6) **912**

1. United States—Maps 2. Atlases

ISBN 0-528-83362-6

"States, alphabetically arranged, each get a double-page spread. A state map, with relief and political features . . . takes up about half of the right-hand page. A small U.S. map highlights the featured state in color. On the left side are several paragraphs of text, some dealing with history. There is a box with basic data (population, size, etc.) and another with state emblems. Each state is illustrated by one drawing (rather garish) and a photograph. The maps are indexed." Booklist

Rand McNally children's world atlas. Rand McNally 1989 93p il maps $12.95 (4-6) **912**

1. Atlases

ISBN 0-528-83348-0

"The arrangement of material is conventional, with a series of world maps followed by sets for each of the seven continents. There is a helpful section on using the atlas and an index to most places shown on the maps. As might be expected from Rand McNally, map quality is good and information up-to-date. Color is used extensively, and the quality of printing is quite satisfactory. A unique feature designed for the younger audience is a series of double-page artwork maps showing economic activities and characteristic animal species for each of the continents." Am Ref Books Annu, 1990

For a fuller review see: Booklist, Dec. 15, 1989

Rand McNally cosmopolitan world atlas. Rand McNally il maps $55 **912**

1. Atlases

First published 1949. Periodically revised

This atlas includes 1980 census information for U.S. cities and towns, a special section entitled "Human patterns and imprints," as well as state, regional, metropolitan, international and global maps

917.3 Geography of and travel in the United States

Adventures in your national parks. National Geographic Soc. 1988 95p il $8.50 (4 and up) **917.3**

1. National parks and reserves 2. Outdoor recreation LC 88-31473

"Books for world explorers"

Adventures in your national parks — *Continued*

Editor: Donald J. Crump

Provides an introduction to the national parks of the United States and Canada through the adventures of various young people as they explore Yellowstone, Yosemite, the Everglades, Cape Cod, Pacific Rim, Crater Lake, and Grand Canyon

Includes bibliography

Young, Donald

The Sierra Club book of our national parks; [by] Donald Young with Cynthia Overbeck Bix. Sierra Club Bks.; Little, Brown 1990 64p il map $14.95 (4 and up) **917.3**

1. National parks and reserves

ISBN 0-316-97744-6 LC 89-60740

"The work and writings of early preservationists such as John Muir, William Gladstone Steel, and Enos Mills are described, and Theodore Roosevelt's role in advancing the national park cause is cited as well. Later chapters describe what today's parks have to offer and look at the environmental problems some of them face today." Booklist

"This laudatory and noncritical overview of the history of U.S. National Parks is not so much a guide as an attractive essay on the development of the park system. . . . Excellent quality historical black-and-white and contemporary color photographs highlight the text and showcase the splendor of the parks." SLJ

920 BIOGRAPHY

Books of biography are arranged as follows: 1. Biographical collections (920) 2. Biographies of individuals alphabetically by name of biographee (92)

Aaseng, Nathan, 1956-

From rags to riches; people who started businesses from scratch. Lerner Publs. 1990 80p il lib bdg $11.95 (5 and up) **920**

1. Business people 2. Corporations

ISBN 0-8225-0679-3 LC 89-13059

Presents brief biographies of the enterprising individuals who started such products and companies as Apple computers, Sears, the Dow Jones Index and The Wall Street Journal, J.C. Penney, Hershey's chocolate, and Kinney shoes

Includes bibliography

The problem solvers. Lerner Publs. 1989 80p il lib bdg $11.95 (5 and up) **920**

1. Business people

ISBN 0-8225-0675-0 LC 88-695

"This brief book tells the stories of people who found ways to turn problems into useful products. The names of the companies and products they started are famous now and include Evinrude, Kitchen-Aid, Prudential Insurance, Polaroid, and Astro-Turf. Each story is briefly told in about seven pages with one full page or more of illustrations and pictures of the inventors and the products." Sci Books Films

Includes glossary and bibliography

The unsung heroes. Lerner Publs. 1989 80p il lib bdg $11.95 (5 and up) **920**

1. Business people

ISBN 0-8225-0676-9 LC 88-3022

Introduces little-known individuals responsible for advancing well-known business products, including the originators of Coca-Cola, Hoover vacuum cleaners, and Bingo

Includes bibliography

Altman, Susan R.

Extraordinary black Americans; from colonial to contemporary times; [by] Susan Altman. Childrens Press 1988 208p il lib bdg $30.90 (5 and up) **920**

1. Blacks—Biography

ISBN 0-516-00581-2 LC 88-11977

A "collection of 85 short biographies interspersed with explanations of key historical (particularly civil rights) events. The scope is wide ranging: Altman's subjects are men and women recognized for their achievements in exploration, invention, literature, theater, the military, education, politics, science, medicine, music, and sports. . . . A priority choice for black-studies collections." Booklist

Includes bibliography

Ashabranner, Brent K., 1921-

People who make a difference; [by] Brent Ashabranner; photographs by Paul Conklin. Cobblehill Bks. 1989 135p il $15.95 (5 and up) **920**

1. United States—Biography

ISBN 0-525-65009-1 LC 89-34593

"The fourteen people interviewed here demonstrate a wide variety of concerns, but all share an unwavering commitment to their chosen causes. . . . Mary Joan Willard trains capuchin monkeys to assist quadraplegics; Frank Trejo teaches karate to handicapped children; Beverly Thomas is the principal of an inner-city high school in Detroit that sends its graduates on to Ivy League colleges. Like these heroes, the rest of the subjects—some young people themselves—seem to have been chosen not only as worthy role models, but as people whose accomplishments will have a special meaning for young adults." Bull Cent Child Books

Includes bibliography

Beard, Charles Austin, 1874-1948

Charles A. Beard's The presidents in American history. Messner il lib bdg $12.98; pa $5.95 (5 and up) **920**

1. Presidents—United States

First published 1935 and periodically revised to include new Presidents and administrations

"A standard juvenile reference on the American presidency. . . . The narrative text profiles the life of each President and gives basic facts about his presidency such as names of the vice president and cabinet mem-

Beard, Charles Austin, 1874-1948 — *Continued*

bers; includes a black-and-white portrait of each President. Additional information consists of overviews of the elections and administrations of each President." Wynar. Guide to Ref Books for Sch Media Cent. 3d edition

Blassingame, Wyatt

The look-it-up book of presidents. Random House il $10.95; lib bdg $11.99; pa $5.95 (5 and up) **920**

1. Presidents—United States

First published 1968 and periodically revised to include new Presidents and administrations

"Each president is (allotted) several pages of readable text that cover his politics and policies and touch upon his personal life. The good-sized print and well-chosen illustrations (black-and-white photographs, lithographs, and cartoons) combine in an easy-to-peruse layout. This will be practical for students needing to use sources other than encyclopedias." Booklist

Breen, Karen, 1943-

Index to collective biographies for young readers. 4th ed. Bowker 1988 xxxiii, 494p $44.95 **920**

1. Biography—Indexes 2. Biography—Bibliography
ISBN 0-8352-2348-5 LC 88-19410

First edition edited by Judith Silverman published 1970 with title: An index to young readers' collective biographies

Alphabetical and subject access to 9,773 people found in 1,129 collective biographies

For a fuller review see: Booklist, March 1, 1989

Drimmer, Frederick

Born different; amazing stories of very special people. Atheneum Pubs. 1988 182p il $13.95 (6 and up) **920**

1. Physically handicapped—Biography
ISBN 0-689-31360-8 LC 87-33354

"A collective biography of seven people (six accounts, since one includes Chang and Eng, Siamese twins) whose anatomical anomalies made them prominent; among them are the midget known as Tom Thumb, Robert Wadlow (the tallest man who ever lived, according to medical records) and the tragic 'elephant man.'" Bull Cent Child Books

"Drimmer relates each well-documented story sympathetically, explains the causes of his subjects' various birth defects and shows that no matter what their deformity most led happy, dignified lives." Booklist

Includes bibliography

Freedman, Russell

Indian chiefs. Holiday House 1987 151p il map lib bdg $16.95 (6 and up) **920**

1. Indians of North America—Biography
ISBN 0-8234-0625-3 LC 86-46198

This "book chronicles the lives of six renowned Indian chiefs, each of whom served as a leader during a critical period in his tribe's history. . . . The text relates information about the lives of each chief and aspects of Indian/white relationships that illuminate his actions. . . . The illustrations and photographs and an especially clear map augment the text well and add to the overall appeal of the book." Horn Book

Goffstein, M. B.

Lives of the artists. Farrar, Straus & Giroux 1981 unp il $10.95 (5 and up) **920**

1. Artists
ISBN 0-374-34628-3 LC 81-68932

"Goffstein presents poetic reflections on the life and work of five artists: Rembrandt, Guardi, Van Gogh, Bonnard, Nevelson. Each is represented by two illustrations, one in color and one in black and white, accompanying a brief text. For readers who know the artist already, the author sets out a satisfying, fresh summary of their genius. Those encountering an artist for the first time will find narrative and pictures working together as a tantalizing introduction." SLJ

Greene, Carol

Presidents. Childrens Press il lib bdg $13.27; pa $4.95 (2-4) **920**

1. Presidents—United States

"A New true book"

First published 1984 and periodically revised to include new Presidents and administrations

This book "explains the job of the U.S. president, requirements for the position, and the oath of office. Of particular interest is a complete list of presidents with their pictures and a few sentences covering the highlights of each administration." Booklist

Includes glossary

Greenfield, Eloise, 1929-

Childtimes: a three-generation memoir; by Eloise Greenfield and Lessie Jones Little; with material by Pattie Ridley Jones; drawings by Jerry Pinkney and photographs from the authors' family albums. Crowell 1979 175p il lib bdg $12.89 (4 and up) **920**

1. Black women
ISBN 0-690-03875-5 LC 77-26581

Childhood memoirs of three black women—grandmother, mother, and daughter—who grew up between the 1880's and the 1950's

"A carefully considered and thoughtful book, moving deliberately, constructed with loving care. The authors respect their child-readers (or listeners) and honor them with candor and honesty, tragedy and tears, providing chuckles and smiles as well." Interracial Books Child Bull

Jacobs, William Jay

Great lives: human rights. Scribner 1990 278p il $22.95 (5 and up) **920**

1. Reformers 2. Civil rights 3. United States—Biography

ISBN 0-684-19036-2 LC 89-37211

This volume presents "biographical portraits of thirty defenders of human rights throughout American history, from Thomas Paine and Anne Hutchinson to Cesar Chavez and Martin Luther King, Jr." Horn Book Guide

"The biographies are well written and paced to keep the reader interested. They convey significant facts with clarity and include curious and exciting anecdotes." Voice Youth Advocates

Includes bibliography

Morey, Janet (Janet Nomura)

Famous Mexican Americans; [by] Janet Morey & Wendy Dunn; illustrated with photographs. Cobblehill Bks. 1989 176p il $14.95 (5 and up) **920**

1. Mexican Americans—Biography

ISBN 0-525-65012-1 LC 89-7218

This biography "gives sketches of the lives of fourteen contemporary Mexican Americans; the men and women who are discussed represent such diverse fields as the law, sports, entertainment, business, and public service at the local or federal level." Bull Cent Child Books

"While the intent of the book is to showcase the outstanding contributions of the selected Mexican Americans, the book also provides young readers with role models to be admired and emulated." SLJ

Includes bibliography

Provensen, Alice, 1918-

The buck stops here: the presidents of the United States. Harper & Row 1990 unp il $17.95; lib bdg $17.89 (3-6) **920**

1. Presidents—United States—Pictorial works

ISBN 0-06-024786-X; 0-06-024787-8 (lib bdg) LC 88-35036

"Provensen introduces the presidents through a series of colorful, period tableaux accompanied by pithy, rhymed couplets. Within the illustrations, symbols and words re-create events and characteristics of each presidency. While suggesting American primitive portraiture through static figures, flattened perspective, and the use of significant objects to enlarge upon the subject, Provensen puts her unique stamp on the full-color artwork." Booklist

Includes bibliography

Richards, Norman, 1932-

Dreamers & doers: inventors who changed our world. Atheneum Pubs. 1984 153p il $12.95 (6 and up) **920**

1. Inventors

ISBN 0-689-30914-7 LC 81-21029

Discusses the lives and achievements of four outstanding American inventors: Robert Goddard, Charles Goodyear, Thomas Edison, and George Eastman

"The writing is smooth and there are enough personal details to keep the subject quite human, even though the enormity of their contributions is also clear-cut. With well-chosen and -reproduced black-and-white photographs, this is a polished introduction to these men and their singular achievements." Booklist

Sills, Leslie

Inspirations; stories about women artists: Georgia O'Keeffe, Frida Kahlo, Alice Neel, Faith Ringgold. Whitman, A. 1989 49p il lib bdg $16.95 (5 and up) **920**

1. Women artists 2. Artists, American

ISBN 0-8075-3649-0 LC 88-80

"Here are stories about Georgia O'Keeffe, Frida Kahlo, Alice Neel and Faith Ringgold, four 20th-century women artists of great talent. There are photographs of the artists as children and adults, and well-chosen examples of their work reproduced in full color." N Y Times Book Rev

"Sensitively written, the book is also beautifully designed. . . . While the title refers to the artists' inspirations, this thoughtful volume will also inspire readers, especially girls, who may need the reinforcement most." Booklist

Includes bibliography

920.003 Biographical reference works

Authors of books for young people; by Martha E. Ward [et al.] 3rd ed. Scarecrow Press 1990 780p $59.50 **920.003**

1. Authors—Dictionaries 2. Children's literature—Bio-bibliography

ISBN 0-8108-2293-8 LC 90-32569

First published 1964

This compendium lists more than 3,700 authors, providing for each a brief biography and citations for the author's works

For a fuller review see: Booklist, May 1, 1991

Children's authors and illustrators: an index to biographical dictionaries. Gale Res. (Gale biographical index ser) $140 **920.003**

1. Authors—Dictionaries—Indexes 2. Illustrators—Dictionaries—Indexes

First published 1976

"Provides over 145,000 citations to biographical sketches of over 25,000 authors and illustrators found in 450 reference sources. Comprehensive; non-judgmental." N Y Public Libr. Ref Books for Child Collect

Fifth book of junior authors & illustrators; edited by Sally Holmes Holtze. Wilson, H.W. 1983 357p il (Authors ser) $40 **920.003**

1. Authors—Dictionaries 2. Illustrators—Dictionaries 3. Children's literature—Bio-bibliography

ISBN 0-8242-0694-0 LC 83-21828

Fifth book of junior authors & illustrators *—Continued*

Information on 243 outstanding creators of children's literature who achieved distinction between 1978 and 1983

Fourth book of junior authors and illustrators; edited by Doris de Montreville and Elizabeth D. Crawford. Wilson, H.W. 1978 370p il (Authors ser) $38 **920.003**

1. Authors—Dictionaries 2. Illustrators—Dictionaries 3. Children's literature—Bio-bibliography
ISBN 0-8242-0568-5 LC 78-115

Provides biographical or autobiographical sketches of some 250 authors and illustrators, most of whom have come into prominence since 1972

The **Junior** book of authors; edited by Stanley J. Kunitz and Howard Haycraft. 2nd ed rev. Wilson, H.W. 1951 309p (Authors ser) $32 **920.003**

1. Authors—Dictionaries 2. Illustrators—Dictionaries 3. Children's literature—Bio-bibliography
ISBN 0-8242-0028-4

First published 1934. Continued by the following volumes in this series: More junior authors; Third book of junior authors; Fourth book of junior authors and illustrators; Fifth book of junior authors and illustrators; and Sixth book of junior authors and illustrators, each entered separately in this catalog

This foundation volume in the series presents biographical and autobiographical sketches of 289 authors and illustrators of books for children and young people

More junior authors; edited by Muriel Fuller. Wilson, H.W. 1963 235p il (Authors ser) $28 **920.003**

1. Authors—Dictionaries 2. Illustrators—Dictionaries 3. Children's literature—Bio-bibliography
ISBN 0-8242-0036-5 LC 63-11816

Offers biographical and autobiographical sketches of 268 noted children's authors and illustrators

Rollock, Barbara T., 1924-

Black authors and illustrators of children's books; a biographical dictionary; by Barbara Rollock. Garland 1988 130p il (Garland reference lib. of the humanities) lib bdg $25 **920.003**

1. Children's literature—Bio-bibliography 2. Black authors—Bio-bibliography 3. Illustrators
ISBN 0-8240-8580-9 LC 87-25748

This is a collection of "biographical sketches of black authors and illustrators whose books have been published in the United States. . . .The sketches are arranged in alphabetical order by the person's name and include a list of the artist's work." Horn Book

For a fuller review see: Booklist, April 1, 1989

Sixth book of junior authors & illustrators; edited by Sally Holmes Holtze. Wilson, H.W. 1989 345p il $40 **920.003**

1. Authors—Dictionaries 2. Illustrators—Dictionaries 3. Children's literature—Bio-bibliography
ISBN 0-8242-0777-7 LC 89-14815

"Lists autobiographical or biographical entries for 236 authors and illustrators of notable children's books. The index is cumulative, and entries are alphabetically arranged by subject's last name; most include a photograph, date of birth, autograph, selected works and additional sources of biographical information." SLJ

"This series belongs on every school and public library shelf as a valuable reference tool." Booklist

Something about the author; facts and pictures about authors and illustrators of books for young people; edited by Anne Commire. Gale Res. il ea $74 **920.003**

1. Authors—Dictionaries 2. Illustrators—Dictionaries 3. Children's literature—Bio-bibliography
ISSN 0276-816X LC 72-27107

First published 1971. Frequency varies

"Each entry includes personal and career information, photographs, bibliography and biographical sources. Starting with V. 15, it includes authors of all periods although focus remains on those currently active. . . . Attractive, profusely illustrated, useful as supplementary reference." N Y Public Libr. Ref Books for Child Collect

Something about the author: autobiography series. Gale Res. il ea $74 **920.003**

1. Authors—Dictionaries 2. Illustrators—Dictionaries 3. Children's literature—Bio-bibliography
ISSN 0885-6842

First published 1986

Editors vary

This series is intended to "complement the publisher's Something about the Author. . . . Each volume in this new series will contain essays by 20 established authors and illustrators of books for young people. The purpose of the set is to allow authors who may never write a full-length autobiography to introduce themselves to their readers. They discuss their lives, careers, and specific published works; some include advice for would-be authors." Booklist

Third book of junior authors; edited by Doris de Montreville and Donna Hill. Wilson, H.W. 1972 320p il (Authors ser) $32 **920.003**

1. Authors—Dictionaries 2. Illustrators—Dictionaries 3. Children's literature—Bio-bibliography
ISBN 0-8242-0408-5 LC 75-149381

Contains 255 autobiographical or biographical profiles of outstanding authors and illustrators who achieved distinction after 1963

Twentieth-century children's writers; with a preface by Naomi Lewis; editor, Tracy Chevalier; consulting editor, D.L. Kirkpatrick. 3rd ed. St. James Press 1989 xxi, 1288p (Twentieth-century writers of the English language) $95 **920.003**

1. Authors—Dictionaries 2. Children's literature—Bio-bibliography 3. Children's literature—History and criticism

ISBN 0-912289-95-3 LC 90-171621

First published 1978 by St. Martin's Press

Includes approximately "840 entries on twentieth-century English-language authors. . . . Their entries summarize key biographical facts in Who's Who fashion; lists works for children as well as other works; sometimes include a brief comment by the author on herself or himself; and conclude with a signed critical essay. These essays zero in on the works themselves and assess each author's contribution to children's literature." Wilson Libr Bull

For a fuller review see: Booklist, May 1, 1990

Webster's new biographical dictionary. Merriam-Webster $21.95 **920.003**

1. Biography—Dictionaries

Replaces: Webster's biographical dictionary, first published 1943

"Brief, condensed biographical sketches of more than 40,000 persons from all nations and all periods with emphasis on Americans and the British; lists of popes, American government officials and heads of foreign states; frequently slightly revised." N Y Public Libr. Ref Books for Child Collect

92 Individual biography

Lives of individuals are arranged alphabetically under the name of the person written about. A number of subject headings have been added to the entries in this section to aid in curriculum work. It is not necessarily recommended that these subjects be used in the library catalog.

Adams, John Quincy, 1767-1848

Kent, Zachary. John Quincy Adams, sixth president of the United States. Childrens Press 1987 98p il (Encyclopedia of presidents) lib bdg $15.93; pa $6.95 (4 and up) **92**

1. Presidents—United States

ISBN 0-516-01386-6 (lib bdg); 0-516-41386-4 (pa) LC 86-31022

A biography of the president who continued the family dedication to public service begun by his father, John Adams

"Frequent illustrations include reproductions of historical art, photos, letters, newspapers, and documents, all of which add interest and authenticity to the text. The writing style is easy to read, marked by short declarative sentences. [The] volume includes a fairly comprehensive index, plus a useful 'Chronology of American History,' a list of important events from 982 A.D. to the present." SLJ

Adams, Samuel, 1722-1803

Fritz, Jean. Why don't you get a horse, Sam Adams? illustrated by Trina Schart Hyman. Coward, McCann & Geoghegan 1974 47p il $9.95; pa $5.95 (3-5) **92**

1. United States—History—1775-1783, Revolution—Biography

ISBN 0-698-20292-9; 0-698-20545-6 (pa) LC 73-88023

A brief biography of Samuel Adams describing his activities in stirring up the revolt against the British and how he was finally persuaded to learn to ride a horse

"A piece of history far more entertaining and readable than most fiction. . . . The author has humanized a figure of the Revolution: Adams emerges a marvelously funny and believable man. The illustrations play upon his foibles; they are, in fact, even more outrageously mocking than the text. A tour de force, for both author and illustrator." Horn Book

Appleseed, Johnny, 1774-1845

Aliki. The story of Johnny Appleseed; written and illustrated by Aliki. Prentice-Hall 1963 unp il lib bdg $11.95 (k-3) **92**

1. Frontier and pioneer life

ISBN 0-13-850800-3 LC 63-8507

This is a picture-story of "Johnny Appleseed, the New Englander who wandered through the Middle West in the early days distributing seeds of apple trees for planting, and remaining to share his love for wild creatures, pioneer folk, and nature." Christ Sci Monit

Kellogg, Steven. Johnny Appleseed; a tall tale retold and illustrated by Steven Kellogg. Morrow Junior Bks. 1988 unp il $14.95; lib bdg $14.88 (2-4) **92**

1. Frontier and pioneer life

ISBN 0-688-06417-5; 0-688-06418-3 (lib bdg) LC 87-27317

"Oversize pages have given Kellogg a fine opportunity for pictures that are on a large scale, colorful and animated if often busy with details. His version of Chapman's life is more substantial than the subtitle (*A Tall Tale*) would indicate, since the text makes clear the difference between what Chapman really did and what myths grew up about his work, his life, his personality, and his achievements. There's some exaggeration, but on the whole the biography is factual and written with clarity." Bull Cent Child Books

Armstrong, Louis, 1900-1971

Collier, James Lincoln. Louis Armstrong: an American success story. Macmillan 1985 165p il $12.95 (5 and up) **92**

1. Jazz musicians

ISBN 0-02-722830-4 LC 84-42982

"Evokes Armstrong's life as a poverty-stricken boy from a broken home in New Orleans, a poor, struggling black musician in the South, and one of the outstanding jazz musicians of all time. An intriguing, absorbing portrait that reveals musical genius that could not be denied in an artist who never had a music lesson. Information about recordings is combined with a short annotated bibliography." Soc Educ

Arthur, Chester Alan, 1830-1886

Simon, Charnan. Chester A. Arthur: twenty-first president of the United States. Childrens Press 1989 98p il (Encyclopedia of presidents) lib bdg $15.93 (4 and up) **92**

1. Presidents—United States
ISBN 0-516-01369-6 LC 89-35386

This book traces the early life, influences, and career of the president "in a straightforward manner with black-and-white photographs or drawings on nearly every page. . . . Includes a chronology of American history." Booklist

Banneker, Benjamin, 1731-1806

Ferris, Jeri. What are you figuring now? a story about Benjamin Banneker; illustrations by Amy Johnson. Carolrhoda Bks. 1988 64p il (Carolrhoda creative minds bk) lib bdg $9.95 (3-5) **92**

1. Astronomers 2. Blacks—Biography
ISBN 0-87614-331-1 LC 88-7267

A biography of the Afro-American farmer and self-taught mathematician, astronomer, and surveyor for the new capital city of the United States in 1791, who also calculated a successful almanac notable for its preciseness

"Ferris' judicious use of dialogue and Johnson's full-page gray washes enhance this smooth, engaging biographical story; the mature style and succinct text make this a good choice for reluctant readers." Booklist

Beaumont, William, 1785-1853

Epstein, Sam. Dr. Beaumont and the man with the hole in his stomach; by Sam and Beryl Epstein; illustrated by Joseph Scrofani. Coward, McCann & Geoghegan 1978 57p il map (Science discovery bk) lib bdg $6.99 (4-6) **92**

1. St. Martin, Alexis 2. Physicians 3. Digestion
ISBN 0-698-30680-5 LC 77-8236

A biography of a curious physician and Alexis St. Martin, the unusual patient who enabled him to carry out experiments concerning digestion

"The personalities of the two men are especially well delineated, both in the text and in Scrofani's rugged black-and-white line drawings." SLJ

Includes bibliography

Bethune, Mary Jane McLeod, 1875-1955

Greenfield, Eloise. Mary McLeod Bethune; illustrated by Jerry Pinkney. Crowell 1977 32p il (Crowell biography) lib bdg $14.89 (2-5) **92**

1. Black educators 2. Black women
ISBN 0-690-01129-6 LC 76-11522

"Details the life of Mary McLeod Bethune from her childhood in South Carolina to the founding of her school and her active role in the National Youth Administration under Franklin D. Roosevelt." Horn Book

"Written with a simple, natural flow, this biography for younger readers does not have all the fascinating details of the life of the great educator, but it gives salient facts and is nicely balanced in treatment." Bull Cent Child Books

McKissack, Patricia C. Mary McLeod Bethune: a great American educator. Childrens Press 1985 111p il (People of distinction biographies) lib bdg $17.27 (4 and up) **92**

1. Black educators 2. Black women
ISBN 0-516-03218-6 LC 85-12843

Recounts the life of the black educator, from her childhood in the cotton fields of South Carolina to her success as teacher, crusader, and presidential adviser

This "is a warm story that gives a good view of a slave's life both before and after slaves were freed. Bethune's talents are well described, but her humanness shows through. . . . Photographs and letters . . . are excellent, and time lines are helpful, covering not only the subject's life but also major world events of that time. Indexes are thorough." SLJ

Black, Shirley Temple, 1928-

Haskins, James. Shirley Temple Black; actress to ambassador; illustrated by Donna Ruff. Viking Kestrel 1988 57p il (Women of our time) $10.95; Penguin Bks. pa $3.95 (4 and up) **92**

1. Actors and actresses 2. Diplomats
ISBN 0-670-81957-3; 0-14-032491-7 (pa) LC 87-34076

A biography of the child actress who was known as "America's Sweetheart" and who, as an adult, became active in politics and served as Ambassador to Ghana and as the first woman Chief of Protocol at the White House

The author "introduces such important issues as the treatment of blacks in the movies and describes how, in Palm Springs, Bill Robinson, little Shirley's co-star in several films, had to live with his chauffeur in servant's quarters while they rehearsed. An accessible biography." Booklist

Blackwell, Elizabeth, 1821-1910

Wilson, Dorothy Clarke. I will be a doctor! the story of America's first woman physician. Abingdon Press 1983 160p pa $7.95 (5 and up) **92**

1. Women physicians
ISBN 0-687-19727-9 LC 83-3862

"This compact, mildly fictionalized biography devotes considerable space to Blackwell's childhood in England and America and to the progressive ideas of her sugar-merchant father that would influence her so profoundly. Her famous progress through the Geneva Medical School, her training in Europe and tragic loss of one eye, and her prominence in America as a physician, educator, and social worker are ably recounted." Booklist

Blegvad, Erik

Blegvad, Erik. Self-portrait: Erik Blegvad; written and illustrated by Erik Blegvad, with pictures also by Harald Blegvad [et al.] Harper & Row 1985 c1979 27p il lib bdg $12.70 (4 and up) **92**

1. Illustrators
ISBN 0-201-00498-4 LC 84-43134

A reissue of the title first published 1979 by Addison-Wesley

The illustrator discourses on himself, his life, and his work

To both his "art and the concise narration that accompanies it Mr. Blegvad brings quiet humor, a gifted hand and a generous spirit." N Y Times Book Rev

Blériot, Louis, 1872-1936

Provensen, Alice. The glorious flight: across the Channel with Louis Blériot, July 25, 1909; [by] Alice and Martin Provensen. Viking 1983 39p il lib bdg $13.95 (1-4) **92**

1. Air pilots 2. Airplanes—Design and construction
ISBN 0-670-34259-9 LC 82-7034

Awarded the Caldecott Medal, 1984

This book "recounts the persistence of a Frenchman, Louis Blériot, to build a flying machine to cross the English Channel. For eight years (1901-1909) he tries and tries again to create a kind of contraption light enough to lift him off the ground and yet strong enough to keep from falling apart." SLJ

"A pleasing text recounts Bleriot's adventures with gentle humor and admiration for his earnest, if accident-prone, determination. Best of all, the pictures shine with the illustrator's delight in the wondrous flying machines themselves. Each strut, fin, and wing is lovingly depicted; but the book also tells the story of Bleriot's loyal family; careful readers will observe the five children growing up as they share the ups and downs of Papa's glorious career." Horn Book

Borglum, Gutzon, 1867-1941

St. George, Judith. The Mount Rushmore story. Putnam 1985 128p il map $13.95 (6 and up) **92**

1. Mount Rushmore National Memorial (S.D.) 2. Sculptors, American
ISBN 0-399-21117-9 LC 84-24963

The author "weaves together the history of the region—nearly the geographic center of the United States and the heart of Sioux territory—with the biography of Gutzon Borglum, the sculptor. She candidly treats Borglum's difficult personality, the project's financial problems, the controversies surrounding the conservation philosophy, and the artistic criticism leveled at Borglum." Horn Book

"The smooth narrative and solid research give the book substance—the many fascinating black-and-white photographs of the work in progress are the icing on the cake. Map, glossary, and an extensive bibliography are appended." Booklist

Bridgman, Laura Dewey, 1829-1889

Hunter, Edith Fisher. Child of the silent night; illustrated by Bea Holmes. Houghton Mifflin 1963 124p il $14.95; Dell pa $2.50 (3-5) **92**

1. Blind 2. Deaf
ISBN 0-395-06835-5; 0-440-41223-4 (pa) LC 63-14523

"Biographies of persons who have overcome physical handicaps can often reassure and inspire. This is the story of Laura Bridgman, a blind-deaf child whose successful attempts at communication paved the way for Helen Keller." Cincinnati Public Libr

Buck, Pearl S. (Pearl Sydenstricker), 1892-1973

Mitchell, Barbara. Between two worlds: a story about Pearl Buck; illustrations by Karen Ritz. Carolrhoda Bks. 1988 64p il (Carolrhoda creative minds bk) lib bdg $9.95 (3-5) **92**

1. Authors, American 2. Women authors
ISBN 0-87614-332-X LC 88-6095

"Pearl Buck, author of more than 65 books, was awarded both the Pulitzer and Nobel prizes for her literature. Raised in China by her American missionary parents, her goal was to promote understanding between East and West. This book tells the story of a woman who brought together two different worlds." Publisher's note

Includes bibliography

Bulla, Clyde Robert, 1914-

Bulla, Clyde Robert. A grain of wheat: a writer begins. Godine 1985 49p il $10.95; pa $6.95 (3-5) **92**

1. Authors, American 2. Farm life—Missouri
ISBN 0-87923-568-3; 0-87923-717-1 (pa) LC 84-48750

The author describes "the first ten years of his life on a farm in Missouri. Childhood pranks, accidents, the first day of school (his sister was the teacher) and the death of a pet are some of the memories the author shares, as well as his early decision to be a writer. The book concludes with ten-year-old Clyde winning a dollar in a writing contest." SLJ

"Children familiar with Bulla's books . . . will be pleased, and those coming across this while looking for biographies will be equally intrigued, but the book's greatest use probably will be by librarians seeking ways to introduce the writing of a noteworthy author. A few photographs of Bulla as a child are included." Booklist

Burns, Anthony, 1834-1862

Hamilton, Virginia. Anthony Burns: the defeat and triumph of a fugitive slave. Knopf 1988 193p $11.95; lib bdg $12.99 (5 and up) **92**

1. Slavery—United States 2. Blacks—Biography
ISBN 0-394-88185-0; 0-394-98185-5 (lib bdg) LC 87-38063

Burns, Anthony, 1834-1862—*Continued*

A biography of the slave who escaped to Boston in 1854, was arrested at the instigation of his owner, and whose trial caused a furor between abolitionists and those determined to enforce the Fugitive Slave Act

"This book does exactly what good biography for children ought to do: takes readers directly into the life of the subject and makes them feel what it is like to be that person in those times." Horn Book

Includes bibliography

Bush, George, 1924-

Kent, Zachary. George Bush: forty-first president of the United States. Childrens Press 1989 98p il (Encyclopedia of presidents) lib bdg $15.93; pa $6.95 (4 and up) **92**

1. Presidents—United States
ISBN 0-516-01374-2 (lib bdg); 0-516-41374-0 (pa)
LC 89-33744

A biography emphasizing the political career of the forty-first president

Sullivan, George. George Bush. Messner 1989 169p il lib bdg $11.98; pa $5.95 (5 and up) **92**

1. Presidents—United States
ISBN 0-671-64599-4 (lib bdg); 0-671-67814-0 (pa)
LC 89-8349

"This is standard biographical fare, with the accent on Bush's early life, his experiences during World War II, and his varied careers in public service; the book ends with his election win over Michael Dukakis. Black-and-white photographs pepper the text, though they are not especially exciting. A useful, though uninspired text." Booklist

Includes bibliography

Carson, Rachel, 1907-1964

Harlan, Judith. Sounding the alarm: a biography of Rachel Carson. Dillon Press 1989 128p il (People in focus bk) lib bdg $12.95 (5 and up) **92**

1. Women scientists
ISBN 0-87518-407-3 LC 88-35909

"In this account of the founder of the modern ecology movement, Harlan captures Carson's integrity, vitality, and ability to cherish the most-minute aspects of the natural world. Although the biographer covers Carson's closeknit family, schooling, and dual career (writing and biology), what really emerges is the passionate force of Carson's efforts to try and effect change. It was, for example, the threat of the pesticide DDT and toxic waste pollution that drove her into the all-consuming, personal crusade that resulted in the 1962 publication of *Silent Spring*. [A] well-focused portrait, with an impressive bibliography appended." Booklist

Kudlinski, Kathleen V. Rachel Carson: pioneer of ecology; illustrated by Ted Lewin. Viking Kestrel 1988 55p il (Women of our time) lib bdg $10.95; Puffin Bks. pa $3.95 (4 and up) **92**

1. Women scientists
ISBN 0-670-81488-1 (lib bdg); 0-14-032242-6 (pa)
LC 87-40671

A biography of the scientist and writer whose book Silent spring warned of the dangers of pesticides and launched a popular movement to control their use

"The tone is appreciative rather than reverential, the balance between Carson's personal and professional lives is nicely maintained, and the writing is clear, direct, and informative." Bull Cent Child Books

Carter, Jimmy, 1924-

Wade, Linda R. James Carter: thirty-ninth president of the United States. Childrens Press 1989 100p il (Encyclopedia of presidents) lib bdg $15.93 (4 and up) **92**

1. Presidents—United States
ISBN 0-516-01372-6 LC 89-33754

Describes the life and achievements of the relatively unknown governor from Georgia who became president of the United States in 1977

Carver, George Washington, 1864?-1943

Aliki. A weed is a flower: the life of George Washington Carver; written and illustrated by Aliki. Simon & Schuster Bks. for Young Readers 1988 32p il lib bdg $12.95; pa $5.95 (k-3) **92**

1. Scientists 2. Blacks—Biography
ISBN 0-671-66118-3 (lib bdg); 0-671-66490-5 (pa)
LC 87-22864

First published 1965 by Prentice-Hall

Text and pictures present the life of the man, born a slave, who became a scientist and devoted his entire life to helping the South improve its agriculture

Mitchell, Barbara. A pocketful of goobers: a story about George Washington Carver; illustrations by Peter E. Hanson. Carolrhoda Bks. 1986 64p il (Carolrhoda creative minds bk) lib bdg $9.95; pa $4.95 (3-5) **92**

1. Scientists 2. Blacks—Biography
ISBN 0-87614-292-7 (lib bdg); 0-87614-474-1 (pa)
LC 86-2690

Relates the scientific efforts of George Washington Carver, especially his production of more than 300 uses for the peanut

"This book tells his remarkable story accurately, sympathetically, and felicitously." Sci Books Films

Chaka, Zulu Chief, 1787?-1828

Stanley, Diane. Shaka, king of the Zulus; [by] Diane Stanley and Peter Vennema; illustrated by Diane Stanley. Morrow Junior Bks. 1988 unp il $13.95; lib bdg $13.88 (2-4) **92**

1. Zulus
ISBN 0-688-07342-5; 0-688-07343-3 (lib bdg)
LC 87-27376

A biography of the nineteenth-century military genius and Zulu chief

"Diane Stanley and Peter Vennema have culled the massive amount of historical material that exists about this strange and fascinating figure. Their text is lucid; the incidents are tactfully within the scope and decorum of a children's book but representative and true to the facts. . . . The rhythm of the illustrations . . . makes each page not only a realistic representation but also an artistic composition." N Y Times Book Rev

Includes bibliography

Chaplin, Charlie, 1889-1977

Kamen, Gloria. Charlie Chaplin. Atheneum Pubs. 1982 70p il $12.95 (4 and up) **92**

1. Actors and actresses 2. Comedians
ISBN 0-689-30925-2 LC 82-1674

"The dramatic story of the life of the legendary silent film clown from his youth on the streets of London until his death on Christmas, 1977, is recounted here. His rise in music halls and eventually cinema, his trouble with marriage and politics and the press which pursued him are all described. The emphasis is on his work." SLJ

"The writing is simple and even; the author's black-and-white illustrations are very apt and well thought out, but since Chaplin is an important film figure, one wishes for photographs instead. Nonetheless, this works very well as a crisp elementary introduction." Booklist

Includes bibliography and filmography

Columba, Saint, 521-597

Fritz, Jean. The man who loved books; illuminated by Trina Schart Hyman. Putnam 1981 unp il $9.95 (3-5) **92**

1. Christian saints
ISBN 0-399-20715-5 LC 80-12614

A biography of the Irish saint who was known for his love of books and his missionary work throughout Scotland

"The telling is direct and spirited, lilting and sensitively balanced. . . . The episodes in [Columba's] adventurous life are humorously reflected in full-page and half-page drawings washed with shades of brown." Horn Book

Columbus, Christopher

D'Aulaire, Ingri. Columbus; [by] Ingri & Edgar Parin D'Aulaire. Doubleday 1955 56p il o.p. paperback available $8.95 (1-4) **92**

1. Explorers 2. America—Exploration
ISBN 0-385-24106-2 (pa) LC 55-9011

"This is an account of Columbus' four voyages to the New World. . . . The authors have a lively enthusiasm for their subject, and have imbued this biography with the excitement of exploring the unknown, and they have successfully brought to life the restless ambitious spirit, which sent Columbus out into the 'trackless waste of the sea.' The illustrations are striking full-page lithographs, some in colour and some in black and white, and imaginative marginal drawings." Ont Libr Rev

Fritz, Jean. Where do you think you're going, Christopher Columbus? pictures by Margot Tomes. Putnam 1980 80p il maps $13.95; pa $7.95 (3-5) **92**

1. Explorers 2. America—Exploration
ISBN 0-399-20723-6; 0-399-20734-1 (pa)
LC 80-11377

"Reducing a life as well-documented as Columbus's to 80 pages must result in some simplifications of fact or context, but in this case they are not readily apparent. Mrs. Fritz's breezy narrative gives us a highly individual Columbus. . . . Margot Tomes's three-color illustrations are attractive, amusing and informative." N Y Times Book Rev

Levinson, Nancy Smiler. Christopher Columbus: voyager to the unknown. Lodestar Bks. 1990 118p il maps $16.95 (4 and up) **92**

1. Explorers 2. America—Exploration
ISBN 0-525-67292-3 LC 89-32254

This "biography begins with Columbus's early life, his interest in the sea route to the East Indies, and his fight to get his trip funded. The historic 1492 voyage is discussed in detail, but the book covers his later voyages, his loss of respect and wealth and his death as a forgotten man." Child Book Rev Serv

"Historical imprints, maps, and occasional excerpts from Columbus' log and letters provide a sense of immediacy." Bull Cent Child Books

Includes bibliography

Cosby, Bill, 1937-

Haskins, James. Bill Cosby: America's most famous father; by Jim Haskins. Walker & Co. 1988 138p il $13.95; lib bdg $14.85 (5 and up) **92**

1. Black entertainers
ISBN 0-8027-6785-0; 0-8027-6786-9 (lib bdg)
LC 87-33951

"Unlike most juvenile biographies of celebrities, this one deals extensively with the problems Bill Cosby faced, both as a youngster growing up in an impoverished family and as a comedian who refused to use race as a source for his material. Prolific writer Jim Haskins has written a biography that gives its readers something to think about as they learn about one of their favorites." Child Book Rev Serv

Includes bibliography

Crockett, Davy, 1786-1836

Quackenbush, Robert M. Quit pulling my leg! a story of Davy Crockett; [by] Robert Quackenbush. Prentice-Hall Bks. for Young Readers 1987 36p il $11.95; pa $3.95 (2-4) **92**

1. Frontier and pioneer life
ISBN 0-671-66516-2; 0-671-69441-3 (pa) LC 86-21795

A brief illustrated biography of the renowned American frontiersman

The author "captures the essence of his subject through a straightforward writing style with little fictionalization. . . . Two-tone pen-and-ink drawings are appropriate to the subject and text." SLJ

Darwin, Charles, 1809-1882

Hyndley, Kate. The voyage of the Beagle; illustrated by Peter Bull. Bookwright Press 1989 32p il map (Great journeys) lib bdg $11.90 (4 and up) **92**

1. Beagle Expedition (1831-1836) 2. Scientists
ISBN 0-531-18272-X LC 88-28695

An account of the five years that English naturalist Charles Darwin spent traveling around the world on the HMS Beagle, a voyage that led him to develop his theory of the evolution of the species

"The text is clear and concise and the drawings depicting Darwin in the various countries are interspersed with color photographs of the same places today, which helps familiarize the reader with these areas of the world. This is an informative text." Appraisal

Includes glossary and bibliography

De Mille, Agnes

Gherman, Beverly. Agnes de Mille: dancing off the earth. Atheneum Pubs. 1990 138p il $13.95 (5 and up) **92**

1. Dancers
ISBN 0-689-31441-8 LC 89-6888

The life and accomplishments of the choreographer, dancer and author best known for the ballets she created on American themes and for the choreography of the musical "Oklahoma"

"In a judicious blend of well-researched text and pithy, candidly revealing quotes from de Mille, the author infuses splendid vitality into her biography of one of America's greatest choreographers." Booklist

Includes bibliography

Douglass, Frederick, 1817?-1895

McKissack, Patricia C. Frederick Douglass: the black lion; by Patricia and Fredrick McKissack. Childrens Press 1987 136p il (People of distinction biographies) lib bdg $17.27 (4 and up) **92**

1. Abolitionists 2. Blacks—Biography
ISBN 0-516-03221-6 LC 86-32695

"The McKissacks supply a sympathetic yet balanced portrait of the Black Lion, as Douglass was called, as they chart the man's life from his birth as a slave through his death as an accomplished writer, orator, and leader in the antislavery movement. . . . Although the authors are careful to identify their material and quotations in the body of their text, they have not included any source notes or bibliography. Scattered black-and-white line drawings are included and a chronology is appended." Booklist

Miller, Douglas T. Frederick Douglass and the fight for freedom. Facts on File 1988 152p il (Makers of America) lib bdg $16.95 (6 and up) **92**

1. Abolitionists 2. Blacks—Biography
ISBN 0-8160-1617-8 LC 87-28806

Traces the life of the black abolitionist, from his early years in slavery to his later success as a persuasive editor, orator, and writer

"This biography is clearly organized and provides a fast-paced narrative which, in addition to being an excellent study of Douglass, presents the issues of south vs. north, slave owners vs. abolitionists, whites vs. blacks. . . . Miller's readable and reliable life of Frederick Douglass is a fine example of biographical writing." SLJ

Includes bibliography

Dunbar, Paul Laurence, 1872-1906

McKissack, Patricia C. Paul Laurence Dunbar, a poet to remember. Childrens Press 1984 127p il (People of distinction biographies) lib bdg $17.27 (4 and up) **92**

1. Poets, American 2. Black authors
ISBN 0-516-03209-7 LC 84-7625

A biography of the turn-of-the-century black poet and novelist whose works were among the first to give an honest presentation of black life

The author "makes a good case for the enduring value of Dunbar's dialect poetry, illustrating with excerpts and her own commentary the sensitivity and appreciation which Dunbar expressed for the language and the people who spoke it." SLJ

Dunham, Katherine

Haskins, James. Katherine Dunham. Coward, McCann & Geoghegan 1982 158p il $10.95 (5 and up) **92**

1. Black dancers 2. Black women
ISBN 0-698-20549-9 LC 81-15178

"Katherine Dunham is world-famous as a performer, teacher, and choreographer. In this well-balanced biography, there is a good mixture of material about her professional experiences, her personal life, her role as a champion of black culture, and her devotion to the Performing Arts Training Center that she established in East St. Louis in the 1960's." Bull Cent Child Books

Earhart, Amelia, 1898-1937

Lauber, Patricia. Lost star: the story of Amelia Earhart. Scholastic 1988 106p il maps $10.95; pa $2.75 (5 and up) **92**

1. Women air pilots
ISBN 0-590-41615-4; 0-590-41159-4 (pa) LC 88-3043

Earhart, Amelia, 1898-1937—*Continued*

"Earhart's early life is covered succinctly, including the family problems that resulted from her father's alcoholism. Close to half of the book is concerned with the details of the last flight around the world and the mysterious disappearance, sure to hold the attention of readers. Small but very clear black-and-white photographs are included." SLJ

Includes bibliography

Quackenbush, Robert M. Clear the cow pasture, I'm coming in for a landing!: a story of Amelia Earhart; [by] Robert Quackenbush. Simon & Schuster Bks. for Young Readers 1990 36p il $11.95; pa $3.95 (2-4) **92**

1. Women air pilots
ISBN 0-671-68548-1; 0-671-69218-6 (pa) LC 89-6164

A biography of the courageous aviatrix who became the first woman to cross the Atlantic by air

"Concisely and amusingly worded, the book includes three separate illustrative styles that complement the volume's admiring yet lighthearted tone. The first consists of single-page scenes picturing Earhart's life; the second is a series of cartoons, set in page corners, that depicts a mother bird introducing the concept of flight to her two babies. The third style is featured on the endpapers, which show a map of Earhart's final, incomplete flight route with added diagrams of aerial maneuvers." Booklist

Eastman, George, 1854-1932

Mitchell, Barbara. CLICK!: a story about George Eastman; illustrations by Jan Hosking Smith. Carolrhoda Bks. 1986 56p il (Carolrhoda creative minds bk) lib bdg $9.95; pa $4.95 (3-5) **92**

1. Inventors 2. Photography—History
ISBN 0-87614-289-7 (lib bdg); 0-87614-472-5 (pa)
LC 86-2672

Follows the life and career of the man who revolutionized photography by developing a camera simple enough for anyone to use

Edmonds, S. Emma E. (Sarah Emma Evelyn), 1841-1898

Reit, Seymour. Behind rebel lines: the incredible story of Emma Edmonds, Civil War spy. Harcourt Brace Jovanovich 1988 102p $12.95 (4 and up) **92**

1. United States—History—1861-1865, Civil War—Biography 2. Spies
ISBN 0-15-200416-5 LC 87-28079

"Gulliver books"

This biography tells of a Canadian-born woman who assumed male dress and served in the Union Army, first in a tent hospital, and then as a spy behind Confederate lines under various disguises

"Working from Emma's memoirs, U.S. Army records, and National Archives files, Reit has woven a suspense-filled account of a brave and loyal feminist." Booklist

Includes bibliography

El Chino

Say, Allen. El Chino. Houghton Mifflin 1990 32p il $14.95 (2-5) **92**

1. Bullfights—Biography
ISBN 0-395-52023-1 LC 90-35026

A biography of Bill Wong, a Chinese American who became a famous bullfighter in Spain

"Say's text renders Billy's complex story with simplicity and grace, presenting Billy as an endearing, determined hero; Say's watercolors are luminous, filled with harmonious detail. The first several pages of the book are reproduced in sepia tones, but when Billy attends his first bullfight, the pictures burst into full color." Publ Wkly

Eleanor, Queen, consort of Henry II, King of England, 1122?-1204

Brooks, Polly Schoyer. Queen Eleanor: independent spirit of the medieval world; a biography of Eleanor of Aquitaine. Lippincott 1983 183p il map lib bdg $13.89 (6 and up) **92**

1. Great Britain—Kings, queens, rulers, etc. 2. France—Kings, queens, rulers, etc.
ISBN 0-397-31995-9 LC 82-48776

A biography of the twelfth-century queen, first of France, then of England, who was the very lively wife of Henry II and mother of several notable sons, including Richard the Lionhearted

"The biographer has captured the subject's personality in a narrative as elegant and vivacious as Eleanor herself. And while obviously enthusiastic, the author nevertheless presents a balanced portrait: legend is separated from known facts; gossip from evidence." Horn Book

Includes bibliography

Elizabeth I, Queen of England, 1533-1603

Stanley, Diane. Good Queen Bess: the story of Elizabeth I of England; by Diane Stanley and Peter Vennema; illustrated by Diane Stanley. Four Winds Press 1990 unp il $14.95 (3-5) **92**

1. Great Britain—Kings, queens, rulers, etc.
ISBN 0-02-786810-9 LC 88-37501

Follows the life of the strong-willed queen who ruled England in the time of Shakespeare and the defeat of the Spanish Armada

"The handsome illustrations . . . are worthy of their subject. Although the format suggests a picture-book audience, this biography needs to be introduced to older readers who have the background to appreciate and understand this woman who dominated and named an age." SLJ

Includes bibliography

Ford, Gerald R., 1913-

Sipiera, Paul P. Gerald Ford: thirty-eighth president of the United States. Childrens Press 1989 100p il (Encyclopedia of presidents) lib bdg $15.93 (4 and up) **92**

1. Presidents—United States
ISBN 0-516-01371-8 LC 89-33745

Ford, Gerald R., 1913-—*Continued*

Examines the life of the first president to be sworn into office as a result of his predecessor's resignation

Ford, Henry, 1863-1947

Mitchell, Barbara. We'll race you, Henry: a story about Henry Ford; illustrations by Kathy Haubrich. Carolrhoda Bks. 1986 56p il (Carolrhoda creative minds bk) lib bdg $9.95; pa $4.95 (3-5) **92**

1. Automobile industry 2. Inventors
ISBN 0-87614-291-9 (lib bdg); 0-87614-471-7 (pa) LC 86-2691

A brief biography of Henry Ford with emphasis on how he came to develop fast, sturdy, and reliable racing cars that eventually gave him the idea for his Model T

"This book stands out from the general run of biographies for children because of the successful integration of a goodly amount of technological information with accurate and interesting biographical information." Appraisal

Foreman, Michael, 1938-

Foreman, Michael. War boy: a country childhood. Arcade Pub. 1990 1989 92p il $16.95 (5 and up) **92**

1. Authors, English 2. Illustrators 3. World War, 1939-1945—Great Britain—Personal narratives
ISBN 1-55970-049-1 LC 89-48501

First published 1989 in the United Kingdom

"War memories of a childhood spent on the frontline of World War II on the Suffolk coast of England are related . . . by text and illustrations." Child Book Rev Serv

"The stories meander among small, intriguing details. Bomb shelters, local characters and sweetshop treats are remembered and enlivened with beautiful, evocative illustrations. Foreman's sketches and full-color watercolors are sprinkled across the wide format, while reproductions of airplane specifications and other period details keep this from looking like just another picture book." Publ Wkly

Fortune, Amos, 1709 or 10-1801

Yates, Elizabeth. Amos Fortune, free man; illustrations by Nora S. Unwin. Dutton 1950 181p il $12.95; Penguin Bks. pa $3.95 (4 and up) **92**

1. Blacks—Biography 2. Slavery—United States
ISBN 0-525-25570-2; 0-14-034158-7 (pa) LC 50-7154

Awarded the Newbery Medal, 1951

"Born free in Africa, Amos Fortune was sold into slavery in America in 1725. After more than 40 years of servitude Amos was able to purchase his freedom and, in time, that of several others. He died a tanner of enviable reputation, a landowner, and a respected citizen of his community. Based on fact, this is a . . . story of a life dedicated to the fight for freedom and service to others." Booklist

Francis, of Assisi, Saint, 1182-1226

Cole, Joanna. A gift from Saint Francis; the first crèche; written by Joanna Cole; illustrated by Michèle Lemieux. Morrow Junior Bks. 1989 unp il $13.95; lib bdg $13.88 (2-4) **92**

1. Christian saints
ISBN 0-688-06502-3; 0-688-06503-1 (lib bdg) LC 88-22048

This book emphasizes Francis of Assisi's "connection with the celebration of Christmas. A brief biography nicely conveys the essence of the man—his humility, devotion to poverty, love of fellow creatures, and joyous religious fervor. Then, slightly embellishing the historical facts, Joanna Cole tells how in 1223 Francis was inspired to re-enact the Nativity outside the little town of Greccio. . . . A handsome work of visual storytelling that incorporates details echoing the art of the early Renaissance." Horn Book

De Paola, Tomie. Francis, the poor man of Assisi; written and illustrated by Tomie de Paola. Holiday House 1982 unp il lib bdg $14.95; pa $6.95 (3-5) **92**

1. Clare, of Assisi, Saint, 1194-1253 2. Christian saints
ISBN 0-8234-0435-8 (lib bdg); 0-8234-0812-4 (pa) LC 81-6984

The text "describes how Francis of Assisi changed from a roistering youth, son of a rich merchant, to a beggar for God. There are stories about the miracles that influenced him, of miracles he performed as he inspired others to join his mendicant band. The author also tells about Clare who heard Francis speak and left home to found the order still known as the Little Sisters of the Poor and of the miracles she performed." Publ Wkly

"Tomie de Paola captures the sweetness and gentleness of St. Francis, particularly in the illustrations, whose flattened perspective and muted earth, green and rust tones are obviously inspired by Giotto. . . . The inclusion of the text of Francis' 'Song to the Sun' makes a charming conclusion for the book." N Y Times Book Rev

Frank, Anne, 1929-1945

Frank, Anne. The diary of a young girl; translated from the Dutch by B. M. Mooyaart-Doubleday; with an introduction by Eleanor Roosevelt (6 and up) **92**

1. World War, 1939-1945—Jews 2. Netherlands—History—1940-1945, German occupation 3. Jews—Netherlands

Some editions are:
Amereon $15.95 (ISBN 0-89190-223-6)
Cornerstone Bks. $14.95 (ISBN 1-55736-098-7) large print edition
Doubleday $21.95 (ISBN 0-385-04019-9)
Modern Lib. $8.95 (ISBN 0-394-60451-2)
Pocket Bks. pa $4.95 (ISBN 0-671-70761-2)

This is the diary of a "German-Jewish girl who hid from the Nazis with her parents, their friends, and some other fugitives in an Amsterdam warehouse from 1942 to 1944. Her diary, covering the years of hiding, was found by friends and published as *Het achterhus* (1947); it was later published in English as *The Diary of a Young Girl* (1952). Against the background of the mass

Frank, Anne, 1929-1945—*Continued*
murder of European Jewry, the book presents an impressive picture of a group of hunted people forced to live together in almost intolerable proximity. Written with humor as well as insight, it shows a growing girl with all the preoccupations of adolescence and first love. The diary ends three days before the Franks and their group were discovered by the Nazis." Reader's Ency. 3d edition

Hurwitz, Johanna. Anne Frank: life in hiding; illustrated by Vera Rosenberry. Jewish Publ. Soc. 1988 62p il map $10.95 (3-5) **92**

1. Jews—Netherlands 2. Holocaust, Jewish (1933-1945)

ISBN 0-8276-0311-8 LC 87-35263

The author "gives a concise explanation of the political and economic background to the Holocaust and provides a map of Europe and a chronology. She ably covers the events of Anne's life before, during, and after the period covered by the 'Diary of Anne Frank,' explaining the significance and importance of the 'Diary' throughout the world." SLJ

Franklin, Benjamin, 1706-1790

Adler, David A. A picture book of Benjamin Franklin; illustrated by John & Alexandra Wallner. Holiday House 1990 unp il $13.95 (1-3) **92**

ISBN 0-8234-0792-6 LC 89-20059

Surveys the life of Benjamin Franklin, highlighting his work as an inventor and statesman

"The Wallners' full-color, softly painted illustrations are well executed and add informative details to the text. None of Franklin's life is dealt with in detail. . . . Adler's book will provide an excellent resource for primary readers." SLJ

Aliki. The many lives of Benjamin Franklin; written down and illustrated by Aliki. Simon & Schuster Bks. for Young Readers 1988 unp il $12.95; pa $5.95 (1-3) **92**

ISBN 0-671-66119-1; 0-671-66491-3 (pa) LC 87-22872

First published 1977 by Prentice-Hall

Recounts the story of Benjamin Franklin's life and his many activities and achievements

"Aliki's captioned cartoons—lightly lined and washed—expand or punctuate her easy text. . . . An efficient, lightweight introduction for picturebook readers." Booklist

D'Aulaire, Ingri. Benjamin Franklin; [by] Ingri & Edgar Parin D'Aulaire. Doubleday 1950 48p il o.p. paperback available $9.95 (2-4) **92**

ISBN 0-385-24103-8 (pa) LC 50-10503

"Incidents chosen for special appeal to young children make up this picture-biography of Franklin. The large, colored lithographs and marginal drawings dramatize the story and add details of eighteenth-century American life." Hodges. Books for Elem Sch Libr

Fritz, Jean. What's the big idea, Ben Franklin? illustrated by Margot Tomes. Coward, McCann & Geoghegan 1976 46p il $9.95; pa $5.95 (3-5) **92**

ISBN 0-698-20365-8; 0-698-20543-X (pa) LC 75-25902

The text "focuses on Franklin's multifaceted career but also gives personal details and quotes some of his pithy sayings. Enough background information about colonial affairs is given to enable readers to understand the importance of Franklin's contributions to the public good but not so much that it obtrudes on his life story. Although the text is not punctuated by references or footnotes, a page of notes (with numbers for pages referred to) is appended." Bull Cent Child Books

Friedan, Betty

Meltzer, Milton. Betty Friedan: a voice for women's rights; illustrated by Stephen Marchesi. Viking Kestrel 1985 57p il (Women of our time) lib bdg $10.95 (4 and up) **92**

1. Feminism

ISBN 0-670-80786-9 LC 85-40441

Focuses on the childhood and youth of the writer, thinker, and activist Betty Friedan

"The tone leans to admiration without adulation; the book offers perspective with its compact summary of the times that nurtured spontaneous consciousness-raising during the late 60s and early 70s. Black-and-white pencil sketches add to an accessible text." Bull Cent Child Books

Fritz, Jean

Fritz, Jean. Homesick: my own story; illustrated with drawings by Margot Tomes and photographs. Putnam 1982 176p il $13.95; Dell pa $3.25 (5 and up) **92**

1. China

ISBN 0-399-20933-6; 0-440-43683-4 (pa) LC 82-7646

Also available ABC-CLIO large print edition $15.95 (ISBN 1-55736-070-7)

A Newbery Medal honor book, 1983

Companion volume to: China homecoming, entered in class 951.05

This is a somewhat fictionalized memoir of the author's childhood in China. "Born in Hankow, where her father was director of the YMCA, Jean loved the city. . . . But she knew she 'belonged on the other side of the world'—in Pennsylvania with her grandmother and her other relations." Horn Book

"No seams are visible; the story flows smoothly, richly, intimately. The descriptions of places and the times are vivid in a book that brings to the reader, with sharp clarity and candor, the yearnings and fears and ambivalent loyalties of a young girl." Bull Cent Child Books

Gallaudet, T. H. (Thomas Hopkins), 1787-1851

Neimark, Anne E. A deaf child listened: Thomas Gallaudet, pioneer in American education. Morrow 1983 116p $11.95 (6 and up) **92**

1. Deaf—Education
ISBN 0-688-01719-3 LC 82-23942

This biography of the man who established the first school for the deaf in the United States "is both a record of Gallaudet's life and his battles on behalf of deaf children, and a record of the status of treatment and education of the deaf as they changed over the centuries." Bull Cent Child Books

The author presents "a thorough sketch of the man, personally and professionally. She does not end the book with Gallaudet's death, but with the progress deaf education has made . . . including a synopsis of Gallaudet College. A well-researched, readable book." SLJ

Includes bibliography

Gannett, Deborah Sampson, 1760-1827

McGovern, Ann. The secret soldier: the story of Deborah Sampson; illustrated by Ann Grifalconi. Four Winds Press 1987 c1975 62p il $12.95; Scholastic pa $2.50 (3-5) **92**

1. United States—History—1775-1783, Revolution—Biography 2. Soldiers—United States 3. Women soldiers
ISBN 0-02-765780-9; 0-590-43052-1 (pa)
LC 75-15819

A reissue of the title first published 1975

A "biography of Deborah Sampson who, disguised as a boy, fought for one and a half years in the Continental army until her true identity was discovered (Deborah then became a wife and mother but still continued to defy convention by traveling and lecturing). History and biography from childhood to young adulthood, paralleling the young nation's fight for freedom with Deborah's own desire for independence and selfhood." SLJ

George III, King of Great Britain, 1738-1820

Fritz, Jean. Can't you make them behave, King George? pictures by Tomie de Paola. Coward, McCann & Geoghegan 1977 45p il $9.95; pa $5.95 (3-5) **92**

1. Great Britain—Kings, queens, rulers, etc.
ISBN 0-698-20315-1; 0-698-20542-1 (pa)
LC 75-33722

"As a boy, George is seen to have had struggles in deportment; as King George III, he is mystified that the colonists refuse to be taught. Bits of history, a sense of George's personality, and the loneliness of being king are all conveyed with good humor. The artist's drawings evoke more chuckles." LC. Child Books, 1977

Geronimo, Apache Chief, 1829-1909

Shorto, Russell. Geronimo and the struggle for Apache freedom; written by Russell Shorto; introduction by Alvin M. Josephy, Jr.; illustrated by L.L. Cundiff. Silver Burdett Press 1989 131p il maps (Alvin Josephy's biography ser. of American Indians) lib bdg $12.98; pa $7.95 (5 and up) **92**

1. Apache Indians
ISBN 0-382-09571-5 (lib bdg); 0-382-09760-2 (pa)
LC 88-33687

Recounts the life story of the Apache chief who led one of the last great Indian uprisings

Includes bibliography

Gershwin, George, 1898-1937

Mitchell, Barbara. America, I hear you: a story about George Gershwin; illustrations by Jan Hosking Smith. Carolrhoda Bks. 1987 56p il (Carolrhoda creative minds bk) lib bdg $9.95 (3-5) **92**

1. Composers, American
ISBN 0-87614-309-5 LC 87-6544

Focuses on the life and musical career of the composer who wrote a number of popular musicals and brought jazz into the realm of acceptable and respectable music

Gish, Lillian, 1896?-

Gish, Lillian. An actor's life for me; [by] Lillian Gish as told to Selma Lanes; illustrations by Patricia Henderson Lincoln. Viking Kestrel 1987 73p il lib bdg $14.95 (3-5) **92**

1. Actors and actresses
ISBN 0-670-80416-9 LC 87-8197

"Discipline acquired early is the rock on which Gish built her singular success. But she still enjoyed many good times and adventures while growing up and traveling around the country with fellow performers. Lincoln's illustrations add color. . . . From the outset, the lively telling will engage readers who will discover that Lanes's script of this actor's life is informative and charming." Publ Wkly

Goodall, Jane

Goodall, Jane. My life with the chimpanzees. Pocket Bks. 1988 123p il map pa $2.95 (3-6) **92**

1. Zoologists 2. Chimpanzees
ISBN 0-671-66095-0

"A Byron Preiss book. A Minstrel book"

This autobiography "follows Goodall from her early years in London through her schooling . . . her fortuitous meeting and subsequent work with Louis Leakey, happenings in her personal life, and her . . . studies of chimpanzee behavior." Sci Books Films

"Family snapshots add to the special feeling of being let into Goodall's circle of friends as the famous scientist

Goodall, Jane—*Continued*
recounts her adventures with the chimps and illustrates many of her subjects' distinctive personalities. . . . This outstanding autobiography will be a noteworthy choice for school and public libraries." Booklist

Gorbachev, Mikhail

Caulkins, Janet (Janet Hillier). The picture life of Mikhail Gorbachev. 2nd ed. Watts 1989 64p il map lib bdg $7.99 (4 and up) **92**

1. Soviet Union—Politics and government
ISBN 0-531-10694-2 LC 88-39141
First published 1985

An illustrated biography of the leader of the Soviet Union, including a chronology of important dates in his life and a glossary of political words

Guevara, Ernesto, 1928-1967

Neimark, Anne E. Ché! Latin America's legendary guerilla leader. Lippincott 1989 113p il maps $13.95; lib bdg $13.89 (6 and up) **92**

1. Guerrillas
ISBN 0-397-32308-5; 0-397-32309-3 (lib bdg) LC 88-23137

Traces the life of the Latin American revolutionary and guerilla fighter, from his days as a student to his death in Bolivia

"While the language of this well-researched biography . . . is colorful and perhaps romantic, the story is efficiently and accurately told." N Y Times Book Rev

Includes bibliography

Halley, Edmond, 1656-1742

Heckart, Barbara Hooper. Edmond Halley, the man and his comet. Childrens Press 1984 111p il (People of distinction biographies) lib bdg $17.27 (4 and up) **92**

1. Halley's comet 2. Astronomers
ISBN 0-516-03202-X LC 83-24000

Presents the life of the seventeenth-century scientist who made predictions about the comet which bears his name and discusses many other important scientific contributions he made

"Choppy writing slows the pace from time to time . . . but Heckart's collection of facts on Halley's studies, theories and experiments is dazzling." SLJ

Includes glossary and bibliography

Hancock, John, 1737-1793

Fritz, Jean. Will you sign here, John Hancock? pictures by Trina Schart Hyman. Coward, McCann & Geoghegan 1976 47p il $9.95; pa $6.95 (3-5) **92**

1. United States—History—1775-1783, Revolution—Biography
ISBN 0-698-20308-9; 0-698-20539-1 (pa) LC 75-33243

"A straightforward biography of the rich Boston dandy with the gigantic signature. When he signed the Declaration of Independence he quipped, 'There! George the Third can read "that" without his spectacles. Now he can double his reward for my head.'" Saturday Rev

"An affectionate look at a flamboyant, egocentric, but kindly, patriot, the book is a most enjoyable view of history. The delightful illustrations exactly suit the times and the extraordinary character of John Hancock." Horn Book

Henry, Patrick, 1736-1799

Fritz, Jean. Where was Patrick Henry on the 29th of May? illustrated by Margot Tomes. Coward, McCann & Geoghegan 1975 47p il $9.95; pa $5.95 (3-5) **92**

1. United States—History—1600-1775, Colonial period—Biography
ISBN 0-698-20307-0; 0-698-20544-8 (pa) LC 74-83014

A "portrait of a founding father. Patrick Henry was born on May 29, and the author uses this date to focus on significant periods in his life. Henry's skill at oratory is shown in development as well as his anger at English laws, until they peak in his famous speech." Child Book Rev Serv

"The color pictures are artful evocations of the [18th] century in America and the text presents Patrick Henry as a human being—not a sterilized historic 'figure.'" Publ Wkly

Henson, Matthew Alexander, 1866-1955

Ferris, Jeri. Arctic explorer: the story of Matthew Henson. Carolrhoda Bks. 1989 80p il maps lib bdg $11.95; pa $5.95 (3-6) **92**

1. Explorers 2. North Pole 3. Blacks—Biography
ISBN 0-87614-370-2 (lib bdg); 0-87614-507-1 (pa) LC 88-34449

"A high adventure biography of Matthew Henson, the black explorer who accompanied Robert Peary on six expeditions to the North Pole. Henson's great courage, determination, and adaptability were crucial elements in the success of the expeditions. Black-and-white photographs supplement well-written text." Sci Child

Includes bibliography

Hiawatha, 15th cent.

McClard, Megan. Hiawatha and the Iroquois league; written by Megan McClard, George Ypsilantis; introduction by Alvin M. Josephy, Jr.; illustrated by Frank Riccio. Silver Burdett Press 1989 123p il maps (Alvin Josephy's biography ser. of American Indians) lib bdg $12.98; pa $7.95 (5 and up) **92**

1. Iroquois Indians
ISBN 0-382-09568-5 (lib bdg); 0-382-09757-2 (pa) LC 88-37503

Follows the life of the Iroquois leader who contributed to the formation of a league of Indian nations and discusses the actions and effects of this league as it interacted with the white colonists up through the eighteenth

Hiawatha, 15th cent.—*Continued*
century

Includes bibliographic references

Houston, Samuel, 1793-1863

Fritz, Jean. Make way for Sam Houston; illustrations by Elise Primavera. Putnam 1986 109p il map $12.95; pa $5.95 (4 and up) **92**

1. United States—History—1800-1899 (19th century)—Biography
ISBN 0-399-21303-1; 0-399-21304-X (pa) LC 85-25601

This is a biography of the "lawyer, governor of Tennessee, general in the wars against Santa Anna, president of the Republic of Texas, and finally U.S. senator and governor of the state of Texas." Horn Book

"Artfully weaving the threads of fact, Fritz creates a biography that is both interesting and informative. Developing Houston as a human character that readers can identify with as well as admire, and drawing him against the scene of America's own political turmoil, Fritz gives us a book to be read and to be felt." Voice Youth Advocates

Includes bibliography

Hughes, Langston, 1902-1967

Walker, Alice. Langston Hughes, American poet; illustrated by Don Miller. Crowell 1974 33p il (Crowell biography) lib bdg $12.89 (2-5) **92**

1. Poets, American 2. Black authors
ISBN 0-690-00219-X LC 73-9565

In this biography of the beloved black writer, the author traces Langston Hughes' childhood in Kansas, the discovery of his poems by Vachel Lindsay, his later fame as a writer, and his efforts to bring his work directly to the people

The author "includes a candid assessment of the poet's bitter, biased father that is not usually found in books about Hughes written for children. The illustrations are adequate, the biography as substantial as one for the primary grades reader can be." Bull Cent Child Books

Huynh, Quang Nhuong

Huynh, Quang Nhuong. The land I lost: adventures of a boy in Vietnam; with pictures by Vo-Dinh Mai. Harper & Row 1982 115p il $12.95; lib bdg $12.89; pa $3.50 (4 and up) **92**

1. Vietnam—Social life and customs
ISBN 0-397-32447-2; 0-397-32448-0 (lib bdg); 0-06-440183-9 (pa) LC 80-8437

"Each chapter in this book of reminiscence about the author's boyhood in a hamlet in the Vietnamese highlands, is a separate episode, although the same characters appear in many of the episodes. . . . The writing has an ingenuous quality that adds to the appeal of the strong sense of familial and communal ties that pervades the story." Bull Cent Child Books

Hyman, Trina Schart, 1939-

Hyman, Trina Schart. Self-portrait: Trina Schart Hyman; written and illustrated by Trina Schart Hyman. HarperCollins Pubs. 1981 unp il lib bdg $12.89 (4 and up) **92**

1. Illustrators 2. Women artists
ISBN 0-06-022766-4 LC 80-26662

First published by Addison-Wesley

"Hyman's sense of humor is as evident in her writing as in her drawing as she describes her childhood, her marriage while an art student, the year she and her husband spent in Sweden, where she had her first commission: illustrating a children's book at the behest of editor Astrid Lindgren. . . . Interspersed throughout the personal material are facts about books and other assignments on which Trina Hyman worked. A lively and informative book." Bull Cent Child Books

Ishi

Kroeber, Theodora. Ishi, last of his tribe; drawings by Ruth Robbins. Parnassus Press 1964 209p il maps o.p.; Bantam Bks. paperback available $3.50 (5 and up) **92**

1. Yana Indians
ISBN 0-553-24898-7 (pa) LC 64-19401

"The true story of a California Yahi Indian [discovered in 1911 by anthropologists] who survives the invasion by the white man, while the rest of his tribe die off." Notable Books, 1964

Written "with a grave simplicity . . . utterly right for the subject. The cultural details are quite unobtrusive: they are simply there, an evidence of the author's knowledge and empathy." Bull Cent Child Books

Includes glossary

Jackson, Jesse L., 1941-

McKissack, Patricia C. Jesse Jackson: a biography. Scholastic 1989 108p il $11.95 (4 and up) **92**

1. Blacks—Biography
ISBN 0-590-43181-1 LC 89-10133

A biography of the Afro-American minister and civil rights worker who ran for the Democratic presidential nomination in 1984 and 1988

"Occasionally the tone is adulatory, as in the implication that Jackson's advocacy is responsible for the drop in sickle cell anemia rates. However, the information is factually solid without becoming too detailed, and, in spite of a few stylistic flaws, the text is accessible and easy to read. Although it would have been helpful for students doing research to have source notes included, especially for quotes, there is a bibliography and index. Illustrated with black-and-white photographs." Bull Cent Child Books

Jackson, Mahalia, 1911-1972

Jackson, Jesse. Make a joyful noise unto the Lord! The life of Mahalia Jackson, queen of gospel singers; illustrated with photographs. Crowell 1974 160p il (Women of America) $12.95 (5 and up) **92**

1. Black singers 2. Singers
ISBN 0-690-43344-1 LC 72-7549

"An often moving portrait of 'Sister Haley'. From choir girl in New Orleans to world-renowned artist, she never let European music destroy her Afro-American roots. . . . Parallel to the story of her rise to fame are the accounts of major developments in the civil rights movements of the 1950's and 1960's and her increasing support of them up to her death in 1972." Horn Book

Includes bibliography

Jackson, Stonewall, 1824-1863

Fritz, Jean. Stonewall; with drawings by Stephen Gammell. Putnam 1979 152p il map $14.95; Penguin Bks. pa $3.95 (4 and up) **92**

1. Generals 2. United States—History—1861-1865, Civil War
ISBN 0-399-20698-1; 0-14-032937-4 (pa) LC 79-12506

A biography of the brilliant southern general who gained the nickname Stonewall by his stand at Bull Run during the Civil War

"Fritz's trenchant, compassionate life of General Thomas Jonathan Jackson grips the reader and makes one understand why Stonewall is an honored legend in American history. . . . The tragic irony of his death at age 39 is movingly described." Publ Wkly

Includes bibliography

Jefferson, Thomas, 1743-1826

Adler, David A. A picture book of Thomas Jefferson; illustrated by John & Alexandra Wallner. Holiday House 1990 unp il $13.95 (1-3) **92**

1. Presidents—United States
ISBN 0-8234-0791-8 LC 89-20076

Traces the life and achievements of the architect, bibliophile, president, and author of the Declaration of Independence

"The book includes an amazing amount of material. An appealing package with simple language and detailed drawings." Horn Book

Quackenbush, Robert M. Pass the quill, I'll write a draft: a story of Thomas Jefferson; [by] Robert Quackenbush. Pippin Press 1989 36p il lib bdg $12.95 (2-4) **92**

1. Presidents—United States
ISBN 0-945912-07-2 LC 89-8439

Follows the life and accomplishments of the third president, from his birth in 1743 to his retirement to Monticello

"Quackenbush's drawings are witty, expressive, and for the most part appealing. A full-page illustration faces each page of text; small cartoons appear at the bottom of each printed page. . . . These cartoons extend the text with interesting odd facts about Jefferson's many inventions." SLJ

Joplin, Scott, 1868-1917

Mitchell, Barbara. Raggin': a story about Scott Joplin; illustrations by Hetty Mitchell. Carolrhoda Bks. 1987 55p il (Carolrhoda creative minds bk) lib bdg $9.95 (3-5) **92**

1. Composers, American 2. Black musicians
ISBN 0-87614-310-9 LC 87-9310

The life story of the black Texan who became a popular composer and sought to elevate ragtime to the level of classical music, only to have his talents fully recognized after his death

Jordan, Michael

Deegan, Paul Joseph. Michael Jordan: basketball's soaring star; [by] Paul J. Deegan. Lerner Publs. 1988 55p il (Achievers) lib bdg $8.95; pa $3.95 (4 and up) **92**

1. Basketball—Biography 2. Black athletes
ISBN 0-8225-0492-8 (lib bdg); 0-8225-9548-6 (pa) LC 87-29669

Describes the life and career of the Chicago Bulls basketball player who became the first player in twenty-four years to score more than 3,000 points in one season

Keller, Helen, 1880-1968

Peare, Catherine Owens. The Helen Keller story. Crowell 1959 183p il $12.95; lib bdg $13.89 (5 and up) **92**

1. Blind 2. Deaf
ISBN 0-690-37520-4; 0-690-04793-2 (lib bdg) LC 59-10979

"Biography of Helen Keller, the child who was deaf and blind, and therefore mute, who became, with the loving, intelligent guidance of Anne Sullivan Macy, a graduate of Radcliffe College, a most potent force in coordinating the work with the blind as both writer and lecturer and an outstanding woman of the world." Bookmark

"Although the style is somewhat fictional, this is nevertheless a well documented account." Chicago Sunday Trib

Includes bibliography

Kenny, Elizabeth, 1886-1952

Crofford, Emily. Healing warrior: a story about Sister Elizabeth Kenny; illustrations by Steve Michaels. Carolrhoda Bks. 1989 64p il (Carolrhoda creative minds bk) lib bdg $9.95 (3-5) **92**

1. Nurses
ISBN 0-87614-382-6 LC 89-33474

"This biography traces Sister Kenny's life from childhood, through her nursing career, to her death at age 72 in 1952. Known as the founder of modern physical rehabilitation, the Australian nurse was instrumental in improving treatment of polio patients." Sci Child

This book is "well written and, while a bit of dialogue may have been invented, on the whole, [it] seems to

Kenny, Elizabeth, 1886-1952—*Continued*
be authoritative and objective. . . . [A] good introduction to [an] admirable medical pioneer that will attract recreational readers and be useful for reports." SLJ

Kherdian, Veron, 1907-

Kherdian, David. The road from home; the story of an Armenian girl. Greenwillow Bks. 1979 238p il map $13; lib bdg $12.88; Penguin Bks. pa $4.95 (6 and up) **92**

1. Armenians—Turkey 2. Armenian massacres, 1915-1923
ISBN 0-688-80205-2; 0-688-84205-4 (lib bdg); 0-14-032524-7 (pa) LC 78-72511

A Newbery Medal honor book, 1980

The author presents a "biography of his mother's early life as a young Armenian girl. Veron Dumehjian was part of a prosperous Armenian family in Turkey, but the Armenian minority undergoes a holocaust when the Turkish government persecutes its Christian minorities. In 1915 Veron and her family are deported and, as refugees, live through hardships of disease, starvation, bombing, and fire until, at sixteen, Veron is able to go to America as a 'mail-order' bride." Babbling Bookworm

King, Martin Luther, 1929-1968

Adler, David A. Martin Luther King, Jr.: free at last; illustrated by Robert Casilla. Holiday House 1986 48p il lib bdg $12.95; pa $4.95 (2-4) **92**

1. Blacks—Biography 2. Blacks—Civil rights
ISBN 0-8234-0618-0 (lib bdg); 0-8234-0619-9 (pa) LC 86-4670

"A short, chronological account of the life and major activities of this Civil Rights leader. . . . Preceded by a chronology of the major dates in King's life, the text is divided into four chapters and illustrated very fully with black-and-white paintings. . . . The book is pleasing in appearance, and the didactic thrust of explaining background issues and the value of King's beliefs and actions is well modulated." Horn Book

Adler, David A. A picture book of Martin Luther King, Jr. written by David A. Adler; illustrated by Robert Casilla. Holiday House 1989 unp il $13.95; pa $5.95 (1-3) **92**

1. Blacks—Biography 2. Blacks—Civil rights
ISBN 0-8234-0770-5; 0-8234-0847-7 (pa) LC 89-1930

This "biography takes a look at the life, leadership, and ideals of Dr. Martin Luther King, Jr. Adler examines King's family background, leadership of the Montgomery bus boycott, and the 1963 march on Washington, D.C. By focusing primarily on these events, Adler provides young readers with enough basic information to form a well-rounded picture of King and his ideals. However, the outstanding feature of this book is the vivid watercolor illustrations, which are sure to capture readers' attention. Casilla dramatically reveals the mood and feelings of the era." SLJ

Darby, Jean. Martin Luther King, Jr. Lerner Publs. 1990 144p il lib bdg $14.95 (5 and up) **92**

1. Blacks—Biography 2. Blacks—Civil rights
ISBN 0-8225-4902-6 LC 89-36797

This book "provides an indepth look into King's life and the racial strife and civil rights movement of the sixties. It begins with his childhood and shows the impact that his college and theological education had on his beliefs, actions, and strategies for leadership. This moving account in highly readable prose captures King's spirit, genius, and determination. Frequent and varied black-and-white photos add dramatic appeal." Booklist

Includes glossary and bibliography

Haskins, James. The life and death of Martin Luther King, Jr. Lothrop, Lee & Shepard Bks. 1977 176p il lib bdg $12.88 (5 and up) **92**

1. Blacks—Biography 2. Blacks—Civil rights
ISBN 0-688-51802-8 LC 77-3157

The author "writes about the civil rights leader in a simple, readable manner. Part one describes the development of the civil rights movement; part two describes the assassination, and an inordinate amount of space is given to James Earl Ray and the theory of a conspiracy behind the murder." Horn Book

McKissack, Patricia C. Martin Luther King, Jr., a man to remember; by Patricia McKissack. Childrens Press 1984 128p il (People of distinction biographies) lib bdg $17.27 (4 and up) **92**

1. Blacks—Biography 2. Blacks—Civil rights
ISBN 0-516-03206-2 LC 83-23933

Includes index

"McKissack addresses King's relationship with other black leaders, movements, politicians, and the FBI as well as allegations of Communism. King's uncertainties and concerns, particularly with the rise of Black Power, are portrayed in a way that makes his character understandable. Chapters are introduced with poems from various black authors that set the tone for what follows. A time line at the end places King in the perspective of world affairs." SLJ

Patrick, Diane. Martin Luther King, Jr. Watts 1990 64p il lib bdg $10.90 (4 and up) **92**

1. Blacks—Biography 2. Blacks—Civil rights
ISBN 0-531-10892-9 LC 89-24800

"A First book"

"King's family life, childhood, and schooling are described, along with the major events that established him as a leader. The information provided is general, and terms that readers might not understand are fully explained. . . . Numerous photographs supplement the text, which is arranged in an attractive manner. This book is a good, basic introduction to King." SLJ

King, Martin Luther, 1929-1968 — *Continued*

Patterson, Lillie. Martin Luther King, Jr., and the freedom movement. Facts on File 1989 178p il (Makers of America) $15.95 (6 and up) **92**

1. Blacks—Biography 2. Blacks—Civil rights
ISBN 0-8160-1605-4 LC 88-26051

"This political biography of King is also a dramatic account of the civil rights movement he led. Beginning with the Montgomery bus boycott in the mid-1950s, through the sit-ins, freedom rides, the march on Washington, the Nobel Prize, Selma, and the Voting Rights Act of 1965, Patterson presents King as a heroic figure." Booklist

Kipling, Rudyard, 1865-1936

Kamen, Gloria. Kipling, storyteller of East and West. Atheneum Pubs. 1985 72p il $13.95 (3-5) **92**

1. Authors, English
ISBN 0-689-31195-8 LC 85-7945

This biography traces Kipling's life from his early years in India and schooling in England to his later success as reporter, poet, and short story writer

"Lively and fluent, Kamen's writing brings the subject to life through vivid details and vignettes, yet avoids the false ring of fictionalization. . . . Kamen has written an excellent biography for children." Booklist

Includes glossary and bibliography

Koehn, Ilse, 1929-1991

Koehn, Ilse. Mischling, second degree: my childhood in Nazi Germany; with a foreword by Harrison E. Salisbury. Greenwillow Bks. 1977 240p lib bdg $12.88; Penguin Bks. pa $4.95 (6 and up) **92**

1. World War, 1939-1945—Jews 2. Germany—History—1933-1945 3. Jews—Germany
ISBN 0-688-84110-4; 0-14-034290-7 (pa) LC 77-6189

This story "is told in retrospect by an author who did not know why her loving parents separated until after the war, when she learned that it had helped her and her mother avoid the consequences of the fact that her father had one Jewish parent. Liberals and intellectuals, the Koehns coped, as many did, with a government and a philosophy they detested. And Ilse, a young adolescent, was drafted into the Hitler Youth, forced to go through the motions of devotion." Bull Cent Child Books

Lange, Dorothea, 1895-1965

Meltzer, Milton. Dorothea Lange: life through the camera; illustrations by Donna Diamond; photographs by Dorothea Lange. Viking Kestrel 1985 57p il (Women of our time) lib bdg $10.95; Puffin Bks. pa $3.95 (4 and up) **92**

1. Women photographers
ISBN 0-670-28047-X (lib bdg); 0-14-032105-5 (pa) LC 84-13124

A biography of Dorothea Lange, whose photographs of migrant workers and rural poverty helped bring about important social reforms

This "volume is smoothly written, although there are occasional comments that could be clarified. Still, the combination of a competent and careful biographer and a fascinating subject make accessible to readers the story of a strong contemporary artist they may not have known." Bull Cent Child Books

Lavoisier, Antoine Laurent, 1743-1794

Grey, Vivian. The chemist who lost his head: the story of Antoine Laurent Lavoisier. Coward, McCann & Geoghegan 1982 112p il $9.95 (5 and up) **92**

1. Chemists
ISBN 0-698-20559-6 LC 82-1571

A "description of the life and science of Antoine Laurent Lavoisier who became known as the 'father of chemistry,' but who was beheaded in 1794 as one of the King's tax collectors. The story tells both of aristocratic life in France before and during the French Revolution, as well as of the revolution in chemistry which Lavoisier headed. He brought together chemical principles as a scientific system." Appraisal

Lee, Robert E. (Robert Edward), 1807-1870

Weidhorn, Manfred. Robert E. Lee. Atheneum Pubs. 1988 150p il map $13.95 (5 and up) **92**

1. Generals 2. United States—History—1861-1865, Civil War—Biography
ISBN 0-689-31340-3 LC 87-14500

"Opening with Lee's decision, in 1861, to resign from the U.S. army rather than accept an offer to command it, Weidhorn flashes back with a brief overview of the Virginian's life. The rest of the book is devoted to Lee's leadership of Confederate forces throughout the Civil War, with two final chapters on his 'reconciliation' and years as a college president." Bull Cent Child Books

"With a quick, fluid pace and sustained tension, Weidhorn describes the battles in a big-picture sense, analyzing Lee's part in the outcome, win or lose, and capturing for the reader Lee's penetrating insight, brilliant maneuvers, and strategy." Booklist

Includes bibliography

Leeuwenhoek, Antoni van, 1632-1723

Kumin, Maxine. The microscope; pictures by Arnold Lobel. Harper & Row 1984 c1968 unp il $11.95; lib bdg $11.89; pa $2.95 (k-3) **92**

1. Microscope and microscopy 2. Scientists
ISBN 0-06-023523-3; 0-06-023524-1 (lib bdg); 0-06-443136-3 (pa) LC 82-47728

First published 1968 in the author's collection: The wonderful babies of 1809 and other years

Relates in rhyme the famous Dutch scientist's penchant for viewing things with a microscope, through which he made remarkable observations

This "short, amusing poem . . . deftly sketches Leeuwenhoek's adventures and the wondrous, miniscule world that wriggled to life before his astonished eyes.

Leeuwenhoek, Antoni van, 1632-1723—*Continued*

The somber pen-and-ink drawings, handsomely printed on creamy beige paper, are often humorous parodies of the Dutch painters of Leeuwenhoek's era." Horn Book

Leonardo, da Vinci, 1452-1519

Provensen, Alice. Leonardo da Vinci: the artist, inventor, scientist; in three-dimensional, movable pictures by A. & M. Provensen. Viking 1984 unp il $16.95 (3 and up) **92**

1. Artists, Italian 2. Inventors 3. Scientists
ISBN 0-670-42384-X LC 83-26005

This "book contains eight 'pop-up' or movable paintings that dynamically illustrate some of Leonardo da Vinci's great inventions and paintings. The controls on the 'pop-ups' work well and each resulting movement displays some facet of Leonardo's inventiveness. . . . The brief text tells facts and stories about da Vinci." Sci Child

Lincoln, Abraham, 1809-1865

Adler, David A. A picture book of Abraham Lincoln; written by David A. Adler; illustrated by John & Alexandra Wallner. Holiday House 1989 unp il lib bdg $13.95 (1-3) **92**

1. Presidents—United States
ISBN 0-8234-0731-4 LC 88-16393

Follows the life of the popular president, from his childhood on the frontier to his assassination after the end of the Civil War

"While the author does include details that make the narratives more specific or realistic, he avoids fictionalizing. The Wallners' attractive line-and-watercolor illustrations evoke the past with the narrative quality of American naive painting and a certain gentle charm all their own." Booklist

D'Aulaire, Ingri. Abraham Lincoln; by Ingri & Edgar Parin d'Aulaire. Doubleday 1957 unp il $10.95; lib bdg $12.95; pa $9.95 (2-4) **92**

1. Presidents—United States
ISBN 0-385-07669-X; 0-385-07674-6 (lib bdg); 0-385-24108-9 (pa) LC 57-2502

Awarded the Caldecott Medal, 1940

First published 1939

"The story devotes itself more to pioneer phases than to darker scenes of Lincoln's later life, and it closes before he has started for Ford's Theater." N Y Her Trib Books

Presented "in a brief, direct, semiwhimsical text and in notable lithographic drawings by the authors, some of which have soft rich color, others being reproduced in black and white. The illustrations, detailed and faithful to the atmosphere of the various settings are both tender and humorous in their interpretation. . . . A distinguished piece of bookmaking." Bookmark

Freedman, Russell. Lincoln: a photobiography. Clarion Bks. 1987 150p il $16.95; Houghton Mifflin pa $7.95 (4 and up) **92**

1. Presidents—United States
ISBN 0-89919-380-3; 0-395-51848-2 (pa) LC 86-33379

Awarded the Newbery Medal, 1988

The author "begins by contrasting the Lincoln of legend to the Lincoln of fact. His childhood, self-education, early business ventures, and entry into politics comprise the first half of the book, with the rest of the text covering his presidency and assassination." SLJ

This is "a balanced work, elegantly designed and enhanced by dozens of period photographs and drawings, some familiar, some refreshingly unfamiliar." Publ Wkly

Includes bibliography

Gross, Ruth Belov. True stories about Abraham Lincoln; illustrated by Jill Kastner. Lothrop, Lee & Shepard Bks. 1990 c1973 46p il $12.95; lib bdg $12.88 (2-4) **92**

1. Presidents—United States
ISBN 0-688-08797-3; 0-688-08798-1 (lib bdg) LC 89-45899

A newly illustrated edition of the title first published 1973 in paperback by Scholastic

"Twenty-two one-page chapters, each facing a full-page watercolor painting, describe episodes in Lincoln's life. . . . The illustrations are strong in color and composition, though some of the facial expressions seem stilted. . . . Nevertheless, the overall visual effect is an inviting one, well supported by the solid introductory narrative." Bull Cent Child Books

North, Sterling. Abe Lincoln: log cabin to White House. Random House 1987 c1956 150p lib bdg $8.99; pa $2.95 (5 and up) **92**

1. Presidents—United States
ISBN 0-394-90361-7 (lib bdg); 0-394-89179-1 (pa) LC 87-4654

"Landmark books"

A reissue of the title first published 1956

A biography of Abraham Lincoln, focusing on his childhood spent in poverty on the Midwestern frontier, and chronicling his rise to the Presidency and the highlights of his tenure

"Mr. North has complimented his readers by refraining from fictional dialogue or introspection—the facts are impressive enough—and he has quoted briefly from Lincoln's own writings and speeches and from his contemporaries' recollections." N Y Times Book Rev

Sandburg, Carl. Abe Lincoln grows up; with illustrations by James Daugherty. Harcourt Brace Jovanovich 1985 c1928 222p il $19.95; pa $4.95 (5 and up) **92**

ISBN 0-15-201037-8; 0-15-602615-5 (pa) LC 74-17180

A reissue of the title first published 1928

"Drawn from Sandburg's *Abraham Lincoln: The Prairie Years* (published in 1926), this includes the earlier chapters on Lincoln's boyhood. Beginning with the story of Abe's forebears and a picture of the Midwest during

Lincoln, Abraham, 1809-1865—*Continued*

the early days of our country, Sandburg follows young Lincoln to the age of 19, when he says good-bye to his family and sets off for New Salem, Illinois, to seek his fortune. Bold illustrations by Daugherty add strength." Booklist

Lindgren, Astrid, 1907-

Hurwitz, Johanna. Astrid Lindgren: storyteller to the world; illustrated by Michael Dooling. Viking Kestrel 1989 54p il (Women of our time) lib bdg $10.95 (4 and up) 92

1. Authors, Swedish 2. Women authors
ISBN 0-670-82207-8 LC 89-33913

Examines the life of the Swedish storyteller who created the well-known Pippi Longstocking for her sick daughter and saw the story go on to be published in fifty languages

"Peppering the text with lively details, anecdotes, and quotations, Hurwitz affectionately introduces Lindgren without gushing or fictionalizing. Readers who enjoy Pippi and other Lindgren books will welcome this window into her world. Illustrated with softly shaded black pencil drawings." Booklist

Little, Jean, 1932-

Little, Jean. Little by Little; a writer's education. Viking Kestrel 1988 c1987 233p il $11.95 (5 and up) 92

1. Authors, Canadian 2. Women authors
ISBN 0-670-81649-3

First published 1987 in Canada

This autobiography covers the life of the Canadian author of children's literature from preschool memories to the publication of her first book

"Jean Little's story is a remarkable one, for it is a celebration of the human spirit. By turns touching and humorous, her autobiographical reminiscence should equal or surpass her fictional works in appeal, for it has the same flow, the same emotional power, the same warm tone as her novels." Horn Book

Louis XIV, King of France, 1638-1715

Aliki. The King's day: Louis XIV of France. Crowell 1989 unp il $13.95; lib bdg $13.89 (3-5) 92

1. France—Kings, queens, rulers, etc.
ISBN 0-690-04588-3; 0-690-04590-5 (lib bdg)
LC 88-38179

This book "introduces Louis XIV, his palaces and his family. It follows him through a typical day from his getting up ritual, to chapel, council, his huge dinner and riding or hunting. After a rest, he entertains and has supper with the royal family before his going to bed ceremony." Child Book Rev Serv

"The book design combines the appeal of a comic format with carefully researched illustration, including elaborate indoor and outdoor scenes of Versailles. A chronology and list of definitions (without pronunciation) for French words are appended. On balance, this is lively and informative biography." Bull Cent Child Books

Low, Juliette Gordon, 1860-1927

Kudlinski, Kathleen V. Juliette Gordon Low: America's first Girl Scout; illustrated by Sheila Hamanaka. Viking Kestrel 1988 55p il (Women of our time) lib bdg $10.95; Puffin Bks. pa $3.95 (4 and up) 92

1. Girl Scouts of the United States of America
ISBN 0-670-82208-6 (lib bdg); 0-14-032691-X (pa)
LC 88-17428

Presents an illustrated biography of the founder of the Girl Scout movement

"Although there are traces of adulatory writing, the author has . . . done a good job of pulling together facts about her subject, providing information about Low's role as founder of the Girl Scout movement as well as giving a picture of her as a person, and noting, in the closing pages, how the research was done. The author's note is as simply written as the book itself, and is equally brief and clear." Bull Cent Child Books

Madison, James, 1751-1836

Fritz, Jean. The great little Madison. Putnam 1989 159p il $15.95 (5 and up) 92

1. Presidents—United States
ISBN 0-399-21768-1 LC 88-31584

"Small, soft-spoken, and by nature diffident, James Madison found it difficult to speak in the midst of controversy, but his zeal and his convictions in the struggle between Republicans and Federalists gave him confidence, and his successes brought him to the presidency. Fritz has given a vivid picture of the man and an equally vivid picture of the problems—especially the internal dissension—that faced the leaders of the new nation in the formative years after the appearance of the Declaration of Independence and the turmoil of the several decades that followed the ratification of the Constitution. Notes by the author and a bibliography are appended." Bull Cent Child Books

Malcolm X, 1925-1965

Adoff, Arnold. Malcolm X; illustrated by John Wilson. Crowell 1970 41p il (Crowell biography) hardcover o.p. paperback available $4.95 (2-5) 92

1. Blacks—Biography
ISBN 0-06-446015-0 (pa) LC 70-94787

"This short forthright biography vividly outlines the events, both tragic and rewarding, which influenced the life and thought of Malcolm X from childhood to death and clearly evinces his significance as a black leader. The account describes the adverse effects of Malcolm's bitter childhood experiences, the changes which began during his incarceration in the Norfolk Prison Colony, his association with the Black Muslims and his later break with them, and the hostility of both black and white groups toward his Organization of Afro-American Unity." Booklist

Matzeliger, Jan

Mitchell, Barbara. Shoes for everyone: a story about Jan Matzeliger; illustrations by Hetty Mitchell. Carolrhoda Bks. 1986 63p il (Carolrhoda creative minds bk) lib bdg $9.95; pa $4.95 (3-5) **92**

1. Shoe industry 2. Inventors 3. Blacks—Biography
ISBN 0-87614-290-0 (lib bdg); 0-87614-473-3 (pa)
LC 86-4157

A biography of the half-Dutch half-black Surinamese man who, despite the hardships and prejudice he found in his new Massachusetts home, invented a shoe-lasting machine that revolutionized the shoe industry in the late nineteenth century

This is "a compelling story of human endeavor. A clear text blessedly allows the extraordinary individual in focus, Jan Matzeliger, . . . to emerge without undue exclamatory adulation." Bull Cent Child Books

Meir, Golda, 1898-1978

Adler, David A. Our Golda: the story of Golda Meir; illustrated by Donna Ruff. Viking 1984 52p il $11.95; Puffin Bks. pa $3.95 (3-5) **92**

1. Women politicians 2. Israel—Politics and government 3. Zionism
ISBN 0-670-53107-3; 0-14-032104-7 (pa)
LC 83-16798

"Adler's biography covers Golda Meir's life, including her Russian birth and American upbringing, through her resignation from the office of Prime Minister of Israel in 1974. Golda's strong-willed personality is Adler's primary focus." SLJ

This is a "compact, thoughtful biography. . . . [The] well-researched narrative exhibits a sensitivity for time and place that is echoed in accompanying soft-pencil drawings." Booklist

Merrick, Joseph Carey, 1862 or 3-1890

Howell, Michael. The elephant man; [by] Michael Howell and Peter Ford; illustrated by Robert Geary. Allison & Busby; distributed by Schocken Bks. 1984 c1983 64p il $9.95 (4 and up) **92**

1. Physically handicapped
ISBN 0-8052-8160-6 LC 85-107627

First published 1983 in the United Kingdom

Follows the life of Joseph Merrick, called the Elephant Man because of a deformity, from his early years as a sideshow attraction to his death in a London hospital in 1890

Michelangelo Buonarroti, 1475-1564

Ventura, Piero. Michelangelo's world. Putnam 1988 38p il $13.95 (5 and up) **92**

1. Artists, Italian
ISBN 0-399-21593-X LC 88-18535

Recounts the life of the famous sculptor, painter, poet, and architect who flourished during the Italian Renaissance

The author "spices the narrative with colorful details that make Michelangelo into a distinctive character. . . . Unfortunately, there are no notes to address what is fact and what is fiction; one hopes such invigorating detail is grounded in truth. Ventura's miniature pen-and ink drawings decorate the large pages, fashioning scenes described in the narrative and injecting notes of humor here and there. . . . Absorbing, though the lack of documentation is irritating." Booklist

Miller, Bertha E. Mahony

Ross, Eulalie Steinmetz. The spirited life: Bertha Mahony Miller and children's books; selected bibliography compiled by Virginia Haviland. Horn Bk. 1973 274p il $12.95 **92**

1. Children's literature—History and criticism
ISBN 0-87675-057-9 LC 73-84132

This is "a stately, detailed, and sometimes nostalgic trip into early crusading for children's literature. Bertha Mahony Miller's intense creative energy, her feminine independence and her optimistic sense of wonder are highlighted throughout the account of her childhood, her founding of the successful Bookshop for Boys and Girls in Boston, the launching and long, fruitful editorship of 'The Horn Book,' and her contribution to publications on children's literature." Booklist

Mitchell, Arthur, 1934-

Tobias, Tobi. Arthur Mitchell; illustrated by Carole Byard. Crowell 1975 32p il (Crowell biography) lib bdg $12.89 (2-5) **92**

1. Dance Theatre of Harlem 2. Ballet dancers 3. Black dancers
ISBN 0-690-00662-4 LC 74-13730

A biography of the black ballet dancer who gave up his career as a star with the New York City Ballet to found the Dance Theatre of Harlem

"An attractive format—large, clean type and sepia pastel drawings overlayed with yellow and blue—enhances this fine biography." SLJ

Moses, Grandma, 1860-1961

Oneal, Zibby. Grandma Moses: painter of rural America; illustrated by Donna Ruff; paintings by Grandma Moses. Viking Kestrel 1986 58p il (Women of our time) lib bdg 10.95; Penguin Bks. pa $3.95 (4 and up) **92**

1. Artists, American 2. Women artists
ISBN 0-670-80664-1 (lib bdg); 0-14-032220-5 (pa)
LC 86-4071

A biography focusing on the early years of Grandma Moses, who was known for her paintings of rural America

"Though short, this biographical sketch brims with the energy of both the woman and the artist. . . . Oneal does an exemplary job of interpreting the artist's work, giving a semblance of the style and flavor in a brisk, evocative narrative. Recommended not only as a biography of a woman who succeeded in her craft but also as an inspirational source for fledgling artists." Booklist

Muir, John, 1838-1914

Force, Eden. John Muir. Silver Burdett Press 1990 145p il (Pioneers in change) $13.98; pa $7.95 (5 and up) **92**

1. Naturalists 2. Nature conservation
ISBN 0-382-09965-6; 0-382-09970-2 (pa) LC 90-34464

"An inspirational biography of the turn-of-the-century naturalist and conservationist responsible for the establishment of Yosemite National Park, the founding of the Sierra Club, and the creation of the U.S. National Park Service, describes John Muir's boyhood, explorations, publications, and adult life. Includes a chronology." Sci Child

Includes bibliographic references

Nesbit, E. (Edith), 1858-1924

Nesbit, E. (Edith). Long ago when I was young; watercolor illustrations by George Buchanan; line drawings by Edward Ardizzone; introduction by Noel Streatfeild. Dial Bks. 1987 127p il $14.95 (5 and up) **92**

1. Authors, English 2. Women authors
ISBN 0-8037-0476-3 LC 87-8974

A reissue with some new illustrations of the title first published 1966 in the United Kingdom

An autobiographical account by the author of The Railway Children and other children's books, in which she describes a childhood spent sometimes within the security of her family and sometimes apart from them in schools she detested

This edition "retains Ardizzone's ink drawings from the 1966 edition (o.p.) and adds Buchanan's seven watercolors. . . . Not only is the book a natural for children who love Nesbit's classic novels, but also it's good choice for students with autobiography assignments." Booklist

Oakley, Annie, 1860-1926

Quackenbush, Robert M. Who's that girl with the gun? a story of Annie Oakley; [by] Robert Quackenbush. Prentice-Hall Bks. for Young Readers 1988 36p il $11.95 (2-4) **92**

ISBN 0-671-66379-8 LC 87-11545

This biography "traces the famous sharpshooter's life from early childhood in the 1860s to her death in 1926. Writing in a simple but factual style and avoiding fictionalized dialogue, the author devotes the majority of his brief biography to the difficulties in Oakley's childhood and the excitement and rewards of her years performing with Buffalo Bill's Wild West Show. Two pages detail the events of the final third of Oakley's life. Quackenbush's full-page illustrations, cartoon-like figures executed in black ink and gray and yellow washes, appropriately call to mind circus or rodeo posters from the turn of the century." SLJ

O'Keeffe, Georgia, 1887-1986

Gherman, Beverly. Georgia O'Keeffe; the "wideness and wonder" of her world. Atheneum Pubs. 1986 131p il $13.95 (5 and up) **92**

1. Painters, American 2. Women artists
ISBN 0-689-31164-8 LC 85-26860

"A reverential, chronological history of a major American painter. Gherman tells O'Keeffe's story, from infancy to old age, simply and with the sorts of interpretation of recorded events and characteristic anecdotes in a way that animates the pages. She addresses the artist's development, a bit about her personal relations and even more about the evolution of the modern art movement in America and her role as a woman in it." SLJ

Includes bibliography

O'Kelley, Mattie Lou

O'Kelley, Mattie Lou. From the hills of Georgia: an autobiography in paintings. Little, Brown 1983 32p il $14.95; pa $6.95 (2-4) **92**

1. Painters, American 2. Women artists
ISBN 0-316-63800-5; 0-316-63799-8 (pa) LC 83-9414

"An Atlantic Monthly Press book"

"Re-creating not only her own childhood in rural Georgia but a vanished mode of American life, Mattie O'Kelley, the seventh of eight children, begins with her own birth in 1908. In plain, conversational language and in joyous primitive paintings, she informally describes and visually elaborates on the endless round of farm work; family events, pastimes, and celebrations; childhood school and play; and community life—all linked to the ever-changing seasons. Words and wonderfully detailed pictures function in total harmony in an organically unified book." Horn Book

Peet, Bill

Peet, Bill. Bill Peet: an autobiography. Houghton Mifflin 1989 190p il lib bdg $16.95 (4 and up) **92**

1. Walt Disney Productions 2. Authors, American 3. Illustrators
ISBN 0-395-50932-7 LC 88-37067

A Caldecott Medal honor book, 1990

This memoir "describes the life of the well-known children's book author who worked as an illustrator for Walt Disney from the making of 'Dumbo' until 'Mary Poppins.'" N Y Times Book Rev

"Every page of this oversized book is illustrated with Peet's unmistakable black-and-white drawings of himself and the people, places, and events described in the text. Familiar characters from his books and movies appear often. The fascinating subject matter will encourage readers to finish the lengthy text. The pictures tell their own story and can be appreciated on many levels. An excellent choice for inspiring young gifted and talented students as well as for general readers." SLJ

Peter I, the Great, Emperor of Russia, 1672-1725

Stanley, Diane. Peter the Great. Four Winds Press 1986 32p il $13.95 (3-5) **92**

1. Soviet Union—Kings, queens, rulers, etc.
ISBN 0-02-786790-0 LC 85-13060

A biography of the tsar who began the transformation of Russia into a modern state in the late seventeenth-early eighteenth centuries

The author's "material is presented with a modicum of oversimplification and a plethora of details that are sure to fascinate children. But what really makes this biography shine are its breathtaking illustrations. The meticulously researched, vivid scenes of Russian life during Peter's reign—courts, countryside, architecture, costumes—are beautifully rendered. The illustrations do not merely picture the text; they accompany it, providing a counterpoint melody of visual harmony and details." Publ Wkly

Philip, Sachem of the Wampanoags, d. 1676

Cwiklik, Robert. King Philip and the war with the colonists; written by Robert Cwiklik; introduction by Alvin M. Josephy, Jr.; illustrated by Robert L. Smith. Silver Burdett Press 1989 131p il (Alvin Josephy's biography ser. of American Indians) lib bdg $11.98; pa $7.95 (5 and up) **92**

1. Wampanoag Indians 2. King Philip's War, 1675-1676
ISBN 0-382-09573-1 (lib bdg); 0-382-09762-9 (pa)
LC 89-5952

Examines the life and fortunes of the Wampanoag Indian leader who led an uprising against the New England colonists in the seventeenth century

Includes bibliography

Pinkerton, Allan, 1819-1884

Wormser, Richard. Pinkerton: America's first private eye. Walker & Co. 1990 119p il $17.95; lib bdg $18.85 (5 and up) **92**

1. Detectives
ISBN 0-8027-6964-0; 0-8027-6965-9 (lib bdg)
LC 90-12362

Examines the life of the detective who founded his own agency and introduced a system to help track criminals down and tie them to crimes

"An intriguing subject, lively prose, and in-depth analysis combine to make this a first-rate biography. . . . Wormser never tries to paper over the contradictions or erase Pinkerton's warts. He makes abundant anecdotal use of Pinkerton's detective cases, and the result is fresh and thought provoking, engrossing despite a high ratio of text to illustration." Booklist

Includes bibliography

Pocahontas, d. 1617

D'Aulaire, Ingri. Pocahontas; by Ingri & Edgar Parin d'Aulaire. Doubleday 1946 unp il $13.95; pa $7.95 (2-4) **92**

1. Powhatan Indians
ISBN 0-385-07454-9; 0-385-26607-3 (pa)
LC 46-11835

With "simplicity and dignity, the . . . authors have told the story of Pocahontas and Captain John Smith, bringing in the romantic and courageous elements as well as authentic historical fact. The lithographs are colourful, primitive in design and picture the story of Pocahontas from her childhood [in the Virginia wilderness] to her reception as a princess in England." Ont Libr Rev

Fritz, Jean. The double life of Pocahontas; with illustrations by Ed Young. Putnam 1983 96p il $12.95; Puffin Bks. pa $3.95 (4 and up) **92**

1. Powhatan Indians 2. Jamestown (Va.)—History
ISBN 0-399-21016-4; 0-14-032257-4 (pa) LC 83-9662

"Pocahontas, the daughter of the seventeenth century Indian chief Powhatan, . . . saved the life of Captain John Smith and later married John Rolfe. In tracing the girl's life, the author has explored the history of the Jamestown colony from 1607 to 1622 and has given [an] . . . account of the often unhappy relationship between the colonists and the Indians." Horn Book

Includes bibliography

Polo, Marco, 1254-1323?

Ceserani, Gian Paolo. Marco Polo; illustrated by Piero Ventura. Putnam 1982 unp il maps $9.95 (3-6) **92**

1. Explorers 2. Voyages and travels 3. Asia—Description and travel
ISBN 0-399-20843-7 LC 81-15685

This "account of the life and travels of Marco Polo is presented in picture-book format. Full-page illustrations or double-page spreads are set along with the text, which traces Marco Polo's journey with his father and uncle from medieval Venice to the court of Kublai Khan in China and home again by a different route." Horn Book

Potter, Beatrix, 1866-1943

Collins, David R. The country artist: a story about Beatrix Potter; illustrations by Karen Ritz. Carolrhoda Bks. 1989 56p il (Carolrhoda creative minds bk) lib bdg $9.95; pa $4.95 (3-5) **92**

1. Authors, English 2. Illustrators 3. Women authors 4. Women artists
ISBN 0-87614-344-3 (lib bdg); 0-87614-509-8 (pa)
LC 88-27417

A biography of the English author and illustrator who grew up during the Victorian era and whose detailed drawings of plants and animals found their way into her famous picture books

Potter, Beatrix, 1866-1943—*Continued*

Taylor, Judy. Beatrix Potter: artist, storyteller and countrywoman. Warne 1987 c1986 224p il $24.95 **92**

1. Authors, English 2. Illustrators 3. Women authors 4. Women artists
ISBN 0-7232-3314-4 LC 86-50799

First published 1986 in the United Kingdom

"In this brief but copiously illustrated biography, Judy Taylor adds much fresh information to what was previously known about her sanguine-spirited and intensely private subject's life. . . . Further insights may be gleaned from the more than 200 illustrations reproduced in this attractive volume, including dozens of family photographs . . . and an abundant sampling of Potter landscapes, botanical studies, picture letters, rough sketches and finished book art." N Y Times Book Rev

Includes bibliography

Reagan, Ronald, 1911-

Kent, Zachary. Ronald Reagan, fortieth president of the United States; consultant, Charles Abele. Childrens Press 1989 99p il (Encyclopedia of presidents) lib bdg $15.93; pa $6.95 (4 and up) **92**

1. Presidents—United States
ISBN 0-516-01373-4 (lib bdg); 0-516-41373-2 (pa) LC 89-33746

A biography of the former motion picture actor who served two terms as the fortieth president of the United States

Reiss, Johanna

Reiss, Johanna. The upstairs room. Crowell 1972 196p $12.95; lib bdg $12.89; Harper & Row pa $3.50 (4 and up) **92**

1. World War, 1939-1945—Jews 2. Netherlands—History—1940-1945, German occupation 3. Jews—Netherlands
ISBN 0-690-85127-8; 0-690-04702-9 (lib bdg); 0-06-440370-X (pa) LC 77-187940

A Newbery Medal honor book, 1973

"In a vital, moving account the author recalls her experiences as a Jewish child hiding from the Germans occupying her native Holland during World War II. . . . Ten-year-old Annie and her twenty-year-old sister Sini, . . . are taken in by a Dutch farmer, his wife, and mother who hide the girls in an upstairs room of the farm house. Written from the perspective of a child the story affords a child's-eye-view of the war." Booklist

Followed by: The journey back (1976)

Revere, Paul, 1735-1818

Fritz, Jean. And then what happened, Paul Revere? pictures by Margot Tomes. Coward, McCann & Geoghegan 1973 45p il $9.95; pa $4.95 (2-4) **92**

1. United States—History—1775-1783, Revolution—Biography
ISBN 0-698-20274-0; 0-698-20541-3 (pa) LC 73-77423

This "description of Paul Revere's ride to Lexington is funny, fast-paced, and historically accurate; it is given added interest by the establishment of Revere's character: busy, bustling, versatile, and patriotic, a man who loved people and excitement. The account of his ride is preceded by a description of his life and the political situation in Boston, and it concludes with Revere's adventures after reaching Lexington." Bull Cent Child Books

Lee, Martin. Paul Revere. Watts 1987 95p il lib bdg $10.40 (5 and up) **92**

1. United States—History—1775-1783, Revolution—Biography
ISBN 0-531-10312-9 LC 86-23362

"A First book"

This book "has a straightforward writing style that relates what's known of Revere's childhood, youth, and young adulthood. His silversmithing . . . , his political activities, and his famous ride are all described. While these broad essentials of Revere's life are common knowledge, Lee includes information that is less well known; for example, in Revere's later years he was a prosperous businessman who operated copper mills and bell foundries." Booklist

Includes bibliography

Robeson, Paul, 1898-1976

Greenfield, Eloise. Paul Robeson; illustrated by George Ford. Crowell 1975 32p il (Crowell biography) lib bdg $12.89 (2-5) **92**

1. Blacks—Biography
ISBN 0-690-00660-8 LC 74-13663

A biography of the black man who became a famous singer, actor, and spokesman for equal rights for his people

"This format and style are appealing to the beginning reader and useful for the high-interest-low-reading level that many teachers and librarians encounter." Child Book Rev Serv

Robinson, Jackie, 1919-1972

Adler, David A. Jackie Robinson: he was the first; written by David A. Adler; illustrated by Robert Casilla. Holiday House 1989 48p il (First biography) lib bdg $12.95; pa $4.95 (3-5) **92**

1. Baseball—Biography 2. Black athletes
ISBN 0-8234-0734-9 (lib bdg); 0-8234-0799-3 (pa) LC 88-23294

Traces the life of the talented and determined athlete who broke the color barrier in major league baseball in 1947 by joining the Brooklyn Dodgers

This biography is "clearly written, admiring but not adulatory, and succinct without being terse. . . . Adler does a good job in covering the highlights of Robinson's career and maintains a balance between facts about that career and about Robinson's personal life; the information is accurate, the tone subdued, so that any tension and action speak the more volubly for themselves." Bull Cent Child Books

Robinson, Jackie, 1919-1972—*Continued*

Golenbock, Peter. Teammates; written by Peter Golenbock; designed and illustrated by Paul Bacon. Harcourt Brace Jovanovich 1990 unp il lib bdg $15.95; pa $5.95 (1-4) **92**

1. Reese, Pee Wee, 1919- 2. Brooklyn Dodgers (Baseball team) 3. Baseball—Biography 4. Black athletes

ISBN 0-15-200603-6 (lib bdg); 0-15-284285-3 (pa) LC 89-38166

"Gulliver books"

Describes the racial prejudice experienced by Jackie Robinson when he joined the Brooklyn Dodgers and became the first black player in Major League baseball and depicts the acceptance and support he received from his white teammate Pee Wee Reese

"Golenbock's bold and lucid style distills this difficult issue, and brings a dramatic tale vividly to life. Bacon's spare, nostalgic watercolors, in addition to providing fond glimpses of baseball lore, present a haunting portrait of one man's isolation. Historic photographs of the major characters add interest and a touch of stark reality to an unusual story, beautifully rendered." Publ Wkly

Scott, Richard. Jackie Robinson. Chelsea House 1987 110p (Black Americans of achievement) lib bdg $16.95; pa $9.95 (5 and up) **92**

1. Baseball—Biography 2. Black athletes

ISBN 1-55546-609-5 (lib bdg); 0-7910-0200-4 (pa) LC 87-745

"The life of Jackie Robinson, the first black baseball player in the National League, is presented along with black-and-white photographs depicting events from his successes. A forward by Coretta Scott King and a chronology, along with the accurate and smooth flowing text, provide insights into Robinson's personal and professional struggles to succeed." SLJ

Includes bibliography

Roosevelt, Eleanor, 1884-1962

Faber, Doris. Eleanor Roosevelt: first lady of the world; illustrated by Donna Ruff. Viking Kestrel 1985 57p il (Women of our time) lib bdg $10.95; Puffin Bks. pa $13.95 (4 and up) **92**

1. Presidents—United States—Spouses

ISBN 0-670-80551-3 (lib bdg); 0-14-032103-9 (pa) LC 84-20861

A biography emphasizing the early years of Eleanor Roosevelt, who had enormous political influence and won love and respect as America's first lady

The author "manages to convey the basic events and experience of her subject's life in a clear, interesting and understanding manner." SLJ

Sasaki, Sadako, 1943-1955

Coerr, Eleanor. Sadako and the thousand paper cranes; paintings by Ronald Himler. Putnam 1977 64p il $13.95; Dell pa $2.75 (3-6) **92**

1. Leukemia 2. Atomic bomb—Physiological effect 3. Hiroshima (Japan)—Bombardment, 1945

ISBN 0-399-20520-9; 0-440-47465-5 (pa) LC 76-9872

"A story about a young girl of Hiroshima who died from leukemia ten years after the dropping of the atom bomb. Her dreams of being an outstanding runner are dimmed when she learns she has the fatal disease. But her spunk and bravery, symbolized in her efforts to have faith in the story of the golden crane, are beautifully portrayed by the author. Sadako was a real person for whom a statue has been erected in the Hiroshima Peace Park. Her legend has been alive to the Japanese for many years and this sensitive book now enables young Americans to share her story." Babbling Bookworm

Sequoyah, 1770?-1843

Cwiklik, Robert. Sequoyah and the Cherokee alphabet; written by Robert Cwiklik; introduction by Alvin M. Josephy, Jr.; illustrations by T. Lewis. Silver Burdett Press 1989 129p il (Alvin Josephy's biography ser. of American Indians) lib bdg $11.98; pa $7.95 (5 and up) **92**

1. Cherokee Indians

ISBN 0-382-09570-7 (lib bdg); 0-382-09759-9 (pa) LC 89-30737

A biography of the Cherokee Indian who invented a method for his people to write and read their own language

Includes bibliography

Singer, Isaac Bashevis, 1904-1991

Kresh, Paul. Isaac Bashevis Singer: the story of a storyteller; illustrated by Penrod Scofield. Dutton 1984 149p il (Jewish biography ser) $13.95 (6 and up) **92**

1. Authors, American

ISBN 0-525-67156-0 LC 84-10271

"Lodestar books"

The author "traces Singer's life from the shtetls of Poland, through the ghettos of Warsaw, to his life in the United States where he found literary acceptance and financial reward. . . . An author who received little notice or recognition until he was in his 40s, he eventually went on to receive the Nobel Prize for literature." Booklist

"Kresh gives full and balanced coverage to personal and literary aspects of Singer's life . . . writing in a straightforward, capable style. A divided bibliography of Singer's writings is provided." Bull Cent Child Books

Stevenson, James, 1929-

Stevenson, James. Higher on the door. Greenwillow Bks. 1987 unp il $11.75; lib bdg $11.88 (k-2) **92**

1. Authors, American 2. Illustrators
ISBN 0-688-06636-4; 0-688-06637-2 (lib bdg)
LC 86-14925

This is "Stevenson's recollection of growing up in a small town not too far from New York City." Booklist

"The vigor of the remembrance is in the paintings. The artist's strokes of color are unaffected and abstract: mere blots of paint represent children in one context and entire forests in another. There is humor and the tender irony of hindsight. . . . Stevenson touches on the color-filled moments of childhood that are at once particular and universal." Publ Wkly

Stevenson, James. July. Greenwillow Bks. 1990 unp il $12.95; lib bdg $12.88 (k-2) **92**

1. Authors, American 2. Illustrators
ISBN 0-688-08822-8; 0-688-08823-6 (lib bdg)
LC 88-37584

The author "looks back to when, as a boy, he and his brother happily spent the month of July with their grandparents, who lived near the beach." Booklist

"This book of gentle reminiscence combines past yet timeless joys into one perfect summer memory. . . . This lovingly executed book avoids heavy nostalgia by skillfully evoking universal pleasures of the season. Soft, evocative watercolors capture various moods with minimum detail but maximum emotional impact. With a few splashes and lines of color, Stevenson reveals the pure exuberance of racing bicycles along the boardwalk." SLJ

Stevenson, James. When I was nine. Greenwillow Bks. 1986 unp il $12.95; lib bdg $12.88 (k-2) **92**

1. Authors, American 2. Illustrators
ISBN 0-688-05942-2; 0-688-05943-0 (lib bdg)
LC 85-9777

"An autobiographical snippet from the prolific children's writer and cartoonist for The New Yorker. The illustrations are graceful watercolor washes—slightly faded, too, like memories. The spare text, about everyday life when he was a boy and then a special vacation trip to New Mexico, is wry and haunting." N Y Times Book Rev

Strauss, Levi, 1829-1902

Henry, Sondra. Everyone wears his name: a biography of Levi Strauss; [by] Sondra Henry and Emily Taitz. Dillon Press 1990 128p il (People in focus bk) lib bdg $12.95 (5 and up) **92**

1. Levi Strauss & Co. 2. Clothing trade
ISBN 0-87518-375-1 LC 87-32455

Traces the life of the immigrant Jewish peddler who went on to found Levi Strauss & Co., the world's first and largest manufacturer of denim jeans

"The authors set Strauss squarely within the milieu of nineteenth-century San Francisco, noting the impact of economic and political developments within the city, state, and nation. . . . A competent, thorough, and well-illustrated presentation." SLJ

Includes bibliography

Szold, Henrietta, 1860-1945

Kustanowitz, Shulamit E. Henrietta Szold: Israel's helping hand; by Shulamit Kustanowitz; illustrated by Robert Masheris. Viking 1990 58p il (Women of our time) lib bdg $10.95 (4 and up) **92**

1. Zionism
ISBN 0-670-82518-2 LC 89-70656

"A first-generation American, Szold organized what became the first official night school in the U.S. so that immigrants could learn English and still put in a day's work. She also founded Hadassah, an organization of American women dedicated to promoting health services in what was then Palestine. With the rise of nazism, Szold was instrumental in resettling as many Jewish youngsters in the Holy Land as could escape Europe." Booklist

"Kustanowitz captures Szold's indomitable spirit, and adeptly integrates necessary background on Judaism and the Holocaust into the smooth-flowing text." SLJ

Tecumseh, Shawnee Chief, 1768-1813

Shorto, Russell. Tecumseh and the dream of an American Indian nation; written by Russell Shorto; introduction by Alvin M. Josephy, Jr.; illustrations by Tim Sisco. Silver Burdett Press 1989 123p il maps (Alvin Josephy's biography ser. of American Indians) lib bdg $11.98; pa $7.95 (5 and up) **92**

1. Shawnee Indians
ISBN 0-382-09569-3 (lib bdg); 0-382-09758-0 (pa)
LC 88-32656

A biography of the Shawnee warrior, orator, and leader who united a confederacy of Indians in an effort to save Indian land from the advance of white soldiers and settlers

Includes bibliography

Thoreau, Henry David, 1817-1862

Burleigh, Robert. A man named Thoreau; illustrated by Lloyd Bloom. Atheneum Pubs. 1985 31p il lib bdg $12.95 (3-5) **92**

1. Authors, American
ISBN 0-689-31122-2 LC 85-7947

"An intriguing blend of biographical fact and philosophical summary, this has more substance than its picture-book format might imply. The author has smoothly interwoven quotes from Walden, particularly, into a pithy development of Thoreau's thinking there. . . . Bloom's subtly valued pencil drawings facing every page of text lend further dimension. The list of important dates and bibliography are unusual features in a book for this audience." Bull Cent Child Books

Thoreau, Henry David, 1817-1862 — *Continued*

Stern, Philip Van Doren. Henry David Thoreau: writer and rebel. Crowell 1972 183p $12.95 (5 and up) **92**

1. Authors, American
ISBN 0-690-37715-0 LC 74-139108

This biography follows the growth of Thoreau as thinker and writer, placing him within the distinguished intellectual circle of early nineteenth century America

This book "is clearly and succinctly written and supported by well selected incidents and quotations. [The author's] balanced discussion of both Thoreau's life and his works convincingly portrays a man whose thoughts are relevant to all ages." Libr J

Includes bibliography

Trenary, Jill

Trenary, Jill. Time of my life: Jill Trenary; the day I skated for the gold; by Jill Trenary with Dale Mitch; photographs by Dino Ricci. Simon & Schuster Bks. for Young Readers 1989 60p il hardcover o.p. paperback available $5.95 (4 and up) **92**

1. Ice skating—Biography 2. Olympic games 3. Women athletes
ISBN 0-671-73348-6 (pa) LC 89-30554

Photographs and text follow American figure skater Jill Trenary's final day of competition at the 1988 Olympic Winter Games, where she placed fourth out of thirty-one competitors from around the world

"While a little too perky, Jill Trenary's story is direct, focused and as informative about the world of figure-skating as it is about the skater herself. . . . She provides plenty of technical detail, shows generosity to her peers, and is candid about her own performance. . . . Plenty of colorful action shots add glamour and excitement." Bull Cent Child Books

Truth, Sojourner, d. 1883

Ferris, Jeri. Walking the road to freedom: a story about Sojourner Truth; illustrations by Peter E. Hanson. Carolrhoda Bks. 1988 64p il (Carolrhoda creative minds bk) lib bdg $9.95; pa $4.95 (3-5) **92**

1. Black women 2. Feminism 3. Abolitionists
ISBN 0-87614-318-4 (lib bdg); 0-87614-505-5 (pa) LC 87-18277

"Truth, born into slavery in New York in about 1797, survived several wrenching sales as a child. Securing her freedom, she determined to 'walk up and down the land, telling others about God's goodness.' She sang and spoke out against slavery and in support of women's rights throughout the Midwest, becoming well known and widely respected. . . . Hanson's [illustrations] are more impressionistic, with muted backgrounds." Booklist

Ortiz, Victoria. Sojourner Truth, a self-made woman. Lippincott 1974 157p il lib bdg $11.89 (6 and up) **92**

1. Black women 2. Feminism 3. Abolitionists
ISBN 0-397-32134-1 LC 73-22290

The author "goes far beyond the well-known 'Ain't I a Woman?' speech to present evidence of this woman's understanding of people and institutions and her uncanny ability to transmit that understanding to others. Unfortunately there is no bibliography, but the fine writing style and insightful portrayal make this valuable for Black studies and women's rights collections." SLJ

Tubman, Harriet, 1815?-1913

Ferris, Jeri. Go free or die: a story about Harriet Tubman; illustrations by Karen Ritz. Carolrhoda Bks. 1988 63p il (Carolrhoda creative minds bk) hardcover o.p. paperback available $4.95 (3-5) **92**

1. Black women 2. Underground railroad
ISBN 0-87614-504-7 (pa) LC 87-18279

This is "the story of Harriet Tubman, born a slave in Maryland in 1820. Fiercely determined to 'go free or die,' Tubman, aided by the Quakers, mastered the intricate maneuvering of the Underground Railroad, and from 1850 to 1861 made 19 trips leading more than 300 slaves to freedom, never losing one. Using a clear direct style, Ferris does not dwell on the brutal injustices . . . but rather on [her] against-all-odds perseverance to fight for equal rights. Ritz' illustrations have a haunting antique-photo quality." Booklist

Verne, Jules, 1828-1905

Quackenbush, Robert M. Who said there's no man on the moon? a story of Jules Verne; [by] Robert Quackenbush. Prentice-Hall 1985 36p il lib bdg $11.95 (2-4) **92**

1. Authors, French
ISBN 0-671-66848-X LC 84-22314

A biography of the nineteenth-century author whose novels of science fiction adventure predicted space travel, the submarine, and other modern achievements

"Quackenbush writes with a light touch that will grab readers right from the beginning. The numerous monochromatic wash drawings expand the humor and extend the story line. Actually, little is known about Verne's life, and the author illustrates this through a continuing interview between a reporter and Verne, which runs at the bottom of the page in captioned cartoon drawings." Booklist

Washington, George, 1732-1799

Adler, David A. A picture book of George Washington; written by David A. Adler; illustrated by John & Alexandra Wallner. Holiday House 1989 unp il lib bdg $13.95; pa $5.95 (1-3) **92**

1. Presidents—United States
ISBN 0-8234-0732-2 (lib bdg); 0-8234-0800-0 (pa) LC 88-16384

"Straightforward and informative, the brief text moves easily from Washington's childhood, when 'his favorite subject was arithmetic,' through his early career as a surveyor and later years as revolutionary and President. The sweetness of the book is greatly enhanced by John and Alexandra Wallner's gentle, colorful and sometimes

Washington, George, 1732-1799—*Continued*
amusing illustrations. . . . This book is an excellent resource for a first or second grade classroom or for library use." N Y Times Book Rev

D'Aulaire, Ingri. George Washington; by Ingri & Edgar Parin d'Aulaire. Doubleday 1936 unp il $13.95; pa $8.95 (2-4) **92**

1. Presidents—United States
ISBN 0-385-07306-2; 0-385-24107-0 (pa)
LC 36-27417

"Using their usual technique of lithographing on stone the d'Aulaires have done a gay, stylized picture book in five colors showing Washington's life. Familiar incidents have been chosen. The most appealing small animals find their way into many of the pictures. The text is a simple recounting of his life." Booklist

Meltzer, Milton. George Washington and the birth of our nation. Watts 1986 188p il maps lib bdg $13.90 (5 and up) **92**

1. Presidents—United States
ISBN 0-531-10253-X LC 86-9222

A biography of our first President, from his growing-up years in Virginia to his death at Mount Vernon

This "is a competently written and carefully documented book, well illustrated with reproductions of historic art, manuscript pages, and maps." Bull Cent Child Books

Includes bibliographic references

West, Benjamin, 1738-1820

Henry, Marguerite. Benjamin West and his cat Grimalkin; by Marguerite Henry and Wesley Dennis. Macmillan 1987 c1947 147p il $12.95 (4 and up) **92**

1. Painters, American 2. Cats 3. Society of Friends
ISBN 0-02-743660-8 LC 86-28658

A reissue of the title first published 1947 by Bobbs-Merrill

"As a small boy, Quaker-born Benjamin West, known as the 'father of American painting,' wanted so much to paint that he made his own brushes from his cat's tail, made his colors from earth and clay, and used boards for paper. This is a well-written story, touched with humor and tenderness, of Benjamin's boyhood at his father's inn near Philadelphia, of his early experiences and training in painting, and of his adventures with his remarkable cat, Grimalkin." Booklist

Wilder, Laura Ingalls, 1867-1957

Wilder, Laura Ingalls. West from home; letters of Laura Ingalls Wilder to Almanzo Wilder, San Francisco, 1915; edited by Roger Lea MacBride; historical setting by Margot Patterson Doss. Harper & Row 1974 124p il $13.95; lib bdg $13.89; pa $3.50 (6 and up) **92**

1. San Francisco (Calif.)—Description 2. Authors, American 3. Women authors
ISBN 0-06-024110-1; 0-06-024111-X (lib bdg); 0-06-440081-6 (pa) LC 73-14342

This collection is "edited from letters sent to her beloved husband while Laura spent two months in late 1915 visiting their daughter and immersing herself in the sights of bustling San Francisco and the exciting Panama-Pacific Exposition. Wilder readers of all ages will lose themselves in this trip—the adults with nostalgia and wholesome pleasure, the youth with wonder and awe over the sights vividly described in her inimitable combination of homespun literary and journalistic styles." Child Book Rev Serv

Williams, Daniel Hale

Patterson, Lillie. Sure hands, strong heart: the life of Daniel Hale Williams. Abingdon Press 1981 159p il $8.95 (4 and up) **92**

1. Physicians 2. Blacks—Biography
ISBN 0-687-40700-1 LC 81-2660

A biography of the black surgeon who, among other achievements, was the first to perform open heart surgery

"Patterson selects details significant to a young audience without sacrificing important issues. . . . The invented dialogue is occasionally wooden, but the book's readability, its scope and its humanity should appeal to a wide audience. David Scott Brown's full-page pen-and-ink drawings are pleasing and show accurate and sensitive portraiture." SLJ

Includes bibliography

Yeager, Chuck, 1923-

Levinson, Nancy Smiler. Chuck Yeager: the man who broke the sound barrier; a science biography. Walker & Co. 1988 133p il $13.95; lib bdg $14.85 (5 and up) **92**

1. Air pilots
ISBN 0-8027-6781-8; 0-8027-6799-0 (lib bdg)
LC 87-25431

"Well-written text describes the boyhood, war experiences, years as a test pilot, and goals and ambitions of the then Air Force captain who first broke the sound barrier." Sci Child

Includes glossary and bibliography

Zaharias, Babe Didrikson, 1911-1956

Knudson, R. Rozanne. Babe Didrikson: athlete of the century; by R.R. Knudson; illustrated by Ted Lewin. Viking Kestrel 1985 57p il (Women of our time) o.p.; Puffin Bks. paperback available $3.95 (4 and up) **92**

1. Women athletes
ISBN 0-14-032095-4 (pa) LC 84-17411

A biography, emphasizing the early years, of Babe Didrikson, who broke records in golf, track and field, and other sports, at a time when there were few opportunities for female athletes

"Knudson comes forth with all sorts of little-known information about one of the greatest athletes of this century. The book's lively, contemporary style will encourage young readers' respect for and admiration of the exuberant Babe. A pleasant addition to any library." Child Book Rev Serv

929 Genealogy, names, insignia

Cooper, Kay

Where did you get those eyes? a guide to discovering your family history; illustrated by Anthony Accardo. Walker & Co. 1988 68p il (Walker's American history ser. for young people) $13.95; lib bdg $14.85 (5 and up) **929**

1. Genealogy
ISBN 0-8027-6802-4; 0-8027-6803-2 (lib bdg)
LC 88-149

An "introduction to the forms and processes involved in researching one's family history. After a short explanation of why family history is both interesting and educational, Cooper outlines the procedures often followed. . . . She ends with pieces written by young people about the results of their genealogical searches, followed by a brief directory of official information sources and an index." SLJ

Perl, Lila

The great ancestor hunt; the fun of finding out who you are; drawings by Erika Weihs; illustrated with photographs. Clarion Bks. 1989 104p il $15.95 (5 and up) **929**

1. Genealogy
ISBN 0-89919-745-0 LC 88-36211

The author "weaves the how-to of genealogy with a historical perspective on immigration. All the basics are covered: drawing an ancestry chart, conducting interviews with relatives, finding family memorabilia, and, for those who wish to continue their quest, writing away for documentation. The format is also a plus. Interesting black-and-white photos alternate with charts, diagrams, and a few (softly executed) drawings by Erika Weihs." Booklist

Includes bibliography

929.4 Personal names

Lee, Mary Price

Last names first; —and some first names too; by Lee, Mary Price and Lee, Richard S.; illustrated by Weber, Debora. Westminster Press 1985 119p il $11.95 (5 and up) **929.4**

1. Names, Personal
ISBN 0-664-32719-2 LC 84-20860

Discusses various kinds of personal names such as nicknames and names after marriage and describes how names changed as they traveled overseas and were passed down through generations. Includes a dictionary of common last names and their meanings

Although the authors "concentrate on the West, African and Eastern customs and names are also discussed. The checklist of steps to take in researching family names is well-organized and thorough. Anecdotal material discusses amusing nicknames, spies' code names, aliases and the way technology is effecting the use of names and numbers for personal identity. . . . The bibliography lists both magazine articles and books on geneology and names." SLJ

Meltzer, Milton, 1915-

A book about names; drawings by Mischa Richter. Crowell 1984 128p il $13.95; lib bdg $13.89 (5 and up) **929.4**

1. Names, Personal 2. Nicknames
ISBN 0-690-04380-5; 0-690-04381-3 (lib bdg)
LC 83-45241

"In which custom, tradition, law, myth, history, folklore, foolery, legend, fashion, nonsense, symbol, taboo help explain how we got our names and what they mean." Title page

"A delight for browsing. . . . Meltzer goes all over the world for his information, back and forth through history. He looks at the naming practices of Jews, native Americans, Anglo-Saxons, Chinese, Christians, famous people, the rich and the poor." Booklist

Shankle, George Earlie

American nicknames; their origin and significance. 2nd ed. Wilson, H.W. 1955 524p $38 **929.4**

1. Nicknames 2. Names, Personal—United States 3. Names, Geographical—United States
ISBN 0-8242-0004-7 LC 55-5038

First published 1937

"Not limited to nicknames of persons, but includes also those applied to places, institutions, or objects, arranged by real names with cross references from nicknames. Information under the real names includes some explanation of the nicknames and their origin, and gives references to sources of information in footnotes." Sheehy. Guide to Ref Books. 10th edition

929.9 Flags

Crampton, W. G. (William G.)

Flag; written by William Crampton. Knopf 1989 63p il (Eyewitness bks) $13.95; lib bdg $14.99 (4 and up) **929.9**

1. Flags
ISBN 0-394-82255-2; 0-394-92255-7 (lib bdg)
LC 88-27174

A photographic essay about flags from countries all over the world and such special flags as signal flags for ships and boats, flags for special festivals and sports, political flags and coats of arms. Also includes information about the meaning of shapes and colors on flags

Haban, Rita D.

How proudly they wave; flags of the fifty states. Lerner Publs. 1989 111p il lib bdg $16.95 (4 and up) **929.9**

1. Flags—United States
ISBN 0-8225-1799-X LC 89-2302

"Haban presents full-color pictures of the 50 state flags. . . . Two-page descriptions explain who designed the flag, what the design means, and when each flag was officially adopted. . . . A glossary lists flag-related terms, and an accompanying diagram shows the parts of a flag. An enormously useful reference source for both school and public librarians." Booklist

930 The ancient world to ca. 499 A.D.

Briquebec, John

The ancient world; from the earliest civilizations to the Roman Empire. Warwick Press 1990 c1989 47p il maps (Historical atlas ser) lib bdg $13.90 (4 and up) **930**

1. History, Ancient
ISBN 0-531-19073-0 LC 89-24915

First published 1989 in the United Kingdom

This book "introduces the people of the fertile crescent, China and Greece, the early Americas, and Australia, tracing their history and showing how they conducted their lives. There is also an opening chapter on archaeologists that explains how they do their exacting work." Booklist

"Beautifully illustrated, nearly every page is filled with color. . . . Each two-page layout has one column of text, while each illustration or map is accompanied by explanations ranging from one or two sentences to one or two paragraphs." SLJ

Includes glossary

Gallant, Roy A.

Lost cities. Watts 1985 64p il maps lib bdg $10.40 (4 and up) **930**

1. Cities and towns, Ruined, extinct, etc. 2. Archeology 3. Civilization, Ancient
ISBN 0-531-04914-0 LC 84-17422

"A First book"

"The rediscoveries of five ancient cities—Crete, Mycenae, Troy, Pompeii and Chichen Itza—are highlighted in this . . . introduction to archaeology. Gallant's emphasis is on the various information and methods used by the archaeologists to pinpoint the sites. . . . The book is visually appealing with bold type, clear maps and high quality black-and-white photographs and reproductions. An objective, well-researched overview which brings alive the romance and serendipity of archaeology." SLJ

Includes bibliography

930.1 Archaeology

Anderson, Joan

From map to museum; uncovering mysteries of the past; photographed by George Ancona; introduction by David Hurst Thomas. Morrow Junior Bks. 1988 63p il maps $12.95; lib bdg $12.88 (5 and up) **930.1**

1. Indians of North America—Antiquities 2. Archeology
ISBN 0-688-06914-2; 0-688-06915-0 (lib bdg) LC 87-31307

"An enjoyable, informative photo essay about the exploration of the site of a Spanish mission off the coast of Georgia enhances the reader's understanding of the relationship between museums and archaeology. Includes an introduction by the archaeologist responsible for the find." Sci Child

Includes glossary

Early humans; [project editor, Phil Wilkinson; editorial consultant, Nick Merriman; special photography by Dave King] Knopf 1989 63p il maps (Eyewitness bks) $13.95; lib bdg $14.99 (4 and up) **930.1**

1. Man, Prehistoric 2. Civilization, Ancient
ISBN 0-394-82257-9; 0-394-92257-3 (lib bdg) LC 88-13431

Text and photographs present a description of early humans: their origins; their tools and weapons; how they hunted and foraged for food; and the role of family life, money, religion, and magic

"The book is beautifully illustrated, with a paragraph of text at the beginning of each two-page section and an explanatory caption for each artifact pictured. The 25 sections range in topic from the toolmakers to the first artists to bronzeworking. In addition, there is a liberal sprinkling of small drawings showing early humans using many of the artifacts pictured." Sci Books Films

Hackwell, W. John

Digging to the past: excavations in ancient lands. Scribner 1986 50p il $13.95 (4 and up) **930.1**

1. Archeology 2. Civilization, Ancient
ISBN 0-684-18692-6 LC 86-13115

The author "describes the painstaking process of excavating clues to the past. He sets his story in the Middle East, and outlines the participants, the hardships, the excitement, and the satisfaction. . . . The book includes archeological vocabulary defined in context . . . and words from the local culture surrounding the dig." Appraisal

"Although this has the horizontal shape of a picture book and is chock-full of handsome full-color and black-and-white illustrations, Hackwell's introduction to archaeology is actually quite sophisticated." Booklist

Lauber, Patricia, 1924-

Tales mummies tell; illustrated with photographs. Crowell 1985 118p il $12.95; lib bdg $12.89 (5 and up) **930.1**

1. Mummies 2. Archeology 3. Civilization
ISBN 0-690-04388-0; 0-690-04389-9 (lib bdg) LC 83-46172

"Lauber describes the various ways, intentional or accidental, that animals and human beings have become mummies, and she discusses the various ways (carbon-14 dating, x-rays, analysis of body tissue and stomach contents) that scientists use to establish facts about the individual or the culture or changes over the centuries. Clearly written and well-organized, this is an informative and eminently readable text." Bull Cent Child Books

Includes bibliography

932 Egypt to 640 A.D.

Bendick, Jeanne, 1919-

Egyptian tombs. Watts 1989 64p il lib bdg $11.40 (4 and up) **932**

1. Tombs 2. Pyramids 3. Egypt—Antiquities
ISBN 0-531-10462-1 LC 87-27918

"A First book"

The author discusses the design, purpose, and excavation of the pyramids of ancient Egypt, the Egyptians' beliefs about death, how mummies were made, and some legends about the pyramids

"Full-color artwork enlivens the pages, and there are numerous color and black-and-white photos, many bordered in orange. Pronunciations are included in the text (though this does interrupt the flow of the narrative)." Booklist

Includes glossary

Cohen, Daniel, 1936-

Ancient Egypt; illustrated by Gary A. Lippincott. Doubleday 1989 45p il $10.95; lib bdg $11.99 (3-6) **932**

1. Egypt—History 2. Egypt—Civilization
ISBN 0-385-24586-6; 0-385-24587-4 (lib bdg)
LC 88-12146

This "volume consists of short essays on the art, religion, history, geography, agriculture and way of life of the ancient Egyptians." Publ Wkly

"In his brief overview covering more than 3,000 years, Cohen has managed to bring a coherent unity to his topic. . . . Readers will find a clear, direct text combined with oversized illustrations that brings a lively immediacy to the subjects." SLJ

Hart, George, 1945-

Ancient Egypt; written by George Hart. Knopf 1990 63p il (Eyewitness bks) $13.95; lib bdg $14.99 (4 and up) **932**

1. Egypt—Civilization 2. Egypt—Antiquities
ISBN 0-679-80742-X; 0-679-90742-4 (lib bdg)
LC 90-4106

A photo essay on ancient Egypt and the people who lived there, documented through the mummies, pottery, weapons, and other objects they left behind. Describes their society, religion, obsession with the afterlife, and methods of mummification

"Dazzles the eye with hundreds of color photographs and illustrations. Each two-page spread treats one particular aspect of the civilization. . . . All items pictured are identified with brief captions and clear definitions." SLJ

Exploring the past: ancient Egypt; illustrated by Stephen Biesty. Harcourt Brace Jovanovich 1989 c1988 64p il map $13.95 (4 and up) **932**

1. Egypt—History 2. Egypt—Civilization
ISBN 0-15-200449-1 LC 88-30065

"Gulliver books"

First published 1988 in the United Kingdom

Presents an overview of life in ancient Egypt discussing such topics as the Pharaoh, religion, mummification and afterlife, the role of scribes and craftsmen, home and family, and common occupations

"Overall, the book is worth acquiring on the basis of the illustrations alone. The text, though brief, is useful and well written. As an invitation to young readers to explore ancient Egypt further, the book succeeds nicely." Sci Books Films

937 Roman Empire

Corbishley, Mike

Ancient Rome; [by] Michael Corbishley. Facts on File 1989 96p il maps (Cultural atlas for young people) $17.95 (5 and up) **937**

1. Rome—Civilization 2. Rome—Antiquities
ISBN 0-8160-1970-3 LC 88-31687

"An Equinox book"

Text, maps, illustrations, charts, tables, and chronologies depict the history, society, and political life of ancient Rome and its vast empire

For a fuller review see: Booklist, Apr. 1, 1990

Includes glossary and bibliographic references

Goor, Ron, 1940-

Pompeii: exploring a Roman ghost town; [by] Ron and Nancy Goor. Crowell 1986 118p il maps $13.95; lib bdg $13.89 (5 and up) **937**

1. Pompeii (Ancient city) 2. Excavations (Archeology)
ISBN 0-690-04515-8; 00690-04516-6 (lib bdg)
LC 85-47895

"A concise overview of the social, political, cultural, and religious life in the ancient Roman city of Pompeii that was destroyed and preserved by the eruption of Mt. Vesuvius in A.D. 79. Rediscovery in 1748, Pompeii offers a unique glimpse of everyday life in a Roman city." Soc Educ

Humphrey, Kathryn Long

Pompeii; nightmare at midday. Watts 1990 64p il maps lib bdg $10.90 (4 and up) **937**

1. Pompeii (Ancient city) 2. Excavations (Archeology)
ISBN 0-531-10895-3 LC 89-39711

"A First book"

Describes the destruction of Pompeii by the eruption of Mount Vesuvius in 79 A.D. and modern efforts to excavate and reconstruct the site of the ancient city

"This will be useful for classes studying ancient history, Italy, or volcanoes." Booklist

Includes bibliography

James, Simon

Ancient Rome; written by Simon James. Knopf 1990 62p il (Eyewitness bks) $13.95; lib bdg $14.99 (4 and up) **937**

1. Rome—Civilization 2. Rome—Antiquities
ISBN 0-679-80741-1; 0-679-90741-6 (lib bdg) LC 90-4111

A photo essay documenting ancient Rome and the people who lived there as revealed through the many artifacts they left behind, including shields, swords, tools, toys, cosmetics, and jewelry

Mulvihill, Margaret

Roman forts. Gloucester Press 1990 32p il maps (History highlights) lib bdg $11.90 (5 and up) **937**

1. Fortification 2. Rome—History, Military
ISBN 0-531-17201-5 LC 89-28778

Examines the structure and defenses of an ancient Roman fort, Roman military life, and the campaigns waged by the Roman Empire against its enemies

"Visualized in colorful, realistic illustrations that splash across the pages and complemented by photographs of Roman relics, the chapters also touch on religion, government, and citizenship. The final sections consider the empire's decline and its remaining traces today; a date chart and a glossary round out this informative presentation." Booklist

938 Greece to 323 A.D.

Coolidge, Olivia Ensor, 1908-

The golden days of Greece; by Olivia Coolidge; illustrated by Enrico Arno. Crowell 1968 211p il lib bdg $14.89 (4-6) **938**

1. Greece—History 2. Civilization, Greek
ISBN 0-690-04795-9 LC 68-21599

"Highlights of Greek history combined with anecdotes depicting the exploits of gods and men and accounts describing the lives and accomplishments of Greek philosophers, artists, poets, and playwrights provide a lively, illuminating introduction to ancient Greek civilization." Booklist

Includes glossary

Odijk, Pamela, 1942-

The Greeks. Silver Burdett Press 1989 47p il map (Ancient world) lib bdg $16.98 (5 and up) **938**

1. Greece—History 2. Civilization, Greek
ISBN 0-382-09884-6 LC 89-33859

Discusses the civilization of ancient Greece, including the hunting, medicine, clothing, religion, laws, legends, and recreation

This book "will prove just the thing at report time. The information . . . is arranged the way young researchers like it. . . . Each topic gets a page or so, and the information is clearly and concisely presented. Especially nice are the color photographs and historical reproductions." Booklist

Includes glossary

940.1 Europe—Early history to 1453

Lyttle, Richard B.

Land beyond the river; Europe in the age of migration; with illustrations by the author. Atheneum Pubs. 1986 175p il maps $14.95 (6 and up) **940.1**

1. Europe—History
ISBN 0-689-31199-0 LC 85-28758

"The author aims to show how Europe was affected by Huns, Goths, Vandals, Anglo-Saxons, Vikings, Mongols, and other migrating groups." Voice Youth Advocates

Includes bibliography

940.53 World War II, 1939-1945

Leckie, Robert

The story of World War II. Random House 1964 193p il maps lib bdg $13.99 (5 and up) **940.53**

1. World War, 1939-1945
ISBN 0-394-90295-5 LC 64-21721

"Landmark books"

"The author, who served in the Pacific as a member of the First Marine Division, tells of World War II from the rise of Adolph Hitler to the surrender of Japan." Libr J

The author "has written a very good [book] on World War II for younger readers. The text is exciting, and the maps are particularly good—handsome and easy to follow. . . . His treatment of the war itself is simplified somewhat—as it must be in a book of this length—yet it more than adequately covers the main actions in both the Pacific and European theaters. . . . The photographs are extensive and well chosen." N Y Times Book Rev

Snyder, Louis Leo, 1907-

World War II; by Louis L. Snyder. rev ed. Watts 1981 90p il maps lib bdg $10.40 (4 and up) **940.53**

1. World War, 1939-1945
ISBN 0-531-04333-9 LC 81-5021

"A First book"

First published 1958 with title: The first book of World War II

This book discusses the causes, conduct, battles, personalities, and effects of World War II

Includes glossary

940.54 World War II, 1939-1945 (Military conduct of the war)

Abells, Chana Byers

The children we remember; photographs from the Archives of Yad Vashem, the Holocaust Martyrs' and Heroes' Remembrance Authority, Jerusalem, Israel. Greenwillow Bks. 1986 unp il $9.95; lib bdg $10.88 (3-6) **940.54**

1. Holocaust, Jewish (1933-1945)—Pictorial works
ISBN 0-688-06371-3; 0-688-06372-1 (lib bdg)
LC 85-24876

Text and photographs briefly describe the fate of Jewish children after the Nazis began to control their lives

"This is a book of few words, assuming some background knowledge of World War II and the Holocaust. And in this case, less is more, for the carefully selected photos dominate the unobtrusive statements describing scenes of children helping each other, children dying, children surviving. In acknowledging, along with the book jacket, that this is 'a story that must be told to all of today's children,' one also hopes there is an adult nearby to help share the shock of scenes like the one in which a soldier is shooting a mother and her baby." Bull Cent Child Books

Bliven, Bruce, 1916-

The story of D-Day: June 6, 1944; illustrated by Albert Orbaan. Random House 1956 180p il map lib bdg $8.99 (5 and up) **940.54**

1. Normandy (France), Attack on, 1944
ISBN 0-394-90362-5 LC 56-5458
"Landmark books"

An account of the planning and resources of the Allied invasion of Normandy which was the turning point of the Second World War, and of the brave men who implemented it

"A brief, dramatic account . . . recommended for reluctant older readers." Hodges. Books for Elem Sch Libr

Chaikin, Miriam, 1928-

A nightmare in history; the Holocaust 1933-1945. Clarion Bks. 1987 150p il $14.95 (5 and up) **940.54**

1. Holocaust, Jewish (1933-1945)
ISBN 0-89919-461-3 LC 86-17617

Traces the history of anti-semitism from biblical times through the twelve years of the Nazi era, 1933-1945 and describes Hitler's plans to annihilate European Jews by focusing on the Warsaw Ghetto and the Auschwitz-Birkenau concentration camps

"With her simple, elegant style, the widely praised writer on Jewish themes turns to the hardest subject of all. Her contribution is unique, both as a study of Hitler, . . . and as an exploration . . . of how anti-Semitism began." Publ Wkly

Includes bibliography

Davis, Daniel S.

Behind barbed wire: the imprisonment of Japanese Americans during World War II. Dutton 1982 166p il $15.95 (5 and up) **940.54**

1. Japanese Americans—Evacuation and relocation, 1942-1945 2. World War, 1939-1945—United States
ISBN 0-525-26320-9 LC 81-3126

"The author points to a history of anti-Asian feeling in America as background to a sensitive, well-organized examination of the incarceration of some 120,000 Japanese and Japanese Americans in U.S. internment camps during World War II. . . . Davis describes conditions in the camps as well as the difficulties the inmates encountered reentering society." Booklist

Includes bibliography

Finkelstein, Norman H.

Remember not to forget; a memory of the Holocaust; illustrations by Lois and Lars Hokanson. Watts 1985 31p il lib bdg $10.90 (3-5) **940.54**

1. Holocaust, Jewish (1933-1945)
ISBN 0-531-04892-6 LC 84-17315

"This spare, starkly illustrated book explains what the Holocaust was and how it is remembered on Yom Hashoa, Holocaust Remembrance Day. The explanation reaches back to the explusion of the Jews from Jerusalem in A.D. 70 and describes how Jews, strangers in many lands became targets of anti-Semitism, which culminated in the systematic murder of six million by the Nazis in World War II. The tone is straightforward and matter-of-fact. Black-and-white woodcuts accompany the text with somber scenes reflective of the narrative. A useful explanation for younger readers, especially the non-Jews among them." Booklist

Graff, Stewart

The story of World War II. Dutton 1978 88p il maps $10.95 (4-6) **940.54**

1. World War, 1939-1945
ISBN 0-525-40355-8 LC 77-7522

This book describes "Hitler's invasion of Poland, his march on Russia, the opening of the Pacific theater with Japan's attack on Pearl Harbor, the North Atlantic sea battles, the North African front, etc.—without getting bogged down in sideline detail. With black-and-white war photographs and an index for easy access." Booklist

Humble, Richard, 1945-

U-boat. Watts 1990 32p il map (Fighting ships) lib bdg $11.90 (4 and up) **940.54**

1. World War, 1939-1945—Naval operations 2. World War, 1939-1945—Atlantic Ocean 3. Submarines
ISBN 0-531-14023-7 LC 89-35888

A brief history of German submarine warfare during World War II and the measures taken by the Allies to combat the U-boats

"The art of illustrating nonfiction for young readers is well-demonstrated here; full-color sketches show action scenes, while cut-away drawings clearly and correctly depict the interior of the U-boat. Interspersed with the drawings are fascinating photographs from the Imperial

Humble, Richard, 1945-—*Continued*
War Museum." SLJ

Includes glossary

Marrin, Albert, 1936-

Victory in the Pacific. Atheneum Pubs. 1983 217p il map $13.95 (6 and up) **940.54**

1. World War, 1939-1945—Naval operations 2. World War, 1939-1945—Pacific Ocean

ISBN 0-689-30948-1 LC 82-6707

"From the attack on Pearl Harbor to Japan's surrender the book follows major battles fought by the Navy and the Marines in the Pacific. Fast-paced accounts of Doolittle's raid on Tokyo and the air, land, and sea action at Midway, Guadalcanal, Iwo Jima, and Okinawa give a broad, dramatic overview of Japanese and American strategies." Horn Book

Includes bibliography

Maruki, Toshi, 1912-

Hiroshima no pika; words and pictures by Toshi Maruki. Lothrop, Lee & Shepard Bks. 1982 c1980 unp il $13 **940.54**

1. Hiroshima (Japan)—Bombardment, 1945 2. World War, 1939-1945—Japan

ISBN 0-688-01297-3 LC 82-15365

First published 1980 in Japan

"Impressionistic paintings accompany a realistic account of one child's suffering on the day the atomic bomb was dropped on Hiroshima." Booklist

"The publisher suggests that the book is suitable for twelve-year-olds and up, but twelve-years-olds do not read picture books on their own. I would use this book with grades two and up, and it could also be used with even younger children. . . . Other adults who have read the book to eight-year-olds also report no nightmares, just feelings of deep sorrow. I would not suggest reading the book to large groups of children, however, unless there was a great deal of prior discussion and mood-setting." Interracial Books Child Bull

Meltzer, Milton, 1915-

Never to forget: the Jews of the Holocaust. Harper & Row 1976 217p maps lib bdg $14.89; Dell pa $2.50 (6 and up) **940.54**

1. Holocaust, Jewish (1933-1945)

ISBN 0-06-024175-6 (lib bdg); 0-440-96070-3 (pa) LC 75-25409

"The mass murder of six million Jews by the Nazis during World War II is the subject of this compelling history. Interweaving background information, chilling statistics, individual accounts and newspaper reports, it provides an excellent introduction to its subject." Interracial Books Child Bull

Includes bibliography

Rescue: the story of how Gentiles saved Jews in the Holocaust. Harper & Row 1988 168p maps $12.95; lib bdg $12.89 (6 and up) **940.54**

1. World War, 1939-1945—Jews 2. Holocaust, Jewish (1933-1945)

ISBN 0-06-024209-4; 0-06-024210-8 (lib bdg) LC 87-47816

A recounting drawn from historic source material of the many individual acts of heroism performed by righteous gentiles who sought to thwart the extermination of the Jews during the Holocaust

"This is an excellent portrayal of a difficult topic. Meltzer manages to both explain without accusing, and to laud without glorifying. The reader does not forget that the heroes, victims and villains were real people. The discussion of the complicated relations between countries are clear, but not simplistic. An impressive aspect of this book is its lack of didacticism." Voice Youth Advocates

Includes bibliography

Morimoto, Junko

My Hiroshima. Viking 1990 unp il $12.95 (2-4) **940.54**

1. Hiroshima (Japan)—Bombardment, 1945 2. World War, 1939-1945—Japan—Personal narratives

ISBN 0-670-83181-6

First published 1987 in the United Kingdom

"The narrator describes her pre-war childhood before detailing the events of August 6, 1945, when she and her family were lucky enough to survive the blast that destroyed her home. . . . A last page gives facts about the bombing of Hiroshima, and endpapers include historical black-and-white photographs together with an author's note to parents and teachers." Bull Cent Child Books

"This nonfiction title in picture-book format is a frank, powerful story in which both text and illustration work together without sentimentality or sensationalism to show the horror of war." SLJ

Rossel, Seymour

The Holocaust; the fire that raged. Watts 1989 124p il maps lib bdg $12.40 (5 and up) **940.54**

1. Holocaust, Jewish (1933-1945)

ISBN 0-531-10674-8 LC 88-26718

"A Venture book"

A new version, for younger readers, of the title first published 1981

The author "chronicles Hitler's rise to power and his relentless, systematic persecution and killing of Jews. Afterward, he warns that such an event can happen again unless people resist propaganda and stand together against prejudice and hatred. Photographs and a few maps are interspersed through the narrative. A chronology of Holocaust events and a list of further reading appended." Booklist

Skipper, G. C., 1939-
Pearl Harbor. Childrens Press 1983 47p il (World at war) lib bdg $14.60 (4 and up) **940.54**

1. Pearl Harbor (Oahu, Hawaii), Attack on, 1941
ISBN 0-516-04774-4 LC 83-6569

Describes the Japanese surprise attack on the United States naval base at Pearl Harbor, which resulted in the deaths of more than 2,000 American officers and servicemen and an immediate declaration of war on Japan

"This overview is a fine introduction that stands alone or can be used as a jumping-off point for those who want to delve more deeply into it. . . . Carefully chosen photographs . . . and an easy-to-read style . . . [make it] suitable for reluctant readers." Booklist

Taylor, Theodore, 1921 or 2-
Air raid—Pearl Harbor! the story of December 7, 1941; illustrated by W. T. Mars. Crowell 1971 185p il maps $12.95 (5 and up) **940.54**

1. Pearl Harbor (Oahu, Hawaii), Attack on, 1941
ISBN 0-690-05373-8 LC 76-132303

"Well-documented and written with all the suspense of a mystery story, this is a detailed account of the events that led up to the disaster of Pearl Harbor. The story is told both from the American and the Japanese viewpoint, with all of the errors in planning, the gaps in communication, the secrecy of tactics and strategy." Bull Cent Child Books

Includes bibliography

Battle in the Arctic seas; the story of convoy PQ 17; illustrated by Robert Andrew Parker. Crowell 1976 151p il $12.95 (5 and up) **940.54**

1. World War, 1939-1945—Naval operations 2. World War, 1939-1945—Arctic Ocean
ISBN 0-690-01084-2 LC 75-33655

"A Guild book"

"World War II's Convoy PQ 17 was slated to carry much-needed military supplies to Russians engaged in holding back German forces. The convoy's course took it through Arctic waters patrolled by German air and sea craft. . . . [The author] charts the converging events that influenced Allied commanders in their decision to abandon protective measures for the convoy. The order for them to 'scatter' ensured German attack and when it came the results were disastrous. . . . Reportage of this 'bitter military lesson' is succinct yet many-sided." Booklist

Includes bibliography

941.1 Scotland

Meek, James
The land and people of Scotland. Lippincott 1990 244p il maps (Portraits of the nations ser) $17.95; lib bdg $14.89 (5 and up) **941.1**

1. Scotland
ISBN 0-397-32332-8; 0-397-32333-6 (lib bdg) LC 88-27215

Introduces the history, geography, people, culture, government, and economy of Scotland

Includes bibliography

941.5 Ireland

Fradin, Dennis B.
The Republic of Ireland. Childrens Press 1984 123p il maps (Enchantment of the world) lib bdg $23.93 (4 and up) **941.5**

1. Ireland
ISBN 0-516-02767-0 LC 83-20960

The author "recounts Irish history, highlighting the words and deeds of local heros and patriots who strove against, primarily, British religious and political dominance. The continuing conflict over unification of Northern Ireland with the Republic of Ireland is clearly developed and briefly described. Irish government, people, culture and famous citizens . . . are presented." SLJ

942 England and Wales

England—in pictures; prepared by Geography Department. Lerner Publs. 1990 64p il maps (Visual geography ser) lib bdg $11.95 (5 and up) **942**

1. England
ISBN 0-8225-1874-0 LC 89-78070

Revised edition of the title prepared by James Nach, published 1977 by Sterling

Introduces the topography, history, society, economy, and governmental structure of England

Includes bibliographic references

Goodall, John S., 1908-
The story of a castle. Margaret K. McElderry Bks. 1986 29p il $14.95 (3-6) **942**

1. Castles—Pictorial works 2. England—Social life and customs—Pictorial works
ISBN 0-689-50405-5 LC 86-70130

"A British castle is the subject of a sequence of paintings aimed at showing the building's history. There is no text; specifics are related in a page of front matter that identifies each of the castle's eras. . . . The paintings are typical of Goodall's style: quick, detailed, and strong in color and composition. The book's design, with half pages advancing the action, will be familiar as well. A wordless lesson that can play to a wider audience, including middle graders studying medieval history or castles." Booklist

The story of a farm. Margaret K. McElderry Bks. 1989 34p il $14.95 (3-6) **942**

1. Farm life—England—Pictorial works 2. England—Social life and customs—Pictorial works
ISBN 0-689-50479-9 LC 88-13398

By following the changes in one house over centuries, the development of farm life in England is depicted

Goodall's "watercolors capture both particular details

Goodall, John S., 1908-—*Continued*
and larger impressions, and finely convey a sense of time's inexorable passage. In addition, he makes ingenious use of half-page flaps to portray two faces of a single scene." Publ Wkly

The story of a main street. Margaret K. McElderry Bks. 1987 58p il $14.95 (3-6) **942**

1. Cities and towns—England—Pictorial works 2. England—Social life and customs—Pictorial works
ISBN 0-689-50436-5 LC 87-60644

In this wordless picture book "the artist traces the evolution of an English Main Street. Medieval wattle-and-daub houses give way to overhanging Tudor structures, which in turn are replaced by the buildings of succeeding eras up through the present. Goodall's watercolors portray Main Street, in all its incarnations, as a vital, dynamic center of activity." Publ Wkly

The story of an English village. Atheneum Pubs. 1979 c1978 unp il $12.95 (3-6) **942**

1. Cities and towns—England—Pictorial works 2. England—Social life and customs—Pictorial works
ISBN 0-689-50125-0 LC 78-56242

"A Margaret K. McElderry book"

First published 1978 in the United Kingdom

"Beginning with a fourteenth-century rural site that includes a wayside cross, a church, and a thatched cottage—all dominated by a castle stronghold—the wordless illustrations show the same place and the same house, both interior and exterior, over a period of six hundred years. . . . Not only the inanimate objects but the people as well—their activities, costumes, and general demeanor—reflect the shifting pattern of life over the centuries." Horn Book

942.03 England—Period of House of Plantagenet, 1154-1399

Sancha, Sheila, 1924-
The Luttrell village; country life in the Middle Ages. Crowell 1983 c1982 64p il $13.95; lib bdg $13.89 (6 and up) **942.03**

1. England—Social life and customs 2. Country life—England 3. Civilization, Medieval
ISBN 0-690-04323-6; 0-690-04324-4 (lib bdg) LC 82-45588

First published 1982 in Scotland

"Between 1320 and 1340 Sir Geoffrey Luttrell commissioned an artist to make drawings of daily life in his village; it is from this psalter . . . as well as other sources, that Sancha has created this book. . . . She introduces children to a typical year in 14th-Century Gerneham." SLJ

"Elaborate ink-and wash illustrations—many clearly labeled—fill the pages, showing countryside panoramas, cutaway buildings and the countryfolk themselves working at various tasks. . . . The book presents an exceptionally fine portrait of medieval life." Horn Book

Includes glossary

Walter Dragun's town; crafts and trade in the Middle Ages. Crowell 1989 c1987 64p il $13.95; lib bdg $13.89 (6 and up) **942.03**

1. England—Social life and customs 2. Handicraft 3. Civilization, Medieval
ISBN 0-690-04804-1; 0-690-04806-8 (lib bdg) LC 88-34066

First published 1987 in the United Kingdom

"This is a superb resource book with engaging text and line art that looks closely, with a great deal of in-depth detail, at life in the English town of Stanford on the river Weland in the year 1274. Events, architecture, cast of characters, are all based on facts found in still-existing Public Records; Ms. Sancha has fashioned these facts into an intimate history covering a few busy days in August. Introduction, epilogue, word origins for place-names and surnames, and glossary add their value to this brief-but-compact oversize volume." Child Book Rev Serv

942.1 London

Fisher, Leonard Everett, 1924-
The Tower of London. Macmillan 1987 unp il $13.95 (4 and up) **942.1**

1. Tower of London (England) 2. London (England)—History
ISBN 0-02-735370-2 LC 87-1629

"Fisher introduces the history-laden Tower of London and recounts 13 episodes from its bloody history. . . . The tellings are succinct while capturing the essence of the famous structure. Kids will be enticed by the gory goings-on. . . . Fisher provides bold black-and-white artwork throughout in double-page spreads; impressive and dramatic, they add strong flavor to the narrative." Booklist

Munro, Roxie, 1945-
The inside-outside book of London. Dutton 1989 unp il $13.95 (2-4) **942.1**

1. London (England)—Description
ISBN 0-525-44522-6 LC 89-12023

Captioned illustrations depict noted sights in London as seen from the outside and inside. Includes the British Museum, Houses of Parliament, Tower of London, Waterloo Station, St. Paul's Cathedral, and others. Includes a section of text in the back of the book providing information on each sight

"The book displays a high level of craftsmanship and careful research, offering a uniquely personal yet informative view of the city's treasures." SLJ

942.9 Wales

Sutherland, Dorothy B.
Wales. Childrens Press 1987 128p il maps (Enchantment of the world) lib bdg $23.93 (4 and up) **942.9**

1. Wales
ISBN 0-516-02794-8 LC 86-29954

Explores the geography, history, industry, arts, and everyday life of Wales

943.086 Germany—Period of Third Reich, 1933-1945

Shirer, William L. (William Lawrence)
The rise and fall of Adolf Hitler. Random House 1961 185p il map lib bdg $7.99 (6 and up) **943.086**
1. Hitler, Adolf, 1889-1945
2. Germany—History—1933-1945
3. Germany—Politics and government—1933-1945
4. National socialism
ISBN 0-394-90547-4 LC 61-7317
"World landmark books"
"Not, as might be supposed, merely an instant, small-package version of Shirer's massive bestseller The Rise and Fall of the Third Reich. This book is more sharply and dramatically focused on the man rather than the world he terrorized." Time

943.087 Germany—1945-

Stewart, Gail, 1949-
Germany; by Gail B. Stewart. Crestwood House 1990 48p il map (Places in the news) $10.95 (4 and up) **943.087**
1. Germany—History
ISBN 0-89686-548-7 LC 90-2244
Examines the historical and political situation which led to the dividing of Germany, the problems caused by this change, recent events such as the lowering of the Berlin Wall, and possible future developments
"This is a good book for basic information on recent events. . . . Students may find it useful for assignments and inquiries regarding the topic of the Berlin Wall, but it will not be useful for term papers. Color and black and white photographs, a glossary, an index, and simple and clear language make it appealing for reluctant readers." Voice Youth Advocates

943.9 Hungary

Hintz, Martin, 1945-
Hungary. Childrens Press 1988 127p il maps (Enchantment of the world) lib bdg $23.93 (4 and up) **943.9**
1. Hungary
ISBN 0-516-02707-7 LC 88-10899
This illustrated introduction to the land and peoples of Hungary discusses the nation's history, geography, culture, and economics

944 France and Monaco

Harris, Jonathan, 1921-
The land and people of France. Lippincott 1989 244p il maps (Portraits of the nations ser) $17.95; lib bdg $14.89 (5 and up) **944**
1. France
ISBN 0-397-32320-4; 0-397-32321-2 (lib bdg) LC 88-19211
"A history of France that includes early language, Greek and Roman influence, early kings, the Revolution, and five successive Republics. Material on the French government is the most comprehensive and informative. . . . The organization is excellent. The book has a clean, open format and is illustrated with many clear black-and-white photographs." SLJ
Includes bibliography

945 Italian Peninsula and adjacent islands. Italy

Hubley, Penny
A family in Italy; [by] Penny and John Hubley. Lerner Publs. 1987 c1986 31p il maps lib bdg $9.95 (3-5) **945**
1. Italy 2. Family life
ISBN 0-8225-1673-X LC 86-27228
First published 1986 in the United Kingdom with title: Italian family
Describes the home, school, amusements, customs, and work of an eight-year-old girl and her family living in a small town outside of Florence

Italy; photography by Laura Drighi; edited by Rhoda Irene Sherwood. Stevens, G. 1988 64p il maps (Children of the world) lib bdg $12.95 (3-5) **945**
1. Children—Italy 2. Italy—Social life and customs
ISBN 1-55532-404-5 LC 87-42640
Presents the life of a young girl living in Florence, Italy, describing her family, home, school, and amusements and some of the traditions and celebrations of her country
Includes glossary and bibliography

James, Ian
Italy; photography: Chris Fairclough. Watts 1988 32p il maps (Inside) lib bdg $11.90 (4-6) **945**
1. Italy
ISBN 0-531-10613-6 LC 88-50193
Partial contents: The land; The people and their history; Towns and cities; Family life; Food; Sports and pastimes; The arts; Farming; Industry; Looking to the future

Ventura, Piero
Venice, birth of a city; English translation/adaptation by John Grisewood. Putnam 1988 unp il $13.95 (4-6) **945**
1. Venice (Italy)—History
ISBN 0-399-21531-X LC 87-25892
This "book traces the history of the Italian city that straddles tiny islands in the Lagoon of Venice. The emphasis is on the 15th and 16th centuries, when 'La Serenissima' was the richest and one of the most important trading cities in the world." N Y Times Book Rev
"A fine example of presenting history through pictures, this is remarkable for its beauty and its use of perspective; the book closes with a four-page fold-out that shows

Ventura, Piero—*Continued*
much of that part of Venice that is most famous." Bull Cent Child Books

946 Iberian Peninsula and adjacent islands. Spain

Lye, Keith
Passport to Spain. Watts 1987 48p il lib bdg $12.90 (5 and up) **946**

1. Spain
ISBN 0-531-10402-8 LC 86-51662

This book contains "two-page spreads devoted to topics such as land, people, home life, farming, transportation, language, education, and the arts." Booklist

Spain; photography by Masami Yokoyama; edited by MaryLee Knowlton & Mark J. Sachner. Stevens, G. 1987 63p il (Children of the world) lib bdg $12.95 (3-5) **946**

1. Children—Spain 2. Spain—Social life and customs
ISBN 1-55532-163-1 LC 86-42808

Presents the life of a girl and her family in a village in southern Spain, describing her home activities and the festivals, religious ceremonies, and national holidays of her country

Includes glossary and bibliography

946.081 Spain—Period of Second Republic, 1931-1939

Katz, William Loren
The Lincoln Brigade; a picture history; by William Loren Katz and Marc Crawford. Atheneum Pubs. 1989 84p il map $14.95 (5 and up) **946.081**

1. Spain—History—1936-1939, Civil War
ISBN 0-689-31406-X LC 88-27522

Recounts the story of the American contingent which joined other International Brigades in fighting with the Loyalists during the Spanish Civil War

This book "bills itself as 'a picture history.' The handsome book is that—and many of the photos have never before been published—but it also has a substantial text. It does not focus on any one hero. Rather, this politically aware book gives emphasis to the black volunteers who, for the first time in the history of an American armed force, served side-by-side with whites." N Y Times Book Rev

Includes bibliography

947 Soviet Union. Eastern Europe

Andrews, William George, 1930-
The land and the people of the Soviet Union; by William G. Andrews. HarperCollins Pubs. 1991 304p il maps (Portraits of the nations ser) $17.95; lib bdg $17.89 (5 and up) **947**

1. Soviet Union
ISBN 0-06-020034-0; 0-06-020035-9 (lib bdg) LC 90-5746

Introduces the history, geography, people, culture, government, and economy of the Soviet Union

Includes bibliography

948.1 Norway

Norway—in pictures; prepared by Geography Department. Lerner Publs. 1990 64p il maps (Visual geography ser) lib bdg $11.95 (5 and up) **948.1**

1. Norway
ISBN 0-8225-1871-6 LC 89-12118

Revised edition of the title prepared by John B. Burks, published 1980 by Sterling

An introduction to the geography, history, economy, government, culture, and people of Norway

948.97 Finland

Lander, Patricia Slade
The land and people of Finland; by Patricia Slade Lander and Claudette Charbonneau. Lippincott 1990 212p il maps (Portraits of the nations ser) $14.95; lib bdg $14.89 (5 and up) **948.97**

1. Finland
ISBN 0-397-32357-3; 0-397-32358-1 (lib bdg) LC 88-27144

Introduces the history, geography, people, culture, government, and economy of Finland

Includes bibliography

949.12 Iceland

Lepthien, Emilie U. (Emilie Utteg)
Iceland. Childrens Press 1987 126p il maps (Enchantment of the world) lib bdg $23.93 (4 and up) **949.12**

1. Iceland
ISBN 0-516-02775-1 LC 86-29966

Discusses the history, geography, wildlife, social life and customs, agriculture, industry, and culture of the small island nation known as the land of fire and ice

949.3 Southern Low Countries. Belgium

Hargrove, Jim, 1947-
Belgium. Childrens Press 1988 127p il maps (Enchantment of the world) lib bdg $23.93 (4 and up) **949.3**
1. Belgium
ISBN 0-516-02701-8 LC 87-36753
An introduction to the geography, history, government, economy, culture, and people of this small country that is often called the "crossroads of Europe"

949.35 Luxembourg

Lepthien, Emilie U. (Emilie Utteg)
Luxembourg. Childrens Press 1989 125p il (Enchantment of the world) lib bdg $23.93 (4 and up) **949.35**
1. Luxembourg
ISBN 0-516-02714-X LC 89-34664
An introduction to the geography, history, government, economy, culture, and people of one of the smallest and oldest independent countries in Europe

949.5 Greece

Stein, R. Conrad, 1937-
Greece. Childrens Press 1987 127p il maps (Enchantment of the world) lib bdg $23.93 (4 and up) **949.5**
1. Greece
ISBN 0-516-02759-X LC 87-13225
Describes the geography, history, government, culture, and people of Greece

949.8 Romania

Carran, Betty
Romania. Childrens Press 1988 124p il maps (Enchantment of the world) lib bdg $23.93 (4 and up) **949.8**
1. Romania
ISBN 0-516-02703-4 LC 87-35423
An introduction to the geography, history, government, economy, culture, and people of the only Eastern European country that traces its origins back to the Romans

951 China and adjacent areas

Fisher, Leonard Everett, 1924-
The Great Wall of China. Macmillan 1986 30p il map $12.95 (4 and up) **951**
1. China—History
ISBN 0-02-735220-X LC 85-15324
A brief history of the Great Wall of China, begun about 2,200 years ago to keep out Mongol invaders
"The combination of stunning black-and-white illustrations, calligraphy and the artist's chops (signature seal) in red, plus a spare, narrative text makes this an exciting introduction to one of history's great building projects." N Y Times Book Rev

Haskins, James, 1941-
Count your way through China; by Jim Haskins; illustrations by Dennis Hockerman. Carolrhoda Bks. 1987 unp il lib bdg $11.95 (2-4) **951**
1. China
ISBN 0-87614-302-8 LC 87-5177
Using the numbers from one to ten, this book presents facts about China and Chinese culture. Each double-page spread shows the number, the character for it, the pronunciation, and a full-color illustration

Major, John S.
The land and people of China. Lippincott 1989 298p il maps (Portraits of the nations ser) $17.95; lib bdg $14.89 (5 and up) **951**
1. China
ISBN 0-397-32336-0; 0-397-32337-9 (lib bdg) LC 88-23427
An "account of Chinese history, philosophy, and government. Science and technology (clearly delineated), art, literature, etc. have short chapters to themselves, and are brought into the larger historical narrative as well. Two concluding paragraphs update recent events through June 4, 1989." SLJ
Includes bibliography

McLenighan, Valjean, 1947-
China, a history to 1949. Childrens Press 1983 127p il maps (Enchantment of the world) lib bdg $23.93 (4 and up) **951**
1. China—History
ISBN 0-516-02754-9 LC 83-14260
A history of China up to the establishment of the communist state in 1949

951.04 China—Period of Republic, 1912-1949

Fritz, Jean
China's Long March; 6,000 miles of danger; with illustrations by Yang Zhr Cheng. Putnam 1988 124p il maps $14.95 (6 and up) **951.04**
1. China—History—1912-1949
ISBN 0-399-21512-3 LC 87-31171
Describes the events of the 6,000 mile march undertaken by Mao Zedong and his Communist followers as they retreated before the forces of Chiang Kai-shek
"Because Fritz is adept at gauging her intended audience, and because most of her material is based on interviews with survivors, the writing has an easy flow and an immediacy that make the ordeal vivid and personal. Jean Fritz loves the country where she spent most of her childhood, and her book is a felicitous blend of

Fritz, Jean—*Continued*
sympathetic understanding and an objective assessment of historical events." Bull Cent Child Books

Includes bibliography

951.05 China—Period of People's Republic, 1949-

Fritz, Jean

China homecoming; with photographs by Michael Fritz. Putnam 1985 143p il $13.95 (6 and up) **951.05**

1. China
ISBN 0-399-21182-9 LC 84-24775

Companion volume to: Homesick: my own story, entered in class 92

The author "describes her return to Hankou, her home town, four decades later. Although she no longer spoke as fluently, she still spoke Chinese. This is, therefore, a record of a very personal search for roots and memories. It is also a rarely candid and objective picture of contemporary China." Bull Cent Child Books

This "is intended for a slightly older readership than 'Homesick' . . . as it is not only an autobiography, but also a glimpse of Chinese history and a social commentary. It is, however, a book to be read and reread." SLJ

Includes bibliography

951.7 Mongolia

Major, John S.

The land and people of Mongolia. Lippincott 1990 200p il maps (Portraits of the nations ser) $15.95; lib bdg $15.89 (5 and up) **951.7**

1. Mongolia
ISBN 0-397-32386-7; 0-397-32387-5 (lib bdg)
LC 89-37790

Introduces the history, geography, people, culture, government, and economy of Mongolia

Includes bibliography

951.9 Korea

Jacobsen, Karen

Korea. Childrens Press 1989 45p il maps lib bdg $13.27; pa $4.95 (2-4) **951.9**

1. Korea
ISBN 0-516-01174-X (lib bdg); 0-516-41174-8 (pa)
LC 89-10043

Introduces the geography, history, people, and culture of the country known as "the land of morning calm"

Includes glossary

Solberg, S. E. (Sammy Edward), 1930-

The land and people of Korea. HarperCollins Pubs. 1991 216p il maps (Portraits of the nations ser) $17.95; lib bdg $17.89 (5 and up) **951.9**

1. Korea
ISBN 0-06-021648-4; 0-06-021649-2 (lib bdg)
LC 90-5952

An introduction to the history, government, traditions, and way of life of the people of Korea

Includes bibliography

South Korea—in pictures; prepared by Geography Department. Lerner Publs. 1989 64p il maps (Visual geography ser) lib bdg $11.95 (5 and up) **951.9**

1. Korea
ISBN 0-8225-1868-6 LC 89-2283

Revised edition of: Korea in pictures, prepared by William H. Mathews, published 1968 by Sterling

Describes the geography, history, government, people, and economy of South Korea

952 Japan

Birmingham, Lucy, 1956-

Japan; edited by Meredith Ackley, Susan Taylor-Boyd, and Rhoda Irene Sherwood. Stevens, G. 1990 64p il map (Children of the world) lib bdg $12.95 (3-5) **952**

1. Children—Japan 2. Japan—Social life and customs
ISBN 0-8368-0121-0 LC 89-11493

First published 1989 in Japan in shortened form

Text and photographs present the lives of two children in Tokyo and a reference section presents Japan's history, geography, culture, industry, and natural resources

Includes glossary and bibliography

Blumberg, Rhoda, 1917-

Commodore Perry in the land of the Shogun. Lothrop, Lee & Shepard Bks. 1985 144p il map lib bdg $13 (5 and up) **952**

1. Perry, Matthew Calbraith, 1794-1858 2. United States Naval Expedition to Japan (1852-1854) 3. United States—Foreign relations—Japan 4. Japan—Foreign relations—United States
ISBN 0-688-03723-2 LC 84-21800

A Newbery Medal honor book, 1986

"With fascinating detail, the diplomatic expeditions of Commodore Matthew C. Perry to secure a treaty to provide for U.S. trade with Japan are described. The black-and-white period illustrations and informative text provide an in-depth and intimate view of nineteenth century Japan, Japanese and U.S. values and attitudes, and treaty negotiations." Soc Educ

Includes bibliography

Haskins, James, 1941-
Count your way through Japan; by Jim Haskins; illustrations by Martin Skoro. Carolrhoda Bks. 1987 unp il lib bdg $11.95; pa $4.95 (2-4) **952**

1. Japan
ISBN 0-87614-301-X (lib bdg); 0-87614-485-7 (pa) LC 87-6398

Presents the numbers one to ten in Japanese, using each number to introduce concepts about Japan and its culture

Japan—in pictures; prepared by Geography Department. Lerner Publs. 1989 64p il maps (Visual geography ser) lib bdg $11.95 (5 and up) **952**

1. Japan
ISBN 0-8225-1861-9 LC 88-30461

Revised edition of the title prepared by Robert V. Masters [i.e. David A. Boehm] published 1973 by Sterling

Introduces Japan's geography, history, society, economy, and government structure

953 Arabian Peninsula and adjacent areas

Dutton, Roderic
An Arab family; photographs by John B. Free. Lerner Publs. 1985 31p il maps (Families the world over) lib bdg $9.95 (3-5) **953**

1. Oman—Social life and customs 2. Family life
ISBN 0-8225-1660-8 LC 85-10272

Revised edition of: An Arab village, published 1980

"Mohammed and Zainab have nine children and live in a village on the coast of Oman, a country south of Saudi Arabia. The family has a very small farm with date, lime, banana, and mango trees. Their life has changed since oil was discovered in Oman." Publisher's note

Jacobsen, Peter Otto
A family in the Persian Gulf; [by] Peter Otto Jacobsen, Preben Sejer Kristensen. Bookwright Press 1985 32p il maps (Families around the world) lib bdg $11.90 (2-4) **953**

1. Bahrain—Social life and customs
ISBN 0-531-18003-4 LC 84-73579

Text and photographs present the home, work, recreation, and day-to-day activities of the Al-Alrifi family who live in Bahrain on the Persian Gulf

Includes glossary

Kuwait—in pictures; prepared by Geography Department. Lerner Publs. 1989 64p il maps (Visual geography ser) lib bdg $11.95 (5 and up) **953**

1. Kuwait
ISBN 0-8225-1846-5 LC 88-9445

Revised edition of the title prepared by Camille Mirepoix, published 1970 by Sterling

Photographs and text introduce the geography, history, government, people, culture, and economy of the small oil-rich country on the Persian Gulf

953.8 Saudi Arabia

Al Hoad, Abdul Latif
We live in Saudi Arabia. Bookwright Press 1987 c1986 60p il (Living here) lib bdg $9.49 (4-6) **953.8**

1. Saudi Arabia—Social life and customs
ISBN 0-531-18089-1 LC 87-124748

First published 1986 in the United Kingdom

Saudi Arabians, ranging from schoolchildren to laborers, professionals, and military personnel, speak about their own lives. The book includes a section with information about the nation's government, education, climate, and other topics

Lye, Keith
Take a trip to Saudi Arabia; general editor: Henry Pluckrose. Watts 1984 32p il map lib bdg $7.99 (1-3) **953.8**

1. Saudi Arabia
ISBN 0-531-04872-1 LC 84-50611

Published in the United Kingdom with title: Let's go to Saudi Arabia

This book describes the country's "desert location, its oil-producing economy, its monarchy, and something of its schools and changing living standards as oil money supports the nation's development. There is little comment on the status of women except that most, outside fields such as medicine or teaching, still wear the veil. Full-color photographs are a plus, and students will find the requisite pictures of stamps and currency helpful." Booklist

Saudi Arabia—in pictures; prepared by Geography Department. Lerner Publs. 1989 64p il maps (Visual geography ser) lib bdg $11.95 (5 and up) **953.8**

1. Saudi Arabia
ISBN 0-8225-1845-7 LC 88-7335

Revised edition of the title prepared by Eugene Gordon, published 1973 by Sterling

Introduces the geography, history, economy, culture, and people of the large middle eastern country that occupies most of the Arabian Peninsula

954 South Asia. India

India—in pictures; prepared by Geography Department. Lerner Publs. 1989 64p il maps (Visual geography ser) lib bdg $11.95 (5 and up) **954**

1. India
ISBN 0-8225-1852-X LC 88-9018

Revised edition of the title prepared by Elizabeth Katz, published 1961 by Sterling

Photographs and text introduce the geography, history, government, society, and economy of this diverse nation

954.91 Pakistan

Pakistan—in pictures; prepared by Geography Department. Lerner Publs. 1989 64p il maps (Visual geography ser) lib bdg $11.95 (5 and up) **954.91**

1. Pakistan
ISBN 0-8225-1850-3 LC 88-13589

Revised edition of title prepared by Jon A. Teta, published 1968 by Sterling

Photographs and text introduce the geography, history, government, people, and economy of Pakistan

954.93 Sri Lanka

Sri Lanka—in pictures; prepared by Geography Department. Lerner Publs. 1989 64p il maps (Visual geography ser) lib bdg $11.95 (5 and up) **954.93**

1. Sri Lanka
ISBN 0-8225-1853-8 LC 88-15888

Revised edition of: Ceylon (Sri Lanka) by E. W. Egan, published 1967 by Sterling

Sri Lanka's topography, history, society, economy, and government are concisely described, augmented by photographs, maps, charts, and captions

954.96 Nepal

Nepal—in pictures; prepared by the Geography Department. Lerner Publs. 1989 64p il maps (Visual geography ser) lib bdg $9.95 (5 and up) **954.96**

1. Nepal
ISBN 0-8225-1851-1 LC 88-8347

Revised edition of: Nepal, Sikkim and Bhutan (Himalayan kingdoms) in pictures, prepared by Eugene Gordon, published 1972 by Sterling

Discusses the land, history, government, people, and economy of the country whose diverse topography contains the world's highest peak and also lush tropical lowlands

Pitkänen, Matti A.
The children of Nepal; [by] Matti A. Pitkänen, with Reijo Härkönen. Carolrhoda Bks. 1990 48p il map (World's children) lib bdg $14.95 (2-4) **954.96**

1. Nepal 2. Children—Nepal
ISBN 0-87614-395-8 LC 89-23923

Original Finish edition, 1985

An introduction to the history, geography, and people of Nepal with emphasis on the day-to-day life of the children

"This book will make readers fall in love with Nepal. Fifty-nine full-color photographs provide a dazzling introduction to the home of Mt. Everest and the abominable snowman." SLJ

955 Iran

Iran—in pictures; prepared by Geography Department. Lerner Publs. 1988 64p il maps (Visual geography ser) lib bdg $11.95 (5 and up) **955**

1. Iran
ISBN 0-8225-1848-1 LC 88-6818

Revised edition of: Iran (Persia) in pictures, prepared by Jon A. Teta, published 1968 by Sterling

Iran's topography, history, society, economy, and government are concisely described, augmented by photographs, maps, charts, and captions

Tames, Richard
Take a trip to Iran. Watts 1989 32p il maps lib bdg $7.99 (1-3) **955**

1. Iran
ISBN 0-531-10650-0 LC 88-51323

Published in the United Kingdom with title: Let's go to Iran

A brief introduction to the geography, history, natural resources, economy, people, and culture of the Islamic republic

956 Middle East

Alotaibi, Muhammad
Bedouin: the nomads of the desert. Rourke Publs. 1989 48p il maps (Original peoples) lib bdg $15.33 (5 and up) **956**

1. Bedouins 2. Arab countries—Social life and customs
ISBN 0-86625-265-7 LC 88-15074

First published 1985 in the United Kingdom

"Describes the traditional lifestyle of the group, its history, culture, religion, and the adaptations that it has made for survival in the modern world." SLJ

Includes glossary and bibliography

956.1 Turkey

Feinstein, Steve
Turkey—in pictures; prepared by Steve Feinstein. Lerner Publs. 1988 64p il maps (Visual geography ser) lib bdg $11.95 (5 and up) **956.1**
1. Turkey
ISBN 0-8225-1831-7 LC 87-26475
Revised edition of the title prepared by James Nach, published 1976 by Sterling
Text and photographs introduce the geography, history, government, people, culture, and economy of Turkey

Lye, Keith
Take a trip to Turkey. Watts 1987 32p il maps lib bdg $7.99 (1-3) **956.1**
1. Turkey
ISBN 0-531-10366-8 LC 86-51549
Published in the United Kingdom with title: Let's go to Turkey
Text and photographs introduce the history, people, and customs of Turkey. Includes photographs of stamps and currency, and a list of facts and statistics

Spencer, William
The land and people of Turkey. Lippincott 1990 208p il maps (Portraits of the nations ser) $14.95; lib bdg $14.89 (5 and up) **956.1**
1. Turkey
ISBN 0-397-32363-8; 0-397-32364-6 (lib bdg) LC 89-2421
Introduces the history, geography, people, culture, government, and economy of Turkey
"In the manner of a sensitive teacher, Spencer is enthusiastic without being overbearing; authoritative without being condescending; and like a good teacher, he relates both fact and fiction and thus engenders belief, concern, and interest." Voice Youth Advocates
Includes bibliography

Turkey; photography by Takako Tozuka; edited by Scott Enk. Stevens, G. 1989 64p il maps (Children of the world) lib bdg $12.95 (3-5) **956.1**
1. Children—Turkey 2. Turkey—Social life and customs
ISBN 1-55532-851-2 LC 88-32745
Presents the life of an eleven-year-old girl and her family living in Nevsehir, the largest city in the Cappadocia area of Turkey, describing her home and school, daily activities, amusements, and some of the customs and celebrations of her country
Includes glossary and bibliography

956.7 Iraq

Iraq—in pictures; prepared by Geography Department. Lerner Publs. 1990 64p il maps (Visual geography ser) lib bdg $11.95 (5 and up) **956.7**
1. Iraq
ISBN 0-8225-1847-3 LC 89-8351
Revised edition of the title prepared by Jon A. Teta, published 1976 by Sterling
Photographs and text introduce the geography, history, government, people, and economy of Iraq, the cradle of civilization

Tames, Richard
Take a trip to Iraq. Watts 1989 32p il maps lib bdg $7.99 (1-3) **956.7**
1. Iraq
ISBN 0-531-10651-9 LC 88-51322
Published in the United Kingdom with title: Let's go to Iraq
Text and photographs introduce the geography, history, natural resources, people, and culture of the oil-rich Middle Eastern country

956.91 Syria

Beaton, Margaret
Syria. Childrens Press 1988 125p il maps (Enchantment of the world) lib bdg $23.93 (4 and up) **956.91**
1. Syria
ISBN 0-516-02708-5 LC 88-18697
Discusses the geography, history, people, economy, and customs of the ancient land of Syria

Lye, Keith
Take a trip to Syria. Watts 1988 32p il maps lib bdg $7.99 (1-3) **956.91**
1. Syria
ISBN 0-531-10560-1 LC 87-51699
Published in the United Kingdom with title: Let's go to Syria
A simple introduction to the geography, history, resources, economy, government, culture, and people of the southwestern Asian country whose coastal region was once part of ancient Phoenicia

Syria—in pictures; prepared by Geography Department. Lerner Publs. 1990 64p il maps (Visual geography ser) lib bdg $11.95 (5 and up) **956.91**
1. Syria
ISBN 0-8225-1867-8 LC 89-13655
Describes the topography, history, society, economy, and governmental structure of Syria

956.92 Lebanon

Lebanon—in pictures; prepared by Geography Department. Lerner Publs. 1988 64p il maps (Visual geography ser) lib bdg $11.95 (5 and up) **956.92**

1. Lebanon

ISBN 0-8225-1832-5 LC 87-25997

Revised edition of the title by Camille Mirepoix, published 1978 by Sterling

Lebanon's topography, history, society, economy, and government are concisely described, augmented by photographs, maps, charts, and captions

Tames, Richard

Take a trip to Lebanon. Watts 1989 32p il maps lib bdg $7.99 (1-3) **956.92**

1. Lebanon

ISBN 0-531-10652-7 LC 88-51324

Published in the United Kingdom with title: Let's go to Lebanon

An introduction to a beautiful but war-torn Mediterranean country

956.94 Palestine. Israel

Burstein, Chaya M.

A kid's catalog of Israel; written and illustrated by Chaya M. Burstein. Jewish Publ. Soc. 1988 279p il pa $12.95 (4 and up) **956.94**

1. Israel

ISBN 0-8276-0263-4 LC 85-24190

Examines the history, customs, language, crafts, recipes, geography, and music of Israel

The author "packs the pages with such excitement that casual readers will be drawn right in; the book can be read cover to cover easily, but will probably inspire browsing, as there is definitely something for everyone. . . . Lively pencil drawings throughout create interest and add energy to the whole." SLJ

Includes glossary and bibliography

Israel—in pictures; prepared by Steve Feinstein. Lerner Publs. 1988 64p il maps (Visual geography ser) lib bdg $11.95 (5 and up) **956.94**

1. Israel

ISBN 0-8225-1833-3 LC 87-26476

Revised edition of the title prepared by Peggy Mann and Nina Brodsky, published 1979 by Sterling

Text and photographs introduce the ancient and modern history, geography, people, government, economy, and culture of the biblical country reborn in modern times

Jones, Helen Hinckley, 1903-

Israel. Childrens Press 1986 124p il maps (Enchantment of the world) lib bdg $23.93 (4 and up) **956.94**

1. Israel

ISBN 0-516-02766-2 LC 85-5740

This history and description of Israel "emphasizes the biblical background of that country and the Jews' long history of persecution, leading up to the creation of an independent state. While the claims of other religions and peoples to the land are briefly discussed, there is little reference to the plight of uprooted Arab people." Booklist

Kuskin, Karla

Jerusalem, shining still; illustrations by David Frampton. Harper & Row 1987 27p il $13.95; lib bdg $13.89; pa $5.50 (2-4) **956.94**

1. Jerusalem

ISBN 0-06-023548-9; 0-06-023549-7 (lib bdg); 0-06-443243-2 (pa) LC 86-25841

"A Charlotte Zolotow book"

"A hommage to the holy city of Jerusalem, home of the three major religions. Four thousand years of the city's history are described, beginning with King David's conquest over Goliath, continuing through the Six Day War. . . . It is to Kuskin's credit that she describes the city's 4000 year history in such a brief form, while still conveying a personal sense of the place. She sometimes interweaves verses with the rhythmic prose. Frampton's woodcuts . . . are elegantly composed and radiant." SLJ

Lawton, Clive

Passport to Israel; [by] Clive A. Lawton. Watts 1987 48p il maps lib bdg $12.90 (5 and up) **956.94**

1. Israel

ISBN 0-531-10494-X LC 87-50891

The author covers "topics such as agriculture, transportation, education, natural resources, and technology, as well as home life, food, and recreation." SLJ

This book is "useful, and in a format that will make research attractive." Booklist

Rutland, Jonathan

Take a trip to Israel; text and photographs by Jonathan Rutland; general editor: Henry Pluckrose. Watts 1981 32p il lib bdg $7.99 (1-3) **956.94**

1. Israel

ISBN 0-531-04318-5 LC 81-50030

Published in the United Kingdom with title: Let's go to Israel

A brief introduction to the geography, history, culture and people of Israel

Taitz, Emily
Israel; a sacred land; by Emily Taitz & Sondra Henry. Dillon Press 1987 159p il maps (Discovering our heritage) lib bdg $14.95 (4 and up) **956.94**
1. Israel
ISBN 0-87518-364-6 LC 87-13449
"This overview of Israel includes some history and contemporary politics; a dollop of social customs and travel information; and a taste of the flavor of the country, figuratively and literally. Recipes are given for Humus, Eggplant Salad, and Chicken Soup. . . . A detailed index, a glossary with pronunciation, a list of Israeli Consulates in the United States and Canada, and a short bibliography add to the book's usefulness. The photographs, which are mostly in color, contribute to its attractiveness." SLJ

Taylor, Allegra
A kibbutz in Israel; photographs by Nancy Durrell McKenna. Lerner Publs. 1987 31p il maps (Families the world over) lib bdg $9.95 (3-5) **956.94**
1. Collective settlements—Israel 2. Israel—Social life and customs
ISBN 0-8225-1678-0 LC 87-3473
Published in the United Kingdom with title: Tal Niv's kibbutz
Describes the life of a ten-year-old Israeli boy who lives with his family on a kibbutz

956.95 Jordan

Jordan—in pictures; prepared by Geography Department. Lerner Publs. 1988 64p il maps (Visual geography ser) lib bdg $11.95 (5 and up) **956.95**
1. Jordan
ISBN 0-8225-1834-1 LC 87-26455
Revised edition of the title prepared by Camille Mirepoix, published 1976 by Sterling
Text and photographs introduce the geography, history, government, people, and economy of Jordan

957 Siberia

Anderson, Madelyn Klein
Siberia. Dodd, Mead 1988 c1987 148p il maps lib bdg $13.95 (5 and up) **957**
1. Siberia (Soviet Union)
ISBN 0-396-08662-4 LC 87-19922
The book "begins with a discussion of the 1908 explosion that charred miles of Siberian territory. . . . Anderson then goes on to describe the history and people, as well as the part Siberia has played as the Soviet prison." Booklist

958.1 Afghanistan

Afghanistan—in pictures; prepared by Geography Department. Lerner Publs. 1989 64p il maps (Visual geography ser) lib bdg $11.95 (5 and up) **958.1**
1. Afghanistan
ISBN 0-8225-1849-X LC 88-13587
Revised edition of the title by Camille Mirepoix, published 1971 by Sterling
An introduction to the geography, history, government, people, and economy of this landlocked country with a long history of warfare and conquest

Clifford, Mary Louise
The land and people of Afghanistan. Lippincott 1989 225p il maps (Portraits of the nations ser) $17.95; lib bdg $14.89 (5 and up) **958.1**
1. Afghanistan
ISBN 0-397-32338-7; 0-397-32339-5 (lib bdg) LC 88-21419
Introduces the history, geography, people, culture, government, and economy of the Central Asian nation that has had a history of invasion and conquest by its powerful neighbors
Includes bibliography

959.3 Thailand

Jacobsen, Karen
Thailand. Childrens Press 1989 45p il maps lib bdg $13.27; pa $4.95 (2-4) **959.3**
1. Thailand
ISBN 0-516-01179-0 (lib bdg); 0-516-41179-9 (pa) LC 89-34413
Introduces the history, land, people, religion, and culture of this exotic country in Southeast Asia
Includes glossary

McNair, Sylvia
Thailand. Childrens Press 1987 127p il (Enchantment of the world) lib bdg $23.93 (4 and up) **959.3**
1. Thailand
ISBN 0-516-02792-1 LC 86-29933
Explores the geography, history, arts, religion, and everyday life of Thailand

959.4 Laos

Diamond, Judith
Laos. Childrens Press 1989 127p il (Enchantment of the world) lib bdg $23.93 (4 and up) **959.4**
1. Laos
ISBN 0-516-02713-1 LC 89-34279

Diamond, Judith—*Continued*
Discusses the geography, history, people, and culture of the only landlocked country of the Indochinese peninsula

959.5 Commonwealth of Nations territories. Malaysia

Wright, David K.
Malaysia. Childrens Press 1988 128p il (Enchantment of the world) lib bdg $23.93 (4 and up) **959.5**
1. Malaysia
ISBN 0-516-02702-6 LC 87-33784
This introduction to the small independent tropical nation describes "country and people, giving information on history, government, economics, and travel." SLJ

959.57 Singapore

Brown, Marion Marsh
Singapore. Childrens Press 1989 125p il (Enchantment of the world) lib bdg $23.93 (4 and up) **959.57**
1. Singapore
ISBN 0-516-02715-8 LC 89-34280
Discusses the history, geography, people, and culture of the island republic which is Asia's smallest independent state, yet plays a major political and economic role in the East

959.6 Cambodia (Kampuchea)

Chandler, David P.
The land and people of Cambodia. HarperCollins Pubs. 1991 210p il maps (Portraits of the nations ser) $17.95; lib bdg $17.89 (5 and up) **959.6**
1. Cambodia
ISBN 0-06-021129-6; 0-06-021130-X (lib bdg) LC 90-5907
Introduces the history, geography, people, culture, government, and economy of Cambodia
Includes bibliography

959.704 Vietnam—1949-

Ashabranner, Brent K., 1921-
Always to remember; the story of the Vietnam Veterans Memorial; [by] Brent Ashabranner; photographs by Jennifer Ashabranner. Dodd, Mead 1988 101p il lib bdg $14.95 (5 and up) **959.704**
1. Vietnam War, 1961-1975 2. Vietnam Veterans Memorial (Washington, D.C.)
ISBN 0-399-22031-3 LC 87-33110
"Beginning with a concise (and fair) chapter on the Vietnam War, the author then recounts the hard work of Jan Scruggs, the vet who began the Vietnam Veterans Memorial Fund, and Maya Lin, the 21-year-old architecture student who won the contest to design the monument. While there is plenty in this book to bring tears, Ashabranner is unobtrusive, allowing the veterans, families, and the memorial to speak for themselves. . . . Jennifer Ashabranner's photographs capture the details of flowers and fatigues left along the base of the monument wall but, as the architect intended, viewers will find their attentions primarily caught by the endless rows of names." Bull Cent Child Books

Garland, Sherry
Vietnam, rebuilding a nation. Dillon Press 1990 127p il map (Discovering our heritage) lib bdg $14.95 (4 and up) **959.704**
1. Vietnam
ISBN 0-87518-422-7 LC 89-29212
The author offers an "overview of Vietnam, describing its landscape, peoples, history, and culture in a text that is aimed at middle graders on the lookout for report material. Color and black-and-white photos support the information. . . . Also included is a chapter on the boat people and the struggles of Vietnamese immigrants making a new life in the U.S." Booklist
Includes glossary and bibliographic references

Lawson, Don
An album of the Vietnam War. Watts 1986 88p il map lib bdg $13.90 (5 and up) **959.704**
1. Vietnam War, 1961-1975
ISBN 0-531-10139-8 LC 85-26624
An illustrated history, with emphasis on American involvement, of the war in Vietnam from Ho Chi Minh's declaration of independence to the withdrawal of United States troops
The author "does a fine job of explaining the origins of the conflict and how the war esclated, while at the same time balancing the viewpoints of those for and against America's involvement." Booklist

959.8 Indonesia

Indonesia—in pictures; prepared by Geography Department. Lerner Publs. 1990 64p il maps (Visual geography ser) lib bdg $11.95 (5 and up) **959.8**
1. Indonesia
ISBN 0-8225-1860-0 LC 89-36540
Revised edition of the title prepared by Tom Gerst, published 1974 by Sterling
Text and photographs introduce the topography, history, society, economy, and governmental structure of Indonesia

960 Africa

Chiasson, John C.
African journey; [by] John Chiasson. Bradbury Press 1987 55p il map $16.95 (4 and up) **960**
1. Africa—Social life and customs 2. Ethnology—Africa
ISBN 0-02-718530-3 LC 86-8233
"Text describes the culture and habitat of the people in six regions, beginning with the Twareg and WoDaaBe, two herding tribes in desert areas of Niger." Horn Book
"Chiasson creates a stark, compelling picture of this continent. . . . The images themselves are involving and immediate; this is a photoessay deserving of high honors." Publ Wkly

Musgrove, Margaret, 1943-
Ashanti to Zulu: African traditions; pictures by Leo and Diane Dillon. Dial Bks. for Young Readers 1976 unp il $15.95; lib bdg $15.89; pa $4.95 (3-6) **960**
1. Africa—Social life and customs 2. Ethnology—Africa
ISBN 0-8037-0357-0; 0-8037-0358-9 (lib bdg); 0-8037-0308-2 (pa) LC 76-6610
Awarded the Caldecott Medal, 1977
"In brief texts arranged in alphabetical order, each accompanied by a large framed illustration, the author introduces 'the reader to twenty-six African peoples by depicting a custom important to each.' . . . In most of the paintings the artists 'have included a man, a woman, a child, their living quarters, an artifact, and a local animal' and have, in this way, stressed the human and the natural ambience of the various peoples depicted." Horn Book
"The writing is dignified and the material informative, but it is the illustrations that make the book outstanding." Bull Cent Child Books

961.1 Tunisia

Tunisia—in pictures; prepared by Geography Department. Lerner Publs. 1989 64p il maps (Visual geography ser) lib bdg $11.95 (5 and up) **961.1**
1. Tunisia
ISBN 0-8225-1844-9 LC 88-12965
Revised edition of the title prepared by Coleman Lollar, published 1972 by Sterling
Introduces the land, history, government, economy, people, and culture of this North African country that was once the site of the ancient city of Carthage

961.2 Libya

Targ-Brill, Marlene
Libya. Childrens Press 1987 127p il maps (Enchantment of the world) lib bdg $23.93 (4 and up) **961.2**
1. Libya
ISBN 0-516-02776-X LC 87-13192
Discusses the geography, history, religion, economy, people, and everyday life of the North African country

962 Egypt and Sudan

Bennett, Olivia
A family in Egypt; photographs by Liba Taylor. Lerner Publs. 1985 c1983 31p il map (Families the world over) lib bdg $9.95 (3-5) **962**
1. Egypt—Social life and customs 2. Family life
ISBN 0-8225-1652-7 LC 84-19468
First published with title: Village in Egypt
Describes the life of a ten-year-old Egyptian boy who lives in a large village near Cairo with his farmer grandfather, his camel driver father, and the rest of his extended family

Cross, Wilbur, 1918-
Egypt. Childrens Press 1982 124p il maps (Enchantment of the world) lib bdg $23.93 (4 and up) **962**
1. Egypt
ISBN 0-516-02762-X LC 82-9465
Discusses the history, physical characteristics, economy, and culture of the land which has been called the gift of the Nile

Egypt—in pictures; prepared by Stephen C. Feinstein. Lerner Publs. 1988 64p il maps (Visual geography ser) lib bdg $11.95 (5 and up) **962**
1. Egypt
ISBN 0-8225-1840-6 LC 87-27038
Revised edition of the title prepared by Camille Mirepoix, published 1979 by Sterling
Introduces the history, geography, economy, government, culture, and people of the Arab nation whose history dates back more than 5000 years

Kristensen, Preben Sejer
We live in Egypt; [by] Preben Kristensen and Fiona Cameron. Bookwright Press 1987 c1986 60p il (Living here) lib bdg $9.49 (4-6) **962**
1. Egypt—Social life and customs
ISBN 0-531-18087-5 LC 86-70994
First published 1986 in the United Kingdom
Presents various aspects of life in Egypt through interviews with twenty-six people representing different age groups, occupations, and regions. Also includes a section of brief facts about the country and a glossary

Kristensen, Preben Sejer—*Continued*
"For example, a 63-year-old midwife discusses her life's work; a wealthy Bedouin describes his business, his several homes, and his two wives; and a 42-year-old woman tells about her chain of shops dedicated to preserving traditional Egyptian arts and crafts." Booklist

963 Ethiopia

Ethiopia—in pictures; prepared by Daniel Abebe. Lerner Publs. 1988 64p il maps (Visual geography ser) lib bdg $11.95 (5 and up) **963**
1. Ethiopia
ISBN 0-8225-1836-8 LC 87-27034
Revised edition of the title prepared by Alfred Allotey Acquaye, published 1973 by Sterling
Brief text and photographs introduce the geography, history, government, people, and economy of Ethiopia

Fradin, Dennis B.
Ethiopia; by Dennis Brindell Fradin. Childrens Press 1988 125p il maps (Enchantment of the world) lib bdg $23.93 (4 and up) **963**
1. Ethiopia
ISBN 0-516-02706-9 LC 88-10882
Discusses the geography, history, government, people, and culture of this east African country

964 Northwest African coast and offshore islands. Morocco

Hintz, Martin, 1945-
Morocco. Childrens Press 1985 127p il maps (Enchantment of the world) lib bdg $23.93 (4 and up) **964**
1. Morocco
ISBN 0-516-02774-3 LC 84-23269
Presents the history, geography, natural history, economy, customs, and people of this diverse North African country

Lye, Keith
Take a trip to Morocco. Watts 1988 32p il maps lib bdg $7.99 (1-3) **964**
1. Morocco
ISBN 0-531-10467-2 LC 87-51068
Published in the United Kingdom with title: Let's go to Morocco
An introduction to the geography, history, economy, government, culture, and people of Morocco

Morocco—in pictures; prepared by Geography Department. Lerner Publs. 1989 64p il maps (Visual geography ser) lib bdg $11.95 (5 and up) **964**
1. Morocco
ISBN 0-8225-1843-0 LC 88-9126
Revised edition of the title prepared by Noel Sheridan, published 1967 by Sterling
An introduction to the geography, history, government, economy, culture, and people of the north African country that is ten miles away from Spain

Stewart, Judy, 1948-
A family in Morocco; photographs by Jenny Matthews. Lerner Publs. 1986 c1985 31p il maps (Families the world over) lib bdg $9.95 (3-5) **964**
1. Morocco—Social life and customs 2. Family life
ISBN 0-8225-1664-0 LC 86-54
First published 1985 in the United Kingdom with title: Moroccan family
Text and photographs present the life of twelve-year-old Malika and her family, residents of Tangier, Morocco

966.23 Mali

Mali—in pictures; prepared by Thomas O'Toole. Lerner Publs. 1990 64p il maps (Visual geography ser) lib bdg $11.95 (5 and up) **966.23**
1. Mali
ISBN 0-8225-1869-4 LC 89-34527
Text and photographs introduce the topography, history, society, economy, and governmental structure of Mali

966.3 Senegal

Senegal—in pictures; prepared by Geography Department. Lerner Publs. 1988 64p il maps (Visual geography ser) lib bdg $11.95 (5 and up) **966.3**
1. Senegal
ISBN 0-8225-1827-9 LC 87-21347
Revised edition of the title prepared by Eugene Gordon, published 1977 by Sterling
Introduces the land, history, government, natural resources, culture, and people of the Republic of Senegal, situated on the westernmost bulge of the African continent

966.62 Liberia

Liberia—in pictures; prepared by Jo M. Sullivan. Lerner Publs. 1988 64p il maps (Visual geography ser) lib bdg $11.95 (5 and up) **966.62**
1. Liberia
ISBN 0-8225-1837-6 LC 87-26470
Revised edition of the title prepared by Camille Mirepoix, published 1973 by Sterling
Describes the land, climate, history, government, economy, culture, and people of the west African country settled by freed American slaves

966.68 Ivory Coast

Cote d'Ivoire (Ivory Coast)—in pictures; prepared by Geography Department. Lerner Publs. 1988 64p il maps (Visual geography ser) lib bdg $11.95 (5 and up) **966.68**

1. Ivory Coast
ISBN 0-8225-1828-7 LC 87-17266

Revised edition of: The Ivory Coast in pictures, prepared by Albert Rossellini, published 1976 by Sterling

Text and photographs introduce the geography, history, government, people, and economy of Ivory Coast

966.7 Ghana

Ghana—in pictures; prepared by Geography Department. Lerner Publs. 1988 64p il maps (Visual geography ser) lib bdg $11.95 (5 and up) **966.7**

1. Ghana
ISBN 0-8225-1829-5 LC 87-17260

Revised edition of the title prepared by Lydia Verona Zemba, published 1975 by Sterling

Describes the history, geography, government, economy, culture, and people of the African country once known as the Gold Coast

Hintz, Martin, 1945-
Ghana. Childrens Press 1987 127p il maps (Enchantment of the world) lib bdg $23.93 (4 and up) **966.7**

1. Ghana
ISBN 0-516-02773-5 LC 86-29935

"A discussion of Ghana's prehistory, history, geography, political organization, economy, social and cultural life SLJ

966.9 Nigeria

Nigeria—in pictures; prepared by Geography Department. Lerner Publs. 1988 64p il maps (Visual geography ser) lib bdg $11.95 (5 and up) **966.9**

1. Nigeria
ISBN 0-8225-1826-0 LC 87-17267

Revised edition of the title prepared by John Schultz, published 1975 by Sterling

Introduces the land, history, government, people, and economy of Nigeria

967.62 Kenya

Kenya—in pictures; prepared by Geography Department. Lerner Publs. 1988 64p il maps (Visual geography ser) lib bdg $11.95 (5 and up) **967.62**

1. Kenya
ISBN 0-8225-1830-9 LC 87-17261

Revised edition of the title prepared by Joel Reuben, published 1976 by Sterling

Text and photographs introduce the geography, history, government, people, and economy of the thirty-fourth African nation to gain independence

Maren, Michael
The land and people of Kenya. Lippincott 1989 191p il maps (Portraits of the nations ser) $17.95; lib bdg $14.89 (5 and up) **967.62**

1. Kenya
ISBN 0-397-32334-4; 0-397-32335-2 (lib bdg) LC 88-22959

Introduces the history, geography, people, culture, government, and economy of Kenya

Includes bibliography

968 Southern Africa. Republic of South Africa

Jacobsen, Karen
South Africa. Childrens Press 1989 45p il lib bdg $13.27; pa $4.95 (2-4) **968**

1. South Africa
ISBN 0-516-01176-6 (lib bdg); 0-516-41176-4 (pa) LC 89-10044

Discusses South Africa's geography, history, people, government, and anti-apartheid movement

Includes glossary

Paton, Jonathan
The land and people of South Africa. Lippincott 1990 288p il maps (Portraits of the nations ser) $17.95; lib bdg $14.89 (5 and up) **968**

1. South Africa
ISBN 0-397-32361-1; 0-397-32362-X (lib bdg) LC 89-2477

An introduction to the history, economy, geography, politics, art, and culture of South Africa

The author "portrays the beauty of the land along with the tragedy of a people at war with one another. His explanations and descriptions are clear, and his use of the poetry and prose literature of native South Africans, both black and white, adds depth to the text and increases understanding." SLJ

Includes bibliography

968.83 Botswana

Botswana—in pictures; prepared by Thomas O'Toole. Lerner Publs. 1990 64p il maps (Visual geography ser) lib bdg $11.95 (5 and up) **968.83**

1. Botswana
ISBN 0-8225-1856-2 LC 89-13103

An introduction to the geography, history, government, economy, culture, and people of Botswana, a landlocked country located in southern Africa

"The visual material in this book is particularly rich and thoughtfully used. Full-color and black-and-white pictures illustrate key concepts, and the captions extend and highlight supplementary detail. . . . The writing style is straightforward, using short sentences." SLJ

968.91 Zimbabwe

Cheney, Patricia

The land and people of Zimbabwe. Lippincott 1990 242p il maps (Portraits of the nations ser) $15.95; lib bdg $15.89 (5 and up) **968.91**

1. Zimbabwe
ISBN 0-397-32392-1; 0-397-32393-X (lib bdg) LC 89-36244

An introduction to the history, geography, economy, culture, and people of Zimbabwe

"A fairly even account of Zimbabwe's struggle to regain its independence. . . . Detailed but not overburdened with facts, this is a straightforward account that has interesting incidents and information." SLJ

Includes bibliography

Lauré, Jason, 1940-

Zimbabwe. Childrens Press 1988 127p il maps (Enchantment of the world) lib bdg $23.93 (4 and up) **968.91**

1. Zimbabwe
ISBN 0-516-02704-2 LC 87-35426

A survey of the land and people of Zimbabwe (formerly Rhodesia). Topics covered include culture, industry, farming, economics and the everyday life of the people

Zimbabwe—in pictures; prepared by Thomas O'Toole. Lerner Publs. 1988 64p il maps (Visual geography ser) lib bdg $11.95 (5 and up) **968.91**

1. Zimbabwe
ISBN 0-8225-1825-2 LC 87-21348

Revised edition of the title: Rhodesia in pictures, prepared by Bernadine Bailey, published 1977 by Sterling

Introduces the land, history, government, people, and economy of one of Africa's most controversial countries

968.94 Zambia

Lauré, Jason, 1940-

Zambia. Childrens Press 1989 126p il (Enchantment of the world) lib bdg $23.93 (4 and up) **968.94**

1. Zambia
ISBN 0-516-02716-6 LC 89-34281

Introduces the geography, climate, history, people, industry, and culture of Zambia

970.004 North American native peoples

Baylor, Byrd

When clay sings; illustrated by Tom Bahti. Scribner 1972 unp il $11.95; pa $3.95 (1-4) **970.004**

1. Indians of North America—Art 2. Indians of North America—Southwestern States 3. Pottery
ISBN 0-684-18829-5; 0-689-71106-9 (pa) LC 70-180758

A Caldecott Medal honor book, 1973

"A lyrical tribute to an almost forgotten time of the prehistoric Indian of the desert West presents broken bits of pottery from this ancient time. The designs and drawings, done in rich earth tones, are derived from prehistoric pottery found in the American Southwest." Read Ladders for Hum Relat. 6th edition

Bealer, Alex W.

Only the names remain; the Cherokees and the Trail of Tears; illustrated by William Sauts Bock. Little, Brown 1972 88p il lib bdg $14.95 (4-6) **970.004**

1. Cherokee Indians
ISBN 0-316-08520-0 LC 71-169008

The author describes "the rise of the Cherokee Nation, with its written language, constitution, and republican form of government, and its tragic betrayal in the 1830s." Chicago Public Libr

"The author's narrative style, which is dramatic and immediate, is intensified by the illustrator's meticulous and evocative black-and-white illustrations. A helpful index is appended." Horn Book

Ehrlich, Amy, 1942-

Wounded Knee: an Indian history of the American West; adapted for young readers by Amy Ehrlich from Dee Brown's Bury my heart at Wounded Knee. Holt & Co. 1974 202p il maps o.p.; Dell paperback available $1.50 (6 and up) **970.004**

1. Indians of North America—West (U.S.) 2. Indians of North America—Wars 3. West (U.S.)—History
ISBN 0-440-95768-0 (pa) LC 73-21821

This book traces the plight of the Navaho, Apache, Cheyenne and Sioux Indians in their struggles against the white man in the West between 1860 and 1890. It recounts battles and their causes, participants, and conse-

Ehrlich, Amy, 1942-—*Continued*

quences during this era

"Some chapters [of the original] have been deleted, others condensed, and in some instances sentence structure and language have been simplified. The editing is good, and this version is interesting, readable, and smooth. " SLJ

Includes bibliographies

Fradin, Dennis B.

The Cheyenne. Childrens Press 1988 45p il lib bdg $13.27; pa $4.95 (2-4) **970.004**

1. Cheyenne Indians
ISBN 0-516-01211-8 (lib bdg); 0-516-41211-6 (pa) LC 87-33792

"A New true book"

"Fradin covers in short chapter segments topics such as the early history of the tribe, their beliefs, social and family life, Indian-white relations, and the Cheyenne today. The volume contains color as well as black-and-white photographs." SLJ

Includes glossary

The Pawnee. Childrens Press 1988 45p il map lib bdg $13.27; pa $4.95 (2-4) **970.004**

1. Pawnee Indians
ISBN 0-516-01155-3 (lib bdg); 0-516-41155-1 (pa) LC 88-11820

"A New true book"

Discusses Pawnee Indian customs, villages, warfare, religious beliefs, family life, and their place in contemporary American society

Includes glossary

The Shoshoni. Childrens Press 1988 47p il maps lib bdg $13.27; pa $4.95 (2-4) **970.004**

1. Shoshoni Indians
ISBN 0-516-01156-1 (lib bdg); 0-516-41156-X (pa) LC 88-11821

"A New true book"

Describes the history, beliefs, customs, homes, and day-to-day life of the Shoshoni Indians. Also discusses how they live today

Includes glossary

Freedman, Russell

Buffalo hunt. Holiday House 1988 52p il lib bdg $16.95 (4 and up) **970.004**

1. Indians of North America—Great Plains 2. Bison
ISBN 0-8234-0702-0 LC 87-35303

The author discusses the importance of the buffalo in the lore and day-to-day life of the Indian tribes of the Great Plains. He describes hunting methods, the uses found for each part of the animal, and the near disappearance of the buffalo as white hunters, traders and settlers moved west

"Freedman has hit his stride in terms of selection, style, and illustration: the color reproductions of historical art work form a stunning complement to the carefully researched, graceful presentation of information." Bull Cent Child Books

Hoyt-Goldsmith, Diane

Totem pole; photographs by Lawrence Migdale. Holiday House 1990 30p il lib bdg $14.95 (3-5) **970.004**

1. Indians of North America—Northwest coast of North America 2. Totems and totemism
ISBN 0-8234-0809-4 LC 89-26720

A Tsimshian Indian boy proudly describes how his father carved a totem pole for the Klallman tribe and the subsequent ceremonial celebration

"The writing is simple and direct, the tone of pride is strong, the information is not often found in books for children, and the book is imbued with cultural dignity and a sense of the value of the extended family and community." Bull Cent Child Books

Includes glossary

Jenness, Aylette

In two worlds: a Yup'ik Eskimo family; [by] Aylette Jenness and Alice Rivers; photographs by Aylette Jenness. Houghton Mifflin 1989 84p il $13.95 (4 and up) **970.004**

1. Inuit
ISBN 0-395-42797-5 LC 88-13887

Text and photographs document the life of a Yup'ik Eskimo family, residents of a small Alaskan town on the coast of the Bering Sea, detailing the changes that have come about in the last fifty years

"More descriptive than analytical, the book includes details of hunting, fishing, trapping and skinning, schooling, family life, and recreation, which includes both women's basketball and traditional dancing. The writing is generally clear although sometimes oddly constructed, and the many black-and-white photographs lack captions but are usually well-placed." Bull Cent Child Books

Includes bibliography

Lepthien, Emilie U. (Emilie Utteg)

The Choctaw. Childrens Press 1987 45p il maps lib bdg $13.27; pa $4.95 (2-4) **970.004**

1. Choctaw Indians
ISBN 0-516-01240-1 (lib bdg); 0-516-41240-X (pa) LC 87-14583

"A New true book"

"The book begins with a brief history of the Choctaw and their legends of how they came to settle in the area that is now Alabama and Mississippi. Descriptions of their daily lives are given, telling what they ate, their respect for nature, and methods of building homes. There is a short chronology of the Choctaw up to present times. . . . Problems and accomplishments of modern life are mentioned, making this a valuable book for native American studies." SLJ

Includes glossary

The Mandans. Childrens Press 1989 45p il lib bdg $13.27; pa $4.95 (2-4) **970.004**

1. Mandan Indians
ISBN 0-516-01180-4 (lib bdg); 0-516-41180-2 (pa) LC 89-22235

"A New true book"

Lepthien, Emilie U. (Emilie Utteg)—*Continued*

"Filled with attractive contemporary photographs and informative historical materials such as sketches by George Catlin and N.C. Wyeth, this attractive book contains historical background of the Mandans and their neighbors, the Hidatsa and the Arikara. . . . Well organized, the book offers historical accuracy and readability." SLJ

Includes glossary

McKissack, Patricia C., 1944-

The Apache; by Patricia McKissack. Childrens Press 1984 45p il lib bdg $13.27; pa $4.95 (2-4) **970.004**

1. Apache Indians
ISBN 0-516-01925-2 (lib bdg); 0-516-41925-0 (pa) LC 84-7803

"A New true book"

Describes the history, customs, religion, government, homes, and day-to-day life of the Apache people of the Southwest

Osinski, Alice

The Chippewa. Childrens Press 1987 45p il maps lib bdg $13.27; pa $4.95 (2-4) **970.004**

1. Chippewa Indians
ISBN 0-516-01230-4 (lib bdg); 0-516-41230-2 (pa) LC 86-32687

"A New true book"

Presents a brief history of the Chippewa Indians describing their customs and traditions and how they are maintained in the modern world

Includes glossary

The Navajo. Childrens Press 1987 45p il maps lib bdg $13.27; pa $4.95 (2-4) **970.004**

1. Navajo Indians
ISBN 0-516-01236-3 (lib bdg); 0-516-41236-1 (pa) LC 86-30978

"A New true book"

A brief history of the Navajo Indians describing customs, interactions with white settlers, and changes in traditional ways of life brought on by modern civilization

The author "doesn't back away from the facts; detailing, for example, the 'Long Walk' forced upon the Navajos in 1864-65 as well as discussing the difficulties many native Americans face in today's world." Booklist

Includes glossary

The Nez Perce. Childrens Press 1988 45p il map lib bdg $13.27; pa $4.95 (2-4) **970.004**

1. Nez Percé Indians
ISBN 0-516-01154-5 (lib bdg); 0-516-41154-3 (pa) LC 88-11822

"A New true book"

A brief history of the Nez Percé Indians describing their customs, religious beliefs and their place in contemporary society

Includes glossary

The Sioux. Childrens Press 1984 40p il lib bdg $13.27; pa $4.95 (2-4) **970.004**

1. Dakota Indians
ISBN 0-516-01929-5 (lib bdg); 0-516-41929-3 (pa) LC 84-7629

"A New true book"

A brief history of the Sioux, or Dakota, Indians of the Great Plains describing their tribal organization, customs, religion, and their encounter with the white settlers

Tomchek, Ann Heinrichs

The Hopi. Childrens Press 1987 45p il maps lib bdg $13.27; pa $4.95 (2-4) **970.004**

1. Hopi Indians
ISBN 0-516-01234-7 (lib bdg); 0-516-41234-5 (pa) LC 87-8037

"A New true book"

A brief history of the Hopi Indians describing their customs, religious beliefs, interactions with other tribes, and the changes modern civilization has brought to their traditional way of life

Includes glossary

Trimble, Stephen, 1950-

The village of blue stone; words by Stephen Trimble; illustrations by Jennifer Owings Dewey and Deborah Reade. Macmillan 1990 58p il maps $13.95 (4-6) **970.004**

1. Pueblo Indians—Social life and customs 2. Cliff dwellers and cliff dwellings 3. Chaco Culture National Historical Park (N.M.)
ISBN 0-02-789501-7 LC 88-34194

Recreates, in text and illustrations, the day-to-day life throughout a full year in a Chaco Culture Anasazi pueblo, located in what is now New Mexico, in 1100 A.D

"An impressive amount of material is packed into the slim volume. . . . The modest format is pleasant, and, although the fictional-looking narrative will deter some information seekers, the account conveys . . . a respectful view of an intriguing way of life." Horn Book

Includes glossary and bibliography

Wheeler, Mary Jo

First came the Indians; [by] M.J. Wheeler; illustrated by James Houston. Atheneum Pubs. 1983 unp il lib bdg $11.95 (2-4) **970.004**

1. Indians of North America
ISBN 0-689-50258-3 LC 82-13916

"A Margaret K. McElderry book"

"The focus of this book is the culture of six (the Creek, Iroquois, Ojibwa, Makah, Sioux and Hopi) North American Indian tribes that are representative of their particular geographical area. Each tribe is given three or four pages of description about ways of living and how particular ways suited particular geographical areas." Child Book Rev Serv

"This is not a comprehensive book; there are

Wheeler, Mary Jo—*Continued*
references to 'fighting wars' and 'enemies' but no discussion of tribal conflict or cultural conflict. . . . This is otherwise well-written, at times poetic, and a good introduction to the diversity and richness of Indian life styles." Bull Cent Child Books

Wolfson, Evelyn
From Abenaki to Zuni; a dictionary of native American tribes; illustrated by William Sauts Bock. Walker & Co. 1988 215p il maps $17.95; lib bdg $18.85 (4 and up) **970.004**
1. Indians of North America—Dictionaries
ISBN 0-8027-6789-3; 0-8027-6790-7 (lib bdg) LC 87-27875
An alphabetical identification of sixty-eight of the larger North American Indian tribes, describing their habitats, social life and customs, food, means of travel, and modern descendants
"Although, as the author notes, the book is not exhaustive in terms of tribes covered, Wolfson has provided help for researchers by pulling together data on so many native peoples in such a handy format. Students will be pleased with the concise summaries of information needed for school reports." Booklist
Includes bibliography

Yue, Charlotte
The Pueblo; [by] Charlotte and David Yue. Houghton Mifflin 1986 117p il $12.95 (4 and up) **970.004**
1. Pueblo Indians
ISBN 0-395-38350-1 LC 85-27087
"A look at the many facets of Pueblo life, not often covered in the many books on Native Americans. Filled with illustrations and diagrams that expand and clarify, it emphasizes the relationship between the people and the land. Superb nonfiction and a boon to report writers." SLJ
Includes bibliography

970.01 North America—Early history to 1599

Krensky, Stephen, 1953-
Who really discovered America? illustrated by Steve Sullivan. Hastings House 1987 60p il maps lib bdg $12.95 (4-6) **970.01**
1. America—Exploration
ISBN 0-8038-9306-X LC 87-15000
Examines the races, tribes, wanderers, and explorers who may have found America before Columbus, including the prehistoric nomads who crossed the land bridge from Asia and possible Polynesian, Phoenician, and European visitors by sea
"A light-handed writing style and spacious format make the information widely accessible. Full-page black-and-white drawings and maps elucidate the text. Although this doesn't provide indepth information about explorers, students wanting a broad perspective may find it useful." SLJ

971 Canada

Shepherd, Jenifer A.
Canada; by Jenifer Shepherd. Childrens Press 1987 144p il maps (Enchantment of the world) lib bdg $23.93 (4 and up) **971**
1. Canada
ISBN 0-516-02757-3 LC 87-14626
"The first chapter accounts for Canada's cultural diversity by giving an historical overview of immigration and settlement. Subsequent chapters outline Canada's geography, history, economy, government, and society. . . . Many color photographs brighten the pages and add interest, if not information, to the functional text." SLJ

971.01 Canada—Early history to 1763

Anderson, Joan
Pioneer settlers of New France; photographs by George Ancona. Lodestar Bks. 1990 unp il map $15.95 (3-5) **971.01**
1. Frontier and pioneer life—Canada
2. Canada—History—0-1763 (New France)
ISBN 0-525-67291-5 LC 89-34991
"Black-and-white photographs of costumed actors are scattered profusely in this brief look at Louisbourg, Nova Scotia, during the final years of King George's war. Together, the illustrations and the fictionalized dialogue make this historical period come alive." SLJ

971.27 Manitoba

Kurelek, William, 1927-1977
A prairie boy's summer; paintings and story by William Kurelek. Houghton Mifflin 1975 unp il o.p.; Tundra Bks. reprint available $14.95 (3-5) **971.27**
1. Children—Canada 2. Farm life—Canada
3. Summer
ISBN 0-88776-058-9 LC 74-32137
This book shows "many details of the artist's life when he was a boy growing up on a farm in Western Canada." Horn Book
"It is, of course, the pictures by this distinguished Canadian artist that give the book its distinction; each full-color page glows with life and vigor, and the paintings have both a felicity of small details and a remarkable evocation of the breadth and sweep of the Manitoba prairie." Bull Cent Child Books

A prairie boy's winter; paintings and story by William Kurelek. Houghton Mifflin 1973 unp il $13.95; pa $4.95 (3-5) **971.27**
1. Children—Canada 2. Farm life—Canada 3. Winter
ISBN 0-395-17708-1; 0-395-36609-7 (pa) LC 73-8913
The author depicts the rigors and pleasures of boyhood winters on a Manitoba farm in the 1930's including hauling hay, playing hockey, and surviving a blizzard

971.9 Northern territories of Canada

Cooper, Michael, 1950-
Klondike fever; the famous gold rush of 1898; illustrated with photographs. Clarion Bks. 1989 80p il $14.95 (5 and up) **971.9**
1. Klondike River Valley (Yukon)—Gold discoveries
ISBN 0-89919-803-1 LC 89-31117
Traces the history of the Klondike gold rush of the late 1890s, describing the men responsible for the initial discovery, the trail to the Klondike gold fields, and the explosive growth and rapid demise of the gold rush town of Dawson
"An oversize book, profusely illustrated with contemporary photographs, with a bibliography and a good index. The provision and arrangement of the material are quite adequate." Bull Cent Child Books

Ray, Delia
Gold! the Klondike adventure. Lodestar Bks. 1989 90p il maps $14.95 (5 and up) **971.9**
1. Klondike River Valley (Yukon)—Gold discoveries
ISBN 0-525-67288-5 LC 89-31823
The author begins by "telling of the adventures and encounters of the colorful personalities involved in the beginnings of the Canadian gold rush. [She] even includes conversations taken, presumably, from memoirs, but no sources are cited. The remaining sections . . . are straightforward recountings of historical fact, but the telling remains lively and interesting." Horn Book
Includes glossary

972 Middle America. Mexico

Beck, Barbara L.
The ancient Maya. rev ed, revised by Lorna Greenberg. Watts 1983 64p il map lib bdg $10.40 (4 and up) **972**
1. Mayas
ISBN 0-531-04529-3 LC 82-17672
"A First book"
First published 1965 with title: The first book of the ancient Maya
This book discusses the Mayan culture, its discovery by Spaniards, and its eventual collapse, and describes the ruins existing today
Includes bibliography

The Aztecs. rev ed, revised by Lorna Greenberg. Watts 1983 64p il map lib bdg $10.40 (4 and up) **972**
1. Aztecs
ISBN 0-531-04522-6 LC 82-16013
"A First book"
First published 1966 with title: The first book of the Aztecs
This book discusses the beginnings of the ancient American civilization, its people and their ways of life, and coming of the Spanish conquistadores
Includes bibliography

Casagrande, Louis B.
Focus on Mexico; modern life in an ancient land; [by] Louis B. Casagrande, Sylvia A. Johnson; photographs by Phillips Bourns. Lerner Publs. 1986 96p il lib bdg $14.95 (4 and up) **972**
1. Mexico
ISBN 0-8225-0645-9 LC 85-23829
"After a brief history and introduction to Mexico's diverse cultures, the authors spotlight various young people from different backgrounds. . . . Period photographs . . . are included, as well as numerous color and black-and-white photographs. A good overview of modern day Mexico with photographs and illustrations that are exceptional." SLJ

Fisher, Leonard Everett, 1924-
Pyramid of the sun, pyramid of the moon. Macmillan 1988 unp il map $13.95 (4 and up) **972**
1. Aztecs 2. Toltecs 3. Teotihuacán site (San Juan Teotihuacán, Mexico)
ISBN 0-02-735300-1 LC 88-1410
Fisher discusses the history of the pyramids of Teotihuacan, built by the Toltecs and later sacred to the Aztecs. He describes how the Aztecs lived and worshipped, and how they were overcome by the Spaniards
"Shadowy paintings in black, white, and gray—punctuated with brick-red symbols—depict events and ceremonies of monumental grandeur. The book has an abstract quality, which is just as well for dealing with the cruelties that marked the Aztec sacrifice of prisoners and the Spaniards' destruction of Montezuma's city, Tenochtitlan. A dramatic, well-designed introduction." Bull Cent Child Books

Moran, Tom, 1943-
A family in Mexico. Lerner Publs. 1987 31p il maps (Families the world over) lib bdg $9.95 (3-5) **972**
1. Mexico—Social life and customs 2. Family life
ISBN 0-8225-1677-2 LC 87-3482
Describes the life of a Mexican family, resident of a suburb of Oaxaca, following expecially the activities of nine-year-old Paula Maria

972.84 El Salvador

Bachelis, Faren Maree
El Salvador. Childrens Press 1990 127p il maps (Enchantment of the world) lib bdg $23.93 (4 and up) **972.84**
1. El Salvador
ISBN 0-516-02718-2 LC 89-25419
This "book has as its mainstay information on the country's geography, history, people, and culture. The author also provides a glimpse into El Salvador's complex political life and delicate relationship with the U.S. . . . A combination of black-and-white and full-color photographs points up the beauty of the country as well as its poverty and violence." Booklist

972.87 Panama

St. George, Judith, 1931-
Panama Canal; gateway to the world; illustrated with photographs. Putnam 1989 159p il maps $15.95 (5 and up) **972.87**

1. Panama Canal
ISBN 0-399-21637-5 LC 88-11617

Presents a history of the Panama Canal from the time Columbus first anchored off the coast of Panama through the signing of the 1977 United States-Panama treaties

"Based on carefully chosen material from newspapers and other writing of the time, the absorbing, balanced narrative incorporates both humorous and sobering ideas as it blends descriptions of social history, technology, and the characters of the principal figures. A fine assortment of photographs, and extensive bibliography, and a statistical table extend the informative treatment and add to the pleasure of a handsomely designed volume." Horn Book

973 United States

America the beautiful. Childrens Press 1987-1991 48v il maps lib bdg ea $25.27 (4 and up) **973**

Contents: Alabama, by S. McNair; Alaska, by A. Heinrichs; Arizona, by A. Heinrichs; Arkansas, by A. Heinrichs; California, by R. C. Stein; Colorado, by D. Kent; Connecticut, by D. Kent; Delaware, by D. Kent; Florida, by L. M. Stone; Georgia, by Z. Kent; Hawaii, by S. McNair; Idaho, by Z. Kent; Illinois, by R. C. Stein; Indiana, by R. C. Stein; Iowa, by D. Kent; Kansas, by Z. Kent; Kentucky, by S. McNair; Louisiana, by D. Kent; Maine, by T. Harrington; Maryland, by D. Kent; Massachusetts, by D. Kent; Michigan, by R. C. Stein; Minnesota, by R. C. Stein; Mississippi, by R. Carson; Missouri, by W. R. Sanford; Montana, by A. Heinrichs; Nebraska, by J. Hargrove; Nevada, by D. Lillegard and W. Stoker; New Jersey, by D. Kent; New Mexico, by R. C. Stein; New York, by R. C. Stein; North Carolina, by R. C. Stein; North Dakota, by M. S. Herguth; Ohio, by D. Kent; Oklahoma, by A. Heinrichs; Oregon, by R. C. Stein; Pennsylvania, by D. Kent; Rhode Island, by A. Heinrichs; South Carolina, by D. Kent; South Dakota, by E. U. Lepthien; Tennessee, by S. McNair; Texas, by R. C. Stein; Utah, by B. McCarthy; Vermont, by S. McNair; Virginia, by S. McNair; Washington, D. C., by D. Kent; West Virginia, by R. C. Stein; Wisconsin, by R. C. Stein

In this series, "topics covered include geography, history from the pioneer times to today, government and the economy, industry, arts and leisure, and historic sites. Whether utilized for a quick report, appreciative browsing of the outstanding photography, historical research, or armchair-vacation planning, these books are top-notch presentations. Each 30-page reference section is a veritable gold mine—besides the expected statistics, maps, dates, and descriptions there are biographical sketches with accompanying photos." Booklist

Brandt, Sue R., 1916-
Facts about the fifty states. 2nd rev ed. Watts 1988 72p il maps lib bdg $10.40 (4 and up) **973**

1. United States
ISBN 0-531-10476-1 LC 87-25437
"A First book"
First published 1970

Answers questions on the geography, population, history, products, and many other aspects of the fifty states

Scott, John Anthony, 1916-
The story of America: a National Geographic picture atlas. National Geographic Soc. 1984 324p il maps $19.95; lib bdg $21.95 (5 and up) **973**

1. United States—History
ISBN 0-87044-508-1; 0-87044-535-9 (lib bdg) LC 84-2018

"Beginning with the Paleo-Indians of 40,000 years ago and extending through the Vietnam era, [this volume] presents the history of people and events in the land that is now the continental United States." Booklist

"The story flows smoothly, and continuity is maintained. . . . The numerous captioned illustrations, predominantly reprints of period art and photographs, are of the highest quality." SLJ

Tunis, Edwin, 1897-1973
The young United States, 1783 to 1830; a time of change and growth; a time of learning democracy; a time of new ways of living, thinking, and doing; written and illustrated by Edwin Tunis. Crowell 1976 c1969 159p il $24.95 (5 and up) **973**

1. United States—Social life and customs 2. United States—History—1783-1865
ISBN 0-690-01065-6 LC 75-29613

A reissue of the title first published 1969 by World Publishing Company

"Portrait of the first fifty years of the republic. Family life, city and town life and important historical events are discussed. Detailed descriptions and illustrations of clothing, homes, furniture, etc." N Y Public Libr. Ref Books for Child Collect

Weitzman, David L.
My backyard history book; written by David Weitzman; illustrated by James Robertson. Little, Brown 1975 128p il $14.95; pa $7.95 (4 and up) **973**

1. United States—History—Miscellanea 2. United States—History, Local
ISBN 0-316-92901-8; 0-316-92902-6 (pa) LC 75-6577
"A Brown paper school book"

Activities and projects, such as making time capsules and rubbings and tracing genealogy, demonstrate that learning about the past begins at home

"Full of fascinating social studies activities to be pursued 'scientifically' by elementary children. The clever, down-to-earth tasks will not only keep children happy

Weitzman, David L.—*Continued*
and busy for weeks, but will give them a taste of historical research techniques. The illustrations are clear and concise. The humor injected into every page is the kind of slapstick hilarity kids love." Sci Books Films

973.05 United States—History—Serial publications

Cobblestone; the history magazine for young people. Cobblestone Pub. $22.95 per year **973.05**

1. United States—History—Periodicals
ISSN 0199-5197

Monthly. Forst published 1980

"Each issue explores a single theme, drawing from the political, business, scientific, artistic, and literary areas of life in the period covered. It presents U.S. history in a fresh, new way: through firsthand accounts, biographies, stories, maps, poems, games, puzzles, songs, recipes, and book and film sources for futher study. Clear black-and-white illustrations and photographs, many from museums and historical societies, add another dimension to this excellent periodical." Katz. Mag for Sch Libr

973.2 United States—Colonial period, 1607-1775

Alderman, Clifford Lindsey
The story of the thirteen colonies; illustrated by Leonard Everett Fisher. Random House 1966 187p il lib bdg $8.99 (5 and up) **973.2**

1. United States—History—1600-1775, Colonial period
ISBN 0-394-90415-X LC 67-641

"Landmark books"

The author "describes the events leading up to the establishment of the colonies, including the lives and characters of the men most important in each colony's history." Libr J

"Mr. Alderman writes smoothly, and the book will (hopefully) stimulate young Americans to discover more about the lively, complex world that existed here before 1776." N Y Times Book Rev

Includes bibliography

Siegel, Beatrice
A new look at the Pilgrims; why they came to America; illustrated by Douglas Morris. Walker & Co. 1977 82p il lib bdg $12.85 (4-6) **973.2**

1. Pilgrims (New England colonists)
ISBN 0-8027-6292-1 LC 76-57060

In a question-and-answer format "the author traces the separatist movement that led people from England to Holland to America. Background information on seventeenth-century England and Holland sets the scene for the future pilgrims' discontent and tells why they felt forced to emigrate and seek a new land where they were free to worship and live as they chose. How they organized, financed, and finally completed their voyage are concisely chronicled." Child Book Rev Serv

"A handy, workable introduction, with a descriptive table of contents rather than an index, and softened, articulate black-and-white illustrations." Booklist

Includes bibliography

Tunis, Edwin, 1897-1973
Colonial living; written and illustrated by Edwin Tunis. Crowell 1976 c1957 155p il $24.95 (5 and up) **973.2**

1. United States—Social life and customs—1600-1775, Colonial period
ISBN 0-690-01063-X LC 75-29611

A reissue of the title first published 1957 by The World Publishing Company

"Common everyday aspects of colonial living from 1564-1770 are highlighted by the detailed descriptions and numerous black and white illustrations of items such as tools, home furnishings, clothing, etc." N Y Public Libr. Ref Books for Child Collect

The tavern at the ferry; illustrated by the author. Crowell 1973 109p il $24.95 (5 and up) **973.2**

1. United States—Social life and customs—1600-1775, Colonial period
ISBN 0-690-00099-5 LC 73-4488

"Baker's Ferry on the Delaware River is the focal point for a . . . recreation of American life from the 17th to the 19th century, and also the scene of dramatic events during the Revolutionary War." Publisher's note

This book "is profusely illustrated with pictures that give, in their meticulous detail, authoritative information about clothing, buildings, weapons, vehicles, and other artifacts of the period." Bull Cent Child Books

973.3 United States—Periods of Revolution and Confederation, 1775-1789

The **American** revolutionaries: a history in their own words, 1750-1800; edited by Milton Meltzer. Crowell 1987 210p il $13.95; lib bdg $13.89 (6 and up) **973.3**

1. United States—History—1775-1783, Revolution
2. United States—History—1755-1763, French and Indian War
ISBN 0-690-04641-3; 0-690-04643-X (lib bdg) LC 86-47846

"Meltzer has assembled a collage of eyewitness accounts, speech and diary excerpts, letters, and other documents for a chronological account of the half century that included the American Revolution. . . . The voices of women who accompanied the troops and of blacks who fought with the army are both represented." Bull Cent Child Books

Bliven, Bruce, 1916-
The American Revolution, 1760-1783; illustrated by Albert Orbaan. Random House 1958 182p il maps lib bdg $8.99; pa $3.95 (5 and up) **973.3**
1. United States—History—1775-1783, Revolution
ISBN 0-394-90383-8 (lib bdg); 0-394-84696-6 (pa) LC 58-6183
"Landmark books"
An "overview of the causes, battles, and results of the Revolution." Hodges. Books for Elem Sch Libr

Dalgliesh, Alice, 1893-1979
The Fourth of July story; illustrated by Marie Nonnast. Scribner 1956 unp il lib bdg $13.95; pa $3.95 (2-4) **973.3**
1. United States. Declaration of Independence 2. Fourth of July
ISBN 0-684-13164-1 (lib bdg); 0-689-71115-8 (pa) LC 56-6138
The author "tells briefly and succinctly of the events that led up to the decision of the colonies to break with England, of the actual writing of the Declaration of Independence, and of its reception by the people of the colonies. The text, written at an upper third grade reading level, is excellently suited to reading aloud at any age level. . . . Colorful illustrations add greatly to the attractiveness and appeal of the book." Bull Cent Child Books

Davis, Burke, 1913-
Black heroes of the American Revolution; foreword by Edward W. Brooke. Harcourt Brace Jovanovich 1976 80p il $14.95 (5 and up) **973.3**
1. United States—History—1775-1783, Revolution 2. Black soldiers
ISBN 0-15-208560-2 LC 75-42218
"In a very readable style, the author relates the stories of a few of the approximately 5000 Black soldiers who participated in the Revolution, emphasizing their unselfishness fighting a war from which few of them would substantially benefit. In addition, there is an excellent chapter on the exploits of several predominantly Black infantry companies." SLJ
Includes bibliography

Morris, Richard Brandon, 1904-1989
The American Revolution; [by] Richard B. Morris; illustrations by Leonard Everett Fisher. rev ed. Lerner Publs. 1985 66p il maps (American history topic bks) lib bdg $8.95 (4-6) **973.3**
1. United States—History—1775-1783, Revolution
ISBN 0-8225-1701-9 LC 85-12878
First published 1956 by Watts with title: The first book of the American Revolution
Presents the causes and events of the Revolution
"Most of the writing is lively, and the personalities of the great men are vividly portrayed. Good, simple maps and excellent woodblock illustrations." Child Book Rev Serv

Phelan, Mary Kay
The story of the Boston Massacre; illustrated by Allan Eitzen. Crowell 1976 146p il maps $13.95; lib bdg $13.89 (5 and up) **973.3**
1. Boston Massacre, 1770
ISBN 0-690-00716-7; 0-690-04883-1 (lib bdg) LC 75-25961
"In a present-tense narrative that evokes the tense mood of Boston in the months before the Massacre, the author objectively portrays the underlying causes and graphically describes the event. Also included is the town's angry reaction and details of the soldiers' trial. Generous use of primary sources and colorful descriptions of the famous patriots involved make this a very appealing account." SLJ
Includes bibliography

973.4 United States—Constitutional period, 1789-1809

Fisher, Leonard Everett, 1924-
Monticello. Holiday House 1988 64p il $13.95 (4 and up) **973.4**
1. Jefferson, Thomas, 1743-1826—Homes and haunts
ISBN 0-8234-0688-1 LC 87-25219
"The text opens with summary background on the development of English and American architecture, the specific buildings that influenced Jefferson, and his early planning. Various stages of construction and modification demonstrate Jefferson's ingenuity and wide-ranging intelligence as he adapted classical structures to local landscape. The decay of the property after Jefferson's death and its eventual renovation give as much sense of history as the building's conception. The photographs, reproductions, diagrams, and drawings are a masterly mix of graphic information." Bull Cent Child Books

Phelan, Mary Kay
The story of the Louisiana Purchase; illustrated by Frank Aloise. Crowell 1979 149p il map $13.95 (5 and up) **973.4**
1. Louisiana Purchase 2. United States—History—1783-1809
ISBN 0-690-03955-7 LC 78-22505
"The political maneuvering and delicate diplomacy which led to the purchase of the land are shown through conversations—which the author based on reports by the participants—and excerpts from letters, diaries, and newspapers of the era. The writing style of the present-tense narrative is unexceptional, but the dialogue is smooth and believable and gives enticing glimpses into the personalities of such men as Thomas Jefferson, James Monroe, and Napoleon Bonaparte. Bibliography and index." Horn Book

Siegel, Beatrice
George and Martha Washington at home in New York; illustrated by Frank Aloise. Four Winds Press 1989 74p il $12.95 (4-6) **973.4**
1. Washington, Martha, 1731-1802 2. New York (N.Y.)—History
ISBN 0-02-782721-6 LC 88-24534
Describes the life shared by George and Martha Washington, with an emphasis on the government activities, historical events, and social and sociological aspects of their residence in New York City during the seventeen months when it was the nation's first capital
"This excellent social and political history of life in New York City, from the point of view of the Washingtons, is a breath of fresh air. The narrative brings New York City and the Washington family vividly alive." SLJ
Includes bibliography

973.6 United States—1845-1861

Baker, Betty, 1928-1987
The Pig War; pictures by Robert Lopshire. Harper & Row 1969 64p il map (I can read history bk) lib bdg $10.89 (k-2) **973.6**
1. Pacific Northwest 2. United States—History—1815-1861
ISBN 0-06-020333-1 LC 69-10212
It is the year 1859, and on a tiny Pacific coast island between the United States and British Canada, "a war almost begins when British pigs raid an American garden. All ends well when the islanders unite to get rid of the soldiers of both sides." Minnesota. Dept of Educ. Libr Div

973.7 United States—Administration of Abraham Lincoln, 1861-1865. Civil War

Carter, Alden R.
The Battle of Gettysburg. Watts 1990 64p il maps lib bdg $10.90 (4 and up) **973.7**
1. Gettysburg (Pa.), Battle of, 1863
ISBN 0-531-10852-X LC 89-37033
"A First book"
Describes the Confederate Army's northern campaign, its defeat at the Battle of Gettysburg, and the subsequent effect on the course of the Civil War
Includes bibliography

Johnson, Neil
The Battle of Gettysburg; with photographs from the 125th anniversary reenactment. Four Winds Press 1989 56p il maps $14.95 (5 and up) **973.7**
1. Gettysburg (Pa.), Battle of, 1863
ISBN 0-02-747831-9 LC 88-30414
Text recounts the historic Civil War battle at Gettysburg and photographs capture a reenactment of that encounter, performed in 1988 in honor of the 125th anniversary
"Johnson's camera captures an intriguing slice of the action while his text explains how the battle unfolded, skirmish by skirmish, ridge by ridge. . . . Of obvious use to students researching assignments, this handsomely designed photo essay will also appeal to Civil War buffs." Booklist
Includes bibliography

Jordan, Robert Paul
The Civil War; produced by the Special Publications Division, National Geographic Society. National Geographic Soc. 1982 c1969 215p il maps $7.95 (6 and up) **973.7**
1. United States—History—1861-1865, Civil War
ISBN 0-87044-077-2 LC 82-18807
First published 1969
This account of the American Civil War offers an historical survey of the decades before the clash and descriptions of numerous battles, leaders and personalities
"A magnificent book. . . . Fascinating drawings, photographs, and paintings supplement the absorbing text." Keating. Build Bridges of Understanding Between Cultures
Includes bibliography

Voices from the Civil War; a documentary history of the great American conflict; edited by Milton Meltzer. Crowell 1989 203p il $14.95; lib bdg $14.89 (6 and up) **973.7**
1. United States—History—1861-1865, Civil War—Sources
ISBN 0-690-04800-9; 0-690-04802-5 (lib bdg) LC 88-34067
Letters, diaries, memoirs, interviews, ballads, newspaper articles, and speeches depict life and events during the four years of the Civil War
"Meltzer has incorporated a good cross-section of material documenting both the Northern and Southern viewpoints. . . . The open format, clean pages, and outstanding black-and-white photographs make this an attractive book that will be a fine resource for reports, as well as informative recreational reading for history buffs." SLJ
Includes bibliography

974.4 Massachusetts

Anderson, Joan
The first Thanksgiving feast; photographed by George Ancona. Clarion Bks. 1984 unp il $14.95; pa $5.95 (3-5) **974.4**
1. Massachusetts—History—1600-1775, Colonial period 2. Pilgrims (New England colonists) 3. Thanksgiving Day
ISBN 0-89919-287-4; 0-395-51886-5 (pa) LC 84-5804
Recreates the first harvest feast celebrated by the Pilgrims in 1621 using the Pilgrim and Indian actors and the seventeenth-century setting of Plimoth Plantation, a

Anderson, Joan—*Continued*
living history museum in Plymouth, Massachusetts

"Narrative and illustrations work together to create a real sense of the people, daily life and culture in 1620s Plymouth. The personalized dialogue and sensitive photographs humanize and enliven a historical legend that has become static and empty from too many textbook tellings." SLJ

Dalgliesh, Alice, 1893-1979

The Thanksgiving story; with illustrations by Helen Sewell. Scribner 1988 c1954 unp il map lib bdg $13.95; pa $4.95 (k-2) **974.4**

1. Massachusetts—History—1600-1775, Colonial period 2. Pilgrims (New England colonists) 3. Thanksgiving Day

ISBN 0-684-18999-2 (lib bdg); 0-689-71053-4 (pa) LC 88-4448

A Caldecott Medal honor book, 1955

A reissue of the title first published 1954

A "picture book that tells the story of Thanksgiving through the experiences of one family on the Mayflower, the hardships of their first winter, the birth of the new baby, spring planting, harvest, and the giving of thanks." Wis Libr Bull

"It is told briefly and directly in the words that will be easy for the youngest readers to enjoy for themselves and in pictures which are in the character of American primitives and at the same time have strength and drama." Saturday Rev

Fritz, Jean

Who's that stepping on Plymouth Rock? illustrated by J. B. Handelsman. Coward, McCann & Geoghegan 1975 30p il $8.95 (3-5) **974.4**

1. Plymouth Rock

ISBN 0-698-20325-9 LC 74-30593

An "account of the Rock which is visited yearly by about one and a half million people. It stands now under a monument on the waterfront of Plymouth, Massachusetts, sacred to the memory of the First Comers (Pilgrims) but it has figured in many adventures since the Pilgrims did—or did not—step upon it in 1620." Publ Wkly

"Both a delightful story and a perceptive commentary on how the mythmaking process works in American history." N Y Times Book Rev

Sewall, Marcia, 1935-

The pilgrims of Plimoth; written and illustrated by Marcia Sewall. Atheneum Pubs. 1986 48p il $14.95 (3-6) **974.4**

1. Pilgrims (New England colonists) 2. Massachusetts—History—1600-1775, Colonial period

ISBN 0-689-31250-4 LC 86-3362

"In journal-like passages that include quotes from original sources, Sewall . . . reconstructs the lives of the pilgrims. She takes readers from the journey out of England, financed by English merchants . . . and to the building of many new townships around the original. The text is broken into sections: Pilgrims, Menfolk, Womenfolk, Children and Youngfolk, Plantation and Glossary." Publ Wkly

"Translating narrative and descriptive details into visual images, the illustrations accompany every page of text, occasionally overspreading double pages for panoramic effects. Combining subtle, modulating color with a spiritual as well as an actual luminosity, the paintings—done in gouache—are vibrant with the daily pulse of life among an energetic, enterprising people." Horn Book

974.7 New York

Burchard, Sue

The Statue of Liberty; birth to rebirth; illustrated with photographs. Harcourt Brace Jovanovich 1985 199p il maps $13.95 (5 and up) **974.7**

1. Statue of Liberty (New York, N.Y.)

ISBN 0-15-279969-9 LC 85-5525

Traces the history of the Statue of Liberty from its conception to its centennial with emphasis on the statue's restoration and its significance through the years

Includes bibliography

Costabel, Eva Deutsch, 1924-

The Jews of New Amsterdam; written and illustrated by Eva Deutsch Costabel. Atheneum Pubs. 1988 32p il $13.95 (2-4) **974.7**

1. Jews—New York (N.Y.) 2. New York (N.Y.)—History

ISBN 0-689-31351-9 LC 87-27873

Traces the events leading to the arrival of the first group of Jews in the Dutch colony of New Amsterdam in 1654 and describes how they adapted and eventually prospered under Dutch, and later British, rule

"Sprightly hued watercolors alternate with striking black-and-white line drawings as Costabel authentically evokes seventeenth-century New Amsterdam. Alongside her quaint illustrations are brief chapters studded with fascinating historical anecdotes about the Jews' settlements of the colony and the Dutch-influenced life-style they adopted there. This invitingly instructive presentation brightly illuminates one aspect of early American history and the roots of religious tolerance." Booklist

Includes glossary and bibliography

Fisher, Leonard Everett, 1924-

The Statue of Liberty. Holiday House 1985 64p il lib bdg $13.95 (4 and up) **974.7**

1. Statue of Liberty (New York, N.Y.)

ISBN 0-8234-0586-9 LC 85-42878

Recounts the history of one of the largest monuments in the world, including how it was executed in France, shipped to America, and erected in New York Harbor

Fradin, Dennis B.
The New York Colony. Childrens Press 1988 159p il lib bdg $22.60 (4 and up) **974.7**

1. New York (State)—History
ISBN 0-516-00389-5 LC 87-35803

"Beginning with the 1300s, when the Algonquian and Iroquois Indians were the dominant tribes, Fradin traces the development of New York state. . . . Fradin's lively word pictures chronicle everyday life as the colony moves from Dutch to English domination, and his account ends in 1790 with the relocation of the nation's capital from New York to Philadelphia. Biographical sketches of historical state figures are interspersed, and the crisply designed book includes a liberal use of portraits and engravings. A colonial America time line is a handy reference; overall, a competent, attractive offering." Booklist

Haskins, James, 1941-
The Statue of Liberty: America's proud lady; [by] Jim Haskins. Lerner Publs. 1986 48p il lib bdg $9.95 (4 and up) **974.7**

1. Statue of Liberty (New York, N.Y.)
ISBN 0-8225-1706-X LC 85-18061

"A straightforward account of the people and ideas which inspired Bartholdi's arduous battle to make the Statue of Liberty a reality. The book's many black-and-white photographs and prints are effectively dramatic. The paper is of high quality, and the layout and design are superb. Included is information about vital statistics and a plan of repairs. The index is thorough and makes this an excellent book for beginning researchers." SLJ

Includes glossary

Maestro, Betsy, 1944-
The story of the Statue of Liberty; [by] Betsy & Giulio Maestro. Lothrop, Lee & Shepard Bks. 1986 39p il $13; lib bdg $12.88; pa $5.95 (k-3) **974.7**

1. Bartholdi, Frédéric Auguste, 1834-1904 2. Statue of Liberty (New York, N.Y.)
ISBN 0-688-05773-X; 0-688-05774-8 (lib bdg); 0-688-08746-9 (pa) LC 85-11324

"Although Maestro simplifies the story—including only the most important people's names, for example—she still presents an accurate account of what happened. The exceptional drawings are visually delightful—primarily in the blue-green range, although they are in full color—and cover most of every page. Human figures—workers, tourists—are included in many drawings, indicating the statue's tremendous scale. Further, the drawings involve viewers through the use of unusual perspectives and angles and by placing the statue in scenes of city life." SLJ

Includes bibliography

Munro, Roxie, 1945-
The inside-outside book of New York City. Dodd, Mead 1985 unp il $13.95 (2-4) **974.7**

1. New York (N.Y.)—Description
ISBN 0-396-08513-X LC 85-7085

"Paired pictures explore exterior and interior views of various sites in Manhattan (plus the Bronx Zoo)." Bull Cent Child Books

"The book thoughtfully includes a one-page reprise, summarizing salient and interesting facts about each site. Notable for the skill with which design elements emphasize the structural significance and relationship of parts to whole, the book is a stylish yet very human approach to this quintessential metropolis." Horn Book

Shapiro, Mary J.
How they built the Statue of Liberty; illustrated by Huck Scarry. Random House 1985 61p il $9.95; lib bdg $9.99 (4 and up) **974.7**

1. Statue of Liberty (New York, N.Y.)
ISBN 0-394-86957-5; 0-394-96957-X (lib bdg) LC 85-42720

"This handsome volume is an absorbing account of the conception and creation of the well-known statue, with emphasis on the engineering processes involved. Huck Scarry's many detailed and well-researched drawings, with their lucid captions, are an integral part of the explanation of how the Statue of Liberty came to stand in New York Harbor." Sci Child

974.8 Pennsylvania

Fradin, Dennis B.
The Pennsylvania colony. Childrens Press 1988 160p il maps lib bdg $22.60 (4 and up) **974.8**

1. Pennsylvania—History
ISBN 0-516-00390-9 LC 88-11975

A history of the colony of Pennsylvania, from the time of the earliest European settlers to the aftermath of the battle for independence that resulted in statehood. Includes biographical sketches of some individuals prominent in Pennsylvania history

975.3 District of Columbia (Washington)

Fisher, Leonard Everett, 1924-
The White House. Holiday House 1989 96p il $14.95 (4 and up) **975.3**

1. White House (Washington, D.C.)
ISBN 0-8234-0774-8 LC 89-1990

"A fresh, captivating commentary of the conception and evolution of America's most famous residence. Through anecdotal prose and wonderful historical photos, Fisher demystifies the prestigious monument by showing it to be a home—complete with its foibles, quirks, and inconveniences." SLJ

Krementz, Jill

A visit to Washington, D.C. Scholastic 1987 unp il $13.95; pa $3.95 (k-2) **975.3**

1. Washington (D.C.)
ISBN 0-590-40582-9; 0-590-40583-7 (pa)

LC 86-27973

Six-year-old "Matt and his family visit a variety of usual and unusual points of interest in Washington." Child Book Rev Serv

"Endpapers add to the usefulness of this introductory guide to Washington by providing maps that clearly indicate all sites mentioned in the text. The color photographs are of excellent quality, and the scenes commented on by the six-year-old protagonist are ones that would interest a child." Bull Cent Child Books

Munro, Roxie, 1945-

The inside-outside book of Washington, D.C. Dutton 1987 unp il $13.95 (2-4) **975.3**

1. Washington (D.C.)—Description
ISBN 0-525-44298-7 LC 86-24267

"Views of familiar—and some less familiar—landmarks in our national capitol are recreated in a series of wonderfully effective, colorful pictures. Using a variety of perspectives and an awe-inspiring multiplicity of detail, the illustrator captures the often ponderous lavishness of Federal buildings with careful attention to architectural motifs and just a touch of humor." Horn Book

St. George, Judith, 1931-

The White House; cornerstone of a nation. Putnam 1990 160p il map $16.95 (5 and up) **975.3**

1. White House (Washington, D.C.)
ISBN 0-399-22186-7 LC 89-27005

Discusses some of the changes and the events occurring over two centuries in the building that represents the power and majesty of the presidency

"A handsome format with spacious margins and well-chosen photographs complements the appealing presentation. Not intended as a comprehensive account, the blend of ideas and facts in graceful prose, skillfully threading heritage and ongoing history into an interesting story, makes this a pleasing and memorable book." Horn Book

Includes bibliographic references

Sullivan, George, 1927-

How the White House really works. Lodestar Bks. 1989 117p il $15.95; Scholastic pa $2.95 (5 and up) **975.3**

1. White House (Washington, D.C.)
2. Presidents—United States
ISBN 0-525-67266-4; 0-590-43403-9 (pa)

LC 88-16409

Provides a behind-the-scenes look at life in the official residence of the president of the United States, describing how the staff and facilities affect that key official's daily life

"Black-and-white photographs of post-World War II presidents and their staffs offer candid views of the official residence. . . . [The book includes] a chapter on a subject about which many readers will be curious: the president's Secret Service protection. An eye-opening and engaging choice." Booklist

975.8 Georgia

Fradin, Dennis B.

The Georgia colony; by Dennis Brindell Fradin. Childrens Press 1990 143p il lib bdg $22.60 (4 and up) **975.8**

1. Georgia
ISBN 0-516-00392-5 LC 89-34954

A historical account of Georgia's early days, from its creation as a colony for debtors in the 1700's until its admission as the fourth state in 1788

"The format features large print, wide margins, and a liberal use of portraits, photos, and engravings. Biographical sketches, set off from the main text, will be a boon to report writers. Because the text reads easily, it will be a good choice for reluctant researchers." Booklist

976.4 Texas

Fisher, Leonard Everett, 1924-

The Alamo. Holiday House 1987 64p il maps $13.95 (4 and up) **976.4**

1. Alamo (San Antonio, Tex.) 2. Texas—History
ISBN 0-8234-0646-6 LC 86-46204

"Some of Mexico's turbulent history and the rise of the Texas in dependence movement are described along with what's known of the battle." Booklist

"The oversize format of this detailed history of the Alamo gives ample opportunity for large-scale maps, reproductions of old prints and photographs, and some of Fisher's own distinctive and dramatic scratchboard drawings. Although no sources are cited, Fisher has clearly done intensive research. . . . The tone is serious, the writing style sober, the material dramatic." Bull Cent Child Books

977 North Central United States. Lake states

Crisman, Ruth

The Mississippi. Watts 1984 64p il map lib bdg $10.40 (4 and up) **977**

1. Mississippi River valley 2. Mississippi River
ISBN 0-531-04826-8 LC 84-7233

"A First book"

The author "takes readers on a grand tour of the central United States, riding the river from Minnesota down to the Gulf of Mexico, looking at the historic cities and ports, the various river economies and the massive flood containment systems." SLJ

McCall, Edith S.

Biography of a river: the living Mississippi; [by] Edith McCall. Walker & Co. 1990 162p il maps $16.95; lib bdg $17.85 (6 and up) **977**

1. Mississippi River
ISBN 0-8027-6914-4; 0-8027-6915-2 (lib bdg) LC 89-70698

Traces the history of the Mississippi River, presents stories of people whose lives were affected by the river, and describes how humans have changed the Mississippi

The author "writes clearly and comprehensively of people and events. . . . She is very objective in her treatment of native Americans. Black-and-white period illustrations and photos show how people have viewed the river throughout history." SLJ

Includes glossary

978 Western United States

Blumberg, Rhoda, 1917-

The incredible journey of Lewis and Clark. Lothrop, Lee & Shepard Bks. 1987 143p il maps $17.95 (5 and up) **978**

1. Lewis, Meriwether, 1774-1809 2. Clark, William, 1770-1838 3. Lewis and Clark Expedition (1804-1806) 4. West (U.S.)—Exploration
ISBN 0-688-06512-0 LC 87-4235

Describes the expedition led by Lewis and Clark to explore the unknown western regions of America at the beginning of the nineteenth century

"Blumberg's writing is dignified but never dry, and her sense of narrative makes familiar history an exciting story." Bull Cent Child Books

Includes bibliography

Freedman, Russell

Children of the wild West. Clarion Bks. 1983 104p il map $14.95 pa $5.95 (4 and up) **978**

1. Children—West (U.S.) 2. Frontier and pioneer life—West (U.S.) 3. West (U.S.)—History
ISBN 0-89919-143-6; 0-395-54785-7 (pa) LC 83-5133

"A smooth narrative and numerous historical photographs combine for an intriguing backward look at how children fared in pioneer times." Booklist

Cowboys of the wild West. Clarion Bks. 1985 103p il map lib bdg $15.95 (4 and up) **978**

1. Cowhands 2. Frontier and pioneer life—West (U.S.) 3. West (U.S.)—History
ISBN 0-89919-301-3 LC 85-4200

"Freedman describes the herders' duties on the open range roundups and trail rides, their ranch and line-camp life, the clothes and equipment dictated by their work, and the economic necessities that defined the job in its heyday, from the 1860s to the 1890s." Bull Cent Child Books

"The author does a fine job of presenting us with information without belittling the real place the cowboy has in both history and fiction. Bibliography and index." Horn Book

Tunis, Edwin, 1897-1973

Frontier living; written and illustrated by Edwin Tunis. Crowell 1976 c1961 165p il maps $24.95 (5 and up) **978**

1. Frontier and pioneer life—West (U.S.) 2. West (U.S.)—History
ISBN 0-690-01064-8 LC 75-29639

A Newbery Medal honor book, 1962

Companion volume to: Colonial living, entered in class 973.2

A reprint of the title first published 1961 by World Publishing Company

This volume "portrays the manners and customs of the frontiersman and his family from the beginning of the westward movement through the 19th century in . . . text and more than 200 drawings." Wis Libr Bull

978.9 New Mexico

Ashabranner, Brent K., 1921-

Born to the land: an American portrait; by Brent Ashabranner; photographs by Paul Conklin. Putnam 1989 134p il $14.95 (5 and up) **978.9**

1. Ranch life 2. Agriculture 3. New Mexico
ISBN 0-399-21716-9 LC 88-26414

This book "examines the contemporary situation of ranchers, and, to a lesser extent, farmers, in southwestern New Mexico. . . . Scant attention is paid to the Mexican-American inhabitants of Luna County—it is not until the end of the book that we are told Hispanics constitute half the county population. . . . Although Ashabranner is usually better at providing social and political context, his (and Conklin's) gift for detail serves them well when describing the actual work of a ranch: branding, corralling, selling cattle, and always praying for rain." Bull Cent Child Books

Includes bibliography

979.4 California

Blumberg, Rhoda, 1917-

The great American gold rush. Bradbury Press 1989 135p il $16.95 (5 and up) **979.4**

1. California—Gold discoveries 2. Overland journeys to the Pacific (U.S.) 3. Frontier and pioneer life—California
ISBN 0-02-711681-6 LC 89-736

Describes the emigration of people from the East Coast of the United States and from foreign countries to California to pursue the dream of discovering gold

"Profusely illustrated with cartoons and sketches from publications of the gold rush years, 1848-1852, this oversize book is an impressive combination of good bookmaking, thorough (and documented) research, a lively writing style, and logical arrangement of material. Source material, cited in an appended section by chapters, is used within the text; an extensive relative index is provided, as is a bibliography that is divided into primary and secondary sources. It is rare to find so illuminating a new book on an old subject." Bull Cent Child Books

Climo, Shirley, 1928-
City! San Francisco; photographs by George Ancona. Macmillan 1990 57p il maps $15.95 (4 and up) **979.4**
1. San Francisco (Calif.)
ISBN 0-02-719030-7 LC 89-32912
"The author's suggestions for tourist activities in and around San Francisco are as diversified as they are interesting, and the book offers much more besides. The author has chosen and arranged her material to produce a superbly clear picture of the city - its geographical location, history, ethnic composition, and relationship to other cities that together with San Francisco make up the San Francisco Bay Area. The design is attractive and enticing. . . . Ancona's photographs catch San Francisco's lively flavor, its diversity, and its breathtaking views." Horn Book

982 Argentina

Fox, Geoffrey
The land and people of Argentina. Lippincott 1990 238p il maps (Portraits of the nations ser) $16.95; lib bdg $16.89 (5 and up) **982**
1. Argentina
ISBN 0-397-32380-8; 0-397-32381-6 (lib bdg) LC 89-37811
Introduces the history, geography, people, culture, government, and economy of Argentina
Includes bibliography

983 Chile

Hintz, Martin, 1945-
Chile. Childrens Press 1985 128p il (Enchantment of the world) lib bdg $23.93 (4 and up) **983**
1. Chile
ISBN 0-516-02755-7 LC 84-23104
Describes the landscape, history, economy, culture, and people of this extraordinarily long, narrow country

984 Bolivia

Blair, David Nelson
The land and people of Bolivia. Lippincott 1990 208p il maps (Portraits of the nations ser) $15.95; lib bdg $15.89 (5 and up) **984**
1. Bolivia
ISBN 0-397-32382-4; 0-397-32383-2 (lib bdg) LC 89-39721
Introduces the history, geography, people, culture, government, and economy of Bolivia
Includes bibliography

Morrison, Marion
Bolivia. Childrens Press 1988 128p il maps (Enchantment of the world) lib bdg $23.93 (4 and up) **984**
1. Bolivia
ISBN 0-516-02705-0 LC 88-10877
Discusses the geography, history, people, culture, politics, daily life, and economy of Bolivia
"The cocaine trade receives open discussion, with a good tie-in to its roots in the impoverished Bolivian economy." SLJ

985 Peru

Beck, Barbara L.
The Incas. 2nd ed, revised by Lorna Greenberg. Watts 1983 64p il maps lib bdg $10.40 (4 and up) **985**
1. Incas
ISBN 0-531-04528-5 LC 82-17657
"A First book"
First published 1966 with title: The first book of the Incas
This book "uses archaeological and historical research to trace the development and demise of a fascinating culture. From prehistory to Spanish conquest, the Incas' history, culture, social structure, and daily life are described. Complete with index, chronology, map, reading list, and black-and-white photographs . . . this book will satisfy curiosity and class assignments." Booklist
Includes bibliography

986.6 Ecuador

Lephien, Emilie U. (Emilia Utteg)
Ecuador. Childrens Press 1986 127p il maps (Enchantment of the world) lib bdg $23.93 (4 and up) **986.6**
1. Ecuador
ISBN 0-516-02760-3 LC 85-26967
An introduction to the geography, history, culture, industries, resources, and people of one of the smallest countries in South America

993 New Zealand

Higham, Charles
The Maoris; published in cooperation with Cambridge University Press. Lerner Publs. 1983 c1981 51p il maps lib bdg $8.95 (5 and up) **993**
1. Maoris
ISBN 0-8225-1229-7 (lib bdg) LC 83-1856
"A Cambridge topic book"
First published 1981 in the United Kingdom
"Illustrated with engravings and photos of artifacts, this history offers a comprehensive picture of the Maoris, inhabitants of New Zealand from about A.D. 1000. Because the Maoris left no written records, interpretation of the archaeological evidence is crucial to an understanding of their life-style and social conventions. The

Higham, Charles—*Continued*
account is chronological, beginning with the earliest known settlements and ending with Maori traditions that survive to this day." Booklist

Includes glossary

New Zealand—in pictures; prepared by Geography Department. Lerner Publs. 1990 64p il maps (Visual geography ser) lib bdg $11.95 (5 and up) **993**

1. New Zealand
ISBN 0-8225-1862-7 LC 89-36541

Revised edition of the title prepared by Michael Robson, published 1979 by Sterling

Text and photographs introduce the topography, history, society, economy, and governmental structure of New Zealand

994 Australia

Australia—in pictures; prepared by Geography Department. Lerner Publs. 1990 64p il maps (Visual geography ser) lib bdg $11.95 (5 and up) **994**

1. Australia
ISBN 0-8225-1855-4 LC 89-29199

Revised edition of the title prepared by Jo McDonald and Reven Uihlein, published 1979 by Sterling

An introduction to the land, history, government, economy, people, and culture of Australia

998 Arctic islands and Antarctica

Cowcher, Helen

Antarctica. Farrar, Straus & Giroux 1990 unp il $13.95 (1-3) **998**

1. Antarctic regions 2. Penguins 3. Seals (Animals) 4. Wildlife conservation
ISBN 0-374-30368-1

"In story form, Cowcher attempts to describe life for emperor and Adélie penguins and Weddell seals during one Antarctic winter and spring as they nest, give birth, and raise their young. Harsh weather makes survival difficult, but the true enemy may be the men who have a base camp near the Adélies' nesting area; their helicopter frightens the penguins away, allowing the predatory skuas access to their eggs." SLJ

"The superb pictures, with stunning closeups of birds and mammals in colours glowing against the blue and green of ice and water, hold the eye while the mind takes in the crucial conservation message. Grow Point

Ekoomiak, Normee

Arctic memories. Holt & Co. 1990 c1988 unp il $15.95 (3-5) **998**

1. Inuit 2. Québec (Province) 3. Arctic regions
ISBN 0-8050-1254-0 LC 89-39194

First published 1988 in Canada

"Ekoomiak, an Inuit who grew up in the James Bay area of Arctic Quebec, depicts scenes from his childhood in a picture book that is essentially a personalized record of a way of life that is now all but extinct. The text is written in both English and Inuktitut, the language of the Inuit people." Horn Book

"These simple commentaries become an unexpectedly resonant voice. . . . Ekoomiak's art is spare and elemental. Clean shapes and stylized figures are the rule, though compositions can become agreeably busy and even complex." Booklist

Gilbreath, Alice (Alice Thompson)

The Arctic and Antarctica; roof and floor of the world. Dillon Press 1988 127p il maps (Ocean world lib) lib bdg $11.95 (4 and up) **998**

1. Polar regions
ISBN 0-87518-373-5 LC 87-32448

Describes various aspects of the Arctic and Antarctica including the animals that live there, the people who have explored them, and the changes brought to these faraway regions by modern technology and the search for new energy sources

"A workman-like job with a pleasant open format and many excellent color photos." SLJ

Includes glossary and bibliography

Swan, Robert

Destination: Antarctica; photographs by Roger Mear, Robert Swan, and Rebecca Ward. Scholastic 1988 unp il $13.95; pa $3.95 (4-6) **998**

1. Scott, Robert Falcon, 1868-1912 2. Antarctic regions 3. Explorers
ISBN 0-590-41285-X; 0-590-41286-8 (pa) LC 87-20793

Follows the British adventurer Robert Swan and two other explorers on an exciting and dangerous 900-mile trek to the South Pole as they retrace Robert Scott's 1912 expedition

"This gripping account of perseverance is further enhanced by photographs of the stunning terrain and fascinating glimpses of campsite living. Front and back endpapers, a double-page map of Antarctica, add further dimension to this dramatic quest." Booklist

Fic FICTION

A number of subject headings have been added to the books in this section to aid in curriculum work. It is not necessarily recommended that these subjects be used in the library catalog.

Adams, Richard, 1920-

Watership Down. Macmillan 1974 c1972 429p $29.95; Avon Bks. pa $5.50 (6 and up) **Fic**

1. Rabbits—Fiction 2. Allegories
ISBN 0-02-700030-3; 0-380-00293-0 (pa) LC 73-6044

First published 1972 in the United Kingdom

"Faced with the annihilation of its warren, a small group of male rabbits sets out across the English downs in search of a new home. Internal struggles for power surface in this intricately woven, realistically told adult adventure when the protagonists must coordinate tactics

Adams, Richard, 1920-—*Continued*
in order to defeat an enemy rabbit fortress. It is clear that the author has done research on rabbit behavior, for this tale is truly authentic." Shapiro. Fic for Youth. 2d edition

Ahlberg, Allan

Ten in a bed; illustrated by André Amstutz. Viking Kestrel 1989 c1983 94p il $11.95; Puffin Bks. pa $3.95 (3-5) **Fic**

1. Fairy tales
ISBN 0-670-82042-3; 0-14-032531-X (pa)

First published 1983 in the United Kingdom

"Dinah Price's daytimes may be ordinary but her bedtimes are fantastic. As the sun sets on each of eight consecutive nights, she climbs the stairs and finds in her bed at least one well-known character: the three bears, the Wicked Witch, the cat of 'Hey Diddle, Diddle' fame, Sleeping Beauty, the Big Bad Wolf, Simple Simon, the Frog Prince, or a giant. Each feels right at home beneath Dinah's covers, and it takes all of her inventive powers and patience to chase them out." Booklist

"André Amstutz' illustrations are charming black-and-white line drawings, scattered throughout the text—a benign complement to the wacky stories, and pleasantly moderate in comparison." N Y Times Book Rev

Ahlberg, Janet

Jeremiah in the dark woods; [by] Janet and Allan Ahlberg. Viking 1978 c1977 47p il lib bdg $11.95; Penguin Bks. pa $3.95 (1-3) **Fic**

1. Fairy tales 2. Humorous stories
ISBN 0-670-40637-6 (lib bdg); 0-14-032811-4 (pa)
LC 77-6641

First published 1977 in the United Kingdom

A little boy sets out to find the thief of his grandmother's strawberry tarts and meets a number of unusual characters on his search

"Familiar nursery rhyme characters appear in zany new roles in this amusing, illustrated story." Booklist

Aiken, Joan, 1924-

Arabel and Mortimer; illustrated by Quentin Blake. Doubleday 1981 143p il o.p. (4-6) **Fic**

1. Ravens—Fiction LC 79-6577

Available ABC-CLIO large print edition $14.95 (ISBN 1-85089-978-9)

Sequel to: Arabel's raven (1974)

"The pet of an English girl, Arabel, Mortimer is an irrepressible raven that does as he pleases, to the consternation of the humans around him. His one-word vocabulary, 'Nevermore!', does not prevent him from wreaking havoc on a cruise ship, at a zoo and at an archaeological site. The episodes begin with ordinary situations that quickly escalate into absurdity. The characters are individuals—each is defined by a distinct mannerism or pattern of speech—and the plots are fast-paced and inventive. . . . The cartoon-like, black-and-white illustrations reflect the cheerfully nonsensical spirit of the book." SLJ

Other available titles about Arabel and Mortimer are:
Mortimer says nothing (1989)
Mortimer's cross (1984)

Bridle the wind. Delacorte Press 1983 242p $14.95 (6 and up) **Fic**

1. Adventure and adventurers—Fiction 2. Friendship—Fiction 3. France—Fiction 4. Spain—Fiction
ISBN 0-385-29301-1 LC 83-5355

Sequel to: Go saddle the sea (1977)

"Shipwrecked in France, 13-year-old Felix is rescued by monks and finds himself threatened by an evil Abbot who seems possessed by demoniac powers. Escape leads to encounters with primitive inhabitants of the Pyrenees, gypsies and bandits while, always, the villainous Abbot pursues Felix and his young companion, Juan. Readers will quickly guess that Juan is a girl in disguise, although Felix remains unaware until the end of the story." SLJ

"Only Joan Aiken can carry off such feats of the imagination; the breathtaking story is an outstanding example of the picaresque novel for children." Horn Book

Midnight is a place. Viking 1974 287p o.p.; Dell paperback available $3.50 (5 and up) **Fic**

1. Orphans—Fiction 2. Great Britain—Fiction
ISBN 0-440-45634-7 (pa) LC 74-760

Fourteen-year-old Lucas leads a lonely, monotonous life in the house of his unpleasant guardian until the unexpected arrival of an unusual little girl presages a series of events that completely change his life

"With her customary vivacity and inventiveness, the author has created another novel steeped in nineteenth-century literary traditions and devices. . . . The melodrama, which manages to avoid even a hint of sentimentality, never flags as it goes from incident to incident and reaches a happy ending." Horn Book

The shadow guests. Delacorte Press 1980 150p $11.95; Dell pa $2.95 (5 and up) **Fic**

1. Ghosts—Fiction 2. Great Britain—Fiction
ISBN 0-385-28889-1; 0-440-48226-7 (pa)
LC 80-11984

"After the disappearance of his mother and older brother, Cosmo Curtoys goes to England to live with his cousin Eunice. Upon his arrival at the ancestral family home, Cosmo begins having inexplicable visions, and supernatural events begin to occur at the house." Child Book Rev Serv

"The core of the book, a boy's brave reconciliation to grief and his consequent emotional growth, is enclosed in scenes that are by turns comic, macabre, matter-of-fact or richly descriptive. The maturity and wisdom of the book reflects a respect for and understanding of the young." Grow Point

The wolves of Willoughby Chase; illustrated by Pat Marriott. Doubleday 1963 c1962 168p il $13.95; Dell pa $3.50 (5 and up) **Fic**

1. Great Britain—Fiction
ISBN 0-385-03594-2; 0-440-49603-9 (pa)
LC 63-18034

First published 1962 in the United Kingdom

Aiken, Joan, 1924-—*Continued*

"In this burlesque of a Victorian melodrama, two London children are sent to a country estate while their parents are away. Here they outwit a wicked governess, escape from packs of hungry wolves, and restore the estate to its rightful owner." Hodges. Books for Elem Sch Libr

"Plot, characterization, and background blend perfectly into an amazing whole. . . . Highly recommended." SLJ

Other available titles about Dido Twite and Simon are:
Black hearts in Battersea (1964)
Dido and Pa (1986)
Nightbirds on Nantucket (1966)

Alcock, Vivien, 1924-

The cuckoo sister. Delacorte Press 1986 c1985 160p $14.95 (6 and up) **Fic**

1. Sisters—Fiction 2. London (England)—Fiction
ISBN 0-385-29467-0 LC 85-20648

Also available G.K. Hall large print edition $14.95 (ISBN 0-7451-0586-6)

First published 1985 in the United Kingdom

"Eleven year old Kate Seton becomes very upset when an underfed 13-year-old shows up at her parents' home with a letter stating that she is Kate's sister—stolen from a pram outside a store where Mrs. Seton had been shopping. Rosie doesn't believe the story that she is Emma Seton and frantically tries to find her mother who has left with no trace. Kate eventually comes to love Rosie and tries to provide a clue that will enable her to stay. Characterizations are very vivid and although it definitely has a British flavor, students will empathize with Kate and Rosie." Voice Youth Advocates

The monster garden. Delacorte Press 1988 134p $13.95; Dell pa $2.95 (4 and up) **Fic**

1. Monsters—Fiction 2. Fathers and daughters—Fiction 3. Science fiction
ISBN 0-440-50053-2; 0-440-40257-3 (pa) LC 88-6900

"The story of a young girl who unexpectedly finds herself nurturing a creature of unknown origin. Frankie Stein is the daughter of a scientist whose preoccupation with his work drives a wedge among the family members. When Frankie obtains some unknown genetic 'material,' she finds herself having to cope with a growing 'monster.'" SLJ

"*The Monster Garden* is a deft fantasy; it is also a story of compassionate love and growing self-reliance." Bull Cent Child Books

The stonewalkers. Delacorte Press 1983 c1981 151p $12.95 (5 and up) **Fic**

1. Monuments—Fiction 2. Horror—Fiction 3. Great Britain—Fiction
ISBN 0-385-29233-3 LC 82-13956

First published 1981 in the United Kingdom

"Virtually friendless, Poppy makes a confidante of the statue she names Belladonna. . . . A sudden bolt of lightning . . . somehow brings the statue to life. To Poppy's horror, it quickly loses its friendly innocence, becoming instead a destructive force. The girl enlists the aid of a schoolmate in an effort to impede the statue's progress as the now malevolent Belladonna recruits an army of stone figures from churchyards and gardens." Horn Book

"The blending of suspenseful fantasy and elements of the contemporary problem novel works remarkably well here, and may appeal to children not ordinarily attracted to fantasy literature." SLJ

Alcott, Louisa May, 1832-1888

Little women; or Meg, Jo, Beth and Amy (5 and up) **Fic**

1. Family life—Fiction 2. New England—Fiction

Some editions are:
Golden Bks. (Golden classics) $9.95 Illustrated by Michael Adams (ISBN 0-307-17116-7)
Knopf (Knopf children's classics) $18.95 Illustrated By Derek James (ISBN 0-394-56279-8)
Little, Brown $17.95 With illustrations in color by Jessie Willcox Smith (ISBN 0-316-03095-3)
Macmillan pa $3.95 (ISBN 0-02-041240-1)
Messner (Messner classics ser) lib bdg $14.79 Illustrated by Judith Cheng (ISBN 0-671-45651-2)
Penguin Bks. (Penguin classics) pa $5.95 Edited with an introduction by Elaine Showalter and with notes by Siobhan Kilfeather and Vinca Showalter (ISBN 0-14-039069-3)
Putnam Pub. Group pa $9.95 (ISBN 0-448-11019-9)
Wanderer Bks. (Simon and Schuster classics) $15.95 Illustrated by Judith Cheng (ISBN 0-671-44447-6)

First published 1868

The story of the New England home life of the four March sisters. Each 'little woman's' personality differs: Jo's quick temper and restless desire for the freedom of a boy's life; Meg's hatred of poverty and her longing for pretty clothes; Amy's all-engulfing self-interest; and gentle Beth's love of home and family

The tale is "related with sympathy, humour, and sincerity. This lively natural narrative of family experience is as well-loved today as when it first appeared." Toronto Public Libr. Books for Boys & Girls

Other available titles about members of the March family are:
Eight cousins (1875)
Jo's boys (1886)
Little men (1871)
Rose in bloom (1876)

An old-fashioned Thanksgiving (3-5) **Fic**

1. Family life—Fiction 2. Thanksgiving Day—Fiction 3. New England—Fiction

Some editions are:
Holiday House $14.95 Illustrated by Michael McCurdy (ISBN 0-8234-0772-1)
Lippincott $12.95 Illustrated by Holly Johnson (ISBN 0-397-31515-5)

"In this story, which first appeared in 'St. Nicholas' magazine in 1881, Alcott recounts the escapades of a New Hampshire farm family in the 1820s. When the parents are unexpectedly called away on Thanksgiving Day, the children pitch in to make their version of the traditional holiday feast and, with little knowledge and less caution, bumble along toward a culinary catastrophe reminiscent of Meg and Jo's dinner in 'Little Women.'" Booklist

Alexander, Lloyd

The book of three. Holt & Co. 1964 217p il $12.95; Dell pa $3.50 (5 and up) **Fic**

1. Fantastic fiction
ISBN 0-8050-0874-8; 0-440-90702-0 (pa) LC 68-11833

Alexander, Lloyd—*Continued*

"The first of five books about the mythical land of Prydain finds Taran, an assistant pig keeper, fighting with Prince Gwydion against the evil which theatens the kingdom." Hodges. Books for Elem Sch Libr

"Related in a simple, direct style, this fast-paced tale of high adventure has a well-balanced blend of fantasy, realism, and humor. Although the Welsh Mabinogion is the inspiration for the story and some of the characters, the incidents, mood, and characterizations are more reminiscent of Tolkien's trilogy." SLJ

Other available titles about the mythical land of Prydain are:
The black cauldron (1965)
The castle of Llyr (1966)
Taran Wanderer (1967)

Final volume about Prydain: The High King, entered below

The cat who wished to be a man. Dutton 1973 107p $14.95 (4-6) **Fic**

1. Cats—Fiction
ISBN 0-525-27545-2 LC 73-77447

When he begins dealing with humanity, Lionel the cat begins to understand why his wizard master was reluctant to change him into a man

This is "a comic and ebullient fantasy; just right for reading aloud." Horn Book

The first two lives of Lukas-Kasha. Dutton 1978 213p $14.95; Dell pa $2.25 (4 and up) **Fic**

1. Fairy tales
ISBN 0-525-29748-0; 0-440-42784-3 (pa)
LC 77-26699

"High adventure in the kingdom of Abadan as Lukas-Kasha enters from the sea and is declared king by the court astrologer. The evil vizier wants no king but himself and plots to do away with Lukas, who escapes with the help of a poet and a slave girl." Child Book Rev Serv

"What gives the story its final high gloss are the depth and nuance of the serious conversation and the transfusion of pithy ideas into the derring-do setting, ideas that are universally applicable. That's the frosting: it crowns a confection of polished style, well-paced plot, and engaging wit." Bull Cent Child Books

The High King. Holt & Co. 1968 285p il lib bdg $16.95; Dell pa $3.50 (5 and up) **Fic**

1. Fantastic fiction
ISBN 0-8050-1114-5 (lib bdg); 0-440-43574-9 (pa)
LC 68-11833

Awarded the Newbery Medal, 1969

Concluding title in the chronicles of Prydain which include: The book of three, The black cauldron, The castle of Llyr, and Taran Wanderer, entered above

In this final volume Taran, the assistant pig-keeper "becomes High King of Prydain, Princess Eilonwy becomes his queen, the predictions of Taran's wizard guardian Dallben are fulfilled, and the forces of black magic led by Arawn, Lord of Annuvin, Land of the Dead, are vanquished forever." SLJ

"For those who have learned to love the land of Prydain, reading this last volume in the cycle will be a bittersweet experience. . . . The fantasy has the depth and richness of a medieval tapestry, infinitely detailed and imaginative." Saturday Rev

The Illyrian adventure. Dutton 1986 132p $13.95; Dell pa $3.50 (5 and up) **Fic**

1. Adventure and adventurers—Fiction
ISBN 0-525-44250-2; 0-440-40297-2 (pa)
LC 85-30762

"Sixteen-year-old Vesper Holly drags her long-suffering guardian, Brinnie, off to Illyria to vindicate her late father's reputation as a scholar. With humor, beguiling charm, and intelligence she manages to find a treasure, thwart a conspiracy to murder Illyria's King Osman, and guide two rival factions to the peace table." Wilson Libr Bull

"Alexander's archeological mystery has intricate plotting and witty wording—a romp of a read-aloud for Raiders of the Lost Ark fans." Bull Cent Child Books

Other available adventure titles featuring Vesper Holly are:
The Drackenberg adventure (1988)
The El Dorado adventure (1987)
The Jedera adventure (1989)
The Philadelphia adventure (1990)

The marvelous misadventures of Sebastian; grand extravaganza, including a performance by the entire cast of the Gallimaufry-Theatricus. Dutton 1970 204p $14.95 (4 and up) **Fic**

1. Adventure and adventurers—Fiction 2. Musicians—Fiction
ISBN 0-525-34739-9 LC 70-116879

"Sebastian, a teenage fiddler, gets involved in court intrigue and muddles his way to eventual success in ousting a cruel usurper from the throne." Natl Counc of Teach of Engl. Adventuring with Books

"The intricacy of plot, the humor and allusiveness of the writing, the exaggerated characterization, and the derring-do of romantic adventures are knit into a lively and elaborate tale that can be enjoyed for its action and appreciated for its subtler significance." Sutherland. The Best in Child Books

Westmark. Dutton 1981 184p $15.95; Dell pa $3.25 (5 and up) **Fic**

1. Adventure and adventurers—Fiction
ISBN 0-525-42335-4; 0-440-99731-3 (pa)
LC 80-22242

A boy fleeing from criminal charges falls in with a charlatan, his dwarf attendant, and an urchin girl, travels with them about the kingdom of Westmark, and ultimately arrives at the palace where the king is grieving over the loss of his daughter

The author "peoples his tale with a marvelous cast of individuals, and weaves an intricate story of high adventure that climaxes in a superbly conceived conclusion, which, though predictable, is reached through carefully built tension and subtly added comic relief." Booklist

Other available titles about the kingdom of Westmark are:
The beggar queen (1984)
The Kestrel (1982)

Almedingen, E. M. (Edith Martha), 1898-1971

The crimson oak. Coward-McCann 1983 c1981 112p $9.95 (5 and up) **Fic**

1. Elizabeth, Empress of Russia, 1709-1762—Fiction 2. Soviet Union—Fiction

ISBN 0-698-20569-3 LC 82-12556

First published 1981 in the United Kingdom

"This historical novel is set in Russia in 1739, when the Princess Elizabeth, heir to the throne, had been sent into the countryside. . . . Peter, a peasant boy of twelve meets her in the woods and saves her from a marauding bear, earning her promise to help him if it is ever within her power. She fulfills her promise when she comes to the throne, granting the boy's dearest wish: an education." Bull Cent Child Books

"The narrative, which depends on the political situation in Russia during the 1730s, speaks frankly about the ferociously bureaucratic tyranny of the era. . . . On the other hand, the fulfillment of Peter's wish, based on his chance encounter with the Princess Elizabeth, gives the story—with its sensitive and lively description of eighteenth-century Russian life—the quality of a fairy tale." Horn Book

Andersen, Hans Christian, 1805-1875

The emperor's new clothes; designed and illustrated by Virginia Lee Burton. Houghton Mifflin 1949 43p il hardcover o.p. paperback available $5.95 (2-5) **Fic**

1. Fairy tales

ISBN 0-395-28594-1 (pa) LC 49-10479

A tale about the vain emperor whose only concern was his wardrobe. It tells of the clever rascals who pocketed the money given them to weave beautiful cloth for the emperor but did not weave any, his flattering courtiers who dared not voice their own opinions, and the child who pointed out the deceit as the emperor paraded proudly with nothing on

"Delightfully illustrated with humorous pictures. Lends itself equally well to looking, listening, and discussion." Hodges. Books for Elem Sch Libr

Hans Christian Andersen's The fir tree; illustrated by Nancy Ekholm Burkert. Harper & Row 1970 34p il $13.95; lib bdg $13.89 (2-5) **Fic**

1. Christmas—Fiction

ISBN 0-06-020077-4; 0-06-020078-2 (lib bdg) LC 73-121800

This translation of the fairy tale is by H. W. Dulcken

Surrounded by the beauties of the forest, the little fir tree was unhappy and longed for its moment of glory. It came one Christmas Eve but it was neither what the tree expected nor wanted

"The delicacy and meticulousness of the illustrative details of this edition, beautiful in soft colors or in black and white, should please old fans and the felicity of mood should attract new ones." Bull Cent Child Books

The little match girl; illustrated by Blair Lent. Houghton Mifflin 1968 43p il lib bdg $12.95 (2-5) **Fic**

ISBN 0-395-21625-7 LC 68-28050

Also available from Putnam in an edition with illustrations by Rachel Isadora in paperback for $5.95 (ISBN 0-399-22007-0)

This is the "touching story of the lonely, shivering child who sees visions in the flames of the matches she cannot sell, and whose last vision is the loving grandmother who is dead and who comes to take the child. The illustrations are tremendously effective, the tiny figure lost and lorn against towering grey buildings and driving snow; even the glorious warmth and comfort of the hallucinations are pictured in muted tones." Sutherland. The Best in Child Books

The nightingale (2-5) **Fic**

1. Nightingales—Fiction 2. Fairy tales

Some editions are:

Barron's Educ. Ser. $7.95 Illustrated by Francois Crozat; translated from the original Danish text by Marlee Alex (ISBN 0-8120-5718-X)

Doubleday $13.95, lib bdg $14.99 Illustrated by Alison Claire Darke (ISBN 0-385-26081-4; 0-385-26082-2)

Harcourt Brace Jovanovich pa $3.95 Illustrated by Demi (ISBN 0-15-257428-X)

Harper & Row $13.95, lib bdg $14.89, pa $7.95 Translated by Eva Le Gallienne; designed and illustrated by Nancy Ekholm Burkert (ISBN 0-06-023780-5; 0-06-023781-3; 0-06-443070-7)

Picture Bk. Studio $14.95 Illustrated by Lisbeth Zwerger; translated by Anthea Bell (ISBN 0-907234-57-7)

This is the "story of the Emperor's nightingale which entertained him with exquisite song. Replaced by a gorgeous jewel-encrusted artificial bird, the nightingale is banished from the empire, only to return later to save the Emperor from sure death." Publ Wkly

The princess and the pea (1-4) **Fic**

1. Fairy tales

Some editions are:

Clarion Bks. $11.95 Illustrated by Paul Galdone (ISBN 0-395-28807-X)

North-South Bks. $14.95 Illustrated by Dorothee Duntze (ISBN 1-55858-034-4)

Picture Bk. Studio $13.95 Translated by Anthea Bell; illustrated by Eve Tharlet (ISBN 0-88708-052-9)

A "well-known prince seeks in vain for a bride but finds no princess who seems real in all the world. When a pretty unknown girl shows up at the royal castle and asks for shelter from a storm . . . [the queen] plans to test the princess for sensitivity. Of course, the stranger becomes the prince's bride when she passed a sleepless night because of the pea under the 20 mattresses and 20 featherbeds towering over her four-poster." Publ Wkly

The Snow Queen (4-6) **Fic**

1. Fairy tales

Some editions are:

HarperCollins Pubs. $14.95, lib bdg $14.89 Translated by Eve Le Gallienne; illustrations by Arieh Zeldich (ISBN 0-06-023694-9; 0-06-023695-7)

Holt & Co. $15.95 Translated by Naomi Lewis; illustrated by Angela Barrett (ISBN 0-8050-0830-6)

Lothrop, Lee & Shepard Bks. $14.95, lib bdg $14.88 Illustrated by Sally Holmes; English version by Neil Philip (ISBN 0-688-09047-8; 0-688-09048-6)

"The devil makes a mirror which causes everything good to appear unpleasant and vice versa. The mirror shatters and splinters of its glass fly about the world. Two enter the eyes and heart of Kai, a little boy, who becomes cynical and hard in character, beginning to turn

Andersen, Hans Christian, 1805-1875—*Continued*

against his former playfellow, the little girl Gerda. Soon he is carried off by the icily beautiful but cruel Snow Queen. Gerda goes in search of him, and has many strange adventures before she finds him and melts the splinters and his frozen heart with her tears." Oxford Companion to Child Lit

The steadfast tin soldier (1-4) **Fic**

1. Toys—Fiction 2. Fairy tales

Some editions are:

Houghton Mifflin $14.95 Illustrated by Paul Galdone (ISBN 0-395-28964-5)

Prentice-Hall $8.95 Illustrated by Thomas DiGrazia (ISBN 0-13-846295-X)

Scribner edition published 1953 translated by M. R. James and illustrated by Marcia Brown (Caldecott Medal honor book, 1954) is o.p.

A favorite among Hans Christian Andersen's stories, this tells the adventures of a tin soldier and his love for a little toy dancer

The swineherd; translated by Naomi Lewis; illustrated by Dorothée Duntze. North-South Bks. 1987 unp il $14.95 (1-4) **Fic**

1. Fairy tales

ISBN 1-55858-038-7 LC 86-62521

A prince disguises himself as a swineherd and learns the true character of the princess he desires

"The large-format picture book is dominated by Duntze's elegant watercolors. Exquisitely rendered in a formal, somewhat surreal style, the illustrations point up the foibles of the princess' artificial court. . . . The sunny, gentle hues of the artist's palette lend an air of warmth to the paintings." Booklist

Thumbeline; illustrated by Lisbeth Zwerger; translated by Anthea Bell. Picture Bk. Studio 1985 unp il $14.95 (1-4) **Fic**

1. Fairy tales

ISBN 0-88708-006-5 LC 85-12062

"The delightful adventures of a tiny girl no bigger than a thumb and her many animal friends . . . evocatively interpreted by Austrian illustrator Lisbeth Zwerger." Booklist

The ugly duckling; illustrated by Alan Marks; translated by Anthea Bell. Picture Bk. Studio 1989 unp il $14.95 (1-4) **Fic**

1. Swans—Fiction

ISBN 0-88708-116-9 LC 89-3975

An ugly duckling spends an unhappy year ostracized by the other animals before he grows into a beautiful swan

"Bell's smoothly translated text fills the left-hand pages of this book, with full-color washes by Marks on the right. His illustrations have an earthy quality, with ruddy colors and bold action." Booklist

The wild swans; English version by Naomi Lewis; illustrated by Angela Barrett. Bedrick Bks. 1984 unp il hardcover o.p. paperback available $6.95 (2-5) **Fic**

1. Fairy tales

ISBN 0-87226-232-4 (pa) LC 83-15805

This is "the story of eleven brothers who were turned into swans and their sister who breaks the spell through courage and sacrifice." SLJ

"The detailed vivid story has inspired equally complex and intense pictures. Composition is striking, with perspective used to dramatize effect and elaborate line work creating some densely detailed interiors and woodland greenery. . . . The text is modern but formal, with spare use of dialogue." Booklist

Angell, Judie, 1937-

Dear Lola; or, How to build your own family; a tale. Bradbury Press 1980 166p o.p.; Dell paperback available $1.95 (4-6) **Fic**

1. Orphans—Fiction 2. Runaway children—Fiction

ISBN 0-440-91787-5 (pa) LC 80-15111

"Eighteen-year-old Arthur Beniker, who makes his living writing a Dear Lola column, shepherds six parentless children to a small town where they all live happily with their own idiosyncrasies when not avoiding nosy townspeople. Do-gooders nearly destroy their happy home, however, necessitating a quick exit." Booklist

"Patient, loving, wise, and compassionate, Lola is one of the nicest father figures in fiction; if the story isn't wholly believable, it's still wholly beguiling: good style, good characters, a fresh plot, and the perennial appeal of a dream come true." Bull Cent Child Books

A home is to share—and share—and share—. Bradbury Press 1984 151p $11.95; Berkley Bks. pa $2.50 (4-6) **Fic**

1. Pets—Fiction 2. Brothers and sisters—Fiction

ISBN 0-02-705830-1; 0-425-09176-7 (pa) LC 83-21356

The three Muchmore children "are great animal lovers and when they learn that the local animal shelter is to close, they try various ingenious schemes to find homes for the stray dogs, cats, and monkey who live there." Child Book Rev Serv

The author "captures readers with a fast-paced plot, funny dialogue and warm-blooded characters. Subtle messages on family life are conveyed, particularly the special place of adopted children and the importance of caring and sharing." SLJ

Tina Gogo. Bradbury Press 1978 196p o.p.; Dell paperback available $1.75 (6 and up) **Fic**

1. Friendship—Fiction 2. Foster home care—Fiction

ISBN 0-440-98738-5 (pa) LC 77-16439

The story revolves around eleven-year-old Tina Gogolavsky, who is "a problem foster child and her giant leap into maturity one summer when she befriends another girl and her 'typical' family in a small community around a lake resort." Child Book Rev Serv

"In a well-paced plot that is never melodramatic, Angell gingerly peels away the layers of hurt and mistrust beneath which Tina . . . has buried herself revealing

Angell, Judie, 1937-—*Continued*
a miraculously resilient and sturdy core. . . . Relationships between the characters are skillfully drawn and this is, altogether, nicely done." SLJ

Arkin, Alan, 1934-
The lemming condition; illustrated by Joan Sandin. Harper & Row 1976 57p il $12.95; lib bdg $11.89 (5 and up) **Fic**
1. Lemmings—Fiction
ISBN 0-06-020133-9; 0-06-020134-7 (lib bdg) LC 75-6296
"Disturbed that no other lemming can answer his question of whether or not lemmings can swim, Bubber decides to find out himself. Two feet stuck uncomfortably into a nearby pond tell him all he needs to know, and now he anxiously ponders the fate of his family and friends—indeed all the lemmings who feel moved to travel west to the sea that afternoon. . . . Facile, upbeat dialogue among Bubber's family and friends serves to quickly delineate common attitudes, and Arkin manages to mesh the biological habits of lemmings with the human characteristics he imposes upon them. The resulting contemporary parable is arch but solid enough to provoke its share of discussion." Booklist

Armstrong, William Howard
Sounder; [by] William H. Armstrong; illustrations by James Barkley. Harper & Row 1969 116p il $13.95; lib bdg $13.89; pa $3.95 (5 and up) **Fic**
1. Dogs—Fiction 2. Blacks—Fiction 3. Family life—Fiction
ISBN 0-06-020143-6; 0-06-020144-4 (lib bdg); 0-06-080975-2 (pa) LC 70-85030
Also available ABC-CLIO large print edition $13.95 (ISBN 1-55736-003-0)
Awarded the Newbery Medal, 1970
"Set in the South in the era of sharecropping and segregation, this succinctly told tale poignantly describes the courage of a father who steals a ham in order to feed his undernourished family; the determination of the eldest son, who searches for his father despite the apathy of prison authorities; and the devotion of a coon dog named Sounder." Shapiro. Fic for Youth. 2d edition

Atwater, Richard Tupper, 1892-1948
Mr. Popper's penguins; [by] Richard and Florence Atwater; illustrated by Robert Lawson. Little, Brown 1938 138p il $14.95; Dell pa $3.25 (3-5) **Fic**
1. Penguins—Fiction
ISBN 0-316-05842-4; 0-440-45934-6 (pa) LC 38-27840
A Newbery Medal honor book, 1939
When Mr. Popper, a mild little painter and decorator with a taste for books and movies on polar explorations, was presented with a penguin, he named it Captain Cook. From that moment on life was changed for the Popper family
"To the depiction of the penguins in all conceivable moods Robert Lawson [the] artist has brought not only his skill but his individual humor, and his portrayal of the wistful Mr. Popper is memorable." N Y Times Book Rev

Auch, Mary Jane
Kidnapping Kevin Kowalski. Holiday House 1990 124p $13.95 (4-6) **Fic**
1. Friendship—Fiction 2. Mothers and sons—Fiction 3. Kidnapping—Fiction
ISBN 0-8234-0815-9 LC 89-46065
When a terrible accident partially disables Kevin and makes his mother overprotective of him, his best friends Ryan and Mooch decide that the only way to liberate him is to kidnap him
"With a practiced blend of fast-moving storytelling, believable characters, and ethical questions that inform but do not overwhelm the story, this has guaranteed appeal for middle-grade boys." Bull Cent Child Books

Avi, 1937-
The fighting ground. Lippincott 1984 157p $12.95; lib bdg $12.89 (5 and up) **Fic**
1. United States—History—1775-1783, Revolution—Fiction
ISBN 0-397-32073-6; 0-397-32074-4 (lib bdg) LC 82-47719
"It's April 1776, and the fighting ground is both the farm country of Pennsylvania and the heart of a boy which is 'wonderful ripe for war.' Twenty-four hours transform Jonathan from a cocky 13-year-old, eager to take on the British, into a young man who now knows the horror, the pathos, the ambiguities of war." Voice Youth Advocates
The author "has written a taut, fast-paced novel that builds to a shattering climax. His protagonist's painful, inner struggle to understand the intense and conflicting emotions brought on by a war that spares no one is central to this finely crafted novel." ALAN

S.O.R. losers. Bradbury Press 1984 90p $11.95; Avon Bks. pa $2.75 (5 and up) **Fic**
1. Soccer—Fiction 2. School stories
ISBN 0-02-793410-1; 0-380-69993-1 (pa) LC 84-11022
Each member of the South Orange River eighth-grade soccer team has qualities of excellence, but not on the soccer field
"Short, pithy chapters highlighting key events maintain the pace necessary for successful comedy. . . . The style is vivid, believably articulate, for the narrator and his teammates may be deficient athletically but not intellectually. Certainly, the team manifesto 'People have a right to be losers' is as refreshing as it is iconoclastic." Horn Book

The true confessions of Charlotte Doyle; decorations by Ruth E. Murray. Orchard Bks. 1990 215p $14.95; lib bdg $14.99 (6 and up) **Fic**
1. Sea stories
ISBN 0-531-05893-X; 0-531-08493-0 (lib bdg) LC 90-30624
A Newbery Medal honor book, 1991
"A Richard Jackson book"

Avi, 1937—*Continued*

This is a "seafaring adventure, set in 1832. Charlotte Doyle, 13, returning from school in England to join her family in Rhode Island, is deposited on a seedy ship with a ruthless, mad captain and a mutinous crew. Refusing to heed warnings about Captain Jaggery's brutality, Charlotte seeks his guidance and approval only to become his victim, a pariah to the entire crew, and a convicted felon for the murder of the first mate." SLJ

The author has "fashioned an intriguing, suspenseful, carefully crafted tale, with nonstop action on the high seas." Booklist

Babbitt, Natalie

The eyes of the Amaryllis. Farrar, Straus & Giroux 1977 127p $12.95; pa $3.50 (5 and up) **Fic**

1. Sea stories 2. Grandmothers—Fiction
ISBN 0-374-32241-4; 0-374-42238-9 (pa)
LC 77-11862

"The sea holds countless mysteries and gives up very few secrets; when she does, it is truly a remarkable event, an event that eleven-year-old Geneva Reade experiences when she visits her grandmother who lives in a house by the water's edge. Sent for to tend her Gran through a broken leg, Jenny is put to work, at once, combing the beach for a sign from her grandfather, a captain lost at sea with his ship and crew thirty years ago." Child Book Rev Serv

The story "has as its central theme the idea that love can be mistaken or misunderstood but that it can never be fully satisfied or completely destroyed. . . . An intricate combination of patterns . . . the book succeeds as a well-wrought narrative in which a complex philosophic theme is developed through the balanced, subtle use of symbol and imagery. It is a rare story." Horn Book

Goody Hall; story and pictures by Natalie Babbitt. Farrar, Straus & Giroux 1971 176p il hardcover o.p. paperback available $3.50 (4-6) **Fic**

1. Mystery and detective stories
ISBN 0-374-42767-4 (pa) LC 73-149221

In this Gothic mystery "Hercules Feltwright, a would-be actor, comes to a magnificent house—Goody Hall—to tutor the young master, Willet Goody. The boy soon announces his firm conviction that his father is not dead and interred in the family tomb. In trying to find an answer for Willet, Hercules' way is marked by chilling events, including a gypsy seance on a rainy night and a thrilling descent into Mr. Goody's burial vault." Wis Libr Bull

"Lightened by humor and colored by suspense, the story whirls its delightfully just-short-of-burlesqued characters in a triumphant gavotte of melodrama." Saturday Rev

Kneeknock Rise; story and pictures by Natalie Babbitt. Farrar, Straus & Giroux 1970 117p il hardcover o.p. paperback available $3.45 (4-6) **Fic**

1. Allegories 2. Superstition—Fiction
ISBN 0-374-44260-6 (pa) LC 79-105622

A Newbery Medal honor book, 1971

"Did you ever meet a Megrimum? There is one in KneeKnock Rise, and on stormy nights the villagers of Instep tremble in delicious delight as its howls echo over the Mammoth Mountains. Egan learns a lesson when he climbs to meet and conquer the Megrimum." Best Sellers

"An enchanting tale imbued with a folk flavor, enlivened with piquant imagery and satiric wit." Booklist

The search for delicious. Farrar, Straus & Giroux 1969 167p il $12.95; pa $3.50 (5 and up) **Fic**

ISBN 0-374-36534-2; 0-374-46536-3 (pa)
LC 69-20374

"An Ariel book"

The Prime Minister is compiling a dictionary and when no one at court can agree on the meaning of delicious, the King sends his twelve-year-old messenger to poll the country

"The theme, foolish arguments can lead to great conflict, may not be clear to all children who will enjoy this fantasy." Best Sellers

Tuck everlasting. Farrar, Straus & Giroux 1975 139p $12.95; pa $3.50 (5 and up) **Fic**

1. Fantastic fiction
ISBN 0-374-37848-7; 0-374-48009-5 (pa)
LC 75-33306

Also available ABC-CLIO large print edition $14.95 (ISBN 1-55736-050-2)

The Tuck family is confronted with an agonizing situation when they discover that a ten-year-old girl and a malicious stranger now share their secret about a spring whose water prevents one from ever growing any older

"The story is macabre and moral, exciting and excellently written." N Y Times Book Rev

Bagnold, Enid

National Velvet; illustrations by Ted Lewin. Morrow 1985 c1935 258p il lib bdg $15.95; Pocket Bks. pa $2.95 (5 and up) **Fic**

1. Horses—Fiction 2. Great Britain—Fiction
ISBN 0-688-05788-8 (lib bdg); 0-671-69388-3 (pa)
LC 85-2982

Also available ABC-CLIO large print edition $15.95 (ISBN 1-55736-175-4)

First published 1935; first Morrow edition illustrated by Paul Brown published 1949

An English girl, Velvet Brown, wins a magnificent piebald horse in a lottery and determines to enter and win the Grand National Steeplechase even though girls are not allowed to ride in that race

"Numerous vibrant, full-page watercolors and some in shaded, pale washes of gray add new spirit while still keeping the original flavor of the story. An inviting piece." Booklist

Bailey, Carolyn Sherwin, 1875-1961

Miss Hickory; with lithographs by Ruth Gannett. Viking 1946 120p il $13.95; Puffin Bks. pa $3.95 (3-5) **Fic**

1. Dolls—Fiction 2. New Hampshire—Fiction
ISBN 0-670-47940-3; 0-14-030956-X (pa) LC 46-7275

Awarded the Newbery Medal, 1947

"With her hickory nut head glued to a body made of an apple-wood twig, Miss Hickory may have seemed to be merely a country doll—but actually, she was a real person, who had all sorts of exciting adventures after Great-Granny Brown closed her New Hampshire home for the winter." Bookmark

"Fascinating and harmonious lithographs adorn this imaginative and delightful story." Horn Book

Baker, Betty, 1928-1987

Walk the world's rim. Harper & Row 1965 168p il lib bdg $13.89 (5 and up) **Fic**

1. Estevan, d. 1539—Fiction 2. Nuñez Cabeza de Vaca, Alvar, 16th cent.—Fiction 3. America—Exploration—Fiction
ISBN 0-06-020381-1 LC 65-11458

Chakho, an Indian boy, travels from Texas to Mexico City with the black slave Esteban, Cabeza de Vaca, and two other Spanish explorers in the 16th century

"Told against an authentic background, the story has much to say about freedom and human dignity." Hodges. Books for Elem Sch Libr

Baker, Olaf

Where the buffaloes begin; drawings by Stephen Gammell. Warne 1981 unp il o.p.; Puffin Bks. paperback available $5.95 (2-4) **Fic**

1. Indians of North America—Fiction 2. Bison—Fiction
ISBN 0-14-050560-1 (pa) LC 80-23319

A Caldecott Medal honor book, 1982

"Originally published in 1915 in 'St. Nicholas Magazine,' the story tells in four short chapters of the adventure of Little Wolf, a ten-year-old Indian boy. He was fascinated by a tribal legend about a lake to the south, a sacred spot where the buffaloes were said to originate. . . . Narrated in cadenced prose rich in images, the story evokes the Plains Indians' feelings of reverence for the buffalo." Horn Book

The illustrations "are an example of the best kind of book art, pictures that extend and complement the story, that are appropriate in mood, and that are distinctive in themselves." Bull Cent Child Books

Barrie, J. M. (James Matthew), 1860-1937

Peter Pan (3-5) **Fic**

1. Fairy tales

Some editions are:

ABC-CLIO $14.95 Large print edition (ISBN 0-85089-949-5)
Holt & Co. $16.95 Illustrated by Michael Hague (ISBN 0-8050-0276-6)
Potter $12.95 Illustrated by Michael Foreman (ISBN 0-517-56837-3) Has title: Peter Pan & Wendy
Random House lib bdg $8.99; pa $8.95 Illustrated by Diane Goode; edited by Josette Frank (ISBN 0-394-95717-2; 0-394-85717-8)
Scribner $18.95 Illustrations by Trina Schart Hyman (ISBN 0-684-16611-9)

First published 1911 by Scribner with title: Peter and Wendy

This is the story of "how Wendy, John, and Michael flew with Peter Pan, the boy who never grows up, to adventures in the Never-Never Land with pirates, red-skins, and the fairy Tinker Bell. [It is] in Barrie's inimitable style, pleasing the child with delightful absurdities and the adult with good-humored satire." Right Book for the Right Child

Base, Graeme, 1958-

The eleventh hour; a curious mystery. Abrams 1989 unp il $14.95 (4-6) **Fic**

1. Animals—Fiction 2. Birthdays—Fiction 3. Mystery and detective stories 4. Stories in rhyme
ISBN 0-8109-0851-4 LC 89-167

"This picture book is a puzzle mystery written in verse. When Horace the elephant turns 11, he decides to throw an elaborate birthday party and invites 11 friends. The animal guests arrive in costume, and entertain themselves with a variety of activities until it is time to eat. When the 11th hour arrives, however, they are horrified to find that the entire feast has been eaten. . . . What remains is for readers to discover the culprit. 'The Inside Story,' a sealed section of pages containing the solution to the mystery and explanations of the . . . clues and puzzles in the book, follows the story." SLJ

"Younger children may enjoy looking at the bursting-to-overflowing pictures, but this offering definitely fits into the picture-books-for-older-readers category. . . . Hours of intriguing entertainment for young sleuths." Booklist

Bauer, Marion Dane

On my honor. Clarion Bks. 1986 90p $12.95; Dell pa $2.75 (4 and up) **Fic**

1. Accidents—Fiction
ISBN 0-89919-439-7; 0-440-46633-4 (pa) LC 86-2679

Also available G.K. Hall large print edition $13.95 (ISBN 0-8161-4646-2)

A Newbery Medal honor book, 1987

When his best friend drowns while they are both swimming in a treacherous river that they had promised never to go near, Joel is devastated and terrified at having to tell both sets of parents the terrible consequences of their disobedience

"Bauer's association of Joel's guilt with the smell of the polluted river on his skin is particularly noteworthy. Its miasma almost rises off the pages. Descriptions are vivid, characterization and dialogue natural, and the style taut but unforced. A powerful, moving book." SLJ

Rain of fire. Clarion Bks. 1983 153p $13.95 (5 and up) **Fic**

1. World War, 1939-1945—Fiction 2. Brothers—Fiction 3. Veterans—Fiction
ISBN 0-89919-190-8 LC 83-2065

Bauer, Marion Dane—*Continued*

"Steve wants to hear about his older brother's World War II experiences, but Matthew is too upset by them to oblige. Steve makes up stories to cover for Matthew, but each story plunges him deeper into trouble. A moral story about the dangers of lying as well as a book that shows the difficulties in adjusting faced by returning veterans." Child Book Rev Serv

"This is a trenchant story of the ways in which children's attitudes toward war, enemies, heroism, and ethical conduct are shaped by events, by the ideas of adults, and by their own needs to be accepted and feel secure . . . it has good pace and momentum within its tight frame." Bull Cent Child Books

Shelter from the wind. Clarion Bks. 1976 108p $13.95 (5 and up) **Fic**

1. Runaway children—Fiction 2. Oklahoma—Fiction
ISBN 0-395-28890-8 LC 75-28184

First published by Seabury Press

"An interesting setting: the Oklahoma panhandle, windy, dusty, lonely. A promising situation: Stacy, left out when her father remarries and a baby is due, runs away and is befriended by an abandoned old woman who survives isolation by her love for her dogs and her land. Stacy delivers puppies and learns about death and abandonment." Child Book Rev Serv

"The powerful concrete imagery and strong realistic characterization allow the author to explore such subjects as alcoholism and childbirth with rare sensitivity and unflinching avoidance of sentimentality." SLJ

Baum, L. Frank (Lyman Frank), 1856-1919

The Wizard of Oz (3-6) **Fic**

1. Fantastic fiction

Some editions are:

ABC-CLIO lib bdg $13.95 With pictures by W. W. Denslow Large print edition (ISBN 1-55736-013-8) Has title: The wonderful Wizard of Oz

Golden Bks. (Golden classics) $8.95 Illustrated by Kathy Mitchell (ISBN 0-307-17115-9)

Holt & Co. $18.95 Illustrated by Michael Hague (ISBN 0-03-061661-1)

Morrow lib bdg $19.95 With pictures by W. W. Denslow (ISBN 0-688-06944-4) Has title: The wonderful Wizard of Oz

Penguin Bks. (Puffin classics) pa $2.25 (ISBN 0-14-035001-2)

First published 1900 with title: The wonderful Wizard of Oz

Here are the adventures of Dorothy who, in her dreams, escapes from her bed in Kansas to visit the Emerald City and to meet the wonderful Wizard of Oz, the Scarecrow, the Tin Woodman, and the Cowardly Lion

Other available titles about the land of Oz are:
Dorothy and the Wizard in Oz (1908)
The land of Oz (1904)
Little Wizard stories of Oz (1985)
The magic of Oz (1919)
The marvelous land of Oz (1904)
Ozma of Oz (1907)
The patchwork girl of Oz (1913)
The tin woodsman of Oz (1918)

Bawden, Nina, 1925-

Carrie's war. Lippincott 1973 159p il lib bdg $13.89; Puffin Bks. pa $4.95 (4 and up) **Fic**

1. Wales—Fiction
ISBN 0-397-31450-7 (lib bdg); 0-440-40142-9 (pa) LC 72-13253

"Carrie, recently widowed, takes her children to the small Welsh mining town where she and her younger brother, Nick, had been evacuated during World War II. Carrie is tormented by her mistaken belief that she caused a fire at the time which may have killed people she loved. For the most part, the story revolves around Carrie and Nick's days spent in the home of rigid, strict Mr. Evans and his kindly sister, their friendship with Hepzibah Green, who may have been a witch, and Albert Sandwich, another evacuee." Libr J

"The pace and the dialogue and the characterization all add up to a whole which could be read with interest and pleasure by any age, and in which the lessons are implied, delicately in the behaviour and relationships of the principal actors, never rammed home." New Statesman

The finding. Lothrop, Lee & Shepard Bks. 1985 153p $11.95; Dell pa $2.95 (4 and up) **Fic**

1. Orphans—Fiction 2. Runaway children—Fiction 3. Great Britain—Fiction
ISBN 0-688-04979-6; 0-440-40004-X (pa) LC 84-25069

When an unexpected inheritance threatens to change his life with his adopted family in London, an eleven-year-old foundling runs away from home

"In the hands of a lesser writer, the situation and developments used here could easily have become maudlin or melodramatic. Bawden, however, has firm control over her material and discrimination about its treatment. . . . [The] crisis is deftly handled, with a building of suspense as the story moves back and forth from the plight of the runaway to the fearful apprehension of his family. Characterization and dialogue are excellent." Bull Cent Child Books

Henry; illustrated by Joyce Powzyk. Lothrop, Lee & Shepard Bks. 1988 119p il $13; Dell pa $3.25 (5 and up) **Fic**

1. World War, 1939-1945—Fiction 2. Squirrels—Fiction
ISBN 0-688-07894-X; 0-440-40309-X (pa) LC 87-29339

"Henry is a baby squirrel adopted by a family waiting out the London Blitz on a country farm during World War II. With her characteristic subtlety of craft, Bawden develops scenes and dialogue that bring the reader to realize what Henry means to the narrator, her two brothers, and her mother as they all await her father's return from naval duty. The youngest, Charlie, is particularly touching in his desperate attachments to any strong male figure—a farm hand, an Italian prisoner of war—and in his vague fears about the father he can't quite remember. . . . This is a story that speaks of family unity in the face of dislocation and separation." Bull Cent Child Books

Bawden, Nina, 1925-—*Continued*

The outside child. Lothrop, Lee & Shepard Bks. 1989 232p $12.95 (5 and up) **Fic**

1. Brothers and sisters—Fiction
ISBN 0-688-08965-8 LC 88-27349

"Suddenly and accidentally, thirteen-year-old Jane Tucker learns that her widowed father—a ship's engineer whom she rarely sees—is remarried and has two younger children. Inevitably, she defies her adoptive aunts to locate her half-sister and brother. What she doesn't expect to find is a dark secret that seems to spark violent hostility from her stepmother." Bull Cent Child Books

The author has a "remarkable gift for combining subtlety and clarity in her writing for children; superb characterizations, the interplay of human relationships, and powerful emotions that lie beneath the surface of everyday life are presented wholly from the girl's ingenuous perspective." Horn Book

The peppermint pig; frontispiece by Charles Lilly. Lippincott 1975 191p lib bdg $13.89; Dell pa $4.95 (5 and up) **Fic**

1. Pigs—Fiction 2. Family life—Fiction 3. Great Britain—Fiction
ISBN 0-397-31618-6; 0-440-40122-4 (pa) LC 74-26922

Also available G.K. Hall large print edition $11.95 (ISBN 0-7451-0447-9)

"Nine-year-old Poll feels things more deeply than her brothers and sisters. When her father quits his job because of a theft, some people believe the worst. In turn-of-the-century England, when father leaves for America to seek his fortune, mother does dressmaking at home. Mama buys the pig to make them smile during this time of unanswered questions." Child Book Rev Serv

"The story is historical rather than contemporary, subtle rather than mysterious; and its plot is more relaxed than suspenseful. Time and setting come sharply through the writing, which is typically graceful, witty, clear, and fluid." Horn Book

The robbers. Lothrop, Lee & Shepard Bks. 1979 155p $12.95; Dell pa $3.25 (5 and up) **Fic**

1. Grandmothers—Fiction 2. Family life—Fiction 3. London (England)—Fiction 4. Friendship—Fiction
ISBN 0-688-41902-X; 0-440-40316-2 (pa) LC 79-4152

"Solitary and happy, nine-year-old Philip lived with his grandmother in an apartment in a seaside castle; his mother was dead, his father a peripatetic television reporter. When his father married an American, Philip went to London for what he thought was a visit; it proved to be a long stay. Precocious and articulate, Philip made only one friend, Darcy, a street-wise boy whose family . . . made Philip welcome." Bull Cent Child Books

"It is always character that counts with Nina Bawden. Motive, action, setting —everything is simple, clear-cut and selective, and totally adequate for the task of creating a particular corner of London in which believable people speak, act, suffer and learn from their mistakes." Grow Point

Squib; illustrated by Hank Blaustein. Lothrop, Lee & Shepard Bks. 1982 c1971 159p il $12.95; Dell pa $3.25 (5 and up) **Fic**

1. Child abuse—Fiction
ISBN 0-688-01299-X; 0-440-40326-X (pa) LC 82-75

A newly illustrated reissue of the title first published 1971

"When a shy, pale boy appears at the playground, 12-year-old Kate Pollack is haunted by his looks and compelled to discover his origins. Hoping he may be her younger brother—lost in a swimming accident four years before—Kate pursues the mystery and saves the boy, Squib, from abusive relatives. . . . The artist, Hank Blaustein, has obviously read the story carefully. His loose and lively ink drawings reinforce the action and his honest portrayal of Bawden's vivid characters adds much to the enjoyment of this popular and highly regarded book." SLJ

The witch's daughter. Lippincott 1966 181p o.p. (4 and up) **Fic**

1. Blind—Fiction 2. Scotland—Fiction LC 66-7115

Available G.K. Hall large print edition $15.95 (ISBN 0-7451-0654-4)

This story, set on the Scottish island of Skua, involves "much more than the capture of jewel thieves. Perdita, a lonely orphan, is rejected by the other children because of her unusual power to see into the future. Through the arrival of a blind girl, Janey, and Janey's brother Tim, Perdita comes to realize that her powers are not a sign of witchcraft, but a special talent." Read Ladders for Hum Relat. 6th edition

"A credible suspense story, with a likeable and resourceful cast. A plausible plot, superior dialogue and an appropriate setting." N Y Times Book Rev

Baylor, Byrd

I'm in charge of celebrations; pictures by Peter Parnall. Scribner 1986 unp il $13.95 (3-6) **Fic**

1. Deserts—Fiction
ISBN 0-684-18579-2 LC 85-19633

A dweller in the desert celebrates a triple rainbow, a chance encounter with a coyote, and other wonders of the wilderness

Baylor writes in a "conversational, poetic prose that begs to be read aloud. Sky blues, cactus greens, searing sun yellows, desert browns, and bright to burnt oranges are jabbed, streaked, and swirled around Parnall's arresting, expressionistic impressions of Baylor's experiences." Booklist

Beatty, Patricia

Charley Skedaddle. Morrow 1987 186p $12.95 (5 and up) **Fic**

1. United States—History—1861-1865, Civil War—Fiction 2. Farm life—Fiction 3. Virginia—Fiction
ISBN 0-688-06687-9 LC 87-12270

"12-year-old Charley Quinn, a cocky boy from the Bowery, runs away and finagles a job as a drummer in the Union army. In his first battle he meets the horrors of war face to face and, without thought to an

Beatty, Patricia—*Continued*

injured friend, 'skedaddles' into the Virginia mountains." Booklist

"The author notes that she has based Charley's fictional adventures on actual accounts, and her reading and research lend authenticity to her story. . . . Told without the exuberant tall-tale quality of some of Beatty's books, Charley's Civil War adventures . . . move at a lively pace and offer an entertaining account of a young city slicker's growing respect for his new surroundings." Horn Book

Eight mules from Monterey. Morrow 1982 192p $12.95 (5 and up) **Fic**

1. Libraries—Fiction 2. California—Fiction

ISBN 0-688-01047-4 LC 81-22284

"The time is 1916, the place is the Santa Lucia mountains of California, and the story describes the trip that [thirteen-year-old] Fayette and her younger brother take with their widowed mother, who has just graduated from library school, as she travels the mountain trails (by mule) to set up library outposts." Bull Cent Child Books

The author "has created a warm story of perserverance coupled with well-developed believable characters, set in an unusual time period. Her use of slang terms in character conversation is true to the period making this a good book to use in history classes." Voice Youth Advocates

Turn homeward, Hannalee. Morrow 1984 193p $12.95 (5 and up) **Fic**

1. United States—History—1861-1865, Civil War—Fiction 2. Georgia—Fiction 3. Children—Employment—Fiction

ISBN 0-688-03871-9 LC 84-8960

This "historical fiction shows how the Civil War affected one segment of the population—the southern mill workers—and is based on fact. . . . The protagonists are Hannalee and Jem, twelve and ten, who are shipped from their Georgia town (and their recently widowed, pregnant mother) to Indiana, where they are offered as workers to anyone who wants them." Bull Cent Child Books

"The story is vintage Beatty, with a forthright, plainspoken heroine who has gumption to spare. As a period piece, it is a vivid, seemingly authentic picture of what times might have been like for a hardworking, white, Southern family." Booklist

Bell, Anthea

The nutcracker; [by] E.T.A. Hoffmann; retold by Anthea Bell; illustrated by Lisbeth Zwerger. Picture Bk. Studio 1987 unp il $14.95 (2-4) **Fic**

1. Fairy tales 2. Christmas—Fiction

ISBN 0-88708-051-0 LC 87-15249

"A Michael Neugebauer book"

First published 1983 by Neugebauer Press with a longer text with title: The nutcracker and the mouse-king

After hearing how her toy nutcracker got his ugly face, a little girl helps break the spell and changes him into a handsome prince

This book "features full pages of text alternating with Lisbeth Zwerger's beautiful full-page, full-color illustrations, including one double-page spread. . . . Anthea Bell's translation for this book is a slightly condensed version of the original story, which, of course, differs substantially from the ballet version." Horn Book

Bellairs, John

The curse of the blue figurine. Dial Bks. for Young Readers 1983 200p $11.95; lib bdg $11.89; Bantam Bks. pa $2.95 (5 and up) **Fic**

1. Mystery and detective stories

ISBN 0-8037-1119-0; 0-8037-1265-0 (lib bdg); 0-553-15540-7 (pa) LC 82-73217

"The terror for young Johnny Dixon begins when cranky eccentric Professor Childermass tells him that St. Michael's Church is haunted by Father Baart, an evil sorcerer who mysteriously disappeared years ago. When Johnny finds a blue Egyptian figurine hidden in the church basement, he takes it home in spite of the warning note from Father Baart threatening harm to anyone who removes it from the church." SLJ

The author "intertwines real concerns with sorcery in a seamless fashion, bringing dimension to his characters and events with expert timing and sharply honed atmosphere." Booklist

Other available titles about Johnny Dixon and Professor Childermass are:

The chessmen of doom (1989)
The eyes of the killer robot (1986)
The mummy, the will and the crypt (1983)
The revenge of the wizard's ghost (1985)
The secret of the underground room (1990)
The spell of the sorcerer's skull (1984)
The trolley to yesterday (1989)

The house with a clock in its walls; pictures by Edward Gorey. Dial Bks. for Young Readers 1973 179p il $13.95; lib bdg $13.89; Dell pa $3.25 (5 and up) **Fic**

1. Witchcraft—Fiction

ISBN 0-8037-3821-8; 0-8037-3823-4 (lib bdg); 0-440-43742-3 (pa) LC 72-7600

In 1948, Lewis, a ten-year-old orphan, goes to New Zebedee, Michigan with his warlock Uncle Jonathan, who lives in a big mysterious house and practices white magic. Together with their neighbor, Mrs. Zimmerman, a witch, they search to find a clock that is programmed to end the world and has been hidden in the walls of the house by the evil Isaac Izard

"Bellairs's story and Edward Gorey's pictures are satisfyingly frightening." Publ Wkly

Other available titles about Lewis are:

The figure in the shadows (1975)
The letter, the witch, and the ring (1976)

The treasure of Alpheus Winterborn; illustrated by Judith Gwyn Brown. Harcourt Brace Jovanovich 1978 180p il o.p.; Bantam Bks. paperback available $3.50 (5 and up) **Fic**

1. Buried treasure—Fiction

ISBN 0-553-15629-2 (pa) LC 77-88959

"His parents' continual quarrels and his father's subsequent heart attack trigger Anthony's determination to find the eccentric Alpheus Winterborn's legacy, supposedly hidden within the town. While working with his good friend Miss Eells, the local librarian, he finds clues point-

Bellairs, John—*Continued*

ing first to the old Winterborn mansion and then to the library itself. Anthony's attempts to play detective boomerang, however, until the night when he is inadvertently trapped in the library with Hugo Philpotts, the sneaky bank vice-president who thinks himself to be the rightful heir." Booklist

Other available titles about Anthony Monday and Miss Eells are:

The dark secret of Weatherend (1984)
The lamp from the warlock's tomb (1988)

Benchley, Nathaniel, 1915-1981

Feldman Fieldmouse; a fable; drawings by Hilary Knight. Harper & Row 1971 96p il lib bdg $11.89 (3-5) **Fic**

1. Mice—Fiction

ISBN 0-06-020484-2 LC 72-135773

Fendall Fieldmouse is befriended by Lonny, a boy who knows how to talk to mice. As a pet, Fendall leads a lazy, contended life. This story tells what happens when Fendall's uncle, Feldman Fieldmouse, appears to take over his nephew's education

"An engaging fanciful tale. . . . The style is delightful, the animal characters amusing, and the dialogue witty." Bull Cent Child Books

Bennett, Anna Elizabeth

Little witch; illustrated by Helen Stone. Lippincott 1953 127p il lib bdg $12.89; Harper & Row pa $3.50 (3-5) **Fic**

1. Witchcraft—Fiction

ISBN 0-397-30261-4 (lib bdg); 0-06-440119-7 (pa) LC 52-13721

"Miniken Snickasee was the daughter of a witch. She could ride on a broom; she could brew magic spells; she didn't have to go to school at all; and yet she wasn't happy. She wanted to be just an ordinary child. In a fresh and imaginative story, full of humor. Miss Bennett tells what happened when Miniken stole away from her mother and set out for school all by herself. Helen Stone's pictures of the 'little witch' and her adventures are exactly right too. Fun to read aloud to both boys and girls in October—or in any other month." Horn Book

Berends, Polly Berrien

The case of the elevator duck; illustrated by James K. Washburn. Random House 1973 54p il lib bdg $7.99 (3-5) **Fic**

1. Ducks—Fiction 2. Apartment houses—Fiction 3. Mystery and detective stories

ISBN 0-394-92115-1 LC 72-158380

Also available in an edition with illustrations by Diane Allison in library binding for $5.99 (ISBN 0-394-92646-3) and paperback for $1.95 (ISBN 0-394-82646-9)

Gilbert finds a lost duck in the elevator of his apartment building, and must do some secret detective work to find its owner, since no pets are allowed in the housing project

A "light mystery for beginning readers. The action is humorously illustrated by Washburn's line sketches; and Berends' first-person, short-sentence story is personable, plausible, and useful for librarians needing simple, satisfying material for their easy mystery shelves." Booklist

Bianco, Margery Williams, 1880-1944

The velveteen rabbit; or, How toys become real; by Margery Williams (2-4) **Fic**

1. Toys—Fiction 2. Rabbits—Fiction 3. Fairy tales

Some editions are:

Doubleday $9.95 With illustrations by William Nicholson (ISBN 0-385-07725-4)
Harcourt Brace Jovanovich $10.95 Illustrated by Ilse Plume (ISBN 0-15-293500-2)
Holt & Co. $11.95 Illustrated by Michael Hague (ISBN 0-8050-0209-X)
Knopf (An Ariel book) $10.95 Illustrated by Allen Atkinson (ISBN 0-394-53221-X)
Running Press lib bdg $12.90; pa $3.95 Illustrated by Michael Green (ISBN 0-89471-127-X; 0-89471-128-8)

First published 1922 by Doran

"The story of a toy rabbit that becomes real through the love of a child and the intervention of a fairy." Bull Cent Child Books

Björk, Christina

Linnea in Monet's garden; text, Christina Björk; drawings, Lena Anderson. R & S Bks. 1987 52p il $10.95 (3-5) **Fic**

1. Monet, Claude, 1840-1926—Fiction 2. Paris (France)—Fiction

ISBN 91-29-58314-4 LC 87-45163

Original Swedish edition, 1985

"Linnea and her elderly friend Mr. Bloom travel to Paris, visit Monet's home in Giverny, picnic in the artist's garden, and admire the waterlilies and the Japanese bridge which he often painted. In Paris, the two companions stop at a museum to see Impressionist paintings, view the sunlight over the Seine, and chatter about the life and times of the artist. The book ends with a page of information about things to do and see in Paris." SLJ

"In addition to the long but smooth text peppered with dialogue are photographs of Monet's paintings, house, and family as well as colorful drawings of the little girl's excursion. . . . A splendid way to introduce children to impressionism and to the man behind the masterpieces." Booklist

Blades, Ann

Mary of Mile 18; story and pictures by Ann Blades. Tundra Bks. 1971 unp il $11.95; pa $6.95 (2-4) **Fic**

1. Canada—Fiction 2. Farm life—Fiction 3. Wolves—Fiction 4. Mennonites—Fiction

ISBN 0-88776-015-5; 0-88776-059-7 (pa) LC 79-179430

"In the simple story Mary Fehr finds a wolf pup which her father doesn't want her to keep until it alerts him to a chicken-thieving coyote. Blades' appreciation of the Canadian wilderness and of those who eke out a living there is apparent in her richly colored and textured primitive watercolors. Providing a breathtaking backdrop to the story, they contrast the stark frozen landscape

Blades, Ann—*Continued*
with the cozy warmth of the seven-member Fehr family inside their rustic farmhouse." SLJ

Blos, Joan W.

A gathering of days: a New England girl's journal, 1830-32; a novel. Scribner 1979 144p $12.95; pa $3.95 (6 and up) **Fic**

1. New Hampshire—Fiction
ISBN 0-684-16340-3; 0-689-70750-9 (pa)
LC 79-16898

Awarded the Newbery Medal, 1980

The journal of a 14-year-old girl, kept the last year she lived on the family farm, records daily events in her small New Hampshire town, her father's remarriage, and the death of her best friend

"The 'simple' life on the farm is not facilely idealized, the larger issues of the day are felt . . . but it is the small moments between parent and child, friend and friend that are at the fore, and the core, of this lowkey, intense, and reflective book." SLJ

Blume, Judy

Are you there God? it's me, Margaret. Twentieth anniversary ed. Bradbury Press 1990 c1970 149p $12.95; Dell pa $3.25 (5 and up) **Fic**

1. Adolescence—Fiction 2. Religions—Fiction
ISBN 0-02-710991-7; 0-440-40419-3 (pa)
LC 90-44484

First published 1970

"A perceptive story about the emotional, physical, and spiritual ups and downs experienced by 12-year-old Margaret, child of a Jewish-Protestant union." Natl Counc of Teach of Engl. Adventuring with Books. 2d edition

"The writing style is lively, the concerns natural, and the problems are treated with both humor and sympathy, but the story is intense in its emphasis on the four girls' absorption in, and discussions of, menstruation and brassieres." Bull Cent Child Books

Freckle juice; illustrated by Sonia O. Lisker. Four Winds Press 1971 40p il lib bdg $12.95; Dell pa $2.95 (2-4) **Fic**

ISBN 0-02-711690-5 (lib bdg); 0-440-42813-0 (pa)
LC 74-161016

"A gullible second-grader pays 50¢ for a recipe to grow freckles." Best Books for Child

"Spontaneous humor, sure to appeal to the youngest reader." Horn Book

It's not the end of the world. Bradbury Press 1972 169p $12.95; Dell pa $3.50 (4-6) **Fic**

1. Divorce—Fiction 2. Parent and child—Fiction
ISBN 0-02-711050-8; 0-440-94140-7 (pa)
LC 70-181739

Unwilling to adjust to her parents' impending divorce, twelve-year-old Karen Newman attempts a last ditch effort at arranging a reconciliation. This story tells how her scheme goes awry when an unplanned confrontation between her parents sharply illuminates for Karen the reality of the situation

"A believable first-person story with good characterization, particularly of twelve-year-old Karen, and realistic treatment of the situation." Booklist

Just as long as we're together. Orchard Bks. 1987 296p $12.95; lib bdg $12.99 (5 and up) **Fic**

1. Friendship—Fiction 2. Family life—Fiction
ISBN 0-531-05729-1; 0-531-08329-2 (lib bdg)
LC 87-7980

"The narrator is Stephanie, who's in her first year of junior high, who's distressed by her parents' trial separation (and, when she visits Dad, by his friend Iris), and who finds that best friends are not infallibly understanding or tolerant. Rachel has always been her friend, but both of them like a newcomer (Alison, a Vietnamese adoptee) enough to make it a triumvirate." Bull Cent Child Books

"As usual, Blume addresses many issues about growing up that make some adults nervous and ill at ease: menstruation, budding sexuality, and that inevitable first kiss. But she offers more: a family in a painful state of flux that can still function effectively." Wilson Libr Bull

Otherwise known as Sheila the Great. Dutton 1972 188p lib bdg $10.95; Dell pa $3.25 (4-6) **Fic**

1. Fear—Fiction
ISBN 0-525-36455-2 (lib bdg); 0-440-46701-2 (pa)
LC 72-78082

Ten-year-old Sheila is secretly afraid of dogs, spiders, bees, ghosts and the dark. When she and her family leave New York for their summer home, she has to face up to her problems

"An unusual and merry treatment of the fears of a young girl. . . . This is a truly appealing book in which the author makes her points without a single preachy word." Publ Wkly

Tales of a fourth grade nothing; illustrated by Roy Doty. Dutton 1972 120p il $10.95; Dell pa $3.25 (3-6) **Fic**

1. Brothers—Fiction 2. Family life—Fiction
ISBN 0-525-40720-0; 0-440-48474-X (pa)
LC 70-179050

Also available ABC-CLIO large print edition $14.95 (ISBN 1-55736-015-4)

This story describes the trials and tribulations of nine-year-old Peter Hatcher who is saddled with a pesky two-year-old brother named Fudge who is constantly creating trouble, messing things up, and monopolizing their parents' attention. Things come to a climax when Fudge gets at Peter's pet turtle

"The episode structure makes the book a good choice for reading aloud." Saturday Rev

Other available titles about Peter and Fudge are:
Fudge-a-mania (1990)
Superfudge (1980)

Then again, maybe I won't; a novel. Bradbury Press 1971 164p $12.95; Dell pa $3.25 (5 and up) **Fic**

1. Adolescence—Fiction
ISBN 0-02-711090-7; 0-440-48659-9 (pa)
LC 77-156548

Also available G.K. Hall large print edition $13.95 (ISBN 0-8161-4417-6)

Blume, Judy—*Continued*

"Thirteen-year-old Tony is not as thrilled as his parents are when the family's finances improve and they move to affluent suburbia. The 'nice' boy next door (of whom Tony's mother heartily approves) proves to be an inveterate shoplifter. Tony is, in fact, bothered by the eagerness of his parents to live up to their surroundings. He's also just discovered how he reacts to sexual provocation—and he worries about that, too. . . . Deftly handled, Tony's dilemma is really that he has become mature enough to see the conflicts and imperfections in his own life and in those around him, and he is sensitive enough to accept compromise." Bull Cent Child Books

Bond, Michael, 1926-

A bear called Paddington; with drawings by Peggy Fortnum. Houghton Mifflin 1960 c1958 128p il $12.95; Dell pa $2.95 (2-5) **Fic**

1. Bears—Fiction 2. Great Britain—Fiction
ISBN 0-395-06636-0; 0-440-40483-5 (pa) LC 60-9096

First published 1958 in the United Kingdom

"Mr. and Mrs. Brown first met Paddington on a railway platform in London. Noticing the sign on his neck reading 'Please look after this bear. Thank you,' they decided to do just that. From there on home was never the same though the Brown children were delighted." Publ Wkly

Other available titles about Paddington Bear are:
More about Paddington
Paddington abroad
Paddington at large
Paddington at the fair
Paddington at the seaside
Paddington at the tower
Paddington at the zoo
Paddington at work
Paddington Bear
Paddington goes to town
Paddington helps out
Paddington marches on
Paddington on screen
Paddington on top
Paddington takes the air
Paddington takes the test
Paddington takes to TV
Paddington's art exhibition
Paddington's lucky day

Another book about Paddington Bear with the title: Paddington's storybook, is entered in the Story Collections section

The complete adventures of Olga da Polga; illustrated by Hans Helweg. Delacorte Press 1983 511p il $16.95 (2-5) **Fic**

1. Guinea pigs—Fiction
ISBN 0-440-00981-2 LC 82-72753

A combined edition of the following four titles: The tales of Olga da Polga (entered below), Olga meets her match, Olga carries on, and Olga takes charge

The tales of Olga da Polga; illustrated by Hans Helweg. Macmillan 1989 c1971 113p il $11.95 (2-5) **Fic**

1. Guinea pigs—Fiction
ISBN 0-02-711731-6 LC 88-31444

A reissue of the title first published 1971 in the United Kingdom; first United States edition, 1973

The adventures of Olga da Polga, a vain and talented guinea pig, as she leaves the pet shop to enter the world of the Sawdust People (guinea pigs' name for humans)

"The book will delight . . . [children] who like to imagine that their pets have their own lives and personalities. The style is easy and the characters flow from the author's pen, but he sketches his animal friends with a much surer stroke than the humans." Jr Bookshelf

Followed by: Olga meets her match (1975 c1973); Olga carries on (1977 c1976); and Olga takes charge (1982)

Bond, Nancy

A place to come back to. Atheneum Pubs. 1984 187p $13.95 (6 and up) **Fic**

1. Friendship—Fiction 2. Death—Fiction
ISBN 0-689-50302-4 LC 83-48745

Sequel to: The best enemies (1978)

"A Margaret K. McElderry book"

When Charlotte's friend Oliver's life is shattered by the death of his eighty-two-year-old great-uncle and guardian, Oliver turns to Charlotte with urgent demands she finds herself unprepared to meet

The author "has written a fine novel touching on the feelings that surround the death of a loved one, the disbelief, the hurt, the anger, the emptiness, and the sorrow." Voice Youth Advocates

A string in the harp. Atheneum Pubs. 1976 370p il $12.95 (6 and up) **Fic**

1. Taliesin—Fiction 2. Fantastic fiction 3. Wales—Fiction
ISBN 0-689-50036-X LC 75-28181

"A Margaret K. McElderry book"

"Present-day realism and the fantasy world of sixth-century Taliesin meet in an absorbing novel set in Wales. The story centers around the Morgans—Jen, Peter, Becky, and their father—their adjustment to another country, their mother's death, and especially, Peter's bitter despair, which threatens them all." LC. Child Books, 1976

Boston, L. M. (Lucy Maria), 1892-1990

The children of Green Knowe; with illustrations by Peter Boston. Harcourt Brace 1955 157p il o.p. paperback available $3.95 (4-6) **Fic**

1. Fantastic fiction 2. Great Britain—Fiction
ISBN 0-15-217151-7 (pa) LC 55-7608

First published 1954 in the United Kingdom

"Tolly comes to live with his great-grandmother at Green Knowe, her ancestral mansion in the English countryside. Here the present blends with the past, and the children of another era become his playmates and help him to break the curse put upon the house by a gypsy." Hodges. Books for Elem Sch Libr

"A special book for the imaginative child, in which mood predominates and fantasy and realism are skillfully blended; not the least of the book's charm is the rapport that exists between the lonely little boy and the understanding old woman who lives with her memories." Booklist

Boston, L. M. (Lucy Maria), 1892-1990— *Continued*

Other available titles about Green Knowe are:
An enemy at Green Knowe (1964)
The river at Green Knowe (1959)
A stranger at Green Knowe (1961)
Treasure of Green Knowe (1958)

The sea egg; illustrated by Peter Boston. Harcourt Brace Jovanovich 1967 94p il $8.95 (3-5) **Fic**

1. Fantastic fiction 2. Seashore—Fiction
ISBN 0-15-271050-7 LC 67-3334

"This exquisitely written little fantasy is woven around an episode in the lives of two boys. While on a seaside vacation Toby and Joe purchase an egg-shaped stone which they put in a deep tide pool in the hope that it will hatch a rare sea creature. The egg disappears and two days later the boys see a child merman or triton living with the seals. Mood rather than action dominates the description of their play in the sea and the special night swim which the boys share with their unusual companion. Probably limited in appeal to the highly imaginative reader." Booklist

Boyd, Candy Dawson, 1946-

Charlie Pippin. Macmillan 1987 182p $12.95; Penguin Bks. pa $3.95 (4-6) **Fic**

1. Fathers and daughters—Fiction 2. Vietnam War, 1961-1975—Fiction 3. Blacks—Fiction
ISBN 0-02-726350-9; 0-14-032587-5 (pa) LC 86-23780

"Charlie (Chartreuse) Pippin is eleven, jealous of her older sister Sienna, baffled by her father's stern intransigence. She's black and bright; she's often in trouble at school (and that makes even more trouble at home) because she sets up businesses in school. Charlie wonders why her father is so angry, why he is irked by her school project, which entails a study of the Vietnam War in which he served." Bull Cent Child Books

"Boyd's story probes sensitive issues with remarkable balance. While the story's theme is decidedly antiwar, it presents an affecting portrayal, from a child's standpoint, of the anger, concerns, and painful emotional wounds that many returned veterans still bear. Charlie's family is black, but their relationships and emotional pain reach beyond color, and the story's impact won't quickly fade." Booklist

Branscum, Robbie

The adventures of Johnny May; illustrated by Deborah Howland. Harper & Row 1984 87p il $12.89 (4-6) **Fic**

1. Arkansas—Fiction 2. Family life—Fiction 3. Grandparents—Fiction
ISBN 0-06-020615-2 (lib bdg) LC 83-49464

Sequel to: Johnny May (1975)

"There are two threads in this Arkansas story, told in regional dialect by eleven-year-old Johnny May; there's the problem of keeping the grandparents for whom she's responsible fed and possibly to observe Christmas with them despite the family's poverty, and there's the problem of what to do about Homer, a kind and popular man she's seen shoot another man, boastful Tom Satterfield." Bull Cent Child Books

"The mystery presented at the outset will keep readers dangling nicely, but the conclusion may raise a few eyebrows. . . . The story's finish could be used to spark a hearty discussion. Whether one considers it flawed or not, the story will prove quite absorbing." Booklist

Brenner, Barbara

On the frontier with Mr. Audubon. Coward-McCann 1977 96p il $8.95 (4 and up) **Fic**

1. Mason, Joseph, 1807-1883—Fiction 2. Audubon, John James, 1785-1851—Fiction
ISBN 0-698-20385-2 LC 76-41601

"Thirteen-year-old Joseph Mason describes his travels down the Mississippi River and in the Southern swamps and forests and cities. As pupil-assistant, Joseph helped shoot specimens of birds never before pictured in guide books, helped paint some of the details or background, and suffered with Audubon through poverty, illness, and home-sickness. Whether describing life on a flatboat or on the crowded docks of New Orleans, the narrative (based on thorough research) is lively and natural, and through Joseph's eyes Brenner draws a perceptive, candid picture of the great artist who had been jailed for debt, branded a wastrel, and gone from a pampered childhood in France to near penury in America. Joseph's journal is a fictional device, but the facts it records are documented, and it gives a memorable picture of the artist and his work." Bull Cent Child Books

Bridgers, Sue Ellen, 1942-

All together now; a novel. Knopf 1979 238p lib bdg $13.99; Bantam Bks. pa $3.50 (6 and up) **Fic**

1. Grandparents—Fiction 2. Mentally handicapped—Fiction 3. Friendship—Fiction
ISBN 0-394-94098-9 (lib bdg); 0-553-24530-9 (pa) LC 78-12244

"Because her father is a pilot serving in the Korean War and her mother is busy holding down two jobs, twelve year old Casey Flanagan spends the summer vacation with her grandparents in a small southern town. Shy, lonely and somewhat resentful, the youngster slowly begins to respond to her environment and to become involved in the lives of those around her. Among the people who contribute to Casey's emotional growth are her devoted grandparents, her fun-loving uncle and his earthy girl friend, a warm-hearted spinster, a middle-aged 'dancin man,' and, most important of all, Dwayne, a thirty-three year old man with the mind of a child." Best Sellers

"It is the delicacy with which Bridgers weaves together the various strains of her story that creates the beauty of the book." Christ Sci Monit

Home before dark; a novel. Knopf 1976 176p lib bdg $13.99; Bantam Bks. pa $2.50 (6 and up) **Fic**

1. Migrant labor—Fiction 2. Family life—Fiction
ISBN 0-394-93299-4 (lib bdg); 0-553-26432-X (pa) LC 76-8661

"After years as a migrant laborer, James Earl brings his family to settle down and work on the tobacco farm inherited by his younger brother Newt. Fourteen-year-old Stella is particularly pleased; she's anxious to have a better life, to make something more of herself than her

Bridgers, Sue Ellen, 1942-—*Continued*
timid, fearful mother has. Stella admires Newt's brisk wife, is admired by two boys and learns to care for one of them, and resists (eventually succumbing) the genuinely affectionate overtures made by her stepmother after her mother's death and James Earl's rather hasty second marriage." Bull Cent Child Books

"No summary can convey the tremendous integrity of a book like 'Home Before Dark.' The author speaks with a voice that is intensely lyrical yet wholly un-self-conscious. Character and theme have been developed with such painstaking attention that each episode seems inevitable and right." N Y Times Book Rev

Briggs, Katharine Mary

Kate Crackernuts; [by] K. M. Briggs. Greenwillow Bks. 1980 c1979 223p $13.50 (6 and up) **Fic**

1. Witchcraft—Fiction 2. Scotland—Fiction 3. Good and evil—Fiction

ISBN 0-688-80240-0 LC 79-9229

First published 1979 in the United Kingdom

"Two Kates, Katherine Lindsay and Kate Maxwell, met when they were quite young and a deep and enduring friendship developed. Later, when Katherine was twelve her father married Kate's mother. Unfortunately for Katherine her stepmother was very jealous of her and not only made her life most unpleasant but used her black arts against her. A high-spirited girl, Kate does her best to shield her stepsister from a witch's wrath. . . . The setting is Scotland in the 17th century during a Scottish/English war." Best Sellers

"History and folklore are melded into a strong, anguished story of evil incarnate pitted against compassion and love. Some difficulties are posed by the complexity of the background events and by the unfamiliar Lowland Scots speech, but with encouragement capable older readers should be able to transcend the obstacles." Horn Book

Brink, Carol Ryrie, 1895-1981

The bad times of Irma Baumlein; pictures by Trina Schart Hyman. Macmillan 1972 134p il $14.95; pa $3.95 (4-6) **Fic**

1. Dolls—Fiction 2. Truthfulness and falsehood—Fiction

ISBN 0-02-714220-5; 0-02-041900-7 (pa) LC 76-182018

"Irma's bad times begin when she tries to impress her classmates in a new school by claiming to own the biggest doll in the world. When she's asked to exhibit it at the school fair, she panics and 'borrows' a dummy from her family's store." Publ Wkly

"The characterization is adequate, the plot far-fetched here and there, but the story has plenty of action, humor, and the perennial appeal of a protagonist in a predicament with which readers can identify." Bull Cent Child Books

Caddie Woodlawn; illustrated by Trina Schart Hyman. Macmillan 1973 275p il $13.95; pa $3.95 (4-6) **Fic**

1. Frontier and pioneer life—Fiction 2. Wisconsin—Fiction

ISBN 0-02-713670-1; 0-689-71370-3 (pa) LC 73-588

Also available ABC-CLIO large print edition $15.95 (ISBN 1-55736-043-X)

Awarded the Newbery Medal, 1936

First published 1935

Caddie Woodlawn was eleven in 1864. Because she was frail, she had been allowed to grow up a tomboy. Her capacity for adventure was practically limitless, and there was plenty of adventure on the Wisconsin frontier in those days. The story covers one year of life on the pioneer farm, closing with the news that Mr. Woodlawn had inherited an estate in England, and the unanimous decision of the family to stay in Wisconsin. Based upon the reminiscences of the author's grandmother

The typeface "is eminently clear and readable, and the illustrations in black and white . . . are attractive and expressive." Wis Libr Bull

Brittain, Bill

All the money in the world; illus. by Charles Robinson. Harper & Row 1979 150p il lib bdg $12.89; pa $3.50 (4-6) **Fic**

1. Money—Fiction

ISBN 0-06-020676-4 (lib bdg); 0-06-440128-6 (pa) LC 77-25635

"The consequences of having all the money in the world deposited in your backyard include a humorous encounter with the army, a kidnapping and an interview with the President of the United States. A delightful fantasy with some hilarious moments shared by an interracial group of friends." Read Teach

Devil's donkey; drawings by Andrew Glass. Harper & Row 1981 120p il lib bdg $13.89; pa $3.50 (3-6) **Fic**

1. Witches—Fiction 2. Devil—Fiction 3. New England—Fiction

ISBN 0-06-020683-7 (lib bdg); 0-06-440129-4 (pa) LC 80-7907

Young Dan'l Pitt scoffs at warnings about local witches by his guardian, storekeeper Stewart Meade (Stew Meat), who tells the story. "Having offended Old Magda, the last witch left in the New England town of Coven Tree the boy is put under a spell that turns him into a donkey. . . . The shrewd and courageous efforts of Stew Meat and of a farm girl not only succeed in changing Dan'l back, but culminate in a risky contest in which they win a bet with the devil." SLJ

"Notable for color and grace in the telling and with distinction of format, [this is a] highly original fantasy. . . . The wonder and humor of the story are finely evoked by animated charcoal drawings conveying atmosphere and sense of mystery." Horn Book

Other available titles about Coven Tree are:
Dr. Dredd's wagon of wonders (1987)
The wish giver (1983)

Brooks, Walter R., 1886-1958

Freddy the detective; with illustrations by Kurt Wiese. Knopf 1987 c1932 263p il lib bdg $9.99; pa $4.95 (3-5) **Fic**

1. Pigs—Fiction 2. Mystery and detective stories

ISBN 0-394-98885-X (lib bdg); 0-394-88885-5 (pa) LC 86-40422

A reissue of the title first published 1932

Brooks, Walter R., 1886-1958—*Continued*

This is a story about the animals on Mr. Bean's farm. Freddy, the pig, sets up in business as a detective, after reading the stories of Sherlock Holmes. He then solves a number of very mysterious cases

"This book will be great fun for all who have not outgrown the gift of fitting becoming personalities to our animal friends." N Y Her Trib Books

Other available titles about Freddy are:
Freddy and the men from Mars (1954)
Freddy and the perilous adventure (1942)
Freddy goes camping (1948)
Freddy goes to Florida (1949)
Freddy the cowboy (1950)
Freddy the politician (1948)

Bulla, Clyde Robert, 1914-

The cardboard crown; illustrated by Michele Chessare. Crowell 1984 78p il $12.95; lib bdg $13.89 (3-5) **Fic**

1. Friendship—Fiction 2. Parent and child—Fiction
ISBN 0-690-04360-0; 0-690-04361-9 (lib bdg) LC 83-45049

"A strange girl arrives at the farmhouse where Adam, 11, lives with his father. Wearing a golden crown and a shimmering dress, the girl says she's Olivia, a lost princess, and asks for shelter. Adam's father lets her stay but in the morning, he learns that the 'princess' had been sent by her father to stay with his sister, Jen, a neighbor whom Adam dislikes. So does Olivia and she's unhappy at her aunt's house, even with Adam as a friend and morale booster. When Olivia asks him to help her run away, he does." Publ Wkly

"The problem of parent-child relationships is familiar, but the author tells the story with a limpid simplicity in terse sentences that fit the stark, rural setting and the laconic characters." Horn Book

A lion to guard us; illustrated by Michele Chessare. Crowell 1981 117p il $13.95; lib bdg $13.89 (3-5) **Fic**

1. London (England)—Fiction 2. Voyages and travels—Fiction
ISBN 0-690-04096-2; 0-690-04097-0 (lib bdg) LC 80-2455

"This is a tale with a nugget of historical basis: the voyage of a small fleet from England to the Virginia colony. Here the protagonists are three motherless children whose father has been in Jamestown for three years; there are problems in London and en route, and the children find their father alone and ill in an almost deserted settlement, but they are reunited. The 'lion' of the title is a doorknocker in the shape of a lion's head, a memento the children regard as their talisman." Bull Cent Child Books

"Secondary characters, including a nasty guardian who keeps the children's money and a good-hearted doctor who sails with them, strengthen the blend of history, adventure, and human interest. With evocative gray watercolors." Booklist

Shoeshine girl; illustrated by Leigh Grant. Crowell 1975 84p il $12.95; lib bdg $13.89 (3-5) **Fic**

ISBN 0-690-00758-2; 0-690-04830-0 (lib bdg) LC 75-8516

"When ten-and-a-half Sara Ida, a spirited defiant youngster, becomes involved with a friend who steals for kicks, her parents send her to an aunt for the summer. Denied an allowance (for discipline), Sara Ida finds a job as a shoeshine girl and discovers the satisfaction of earning her own pocket money and becomes less self-centered." Child Book Rev Serv

"The willful young heroine is appealing in spite of her bristly disposition; the setting is realistic and the storytelling smooth and economical." Horn Book

The sword in the tree; illustrated by Paul Galdone. Crowell 1956 113p il lib bdg $12.89 (2-5) **Fic**

1. Arthur, King—Fiction 2. Knights and knighthood—Fiction
ISBN 0-690-79909-8 LC 56-5699

A story of England in King Arthur's days. Shan, the son of Lord Weldon, takes on the duties of a knight and seeks redress against his uncle, who had usurped his father's rights. A picture of the Knights of the Round Table and King Arthur develops

"A good story for beginning readers, this is also excellent for the older child who is a slow reader, because of the stimulating combination of exciting adventure, short sentences, and easy vocabulary." N Y Times Book Rev

Bunting, Eve, 1928-

Our sixth-grade sugar babies. Lippincott 1990 147p $12.95; lib bdg $12.89 (4-6) **Fic**

1. School stories
ISBN 0-397-32451-0; 0-397-32452-9 (lib bdg) LC 90-5487

Vicki and her best friend fear that their sixth grade project, carrying around five-pound bags of sugar to learn about parental responsibility, will make them look ridiculous in the eyes of the seventh grade boy they both love

"Responsibility and honesty are major themes here, but Bunting's light touch makes them easily digestible lessons. Parental estrangement (Mom and Dad are divorced) and mother-daughter conflict are both honestly dealt with. Characters are convincingly developed, and Bunting shows a genuine understanding for pre-teen angst." Bull Cent Child Books

Burch, Robert, 1925-

Christmas with Ida Early. Viking 1983 157p $12.95; Puffin Bks. pa $3.95 (4 and up) **Fic**

1. Christmas—Fiction 2. Georgia—Fiction 3. Country life—Fiction
ISBN 0-670-22131-7; 0-14-031971-9 (pa) LC 83-5792

Sequel to: Ida Early comes over the mountain, entered below

"Life for the Suttons has never been the same since the zesty Ida Early came to be their cook, housekeeper, and friend. . . . Her eccentric antics and tall tales ramble through one family escapade after another, all recounted with good humor from 12-year-old Randall's point of view. When the new preacher decides to put on a living Christmas tableau that involves some real animals—and

Burch, Robert, 1925-—*Continued*
Ida—readers can be sure that the festivities will be far from normal." Booklist

Ida Early comes over the mountain. Viking 1980 145p $12.95; Puffin Bks. pa $3.95 (4 and up) **Fic**

1. Depressions, Economic—Fiction 2. Country life—Fiction 3. Georgia—Fiction
ISBN 0-670-39169-7; 0-14-034534-5 (pa)
LC 79-20532

"A strong but rather eccentric non-conforming female character is central to this whimsical novel set in the mountains of rural Georgia during the Depression. Ida Early arrives one day to the motherless Sutton family of four children. Mr. Sutton agrees to hire her as a temporary housekeeper. So the adventure begins." Interracial Books Child Bull

"The book works on two levels—the hilarious account of Ida Early's exotic housekeeping in which real cleverness and skill is as effective and amazing as any fantasy magic, and the gentle, touching story of an ungainly woman's longing for beauty and femininity. That both levels meet, resolve themselves satisfactorily, and leave the characters deeply changed is the true success of this fine book." SLJ

Followed by Christmas with Ida Early, entered above

Queenie Peavy; illustrated by Jerry Lazare. Viking 1966 159p il o.p.; Puffin Bks. paperback available $3.95 (5 and up) **Fic**

1. Parent and child—Fiction 2. Georgia—Fiction
ISBN 0-14-032305-8 (pa) LC 66-15649

"Defiant, independent and intelligent, 13-year-old Queenie idolized her father who was in jail and was neglected by her mother who had to work all the time. Growing up in the [Depression] 1930's in Georgia, Queenie eventually understands her father's real character, herself and her relationships to those about her." Wis Libr Bull

"There is no straining here to formulate a story about a problem child. On the surface the account is as dispassionate as a case study, but considerably more convincing, and Queenie is so real that the reader becomes deeply involved in everything that concerns her." Horn Book

Burnett, Frances Hodgson, 1849-1924

A little princess; pictures by Tasha Tudor. Lippincott 1963 240p il $12.95; lib bdg $12.89; Dell pa $3.50 (4-6) **Fic**

1. School stories 2. Great Britain—Fiction
ISBN 0-397-30693-8; 0-397-31339-X (lib bdg); 0-440-44767-4 (pa) LC 63-15435

First American edition published 1892 by Scribner in shorter form with title: Sara Crewe

The story of Sara Crewe, a girl who is sent from India to a boarding school in London, left in poverty by her father's death, and rescued by a mysterious benefactor

"The story is inevitably adorned with sentimental curlicues but the reader will hardly notice them since the story itself is such a satisfying one. Tasha Tudor's gentle, appropriate illustrations make this a lovely edition." Publ Wkly

The secret garden (4-6) **Fic**

Some editions are:

ABC-CLIO $13.95 Large print edition (ISBN 1-85089-908-8)

Godine $16.95 Illustrated by Graham Rust (ISBN 0-87923-649-3)

Harper & Row $12.95; lib bdg $12.89; pa $3.50 Illustrated by Tasha Tudor (ISBN 0-397-32165-1; 0-397-32162-7; 0-06-440-188-X)

Holt & Co. $18.95 Illustrated by Micheal Hague (ISBN 0-8050-0277-4)

Knopf $18.95 Illustrated by Ruth Sanderson (ISBN 0-394-55431-0)

Viking $18.95 Illustrated by Shirley Hughes (ISBN 0-670-82571-9)

First published 1909 by Stokes

"Neglected by his father because of his mother's death at his birth, Colin lives the life of a spoilt and incurable invalid until, on the arrival of an orphaned cousin, the two children secretly combine to restore his mother's locked garden and Colin to health and his father's affection." Four to Fourteen

Burnford, Sheila, 1918-1984

The incredible journey (4 and up) **Fic**

1. Cats—Fiction 2. Dogs—Fiction 3. Canada—Fiction

Some editions are:

Amereon $13.95 (ISBN 0-88411-099-0)

Bantam Bks. $14.95; pa $2.95 (ISBN 0-553-05874-6; 0-553-26218-1)

First published 1961 by Little, Brown

"A half-blind English bull terrier, a sprightly yellow Labrador retriever, and a feisty Siamese cat have resided for eight months with a friend of their owners, who are away on a trip. Then their temporary caretaker leaves them behind in order to take a short vacation. The lonely trio decides to tackle the harsh 250-mile hike across the Canadian wilderness in search of home, despite the human and wild obstacles the group will encounter." Shapiro. Fic for Youth. 2d edition

Butterworth, Oliver, 1915-1990

The enormous egg; illustrated by Louis Darling. Little, Brown 1956 187p il $14.95; Dell pa $3.25 (4 and up) **Fic**

1. Dinosaurs—Fiction
ISBN 0-316-11904-0; 0-440-42337-6 (pa) LC 56-5622

"Up in Freedom, New Hampshire, one of the Twitchell's hens laid a remarkable egg—long, leathery-shelled, and so enormous that she could neither cover it nor turn it. Six weeks later when a live dinosaur hatched from the egg, the hen was dazed and upset, the Twitchells dumbfounded, and the scientific world went crazy. Twelve-year-old Nate who had taken care of the egg and made a pet out of the triceratops tells of the hullabaloo." Booklist

Nate's story, "is not only great fun but, one might say, educational—in a painless way, of course. And if you have any trouble visualizing a Triceratops moving placidly through the twentieth-century world you need only turn to Louis Darling's illustrations to believe." NY Times Book Rev

Byars, Betsy Cromer, 1928-

The 18th emergency; [by] Betsy Byars; illustrated by Robert Grossman. Viking 1973 126p il lib bdg $12.95; Puffin Bks. pa $3.95 (4-6) **Fic**

1. Fear—Fiction
ISBN 0-670-29055-6; 0-14-031451-2 (pa) LC 72-91399

Timid Benjie, whose nickname is Mouse, spends two days worrying about Marv a big sixth grader who threatens to beat him up. Mouse "finally confronts Marv and takes two to the stomach, one to the breastbone, and two to the face without landing a punch on his opponent. Standing up like a man (not a Mouse) so impresses his peers that they begin to call him Benjie." Libr J

"For its skillful portrayal of the loneliness of fear as well as a boy's emotional battle with himself—his frantic thoughts, his fantasies of escape, his gradual awakening to the way things are as against the way he wishes they were—'The 18th Emergency' weighs in . . . as a bantam champion." N Y Times Book Rev

After the Goat Man; [by] Betsy Byars; illustrated by Ronald Himler. Viking 1974 126p il $13.95; Penguin Bks. pa $3.95 (5 and up) **Fic**

ISBN 0-670-10908-8; 0-14-031533-0 (pa) LC 74-8200

Figgy's "grandfather, the town's oddball nicknamed the Goat Man, has barricaded himself with his shotgun in their old cabin in a last ditch attempt to halt the wrecking crew from flattening their home for a superhighway. In a crisis which develops when they set out to talk the old man away from the cabin, Ada, Figgy, [overweight] Harold and the Goat Man become linked by their mutual caring, generosity and gentleness." N Y Times Book Rev

"The restrained plot, developed through spare, unsentimental prose, effectively and clearly delineates the need to recognize individual dignity and the pangs of adolescence. A compassionate and artistic treatment of human problems." Horn Book

The animal, the vegetable, and John D Jones; [by] Betsy Byars; illustrated by Ruth Sanderson. Delacorte Press 1982 150p il o.p.; Dell paperback available $2.95 (5 and up) **Fic**

1. Parent and child—Fiction 2. Vacations—Fiction 3. Family life—Fiction
ISBN 0-440-40356-1 (pa) LC 81-69665

"Sam Malcolm and Dolores Jones have decided to spend their vacation together at the beach. Sam's two daughters, Denise and Clara, know their two-week vacation is going to be terrible. John D. Jones, Dolores' son, is sure the whole venture will be a dead loss. Sam is divorced from the girl's mother; Dolores' husband has been dead for many years. . . . A near tragedy brings a new awareness to the youngsters." Child Book Rev Serv

"Notable for its probing of adolescent psyches, the novel creates believable characters—flawed human beings, whose punishment for misbehavior is living with the consequences of their actions. Spare and wryly humorous, the novel maintains a brisk pace while preserving intensity." Horn Book

Beans on the roof; [by] Betsy Byars; illustrated by Melodye Rosales. Delacorte Press 1988 65p il $13.95; Dell pa $2.95 (2-4) **Fic**

1. Family life—Fiction
ISBN 0-440-50055-9; 0-440-40314-6 (pa) LC 88-6907

"George Bean wants to play on the roof, but his mother says no. His sister Anna is writing a poem up there, a roof poem, which she hopes will be published in a book at school. Intrigued, George tries his hand at a roof poem, but nothing comes to mind. When everyone in the family—Papa, Mama, younger sister Jenny, and Anna—all write roof poems, George feels awful until he devises a two-liner of his own." Booklist

"Character, setting and mood are created through a subtle and masterful use of dialogue. Like a poem, this distills the feelings of the characters and reflects their regard and caring for one another." Publ Wkly

The burning questions of Bingo Brown; [by] Betsy Byars. Viking 1988 166p lib bdg $12.95; Puffin Bks. pa $3.95 (4 and up) **Fic**

1. School stories
ISBN 0-670-81932-8 (lib bdg); 0-14-032479-8 (pa) LC 87-21022

Also available G.K. Hall large print edition $14.95 (ISBN 0-8161-4770-1)

A boy is puzzled by the comic and confusing questions of youth and worried by disturbing insights into adult conflicts

"A fully worked out novel. . . . Readers will recognize the pitfalls, agonies, and joys of elementary school life in this book. . . . The short chapters and comic style are designed to appeal to young readers and to move them right into other books." Christ Sci Monit

Other available titles about Bingo Brown are:
Bingo Brown and the language of love (1989)
Bingo Brown, gypsy lover (1990)

The cartoonist; [by] Betsy Byars; illustrated by Richard Cuffari. Viking 1978 119p il $12.95; Puffin Bks. pa $3.95 (4 and up) **Fic**

1. Family life—Fiction
ISBN 0-670-20556-7; 0-14-032309-0 (pa) LC 77-12782

"Alfie seeks refuge from the rest of the world, especially his shrill-voiced, TV-addicted mother, in the attic of their dilapidated house, where he creates wry cartoons. When it appears that his older brother Bubba and wife will move into the attic, Alfie locks himself in, determined not to allow this assault on his being. . . . Bubba [finally] decides to move in with the other in-laws, and Alfie 'wins' by default, realizing, as he emerges, that the only real victory lies in his ability to deal with reality." Child Book Rev Serv

"Alfie's ultimate reconciliation of his real and imaginary worlds is conveyed with extraordinary sensitivity to the thoughts and emotions of a child. Yet the tone of the book is neither serious nor somber; humorous dialogue is used throughout both to characterize and to narrate." Horn Book

Byars, Betsy Cromer, 1928-—*Continued*

Cracker Jackson; by Betsy Byars. Viking Kestrel 1985 147p $11.95; Puffin Bks. pa $3.95 (5 and up) **Fic**

1. Wife abuse—Fiction 2. Child abuse—Fiction
ISBN 0-670-80546-7; 0-14-031881-X (pa)
LC 84-24684

Also available G.K. Hall large print edition $13.95 (ISBN 0-7451-0493-2)

"Young Jackson discovers that his ex-baby sitter has been beaten by her husband; and, spurred by affection for her, the boy enlists his friend Goat to help drive her to a home for battered women. The pathetic story of Alma, with her adored baby, tidy home, and treasured collection of Barbie dolls, is relieved by flashbacks to the two boys' antics at school and by their hilarious, if potentially lethal, attempt to drive her to safety." Horn Book

"Suspense, danger, near-tragedy, heartbreak and tension-relieving, unwittingly comic efforts at seriously heroic action mark this as the best of middle-grade fiction to highlight the problems of wife-battering and child abuse." SLJ

The Cybil war; [by] Betsy Byars; illustrated by Gail Owens. Viking 1981 126p il $12.95; Puffin Bks. pa $3.95 (4-6) **Fic**

1. Friendship—Fiction
ISBN 0-670-25248-4; 0-14-034356-3 (pa)
LC 80-26912

"Simon is deeply smitten by Cybil, a fourth-grade classmate, and just as deeply angered by his once-closest friend Tony, a blithely inventive liar who persists in telling fibs to and about Cybil to strengthen his cause: Tony is also smitten by Cybil." Bull Cent Child Books

"In her gently comic style, Byars presents Simon and the other people in her . . . story (even nasty Tony) as subteens who are people dealing with real problems. . . . Owens has illustrated sympathetically, making up a book that readers will take to their hearts." Publ Wkly

The house of wings; [by] Betsy Byars; illustrated by Daniel Schwartz. Viking 1972 142p il lib bdg $13.95; Puffin Bks. pa $3.95 (4-6) **Fic**

1. Cranes (Birds)—Fiction 2. Grandfathers—Fiction
ISBN 0-670-38025-3 (lib bdg); 0-14-031523-3 (pa)
LC 77-183033

"A young boy reeling from the pain of temporary parental abandonment forges a relationship with an eccentric grandfather whom he despises. In attempting to rescue and mend a wounded crane, they come to respect each other for what they are, and as men." Book World

This story "has an unsentimental and potent message about wildlife and draws a telling portrait of a human relationship. Save for the brief appearance of the parents, Sammy and his grandfather are the only characters. The book's spare construction makes it strong." Saturday Rev

The midnight fox; [by] Betsy Byars; illustrated by Ann Grifalconi. Viking 1968 157p il lib bdg $13.95; Puffin Bks. pa $3.95 (4-6) **Fic**

1. Foxes—Fiction
ISBN 0-670-47473-8 (lib bdg); 0-14-031450-4 (pa)
LC 68-27566

"City-bred Tommy hates the idea of spending the summer on Aunt Millie's farm while his parents bicycle through Europe. Once he is there, however, a black fox shatters his conviction that he and animals share a mutual antipathy; fascinated, he stalks and watches the wild creature for two months—until it steals some of Aunt Millie's poultry and has to be hunted down." Booklist

"What distinguishes the story from many others on the same theme is the simplicity and beauty of the writing and the depth of the characterization." Horn Book

The night swimmers; by Betsy Byars; illustrated by Troy Howell. Delacorte Press 1980 131p il o.p.; Dell paperback available $2.95 (5 and up) **Fic**

1. Single parent family—Fiction 2. Brothers and sisters—Fiction
ISBN 0-440-45857-9 (pa) LC 79-53597

Also available ABC-CLIO large print edition $15.95 (ISBN 1-55736-177-0)

With their mother dead and their father working nights, Retta tries to be mother to her two younger brothers but somehow things just don't seem to be working right

"The plot moves a little slowly but characterization is good." Voice Youth Advocates

The not-just-anybody family; [by] Betsy Byars; illustrated by Jacqueline Rogers. Delacorte Press 1986 149p il $13.95; Dell pa $2.95 (5 and up) **Fic**

1. Brothers and sisters—Fiction 2. Family life—Fiction
ISBN 0-385-29443-3; 0-440-45951-6 (pa)
LC 85-16184

"It's an ordinary day in the Blossom family: Junior, with Maggie and Vernon watching, is poised to fly off the barn in homemade wings; Mom's on the rodeo circuit; and Pap and his dog, Mud, are in town. By evening, Pap's in jail; Junior's in the hospital; Mud is gone; and Maggie helps Vernon break into jail to be with their grandfather." Publisher's note

"The author has a sure hand with the telling details and desperate problems of people living at the poverty level—what they eat and wear, why they avoid authority—and a gift for short, pithy, authentic characterizations. The story of the pathetically self-reliant, eccentric, but deeply loving family makes a book that is funny and sad, warm and wonderful." Horn Book

Other available titles about the Blossom family are:
The Blossoms meet the Vulture Lady (1986)
The Blossoms and the Green Phantom (1987)
A Blossom promise (1987)

The pinballs; [by] Betsy Byars. Harper & Row 1977 136p $12.95; lib bdg $12.89; pa $2.95 (5 and up) **Fic**

1. Foster home care—Fiction 2. Friendship—Fiction
ISBN 0-06-020917-8; 0-06-020918-6 (lib bdg); 0-06-440198-7 (pa) LC 76-41518

Also available ABC-CLIO large print edition $15.95 (ISBN 1-55736-028-6)

"Three lonely foster children, each scarred by parental abuse or neglect, come together in a supportive home where they begin to understand themselves and to care

Byars, Betsy Cromer, 1928-—*Continued*
for one another." LC. Child Books, 1977

"The economically told story, liberally spiced with humor, is something of a tour de force. . . . A deceptively simple, eloquent story, its pain and acrimony constantly mitigated by the author's light, offhand style and by Carlie's wryly comic view of life." Horn Book

The summer of the swans; [by] Betsy Byars; illustrated by Ted CoConis. Viking 1988 c1970 185p il o.p. (5 and up) **Fic**

1. Slow learning children—Fiction 2. Brothers and sisters—Fiction LC 87-29014

Available ABC-CLIO large print edition $15.95 (ISBN 1-55736-030-8)

Awarded the Newbery Medal, 1971

"The thoughts and feelings of a young girl troubled by a sense of inner discontent which she cannot explain are tellingly portrayed in the story of two summer days in the life of fourteen-year-old Sara Godfrey. Sara is jolted out of her self-pitying absorption with her own inadequacies by the disappearance of her ten-year-old retarded brother who gets lost while trying to find the swans he had previously seen on a nearby lake. Her agonizing, albeit ultimately successful, search for Charlie and the reactions of others to this traumatic event help Sara gain a new perspective on herself and life." Booklist

Trouble River; [by] Betsy Byars; illustrated by Rocco Negri. Viking 1969 158p il $13.95 (4-6) **Fic**

1. Frontier and pioneer life—Fiction 2. Rivers—Fiction

ISBN 0-670-73257-5 LC 69-18260

Dewey Martin and his grandmother must make their way down the Trouble River on a home-made raft to escape the danger of hostile Indians. They find the raft hard to navigate on the river, but they persevere and eventually reach Hunter City and safety

"A philosophy of not giving up amid hardships and a sense of real love and family solidarity predominate." Read Ladders for Hum Relat. 6th edition

The TV kid; [by] Betsy Byars; illustrated by Richard Cuffari. Viking 1976 123p il $12.95; Puffin Bks. pa $3.95 (4-6) **Fic**

1. Television and children—Fiction

ISBN 0-670-73331-8; 0-14-032308-2 (pa) LC 75-37944

"TV addict Lennie scores low on his school tests, but in his fantasies he's big winner of every sort of giveaway quiz show. He lives with his mother in a decrepit motel and his lonely hobby is breaking into nearby summer cottages. Bitten by a rattler while hiding under a cottage during a neighborhood police check, Lennie is rescued barely in time for the anti-venom shots to save him. . . . The long and painful recovery is Lennie's reality cure." SLJ

"Byars avoids what could be a melodramatic ending for Lennie-the-TV-star with well-developed characters, splurges of humor, and a suspenseful but believable plot. She also successfully uses satire that children can relate to, which is rarely found in a children's book." Booklist

The two-thousand-pound goldfish; [by] Betsy Byars. Harper & Row 1982 153p $11.95; lib bdg $11.89 (5 and up) **Fic**

1. Family life—Fiction 2. Horror films—Fiction

ISBN 0-06-020889-9; 0-06-020890-2 (lib bdg) LC 81-48652

"Warren has problems. His mother is underground, a fugitive in a radical peace group. Her commitments do not include her children—she has called them once in five years. Warren wants her around and spends a great deal of time fantasizing about her and a reunion. For diversion, Warren watches horror films and writes horror scripts. After the death of his grandmother, Warren gets a better grip on reality, but continues to enjoy his horror films." Child Book Rev Serv

"Evoking empathy, the plot is not overly melodramatic, and the action of the story line, the lively film scripts and the explanatory flashbacks are well integrated." SLJ

Calhoun, Mary, 1926-

Katie John; pictures by Paul Frame. Harper & Row 1960 134p il lib bdg $12.89; pa $3.50 (4-6) **Fic**

1. Houses—Fiction

ISBN 0-06-020951-8 (lib bdg); 0-06-440028-X (pa) LC 60-5775

"When the Tuckers inherited an old house in a Missouri town, they decided to live in it until they could get it ready to sell. Ten-year-old Katie John was gloomy at the prospect—until she made a new friend, helped to solve a mystery, and learned to love the house." Hodges. Books for Elem Sch Libr

A "story with a likable heroine, lively doings, and a credible ending." Booklist

Other available titles about Katie John are:
Depend on Katie John (1961)
Honestly, Katie John (1963)
Katie John and Heathcliff (1980)

Callen, Larry

Pinch; illustrated by Marvin Friedman. Little, Brown 1975 179p il $14.95 (5 and up) **Fic**

1. Country life—Fiction 2. Pigs—Fiction

ISBN 0-316-12495-8 LC 75-25618

"An Atlantic Monthly Press book"

"Pinch Grimball, who tells the story, is an adolescent whose father is the best trainer of hunting pigs in Louisiana. . . . Pinch's pig Homer, trained by Dad . . . is coveted, stolen, recovered, lied about, and wins a hunting contest." Bull Cent Child Books

"The events are hilarious. . . . Readers will alternately admire and sympathize with Pinch as he relates his adventures in a plain, open style. Definitely worth recommending to reluctant readers, too!" SLJ

Cameron, Ann, 1943-

The most beautiful place in the world; drawings by Thomas B. Allen. Knopf 1988 57p il $11.95; lib bdg $11.99 (2-4) **Fic**

1. Grandmothers—Fiction 2. Guatemala—Fiction
ISBN 0-394-89463-4; 0-394-99463-9 (lib bdg)
LC 88-532

Growing up with his grandmother in a small Central American town, seven-year-old Juan discovers the value of hard work, the joy of learning, and the location of the most beautiful place in the world

"The easy-to-read text, the handsome pencil drawings, and a setting that will take U.S. children into lives led elsewhere make this a winning choice for reading aloud or alone." Bull Cent Child Books

The stories Julian tells; illustrated by Ann Strugnell. Pantheon Bks. 1981 71p il $8.95; lib bdg $8.99; pa $2.95 (2-4) **Fic**

1. Family life—Fiction 2. Blacks—Fiction
ISBN 0-394-84301-0; 0-394-94301-5 (lib bdg); 0-394-82892-5 (pa) LC 80-18023

"When seven-year-old Julian tells his little brother, Huey, that cats come from catalogues, Huey believes him. But when he flips the pages of the catalogue and doesn't find any cats, he begins to cry and Julian has some fast explaining to do. He also has to think fast when one lick of the pudding his father made leads to another lick then another. A loving family is the center for six happy stories about catalog cats, strange teeth, a garden, a birthday fig tree and a new friend." West Coast Rev Books

"Strugnell's delightful drawings depict Julian, his little brother Huey and their parents as black, but they could be members of any family with a stern but loving and understanding father." Publ Wkly

Other available titles about Julian and his family are:
Julian, dream doctor (1990)
Julian, secret agent (1988)
Julian's glorious summer (1987)
More stories Julian tells (1986)

Cameron, Eleanor, 1912-

Beyond silence. Dutton 1980 197p $9.95 (6 and up) **Fic**

1. Death—Fiction 2. Space and time—Fiction 3. Scotland—Fiction
ISBN 0-525-26463-9 LC 80-10350

Troubled by a recurring nightmare following his brother's death, Andrew accompanies his father to the family castle in Scotland where he has several encounters with one of his forebears

"A kind of psychological science fiction, the novel presents a warping of reality, explained in terms of theories of the unconscious mind and recognition as well as of revised notions about time-space, cause and effect, and coincidence. A definite literary style flavors the book." Horn Book

The court of the stone children. Dutton 1973 191p $13.95; Puffin Bks. pa $3.95 (5 and up) **Fic**

1. Museums—Fiction 2. Mystery and detective stories
ISBN 0-525-28350-1; 0-14-034289-3 (pa)
LC 73-77451

In a San Francisco museum of French art and furniture, Nina encounters the ghost of Dominique, a girl who lived in the nineteenth-century. Spurred on by the appearance of the ghost, Nina sets out to untangle a murder mystery which had remained unsolved since Napoleon's day

"A nice concoction of mystery, fantasy, and realism adroitly blended in a contemporary story. . . . The characters are interesting, the plot threads nicely integrated." Bull Cent Child Books

A room made of windows; illustrated by Trina Schart Hyman. Little, Brown 1971 271p il $15.95; Puffin Bks. pa $4.95 (5 and up) **Fic**

ISBN 0-316-12523-7; 0-14-034156-0 (pa)
LC 77-140479

"An Atlantic Monthly Press book"

"This is the tale of Julia, an aspiring young author, who is highly intelligent but emotionally immature. Although she revels in the satisfactions of good friends and progress in her writing, she is troubled by her mother's desire to remarry, the death of a much-loved elderly friend, and problems of those around her." Wis Libr Bull

"The portrayal and interaction of interesting and diverse characters are given unity and meaning by the genius of a fine storyteller." J Youth Serv Libr

Other available titles about Julia Redfern are:
Julia and the hand of God (1977)
Julia's magic (1984)
The private worlds of Julia Redfern (1988)
That Julia Redfern (1982)

To the green mountains. Dutton 1975 180p $9.95 (6 and up) **Fic**

1. Ohio—Fiction
ISBN 0-525-41355-3 LC 75-6758

"This story of Kath Rule, who is growing up during World War I, evokes the past in Midwest America. Kath's mother . . . manages a hotel in Columbus, Ohio, and Kath is tenderly treated by the staff, especially Grant and his wife, Tissy, a black couple. Mrs. Rule gets law books into Grant's hands and encourages him to study. She endures pangs of conscience when her help leads to a crisis and tragedy. The story brings all the people in the girl's circle to brilliant life and it is through her eyes and ears that we know them, and her with her longings for a 'proper' home, far away in the hills where her grandmother lives." Publ Wkly

The wonderful flight to the Mushroom Planet; with illustrations by Robert Henneberger. Little, Brown 1954 214p il $14.95; pa $4.95 (4-6) **Fic**

1. Science fiction
ISBN 0-316-12537-7; 0-316-12540-7 (pa) LC 54-8310

"An Atlantic Monthly Press book"

Two boys help a neighbor build a space ship in answer to an ad and take off for the dying planet of Basidium. There they help the inhabitants to restore an essential food to their diets and thereby save the life of the planet

"Scientific facts are emphasized in this well-built story. Since they are necessary to the development of the story the reader absorbs them naturally as he soars with the boys on the mission." N Y Times Book Rev

Cameron, Eleanor, 1912-—*Continued*

Other available titles about the Mushroom Planet, the boys and Mr. Bass are:
Mr. Bass's planetoid (1958)
Stowaway to the Mushroom Planet (1956)
Time and Mr. Bass (1967)

Capote, Truman, 1924-1984

A Christmas memory; illustrated by Beth Peck. Knopf 1989 unp il lib bdg $12.95 (3-5) **Fic**

1. Christmas—Fiction
ISBN 0-679-80040-9 LC 88-36452

Text first published 1956

A reminiscence of a Christmas shared by a seven-year-old boy and a sixtyish childlike woman, with enormous love and friendship between them

"Peck's watercolor-and-ink full-page illustrations greatly enhance the text. Her use of lighter shades, tawny colors, and fine lines plus a background wash which suggests rather than delineates detail is perfect for this holiday memory of Christmas celebrated in rural Alabama in the early 1930s." SLJ

Carlson, Natalie Savage

The family under the bridge; pictures by Garth Williams. Harper & Row 1958 99p il lib bdg $14.89 (3-5) **Fic**

1. Tramps—Fiction 2. Christmas—Fiction 3. Paris (France)—Fiction
ISBN 0-06-020991-7 LC 58-5292

A Newbery Medal honor book, 1959

"Old Armand, a Parisian hobo, enjoyed his solitary, carefree life. . . . Then came a day just before Christmas when Armand, who wanted nothing to do with children because they spelled homes, responsibility, and regular work, found that three homeless children and their working mother had claimed his shelter under the bridge. How the hobo's heart and life become more and more deeply entangled with the little family and their quest for a home is told." Booklist

"Garth Williams' illustrations are perfect for this thoroughly delightful story of humor and sentiment which includes a Christmas Eve party given by the ladies of Notre Dame for the homeless of Paris and an inside view of a gypsy encampment." Libr J

The happy orpheline; pictures by Garth Williams. Harper & Row 1957 96p il lib bdg $13.89; Dell pa $2.75 (3-5) **Fic**

1. Orphans—Fiction 2. France—Fiction
ISBN 0-06-021007-9 (lib bdg); 0-440-43455-6 (pa)
LC 57-9260

"Twenty orphan girls dread adoption because it will mean separation. One gets lost and involved in adventures with the 'queen of France' who threatens to adopt her." SLJ

"Garth Williams' strong pen-and-ink sketches, full of life and laughter, match the imagination and French flavor of the writing." Horn Book

Other available titles about the orphelines are:
A brother for the orphelines (1959)
A grandmother for the orphelines (1980)
The orphelines in the enchanted castle (1964)
A pet for the orphelines (1962)

Carrick, Carol

Stay away from Simon! pictures by Donald Carrick. Clarion Bks. 1985 63p il lib bdg $12.95 (3-5) **Fic**

1. Mentally handicapped—Fiction
ISBN 0-89919-343-9 LC 84-14289

"In a story set on Martha's Vineyard in the 1830's, the children of the Village echo the ignorance of the period and their fear of, and misunderstanding about, those who are retarded. Lucy, eleven, is already afraid of big, shambling Simon and is terrified when she finds he is following her as she stumbles homeward through a snowstorm with her weeping little brother. It is then that Simon saves them, leading the way to the road and carrying Josiah." Bull Cent Child Books

"Because the story is set in a different era and features an intrinsically interesting adventure, its message comes across without being didactic. Involving and moving, the tale also comes alive through Donald Carrick's finely crafted pencil drawings that set the mood as well as the scene. This will work especially well as a class read-aloud because of its adventure, its characterizations, and the discussion it could provoke." Booklist

What a wimp! drawings by Donald Carrick. Clarion Bks. 1983 89p il lib bdg $12.95; pa $4.95 (3-5) **Fic**

1. School stories 2. Divorce—Fiction
ISBN 0-89919-139-8 (lib bdg); 0-89919-703-5 (pa)
LC 82-9597

"After their parents were divorced, Barney and his brother Russ moved to the small town where his mother had spent her childhood summers. Barney finds now that coping with a bully in his class, Lenny, makes him unhappy about everything else. . . . Barney knows he can't expect his mother or brother to fight his battles, but their sympathy does help . . . but in the end it is Barney who decides that if he stops running, he can't be chased, and who learns that a bully will often back down when confronted." Bull Cent Child Books

"Prose and illustrations excel at capturing the classrooom and playground atmosphere of a primary school." SLJ

Carris, Joan Davenport, 1938-

Pets, vets, and Marty Howard; [by] Joan Carris; illustrated by Carol Newsom. Lippincott 1984 186p il lib bdg $12.89; Dell pa $2.95 (5 and up) **Fic**

1. Veterinary medicine—Fiction 2. Animals—Fiction
ISBN 0-397-32093-0 (lib bdg); 0-397-32093-0 (pa)
LC 84-47635

Sequel to: When the boys ran the house (1982)

"Twelve-year-old Marty Howard is proud of his job at the veterinary clinic. He helps the doctors, cleans up, and finds himself the unofficial seeker of homes for deserted animals. As his proficiency in veterinary techniques increases, he begins to wonder if he is as set in his career choice as he thought." Booklist

"The soft, cuddly animals are great, but abandoned pets, euthanasia, and some operations are less pleasant. . . . Well-done and told realistically with humor." Child Book Rev Serv

Carroll, Lewis, 1832-1898

Alice's adventures in Wonderland (4 and up) **Fic**

1. Fantastic fiction

Some editions are:

Crown (Children's classics) $10.99 With illustrations in color by Bessie Pease Gutmann and black and white illustrations by John Tenniel (ISBN 0-517-65961-1)
Holt & Co. $14.95 Illustrated by Michael Hague (ISBN 0-8050-0212-X)
Knopf $17.95 Illustrated by S. Michelle Wiggins (ISBN 0-394-53227-9)
Knopf $19.95, lib bdg $19.99 Illustrated by Anthony Browne (ISBN 0-394-80592-5; 0-394-90592-X)
Philomel Bks. $19.95 Illustrated by Peter Weevers (ISBN 0-399-22241-3)
St. Martin's Press $9.95 Illustrated by Sir John Tenniel (ISBN 0-312-01821-5)

"First told in 1862 to the little Liddell girls. Written out for Alice Liddell, published, and first copy given to her in 1865." Arnold

"A rabbit who took a watch out of his waistcoat pocket seemed well-worth following to Alice so she hurried after him across the field, down the rabbit hole, and into a series of adventures with a group of famous and most unusual characters." Let's Read Together

This fantasy "is one of the most quoted books in the English language. Every child should be introduced to Alice, though its appeal will not be universal." Natl Counc of Teach of Engl. Adventuring with Books

Followed by: Through the looking glass, and what Alice found there, entered below

Alice's adventures in Wonderland, and Through the looking glass (4 and up) **Fic**

1. Fantastic fiction

Some editions are:

Contemporary Bks. (A Calico book) pa $7.95 Illustrated by T. Lewis; foreword by Hilma Wolitzer (ISBN 0-8092-4488-8)
Dent (Children's illustrated classics) $11 With the original engravings by John Tenniel, of which 8 have been redrawn in colour by Diana Stanley (ISBN 0-460-05029-X)
Golden Bks. (Golden classic) $8.95 Illustrated by Kathy Mitchell (ISBN 0-307-17111-6) Has title: Alice in Wonderland & Through the looking glass
Messner lib bdg $14.79 Illustrations by John Speirs (ISBN 0-671-45649-0) Has title: Alice in Wonderland, and Through the looking glass

An omnibus edition of the two titles listed separately

Through the looking glass, and what Alice found there. (4 and up) **Fic**

1. Fantastic fiction

Some editions are:

Knopf $17.95 Illustrated by S. Michelle Wiggins (ISBN 0-394-53228-7)
Schocken Bks. $16.95 Illustrated by Justin Todd (ISBN 0-8052-4036-5)
St. Martin's Press $8.95 Illustrated by Sir John Tenniel (ISBN 0-312-80374-5)

First published 1872

In this sequel to Alice's adventures in Wonderland, entered above, Alice climbs through a looking glass into a country where "everything is reversed, just as reflections are reversed in a mirror. Brooks and hedges divide the land into a checkerboard and Alice finds herself a white pawn in the whimsical and fantastic game of chess that constitutes the bulk of the story. . . . The ballad 'Jabberwocky' is found in the tale." Reader's Ency

Cassedy, Sylvia, 1930-1989

Behind the attic wall. Crowell 1983 315p $12.95; lib bdg $12.89 (5 and up) **Fic**

1. Uncles—Fiction 2. Orphans—Fiction 3. Ghosts—Fiction

ISBN 0-690-04336-8; 0-690-04337-6 (lib bdg) LC 82-45922

Maggie, a rebellious twelve-year-old "orphan, had been ejected from every boarding school she'd ever attended. Now she is sent to stay with two elderly great-aunts; like other guardians they are horrified by the behavior of the . . . hostile child . . . who throws away the doll . . . they have bought her. That is the realistic matrix for a fantasy world behind the attic wall, where Maggie finds two dolls who are articulate and who draw her into their world so that she becomes engaged and protective." Bull Cent Child Books

"Maggie's harsh dislike for the people about her vividly contrasts with the love and tenderness she is finally able to lavish on the dolls. . . . The gradual merging of the story into fantasy, detail by telling detail, demands patience and attention on the part of the reader, but the wonderfully strange denouement will reward perseverance." Horn Book

Lucie Babbidge's house. Crowell 1989 242p $12.95; lib bdg $12.89 (4-6) **Fic**

1. Dolls—Fiction 2. Orphans—Fiction

ISBN 0-690-04796-7; 0-690-04798-3 (lib bdg) LC 89-1296

Having found a dollhouse full of dolls in the orphanage where she leads an unhappy existence, Lucie creates a secret life for herself

"An ambitious and highly satisfying novel for readers who delight in complex characterization, and the inventive use of language and plotting." SLJ

M.E. and Morton. Crowell 1987 312p $13.95; lib bdg $13.89; HarperCollins Pubs. pa $3.95 (6 and up) **Fic**

1. Brothers and sisters—Fiction 2. Learning disabilities—Fiction 3. Friendship—Fiction

ISBN 0-690-04560-3; 0-690-04562-X (lib bdg); 0-06-440306-8 (pa) LC 85-48251

"M.E., short for Mary Ellen, is an excellent student at the private school she attends on scholarship, but she has few friends because she is ashamed of her learning disabled brother. When Polly, a strange new girl, moves into the neighborhood and becomes friends with M.E. and her brother, their summer is filled with imaginative games." Child Book Rev Serv

"What makes the story special is the complete uniqueness of M.E. and her view of the world. . . . Her voice, the only one heard directly, is occasionally self-centered and sometimes outrightly cruel; it is also completely original and by the story's finish considerably richer in compassion." Booklist

Caudill, Rebecca, 1899-1985

A certain small shepherd; with illustrations by William Pène Du Bois. Holt & Co. 1965 48p il lib bdg $9.95; Dell pa $2.75 (4 and up) **Fic**

1. Physically handicapped children—Fiction 2. Christmas—Fiction 3. Appalachian Mountains—Fiction
ISBN 0-03-089755-6 (lib bdg); 0-440-41194-7 (pa)
LC 65-17604

The author tells of "the singleminded enthusiasm of [Jamie], a little mute boy, who is given the part of one of the shepherds in a church celebration. . . . The pageant never takes place as a blizzard immobilizes the poor mountain community where the child lives, but the small shepherd is so deeply committed to his part that he acts it out impulsively [and speaks] when a baby is born to a family of travelers, caught by the storm and obliged to take refuge in the church." Book Week

"Set in the mountains of Appalachia, the tender, moving story, illustrated with poignantly interpretive drawings, expresses anew the age-old Christmas message of love and wonder." Booklist

Did you carry the flag today, Charley? illustrated by Nancy Grossman. Holt & Co. 1966 94p il lib bdg $9.95; pa $3.95 (2-4) **Fic**

1. School stories 2. Appalachian Mountains—Fiction
ISBN 0-03-089753-X (lib bdg); 0-03-086620-0 (pa)
LC 66-11422

A "story about a small and lively boy, just turned five, who has his first encounter with the necessary strictures of the classroom at a summer school in Appalachia. Charley, obstreperous youngest in a family of ten, is given a full picture of the joys and the responsibilities he will encounter; his brothers and sisters tell him that one child 'who has been specially good that day' has the honor of carrying the flag at the head of the line to the bus. They ask every day, but they hardly expect Charley to carry the flag, since he has an affinity for trouble, usually emanating from curiosity. He does, of course, carry the flag in the last episode. This is a realistic and low-keyed story with good dialogue, although Charley seems precocious, and excellent classroom scenes." Bull Cent Child Books

Chaikin, Miriam, 1928-

Finders weepers; drawings by Richard Egielski. Harper & Row 1980 120p il lib bdg $12.89 (3-5) **Fic**

1. Jews—New York (N.Y.)—Fiction 2. Family life—Fiction 3. Brooklyn (New York, N.Y.)—Fiction
ISBN 0-06-021177-6
LC 79-9608

Sequel to: I should worry, I should care (1979)

A "portrayal of a Jewish family in Brooklyn in the late 1930s. . . . Heroine Molly is pleased with a ring she picks up on a playground—until she finds out it belongs to a Hebrew school classmate, a refugee from Nazi Germany. Faced with both a moral and physical dilemma (she can't get the ring off her finger), Molly ponders her situation in the midst of family preparations for the High Holidays, her baby brother's illness, ever-present concern for the plight of European Jews, and the day-to-day traumas and joys of family and school." SLJ

"The writing style has a casual lilt, but it is the humor, the dialogue that is so right for the time and place, and the warmth of familial relationships that are most appealing." Bull Cent Child Books

Other available titles about Molly are:
Friends forever (1988)
Getting even (1982)
Lower! Higher! You're a liar! (1984)

Yossi asks the angels for help; pictures by Petra Mathers. Harper & Row 1985 52p il $11.95; lib bdg $11.89 (3-5) **Fic**

1. Hanukkah—Fiction 2. Jews—Fiction
ISBN 0-06-021195-4; 0-06-021196-2 (lib bdg)
LC 84-48351

Sequel to: How Yossi beat the evil urge (1983)

When he loses the Hanukkah money he planned to use for presents for his sister and parents, Yossi prays to the angels for help

"Underneath this small plot is lots of discussion about Hannukah which is informative for children who know little or nothing about Jewish faith and celebrations. Humor is present in the exchanges between Yossi and Rebbe, proving that school boys are the same regardless of the instructional situation." Okla State Dept of Educ

Other available titles about Yossi are:
Feathers in the wind (1989)
Yossi tries to help God (1987)

Chang, Margaret Scrogin

In the eye of war; [by] Margaret and Raymond Chang. Margaret K. McElderry Bks. 1990 198p $14.95 (4 and up) **Fic**

1. Sino-Japanese Conflict, 1937-1945—Fiction 2. Family life—Fiction 3. Shanghai (China)—Fiction
ISBN 0-689-50503-5
LC 89-38027

"Based on Raymond Chang's childhood in Japanese-occupied Shanghai during WW II, this first novel focuses on Shao-Shao, a 10-year-old Chinese boy. Even with the war ranging, Shao-Shao leads a somewhat normal life: he goes to school, flies his kite and is coddled by his nurse. But some difficulties prevail: the boy wants to be friends with Li-Sha, but since her father is collaborating with the Japanese, he is not supposed to talk with her. And because of his wartime concerns, Shao-Shao's father is even more distant and harder to please than usual." Publ Wkly

"The book, although not without action, is largely a mood piece, evoking a sense of time and place with the loving details a young boy would notice and appreciate. However, transcending time and place is Shao-shao's tenuous relationship with his father. . . . This is a fascinating glimpse into the mind of a typical boy in unusual circumstances." SLJ

Charbonneau, Eileen

The ghosts of Stony Clove. Orchard Bks. 1988 150p $13.95; lib bdg $13.99 (5 and up) **Fic**

1. Ghosts—Fiction
ISBN 0-531-05739-9; 0-531-08339-X (lib bdg)
LC 87-20321

A "ghost story/romance set in a small town in New York at the beginning of the last century. Asher Woods and Ginny Rockwell are two teenage outsiders in the

Charbonneau, Eileen—*Continued*

small town of Stony Clove. . . . Late one night . . . the two friends venture near the house of Squire Sutherland, an elderly recluse shunned by the town for a murder that he is rumored to have committed as a young man. The ghost of his victim . . . leads Asher and Ginny toward the house and the solution of a crime that took place decades earlier." SLJ

"The author meshes the supernatural and the realistic plot elements with proficiency. . . . A good introduction to historical fiction for readers who are ready for something more substantial than a light romance." Horn Book

Chetwin, Grace

Gom on Windy Mountain. Lothrop, Lee & Shepard Bks. 1986 206p il (Legends of Ulm, bk1) $12.95; Dell pa $3.50 (5 and up) **Fic**

1. Fantastic fiction
ISBN 0-688-05767-5; 0-440-20543-3 (pa) LC 85-18166

"Stig is a mountain man who loves the outdoors as well as singing and composing catchy little tunes. He doesn't feel the need for anyone else in his life until an unusual woman appears in his cabin. Soon they marry, and 'Wife' fulfills all the unspoken dreams of this silent man. After baby Gom arrives, Stig realizes his son has inherited many of his wife's mysterious and magical powers." Child Book Rev Serv

"Chetwin has varied the conflicts so that interest and action are sustained throughout the book. Conflicts rise to a high level when Gom is trapped in the cave awaiting possible death, to a lower level, when Gom must free the frog, Leadbelly, from his brother Horvin. Gom is a fresh, sympathetic character." Voice Youth Advocates

The riddle and the rune; from Tales of Gom in the Legends of Ulm. Bradbury Press 1987 257p $13.95; Dell pa $3.50 (5 and up) **Fic**

1. Fantastic fiction
ISBN 0-02-718312-2; 0-440-20581-6 (pa) LC 87-10284

"This sequel to *Gom on Windy Mountain* [entered above] can stand alone as a fantasy-adventure in itself. Left alone after his father's death, Gom leaves his mountain home to search for his mother, Harga, a great wizard who left him at birth. The rune of the title, his only clue to her existence, is a magical stone he must carry safely to her. The riddle is one that he must solve in order to find her. Gom's ability to speak to animals aids him in his quest, as well as the power he begins to find in the rune. . . . Chetwin enlivens her tale by giving Gom a variety of adventures with very different characters, from talking animals and humorously-drawn farm folk to the evil shape-changer Katak." SLJ

Followed by: The crystal stair (1988) and The starstone (1989)

Childress, Alice, 1920-

A hero ain't nothin' but a sandwich. Coward-McCann 1973 126p o.p.; Avon Bks. paperback available $2.95 (6 and up) **Fic**

1. Drug abuse—Fiction 2. Blacks—Fiction 3. Harlem (New York, N.Y.)—Fiction
ISBN 0-380-00132-2 (pa) LC 73-82035

Also available ABC-CLIO large print edition $14.95 (ISBN 1-55736-112-6)

"At the age of thirteen Benjie Johnson is hooked on 'horse.' He believes that he can break the habit whenever he is ready. When two of Benjie's teachers realize that he is on drugs, they report him to the principal of the school. Then begins his seesaw battle to break his addiction. Using Black English, the author draws a picture of the urban drug scene." Shapiro. Fic for Youth. 2d edition

Christopher, John, 1922-

Empty world. Dutton 1978 c1977 134p $13.95 (5 and up) **Fic**

1. Plague—Fiction 2. Science fiction
ISBN 0-525-29250-0 LC 77-18917

First published 1977 in the United Kingdom

"The world is afflicted by the Calcutta Plague, a blight which kills by aging people prematurely. In quiet Winchelsea, Neil Miller watches helplessly as his familiar world disintegrates. He is fortunate enough to be immune from the disease but he is powerless to help his friends, teachers and family as they wither and die around him. He leaves Winchelsea for London to search for other survivors and finds there two girls who have also escaped the plague." Times Lit Suppl

"Well conceived from both literal and psychological standpoints, this forceful look at the human condition offers much to ponder." Booklist

Fireball. Dutton 1981 148p $11.95 (5 and up) **Fic**

1. Fantastic fiction 2. Space and time—Fiction
ISBN 0-525-29738-3 LC 80-22094

"Simon's hopes for a typical British holiday are dashed when he learns his American cousin Brad is coming to visit. It's especially galling when Brad turns out to be more talented than Simon in many areas. The boys are ready to slug it out when a supernatural fireball transports them to a parallel, but strikingly different England: an England still modeled after the Roman way of life. By introducing the long-bow and saddle stirrup, the two lead a rebellion that changes the world." Voice Youth Advocates

"The author has a final surprise in store; for after the dramatic climax the narrative winds down to a logical but entirely unpredictable conclusion, proving that he is still a master storyteller writing with intelligence, wit, and style." Horn Book

The White Mountains. Macmillan 1967 184p $13.95; pa $3.95 (5 and up) **Fic**

1. Science fiction
ISBN 0-02-718360-2; 0-02-042711-5 (pa) LC 67-1262

"The world of the future is ruled by huge and powerful machine-creatures, the Tripods, who control mankind by implanting metal caps in their skulls when they reach the age of fourteen. Three boys . . . see that the people

Christopher, John, 1922-—*Continued*
about them are mindless conformists [and] decide to flee to the White Mountains (Switzerland), where there is a colony of free men." Saturday Rev

This "remarkable story . . . belongs to the school of science-fiction which puts philosophy before technology and is not afraid of telling an exciting story." Times Lit Suppl

Other available titles about the Tripods are:
The city of gold and lead (1967)
The pool of fire (1968)
When the Tripods came (1988)

Christopher, Matt, 1917-

The hit-away kid; illustrated by George Ulrich. Little, Brown 1988 60p il lib bdg $9.95; pa $2.95 (2-4) **Fic**

1. Baseball—Fiction
ISBN 0-316-13995-5 (lib bdg); 0-316-14007-4 (pa) LC 87-24406

Barry McGee, star batter for the Peach Street Mudders, enjoys winning so much that he has a tendency to bend the rules; then the dirty tactics of the pitcher on a rival team give him a new perspective on sports ethics

"This is predictable in theme if not in plot (Barry's team loses), but kids will get the reading practice they need on a subject that's palatable and popular." Bull Cent Child Books

Tackle without a team; illustrated by Margaret Sanfilippo. Little, Brown 1989 145p il $12.95 (5 and up) **Fic**

1. Football—Fiction 2. Drugs—Fiction 3. Mystery and detective stories
ISBN 0-316-14067-8 LC 88-22644

Unjustly dismissed from the football team for drug possession, Scott learns that only by finding out who planted the marijuana in his duffel bag can he clear himself with his parents

"Christopher's message—that smoking cigarettes or pot is a bummer—comes through loud and clear. Lots of action and enough suspense hold the plot together." Booklist

Takedown; illustrated by Margaret Sanfilippo. Little, Brown 1990 147p $13.95 (6 and up) **Fic**

1. Wrestling—Fiction 2. Stepchildren—Fiction
ISBN 0-316-13930-0 LC 89-31645

As he is helped by an assistant referee to prepare for a wrestling match with the neighborhood bully, Sean begins to wonder if his mentor could be his long-lost father

"Although the story isn't a particularly deep one, and the ending is pat, this is offset by the book's potential to lure sports fans into the world of books. Christopher is well-versed in the sports story genre and he details wrestling with accuracy and color." Publ Wkly

Clapp, Patricia, 1912-

Constance: a story of early Plymouth. Lothrop, Lee & Shepard Bks. 1968 255p o.p.; Penguin Bks. paperback available $4.95 (5 and up) **Fic**

1. Pilgrims (New England colonists)—Fiction 2. Massachusetts—History—1600-1775, Colonial period—Fiction
ISBN 0-14-032030-X (pa) LC 68-14064

The imaginary "journal kept by Constance Hopkins, daughter of Stephen Hopkins and ancestress of Patricia Clapp. Constance began jotting down her impressions and intimate thoughts at the age of fifteen on the eve of the 'Mayflower's' arrival and continued up to the day of her wedding five years later. With disarming candor, quick wit, and sprightliness she tells of her despair at leaving London, the discomforts of the voyage, her instant hatred of the wilderness and fear of the native savages." Horn Book

"The characters come alive, the writing style is excellent, and the historical background is smoothly integrated." Bull Cent Child Books

Jane-Emily. Lothrop, Lee & Shepard Bks. 1969 160p o.p.; Dell paperback available $1.75 (5 and up) **Fic**

1. Ghosts—Fiction
ISBN 0-440-94185-7 (pa) LC 69-14326

"While visiting her grandmother, young Jane finds a crystal ball which reflects the image of Emily, a dead girl. Jane is soon possessed by the ghost of Emily, and the events which follow are chilling." Cincinnati Public Libr

"Well written and with a convincing strong Gothic strain, the story is spellbinding, building up to an exciting climax." Horn Book

Witches' children; a story of Salem. Lothrop, Lee & Shepard Bks. 1982 160p o.p.; Penguin Bks. paperback available $3.95 (6 and up) **Fic**

1. Witchcraft—Fiction 2. Massachusetts—History—1600-1775, Colonial period—Fiction
ISBN 0-14-032407-0 (pa) LC 81-13678

The author "uses a first-person account to give immediacy to events in colonial New England. . . . The tale is told by Mary Warren, a young girl who is bound to service in a Salem household. Like the other restless adolescent girls who are her friends, Mary is at first only curious about Tituba's fortune-telling, aware that it is sly Abigail Williams who is pushing the slave to further titillation. There is nothing new in the story of the mass hysteria and witch-hunting in Salem; what Clapp does is make the role of the participants more comprehensible in a vivid and convincing narrative." Bull Cent Child Books

Clark, Ann Nolan, 1896-

Secret of the Andes; with drawings by Jean Charlot. Viking 1952 130p il $13.95; Puffin Bks. pa $3.95 (4 and up) **Fic**

1. Incas—Fiction 2. Peru—Fiction
ISBN 0-670-62975-8; 0-14-030926-8 (pa) LC 52-8075
Awarded the Newbery Medal, 1953

Clark, Ann Nolan, 1896-—*Continued*

"A young South American Indian boy searches for his destiny, eventually realizing that he wants to be a llama herder just as he has been trained to do. Interwoven into the story is the history of the Spanish conquerors and the value of continuing the ancient Incan traditions." Read Ladders for Hum Relat. 6th edition

It is a "rarely beautiful and subtle story. . . . Perceptive young readers will respond to the beauty of the telling, with mysticism in Incan songs and vivid description of wild and unvisited grandeur in the high Andes." Horn Book

Cleary, Beverly

Dear Mr. Henshaw; illustrated by Paul O. Zelinsky. Morrow 1983 133p il $12.95; lib bdg $12.88; Dell pa $3.25 (4-6) **Fic**

1. Divorce—Fiction 2. Parent and child—Fiction 3. School stories

ISBN 0-688-02405-X; 0-688-02406-8 (lib bdg); 0-440-41794-5 (pa) LC 83-5372

Also available ABC-CLIO large print edition $14.95 (ISBN 1-55736-001-4)

Awarded the Newbery Medal, 1984

"Leigh Botts started writing letters to his favorite author, Boyd Henshaw, in the second grade. Now, Leigh is in the sixth grade, in a new school, and his parents are recently divorced. This year he writes many letters to Mr. Henshaw, and also keeps a journal. Through these the reader learns how Leigh adjusts to new situations, and of his triumphs." Child Book Rev Serv

"The story is by no means one of unrelieved gloom, for there are deft touches of humor in the sentient, subtly wrought account of the small triumphs and tragedies in the life of an ordinary boy." Horn Book

Ellen Tebbits; illustrated by Louis Darling. Morrow 1951 160p il $12.95; lib bdg $12.88; Dell pa $3.25 (3-5) **Fic**

1. School stories

ISBN 0-688-21264-6; 0-688-31264-0 (lib bdg); 0-440-42299-X (pa) LC 51-11430

"Ellen Tebbits is eight years old, takes ballet lessons, wears bands on her teeth, and has a secret—she wears woolen underwear. But she finds a friend in Austine, a new girl in school, who also wears woolen underwear. They have the usual troubles that beset 'best friends' in grade school plus some that are unusual." Carnegie Libr of Pittsburgh

"Their experiences in the third grade are comical and very appealing to children in the middle grades." Hodges. Books for Elem Sch Libr

Henry Huggins; illustrated by Louis Darling (3-5) **Fic**

Also available Morrow Spanish language edition $12.95 (ISBN 0-688-02014-3)

Some editions are:

ABC-CLIO $15.95 Large rpint edition (ISBN 1-55736-148-7)
Dell pa $3.25 (ISBN 0-440-43551-X)
Morrow $12.95; lib bdg $12.88 (ISBN 0-688-21385-5; 0-688-31385-X)

First published 1950 by Morrow

"Henry Huggins is a typical small boy who, quite innocently, gets himself into all sorts of predicaments—often with the very apt thought, 'Won't Mom be surprised.' There is not a dull moment but some hilariously funny ones in the telling of Henry's adventures at home and at school." Booklist

Other available titles about Henry Huggins are:
Henry and Beezus (1952)
Henry and Ribsy (1954)
Henry and the clubhouse (1962)
Henry and the paper route (1957)
Ribsy (1964)

Mitch and Amy; illustrated by George Porter. Morrow 1967 222p il $15.95; lib bdg $15.88; Dell pa $3.25 (3-5) **Fic**

1. Twins—Fiction 2. School stories

ISBN 0-688-21688-9; 0-688-31688-3 (lib bdg); 0-440-45411-5 (pa) LC 67-1293

"The twins Mitch and Amy are in the fourth grade. Mitch is plagued by a bully and by reading difficulties, Amy struggles with multiplication tables, and their patient mother mediates their squabbles." SLJ

"The writing style and dialogue, the familial and peer group relationships, the motivations and characterizations all have the ring of truth. Written with ease and vitality, lightened with humor, the story is perhaps most appealing because it is clear that the author respects children." Bull Cent Child Books

The mouse and the motorcycle; illustrated by Louis Darling. Morrow 1965 158p il $12.95; lib bdg $12.88; Dell pa $3.25 (3-5) **Fic**

1. Mice—Fiction

ISBN 0-688-21698-6; 0-688-31698-0 (lib bdg); 0-440-46075-1 (pa) LC 65-20956

Also available ABC-CLIO large print edition $15.95 (ISBN 0-55736-137-1)

"A fantasy about Ralph, a mouse, who learns to ride a toy motorcycle and goes on wild rides through the corridors of the hotel where he lives. Keith, the boy to whom the motorcycle belongs, becomes fast friends with Ralph and defends him when danger threatens." Hodges. Books for Elem Sch Libr

"The author shows much insight into the thoughts of children. She carries the reader into an imaginative world that contains many realistic emotions." Wis Libr Bull

Other available titles about Ralph are:
Ralph S. Mouse (1982)
Runaway Ralph (1970)

Muggie Maggie; illustrated by Kay Life. Morrow Junior Bks. 1990 70p il $11.95; lib bdg $11.88; pa $3.50 (2-4) **Fic**

1. Handwriting—Fiction 2. School stories

ISBN 0-688-08553-9; 0-688-08554-7 (lib bdg); 0-380-71087-0 (pa) LC 89-38959

Maggie resists learning cursive writing in the third grade, until she discovers that knowing how to read and write cursive promises to open up an entirely new world of knowledge for her

"With the introduction of Maggie Schultz, a feisty and independent third grader, Cleary again gives young readers a real person with whom they can identify and empathize. This deceptively simple story is accessible to primary-grade readers able to read longhand, as some of the text is in script. . . . Everything in this book

Cleary, Beverly—*Continued*
rings true, and Cleary has created a likable, funny heroine about whom readers will want to know more." SLJ

Otis Spofford; illustrated by Louis Darling. Morrow 1953 191p il $12.95; lib bdg $12.88; Dell pa $3.25 (3-5) **Fic**

1. School stories
ISBN 0-688-21720-6; 0-688-31720-0 (lib bdg); 0-440-46651-2 (pa) LC 53-6660

"Otis, a mischievous, fun loving boy, is always getting in and out of trouble. His mother, a dancing teacher, is busy and often leaves Otis on his own. This book tells of several episodes in Otis's life—from his sneaking vitamins to a white rat to 'disprove' a diet experiment, to getting his final 'come-uppance' when a trick on Ellen Tebbits backfires." Read Ladders for Hum Relat. 6th edition

"This writer has her elementary school down pat, and manages to report her growing boys, teachers, and P.T.A. meetings so that parents chuckle and boys laugh out loud." N Y Her Trib Books

Ramona the pest; illustrated by Louis Darling. Morrow 1968 192p il $13.95; lib bdg $13.88; Dell pa $3.25 (3-5) **Fic**

1. Kindergarten—Fiction 2. School stories
ISBN 0-688-21721-4; 0-688-31721-9 (lib bdg); 0-440-47209-1 (pa) LC 68-12981

Also available Spanish language edition $12.95 (ISBN 0-688-02783-0); and ABC-CLIO large print edition $15.95 (ISBN 1-55736-158-4)

"Ramona Quimby comes into her own. Beezus keeps telling her to stop acting like a pest, but Ramona is five now, and she is convinced that she is 'not' a pest; she feels very mature, having entered kindergarten, and she immediately becomes enamoured of her teacher. Ramona's insistence on having just the right kind of boots, her matter-of-fact interest in how Mike Mulligan got to a bathroom, her determination to kiss one of the boys in her class, and her refusal to go back to kindergarten because Miss Binney didn't love her any more—all of these incidents or situations are completely believable and are told in a light, humorous, zesty style." Bull Cent Child Books

Other available titles about Ramona are:
Beezus and Ramona (1955)
Ramona and her father (1977)
Ramona and her mother (1979)
Ramona, forever (1984)
Ramona Quimby, age 8 (1981)
Ramona the brave (1975)

Socks; illustrated by Beatrice Darwin. Morrow 1973 156p il $11.75; lib bdg $11.88; Dell pa $3.25 (3-5) **Fic**

1. Cats—Fiction 2. Infants—Fiction
ISBN 0-688-20067-2; 0-688-30067-7 (lib bdg); 0-440-48256-9 (pa) LC 72-10298

"The Brickers' kitten, Socks, is jealous when they bring a baby home from the hospital. How he copes with this rivalry makes an amusing story true to cat nature." Cleveland Public Libr

"Not being child-centered, this may have a smaller audience than earlier Cleary books, but it is written with the same easy grace, the same felicitous humor and sharply observant eye." Bull Cent Child Books

Cleaver, Vera

Ellen Grae; [by] Vera and Bill Cleaver; illustrated by Ellen Raskin. Lippincott 1967 89p il $12.89 (4-6) **Fic**

1. Truthfulness and falsehood—Fiction 2. Mentally handicapped children—Fiction
ISBN 0-397-30938-4 LC 67-10623

"The wildly colorful tales fabricated by Ellen Grae, an engaging young person, have prepared the community to mistrust her when, in honesty, she shares an ugly tale." Child Books, 1967

"Although the story has poignant moments, it is funny most of the time and perceptive all of the time. . . . Divorce is nicely handled, with Ellen Grae's parents on friendly footing and no less responsible and loving toward their child because they don't live under the same roof." Saturday Rev

Followed by: Lady Ellen Grae, entered below

Grover; [by] Vera and Bill Cleaver; illustrated by Frederic Marvin. Lippincott 1970 125p il $12.95 (4-6) **Fic**

1. Death—Fiction
ISBN 0-397-31118-4 LC 69-12001

Ten-year-old Grover "goes through an agonizing period of adjustment beginning with his mother's sudden departure to the hospital and ending with his eventual acceptance of her death. The strain is increased by adult attempts to 'protect' him from the truth during her illness and by his father's withdrawal into grief after her suicide." Booklist

Although the elements of the story "may sound grim, there's nothing depressing about this book—it seems very real, with its most deeply touching or dramatic moments heightened by superbly comic incidents or dialogue." SLJ

Hazel Rye; [by] Vera and Bill Cleaver. Lippincott 1983 178p $12.95; lib bdg $12.89; HarperCollins Pubs. pa $3.95 (5 and up) **Fic**

ISBN 0-397-31951-7; 0-397-31952-5 (lib bdg); 0-06-440156-1 (pa) LC 81-48603

"Eleven-year-old Hazel Rye is as unusual as her name; a girl of imagination and spirit. When the intellectually curious Poole family arrives at her father's southern citrus farm in need of a place to live, Hazel rents them the small house in a dying orange grove which her father has given her. Hazel and Felder Poole work on improving the grove; this results in conflicts both with her father, who resents the new friendship and feels threatened by it, and in herself as she must confront her own ignorance and inability for the first time." SLJ

"The Cleavers have traced Hazel's development with care, and her gradual metamorphosis is a pleasure to watch. Her strong personality makes for a character easy to stay with. . . . This is the Cleavers at their best." Booklist

The Kissimmee Kid; [by] Vera and Bill Cleaver. Lothrop, Lee & Shepard Bks. 1981 159p lib bdg $12.88 (6 and up) **Fic**

1. Brothers and sisters—Fiction 2. Florida—Fiction
ISBN 0-688-51992-X LC 80-29262

The authors "tell the story of a young girl torn between the importance of justice and family loyalty. Twelve year old Evelyn, who carries her wishes and

Cleaver, Vera—*Continued*
prayers around in a tin box she calls her God box, is sent to spend the summer on the [Florida] ranch where her brother-in-law is employed. With her she takes her younger brother, Buell, and her God box. She worships her brother-in-law and admires his values. She believes that anyone who paints pink birds and princes as he does must be near perfect and would never be involved in criminal activities. As Evelyn accidentally uncovers evidence proving he is a cattle rustler she tries to ignore the facts and envies the innocence of Buell. The summer on the ranch tests Evelyn's moral strength." Voice Youth Advocates

"The book's exposition is masterly; the language, with its light touch of Southern dialect, is just right; and the characters fairly spring forth from the page." Horn Book

Lady Ellen Grae; [by] Vera and Bill Cleaver; illustrated by Ellen Raskin. Lippincott 1968 124p il lib bdg $12.89 (4-6) **Fic**

ISBN 0-397-31012-9 LC 68-10981

In this sequel to Ellen Grae, entered above, the eleven-year-old tomboy is sent from her home in Florida "to Seattle with her . . . Aunt Eleanor and her Cousin Laura to learn how to become a lady." Publisher's note

"Ingenuous and ingenious, Ellen Grae is a marvelous character." Saturday Rev

Queen of hearts; [by] Vera and Bill Cleaver. Lippincott 1978 158p $12.95; HarperCollins Pubs. pa $2.95 (6 and up) **Fic**

1. Grandmothers—Fiction 2. Old age—Fiction 3. Family life—Fiction
ISBN 0-397-31771-9; 0-06-440196-0 (pa) LC 77-18252

Although there is no love lost between them, twelve-year-old Wilma is her willful and peppery grandmother's choice for a companion

"Young readers will find this a quick-flowing novel covering the multiple harassments that many old come to face, along with the unique humor with which they view so many of their experiences. . . . The Cleavers present a realistic view of what it means to grow old and not be fully understood or appreciated for the wealth of experience that often comes from a long life." Best Sellers

Trial Valley; [by] Vera and Bill Cleaver. Lippincott 1977 158p lib bdg $12.89 (5 and up) **Fic**

1. Brothers and sisters—Fiction 2. Orphans—Fiction 3. Appalachian Mountains—Fiction
ISBN 0-397-32246-1 LC 76-54303

"At 16, two years older than she was when she took charge of her siblings in *Where the Lilies Bloom* [entered below], Mary Call Luther faces a new trial in the form of an abused and abandoned waif. . . . Mary Call finds her true calling in caring for the boy, determining in the process that both of her suitors are unsuitable: Gaither Graybeal, the good-hearted down-home boy, is domestic but dim; Thad Yancey is rich and cultivated but his love doesn't embrace those whose lives are entwined with hers." SLJ

"It is a beautiful depiction of a young girl growing up and finding her direction in life. The characters are finely drawn, the mood is poetic at times. A sensitive book for thoughtful readers." Christ Sci Monit

Where the lillies bloom; [by] Vera & Bill Cleaver; illustrated by Jim Spanfeller. Lippincott 1969 $12.95; Harper & Row pa $2.95 (5 and up) **Fic**

1. Orphans—Fiction 2. Brothers and sisters—Fiction 3. Appalachian Mountains—Fiction
ISBN 0-397-31111-7; 0-06-447005-9 (pa) LC 75-82402

"Mary Call Luther [is] fourteen years old and made of granite. When her sharecropper father dies, Mary Call becomes head of the household, responsible for a boy of ten and a retarded, gentle older sister. Mary and her brother secretly bury their father so they can retain their home; tenaciously she fights to keep the family afloat by selling medicinal plants and to keep them together by fending off [Kiser Pease, their landlord], who wants to marry her sister." Saturday Rev

"The setting is fascinating, the characterization good, and the style of the first-person story distinctive." Bull Cent Child Books

Followed by: Trial Valley, entered above

Clements, Bruce
I tell a lie every so often. Farrar, Straus & Giroux 1974 149p il hardcover o.p. paperback available $3.50 (6 and up) **Fic**

1. Truthfulness and falsehood—Fiction 2. Frontier and pioneer life—Fiction
ISBN 0-374-43539-1 (pa) LC 73-22356

"Our hero, 14-year-old Henry Desant, keeps the laughs coming in his account of what happens when he tells a couple of lies (in a worthy cause) to his older brother, Clayton. Fifteen years earlier, in 1833, their cousin, Hanna, had been taken by the Indians. Henry tells Clayton that a young white girl has been reported living in an Indian settlement 500 miles north of their home in St. Louis. This fib sets the two on a boat journey up the Missouri River . . . into and out of wild adventures including . . . a game of wits with the Indians and a stunning encounter with the girl who may or may not be lost Hanna." Publ Wkly

Clifford, Eth, 1915-
The dastardly murder of Dirty Pete; illustrated by George Hughes. Houghton Mifflin 1981 120p il $13.95 (3-5) **Fic**

1. Ghost towns—Fiction 2. Mystery and detective stories 3. West (U.S.)—Fiction
ISBN 0-395-31671-5 LC 81-6316

"While traveling cross-country with their nose-for-a-story father, Mary Rose and Jo-Beth Onetree [featured in Help! I'm a prisoner in the library, entered below] stumble upon a fake ghost town that was once an old movie set. Some spooky events convince the girls that the place is haunted, but when they are lured into a mine and Mr. Onetree is locked in the jail, the situation takes a more sinister turn." Booklist

The author has written a "suspenseful and intriguing adventure story, complete with ghosts, murders, skeletons and treasure, while maintaining the sense of humor and fun familiar to her readers." SLJ

Clifford, Eth, 1915-—*Continued*

Harvey's horrible snake disaster. Houghton Mifflin 1984 108p $13.95 (3-5) **Fic**

1. Cousins—Fiction 2. Snakes—Fiction
ISBN 0-395-35378-5 LC 83-27299

"Harvey is secretly petrified about the upcoming school visit of a herpetologist and his snake menagerie, and things go from bad to worse when the snake program coincides with the arrival of cousin Nora and her timid mother, Aunt Mildred." Booklist

"The light tone and smoothly written text will turn on transitional readers who still need short chapters and a quickly moving story." Child Book Rev Serv

Other available titles about Harvey are:
Harvey's marvelous monkey mystery (1987)
Harvey's wacky parrot adventure (1990)

Help! I'm a prisoner in the library; illustrated by George Hughes. Houghton Mifflin 1979 105p il $13.95; Scholastic pa $2.50 (3-5) **Fic**

1. Libraries—Fiction 2. Blizzards—Fiction
ISBN 0-395-28478-3; 0-590-31591-9 (pa)
LC 79-14447

"Caught in a blinding snowstorm with their car out of gas, Mary Rose and Jo-Beth are told to stay put while their father finds fuel for the stalled vehicle. Jo-Beth, however, develops 'an emergency' and Mary Rose takes her to a nearby library to find a restroom. . . . Without warning the girls find themselves locked in when the building closes early. As the storm worsens, the lights and telephone go out and a series of flying objects, creaking noises, and moaning sounds thoroughly frighten the girls. . . . Upstairs . . . they not only find logical reasons for the happenings but meet a surprising woman as well. With the help of fireworks, they locate their father and complete a marvelous adventure in a blizzard. Clifford uses a light touch while evoking a pleasingly scary atmosphere that children will enjoy. Spirited dialogue and swift pace are an additional plus." Booklist

The remembering box; illustrated by Donna Diamond. Houghton Mifflin 1985 70p il $12.95 (3-5) **Fic**

1. Grandmothers—Fiction 2. Jews—Fiction 3. Death—Fiction
ISBN 0-395-38476-1 LC 85-10851

Nine-year-old Joshua's weekly visits to his beloved grandmother on the Jewish Sabbath give him an understanding of love, family, and tradition which helps him accept her death

"This warm and loving relationship between a boy and his grandmother is beautifully depicted. . . . Diamond's silhouettes, used for the stories that Grandma tells Joshua, are dramatic, and her meticulously detailed black-and-white illustrations of Joshua and his grandmother are both expressive and moving." SLJ

The rocking chair rebellion. Houghton Mifflin 1978 147p $13.95 (6 and up) **Fic**

1. Old age—Fiction 2. Voluntarism—Fiction
ISBN 0-395-27163-0 LC 78-14834

Opie "has no intention of becoming involved with the residents of the Maple Ridge Home for the Aged, but an unexpected turn of events leads her to become a volunteer worker. . . . Several of the more hale and hearty of the inmates buy a house on her street, intending to establish an arrangement for communal living. Bitter opposition arises among the neighbors, but the sale is successfully defended in court by Opie's father." Horn Book

"Using Opie as narrator allows the author to reveal events and issues through the eyes of a bright, articulate adolescent. The treatment of the familiar theme is thoughtful, and Clifford successfully avoids stereotypes in either people or institutions." SLJ

Clifton, Lucille, 1936-

The lucky stone; illustrated by Dale Payson. Delacorte Press 1979 64p il o.p.; Dell paperback available $2.75 (3-5) **Fic**

1. Blacks—Fiction 2. Charms
ISBN 0-440-45110-8 (pa) LC 78-72862

"Four short stories about four generations of Black women and their dealings with a lucky stone. . . . Clifton uses as a frame device a grandmother telling the history of the stone to her granddaughter; by the end the granddaughter has inherited the stone herself. . . . The story is written in Black dialect." SLJ

"This book contains information on various aspects of Black culture—slavery, religion and extended family—all conveyed in a way that is both positive and accurate." Interracial Books Child Bull

Clymer, Eleanor Lowenton, 1906-

The horse in the attic; [by] Eleanor Clymer; illustrated by Ted Lewin. Bradbury Press 1983 87p il $10.95; Dell pa $2.50 (4 and up) **Fic**

1. Horses—Fiction 2. Mystery and detective stories
ISBN 0-02-719040-4; 0-440-43798-9 (pa) LC 83-6377

"Narrated by twelve-year-old Caroline, the novel reconstructs the momentous year when the family moved from their New York apartment to an old house in the country. Exploring the attic, Caroline discovered a painting of a filly entitled 'Sprite. O'Brien up. 1905.' . . . Then, when she revealed her discovery to her family and to her friend Betsy, they shared her excitement and encouraged her to learn more about the artist and the origins of the work." Horn Book

"The writing is direct and controlled, with good pace and adequate characterization; the mystery of the painter's identity adds suspense; what is most effective, however, is the convincing delineation of relationships within a family in which the members are mutually supportive, cooperating and compromising for the general good. The realistic black and white pictures are strong in draughtsmanship and effective in the play of light and shadow." Bull Cent Child Books

Coatsworth, Elizabeth Jane, 1893-1986

The cat who went to heaven; [by] Elizabeth Coatsworth; illustrated by Lynd Ward. Macmillan 1958 62p il $11.95; pa $4.95 (4 and up) **Fic**

1. Cats—Fiction 2. Japan—Fiction
ISBN 0-02-719710-7; 0-02-042580-5 (pa)
LC 58-10917

First published 1930. The 1958 edition is a reprint with new illustrations of the book which won the Newbery Medal award in 1931

Coatsworth, Elizabeth Jane, 1893-1986 — *Continued*

"Watched by his little cat, Good Fortune, a Japanese artist paints a picture of the Buddha receiving homage from the animals. By tradition the cat should not be among them, but the artist risks his reputation by adding Good Fortune and is vindicated by a miracle." Hodges. Books for Elem Sch Libr

"Into this lovely and imaginative story the author has put something of the serenity and beauty of the East and of the gentleness of a religion that has a place even for the humblest of living creatures." N Y Times Book Rev

Cohen, Barbara, 1932-

Canterbury tales; [by] Geoffrey Chaucer; selected, translated, and adapted by Barbara Cohen; illustrated by Trina Schart Hyman. Lothrop, Lee & Shepard Bks. 1988 87p il $17.95 (4 and up) **Fic**

ISBN 0-688-06201-6 LC 86-21045

Contents: The nun's priest's tale; The pardoner's tale; The wife of Bath's tale; The franklin's tale

"Cohen's evident love and respect for Chaucer's writing keep her close to the text. Her writing retains the flavor of the times and the spirit of Chaucer's words while her prose retelling, enriched by Hyman's lively full-color paintings, enhances the book's appeal to young people. . . . An excellent introduction to *The Canterbury Tales* for young readers." Booklist

The carp in the bathtub; illustrated by Joan Halpern. Lothrop, Lee & Shepard Bks. 1972 48p il $12.95; lib bdg $12.88; Kar-Ben Copies pa $4.95 (2-4) **Fic**

1. Jews—New York (N.Y.)—Fiction 2. Fishes—Fiction
ISBN 0-688-41627-6; 0-688-51627-0 (lib bdg); 0-930494-67-9 (pa) LC 72-1079

Set in New York City. "Leah and Harry have made friends of Joe, the appealing carp their mother has swimming in the bathtub, awaiting its execution on the Feast of Seder. Joe will make marvelous 'gefilte' fish but the children are determined to save him. They sneak him into the tub of a neighbor, but alas; his change of scene is only a reprieve, not a pardon. A delightfully warm book with pictures equally appealing." Publ Wkly

Molly's Pilgrim; illustrated by Michael J. Deraney. Lothrop, Lee & Shepard Bks. 1983 unp il $12.95; lib bdg $12.88; Bantam Bks. pa $2.75 (2-4) **Fic**

1. Jews—Fiction 2. School stories 3. Thanksgiving Day—Fiction 4. Immigration and emigration—Fiction
ISBN 0-688-02103-4; 0-688-02104-2 (lib bdg); 0-533-15833-3 (pa) LC 83-797

"It is an unpleasant irony that each generation of Americans demoralizes the incoming immigrant generation and forgets that the Pilgrims were immigrants. Using a Jewish immigrant as the main character, the author develops this irony further, noting that both groups came to this country seeking religious freedom, and that Thanksgiving was a Pilgrim rendering of an Old Testament holiday which Jews call Succos. A sensitive teacher translates this message to the children who torment Molly because of her appearance and lack of familiarity with our Thanksgiving." Child Book Rev Serv

"Pencil drawings, firmly shaded, are strong in characterization and period details. The picture-book format recommends this as a thought-provoking Thanksgiving read-aloud." Booklist

Thank you, Jackie Robinson; drawings by Richard Cuffari. Lothrop, Lee & Shepard Bks. 1974 125p il lib bdg $12.95; Scholastic pa $2.75 (4-6) **Fic**

1. Baseball—Fiction 2. Friendship—Fiction 3. Blacks—Fiction
ISBN 0-688-07909-1 (lib bdg); 0-590-42378-9 (pa) LC 73-17703

"When 60-year-old Davey (Black) comes to work at the inn for Sam's mother, Sam (Jewish and fatherless) gains a friend. Davey takes Sam to see the Brooklyn Dodgers (circa 1945), and an avid, statistic-spouting Dodger fan is born. When Davey becomes ill, Sam gets Jackie Robinson and his teammates to autograph a ball for Davey." Child Book Rev Serv

"Cohen's characters have unusual depth and her story succeeds as a warm, understanding consideration of friendship and, finally, death." Booklist

Cole, Brock, 1938-

The goats; written and illustrated by Brock Cole. Farrar, Straus & Giroux 1987 184p il $11.95; pa $3.50 (5 and up) **Fic**

1. Camps—Fiction 2. Friendship—Fiction
ISBN 0-374-32678-9; 0-374-42575-2 (pa) LC 87-45362

Also available ABC-CLIO large print edition $14.95 (ISBN 1-55736-113-4)

"A boy and the girl have been chosen as 'the goats' at summer camp. Stripped naked, they are marooned on Goat Island, as part of an annual prank played on campers who don't fit in. But the goats have much more spirit than their fellow campers expect, and they decide to disappear completely." Publ Wkly

"This is an unflinching book, and there is a quality of raw emotion that may score some discomfort among adults. Such a first novel restores faith in the cultivation of children's literature." Bull Cent Child Books

Collier, James Lincoln, 1928-

Jump ship to freedom; [by] James Lincoln Collier, Christopher Collier. Delacorte Press 1981 198p $13.95; Dell pa $3.50 (6 and up) **Fic**

1. United States—History—1783-1809—Fiction 2. Slavery—Fiction 3. Blacks—Fiction
ISBN 0-385-28484-5; 0-440-44323-7 (pa) LC 81-65492

Companion volume to: War comes to Willie Freeman and Who is Carrie, both entered below

In 1787 a fourteen-year-old slave, anxious to buy freedom for himself and his mother, escapes from his dishonest master and tries to find help in cashing the soldier's notes received by his father for fighting in the Revolution

"The period seems well researched, and the speech has an authentic ring without trying to imitate a dialect." SLJ

Collier, James Lincoln, 1928-—*Continued*

My brother Sam is dead; by James Lincoln Collier and Christopher Collier. Four Winds Press 1974 216p il $13.95; Scholastic pa $2.50 (6 and up) **Fic**

1. United States—History—1775-1783, Revolution—Fiction

ISBN 0-02-722980-7; 0-590-33694-0 (pa) LC 74-8350

Also available ABC-CLIO large print edition $15.95 (ISBN 1-55736-038-3)

A Newbery Medal honor book, 1975

"In 1775 the Meeker family lived in Redding, Connecticut, a Tory community. Sam, the eldest son, allied himself with the Patriots. The youngest son, Tim watched a rift in the family grow because of his brother's decision. Before the war was over the Meeker family had suffered at the hands of both the British and the Patriots." Shapiro. Fic for Youth. 2d edition

War comes to Willy Freeman; [by] James Lincoln Collier, Christopher Collier. Delacorte Press 1983 178p $13.95; Dell pa $3.25 (6 and up) **Fic**

1. United States—History—1775-1783, Revolution—Fiction 2. Blacks—Fiction 3. Slavery—Fiction

ISBN 0-385-29235-X; 0-440-49504-0 (pa) LC 82-70317

This deals with events prior to those in Jump ship to freedom, entered above, and involves members of the same family. "Willy is thirteen when she begins her story, which takes place during the last two years of the Revolutionary War; her father, a free man, has been killed fighting against the British, her mother has disappeared. Willy makes her danger-fraught way to Fraunces Tavern in New York, her uncle, Jack Arabul, having told her that Mr. Fraunces may be able to help her. She works at the tavern until the war is over, goes to the Arabus home to find her mother dying, and participates in the trial (historically accurate save for the fictional addition of Willy) in which her uncle sues for his freedom and wins." Bull Cent Child Books

Who is Carrie? by James Lincoln Collier and Christopher Collier. Delacorte Press 1984 158p $14.95; Dell pa $3.25 (6 and up) **Fic**

1. United States—History—1783-1809—Fiction 2. Slavery—Fiction 3. Blacks—Fiction

ISBN 0-385-29295-3; 0-440-49536-9 (pa) LC 83-23947

Companion volume to: Jump ship to freedom, and War comes to Willy Freeman, both entered above

Carrie "is a kitchen slave in Samuel Fraunces Tavern. It isn't a perfect existence, but it is bearable. She keeps in touch with her special friend, Dan Arabus, and he enlists Carrie's help in finding out if the new government will honor the notes with which Dan hopes to purchase his mother's freedom. In so doing, Carrie finds out the truth about herself." Child Book Rev Serv

"This is historical fiction at its best. The Collier's familiar 'How Much of This Book is True' addendum fills readers in on the essentials concerning fictional and factual elements of the plot, as well as the research involved in its composition. Useful application in a middle grades black history curriculum or simply for enjoyable reading that provides a look at the life and times in late 18th century America." SLJ

Collodi, Carlo, 1826-1890

The adventures of Pinocchio (36) **Fic**

1. Puppets and puppet plays—Fiction 2. Fairy tales

Some editions are:

Holt & Co. $16.95 Translated and illustrated by Francis Wainwright (ISBN 0-8050-0027-5)

Knopf $18.95 Illustrated by Roberto Innocenti translated by E. Harden (ISBN 0-394-82110-6)

Macmillan $24.95 Translated from the Italian by Carol Della Chiesa; illustrated by Attilio Mussino (ISBN 0-02-722821-5)

An Italian classic for children, written late in the 19th century

"When Geppetto discovered a piece of wood which talked, he carved it into a marionette and named him Pinocchio. Although he is a wooden boy, Pinocchio has a lively and nimble mind and an ardent curiosity which lead to unexpected and extraordinary results. A light-hearted and original fantasy in which children can identify themselves with Pinocchio and grasp the simple and practical morality which underlies the story." Toronto Public Libr. Books for Boys & Girls

Cone, Molly

Mishmash; illustrated by Leonard Shortall. Houghton Mifflin 1962 114p il $13.95; Pocket Bks. pa $2.95 (3-5) **Fic**

1. Dogs—Fiction

ISBN 0-395-06711-1; 0-671-70937-2 (pa) LC 62-10016

The dog Mishmash moved like a cyclone into Pete's heart, his family's new house, the neighbor's gardens and life was never the same again! Pete, who was new in town, found that suddenly good old Mish had introduced him to practically everybody. But Pete had to solve the problem of troublesome Mish, also the problem of what to give his teacher

"Sprightly and enjoyable [the book's] charm [is] enhanced by Leonard Shortall's lively pictures." N Y Her Trib Books

Other available titles about Mishmash are:

Mishmash and the big fat problem (1982)
Mishmash and the robot (1981)
Mishmash and the sauerkraut mystery (1965)
Mishmash and the substitute teacher (1963)

Conford, Ellen

And this is Laura. Little, Brown 1977 179p $14.95; Pocket Bks. pa $2.75 (4-6) **Fic**

1. Extrasensory perception—Fiction 2. Family life—Fiction

ISBN 0-316-15300-1; 0-671-67879-5 (pa) LC 76-53583

"Preadolescent Laura Hoffman is convinced that she is an ordinary run-of-the-mill person in a family of superachievers. . . . Only Laura, who relates the story, has no special talent until she accidently discovers her psychic powers and . . . she wonders if this newly emerged gift is as much a liability as it is an asset. She finally resolves the problem and, at the same time, realizes that parental love is more than mere pride in the accomplishments of one's children." Horn Book

"The validity of ESP is not questioned (it's just a trendy peg on which to hang a familiar message), but

Conford, Elen—*Continued*
the story is lively, fast-paced, and written in natural dialogue (inclding an occasional 'hell' or 'dammit')." SLJ

A case for Jenny Archer; illustrated by Diane Pamisciano. Little, Brown 1988 61p il lib bd $10.95; pa $2.95 (2-4) **Fic**

1. Humorous stories
ISBN 0-16-15266-8 (lib bdg); 0-316-15352-4 (pa) LC 88-14169

"A Sprigboard book"

After reding three mysteries in a row, Jenny becomes convinced hat the neighbors across the street are up to no good nd decides to investigate

Other aailable titles about Jenny Archer are:
Jenny Aner, author (1989)
A job fc Jenny Archer (1988)
What's coking, Jenny Archer? (1989)
Jenny Acher to the rescue (1990)

Dea Lovey Hart: I am desperate. Little, Browr 1975 170p $14.95; Scholastic pa $2.50 (6 and up) **Fic**

1. ollege and school journalism—Fiction 2. School stors
ISB 0-316-15306-0; 0-590-40721-X (pa) LC 75-16238

"Crie is having a great time writing a column of advic to the lovelorn for her school paper. An added bene: is that she gets to be around Chip, the paper's hancome editor. But when the letters to 'Lovey Hart' becoe more serious, Carrie does not know what to do. Peoe are taking her advice, and trouble is usually the resu. What is worse, though, is that Chip seems to be intested in Carrie's best friend Claudia. Now Carrie fee she needs some advice!" Your Read

ollowed by: We interrupt this semester for an importa bulletin (1979)

Dreams of victory; illustrated by Gail Bockwell. Little, Brown 1973 121p il $14.95 (-6) **Fic**

ISBN 0-316-15294-3 LC 72-8437

"Victory Benneker couldn't dance; she couldn't skate; e got only six votes in an election for class president; nd she was a miserable failure in an unimportant role n the class play. Despite the optimistic name her mother ad given her, nothing came out to her satisfaction. But Vicky had a wonderful safeguard. She could daydream." Horn Book

"The dialog is amusing, the class characters alarmingly familiar, and Vicky's relationship with her parents delightful—two adults and a child who can laugh at each other and themselves." Booklist

Felicia the critic; illustrated by Arvis Stewart. Little, Brown 1973 145p il $13.95; Pocket Bks. pa $2.25 (4-6) **Fic**

ISBN 0-316-15295-1; 0-671-60039-7 (pa) LC 73-7831

"When her negative communications meet with looks of loathing, Felicia, mostly undaunted and with good intentions, embarks on a career as a constructive critic, hoping that she will be valued for her talent. . . . Felicia's audacity continues to be regarded with coldness by her family, her friends, and many of her victims. Nevertheless, she is so often on target that some people find themselves taking up her advice in spite of themselves." Booklist

"Fresh, entertaining, and percipient. . . . It all adds up to a deft, sympathetic portrait of a real child—a loner aware of the obtuseness and supercritical responses of other people." Horn Book

Genie with the light blue hair. Bantam Bks. 1989 150p $13.95; pa $3.50 (5 and up) **Fic**

ISBN 0-553-05806-1; 0-553-28484-3 (pa) LC 88-7777

When Jean finds a wish-granting genie in the lamp she receives for her birthday, she discovers that having all her wishes come true isn't as wonderful as she thought it would be

"The plot is featherweight, but it probably won't diminish the enthusiasm of Conford fans, who expect humor, good dialogue, a pleasant writing style, and only enough characterization to lend credence to the action. That's what they'll find here, a capably written story that's entertaining." Bull Cent Child Books

Lenny Kandell, smart aleck; illustrations by Walter Gaffney-Kessell. Little, Brown 1983 120p il $12.95; Pocket Bks. pa $2.50 (4 and up) **Fic**

ISBN 0-316-15313-3; 0-671-64190-5 (pa) LC 83000089

"Wisecracking Lenny Kandell dreams of being a standup comic one day. He's always rehearsing routines with his friend Artie, who is his best audience. Meanwhile, life goes on in everyday fashion with Lenny getting himself in scrapes as the result of either his smart mouth or his irresponsibility." Booklist

"A brisk tempo and an entertaining picture of boyhood in the forties complement the predicaments, jokes, and comic patter that keep Lenny squarely on center stage. Lenny and Artie, a study in friendship, are a pair to call back for an encore." Horn Book

The luck of Pokey Bloom; illustrated by Bernice Lowenstein. Little, Brown 1975 135p il $14.95; Pocket Bks. pa $2.50 (3-6) **Fic**

1. Family life—Fiction
ISBN 0-316-15305-2; 0-671-63667-7 (pa) LC 74-26556

"Pokey is an inveterate contestant. . . . When Pokey finally wins a prize, after many defeats, she learns that the victory is not a matter of luck but the result of her own efforts." Publ Wkly

"The book is well-crafted, fast-paced, and freshly imagined; Pokey's tribulations and triumphs are the warp and woof of a richly comic, thoroughly believable, contemporary family story." Horn Book

Me and the terrible two; illustrated by Charles Carroll. Little, Brown 1974 117p il $14.95 (3-6) **Fic**

1. Friendship—Fiction 2. Twins—Fiction
ISBN 0-316-15303-6 LC 73-18393

"Dorrie, a sixth-grader . . . not only loses her best friend when the family next door moves to Australia, but must be plagued by the new incumbents—a pair of zany, prankish, totally self-sufficient, identical twin boys. Dorrie, predictably, not only manages to survive, but ultimately settles into a three-way friendship with her tormentors." Horn Book

Conford, Ellen—*Continued*

"A witty, brisk and altogether effective story." Publ Wkly

A royal pain. Scholastic 1986 171p $11.95; pa $2.75 (6 and up) **Fic**

ISBN 0-590-33269-4; 0-590-43437-3 (pa)

LC 85-26226

A sixteen-year-old in Kansas, who discovers she is really a princess, is taken to a tiny European monarchy to assume her duties and marry a distasteful neighboring prince, and in the ensuing weeks tries to become such a "royal pain" that everyone will want to be rid of her

"What makes the book so irresistibly funny are the gut-level adolescent responses, word plays and banter that this decidedly modern princess engages in on her trip to and from the throne. Author Conford has a great knack for these sometimes wry and often devastatingly funny asides tossed out by our heroine in the midst of one crazy situation after another. They really ring true." Voice Youth Advocates

Seven days to a brand-new me. Little, Brown 1981 136p $14.95; Scholastic pa $2.50 (6 and up) **Fic**

1. School stories

ISBN 0-316-15311-7; 0-590-40729-5 (pa)

LC 80-25994

Maddy, a shy girl follows the suggestions in a self-help book to win the attentions of the handsome new boy whose locker is next to hers

"Basically, this is a girl-meets-boy story, but it's balanced by the warmth of the relationships between Maddy and her friends and the less frequent but equally affectionate exchanges between Maddy and her mother. Above all, it's the lively style, especially in the dialogue, that makes the book enjoyable." Bull Cent Child Books

Why me? Little, Brown 1985 145p $14.95; Pocket Bks. pa $2.75 (5 and up) **Fic**

ISBN 0-316-15326-5; 0-671-62841-0 (pa) LC 85-214

Thirteen-year-old Hobie, hoping to sweep women off their feet in the manner of his spy novel hero, runs into complications when he encounters a girl who has studied the bestseller, "How to Make Men Crazy"

The author "keeps everything light and breezy thanks to an ear for natural dialogue and a well-developed sense of humor." Booklist

Conly, Jane Leslie

R-T, Margaret, and the rats of NIMH; illustrations by Leonard Lubin. Harper & Row 1990 260p il $12.95; lib bdg $12.89 (4 and up) **Fic**

1. Mice—Fiction 2. Rats—Fiction

ISBN 0-06-021363-9; 0-06-021364-7 (lib bdg)

LC 89-19968

Sequel to: Racso and the rats of NIMH, entered below

The intelligent young rat Racso and his friends Christopher and Isabella try to ensure the survival of their secret community in Thorn Valley after its accidental discovery by two human children

"Though too many of the relationships among Conly's minor characters spark briefly only to fizzle out—demanding less emotional commitment than earlier installments in the Rats of NIMH saga—the novel proves enjoyable for its excitement and believably drawn characterizations of the children and their amazing rodent friends." Publ Wkly

Racso and the rats of NIMH; illustrations by Leonard Lubin. Harper & Row 1986 278p il $12.95; lib bdg $12.89; pa $3.50 (4 and up) **Fic**

1. Mice—Fiction 2. Rats—Fiction

ISBN 0-06-021361-2; 0-06-021362-0 (lib bdg); 0-06-440245-2 (pa) LC 85-42634

Sequel to: Mrs. Frisby and the rats of NIMH by Robert C. O'Brien, entered below

This book "continues the NIMH saga with a focus on the second rodent generation: Timothy, Mrs. Frisby's son, and Racso, son of the rebel rat Jenner. On his way to classes at Thorn Valley, Timothy saves Racso's life but is himself severely injured. Both reach the Utopian colony only to discover that the valley and surrounding farms are to be turned into a tourist lake and campgrounds. Insecure and arrogant when he first arrives, Racso learns more than just how to read. In fact it is he who suggests a plan to save the colony—sabotaging the dam site computer." SLJ

"The book suffers slightly from too many themes—city life versus country life, the importance of conservation of wild land, and the nature of heroism. But Racso is a charmingly cheeky hero, and his friend Timothy and the other rats of NIMH are remarkably intelligent and sensible. The book is cleverly and gracefully built upon both the philosophy of self-sufficiency and the details of the plot of its predecessor. Given the difficulty of writing good sequels, *Racso and the Rats of NIMH* is an outstanding success." Horn Book

Followed by: R-T, Margaret, and the rats of NIMH, entered above

Conrad, Pam, 1947-

My Daniel. Harper & Row 1989 137p $12.95; lib bdg $12.89 (5 and up) **Fic**

1. Brothers and sisters—Fiction 2. Nebraska—Fiction

ISBN 0-06-021313-2; 0-06-021314-0 (lib bdg)

LC 88-19850

"When she's 80 years old, Julia Summerwaithe decides to visit her grandchildren, Ellie and Stevie, in New York City, for the first time. She has something important to show them; in the Natural History Museum is the dinosaur she and her brother discovered on their farm in Nebraska when they were young. But even more important to Julia than seeing the dinosaur is sharing her memories of the discovery and excavation with her grandchildren." SLJ

"The structure of the story is teasing; it tautly builds suspense and culminates in a scene of epiphanic intensity as the elderly Julia is reunited with her Daniel in a place called memory. Rendering scenes from both the past and the present with equal skill, Conrad is at the peak of her storytelling powers." Publ Wkly

Prairie songs; illustrations by Darryl S. Zudeck. Harper & Row 1985 167p il $12.95; lib bdg $12.89; pa $3.50 (5 and up) **Fic**

1. Frontier and pioneer life—Fiction 2. Nebraska—Fiction

ISBN 0-06-021336-1; 0-06-021337-X (lib bdg); 0-06-440206-1 (pa) LC 85-42633

Conrad, Pam, 1947-—*Continued*

"The deterioration of the frail, young wife of a doctor who is unable to adapt to the harshness of prairie life is made more vivid because the reader views it through the eyes of an adolescent girl who lives nearby. Set in Nebraska at the turn of the century, this story is rich with detail about the beauty and hardships of pioneer life in the American West." Soc Educ

Staying nine; illustrated by Mike Wimmer. Harper & Row 1988 70p il $12.95; lib bdg $12.89; pa $3.25 (3-5) **Fic**

1. Birthdays—Fiction 2. Family life—Fiction
ISBN 0-06-021319-1; 0-06-021320-5 (lib bdg); 0-06-440377-7 (pa) LC 87-45862

Nine-year-old Heather doesn't want to turn ten until wacky Rosa Rita shows her that growing up isn't so bad

"Conrad captures a pivotal few days in a young girl's life with perception and touching reality, bringing off a contemporary, individualized protagonist through some memorable detailing. Family relationships are naturally drawn and events ring true in a story delivered with a grace and depth rarely found in so short a novel." Booklist

Stonewords; a ghost story. Harper & Row 1990 130p $12.95; lib bdg $12.89 (5 and up) **Fic**

1. Ghosts—Fiction 2. Space and time—Fiction
ISBN 0-06-021315-9; 0-06-021316-7 (lib bdg) LC 89-36382

Zoe discovers that her house is occupied by the ghost of an eleven-year-old girl, who carries her back to the day of her death in 1870 to try to alter that tragic event

"The supernatural and time-travel elements of the book are viscerally convincing, and the desperate neediness of both girls is fierce and real. The disquieting ending is in the richest gothic tradition, resolving one mystery only to reveal another even more frightening. This is a very scary book." Bull Cent Child Books

Cooper, Susan, 1935-

Dawn of fear; illustrated by Margery Gill. Harcourt Brace Jovanovich 1970 157p il $14.95; Aladdin Bks. (NY) pa $3.95 (5 and up) **Fic**

1. Great Britain—Fiction 2. World War, 1939-1945—Fiction
ISBN 0-15-266201-4; 0-689-71327-4 (pa) LC 71-115755

During World War II, three English boys' fearless unconcern with the enemy planes that flew daily on their way to bomb London, gradually underwent a change as the night raids grew more severe. This is the story of how, through the destruction—not by bombs—of the secret camp they were building, the boys came face-to-face with grown-up hatred, and then they knew the meaning of fear

"The characterization [is] deft and the dialogue natural [and] the relationship between the boys and a young man who is about to enter the Merchant Navy [is] particularly perceptive." Sutherland. The Best in Child Books

The grey king; illustrated by Michael Heslop. Atheneum Pubs. 1975 208p il $13.95; pa $2.95 (5 and up) **Fic**

1. Good and evil—Fiction 2. Fantastic fiction 3. Wales—Fiction
ISBN 0-689-50029-7; 0-689-71089-5 (pa) LC 75-8526

Also available ABC-CLIO large print edition $14.95 (ISBN 1-85089-935-5)

Awarded the Newbery Medal, 1976

"A Margaret K. McElderry book"

"In the fourth of Cooper's Arthurian fantasies [series entered below] Will Stanton, last and youngest of the Old Ones, the strange Welsh boy, Bran, and the sheep dogs and ghostly gray foxes of the mountains are drawn into the epic struggles of a world beyond time." SLJ

"So well-crafted that it stands as an entity in itself, the novel . . . is nevertheless strengthened by its relationship to the preceding volumes—as the individual legends within the Arthurian cycles take on deeper significance in the context of the whole. A spellbinding tour de force." Horn Book

Over sea, under stone; illustrated by Margery Gill. Harcourt Brace Jovanovich 1966 c1965 252p il $14.95; Collier Bks. pa $2.95 (5 and up) **Fic**

1. Fantastic fiction 2. Good and evil—Fiction 3. Great Britain—Fiction
ISBN 0-15-259034-X; 0-02-042785-9 (pa) LC 66-11199

Also available ABC-CLIO large print edition $14.95 (ISBN 1-85089-932-0)

First published 1965 in the United Kingdom

In this series about the "conflict between the good of the Servants of Light and the evil of the Powers of Dark, Cooper has created an intricate fantasy. Ancient lore and mythology are believably interwoven into a modern setting. Ostensibly, the three Drew children, on a holiday in Cornwall, find an old map and, aided by their uncle, they begin a search for an ancient treasure linked with King Arthur. With each book, more reliance is placed on folklore and legend. There is much action and excitement included in the carefully wrought stories." Roman. Sequences

Other available titles in the Dark is rising series are:
The dark is rising (1973)
Greenwitch (1974)
Silver on the tree (1977)

Fourth title in series: The grey king, entered above

Seaward. Atheneum Pubs. 1983 167p $10.95; pa $3.95 (6 and up) **Fic**

1. Fantastic fiction
ISBN 0-689-50275-3; 0-02-042190-7 (pa) LC 83-7055

"A Margaret K. McElderry book"

"Fleeing from unhappiness, two young people are cast into a different reality. . . . Cally and West are the two young people. Cally's ancestors may have been seals; West's were probably Shamana. Having nothing better to do, the two set off for the sea, where they expect to find their parents. As they travel, they are hounded by strange creatures. However, they survive and reach the sea where they learn that Life and Death are related by necessity and where they learn to embrace the reality from which they once fled." ALAN

"This metaphysical adventure has appeal for beginning fantasy readers. Cooper's fans however, will find only

Cooper, Susan, 1935-—*Continued*
hints of the rich mythic and folkloric detail they have come to expect of her." SLJ

Corbett, Scott, 1913-

The deadly hoax. Dutton 1981 86p $9.25 (5 and up) **Fic**

1. Horror—Fiction 2. Science fiction
ISBN 0-525-28585-7 LC 80-26552

"A Unicorn book"

"In this science-fiction book that borders on reality, two friends turn the tables on aliens from outer space who are planning to command the earthlings by destroying a nuclear plant. How the aliens control a computer and force the boys to join them in a space flight is revealed in this fast-paced story that will appeal to both computer and science-fiction fans." Child Book Rev Serv

"Despite the rapid pace, Corbett is able to make his characters credible. The aliens are properly enigmatic, and the book leaves one wanting to know more about the origin and culture of the strange creatures. The book's short length and fast action should appeal to older reluctant readers as well, although Corbett does not make concessions in vocabulary." SLJ

The discontented ghost. Dutton 1978 180p $10.64 (6 and up) **Fic**

1. Ghosts—Fiction 2. Great Britain—Fiction
ISBN 0-525-28775-2 LC 78-18013

"A Unicorn book"

A "retelling of Oscar Wilde's 'The Canterville Ghost'—from the ghost's point of view. Sir Simon de Canterville is the resident haunt, having stayed on at his ancestral home some 300 years after his death, and by 1884 quite proud of his record. His wife (whom he is said to have murdered but did not) has performed the services of an assistant, playing the housekeeper. Though somewhat weary of his role, Sir Simon has little doubt that he will roust out the new American family who buys his home and is stunned to find that one set of twins, Yankee common sense, and 'Pinkerton's Champion Stain Remover and Paragon Detergent' prove more than a self-respecting ghost can handle." SLJ

"This is the most sophisticated of Corbett's ghost stories, a well-written comedy with carefully developed characters and a beguiling plot that doesn't lose out by having its ends tied up neatly." Booklist

Grave doubts. Little, Brown 1982 157p $14.95 (4 and up) **Fic**

1. Mystery and detective stories
ISBN 0-316-15659-0 LC 82-10050

"An Atlantic Monthly Press book"

"Wally Brenner and Les Cunningham turn detective following their unusual meeting with elderly Mr. Canby and his surprise death later that night. The boys are called in to help Shapley Hobson, a man despised by Canby, to complete an inventory of some of Canby's possessions. The mystery begins when Les and Wally overhear Mr. Canby, a puzzle lover, hint to his nephew Otis that when he works out a puzzle he has given him, he will find something very valuable. That plus the suspicious death raise 'grave doubts' in the boys' minds, so they set out to unravel the mystery." Voice Youth Advocates

"Puzzle fans should enjoy Corbett's insertion of some facts about cryptic crossword puzzles, and mystery fans should enjoy the suspense that's built into a story that's capably plotted and written." Bull Cent Child Books

The lemonade trick; illustrated by Paul Galdone. Little, Brown 1960 103p il lib bdg $14.95; Scholastic pa $2.50 (3-5) **Fic**

1. Fantastic fiction
ISBN 0-316-15694-9 (lib bdg); 0-590-32197-8 (pa) LC 59-7361

"An Atlantic Monthly Press book"

A brew from his Feats O'Magic chemistry set, given to him by the mysterious Mrs. Graymalkin, changes Kerby into a perfect gentleman; unfortunately, it has the opposite effect on good boys

"An ingenious bit of magic has been mixed by [the author] and dashingly illustrated . . . to please eight-year-old readers . . . and even some a bit older who like a fairly simple story that doesn't take too long to read." N Y Her Trib Books

Other available titles in this series are:
The disappearing dog trick (1963)
The hairy horror trick (1969)
The hangman's ghost trick (1977)
The mailbox trick (1961)

Corbett, W. J.

The song of Pentecost; illustrated by Martin Ursell. Dutton 1983 c1982 215p il $10.95; Dell pa $3.25 (5 and up) **Fic**

1. Mice—Fiction 2. Animals—Fiction 3. Allegories
ISBN 0-525-44051-8; 0-440-48092-2 (pa) LC 83-1712

First published 1982 in the United Kingdom

"An extended family of Harvest Mice, over whose living quarters the city has grown, agree to help gullible Snake recover his inheritance from an impostor Cousin in return for his help in finding a new home. Under the leadership of earnest young Pentecost Mouse, the group has mildly suspenseful, action-filled adventures as they make their way . . . over the countryside." Child Book Rev Serv

"Although Corbett tends to write ornately, his style is saved from pomposity by the wit of the dialogue, the humor of the exposition, and the acuteness and color of the characterization, with its quick establishment of strong personalities." Bull Cent Child Books

Corcoran, Barbara, 1911-

Annie's monster. Atheneum Pubs. 1990 188p $13.95 (5 and up) **Fic**

1. Dogs—Fiction 2. Mentally ill—Fiction 3. Clergy—Fiction 4. Homeless people—Fiction
ISBN 0-689-31632-1 LC 89-28121

"A Jean Karl book"

"Annie's monster is an Irish wolfhound named Flanagan, whose size and exuberance have frightened some of the people in the small New England town where they live. When the dog leads her to the hiding place of a mentally ill woman, Annie must decide what to do. Cora has been turned out of the state hospital and has run away from an inadequate halfway house, and good-hearted Annie is afraid that her stern father, an Episcopalian priest, will send her back." Horn Book

"Spun with the kind of practiced ease that smoothes over most rough spots, the story is absorbing as well

Corcoran, Barbara, 1911-—*Continued*
as entertaining and will leave readers thinking about society's obligations to the Coras of the world." Booklist

Coren, Alan, 1938-

Arthur the Kid; illustrated by John Astrop. Little, Brown 1978 c1977 73p il $12.95; Bantam Bks. pa $2.25 (3-5) **Fic**

1. West (U.S.)—Fiction 2. Robbers and outlaws—Fiction

ISBN 0-316-15734-1; 0-553-15169-X (pa)

First published 1976 in the United Kingdom

"Derby-sporting [ten-year-old] Arthur responds to a newspaper ad from the bungling Black Hand Gang. . . . With Arthur in charge, instead of robbing a Wells Fargo office, the gang members, dressed as women, hand over one hundred thousand dollars to Wells Fargo officials, collect a big reward, and ultimately turn away from criminal pursuits." SLJ

"Coren's funny situations, broadened by comical drawings and heightened by clever dialogue, entertain from start to finish." Booklist

Coutant, Helen

First snow; pictures by Vo-Dinh. Knopf 1974 30p il lib bdg $6.99 (2-4) **Fic**

1. Death—Fiction 2. Vietnamese—United States 3. Family life—Fiction

ISBN 0-394-92831-8 LC 74-1187

This is the "story of a Vietnamese family's first winter in New England. The excitement and happiness of the impending first snow is mingled with the uncertainty and sadness of Grandmother's dying. Young Lien soon sees dying as a natural process: a change—just as in the life of a snowflake." Child Book Rev Serv

"So 'that' was dying, something disappeared and in its place came something else! This is the Buddhist view, the oneness of life and death. . . . The story has a quiet serenity and delivers effectively its message of the continuity of the life-death cycle." Bull Cent Child Books

The gift; drawings by Vo-Dinh Mai. Knopf 1983 unp il $9.95 (2-5) **Fic**

1. Friendship—Fiction 2. Old age—Fiction 3. Blind—Fiction

ISBN 0-394-85499-3 LC 82-7810

After much deliberation, Anna finally decides on the perfect present for her special friend, Nana Marie, an old lady who has suddenly gone blind

"Although the book is very short, the characters are treated with warmth and humanity. The issue of blindness is handled naturally, with simplicity and dignity. . . . The soft grey drawings complement the text." SLJ

Cresswell, Helen

Dear Shrink. Macmillan 1982 186p $12.95 (5 and up) **Fic**

1. Brothers and sisters—Fiction 2. Foster home care—Fiction

ISBN 0-02-725560-3 LC 82-7728

"A fictional diary written by Oliver Saxon. In it, Oliver details the adventures he and his brother and sister have when they are left in London by their botanist parents, who have gone to study in the Amazon. The three children are farmed out to foster homes when the woman caring for them dies. The ups and downs of their experiences and the final reunion of the family makes for rewarding reading." Child Book Rev Serv

"Despite the pat ending, the story is very readable, with the plot developing at a good pace. People's reactions to death are astutely handled. . . . Elsewhere the humour is characteristic of Helen Cresswell and the technique of letters to a 'psychological friend' enables her to pose some serious social and psychological questions with a pleasing lightness of touch." Times Lit Suppl

Ordinary Jack. Macmillan 1977 195p $12.95; Penguin Bks. pa $3.95 (5 and up) **Fic**

1. Family life—Fiction

ISBN 0-02-725540-9; 0-14-031176-9 (pa) LC 77-5146

Also available ABC-CLIO large print edition $14.95 (ISBN 0-85089-913-3)

Eleven-year-old Jack, the only "ordinary" member of the talented and eccentric Bagthorpe family, concocts a scheme to distinguish himself as a modern-day prophet

Other available titles about the Bagthorpe family are:
Absolute zero (1978)
Bagthorpes abroad (1984)
Bagthorpes haunted (1985)
Bagthorpes liberated (1989)
Bagthorpes unlimited (1978)
Bagthorpes v. the world (1979)

The secret world of Polly Flint; illustrated by Shirley Felts. Macmillan 1984 c1982 176p il $11.95; Penguin Bks. pa $3.50 (4-6) **Fic**

1. Space and time—Fiction 2. Fantastic fiction

ISBN 0-02-725400-3; 0-14-031542-X (pa) LC 83-24861

First published 1982 in the United Kingdom

"Polly Flint, a girl who sees things other people can't, finds herself involved with the 'time gypsies' of Grimstone, inhabitants of a lost village who have become trapped in a time not their own." Bull Cent Child Books

"Cresswell's shimmering novel is steeped in a potent aura of magic, brilliantly drawing on many classic fantasy motifs. Readers may wonder at impetuous Polly's hesitance to meet the magic head-on, and the story's logic must be followed attentively. But the inviting cover painting, which echoes sensitive pen-and-ink drawings inside, and the story's bewitching time-slip appeal should attract younger fantasy readers in droves, particularly where Cresswell's previous work has found favor." Booklist

Crosher, G. R.

The awakening water; [by] G. R. Kesteven. Hastings House 1979 c1977 160p $9.95 (5 and up) **Fic**

1. Science fiction

ISBN 0-8038-0471-7 LC 78-27186

First published 1977 in the United Kingdom

"In the early years of the 21st-Century, after the 'devastation' of 1997, a 13-year-old boy tastes fresh water for the first time. He then begins to question his life and runs away to join others who have previously escaped the 'Party.' The story of how this resourceful group of youngsters survive is enjoyable, and the contrast

Crosher, G. R.—*Continued*

between the 'doped' masses and the group of 'lost ones' is well drawn. . . . Kesteven's latest has well-developed characters and plot and an unexpected, but plausible and optimistic, ending." SLJ

Dahl, Roald

James and the giant peach; illustrated by Nancy Ekholm Burkert. Knopf 1961 118p il $17.95; lib bdg $17.99; Bantam Bks. pa $2.95 (4-6) **Fic**

1. Fantastic fiction
ISBN 0-394-81282-4; 0-394-91282-9 (lib bdg); 0-553-15317-X LC 61-8127

Also available ABC-CLIO large print edition $14.95 (ISBN 1-55736-155-X)

After the death of his parents, little James is forced to live with Aunt Sponge and Aunt Spike, two cruel old harpies. A magic potion causes the growing of a giant-sized peach on a puny peach tree. James sneaks inside the peach and finds a new world of insects. With his new family, James heads for many adventures

"A 'juicy' fantasy, 'dripping' with humor and imagination." Commonweal

Matilda; illustrations by Quentin Blake. Viking Kestrel 1988 240p il $14.95; Puffin Bks. pa $3.95 (4-6) **Fic**

1. School stories
ISBN 0-670-82439-9; 0-14-034294-X (pa) LC 88-40312

Also available ABC-CLIO large print edition $15.95 (ISBN 1-55736-123-1)

"Matilda knows how to be extremely and creatively naughty—lining her father's hat with super glue, putting her mother's hair bleach in her father's hair tonic bottle, for example. This streak of imaginative wickedness not only allows her to make a loyal friend, Lavender, but also to wreak revenge on her unloving parents, defeat the fiendish headmistress, Miss Turnbull, and return her victimized teacher, the enchanting Miss Honey, to her rightful place in the world. Having saved the day, Matilda is released from her parents and has the prospect of living happily ever after." N Y Times Book Rev

"Dahl has written another fun and funny book with a child's perspective on an adult world. As usual, Blake's comical sketches are the perfect complement to the satirical humor." SLJ

Dalgliesh, Alice, 1893-1979

The bears on Hemlock Mountain; illustrated by Helen Sewell. Scribner 1990 c1952 unp il $12.95; pa $3.95 (1-4) **Fic**

1. Bears—Fiction
ISBN 0-684-19169-5; 0-689-70497-6 (pa) LC 89-27651

A Newbery Medal honor book, 1953

A reissue of the title first published 1952

"This is the story of a little boy sent by his mother to borrow an iron from an aunt who lived on the other side of Hemlock Mountain—really only a hill. Jonathan's mother did not believe that there were bears on Hemlock Mountain but Jonathan did. . . . The two-color, somewhat stylized illustrations seem right for the story." Booklist

"Jonathan's adventure is a tall tale passed down in Pennsylvania, which might have happened to a pioneer boy almost anywhere. Full of suspense and humor, it will make good reading aloud." N Y Her Trib Books

The courage of Sarah Noble; illustrations by Leonard Weisgard. Scribner 1986 c1954 52p il $12.95; pa $4.95 (2-4) **Fic**

1. Frontier and pioneer life—Fiction 2. Indians of North America—Fiction 3. Connecticut—Fiction
ISBN 0-684-18830-9; 0-689-71057-7 (pa) LC 54-5922

A Newbery Medal honor book, 1955

"Sarah, though only eight, cooked for her father while he made a new home for the family in the Connecticut wilderness of 1707. When Mr. Noble returned to Massachusetts for the rest of the family, leaving Sarah with a friendly Indian, her courage was sorely tested." Hodges. Books for Elem Sch Libr

"Based on a true incident in Connecticut history—the founding of New Milford—this story is one to be long remembered for its beautiful simplicity and dignity. Leonard Weisgard's pictures add just the right sense of background." N Y Times Book Rev

Danziger, Paula, 1944-

The cat ate my gymsuit. Delacorte Press 1974 147p $14.95; lib bdg $14.95; Dell pa $3.25 (5 and up) **Fic**

1. School stories 2. Teachers—Fiction
ISBN 0-385-28183-8; 0-385-28194-3 (lib bdg); 0-440-41612-4 (pa)

Also available ABC-CLIO large print edition $14.95 (ISBN 1-55736-068-5)

Marcy Lewis is bored by school and tyrannized by her father. With the help of an unconventional teacher, she conquers many of her feelings of insecurity and, in turn, rallies the student body in support of the teacher who was fired because of her behavior

"A sad-funny novel. . . . Ms. Danziger has an attractive style; her prose sparkles with wit and originality." Publ Wkly

Followed by: There's a bat in bunk five, entered below

Everyone else's parents said yes. Delacorte Press 1989 115p $13.95; Dell pa $3.50 (4-6) **Fic**

1. Family life—Fiction 2. School stories
ISBN 0-385-29805-6; 0-440-40333-2 (pa) LC 88-37540

Matthew cannot resist the temptation to play practical jokes on his older sister and all the girls in his class at school, so by the time of the big party for his eleventh birthday they have all declared war on him

"Danziger does display a keen sensitivity to the typical concerns and sense of humor of her target audience. Brisk in style and pacing, this lighthearted offering is sure to be popular." Booklist

Make like a tree and leave. Delacorte Press 1990 117p $13.95 (4-6) **Fic**

1. Family life—Fiction 2. School stories
ISBN 0-385-30151-0 LC 89-71481

Sequel to: Everyone else's parents said yes, entered above

Danziger, Paula, 1944-—*Continued*

Sixth-grader Matthew gets into trouble at home and at school, spars with his older sister, and helps save an elderly friend's property from the hands of a developer

"In addition to her customarily funny, energetic writing, Danziger offers valid insights into the tensions created in a town between those who want to preserve the land and those who want to develop it." Publ Wkly

There's a bat in bunk five. Delacorte Press 1980 150p lib bdg $14.95; Dell pa $2.95 (5 and up) **Fic**

1. Camps—Fiction
ISBN 0-385-29015-2 (lib bdg); 0-440-40098-8 (pa) LC 80-15581

Also available ABC-CLIO large print edition $15.95 (ISBN 1-55736-047-2)

"A thinner Marcy than appeared in 'The Cat ate My Gymsuit' [entered above] here eagerly accepts an invitation from Ms. Finney, her favorite teacher, to work as a counselor-in-training at a summer camp. Though wanting to do a good job, particulrly in reaching the abrasive and uncooperative Ginger, Marcy also indulges in a romance with fellow camper Ted and spends time sorting out her own inner conflicts." Booklist

"In some ways this is the usual camping story of pranks, bunkmates, adjustment to separation from parents, etc. This doesn't, however, follow a formula plot; it has depth in the relationships and characterizations; and it's written with vigor and humor." Bull Cent Child Books

De Angeli, Marguerite Lofft, 1889-1987

The door in the wall; by Marguerite de Angeli. Doubleday 1989 c1949 120p il $14.95; Dell pa $3.50 (4-6) **Fic**

1. Physically handicapped children—Fiction 2. Great Britain—History—1154-1399, Plantagenets—Fiction
ISBN 0-385-07283-X; 0-440-40283-2 (pa) LC 64-7025

Awarded the Newbery Medal, 1950

First published 1949

Robin, a crippled boy in fourteenth-century England, proves his courage and earns recognition from the King

"An enthralling and inspiring tale of triumph over handicap. Unusually beautiful illustrations, full of authentic detail, combine with the text to make life in England during the Middle Ages come alive." N Y Times Book Rev

DeClements, Barthe, 1920-

6th grade can really kill you. Viking Kestrel 1985 146p $11.95; Scholastic pa $2.50 (5 and up) **Fic**

1. Learning disabilities—Fiction 2. School stories
ISBN 0-670-80656-0; 0-590-40180-7 (pa) LC 85-40382

Also available ABC-CLIO large print edition $15.95 (ISBN 0-55736-108-8)

"Helen dreads the first day in sixth grade. Good in math and gifted on the pitcher's mound, she is a non-reader diagnosed as a behavior problem. Against the slice-of-life background of a skating party, pierced ears and overnights at friend Louise's, Helen loses the battle with the printed word." SLJ

This is "a story that amply compensates for its uneven pace by the natural quality of the relationships and the dialogue in the classroom environment and by the insight gained through the first person treatment of a learning disability." Bull Cent Child Books

DeFelice, Cynthia C.

Weasel; [by] Cynthia DeFelice. Macmillan 1990 119p $12.95 (4 and up) **Fic**

1. Frontier and pioneer life—Fiction 2. Ohio—Fiction
ISBN 0-02-726457-2 LC 89-37794

Alone in the Ohio frontier wilderness in the winter of 1839 while his father is recovering from an injury, eleven-year-old Nathan runs afoul of the renegade killer known as Weasel and makes a surprising discovery about the concept of revenge

"Aimed at relatively young readers, whose frame of reference for complex issues is limited, this novel's highest virtue is that a complicated issue is put in terms young thinkers can understand and grapple with—and grapple they will. Despite its clear point of view, the book is ideal for discussion and debate—a fine choice as a novel to teach in a literature-based curriculum, where children can be stimulated to think about moral choices and about some of the unhappy truths of frontier settlement." Booklist

Defoe, Daniel, 1661?-1731

Robinson Crusoe (5 and up) **Fic**

1. Survival (after airplane accidents, shipwrecks, etc.)—Fiction

Some editions are:

Amereon $21.95 (ISBN 0-88411-594-1)
Bantam Bks. pa $2.25 (ISBN 0-553-21373-3)
Buccaneer Bks. $21.95 (ISBN 0-89966-403-2)
New Am. Lib. pa $2.25 (ISBN 0-451-52236-2)
Penguin Bks. pa $2.50 (ISBN 0-14-043007-5)
Scribner $22.50 With illustrations by N. C. Wyeth (ISBN 0-684-17946-6)

First published 1719

"A minutely circumstantial account of the hero's shipwreck and escape to an uninhabited island, and the methodical industry whereby he makes himself a comfortable home. The story is founded on the actual experiences of Alexander Selkirk, who spent four years on the island of Juan Fernandez in the early 18th century." Lenrow. Reader's Guide to Prose Fic

A "world-famous tale of adventure. . . . The simplicity of style, and the realistic atmosphere which pervades the narrative, have caused the popularity of this book to remain unimpaired." Keller. Reader's Dig of Books

DeJong, Meindert, 1906-

The house of sixty fathers; pictures by Maurice Sendak. Harper & Row 1956 189p il lib bdg $13.89; pa $3.50 (4-6) **Fic**

1. Sino-Japanese Conflict, 1937-1945—Fiction 2. China—Fiction
ISBN 0-06-021481-3 (lib bdg); 0-06-440200-2 (pa) LC 56-8148

A Newbery Medal honor book, 1957

"A vividly realistic story of China during the early days of the Japanese invasion. Tien Pao, a small Chinese boy, and his family fled inland on a sampan when the Japanese attacked their coastal village, but Tien Pao was separated from his parents during a storm and swept

DeJong, Meindert, 1906-—*Continued*

back down the river on the sampan. . . . Once again the author has shown his ability to paint starkly realistic word pictures that give the reader the full impact of the terror, pain, hunger and finally the joy that Tien Pao knew during his search for his family." Bull Cent Child Books

The wheel on the school; pictures by Maurice Sendak. Harper & Row 1954 298p il $13.95; lib bdg $13.89; pa $3.50 (4-6) **Fic**

1. Storks—Fiction 2. School stories 3. Netherlands—Fiction

ISBN 0-06-021585-2; 0-06-021586-0 (lib bdg); 0-06-440021-2 (pa) LC 54-8945

Awarded the Newbery Medal, 1955

"Six Dutch children encouraged by a sensitive schoolmaster search for a wheel to place on the schoolhouse roof as a nesting place for storks. Their efforts and ultimate success lead to better understanding among the children and closer ties to older members of the community." Read Ladders for Hum Relat

"This author goes deeply into the heart of childhood and has written a moving story, filled with suspense and distinguished for the quality of its writing." Child Books Too Good To Miss

"It is difficult to imagine drawings more in tune with the text than these unforgettable ones by Maurice Sendak." N Y Times Book Rev

Delton, Judy

Angel's mother's wedding; illustrated by Margot Apple. Houghton Mifflin 1987 166p il $12.95; Dell pa $2.95 (3-5) **Fic**

1. Weddings—Fiction 2. Family life—Fiction

ISBN 0-395-44470-5; 0-440-40281-6 (pa) LC 87-16937

"Angel's capacity for worry, added to her friend Edna's knowledge of how a wedding should be properly organized, leads to confusions and misunderstandings that reach almost epic proportions. . . . Humor, affection, and action narrowly skirting disaster mark each chapter in the progress from bridal shower to wedding march. Angel, her family, and friends are all pleasantly ordinary folk with a singular capacity to bring near-chaos into the normally quiet routines and celebrations of their daily life." Horn Book

Other available titles about Angel are:
Angel in charge (1985)
Angel's mother's baby (1989)
Angel's mother's boyfriend (1986)
Back yard Angel (1983)

Kitty from the start. Houghton Mifflin 1987 141p il $12.95 (2-4) **Fic**

1. Catholics—United States—Fiction 2. Moving, Household—Fiction 3. School stories

ISBN 0-395-42847-5 LC 86-21481

"A prequel to *Kitty in the Middle* recounts Kitty's first weeks in the third grade as an apprehensive and, at least to herself, conspicuous new student. Immediately Kitty is befriended on the one hand by the devout and oh-so-proper Margaret Mary and on the other by the free-spirited Eileen. Kitty is drawn to the secure if occasionally irritating conformity of Margaret Mary and at the same time warily attracted to Eileen's wilder ways and offhand attitude toward the Sisters and rules of the strict Catholic school." Horn Book

"As with the other Kitty stories, this has a heartfelt honesty about it, yet there's always plenty of room for humor. Although Kitty's theological debates with herself (Will she go to hell for playing confession with Eileen?) may offend a few, most readers will find this a delightful re-creation of a bygone era, which is filled with simple, eternal truths." Booklist

Other available titles about Kitty are:
Kitty in high school (1984)
Kitty in the middle (1979)
Kitty in the summer (1980)

Dickens, Charles, 1812-1870

A Christmas carol in prose (4 and up) **Fic**

1. Christmas—Fiction 2. Ghosts—Fiction 3. Great Britain—Fiction

Some editions are:
Dial Bks. for Young Readers $14.95 With illustrations by Michael Foreman (ISBN 0-8037-0032-6)
Holiday House $14.95 Illustrated by Trina Schart Hyman (ISBN 0-8234-0486-2)
Penguin Bks. pa $4.95 With illustrations by John Leech (ISBN 0-14-007120-2)
Picture Bk. Studio $19.95 Illustrated by Lisbeth Zwerger (ISBN 0-88708-069-3)
Simon & Schuster $14.95 Illustrated by Greg Hildebrandt (ISBN 0-671-45599-0)
Stewart, Tabori & Chang $25 Illustrated by Roberto Innocenti (ISBN 1-55670-161-6)

Written in 1843

"This Christmas story of nineteenth century England has delighted young and old for generations. In it, a miser, Scrooge, through a series of dreams, finds the true Christmas spirit. . . . The story ends with the much-quoted cry of Tiny Tim, the crippled son of Bob Cratchit, whom Scrooge now aids: 'God bless us, every one!'" Haydn. Thesaurus of Book Dig

"There is perhaps no story in English literature better known and loved, or one that carries a more potent appeal to the Christmas sentiment." Springfield Repub

Dickinson, Peter, 1927-

Merlin dreams; illustrated by Alan Lee. Delacorte Press 1988 166p il $19.95 (5 and up) **Fic**

1. Merlin (Legendary character)—Fiction 2. Fantastic fiction

ISBN 0-440-50067-2 LC 88-3985

"While trapped under a rock, the Arthurian prophet and magician Merlin dreams, spinning nine tales of medieval enchantment leavened with quiet comedy. . . . Dickinson evokes a world of dragons, maidens and myth vividly enough to reach readers young and old; Lee's watercolors and pencil drawings dwell with uncommon delicacy on the legendary romance of the tales." Publ Wkly

Dicks, Terrance

The Baker Street Irregulars in the case of the missing masterpiece. Elsevier/Nelson Bks. 1979 c1978 141p $7.95 (5 and up) **Fic**

1. Mystery and detective stories
ISBN 0-525-66656-7 LC 79-18861

First published 1978 in the United Kingdom with title: The case of the missing masterpiece

"It's because of a challenge from a hostile bully that Dan, a Conan Doyle fan, announces that he will solve the mystery of a stolen painting by the time school resumes after a half-term holiday. With the help of three friends, all of whom expose themselves to danger, he and they find clues that lead Dan to deduce the villain, understand how the crime took place, and prevent a murder." Bull Cent Child Books

Other available titles about the Baker Street Irregulars are:
The Baker Street Irregulars in the case of the blackmail boys (1980)
The Baker Street Irregulars in the case of the cinema swindle (1981)
The Baker Street Irregulars in the case of the cop catchers (1982)
The Baker Street Irregulars in the case of the crooked kids (1980)
The Baker Street Irregulars in the case of the ghost grabbers (1981)

Dodge, Mary Mapes, 1830-1905

Hans Brinker; or, The silver skates (4 and up) **Fic**

1. Ice skating—Fiction 2. Netherlands—Fiction
LC 63-6890

Some editions are:
Crown (Children's classics) $12.99 Illustrated by Edna Cooke and Maginel Wright Enright (ISBN 0-517-68798-4)
Dell pa $4.95 (ISBN 0-440-43446-7)
Puffin Bks. pa $2.25 (ISBN 0-14-035042-X)
Scholastic pa $2.95 (ISBN 0-590-41295-7)

First published 1865

A new friend gives Hans and his sister Gretel enough money for one pair of ice skates, so Hans insists that Gretel enter the grand competition for silver skates, while he seeks the great Doctor who consents to try to restore their father's memory

Doherty, Berlie

White Peak Farm. Orchard Bks. 1990 c1984 102p $12.95; lib bdg $12.99 (5 and up) **Fic**

1. Farm life—Fiction 2. England—Fiction
ISBN 0-531-05867-0; 0-531-08467-1 (lib bdg)
LC 89-23060

Companion volume to: Granny was a buffer girl (1988)

First published 1984 in the United Kingdom

"This is an account by adolescent Jeannie of the strong bonds and major events in the life of her family, living in comparative isolation on their Derbyshire farm. . . . Older sister Kathleen marries the son of a family enemy; brother Martin wants to leave and study art." Bull Cent Child Books

"The spare writing does its job quietly, creating characters who are both memorable and utterly believable. Words are never wasted here: even the most insignificant-seeming details add their weight to the story's momentum. It is the telling of the tale, perhaps even more than the tale itself, that makes Doherty's work invite rereading." Publ Wkly

Dragonwagon, Crescent

Winter holding spring; illustrated by Ronald Himler. Macmillan 1990 31p il $11.95 (2-4) **Fic**

1. Death—Fiction 2. Parent and child—Fiction 3. Seasons—Fiction
ISBN 0-02-733122-9 LC 88-13747

In discussing her mother's death with her father, eleven-year-old Sarah comes to see that in endings there are new beginnings, that in winter there is the promise of spring, and that everything comes full circle

"The father-daughter relationship is a tender, well-drawn one with plenty of details, thoughtful dialogue, and glimpses of the father's different, but also real sense of loss." SLJ

"Rough charcoal drawings illustrate the story, paying special attention to the father-daughter connection." Booklist

Du Bois, William Pène, 1916-

The twenty-one balloons; written and illustrated by William Pène Du Bois. Viking 1947 179p il $12.95; Dell pa $2.75 (5 and up) **Fic**

1. Balloons—Fiction
ISBN 0-670-73441-1; 0-440-49183-5 (pa) LC 47-2533

Awarded the Newbery Medal, 1948

"Professor Sherman set off on a flight across the Pacific in a giant balloon, but three weeks later the headlines read 'Professor Sherman in wrong ocean with too many balloons.' This book is concerned with the professor's explanation of this phenomenon. His account of his one stopover on the island of Krakotoa which blew up with barely a minute to spare to allow time for his escape, is the highlight of this hilarious narrative." Ont Libr Rev

Duder, Tessa

Jellybean. Viking Kestrel 1986 c1985 112p $10.95; Penguin Bks. pa $3.95 (5 and up) **Fic**

1. Single parent family—Fiction 2. Mothers and daughters—Fiction 3. Musicians—Fiction
ISBN 0-670-81235-8; 0-14-032114-4 (pa) LC 86-5553

First published 1985 in New Zealand

"As an only child of a single musician, Geraldine (nicknamed Jellybean) has always played second fiddle to her mother's career. Resentful and lonely, she has arranged her life around her mother's rehearsal and performance schedule as a concert cellist. A man from her mother's past helps Geraldine discover her own passion for music and helps her to better understand her mother and herself." SLJ

"The writing here is beautifully crafted . . . the characters closely portrayed, the scenes intensely played. . . . Although the setting is Auckland, New Zealand,

Duder, Tessa—*Continued*
the novel has immediate appeal by virtue of its depths and development." Bull Cent Child Books

Eager, Edward, 1911-1964
Half magic; drawings by N. M. Bodecker. Harcourt Brace Jovanovich 1954 217p il $12.95; pa $3.95 (4-6) **Fic**

1. Fantastic fiction
ISBN 0-15-233078-X; 0-15-233081-X (pa)
LC 54-5153

"Three sisters, a brother and widowed mother made up the family. Jane, the eldest, found a magic charm [an ancient coin] which granted half of any wish; after finding that out, and barring accidents, the children wished for twice as much as they wanted. The charm made for a week of adventures including Katharine's defeat of Sir Launcelot in a thoroughly unfair tourney and ending with mother's acquisition of a new husband amid a burst of what Mark called 'love blah.'" N Y Times Book Rev

"The chief effect of such a book is humor, arising from the ridiculous yet logical situations. . . . [It is] a book whose total contribution is one of fun and relaxation." Saturday Rev

Other available titles in this series are:
Knight's castle (1956)
Magic by the lake (1957)
The time garden (1958)

Seven-day magic; illustrated by N. M. Bodecker. Harcourt Brace 1962 156p il o.p. paperback available $3.95 (4-6) **Fic**

1. Fantastic fiction
ISBN 0-15-272916-X (pa) LC 62-17040
Also available in hardcover from Smith, P. $15.75 (ISBN 0-8446-6381-6)

"A sophisticated fantasy in which five children find a magic book that describes themselves, and realize that they can create their own magic by wishing with the book. In one episode . . . they disrupt a telecast by silencing all the cast except for one member of a male quartet. The children are lively and a bit precocious. . . . [The book has] humor, and some fresh and imaginative situations." Bull Cent Child Books

Eckert, Allan W.
Incident at Hawk's Hill; with illustrations by John Schoenherr. Little, Brown 1971 173p il $14.95; Bantam Bks. pa $3.50 (6 and up) **Fic**

1. Badgers—Fiction 2. Wilderness survival—Fiction 3. Saskatchewan—Fiction
ISBN 0-316-20866-3; 0-553-26696-9 (pa)
LC 77-143718

A Newbery Medal honor book, 1972

This account of an actual incident in Saskatchewan at the turn of the century tells of six-year-old Ben Macdonald, more attuned to animals than to people, who gets lost on the prairie and is nurtured by a female badger for two months before being found. Although a strange bond continues between the boy and the badger, the parents' understanding of their son and his communication with them improve as a result of the bizarre experience

"A really beautiful, simple book. . . . The descriptions of life in the wild are magnificent, the dignity of the animal against the greed and foolishness of man is illuminating. It is simply a very deeply moving, well written book which readers of every age will appreciate." Jr Bookshelf

Edmonds, Walter Dumaux, 1903-
Bert Breen's barn; [by] Walter D. Edmonds. Little, Brown 1975 270p il o.p.; Syracuse Univ. Press paperback available $9.95 (6 and up) **Fic**

1. Farm life—Fiction 2. New York (State)—Fiction
ISBN 0-8156-0255-3 (pa) LC 75-2157

The plot of the novel "revolves around young Tom Dolan's acquisition of a sturdy barn and the treasure rumoured to be hidden in it. Tom, his mother, and his two sisters live in turn-of-the-century upstate New York, and are very poor, a condition which Tom resolutely plans to change, beginning with buying and moving the barn on the old Breen place." Child Book Rev Serv

"This is a long, quiet story with strong characters and a well-knit plot, its strength lying in the felicity of details, the full picture it gives of a bygone way of life." Bull Cent Child Books

The matchlock gun; by Walter D. Edmonds; illustrated by Paul Lantz. Dodd, Mead 1941 50p il $14.95 (4-6) **Fic**

1. New York (State)—Fiction 2. United States—History—1755-1763, French and Indian War—Fiction
ISBN 0-399-21911-0 LC 41-17547

Awarded the Newbery Medal, 1942

"New York State during the French and Indian War is the setting for this story of a boy's courage and resourcefulness. In his father's absence, ten-year-old Edward Alstine helps his mother fight off an Indian attack by firing an old Spanish musket." Hodges. Books for Elem Sch Libr

Ehrlich, Amy, 1942-
The Snow Queen; [by] Hans Christian Andersen; pictures by Susan Jeffers; retold by Amy Ehrlich. Dial Bks. for Young Readers 1982 40p il $14.95; lib bdg $14.89; pa $4.95 (2-4) **Fic**

1. Fairy tales
ISBN 0-8037-8011-7; 0-8037-8029-X (lib bdg); 0-8037-0692-8 (pa) LC 82-70199

"A smooth and simplified retelling of Andersen's classic story of the power of love, this is in oversize format that affords the artist an opportunity for stunning paintings, soft and romantic in hues and mood but strong in composition and in the use of imaginative details, often sensuously textured. While the book can be used for reading aloud to younger children, the length of the story and the concept of love's transmuting power indicate the middle grades as prime audience." Bull Cent Child Books

Ellis, Sarah

Next-door neighbors. Margaret K. McElderry Bks. 1990 154p $11.95 (4 and up) **Fic**

1. Friendship—Fiction 2. Family life—Fiction 3. Canada—Fiction

ISBN 0-689-50495-0 LC 89-37923

Her family's move to a new town in Canada leaves shy twelve-year-old Peggy feeling lonely and uncomfortable, until she befriends the unconventional George and the Chinese servant of her imperious neighbor Mrs. Manning

"The theme of prejudicial scapegoating is confidently woven into an essentially optimistic school-and-family story, with neither characterization nor plot succumbing to didacticism. Plenty of gentle humor, an open and inviting style, and a young heroine both exasperating and admirable recommend this to a wide audience." Bull Cent Child Books

Enright, Elizabeth, 1909-1968

Gone-Away Lake; illustrated by Beth and Joe Krush. Harcourt Brace 1957 192p il pa $4.95 (4-6) **Fic**

ISBN 1-15-231649-3 LC 57-5172

Also available from Smith, P. $16 (ISBN 0-8446-6356-5)

A Newbery Medal honor book, 1958

Tale of an exciting summer when Portia, "beginning to be eleven," and her brother Foster, aged six-and-a-half, went to visit an uncle and aunt in the country. On one of Portia's expeditions with her slightly older cousin Julian they discovered a swamp which had once been a lake, with houses, mostly unoccupied, where the summer people had lived. Life became a happy thing from that moment for the rest of the summer

"Excellent writing, clear in setting of scene and details of nature, and strong in appeal for children." Horn Book

Followed by: Return to Gone-Away Lake (1961)

Thimble summer; written and illustrated by Elizabeth Enright. Holt & Co. 1938 124p il $15.95; Dell pa $3.25 (4-6) **Fic**

1. Farm life—Fiction 2. Wisconsin—Fiction

ISBN 0-8050-0306-1; 0-440-48681-5 (pa) LC 38-27586

Awarded the Newbery Medal, 1939

A story about life on a Wisconsin farm. When "Garnet finds a silver thimble near the river just before a much needed rain, she thinks the thimble is an omen of a happy summer." Read Ladders for Hum Relat. 5th edition

Erickson, Russell E.

A toad for Tuesday; pictures by Lawrence Di Fiori. Lothrop, Lee & Shepard Bks. 1974 63p il lib bdg $12.88 (2-4) **Fic**

1. Toads—Fiction 2. Owls—Fiction 3. Mice—Fiction 4. Friendship—Fiction

ISBN 0-688-51569-X LC 73-19900

Warton the toad sets out on skis to visit his aunt during the winter. After rescuing a mouse from danger, he is captured by an owl who threatens to eat him in five days. During this interval, events occur which create friendship between the toad, the owl and a group of mice

The book "stresses friendship, caring for and helping others without motivational self-gain. . . . Real feelings are expressed in this story. Fine illustrations." Child Book Rev Serv

Another available title about Warton and Morton is: Warton and the contest (1968)

Estes, Eleanor, 1906-1988

Ginger Pye. Harcourt Brace 1951 250p il $12.95; pa $3.95 (4-6) **Fic**

1. Dogs—Fiction

ISBN 0-15-230930-6; 0-15-230933-0 (pa) LC 51-10446

Also available ABC-CLIO large print edition $14.95 (ISBN 1-55736-056-1)

Awarded the Newbery Medal, 1952

The Pyes lived in the little New England town of Cranbury. There was Mr. Pye, a famous ornithologist, his pretty young wife, their two children Jerry and Rachel, and Gracie the cat. Later there was the dog Ginger. The story is about the loss of Ginger, and his return to his beloved family, through the cleverness of Uncle Benny, aged three

"Not many writers can give us the mind and heart of a child as Eleanor Estes can. . . . [She] has illustrated [the book] with her own drawings—vivid, amusing sketches that point up and confirm the atmosphere of the story. It is a book to read and reread." Saturday Rev

Followed by: Pinky Pye, entered below

The hundred dresses; illustrated by Louis Slobodkin. Harcourt Brace Jovanovich 1944 80p il $12.95; pa $4.95 (4-6) **Fic**

ISBN 0-15-237374-8; 0-15-642350-2 (pa) LC 44-8963

A Newbery Medal honor book, 1945

"The 100 dresses are just dream dresses, pictures Wanda Petronski has drawn, but she describes them in self-defense as she appears daily in the same faded blue dress. Not until Wanda, snubbed and unhappy, moves away leaving her pictures at school for an art contest, do her classmates realize their cruelty." Books for Deaf Child

"Written with great simplicity it reveals, in a measure, the pathos of human relationships and the suffering of those who are different. Mr. Slobodkin's water-colors interpret the mood of the story and fulfill the quality of the text." N Y Public Libr

The Moffats; illustrated by Louis Slobodkin. Harcourt Brace Jovanovich 1941 290p il $14.95; Dell pa $3.25 (4-6) **Fic**

1. Family life—Fiction

ISBN 0-15-255095-X; 0-440-40177-1 (pa) LC 41-51893

"The Moffats—Mama and her four children—have a fun-filled and satisfying life in spite of being poor. Their little house on New Dollar Street in Cranbury, Connecticut, is the scene of constant activity and surprises. A captivating family story with highly individual characters. Each chapter is a separate episode, suitable for reading aloud." Hodges. Books for Elem Sch Libr

Estes, Eleanor, 1906-1988—*Continued*

Other available titles about the Moffats are:
The middle Moffat (1942)
The Moffat Museum (1983)
Rufus M. (1943)

Pinky Pye; illustrated by Edward Ardizzone. Harcourt Brace Jovanovich 1958 192p il $10.95; pa $1.75 (4-6) **Fic**

1. Cats—Fiction
ISBN 0-15-262076-1; 0-15-671840-5 (pa) LC 58-5708

Sequel to: Ginger Pye, entered above

"Another story about the Pye family who, with cat and dog and four-year-old Uncle Benny, go to Fire Island for a summer of bird watching. The family acquires a new member: a small black kitten who can use the typewriter. . . . The book has the same spontaneity, humor and sincerity as other books by Estes." Bull Cent Child Books

"Edward Ardizzone, though clothing the family in a vaguely British fashion, catches the spirit of every scene marvelously." N Y Her Trib Books

The witch family; illustrated by Edward Ardizzone. Harcourt Brace Jovanovich 1960 186p il hardcover o.p. paperback available $4.95 (2-5) **Fic**

1. Witches—Fiction 2. Halloween—Fiction
ISBN 0-15-298572-7 (pa) LC 60-11250

"Two little girls become intimately involved in the lively 'abracadabra' doings of a family of witches when, through their drawings and imagination, they conjure up wicked Old Witch, the head witch of all the witches, and banish her to a bare, bleak glass hill." Booklist

"Ardizzone's pictures add the perfect illustration to a book full of wonderful fun, excitement, and humor." Libr J

Farjeon, Eleanor, 1881-1965

The glass slipper. Lippincott 1986 c1955 215p $11.95; lib bdg $11.89 (3-6) **Fic**

1. Fairy tales
ISBN 0-397-32180-5; 0-397-32181-3 (lib bdg)
LC 85-45853

A reissue of the title first published 1955 in the United Kingdom, 1956 in the United States. Copyright renewed 1984

"One of the most famous of fairy tales in the Western world—the Cinderella story—is here retold by a talented storyteller. . . . The result is an expanded version—almost novel length—alive with amusing characters and rich in background detail." N Y Times Book Rev

Farley, Walter, 1915-1989

The Black Stallion; illustrated by Keith Ward. Random House 1941 275p il lib bdg $10.99; pa $2.95 (4 and up) **Fic**

1. Horses—Fiction
ISBN 0-394-90601-2 (lib bdg); 0-394-83609-X (pa)
LC 41-21882

A boy and a wild black stallion, the only survivors from a shipwreck, live for a time on an uninhabited island, and somehow manage to exist until they are rescued. Back in the United States the boy and a retired jockey tame the horse and race him to the entire satisfaction of all concerned

Other available titles about the Black Stallion are:
The Black Stallion and Flame (1960)
The Black Stallion and Satan (1949)
The Black Stallion and the girl (1971)
The Black Stallion challenged! (1964)
The Black Stallion legend (1983)
The Black Stallion mystery (1957)
The Black Stallion picture book (1979)
The Black Stallion returns (1945)
The Black Stallion revolts (1953)
The Black Stallion's courage (1956)
The Black Stallion's filly (1952)
The Black Stallion's ghost (1969)
The Black Stallion's sulky colt (1954)
Son of the Black Stallion (1947)
The young Black Stallion (1989)

Ferguson, Alane

Cricket and the crackerbox kid. Bradbury Press 1990 179p $13.95 (4-6) **Fic**

1. Friendship—Fiction 2. Dogs—Fiction 3. School stories
ISBN 0-02-734525-4 LC 89-39291

Pampered eleven-year-old rich kid Cricket thinks she has finally found a friend in Dominic, who lives in the low-income houses called crackerboxes, until they quarrel over ownership of a dog and their classroom becomes a courtroom to decide who is right

"What could be a clinical case-study approach is shaded by Ferguson's light touch. Her well-constructed plot contains thoughtful detail on both sides, and the characters are given realistic emotions. The interwoven themes of friendship, justice, and doing the right thing make this book ideal for classroom discussion." Booklist

Field, Rachel, 1894-1942

Calico bush; with the original wood engravings by Allen Lewis. Macmillan 1987 c1931 201p il $12.95; Dell pa $3.50 (4 and up) **Fic**

1. Frontier and pioneer life—Fiction 2. United States—History—1600-1775, Colonial period—Fiction
ISBN 0-02-734610-2; 0-440-40368-5 (pa)
LC 66-19095

A Newbery Medal honor book, 1932

First published 1931; this is a reissue of the 1966 edition

Maine, in the 1740s, is the setting for this story of a French 13-year-old "bound-out girl" who faces hardship, danger, and tragedy with courage and love

Hitty: her first hundred years; with illustrations by Dorothy P. Lathrop. Macmillan 1929 207p il $13.95; Dell pa $3.95 (4 and up) **Fic**

1. Dolls—Fiction
ISBN 0-02-734840-7; 0-440-40337-5 (pa)
LC 29-22704

Awarded the Newbery Medal, 1930

"Hitty, a doll of real character carved from a block of mountain ash, writes a story of her eventful life from the security of an antique-shop window which she shares with Theobold, a rather over-bearing cat. . . . The

Field, Rachel, 1894-1942—*Continued*
illustrations by Dorothy P. Lathrop are the happiest extension of the text." Cleveland Public Libr

Fine, Anne
My war with Goggle-eyes. Little, Brown 1989 166p $13.95; Bantam Bks. pa $2.95 (5 and up) **Fic**
1. Single parent family—Fiction
ISBN 0-316-28314-2; 0-316-28314-2 (pa) LC 88-31420
"Joy Street books"
Kitty is not pleased with her mother's boyfriend, especially his views on the anti-nuclear issue, until unexpected events prompt her, after all, to help him find his place in the family
"Fine's gentle anti-nuclear subplot never overshadows the main theme of acceptance and tolerance in relationships. Her characters are neither fanatics nor buffoons, but people with a wide range of feelings and reactions; the dialogue is especially expressive and full of feeling. A book that is thoroughly delightful to read." SLJ

Fitzgerald, John D., 1907-1988
The Great Brain; illustrated by Mercer Mayer. Dial Bks. for Young Readers 1967 175p lib bdg $11.89; Dell pa $3.25 (4 and up) **Fic**
1. Utah—Fiction
ISBN 0-8037-3076-4 (lib bdg); 0-440-43071-2 (pa) LC 67-22252
Also available ABC-CLIO large print edition $14.95 (ISBN 1-55736-102-9)
"The Great Brain was Tom Dennis ('T.D.') Fitzgerald, age ten, of Adenville, Utah; the time, 1896. . . . This autobiographical yarn is spun by his brother John Dennis ('J.D.'), age seven . . . who can tell stories about himself and his family with enough tall-tale exaggeration to catch the imagination." Horn Book
Other available titles about the Great Brain are:
The Great Brain at the academy (1972)
The Great Brain does it again (1975)
The Great Brain reforms (1973)
Me and my little brain (1971)
More adventures of the Great Brain (1969)
The return of the Great Brain (1974)

Fitzhugh, Louise, 1928-1974
Harriet the spy; written and illustrated by Louise Fitzhugh. Harper & Row 1964 298p il $14.95; lib bdg $14.89; Dell pa $3.50 (4 and up) **Fic**
1. School stories
ISBN 0-06-021910-6; 0-06-021911-4 (lib bdg); 0-440-43447-5 (pa) LC 64-19711
Also available ABC-CLIO large print edition $13.95 (ISBN 1-55736-012-X)
"Harriet roams her Manhattan neighborhood spying on everyone who interests her and writing down her opinions in a notebook. When fellow sixth-graders find her notes and read her caustic remarks about them, she is ostracized until she finds a way to make a place for herself in the school." Hodges. Books for Elem Sch Libr
"A very, very funny and a very, very affective story; the characterizations are marvelously shrewd, the pictures of urban life and of the power structure of the sixth grade class are realistic." Bull Cent Child Books

The long secret; written and illustrated by Louise Fitzhugh. Harper & Row 1965 275p il $13.70; lib bdg $13.89; Dell pa $3.50 (4 and up) **Fic**
ISBN 0-06-021410-4; 0-06-021411-2 (lib bdg); 0-440-44977-4 (pa) LC 65-23370
Sequel to: Harriet the spy, entered above
Investigating a mysterious series of anonymous notes warning various members of the small Long Island beach community to mend their ways, Harriet learns that her summer friend, Beth Ellen Hansen, is the culprit

Nobody's family is going to change. Farrar, Straus & Giroux 1974 221p il $13.95; pa $3.50 (5 and up) **Fic**
1. Family life—Fiction 2. Blacks—Fiction
ISBN 0-374-35539-8; 0-374-45523-6 (pa) LC 74-19152
This story about a conventional middle class black family focuses on the ambition of eleven-year-old Emma to be a lawyer, and her brother Willie's desire to become a dancer despite strong parental disapproval
"There's some wit and certainly much sophistication in the writing, a metallic polish that is right for the setting and the people." Bull Cent Child Books

Fleischman, Paul
The birthday tree; pictures by Marcia Sewall. Harper & Row 1979 unp il lib bdg $12.89 (2-4) **Fic**
1. Trees—Fiction
ISBN 0-06-021916-5 LC 78-22155
"After losing three sons to the sea, a sailor and his wife pack their meager belongings and head inland. Soon a son, Jack, is born and they attempt to root him to the land via a seedling planted to celebrate the event. 'The Birthday Tree' and Jack flourish until the boy runs off to sea and is wrecked upon a desert island. . . . The style is fine for independent reading but the imagery would find its due in the hands of a good storyteller. Marcia Sewall's blunt-faced characters and sparse illustrations evoke the rustic spirit of the words. The pencil sketches and subdued backgrounds are simple reinforcements for a well-told tale." SLJ

Finzel the farsighted; illustrated by Marcia Sewall. Dutton 1983 46p il $11.95 (2-4) **Fic**
1. Fortune telling—Fiction
ISBN 0-525-44057-7 LC 83-1416
"A Unicorn Book"
"Finzel can predict the future, but his eyesight is so poor that he is chronically in error about the present. . . . Finzel tells the fortune of Pavel, the simpleton, but there's a mixup: Pavel gets someone else's fortune and becomes erroneously convinced that he's deathly ill. Next, Pavel's greedy brother Osip tricks Finzel into revealing the location of his treasure and steals it. But this time Finzel's mistake reverses the trickster's trick and Osip is caught." SLJ
"The clever story is neatly told with a judicious blend

Fleischman, Paul—*Continued*
of narrative and dialogue. Sewall's charcoal sketches show quick lines and faces with distinct character." Booklist

The Half-a-Moon Inn; illustrated by Kathy Jacobi. Harper & Row 1980 88p il lib bdg $12.89 (4-6) **Fic**

1. Kidnapping—Fiction 2. Physically handicapped children—Fiction 3. Hotels, motels, etc.—Fiction
ISBN 0-06-021918-1 LC 79-2010

"A mute boy, Aaron, leaves the cottage he shares with his mother to search for her when she is days late returning from market. Lost in a blizzard, he seeks shelter at the Half-A-Moon Inn. Here the evil crone Miss Grackle, who owns the place, forces Aaron to abet her thieving. The boy tries to warn guests against Miss Grackle but none of them can read his hastily written notes. . . . The ending is a terrific twist." Publ Wkly

"Despite the grimness of Aaron's predicament, accentuated by dark scratch drawings of figures in grotesque proportion, the story's tone is hopeful and its style concrete and brisk. Elements of folklore exist in the story's characterization, structure, and narration." SLJ

Saturnalia. Harper & Row 1990 113p $12.95; lib bdg $12.89 (5 and up) **Fic**

1. Narraganset Indians—Fiction 2. Apprentices—Fiction 3. Prejudices—Fiction 4. Boston (Mass.)—Fiction
ISBN 0-06-021912-2; 0-06-021913-0 (lib bdg)
LC 89-36380

"A Charlotte Zolotow book"

This novel is set in Boston in 1681. Fourteen-year-old William, a Narraganset Indian captured six years earlier in a raid, is apprenticed to Mr. Currie, a printer. "William's accomplishments enrage Mr. Baggot, the tithingman whose grandsons were killed by Indians. . . . William often wanders the streets after curfew playing an Indian melody on a small bone flute in the hope of finding his lost brother. One night, the melody does bring him to an uncle and young cousin, now servants of a cruel eyeglass maker. When the eyeglass maker is found murdered, . . . [Mr. Baggot] accuses William of the crime." Horn Book

"While William is the main focus of the story, there are several bubbling subplots that illuminate the texture of Puritan colonial life. . . . Especially welcome as a support for history units, this absorbing story exemplifies Fleischman's graceful, finely honed use of the English language." Booklist

Fleischman, Sid, 1920-

By the Great Horn Spoon! illustrated by Eric von Schmidt. Little, Brown 1963 193p il $14.95; pa $4.95 (4-6) **Fic**

1. California—Gold discoveries—Fiction
ISBN 0-316-28577-3; 0-316-28612-5 (pa)
LC 63-13459

"An Atlantic Monthy Press book"

"Jack and his aunt's butler, Praiseworthy, stow away on a ship bound for California. Here are their adventures aboard ship and in the Gold Rush of '49." Publ Wkly

Chancy and the grand rascal; illustrated by Eric von Schmidt. Little, Brown 1966 179p il $14.95; pa $4.95 (4-6) **Fic**

1. Frontier and pioneer life—Fiction
ISBN 0-316-28575-7; 0-316-26012-6 (pa)
LC 66-14903

"An Atlantic Monthly Press book"

"A young boy sets out to find his brothers and sisters, separated by the death of their parents in the Civil War, and meets a 'Grand Rascal' who leads him through many adventures in the battle of wits and colorful tall-talking." Bruno. Books for Sch Libr, 1968

"This is one of those rare children's books where language and story are one. It is a world of hyperbole and homely detail, an ebullient, frontier, Bunyanesque world." Christ Sci Monit

The ghost on Saturday night; illustrated by Eric von Schmidt. Little, Brown 1974 57p il $13.95 (3-5) **Fic**

1. Robbers and outlaws—Fiction
ISBN 0-316-28583-8 LC 73-14751

"An Atlantic Monthly Press book"

Opie is working as a guide in order to earn $17.59 for a saddle. He gets the saddle free, however, when he guides a fraudulent ghost-raising bank robber straight into the sheriff's arms

"The short scenario, illustrated with figures as overstated and caricatured as those in the text, is filled with the same kind of hyperbole, piquant phrasing, and bravura that have made the author's other books so delightful and so much fun to read." Horn Book

Humbug Mountain; illustrated by Eric von Schmidt. Little, Brown 1978 149p il o.p. paperback available $4.95 (4-6) **Fic**

1. West (U.S.)—Fiction 2. Frontier and pioneer life—Fiction
ISBN 0-316-28613-3 LC 78-9419

"An Atlantic Monthly Press book"

"Moving from place to place with his family at the turn of the century . . . Wiley finds himself in the midst of outlaws and con-men in what his grandfather has said is a prosperous city on the Missouri River but which turns out to be empty of any amenities—as well as of Grandpa. . . . False rumors of gold and business and building boom abound and the rascals almost win—but Grandpa shows up just in time, bringing riches and rescue." SLJ

"There's a lot going on here. Twists, turns, unexpected surprises. The style is straightforward and the spoken language is Twainish." N Y Times Book Rev

McBroom tells the truth; illustrated by Walter Lorraine. Little, Brown 1981 42p il $12.45 (3-5) **Fic**

1. Farm life—Fiction
ISBN 0-316-28550-1 LC 81-1035

"An Atlantic Monthly Press book"

A reissue with new illustrations of the title first published 1966 by Norton

"A hilarious yarn about a New England farmer who is duped into buying a piece of land 80 acres deep with a pond on top. When a freak drought dries up the pond, however, McBroom discovers the soil underneath is so

Fleischman, Sid, 1920-—*Continued*
fertile it will produce four crops of vegetables a day. Beans grow so fast that McBroom has to step lively to keep from getting entangled in the vines and his 11 children have great fun riding pumpkins and using corn stalks as pogo sticks." Booklist

Other available titles about McBroom are:
McBroom and the big wind (1967)
McBroom and the great race (1980)
McBroom tells a lie (1976)
McBroom's almanac (1984)

The midnight horse; illustrations by Peter Sis. Greenwillow Bks. 1990 84p il $12.95 (3-6) **Fic**

1. Magicians—Fiction 2. Ghosts—Fiction 3. Orphans—Fiction
ISBN 0-688-09441-4 LC 89-23441

Touch enlists the help of The Great Chaffalo, a ghostly magician, to thwart his great-uncle's plans to put Touch into the orphan house and swindle The Red Raven Inn away from Miss Sally

"The prose is colorful and earthy. . . . Good and bad are clearly defined, a happy ending is never in doubt, and the reader must accept in good faith the capricious appearances of a deceased but still-practicing magician. The enjoyment of the book lies in Fleischman's exuberant narrative flow and his ingenuity in dispatching his scoundrels. Sis's black-and-white illustrations enhance the earnest if tongue-in-cheek battle of good against evil." Horn Book

Mr. Mysterious & Company; illustrated by Eric von Schmidt. Little, Brown 1962 151p il $14.95; pa $4.95 (4-6) **Fic**

1. Magic—Fiction 2. Frontier and pioneer life—Fiction
ISBN 0-316-28578-1; 0-316-28614-1 (pa) LC 62-7105

"An Atlantic Monthly Press book"

"An engaging story of a traveling magic show during the 1880's in which Pa is Mr. Mysterious and the whole family performs. A sound philosophy of good will and common sense underlies their sheer, happy bravado as they play the frontier towns westward to California." Chicago Public Libr

The whipping boy; illustrations by Peter Sis. Greenwillow Bks. 1986 90p il $11.75 (5 and up) **Fic**

1. Robbers and outlaws—Fiction 2. Adventure and adventurers—Fiction
ISBN 0-688-06216-4 LC 85-17555

Also available ABC-CLIO large print edition $14.95 (ISBN 1-55736-115-0)

Awarded the Newbery Medal, 1987

"A round tale of adventure and humor, this follows the fortunes of Prince Roland (better known as Prince Brat) and his whipping boy, Jemmy, who has received all the hard knocks for the prince's mischief. When Roland decides to run away from boring palace life, he also decides that he requires Jemmy's assistance in carrying his lunch basket. The two are shortly apprehended by scoundrels, who kidnap them and place Jemmy in a tight spot between their greedy demands of the king and the king's assumption that Jemmy is the kidnapper. . . . There's not a moment's lag in pace, and the stock characters, from Hold-Your-Nose Billy to Betsy's dancing bear Petunia, have enough inventive twists to project a lively air to it all." Bull Cent Child Books

Fleming, Ian, 1908-1964

Chitty-Chitty-Bang-Bang; the magical car; illustrated by John Burningham. Random House 1964 111p il o.p.; Amereon reprint available $15.95 (4-6) **Fic**

1. Automobiles—Fiction
ISBN 0-88411-983-1 LC 64-21282

"An ingenious nonsense tale about an English family and their remarkable old car. Gifted with the ability to navigate land, sea, and air, Chitty-Chitty-Bang-Bang rescues the family from floods, traffic jams, and gangsters." Hodges. Books for Elem Sch Libr

Foley, Patricia

John and the fiddler; illustrated by Marcia Sewall. Harper & Row 1990 63p il $12.95; lib bdg $12.85 (3-5) **Fic**

1. Violinists, violoncellists, etc.—Fiction
2. Friendship—Fiction 3. Death—Fiction
ISBN 0-06-021841-X; 0-06-021842-8 (lib bdg)
LC 89-34514

John befriends Sean MacLoegaire, an old violin maker who teaches him the beauty of music and friendship. When Sean dies of pneumonia, he leaves his fiddle to John

"Told with simplicity and grace, the story . . . has the power of deeply held memory. Sewall's unadorned line-and-wash drawings, as well as the book's pristine layout, are the perfect accompaniment to the purity of a tale whose messages about the bonds of fellowship will be instinctively understood by children." Booklist

Fonteyn, Dame Margot, 1919-1991

Swan lake; as told by Margot Fonteyn and illustrated by Trina Schart Hyman. Harcourt Brace Jovanovich 1988 unp il $14.95 (3-5) **Fic**

1. Ballets—Stories, plots, etc. 2. Fairy tales
ISBN 0-15-200600-1 LC 87-7573

"Gulliver books"

"In the story, Prince Siegfried has fallen in love with Odette, a queen turned swan by an evil owl-magician. When the owl-magician's daughter appears at a ball disguised as Odette, Siegfried pledges his troth, only to discover the deception too late." Bull Cent Child Books

"Both prose and paintings are haunting in their elegant evocation of this sad, mysterious tale. An uncommonly fine ballet book for children, this communicates not only the story but a touch of the magic as well." Booklist

Forbes, Esther, 1891-1967

Johnny Tremain; a novel for old & young; with illustrations by Lynd Ward. Houghton Mifflin 1943 256p il $13.95; Dell pa $3.50 (5 and up) **Fic**

1. United States—History—1775-1783, Revolution—Fiction 2. Boston (Mass.)—Fiction
ISBN 0-395-06766-9; 0-440-44250-8 (pa)
LC 43-16483

Awarded the Newbery Medal, 1944

This story of a young Boston apprentice during the exciting year of the Tea Party, culminates in the Battle of Lexington. It is a story of Boston in revolt—and a very young man in love—as seen through the experiences of a courier for the revolutionary Committee of Public Safety

"This is Esther Forbes at her brilliant best. She has drawn the character of Johnny Tremain with such sympathy and insight that he may well take his place with Jim Hawkins, Huck Finn and other young immortals. . . . Youth, particularly, will get from it [a] live and clear and significant picture of a great period in American history." Book Week

Fox, Paula

How many miles to Babylon? a novel; illustrated by Paul Giovanopoulos. Bradbury Press 1980 c1967 117p il $12.95 (4-6) **Fic**

1. Blacks—Fiction 2. Brooklyn (New York, N.Y.)—Fiction
ISBN 0-02-735590-X LC 79-25802

First published 1967 by D. White Co.

Ten-year-old James Douglas, a black boy who lives in Brooklyn, knows his mother is in the hospital but fantasizes that she has gone to Africa, home of his ancestors. He runs away from his aunts to find his mother. After a harrowing encounter with three dog thieves, he returns home to find his mother back in their room

"A realistic little novel of ghetto life in Brooklyn." N Y Public Libr. Black Exper in Child Books

A likely place; illustrated by Edward Ardizzone. Macmillan 1987 c1967 57p il $10.95 (3-5) **Fic**

1. Baby sitters—Fiction
ISBN 0-02-735761-9 LC 87-5542

A reissue of the title first published 1967

Both at home and at school, nine-year-old "Lewis suffers from the over-solicitude of hovering parents and concerned teachers. The big change comes when his parents go off on a trip, leaving him in the care of Miss Fitchlow, who practices yoga, eats yoghurt, and allows him to go to the park alone." Libr J

"Paula Fox knows how children talk, think and act. Edward Ardizzone's illustrations convey in masterly fashion the oddities of character and situation that bring perplexity, purpose and wonder into an imaginative child's daily life." N Y Times Book Rev

One-eyed cat; a novel. Bradbury Press 1984 216p $11.95; Dell pa $3.50 (5 and up) **Fic**

1. Firearms—Fiction 2. Cats—Fiction
ISBN 0-02-735540-3; 0-440-46641-5 (pa)
LC 84-10964

A Newbery Medal honor book, 1985

"Told by his father that he's too young for the air rifle an uncle gives him as a bithday present, Ned sneaks the gun out one night and takes a shot at a shadowy creature. He is subsequently smitten with guilt when he sees a one-eyed feral cat, and the knowledge that he may have been responsible as well as [having disobeyed] his father colors all his days." Bull Cent Child Books

The author's "writing is sure. Her characterization is outstanding, and she creates a strong sense of place and mood. The relationships among the characters are complex and ring true, while often filling readers with a sense of despair. 'One-Eyed Cat' is a deep and demanding psychological novel. Its slow pace may limit its appeal, but those who persevere will be rewarded." SLJ

The slave dancer; a novel; with illustrations by Eros Keith. Bradbury Press 1973 176p il $13.95; Dell pa $3.25 (5 and up) **Fic**

1. Slave trade—Fiction 2. Sea stories
ISBN 0-02-735560-8; 0-440-96132-7 (pa)
LC 73-80642

Awarded the Newbery Medal, 1974

"Thirteen-year-old Jessie Bollier is kidnapped from New Orleans and taken aboard a slave ship. Cruelly tyrannized by the ship's captain, Jessie is made to play his fife for the slaves during the exercise period into which they are forced in order to keep them fit for sale. When a hurricane destroys the ship, Jessie and Ras, a young slave, survive. They are helped by an old black man who finds them, spirits Ras north to freedom, and assists Jessie to return to his family." Shapiro. Fic for Youth. 2d edition

The stone-faced boy; illustrated by Donald A. Mackay. Bradbury Press 1968 106p il $12.95; Macmillan pa $3.95 (4-6) **Fic**

1. Brothers and sisters—Fiction 2. Family life—Fiction
ISBN 0-02-735570-5; 0-689-71127-1 (pa) LC 68-9053

"The story is a perceptive character study of a lonely, timid middle child in a family of five self-possessed, individualistic children. To save himself from teasing by classmates and siblings, Gus Oliver has learned to mask his feelings so well that he has lost all ability to show emotion. Even the startling and unexpected arrival of an eccentric, outspoken great-aunt appears to leave Gus unmoved but the night his sister inveigles him into going out in the dark and the cold to rescue a stray dog, he gains a new-found confidence in himself." Booklist

The village by the sea. Orchard Bks. 1988 147p $13.95; lib bdg $13.99; Dell pa $3.50 (5 and up) **Fic**

1. Aunts—Fiction
ISBN 0-531-05788-7; 0-531-08388-8 (lib bdg); 0-440-40299-9 (pa) LC 88-60099

"A Richard Jackson book"

Fox, Paula—*Continued*

"Emma is sent to stay with her fractious aunt and eccentric uncle, where she experiences the devastating effects of envy and the power of love and forgiveness." SLJ

"Fox's style is compressed without seeming dense, each scene and image allowed space for clean effect. Although the emotional layering is sophisticated, the viewpoint is unfalteringly that of the child. The novel is easy to read and complex to consider, an encounter that moves the reader from Gothic narrative suspense to compassionate illumination of the dark in human nature." Bull Cent Child Books

Fritz, Jean

The cabin faced west; illustrated by Feodor Rojankovsky. Coward-McCann 1958 124p il $8.95; Puffin Bks. pa $3.95 (3-6) **Fic**

1. Scott, Ann Hamilton—Fiction 2. Frontier and pioneer life—Fiction 3. Pennsylvania—Fiction
ISBN 0-698-20016-0; 0-14-032256-6 (pa)
LC 57-10714

"Ann is unhappy when her family moves from Gettysburg to the Pennsylvania frontier, but she soon finds friends and begins to see that there is much to enjoy about her new home—including a visit from General Washington." Hodges. Books for Elem Sch Libr

Early thunder; illustrated by Lynd Ward. Coward-McCann 1967 255p il $9.95; Puffin Bks. pa $3.95 (6 and up) **Fic**

1. United States—History—1600-1775, Colonial period—Fiction 2. Salem (Mass.)—Fiction
ISBN 0-698-20036-5; 0-14-032259-0 (pa)
LC 67-24217

"The political conflict in Salem, Mass., 1774-75, is realized in the agony of David, the 14-year-old son of a Tory doctor, who struggles to determine where his own allegiance lies." Coughlan. Creating Independence, 1763-1789

"The period details and the historical background are excellent, both in themselves and in the easy way they are incorporated into the story." Bull Cent Child Books

George Washington's breakfast; Paul Galdone drew the pictures. Coward-McCann 1969 unp il o.p. paperback available $5.95 (2-4) **Fic**

1. Washington, George, 1732-1799—Fiction
ISBN 0-698-20616-9 (pa) LC 69-11475

George W. Allen "was named for George Washington and he had the same birthday. It made him feel almost related. So related he wanted to know everything he could about George Washington. . . . [He especially wanted to] know what George Washington ate for breakfast. He got his grandmother to promise she'd cook George Washington's breakfast if he found out what it was, and he was going to find out—no matter what." About the book

"Paul Galdone's red, white, and blue illustrations don't equal many of his earlier ones, but they are appropriate to the story and, like it, are not overstated. Younger and reluctant readers may enjoy this, as it offers a painless way of picking up information." SLJ

Gage, Wilson, 1922-

Mike's toads; illustrated by Glen Rounds. Greenwillow Bks. 1990 85p il $12.95 **Fic**

ISBN 0-688-08834-1 LC 88-34907

A newly illustrated edition of the title first published 1970 by World Pub. Co.

A sixth-grade boy volunteers his brother's services once too often without consulting him and ends up having to spend the summer vacation caring for a friend's toads himself

Gannett, Ruth Stiles, 1923-

My father's dragon; illustrated by Ruth Chrisman Gannett. Random House 1948 86p il lib bdg $12.99; pa $3.95 (1-4) **Fic**

1. Dragons—Fiction 2. Fantastic fiction 3. Animals—Fiction
ISBN 0-394-91438-4 (lib bdg); 0-394-89048-5 (pa)
LC 48-6521

A Newbery Medal honor book, 1949

This is a combination of fantasy, sense, and nonsense. It describes the adventures of a small boy, Elmer Elevator, who befriended an old alley cat and in return heard the story of the captive baby dragon on Wild Island. Right away Elmer decided to free the dragon. The tale of Elmer's voyage to Tangerina and his arrival on Wild Island, his encounters with various wild animals, and his subsequent rescue of the dragon follows

Followed by: Elmer and the dragon (1950) and The dragons of Blueland (1951)

Gardam, Jane

The hollow land; illustrated by Janet Rawlins. Greenwillow Bks. 1982 c1981 152p il $10.25 (5 and up) **Fic**

1. Farm life—Fiction 2. Friendship—Fiction 3. Great Britain—Fiction
ISBN 0-688-00873-9 LC 81-6620

First published 1981 in the United Kingdom

The episodes in this story about two families "focus on the relationship between the Teesdales, a local farming family, and the Batemans, a London family who rents a house from the Teesdales and continues to return for part of every year. The enduring friendship between Bell Teesdale, a boy of eight at the beginning of the first narrative, and Harry Bateman, two or three years younger, rounds out the story." Horn Book

"With humor and mystery and realistic detail Gardam lovingly evokes the Cumbrian fells area in northern England." SLJ

A long way from Verona. Macmillan 1988 190p $12.95 (6 and up) **Fic**

1. World War, 1939-1945—Fiction 2. Great Britain—Fiction
ISBN 0-02-735781-3 LC 88-5254

A reissue of the title first published 1971

"Using the matter-of-fact tone of an aspiring author writing in her diary, the book gives us a meaty slice of a young girl's life in World War II England. Jessica is a no-nonsense teenager who wisely and humorously observes and records her own struggle for autonomy in the face of staid family, eccentric teachers, fickle class-

Gardam, Jane—*Continued*
mates, a befuddled boyfried, and even a surprised prisoner of war." Voice Youth Advocates

Gardiner, John Reynolds, 1944-
Stone Fox; illustrated by Marcia Sewall. Crowell 1980 81p il $11.95; lib bdg $11.89; pa $2.95 (2-5) **Fic**

1. Sled dog racing—Fiction 2. Dogs—Fiction
ISBN 0-690-03983-2; 0-690-03984-0 (lib bdg); 0-06-440132-4 (pa) LC 79-7895

"When his usually spry grandfather won't get out of bed Willy searches for a remedy. Back taxes are the problem and the only way to get the money is to win the dogsled race. Stone Fox, a towering Indian who has never lost a race, is primary competition. Both want the prize money for the government—Willy for taxes and Stone Fox to buy his native land back." SLJ

This story "is rooted in a Rocky Mountain legend, a locale faithfully represented in Sewall's wonderful drawings. . . . In Gardiner's bardic chronicle, the tension is teeth rattling, with the tale flying to a conclusion that is almost unbearably moving, one readers won't soon forget." Publ Wkly

Garfield, Leon
The December Rose. Viking Kestrel 1987 c1986 207p $12.95; Penguin Bks. pa $3.95 (5 and up) **Fic**

1. Adventure and adventurers—Fiction 2. London (England)—Fiction
ISBN 0-670-81054-1; 0-14-032070-9 (pa)

Also available G.K. Hall large print edition $14.95 (ISBN 0-7451-0588-2)

First published 1986 in the United Kingdom

"Barnacle, the chimney sweep's boy, got his name because of his amazing holding powers. But one day his grip gives out and he tumbles into a room where a nefarious quartet is discussing a dastardly plot. Unwittingly, he grabs a decorative locket embossed with an eagle and runs out of the room. Little does he know that the locket is the key to an operation that involves espionage and murder. . . . Garfield's swiftly moving story and finely tuned Victorian setting will quickly enmesh readers in the events. The authentic English dialect may trip up a few, and the mystery itself becomes a bit convoluted, but better readers will stick with this to the end and thoroughly enjoy the adventure." Booklist

Young Nick and Jubilee; illustrated by Ted Lewin. Delacorte Press 1989 134p il $13.95 (5 and up) **Fic**

1. Orphans—Fiction 2. Brothers and sisters—Fiction 3. Robbers and outlaws—Fiction 4. London (England)—Fiction
ISBN 0-385-29777-7 LC 89-1604

"Orphaned siblings (Nick is ten, Jubilee nine) live precariously in 18th century London, and, through the offices of Mr. Owen (a thief) are accepted as scholars at a charity school. The arrangement benefits the children and Owen, whom they mendaciously claim as their father. In the Dickensian picture of a segment of Westminster life, it is almost inevitable that a tenderness enters the relationship and fosters affection between Owen and the children." Bull Cent Child Books

"With its rich London background and lively flow of Cockney speech patterns, the story follows the two children through their madcap adventures to a heartwarming conclusion." Horn Book

Gates, Doris, 1901-
Blue willow; illustrated by Paul Lantz. Viking 1940 172p il $13.95; Penguin Bks. pa $3.95 (4 and up) **Fic**

1. Migrant labor—Fiction 2. California—Fiction
ISBN 0-670-17557-9; 0-14-030924-1 (pa) LC 40-32435

"Having to move from one migrant camp to another intensifies Janey Larkin's desire for a permanent home, friends, and school. The only beautiful possession the family has is a blue willow plate handed down from generation to generation. It is a reminder of happier days in Texas and represents dreams and promises for a better future. Reading about this itinerant family's ways of life, often filled with despair and yet always hopeful, leaves little room for the reader's indifference." Read Ladders for Hum Relat. 6th edition

Gauch, Patricia Lee
This time, Tempe Wick? illustrated by Margot Tomes. Coward, McCann & Geoghegan 1974 43p il $6.95 (3-5) **Fic**

1. Wick, Tempe—Fiction 2. United States—History—1775-1783, Revolution—Fiction
ISBN 0-698-20300-3 LC 74-79706

Based on a Revolutionary War legend about a real girl, this story tells how Tempe Wick helped feed and clothe the thousands of American soldiers who spent the winters of 1780 and 1781 in Jockey Hollow, New Jersey. When the soldiers mutinied, Tempe had to use her wits and courage to prevent two of them from stealing her horse

"The book presents a realistic and humane view of the war and of the people who fought it. . . . The writing is the perfect vehicle for the illustrations—in the artist's inimitable style—which capture the down-to-earth, unpretentious, and humorous quality of the storytelling." Horn Book

George, Jean Craighead, 1919-
Julie of the wolves; pictures by John Schoenherr. Harper & Row 1972 170p il $14.95; lib bdg $14.89; pa $3.95 (6 and up) **Fic**

1. Inuit—Fiction 2. Wolves—Fiction 3. Arctic regions—Fiction 4. Wilderness survival—Fiction
ISBN 0-06-021943-2; 0-06-021944-0 (lib bdg); 0-06-440058-1 (pa) LC 72-76509

Awarded the Newbery Medal, 1973

"Lost in the Alaskan wilderness thirteen-year old Miyax [Julie in English] an Eskimo girl, is gradually accepted by a pack of Arctic wolves that she comes to love." Booklist

"The superb narration includes authentic descriptions and details of the Eskimo way-of-life and of Eskimo rituals. . . . The story graphically pictures the seasonal changes of the vast trackless tundra and reveals Miyax's awakening to the falseness of the white man's world. Through the eyes of Julie, who survives for months in

George, Jean Craighead, 1919-—*Continued*
the wilderness with the wolves, the author lovingly describes the wildlife: the golden plover, the snow buntings, the snowshoe rabbits, as well as the wolves. She evokes in full measure the terrors of losing directions and facing storms in abysmal temperatures. The whole book has a rare, intense reality which the artist enhances beautifully with animated drawings." Horn Book

My side of the mountain; written and illustrated by Jean Craighead George. Dutton 1988 177p il $12.95; pa $4.95 (5 and up) **Fic**

1. Outdoor life—Fiction 2. Catskill Mountains (N.Y.)—Fiction
ISBN 0-525-44392-4; 0-525-44395-9 (pa)
LC 87-27556

A reissue of the title first published 1959

"Sam Gribley feels closed in by the city and his large family so he runs away to the Catskills and the land that had belonged to his grandfather. He tells the story of his year in the wilderness—the loneliness, the struggle to survive, and the need for companionship." Read Ladders for Hum Relat. 6th edition

"The book is all the more convincing for the excellence of style, the subtlety of humor, aptness of phrases, and touches of poetry. . . . [It] brings a great deal to children; emphasis on the rewards of courage and determination and an abundance of scientific knowledge, certainly, but, far more important, unforgettable experiences in the heart of nature." Horn Book

Followed by: On the far side of the mountain, entered below

On the far side of the mountain; written and illustrated by Jean Craighead George. Dutton Children's Bks. 1990 170p il $13.95 (5 and up) **Fic**

1. Outdoor life—Fiction 2. Catskill Mountains (N.Y.)—Fiction
ISBN 0-525-44563-3 LC 89-25988

Sam's peaceful existence in his wilderness home is disrupted when his sister runs away and his pet falcon is confiscated by a conservation officer

"A tense, believable plot; likable characters; and a strong, positive message about the joys and beauty of the mountains . . . combine to make this story a jewel." Booklist

Water sky. Harper & Row 1987 208p $12.95; lib bdg $12.89; pa $3.95 (5 and up) **Fic**

1. Inuit—Fiction 2. Whaling—Fiction 3. Alaska—Fiction
ISBN 0-06-022198-4; 0-06-022199-2 (lib bdg); 0-06-440202-9 (pa) LC 86-45496

"Because his father had so enjoyed his own stay, when young, with an Eskimo family, he has sent Lincoln to Alaska. Caught up in the beauty of Eskimo culture, the excitement of whale hunting (Eskimo style) and a first shy love affair, Lincoln almost forgets that he is determined to find the beloved uncle who had disappeared in the vicinity. The characters are strong, the plot is smoothly developed, and the setting vividly drawn in a novel imbued with understanding and respect for the rich traditions of Eskimo life." Bull Cent Child Books

Who really killed Cock Robin? an ecological mystery. HarperCollins Pubs. 1991 160p $14.95; lib bdg $14.89 (3-7) **Fic**

1. Ecology—Fiction
ISBN 0-06-021980-7; 0-06-021981-5 (lib bdg)
LC 90-38659

A reprint with a new introduction of the title first published 1971 by Dutton

"The residents of Saddleboro were ecology conscious and none more so than the mayor, whose particular pride was the robins nesting in a hat on his front porch. Nevertheless, despite the carefulness of its citizens, the town is subject to some undetected pollutant, for one day the father robin is found dead. Young Tony Isidoro, assisted by his friend Mary Alice, decides to investigate the cause." Saturday Rev

"A great deal of sound ecological information is presented, and the story is timely and entertaining. Above all, the message is clear: 'The Earth is one ecosystem.'" Horn Book

Giff, Patricia Reilly

The gift of the pirate queen; illustrated by Jenny Rutherford. Delacorte Press 1982 164p il o.p.; Dell paperback available $3.25 (4-6) **Fic**

1. Diabetes—Fiction 2. Irish Americans—Fiction 3. Courage—Fiction
ISBN 0-440-43046-1 (pa) LC 82-70310

"Motherless Grace O'Malley looks forward with some trepidation to the arrival of cousin Fiona from Ireland. Fiona is coming to take care of Grace and her younger sister, Amy, a diabetic who is negligent about her diet. At the same time, Grace is trying to handle another problem; she has broken her teacher's favorite possession, a Christmas bell, and does not have the courage to confess the deed." Booklist

The story "has good pace and balance, believable characters and dialogue, and just enough sentiment to sweeten the tale without making it sugary." Bull Cent Child Books

Loretta P. Sweeny, where are you? illustrated by Anthony Kramer. Delacorte Press 1983 131p il $11.95; lib bdg $11.95; Dell pa $2.95 (4-6) **Fic**

1. Mystery and detective stories
ISBN 0-385-29298-8; 0-385-29299-6 (lib bdg); 0-440-44926-X (pa)

Determined crime-solver Abby finds a purple and orange wallet that she thinks may belong to a murderer

"The action is fast paced, the dialogue snappy, and the humorous plot builds real suspense." SLJ

Love, from the fifth-grade celebrity; illustrated by Leslie Morrill. Delacorte Press 1986 117p il $13.95; Dell pa $2.75 (4-6) **Fic**

1. Friendship—Fiction 2. School stories
ISBN 0-385-29486-7; 0-440-44948-0 (pa)
LC 85-46075

Casey enjoyed Tracy's company during summer vacation but becomes increasingly jealous of her irrepressible new friend when she joins Casey's fifth-grade class

"This pleasant book appealingly presents the ups and

Giff, Patricia Reilly—*Continued*

downs of friendship—how it can founder on jealousy and misunderstanding. A subplot underscores conflicting feelings children may have when a new baby joins the family." Publ Wkly

Gilson, Jamie, 1933-

4B goes wild; illustrated by Linda Strauss Edwards. Lothrop, Lee & Shepard Bks. 1983 160p il lib bdg $12.95; Pocket Bks. pa $2.75 (4-6) **Fic**

1. Camping—Fiction 2. School stories
ISBN 0-688-02236-7 (lib bdg); 0-671-68063-3 (pa) LC 83-948

"Hobie Hanson, a sensitive fourth grader, tells of the time two fourth grade classes went on a three day camping trip. Along with learning about the country, they learned how to work together, and developed new relationships with each other and the adults with them." Child Book Rev Serv

"There are sustaining threads, but the plot is episodic; the writing style is breezy and comic, occasionally a bit cute; the characters are drawn with variable depth and some exaggeration; the dialogue is natural, one of the strong points of Gilson's writing." Bull Cent Child Books

Other available titles about Hobie Hanson are:
Double dog dare (1988)
Hobie Hanson, greatest hero of the mall (1989)
Hobie Hanson, you're weird (1987)
Thirteen ways to sink a sub (1982)

Do bananas chew gum? Lothrop, Lee & Shepard Bks. 1980 158p $11.95; lib bdg $11.88; Pocket Bks. pa $2.95 (4-6) **Fic**

1. Reading—Fiction 2. Learning disabilities—Fiction
ISBN 0-688-41960-7; 0-688-51960-1 (lib bdg); 0-671-70926-7 (pa) LC 80-11414

Able to read and write at only a second grade level, sixth-grader Sam Mott considers himself dumb until he is prompted to cooperate with those who think something can be done about his problem

"This is a wonderfully written story, with real situations and a main character for whom the reader feels anguish at his fear of his learning disability being discovered, but also exultation when he correctly reads a long and difficult word. . . . This is a story that leaves you feeling good." Voice Youth Advocates

Hello, my name is Scrambled Eggs; illustrated by John Wallner. Lothrop, Lee & Shepard Bks. 1985 159p il $11.95; Pocket Bks. pa $2.75 (4 and up) **Fic**

1. Vietnamese—United States—Fiction
ISBN 0-688-04095-0; 0-671-67039-5 (pa) LC 84-10075

"A humorous account of what happens when a Vietnamese family, sponsored by the church, moves into Harvey's home temporarily. To make himself feel more important, Harvey decides to make educating and Americanizing the 12-year-old boy his project. By the end of the book, Tuan is not the only one who has received an education. . . . Child characters are believable and intuitive because they understand the sense of isolation that Tuan's father and grandmother feel about being in a strange culture with a different language, customs and food. Adult characters are well-meaning and kindly but not as strongly portrayed as the children." SLJ

Another available title about Harvey is:
Harvey, the beer can king (1978)

Gipson, Frederick Benjamin, 1903-1973

Old Yeller; [by] Fred Gipson; drawings by Carl Burger. Harper & Row 1956 158p il $19.95; lib bdg $14.89; pa $4.50 (6 and up) **Fic**

1. Dogs—Fiction 2. Texas—Fiction 3. Frontier and pioneer life—Fiction
ISBN 0-06-011545-9; 0-06-011546-7 (lib bdg); 0-06-080002-X (pa) LC 56-8780

A Newbery Medal honor book, 1957

"Travis at fourteen was the man of the family during the hard summer of 1860 when his father drove his herd of cattle from Texas to the Kansas market. It was the summer when an old yellow dog attached himself to the family and won Travis' reluctant friendship. Before the summer was over, Old Yeller proved more than a match for thieving raccoons, fighting bulls, grizzly bears, and mad wolves. This is a skilful tale of a boy's love for a dog as well as a description of a pioneer boyhood and it can't miss with any dog lover." Horn Book

Girion, Barbara, 1937-

A handful of stars. Scribner 1981 179p o.p.; Dell paperback available $2.95 (6 and up) **Fic**

1. Epilepsy—Fiction
ISBN 0-440-93642-X (pa) LC 81-14476

Julie, a busy high school sophomore suddenly stricken with epileptic seizures, must learn to live with her condition as the doctors attempt to control it through medication

"Told in retrospect on the night of high school graduation, this is a moving and perceptive story that is candid in dealing with the resentment, despair, and anger that Julie must overcome if she is to adjust (as she does) and take a positive attitude toward her liability and her future." Bull Cent Child Books

Gleeson, Libby

Eleanor, Elizabeth. Holiday House 1990 c1984 129p $13.95 (5 and up) **Fic**

1. Grandmothers—Fiction 2. Australia—Fiction
ISBN 0-8234-0804-3 LC 89-36009

First published 1984 in Australia

Having left the town and the friends of her childhood, Eleanor, a twelve-year-old Australian girl, finds the land and the house of her grandmother to be an alien place, full of other people's memories

"This story mixes universal feelings with a beautifully blended intergenerational connection. However, the use of italics (to denote Eleanor's thoughts) and narrow columns (for the diary entries) demands more than casual attention from the reader. Regardless, Gleeson has an effective voice that speaks clearly across the seas." Booklist

Goble, Paul

Beyond the ridge; story and illustrations by Paul Goble. Bradbury Press 1989 unp il $13.95 (2-4) **Fic**

1. Indians of North America—Fiction
ISBN 0-02-736581-6 LC 87-33113

At her death an elderly Plains Indian woman experiences the afterlife believed in by her people, while the surviving family members prepare her body according to their custom

"Goble's illustrations—in a double spread of gray rocks, smoothly surfaced in a skyscape of flying vultures—make a dignified context for a moving, direct discussion of death. Goble has managed to make personal what might have been anthropological." Bull Cent Child Books

Godden, Rumer, 1907-

The doll's house; illustrated by Tasha Tudor. Viking 1962 c1947 136p il o.p.; Puffin Bks. paperback available $3.95 (2-4) **Fic**

1. Dollhouses—Fiction 2. Dolls—Fiction
ISBN 0-14-030942-X (pa)

First published 1947 in the United Kingdom; first United States edition illustrated by Dana Saintsbury published 1948

Adventures of a brave little hundred-year-old Dutch farthing doll, her family, their Victorian dollhouse home and the two little English girls to whom they all belonged. Tottie's great adventure was when she went to the exhibition, Dolls through the ages, and was singled out for notice by the Queen who opened the exhibition

"Each doll has a firmly drawn, recognizably true character; the children think and behave convincingly; only the grown-ups are remote and Olympian, as grown-ups must be. The story is enthralling, and complete in every detail. . . . This is an exceptionally good book." Spectator

Fu-dog; illustrated by Valerie Littlewood. Viking 1990 c1989 unp il $14.95 (1-3) **Fic**

1. Children of intermarriage—Fiction 2. Chinese—Great Britain
ISBN 0-670-82300-7 LC 89-50858

First published 1989 in the United Kingdom

"Although Li-la's grandmother was Chinese, Li-la's father had not liked her mother's family. . . . Li-la's only contact with them is a collection of exotic presents from her Great Uncle in London's Chinatown. When he sends her a Fu-Dog, an embroidered satin, dragonlike dog, she finds that it talks to her. Its advice leads Li-la and her brother on an adventure that climaxes at the dragon dance on Chinese New Year and leads to the reconciliation of both sides of her family." Booklist

"Rumer Godden's smooth, graceful prose with its casual, slithery dialogue and its drifting sentences of description reflect a London of colour and movement reinforced by illustrations . . . in which Chinese motifs are used with fine decorative effect." Grow Point

Goffstein, M. B.

Goldie the dollmaker. Farrar, Straus & Giroux 1969 55p il $8.95; pa $3.45 (3-5) **Fic**

1. Dolls—Fiction 2. Lamps—Fiction
ISBN 0-374-32739-4; 0-374-42740-2 (pa) LC 79-85369

"An Ariel book"

"Living alone, Goldie lavishes her love on the dolls she makes, painting into each little wooden face her own gentle smile. Shopping one day, Goldie sees an expensive Chinese lamp and extravagantly buys it. A friend tells her she's crazy, but Goldie is consoled by a dream of the man who made the lamp. 'I made the lamp for you, whoever you are,' the voice says, and the little dollmaker, listening, is comforted, knowing well that happiness can lie in the making of beauty." Saturday Rev

"What seems at first to be a simple picture story about dolls is really an attempt to define the nature of art and to explain the compulsion that forces the artist to be faithful to his own inner vision." Horn Book

Two piano tuners. Farrar, Straus & Giroux 1970 65p il $9.95 (3-5) **Fic**

1. Piano—Fiction 2. Grandfathers—Fiction
ISBN 0-374-38019-8 LC 71-106399

"Little orphaned Debbie Weinstock comes to live with her Grandpa Reuben, the world's best piano tuner, who wants her to become a concert pianist like the famous Isaac Lipman with whom he used to travel. Debbie dutifully practices her piano lessons but is interested only in becoming a piano tuner like her grandfather. After Grandpa Reuben takes her to hear the great artist play and finds that Debbie is impressed only by the fact that the piano stays in tune no matter how hard Mr. Lipman plays, he relents and agrees to teach her piano tuning. The understated humor and warmth of the story are enhanced by the author's spare line drawings." Booklist

Grahame, Kenneth, 1859-1932

The open road (2-5) **Fic**

1. Animals—Fiction

Some editions are:

Scribner $11.95 Illustrated by Beverley Gooding (ISBN 0-684-16471-X)

Wanderer Bks. pa $2.25 Illustrated by Val Biro (ISBN 0-671-63626-X)

"In this second chapter of Kenneth Grahame's 'Wind in the Willows,' [entered below] Rat, Mole and Toad of Toad Hall wander off in a gypsy caravan which is eventually replaced by a motorcar." SLJ

The reluctant dragon (3-5) **Fic**

1. Dragons—Fiction 2. Fairy tales

Some editions are:

Holiday House $8.95; pa $4.95 Illustrated by Ernest H. Shepard (ISBN 0-8234-0093-X; 0-8234-0755-1)

Holt & Co. $14.95; pa $5.95 Illustrated by Michael Hague (ISBN 0-8050-1112-9; 0-8050-0802-0)

This chapter from Dream days was first published 1938 by Holiday House

This "is the droll tale of a peace-loving dragon who is forced to fight St. George. The dragon's friend, called simply the Boy, arranges a meeting between St. George and the dragon, and a mock fight is planned. St. George is the hero of the day, the dragon is highly entertained

Grahame, Kenneth, 1859-1932—*Continued*
at a banquet, and the Boy is pleased to have saved both the dragon and St. George." Huck. Child Lit in the Elem Sch. 3d edition

The wind in the willows (4-6) **Fic**

1. Animals—Fiction

Some editions are:

Adama Bks. $12.95 With illustrations from the Cosgrove Hall production [film] (ISBN 0-915361-32-9)

Holt & Co. $19.95 Illustrated by Michael Hague (ISBN 0-8050-0213-8)

Scribner $18.95; pa $3.95 Illustrated in color and black and white by Ernest H. Shepard Seventy-fifth anniversary edition (ISBN 0-684-17957-1; 0-684-18025-1)

Viking $15.75 Pictures by John Burningham (ISBN 0-670-77120-1)

First published 1908 by Scribner

In this fantasy "the characters are Mole, Water Rat, Mr. Toad, and other small animals, who live and talk like humans but have charming individual characters. The book is a tender portrait of the English countryside." Reader's Ency

Greene, Bette, 1934-

Get on out of here, Philip Hall. Dial Bks. for Young Readers 1981 150p $14.95; lib bdg $13.89; Dell pa $2.75 (4-6) **Fic**

1. Friendship—Fiction 2. Blacks—Fiction 3. Arkansas—Fiction

ISBN 0-8037-2871-9; 0-8037-2872-7 (lib bdg); 0-440-43038-0 (pa) LC 80-22775

Sequel to: Philip Hall likes me, I reckon maybe, entered below

While trying to outdo Philip Hall, Beth learns an important but painful lesson about leadership

"It's rare to encounter a children's book that conveys the ambiance of the rural South as faithfully as . . . the story of Beth Lambert, her family, friends and life in the small community of Pocahontas, Arkansas. Through Beth's experiences we feel the pulse of life in a rural African American Southern community. The vivid metaphorical speech of Southern African Americans is skillfully woven into the dialog and narrative; this humorous, perceptive and original mode of speech will be novel and amusing to some readers and pleasantly familiar to others." Interracial Books Child Bull

Philip Hall likes me, I reckon maybe; pictures by Charles Lilly. Dial Bks. for Young Readers 1974 135p il $13.95; lib bdg $13.89; Dell pa $3.25 (4-6) **Fic**

1. Friendship—Fiction 2. Blacks—Fiction 3. Arkansas—Fiction

ISBN 0-8037-6098-1; 0-8037-6096-5 (lib bdg); 0-440-45755-6 (pa)

Also available ABC-CLIO large print edition $15.95 (ISBN 1-55736-106-1)

A Newbery Medal honor book, 1975

This "story tells of a year in the life of a bright and lively black girl whose only real problems resulted from her infatuation with the boy from the next farm. . . The book . . . deals chiefly with Beth's minor trials and triumphs: She tracks down a pair of turkey thieves, discovers that she is allergic to dogs, embarks on a vegetable-selling business venture, rescues Philip when he injures his leg on a mountaintop, and, finally, wins first prize in a calf-raising contest." Horn Book

"The action is sustained; the narration, in first person Black dialect, is good or bad, depending on your linguistic stance; the illustrations are excellent black-and-white pencil sketches. This is a pleasant, undemanding little tale, good for a rainy afternoon." Read Teach

Followed by: Get on out of here, Philip Hall, entered above

Summer of my German soldier. Dial Bks. for Young Readers 1973 230p $14.95; Bantam Bks. pa $3.50 (6 and up) **Fic**

1. World War, 1939-1945—Fiction 2. Prisoners of war, German—Fiction 3. Arkansas—Fiction

ISBN 0-8037-8321-3; 0-553-27247-0 (pa) LC 73-6025

Also available ABC-CLIO large print edition $15.95 (ISBN 1-55736-134-7)

"Patty knows the pain of loneliness, rejection, and beatings in a family where she is the ugly duckling, unable to gain her parents' love. This is in contrast to the affection shown to her beautiful and submissive sister. Anton Reiker is a German prisoner-of-war in a camp outside of Jenkinsville, Arkansas, and when he escapes, Patty helps him. Because her family is Jewish, she pays dearly for this intervention." Shapiro. Fic for Youth. 2d edition

Greene, Constance C.

Ask anybody. Viking 1983 150p o.p.; Dell paperback available $2.75 (5 and up) **Fic**

1. Friendship—Fiction 2. Divorce—Fiction

ISBN 0-440-40330-8 (pa) LC 82-17624

"This is Schuyler Sweet's story about Nell, an unusual girl who comes with her family to a quiet town in Maine. In a parallel story, Schuyler's divorced artist parents live at opposite ends of the same rambling house, but Schuyler is worried about the future as it looks as if her mother is falling in love." Child Book Rev Serv

"Greene, a master at character portrayals, underscores her theme with sharp, witty dialogue and narrative, packing more insights and perceptions into this spare, highly readable novel that can be found in many a longer book." Booklist

Beat the turtle drum; illustrated by Donna Diamond. Viking 1976 119p il $13.95; Dell pa $2.95 (5 and up) **Fic**

1. Sisters—Fiction 2. Death—Fiction

ISBN 0-670-15241-2; 0-440-40875-X (pa) LC 76-14772

Also available ABC-CLIO large print edition $15.95 (ISBN 1-55736-039-1)

"Joss saves money for her 11th birthday so that she can rent a horse for a week. She and her older sister, who narrates the story, have the happiest week of their lives until Joss falls from the apple tree and breaks her neck. Joss's death stuns the family. Mother lies in bed sedated by tranquilizers, Dad takes to drink, and 13-year-old Kate is left to her own resources. Slowly she gathers strength from her older cousin Mona, the wife of the man who rented the horse and a former teacher." SLJ

"In this sensitive and realistic story the author examines one family's handling of what may well be the ultimate family crisis—the death of one [of] the children.

Greene, Constance C.—*Continued*
Both the narrator, Kate, and the younger sister, Joss, are believable girls who quickly gain the reader's empathy. Joss's absorption in horses will attract many children to this book. Kate's reactions to Joss's death and to the family's dealing with it are likely to be touching and fascinating to the middle-school-age children." Child Book Rev Serv

Double-dare O'Toole. Viking 1981 158p o.p.; Puffin Bks. paperback available $3.95 (4 and up) **Fic**

ISBN 0-14-034541-8 (pa) LC 81-5102

"Francis Xavier (Fex) O'Toole is your nice, all-around American boy complete with understanding parents, a younger brother whom he likes, and an older brother whom he tolerates. There is even Audrey, the girl next door. But Fex is plagued by one weakness—he cannot refuse a double-dare—which leads him into painful scrapes." Horn Book

"Fex's triumph over his 'double-dare' problems is smoothly accomplished, with Greene masterfully capturing the ups and downs of preteen adolescence with a witty, light-but-sure touch. As in the past her characters are believable and likeable, and readers will find this an amusing trip into an 11-year-old's head." Booklist

A girl called Al; illustrated by Byron Barton (5 and up) **Fic**

1. Friendship—Fiction

Some editions are:
ABC-CLIO $15.95 Large print books (ISBN 1-55736-145-2)
Dell pa $2.95 (ISBN 0-440-42810-6)
Puffin Bks. pa $3.95 (ISBN 0-14-034681-3)
Viking $12.95 (ISBN 0-670-34153-3)

First published 1969 by Viking

"Written in an amusing first-person style, this is the story of a friendship between two seventh grade girls. Al (short for Alexandra) and the unnamed narrator of the story learn much from Mr. Richards, the elderly assistant superintendent of their apartment house, as he helps build their self-confidence and reveals his own ability to accept life's problems as well as its joys." Read Ladders for Hum Relat. 6th edition

Other available titles about Al are:
Al(exandra) the Great (1982)
Al's blind date (1989)
I know you, Al (1975)
Just plain Al (1986)
Your old pal, Al (1979)

I and Sproggy; illustrated by Emily McCully. Viking 1978 155p il o.p.; Dell paperback available $1.95 (5 and up) **Fic**

1. Brothers and sisters—Fiction 2. New York (N.Y.)—Fiction
ISBN 0-440-43986-8 (pa) LC 78-6096

"Adam is almost 11, living with his divorced mother near Gracie Mansion (home of New York City's mayor) and fostering two major ambitions. He wants to be the mayor's honored guest and to get rid of a new stepsister, Sproggy. She has come from England with Adam's father and second wife and the girl has many sins. She is closer to 11 than Adam, she has a crazy accent and Adam's dog likes her." Publ Wkly

"Especially notable are the understated description of Adam's relationship with his parents and friends; the realistic, pleasant picture of one aspect of life in New York City; and the many natural, humorous episodes characteristic of the author's work." Horn Book

Isabelle the itch; illustrated by Emily A. McCully. Viking 1973 126p il lib bdg $12.95; Dell pa $2.95 (4-6) **Fic**

ISBN 0-670-40177-3 (lib bdg); 0-440-44345-8 (pa) LC 72-91404

Isabelle, a hyperactive fifth grader, spends a great deal of time getting nowhere, until she realizes that she must channel her energy in order to reach her goals, which include taking over her brother's paper route and winning the fifty-yard dash at school

"This has lively characters described in good style and is written with abundant humor." Bull Cent Child Books

Other available titles about Isabelle are:
Isabelle and little orphan Frannie (1988)
Isabelle shows her stuff (1984)

Greenfield, Eloise, 1929-

Sister; drawings by Moneta Barnett. Crowell 1974 83p il $13.95; Harper & Row pa $3.50 (4 and up) **Fic**

1. Sisters—Fiction 2. Single parent family—Fiction 3. Blacks—Fiction
ISBN 0-690-00497-4; 0-06-440199-5 (pa) LC 73-22182

A 13-year-old black girl whose father is dead watches her 16-year-old sister drifting away from her and her mother and fears she may fall into the same self-destructive behavior herself. While waiting for her sister's return home, she leafs through her diary, reliving both happy and unhappy experiences while gradually recognizing her own individuality

"The book is strong . . . strong in perception, in its sensitivity, in its realism." Bull Cent Child Books

Greenwald, Sheila

Give us a great big smile, Rosy Cole. Little, Brown 1981 76p il $12.95; Dell pa $2.50 (3-5) **Fic**

1. Violinists, violoncellists, etc.—Fiction 2. Photographers—Fiction
ISBN 0-316-32672-0; 0-440-42923-4 (pa) LC 80-24319

"An Atlantic Monthly Press book"

"Rosy's uncle, an author-photographer, has made Rosy's sisters, with their dancing and equestrian talents, the subject of two famous books. Now, to her dismay, it's 10-year-old Rosy's turn to gild Uncle Ralph's bank account, and he begins making regular visits to her violin class with his camera." Booklist

"The author never loses touch with her heroine, a refreshingly ordinary child whose basic good sense saves her from the foibles of adults. Lively, scratchy ink drawings extending the text's considerable humor, aptly picture Rosy's true feelings as she is led down the path to stardom." Horn Book

Other available titles about Rosy Cole are:
Rosy Cole's great American guilt club (1985)
Rosy's romance (1989)
Valentine Rosy (1984)
Write on, Rosy! (1988)

Greenwald, Sheila—*Continued*

It all began with Jane Eyre; or, The secret life of Franny Dillman. Little, Brown 1980 117p il $14.95; Dell pa $1.75 (6 and up) **Fic**

1. Books and reading—Fiction
ISBN 0-316-32671-2; 0-440-94136-9 (pa) LC 79-26901

"An Atlantic Monthly Press book"

Avid reading and a vivid imagination get Franny Dillman into hot water when she turns from the classics to modern teenage novels

This is a "fast-paced, light-hearted spoof that pokes fun at the tedious seriousness and monotonous dilemmas of contemporary teenage novels. The plot is original and well developed, acted by humorous but believable characters. Franny, an over-weight bookworm, and her unrestrained imagination are delightful; she offers a much-needed antidote to the simpering, self-absorbed teenage heroines of the very books the author parodies." Horn Book

Mariah Delany's Author-of-the-Month Club. Little, Brown 1990 124p il $13.95 (4-6) **Fic**

1. Authors—Fiction 2. Clubs—Fiction
ISBN 0-316-32713-1 LC 89-49508

Sequel to: The Mariah Delany Lending Library disaster (1977)

"Joy Street books"

Mariah invites authors to speak at her Author of the Month Club with near disastrous results

"Arch and amusing, this is a story that sparkles with originality." Booklist

Will the real Gertrude Hollings please stand up? Little, Brown 1983 162p o.p.; Dell paperback available $2.95 (5 and up) **Fic**

1. Dyslexia—Fiction 2. Cousins—Fiction
ISBN 0-440-49553-9 (pa) LC 83-974

"An Atlantic Monthly Press book"

"Eleven-year-old Gertrude Hollings has been labeled 'learning disabled' by her teachers, yet at home she creates owl games. Gertrude isn't too thrilled about having to spend three weeks with her overachieving cousin Albert until she realizes she must prepare Albert for being a brother." Bull Cent Child Books

Gertrude "not only wreaks havoc on her relatives' tightly organized household but changes the pattern of Albert's sober, unimaginative existence. Adept at portraying the predicaments of children overwhelmed by well-meaning adults, the author makes the most of the irony of the situation in a sensitive, humorous book." Horn Book

Greer, Gery

Max and me and the time machine; by Gery Greer and Bob Ruddick. Harcourt Brace Jovanovich 1983 114p $13.95; Harper & Row pa $2.95 (5 and up) **Fic**

1. Space and time—Fiction 2. Middle Ages—Fiction 3. Knights and knighthood—Fiction
ISBN 0-15-253134-3; 0-06-440222-3 (pa) LC 82-48762

"Steve and Max come into possession of a time machine and end up spending three days in England during the Middle Ages. Steve is transported into the body of a knight, Sir Robert, while Max spends his time in the body of Sir Robert's horse and his squire." Child Book Rev Serv

"The greatest asset of this title, which serves to differentiate it from similar 'time machine' themes, is its tongue-in-cheek humor which permeats and diffuses the title's action. This humorous bent allows it to become more than a typical science fiction story, elevating it to the status of a humorous adventure tale that younger readers should thrill to a chuckle over." Voice Youth Advocates

Grove, Vicki

Good-bye, my wishing star. Putnam 1988 128p $12.95; Scholastic pa $2.75 (5 and up) **Fic**

1. Farm life—Fiction 2. Family life—Fiction 3. Moving, Household—Fiction 4. Poverty—Fiction
ISBN 0-399-21532-8; 0-590-42152-2 (pa) LC 87-29099

Twelve-year-old Jens, who adores the farm where she has lived all her life, is devastated when severe financial problems may force her family to sell out and move to the city

"This is a quiet, steady book, which aspires not to preach or overdramatize the farmers' plights, but to observe the bittersweet passing of an era. By the time the family moves, Jen's heartfelt plea to 'appreciate every minute and every second of what you've got' resonates with dignity and simplicity." Publ Wkly

Hahn, Mary Downing, 1937-

Daphne's book. Clarion Bks. 1983 177p $13.95; Bantam Bks. pa $2.50 (5 and up) **Fic**

1. School stories 2. Friendship—Fiction 3. Authorship—Fiction 4. Family life—Fiction
ISBN 0-89919-183-5; 0-553-15360-9 (pa) LC 83-7348

As author Jessica and artist Daphne collaborate on a picture book for a seventh-grade English class contest, Jessica becomes aware of conditions in Daphne's home life that seem to threaten her health and safety

"The story is compelling in its portrayal of peer group cruelty and the disturbing dilemma Daphne faces. Jessica's own conflict about how long to shield Daphne will provoke its share of thought too. Characterizations are strong and the situations pressing, so that although the development has a weak spot or two, the story's capacity to move a reader is strong." Booklist

The dead man in Indian Creek. Clarion Bks. 1990 130p $13.95; Avon Bks. pa $2.95 (5 and up) **Fic**

1. Mystery and detective stories
ISBN 0-395-52397-4; 0-380-71362-4 (pa) LC 89-22162

When Matt and Parker learn the body they found in Indian Creek is a drug-related death, they fear Parker's mother may be involved

"Though readers will respond viscerally to the action, what sets the book apart are Hahn's insightful character sketches, especially her portrayal of Matt, whose first-

Hahn, Mary Downing, 1937-—*Continued*
person musings will both entertain and give pause." Booklist

December stillness. Clarion Bks. 1988 181p $13.95; Avon Bks. pa $2.95 (6 and up) **Fic**

1. Veterans—Fiction 2. Homeless people—Fiction 3. Vietnam Veterans Memorial (Washington, D.C.)—Fiction

ISBN 0-89919-758-2; 0-380-70764-0 (pa) LC 88-2572

Thirteen-year-old Kelly tries to befriend Mr. Weems, a disturbed, homeless Vietnam War veteran who spends his days in her suburban library, though the man makes it clear he wants to be left alone

"The author's skillful use of dialogue in defining her characters rescues what could have been a maudlin ending to a fine story, and her depiction of teenagers and their concerns is, as always, right on the mark." Horn Book

The doll in the garden; a ghost story. Clarion Bks. 1989 128p $13.95; Avon Bks. pa $2.95 (4-6) **Fic**

1. Space and time—Fiction 2. Ghosts—Fiction

ISBN 0-89919-848-1; 0-380-70865-5 (pa) LC 88-20365

"After the death of her father, Ashley and her mother move to a new town to start over. Ashley doesn't mind their small, second-floor apartment, but she takes an immediate dislike to grumpy Miss Cooper, the owner of the house. Fascinated by the tangled, overgrown rose garden in the back yard, Ashley and her new friend Kristi explore the neglected, forbidden area. When she and Kristi unearth an antique doll buried beneath one of the bushes, Ashley soon finds herself entangled in a ghostly past and its ties to the present." Publ Wkly

"The girls' friendship is realistically knotty, and Ashley's pain at her father's death is emotionally convincing as well as neatly meshed in the mystery." Bull Cent Child Books

Wait till Helen comes; a ghost story. Clarion Bks. 1986 184p $12.95; Avon Bks. pa $2.95 (4-6) **Fic**

1. Ghosts—Fiction 2. Stepchildren—Fiction

ISBN 0-89919-453-2; 0-380-70442-0 (pa) LC 86-2648

Molly and Michael dislike their spooky new stepsister Heather but realize that they must try to save her when she seems ready to follow a ghost child to her doom

"Hahn builds her plot in the best horror story tradition. Her vivid descriptions add to the creepiness, and more than once readers may find themselves putting down the book and looking over their shoulders; the malevolence is that palpable. Intertwined with the ghost story is the question of Molly's moral imperative to save a child she truly dislikes. Though the emotional turnaround may be a bit quick for some, this still scores as a first-rate thriller." Booklist

Hall, Donald, 1928-

The man who lived alone; illustrated by Mary Azarian. Godine 1984 33p il $12.50 (2-4) **Fic**

1. Country life—Fiction 2. New England—Fiction

ISBN 0-87923-538-1 LC 84-47655

This "narrative poem relates the hard but satisfying life of a man who suffered abuse as a child, settled in with kind relatives until the return of his cruel father, ran away to see the world, and returned home for a quirky middle to old age in the place where he had been happiest." Booklist

"Here is a book as sturdy, genuine and beautiful as a Shaker bench. . . . Hall keeps the narrative moving, telling what he sees with restraint, without judgment. . . . Azarian's remarkable woodcuts draw readers through light and dark into the mystery of ordinary life. . . . Hall and Azarian are an inspired team with firm roots in New England. Their work is steeped in its rhythm and temperament." SLJ

Hall, Lynn, 1937-

Dagmar Schultz and the angel Edna. Scribner 1989 86p $11.95 (6 and up) **Fic**

1. Adolescence—Fiction 2. Humorous stories

ISBN 0-684-19097-4 LC 88-36862

"Dagmar Schultz, the girl from New Berlin, Iowa, who has had more than her share of supernatural adventures, meets her guardian angel. . . . Fast-talking Dagmar is turning 13 and ready for a boyfriend, but her plans are stymied when long-dead Aunt Edna suddenly materializes." Booklist

"The book is written, as are the others about Dagmar, in a chatty, friendly style—a cross between recounting adventures to a best friend and musing aloud. Dagmar's hilarious and frustrating ventures into the new world of being a teenager at long last and finding her very first boyfriend are sure to be a hit with preteens." SLJ

Other available titles about Dagmar Schultz are:
Dagmar Schultz and the powers of darkness (1989)
The secret life of Dagmar Schultz (1988)

Hamilton, Virginia, 1936-

The bells of Christmas; illustrations by Lambert Davis. Harcourt Brace Jovanovich 1989 59p $16.95 (4-6) **Fic**

1. Christmas—Fiction 2. Family life—Fiction 3. Blacks—Fiction 4. Ohio—Fiction

ISBN 0-15-206450-8 LC 89-7468

"On Christmas Day, 1890, in Ohio, the Bell family comes along the National Road to spend the holiday with Jason and his family. The gentle story is stuffed like a proper plum pudding with specific details of rural life almost a century ago." N Y Times Book Rev

"Hamilton laces her story with deliberate bits of history that call attention to the National Road (the thoroughfare connecting the East to what was then the frontier) and to the prosperous status of this black family whose household is headed by a master carpenter on the verge of starting his own business. Davis' quiet, studied pictures of the house's interior and outdoor settings lend a dignified tone. A proud, loving story of a wonderful Christmas past." Booklist

Cousins. Philomel Bks. 1990 125p $14.95 (5 and up) **Fic**

1. Death—Fiction 2. Cousins—Fiction 3. Grandmothers—Fiction 4. Blacks—Fiction

ISBN 0-399-22164-6 LC 90-31451

"Cammy feels things strongly, whether it's the immeasurable love she has for her Gram Tut, or the jealousy and anger she feels for her perfect, sometimes

Hamilton, Virginia, 1936—*Continued*

patronizing cousin Patty Ann. But while those intense emotions make her a strong-willed, feisty girl, they also cause her a great deal of pain when Patty Ann drowns saving another cousin. Only through the wisdom and love of Gram and the return of her estranged father is Cammy able to work her way through the guilt and grief." SLJ

"The book deals essentially with emotions and sensations, and the writing reverberates with honesty and truth. Virginia Hamilton encases the story in family tradition, which offsets the instabilities of contemporary life, and she beautifully counterposes superstition and rationality, separation and reconciliation, love and death." Horn Book

The house of Dies Drear; illustrated by Eros Keith. Macmillan 1968 246p il $13.95; pa $3.95 (5 and up) **Fic**

1. Blacks—Fiction 2. Mystery and detective stories 3. Ohio—Fiction

ISBN 0-02-742500-2; 0-02-043520-7 (pa) LC 68-23059

"A hundred years ago, Dies Drear and two slaves he was hiding in his house, an Underground Railroad station in Ohio, had been murdered. The house, huge and isolated, was fascinating, Thomas thought, but he wasn't sure he was glad Papa had bought it—funny things kept happening, frightening things. The caretaker was forbidding, the neighbors unfriendly." Bull Cent Child Books

"The answer to the mystery comes in a startling dramatic dénouement that is pure theater. This is gifted writing; the characterization is unforgettable, the plot imbued with mounting tension." Saturday Rev

Followed by: The mystery of Drear House, entered below

M. C. Higgins the great. Macmillan 1974 278p $14.95; pa $3.95 (6 and up) **Fic**

1. Blacks—Fiction 2. Family life—Fiction 3. Appalachian Mountains—Fiction

ISBN 0-02-742480-4; 0-02-043490-1 (pa) LC 72-92439

Also available ABC-CLIO large print edition $15.95 (ISBN 1-55736-075-8)

Awarded the Newbery Medal, 1975

M.C. Higgins, a 13-year-old black boy "dreams of saving his family's house from an Ohio strip mining slag heap and finds that the answer to his dreams lies in coming to terms with his family heritage and his own identity." Publisher's note

"This is a deeply involving story possessing a folklorish quality. Superstition and magic are deeply rooted in its telling. Characterizations are highly original. The unusual setting and uniqueness of story line make this outstanding juvenile literature." Child Book Rev Serv

The magical adventures of Pretty Pearl. Harper & Row 1983 311p $12.95; lib bdg $17.89; pa $5.50 (6 and up) **Fic**

1. Blacks—Fiction 2. Fantastic fiction

ISBN 0-06-022186-0; 0-06-022187-9 (lib bdg); 0-06-440178-2 (pa) LC 82-48629

"A Charlotte Zolotow book"

Pretty Pearl, a spirited young African god child eager to show off her powers, travels to the New World where, disguised as a human, she lives among a band of free blacks who created their own separate world deep inside a forest

"The author interweaves black folklore with her own family history in a tale remarkable for its total integration of the novel with the imaginative possibilities of legend; and she establishes and illuminates the symbolic structure of many of her previous books." Horn Book

The mystery of Drear House; the conclusion of the Dies Drear chronicle. Greenwillow Bks. 1987 217p $11.75; Macmillan pa $3.95 (5 and up) **Fic**

1. Blacks—Fiction 2. Buried treasure—Fiction 3. Mystery and detective stories 4. Buried treasure—Fiction

ISBN 0-688-04026-8; 0-02-043480-4 (pa) LC 86-9829

"This is the sequel to 'The house of Dies Drear' [entered above] featuring young Thomas Small and his family who are living in the Drear house, once owned by an abolitionist and part of the Underground Railroad, offering shelter to escaping slaves. Professor Small, Thomas' father is engaged in cataloging a treasure house of antiques which have been hidden in one of the caverns on the property, which is a maze of tunnels and caves. He must protect these treasures from discovery by a neighboring family who are searching for them in order to sell them." Voice Youth Advocates

"Ingredients such as secret rooms and passages, moving walls, and awesome treasure will play well to a popular audience; yet substantive portrayals of characters and relationships provide the depth one associates with Hamilton. This solid tale displays a sensitivity toward feelings, emotions, and conflicting values—all in the context of a fantastic mystery laid to rest." Booklist

The planet of Junior Brown. Macmillan 1971 210p $14.95; pa $3.95 (6 and up) **Fic**

1. Friendship—Fiction 2. Blacks—Fiction

ISBN 0-02-742510-X; 0-02-043540-1 (pa) LC 71-155264

Also available G.K. Hall large print edition $13.95 (ISBN 0-8161-4642-4)

"This is the story of a crucial week in the lives of two black, eighth-grade dropouts who have been spending their time with the school janitor. Each boy is presented as a distinct individual. Jr. is a three-hundred pound musical prodigy as neurotic as his overprotective mother. Buddy has learned to live by his wits in a world of homeless children. Buddy becomes Jr. Brown's protector and says to the other boys, 'We are together because we have to learn to live for each other.'" Read Ladders for Hum Relat. 6th edition

Willie Bea and the time the Martians landed. Greenwillow Bks. 1983 208p $14; Aladdin Bks. (NY) pa $3.95 (5 and up) **Fic**

1. Family life—Fiction 2. Blacks—Fiction 3. Halloween—Fiction

ISBN 0-688-02390-8; 0-689-71328-2 (pa) LC 83-1659

"Set in Ohio in 1938, this is the story of Willie Bea and her family, who have gathered for a festive Sunday dinner. Willie Bea and her cousins are anticipating Halloween trick or treating, but the evening takes an unexpected turn as Orson Welles' radio broadcast 'War of the Worlds' terrifies Willie Bea's family. A wonderful portrayal of a warm, extended black family." Soc Educ

Hamilton, Virginia, 1936-—*Continued*

Zeely; illustrated by Symeon Shimin. Macmillan 1967 122p il $12.95; pa $3.95 (4 and up) **Fic**

1. Blacks—Fiction
ISBN 0-02-742470-7; 0-689-71110-7 (pa)
LC 66-31616

"Imaginative eleven-year-old Geeder is stirred when she sees Zeely Tayber, who is dignified, stately, and six-and-a-half feet tall. Geeder thinks Zeely looks like the magazine picture of the Watusi queen. Through meeting Zeely personally and getting to know her, Geeder finally returns to reality." Read Ladders for Hum Relat. 5th edition

Hansen, Joyce

The gift-giver. Clarion Bks. 1980 118p $13.95; Ticknor & Fields pa $3.95 (4-6) **Fic**

1. School stories 2. Blacks—Fiction 3. New York (N.Y.)—Fiction
ISBN 0-395-29433-9; 0-89919-852-X (pa)
LC 80-12969

"Ten-year-old Doris lives in the ghetto, but has a loving family and teachers and parents who set forth important values in her life. In fact, Doris believes her life is too protected and restricted until Amir moves into the neighborhood. Amir shows her that she does not have to be exactly like everyone else and helps Doris and others in their class to develop their own special talents. The author gives a non-stereotypical view of life in a ghetto." Read Ladders for Hum Relat. 6th edition

Followed by: Yellow Bird and me (1985)

Härtling, Peter, 1933-

Crutches; translated from the German by Elizabeth D. Crawford. Lothrop, Lee & Shepard Bks. 1988 163p $12.95 (5 and up) **Fic**

1. Friendship—Fiction 2. Austria—Fiction
ISBN 0-688-07991-1 LC 88-80400

Original German edition, 1986

A young boy, searching vainly for his mother in post-war Vienna, is befriended by a man on crutches, a former German officer, and together they find hope for the future

"Because of its pacing, the book, while re-creating a specific time in history, has the intensity of an adventure story; it is equally remarkable for its development of theme without sacrificing believability or sense of story. When Thomas is finally reunited with his mother, for example, the moment is tinged with sadness, as it means that he will be parted from Crutches. The bittersweet ending is poignant but not manipulative." Horn Book

Old John; translated from the German by Elizabeth D. Crawford. Lothrop, Lee & Shepard Bks. 1990 120p lib bdg $11.95 (4 and up) **Fic**

1. Grandfathers—Fiction 2. Old age—Fiction 3. Death—Fiction
ISBN 0-688-08734-3 LC 89-12976

Original German edition, 1981

"When Jacob's family invite their 75-year-old maternal grandfather, Old John, to come and live with them, he's hale and hearty, asserting himself in ways the family finds eccentric, but tolerable. Old John makes a place for himself within his family and about the town, even enjoying a romance. Then one fateful day, he has a stroke, and though he returns home from the hospital, he never regains his former strength." Booklist

"Härtling deftly sketches simple chapters, each unfolding into the next, with an economy of vocabulary and a storyteller's sense of timing. Even in translation the story crackles with energy and poignancy. A book to be savored, read aloud, and used to entice older but less skillful readers." SLJ

Harvey, Brett

Cassie's journey; going West in the 1860s; illustrated by Deborah Kogan Ray. Holiday House 1988 unp il lib bdg $12.95 (2-4) **Fic**

1. Overland journeys to the Pacific (U.S.)—Fiction 2. Frontier and pioneer life—Fiction 3. West (U.S.)—Fiction
ISBN 0-8234-0684-9 LC 87-23599

A young girl relates the hardships and dangers of traveling with her family in a covered wagon from Illinois to California during the 1860's

"Harvey has based this story of westward migration on the diaries of pioneer women; the events that occur as Cassie and her family travel to California actually happened to people—making this a fascinating piece of historical fiction in picture-book format. . . . Ray's soft charcoal drawings carry a solemnity that gives the account a serious edge while evoking the loneliness and breadth of the landscape; the essentially happy finish makes sure that positive emotions have the upper hand." Booklist

Haugaard, Erik Christian

Leif the unlucky. Houghton Mifflin 1982 206p $9.95 (6 and up) **Fic**

1. Vikings—Fiction 2. Greenland—Fiction
ISBN 0-395-32156-5 LC 82-1053

This novel concerns "the last remnants of the Greenland colony in the early fifteenth century, a group of farmers whose lives were being strangled by the increasingly bitter cold winters, whose dreams of returning to Norway were thwarted because they had neither ships nor wood to build them. Leif, aware that the older members of the community have lost all initiative, gathers a group of young people to battle another such group led by the power-hungry Egil." Bull Cent Child Books

"Spare, taut, almost unemotional in tone, the story of desolation and retribution resembles the Icelandic sagas in its feeling of tragic inevitability and resignation." Horn Book

Hautzig, Esther Rudomin

A gift for Mama; [by] Esther Hautzig; illustrated by Donna Diamond. Viking 1981 56p il o.p.; Puffin Bks. paperback available $3.95 (3-6) **Fic**

1. Gifts—Fiction 2. Jews—Poland—Fiction 3. Poland—Fiction

ISBN 0-14-032384-8 (pa) LC 80-24973

"Sara, an only child, determines to buy her mother a gift for Mother's Day rather than make one as she has in the past. . . . She manages to earn the nine zlotys for the satin slippers with blue leather trim by mending and repairing the clothes of her aunt's friends at the university." Child Book Rev Serv

"The book is set in Poland [in the 1930s] the author's homeland, and the reader learns much about Jewish customs and Polish lifestyle. The illustrations are beautiful, high-quality monoprints, which are pictures painted on glass and then transferred to paper by using an etching press." Interracial Books Child Bull

Haywood, Carolyn, 1898-1990

"B" is for Betsy; written and illustrated by Carolyn Haywood. Harcourt Brace 1939 159p il $12.95; pa $3.95 (2-4) **Fic**

1. School stories

ISBN 0-15-204975-4; 0-15-204977-0 (pa) LC 39-6264

"The first day of school is a momentous one. For Betsy it would have been overwhelming but for the comforting knowledge of the presence of Koala bear in her schoolbag and the new friendship with Ellen. A simple, direct story of a six-year-old girl's first year in school; the incidents chosen are the commonplace ones which loom large in a child's life. . . . Appealing black-and-white illustrations; large type, well leaded." Booklist

Other available titles about Betsy are:
Back to school with Betsy (1943)
Betsy and Billy (1941)
Betsy and Mr. Kilpatrick (1967)
Betsy and the boys (1945)
Betsy and the circus (1954)
Betsy's busy summer (1956)
Betsy's little star (1950)
Betsy's play school (1977)
Betsy's winterhouse (1958)
Merry Christmas from Betsy (1970)
Snowbound with Betsy (1962)

Little Eddie; written and illustrated by Carolyn Haywood. Morrow 1947 160p il o.p.; Beech Tree Bks. paperback available $3.95 (2-4) **Fic**

ISBN 0-688-10074-0 (pa) LC 47-30839

Seven-year-old Eddie Wilson is a little boy who knows what he wants and goes after it. Collecting—stray animals and junk—is his favorite activity. His projects, which sometimes inconvenience his parents, are graphically told. Betsy and some of the other playmates from the author's series entered above reappear here

Other available titles about Eddie are:
Eddie and his big deals (1955)
Eddie and the fire engine (1949)
Eddie's menagerie (1978)
Eddie's valuable property (1975)
Merry Christmas from Eddie (1986)

Heide, Florence Parry, 1919-

The shrinking of Treehorn; drawings by Edward Gorey. Holiday House 1971 unp il lib bdg $10.95 (2-5) **Fic**

ISBN 0-8234-0189-8 LC 78-151753

Treehorn spends an unhappy day and night shrinking. Yet when he tells his mother, father, teacher and principal of his problem they're all too busy to do anything about it. To Treehorn's great relief he finally discovers a magical game that restores him to his natural size, but then he starts turning green!

This "is an imaginative little whimsy, whose sly humor and macabre touches are perfectly matched in Edward Gorey's illustrations." Book World

Other available titles about Treehorn are:
The adventures of Treehorn (1983)
Treehorn's treasure (1981)
Treehorn's wish (1984)

Henry, Marguerite, 1902-

Black Gold; illustrated by Wesley Dennis. Rand McNally 1957 172p il $8.95; Macmillan pa $3.95 (4-6) **Fic**

1. Black Gold (Race horse)—Fiction 2. Horse racing—Fiction

ISBN 0-528-82130-X; 0-02-688754-1 (pa) LC 57-14557

The story "of a black stallion, [a Kentucky Derby winner] whose splendid turf record put him in the front rank of champions. Black Gold's courage and will to win were strengthened by the faith which two people, his trainer and his rider, held in him. Marguerite Henry tells their story with conviction, and with a sympathetic knowledge of horses and the people who care for them. Black and white illustrations by Wesley Dennis are full of action." Ont Libr Rev

Brighty of the Grand Canyon; illustrated by Wesley Dennis. Rand McNally 1953 222p il $8.95; Atheneum Pubs. pa $3.95 (4 and up) **Fic**

1. Donkeys—Fiction 2. Grand Canyon (Ariz.)—Fiction

ISBN 0-528-82150-4; 0-689-71485-8 (pa) LC 53-7233

Drawn from a real-life incident, this is the story of "Brighty, the shaggy little burro who roamed the canyons of the Colorado River [and] had a will of his own. He liked the old prospector and Uncle Jim and he helped solve a mystery, but chiefly he was the freedom loving burro." Chicago Public Libr

"Only those who are unfamiliar with the West would say it is too packed with drama to be true. And the author's understanding warmth for all of God's creatures still shines through her superb ability as a story teller making this a vivid tale." Christ Sci Monit

Justin Morgan had a horse; illustrated by Wesley Dennis. Rand McNally 1954 169p il $8.95; pa $2.95 (4 and up) **Fic**

1. Horses—Fiction 2. Morgan horse—Fiction 3. Vermont—Fiction

ISBN 0-528-82255-1; 0-528-87682-1 (pa) LC 54-8903

A Newbery Medal honor book, 1946

An expanded version of the book first published 1945 by Wilcox & Follett

Henry, Marguerite, 1902-—*Continued*

Story of the brave little Vermont work horse from which came the famous American breed of Morgan horses. Justin Morgan first owned the horse, but it was the boy Joel Goss who loved 'Little Bub', later called 'Justin Morgan', followed him through his career, rescued him from a cruel master, and finally had the pleasure of having him ridden by James Monroe when he was President of the United States

A horse story "in a book that is rich in human values—the sort of book that makes you proud and sometimes brings a lump to your throat." Book Week

King of the wind; illustrated by Wesley Dennis. Macmillan 1988 c1948 172p il $12.95; Atheneum Pubs. pa $3.95 (4 and up) **Fic**

1. Horses—Fiction
ISBN 0-02-689089-5; 0-689-71486-6 (pa) LC 88-22934

Awarded the Newbery Medal, 1949

A reissue of the title first published 1948 by Rand McNally

"A beautiful, sympathetic story of the famous [ancestor of a line of great thoroughbred horses] . . . and the little mute Arabian stable boy who accompanies him on his journey across the seas to France and England [in the eighteenth century]. The lad's fierce devotion to his horse and his great faith and loyalty are skillfully woven into an enthralling tale which children will long remember. The moving quality of the writing is reflected in the handsome illustrations." Wis Libr Bull

Misty of Chincoteague; illustrated by Wesley Dennis. Macmillan 1947 173p il $12.95; pa $2.95 (4 and up) **Fic**

1. Ponies—Fiction 2. Chincoteague Island (Va.)—Fiction 3. Assateague Island National Seashore (Md. and Va.)—Fiction
ISBN 0-02-689090-9; 0-02-688759-2 (pa) LC 47-11404

A Newbery Medal honor book, 1948

First published by Rand McNally

"The islands of Chincoteague and Assateague, just off the coast of Virginia, are the setting. . . . Two children have their hearts set on owning a wild pony and her colt, descendants, so legend says, of the Moorish ponies who were survivors of a Spanish galleon wrecked there long ago." Booklist

"The beauty and pride of the wild horses is the highpoint in the story, and skillful drawings of them reveal their grace and swiftness." Ont Libr Rev

Other available titles about the ponies of Chincoteague Island are:
Sea star, orphan of Chincoteague (1949)
Stormy, Misty's foal (1963)

Mustang, wild spirit of the West; illustrated by Robert Lougheed. Rand McNally 1966 222p il $8.95; Macmillan pa $3.95 (5 and up) **Fic**

1. Johnston, Annie Bronn—Fiction 2. Horses—Fiction
ISBN 0-528-82327-2; 0-02-688760-6 (pa) LC 66-8847

The "story of how Wild Horse Annie Johnston successfully led the . . . fight to save the mustangs from virtual extinction. Tells of her lifelong fight, first in Nevada and then on a national level, against the cruel practices of mustangers who hunt their prey in planes and trucks." Natl Counc of Teach of Engl. Adventuring with Books. 2d edition

"Engrossing as a story of the preservation of wild animals and truly moving as a story of a dauntless woman." Bull Cent Child Books

San Domingo: the medicine hat stallion; illustrated by Robert Lougheed. Rand McNally 1972 230p il $8.95; Macmillan pa $3.95 (4-6) **Fic**

1. Ponies—Fiction 2. Frontier and pioneer life—Fiction
ISBN 0-528-82443-0; 0-02-689415-7 (pa) LC 72-7416

The author "traces twelve-year-old Peter's coming of age in the rough Nebraska Territory of the mid 1800's. In spite of his father's cruelty, which never basically changes, Peter finds staunch allies in his sympathetic mother, a lively old surveyor named Brislawn, and a faithful Dalmation. But Peter's first love and constant companion is an Indian pony, San Domingo, who shared his boyhood adventures and dies carrying him to safety as a Pony Express rider. Robert Lougheed's vivid drawings and paintings add to the historical setting." Booklist

Henry, O., 1862-1910

The gift of the Magi (5 and up) **Fic**

1. Christmas—Fiction

Some editions are:

Macmillan $7.95 Original illustrations by Shelley Freshman (ISBN 0-672-52296-9)

Picture Bk. Studio $16.95 Illustrations by Lisbeth Zwerger; script by Michael Neugebauer (ISBN 0-907234-17-8)

Simon & Schuster Bks. for Young Readers $12.95 Illustrated by Kevin King (ISBN 0-671-64706-7)

"The tale of a poor young couple who sacrifice their dearest possessions to buy each other Christmas gifts." Bull Cent Child Books

Herman, Charlotte

The house on Walenska Street; illustrated by Susan Avishai. Dutton 1990 78p il $11.95 (3-5) **Fic**

1. Jews—Soviet Union—Fiction 2. Single parent family—Fiction
ISBN 0-525-44519-6 LC 89-33505

"This gentle family story conveys the hard reality of Jewish life in a small Russian town in 1918. After the death of her father, eight-year-old Leah must help with her two younger sisters so their mother can support the family. The tension in their lives is balanced by the natural exuberance of three well-loved children." Horn Book Guide

Millie Cooper, 3B; illustrated by Helen Cogancherry. Dutton 1985 73p il $11.95; Puffin Bks. pa $3.95 (3-5) **Fic**

1. School stories
ISBN 0-525-44157-3; 0-14-032072-5 (pa) LC 84-25951

Herman, Charlotte—*Continued*

"Based on the author's childhood, this is a low-keyed, episodic story about a third grader who yearns for distinction; she isn't sure how to achieve it, but Millie wants to be special in some way. There is nothing dramatic here, just a series of realistic small events that end in Millie happily realizing that there are some ways in which she is indeed special. This is simply written, a bit rambling, pleasant, and believable." Bull Cent Child Books

Another available title about Millie Cooper, is entered below

Millie Cooper, take a chance; illustrated by Helen Cogancherry. Dutton 1988 100p il $11.95; Puffin Bks. pa $3.95 (3-5) **Fic**

ISBN 0-525-44442-4; 0-14-034119-6 (pa)

LC 88-11081

In 1947, after trying two different ways to win a bicycle and forcing herself to read a poem in front of her third grade class, Millie recognizes the importance of taking chances to make her life more interesting and satisfying

"This bright, episodic story proves that life in 1947 is not much different than it is today, and that taking chances is important to succeeding in life. Herman peppers her story with humorous and nostalgic references that texture the tale and will spark a chain of memories in readers' parents." Booklist

Hermes, Patricia, 1936-

Friends are like that. Harcourt Brace Jovanovich 1984 123p $12.95; Scholastic pa $2.50 (5 and up) **Fic**

1. School stories 2. Friendship—Fiction

ISBN 0-15-229722-7; 0-590-40757-0 (pa)

LC 83-18407

"Thirteen-year-old Tracy has a chance to join the most popular clique at school. All she has to do is drop unconventional Kelly, her best friend since first grade, whom the ringleader of the group thinks is 'weird.' Tracy's quandary is that although she wants to be part of the popular crowd, she feels guilty about abandoning her best friend." SLJ

"Though this has some features of the typical junior high school friendship story, it also has an original, touching element in a story Kelly writes, which helps her to express her ideas and emotions, and gives Tracy insight into the meaning of their friendship." SLJ

I hate being gifted. Putnam 1990 122p $14.95 (5 and up) **Fic**

1. Gifted children—Fiction 2. Friendship—Fiction 3. School stories

ISBN 0-399-21687-1 LC 90-8516

"Being in the sixth grade is difficult enough, but when KT is placed in the gifted program and gets the weirdest teacher in school, she feels her life is falling apart. Her dearest friends, Melinda and Chrissy, start a new friendship with Erica, a pushy, upbeat girl who seems to be edging KT out of the group. In addition, many of her classmates make fun of the gifted students." Voice Youth Advocates

"Hermes' insight into the problem of cliques lets her create not only characters, but also situations that are true to life. The writing is accessible and the dialogue is accurate, right down to the all-too-familiar ungrammatical sentence structure." SLJ

Kevin Corbett eats flies; illustrated by Carol Newsom. Harcourt Brace Jovanovich 1986 160p il $13.95; Pocket Bks. pa $2.95 (4 and up) **Fic**

1. Friendship—Fiction 2. Moving, Household—Fiction 3. Fathers and sons—Fiction

ISBN 0-15-242290-0; 0-671-69183-X (pa)

LC 85-27086

Kevin and his friend Bailey conspire to prevent Kevin's widowed father from moving himself and Kevin once again

"Kevin has made a staunch friend . . . in the form of a daring defiant fosterchild named Bailey, who helps him plan a romance between Kevin's father and their fifth-grade teacher, to prevent any further moves. The children's scheming toward a dinner party has much ring of truth, as do the classroom scenes and the comradely discussions between Kevin and his loving father. There's lots to laugh about here and, in the end, something to think about as well." Bull Cent Child Books

You shouldn't have to say good-bye. Harcourt Brace Jovanovich 1982 117p $11.95; Scholastic pa $2.50 (5 and up) **Fic**

1. Mothers—Fiction 2. Parent and child—Fiction 3. Death—Fiction

ISBN 0-15-299944-2; 0-590-41359-7 (pa)

LC 82-47933

"When 12-year-old Sarah Morrow learns her mother is dying, her world seems to come apart. Sometimes Sarah refuses to think about anything but her own immediate concerns, sometimes she is frightened and at other times she is terribly angry. Mrs. Morrow's cancer spreads rapidly and she dies at Christmas leaving a book she has written for her daughter in which she offers some guidance for understanding and dealing with her feelings. In her best work to date, Hermes explores the death of a parent, treating it as a crisis for the entire family. The difficulties the adults have in coping with this tragedy are explored as are the problems experienced by the child. Characters are credible and their behaviors realistic." SLJ

Herriot, James

Moses the kitten; illustrated by Peter Barrett. St. Martin's Press 1984 unp il $10.95 (2-4) **Fic**

1. Cats—Fiction 2. Farm life—Fiction

ISBN 0-312-54905-9 LC 84-50930

"Found by Herriot among the frozen rushes, the kitten was quickly adopted by a farm family, warmed back to liveliness in an [open] oven, and named Moses. What the veterinarian-author found, on his next visit, was that Moses had inserted himself into a litter of piglets and been accepted as one of the family, both at feeding times and at sleep-in-a-heap naptime." Bull Cent Child Books

"Patience, kindness and caring are the dominant themes here, and the storyline and characterizations never deviate from this. The text is complemented throughout with appropriate, well-placed soft pastel watercolors [depicting] in detail the northern English countryside." SLJ

Hildick, E. W. (Edmund Wallace), 1925-

The case of the purloined parrot. Macmillan 1990 133p il $12.95 (3-6) **Fic**

1. Mystery and detective stories
ISBN 0-02-743965-8 LC 89-37924

"A McGurk mystery"

"The McGurk Organization, headed by the group's namesake, includes four boys and two girls, one of whom is a Japanese-American. In this [mystery] they foil the cat rustlers who've been kidnapping pets. As in the other books [in this series] the humorous plot moves along at a brisk pace." SLJ

Other available titles in this series are:
The case of the muttering mummy (1986)
The case of the phantom frog (1979)
The case of the wandering weathervanes (1988)

The Ghost Squad breaks through. Dutton 1984 138p $12.95; TOR Bks. pa $1.95 (5 and up) **Fic**

1. Ghosts—Fiction 2. Mystery and detective stories
ISBN 0-525-44097-6; 0-8125-6850-8 (pa) LC 84-3985

"A Ghost Squad book"

When one of them finds a successful way to communicate with a live person, four young ghosts decide to band together to help solve and prevent crimes

"The idea of a ghost squad may at first seem an unsavory idea. . . . But Hildick handles all of this in the most matter-of-fact way and provides readers with an exciting adventure in the bargain. . . . The story is filled with fascinating details of what life is like on the other side; ghosts wear clothes they felt most comfortable in before they died, and they don't get wet in the rain. All of this is presented in a perfectly plausible manner, which is part of the book's appeal." Booklist

Other available titles about the Ghost Squad are:
The Ghost Squad and the Ghoul of Grunberg (1986)
The Ghost Squad and the Halloween conspiracy (1985)
The Ghost Squad and the menace of the Malevs (1988)
The Ghost Squad and the prowling hermits (1987)
The Ghost Squad flies Concorde (1985)

Hoban, Russell

The mouse and his child; pictures by Lillian Hoban. Harper & Row 1967 181p il lib bdg $13.89; Dell pa $3.50 (4-6) **Fic**

1. Fantastic fiction
ISBN 0-06-022378-2; 0-440-40293-X (pa)
LC 67-19624

Also available G. K. Hall large print edition $17.95 (ISBN 0-7451-1104-1)

A fantasy "that chronicles the hazardous and heroic adventures of a broken windup mouse child and his father in search of happiness and security. Love and valor ultimately triumph over violence and evil in a realistically created world of humanly characterized wind-up toys and real animals. . . . Limited in appeal but for the special reader a rare treat and for the perceptive adult a delight to share. Small black-and-white drawings fittingly complement the spirit of the story." Booklist

Hoffmann, E. T. A. (Ernst Theodor Amadeus), 1776-1822

Nutcracker (3 and up) **Fic**

1. Fairy tales 2. Christmas—Fiction

Some editions are:
Crown $24.95 Pictures by Maurice Sendak; translated by Ralph Manheim (ISBN 0-517-55285-X)
Knopf $14.95 Translated by Andrea Clarke Madden; illustrated by Carter Goodrich (ISBN 0-394-55384-5)

After hearing how her toy nutcracker got his ugly face, a little girl helps break the spell and changes him into a handsome prince

Holland, Isabelle

The journey home. Scholastic 1990 312p $13.95 (4 and up) **Fic**

1. Orphans—Fiction 2. Sisters—Fiction 3. West (U.S.)—Fiction
ISBN 0-590-43110-2 LC 90-32175

"After their mother dies, Maggie Lavin, 12, and her younger sister, Annie, leave the slums of New York City on one of the orphan trains that delivered thousands of tenement youngsters to adoptive homes during the second half of the 19th century. Taken in by a childless couple, they begin a new life on the Kansas prairie." SLJ

"Holland, who has peopled her novel with wonderfully complex and distinct characters, shows a subtle instinct for both the insecurities of orphanhood and the tensions generated by cultural difference. Maggie is hardly perfect but fully engaging, making her a welcome addition to the ranks of prairie heroines." Booklist

Holling, Holling C., 1900-1973

Minn of the Mississippi; written and illustrated by Holling Clancy Holling. Houghton Mifflin 1951 85p il $16.95; pa $7.95 (4-6) **Fic**

1. Turtles—Fiction 2. Mississippi River—Fiction
ISBN 0-395-17578-X; 0-395-27399-4 (pa) LC 51-6290

A Newbery Medal honor book, 1952

Minn of the Mississippi is a tough snapping turtle. The story of the Mississippi River is here told in text and pictures as Minn is carried from the Minnesota headwaters of the Mississippi to the Gulf of Mexico. The time required in Minn's life is twenty-five years but the story reaches back into history to make the tale complete

"In telling the story of Minn, a snapping turtle, the author touches on the geography, history, geology and climate of the Mississippi River. . . . Illustrated with full page pictures in color and many marginal pencil drawings." Los Angeles. Sch Libr

Paddle-to-the-sea; written and illustrated by Holling Clancy Holling. Houghton Mifflin 1941 unp il lib bdg $16.95; pa $7.95 (4-6) **Fic**

1. Great Lakes region—Fiction
ISBN 0-395-15082-5 (lib bdg); 0-395-29203-4 (pa)
LC 41-13399

A Caldecott Medal honor book, 1942

A toy canoe with a seated Indian figure is launched in Lake Nipigon by the Indian boy who carved it and in four years travels thru all the Great Lakes and the St. Lawrence River to the Atlantic. An interesting picture of the shore life of the lakes and the river with striking full page pictures in bright colors and marginal pencil drawings

"The canoe's journey is used to show the flow of

Holling, Holling C., 1900-1973—*Continued*

currents and of traffic, and each occurrence is made to seem plausible. . . . There are also diagrams of a sawmill, a freighter, the canal locks at the Soo, and Niagara Falls." Libr J

Seabird; written and illustrated by Holling Clancy Holling. Houghton Mifflin 1948 58p il lib bdg $15.95; pa $5.95 (4-6) **Fic**

1. Whaling—Fiction 2. Sea stories
ISBN 0-395-18230-1 (lib bdg); 0-395-26681-5 (pa)
LC 48-7832

A Newbery Medal honor book, 1949

Seabird is an ivory gull carved by Ezra Brown when he was just a boy while on a whaler in 1832. It brought luck and good sailing to him and to his descendants on all the seven seas, and through many years of thrilling sea adventures

"Through four generations of seamen Seabird saw the whaler give way to the clipper, the clipper yield to steam, the airplane succeed both. The subject takes the reader over the globe and provides room for imagination to aid history in vitalizing the period. The beauty of the illustrations gives the book distinction." Horn Book

Tree in the trail; written and illustrated by Holling Clancy Holling. Houghton Mifflin 1942 unp il lib bdg $16.95; pa $7.95 (4 and up) **Fic**

1. Trees—Fiction 2. Santa Fe Trail—Fiction
ISBN 0-395-18228-X (lib bdg); 0-395-54534-X (pa)
LC 42-25811

"The story of a cottonwood tree that watched the pageant of history on the Santa Fe trail where it stood, a landmark to travelers and a peace-medicine tree to Indians, for over 200 years." Booklist

"The care with which this [book] is documented by pictures gives it exceptional usefulness. Besides the large color plates, every important detail in the story appears in small pencil studies on the wide margins of facing pages." N Y Her Trib Books

Holm, Anne, 1922-

North to freedom; translated from the Danish by L. W. Kingsland. Harcourt Brace 1965 190p hardcover o.p. paperback available $3.95 (6 and up) **Fic**

1. Refugees—Fiction
ISBN 0-15-257553-7 (pa) LC 65-12612

First published 1963 in Denmark; first United States edition published 1965

"Twelve-year-old David, whose only memory is of life in a prison camp, escapes and makes his way across Europe alone. Before he is reunited with his mother, his prison-bred fear of people has gradually faded, and he has learned that goodness as well as evil exists in the world." Hodges. Books for Elem Sch Libr

Holman, Felice

Secret City, U.S.A. Scribner 1990 199p $13.95 (6 and up) **Fic**

1. Homeless people—Fiction 2. Poor—Fiction
ISBN 0-684-19168-7 LC 89-39841

"Benno and his friends are poor, living in overcrowded tenements and even the streets and suffering all the consequences of a life where the barest necessities are hard to come by. They find relief in an unlikely spot—a razed portion of the city where rubble and debris conceal a still-sturdy house that Benno and his friends take over. Here, they make themselves a home and envision a wider scope of reclamation whereby others like themselves can have a decent place to live." SLJ

"While the boys' modest successes may be romanticized and the ending more hopeful than reality might allow, the author paints an uncompromising picture of the misery and squalor of our cities." Horn Book

Slake's limbo. Scribner 1974 117p $12.95; Macmillan pa $3.95 (6 and up) **Fic**

1. Runaway children—Fiction 2. Subways—Fiction 3. New York (N.Y.)—Fiction
ISBN 0-684-13926-X; 0-689-71066-6 (pa)
LC 74-11675

Aremis Slake, at the age of thirteen, takes to the New York City subways as a refuge from an abusive home life and oppressive school system

"The economically told chronicle of Slake's adventures is more than a survival saga: it is also an eloquent study of poverty, of fear, and finally of hope." Horn Book

Honeycutt, Natalie

The all new Jonah Twist. Bradbury Press 1986 110p $10.95; Avon Bks. pa $2.95 (3-5) **Fic**

1. School stories 2. Friendship—Fiction
ISBN 0-02-744840-1; 0-380-70317-3 (pa)
LC 85-28048

Jonah's efforts to survive the third grade are complicated by the new boy in class, who has the potential for either becoming a friend or beating him up

"Although things fall predictably into place at the end, the novel is satisfying in its depiction of third-grade culture in general and Jonah in particular. Other characters are drawn in a more cursory fashion, but in Jonah, Honeycutt creates a sympathetic figure who grows with the help of circumstances, friends, and his own will to change. With only 110 pages and a dash of humor, this novel will be a welcome addition to many collections." Booklist

Another available title about Jonah Twist is entered below

The best-laid plans of Jonah Twist. Bradbury Press 1988 115p $11.95; Avon Bks. pa $2.95 (3-5) **Fic**

1. School stories 2. Family life—Fiction
ISBN 0-02-744850-9; 0-380-70762-4 (pa) LC 88-7288

"As the story opens, third-grade Jonah's first 'best-laid plan,' to convince his mother to let him keep a kitten, runs into difficulties. The kitten does stay, but is accused of devouring Woz, a hamster belonging to Jonah's older brother. When Jonah and Granville plan to be partners for an animal habitat study, they are assigned to work with the bossiest girl in class. When Jonah goes to visit an elderly neighbor, the neighbor is missing. Well-rounded characters and many themes are comfortably woven into the plot." SLJ

Honeycutt, Natalie—*Continued*

Invisible Lissa. Bradbury Press 1985 168p $11.95; Avon Bks. pa $2.75 (3-5) **Fic**

1. School stories 2. Clubs—Fiction
ISBN 0-02-744360-4; 0-380-70120-0 (pa)
LC 84-20466

"Not only is Lissa the victim of Debra's snubbing campaign, but also the only girl in fifth grade excluded from the secret 'FUNCHY' club. Even friends Katie and Joel seem to have succumbed to Debra's phony charms. Hurt and isolated, Lissa throws herself into a school project that leads to a decisive confrontation and brings her back to social visibility." Publisher's note

"There are many middle-grades stories about classroom power struggles; this is not unusual in structure but it is better written than most, is nicely balanced by other facets of Lissa's life, and has a cheerful, lively tone." Bull Cent Child Books

Hooks, William H.

The ballad of Belle Dorcas; illustrated by Brian Pinkney. Knopf 1990 unp il $13.95; lib bdg $14.99 (3-5) **Fic**

1. Blacks—Fiction 2. Slavery—Fiction 3. Magic—Fiction
ISBN 0-394-84645-1; 0-394-94645-6 (lib bdg)
LC 89-2715

"Belle Dorcas, a free issue, marries Joshua, a slave. When his master decides to sell him, Belle Dorcas seeks the help of Granny Lizzard, a conjure woman. A tree by day, Joshua is transformed back into a man each night so he can be reunited with his love. Both are happy until the master cuts down the Joshua tree and uses the lumber to build a smokehouse." Child Book Rev Serv

"Hooks's graceful prose captures all the drama and poignancy of this tale of star-crossed lovers, and Pinkney's brooding illustrations, reminiscent of woodcuts, provide the perfect accompaniment." Publ Wkly

Circle of fire. Atheneum Pubs. 1982 147p $12.95 (5 and up) **Fic**

1. Ku Klux Klan—Fiction 2. North Carolina—Fiction 3. Prejudices—Fiction
ISBN 0-689-50241-9 LC 82-3982

"A Margaret K. McElderry book"

"Harrison Hawkins is an eleven-year-old white boy growing up in 1936 rural coastal North Carolina. His best friends are Kitty Fisher, an eleven-year-old black boy, and Kitty's sister, Scrap. A band of gypsies camps in his father's hollow. Harrison overhears a local bigot planning a Ku Klux Klan attack on the tinkers, the gypsies' name for themselves, on Christmas. Harrison begins to suspect his father is involved in the Klan plot. He wrestles with his conscience over whether or not to warn the gypsies." Voice Youth Advocates

The story "is crisp with dialogue and beautifully shaded with a variety of vivid characters. Its mystery aspects propel the story's momentum, while the ethical decisions inherent in the plot give readers a sense of history and of moral obligation." Booklist

Hoover, H. M., 1935-

Away is a strange place to be. Dutton 1989 167p $14.95 (4-6) **Fic**

1. Science fiction
ISBN 0-525-44505-6 LC 89-34455

When she is kidnapped from the Earth in 2349 to serve as slave labor on an artificial world under construction, twelve-year-old Abby must cooperate with her fellow prisoner Bryan, a spoiled rich boy, in order to plan an escape

"Hoover's crisp writing creates a gripping story with believable settings." Publ Wkly

Orvis. Viking Kestrel 1987 186p $12.95; Puffin Bks. pa $3.95 (5 and up) **Fic**

1. Science fiction 2. Robots—Fiction
ISBN 0-670-81117-3; 0-14-032113-6 (pa)
LC 86-28298

"The time is the distant future, the setting an Earth that is only partially settled, since most Terran descendants have lived for generations in space ships or space colonies. Toby is attending an Earth school and is unhappy because her domineering grandmother has decided to transfer her to a school on Mars. With a younger friend, Thaddeus, and the highly intelligent old robot Orvis, she decides to visit the great-grandmother who lives near Lake Erie and whom she's never seen. . . . Hoover is deft and consistent in her creation of a not-so-brave new world; her characters are solidly defined by their words and actions, and she maintains a brisk pace while subtly incorporating some thoughtful comments on human behavior." Bull Cent Child Books

The shepherd moon; a novel of the future. Viking 1984 149p $11.95; Penguin Bks. pa $3.95 (6 and up) **Fic**

1. Science fiction
ISBN 0-670-63977-X; 0-14-032611-1 (pa)
LC 83-16784

"While vacationing at her grandfather's isolated estate in the forty-eighth century, lonely, 13-year-old Merry witnesses the arrival of what is thought to be a meteorite but is, in fact, a conveyance carrying Mikel, an alien from one of Earth's artificial moons long thought to have been abandoned. Mikel's strange powers are frightening, and when he flees, Merry and her grandfather try to unravel the mystery surrounding him." Booklist

"Despite an occasional narrative unevenness induced by a shifting point of view, the book is notable for its depiction of the innocent-appearing yet malevolently amoral space visitor." Horn Book

Houston, James A., 1921-

Frozen fire; a tale of courage; by James Houston; drawings by the author. Atheneum Pubs. 1977 149p il $12.95 (6 and up) **Fic**

1. Wilderness survival—Fiction 2. Arctic regions—Fiction 3. Inuit—Fiction
ISBN 0-689-50083-1 LC 77-6366

"A Margaret K. McElderry book"

"Based on the true and dramatic ordeal of an Eskimo boy in the 1960's, this adventure story is set . . . in the far north. Kayak, a classmate of Matthew Morgan's in their Baffin Island school, suggests to his new friend

Houston, James A., 1921-—*Continued*
Mattoosie (Matthew) that they take a snowmobile and go to the rescue of Mattoosie's father when the latter, a prospector, disappears. The spare can of gasoline leaks, and the two boys face a homeward trek through seventy-five miles of whirling snow and bitter cold." Bull Cent Child Books

"Convincing dialogue, good pace, and lean style mark this as first-class adventure with a partial basis in fact." SLJ

Followed by: Black diamonds (1982) and Ice swords: an undersea adventure (1985)

Howard, Ellen

Circle of giving. Atheneum Pubs. 1984 99p lib bdg $11.95 (4-6) **Fic**

1. Cerebral palsy—Fiction 2. Friendship—Fiction
ISBN 0-689-31027-7 LC 83-15631

"When Marguerite and Jeannie move to Los Angeles in the late 1920's, they find their lives changed. The popular, outgoing Marguerite suddenly becomes shy, withdrawn, and ill at ease. When a new family moves to the block, Marguerite meets Francie, a girl with cerebral palsy. Francie's mother thinks she is a burden, a child to curb her pride, a child that cannot learn. Francie demonstrates her skills with a touching Christmas gift to her mother and brings the dull, uninteresting members of the community together into a family-like relationship." Child Book Rev Serv

"The novel is based on a true happening related to the author by her mother and grandmother, which helps to account for the warmly personal tone that makes the narrative so affecting." Booklist

Edith herself; illustrated by Ronald Himler. Atheneum Pubs. 1987 131p il $12.95 (4-6) **Fic**

1. Epilepsy—Fiction 2. Farm life—Fiction 3. Orphans—Fiction
ISBN 0-689-31314-4 LC 86-10826

"A Jean Karl book"

Orphaned by her mother's death, Edith goes to live with her older sister and dour brother-in-law in their stern Christian farming household, where the strain of adjusting seems to aggravate Edith's epileptic seizures

"The black-and-white drawings which head each chapter lend an old-fashioned, homespun touch to the quiet appeal of a young girl's triumph over her handicap and her ability to find joy and pleasure in her new surroundings." Horn Book

Her own song. Atheneum Pubs. 1988 160p $12.95 (4 and up) **Fic**

1. Adoption—Fiction 2. Chinese Americans—Fiction
ISBN 0-689-31444-2 LC 88-3393

"A Jean Karl book"

"Mellie, who lives with a childless couple in turn-of-the-century Oregon, is friendless and lonely, teased by her classmates for being adopted. Because her adopted mother is dead, Mellie is raised by her father, Bill, a stern and undemonstrative man, and by her aunt. But Mellie has a recurring dream of another place, and feels a strange kinship for the Chinese laundryman everyone else despises. It is only when—through the laundryman—Mellie discovers the truth behind her dreams that she also gains a new sense of self-worth. Although it has a warm and sensitive ending, the book has some stylistic problems, such as an overuse of flashbacks. But it also offers an unusual glimpse into life-styles and historical incidents not often addressed in children's books, and for that it must be valued." Publ Wkly

Howe, Deborah, 1946-1978

Bunnicula; a rabbit-tale of mystery; by Deborah and James Howe; illustrated by Alan Daniel. Atheneum Pubs. 1979 98p il $11.95; Avon Bks. pa $2.95 (4-6) **Fic**

1. Animals—Fiction 2. Mystery and detective stories
ISBN 0-689-30700-4; 0-380-51094-4 (pa)
LC 78-11472

"When the Monroes add a new pet to their household and vegetables are drained of their juices and turn white overnight, all the clues point to the little bunny they found in the theater the night they went to see a Dracula movie. The Monroes do not suspect Bunnicula, but their bookish cat, Chester, does. He sits up late reading Edgar Allan Poe and 'The Mark of the Vampire.' and he enlists the help of Harold, the dog, in getting to the bottom of the mystery." Child Book Rev Serv

"The plot is less important in the story than the style: blithe, sophisticated, and distinguished for the wit and humor of the dialogue. If readers like shaggy dog stories at all, they'd have to search hard for a funnier one." Bull Cent Child Books

Other available titles about Harold and Chester are entered below under James Howe; titles in picture book format are entered in Easy Section

Howe, James, 1946-

The celery stalks at midnight; illustrated by Leslie Morrill. Atheneum Pubs. 1983 111p il $11.95; Avon Bks. pa $2.95 (4-6) **Fic**

1. Animals—Fiction 2. Mystery and detective stories
ISBN 0-689-30987-2; 0-380-69054-3 (pa) LC 83-2665

"Convinced that Bunnicula, the Monroe family's pet rabbit, is a kind of vegetarian vampire, Chester becomes alarmed when the object of his suspicions mysteriously disappears. His overworked imagination begins to envision the possible consequences of Bunnicula's appetite for vegetable juices. . . . With his two canine companions—Harold, the narrator, and Howie, a naîve dachshund—Chester sets forth to locate Bunnicula and to save the victims." Horn Book

"The amusing and skillful black-and-white sketches capture the animals' antics and expressions of alternating doubt, skepticism, disgust and worry in this clever tale abounding with puns, wild chases and slapstick humor." SLJ

Other available titles about Harold and Chester are:
Howliday Inn (1982)
Nighty-nightmare (1987)

Dew drop dead; a Sebastian Barth mystery. Atheneum Pubs. 1990 156p $12.95 (4-6) **Fic**

1. Mystery and detective stories 2. Homeless people—Fiction
ISBN 0-689-31425-6 LC 89-34697

"A Jean Karl book"

Howe, James, 1946-—*Continued*

"Sebastian Barth and his friends Corrie and David discover what appears to be a dead body in the long-abandoned Dew Drop Inn. But when they return with the police, the body has vanished. Police theory—that the 'body' was a homeless man passed-out drunk—is refuted when the kids find the body again in the woods, undeniably dead and possibly murdered." SLJ

"The story is well crafted and has substance beyond escapist fare as a result of Howe's inclusion of secondary storylines involving the homeless and Sebastian's own worries about his father's pending job loss." Booklist

Other available titles about Sebastian Barth are:
Eat your poison, dear (1986)
Stage fright (1986)
What Eric knew (1985)

A night without stars. Atheneum Pubs. 1983 178p $13.95; Avon Bks. pa $2.95 (5 and up) **Fic**

1. Hospitals—Fiction 2. Physically handicapped children—Fiction 3. Friendship—Fiction
ISBN 0-689-30957-0; 0-480-69877-3 (pa) LC 82-16278

"Admitted to the hospital for heart surgery, 11-year-old Maria Tirone encounters 'Monster Man'—Donald Harris—whose burns have scarred his psyche as well as his face. Donald, rejected by the other pediatric patients, responds to Maria's fears about surgery, and the two become close friends." SLJ

"The plot is of less importance in this story than the perceptive handling of relationships, not only the friendship between Maria and Donald, but the supportive family relationships and the easy familiarity among the girls who are patients." Bull Cent Child Books

Howker, Janni

Isaac Campion. Greenwillow Bks. 1986 83p $10.25; Dell pa $2.95 (5 and up) **Fic**

1. Fathers and sons—Fiction 2. Great Britain—Fiction
ISBN 0-688-06658-5; 0-440-40280-8 (pa) LC 86-9843

Also available ABC-CLIO large print edition $14.95 (ISBN 1-85089-944-4)

"A first-person narrative, set between two letters to the author, [this] is the reminiscence of a ninety-six-year-old man recalling the tragic death of his older brother in 1901. . . . Perhaps in no other book for children have the reality of poverty and its effects on family relationships been so movingly portrayed, but the book is not a diatribe pro or con economic theories. Rather, it is a gut-wrenching view of a particular time, uncompromising yet not without humor." Horn Book

Hughes, Dean, 1943-

Family pose. Atheneum Pubs. 1989 184p $13.95 (5 and up) **Fic**

1. Orphans—Fiction 2. Runaway children—Fiction
ISBN 0-689-31396-9 LC 88-28501

"Eleven year old David runs away from his uncaring foster family and ends up sleeping in the warm hallway of the Hotel Jefferson. Paul, a struggling reformed alcoholic and the night bellboy, finds David there. Even though it means risking his job, Paul lets David sleep in an unused room, and eventually gets David to reveal his name and why he is a runaway on the Seattle streets. Paul's other co-workers are very good to David, and he begins to trust them. But the time comes to talk to a friend of Paul's at Social Services about David's future." Voice Youth Advocates

"The interaction of the characters and the clear definition of their quirks, clothing, and conversation hold the reader's interest. The young boy's naive but stubborn efforts to survive on his own and the growing affection between Paul and David are well presented and give the book considerable emotional impact." Horn Book

Hunt, Irene, 1907-

Across five Aprils. Follett 1964 223p o.p.; Berkley Bks. paperback available $2.75 (5 and up) **Fic**

1. United States—History—1861-1865, Civil War—Fiction 2. Illinois—Fiction 3. Farm life—Fiction
ISBN 0-425-10241-6 (pa) LC 64-17209

A Newbery Medal honor book, 1965

"Jethro Creighton, a boy of nine when the story begins, watches five Aprils come and go while his southern Illinois family is caught up emotionally and physically in the terrible conflict of the Civil War. Authentic background, a feeling for the people of that time, and a story that never loses the reader's interest." Wilson Libr Bull

Up a road slowly; cover painting by Don Bolognese. Follett 1966 192p o.p.; Berkley Bks. paperback available $2.75 **Fic**

ISBN 0-425-10003-0 (pa) LC 66-16937

Awarded the Newbery Medal, 1967

"Julie Trelling describes her life from the time her mother dies until her high school graduation: ten years. Aunt Cordelia's ramrod soul seems hard to live with, but Julie finds, to her surprise, when her father remarries and wants his daughter at home again, that she has become used to Aunt Cordelia and loves her dearly. The problems of jealousy, first love, parental relations, and snobbishness are handled with ease and honesty; the more serious problems of alcoholism and of emotional disturbance in adult characters are handled with dignity. A moving and beautifully written book." Sutherland. The Best in Child Books

Hunter, Mollie, 1922-

The haunted mountain; a story of suspense; illustrated by Laszlo Kubinyi. Harper & Row 1972 125p il lib bdg $12.89 (5 and up) **Fic**

1. Fantastic fiction 2. Scotland—Fiction
ISBN 0-06-022667-6 LC 77-183164

This "is the story of brave MacAllister's defiance of the magical creatures of the mountain, of his long years of captivity, and of his rescue by a doughty son and an old dog. The dog, indeed, gives its life to save MacAllister in his final confrontation with the blind ghost, the huge grey stone man who haunts the mountain and guards its treasure." Sutherland. The Best in Child Books

Hunter, Mollie, 1922-—*Continued*

The kelpie's pearls; illustrated by Joseph Cellini. Funk & Wagnalls 1966 c1964 112p il o.p. (4-6) **Fic**

1. Fairy tales 2. Scotland—Fiction LC 66-8355

Available G.K. Hall large print edition $16.50 (ISBN 0-7451-0758-3)

First published 1964 in the United Kingdom

"A kelpie who can change into a black horse with flaming eyes, the Loch Ness monster, a good witch . . . and Tirnan-Og (the land of eternal youth) are woven into [this] . . . fantasy. Morag MacLeod, a lonely old woman, befriends a kelpie and Torquil, a boy who understands animals so well he can almost talk to them, but she makes an enemy of wicked Alasdair, the trapper, because she will not help him steal the kelpie treasure horde of pearls." SLJ

"This is so enchantingly told in the gentle dialect of the Highlands that it is a spellbinder from first to last. Read it aloud—in school, home or library." Horn Book

The mermaid summer. Harper & Row 1988 118p $13.95; lib bdg $12.89; pa $3.50 (4 and up) **Fic**

1. Mermaids and mermen—Fiction 2. Grandfathers—Fiction
ISBN 0-06-022627-7; 0-06-022628-5 (lib bdg); 0-06-440344-0 (pa) LC 87-45984

"A Charlotte Zolotow book"

With the help of her brother, Jon, nine-year-old Anna daringly seeks to discover the secret means to undo a mermaid's curse upon their grandfather

"Hunter's atmospherically rich story, set about a century ago, unfolds against a tapestry of local color. The delicately intertwining plot skeins reveal both tightly controlled suspense and an intriguing puzzle. Characters are well realized and fit the time and setting as well as the folkloric mold that Hunter once again uses to thoroughly enchant her readers." Booklist

A sound of chariots. Harper & Row 1972 242p $12.95; lib bdg $12.89; pa $3.95 (5 and up) **Fic**

1. Death—Fiction 2. Authorship—Fiction 3. Scotland—Fiction
ISBN 0-06-022668-4; 0-06-022669-2 (lib bdg); 0-06-440235-5 (pa) LC 72-76523

A story set in post World War I Scotland. Bridie McShane's happy early childhood is interrupted by the death of her beloved father whose favorite child she was. Her sorrow colors her life as she matures, leading her to morbid reflections on time and death which she finally learns to deal with through her desire to write poetry

"The rich flavor of time and place, the details of poverty, hard work, and religious and political fervor add strength to the story." Horn Book

A stranger came ashore; a story of suspense. Harper & Row 1975 163p lib bdg $13.89; pa $3.50 (6 and up) **Fic**

1. Animals, Mythical—Fiction 2. Shetland (Scotland)—Fiction
ISBN 0-06-022652-8 (lib bdg); 0-06-440082-4 (pa) LC 75-10814

The author "mingles the reality of the lives of fishermen-crofters and the legends of the Selkies, the seal-folk of the Shetland Islands. A young man, Finn Learson, appears during a fierce storm. Is he the lone survivor of a shipwreck or is he—as young Rob suspects—a seal-man who plans to take Rob's sister to his ocean home? The folklore of the Selkies and the customs of the islands are woven throughout the tale, which culminates in a suspense-filled struggle between the forces of good and evil." Bull Cent Child Books

The wicked one; a story of suspense. Harper & Row 1977 136p lib bdg $12.89; pa $1.95 (4 and up) **Fic**

1. Fairy tales 2. Scotland—Fiction
ISBN 0-06-022648-X (lib bdg); 0-06-440117-0 (pa) LC 76-41515

"The Grollican, an otherworld creature, delights in tormenting fiery-tempered Colin Grant. Even a trip from Scotland to America doesn't rid the crofter of this persistent, almost likeable, pest." LC. Child Books, 1977

"The book exudes a fine Highland flavor and is an excellent example of the author's ability to interplay strong, solid characters with creatures from the Otherworld in tales of excitement and humor." Horn Book

Hurwitz, Johanna

The adventures of Ali Baba Bernstein; illustrated by Gail Owens. Morrow 1985 82p il $12.95; lib bdg $12.88; Scholastic pa $2.50 (2-4) **Fic**

1. Names, Personal—Fiction 2. Humorous stories
ISBN 0-688-04161-2; 0-688-04345-3 (lib bdg); 0-590-42011-9 (pa) LC 84-27387

"Tired of his ordinary name, David Bernstein, age eight, decides he wants to be called Ali Baba, and he has a series of . . . adventures, culminating in a birthday party to which he invites every David Bernstein in the Manhattan telephone directory. That's when he realizes how different people with the same name can be, and he decides that some day he might go back to calling himself David." Bull Cent Child Books

"Hurwitz' characters, as always, are believable, the situations realistic and the plot well developed." SLJ

Another available title about Ali Baba Bernstein is: Hooray for Ali Baba Bernstein (1989)

Baseball fever; illustrated by Ray Cruz. Morrow 1981 128p il $12.95; lib bdg $12.88; Dell pa $2.95 **Fic**

1. Baseball—Fiction 2. Fathers and sons—Fiction
ISBN 0-688-00710-4; 0-688-00711-2 (lib bdg); 0-440-40311-1 (pa) LC 81-5633

"Ten-year-old Ezra suffers from 'Baseball Fever' and a father who has no interest in the sport. Mr. Feldman is constantly nagging Ezra to show an interest in chess. A weekend trip that takes the pair to Cooperstown and the Hall of Fame sets the stage for father-and-son rapprochement." SLJ

"A brisk, breezy story about a believable family is told with warmth and humor." Bull Cent Child Books

Busybody Nora; illustrated by Lillian Hoban. Morrow Junior Bks. 1990 63p il $12.95; lib bdg $12.88 (2-4) **Fic**

1. Apartment houses—Fiction 2. New York (N.Y.)—Fiction
ISBN 0-688-09092-3; 0-688-09093-1 (lib bdg) LC 89-13649

Hurwitz, Johanna—*Continued*

A newly illustrated edition of the title first published 1976

"To five-year-old Nora and her little brother Teddy, their large apartment building in New York City is an exciting place to be. After learning there are as many as 200 people living 'in the same house,' Nora resolves to learn all their names and bring everyone together like one big happy family. Readers view big and little episodes in Nora and Teddy's lives through a nearly unblemished window on childhood." Booklist

Other available titles about Nora are:
New neighbors for Nora (1979)
Nora and Mrs. Mind-Your-Own-Business (1977)

Class clown; illustrated by Sheila Hamanaka. Morrow 1987 98p il $11.95; Scholastic pa $2.50 (2-4) **Fic**

1. School stories
ISBN 0-688-06723-9; 0-590-41821-1 (pa) LC 86-23624

Lucas Cott "is the problem child in class; although extremely bright, he acts out involuntarily at the most inopportune moments. Even when he is trying his best to do assignments properly, things go wrong." Horn Book

"Once again Hurwitz exhibits her talent for creating characters who talk, act, and think just like real kids. Adults are also given three-dimensional treatment. . . . There are some very funny moments here, as well as some gentle and touching ones. . . . Realistic dialogue, short sentences in large print, and commonplace situations that sparkle with humor combine to make this a fine choice for children just beginning chapter books." SLJ

Other available titles in this series are:
Class president (1990)
Teacher's pet (1988)

DeDe takes charge; illustrated by Diane de Groat. Morrow 1984 121p il $12.95; Scholastic pa $2.75 (3-5) **Fic**

1. Divorce—Fiction 2. Single parent family—Fiction
ISBN 0-688-03853-0; 0-590-43128-5 (pa) LC 84-9085

"DeDe has adjusted to her parents' divorce, although she often misses her father and finds it embarrassing to be the only 'divorced kid' in her class. It's her mother who's had trouble adjusting. . . . In a series of linked, episodic chapters DeDe tries to help and in fact is fairly successful." Bull Cent Child Books

"The easygoing story does a nice job of sketching out the turmoil of postdivorce life without losing a sense of humor. . . . Like other Hurwitz stories, this is both natural and to the point." Booklist

The hot & cold summer; illustrated by Gail Owens. Morrow 1984 160p il lib bdg $12.95; Scholastic pa $2.75 (3-5) **Fic**

1. Friendship—Fiction
ISBN 0-688-02746-6 (lib bdg); 0-590-42858-6 (pa) LC 83-19336

"Ten-year-olds Rory and Dere are best friends—a unit that does not need outsiders. So when their neighbor tells them that her neice is coming for the summer and that she expects they'll be great chums, Rory decides that the best attack is to ignore the girl from the start. But Bolivia . . . is not to be shunted aside. With the help of her talking parrot, she knows how to get attention and, once gotten, how to keep it. . . . This episodic novel is cheerful and perceptive—right on target for both boys and girls." Booklist

Another available title about Rory, Derek, and Bolivia is:
The cold & hot winter (1988)

Hurricane Elaine; [illustrated by Diane de Groat] Morrow 1986 99p il $12.95 (4-6) **Fic**

1. Family life—Fiction
ISBN 0-688-06461-2 LC 86-12409

Fifteen-year-old Elaine Sossi suddenly finds her life very interesting, as her family deals with the death of a cat, her little brother Aldo (featured in Much ado about Aldo) gets five dogs for his birthday, and she begins a promising romance

"Hurricane Elaine's mistakes are alternately funny, touching and exciting; a sweet teen at heart, she learns from each fall. It's good to find her breezy instead of stormy in the final surprise that ends the adventures." Publ Wkly

Much ado about Aldo; pictures by John Wallner. Morrow 1978 95p il lib bdg $13.88; Puffin Bks. pa $3.95 (3-5) **Fic**

1. Vegetarianism—Fiction
ISBN 0-688-32160-7 (lib bdg); 0-14-034082-3 (pa) LC 78-5434

"Aldo ponders on the meanings of everything in his orbit, especially relationships. He enters enthusiastically into a class project, a terrarium with crickets. When the teacher adds chameleons to the tank, however, Aldo realizes the purpose of the project: to teach how living things feed on each other. In shock and horror, Aldo becomes a vegetarian and gets into a fix when he stealthily rescues the crickets." Publ Wkly

"Aldo is an earnest and likeable character in a convincing family story with a pleasant urban setting. The author has a remarkable ability to project the amusements and worries of childhood, conveying them in a deceptively simple style." Horn Book

Other available titles about Aldo are:
Aldo Applesauce (1979)
Aldo Ice Cream (1981)
Aldo Peanut Butter (1990)

Rip-roaring Russell; illustrated by Lillian Hoban. Morrow 1983 80p il $12.95; lib bdg $12.88; Puffin Bks. pa $3.95 (2-4) **Fic**

1. Family life—Fiction 2. School stories 3. Nursery schools—Fiction
ISBN 0-688-02347-9; 0-688-02348-7 (lib bdg); 0-14-032939-0 (pa) LC 83-1019

Russell the four-year-old neighbor of Busybody Nora, entered above "faces the challenges of growing up in his own inimitable way. . . . Being a big brother disturbs him because baby Elisa takes altogether too much of his mother's time, but by the book's end, he decides that it isn't so bad." SLJ

"The action is low-keyed. . . . This is both realistic and sunny, with good adult-child relationships, the appeal of everyday life experiences, and a light, humorous treatment." Bull Cent Child Books

Other available titles about Russell are:
Russell and Elisa (1989)
Russell rides again (1985)
Russell sprouts (1987)

Hurwitz, Johanna—*Continued*

Superduper Teddy; illustrated by Lillian Hoban. Morrow Junior Bks. 1990 80p il $12.95; lib bdg $12.88 (2-4) **Fic**

1. Brothers and sisters—Fiction 2. New York (N.Y.)—Fiction

ISBN 0-688-09094-X; 0-688-09095-8 (lib bdg) LC 89-13592

A newly illustrated edition of the title first published 1980

Encouraged by his gregarious sister, featured in Busybody Nora, entered above, and his trusty Superman cape, five-year-old Teddy takes his first steps toward independence

"Hurwitz has a good focus on the feelings of a five-year-old; the author's relaxed manner of storytelling will make readers truly comfortable while it entertains them." Booklist

Hutchins, Pat, 1942-

Rats! illustrated by Lawrence Hutchins. Greenwillow Bks. 1989 96p il $11.95 (2-4) **Fic**

1. Rats—Fiction 2. Pets—Fiction 3. Family life—Fiction

ISBN 0-688-07776-5 LC 88-11287

Sam's insistence on getting a pet rat eventually changes his family's entire daily routine and brings an exciting surprise

"Hutchins's intimately detailed descriptions of pained and helpless parents being swept up by events hint at an autobiographical knowledge of her subject, but even with the focus so much on adults, children will appreciate the humor in the story and will surely understand and empathize with Sam's loyal devotion to his pet." Horn Book

Innocenti, Roberto

Rose Blanche; text by Christophe Gallaz and Roberto Innocenti; English translation Martha Coventry and Richard Graglia. Creative Educ. 1985 unp il $16.95 (5 and up) **Fic**

1. World War, 1939-1945—Fiction 2. Concentration camps—Fiction

ISBN 0-87191-944-X LC 85-70219

Set during "World War II. The story's namesake, Rose Blanche, is a young German girl who watches the escalating war activities with youthful detachment until the day she hikes out of town and discovers a concentration camp in the adjacent woods. She sees hungry children there and takes it upon herself to bring them food. One day, when the tide of the war shifts and the Germans are being routed, Rose Blanche is again making her way to the camp, only to be killed in the crossfire." Booklist

"The abrupt change in narrator [near the end of the book] is the one weak note in a powerful, disturbing, and unforgettable book. The text functions primarily as a commentary on the paintings—each a carefully planned vignette, creating story through somber colors, striking composition, and precise detail. The images are recognizable, drawn from the artist's memory and the collective memory of those familiar with historical documents." Horn Book

Irving, Washington, 1783-1859

Rip Van Winkle; pictures & decorations by N.C. Wyeth. Morrow 1987 94p il lib bdg $15 (5 and up) **Fic**

1. New York (State)—Fiction

ISBN 0-688-07459-6 LC 87-60720

A reissue of the title first published 1921 by David McKay Company; the story first appeared 1819-1820 in Irving's: The sketch book of Geoffrey Crayon, Gent.

Rip Van Winkle "is based on a folk tale. Henpecked Rip and his dog Wolf wander into the Catskill mountains before the Revolutionary War. There they meet a dwarf, whom Rip helps to carry a keg. They join a group of dwarfs playing ninepins. When Rip drinks from the keg, he falls asleep and wakes 20 years later, an old man. Returning to his town, he discovers his termagant wife dead, his daughter married, and the portrait of King George replaced by one of George Washington. Irving uses the folk tale to present the contrast between the new and old societies." Reader's Ency. 3d edition

Irwin, Patricia Kathleen Page, 1916-

A flask of sea water; [by] P.K. Page; illustrated by Laszlo Gal. Oxford Univ. Press 1989 unp il $15.95 (2-4) **Fic**

1. Fairy tales

ISBN 0-19-540704-0

"The goatherd, deeply in love with the princess after only a brief glance at her face, becomes a competitor for her hand in marriage along with two others. A smoothly written, attractive book." Horn Book Guide

Jacobs, Paul Samuel

Born into light. Scholastic 1988 149p $11.95; pa $2.75 (6 and up) **Fic**

1. Science fiction 2. New England—Fiction

ISBN 0-590-40710-4; 0-590-40622-1 (pa) LC 87-20792

"This science fiction period piece depicts a quiet New England community near the turn of the century as it is visited and changed by a handful of strange unearthly beings, one of whom is taken in by the Westwood family and becomes young Roger's Westwood's brother. . . . The story unfolds through the eyes of elderly Roger Westwood. Although this technique of an adult looking back on childhood events may limit the book's accessibility for some readers, the vividly visual language makes the novel a very finely crafted work. Gradual revelations about the nature of these beings and their origin should tantalize and beguile readers, and with its fascinating plot, the book should appeal to many." SLJ

Jacques, Brian

Mattimeo; illustrated by Gary Chalk. Philomel Bks. 1990 446p il $16.95 (6 and up) **Fic**

1. Mice—Fiction 2. Animals—Fiction 3. Fantastic fiction

ISBN 0-399-21741-X LC 89-37005

Sequel to: Redwall, entered below

Mattimeo, the son of the warrior mouse Matthias, learns to take up the sword and joins the other animal inhabitants of Redwall Abbey in resisting Slagar the fox

Jacques, Brian—*Continued*
and his band of marauders

"This final book in the Redwall trilogy is a truly thrilling conclusion to a swashbuckling, heroic adventure. Jacques's realistically drawn characters are full of personality, from the most humble bankvole to the foppish, lop-eared rabbit and the vicious, back-stabbing fox. The fierceness with which the Redwallers fight back to save their young lends the story credibility within the realm of the animal kingdom, while at the same time taking wonderful liberties with the imagination." Publ Wkly

Redwall; illustrated by Gary Chalk. Philomel Bks. 1986 351p il $15.95; Avon Bks. pa $4.50 (6 and up) **Fic**

1. Mice—Fiction 2. Animals—Fiction 3. Fantastic fiction
ISBN 0-399-21424-0; 0-380-70827-2 (pa)
LC 86-25467

Also available: Mossflower, a prequel published 1988

"Only the lost sword of Martin the Warrior can save Redwall Abbey from the evil rat Cluny and his greedy horde. The young mouse Matthias (formerly Redwall's most awkward novice) vows to recover the legendary weapon." Publ Wkly

"Thoroughly engrossing, this novel captivates despite its length. Some readers may argue that there is one too many capture-and-escape episodes and that some paring of the incidents would have resulted in a tighter narrative, and some librarians might wish that this exciting three-part story had appeared as a trilogy to better attract less-capable readers. But the nonstop action and finely honed characters more than compensate, and the theme will linger long after the story is finished." Booklist

Followed by: Mattimeo, entered above

James, Mary, 1927-

Shoebag. Scholastic 1990 135p $10.95 (5 and up) **Fic**

1. Cockroaches—Fiction 2. Fantastic fiction
ISBN 0-590-43029-7 LC 89-10828

Shoebag, a happy young cockroach who finds himself suddenly changed into a little boy, changes the lives of those around him before returning to his former life as an insect

"Fans of the improbable will find this cockroach fantasy holds appeal, while the combination of humor and possible discussion topics offers opportunities for interchange." Booklist

James, Will, 1892-1942

Smoky, the cow horse; illustrated by the author. Scribner 1929 263p il $12.95; pa $5.95; Aladdin Bks. (NY) pa $3.95 (6 and up) **Fic**

1. Cowhands—Fiction 2. Horses—Fiction
ISBN 0-684-12875-6; 0-684-17145-7 (pa); 0-689-71171-9 (pa) LC 29-19426

Awarded the Newbery medal, 1927

"Scribner illustrated classics"

First published 1926

"The story of a cowpony from his wild colthood on the range through varied incidents of his life. . . . Told in Will James' graphic cowboy language and fully illustrated with pencil sketches." Wis Libr Bull

Jarrell, Randall, 1914-1965

The animal family; decorations by Maurice Sendak. Pantheon Bks. 1985 c1965 179p il $16.95; Knopf pa $4.95 (4 and up) **Fic**

1. Animals—Fiction
ISBN 0-394-81043-0; 0-394-88964-9 (pa)
LC 65-20659

A Newbery Medal honor book, 1966

A reissue of the title first published 1965

A "tale about a lonely hunter who acquires an amazing family. One by one, he takes into his log cabin by the sea a mermaid, a bear cub, a lynx, and a small boy washed ashore from a shipwreck. The arrival and adjustment of each new member to this extraordinary family circle are sensitively related with touches of humor and wisdom." Booklist

"Simple enough to read aloud to children too young to read the book by themselves, the story is probably best suited to the sensitive reader who can appreciate the perceptive writing." Bull Cent Child Books

The bat-poet; pictures by Maurice Sendak. Macmillan 1964 42p il $13.95; Aladdin Bks. (NY) pa $4.95 **Fic**

1. Bats—Fiction
ISBN 0-02-747640-5; 0-02-043910-5 (pa)
LC 64-16812

The bat-poet, a little brown bat, "opened his eyes to the daytime and began to see the world in another light. . . . He made up poems about the daytime world's sights and sounds, and recited them to the unappreciative ears of his fellow bats and then hunted around for more receptive listeners." Toronto Public Libr

"Fortunately, the book does not come right out and baldly make its points about poetry, one, two, three. But like a good poem, it uses words, to make the reader thing and feel the ideas, rather than just hear them. A lovely book, perfectly illustrated—one well worth a child's attention and affection." Publ Wkly

Johansen, Hanna, 1939-

7 x 7 tales of a sevensleeper; illustrated by Käthi Bhend. Dutton 1989 95p il $12.95 (2-4) **Fic**

1. Family life—Fiction
ISBN 0-525-44491-2 LC 89-11805

First published 1985 in Switzerland

A seven-year-old boy identifies with sevensleepers, little squirrel-like creatures who sleep for seven months, and he insists on doing everything in sevens, including going to bed at seven o'clock, eating seven potatoes, and taking seven minutes to wash his face with seven drops of water

"The book is unusual in format as well as content. Artwork, well integrated with the text, appears on every page; fairly large type in vertical columns with unjustified right margins gives a feeling of free verse. While the whimsical prose will strike some readers as too precious,

Johansen, Hanna, 1939-—*Continued*
others will find its brand of imagination engaging." Booklist

Johnson, Annabel, 1921-

The grizzly; pictures by Gilbert Riswold. Harper & Row 1964 160p il lib bdg $13.89; pa $3.50 (5 and up) **Fic**

1. Bears—Fiction 2. Camping—Fiction 3. Parent and child—Fiction
ISBN 0-06-22871-7 (lib bdg); 0-06-440036-0 (pa)
LC 64-11831

"Eleven-year-old David, living with his divorced mother, is doubtful about going on a camping trip with his father. When a grizzly injures the father and disables the truck, David surprises both himself and his father by his resourcefulness." Hodges. Books for Elem Sch Libr

"Through a fine balance of descriptive detail and dialogue between the characters, the authors offer much insight into human relationships, especially those between father and son." Adventuring with Books. 2d edition

Jones, Diana Wynne

Archer's goon. Greenwillow Bks. 1984 241p $10.25; Berkley Bks. pa $2.95 (6 and up) **Fic**

1. Science fiction
ISBN 0-688-02582-X; 0-425-09888-5 (pa)
LC 83-17199

"When Quentin Sykes refuses to write his quarterly quota of words for the mysterious Mountjoy, he and his family learn it can be inconvenient—and even dangerous—to defy the commands of imperious magicians." SLJ

"Besides the inventive magic the author is able to develop a dozen zany, but complex characters whose interrelationships teach us something about Jones' favorite topic, the complexity of love and family ties. Highly recommended." BAYA Book Rev

Dogsbody. Greenwillow Bks. 1988 c1975 242p $11.95; Bullseye Bks. pa $3.50 (6 and up) **Fic**

1. Dogs—Fiction 2. Fantastic fiction
ISBN 0-688-08191-6; 0-394-82031-2 (pa)
LC 76-28715

A reissue of the title first published 1975 in the United Kingdom; 1977 in the United States

"Sirius, the Dog Star, falsely accused in the heavens of losing the Zoi, is sentenced to earth as a pup in order to search for this sacred object, which has fallen as a meteorite. Rescued from drowning by Kathleen, an Irish waif abused by her uncle's family, Sirius develops a close bond of affection with the girl. However, it is the search for the Zoi that compels Sirius, a quest that seems futile until help comes from Sol, Earth, and Moon. [The author] . . . intricately weaves contemporary family tensions with the evil powers' struggle to gain control of the Zoi and incidentally portrays a touching child-dog relationship. Her ability to tell the story through a dog's eyes in a believable way is to her credit." Booklist

Eight days of Luke. Greenwillow Bks. 1988 c1975 150p lib bdg $11.95; Knopf pa $3.50 (5 and up) **Fic**

1. Fantastic fiction
ISBN 0-688-08006-5 (lib bdg); 0-394-84339-8 (pa)
LC 88-220

First published 1975 in the United Kingdom

"David Allard is a young orphan forced to stay with a set of perfectly horrid relations. After a particularly trying day, he tries to lay a curse on them by speaking random words and syllables. Instead of finding a curse, he stumbles on an unlocking spell which releases a young redhead named Luke from a dreadful prison. Luke's appearance is followed by a series of strangers, including one-eyed Mr. Wedding, who want to find Luke and send him back to his prison. To keep his friend free, David undertakes a quest to find an object which has been stolen, but because of a hiding charm . . . placed on it, the searcher cannot know what it is he's looking for, or to whom it belongs." SLJ

"Jones' taut fantasy spins out with the ultimate revelation that David has become entangled with the Norse gods. . . . A rich complexity distinguishes Jones' storytelling, and an ingenious plot will reward the good reader." Booklist

Howl's moving castle. Greenwillow Bks. 1986 212p $10.25; Ace Bks. pa $3.50 (6 and up) **Fic**

1. Fantastic fiction
ISBN 0-688-06233-4; 0-441-34664-2 (pa)
LC 85-21981

"When the wicked Witch of the Waste turns Sophie Hatter into an ugly crone, the girl seeks refuge in Wizard Howl's moving castle. To her surprise and dismay, she finds herself embroiled in a contest between the witch and the wizard, in the tangled love affairs of the wizard, and in a perplexing mystery." Child Book Rev Serv

"Satisfyingly, Sophie meets a fate far exceeding her dreary expectations. This novel is an exciting, multifaceted puzzle, peopled with vibrant, captivating characters. A generous sprinkling of humor adds potency to this skillful author's spell." Voice Youth Advocates

Jones, Janice Beare

Secrets of a summer spy. Bradbury Press 1990 175p $13.95 (5 and up) **Fic**

1. Friendship—Fiction 2. Old age—Fiction 3. Islands—Fiction
ISBN 0-02-747861-0 LC 89-38156

Thirteen-year-old Ronnie, part of a trio of best friends that seems to be falling apart because Amy and Jimmy are growing up faster than she is, finds solace in the company of her island's eccentric catlady, an eighty-three-year-old retired concert pianist

"Jones manages to overcome some obvious turn-of-events with her vivid, evocative descriptions and characterizations. Ronnie's impulsive actions, her discomfort with the changes in her friends, and her need to find new companionship will be understood by many middle-school age readers." Voice Youth Advocates

Jones, Rebecca C., 1947-

The Believers. Arcade Pub. 1989 176p lib bdg $13.95; Knopf pa $3.95 (5 and up) **Fic**

1. Adoption—Fiction 2. Religion—Fiction 3. Fanaticism—Fiction
ISBN 1-55970-035-1 (lib bdg); 0-679-80594-X (pa) LC 89-84223

"Tibby rarely sees her adoptive mother Veronica, a glamorous TV reporter, and has become adept at sneaking around Aunt Evelyn, who cares for Tibby when Veronica is out of town. Tibby knows she's supposed to stay away from 'the Believers,' a fundamentalist sect that meets in a nearby barn, but she is drawn because of a budding friendship with Veri, a boy in the group, and because she hopes for a miracle that will bring her mother home to stay." Bull Cent Child Books

"This fast-paced, absorbing story . . . features skillful characterization and avoids the stereotyping that is suggested by the themes of parental neglect and religious fanaticism. While Tibby's acceptance of the love and devotion of her Aunt Evelyn as a substitute for her mother's is only hinted at, the book ends on a note of hope. A well-written, involving novel." SLJ

Germy blew the Bugle. Arcade Pub. 1990 136p $13.95 (4-6) **Fic**

1. School stories 2. Newspapers—Fiction
ISBN 1-55970-088-2 LC 90-81535

Jeremy Bluett, known to his friends as Germy Blew It, starts a school newspaper with dreams of making a fortune; but as usual, his grand plans backfire

"Intermingled with all Germy's woes are wonderfully amusing flights of fancy that depict the way things would be going in a world that appreciates Germy. Clever and funny, this one also tucks in a few messages about journalistic responsibility." Booklist

Other available titles about Germy are:
Germy Blew It (1987)
Germy Blew It—again! (1988)

Jones, Weyman

Edge of two worlds; illustrated by J. C. Kocsis. Dial Bks. for Young Readers 1968 143p il $7.95 (5 and up) **Fic**

1. Sequoyah, 1770?-1843—Fiction 2. Frontier and pioneer life—Fiction 3. Texas—Fiction 4. Cherokee Indians—Fiction
ISBN 0-8037-2211-7 LC 68-15256

Based on incidents in the life of Sequoyah, creator of the Cherokee's written language. "This is a story of a young Missouri boy and an old Cherokee Indian [Sequoyah] who face a long and difficult journey across the plains together; first as enemies, then as comrades in peril." Publ Wkly

"The writing is taut and sustained and will especially be enjoyed by better readers." Wis Libr Bull

Jordan, June, 1936-

Kimako's story; illustrated by Kay Burford. Houghton Mifflin 1981 42p il lib bdg $6.95 (2-4) **Fic**

1. Blacks—Fiction 2. Dogs—Fiction 3. New York (N.Y.)—Fiction
ISBN 0-395-31604-9 LC 81-2894

"Kimako lives in New York City and enjoys exploring the world around her. Her explorations are limited (for reasons of safety) until one week during the summer vacation when she becomes a 'sitter' for a neighbor's Airedale." Child Book Rev Serv

Jordan, MaryKate

Losing Uncle Tim; illustrated by Judith Friedman. Whitman, A. 1989 unp il $12.95 (2-4) **Fic**

1. AIDS (Disease)—Fiction 2. Death—Fiction 3. Uncles—Fiction
ISBN 0-8075-4756-5 LC 89-5280

When his beloved Uncle Tim dies of AIDS, Daniel struggles to find reassurance and understanding and finds that his favorite grown-up has left him a legacy of joy and courage

"The softly colored gouache illustrations have a pensive tenderness and an air of melancholy that perfectly suit the plot, mood, and theme of the text. The first-person narrative is conversational and readable, appropriate to the young school-age boy telling the story. Uncle Tim is shown as a loving, brave, gentle person. Although obviously written to teach about illness, grief, and death, the book is involving as well as honest and positive, filling a need for AIDS material at this age level." SLJ

Jukes, Mavis

Blackberries in the dark; pictures by Thomas B. Allen. Knopf 1985 unp il $10.95; lib bdg $11.99; Dell pa $2.50 (2-4) **Fic**

1. Grandmothers—Fiction 2. Death—Fiction
ISBN 0-394-87599-0; 0-394-97599-5 (lib bdg); 0-440-40647-1 (pa) LC 85-4259

Nine-year-old Austin visits his grandmother the summer after his grandfather dies and together they try to come to terms with their loss

"This spare story vividly captures the emotions of painful times and shows how they ease with sharing and remembering. . . . Poignant and perceptive, this has impressive resonance for so brief a story, and readers won't easily shed its warm afterglow. Heavily shaped pencil drawings are scattered throughout." Booklist

Like Jake and me; pictures by Lloyd Bloom. Knopf 1984 unp il $12.95; lib bdg $13.99; pa $4.95 (2-4) **Fic**

1. Stepfathers—Fiction 2. Spiders—Fiction
ISBN 0-394-85608-2; 0-394-95608-7 (lib bdg); 0-394-89263-1 (pa) LC 83-8380

A Newbery Medal honor book, 1985

In this book "timid Alex strives to be like his rugged cowboy stepfather, and the two find a common bond when Alex demonstrates his bravery by 'rescuing' Jake from a wolf spider that is crawling on his clothes." SLJ

"The humorous short story is illustrated picture-book fashion with a series of misty, soft-edged paintings that pose slightly caricatured figures largely on the pages. The story might be an excellent springboard for discussion of relationships and emotions; at the very least it's a satisfying vignette of the tender spots left when families take new shapes." Booklist

Juster, Norton, 1929-
The phantom tollbooth; illustrated by Jules Feiffer. Random House 1961 255p il $15.95; pa $3.95; Knopf pa $3.95 (5 and up) **Fic**

1. Fantastic fiction
ISBN 0-394-81500-9; 0-394-82199-8 (pa); 0-394-82037-1 (pa) LC 61-13202

Also available G.K. Hall large print edition $14.95 (ISBN 0-8161-4801-5)

"Milo, a boy who receives a surprise package which, when put together, is a toll-booth, goes off in a toy automobile on a tour of an imaginary country." Bull Cent Child Books

"It's all very clever. The author plays most ingeniously on words and phrases . . . and on concepts of averages and infinity and such . . . while the pictures are even more diverting than the text, for they add interesting details." N Y Her Trib Books

Karl, Jean, 1927-
Beloved Benjamin is waiting; by Jean E. Karl. Dutton 1978 150p lib bdg $10.75 (4-6) **Fic**

1. Family life—Fiction 2. Fantastic fiction
ISBN 0-525-26372-1 LC 77-25286

Hounded by a gang of kids after her mother's disappearance leaves her on her own, Lucinda hides in the abandoned caretaker's house in the local cemetery where she makes contact with intelligent beings from another galaxy

"Karl's . . . novel successfully combines space fantasy of the alien-contact variety with a suspenseful adventure of the grimly down-to-earth sort. . . . Lucinda is an appealing character, and her successful coping with an unusual survival situation will hold young readers' interest." SLJ

Kehret, Peg
Sisters, long ago. Cobblehill Bks. 1990 149p $14.95 (5 and up) **Fic**

1. Reincarnation—Fiction 2. Sisters—Fiction
3. Leukemia—Fiction
ISBN 0-525-65021-0 LC 89-38677

When Willow Paige nearly drowns, she envisions scenes from a past life which lead to an exploration of reincarnation and mental telepathy and set her on a quest to help give hope and strength to her sister who has leukemia

"This appealing story moves along briskly, with all the various pieces of the plot hanging nicely together, Willow and her best friend are likeable, interesting characters in their own right. . . . Suspense is maintained up to the very end, making this a page-turner." SLJ

Keith, Harold, 1903-
Rifles for Watie. Crowell 1957 332p $13.95; Harper & Row pa $3.50 (6 and up) **Fic**

1. Watie, Stand, 1806-1871—Fiction 2. United States—History—1861-1865, Civil War—Fiction
ISBN 0-690-70181-0; 0-06-447030-X (pa) LC 57-10280

Awarded the Newbery Medal, 1958

"Young Jeff Bussey longs for the life of a Union soldier during the Civil War, but before long he realizes the cruelty and savagery of some men in the army situation. The war loses its glamor as he sees his very young friends die. When he is made a scout, his duties take him into the ranks of Stand Watie, leader of the rebel troops of the Cherokee Indian Nation, as a spy." Stensland. Lit By & About the Am Indian

Kelleher, Victor, 1939-
The red king. Dial Bks. 1990 185p $14.95 (6 and up) **Fic**

1. Fantastic fiction
ISBN 0-8037-0758-4 LC 89-23745

Aided only by a trained bear and a monkey, Petie, a magician and thief, and, Tinkin, a female acrobat, challenge the power of the evil Red King who rules the Forest Lands by spreading the red fever to those who refuse to pay him tribute

"Excitement and suspense are maintained throughout the story; readers will anxiously turn the pages, eager to discover the outcome. . . . Fantasy lovers will find this to be an intriguing tale that provides not only high adventure but also some challenging food for thought about the nature of good and evil." SLJ

Kelly, Eric Philbrook, 1884-1960
The trumpeter of Krakow; [by] Eric P. Kelly; decorations by Janina Domanska; foreword by Louise Seaman Bechtel. Macmillan 1966 208p il $13.95; pa $3.95 (5 and up) **Fic**

1. Poland—Fiction
ISBN 0-02-750140-X; 0-02-044150-9 (pa) LC 66-16712

Awarded the Newbery Medal, 1929

"A reissue of a book first published 1928, in a new handsomely designed and illustrated format." Booklist

"How the commemoration of an act of bravery and self-sacrifice in ancient Krakow saved the lives of a family two centuries later. In this story of Poland, there is adventure and mystery aplenty." St Louis Public Libr

Kendall, Carol
The Gammage cup; illustrated by Erik Blegvad. Harcourt Brace 1959 221p il hardcover o.p. paperback available $3.95 (5 and up) **Fic**

1. Fantastic fiction
ISBN 0-15-230575-0 (pa)

A Newbery Medal honor book, 1960

A handful of Minnipins, a sober and sedate people, rise up against the Periods, the leading family of an isolated mountain valley, and are exiled to a mountain where they discover that the ancient enemies of their people are preparing to attack

Followed by: The whisper of Glocken (1965)

Kendall, Jane F.

Miranda and the movies; [by] Jane Kendall with illustrations by the author. Crown 1989 208p il $14.95; lib bdg $14.99 (6 and up) **Fic**

1. Motion pictures—Fiction 2. New Jersey—Fiction
ISBN 0-517-57301-6; 0-517-57357-1 (lib bdg)
LC 89-1515

The arrival of a band of moviemaking visionaries in peaceful Leewood Heights enlivens the summer of 1914 for twelve-year-old Miranda

"With its excellent period detail, this novel makes a little-known part of cinema live again. Miranda sparkles, and the various personalities of the American Film Company shine realistically. Subplots and conflicts flesh out the story into a very satisfying novel." Publ Wkly

Kendall, Sarita

The Bell Reef; illustrated by Mark Hudson. Houghton Mifflin 1990 c1989 134p il $13.95 (5 and up) **Fic**

1. Buried treasure—Fiction 2. Adventure and adventurers—Fiction 3. Colombia—Fiction 4. Dolphins—Fiction
ISBN 0-395-53354-6 LC 89-24708

First published 1989 in the United Kingdom

Anxious to recover the sunken treasure of a famous pirate ship, Daniel, a Colombian boy, and Vicky, an American girl, enlist the help of a trained dolphin and determine to carry out their hunt despite the ghost stories and mysterious underwater noises surrounding the Bell Reef

"Short chapters and fairly large print make this easy reading. Details about dolphin training, the history of Colombia, pirates and Spanish conquerors add depth to this story that contains a dash of magical realism so characteristic of South American literary tradition." Child Book Rev Serv

Kennedy, Richard, 1932-

Amy's eyes; illustrations by Richard Egielski. Harper & Row 1985 437p il $14.95; lib bdg $14.89; pa $6.95 (5 and up) **Fic**

1. Fantastic fiction 2. Buried treasure—Fiction 3. Pirates—Fiction 4. Adventure and adventurers—Fiction
ISBN 0-06-023219-6; 0-06-023220-X (lib bdg); 0-06-440220-7 (pa) LC 82-48841

A girl who has changed into a doll and a doll who has changed into a sea captain sail the pirate-ridden high seas with a crew of Mother Goose animals, in search of gold treasure

"This vital sense of life, both as possibility and meaning, is this big book's wonderful achievement, and it is handsomely complemented by the strong and vivid full-color jacket, two full-color and two black-and-white illustrations by Richard Egielski." N Y Times Book Rev

Kennedy, X. J.

The Owlstone crown; illustrated by Michele Chessare. Atheneum Pubs. 1983 209p $11.95; Bantam Bks. pa $2.50 (5 and up) **Fic**

1. Fantastic fiction
ISBN 0-689-50207-9; 0-553-15349-8 (pa) LC 81-3513

"A Margaret K. McElderry book"

Orphans Timothy and Verity are cruelly treated by their foster parents before escaping to another world where they are caught up in a struggle against a despicable tyrant and his wicked ally

This "is a fast-paced fantasy with strong whimsical characterizations. . . . Rich with amusing detail and poetic imagery, this will make an excellent read aloud." SLJ

Kerr, Judith

When Hitler stole Pink Rabbit; illustrated by the author. Coward-McCann 1972 c1971 191p il $8.95; Dell pa $3.25 (4 and up) **Fic**

1. Refugees, Jewish—Fiction
ISBN 0-698-20182-5; 0-440-49017-0 (pa)
LC 71-185765

First published 1971 in the United Kingdom

"Anna, aged nine, finds that her family suddenly has to leave Berlin for Switzerland because the Nazis have won an election. In packing, she has to choose between two stuffed animals—an old beloved pink rabbit and a new dog. She chooses the dog, assuming that their exile will be temporary. Only gradually as her family moves from Switzerland to France to England in search of a meager living does she realize that she will never return to Germany and that she will never see the rabbit again." Economist

"This tale of a refugee family is based on the author's childhood experience and, although anti-Semitism in Germany and financial depression everywhere are a somber backdrop, the book is warm and cozy, filled with the small, homely details of events that are important in a child's life." Saturday Rev

Followed by: The other way around (1975) o.p.

Key, Alexander, 1904-1979

Escape to Witch Mountain; illustrated by Leon B. Wisdom, Jr. Westminster Press 1968 172p il $10.95; Simon & Schuster pa $1.75 (5 and up) **Fic**

1. Fantastic fiction
ISBN 0-664-32417-7; 0-671-56044-1 (pa)
LC 68-11206

Orphaned "Tony and his sister Tia, who is mute to others but able to communicate with him . . . [are] menaced by a thug with a custody order. They flee to the town shown on their map, which is located deep in the Great Smokies. Closely pursued, their need for sanctuary prompts them to piece together out of deeply repressed memories the story of a trip . . . from a disintegrating planet to a carefully prepared new home on earth." SLJ

"Action, mood, and characterization never falter in this superior science fiction novel." Libr J

Followed by: Return to Witch Mountain (1978) o.p.

Key, Alexander, 1904-1979—*Continued*

The forgotten door. Westminster Press 1965 126p o.p.; Scholastic paperback available $2.75 (5 and up) **Fic**

1. Fantastic fiction
ISBN 0-590-43130-7 (pa) LC 65-10170

"Little John is discovered in a mossy cave by a kind family, the Beans. As they care for him they discover that he cannot speak English but can communicate with animals and humans. Little John, after some breathtaking experiences, takes his new friends through the forgotten door into the world where humans are friends with the animals as well as with one another." Read Ladders for Hum Relat. 5th edition

Kherdian, David, 1931-

A song for Uncle Harry; illustrated by Nonny Hogrogian. Philomel Bks. 1989 76p il $13.95 (4-6) **Fic**

1. Armenian Americans—Fiction 2. Uncles—Fiction
ISBN 0-399-21895-5 LC 89-3700

A young boy, Pete, relates his special friendship with his Armenian uncle Harry

"Though the story is set in the 1930s, the relationship between Pete and Harry is timeless. Every kid needs an Uncle Harry; those who don't can find one between these carefully phrased pages. Hogrogian's black-and-white drawings are scattered throughout. A joyous dust jacket sets the tone." Booklist

Kimmel, Margaret Mary

Magic in the mist; illustrated by Trina Schart Hyman. Atheneum Pubs. 1975 unp il $11.95 (1-4) **Fic**

1. Dragons—Fiction 2. Magic—Fiction 3. Wales—Fiction
ISBN 0-689-50026-2 LC 74-18186

"A Margaret K. McElderry book"

"Practicing to be a wizard, a boy named Thomas lived alone in a damp, cold Welsh cottage with his pet toad. One day a great mist came and Thomas found a tiny dragon in the grass; the dragon breathed on the fire and the logs burned brightly as they never had. The next day the dragon was gone, but the fire has burned cheerfully ever since." Bull Cent Child Books

"Hyman's pen-and-ink drawings effectively convey the chill starkness of marshlands and bogs." SLJ

King-Smith, Dick, 1922-

Babe; the gallant pig; written by Dick King-Smith, illustrated by Mary Rayner. Crown 1985 c1983 118p il $11.95 (3-5) **Fic**

1. Pigs—Fiction
ISBN 0-517-55556-5 LC 84-11429

First published 1983 in the United Kingdom with title: The sheep-pig

A piglet destined for eventual butchering arrives at the farmyard, is adopted by an old sheep dog, and discovers a special secret to success

"Mary Rayner's engaging black-and-white drawings capture the essence of Babe and the skittishness of sheep and enhance this splendid book—which should once and for all establish the intelligence and nobility of pigs." Horn Book

The fox busters; illustrated by Jon Miller. Delacorte Press 1988 c1978 117p il $13.95; Dell pa $2.95 (3-5) **Fic**

1. Chickens—Fiction 2. Foxes—Fiction
ISBN 0-440-50064-8; 0-440-40288-3 (pa) LC 87-37409

First published 1978 in the United Kingdom

"The fox busters are three extraordinary pullets, whose heritage, upbringing and intelligence combine to make them attempt a daring plan. Their enemies, four smart poultry-loving foxes, have hatched a murderous plan of their own. While the odds seem to favor the carnivores, the chickens have discovered an ingenious way to harden their unlaid eggs and to use them as weapons. Suspenseful, engrossing, and so carefully structured as to render it entirely believable, the story is an ideal read-aloud." Publ Wkly

Harry's Mad; pictures by Jill Bennet [sic] Crown 1987 c1984 123p il $11.95; Dell pa $3.25 (3-5) **Fic**

1. Inheritance and succession—Fiction 2. Parrots—Fiction
ISBN 0-517-56254-5; 0-440-40112-7 (pa) LC 86-6177

Also available G.K. Hall large print edition $14.95 (ISBN 0-7451-1101-7)

First published 1984 in the United Kingdom

"Harry, when he heard that a great-uncle in America had left him a prize possession, did a lot of fantasizing about what it could be. He never expected a parrot, nor was he pleased with his inheritance. That is, he wasn't pleased until he learned that Madison, the parrot, could talk—not 'Pretty Polly,' but talk as humans did. The removal of Madison by a frustrated burglar and the complex mishaps that ensue before the reunion of Harry and his Mad are lively, funny, fast-paced, and adroitly told. King-Smith is a master of word-play, and his deft comic writing is multilevel." Bull Cent Child Books

Magnus Powermouse; illustrated by Mary Rayner. Harper & Row 1984 c1982 120p il lib bdg $11.89 (4-6) **Fic**

1. Mice—Fiction
ISBN 0-06-023232-3 LC 83-48435

First published 1982 in the United Kingdom

"Madeleine Mouse ate Pennyfeather's Patent Porker Pills while she was pregnant and her son Magnus just grows and grows. How he grows from a greedy baby constantly demanding food to a Powermouse who can fight cats and spring traps makes an entertaining tale." Child Book Rev Serv

"Some aspects of the urbane, lightly satiric story—for instance, the shrewd humorous depiction of marriage and parenthood—may elude children; yet they are likely to be amused by the brisk story's witty views of gluttony, growth, and devotion." Horn Book

Martin's mice; illustrations by Jez Alborough. Crown 1989 c1988 122p il $11.95; Dell pa $2.95 (3-5) **Fic**

1. Cats—Fiction 2. Mice—Fiction
ISBN 0-517-57113-7; 0-440-40380-4 (pa) LC 88-20359

King-Smith, Dick, 1922-—*Continued*

Also available G.K. Hall large print edition $15.50 (ISBN 0-7451-0956-X)

First published 1988 in the United Kingdom

"Martin, a kitten, is branded 'wimp' by his siblings and 'stupid' by other farm animals for his friendly interest in mice. When he captures the pregnant mouse Drusilla, he makes her and her eventual brood his pets. He loves caring for them and can't understand their desire for freedom. Only when he becomes the pet of a big city apartment dweller does he realize why his pets deserted him." SLJ

"Dick King-Smith is at his anthropomorphic jolliest and the perspective of the farmyard allows him to explore a number of issues, such as the relationship between humans and animals. . . . Martin is also the kind of child/kitten who constantly asks questions. As a result, this book will teach you the differences between omnivores, herbivores and carnivores; the relative intelligence of sheep, cows and pigs; and how to keep a pet mouse." Times Lit Suppl

Pigs might fly; a novel; drawings by Mary Rayner. Viking 1982 158p il $12.95; Penguin Bks. pa $3.95 (4-6) **Fic**

1. Pigs—Fiction 2. Farm life—Fiction 3. Physically handicapped—Fiction 4. Great Britain—Fiction
ISBN 0-670-55506-1; 0-14-034537-X (pa); 0-590-40839-9 (pa) LC 81-11525

First published 1980 in the United Kingdom with title: Daggie Dogfoot

"Daggie Dogfoot (his front trotters are formed like paws) is the nickname bestowed on the runt of a litter born on a pig farm in England. Daggie overhears, out of its ironic context, the comment that 'pigs might fly' and this becomes his goal. His attempts to fly lead to his learning how to swim, with the help of a Muscovy duck and a happy-go-lucky otter. After a fierce rainstorm bursts the dam upstream, flooding most of the farm and carrying the food-storage shed downstream, it is Daggie who must swim to get help." SLJ

"Written with wit and controlled ebullience, this has excellent characterization, pithy dialogue, good pace, and admirable line drawings." Bull Cent Child Books

Sophie's snail; illustrated by Claire Minter-Kemp. Delacorte Press 1989 c1988 65p il $11.95 (3-5) **Fic**

1. Great Britain—Fiction
ISBN 0-385-29824-2 LC 89-1098

First published 1988 in the United Kingdom

"Sophie, a British girl, stars in five vignettes that show her independence and determination. In the first, Sophie and her brother's snail race teach her that slow and steady can win. In another, Sophie decides to be a lady farmer and nothing will change her ambition." Booklist

The author has "conceived a four-year-old heroine who is amusing and endearing without being the slightest bit winsome or cute. Independent readers can read this with no embarrassment, because the style is sophisticated in the true sense and because there is a tart humor throughout the episodic chapters that describe small but important events in the life of Sophie." Bull Cent Child Books

Kinsey-Warnock, Natalie

The Canada geese quilt; illustrated by Leslie W. Bowman. Dutton 1989 60p il $12.95 (3-5) **Fic**

1. Quilts—Fiction 2. Grandmothers—Fiction 3. Family life—Fiction 4. Vermont—Fiction
ISBN 0-525-65004-0 LC 88-32661

Worried that the coming of a new baby and her grandmother's serious illness will change the warm familiar life on her family's Vermont farm, ten-year-old Ariel combines her artistic talent with her grandmother's knowledge to make a very special quilt

"Written in simple language, this intergenerational love story succeeds in touching the heart through its rare combination of sensitivity and grit. Bowman's softly shaded pencil drawings subtly suggest the 1940s Vermont setting, characters, and mood." Booklist

Kipling, Rudyard, 1865-1936

The beginning of the armadilloes (1-4) **Fic**

1. Armadillos—Fiction

Some editions are:

Bedrick Bks. lib bdg $10.95 Illustrated by Charles Keeping (ISBN 0-911745-03-3)

Harcourt Brace Jovanovich $14.95; pa $3.95 Illustrated by Lorinda Bryan Cauley (ISBN 0-15-206380-3; 0-15-206381-1)

Story originally published 1902 as part of Kipling's Just so stories

A tortoise and a hedgehog combine their natural assets and transform themselves into armadillos to escape the hungry attention of a young jaguar

"Charles Keeping's handsomely illustrated version uses strong blues and greens, highly patterned shapes and bold design to render this jungle tale. Cauley's version features nearly twice the number of illustrations, which makes the action plain to young readers. At the same time, her anthropomorphized animals reflect well Kipling's gentle mocking of the bouncy Jaguar and provide a warmth which the Keeping version lacks." SLJ

The butterfly that stamped; illustrated by Alan Baker. Bedrick Bks. 1988 c1982 31p il lib bdg $10.95 (1-4) **Fic**

1. Butterflies—Fiction
ISBN 0-911745-04-1 LC 83-71482

Story originally published 1902 as part of Kipling's Just so stories, this edition first published 1982 in the United Kingdom

A butterfly and his wife help a mighty king control his quarreling wives

The book "gleams with rich color, biblical motifs and costumes." SLJ

The cat that walked by himself; illustrated by William Stobbs. Bedrick Bks. 1983 c1982 31p il lib bdg $10.95 (1-4) **Fic**

1. Cats—Fiction
ISBN 0-911745-05-X LC 83-71483

Story originally published 1902 as part of Kipling's Just so stories, this edition first published 1982 in the United Kingdom

A Just so story that humorously relates the evolution of feline independence

Kipling, Rudyard, 1865-1936—*Continued*

The crab that played with the sea; illustrated by Michael Foreman. Bedrick Bks. 1983 c1982 31p il lib bdg $10.95 (1-4) **Fic**

1. Crabs—Fiction
ISBN 0-911745-06-8 LC 83-71484

Story originally published 1902 as part of Kipling's Just so stories, this edition first published 1982 in the United Kingdom

Relates how the crab came to live both in the sea and on land and to lose its hard shell once a year

This book "reflects the deep color of the primordial ocean and the frailty of human life in confrontation with Eldest Magician's huge creations." SLJ

The elephant's child (1-4) **Fic**

1. Elephants—Fiction

Some editions are:

Bedrick Bks. lib bdg $10.95 Illustrated by Louise Brierley (ISBN 0-87226-030-5)
Harcourt Brace Jovanovich $13.95; pa $3.95 Illustrated by Lorinda Bryan Cauley (ISBN 0-15-225385-8; 0-15-225386-6)
Knopf $11.95 Illustrated by Tim Raglin (ISBN 0-394-88401-9)
Prentice Hall Press lib bdg $13.95 Illustrated by Edward Frascino (ISBN 0-13-273640-3)
Walker & Co. $7.95 Illustrated by Leonard Weisgard (ISBN 0-8027-6020-1)
Warne $4.95 Illustrated by Krystyna Turska (ISBN 0-7232-3449-3)

Originally published 1902 as part of Kipling's Just so stories

"This well-known whimsical fantasy that explains how the insatiably curious elephant child got his trunk is a fine example of one of Kipling's greatest classics." Adventuring with Books

How the camel got his hump (1-4) **Fic**

1. Camels—Fiction

Some editions are:

Bedrick Bks. lib bdg $10.95 Illustrated by Quentin Blake (ISBN 0-87226-029-1)
Picture Bk. Studio $14.95 Illustrated by Tim Raglin (ISBN 0-88708-096-0)
Putnam $5.95 Illustrated by Jonathan Langley (ISBN 0-399-21553-0)
Warne $4.95 Illustrated by Krystyna Turska (ISBN 0-7232-3450-7)

Originally published 1902 as part of Kipling's Just so stories

Relates how the idle camel got a hump on his back

Kjelgaard, Jim, 1910-1959

Big Red; illustrated by Bob Kuhn. new ed. Holiday House 1956 c1945 254p il $14.95; Bantam Bks. pa $2.95 (4 and up) **Fic**

1. Dogs—Fiction
ISBN 0-8234-0007-7; 0-553-15434-6 (pa) LC 66-2767

First published 1945

"The story of a champion Irish setter and a trapper's son who grew up together, roaming the wilderness." Title page

Together they conquered blizzards and varmints, and eventually tracked down Old Majesty, the great outlaw bear. In the process boy and dog grew to real maturity, and found a place for themselves

"A tale which paints the stern life of the Wintapi wilderness in strong, clear strokes." N Y Times Book Rev

Other available titles about Big Red's offspring are:
Irish Red (1951)
Outlaw Red (1953)

Klaveness, Jan O'Donnell

The Griffin legacy. Macmillan 1983 184p o.p.; Dell paperback available $3.25 (6 and up) **Fic**

1. Ghosts—Fiction 2. Mystery and detective stories 3. United States—History—1775-1783, Revolution—Fiction
ISBN 0-440-43165-4 (pa) LC 83-9353

Amy Enfield becomes involved with the spirit of her ancestor Lucy Griffin and undertakes a quest for silver stolen from the parish church by Lucy's lover during the American Revolution

"The story is somewhat weighted down with the familiar paraphernalia of special fantasy: mirrored apparitions, dream voices, cryptic messages. But riddles of plot and character absorb the reader, and the urgency of the quest carries the mystery forward at a breathless pace." Horn Book

Klein, Robin, 1936-

Enemies; illustrated by Noela Young. Dutton 1989 c1985 68p il $11.95 (3-5) **Fic**

1. Friendship—Fiction 2. Australia—Fiction
ISBN 0-525-44479-3 LC 88-27318

First published 1985 in Australia

Mary-Anna Clutterworth and Sandra Sutton are bitter enemies, until they have to spend an afternoon in town together and get lost

"Never one to seize a sledgehammer when a gentle pat will do the job, Robin Klein has once again subtly demonstrated her insightfulness into the emotions of the young. Both Mary-Anna andd Sandra are real-seeming, believable little girls, who have their own individual shortcomings and attributes along with an amazing propensity for hateful remarks. . . . The book, with its familiar situation and vivid characters, will undoubtedly ring true for many readers." Horn Book

Kline, Suzy, 1943-

Herbie Jones; illustrated by Richard Williams. Putnam 1985 95p il $12.95; Puffin Bks. pa $3.95 (3-5) **Fic**

1. School stories
ISBN 0-399-21183-7; 0-14-032071-7 (pa) LC 84-24915

Herbie's experiences in the third grade include finding bones in the boy's bathroom, wandering away from his class on their field trip, and being promoted to a higher reading group

"This should be encouraging to children who are having reading problems, should make readers who aren't

Kline, Suzy, 1943-*—Continued*
having such problems more sympathetic, and should amuse both groups equally. The story of third-grade Herbie focuses on his upward mobility in the stratified reading sub-groups of his classroom, but it's filled with light humor in its accounts of classroom incidents." Bull Cent Child Books

Other available titles about Herbie Jones are:
Herbie Jones and Hamburger Head (1989)
Herbie Jones and the class gift (1987)
Herbie Jones and the monster ball (1988)
What's the matter with Herbie Jones? (1986)

Horrible Harry in room 2B; pictures by Frank Remkiewicz. Viking Kestrel 1988 56p il lib bdg $10.95; Puffin Bks. pa $2.95 (2-4) **Fic**

1. School stories
ISBN 0-670-82176-4 (lib bdg); 0-14-032825-4 (pa)
LC 88-14204

Harry "is the devilish second grader who plays pranks and gets into mischief but can still end up a good friend. In a series of brief scenes, children meet Harry as he shows a garter snake to Song Lee and later ends up being a snake himself for Halloween. His trick to make scary people out of pencil stubs backfires when no one is scared, and his budding romance with Song Lee goes nowhere on the trip to the aquarium. Told by his best friend, Doug, this story should prove to be popular with those just starting chapter books or looking for a new male character." SLJ

Other available titles about Horrible Harry are:
Horrible Harry and the ant invasion (1989)
Horrible Harry and the green slime (1989)
Horrible Harry's secret (1990)

Konigsburg, E. L.

About the B'nai Bagels; written and illustrated by E. L. Konigsburg. Atheneum Pubs. 1969 172p il $13.95; Dell pa $2.95 (4-6) **Fic**

1. Jews—United States—Fiction 2. Baseball—Fiction
ISBN 0-689-20631-3; 0-440-40034-1 (pa)
LC 69-13529

A "story of a Jewish Little League team. Twelve-year-old Mark Stezer has problems: his mother is manager of the team; his brother is coach. This makes some sticky situations and 'overlaps' in his life. And he has worries about losing his best friend. Mark matures, having to make some difficult decisions on his own." Read Ladders for Hum Relat. 5th edition

"Penetrating characterizations emerge by implication; and the author's unfailing humor and her deep understanding of human nature are as noticeable as ever." Horn Book

From the mixed-up files of Mrs. Basil E. Frankweiler; written and illustrated by E. L. Konigsburg. Atheneum Pubs. 1967 162p il $12.95; Dell pa $3.25 (4 and up) **Fic**

1. Metropolitan Museum of Art (New York, N.Y.)—Fiction
ISBN 0-689-20586-4; 0-440-43180-8 (pa)
LC 67-18988

Also available ABC-CLIO large print edition $15.95 (ISBN 1-55736-092-8)

Awarded the Newbery Medal, 1968

"Claudia, feeling misunderstood at home, takes her younger brother and runs away to New York where she sets up housekeeping in the Metropolitan Museum of Art, making ingenius arrangements for sleeping, bathing, and laundering. She and James also look for clues to the authenticity of an alleged Michelangelo statue, the true story of which is locked in the files of Mrs. Frankweiler, its former owner. Claudia's progress toward maturity is also a unique introduction to the Metropolitan Museum." Moorachian. What is a City?

Jennifer, Hecate, Macbeth, William McKinley, and me, Elizabeth; written and illustrated by E. L. Konigsburg. Atheneum Pubs. 1967 117p il $12.95; Dell pa $2.95 (4-6) **Fic**

1. Friendship—Fiction 2. Witchcraft—Fiction
3. Blacks—Fiction
ISBN 0-689-30007-7; 0-440-44162-5 (pa)
LC 67-10458

Also available ABC-CLIO large print edition $15.95 (ISBN 1-55736-143-6)

A Newbery Medal honor book, 1968

"Two fifth grade girls, one of whom is the first black child in a middle-income suburb, play at being apprentice witches in this amusing and perceptive story." NY Public Libr. Black Exper in Child Books

Journey to an 800 number. Atheneum Pubs. 1982 138p $12.95; Dell pa $2.95 (4 and up) **Fic**

1. Fathers—Fiction 2. Parent and child—Fiction
3. Social classes—Fiction
ISBN 0-689-30901-5; 0-440-44264-8 (pa)
LC 81-10829

Bo learns about kindness, love, loyalty, appearances, and pretense from the unusual characters he meets when he is sent to live with his father after his mother decides to remarry

"With a fine display of irony yet without aiming over the heads of young readers, the author has written a splendid satire on modern American life and has peopled it with some of her most original and eccentric characters." Horn Book

A proud taste for scarlet and miniver; written and illustrated by E. L. Konigsburg. Atheneum Pubs. 1973 201p il $13.95; Dell pa $3.25 (5 and up) **Fic**

1. Eleanor, Queen, consort of Henry II, King of England, 1122?-1204—Fiction
ISBN 0-689-30111-1; 0-440-47201-6 (pa)
LC 73-76320

This is an historical novel about the 12th century queen, Eleanor of Aquitaine, wife of kings of France and England and mother of King Richard the Lion Heart and King John. Impatiently awaiting the arrival of her second husband, King Henry II, in heaven, she recalls her life with the aid of some contemporaries

The author "has succeeded in making history amusing as well as interesting. . . . The characterization is superb—not only of Eleanor, who dominates the Tales, but of aesthetic Abbot Suger, who was responsible for the invention of Gothic architecture, and of William the Marshal, who always backed the winning Plantagenet. . . . The black-and-white drawings are skillfully as well

Konigsburg, E. L.—*Continued*

as appropriately modeled upon medieval manuscript illuminations and add their share of joy to the book." Horn Book

Up from Jericho Tel. Atheneum Pubs. 1986 178p $13.95; Dell pa $2.95 (5 and up) **Fic**

1. Actors and actresses—Fiction 2. Mystery and detective stories
ISBN 0-689-31194-X; 0-440-49142-8 (pa) LC 85-20061

"Jeanmarie and Malcolm are both unpopular, both bossy, both latchkey children, both live in a trailer park, and both want to be famous. Jeanmarie knows that she will be a famous actress and that Malcolm will one day be a famous scientist. These two friends embark on a series of adventures encouraged by the spirit of the long dead actress, Tallulah. Yes, presumbably 'the' Tallulah! Tallulah, as a ghost, has the ability to make them invisible, and in that state the kids are sent to find the missing Regina Stone." Voice Youth Advocates

"Whether she is writing a realistic or a fanciful story, Konigsburg always provides fresh ideas, tart wit and humor, and memorable characters. As for style, she is a natural and gifted storyteller. . . . This is a lively, clever, and very funny book." Bull Cent Child Books

Kortum, Jeanie

Ghost vision; pictures by Dugald Stermer. Pantheon Bks. 1983 143p il $10.95 (5 and up) **Fic**

1. Inuit—Fiction 2. Greenland—Fiction
ISBN 0-394-86190-6 LC 83-4706

"A Sierra Club book"

"On a hunting trip in Northern Greenland, an Inuit boy finds he is having visions of the past and can communicate with the people of Inuit legend. His father, however, believes in a modern Greenland with no place for what he calls nostalgia. In the end Panipaq must convince his father in order to save his life." Child Book Rev Serv

"The book gives an effective picture of cultural conflict among the contemporary Inuit of Greenland as well as of some of the cultural patterns, but its focus is on the legendary; as a fantasy it is slow-paced, the realistic matrix vying for attention rather than serving as a base for the fantastic." Bull Cent Child Books

Kropp, Paul, 1948-

Moonkid and Liberty. Little, Brown 1990 c1988 167p $13.95 (6 and up) **Fic**

1. Moving, Household—Fiction 2. School stories 3. Brothers and sisters—Fiction 4. Divorce—Fiction
ISBN 0-316-50485-8 LC 89-27192

"Joy Street books"

First published 1988 in Canada

While Libby and Ian, who live with their nonconformist father, experience the problems of starting over at a new high school, their mother resurfaces in their lives and wants them to come and live with her in California

"Told from two points of view, this funny book deals nicely with growing up, fitting in, and working on priorities. . . . How Ian and Liberty deal with their mother, father and friends makes for an enjoyable and surprisingly suspenseful read." BAYA Book Rev

Krumgold, Joseph, 1908-1980

—and now Miguel; illustrated by Jean Charlot. Crowell 1953 245p il $13.95; lib bdg $13.89; Harper & Row pa $3.50 (6 and up) **Fic**

1. Shepherds—Fiction 2. Sheep—Fiction 3. New Mexico—Fiction
ISBN 0-690-09118-4; 0-690-04696-0 (lib bdg); 0-06-440143-X (pa) LC 53-8415

Awarded the Newbery Medal, 1954

The "story of a family of New Mexican sheepherders, in which Miguel, neither child nor man, tells of his great longing to accompany men and sheep to summer pasture, and expresses his need to be recognized as a maturing individual." Cincinnati Public Libr

The "seasonal life of the shepherds is realistically and sensitively drawn. Nevertheless the book's appeal is likely to be limited because of the introspective character that the author has given to Miguel and because of the stylized form in which the tale is told." Ont Libr Rev

Onion John; illustrated by Symeon Shimin. Crowell 1959 248p il $12.95; lib bdg $14.89; Harper & Row pa $3.95 (5 and up) **Fic**

1. Friendship—Fiction
ISBN 0-690-59957-9; 0-690-04698-7 (lib bdg); 0-06-440144-8 (pa) LC 59-11395

Awarded the Newbery Medal, 1960

The story "at once humorous and compassionate, of Andy Rusch, twelve, and European-born Onion John, the town's odd-jobs man and vegetable peddler who lives in a stone hut and frequents the dump. Andy . . . tells of their wonderful friendship and of how he and his father, as well as Onion John, are affected when the Rotary Club, at his father's instigation, attempts to transform Onion John's way of life." Booklist

"The writing has dignity and strength. There is conflict, drama, and excellent character portrayal." SLJ

Lamorisse, Albert, 1922-1970

The red balloon. Doubleday 1957 c1956 unp il $13.95; pa $6.95 (1-4) **Fic**

1. Balloons—Fiction 2. Paris (France)—Fiction
ISBN 0-385-00343-9; 0-385-14297-8 (pa) LC 57-9229

Original French edition, 1956

"The chief feature of this book is the stunning photographs, many in color, which were taken during the filming of the French movie of the same name. A little French schoolboy Pascal catches a red balloon which turns out to be magic. The streets of Paris form a backdrop for a charming story and superb photographs." Libr J

Lampman, Evelyn Sibley

White captives. Atheneum Pubs. 1975 181p $6.95 (5 and up) **Fic**

1. Oatman, Olive Ann—Fiction 2. Indians of North America—Fiction
ISBN 0-689-50023-8 LC 74-18187

Lampman, Evelyn Sibley—*Continued*

"A Margaret K. McElderry book"

"The story of Olive Oatman's five years of slavery among the Apache and Mohave Indians was first recorded in 1857, a year after her return to white society. At that time, the account became a relative best-seller and fanned the flames of anti-Indian feeling. Lampman's current version, told mainly from Olive's viewpoint but shifting at times to those of a few of the Indian characters, affords readers a degree of insight into the world of the two tribes, depicting the Apaches and Mohave as neither heartless nor holy. The narrative itself is well paced, though often depressing, and the characters are convincing enough to sustain reader involvement." Booklist

Langton, Jane

The fledgling. Harper & Row 1980 182p il lib bdg $12.89; pa $3.50 (5 and up) **Fic**

1. Geese—Fiction 2. Fantastic fiction
ISBN 0-06-023679-5 (lib bdg); 0-06-440121-9 (pa)
LC 79-2008

A Newbery Medal honor book, 1981

"An Ursula Nordstrom book"

"Quiet, introspective Georgie . . . yearns to fly. An encounter with a large, old Canadian goose, which stops at Walden Pond on its migratory journey south, brings her that chance. . . . Then neighboring Mr. Preek, who tries to save Georgie from what he thinks is an attacking predator, and Miss Prawn, who sees the girl's feat as a saintly sign, interfere. . . . In the end, Mr. Preek seemingly wins as he brings the goose down with a blast from his gun, but Georgie still has the Goose Prince's present (a rubber ball that is magically transformed before her eyes into an image of the earth)." Booklist

The writing is alternately solemn and funny, elevated and colloquial. It is mythic, almost sacred, in passages involving Georgie and the goose; it is satiric, almost irreverent, when it relates to Mr. Preek and Miss Prawn." Horn Book

The fragile flag. Harper & Row 1984 275p il $12.95; lib bdg $12.89; pa $4.95 (5 and up) **Fic**

1. Protests, demonstrations, etc.—Fiction 2. Arms control—Fiction
ISBN 0-06-023698-1; 0-06-023699-X (lib bdg); 0-06-440311-4 (pa) LC 83-49471

A nine-year-old girl leads a march of children from Massachusetts to Washington, in protest against the President's new missile which is capable of destroying the Earth

"There may be differences of opinion about the political-military implications of the story; there can be little disagreement about its effectiveness as a piece of dramatic and polished writing. The book has good pace, momentum, strong characters, and a sturdy story line." Bull Cent Child Books

Lattimore, Deborah Nourse

The dragon's robe. Harper & Row 1990 unp il $14.95; lib bdg $19.89 (3-5) **Fic**

1. China—Fiction 2. Fairy tales
ISBN 0-06-023719-8; 0-06-023723-6 (lib bdg)
LC 89-34512

Kwan Yin, a young weaver in medieval China, saves her people from drought and foreign invasion by weaving the imperial dragon's robe

"Elegantly told in the manner of a classic fairy tale. . . . In burnished tones of brown and gold, Lattimore's intricate, sumptuous paintings transform each spread into a rich tapestry." Publ Wkly

Lawson, Robert, 1892-1957

Ben and me; a new and astonishing life of Benjamin Franklin, as written by his good mouse Amos; lately discovered, edited and illustrated by Robert Lawson. Little, Brown 1939 113p il $14.95; pa $4.95 (5 and up) **Fic**

1. Franklin, Benjamin, 1706-1790—Fiction 2. Mice—Fiction
ISBN 0-316-51732-1; 0-316-51730-5 (pa)
LC 39-24448

"How Amos, a poor church mouse, oldest son of a large family, went forth into the world to make his living, and established himself in Benjamin Franklin's old fur cap, 'a rough frontier-cabin type of residence,' and made himself indispensable to Ben with his advice and information, and incidentally let himself in for some very strange experiences is related here in a merry compound of fact and fancy." Bookmark

"The sophisticated and clever story is illustrated by even more sophisticated and clever line drawings." Roundabout of Books

Mr. Revere and I; set down and embellished with numerous drawings by Robert Lawson. Little, Brown 1953 152p il $14.95; pa $4.95 (5 and up) **Fic**

1. Revere, Paul, 1735-1818—Fiction 2. Horses—Fiction 3. United States—History—1775-1783, Revolution—Fiction
ISBN 0-316-51739-9; 0-316-51729-1 (pa)
LC 52-10952

"Being an account of certain episodes in the career of Paul Revere, Esq., as recently revealed by his horse, Scheherazade, late pride of His Royal Majesty's 14th Regiment of Foot." Subtitle

"A delightful tale which is perfect for reading aloud to the whole family. The make-up is excellent, illustrations are wonderful, and the reader will get a very interesting picture of the American Revolution." Libr J

Rabbit Hill. Viking 1944 127p il lib bdg $12.95; Puffin Bks. pa $3.95 (3-6) **Fic**

1. Rabbits—Fiction 2. Animals—Fiction
ISBN 0-670-58675-7 (lib bdg); 0-14-031010-X (pa)
LC 44-8234

Awarded the Newbery Medal, 1945

"Story of the great rejoicing among the wild creatures when the news goes round that new people are coming to live in the big house. For people in the big house

Lawson, Robert, 1892-1957—*Continued*
will mean a garden and a garden means food. Their hopes are rewarded. The new people are 'planting folks' and the garden is big enough to provide for all." Wis Libr Bull

"Robert Lawson, because he loves the Connecticut country and the little animals of field and wood and looks at them with the eye of an artist, a poet and a child, has created for the boy and girl, indeed for the sensitive reader of any age, a whole, fresh, lively, amusing world." N Y Times Book Rev

Followed by: The tough winter, entered below

The tough winter. Viking 1954 128p il o.p.; Puffin Bks. paperback available $3.95 (3-6) **Fic**

1. Rabbits—Fiction 2. Animals—Fiction
ISBN 0-14-031215-3 (pa) LC 54-4416

Sequel to: Rabbit Hill, entered above

"When the 'folks' go south for the winter and the caretaker arrives with a 'mean and ornery' dog, the small animals experience a tough winter that is made bearable by the spirit of friendliness among them." Natl Counc of Teach of Engl. Adventuring with Books. 2d edition

Le Guin, Ursula K., 1929-

Catwings; illustrations by S. D. Schindler. Orchard Bks. 1988 39p il $11.95; lib bdg $11.99; Scholastic pa $2.50 (2-4) **Fic**

1. Cats—Fiction
ISBN 0-531-05759-3; 0-531-08359-4 (lib bdg); 0-590-42833-0 (pa) LC 87-33104

"A Richard Jackson book"

"When four kittens with wings are born in a rough city neighborhood, their mother nurtures and protects them as they grow and learn to fly. At her urging they soon escape the dangerous streets and alleys, flying to a forest where they find more enemies but, finally, new friends." Booklist

"Le Guin's adroit writing style, the well-observed feline detail, the thematic concern for natural victims of human environment, and the gentle humor make this a prime choice for reading aloud, although one would not want children to miss the fine-line hatch drawings that further project the satisfying sense of reality." Bull Cent Child Books

Followed by: Catwings return, entered below

Catwings return; illustrations by S. D. Schindler. Orchard Bks. 1989 48p il $11.95; lib bdg $11.99 (2-4) **Fic**

1. Cats—Fiction
ISBN 0-531-05803-4; 0-531-08403-5 (lib bdg)
LC 88-17902

"A Richard Jackson book"

"Two of the four cats in *Catwings* [entered above] decide to visit their mother, Mrs. Jane, in the city. They find the old neighborhood under attack by wrecking balls and barely rescue Mrs. Jane's last kitten, winged and black, before saying good-bye to their aging mother, who has been adopted by a benefactor." Bull Cent Child Books

"Le Guin's precise prose keeps the fantasy so securely rooted in reality that the magic is all the more convincing. Similar to the earlier book in format, this small, well-designed volume will please young readers with its many illustrations. Few artists use full-color washes with as much restraint as Schindler or to such good effect." Booklist

A wizard of Earthsea; drawings by Ruth Robbins. Parnassus Press 1968 205p il o.p.; Bantam Bks. paperback available $3.95 (6 and up) **Fic**

1. Fantastic fiction
ISBN 0-553-26250-5 (pa) LC 68-21992

"An imaginary archipelago is the setting for . . . [this] fantasy about a talented but proud, overzealous student of wizardry. In a willful misuse of his limited powers, the novice wizard unleashes a shadowy, malevolent creature that endangers his life and the world of Earthsea. To atone for his misdeed, Ged goes on a perilous journey through the island kingdom to find the baleful beast and destroy its evil influence." Booklist

A "powerful fantasy-allegory. Though set as prose, the rhythms of the language are truly and consistently poetical." Read Ladders for Hum Relat. 6th edition

Other available titles in this series are:
The farthest shore (1972)
Tehanu (1990)
The Tombs of Atuan (1971)

L'Engle, Madeleine, 1918-

Meet the Austins. Vanguard Press 1960 191p o.p.; Dell paperback available $3.25 (5 and up) **Fic**

1. Family life—Fiction 2. Orphans—Fiction
ISBN 0-440-95777-X (pa) LC 60-9726

A "story of the family of a country doctor, told by the twelve-year-old daughter, during a year in which a spoiled young orphan, Maggy, comes to live with them. . . . [This is an] account of the family's adjustment to Maggy and hers to them." Horn Book

A ring of endless light. Farrar, Straus & Giroux 1980 324p $14.95; Dell pa $3.50 (5 and up) **Fic**

1. Death—Fiction 2. Dolphins—Fiction
ISBN 0-374-36299-8; 0-440-97232-9 (pa)
LC 79-27679

A Newbery Medal honor book, 1981

Vicky Austin, who appeared in Meet the Austins (entered above) and The moon by night (1963), "is now sixteen and saddened by the fact that her beloved grandfather has terminal cancer; her summer is further disturbed because a family friend has lost his life rescuing a would-be suicide, the latter a rich, unhappy young man who makes demands on Vicky's time and affections. She is, however, more responsive to Adam [a character who previously appeared in The arm of the starfish (1965)] who works at a marine biology station and who is the first to realize that Vicky has telepathic powers and can communicate with the dolphins he's using in experiments." Bull Cent Child Books

A wrinkle in time. Farrar, Straus & Giroux 1962 211p $13.95; Dell pa $3.50 (5 and up) **Fic**

1. Fantastic fiction
ISBN 0-374-38613-7; 0-440-49805-8 (pa)

L'Engle, Madeleine, 1918-—*Continued*
Also available ABC-CLIO large print edition $14.95 (ISBN 1-55736-059-6)

Awarded the Newbery Medal, 1963

"A brother and sister, together with a friend, go in search of their scientist father who was lost while engaged in secret work for the government on the tesseract problem. A tesseract is a wrinkle in time. The father is a prisoner on a forbidding planet, and after awesome and terrifying experiences, he is rescued, and the little group returns safely to Earth and home." Child Books Too Good To Miss

"It makes unusual demands on the imagination and consequently gives great rewards." Horn Book

Other available titles in this series are:
Many waters (1986)
A swiftly tilting planet (1978)
A wind in the door (1973)

Lenski, Lois, 1893-1974

Strawberry girl; written and illustrated by Lois Lenski. Lippincott 1945 193p il $15.95; lib bdg $15.89; Dell pa $3.50 (4-6) **Fic**

1. Florida—Fiction
ISBN 0-397-30109-X; 0-397-30110-3 (lib bdg); 0-440-48347-6 (pa) LC 45-7609

Awarded the Newbery Medal, 1946

"A strong sense of place pervades this story of Birdie Boyer, a little Cracker girl who helps her Florida family to raise strawberries and to cope with the shiftless Slaters next door." Hodges. Books for Elem Sch Libr

"An authentic regional tale told with humor and vigor." Child Books Too Good to Miss

Levin, Betty, 1927-

Brother moose. Greenwillow Bks. 1990 213p lib bdg $12.95 (5 and up) **Fic**

1. Orphans—Fiction 2. Frontier and pioneer life—Fiction 3. Indians of North America—Fiction
ISBN 0-688-09266-7 LC 89-34437

"Orphans Nell and Louisa, on their way to foster homes in rural Canada in the late nineteenth century, find their journey unexpectedly curtailed. They face the prospect of surviving winter with a runaway Indian and his grandson in the northern Maine wilderness. A singular, fascinating survival story based on some little-known aspects of American social history." Horn Book Guide

Levitin, Sonia, 1934-

The return. Atheneum Pubs. 1987 213p map $12.95; Fawcett Bks. pa $2.95 (6 and up) **Fic**

1. Jews—Ethiopia—Fiction 2. Antisemitism—Fiction
ISBN 0-689-31309-8; 0-449-70280-4 (pa) LC 86-25891

"In a docunovel of a Jewish Ethiopian family's flight to Israel, Levitin focuses on an orphan, Desta, whose older brother, Joas, persuades her to leave the village where hunger and political recriminations constantly threaten their lives." Bull Cent Child Books

"A vivid and compelling book about a subject untouched in children's literature. . . . Levitin's tour de force is sensitively written; her command of the language is impressive and she uses Ethiopian terms effectively, interspersing them in ways readers will understand. Whatever their religious persuasion, young people will be touched." Booklist

Silver days. Atheneum Pubs. 1989 185p $13.95 (5 and up) **Fic**

1. United States—Immigration and emigration—Fiction 2. Jews—United States—Fiction 3. World War, 1939-1945—Fiction
ISBN 0-689-31563-5 LC 88-27491

Sequel to: Journey to America (1970)

"Once prosperous, a Jewish family that has fled Nazi Germany finds life difficult in Manhattan and moves to California, where Papa insists that he will be able to make a decent living. The story is told by the middle daughter (Lisa, 13) and the narration is punctuated by her italicized journal entries." Bull Cent Child Books

"Levitin's novel ends on a positive note, with narrator Lisa and her older sister Ruth well settled into American life. Her story moves forward easily through incident and detail. The sense of the times is strong, both in terms of the war's reaching shadow and the prejudices that are quickly displayed." Booklist

Levoy, Myron

Alan and Naomi. Harper & Row 1977 192p lib bdg $12.89; pa $3.95 (6 and up) **Fic**

1. Friendship—Fiction 2. Jews—New York (N.Y.)—Fiction 3. Mentally ill—Fiction 4. World War, 1939-1945—Fiction
ISBN 0-06-023800-3 (lib bdg); 0-06-440209-6 (pa) LC 76-41522

"After reluctantly agreeing to befriend Naomi, a disturbed war refugee who has crumbled under the memory of seeing her father beaten to death by Nazis, Alan breaks through her defenses and begins truly to like her—only to lose her when a violent incident shatters her fragile sanity." Booklist

"This warming story with its ethnic humor, its compassionate families, and its heart-wrenching ending is one of the more honest approaches to the repercussions of W.W.II." SLJ

Lewis, C. S. (Clive Staples), 1898-1963

The lion, the witch and the wardrobe; illustrated by Pauline Baynes. Macmillan 1988 c1950 154p il $12.95; pa $5.95 (4 and up) **Fic**

1. Fantastic fiction
ISBN 0-02-758120-9; 0-02-044490-7 (pa) LC 87-31326

Also available in a gift edition illustrated by Michael Hague for $21.50 (ISBN 0-02-758200-0)

A reissue of the title first published 1950

This begins "the 'Narnia' stories, outstanding modern fairy tales with an underlying theme of good overcoming evil. In the first title, four English children walk through the wardrobe in a strange home they are visiting and enter the cold, wintry land of Narnia, which is suffering under the spell of the White Witch. They are guided to the noble lion Aslan and loyally aid him in freeing Narnia and its inhabitants from their unhappy fate." Child Books Too Good to Miss

Lewis, C. S. (Clive Staples), 1898-1963— *Continued*

Other available titles about Narnia are:
The horse and his boy (1954)
The last battle (1956)
The magician's nephew (1955)
Prince Caspian (1951)
The silver chair (1953)
The voyage of the Dawn Treader (1952)

Lindgren, Astrid, 1907-

Lotta on Troublemaker Street; illustrated by Julie Brinckloe. Macmillan 1984 c1963 57p il lib bdg $9.95 (1-3) **Fic**

1. Family life—Fiction
ISBN 0-02-759040-2 LC 83-25619

Original Swedish edition, 1962; this is a newly illustrated reissue of the translation first published 1963

Angry because everyone at home is so mean, five-year-old Lotta takes her favorite toy and goes to live in a neighbor's attic

"Lindgren has a finely tuned sense of child behavior. Lotta's musings and petulance ring very true—and so does her improved behavior. Such resonance gives the book dual appeal; both children and adults will respond to the veracity of Lotta's childish deed and resulting fit of independence." Booklist

Pippi Longstocking; translated from the Swedish by Florence Lamborn; illustrated by Louis S. Glanzman. Viking 1950 158p il lib bdg $11.95; Puffin Bks. pa $3.95 (3-6) **Fic**

1. Sweden—Fiction
ISBN 0-670-55745-5 (lib bdg); 0-14-030957-8 (pa)

Also available ABC-CLIO large print edition $13.95 (ISBN 1-85089-906-1)

Original Swedish edition, 1945

"There were no more dull days for Tommy and Annika after they made the acquaintance of Pippi Longstocking. Pippi was nine years old, her strength—and her imagination—was prodigious, and except for her monkey and horse, she lived alone unrestrained by adults." Booklist

Other available titles about Pippi Longstocking are:
Pippi goes on board (1957)
Pippi in the South Seas (1959)

Ronia, the robber's daughter; translated by Patricia Crampton. Viking 1983 c1981 176p il o.p.; Puffin Bks. paperback available $3.95 (4-6) **Fic**

1. Robbers and outlaws—Fiction 2. Middle Ages—Fiction
ISBN 0-14-031720-1 (pa) LC 82-60081

Original Swedish edition, 1981

"Ronia, the robber's daughter, meets Birk, son of her father's rival, and the result is a benefit to all in both camps. Thanks to a shrewd older friend, the young people bring about the union of their parents' forces and, even better, learn to make a living legally." Publ Wkly

"The book is full of high adventure, hairsbreadth escapes, droll earthy humor, and passionate emotional energy; and cast over the whole narrative is a primitive, ecstatic response to the changing seasons and the wonders of nature." Horn Book

Lippincott, Joseph Wharton, 1887-1976

Wilderness champion; the story of a great hound; illustrated by Paul Bransom. Lippincott 1944 195p il $11.95 (5 and up) **Fic**

1. Dogs—Fiction 2. Wolves—Fiction 3. Canada—Fiction
ISBN 0-397-30099-9 LC 44-9586

"On the way to his ranger cabin in the Alberta mountains, Johnny loses his favorite pup, Reddy, and this . . . story tells how Reddy becomes the running mate of King, an old black wolf, how he returns to Johnny, wins fame as a hunter and then goes back to stay with King, his 'first loyalty,' until the old wolf's death." Booklist

Lisle, Janet Taylor, 1947-

Afternoon of the elves. Orchard Bks. 1989 122p $12.95; lib bdg $12.99 (4-6) **Fic**

1. Friendship—Fiction 2. Mentally ill—Fiction
ISBN 0-531-05837-9; 0-531-08437-X (lib bdg)
LC 88-35099

A Newbery Medal honor book, 1990

"Nine-year-old Hillary has a happy home, all the material possessions she wants, and plenty of friends at school. Eleven-year-old Sara-Kate is an outcast, thin, poorly dressed, with failing grades, a decrepit house, and a weedy yard adjoining Hillary's neat garden. But Sara-Kate has an elf village, and with it she hooks Hillary into a friendship that thrives on elf stories but suffers from Sara-Kate's stormy moods and prickly pride. It is for Hillary to discover that Sara-Kate alone is caring for a mother who is mentally ill, penniless, and unable to provide the most basic physical or emotional necessities." Bull Cent Child Books

The author has "chosen to write about territory that will seem familiar to some readers, but she has clearly made it her own. As a result, 'Afternoon of the elves' is a distinctive portrayal of the way children figure out ways to inhabit the world when there aren't any adults around." N Y Times Book Rev

Litchfield, Ada Bassett

Making room for Uncle Joe; [by] Ada B. Litchfield; illustrated by Gail Owens. Whitman, A. 1984 unp il lib bdg $10.95 (2-5) **Fic**

1. Mentally handicapped—Fiction
ISBN 0-8075-4952-5 LC 83-17036

This "book is about an adult with Down's syndrome, Uncle Joe, who must leave the institution where he has been living to move in with his sister's family. The story is told through the eyes of the 10-year-old nephew . . . and it is largely about how the children overcome their prejudices about retarded people, how the children and Uncle Joe accommodate each other, and how they come to like each other." Sci Books Films

"Although the family's acceptance of Uncle Joe is too easy, the author does not neglect the real feelings of embarrassment and frustration that are involved." SLJ

Little, Jean, 1932-

Different dragons; illustrated by Laura Fernandez. Viking Kestrel 1987 c1986 123p il $14.95; Puffin Bks. pa $3.95 (3-5) **Fic**

1. Fear—Fiction 2. Dogs—Fiction
ISBN 0-670-80836-9; 0-14-031998-0 (pa)
LC 86-50710

First published 1986 in the United Kingdom

"On his first stay away from home without his family, timid Ben faces many challenges: Aunt Rose, whom his brother said was mean; sleeping alone; the bossy girl next door; a thunderstorm; but most of all—a big dog." SLJ

"Simply told, this features a true-to-life situation with very realistic characters. The story is compact, taking place over just one weekend; the rapid movement of events and the handling of a common problem—childhood fears—ensure a ready audience." Booklist

From Anna; pictures by Joan Sandin. Harper & Row 1972 201p il $12.89; pa $3.95 (4-6) **Fic**

1. Vision disorders—Fiction 2. Family life—Fiction 3. Germans—Canada—Fiction
ISBN 0-06-023912-3; 0-06-440044-1 (pa)
LC 72-76505

"Often ridiculed by her older brothers and sisters and chided by her mother for her awkwardness and lack of ability nine-year-old Anna is prickly and uncommunicative, but when her family moves to Canada in 1933 to get away from the growing oppression in their native Germany a doctor discovers that Anna has an acute vision problem. Fitted with glasses and sent to a special school for visually handicapped children Anna is slowly drawn out of her shell by an understanding teacher and new friends. Despite the implausibility of Anna's parents' never even suspecting her difficulty in seeing and the borderline sentimentality of the climax this is an engaging story of Anna's adjustment to life and her family's to a new homeland." Booklist

Followed by: Listen for the singing (1977)

Kate. Harper & Row 1971 162p lib bdg $12.89; pa $3.95 (4-6) **Fic**

1. Jews—Fiction 2. Friendship—Fiction
ISBN 0-06-023914-X (lib bdg); 0-06-440037-9 (pa)
LC 70-148419

Sequel to: Look through my window, entered below

"Eight-year-old Susannah (Susan Rosenthal) . . . helps a young adolescent girl, Kate Bloomfield, to come to terms with the meaning of her Jewishness, her place within her unconventional family, and the depth and value of her relationship with her long time Protestant friend Emily." Libr J

"The story is balanced by a continuation of the friendship with Emily, and by Kate's delighted appreciation of a younger child she finds endearing. Stimulating and smoothly written, the book has fine characterization and relationships and a realistic development of a modest but significant plot." Bull Cent Child Books

Look through my window; pictures by Joan Sandin. Harper & Row 1970 258p il lib bdg $12.89 (4-6) **Fic**

1. Family life—Fiction 2. Friendship—Fiction
ISBN 0-06-023924-7 LC 71-105470

Emily's very predictable life as an only child suddenly changes when her family moves into an eighteen-room house and her cousins come to stay with them. She discovers that life in a big family can be rewarding if sometimes exasperating and after meeting Kate she discovers both the hurts and the joys of true friendship

"The small but absorbing crises of family life are described with vitality, and the book is garlanded with Emily's and Kate's rapt discussions of books and their candid exploration of what it means to be Jewish (as Kate is)." Saturday Rev

Followed by: Kate, entered above

Mama's going to buy you a mockingbird. Viking Kestrel 1985 c1984 213p $12.95; Penguin Bks. pa $3.95 (5 and up) **Fic**

1. Cancer—Fiction 2. Death—Fiction
ISBN 0-670-80346-4; 0-14-031737-6 (pa)
LC 84-20877

First published 1984 in the United Kingdom

"Jeremy Talbot is unsettled when his father, Adrian, has to forgo their annual cottage stay to remain in the city for an operation. But the world crashes around him when he learns that Adrian has cancer and will soon die." Booklist

"The story has depth and insight, and it ends on a convincingly positive note. Little has good command of the elements of her writing, so that there is a smooth narrative flow and enough balance of subplots to highlight, rather than compete with, the thrust of the story line." Bull Cent Child Books

Mine for keeps; with illustrations by Lewis Parker. Little, Brown 1962 186p il hardcover o.p. paperback available $4.95 (4-6) **Fic**

1. Cerebral palsy—Fiction 2. Physically handicapped children—Fiction
ISBN 0-316-52800-5 (pa) LC 62-12381

"Sally Copeland adjusts to living at a special school for children with physical handicaps. When she learns she is going home to live, she is filled with fear and apprehension for she knows being the only cerebral palsied child in a family and a school would cause many difficulties. With the help of an understanding family, she acquires new attitudes about herself, and when she begins to be thoughtful of others her life becomes more satisfying." Read Ladders for Hum Relat. 6th edition

Lively, Penelope, 1933-

Fanny's sister; illustrated by Anita Lobel. Dutton 1980 56p il $7.95 (3-5) **Fic**

1. Brothers and sisters—Fiction 2. Infants—Fiction 3. Great Britain—Fiction
ISBN 0-525-29618-2 LC 79-20118

Text first published 1976 in the United Kingdom

"Since there has been a new sibling every year, Fanny, a Victorian girl, decides that she hates babies and prays that God will take her newest sister back. Later she regrets this action and runs away to become a kitchen maid at the vicarage. She and the Vicar have a long talk and Fanny comes to terms with being the oldest child." Child Book Rev Serv

"A small gem, this Victorian story that takes place in just a day, sees into a child's mind, captures the essence of family life in England's middle class, and is beguiling without being saccharine. The writing is polished, with overtones of humor, and the illustrations

Lively, Penelope, 1933-—*Continued*

fit the story perfectly: grave, sedate, plush, with just a trace of humor. . . . This may be too restrained a story for some children, but it is highly probable that those who enjoy it will enjoy it with a passion." Bull Cent Child Books

The ghost of Thomas Kempe; illustrated by Antony Maitland. Dutton 1973 186p il $14.95; Pacer Bks. pa $2.50 (4-6) **Fic**

1. Ghosts—Fiction 2. Great Britain—Fiction
ISBN 0-525-30495-9; 0-425-09419-7 (pa)

LC 73-77456

"Workmen getting an English cottage ready for its new tenants break an old bottle and let loose the spirit of Thomas Kempe, a sorcerer whose mortal remains have been buried since 1639. Thus begin the persecutions and perils of young James Harrison, a prankish boy who moves into the house and is blamed for the high jinks of the ghost. Aware that he can't convince his pragmatic parents that the house is haunted and that he is not to blame for the tricks played when the vicar comes to call, as well as other disasters, Jim seeks out an exorcist." Publ Wkly

"Although the British vocabulary and spelling may seem strange at times to middle graders, they are sure to enjoy this exciting and involving tale of the supernatural." SLJ

Lobel, Arnold

Fables; written and illustrated by Arnold Lobel. Harper & Row 1980 40p il $12.95; lib bdg $12.89; pa $5.95 (3-5) **Fic**

1. Animals—Fiction
ISBN 0-06-023973-5; 0-06-023974-3 (lib bdg); 0-06-443046-4 (pa)

LC 79-2004

Awarded the Caldecott Medal, 1981

"Short, original fables, complete with moral, poke subtle fun at human foibles through the antics of 20 memorable animal characters. . . . Though generally witty and provocative, the tales are uneven, especially in their appeal to young children, and will need adult interpretation. Despite the large picture-book format, the best audience will be older readers who can understand the innuendos and underlying messages. Children of all ages, however, will appreciate and be intrigued by the artist's fine, full-color illustrations. Tones are deftly blended to luminescent shadings, and the pictorial simplicity of ideas, droll expressions, and caricature of behavior work in many instances as complete and humorous stories in themselves." Booklist

London, Jack, 1876-1916

The call of the wild (5 and up) **Fic**

1. Dogs—Fiction 2. Alaska—Fiction

Some editions are:

ABC-CLIO $15.50 Large print edition (ISBN 1-85089-113-3)
Macmillan $12.95 (ISBN 0-02-759510-2)
Pocket Bks. pa $3.50 (ISBN 0-671-70494-X)
Vintage Bks. pa $8.50 (ISBN 0-679-72535-0)

First published 1903 by Macmillan

"The dog hero, Buck, is stolen from his comfortable home and pressed into service as a sledge dog in the Klondike. At first he is abused by both men and dogs, but he learns to fight ruthlessly and finally finds in John Thornton a master whom he can respect and love. When Thornton is murdered, he breaks away to the wilds and becomes the leader of a pack of wolves." Reader's Ency

White Fang (5 and up) **Fic**

1. Dogs—Fiction 2. Alaska—Fiction

Some editions are:

Puffin Bks. pa $2.25 (ISBN 0-14-035045-4)
Scholastic pa $2.50 (ISBN 0-590-40523-3)

First published 1906

White Fang "is about a dog, a cross-breed, sold to Beauty Smith. This owner tortures the dog to increase his ferocity and value as a fighter. A new owner Weedom Scott, brings the dog to California, and, by kind treatment, domesticates him. White Fang later sacrifices his life to save Scott." Haydn. Thesaurus of Book Dig

Lord, Bette Bao

In the Year of the Boar and Jackie Robinson; illustrations by Marc Simont. Harper & Row 1984 169p il $12.95; lib bdg $12.89 (4-6) **Fic**

1. Chinese Americans—Fiction 2. School stories
ISBN 0-06-024003-2; 0-06-024004-0 (lib bdg)

LC 83-48440

"In a story based in part on the author's experience as an immigrant, Shirley Temple Wong . . . arrives in Brooklyn and spends her first year in public school." Bull Cent Child Books

"Warm-hearted, fresh, and dappled with humor, the episodic book, which successfully encompasses both Chinese dragons and the Brooklyn Dodgers, stands out in the bevy of contemporary problem novels. And the unusual flavor of the text infiltrates the striking illustrations picturing the pert, pigtailed heroine making her way in 'Mei Guo'—her new 'Beautiful Country.'" Horn Book

Lovelace, Maud Hart, 1892-

Betsy-Tacy; illustrated by Lois Lenski. Crowell 1940 112p il lib bdg $12.89; HarperCollins Pubs. pa $2.95 (2-4) **Fic**

1. Friendship—Fiction 2. Minnesota—Fiction
ISBN 0-690-13805-9 (lib bdg); 0-06-440096-4 (pa)

LC 40-30965

Betsy and Tacy (short for Anastacia) were two little five-year-olds, such inseparable friends that they were regarded almost as one person. This is the story of their friendship in a little Minnesota town in the early 1900's

The author "has written a story about two very natural, very appealing little girls. More than this, she has written a story of real literary merit as well as one with good story interest." Libr J

Other available titles about Betsy through adolescence and young womanhood with reading levels of grade 5 and up are:

Betsy and Joe (1948)
Betsy and Tacy go downtown (1943)
Betsy and Tacy go over the big hill (1942)
Betsy and the great world (1952)
Betsy in spite of herself (1946)
Betsy-Tacy and Tib (1941)
Betsy was a junior (1947)
Betsy's wedding (1955)
Heaven to Betsy (1945)

Lowry, Lois

Anastasia Krupnik. Houghton Mifflin 1979 113p $12.95; Bantam Bks. pa $2.75 (4-6) **Fic**

1. Family life—Fiction
ISBN 0-395-28629-8; 0-553-15534-2 (pa)

Also available ABC-CLIO large print edition $15.95 (ISBN 1-55736-073-1)

This book describes the tenth year in the life of fourth-grader Anastasia. As she "experiences rejection of a long labored-over poem, fights acceptance of the coming arrival of a baby sibling, deliberates about becoming Catholic (in order to change her name), has a crush on Washburn Cummings who constantly dribbles an imaginary basketball, and learns to understand her senile grandmother's inward eye, she grows and matures." Booklist

"Although the episodic story is somewhat slight, Anastasia's father and mother—an English professor and an artist—are among the most humorous, sensible, and understanding parents to be found in . . . children's fiction, and Anastasia herself is an amusing and engaging heroine." Horn Book

Other available titles about Anastasia Krupnik and her family are:
All about Sam (1988)
Anastasia again! (1981)
Anastasia, ask your analyst (1984)
Anastasia at your service (1982)
Anastasia has the answers (1986)
Anastasia on her own (1985)
Anastasia's chosen career (1987)

Autumn Street. Houghton Mifflin 1980 188p $13.95; Dell pa $2.95 (4 and up) **Fic**

1. World War, 1939-1945—Fiction 2. Friendship—Fiction
ISBN 0-395-27812-0; 0-440-40344-8 (pa) LC 80-376

"Elizabeth, the teller of the story, feels danger around her when her father goes to fight in World War II. She, her older sister, and her pregnant mother go to live with her grandparents on Autumn Street. Tatie, the black cook-housekeeper, and her street-wise grandson Charley love Elizabeth and reassure her during this difficult time." Child Book Rev Serv

"Characters, dialogue, believable plot combine in this well written story to capture the mind and heart of all who read this memorable and touching book." Voice Youth Advocates

Number the stars. Houghton Mifflin 1989 137p $12.95 (4 and up) **Fic**

1. World War, 1939-1945—Fiction 2. World War, 1939-1945—Jews 3. Friendship—Fiction 4. Denmark—Fiction
ISBN 0-395-51060-0 LC 88-37134

Awarded the Newbery Medal, 1990

"Best friends Annemarie Johansen and Ellen Rosen must suddenly pretend to be sisters one night when Ellen's parents go into hiding to escape a Nazi roundup in wartime Copenhagen. With the help of a young resistance fighter, the Johansens smuggle the Rosens aboard Annemarie's uncle's fishing boat bound for freedom in Sweden. But it is Annemarie who actually saves all their lives by transporting a handkerchief coated with blood and cocaine to deaden the search dogs' sense of smell." Bull Cent Child Books

"The appended author's note details the historical incidents upon which Lowry bases her plot. By employing the limited omniscient third-person perspective, she draws the reader into the intensity of the situation as a child of Annemarie's age might perceive it. The message is so closely woven into the carefully honed narrative that the whole work is seamless, compelling, and memorable." Horn Book

The one hundredth thing about Caroline. Houghton Mifflin 1983 150p $10.95; Dell pa $2.95 (5 and up) **Fic**

1. Single parent family—Fiction 2. Brothers and sisters—Fiction
ISBN 0-395-34829-3; 0-440-46625-3 (pa) LC 83-12629

"Caroline, fascinated by dinosaurs, spends much of her free time prowling New York's Museum of Natural History; her best friend, Stacy, practices being an investigative reporter. The combination proves disastrous when Caroline's mother becomes interested in Frederick Fiske, the mysterious man in the fifth-floor apartment who looks, Caroline is convinced, like the evil 'Tyrannosaurus rex' and who seemingly wants to eliminate Caroline and her brother, J.P." Booklist

"Lowry's style is bright, fast-paced and funny, with skillfully-drawn, believable characters." SLJ

Followed by: Switcharound, entered below

Rabble Starkey. Houghton Mifflin 1987 192p $12.95; Dell pa $3.25 (5 and up) **Fic**

1. Friendship—Fiction 2. Mothers and daughters—Fiction
ISBN 0-395-43607-9; 0-440-40056-2 (pa) LC 86-27542

Also available G.K. Hall large print edition $14.95 (ISBN 0-8161-4776-0)

"Parable Starkey and her mother, Sweet Hosanna, move into the Bigelows' house to take charge of the children after Mrs. Bigelow's hospitalization for mental illness. That suits Rabble just fine; Veronica Bigelow is her best friend in sixth grade, little Gunther Bigelow is her favorite kid, and Mr. Bigelow is both wise and generous. . . . Rabble and Veronica's relationships with each other, with the cranky old neighbor they try to help, and with a delinquent boy down the street are well developed in a smooth first-person narrative that quietly takes on class as well as individual differences. In the end, Lowry has managed to portray a large, diverse cast by carefully and consistently focusing the point of view as one of a maturing observer." Bull Cent Child Books

A summer to die; illustrated by Jenni Oliver. Houghton Mifflin 1977 154p il $13.95; Bantam Bks. pa $2.95 (3-6) **Fic**

1. Sisters—Fiction 2. Death—Fiction
ISBN 0-395-25338-1; 0-553-26297-1 (pa) LC 77-83

"Meg, 13, envies her older sister's popularity and prettiness and finds it difficult to cope with Molly's degenerating illness and eventual death." Booklist

"As told by Meg, the chronicle of this experience is a sensitive exploration of the complex emotions underlying the adolescent's first confrontation with human mortality; the author suggests nuances of contemporary conversation and situations without sacrificing the finesse with which she limns her characters. . . . The book is memorable as a well-crafted reaffirmation of universal values." Horn Book

Lowry, Lois—*Continued*

Switcharound. Houghton Mifflin 1985 118p il $12.95; Dell pa $2.95 (5 and up) **Fic**

1. Brothers and sisters—Fiction 2. Family life—Fiction
ISBN 0-395-39536-4; 0-440-48415-4 (pa) LC 85-14576

Sequel to: The one hundredth thing about Caroline, entered above

"Caroline Tate and her brother rarely agree on anything, but when their father asks them to spend the summer in Des Moines, they suddenly sound like the 'Mormon Tabernacle Choir.' Leaving New York means that Caroline won't have the Museum of Natural History and J.P.'s summer computer project will have to be postponed. It also means that J.P. will have to play baseball and they'll both have to put up with their father's three kids, Poochie and twin baby girls." SLJ

"Caroline's wry commentary on babies, J.P.'s distaste for athletics, and their observations of an energetic, enthusiastic father blend together effectively in a book worth reading for the hilarious descriptions of baseball games alone." Horn Book

Taking care of Terrific. Houghton Mifflin 1983 168p $13.95; Dell pa $2.95 (5 and up) **Fic**

1. Baby sitters—Fiction 2. Boston (Mass.)—Fiction
ISBN 0-395-34070-5; 0-440-48494-4 (pa) LC 82-23331

Also available ABC-CLIO large print edition $15.95 (ISBN 1-55736-119-3)

Fourteen-year-old Enid Crowley is "bored by the prospect of a Boston summer. That's before she begins taking care of a precocious . . . four-year-old, Joshua Warwick Cameron IV, who prefers to be called Tom Terrific, before she meets the friendly black musician in the Public Garden, or the bag ladies, before she discovers that that pest of a classmate, Seth, is really a very nice boy." Bull Cent Child Books

"Although the plot seems incredible, the book as a whole is somehow satisfying. The Boston setting is vividly evoked, and the diverse cast of characters adds variety and flavor to the narrative." Horn Book

Us and Uncle Fraud. Houghton Mifflin 1984 148p $10.95; Dell pa $2.95 (4 and up) **Fic**

1. Uncles—Fiction
ISBN 0-395-36633-X; 0-440-49185-1 (pa) LC 84-12783

Mysterious things begin to happen after Uncle Claude comes to stay with his sister's family. Is Uncle Claude a thief, an imposter, or just a dream weaver?

The author "lightens tension with her . . . high-grade humor and brings thoughtful perceptions to a story that is also full of drama and adventure. However, Uncle Claude, or Uncle Fraud as Louise and Marcus sometimes refer to him, is the most tantalizing element." Booklist

Your move, J.P.! Houghton Mifflin 1990 122p $13.95 (5 and up) **Fic**

1. School stories
ISBN 0-395-53639-1 LC 89-24707

Caroline's older brother, twelve-year-old J.P. Tate who appeared in The one hundredth thing about Caroline and Switcharound (both entered above), has a "crush on Angela Galsworthy, newly arrived at his private school from London, England. . . . Anxious to sustain Angela's interest, J.P. tells her that he is suffering from triple framosis, a rare but fatal disease. Angela believes him and J.P. is stuck with his lie." Bull Cent Child Books

"The author makes the most of the humor in J.P.'s antics but maintains a rueful sympathy throughout for his plight and for his eventual admission of truth." Horn Book

Lunn, Janet Louise Swoboda, 1928-

The root cellar; [by] Janet Lunn. Scribner 1983 c1981 229p $13.95; Puffin Bks. pa $3.95 (5 and up) **Fic**

1. Space and time—Fiction 2. Orphans—Fiction 3. Farm life—Fiction 4. United States—History—1861-1865, Civil War—Fiction
ISBN 0-684-17855-9; 0-14-031835-6 (pa) LC 83-3246

First published 1981 in Canada

"Rose, a twelve-year-old orphan, is unhappy in her new home. When she goes down into the root cellar she finds herself back in Civil War days. She makes friends with the former tenants of the old house and becomes involved in their war-torn lives. She finally decides she belongs in modern times and returns with a better spirit." Child Book Rev Serv

"It's hard not to feel for Rose as she learns, for the first time in her life, how to be part of a family and have companions her own age. The descriptions of the physical surroundings and conditions in the post-Civil War time period are particularly vivid, and the pieces fit together well in this fast-paced, readable novel." SLJ

Lyon, George Ella, 1949-

Borrowed children. Orchard Bks. 1988 154p $12.95; lib bdg $12.99; Bantam Bks. pa $2.95 (5 and up) **Fic**

1. Depressions, Economic—Fiction 2. Family life—Fiction 3. Kentucky—Fiction
ISBN 0-531-05751-8; 0-531-08351-9 (lib bdg); 0-553-28380-4 (pa) LC 87-22700

"A Richard Jackson book"

"Twelve-year-old Amanda, the oldest girl in a large, poor Kentucky family during the Depression, has to quit school to take care of the house and new baby after her mother's difficult delivery. As a reward, she's sent to her grandparents' comfortable home in Memphis for a [rest]. Observing her alcoholic aunt's unhappy marriage makes her realize how rich her mountain background is." Bull Cent Child Books

"There is a tender and unusual quality to both Amanda's story and the novel itself. The author has imbued her narrator with lyricism, which somehow doesn't feel out of place. Instead, it helps create a sense of the past: slightly formal and suggestively nostalgic." N Y Times Book Rev

MacDonald, Betty, d. 1958

Mrs. Piggle-Wiggle; illustrated by Hilary Knight. Lippincott 1957 c1947 118p il $12.95; pa $3.50 (2-4) **Fic**

ISBN 0-397-31712-3; 0-06-440148-0 (pa) LC 47-1876

First published 1947

Chapters follow "the amazing versatility of Mrs. Piggle-Wiggle who loves children good or bad, who never scolds but who has positive cures for 'Answer-Backers,' 'Never-Want-To-Go-To-Bedders,' and other children with special problems." Books for Deaf Child

The author "mixes a little psychology with a lot of common sense, and seasons with nonsense, to produce the most palatable type of lecture on good behavior. Hilary Knight's illustrations catch the mood of the whole delightful business." Chicago Sunday Trib

Other available titles about Mrs. Piggle-Wiggle are:
Hello, Mrs. Piggle-Wiggle (1957)
Mrs. Piggle-Wiggle's farm (1954)
Mrs. Piggle-Wiggle's magic (1949)

MacDonald, George, 1824-1905

At the back of the North Wind (4-6) **Fic**

1. Fairy tales

Some editions are:
Godine $18.95 Illustrated by Lauren A. Mills (ISBN 0-87923-703-1)
Morrow lib bdg $17.95 Illustrated by Jessie Willcox Smith (ISBN 0-688-07808-7)
Puffin Bks. pa $2.25 (ISBN 0-14-035030-6)
Schocken Bks. pa $8.95 With illustrations by Charles Mozley (ISBN 0-8052-0595-0)

First published 1871

"There is a rare quality in Macdonald's lovely fairy tales which relates spiritual ideals with the everyday things of life. This one tells of Diamond, the little son of a coachman, and his friendship with the North Wind who appears to him in various guises." Toronto Public Libr. Books for Boys & Girls

The light princess; with pictures by Maurice Sendak. 2nd ed. Farrar, Straus & Giroux 1977 c1969 110p il $10.95; pa $3.45 (3-6) **Fic**

1. Fairy tales

ISBN 0-374-34455-8; 0-374-44458-7 (pa) LC 69-14981

"An Ariel book"

This fairy story originally appeared 1864 in the author's novel Adela Cathcart and was reprinted in his 1867 story collection Dealings with the fairies. First published with these illustrations in 1969

"The problems of the princess who had been deprived, as an infant, of her gravity and whose life hung in the balance when she grew up are amusing as ever and the sweet capitulation to love that brings her (literally) to her feet, just as touching. All of the best of Macdonald is reflected in the Sendak illustrations: the humor and wit, the sweetness and tenderness, and the sophistication—and they are beautiful." Sutherland. The Best in Child Books

The princess and the goblin (3-6) **Fic**

1. Fairy tales

Some editions are:
ABC-CLIO lib bdg $13.95 With the original illustrations by Arthur Hughes Large print edition (ISBN 0-85089-915-0)
Dell pa $4.95 With an afterword by Andre Norton (ISBN 0-440-47189-3)
Grosset & Dunlap (Illustrated junior lib) $13.95 Illustrated by Jos. A. Smith (ISBN 0-448-18973-9)
Morrow $17.94 Illustrated by Jessie Willcox Smith (ISBN 0-688-06604-6)

First published 1872

"Living in a great house on the side of a mountain in a country where hideous spiteful goblins inhabit the dark caverns below the mines, little Princess Irene and Curdie the miner's son have many strange adventures. . . . To adults Macdonald's stories have an allegorical significance, to each succeeding generation of children they are wonderful fairytale adventures." Four to Fourteen

Followed by: The princess and Curdie

MacLachlan, Patricia

Arthur, for the very first time; illustrated by Lloyd Bloom. Harper & Row 1980 117p il lib bdg $13.89; pa $3.50 (4-6) **Fic**

ISBN 0-06-024047-4 (lib bdg); 0-06-440288-6 (pa) LC 79-2007

Also available ABC-CLIO large print edition $15.95 (ISBN 1-55736-169-X)

A "recounting of ten-year-old Arthur's activities and introspections during a summer spent with a great-uncle and a great-aunt. The offbeat relatives cultivate equally offbeat friends, climb trees, and speak French to their pet chicken. Arthur also enjoys the companionship of a veterinarian's granddaughter, although she delights in teasing him and calls him by name only at the end of the book." Horn Book

"Good-hearted good humor relieves this from the mawkishness of therapeutic novels about kids with problems who invariably get transformed. . . . The colorfulness of the characters is unrelenting; each is more exaggeratedly unique and zany than the other. But the intensity of their collective impact does make Arthur's reprogramming plausible—and fun." SLJ

Cassie Binegar. Harper & Row 1982 120p lib bdg $11.89; pa $3.50 (4-6) **Fic**

1. Family life—Fiction

ISBN 0-06-024034-2 (lib bdg); 0-06-440195-2 (pa) LC 81-48641

"A Charlotte Zolotow book"

"Cassie—whose family is loving, boisterous and original—longs to have a family life like her friend Margaret Mary. MM's parents are coldly unimaginative bores, but Cassie finds them 'serene.' Meanwhile, proper MM basks in the warmth of Cassie's casual but big-hearted clan. The problem is that Cass is changing—aware for the first time of other people, and feeling the natural 'anguish' of growing up." SLJ

"It is not the plot (there really isn't one) that makes this so readable and distinctive a novel, but the flow of the writing, the easy mingling of exposition and dialogue, the polished merging of colorful characters and shifting relationships and Cassie's continuing and believable growth in understanding herself and others." Bull Cent Child Books

MacLachlan, Patricia—*Continued*

The facts and fictions of Minna Pratt. Harper & Row 1988 136p $11.95; lib bdg $11.89; pa $3.50 (4 and up) **Fic**

1. Musicians—Fiction
ISBN 0-06-024114-4; 0-06-024117-9 (lib bdg); 0-06-440265-7 (pa) LC 85-45388

"A Charlotte Zolotow book"

"Minna Pratt plays the cello and wishes she would get her vibrato. She wishes someone would answer her questions about herself and life and love. She wishes her mother would ask her regular questions about school and not questions like 'What is the quality of beauty?' for the book she's writing. Then she meets Lucas Ellerby. His life seems so perfect and he has a vibrato. As their friendship develops Minna finds that life is not always as it seems and even when you think you know someone or something there may be a hidden side that will surprise you." Voice Youth Advocates

"Ms. MacLachlan's skillful handling of her subject, and above all her vivid characterization . . place her story in the ranks of outstanding middle-grade fiction." N Y Times Book Rev

Sarah, plain and tall. Harper & Row 1985 58p $10.95; lib bdg $10.89; pa $2.50 (3-5) **Fic**

1. Stepmothers—Fiction 2. Frontier and pioneer life—Fiction
ISBN 0-06-024101-2; 0-06-024102-0 (lib bdg); 0-06-440205-3 (pa) LC 83-49481

Also available ABC-CLIO large print edition $15.95 (ISBN 1-55736-080-4)

Awarded the Newbery Medal, 1986

"A Charlotte Zolotow book"

When their father invites a mail-order bride to come live with them in their prairie home, Caleb and Anna are captivated by their new mother and hope that she will stay

"It is the simplest of love stories expressed in the simplest of prose. Embedded in these unadorned declarative sentences about ordinary people, actions, animals, facts, objects and colors are evocations of the deepest feelings of loss and fear, love and hope." N Y Times Book Rev

Seven kisses in a row; pictures by Maria Pia Marrella. Harper & Row 1983 56p il $12.95; lib bdg $12.89; pa $2.50 (2-4) **Fic**

1. Aunts—Fiction 2. Uncles—Fiction 3. Family life—Fiction
ISBN 0-06-024083-0; 0-06-024084-9 (lib bdg); 0-06-440231-2 (pa) LC 82-47718

"A Charlotte Zolotow book"

"How different life is for Emma and Zachary when Aunt Evelyn and Uncle Elliott babysit for them while their parents attend an 'eyeball meeting'! No seven kisses before breakfast or divided grapefruit with cherry. Nevertheless both learn from the others—Emma learns to eat broccoli and her aunt and uncle learn about babies and what they do." Child Book Rev Serv

"The brief understated story makes few demands on the reader, but it is full of humor and the warmth of family caring and mutual affection. Informal, offhand pen-and-ink drawings reflect the tone of both story and style." Horn Book

Unclaimed treasures. Harper & Row 1984 118p $12.95; lib bdg $12.89; pa $2.95 (5 and up) **Fic**

ISBN 0-06-024093-8; 0-06-024094-6 (lib bdg); 0-06-440189-8 (pa) LC 83-47714

"A Charlotte Zolotow book"

This story "describes the summer when Willa, aged eleven, longs to find her true love. This search she knows has nothing to do with her parents' comfortable relationship but a lot to do . . . with her infatuation with her friend Horace's father—a painter for whom she poses—and with Ted and Wanda, the self-absorbed characters in a mindless romance written by one of her father's students." Horn Book

The author "has crafted an extraordinary story from ordinary daily events and filled it with unique neighborhood characters. . . . MacLachlan's penetration into the dreams of youth merges with her keen sense of humor and fluid writing style." SLJ

Magorian, Michelle, 1947-

Good night, Mr. Tom. Harper & Row 1981 318p $13.95; lib bdg $13.89; pa $3.95 (6 and up) **Fic**

1. Child abuse—Fiction 2. Adoption—Fiction 3. Great Britain—Fiction
ISBN 0-06-024078-4; 0-06-024079-2 (lib bdg); 0-06-440174-X (pa) LC 80-8444

"When children are evacuated from London during World War II, Tom Oakley, a taciturn near-recluse who has never recovered from the deaths of his wife and child, takes in and forms a mutually healing relationship with eight-year-old Willie, a sickly, quiet boy who bears the marks of brutal beatings." Booklist

"The ending is tense, dramatic, believable, and satisfying, a happy ending to a touching story of love. Magorian uses dialogue and dialect well, giving local color as well as using them to establish character. Save for the reflection of the current interest in the problems of child abuse, this is an old-fashioned story with timeless appeal." Bull Cent Child Books

Mahy, Margaret

The blood-and-thunder adventure on Hurricane Peak; illustrated by Wendy Smith. Margaret K. McElderry Bks. 1989 132p il $12.95 (4-6) **Fic**

1. School stories 2. Magic—Fiction
ISBN 0-689-50488-8 LC 89-8098

Relates the tangled events that lead the students of the Unexpected School on Hurricane Peak to foil the wicked Sir Quincey and his accomplices and to solve several mysteries

"Oversize events unfold in a high-energy manner that will keep kids turning the pages. The droll telling suits the story well, as do Smith's scrawled line drawings." Booklist

The great piratical rumbustification & The librarian and the robbers; illustrated by Quentin Blake. Godine 1986 c1978 63p il $11.95 (3-6) **Fic**

ISBN 0-87923-629-9 LC 85-45966

First published 1978 in the United Kingdom

Mahy, Margaret—*Continued*

A "pair of humorous pieces, one a novella, the other a short story. In *The Great Piratical Rumbustification,* the boys of the Terrapin family find themselves with a pirate babysitter who wants to use their house for a long-delayed pirate party. In *The Librarian and the Robbers,* Serena Laburnum, the beautiful librarian, is kidnapped and held for ransom by a gang of ill-read robbers." SLJ

"These are splendid read-alouds, but listeners should not miss Quentin Blake's exuberantly ridiculous, black-and-white cartoons, which tumble across the pages with much the same verve as Mahy's text—a matchless combo of childlike irreverence." Bull Cent Child Books

The haunting. Atheneum Pubs. 1983 c1982 135p $11.95 (5 and up) **Fic**

1. Extrasensory perception—Fiction
ISBN 0-689-50243-5 LC 82-3983

"A Margaret K. McElderry book"

"Barney, eight, is terrified by the repetition of images and messages that proclaim 'Barney is dead,' but . . . he discovers that he had had a great-uncle who had been a 'magician,' not only having ESP but able to evoke illusions. This was Cole, who had a beloved brother, another Barney. Presumed dead for many years, Cole suddenly appears and there is an interfamilial confrontation." Bull Cent Child Books

The principal characters "are beautifully drawn, and perhaps because they care so much for each other, readers care for them, too. Their growth and development as individuals and as members of a family unit are as important to the story as its supernatural chills, thrills and puzzlements, a fact that lends this genre book unusual richness." SLJ

Manes, Stephen, 1949-

Some of the adventures of Rhode Island Red; illustrated by William Joyce. Lippincott 1990 117p il $10.95; lib bdg $10.89 (3-6) **Fic**

1. Chickens—Fiction 2. Rhode Island—Fiction
ISBN 0-397-32347-6; 0-397-32348-4 (lib bdg) LC 89-35397

A diminutive red-haired man no bigger than a hen's egg, Rhode Island Red leaves his home among the chickens and travels throughout Rhode Island, becoming a legendary figure through his many heroic exploits

"The illustrations, black-and-white pencil drawings, are in keeping with the exaggerated humor of the text. The story bounces along, effortlessly sustained by an abundance of chicken jokes and size puns." Bull Cent Child Books

Mark, Jan

Thunder and Lightnings; illustrated by Jim Russell. Crowell 1979 c1976 181p il $11.95 (5 and up) **Fic**

1. Airplanes—Fiction 2. Friendship—Fiction 3. Great Britain—Fiction
ISBN 0-690-03901-8 LC 78-4778

First published 1976 in the United Kingdom

Set in Norfolk, this is a "perceptive story of an unusual friendship between two boys of unlike backgrounds and personalities. . . . Victor, the more unusual character, is slow in school but sophisticated in his ability to identify airplanes. He is friendly to the newcomer Andrew, a racing-car devotee, and they become companions in plane-watching. Little details sharply define their different home backgrounds—Victor's so sterile with cleanliness and order, Andrew's so welcoming and comfortable. Humorous conversations lighten the pictures of domestic life and reveal the boys' attitudes toward their contrasting lifestyles, but their passionate interest in aircraft is the focus of the story." Horn Book

Masefield, John, 1878-1967

The box of delights; or, When the wolves were running; abridged by Patricia Crampton; illustrated by Faith Jaques. Macmillan 1984 167p o.p.; Dell paperback available $2.95 (5 and up) **Fic**

1. Fantastic fiction 2. Great Britain—Fiction
ISBN 0-440-40853-9 (pa) LC 84-14404

An abridgment of the title first published 1935

"Kay Harker, the protagonist, is given the box of the title by a mysterious old man who comes and goes throughout the story, as obviously on the side of the angels as Abner is a representation of evil. The Box of Delights makes it possible for Kay to achieve time-travel and to teleport." Bull Cent Child Books

"This new abridgment . . . features a clear text and charming full-color plates and illustrations." SLJ

Matas, Carol, 1949-

Lisa's war. Scribner 1989 c1987 111p $12.95 (5 and up) **Fic**

1. World War, 1939-1945—Fiction 2. World War, 1939-1945—Jews 3. Denmark—Fiction
ISBN 0-684-19010-9 LC 88-29525

During the Nazi occupation of Denmark, Lisa and other teenage Jews become involved in an underground resistance movement and eventually must flee for their lives

"'Lisa's War' poses such sophisticated concerns with an honorable simplicity rare even in adult fiction. And at the same time it builds a great deal of excitement, as the German menace spreads and intensifies, growing from a sinister fear to lethal reality. As it does, Lisa's involvement in the resistance also grows from a first, comically terrified attempt to leave contraband leaflets on the streetcar to a central role in guarding her fellow Jews as they wait to go to Sweden." N Y Times Book Rev

Mathis, Sharon Bell, 1937-

Sidewalk story; illustrated by Leo Carty. Viking 1971 71p il o.p.; Penguin Bks. paperback available $3.95 (3-5) **Fic**

1. Friendship—Fiction 2. Blacks—Fiction
ISBN 0-14-032165-9 (pa) LC 86-4075

"An affecting easy-to-read story of a persistent little black girl to whom friendship means caring and helping a friend in trouble. Upset because her best friend Tanya and her family are being evicted and their belongings piled on the sidewalk and frustrated by her own mother's unwillingness to become involved, Lilly Etta phones first the police and then the newspaper for help and in the night creeps out to cover the things with sheets and

Mathis, Sharon Bell, 1937-—*Continued*

blankets—and herself—to protect them from the wind and rain. Enhanced by several sensitive double-spread paintings in black and white." Booklist

Mazer, Norma Fox, 1931-

A figure of speech. Delacorte Press 1973 197p o.p.; Dell paperback available $2.95 (6 and up) Fic

1. Grandfathers—Fiction 2. Old age—Fiction
ISBN 0-440-94374-4 (pa) LC 73-6239

"Certain that she was an unwanted child when she was born, Jenny Pennoyer has always found it difficult to relate to the rest of the family. All except Grandpa, who practically raised her. When she learns that her parents are secretly planning to move Grandpa into an old folks' home to make room for Jenny's older brother . . . she is shocked. She tells the old man what her parents have in store for him, setting in motion a chain of events that will lead to tragedy." Publisher's note

"In this touching, realistic story of a child's love of her grandfather, the author shows a situation that is common in our time: the old person who is tolerated, unwanted, and then pushed aside." Bull Cent Child Books

McCaffrey, Anne

Dragonsong. Atheneum Pubs. 1976 202p $14.95; Bantam Bks. pa $3.50 (6 and up) Fic

1. Fantastic fiction
ISBN 0-689-30507-9; 0-553-23460-9 (pa)
LC 75-30530

"Forbidden by her stern father to make the music she loves, Menolly runs away from Half-Circle Sea Hold on the Planet Pern, takes shelter with fire lizards, and finds a new life opening up for her." LC. Child Books, 1976

"The author explores the ideas of alienation, rebellion, love of beauty, the role of women and the role of the individual in society with some sensitivity in a generally well-structured plot with sound characterizations." SLJ

Others available titles in the Harper Hall series are:
Dragondrums (1979)
Dragonsinger (1977)

McCloskey, Robert, 1914-

Centerburg tales. Viking 1951 190p il $14.95; Puffin Bks. pa $3.95 (4-6) Fic

ISBN 0-670-20977-5; 0-14-031072-X (pa)
LC 51-10675

Sequel to: Homer Price, entered below

In Centerburg, "preposterous things are still happening, no doubt because Homer Price, Grandpa Hercules, Freddy, Uncle Ulysses, and the others still live there. Uncle Ulysses' lunchroom has a new juke box but otherwise is the same as ever, and Grandpa Herc's tales, which make up the first part of the book, are even taller and better than ever." Booklist

"Pictures and story show a real, live American boy with a knack for getting into hilarious adventures that make perfect reading aloud for children from eight to twelve." Horn Book

Homer Price. Viking 1943 149p il $13.95; Puffin Bks. pa $3.95 (4-6) Fic

ISBN 0-670-37729-5; 0-14-030927-6 (pa)
LC 43-16001

Six "stories about the exploits of young Homer Price, who divides his time between school and doing odd jobs at his father's filling station and in his mother's tourist lunchroom two miles outside of Centerburg." Bookmark

"Text and pictures are pure Americana, hilarious and convincing in their portrayal of midwestern small-town life." Child Books Too Good to Miss

Followed by: Centerburg tales, entered above

McDonnell, Christine, 1949-

Don't be mad, Ivy; pictures by Diane de Groat. Dial Bks. 1981 77p il lib bdg $8.89; Puffin Bks. pa $3.95 (2-4) Fic

1. Friendship—Fiction
ISBN 0-8037-2128-5 (lib bdg); 0-14-032329-5 (pa)
LC 81-65850

"Believable and engaging, Ivy is the central character in six appealing glimpses of the special world of childhood. She is independent and ingenious, and her triumphs and trials are appropriately scaled to younger readers; the problems are childsized, and the tone is warm and reassuring. . . . The childlike perspective is extended through the softly shadowed drawings, representational in style, which effectively capture nuances of expression." Horn Book

Followed by: Toad food & measle soup and Lucky charms & birthday wishes, both entered below

Friends first. Viking 1990 171p $11.95 (6 and up) Fic

ISBN 0-670-81923-9 LC 89-70578

"Miranda and her upstairs neighbor, Gus, have been best friends since they were babies. The two have shared outings and sleepovers as naturally as siblings, but, as both approach adolescence, uncertainty and troublesome emotions upset their placid companionship. Miranda . . . is first jolted by the sexual overtones in the threats of a street gang encountered while trick-or-treating and devastated still further by an attack and near rape on her own doorstep." Horn Book

"Sharp, sensitive details and clever analogies highlight the narrative, as McDonnell candidly yet delicately explores what reaching adolescence means for a girl in today's world. Although the dialogue is occasionally stiff, both characters and plot are infused with credibility." Publ Wkly

Lucky charms & birthday wishes; pictures by Diane de Groat. Viking 1984 84p il $11.95; Puffin Bks. pa $3.95 (2-4) Fic

1. Friendship—Fiction 2. School stories
ISBN 0-670-44430-8; 0-14-031886-0 (pa)
LC 83-19861

"Five more stories by the author of 'Don't Be Mad, Ivy' and 'Toad Food and Measle Soup' [entered above and below respectively] feature many of the characters from earlier books, although this time the episodes revolve around Emily Mott, a more reserved protagonist than either Ivy Adams or Leo Nolan. Beginning a new school year, Emily experiences familiar fears about settling in but soon makes friends—eventually even with the class bully." Horn Book

McDonnell, Christine, 1949-—*Continued*

"Rich in characterization and creative detail, this story is brimming with life; yet, beneath the bubbling current, there is a quiet appreciation for personal relationships." SLJ

Toad food & measle soup; pictures by Diane de Groat. Dial Bks. 1982 109p il $10.95; lib bdg $10.89; Puffin Bks. pa $3.95 (2-4) **Fic**

1. Family life—Fiction
ISBN 0-8037-8476-7; 0-8037-8488-0 (lib bdg); 0-14-031724-4 (pa) LC 82-70204

"Leo, introduced as a supporting player in 'Don't Be Mad, Ivy' [entered above] is the star of these five . . . episodes. In one, Leo's imagination gets him in trouble; in another, he is dissatisfied with his longed-for pet chameleon. But the funniest chapter is the first, in which Leo's mom becomes a vegetarian cook and introduces the family to what Leo thinks is toad food and measle soup ('tofu and miso soup')." Booklist

"The author presents a very human boy, beset by the insecurities of youth, but helped by loving parents and she does so with clever, gentle humor. McDonnell is particularly good at describing Leo's thoughts and feelings, and the text is illustrated with 11 realistic pencil drawings." SLJ

Followed by: Lucky charms & birthday wishes, entered above

McKillip, Patricia A., 1948-

The riddle-master of Hed. Atheneum Pubs. 1976 228p il o.p.; Ballantine Bks. paperback available $3.95 (5 and up) **Fic**

1. Fantastic fiction
ISBN 0-345-33104-4 (pa) LC 76-5492

"Morgon, Prince of Hed, goes in pursuit of an explanation for the three stars on his forehead. Accompanied by Deth, the harpist, Morgon ultimately is led to the High One himself." Roman. Sequences

"Many of the elements and the names appear to be drawn from Welsh mythology, but the author has the ability to deal with familiar themes in a fresh manner and a poetic facility in description." Horn Book

Other available titles in this series are:
Harpist in the wind (1977)
Heir of sea & fire (1977)

McKinley, Robin

Beauty: a retelling of the story of Beauty & the beast. Harper & Row 1978 247p $13.95; lib bdg $13.89 (5 and up) **Fic**

1. Fairy tales
ISBN 0-06-024149-7; 0-06-024150-0 (lib bdg) LC 77-25636

"McKinley's version of this folktale is embellished with rich descriptions and settings and detailed characterizations. The author has not modernized the story but varied the traditional version to attract modern readers. The values of love, honor, and beauty are placed in a magical setting that will please the reader of fantasy." Shapiro. Fic for Youth. 2d edition

The hero and the crown. Greenwillow Bks. 1985 246p lib bdg $13.95; Ace Bks. pa $3.50 (6 and up) **Fic**

1. Fantastic fiction
ISBN 0-688-02593-5 (lib bdg); 0-441-32809-1 (pa) LC 84-4074

Also available ABC-CLIO large print edition $15.95 (ISBN 1-55736-078-2)

Awarded the Newbery Medal, 1985

"A prequel rather than sequel to 'The Blue Sword' [1982] McKinley's second novel set in the . . . mythical kingdom of Damar centers on Aerin, daughter of a Damarian king and his second wife, a witchwoman from the feared, demon-ridden North. The narrative follows Aerin as she seeks her birthright, becoming first a dragon killer and eventually the savior of the kingdom." Booklist

The author "has in this suspenseful prequel . . . created an utterly engrossing fantasy, replete with a fairly mature romantic subplot as well as adventure. She transports the reader into a beguiling realm of pseudomedieval pageantry and ritual where the supernatural is never far below the surface of the ordinary." N Y Times Book Rev

Menotti, Gian Carlo, 1911-

Amahl and the night visitors; illustrated by Michèle Lemieux. Morrow 1986 64p il $15; lib bdg $14.88 (2-4) **Fic**

1. Jesus Christ—Nativity—Fiction 2. Magi
ISBN 0-688-05426-9; 0-688-05427-7 (lib bdg) LC 84-27196

Relates how a crippled young shepherd comes to accompany the three Kings on their way to pay hommage to the newborn Jesus

"Some of the pictures, which are dominated by reddish brown, have rich tension and composition, as in the one of Amahl's mother contemplating theft, or in the portrait of Melchior describing the Christ child. Others stay smoothly on the surface or stray toward cliche, or, in the unfortunate case of the three kings' appearance at Amahl's doorway, fall into the gutter. Still, there is a great deal to look at, and the story, popular since the opera's 1951 debut, has sentimental appeal, humor, and some commanding moments." Bull Cent Child Books

Merrill, Jean, d. 1985

The pushcart war; with illustrations by Ronni Solbert. Harper & Row 1964 222p il (5 and up) **Fic**

1. Trucks—Fiction 2. New York (N.Y.)—Fiction

Also available from Smith, P. $14.50 (ISBN 0-8446-6251-8)

In the near future, "arrogant, mammoth trucks threaten to crowd people, small cars, pushcarts, and peddlers off the streets of New York. When a truck contemptuously runs down a pushcart, the peddlers rebel and wage a guerrilla war against the trucks, using a primitive, but effective, secret weapon. Funny, dramatic, tongue-in-cheek satire on the sheer bigness which is overwhelming urban life but which is here, for once, defeated by the little people who 'are' the city." Moorachian. What is a City?

Merrill, Jean, d. 1985—*Continued*

The toothpaste millionaire; prepared by the Bank Street College of Education. Houghton Mifflin 1974 c1972 90p il $13.95 (4-6) **Fic**

1. Business—Fiction
ISBN 0-395-18511-4 LC 73-22055

First copyright 1972

Illustrated by Jan Palmer

The author recounts the adventures of twelve-year-old Rufus Mayflower who starts manufacturing and selling toothpaste when he is in the sixth grade. By the time he is an eighth grader, he is a millionaire and ready to retire

This story "is laden rather heavily with arithmetic and business details, but rises above it. . . . The illustrations are engaging, the style is light, the project interesting (with more than a few swipes taken at advertising and business practices in our society) and Rufus a believable genius." Bull Cent Child Books

Meyers, Susan

P.J. Clover, private eye: the case of the Halloween hoot; illustrated by Gioia Fiammenghi. Lodestar Bks. 1990 132p il $13.95 (4-6) **Fic**

1. Mystery and detective stories 2. School stories 3. Halloween—Fiction
ISBN 0-525-67297-4 LC 89-36178

While designing the perfect costumes for a Halloween contest, P.J. and Stacy try to clear their school custodian's name by tracking down the thief who entered the school after hours and stole an antique samovar

"Meyers keeps her pace brisk and drops plenty of hints for observant readers. Fans of this spunky duo as well as newcomers to the series will enjoy the deftly plotted mystery." Booklist

Other available titles about P.J. Clover are:
P.J. Clover, private eye: the case of the borrowed baby (1988)
P.J. Clover, private eye: the case of the missing mouse (1985)
P.J. Clover, private eye: the case of the stolen laundry (1981)

Miles, Betty

The trouble with thirteen. Knopf 1979 108p $6.95; lib bdg $10.99; pa $2.95 (5 and up) **Fic**

1. Friendship—Fiction
ISBN 0-394-83930-7; 0-394-93930-1 (lib bdg); 0-394-82043-6 (pa) LC 78-31678

"Annie, who tells the story, and her best friend Rachel are twelve and in no hurry to grow up too fast. . . . When Rachel's parents decide to get a divorce, Rachel and her mother move to the city. While Annie's adjustment to her friend's departure, to the fact that they are each going to have other close friends, and to the death of a beloved pet gives the story some continuity, this is primarily an account of changes that are peculiar to adolescent girlhood." Bull Cent Child Books

"Annie and Rachel are distinct, fully drawn characters, not meant to stand for Everygirl nor needlessly quirky. They are authentic, the plot is balanced and believable, the pace is sure, and the book is a winner." SLJ

Miles, Miska, 1899-1986

Annie and the Old One; illustrated by Peter Parnall. Little, Brown 1971 44p il $13.95; pa $5.95 (1-4) **Fic**

1. Navajo Indians—Fiction 2. Death—Fiction
ISBN 0-316-57117-2; 0-316-57120-2 (pa) LC 79-129900

A Newbery Medal honor book, 1972

"An Atlantic Monthy Press book"

"Annie, a young Navajo girl, struggles with the realization that her grandmother, the Old One, must die. Slowly and painfully, she accepts the fact that she cannot change the cyclic rhythms of the earth to which the Old One has been so sensitively attuned." Wis Libr Bull

This is "a poignant, understated, rather brave story of a very real child, set against a background of Navajo traditions and contemporary Indian life. Fine expressive drawings match the simplicity of the story." Horn Book

Mills, Claudia, 1954-

Dynamite Dinah. Macmillan 1990 120p $12.95 (3-5) **Fic**

1. Friendship—Fiction 2. School stories 3. Infants—Fiction
ISBN 0-02-767101-1 LC 89-13300

Mischievous Dinah struggles to remain the center of attention when her baby brother comes home from the hospital and her best friend gets a lead role in the class play

"The writing is both savvy and sparkling, making Dinah a distinctive and memorable individual with broad appeal." Bull Cent Child Books

Milne, A. A. (Alan Alexander), 1882-1956

The house at Pooh Corner; with decorations by Ernest H. Shepard. Dutton 1961 c1928 180p il $9.95 (1-4) **Fic**

1. Bears—Fiction 2. Animals—Fiction 3. Toys—Fiction
ISBN 0-525-32302-3 LC 61-16260

First published 1928

"Pooh and Piglet built a house for Eeyore at Pooh Corner. They called it that because it was shorter and sounded better than did Poohanpiglet Corner. Christopher Robin, Rabbit, and other old acquaintances of 'Winnie-the-Pooh' appear, and a new friend, Tigger, is introduced." Carnegie Libr of Pittsburgh

"It is hard to tell what Pooh Bear and his friends would have been without the able assistance of Ernest H. Shepard to see them and picture them so cleverly. . . . They are, and should be, classics." N Y Times Book Rev

The Pooh story book; with decorations and illustrations in full color by E. H. Shepard. Dutton 1965 77p il $11.95 (1-4) **Fic**

1. Bears—Fiction 2. Animals—Fiction 3. Toys—Fiction
ISBN 0-525-37546-5 LC 65-19580

Excerpts from: The house at Pooh Corner and Winnie-the-Pooh

Milne, A. A. (Alan Alexander), 1882-1956
—Continued

Contents: In which a house is built at Pooh Corner for Eeyore; In which Piglet is entirely surrounded by water; In which Pooh invents a new game and Eeyore joins in

Winnie-the-Pooh; illustrated by Ernest H. Shepard, colored by Hilda Scott. Dutton 1974 c1926 161p il $9.95; Dell pa $5.95 (1-4) **Fic**

1. Bears—Fiction 2. Animals—Fiction 3. Toys—Fiction

ISBN 0-525-44443-2; 0-440-40116-X (pa) LC 74-7215

First published 1926

"The kindly, lovable Pooh is one of an imaginative cast of animal characters which includes Eeyore, the wistfully gloomy donkey, Tigger, Piglet, Kanga, and Roo, all living in a fantasy world presided over by Milne's young son, Christopher Robin. Many of the animals are drawn from figures in Milne's life, though each emerges as a universally recognizable type." Reader's Ency

The world of Pooh; the complete Winnie-the-Pooh and The House at Pooh Corner; with decorations and new illustrations in full color by E. H. Shepard. Dutton 1957 314p il $15.95 (1-4) **Fic**

1. Bears—Fiction 2. Animals—Fiction 3. Toys—Fiction

ISBN 0-525-44447-5 LC 57-8986

Also available as part of a boxed set together with: The world of Christopher Robin, entered separately in class 821, for $29.95 (ISBN 0-525-43348-1)

This combined edition of the two titles entered separately above contains the original black and white "illustrations and eight delightful new full-page pictures printed in lovely soft colors." Publ Wkly

Moeri, Louise

The forty-third war. Houghton Mifflin 1989 208p $13.95 (6 and up) **Fic**

ISBN 0-395-50215-2 LC 89-31178

"Twelve-year-old Uno Ramirez and his best friend Lolo are conscripted from their Central American village by guerillas who hold them in a mountain fortress, train them quickly, and send them into battle. . . . Uno's father has already been killed and his sister raped; while he's on a reconaissance patrol, he and other recruits discover the bodies of a whole village slaughtered by government troops. Convinced by what he sees and by heroic Captain Mendoza, who commands his unit, Uno commits himself to the revolution." Bull Cent Child Books

This "is a piece of political fiction highly suitable for adjunct classroom reading in a curriculum focusing on the history of that area. . . . A fine discussion book." SLJ

Save Queen of Sheba. Dutton 1981 116p $14.95; Avon Bks. pa $2.95 (4 and up) **Fic**

1. Survival (after airplane accidents, shipwrecks, etc.)—Fiction 2. Brothers and sisters—Fiction 3. West (U.S.)—Fiction

ISBN 0-525-33202-2; 0-380-71154-0 (pa) LC 80-23019

"A marauding band of Sioux have botched the job of scalping twelve-year-old King David. He awakes with a massive head wound to find that he is alone amidst the wreckage of the wagon train and the bodies of the other travelers. Searching desperately, he finds his six-year-old sister, Queen of Sheba, unharmed but mightily unhappy. Collecting scant food supplies, a rifle, and a plow horse who has returned, the two children set off across the prairie to seek the remnants of a wagon train that might be a few days ahead." Child Book Rev Serv

"Vivid scenes are held taut by a continuity of background. . . . Memorable for reading aloud, with discussion, or alone." Booklist

Mohr, Nicholasa, 1935-

Felita; pictures by Ray Cruz. Dial Bks. for Young Readers 1979 112p il lib bdg $12.89; Bantam Bks. pa $2.75 (3-5) **Fic**

1. City life—Fiction 2. Puerto Ricans—New York (N.Y.)—Fiction

ISBN 0-8037-3144-2 (lib bdg); 0-553-15792-2 (pa) LC 79-50151

"When nine-year-old Felita's Puerto Rican family moves to a better neighborhood, she is sad about leaving old friends. Their new neighbors are hate-filled, prejudiced people. The family returns to the old area. Throughout their ordeal, Felita's grandmother helps her understand her problems." Child Book Rev Serv

"The candid message is practical: 'You must feel strength inside.' A few words in Spanish and Ray Cruz's art work fit in perfectly. Mohr scores with her first story for younger readers, capturing the spirit of family and neighborhood." SLJ

Another available title about Felita is:
Going home (1986)

Montgomery, L. M. (Lucy Maud), 1874-1942

Anne of Green Gables (5 and up) **Fic**

Some editions are:
Bantam Bks. pa $2.95 (ISBN 0-553-15327-7)
Crown (Children's classics) $10.99 Illustrated in color by Troy Howell (ISBN 0-517-65958-1)
Godine $22.50 Illustrated by Lauren Mills (ISBN 0-87923-783-X)
Grosset & Dunlap (Illustrated junior lib) $12.95 Illustrated by Jody Lee (ISBN 0-448-06030-2)

First published 1908 by Page

"Daily doings and dreams from her 10th to 17th year of a lively, imaginative child, adopted by an elderly brother and sister on a Prince Edward island farm." NY State Libr

Other available titles about Anne are:
Anne of Avonlea (1909)
Anne of Ingleside (1939)
Anne of the island (1915)
Anne of Windy Poplars (1936)
Anne's house of dreams (1917)

Morey, Walt, 1907-

Gentle Ben; illustrated by John Schoenherr. Dutton 1965 191p il $12.95; Avon Bks. pa $2.95 (5 and up) **Fic**

1. Bears—Fiction 2. Alaska—Fiction
ISBN 0-525-30429-0; 0-380-00743-6 (pa)
LC 65-21290

Set in Alaska before statehood, this is the story of 13-year-old Mark Anderson who befriends a huge brown bear which has been chained in a shed since it was a cub. Finally Mark's father buys the bear, but Orca City's inhabitants eventually insist that the animal, named Ben, be shipped to an uninhabited island. However, the friendship of Mark and Ben endures

The author "has written a vivid chronicle of Alaska, its people and places, challenges and beauties. Told with simplicity and dignity which befits its characters, human and animal, [it] is a memorable reading experience." SLJ

Moser, Barry

The tinderbox; [by] Hans Christian Andersen; adapted, illustrated, and designed by Barry Moser. Little, Brown 1990 29p il $14.95 **Fic**

1. Fairy tales 2. Tennessee—Fiction
ISBN 0-316-03938-1 LC 90-30279

"Moser retells Andersen's classic fairy tale as it might have happened in the Tennessee mountains just after the Civil War. A young soldier on his way home meets an old codger (rather than the traditional witch). The mountain man lowers the soldier down a rock cliff to a cave where he finds three magical dogs atop their treasure chests and, of course, the tinderbox. Preserving the main elements of the story, Moser uses dialogue along with the illustrations to create the Southern setting." Booklist

"Moser's superb watercolors are chiefly portraits of the principals: the old codger; the country girl; the open-faced hero, Yoder Ott—and the three dogs, whose eyes are not *quite* as big as wagon wheels or windmills. Their vivid individuality convincingly links the real, the historic, and the fantastic, giving a new, distinctly American life to the tale." SLJ

Myers, Walter Dean, 1937-

Fast Sam, Cool Clyde, and Stuff. Viking 1975 190p $12.95; Penguin Bks. pa $3.95 (6 and up) **Fic**

1. Friendship—Fiction 2. Blacks—Fiction 3. Harlem (New York, N.Y.)—Fiction
ISBN 0-670-30874-9; 0-14-032613-8 (pa)
LC 74-32383

"In an affectionate, colloquial narrative, Stuff, now 18, recalls the time when he was 13, hanging out on 116th Street, and enjoying being part of a circle of dependable friends, the best of whom were Fast Sam and Cool Clyde." Booklist

"A funny, fast-paced story of teenagers in the ghetto. The characters are memorable: amusing, troubled, embarrassed, triumphant, angry—they run the gamut of adolescent emotions. The plot is an exciting one revolving around a dope ring; the day-to-day episodes of life at school and at home are done well. This is an excellent portrayal of warm relationships of family and friends, and a fine stimulus to discussion and personal writing." Read Teach

Me, Mop, and the Moondance Kid; illustrated by Rodney Pate. Delacorte Press 1988 154p il $13.95 (4-6) **Fic**

1. Baseball—Fiction 2. Adoption—Fiction 3. Friendship—Fiction
ISBN 0-440-50065-6 LC 88-6503

"Eleven-year-old T. J. and his younger brother Billy, a.k.a. the Moondance Kid, have been living with their adoptive parents for about six months, and are settling in well. They are worried that their friend Mop, a girl who has not yet been adopted, may be transferred to an orphanage some distance away. Mop decides to join T. J.'s little league team in order to get close to the coach and his wife, whom she suspects are interested in adopting her." SLJ

"Myers's keen sense of humor, quick, natural dialogue and irresistible protagonists make this novel a winner." Publ Wkly

The Mouse rap. Harper & Row 1990 186p $12.95; lib bdg $12.88 (6 and up) **Fic**

1. Blacks—Fiction 2. Buried treasure—Fiction 3. Harlem (New York, N.Y.)—Fiction
ISBN 0-06-024343-0; 0-06-024344-9 (lib bdg)
LC 89-36419

During an eventful summer in Harlem, fourteen-year-old Mouse and his friends fall in and out of love and search for a hidden treasure from the days of Al Capone

"A crisp rap beat, an intriguing, intergenerational cast of characters, and the zaniness of events make this story of fourteen-year-old Mouse and his friends a very upbeat adventure." Horn Book Guide

Scorpions. Harper & Row 1988 216p $12.95; lib bdg $12.89 (6 and up) **Fic**

1. Blacks—Fiction 2. Juvenile delinquency—Fiction 3. Harlem (New York, N.Y.)—Fiction
ISBN 0-06-024364-3; 0-06-024365-1 (lib bdg)
LC 85-45815

A Newbery Medal honor book, 1989

"Set in present day Harlem, this . . . story presents a brutally honest picture of the tragic influence of gang membership and pressures on a young black adolescent. Jamal Hicks, age twelve, reluctantly follows the orders of his older brother, now serving time in prison for robbery, and takes his place as leader of the Scorpions. When Jamal's leadership is challenged, disaster follows and Jamal learns some tragic lessons about friendship and owning a gun. Written by a true master of the genre, 'Scorpions' deals with issues that are 'in touch' with what is happening now." Child Book Rev Serv

The young landlords. Viking 1979 197p o.p.; Penguin Bks. paperback available $3.95 (6 and up) **Fic**

1. Blacks—Fiction 2. Landlord and tenant—Fiction 3. Harlem (New York, N.Y.)—Fiction
ISBN 0-14-034244-3 (pa) LC 79-13264

Coretta Scott King Award for text, 1980

"This is the story of a group of black teenagers living in New York City who become the owners of a run-down slum building. Led by Paul (the narrator) and his soon-to-be girl friend Gloria, they try to cope with the day-to-day (and night-to-night) pressures of running the building." SLJ

"The story is presented with a masterful blend of

Myers, Walter Dean, 1937-—*Continued*
humor and realism; dialogue is lively and authentic, and the many characters are drawn with compassion. The author has once again demonstrated his keen sensitivity to the joys and frustrations of adolescence as well as his thorough knowledge of the New York City street scene." Horn Book

Naidoo, Beverley

Chain of fire; illustrations by Eric Velasquez. Lippincott 1990 c1989 245p il $12.95; lib bdg $12.89 (5 and up) **Fic**

1. South Africa—Race relations—Fiction
ISBN 0-397-32426-X; 0-397-32427-8 (lib bdg)
LC 89-27551

First published 1989 in the United Kingdom

"The political awakening of fifteen-year-old Naledi, who first appeared in *Journey to Jōburg* [entered below], is recounted with passion and eloquence as the author describes the resettling of Black villagers to their new and barren 'homeland'—the result of South Africa's policy of aparthied." Horn Book Guide

Journey to Jo'burg; a South African story; illustrations by Eric Velasquez. Lippincott 1986 80p il $11.95; lib bdg $11.89 (5 and up) **Fic**

1. South Africa—Race relations—Fiction
ISBN 0-397-32168-6; 0-397-32169-4 (lib bdg)
LC 85-45508

"This touching novel graphically depicts the plight of Africans living in the horror of South Africa. Thirteen-year-old Maledi and her 9-year-old brother leave their small village, take the perilous journey to the city, and encounter, firsthand, the painful struggle for justice, freedom, and dignity in the 'City of Gold.' A provocative story with a message readers will long remember." Soc Educ

Followed by: Chain of fire, entered above

Naylor, Phyllis Reynolds, 1933-

The agony of Alice. Atheneum Pubs. 1985 131p $12.95 (5 and up) **Fic**

1. Teachers—Fiction 2. School stories
ISBN 0-689-31143-5 LC 85-7957

Eleven-year-old, motherless Alice decides she needs a gorgeous role model who does everything right; and when placed in homely Mrs. Plotkins's class she is greatly disappointed until she discovers it's what people are inside that counts

"The lively style exhibits a deft touch at capturing the essence of an endearing heroine growing up without a mother." SLJ

Another available title about Alice is entered below

Alice in rapture, sort of. Atheneum Pubs. 1989 166p $12.95 (5 and up) **Fic**

ISBN 0-689-31466-3 LC 88-8174

"A Jean Karl book"

The summer before she enters the seventh grade becomes the summer of Alice's first boyfriend, and she discovers that love is about the most mixed-up thing that can possibly happen to you, especially since she has no mother to go to for advice

"The dynamics between Alice and her two best girlfriends, Alice's yearning for her dead mother to help with the ordinary and extraordinary problems of growing up, and her individualistic approach to dating are smoothly blended into a funny, sometimes poignant narrative." Bull Cent Child Books

Bernie and the Bessledorf ghost. Atheneum Pubs. 1990 132p $12.95 (4-6) **Fic**

1. Ghosts—Fiction 2. Mystery and detective stories 3. Hotels, motels, etc.—Fiction
ISBN 0-689-31499-X LC 88-29389

"A Jean Karl book"

Living at the Bessledorf Hotel where his father works as the manager, Bernie tries to solve the mystery of a troubled, young ghost who wanders the halls of the hotel at night

"The ghost is appropriately spooky, but the story is liberally laced with humor; the plot flows along nicely, with enough suspense to keep the pages turning." SLJ

Another available title about the Bessledorf Hotel is: The bodies in the Bessledorf Hotel (1986)

Maudie in the middle; [by] Phyllis Reynolds Naylor and Lura Schield Reynolds; illustrated by Judith Gwyn Brown. Atheneum Pubs. 1988 161p il $13.95; Dell pa $3.25 (3-5) **Fic**

1. Family life—Fiction 2. Iowa—Fiction
ISBN 0-689-31395-0; 0-440-40324-3 (pa) LC 87-3470

"A Jean Karl book"

"Maudie, who is eight when the story begins, is the middle child of seven, either too young or too old for everything, she feels. And, since she is a lively child and often in trouble, she despairs of ever being appreciated, or being special in any way. This turn-of-the-century family story is based on the childhood of Lura Reynolds, Phyllis Naylor's mother, and it's adequately told and structured but expectably episodic in the way most reminiscences are. Intermittently, this is a bit sugary, but it's an amicable period piece." Bull Cent Child Books

The witch's eye; illustrated by Joe Burleson. Delacorte Press 1990 179p il $13.95 (5 and up) **Fic**

1. Witchcraft—Fiction
ISBN 0-385-30157-X LC 89-77237

Though suspected witch-neighbor Mrs. Tuggle has died, her glass eye resurfaces, bringing new dangers and terrors to Lynn's family

"The quality of writing and characterization makes this a truly scary story, much more so than the many series that are attempting to exploit the popularity of horror. The personaity changes of characters who come under the influence of the witch or her eye sustain a convincingly threatening atmosphere." SLJ

Other available titles about Lynn, Mouse, and Mrs. Tuggle are:
The witch herself (1978)
Witch water (1977)
Witch's sister (1975)

Nelson, Theresa, 1948-

The 25¢ miracle. Bradbury Press 1986 214p $13.95 (5 and up) **Fic**

1. Fathers and daughters—Fiction
ISBN 0-02-724370-2 LC 85-17061

"Complex characterizations illuminate the anguish of a widowed father and his plucky motherless daughter, unable to discuss their true feelings. It's a story filled with childhood angst, heartache, and joy." SLJ

And one for all. Orchard Bks. 1989 182p $12.95; lib bdg $12.99 (6 and up) **Fic**

1. Vietnam War, 1961-1975—Fiction 2. Brothers and sisters—Fiction
ISBN 0-531-05804-2; 0-531-08404-3 (lib bdg) LC 88-22490

"A Richard Jackson book"

Geraldine, the twelve-year-old narrator of this Vietnam War novel, tells the story of her older brother Wing who enlists in the Marines, and his best friend Sam, an antiwar activist. When Wing is killed at Khe Sanh, "Geraldine blames Sam and hops a bus to Washington, D.C., where she confronts him among peace protestors at the foot of the Washington Monument. Finally, her grief and fury give way to understanding that Sam was always on Wing's side in trying to end the war." SLJ

"Plot, dialogue, and setting are effortlessly authentic and never overwhelmed by the theme. . . . Smoothly written and easily read, this also manages to challenge assumptions in a thought-provoking probe of the past." Bull Cent Child Books

Neufeld, John, 1938-

Edgar Allan. Phillips 1968 95p $17.95; New Am. Lib. pa $2.95 (5 and up) **Fic**

1. Adoption—Fiction 2. Race relations—Fiction 3. Family life—Fiction
ISBN 0-87599-149-1; 0-451-15870-9 (pa) LC 68-31175

"A California Protestant minister's family adopts three-year-old Edgar Allan. Because Edgar is black and the family is white, there are many and varied reactions to the adoption, both within the family and in the community. Stark, terse telling of a memorable event." Adventuring with Books. 2d edition

Neville, Emily Cheney, 1919-

It's like this, Cat; [by] Emily Neville; pictures by Emil Weiss. Harper & Row 1963 180p il $14.95; lib bdg $14.98; pa $3.50 (5 and up) **Fic**

1. Cats—Fiction 2. New York (N.Y.)—Fiction
ISBN 0-06-024390-2; 0-06-024391-0 (lib bdg); 0-06-440073-5 (pa) LC 62-21292

Awarded the Newbery Medal, 1964

This is the "story of a fourteen-year-old growing up in the neighborhood of Gramercy Park in New York City. He tells of life in the city and his relationships with his parents, neighbors, and friends. It is his pet, a stray tom cat whom he adopts, that brings him two new friends, one a troubled boy and the other his first girl." Wis Libr Bull

"A story told with a great amount of insight into human relationships. . . . This all provides a wonderfully real picture of a city boy's outlets and of one likable adolescent's inner feelings. An exceedingly fresh, honest, and well-rounded piece of writing." Horn Book

Newman, Robert, 1909-1988

The case of the Baker Street Irregular; a Sherlock Holmes story. Atheneum Pubs. 1978 216p hardcover o.p. paperback available $3.95 (5 and up) **Fic**

1. Mystery and detective stories 2. London (England)—Fiction
ISBN 0-689-70766-5 (pa) LC 77-15463

Brought to London under mysterious circumstances by his tutor, young Andrew Tillett seeks the help of Sherlock Holmes when his tutor is kidnapped and he himself is threatened with the same fate

"The author is as urbane and fluent as the legendary Mr. Holmes; he seems thoroughly comfortable with the characters, the atmosphere, and the turn-of-the century London setting; and the story moves along with unflagging energy." Horn Book

Other available titles involving Andrew Tillett, his friend Sara Wiggins and Scotland Yard's Inspector Peter Wyatt are:

The case of the watching boy (1987)
The case of the Indian curse (1986)
The case of the threatened king (1982)
The case of the murdered players (1985)
The case of the vanishing corpse (1980)

Nilsson, Ulf, 1948-

If you didn't have me; illustrated by Eva Eriksson; translated from the Swedish by Lone Thygesen Blecher and George Blecher. Margaret K. McElderry Bks. 1987 113p il $10.95 (3-5) **Fic**

1. Farm life—Fiction 2. Sweden—Fiction
ISBN 0-689-50406-3 LC 86-21327

"A young boy and his baby brother are deposited with their widowed grandmother on a farm in southern Sweden while their parents build a new house in a distant town. In each chapter of this episodic novel, the boy describes an incident in which he interacts with the rural residents." SLJ

"Sights, sounds and smells . . . are evoked with charm and immediacy. Everyday events, from feeding chickens to resting under a tree, are shown to have potentially vast significance to a small boy with imagination and minimal adult interference. Told in short, episodic chapters, this child's-eye view of rural life in Sweden will make a dandy read-aloud." Publ Wkly

Nixon, Joan Lowery, 1927-

A family apart. Bantam Bks. 1987 162p $14.95; pa $2.95 (5 and up) **Fic**

1. Foster home care—Fiction 2. Brothers and sisters—Fiction 3. United States—History—1783-1865—Fiction
ISBN 0-553-05432-5; 0-553-27478-3 (pa) LC 87-12563

"The first volume in the *Orphan Train* quartet, this is based on a real program, the Children's Aid Society's placement of orphans who travelled from New York City

Nixon, Joan Lowery, 1927-—*Continued*
to the West to be adopted by residents there. In this story, set in 1860, widowed Mrs. Kelley realizes she cannot support her six children and gives them up for adoption. The protagonist is the oldest girl, Frances, who disguises herself as a boy so that she can be paired with her baby brother for adoption, and they are indeed taken together by a very nice family." Bull Cent Child Books

"The plot is rational and well paced; the characters are real and believable; the time setting important to U.S. history, and the values all that anyone could ask for." Voice Youth Advocates

Other titles available in the Orphan train quartet are:
Caught in the act (1988)
In the face of danger (1988)
A place to belong (1989)

Nordstrom, Ursula, 1910-1988

The secret language; pictures by Mary Chalmers. Harper & Row 1960 167p il lib bdg $12.89; pa $3.50 (3-5) **Fic**

1. School stories
ISBN 0-06-024576-X (lib bdg); 0-06-440022-0 (pa)
LC 60-7701

A "story about two eight-year-old girls at boarding school. None of the experiences that Vicky and Martha have are unusual; none dramatic; yet all of the details of their year make absorbing reading. Vicky is homesick and Martha is a rebel; as they adjust to each other and as they adapt themselves to the pattern of school life, both girls find satisfactions and both grow up a little. The writing style has a gentle humor, a warm understanding, and an easy narrative flow that seems effortless." Bull Cent Child Books

Norton, Mary, 1903-

Bed-knob and broomstick; illustrated by Erik Blegvad. Harcourt Brace 1957 189p il o.p. paperback available $3.95 (3-5) **Fic**

1. Fantastic fiction 2. Witches—Fiction
ISBN 0-15-206231-9 LC 57-11341

Also available G.K. Hall large print edition $14.95 (ISBN 0-8161-4786-8)

A combined edition of: The magic bed-knob, first published 1943 by Putnam and Bonfires and broomsticks, first published 1947 in the United Kingdom

The story is about "two brothers and a sister who receive from their neighbor Miss Price, because they have uncovered her secret efforts to become a witch, a magic bed-knob which can grant their wishes to be anywhere in the present or, with a different twist, in the past." Horn Book

"While there is one unpleasant note in text and illustration of Negroid cannibals, the story has the same quiet humor and calm acceptance of the fantastic as does 'The Borrowers' [entered below]." Bull Cent Child Books

The Borrowers; illustrated by Beth and Joe Krush. Harcourt Brace 1953 180p il $12.95; pa $3.95 (3-6) **Fic**

1. Fairy tales
ISBN 0-15-209987-5; 0-15-209990-5 (pa) LC 53-7870

First published 1952 in the United Kingdom

A "fascinating fantasy about a tiny family that lived beneath the kitchen floor of an old English country house and 'borrowed' from the larger human residents to fill their modest needs. Their sudden discovery by a small boy visitor almost proves to be their undoing. The imaginative details about the activities of the miniature people have tremendous appeal for children." Child Books Too Good to Miss

Other available titles about the Borrowers are:
The Borrowers afield (1955)
The Borrowers afloat (1959)
The Borrowers aloft (1961)
The Borrowers avenged (1982)
Poor Stainless (1966)

O'Brien, Robert C.

Mrs. Frisby and the rats of NIMH; illustrated by Zena Bernstein. Atheneum Pubs. 1971 223p il lib bdg $14.95; pa $3.95 (4 and up) **Fic**

1. Mice—Fiction 2. Rats—Fiction
ISBN 0-689-20651-8 (lib bdg); 0-689-71068-2 (pa)
LC 74-134818

Awarded the Newbery Medal, 1972

"Mrs. Frisby, a widowed mouse, is directed by an owl to consult with the rats that live under the rosebush about her problem of moving her sick son from the family's endangered home. Upon entering that rats' quarters, Mrs. Frisby discovers to her astonishment that the rats are not ordinary rodents, but highly intelligent creatures that escaped from an NIMH laboratory after being taught to read. How the rats help Mrs. Frisby and she, in turn, helps them from being captured, is told in a thoroughly enjoyable animal fantasy." Booklist

"The story is fresh and ingenious, the style witty, and the plot both hilarious and convincing." Saturday Rev

Followed by: Racso and the rats of NIMH and R-T, by Jane Leslie Conly, entered above

O'Connor, Jane, 1947-

Yours till Niagara Falls, Abby; illustrated by Margot Apple. Hastings House 1979 128p il o.p.; Scholastic paperback available $2.50 **Fic**

1. Camps—Fiction 2. Friendship—Fiction
ISBN 0-590-41119-5 (pa) LC 79-19782

Ten-year-old Abby faces two months of summer camp without her best friend

"The material isn't unusual, but the writing style is yeasty, and the characterization and dialogue sound; the action and the humor should appeal to readers." Bull Cent Child Books

O'Dell, Scott, 1903-1989

The black pearl; illustrated by Milton Johnson. Houghton Mifflin 1967 140p il $13.95; Dell pa $2.95 (6 and up) **Fic**

1. Pearlfisheries—Fiction 2. Baja California (Mexico: Peninsula)—Fiction
ISBN 0-395-06961-0; 0-440-90803-5 (pa)
LC 67-23311

A Newbery Medal honor book, 1968

O'Dell, Scott, 1903-1989—*Continued*

"The people of Baja California feared a demon creature, a giant ray—El Manta Diablo. He was believed to live in a cave at the end of a lagoon, and though a few Indians who 'had a pact with El Manta Diablo' dared to dive for pearls, no one had searched in the cave. A pearl taken from the Manta would bring only ill fortune. Yet Ramón Salazar, goaded by the taunts of the greatest pearl diver of his father's fleet, dared to enter the cave to dive for a pearl even more wonderful than the one El Sevillano had boasted of. And he found it—the Paragon of Pearls, the Pearl of Heaven. Then came the encounter with the Manta." Horn Book

"The stark simplicity of the story and the deeper significance it holds in the triumph of good over evil add importance to the book, but even without that the book would be enjoyable as a rousing adventure tale with supernatural overtones and beautifully maintained tempo and suspense." Bull Cent Child Books

The captive. Houghton Mifflin 1979 210p $14.95 (6 and up) **Fic**

1. Mayas—Fiction 2. Mexico—Fiction
ISBN 0-395-27811-2 LC 79-15809

This story set in the 16th century, "centers on the adventures of a young Jesuit seminarian who goes to the New World as part of a Spanish expedition. Full of Christian idealism, Julián Escobar believes his role is to convert the savages. Instead, he succumbs to the temptation to pose as the reincarnated Mayan deity [Kukulcán]." Child Book Rev Serv

"Characterizations are all finely drawn, and Julián's transformation from insecure, humane seminarian to pretend god is remarkable in its honest development." SLJ

Other available titles in The City of the Seven Serpents series are:
The amethyst ring (1983)
The feathered serpent (1981)

Island of the Blue Dolphins; illustrated by Ted Lewin. Houghton Mifflin 1990 181p il $18.95 (5 and up) **Fic**

1. Indians of North America—Fiction 2. Wilderness survival—Fiction 3. San Nicolas Island (Calif.)—Fiction
ISBN 0-395-53680-4 LC 90-35331

Also available ABC-CLIO large print edition $14.95 (ISBN 1-55736-002-2)

Awarded the Newbery Medal, 1961

A reissue with new illustrations of the title first published 1960

"Unintentionally left behind by members of her California Native American tribe who fled a tragedy-ridden island, young Karana must construct a life for herself. Without bitterness or self-pity, she is able to extract joy and challenge from her eighteen years of solitude." Shapiro. Fic for Youth. 2d edition

Followed by: Zia, entered below

The King's fifth; decorations and maps by Samuel Bryant. Houghton Mifflin 1966 264p $14.95 (5 and up) **Fic**

1. Estevan, d. 1539—Fiction 2. Mexico—Fiction
ISBN 0-395-06963-7 LC 66-7763

A Newbery Medal honor book, 1967

"Fifteen-year-old Esteban sailed with Admiral Alarcon as a cartographer; carrying supplies for Coronado, the expedition went astray and a small group was put ashore to find Coronado's camp. Thus begins a harrowing story of the exciting and dangerous journey in search of the fabled gold of Cibola." Sutherland. The Best in Child Books

My name is not Angelica. Houghton Mifflin 1989 130p $14.95; Dell pa $3.50 (5 and up) **Fic**

1. Slavery—Fiction 2. West Indies—Fiction
ISBN 0-395-51061-9; 0-440-40379-0 (pa) LC 89-1864

"Raisha is renamed Angelica by the slaveowners who purchase her for their plantation on St. John, an island in the Danish West Indies (now the U.S. Virgin Islands). Both Raisha and her betrothed, Konje, have been captured and sold into slavery by a rival African king, and soon after landing in St. John, Konje escapes to a hidden colony of runaways intent upon revolt." Bull Cent Child Books

"O'Dell's thoroughly researched and deftly written novel is historical fiction at its best. He magnifies the slave issue by building characters with resolve using different perspectives, and keeping emotions taut." Booklist

Sarah Bishop. Houghton Mifflin 1980 184p $13.95; Scholastic pa $2.75 (6 and up) **Fic**

1. United States—History—1775-1783, Revolution—Fiction 2. American loyalists—Fiction 3. New York (State)—Fiction
ISBN 0-395-29185-2; 0-590-42298-7 (pa) LC 79-28394

"Surrounded by war, prejudice, and fear, fifteen-year-old Sarah Bishop quietly determines to live her own kind of life in the wilderness that was Westchester County, New York, during the Revolution. Orphaned Sarah plucks up her courage when she is wrongfully dealt with by both the American and British forces, and she creates a home for herself and her animal friends in the forest near Long Pond." Child Book Rev Serv

"Despite a series of highly dramatic incidents, the story line is basically sharp and clear; O'Dell's messages about the bitterness and folly of war, the dangers of superstition, and the courage of the human spirit are smoothly woven into the story, as are the telling details of period and place." Bull Cent Child Books

Sing down the moon. Houghton Mifflin 1970 137p $13.95; Dell pa $2.95 (5 and up) **Fic**

1. Navajo Indians—Fiction
ISBN 0-395-10919-1; 0-440-97975-7 (pa) LC 71-98513

Also available ABC-CLIO large print edition $15.95 (ISBN 1-55736-142-8)

A Newbery Medal honor book, 1971

This story is told "through the eyes of a young Navaho girl as she sees the rich harvest in the Canyon de Chelly in 1864 destroyed by Spanish slavers and the subsequent destruction by white soldiers which forces the Navahos on a march to Fort Sumner." Publ Wkly

"There is a poetic sonority of style, a sense of identification, and a note of indomitable courage and stoicism that is touching and impressive." Saturday Rev

O'Dell, Scott, 1903-1989—*Continued*

Streams to the river, river to the sea; a novel of Sacagawea. Houghton Mifflin 1986 191p $14.95; Macmillan pa $3.95 (5 and up) **Fic**

1. Sacagawea, 1786-1884—Fiction 2. Lewis and Clark Expedition (1804-1806)—Fiction 3. Indians of North America—Fiction

ISBN 0-395-40430-4; 0-02-044665-9 (pa) LC 86-936

Also available G.K. Hall large print edition $14.95 (ISBN 0-8161-4811-2)

"This is the story of the Shoshone girl who served as an interpreter for the Lewis & Clark expedition. Sacagawea narrates the story, beginning with her abduction, as a young teenager, by the Minnetarees. From this tribe she is married to a French trader, Toussaint Charbonneau, with whom she has a child. When Lewis & Clark arrive at the Indian camp on their way up the Mississippi River, they hire Charbonneau as a guide, and Sacagawea accompanies the expedition to interpret while traveling through Shoshone territory. She relates the ordeals of the trip, descriptions of the land and Indian life, and her growing feelings for Captain Clark." Voice Youth Advocates

"An informative and involving choice for American history students and pioneer-adventure readers." Bull Cent Child Books

Zia. Houghton Mifflin 1976 179p $14.95; Dell pa $2.95 (5 and up) **Fic**

1. Indians of North America—Fiction 2. Missions, Christian—Fiction

ISBN 0-395-24393-9; 0-440-99904-9 (pa) LC 75-44156

Sequel to: Island of the Blue Dolphins, entered above

"Taking the point of view that Karana is still on the island, [the author] invents a niece for her in the character of Zia, a young Indian who lives at the Santa Barbara Mission and who dreams of sailing to the island to rescue her aunt. After one thwarted attempt to get there, and imprisonment for helping some fellow Indians flee the Mission, Zia finds her dream realized." N Y Times Book Rev

"Zia is an excellent story in its own right, written in a clear, quiet, and reflective style which is in harmony with the plot and characterization." SLJ

Oneal, Zibby, 1934-

A long way to go; illustrated by Michael Dooling. Viking 1990 54p il (Once upon America) $11.95 (3-5) **Fic**

1. Women—Suffrage—Fiction 2. Sex role—Fiction 3. World War, 1914-1918—United States—Fiction

ISBN 0-670-82532-8 LC 89-48760

"This short novel about the women's suffrage movement is told from the perspective of Lila, a 10-year-old girl living in New York City in 1917." N Y Times Book Rev

"Nicely structured, with succinct plot and a smooth narrative flow, this has as much message and as much characterization as its brevity permits." Bull Cent Child Books

Orgel, Doris

The devil in Vienna. Dial Bks. for Young Readers 1978 246p $8.95; Puffin Bks. pa $3.95 (6 and up) **Fic**

1. Austria—Fiction 2. Jews—Austria—Fiction 3. Holocaust, Jewish (1933-1945)—Fiction 4. Friendship—Fiction

ISBN 0-8037-1920-5; 0-14-032500-X (pa) LC 78-51319

"Although fictional, the events in this story about the Nazi occupation of Austria are based on the author's experiences as a child in Vienna. Inge is Jewish, her best friend Lieselotte is the daughter of a Nazi officer so devoted to Hitler that he had moved his family to Germany, returning only after the anschluss. Although the girls have been forbidden to meet by both sets of parents, Inge knows her friend is loyal; when her parents are having difficulty in leaving the country, Inge turns to Lieselotte's uncle, a Catholic priest, for help. The story ends with the refugees' safe arrival in Yugoslavia." Bull Cent Child Books

"The book arouses in its readers anguish, fury, admiration, scorn—it couldn't be a more effective story or a more powerful illustration of the reason 'never to forget.'" Publ Wkly

Orlev, Uri, 1931-

The island on Bird Street; translated by Hillel Halkin. Houghton Mifflin 1984 162p $13.95 (5 and up) **Fic**

1. Holocaust, Jewish (1933-1945)—Fiction 2. Jews—Poland—Fiction 3. World War, 1939-1945—Fiction 4. Poland—Fiction

ISBN 0-395-33887-5 LC 83-26524

Original Hebrew edition, copyright 1981

This is the "story of an 11-year-old boy's life during the Holocaust. Alex, entirely on his own in an empty Polish ghetto, is sustained by his father's admonition to wait for him. Over rooftops, through attics and basements he traverses the deserted sector in his struggle for life." SLJ

"The author has written a book that offers on one level a first-rate survival story and on another a haunting glimpse of the war's effects on individual people. . . . While fully aware of his chances of survival, Alex thought of his experience as an adventure akin to Robinson Crusoe's; and although the tone of the book reflects the boy's cheerful, logical disposition, the loneliness and utter desperation of his situation come through with a piercing clarity." Horn Book

Park, Barbara, 1947-

Almost starring Skinnybones. Knopf 1988 108p $10.95; lib bdg $11.99; pa $2.95 (4-6) **Fic**

1. School stories

ISBN 0-394-89831-1; 0-394-99831-6 (lib bdg); 0-394-82591-8 (pa) LC 87-28752

Sequel to: Skinnybones, entered below

"Alex Frankovitch figures that he has finally made it. Having won the National Kitty Fritters Commercial Contest, he hopes to impress the folks back home. At last, he thinks, he will shed his humiliating nickname 'Skinnybones'. . . . There is just one hitch: Alex's big break into commercials is as a wimpy, six-year-old weak-

Park, Barbara, 1947-—*Continued*
ling, wearing a Davy Crockett cap and pulling a red wagon." Publ Wkly

"Readers will respond to the hilarious dialogue, realistic situations, and even to Alex's brief moments of humanity. With plenty of action and characters that are predictable but never flat, the book is a good choice for that next request for a short, funny book." Horn Book

Beanpole; by Barbara Park. Knopf 1983 147p $10.95; lib bdg $10.99; pa $3.50 (5 and up) **Fic**

ISBN 0-394-85811-5; 0-394-95811-X (lib bdg); 0-394-84746-6 (pa) LC 83-111

"Lillian begins her plaintive, often funny, story just as she turns thirteen; five feet six, she's called 'Beanpole' by her classmates in seventh grade. She has a three-part birthday wish; to get a bra, to dance with a boy, to become a member of the Pom Squad. Her wishes are granted, to an extent: Mom buys the bras Lillian doesn't really need, she does dance with a boy but learns he's been paid to do it, and her strenuous efforts at Pom Squad tryouts fail. . . . By the time the story ends Lillian has learned to laugh about her problems." Bull Cent Child Books

"Told in a first-person rambling style, 'Beanpole' features common sense outlined in humor with a three-dimensional supporting cast of relatives and friends. Park clearly depicts Lillian's need to stretch toward maturity while at the same time fearing to let go of a child's faith in magic wishes." SLJ

The kid in the red jacket. Knopf 1987 113p $9.95; lib bdg $9.99; pa $2.95 (4-6) **Fic**

1. Moving, Household—Fiction
ISBN 0-394-88189-3; 0-394-98189-8 (lib bdg); 0-394-80571-2 (pa) LC 86-20113

When ten-year-old Howard has to move with his family to a distant state, he is forced to live on a street named Chester Pewe, adjust to a new school, and get used to being shadowed by the little girl in a nearby house

"A short, funny, sympathetic, and ultimately reassuring book on the problems of moving and readjustment." Horn Book

Maxie, Rosie, and Earl—partners in grime; illustrations by Alexander Strogart. Knopf 1990 117p il $12.95; lib bdg $13.99 (3-5) **Fic**

1. School stories
ISBN 0-679-80212-6; 0-679-90212-0 (lib bdg) LC 89-28027

"Three misfits come together in the principal's office. Earl Wilber is a new boy, a hypochondriac, who makes a fatal mistake when he is reading aloud. . . . Rosie is a tattletale, whose teacher is fed up with her, and Maxie, a wiseguy, has cut a hole in Daniel W.'s shirt. When Mr. Shivers doesn't have time for them, the unlikely trio decide to cut the rest of their classes—and then worry for the rest of the weekend they will be found out." Booklist

"Light-hearted, not quite believable (because of contrivance or coincidence) but quite enjoyable, this story of the accidental meeting of three loners bounces along amicably to reach a conclusion most readers will expect: a triangular friendship." Bull Cent Child Books

My mother got married (and other disasters). Knopf 1989 138p $10.95; lib bdg $11.99; pa $3.50 (4-6) **Fic**

1. Stepfamilies—Fiction
ISBN 0-394-82149-1; 0-394-92149-6 (lib bdg); 0-394-85059-9 (pa) LC 88-27257

Twelve-year-old Charles experiences many difficulties in adjusting to a new stepfather, stepsister, and stepbrother

"Stories about divorce are nothing new, but Parks does a superb job of giving this one a fresh feel. Charlie's first-person dialogue is humorous but also realistically bitter. In too many problem novels, the protagonist sees the error of his ways and drops previously unsympathetic behavior. Not Charlie. This kid is mad, and he is not willing to give up his anger until a near tragedy tempers his feelings. . . . A story of surprising depth." Booklist

Skinnybones. Knopf 1982 112p $9.95; lib bdg $9.99; pa $2.95 (4-6) **Fic**

1. School stories 2. Baseball—Fiction
ISBN 0-394-84988-4; 0-394-94988-9 (lib bdg); 0-394-94988-9 (pa) LC 81-20791

The novel's hero "Alex Frankovitch (short, thin 'Skinnybone'), is a realist who knows that winning the Most Improved Player awards for six years only means that each year he has started out 'stink-o' and gone to 'smelly.' His particular nemesis this year is T.J. Stoner; T.J.'s brother plays for the Chicago Cubs, and T.J.'s so good he could be suiting up with them momentarily himself. At least that's the way it seems to Alex, who always manages to be on T.J.'s wrong side and in the middle of a disaster because of it. Alex finally comes into his own when he wins the Kitty Fritters TV Contest and thus gets his own taste of what being a celebrity is like." Booklist

Followed by: Almost starring Skinnybones, entered above

Park, Ruth

Playing Beatie Bow. Atheneum Pubs. 1982 c1980 196p $13.95; Penguin Bks. pa $3.95 (5 and up) **Fic**

1. Family life—Fiction 2. Space and time—Fiction 3. Australia—Fiction
ISBN 0-689-30889-2; 0-14-031460-1 (pa) LC 81-8097

"An Argo book"

First published 1980 in Australia

"'Beatie Bow' is the name of a game that Abigail sees younger children playing, and she notices one waif-like girl who watches but never joins the play. Abigail's fourteen, resenting the fact that her mother is more than willing to take back the husband who'd deserted her for another woman, resenting even more her parents' decision to move from Sydney to Norway. . . . [In this] time-slip story, the waif proves to be the Beatie Bow for whom the game was named—but she doesn't know why her name is known. Only when Abigail goes back to Beatie's time, a century ago, does a pattern emerge that answers both their questions." Bull Cent Child Books

Pascal, Francine, 1938-
Hangin' out with Cici. Viking 1977 152p $12.95; Dell pa $2.95 (5 and up) **Fic**

1. Mothers and daughters—Fiction 2. Space and time—Fiction
ISBN 0-670-36045-7; 0-440-93364-1 (pa)
LC 76-57700

"Victoria, a 14-year-old with an unfortunate penchant for trouble, bumps her head while riding on a train and travels back in time to 1944, where she meets Cici. After several hilarious escapades, Victoria realizes that Cici is her own mother, and the discovery gives her a new perspective on her own problems." SLJ

"Here is a humorous and touching story that deals head on with a painful conflict between an adolescent girl and her mother. The author has contrived an ingenious plot, cleverly maneuvered with exquisite detail and realism." Child Book Rev Serv

Paterson, Katherine
Bridge to Terabithia; illustrated by Donna Diamond. Crowell 1977 128p il $12.95; pa $2.95 (4 and up) **Fic**

1. Friendship—Fiction 2. Death—Fiction 3. Virginia—Fiction
ISBN 0-690-01359-0; 0-06-440184-7 (pa) LC 77-2221

Also available ABC-CLIO large print edition $14.95 (ISBN 1-55736-010-3)

Awarded the Newbery Medal, 1978

The life of Jess, a ten-year-old boy in rural Virginia expands when he becomes friends with a newcomer who subsequently meets an untimely death trying to reach their hideaway, Terabithia, during a storm

"Jess and his family are magnificently characterized; the book abounds in descriptive vignettes, humorous sidelights on the clash of cultures, and realistic depictions of rural school life." Horn Book

Come sing, Jimmy Jo. Lodestar Bks. 1985 193p $12.95; Avon Bks. pa $2.95 (5 and up) **Fic**

1. Country music—Fiction 2. Family life—Fiction
ISBN 0-525-67167-6; 0-380-70052-5 (pa)
LC 84-21123

When his family becomes a successful country music group and makes him a featured singer, eleven-year-old James has to deal with big changes in all aspects of his life, even his name

"What Katherine Paterson does so well is catch the cadence of the locale without sounding fake. There isn't a false note in her diction. She has created a West Virginian world that is entirely believable: homely, honest, goodhearted. . . . This book is James's personal inward journey, and it is deeply felt." Christ Sci Monit

The great Gilly Hopkins. Crowell 1978 148p $12.70; lib bdg $12.95; pa $3.50 (5 and up) **Fic**

1. Foster home care—Fiction
ISBN 0-690-03837-2; 0-690-03838-0 (lib bdg); 0-06-440201-0 (pa) LC 77-27075

Also available ABC-CLIO large print edition $13.95 (ISBN 1-55736-011-1)

"Cool, scheming, and deliberately obstreperous, 11-year-old Gilly is ready to be her usual obnoxious self when she arrives at her new foster home. . . . But Gilly's old tricks don't work against the all-encompassing love of the huge, half-illiterate Mrs. Trotter. . . . Determined not to care she writes a letter full of wild exaggerations to her real mother that brings, in return, a surprising visit from an unknown grandmother." Booklist

"Paterson's development of the change in Gilly is brilliant and touching, as she depicts a child whose tough protective shield dissolves as she learns to accept love and to give it. A well-structured story [this] has vitality of writing style, natural dialogue, deep insight in characterization, and a keen sense of the fluid dynamics in human relationships." Bull Cent Child Books

The master puppeteer; illus. by Haru Wells. Crowell 1976 c1975 179p il $14.95; Harper & Row pa $3.50 (6 and up) **Fic**

1. Puppets and puppet plays—Fiction 2. Japan—Fiction
ISBN 0-690-00913-5; 0-06-440281-9 (pa) LC 75-8614

"In 18th-century Osaka, Japan, Jiro, son of a starving puppetmaker, runs away from home to apprentice himself to Yoshida, the ill-tempered master of the Hanaza puppet theater. As Jiro works to learn the art of the puppeteer and travels among the savage, hunger-crazed bands of night rovers in search of his parents, he becomes aware of a mysterious connection between Saboro, a Robin Hood-like figure, and the Hanaza theater itself." SLJ

"The make-believe world of the Japanese puppet theatre merges excitingly with the hungry, desperate realities of 18th century Osaka in this better-than-average junior novel." Bull Cent Child Books

Of nightingales that weep; illustrated by Haru Wells. Crowell 1974 170p $13.95; Harper & Row pa $3.50 (6 and up) **Fic**

1. Japan—Fiction
ISBN 0-690-00485-0; 0-06-440282-7 (pa) LC 74-8294

"Takiko, daughter of a famous samurai killed in the wars, is taken into the court of the boy emperor Antoku as a musician and personal servant. Takiko's conflicting loyalties to the Heike-supported court, a dashing Genji warrior, and her physically grotesque but goodhearted peasant stepfather form the impetus for her internal development while the war rages around her." Booklist

Park's quest. Lodestar Bks. 1988 148p $12.95; Penguin Bks. pa $3.95 (5 and up) **Fic**

1. Farm life—Fiction 2. Vietnamese Americans—Fiction
ISBN 0-525-67258-3; 0-14-034262-1 (pa)
LC 87-32422

Eleven-year-old Park makes some startling discoveries when he travels to his grandfather's farm in Virginia to learn about his father who died in the Vietnam War and meets a Vietnamese-American girl named Thanh

The author "confronts the complexity, the ambiguity, of the war and the emotions of those it involved with an honesty that young readers are sure to recognize and appreciate. But what is even more remarkable is that she has fashioned from this complexity a story for young adults that does not offer an antidote, or even a resolution, for the irreversible damages of this war but that speaks instead of the opportunity for healing; the possbility, despite the damage, of sharing the grief without ever shedding it, and going on." N Y Times Book Rev

Paton Walsh, Jill, 1937-

Fireweed. Farrar, Straus & Giroux 1970 c1969 133p $14.95; pa $3.50 (5 and up) **Fic**

1. World War, 1939-1945—Fiction 2. London (England)—Fiction
ISBN 0-374-32310-0; 0-374-42316-4 (pa)
LC 73-109554

First published 1969 in the United Kingdom

During World War II, "Bill and Julie had found each other by chance, each of them lurking around London after having started off with a group of children being evacuated. Julie had money, Bill could cope, and together the two made a clandestine home in the rubble of a building. Only when Julie was caught by a raid did Bill, staring in anguish at the fresh ruins, realize how important she had become to him." Saturday Rev

"The development of a relationship . . . is one of the two main achievements of this book: a touchingly real and beautifully understated picture of a growth of feeling, almost unrealized and quite unconsummated, between two innocent and very different adolescents. The second achievement is the setting, the picture given without squeamishness or apparent over-emphasis of London in the blitz—the humour, the fear, the misery, the sometimes uncanny normality." Times Lit Suppl

Gaffer Samson's luck; illustrations by Brock Cole. Farrar, Straus & Giroux 1984 118p il $11.95; pa $3.50 (4-6) **Fic**

1. Great Britain—Fiction
ISBN 0-374-32498-0; 0-374-42513-2 (pa)
LC 84-10180

"Descriptive, often metaphorical, images lend richness and vigor to the storytelling, but the book is no mere exercise in fine writing. Imbuing the narrative with a graphic, insistent sense of place, the author has also woven into it patterns of social custom, human behavior, and childhood feelings, giving the brief novel both sensibility and suspense. Line drawings reflect the atmosphere and the crucial episodes." Horn Book

Lost and found; story by Jill Paton Walsh; illustrations by Mary Rayner. Deutsch 1985 c1984 unp il $11.95 (2-4) **Fic**

1. Great Britain—Fiction
ISBN 0-233-97672-8

First published 1984 in the United Kingdom

This "is an intriguing progression of four tales in one, linked by their themes, their setting (the same hillside in Britain) and by a series of objects lost and found. . . . Although called by different names and used in different ways, the land serves to connect one age to the next." SLJ

"Rayner's softly hued paintings illustrate beautifully the characters and their vastly different locales." Publ Wkly

Unleaving. Farrar, Straus & Giroux 1976 145p $11.95; pa $3.50 (6 and up) **Fic**

1. Cornwall (England)—Fiction
ISBN 0-374-38042-2; 0-374-48068-0 (pa) LC 76-8857

Sequel to: Goldengrove (1972)

"Young Madge rents most of her house for the summer to two college professors, their families, and students for an intellectual retreat. She becomes friendly with the group, especially Patrick and his young mongoloid sister, and enters into their discussions of life, death, and God. Woven in are episodes of Gran, now years later, again at summertime, sharing the same house with her family and examining the same topics as the young Madge did." Child Book Rev Serv

"Drawing upon the changing surface of the ocean by the beach house, Walsh creates intense descriptive passages which provide a shimmering background for the constantly shifting perspectives of the plot. The result is a tantalizing evocative book, skillfully interweaving themes of love, death, and the continuity of the soul." SLJ

Patterson, Nancy Ruth

The Christmas cup; illustrated by Leslie Bowman. Orchard Bks. 1989 71p il $13.95; lib bdg $13.99 (3-5) **Fic**

1. Gifts—Fiction 2. Christmas—Fiction 3. Grandmothers—Fiction
ISBN 0-531-05821-2; 0-531-08421-3 (lib bdg)
LC 88-29112

"As 8-year-old Megan and her grandmother secretly collect coins in a cup and select possible recipients of an anonymous Christmas gift, they learn to understand people in their community who are often overlooked or misunderstood." Soc Educ

"Patterson's narrative has a precious air, but the story, though somewhat sentimental, clearly depicts the joy of giving, a theme that many will welcome for the holiday season." Booklist

Paulsen, Gary

The boy who owned the school; a comedy of love. Orchard Bks. 1990 85p $11.95; lib bdg $11.99 (6 and up) **Fic**

1. School stories
ISBN 0-531-05865-4; 0-531-08465-5 (lib bdg)
LC 89-23048

"A Richard Jackson book"

This "novel relates Jacob Freisten's quest to survive high school unnoticed by classmates, teachers, *anyone.* He would have succeeded except for his love for Maria Tresser, the most beautiful, most popular, most talented girl in school. Lost in his love fog, Jacob begins to wave at kids, answer correctly in class, and even walk in the front door of the school. To complicate matters, Jacob is assigned to work with Maria on the school play and the results are unexpected and disastrous. A quick, funny, delightful book that will be great to booktalk." Voice Youth Advocates

Dogsong. Bradbury Press 1985 177p $11.95; Penguin Bks. pa $3.95 (6 and up) **Fic**

1. Inuit—Fiction 2. Arctic regions—Fiction
ISBN 0-02-770180-8; 0-14-032235-3 (pa)
LC 84-20443

A Newbery Medal honor book, 1986

A fourteen-year-old Eskimo boy who feels assailed by the modernity of his life takes a 1400-mile journey by dog sled across ice, tundra, and mountains seeking his

Paulsen, Gary—*Continued*
own "song" of himself

The author's "mystical tone and blunt prose style are well suited to the spare landscape of his story, and his depictions of Russell's icebound existence add both authenticity and color to a slick rendition of the vision-quest plot, which incorporates human tragedy as well as promise." Booklist

The winter room. Orchard Bks. 1989 103p $11.95; lib bdg $11.99 (5 and up) **Fic**

1. Farm life—Fiction 2. Minnesota—Fiction
ISBN 0-531-05839-5; 0-531-08439-6 (lib bdg) LC 89-42541

A Newbery Medal honor book, 1990

"A Richard Jackson book"

A young boy growing up on a northern Minnesota farm describes the scenes around him and recounts his old Norwegian uncle's tales of an almost mythological logging past

"While this seems at first to be a collection of anecdotes organized around the progression of the farm calendar, Paulsen subtly builds a conflict that becomes apparent in the last brief chapters, forceful and well-prepared. . . . Lyrical and only occasionally sentimental, the prose is clean, clear, and deceptively simple." Bull Cent Child Books

Pearce, Philippa, 1920-

The battle of Bubble and Squeak; illustrated by Alan Baker. Deutsch 1979 c1978 88p il $10.95 (3-6) **Fic**

1. Gerbils—Fiction 2. Family life—Fiction
ISBN 0-233-96986-1 LC 78-318736

First published 1978 in the United Kingdom

"When two gerbils—Bubble and Squeak—come to live at the Parkers, the reaction is mixed. Sid's mum hates them 'like rats!'; Sid's stepfather is understanding of Mum but remembers the white mice he had as a boy; Sid's small sister adores them; and Sid himself, well, the gerbils are the most special thing that's ever happened to him." SLJ

The "question of whether the gerbils are kept or not is—while appealing in itself—not the core of the story. The core is really in the delicate balance of the parent-child relationship, and the facets here are explored with sympathy and percipience." Bull Cent Child Books

Tom's midnight garden; illustrated by Susan Einzig. Lippincott 1959 c1958 229p il $13.95; Dell pa $4.95 (4 and up) **Fic**

1. Fantastic fiction 2. Space and time—Fiction
ISBN 0-397-30475-7; 0-440-48819-2 (pa) LC 59-16380

Also available ABC-CLIO large print edition $13.95 (ISBN 1-85089-914-2)

First published 1958 in the United Kingdom

"Daytime life for Tom at his aunt's home in England is dull, but each night he participates through fantasy in the lives of the former inhabitants of the interesting old house in which he is spending an enforced vacation. The book is British in setting and atmosphere. The element of mystery is well sustained, and the reader is left to make his own interpretation of the reality of the story." Natl Counc of Teach of Engl. Adventuring with Books

The way to Sattin Shore; illustrated by Charlotte Voake. Greenwillow Bks. 1983 182p il o.p.; Puffin Bks. paperback available $3.95 (5 and up) **Fic**

1. Mystery and detective stories
ISBN 0-14-031644-2 (pa) LC 83-14152

When a tombstone with her father's name suddenly disappears from the graveyard, Kate, an English school girl, witnesses the unraveling of a mystery surrounding the death of her father

"The story is tightly woven, blending eerie events with everyday happenings, but it is much more than a mystery tale. Pearce skillfully develops Kate's growth as she moves from isolation and bewilderment to a confidence based upon an honesty that generates the determination to learn who she is, as an individual and as part of a family." SLJ

Pearson, Kit

The sky is falling. Viking 1990 248p il $12.95 (6 and up) **Fic**

1. Brothers and sisters—Fiction 2. World War, 1939-1945—Fiction
ISBN 0-670-82849-1

The experiences of Norah, a young British girl and her small brother Gavin who are evacuated to Canada at the beginning of World War II and find that they will be staying with complete strangers

"One of the strengths of the story is that Pearson sees her characters with perspective and depicts them with nuance; nobody is all bad or all good, or all wise or all foolish. The pace is well maintained, and the changes that occur as Norah gains insight are natural." Bull Cent Child Books

Peck, Richard

The ghost belonged to me; a novel. Viking 1975 183p $13.95; Dell pa $3.25 (5 and up) **Fic**

1. Ghosts—Fiction
ISBN 0-670-33767-6; 0-440-42861-0 (pa) LC 74-34218

Also available ABC-CLIO large print edition $15.95 (ISBN 1-55736-116-9)

"Although he tries to avoid her, thirteen-year-old Alexander Armsworth relates how his classmate and neighbor, Blossom Culp, involves him in a ghost mystery. Later, Blossom relates her own stories with a most convincing air. Humor and excitement play a big role in the stories, which are set in 1913. The characters are unusual and unforgettable. Peck writes with a flair for the dramatic." Roman. Sequences

Other available titles about Blossom Culp are:
Blossom Culp and the sleep of death (1986)
The dreadful future of Blossom Culp (1983)
Ghosts I have been (1977)

Peck, Robert Newton, 1928-

Arly. Walker & Co. 1989 153p $16.95 (5 and up) **Fic**

1. Teachers—Fiction 2. Florida—Fiction
ISBN 0-8027-6856-3 LC 88-24339

Peck, Robert Newton, 1928-—*Continued*

"Set in 1927 in a migrant camp in Jailtown, Florida, the story features 11-year-old Arly Poole, who lives with his father in Shack Row. Arly would live and die illiterate if not for the stranger who arrives one Sunday on the *Caloosahatchee Queen*. The delicate and restrained demeanor of Miss Binnie Hoe belie the underlying feistiness, good humor, and invincible will of this teacher who has come to start a school." Booklist

"Peck has given his readers a true hero, compassionate and self-effacing, yet blazing with determination and courage. Arly's adventures at school, his encounters with evil, his moments of grief and despair, remain vivid long after the last page has been turned." SLJ

A day no pigs would die. Knopf 1973 c1972 150p $16.95; Dell pa $3.50 (6 and up) **Fic**

1. Shakers—Fiction 2. Farm life—Fiction 3. Vermont—Fiction

ISBN 0-394-48235-2; 0-440-92083-3 (pa) LC 72-259

Also available ABC-CLIO large print edition $14.95 (ISBN 1-55736-058-8)

"Rob lives a rigorous life on a Shaker farm in Vermont in the 1920s. Since farm life is earthy, this book is filled with Yankee humor and explicit descriptions of animals mating. A painful incident that involves the slaughter of Rob's beloved pet pig is instrumental in urging him toward adulthood. The death of his father completes the process of his accepting responsibility." Shapiro. Fic for Youth. 2d edition

Soup; illustrated by Charles C. Gehm. Knopf 1974 96p il lib bdg $9.99; Dell pa $2.95 (5 and up) **Fic**

1. Friendship—Fiction 2. Vermont—Fiction

ISBN 0-394-92700-1 (lib bdg); 0-440-48186-4 (pa) LC 73-15117

"Soup was Robert Peck's best friend during his boyhood, and this is an episodic account of some of the ploys and scrapes the two shared when they were in elementary school." Bull Cent Child Books

"Rural Vermont during the 1920's is the setting for this nostalgic account. . . . In a laconic and wryly humorous style, the author relates the activities of the mischievous twosome. . . . The black-and-white pencil drawings, artistically executed in the manner of Norman Rockwell, reflect the understated story." SLJ

Other available titles about the author and his friend Soup are:

Soup & me (1975)
Soup for president (1978)
Soup in the saddle (1983)
Soup on fire (1987)
Soup on ice (1985)
Soup on wheels (1981)
Soup's drum (1980)
Soup's goat (1984)
Soup's hoop (1990)
Soup's uncle (1988)

Petry, Ann Lane, 1911-

Tituba of Salem Village; [by] Ann Petry. Crowell 1964 254p lib bdg $14.89 (6 and up) **Fic**

1. Tituba—Fiction 2. Salem (Mass.)—Fiction 3. Witchcraft—Fiction 4. Blacks—Fiction

ISBN 0-690-04766-5 LC 64-20691

"From the beauty of the island of Barbados, Tituba is uprooted to the dreary, gray cold of Boston. As the slave in the household of the minister, Samuel Parris, Tituba cooks, nurses, and attends to his sickly wife, daughter, and niece. When the minister moves to a new post in Salem Village, Tituba becomes the central figure in a witchcraft trial." Shapiro. Fic for Youth. 2d edition

Pevsner, Stella

And you give me a pain, Elaine. Clarion Bks. 1978 182p $12.95; Pocket Bks. pa $2.75 (4 and up) **Fic**

1. Brothers and sisters—Fiction 2. Family life—Fiction

ISBN 0-395-28877-0; 0-671-68838-3 (pa) LC 78-5857

First published by Seabury Press

"Thirteen-year-old Andrea, who tells the story, is the youngest of three; her adored brother Joe is away at college and her sister Elaine, sixteen, is the bane of Andrea's life, a sulky and rebellious adolescent who can't get along with Andrea or with their parents. Depressed by her own plodding personality and resentful of the attention Elaine gets when she defies her parents, Andrea is jolted into despair when Joe is killed in a motorcycle accident. This isn't a book with a strong story line, but it is strong in every other way: it is convincing as a first-person record, it is perceptive in establishing the fluctuations in personal relationships, it has excellent dialogue, and it balances nicely the several aspects of Andrea's life." Bull Cent Child Books

Keep stompin' till the music stops. Clarion Bks. 1977 136p $13.95 (4 and up) **Fic**

1. Learning disabilities—Fiction 2. Family life—Fiction

ISBN 0-395-28875-4 LC 76-27845

First published by Seabury Press

"Richard is 12 and painfully coming to grips with his dyslexia. His great-grandfather—a sympathetic character—is about to be shipped off to a retirement trailer-village in Florida. Four generations gather for several days in his Galena, Illinois home where bossy Aunt Violet will break the news to the old man. But Grandpa rebels and solves the problem by making arangements of his own to preserve his home and his independence. Richard also seems to accept his learning disability and gain some confidence." SLJ

The author "peppers her perceptive story with witty dialogue as she successfully reaches into the head of a young boy grappling with a problem." Booklist

Pinkwater, Daniel Manus, 1941-

Alan Mendelsohn, the boy from Mars; by Daniel M. Pinkwater. Dutton 1979 248p $14.95 (5 and up) **Fic**

1. Science fiction
ISBN 0-525-25360-2 LC 78-12052

"The author introduces Leonard Neeble and Alan Mendelsohn, both new to Bat Masterson Junior High School. The boys, looking for additions to Alan's massive collection of comic books, discover a shop which deals in occult materials. Pooling their resources, they purchase a portable Omega Meter and the first volume of the Klugarsh Mind Control Course. . . . Using the incredible new power they gain, they succeed in achieving an adventure on the lost continent of Waka-Waka." Horn Book

"In this exaggerated, tongue-in-cheek story of time-slips and thought control, Pinkwater lampoons con men and dupes, psychic powers, quack medicos, natural food faddists and assorted weird characters with great humor if, occasionally, at great length." Bull Cent Child Books

Blue moose; [by] Manus Pinkwater. Dodd, Mead 1989 c1975 47p il $10.95 (1-3) **Fic**

1. Moose—Fiction 2. Restaurants, bars, etc.—Fiction
ISBN 0-396-07151-1 LC 88-32207

A reissue of the title first published 1975

"Mr. Breton owns a restaurant and is a very good cook who feels he's not appreciated by his customers. He hates the cold, snowy winter—until the day he meets a talking blue moose who comes in to warm himself, tries the clam chowder, and finds it so delectable that he stays on as headwaiter (and star attraction) at the restaurant." Natl Counc of Teach of Engl. Adventuring with Books

"Serio-comic narration is perfectly complemented by black-and-white line drawings of a very professional moose—mittens drying on his antlers, serving bowls line up properly between the antler tips, etc. A quietly pleasing and most rewarding book." SLJ

Fat men from space; written and illustrated by Daniel Manus Pinkwater. Dodd, Mead 1977 57p il lib bdg $9.95; Dell pa $2.95 (3-6) **Fic**

1. Food—Fiction 2. Science fiction
ISBN 0-396-07461-8 (lib bdg); 0-440-44542-6 (pa)
LC 77-6091

"Young William goes to the dentist and comes out with a filling that receives radio programs. Exploring the infinite possibilities of a tooth radio, he attaches a wire to a chainlink fence, touches it to his molar, and tunes in on an invading 'spaceburger' from the planet Spiegel. Before he can warn anyone of earth's peril, he is captured and 'floated' up to the spaceburger where he meets the invaders—fat men with glasses, wearing plaid sport jackets. Their raid is successful—Earth is stripped of all its junk food." SLJ

"Message books aren't usually this much fun, but Pinkwater makes his a polished romp." Bull Cent Child Books

Another available title in this series is:
The Magic Moscow (1980)

The Hoboken chicken emergency; by D. Manus Pinkwater. Prentice-Hall 1977 83p il lib bdg $10.95; pa $4.95 (3-6) **Fic**

1. Chickens—Fiction
ISBN 0-13-392514-5 (lib bdg); 0-671-66447-6 (pa)
LC 76-41910

Arthur goes to pick up the turkey for Thanksgiving dinner but comes back with a 260-pound chicken

"A contemporary tall tale that will stretch middle graders' imagination, sense of humor, and enthusiasm for reading. For absurdity with perfect timing, not many can match the author." Booklist

I was a second grade werewolf; by Daniel Pinkwater. Dutton 1983 unp il lib bdg $12.95; pa $3.95 (1-3) **Fic**

1. Werewolves—Fiction
ISBN 0-525-44038-0 (lib bdg); 0-525-44194-8 (pa)
LC 82-17715

"Lawrence Talbot changes into a werewolf one morning but nobody at home or in school notices, even though Lawrence snarls, bites, growls and eats his milk carton and a Twinkie with the cellophane on it and a pencil." Publ Wkly

"Pinkwater has stepped right into a little boy's imagination and has illustrated the episode in his own inimitable style. The good-size pictures are brightly colored and funny enough to make kids laugh out loud. And in keeping with the title, a strong second-grade reader should be able to handle this one alone." Booklist

Lizard music; written and illustrated by D. Manus Pinkwater. Dodd, Mead 1976 157p il o.p.; Bantam Bks. paperback available $2.95 (4 and up) **Fic**

1. Science fiction
ISBN 0-553-15605-5 (pa) LC 76-12508

Also available from Smith, P. $14.50 (ISBN 0-8446-6472-3)

"Left alone when his parents go on a vaction, Victor discovers, through late-night TV, a community of intelligent lizards and the Chicken Man. The succeeding adventures take Victor through some strange but thought-provoking escapades. Children associate with the ending—a return to normal but dull life when the rest of the family returns. A good read-aloud book." Read Teach

Pinkwater, Jill

Buffalo Brenda. Macmillan 1989 203p $13.95 (5 and up) **Fic**

1. School stories
ISBN 0-02-774631-3 LC 88-31929

Determined to make their mark on their high school, ninth graders India Ink and her zany best friend Brenda Tuna organize an underground newspaper and then provide a live buffalo as a mascot for the football team

"Pinkwater snappily sends up suburban upper-middle-class values and ex-hippies while tenderly eulogizing the importance of friendship in this rollicking modern tall tale." Publ Wkly

Pope, Elizabeth Marie, 1917-

The Perilous Gard; illustrated by Richard Cuffari. Houghton Mifflin 1974 280p il $13.95; Ace Bks. pa $2.25 (6 and up) **Fic**

1. Great Britain—Fiction 2. Druids and Druidism—Fiction 3. Fantastic fiction
ISBN 0-395-18512-2; 0-441-65956-X (pa)

LC 73-21648

A Newbery Medal Honor book, 1975

In 1558 while imprisoned in a remote castle, a young girl becomes involved in a series of events that leads to an underground labyrinth peopled by the last practitioners of Druidic magic.

"The description of the Fairy Folk's life and customs is fascinating and the plot is mystical and exciting enough for all fantasy lovers." SLJ

Porte-Thomas, Barbara Ann

Ruthann and her pig; [by] Barbara Ann Porte; pictures by Suçie Stevenson. Orchard Bks. 1989 84p il $14.99; lib bdg $14.95 (3-5) **Fic**

1. Pigs—Fiction 2. Family life—Fiction
ISBN 0-531-05825-5; 0-531-08425-6 (lib bdg)

LC 88-31452

"Ruthann's mother is not particularly happy that Ruthann has a pig for a pet, but it's certainly better than her previous choice—a squash. Ruthann loves her pig, named, after many experiments, Henry Brown. Her cousin Frank, who is allergic to furry animals, also loves Henry Brown and yearns to have him come visit and be an 'attack pig' to help him with the bullies on the school bus." Horn Book

"The full-color cartoon drawings are light without being cute, and the book design is broken up for a user-friendly look without being obtrusively easy. Distinctively done and lots of fun to read out loud." Bull Cent Child Books

Price, Susan, 1955-

The ghost drum; a cat's tale. Farrar, Straus & Giroux 1987 167p $12.95; pa $3.50 (4 and up) **Fic**

1. Witches—Fiction
ISBN 0-374-32538-3; 0-374-42547-7 (pa)

LC 86-46032

Chingis, "a gifted shaman meets a Czar's son who has been imprisoned in his windowless room, and the two bond together to fight fearful enemies." SLJ

"This quasi-Russian world is shot through with magic, rendered with an incantatory repetition of both language and story patterns." Bull Cent Child Books

Procházková, Iva

The season of secret wishes; translated by Elizabeth D. Crawford. Lothrop, Lee & Shepard Bks. 1989 213p $12.95 (4-6) **Fic**

1. Czechoslovakia—Fiction
ISBN 0-688-08735-3

LC 89-45291

Original German edition, 1988

"In a story that has vitality and immediacy (qualities that are preserved by the translator) eleven-year-old Kapka describes the events and people of a springtime when her family has just moved to a new neighborhood in Prague. Her father is an artist whose work has been rejected by the authorities, and it is Kapka and her new friends (all ages) who help mount a street show of Papa's sculpture. This is not a bitter indictment, but a soft impeachment, of an authoritarian regime." Bull Cent Child Books

Quackenbush, Robert M., 1929-

Express train to trouble; a Miss Mallard mystery; [by] Robert Quackenbush. Prentice-Hall 1981 48p il $9.95 (2-4) **Fic**

1. Ducks—Fiction 2. Mystery and detective stories
ISBN 0-13-298067-3

LC 81-8477

When troublesome George Ruddy Duck disappears on the express train to Cairo, Miss Mallard applies her detective genius to find out what happened and save the reputation of the train

"Imagine a takeoff on 'Murder on the Orient Express' in which all the passengers are ducks including the detective, a Marple-like knitter names Miss Mallard. The plot . . . is fairly straightforward. More appealing are the written and illustrated characterizations of the birds gathered for the journey. . . . Most readers will be too young to make the Christie connection, but its merriment is able to stand alone." Booklist

Other available titles about Miss Mallard are:
Bicycle to treachery (1985)
Cable car to catastrophe (1982)
Danger in Tibet (1989)
Dig to disaster (1982)
Dogsled to dread (1987)
Gondola to danger (1983)
Lost in the Amazon (1990)
Rickshaw to horror (1984)
Stage door to terror (1985)
Stairway to doom (1983)
Surfboard to peril (1986)
Taxi to intrigue (1984)
Texas trail to calamity (1986)

Rabe, Berniece

Margaret's moves; illustrated by Julie Downing. Dutton 1987 105p il $10.95; Scholastic pa $2.50 (3-6) **Fic**

1. Physically handicapped children—Fiction 2. Brothers and sisters—Fiction
ISBN 0-525-44271-5; 0-590-41667-7 (pa)

LC 86-11592

Nine-year-old Margaret, confined to a wheelchair by spina bifida, longs for a new, lightweight 'sportsmodel' chair so that she can speed around as fast as the athletic brother with whom she has an ongoing rivalry

"This is singleminded fiction, sometimes strained, but the family dynamics—especially Margaret's relationship with her two younger brothers—are authentic enough to relieve the focus on Margaret's disability. There is also child appeal in the youngsters' everyday activities and in the happy ending." Bull Cent Child Books

Another available title about Margaret, The balancing girl, is entered in Easy section

Raskin, Ellen, 1928-1984

Figgs & phantoms. Dutton 1989 c1974 152p il lib bdg $15.95; Puffin Bks. pa $4.95 (5 and up) **Fic**

1. Family life—Fiction
ISBN 0-525-29680-8; 0-14-032944-7 (pa) LC 88-29910

A Newbery Medal honor book, 1974

A reissue of the title first published 1974

"This concerns Mona Lisa Newton, fat and frustrated member of the Figg Newton family in the town of Pineapple. Of the Figg Newton family, which includes ex-variety show stars Truman the Human Pretzel and uncles Romulus and Remus, Mona loves only Uncle Florence Italy Figg—a book dealer who dreams of dying and going to Capri, the Figg fantasy heaven. When Florence dies, Mona embarks on a clue-solving search for Capri, takes a wild mind trip, and returns a wiser and happier person." Booklist

The mysterious disappearance of Leon (I mean Noel). Dutton 1989 149p il lib bdg $14.95; Puffin Bks. pa $3.95 (4 and up) **Fic**

1. New York (N.Y.)—Fiction 2. Mystery and detective stories
ISBN 0-525-35540-5; 0-14-032945-5 (pa) LC 88-30658

A reissue of the title first published 1971

"Wed at the age of five to a seven-year-old husband (it solved a business difficulty for their two families), the very young Mrs. Leon Carillon immediately loses her spouse, who is sent off to boarding school. This is the hilarious account of her search for Leon, aided by adopted twins, when she is older. With clever clues to stimulate the reader's participation, the story is a bouquet of wordplay garnished with jokes, sly pokes at our society, daft characters, and soupcon of slapstick. Fresh and funny, it's the kind of book that passes from child to child." Saturday Rev

The tattooed potato and other clues. Dutton 1975 170p lib bdg $15.95; Puffin Bks. pa $3.95 (5 and up) **Fic**

1. Mystery and detective stories
ISBN 0-525-40805-3; 0-14-032980-3 (pa) LC 74-23764

"A baffled Chief of Detectives in New York City turns repeatedly to the painter Garson, who uses brilliant deductive powers to solve a series of crimes (all ridiculous) while apparently oblivious to the menacing tenants who frighten his assistant, Dickery Dock (she's seventeen and the protagonist) and who bear such names as Shrimps Marinara and Manny Mallomar. And there's a mystery about Garson himself." Bull Cent Child Books

"The preposterous plot, madcap characters, and comic shticks never conceal the home truths about dreams and disguises, artists and con artists." SLJ

The Westing game. Dutton 1978 185p lib bdg $14.95; Avon Bks. pa $2.95 (5 and up) **Fic**

1. Mystery and detective stories
ISBN 0-525-42320-6; 0-380-67991-4 LC 77-18866

Also available ABC-CLIO large print edition $15.95 (ISBN 1-55736-031-6)

Awarded the Newbery Medal, 1979

"This mystery puzzle . . . centers on the challenge set forth in the will of eccentric multimillionaire Samuel Westing. Sixteen heirs of diverse backgrounds and ages are assembled in the old 'Westing house,' paired off, and given clues to a puzzle they must solve—apparently in order to inherit." SLJ

"The rules of the game make eight pairs of the players; each oddly matched couple is given a ten thousand dollar check and a set of clues. The result is a fascinating medley of word games, disguises, multiple aliases and subterfuges—in a demanding but rewarding book." Horn Book

Rawlings, Marjorie Kinnan, 1896-1953

The yearling; with pictures by N. C. Wyeth. Scribner 1985 c1938 400p il $24.95; Collier Bks. pa $4.95 (6 and up) **Fic**

1. Deer—Fiction 2. Florida—Fiction
ISBN 0-684-18461-3; 0-02-044931-3 (pa) LC 85-40301

First published 1938; this is a reissue of the 1939 edition; copyright renewed 1966

"Young Jody Baxter lives a lonely life in the scrub forest of Florida until his parents unwillingly consent to his adopting an orphan fawn. The two become inseparable until the fawn destroys the meager crops. Then Jody realizes that this situation offers no compromise. In the sacrifice of what he loves best, he leaves his own yearling days behind." Read Ladders for Hum Relat. 5th edition

Rawls, Wilson, 1913-

Where the red fern grows; the story of two dogs and a boy. Doubleday 1961 212p $14.95; lib bdg $11.95; Bantam Bks. pa $3.25 **Fic**

1. Dogs—Fiction 2. Ozark Mountains—Fiction
ISBN 0-385-02059-7; 0-385-05619-2 (lib bdg); 0-553-25585-1 (pa) LC 61-9201

Also available ABC-CLIO large print edition $14.95 (ISBN 1-55736-057-X)

"Looking back more than 50 years to his boyhood in the Ozarks, the narrator recalls how he achieved his heart's desire in the ownership of two redbone hounds, how he taught them all the tricks of hunting, and how they won the championship coon hunt before Old Dan was killed by a mountain lion and Little Ann died of grief. Although some readers may find this novel hackneyed and entirely too sentimental, others will enjoy the fine coon-hunting episodes and appreciate the author's feelings for nature." Booklist

Reeder, Carolyn

Shades of gray. Macmillan 1989 152p $13.95 (4 and up) **Fic**

1. Orphans—Fiction 2. Uncles—Fiction 3. United States—History—1861-1865, Civil War—Fiction
ISBN 0-02-775810-9 LC 89-31976

At the end of the Civil War, twelve-year-old Will, having lost all his immediate family, reluctantly leaves his city home to live in the Virginia countryside with his aunt and the uncle he considers a "traitor" because

Reeder, Carolyn—*Continued*
he refused to take part in the war
"Reeder develops, believably, a change in Will's attitude as he comes to realize that neutrality is not treason and that it has taken enormous courage for Uncle Jed to stand firm in his pacific conviction. Minor plot threads (Will's adjustment to rural life, his relationships with the local boys and his affection for his cousin Meg) provide changes of tone and tempo in a novel that has, despite an uneven pace, both momentum and nuance." Bull Cent Child Books

Reid Banks, Lynne, 1929-
The Indian in the cupboard. Doubleday 1980 181p il $13.95; Avon Bks. pa $3.25 (5 and up) **Fic**

1. Indians of North America—Fiction 2. Fantastic fiction
ISBN 0-385-17051-3; 0-380-60012-9 (pa) LC 79-6533
Also available ABC-CLIO large print edition $15.95 (ISBN 0-55736-034-0)
Illustrated by Brock Cole
A nine-year-old boy receives a plastic Indian, a cupboard, and a little key for his birthday and finds himself involved in adventure when the Indian comes to life in the cupboard and befriends him
Other available titles in this series are:
The return of the Indian (1986)
The secret of the Indian (1989)

Reuter, Bjarne
Buster's world; translated by Anthea Bell. Dutton 1989 154p il $12.95 (4 and up) **Fic**

1. Denmark—Fiction
ISBN 0-525-44475-0 LC 89-11919
Original Danish edition, 1980
Buster's magic tricks get him in and out of trouble
"Set in a small section of Copenhagen, the story gives vivid glimpses of the frazzled teachers, kindly neighbors, a newly discovered girl, and bullying older boys who move in and out of Buster's world. . . . Frank in its sexual references, the story is episodic in nature, but is unified throughout by Buster's performances, sometimes at highly inappropriate moments, of magic tricks learned from his father. The bustling life of the town and Buster's ingenuous efforts to ingratiate himself with his friends and his girl result in a lively and irresistibly effervescent story of the perils and raptures of a likable and amusing young boy." Horn Book

Riskind, Mary, 1944-
Apple is my sign. Houghton Mifflin 1981 146p $12.95 (5 and up) **Fic**

1. Deaf—Fiction
ISBN 0-395-30852-6 LC 80-29746
"The story is set in Pennsylvania at the time of the first horseless carriages . . . in a school for the deaf. Ten-year-old Harry is at first homesick, but he soon makes friends, becomes excited about learning to draw and learning to talk. Aware that his father is ashamed of his own deafness (both parents are deaf) and that his mother is not, Harry learns to accept his situation as his mother has: a handicap rather than a stigma." Bull Cent Child Books
"In a lengthy note the author explains that she had deaf parents and learned sign language before she learned to speak. She also explores some characteristics of sign language, which has been translated into print via sentence syntax and spelling. A warm, unpretentious story that rises above bibliotherapeutic intent to become simple, effective storytelling." Booklist

Roberts, Willo Davis
The girl with the silver eyes. Atheneum Pubs. 1980 181p $12.95; Scholastic pa $2.50 (4-6) **Fic**

1. Psychokinesis—Fiction
ISBN 0-689-30786-1; 0-590-40950-6 (pa) LC 80-12391
"Silver eyes are not all that set ten-year-old Katie apart from her peers—she's able to move things by thinking about them and talk to animals. Living with her mother for the first time since she was three, Katie tries to adjust to the other adults in the building, to her mom's male friend, and to her own strange situation." SLJ
"Much of the book's first half relies on diverting readers with examples of Katie's powers . . . while the second section builds more suspensefully around her efforts to track down the source of her problem, other children who might share it, and someone who will help her deal with it. . . . Roberts' smooth writing will lure them right to the end." Booklist

Megan's island. Atheneum Pubs. 1988 187p lib bdg $12.95; pa $3.95 (5 and up) **Fic**

1. Mystery and detective stories
ISBN 0-689-31397-7 (lib bdg); 0-689-71387-8 (pa) LC 87-17505
"A Jean Karl book"
"Young Megan is baffled when she and her younger brother [Sandy] are suddenly, secretly moved to their grandfather's cabin in Lakewood, Minnesota. . . . [She then learns that her] father, whom they had presumed dead for many years, recently died in prison. And his father (their other grandfather), who had earlier tried to get custody of the children, has offered a reward to find them. Two men seeking the reward try to kidnap the children, but through Megan's ingenuity the youngsters capture the kidnappers." Christ Sci Monit
"The plot is occasionally turgid, but that's compensated for by the author's fluid writing style, the excitement of the action, and the solidity of the characterization." Bull Cent Child Books

To Grandmother's house we go. Atheneum Pubs. 1990 188p $13.95 (4-6) **Fic**

1. Mystery and detective stories
ISBN 0-689-31594-5 LC 89-34972
"A Jean Karl book"
To avoid foster home care while their mother is recuperating from illness, three children run off to the home of a grandmother they have never seen, where they find a cold reception and a terrible secret
"Roberts offers a real page turner, and even if all the plot elements don't hang together . . . readers will scarcely notice as they race toward the conclusion.

Roberts, Willo Davis—*Continued*
Definitely a book whose whole is more than the sum of its parts." Booklist

The view from the cherry tree. Atheneum Pubs. 1975 181p $14.95; pa $3.95 (5 and up) **Fic**

1. Mystery and detective stories
ISBN 0-689-30483-8; 0-689-71131-X (pa) LC 75-6759

"Thoroughly disgruntled by the furor which accompanies his sister's wedding, eleven-year-old Rob Mallory retires to his favorite perch in the cherry tree. There, he is a horrified witness to the murder of an unpleasant neighborhood recluse. Because of the wedding preparations and the arrival of hordes of relatives, no adult will believe Rob's story. Soon, he finds that someone knows—and is trying to kill him, too." Child Book Rev Serv

"Although written in a direct and unpretentious style, this is essentially a sophisticated story, solidly constructed, imbued with suspense, evenly paced, and effective in conveying the atmosphere of a household coping with the last-minute problems and pressures of a family wedding." Bull Cent Child Books

Robertson, Keith, 1914-

Henry Reed, Inc. illustrated by Robert McCloskey. Viking 1958 239p il lib bdg $14.95; Puffin Bks. pa $3.95 (4-6) **Fic**

ISBN 0-670-36796-6 (lib bdg); 0-14-034144-7 (pa) LC 58-4758

"Henry Reed, on vacation from the American School in Naples, keeps a record of his research into the American free-enterprise system, to be used as a school report on his return. With a neighbor, Midge Glass, he starts a business in pure and applied research, which results in some very free and widely enterprising experiences, all recorded deadpan in his journal. Very funny and original escapades." Hodges. Books for Elem Sch Libr

Other available titles about Henry Reed are:
Henry Reed's babysitting service (1966)
Henry Reed's big show (1970)
Henry Reed's journey (1963)
Henry Reed's think tank (1986)

Robinson, Barbara

The best Christmas pageant ever; pictures by Judith Gwyn Brown. Harper & Row 1972 80p il $13.95; lib bdg $13.89; pa $3.50 (4-6) **Fic**

1. Christmas—Fiction 2. Pageants—Fiction
ISBN 0-06-025043-7; 0-06-025044-5 (lib bdg); 0-06-440275-4 (pa) LC 72-76501

In this story the six Herdmans, "absolutely the worst kids in the history of the world," discover the meaning of Christmas when they bully their way into the leading roles of the local church nativity play

"Although there is a touch of sentiment at the end . . . the story otherwise romps through the festive preparations with comic relish, and if the Herdmans are so gauche as to seem exaggerated, they are still enjoyable, as are the not-so-subtle pokes at pageant-planning in general." Bull Cent Child Books

Robinson, Nancy K., 1942-

Angela, private citizen. Scholastic 1989 146p $10.95; pa $2.75 (3-5) **Fic**

1. Family life—Fiction
ISBN 0-590-41726-6; 0-590-41727-4 (pa) LC 89-5918

Companion volume to: Oh honestly, Angela (1985)

Six-year-old Angela's faith in order and fairness is frequently shaken as she tries to cope with all the mysteries of life that keep turning up in her busy family

Rockwell, Anne F., 1934-

The emperor's new clothes; retold by Anne Rockwell from the nineteenth-century translation by H. W. Dulcken; pictures by Anne Rockwell. Crowell 1982 unp il lib bdg $12.89 (1-4) **Fic**

1. Fairy tales
ISBN 0-690-04149-7 LC 81-43313

Based on the story by Hans Christian Andersen

Two rascals sell a vain emperor an invisible suit of clothes

"This adaptation of Andersen's tale has a modern flavor but largely retains the character and incidents of the original. . . . The illustrations, . . keep to Rockwell's flat, open, sunny style." Booklist

Rockwell, Thomas, 1933-

How to eat fried worms; pictures by Emily McCully. Watts 1973 115p il lib bdg $12.90; Dell pa $3.25 (3-6) **Fic**

1. Worms—Fiction
ISBN 0-531-02631-0 (lib bdg); 0-440-44545-0 (pa) LC 73-4262

Also available ABC-CLIO large print edition $14.95 (ISBN 1-55736-051-0)

"The stakes are high when Alan bets $50 that his friend Billy can't eat 15 worms (one per day). . . . Billy's mother, instead of upchucking, comes to her son's aid by devising gourmet recipes like Alsatian Smothered Worm. Alan wants to win as desperately as Billy, who is itching to buy a used minibike, and few holds are barred in the contest." SLJ

"A hilarious story that will revolt and delight bumptious, unreachable, intermediate-grade boys and any other less particular mortals that read or listen to it. . . . The characters and their families and activities are natural to a T, and this juxtaposed against the uncommon plot, makes for some colorful, original writing in a much-needed comic vein." Booklist

Rodda, Emily, 1948-

The best-kept secret; illustrated by Noela Young. Holt & Co. 1990 c1988 119p il $14.95 (3-5) **Fic**

1. Fantastic fiction
ISBN 0-8050-0936-1 LC 89-26842

First published 1988 in Australia

"Troubled over her parents' plan to sell the only home she has ever known, Jo is unable to sleep. She hears carousel music in the distance and searches for its source the next morning. Her adventures begin as she and several troubled townspeople climb upon the

Rodda, Emily, 1948-—*Continued*

brightly colored horses. In a whirlwind of movement, they are tossed seven years into the future. On her return to the present, Jo faces reality with a sense of hope although she is unable to recall the trip." Child Book Rev Serv

"The 17 short chapters spin by as quickly as the carousel, due to Rodda's skill in drawing readers into the story early and keeping events building at a fast clip. . . . Young's black-and-white drawings, with their rampant carousel horses and time travelers in glowing auras, capture the light spirit of the story. An amusing, optimistic chapter-book fantasy to read alone or aloud." SLJ

Rodgers, Mary

Freaky Friday. Harper & Row 1972 145p $13.95; lib bdg $13.89; pa $3.50 (4 and up) **Fic**

1. Mothers and daughters—Fiction
ISBN 0-06-025048-8; 0-06-025049-6 (lib bdg); 0-06-440046-8 (pa) LC 74-183158

Also available ABC-CLIO large print edition $15.95 (ISBN 1-55736-027-8)

"'When I woke up this morning, I found I'd turned into my mother.' So begins the most bizarre day in the life of 13-year-old Annabel Andrews, who discovers one Friday morning she has taken on her mother's physical characteristics while retaining her own personality. Readers will giggle in anticipation as Annabel plunges madly from one disaster to another trying to cope with various adult situations." Publ Wkly

"There's nothing didactic here; the story bubbles along in fine style as Annabel sees herself as others see her . . . and adjusts to the rigors of her mother's problems and the inevitable complications of changed roles. A fresh, imaginative, and entertaining story." Bull Cent Child Books

Other available titles about Annabel Andrews and her family are:
A billion for Boris (1974)
Summer switch (1982)

Rodowsky, Colby F., 1932-

The gathering room; [by] Colby Rodowsky. Farrar, Straus & Giroux 1981 185p $11.95; pa $3.45 (5 and up) **Fic**

1. Family life—Fiction 2. Cemeteries—Fiction 3. Aunts—Fiction
ISBN 0-374-32520-0; 0-374-42520-5 (pa) LC 81-5360

After Aunt Ernestus comes to visit, a family living in seclusion as caretakers for a cemetery find the time has come to rejoin the mainstream of society

"Lacking in fast-moving action and flawed with a slow start, the story relies on an electric atmosphere and on the carefully developed anticipation of change to gain its considerable hold on the reader's interest." Horn Book

Roth-Hano, Renée, 1931-

Touch wood; a girlhood in occupied France. Four Winds Press 1988 297p $15.95; Puffin Bks. pa $4.95 (6 and up) **Fic**

1. Holocaust, Jewish (1933-1945)—Fiction 2. France—History—1940-1945, German occupation—Fiction 3. Jews—France—Fiction
ISBN 0-02-777340-X; 0-14-034085-8 (pa) LC 87-34326

This "novel in diary format tells the experiences of a pre-adolescent Jewish girl in occupied France. Renée Roth's family has fled from Alsace to find safety in Paris, but the Nazi restrictions and round-ups force her parents to send their three daughters to a convent in Normandy, where they're lonely but cared for in relative comfort until caught in the bombing that fronts the Allied invasion." Bull Cent Child Books

"An immediate and moving memoir, the book adds still another dimension to understanding the impact of the 1940s not only on world events but on the lives of individuals." Horn Book

Ruckman, Ivy, 1931-

Night of the twisters. Crowell 1984 153p $13.95; lib bdg $13.89; pa $3.50 (3-6) **Fic**

1. Tornadoes—Fiction 2. Nebraska—Fiction
ISBN 0-690-04408-9; 0-690-04409-7 (lib bdg); 0-06-440176-6 (pa) LC 83-46168

"Twelve-year-old Dan describes the events leading up to the hour that his town was struck seven times by tornadoes. Alone at home, [in Grand Island, Nebraska] Dan, his baby brother, and his best friend Arthur ride out the storm huddled in the shower stall in Dan's basement and then begin the search for their parents." Sci Child

"Ruckman does a good job of creating and maintaining suspense, produces dialogue that sounds appropriate for a stress situation, and gives her characters some depth and differentiation." Bull Cent Child Books

Rylant, Cynthia

A blue-eyed daisy. Bradbury Press 1985 99p $11.95; Dell pa $2.50 (5 and up) **Fic**

1. Family life—Fiction 2. West Virginia—Fiction
ISBN 0-02-777960-2; 0-440-40927-6 (pa) LC 84-21554

This story "describes a year in a child's life. . . Ellie is eleven, youngest of five girls. She wishes her father didn't drink but understands his frustration. . . . It is a bond between them when they acquire a hunting dog. . . . She also acquires a best friend during the year, gets her first kiss (and is surprised to see that she enjoys it) and adjusts to the fact that some of the events in her life will be sad ones." Bull Cent Child Books

"Episodic in nature, the story captures, as if in a frozen frame, the brief moments between childhood and adolescence." Horn Book

A fine white dust. Bradbury Press 1986 106p $11.95; Dell pa $2.95 (5 and up) **Fic**

1. Religion—Fiction 2. Friendship—Fiction 3. Family life—Fiction
ISBN 0-02-777240-3; 0-440-42499-2 (pa) LC 86-1003

A Newbery Medal honor book, 1987

Rylant, Cynthia—*Continued*

The visit of the traveling Preacher Man to his small North Carolina town gives new impetus to thirteen-year-old Peter's struggle to reconcile his own deeply felt religious belief with the beliefs and non-beliefs of his family and friends

"Blending humor and intense emotion with a poetic use of language, Cynthia Rylant has created a taut, finely drawn portrait of a boy's growth from seeking for belief, through seduction and betrayal, to a spiritual acceptance and a readiness 'for something whole.'" Horn Book

Sachs, Marilyn, 1927-

At the sound of the beep. Dutton Children's Bks. 1990 154p lib bdg $13.95; Puffin Bks. pa $3.95 (4-6) **Fic**

1. Mystery and detective stories
ISBN 0-525-44571-4 (lib bdg); 0-14-034681-3 (pa) LC 89-25655

Distraught at the thought of their parents' divorcing, twins Mathew and Mathilda run away from home and take up residence in Golden Gate Park, where they encounter many homeless people and here there is a murderer loose among them

"Suspense is Sachs's strong suit; only at the very end of the story, after a frightening climax in which Mathilda is nearly poisoned, does the author reveal the identity of the killer. . . . The ending is somewhat abrupt, and the parents' reconciliation is not quite convincing; still, this is a riveting adventure that will be popular with middle-grade readers." Booklist

The bears' house. Dutton 1987 c1971 67p lib bdg $10.95; Avon Bks. pa $2.50 (4-6) **Fic**

1. Family life—Fiction 2. Dollhouses—Fiction
ISBN 0-525-44286-3; 0-380-70582-6 (pa) LC 86-29267

First published 1971 by Doubleday in an illustrated edition

"Life is grim for nine-year-old Fran Ellen. Father has deserted the family, mother has retreated into apathy and tears, and the five children shift for themselves. Fran Ellen's only joy is Baby Flora. Rejected at home and taunted at school, Fran Ellen adopts as her own the classroom doll house, compensating for her unhappiness with . . . fantasies in which its tenants, the three bears, adore her." Saturday Rev

"Superb characterizations and uncommonly skilled writing draw the reader completely into the realities and fantasies of Fran Ellen's world." Libr J

Followed by: Fran Ellen's house, entered below

Fran Ellen's house. Dutton 1987 97p $12.95; Avon Bks. pa $2.75 (4-6) **Fic**

1. Family life—Fiction 2. Dollhouses—Fiction
ISBN 0-525-44345-2; 0-380-70583-4 (pa) LC 87-19951

In this sequel to the title entered above, "the bears' house is not her refuge, but the place where her little sister Felice's imagination takes hold. Fran Ellen is ready not only to pass on that legacy but becomes an independent, curious child who simply must participate in what life offers her. The book's one drawback is that to be fully appreciated, it must be read in conjunction with the first heartbreaking story. Any thoughtful reader will embrace that task and witness a family torn apart healing itself." Publ Wkly

A summer's lease. Dutton 1979 124p $13.95 (5 and up) **Fic**

1. Authors—Fiction 2. Teachers—Fiction
ISBN 0-525-40480-5 LC 78-12486

"Gloria was determined to get to college [and become a writer] despite her widowed mother's insistence that she take a secretarial course and start earning money. She had the backing of her beloved English teacher, Mrs. Horne, and she was sure that Mrs. Horne would select her as assistant editor of the high school literary magazine—and that would be her passport to continuing education. Gloria, who tells, the story, is arrogant, conceited about her literary prowess, jealous of and harsh toward those she considers her rivals. . . . Gloria changes during a summer in which Mrs. Horne invites her and her rival, Jerry, to the Horne summer home to help take care of a group of younger children." Bull Cent Child Books

Saint-Exupéry, Antoine de, 1900-1944

The little prince; written and drawn by Antoine de Saint-Exupéry; translated from the French by Katherine Woods. Harcourt Brace Jovanovich 1943 91p il $12.95; pa $6.95 (4 and up) **Fic**

ISBN 0-15-246503-0; 0-15-646511-6 (pa) LC 67-1144

First published by Reynal & Hitchcock

"This many-dimensional fable of an airplane pilot who has crashed in the desert is for readers of all ages. The pilot comes upon the little prince soon after the crash. The prince tells of his adventures on different planets and on Earth as he attempts to learn about the universe in order to live peacefully on his own small planet. A spiritual quality enhances the seemingly simple observations of the little prince." Shapiro. Fic for Youth. 2d edition

Salten, Felix, 1869-1945

Bambi; a life in the woods il (4-6) **Fic**

1. Deer—Fiction LC 74-124383

Some editions are:

Buccaneer Bks. lib bdg $16.95 (ISBN 0-89966-358-3)
Harmony Raine & Co. lib bdg $16.95 (ISBN 0-89967-032-6)
Pocket Bks. pa $3.50 illustrated by Barbara Cooney (ISBN 0-671-66607-X)

Original German edition, 1923; first United States edition published 1928 by Simon & Schuster

"Bambi is a young deer, growing up in a forest, at first a curious child playing about his mother in glade and meadow, conversing with grasshoppers, squirrels and his own little cousins, Faline and Gobo." N Y Libr

"Felix Stalten's story of deer life in the woods that fringe the Danube is neither sentimental nor used to point a moral. It derives its dramatic value, legitimately, from the animals' fear and terror of their historic enemy—man. . . . In his absorption with details that author has brought his whole forest to life, yet these details are selected with a poet's intuition for delicacy of effect." N Y Her Trib Books

Sargent, Sarah, 1937-

Weird Henry Berg. Crown 1980 113p o.p.; Dell paperback available $2.25 (4-6) **Fic**

1. Dragons—Fiction 2. Fantastic fiction

ISBN 0-440-49346-3 (pa) LC 80-13651

"Henry Berg doesn't know that the 'lizard' he has is a baby dragon; all he knows is that the odd, endearing pet has hatched from an ancient egg that had belonged to his great-grandfather. Elderly Millie Levenson doesn't know Henry, but she gets in touch with him because she has had a visit from a dragon, a sophisticated creature sent over from Wales to find the baby that had been left behind a century ago. Henry wants to keep his pet; Millie, knowing that the dragon is in danger, wants to get him back to Wales." Bull Cent Child Books

"The conjunction of fantasy with reality is made believable by the author's narrative skill and by her ability to suggest character through economical description. A fascinating and original tale." Horn Book

Schlein, Miriam

The year of the panda; illustrated by Kam Mak. Crowell 1990 83p il $12.95; lib bdg $12.89 (3-5) **Fic**

1. Giant panda—Fiction 2. Wildlife conservation—Fiction 3. Endangered species—Fiction 4. China—Fiction

ISBN 0-690-04864-5; 0-690-04866-1 (lib bdg) LC 89-71307

"Lu Yi, son of a farm family, is aware that the daxion mao (giant panda) is a rare species, and he reluctantly tells a government messenger that he has a very young panda he's rescued. To Lu Yi's joy, he's invited to come along when his pet is flown to the Daxion Mao Rescue Center." Bull Cent Child Books

"The clear, concise narrative makes it clear that decisions about how to save the panda are not always straightforward. Brief yet thought-provoking, this sensitively written novel is enhanced by Mak's stirring pencil drawings." Publ Wkly

Sebestyen, Ouida, 1924-

IOU's. Little, Brown 1982 188p $14.95; Dell pa $2.75 (6 and up) **Fic**

1. Mothers—Fiction 2. Parent and child—Fiction

ISBN 0-316-77933-4; 0-440-93986-0 (pa) LC 82-124

"An Atlantic Monthly Press book"

"Reflecting on the summer of his thirteenth year, Stowe Garrett concludes that it has been a time of goodbyes—to the grandfather he has never known, to the childish pranks he has enjoyed with his implusive friend Brownie, and to the relationship he has known with Karla, his first friend, whose metamorphosis into young womanhood is disturbing yet mysteriously enticing. . . . Written from the adolescent's perspective, the story explores . . . the relationship between two remarkable individuals—Stowe and his unconventional mother Annie." Horn Book

The author's "mother-son portrait is a pleasure to watch, and Stowe's sensitivity to the feelings of others springs directly from it. This is a delicate revelation of matters of the heart, and speaks strongly of the power of love." Booklist

Words by heart. Little, Brown 1979 162p $13.95; Bantam Bks. pa $2.95 (5 and up) **Fic**

1. Blacks—Fiction 2. Race relations—Fiction 3. Family life—Fiction

ISBN 0-316-77931-8; 0-553-27179-2 (pa) LC 78-27847

"An Atlantic Monthly Press book"

"It is 1910, and Lena's family is the only black family in her small Southwestern town. When Lena wins a scripture reciting contest that a white boy is supposed to win, her family is threatened. Lena's father tries to make her understand that by hating the people who did this, the problems that cause their behavior are not solved. Only more hatred and violence cause Lena and the village to understand the words of her father." ALAN

Followed by: On fire (1985)

Selden, George, 1929-1989

The cricket in Times Square; illustrated by Garth Williams. Farrar, Straus & Giroux 1960 151p il $13.95; Dell pa $3.25 (3-6) **Fic**

1. Cats—Fiction 2. Crickets—Fiction 3. Mice—Fiction 4. New York (N.Y.)—Fiction

ISBN 0-374-31650-3; 0-440-41563-2 (pa) LC 60-12640

Also available ABC-CLIO large print edition $15.95 (ISBN 1-55736-170-3)

A Newbery Medal honor book, 1961

"An Ariel book"

"A touch of magic comes to Times Square subway station with Chester, a cricket from rural Connecticut. He is introduced to the distinctive character of city life by three friends: Mario Bellini, whose parents operate a newsstand; Tucker, a glib Broadway mouse; and Harry, a sagacious cat. Chester saves the Bellinis' business by giving concerts from the newsstand, bringing to rushing commuters moments of beauty and repose. This modern fantasy shows that, in New York, anything can happen." Moorachian. What is a City?

Other available titles about Chester and his friends are:
Chester Cricket's new home (1983)
Chester Cricket's pigeon ride (1981)
Harry Cat's pet puppy (1974)
Harry Kitten and Tucker Mouse (1986)
The old meadow (1987)
Tucker's countryside (1969)

The genie of Sutton Place. Farrar, Straus & Giroux 1973 175p $12.95 (4 and up) **Fic**

ISBN 0-374-32527-8 LC 72-90531

Adapted from the television play written by the author and Kenneth Heuer

"Tim turns to his dead father's diaries for some occult wisdom to help him keep Sam, a beloved mongrel his aunt has banished from their apartment. What he finds is a spell that summons the genie Abdullah from a thousand years' captivity in a woven carpet." Booklist

"The speedy action and clever dialogue in this witty book are sure to entice readers." SLJ

Sendak, Maurice

Higglety pigglety pop! or, There must be more to life; story and pictures by Maurice Sendak. Harper & Row 1967 69p il lib bdg $13.95; pa $5.95 (2-4) **Fic**

1. Dogs—Fiction
ISBN 0-06-025487-4 (lib bdg); 0-06-443021-9 (pa)
LC 67-18553

In this modern fairy tale "Jennie, the Sealyham terrier, leaves home because 'there must be more to life than having everything.' When she applies for a job as the leading lady of the World Mother Goose Theater, she discovers that what she lacks is experience. What follows are her adventures and her gaining of experience; finally Jennie becomes the leading lady of the play." Wis Libr Bull

"The story has elements of tenderness and humor; it also has . . . typically macabre Sendak touches. . . . The illustrations are beautiful, amusing, and distinctive." Sutherland. The Best in Child Books

Seredy, Kate, 1899-1975

The Good Master; written and illustrated by Kate Seredy. Viking 1935 210p il $13.95; Puffin Bks. pa $4.95 (4-6) **Fic**

1. Farm life—Fiction 2. Hungary—Fiction
ISBN 0-670-34592-X; 0-14-030133-X (pa)
LC 35-17487

A Newbery Medal honor book, 1936

Into this story of Jancsi, a ten-year-old Hungarian farm boy and his little hoyden of a cousin Kate from Budapest, is woven a description of Hungarian farm life, fairs, festivals, and folk tales. Under the tutelage of Jancsi's kind father, called by the neighbors The Good Master, Kate calms down and becomes a more docile young person

"The steady warm understanding of the wise father, the Good Master, is a shining quality throughout." Horn Book

Followed by: The singing tree (1939)

The white stag; written and illustrated by Kate Seredy. Viking 1937 94p il $12.95; Puffin Bks. pa $3.95 (4-6) **Fic**

1. Hungary—Fiction
ISBN 0-670-76375-6; 0-14-031258-7 (pa)
LC 37-37800

Awarded the Newbery Medal, 1938

"Striking illustrations interpret this hero tale of the legendary founding of Hungary, when a white stag and a red eagle led the people to their promised land." Hodges. Books for Elem Sch Libr

Serraillier, Ian, 1912-

The silver sword; illustrated by C. Walter Hodges. Phillips 1959 c1956 187p il $21.95 (5 and up) **Fic**

1. World War, 1939-1945—Fiction 2. Refugees, Polish—Fiction
ISBN 0-87599-104-1
LC 59-6556

First published 1956 in the United Kingdom; first United States edition published 1959 by Criterion Books

"As a result of World War II, the Balicki family of Warsaw are separated from one another. Living in bombed-out cellars or the countryside the children are helped by Edek until his arrest for smuggling and from then on by Jan, a sullen orphan. The privations of each member of the family, especially the children, are graphically described as each works toward their rendezvous, Switzerland, and freedom. A suspense-filled, exciting story." Read Ladders for Hum Relat. 5th edition

Service, Pamela F.

Stinker from space. Scribner 1988 83p $11.95; Fawcett Juniper pa $2.95 (4-6) **Fic**

1. Science fiction
ISBN 0-684-18910-0; 0-449-70330-4 (pa)
LC 87-25266

An agent of the Sylon Confederacy, fleeing from enemy ships, crash lands on Earth, transfers his mind to the body of a skunk, and enlists the aid of two children in getting back to his home planet

"A first-class, funny science fantasy that will hook middle-grade readers right from the first scene. . . . The situation is gratifyingly absurd, the development satisfyingly natural." Bull Cent Child Books

Sewell, Anna, 1820-1878

Black Beauty (4-6) **Fic**

1. Horses—Fiction 2. Great Britain—Fiction

Some editions are:

Crown (Children's illustrated classics) $9.98 With illustrations by Lucy Kemp-Welch (ISBN 0-517-61884-2)
Dell pa $3.50 (ISBN 0-440-40355-3)
Farrar, Straus & Giroux $19.95 Pictures by Charles Keeping (ISBN 0-374-30776-8)
Golden Bks. $8.95 Illustrated by Tony Chen (ISBN 0-307-17112-4) Has subtitle: The autobiography of a horse
Grosset & Dunlap (Illustrated junior lib) $12.95 Illustrated by Fritz Eichenberg (ISBN 0-448-11007-5)
Messner lib bdg $14.79 Illustrated by John Speirs (ISBN 0-671-45650-4) Has subtitle: The autobiography of a horse
Scholastic pa $2.95 (ISBN 0-590-42354-1)
Wanderer Bks. $15.95 Illustrated by John Speirs (ISBN 0-671-43789-5) Has subtitle: The autobiography of a horse

First published 1877 in the United Kingdom; first United States edition, 1891

This is "the most celebrated 'Animal story' of the 19th cent., an account of a horse's experiences at the hands of many owners, ranging from the worthy Squire Gordon to a cruel cab-owner." Oxford Companion to Child Lit

Sharmat, Marjorie Weinman, 1928-

Mysteriously yours, Maggie Marmelstein; pictures by Ben Shecter. Harper & Row 1982 151p il $12.95; lib bdg $12.89; pa $3.50 (3-6) **Fic**

1. Journalism—Fiction 2. School stories
ISBN 0-06-025516-1; 0-06-025517-X (lib bdg); 0-06-440145-6 (pa)
LC 81-48656

Sharmat, Marjorie Weinman, 1928-—*Continued*

"When Maggie wins the contest to be the mystery columnist for the school newspaper, she agrees to remain quiet about her identity. An early article about her close friend Ellen, who is mousy and lacks confidence, changes Ellen's popularity in school, and Maggie is triumphant over the power she thinks she now wields. Her next cause, however, has disastrous results, and Maggie finally realizes that power must be tempered with responsibility." Booklist

Other available titles about Maggie Marmelstein are:
Getting something on Maggie Marmelstein (1971)
Maggie Marmelstein for president (1975)

Sharp, Margery, 1905-

The rescuers; with illustrations by Garth Williams. Little, Brown 1959 149p il o.p.; Dell paperback available $2.95 (3-6) **Fic**

1. Mice—Fiction
ISBN 0-440-47378-0 (pa) LC 59-6477

Also available in hardcover from Smith, P. $15 (ISBN 0-8446-6412-X)

This is "a story featuring animals. The Prisoners' Aid Society of mice [one of whose members is Miss Bianca, the pampered pet of an ambassador's son] want to free a Norwegian poet held captive in the Black Castle in a barbarous country." Publ Wkly

Other available titles about Miss Bianca and her friends are:
Miss Bianca (1962)
Miss Bianca in the salt mines (1966)
The turret (1963)

Shreve, Susan Richards

The flunking of Joshua T. Bates; [by] Susan Shreve; illustrated by Diane de Groat. Knopf 1984 82p il $12.95; lib bdg $12.99; Scholastic pa $2.50 (3-5) **Fic**

1. School stories 2. Teachers 3. Family life—Fiction
ISBN 0-394-86380-1; 0-394-96380-6 (lib bdg); 0-590-41189-6 (pa) LC 83-19636

"Sometimes children, especially boys, are held back in school even if they are smart. To his dismay, Joshua T. Bates was supposed to repeat the whole third grade, but he was lucky enough to have a very sympathetic teacher." N Y Times Book Rev

"In addition to the warm depiction of a teacher-pupil relationship, the story has other relationships, astutely drawn: Joshua's parents, the former classmate who teases Joshua, the best friend who stoutly defends him. The dialogue is particularly good, often contributing to characterization, just as often crisply humorous." Bull Cent Child Books

Shyer, Marlene Fanta

Welcome home, Jellybean. Scribner 1978 152p o.p. paperback available $3.95 (5 and up) **Fic**

1. Mentally handicapped children—Fiction 2. Brothers and sisters—Fiction
ISBN 0-689-71213-8 (pa) LC 77-17970

"'When my sister turned thirteen the school where she lived got her toilet-trained and my mother decided she ought to come home to live, once and for all.' So begins Neil Oxley's story of how it was to have his profoundly retarded sister re-enter the family circle." Booklist

"Painful, honest, and convincing, this is quietly written and very effective in evoking sympathy and understanding for retarded children and for their families." Bull Cent Child Books

Singer, Isaac Bashevis, 1904-1991

The fools of Chelm and their history; pictures by Uri Shulevitz; translated by the author and Elizabeth Shub. Farrar, Straus & Giroux 1973 57p il $11.95; pa $3.50 (3-6) **Fic**

1. Jews—Fiction
ISBN 0-374-32444-1; 0-374-42429-2 (pa) LC 73-81500

The "town of Chelm is just like every place else, only worse, as numerous shortages, foolish citizens, and inept leaders combine to make life thoroughly miserable. . . . Singer mocks the 'advantages'—such as war, crime, and revolution—that civilization brings to Chelm, as the leadership changes but never improves." Booklist

"An amusing story, well-told. The pen-and-ink illustrations embellish the text, adding droll touches of their own." Horn Book

Singer, Marilyn, 1948-

Charmed. Atheneum Pubs. 1990 219p $14.95 (5 and up) **Fic**

1. Fantastic fiction
ISBN 0-689-31619-4 LC 90-518

Twelve-year-old Miranda and her companion Bastable, an invisible catlike creature from another world, discover that they are part of the Correct Combination, a team that must stop the evil Charmer from taking over the universe

"The fantasy serves as an obvious metaphor for dangers currently facing society, but excitement abounds, tension remains high and the cast is engaging." Child Book Rev Serv

Sleator, William

Among the dolls; illustrated by Trina Schart Hyman. Dutton 1975 70p il $11.95 (4 and up) **Fic**

1. Dollhouses—Fiction 2. Dolls—Fiction 3. Fantastic fiction
ISBN 0-525-25563-X LC 75-5944

"For her birthday Vicky gets a dollhouse which she doesn't want but is powerfully drawn to as she projects some angry feelings and conflicts with her family through her play with the dolls. When she is mysteriously shrunk and trapped among the dolls, they treat her as cruelly as she has them, and she barely escapes after discovering their own tiny dollhouse, and exact replica of her home and family through which the dolls have revenged themselves on her real world. . . . The plot is airtight, the suspense clutching, the doll personalities real, and the implications scary." Booklist

Sleator, William—*Continued*

The boy who reversed himself. Dutton 1986 167p $13.95; Bantam Bks. pa $2.95 (5 and up) **Fic**

1. Science fiction 2. Space and time—Fiction
ISBN 0-525-44276-6; 0-553-28570-X (pa) LC 86-19700

When Laura discovers that the unpopular boy living next door to her has the ability to go into the fourth dimension, she makes the dangerous decision to accompany him on his journeys there

"What follows is a terrifying trip into the fourth dimension, populated by some of Sleator's most unusual characters to date. An utterly fantastic and ultimately satisfying novel by a master storyteller." SLJ

The duplicate. Dutton 1988 154p $12.95 (6 and up) **Fic**

1. Science fiction
ISBN 0-525-44390-8 LC 87-30562

Sixteen-year-old David, finding a strange machine that creates replicas of living organisms, duplicates himself and suffers the horrible consequences when the duplicate turns against him

"There are some points in the story when the roles of the clones (referred to as Duplicates A and B) become congested to the detriment of the book's pace, but fantasy fans will doubtless find the concept fresh enough and eerie enough to compensate for this, and Sleator is, as always, economical in casting and structuring his story." Bull Cent Child Books

The green futures of Tycho. Dutton 1981 133p $14.95 (5 and up) **Fic**

1. Science fiction 2. Space and time—Fiction 3. Good and evil—Fiction
ISBN 0-525-31007-X LC 80-23020

"Eleven year old Tycho Tithonus, while digging a vegetable garden, uncovers an egg-shaped object, which he quickly learns to use to travel back and forth in time. In one future encounter, Tycho meets an older version of himself. Older Tycho warns young Tycho to wear a watch each time he leaves the present: 'Think what would happen if you came back before you left.' Young Tycho grapples with several possible futures in which older versions of himself become . . . distorted and evil." N Y Times Book Rev

The author's "expert blend of future and horror fiction is unusually stark, dark and intriguing; and the breakneck pace he sets never falters." SLJ

House of stairs. Dutton 1974 166p $14.95 (5 and up) **Fic**

1. Science fiction 2. Behavior modification—Fiction
ISBN 0-525-32335-X LC 73-17417

"Five 15-year-old orphans with widely ranging personality characteristics are involuntarily placed in a house of endless stairs and subjected to psychological experiments on conditioned human responses." Booklist

"The setting is bleak, dramatic and convincing; the interaction and development of the five young people as characters trapped in an abrasive situation are compelling. A very effective and provocative suspense story that can be read for plot alone or doubly enjoyed for the mystery and the message." Bull Cent Child Books

Interstellar pig. Dutton 1984 197p $12.95; Bantam Bks. pa $2.95 (5 and up) **Fic**

1. Science fiction
ISBN 0-525-44098-4; 0-553-25564-9 (pa) LC 84-4132

"Solitary and bored, Barney is quickly attracted by the exotic appearance and protean personalities of Zena, Manny, and Joe, who have rented the summer house next door. The interest of the sophisticated adults in sixteen-year-old Barney at first flatters, then intrigues, and finally terrifies him as he becomes absorbed in their compulsion to possess 'The Piggy.' When he realizes that the talisman has power, the game expands in significance." Horn Book

The author "draws the reader in with intimations of danger and horror, but the climactic battle is more slapstick than horrific, and the victor's prize could scarcely be more ironic. Problematic as straight science fiction but great fun as a spoof on human-alien contact." Booklist

Into the dream; illustrated by Ruth Sanderson. Dutton 1979 137p il $13.95 (5 and up) **Fic**

1. Extrasensory perception—Fiction 2. Psychokinesis—Fiction 3. Unidentified flying objects—Fiction
ISBN 0-525-32583-2 LC 78-11825

When two youngsters realize they are having the same frightening dream, they begin searching for an explanation for this mysterious coincidence

"Tightly woven suspense and an ingenious, totally involving plot line . . . make this a thriller of top-notch quality." Booklist

Strange attractors. Dutton 1990 169p $13.95 (5 and up) **Fic**

1. Space and time—Fiction 2. Science fiction
ISBN 0-525-44530-7 LC 89-33840

"The strange attractors are people from a parallel universe: a brilliant scientist, Sylvan, and his beautiful daughter, Eve, whose reckless manipulation of time travel has plunged their timeline into chaos. Their search for a stable timeline brings them to our world, where they must destroy their doppelgängers, the 'real' Sylvan and Eve, or drag this world into chaos, too. Max, a teenage science student, is forced to become their unwilling ally or be destroyed himself." SLJ

"Sleator's talent for fascinating scientific manipulation is fully in evidence and exceptionally well conceived here. . . . Along with the clever science, Sleator turns in some good suspense as Max plays hide-and-seek with his pursuers and struggles between the lure of illicit excitement and the mundane acceptance of the honorable. His final choice, a compromise of sorts, seems exactly right." Booklist

Slepian, Jan, 1921-

The Alfred summer. Macmillan 1980 119p $11.95 (5 and up) **Fic**

1. Friendship—Fiction 2. Handicapped children—Fiction 3. Brooklyn (New York, N.Y.)—Fiction
ISBN 0-02-782920-0 LC 79-24097

The story is "set in Brooklyn in 1937. . . . Lester, who suffers from cerebral palsy; Alfred, who is crippled and mentally retarded; Myron, clumsy and ineffectual—along with Claire, their athletic tomboy friend, find

Slepian, Jan, 1921-—*Continued*
friendship and spend a happy summer building a boat." Horn Book

"The narrator's intelligent voice, with its youthful, touching irony, is the perfect voice. . . . Most remarkable is that the author is not handing out leaflets and guilt. She is not talking about US and Them. . . . She is saying that we are all a little bent somewhere, a little palsied. . . . A point worth making, a book worth reading." N Y Times Book Rev

Followed by: Lester's turn (1981)

The Broccoli tapes. Philomel Bks. 1989 157p $13.95; Scholastic pa $2.75 (5 and up) **Fic**

1. Cats—Fiction 2. Death—Fiction 3. Brothers and sisters—Fiction 4. Hawaii—Fiction
ISBN 0-399-21712-6; 0-590-43473-X (pa)
LC 88-25490

"Both 12-year-old Sara and her 13-year-old brother, Sam, have trouble adjusting to Hawaii during the five months that their family is living there. . . . When Sara and Sam rescue a wild cat (who is later named Broccoli), they meet Eddie Nutt. At first Eddie is as suspicious and untrusting as Broccoli until the bonds of friendship gradually develop. The story unfolds through Sara's cassette tapes sent to her teacher and classmates back home." SLJ

"Slepian is a fine writer, and the elements of her story are smoothly meshed, the action and characterization mutually affective. The message that love is worth the chance of pain is given by the people in her story, not didactically imposed by the author." Bull Cent Child Books

The night of the Bozos. Dutton 1983 152p lib bdg $10.95 (6 and up) **Fic**

1. Amusement parks—Fiction 2. Friendship—Fiction
ISBN 0-525-44070-4
LC 83-5564

"George, an introverted thirteen-year-old whose life revolves around music, and his twenty-three-year-old Uncle Hibble, who stutters badly, meet a tattooed girl from a carnival. Invited behind the scenes, they begin to learn from the philosophies of the carneys that while people can hurt you, they can also give you strength." Bull Cent Child Books

"The author's use of the carnival as a device for providing the story with the necessary characters may seem obvious, but the individual personalities are clearly and consistently revealed with the ease and style of an able writer. Vivid, unexpected details foreshadow the outcome of the plot; the story, which celebrates quiet determination and the restorative energy of friendship, is at once humorous, grotesque, and poignant." Horn Book

Risk 'n' roses. Philomel Bks. 1990 175p $14.95 (5 and up) **Fic**

1. Friendship—Fiction 2. Mentally handicapped children—Fiction 3. Sisters—Fiction
ISBN 0-399-22219-7
LC 90-31460

In this "novel set after World War II, Skip, eleven, is as enthralled as the other neighborhood children with Jean, who is tough, daring, and domineering. Sharp-tongued Jean is a manipulator, and one of the people she manipulates is Angela, the beautiful and retarded older sister of Skip. Slepian is an astute and perceptive observer of group dynamics, and her skillfully written story explores the intricacies of the relationships among the children, the cruelty of Jean to Angela, and the way it moves Skip to a new perspective on her feeling for her sister. The characterizations of Angela's overprotective mother and of the elderly neighbor (a victim of Nazi persecution) who is persecuted by Jean are powerful, both adding to the suspense of a story about the effect on others of an unhappy, vindictive child." Bull Cent Child Books

Slote, Alfred

Matt Gargan's boy. Lippincott 1975 159p o.p.; HarperCollins Pubs. paperback available $3.50 (4-6) **Fic**

1. Baseball—Fiction 2. Divorce—Fiction
ISBN 0-06-440154-5 (pa)
LC 74-26669

"Baseball-playing Danny Gargan's chief concern is keeping his divorced mother from dating other men so that when his father retires from major league baseball the two can get back together again. His plans begin to go awry with the appearance of the Warren family; not only does his mother obviously like Mr. Warren, a widower, but one of his daughters is a competent ballplayer who wants to try out for Danny's team. Danny's eventual coming to terms with situations that he cannot change is well handled; and Slote's able use of first-person narrative fosters some apt characterizations as well as added insight into the mechanics of Danny's diminishing egotistical and male chauvinistic streaks." Booklist

Moving in. Lippincott 1988 167p $14.95; lib bdg $14.89; HarperCollins Pubs. pa $3.50 (4-6) **Fic**

1. Moving, Household—Fiction 2. Fathers—Fiction
ISBN 0-397-32261-5; 0-397-32262-3 (lib bdg); 0-06-440294-0 (pa)
LC 87-45569

Eleven-year old Robbie and his thirteen-year-old sister, Peggy, involve themselves in some elaborate schemes to discourage their widowed father's budding romance and to persuade him to move back to their old hometown

"In this novel humor derives from a child's perception of the dynamics at work in people's interconnecting lives. Well-paced and solidly written, it is a book young readers will enjoy and identify with." Christ Sci Monit

The trading games. Lippincott 1990 200p $13.95; lib bdg $13.89 (4-6) **Fic**

1. Baseball cards—Fiction 2. Fathers and sons—Fiction 3. Grandfathers—Fiction
ISBN 0-397-32397-2; 0-397-32398-0 (lib bdg)
LC 89-12851

"Andy Harris' baseball-card collection, inherited from his recently deceased father, contains some valuable items, including a 1952 Mickey Mantle card worth $2500. He's willing, however, to trade Mantle for a 25-cent card that pictures his grandfather, Jim 'Ace 459' Harris, whom Andy idolizes. . . . It's not until Grampa coaches Andy that he learns why the relationship between his father and grandfather was strained." SLJ

"Slote does a masterful job grounding the moral dilemmas of growing up within the rigorously measured world of the baseball diamond. Friendship, father-son intimacy, and the rough edges of adult life are all examined and filtered through the eyes of a boy who instinctively understands more than he knows." Booklist

Smith, Doris Buchanan

The first hard times. Viking 1983 137p $12.95; Dell pa $2.50 (4-6) **Fic**

1. Stepfathers—Fiction 2. Family life—Fiction 3. Missing in action—Fiction
ISBN 0-670-31571-0; 0-440-42532-8 (pa)
LC 82-60084

This companion volume to Last was Lloyd, features Lloyd in the supporting role of friend to twelve-year-old Ancil who has difficulty accepting her new stepfather because she remains convinced her MIA father will return someday

The author is "astute in her understanding and depiction of the intricacies of familiar relationships and realistic in depicting the changes in Ancil. The characters are drawn with depth and conviction, and the style is fluent, marked by good pace and natural dialogue." Bull Cent Child Books

Kelly's creek; illustrated by Alan Tiegreen. Crowell 1975 69p il lib bdg $12.89 (4-6) **Fic**

1. Learning disabilities—Fiction 2. Marshes—Fiction
ISBN 0-690-04774-6 LC 75-6761

"A learning disability blocks Kelly's progress at school. His worried parents insist that he try harder to do his exercises and improve, and until he does, they make his daily sojourns to the nearby marsh off limits. Kelly finds the curb intolerable, for the marsh is the one place where he doesn't feel 'dumb.' He knows the terrain and with the help of Phillip, a marine biology student who is conducting a study there, has begun to learn about the wildlife surrounding him. Kelly's unique knowledge proves to be his saving grace. . . . A simple story, perhaps resolved a little too easily, but instructive in its portrayal of a boy with learning problems and appealing enough to keep readers along for the story alone." Booklist

Last was Lloyd. Viking 1981 124p $12.95; Puffin Bks. pa $3.95 (4-6) **Fic**

1. Parent and child—Fiction 2. Friendship—Fiction
ISBN 0-670-41921-4; 0-14-034444-6 (pa)
LC 80-29468

Companion volume to: The first hard times, entered above

A friendless, overweight 12-year-old with an overprotective mother begins to change the monotonous pattern of his life

This "tersely written novel shows a striking verisimilitude and acute psychological pereception as it reveals Lloyd's struggle to achieve independence." SLJ

Return to Bitter Creek; a novel. Viking Kestrel 1986 174p $12.95; Penguin Bks. pa $3.95 (5 and up) **Fic**

1. Family life—Fiction 2. Appalachian Mountains—Fiction
ISBN 0-670-80783-4; 0-14-032223-X (pa)
LC 85-40838

"After living in Colorado for most of her life, twelve-year-old Lacey returns with her mother, Campbell, and her mother's friend, David, to the North Carolina mountain village where she was born. Life is difficult there, for Lacey's grandmother has never forgiven her daughter for being an unwed mother and for taking her granddaughter away from her. The two women bicker constantly, and Lacey is caught between them. Lacey slowly begins to fit in when David, the only father she has ever known, is killed." Child Book Rev Serv

As mother and daughter "struggle to begin life without David, it is Grandmom who ultimately and believably emerges as the most profoundly changed by David's short-lived presence. Neither harsh in the portrayal of Grandmom's stubborn conventionality nor critical of Campbell's waywardness, the author shows that love survives in unlikely surroundings and that acknowledging its existence can be almost as difficult as grieving for its absence." Horn Book

A taste of blackberries; illustrated by Charles Robinson. Crowell 1973 58p il lib bdg $12.89; HarperCollins Pubs. pa $2.95 (4-6) **Fic**

1. Death—Fiction 2. Friendship—Fiction
ISBN 0-690-80512-8 (lib bdg); 0-06-440238-X (pa)
LC 72-7558

A "portrayal of the death of a close friend. While gathering Japanese beetles to help a neighbor, Jamie is stung by a bee and falls screaming and writhing to the ground. His best friend (never named) disgustedly stalks off, only to find later that Jamie is dead of the bee sting. The boy feels guilty because he thought Jamie was clowning and didn't try to help. The boy is very withdrawn the week of the funeral, but comes to grips with the tragedy and learns to manage his grief." SLJ

"A difficult and sensitive subject, treated with taste and honesty, is woven into a moving story about a believable little boy. The black-and-white illustrations are honest, affective, and sensitive." Horn Book

Smith, Janice Lee, 1949-

The kid next door and other headaches; stories about Adam Joshua; drawings by Dick Gackenbach. Harper & Row 1984 143p il $12.95; lib bdg $12.89; pa $2.95 (2-4) **Fic**

1. Friendship—Fiction
ISBN 0-06-025792-X; 0-06-025793-8 (lib bdg); 0-06-440182-0 (pa) LC 83-47689

"Adam Joshua and Nelson, who are best friends as well as next-door neighbors, play and battle as best friends do. Their finest hour is coping with a visit from Nelson's truly horrid cousin Cynthia." N Y Times Book Rev

"This book has all the ingredients necessary for the often reluctant transition from easy readers to chapter books: large print and an ample supply of dialogue, humor and wonderfully funny black-and-white illustrations." SLJ

Other available titles about Adam Joshua are:
It's not easy being George (1989)
The monster in the third dresser drawer and other stories about Adam Joshua (1981)
The show-and-tell war and other stories about Adam Joshua (1988)
The turkeys' side of it (1990)

Smith, Robert Kimmel, 1930-

Bobby Baseball; illustrated by Alan Tiegreen. Delacorte Press 1989 165p il $13.95 (4-6) **Fic**

1. Fathers and sons—Fiction 2. Baseball—Fiction
ISBN 0-385-29807-2 LC 89-1175

Ten-year-old Bobby is passionate about baseball and convinced that he is a great player. The only problem is to get a chance to prove his skill, especially to his father

"Baseball fans who share Bobby's fantasies will admire his determination and empathize with his stinging realization. Smith's crisp dialogue vivifies the book's appealing characters, and Tiegreen's illustrations lend an antic touch to Bobby's predicaments. This is an upbeat, refreshing celebration of the spirit of our national pastime." Publ Wkly

Chocolate fever; illustrated by Gioia Fiammenghi. Putnam 1989 c1972 93p il $10.99; Dell pa $2.95 (4-6) **Fic**

ISBN 0-399-61224-6; 0-440-41369-6 (pa)
LC 88-23508

A reissue of the title first published 1972 by Coward-McCann

"You've heard of too much of a good thing? You've never heard of it the way it happens to Henry Green. Henry's a chocolate maven, first class. No, that's too mild. Henry's absolutely freaky over chocolate, loco over cocoa. He can't get enough, until—aaarrrfh! Brown spots, brown bumps all over Henry. It's (gulp) 'Chocolate Fever.'" N Y Times Book Rev

"It's all quite preposterous and lots of laughs, and so are the cartoon illustrations." Publ Wkly

The war with Grandpa; illustrated by Richard Lauter. Delacorte Press 1984 141p il $12.95; lib bdg $12.95; Dell pa $2.95 (4-6) **Fic**

1. Grandfathers—Fiction 2. Family life—Fiction
ISBN 0-385-29312-7; 0-385-29314-3 (lib bdg); 0-440-49276-9 (pa) LC 83-14366

"Pete's Grandpa comes to live with the family and bumps Pete out of the room he's had 'forever.' Egged on by his buddies, Pete starts a war of notes and practical jokes. To his surprise, Grandpa enjoys the skirmishes and the two carry on a quiet campaign for a while. In the final episode, Pete realizes just how wrong he has been and Grandpa comes up with a happy solution. This should be a winner with the middle grade set." Child Book Rev Serv

Snyder, Zilpha Keatley

And condors danced. Delacorte Press 1987 211p $14.95; Dell pa $3.95 (5 and up) **Fic**

1. Ranch life—Fiction 2. California—Fiction
ISBN 0-385-29575-8; 0-440-40153-4 (pa) LC 87-5364

"Eleven-year-old Carly's world is circumscribed by a stern, intolerant father and an oblivious, ailing mother. But Carly is filled with resourcefulness, and she knows who loves her: her older siblings, her friend Matt, and especially Great-aunt Mehitabel and her Chinese housekeeper." SLJ

"This novel blends emotional insight and a joyous sense of play to create a lively, compelling tale." Publ Wkly

Below the root; illustrated by Alton Raible. Atheneum Pubs. 1975 231p il o.p.; TOR Bks. paperback available $2.95 (5 and up) **Fic**

1. Fantastic fiction
ISBN 0-8125-5476-0 (pa) LC 74-19489

Chosen to become one of a group of civil and religious leaders ruling the land of Green-Sky, thirteen-year-old Raamo's experiences make him question their teachings and lead him to uncover age-old deceptions

"There are long passages of description and explanation establishing Green Sky as a believable world, and though at times the allegory is a little heavy-handed, this is still an interesting suspenseful fantasy." SLJ

Other available titles about the land of Green-Sky are:
And all between (1976)
Until the celebration (1977)

The changeling; illustrated by Alton Raible. Atheneum Pubs. 1970 220p il o.p.; Dell paperback available $3.25 (5 and up) **Fic**

1. Friendship—Fiction
ISBN 0-440-41200-5 (pa) LC 79-115075

"Establishment pressures make it difficult for Martha to be friends with Ivy, whose family is notorious and unsettled. But Ivy opens up for Martha a world of make-believe and a realization of her special talents. Done in flashback technique, the story covers the girls' relationship from ages six to fifteen." SLJ

"The characterization is excellent, the writing style smooth and vigorous." Sutherland. The Best in Child Books

The Egypt game; drawings by Alton Raible. Atheneum Pubs. 1967 215p il $13.95; Dell pa $3.25 (5 and up) **Fic**

ISBN 0-689-30006-9; 0-440-42225-6 (pa) LC 67-2717

A Newbery Medal honor book, 1968

"Six children of different ethnic backgrounds secretly play a game invented by a white girl and a [black] girl who are fascinated by their own imaginations and by ancient Egypt. The Egypt game helps solve one girl's personal problems and it leads to the capture of a mentally ill murderer who attacks one of the girls." Wis Libr Bull

This book "is strong in characterization, the dialogue is superb, the plot is original, and the sequences in which the children are engaged in sustained imaginative play are fascinating, and often very funny. . . . In this story, the fact that the children are white, [black], and Oriental seems not a device but a natural consequence of grouping in a heterogeneous community. [This] is a distinguished book." Saturday Rev

The headless cupid; illustrated by Alton Raible. Atheneum Pubs. 1971 203p il $14.95; Dell pa $3.25 (5 and up) **Fic**

1. Occult sciences—Fiction
ISBN 0-689-20687-9; 0-440-43507-2 (pa)
LC 78-154763

A Newbery Medal honor book, 1972

Snyder, Zilpha Keatley—*Continued*

"Story of an unhappy adolescent's preoccupation with the occult, her relationships with her step-siblings, and her eventual acceptance of the tangible world. Set in present-day California." Publisher's note

"The author portrays children with acute understanding, evident both in her delineation of Amanda and David and of the distinctively different younger children. Good style, good characterization, good dialogue, good story." Sutherland. The Best in Child Books

Other available titles about the Stanley family are:
Blair's nightmare (1984)
The famous Stanley kidnapping case (1979)
Janie's private eyes (1989)

Libby on Wednesdays. Delacorte Press 1990 196p $14.95 (5 and up) **Fic**

1. Authorship—Fiction 2. Friendship—Fiction 3. School stories

ISBN 0-385-29979-6 LC 89-34959

"Libby, age eleven, very bright and the only child in an unconventional but strong household, has heretofore been home-educated. She is enrolled in public school for 'socialization' but soon finds that her peers tease her and mock her enormous wealth of knowledge. Only when she is selected for a writer's group does she forge ties to some equally gifted students." Child Book Rev Serv

"Vivid descriptions and clear portraits of the characters give an honest, forthright picture of these classmate-turned-friends who come to accept their difficulties and to care about each other. It's an absorbing story, filled with real young people and genuine concerns." SLJ

The velvet room; drawings by Alton Raible. Atheneum Pubs. 1965 216p il o.p.; Dell paperback available $3.25 (5 and up) **Fic**

1. Migrant labor—Fiction 2. Depressions, Economic—Fiction 3. California—Fiction

ISBN 0-440-40042-2 (pa) LC 65-10474

"Beset by the problems of growing up [in California during the Depression] in a migrant worker's family, Robin finds refuge from the real world in a deserted mansion with a book-lined room and a mysterious past." Natl Counc of Teach of Engl. Adventuring with Books. 2d edition

The witches of Worm; illustrated by Alton Raible. Atheneum Pubs. 1972 183p il $13.95; Dell pa $3.25 (5 and up) **Fic**

1. Witchcraft—Fiction 2. Cats—Fiction

ISBN 0-689-30066-2; 0-440-49727-2 (pa) LC 72-75283

A Newbery Medal honor book, 1973

Jessica, the neglected child of a divorcee, "finds a deserted, new-born kitten which she calls 'Worm' since it is virtually hairless and blind. When this Worm turns—daily becoming more dominant over its mistress—Jessica is convinced she is in the grip of a hellish force that makes her play harmful tricks on her mother and on her few friends." Publ Wkly

"This is a haunting story of the power of mind and ritual, as well as of misunderstanding, anger, loneliness and friendship. It is written with humor, pace, a sure feeling for conversation and a warm understanding of human nature." Commonweal

Sobol, Donald J., 1924-

Encyclopedia Brown, boy detective; illustrated by Leonard Shortall. Dutton Children's Bks. 1963 88p il $11.95; Bantam Bks. pa $2.95 (3-5) **Fic**

1. Mystery and detective stories

ISBN 0-525-67200-1; 0-553-15724-8 (pa) LC 63-9632

First published by Thomas Nelson

"Leroy Brown earns his nickname by applying his encyclopedic learning to community mysteries. The reader is asked to anticipate solutions before checking them in the back of the book." Natl Counc of Teach of Engl. Adventuring with Books. 2d edition

"The answers are logical; some are tricky, but there are no trick questions, and readers who like puzzles should enjoy the . . . challenge. The episodes are lightly humorous, brief, and simply written." Bull Cent Child Books

Other available titles about Encyclopedia Brown are:
Encyclopedia Brown and the case of the dead eagles (1975)
Encyclopedia Brown and the case of the disgusting sneakers (1990)
Encyclopedia Brown and the case of the exploding plumbing (1976)
Encyclopedia Brown and the case of the midnight visitor (1977)
Encyclopedia Brown and the case of the mysterious handprints (1985)
Encyclopedia Brown and the case of the secret pitch (1965)
Encyclopedia Brown and the case of the treasure hunt (1988)
Encyclopedia Brown carries on (1980)
Encyclopedia Brown finds the clues (1966)
Encyclopedia Brown gets his man (1967)
Encyclopedia Brown keeps the peace (1969)
Encyclopedia Brown lends a hand (1974)
Encyclopedia Brown saves the day (1970)
Encyclopedia Brown sets the pace (1982)
Encyclopedia Brown shows the way (1972)
Encyclopedia Brown solves them all (1968)
Encyclopedia Brown takes the cake! (1983)
Encyclopedia Brown takes the case (1973)
Encyclopedia Brown tracks them down (1971)

Sorensen, Virginia Eggertsen, 1912-

Miracles on Maple Hill; illustrated by Beth and Joe Krush. Harcourt Brace 1956 232p il hardcover o.p. paperback available $3.95 (4 and up) **Fic**

1. Family life—Fiction

ISBN 0-15-254561-1 (pa) LC 56-8358

Awarded the Newbery Medal, 1957

"Ever since Father had returned from a prison camp, weary, hurt and discouraged, home had been an unhappy place with everyone irritable and worried. Hoping that the outdoor life would help Father, ten-year-old Marly, who believed in miracles, and her family moved from the city to Maple Hill to open and live in Grandmother's old Pennsylvania farm house. This heartwarming, memorable family story tells of the miracles that happened during a year from one sugaring time to the next—the miracles of nature and the changing seasons, wonderful neighbors, and, best of all, Father's steady improvement and the family's drawing together again in understanding and happiness." Booklist

Southall, Ivan, 1921-

Let the balloon go. Bradbury Press 1985 c1968 136 p $11.95 (4 and up) **Fic**

1. Cerebral palsy—Fiction 2. Physically handicapped children—Fiction
ISBN 0-02-786220-8 LC 84-5984

First published 1968 by St. Martin's Press

Handicapped by cerebral palsy and overprotected by his parents, a twelve-year-old, left alone for the first time, in a desperate need to exert his independence, does precisely what he has been forbidden to do

"Librarians looking for novels about children with physical disabilities will find this noteworthy." Booklist

Speare, Elizabeth George, 1908-

The bronze bow. Houghton Mifflin 1961 255p $13.95; pa $7.95 (6 and up) **Fic**

1. Jesus Christ—Fiction 2. Christianity—Fiction 3. Palestine—Fiction
ISBN 0-395-07113-5; 0-395-13719-5 (pa) LC 61-10640

Awarded the Newbery Medal, 1962

"A book about the days of the early Christians. A vividly written story of a young Jewish rebel who was won over to the gentle teachings of Jesus. Daniel had sworn vengence against the Romans who had killed his parents, and he had become one of a band of outlaws. Forced to return to the village to care for his sister, Daniel found ways—dangerous ways—to work against the Roman soldiers. Each time he saw the Rabbi Jesus, the youth was drawn to his cause; at last he resolved his own conflict by giving up his hatred and, as a follower of the Master, accepting his enemies. The story has drama and pace, fine characterization, and colorful background detail; the theme of conflict and conversion is handled with restraint and perception." Bull Cent Child Books

The sign of the beaver. Houghton Mifflin 1983 135p $12.95; Dell pa $3.50 (5 and up) **Fic**

1. Frontier and pioneer life—Fiction 2. Indians of North America—Fiction 3. Friendship—Fiction
ISBN 0-395-33890-5; 0-440-47900-2 (pa) LC 83-118

Also available ABC-CLIO large print edition $15.95 (ISBN 1-55736-037-5)

A Newbery Medal honor book, 1984

Left alone to guard the family's wilderness home in eighteenth-century Maine, Matt is hard-pressed to survive until local Indians teach him their skills

Matt "begins to understand the Indians' ingenuity and respect for nature and the devastating impact of the encroachment of the white man. In a quiet but not unsuspenseful story . . . the author articulates historical facts along with the adventures and the thoughts, emotions, and developing insights of a young adolescent." Horn Book

The witch of Blackbird Pond. Houghton Mifflin 1958 249p $13.95; Dell pa $3.50 (6 and up) **Fic**

1. Connecticut—History—1600-1775, Colonial period—Fiction 2. Witchcraft—Fiction 3. Puritans—Fiction
ISBN 0-395-07114-3; 0-440-99577-9 (pa) LC 58-11063

Also available ABC-CLIO large print edition $15.95 (ISBN 1-55736-138-X)

Awarded the Newbery Medal, 1959

"Headstrong and undisciplined, Barbados-bred Kit Tyler is an embarrassment to her Puritan relatives, and her sincere attempts to aid a reputed witch soon bring her to trial as a suspect." Child Books Too Good to Miss

Sperry, Armstrong, 1897-

Call it courage; illustrations by the author. Macmillan 1940 95p il $11.95; pa $3.95 (5 and up) **Fic**

1. Polynesia—Fiction
ISBN 0-02-786030-2; 0-689-71391-6 (pa) LC 40-4229

Also available ABC-CLIO large print edition $15.95 (ISBN 1-55736-147-9)

Awarded the Newbery Medal, 1941

"Because he fears the ocean, a Polynesian boy is scorned by his people and must redeem himself by an act of courage. His lone journey to a sacred island and the dangers he faces there earn him the name Mafatu, 'Stout Heart.' Dramatic illustrations add atmosphere and mystery." Hodges. Books for Elem Sch Libr

Spinelli, Jerry, 1941-

Maniac Magee; a novel. Little, Brown 1990 184p $13.95 (5 and up) **Fic**

1. Orphans—Fiction 2. Homeless people—Fiction 3. Race relations—Fiction
ISBN 0-316-80722-2 LC 89-27144

Awarded the Newbery Medal, 1991

"Orphaned at three, Jeffery Lionel Magee, after eight unhappy years with relatives, one day takes off running. A year later, he ends up 200 miles away in Two Mills, a highly segregated community. Part tall tale and part contemporary realistic fiction, this unusual novel magically weaves timely issues of homelessness, racial prejudice, and illiteracy into an energetic story that bursts with creativity enthusiasm, and hope for the future. In short, it's a celebration of life." Booklist

Spyri, Johanna, 1827-1901

Heidi (4 and up) **Fic**

1. Alps—Fiction 2. Switzerland—Fiction

Some editions are:

Crown $12.99 Illustrated by Jessie Willcox Smith (ISBN 0-517-61814-1)
Delacorte Press $19.95 Translated by Helen B. Dole with emendations and revisions by John Githens (ISBN 0-385-30244-4) Has title: Tomi Ungerer's Heidi
Golden Bks. (Golden classics) $8.95 Translated by Helen B. Dole; illustrated by Judith Cheng (ISBN 0-307-17114-0)
Knopf $18.95 Illustrations by Ruth Sanderson (ISBN 0-394-53820-X)
Messner lib bdg $14.79 Illustrated by Troy Howell (ISBN 0-671-45652-0)

First published 1880

"The story of Heidi is the story of the greatness of her affection for her pet goats, for Peter and her grandfather, and for her mountain home. Permeating the whole tale is the play of sunshine and shadow on the slopes of the jagged peaks of the great, glittering, snow-

Spyri, Johanna, 1827-1901—*Continued*
capped mountains of Heidi's [Swiss] Alpine home. A book which finds a responsive chord in every young heart." Toronto Public Libr

Stannard, Russell
The time and space of Uncle Albert. Holt & Co. 1990 c1989 120p il $14.95 (5 and up) **Fic**

1. Relativity (Physics)—Fiction 2. Uncles—Fiction 3. Science fiction
ISBN 0-8050-1309-1 LC 89-24653

First published 1989 in the United Kingdom

"Young Gedanken's Uncle Albert sends her on a series of trips into space in a 'thought bubble' created by his powerful imagination. As she approaches the speed of light, they find that light, weight, and even time act strangely and they try to figure out why." Booklist

"Though not always successful as a novel, Gedanken's school science project and Uncle Albert's research provide an excellent introduction to Einstein's theory. Includes a brief discussion of Einstein's contributions to science." Sci Child

Includes bibliography

Steig, William, 1907-
Abel's island. Farrar, Straus & Giroux 1976 117p il o.p. paperback available $3.50 (3-6) **Fic**

1. Mice—Fiction 2. Survival (after airplane accidents, shipwrecks, etc.)—Fiction
ISBN 0-374-40016-4 (pa) LC 75-35918

"Abel is a mouse who lives in cultured comfort on an inherited income and dotes on his bride Amanda. Ever gentlemanly, Abel leaves the safety of a cave (they've taken shelter while on a picnic) to rescue Amanda's gauzy scarf. He is swept off by wind and rain, catapulted into a torrent of water, and lands on an island. This is really sort of a Robinson Crusoe Tale, as the heretofore pampered and indolent Abel learns to cope with solitude, find food and shelter, avoid a predatory owl, and eventually find his way back—a year later—to his loving wife and luxurious home." Bull Cent Child Books

"The line drawings washed with gray faithfully and delightfully record not only the rigors of Abel's experiences but the refinement of his domestic existence." Horn Book

Dominic; story and pictures by William Steig. Farrar, Straus & Giroux 1972 145p il o.p. paperback available $3.50 (4 and up) **Fic**

1. Dogs—Fiction
ISBN 0-374-41826-8 (pa) LC 70-188272

Dominic, a gregarious dog, sets out on the high road one day, going no place in particular, but moving along to find whatever he can. And that turns out to be plenty, including an invalid pig who leaves Dominic his fortune; a variety of friends and adventures; and even—in the end—his life's companion

"A singular blend of naîveté and sophistication, comic commentary and philosophizing, the narrative handles situation clichés with humor and flair—perhaps because of the author's felicitous turn of phrase, his verbal cartooning, and his integration of text and illustrations. A chivalrous and optimistic tribute to gallantry and romance." Horn Book

The real thief; story and pictures by William Steig. Farrar, Straus & Giroux 1973 58p il hardcover o.p. paperback available $2.95 (2-5) **Fic**

1. Animals—Fiction 2. Robbers and outlaws—Fiction
ISBN 0-374-46208-9 (pa) LC 73-77910

"Proud of his job as guard to the Royal Treasury, loyal to his king (Basil the bear) Gawain the goose is baffled by the repeated theft of gold and jewels from the massive building to which only Gawain and Basil have keys. He is heartsick when the king dismisses him publicly and calls him a disgrace to the kingdom. Sentenced to prison, the goose flies off to isolation. The true thief, a mouse, is penitent and decides that he will go on stealing so that the king will know Gawain is innocent." Bull Cent Child Books

"Steig's gray line-and-wash drawings provide a charming accompaniment to a wholly winning story." SLJ

Stevenson, Laura Caroline, 1946-
Happily after all. Houghton Mifflin 1990 252p $14.95 (4 and up) **Fic**

1. Mothers and daughters—Fiction 2. Vermont—Fiction
ISBN 0-395-50216-0 LC 89-24709

"When Becca's father dies, she's sent from California to Vermont to live with her mother. The change is drastic and difficult for several reasons, not the least of which is Becca's belief that her mother had abandoned her when she was two years old." Booklist

"Using the rugged Vermont mountains as her backdrop, Stevenson weaves a rich tapestry, colored with adventure and textured with emotions. Her descriptions are simple and remarkably clear; her characterizations are sharply defined." Publ Wkly

Stevenson, Robert Louis, 1850-1894
Treasure Island (6 and up) **Fic**

1. Buried treasure—Fiction 2. Pirates

Some editions are:

Grosset & Dunlap (Illustrated junior lib) $10.95 Illustrated by Norman Price (ISBN 0-448-06025-6)
Schocken Bks. pa $4.95 Drawings by Mervyn Peake (ISBN 0-8052-0620-5)
Scribner $20.95 Illustrated by N. C. Wyeth (ISBN 0-684-17160-0)

First published 1882

Young Jim Hawkins discovers a treasure map in the chest of an old sailor who dies under mysterious circumstances at his mother's inn. He shows it to Dr. Livesey and Squire Trelawney who agree to outfit a ship and sail to Treasure Island. Among the crew are the pirate Long John Silver and his followers who are in pursuit of the treasure

"A masterpiece among romances. . . . Pew, Black Dog, and Long John Silver are a villainous trio, strongly individualized, shedding an atmosphere of malignancy and terror. The scenery of isle and ocean contrasts vividly with the savagery of the action." Baker. Guide to the Best Fic

Stockton, Frank, 1834-1902

The Bee-man of Orn; pictures by Maurice Sendak. Harper & Row 1986 c1964 44p il $13.95; lib bdg $13.89; pa $4.95 (4-6) **Fic**

1. Fairy tales

ISBN 0-06-025818-7; 0-06-025819-5 (lib bdg); 0-06-433125-8 (pa) LC 85-45813

A reissue of the title first published 1964 by Holt, Rinehart & Winston; the story originally appeared in the author's The Bee-man of Orn, and other fanciful tales, published 1887 by Scribner

"Completely content, living a simple and busy life with his omnipresent bees, the Bee-Man becomes perturbed when a Junior Sorcerer informs him that he has undoubtedly been transformed from some other sort of being. What kind of being that is, he is not qualified to say—so the Bee-Man sets out to find his previous incarnation." Bull Cent Child Books

The story "has been illustrated to perfection. . . . A delightful and imaginative piece of bookmaking." Publ Wkly

The Griffin and the Minor Canon; by Frank R. Stockton; with illustrations by Maurice Sendak. Harper & Row 1986 c1963 55p il $13.95; lib bdg $13.89; pa $4.95 (3-5) **Fic**

1. Animals, Mythical

ISBN 0-06-025816-0; 0-06-025817-9 (lib bdg); 0-06-443126-6 (pa) LC 85-45827

A reissue of the title first published 1963 by Holt; the story originally appeared in the author's Fanciful tales, published 1894 by Scribner

"The last of the griffins visits a medieval cathedral town and through his ferocity, and his friendship for the gentle minor canon, reforms both young and old alike." Commonweal

"The fine flow of language . . . will please those who read aloud to children as well as the children themselves; and on their own the fairy tale ages will be drawn naturally to this fully illustrated book. Sendak's carefully detailed gothic sketches and his prefacing words reveal his work to have been a labor of love." Horn Book

Stolz, Mary, 1920-

Cat walk; with drawings by Erik Blegvad. Harper & Row 1983 120p il $12.95; lib bdg $12.89; pa $2.95 (3-6) **Fic**

1. Cats—Fiction

ISBN 0-06-025974-4; 0-06-025975-2 (lib bdg); 0-06-440155-3 (pa) LC 82-47576

Yearning to be more than just a barnyard rat catcher, a young cat in search of a name embarks on a journey that finally leads him to a special place he can call a home

"Children may object to the fact that while the adults in this well-written book are uniformly kind to the cat, every child is intentionally or unintentionally cruel to him. In spite of that, this is a perceptive story, simple in its realistic portrayal of one cat's venture through life. The illustrations by Erik Blegvad are a delight and an asset to the story." SLJ

The cuckoo clock; illustrated by Pamela Johnson. Godine 1987 c1986 84p il $12.95 (4-6) **Fic**

1. Orphans—Fiction 2. Clocks and watches—Fiction 3. Magic—Fiction

ISBN 0-87923-653-1 LC 86-45538

"Fiction with a fairy tale quality, this is the story of Erich the foundling's friendship with an old clockmaker, Ula, in the Black Forest 'once upon a time.' . . . Stolz' writing is characteristically careful and clean, with the fantasy elements—a wooden cuckoo's coming to life and Ula's ascension to heaven—skillfully built into the reality of the story. The book design and fine textured pencil drawings are equally strong, creating the total effect of an old-fashioned scene in cameo." Bull Cent Child Books

A dog on Barkham Street; pictures by Leonard Shortall. Harper & Row 1960 184p il lib bdg $14.89; pa $2.50 (4-6) **Fic**

1. Dogs—Fiction

ISBN 0-06-025841-1 (lib bdg); 0-06-440160-X (pa) LC 60-5787

"Fifth-grader Edward Frost has two seemingly insurmountable problems—to rid himself of the constant tormenting by the bully who lives next door and to convince his parents that he is responsible enough to have a dog. It is the coming of his irresponsible vagabond uncle with a beautiful young collie that precipitates the solution of Edward's problems." Booklist

"Simple, everyday events and very familiar people make up this story, but there is nothing ordinary about the way those ingredients are assembled. . . . This author has a remarkable ability to get inside her characters, whether they are young boys, adolescent girls, parents or hobos, and the result in this book is a reading experience as sharp as reality." Horn Book

Other available titles about Edward Frost and Martin Hastings are:

The bully of Barkham Street (1963)
The explorer of Barkham Street (1985)

Quentin Corn; illustrated by Pamela Johnson. Godine 1985 121p il $12.95; Dell pa $2.75 (4-6) **Fic**

1. Pigs—Fiction

ISBN 0-87923-553-5; 0-440-40043-0 (pa) LC 84-48321

Realizing his fate is to be spareribs, a pig disguises himself as a boy, runs away, finds employment, and becomes friends with a little girl

"As expected, Stolz casts a spell over readers, mesmerizing them with the latest of her beautifully written and convincing fantasies. Johnson's drawings add zip to the story of a smart, genteel pig who escapes a waiting oven and passes as a human boy." Publ Wkly

Zekmet, the stone carver; a tale of ancient Egypt; illustrated by Deborah Nourse Lattimore. Harcourt Brace Jovanovich 1988 unp il $13.95 (2-4) **Fic**

1. Egypt—Fiction

ISBN 0-15-299961-2 LC 86-22931

Chosen to design a magnificent monument for a vain and demanding Pharaoh, an Egyptian stone carver conceives of and begins work on the Sphinx

"The clear prose and hieroglyphic-like illustrations

Stolz, Mary, 1920-—*Continued*
make this an easily accessible story that will appeal as a simple fable and as a satirical commentary upon the nature of human glory." Child Book Rev Serv

Streatfeild, Noel, 1895-1986

Theatre shoes, or other people's shoes; illustrated by Richard Floethe. Random House 1945 282p il o.p.; Dell paperback available $2.95 (5 and up) **Fic**

1. Great Britain—Fiction
ISBN 0-440-48791-9 (pa) LC 45-9989

"Sorrel, Mark, and Holly Forbes are sent to their maternal grandmother's when their father's plane is shot down during World War II. They are thrust into the middle of a theatrical family, none of whom they know, but the children's own talents manage to come to light. Solid family fare." Booklist

Thursday's child; illustrated by Peggy Fortnum. Random House 1971 c1970 275p il o.p.; Dell paperback available $3.50 (4 and up) **Fic**

1. Orphans—Fiction 2. Great Britain—Fiction
ISBN 0-440-48687-4 (pa) LC 71-123073

First published 1970 in the United Kingdom

Ten-year-old Margaret Thursday, an "orphan of turn-of-the-century England refuses to be subdued by anybody—or anything. For openers, she becomes the first runaway from St. Luke's orphanage [taking two little orphan boys with her;] the first girl to work as a 'legger' on the canals; and as the story ends she has started a career as actress (playing Little Lord Fauntleroy) . . . with a repertory theater group." Best Sellers

"Although the setting and situations are in the turn-of-the-century tradition of 'orphan stories,' the heroine is a remarkably contemporary character whose final decision to remain independent of her would-be benefactors is logical and consistent with a fully realized personality." Horn Book

Sutcliff, Rosemary, 1920-

Flame-colored taffeta. Farrar, Straus & Giroux 1986 129p $11.95; pa $3.50 (5 and up) **Fic**

1. Smuggling—Fiction 2. Great Britain—History—0-1066—Fiction
ISBN 0-374-32344-5; 0-374-42341-5 (pa)
LC 86-18351

This is a "tale of a girl who rescues a mysterious, wounded man. Twelve-year-old Damaris, who lives on a seaside Sussex farm, discovers a young man who has been shot in the leg. She and 13-year-old Peter hide the man, who calls himself Tom Wildgoose, in their secret meeting place—a half-ruined cottage in the forest." Publ Wkly

"Unlike much fiction set in the past, the suspenseful story involves its characters less in historical events than in personal interplay; Damaris and Peter are passionately concerned with Tom's survival and safety rather than with his hopeless cause." Horn Book

Frontier Wolf. Dutton 1981 c1980 196p $11.50 (6 and up) **Fic**

1. Great Britain—History—0-1066—Fiction
ISBN 0-525-30260-3 LC 80-39849

First published 1980 in the United Kingdom

As punishment for his poor judgment, a young, inexperienced Roman army officer is sent to Northern England to assume the command of a motley group known as the Frontier Wolves

"This is an exciting adventure story full of action and blood. It is also a tale of courage and perseverance. . . . Good booktalking material." Voice Youth Advocates

Sun horse, moon horse; decorations by Shirley Felts. Dutton 1978 c1977 111p $9.95 (5 and up) **Fic**

1. Great Britain—History—0-1066—Fiction
ISBN 0-525-40495-3 LC 77-25440

First published 1977 in the United Kingdom

"Lubrin Dhu is the small dark son of an Iron Age chieftain who dies defending the clan against a tribe retreating before the Roman menace. Lubrin frees his clan by creating for his captors a vast horse image on the side of the chalk hills, knowing as he does so that only his death will breathe true life into the horse." Times Lit Suppl

"Sutcliff country is austere and ennobling; her characters are dwarfed by a sense of their historical and mythical significance. But as always, the story is fast-moving and brilliantly vivid, and Lubrin Dhu is a likeable hero." Christ Sci Monit

Tate, Eleanora E., 1948-

Just an overnight guest. Dial Bks. for Young Readers 1980 182p $8.95; lib bdg $8.44 (4-6) **Fic**

1. Family life—Fiction 2. Blacks—Fiction
ISBN 0-8037-4225-8; 0-8037-4223-1 (lib bdg)
LC 80-12970

"The story is told by nine-year-old Margie, who is . . . appalled . . . when Momma brings a hostile, obstreperous four-year-old to their home. Margie can't stand little Ethel, resents sharing her bed, resents even more sharing her mother's attention, and is sure that when Daddy (driver for a long-distance moving company) gets home, Ethel will be ousted. What she learns is that Ethel is the child of her uncle and a white woman; the latter has decamped." Bull Cent Child Books

"In this first novel, [the author] does a fine job presenting the emotional complexities of Margie's initiation into adult life's moral ambiguities. She does so with sympathy and sensitivity. If she drives home her point with a slightly heavy hand—or if some of the characters come across as types rather than people, Miss Tate has imbued the situation with enough realism to make it plausible." N Y Times Book Rev

Taylor, Mildred D.

The gold Cadillac; pictures by Michael Hays. Dial Bks. for Young Readers 1987 43p il $11.95; lib bdg $11.89 (3-5) **Fic**

1. Blacks—Fiction 2. Prejudices—Fiction 3. Race relations—Fiction
ISBN 0-8037-0342-2; 0-8037-0343-0 (lib bdg)
LC 86-11526

Taylor, Mildred D.—*Continued*

"The shiny gold Cadillac that Daddy brings home one summer evening marks a stepping stone in the lives of Wilma and 'lois, two black sisters growing up in Ohio during the fifties. At first neighbors and relatives shower them with attention. But when the family begins the long journey to the South to show off the car to their Mississippi relatives, the girls, for the first time, encounter the undisguised ugliness of racial prejudice." Horn Book

"Full-page sepia paintings effectively portray the characters, setting, and mood of the story events as Hays ably demonstrates his understanding of the social and emotional environments which existed for blacks during this period." SLJ

Roll of thunder, hear my cry; frontispiece by Jerry Pinkney. Dial Bks. for Young Readers 1976 276p $14.95; Bantam Bks. pa $3.50 (4 and up) **Fic**

1. Blacks—Fiction 2. Depressions, Economic—Fiction 3. Mississippi—Fiction
ISBN 0-8037-7473-7; 0-553-25450-2 (pa) LC 76-2287

Also available ABC-CLIO large print edition $15.95 (ISBN 1-55736-140-1)

Awarded the Newbery Medal, 1977

"The time is 1933. The place is Spokane, Mississippi where the Logans, the only black family who own their own land, wage a courageous struggle to remain independent, displeasing a white plantation owner bent on taking their land. But this suspenseful tale is also about the story's young narrator, Cassie, and her three brothers who decide to wage their own personal battles to maintain the self-dignity and pride with which they were raised. . . . Ms. Taylor's richly textured novel shows a strong, proud black family . . . resisting rather than succumbing to oppression." Child Book Rev Serv

Followed by: Let the circle be unbroken, entered below under Song of the trees

Song of the trees; pictures by Jerry Pinkney. Dial Bks. for Young Readers 1975 48p il $12.95; lib bdg $12.89; Bantam Bks. pa $2.75 (4 and up) **Fic**

1. Blacks—Fiction 2. Depressions, Economic—Fiction 3. Mississippi—Fiction
ISBN 0-8037-5452-3; 0-8037-5453-1 (lib bdg); 0-553-27587-9 (pa) LC 74-18598

The friendship, Let the circle be unbroken, and The road to Memphis were awarded the Coretta Scott King Award for text in 1988, 1982, and 1991 respectively

"True story of how a black family leaving Mississippi during the Depression was cheated into selling for practically nothing valuable and beautiful giant old pines and hickories, beeches and walnuts in the forest surrounding their house." Natl Counc of Teach of Engl. Adventuring with Books

Other available titles about Cassie Logan and her family are:
The friendship (1987)
Let the circle be unbroken (1981)
Mississippi bridge (1990)
The road to Memphis (1990)

Roll of thunder, hear my cry, chronologically following Song of the trees, is entered above

Taylor, Sydney, 1904-

All-of-a-kind family; illustrated by Helen John. Follett 1951 192p il o.p.; Taylor Productions reprint available $11.95 (4-6) **Fic**

1. Jews—New York (N.Y.)—Fiction 2. New York (N.Y.)—Fiction
ISBN 0-929093-00-3 LC 51-13398

"Five little Jewish girls grow up in New York's lower east side in a happy home atmosphere before the first World War." Carnegie Libr of Pittsburgh

"A genuine and delightful picture of a Jewish family . . . with an understanding mother and father, rich in kindness and fun though poor in money. The important part the public library played in the lives of these children is happily evident; and the Jewish holiday celebrations are particularly well described." Horn Book

Other available titles about this family are:
All-of-a-kind family downtown (1957)
All-of-a-kind family uptown (1957)
Ella of all-of-a-kind family (1978)
More all-of-a-kind family (1954)

Taylor, Theodore, 1921 or 2-

The cay. Doubleday 1969 137p $13.95; Avon Bks. pa $3.50 (5 and up) **Fic**

1. Race relations—Fiction 2. Caribbean region—Fiction 3. Survival (after airplane accidents, shipwrecks, etc.)—Fiction 4. Blind—Fiction
ISBN 0-385-07906-0; 0-380-01003-8 (pa) LC 69-15161

Also available ABC-CLIO large print edition $15.95 (ISBN 1-55736-163-0)

"When the freighter which was to take Phillip and his mother from wartime Curacao to the United States is torpedoed, Phillip finds himself afloat on a small raft with a hugh, old, very black West Indian man. Phillip becomes blind from injuries and resents his dependence upon old Timothy. Through exciting adventures on a very small cay (coral island), Phillip learns to overcome his prejudice toward Timothy and to see him as a man and a friend. Following the aftermath of a fierce tropical storm, Timothy dies. Phillip survives to live a more complete life because of his friend and because he has grown with the changes that occurred in his life." Read Ladders for Hum Relat. 5th edition

"Starkly dramatic, believable and compelling." Saturday Rev

Terris, Susan

Author! Author! Farrar, Straus & Giroux 1990 167p $13.95 (6 and up) **Fic**

1. Authors—Fiction 2. Parent and child—Fiction 3. Adolescence—Fiction
ISBN 0-374-34995-9

"Valerie, 12, has just had her first children's book published, under the mentorship of poet Tekla Reis, and in the process has alienated her parents, her friends, and her editor. . . . Valerie seeks out the company of 45-year-old Tekla, longtime friend of her parents, and immerses herself in the mystery of her true parentage, having convinced herself that her parents, stressed-out bankers, couldn't possibly have produced her, a talented writer." SLJ

"As a preteen, Valerie is quite believable: moody, eager to be grown-up, embarrassed by parents, and prone

Terris, Susan—*Continued*
to eavesdropping on adult conversations and drawing her own conclusions. . . . The San Francisco setting adds color to the novel and younger readers will enjoy Terris' light tale of fame at an early age." Voice Youth Advocates

Thiele, Colin, 1920-
Shadow shark. Harper & Row 1988 c1985 214p $13.95; lib bdg $13.89 (5 and up) **Fic**
1. Sharks—Fiction 2. Sea stories 3. Australia—Fiction
ISBN 0-06-026178-1; 0-06-026179-X (lib bdg)
LC 87-45566

First published 1985 in Australia with title: Seashores and shadows

Two fourteen-year-old cousins join a group of fishermen in pursuit of a massive shark off the coast of Southern Australia

"The hunt itself is exciting, but never romanticized. . . . Any combination of shark hunting and survival story has tremendous appeal, of course, and both parts of the novel are filled with you-are-there detail and immediacy." Bull Cent Child Books

Thomas, Jane Resh, 1936-
The comeback dog; drawings by Troy Howell. Clarion Bks. 1981 62p il $13.95 (3-5) **Fic**
1. Dogs—Fiction 2. Farm life—Fiction
ISBN 0-395-29432-0 LC 80-12886

"Grieving over the loss of his dog, Daniel claims he doesn't want another dog, but when he finds one that is near death, he takes her home and gives her loving care. The dog, Lady, gets well but seems fearful and hostile; irritated, Daniel lets her off the leash to run away. When she comes back, some weeks later, her face bristling with porcupine quills, he's again irritated but quickly decides to help Lady and is then gratified when she shows trust and affection." Bull Cent Child Books

"The matter-of-fact, life-must-go-on attitude of Daniel's concerned parents is particularly well communicated. . . . Numerous soft pencil drawings greatly enhance the exceptionally gentle, poignant story." Horn Book

Thurber, James, 1894-1961
Many moons; illustrated by Louis Slobodkin. Harcourt Brace 1943 unp il $14.95; pa $4.95 (1-4) **Fic**
1. Fairy tales
ISBN 0-15-251873-8; 0-15-251877-9 (pa)
LC 43-51250

Also available with illustrations by Marc Simont for $14.95 (ISBN 0-15-251872-X)

Awarded the Caldecott Medal, 1944

This is "the story of a little princess who fell ill of a surfeit of raspberry tarts and would get well only if she could have the moon. The solving of this baffling court problem, how to get the moon, results in an original and entertaining picture-storybook." Booklist

"Louis Slobodkin's pictures float on the pages in four colors: black and white cannot represent them. They are the substance of dreams . . . the long thoughts little children, and some adults wise as they, have about life." N Y Her Trib Books

Titus, Eve
Basil of Baker Street; illustrated by Paul Galdone. McGraw-Hill 1958 96p il lib bdg $8.95; Pocket Bks. pa $2.50 (3-5) **Fic**
1. Doyle, Sir Arthur Conan, 1859-1930—Parodies, travesties, etc. 2. Mice—Fiction 3. Mystery and detective stories
ISBN 0-07-064907-3 (lib bdg); 0-318-37408-0 (pa)
LC 58-8050

"Whittlesey House publications"

"Basil of Baker Street is the Sherlock Holmes of the mouse world, having studied scientific sleuthing at the feet of the famous English detective. Here in an entertaining, delightfully illustrated story Basil's assistant, Dr. Dawson, tells how the great Basil solves a baffling kidnapping case, restores the children to their parents, and brings the dangerous kidnappers to justice. Acquaintance with Sherlock Holmes and Dr. Watson is not essential to the enjoyment of this small-scale detective story." Booklist

Other available titles about Basil are:
Basil and the lost colony (1964)
Basil and the pygmy cats (1971)
Basil in Mexico (1976)
Basil in the Wild West (1982)

Tolkien, J. R. R. (John Ronald Reuel), 1892-1973
The hobbit; or, There and back again; illustrated by the author. Houghton Mifflin 1938 310p il $13.95; Ballantine Bks. pa $5.95 (4 and up) **Fic**
1. Fantastic fiction
ISBN 0-395-07122-4; 0-345-33968-1 (pa) LC 38-5859

Also available from Houghton Mifflin in an edition with illustrations by Michael Hague for $24.95 (ISBN 0-395-36290-3)

First published 1937 in the United Kingdom

"This fantasy features the adventures of hobbit Bilbo Baggins, who joins a band of dwarfs led by Gandalf the Wizard. Together they seek to recover the stolen treasure that is hidden in Lonely Mountain and guarded by Smaug the Dragon." Shapiro. Fic for Youth. 2d edition

Followed by: The lord of the rings, a trilogy intended for older readers

Townsend, John Rowe
Dan alone. Lippincott 1983 214p $10.95; lib bdg $10.89 (6 and up) **Fic**
1. Abandoned children—Fiction 2. Family life—Fiction 3. Great Britain—Fiction
ISBN 0-397-32053-1; 0-397-32054-X (lib bdg)
LC 82-49051

"A novel set in an industrial town in England in the 1920s. After his mother abandons him (he has never known his real father), and after some time spent among pickpockets and other scoundrels, young Dan finally finds the real family of his fantasies." Soc Educ

"Reminiscent of 'Oliver Twist' and 'Nicholas Nickleby'. . . this will engross readers from the onset. . .

Townsend, John Rowe—*Continued*

. This is a meaty, satisfying tale with characters and an ambience that will long be remembered." Booklist

The visitors. Lippincott 1977 221p $12.25 (6 and up) **Fic**

1. Science fiction 2. Great Britain—Fiction
ISBN 0-397-31752-2 LC 77-7197

Published in the United Kingdom with title: The Xanadu Manuscript

"John Dunham, teen-age narrator, and his family become involved with the Wyatts, parents and daughter who have time-traveled from the year 2149 to present-day Cambridge, England." Child Book Rev Serv

This fantasy "displays the author's ability to design a substantial plot, his skill in portraying major and minor characters and dramatizing their interrelationships, and his crisp, confident storytelling." Horn Book

Travers, P. L. (Pamela L.), 1906-

Mary Poppins; illustrated by Mary Shepard. rev ed. Harcourt Brace Jovanovich 1981 206p il $14.95 (4-6) **Fic**

1. Fantastic fiction
ISBN 0-15-252408-8 LC 81-7273

First published 1934

"The chapter 'Bad Tuesday,' in which Mary and the Banks children travel to the four corners of the earth and meet the inhabitants, has been criticized for portraying minorities in an unfavorable light. In 1971 when the paperback edition came out, Travers altered the language of the Africans but has felt it necessary to revise the chapter completely in order to eliminate the negative stereotypical elements. The revised edition accomplishes this by having the entourage meet up with a polar bear, macaw, panda, and dolphin instead of Eskimos, Africans, Chinese, and American Indians. The change is fortuitous, and should put the matter to rest." Booklist

Other available titles about Mary Poppins are:
Mary Poppins and the house next door (1989)
Mary Poppins comes back (1935)
Mary Poppins from A to Z (1962)
Mary Poppins in Cherry Tree Lane (1982)
Mary Poppins opens the door (1943)

Treviño, Elizabeth Borton de, 1904-

El Güero; a true adventure story; pictures by Leslie W. Bowman. Farrar, Straus & Giroux 1989 99p il $12.95 (5 and up) **Fic**

1. Baja California (Mexico: Peninsula)—Fiction
ISBN 0-374-31995-2 LC 88-46133

"Set in the turbulent mid-1800s in Baja California, this adventure is based on the childhood of the author's father-in-law, the son of a judge exiled when Porfirio Diaz seized power in Mexico in 1876. Portrays in detail the land, people, and life in rugged, unsettled Baja." Soc Educ

"The soft pencil sketches add depth and historic perspective to the simple, first-person narrative." Horn Book

I, Juan de Pareja. Farrar, Straus & Giroux 1965 180p o.p. paperback available $3.50 (6 and up) **Fic**

1. Juan, de Pareja—Fiction 2. Velázquez, Diego, 1599-1660—Fiction
ISBN 0-374-43525-1 (pa) LC 65-19330

Awarded the Newbery Medal, 1966

"Bell books"

The black slave boy, Juan de Pareja, "began a new life when he was taken into the household of the Spanish painter, Velázquez. As he worked beside the great artist learning how to grind and mix colors and prepare canvases, there grew between them a warm friendship based on mutual respect and love of art. Created from meager but authentic facts, the story, told by Juan, depicts the life and character of Velázquez and the loyalty of the talented seventeenth-century slave who eventually won his freedom and the right to be an artist." Booklist

Tunis, John R., 1889-1975

The kid from Tomkinsville. Harcourt Brace Jovanovich 1987 278p (Baseball diamonds, 1) $14.95; pa $3.95 (5 and up) **Fic**

1. Baseball—Fiction
ISBN 0-15-242568-3; 0-15-242567-5 (pa) LC 86-27104

Also available from Smith, P. $15.75 (ISBN 0-8446-6353-0)

A reissue of the title first published 1943

As the newest addition to the Brooklyn Dodgers, young Roy Tucker's pitching helps pull the team out of a slump; but, when a freak accident ends his career as a pitcher, he must try to find another place for himself on the team

Other available titles about Roy Tucker and the Brooklyn Dodgers are:
Keystone kids (1943)
Rookie of the year (1944)
World Series (1941)

Turner, Ann Warren

Grasshopper summer. Macmillan 1989 166p $13.95 (4-6) **Fic**

1. Frontier and pioneer life—Fiction 2. South Dakota—Fiction
ISBN 0-02-789511-4 LC 88-13847

In 1874 eleven-year-old Sam and his family move from Kentucky to the southern Dakota Territory, where harsh conditions and a plague of hungry grasshoppers threaten their chances for survival

"Carefully selected details, skillfully woven into the story line, evoke a sense of place and time by documenting the building of a sod house, the distances between neighbors, the grandeur of the Dakota landscape, the modest pleasures of a celebration, and the destructive force of a locust plague. This latter event is a particularly fine example of exposition as an integral part of plot, for it builds to the dénouement even as it provides further insight into character. Both a family story and an account of pioneer living, the book is accessible as well as informative." Horn Book

Turner, Ann Warren—*Continued*

Nettie's trip South; [by] Ann Turner; illustrated by Ronald Himler. Macmillan 1987 unp il $11.95 (3-5) **Fic**

1. Slavery—Fiction
ISBN 0-02-789240-9 LC 86-18135

"In 1859 Nettie is allowed to accompany her brother, who has been assigned his first newspaper story, and an older sister on the trip from Albany, New York, to Richmond. The text appears in the form of a letter Nettie writes to a friend, and while more smoothly written and articulate than one might expect from the young girl depicted in the illustrations, the story recounts her poignantly felt reactions to the viewing of slave quarters and an auction of black men and women." Horn Book

"Himler's charcoal drawings fashion scenes rich with character and emotion. In this case, black and white is as powerful as color. A vivid piece of history for early elementary students or older picture-book audiences." Booklist

Twain, Mark, 1835-1910

The adventures of Huckleberry Finn (5 and up) **Fic**

1. Mississippi River—Fiction 2. Missouri—Fiction

Some editions are:

HarperCollins Pubs. $11.45; lib bdg $9.87 (ISBN 0-06-014376-2 ; 0-06-014377-0)
Houghton Mifflin pa $7.16 (ISBN 0-395-05114-2)
New Am. Lib. pa $1.75 (ISBN 0451-51912-4)
Penguin Bks. pa $2.25 (ISBN 0-14-039046-4)
Running Press lib bdg $12.90, pa $4.95 (ISBN 0-89471-477-5; 0-89471-476-7)
University of Calif. Press $32.50. Illustrated by Barry Moser (ISBN 0-520-05338-9)
Washington Sq. Press pa $2.95 (ISBN 0671-49948-3)

Companion volume to: The adventures of Tom Sawyer, entered below

First published in 1885

"Huck, escaping from his blackguardly father, who had imprisoned him in a lonely cabin, meets Jim, a runaway slave, on Jackson's Island in the Mississippi River. Together they float on a raft down the mighty stream. . . . Two confidence men join them and they drift into many extraordinary adventures, in the course of which Tom Sawyer reappears. Tom's Aunt Sally wants to adopt Huck, who decides he had better disappear again, lest he be 'sivilized'. . . . The struggle in Huck's soul between his 'respectable' Southern prejudices and his growing appreciation of Jim's value and dignity as a human being is an ironic and powerful indictment of the moral blindness of a slaveholding society." Herzberg. Reader's Ency of Am Lit

The adventures of Tom Sawyer (5 and up) **Fic**

1. Mississippi River—Fiction 2. Missouri—Fiction

Some editions are:

Bantam Bks. pa $1.95 (ISBN 0-553-21128-5)
HarperCollins Pubs. $11.49, pa $7.87 (ISBN 0-06-014465-3; 0-06-014427-0)
Messner lib bdg $14.79 (ISBN 0-671-45647-4)
Morrow $21.95 (ISBN 0-688-07510-X)
New Am. Lib. pa $3.95 (ISBN 0-451-51966-3)
Penguin Bks. pa $2.25 (ISBN 0-14-035003-9)
Running Press lib bdg $12.90, pa $4.95 (ISBN 0-89471-542-9; 0-89471-541-0)
University of Calif. Press $22.50, pa $7.95 (ISBN 0-520-04558-0; 0-520-04559-9)
Washington Sq. Press pa $2.95 (ISBN 0-317-56778-0)

Companion volume to: The adventures of Huckleberry Finn, entered above

First published 1876

The plot "is episodic, dealing in part with Tom's pranks in school, Sunday school, and the respectable world of his Aunt Polly, and in part with his adventures with Huck Finn, the outcaste son of the local ne'er-do-well. . . . Tom and Huck witness a murder and, in terror of the murderer, Injun Joe, secretly flee to Jackson's island. They are searched for, are finally mourned for dead, and return to town in time to attend their own funeral. Tom and his sweetheart, Becky Thatcher get lost in a cave in which Injun Joe is hiding. . . . The story closely follows incidents involving Twain and his friends that occured in Hannibal, Mo." Herzberg. Reader's Ency of Am Lit

Followed by two sequels: Tom Sawyer abroad (1984) and Tom Sawyer, detective (1896)

Uchida, Yoshiko

A jar of dreams. Atheneum Pubs. 1981 131p $11.95; pa $3.95 (5 and up) **Fic**

1. Japanese Americans—Fiction 2. Family life—Fiction 3. Prejudices—Fiction 4. California—Fiction
ISBN 0-689-50210-9; 0-689-71041-0 (pa) LC 81-3480

"A Margaret K. McElderry book"

"A story of the Depression Era is told by eleven-year-old Rinko, the only girl in a Japanese-American family living in Oakland and suffering under the double burden of financial pressure and the prejudice that had increased with the tension of economic competition. Into the household comes a visitor who is a catalyst for change." Bull Cent Child Books

"Rinko in her guilelessness is genuine and refreshing, and her worries and concerns seem wholly natural, honest, and convincing." Horn Book

Other available titles about Rinko Tsujimura and her family are:

The best bad thing (1983)
The happiest ending (1985)

Journey home; illustrated by Charles Robinson. Atheneum Pubs. 1978 131p il $12.95; pa $3.95 (5 and up) **Fic**

1. Japanese Americans—Fiction 2. Prejudices—Fiction 3. Family life—Fiction
ISBN 0-689-50126-9; 0-689-70755-X (pa) LC 78-8792

Sequel to: Journey to Topaz, entered below

"A Margaret K. McElderry book"

"The bittersweet story of a Japanese-American family's struggle to return to a normal life after their relocation camp experience in Utah. . . . Seen through the eyes of twelve-year-old Yuki, the plight of her parents, who want to return to California, the disillusionment of her brother, who returns from the war with shattered dreams, and the despair of her friends, who want to rebuild their lives in spite of the hostility outside the camp, take on a special poignancy." Child Book Rev Serv

Uchida, Yoshiko—*Continued*

Journey to Topaz; a story of the Japanese-American evacuation; illustrated by Donald Carrick. Scribner 1971 149p il o.p.; Creative Art Publs. paperback available $7.95 **Fic**

1. Japanese Americans—Evacuation and relocation, 1942-1945—Fiction
ISBN 0-916870-85-5 (pa) LC 75-162730

This is the story of eleven-year-old Yuki, her eighteen-year-old brother and her mother, who were uprooted, evacuated and interned in Topaz, the War Relocation Center in Utah during World War II

"This tragic herding of innocent people is described with dignity and a sorrowful sense of injustice that never becomes bitter." Saturday Rev

Followed by: Journey home, entered above

Van Leeuwen, Jean

The great Christmas kidnapping caper; pictures by Steven Kellogg. Dial Bks. for Young Readers 1975 133p il $12.95; Penguin Bks. pa $3.95 (3-5) **Fic**

1. Mice—Fiction 2. Christmas—Fiction 3. New York (N.Y.)—Fiction
ISBN 0-8037-5415-9; 0-14-034287-7 (pa) LC 75-9201

Sequel to: The great cheese conspiracy (1969)

"Narrated by one mouse named Marvin the Magnificent, it tells of the disappearance of Mr. Dunderhoff, Macy's Santa Claus for 18 years. It happens just after Marvin and his two friends . . . have moved into a dollhouse in the toy department and made friends with the kindly gentleman." N Y Times Book Rev

"Steven Kellogg makes the most of his endearing subjects in pictures which are as zestful and surprising as the author's make-believe." Publ Wkly

The great rescue operation; pictures by Margot Apple. Dial Bks. for Young Readers 1982 167p il $10.95; Penguin Bks. pa $3.95 (3-5) **Fic**

1. Mice—Fiction 2. New York (N.Y.)—Fiction
ISBN 0-8037-3139-6; 0-14-034287-7 (pa)
LC 81-65851

Sequel to: The great Christmas kidnapping caper, entered above

"Marvin the Magnificent (mouse) and his friends Fats and Raymond . . . are bored now in the post-holiday lull of Macy's department store. That is, until Fats' favorite napping place is sold—with Fats in it. Some shrewd detective work puts Marvin and Raymond on his trail, leading to an apartment on Manhattan's Upper East Side. To their surprise, they find Fats happily installed as friend to the lonely Emily, and it takes the endeavors of all three to maneuver a change in the young girl's life." Booklist

"The three mice are distinct—if exaggerated—personalities, the style is colorful and breezy, the plot—deliberately unrestrained—is nicely structured and paced." Bull Cent Child Books

I was a 98-pound duckling. Dial Press 1972 102p o.p.; Bantam Bks. paperback available $2.75 (6 and up) **Fic**

ISBN 0-553-15523-7 (pa) LC 72-714

"Kathy McGruder tells how her life changed overnight and she became a new person just as the 'Allure' magazine article said was possible. As the story opens Kathy is bemoaning her hair, and other beauty problems as well as her lack of dates. Then at the Saturday night square dance which she attends with reluctance she is approached by a dashing stranger and her brief idyllic encounter with this handsome junior counselor from a camp not only enhances her own self-image but launches her social life. Frothy, amusing fare with bright characterizations." Booklist

Verne, Jules, 1828-1905

Twenty thousand leagues under the sea (5 and up) **Fic**

1. Submarines—Fiction 2. Sea stories 3. Science fiction

Some editions are:
Bantam Bks. pa $2.50 (ISBN 0-553-21252-4)
Dent $11; pa $2.50 (Everyman's lib) (ISBN 0-460-05071-0; 0-460-01319-X)
New Am. Lib. pa $2.50 (ISBN 0-451-51849-7)
Penguin Bks. pa $2.25 (ISBN 0-14-035053-5)

Original French edition, 1869

This romance is "remarkable for its prognostication of the invention of submarines. The central characters of the tale, in the process of exploring marine disturbances, are captured by the megalomaniacal Captain Nemo. An underseas tour in a strange craft and their ensuing escape conclude the work." Reader's Ency

Vining, Elizabeth Gray, 1902-

Adam of the road; illustrated by Robert Lawson. Viking 1942 317p il $14.95; Puffin Bks. pa $4.95 (5 and up) **Fic**

1. Minstrels—Fiction 2. Middle Ages—Fiction 3. Great Britain—Fiction
ISBN 0-670-10435-3; 0-14-032464-X (pa)
LC 42-10681

Awarded the Newbery Medal, 1943

Tale of a minstrel and his son Adam, who wandered through southeastern England in the thirteenth century. Adam's adventures in search of his lost dog and his beloved father led him from St. Alban's Abbey to London, and thence to Winchester, back to London, and then to Oxford where the three were at last reunited

Voigt, Cynthia

Come a stranger. Atheneum Pubs. 1986 190p $13.95; Fawcett Bks. pa $3.50 (6 and up) **Fic**

1. Blacks—Fiction 2. Race relations—Fiction
ISBN 0-689-31289-X; 0-449-70246-4 (pa) LC 86-3610

"Mina Smiths, the assertive, intelligent young black girl whom readers caught a glimpse of in 'Dicey's Song' [entered below] is the central figure in this thoughtful coming-of-age novel. Mina is young, only 11 at the story's beginning, and thoroughly involved in ballet. She attends a special ballet camp on a scholarship but is

Voigt, Cynthia—*Continued*
bounced out the following year; in the midst of puberty she has become ungainly—but she wonders if the real reason is that she is black. The shock of rejection and the resulting preoccupation with her identity as a young black woman shadow Mina as her life proceeds on a new course centered on family and friends; there is also her quiet, intense but hopeless love for Tamer Shipp, the summer replacement minister who understands her heart in a way no one else can." Booklist

Dicey's song. Atheneum Pubs. 1982 196p $12.95; Fawcett Bks. pa $3.95 (6 and up) **Fic**

1. Grandmothers—Fiction 2. Brothers and sisters—Fiction
ISBN 0-689-30944-9; 0-449-70276-6 (pa) LC 82-3882

Also available ABC-CLIO large print edition $15.95 (ISBN 1-55736-166-5)

Awarded the Newbery Medal, 1983

Sequel to: Homecoming, entered below

Dicey "had brought her siblings to the grandmother they'd never seen when their mother (now in a mental institution) had been unable to cope. This is the story of the children's adjustment to Gram (and hers to them) and to a new school and a new life—but with some of the old problems. Dicey, in particular, has a hard time since she must abandon her role of surrogate mother and share the responsibility with Gram." Bull Cent Child Books

"The vividness of Dicey is striking; Voigt has plumbed and probed her character inside out to fashion a memorable protagonist. Unlike most sequels, this outdoes its predecessor by being more fully realized and consequently more resonant. A must for those who've read 'Homecoming' but independent enough to stand alone." Booklist

Homecoming. Atheneum Pubs. 1981 312p $13.95; Fawcett Bks. pa $3.95 (6 and up) **Fic**

1. Brothers and sisters—Fiction 2. Abandoned children—Fiction
ISBN 0-689-30833-7; 0-449-70254-5 (pa) LC 80-36723

"When their momma abandons them in a shopping center, Dicey Tillerman and her three younger brothers and sisters set out on foot for where momma was ostensibly taking them—to Great-Aunt Cilla's in Bridgeport, Connecticut. They arrive to find only Cousin Eunice; Priscilla has died. Eunice, mindlessly religious and insensitive to their needs, agrees to look after them. But Dicey knows she has to take another chance and another journey, this time to Crisfield, Maryland, where she hopes their unknown grandmother might provide a better home." Booklist

"The characterizations of the children are original and intriguing, and there are a number of interesting minor characters encountered in their travels. . . . The only real problem with the story is that it's just too long, and despite the built-in suspense of the plot, the onging tension suffers in the multitude of crises." SLJ

Followed by: Dicey's song, entered above

Izzy, willy-nilly. Atheneum Pubs. 1986 258p $14.95; Fawcett Bks. pa $3.50 (6 and up) **Fic**

1. Physically handicapped—Fiction
ISBN 0-689-31202-4; 0-449-70214-6 (pa) LC 85-22933

A car accident causes fifteen-year-old Izzy to lose one leg, and face the need to start building a new life as an amputee

"Voigt shows unusual insight into the workings of a 15-year-old girl's mind. Izzy faces the shock of loss, her friends' inability to cope with that loss, a bungling but bright classmate whose directness helps Izzy face reality, and a supportive, loving family who make her homecoming bearable. Just as Voigt's perceptive empathy brings Izzy to life, other characterizations are memorable, whether of Izzy's shallow former friends or of her egocentric 10-year-old sister." Publ Wkly

Wagner, Jane
J. T. With pictures by Gordon Parks, Jr. Van Nostrand Reinhold 1969 63p il o.p.; Dell paperback available $3.25 (3-6) **Fic**

1. Cats—Fiction 2. Blacks—Fiction 3. Harlem (New York, N.Y.)—Fiction
ISBN 0-440-44275-3 (pa)

"J. T., a constant worry to his anxious mother since his father has left, is running from neighborhood toughs [who are] after the radio he has stolen, when he finds a badly wounded one-eyed alley cat. Secretly and ingeniously J. T. builds a shelter for the cat in an abandoned stove and feeds and nurses it until it is killed by a car. His brief association with the cat and the resultant understanding of the adults in his life are sharply felt." Booklist

Walter, Mildred Pitts, 1922-
Have a happy—; a novel; illustrated by Carole Byard. Lothrop, Lee & Shepard Bks. 1989 106p il $12.95; lib bdg $12.88; Avon Bks. pa $2.95 (4-6) **Fic**

1. Blacks—Fiction 2. Birthdays—Fiction 3. Christmas—Fiction 4. Family life—Fiction
ISBN 0-688-06923-1; 0-688-06924-X (lib bdg); 0-380-71314-4 (pa) LC 88-8962

Upset because his birthday falls on Christmas and will therefore be eclipsed as usual, and worried that there is less money because his father is out of work, eleven-year-old Chris takes solace in the carvings he is preparing for Kwanzaa, the Afro-American celebration of their cultural heritage

"This is a book that has warmth, strong ethical concepts, and a satisfying ending." Bull Cent Child Books

Justin and the best biscuits in the world; with illustrations by Catherine Stock. Lothrop, Lee & Shepard Bks. 1986 122p il $11.95; Knopf pa $3.25 (3-6) **Fic**

1. Sex role—Fiction 2. Grandfathers—Fiction 3. Family life—Fiction 4. Blacks—Fiction
ISBN 0-688-06645-3; 0-679-80346-7 (pa) LC 86-7148

Coretta Scott King Award for text, 1987

Walter, Mildred Pitts, 1922-—*Continued*

"Justin can't seem to do anything right at home. His sisters berate his dishwashing and his mother despairs of his ever properly tidying his room. As for Justin, he angrily rejects the tasks as 'women's work.' Enter now Justin's widowed grandfather, who sizes up the situation, invites Justin for a visit to his ranch, and through daily routines quietly shows Justin that 'it doesn't matter who does the work, man or woman, when it needs to be done." Booklist

"The strong, well-developed characters and humorous situations in this warm family story will appeal to intermediate readers; the large print will draw slow or reluctant readers." SLJ

Mariah keeps cool. Bradbury Press 1990 139p il $12.95 (3-5) **Fic**

1. Family life—Fiction 2. Sisters—Fiction 3. Blacks—Fiction

ISBN 0-02-792295-2 LC 89-23981

Sequel to: Mariah loves rock (1988)

Twelve-year-old Mariah envisions a great summer competing as a diver and planning a surprise party for her sister Lynn but half-sister Denise proves a cloud in Mariah's sunny summer

"The story plays out comfortably. . . . The strong portayal of a warm, close-knit family is a real virtue, and Mariah's character will have broad appeal." Booklist

Ward, Lynd Kendall, 1905-1985

The silver pony; a story in pictures; by Lynd Ward. Houghton Mifflin 1973 174p il $14.95 (2-4) **Fic**

1. Horses—Fiction 2. Stories without words

ISBN 0-395-14753-0 LC 72-5402

"Eighty pictures in shades of gray, black, and white tell the story of a lonely farm boy whose dreams of his adventures on a winged horse become confused with reality. One night the boy leans out his window fantasizing that the horse is carrying him to the moon; but the dream turns into a nightmare as rockets and missiles fill the air around them, then explode, killing the horse and sending the boy hurtling through space—really out the window to his own yard below. The boy recovers physically and, with the help of his parents, doctor, and a real colt, emotionally. This is a complex story subtly conveyed without words—a unique experience for readers and nonreaders alike." Booklist

Watkins, Yoko Kawashima

So far from the bamboo grove. Lothrop, Lee & Shepard Bks. 1986 183p map $11.95; Penguin Bks. pa $3.95 (6 and up) **Fic**

1. World War, 1939-1945—Fiction 2. Korea—Fiction 3. Japan—Fiction

ISBN 0-688-06110-9; 0-14-032385-6 (pa) LC 85-15939

A fictionalized autobiography in which eight-year-old Yoko escapes from Korea to Japan with her mother and sister at the end of World War II

"The tale is simply but compellingly told. Violence is not disguised and becomes, in the madly disrupted life of a refugee, part of everyday experience. Yoko makes no excuses for her own whining and weeping or for her frequent anger toward [her sister] Ko's drive to survive. Even their hard-won escape to Japan does not provide the security they have anticipated. Their grandparents have been killed in the American bombings, and their gentle, heroic mother dies, too. Their grit, determination, and ingenuity summon up a new respect for the resources of the human spirit in an admirably told and absorbing novel." Horn Book

Wells, Rosemary, 1943-

Through the hidden door; with drawings by the author. Dial Bks. for Young Readers 1987 264p il $14.95; Scholastic pa $2.75 (5 and up) **Fic**

1. Fantastic fiction 2. Friendship—Fiction

ISBN 0-8037-0276-0; 0-590-41786-X (pa) LC 86-24273

"When five brutish boys feel that Barney has betrayed them, he becomes a pariah in the small world of a boarding school for younger boys and eventually more than ready to receive the offer of friendship from another outcast, Snowy Cobb. Snowy offers more than friendship; he shares a prized and extraordinary discovery, a secret cave which houses the remains of a miniature civilization." Horn Book

"Like the meshed cogs of two wheels, the small but important element of fantasy and the larger one of reality together spin smoothly to create a story that has pace and suspense, strong relationships, and a sturdy structure." Bull Cent Child Books

Westall, Robert, 1929-

Ghost abbey. Scholastic 1989 c1988 169p $12.95; pa $2.95 (5 and up) **Fic**

1. Ghosts—Fiction 2. Great Britain—Fiction

ISBN 0-590-41692-8; 0-590-41693-6 (pa) LC 88-23945

First published 1988 in the United Kingdom

"When Dad accepts a job repairing a run-down old manor house, Maggi is delighted. She hopes the absorbing work will help him recover from Mum's death and that the move out of the city will keep her mischievious twin brothers out of trouble. None of them know that the old house has its own plans for effecting its restoration and preservation." Horn Book

"Here's a haunted house story that, from the spooky cover to the happy but unsettling ending, delivers the goods. . . . While providing all requisite thrills, this is gentler than most of Westall's fiction, even to the characterization of the Abbey, which is really the main character here." Bull Cent Child Books

The machine gunners. Greenwillow Bks. 1976 c1975 186p lib bdg $11.88; McKay, D. pa $3.50 (6 and up) **Fic**

1. World War, 1939-1945—Fiction 2. Great Britain—Fiction

ISBN 0-688-84055-8 (lib bdg); 0-679-80130-8 (pa) LC 76-13630

First published 1975 in the United Kingdom

"Garmouth, England, is under constant bombing attack by the Germans in World War II. Charles McGill finds a machine gun in a downed German plane and, with that weapon as protection, he and his friends construct a fortress in preparation for an enemy attack. They cap-

Westall, Robert, 1929-—*Continued*
ture a German soldier who becomes their friend. Instead of the expected Nazis, other gangs and their families become the enemy. An attack mistakenly thought to be by Nazis leaves their only ally, the German soldier, dead." Shapiro. Fic for Youth. 2d edition

Followed by: Fathom five (1980)

White, E. B. (Elwyn Brooks), 1899-1985

Charlotte's web; pictures by Garth Williams. Harper & Row 1952 184p il $11.95; lib bdg $11.89; pa $2.95 (3-6) **Fic**

1. Pigs—Fiction 2. Spiders—Fiction
ISBN 0-06-026385-7; 0-06-026386-5 (lib bdg); 0-06-440055-7 (pa) LC 52-9760

A Newbery Medal honor book, 1953

The story of a little girl who could talk to animals, but especially the story of the pig, Wilbur, and his friendship with Charlotte, the spider, who could not only talk but write as well

"Illustrated with amusing sketches . . . [this] story is a fable for adults as well as children and can be recommended to older children and parents as an amusing story and a gentle essay on friendship." Libr J

Stuart Little; pictures by Garth Williams. Harper & Row 1945 131p il $11.95; lib bdg $11.89; pa $2.95 (3-6) **Fic**

1. Mice—Fiction
ISBN 0-06-026395-4; 0-06-026396-2 (lib bdg); 0-06-440056-5 (pa) LC 45-9585

Also available G. K. Hall large print edition $13.95 (ISBN 0-8161-4490-7)

This is "the story of a 'Tom Thumb'-like child born to a New York couple who is to all intents and purposes a mouse. . . . The first part of the book explores, with dead-pan humour, the advantages and disadvantages of having a mouse in one's family circle. Then Stuart sets out on a quest in search of his inamorata, a bird named Margalo, and the story ends in mid-air. The book is outstandingly funny and sometimes touching." Oxford Companion to Child Lit

The trumpet of the swan; pictures by Edward Frascino. Harper & Row 1970 210p il $11.95; lib bdg $11.89; pa $2.95 (3-6) **Fic**

1. Swans—Fiction
ISBN 0-06-026397-0; 0-06-026398-9 (lib bdg); 0-06-440048-4 (pa) LC 72-112484

"The focus of this book is Louis, a trumpeter swan who was born mute. Unable to court a lovely swan, Serena, Louis is saved from a lonely fate by his father, who steals a trumpet so that his son may communicate better. Because he is talented and resourceful, Louis is able to earn enough money as a professional musician to pay for the instrument, and most importantly, to win Serena." Wis Libr Bull

The author "deftly blends true birdlore with fanciful adventures in a witty, captivating fantasy." Booklist

Wibberley, Leonard, 1915-1983

John Treegate's musket. Farrar, Straus & Giroux 1959 188p hardcover o.p. paperback available $3.95 (6 and up) **Fic**

1. United States—History—1775-1783, Revolution—Fiction 2. Boston (Mass.)—Fiction
ISBN 0-374-43788-2 (pa) LC 59-10188

The first of a series of books about the Treegate family set during the Revolutionary War. Other titles: Peter Treegate's war (1960), Sea captain from Salem (1961) and Treegate's raiders (1962)

In 1769, just after his pro-Royalist father has sailed for England on business, 11-year-old Peter Treegate of Boston unwittingly becomes involved in a dock murder. Fleeing arrest, he takes refuge on an American cargo ship which is subsequently wrecked off the South Carolina coast. Peter is rescued by a Scotsman who, in 1775, helps him rejoin his father, now an embattled American patriot, ready to fight at Bunker Hill

An "unusually clear presentation of the political and military mind of the period." Bookmark

Wiggin, Kate Douglas Smith, 1856-1923

The Bird's Christmas Carol; by Kate Douglas Wiggin; illustrated by Jessie Gillespie. Memorial ed. Houghton Mifflin 1941 84p il $13.95 (3-5) **Fic**

1. Christmas—Fiction
ISBN 0-395-07205-0 LC 41-52029

First published 1888

"The story of Carol Bird, an invalid girl so named because she was born at Christmas." Oxford Companion to Child Lit

Wilde, Oscar, 1854-1900

The selfish giant; [illustrated by] Lisbeth Zwerger. Picture Bk. Studio 1984 [24]p col il $15.95 (2-5) **Fic**

1. Fairy tales 2. Giants—Fiction
ISBN 0-907234-30-5 LC 83-24930

This is the "story of a giant whose garden is wrapped in winter until he shares it with the children who live nearby." Booklist

"The familiar, touching tale gains a new dimension by means of the lovely illustrations." Horn Book

Wilder, Laura Ingalls, 1867-1957

Little house in the big woods; illustrated by Garth Williams. newly illustrated, uniform ed. Harper & Row 1953 237p il $13.70; lib bdg $13.89 (4-6) **Fic**

1. Frontier and pioneer life—Fiction 2. Wisconsin—Fiction
ISBN 0-06-026430-6; 0-06-026431-4 (lib bdg) LC 52-7525

Also available ABC-CLIO large print edition $14.95 (ISBN 1-85089-913-4)

First published 1932

This book "tells the story of the author's earliest days 'in the Big Woods of Wisconsin, in a little grey house made of logs.' The style of narrative is simple, almost naive, but the pioneer life is described unsqueamishly,

Wilder, Laura Ingalls, 1867-1957 — *Continued*

with attention to such details as the butchering of the family hog. As in later books, the author refers to herself in the third person as 'Laura.' The record of daily life far from any town is punctuated with stories told in the evenings by Pa, who is also a great singer of folk-songs." Oxford Companion to Child Lit

Other available titles in the Little House series are:
By the shores of Silver Lake (1939)
Farmer boy (1933)
The first four years (1971)
Little house on the prairie (1935)
Little town on the prairie (1941)
The long winter (1940)
On the banks of Plum Creek (1937)
These happy golden years (1943)

Wilkinson, Brenda Scott, 1946-

Ludell; by Brenda Wilkinson. Harper & Row 1975 170p lib bdg $12.89; Bantam Bks. pa $2.50 (6 and up) **Fic**

1. Blacks—Fiction 2. Georgia—Fiction
ISBN 0-06-026492-6 (lib bdg); 0-553-26433-8 (pa) LC 75-9390

"For Ludell Wilson, a black girl in the rural town of Waycross, Georgia, life was not easy materially. Because her mother was living up north in New York, Ludell's grandmother took care of her. The warmth of her love made up for the discipline she imposed, which was much too strict, in Ludell's opinion. We follow Ludell for three years, observing her in school and seeing her become interested in a boyfriend and involved with neighboring families and their troubles. The changes in Ludell afford the reader both laughs and sighs." Shapiro. Fic for Youth. 2d edition

Another available title about Ludell Wilson is:
Ludell and Willie (1977)

Willard, Nancy

The high rise glorious skittle skat roarious sky pie angel food cake; illustrated by Richard Jesse Watson. Harcourt Brace Jovanovich 1990 unp il $15.95 (2-4) **Fic**

1. Cake—Fiction 2. Birthdays—Fiction 3. Mothers and daughters—Fiction
ISBN 0-15-234332-6 LC 89-15230

"A young girl, wishing to make her mother a birthday surprise, searches for her great-grandmother's secret recipe for the cake of the title. The recipe is found in an old diary, the secret ingredient turns up under the grand piano, and at midnight the cake is baked. Following directions, the girl spells LOVE backwards in the sugar, and three angels appear in the kitchen to add a spectacular icing and a golden thimble to the birthday morning surprise." SLJ

"Setting off the tale are Watson's paintings that range from precisely drafted pictures of objects and people (and some very original angels) to drifts of eclectic images that float freely across the page. A fresh, amusing piece that's also handsomely designed." Booklist

Williams, Karen Lynn

Baseball and butterflies; illustrated by Linda Storm. Lothrop, Lee & Shepard Bks. 1990 79p il $12.95 (2-4) **Fic**

1. Brothers—Fiction 2. Butterflies—Fiction 3. Baseball—Fiction
ISBN 0-688-09489-9 LC 90-5713

"Daniel is anxiously awaiting summer vacation, during which he plans to read and add to his butterfly collection. Problems arise when he discovers that his younger brother Joey is not only a nuisance and a tattletale, but also a better baseball player than Daniel. . . . Essentially a story about the discoveries children make about each other when they learn to communicate, the book has no conflicts or major social problems." SLJ

"This is light fare with the kinds of ups and downs that keep younger readers actively engaged. A nice choice for those new to novels." Booklist

Winthrop, Elizabeth

Belinda's hurricane; pictures by Wendy Watson. Dutton 1984 54p il $10.95; Penguin Bks. pa $3.95 (2-4) **Fic**

1. Hurricanes—Fiction 2. Grandmothers—Fiction
ISBN 0-525-44106-9; 0-14-032985-4 (pa) LC 84-8028

While waiting out a fierce hurricane in her grandmother's house on Fox Island, Belinda has a chance to get to know her grandmother's reclusive neighbor Mr. Fletcher

"Ten full-page pencil sketches by Wendy Watson illustrate the text, bring the characters into focus, and make the book more appealing. Well-written books that fall between easy readers and full-length novels are always welcome. Winthrop has turned the limitations of the form into virtues." Booklist

The castle in the attic; frontispiece and chapter title decorations by Trina Schart Hyman. Holiday House 1985 179p il $13.95; Scholastic pa $2.75 (4-6) **Fic**

1. Fantastic fiction
ISBN 0-8234-0579-6; 0-318-37103-0 (pa) LC 85-5607

"William is ten, both of his parents work, and he has always been taken care of by Mrs. Phillips; when she tells him she is going home to England, he is distraught, even though her farewell gift is a large replica of a castle, a toy that has been in her family for generations. There's one little figurine, Sir Simon, and a tale that he will some day come to life. For William, he does, and the boy becomes completely involved with Sir Simon and then with a Mrs. Phillips that William has caused to shrink, by a magic token, to Sir Simon's size. The only way that he can show repentance and rescue her is to shrink himself." Bull Cent Child Books

"Well-crafted, easy to follow, this excursion into knightly times and affairs is further enhanced by the cover art, chapter decorations, and, most important of all, a thoughtful floor plan of the castle." Horn Book

Wise, William, 1923-

The black falcon; a tale from the Decameron; retold by William Wise; illustrated by Gillian Barlow. Philomel Bks. 1990 unp il $14.95 (3-6) **Fic**

1. Falcons—Fiction
ISBN 0-399-21676-6 LC 88-22566

"This adaptation tells of the impoverished knight who falls in love with a rich young widow. To honor her, he serves her his most precious possession, his falcon, for dinner, unaware that her dying son has sent her to request the bird as a gift." Child Book Rev Serv

"Wise's retelling of one of Boccaccio's more ironic tales will appeal to romantics, while giving them an inkling of a different age, the fourteenth century. . . . Barlow's haunting watercolor paintings aptly express the dignity and vitality of the writing. Seen against a background of richly colored Italian landscapes and interiors, the characters seem apart from our time, yet sympathetic. From their portrayal to the quality of light and shadow within the scenes, the artist suggests another time, another place." Booklist

Wiseman, David, 1916-

Jeremy Visick. Houghton Mifflin 1981 170p $12.95 (5 and up) **Fic**

1. Space and time—Fiction 2. Supernatural—Fiction 3. Miners—Fiction 4. Great Britain—Fiction
ISBN 0-395-30449-0 LC 80-28116

"Sent by his teacher to explore some local gravestones, Matthew is inexorably drawn to the message on the 1852 Visick family marker, with its tragic tag line, 'And to Jeremy Visick, . . . aged 12 years, whose body still lies in Wheal Maid.' Numerous nocturnal ramblings find Matthew firmly entrenched in the long-dead family's affairs and their work in the Wheal Maid mine. One night, Matthew compulsively follows young Jeremy into the mine, where he learns how the boy died and, though barely escaping death himself, finally brings peace to the boys restless ghost." Booklist

"This story blends the mystery and awe of the supernatural with the real terror and peril of descending the shaft of an 1850 Cornish copper mine." SLJ

Wojciechowska, Maia, 1927-

Shadow of a bull; drawings by Alvin Smith. Atheneum Pubs. 1964 165p il $12.95; pa $3.95 (6 and up) **Fic**

1. Bullfights—Fiction 2. Spain—Fiction
ISBN 0-689-30042-5; 0-689-71132-8 (pa)
LC 64-12563

Awarded the Newbery Medal, 1965

"Manolo was the son of the great bullfighter Juan Olivar. Ever since his father's death the town of Arcangel [Spain] has waited for [the time] when Manolo would be twelve and face his first bull. From the time he was nine and felt in his heart that he was a coward, Manolo worked and prayed that he might at least face this moment with honor, knowing it could well bring his death." Publ Wkly

"In spare, economical prose [the author] makes one feel, see, smell the heat, endure the hot Andalusian sun and shows one the sand and glare of the bullring. Above all, she lifts the veil and gives glimpses of the terrible loneliness in the soul of a boy. . . . Superbly illustrated." N Y Times Book Rev

Wrede, Patricia C.

Dealing with dragons. Harcourt Brace Jovanovich 1990 212p $15.95 (6 and up) **Fic**

1. Fairy tales 2. Dragons—Fiction
ISBN 0-15-222900-0 LC 89-24599

"A Jane Yolen book"

Bored with traditional palace life, a princess goes off to live with a group of dragons and soon becomes involved with fighting against some disreputable wizards who want to steal away the dragons' kingdom

"A decidedly diverting novel with plenty of action and many slightly skewed fairy-tale conventions that add to the laugh-out-loud reading pleasure and give the story a wide appeal. The good news is that this is book one in the Enchanted Forest Chronicles." Booklist

Wright, Betty Ren

The dollhouse murders. Holiday House 1983 149p $13.95; Scholastic pa $2.75 (4-6) **Fic**

1. Mystery and detective stories
ISBN 0-8234-0497-8; 0-590-43461-6 (pa) LC 83-6147

A dollhouse filled with a ghostly light in the middle of the night and dolls that have moved from where she last left them lead Amy and her retarded sister to unravel the mystery surrounding grisly murders that took place years ago

"More than just a mystery, this offers keen insight into the relationship between handicapped and nonhandicapped siblings and glimpses into the darker adult emotions of guilt and anger. A successful, full-bodied work." Booklist

Wrightson, Patricia, 1921-

Balyet. Margaret K. McElderry Bks. 1989 132p $12.95; Penguin Bks. pa $3.95 (5 and up) **Fic**

1. Supernatural—Fiction 2. Australian aborigines—Fiction 3. Australia—Fiction
ISBN 0-689-50468-3; 0-14-034339-3 (pa) LC 88-8298

Despite the precautions of the old aborigine woman she calls Granny, fourteen-year-old Jo falls under the spell of a secret thing in the Australian hills, a girl endlessly alive and crying for the death that will not take her

"Through her widsom, respect, and compasssion and through the beauty of her writing, Patricia Wrightson brilliantly weaves a modern analogue into the fabric of a primordial story, transposing the significance of Aboriginal myth into contemporary reality." Horn Book

A little fear. Atheneum Pubs. 1983 110p $12.95; Penguin Bks. pa $3.95 (5 and up) **Fic**

1. Fantastic fiction 2. Australia—Fiction
ISBN 0-689-50291-5; 0-14-031847-X (pa) LC 83-2784

"A Margaret K. McElderry book"

Wrightson, Patricia, 1921-—*Continued*

Set in the Australian countryside this novel "tells of an elderly woman's battle with an ancient gnome, the Njimbin. Mrs. Tucker has run away from the security of Sunset House, an old people's home, to an isolated cottage left to her by her brother. The Njimbin resents her intrusion. . . . As their struggle progresses, Mrs. Tucker begins to realize the powers the old gnome can call up." SLJ

"This has a taut, economical structure, suspense in the conflict, good pace and atmosphere, and a polished narrative style." Bull Cent Child Books

The Nargun and the stars. Margaret K. McElderry Bks. 1986 c1970 184p $11.95; Penguin Bks. pa $3.95 (5 and up) **Fic**

1. Fantastic fiction 2. Australia—Fiction
ISBN 0-689-50403-9; 0-14-030780-X (pa)
LC 86-10600

A reissue of the title first published 1973 in the United Kingdom; first American edition published 1974 by Atheneum Pubs.

This is a fantasy set in Northern Australia. An ancient stone monster called the Nargun "threatens to crush the home of orphaned Simon's middle-aged cousins, Charlie and Edie. To rid themselves of the Nargun they seek help from other supernatural beings." Libr J

"The characters, seemingly plain and uncomplicated people, subtly come to life as complex human beings; and the essentially simple plot is worked into the rich fabric of a story that begins serenely, arches up to a great crescendo of suspense, and then falls away at the end to 'a whisper in the dark.'" Horn Book

Wyss, Johann David

The Swiss family Robinson (5 and up) **Fic**

1. Survival (after airplane accidents, shipwrecks, etc.)—Fiction

Some editions are:
Buccaneer Bks. $21.95 (ISBN 0-89966-421-0)
Dell pa $3.25 (ISBN 0-440-98440-8)
Dent (Children's illustrated classics) $13.95 (ISBN 0-460-05008-7)
Grosset & Dunlap $7.95 (ISBN 0-448-11022-9)
Penguin Bks. $2.25 (ISBN 0-14-035044-6)

Originally published 1813 in Switzerland

"A Swiss family—a pastor, his wife, and four boys—are shipwrecked on an uninhabited island. They gradually establish an attractive way of life for themselves, and their many adventures are used by their father to form the basis of lessons in natural history and the physical sciences." Oxford Companion to Child Lit

Yarbrough, Camille, 1948-

The shimmershine queens. Putnam 1988 142p $13.95; Knopf pa $3.50 (4-6) **Fic**

1. Blacks—Fiction 2. School stories 3. Prejudices—Fiction
ISBN 0-399-21465-8; 0-679-80147-2 (pa)
LC 88-11539

"Angie and her friend Michelle are in fifth grade, where Angie is taunted because her skin is so dark. It's an elderly visiting relative . . . who makes Angie feel her own worth and who explains 'shimmershine' as the glow you get when you feel good about yourself." Bull Cent Child Books

"Yarbrough offers a vivid depiction of the troubles facing students in some inner-city schools. Sensitive intraracial prejudices and the inverted values that make scholastic achievement something to scorn are portrayed in several riveting scenes of student disruption. This story carries a clear message about the dire need for students to respect themselves, each other, and education. The dialogue (rendered in black English) rings true, and the characterizations have depth—even the troublemakers have unexpected dimension. A brave book." Booklist

Yep, Laurence

Child of the owl. Harper & Row 1977 217p lib bdg $12.89; pa $3.95; Dell pa $3.25 (5 and up) **Fic**

1. Chinese Americans—Fiction 2. Grandmothers—Fiction 3. San Francisco (Calif.)—Fiction
ISBN 0-06-026743-7 (lib bdg); 0-06-440336-X (pa); 0-440-91230-X (pa)
LC 76-24314

"Casey, a twelve-year-old Chinese American girl, is more American than Chinese. When her father, a compulsive gambler, is hospitalized after a severe beating, Casey moves in with her grandmother in San Francisco's Chinatown. Although she is a street-smart child, Casey finds that she is an outsider in this community. Her grandmother teaches her something of her heritage and what it means to be 'a child of the owl.'" Shapiro. Fic for Youth. 2d edition

Dragonwings. Harper & Row 1975 248p lib bdg $12.89; pa $3.50 (5 and up) **Fic**

1. Chinese Americans—Fiction 2. San Francisco (Calif.)—Fiction 3. Fathers and sons—Fiction
ISBN 0-06-026738-0 (lib bdg); 0-06-440085-9 (pa)
LC 74-2625

Also available ABC-CLIO large print edition $15.95 (ISBN 1-55736-168-1)

"In 1903 Moon Shadow, eight years old, leaves China for the 'Land of the Golden Mountains,' San Francisco, to be with his father, Windrider, a father he has never seen. There, beset by the trials experienced by most foreigners in America, Moonrider shares his father's dream—to fly. This dream enables Windrider to endure the mockery of the other Chinese, the poverty he suffers in this hostile place—the land of the white demons—and his loneliness for his wife and his own country." Shapiro. Fic for Youth. 2d edition

The serpent's children. Harper & Row 1984 277p lib bdg 13.89 (6 and up) **Fic**

1. Family life—Fiction 2. China—Fiction
ISBN 0-06-026812-3
LC 82-48855

"Explores the large events of the Taiping Rebellion, opium pushing and Manchu/foreign battles and their effects on a small village (in China's south coastal province of Kwang-tung) that is more directly troubled by drought and bandits. The story is told by Cassia, one of two spirited children whose independent ways are derided as signs of 'serpent blood' inherited from a legendary ancestress of their non-village mother. The slur becomes a bond between Cassia and her brother after their mother's death and their father's eventual estrangement from the son, whose exodus to the demon's goldfields secures the family fortunes." SLJ

The author's "style has dignity and the story is rich

Yep, Laurence—*Continued*
in the depiction of the history, folklore, and customs of China of more than a century ago." Best Sellers

Sweetwater; pictures by Julia Noonan. Harper & Row 1973 201p il o.p. paperback available $3.50 (6 and up) **Fic**

1. Science fiction
ISBN 0-06-440135-9 (pa) LC 72-9867

"Young Tyree is torn between pursuing an interest in music encouraged by Amadeus, an Argan (the oldest race on the planet Harmony), and obeying his father, elected captain of the Silkies, descendants of the starship crews from Earth, who are fighting for a life in harmony with the dominant sea. A distinctive narrative that unexpectedly and winningly combines a richly imagined world and its ecology, a boy's rite of passage, and wide-ranging allusions to music and the Old Testament." Anatomy of Wonder. 3d edition

Yolen, Jane
The devil's arithmetic. Viking Kestrel 1988 170p $12.95 (4 and up) **Fic**

1. Jews—Fiction 2. Holocaust, Jewish (1933-1945)—Fiction
ISBN 0-670-81027-4 LC 88-14235

"During a Passover Seder, 12-year-old Hannah finds herself transported from America in 1988 to Poland in 1942, where she assumes the life of young Chaya. Within days the Nazis take Chaya and her neighbors off to a concentration camp, mere components in the death factory. As days pass, Hannah's own memory of her past, and the prisoners' future, fades until she is Chaya completely." Publ Wkly

"Through Hannah, with her memories of the present and the past, Yolen does a fine job of illustrating the importance of remembering. She adds much to children's understanding of the effects of the Holocaust." SLJ

The dragon's boy. Harper & Row 1990 120p $13.95; lib bdg $13.89 (5 and up) **Fic**

1. Arthur, King—Fiction 2. Merlin (Legendary character)—Fiction
ISBN 0-06-026789-5; 0-06-026790-9 (lib bdg) LC 89-24642

"This is a retelling of the education and coming of age of 13-year-old Artos (Arthur). Old Linn (Merlin) is to be his teacher, but, doubting he can command the boy's attention, he constructs a fire-breathing dragon as a façade." SLJ

"Scattered throughout the book are broad hints of Artos's identity, but even children unfamiliar with the legendary King Arthur should find the crisply told story accessible and entertaining." Horn Book

The seeing stick; pictures by Remy Charlip and Demetra Maraslis. Crowell 1977 unp il lib bdg $13.89 (2-4) **Fic**

1. Blind—Fiction 2. China—Fiction
ISBN 0-690-00596-2 LC 75-6949

"Yolen tells a sensitive and graceful story of a small, blind [Chinese] princess whose rich, powerful father, the Emperor, cannot give her the most precious gift of all—her sight. A tattered, old wood carver brings her the wide world, however, by telling stories of wonders he has seen on his travels and carving them into the golden wood of a stick. As he invites her to feel not only the cane but objects surrounding her, she begins to see with 'eyes on the tips of her fingers.'" SLJ

"The illustrators worked in concert to create pencil drawings and misty pastel-crayon scenes that look like watercolors." Publ Wkly

Sleeping ugly; by Jane Yolen; pictures by Diane Stanley. Coward, McCann & Geoghegan 1981 64p il lib bdg $10.99; pa $6.95 (2-4) **Fic**

1. Fairy tales
ISBN 0-698-30721-6 (lib bdg); 0-698-20617-7 (pa) LC 81-489

"A Break-of-day book"

When beautiful Princess Miserella, Plain Jane, and a fairy fall under a sleeping spell, a prince undoes the spell in a surprising way

"Diane Stanley's expressive illustrations, jumping from once upon a time to right now, add an intriguing perspective to the tale's witty text and humorous play with fairy tale conventions." SLJ

Zhitkov, Boris, 1882-1938
How I hunted the little fellows; translated from the Russian by Djemma Bider; illustrated by Paul O. Zelinsky. Dodd, Mead 1979 unp il $8.95 (2-4) **Fic**

1. Ships—Models—Fiction 2. Soviet Union—Fiction
ISBN 0-396-07692-0 LC 79-11738

The story is set in "a long-gone Russian town where little Boria (the narrator) visits his grandmother. Generous and loving, the woman nevertheless forbids Boria to touch her treasure, a marvelously complete miniature steamship—her 'dear memory.' But the boy is obsessed by finding tiny sailors he envisions inside the ship. When he's alone, he pulls the graceful thing apart and can't put it together again." Publ Wkly

"The carefully detailed and shaded hatched drawings on practically every page evoke a mood of late nineteenth-century domesticity and successfully portray the steamship and its imaginary little crew." Horn Book

S C STORY COLLECTIONS

Books in this class include collections of short stories by one author and collections by more than one author. Folk tales are entered in class 398.2. Collections of general literature, American literature, English literature, etc.—which may include but are not limited to short stories—are entered in classes 808.8, 810.8, 820.8, etc.

Aiken, Joan, 1924-
Give yourself a fright: thirteen tales of the supernatural. Delacorte Press 1989 180p $14.95 (6 and up) **S C**

1. Horror—Fiction 2. Short stories
ISBN 0-440-50120-2 LC 88-20366

"A magic duck, ghosts, the devil, a confused muse, and human evil haunt these 13 unusual stories that hover between fantasy and reality; humor and psy-

Aiken, Joan, 1924-—*Continued*
chological terror. The styles vary, giving an interesting texture to the collection." SLJ

Past eight o'clock; goodnight stories; pictures by Jan Pieńkowski. Viking Kestrel 1987 c1986 128p il $14.95 (3-6) **S C**

1. Short stories
ISBN 0-670-81636-1

First published 1986 in the United Kingdom

"Inspired by popular nursery rhymes and lullabies, Aiken has created a magical collection of fairy tales that beg to be read aloud. Her language is rich and spellbinding as she tells eight stories about the night, dreams, and sleeping. . . . Aiken's beautiful words are perfectly complemented by Pieńkowski's elegant silhouette illustrations which dance imaginatively across the pages." SLJ

Up the chimney down, and other stories. Harper & Row 1985 c1984 248p $12.95; lib bdg $12.89 (5 and up) **S C**

1. Short stories
ISBN 0-06-020036-7; 0-06-020037-5 (lib bdg) LC 85-42642

"A Charlotte Zolotow book"

"Although the setting of these 11 short stories moves between New York, London and Paris, the real locale is Aiken country where a baker makes cakes for the wind, a rare bird is saved from extinction and a rainbow makes itself comfortable in a small house in a 'rather wild part of London.'" SLJ

"In each of the eleven tales the author's talent for description creates memorable moments and vivid impressions. . . . As a group, the tales demonstrate continuing growth without sacrificing the vivacity, pace, and flamboyant imagination which are the hallmarks of Aiken's work." Horn Book

Alcock, Vivien, 1924-
Ghostly companions; a feast of chilling tales. Delacorte Press 1987 c1984 132p o.p.; Dell paperback available $2.95 (5 and up) **S C**

1. Ghosts—Fiction 2. Short stories
ISBN 0-440-40276-X (pa) LC 86-16229

First published 1984 in the United Kingdom

"Alcock's fans will be well-spooked by the strange events in this anthology of [ten] wonderfully eerie stories. . . . Highly inventive, the tales have ordinary countryside settings—behind which lurks the darkness of beckoning spirits and misdirected intentions." Publ Wkly

Alexander, Lloyd
The town cats, and other tales; illustrated by Laszlo Kubinyi. Dutton 1977 126p il lib bdg $14.95; Dell pa $3.25 (3-5) **S C**

1. Cats—Fiction 2. Fairy tales 3. Short stories
ISBN 0-525-41430-4; 0-440-48989-X (pa) LC 76-13647

"A collection of eight original stories about outstanding felines. The stories appear to be set in various countries and resemble European folk tales; each one shows a cat as a devoted, loyal, but independent creature—and wiser than human beings." Horn Book

"There's great style to these cat stories in the fairy tale mode. Alexander is a master of the form and his language flows easily, effortlessly." Booklist

Andersen, Hans Christian, 1805-1875
Hans Andersen: his classic fairy tales; from the new translation by Erik Haugaard; illustrated by Michael Foreman. Doubleday 1978 c1976 185p il $15.95 (3-6) **S C**

1. Fairy tales 2. Short stories
ISBN 0-385-13364-2 LC 78-107654

First published 1976 in the United Kingdom

"The stories are some of the best known and most asked for . . . plus a few less familiar, like the humorous satire, 'The Dung Beetle.'" SLJ

Illustrated "with 18 full-color and 21 black-and-white drawings. The enchantment of Andersen's fairy world reverberates through Foreman's interpretations." Booklist

Babbitt, Natalie
The Devil's other storybook; stories and pictures by Natalie Babbitt. Farrar, Straus & Giroux 1987 81p il $10.95 (4-6) **S C**

1. Devil—Fiction 2. Short stories
ISBN 0-374-31767-4 LC 86-32760

"Michael di Capua books"

Featuring the same creature as in The Devil's storybook, entered below, this companion volume contains 10 additional tales

The Devil's storybook; stories and pictures by Natalie Babbitt. Farrar, Straus & Giroux 1974 101p il $10.95; pa $3.50 (4-6) **S C**

1. Devil—Fiction 2. Short stories
ISBN 0-374-31770-4; 0-374-41708-3 (pa) LC 74-5488

Ten "stories about the machinations of the Devil to increase the population of his realm. He is not always successful and, despite his clever ruses, meets frustration as often as his intended victims do." Horn Book

"Twists of plot within traditional themes and a briskly witty style distinguish this book, illustrated amusingly with black-and-white line drawings." Booklist

Bond, Michael, 1926-
Paddington's storybook; illustrated in color and black and white by Peggy Fortnum. Houghton Mifflin 1984 c1983 159p il $15.95 (2-5) **S C**

1. Bears—Fiction 2. Great Britain—Fiction 3. Short stories
ISBN 0-395-36667-4 LC 84-12900

For other titles about Paddington see Fiction Section

First published 1983 in the United Kingdom

"A selection of some of the very best stories about a very fine bear published over the past 25 years. Watercolor has been added to the original line drawings." NY Times Book Rev

Brooke, William J.

A telling of the tales: five stories; drawings by Richard Egielski. Harper & Row 1990 132p il $12.95; lib bdg $12.89 (4-6) **S C**

1. Short stories
ISBN 0-06-020688-8; 0-06-020689-6 (lib bdg) LC 89-36588

A retelling of five classic folk/fairy tales, including Cinderella, Sleeping Beauty, Paul Bunyan, John Henry, and Jack and the Beanstalk, from a contemporary perspective

"Brooke has succeeded in making these old familiar tales his own, softening their make-believe, playing with their meanings, but leaving their magic utterly intact. . . . A perceptive and engaging collection that's ideal for reading aloud." SLJ

Carlson, Natalie Savage

The talking cat, and other stories of French Canada; retold by Natalie Savage Carlson; pictures by Roger Duvoisin. Harper & Row 1952 87p il lib bdg $12.89 (3-6) **S C**

1. French Canadians—Fiction 2. Canada—Fiction 3. Short stories
ISBN 0-06-021081-8 LC 52-5429

"These seven once-in-another-time tales of French Canada were told first by the author's great-great uncle, . . . handed down in her family and now retold in an enchanting manner that will appeal to today's storytellers." Wis Libr Bull

"They are not, I am glad to say, written in dialect. Easy for the children to read themselves and perfect for the story hour." Horn Book

Connections: short stories by outstanding writers for young adults; edited by Donald R. Gallo. Delacorte Press 1989 226p $14.95 (6 and up) **S C**

1. Short stories
ISBN 0-385-29815-3 LC 89-1126

A collection of seventeen short stories by such writers as Gordon Korman, Chris Crutcher, T. Ernesto Bethancourt, Richard Peck, and M. E. Kerr, spanning subjects that include penpals, the first day of high school, computers, and family life

"This superb collection should have instant appeal to most teens, and the boy-meets-girl theme should attract reluctant readers." SLJ

Face to face: a collection of stories by celebrated Soviet and American writers; [by] Robert Cormier [et al.]; designed by Barry Moser; edited by Thomas Pettepiece and Anatoly Aleksin. Philomel Bks. 1990 233p $15.95 (5 and up) **S C**

1. Soviet Union—Fiction 2. Short stories
ISBN 0-399-21951-X LC 89-3874

"Brought together in this . . . anthology are 18 examples of Soviet and American literature by such authors as Yuri Yakovlev, Robert Cormier, Anatoly Aleksin, Scott O'Dell, Jane Yolen and Cynthia Rylant. Carefully selected and impeccably arranged, the stories offer a wide variety of writing styles, moods, characters and settings which reflect life in different regions of both nations. Rather than focusing on the contrasts between cultures, the collection affirms the universality of young people's experiences." Publ Wkly

Fleischman, Paul

Coming-and-going men; four tales; illustrations by Randy Gaul. Harper & Row 1985 147p il lib bdg $12.89 (6 and up) **S C**

1. New England—Fiction 2. Short stories
ISBN 0-06-021884-3 LC 84-48336

"A Charlotte Zolotow book"

"Four loosely connected stories present the adventures of itinerant artisans and tradesmiths as they travel through the small town of New Canaan, Vermont, in the year 1800. Each tale involves a young person as a major character, and Fleischman creates a pleasing motif by setting each adventure in a different season." SLJ

Graven images; 3 stories; illustrations by Andrew Glass. Harper & Row 1982 85p il $12.95; lib bdg $12.89; pa $3.50 (6 and up) **S C**

1. Supernatural—Fiction 2. Short stories
ISBN 0-06-021906-8; 0-06-021907-6 (lib bdg); 0-06-440186-3 (pa) LC 81-48649

A Newbery Medal honor book, 1983

"A Charlotte Zolotow book"

Three stories about people whose lives are influenced by sculptured figures. In Saint Crispin's follower, "Nicholas, an apprentice cobbler, believes the statue of St. Crispin in his village square is guiding him to a successful courtship with a comely lass. . . . The other two tales are grim examples of retribution. A wooden figurehead, 'The Binnacle Boy,' unmasks a killer in an old whaling port, and a statue commissioned by a ghost proves that a father has murdered his son in 'The Man of Influence.'" Publ Wkly

Garfield, Leon

The apprentices. Viking 1978 315p o.p.; Penguin Bks. paperback available $4.95 (6 and up) **S C**

1. Apprentices—Fiction 2. London (England)—Fiction 3. Short stories
ISBN 0-14-031595-0 (pa) LC 77-21770

A "linked series of twelve tales about apprentices set in successive months, so that the book covers one year; each tale has a relationship to at least one of the others and each deals with a different craft. . . . The sights, the sounds, and especially the smells of eighteenth-century London are vividly presented, making a brilliantly impressionistic and amusing book." Horn Book

Godden, Rumer, 1907-

Four dolls; illustrated by Pauline Baynes. Greenwillow Bks. 1984 c1983 137p il $13; Dell pa $4.95 (3-5) **S C**

1. Dolls—Fiction 2. Short stories
ISBN 0-688-02801-2; 0-440-42568-9 (pa)
LC 83-14157

This collection was first published 1983 in the United Kingdom; the stories were originally published separately

Impunity Jane (1955); The fairy doll (1956); The story of Holly and Ivy (1959); Candy Floss (1960)

These "are timeless tales featuring plucky little dolls and their resourceful owners. The new black-and-white and color artwork is not terribly exciting but serves pleasantly." Booklist

Gorog, Judith, 1938-

Three dreams and a nightmare, and other tales of the dark. Philomel Bks. 1988 156p lib bdg $13.95 (5 and up) **S C**

1. Fantastic fiction 2. Short stories
ISBN 0-399-21578-6 LC 88-4036

"The macabre and the fantastic pervade the usually down-to-earth matrices of a collection of short stories that are unusual in their pace and plot, impressive save for the occasional flat, non-sequential ending. The style is polished, and the wit in exposition as well as in dialogue may be as appealing to readers as the drama and suspense of that brief gem, 'The Perfect Solution,' in which an amateur chemist discovers a way to mend torn sweat shirts—or the reversal of a standard role for a giant in 'Hedwig the Wise.'" Bull Cent Child Books

Hunter, Mollie, 1922-

A furl of fairy wind: four stories; drawings by Stephen Gammell. Harper & Row 1977 58 p il lib bdg $12.95 (2-5) **S C**

1. Fairy tales 2. Short stories
ISBN 0-06-022675-7 LC 76-58732

"The first of these four stories "introduces a genuine Scottish Brownie who must receive his bowl of hot porridge every night—and wreaks havoc in the household if not so indulged. In the second story a boy foolishly enters the fairy world on Midsummer's Eve, when the little people do not like to have strangers among them. The third story tells of a peddler who receives from a fairy woman an extravagant reward for one of his ordinary pots; and in the last tale, an orphan girl has forgotten how to smile, until a 'furl of fairy wind' blows around the house." Horn Book

Hunter "writes entrancingly, as expected, infusing the tales with warmth and gentle humor. And Gammell graces the collection with wonderful scenes of people and places in the dream landscapes." Publ Wkly

Kennedy, Richard, 1932-

Richard Kennedy: collected stories; illustrations by Marcia Sewall. Harper & Row 1987 270p il $14.95; lib bdg $14.89 (3-5) **S C**

1. Short stories
ISBN 0-06-023255-2; 0-06-023256-0 (lib bdg)
LC 86-45495

A collection of two poems and 14 stories, previously published separately in picture book format

Kennedy "introduces each story with a brief paragraph answering the inevitable question, 'Where do you get your ideas?' As individual as its source, each story is remarkably different from the others which surround it. . . . What the stories *do* have in common—aside from the richness of their language—is vivid and loving characterization, levels of meaning which speak to a multi-generational audience, the timeless, enduring appeal of stories which have been told around long generations of campfires, and an astonishing gift of imagination." SLJ

Kipling, Rudyard, 1865-1936

The jungle books (4 and up) **S C**

1. Animals—Fiction 2. India—Fiction 3. Short stories

Also available in two separate volumes from various publishers

Some editions are:

Airmont pa $1.95 (ISBN 0-8049-0109-0)
New Am. Lib. pa $3.95; 0-451-52340-7)
Penguin Bks. pa $2.95; 0-14-043282-5)

A collection of fifteen animal stories first published 1894 and 1895 in two volumes by Macmillan with titles: The jungle book and The second jungle book

The central figure in the stories is the human Mowgli, brought up in the jungle in India by Mother Wolf

Just so stories (3-6) **S C**

1. Animals—Fiction 2. India—Fiction 3. Short stories

Some editions are:

Holt & Co. $16.95 Illustrated by Safaya Salter (ISBN 0-8050-0439-4)
Viking Kestrel $12.95 Illustrated by Michael Foreman; 0-670-80242-5)

The book consists of twelve animal fables

"While Kipling's original and humorous elucidation of how the elephant got his trunk and the leopard his spots are barely believable, he has nevertheless drawn animal characteristics and habits 'just so.' First published in 1902." Toronto Public Libr. Books for Boys & Girls

Several of the Just so stories are entered separately in the Fiction Section

Konigsburg, E. L.

Altogether, one at a time; illustrated by Gail E. Haley [et al.] Atheneum Pubs. 1971 79p il $12.95; pa $2.95 (4-6) **S C**

1. Short stories
ISBN 0-689-20638-0; 0-689-71290-1 (pa)
LC 70-134814

"Compelled to invite a child he doesn't want to his birthday party in 'Inviting Jason,' Stanley likes the boy even less afterwards, but for a different reason. A 10-year-old boy learns something about old age in 'The Night of the Leonids' when he realizes his grandmother has lost her chance to see a shower of stars that occurs

Konigsburg, E. L.—*Continued*

only once every 33⅓ years. The spirit of a long dead camp counselor helps an obese girl make up her mind that she will never have to attend Camp Fat again. In 'Momma at the Pearly Gates,' Momma tells the story of how, as a girl, she was called a 'dirty nigger' by a white classmate." Libr J

Throwing shadows. Atheneum Pubs. 1979 151p hardcover o.p. paperback available $3.95 (5 and up) **S C**

1. Short stories
ISBN 0-02-044140-1 (pa) LC 79-10422

"This is a collection of five original short stories. Each of the stories is told in the first person and concerns a pre-adolescent boy as he learns a little about his identity. The boys come from a variety of geographical backgrounds, races, and cultures. . . . As each boy discovers a new facet of his personality or accepts an old one, he throws a shadow that is uniquely his own." Child Book Rev Serv

"The stories each occupy about 30 pages but have the spacious quality of a novel; characters and events have a chance to develop naturally rather than seeming pushed along." SLJ

Levoy, Myron

The witch of Fourth Street, and other stories; pictures by Gabriel Lisowski. Harper & Row 1972 110p il hardcover o.p. paperback available $3.95 (4-6) **S C**

1. New York (N.Y.)—Fiction 2. Short stories
ISBN 0-06-440059-X (pa) LC 74-183174

Also available Smith, P. $15.25 (ISBN 0-8446-6450-2)

"The eight stories [set on the Lower East Side of New York in the 1920's] tell about a group of neighbors, young and old. . . . Tales and characters are highly original, sometimes humorous, sometimes poignant, and often profound. . . . The soft drawings are exactly right." Horn Book

Lively, Penelope, 1933-

Uninvited ghosts, and other stories; illustrated by John Lawrence. Dutton 1985 c1984 119p il lib bdg $11.95 (4 and up) **S C**

1. Supernatural—Fiction 2. Short stories
ISBN 0-525-44165-4 LC 84-26035

First published 1984 in the United Kingdom

"Bizarre creatures invade prosaic daily life in eight hilarious original short stories. . . . In the title story, ghosts come oozing out of the chest of drawers on the children's first night in a new house. 'The Disastrous Dog' is about a pup who communicates with a boy by telepathy and who turns out to be domineering, lazy, sulky, and manipulative, much like any demanding houseguest. The stories' humor lies in the sharp characterizations—both of the human and supernatural creatures—and in the brisk, commonsense tone that combines the routines and squabbles of family life with outlandish experiences. With a few substitutions for unfamiliar British terms . . . these immediate and dramatic stories will be wonderful for reading aloud." Booklist

MacDonald, George, 1824-1905

The complete fairy tales of George Macdonald; with original illustrations by Arthur Hughes; introduction by Roger Lancelyn Green. Schocken Bks. 1977 c1961 288p il hardcover o.p. paperback available $8.95 (4 and up) **S C**

1. Fairy tales 2. Short stories
ISBN 0-8052-0579-9 (pa) LC 77-80272

First published 1961 in the United Kingdom with title: The light princess, and other tales

"A collection of eight short fairy tales . . . includes the original woodcuts, intricately executed by the painter Arthur Hughes. A short introduction traces Macdonald's life and work, commenting briefly on the backgrounds of the included selections. . . . Format makes this more a candidate for adults wanting tales to tell or read aloud." Booklist

MacLachlan, Patricia

Tomorrow's wizard; illustrations by Kathy Jacobi. Harper & Row 1982 80p il $12.95; lib bdg $12.89 (3-6) **S C**

1. Witchcraft—Fiction 2. Short stories
ISBN 0-06-024073-3; 0-06-024074-1 (lib bdg) LC 81-47733

"A Charlotte Zolotow book"

This collection of six stories "follows the adventures of three . . . characters: Tomorrow's Wizard, his young apprentice Murdoch and a philosophical horse saved from an ill-tempered owner. The Wizard and Murdoch are charged with fulfulling the most important wishes and curses uttered by the humans who inhabit the nearby villages of this unnamed land. Watched over by the High Wizard, the three companions go about making surprising matches between very different individuals." SLJ

This "is a quietly stunning book, filled with poetry and parables. Kathy Jacobi's illustrations perfectly complement Patricia MacLachlan's lyrical storytelling. A book that should stand permanently on every child's shelf." Christ Sci Monit

Paterson, Katherine

Angels & other strangers: family Christmas stories. Crowell 1979 118p $13.95; pa $3.50 (5 and up) **S C**

1. Christmas—Fiction 2. Short stories
ISBN 0-690-03992-1; 0-06-440283-5 (pa) LC 79-63797

"The author weaves stories about miracles of the Christmas season—miracles that take place on a truly human level. Each story is based on the Christian message of the birth of Christ and the significance that message takes on for the characters. She writes of the poor, the desolate, and the lonely as well as of the arrogant, the complacent, and the proud." Horn Book

Porte-Thomas, Barbara Ann

Jesse's ghost, and other stories; [by] Barbara Ann Porte. Greenwillow Bks. 1983 105p lib bdg $10.25 (5 and up) **S C**

1. Supernatural—Fiction 2. Short stories
ISBN 0-688-02301-0 LC 83-1451

In these eleven supernatural tales a hurried child grows old before her time, one ghost falls from the sky, another ghost follows a woman home, and a third lies buried in his bed. In one story love plays a trick on death, and in another Cinderella comes into the twentieth century

"The unifying device is the storyteller who introduces each story and 'sits where three worlds meet, before and now and after.' The title 'Jesse's Ghost' may mislead readers, for compared to the overtly grisly media fare available, Porte's works will evoke little stronger response than a slight grimace and a shudder. These are definitely for thoughtful, sensitive children." SLJ

Roach, Marilynne K.

Encounters with the invisible world; being ten tales of ghosts, witches, & the devil himself in New England; written and illustrated by Marilynne K. Roach. Crowell 1977 131p il o.p.; Amereon reprint available $13.95 (5 and up) **S C**

1. Ghosts—Fiction 2. New England—Fiction 3. Short stories
ISBN 0-89190-874-9 LC 76-22186

"Adapted from New England legends, the colloquial narration, simple dialogue, and old Yankee settings give . . . [a] regional backdrop to universal motifs like a bargain struck with the devil, a ghostly peddler's tragic end, and a witch spinning the fates of men." SLJ

Rylant, Cynthia

Children of Christmas; stories for the season; drawings by S. D. Schindler. Orchard Bks. 1987 38p il $11.95; lib bdg $11.99 (4 and up) **S C**

1. Christmas—Fiction 2. Short stories
ISBN 0-531-05706-2; 0-531-08306-3 (lib bdg)
LC 87-1690

These Christmas stories are "about lost things: a stray cat, a stray bachelor, a grandfather who has lost the connection to the youngest generation, a misunderstood boy who receives a cowboy set instead of a doctor kit and who tries to hold onto a lost dream." Read Teach

"Rylant's Christmas is a sad and lonely one, but her ability to summon the joys of the season through her writing is extraordinary. Schindler's illustrations, appropriately, are both reserved and inciting." Publ Wkly

Every living thing; stories; decorations by S. D. Schindler. Bradbury Press 1985 81p $10.95; Aladdin Bks. (NY) pa $3.50 (5 and up) **S C**

1. Animals—Fiction 2. Short stories
ISBN 0-02-777200-4; 0-689-71263-4 (pa) LC 85-7701

"This book tells twelve stories about lonely people whose lives have been changed for the better by an association with an animal. Many of the stories are heartwarming and meant to be read aloud. Through a parrot, a twelve-year-old boy learns how much his father loves him; a retired schoolteacher and an old collie renew their life by becoming friends with young children. While some of the stories are overly sentimental, the majority realistically show the importance of animals in our lives." Okla State Dept of Educ

Sandburg, Carl, 1878-1967

Rootabaga stories; illustrated by Michael Hague. Harcourt Brace Jovanovich 1988-1989 2v il ea $19.95; pa $3.95 **S C**

1. Fairy tales 2. Short stories
ISBN 0-15-269061-1 (v1); 0-15-269065-4 (v1 pa); 0-15-269062-X (v2); 0-15-269063-8 (v2 pa)
LC 88-935

A newly illustrated combined edition of Rootabaga stories and Rootabaga pigeons, first published separately 1922 and 1923 respectively

The stories combine "the realism of the American middle West with a great deal of fancy and symbolism. A certain amount of repetition and the use of mouth-filling words create a rhythm and a singing quality which make the stories particularly suitable for reading aloud." Right Book for the Right Child

"The illustrations are a good match to the lively prose of these highly imaginative tales." SLJ

Sholem Aleichem, 1859-1916

Holiday tales of Sholom Aleichem; selected and translated by Aliza Shevrin; illustrated by Thomas di Grazia. Scribner 1979 145p il hardcover o.p. paperback available $5.95 (5 and up) **S C**

1. Jews—Fiction 2. Fasts and feasts—Judaism—Fiction 3. Short stories
ISBN 0-689-71034-8 (pa) LC 79-753

The "translator has chosen seven [stories] for young readers, partly because she considers them to be among [the author's] finest work and also because they show how Jews celebrated holidays—not only as religious observances but as family festivals. Six of them are first-person narratives presented from a boy's point of view; all seven deal not with solemn holy days but with joyous holidays—three center on Passover, two on Sukkos, one on Chanukah, and one on Purim." Horn Book

Singer, Isaac Bashevis, 1904-1991

Naftali the storyteller and his horse, Sus, and other stories; pictures by Margot Zemach. Farrar, Straus & Giroux 1976 129p il $13.95; Dell pa $1.50 (4 and up) **S C**

1. Jews—Poland—Fiction 2. Poland—Fiction 3. Short stories
ISBN 0-374-35490-1; 0-440-46642-3 (pa)
LC 76-26917

Three of the stories "continue the adventures of the fools of Chelm, characters whose zaniness has tickled readers of all ages in earlier collections by the author [including The fools of Chelm and their history, entered in the Fiction Section]. The title story, however, is a moving account of Naftali who lived long ago in Poland, of his inordinate love of stories." Publ Wkly

Singer, Isaac Bashevis, 1904-1991 — *Continued*

The power of light; eight stories for Hanukkah; with illustrations by Irene Lieblich. Farrar, Straus & Giroux 1980 86p il $13.95; pa $6.95 (4 and up) **S C**

1. Hanukkah—Fiction 2. Jews—Fiction 3. Short stories

ISBN 0-374-36099-5; 0-374-45984-3 (pa) LC 80-20263

"The stories, bound together by recurring Hanukkah motifs—the lamp, the dreidel, and the pancakes, tell chiefly of events affecting the lives of Eastern European Jews. Ranging from such somber happenings as the drafting of small Jewish boys to serve in the Russian army during the nineteenth century through the bombing and burning of the Warsaw ghetto, the harrowing events are seen in the context of the celebration of Hanukkah." Horn Book

"The stories vary from realism to incorporation of the miraculous . . . but are united in their strong piety as they are in the polished craftsmanship and warmth with which they are written." Bull Cent Child Books

Stories for children. Farrar, Straus & Giroux 1984 337p $16.95; pa $7.95 (4 and up) **S C**

1. Jews—Fiction 2. Short stories

ISBN 0-374-37266-7; 0-374-46489-8 (pa) LC 84-13612

This collection of thirty-six stories includes "parables, beast fables, allegories and reminiscences. Some stories are silly and charming, while others are wildly fantastic, dealing with savagery and miracles in mythical, medieval Poland. Frequently they are about scary situations, but all tend to end happily, with an edifying idea. Most appealing is the Nobel Prize winner's sheer story-telling power. In this respect, he has no equal among contemporaries." N Y Times Book Rev

Soto, Gary

Baseball in April, and other stories. Harcourt Brace Jovanovich 1990 111p $14.95 (5 and up) **S C**

1. Mexican Americans—Fiction 2. California—Fiction 3. Short stories

ISBN 0-15-205720-X LC 89-36460

A collection of eleven short stories focusing on the everyday adventures of Hispanic young people growing up in Fresno, California

Each story "gets at the heart of some aspect of growing up. The insecurities, the embarrassments, the triumphs, the inequities of it all are chronicled with wit and charm. Soto's characters ring true and his knowledge of, and affection for, their shared Mexican-American heritage is obvious and infectious." Voice Youth Advocates

Things that go bump in the night; a collection of original stories; edited by Jane Yolen & Martin H. Greenberg. Harper & Row 1989 280p $13.95; lib bdg $13.89 (5 and up) **S C**

1. Horror—Fiction 2. Fantastic fiction 3. Short stories

ISBN 0-06-026802-6; 0-06-026803-4 (lib bdg) LC 88-34065

"A collection of eighteen short stories whose horror quotient ranges from mild to nail-biting. The authors include a few familiar names like William Sleator, Diana Wynne Jones, Jane Yolen, and Bruce Coville; the rest of the collection contains contributions by less well-known writers. . . . Although all the selections fall loosely under the heading of horror story, they vary widely in tone, subject matter, and style, offering something for almost everyone." Horn Book

Where angels glide at dawn; new stories from Latin America; edited by Lori M. Carlson and Cynthia Ventura; introduction by Isabel Allende; illustrations by José Ortega. Lippincott 1990 114p il $13.95; lib bdg $13.89 (5 and up) **S C**

1. Latin America—Fiction 2. Short stories

ISBN 0-397-32424-3; 0-397-32425-1 (lib bdg) LC 90-6697

"Tinged with the surreal quality of dreams and fairy tales, this collection of translated stories amplifies the richness of Latin American culture. Reflecting a history of social upheaval and political changes, the selections reveal the quiet wisdom and deep emotions of a strong, enduring people. . . . Bolstered by a glossary of terms and brief explanations of each entry's setting, these 10 tales are as accessible as they are intriguing." Publ Wkly

Wilde, Oscar, 1854-1900

The Happy Prince, and other stories; illustrated with four colour plates and line drawings by Peggy Fortnum. Dent 1968 154p il $11 (3-6) **S C**

1. Fairy tales 2. Short stories

ISBN 0-460-05075-3 LC 68-95987

"Children's illustrated classics"

A combined edition, first published 1952 in the United Kingdom, of The Happy Prince, and other stories (1888) and A house of pomegranates (1891)

"Writing his [nine] fairy tales to express his ideas and feelings about the world and the people in it, Oscar Wilde has imbued them with a beauty and charm of his own that appeals to grown-ups and boys and girls alike." Toronto Public Libr. Books for Boys & Girls

Yee, Paul

Tales from Gold Mountain; stories of the Chinese in the New World; paintings by Simon Ng. Macmillan 1989 64p il $14.95 (4 and up) **S C**

1. Chinese—North America—Fiction 2. Short stories

ISBN 0-02-793621-X LC 89-12643

Yee, Paul—*Continued*

"The eight stories in this collection are . . . rooted in the real experiences of the Chinese who came to North America seeking the prosperity of Gold Mountain. Though Mr. Yee has drawn on tales he heard growing up in Vancouver's Chinatown and on research into the lives of the Chinese who settled in Canada, the stories contain many parallels with the experiences of the Chinese in the United States." Horn Book

These "brief, pithy tales strikingly reflect traditional Chinese beliefs and customs in new world circumstances. . . . Romance, family loyalty, and justice are important themes, and an element of surprise is never far away. Ng's cool, brooding full-page paintings have an intense presence that enhances the stories' exotic flavor." Booklist

Yolen, Jane

The faery flag; stories and poems of fantasy and the supernatural. Orchard Bks. 1989 120p $15.95; lib bdg $15.99 (5 and up) **S C**

1. Supernatural—Fiction 2. Supernatural—Poetry 3. Short stories

ISBN 0-531-05838-7; 0-531-08438-8 (lib bdg)

LC 88-34866

"The nine stories and six poems have been drawn from the author's rich imagination and are well-matched fusing of folklore and fantasy. Set in such diverse places as Japan, the Hebrides, and India, the stories vary somewhat in quality. The poems, which flow with more spontaneity, sparkle with fresh and vivid imagery and are nicely touched with both humor and moments of gentle melancholy." Horn Book

E Easy Books

This section consists chiefly of fiction books that would interest children from pre-school through third grade. Easy books that have a definite nonfiction subject content are usually classified with other nonfiction books. Easy books listed here include:

1. Picture books, whether fiction or nonfiction, that the young child can use independently
2. Fiction books with very little or scattered text, with large print and with vocabulary suitable for children with reading levels of grades 1-3
3. Picture storybooks with a larger amount of text to be used primarily by or with children in pre-school through grade 3

Ackerman, Karen, 1951-

Song and dance man; illustrated by Stephen Gammell. Knopf 1988 unp il $11.95; lib bdg $13.99 **E**

1. Entertainers—Fiction 2. Grandfathers—Fiction

ISBN 0-394-89330-1; 0-394-99330-6 (lib bdg)

LC 87-3200

Awarded the Caldecott Medal, 1989

"Grandpa takes three grandchildren up to the attic, where he arranges lights and gives a performance that enchants his audience. They tell him they wish they could have seen him dance in 'the good old days' but he says he wouldn't trade a million good old days for the time he spends with the narrators." Bull Cent Child Books

The illustrator "captures all the story's inherent joie de vivre with color pencil renderings that fairly leap off the pages. Bespectacled, enthusiastic Grandpa clearly exudes the message that you're only as old as you feel, but the children respond—as will readers—to the nostalgia of the moment." Booklist

Adams, Adrienne

The Easter egg artists. Scribner 1976 unp il $13.95; pa $4.95 **E**

1. Rabbits—Fiction 2. Easter—Fiction 3. Egg decoration—Fiction

ISBN 0-684-14652-5; 0-684-71481-5 (pa)

LC 75-39301

"The Abbotts, rabbits who design Easter Eggs, are worried that son Orson will not follow the family trade. On a winter vacation Orson and the family paint a car, a house, an airplane, a bridge, and Orson becomes a committed Easter Egg Artist. Children rated this charming story with its lovely illustrations one of the most beautiful picture books of the year." Read Teach

Adoff, Arnold, 1935-

Black is brown is tan; pictures by Emily Arnold McCully. Harper & Row 1973 31p il $13.70; lib bdg $13.89 **E**

1. Stories in rhyme 2. Family life—Fiction 3. Race relations—Fiction

ISBN 0-06-020083-9; 0-06-020084-7 (lib bdg)

LC 72-9855

This story in rhyme describes "a warm, racially-mixed family who reads, cuts wood, plays, and eats together." Booklist

"Arnold Adoff's spare free verse combines familiar images in a startling original way . . . and Emily McCully's beautiful watercolors are radiant with feeling and life." SLJ

Agard, John, 1949-

The calypso alphabet; illustrated by Jennifer Bent. Holt & Co. 1989 unp il $13.95 **E**

1. Alphabet 2. Caribbean region—Social life and customs

ISBN 0-8050-1177-3 LC 89-045617

"Combines short, lilting text built around alphabetically arranged words indigenous to the Caribbean Islands with bright, scratchboard illustrations to give a lively picture of island life." Soc Educ

Agee, Jon

The incredible painting of Felix Clousseau. Farrar, Straus & Giroux 1988 unp il $13.95 **E**

ISBN 0-374-33633-4 LC 87-046072

"When the Royal Palace holds a competition, Clousseau . . . is ridiculed for his simple painting of a duck—until it goes 'QUACK!' and walks out of the frame. . . . Suddenly Paris is agog, all of the man's paintings are coming alive—'The Sleeping Boa Constrictor' awakens and slithers off to meet its owner, waterfalls fall, volcanoes erupt, cannons discharge, and poor Clousseau

Agee, Jon—*Continued*

winds up in prison. However, when a ferocious dog in one of his paintings reaches out and catches a notorious jewel thief, Clousseau is restored to the king's good graces." Booklist

"A well-defined drawing style is enhanced by dark, rich colors, thickly and boldly applied. Agee provides much food for the spirit with his spare storytelling and distinctive artwork." Publ Wkly

Ahlberg, Janet

The baby's catalogue; [by] Janet and Allan Ahlberg. Little, Brown 1982 unp il $14.95; pa $5.95 **E**

1. Infants—Fiction 2. Vocabulary

ISBN 0-316-02037-0; 0-316-02038-9 (pa) LC 82-9928

"An Atlantic Monthly press book"

"Titles and labels are the only print on the pages of a book that begins with a page headed 'Babies' and goes through the objects and activities and people that most babies see on a typical day. There are Moms, Dads, brothers and sisters, toys, high chairs, diapers, meals, books, baths, bedtimes, etc. The softly colored paintings are cheerful and amusing, the format is clean and uncluttered, and the whole should provide hours of pointing, identification, and naming." Bull Cent Child Books

Each peach pear plum; an 'I spy' story; [by] Janet and Allan Ahlberg. Viking 1979 c1978 unp il $12.95; Penguin Bks. pa $3.95 **E**

1. Stories in rhyme

ISBN 0-670-28705-9; 0-14-050639-X (pa) LC 78-16726

First published 1978 in the United Kingdom

This book "invites children to play 'I spy' and point out nursery rhyme and story characters such as Jack and Jill, the Three Bears, Cinderella, etc. who are semi-hidden within . . . [the] illustrations." SLJ

The characters hide "in a pleasant, rural, watercolor world that's decorative but never precious or self-regarding. This is a lovely small book, well-conceived and very well drawn, gentle, humorous, unsentimental." N Y Times Book Rev

Funnybones; [by] Janet and Allan Ahlberg. Greenwillow Bks. 1981 c1980 unp il $12.88; lib bdg $11.88; Mulberry Bks. pa $3.95 **E**

1. Skeleton—Fiction

ISBN 0-688-80238-9; 0-688-84238-0 (lib bdg); 0-688-09927-0 (pa) LC 79-24872

Three skeletons—a grown-up, a child, and a dog—live in a dark cellar. They wake one night and decide "to go out and frighten someone, and though no one is in the park, the adult and child skeletons have a good time on the swings." SLJ

"What happens in the story is of less importance than the basic situation and the way in which the story's told, in a book in comic strip format. . . . The Ahlbergs have fun with words and with the concept of skeletons at play, and their communicable zest precludes any note of the macabre." Bull Cent Child Books

Peek-a-boo! by Janet & Allan Ahlberg. Viking 1981 unp il $11.95; pa $4.95; Penguin Bks. pa $3.95 **E**

1. Infants—Fiction 2. Family life—Fiction 3. Stories in rhyme

ISBN 0-670-54598-8; 0-670-82383-9 (pa); 0-14-050107-X (pa) LC 81-1925

Published in the United Kingdom with title: Peepo!

Brief rhyming clues invite the reader to look through holes in the pages for a baby's view of the world from breakfast to bedtime

"Perfectly tuned for a first-book experience. . . . The full-color paintings reveal a reassuringly disorganized but loving family in pastel-framed scenes that feature tiny familiar objects as part of the border. The baby's postures are droll and realistic and his position in the center of a clean white page, alternated with the ordinary but exciting activities he sees through his peephole eye, are ingeniously conceived." Booklist

Starting school; [by] Janet and Allan Ahlberg. Viking Kestrel 1988 unp il $11.95; Penguin Bks. pa $3.95 **E**

1. School stories

ISBN 0-670-82175-6; 0-14-050843-0 (pa) LC 88-50053

"The first four months of school for eight first graders are chronicled in wonderful watercolor detail. Lines of text interrupted by numerous small pictures, perfect for sharing in laps or small groups, show a multi-racial class of children getting used to things." SLJ

Alderson, Sue Ann, 1940-

Ida and the wool smugglers; pictures by Ann Blades. Margaret K. McElderry Bks. 1988 c1987 unp il $12.95 **E**

1. Sheep—Fiction 2. Smuggling—Fiction

ISBN 0-689-50440-3 LC 87-15487

First published 1987 in Canada

This "adventure tells how young Ida, carrying bread to a neighbor's farm, stops to pet her favorite sheep and its twin lambs. Warned that smugglers are often lurking in the woods, and hearing their signals, Ida rescues the sheep by skillfully driving them ahead of her to the safety of the neighbor's property." SLJ

"The folk-art style illustrations complement the text. In places they appear static but illustrate the story with warmth and simplicity. Children will chant right along with Ida as she moves her sheep to a rhythmic 'Soo-ey! Shoo! Scat! Clap! Clappety-clap!' The book's Canadian coastal setting adds to its charm." Horn Book

Alexander, Martha G.

Bobo's dream; by Martha Alexander. Dial Bks. for Young Readers 1970 unp il $7.95; lib bdg $7.89 **E**

1. Dogs—Fiction 2. Blacks—Fiction 3. Stories without words

ISBN 0-8037-0686-3; 0-8037-0687-1 (lib bdg) LC 73-102825

This story without words tells "how a black boy and his dachshund feel about each other. Boy and dog settle under a shady tree to enjoy a book, a bone, and companionship. A large dog tries to steal the dachshund's

Alexander, Martha G.—*Continued*
bone, but the boy retrieves the bone. The grateful dog dreams of daring exploits in which he comes to the rescue of his master." Keating. Build Bridges of Understanding Between Cultures

"Unpretentious three-color drawings, childlike and humorous, show that might does not make right." Horn Book

Even that moose won't listen to me; by Martha Alexander. Dial Bks. for Young Readers 1988 unp il $9.95; lib bdg $9.89 E

1. Moose—Fiction
ISBN 0-8037-0187-X; 0-8037-0188-8 (lib bdg) LC 85-4338

"As a moose calmly munches his way through the family vegetable garden, Rebecca's urgent pleas for intervention are dismissed by each member of her family; even the moose, when she tries to frighten him off, ignores Rebecca. When, too late, the others see the destruction in the garden and ask Rebecca what in the world happened, she answers 'I'm busy now,' and promises to tell them when she finishes building her toy rocket ship." Bull Cent Child Books

This story is "simply told, gently humorous, superbly illustrated, and perfectly attuned to the thoughts and feelings of children." SLJ

How my library grew, by Dinah; story and pictures by Martha Alexander. Wilson, H.W. 1983 unp il $18 E

1. Libraries—Fiction
ISBN 0-8242-0679-7 LC 82-20204

"Told through the eyes of a young girl talking to her stuffed friend, Teddy, this softly colored, child-like story describes a library being built across the street. Through the seasons, Dinah and Teddy watch a hole being dug and the building going up; they wonder about its use and delight in designing a surprise for opening day. . . . Small vignettes, often grouped two or three to a page, enticingly depict the library's construction and open-for-business scenes, making the library a very inviting and stimulating place to be." Booklist

Move over, Twerp; story and pictures by Martha Alexander. Dial Bks. for Young Readers 1981 unp il $11.95; pa $3.95 E

1. School stories
ISBN 0-8037-6139-2; 0-8037-5814-6 (pa) LC 80-21405

"Young Jeffrey's first day on the school bus ends in disaster when the older kids oust him from his chosen seat. Dad counsels stubborness . . . while big sister advises combat. . . . Neither solution is a success, and it is Jeffrey who comes up with the appropriate weapon: humor, which simultaneously saves his seat and wins him a slot in the pecking order." SLJ

"Tones of green and yellow add brightness to the neat, small-scale drawings of children in a heartening little story in which a very small boy outwits a bully. . . . Simply, lightly told in monologue or dialogue, a story that should satisfy the youngest set." Bull Cent Child Books

Nobody asked me if I wanted a baby sister; story and pictures by Martha Alexander. Dial Bks. for Young Readers 1971 unp il $10.95; lib bdg $10.89; pa $3.95 E

1. Brothers and sisters—Fiction 2. Infants—Fiction
ISBN 0-8037-6401-4; 0-8037-6402-2 (lib bdg); 0-8037-6410-3 (pa) LC 78-173731

Companion volume to: When the new baby comes, I'm moving out, entered blow

"Jealous of the fuss made over his baby sister, Oliver bundles Bonnie into his wagon and, wheeling her around the neighborhood, tries to give her away. He changes his mind, however, and decides to keep her when the baby, unhappy at being held by strangers, cries until he takes her." Booklist

"Not a brand-new theme, but pictures and text together make a charming variation, the precise little drawings affectionate and humorous, the writing ingenious and direct." Bull Cent Child Books

We're in big trouble, Blackboard Bear; story and pictures by Martha Alexander. Dial Bks. for Young Readers 1980 unp il $9.95; pa $3.50 E

1. Bears—Fiction
ISBN 0-8037-9741-9; 0-8037-9583-1 (pa) LC 79-20631

A "slate-colored bear materializes one night out of a drawing sketched on a child's blackboard. Unbeknown to his young owner, Blackboard Bear walks off the blackboard at night, climbs out the window, and raids the neighborhood goldfish bowls and honey pots. Happily, however, the bear soon mends the error of his ways by drawing the missing items on the blackboard (which then turn to tangible objects) and returning them to their proper places." Christ Sci Monit

"Alexander's soft, uncluttered, gently expressive drawings perfectly match her understated text. This could be a reassuring story for children, who might have experiences similar to Bear's, to know that they will not lose a parent's love by making a mistake, but also that they will in some fashion have to make amends." SLJ

Other available titles about Blackboard Bear are:
And my mean old mother will be sorry, Blackboard Bear (1972)
Blackboard Bear (1969)
I sure am glad to see you, Blackboard Bear (1976)

When the new baby comes, I'm moving out; story and pictures by Martha Alexander. Dial Bks. for Young Readers 1979 unp il $9.95; lib bdg $9.89; pa $3.95 E

1. Brothers and sisters—Fiction 2. Infants—Fiction
ISBN 0-8037-9557-2; 0-8037-9558-0 (lib bdg); 0-8037-9563-7 (pa) LC 79-4275

"Although this is a companion to 'Nobody asked me if I wanted a baby sister,' [entered above] the action precedes the first book in that the object of Oliver's sibling jealousy hasn't been born yet. Mom is due any day and Oliver is feeling hostile. So hostile in fact, that he fantasizes stuffing his pregnant mother into a garbage can and taking it to the dump. When Mom isn't fond of that idea, Oliver threatens to run away. Finally, Oliver is persuaded to stay at home because, after all, big brothers get to do very special things. In the book these

Alexander, Martha G.—*Continued*
'special things' are unstated and left up to Mom's and Oliver's individual imaginations." SLJ

"The clean, small-scale pictures echo the warmth and humor of the story." Bull Cent Child Books

Alexander, Sue, 1933-

Nadia the Willful; pictures by Lloyd Bloom. 1st ed. Pantheon Bks. 1983 unp il lib bdg $12.99 E

1. Bedouins—Fiction 2. Death—Fiction 3. Brothers and sisters—Fiction
ISBN 0-394-95265-0 LC 82-12602

When her favorite brother disappears in the desert forever, Nadia refuses to let him be forgotten, despite her father's bitter decree that his name shall not be uttered

"The message is clear: a person is not truly dead unless forgotten. The language is as soft and fluid as the full-page black-and-white illustrations. These drawings achieve a sense of the changing desert and of the life and sorrow of its people. Simple borders confine both text and illustration giving the feeling of looking into another world while the text affirms universal emotions." SLJ

Aliki

Overnight at Mary Bloom's. Greenwillow Bks. 1987 unp il $11.75; lib bdg $11.88 E

1. Friendship—Fiction 2. Night—Fiction
ISBN 0-688-06764-6; 0-688-06765-4 (lib bdg) LC 86-7719

"'Come spend the night,' says Mary Bloom to her young friend, and the excited child packs her bags as quickly as she can. As in *At Mary Bloom's* [1976, o.p.] plenty happens, here in the company of the cheerful grown-up who relishes her young visitor." Booklist

"A visit with Mary Bloom is a kid's idea of adventure, creative play and independence. Aliki's now-familiar technique of full color with ink outline conveys the fun and excitement of every kid's sleepover dream." Publ Wkly

The two of them; written and illustrated by Aliki. Greenwillow Bks. 1979 unp il $12.95; lib bdg $12.88; pa $4.95 E

1. Grandfathers—Fiction 2. Death—Fiction
ISBN 0-688-80225-7; 0-688-84225-9 (lib bdg); 0-688-07337-9 (pa) LC 79-10161

Describes the relationship of a grandfather and his granddaughter from her birth to his death

"The eloquent illustrations in muted full color and the smaller soft-pencil drawings show the life the two shared as well as the tenderness and pure pleasure implicit in their relationship. . . . The book transcends the labored introductions to geriatrics which have proliferated in contemporary children's literature and describes with sensitivity and truth the changing seasons of human life." Horn Book

Use your head, dear. Greenwillow Bks. 1983 unp il $10.25; lib bdg $10.88 E

1. Alligators—Fiction
ISBN 0-688-01811-4; 0-688-01812-2 (lib bdg) LC 82-11911

Charles, a young alligator, means well, but gets things mixed up until his father gives him an invisible thinking cap for his birthday

"Both text and illustrations are notable for the care with which they develop the thoroughly childlike story. The words are fresh and funny, precise complements for expressive line drawings highlighted by the authoritative green shapes of the alligator characters and by the quarter-inch borders defining each double-page spread. As winsome as its reptilian protagonist, the book readily demonstrates that the most effective picture book is not necessarily the most elaborate, that there is artistic merit in restraint and enduring appeal in simplicity." Horn Book

We are best friends. Greenwillow Bks. 1982 unp il $14.95; lib bdg $14.88 E

1. Friendship—Fiction
ISBN 0-688-00822-4; 0-688-00823-2 (lib bdg) LC 81-6549

When Robert's best friend Peter moves away, both are unhappy, but they learn that they can make new friends and still remain best friends

"Brightly lit pictures in cheerful primary colors portray with just a stroke of the pen the misery of losing a friend who must move away and the tentative beginnings of a new companionship. . . . Details of school and home abound in the lively pictures." Horn Book

Welcome, little baby. Greenwillow Bks. 1987 unp il $11.95; lib bdg $11.88 E

1. Infants—Fiction 2. Mothers—Fiction
ISBN 0-688-06810-3; 0-688-06811-1 (lib bdg) LC 86-7648

A mother welcomes her newborn infant, and tells what life will be like as the child grows older

"Tender pictures in pastel colors are appropriate for a minimal text, not substantial but effective in its message of love." Bull Cent Child Books

Allard, Harry, 1928-

Bumps in the night; pictures by James Marshall. Doubleday 1979 32p il o.p.; Bantam Bks. paperback available $2.25 E

1. Ghosts—Fiction 2. Animals—Fiction
ISBN 0-553-15284-X (pa) LC 78-22301

"Marshall's chunky, silly animal figures add humor to a friendly-ghost story for the read-aloud audience. Dudley the stork is terrified by a bumping noise and something wet touching his cheek; his best friend Trevor Hog advises having a medium preside at a séance. Madame Kreep comes, goes into a trance, and the ghost appears; he's a horse named Donald who used to live in the house and is now lonely. Donald soon becomes a friend to all, helping Trevor with his arithmetic, telling Dudley funny stories when he can't sleep, showing Dagmar the Baboon how to dance a jig, etc." Bull Cent Child Books

Allard, Harry, 1928-—*Continued*

Miss Nelson is missing! [by] Harry Allard, James Marshall. Houghton Mifflin 1977 32p il $12.95; pa $3.95 **E**

1. School stories 2. Teachers—Fiction
ISBN 0-395-25296-2; 0-395-40146-1 (pa)
LC 76-55918

Illustrated by James Marshall

"The kids in room 207 were so fresh and naughty that they lost their sweet-natured teacher, the blonde Miss Nelson, and got in her place the sour-souled Miss Swamp." N Y Times Book Rev

"Humor and suspense fill the pages of [this book]. . . . On one page I found the drawings a treat and the text great. Then I turned the page to find the drawings great, and the text a treat. Appreciation of teachers shines through it all with imagination and great humor." Christ Sci Monit

Other available titles about Miss Nelson are:
Miss Nelson has a field day (1985)
Miss Nelson is back (1982)

Allen, Pamela

Bertie and the bear. Coward-McCann 1984 unp il $10.95; pa $4.95 **E**

1. Bears—Fiction
ISBN 0-698-20600-2; 0-698-20607-X (pa)
LC 83-19044

"A cumulative story that begins with a bear chasing little Bertie, predatory gleam in eye. The queen (plump woman, red crown) chases after the bear, the king after the queen, the admiral (his gong rivalling the king's trumpet blare) after the king, et cetera. 'All this for me?' The bear is so flattered he bows, turns cartwheels, and dances." Bull Cent Child Books

"Like all books in which plot is enhanced by sound, this one must be read aloud for full appreciation. However, the multicolored words that flow above the scenes are almost visual sounds, and the bear's impromptu ballet is delightful. Large, uncluttered illustrations and sparse text make this a natural for story hours." SLJ

Andersen, Karen Born

What's the matter, Sylvie, can't you ride? story and pictures by Karen Born Andersen. Dial Bks. for Young Readers 1981 unp il $9.95; lib bdg $9.89 **E**

1. Bicycles and bicycling—Fiction
ISBN 0-8037-9607-2; 0-8037-9621-8 (lib bdg)
LC 80-12514

Sylvie experiences the trials and tribulations of learning to ride her two-wheel bicycle

"The illustrations washed with tones of red and blue capture the frustrations and disappointment of the small heroine as well as the studiously casual, superior attitude of her friends. The softly limned backgrounds suggest a comfortable suburban community whose pleasant vistas offer an effective contrast to Sylvie's darkening moods. Together, text and pictures create a real-life minidrama drawn from a situation familiar to young children." Horn Book

Andrews, Jan, 1942-

Very last first time; illustrated by Ian Wallace. Atheneum Pubs. 1986 unp il lib bdg $14.95 **E**

1. Inuit—Fiction
ISBN 0-689-50388-1
LC 85-71606

"A Margaret K. McElderry book"

"In her Inuit village in northern Canada, Eva Padlyat prepares to 'walk on the bottom of the sea' alone for the first time. For years, after the tide goes out, she and her mother have gone under the ice to collect mussels, but doing it by herself is a rite of passage that becomes a mini-adventure when she goes exploring, forgets the time, drops her candle, and barely beats the sea water back to her ice hole. The paintings, dominated by deep purple glinting here and there with gold or green, are impressionistic in texture and give an eerie sense of the shadowy shapes, crevasses, and sense of isolation surrounding the child. A unique experience for young listeners and an intriguing introduction to another culture." Bull Cent Child Books

Anholt, Catherine

Tom's rainbow walk. Little, Brown 1990 c1989 unp il lib bdg $12.95 **E**

1. Color—Fiction
ISBN 0-316-04261-7
LC 89-83660

"Joy Street books"

First published 1989 in the United Kingdom

"Grandma is knitting a new sweater for Tom, but he can't make up his mind about the color. At naptime, he dreams about a giant ball of yarn that unwinds as it makes its way through a fox's lair, a chicken's yard, and a frog's pond, where each animal suggests a color for the sweater. When Tom wakes up, he knows what color he wants, but Grandma has already come up with the same idea—a multicolored sweater featuring every hue in the rainbow." Booklist

"Anholt's whimsical watercolor washes are warm and comforting, featuring round and smiling characters." SLJ

Anno, Mitsumasa, 1926-

All in a day; by Mitsumasa Anno and Raymond Briggs. Philomel Bks. 1986 unp il $14.99 **E**

1. Children
ISBN 0-399-61292-0
LC 86-5011

Brief text and illustrations by ten internationally well-known artists reveal a day in the lives of children in eight different countries showing the similarities and differences and emphasizing the commonality of humankind

"The variety of illustrative styles and interpretations by the artists will require many examinations before children will be able to integrate them. Complex in concept, minimal in plot, *All in a Day* is nonetheless a great success at conveying the warmth, richness, and variety of people." SLJ

Anno, Mitsumasa, 1926—*Continued*

Anno's alphabet; an adventure in imagination. Crowell 1975 c1974 unp il $13.95; lib bdg $13.89; Harper & Row pa $5.95 E

1. Alphabet
ISBN 0-690-00540-7; 0-690-00541-5 (lib bdg); 0-06-443190-8 (pa) LC 73-21652

"In this unusual alphabet book, large letters, painted to look like carved wood, have a three-dimensional, optically challenging appearance. Borders, embellished with plants and hidden creatures, surround the pictured letters and objects." LC. Child Books, 1975

Anno's Britain. Philomel Bks. 1982 c1981 unp il $11.95 E

1. Great Britain—Pictorial works 2. Stories without words
ISBN 0-399-20861-5 LC 81-21058

This wordless picture book follows Anno's traveler on horseback through British villages and countryside, "as the solitary wayfarer sees such sights as the construction of a medieval castle, the Beatles performing in a village square, and St. Paul's Cathedral and Westminster Abbey." Horn Book

This book "needs no words; the journey is sufficient narrative. Each double page, a tapestry of tiny easy brush strokes, is alive with surprises. . . . [Anno is] a skilled draughtesman with a faultless sense of scale and design." N Y Times Book Rev

Anno's counting book. Crowell 1977 c1975 unp il $13.95; lib bdg $13.89; Harper & Row pa $5.95 E

1. Counting 2. Seasons—Fiction 3. Stories without words
ISBN 0-690-01287-X; 0-690-01288-8 (lib bdg); 0-06-443123-1 (pa) LC 76-28977

Original Japanese edition, 1975

"A distinctive, beautifully conceived counting book in which twelve full-color doublespreads show the same village and surrounding countryside during different hours (by the church clock) and months. Both the seasons and community changes are studied, as such components of the scene as flowers, trees, animals, people, and buildings increase from one to twelve." LC. Child Books, 1977

Anno's counting house. Philomel Bks. 1982 unp il $12.95 E

1. Counting 2. Moving, Household—Fiction 3. Stories without words
ISBN 0-399-20896-8 LC 82-617

One by one, ten children move from their old house into their new house with all their possessions. Die-cut windows reveal the interiors of the houses and the book can also be read from back to front

"The paintings are precisely and beautifully detailed, and the book has a game element that should appeal to children although the initial interest may depend on guidance. A note to adults is appended, discussing the fostering of mathematical concepts in the early years." Bull Cent Child Books

Anno's flea market. Philomel Bks. 1984 unp il $11.95 E

1. Stories without words
ISBN 0-399-21031-8 LC 83-21954

The treasures and trash of a flea market are depicted, one Saturday morning in the town square, as men, women, and children buy and sell everything imaginable

"As children walk through these pages, they will take delight in the rich display of handcrafted wares and the worlds these artifacts represent. The book encourages an eye for detail and appreciation for the artistic nature of life." Child Book Rev Serv

Anno's journey. Philomel Bks. 1981 c1977 unp il $12.95; pa $7.95 E

1. Europe—Pictorial works 2. Stories without words
ISBN 0-399-20762-7; 0-399-20952-2 (pa)

Original Japanese edition, 1977; first United States edition published 1978 by Collins

"In a panorama which unrolls wordlessly, a traveler rides horseback over a landscape that seems distinctly European, shown in meticulously detailed illustrations of everyday life, artifacts, and architecture. Hints and fragments of stories abound, carried from scene to scene; one sees anachronisms and visual jokes, children and grown-ups at games and sports, and characters from classics like 'Red Riding Hood' and 'The Pied Piper of Hamelin' all the way to 'Sesame Street.' Suggestions of famous paintings are casually inserted into natural settings." Horn Book

"Most children will need the help of informed adults to decipher the puzzles. But even beginners should enjoy turning the pages of an exceptional book and responding to the beauties depicted." Publ Wkly

Anno's U.S.A. Philomel Bks. 1983 unp il $11.95; pa $4.95 E

1. United States—Pictorial works 2. Stories without words
ISBN 0-399-20974-3; 0-399-21595-6 (pa) LC 83-13107

In wordless panoramas a lone traveler approaches the New World from the West in the present day and journeys the width of the country backward through time, departing the east coast as the Santa Maria appears over the horizon

"Anno deliberately mixes costumes, vehicles, and other representations of various periods in the handsome double-page spreads that are beautifully composed; his use of color and perspective are admirable; his command of architectural drawing is impressive. What may appeal most to readers, however, are the small visual jokes that enliven the pages." Bull Cent Child Books

Topsy-turvies; pictures to stretch the imagination. Philomel Bks. 1989 c1970 unp il $13.95 E

1. Puzzles 2. Optical illusions 3. Stories without words
ISBN 0-399-21557-3 LC 71-96054

Companion volume to: Upside-downers, entered below

Original Japanese edition, 1968; first United States edition published 1970 by Weatherhill

"In pictures of deceptive simplicity, optical illusions form structures in which curious little men can go up stairs to get to a lower place, hang pictures on the ceiling, and walk on walls." LC. Child Books, 1970

Anno, Mitsumasa, 1926-—*Continued*

Upside-downers; more pictures to stretch the imagination. Philomel Bks. 1988 c1971 27p il $13.95 **E**

1. Puzzles 2. Optical illusions 3. Stories without words
ISBN 0-399-21522-0 LC 71-157269

Original Japanese edition, 1969; first United States edition published 1971 by Weatherhill

"In a companion volume to Topsy-Turvies [entered above] the artist performs further feats of optical ingenuity with the same joyous dexterity that characterized the earlier book. . . . A kind of mad logic runs through the book." Horn Book

Archambault, John

Counting sheep; illustrated by John Rombola. Holt & Co. 1989 unp il $14.95 **E**

1. Counting 2. Sleep—Fiction 3. Stories in rhyme
ISBN 0-8050-1135-8 LC 89-11163

"A counting book is combined with a bedtime theme to create a story with unusual style and flair. Unable to sleep, but tired of counting sheep, a boy finds other animals to amuse him and to encourage him to slumber. . . . The sprightly verse is matched by vibrant illustrations, inspired by folk art and executed in dazzlingly bright colors." Horn Book

Arnosky, Jim

Deer at the brook. Lothrop, Lee & Shepard Bks. 1986 unp il $12.95; lib bdg $12.88 **E**

1. Deer
ISBN 0-688-04099-3; 0-688-04100-0 (lib bdg) LC 84-12239

The "illustrations are everything here, amplifying the sparest of texts with dramatic scenes of deer coming to a woodland brook to drink, eat, play, and nap. The full-color pictures are soft and compelling, focusing on a doe and her two fawns, which are masterfully drawn and imbued with nearly as much presence as real-life creatures would have. Other wildlife are artistically integrated into the drawings." Booklist

Raccoons and ripe corn. Lothrop, Lee & Shepard Bks. 1987 unp il $13; lib bdg $12.88 **E**

1. Raccoons
ISBN 0-688-05455-2; 0-688-05456-0 (lib bdg) LC 87-4243

"A mother raccoon and two older kits come in autumn dusk to a farmer's field, enjoy a star-lit romp and feed, then skulk off at dawn. A trail of fall leaves across the title pages leads to 11 double-spreads of open pencil sketches and color washes of woods and farm." SLJ

"Arnosky's pictures have a way of making nature larger than life. His raccoons are a strong focus of attention, and the hushed nighttime mood is almost palpable. The nature lesson implicit in the depicted episode is not romantic; these raccoons are greedy and somewhat destructive." Booklist

Aruego, Jose

Look what I can do. Scribner 1971 unp il o.p. paperback available $3.95 **E**

1. Water buffalo—Fiction
ISBN 0-689-71205-7 (pa) LC 73-158880

"The story of two carabaos who get carried away trying to outdo each other and almost come to a sad end." Booklist

"There are just fifteen words in this story . . . whose valuable message should be intelligible to the young non-reader. . . . Sprightly, cartoon-like drawings are the focal point." Book World

We hide, you seek; by Jose Aruego and Ariane Dewey. Greenwillow Bks. 1979 unp il $13.95; lib bdg $13.88; pa $3.95 **E**

1. Camouflage (Biology)—Fiction
ISBN 0-688-80201-X; 0-688-84201-1 (lib bdg); 0-688-07815-X (pa) LC 78-13638

"An oafishly good-natured rhino, invited into a jungle-wide game of hide and seek, bumbles from one scene to the next, accidentally exposing would-be hiders (leopards, crocodiles, lions) at every stop; then turning the tables on his playmates, cleverly hides himself. Readers are served up a wealth of information in 27 words (plus end-papers that give a page-by-page identification of the species pictured) and droll scenes drenched in the vibrant tones of an East African palette." SLJ

Asch, Frank

Here comes the cat! [by] Frank Asch and Vladimir Vagin. Scholastic 1988 unp il $11.95 **E**

1. Cats—Fiction 2. Mice—Fiction
ISBN 0-590-41859-9 LC 88-3083

"The plot is simple. A mouse travels throughout the land, á la Paul Revere, announcing, in both English and Russian, Roman and Cyrillic letters, 'Here comes the cat!' Indeed, a cat looms and finally appears. The surprise is that the cat is bearing a tremendous wheel of cheese. The mice, with relief and relish, munch the cheese while the benign cat lounges, eyes closed in contentment. On the final page, the messenger mouse, no longer a doomsayer, rides off into the sunset on the cat's back." N Y Times Book Rev

"The spreads feature pure colors and sturdy shapes that sometimes escape the pictures' thin borders. The book may be used by beginning readers, as a read-aloud, and, of course, as a jumping-off point for discussion." Booklist

Sand cake; a Frank Asch bear story. Parents Mag. Press 1979 c1978 unp il $5.95; lib bdg $5.95; Grosset & Dunlap pa $2.95 **E**

1. Bears—Fiction 2. Beaches—Fiction 3. Fathers and sons—Fiction
ISBN 0-8193-0985-0; 0-8193-0986-9 (lib bdg); 0-448-04341-6 (pa) LC 78-11183

Papa Bear uses his culinary skills and a little imagination to concoct a sand cake

Other available titles about Baby Bear and his family are:

Bread and honey (1982)
Goodbye house (1985)
Just like Daddy (1981)

Asch, Frank—*Continued*
Milk and cookies (1982)
Other available titles about a similar looking character called Bear are:
Bear shadow (1985)
Bear's bargain (1985)
Happy birthday, Moon (1982)
Moongame (1984)
Skyfire (1984)

Asher, Sandy, 1942-
Princess Bee and the royal good-night story; pictures by Cat Bowman Smith. Whitman, A. 1990 unp il $12.95 E
1. Sleep—Fiction
ISBN 0-8075-6624-1 LC 89-35790
"A lighthearted look at separation anxiety that succeeds as a pre-school read-aloud or a bedtime story. When the queen goes on a trip, young Princess Bee cannot fall asleep. Her brother and sister try to help, but their stories are too short. . . . Comforting words from her father encourage Bee to find the solution to her problem within herself. Asher's lilting text begs to be read aloud. . . . The humorous watercolors add to the appeal." SLJ

Aylesworth, Jim, 1943-
Hanna's hog; illustrated by Glen Rounds. Atheneum Pubs. 1988 unp il $13.95 E
1. Farm life—Fiction 2. Pigs—Fiction
ISBN 0-689-31367-5 LC 87-11559
"Hanna Brodie suspects her neighbor of stealing her chickens and her hog. Hanna gives Kenny Jackson a dose of his own medicine by convincing him there is a bear in the back woods." Child Book Rev Serv
"Rounds' scribbly, fluent illustrations capture the characters—Hanna's no-nonsense stride and ferocious scowl, Kenny's nervousness, and even the hog's porcine cheer—perfectly." SLJ

One crow; a counting rhyme; illustrated by Ruth Young. Lippincott 1988 unp il $12.95; lib bdg $12.89; Harper & Row pa $4.95 E
1. Counting 2. Animals—Fiction 3. Stories in rhyme
ISBN 0-397-32174-0; 0-397-32175-9 (lib bdg); 0-06-443242-4 (pa) LC 85-45856
"Simple four-line counting rhymes from one to ten (zero's there, too, but without a verse) take readers on a morning-to-night barnyard tour twice, once for a sunny summer day and once for a cold, snowy winter day. The first two lines of each quatrain focus on the animals representing the given number, while the second two comment on some aspect of nature in the setting. . . . The clear colors, clean line, and open composition of the illustrations convey a cheerful mood that's in keeping with the text." SLJ

Azarian, Mary
A farmer's alphabet. Godine 1981 61p il $16.95; pa $12.95 E
1. Alphabet 2. Farm life—Fiction
ISBN 0-87923-394-X; 0-87923-397-4 (pa) LC 80-84938
"Large, bold woodcuts make up an album of farming scenes obviously from New England—for example, 'M' is for maple sugar. A few scenes look cold and stern—showing winter and icicles—but there are children jumping in hay and flying a kite as well as . . . 'N' for neighbor and 'G' for a garden bursting with vegetables." Horn Book

Babbitt, Natalie
Nellie: a cat on her own; story and pictures by Natalie Babbitt. Farrar, Straus & Giroux 1989 unp il $11.95 E
1. Cats—Fiction
ISBN 0-374-35506-1 LC 89-61248
"Michael Di Capua books"
"Nellie is a marionette who can only dance when the old woman pulls her strings. Big Tom is a real cat who dashes in and out at all times leaving Nellie to wonder where he goes. When the old woman dies, Tom leads Nellie into the world to meet his friends. She becomes inspired to learn to dance in the moonshine by herself." Child Book Rev Serv
"This tale of independence achieved, certainly the epitome of catlike behavior, is enhanced by delicate watercolors of the dubious Nellie and competent Big Tom. A small tale, charmingly rendered." Horn Book

The something; story and pictures by Natalie Babbitt. Farrar, Straus & Giroux 1970 unp il $6.95; pa $2.95 E
1. Night—Fiction 2. Fear—Fiction
ISBN 0-374-37137-7; 0-374-46464-2 (pa) LC 70-125143
"Mylo is an ugly, hair-covered, bucktoothed little boy who is afraid of an indefinable Something coming in through his window at night. Given some modeling clay by his concerned mother, Mylo finally succeeds in making a statue of the Something but it is not until he meets the Something—an attractive little girl—in a dream that he discovers he is no longer afraid. Illustrated with drawings that endow the grotesque Mylo and his mother with endearing charm and printed on soft yellow pages except for the dream sequence which appears on gray pages, the clever, ironic story interprets common childhood fears of the dark in a way that should prove highly amusing to many small children." Booklist

Baker, Barbara, 1947-
Digby and Kate again; pictures by Marsha Winborn. Dutton 1989 44p il $9.95 E
1. Dogs—Fiction 2. Cats—Fiction
ISBN 0-525-44477-7 LC 88-25677
Sequel to: Digby and Kate (1988)
Digby the dog and Kate the cat share four adventures: hunting, bicycling, letter-writing, and raking the leaves
"Short snappy dialogue and a brisk pace mesh well with Winborn's cheery watercolors, reflecting the duo's spirit of adventure." Booklist

Baker, Jeannie

Home in the sky; story and pictures by Jeannie Baker. Greenwillow Bks. 1984 unp il $13; lib bdg $11.96 **E**

1. Pigeons—Fiction 2. New York (N.Y.)—Fiction
ISBN 0-688-03841-7; 0-688-03842-5 (lib bdg) LC 83-25379

"The story of a day in the life of a New York City pigeon recounts his trauma as he faces the perils of the weather and the subway system before being united with the gentle Black man who feeds him. Although the story is totally uninspired, the illustrations are utterly fascinating. Made of such items as grasses, leaves, pigeon feathers, fabric, and human hair and then painted, these collage constructions give an incredible feeling of three dimensions to the two-dimensional surface of the page: At times the viewer almost feels able to walk through the scenes." Horn Book

Where the forest meets the sea; story and pictures by Jeannie Baker. Greenwillow Bks. 1988 c1987 unp il $13.95; lib bdg $13.88 **E**

1. Australia—Fiction 2. Rain forests—Fiction
ISBN 0-688-06363-2; 0-688-06364-0 (lib bdg) LC 87-7551

First published 1987 in the United Kingdom

On a camping trip in an Australian rain forest with his father, a young boy thinks about the history of the plant and animal life around him and wonders about their future

"The illustrations, which translate the text into an extraordinary visual experience, are exciting as individual works of art yet do not violate the basic requirements of the picture-story concept. They are relief collages 'constructed from a multitude of materials, including modeling clay, papers, textured materials, preserved natural materials, and paints.' Integrated by the artist's vision, the collages create three-dimensional effects on two-dimensional pages drawing the reader into each scene as willing observer and explorer." Horn Book

Baker, Keith, 1953-

The magic fan; written and illustrated by Keith Baker. Harcourt Brace Jovanovich 1989 unp il $14.95 **E**

1. Japan—Fiction
ISBN 0-15-250750-7 LC 88-18727

Despite the laughter of his fellow villagers, Yoshi uses his building skills to make a boat to catch the moon, a kite to reach the clouds, and a bridge that mimics the rainbow

"The artwork, acrylics on illustration board, is framed within the outline of an open fan. The text appears outside this frame, and fan-shaped die-cuts allow the reader to turn the inner page and see a second picture on each double-page spread. . . . An entertaining tale as well as an elegant addition to the picture-book shelf." Booklist

Baker, Leslie A.

Morning beach; [by] Leslie Baker. Little, Brown 1990 unp il $14.95 **E**

1. Vacations—Fiction 2. Seashore—Fiction
ISBN 0-316-07835-2 LC 88-25836

"Set on Martha's Vineyard, the book begins with a girl waking up in Grandma's house. She and her Mom are to take their annual first trip to the beach, as 'Grandma took Mom when she was a little girl.'" Publ Wkly

"Lovely, warm tale of the joy of rediscovering a favorite place. The wonderful watercolors add just the right dreamy-kind of touch." Child Book Rev Serv

Balian, Lorna

Humbug witch. Abingdon Press 1965 unp il $5.95 **E**

1. Witches—Fiction
ISBN 0-687-37105-8 LC 65-14089

This book is about "a little witch and her unsuccessful attempts at witchcraft. One evening she wearily takes off piece after piece of comical attire—the last of which proves to be a mask, revealing a hilarious little girl underneath! Too good to miss." Adventuring with Books. 2d edition

Bang, Molly

Delphine. Morrow Junior Bks. 1988 unp il $12.95; lib bdg $12.88 **E**

1. Gifts—Fiction
ISBN 0-688-05636-9; 0-688-05637-7 (lib bdg) LC 87-34958

"Delphine, giant in proportion to a tiny mailman, receives a message that Gram has a present waiting for her at the Post Office. She sets out in her symbolic baby buggy with her pet wolf and mountain lion to cross gorges, run rapids, and risk lightning with aplomb, all the while expressing nervousness about what she suspects will be a bicycle. Needless to say, she learns to stay on, steer, and stop the bike in one double-page spread." Bull Cent Child Books

"The vibrant pictures and the sparse, direct text are interdependent, while the interspersion of wordless pages that carry the story adds a creative and unusual aspect." Publ Wkly

The Grey Lady and the Strawberry Snatcher. Four Winds Press 1980 unp il $14.95 **E**

1. Strawberries—Fiction 2. Stories without words
ISBN 0-02-708140-0 LC 79-21243

A Caldecott Medal honor book, 1981

The strawberry snatcher tries to wrest the strawberries from the grey lady but as he follows her through shops and woods he discovers some delicious blackberries instead

"The award-winning artist has conceived and realized an extraordinary picture book. Bang's illustrations are unparalleled in effects, full-color paintings and collages in which the surrealistic and the representational combine to tell a story without words." Publ Wkly

Bang, Molly—*Continued*

The paper crane. Greenwillow Bks. 1985 unp il $13; lib bdg $12.88; pa $4.95 **E**

ISBN 0-688-04108-6; 0-688-04109-4 (lib bdg); 0-688-07333-6 (pa) LC 84-13546

"Bang gives a modern setting and details to the consoling story of a good man, deprived by unlucky fate of his livelihood, whose act of kindness and generosity is repaid by the restoration of his fortunes, through the bringing to life of a magical animal—the paper crane." SLJ

"Every detail of the restaurant interior, from the strawberries on the cake to the floral centerpieces, is a delight to the eye and imagination. The warm, amber backgrounds and vibrant colors of the crowded restaurant strikingly contrast with the stark simplicity of the climactic scene. The double-page spread of the old man and the dancing crane has the quality of a fine old Japanese screen. The book successfully blends Asian folklore themes with contemporary Western characterization." Horn Book

Ten, nine, eight. Greenwillow Bks. 1983 unp il $13.95; lib bdg $13.88; pa $3.95 **E**

1. Lullabies 2. Counting
ISBN 0-688-00906-9; 0-688-00907-7 (lib bdg); 0-688-10480-0 (pa) LC 81-20106

A Caldecott Medal honor book, 1984

"In countdown style, the text of this counting book begins with '10 small toes all washed and warm,' and ends with '1 big girl all ready for bed.' The captions rhyme . . . and the pictures—warm, bright paintings—show a black father and child snuggling in a chair, the child yawning, and the child hugging her toy bear after some loving good night kisses." Bull Cent Child Books

"The author-artist has devised an appealing countdown book . . . in direct, lilting rhymes accompanied by handsome full-page paintings executed in rich, intense colors. The style is representational, the composition uncluttered; the total effect is one of elegance and warmth." Horn Book

Banks, Kate, 1960-

Alphabet soup; pictures by Peter Sis. Knopf 1988 unp il $12.95; lib bdg $11.99 **E**

1. Bears—Fiction
ISBN 0-394-89151-1; 0-394-99151-6 (lib bdg) LC 87-3191

"A young schoolboy dawdles over his lunchtime bowl of noodle soup. After his mother urges him to eat, he spoons the letters B-E-A-R from the soup, and instantly a bear appears, looking somewhat like the honey container on the table. The boy and the bear begin a series of adventures, all of which involve items from the lunch table—a salt shaker becomes a wizard; a teacup becomes a sailboat; a bowl of fruit, a mountain. All of these appear when the boy fishes out appropriate letters from his soup. Illustrations add a dreamy quality to the narration. Soft pastels are washed with textured blue oil paint. Text is printed on honey-colored panels, over which tumble alphabet noodles. An exciting adventure with extra appeal to daydreamers." SLJ

Banks, Merry

Animals of the night; pictures by Ronald Himler. Scribner 1990 unp il $13.95 **E**

1. Animals—Fiction 2. Night—Fiction
ISBN 0-684-19093-1 LC 89-6194

"This book describes various nocturnal animals and some of their activities. At the end of the day, sleepy farm children go to bed, and the night animals appear. At sunrise, the animals get ready for sleep as the children awaken to start the new day." SLJ

"Because the text is simple without becoming either boring or cloying, and because the watercolor paintings are deeply involving, this is one of those rare bedtime mood pieces that does indeed cast a spell. . . . The skillfully varied pictorial frames, the convincing perspectives, and the fine animal drafting invite a long look, while the words will soothe many a fear of the shadowed world beyond reach of electric lights." Bull Cent Child Books

Barber, Antonia, 1932-

The Mousehole cat; illustrated by Nicola Bayley. Macmillan 1990 unp il $14.95 **E**

1. Cats—Fiction 2. Sea stories
ISBN 0-02-708331-4 LC 90-31533

"In the village of Mowzel lives a proud, determined cat named Mowzer. Her 'pet' is an old fisherman who provides her with succulent fresh fish. When the Storm Cat blocks the village, Tom and Mowzer venture forth anyhow. Mowzer's eloquent purring tames the ferocious giant and enables Tom to pull in a boat-load of fish." Child Book Rev Serv

"This delicate, charming tale and the exquisite illustrations of stormy seas, gleaming fish, and delightful cats and townspeople make an extremely handsome book, splendid for reading aloud." Horn Book

Barracca, Debra

The adventures of Taxi Dog; by Debra and Sal Barracca; pictures by Mark Buehner. Dial Bks. for Young Readers 1990 30p il $12.95; lib bdg $12.89 **E**

1. Dogs—Fiction 2. Stories in rhyme
ISBN 0-8037-0671-5; 0-8037-0672-3 (lib bdg) LC 89-1056

"In snappy, rhymed lines, Maxi recalls his days as a stray and his adoption by taxi-driving Jim. Applying oil paint over acrylics, Buehner creates color with lush character. The hues' intense depth, coupled with the artist's finesse with perspective, will draw readers into the action." Booklist

Barrett, Judi, 1941-

Benjamin's 365 birthdays; written by Judi Barrett and drawn by Ron Barrett. Atheneum Pubs. 1974 unp il hardcover o.p. paperback available $4.95 **E**

1. Birthdays—Fiction
ISBN 0-689-70443-7 (pa) LC 72-86926

"Benjamin loves birthdays so much that the thought of waiting a whole year after his ninth till his next one makes him weep and then inspires him to rewrap his presents, one each day, and go on to wrap everything

Barrett, Judi, 1941-—*Continued*
in his house." Booklist

Benjamin's "solution to prolonging pleasure will amuse preschoolers familiar with post-party blues. . . . The theme is familiar, but its execution both in text and humorously detailed illustrations is fresh and spontaneous." Horn Book

Barton, Byron

Bones, bones, dinosaur bones. Crowell 1990 unp il $9.95; lib bdg $12.89 **E**

1. Dinosaurs—Fiction
ISBN 0-690-04825-4; 0-690-04827-0 (lib bdg) LC 89-71306

"From the field search for dinosaur bones to reconstructed skeletons for museum display, paleontology as process is revealed in simple text, bold print, and flat illustrations with heavy, black outlines. Includes labeled illustrations of eight dinosaurs." Sci Child

Bate, Lucy

How Georgina drove the car very carefully from Boston to New York; illustrated by Tamar Taylor. Crown 1989 unp il $12.95 **E**

1. Automobile drivers—Fiction
ISBN 0-517-57142-0 LC 88-22861

Young Georgina pretends she drives her family all the way from Boston to Grandma's house in New York City

"Younger readers and listeners are sure to respond in kind to Georgina's glee as they enjoy this short, rhythmic tale with its cautionary refrain. The prose has an authentically child-like sound, perfectly complemented by Taylor's cheery watercolors; tiny-wheeled cars and stylized figures with fixed smiles suggest a child's hand. A natural read-aloud—funny, imaginative, and satisfying." SLJ

Bayer, Jane, d. 1985

A my name is Alice; pictures by Steven Kellogg. Dial Bks. for Young Readers 1984 unp il $14.95; lib bdg $14.89; pa $4.95 **E**

1. Stories in rhyme 2. Alphabet
ISBN 0-8037-0123-3; 0-8037-0124-1 (lib bdg); 0-8037-0130-6 (pa) LC 84-7059

"Each page contains (in the border above the illustration) the name of an animal ('A my name is Alice') and its spouse ('and my husband's name is Alex.'), their locale ('We come from Alaska') and occupation ('and we sell ants.'). Two sentences appear beneath the illustrations on each page identifying the kind of animals in the verse ('Alice is an 'Ape.' Alex is an 'Anteater.')." SLJ

"It is a superlative blend of visual and textual nonsense because the visual surprises keep the repetitive pattern in the text from becoming tedious. The verbal parts gradually expand in their ludicrousness, in their cataloging of zany characters and occupations." Wilson Libr Bull

Baylor, Byrd

The best town in the world; pictures by Ronald Himler. Scribner 1983 unp il $13.95; Aladdin Bks. (NY) pa $3.95 **E**

1. Texas—Fiction
ISBN 0-684-18035-9; 0-689-71086-0 (pa) LC 83-9033

"The text describes the way the author's father talked about his home town in Texas, the best town in the world, viewed with nostalgia." Bull Cent Child Books

The author "has written many prose poems celebrating her Southwest. . . . All have been works of power and grace, but none come close to this one, her most personal, accessible, and lively. . . . Ronald Himler's water color scenes, at first glance typically dreamy, gradually reveal a solid beauty, that of ordinary people and extraordinary space." N Y Times Book Rev

Guess who my favorite person is; illustrated by Robert Andrew Parker. Scribner 1977 unp il o.p.; Aladdin Bks. (NY) paperback available $4.95 **E**

ISBN 0-689-71052-6 (pa) LC 77-7151

A "book celebrating the pleasures of favorite things. A young man and a little girl who chance to meet in an alfalfa field take turns choosing sounds, places to live, dreams, colors, and smells—'We must have named a hundred favorite things that afternoon.' The combination of thoughtfulness, friendliness, and sensitivity in the text with the peaceful, subtle watercolors—including a magnificent illustration of falling stars—makes the book a unique experience." Horn Book

Hawk, I'm your brother; illustrated by Peter Parnall. Scribner 1976 unp il lib bdg $12.95; Aladdin Bks. (NY) pa $3.95 **E**

1. Hawks—Fiction
ISBN 0-684-14571-5 (lib bdg); 0-689-71102-6 (pa) LC 75-39296

A Caldecott Medal honor book, 1977

"Driven by the desire to fly, Rudy Soto steals a baby hawk from its nest in the hope that having a hawk as his 'brother' will somehow enable him to take flight. Seeing the hawk's frustration in confinement, the boy finally releases it. But the hawk remembers Rudy and the two call back and forth to each other across the mountains. Through their communication, Rudy begins to experience flying vicariously. . . . Now the hawk is truly his brother." Interracial Books Child Bull

"In the poetic simplicity of the writing, Baylor echoes the quietness of the desert and she captures the essence of the desert people's affinity for natural things. Both are reflected in Parnall's spacious illustrations, as clean and poetic as is the writing." Bull Cent Child Books

The other way to listen; by Byrd Baylor and Peter Parnall. Scribner 1978 unp il $13.95 **E**

ISBN 0-684-16017-X LC 78-23430

Illustrated by Peter Parnall

The text is "spoken by a child, who remembers . . . conversations with the old man who could hear the cactus flowers blooming or the rock murmuring to the lizard perching on it. There was no way, he said, to teach such listening, but one must feel that each object or creature is important, and one must be silent and patient. The child tried and tried to no avail, and then

Baylor, Byrd—*Continued*
one morning, singing to the hills, heard the hills sing too. And, as the old man had said, it wasn't surprising at all, but seemed the most natural thing in the world." Bull Cent Child Books

"Set in pages of varied design, the book is a tribute to the idea that spareness is effective. The flowing sketches with minimal lines are brightened by the addition of yellowish orange; the short text does not have an unnecessary word." Horn Book

Bemelmans, Ludwig, 1898-1962

Madeline; story and pictures by Ludwig Bemelmans. Viking 1985 c1939 unp il $13.95; Penguin Bks. pa $3.95 E

1. Paris (France)—Fiction 2. Stories in rhyme
ISBN 0-670-44580-0; 0-14-050198-3 (pa)

A Caldecott Medal honor book, 1940

A reissue of the title first published 1939 by Simon & Schuster

"Madeline is a nonconformist in a regimented world—a Paris convent school. This rhymed story tells how she made an adventure out of having appendicitis." Hodges. Books for Elem Sch Libr

Other available titles about Madeline are:
Madeline and the bad hat (1957)
Madeline and the gypsies (1959)
Madeline in London (1961)
Madeline's Christmas (1985)

Another available title about Madeline is: Madeline's rescue, entered below

Madeline's rescue; story and pictures by Ludwig Bemelmans. Viking 1985 c1953 unp il $13.95; Penguin Bks. pa $3.95 E

1. Dogs—Fiction 2. Paris (France)—Fiction 3. Stories in rhyme
ISBN 0-670-44716-1; 0-14-050207-6 (pa)

Awarded the Caldecott Medal, 1954

Sequel to: Madeline, entered above

First published 1953

A picture-story book with rhymed text about little Madeline in Paris. This time she falls into the Seine and is rescued by 'a dog that kept its head.' The dog, named Genevieve, was promptly adopted by Madeline's boarding school mistress and her twelve pupils. When Genevieve was turned out by snobbish trustees the little girls were inconsolable, until Genevieve solved their problem

Benchley, Nathaniel, 1915-1981

A ghost named Fred; pictures by Ben Shecter. Harper & Row 1968 unp il lib bdg $10.89; pa $3.50 E

1. Ghosts—Fiction
ISBN 0-06-020474-5 (lib bdg); 0-06-444022-2 (pa)
LC 68-24322

"An I can read mystery"

"George, an imaginative child used to playing alone, went into an empty house to get out of the rain; there he met an absent-minded ghost named Fred, who knew there was a treasure but had forgotten where. Only when Fred opened an umbrella for George's homeward journey did the treasure materialize." Bull Cent Child Books

"More humorous than scary . . . this is a pleasing and acceptable ghost story for beginning readers." Booklist

Berenstain, Stan, 1923-

Bears on wheels. Random House 1969 unp il $6.95; lib bdg $7.99 E

1. Bears—Fiction 2. Counting
ISBN 0-394-80967-X; 0-394-90967-4 (lib bdg)
LC 72-77840

"A Bright & early book"

The authors' illustrations are used with numbers in this counting book which tells the story of a small bear who goes out for a ride on one small wheel. As the bear rides on, traffic and unwanted passengers accumulate

Berenzy, Alix

A Frog Prince; written and illustrated by Alix Berenzy. Holt & Co. 1989 unp il $13.95 (2-4) E

1. Fairy tales 2. Frogs—Fiction
ISBN 0-8050-0426-2 LC 88-29628

"Based on the original story: Der Froschkönig." Verso of title page

"Beginning like Grimm's fairy tale 'The Frog Prince,' this story takes an unusual twist, leading to new adventures and a surprise ending. Told from the frog's point of view . . . the story progresses along expected lines until the princess flings the frog against the wall. Rather than changing into a prince, he remains a broken-hearted frog . . . he appeals to the king, who . . . outfits him and sends him off to seek his fortune. After rescuing several hapless creatures who help him along his way, the frog discovers a true princess, a golden-eyed, green, amphibious beauty who loves him as he is." Booklist

"Elegant composition and attention to detail pull the eye into the pictures and reward repeated scrutiny. Several of the pictures are simply breathtaking, conveying an unusual depth of emotion. . . . Berenzy's palette of deep rich color, alternately gilded with light and cloaked in darkness, displays a magnificent utilization of light and shadow. A wonderful book—wry, touching, funny, and completely satisfying." SLJ

Berger, Barbara, 1945-

Grandfather Twilight. Philomel Bks. 1984 unp il $14.95 E

1. Night—Fiction
ISBN 0-399-20996-4 LC 83-19490

"The coming of night is fancifully explained via the glowing figure of Grandfather Twilight, a benign, mysterious figure who walks shimmering through the woods to the seaside to release an incandescent pearl that becomes the moon. The slight story gets a lift from the attractive illustrations, which are full-color paintings with soft textures, and deep, rich color. Grandfather Twilight's ethereal form is an intriguing presence who radiates calm and warmth. An image poetically and graphically extended for quiet one-on-one sharing." Booklist

Berry, Christine

Mama went walking; illustrated by María Cristina Brusca. Holt & Co. 1990 unp il $14.95 **E**

1. Mothers and daughters—Fiction
ISBN 0-8050-1261-3 LC 89-39789

Sarah saves her mother from a series of imaginary dangers, from lions in the Jaba-Jaba Jungle to scritchy-witchy things in the Gonagetcha Forest

"Illustrated with fanciful, imaginative paintings, this story of make-believe adventure, danger, and rescue rollicks along in a rhythmic text that will seem fresh through many rereadings." Horn Book

Beskow, Elsa, 1874-1953

Pelle's new suit; picture book by Elsa Beskow; translated by Marion Letcher Woodburn. Harper & Row 1929 unp il lib bdg $13.89 **E**

1. Sweden—Fiction
ISBN 0-06-020496-6

"Charming pictures tell the story of how Pelle earned his new suit. He is shown raking hay, bringing in wood, feeding pigs, going on errands and at the same time, each process in the making of the suit is followed, beginning with the shearing of the lamb. The coloring of the pictures (which show both Swedish peasant house interiors and out-of-door scenes) is quite lovely." N Y Public Libr

Birdseye, Tom

Airmail to the moon; illustrated by Stephen Gammell. Holiday House 1988 unp il lib bdg $13.95; pa $5.95 **E**

1. Teeth—Fiction
ISBN 0-8234-0683-0 (lib bdg); 0-8234-0754-3 (pa)
LC 87-21199

"Ora Mae, better known as Oreo because she's such a sweet cookie, has been worrying at a loose tooth like mad until, finally, one night it plops into her plate of spaghetti. Hurrying to bed to dream of all the wonderful things she'll buy with the tooth fairy's money, she's outraged in the morning to find that her tooth has been stolen. From one member of her family to the next, Oreo investigates the dastardly deed, vowing that when she catches the villain she'll 'open up a can of gotcha and send 'em airmail to the moon!'" Horn Book

"Gammell's colorful pencil drawings carry out the down-home rickety flavor from the title page outhouse to the pig waller. If the country flavor is spread a bit thick, the underlying story does work." SLJ

Blaine, Marge

The terrible thing that happened at our house; pictures by John C. Wallner. Four Winds Press 1986 c1975 unp il $12.95 **E**

1. Children of working parents—Fiction 2. Family life—Fiction
ISBN 0-02-710720-5 LC 86-4827

A reissue of the 1975 edition published by Parents Magazine Press

A story "about the plaint of a young girl who longs for life as it used to be before her mother returned to work. Before that 'terrible thing' happened, life was calm and orderly. . . . After Mother goes back to teaching science . . . the chaos of rushed breakfasts and lost sneakers ensues. But Mother doesn't quit her job. Instead, they work out cooperative compromises in which the children share some chores and the story ends with the family spending leisure time together again." SLJ

Blake, Quentin, 1932-

Quentin Blake's ABC. Knopf 1989 unp il $11.95; lib bdg $12.99 **E**

1. Alphabet
ISBN 0-394-84149-2; 0-394-94149-7 (lib bdg)
LC 88-26621

"Each page playfully introduces a letter of the alphabet, a word beginning with that letter, and a phrase describing the word. Many pages are humorous. . . . Blake's zany watercolor illustrations, loosely outlined in black ink, are vibrant and whimsical. The oversized format and the large, bold print add visual appeal." Publ Wkly

Blegvad, Lenore

Anna Banana and me; illustrated by Erik Blegvad. Atheneum Pubs. 1985 unp il lib bdg $10.95; pa $3.95 **E**

1. Fear—Fiction
ISBN 0-689-50274-5 (lib bdg); 0-689-71114-X (pa)
LC 84-457

"A Margaret K. McElderry book"

"Small, deft, softly-tinted sketches add measurably to the appeal of a short book that captures the insecurity of a small boy and his admiration for the intrepid playmate he calls Anna Banana. The boy, who is the narrator, describes a series of encounters in which Anna Banana takes the lead and he follows. In the final episode, she frightens him with a story about a goblin and runs off; the boy is almost paralyzed with apprehension until he finds a feather, when he remembers that Anna Banana had said a feather was magic, takes heart, and happily trots off toward home. A nicely told story that reverses stereotypical sex roles." Bull Cent Child Books

Blood, Charles L., 1929-

The goat in the rug; as told to Charles L. Blood & Martin Link by Geraldine; illustrated by Nancy Winslow Parker. Four Winds Press 1980 1976 unp il $14.95; Aladdin Bks. (NY) pa $3.95 **E**

1. Goats—Fiction 2. Navajo Indians—Fiction 3. Rugs—Fiction
ISBN 0-02-710920-8; 0-689-71418-1 (pa)
LC 80-17315

A reissue of the 1976 edition published by Parents Magazine Press

"A goat's-eye view of how a Navajo rug is made, from the shearing of our supposed narrator ('Geraldine') to the dyeing and weaving. By the time the rug is finished, Geraldine has grown enough wool to start another one." Saturday Rev

Blood, Charles L., 1929-—*Continued*

"Parker's vivid primary colored illustrations are as enjoyable and humorous as the instructive text." SLJ

Blos, Joan W.

The grandpa days; illustrated by Emily Arnold McCully. Simon & Schuster Bks. for Young Readers 1989 unp il $8.95 E

1. Grandfathers—Fiction
ISBN 0-671-64640-0 LC 88-19801

Philip comes up with just the right project to build with Grandpa during their week together, but first he has to learn the difference between wishes and good planning

"Besides celebrating the link between old and young, the story also explores the creative process in a fashion young children can easily understand. McCully's pen-and-wash drawings capture the good feelings between Philip and his Grandpa in warm scenes of the two planning, working, and puttering about. Unassuming and sweet." Booklist

Old Henry; illustrated by Stephen Gammell. Morrow 1987 unp il $13.95; lib bdg $13.88 E

1. Stories in rhyme
ISBN 0-688-06399-3; 0-688-06400-0 (lib bdg) LC 86-21745

A "poem-portrait of an old man who offends the neighbors with his raggedy house and renegade ways. When Old Henry moves in, people expect him 'to fix things up a bit. He did not think of it.' Instead, he spreads his paraphernalia over the uncut grass, rejects offers of help shoveling snow, and finally moves out. Amazingly, he and the community come to miss each other." Bull Cent Child Books

"This very lightly told story about social tolerance and the merits of diversity is deftly illustrated in soft, colored-pencil drawings that capture the characters perfectly." N Y Times Book Rev

Blume, Judy

The Pain and the Great One; illustrations by Irene Trivas. Bradbury Press 1984 unp il lib bdg $12.95; Dell pa $3.95 E

1. Brothers and sisters—Fiction
ISBN 0-02-711100-8 (lib bdg); 0-440-46819-1 (pa) LC 84-11009

A six-year-old (The Pain) and his eight-year-old sister (The Great One) see each other as troublemakers and the best-loved in the family

"Young readers, depending on their position within the family, will readily identify with either character and may learn empathy for the other. Used in a group, this will provide much healthy discussion. . . . Trivas' vibrant colors add depth and humor to a valuable book on sibling relationships." SLJ

Bogart, Jo Ellen

Daniel's dog; illustrated by Janet Wilson. Scholastic 1990 30p il $11.95; lib bdg $11.95 E

1. Imaginary playmates—Fiction 2. Brothers and sisters—Fiction 3. Blacks—Fiction
ISBN 0-590-43402-0; 0-590-73344-3 (lib bdg) LC 89-35258

A young black boy adjusts to the arrival of his new baby sister with the help of his imaginary dog Lucy

"Wilson's realistic illustrations ingeniously capture Daniel's facial expressions as he plays with his imaginary pet and learns to take care of his tiny sibling. According to dust-jacket copy, this story was inspired by tales of dog ghosts, part of the Afro-American oral tradition. The story will also speak to children's penchant for inventing imaginary friends." Booklist

Bollen, Marilyn Sadler

Alistair's elephant; [by] Marilyn Sadler; illustrated by Roger Bollen. Prentice-Hall 1983 unp il $12.95; pa $5.95 E

1. Elephants—Fiction
ISBN 0-671-66680-0; 0-13-022773-0 (pa) LC 82-23091

"Alistair Grittle is an extremely intelligent, highly organized little boy who, we are told, has 'no time for nonsense.' Into his carefully structured existence comes an elephant, who follows Alistair home from the zoo one Saturday and proceeds to make the following week a bewildering series of frustrations for Alistair. The elephant follows him everywhere, even to school, and is not only nosy but midly destructive. At the end of the week, having taught the elephant a few manners, Alistair returns him to the zoo and gratefully heads for home . . . only to be followed by a giraffe." SLJ

"The story has the sort of humor children find appealing, and the full-color illustrations are bright and clean." Booklist

Other available titles about Alistair are:
Alistair in outer space (1984)
Alistair underwater (1990)
Alistair's time machine (1986)

Bond, Felicia, 1954-

Poinsettia & her family. Crowell 1981 32p il lib bdg $13.89; Harper & Row pa $4.95 E

1. Family life—Fiction 2. Pigs—Fiction
ISBN 0-690-04145-4 (lib bdg); 0-06-443076-6 (pa) LC 81-43035

"Irritated when all her favorite retreats . . . have been pre-empted by one or another of her six brothers and sisters, Poinsettia Pig makes herself thoroughly disagreeable and is sent to bed early 'for general misbehavior.' But when, on the following day, father pig announces that they will look for a new and larger home, she deliberately remains behind, convinced that the size of the family, not the size of the house, is responsible for their discomfort." Horn Book

"What makes this . . . story unexpectedly entertaining is Bond's slightly potty pen-and-wash drawings and her success at portraying Poinsettia as a connoisseur of privacy. . . . A light confection, but one with a special sense of truth." Booklist

Bond, Felicia, 1954-—*Continued*

Another available title about Poinsettia is entered below

Poinsettia and the firefighters. Crowell 1984 32p il lib bdg $12.89; Harper & Row pa $3.95 **E**

1. Night—Fiction 2. Fear—Fiction 3. Fire fighters—Fiction 4. Pigs—Fiction
ISBN 0-690-04401-1 (lib bdg); 0-06-443160-6 (pa) LC 83-46169

Lonely and afraid of the dark in her new room, Poinsettia Pig is comforted when she discovers that the firefighters are awake and keep watch during the night

"Enlivened by Bond's sprightly pictures, this comforting story should take some of the spookiness out of night frights for many young readers." Publ Wkly

Bonsall, Crosby Newell, 1921-

The amazing, the incredible super dog; by Crosby Bonsall. Harper & Row 1986 32p il $11.95; lib bdg $11.89 **E**

1. Dogs—Fiction 2. Cats—Fiction
ISBN 0-06-020590-3; 0-06-020591-1 (lib bdg) LC 85-45811

"A girl tries unsuccessfully to get her dog to perform a variety of tricks, meanwhile unaware that her cat is doing them perfectly and that a nearby bird is attempting them as well. The brightly-colored illustrations amplify the story's amusing antics." Child Book Rev Serv

The day I had to play with my sister. Harper & Row 1972 32p il lib bdg $9.89; pa $3.50 **E**

1. Brothers and sisters—Fiction
ISBN 0-06-020576-8 (lib bdg); 0-06-444117-2 (pa) LC 72-76507

"An Early I can read book"

A young boy finds trying to teach his little sister to play hide-and-seek very frustrating

"The extremely simple text, written from the boy's point of view, is one with which children can readily identify. Pastel illustrations on every page add touches of humor to the text, which is divided into chapters. The realistic atmosphere makes Bonsall's book an excellent addition to the very early reading shelves." SLJ

Piggle; by Crosby Bonsall. Harper & Row 1973 63p il lib bdg $10.89 **E**

1. Games—Fiction 2. Animals—Fiction
ISBN 0-06-020580-6 LC 73-5478

"An I can read book"

"Rebuffed by his four sisters—Lolly, Molly, Polly, and Dolly—who are playing Pin the Tail, Homer goes in search of someone who will play a game with him. . . . Homer and Bear play Piggle, a fascinating word game; and soon Homer's four sisters, Rabbit, and Duck are also playing. Only Pig, after whom the game was named, can't understand how to play it." Horn Book

"Light-hearted and nicely gauged for the primary audience, the story is, despite the easy vocabulary, not too stilted—as many books for beginning readers are—to read aloud to preschool children." Bull Cent Child Books

Another available title about Homer is: Who's a pest, entered below

Tell me some more; by Crosby Bonsall; pictures by Fritz Siebel. Harper & Row 1961 64p il lib bdg $10.89 **E**

1. Libraries—Fiction
ISBN 0-06-020601-2 LC 61-5773

"An I can read book"

"A fresh and original introduction to the public library, a special place where one can hold an elephant, pat a lion on the nose, tickle a seal, and do all sorts of unusual things. At least that's what Andrew told Tim, and Tim always answered 'Tell me some more.' The artist has caught the small boys' delight in books." Bull Cent Child Books

"Highly original and full of fun. . . . Humorous sketches in which the children appear in black line only, although bright color is added for backgrounds and animals." Horn Book

Who's a pest? Harper & Row 1962 64p il lib bdg $10.89; pa $3.50 **E**

ISBN 0-06-020621-7 (lib bdg); 0-06-444099-0 (pa) LC 62-13310

"An I can read book"

"In this truly funny . . . book a small boy named Homer proves that he is not a pest as his four sisters, a rabbit, chipmunk, and lizard claim. The drawings are as laughable as the text and the tongue-twisting dialog begs to be read aloud." Booklist

Who's afraid of the dark? by Crosby Bonsall. Harper & Row 1980 32p il $9.95; lib bdg $9.89; pa $2.95 **E**

1. Night—Fiction 2. Fear—Fiction
ISBN 0-06-020598-9; 0-06-020599-7 (lib bdg); 0-06-444071-0 (pa) LC 79-2700

"An Early I can read book"

"In a variation on an old theme a little boy describes to a friend the nighttime fears of his dog Stella. Stella shivers in the dark, he claims; she sees shapes and hears scary sounds. The doubting but sympathetic friend offers a suggestion—hug Stella in the night and comfort her until her fears go away. When the boy tries this method of solving the problem, he finds that it works perfectly. The illustrations in shades of light blue and brown are filled with as much life and warmth as ever. As the little boy describes Stella's fears, full-page pictures on alternating pages show the real story. While Stella sleeps peacefully, the heroic protagonist shivers under his covers." Horn Book

Boynton, Sandra

A is for angry. Workman 1983 42p il o.p. paperback available $5.95 **E**

1. Alphabet
ISBN 0-89480-507-X (pa) LC 83-40038

"Boynton's alphabet book introduces preschoolers to adjectives and animals beginning with each letter of the alphabet (except X): an angry anteater peers through the letter A while an angry ant is perched atop it. . . . Some of the adjectives used are very common, such as 'clean' or 'dirty,' while others are much more sophisticated, such as 'vain, jazzy, rotund.'" SLJ

"Young children unfamiliar with Boynton's greeting-card menagerie will find these animals fresh and funny as they cavort in and around strikingly colored, page-

Boynton, Sandra—*Continued*
filling capital letters demonstrating various states of mind and/or body." Booklist

Brandenberg, Franz, 1932-

Aunt Nina and her nephews and nieces; illustrated by Aliki. Greenwillow Bks. 1983 unp il $11.75; lib bdg $11.88 **E**

1. Aunts—Fiction 2. Parties—Fiction 3. Birthdays—Fiction 4. Cats—Fiction
ISBN 0-688-01869-6; 0-688-01870-X (lib bdg) LC 82-12004

"Fun-loving Aunt Nina, who lives alone, invites her six nephews and nieces to a birthday celebration for her cat, Fluffy. When the honored guest fails to appear, the children search the house for her, from cellar to attic, and have more fun doing it than if they had gone to the zoo, toy shop, theater, or haunted house as Aunt Nina had suggested. After lunch, they prepare for naps and discover the missing Fluffy in Aunt Nina's bed with six newborns that look just like her." Child Book Rev Serv

"Aliki's chipper, brightly colored watercolor paintings of children making the most of Aunt Nina's cozy home underscore the story's warmth." Booklist

Other available titles about Aunt Nina are:
Aunt Nina, goodnight (1989)
Aunt Nina's visit (1984)

Leo and Emily; illustrated by Aliki. Greenwillow Bks. 1981 55p il $12.95 **E**

1. Friendship—Fiction
ISBN 0-688-80292-3 LC 80-19657

"A Greenwillow read-alone book"

"Emily often wakes her pal Leo before dawn, encouraging him to dress in the dark and join her to swap treasures (a rabbit for Grandmother's wig) or just to talk. Dressing in the dark results in inside-out clothes, untied spaghetties (shoestrings) and the omission of socks. Emily's grandmother is so understanding about her wig being borrowed, she buys Emily her own rabbit and Leo and Emily put on a magic show." SLJ

"In three chapters, this book for beginning independent readers incorporates humor, friendship values, enterprise, and some excellent familial relationships. . . . Aliki's people are small, brisk, and amusing; a nice integration—both in mood and in page layout—of drawings and text." Bull Cent Child Books

Other available titles about Leo and Emily are:
Leo and Emily and the dragon (1984)
Leo and Emily's big ideas (1982)
Leo and Emily's zoo (1988)

Nice new neighbors; illustrated by Aliki. Greenwillow Bks. 1977 56p il lib bdg $13.88; Scholastic pa $2.75 **E**

1. Friendship—Fiction 2. Mice—Fiction
ISBN 0-688-84105-8 (lib bdg); 0-590-44117-5 (pa) LC 77-1651

"A Greenwillow read-alone book"

"A newly moved-in family of fieldmouse children makes vain attempts to join other youngsters in game playing. After being rebuffed by juvenile representatives of each nearby household, the resourceful mouse children decide to create their own play, based on the old favorite 'Three Blind Mice.' Suddenly, they become very popular and end up with a grand production in which all the neighborhood children take part." Booklist

"Aliki uses pale pinks and greens in combination with black and white for her lively, scrawly drawings of small animals; her illustrations have some touches (balloon captions, framed sequence drawing for a play) that will be familiar to cartoon-conscious beginning independent readers." Bull Cent Child Books

Brenner, Barbara

Wagon wheels; pictures by Don Bolognese. Harper & Row 1978 64p il $11.95; lib bdg $10.89; pa $3.50 **E**

1. Frontier and pioneer life—Fiction 2. Blacks—Fiction
ISBN 0-06-020668-3; 0-06-020669-1 (lib bdg); 0-06-444052-4 (pa) LC 76-21391

"An I can read history book"

A "frontier story for beginning independent readers describes the experiences of a black family which comes from Kentucky to Kansas in the 1870's. The story is told by one of the three boys; the writing is simple and direct, yet it has a narrative flow and gives a vivid picture of both the hardships of pioneer life and of the love and courage of the family. The book is based on fact: Nicodemus, Kansas, was a black community and there really was an Ed Muldie who journeyed there and who left the younger boys in the hands of eleven-year-old Johnny while he went ahead to find better land; there really was a famine in Nicodemus that ended because of the kindness of some Osage Indians, and the three boys really did strike out alone to join their father, following his directions and having a happy reunion." Bull Cent Child Books

Brett, Jan, 1949-

Annie and the wild animals; written and illustrated by Jan Brett. Houghton Mifflin 1985 unp il lib bdg $13.95; pa $3.95 **E**

1. Animals—Fiction 2. Cats—Fiction
ISBN 0-395-37800-1 (lib bdg); 0-395-51006-6 (pa) LC 84-19818

When Annie's cat disappears, she attempts friendship with a variety of unsuitable woodland animals, but with the emergence of Spring, everything comes right

"Miss Brett uses colorful borders filled with detail to provide miniature previews of the narrative action and a story around a story, so that the reader instantly becomes an insider. The small glimpses of the world outside Annie's cottage move the tale forward and embellish the pages with grace and skill. It is foretold in the borders, for instance, and therefore no great surprise when it happens, that Taffy will return with three kittens." N Y Times Book Rev

The wild Christmas reindeer; written and illustrated by Jan Brett. Putnam 1990 unp il $14.95 **E**

1. Reindeer—Fiction 2. Christmas—Fiction
ISBN 0-399-22192-1 LC 89-36095

"Don't look for Dasher or Prancer or even Rudolph in this story. Brett introduces a whole new crew of Santa's reindeer, wild ones, who may be unwilling to come in from the tundra and pull Santa's sleigh. The story's heroine is Teeka, who is asked by Santa to get the reindeer ready to fly. Theatrical spreads depict Teeka's

Brett, Jan, 1949-—*Continued*

struggle with the reindeer, who don't respond to her yelling. Only when she realizes that hugging works better than bossing, do the reindeer unite into the working team that Santa needs to bring Christmas to the world. While the story is nothing extraordinary, the artwork surely is." Booklist

Briggs, Raymond

Father Christmas. Coward-McCann 1973 unp il $9.95; Penguin Bks. pa $3.95 **E**

1. Santa Claus—Fiction 2. Christmas—Fiction
ISBN 0-698-20272-4; 0-14-050125-8 (pa)
LC 73-77885

Illustrated by the author in cartoon format, this book "portrays Christmas Eve as Santa sees it. Dreaming of tropic weather, he grumbles his way through the preparations for a long, cold night of work: feeding the animals, loading the sleigh, packing a snack. He grumbles at chimneys, catches cold, wearily distributes gifts, and rides home to a steaming bath and a solitary Christmas dinner." Bull Cent Child Books

"Each small picture is precisely detailed, convincingly well-drawn, and alive with action; the longer and larger frames—including some full-page spreads—offer a lot of visual contrast in size, color, and contents." Booklist

The snowman. Random House 1978 unp il $12.95 **E**

1. Stories without words 2. Dreams—Fiction 3. Snow—Fiction
ISBN 0-394-83973-0 LC 78-55904

A "wordless picture book about a small boy who expertly fashions a snowman and then dreams that his splendid creation comes alive. Affably greeting the child, the snowman enters the house and is introduced to the delights and dangers of gadgetry. . . . Finally, no longer earthbound, the two friends go soaring over city and countryside, magical in their snowy beauty." Horn Book

"The pastel-toned pencil-and-crayon pictures in their neat rectangular frames will hold the attention of primary 'readers.'" SLJ

Bright, Robert, 1902-1988

Georgie. Doubleday 1944 unp il $7.95; Scholastic pa $1.50 **E**

1. Ghosts—Fiction
ISBN 0-385-07307-0; 0-590-01617-2 (pa) LC 44-7589

"Georgie is an extremely personable little ghost who lives with the Whittakers and haunts their house. Trouble begins for Georgie when he feels it necessary to find another house to haunt. Every house already has a ghost. The friendliness of little Georgie and the just pleasantly spooky-looking pictures make this the perfect Halloween picture storybook for little children." Booklist

Another available title about Georgie is:
Georgie and the robbers (1963)

My red umbrella. Morrow 1985 c1959 unp il $8.95; pa $3.95 **E**

1. Umbrellas and parasols—Fiction
ISBN 0-688-05249-5; 0-688-05250-9 (pa) LC 59-7928

A reissue of the title first published 1959

"A good read-aloud story for very young listeners, about a little girl whose red umbrella grew to accomodate all the creatures who sought shelter under it. Cheerful colored pictures by the author." Hodges. Books for Elem Sch Libr

Brinckloe, Julie

Fireflies! story and pictures by Julie Brinckloe. Macmillan 1985 unp il $12.95; pa $3.95 **E**

1. Fireflies—Fiction
ISBN 0-02-713310-9; 0-689-71055-0 (pa)
LC 84-20158

A young boy is proud of having caught a jar full of fireflies, which seems to him like owning a piece of moonlight, but as the light begins to dim he realizes he must set the insects free or they will die

"The delicate, sensitive story reflects a classic theme in children's literature—the need to set something free in order to keep it. . . . The tale is embellished with lovely, wistful pencil drawings of the boy and his friends leaping about in the twilight and of his expressive face showing his mingled joy and sadness. A simple, basic story, very gracefully presented." Horn Book

Brown, Jeff, 1926-

Flat Stanley; pictures by Tomi Ungerer. Harper & Row 1964 unp il lib bdg $12.89; pa $4.95 **E**

ISBN 0-06-020681-0 (lib bdg); 0-06-440293-2 (pa)
LC 63-17525

"When an enormous bulletin board fell on him as he lay in bed Stanley Lambchop emerged as flat as a pancake. Once he got used to his half-inch thickness Stanley came to enjoy it and so did his parents— he could be lowered through sidewalk gratings, mailed to California, rolled up like wallpaper and tied with a string for carrying, and disguised as a framed picture to help catch art thieves in the museum. Comical colored pictures accentuate the humor of this rib-tickling story." Booklist

Brown, Marc Tolon

Arthur's nose; by Marc Brown. Little, Brown 1976 32p il $14.95; pa $4.95 **E**

1. Nose—Fiction 2. Aardvark—Fiction
ISBN 0-316-11193-7; 0-316-11070-1 (pa)
LC 75-30610

"An Atlantic Monthly Press book"

"Arthur the aardvark is unhappy with his long nose. When he finally decides to visit a rhinologist to have it changed, he discovers that he can't come up with a different kind of nose that suits him. No alterations are done, for Arthur comes to realize that 'I'm just not me without my nose.' The overworked lesson is pleasantly conveyed with surprisingly little text and large and colorful illustrations so that independent readers may be tempted to pick this up." SLJ

Other available titles about Arthur are:
Arthur goes to camp (1982)
Arthur's April Fool (1983)
Arthur's baby (1987)
Arthur's birthday (1989)
Arthur's Christmas (1985)

Brown, Marc Tolon—*Continued*
Arthur's eyes (1979)
Arthur's Halloween (1982)
Arthur's pet business (1990)
Arthur's teacher trouble (1986)
Arthur's Thanksgiving (1983)
Arthur's tooth (1985)
Arthur's valentine (1980)

D.W. all wet; [by] Marc Brown. Little, Brown 1988 unp il $10.95 E

1. Beaches—Fiction 2. Brothers and sisters—Fiction
ISBN 0-316-11077-9 LC 87-15752

"Joy Street books"

"Arthur the Aardvark's little sister D.W. stars in the second book (the first was D.W. flips [1987]) of her own series that features the likable, cheeky young heroine. This time D.W. . . . announces, 'I don't like the beach, and I don't like to get wet.' She asks to leave the minute she arrives, she won't play and she's afraid of getting sunburned. It's Arthur who helps change D.W.'s mind about the beach by unexpectedly tossing her into very shallow water." Publ Wkly

"A simple, even predictable vignette, but entertaining nonetheless because of Brown's warm pictures." Booklist

Brown, Margaret Wise, 1910-1952

Baby animals; illustrated by Susan Jeffers. Random House 1989 unp il $10.95; lib bdg $11.99 E

1. Animals—Fiction
ISBN 0-394-82040-1; 0-394-92040-6 (lib bdg) LC 88-18481

Text originally published 1941 in longer version

Relates the morning, noon, and evening activities of several young animals and a little girl

"Paintings and text are interspersed on each page, creating a lovely whole. Illustrations range from full-page and double-page spreads to several smaller ones on a page surrounded by crisp white space. Young children will delight in the lilting, often repetitive, question-and-answer format of the text." SLJ

Big red barn; pictures by Felicia Bond. Newly illustrated ed. Harper & Row 1989 unp il $11.95; lib bdg $11.89 E

1. Domestic animals—Fiction 2. Farm life—Fiction 3. Stories in rhyme
ISBN 0-06-020748-5; 0-06-020749-3 (lib bdg) LC 85-45814

A newly illustrated edition of the title first published 1956

Rhymed text and illustrations introduce the many different animals that live in the big red barn

"The large illustrations are somewhat stylized, but still have a strong sense of detail and reality. The bright colors will attract young readers. The short text on each page is superimposed on the picture, but always in a way that is easy to read. Children will enjoy studying each of the pages as the day progresses from early morning to night." SLJ

Goodnight moon; pictures by Clement Hurd. Harper & Row 1947 unp il $9.95; lib bdg $9.89; pa $3.95 E

1. Rabbits—Fiction 2. Night—Fiction 3. Stories in rhyme
ISBN 0-06-020705-1; 0-06-020706-X (lib bdg); 0-06-443017-0 (pa) LC 47-30762

Written in rhymed verse

"The coming of night is shown in pictures which change from bright to dark as a small rabbit says good night to the familiar things in his nest." Hodges. Books for Elem Sch Libr

"A clever goodnight book in which pages are progressively darker as the leaves are turned. There are many objects to identify and children enjoy picking out familiar words." Books for Deaf Child

Margaret Wise Brown's A child's good night book; illustrated by Jean Charlot. Harper & Row 1985 c1943 unp il lib bdg $12.89; pa $3.95 E

1. Night—Fiction
ISBN 0-06-020752-3 (lib bdg); 0-06-443114-2 (pa) LC 84-43123

A Caldecott Medal honor book, 1944

First published 1943 by W.R. Scott

As an invitation to sleepiness the author writes of birds and animals, sailboats, automobiles and little children as they settle down for the night

The brief text is accompanied by full-page softly colored lithographs

The runaway bunny; pictures by Clement Hurd. Harper & Row 1972 c1942 unp il $9.95; lib bdg $9.89; pa $3.95 E

1. Rabbits—Fiction
ISBN 0-06-020765-5; 0-06-020766-3 (lib bdg); 0-06-443018-9 (pa) LC 71-183168

A reissue, with some illustrations redrawn, of the title first published 1942

"Within a framework of mutual love, a bunny tells his mother how he will run away and she answers his challenge by indicating how she will catch him." SLJ

"The text has the simplicity of a folk tale and the illustrations are black and white or double page drawings in startling colour." Ont Libr Rev

Wait till the moon is full; pictures by Garth Williams. Harper & Row 1948 unp il $12.95; lib bdg $12.89; pa $3.95 E

1. Raccoons—Fiction 2. Night—Fiction
ISBN 0-06-020800-7; 0-06-020801-5 (lib bdg); 0-06-443222-X (pa) LC 48-9278

"The mystery and wonder of nighttime is presented here in a way to sharpen the awareness of the very young child and to dispel any fears of it which the more timorous may have. . . . This is very slight, but the words, the rhythm and the mood have a great deal of charm and humor, which is matched by Garth Williams' pictures of a cozy, well-furnished raccoon home and the moonlit world waiting outside." N Y Times Book Rev

Brown, Margaret Wise, 1910-1952 — *Continued*

Wheel on the chimney; illustrated by Tibor Gergely. Lippincott 1985 c1954 unp il $13.95; lib bdg $13.89 **E**

1. Storks—Fiction
ISBN 0-397-30288-6; 0-397-30296-7 (lib bdg)
LC 84-48379

A Caldecott Medal honor book, 1955

A reissue of the title first published 1954

"First there was one stork, then there were two. They built their nest on a wheel on the chimney of a little Hungarian house, thus promising good luck to the family. This annual ritual inspired Gergely's tracing of the stork's migration from their summer European habitat to their winter sojourn in Africa." Second Educ Board

"The simple text tells of the ways of storks and of the hazards of their long flight south, while the illustrations in strong contrasting colours show much of the beauty and interest of the seas and continents the great birds cross in their journey." Ont Libr Rev

Brown, Ruth

The big sneeze. Lothrop, Lee & Shepard Bks. 1985 unp il $13.95; lib bdg $12.88 **E**

1. Farm life—Fiction
ISBN 0-688-04665-7; 0-688-04666-5 (lib bdg)
LC 84-23385

A farmer sneezes a fly off his nose and causes havoc in the barnyard

"The deep, rich colour and naturalistic style of the illustrations lead the eye agreeably along the line of cumulative disaster in an energetic and diverting picture-book." Grow Point

A dark, dark tale; story and pictures by Ruth Brown. Dial Bks. for Young Readers 1981 unp il $11.95; lib bdg $11.89 **E**

1. Cats—Fiction
ISBN 0-8037-1672-9; 0-8037-1673-7 (lib bdg)
LC 81-66798

In a "style used by storytellers of ghostly tales, Brown begins 'Once upon a time there was a dark, dark moor' and goes on to describe the 'dark, dark wood' on the moor, the 'dark, dark house' in the wood and the stygian rooms in the huge place. A nimble black cat accompanies explorers of the mansion and leaps with them in gleeful terror when the final 'dark, dark thing' is discovered." Publ Wkly

The author's "spooky read-aloud book pretends to be scarier than it is: even the youngest listener should be delighted by the punch line. The book's mysterious power is engendered by the illustrations of weed-choked gardens and abandoned, echoing halls, of mullioned windows and blowing curtains—a child's portion of gothica, easy on the 'frissons.'" Time

Browne, Anthony

Gorilla. Knopf 1985 c1983 unp il $12.95; lib bdg $13.99 **E**

1. Gorillas—Fiction 2. Fathers and daughters—Fiction
ISBN 0-394-87525-7; 0-394-97525-1 (lib bdg)
LC 85-13

First published 1983 in the United Kingdom

Neglected by her busy father, a lonely young girl receives a toy gorilla for her birthday and together they take a miraculous trip to the zoo

"Despite the fantasy, Browne has created a picture book that explores real emotions with a beautifully realized child protagonist. Using his artistic skills, he's fashioned the visual metaphors that help us transcend superficial meanings and feel the power of the more archetypical emotions that bind children to parents and people to the other animals." Horn Book

I like books. Knopf 1988 unp il lib bdg $10.99; pa $3.95 **E**

1. Chimpanzees—Fiction 2. Books and reading—Fiction
ISBN 0-394-94186-1 (lib bdg); 0-394-84186-7 (pa)
LC 88-8471

"Dragonfly books"

A young chimp declares his love for all kinds of books, from funny books and scary books to song books and strange books

"Browne's inventive illustrations contribute a great deal of gentle humor to this brief recitation; his drawing for counting books shows the monkey climbing steps of books—first one, then two, then a pile of three books—while the border incorporates the same numerals in the four corners. Similarly, the cover of a song book appears to be an echo of the chimp's singing face, with open mouth and closed eyes." Horn Book

Things I like. Knopf 1989 unp il lib bdg $10.99; pa $3.95 **E**

1. Chimpanzees—Fiction
ISBN 0-394-94192-6 (lib bdg); 0-394-84192-1 (pa)
LC 88-26632

"Dragonfly books"

A young chimp enumerates favorite playtime activities, from painting and riding a bike to paddling in the sea and partying with friends

"Executed in . . . bright yet gentle and appealing mix of watercolor, pen, and crayon and placed as they are on nondistracting white backgrounds, the pictures perfectly suit the youngest in every audience." Horn Book

The tunnel. Knopf 1990 c1989 unp il $11.95; lib bdg $12.99 **E**

1. Brothers and sisters—Fiction 2. Fear—Fiction
ISBN 0-394-84582-X; 0-394-94582-4 (lib bdg)
LC 88-31923

First published 1989 in the United Kingdom

"Rose likes to stay alone inside and read fairy stories, while her brother Jack prefers to play outside with the other boys. Forced to spend a morning with his sister, Jack intimidates her into following him down a tunnel that is 'dark, and damp, and slimy, and scary.' Finding herself in a spooky wood, Rose discovers that her brother has been turned to stone. Crying, she throws her arms around the cold figure and holds on until it becomes 'softer and warmer'; the transformation complete, her brother is alive again." Booklist

"The whole book is suffused with a surreal feeling;

Browne, Anthony—*Continued*
the most innocuous blade of grass to acquire a menacing air. A fascinating, unsettling evocation of a common childhood relationship, demanding careful scrutiny." Horn Book

Willy the champ. Knopf 1986 c1985 unp il lib bdg $9.99 E

1. Chimpanzees—Fiction
ISBN 0-394-97907-9 LC 85-10053

First published 1985 in the United Kingdom

Not very good at sports or fighting, mild-mannered Willy nevertheless proves he's the champ when the local bully shows up

"Browne's effective use of the full-color palette uses emphatic colors for emphatic situations and portrays Willy's innate equilibrium with constant, realistic hues all the way to his accidental, blushing triumph. There's play on pop culture, with muscle-bound pool-lurkers decked in gold and a flashy dancer in red high heels. Although the book's story line is simple, its visual sophistication makes it most accessible to older picture book readers, who will relate to Willy's self-contained success." SLJ

Brunhoff, Jean de, 1899-1937

The story of Babar, the little elephant; translated from the French by Merle S. Haas. Random House 1937 c1933 47p il $9.95; lib bdg $7.99; pa $4.95 E

1. Elephants—Fiction
ISBN 0-394-80575-5; 0-394-90575-X (lib bdg); 0-394-82940-9 (pa) LC 33-30566

Also available facsmile reprint of the original oversized United States edition $18.95 (ISBN 0-394-86823-4)

Original French edition, 1931; this is a reduced format version of the 1933 United States edition

"Babar runs away from the jungle and goes to live with an old lady in Paris, where he adapts quickly to French amenities. Later he returns to the jungle and becomes king. Much of the charm of the story is contributed by the author's gay pictures." Hodges. Books for Elem Sch Libr

Other available titles about Babar by Jean de Brunhoff are:

Babar and Father Christmas (1940)
Babar and his children (1938)
Babar and Zephir (1942)
Babar the king (1935)
Travels of Babar (1934)

Other available titles about Babar by Laurent de Brunhoff are:

Babar and the ghost (1981)
Babar learns to cook (1978)
Babar loses his crown (1967)
Babar saves the day (1976)
Babar visits another planet (1972)
Babar's ABC (1983)
Babar's anniversary album (1981)
Babar's birthday surprise (1970)
Babar's book of color (1984)
Babar's bookmobile (1974)
Babar's busy year (1989)
Babar's counting book (1986)
Babar's French lessons (1963)
Babar's little circus star (1988)
Babar's little girl (1987)
Babar's mystery (1978)
Babar's trunk (1969)
Meet Babar and his family (1973)

Bulla, Clyde Robert, 1914-

The chalk box kid; illustrated by Thomas B. Allen. Random House 1987 unp il $5.99; pa $1.95 E

ISBN 0-394-99102-8; 0-394-89102-3 (pa) LC 87-4683

"Gregory's family moves to a smaller house in a poorer part of town; the father has lost his factory job. There is no yard at the new house in which to play, but Gregory explores a nearly burnt-out building that formerly was a chalk factory. Gregory finds plenty of chalk in the debris as he cleans up, and the artist in him soars." Publ Wkly

"As usual, Bulla manages a poignant depth within the confines of simple style and narrative. Understated and easy to read, this nevertheless tackles problems that are not easy to solve without exercising the imagination." Bull Cent Child Books

The Christmas coat; pictures by Sylvie Wickstrom. Knopf 1990 unp il $13.95; lib bdg $14.99 E

1. Brothers—Fiction 2. Christmas—Fiction
ISBN 0-394-89385-9; 0-394-99385-3 (lib bdg) LC 88-2380

"The story of battling sibling brothers. Even though their exasperated mother divides their room with a line, they still manage to tear apart a coat meant as a Christmas present for a sick child. There is a peaceful resolution as the true meaning of Christmas as a giving season is portrayed." Child Book Rev Serv

"Wickstrom's pictures with their soft colors and old-world quality, impart an elegant look to Bulla's story." Publ Wkly

Daniel's duck; pictures by Joan Sandin. Harper & Row 1979 60p il $10.95; lib bdg $10.89; pa $3.50 E

1. Wood carving—Fiction
ISBN 0-06-020908-9; 0-06-020909-7 (lib bdg); 0-06-444031-1 (pa) LC 77-25647

"An I can read book"

"Daniel, who lived in 'a cabin on a mountain in Tennessee,' wanted 'to make something for the spring fair,' as the rest of the family were doing. Using the block of wood and the knife his father gave him, the boy carved a duck with its head looking backward. At the fair, people laughed when they saw the carving, and Daniel thought his work was being ridiculed: but he was more than consoled by a famous local wood-carver, who not only praised Daniel's duck but offered to buy it. The easy-to-read story and the simple format are excellently served by the subdued three-color illustrations, which round out the account of a traditional Appalachian family." Horn Book

Bunting, Eve, 1928-

Ghost's hour, spook's hour; illustrated by Donald Carrick. Clarion Bks. 1987 unp il lib bdg $12.95; Houghton Mifflin pa $4.95 E

1. Night—Fiction 2. Fear—Fiction
ISBN 0-89919-484-2 (lib bdg); 0-395-51583-1 (pa) LC 86-31674

Bunting, Eve, 1928-—*Continued*

"A little boy, frightened by a howling wind and by a bedside lamp that doesn't turn on, creeps down to his parents' room only to find their bed empty and to hear more strange slitherings and thumpings on their window." Horn Book

"Bunting masterfully paces her story, with each fear of the child climaxing in his discovery of the basis for the sound. . . . The text is extended by Carrick's paintings, most of which brood with the darkness and . . . change completely when the boy, with his parents, is no longer afraid: warm, comforting gold tones then enrobe the family. A book that provides the perfect blend of chills and comfort." SLJ

How many days to America? a Thanksgiving story; illustrated by Beth Peck. Clarion Bks. 1988 unp il lib bdg $14.95; Houghton Mifflin pa $5.95 E

1. Refugees—Fiction 2. Thanksgiving Day—Fiction
ISBN 0-89919-521-0; 0-395-54777-6 (pa) LC 88-2590

Refugees from an unnamed Caribbean island embark on a dangerous boat trip to America where they have a special reason to celebrate Thanksgiving

"Bunting's simple tale focuses on the hardships of the journey and on the American ideals of freedom and safety. She wisely leaves aside the issues of politics in the homeland or in this country. Her prose is poetically spare. . . . Peck's richly colored crayon drawings yield added enjoyment. . . . A poignant story and a thought-provoking discussion starter." SLJ

In the haunted house; illustrated by Susan Meddaugh. Clarion Bks. 1990 unp il $13.95 E

1. Halloween—Fiction
ISBN 0-395-51589-0 LC 89-77663

"Skeletons pop out of closets and a bandaged mummy winks at two people—identified only by their red and blue high-top sneakers—as they explore a haunted house. Accompanying the pictures of green-faced witches and swirling ghosts is a rhyming text that relates what the two are seeing and their mutual assurances that they are really not frightened at all. Nice details in the pictures add to the ghoulish fun." Horn Book

The man who could call down owls; illustrated by Charles Mikolaycak. Macmillan 1984 unp il $12.95 E

1. Owls—Fiction
ISBN 0-02-715380-0 LC 83-17568

"Every evening an old man carrying a willow wand, wearing a flowing white cape and a large hat, walks into the woods and calls the owls to him. And every evening a boy watches him, marveling at his mastery of the mysterious birds. An evil stranger, covetous but not respectful of the power the man wields, kills the owl-man and attempts to use his secrets, but it is the boy who inherits the cape at the end of the tale." Horn Book

"A haunting story, lyrically narrated, is realized in powerful pencil drawings that effortlessly draw viewers into their spell. Mikolaycak's exquisite draftsmanship is never more apparent than in his black-and-white work, and the intricate patterns formed by the owls' feathers are echoed in the owl man's garb and in contrasting textures that contribute visual interest and pictorial rhythm." Booklist

The Mother's Day mice; illustrated by Jan Brett. Clarion Bks. 1986 unp il lib bdg $12.95; pa $4.95 E

1. Gifts—Fiction 2. Mice—Fiction
ISBN 0-89919-387-0 (lib bdg); 0-89919-702-7 (pa) LC 85-13991

"Three little mice go out on a spring morning in search of Mother's Day presents. After suitable adventures they return with a dandelion, a strawberry and a song." N Y Times Book Rev

"The story is a sweet one, saved from being too sugary by Brett's wonderful full-color illustrations. Each two-page spread totally fills up the space, giving the effect of a movie screen. Moreover, the art has a high-quality, animated-picture look, each 'frame' exquisitely detailed and technicolor bright. A book as endearing as the three little mice who star in it." Booklist

No nap; illustrated by Susan Meddaugh. Clarion Bks. 1989 unp il $13.95 E

1. Bedtime—Fiction 2. Sleep—Fiction
ISBN 0-89919-813-9 LC 88-35256

Dad tries various activities to get Susie tired enough to take her nap, but they only exhaust him

"This is one of those slices of life that acquires creative buoyancy by virtue of humorous illustrations. Susie's not cute; she's one of those diminutive but determined kids who rules her parents with a firm hand and exhausts everyone in the process. Meddaugh has used scraggly lines and contrasting colors to convey her main character's energy." Bull Cent Child Books

Scary, scary Halloween; pictures by Jan Brett. Clarion Bks. 1986 unp il $12.95; pa $4.95 E

1. Halloween—Fiction 2. Cats—Fiction 3. Stories in rhyme
ISBN 0-89919-414-1; 0-89919-799-X (pa) LC 86-2642

A band of trick-or-treaters and a mother cat and her kittens spend a very scary Halloween

"Tailored for nursery and pre-school holiday read-aloud sessions, this is a slightly spooky picturebook with bright graphics on a black background showing costumed creepies prancing through the night, all watched by four pairs of green eyes hiding under a porch. . . . The faces on the creatures, the pumpkins, and even the trees will inspire shivers of delight in any darkened room." Bull Cent Child Books

The Wall; illustrated by Ronald Himler. Clarion Bks. 1990 unp il $13.95 E

1. Fathers and sons—Fiction 2. Vietnam Veterans Memorial (Washington, D.C.)—Fiction
ISBN 0-395-51588-2 LC 89-17429

"A father and his young son come to the Vietnam Veterans Memorial to find the name of the grandfather the boy never knew. This moving account is beautifully told from a young child's point of view; the watercolors capture the impressive mass of the wall of names as well as the poignant reactions of the people who visit there." Horn Book Guide

Bunting, Eve, 1928-—*Continued*

The Wednesday surprise; illustrated by Donald Carrick. Clarion Bks. 1989 unp il lib bdg $13.95; Houghton Mifflin pa $4.95 **E**

1. Grandmothers—Fiction 2. Reading—Fiction
ISBN 0-89919-721-3 (lib bdg); 0-395-54776-8 (pa)
LC 88-12117

This "first-person account tells of the special gift that seven-year-old Anna and her grandmother have planned for her dad's birthday: secretly, the two read books together until finally, the grandmother has learned to read." SLJ

"Bunting's writing is simple and warm and direct, showing rather than telling the book's audience that reading is both a skill and a joy. Carrick's pictures echo the warmth, especially in the faces of the family, painted in realistically detailed watercolors with a careful attention to familial resemblance. A gentle charmer." Bull Cent Child Books

Burningham, John, 1936-

Come away from the water, Shirley. Crowell 1977 unp il $13.95; lib bdg $13.89; Harper & Row pa $5.95 **E**

1. Pirates—Fiction 2. Beaches—Fiction
ISBN 0-690-01360-4; 0-690-01361-2 (lib bdg); 0-06-443039-1 (pa) LC 77-483

"A little girl uses her imagination to rise above all-too-familiar parental warnings at the beach." LC. Child Books, 1977

Another available title about Shirley is: Time to get out of the bath, Shirley, entered below

Granpa. Crown 1985 c1984 unp il $8.95 **E**

1. Grandfathers—Fiction
ISBN 0-517-55643-X LC 84-17464

First published 1984 in the United Kingdom

"The special relationship between a little girl and her grandfather is lovingly portrayed in a series of double-page vignettes. . . . Text is minimal; it is the illustrations in pastel crayon and pen-and-ink that bring to life the activities of the two and their love for each other. The book is an exaltation of a glorious relationship with the life/continuum viewed as the natural progression of things." SLJ

Hey! get off our train. Crown 1990 c1989 unp il $14.95; lib bdg $14.99 **E**

1. Railroads—Fiction 2. Rare animals—Fiction 3. Dreams—Fiction
ISBN 0-517-57638-4; 0-517-57643-0 (lib bdg)
LC 89-15802

First published 1989 in the United Kingdom with title: Oi! get off our train

"In a dream sequence, a boy and his canine companion board his toy train for a trip around the world. They interrupt their journey to get off the train and play, but when they return they discover that an uninvited elephant has come on board. The pair are indignant—until they learn of the elephant's plight: He has become an endangered species because of his tusks. In their travels, they in turn encounter a seal, a crane, a tiger, and a polar bear, each recounting the environmental hazards that threaten its survival. The animals are then welcomed aboard." SLJ

"The book is gorgeous; the illustrations—magnificent impressions of landscapes, wittily juxtaposed with wonderfully limned washed-line drawings of the animals—are among the best that Burningham has ever produced." Horn Book

John Patrick Norman McHennessy—the boy who was always late. Crown 1988 c1987 unp il $12.95 **E**

1. School stories
ISBN 0-517-56805-5 LC 87-20165

First published 1987 in the United Kingdom

A schoolmaster who punishes John Patrick each time the boy gives implausible excuses for being late comes to regret his incredulity

"Burningham's use of scale, size and comic shape, the serenely realistic trees, bridges, river and meadows backing strange events and the inimitable defence of free fancy, add one more masterpiece to his repertoire." Grow Point

Mr. Gumpy's motor car. Crowell 1976 c1973 unp il lib bdg $13.89; Puffin Bks. pa $3.50 **E**

1. Automobile drivers—Fiction
ISBN 0-690-00799-X (lib bdg); 0-14-050300-5 (pa)
LC 75-4582

First published 1973 in the United Kingdom

An aging touring car "is crowded with children and animals, there's a spot of trouble, but all ends happily." Bull Cent Child Books

"The strength here is in the rural simplicity and in the colorful illustrations of amiable animals, the countryside in sunshine and under lowering clouds. Those things and the bold type which carries words and phrases for the reader to chew on and roll around on the tongue—'slipped and slithered and squelched.' Yes, good man, this Gumpy; Burningham, too." N Y Times Book Rev

Another available title about Mr. Grumpy is entered below

Mr. Gumpy's outing. Holt & Co. 1971 c1970 unp il $14.95; pa $5.95; Penguin Bks. pa $3.95 **E**

1. Animals—Fiction
ISBN 0-8050-0708-3; 0-8050-1315-6 (pa); 0-14-050254-8 (pa) LC 77-159507

First published 1970 in the United Kingdom

"Mr. Gumpy is about to go off for a boat ride and is asked by two children, a rabbit, a cat, a dog, and other animals if they may come. To each Mr. Gumpy says yes, if—if the children don't squabble, if the rabbit won't hop, if the cat won't chase the rabbit or the dog tease the cat, and so on. Of course each does exactly what Mr. Gumpy forbade, the boat tips over, and they all slog home for tea in friendly fashion." Sutherland. The Best in Child Books

The shopping basket. Crowell 1980 unp il $13.95; lib bdg $12.89 **E**

1. Animals—Fiction
ISBN 0-690-04082-2; 0-690-04083-0 (lib bdg)
LC 80-7987

Burningham, John, 1936-—*Continued*

Steven "is sent by his mother to buy some groceries. On the way he has a succession of threatening encounters—with a bear, a monkey, a kangaroo, a goat, a pig, and finally an elephant. . . . The boy calmly outwits them all and arrives home safely with his purchases; but his mother chides him for taking so long: 'Where on earth have you been Steven?'" Horn Book

"A mild foray into mathematical concepts is incorporated into a blithe story. . . . In each case, a page that shows the items in inverse pyramid has one egg or banana or apple missing. . . . A brisk, fresh story with just enough nonsense to keep it entertaining rather than silly, this is illustrated with nicely composed line and wash drawings that have an understated humor." Bull Cent Child Books

Slam bang. Viking 1985 c1984 unp il $4.95 **E**

1. Vocabulary
ISBN 0-670-65076-5 LC 83-23549

"Noisy words"

This book "shows [a] child and his dog out for an eventful car ride. Here, a door slams, wheels squeal, a flattened tire bangs, and brakes screech as the pair make their bumpy way. The books will be useful with preschoolers and babies for naming objects or for building stories around the bare-bones events. Burningham's skillful hand ensures that the visual interest is high. His light textures and whimsical lines create a strong sense of fun that children should have no trouble exploiting." Booklist

Other available titles in the Noisy words series are:
Sniff shout (1984)
Wobble pop (1984)

Time to get out of the bath, Shirley. Crowell 1978 unp il $13.95; lib bdg $13.89 **E**

1. Baths—Fiction
ISBN 0-690-01378-7; 0-690-01379-5 (lib bdg) LC 76-58503

"Shirley is sitting in the bathtub when her mother comes barging in to tidy things up and give unsolicited advice such as, 'You really ought to have a bath more often, Shirley.' Shirley immediately fantasizes a trip down the bathtub drain into a medieval world complete with knights, a castle, and a royal family." SLJ

The author uses "pallid pastel colors . . . to characterize the nature of family life while boldly contrasted deep colors and forceful shapes triumphantly express the power of Shirley's personal universe." Horn Book

Burstein, Fred

Rebecca's nap; pictures by Helen Cogancherry. Bradbury Press 1988 unp il $12.95 **E**

1. Sleep—Fiction
ISBN 0-02-715620-6 LC 88-1041

Rebecca, Daddy, and Mommy have different ideas about naptime

"The short, simple text, made up almost entirely of dialogue, has a natural flow and captures the warmth of this young family. The story is really brought to life, however, by Cogancherry's soft, highly expressive watercolor and pencil illustrations. Toddlers are sure to relate to Rebecca's experiences and enjoy them in story hour." SLJ

Burton, Virginia Lee, 1909-1968

Katy and the big snow; story and pictures by Virginia Lee Burton. Houghton Mifflin 1943 32p il $13.95; pa $4.95 **E**

1. Tractors—Fiction 2. Snow—Fiction
ISBN 0-395-18155-0; 0-395-18562-9 (pa) LC 43-18856

"Katy was a beautiful red crawler tractor. In summer she wore a bulldozer to push dirt with. In winter she wore a snowplow. She was big and strong and the harder the job the better she liked it. When the Big Snow covered the city of Geoppolis like a thick blanket, Katy cleared the city from North to South and East to West." Ont Libr Rev

The little house; story and pictures by Virginia Lee Burton. Houghton Mifflin 1942 40p il $13.95; pa $4.95 **E**

1. Houses—Fiction 2. Cities and towns—Fiction
ISBN 0-395-18156-9; 0-395-25938-X (pa) LC 42-24744

Awarded the Caldecott Medal, 1943

"The little house was very happy as she sat on the quiet hillside watching the changing seasons. As the years passed, however, tall buildings grew up around her, and the noise of city traffic disturbed her. She became sad and lonely until one day someone who understood her need for twinkling stars overhead and dancing apple blossoms moved her back to just the right little hill." Child Books Too Good to Miss

Mike Mulligan and his steam shovel; story and pictures by Virginia Lee Burton. Houghton Mifflin 1939 unp il $12.95; lib bdg $11.95; pa $3.95 **E**

1. Steam-shovels—Fiction
ISBN 0-395-16961-5; 0-395-06681-6 (lib bdg); 0-395-25939-8 (pa) LC 39-30335

"Mike Mulligan remains faithful to his steam shovel, Mary Anne, against the threat of the new gas and Diesel-engine contraptions and digs his way to a surprising and happy ending." New Yorker

"One of the most convincing personifications of a machine ever written. Lively pictures, dramatic action, and a satisfying conclusion." Adventuring with Books. 2d edition

Butler, Dorothy, 1925-

My brown bear Barney; illustrated by Elizabeth Fuller. Greenwillow Bks. 1989 unp il $11.95; lib bdg $11.88 **E**

1. Teddy bears—Fiction
ISBN 0-688-08567-9; 0-688-08568-7 (lib bdg) LC 88-21199

First published 1988 in New Zealand

"As a wide-eyed, straight-haired little girl enumerates all the places she takes her brown bear, Barney, her faithful teddy is spied amid the weeds in the wheelbarrow, sunning at the beach, and—of course—tucked into bed (sporting matching nightcap and pajamas). But when the youngster itemizes the things she'll carry to school,

Butler, Dorothy, 1925-—*Continued*

the omnipresent Barney is conspicuously absent." Booklist

"Every item on the little girl's checklists is first pictured clearly for easy identification and then imaginatively placed in its proper narrative context in an inviting, bright full-page illustration with just enough detail to fascinate but not overwhelm. The child's own ingenuous voice validates the unencumbered, well-timed storytelling, which makes the most of its unexpected ending." Horn Book

Byars, Betsy Cromer, 1928-

Go and hush the baby; by Betsy Byars; illustrated by Emily A. McCully. Viking 1971 unp il $11.95; pa $3.95 **E**

1. Brothers and sisters—Fiction 2. Infants—Fiction
ISBN 0-670-34270-X; 0-14-050396-X (pa)
LC 72-136825

"Just as he is about to leave the house, bat in hand, Will is asked by his mother to pacify the baby. He performs and the baby smiles, but as soon as Will leaves the crying resumes. Play a game, mother suggests. Finally Will launches on a story that quiets the baby and so intrigues the storyteller that he is surprised when he loses his audience to a nursing bottle. 'Well, I have to play this game of baseball anyway,' he announces as he goes off." Bull Cent Child Books

"A charming little picture book, told with simplicity and illustrated with appealing two-color drawings." Booklist

The Golly Sisters go West; by Betsy Byars; pictures by Sue Truesdell. Harper & Row 1986 c1985 64p il $10.95; lib bdg $10.89; pa $3.50 **E**

1. Entertainers—Fiction 2. Frontier and pioneer life—Fiction 3. West (U.S.)—Fiction
ISBN 0-06-020883-X; 0-06-020884-8 (lib bdg); 0-06-444132-6 (pa) LC 84-48474

"An I can read book"

May-May and Rose, the singing, dancing Golly sisters, travel west by covered wagon, entertaining people along the way

"In the first story, they learn the hard way how to make a horse move forward; in the second, they give their first road show to an audience of two dogs; in the third, they get lost; in the fourth, try to inncorporate the horse into their act; in the fifth, make up after one of their constant arguments; in the sixth, talk themselves out of a nighttime scare. The dialogue and antics are convincingly like those of rivalrous young siblings anywhere on the block. The story lines are cleverer than much easy-to-read fare, and the old-West setting adds flair. The accompanying water colors, too, add a generous dollop of humor, especially in the horse's expressions and the riotous postures of the two main characters." Bull Cent Child Books

Another available title about the Golly sisters is entered below

Hooray for the Golly sisters! by Betsy Byars; pictures by Sue Truesdell. Harper & Row 1990 64p il $11.95; lib bdg $11.89 **E**

1. Sisters—Fiction 2. Entertainers—Fiction 3. Frontier and pioneer life—Fiction 4. West (U.S.)—Fiction
ISBN 0-06-020898-8; 0-06-020899-6 (lib bdg)
LC 89-48147

"An I can read book"

"In five short stories, Rose and May-May Golly, two pioneering showgirls—er, thespians—who now seem to have mastered the art of driving their covered wagon, cross a big river . . . find out that pigs don't substitute very well for rabbits in a magic act . . . brave their way through a swamp, devise a high-wire act on the ground, and deviously entice a crowd to yell 'Hooray for the Golly Sisters!'" Bull Cent Child Books

"This zany comedy [is] sure to delight emerging readers. Varying levels of humor make the title appealing to slightly older, less able readers as well. Truesdell's fluid watercolor illustrations enhance and expand on each episode. . . . The adventuresome gals' pioneer spirit and sibling affection are convincing and true to life, but most of all, the stories are full of gentle fun." SLJ

Byers, Rinda M.

Mycca's baby; pictures by David Tamura. Orchard Bks. 1990 unp il $13.95; lib bdg $13.99 **E**

1. Aunts—Fiction 2. Infants—Fiction 3. Family life—Fiction
ISBN 0-531-05828-X; 0-531-08428-0 (lib bdg)
LC 88-27320

"A young Thai girl tells of happenings in her family as she awaits the birth of Aunt Rose's baby. Softly-colored illustrations and simple language patterns are consistent with story setting and content. Feelings of warmth, caring and close family ties emerge. A good choice for adding cultural diversity to classroom libraries." Child Book Rev Serv

Caines, Jeannette Franklin, 1938-

Abby; pictures by Steven Kellogg. Harper & Row 1973 32p il lib bdg $12.89; pa $3.95 **E**

1. Adoption—Fiction 2. Brothers and sisters—Fiction 3. Blacks—Fiction
ISBN 0-06-020922-4 (lib bdg); 0-06-443049-9 (pa)
LC 73-5480

Abby, an adopted pre-schooler, "loves to look at her baby book, even more, to listen to stories told by her mother and by her brother, Kevin, about the day she became part of the family. . . . A crisis arises when Kevin announces he can't be bothered with her because she's a girl. But the clouds roll by when big brother says he was only fooling and that he loves her. In fact, he will even take her to school with him and feature Abby at show-and-tell time." Publ Wkly

This "story of a warm and loving black family living in a city apartment could be used to introduce the subject of adoption. . . . Shaded drawings showing the family at home perfectly complement the story." SLJ

Caines, Jeannette Franklin, 1938- — *Continued*

Daddy; by Jeannette Caines; pictures by Ronald Himler. Harper & Row 1977 32p il lib bdg $12.89 E

1. Fathers and daughters—Fiction 2. Divorce—Fiction
ISBN 0-06-020924-2 LC 76-21388

"Even though Windy and her father live apart, they have a special relationship. Every Saturday, her father comes to visit, and . . . share happy experiences. They play hide and seek, make funny faces with shaving cream, go to the supermarket, make chocolate pudding, color in coloring books." Interracial Books Child Bull

"The warm text and sensitive drawings will give children of divorced parents a strong sense of identity and a positive perspective from which to review their own family situations. Easy reading. 'Daddy' is an important book." Child Book Rev Serv

I need a lunch box; by Jeannette Caines; pictures by Pat Cummings. Harper & Row 1988 unp il $12.95; lib bdg $12.89 E

1. Blacks—Fiction
ISBN 0-06-020984-4; 0-06-020985-2 (lib bdg)
LC 85-45829

"A little boy's big sister has just gotten a lunch box, and he wants one too. Mama says no, because unlike his sister, he isn't about to start school. Still, the boy covets one, thinking about what he could keep in it—his crayons, marbles, bug collection, or toy animals—and dreaming of a different model for each day of the week. . . . The family portrayed here is black, but their experience is universal. Cummings' pictures are exuberant paintings that don't stint on strident displays of strong color." Booklist

Just us women; by Jeannette Caines; illustrated by Pat Cummings. Harper & Row 1982 32p il $14.95; lib bdg $14.89 E

1. Aunts—Fiction 2. Travelers—Fiction 3. Blacks—Fiction
ISBN 0-06-020942-9; 0-06-020941-0 (lib bdg)
LC 81-48655

The "story of a Black little girl planning a long car trip with her favorite aunt. Enjoying being together, 'no boys and no men, just us women,' they pack carefully and buy two road maps (because last year Aunt Martha forgot their lunch and the map on the kitchen table). But the special delight of the trip is the escape from fixed routes, timetables and routine, and from those who see no reason to 'mosey down the back roads' and walk in the rain." SLJ

"The pleasure of that trip and the warm relationship it represents shine through in realistic, sometimes photograph-like pictures. The two-color drawings have airbrush-effect shadings and occasional deco details. Aunt Martha, a polished-looking young woman, and her pretty niece look like their day of fun is something worth sharing." Booklist

Calhoun, Mary, 1926-

Cross-country cat; illustrated by Erick Ingraham. Morrow 1979 unp il $12.95; lib bdg $12.88; pa $3.95 E

1. Cats—Fiction
ISBN 0-688-22186-6; 0-688-32186-0 (lib bdg); 0-698-06519-8 (pa) LC 78-31718

When he becomes lost in the mountains, a cat with the unusual ability of walking on two legs finds his way home on cross-country skis

"Only the careful blending of skills by a talented author and illustrator could turn such a farfetched plot into a warm, rich, and rewarding story. The realistic illustrations seem to be enveloped in a glowing light and invite the reader to step right into the story." Child Book Rev Serv

Another available title about Henry is entered below

Hot-air Henry; illustrated by Erick Ingraham. Morrow 1981 unp il $12.95; lib bdg $12.88; pa $3.95 E

1. Cats—Fiction 2. Balloons—Fiction
ISBN 0-688-00501-2; 0-688-00502-0 (lib bdg); 0-688-04068-3 (pa) LC 80-26189

Henry "tries to stow away on The Man's first hot-air balloon, accidently fires the burner and takes his own solo flight instead. By trial and error, he learns how to control the balloon and makes the most of his chance to invade the realm of birds." SLJ

"Ingraham's accompanying illustrations are exquisite and strikingly original in their play with complex height perspectives." Booklist

Carle, Eric

Do you want to be my friend? Crowell 1971 unp il $13.95; lib bdg $13.89 E

1. Mice—Fiction 2. Stories without words
ISBN 0-690-24276-X; 0-690-01137-7 (lib bdg)
LC 70-140643

"The only text is the title question at the start and a shy 'Yes' at the close. The pictures do the rest, as the hopeful mouse overtakes one large creature after another. With each encounter, the mouse sees (on the right-hand page) an interesting tail. Turn the page, and there is a huge lion, or a malevolent fox, or a peacock, and then, at last another wee mouse." Saturday Rev

"Good material for discussion and guessing games. . . . The pictures tell an amusing story and they are good to look at as well." Times Lit Suppl

The grouchy ladybug. Crowell 1977 unp il $13.70; lib bdg $13.95 E

1. Ladybirds—Fiction
ISBN 0-690-01391-4; 0-690-01392-2 (lib bdg)
LC 77-3170

"Hour by hour, a hungry, irritable ladybug challenges everyone she meets to a fight. As the creatures encountered by the ladybug become larger, so do the pages and the accompanying print. The climax is reached on the tail of a Blue Whale. The story is resolved with the ladybug returning to her starting point, contrite and pleasant at last." Child Book Rev Serv

"The finger paint and collage illustrations—as bold as the feisty hero—are satisfyingly placed on pages sized to suit the successsive animals that appear (one is cut in the fan shape of the whale's tail). Tiny clocks show

Carle, Eric—*Continued*
the time of each enjoyable encounter, with the sun rising and setting as the action proceeds." SLJ

A house for Hermit Crab. Picture Bk. Studio 1988 c1987 unp il $15.95 **E**

1. Crabs—Fiction
ISBN 0-88708-056-1 LC 87-29261

"Hermit Crab, having outgrown his old shell, sets out to find a new one. He's a bit frightened at first, but over the course of the next year acquires not only a shell, but also an array of sea creatures to decorate, clean, and protect his new home. The story ends with him once again outgrowing his shell." SLJ

"The bright illustrations in Carle's familiar style, which seems particularly suited to undersea scenes, and the cumulative story are splendid, and one of the book's greatest strengths is the encouraging, hopeful view that the outside world is full of exciting possibilities." Horn Book

The mixed-up chameleon; by Eric Carle. Crowell 1984 unp il $13.95; lib bdg $13.89 **E**

1. Chameleons—Fiction
ISBN 0-690-04396-1; 0-690-04397-X (lib bdg) LC 83-45950

A revised and newly illustrated edition of the title first published 1975

"A chameleon goes to a zoo where it wishes it could become like the different animals it sees. It does, but then isn't happy until it wishes it could be itself again." Child Book Rev Serv

The author "has replaced the heavy-lined, childlike, scrawled colors with crisp, appealing collages and has streamlined the text. The cutaway pages have been retained, and none of the humor has been lost. The simpler text results in a smoother flow, and children will enjoy the resulting repetition." Booklist

Rooster's off to see the world. Picture Bk. Studio 1987 unp il $15.95 **E**

1. Counting 2. Animals—Fiction
ISBN 0-88708-042-1 LC 86-25509

A reissue of the title first published 1972 by Watts with title: The rooster who set out to see the world

"A rooster who wants to see the world entices two cats, three frogs, four turtles, and five fishes to accompany him. But when night falls with no provisions for food or shelter, the morale of the traveling companions deteriorates dramatically, and five, four, three, two, they abandon their leader to his own devices. Not surprisingly, the rooster goes back home—to dream about a trip around the world." Horn Book

"The pictures are fetching and colourful, and organized so as to show how the different numbers relate to one another." Times Lit Suppl

The very busy spider. Philomel Bks. 1984 unp il $16.95; pa $4.95 **E**

1. Spiders—Fiction
ISBN 0-399-21166-7; 0-399-21592-1 (pa) LC 84-5907

"Blown by the wind across the book's first pages and onto a fence post near a farm yard, a spider begins to spin a web. Her task allows her no time to answer barnyard animals, each of whom invites her to join in a favorite activity. Finally, her web completed, she snags the pesty fly that's been annoying all of the animals and, exhausted, falls asleep." SLJ

This book "has a disarming ingenuousness and a repetitive structure that will capture the response of preschool audiences. Of special note is the book's use of raised lines for the spider, its web, and an unsuspecting fly. Both sighted and blind children will be able to follow the action with ease." Booklist

The very hungry caterpillar. Philomel Bks. 1981 c1970 unp il $15.95 **E**

1. Caterpillars—Fiction
ISBN 0-399-20853-4

First published 1970 by World Publishing Company

"This caterpillar is so hungry he eats right through the pictures on the pages of the book—and after leaving many holes emerges as a beautiful butterfly on the last page." Best Books for Child, 1972

Carlson, Nancy L., 1953-

I like me! [by] Nancy Carlson. Viking Kestrel 1988 unp il lib bdg $12.95; Penguin Bks. pa $3.95 **E**

1. Pigs—Fiction
ISBN 0-670-82062-8 (lib bdg); 0-14-050819-8 (pa) LC 87-32616

By admiring her finer points and showing that she can take care of herself and have fun even when there's no one else around, a charming pig proves the best friend you can have is yourself

This book is "visually interesting, with sturdy animals drawn in a deliberately artless style. Simple shapes, strong lines, and clear colors, with lots of pattern mixing, show what is not described in the minimal text. The text is hand-lettered." SLJ

Carlson, Natalie Savage

Spooky night; illustrated by Andrew Glass. Lothrop, Lee & Shepard Bks. 1982 unp il $13.95; lib bdg $13.88 **E**

1. Cats—Fiction 2. Witches—Fiction
3. Halloween—Fiction
ISBN 0-688-00934-4; 0-688-00935-2 (lib bdg) LC 82-54

A witch's black cat who wishes to become a family pet must perform one last bit of magic before he can be free

"Just the right ingredients—a cat, a witch, and a spooky night—are brewed into a gentle Halloween story. . . . The shadowy crosshatched illustrations show to advantage the dark night with shooting stars, the mean witch, and Spooky's emerald green eyes." Horn Book

Carlstrom, Nancy White, 1948-

Blow me a kiss, Miss Lilly; illustrations by Amy Schwartz. Harper & Row 1990 unp il $12.95; lib bdg $12.89 **E**

1. Friendship—Fiction 2. Old age—Fiction
3. Death—Fiction
ISBN 0-06-021012-5; 0-06-021013-3 (lib bdg) LC 89-34505

Carlstrom, Nancy White, 1948—*Continued*

"Miss Lilly and her cat Snug live across the street from Sara, who spends a great deal of time there. . . . Whenever it's time for Sara to leave, she and Miss Lilly blow kisses as their special way of saying they will always be friends. . . . Her friend dies and Sara is terribly sad. Caring for Snug helps, and when spring comes, seeing Miss Lilly's garden blooming reminds Sara of their wonderful times together." SLJ

"Illustrated with trim but unfussy spring-colored pictures, this is a gentle if excessively charming introduction to mortality." Bull Cent Child Books

Grandpappy; illustrated by Laurel Molk. Little, Brown 1990 unp il lib bdg $13.95 **E**

1. Grandfathers—Fiction 2. Maine—Fiction
ISBN 0-316-12855-4 LC 88-38819

Nate's visit to Grandpappy's house in Maine is filled with such everyday adventures as finding a four-leaf clover, watching a Great Egret, and shopping for supplies

"Lovely pastels provide just the right feeling for the warm, sensitive relationship between a grandfather and his grandson. Verbal expressions are particularly eloquent when they describe the old man's laugh. A thought-provoking look at these two characters will prove stimulating to readers. Exceptional." Child Book Rev Serv

Jesse Bear, what will you wear? illustrations by Bruce Degen. Macmillan 1986 unp il $12.95 **E**

1. Bears—Fiction 2. Stories in rhyme
ISBN 0-02-717350-X LC 85-10610

"The happy, singsong verse of the title follows Jesse Bear through the changes of clothes and activities of his day, even to bath and bed." N Y Times Book Rev

"The big, cheerful watercolor paintings show the baby bear in loving relation to his family and world. Without crossing the line into sentimentality, this offers a happy, humorous soundfest that will associate reading aloud with a sense of play." Bull Cent Child Books

Other available titles about Jesse Bear are:
Better not get wet, Jesse Bear (1988)
It's about time, Jesse Bear, and other rhymes (1990)

Carrick, Carol

Ben and the porcupine; pictures by Donald Carrick. Houghton Mifflin 1981 unp il lib bdg $13.95; pa $4.95 **E**

1. Dogs—Fiction 2. Porcupines—Fiction
ISBN 0-395-30171-8 (lib bdg); 0-89919-348-X (pa) LC 80-21402

"A Clarion book"

After his dog tangles with a porcupine, Christopher fears for his pet's safety until he thinks of a way to pacify the porcupine

"This simple unadorned prose serves as a libretto for the full-page and double-page spread ink-and-wash drawings in tones of brown, green, and gray. Realistic scenes of house and country by day and by night dominate the book, and Ben—with quills in his muzzle—is skillfully portrayed on a page by himself, an unsentimentalized picture of animal pathos." Horn Book

Other available titles about Christopher are:
Dark and full of secrets (1984)
The foundling (1977)
Left behind (1988)
Sleep out (1973)
The washout (1978)

Big old bones; a dinosaur tale; illustrated by Donald Carrick. Clarion Bks. 1989 unp il $13.95 **E**

1. Fossils—Fiction
ISBN 0-89919-734-5 LC 88-16967

"In this tale the learned professor Potts and his family are traveling out West when he finds a fascinating site with quantities of very large, very old bones. He takes them home and tries different ways of assembling them, but the resulting skeletons are too absurd to be believed. . . . The book is a gentle spoof of early paleontologists who were a little unsure of exactly what they had found. It will be a treat for almost every child over the age of three, who will have an enjoyable feeling of superiority as the professor bungles about, making ridiculous mistakes." Horn Book

In the moonlight, waiting; illustrated by Donald Carrick. Clarion Bks. 1990 unp il lib bdg $13.95 **E**

1. Sheep—Fiction 2. Farm life—Fiction
ISBN 0-89919-867-8 LC 89-17430

In the spring during lambing time, a family wakes in the middle of the night to welcome Clover the sheep's new baby

"The story—full of a sense of life and the renewal of spring—captures the shivery excitement of waking during the night for a special event. The watercolor sketches made by Donald Carrick before his death have a fresh, spontaneous, and unformed quality that heightens the emotional intensity of newness and birth." Horn Book

Patrick's dinosaurs; pictures by Donald Carrick. Clarion Bks. 1983 unp il $13.95 **E**

1. Dinosaurs—Fiction 2. Brothers—Fiction
ISBN 0-89919-189-4 (lib bdg) LC 83-2049

"During a zoo visit, Patrick's older brother Hank compares the size, habits, and ferocity of dinosaurs to the animals in the zoo, blithely unaware that Patrick is becoming increasingly afraid. Even on the way home Hank continues to spout facts—'A stegosaurus was bigger than one of those cars'—until Patrick begins to see the enormous creatures at every turn. Only at home over peanut-butter-and-jelly sandwiches, when Hank assures him that 'dinosaurs have been gone for sixty million years,' can Patrick relax." Booklist

"The Carricks do a particularly good job of creating an impressive array of creatures both in text and illustrations—realistic pencil drawings washed in muted greens, browns and oranges." SLJ

Another available title about Patrick is entered below

Paul's Christmas birthday; pictures by Donald Carrick. Greenwillow Bks. 1978 unp il lib bdg $11.88 **E**

1. Birthdays—Fiction 2. Christmas—Fiction
ISBN 0-688-84159-7 LC 77-28408

"When Paul comes home from school complaining that nobody talks about anything but Christmas, and he wishes that the day before Christmas weren't his birthday, his mother comes up with a plan. All his firends get invitations to a birthday party where they will 'meet

Carrick, Carol—*Continued*
someone from outer space,' and that someone turns out to be Santa Claus." Bull Cent Child Books

"The watercolor and charcoal scenes are full and happy, showing wintry small-town landscapes and snug early American interiors. The family cat, perched above Paul as he reads a book or looking on as he blows his birthday candles out is an especially homey, humorous inclusion." Booklist

What happened to Patrick's dinosaurs? pictures by Donald Carrick. Clarion Bks. 1986 unp il lib bdg $12.95; pa $4.95 E

1. Dinosaurs—Fiction 2. Brothers—Fiction
ISBN 0-89919-406-0 (lib bdg); 0-89919-402-8 (pa)
LC 85-13989

"While he and his brother Hank rake leaves, Patrick unfolds the true life and times of dinosaurs. They were friends with people once, you see, picnicking and fishing, building houses, operating car wind-up (not fill-up) service stations and presenting carnival shows to bored humans. Patrick recounts the sad fact that people did not want to learn from the dinosaurs, as they were only interested in recess and lunch, so the dinosaurs left on a spaceship, keeping a celestial check on the people they miss so dearly." SLJ

"A kindly, funny book, wonderfully evocative of the imagination of children, with a theme that will appear perfectly probable to young readers." Horn Book

Carrick, Donald

Harald and the great stag. Clarion Bks. 1988 unp il lib bdg $14.95; Houghton Mifflin pa $4.95 E

1. Deer—Fiction 2. Hunting—Fiction 3. Middle Ages—Fiction
ISBN 0-89919-514-8; 0-395-52596-9 (pa)
LC 87-17875

Sequel to: Harald and the giant knight (1982)

When Harald, who lives in medieval England, hears that the Baron and his royal guests are planning to hunt the legendary Great Stag, he devises a clever scheme to protect the animal

"The clear antihunting statement reaches across the ages. Carrick's rendering of the characters and details of the period add depth to the simple tale. In full color the illustrations capture the lush forest from misty morning through sunset." Horn Book

Caseley, Judith, 1951-

The cousins. Greenwillow Bks. 1990 unp il $12.95; lib bdg $12.88 E

1. Cousins—Fiction
ISBN 0-688-08433-8; 0-688-08434-6 (lib bdg)
LC 88-34903

"Moving from declaring their children are 'as opposite as can be' to realizing they are both 'one of a kind', first cousins' mothers discover and learn to appreciate their daughters in this unusual romp. The story is delightful, the language and dialogue snappy, and the illustrations detailed and imaginatively vignetted." Child Book Rev Serv

When Grandpa came to stay. Greenwillow Bks. 1986 unp il $11.75; lib bdg $11.88 E

1. Grandfathers—Fiction 2. Jews—Fiction 3. Death—Fiction
ISBN 0-688-06128-1; 0-688-06129-X (lib bdg)
LC 85-12616

When Grandpa comes to his house to stay, Benny enjoys his company and helps him cope with Grandma's death

"A story of the aged and bereavement with characters and relationships that come to life and that have appeal for younger children. . . . The presentation is honest and forthright, without sentimentality, and with light, humorous touches and an upbeat ending. Small pictures, done in mostly pastel shades of yellow, orange, pink, brown and green, have a comforting charm and convey well a happy family environment. . . . A useful book, but more important, an enjoyable one." SLJ

Catalanotto, Peter

Dylan's day out; story and paintings by Peter Catalanotto. Orchard Bks. 1989 unp il $14.95; lib bdg $14.99 E

1. Dogs—Fiction
ISBN 0-531-05829-8; 0-531-08429-9 (lib bdg)
LC 88-36440

"A Richard Jackson book"

"Dylan, a bored Dalmatian, finds the door open one day and escapes into a hotly contested soccer match between the penguins and the skunks. Middle elementary school children will enjoy finding all of the black and white items that Catalanotto has cleverly woven into this improbable and thoroughly delightful tale of a dog's best day." Read Teach

Caudill, Rebecca, 1899-1985

A pocketful of cricket; illustrated by Evaline Ness. Holt & Co. 1964 unp il $14.95 E

1. Crickets—Fiction 2. Farm life—Fiction
ISBN 0-8050-1200-1 LC 64-12617

A Caldecott Medal honor book, 1965

"A six-year-old Kentucky farm boy on his way home with the cows one afternoon catches a cricket, makes a pet and friend of it, and on the first day of school takes it along in his pocket. Happily the teacher understands about friends and instead of putting Cricket out lets Jay introduce Cricket in the first 'Show and tell.'" Booklist

"A perspective nature story with distinctively designed pictures of farm life. Excellent for reading aloud." Hodges. Books for Elem Sch Libr

Cazet, Denys, 1938-

Big Shoe, Little Shoe. Bradbury Press 1984 unp il $12.95 E

1. Rabbits—Fiction 2. Grandfathers—Fiction
ISBN 0-02-717820-X LC 83-21362

"When Grandma insists that it's time for Grandpa to deliver the laundry to their customers, Louie asks to go along. Grandpa demurs, so Louie comes up with another idea; he finds his grandfather's missing shoes,

Cazet, Denys, 1938-—*Continued*
puts them on, and insists in his deepest voice that he is Big Shoe, the delivery man. Grandpa plays right along and stuffs his feet into Louie's shoes, becoming the squeaky-voiced Little Shoe." Booklist

"Children will appreciate this warm story about close relationships between grandparents and grandchildren. It's nicely told without becoming cloying. The illustrations are softly colored; the rabbit characters beguiling and lovable." SLJ

"Never spit on your shoes". Orchard Bks. 1990 unp il $14.95; lib bdg $14.99 E

1. School stories
ISBN 0-531-05847-6; 0-531-08447-7 (lib bdg) LC 89-35164

"A Richard Jackson book"

First grader Arnie tells his mother about his tiring first day at school, while the illustrations reveal the mayhem he is leaving out of his account

"The humor comes not from Arnie's understated commentary, which appears in an orderly inset on each page, but rather from the chaotic mayhem that he omits, shown in the full-page illustrations surrounding the boxed narratives. Here we find assorted animal children eating paste, sticking straws up their nostrils at the lunch table, counting with fingers and toes, and blowing bubbles into the fish bowl. A few jokes may pass right over the intended audience . . . but for the most part Cazet is right on target." Booklist

Chalmers, Mary, 1927-

Throw a kiss, Harry; story and pictures by Mary Chalmers. new ed. Harper & Row 1990 30p il $12.95; lib bdg $12.89 E

1. Cats—Fiction
ISBN 0-06-021246-2; 0-06-021245-4 (lib bdg) LC 89-49064

First published 1958

Wandering away from his mother, Harry the Cat gets stuck in a tree until a fireman comes to his rescue

"Some of Chalmers' fans will insist that the now out-of-print edition (1958), a diminutive volume with line drawings and washes in gray and blue, was perfect in every way. But only a purist could refuse this radiant new version. Somewhat larger in format and bright with full-color artwork, it will soon become a favorite for preschool and library story times as well as for home read-aloud sessions." Booklist

Other available titles about Harry are:
Come to the doctor, Harry (1981)
Merry Christmas, Harry (1977)
Take a nap, Harry (1964)

Charlip, Remy

Thirteen. Four Winds Press 1975 unp il $12.95 E

1. Stories without words
ISBN 0-02-718120-0

First published by Parents Magazine Press

"Each double-page spread contains thirteen different illustrations that are part of thirteen graphic sequences. Some of these are narrative, but most of them are concerned with changing and evolving visual forms. . . . All of these images, beautifully executed in pastels, have been carefully arranged on the pages. The book may have to be introduced to children because it is not immediately obvious." Horn Book

Cherry, Lynne, 1952-

The great kapok tree; a tale of the Amazon rainforest. Harcourt Brace Jovanovich 1990 unp il $14.95 E

1. Rain forests—Fiction 2. Conservation of natural resources—Fiction
ISBN 0-15-200520-X LC 89-2208

"Gulliver books"

The many different animals that live in a great kapok tree in the Brazilian rainforest try to convince a man with an ax of the importance of not cutting down their home

"A carefully researched picture book about the Brazilian rain forest is strikingly illustrated and presented in a large format. Cherry captures the Amazonian proportions of the plants and animals that live there by using vibrant colors, intricate details, and dramatic perspectives. . . . The writing is simple and clear, yet makes a serious point about humans' destructive ways." Booklist

Who's sick today? Dutton 1988 unp il $11.95 E

1. Sick—Fiction 2. Animals—Fiction 3. Stories in rhyme
ISBN 0-525-44380-0 LC 87-22185

Rhyming text and illustrations introduce a variety of animals with different ailments

"On each double page, Cherry pictures a patient, either in a cheerful bedroom, a doctor's office, or a bright hospital room. Attentive mom and dad animals and the doctor, a wise-looking stork with a gray fringe of hair and tiny spectacles, are nearby. The minimal text may produce some giggles, but the real charm lies in the softly shaded, carefully detailed pictures." SLJ

Chetwin, Grace

Box and Cox; illustrated by David Small. Bradbury Press 1990 unp il $13.95 E

1. Humorous stories
ISBN 0-02-718314-9 LC 88-35337

This "story concerns the landlady Mrs. Bouncer, who rents the same room to two unsuspecting gentlemen boarders, one who sleeps there at night and one who sleeps there during the day. She . . . rearranges the room twice daily to prevent Box and Cox from finding out about each other. But after she promises to marry each man, the secret is out." SLJ

"Ms. Chetwin, who is the author of five novels for older readers, moves the story with the clockwork precision and suspense of a Victorian farce. David Small's highly stylized illustrations, done in subtle Victorian colors with theatrical lighting effects, create the illusion of a stage set of the era perfectly. This book should appeal to any child over the age of 5—and to more than a few parents." N Y Times Book Rev

Chorao, Kay

Cathedral mouse. Dutton 1988 unp il lib bdg $12.95 E

1. Mice—Fiction 2. Cathedrals—Fiction
ISBN 0-525-44400-9 LC 87-33398

"Mouse runs away from a pet shop to find a home of his own, but when he arrives at a cathedral it is not quite the sanctuary he hoped it would be. Despite its beauty, danger lurks everywhere—a dropped book, a pack of unfriendly rats, a human hand, all mean trouble. Still, someone is watching out for Mouse as evinced by the periodic gifts of cheese and bread he receives. Finally, his benefactor makes himself known; he's one of the stone carvers working on the cathedral." Booklist

"Softly colored pencil sketches capture the architectural detail, the wonderful light and atmosphere of the cathedral." SLJ

Kate's box. Dutton 1982 unp il $3.95 E

1. Elephants—Fiction
ISBN 0-525-44010-0 LC 82-2403

This book "begins with Kate hiding in a box while her infant cousin Otto visits and steals the show from her. Everyone makes a fuss over Otto until his howling sends them all into another room, whereupon Kate ventures out of her box and, in jig time, finds she loves the squalling baby and he loves her, his friend for life when she plays peek-a-boo with him." Publ Wkly

"Simplicity of plot and vocabulary combine with genuine insight into . . . young children to make an enjoyable reading experience. . . . Because the books are small (4 ½ X 5 ⅞), they will make grand companions for intimate reading as well as for children just reading on their own." SLJ

Other available titles about Kate are:
George told Kate (1987)
Kate's car (1982)
Kate's quilt (1982)
Kate's snowman (1982)

Ups and downs with Oink and Pearl. Harper & Row 1986 63p il $8.95; lib bdg $9.89 E

1. Pigs—Fiction
ISBN 0-06-021274-8; 0-06-021275-6 (lib bdg) LC 85-45264

"An I can read book"

Piglet Oink concocts an unusual birthday present for his sister Pearl, helps her escape from a witch, and ignores her advice on a mail-order movie projector

"The give-and-take earnestness of brother and sister is quite genuine; Chorao's gleeful pictures give these stories both humor and heart." Publ Wkly

Christelow, Eileen, 1943-

Five little monkeys jumping on the bed; retold and illustrated by Eileen Christelow. Clarion Bks. 1989 unp il $13.95 E

1. Monkeys—Fiction 2. Counting
ISBN 0-89919-769-8 LC 88-22839

A counting book in which one by one the little monkeys jump on the bed only to fall off and bump their heads

"Squiggling, swirling lines of color capture the sense of unbridled motion as the monkeys bounce and, one by one, topple from the bed. After all five bandaged youngsters finally fall asleep, a relaxed mama gratefully retires to her room . . . to bounce on 'her' bed. An amusingly presented counting exercise." Booklist

Christiansen, C. B.

My mother's house, my father's house; illustrated by Irene Trivas. Atheneum Pubs. 1989 unp il $12.95 E

1. Divorce—Fiction 2. Parent and child—Fiction
ISBN 0-689-31394-2 LC 88-16802

"A child of divorce speaks of what it's like at her mother's house, where she lives for four days of the week, and at her father's house, where she lives for three days. Both places are home, but neither parent will enter the home of the other." Bull Cent Child Books

"Irene Trivas's comfortably messy watercolor pictures add a great deal to the feeling that the two houses are homes, where the heroine can feel that she belongs and is safe and cared for." N Y Times Book Rev

Cleary, Beverly

The real hole; illustrated by DyAnne DiSalvo-Ryan. Morrow 1986 c1960 unp il $11.95; lib bdg $11.88 E

1. Twins—Fiction
ISBN 0-688-05850-7; 0-688-05851-5 (lib bdg) LC 85-18815

A reissue with new illustrations of the title first published 1960

With interference and suggestions from his twin sister, Janet, four-year-old Jimmy sets out to dig the biggest hole in the world

This book "feature[s] updated illustrations—pencil-and-wash drawings with a slightly scruffy, down-to-earth look that glow with sprightly color. Pleasantly true to life." Booklist

Climo, Shirley, 1928-

The cobweb Christmas; illustrated by Joe Lasker. Crowell 1982 unp il $12.95; lib bdg $12.89 E

1. Christmas—Fiction 2. Spiders—Fiction
ISBN 0-690-04215-9; 0-690-04216-7 (lib bdg) LC 81-43879

"Every year Tante shooed the animals and spiders from her cottage so that she could prepare for Christmas. But every year, after sharing her decorated tree with the village children, she would ask the animals back to her cottage, for she had heard that on Christmas Eve they might speak. . . . This year, as always, the old woman—exhausted from her labors—fell asleep. She never heard 'the rusty, squeaky voices' of the neglected spiders, hoping to be let in. But Christkindel, passing by, opened the door for the spiders, who covered the tree with sticky webs; then, dismayed at the mess, Christkindel transformed the webs into strands of gold and silver." Horn Book

"Lasker's watercolor paintings fill each page they occupy with glowing color. The scenes he sets are contained but full, with sparely composed rustic interiors and appropriate touches of glory when Christkindel works his magic. A good-looking, involving story for the Christmas shelf." Booklist

Coatsworth, Elizabeth Jane, 1893-1986

Under the green willow; by Elizabeth Coatsworth; etchings by Janina Domanska. Greenwillow Bks. 1984 c1971 unp il $9.25; lib bdg $8.59 **E**

1. Animals—Fiction
ISBN 0-688-03845-X; 0-688-03846-8 (lib bdg)
LC 84-1471

A reissue of the title first published 1971 by Macmillan

"The story, in which various pond creatures gather under a willow tree waiting to be fed crumbs, boasts stylized illustrations in sprightly yellow-and-green tones. A nice introduction to pond life for the very young." Booklist

Coerr, Eleanor, 1922-

The big balloon race; pictures by Carolyn Croll. Harper & Row 1981 62p il $7.95; lib bdg $7.89 **E**

1. Balloons—Fiction 2. Parent and child—Fiction
ISBN 0-06-021352-3; 0-06-021353-1 (lib bdg)
LC 80-8368

"An I can read book"

The author "recounts the winning of a hydrogen balloon race by Carlotta Myers, a famous aeronaut, and her stowaway daughter Ariel. Balloon facts are slipped naturally and painlessly into the story, which moves cogently along. The novel subject matter, straightforward mother-daughter relationship, and clear composition of the orange, blue and gray illustrations . . . make for a high-flying new look at a piece of the past." SLJ

Chang's paper pony; pictures by Deborah Kogan Ray. Harper & Row 1988 64p il $11.95; lib bdg $11.89 **E**

1. Chinese Americans—Fiction 2. Ponies—Fiction 3. Gold mines and mining—Fiction
ISBN 0-06-021328-0; 0-06-021329-9 (lib bdg)
LC 87-45679

"An I can read book"

This story is "set at the time of California's Gold Rush. Chang and his grandfather work in the kitchen of a mining camp. As a result of hard work and honesty, not to mention fair play by one of the miners, Chang gets the pony of his dreams. But the story does not prettify the ugly way many immigrant Chinese were treated." N Y Times Book Rev

"Ray's forceful drawings support the text well and firmly establish the dusty mining-town environment. She is particularly adept at showing the vulnerability of children, as well as the ways in which large and small joys affect them." Publ Wkly

The Josefina story quilt; pictures by Bruce Degen. Harper & Row 1986 64p il $8.95; lib bdg $9.89 **E**

1. Quilts—Fiction 2. Overland journeys to the Pacific (U.S.)—Fiction
ISBN 0-06-021348-5; 0-06-021349-3 (lib bdg)
LC 85-45260

"An I can read book"

While traveling west with her family in 1850, a young girl makes a patchwork quilt chronicling the experiences of the journey and reserves a special patch for her pet hen Josefina

"The story makes the history go down easily, and an author's note at the end fills in facts about the western trip and the place of quilts as pioneer diaries. The charcoal and blue/yellow wash illustrations are clear and natural but little attention is paid to matching up quilt squares with the story's action. On the whole, a good introduction to historical fiction that children can read for themselves." SLJ

Cohen, Miriam

See you in second grade! story by Miriam Cohen; pictures by Lillian Hoban. Greenwillow Bks. 1989 unp il $13.95; lib bdg $13.88; Dell pa $2.95 **E**

1. School stories
ISBN 0-688-07138-4; 0-688-07139-2 (lib bdg); 0-440-40303-0 (pa)
LC 87-14869

"In this title Cohen's familiar and popular group of multi-ethnic students reminisce about past experiences and look forward with both anticipation and trepidation to second grade as they embark on an end-of-the-year class trip to the beach." SLJ

"There's a dash of poignant nostalgia, but no sentimentality, as they remember events of the year and say goodbye to their beloved teacher and to each other." Bull Cent Child Books

Other available titles about Jim and his classmates are:
"Bee my valentine!" (1978)
Best friends (1971)
Don't eat too much turkey! (1987)
First grade takes a test (1980)
It's George! (1988)
Jim meets The Thing (1981)
Jim's dog Muffins (1984)
Liar, liar, pants on fire! (1985)
Lost in the museum (1979)
The new teacher (1972)
No good in art (1980)
The real skin rubber monster mask (1990)
See you tomorrow, Charles (1983)
So what? (1982)
Starring first grade (1985)
When will I read? (1977)
Will I have a friend? (1967)

Cohn, Janice

I had a friend named Peter; talking to children about the death of a friend; illustrated by Gail Owens. Morrow 1987 unp il $13; lib bdg $12.88 **E**

1. Death—Fiction
ISBN 0-688-06685-2; 0-688-06686-0 (lib bdg)
LC 86-31150

An "account of the feelings and questions that arise when a child's playmate dies is presented in this gently-told story. Peter is run over while chasing a ball into the street, and Betsy's parents have the sad task of telling their daughter and helping her cope with the tragedy." SLJ

"Betsy's parents and teacher are role models of supportive adults, understanding and accepting her concerns. A lengthy, useful introduction to parents explains how to help children understand death and grieving. The story does not take a religious or metaphysical line of any kind, leaving these issues open for personal comment according to one's own beliefs. Illustrated in soft shades of full color, this book will

Cohn, Janice—*Continued*
be helpful to parents and teachers who want to talk with children about death." Booklist

Cole, Babette

The silly book. Doubleday 1990 unp il $12.95; lib bdg $13.99 E

1. Humorous stories 2. Stories in rhyme
ISBN 0-385-41237-1; 0-385-41238-X (lib bdg)
LC 89-17172

"In a series of vignettes, a parade of people and an animal or two show off goofy walks, heads, pets, food, and behavior. Held together by the occasional appearance of the child narrator, the book is a collection of observations in verse on the foibles of the ordinary and nonsensical in life." SLJ

"The well balanced combination of text and artwork engenders utter lunacy on a scale that defies description." Publ Wkly

Cole, Brock, 1938-

No more baths; written and illustrated by Brock Cole. Doubleday 1980 unp il $10.95; lib bdg $11.95 E

1. Baths—Fiction 2. Animals—Fiction
ISBN 0-385-14714-7; 0-385-14715-5 (lib bdg)
LC 78-22790

"When Jessie McWhistle's unreasonable family tries to make her have a bath 'in the middle of the day,' the outrage is too much, and she decides to leave home. She tries being a chicken 'frazzling' in the sand but it makes her feel gritty. Next she tries copying her cat, licking her paws and smoothing her hair; that doesn't work either. So she attempts to follow the example of the happy pig in her deep, oozy wallow, with predictably uncomfortable results. At last, Jessie gives up the unequal struggle, marches home, and surrenders to the hot bath, the shampoo, the towel." SLJ

"The author-artist tells a fresh, funny story with a clear text, well-paced for reading aloud. The watercolor illustrations add detail and humor and help create a lively sense of farm life." Horn Book

The winter wren. Farrar, Straus & Giroux 1984 unp il $12.95 E

1. Spring—Fiction
ISBN 0-374-38454-1 LC 84-1583

"It's bitter cold and the seasons are late in turning when young Simon and his little sister, Meg, go out looking for Spring, who is sleeping at Winter's farm. Old Man Winter is snowing sleet, but the Winter Wren tells the children to sow meal behind him, and lo, Spring finally comes." N Y Times Book Rev

"The shading of hues and delicate airiness afforded by watercolors are fully realized in Cole's artistic evocation of this original story. Told in well-turned phrases." Booklist

Cole, Joanna

Don't tell the whole world! illustrated by Kate Duke. Crowell 1990 32p il $13.95; lib bdg $13.89 E

1. Buried treasure—Fiction
ISBN 0-690-04809-2; 0-690-04811-4 (lib bdg)
LC 89-29283

"Farmer John's wife, Emma, never means to tell things, but she just can't keep a secret. So when John and his ox plow up a money box that will pay the rent and then some, he has to think pretty creatively about dealing with Emma's loose tongue." Horn Book

"Duke's pastel palette and affable characters lend snappy support to Cole's amusing text. This is fine storytelling, charmingly illustrated." Publ Wkly

Collington, Peter

The angel and the soldier boy. Knopf 1987 unp il $9.95; lib bdg $10.99 E

1. Dreams—Fiction 2. Stories without words
ISBN 0-394-88626-7; 0-394-98626-1 (lib bdg)
LC 86-20169

This wordless picture book "begins with the bedtime of a little girl who clutches a tiny tin soldier and toy angel while she listens to her mother read about pirates. As soon as she is asleep, a miniature pirate robs her piggy bank and captures the soldier, who has tried to stop him. The angel tracks them to a model ship, avoiding the claws of the family cat, and rescues the soldier, retrieves the coin, and sees that they are safely settled back in the child's hands." Bull Cent Child Books

"Pastel watercolors and colored pencil tell this wordless story with great flair. . . . It is the realistic detail in this book which sets it apart from the many wordless picture books." SLJ

Conrad, Pam, 1947-

The Tub People; illustrations by Richard Egielski. Harper & Row 1989 unp il $13.95; lib bdg $13.89 E

1. Toys—Fiction
ISBN 0-06-021340-X; 0-06-021341-8 (lib bdg)
LC 88-32804

"The Tub People are a family of seven wooden toys that are always perched on the edge of the bathtub. One evening during one of their favorite games, the Tub Child is sucked down the drain. Fortune arrives in the form of a plumber who rescues the tired Tub Child. The whole family is given a new, safer (and dry) home where some things are very different." Child Book Rev Serv

"In its combination of the dramatic and the subtle, this is a masterful picture book. The narrative takes for its patterns the rituals of play, heightening the reality and injecting it with drama by excluding humans from the action. The art, too, juggles the effects of order and chaos, the neat shapes offset by strong color contrasts and lively patterns." Bull Cent Child Books

Cooney, Barbara, 1917-

Chanticleer and the fox; adapted and illustrated by Barbara Cooney. Crowell 1958 unp il $13.95; lib bdg $13.89; pa $3.80 **E**

1. Fables 2. Foxes—Fiction 3. Roosters—Fiction
ISBN 0-690-18561-8; 0-690-18562-6 (lib bdg); 0-690-04318-X (pa) LC 58-10449

Awarded the Caldecott Medal, 1959

"Adaptation of the 'Nun's Priest's Tale' from the Canterbury Tales." Verso of title page

"Chanticleer, the rooster, learns the pitfalls of vanity, while the fox who captures, then loses him, learns the value of self-control." Books for Deaf Child

This adaptation "retains the spirit of the original in its telling and in the beautiful, strongly colored illustrations softened by detailed lines. . . . [It] will be excellent for reading aloud to children." Libr J

Hattie and the wild waves. Viking 1990 unp il $14.95 **E**

1. Beaches—Fiction 2. Artists—Fiction
ISBN 0-670-83056-9 LC 90-32577

"A little girl recounts the story of her family's life in Brooklyn at the beginning of the century. Her prosperous father builds houses so they can afford to vacation on Coney Island and Long Island, where her imagination blooms. She wishes with the waves and decides to pursue her love of drawing and become an artist when she grows up." SLJ

"The exquisite paintings, done in acrylics and pastels, reflect the solid comfort and cultivation of turn-of-the-century affluent life in Brooklyn." Horn Book

Island boy; story and pictures by Barbara Cooney. Viking Kestrel 1988 unp il lib bdg $14.95 **E**

1. Islands—Fiction 2. Growth—Fiction 3. Family life—Fiction
ISBN 0-670-81749-X LC 88-175

"Lyrical in its telling and flawless in its visualization, Cooney's book shows the interdependence of three generations of life off the New England coast. This island is a treasure." SLJ

Miss Rumphius; story and pictures by Barbara Cooney. Viking 1982 unp il $13.95; Penguin Bks. pa $4.95 **E**

ISBN 0-670-47958-6; 0-14-050539-3 (pa) LC 82-2837

As a child Great-aunt Alice Rumphius resolved that when she grew up she would go to faraway places, live by the sea in her old age, and do something to make the world more beautiful—and she does all those things, the last being the most difficult of all

"The idea of offering beauty as one's heritage is appealing, the story is nicely told, and the illustrations are quite lovely, especially the closing scenes of a hill covered with flowers being gathered by children." Bull Cent Child Books

Cooney, Nancy Evans, 1932-

Go away monsters, lickety split! pictures by Maxie Chambliss. Putnam 1990 unp il $13.95 **E**

1. Bedtime—Fiction 2. Night—Fiction 3. Fear—Fiction
ISBN 0-399-21935-8 LC 89-10515

"When night falls at his new house, Jeffrey is scared there may be monsters lurking in his room. None of his parents' responses—leaving the hall light on; using a nightlight; or keeping a flashlight ready—seems to help. Then Jeffrey's grandmother visits with a small, furry solution." Publisher's note

"The illustrations are in simple watercolor washes, capturing and supporting the spirit of the story. Not only will this be an appropriate selection for those children experiencing the trauma of a move, but it also makes a reassuring bedtime story for all children." SLJ

Couture, Susan Arkin

The block book; illustrated by Petra Mathers. Harper & Row 1990 unp il $13.95; lib bdg $13.89 **E**

1. Toys—Fiction 2. Stories in rhyme
ISBN 0-06-020523-7; 0-06-020524-5 (lib bdg) LC 89-34504

"Pack rats everywhere will have no trouble identifying with Betsy and Ben, a pair of blocks whose home is so overflowing with found objects (from yo-yos to worn-out appliances) that they are reduced to camping out in their yard under a Valentine's Day card. Yet when a neighbor's house burns down, it's Betsy and Ben—and their junk—who come to the rescue and help him rebuild." Publ Wkly

"The simplicity of the rhyming text, set sparely on a page facing the illustrations, makes the text itself accessible. The crayon figures on watercolor-washed backgrounds are full of deep fantasy colors and vibrant tones, and hold much detailed, intriguing junk." SLJ

Craft, Ruth

The winter bear; illustrated by Erik Blegvad. Atheneum Pubs. 1975 c1974 25p il $13.95; pa $3.95 **E**

1. Toys—Fiction 2. Winter—Fiction 3. Stories in rhyme
ISBN 0-689-50017-3; 0-689-70456-9 (pa) LC 74-18178

"A Margaret K. McElderry book"

First published 1974 in the United Kingdom

"An abandoned knitted bear, found in a tree by three children on a winter's afternoon, is lovingly dried, dressed, and given a home." LC. Child Books, 1975

"A simple but concrete text characterized by unforced rhyme and unobtrusive rhythm. . . . The exquisite watercolor illustrations, detailed in fine pen-and-ink lines, underscore the gentle drama." Horn Book

Crampton, Patricia

Peter and the wolf; [by] Sergei Prokofiev; illustrated by Josef Paleček; retold by Patricia Crampton. Picture Bk. Studio 1987 unp il $13.95; pa $3.95 **E**

1. Wolves—Fiction 2. Fairy tales
ISBN 0-88708-049-9; 0-14-050633-0 (pa)
LC 87-13915

"A Michael Neugebauer book"

Retells the orchestral fairy tale of the boy who, ignoring his grandfather's warnings proceeds to capture a wolf

"Palaček uses warm, bright colors; flat backgrounds; and exaggerated expressionistic forms." SLJ

Crews, Donald

Carousel. Greenwillow Bks. 1982 unp il lib bdg $12.88 **E**

ISBN 0-688-00909-3 (lib bdg) LC 82-3062

"Crews uses both color photography of words and paintings in Art Deco style of the carousel; a brief text describes the ride, from the horses waiting, silent and still, to the end of a whirling ride. The speeded, blurred pictures of the carousel in motion and of the words (boom, too) that signify the calliope sounds are very effective. Despite the lack of story line, this should appeal to children because of the brilliant color, the impression of speed, and the carousel itself." Bull Cent Child Books

Freight train. Greenwillow Bks. 1978 unp il $12.95; lib bdg $11.88; Puffin Bks. pa $3.95 **E**

1. Railroads 2. Color
ISBN 0-688-80165-X; 0-688-84165-1 (lib bdg); 0-14-050480-X (pa) LC 78-2303

A Caldecott Medal honor book, 1979

"Crews, with a minimum of descriptive words, has drawn a stylized freight train passing by, slowly at first, then in a blur of black and bright color." Babbling Bookworm

"The young child can learn to identify the engine, the caboose and the different cars. . . . A delightful introduction to railroad transportation and to the colors in the spectrum." America

Harbor. Greenwillow Bks. 1982 unp il $11.75; lib bdg $11.88 **E**

1. Harbors 2. Ships
ISBN 0-688-00861-5; 0-688-00862-3 (lib bdg)
LC 81-6607

"Liners, tankers, barges, and freighters move in and out. Ferryboats shuttle from shore to shore. Busiest of all are the tugboats as they push and tow the big ships to their docks. The New York harbor is full of action." Publisher's note

This book "is an exciting, educational and beautiful show-and-tell. . . . The full-page, full-color paintings will delight children. . . . Crew's outstanding feat here . . . is demonstrating the widely different sizes of the boats in pictures matching and contrasting them with trucks and other land vehicles." Publ Wkly

Parade. Greenwillow Bks. 1983 unp il $13.95; lib bdg $13.88 **E**

1. Parades
ISBN 0-688-01995-1; 0-688-01996-X (lib bdg)
LC 82-20927

"Full-color illustrations and a brief text combine to present the various elements of a city parade. Beginning with an early morning empty street and then readying street vendors, excitement mounts as crowds swell to greet a parade of bright images; flags, floats, a marching band, baton twirlers, antique cars and bicycles and a new fire engine. The parade ends and crowds thin; a street cleaning machine sweeps up the remains." SLJ

The author/illustrator's "refined poster-art approach to evoking an event works again here. . . . A polished assembly of crisp shapes, effective compositions, and pure, bright color." Booklist

School bus. Greenwillow Bks. 1984 unp il $13.95; lib bdg $13.88; Penguin Bks. pa $3.95 **E**

1. School stories 2. Buses—Fiction
ISBN 0-688-02807-1; 0-688-02808-X (lib bdg); 0-14-050549-0 (pa) LC 83-18681

"The book takes readers through the morning hours, when the buses roll to collect children from their parents and deposit them at different schools, to the end of the day, when they return to gather their riders together again and bring them back to the corners where mothers and fathers are awaiting the homeward-bound scholars." Publ Wkly

"The author-artist cleverly avoids monotony in his subject matter by using different size buses and a pleasing variety of background, perspectives, and the directions in which they travel. Even the potentially tiresome yellow of the buses provides both a unifying element and a contrast for the cheerful colors of the children's clothing and for the bustle of city streets." Horn Book

Ten black dots. rev ed. Greenwillow Bks. 1986 unp il $12.95; lib bdg $12.88 **E**

1. Counting 2. Stories in rhyme
ISBN 0-688-06067-6; 0-688-06068-4 (lib bdg)
LC 85-14871

A revision of the title first published 1968

"In this basic counting book . . . large black dots appear as an integral part of each illustrated subject. For example, 'Five dots can make buttons on a coat . . . or the port-holes of a boat.' This simple concept succeeds admirably through the bold, flat colors and briskly delineated graphics of Crews' illustrations." Booklist

Truck. Greenwillow Bks. 1980 unp il $12.95; lib bdg $12.88; Penguin Bks. pa $3.95 **E**

1. Trucks
ISBN 0-688-80244-3; 0-688-84244-5 (lib bdg); 0-14-050506-7 (pa) LC 79-19031

A Caldecott Medal honor book, 1981

A bright red tractor-trailer truck "sporting a chalk-white 'Trucking' label affixed to its side . . . pushes its way across the United States to deliver its prized cargo of tricycles. . . . [It rolls] through a network of crowded highways, dank tunnels, all-night truck stops, rain-splattered city streets, Los Angeles spider freeways, over . . . the Golden Gate Bridge, until at last 'Trucking'

Crews, Donald—*Continued*

finds its way to the warehouse awaiting its [cargo]." Christ Sci Monit

"Although there is no text, the story is far from wordless; trucks, buses, and vans are emblazoned with letters and emblems, the streets are lined with familiar traffic signs, and a truck stop is festooned with advertisements in neon lights. The artist depicts no people; the silent red truck is the main character of an imaginative, almost pop-art view of mobile America." Horn Book

We read: A to Z. Greenwillow Bks. 1984 c1967 26p il $14.95; lib bdg $14.88 **E**

1. Alphabet
ISBN 0-688-03843-3; 0-688-03844-1 (lib bdg)
LC 83-25453

A reissue of the title first published 1967 by Harper & Row

"An indispensable book that will provide days of fun for children. Instead of the conventional approach to the alphabet, the author has combined the letters and the illustrations with definite concepts that a child can see and use. The format is good, the print excellent, and the use of colors unusual and very appealing to a child's imagination." Bruno. Books for Sch Libr, 1968

Crowe, Robert L.

Clyde monster; illustrated by Kay Chorao. Dutton 1976 unp il $12.95; pa $3.95 **E**

1. Monsters—Fiction 2. Night—Fiction 3. Fear—Fiction
ISBN 0-525-28025-1; 0-525-44289-8 (pa)
LC 76-10733

"In an amusing reversal of roles, a young monster is afraid of the dark because he believes that a person may be lurking under the bed or in a corner." LC. Child Books, 1976

"The now familiar table-turning theme for children afraid of monsters takes on effective, rational proportions in a very amusing tale. . . . Chorao's softly grotesque portraits add character without chill, though the use of blue skyground and glaring yellow moon seems gratuitous among the figuratively colorful black-and-white drawings." Booklist

Cushman, Doug

Possum stew. Dutton 1990 unp il $12.95 **E**

1. Animals—Fiction
ISBN 0-525-44566-8
LC 89-34481

"Old Possum is full of devilment, always playing tricks on everyone in the swamp. One day he tricks Bear and Gator once too often, and they decide to get even. Their revenge is so sweet and Possum so scared that he never bothers them again." Horn Book Guide

"Written in a drawl that youngsters will love imitating, the book's equally engaging pictures feature brightly colored swamp scenes that set just the right cornpone ambience for this knee-slapping tale." Booklist

Cuyler, Margery

Baby Dot: a dinosaur story; illustrated by Ellen Weiss. Clarion Bks. 1990 unp il $13.95 **E**

1. Dinosaurs—Fiction 2. School stories
ISBN 0-395-51934-9
LC 89-77726

"Polka-dotted Dot is just a little spoiled and does not take well to school. She won't play cooperatively, and she throws the occasional tantrum. Her parents decide to keep her home, and she soon becomes bored. Thus, Dot tries school again with a new attitude." SLJ

"Weiss' primitive-style, pastel illustrations are playful and amusing, as is Cuyler's story. The combination is bound to please when the inevitable preschool dinosaurmania strikes." Booklist

Daly, Niki, 1946-

Not so fast, Songololo; written & illustrated by Niki Daly. Atheneum Pubs. 1986 c1985 unp il $13.95; Puffin Bks. pa $3.50 **E**

1. Blacks—Fiction 2. Grandmothers—Fiction 3. South Africa—Fiction
ISBN 0-689-50367-9; 0-14-050715-9 (pa)
LC 85-71034

"A Margaret K. McElderry book"

First published 1985 in the United Kingdom

"The setting is South Africa and the names of the people are like poetry: Uzuti, Mongi, Mr. Motiki. Malusi is now old enough to accompany his grandmother, Gogo, into the city to shop. She is an old woman—ample, proud, not quite in step with modern technology, and she no longer moves quickly. Malusi (Songololo to his grandmother) helps her with her shopping." Publ Wkly

"The watercolor illustrations are splendidly evocative of the affection between the generations and of the South African city scene, which, surprisingly, is hardly distinguishable from an American city. The beautiful, gentle book about the ordinary occurrences of daily life has an extraordinary effect." Horn Book

Daugherty, James Henry, 1887-1974

Andy and the lion; by James Daugherty. Viking 1938 unp il $13.95; Penguin Bks. pa $3.95 **E**

1. Lions—Fiction
ISBN 0-670-12433-8; 0-14-050277-7 (pa)
LC 38-27390

A Caldecott Medal honor book, 1939

A modern picture story of Androcles and the lion in which Andy, who read a book about lions, was almost immediately plunged into action. The next day he met a circus lion with a thorn in his paw. Andy removed the thorn and earned the lion's undying gratitude

"This is a tall tale for little children. It is typically American in its setting and its fun. The large full page illustrations are in yellow, black and white and the brief, hand-lettered text on the opposite page is clear and readable." Libr J

Day, Alexandra

Carl goes shopping. Farrar, Straus & Giroux 1990 unp il $9.95 **E**

1. Dogs—Fiction 2. Department stores—Fiction 3. Stories without words
ISBN 0-374-31111-0 LC 88-46216

Carl, featured in Good dog, Carl (1985) "is left to mind his owner's baby in the lobby of an elegant department store. The diapered toddler, who climbs out of her carriage and onto the dog's back, is transported by elevator to the upper floors where she and Carol innocently explore different departments and leave a hilariously incriminating trail behind them." Horn Book

"While their antics are pure fantasy, Day's characters have real faces and personalities. Painted with rich texture and subdued colors, the illustrations tell the largely wordless story with ample action and humor to sustain children's and adults' repeated enjoyment." Booklist

Frank and Ernest. Scholastic 1988 unp il $12.95; pa $3.95 **E**

1. Elephants—Fiction 2. Bears—Fiction 3. Restaurants, bars, etc.—Fiction
ISBN 0-590-41557-3; 0-590-41556-5 (pa) LC 88-1966

"Frank, a bear, and Ernest, an elephant, specialize in taking care of small businesses while the owner is away. When Mrs. Miller hires them to run her diner for three days, they assure her that they will take good care of it. Then Frank decides they must learn diner lingo before they begin." Publ Wkly

"A four-page glossary of restaurant language may encourage children to invent their own picturesque nomenclature. Carrying the text are the watercolor illustrations, rich in diner detail and humor. A novelty offering with nostalgia appeal." Booklist

Another available title about Frank and Ernest is entered below

Frank and Ernest play ball. Scholastic 1990 unp il lib bdg $12.95 **E**

1. Elephants—Fiction 2. Bears—Fiction 3. Baseball—Fiction
ISBN 0-590-42548-X LC 89-10312

Frank and Ernest have "agreed to manage a baseball team for a single game in the owners' absence. The pair admit to knowing little about the game, but conscientiously do their homework and with the help of a Dictionary of Baseball, set about to learn the lingo." SLJ

"Day's rich watercolors nicely capture the pastoral quality of the game (there's green in every picture), and young fans will enjoy Frank and Ernest's determined efforts to learn new meanings for old words. It's never too early, after all, to appreciate the poetry of baseball." Booklist

Day, Edward C.

John Tabor's ride; illustrated by Dirk Zimmer. Knopf 1989 unp il $12.95; lib bdg $13.99 **E**

1. Tall tales 2. Whaling—Fiction 3. Voyages and travels—Fiction
ISBN 0-394-88577-5; 0-394-98577-X (lib bdg) LC 88-9065

"This sea-faring yarn tells a fantastic tale of a young whaler from Taborstown. Although young John springs from a whaling family, he is not a happy sailor. He does nothing but complain. Finally, a little old man literally takes him on a 'whale' of a ride around the world. Young John is so frightened that he learns his lesson and becomes the jolliest sailor around." Child Book Rev Serv

"Shaded with scratched lines and cross-hatching reminiscent of scrimshaw, Zimmer's artwork features vivid colors tempered with sea greens and blues. Varied in composition, humorously exaggerated in characterization, and enlivened with many amusing details, the illustrations will capture children's attention and lead their imaginations in new directions." Booklist

De Paola, Tomie, 1934-

The art lesson; written and illustrated by Tomie dePaola. Putnam 1989 unp il $13.95 **E**

ISBN 0-399-21688-X LC 88-27617

Having learned to be creative in drawing pictures at home, young Tommy is dismayed when he goes to school and finds the art lesson there much more regimented

"How Tommy learns to express his own individuality and listen to his own creative impulses and imagination makes for engrossing reading. DePaola's characteristic bright illustrations complement and enliven his tale of growing up." Horn Book

Bill and Pete; story and pictures by Tomie de Paola. Putnam 1978 unp il $13.95; pa $5.95 **E**

1. Crocodiles—Fiction 2. Birds—Fiction
ISBN 0-399-20646-9; 0-399-20650-7 (pa)

"Near the Nile River, long ago, William Everett Crocodile chooses Pete the plover for his toothbrush, and they become friends as well. When the reptile scholar despairs of writing all the letters in his name, Pete has an idea and William passes the test by penning 'Bill.' Then, the Bad Guy (a human trapper) captures Bill and plans to make a suitcase of him. The solution to that problem is heady fun." Publ Wkly

"De Paola has again created an imaginative, humorous tale which he illustrates in happy pinks, greens, yellows, and blues." SLJ

Another available title about Bill and Pete is entered below

Bill and Pete go down the Nile; written and illustrated by Tomie dePaola. Putnam 1987 unp il lib bdg $12.95; pa $5.95 **E**

1. Crocodiles—Fiction 2. Birds—Fiction 3. Egypt—Fiction
ISBN 0-399-21395-3 (lib bdg); 0-399-21396-1 (pa)
LC 86-12258

"On Monday Bill Crocodile learns about his hometown on the River Nile from a spectacled Ms. Ibis; on Tuesday, about the Sphinx; Pharaohs, burial chambers and pyramids on Wednesday; Thursday is the day for the Sacred Eye of Isis. Finally, on Friday, he sees it all on a class trip to the Royal Museum, where Bill and Pete doughtily save the famous Isis jewel from 'Bad Guy'." Publ Wkly

"DePaola includes all sorts of clever minutiae in both text and pictures. . . . The whole thing is suspiciously simple, amazingly complicated, and quietly creative." Wilson Libr Bull

De Paola, Tomie, 1934-—*Continued*

An early American Christmas; written and illustrated by Tomie dePaola. Holiday House 1987 unp il lib bdg $14.95 **E**

1. Christmas—Fiction 2. German Americans
ISBN 0-8234-0617-2 LC 86-3102

"A German family moves from the old country to a small New England town in the 1800's. The town doesn't celebrate Christmas, but the family forges ahead with bayberry candles, evergreen decorations, a Christmas tree in the parlor, and carols on the night air. Gradually, all the households become 'Christmas families'." Child Book Rev Serv

"This provides a fascinating look at Christmas as it once was: a holiday whose customs were entwined with the season's natural bounty. The emphasis is on the joys of preparation and of quiet, heartfelt observance; refreshingly, gift-giving is not a concern. This is a warm and beautifully realized tribute to the spirit and traditions of the season." Publ Wkly

Helga's dowry; a troll love story; story and pictures by Tomie de Paola. Harcourt Brace Jovanovich 1977 unp il $13.95; pa $3.95 **E**

1. Fairy tales
ISBN 0-15-233701-6; 0-15-640010-3 (pa) LC 76-54953

"Helga . . . is 'the loveliest Troll in three parishes' but she is also the poorest. Handsome Lars loves her—but not enough to resist the lure of Plain Inge's enormous dowry. Upon hearing the news of their engagement . . . she clomps off to earn, through the use of her wits . . . an estate fit for a queen—which she promptly becomes, after a hilarious confrontation with her rival." SLJ

"Humor bubbles through text and pictures with squatty, buck-toothed, detailed trolls amd bemused bystanders cavorting across richly colored paintings trimmed with hearts-and-flowers. An amusing tale from an accomplished hand." Booklist

The knight and the dragon; story and pictures by Tomie de Paola. Putnam 1980 unp il $10.95; pa $5.95 **E**

1. Knights and knighthood—Fiction 2. Dragons—Fiction
ISBN 0-399-20707-4; 0-399-20708-2 (pa) LC 79-18131

"A boy knight feels he really ought to fight a dragon and, in a cave far away, a dragon begins to feel he ought to defend his species' honor by a duel with a knight. . . . When the foes finally meet, the encounter becomes something else." Publ Wkly

"Very few words and typical de Paola illustrations make this lighthearted jest . . . superb for young listeners and readers. There's a chuckle on every page, especially for librarians, as the castle librarian saves both warriors from disgrace with the right books from her horse-drawn bookmobile!" Child Book Rev Serv

The mysterious giant of Barletta; an Italian folktale; adapted and illustrated by Tomie DePaola. Harcourt Brace Jovanovich 1984 unp il $12.95 **E**

1. Giants—Fiction 2. Folklore—Italy
ISBN 0-15-256347-4 (lib bdg) LC 83-18445

"A statue of a colossal youth comes to life and saves the town from an invading army by persuading the marauders that he is really the smallest and weakest of the town's schoolboys." SLJ

"A fine sense of humor lightens the story, which the author says is based on an Italian legend, while the expedient blend of Christian and pagan faiths reflects its peasant unself-consciousness." Horn Book

Nana Upstairs & Nana Downstairs; story and pictures by Tomie de Paola. Putnam 1973 unp il $11.95; Puffin Bks. pa $3.95 **E**

1. Grandmothers—Fiction 2. Death—Fiction
ISBN 0-399-21417-8; 0-14-050290-4 (pa) LC 72-77965

"Small Tommy calls his ninety-four-year-old grandmother 'Nana Upstairs' because she is bedridden; downstairs her daughter is busily keeping house, she's 'Nana Downstairs.' When great-grandmother dies, Tommy learns about death and, years later, he is better prepared when Nana Downstairs dies in her old age." Bull Cent Child Books

"In a quietly touching story, the author-illustrator depicts loving family relationships so that even the very young reader can understand the concepts." Publ Wkly

Now one foot, now the other; story and pictures by Tomie de Paola. Putnam 1981 unp il $11.95; pa $5.95 **E**

1. Grandfathers—Fiction
ISBN 0-399-20774-0; 0-399-20775-9 (pa) LC 80-22239

"Bobby's much loved grandfather has had a stroke. After a long hospitalization, the man returns home unable to speak, walk or care for himself. . . . Their roles reversed, the youngster helps his grandfather learn to walk again 'now one foot, now the other.'" SLJ

"In this warmly told companion to the grandmother's book, 'Nana Upstairs and Nana Downstairs' [entered above] de Paola sensitively provides an understanding portrayal about grandparents' illness, an often puzzling situation for children. Soft blues and tans, textured with pencil shadings, provide a tranquil backdrop for the emotion-filled faces that expressively suggest the changing relationship of the old man and the boy." Booklist

Sing, Pierrot, sing; a picture book in mime. Harcourt Brace Jovanovich 1983 unp il lib bdg $12.95; pa $3.95 **E**

1. Stories without words
ISBN 0-15-274988-8 (lib bdg); 0-15-274989-6 (pa) LC 83-8403

"This wordless take-off on the familiar story finds pantalooned clown Pierrot wooing his beloved, coquettish Columbine beneath the silvery moon, unaware that her lover, Harlequin, shares her balcony room. The friendship of the Renaissance village children sustains him in his misery and gives him renewed purpose in life." Child Book Rev Serv

"Unusually pleasing illustrations in glowing colors show to perfection a pensive Pierrot usually accompanied by a cat, a dog, and a rabbit as well as by a Botticelli-like Columbine and an enormous brilliant moon." Horn Book

De Regniers, Beatrice Schenk

A little house of your own; illustrated by Irene Haas. Harcourt Brace Jovanovich 1987 c1982 unp il $9.95 E

ISBN 0-15-245787-9 LC 86-27013

A reissue of the title first published 1954

"This book describes and explains the need to be alone at times. Everyone must have a 'house of his own,' boys and girls, mothers and fathers." Read Ladders for Hum Relat. 5th edition

"This is a delightful book by an author who obviously understands children well and has observed them very carefully. . . . The illustrations are perfectly matched to the text." Publ Wkly

May I bring a friend? illustrated by Beni Montresor. Atheneum Pubs. 1964 unp il $13.95; pa $3.95 E

1. Animals—Fiction
ISBN 0-689-20615-1; 0-689-71353-3 (pa) LC 64-19562

Awarded the Caldecott Medal, 1965

"Each time the little boy in this picture book is invited to take tea or dine with the King and Queen, he brings along a somewhat difficult animal friend. Their Highnesses always cope and are wonderfully rewarded in the end." Publ Wkly

"Rich color and profuse embellishment adorn an opulent setting. Absurdities and contrasts are so imaginatively combined in a hilarious comedy of manners that the merriment can be enjoyed on several levels." Horn Book

So many cats! illustrated by Ellen Weiss. Clarion Bks. 1985 unp il lib bdg $13.95; pa $4.95 E

1. Cats—Fiction 2. Counting 3. Stories in rhyme
ISBN 0-89919-322-6; 0-89919-700-0 (pa) LC 85-3739

Counting verses explain how a family ended up with a dozen cats

"Because the cats are counted and recounted each time there is an addition, every cat is recognizable and distinctive, relaxed or playful, inscrutable or attentive; they are drawn in flat outline and light color. But the humans, as befits an inferior species, are almost invisible, showing only an odd leg or the top of a head. Clearly a cat's paradise and certainly enjoyable for young counters and cat-lovers." Horn Book

Waiting for Mama; illustrated by Victoria de Larrea. Clarion Bks. 1984 unp il lib bdg $9.95 E

ISBN 0-89919-222-X LC 83-14982

"A little girl sits under a tree, as she is told to, and imagines a whole lifetime passing by while she waits for her mother to finish an errand. She might grow up, get married, have children, even grandchildren before the shopping is finally done." N Y Times Book Rev

"The cheerful pen-and-wash drawings in shades of pink, orange, and yellow have a light touch even when Amy's burgeoning fantasy makes for complicated compositions. An amusing depiction that's well in tune with childhood emotions." Booklist

Degen, Bruce, 1945-

Jamberry; story and pictures by Bruce Degen. Harper & Row 1983 unp il $12.95; pa $3.95 E

1. Stories in rhyme 2. Berries—Fiction
ISBN 0-06-021416-3; 0-06-443068-5 (pa) LC 82-47708

"Boy meets bear, and together they go berry-picking by canoe, through fields and by pony and 'Boys-in-Berries' train, all the way to Berryland." Child Book Rev Serv

"Berries and jam are roundly celebrated in a lilting rhyme that, coupled with the jaunty colored pictures, makes it . . . a good pick for sharing one on one, or fun to read aloud as a poetry introduction." Booklist

Delton, Judy

I'm telling you now; illustrated by Lillian Hoban. Dutton 1983 unp il $9.95; pa $3.95 E

1. Parent and child—Fiction
ISBN 0-525-44037-2; 0-525-44221-9 (pa) LC 82-17714

"A little boy gets into trouble just because his mother didn't always specify what he could 'not' do. She did tell him 'NOT' to cross the road, so he climbed a ladder to the roof." Child Book Rev Serv

"This amusing picture book depicts a situation with which children will instantly identify. . . . Hoban's bright full-color illustrations peopled with her trademark round-faced characters perfectly suit this story of the trials and errors of a preschooler's growing sense of independence and curiosity." SLJ

The new girl at school; illustrated by Lillian Hoban. Dutton 1979 unp il $12.95 E

1. School stories
ISBN 0-525-35780-7 LC 79-11409

"When Mother gets a new job, Marcia gets a new school. No one notices her octopus dress and she sits alone in the bus seats for two. She threatens to run away and get the mumps, but gradually she makes friends, learns subtraction, and life is again good." SLJ

"The feelings presented are very real. . . . Hoban's sketches adequately depict the school setting and the main character's adjustment to it." Child Book Rev Serv

Demi, 1942-

Demi's Count the animals 1 2 3. Grosset & Dunlap 1986 unp il $9.95; pa $5.95 E

1. Counting 2. Animals—Fiction
ISBN 0-448-18980-1; 0-448-19166-0 (pa) LC 85-81653

"Each number from 1 to 20 gets a double-page color illustration, the numeral and number word, a short rhyme, and instructions on what to count on that page. The bright, colorful drawings often show the animals covered in paisley, flower patterns, or in small versions of the same animal." Child Book Rev Serv

"Here's a counting book that is an effective teaching tool, with clear correlation between words, digits, and pictures and with attractive illustrations of animals. . . . Color, humor, and the appeals of rhyme, rhythm, and

Demi, 1942-—*Continued*
a parade of animals equal a winner." Bull Cent Child Books

Demi's Find-the-animal A.B.C.; an alphabet-game book. Grosset & Dunlap 1985 unp il $9.95; pa $5.95 **E**

1. Alphabet 2. Animals—Fiction
ISBN 0-448-18970-4; 0-448-19165-2 (pa)
LC 85-70285

The author/illustrator uses animals from A to Z to introduce the letters of the alphabet. Readers are also asked to spot additional animals hidden in the illustrations

"Not just a showcase for the artist's talent, this engaging puzzle book will sharpen the basic prereading skill of discrimination. . . . Alternating with well-designed black-and-white spreads are those in color, their bright but harmonious hues adding gaiety to the already animated scenes. A hide-and-seek lover's dream, this will not be a story-hour choice because the viewer needs to be close enough to point to the animals. However, children will enjoy poring over this exuberant picture book individually or sharing the challenge and the fun with a partner." Booklist

Dennis, Wesley

Flip and the cows; story and pictures by Wesley Dennis. Linnet Bks. 1989 c1942 unp il $15 **E**

1. Horses—Fiction 2. Cattle—Fiction
ISBN 0-208-02240-6
LC 88-39705

A reissue of the title first published 1942 by Viking. Copyright renewed 1970

A curious colt overcomes his fear of cows and their sharp horns by backing out of trouble

Denslow, Sharon Phillips

Night owls; illustrated by Jill Kastner. Bradbury Press 1990 unp il $12.95 **E**

1. Night—Fiction 2. Aunts—Fiction
ISBN 0-02-728681-9
LC 89-33937

"On a memorable summer visit, William is persuaded to join Aunt Charlene for a late evening picnic and the slightly scary adventure of climbing a tree in the dark. The special enchantment of being awake while others sleep is evident in both the pictures and the text." Horn Book Guide

Dewey, Ariane

The narrow escapes of Davy Crockett; from a bear, a boa constrictor, a hoop snake, an elk, an owl, eagles, rattlesnakes, wildcats, trees, tornadoes, a sinking ship, and Niagara Falls. Greenwillow Bks. 1990 48p il $13.95; lib bdg $13.88 **E**

1. Crockett, Davy, 1786-1836 2. Tall tales
ISBN 0-688-08914-3; 0-688-08915-1 (lib bdg)
LC 88-34902

Recounts the wild adventures of Davy Crockett, including his tangles with a wrestling bear, eagles that wish to pull out his hair, and an alligator he rides up Niagara Falls

"The illustrations are crisp and colorful and the brief text moves along swiftly." Publ Wkly

Dodds, Dayle Ann

Wheel away! illustrations by Thacher Hurd. Harper & Row 1989 unp il $13.95; lib bdg $13.89 **E**

1. Wheels—Fiction 2. Stories in rhyme
ISBN 0-06-021688-3; 0-06-021689-1 (lib bdg)
LC 87-27091

A runaway wheel takes a bouncy, bumpy, amusing journey through town

"A triumphant melding of content, sound, and illustration, the book is a production that is as thoroughly entertaining as it is thoughtfully designed." Horn Book

Downing, Julie

White snow, blue feather. Bradbury Press 1989 unp il $13.95 **E**

1. Snow—Fiction 2. Winter—Fiction 3. Animals—Fiction
ISBN 0-02-732530-X
LC 89-815

"A young boy takes a walk in the woods to feed the birds on a snowy day. His adventures reveal the pleasures of wintertime observance of nature." Sci Child

"A soothing story, meant to be read by the fire on a cold winter's day. The watercolors capture the soft tone of the story." Child Book Rev Serv

Dragonwagon, Crescent

Half a moon and one whole star; illustrations by Jerry Pinkney. Macmillan 1986 unp il $13.95 **E**

1. Night—Fiction 2. Sleep—Fiction 3. Stories in rhyme
ISBN 0-02-733120-2
LC 85-13818

The summer night is full of wonderful sounds and scents as Susan falls asleep

"The poem has some lilting phrases and some sharp images; occasionally the rhyme or meter falters, but the concept of night activity and the sleeping household should appeal to the read-aloud audience." Bull Cent Child Books

Drescher, Henrik, 1955-

Simon's book. Lothrop, Lee & Shepard Bks. 1983 unp il $13.95; lib bdg $13.88 **E**

1. Drawing—Fiction 2. Monsters—Fiction
ISBN 0-688-02085-2; 0-688-02086-0 (lib bdg)
LC 82-24931

"A frightening yet humorous-looking monster . . . chases young Simon through the pages of his drawing pad. Despite the aid of snake-like pens and an antennae-equipped ink bottle, Simon eventually becomes trapped at the bottom of the page. Surprisingly, a big sloppy kiss reveals the beast's friendly feelings, so boy, beast, pens and ink can relax and peacefully retire. A finished book—'Simon's Book'—is left upon the table for the real Simon to discover when he wakes in the morning." SLJ

"Using the story-within-a-story format, the author-artist

Drescher, Henrik, 1955-—*Continued*
embarks on an exhilarating exploration, in a childlike yet sophisticated manner, of the elusive border separating dream and reality. . . . Original, fresh, and engaging, the book is deliciously thrilling but never terrifying." Horn Book

Dubanevich, Arlene, 1950-
Pigs in hiding. Four Winds Press 1983 unp il $13.95; Scholastic pa $2.95 **E**
1. Pigs—Fiction
ISBN 0-02-732140-1; 0-590-42294-4 (pa) LC 83-1409
"One pig initiates a game of hide-and-seek. He's 'it' while the other 99 porkers go and hide among the house's swine artifacts. He can't find his friends anywhere until he gets an idea. Laying out a spread of tasty goodies he lures his fellows from their nooks and crannies while he hides under a nearby umbrella. When they have assembled, he gleefully shouts he has found them all." Booklist
"The imagination displayed in the sharply detailed, bravely colored pictures and the whirling happenings can't fail to make readers laugh out loud." Publ Wkly

Duke, Kate
The guinea pig ABC. Dutton 1983 unp il lib bdg $11.95; pa $3.95 **E**
1. Alphabet 2. Guinea pigs
ISBN 0-525-44058-5 (lib bdg); 0-525-44274-X (pa) LC 83-1410
Each letter of the alphabet is illustrated by a word which applies to pictured guinea pigs

Guinea pigs far and near. Dutton 1984 unp il $9.95 **E**
1. Guinea pigs
ISBN 0-525-44112-3 LC 84-1580
Illustrations of guinea pigs engaged in a variety of activities are accompanied by the word they depict

Dunrea, Olivier, 1953-
Deep down underground. Macmillan 1989 unp il $13.95 **E**
1. Animals 2. Counting
ISBN 0-02-732861-9 LC 88-13534
Animals present the numbers from one to ten, as earthworms, toads, ants, and others march and burrow, scurry and scooch deep down underground
"The reader chants the cumulative, repetitive words, counting from 1 to 10 and back again. Delightful, full-color illustrations depict the dwellings of underground creatures." Sci Child

Durán, Cheli
Hildilid's night; by Cheli Durán Ryan; illustrated by Arnold Lobel. Macmillan 1986 c1971 unp il $9.95 **E**
1. Night—Fiction
ISBN 0-02-777260-8 LC 86-5294
A Caldecott Medal honor book, 1972
A reissue of the title first published 1971
"Hating the night, [an old woman named] Hildilid tries to sweep it away with a broom, spanks it, digs a grave for it, tries to stuff it into a sack, and so on. Exhausted by her vain endeavors, she falls asleep just as the sun comes up and the detested darkness is gone." Bull Cent Child Books
"The black-and-white line drawings, into which yellow is occasionally but strategically inserted, perfectly illustrate the rhythmically narrative lines." Horn Book

Duvoisin, Roger, 1904-1980
Petunia; written and illustrated by Roger Duvoisin. Knopf 1950 unp il lib bdg $8.99; pa $3.95 **E**
1. Geese—Fiction
ISBN 0-394-90865-1 (lib bdg); 0-394-82589-6 (pa) LC 50-10286
A picture story book about Petunia, the silly goose, who found a book and carried it around because she thought it would make her wise. After a catastrophe brought on by Petunia's silliness she suddenly discovered that it's what is inside the book that counts
"Not since 'The Little Red Hen' has there been written such an engaging story of a poultry heroine. . . . Delightfully illustrated by the author in black-and-white and color wash." Libr J
Other available titles about Petunia are:
Petunia, beware! (1958)
Petunia, I love you (1965)
Petunia takes a trip (1953)
Petunia the silly goose stories (1987)
Petunia's Christmas (1952)

Veronica; written and illustrated by Roger Duvoisin. Knopf 1961 unp il lib bdg $13.99 **E**
1. Hippopotamus—Fiction
ISBN 0-394-91792-8 LC 61-6051
"Longing to be different, a hippopotamus named Veronica left the herd where nobody noticed her and walked until she reached a city. There she was not just different, she was gloriously conspicuous, so conspicuous in fact that she ended in jail. Veronica's misadventures in the city and her return to the mudbank and the acclaim of the herd are recounted in a diverting picture book illustrated with laughable drawings in color and in black and white." Booklist
Another available title about Veronica is:
Our Veronica goes to Petunia's farm (1962)

Eastman, P. D. (Philip D.), 1909-1986
Are you my mother? written and illustrated by P. D. Eastman. Beginner Bks. 1960 63p il $6.95; lib bdg $7.99 **E**
1. Birds—Fiction
ISBN 0-394-80018-4; 0-394-90018-9 (lib bdg) LC 60-13495
Also available Spanish-English edition $8.95 (ISBN 0-394-81596-3)
"A small bird falls from his nest and searches for his mother. He asks a kitten, a hen, a dog, a cow, a boat, [and] a plane . . . 'Are you my mother?' Repetition of words and phrases and funny pictures are just right for beginning readers." Chicago. Public Libr

Ehlert, Lois, 1934-

Color farm. Lippincott 1990 unp il $12.95; lib bdg $12.89 **E**

1. Color 2. Size and shape
ISBN 0-397-32440-5; 0-397-32441-3 (lib bdg)
LC 89-13561

"A delightful die-cut exploration of how shapes and colors can be layered and overlapped to create the faces of farm animals. Includes geometric pictures of a rooster, a chicken, a goose, a duck, a cat, a dog, a sheep, a pig, and a cow." Sci Child

Color zoo. Lippincott 1989 unp il $12.95; lib bdg $12.89 **E**

1. Color 2. Size and shape
ISBN 0-397-32259-3; 0-397-32260-7 (lib bdg)
LC 87-17065

A Caldecott Medal honor book, 1990

This "book features a series of cutouts stacked so that with each page turn, a layer is removed to reveal yet another picture. Each configuration is an animal: a tiger's face (a circle shape) and two ears disappear with a page turn to leave viewers with a square within which is a mouse. . . . There are three such series, and each ends with a small round-up of the shapes used so far. . . . On the reverse of the turned page is the shape cutout previously removed with the shape's printed name." SLJ

"Not only an effective method for teaching basic concepts, the book is also a means for sharpening visual perception, which encourages children to see these shapes in other contexts." Horn Book

Eating the alphabet; fruits and vegetables from A to Z. Harcourt Brace Jovanovich 1989 unp il $13.95 **E**

1. Alphabet 2. Fruit 3. Vegetables
ISBN 0-15-224435-2 LC 88-10906

An alphabetical tour of the world of fruits and vegetables, from apricot and artichoke to yam and zucchini

"The objects depicted, shown against a white ground, are easily identifiable for the most part, and represent the more common sounds of the letter shown. . . . Both upper- and lower-case letters are printed in large, black type. A nice added touch is the glossary which includes the pronunciation and interesting facts about the origin of each fruit and vegetable, how it grows, and its uses. An exuberant, eye-catching alphabet book." SLJ

Feathers for lunch. Harcourt Brace Jovanovich 1990 unp il $13.95 **E**

1. Cats—Fiction 2. Birds—Fiction 3. Stories in rhyme
ISBN 0-15-230550-5 LC 89-29459

This "book is both a story and a beginning nature guide. A pet cat wants to vary his diet with wild birds, but each attempt gains him only feathers. Twelve different bird species are . . . illustrated. . . . On each page, the bird's typical call is printed and plants pictured are named." SLJ

"Ehlert has attempted many things in these pages—for instance, the birds are all drawn life-size—and has succeeded in all of them; her lavish use of bold color against generous amounts of white space is graphically appealing, and the large type, nearly one-half-inch tall, invites attempts by those just beginning to read. An engaging, entertaining, and recognizably realistic story." Horn Book

Growing vegetable soup; written and illustrated by Lois Ehlert. Harcourt Brace Jovanovich 1987 unp il $13.95; pa $4.95 **E**

1. Vegetable gardening—Fiction
ISBN 0-15-232575-1; 0-15-232580-8 (pa)
LC 86-22812

"Brightly-colored large illustrations and a boldly-worded text show how to plant and grow vegetables for Dad's soup. Shocking pinks, reds and greens give the illustrations an almost three-dimensional quality and will be good for large audiences of preschoolers." Child Book Rev Serv

Planting a rainbow; written and illustrated by Lois Ehlert. Harcourt Brace Jovanovich 1988 unp il lib bdg $14.95 **E**

1. Gardening—Fiction 2. Flowers—Fiction
ISBN 0-15-262609-3
LC 87-8528

A mother and daughter plant a rainbow of flowers in the family garden

"The stylized forms of the plants are clearly and beautifully designed, and the primary, blazing colors of the blossoms dazzle in their resplendence. The minimal text, in very large print, is exactly right to set off the glorious illustrations, making a splendid beginning book of colors and flowers cleverly arranged for young readers." Horn Book

Ehrlich, Amy, 1942-

Leo, Zack, and Emmie; pictures by Steven Kellogg. Dial Bks. for Young Readers 1981 64p il lib bdg $9.89; pa $4.95 **E**

1. School stories 2. Friendship—Fiction
ISBN 0-8037-4761-6 (lib bdg); 0-8037-4760-8 (pa)
LC 81-2604

"An Easy-to-read book"

"Leo, Zack, and Emmie become friends when Emmie moves into the boys' class, but not without some typical second-grade turf problems and talent rivalries." SLJ

"The light, merry tone of the text is echoed by the brisk and cheerful drawings, softly tinted drawings of the three slightly grubby and quite engaging children." Bull Cent Child Books

Another available title about Leo, Zack and Emmie is entered below

Leo, Zack, and Emmie together again; pictures by Steven Kellogg. Dial Bks. for Young Readers 1987 56p il $9.95; lib bdg $9.89; pa $3.95 **E**

1. Friendship—Fiction
ISBN 0-8037-0381-3; 0-8037-0382-1 (lib bdg); 0-8037-0837-8 (pa)
LC 86-16810

"An Easy-to-read book"

In this title "the three second graders are involved . . . in four loosely connected episodes that take place in the winter: they play in the snow, meet Santa Claus, suffer through chicken pox . . . and make Valentine cards. . . . Ehrlich's writing is direct and uncluttered. There is just enough conflict in the plot to create interest. Kellogg's full-color illustrations consistently add humor to the text and make this book hard to put down." SLJ

Ehrlich, Amy, 1942-—*Continued*

The wild swans; [by] Hans Christian Andersen; pictures by Susan Jeffers; retold by Amy Ehrlich. Dial Bks. for Young Readers 1981 40p il $14.95; lib bdg $14.89 **E**

1. Fairy tales
ISBN 0-8037-9381-2; 0-8037-9391-X (lib bdg) LC 81-65843

"An extra-large but truly magnificent version of this old favorite. The illustrations superbly convey the tale of a young princess trying to free her eleven brothers from a spell. With this lively adaptation [of the tale entered under Andersen in the Fiction Section] youngsters will be thrilled anew by this story." Child Book Rev Serv

Eichenberg, Fritz, 1901-1990

Ape in a cape; an alphabet of odd animals. Harcourt Brace 1952 unp il $12.95; pa $3.95 **E**

1. Animals—Pictorial works 2. Alphabet
ISBN 0-15-203722-5; 0-15-607830-9 (pa) LC 52-6908

A Caldecott Medal honor book, 1953

"Each letter of the alphabet from A for ape to Z for zoo is represented by a full-page picture of an animal with a brief nonsense rhyme caption explaining it. For example: mouse in a blouse, pig in a wig, toad on the road, whale in a gale." Publ Wkly

"The skill of a craftsman distinguishes this picture book illustrated with bold and lively drawings printed in three colors." N Y Public Libr

Dancing in the moon; counting rhymes. Harcourt Brace 1955 20p il hardcover o.p. paperback available $3.95 **E**

1. Animals—Pictorial works 2. Counting
ISBN 0-15-623811-X (pa) LC 55-8674

This book "introduces numbers up to twenty, from '1 raccoon dancing in the moon' to '20 fishes juggling dishes.' The three-color wonderfully detailed and humorous drawings show gay and serious animals and birds who can be examined with fun again and again. . . . And the irresistible rhyming lines are likely to be chanted over and over." Horn Book

Emberley, Ed

Ed Emberley's ABC. Little, Brown 1978 unp il lib bdg $15.95 **E**

1. Alphabet
ISBN 0-316-23408-7 LC 77-28099

Animals engaged in a variety of activities introduce the letters of the alphabet

Emberley's "pictures are filled with enough goings-on and detail to invite concentrated examination; indeed, a few of them are almost too jammed with energetic busyness. But the pages show great ingenuity of conception and design, the color work is strikingly beautiful and subtle, and the whole book—including jacket, binding, end papers, and hand-lettered text—constitutes a handsome, unified production." Horn Book

The wing on a flea; a book about shapes; written and illustrated by Ed Emberley. Little, Brown 1961 48p il $14.95 **E**

1. Size and shape
ISBN 0-316-23600-4 LC 61-6570

"A read-aloud picture book that encourages children to recognize shapes to be found in familiar objects; the rhyming text concentrates on the triangle, the rectangle (some of those illustrated being almost squares), and the circle. The author-illustrator uses color boldly to point out the shape within black and white illustrations that are an interesting combination of ornate detail balanced by large areas of white space." Bull Cent Child Books

Emberley, Michael, 1960-

Ruby. Little, Brown 1990 unp il lib bdg $14.95 **E**

1. Mice—Fiction 2. Cats—Fiction
ISBN 0-316-23643-8 LC 89-12108

"Ruby [a mouse] is given some pies to deliver to her sick grandmother and to a neighbor, Mrs. Mastiff. She is warned not to talk to strangers and especially never to trust a cat. Of course, Ruby forgets this sound advice and gets smart-alecky with a slimy reptile who steals her goodie bag. She is rescued by a well-dressed, smooth-talking cat whose drool drips down his whiskers at the sight of Ruby. When Ruby tells the cat exactly where her grandma lives, readers will be aghast, yet Ruby has a plan. All ends well—except for the cat." SLJ

"Emberley brings this urbanized Red Riding Hood vividly to life, with multicolored, intensely detailed paintings capturing the clutter and constant motion of city life." Booklist

Ernst, Lisa Campbell, 1957-

Sam Johnson and the blue ribbon quilt. Lothrop, Lee & Shepard Bks. 1983 32p il $12.95; lib bdg $12.88 **E**

1. Quilting—Fiction
ISBN 0-688-01516-6; 0-688-01517-4 (lib bdg) LC 82-9980

While mending the awning over the pig pen, Sam discovers that he enjoys sewing the various patches together but meets with scorn and ridicule when he asks his wife if he could join her quilting club

The illustrations "bring an old-timey, bucolic scene to life and show steps in an equal-rights issue." Publ Wkly

When Bluebell sang. Bradbury Press 1989 unp il $12.95 **E**

1. Cattle—Fiction
ISBN 0-02-733561-5 LC 88-22262

Bluebell the cow's talent for singing brings her stardom but she soon longs to be back at the farm—if she can get away from her greedy manager

"An amusing, lighthearted tale ideal for early grades' story hours, and also an enjoyable read-alone for third and fourth graders. The pastel-hued, cartoon-like illustrations are humorous without being silly. The text, which appears opposite the illustrations, is decorated with drawings of Bluebell's mementos—photos, tickets and posters—which add to the fun." SLJ

Ets, Marie Hall, 1893-

Gilberto and the Wind. Viking 1963 32p il $12.95; Puffin Bks. pa $3.95 E

1. Winds—Fiction

ISBN 0-670-34025-1; 0-14-050276-9 (pa) LC 63-8527

"I am Gilberto and this is the story of me and the Wind." Title page

"A little Mexican boy thinks aloud about all the things his playmate the wind does with him, for him, and against him. The wind calls him to play, floats his balloon, refuses to fly his kite, blows his soap bubble into the air, races with him, and rests with him under a tree." SLJ

"In brown, black, and white against soft gray pages, this author-artist has caught in a very appealing book . . . the emotions and attitudes of childhood." Horn Book

In the forest; story and pictures by Marie Hall Ets. Viking 1944 unp il o.p.; Puffin Bks. paperback available $3.95 E

1. Animals—Fiction

ISBN 0-14-050180-0 (pa) LC 44-7727

A Caldecott Medal honor book, 1945

This is the story of "a very small boy with a new horn and paper hat who goes for a walk in a great big forest. Along with him go a wild lion, two elephant babies, two brown bears, three kangaroos, two little monkeys, a stork and a rabbit, making quite a parade. But strangely enough, when Dad comes hunting for him and he opens his eyes, there are no animals at all!" Bookmark

"The drawings are soft and lovely. There is a strange impression conveyed, as if one really moved through a great dim forest." Libr J

Just me; written and illustrated by Marie Hall Ets. Viking 1965 32p il $13.95; Penguin Bks. pa $3.95 E

ISBN 0-670-41109-4; 0-14-050325-0 (pa) LC 65-13349

A Caldecott Medal honor book, 1966

"A little boy plays a game commonly enjoyed by small children for its imaginative as well as muscular demands. He goes from one animal to another, mimicking its ambulation, moving 'just like' it. When there is a chance to take a boat ride with Dad, the game ends abruptly, and another kind of imitation begins—emulation of father." Horn Book

"Strong, simply designed illustrations and brief, rhythmic text." LC. Child Books, 1965

Play with me; story and pictures by Marie Hall Ets. Viking 1955 31p il $13.95; Puffin Bks. pa $3.95 E

1. Animals—Fiction

ISBN 0-670-55977-6; 0-14-050178-9 (pa) LC 55-14845

A Caldecott Medal honor book, 1956

On a sunny morning in the meadow an excited little girl tries to catch the meadow creatures and play with them. But, one by one, they all run away. Finally, when she learns to sit quietly and wait, there is a happy ending

The "pictures done in muted tones of brown, gray and yellow . . . accurately reflect the little girl's rapidly changing moods of eagerness, bafflement, disappointment and final happiness." N Y Times Book Rev

Fair, Sylvia

The bedspread. Morrow 1982 unp il $14.95 E

1. Embroidery—Fiction 2. Sisters—Fiction

ISBN 0-688-00877-1 LC 81-11152

Two elderly sisters embroider the house of their childhood at either end of a white bedspread, each as she remembers it, with results that surprise them

"The subject of old women doing needlework is an unusual one for a picture book; but the characters are lively and appealing, and their sisterly differences can be appreciated by many different ages. The flowing style of the story makes it a fine one to read aloud, and the illustrations are special. The neat, intricate needlework of lean Maud and the happy, comfortable stitching of plump Amelia are done in detailed full-color pictures. They fit the text beautifully and create an atmosphere that makes the story seem quite believable." SLJ

Fatio, Louise

The happy lion; pictures by Roger Duvoisin. McGraw-Hill 1954 unp il o.p.; Scholastic paperback available $3.95 E

1. Lions—Fiction 2. France—Fiction

ISBN 0-590-41936-6 (pa) LC 54-6732

"A Whittlesey House publication"

"A lion in a zoo in France is everybody's favorite—until he escapes. Then his only friend is a little boy who leads him back to his cage." Hodges. Books for Elem Sch Libr

"A merry nonsense story, whose pictures have captured an air of irresponsible gaiety." Ont Libr Rev

Other titles about the happy lion o.p.

Feelings, Muriel, 1938-

Jambo means hello; Swahili alphabet book; pictures by Tom Feelings. Dial Bks. for Young Readers 1981 unp il $13.95; lib bdg $13.89; pa $3.50 E

1. Alphabet 2. Swahili language 3. Africa, East

ISBN 0-8037-4346-7; 0-8037-4350-5 (lib bdg); 0-8037-4428-5 (pa) LC 73-15441

A Caldecott Medal honor book, 1975

This book "gives a word for each letter of the alphabet (the Swahili alphabet has 24 letters) save for 'q' and 'x', and a sentence or two provides additional information. A double-page spread of soft black and white drawings illustrates each word. . . . The text gives a considerable amount of information about traditional East African life as well as some acquaintance with the language that is used by approximately 45 million people." Bull Cent Child Books

"Integrated totally in feeling and mood, the book has been engendered by an intense personal vision of Africa—one that is warm, all-enveloping, quietly strong and filled with love." Horn Book

Feelings, Muriel, 1938-—*Continued*

Moja means one; Swahili counting book; pictures by Tom Feelings. Dial Bks. for Young Readers 1971 unp il $13.95; lib bdg $13.89 **E**

1. Counting 2. Swahili language 3. Africa, East
ISBN 0-8037-5776-X; 0-8037-5777-8 (lib bdg) LC 76-134856

A Caldecott Medal honor book, 1972

The book "uses double-page spreads for each number, one to ten, with beautiful illustrations that depict aspects of East African culture as well as numbers of objects in relation to the various numbers." Publ Wkly

"A short introduction explaining the importance of Swahili and providing a map of the areas in which it is spoken expands the book's use beyond the preschool level of the text into the first three school grades." SLJ

Fisher, Aileen Lucia, 1906-

Listen, rabbit; by Aileen Fisher; illustrated by Symeon Shimin. Crowell 1964 unp il lib bdg $12.89 **E**

1. Rabbits—Fiction 2. Stories in rhyme
ISBN 0-690-49592-7 LC 64-10860

In this rhyming narrative "a little boy tells the story of how he wanted a pet. When he saw a wild rabbit, he hoped it might be his pet; but if the rabbit didn't want to leave the fields, just to be friends would be enough. It is difficult, though, to get to be friends with a rabbit. There are too many things to frighten it away. However, patience and love are rewarded." Christ Sci Monit

"Sunset, rainy, snowy, moonlit, and pale-green spring scenes have a maximum of atmosphere and lovely color with the jumping or hiding rabbit always an appealing focus." Horn Book

Fisher, Leonard Everett, 1924-

Look around; a book about shapes. Viking Kestrel 1987 unp il $11.95 **E**

1. Size and shape
ISBN 0-670-80869-5 LC 86-40367

"Most of Fisher's text and illustration focus on four shapes: square, circle, triangle, and rectangle. As does any good concept book, this reinforces by repeating an idea in more than one way. . . . A simple way of suggesting observation and comparison is effective in a book with bold, clean design and use of color." Bull Cent Child Books

Flack, Marjorie, 1897-1958

Angus and the ducks; told and pictured by Marjorie Flack. Doubleday 1930 unp il $12.95; lib bdg $13.99; pa $4.95 **E**

1. Dogs—Fiction 2. Ducks—Fiction
ISBN 0-385-07213-9; 0-385-07600-2 (lib bdg); 0-385-26669-3 (pa) LC 30-26829

A "picture book describing the amusing experiences of Angus, a Scotch terrier puppy, when curiosity led him to slip under the hedge." Cleveland Public Libr

This book "stands out for good and sufficient reasons. It is good to look at, it is delightful to read aloud, it is a convenient size for small hands to hold, and above all it has an inner and outer harmony." N Y Her Trib Books

Other available titles about Angus are:
Angus and the cat (1931)
Angus lost (1932)

Ask Mr. Bear. Macmillan 1958 c1932 unp il $10.95; pa $3.95 **E**

1. Animals—Fiction 2. Birthdays—Fiction
ISBN 0-02-735390-7; 0-02-043090-6 (pa) LC 58-8370

First published 1932

Danny did not know what to give his mother for a birthday present, so he set out to ask various animals—the hen, the duck, the goose, the lamb, the cow and others, but he met with very little success until he met Mr. Bear

This "will have a strong appeal to very young children because of its repetition, its use of the most familiar animals, its gay pictures and the cumulative effect of the story." N Y Times Book Rev

The story about Ping; by Marjorie Flack and Kurt Wiese. Viking 1933 unp il lib bdg $11.95; Puffin Bks. pa $6.95 **E**

1. Ducks—Fiction 2. China—Fiction
ISBN 0-670-67223-8 (lib bdg); 0-14-095038-9 (pa) LC 33-29356

The story of Ping, a duck who lived on a houseboat in the Yangtze River

"An irresistible picture book with so much atmosphere and kindly humor that its readers of any age will unconsciously add to their understanding and appreciation of a far distant country. . . . Few books for little children have the genuinely artistic quality of this one." N Y Times Book Rev

Fleischman, Paul

Shadow play; story by Paul Fleischman; pictures by Eric Beddows. Harper & Row 1990 33p il $14.95; lib bdg $14.89 **E**

1. Shades and shadows—Fiction 2. Puppets and puppet plays—Fiction 3. Fairy tales
ISBN 0-06-021858-4; 0-06-021865-7 (lib bdg) LC 89-26874

"A Charlotte Zolotow book"

"A boy and girl use their last dimes to enter Monsieur LeGrand's shadow-puppet play of *Beauty and the Beast*, during which the audience is treated to an elaborate, elegantly narrated production with many characters and scene changes. The climax of the play finds Beauty changing the rampaging wild beast, a bull, into a docile creature." SLJ

"Fleischman and Beddows have wrought a sophisticated interchange of text and art (appropriately in black, white, and shades of gray), and adults will notice a few Greek statues that seem to recall Cocteau's film of 'Beauty and the Beast.' . . . The actual power of the book—besides imaginative crafting on the part of both author and artist—is leaving mystery to be explored instead of explained." Bull Cent Child Books

Fleischman, Sid, 1920-

The scarebird; pictures by Peter Sis. Greenwillow Bks. 1988 unp il $13.95; lib bdg $13.88 **E**

1. Friendship—Fiction 2. Farm life—Fiction
ISBN 0-688-07317-4; 0-688-07318-2 (lib bdg)
LC 87-4099

A lonely old farmer realizes the value of human friendship when a young man comes to help him and his scarecrow with their farm

"The oil paintings by Peter Sis are wonderfully evocative. They capture the quiet dignity of the sturdy old farmer and of the farm set in a vast expanse of field and sky. Together, words and pictures create a memorable portrait of a loving human being." Horn Book

Flora, James, 1914-

The great green Turkey Creek monster; story and pictures by James Flora. Atheneum Pubs. 1976 unp il $14.95 **E**

ISBN 0-689-50060-8 LC 75-43894

"A Margaret K. McElderry book"

"Ernie Bogwater's store in Turkey Creek is invaded by a monster vine which snakes out of all the emporium's apertures and into further mischief. . . . Finally a trombone-playing boy stops the growth but the local children persuade the authorities to spare the vine's life and let it out, each year, to help celebrate the Fourth of July." Publ Wkly

"Like his vine, Flora's tall tale grows at a rapid good-humored rate, and the ink-and-wash illustrations are cleverly matched to the text." SLJ

Florian, Douglas, 1950-

City street. Greenwillow Bks. 1990 32p il $12.95; lib bdg $12.88 **E**

1. City life—Fiction
ISBN 0-688-09543-7; 0-688-09544-5 (lib bdg)
LC 89-28694

Pictures and minimal text present life on a city street, where skateboards roll, pigeons fly, and traffic moves

"The sights and sounds, the bustling activity and rare quiet moments are depicted with precision and élan. . . . Whether at work or play, Florian's thickly defined figures capture just the right city attitudes. In a style that seems both childlike and sophisticated, his vibrant palette washes each scene with a rainbow of color." Publ Wkly

Nature walk. Greenwillow Bks. 1989 32p il $12.95; lib bdg $12.88 **E**

1. Nature—Pictorial works
ISBN 0-688-08266-1; 0-688-08269-6 (lib bdg)
LC 88-39430

"A walk through the forest in simple, rhyming text and black pen and crayon drawings. Trail-side discoveries identified on the last page encourage rereading and observation." Sci Child

Turtle day. Crowell 1989 unp il $12.95; lib bdg $12.89 **E**

1. Turtles—Fiction
ISBN 0-690-04743-6; 0-690-04745-2 (lib bdg)
LC 88-30321

"A turtle's typical day is recounted in simple, predictable text and childlike, full-color drawings. Format invites readers to anticipate what the turtle will do next." Sci Child

A year in the country. Greenwillow Bks. 1989 unp il $12.95; lib bdg $12.88 **E**

1. Farm life—Pictorial works 2. Seasons—Pictorial works
ISBN 0-688-08186-X; 0-688-08187-8 (lib bdg)
LC 88-16026

"Utilizing a single landscape, Florian visually chronicles the monthly changes that occur on a farm and its surrounding countryside. The name of each month appears in boldface type in the upper left-hand corner of each double-page watercolor-and-ink spread." SLJ

"The simple drawn pictures, bask in a golden glow year round. Florian once again demonstrates that less can be more." Booklist

Flournoy, Valerie, 1952-

The patchwork quilt; pictures by Jerry Pinkney. Dial Bks. for Young Readers 1985 unp il $11.95; lib bdg $11.89 **E**

1. Quilting—Fiction 2. Family life—Fiction 3. Blacks—Fiction
ISBN 0-8037-0097-0; 0-8037-0098-9 (lib bdg)
LC 84-1711

Coretta Scott King Award for illustrations, 1986

Using scraps cut from the family's old clothing, Tanya helps her grandmother and mother make a beautiful quilt that tells the story of her Afro-American family's life

"Plentiful full-page and double-page paintings in pencil, graphite and watercolor are vivid yet delicately detailed, bespeaking the warm physical bonds among members of this family. Giving a sense of dramatization to the text, which is longer than most picture books, the illustrations provide just the right style and mood for the story and are well placed within the text." SLJ

Folsom, Michael

Easy as pie; a guessing game of sayings; by Marcia and Michael Folsom; pictures by Jack Kent. Clarion Bks. 1985 unp il lib bdg $13.95; pa $5.95 **E**

1. Alphabet
ISBN 0-89919-303-X (lib bdg); 0-89919-351-X (pa)
LC 84-14978

Introduces the letters of the alphabet with such familiar sayings as A "Straight as an arrow", B "Snug as a bug in a rug"

"The collection is . . . infused with freshness and vitality by artful Kent's color cartoons. He illustrates 'Crazy as a loon' with the dippiest bird conceivable. Then there is the disconcerted scuba diver who loses his catch and finds out just what 'Slippery as an eel' means. There is the zest of discovery in other choices that can stimulate interest in the power of images. In the authors' note, a discussion of comparisons ends with

Folsom, Michael—*Continued*
examples that encourage young people to make up new 'old sayings' instead of using inherited ones." Publ Wkly

Fox, Mem, 1946-

Hattie and the fox; illustrated by Patricia Mullins. Bradbury Press 1987 c1986 unp il $12.95 **E**

1. Chickens—Fiction 2. Foxes—Fiction
ISBN 0-02-735470-9 LC 86-18849

First published 1986 in Australia

"Hattie is a fine, portly, and observant hen, and she knows there is something wrong when she spies a sharp foxy nose in the bushes. Her alarmist and ever escalating announcements, however, bring nothing but bored and languid replies." Horn Book

"Bright, whimsical tissue collage and crayon illustrations add zest to this simple cumulative tale, and reveal more action than is expressed by the text alone. . . . *Hattie and the Fox* combines a refreshing visual presentation with a classic form to make a terrific choice for reading aloud to very young children, or for those just beginning to read on their own." SLJ

Koala Lou; illustrated by Pamela Lofts. Harcourt Brace Jovanovich 1989 c1988 unp il $13.95 **E**

1. Koalas—Fiction
ISBN 0-15-200502-1 LC 88-26810

"Gulliver books"

First published 1988 in Australia

This story is "set in the Australian bush. Koala Lou feels bereft when her mother becomes preoccupied with a growing brood of younger koala children. In her desire to recapture her mother's attention and affection, the enterprising Koala Lou decides to become a contestant in the Bush Olympics." Horn Book

"A reassuring story for the child who feels neglected when siblings arrive." Child Book Rev Serv

Night noises; written by Mem Fox; illustrated by Terry Denton. Harcourt Brace Jovanovich 1989 unp il $13.95 **E**

1. Night—Fiction 2. Sleep—Fiction
ISBN 0-15-200543-9 LC 89-2162

"Gulliver books"

Old Lily Laceby dozes by the fire with her faithful dog Butch Aggie at her feet as strange night noises herald a surprising awakening

"With an almost joltingly bright palette, reminiscent of that of Thacher Hurd, Denton has divided up many of the double-page spreads into three scenes: the main one depicting Lily Laceby and Butch Aggie in various stages of alertness, another showing the chronology of Lily's life, and the third cleverly revealing clues to the mysterious activity outdoors. The text, in Mem Fox's Houdini-like hands, reads beautifully—the language, pacing, tension, and sparks of excitement absolutely at one with the artwork." Horn Book

Shoes from Grandpa; illustrated by Patricia Mullins. Orchard Bks. 1990 unp il $13.95; lib bdg $13.99 **E**

1. Clothing and dress—Fiction 2. Stories in rhyme
ISBN 0-531-05848-4; 0-531-08448-5 (lib bdg)
LC 89-35401

First published 1989 in Australia

In a cumulative rhyme, family members describe the clothes they intend to give Jessie to go with her shoes from Grandpa

"The illustrations, torn-paper collages, are as lively as the text, giving concrete reality to the catalogue of garments. The choice of medium was inspired, for it allows the artist to extend the text, adding subtly to the characterization of each participant through his or her selections." Horn Book

Freeman, Don, 1908-1978

Beady Bear; story and pictures by Don Freeman. Viking 1954 48p il $11.95; Penguin Bks. pa $3.95 **E**

1. Teddy bears—Fiction
ISBN 0-670-15056-8; 0-14-050197-5 (pa)
LC 54-12295

A picture-story book about a toy Teddy bear who tried living in a cave, but found it not to his liking. Beady Bear was glad to be rescued by the little boy who had the much-needed key

"With simple page-by-page black and white scratchboard illustrations for each rhythmic sentence, this is the kind of book small children will delight in 'reading' to themselves after a couple of out-loud readings." N Y Times Book Rev

Corduroy; story and pictures by Don Freeman. Viking 1968 32p il lib bdg $11.95; Puffin Bks. pa $3.95 **E**

1. Teddy bears—Fiction
ISBN 0-670-24133-4 (lib bdg); 0-14-050173-8 (pa)
LC 68-16068

"One day Corduroy, a toy bear who lives in a big department store, discovers he has lost a button. That night he goes to look for it and in his search he sees many strange and wonderful things. He does not find his button, but the following morning he finds what he has always wanted—a friend, Lisa." Read Ladders for Hum Relat. 6th edition

"The art and story are direct and just right for the very young who like bears and escalators." Book World

Another available title about Corduroy is: A pocket for Corduroy, entered below

Dandelion; story and pictures by Don Freeman. Viking 1964 48p il lib bdg $12.95; Puffin Bks. pa $3.95 **E**

1. Lions—Fiction
ISBN 0-670-25532-7 (lib bdg); 0-14-050218-1 (pa)
LC 64-21472

"Dandelion, properly invited by note to Jennifer Giraffe's tea-and-taffy party, pays no heed to the words, 'Come as you are.' At his regular haircut appointment he allows Lou Kangaroo and helper to do him up properly, according to the new fashions for lions. But pride goeth before a fall—and it is not surprising that Jennifer's tall door is closed on the unrecognizable stranger; nor that after being restored by a heavy rainfall

Freeman, Don, 1908-1978—*Continued*

to something nearer his usual state, he makes the party, after all. Mr. Freeman cleverly depicts an assortment of personalities in his many animal characters. The party scenes and the barber shop are wonderfully amusing." Horn Book

Norman the doorman. Viking 1959 64p il lib bdg $13.95; Puffin Bks. pa $4.95 **E**

1. Mice—Fiction 2. Museums—Fiction
ISBN 0-670-51515-9 (lib bdg); 0-14-050288-2 (pa)
LC 59-16171

"Norman, the mouse doorman at the basement of the museum, wins an award with a 'sculpture' made from mousetrap parts. Full-color lithographs by the author are as full of fun as the imaginative text." Hodges. Books for Elem Sch Libr

A pocket for Corduroy; story and pictures by Don Freeman. Viking 1978 unp il lib bdg $11.95; Puffin Bks. pa $3.95 **E**

1. Teddy bears—Fiction 2. Laundry—Fiction
ISBN 0-670-56172-X (lib bdg); 0-14-050352-8 (pa)
LC 77-16123

Corduroy "overhears a conversation about pockets and off he goes in search of one. . . . After a series of adventures within a laundromat, he ends up being left there overnight. In the morning he is reunited with Lisa, his owner, who, upon hearing about his quest, promptly sews on a pocket, complete with name card." Child Book Rev Serv

"The merry tale gets added interest from the author's expert and lively portrayals of the setting, a multiethnic urban neighborhood, of cuddly Corduroy and his pal Lisa, a black child and her attractive mother." Publ Wkly

Friedman, Ina R.

How my parents learned to eat; illustrated by Allen Say. Houghton Mifflin 1984 30p il $13.95; pa $3.95 **E**

1. Dinners and dining—Fiction 2. Japan—Fiction
ISBN 0-395-35379-3; 0-395-44235-4 (pa)
LC 83-18553

An American sailor courts a Japanese girl and each tries, in secret, to learn the other's way of eating

"The illustrations have precise use of line and soft colors, and the composition is economical. A warm and gentle story of an interracial family." Bull Cent Child Books

Gackenbach, Dick, 1927-

What's Claude doing? Clarion Bks. 1984 unp il lib bdg $13.95; pa $4.95 **E**

1. Dogs—Fiction
ISBN 0-89919-224-6 (lib bdg); 0-89919-464-8 (pa)
LC 83-14983

"Claude, a 'do-good' hound, can't be persuaded by his friends to come outside and join their fun. Suspense builds as the animals (and children) wonder just what Claude is doing." SLJ

"Large three-color pictures featuring a perky cast of animal characters and a pared-down text make this cozy, mildly suspenseful winter story a prime read-aloud choice for the toddler set." Booklist

Gág, Wanda, 1893-1946

The A B C bunny; hand lettered by Howard Gág. Coward-McCann 1933 unp il $12.95; pa $5.95 **E**

1. Rabbits—Fiction 2. Alphabet 3. Stories in rhyme
ISBN 0-698-20000-4; 0-698-20465-4 (pa)
LC 33-27359

A Newbery Medal honor book, 1934

An alphabet book which tells in verse and pictures the story of a little rabbit's adventures. The verse has been set to music by the author's sister

"The book has the freshness of invention, and the drawings, the beauty, humor and originality characteristic of this artist's work. The illustrations are original lithographs." N Y Times Book Rev

Millions of cats. Coward-McCann 1928 unp il $9.95; pa $4.95 **E**

1. Cats—Fiction
ISBN 0-698-20091-8; 0-698-20637-1 (pa)
LC 28-21571

A Newbery Medal honor book, 1929

"An unusual story-picture book about a very old man and a very old woman who wanted one little cat and who found themselves with 'millions and billions and trillions of cats.'" St Louis Public Libr

It is "a perennial favorite among children and takes a place of its own, both for the originality and strength of its pictures and the living folktale quality of its text." N Y Her Trib Books

Nothing At All. Coward-McCann 1941 unp il lib bdg $6.99 **E**

1. Dogs—Fiction
ISBN 0-688-30264-8
LC 41-19723

A Caldecott Medal honor book, 1942

Nothing At All was an invisible orphan puppy, with two visible and loving brother puppies. With the help of a jackdaw, some magic, and a great deal of strenuous effort, little Nothing At All achieved visibility and all three were adopted by two kindly children. And the other puppies remarked how nice it was to see Something-after-all

"In a series of lithographic drawings in colors, Wanda Gag has invested the unseen with a reality that goes straight to the heart of child or grownup. Here are humor, beauty, strength of draughtsmanship and a fresh child-like conception of life most reassuring in a world even more upset for animals than for human beings." Horn Book

Gage, Wilson, 1922-

Cully Cully and the bear; pictures by James Stevenson. Greenwillow Bks. 1983 unp il lib bdg $10.88 **E**

1. Hunting—Fiction 2. Bears—Fiction
ISBN 0-688-01769-X
LC 82-11715

"Cully Cully, a hunter armed with bow and arrows, decided he needed a bearskin to lie on. Nicking a bear's nose with an arrow, the hunter became fearful and tried to run away. Man and beast began to chase each other around the trunk of a huge tree, each never completely certain as to who was chasing whom. Ultimately, the bear walked away, and Cully Cully was happy to lie on the rough ground." Horn Book

"Stevenson's robust pictures are a great asset, and the

Gage, Wilson, 1922-—*Continued*
book is a guaranteed story-hour success." Child Book Rev Serv

Mrs. Gaddy and the ghost; by Wilson Gage; pictures by Marylin Hafner. Greenwillow Bks. 1979 55p il $10.95 **E**

1. Ghosts—Fiction
ISBN 0-688-80179-X LC 78-16366

"A Greenwillow read-alone book"

"Plump Mrs. Gaddy is very happy living on her farm; she has fields and a meadow, chickens and a mule. . . . But she also has an unwanted boarder—a hungry ghost who keeps her awake with its nocturnal feasting. Mrs. Gaddy tries many ploys to rid her house of 'the ghosty thing,' including bug spray and a trap baited with gingerbread. Finally she writes a polite letter asking it to haunt another house in the neighborhood. But the ghost—who is really a benign creature—bursts into tears upon reading the letter, and Mrs. Gaddy allows it to stay. . . . The simple text is spiced with such colorful expression as 'bless my big toe!' and 'tarnation.' The illustrations in warm tones of pink and sepia ink are full of witty and imaginative detail." Horn Book

Other available titles about Mrs. Gaddy are:
The crow and Mrs. Gaddy (1984)
Mrs. Gaddy and the fast-growing vine (1985)

Galbraith, Kathryn Osebold

Laura Charlotte; by Kathryn O. Galbraith; illustrated by Floyd Cooper. Philomel Bks. 1989 unp il $14.95 **E**

1. Toys—Fiction 2. Mothers and daughters—Fiction
ISBN 0-399-21613-8 LC 88-9898

A mother describes her love for a toy elephant she was given as a child, a gift she has now passed on to her daughter

"The story's simple declarations and sure details draw readers into an authentic shared familiarity. Cooper's pictures are endearing, filling the pages with photographlike re-creations of Mama's past and of the story's present. The twilight colors, rendered with high graininess, perfectly suit the moods of bedtime and of reminiscence." SLJ

Gantos, Jack

Rotten Ralph; written by Jack B. Gantos; illustrated by Nicole Rubel. Houghton Mifflin 1976 unp il lib bdg $13.95; pa $4.95 **E**

1. Cats—Fiction
ISBN 0-395-24276-2 (lib bdg); 0-395-29202-6 (pa) LC 75-34101

"The protagonist of this story is a mean and nasty cat, Ralph. As his young owner, Sarah, and her family say, he is very difficult to love. Finally on a trip to the circus his behavior becomes unforgivable and they leave him. There he is treated as miserably as he has treated everyone else and he comes home a week later a wiser, more benevolent cat—well, almost." Child Book Rev Serv

The "bright watercolor scenes . . . capturing Ralph's demonic meanness and his family's chagrin are a perfect complement to the text." SLJ

Other available titles about Ralph the cat are:
Happy birthday Rotten Ralph (1990)
Rotten Ralph's rotten Christmas (1984)
Rotten Ralph's show and tell (1989)
Rotten Ralph's trick or treat! (1986)
Worse than rotten, Ralph (1978)

Gardner, Beau, 1941-

Can you imagine—? a counting book; text and graphics by Beau Gardner. Dodd, Mead 1987 unp il $12.95 **E**

1. Counting 2. Animals
ISBN 0-396-09001-X LC 87-13520

Rhyming text introduces animals and numbers from one whale wearing a veil to twelve swans twirling batons

"Each pairing is set upon a glistening surface, in bold, often overbright colors and abstract shapes." Publ Wkly

Have you ever seen—? an ABC book; text and graphics by Beau Gardner. Dodd, Mead 1986 unp il $10.95 **E**

1. Alphabet
ISBN 0-396-08825-2 LC 86-4612

"Gardner presents one letter per page, each printed in upper and lower case, . . . followed by an illustration to match the letter and a simple phrase at the bottom. The question asked in the title, Have You Ever Seen. . . ?, is answered by phrases such as 'a Monster wearing Mittens,' 'a Nose like a Noodle,' 'a Vampire playing a Violin' and so on." SLJ

"Gardner has created a bold and sparkling alphabet book with strong graphics that shout from the pages in rich primary colors. To the clarity of the images he has added a zany twist of humor that should tickle the funny bone of preschoolers, who will enjoy the book the most." Horn Book

Gauch, Patricia Lee

Christina Katerina and the time she quit the family; illustrated by Elise Primavera. Putnam 1987 unp il $12.95 **E**

1. Family life—Fiction
ISBN 0-399-21408-9 LC 86-18658

"It all begins on a 'perfectly good' Saturday morning when Christina Katerina, who has been unjustly accused of just about everything, changes her name to Agnes and quits on the spot. 'You go your way. We'll go ours,' announces Mildred (a k a Mother)." N Y Times Book Rev

"Parents will admire Mom's forbearance, but kids will identify totally with Christina and the up-and-down sides of her decision to go it alone. Primavera's spiffy watercolors pulse with reality, and although the scenarios are at times inevitably exaggerated, no one should mind the dramatic license when the situation, in words and pictures, comes right from the heart." Booklist

Other available titles about Christina Katerina are:
Christina Katerina & the box (1971)
Christina Katerina and the great bear train (1990)

Dance, Tanya; [illustrations by] Satomi Ichikawa; story by Patricia Lee Gauch. Philomel Bks. 1989 unp il $13.95 **E**

1. Ballet—Fiction
ISBN 0-399-21521-2 LC 88-9935

Gauch, Patricia Lee—*Continued*

Tanya loves ballet dancing, repeating the moves she sees her older sister using when practicing for class or a recital, and soon Tanya is big enough to go to ballet class herself

"Gauch's sweet story gains strength from Ichikawa's soft watercolor paintings, which celebrate Tanya's enthusiasm with a sharp sense of how small children move. Even though the story and pictures are amusing (especially the tutu-clad teddy bear following in Tanya's wake), a wholehearted respect for Tanya's earnest dedication is evident. A gentle, knowing book." Booklist

Geisert, Arthur

Pigs from A to Z. Houghton Mifflin 1986 unp il $15.95 **E**

1. Alphabet 2. Pigs—Fiction
ISBN 0-395-38509-1 LC 86-18542

Seven piglets cavort through a landscape of hidden letters as they build a tree house

"At the back of the book is a key that shows where the artist has secreted all the letters in each illustration; some are plain, some are subtle and every picture has, in addition to its principal letter, one or two from the alphabetical surroundings: the W page will yield up a V and an X in addition to five W's. So 'Pigs From A to Z' succeeds as narrative, alphabet book, counting book (are all seven piglets in each etching?), puzzle book and as art. The etchings are distinctive, and though they may be just a trace somber or moody, they are also strange enough, I would think, to catch the attention of young and old alike." N Y Times Book Rev

George, William T.

Box Turtle at Long Pond; pictures by Lindsay Barrett George. Greenwillow Bks. 1989 unp il $12.95; lib bdg $12.88 **E**

1. Turtles—Fiction
ISBN 0-688-08184-3; 0-688-08185-1 (lib bdg) LC 88-18787

Companion volume to: Beaver at Long Pond (1988)

On a busy day at Long Pond, Box Turtle searches for food, basks in the sun, and escapes a raccoon

"A beautifully illustrated book that introduces a pond environment. The simple text follows the daily activities of a box turtle as it searches for food, rests, and escapes danger. The reader learns of other plants, animals, and insects that inhabit the pond." Sci Child

Geringer, Laura

A three hat day; pictures by Arnold Lobel. Harper & Row 1985 30p il $12.95; lib bdg $12.89; pa $3.95 **E**

1. Hats—Fiction
ISBN 0-06-021988-2; 0-06-021989-0 (lib bdg); 0-06-443157-6 (pa) LC 85-42640

This "is about R.R. Pottle the Third, an inveterate collector of hats. Wearing one at a time usually suits him, but on days when he is depressed, he wears three all at once. It is on such a day that he meets Ida, the shop clerk, and not long after, R.R. Pottle the Fourth is born—an inveterate collector of shoes." Wilson Libr Bull

"The theme is not romantic love so much as loneliness and the satisfaction of finding someone who understands and cares. Lobel's energetic line drawings with warm, full-color washes contribute their own dignity and humor to the characters. . . . With its light touch, good pacing, and satisfying symmetry, this is a pleasing choice to read aloud." Booklist

Gerrard, Roy, 1935-

Mik's mammoth. Farrar, Straus & Giroux 1990 unp il $13.95 **E**

1. Cave dwellers—Fiction 2. Mammoths—Fiction 3. Stories in rhyme
ISBN 0-374-31891-3 LC 90-55189

"Mik the caveman is a timid sort who befriends a woolly mammoth. He and the beast save the tribe from 'hordes of hairy men,' and Mik becomes their leader." SLJ

"Gerrard's . . . paintings, subtly shaded watercolors on a white ground, create a sturdy, pleasing, understated vision of the tale. Handsomely illustrated in full color, the book is sophisticated in design and disarmingly childlike in content. Touches of droll humor in both artwork and verse will endear it to readers young and old." Booklist

Gerstein, Mordicai, 1935-

Arnold of the Ducks; by Mordicai Gerstein. Harper & Row 1983 unp il $12.95; lib bdg $12.89; pa $3.95 **E**

1. Ducks—Fiction
ISBN 0-06-022002-3; 0-06-022003-1 (lib bdg); 0-06-443080-4 (pa) LC 82-47735

"Snatched as an infant by a pelican, Arnold is dropped from the bird's beak into a nest of ducklings, and adopted by Mrs. Leda Duck as one of her own. An odd duckling, but she loves him. With mud and marsh slime, the others paste feathers over Arnold so that he won't look so odd, and that's how Arnold is able to fly. Alas, investigating a kite one day (although his 'mother' has told him to stay away from it) Arnold's caught. He falls, is rescued by a huge dog, taken to a house, and cleaned by the people who live there and who recognize him as their own boy. Nicely told, with a wistful ending that rounds out the concept of the fantasy." Bull Cent Child Books

The mountains of Tibet. Harper & Row 1987 unp il $13.95; lib bdg $13.89; pa $4.95 **E**

1. Reincarnation—Fiction 2. Tibet (China)—Fiction
ISBN 0-06-022144-5; 0-06-022149-6 (lib bdg); 0-06-443211-4 (pa) LC 85-45684

The author "has created a tale of reincarnation inspired by his reading of the *Tibetan Book of the Dead.* A little boy is born in a valley high in the mountains of Tibet. 'He loved to fly kites.' Looking at the stars, he dreams of visiting other worlds and seeing other countries and peoples. But he grows up, raises a family, grows old, and never leaves his valley. After his death a voice offers him a chance to live another life; he chooses from the galaxies, star systems, planets, and life forms. With his final choice the cycle of life is completed." Horn Book

"As the illustrator of his own spare text, Mr. Gerstein . . . makes tasteful allusions to Tibetan art, creating a

Gerstein, Mordicai, 1935-—*Continued*
colorful, well-balanced picture book in the classic mold. Every element complements the story or, indeed, adds to it." N Y Times Book Rev

Roll over! by Mordicai Gerstein. Crown 1984 unp il $8.95 E

1. Nursery rhymes 2. Counting
ISBN 0-517-55209-4 LC 83-18884

The author "injects fresh jollity into the old counting chant. A yawning tyke in pajamas approaches his huge bed where 10 'guests' are already snuggled and the 'little one said,' 'ROLL OVER!'" Publ Wkly

"The book's design features a folded-over flap on the right-hand side; youngsters will have the surprise of peeking beneath to see who the latest ejected creature is. Full-color pen-and-wash drawings create a cozy-looking, very broad bed with a star-and moon-covered quilt." Booklist

Gibbons, Gail

The seasons of Arnold's apple tree. Harcourt Brace Jovanovich 1984 unp il $13.95; pa $3.95 E

1. Seasons—Fiction 2. Trees—Fiction
ISBN 0-15-271246-1; 0-15-271245-3 (pa) LC 84-4484

"Arnold enjoys his apple tree through the changing year: its springtime blossoms, the swing and tree-house it supports, its summer shade, its autumn harvest; in the winter, the tree's branches hold strings of popcorn and berries for the birds

"Two major concepts emerge here, the first being the passage of the seasons, the second the valuable resource Arnold has in his apple tree. . . . Gibbons' crisp pictures ensure that the multifaceted lesson is explicit, bright and cheery." Booklist

Giff, Patricia Reilly

Watch out, Ronald Morgan! illustrated by Susanna Natti. Viking Kestrel 1985 24p il $10.95; Puffin Bks. pa $3.95 E

1. Eyeglasses—Fiction 2. School stories
ISBN 0-670-80433-9; 0-14-050638-1 (pa)
LC 84-19623

Ronald has many humorous mishaps until he gets a pair of eyeglasses. Includes a note for adults about children's eye problems

"Told in a forthright manner but with appreciation for children's candor, the book's dialogue rings true with catchy humor. Giff obviously recognizes Ronald's need to feel unique and be cherished for his uniqueness. Natti's illustrations show the characters to be bright, colorful informal figures who move with the text." SLJ

Other available titles about Ronald Morgan are:
Happy birthday, Ronald Morgan! (1986)
Ronald Morgan goes to bat (1988)

Giganti, Paul, Jr.

How many snails? a counting book; by Paul Giganti, Jr.; pictures by Donald Crews. Greenwillow Bks. 1988 unp il $11.95; lib bdg $11.88 E

1. Counting
ISBN 0-688-06369-1; 0-688-06370-5 (lib bdg)
LC 87-26281

"Instead of inviting children to count static objects, Mr. Giganti poses a series of simple, direct questions designed to encourage youngsters to determine the often subtle differences between those objects. Donald Crews . . . concentrates here on decorating each page with objects that supply the necessary links to the text. Some of the pages—depicting a collection of motley dogs at the park or beautiful toy boats and trucks, cars and airplanes at a toy store—are a joy to look at." N Y Times Book Rev

Ginsburg, Mirra

The chick and the duckling; translated [and adapted] from the Russian of V. Suteyev; pictures by Jose & Ariane Aruego. Macmillan 1972 unp il $14.95; Atheneum Pubs. pa $4.95 E

1. Ducks—Fiction 2. Chickens—Fiction
ISBN 0-02-735940-9; 0-689-71226-X (pa)
LC 74-188773

"The adventures of a duckling who is a leader and a chick who follows suit. When the chick decides that an aquatic life is not for him, this brief selection for reading aloud comes to a humorous conclusion." Wis Libr Bull

"The sunny simplicity of the illustrations is just right for a slight but engaging text, and they add a note of humor that is a nice foil for the bland directness of the story. . . . Easy enough to be read by a beginning reader, but too right (by length, subject, and level of concept) for the lap audience not to be directed primarily at them." Bull Cent Child Books

Good morning, chick; by Mirra Ginsburg, adapted from a story by Korney Chukovsky; pictures by Byron Barton. Greenwillow Bks. 1980 unp il lib bdg 12.88; pa $3.95 E

1. Chickens—Fiction
ISBN 0-688-84284-4 (lib bdg); 0-688-08741-8 (pa)
LC 80-11352

"In this simple preschool tale . . . a chick hatches out of an egg ('like this'), learns to eat worms ('like this'), is scared by a cat ('like this'), falls in a pond ('like this'), and is coddled back to fluffiness by Mom ('like this')." SLJ

"Based upon a tale by the great Russian poet and storyteller, the totally childlike picture book for the very young employs an engaging device: The text, illustrated with a bright vignette, appears on each of the left-hand pages; then, after pausing briefly and leading the eye to the right, a sentence runs to completion on the opposite page with two words contained in a large storytelling picture done in bold, brilliant color." Horn Book

Ginsburg, Mirra—*Continued*

The sun's asleep behind the hill; adapted from an Armenian song by Mirra Ginsburg; illustrated by Paul O. Zelinsky. Greenwillow Bks. 1982 unp il $12.95; lib bdg $12.88 E

1. Night—Fiction 2. Stories in rhyme
ISBN 0-688-00824-0; 0-688-00825-9 (lib bdg)
LC 81-6615

In this adaptation of an Armenian lullaby the sun, the breeze, the leaves, the bird, the squirrel, and the child all grow tired after a long day and go to sleep

Where does the sun go at night? adapted from an Armenian song by Mirra Ginsburg; pictures by Jose Aruego and Ariane Dewey. Greenwillow Bks. 1981 unp il $10.95; lib bdg $10.88 E

1. Sun—Fiction 2. Animals—Fiction
ISBN 0-688-80245-1; 0-688-84245-3 (lib bdg)
LC 79-16151

"Aruego and Dewey's familiar humorous animals watch the sun set, and the first of a series of childlike questions is asked, 'Where does the sun go at night?' The sun goes to his grandmother's house in the 'deep blue sky' where it sleeps in a 'woolly cloud.' We see the animals burrowed into clouds, too, and their comic presence is a nice juxtaposition to the quiet rhythm of the words. . . . The most comic illustration shows the drowsy creatures being wakened by the morning's alarm clock. 'Who is the clock? The village cock.' A colorful flight of fancy produced by a winning author-illustrator team." SLJ

Goble, Paul

Death of the iron horse; story and illustrations by Paul Goble. Bradbury Press 1987 unp il $12.95 E

1. Cheyenne Indians—Fiction 2. Railroads—Fiction
ISBN 0-02-737830-6 LC 85-28011

The author "has taken several accounts of the 1867 Cheyenne attack of a Union Pacific freight train . . . and combined them into a story from the Indians' viewpoint. As the Cheyenne Prophet Sweet Medicine had foretold, strange hairy people were invading the land, killing women and children and driving off the horses. Descriptions of the iron horse inspired curiosity and fear in the young braves who decided to go out and protect their village from this new menace. Keeping fairly close to actual Indian accounts, Goble presents the braves' bold attack on the train, glossing over the deaths of the train crew." SLJ

Dream wolf; story and illustrations by Paul Goble. Bradbury Press 1990 unp il $14.95 E

1. Indians of North America—Fiction 2. Wolves—Fiction
ISBN 0-02-736585-9 LC 89-687

Revised edition of: The friendly wolf, published 1974

When two Plains Indian children become lost, they are cared for and guided safely home by a friendly wolf

"*Dream Wolf* is filled with glowing imagery—the illustrations showing nightfall, the children's search for shelter and the wolf's first, dreamlike appearance are particularly riveting. Once again, Goble has captured the lives and legends of this tribe in a magnificent picture book." Publ Wkly

The girl who loved wild horses; story and illustrations by Paul Goble. Bradbury Press 1978 unp il $13.95; Atheneum Pubs. pa $3.95 E

1. Indians of North America—Fiction 2. Horses—Fiction
ISBN 0-87888-121-2; 0-689-71082-8 (pa)
LC 77-20500

Awarded the Caldecott Medal, 1979

"After becoming lost in a storm, a young Indian girl joins and lives with a herd of wild horses until finally, she becomes one herself." SLJ

"Elaborate double-page spreads burst with life, revealing details of flowers and insects, animals and birds. . . . The story is told in simple language, and the author has included verses of a Navaho and Sioux song about horses. Both storytelling and art express the harmony with and the love of nature which characterize Native American culture." Horn Book

Godden, Rumer, 1907-

The story of Holly and Ivy; pictures by Barbara Cooney. Viking Kestrel 1985 31p il lib bdg $13.95; Puffin Bks. pa $4.95 E

1. Orphans—Fiction 2. Christmas—Fiction 3. Dolls—Fiction
ISBN 0-670-80622-6 (lib bdg); 0-14-050723-X (pa)
LC 84-25799

A newly illustrated edition of the title first published 1959, and entered in the author's collection: Four dolls, class S C

Orphaned Ivy finds her Christmas wish fulfilled with the help of a lonely couple and a doll named Holly

"One of the author's most winsome doll stories has been revitalized by an abundance of luminous new paintings, precisely detailed and full of authentic atmosphere, sensitivity, and beauty." Horn Book

Goffstein, M. B.

Fish for supper. Dial Bks. for Young Readers 1976 unp il lib bdg $8.89; pa $3.95 E

1. Grandmothers—Fiction 2. Fishing—Fiction
ISBN 0-8037-2572-8 (lib bdg); 0-8037-0284-1 (pa)
LC 75-27598

A Caldecott Medal honor book, 1977

"Grandmother's routine, beginning at five A.M., involves getting ready to go fishing, rowing her boat, catching some fish, cleaning, cooking and eating the fish and then going to bed to rest up for the next day's fishing. Grandmother is a happy loner who will bring smiles to young and old alike." Interracial Books Child Bull

"With her economy of line and of words, the author-artist is mistress of understatement. The tidy drawings, without a single superfluous stroke of the pen, balance perfectly with the reticent storytelling." Horn Book

Goffstein, M. B.—*Continued*

My Noah's ark; story and pictures by M. B. Goffstein. Harper & Row 1978 unp il $13.95 E

1. Toys—Fiction
ISBN 0-06-022022-8 LC 77-25666

During her childhood the narrator "received a wooden ark and tiny animals, which her father had carved. 'Two spotted leopards, two meek sheep, two gray horses, and two white doves' were joined by other creatures over the years. She kept them through marriage and motherhood, sharing the story—both of Noah's ark and of her tiny one—with children and grandchildren. Then as an old woman in her nineties, she reflects, '[E]veryone is gone, and the ark holds their memories.' . . . The author's rich imagination endows inanimate objects with a life all their own. Typically restrained, naive drawings share in telling the quiet story which manages to capture deep emotion." Horn Book

Goldin, Barbara Diamond

Just enough is plenty: a Hanukkah tale; paintings by Seymour Chwast. Viking Penguin 1988 unp il lib bdg $12.95 E

1. Hanukkah—Fiction 2. Jews—Fiction
ISBN 0-670-81852-6 LC 88-3953

"Malka's family is too poor to have a proper Hanukkah celebration, but when a mysterious stranger knocks on their door, he is welcomed in anyway. He rewards their generosity by weaving enough stories and magic to last a lifetime. The stranger's sudden disappearance leaves everyone wondering if they had not been blessed by a visit from the prophet Elijah." Child Book Rev Serv

"Goldin's tale and Chwast's vibrant, primitive paintings are masterfully combined." Publ Wkly

Goodall, John S., 1908-

Creepy castle. Atheneum Pubs. 1975 unp il $10.95 E

1. Mice—Fiction 2. Castles—Fiction 3. Stories without words
ISBN 0-689-50027-0 LC 74-16838

"A Margaret K. McElderry book"

In this wordless adventure a brave young mouse and his lady fair venture into a deserted castle, unaware that a villainous outlaw has been skulking behind them

"The story is clear, the plot sturdy, the pictures exciting and romantic. Great fun." Bull Cent Child Books

Naughty Nancy goes to school; by John Goodall. Atheneum Pubs. 1985 unp il $8.95 E

1. Mice—Fiction 2. Stories without words
ISBN 0-689-50329-6 LC 85-70230

"A Margaret K. McElderry book"

A mischievous Victorian mouse, Nancy's naughtiness in school is alleviated by a courageous act during a school trip to the seashore

"All this action plays out in vintage Goodall wordless format. Scenes unfold through right-hand half pages. Richly colored paintings full of action provide lots to look at. The Victorian setting might excuse the somewhat stereotypical portrayal of Nancy's stern, humorless teacher; mischievous Nancy is the opposite extreme." Booklist

Paddy to the rescue; [by] John Goodall. Atheneum Pubs. 1985 unp il $8.95 E

1. Pigs—Fiction 2. Stories without words
ISBN 0-689-50330-X LC 85-70231

"A Margaret K. McElderry book"

Paddy pursues "a robber rat who has just stolen a mistress pig's jewels (from around her neck no less!). Paddy chases him over the rooftops and down to the dockside, to the point of brandishing oars from rowboats in the harbor." SLJ

"The wordless adventure is easy to follow, and Goodall's half-page inserts continue to be a useful gimmick for increasing the suspense in the visual sequences. Rich, warm colors, true lines, and a charming bit of untidiness to the shadings and textures give the artist's illustrations a distinctive character." Booklist

Other available titles about Paddy Pork are:
Paddy goes traveling (1982)
Paddy under water (1984)

Gould, Deborah

Aaron's shirt; illustrated by Cheryl Harness. Bradbury Press 1989 unp il $12.95 E

1. Clothing and dress—Fiction
ISBN 0-02-736351-1 LC 88-10414

"Aaron really likes the red-and-white striped shirt he's chosen at a department store. He gives it up only through necessity (laundering or seasonal storage) and wears it until it's uncomfortably tight. Eventually he admits defeat, passing the shirt on to his stuffed bear." Bull Cent Child Books

"Vivid watercolors believably portray Aaron's growth over three years. Dealing with change and parting with favorite things are familiar themes, and children will recognize Aaron's dilemma and solution as just right." SLJ

Graham, Lorenz B., 1902-1989

Song of the boat; by Lorenz Graham; pictures by Leo and Diane Dillon. Crowell 1975 unp il lib bdg $12.89 E

1. Africa—Fiction
ISBN 0-690-75232-6 LC 74-5183

"Graham draws on the idiomatic English of West Africa to tell of Flumbo, who goes with his son Momolu to search for a tree he can fashion into a new canoe. The quest is realized through a dream of Momolu's in which the spirit people reveal to him 'one fine tree, fine past all he ever see before.' Out of it Flumbo makes a magnificent canoe, and after crediting Momolu, takes his family for a ride down the river." Booklist

"The woodcuts—some black and white and some colored with magenta and orange—present solid, often massive, figures against settings articulated with bold line. Like the text, the woodcuts feel indigenous to Africa, but, at the same time, both text and pictures retain a universal element." Horn Book

Gramatky, Hardie, 1907-1979

Little Toot; pictures and story by Hardie Gramatky. Putnam 1939 unp il $8.95; lib bdg $9.99; pa $5.95 **E**

1. Tugboats—Fiction

ISBN 0-399-20144-0; 0-399-60422-7 (lib bdg); 0-399-20649-3 (pa) LC 39-24222

Story and pictures describe the early career of a saucy little tug-boat too pleased with himself to do any real work until one day when he found himself out on the ocean in a storm. Then Little Toot earned the right to be called a hero

"Mr. Gramatky tells his story with humor and enjoyment, giving, too, a genuine sense of the water front in both pictures and story." Horn Book

Another available title about Little Toot is:
Little Toot and the Loch Ness monster (1989)

Green, Norma

The hole in the dike; retold by Norma Green; pictures by Eric Carle. Crowell 1975 c1974 unp il $14.95; lib bdg $14.89 **E**

1. Netherlands—Fiction

ISBN 0-690-00734-5; 0-690-00676-4 (lib bdg) LC 74023562

Adapted from a story which was first published in Hans Brinker; or, The silver skates, by M. M. Dodge, entered in the Fiction Section

The "tale of the brave lad who saved Holland from disaster by using his finger to plug a leak in the dike." Child Book Rev Serv

"Almost all of the full-color collage and paint illustrations are doublespreads with bold, angular forms and with profusely brush-stroked patterns. They add a strong element of visual drama to the simple, traditional story." Horn Book

Greenfield, Eloise, 1929-

Africa dream; illustrated by Carole Byard. Crowell 1977 unp il lib bdg $12.89 **E**

1. Africa—Fiction

ISBN 0-690-04776-2 LC 77-5080

Coretta Scott King Award, 1978

"As ethereal as the title implies, this sparsely worded prose-poem relates the benign dream experience of a young child who transports her mind to 'Long-ago Africa.'" Booklist

Grandmama's joy; illustrated by Carole Byard. Philomel Bks. c1980 unp il $12.95 **E**

1. Blacks—Fiction 2. Grandmothers—Fiction

ISBN 0-399-21064-4 LC 79-11403

First published 1980 by Collins

This is the story of the relationship between Grandmama and Rhondy. Rhondy has lived with Grandmama since she "was a baby and her parents died in a car accident. Rhondy's attempts to cheer the sad woman fail, and Rhondy learns why; they must move to a cheaper home. But the girl is persistent and cheers her by reminding her of the love they share." SLJ

"This extremely gifted and sensitive writer consistently . . . illuminates key aspects of the Black experience in a way that underlines both its uniqueness and universality. . . . You have to care about the people Eloise Greenfield writes about. You have to feel about them. . . . Carole Byard's beautiful expressive drawings match the tone of the story." Interracial Books Child Bull

Grandpa's face; illustrated by Floyd Cooper. Philomel Bks. 1988 unp il lib bdg $13.95 **E**

1. Grandfathers—Fiction 2. Actors and actresses—Fiction

ISBN 0-399-21525-5 LC 87-16729

"Tamika fears that her grandfather, an actor, is incapable of loving her when she sees him practicing a cruel expression. The young girl's turmoil and its resolution are keenly felt through evocative text and striking pictures." SLJ

Me and Neesie; illustrated by Moneta Barnett. Crowell 1975 unp il lib bdg $12.89 **E**

1. Blacks—Fiction 2. Imaginary playmates—Fiction

ISBN 0-690-00715-9 LC 74-23078

"An enjoyable story of a little girl and her imaginary, mischievous friend. Janell's mother wishes she would abandon her modern day 'Binker,' but it's not until Janell goes to school where she meets many new friends that Neesie disappears from her life." SLJ

"This story about a Black family has a very warm texture. Janell's mother and father are portrayed as being sensitive and sympathetic regarding their daughter's growing pains. Moneta Barnett's illustrations are lively and expressive." Interracial Books Child Bull

She come bringing me that little baby girl; illustrated by John Steptoe. Lippincott 1974 unp il $12.95; lib bdg $12.89 **E**

1. Brothers and sisters—Fiction 2. Infants—Fiction 3. Blacks—Fiction

ISBN 0-397-31586-4; 0-397-32478-2 (lib bdg) LC 74-8104

"For Kevin, who had wanted a baby brother, the arrival of his pink-shawled baby sister proved a bitter disappointment. Not only was she the wrong sex, she also cried too much, had too many wrinkles to look new, and most provoking of all she occupied everyone's attention. How he changed his opinion about his sister is developed in a sensitive first-person text, complemented and extended by the poignant, darkly brilliant, three-color illustrations. A familiar situation handled with rare charm, culminating in a visual and verbal paean to familial love." Horn Book

Gretz, Susanna

Teddy bears go shopping. Four Winds Press 1982 unp il $12.95 **E**

1. Teddy bears—Fiction 2. Shopping—Fiction

ISBN 0-02-737310-X LC 82-70418

The teddy bears "are as scatty as ever and portrayed in cheerfully bright colors as they invade a supermarket on a Saturday morning. 'Ice cream and cheese, soap and peas, marmalade and pears, toothpaste for bears,' runs the list that the providers lose, of course. It happens that John William and Robert—separated from Charles—buy the same things he does and everyone forgets important staples, like food for their Dalmatian Fred. Back

Gretz, Susanna—*Continued*
home, Fred expresses his irritation by taking a couple of nips out of the forgetful ones. But everything is fine when Andrew, who's been on a long journey, comes home with gifts for everyone and particularly toothsome biscuits for Fred. A winner." Publ Wkly

Other available titles about the teddy bears are:
Teddy bears 1 to 10 (1986)
Teddy bears ABC (1986)
Teddy bears at the seaside (1989)
Teddy bears cure a cold (1984)
Teddy bears' moving day (1981)
Teddy bears stay indoors (1987)
Teddy bears take the train (1987)

Grifalconi, Ann

Darkness and the butterfly. Little, Brown 1987 unp il lib bdg $14.95 **E**

1. Fear—Fiction 2. Night—Fiction 3. Africa—Fiction
ISBN 0-316-32863-4 LC 86-27561

Small Osa is fearless during the day, climbing trees or exploring the African valley where she lives, but at night she becomes afraid of the things that might be hiding in the dark

Another available title about Osa is entered below

Osa's pride. Little, Brown 1990 unp il lib bdg $14.95 **E**

1. Africa—Fiction 2. Grandmothers—Fiction
ISBN 0-316-32865-0 LC 88-28828

"Told in retrospect by Osa, this describes the way she had boasted about her father when she was seven; refusing to believe he was dead, she had invented more and more details about his importance. After alienating her friends by her pride, Osa is taught a gentle lesson by her grandmother." Bull Cent Child Books

"Artistically, the book is superb: the pictures capture the community life and Osa's personal struggle with vivid images and rich, vibrant colors." Publ Wkly

Griffith, Helen V.

Alex and the cat; pictures by Joseph Low. Greenwillow Bks. 1982 63p il $13.95; lib bdg $13.88 **E**

1. Dogs—Fiction 2. Cats—Fiction
ISBN 0-688-00420-2; 0-688-00421-0 (lib bdg) LC 81-11608

"A Greenwillow read-alone book"

This is a book "about Alex, a puppy still wet behind the ears, and his wise housemate, the cat. Three chapters in the book reveal the cat as Alex's mentor and champion. In the first, the puppy decides to be a cat. . . . In the second episode, the dog discovers that running away from home isn't all it's cracked up to be, and in the third . . . the cat saves Alex from a furious hen." Publ Wkly

"The stories are appropriate in length, vocabulary difficulty, and concept for the beginning reader, the illustrations are amusing, almost aqueous wash and line. . . . What makes the book a joy to read aloud or alone is the terse humor of the talks between Alex and his blasé companion." Bull Cent Child Books

Followed by: Alex remembers (1983) and More Alex and the cat (1983)

Georgia music; pictures by James Stevenson. Greenwillow Bks. 1986 unp il $12.95; lib bdg $12.88; Morrow pa $3.95 **E**

1. Grandfathers—Fiction
ISBN 0-688-06071-4; 0-688-06072-2 (lib bdg); 0-688-09931-9 (pa) LC 85-24918

"Grandpa introduces the love of music and an appreciation for nature to his 'citified' granddaughter when she summers with him at his country home in Georgia. When the old man is silent and unhappy a year later because he has had to move to the city, the girl plays his harmonica, bringing back those warm southern evenings they had shared. Stevenson's sketches with color washes catch the essence of the lush summer days and are artfully teamed with Griffith's touching story." Child Book Rev Serv

Grandaddy's place; pictures by James Stevenson. Greenwillow Bks. 1987 unp il $13.95; lib bdg $13.88; pa $4.95 **E**

1. Farm life—Fiction 2. Grandfathers—Fiction
ISBN 0-688-06253-9; 0-688-06254-7 (lib bdg); 0-688-10491-6 (pa) LC 86-19573

"In this prequel to *Georgia Music* [entered above], Janetta accompanies her mother to the country to meet her grandfather for the first time. . . . This vacation in the country seems doomed until her grandfather tells of some absolutely incredible incidents that happened to him on this very farm. . . . Imaginative, tall-tale humor abounds throughout the smooth, well-paced text. . . . Watercolor illustrations, executed in warm pastels, lend visual clarity, exuding warmth and satisfaction. . . . This is an eye-catching, heart-grabbing jewel that children won't want to miss." SLJ

Plunk's dreams; pictures by Susan Condie Lamb. Greenwillow Bks. 1990 unp il $12.95; lib bdg $12.88 **E**

1. Dogs—Fiction 2. Dreams—Fiction
ISBN 0-688-08812-0; 0-688-08813-9 (lib bdg) LC 88-34905

John imagines what vivid adventures may lie in the dreams of his dog Plunk

"Lamb's jovial art pictures the honey-colored Plunk in the various scenarios that Griffith describes in a pertly phrased text. . . . Their joyous joint effort at analyzing a dog's dreams from a boy's perspective adds an engaging dimension to books on canines and kids." Booklist

Grindley, Sally

I don't want to! illustrated by Carol Thompson. Little, Brown 1990 unp il $13.95 **E**

1. Nursery schools—Fiction
ISBN 0-316-32893-6 LC 89-85798

"Joy Street books"

"Jim's parents have their hands full trying to get him ready for his first day of nursery school. . . . Jim steadfastly maintains that he doesn't want to go." SLJ

"This appealing book will help assuage those first-day jitters at nursery school or the day-care center. . . . Thompson's pictures, with their cheery pastel palette and comically drawn figures, amplify and give texture to the

Grindley, Sally—*Continued*

sparsely worded text. . . . An uncontrived, upbeat, successful collaboration between author and artist." Horn Book

Gross, Theodore Faro

Everyone asked about you; story by Theodore Faro Gross; pictures by Sheila White Samton. Philomel Bks. 1989 unp il $14.95 **E**

1. Stories in rhyme
ISBN 0-399-21727-4 LC 88-28131

"A red-haired, ebullient boy rides his bike to the pretty cottage of Nora Blue, who is pouting in an upstairs window. In his efforts to cheer her up and coax her outdoors, he tells her increasingly more fanciful tales of those who have asked about her: schoolmates, baseball teams, wild animals of land and sea, children worldwide, and finally creatures from the sky." SLJ

"The accompanying pictures are vigorous, blending cut paper and watercolor into scenes that project a self-assured presence. The sense of fun is unmistakable." Booklist

Guarino, Deborah

Is your mama a llama? illustrated by Steven Kellogg. Scholastic 1989 unp il $11.95 **E**

1. Llamas—Fiction 2. Animals—Fiction 3. Stories in rhyme
ISBN 0-590-41387-2 LC 87-32315

A young llama asks his friends if their mamas are llamas and finds out, in rhyme, that their mothers are other types of animals

"The lines are clean as well as exuberant, the colors well-blended as well as bright, and the compositions uncluttered as well as appealing. An ingenious page design invites choral participation, and the ending will encourage a cozy hiatus for bed/nap time. Both the sights and the sounds in the book are playful, the hide-and-seek motif sure and secure in its appeal to a home, daycare, or toddler-hour audience." Bull Cent Child Books

Gundersheimer, Karen, 1939-

1 2 3, play with me. Harper & Row 1984 unp il $3.95; lib bdg $10.89 **E**

1. Counting 2. Mice—Fiction
ISBN 0-694-00105-8; 0-06-022177-1 (lib bdg)
LC 84-47628

This title "features two mice, Minna and Memo. While Minna shows a card with a number on it, Memo, on the opposite page, plays with the same number of toys: one birthday hat, two fuzzy puppets, etc. Since all the toys are tossed aside as Memo moves on to higher numbers, there is also a fine opportunity to practice visual discrimination skills. This book, like the ABC book [entered below], is an excellent example of learning with material that is playful and fun. And, in addition to the educational content, Gundersheimer's typically whimsical and cozy-looking illustrations will be very appealing to small children." SLJ

A B C, say with me. Harper & Row 1984 unp il lib bdg $10.89 **E**

1. Alphabet
ISBN 0-06-022175-5 LC 84-47627

This book "is bright with primary colors, animating illustrations of words representing letters of the alphabet. Each picture is a miniature story for little children to 'read': an elfin character perches on a red apple beside a begging ant for 'Asking.' The actor grips two balloons as he flies on a butterfly, 'Balancing.'" Publ Wkly

Hader, Berta, 1891-1976

The big snow. Macmillan 1948 unp il $12.95; pa $4.95 **E**

1. Animals—Pictorial works 2. Winter
ISBN 0-02-737910-8; 0-02-043300-X (pa)
LC 48-10240

Awarded the Caldecott Medal, 1949

This book shows "the birds and animals which come for the food put out by an old couple after a big snow." Hodges. Books for Elem Sch Libr

Hall, Donald, 1928-

Ox-cart man; pictures by Barbara Cooney. Viking 1979 unp il $14.95; Puffin Bks. pa $4.95 **E**

1. New England—Fiction
ISBN 0-670-53328-9; 0-14-50441-9 (pa) LC 79-14466

Awarded the Caldecott Medal, 1980

"It is fall and a farmer loads a cart with the year's produce, journeys to market, sells, buys, and returns to his family to begin the year's work anew. The journey, and the ensuing year, unfold at a stately pace against the rich 19th-century New England backdrop alive with the subtly changing colors and activities of the succeeding seasons." SLJ

"The stunning combination of text and illustrations, suggesting early American paintings on wood, depict the countryside through which [the farmer] travels, the jostle of the marketplace, and the homely warmth of family life." Horn Book

Handforth, Thomas, 1897-1948

Mei Li. Doubleday 1938 unp il lib bdg $15.99; pa $14.95 **E**

1. China—Fiction 2. Fairs—Fiction
ISBN 0-385-07401-8 (lib bdg); 0-385-07639-8 (pa)
LC 38-27994

Awarded the Caldecott Medal, 1939

The story "of Mei Li, a little girl of North China, and her day at the Fair in the town and of her part in all the doings along with her brother San Yu, his kitten Igo and her thrush, until at the end of a long day she goes riding home on a camel just in time to greet the Kitchen God at midnight on New Year's Eve." Horn Book

"This gay, brief story, with its really wonderful big black and white drawings . . . will give children a wealth of clear, simple impressions of traditional Chinese life." Saturday Rev

Havill, Juanita

Jamaica tag-along; illustrations by Anne Sibley O'Brien. Houghton Mifflin 1989 unp il $13.95; pa $4.95 **E**

1. Brothers and sisters—Fiction 2. Friendship—Fiction
ISBN 0-395-49602-0; 0-395-54949-3 (pa) LC 88-13478

Sequel to: Jamaica's find (1986)

"Jamaica follows her brother Ossie to the park and tries to join his game of basketball but is told not to tag along. Stung by the rejection, Jamaica spurns little Berto's attempt to help her build a sand castle, then stops herself and teaches him how to help her." Bull Cent Child Books

"O'Brien's watercolors are extraordinarily lifelike and tender. She has a rare gift for capturing the many nuances of expression; her illustrations lend an extra dimension of compassion to the story." Publ Wkly

Hayes, Sarah

Eat up, Gemma; written by Sarah Hayes; illustrated by Jan Ormerod. Lothrop, Lee & Shepard Bks. 1988 unp il lib bdg $13 **E**

1. Infants—Fiction 2. Blacks—Fiction
ISBN 0-688-08149-5 LC 87-36205

Baby Gemma refuses to eat, throwing her breakfast on the floor and squashing her grapes, until her brother gets an inspired idea

"Narrated from the perspective of an adoring older brother, the story is indeed one that rings familiar to most families. . . . Ormerod's bold and vibrant watercolors present a warm and loving portrait of a black family." Horn Book

Another available title about Gemma, Happy Christmas, Gemma, is entered below

Happy Christmas, Gemma; illustrated by Jan Ormerod. Lothrop, Lee & Shepard Bks. 1986 unp il $13 **E**

1. Christmas—Fiction 2. Blacks—Fiction
ISBN 0-688-06508-2 LC 85-23674

A "story of a black family preparing for and celebrating Christmas. It is told from the perspective of the older brother as he contrasts his proper and helpful behavior with that of his mischievous toddler sister, Gemma." SLJ

"Ormerod's clean, brightly-colored illustrations effectively placed against a white background capture the warmth of the black family and of their shared holiday experience along with the pleasure they take in their smallest member." Horn Book

Hazen, Barbara Shook, 1930-

The gorilla did it; illustrated by Ray Cruz. Atheneum Pubs. 1974 unp il $12.95; pa $3.95 **E**

1. Gorillas—Fiction
ISBN 0-689-30138-3; 0-689-71214-6 (pa) LC 73-84828

"An imaginary ape interrupts the boy's nap, and together they make a wreck of his room, to his mother's annoyance. She can hardly believe him when he lays the blame on a gorilla she can't see." Saturday Rev

"The absolute pitch of familiarity in the dialog and line drawings, which contrast the huge, innocent-but-destructive gorilla in blue with everything unimagined in black and white, makes a picture book humorously tuned into a child's fantasy friend without making fun of it." Booklist

Heide, Florence Parry, 1919-

The day of Ahmed's secret; [by] Florence Parry Heide & Judith Heide Gilliland; illustrated by Ted Lewin. Lothrop, Lee & Shepard Bks. 1990 unp il $13.95; lib bdg $13.88 **E**

1. Cairo (Egypt)—Fiction
ISBN 0-688-08894-5; 0-688-08895-3 (lib bdg) LC 90-52694

"Ahmed has monumental news to share with his family, but first he must complete the age-old duties of a butagaz boy, delivering cooking gas to customers all over Cairo. The juxtaposition of old and new is a repeated theme in Heide and Gilliland's thoughtful story of a young boy living in the bustling metropolis surrounded by thousand-year-old walls and buildings. . . . Enhanced by Lewin's distinguished photorealistic watercolors, the sights, sounds, and smells of the exotic setting come to life. . . . At home at last, surrounded by his loving family, Ahmed demostrates his newly acquired facility, proudly writing his name in Arabic." SLJ

Heilbroner, Joan

This is the house where Jack lives; illustrated by Aliki. Harper & Row 1962 62p il $10.89 **E**

1. Nonsense verses
ISBN 0-06-022286-7 LC 62-7311

"An I can read book"

"A city apartment building is the setting for this modern version of the old cumulative nonsense rhyme about Jack and his house." Cincinnati Public Libr

"The illustrations are gay and humorous, echoing in the drawings the cumulative parts of the rhyme." Bull Cent Child Books

Heine, Helme

Friends; written and illustrated by Helme Heine. Atheneum Pubs. 1982 unp il lib bdg $13.95; pa $3.95 **E**

1. Friendship—Fiction 2. Animals—Fiction
ISBN 0-689-50256-7 (lib bdg); 0-689-71083-6 (pa) LC 82-45313

"A Margaret K. McElderry book"

This is an "account of the friendship between three animals, a mouse, a cock and a pig. . . . They do everything together like true friends should, but at bedtime, having all tried in turn the mousehole, the pigsty and the perch, they decide that they are after all quite different, and each sets off to his own bed to dream happy dreams of one another." Times Lit Suppl

"Heine's visual imagination makes the images extraordinary. . . . Watercolors take full advantage of the white page. The double-page scene at dusk with silhouetted cottage and tree is a fine restful transition from the frenetic daytime fun to the final funny efforts to bed down." SLJ

Heine, Helme—*Continued*

The most wonderful egg in the world; written and illustrated by Helme Heine. Atheneum Pubs. 1983 unp il $13.95; pa $3.95 **E**

1. Chickens—Fiction
ISBN 0-689-50280-X; 0-689-71117-4 (pa)
LC 82-49350

"A Margaret K. McElderry book"

"Three proud hens—Dotty, with the most beautiful feathers; Stalky, with the most beautiful legs; and Plumy, with the most beautiful crest—quarrel about which one of them is the most beautiful." Horn Book

"The message here—'What you can do is more important than what you look like'—is conveyed simply but effectively, with the theme of uniqueness and individuality nicely underplayed. The watercolor illustrations, mostly in pale tones with much open white space, are full of fun. . . . Children will be rewarded with new, humorous details on each rereading." SLJ

Hendershot, Judith, 1940-

In coal country; illustrated by Thomas B. Allen. Knopf 1987 unp il $14.95; lib bdg $14.99 **E**

1. Coal mines and mining—Fiction
ISBN 0-394-88190-7; 0-394-98190-1 (lib bdg)
LC 86-15311

A child growing up in a coal mining community finds both excitement and hard work, in a life deeply affected by the local industry

"The power of the book . . . lies in the deep, dark counterpoint that underlies the light melody of the childhood reminiscence. Using charcoal and pastels on earth-tone paper, Thomas Allen creates the illusion that coal dust permeates every illustration. The text is set in a box of grayed color centered on a stark white page. . . . Though the text is spare, the dark, eloquent pictures speak volumes." Horn Book

Henkes, Kevin, 1960-

Chester's way. Greenwillow Bks. 1988 unp il $11.95; lib bdg $11.88 **E**

1. Mice—Fiction
ISBN 0-688-07607-6; 0-688-07608-4 (lib bdg)
LC 87-14882

The mice Chester and Wilson share the exact way of doing things, until Lilly moves into the neighborhood and shows them that new ways can be just as good

"Henkes' charming cartoons are drawn with pen-and-ink, washed over with cheerful watercolors. They give witty expressions to his characters." SLJ

Jessica. Greenwillow Bks. 1989 unp il $11.95; lib bdg $11.88 **E**

1. Imaginary playmates—Fiction
ISBN 0-688-07829-X; 0-688-07830-3 (lib bdg)
LC 87-38087

"A shy preschooler insists that her friend Jessica is not imaginary—and, in the end, she's absolutely correct. Henkes' depiction of play-alone and play-together time brims with buoyant camaraderie in this upbeat story of friendship fulfilled." SLJ

Julius, the baby of the world. Greenwillow Bks. 1990 unp il $12.95; lib bdg $12.88 **E**

1. Mice—Fiction
ISBN 0-688-08943-7; 0-688-08944-5 (lib bdg)
LC 88-34904

Lilly, the girl mouse who debuted in Chester's way, entered above, "may still be the queen of the world, but her new brother 'Julius is the baby of the world.' Suffering from a severe case of sibling-itis, she warns pregnant strangers: 'You will live to regret that bump under your dress.' While her understanding parents shower her with 'compliments and praise and niceties of all shapes and sizes,' nothing works until snooty Cousin Garland comes for a visit." Booklist

"Magically, Henkes conveys a world of expressions and a wide range of complex emotions with a mere line or two upon the engaging mousey faces of Lilly and her family. A reassuring, funny book for all young children who suffer from new-sibling syndrome." SLJ

Sheila Rae, the brave. Greenwillow Bks. 1987 unp il $13.95; lib bdg $13.88 **E**

1. Mice—Fiction
ISBN 0-688-07155-4; 0-688-07156-2 (lib bdg)
LC 86-25761

"A mouse both boastful and fearless, Sheila Rae decides to go home from school by taking a new route. She walks backwards with her eyes closed, growls at dogs and cats, climbs trees, turns new corners and crosses different streets—and ends up in the middle of unfamiliar territory." Publ Wkly

"Bouncy watercolors in spring-like colors with some pen-and-ink detailing highlight Sheila Rae's bravado in an engaging and amusing way, and Henkes provides Sheila Rae, Louise, and their school friends with highly expressive faces. Children will respond to both the humor of the story and the illustrations and to the challenge of facing fears head-on. Librarians can share this one with small groups or recommend it for patrons without fear, for children will love it." SLJ

Hennessy, B. G. (Barbara G.)

A,B,C,D, tummy, toes, hands, knees; pictures by Wendy Watson. Viking Kestrel 1989 unp il lib bdg $12.95; Puffin Bks. pa $3.95 **E**

1. Infants—Fiction 2. Mothers—Fiction 3. Stories in rhyme
ISBN 0-670-81703-1 (lib bdg); 0-14-050739-6 (pa)
LC 88-32225

Listed rhyming words and simple illustrations depict how a mother and baby spend the day together delighting in the world and each other

"Children will have fun filling in the rhyming word in this picture book." Okla State Dept of Educ

The missing tarts; pictures by Tracey Campbell Pearson. Viking Kestrel 1989 unp il $12.95 **E**

1. Stories in rhyme
ISBN 0-670-82039-3
LC 88-28809

When the Queen of Hearts discovers that her strawberry tarts have been stolen, she enlists the help of many popular nursery rhyme characters in order to find them

"Bright colors pick out the scampering figures which

Hennessy, B. G. (Barbara G.)—*Continued*
are sketched in with humor and bubbling vitality and seem to leap from one page to the next. Youngsters will enjoy spotting Bo Peep and Little Jack Horner in the illustrations and confirming their identities in the rhymed text." Horn Book

Hest, Amy

The crack-of-dawn walkers; pictures by Amy Schwartz. Macmillan 1984 unp il $11.95; pa $3.95 **E**

1. Grandfathers—Fiction 2. Walking—Fiction
ISBN 0-02-743710-8; 0-14-050829-5 (pa)
LC 83-19597

"Before anyone else in the neighborhood is up, Sadie and her grandfather begin their biweekly walk to the bakery for onion rolls, to Fabio for cocoa, and to pick up the paper. Next week this treat will be her younger brother's, but now Sadie has her grandfather all to herself." Child Book Rev Serv

"Soft pencil drawings project the tranquil mood of a picture book that communicates the love and companionship of a small girl and her grandfather. . . . The unpretentious, somewhat stylized drawings are well-suited to depicting the details of Sadie's neighborhood." Horn Book

Fancy Aunt Jess; illustrated by Amy Schwartz. Morrow Junior Bks. 1990 unp il $12.95; lib bdg $12.88 **E**

1. Aunts—Fiction 2. Jews—Fiction 3. Brooklyn (New York, N.Y.)—Fiction
ISBN 0-688-08096-0; 0-688-08097-9 (lib bdg)
LC 88-34370

"Becky's Aunt Jess has billowing blond hair, loves new clothes, and doesn't mind talking about her previous boyfriends. A visit to her apartment is an adventure for Becky as the two indulge in special cookies and discuss what it's like to be grownup and in love. The colorful illustrations are bright with the patterned carpets and comfortably overstuffed furniture in Jess's rooms as well as the shops and streets and temple in her Brooklyn neighborhood. When a friendship develops between Becky and a little girl, Nicole, while attending a Friday night shul, a romance also blossoms between Nicole's uncle and Aunt Jess." Horn Book

The midnight eaters; illustrated by Karen Gundersheimer. Four Winds Press 1989 unp il $13.95 **E**

1. Grandmothers—Fiction 2. Old age—Fiction
ISBN 0-02-743630-6 LC 88-24381

Despite the doctor's warning that she is too frail, Samantha's grandmother zestfully joins her in a midnight raid on the kitchen, where they make fabulous ice cream sundaes and look at old photographs

"The neatly contained illustrations rely on selective detailing of interior scenes that consistently highlight the two diminutive characters. The art is quietly toned, befitting secrets." Bull Cent Child Books

The purple coat; pictures by Amy Schwartz. Four Winds Press 1986 unp il $12.95 **E**

1. Coats—Fiction 2. Grandfathers—Fiction
ISBN 0-02-743640-3 LC 85-29186

"Gabrielle has always gotten a navy coat in the fall, but, this year, to Mama's dismay, she yearns for a purple one. Grandpa, their favorite tailor, discovers a solution to please all." Child Book Rev Serv

"Schwartz' signature shapes—round, chunky, and unnaturally elongated—work beautifully here, especially in the city scenes filled with all types of people. The artwork is full color, and the deep shades and vibrant colors (especially that purple) are arresting. The numerous details and patternings catch the eye and make for pictures that can be looked at over and over; each time the story's satisfying conclusion rings sweetly true." Booklist

Heyward, DuBose, 1885-1940

The country bunny and the little gold shoes; as told to Jenifer; pictures by Marjorie Flack. Houghton Mifflin 1939 unp il lib bdg $12.95; pa $4.95 **E**

1. Rabbits—Fiction 2. Easter—Fiction
ISBN 0-395-15990-3 (lib bdg); 0-395-18557-2 (pa)
LC 39-8350

This is an Easter story for young readers which grew out of a story the author has told and retold to his young daughter. It is of the little country rabbit who wanted to become one of the five Easter bunnies, and how she managed to realize her ambition

"It is really imaginative and well written. . . . The colored pictures are just right too." New Yorker

Hines, Anna Grossnickle, 1946-

Big like me. Greenwillow Bks. 1989 unp il $12.95; lib bdg $12.88 **E**

1. Infants—Fiction 2. Brothers and sisters—Fiction
ISBN 0-688-08354-4; 0-688-08355-2 (lib bdg)
LC 88-18772

A boy tells his baby sister all the things he will show her as she grows, from snow and bouncing high to making faces and blowing out candles

"The drawings are not static presentations, but show a range of movements from crawling to bouncing on Mom's knee. Some renderings are a bit off, but the whole is so enjoyable that they do not detract from the overall presentation." SLJ

Daddy makes the best spaghetti. Clarion Bks. 1986 unp il lib bdg $11.95 **E**

1. Fathers—Fiction
ISBN 0-89919-388-9 LC 85-13993

"Corey and his father enjoy a close relationship that is aptly demonstrated in picture and story. He teases Corey and they spend time together doing things such as shopping for groceries and making a pot of spaghetti or being silly at bath time and getting ready for bed. Hines' simple but warm pencil drawings play out the scenes by capitalizing on the incidents described in the text; the strong sense of family (Mother is here too) is evident." Booklist

It's just me, Emily. Clarion Bks. 1987 unp il $12.95 **E**

1. Mothers and daughters—Fiction 2. Stories in rhyme
ISBN 0-89919-487-7 LC 86-34352

Hines, Anna Grossnickle, 1946-—*Continued*

"In this simple rhyming story, young Emily is either squirming under Mother's blanket, splashing around in the tub, or thumping under the table. At each juncture Mother comes up with a fanciful reason for all the noises." Booklist

"The text is full of rhymes and rhythms that will delight children. Hines has added to her story with fine line illustrations filled in with creamy pastel colors on white backgrounds that exhibit the familiar items and environment of a normal preschool child's world. . . . Best for sharing on a one-to-one basis due to its small size, this book should be a big hit with the preschool crowd." SLJ

Mean old Uncle Jack. Clarion Bks. 1990 unp il lib bdg $13.95 **E**

1. Uncles—Fiction 2. Fourth of July—Fiction
ISBN 0-395-52137-8 LC 89-17398

Uncle Jack loves to tease the kids with scary mean faces and growly mean noises, but one Fourth of July his nieces and nephews turn the tables on him

"Hines' soft, color-pencil drawings belie the text's seemingly somber warnings about Uncle Jack and highlight the relaxed extended family fun everyone has on this Independence Day celebration. An affectionate portrayal." Booklist

Hoban, Lillian

Arthur's Christmas cookies; words and pictures by Lillian Hoban. Harper & Row 1972 63p il $10.95; lib bdg $10.89; pa $3.50 **E**

1. Chimpanzees—Fiction 2. Christmas—Fiction 3. Baking—Fiction
ISBN 0-06-022367-7; 0-06-022368-5 (lib bdg); 0-06-444055-9 (pa) LC 72-76496

"An I can read book"

When Arthur decides to make Christmas cookies for his parents, a "disastrous mistake in the ingredients makes the cookies inedible but the story ends happily when Arthur turns them into holiday decorations." Publ Wkly

The characters are chimpanzees but "are endearingly like human children. Their conversation is realistically childlike, as are their actions. The Christmas setting is appealing, the plot has problem, conflict, and solution yet is not too complex for the beginning independent reader, and the simplicity and humor make the book an appropriate one for reading aloud to preschool children also." Bull Cent Child Books

Other available titles about Arthur are:
Arthur's funny money (1981)
Arthur's great big valentine (1989)
Arthur's Halloween costume (1984)
Arthur's Honey Bear (1974)
Arthur's loose tooth (1985)
Arthur's pen pal (1976)
Arthur's prize reader (1978)

It's really Christmas. Greenwillow Bks. 1982 39p il $11.75; lib bdg $11.88 **E**

1. Mice—Fiction 2. Christmas—Fiction
ISBN 0-688-00830-5; 0-688-00831-3 (lib bdg) LC 81-6324

Born in the spring in a box of Christmas decorations, a young mouse eagerly awaits his first real Christmas. But when he becomes gravely ill after a generous and brave act which saves the other attic mice, they, to aid his recovery, stage Christmas in summer for him

"Soft-hued paintings, more detailed and romantic than Hoban's usual work, illustrate a gentle, sentimental story. . . . A little sugary, the story is nicely structured and told, and the wee protagonist should be appealing to the read-aloud audience." Bull Cent Child Books

Hoban, Russell

Bedtime for Frances; illustrated by Garth Williams. Harper & Row 1960 unp il $13.95; lib bdg $13.89; pa $3.95 **E**

1. Badgers—Fiction
ISBN 0-06-022350-2; 0-06-022351-0 (lib bdg); 0-06-443005-7 (pa) LC 60-8347

"A little badger with a lively imagination comes up with one scheme after another to put off going to sleep but father badger proves himself as smart as his daughter." Bookmark

"Nothing at all unusual in this story—but Mr. Williams was inspired to make Frances a small round appealing badger, with kindly badger parents, although badgers are not mentioned in the text. The soft humorous pictures of these lovable animals in human predicaments are delightful." Horn Book

Other available titles about Frances are:
A baby sister for Frances (1964)
A bargain for Frances (1970)
Best friends for Frances (1969)
A birthday for Frances (1968)
Bread and jam for Frances (1964)

Another book about Frances, Egg thoughts, and other Frances songs, is entered in class 811

Dinner at Alberta's; pictures by James Marshall. Crowell 1975 unp il lib bdg $11.89; Dell pa $2.95 **E**

1. Crocodiles—Fiction 2. Etiquette—Fiction
ISBN 0-690-23993-9 (lib bdg); 0-440-41864-X (pa) LC 73-94796

Arthur Crocodile cannot seem to learn table manners until his sister brings her new girlfriend to visit

Arthur's "concentrated practice sessions for dining out according to accepted standards are hilariously documented in an absurd combination of tongue-in-cheek text and droll, brown-toned drawings." Horn Book

Another available title about Arthur is:
Arthur's new power (1978)

The sorely trying day; pictures by Lillian Hoban. Harper & Row 1964 unp il lib bdg $12.89 **E**

1. Family life—Fiction
ISBN 0-06-022421-5 LC 64-11836

"After a sorely trying day the father of a Victorian household comes home to find the place in an uproar. . . . As Father tries to get to the source of the trouble each accuses another until the blame reaches down to the mouse who nobly takes the blame for the whole miserable business; in reverse order admissions of guilt and apologies are made and peace is finally restored." Booklist

"Both children and adults will enjoy the progessively

Hoban, Russell—*Continued*
funny comedy and the subtle humor in the detailed Victorian drawings." SLJ

Hoban, Tana

26 letters and 99 cents. Greenwillow Bks. 1987 unp il $14.95; lib bdg $14.88 **E**

1. Alphabet 2. Counting 3. Coins
ISBN 0-688-06361-6; 0-688-06362-4 (lib bdg)
LC 86-11993

This concept book "is really two books in one. *26 Letters* is a delightful ABC handbook. Each page shows two letters (in both upper- and lowercase) paired with objects from airplane to zipper. Turning the book around reveals the even more creative *99 Cents.* Here Hoban clearly shows youngsters how to count by pairing photos of numbers with pennies, nickels, dimes and quarters in a variety of combinations. The book counts ones from 1¢ to 30¢, by fives from 30¢ to 50¢, by tens from 50¢ to 90¢, culminating in 99¢. . . . An extremely inventive approach that will be hailed by parents, teachers and librarians." Publ Wkly

A, B, see! Greenwillow Bks. 1982 unp il lib bdg $13.88 **E**

1. Alphabet
ISBN 0-688-00833-X LC 81-6890

A collection of black and white silhouette photographs of objects beginning with a particular letter of the alphabet

"Artistically arranged to provide rhythm and balance, the pictures are also exercises in object recognition and visual discrimination—intriguing puzzles to be solved rather than just lessons to be learned. Some objects are instantly recognizable; others demand somewhat sophisticated understanding; and still others require some mental agility to identify. . . . An exciting, original, and carefully conceived book." Horn Book

Circles, triangles and squares. Macmillan 1974 unp il $12.95 **E**

1. Size and shape
ISBN 0-02-744830-4 LC 72-93305

"There is no division of the material into sections and no text here, simply a series of photographs in which the three most familiar geometric forms occur. Often more than one shape appears on the photograph." Bull Cent Child Books

"An imaginative exercise for the development of visual awareness." Horn Book

Dots, spots, speckles, and stripes. Greenwillow Bks. 1987 unp il $11.75; lib bdg $11.88 **E**

ISBN 0-688-06862-6; 0-688-06863-4 (lib bdg)
LC 86-22919

Photographs show dots, spots, speckles, and stripes as found on clothing, flowers, faces, animals, and other places

"Not only are the photos in this title technically superb, but the composition and the subjects are imaginative yet clearly identifiable. . . . The book is wordless, but Hoban needs no text to fascinate and enthrall. Going beyond a concept book on patterns, *Dots, Spots, Speckles, and Stripes* becomes a thought-provoking photo essay that can be appreciated by older children." Horn Book

Exactly the opposite. Greenwillow Bks. 1990 unp il $12.95; lib bdg $12.88 **E**

1. English language—Synonyms and antonyms
ISBN 0-688-08861-9; 0-688-08862-7 (lib bdg)
LC 89-27227

"Using a variety of people, animals, and objects found in outdoor settings of both the city and the country, [the author] introduces and expands on the concept of opposites in this wordless photographic book. The photographs are clear, bright, and enticing. Pairs of opposites are presented on facing pages. . . . As with all of Hoban's books, readers are asked to view their environment in a new light while learning a new concept. A worthy addition to any collection." SLJ

Is it larger? Is it smaller? Greenwillow Bks. 1985 unp il $12.95; lib bdg $12.88 **E**

1. Size and shape
ISBN 0-688-04027-6; 0-688-04028-4 (lib bdg)
LC 84-13719

"In each full-color photograph of the wordless picture book Hoban juxtaposes similar objects of differing size. In the simplest pictures only one kind of object is shown, such as three bright plastic sand cups in graduated sizes or three maple leaves. More complex compositions group several related items: measuring cups, bowls, and utensils; fish, shells, and pebbles in an aquarium. Still others contrast dissimilar objects that have common features. . . . In the photographs, Hoban demonstrates once again her mastery of the elements of composition, such as color, texture, and balance." Horn Book

Is it red? Is it yellow? Is it blue? An adventure in color. Greenwillow Bks. 1978 unp il $13.95; lib bdg $13.88 **E**

1. Color 2. Size and shape
ISBN 0-688-80171-4; 0-688-84171-6 (lib bdg)
LC 78-2549

Illustrations and brief text introduce colors and the concepts of shape and size

"The wordless book is simply designed and opens the eye to the marvelous world of color; each stark-white page contains one photograph which nearly fills it. In the bottom margin the predominant colors in the photograph are indicated by a row of corresponding circles. . . . The book is not a random hodgepodge of photographs—color, movement, and theme are subtly controlled." Horn Book

Is it rough? Is it smooth? Is it shiny? Greenwillow Bks. 1984 unp il $13.95; lib bdg $13.88 **E**

ISBN 0-688-03823-9; 0-688-03824-7 (lib bdg)
LC 83-25460

Color photographs without text introduce objects of many different textures, such as pretzels, foil, hay, mud, kitten, and bubbles

"Extraordinarily crisp, clean color photographs allow Hoban to call attention to textures. . . . There are no words and none needed, for the concrete images will spark plenty to talk about between a child and anyone

Hoban, Tana—*Continued*
sharing the book with him or her. A simple idea executed with the requisite technical skill." Booklist

Look again! Macmillan 1971 unp il $11.95 **E**

ISBN 0-02-744050-8 LC 72-127469

"This captivating book of photographs invites the reader to look once through a two-inch cut-out square at a pattern or portion of something larger. On the next page, the complete picture of the object is revealed. On the verso of the second page is another view of the object. And so, as each set is displayed, one is impelled to look again and again and again." Wis Libr Bull

Look! look! look! Greenwillow Bks. 1988 unp il $12.95; lib bdg $12.88 **E**

ISBN 0-688-07239-9; 0-688-07240-2 (lib bdg) LC 87-25655

Photographs of familiar objects are first viewed through a cut-out hole, then in their entirety

"The author employs an element of trickery that will intrigue older children: for instance, showing a bit of a Ferris wheel that children in a story hour first guessed as the Statue of Liberty. Hoban's photographs are crystal clear, beautifully composed, and a treat to view." Horn Book

One little kitten. Greenwillow Bks. 1979 unp il lib bdg $12.88 **E**

1. Cats—Fiction 2. Stories in rhyme
ISBN 0-688-84222-4 LC 78-31862

This is a "picture book that has a rhyming text and that presents some concepts of position (inside, behind, through). . . . [A] kitten wakes and plays, hides, pounces on string, investigates some shoes, and decides it's time to retire. . . . The book ends as the kitten and its siblings snuggle up to a mother cat. Not substantial, but appealing." Bull Cent Child Books

Over, under & through, and other spatial concepts. Macmillan 1973 unp il $12.95; Atheneum Pubs. pa $3.95 **E**

1. Vocabulary
ISBN 0-02-744820-7; 0-689-71111-5 (pa) LC 72-81055

In brief text and photographs, the author depicts several spatial concepts—over, under, through, on, in, around, across, between, beside, below, against, and behind

"Children who are confused by these concepts may need help understanding that many of the pictures illustrate more than one concept. However, both the photographs and the format, with the words printed large on broad yellow bands at the beginning of each section, are uncluttered and appealing." Booklist

Push pull, empty full; a book of opposites. Macmillan 1972 unp il $12.95 **E**

1. English language—Synonyms and antonyms
ISBN 0-02-744810-X LC 72-90410

Brief text and black and white photographs illustrate fifteen pairs of opposites—push pull, empty full, wet dry, in out, up down, thick thin, whole broken, front back, big little, first last, many few, heavy light, together apart, left right, and day night

"Most of the meanings are immediately apparent from the pictures although some children may have difficulty with thick (elephants) and thin (flamingos)." Booklist

Round & round & round. Greenwillow Bks. 1983 unp il $12.95; lib bdg $12.88 **E**

1. Size and shape
ISBN 0-688-01813-0; 0-688-01814-9 (lib bdg) LC 82-11984

Color photos without text feature objects that are round

"This is a good choice for encouragement of a child's powers of observation as well as to emphasize a concept of shape, and the pictures of a scoop of ice cream, a raccoon peering out of a hole in a tree, bright balloons, irridescent soap bubbles, and a seal balancing a ball should appeal to young children." Bull Cent Child Books

Take another look. Greenwillow Bks. 1981 40p il $13.88 **E**

ISBN 0-688-84298-4 LC 80-21342

By viewing nine subjects both in full-page photos and through die-cut pages, the reader learns that things maybe perceived in different ways

"The objects are as familiar as a daisy, a cat, an umbrella, et cetera, with only one perhaps less familiar object, a lizard. A nice concept book, this has a guessing game appeal." Bull Cent Child Books

Where is it? Macmillan 1974 unp il $11.95 **E**

1. Rabbits—Fiction 2. Easter—Fiction 3. Stories in rhyme
ISBN 0-02-744070-2 LC 73-8573

In this story in rhyme, illustrated with photographs, a rabbit searches for its own Easter basket full of garden vegetables

"The type is large and the scanning lines short while some end words rhyme—all factors considered helpful to the decoding practice of the youngest readers as well as older reluctants." SLJ

Hoff, Syd, 1912-

Danny and the dinosaur; story and pictures by Syd Hoff. Harper & Row 1958 64p il $10.95; lib bdg $10.89; pa $3.50 **E**

1. Dinosaurs—Fiction
ISBN 0-06-022465-7; 0-06-022466-5 (lib bdg); 0-06-444002-8 (pa) LC 58-7754

"An I can read book"

The story is "about an amiable dinosaur who leaves his home in the museum to stroll about town and play with Danny, a small boy who loves dinosaurs. The dinosaur talks (of course) to Danny's friends and plays games with them, visits the zoo, goes to a baseball game and enjoys, with a beatific smile, an ice cream cone." Bull Cent Child Books

"The bold, humorous, colored pictures convey the imaginative story. . . . Because of the simple vocabulary and sentence structure, first-graders can actually read this story." Libr J

Hogrogian, Nonny

The cat who loved to sing. Knopf 1988 unp il music $12.95; lib bdg $13.99 **E**

1. Cats—Fiction
ISBN 0-394-89004-3; 0-394-99004-8 (lib bdg) LC 86-27358

"Hogrogian presents this cumulative tale of a carefree cat who trades with those he meets: a thorn for bread, then for a hen, and so on until he winds up with a mandolin, which he keeps 'for he is a cat who loves to sing'." SLJ

"The words and music of the cat's song conclude the book, which is designed with woodsy endpapers that extend the verdant scenery of the cat's capers. The fused effects of the backgrounds contrast nicely with the penciled lines texturing the cat's fur for a gentle effect to which young listeners will respond by quickly picking up the chant." Bull Cent Child Books

Hoguet, Susan Ramsay

I unpacked my grandmother's trunk; a picture book game. Dutton 1983 unp il $12.95 **E**

1. Alphabet 2. Games
ISBN 0-525-44069-0 LC 83-1701

"This familiar word game is usually played without a book, but Hoguet's rendition is so charmingly illustrated that even veteran players will welcome it. Just a few of the articles that tumble out of the trunk include: a curious bear, a melting igloo, an adept acrobat, and a mimicking kangaroo. Executed in precise pastel drawings, the objects illustrate each letter of the alphabet, provide lots to look at, and cumulatively tell a story of sorts. The clever use of half pages exposes the trunk's contents imaginatively, adding to the fun. Also included are directions for playing the memory game without the book." Booklist

Solomon Grundy. Dutton 1986 32p il $13.95 **E**

1. Nursery rhymes
ISBN 0-525-44239-1 LC 85-20453

"Hoguet uses the familiar nursery rhyme to tell the story of a young boy born to immigrant parents. While a historical perspective is provided through the addition of end notes, younger readers will require considerable discussion to grasp the intent of the story. The charming and colorful illustrations are the most appealing aspect of the book." Child Book Rev Serv

Holabird, Katharine

Angelina ballerina; illustrations by Helen Craig; text by Katharine Holabird. Potter 1983 unp il $9.95 **E**

1. Mice—Fiction 2. Ballet—Fiction
ISBN 0-517-55083-0 LC 83-8233

Also available miniature edition $4.95 (ISBN 0-517-57668-6)

"Though Angelina is a little mouse, she could be any child who has dreamed of taking lessons in a special subject. When she starts ballet class, instead of dreaming and trying, she can concentrate on chores and school. Later, her talent and hard work enable her to become a famous ballerina. Touches of humor, attention to detail, a feel for dance and truly anthropomorphic mice make the illustrations a major part of the book." Child Book Rev Serv

Other available titles about Angelina are:
Angelina and Alice (1987)
Angelina and the princess (1984)
Angelina at the fair (1985)
Angelina on stage (1986)
Angelina's birthday surprise (1989)
Angelina's Christmas (1985)

Horenstein, Henry

Sam goes trucking. Houghton Mifflin 1989 38p il $14.95; pa $4.95 **E**

1. Trucks—Fiction 2. Fathers and sons—Fiction
ISBN 0-395-44313-X; 0-395-54950-7 (pa) LC 88-8321

"A photo essay in color in which Sam accompanies his father during a routine day on the road in Sam's father's big Mack truck." Soc Educ

"Children are endlessly fascinated by big rigs, and this nicely designed, well photographed book will satisfy their curiosity while adding the extra element of a child learning about and sharing his father's job. It will be appreciated by preschoolers along with older truck fans." Horn Book

Houston, Gloria

The year of the perfect Christmas tree; an Appalachian story; pictures by Barbara Cooney. Dial Bks. for Young Readers 1988 unp il $13.95; lib bdg $13.89 **E**

1. Christmas—Fiction 2. Appalachian Mountains—Fiction
ISBN 0-8037-0299-X; 0-8037-0300-7 (lib bdg) LC 87-24551

"It's 1918 in the mountains of North Carolina, and the custom in the village is for one family to select and donate the Christmas tree each year. In the spring Ruthie and her father select a perfect balsam high on a rocky crag. Then Father goes to war. Still, on Christmas Eve the tree is in the church and Ruthie plays the angel. The winning illustrations perfectly match the tone of this affecting story, which comes from the author's family." N Y Times Book Rev

Howard, Elizabeth Fitzgerald

Chita's Christmas tree; illustrated by Floyd Cooper. Bradbury Press 1989 unp il $13.95 **E**

1. Christmas—Fiction 2. Family life—Fiction 3. Blacks—Fiction
ISBN 0-02-744621-2 LC 88-26250

"A turn-of-the-century story begins on the Saturday before Christmas, when Chita and her father go out of the city (Baltimore) to choose a tree. Papa marks it with Chita's name and assures her that Santa Claus will get it to their house. The story continues, quietly, with preparations for the holiday, a dinner for the black family and relatives on Christmas Eve, and Chita's happy discovery the next morning that the big, decorated tree does indeed have her name carved on it." Bull Cent Child Books

"The paintings that surround the almost-poetic text

Howard, Elizabeth Fitzgerald—*Continued*
are softly unfocused and glow with a golden color that suffuses the scenes. Yet despite the dreamy feeling of the art, carefully delineated characters play their parts perfectly in the family scenes." Booklist

The train to Lulu's; illustrated by Robert Casilla. Bradbury Press 1988 unp il $13.95 E

1. Railroads—Fiction 2. Sisters—Fiction 3. Blacks—Fiction
ISBN 0-02-744620-4 LC 86-33429

This story "describes two young sisters' nine-hour train ride from Boston to Baltimore. Although the girls are travelling alone, the Travelers' Aid ladies and conductors assure them safe passage, and it's only boredom that mars the trip. Beppy does her best to entertain Babs, but both are relieved when they finally arrive to be claimed by grandmotherly Lulu for the summer." Bull Cent Child Books

"Even though this story takes place in the late 1930s, its themes of self-reliance and readiness are timeless. . . . Casilla deftly captures the warmth existing in this extended black family and also the appealing aspects of railroad travel." SLJ

Howe, James, 1946-

The day the teacher went bananas; illustrated by Lillian Hoban. Dutton 1984 unp il $11.95; pa $3.95 E

1. Teachers—Fiction 2. School stories 3. Gorillas—Fiction
ISBN 0-525-44107-7; 0-525-44321-5 (pa) LC 84-1536

"A mix-up places a gorilla and a new teacher in the wrong places, and the class of children find that the gorilla is a fine teacher. They learn to count on their toes and swing on trees before the error is matter-of-factly righted, and the following day the class goes to the zoo to have lunch with their favorite teacher." SLJ

"Hoban's artistic perceptions of children are, as usual, right on target, and in a book where integration of text and picture is crucial, the two mesh with colorful vigor and aplomb." Booklist

Pinky and Rex; illustrated by Melissa Sweet. Atheneum Pubs. 1990 38p il $11.95 E

1. Museums—Fiction 2. Friendship—Fiction 3. Toys—Fiction
ISBN 0-689-31454-X LC 89-30786

"Pinky, a boy named for his favorite color, and Rex, a girl whose name reflects her interest in dinosaurs, live next door to each other; they each have twenty-seven stuffed animals and are best friends. . . . They go to the museum and discover that even best friends can vie with each other for the last remaining pink dinosaur in the museum store." Horn Book

"Sweet's gently washed, jovial illustrations reflect the unpretentious sincerity of Rex and Pinky's relationship, while Howe's readable text blending natural dialogue with narrative, is divided into individual chapters." Booklist

Another available title about Pinky and Rex is:
Pinky and Rex get married (1990)

Scared silly: a Halloween treat; illustrated by Leslie Morrill. Morrow Junior Bks. 1989 unp il $13.95; lib bdg $13.88 E

1. Halloween—Fiction 2. Animals—Fiction
ISBN 0-688-07666-1; 0-688-07667-X (lib bdg) LC 88-7837

At head of title: Harold & Chester in

The Monroes leave their cat, Chester, and two dogs, Harold and Howe, alone on Halloween night, unaware that their pets are about to be visited by a strange figure who might be a wicked witch

"Howe's pacing is perfect, and the ending is unexpected. But it is Morrill's artwork that really enhances the drama. Exciting watercolors capture the individuality of the animals and the creepiness of the setting as shadows gradually fall." Booklist

Other picture books about Harold and Chester are:
The fright before Christmas (1988)
Hot fudge (1990)

Other available titles about Harold and Chester are entered in Fiction Section under Deborah Howe and James Howe

Hughes, Shirley

Alfie gets in first. Lothrop, Lee & Shepard Bks. 1982 c1981 unp il $12.95; lib bdg $12.88 E

1. Locks and keys—Fiction
ISBN 0-688-00848-8; 0-688-00849-6 (lib bdg) LC 81-8427

"Alfie, racing ahead of his mother and his baby sister as they return from grocery shopping, reaches the front door first; after Mom has unlocked the door and gone down the steps to get the baby, Alfie dashes into the hall shouting 'I've won!' Unfortunately, he slams the door. Unfortunately, Mom's key is inside with Alfie. Crisis! Just as the milkman brings a ladder for the window cleaner to use in getting to an upstairs window, the door opens: a beaming Alfie has thought of a way to solve the problem." Bull Cent Child Books

"Inventive use of the double spreads establishes the simultaneous display of indoor and outdoor actions. The setting is English and the prose understated, and the illustrations, in full color, manage to be pleasing in a slightly scruffy way." SLJ

Other available titles about Alfie and his family are:
Alfie gives a hand (1983)
Alfie's feet (1982)
An evening at Alfie's (1985)
The big Alfie and Annie Rose storybook (1989)

All shapes and sizes. Lothrop, Lee & Shepard Bks. 1986 unp il $4.95 E

1. Size and shape 2. Stories in rhyme
ISBN 0-688-04205-8 LC 86-2734

Rhyming text describes how familiar things come in different shapes and sizes

"Inviting endpaper pictures, an interracial and variously aged cast, plus a winsome, active three or four year old and her lumpy baby brother are just right." SLJ

Hughes, Shirley—*Continued*

Angel Mae: a tale of Trotter Street. Lothrop, Lee & Shepard Bks. 1989 unp il $12.95; lib bdg $12.88 **E**

1. Infants—Fiction 2. Christmas—Fiction
ISBN 0-688-08538-5; 0-688-08539-3 (lib bdg) LC 89-45288

"Christmas is coming, and so is a new baby for the Morgan family of Trotter Street. Mum, Dad, Grandma, Frankie, and little sister Mae are getting ready for both events, preparing a room, a crib, toys, and more for the baby at home, and rehearsing a Christmas play at school." SLJ

"Set in an English working-class, multiethnic neighborhood, this warm, humorous, well-told story also has holiday appeal. Hughes' pictures are, as always, delightful; realistically rendered in ink and watercolors, they are placed on the page in a pleasantly varied manner, and both art and text are appropriately childlike." Booklist

Other available titles in the Trotter Street series are:
The big concrete lorry (1990)
The snow lady (1990)

Bathwater's hot. Lothrop, Lee & Shepard Bks. 1985 unp il lib bdg $4.95 **E**

1. Stories in rhyme
ISBN 0-688-04202-3 LC 84-14389

This work "shows the little girl of the family and her baby brother exploring a series of opposites." Horn Book

The "pictures have the verve and humour we expect from this artist and the firm individuality with which she can always endow her characters. They are Everyman (so they can be accepted by Anychild) yet each one performs a particular action or shows a particular mood in a way that makes them real people. As a bonus this kind of book, given the vivacity of colour and variety of backgrounds, can start and support those bedtime conversations in which early vocabularies grow and flourish." Grow Point

Other available titles in this series are:
Noisy (1985)
When we went to the park (1985)

Lucy & Tom's a.b.c. Viking Kestrel 1986 c1984 unp il $11.95; Penguin Bks. pa $4.95 **E**

1. Alphabet 2. Brothers and sisters—Fiction
ISBN 0-670-81256-0; 0-14-050697-7 (pa) LC 86-40022

First published 1984 in the United Kingdom

"Lucy and Tom, a cherubic, tousled pair of siblings, are the stars of this alphabetized catalog of everyday items. Each letter is shown in both upper- and lower-case and is accompanied by a short paragraph, often containing more than one word to go along with the letter. While nearly all of the words are readily familiar to preschoolers, one or two may need explanation. . . . Hughes' humorous illustrations are cheerfully cluttered and untidy, and Lucy and Tom are a winning, if sometimes mischievous, pair. Too complex to be a first book on the ABCs, this will nonetheless delight listeners who need or want to reinforce their alphabet skills." SLJ

Lucy & Tom's 1.2.3. Viking Kestrel 1987 unp il $10.95 **E**

1. Counting 2. Brothers and sisters—Fiction
ISBN 0-670-81763-5 LC 86-40596

This "companion volume to *Lucy and Tom's A.B.C.* [entered above] integrates visual and verbal representations of mathematical realities into the proceedings and environments of a busy Saturday. . . . Spirited, detailed paintings imbued with the assurance of family closeness and warmth bring immediacy and verisimilitude to the relaxed, objective text. . . . Seizing every opportunity, she has embodied in her account of a single day's events an impressive variety of mathematical operations and concepts—such as numeration and simple division as well as pairs, sets, odd and even numbers, weight versus quantity, and a surprising hint at infinity." Horn Book

Moving Molly. Lothrop, Lee & Shepard Bks. 1988 c1978 unp il $11.95; lib bdg $11.88 **E**

1. Moving, Household—Fiction
ISBN 0-688-07982-2; 0-688-07984-9 (lib bdg) LC 87-34250

First published 1978 in the United Kingdom; first United States edition published 1979 by Prentice-Hall

Molly is lonely after her family's move from the city to the country but she adjusts with the help of her two new next-door-neighbors

"The illustrations showing comfortable family life are very English in appearance but universal in appeal and add immeasurably to the warm, simple story." Horn Book

Out and about. Lothrop, Lee & Shepard Bks. 1988 unp il $13; lib bdg $12.88 **E**

1. Seasons—Fiction 2. Stories in rhyme
ISBN 0-688-07690-4; 0-688-07691-2 (lib bdg) LC 87-17000

Rhyming text depicts the pleasures of the outdoors in all kinds of weather, through the four seasons

"The children who romp through these non-stop family scenes are rosy, cared-for, active, and enthusiastically messy. Hughes' drawing is always good, but the composition and coloration here mark some of her most cohesive book design and art work." Bull Cent Child Books

Two shoes, new shoes. Lothrop, Lee & Shepard Bks. 1986 unp il $4.95 **E**

1. Clothing and dress—Fiction 2. Stories in rhyme
ISBN 0-688-04207-4 LC 86-2733

"The rhyme informs as the pictures celebrate the pleasures of dressing up: 'Slippers, warm by the fire, lace-ups in the street./Gloves are for hands and socks are for feet.' These are nice for sharing one on one; their down-to-earth ambience is most appealing." Booklist

Hurd, Edith Thacher, 1910-

I dance in my red pajamas; pictures by Emily Arnold McCully. Harper & Row 1982 unp il lib bdg $12.89 **E**

1. Grandparents—Fiction
ISBN 0-06-022700-1 LC 81-47721

Jenny visits with her grandparents and enjoys a beautiful noisy day

"McCully's drawings are buoyant and as lively as the day described. Her pen drawings give form and vibrance, while the colored washes provide the gentleness of a child's view of grandparents." SLJ

Hurd, Edith Thacher, 1910-—*Continued*

Johnny Lion's book; pictures by Clement Hurd. Harper & Row 1965 63p il lib bdg $10.89; pa $3.50 E

1. Lions—Fiction
ISBN 0-06-022706-0 (lib bdg); 0-06-444074-5 (pa) LC 65-14490

"An I can read book"

"A small lion, told to stay home and read his new book while his parents are out hunting, reads about another small lion. Less dutiful than the reader, the lion cub in the book wanders off and is later put to bed early. Johnny Lion pretends to his parents that he has strayed, but quickly informs them that he has really stayed home and read his book." Bull Cent Child Books

The "book-within-a-book technique is admirably handled, though it may be a bit sophisticated for the youngest readers without some guidance. More experienced readers . . . will enjoy the gay pictures and understand the central idea that adventures in a book are almost as exciting and interesting as real ones." N Y Times Book Rev

Other available titles about Johnny Lion are:
Johnny Lion's bad day (1970)
Johnny Lion's rubber boots (1972)

Last one home is a green pig; pictures by Clement Hurd. Harper & Row 1959 63p il lib bdg $10.89 E

1. Ducks—Fiction 2. Monkeys—Fiction
ISBN 0-06-022716-8 LC 59-8972

"An I can read book"

"A duck and a monkey use many ingenious means of transportation when they race each other home." Hodges. Books for Elem Sch Libr

Hurd, Thacher

Axle the freeway cat. Harper & Row 1981 unp il lib bdg $12.89; pa $3.95 E

1. Cats—Fiction 2. Express highways—Fiction
ISBN 0-06-022698-6 (lib bdg); 0-06-443173-8 (pa) LC 80-8432

"A lot of kids would love to live like Axle, in a beat-up wood-panelled station wagon that's snug and just the way he wants it inside. . . . Days, he's a trash picker for the highway department, a job that allows him to find good things, like a harmonica. Nights as he plays harmonica solos with the car windows rolled down the concrete overpass performs acoustical wonders. Content, carefree, Axle almost has it all. Then a racy red vintage MG breaks down in traffic and Axle finds the rest—friendship with a she-cat who also likes fast cars and music. You don't have to be car crazy to like Axle—he's independent, gallant, jaunty. Hurd's prose hums like a well-tuned motor and his watercolors touch the L.A. freeways with . . . transforming magic." SLJ

Little Mouse's big valentine. Harper & Row 1990 unp il $12.95; $12.89 E

1. Mice—Fiction 2. Valentine's Day—Fiction
ISBN 0-06-026192-7; 0-06-026193-5 (lib bdg) LC 89-34515

After several unsuccessful attempts to give his special valentine to someone, Little Mouse finally finds just the right recipient

"The plot of boy mouse meets girl mouse may be simple, but it is offset by delightful characterizations. The book's small size gives it added appeal for its intended audience." Publ Wkly

Mama don't allow; starring Miles and the Swamp Band. Harper & Row 1984 unp il $14.95; lib bdg $14.89; pa $3.95 E

1. Bands (Music)—Fiction 2. Alligators—Fiction
ISBN 0-06-022689-7; 0-06-022690-0 (lib bdg); 0-06-443078-2 (pa) LC 83-47703

Miles and the Swamp Band have the time of their lives playing at the Alligator Ball, until they discover the menu includes Swamp Band soup

"The multi-colored full-spread watercolor illustrations are stunningly bright and full of movement, far outpacing the story line in energy and imagination." SLJ

Mystery on the docks. Harper & Row 1983 unp il $12.95; lib bdg $12.89; pa $3.95 E

1. Mystery and detective stories 2. Rats—Fiction
ISBN 0-06-022701-X; 0-06-022702-8 (lib bdg); 0-06-443058-8 (pa) LC 82-48261

Ralph, a short order cook, rescues a kidnapped opera singer from Big Al and his gang of nasty rats

Hurd "creates real excitement (albeit tongue-in-cheek) with his colorful pictures and fast-paced plot. There's a mysterious aura to the docks, and the stereotyped good and bad guys are hilarious. The unabashed fun and excitement make it perfect for reading aloud." Child Book Rev Serv

The pea patch jig. Crown 1986 unp il $11.95 E

1. Mice—Fiction 2. Gardens—Fiction
ISBN 0-517-56307-X LC 86-2693

"This picture book in three short chapters, inspired by an old fiddle tune of the same name, tells about the midsummer afternoon and evening adventures of Baby Mouse. As her parents get ready for their big party, she is irresistibly drawn to Farmer Clem's garden. The colors are vibrant and lush, the drawings are lively." NY Times Book Rev

Hutchins, Pat, 1942-

1 hunter. Greenwillow Bks. 1982 unp il $12.95; lib bdg $12.88 E

1. Counting 2. Animals—Fiction
ISBN 0-688-00614-0; 0-688-00615-9 (lib bdg) LC 81-6352

This is "a 1 to 10 and back again counting book. . . . Here, a Mr. Magoo-type hunter blunders through the jungle entirely missing the camouflaged elephants (2), giraffes (3), ostriches (4), etc. . . . The animals pop out of hiding in perfect order to be counted only after the hunter's myopic passage, then turn the tables, ganging up in 10-to-1 order to chase him out of the jungle." SLJ

"The hunter marching obliviously and insouciantly through a forest of giraffe legs will undoubtedly bring forth giggles; the endpapers are especially delightful, like a puzzle with all the animals hidden in the bush. Humorous illustrations done in a flat, clear style make an outstanding counting book." Horn Book

Hutchins, Pat, 1942-—*Continued*

Changes, changes. Macmillan 1971 unp il o.p. paperback available $4.95 E

1. Toys—Fiction 2. Dolls—Fiction 3. Stories without words

ISBN 0-689-71137-9 (pa) LC 70-123133

This word-less book shows how two wooden dolls rearrange a child's building blocks to form various objects

"Another book for the very young child who delights in 'reading' by himself, the lack of text amply compensated for by the bright, bold pictures and the imaginative use of blocks and two stiff little dolls." Bull Cent Child Books

Don't forget the bacon! Greenwillow Bks. 1976 unp il $13.95; lib bdg $13.88; pa $4.95 E

ISBN 0-688-80019-X; 0-688-84019-1 (lib bdg); 0-688-08743-4 (pa) LC 75-17935

"Surely anyone could remember four items on a grocery list! A play on words, however, leads the shopper into interesting predicaments. Children gleefully follow the strange replacements that result. A great book for developing visual literacy and word play." Read Teach

The doorbell rang. Greenwillow Bks. 1986 unp il $13.95; lib bdg $13.88 E

ISBN 0-688-05251-7; 0-688-05252-5 (lib bdg) LC 85-12615

"Victoria and Sam are delighted when Ma bakes a tray of a dozen cookies, even though Ma insists that her cookies aren't as good as Grandma's. They count them and find that each can have six. But the doorbell rings, friends arrive and the cookies must be re-divided. This happens again and again, and the number of cookies on each plate decreases as the visitors' pile of gear in the corner of the kitchen grows larger." SLJ

"Bright, joyous, dynamic, this wonderfully humorous piece of realism for the young is presented simply but with style and imagination. It should become a staple for story hours." Horn Book

Good-night, Owl! Macmillan 1972 unp il $12.95 E

1. Owls—Fiction

ISBN 0-02-745900-4 LC 72-186355

Owl takes revenge on the birds and the animals who have not let him sleep during the day

"The ending is perky, the pictures funny, and the simplicity and repetition of pattern in the text are encouraging for the pre-reader." Bull Cent Child Books

Happy birthday, Sam. Greenwillow Bks. 1978 unp il lib bdg $11.88; Puffin Bks. pa $3.50 E

1. Birthdays—Fiction

ISBN 0-688-84160-0 (lib bdg); 0-14-050339-0 (pa) LC 78-1295

Sam "wakes to find that being a year older hasn't changed the fact that he can't reach a light switch, or the clothes in his closet, or the tap above the sink where he'd like to play with the boat he's received as a present from his parents. Then Grandpa's present arrives; it's a small sturdy chair, and it enables Sam to reach everything." Bull Cent Child Books

"Sunny yellow and bright green predominate in this cheerfully stylized, full-color picture book." Booklist

Rosie's walk. Macmillan 1968 unp il $13.95; pa $3.95 E

1. Chickens—Fiction 2. Foxes—Fiction

ISBN 0-02-745850-4; 0-02-043750-1 (pa) LC 68-12090

"In this diverting picture book only 33 words are used to guide the way through the double-spread stylized pictures aglow with sunshiny colors, and even those few words are not actually needed. Rosie the hen goes for a walk around the farm and gets home in time for dinner, completely unaware that a fox has been hot on her heels every step of the way. The viewer knows, however, and is not only held in suspense but tickled by the ways in which the fox is foiled at every turn by the unwitting hen. A perfect choice for the youngest." Booklist

The tale of Thomas Mead. Greenwillow Bks. 1980 31p il $12.95; lib bdg $12.88; pa $2.95 E

1. Reading—Fiction 2. Stories in rhyme

ISBN 0-688-80282-6; 0-688-84282-8 (lib bdg); 0-688-08422-2 (pa) LC 79-6398

"A Greenwillow read-alone book"

"Thomas, who adamantly refuses to learn to read, has a series of disasters that culminate in his causing a multi-vehicle pile-up. (He couldn't read the 'Don't Cross' sign). Jailed for jaywalking, Thomas receives a parental edict: he stays there until he learns to read. He's taught by two hulking cellmates, and learns rather easily; now he reads all the time. But his answer, when told to put his book away, is the same one he had given when he was coaxed to learn to read: 'Why should I?'" Bull Cent Child Books

The author's "strong, clear and lively illustrations take up the greater part of the space and the couplets of verse, one or two per page, are satisfyingly repetitious . . . and run smoothly. . . . This is a book which will be most enjoyed by those who can read it for themselves." Times Lit Suppl

Titch. Macmillan 1971 unp il $12.95 E

1. Brothers and sisters—Fiction

ISBN 0-02-745880-6 LC 77-146622

"How does it feel to be the youngest child in the family? To have an older brother and sister who lead a more exciting life? . . . [The author] has, with a minimum of well-chosen words and bright, engaging illustrations, triumphantly related the story of a small boy who surpasses his brother and sister with one simple action." Publ Wkly

Another available title about Titch is: You'll soon grow into them, Titch, entered below

What game shall we play? Greenwillow Bks. 1990 unp il $12.95; lib bdg $12.88 E

1. Animals—Fiction

ISBN 0-688-09196-2; 0-688-09197-0 (lib bdg) LC 89-34621

Companion volume to: Surprise Party (1969)

"Frog and Duck want to play but can't think of a game, so they search for Fox to ask for help, and so it goes until the animals seek Owl's advice. In their

Hutchins, Pat, 1942—*Continued*

childlike naivete, they don't realize that Owl has been watching them the whole time, and when he suggests a game of 'Hide and Seek,' they enthusiastically agree." SLJ

"Stylized decorative details are incorporated into the animal characters of Hutchins' ink and watercolor pictures. . . . The story line is simple, and young children will enjoy the accumulation of animals, the fact that they have been seeking hidden friends all along, and the fact that they all can easily be seen by Owl from his high perch and by readers from theirs." Bull Cent Child Books

Where's the baby? Greenwillow Bks. 1988 unp il $11.95; lib bdg $11.88 E

1. Monsters—Fiction 2. Infants—Fiction 3. Cleanliness—Fiction

ISBN 0-688-05933-3; 0-688-05934-1 (lib bdg) LC 86-33566

Sequel to: The very worst monster (1985)

When Grandma, Ma, and Hazel Monster want to find Baby Monster, they follow the messy trail he has left

"Delightful. . . . Each brightly decked illustration is cluttered with everyday objects for the young reader to identify and the text is a loping doggerel entirely in keeping with the rough-and-ready storyline." Times Lit Suppl

The wind blew. Macmillan 1974 unp il $13.95; Puffin Bks. pa $3.95 E

1. Winds—Fiction 2. Stories in rhyme

ISBN 0-02-745910-1; 0-14-050236-X (pa) LC 73-11691

"Full-color paintings illustrate a rhymed cumulative text depicting the frantic efforts of unwary pedestrians to recover possessions snatched away by a mischievous and unpredictable wind. . . . Although the brief text is a pleasant, rhythmic accompaniment to the pictures, the story can be 'read' from the doublespread illustrations. A humorous and imaginative treatment of a familiar situation." Horn Book

You'll soon grow into them, Titch. Greenwillow Bks. 1983 unp il $12.95; lib bdg $12.88; Penguin Bks. pa $3.95 E

1. Brothers and sisters—Fiction 2. Clothing and dress—Fiction

ISBN 0-688-01770-3; 0-688-01771-1 (lib bdg); 0-14-050434-6 (pa) LC 82-11755

"Tired of his older siblings' hand-me-downs, young Titch acquires a set of spanking-new duds just in time to turn his own worn-out clothes into hand-me-downs for the new baby that Mother and Father bring home from the hospital." SLJ

"The paintings of the family and their home are clean in line and color, minimally humourous and a shade cartoonish in drawing. The story is slight but gives a sense of the continuum of change and growth in a family; the writing is direct, with most of the brief text carried by dialogue." Bull Cent Child Books

Inkpen, Mick

The blue balloon. Little, Brown 1990 c1989 unp il lib bdg $12.95 E

1. Balloons—Fiction

ISBN 0-316-41886-2 LC 89-84524

First published 1989 in the United Kingdom

"A little boy's dog retrieves a deflated blue ballon—with magical properties—after the boy's birthday party. The delightful book expands and unfolds to demonstrate just what the balloon can do." Horn Book Guide

"Inkpen has created an imaginative, beautifully produced book." Publ Wkly

Isadora, Rachel

Babies. Greenwillow Bks. 1989 unp il $12.95; lib bdg $12.88 E

1. Infants—Fiction

ISBN 0-688-08031-6; 0-688-08032-4 (lib bdg) LC 88-18782

Babies enjoy the activities of the day, from eating and dressing up to bathing, drying, and sleeping

"The illustrations, in watercolors and colored pencil, are fresh, attractive, and energetic. They are filled with familiar, endearing details that children will recognize. [The book has] a good balance of gender and ethnic mixes, and the variety of activities depicted does justice to children's capabilities." SLJ

Ben's trumpet. Greenwillow Bks. 1979 unp il $13 E

1. Musicians—Fiction 2. Blacks—Fiction

ISBN 0-688-80194-3 LC 78-12885

A Caldecott Medal honor book, 1980

This is the story of Ben, a boy whose dream is to be a jazz trumpeter but who is too poor to own an instrument until a real musician, remembering his own dreams, puts one into the boy's hands

"The art is astonishingly varied in its brilliant recreation—in the margins, in the urban backgrounds—of the commercial art of the 20's and 30's." N Y Times Book Rev

City seen from A to Z. Greenwillow Bks. 1983 unp il lib bdg $11.88 E

1. City life—Fiction 2. Alphabet

ISBN 0-688-01803-3 LC 82-11966

Twenty-six black-and-white drawings of scenes of city life suggest words beginning with each letter of the alphabet

"The activities or objects or concepts in this urban alphabet book . . . reflect the multiethnic composition of a city, and they seldom include words that are not easily comprehensible. The first letter of each word (sometimes two words, like 'Roller skate') is in brown, the rest of the word in black, adequately distinguished from, but blending with the soft, soft illustrations that are highly textured, often stippled, dramatic in composition." Bull Cent Child Books

Friends. Greenwillow Bks. 1990 unp il $12.95; lib bdg $12.88 E

1. Friendship—Fiction

ISBN 0-688-08264-5; 0-688-08265-3 (lib bdg) LC 89-11753

Isadora, Rachel—*Continued*

Labeled pictures portray children visiting, building, drawing, laughing, hugging, and engaging in similar friendly pursuits

"The sturdy little bodies totally focused on each activity show all the energetic delight of two-year-olds. . . . [The illustrations are] exuberant and appealing. Both youngsters and parents will like these children and feel closer and happier after sharing their activities." Horn Book

Max; story & pictures by Rachel Isadora. Macmillan 1976 unp il $12.95; pa $3.95 E

1. Baseball—Fiction 2. Ballet—Fiction
ISBN 0-02-747450-X; 0-02-043800-1 (pa) LC 76-9088

Max "is the star of his baseball team. On a Saturday morning, he has time to spare before his game and accepts (with some hidden disdain) the invitation of his sister, Lisa, to watch her ballet class in action. Max is surprised to find himself interested and happy to join the students at teacher's suggestion. . . . The experience pays off at the ball park where Max hits a home run. Now he warms up for the game each week at Lisa's dancing class. The pictures are an ebullient combination of grace and comedy, with the leggy students dipping and soaring, in contrast to Max in his uniform." Publ Wkly

Ivimey, John W. (John William), b. 1868

The complete story of the three blind mice; illustrated by Paul Galdone. Clarion Bks. 1987 unp il lib bdg $13.95; Houghton Mifflin pa $4.95 E

1. Mice—Fiction 2. Stories in rhyme
ISBN 0-89919-481-8 (lib bdg); 0-395-51585-8 (pa) LC 87-689

First published 1909 in the United Kingdom with title: Complete version of ye three blind mice

"Galdone found this story—Ivimey's tale of the three blind mice—in a collection of antique British children's stories and knew he wanted to reillustrate it. . . . The sprightly text is written in the same rhyme as the song (which is given with the music on the dust jacket), making this a perfect read-aloud for story hours. Galdone's familiar, jaunty artwork is done in rich colors and catches all the humorous nuances of a tale that will appeal greatly to young children." Booklist

Iwamatsu, Atushi Jun, 1908-

Crow Boy; [by] Taro Yashima. Viking 1955 37p il lib bdg $13.95; Puffin Bks. pa $3.95 E

1. School stories 2. Japan—Fiction
ISBN 0-670-24931-9 (lib bdg); 0-14-050172-X (pa) LC 55-13626

A Caldecott Medal honor book, 1956

"A young boy from the mountain area of Japan goes to school in a nearby village, where he is taunted by his classmates and feels rejected and isolated. Finally an understanding teacher helps the boy gain acceptance. The other students recognize how wrong they have been and nickname him 'Crow Boy' because he can imitate the crow's calls with such perfection." Adventuring with Books. 2d edition

"A moving story interpreted by the author's distinctive illustrations, valuable for human relations and for its picture of Japanese school life." Hodges. Books for Elem Sch Libr

Umbrella; [by] Taro Yashima. Viking 1958 30p il lib bdg $13.95; Puffin Bks. pa $3.95 E

1. Umbrellas and parasols—Fiction
ISBN 0-670-73858-1 (lib bdg); 0-14-050240-8 (pa) LC 58-14714

A Caldecott Medal honor book, 1959

"Momo, given an umbrella and a pair of red boots on her third birthday, is overjoyed when at last it rains and she can wear her new rain togs." Hodges. Books for Elem Sch Libr

In this simple tale, young children "will be carried along by their identification with the actions of this very real little girl. . . . The beauty of the book makes this worthwhile." Horn Book

Another available title about Momo is entered below

Iwamatsu, Tomoe, 1908-

Momo's kitten; by Mitsu and Taro Yashima. Viking 1961 unp il o.p.; Puffin Bks. paperback available $3.95 E

1. Cats—Fiction
ISBN 0-14-050200-9 (pa) LC 76-54746

"Momo finds a miserable stray kitten, brings it home and cares for it; the cat has a litter of five and Momo is sad that the kittens must be given away; she makes a birth certificate for each departing kitten and is solaced by the fact that her cat is expecting again. Supplemented by the illustrations, the facts of life are presented with candor and the story gives a very nice example of tender loving care of pets." Bull Cent Child Books

James, Betsy

Natalie underneath. Dutton Children's Bks. 1990 unp il $12.95 E

1. Brothers and sisters—Fiction 2. Fathers—Fiction
ISBN 0-525-44591-9 LC 89-23534

Natalie and her brother Thomas enjoy being underneath various things as they play enthusiastically with their patient father

"Natalie and baby brother Thomas joyfully adopt all the funny faces and positions of childhood as they romp with Dad from breakfast to bedtime, where, typically, Dad is asleep while Natalie stays awake. James's bright crayon colors are the perfect medium for this small, intimate book." Publ Wkly

Another available title about Natalie and Thomas is: What's that room for? (1988)

Jeffers, Susan

Wild Robin; retold and illustrated by Susan Jeffers. Dutton 1976 unp il $12.95; pa $3.95 E

1. Tamlane 2. Fairy tales
ISBN 0-525-42787-2; 0-525-44244-8 (pa) LC 76-21343

Jeffers, Susan—*Continued*

"The artist has retold a story from 'Little Prudy's Fairy Book' by Sophie May [pseudonym of Rebecca Sophia Clarke], a story which was loosely based on the well-known folk tale 'Tamlane.' A sly, disobedient boy ran away from home when even his loving sister Janet lost patience with his wild ways. He was captured by the fairies and, although he led a carefree life, he became lonely and homesick. Finally, from an elf whose 'little stone heart was touched,' Janet learned the spell which would free him, and she bravely rescued him." Horn Book

"The text is short. The story is stated and not over-explained. The illustrations are big, graphically rendered, beautifully colored double-page spreads that catch, hold, and bring the eyes back to discover small details and to re-examine and interpret facial expressions." SLJ

Jennings, Linda M.

The Christmas Tomten; by Viktor Rydberg; illustrated by Harald Wiberg. Coward, McCann & Geoghegan 1981 unp il $9.95 **E**

1. Fairy tales 2. Christmas—Fiction
ISBN 0-698-20528-6 LC 81-3225

Freely adapted by Linda M. Jennings from a translation from the Swedish by Lone Thygesen Blecher and George Blecher

"A classic Swedish Christmas story of good and evil. The Tomten, a good troll, takes Vigg on his Christmas rounds while Mother Gertrude searches for gifts for her adopted son." Child Book Rev Serv

"The wide, full-color illustrations evoke a magical mood that is reflected several different ways: in the star-bright, snow-laden landscapes, in the old-fashioned, cozy house interiors, and in the visit to the elaborate Hall of the Mountain King. A good read-aloud choice for the holiday season." Booklist

Other available titles about the Tomten are: The Tomten, and The Tomten and the fox, entered under the adapter: Astrid Lindgren

Jensen, Virginia Allen

Catching; a book for blind and sighted children with pictures to feel as well as to see. Philomel Bks. 1983 23p il $12.95 **E**

1. Blind—Books and reading 2. Size and shape—Fiction
ISBN 0-399-20997-2 LC 83-13152

Tired of being It when they play tag, Little Rough thinks of a plan to fool Little Shaggy. Includes raised, textured pictures in simple, geometric shapes that can be both felt and seen

"The story line is far from exciting even for the littlest child, but the assortment of textures, shapes, and sizes, all of which can be touched, offers challenge and interest to visually impaired children. With a little help, sensitive fingers should easily comprehend the dots and stripes, the small and large circles, the straight and zigzag lines. The paging is printed in braille, but the story itself must be read by a sighted companion." Horn Book

Jernigan, Gisela, 1948-

Agave blooms just once; illustrated by E. Wesley Jernigan. Harbinger House 1989 unp il $12.95; pa $7.95 **E**

1. Alphabet
ISBN 0-943173-46-9; 0-943173-44-2 (pa) LC 89-35428

Illustrated verses present plants and animals of the desert from A to Z

"The pages' stark white backgrounds and boldly defined, almost tropically colored paintings reinforce the sparkling Southwestern flavor. A glossary provides further information on each definition. The Jernigans have provided young readers and teachers with a striking and unusual addition to the ever-increasing roster of alphabet books." Publ Wkly

Johnson, Angela

Do like Kyla; paintings by James E. Ransome. Orchard Bks. 1990 unp il $14.95; lib bdg $14.99 **E**

1. Sisters—Fiction 2. Blacks—Fiction
ISBN 0-531-05852-2; 0-531-08452-3 (lib bdg) LC 89-16229

"A Richard Jackson book"

A little girl imitates her big sister Kyla all day, until in the evening Kyla imitates her

"Ransome's solid oil paintings feature two lively black girls firmly placed in a loving home, with both father and mother, and a neighborhood that pulses with realism. The dustjacket, showing an exhilarated Kyla and her sister making snow angels, is indicative of the rest of the art, which features uncommon perspectives and bold shapings that capture the unbridled motion of childhood. Sweet in the best sense of the word." Booklist

Tell me a story, Mama; pictures by David Soman. Orchard Bks. 1989 unp il $13.95; lib bdg $13.99 **E**

1. Mothers and daughters—Fiction 2. Blacks—Fiction
ISBN 0-531-05794-1; 0-531-08394-2 (lib bdg) LC 88-17917

A young girl and her mother remember together all the girl's favorite stories about her mother's childhood

"Soman's vivid, lively watercolors capture the essence of the mood and message as they deftly portray the quotidian portraits of two generations of a black family. Both language and art are full of subtle wit and rich emotion, resulting in a beautifully realized evocation of treasured childhood and family moments." SLJ

Johnson, Crockett, 1906-1975

Harold and the purple crayon. Harper & Row 1955 unp il $11.95; lib bdg $11.89; pa $2.95 **E**

ISBN 0-06-022935-7; 0-06-022936-5 (lib bdg); 0-06-443022-7 (pa) LC 55-7683

"As Harold goes for a moonlight walk, he uses his purple crayon to draw a path and the things he sees along the way, then draws himself back home." Hodges. Books for Elem Sch Libr

Other available titles about Harold are:
Harold's ABC (1963)
Harold's circus (1959)

Johnson, Crockett, 1906-1975—*Continued*
Harold's trip to the sky (1957)
A picture for Harold's room (1960)

Johnston, Tony

The quilt story; pictures by Tomie dePaola. Putnam 1985 unp il $13.95; pa $5.95 **E**

1. Quilts—Fiction 2. Mothers and daughters—Fiction
ISBN 0-399-21009-1; 0-399-21008-3 (pa) LC 84-18212

A pioneer mother lovingly stitches a beautiful quilt which warms and comforts her daughter Abigail; many years later another mother mends and patches it for her little girl

"DePaola's full-color tempera illustrations add much to the story—the folk-art style matches the text perfectly and will grab the attention of young 'book browsers.' Except for the transition problem [from pioneer times to the present], the text enhances the wonderful pictures—sentences are tightly written and evoke a feeling of calm, warmth and stability which the quilt provides to the two children." SLJ

The vanishing pumpkin; pictures by Tomie dePaola. Putnam 1983 unp il $13.95; pa $4.95 **E**

1. Halloween—Fiction 2. Witches—Fiction
ISBN 0-399-20991-3; 0-399-20992-1 (pa) LC 83-3122

"A 700-year-old woman and an 800-year-old man feel in the mood for some pumpkin pie on Halloween night, but they can't find their pumpkin. Fearing it's been 'snitched,' the two set off to find it." Booklist

"A not-very-scary—but very funny—Halloween story which the youngest trick-or-treaters will enjoy. . . . The illustrations are large and colorful, done in unusual but pleasing shades of green, orange and blue and clearly outlined in black ink." SLJ

The witch's hat; pictures by Margot Tomes. Putnam 1984 unp il $9.95 **E**

1. Witches—Fiction 2. Hats—Fiction
ISBN 0-399-21010-5 LC 84-9948

"The story begins when the witch is stirring her brew and her hat falls in. She tries to fish it out, but her pot is a magic pot, and it has a few tricks of its own." Child Book Rev Serv

"Tomes uses touches of clean pinks and blues to contrast effectively with earthtones in illustrations that are restrainedly comic." Bull Cent Child Books

Yonder; pictures by Lloyd Bloom. Dial Bks. for Young Readers 1988 unp il $12.95; lib bdg $12.89; pa $4.95 **E**

1. Seasons—Fiction 2. Country life—Fiction 3. Family life—Fiction
ISBN 0-8037-0277-9; 0-8037-0278-7 (lib bdg); 0-8037-09870-0 (pa) LC 86-11549

"A young farmer brings a new wife home. The couple plant a tree and say a prayer, then set about being fruitful and multiplying. To commemorate each birth, a new 'tree of life' is planted, and over the years an entire orchard takes root in the fertile soil. The old farmer, by now a grandpa many times over, dies, and it turns out that family deaths are commemorated the same way as births—twin ceremonies based on the author's own family tradition." N Y Times Book Rev

"Lloyd Bloom's lush palette of verdant green and earth tones wakens all the senses. . . . Together, art and text convey an archetypical image of rural American life in an earlier, simpler time." Horn Book

Jonas, Ann

Color dance. Greenwillow Bks. 1989 unp il $13.95; lib bdg $13.88 **E**

1. Color
ISBN 0-688-05990-2; 0-688-05991-0 (lib bdg) LC 88-5446

Three dancers show how colors combine to create different colors

"The clean, spare design of the white background and horizontal spreads makes the contrasting hues all the more striking. An effective picture book for children ready to move beyond mere color labeling." Booklist

Holes and peeks. Greenwillow Bks. 1984 unp il $13.95; lib bdg $13.88 **E**

1. Size and shape—Fiction
ISBN 0-688-02537-4; 0-688-02538-2 (lib bdg) LC 83-14128

"A sparkling, white-tiled bathroom decorated with touches of warm color provides the setting for a preschooler's view of scary holes and welcome peeks in this reassuring story of fears, pleasures and objects common to very young children." SLJ

"The crisp lines of black-and-white tile floor and the horizontally tiled white walls form a patterned expanse against which are set people and objects colored in smooth pastels and bright primary colors. Since the artist utilizes simplified shapes, the effect is not one of confusion but of instant visual appeal." Horn Book

Now we can go. Greenwillow Bks. 1986 unp il $11.75; lib bdg $11.88 **E**

1. Toys—Fiction
ISBN 0-688-04802-1; 0-688-04803-X (lib bdg) LC 85-12614

"The small narrator can't leave the house until he has transferred all his treasures—ball, skates, teddy, book, truck, doll—from their special box to his travel bag." N Y Times Book Rev

"A fine black line, used in conjunction with colored dyes, defines each object with precision and clarity. The colors are bright without being garish; the perspective such that the relative position of each toy in the box or bag is easily discernible. This approach adds still another dimension—predicting which object will be selected next." Horn Book

The quilt. Greenwillow Bks. 1984 unp il $13.95; lib bdg $13.88 **E**

1. Quilts—Fiction
ISBN 0-688-03825-5; 0-688-03826-3 (lib bdg) LC 83-25385

"A little girl is given a new patchwork quilt, and at bedtime she amuses herself by identifying the materials used in its making. Later, she has a colorful dream in which she almost loses her stuffed dog, Sally (a piece of Sally is in the quilt, too)." Child Book Rev Serv

"The intricate illustrations in Jonas's book can be described only in superlatives. Backed by a length of golden-yellow calico imprinted with small red flowers, a quilt fashioned from squares in a variety of colors is

Jonas, Ann—*Continued*
the prize shown to readers by a dear little girl." Publ Wkly

Reflections. Greenwillow Bks. 1987 unp il $13.95; lib bdg $13.88 **E**

1. Seashore—Fiction
ISBN 0-688-06140-0; 0-688-06141-9 (lib bdg) LC 86-33545

"Imaginative book about a day at the seashore. At what is the end in most books, this book is reversed and read from back to front with re-interpreted artwork and new captions. Clever idea executed with skill, flare, and appealing, full-color illustrations. Excellent for encouraging observation and making predictions." Sci Child

Round trip. Greenwillow Bks. 1983 unp il $13.95; lib bdg $13.88; pa $3.95 **E**

1. Cities and towns—Fiction
ISBN 0-688-01772-X; 0-688-01781-9 (lib bdg); 0-688-09986-6 (pa) LC 82-12026

Black and white illustrations and text record the sights on a day trip to the city and back home again to the country. The trip to the city is read from front to back and the return trip, from back to front, upside down

"Although one or two pictures too easily suggest their upside-down images and the device is occasionally strained, the author-artist displays a fine sense of graphic design and balance, and pictorial beauty is never sacrificed for mere cleverness." Horn Book

The trek. Greenwillow Bks. 1985 unp il $13.95; lib bdg $13.88; pa $3.95 **E**

ISBN 0-688-04799-8; 0-688-04800-5 (lib bdg); 0-688-08742-6 (pa) LC 84-25962

The author-illustrator presents the story of a young girl's daydream on her way to school. Familiar objects are transformed by her imagination as the walk turns into a jungle journey where exotic animals lie in wait

"It's up to the reader to find and identify all the animals [the girl] sees lurking on a lawn, along a fence, in a grove of trees, or popping out of a fruit stand. The last two pages picture and identify all the creatures camouflaged in the illustrations, and many a viewer will be forced to flip back for further investigation of a hiding place." Bull Cent Child Books

Two bear cubs. Greenwillow Bks. 1982 unp il lib bdg $11.88 **E**

1. Bears—Fiction
ISBN 0-688-01408-9 LC 82-2860

"Two bear cubs, bent on exploration, stray from their mother in pursuit of adventure (a skunk) and wind up lost. They try their luck getting honey from a bee tree and fish from a stream, and the text repeats, 'Where is their mother?' Mother, meanwhile, appears in the background of each illustration, keeping a watchful eye on the proceedings and revealing herself in the end for a joyful reunion." SLJ

"The illustrations in Jonas's story demonstrate her unerring sense of how to use boldly contrasting colors and uncluttered shapes for maximum effect. Tots will love following two baby bears through an exciting time while parents read the simple text, the few words necessary to explain what the pictures, by themselves, tell." Publ Wkly

When you were a baby. Greenwillow Bks. 1982 unp il $13.95; lib bdg $13.88; Puffin Bks. pa $3.95 **E**

1. Infants
ISBN 0-688-00863-1; 0-688-00864-X (lib bdg); 0-14-050574-1 (pa) LC 81-12800

This book shows, "at the beginning, a baby's plump, brown feet waving in the air above its crib (and looking a bit out of scale) and, at the end, two sturdy legs in socks and shoes planted firmly, independently on the floor. In between, there's a list of all the things you couldn't do when you were a baby: build blocks, make sand molds, eat with a spoon, sail boats in a bathtub, etc. 'But now you can!' the text ends." Bull Cent Child Books

"What a nice simple book, with large primary pictures, to remind a child what it was like to be a baby. Parents may want to use this book to remind children what a new sibling may be like, or to show children how much they have grown." Child Book Rev Serv

Joosse, Barbara M., 1949-

Jam day; pictures by Emily Arnold McCully. Harper & Row 1987 28p il $12.95; lib bdg $12.89 **E**

1. Cookery—Fiction 2. Family life—Fiction
ISBN 0-06-023096-7; 0-06-023097-5 (lib bdg) LC 86-46117

"Ben often wishes that he were part of a large, noisy family instead of a quiet twosome with his mother. When they step off the train for a visit with his grandparents, however, he discovers that he is part of an extended family with plenty of noisy cousins and bustling activities that include berry picking, jam making, and biscuit baking. Only-children without the same advantages may feel jealous! The pen and watercolor illustrations are literal and comfortable, fresh in color if not in concept." Bull Cent Child Books

Jorgensen, Gail

Crocodile beat; written by Gail Jorgensen; illustrated by Patricia Mullins. Bradbury Press 1989 unp il $13.95 **E**

1. Crocodiles—Fiction 2. Lions—Fiction 3. Stories in rhyme
ISBN 0-02-748010-0 LC 89-578

"King Lion leads the animals in a playful jungle romp, but, unbeknownst to them, 'Down by the river in the heat of the day/the crocodile sleeps and awaits his prey.' By forcing the croc to bite his throne, Lion protects all the animals from the reptile's attack. The brief story comes to life in jaunty rhyme, with a variety of animal sounds interspersed. The exceptionally appealing collage illustrations fashioned from tissue paper set the book apart from other similar stories." Horn Book

Joyce, William

A day with Wilbur Robinson. Harper & Row 1990 unp il $13.95; lib bdg $13.89 **E**

ISBN 0-06-022967-5; 0-06-022968-3 (lib bdg) LC 90-4066

Joyce, William—*Continued*

"A young narrator, going to see his best friend Wilbur, remarks, 'His house is the greatest place to visit.' Readers soon see why. Wilbur's large household includes an aunt whose train set is life-sized, an uncle who shares his 'deep thoughts' ('Mississippi spelled with o's. . . would be Mossossoppo!') and a grandfather who trains a dancing frog band. There's not much in the way of formal plot here—save a slight mystery involving Grandfather's missing false teeth—but Joyce's wonderfully strange paintings abound with hilarious, surprising details and leave the impression that a lot has happened." Publ Wkly

Dinosaur Bob and his adventures with the family Lazardo. Harper & Row 1988 unp il $12.95; lib bdg $12.89 **E**

1. Dinosaurs—Fiction
ISBN 0-06-023047-9; 0-06-023048-7 (lib bdg)
LC 87-30796

"The Lazardo family goes on safari to Africa where they find a dinosaur. They name him Bob and take him back to Pimlico Hills. . . . Bob soon becomes famous because he can play the trumpet, dance, and most importantly play baseball." Child Book Rev Serv

"Mr. Joyce has managed the illustrations with considerable panache. His artwork makes it clear why Bob is such a hit with the Lazardos. Whether turning himself into a boat to sail the family down the Nile, riding atop a train to Pimlico Hills or patrolling the outfield for the hometown Pirates, Bob is the most adorable of dinos." N Y Times Book Rev

George shrinks; story and pictures by William Joyce. Harper & Row 1985 unp il $12.95; lib bdg $12.89 **E**

1. Size and shape—Fiction 2. Fantastic fiction
ISBN 0-06-023070-3; 0-06-023071-1 (lib bdg)
LC 83-47697

"A young boy named George awakes from his nap to discover he has become as small as a mouse. . . . Resting against the alarm clock is a piece of poster-size paper on which parental instructions are written telling George all that he should do after getting up. . . . Most of the book's text consists of this note's contents." N Y Times Book Rev

"The colorful illustrations, executed with painstaking attention to detail, create a surreal landscape from an ordinary breakfast-cereal world, as familiar objects become monumental structures through which the diminutive George moves with panache." Horn Book

Jukes, Mavis

Lights around the palm; paintings by Stacey Schuett. Knopf 1987 unp il $12.95; lib bdg $13.99 **E**

1. Brothers and sisters—Fiction 2. Christmas—Fiction 3. Animals—Fiction
ISBN 0-394-88399-3; 0-394-98399-8 (lib bdg)
LC 86-172

"The underlying theme that 'you can believe in a lot of things if you want to' is apparent as Emma, a seven year old who lives on a farm, tries to convince her family that she can teach the farm animals to speak and read English. The story is presented through the use of dialogue between Emma, her family, and the animals. . . . Schuett's full-page color paintings capture the atmosphere of farm life. The use of blue as the predominant color and the slight iridescence that surround Emma and the animals enhance the magical element in the story." SLJ

Kalan, Robert

Blue sea; illustrated by Donald Crews. Greenwillow Bks. 1979 unp il $12.95; lib bdg $12.89 **E**

1. Size and shape—Fiction 2. Fishes—Fiction
ISBN 0-688-80184-6; 0-688-84184-8 (lib bdg)
LC 78-18396

Several fishes of varying size introduce space relationships and size differences

"On a deep-blue background, the words 'blue sea' appear in a paler shade and then the first of Crews's eye-filling paintings, 'little fish,' in bright yellow. While Kalan keeps his text to an irreducible minimum, the pictures increase in color and complexity." Publ Wkly

Jump, frog, jump! pictures by Byron Barton. Greenwillow Bks. 1981 unp il o.p. paperback available $3.95 **E**

1. Frogs—Fiction 2. Stories in rhyme
ISBN 0-688-09241-1 (pa) LC 81-1401

"For the frog, life in the swampy pond was hazardous in the extreme. Everyone, it seemed was out to get him—first a fish; then a snake, a turtle, a net, and finally some boys. The resourceful frog, however, had one big advantage—he was a champion jumper." Horn Book

"The excitement generated by the tale is matched by the humor in Barton's pictures. They resemble naive art but demonstrate superior skill in vibrant juxtaposition of colors and in the masterful composition that intensifies the story's momentum." SLJ

Kalman, Maira

Sayonora, Mrs. Kackleman. Viking Kestrel 1989 unp il $14.95 **E**

1. Japan—Fiction
ISBN 0-670-82945-5 LC 89-9029

"After seeing a performance of The Mikado, Alexander wants to go to Japan, and big sister Lulu, anticipating a piano lesson with the 'dreaded Mrs. Kackleman,' figures this is a good time to get out of town. So off they go . . . on a whirlwind tour, visiting a Japanese school and hotel, taking the bullet train, and experiencing a Zen garden." Bull Cent Child Books

"The story is written in a style that typifies children's dialogue. . . . The illustrations are appealing in their childlike sensitivity to unusual details and perspective. The dialogue is enhanced by the temprapaint illustrations that are typical of grade-school children. The book is an excellent choice for armchair-traveling independent readers. . . . Informative, funny, and lively." Libr J

Kandoian, Ellen

Is anybody up? written and illustrated by Ellen Kandoian. Putnam 1989 unp il $14.95 **E**

ISBN 0-399-21749-5 LC 88-38098

Kandoian, Ellen—*Continued*

"The early morning activities of a young girl on the East Coast of North America and brief descriptions of breakfast for a variety of people and animals that populate the same time zone from Baffin Bay to Antarctica provide an effective introduction to time zones and cultural comparisons." Soc Educ

"The pen-and-wash illustrations are spare and simple, radiant with morning light." Bull Cent Child Books

Kasza, Keiko

When the elephant walks. Putnam 1990 unp il $13.95 **E**

1. Animals—Fiction

ISBN 0-399-21755-X LC 88-26748

When the Elephant walks he scares the Bear who runs away and scares the Crocodile who runs away and scares the Wild Hog in this never-ending animal story

"The large, softly colored illustrations are correctly sized for group presentations. The anthropomorphism is skillfully handled; these amusing critters are true to animal nature if not always to animal behavior. An unpretentious thoroughly engaging book, executed with charm and élan." Horn Book

The wolf's chicken stew. Putnam 1987 unp il $12.95; pa $4.95 **E**

1. Wolves—Fiction 2. Chickens—Fiction

ISBN 0-399-21400-3; 0-399-22000-9 (pa) LC 86-12303

"An old plot takes a new turn after the wolf, determined to fatten a chicken for his stew, bakes goodies for her every day only to find them consumed by a horde of baby chicks who shame 'Uncle Wolf' with their adoring gratitude." Bull Cent Child Books

"Kasza combines quivery line and shaded color to turn Wolf and Chicken into sceptural forms. Landscape images are treated similarly, and produce an open, expansive feeling when placed asymmetrically. Wolf is comically and suspensefully visualized, making the flim-flamming refrains sound just right for such a charismatic rascal." Wilson Libr Bull

Keats, Ezra Jack, 1916-1983

Apt. 3. Macmillan 1971 unp il hardcover o.p. paperback available $3.95 **E**

1. City life—Fiction 2. Brothers—Fiction 3. Blind—Fiction

ISBN 0-689-71059-3 (pa) LC 78-123135

Set in a dingy tenement house, this book describes "the encounter of two young and lonely boys with a blind musician whose beautiful music helps them learn that communication is possible through ways other than words." Wolfe. About 100 Books

"The subtle colors of Keats's paintings and his restrained use of detail to establish atmosphere make Apt. 3 a pleasure to look at, but it is less of a story than a situation picture book." Saturday Rev

Clementina's cactus. Viking 1982 unp il $11.95 **E**

1. Cactus—Fiction 2. Stories without words

ISBN 0-670-22517-7 LC 82-2630

In this wordless picture book "a small girl is intrigued by a prickly cactus, to her father's amusement; she is delighted when, after a heavy rain, her cactus blossoms brilliantly." Bull Cent Child Books

"Showing both the sun-bleached vastness of a desert country as well as its brilliance, the doublepage spreads tell the story without a text. The sketchy drawings washed in watercolor are a departure from some of Keats's more static collages. Contrasts of close-up and distant focus, of interior and exterior landscapes, and of day and night scenes offer a pleasant variety in a book which reveals its simple tale with wonderment and delight." Horn Book

Jennie's hat. Harper & Row 1985 unp il $14.95; lib bdg $14.89; 0064430723 $4.95 **E**

1. Hats—Fiction

ISBN 0-06-023113-0; 0-06-023114-9 (lib bdg); 0-06-443072-3 (pa) LC 66-15683

"Jennie is counting on a new hat from her aunt—and dreaming of its beauty. A very plain hat comes, and after unsuccessful attempts to make herself a hat, Jennie goes to church in the drab one. In the interval she has fed her friends the birds, and they save the day by flying down and trimmming the hat for her." Saturday Rev

This fantasy "has a sense of freshness, of spring, about it. Attractive, colorful pictures make most telling use of collage." Christ Sci Monit

Louie. Greenwillow Bks. 1983 c1975 unp il lib bdg $14.88 **E**

1. Puppets and puppet plays—Fiction

ISBN 0-688-02383-5 LC 75-6766

First published 1975

A shy, withdrawn boy loses his heart to a puppet

"This story is illustrated with the same glowing colors . . . and with some of the postercollage that is the artist's trademark. The aura is touching without being maudlin, the writing simple and informal. . . . The elements of kindness to others, imaginative play, and a fervent wish granted should have a strong appeal to the picture book audience." Sutherland. The Best in Child Books

Other available titles about Louie are:

Louie's search (1980)

Regards to the man in the moon (1981)

The trip (1978)

The snowy day. Viking 1962 31p il lib bdg $11.95; Penguin Bks. pa $3.95 **E**

1. Snow—Fiction

ISBN 0-670-65400-0 (lib bdg); 0-14-050182-7 (pa) LC 62-15441

Awarded the Caldecott Medal, 1963

A small "boy's ecstatic enjoyment of snow in the city is shown in vibrant pictures. Peter listens to the snow crunch under his feet, makes the first tracks in a clean patch of snow, makes angels and a snowman. At night in his warm bed he thinks over his adventures, and in the morning wakens to the promise of another lovely snowy day." Moorachian. What is a City?

Other available titles about Peter and his friends are:

Goggles (1969)

Hi, cat! (1970)

A letter to Amy (1968)

Pet show! (1972)

Peter's chair (1967)

Whistle for Willie (1964)

Keller, Holly

The best present. Greenwillow Bks. 1989 unp il $11.95; lib bdg $11.88 **E**

1. Grandmothers—Fiction 2. Hospitals—Fiction
ISBN 0-688-07319-0; 0-688-07320-4 (lib bdg)
LC 87-38086

"Unable to slip by hospital guards, Rosie asks the elevator man to deliver flowers to her sick grandmother. Grandma Alice keeps Rosie's secret, declaring that the flowers were 'the best present'." Soc Educ

"The story has a warm, dear feeling that will touch young listeners. The uncluttered artwork, watercolors outlined in pen, captures the story's intrinsic compassion, concern, and, of course, love." Booklist

Geraldine's big snow. Greenwillow Bks. 1988 unp il $11.95; lib bdg $11.88 **E**

1. Snow—Fiction 2. Pigs—Fiction
ISBN 0-688-07513-4; 0-688-07514-2 (lib bdg)
LC 87-14936

"Like most young children, plump pig Geraldine waits with impatient anticipation for the first big snowstorm of the season. While the neighbors go about their preparations, stocking shelves and supplementing leisure reading supplies, Geraldine gazes longingly at the still-dry sky." SLJ

"The story, simple in both word and picture, effectively conveys that genuinely childlike sense of anticipation and joy, unmarred by thoughts of shoveling or commuting. In the bright, cheerful watercolors, Holly Keller has created a small, quiet celebration of winter with her small, unquiet heroine." Horn Book

Geraldine's blanket. Greenwillow Bks. 1984 unp il $11.75; lib bdg $11.88; pa $3.95 **E**

1. Blankets—Fiction
ISBN 0-688-02539-0; 0-688-02540-4 (lib bdg); 0-688-07810-9 (pa) LC 83-14062

"Geraldine's pink blanket was a baby present from Aunt Bessie. It's worn now and patched, and when Aunt Bessie sends her a doll, Geraldine preserves and transfers her affections simultaneously by using the scraps for a doll dress." N Y Times Book Rev

"Simply but wonderfully expressive line drawings washed with pastel colors capture the gentleness and humor of the story. Children will enjoy Keller's portrayal of Geraldine's stubborness and her parent's reaction to it. The text is short and the vocabulary easy, making this satisfying story appropriate both for very young children and beginning readers." SLJ

What Alvin wanted. Greenwillow Bks. 1990 unp il $12.95; lib bdg $12.88 **E**

1. Infants—Fiction 2. Baby sitters—Fiction 3. Brothers and sisters—Fiction
ISBN 0-688-08933-X; 0-688-08934-8 (lib bdg)
LC 88-34917

"Though Sam and baby try endlessly to cheer him up, Alvin doesn't want to go to the playground nor does he want cookies and milk. However, the instant she comes home, Mama realizes why Alvin's upset—she forgot to give him a kiss goodbye." Booklist

"Flat simple paintings on the recto pages face a few lines of text on each florally-bordered verso page. Pleasant and direct, but this is a picture of a situation rather than a story." Bull Cent Child Books

Kellogg, Steven, 1941-

Aster Aardvark's alphabet adventures. Morrow 1987 unp il $13.95; lib bdg $13.88 **E**

1. Alphabet 2. Animals—Fiction
ISBN 0-688-07256-9; 0-688-07257-7 (lib bdg)
LC 87-5715

Alliterative text and pictures present adventures of animals from A to Z

"Glowing with bright, harmonious hues, the lively, if sometimes crowded, watercolor scenes display plots, subplots, and myriad details. . . . Children will delight in this zany celebration of the sound and sense of words and will savor the sight of so many silly situations so clearly out of hand. Here's a good way for teachers to lighten up the daily lesson with a spark of humor both for young listeners and middle-grade students." Booklist

Best friends; story and pictures by Steven Kellogg. Dial Bks. for Young Readers 1986 unp il $13.95; lib bdg $13.89; pa $3.95 **E**

1. Friendship—Fiction
ISBN 0-8037-0099-7; 0-8037-0101-2 (lib bdg); 0-8037-0829-7 (pa) LC 85-15971

Kathy feels lonely and betrayed when her best friend Louise goes away for the summer and has a wonderful time

"The watercolor and ink illustrations are appealingly bright and magical. Kathy and Louise's daydreams are vividly and flamboyantly portrayed, with 'reality' just as attractively pictured. If this title is flawed, it is only because Kellogg attempts too much in his plot. There is too much going on for too long, but the charm of the illustrations is enough to minimize this factor." SLJ

Can I keep him? story and pictures by Steven Kellogg. Dial Bks. for Young Readers 1971 unp il $12.95; lib bdg $12.89; pa $3.95 **E**

1. Pets—Fiction
ISBN 0-8037-0988-9; 0-8037-0989-7 (lib bdg); 0-8037-1305-3 (pa) LC 72-142453

"Lonely Arnold wants a playmate but his mother objects to every one he suggests—grandma is allergic to cat fur, bears have a disagreeable odor, pythons shed their skins which clog the vacuum cleaner, and so on." Booklist

"Finely detailed pictures of Arnold's real and imagined pets and an amusing cummulative storyline." Libr J

Much bigger than Martin; story and pictures by Steven Kellogg. Dial Bks. for Young Readers 1976 unp il $11.95; lib bdg $11.89; pa $3.95 **E**

1. Brothers—Fiction
ISBN 0-8037-5809-X; 0-8037-5810-3 (lib bdg); 0-8037-5811-1 (pa) LC 75-27599

"All the frustrations of being younger and smaller than an older sibling come pouring out in this humorous treatment of a very real problem. Henry doesn't like being Martin's little brother when he's victim in games, gets the smallest piece of cake, or finds the basketball loop too high for his shots. Stretching and watering himself doesn't help, while eating a lot of apples only makes him sick; there seems to be no remedy. . . . The

Kellogg, Steven, 1941-—*Continued*

imagination scenes, where Henry perceives himself as a giant towering over Martin, are where Kellogg's touches of subtle humor and whimsical detail are most effective. The black line drawings are washed in hues of gold, green, and blue." Booklist

The mysterious tadpole. Dial Bks. for Young Readers 1977 unp il $13.95; lib bdg $13.89; pa $3.95 E

1. Pets—Fiction
ISBN 0-8037-6245-3; 0-8037-6246-1 (lib bdg); 0-8037-6244-5 (pa) LC 77-71517

"Lively details in the author's full-color illustrations portray the fantastic growth and lovable behavior of a tadpole sent Louis from Loch Ness, Scotland, for his birthday." LC. Child Books, 1977

The mystery of the missing red mitten; story and pictures by Steven Kellogg. Dial Bks. for Young Readers 1974 unp il $8.95; lib bdg $8.89; pa $3.50 E

ISBN 0-8037-6195-3; 0-8037-6194-5 (lib bdg); 0-8037-5749-2 (pa) LC 73-15439

"Annie loses a red mitten and sets out to search for it with her dog, Oscar. She fantasizes about the mitten's possible fate (e.g., 'Do you think that the mouse and his family are using my mitten for a sleeping bag?') and imagines planting her remaining mitten and reaping a multitude from the resultant mitten tree. Annie's search ends when what appears to be the heart of a snowman is revealed to be the missing mitten." SLJ

"Kellogg's imagination extends from a clever story to captivating black-and-white drawings with accents of red. His use of a bubble to show the little gir's thoughts is perfect. And this is a perfect book for a winter day." Babbling Bookworm

Pinkerton, behave! story and pictures by Steven Kellogg. Dial Bks. for Young Readers 1979 unp il $13.95; lib bdg $13.89; pa $3.95 E

1. Dogs—Fiction
ISBN 0-8037-6573-8; 0-8037-6575-4 (lib bdg); 0-8037-7250-5 (pa) LC 78-31794

"Pinkerton is a large dog modeled after the author-artist's harlequin Great Dane. He appears to be untrainable, both at home and at obedience school. Actually, he responds consistently to commands, but when he is told to fetch, he tears the newspaper to shreds; and when he is told to get the burglar, he licks the face of the dummy he is expected to destroy. One day, when a real burglar appears, Pinkerton's small owner remembers the dog's idiosyncracies, commands him to fetch, and all ends well." SLJ

"Kellogg wittily captures expressions and movements of animal and human, wisely allowing the focal humor to emanate through the faces and action and forgoing the background detail usually found in his work." Booklist

Other available titles about Pinkerton are:
Prehistoric Pinkerton (1987)
A Rose for Pinkerton (1981)
Tallyho, Pinkerton! (1982)

Ralph's secret weapon; story and pictures by Steven Kellogg. Dial Bks. for Young Readers 1983 unp il $13.95; lib bdg $12.89; pa $4.95 E

1. Sea monsters—Fiction
ISBN 0-8037-7086-3; 0-8037-7087-1 (lib bdg); 0-8037-0024-5 (pa) LC 82-22115

"Ralph visits his zany Aunt Georgina who insists that the 4th grader learn to play the bassoon during his stay with her. He wins a snake-charming contest with his new-found musical skill, then aids the Navy in teaching a lesson to a bothersome sea serpent." Child Book Rev Serv

The author/illustrator "begins and closes his story on the endpapers, and includes an extravaganza of detail to pore over. Line work, expanded with lively color, leads the eye, and humor electrically explodes from every picture. In the monster department, this one is a tour de force; and to top it off, Kellogg fashions a most clever conclusion" Booklist

Kesselman, Wendy Ann

Emma; illustrated by Barbara Cooney. Doubleday 1980 unp il o.p.; Harper & Row paperback available $4.95 E

1. Painting—Fiction 2. Old age—Fiction
ISBN 0-06-443077-4 (pa) LC 77-15161

This book is "about a lonely grandmother named Emma, who, after her 72d birthday, began to paint pictures, starting with images of the village where she had lived as a girl. The illustrations capture Emma's personal and artistic style with charm." N Y Times Book Rev

Kessler, Ethel

Stan the hot dog man; by Ethel and Leonard Kessler. Harper & Row 1990 64p il $10.95; $10.89 E

1. Old age—Fiction 2. Snow—Fiction
ISBN 0-06-023279-X; 0-06-023280-3 (lib bdg) LC 89-34474

"An I can read book"

After he retires, Stan becomes a hot dog man and finds that his new job helps him come to the rescue during a big snowstorm

"The simple sentences avoid being choppy, and the characterization of Stan is distinctive, even given the restrictions of beginning-to-read vocabulary. His good spirits are catching." Booklist

Kessler, Leonard P., 1920-

Here comes the strikeout; by Leonard Kessler. Harper & Row 1965 64p il hardcover o.p. paperback available $3.50 E

1. Baseball—Fiction
ISBN 0-06-444011-7 (pa) LC 65-10728

Also available Spanish language edition $11.89 (ISBN 0-06-023154-8)

"A Sports I can read book"

Kessler, Leonard P., 1920-—*Continued*

"Bobby, in despair because his batting is weak, tries Willie's lucky hat. No luck! Then Willie coaches Bobby, who practices and practices and finally gets a hit—no instant success, but a combination of hard work and encouragement from Willie. The home attitude is good, too." We Build Together

Another available title about Willie and Bobby is: Last one in is a rotten egg, entered below

Kick, pass, and run; by Leonard Kessler. Harper & Row 1966 64p il hardcover o.p. paperback available $3.50 **E**

1. Football—Fiction
ISBN 0-06-444012-5 (pa) LC 66-18656

"A Sports I can read book"

"Football rules and terms are tackled in easy-to-read, easy-to-remember terms and reinforced by the illustrated glossary that follows the comic story of animal teams imitating the Giants and the Jets." Best Books for Child, 1968

"May [also] appeal to the older reluctant reader." Hodges. Books for Elem Sch Libr

Followed by: On your mark, get set, go! (1972)

Last one in is a rotten egg; by Leonard Kessler. Harper & Row 1969 64p il lib bdg $10.89; pa $3.50 **E**

1. Swimming—Fiction
ISBN 0-06-023158-0 (lib bdg); 0-06-444118-0 (pa) LC 69-10209

"A Sports I can read book"

Because Freddy can't swim, he must stay in the shallow water while his friends have fun diving and racing. Support from his mother and from his friends Bobby and Willy, and lessons from Tom the lifeguard enable Freddy to overcome his fear of the water

Old Turtle's winter games; by Leonard Kessler. Greenwillow Bks. 1983 47p il o.p.; Dell paperback available $2.95 **E**

1. Animals—Fiction 2. Winter sports—Fiction
ISBN 0-440-40261-1 (pa) LC 83-1435

"A Greenwillow read-alone book"

A group of animals organize winter games, and compete in events such as sled races, skating, skiing, and ice hockey

"The variety of sports, short action sequences and lots of dialogue, combined with the blue and gold cartoons, pace the story well and Old Turtle, without being didactic or smarmy, presents an encouraging 'Keep trying' picture of a coach." SLJ

Khalsa, Dayal Kaur

Cowboy dreams. Potter 1990 unp il $13.95; lib bdg $14.99 **E**

1. Cowhands—Fiction
ISBN 0-517-57490-X; 0-517-57491-8 (lib bdg) LC 89-22782

"A young city girl dreams of being a cowgirl and riding horses in the Wild West. Unable to do so, the basement banister, pieces of clothesline and an old blanket become her horse and its trappings." Child Book Rev Serv

"Humorous touches are many. . . . 'Cowboy Dreams' showcases the author-illustrator's special gift for discerning and communicating what is important to children, and since this book is as much about the power of dreams and imagination as it is about the West, it will fascinate young people from coast to coast." Horn Book

How pizza came to Queens. Potter 1989 unp il $13.95 **E**

1. New York (N.Y.)—Fiction
ISBN 0-517-57126-9 LC 88-22452

May, of My family vacation, entered below, is visiting her good friends the Penny sisters. An Italian visitor to their Queens home bemoans the unavailability of pizza until the thoughtful girls enable her to make some

"It is a straightforward little story, with bright, bold, naîve paintings. Any young pizza lover will relish it." N Y Times Book Rev

I want a dog; story and pictures by Dayal Kaur Khalsa. Potter 1987 unp il $13.95 **E**

1. Dogs—Fiction
ISBN 0-517-56532-3 LC 86-30329

"This is the story of a little girl [named May] who desperately wants a dog. Her parents are not too thrilled about the idea, and as a result she pretends that her roller skate is a dog instead. . . . If the plot seems minimal and somewhat static . . . the illustrations are anything but. They are beautiful, inspired, detailed, naîvely drawn and painted and extremely colorful." N Y Times Book Rev

Julian. Potter 1989 unp il $12.95; lib bdg $13.99 **E**

1. Dogs—Fiction 2. Farm life—Fiction
ISBN 0-517-57279-6; 0-517-57410-1 (lib bdg) LC 89-3571

"A dog, brought to a farm to chase groundhogs, chases all the farm animals except the goat and disrupts the quiet rhythms of farm life until he learns to be part of and is accepted into the family. An amusing depiction of rural living." Soc Educ

The "illustrations, executed in brilliant colors with an emphasis on mass and shape, have a direct, artfully crafted simplicity admirably suited to the subject and theme. The scale of the whole suggests the book's appeal for story hours as well as for independent enjoyment." Horn Book

My family vacation. Potter 1988 unp il $13.95 **E**

1. Vacations—Fiction 2. Brothers and sisters—Fiction 3. Florida—Fiction
ISBN 0-517-56697-4 LC 87-25842

"May [featured in I want a dog, entered above] her parents, and her older brother (the one who always wins) set out for a winter vacation in Florida. May is both frightened and excited by the adventure. Khalsa captures this and the delight that a child can take in the smallest details of a new experience. . . . Khalsa's colors blaze like the southern sun with hot pinks and greens. She packs her pictures with detail. From sightseeing excursions to Parrot Jungle, penny arcades, and miniature golf courses, readers will relish May's experiences and enjoy remembering her family vacation." SLJ

Kherdian, David, 1931-

The cat's midsummer jamboree; by David Kherdian and Nonny Hogrogian. Philomel Bks. 1990 unp il $14.95 **E**

1. Animals—Fiction 2. Music—Fiction
ISBN 0-399-22222-7 LC 89-16227

A roaming mandolin-playing cat encounters a number of other musical animals on his travels, and the result is a jamboree in a tree

"Nonny Hogrogian, the designer as well as the illustrator of the beautifully integrated book, has created page after page of well-defined forms and beguiling bright color. Full of dramatic action, imagination, and wit, the illustrations breathe life and energy into the text. The joyous animals, masters of their instruments, look as insouciantly expert as an ensemble of professional musicians." Horn Book

Kimmel, Eric A.

The Chanukkah guest; illustrated by Giora Carmi. Holiday House 1990 unp il $14.95 **E**

1. Hanukkah—Fiction 2. Bears—Fiction
ISBN 0-8234-0788-8 LC 89-20073

On the first night of Chanukkah, Old Bear wanders into Bubba Brayna's house and receives a delicious helping of potato latkes when she mistakes him for the rabbi

"In this comical story, Kimmel captures the kindness of an old woman and the innocence of a hungry bear in an unusual visit. Carmi's airy pastel illustrations shade the tale with a golden glow appropriate for the Festival of Lights." Publ Wkly

Hershel and the Hanukkah goblins; written by Eric A. Kimmel; illustrated by Trina Schart Hyman. Holiday House 1989 unp il $14.95 **E**

1. Hanukkah—Fiction 2. Fairies—Fiction 3. Jews—Fiction
ISBN 0-8234-0769-1 LC 89-1954

A Caldecott Medal honor book, 1990

"The setting is an Eastern European village, and the plot is a little like Halloween Hanukkah—it seems that goblins are occupying the synagogue on the hill. Along comes plucky Hershel of Ostropol, and he cleverly outwits the demons." N Y Times Book Rev

"This will provide relief from the boring, candy-coated read-alouds that so often comprise holiday fare and will fit companionably with haunted castle variants. Hyman is at her best with windswept landscapes, dark interiors, close portraiture, and imaginatively wicked creatures. Both art and history are charged with energy." Bull Cent Child Books

I took my frog to the library; pictures by Blanche Sims. Viking Penguin 1990 unp il $12.95 **E**

1. Pets—Fiction 2. Libraries—Fiction
ISBN 0-670-82418-6 LC 89-37866

"Havoc reigns when Bridgett's animal friends accompany her to the library." SLJ

"Sims plays with the inherent humor of Kimmel's brief story, painting young patrons' horror at a python shedding her skin all over the picture books or their uneasy amusement as a giraffe reads over their shoulders. Finally young Bridgett agrees to the librarian's suggestion that she come alone to the library, leaving her animal friends content at home with the elephant reading to them. A hilariously enjoyable introduction to library manners for young patrons." Booklist

Kimmelman, Leslie

Frannie's fruits; pictures by Petra Mathers. Harper & Row 1989 30p il $12.95; lib bdg $12.89 **E**

ISBN 0-06-023143-2; 0-06-023164-5 (lib bdg)
LC 88-17637

"A warm story about a family fruit stand named after the family dog. Describes simply and vividly the daily operation of the business. The pictures are delicious." Soc Educ

Kitchen, Bert

Animal alphabet. Dial Bks. for Young Readers 1984 unp il o.p. paperback available $4.95 **E**

1. Alphabet 2. Animals
ISBN 0-8037-0431-3 (pa) LC 83-23929

The reader is invited to guess the identity of twenty-six unusual animals illustrating the letter of the alphabet

"Color and line are masterfully manipulated to produce a three-dimensional effect so that each animal seems to have been arrested in motion. Skillful rendering of textures provides effective contrast with the stark, glossy paper, adds visual excitement, and imbues each species with vitality, while the oversized format, allowing for generous expanses of white, is particularly suited to the elegance of the concept. Although a superb choice for story hour participation, the book should appeal to a wide audience and not be limited to young children." Horn Book

Animal numbers. Dial Bks. 1987 unp il $12.95 **E**

1. Counting 2. Animals
ISBN 0-8037-0459-3 LC 87-5365

A counting book in which animals both exotic and familiar are shown with the specified number of infants

"Arranged against starkly white pages, the illustrations combine a scientific authenticity of detail with strong visual appeal. . . . A concluding page of facts about the animals gives brief information for those who would know more, but the appeal of the book lies in its pictorial representations and, as such, is a handsome addition to the number-book genre." Horn Book

Gorilla/Chinchilla and other animal rhymes. Dial Bks. 1990 unp il $13.95; lib bdg $13.89 **E**

1. Animals 2. Stories in rhyme
ISBN 0-8037-0770-3; 0-8037-0771-1 (lib bdg)
LC 89-16851

Rhymed text and illustrations decribe a variety of animals whose names rhyme but are of very different habits and appearance

Kitchen has "produced a book overflowing with stunning, attention-demanding visuals. His realistic renderings of animals are executed with exacting attention to detail." SLJ

Koralek, Jenny

The cobweb curtain; a Christmas story based on a legend told by William Barclay; illustrated by Pauline Baynes. Holt & Co. 1989 unp il $14.95 **E**

1. Jesus Christ—Nativity 2. Spiders—Fiction 3. Christmas—Fiction
ISBN 0-8050-1051-3 LC 88-27035

"This Christmas story is based on William Barclay's *The Legend of the Spider's Web*; as adapted by Koralek, a shepherd who overhears a conversation that threatens the Holy Family whisks them off to a cave in the hills. There a spider who sees the sleepers huddled against the cold protects them by spinning a huge web at the cave's mouth. When the king's soldiers come, they assume that the web would have been broken had anyone come into the cave. Thus Jesus is saved; thus the sparkling web, tossed aside on a small tree, becomes the origin of the practice of decorating Christmas trees with tinsel." Bull Cent Child Books

"Baynes' rounded figures and repetition of shapes and lines visually echo the unobtrusive rhythm of Koralek's cadenced prose. In harmony with the many night scenes, the colors are muted, yet fine-textured and distinct." Booklist

Krahn, Fernando, 1935-

Arthur's adventure in the abandoned house. Dutton 1981 unp il $8.25 **E**

1. Stories without words
ISBN 0-525-25945-7 LC 80-22249

"Arthur, a serious and appealing lad, is naturally curious about an abandoned house. Once inside, he unties a man left in the basement by three sinister gunmen. But when the gang locks up Arthur and his new friend in the crumbling attic, the boy knows just what to do. He sends a paper airplane message out of the hole in the roof and some builders down below come to the rescue. The story unfolds without one word (except for the brief plea for help on the paper plane)—and no text is 'needed,' for Krahn's refreshingly straightforward drawings tell it all." SLJ

Krasilovsky, Phyllis, 1926-

The cow who fell in the canal; illustrated by Peter Spier. Doubleday 1957 unp il $11.95; Harper & Row pa $4.95 **E**

1. Cattle—Fiction 2. Netherlands—Fiction
ISBN 0-385-07585-5; 0-06-443148-7 (pa) LC 56-8236

Picture story about Hendrika, a fat cow living in Holland. Hendrika loved her master and was usually content to eat a great deal and produce rich creamy milk—though she sometimes got bored. But after she fell into the canal and floated down to the distant city on a raft she was never bored again, because she had so much to think about

The artist's "watercolor illustrations are remarkable for details lovingly recalled, panoramic scenes of town and country, and colors as fresh and clean as a newly scrubbed Dutch floor." Cincinnati Public Libr

Kraus, Robert, 1925-

Owliver; pictures by Jose Aruego & Ariane Dewey. Prentice-Hall Bks. for Young Readers 1987 c1974 unp il lib bdg $12.95 **E**

1. Owls—Fiction
ISBN 0-13-647538-8 LC 80-13664

A reissue of the title first published 1974 by Windmill Books

Owliver is "a young owl who loves to act, much to the joy of his mother and the discomfiture of his father, who hopefully gives him doctor and lawyer toys (which Owliver uses to put on a play) with no more chance than readers of guessing what his son will really turn out to be." Booklist

"This is an entertaining spoof on parental guidance with top-notch illustrations." Libr J

Whose mouse are you? pictures by José Aruego. Macmillan 1970 unp il $12.95; pa $4.95 **E**

1. Mice—Fiction 2. Stories in rhyme
ISBN 0-02-751190-1; 0-689-71142-5 (pa) LC 70-89931

A lonely little mouse has to be resourceful in order to bring his family back together

"This is an absolute charmer of a picture book, original, tender, and childlike. The rhyming text is so brief, so catchy, and so right that a child will remember the words after one or two readings, and the large, uncluttered illustrations are gay and appealing." Booklist

Another available title about the mouse and his family is:
Where are you going, little mouse? (1986)

Krause, Ute

Pig surprise; written and illustrated by Ute Krause. Dial Bks. for Young Readers 1989 unp il $11.95 **E**

1. Pigs—Fiction
ISBN 0-8037-0714-2 LC 88-31108

Despite Herman's attempt to be a well-behaved pig, his owner Nina must recognize the fact that he will be happier living outdoors with other pigs

"Krause's ink-and-watercolor illustrations in softly shaded hues deftly capture the story's droll spirit while allowing the text's message about the need to be oneself to shine through. Wrapped in emotion and laced with subtly humorous detail, this richly conceived story will be especially satisfying fare." Booklist

Krauss, Ruth

The carrot seed; pictures by Crockett Johnson. Harper & Row 1989 unp il $11.95; lib bdg $11.89; pa $3.95 **E**

ISBN 0-06-023350-8; 0-06-023351-6 (lib bdg); 0-06-443210-6 (pa) LC 45-4530

Simple text and picture show how the faith of a small boy, who planted a carrot seed, was rewarded

"One of the most satisfying picture books of the year. . . . Crockett Johnson's pictures are perfect and the brief text is just right." Book Week

Krauss, Ruth—*Continued*

The growing story; pictures by Phyllis Rowand. Harper & Row 1947 unp il $11.70 **E**

1. Growth—Fiction
ISBN 0-06-023380-X LC 47-30688

"Watching the animals and plants growing through the seasons, a little boy worries considerably about his own seeming lack of growth—until he puts on last year's clothes and sees actual proof that he too has grown. The subject, the simply written text, and the detailed, stylized pictures should prove satisfying fare for little children." Booklist

A hole is to dig; a first book of first definitions; pictures by Maurice Sendak. Harper & Row 1989 unp il $13.95; lib bdg $13.89; pa $3.95 **E**

ISBN 0-06-023405-9; 0-06-023406-7 (lib bdg); 0-06-443205-X (pa) LC 52-7731

Humorous, unexpected definitions of things and actions which have a place in the child's world. Samples: A hole is to plant a flower; A hole is to sit in; A mountain is to climb to the top; Dishes are to do; A nose is to blow; Steps are to sit on

"A revelation to grownups as to children's impressions, this could also be the basis of a wonderful game of questions and answers which would set children thinking. Maurice Sendak has illustrated it with drawings bouncing with action and good humor." N Y Times Book Rev

A very special house; pictures by Maurice Sendak. Harper & Row 1953 unp il $13.89; pa $4.95 **E**

ISBN 0-06-023456-3; 0-06-443228-9 (pa) LC 53-7115

A Caldecott Medal honor book, 1954

"The very special house is a house which exists in the imagination of a small boy—a house where the chairs are for climbing, the walls for writing on, and the beds for jumping on; a house where a lion, a giant, or a dead mouse is welcome, and where nobody ever says stop. Told in a chanting rhythm that demands participation by the reader; the imaginary characters, objects, and doings are pictured in line drawings almost as a child would scribble them while the real little boy stands out boldly in bright blue overalls." Booklist

Krensky, Stephen, 1953-

Lionel at large; pictures by Susanna Natti. Dial Bks. for Young Readers 1986 56p il $9.95; lib bdg $9.89; pa $4.95 **E**

1. Family life—Fiction
ISBN 0-8037-0240-X; 0-8037-0241-8 (lib bdg); 0-8037-0556-5 (pa) LC 85-15930

"Dial easy-to-read"

"Five simply written stories for the beginning independent reader are illustrated by full-color drawings, line-and-wash, that have a cheerful vitality and humor. Each story is a modest anecdote about Lionel: a visit to the doctor, a confrontation with the necessity of eating vegetables, a nervous hunt for an older sister's pet snake . . . in other words, experiences similar to those most children have. There's a quiet humor in the writing, so that readers can enjoy the joke while they are empathizing with Lionel's problems and with his success in overcoming or tolerating them." Bull Cent Child Books

Other available titles about Lionel are:
Lionel in the fall (1987)
Lionel in the spring (1990)

Kroll, Steven

The biggest pumpkin ever; illustrated by Jeni Bassett. Holiday House 1984 unp il $13.95; Scholastic pa $2.50 **E**

1. Pumpkin—Fiction 2. Halloween—Fiction
3. Mice—Fiction
ISBN 0-8234-0505-2; 0-590-41113-6 (pa) LC 83-18492

"A village mouse and a field mouse fall in love with the same pumpkin. Clayton feeds and waters it by day, while Desmond tends it at night. What a surprise when the two finally bump into each other! Whose pumpkin is it—Clayton's for the pumpkin contest, or Desmond's for a jack-o'-lantern?" Publisher's note

"The cheerful, bright watercolor illustrations are as captivating as the text. Children will delight in reading or hearing this story at any time of the year." Child Book Rev Serv

One tough turkey; a Thanksgiving story; illustrated by John Wallner. Holiday House 1982 unp il lib bdg $13.95 **E**

1. Turkeys—Fiction 2. Thanksgiving Day—Fiction
ISBN 0-8234-0457-9 LC 82-2925

"Sent by the Governor of the Pilgrim colony to hunt turkeys for the first Thanksgiving dinner, the bumbling troop of hunters is outwitted easily by the tough turkey of the title, Solomon. He, his wife Regina, and their children Alfred and Lavinia taunt and trick the hunters, putting up signs (among other ploys) that say 'NO TURKEYS! TURKEYS FLOWN SOUTH FOR THE WINTER!' or 'PILGRIMS GO HOME!' Eventually the weary hunters trudge back and decide to have squash instead of turkey, and that's why, the book ends, 'Everyone just thinks they ate turkey.'" Bull Cent Child Books

"The attractive and lively illustrations complement the story, creating a charming aberration from the usual Thanksgiving tale." Child Book Rev Serv

Santa's crash-bang Christmas; illustrated by Tomie de Paola. Holiday House 1977 unp il $13.95; pa $5.95 **E**

1. Santa Claus—Fiction 2. Christmas—Fiction
ISBN 0-8234-0302-5; 0-8234-0621-0 (pa) LC 77-3025

"As if Santa Claus wasn't having a hard enough time on Christmas Eve with falling out of the sleigh, on top of the fireplace ashes, into the Christmas tree, and against the hanging chandelier, he finds a misplaced polar bear in his pack and Gerald, a stowaway elf, in his sleigh. . . . De Paola extracts full measure from this amusing tale with a clumsy Santa, wide-eyed elf, and lovable polar bear. The three characters are done in red, brown, and white against gray wash until the present-strewn Christmas morning scene splashes forth in full color." Booklist

Kunhardt, Edith

I want to be a farmer. Grosset & Dunlap 1989 unp il $6.95 **E**

1. Farm life
ISBN 0-448-09068-6 LC 88-80427

In this book, a "boy describes his parents' work day on a potato farm, including an introduction to the brooder ('Peep, peep, baby chicks. I see you'), the turkeys ('Gobble, gobble, gobble!) and the geese ('The gander sticks out his neck and hisses at me. Go away, gander. He goes away'). Nathan rides in Daddy's air-conditioned tractor cab and ends the day with dinner ('Baked potatoes! Grandma and Grandpa come over for dessert') and with Daddy reading aloud." Bull Cent Child Books

"Illustrated with sharp, full-color photographs of authentic settings." Publ Wkly

I want to be a fire-fighter. Grosset & Dunlap 1989 unp il $6.95 **E**

1. Fire fighters
ISBN 0-448-09069-4 LC 88-80428

"In *Fire Fighter*, Holly talks about her father's work as a volunteer fire fighter, shows off his equipment, tries on his uniform, and demonstrates procedures for getting out of a burning house. . . . Preschoolers will enjoy browsing through the pictures here, especially in conjunction with day care or nursery school discussions of family occupations." Bull Cent Child Books

Kuskin, Karla

The Dallas Titans get ready for bed; illustrations by Marc Simont. Harper & Row 1986 36p il $11.95; lib bdg $11.89; pa $3.95 **E**

1. Football
ISBN 0-06-023562-4; 0-06-023563-2 (lib bdg); 0-06-443180-0 (pa) LC 83-49470

"A Charlotte Zolotow book"

Follows a fictitious football team off the field, into the locker room, and to their homes, describing the normal routine after a game and examining the uniforms and pieces of equipment as they are removed

As the "players undress, Kuskin and Simont reveal an enormous amount of information about the game and gear, providing at the same time a sophisticated counting book. . . . Kuskin's text throughout is a poetic, energetic romp, and Simon's robust pictures of the big, round players (in the shower they look like 'small wet whales') and the glorious upheaval of the locker room are a perfect match." Bull Cent Child Books

The Philharmonic gets dressed; by Karla Kuskin; illustrations by Marc Simont. Harper & Row 1982 unp il $12.95; lib bdg $12.89; pa $3.95 **E**

1. Clothing and dress 2. Orchestra
ISBN 0-06-023622-1; 0-06-023623-X (lib bdg); 0-06-443124-X (pa) LC 81-48658

"A Charlotte Zolotow book"

"The 105 members of the orchestra (92 men and 13 women) are shown showering, dressing, traveling and setting themselves up on stage for an evening's concert." SLJ

"The vigor and humor of Simont's illustrations add vitality to a direct, simple text." Bull Cent Child Books

Lane, Megan Halsey

Something to crow about; story and pictures by Megan Halsey Lane. Dial Bks. for Young Readers 1989 unp il $10.95; lib bdg $10.89 **E**

1. Chickens—Fiction
ISBN 0-8037-0697-9; 0-8037-0698-7 (lib bdg) LC 88-33394

Two chicks who look just the same find out how different they are when one begins to lay eggs and the other starts to grow

"With a suitably simple text and cheery pictures, Lane teaches this basic lesson of individuality very effectively. Publ Wkly

Lasky, Kathryn

A baby for Max; text by Kathryn Lasky; in the words of Maxwell B. Knight; photographs by Christopher G. Knight. Scribner 1984 48p il $12.95; pa $3.95 **E**

1. Infants 2. Brothers and sisters
ISBN 0-684-18064-2; 0-689-71118-2 (pa) LC 84-5307

Text and photographs record a five-year-old as he awaits the birth of the family's new baby and enjoys her afterward

"Illustrated with photographs of excellent quality by the author's husband, this is a modest photodocumentary about the advent of the couple's second child, as told by five-year-old Max. The text is easy enough for beginning independent readers but so simplified in tone and concept that it seems more appropriate for the preschool child." Bull Cent Child Books

Sea swan; illustrated by Catherine Stock. Macmillan 1988 unp il $13.95 **E**

1. Old age—Fiction 2. Grandmothers—Fiction 3. Swimming—Fiction
ISBN 0-02-751700-4 LC 88-1444

"Elzibah Swan lives quietly on Boston's Beacon Hill with her cat Zanzibar, her housekeeper, and her chauffeur. When her two grandchildren come for a visit she takes them to the beach and marvels at the way they swim. After they leave, she misses them, but the time on her hands prompts an amazing decision: Elzibah herself decides to learn how to swim." Booklist

"This is a quiet, pleasant story, but like Elzibah's life, filled with small surprises. Her courage and determination are delightful and inspiring, especially for the many readers also faced with learning new and difficult skills. Her special relationship with her grandchildren through letters will strike a responsive chord in many. The book is illustrated with wonderful, warm, mostly full-page pencil plus watercolor paintings." SLJ

Lawrence, James

Binky brothers, detectives; pictures by Leonard Kessler. Harper & Row 1968 60p il lib bdg $10.89; pa $3.50 E

1. Mystery and detective stories
ISBN 0-06-023759-7 (lib bdg); 0-06-444003-6 (pa) LC 68-10374

"An I can read mystery"

"Although the detective business in which he and his older brother Pinky are engaged was his idea, Dinky is treated as a helper, not a partner, until he solves the mystery of the missing catcher's mitt and outsmarts Pinky as well. An agreeable story with amusing illustrations." Booklist

Followed by: Binky brothers and the Fearless Four (1970)

Leaf, Margaret

The eyes of the dragon; illustrated by Ed Young. Lothrop, Lee & Shepard Bks. 1987 unp il $13.95; lib bdg $13.88 E

1. Dragons—Fiction 2. Artists—Fiction 3. China—Fiction
ISBN 0-688-06155-9; 0-688-06156-7 (lib bdg) LC 85-11670

"This is the story of a Chinese magistrate who commissions a painter to decorate the new village wall with a dragon. The painter agrees, with the stipulation that the painting be accepted unconditionally. The finished art is breathtaking, but, in spite of warnings, the magistrate insists the artist add eyes to the dragon, whereupon the dragon shakes loose from the wall and flies away in a storm." Bull Cent Child Books

"Powerfully told and touched with humor, the tale works on several levels. . . . The pictures are astonishing. Done in pastels, they are all double-page spreads vibrant with life and color." SLJ

Leaf, Munro, 1905-

The story of Ferdinand; illustrated by Robert Lawson. E

1. Bulls—Fiction 2. Bullfights—Fiction 3. Spain—Fiction

Some editions are:
Buccaneer Bks. $17.95 (ISBN 0-89966-590-X)
Viking $11.95 (ISBN 0-670-67424-9)

First published 1936 by Viking

"Ferdinand was a peace-loving little bull who preferred smelling flowers to making a reputation for himself in the bull ring. His story is told irresistbly in pictures and few words." Wis Libr Bull

"The drawings picture not only Ferdinand but Spanish scenes and characters as well." N Y Public Libr

Lee, Jeanne M.

Bà-Năm; written and illustrated by Jeanne M. Lee. Holt & Co. 1987 unp il $13.95 E

1. Cemeteries—Fiction 2. Old age—Fiction 3. Vietnam—Fiction
ISBN 0-8050-0169-7 LC 86-27127

"The first time Nan goes to honor her ancestors on Thanh-Minh Day, she is frightened by a black-toothed old woman, Ba-Nam, who takes care of the graves. But when Nan and her brother wander off to play, they get lost in a storm that makes Nan glad to see Ba-nam, who guides them through the graveyard in the driving rain and saves Nan from a falling tree. Set in South Vietnam, this is an unpretentious story with full-page paintings effective for their clean, light shapes against smoothly textured color backdrops." Bull Cent Child Books

Lester, Helen

The revenge of the Magic Chicken; illustrated by Lynn Munsinger. Houghton Mifflin 1990 unp il $13.95 E

1. Magic—Fiction
ISBN 0-395-50929-7 LC 89-39597

Sequel to: The wizard, the fairy, and the Magic Chicken (1983)

When the Magic Chicken attempts revenge on his colleagues in spellmaking, the Wizard and the Fairy, he finds his own magic getting out of control

"The text's humor gets the full treatment in Munsinger's raucous art: a chicken dressed as a ballerina, a witch who's been turned into a blueberry muffin, to say nothing of gnarly gnitbats and alligators stuffed in a tree. Sure to appeal to a wide age range." Booklist

Levine, Ellen

I hate English! illustrated by Steve Bjӧrkman. Scholastic 1989 unp il $12.95 E

1. Chinese—United States—Fiction 2. United States—Immigration and emigration—Fiction
ISBN 0-590-42305-3 LC 88-38265

When her family moves to New York from Hong Kong, Mei Mei finds it difficult to adjust to school and learn the alien sounds of English

"This story of cultural adjustment rings true, and Mei Mei's dilemma is strongly affecting. Her disgruntlement with English, the fun of an outing to Jones Beach, to cite two contrasting examples, are brought vividly to life by Bjӧrkman's cartoon-style illustrations (watercolor with pen-and-ink outline). Differentiating carefully between the Asian and Caucasian characters, the breezy humor of the pictures alleviates what otherwise would have been a burdensome bibliotherapeutic message." Publ Wkly

Levinson, Riki

I go with my family to Grandma's; illustrated by Diane Goode. Dutton 1986 unp il $11.95; pa $3.95 E

1. Grandmothers—Fiction 2. Family life—Fiction 3. Transportation—Fiction 4. New York (N.Y.)—Fiction
ISBN 0-525-44261-8; 0-525-44557-9 (pa) LC 86-4490

As five cousins and their families arrive by various means of transportation, Grandma's home in Brooklyn gets livelier and livelier

"With an exceptional elegance of design, each of the five family groups is shown at home, en route, and then being welcomed by the relatives who have already arrived at Grandma's. The warm, pastel-colored drawings

Levinson, Riki—*Continued*
are jam-packed with the most humorous details as each family is hugged, admired, fed, and retrieved from under tables and out of tree branches. . . . In a clever touch the final overleaf has the family portrait in black and white as it would appear in a photograph album and a picture of the five cousins from the five boroughs. The details in the illustrations will be a source of endless fascination to the child reading the book and to the adult lucky enough to share it." Horn Book

Our home is the sea; paintings by Dennis Luzak. Dutton 1988 unp il $13.95 E

1. Hong Kong—Fiction
ISBN 0-525-44406-8 LC 87-36419

A Chinese boy hurries home from school to his family's houseboat in Hong Kong harbor. It is the end of the school year, and he is anxious to join his father and grandfather in their family profession, fishing

"The text is descriptive, minimally weakened by the fact that it seems, at times, to function more as a series of captions for the double-page spreads than as a controlling narrative. What the book does show is the universality of children's interests and concerns. Here the never-named child moves with curiosity and perceptual acuteness through the city scene to the warmth and security of home and family." Bull Cent Child Books

Watch the stars come out; illustrated by Diane Goode. Dutton 1985 unp il $13.95 E

1. United States—Immigration and emigration—Fiction
ISBN 0-525-44205-7 LC 84-28672

Grandma tells about her mama's journey to America by boat, years ago

"The book is ambitious in trying to present to 4-to-8-year-olds both the struggles and joys of new immigrants. And because the story doesn't actually pinpoint the nationality or religion of its characters, it could be read as a portrait of any number of immigrant groups that streamed into this country between the 1880's and 1920's. Unfortunately, children may find the format confusing as it moves without transitions from the child being told a bedtime story by her grandmother to the grandmother's mother's story and back to the child. . . . On the other hand, Diane Goode's beautiful, dreamlike paintings with their charmingly expressive figures manage to capture—even for the very young—the depth and emotion of the immigrant experience." N Y Times Book Rev

Levy, Elizabeth, 1942-

Something queer is going on (a mystery); illustrated by Mordicai Gerstein. Delacorte Press 1973 unp il hardcover o.p. paperback available $2.75 E

1. Mystery and detective stories
ISBN 0-440-47974-6 (pa) LC 72-1385

Also available in hardcover from Smith, P. $14.50 (ISBN 0-8446-6257-7)

"Jill arrives home to find her dog Fletcher missing; armed with sets of identifying pictures of Fletcher from all angles, she and friend Gwen conduct a house-to-house search. The finger of guilt points to television commercial producer Fiedler Fernbach, who denies knowing Fletcher before he has even seen the dog's picture. The next day the girls, accompanied by Jill's mother, follow Fernbach to his television studio where they find Fletcher on camera for a dog food commercial. For the youngest fans a patly plausible story with zany illustrations a la 'Mad' magazine." Booklist

Other available titles in this mystery series are:
Something queer at the ball park (1975)
Something queer at the birthday party (1990)
Something queer at the haunted school (1982)
Something queer at the lemonade stand (1982)
Something queer at the library (1977)
Something queer in rock 'n' roll (1987)
Something queer on vacation (1980)

Lewin, Hugh, 1939-

Jafta; story by Hugh Lewin; pictures by Lisa Kopper. Carolrhoda Bks. 1983 c1981 unp il lib bdg $9.95; pa $3.95 E

1. Animals—Fiction 2. South Africa—Fiction
ISBN 0-87614-207-2 (lib bdg); 0-87614-494-6 (pa)
LC 82-12847

First published 1981 in the United Kingdom

"A small boy in South Africa, Jafta, says 'When I'm happy I purr like a lion cub, or skip like a spider, or laugh like a hyena. And sometimes I want to jump like an impala, and dance like a zebra . . .' and so on. There's no story. The illustrations have no background clutter, showing only the attractive brown child and the appealing animals." Bull Cent Child Books

Other available titles about Jafta are:
Jafta and the wedding (1983)
Jafta—the journey (1984)
Jafta—the town (1984)
Jafta's father (1983)
Jafta's mother (1983)

Lewis, J. Patrick

The tsar & the amazing cow; pictures by Friso Henstra. Dial Bks. for Young Readers 1988 unp il $11.95; lib bdg $11.89 E

1. Soviet Union—Fiction 2. Fairy tales
ISBN 0-8037-0410-0; 0-8037-0411-9 (lib bdg)
LC 86-29255

"An original story with folktale appeal, this relates the fortunes of an old Russian peasant couple whose daughters have died and who have only a cow, Buryonka, left to comfort them. This she does in high style, for her magic milk turns them young again. When the wicked tsar hears of it and commands the couple to bring him their cow, his greed leads him to drink more and more milk, until he's a baby and then . . . nothing!" Bull Cent Child Books

"Chalky illustrations with a peasant flavor capture the humor and conflict of the story and add details to the setting and the characters. This book is to be read and enjoyed many times." Child Book Rev Serv

Lexau, Joan M.

I should have stayed in bed; pictures by Syd Hoff. Harper & Row 1965 48p il lib bdg $13.89 E

1. Blacks—Fiction
ISBN 0-06-023861-5 LC 65-10726

Lexau, Joan M.—*Continued*

"Everything goes wrong for Sam one day—shoes on the wrong feet, late for school, trouble with teacher—until he starts all over at lunch time. Easy and humorous, with inter-racial friendships unobtrusively portrayed." A L A Child Serv Div. Sel Lists of Child Books and Recordings

The rooftop mystery; pictures by Syd Hoff. Harper & Row 1968 64p il lib bdg $10.89 **E**

1. Blacks—Fiction 2. Mystery and detective stories
ISBN 0-06-023865-8 LC 68-16821

"An I can read mystery"

"Sam and Albert are helping Sam's family move to another home within walking distance; unfortunately Sam finds any distance too long in which he can be seen in public carrying his sister's large, conspicuous doll." Sutherland. The Best in Child Books

"The cartoon illustrations show the children to be both blacks and whites." N Y Public Libr. Black Exper in Child Books

Who took the farmer's [hat]? [by] Joan L. Nodset; pictures by Fritz Siebel. Harper & Row 1963 unp il lib bdg $12.89; pa $3.95 **E**

1. Animals—Fiction
ISBN 0-06-024566-2 (lib bdg); 0-06-443174-6 (pa) LC 62-17964

"Away flew the farmer's hat. In his search for it he found that his hat could be many things to many animals including, most permanently, a bird's nest." Publ Wkly

Lindbergh, Reeve

Benjamin's barn; paintings by Susan Jeffers. Dial Bks. for Young Readers 1990 unp il $13.95; lib bdg $13.89 **E**

1. Barns—Fiction 2. Farm life—Fiction 3. Stories in rhyme
ISBN 0-8037-0613-8; 0-8037-0614-6 (lib bdg) LC 88-23690

"One rainy spring day, a small boy named Benjamin sets off for his big red barn, where he spends hours with the flesh-and-blood animals of the farm and the exotic creatures of his imagination. . . . The rhyming text has a comforting circular flow, well-suited to Benjamin's flight of fancy and subsequent return to reality. Jeffers' lifelike illustrations enhance the theme, lending as much reality to the leathery texture of a pterodactyl's wing as to the downy softness of goose feathers." SLJ

The day the goose got loose; pictures by Steven Kellogg. Dial Bks. for Young Readers 1990 unp il $12.95; lib bdg $12.89 **E**

1. Domestic animals—Fiction 2. Stories in rhyme
ISBN 0-8037-0408-9; 0-8037-0409-7 (lib bdg) LC 87-28959

The day the goose gets loose, havoc reigns at the farm as all the animals react

"The line-and-watercolor pictures are active and humorous; they are as out of control as the story, spilling into the margins of each page. The young narrator of the rhyme has the last word, setting herself loose with the goose in a wild and wonderful dream; at the end they both come home to roost in a cozy bed, sleepy and smiling." Horn Book

Lindgren, Astrid, 1907-

The Tomten; adapted by Astrid Lindgren from a poem by Viktor Rydberg; illustrated by Harald Wiberg. Coward-McCann 1961 unp il $8.95; pa $6.95 **E**

1. Winter—Fiction 2. Fairy tales
ISBN 0-698-20147-7; 0-698-20487-5 (pa) LC 61-10658

"Snowy farm pictures and warm scenes inside barn, sheds, and house show the Tomten, a little Swedish troll, going quietly about to the animals on cold winter nights comforting them with the promise that spring will come. The text was adapted from a nineteenth-century poem by Viktor Rydberg, and the pictures are by an outstanding Swedish painter of animals and nature. An unusual and beautiful picture book." Horn Book

Another available title about the Tomten is: The Christmas Tomten, entered under Linda M. Jennings

The Tomten and the fox; adapted by Astrid Lindgren from a poem by Karl-Erik Forsslund; illustrated by Harald Wiberg. Coward-McCann 1966 unp il o.p. paperback available $5.95 **E**

1. Foxes—Fiction 2. Winter—Fiction 3. Fairy tales
ISBN 0-698-20644-4 (pa) LC 65-25501

"When the sly fox comes on Christmas Eve to raid the henhouse, the tomten shares food left for him by the children and sends the fox away content to spare the hens." Hodges. Books for Elem Sch Libr

Lindgren, Barbro, 1937-

Sam's car; illustrated by Eva Eriksson. Morrow 1982 unp il $5.95 **E**

1. Toys—Fiction
ISBN 0-688-01263-9 LC 82-3437

When Sam and Lisa fight over Sam's red car, Sam's mother resolves the conflict by providing another car

"There is but one simple sentence per page, and the facing illustrations portray precisely what the words convey. The language and situations are totally childlike; the pictures are endearing. These are sure to be welcomed by the youngest listeners." Child Book Rev Serv

Other available titles about Sam are:
Sam's ball (1983)
Sam's bath (1983)
Sam's cookie (1982)
Sam's potty (1986)
Sam's teddy bear (1982)
Sam's wagon (1986)

The wild baby; pictures by Eva Eriksson; adapted from the Swedish by Jack Prelutsky. Greenwillow Bks. 1981 unp il lib bdg $13.88 **E**

1. Mothers and sons—Fiction 2. Stories in rhyme
ISBN 0-688-00601-9 LC 81-2151

Lindgren, Barbro, 1937-—*Continued*

"The story of baby Ben: always where he shouldn't be, never where he should. He sleeps in the clock and the chandelier, swims in the sink and wanders off at every opportunity. Things tend to get broken around Ben, but Mama loves him dearly." SLJ

"The Swedish text has been adapted into rhythmic rhymed nonsense verse accompanying a series of lightly caricatured water-color illustrations detailed in pen and ink. The effect is broadly humorous to complement the mood of the situations and reflect the nature of the young protagonist." Horn Book

Other available titles about Baby Ben and his mother are:

The wild baby gets a puppy (1988)
The wild baby goes to sea (1983)

Lionni, Leo, 1910-

Alexander and the wind-up mouse. Pantheon Bks. 1970 c1969 unp il lib bdg $12.99 E

1. Mice—Fiction
ISBN 0-394-90914-3 LC 76-77423

A Caldecott Medal honor book, 1970

"Alexander wants to be a wind-up mouse like Willie, who is the little girl's favorite toy. A magic lizard can change him, but then he learns that Willie's key is broken and decides to turn Willie into a real mouse like himself." Adventuring With Books. 2d edition

The author's "collage illustrations are dazzling in their color and bold design and contribute to a beautiful and appealing picture book." Booklist

The biggest house in the world. Pantheon Bks. 1968 unp il lib bdg $12.99; pa $2.95 E

1. Snails—Fiction
ISBN 0-394-90944-5 (lib bdg); 0-394-82740-6 (pa) LC 68-12646

"In this picture book a small snail has a very large wish. He wants the largest house in the world. But by telling the youngster a story, his wise father helps him to see the impracticality of being encased in a magnificent monstrosity too big to move." Book Week

Cornelius; a fable. Pantheon Bks. 1983 unp il lib bdg $13.99 E

1. Crocodiles—Fiction
ISBN 0-394-95419-X LC 82-6442

"Cornelius is an alligator who walks upright from the time of his birth, learns to stand on his head and swing by his tail with the help of a friendly monkey, and shows off to the other crocodiles, who say 'So what?' but try to do the same as soon as Cornelius has turned his back." Bull Cent Child Books

"Set forth in simple language, the tale is appealing in its directness. The collage technique is used effectively to suggest a tropical backdrop: Lush green leaves hang down to a mottled jungle floor, each shape a carefully placed element in the design. Strolling among the greenery, with his smiling face and unblinking eyes, Cornelius has the dreamy look of a true visionary." Horn Book

Fish is fish. Pantheon Bks. 1970 unp il lib bdg $12.99; pa $2.95 E

1. Frogs—Fiction 2. Fishes—Fiction
ISBN 0-394-90440-0 (lib bdg); 0-394-82799-6 (pa) LC 78-117452

The frog tells the fish all about the world above the sea. The fish, however, can only visualize it in terms of fish-people, fish-birds and fish-cows

"The story is slight but pleasantly and simply told, the illustrations are page-filling, deft, colorful, and amusing." Bull Cent Child Books

Frederick. Pantheon Bks. 1967 unp il $14.95; lib bdg $15.99 E

1. Mice—Fiction
ISBN 0-394-81040-6; 0-394-91040-0 (lib bdg) LC 67-6482

A Caldecott Medal honor book, 1968

"While other mice are gathering food for the winter, Frederick seems to daydream the summer away. When dreary winter comes, it is Frederick the poet-mouse who warms his friends and cheers them with his words." Wis Libr Bull

"This captivating book is about a field mouse, but it sings a hymn of praise to poets in a gentle story that is illustrated with gaiety and charm. The mice are plump little creatures with round, wondering eyes and the backgrounds of the pages echo in soft tones the appropriate colors of the seasons Frederick enjoys." Saturday Rev

Inch by inch. Astor-Honor 1960 unp il $10.95 E

1. Worms—Fiction 2. Birds—Fiction
ISBN 0-8392-3010-9 LC 60-14899

Also available in a French language edition (ISBN 0-8392-3028-1) and a Spanish language edition (ISBN 0-8392-3030-3) for $10.95 each

A Caldecott Medal honor book, 1961

This is a "small tale about an inchworm who liked to measure the robin's tail, the flamingo's neck, the whole of a hummingbird but not a nightingale's song." Christ Sci Monit

"This is a book to look at again and again. The semi-abstract forms are sharply defined, clean and strong, the colors subtle and glowing, and the grassy world of the inchworm is a special place of enchantment." N Y Times Book Rev

It's mine! Knopf 1986 c1985 unp il $14.95; lib bdg $14.99 E

1. Frogs—Fiction
ISBN 0-394-87000-X; 0-394-97000-4 (lib bdg) LC 85-190

Original German edition, 1985

"A picture book that is beautifully simple in line and in language. Three childlike frogs spend their days bickering and baiting each other: It's mine, claims one about the water. Another purports ownership of the earth—or a worm—or a butterfly—or whatever. It isn't until disaster almost stikes and they are saved by a toad that Milton, Rupert and Lydia realize that private ownership isn't that important. . . . Collages of marbled-textured paper, all in cool, crisp, spring-like colors against a stark white background, are a perfect match for this story of selfishness on the pond." SLJ

Lionni, Leo, 1910-—*Continued*

Little blue and little yellow; a story for Pippo and Ann and other children. Astor-Honor 1959 unp il $10.95 **E**

1. Color—Fiction
ISBN 0-8392-3018-4 LC 59-12398

The author uses "splashes of color and abstract forms to tell the story of little blue and his friend little yellow who hugged and hugged each other until they were green—and unrecognizable to their parents." Booklist

"So well are the dots handled on the pages that little blue and little yellow and their parents seem to have real personalities. It should inspire interesting color play and is a very original picture book by an artist." N Y Her Trib Books

Nicolas, where have you been? Knopf 1987 unp il lib bdg $11.99 **E**

1. Mice—Fiction 2. Birds—Fiction
ISBN 0-394-98370-X LC 86-18574

"The story of how Nicolas, a young field mouse, is first abducted by a bird and then befriended by others." N Y Times Book Rev

"Lionni's pristine work corresponds to the early reader's development. He creates a world of adventure and consequence from a wondrously minimal set of objects and words." Publ Wkly

Six crows; a fable. Knopf 1988 unp il $11.95; lib bdg $12.99 **E**

1. Farm life—Fiction
ISBN 0-394-89572-X; 0-394-99572-4 (lib bdg) LC 87-3141

As a "farmer tries to frighten the crows away from his wheat field by building increasingly intimidating scarecrows, the creatures fight back by creating their own bird kite with bark and leaves, so ferocious looking that they soon have the farmer on the run. It is only when the wise old owl advises the adversaries to talk things out that the conflict is resolved to both parties' satisfaction." Booklist

"This is not only an entertaining story filled with big, colorful pictures, it is a lesson in achieving harmony through communication." Child Book Rev Serv

Swimmy. Pantheon Bks. 1991 unp il $14.95; lib bdg $12.99 **E**

1. Fishes—Fiction
ISBN 0-394-81713-3; 0-394-91713-8 (lib bdg) LC 63-8504

A Caldecott Medal honor book, 1964

A reissue of the title first published 1963

"Swimmy, an insignificant fish, escapes when a whole school of small fish are swallowed by a larger one. As he swims away from danger he meets many wonderful, colorful creatures and later saves another school of fish from the jaws of the enemy." Ont Libr Rev

"To illustrate his clever, but very brief story, Leo Lionni has made a book of astonishingly beautiful pictures, full of undulating, watery nuances of shape, pattern, and color." Horn Book

Little, Lessie Jones, 1906-1986

I can do it by myself; by Lessie Jones Little and Eloise Greenfield; illustrated by Carole Byard. Crowell 1978 unp il $12.95; lib bdg $12.89 **E**

1. Birthdays—Fiction 2. Blacks—Fiction
ISBN 0-690-01369-8; 0-690-03851-8 (lib bdg) LC 77-11554

Donny is determined to buy his mother's birthday present all by himself, but he meets a scary challenge on the way home

"The story is well and simply told with enough interesting incidental detail . . . to erase a slight tendency toward wordiness. The drawings using soft pencil and charcoal lines enlivened by pale green washes are especially good at portraying emotion." SLJ

Lobel, Anita, 1934-

Alison's zinnia. Greenwillow Bks. 1990 unp il $14.95; lib bdg $12.88 **E**

1. Flowers—Fiction 2. Alphabet
ISBN 0-688-08865-1; 0-688-08866-X (lib bdg) LC 89-23700

"More than two dozen little girls, a full alphabet of them, pick flowers for their friends: 'Alison acquired an Amaryllis for Beryl' and 'Nancy noticed a Narcissus for Olga' and so on till 'Zena zeroed in on a Zinnia for Alison.' Underneath each large handsome floral illustration is a smaller picture of the named child and her flower. Charming." N Y Times Book Rev

Lobel, Arnold

Frog and Toad are friends. Harper & Row 1970 64p il $10.95; lib bdg $10.89; pa $3.50 **E**

1. Frogs—Fiction 2. Toads—Fiction
ISBN 0-06-023957-3; 0-06-023958-1 (lib bdg); 0-06-444020-6 (pa) LC 73-105492

A Caldecott Medal honor book, 1971

"An I can read book"

Here are five stories . . . which recount the adventures of two best friends—Toad and Frog. The stories are: Spring; The story; A lost button; A swim; The letter

The stories are told "with humor and perception. Illustrations in soft green and brown enhance the smooth flowing and sensitive story." SLJ

Other available titles about Frog and Toad are:
Days with Frog and Toad (1979)
Frog and Toad all year (1976)
Frog and Toad together (1972)

Grasshopper on the road. Harper & Row 1978 62p il $10.95; lib bdg $10.89; pa $3.50 **E**

1. Locusts—Fiction 2. Animals—Fiction
ISBN 0-06-023961-1; 0-06-023962-X (lib bdg); 0-06-444094-X (pa) LC 77-25653

"An I can read book"

"Grasshopper's journey is divided into six chapters. In each chapter he meets a different animal or animals attending to a spectrum of tasks. The chapters weave a tale of habit—doing without questioning. Grasshopper gives his need-for-change reaction to each one, but only a worm in his apple home is open to change." Child Book Rev Serv

Lobel, Arnold—*Continued*

"The contemporary version of the fable of the ant and the grasshopper is told in a repetitive I-Can-Read text and extended in three-color illustrations which delicately capture the grasshopper's microcosmic world view." Horn Book

Ming Lo moves the mountain; written and illustrated by Arnold Lobel. Greenwillow Bks. 1982 unp il lib bdg $13.88; Scholastic pa $2.95 **E**

1. Mountains—Fiction 2. Houses—Fiction
ISBN 0-688-00611-6 (lib bdg); 0-590-33994-X (pa)
LC 81-13327

"Ming Lo and his wife love their house, but not the mountain that overshadows it. So, at his wife's bidding, Ming Lo undertakes to move the mountain by following the advice of a wise man." Child Book Rev Serv

"An original tale utilizing folkloric motifs, the book is Chinese-like rather than Chinese, for the artist has created an imagined landscape. The setting, shown in flowing lines and tones of delicate watercolors, provides a source of inspiration drawn from an ancient artistic tradition; particularly effective in conveying a sense of distance are the panoramic double-page spreads." Horn Book

Mouse soup. Harper & Row 1977 63p il $10.95; lib bdg $10.89 **E**

1. Mice—Fiction
ISBN 0-06-023967-0; 0-06-023968-9 (lib bdg)
LC 76-41517

"In an effort to save himself from a weasel's stew pot, a little mouse tells the weasel four separate stories." West Coast Rev Books

"An artistic triumph with enough suspense, humor and wisdom to hold any reader who has a trace of curiosity and compassion. . . . The little one triumphs over the big one, and every child will rejoice. The exquisite wash drawings in mousey shades of grays, blues, greens and golds, have enough humor and pathos to exact repeated scrutiny. Like the stories, they improve with each reading." N Y Times Book Rev

Mouse tales. Harper & Row 1972 61p il $10.95; lib bdg $10.89; pa $3.50 **E**

1. Mice—Fiction
ISBN 0-06-023941-7; 0-06-023942-5 (lib bdg); 0-06-444013-3 (pa) LC 72-76511

"An I can read book"

Papa Mouse tells seven bedtime stories, one for each of his sons

Contents: The wishing well; Clouds; Very tall mouse and very short mouse; The mouse and the winds; The journey; The odd mouse; The bath

"The illustrations have soft colors and precise, lively little drawings of the imaginative and humorous events in the stories. The themes are familiar to children: cloud shapes, wishing, a tall and a short friend who observe—and greet—natural phenomena on a walk, taking a bath, et cetera." Bull Cent Child Books

On Market Street; pictures by Anita Lobel; words by Arnold Lobel. Greenwillow Bks. 1981 c1980 unp il $13.95; lib bdg $13.88; pa $3.95 **E**

1. Shopping—Fiction 2. Alphabet 3. Stories in rhyme
ISBN 0-688-80309-1; 0-688-84309-3 (lib bdg); 0-688-08745-0 (pa) LC 80-21418

A Caldecott Medal honor book, 1982

In this "alphabet book, a boy trots down Market Street buying presents for a friend, each one starting with a letter of the alphabet. Every letter is illustrated by a figure . . . composed of, for instance, apples or wigs or quilts or Xmas trees." Horn Book

"The artist has adapted the style of old French trade engravings, infusing it with a wonderful sense of color and detail. . . . Arnold Lobel's words ring of old rhymes, but it is these intricate, lovely drawings that take the day, and truly make it brighter." N Y Times Book Rev

On the day Peter Stuyvesant sailed into town. Harper & Row 1971 unp il lib bdg $12.89; pa $4.95 **E**

1. Stuyvesant, Peter, 1592-1672—Fiction 2. New York (N.Y.)—History—Fiction 3. Stories in rhyme
ISBN 0-06-023972-7 (lib bdg); 0-06-443144-4 (pa)
LC 75-148420

This is the "story of Peter Stuyvesant who, arriving in New Amsterdam in 1647, found the whole dirty place a total disgrace, and angrily set the Dutchmen to work transforming the village into a pleasant place in which to live." Booklist

"The illustrations, many framed like Dutch tiles, are done in yellow and blue and have a rhythm and humor that complement the verse exactly. The double-page spread at the end of the book—showing the future of Peter's tidy city—provides an unexpected shock of recognition." Horn Book

Owl at home. Harper & Row 1982 64p il $10.95; lib bdg $10.89; pa $3.50 **E**

1. Owls—Fiction
ISBN 0-06-023948-4; 0-06-023949-2 (lib bdg); 0-06-444034-6 (pa)

"An I can read book"

Five stories describe the adventures of a lovably foolish owl

"A child reader or listener in a kind of one-upmanship over wide-eyed tufted Owl will bristle with anxiety to have him perceive what causes two bewildering bumps under the blanket at the foot of his bed. The best scope for Lobel's inventiveness in drawing is, however, the opening episode where 'poor old' Winter makes a pushy entry into Owl's home. Muted browns and greys are countered by an animation that fully reveals Owl's distresses and contentments." Wash Post Child Book World

The rose in my garden; pictures by Anita Lobel. Greenwillow Bks. 1984 unp il $11.75; lib bdg $12.88; Scholastic pa $2.95 **E**

1. Flowers—Fiction 2. Stories in rhyme
ISBN 0-688-02586-2; 0-688-02587-0 (lib bdg); 0-590-40356-7 (pa) LC 83-14097

"A cumulative poem tells of a lovely garden, starting with 'this is the rose in my garden,' continuing through the lilies, bluebells, daisies, and other flowers, and culminating with a cat chasing a field mouse. A bee on

Lobel, Arnold—*Continued*
the rose awakens and stings the cat, thus allowing the mouse to escape, and the text ends with the opening lines." Horn Book

"A charming diversion, this combination of cumulative verse and rich—also cumulative—paintings of flowers in a profusion of improbably simultaneous bloom. Anita Lobel begins with a luxuriant red rose, adding other flowers and echoing Arnold Lobel's verse story of near-carnage (cat and fieldmouse) in the flower-beds. Lovely to look at, and enjoyable for reading aloud." Bull Cent Child Books

Small pig; story and pictures by Arnold Lobel. Harper & Row 1969 63p il lib bdg $10.89; pa $3.50 **E**

1. Pigs—Fiction
ISBN 0-06-023932-8 (lib bdg); 0-06-444120-2 (pa) LC 69-10213

"An I can read book"

This "is the story of a pig who, finding the clean farm unbearable, runs away to look for mud—and ends up stuck in cement. His facial expressions alone are worth the price of the book; the illustrations, in blue, green, and gold, are a perfect complement to the story. Humor, adventure, and short, simple sentences provide a real treat for beginning readers." SLJ

A treeful of pigs; pictures by Anita Lobel. Greenwillow Bks. 1979 unp il lib bdg $12.88; Scholastic pa $3.95 **E**

1. Pigs—Fiction 2. Farm life—Fiction
ISBN 0-688-84177-5 (lib bdg); 0-590-41280-9 (pa) LC 78-1810

A "story about a farmer's wife who tries everything to pry her lazy husband out of bed. He says he'll come to help her when the pigs grow on trees, fall from the sky, or 'bloom in the garden like flowers.' His wife knows how to work magic, and she makes each one of them happen with the help of a cooperative brood of piglets." Child Book Rev Serv

"The framed, full-color illustrations, characterized by intricately detailed designs in costumes and setting, are as elaborate as the diction is simple. The total effect, however, is one of unity, for the two are combined into a true picture book in which words and illustrations are interdependent." Horn Book

Uncle Elephant. Harper & Row 1981 62p il $10.95; lib bdg $10.89; pa $3.50 **E**

1. Elephants—Fiction
ISBN 0-06-023979-4; 0-06-023980-8 (lib bdg); 0-06-444104-0 (pa) LC 80-8944

"An I can read book"

Uncle Elephant takes care of his nephew whose parents are lost at sea. This book describes the way they lived together until the parents are rescued and little elephant rejoins them

"Nine gentle stories for the beginning independent reader; the soft grey, peach, and green tones of the deft pictures are an appropriate echo of the mood. The nephew and uncle may be elephants, but their relationship speaks effectively of the special bond between young and old and of the comforting fact that other family members can be as loving and supportive as parents are." Bull Cent Child Books

Locker, Thomas, 1937-

The mare on the hill. Dial Bks. for Young Readers 1985 unp il $15.95 **E**

1. Horses—Fiction
ISBN 0-8037-0207-8 LC 85-1684

Grandfather brings home a fearful mare to breed, hoping that his grandsons can teach her to trust people again

"Locker tells a solid story, in a minimum of well-chosen words. . . . Each event is printed on the reader's mind by Locker's ineffable paintings of the matchless terrain of the Hudson River Valley. The artist's rich colors emphasize changes wrought by the four seasons in the country, largely undisturbed by 'progress,' where people live in harmony with nature." Publ Wkly

Sailing with the wind. Dial Bks. for Young Readers 1986 unp il $15; lib bdg $14.89 **E**

1. Sailing—Fiction 2. Uncles—Fiction
ISBN 0-8037-0311-2; 0-8037-0312-0 (lib bdg) LC 85-23381

"A young girl's uncle, a sailor who has been around the world, comes to visit. He arrives by sailboat, having come up the river from the port, where his ship has docked. Ever since his niece was small, Uncle Jack has promised her a sailboat trip to the ocean, and now that promise is about to be fulfilled. Their day begins at dawn; they share a picnic lunch, weather a storm, and then sail back home beneath a red-and-yellow sky." Booklist

"Besides painting exquisite Constable-esque country scenes, Mr. Locker carefully chooses a particular rhythm of Nature to illustrate the passage of time and to provide his palette with the full spectrum of color, light and shadow. What makes his books so spectacularly successful is the harmonious marriage of textual theme and Nature's theme." Child Book Rev Serv

Where the river begins. Dial Bks. for Young Readers 1984 unp il $15; lib bdg $14.89 **E**

1. Grandfathers—Fiction 2. Camping—Fiction 3. Rivers—Fiction
ISBN 0-8037-0089-X; 0-8037-0090-3 (lib bdg) LC 84-1709

"Two young boys journey with their grandfather to find the beginning of the river that flows by their house. In full-page landscape paintings and simple prose, Thomas Locker follows the journey." Sci Child

"Admittedly, the simple narrative text is overshadowed by the magnificence of its illustrations. But their limpid beauty and exquisite detail are—to paraphrase Emerson—their own excuse for being. Reminiscent of the work of great landscape painters like Turner, Constable, and the American George Inness, the paintings follow not only the course of the river but the nearly three-day journey of the old man and the boys." Horn Book

Loh, Morag Jeanette, 1935-

Tucking Mommy in; by Morag Loh; illustrated by Donna Rawlins. Orchard Bks. 1988 c1987 unp il $12.95; lib bdg $12.99 E

1. Sisters—Fiction 2. Mothers and daughters—Fiction 3. Sleep—Fiction
ISBN 0-531-05740-2; 0-531-08340-3 (lib bdg) LC 87-16740

First published 1987 in Australia

Two sisters tuck their mother into bed one evening when she is especially tired

"The amusing turnabout on standard bedtime routines is a sweet reflection of the spontaneous love and generosity children sometimes show. Rawlins' pictures depict a raven-haired family at ease with each other's company. Her scenes show an eye for the dishevelment that follows children's footsteps, and the warm, sunny colors that dominate add to the story's good vibrations." Booklist

Lomas Garza, Carmen

Family pictures; paintings by Carmen Lomas Garza; stories by Carneb Lomas Garza; as told to Harriet Rohmer; version in Spanish, Rosalma Zubizarreta. Children's Bk. Press 1990 30p il $12.95 E

1. Hispanic Americans—Fiction 2. Bilingual books—Spanish-English
ISBN 0-89239-050-6 (lib. bdg.) LC 89-27845

Text in English and Spanish

The author describes her experiences growing up in a Hispanic community in Texas

"An inspired celebration of American cultural diversity. . . . The English text is simple and reads smoothly, but it is Zubizarreta's Spanish rendition that has real verve and style. From the exquisite cut-paper images on the text pages, to the brilliant paintings, to the strong family bonds expressed in the text, Family Pictures/ Cuadros de familia is a visual feast, and an aural delight." SLJ

Lord, John Vernon, 1939-

The giant jam sandwich; story and pictures by John Vernon Lord, with verses by Janet Burroway. Houghton Mifflin 1973 c1972 32p il lib bdg $15.95; pa $3.95 E

1. Wasps—Fiction 2. Stories in rhyme
ISBN 0-395-16033-2 (lib bdg); 0-395-44237-0 (pa) LC 72-13578

First published 1972 in the United Kingdom

This is a story in rhymed verse "about the citizens of Itching Down, who, attacked by four million wasps, make a giant jam sandwich to attract and trap the insects. With dump truck, spades, and hoes the people spread butter and strawberry jam across an enormous slice of bread; then, when the wasps settle, they drop the other slice from five helicopters and a flying tractor." Booklist

"Highly amusing in the details of John Vernon Lord's illustrations. . . . The figures are deliciously grotesque, their expressions wickedly accurate and the colours cheerfully vivid." Jr Bookshelf

Low, Joseph, 1911-

Mice twice; story & pictures by Joseph Low. Atheneum Pubs. 1980 unp il hardcover o.p. paperback available $4.95 E

1. Animals—Fiction
ISBN 0-689-71060-7 (pa) LC 79-23274

A Caldecott Medal honor book, 1981

"A Margaret K. McElderry book"

"The old story of Cat chasing Mouse for dinner has a new twist. Mouse asks to bring a friend when Cat invites her to dinner, and while Cat licks his whiskers at the thought of more than one mouse, Mouse has in mind her friend Dog. And so begins a round of very hospitable and polite dinners with a slightly more outrageous friend brought along every night." SLJ

"Wit triumphant is the motif of an original tale which combines an elegantly crafted text with colorful illustrations. . . . The confrontations are described with eclat; tension is developed through superfically polite conversations contrasting sharply with the real intentions of the protagonists, a contrast intensified by the accompanying illustrations. A humorous and stylish book." Horn Book

Luenn, Nancy, 1954-

Nessa's fish; illustrated by Neil Waldman. Atheneum Pubs. 1990 unp il $13.95 E

1. Inuit—Fiction 2. Grandmothers—Fiction
ISBN 0-689-31477-9 LC 89-15048

"Nessa, an Inuit girl, and her grandmother go on an ice-fishing expedition. When Grandmother falls ill, Nessa uses her wits, her courage, and the remembered advice of her father and her grandfather to defend their catch from a fox, a pack of wolves, and a bear. Luminous watercolor paintings set the action within a remarkable variety of land- and snowscapes seen in the same place at different times of the day and night. . . . Well designed, the book invites readers to linger over its many striking visual images." Booklist

Luttrell, Ida, 1934-

Ottie Slockett; illustrated by Ute Krause. Dial Bks. for Young Readers 1990 40p il $9.95; lib bdg $9.89 E

1. Friendship—Fiction
ISBN 0-8037-0709-6; 0-8037-0711-8 (lib bdg) LC 88-30884

"Dial easy-to-read"

"Ottie Slockett considers himself helpful; other people say he's a 'buttinsky.' He doesn't think twice about telling Mrs. Pepper she should drop a few pounds or informing Mr. Stern that his grass is too high. Then he wonders why his neighbors are so unfriendly. When Ottie makes the mistake of replacing his walls with glass windows (the better to see his neighbors), he learns others can throw stones, too." Booklist

"A humorous story that will capture and hold the interest of beginning readers. . . . Luttrell subtly explores the themes of meddling and learning a lesson, while Krause's comic illustrations perfectly portray Ottie and all his madcap neighbors." SLJ

Lyon, David

The biggest truck. Lothrop, Lee & Shepard Bks. 1988 unp il $12.95; lib bdg $12.88 **E**

1. Trucks—Fiction
ISBN 0-688-05513-3; 0-688-05514-1 (lib bdg) LC 87-22640

"While everyone else is going to bed, Jim, the truck driver, is going to work; he will drive a giant, two-trailored truck full of strawberries to market. The trip takes seven hours, and once he's reached his destination and unloaded, Jim is ready for sleep—just as everyone is waking up." Booklist

"The big truck's night journey is enlivened by Lyon's use of bold, jaunty colors, which illuminate such roadside attractions as the 'Home Cookin' Truck Stop,' where Jim shares a cup of coffee with fellow truckers. An engaging guide to the mysterious flow of goods via the highway, this will please truck fans everywhere." Publ Wkly

Lyon, George Ella, 1949-

A B Cedar; an alphabet of trees; designed and illustrated by Tom Parker. Orchard Bks. 1989 unp il $14.95; lib bdg $14.99 **E**

1. Alphabet 2. Trees
ISBN 0-531-05795-X; 0-531-08395-0 (lib bdg) LC 88-22797

"A Richard Jackson book"

"Here is a grove of trees alphabetically arranged—aspen, butternut, cedar to xolisma, yew and zebrawood. The trees are in silhouette and in proportion to cavorting human beings on the bottom of each page. The leaves and seeds are in larger, fixed scale across the pages." N Y Times Book Rev

"Easily the basis for a nature lesson, this will intrigue children usually considered to old for alphabet books. The art is cleanly executed." Booklist

Come a tide; story by George Ella Lyon; pictures by Stephen Gammell. Orchard Bks. 1990 unp il $14.95; lib bdg $14.99 **E**

1. Floods—Fiction 2. Country life—Fiction
ISBN 0-531-05854-9; 0-531-08454-X (lib bdg) LC 89-35650

"A Richard Jackson book"

"'It'll come a tide,' says Grandma after a four-day deluge. She's right: as the streams and creeks rush down the hill to the river, the water rises, sending residents of the hollows packing. The narrator's family hightails it up the hill to Grandma's house." Booklist

"Capturing the diction and homely imagery of a down-to-earth rural community, the first-person text richly evokes the sturdy qualities of folks who, beset by spring floods, respond to nature's challenges with common sense and wry humor. . . . In combination with Stephen Gammell's energetic illustrations, remarkable for their expressive lines and elegant use of watercolor, it becomes an exemplary picture story book, regional in setting but universal in appeal." Horn Book

A regular rolling Noah; illustrated by Stephen Gammell. Bradbury Press 1986 unp il $13.95; Aladdin Bks. (NY) pa $4.95 **E**

1. Voyages and travels—Fiction 2. Animals—Fiction 3. Railroads—Fiction
ISBN 0-02-761330-5; 0-689-71449-1 (pa) LC 86-8312

"Lyon's story takes the form of a young farmhand's folksy monologue telling about the time he helped a family move their whole farm to Canada. . . . The story's charm comes from its fresh voice and the happy-go-lucky mood of the paintings. Gammell's palette is light and his pictures energetic. Whimsy and humor abound, while a deft sense of composition and color insure that the eye is never bored." Booklist

Together; pictures by Vera Rosenberry. Orchard Bks. 1989 unp il $14.95; lib bdg $14.99 **E**

1. Friendship—Poetry 2. Stories in rhyme
ISBN 0-531-05831-X; 0-531-08431-0 (lib bdg) LC 89-2892

"A Richard Jackson book"

"The poem celebrates friendship, and in the whimsical world evoked by the illustrations, two girls—one black, one white—build a cabin, make a giant-sized ice cream sundae and put out a dragon's flame, among many other activities. Rosenberry's fanciful details add a pixieish touch to this spirited poem." Publ Wkly

Macaulay, David, 1946-

Black and white. Houghton Mifflin 1990 unp il $14.95 **E**

ISBN 0-395-52151-3 LC 89-28888

Awarded the Caldecott Medal, 1990

Four brief "stories" about parents, trains, and cows, or is it really all one story? The author recommends careful inspection of words and pictures to both minimize and enhance confusion

"The magic of *Black and White* comes not from each story, . . . but from the mysterious interactions between them that creates a fifth story. . . . Eventually, the stories begin to merge into a surrealistic tale spanning several levels of reality. . . . *Black and White* challenges the reader to use text and pictures in unexpected ways." Publ Wkly

Why the chicken crossed the road. Houghton Mifflin 1987 31p il lib bdg $13.95 **E**

ISBN 0-395-44241-9 LC 87-2908

"A ridiculous chicken sets off a circular story involving a herd of cows, a bridge, a train, a robber, the fire department and some hydrangeas. Chaos. The illustrations are suitably wild—painted with brilliant color and almost palpable energy." N Y Times Book Rev

Macdonald, Suse, 1940-

Alphabatics. Bradbury Press 1986 unp il $15.95 **E**

1. Alphabet
ISBN 0-02-761520-0 LC 85-31429

A Caldecott Medal honor book, 1987

MacDonald "maneuvers each letter to create a visual image as well as an object that begins with that letter." Child Book Rev Serv

The "*A* tilts, flops over, and literally becomes an ark as it turns itself around. An *N* turns over, glides up a tree trunk, and becomes a nest for three young birds. Crisp, fresh, and totally effective, it's a unique way of looking at the alphabet. This is a book for creative

Macdonald, Suse, 1940-—*Continued*
thinking and sheer enjoyment of MacDonald's precise graphics, rather than for object identification among the very young." SLJ

Numblers; [by] Suse MacDonald, Bill Oakes. Dial Bks. for Young Readers 1988 unp il $13.95; lib bdg $13.89 **E**

1. Counting
ISBN 0-8037-0547-6; 0-8037-0548-4 (lib bdg)
LC 87-32736

On each double-page spread a number from one to ten changes gradually into a familiar object or animal, splitting apart in the process into the appropriate number of parts or pieces. Descriptive text in the back gives clues as to the nature of the thing depicted

"It's a stretch for the imagination and an enjoyable way to introduce children to numbers." SLJ

MacLachlan, Patricia

Mama One, Mama Two; pictures by Ruth Lercher Bornstein. Harper & Row 1982 unp il $12.95; lib bdg $12.89 **E**

1. Foster home care—Fiction 2. Mothers and daughters—Fiction 3. Mental illness—Fiction
ISBN 0-06-024081-4; 0-06-024082-2 (lib bdg)
LC 81-47795

"When Maudie is awakened by the baby's crying, her foster mother tells her the story of how she came to live in this temporary home. Together they describe the girl's mother's increasingly withdrawn behavior that led to the institutionalization of the girl's 'Mama One' and her subsequent placement with Katherine, whom she calls 'Mama Two.' They discuss Maudie's feelings and her hopes for her mother's quick recovery. This articulation of her fears calms the troubled child." SLJ

"Softly-crayoned pastel pictures, simply and tenderly composed and nicely fitting the mood of the story, show the love that is the mortar of the text. . . . There have been other books in which foster parents were sympathetically portrayed; this is the nicest yet for the primary grades reader." Bull Cent Child Books

Maestro, Betsy, 1944-

Ferryboat; by Betsy and Giulio Maestro. Crowell 1986 unp il map $13.95; lib bdg $13.89 **E**

1. Boats and boating—Fiction
ISBN 0-690-04519-0; 0-690-04520-4 (lib bdg)
LC 85-47887

A family crosses the Connecticut River on a ferryboat and observes how the ferry operates

Illustrated with "sunny watercolor paintings in realistically detailed double-page spreads. . . . Children who are familiar with the procedure should enjoy this recreation of their experience, and others may be intrigued. This may also appeal to very young children who are in the any-vehicle-is-a-good-vehicle stage. An appended note gives historical information about the ferry on which the book is based, the Chester-Hadlyme Ferry, which began operating in 1769." Bull Cent Child Books

Snow day; illustrated by Giulio Maestro. Scholastic 1989 unp il $12.95 **E**

1. Snow—Fiction
ISBN 0-590-41283-3
LC 88-19480

Text and illustrations describe what happens after a major snowstorm, from plowing driveways and rescuing stranded motorists to clearing train tracks, airports, and harbors

"The charcoal-and-wash drawings, which nicely carry forth the mood, are realistic in style, in contrast to the bright, slick colors and cartoonlike drawings seen in much of Maestro's other work. An unpretentious wintertime choice." Booklist

Taxi; a book of city words; by Betsy & Giulio Maestro. Clarion Bks. 1989 unp il lib bdg $13.95 **E**

1. Vocabulary 2. City life
ISBN 0-89919-528-8
LC 88-22867

"A taxi moves through a city in the course of an ordinary day. The text describes what happens in the action-oriented pictures. The best illustrations strive to capture a quality of urban motion and lively urban streets." N Y Times Book Rev

Mahy, Margaret

17 kings and 42 elephants; pictures by Patricia MacCarthy. Dial Bks. for Young Readers 1987 26p il $11.95; pa $4.95 **E**

1. Animals—Fiction 2. Stories in rhyme
ISBN 0-8037-0458-5; 0-8037-0781-9 (pa) LC 87-5311

A newly illustrated edition of the title first published 1972 in the United Kingdom

Seventeen kings and forty-two elephants romp with a variety of jungle animals during their mysterious journey through a wild, wet night

"This book takes you on a jungle journey you will never forget. . . . The text is lyrical, humorous, and full of nonsense and fantasy. Children and adults will be charmed by the melodic use of language and the beautiful batik illustrations." Child Book Rev Serv

The boy who was followed home; pictures by Steven Kellogg. Dial Bks. for Young Readers 1986 c1975 unp il $12.95; pa $3.95 **E**

1. Hippopotamus—Fiction 2. Witches—Fiction
ISBN 0-8037-0286-8; 0-8037-0903-4 (pa) LC 75-4866

First published 1975 by Franklin Watts

In this "humorous story, Robert, for some unexplained reason, is adopted by a growing number of hippopotami. His parents are most patient with the situation until the number of hippos reaches twenty-seven. Robert's father calls in the services of a local witch to rid the boy of his rapidly growing horde of friends. The witch solves the problem in an unexpected and delightful (and not totally successful) way." Child Book Rev Serv

"Kellogg is in his element, drawing the perfect details and more; each picture tells a tale of its own while sweeping the story right along. Swathes of lemon yellow and pinkish lavender are balanced with lots of clean white space and fine line work. The artist's sense of the absurd has made connections with an author's experience in what appeals to children." Booklist

Mahy, Margaret—*Continued*

The great white man-eating shark; a cautionary tale; pictures by Jonathan Allen. Dial Bks. for Young Readers 1990 unp il $12.95 **E**

1. Sharks—Fiction
ISBN 0-8037-0749-5 LC 89-1514

Greedy to have the cove where he swims all to himself, Norvin, who looks a bit like a shark, pretends to be one, scaring off the other swimmers and leaving him in happy aquatic solitude—until he is discovered by an amorous female shark

"Mahy's amusing tongue-in-cheek tale meets its match in Allen's droll drawings. Norvin's wonderfully shifty eyes and the vivid expressions on the faces of his victims are certain to tickle funnybones." Publ Wkly

Making friends; illustrated by Wendy Smith. Margaret K. McElderry Bks. 1990 unp il $13.95 **E**

1. Dogs—Fiction 2. Friendship—Fiction
ISBN 0-689-50498-5 LC 89-13246

Small Mrs. de Vere's large dog Titania and large Mr. Derry's small dog Oberon serve as the instruments that bring their masters together in an unexpected but quite successful friendship

"The illustrations are a perfect match for the humor and affection for the nice old couple that suffuse the text. The city's parks and fountains and shops provide a colorful background for the sprightly pair, whose friendship triggers a new lease on life that one might envy at any age." Horn Book

Manushkin, Fran

Latkes and applesauce; a Hanukkah story; illustrated by Robin Spowart. Scholastic 1990 unp il $12.95 **E**

1. Hanukkah—Fiction
ISBN 0-590-42261-8 LC 88-38916

When a blizzard leaves a family housebound one Hanukkah, they share what little food they have with a stray kitten and dog

"To their surprise and delight, the dog digs in the snow and unearths some potatoes, and the kitten has to be rescued from a tree that still has apples on its branches. . . . The two new pets are named Latke and Applesauce. The dark, slightly impressionistic illustrations in warm tones capture the feeling of a time past and of a family that has an abundance of affection. The story of the holiday, a recipe for latkes, instructions for the dreidel game, and the names of a few other books about the holiday are appended." Horn Book

Maris, Ron

Is anyone home? Greenwillow Bks. 1985 unp il lib bdg $11.95 **E**

ISBN 0-688-05899-X LC 85-5436

"Every other page is a half-page door to open. The first half-page is a garden gate to be opened (turned) by the reader. The next door opens to the hen house. The doors lead the reader to the last door which is the door to grandma's house where she is waiting for you to come in and visit. The art work is well done and very colorful. A good book to read aloud, one which lends itself to creative writing as well." Okla State Dept of Educ

Marshall, Edward, 1942-

Fox and his friends; pictures by James Marshall. Dial Bks. for Young Readers 1982 56p il lib bdg $9.89; pa $4.95 **E**

1. Foxes—Fiction
ISBN 0-8037-2669-4 (lib bdg); 0-8037-2668-6 (pa) LC 81-68769

"Dial easy-to-read"

"Fox has one objective—having fun with his motley group of friends. Unfortunately, his desires regularly conflict with his mother's insistence that he care for his younger sister Louise or with his responsibilities when assigned to traffic patrol." Horn Book

"The sibling exchanges and situations are comically true to life, as is Fox's duty/pleasure conflict. The red, green and black illustrations, showing a defiant Louise, a beleaguered Fox, a wonderful assortment of creature friends and a hilariously feeble group of old hounds pick the story up and add character embellishment and humor." SLJ

Other available titles about Fox are:
Fox all week (1984)
Fox at school (1983)
Fox in love (1982)
Fox on wheels (1983)

Other available titles about Fox written by the author using the name James Marshall are:
Fox be nimble (1990)
Fox on the job (1988)

Space case; pictures by James Marshall. Dial Bks. for Young Readers 1980 unp il $13.95; lib bdg $13.89; pa $4.95 **E**

1. Science fiction 2. Halloween—Fiction
ISBN 0-8037-8005-2; 0-8037-8007-9 (lib bdg); 0-8037-8431-7 (pa) LC 80-13369

"The 'thing'—a neon yellow robot-like creature from space—arrives on Halloween for a look around and is promptly mistaken for a costumed trick-or-treater. It spends the night with a friendly child . . . visits at school (the teacher takes it for a science project) and leaves promising to return for the next fun holiday, Christmas." SLJ

"The open ending of the brief story is as satisfying as it is original, for the small space traveler is thoroughly childlike in its insouciance, curiosity, and concern for self-gratification. The text is an economical, tongue-in-cheek accompaniment to the various levels of humor depicted in the illustrations. Transcending the particular holiday, the picture book should be a marvelous vehicle for story hours." Horn Book

Another available title in this series written by the author using the name James Marshall is:
Merry Christmas, space case (1986)

Three by the sea; pictures by James Marshall. Dial Bks. for Young Readers 1981 48p il lib bdg $9.89; pa $4.95 **E**

ISBN 0-8037-8687-5 (lib bdg); 0-8037-8671-9 (pa) LC 80-26097

"Dial easy-to-read"

"When Lolly, on a beach picnic with friends Sam and Spider, reads a story ('The rat saw the cat and the dog.') aloud, it is rated dull. So Sam uses the same rat and

Marshall, Edward, 1942-—*Continued*
cat characters to tell one of his own, and Spider tops Sam's managing to scare the other two with his tale of a monster that passes by the rat and cat to find some tasty kids." SLJ

"What fun, within an easy reader, to find a story that pokes fun at easy readers. . . . The mild lunacy of the illustrations (an almost vertical hill, a neatly striped cat) with their ungainly, comical figures is nicely matched with the bland directness of the writing. This is good-humored and amusing, good practice for the beginning reader, and unusual in its presentation of storytelling within the story." Bull Cent Child Books

Another available title about Spider, Sam, and Lolly is:
Four on the shore (1985)

Another available title about Spider, Sam, and Lolly written by the author using the name James Marshall is:
Three up a tree (1986)

Troll country; pictures by James Marshall. Dial Bks. for Young Readers 1980 56p il lib bdg $9.89; pa $4.95 **E**

1. Fairy tales
ISBN 0-8037-6211-9 (lib bdg); 0-8037-6210-0 (pa)
LC 79-19324

"Dial easy-to-read"

"Elsie's mother—despite her husband's insistence that there are no trolls—tells her daughter how she once met one and bested him. Elsie, when she runs into a mean, green, smelly troll as she returns from an errand, thinks of another way to trick the troll after she's tried her mother's method and been told, 'I have heard 'that' before!'" Bull Cent Child Books

"The artist's familiar style is used to advantage in the illustrations of smugly self-satisfied Elsie, her mother, and the stumpy, unlovely, stupid troll. An amusing book for the beginning reader." Horn Book

Marshall, James, 1942-

The cut-ups. Viking Kestrel 1984 unp il lib bdg $12.95; Puffin Bks. pa $3.95 **E**

ISBN 0-670-25195-X (lib bdg); 0-14-050637-3 (pa)
LC 84-40256

Practical jokers Spud and Joe get away with every trick in the book until the day they meet a little girl named Mary Frances Hooley

"This book may not show the subtle wit of Marshall at his best . . . but it is good-humored fun that will certainly entice readers and listeners." SLJ

Other available titles about Spud and Joe are:
The cut-ups at Camp Custer (1989)
The cut-ups carry on (1990)
The cut-ups cut loose (1987)

George and Martha; written and illustrated by James Marshall. Houghton Mifflin 1972 46p il lib bdg $12.95; pa $4.95 **E**

1. Hippopotamus—Fiction 2. Friendship—Fiction
ISBN 0-395-16619-5 (lib bdg); 0-395-19972-7 (pa)
LC 74-184250

In these five short episodes which include a misunderstanding about split pea soup, invasion of privacy and a crisis over a missing tooth, two not very delicate hippopotamuses reveal various aspects of friendship

"The pale pictures of these creatures and their adventures—in yellows, pinks, greens, and grays—capture the directness and humor of the stories." Horn Book

Other available titles about George and Martha are:
George and Martha back in town (1984)
George and Martha encore (1973)
George and Martha, one fine day (1978)
George and Martha rise and shine (1976)
George and Martha round and round (1988)
George and Martha, tons of fun (1980)

Wings; a tale of two chickens. Viking Kestrel 1986 unp il $12.95; Penguin Bks. pa $3.95 **E**

1. Chickens—Fiction 2. Foxes—Fiction
ISBN 0-670-80961-6; 0-14-050579-2 (pa)
LC 85-40953

Harriet the chicken rescues her foolish, uneducated friend from the clutches of a wily fox

"In a zany series of events, Winnie escapes while her captor is picking up a package of instant dumplings, is recaptured by the fox disguised as a chicken, and is rescued by Harriet disguised as a fox. Marshall's pictures are even roomier and more expressive than usual in a story perfectly suited for the young audience who has just discovered the difference between chickens and foxes and who will therefore delight in these sly reversals. Theatre of the absurd at its most basic level, with vivid color sets." Bull Cent Child Books

Yummers! Houghton Mifflin 1973 30p il lib bdg $12.95; pa $3.95 **E**

1. Pigs—Fiction 2. Turtles—Fiction 3. Reducing—Fiction
ISBN 0-395-14757-3 (lib bdg); 0-395-39590-9 (pa)
LC 72-5400

Worried about her weight, Emily Pig "jumps rope; her friend Eugene [Turtle] suggests a walk as better exercise, but the walk is interrupted by a series of snacks. Emily, who has said 'Yummers,' to everything, finally has a tummy ache. She thinks it must have been due to all the walking, and agrees with Eugene when he suggests that she stay in bed and eat plenty of good food." Bull Cent Child Books

"Corpulent, amiable Emily moves with monumental charm in the humorous, bright pastel pictures." Horn Book

Other available titles about Emily Pig and Eugene Turtle are:
Taking care of Carruthers (1981)
What's the matter with Carruthers? (1972)
Yummers too: the second course (1986)

Martin, Bill, 1916-

Barn dance! by Bill Martin, Jr. and John Archambault; illustrated by Ted Rand. Holt & Co. 1986 unp il $12.95; pa $4.95 **E**

1. Stories in rhyme 2. Dancing—Fiction 3. Country life—Fiction
ISBN 0-8050-0089-5; 0-8050-0799-7 (pa)
LC 86-14225

Unable to sleep on the night of a full moon, a young boy follows the sound of music across the fields and finds an unusual barn dance in progress

"The bouncy rhyme will be a pleasure for listeners and tellers as they pick up the twang and the barn-dance beat. Rand's raucous two-page watercolor spreads are as spirited as the story poem." Booklist

Martin, Bill, 1916-—*Continued*

Chicka chicka boom boom; by Bill Martin, Jr. and John Archambault; illustrated by Lois Ehlert. Simon & Schuster Bks. for Young Readers 1989 unp il $13.95
E

1. Alphabet 2. Stories in rhyme
ISBN 0-671-67949-X LC 89-4315

An alphabet rhyme/chant that relates what happens when the whole alphabet tries to climb a coconut tree

"Ehlert's illustrations—bold, colorful shapes—are contained by broad polka-dotted borders, like a proscenium arch through which the action explodes. Tongue-tingling, visually stimulating, with an insistent repetitive chorus of 'chicka chicka boom boom,' the book demands to be read again and again and again." Horn Book

The ghost-eye tree; by Bill Martin, Jr. and John Archambault; illustrated by Ted Rand. Holt & Co. 1985 unp il $13.95; pa $4.95
E

1. Ghosts—Fiction 2. Fear—Fiction 3. Brothers and sisters—Fiction
ISBN 0-8050-0208-1; 0-8050-0947-7 (pa) LC 85-8422

"On a dark and ghostly night a brother and sister are sent to fetch a pail of milk from the other end of town. They must pass the fearful ghost-eye tree, old and horribly twisted, looking like a monster, with a gap in the branches where the moon shines through like an eye. . . . The story is rhythmically told, sometimes rhyming, always moving ahead, sharp with the affectionate teasing of the brother and sister. The realistic watercolor illustrations are superb—strong, striking, very dark, with highlights of moonlight and lantern light that cast a spooky, scary spell. A splendidly theatrical book for storytelling and reading aloud." Horn Book

Knots on a counting rope; by Bill Martin, Jr. and John Archambault; illustrated by Ted Rand. Holt & Co. 1987 unp il $14.95; pa $4.95
E

1. Indians of North America—Fiction 2. Grandfathers—Fiction 3. Blind—Fiction
ISBN 0-8050-0571-4; 0-8050-1313-X (pa)
LC 87-14858

A different version of the title illustrated by Joe Smith was published in 1966

"Boy-Strength-of-Blue-Horses begs his grandfather to tell him again the story of the night he was born. In a question-and-answer litany, the boy and his grandfather share the telling of the events on that special night." SLJ

"The powerful spare poetic text is done full justice by Rand's fine full-color illustrations, which capture both the drama and brilliance of vast southwestern space and the intimacy of starlit camp-fire scenes. While classified as an Indian story the love, hope, and courage expressed are universal, meriting a wide audience." Booklist

Listen to the rain; by Bill Martin, Jr. and John Archambault; illustrated by James Endicott. Holt & Co. 1988 unp il $13.95
E

1. Rain and rainfall—Fiction 2. Stories in rhyme
ISBN 0-8050-0682-6 LC 88-6502

A "rhyming story about rain. The book is brief, yet each page is so much fun to read that children won't feel shortchanged. Endicott's double-page watercolors in hues of blue and red, capture both the quiet and the angry moods of a rain." SLJ

Up and down on the merry-go-round; by Bill Martin, Jr. and John Archambault; illustrated by Ted Rand. Holt & Co. 1988 unp il lib bdg $12.95
E

1. Stories in rhyme
ISBN 0-8050-0681-8 LC 87-28836

In this rhyming story, children describe the sights and sounds of riding on the merry-go-round

"Martin and Archambault have perfectly captured the joy and freedom a child feels while riding a carousel. . . . Rand's brilliant watercolors enlarge the text to recreate the thrilling ride. The animals on the merry-go-round are lushly drawn, with enough accurate detail to keep readers entranced." Horn Book

Martin, Charles E.

Island winter. Greenwillow Bks. 1984 unp il $10.25; lib bdg $10.88
E

1. Islands—Fiction 2. Winter—Fiction 3. Maine—Fiction
ISBN 0-688-02590-0; 0-688-02592-7 (lib bdg)
LC 83-14098

"Heather faces her first winter on a New England resort island with sadness and concern: what will she do all winter? She is answered through an atmospheric depiction of island days filled with one-room activities, holiday fun, piano lessons, a mailboat at Thanksgiving that also delivers her grandparents, ice skating and January lobstering." SLJ

"The artist has made joyous use of a traditional illustrative style. Subdued full-color paintings, ranging in mood from cheerful busyness to poetic beauty, reflect both the old-fashioned and the contemporary in the activities and the quietude encompassed by the island's circle of seasons." Horn Book

Other available titles about the island children are:
For rent (1986)
Island rescue (1985)
Sam saves the day (1987)
Summer business (1984)

Martin, Rafe, 1946-

Will's mammoth; illustrated by Stephen Gammell. Putnam 1989 unp il $14.95 E

1. Mammoths—Fiction
ISBN 0-399-21627-8 LC 88-11651

"Will loves mammoths—huge, hairy, woolly mammoths. His parents explain that there are no mammoths left in the world, but Will knows better. Off he goes into an iridescent, snowbound world of his own creation, where he quickly finds all manner of woolly prehistoric beasts." SLJ

"Gammell's depiction of a child's rich imagination is illustrated in vivid colors. The fantasy spreads use winter whites and blues as background for subtly individualized animals who move energetically across the pages." Booklist

Marzollo, Jean

Amy goes fishing; pictures by Ann Schweninger. Dial Bks. for Young Readers 1980 56p il lib bdg $5.89; pa $2.25 **E**

1. Fathers and daughters—Fiction 2. Fishing—Fiction
ISBN 0-8037-0109-8 (lib bdg); 0-8037-0111-X (pa)
LC 80-11598

"Dial easy-to-read"

"On a Saturday when the other members of the family are busy, Amy and her father go fishing. At first Amy finds it as boring as her older siblings have said, but the companionship with her father, the delicious lunch, and the triumph of her first catch change her opinion." Bull Cent Child Books

"The pleasant relationship between Amy and her quiet father is realistically shown; he can spin a tall tale with a straight face but also shows his anger when she is disobedient and falls into the water. The text is enhanced by soft water colors . . . but Amy lacks a full range of facial expressions." Horn Book

Close your eyes; pictures by Susan Jeffers. Dial Bks. 1978 unp il $12.95; lib bdg $12.89; pa $4.95 **E**

1. Lullabies
ISBN 0-8037-1609-5; 0-8037-1610-9 (lib bdg); 0-8037-1617-6 (pa) LC 76-42935

A lullaby interspersed with illustrations of a father's efforts to put his reluctant child to bed

"The text is interpreted in magnificent full-color pastel-toned illustrations, remarkable for their clarity, meticulous detail, and delicate line. . . . The book is a charming production in the old-fashioned tradition of a warm and reassuring bedtime story." Horn Book

Pretend you're a cat; pictures by Jerry Pinkney. Dial Bks. for Young Readers 1990 unp il $12.95; lib bdg $12.89 **E**

1. Animals—Fiction 2. Stories in rhyme
ISBN 0-8037-0773-8; 0-8037-0774-6 (lib bdg)
LC 89-34546

"Each double spread consists of a large painting of an animal, a smaller painting—boxed—of children imitating the animal, and of a series of questions [in verse]. Sample 'Can you climb? Can you leap? Can you stretch? Can you sleep? Can you hiss? Can you scat? Can you purr like a cat? What else can you do like a cat?'" Bull Cent Child Books

"The rhymed verses are vivid and straightforward, and Pinkney's inventive watercolor and pencil drawings are as engaging as the characters and animals he portrays." Publ Wkly

Maxner, Joyce

Nicholas Cricket; illustrated by William Joyce. Harper & Row 1989 unp il $13.95; lib bdg $13.89 **E**

1. Crickets—Fiction 2. Bands (Music)—Fiction 3. Animals—Fiction 4. Stories in rhyme
ISBN 0-06-024216-7; 0-06-024222-1 (lib bdg)
LC 88-33076

Nicholas Cricket and the other members of the Bug-a-Wug Cricket Band lead all the forest creatures in a musical celebration of the night

"Joyce's imaginative pictures, . . . depart from the expected by casting much of the action in a decidedly uptown mode. Top-hatted gents squire ladies in gowns in and out of clubs that ooze sophistication—no mean feat, considering these are insects and animals. The palette is dark, the creatures sleek and distinctive—Nicholas and company sport four suit-coated limbs, the better to fiddle and strum. A splendid toe-tapping night for all." Booklist

Mayer, Marianna, 1945-

The unicorn and the lake; pictures by Michael Hague. Dial Bks. for Young Readers 1982 unp il $13.95; lib bdg $13.89; pa $3.95 **E**

1. Unicorns—Fiction 2. Snakes—Fiction
ISBN 0-8037-9337-5; 0-8037-9338-3 (lib bdg); 0-8037-0436-4 (pa) LC 81-5469

When a serpent poisons the lake where all the animals drink, only the unicorn has the power to save them

"Told using dignified and stately language, without mannerisms or excess, the story is ably matched by Michael Hague's illustrations. Full-color double-page spreads, romantic but not sentimental, shimmer with feeling. . . . A lovely book, useful for storytelling or independent reading." SLJ

Mayer, Mercer, 1943-

Appelard and Liverwurst; story by Mercer Mayer; pictures by Steven Kellogg. Morrow Junior Bks. 1990 c1978 34p il $13.95; lib bdg $13.88 **E**

1. Rhinoceros—Fiction
ISBN 0-688-09659-X; 0-688-09660-3 (lib bdg)
LC 89-13803

A reissue of the title first published 1978 by Four Winds Press

Aided by a wayward rhinoceros, Appelard and his motley farm animals finally have a successful harvest

Another available title about Appelard and Liverwurst is entered below

A boy, a dog, and a frog. Dial Bks. for Young Readers 1967 unp il $9.95; lib bdg $9.89; pa $2.95 **E**

1. Frogs—Fiction 2. Stories without words
ISBN 0-8037-0763-0; 0-8037-0767-3 (lib bdg); 0-8037-0769-X (pa) LC 67-22254

"Without the need for a single word, humorous, very engaging pictures tell the story of a little boy who sets forth with his dog and a net on a summer day to catch an enterprising and personable frog. Even very young preschoolers will 'read' the tiny book with the greatest satisfaction and pleasure." Horn Book

Other available titles in this series are:
A boy, a dog, and a friend (1971)
Frog goes to dinner (1974)
Frog on his own (1973)
Frog, where are you? (1969)
One frog too many (1975)

Mayer, Mercer, 1943-—*Continued*

Liverwurst is missing; illustrated by Steven Kellogg. Morrow Junior Bks. 1990 c1981 unp il $13.95; lib bdg $13.88 E

1. Rhinoceros—Fiction 2. Kidnapping—Fiction
ISBN 0-688-09657-3; 0-688-09658-1 (lib bdg)
LC 90-5434

A reissue of the title first published 1981 by Four Winds Press

When Liverwurst the baby rhinosterwurst disappears, Wackatoo Indians, survivors of the 49th Cavalry, and children from the Koala Scouts join the circus company in rescuing him from a burger tycoon interested in creating Rhino-burgers

There's a nightmare in my closet. Dial Bks. for Young Readers 1968 unp il $12.95; lib bdg $12.89; pa $3.95 E

1. Fear—Fiction
ISBN 0-8037-8682-4; 0-8037-8683-2 (lib bdg); 0-8037-8574-7 (pa) LC 68-15250

A young boy confronts the frightening creature lurking in his closet

"Childhood fear of the dark and the resulting exercise in imaginative exaggeration are given that special Mercer Mayer treatment in this dryly humorous fantasy. Young children will easily empathize with the boy and can be comforted by his experience." SLJ

There's an alligator under my bed; written and illustrated by Mercer Mayer. Dial Bks. for Young Readers 1987 unp il $12.95; lib bdg $12.89 E

ISBN 0-8037-0374-0; 0-8037-0375-9 (lib bdg)
LC 86-19944

"The resourceful young hero of *There's a Nightmare in My Closet* [entered above] has a new problem—there's an alligator under his bed. His parents can't see it, but it's there, and to smoke it out the boy trails a line of food that alligators like to eat . . . to the garage, where the boy hopes the creature will stay. . . . The illustrations have a heavy look; dark hues and solid shapes are accented by thick black lines. Nevertheless, the oversize pictures will work well in story-hour groups, as will the short, snappy text." Booklist

Mayne, William, 1928-

The green book of Hob stories; illustrated by Patrick Benson. Philomel Bks. 1984 unp il $7.95 E

1. Fairies—Fiction
ISBN 0-399-21039-3 LC 83-17317

"A whimsical fantasy, this episodic tale [is] about a small, corpulent, self-satisfied household spirit. . . . The adults in a British household cannot see the tiny Hob but children and animals can, and speak of him." Bull Cent Child Books

"The stories are complemented by illustrations that owe something to Sendak but have a character of their own, picturing the pudgy, dumpy little Hob and the comfortable, happy household—very English, with tea cosies and coal fires. The tales are original and beguiling and clamor to be read aloud." Horn Book

Other available titles in this series are:
The blue book of Hob stories (1984)
The red book of Hob stories (1984)

McCloskey, Robert, 1914-

Blueberries for Sal. Viking 1948 54p il $13.95; Puffin Bks. pa $3.95 E

1. Bears—Fiction 2. Maine—Fiction
ISBN 0-670-17591-9; 0-14-050169-X (pa) LC 48-4955

A Caldecott Medal honor book, 1949

"The author-artist tells what happens on a summer day in Maine when a little girl and a bear cub, wandering away from their blueberry-picking mothers, each mistakes the other's mother for its own. The Maine hillside and meadows are real and lovely, the quiet humor is entirely childlike, and there is just exactly the right amount of suspense for small children." Wis Libr Bull

Another available title about Sal is: One morning in Maine, entered below

Burt Dow, deep-water man; a tale of the sea in the classic tradition. Viking 1963 61p il 15.95; Puffin Bks. pa $4.95 E

1. Whales—Fiction 2. Sea stories
ISBN 0-670-19748-3; 0-14-050978-X (pa)
LC 62-15446

"A picture-book yarn about an old retired fisherman who has an astonishing Jonahlike adventure with a whale while he is out fishing one day in his leaky, multicolored boat, the Tidely-Idley." Booklist

"The enchanting scenes of Burt Dow making off with his multi-colored dory into the wild, purple sea and meeting pink-mouthed whales really needs no text at all. It's a deep water voyage into art." Christ Sci Monit

Lentil. Viking 1940 unp il $14.95; Puffin Bks. pa $3.95 E

1. Harmonica—Fiction 2. Ohio—Fiction
ISBN 0-670-42357-2; 0-14-050287-4 (pa) LC 40-8617

Picture-story book about a small boy who could not sing, but who could work wonders on a simple harmonica, especially on the day when the great Colonel Carter returned to his home town

"Big, vigorous, amusing pictures in black-and-white, with an Ohio small-town background." New Yorker

Make way for ducklings. Viking 1941 unp $12.95; Puffin Bks. pa $3.95 E

1. Ducks—Fiction 2. Boston (Mass.)—Fiction
ISBN 0-670-45149-5; 0-14-050171-1 (pa)
LC 41-51868

Awarded the Caldecott Medal, 1942

"A family of baby ducks was born on the Charles River near Boston. When they were old enough to follow, Mother Duck, with some help from a friendly policeman, trailed them through Boston traffic to the pond in the Public Garden." Bookmark

"There are some very beautiful drawings in this book." Horn Book

One morning in Maine. Viking 1952 64p il $13.95; Puffin Bks. pa $3.95 E

1. Maine—Fiction
ISBN 0-670-52627-4; 0-14-050174-6 (pa) LC 52-6983

A Caldecott Medal honor book, 1953

McCloskey, Robert, 1914-—*Continued*

The events of this "story—Sal's discovery of her first loose tooth, the loss of the tooth while digging clams, the consequent wish on a gull's feather, and the wish come true—occur in the course of one morning in Maine. The lovely Maine seacoast scenes and the doings of Sal with her family and friends are drawn with enticing detail in beautiful, big double-spread lithographs printed in dark blue." Booklist

Time of wonder. Viking 1957 63p il $15.95; Puffin Bks. pa $4.95 **E**

1. Maine—Fiction
ISBN 0-670-71512-3; 0-14-050201-7 (pa)
LC 57-14197

Awarded the Caldecott Medal, 1958

"A summer on an island in Maine is described through the simple everyday experiences of children, but also reveals the author's deep awareness of an attachment to all the shifting moods of season and weather, and the salty, downright character of the New England people." Top News

McCully, Emily Arnold

Grandmas at the lake; story and pictures by Emily Arnold McCully. Harper & Row 1990 62p il $10.95; lib bdg $10.89 **E**

1. Grandmothers—Fiction 2. Lakes—Fiction
ISBN 0-06-024126-8; 0-06-024127-6 (lib bdg)
LC 89-36590

"An I can read book"

Pip and Ski have a hard time enjoying themselves at the lake with Pip's two grandmothers, who cannot agree on anything

"The bright cartoon illustrations are sure to appeal to young readers. While the story line is slight and insubstantial, it fulfills its purpose as another of the dependable controlled-vocabulary stories for beginning independent readers." SLJ

Zaza's big break. Harper & Row 1989 unp il $12.95; lib bdg $12.89 **E**

1. Actors and actresses—Fiction 2. Bears—Fiction
ISBN 0-06-024223-X; 0-06-024224-8 (lib bdg)
LC 88-36836

"The bear Zaza is satisfied with life in a successful theatrical family until Hollywood beckons with a screen test. Accompanied by her parents, who fear Tinseltown's jading influence, she experiences life on the backlot with caution. Finally, homesickness and isolation cause her to soundly declare, 'Television is not my cup of tea.'" Booklist

The author "has created a secure, loving story about Zaza and her close-knit family. The pictures express the many emotional moments of each member, as well as the contrasts between the snug theater world and the false glamour of Hollywood." Publ Wkly

Other available titles about Zaza and her family are:
The evil spell (1990)
The show must go on (1987)
You lucky duck! (1988)

McDermott, Gerald

Tim O'Toole and the wee folk; an Irish tale; told and illustrated by Gerald McDermott. Viking 1990 unp il $13.95 **E**

1. Fairy tales 2. Ireland—Fiction
ISBN 0-670-80393-6
LC 89-8913

A very poor Irishman is provided with magical things by the "wee folk", but he must then keep his good fortune out of the hands of the greedy McGoons

"McDermott's characteristic illustrations are a perfect accompaniment to the cheery good humor of the story; flocks of tiny leprechauns resembling fields of shamrocks cavort over the bright green hillsides. The comical folk art and the economical use of language, as well as its slight hint of brogue, will make this book a pleasurable choice for story hour." Horn Book

McKissack, Patricia C., 1944-

Flossie & the fox; pictures by Rachel Isadora. Dial Bks. for Young Readers 1986 unp il $11.95; lib bdg $10.89 **E**

1. Foxes—Fiction 2. Blacks—Fiction
ISBN 0-8037-0250-7; 0-8037-0251-5 (lib bdg)
LC 86-2024

A wily fox notorious for stealing eggs meets his match when he encounters a bold little girl in the woods who insists upon proof that he is a fox before she will be frightened

"The watercolor and ink illustrations, with realistic figures set on impressionistic backgrounds, enliven this humorous and well-structured story which is told in the black language of the rural south. The language is true, and the illustrations are marvelously complementary in their interpretation of the events. This spirited little girl will capture readers from the beginning, and they'll adore her by the end of this delightful story." SLJ

Mirandy and Brother Wind; illustrated by Jerry Pinkney. Knopf 1988 unp il $12.95; lib bdg $13.99 **E**

1. Dancing—Fiction 2. Winds—Fiction 3. Blacks—Fiction
ISBN 0-394-88765-4; 0-394-98765-9 (lib bdg)
LC 87-349

A Caldecott Medal honor book, 1989; Coretta Scott King award for illustrations, 1989

"Mirandy is sure that she'll win the cake walk if she can catch Brother Wind for her partner, but he eludes all the tricks her friends advise. When she finally does catch him with her own quick wits, she ends up wishing instead for her boyfriend Ezel to overcome his clumsiness. Sure enough, the two children finish first in high style." Bull Cent Child Books

"Although this is not a history book, the past lives within these pages. Ms. McKissack and Mr. Pinkney's ebullient collaboration captures the texture of rural life and culture 40 years after the end of slavery. From Brother Wind 'high steppin' ' across the first page to Ezel and Mirandy in 'Sunday best' cakewalking across the last, each page of 'Mirandy and Brother Wind' sparkles with life." N Y Times Book Rev

McKissack, Patricia C., 1944-—*Continued*

Nettie Jo's friends; illustrated by Scott Cook. Knopf 1988 unp il $12.95; lib bdg $13.99 **E**

1. Animals—Fiction 2. Dolls—Fiction
ISBN 0-394-89158-9; 0-394-99158-3 (lib bdg)
LC 87-14080

Nettie Jo desperately needs a needle to sew a new wedding dress for her beloved doll, but the three animals she helps during her search do not seem inclined to give her their assistance in return

"The author successfully blends elements of African American folklore with her special gift for storytelling, and the use of a soft, rhythmic cadence in the dialogue makes this tale engaging. Scott Cook's oil paintings with softly muted orange, green, and blue tones reveal what seems to be a post-Civil War Southern setting." Horn Book

McLeod, Emilie, 1926-1982

The bear's bicycle; by Emilie Warren McLeod; illustrated by David McPhail. Little, Brown 1975 31p il lib bdg $13.95; pa $4.95 **E**

1. Bears—Fiction 2. Bicycles and bicycling—Fiction
ISBN 0-316-56203-3 (lib bdg); 0-316-56206-8 (pa)
LC 74-28282

"An Atlantic Monthly Press book"

"Bicycle safety is demonstrated through colorful pictures leavened by a parallel set of humorous pictures of a teddy-bear-turned-real who takes the hazardous consequences of ignoring the safety rules." Read Teach

McMillan, Bruce

Counting wildflowers. Lothrop, Lee & Shepard Bks. 1986 unp il $12.95; lib bdg $12.88 **E**

1. Counting 2. Wild flowers
ISBN 0-688-02859-4; 0-688-02860-8 (lib bdg)
LC 85-16607

A counting book with photographs of wildflowers illustrating the numbers one through twenty

"Dazzling photographs of twenty-three wildflowers are the major feature of this deftly constructed, multipurpose concept book. On the simplest level this is a counting book. . . . The book is also a simple identification guide, with the popular name of each variety appearing just above the photograph; all the flowers are listed again at the end along with the scientific name, months of blooming, and type of terrain where found. . . . This author-photographer has utilized compound concepts in earlier books . . . but the new book excels in clarity of design and striking presentation of an appealing subject." Horn Book

Growing colors. Lothrop, Lee & Shepard Bks. 1988 32p il $12.95; lib bdg $12.88 **E**

1. Color 2. Vegetables 3. Fruit
ISBN 0-688-07844-3; 0-688-07845-1 (lib bdg)
LC 88-2767

"A colors book using fruits and vegetables of every hue. Each double-page spread has a small photograph of the whole plant and a large close-up of the fruit or vegetable. The colors are announced in bold type tinted in the appropriate shade. . . . At the end of the book, there is a picture glossary of all the colors and plants used." Publ Wkly

"A luscious-looking book that will help children identify colors. . . . This is notably a treat for kids and an example of photography as an art form in picture books." Bull Cent Child Books

Step by step. Lothrop, Lee & Shepard Bks. 1987 unp il $12.95; lib bdg $12.88 **E**

1. Infants—Fiction 2. Growth—Fiction
ISBN 0-688-07233-X; 0-688-07234-8 (lib bdg)
LC 87-4195

"A tiny infant sleeps, rolls over, stands up, walks and then, at 14 months, runs, in this photographic portrait of a child's first moves." Publ Wkly

"Families with one and two year olds will enjoy looking at these familiar moments, unposed and natural. This book works not so much of itself, but because of the response it will call from children looking at it and the opportunity for discussion that may follow." SLJ

McPhail, David M.

Andrew's bath; by David McPhail. Little, Brown 1984 32p il $12.95 **E**

1. Baths—Fiction
ISBN 0-316-56319-6 LC 84-4368

"An Atlantic Monthly Press book"

"Andrew is finally old enough to give himself a bath. Things start out wonderfully . . . but then an assortment of animals climb in through the bathroom window to have some fun. Colorful, amusing illustrations alternate between Andrew's disbelieving parents in the living room and the wild antics in the bathtub." SLJ

The bear's toothache; written and illustrated by David McPhail. Little, Brown 1972 31p il hardcover o.p. paperback available $4.95 **E**

1. Bears—Fiction 2. Teeth—Fiction
ISBN 0-316-56325-0 (pa) LC 79-140482

"An Atlantic Monthly Press book"

"In this delightful fantasy, a small boy receives a nocturnal visit from a bear with a sore tooth. Pulling on the tooth doesn't work, eating fails to loosen it, and hitting it with a pillow breaks a lamp and wakes up father. The boy's cowboy rope is securely fastened to tooth and bedpost and, as the bear jumps out the window, the tooth finally pops out. The grateful bear then gives it to the boy to put under his pillow. The simple text is accompanied by full-page pastel pictures which are filled with action and detail and are superbly suited to this imaginative bedtime tale." SLJ

Fix-it; by David McPhail. Dutton 1984 unp il $10.95; pa $3.95 **E**

1. Bears—Fiction
ISBN 0-525-44093-3; 0-525-44323-1 (pa)
LC 83-16459

"Distraught when the television set won't work, little Emma, a bear, gets her parents out of bed one morning with the demand that they fix the set. They try and fail. Emma weeps. They call a repairman, who also fails

McPhail, David M.—*Continued*
to find out what's wrong. Emma's parents do what they can to distract and amuse her; by the time her father fixes the television set (it had been unplugged) Emma is busy 'reading' to her doll." Bull Cent Child Books
"McPhail's black line and watercolor wash illustrations tell half the story and provide most of the humor." SLJ
Other available titles about Emma are:
Emma's pet (1985)
Emma's vacation (1987)

Lost! [by] David McPhail. Little, Brown 1989 unp il $13.95 **E**
1. Bears—Fiction
ISBN 0-316-56329-3 LC 88-22663
"Joy Street books"
"A bear, bewildered to find himself lost in the big city, . . . is assisted by a young boy who befriends him. None of the patches of trees and water turns out to be the bear's home territory, but a bit of research during a trip to the library helps them locate the correct place on a globe. A long bus ride returns a joyous bear to his home." Horn Book
"The splendid story will satisfy beginning readers who will find the text manageable; it also succeeds as a read-aloud. Splashed with full-color illustrations and enriched with tones of violet, the book has strong eye appeal." SLJ

Pig Pig grows up; by David McPhail. Dutton 1980 unp il $11.95; pa $3.95 **E**
1. Pigs—Fiction
ISBN 0-525-37027-7; 0-525-44195-6 (pa) LC 80-350
"A Unicorn book"
Only when faced with a dire emergency does Pig Pig finally react like a grown-up and admit he is not a baby any more
"Large drawings in subdued full color are uncluttered and go straight to the point; full of humor and action, they virtually tell the story by themselves." Horn Book
Other availables titles about Pig Pig are:
Pig Pig and the magic photo album (1986)
Pig Pig gets a job (1990)
Pig Pig goes to camp (1983)
Pig Pig rides (1982)

Mendez, Phil
The black snowman; illustrated by Carole Byard. Scholastic 1989 unp il $13.95; pa $3.95 **E**
1. Blacks—Fiction 2. Christmas—Fiction
ISBN 0-590-40552-7; 0-590-44873-0 (pa) LC 87-4774
Through the powers of a magical dashiki, a black snowman comes to life and helps young Jacob discover the beauty of his black heritage as well as his own self-worth
"Byard's dramatic illustrations sprawl across the pages in wide-ranging, layered colors, reflecting the story's changing moods: depression, frivolity, amazement, and joy. The use of the 'kente' adds an authentic note. A Christmas story to read all year long." Booklist

Merriam, Eve, 1916-
The Christmas box; illustrated by David Small. Morrow 1985 unp il $12.95; lib bdg $12.88 **E**
1. Christmas—Fiction
ISBN 0-688-05255-X; 0-688-05256-8 (lib bdg) LC 85-5666
"Early on Christmas morning an entire family—parents, grandparents, an aunt, and six children—all rush from their beds to see what presents have been deposited under the tree. To their confusion and dismay, they find only a very long, narrow box, and frantic searching in likely and unlikely places, both indoors and out, produces nothing more. But when the mysterious box is opened, there is revealed to the astonished family a string of appropriate gifts, each one firmly tied to another." Horn Book
"The exaggerated expressions and spritely actions in full color pen and wash are delightful. Together, Merriam and Small have created a special scene of family solidarity and fun that is especially appropriate for Christmas." SLJ

Milhous, Katherine, 1894-1977
The egg tree; story and pictures by Katherine Milhous. Scribner 1950 unp il lib bdg $12.95 **E**
1. Pennsylvania Dutch—Fiction 2. Easter—Fiction 3. Egg decoration—Fiction
ISBN 0-684-12716-4 LC 50-6017
Awarded the Caldecott Medal, 1951
"A seasonal book with the illustrations and 'things to do' aspect of more value than the actual story. A group of children taking part in a Pennsylvania Dutch Easter have an Easter egg hunt and learn how to decorate eggs and hang them on an Easter egg tree. The full page coloured illustrations are Pennsylvania Dutch in character and the smaller ones are decorative Easter egg designs." Ont Libr Rev

Miller, Edna
Mousekin's golden house; story and pictures by Edna Miller. Prentice-Hall 1964 32p il $11.95; lib bdg $9.95; Simon & Schuster pa $5.95 **E**
1. Mice—Fiction 2. Halloween—Fiction
ISBN 0-13-604232-5; 0-13-604421-2 (lib bdg); 0-671-66972-9 (pa) LC 64-16429
"A wood mouse, coming upon an abandoned jack-o-lantern, discovers it can be converted into a cozy nest for the winter. An eye which sees and loves each detail of woodland life illuminates the artist-author's lovely watercolors. The story is neither anthropomorphic nor sentimental." SLJ
Other available titles about Mousekin are:
Mousekin finds a friend (1967)
Mousekin takes a trip (1976)
Mousekin's ABC (1972)
Mousekin's birth (1982)
Mousekin's Christmas Eve (1965)
Mousekin's close call (1978)
Mousekin's Easter basket (1986)
Mousekin's fables (1982)
Mousekin's family (1969)
Mousekin's frosty friend (1990)
Mousekin's mystery (1983)

Miller, Edna—*Continued*
Mousekin's Thanksgiving (1985)
Mousekin's woodland sleepers (1970)

Miller, Jane, 1925-1989

The farm alphabet book. Prentice-Hall 1984 c1981 unp il $8.95; Scholastic pa $2.50 **E**

1. Alphabet
ISBN 0-13-304767-9; 0-590-31991-4 (pa)
LC 83-19277

First published 1981 in the United Kingdom

This "alphabet book surveys animals and objects seen around a farm, from 'apple' to 'zipper.' Shiny black pages set off vivid, crisply focused color photographs to perfection, while the spare text, with a sentence or two of explanation of each word, appears in white." Booklist

Farm counting book. Prentice-Hall 1983 unp il $8.95; pa $4.95 **E**

1. Counting 2. Animals
ISBN 0-13-304790-3; 0-13-304809-8 (pa)
LC 82-21622

"Separate pages show groups of animals (from one kitten on) with ten geese as the last; this is followed by pages that ask either how many (cats, piglets, etc.) are in the picture or that ask such questions as 'Are there more white ducks than brown ducks?' or, with paired pictures, 'How many cats are there? Is there a bowl of milk for each cat?'" Bull Cent Child Books

"The photos of lambs and ponies against the West Country backgrounds of Britain are very appealing; the bright yellow paper on which the photographs are placed and the red numerals are eye-catching." SLJ

Miller, Margaret, 1945-

Who uses this? Greenwillow Bks. 1990 unp il $12.95; lib bdg $12.88 **E**

1. Tools 2. Occupations
ISBN 0-688-08278-5; 0-688-08279-3 (lib bdg)
LC 89-30456

"Brilliant color photographs introducing common objects such as a hammer, a football, and a rolling pin are accompanied by the question, 'Who uses this?' The object is then pictured being used by an adult and by a child. This concept book—quietly nonsexist—is ideal for reading aloud to the youngest listeners." Horn Book Guide

Minarik, Else Holmelund

Little Bear; pictures by Maurice Sendak. Harper & Row 1957 63p il hardcover o.p. paperback available $3.50 **E**

1. Bears—Fiction
ISBN 0-06-444004-4 (pa)
LC 57-9263

Also available Spanish language edition $11.89 (ISBN 0-06-024244-2)

"An I can read book"

Four episodes "about Little Bear, a charming creature who will delight young readers as he persuades his mother to make him a winter outfit—only to discover his fur coat is all he needs; makes himself some birthday soup—and then is surprised with a birthday cake; takes an imaginary trip to the moon, and finally goes happily off to sleep as his mother tells him a story about 'Little Bear.'" Bull Cent Child Books

The pictures "depict all the warmth of feeling and the special companionship that exists between a small child and his mother." Publ Wkly

Other available titles about Little Bear are:
Father Bear comes home (1959)
A kiss for Little Bear (1968)
Little Bear's friend (1960)
Little Bear's visit (1961)

No fighting, no biting! pictures by Maurice Sendak. Harper & Row 1958 62p il $10.95; lib bdg $10.89; pa $3.50 **E**

1. Alligators—Fiction
ISBN 0-06-024290-6; 0-06-024291-4 (lib bdg); 0-06-444015-X (pa)
LC 58-5293

"An I can read book"

"A young lady who is unable to read in peace because of two children squabbling beside her tells them a story about two little alligators whose fighting and biting almost lead to disastrous consequences with a big hungry alligator. Children are sure to accept and enjoy the lesson in this little adventure tale and be amused by the expressive old-fashioned drawings." Booklist

Modell, Frank

Goodbye old year, hello new year. Greenwillow Bks. 1984 unp il lib bdg $10.51 **E**

1. New Year—Fiction
ISBN 0-688-03939-1
LC 84-4020

Marvin and Milton "assemble noisemakers and paper hats to celebrate the coming of the New Year; knowing they won't be allowed to stay up until midnight, they each go to sleep and set an alarm clock. Marvin's doesn't go off, Milton sleeps through the noise; when they wake in the wee hours they celebrate anyway, at least until the neighbors' protests send them back indoors to indulge in cake and milk." Bull Cent Child Books

"Cartoon drawings with watercolor washes provide touches of humor throughout the story." SLJ

One zillion valentines. Greenwillow Bks. 1981 unp il $11.75; lib bdg $11.88; pa $3.95 **E**

1. Valentine's Day—Fiction
ISBN 0-688-00565-9; 0-688-00569-1 (lib bdg); 0-688-07329-8 (pa)
LC 81-2215

"Milton and Marvin decide that valentines are for everybody and proceed to distribute the simple hearts they have drawn up to everyone in the neighborhood. The leftovers they sell for a nickel and with the money they've made, buy a giant box of candy to share." Booklist

"The plot is impeccably logical, and its execution—both in text and drawings—completely childlike. From the opening gambit to a thoroughly satisfying conclusion, the story moves briskly; the author-illustrator captures the essence of youthful optimism in the situation and a comic spirit in the exuberant, cartoonlike illustrations." Horn Book

Modesitt, Jeanne

Vegetable soup; story by Jeanne Modesitt; pictures by Robin Spowart. Macmillan 1988 unp il $13.95 **E**

1. Rabbits—Fiction
ISBN 0-02-767630-7 LC 87-11169

"Elsie and Theodore Rabbit had planned to have boiled carrots, their favorite lunch, for the first meal in their new home, but the carrot sack is empty and the market is closed. They go from neighbor to neighbor, trying to borrow some carrots. None of their new neighbors has carrots, but each offers a substitute. Too polite to refuse the strange foods and having nothing else to eat, they take the offerings and make a soup—which turns out to be delicious." SLJ

"Gentle illustrations and catchy prose make this a delightful storybook." Child Book Rev Serv

Moeri, Louise

Star Mother's youngest child; illustrated by Trina Schart Hyman. Houghton Mifflin 1975 unp il $13.95; pa $4.95 **E**

1. Christmas—Fiction
ISBN 0-395-21406-8; 0-395-29929-2 (pa) LC 75-9743

The grumpy old woman had never properly celebrated Christmas until the year that the Star Mother's youngest child came to earth to find out what Christmas was all about

"Brown-and-white line drawings keep the warm mood of the book, and Hyman's details reflect the changes in the characters as the Old Woman and the Ugly Child experience Christmas together. Word- and picture-perfect." Booklist

Monjo, F. N.

The drinking gourd; pictures by Fred Brenner. Harper & Row 1970 62p il lib bdg $10.89; pa $3.50 **E**

1. Underground railroad—Fiction
ISBN 0-06-024330-9 (lib bdg); 0-06-444042-7 (pa) LC 68-10782

"An I can read history book"

Set in New England in the decade before the Civil War. For mischievous behavior in church, Tommy is sent home to his room, but wanders instead into the barn. There he discovers that his father is helping runaway slaves escape to Canada

"The simplicity of dialogue and exposition, the level of concepts, and the length of the story [makes] it most suitable for the primary grades reader. The illustrations are deftly representational, the whole a fine addition to the needed body of historical books for the very young." Bull Cent Child Books

Montresor, Beni, 1926-

The witches of Venice. Doubleday 1989 unp il $13.95; lib bdg $14.99 **E**

1. Fairy tales 2. Venice (Italy)—Fiction
ISBN 0-385-26354-6; 0-385-26355-4 (lib bdg) LC 88-27158

A newly illustrated edition of the title first published 1963 by Knopf

Though unable "to produce an heir to the throne, the king and queen of Venice reject the tiny boy who is born from a plant brought by two fairies of the lagoon. When the boy, who is being held prisoner by the king, accidentally overhears that there is a flower-girl plant living in the palace of the witches of the Grand Canal, he is determined to escape and find her. He climbs into a large wooden pigeon he has built and, with the help of the wind, journeys bravely past the king's guards, into the witches' palace, past the dragon, and through the crowds of people dancing at the witches' great summer ball to discover and free the flower-plant girl. . . . This original story brings to mind the magical qualities of traditional fairy tales. Montresor's full-page illustrations, in his characteristic watercolor and black line style, are panoramic in scope." Horn Book

Most, Bernard, 1937-

The cow that went oink; written and illustrated by Bernard Most. Harcourt Brace Jovanovich 1990 unp il $9.95 **E**

1. Domestic animals—Fiction
ISBN 0-15-220195-5 LC 89-39896

A cow that oinks and a pig that moos are ridiculed by the other barnyard animals until each teaches the other a new sound

A "delightfully silly picture book with a not-so-silly message about tolerance and determination. . . . Simple and readable, with plenty of repetition and irresistable animal sounds, the book is pure fun, and Most's characteristic bold, flat illustrations are the perfect accompaniment." Horn Book

Whatever happened to the dinosaurs? written and illustrated by Bernard Most. Harcourt Brace Jovanovich 1984 unp il lib bdg $13.95 **E**

1. Dinosaurs—Fiction
ISBN 0-15-295295-0 LC 84-3779

The author "offers various fantastic explanations to answer his title question. 'Did the dinosaurs go to another planet? . . . did a magician make them disappear? . . . Are the dinosaurs in the hospital?'" SLJ

"A hilarious book, sure to be popular for individual reading or with groups." Child Book Rev Serv

Murphy, Jill, 1949-

All in one piece; written and illustrated by Jill Murphy. Putnam 1987 unp il $10.95 **E**

1. Elephants—Fiction
ISBN 0-399-21433-X LC 87-2516

"While Mr. and Mrs. Large get ready for the office dinner dance, the children mess and meddle until the exasperated Mrs. Large shouts, 'Can't I have just one night to myself? One night when I am not covered in jam and poster paint?' As she walks out the door on the arm of her husband, however, sharp observers will note that although she may have a night out, it is not without decoration." SLJ

"Predictable enough, except that the Larges are elephants and the author's appealing paintings of them keep yielding up comic surprises." N Y Times Book Rev

Another available title about the Larges is: Five minutes peace, entered below

Murphy, Jill, 1949-—*Continued*

Five minutes' peace. Putnam 1986 unp il $9.95; pa $3.95 E

1. Elephants—Fiction

ISBN 0-399-21354-6; 0-399-21938-2 (pa) LC 86-643

"Driven from the breakfast table by her unruly offspring, Mrs. Large escapes to the tub with a marmalade-laden tray. Is five minutes much to ask for? Lester, Laura, and the baby think so, and they regale her with tunes, toys, and stories until togetherness becomes torturous." Publisher's note

"The fine-grained color pencil drawings are softly textured and funny; and mother elephant's dilemma is a familiar enough one that children may enjoy it even from her perspective." Bull Cent Child Books

Peace at last. Dial Bks. for Young Readers 1980 unp il $12.95; lib bdg $12.89; pa $3.95 E

1. Night—Fiction 2. Bears—Fiction

ISBN 0-8037-6757-9; 0-8037-6758-7 (lib bdg); 0-8037-6964-4 (pa) LC 80-15659

Mr. Bear spends the night searching for enough peace and quiet to go to sleep

"The story appears on the verso pages with line drawings; facing pages are in full color; the pictures have warmth and humor and the story is told in brisk, forthright style with an appealing refrain that will probably elicit listener-participation, 'Oh, NO! I can't stand THIS.'" Bull Cent Child Books

What next, Baby Bear! Dial Bks. for Young Readers 1984 unp il $13.95 E

1. Bears—Fiction 2. Space flight to the moon—Fiction

ISBN 0-8037-0027-X LC 83-7316

"Baby Bear methodically goes about finding a rocket, space helmet, boots, companionship, and food for his journey to the moon. He returns in time for his bath and bedtime on Earth." Bull Cent Child Books

"The story is simple, yet teases young listeners with the question, was the trip purely imaginary? Baby Bear is, after all, very sooty in the end. But most appealing is the artwork; cleverly wrought black-and-white drawings alternate with charming full-page pictures in jewellike colors." Booklist

Murphy, Shirley Rousseau, 1928-

Tattie's river journey; pictures by Tomie de Paola. Dial Bks. for Young Readers 1983 unp il $11.95; lib bdg $11.89; pa $3.95 E

1. Floods—Fiction

ISBN 0-8037-8767-7; 0-8037-8770-7 (lib bdg); 0-8037-0168-3 (pa) LC 82-45508

"Tattie's life by the river is a quiet one until the day the rains pour down and she is swept away on a journey." Child Book Rev Serv

"De Paola fortifies the story with rich, intense colors and flowing line work that especially capture the swelling river. His folk-art style, particularly in the backgrounds, extends the story's mood and highlights. Tattie is a most beguiling heroine indeed." Booklist

Mwenye Hadithi

Crafty Chameleon; illustrated by Adrienne Kennaway. Little, Brown 1987 unp il lib bdg $12.95 E

1. Chameleons—Fiction

ISBN 0-316-33723-4 LC 87-3867

A chameleon bedeviled by a leopard and a crocodile uses his wits to get them to leave him alone

"The drawings of the animals in the jungle setting are dramatically bold and exciting, and the words add their own rhythmic accent. . . . There are humorous details of jungle life, such as the ants marching in columns along branches. Finding Chameleon as he sits against a background of gray stones, leans from a bush, or hides among green leaves will be a special challenge for young readers." Horn Book

Hot Hippo; illustrated by Adrienne Kennaway. Little, Brown 1986 unp il $12.95 E

1. Hippopotamus—Fiction

ISBN 0-316-33722-6 LC 86-65

"Using the narrative structure of the *pourquoi* tale, Mwenye Hadithi has composed an economical yet marvelously evocative and rhythmic text to describe the circumstances which determined the habitat of the hippopotamus. . . . The illustrations are more than a striking accompaniment to the text; they share equally in the development of plot, setting, and characters. Warm colors, skillfully merging one into another, create a hot, arid atmosphere so that Hippo's longing is thoroughly understandable." Horn Book

My first look at colors. Random House 1990 unp il $6.95 E

1. Color

ISBN 0-679-80535-4 LC 89-63091

"A Dorling Kindersley book"

In this book "children progress from primary colors to a page of black and one of white items. Red objects range from a car to a boxing glove with some attempt to illustrate many different shapes." SLJ

Other available Dorling Kindersley concept books are:
My first look at home
My first look at numbers
My first look at opposites
My first look at seasons
My first look at shapes
My first look at sizes
My first look at touch

Myrick, Mildred

The Secret Three; drawings by Arnold Lobel. Harper & Row 1963 64p il $10.89 E

1. Clubs—Fiction 2. Ciphers—Fiction 3. Seashore—Fiction

ISBN 0-06-024356-2 LC 63-13323

"An I can read book"

"Three boys, two on the mainland and one on an island lighthouse, exchange messages in a bottle carried by the tide. They organize a club with a secret code, handshake, and name. On a trip to the island the boys explore the lighthouse and camp out overnight." SLJ

"The cryptography is elementary enough for the age

Myrick, Mildred—*Continued*
of the readers, and should delight girls as well as boys. The illustrations are charming." Bull Cent Child Books

Neitzel, Shirley
The jacket I wear in the snow; pictures by Nancy Winslow Parker. Greenwillow Bks. 1989 unp il $12.95; lib bdg $12.88 E
1. Clothing and dress—Fiction 2. Snow—Fiction 3. Stories in rhyme
ISBN 0-688-08028-6; 0-688-08030-8 (lib bdg)
LC 88-18767

A young girl names all the clothes that she must wear to play in the snow

"Written in cheerful, cumulative verse that recalls the well-known favorite nursery rhyme 'The House That Jack Built,' the text, with its easy-going rhythm, will be simple for children to recite from memory. . . . The artist's drawings are executed in her familiar style using watercolor, pencil, and pen; they combine with the large typeface and a generous amount of white space to create a tremendously appealing book. An inspired collaboration between author and illustrator." Horn Book

Ness, Evaline, 1911-1986
Sam, Bangs & Moonshine; written and illustrated by Evaline Ness. Holt & Co. 1966 unp il $13.95; pa $4.95 E
ISBN 0-8050-0314-2; 0-8050-0315-0 (pa)
LC 66-10113

Awarded the Caldecott Medal, 1967

Young Samantha, or Sam, "the fisherman's daughter, finally learns to draw the line between reality and the 'moonshine' [her fantasies] in which her mother is a mermaid, she owns a baby kangaroo, and can talk to her cat." Publisher's note

"In this unusually creative story the fantasy in which many, many children indulge is presented in a realistic and sympathetic context. The illustrations in ink and pale color wash (mustard, grayish-aqua) have a touching realism, too. This is an outstanding book." SLJ

Neumeier, Marty
Action alphabet; by Marty Neumeier and Byron Glaser. Greenwillow Bks. 1985 unp il $12.95; lib bdg $12.88 E
1. Alphabet
ISBN 0-688-05703-9; 0-688-05704-7 (lib bdg)
LC 84-25322

The letters of the alphabet appear as parts of pictures representing sample words, such as a drip formed by a D coming out of a faucet and a vampire with two V's for fangs

"This clever concept book, created by an award-winning pair of graphic designers, is bold, brash and as promised by the title, 'full' of action. . . . A mere description doesn't do the smashing graphics justice. To call this alphabet vivid is to understate the case. No matter how many ABC's you have already, you 'need' this one." SLJ

Newberry, Clare Turlay, 1903-1970
Marshmallow; story and pictures by Clare Turlay Newberry. Harper & Row 1990 c1942 unp il $16.95; lib bdg $16.89 E
1. Rabbits—Fiction 2. Cats—Fiction
ISBN 0-06-024460-7; 0-06-024461-5 (lib bdg)
LC 89-20052

A Caldecott Medal honor book

A reissue of the title first published 1942

"A little white bunny, looking as soft as a marshmallow, comes to live in the house with a pampered bachelor cat who at first does not know whether or not to accept so strange a thing. But before long the big black cat and the little white bunny are such friends that, cuddled up together, asleep, and playing, they give the artist an excuse for some of her best work." Bookmark

"It is a delightful combination of beauty, understanding of children and animals, and droll humor." N Y Times Book Rev

Nixon, Joan Lowery, 1927-
Beats me, Claude; story by Joan Lowery Nixon; pictures by Tracey Campbell Pearson. Viking Kestrel 1986 unp il lib bdg $11.95 E
1. Frontier and pioneer life—Fiction
ISBN 0-670-80781-8 LC 86-5465

"In this sequel to *If You Say So, Claude* (1980), Shirley and Claude continue to enjoy their new found peace in the cabin in the great state of Texas. When Shirley, who has never been a very good cook, tries her hand at baking an apple pie, the result is a surprise for her and for readers." SLJ

"Nixon's story has a down-home verve, and Pearson's illustrations of the farfetched antics are as full of spice as a real apple pie." Publ Wkly

Noble, Trinka Hakes
Apple tree Christmas. Dial Bks. for Young Readers 1984 unp il $12.95; lib bdg $12.89; pa $3.95 E
1. Farm life—Fiction 2. Christmas—Fiction 3. Blizzards—Fiction
ISBN 0-8037-0102-0; 0-8037-0103-9 (lib bdg); 0-8037-0552-2 (pa) LC 84-1901

"Katrina's favorite time of year is when the apples are ripe and ready to pick. Then the apple tree becomes her place to dream and draw. But a hard winter comes and the tree has to be chopped down. The thought of losing her special place threatens to spoil the Christmas season until her father preserves a section of the tree as a remembrance." Child Book Rev Serv

"Noble's watercolors of landscapes, storms and domestic settings are more convincing than her people; through her use of cold grays and whites, she exposes readers to the harshness and bleakness of the winter storm, and her warm interiors give a feeling of love and security. A quiet, quaint story that will be enjoyed by children who love a touch of the old-fashioned." SLJ

Noble, Trinka Hakes—*Continued*

The day Jimmy's boa ate the wash; pictures by Steven Kellogg. Dial Bks. for Young Readers 1980 unp il $13.95; lib bdg $13.89; pa $3.95 E

1. Farm life—Fiction 2. Snakes—Fiction 3. School stories
ISBN 0-8037-1723-7; 0-8037-1724-5 (lib bdg); 0-8037-0094-6 (pa) LC 80-15098

"One small girl, reporting to her mother after a class visit to a farm, nonchalantly describes the frenzied day; she works backward from effects to causes, beginning with the statement that the day was kind of dull and boring until the cow started crying. Why? A haystack fell on her. How? The farmer hit it with his tractor. Why? He was busy yelling at the pigs to get off the school bus . . . and she goes on to unfold the tale of how Jimmy's boa escaped, set the hens in a flurry, precipitated an egg-throwing match, and so on." Bull Cent Child Books

"The illustrations, which depict disgruntled chickens, expressive pigs, and smiling cats as well as other individualized animal and human characters, show the artist's flair for humorous detail." Horn Book

Other available titles about Jimmy's boa are:
Jimmy's boa and the big splash birthday bash (1989)
Jimmy's boa bounces back (1984)

Meanwhile back at the ranch; pictures by Tony Ross. Dial Bks. for Young Readers 1987 unp il $11.95; lib bdg $11.89 E

1. Ranch life—Fiction 2. Humorous stories
ISBN 0-8037-0353-8; 0-8037-0354-6 (lib bdg) LC 86-11651

"Rancher Hicks leads a life so uneventful that he takes a trip to town just to see what is happening. Wife Elna stays home. While the rancher is amusing himself with the high life in Sleepy Gulch—getting his whiskers trimmed, having lunch at Millie Mildew's, and watching a turtle cross Main Street—Elna is home winning contests, inheriting fortunes, starring in movies, and entertaining the President." SLJ

"Noble's tongue-in-cheek story fits rollickingly into the tall-tale genre while Ross' exuberant full-color pictures wring every bit of humor from the already funny tale. Exaggeration and slapstick detail are the province of both illustrator and author, and they are in full bloom here. Zany fun." Booklist

Noll, Sally

Watch where you go. Greenwillow Bks. 1990 unp il $12.95; lib bdg $12.88 E

1. Mice—Fiction
ISBN 0-688-08498-2; 0-688-08499-0 (lib bdg) LC 88-35591

"Disregarding dragonfly's warnings, mouse goes wherever he pleases, oblivious to the fact that golden grass is really lion's mane, a tree is elephant's trunk, and a vine is snake's body." Horn Book Guide

"The story's visual game of nothing being what it seems is carried out well in the deeply hued, stylized, collagelike illustrations. The dragonfly's worried asides add just the right amount of drama to keep interest high." Booklist

Numeroff, Laura Joffe

If you give a mouse a cookie; by Laura Numeroff; illustrated by Felicia Bond. Harper & Row 1985 unp il $9.95; lib bdg $11.89 E

1. Mice—Fiction
ISBN 0-06-024586-7; 0-06-024587-9 (lib bdg) LC 84-48343

Relating the cycle of requests a mouse is likely to make after you give him a cookie takes the reader through a young child's day

"Children love to indulge in supposition or to ask 'what will happen if. . .?' and here there is a long, satisfying chain of linked and enjoyably nonsensical causes and effects. . . . The illustrations, neatly drawn, spaciously composed, and humorously detailed, extend the story just the way picture book illustrations should." Bull Cent Child Books

Nunes, Susan, 1937-

Coyote dreams; illustrated by Ronald Himler. Atheneum Pubs. 1988 unp il $13.95 E

1. Coyotes—Fiction 2. Deserts—Fiction
ISBN 0-689-31398-5 LC 87-30288

"In an extended dream sequence a little boy invokes the ancient name for Coyote. As animal shadows appear in the garden of his comfortable, suburban home, the walls and playground equipment fade and become sand and sagebrush, rock and silver hills. The boy joins coyotes in their own desert world, dancing, singing to the moon, and listening to tales of distant times and places." Horn Book

Oakes, Bill

Puzzlers; [by] Bill Oakes, Suse MacDonald. Dial Bks. for Young Readers 1989 unp il $13.95; lib bdg $13.95 E

1. Counting
ISBN 0-8037-0689-8; 0-8037-0690-1 (lib bdg) LC 88-33392

"A colorful menagerie comprising number collages introduces concepts including widest, backward, upside down and sequence. A left-hand page uses three squares to demonstrate the concept of overlap; on the right side, a cow's face is made up of overlapping numbers. A key at the end of the book informs the reader of other things to look for in that cow, such as a pattern and numbers shown back-to-back. MacDonald and Oakes use beautiful marbelized papers in bright hues to create the festive images." Publ Wkly

Oakley, Graham

The church mouse. Atheneum Pubs. 1972 unp il $12.95; pa $4.95 E

1. Mice—Fiction 2. Cats—Fiction
ISBN 0-689-30058-1; 0-689-70475-5 (pa) LC 72-75276

"Arthur, the church mouse at first view seems to live an idyllic existence. . . . He has an easy relationship with the parson—and even with Sampson, the church cat. . . . And he is lonely. One day, while reading 'Exodus' . . . he is inspired to invite all the town mice

Oakley, Graham—*Continued*
to come live with him in the church." N Y Times Book Rev

"Full-color paintings with an abundance of activity and detail contribute much to the telling of the story. . . . Very British allusions give the fulsome text a certain sophistication; but the action and the clever illustrations are wholly childlike in their fun." Horn Book

Other available titles about the church mice and Sampson, the church cat are:
The church cat abroad (1973)
The church mice adrift (1977)
The church mice and the moon (1974)
The church mice at bay (1979)
The church mice at Christmas (1980)
The church mice in action (1983)
The church mice spread their wings (1976)
The diary of a church mouse (1987)

Graham Oakley's magical changes. Atheneum Pubs. 1987 c1980 unp il $5.95 **E**

ISBN 0-689-71179-4 LC 79-2784

In this book "there are no words; there are thirty-two individual, full-color, saddle-stitched pages of art; each page is cut horizontally, leaving a top and bottom that can be mixed and matched in over 4,000 combinations; odd pages have four thick columns; even pages have six thin columns that join the different tops and bottoms." Child Book Rev Serv

"What Oakley has succeeded in doing . . . is to re-create swift dreamlike illusions that are sometimes harrowing, sometimes funny, always surreal. . . . Intriguing, disturbing, ingenious, this book develops a technique hitherto the preserve of the crude spiral-bound joke book, into a new art form." Times Lit Suppl

Hetty and Harriet. Atheneum Pubs. 1982 c1981 unp il $12.95; pa $3.95 **E**

1. Chickens—Fiction
ISBN 0-689-30888-4; 0-689-71061-5 (pa) LC 81-8024
First published 1981 in the United Kingdom

At the "bottom of the peck order, and thoroughly disgruntled, two young hens leave the farmyard but after trying various unsuitable homes, including a fox hole, a bleak derelict windmill and a battery building (where they narrowly escape being slaughtered for inadequate egg-production), they find an ideal refuge— . . . their old home." Grow Point

"Physically, the text is welded with the pictures to make a solid unit. Oakley uses all kinds of pictorial devices to maintain the narrative pace, and double-page spreads are uniquely designed. . . . Details of nature, or tongue-in-cheek signs in town, abound. Both text and illustrations exude the joy of fine storytelling." SLJ

O'Connor, Jane, 1947-
Lulu goes to witch school; pictures by Emily Arnold McCully. Harper & Row 1987 64p il $10.70; lib bdg $10.89; pa $3.50 **E**

1. Witches—Fiction 2. School stories
ISBN 0-06-024628-6; 0-06-024629-4 (lib bdg); 0-06-444138-5 (pa) LC 87-37
"An I can read book"

Lulu starts witch school and meets a classmate who is best at everything

"This story is funny and full of the 'gross' details kids love—like having snake flakes for breakfast and eating lizard tarts. McCully's simple, freehand illustrations, washed in watercolors, add a good dose of silliness to an already absurd and fun idea." Publ Wkly

Another available title about Lulu is:
Lulu and the witch baby (1986)

O'Donnell, Elizabeth Lee
Maggie doesn't want to move; illustrated by Amy Schwartz. Four Winds Press 1987 unp il $13.95; pa $3.95 **E**

1. Moving, Household—Fiction 2. Brothers and sisters—Fiction
ISBN 0-02-768830-5; 0-689-71375-4 (pa) LC 86-23684

Simon expresses his own sad feelings about moving by crediting them to his toddler sister, Maggie

"Schwartz' pen-and-ink and watercolor illustrations perfectly complement the deft and witty text. The prickly stucco houses and the plethora of pastel buildings evoke southern California, while stringy Simon, his equally lean mother, and rounded Maggie are refreshingly expressive." SLJ

Okimoto, Jean Davies, 1942-
Blumpoe the Grumpoe meets Arnold the cat; illustrated by Howie Schneider. Little, Brown 1990 unp il lib bdg $13.95 **E**

1. Hotels, motels, etc. 2. Cats—Fiction
ISBN 0-316-63811-0 LC 88-31436
"Joy Street books"

"The conversion of a midwestern Scrooge begins when Mr. Blumpoe checks into an inn that offers cats as companions for the night. Mr. Blumpoe scorns this creature comfort, but he has reckoned without a scrawny cat named Arnold. This slapstick story of vanquished loneliness and shyness is accompanied by lively, unpretentious illustrations, full of action, humor, and character." Horn Book Guide

Oppenheim, Joanne
Left & right; illustrated by Rosanne Litzinger. Harcourt Brace Jovanovich 1989 unp il $13.95 **E**

1. Brothers—Fiction 2. Shoes—Fiction 3. Stories in rhyme
ISBN 0-15-200505-6 (lib bdg) LC 87-22939
"Gulliver books"

"Two brothers who are constantly bickering master cobblers learn through trial and error that their expertise in left or right footwear makes them better as a team than solo. Invitingly told in a rhythmic rhyme, *Left & Right* confronts cooperation, sibling rivalry, and the concepts of pairs and left and right in an offbeat manner. As the poetic tale entices with its amusing insights on siblings, Litzinger's expressive watercolor and color-pencil illustrations burst from the pages to rivet children's eyes." Booklist

Oppenheim, Shulamith Levey

Waiting for Noah; pictures by Lillian Hoban. Harper & Row 1990 unp il $12.95; lib bdg $12.89 E

1. Birthdays—Fiction 2. Grandmothers—Fiction
ISBN 0-06-024633-2; 0-06-024634-0 (lib bdg) LC 89-35561

"A Charlotte Zolotow book"

"A grandmother recounts to her grandson Noah the often told tale of how she spent a wintry day waiting for the news of his birth. She recalls that she pruned berry canes, baked cookies, shined pots, and dreamed of all the things they would do together someday. Now, on a summer day, Noah eats the berries from those same brambly canes and excitedly waits to hear the part of the story about the phone call in the middle of the night." Horn Book

"Hoban's pastel crayon drawings are particularized enough to make the two characters interesting in themselves, while allowing readers to ask for their own coming-into-the-world stories. Details of cats, countryside, and kitchen add to the story's warmth and honest sentiment, and the warmed reds and oranges of the art convey Noah's delight at his arrival and his place in the world." SLJ

Ormerod, Jan

101 things to do with a baby. Lothrop, Lee & Shepard Bks. 1984 unp il lib bdg $12.88; pa $3.50 E

1. Infants 2. Brothers and sisters
ISBN 0-688-03802-6 (lib bdg); 0-14-050447-8 (pa) LC 84-4401

A six-year-old girl tells 101 things she can do with her baby brother

"Jan Ormerod's illustrations are magnificent—evoking both the tenderness and the tumult with which each day in a two-sibling household is filled. They are also painfully realistic." N Y Times Book Rev

Bend and stretch. Lothrop, Lee & Shepard Bks. 1987 unp il $5.95 E

1. Infants—Fiction 2. Exercise—Fiction
ISBN 0-688-07272-0 LC 87-2604

As in the other titles in this series, this book features a toddler, his pregnant mother, and his cat. The child joins Mom in exercises while the cat looks on

"The simple, minimal text . . . describes the action illustrated, providing just the right narration for sharing with babies and toddlers. . . . A mood of serenity, love, and close companionship pervades. . . . Through the choices of soft watercolors and the expressions and gestures of the mother and her child, a gentle, fun-loving mother/child relationship unfolds." SLJ

Other available titles in this series are:
Making friends (1987)
Mom's home (1987)
This little nose (1987)

Kitten day. Lothrop, Lee & Shepard Bks. 1989 unp il $11.95; lib bdg $11.88 E

1. Cats—Fiction
ISBN 0-688-08536-9; 0-688-08537-7 (lib bdg) LC 88-26687

A girl feeds, plays with, and admires her kitten, who will some day become a grown-up cat, a sit-upon-my-lap cat

Moonlight. Lothrop, Lee & Shepard Bks. 1982 unp il $12.95; lib bdg $12.88; Penguin Bks. pa $3.50 E

1. Stories without words
ISBN 0-688-00846-1; 0-688-00847-X (lib bdg); 0-14-050372-2 (pa) LC 81-8290

"This wordless book about bedtime is a companion to the author's 'Sunshine' [entered below]. In a similar format, with lovely, detailed watercolor paintings that are warm and human, Ormerod describes one bedtime in the life of the same family. Here we see dinner, the making of two boats from fruit leftovers, a bath, a bedtime story and a few not-able-to-sleep ups-and-downs." SLJ

The saucepan game. Lothrop, Lee & Shepard Bks. 1989 unp il $11.95; lib bdg $11.88 E

1. Infants—Fiction 2. Cats—Fiction
ISBN 0-688-08518-0; 0-688-08519-9 (lib bdg) LC 88-12893

"A simple book about a small child, a cat, and the fun they have with a pan and a lid—proof that expensive toys are not necessary to entertain a child." Okla State Dept of Educ

Sunshine. Lothrop, Lee & Shepard Bks. 1981 unp il $12.95; lib bdg $12.88; pa $3.95 E

1. Stories without words
ISBN 0-688-00552-7; 0-688-00553-5 (lib bdg); 0-688-09353-1 (pa) LC 80-84971

"Without benefit of words, this book follows the four or five year old as she rubs her eyes awake . . . and tiptoes into her sleeping parents' bedroom. The book ends with a picture of mother and daughter hand in hand on the way to work and school. The action in between describes all the activities of a first leisurely, then rushed preparation for the day's events." SLJ

"The illustrations are simply composed, with large but quiet areas of color and with realistic details; they are distinctive in the use of light and shadow . . . as the sunlight creeps across the shadowed bedrooms." Bull Cent Child Books

Ormondroyd, Edward

Broderick; illustrated by John Larrecq. Parnassus Press 1969 unp il hardcover o.p. paperback available $4.95 E

1. Mice—Fiction 2. Surfing—Fiction
ISBN 0-395-36170-2 (pa) LC 77-83752

"A young mouse with a fondness for chewing the covers of books becomes an avid reader through the accidental discovery of a book about mice. Inspired by the exploits of such literary mouse personalities as Anatole and Miss Bianca, Broderick determines to make his own mark in the world and by diligent practice wins fame and fortune as a surfer." Booklist

The story is told "with a straight face in polished style, the illustrations matching the deftness and humor of the writing." Sutherland. The Best in Child Books

Ormondroyd, Edward—*Continued*

Theodore; illustrated by John M. Larrecq. Parnassus Press 1966 unp il hardcover o.p. paperback available $4.95 **E**

1. Teddy bears—Fiction
ISBN 0-395-36610-0 (pa) LC 66-10352

"Because Lucy was careless, her poor bear Theodore got mixed up with the clothes in the laundry basket and was taken to the self-service laundry. When he emerged he was so clean that Lucy did not recognize him. But a friendly dog and two disputing cats remedied that situation, and Lucy and Theodore were happily reunited. The simple story, engaging line drawings washed with blue and yellow, and the well-designed format make a book for the youngest children that is all of a piece—unpretentious and charming." Horn Book

Another available title about Theodore is entered below

Theodore's rival; illustrated by John Larrecq. Parnassus Press 1971 unp il hardcover o.p. paperback available $3.95 **E**

1. Teddy bears—Fiction
ISBN 0-395-41669-8 (pa) LC 76-156876

"Dismayed and annoyed when Lucy received a black-and-white bear for her birthday, Theodore was later pleased when Benjamin, the new bear, fell out of the carriage at the supermarket and was lost. But when Lucy began to cry for her lost toy, he became uneasy; and after he heard that Benjamin was a panda, not a teddy bear, he went into action and engineered Benjamin's rescue with great resourcefulness. The book presents settings and situations within the everyday experience of very young children. The humor is delightful, and storytelling illustrations in cheerful blue and yellow add lively details to the birthday-party and the supermarket scenes." Horn Book

Owens, Mary Beth

A caribou alphabet; written & illustrated by Mary Beth Owens. Dog Ear Press 1988 unp il $14.95; Farrar, Straus & Giroux pa $4.95 **E**

1. Caribou 2. Alphabet
ISBN 0-937966-25-8; 0-374-41043-7 (pa)
LC 88-70631

An alphabet book depicting the characteristics and ways of caribou

"A wonderful blending of the impressionist's palette with the graphic designer's authority, the illustrations transcend the utilitarian to become aesthetic statements. The artist has an uncanny ability to execute each so that without distortion the caribou are an essential part of the particular letter." Horn Book

Oxenbury, Helen, 1938-

Beach day. Dial Bks. for Young Readers 1982 unp il $3.50 **E**

1. Beaches—Fiction
ISBN 0-8037-0439-9 LC 81-69273

"Very first books"

Sand play at the beach is featured in this wordless board book

"Youngsters will enjoy the familiar details Oxenbury depicts so humorously without a word. Her clean lines, warm colors, and simple scenes lend themselves to parent-child picture reading." Booklist

The birthday party. Dial Bks. for Young Readers 1983 unp il $5.95 **E**

1. Birthdays—Fiction 2. Parties—Fiction
ISBN 0-8037-0717-7 LC 82-19792

"Out-and-about books"

"A child chooses a present but hates to give it away, is miffed at the casual way the gift is received, has a splendidly messy time, and walks home triumphantly, enjoying the souvenir balloon all the more because it's clear that the birthday child didn't want to give it up." Bull Cent Child Books

"The pictures are humorous and lively, with the left-hand page featuring the central item to be found in the right-hand scene." Publ Wkly

The car trip. Dial Bks. for Young Readers 1983 unp il $3.95 **E**

1. Automobiles—Fiction
ISBN 0-8037-0009-1 LC 83-5255

"Out-and-about books"

"The hapless family in [this story] experiences every mishap imaginable. . . . The contrast between the child's sense of adventure and adult's desire for no surprises couldn't be greater. The bright, exuberant drawings catch each moment at the most emotional peak of each incident. A happy romp sure to prompt discussions about whether delight and disaster are relative terms." SLJ

First day of school. Dial Bks. for Young Readers 1983 unp il $5.95 **E**

1. Nursery schools—Fiction
ISBN 0-8037-0012-1 LC 83-7452

"Out-and-about books"

"On the first day of nursery school, a wailing child is pried away from her mother, makes a friend, and has a fine time. The cleanly drawn, unclutered pictures are small, bright, deft, and hilarious." Bull Cent Child Books

Grandma and Grandpa. Dial Bks. for Young Readers 1984 unp il $3.95 **E**

1. Grandparents—Fiction
ISBN 0-8037-0128-4 LC 84-5830

Previously published as: Gran and granpa

A "depiction of a young girl who visits her grandparents and wears them out. Its situations—playing with Grandma's jewelry, playing doctor ('Grandma and Grandpa let me do anything to them'), or watching TV—are on target with real-life developments." Booklist

Helen Oxenbury's ABC of things. Delacorte Press 1983 unp il lib bdg $13.95; pa $12.95 **E**

1. Alphabet
ISBN 0-385-29291-0 (lib bdg); 0-385-29290-2 (pa)
LC 83-5344

A reissue of the title first published 1971 in the United Kingdom; first United States edition published 1972 by Franklin Watts

Oxenbury, Helen, 1938-—*Continued*

"Large letters and the words that begin them appear on pages bedizened by illustrations in full color of supreme silliness: 'O o' for an ostrich with an otter clinging to its long neck and both looking befuddled by their situation; 'W w' showing the wedding of a weasel and a wolf and the wasp that worries the couple. The originality and fun make this ABC a standout among the numerous offerings in the genre." Publ Wkly

The important visitor. Dial Bks. for Young Readers 1984 unp il $3.95 **E**

ISBN 0-8037-0125-X LC 84-7112

"Out-and-about books"

"Pictures in lively hues illustrate the story told by a little girl. Her mother has stressed the importance of the child's behaving with propriety during a visit from the woman's boss. After the man arrives to talk business, the child tries to be a gracious hostess and turns the occasion into chaos." Publ Wkly

Our dog. Dial Bks. for Young Readers 1984 unp il $5.95 **E**

1. Dogs—Fiction
ISBN 0-8037-0127-6 LC 84-5829

"Out-and-about books"

A small boy and his mother try to cope with a dog that loves to go for walks, jump into dirty water, and roll in mud

Pippo gets lost. Aladdin Bks. (NY) 1989 unp il $5.95 **E**

1. Toys—Fiction
ISBN 0-689-71336-3 LC 89-340

Tom is very worried when he searches the house and can't find his stuffed monkey Pippo

Other available titles about Tom and Pippo are:
Tom and Pippo and the dog (1989)
Tom and Pippo and the washing machine (1988)
Tom and Pippo go for a walk (1988)
Tom and Pippo go shopping (1989)
Tom and Pippo in the garden (1989)
Tom and Pippo in the snow (1989)
Tom and Pippo make a friend (1989)
Tom and Pippo make a mess (1988)
Tom and Pippo read a story (1988)
Tom and Pippo see the moon (1989)
Tom and Pippo's day (1989)

Playing. Wanderer Bks. 1981 unp il $3.95 **E**

ISBN 0-671-42109-3 LC 80-52217

"Baby board books"

Illustrations of objects that infants play with appear alone on one page facing another page showing the baby using them. Included are blocks, a wagon, a pot, a box, a book (held upside down by the fledgling reader), a teddy bear, and a ball

Shopping trip. 2d ed. Dial Bks. for Young Readers 1991 c1982 unp il $3.95 **E**

1. Shopping—Fiction 2. Stories without words
ISBN 0-8037-0997-8 LC 81-69274

"Dial very first books"

First published 1982

The baby in this book "manages to achieve a good bit of independent investigation and some damage, all of which leaves Mama limp by the end of a shopping trip. A foray into a clothes rack, a broken packet of what looks like sugar, a raid on Mama's purse in a fitting booth followed by a sociable pulling back of its curtain, revealing Mama just emerging from the garment she's been trying on. . . . This has no words and needs none; it is drawn with simplicity, humor, and flair." Bull Cent Child Books

Parish, Peggy, 1927-1988

Amelia Bedelia; pictures by Fritz Siebel. Harper & Row 1963 unp il $11.95; lib bdg $11.89; pa $3.50 **E**

ISBN 0-06-024640-5; 0-06-024641-3 (lib bdg); 0-06-443036-7 (pa) LC 63-14367

"Amelia Bedelia is a maid whose talent for interpreting instructions literally results in comical situations, such as dressing the chicken in fine clothes." Hodges. Books for Elem Sch Libr

Other available titles about Amelia Bedelia are:
Amelia Bedelia and the baby (1981)
Amelia Bedelia and the surprise shower (1966)
Amelia Bedelia goes camping (1985)
Amelia Bedelia helps out (1979)
Amelia Bedelia's family album (1988)
Come back, Amelia Bedelia (1971)
Good work, Amelia Bedelia (1976)
Merry Christmas, Amelia Bedelia (1986)
Play ball, Amelia Bedelia (1972)
Teach us, Amelia Bedelia (1977)
Thank you, Amelia Bedelia (1964)

Parker, Nancy Winslow

Love from Aunt Betty. Dodd, Mead 1983 unp il $10.95 **E**

1. Cake—Fiction
ISBN 0-396-08135-5 LC 82-45988

"Aunt Betty sends a chocolate fudge cake recipe: 'I found it in an old trunk in the basement wrapped around this dusty green bottle marked "Dried Carpathian Tree Toads."' It came from Uncle Clyde who got it from 'an aged Gypsy woman who lived in the mountains.' As Aunt Betty's letter continues, Parker's pen-and-ink drawings show her nephew hauling out ingredients and utensils, mixing up the batter (dried toads and all), and popping it into the oven." Booklist

"Very much in the manner of Parker's earlier 'Love from Uncle Clyde' [1977] the situation is underplayed just as the illustrations are freed from unnecessary detail. What is left is uncluttered delight." SLJ

Parkin, Rex

The red carpet; story and pictures by Rex Parkin. Macmillan 1988 c1948 unp il $14.95 **E**

1. Carpets—Fiction 2. Stories in rhyme
ISBN 0-02-770010-0 LC 88-5192

A reissue of the title first published 1948

A tale in rhyme and colorful pictures about a runaway carpet. When it was rolled out of the hotel to receive a visiting duke, it rolled on and on, down the street, along the highway and over the country roads, bringing excitement wherever it went

Parnall, Peter

Feet! written and illustrated by Peter Parnall. Macmillan 1988 unp il $13.95 **E**

1. Foot 2. Animals
ISBN 0-02-770110-7 LC 88-5272

Looks at a variety of animal feet, from big feet and fast feet to cool feet and webbed feet

"Each two-page spread has a close-up, realistic pen-and-ink and watercolor illustration of an animal's foot with a smaller drawing of the whole animal. The animals chosen range from the familiar horse to the more exotic sloth. Parnall's characteristic illustrative style fits the subject well. Color is used sparingly and primarily in the background, accenting but not dominating the pen-and-ink drawings." SLJ

Winter barn; written and illustrated by Peter Parnall. Macmillan 1986 unp il $12.95 **E**

1. Winter—Fiction 2. Animals—Fiction
ISBN 0-02-770170-0 LC 85-23898

A dilapidated old barn shelters a wide variety of animals, including snakes, porcupines, cats, and a skunk, during the sub-zero winter temperature of Maine, while they wait for the first signs of spring

"The double-page charcoal drawings capture the chill as Parnall skillfully manipulates large white spaces. He's able to suggest volumes with hints of black charcoal strokes. His treatment of landforms are most powerful because he seems freer to abstract from nature." SLJ

Patterson, Geoffrey, 1943-

A pig's tale. Deutsch 1983 unp il $9.95 **E**

1. Pigs—Fiction
ISBN 0-233-97477-6 LC 82-72113

"A fat and greedy farmer sends his old sow to market, but she dislikes the poking and prodding and runs away. The hardworking pig finds a small, inviting farm where she's welcomed to spend a comfortable retirement." Publisher's note

Paxton, Tom, 1937-

Engelbert the elephant; written by Tom Paxton; illustrated by Steven Kellogg. Morrow Junior Bks. 1990 unp il $14.95; lib bdg $14.88 **E**

1. Elephants—Fiction 2. Dancing—Fiction 3. Stories in rhyme
ISBN 0-688-08935-6; 0-688-08936-4 (lib bdg)
LC 89-9376

"An unsuspecting elephant receives a surprise invitation to the royal ball (thanks to a pair of prankster mice). Engelbert's arrival startles the stuffy courtiers, who nearly cause a stampede in their panic. But the queen is charmed by the pachyderm's courteous bow, and quickly puts a halt to the mad exit. Wearing one sneaker and one rollerskate, Engelbert turns out to be a veritable Fred Astaire, and is even chosen to squire the queen for the final dance." Publ Wkly

Singer-songwriter Paxton's tune . . . is given new, rambunctious life in this rollicking volume. . . . Though the music for the song is not included, readers can't help but narrate it with a lilt in their voices. Kellogg's frenzied line work and his humorous nuances are the perfect match for such an exuberant text." Booklist

Payne, Emmy, 1919-

Katy No-Pocket; pictures by H. A. Rey. Houghton Mifflin 1944 unp il lib bdg $13.95; pa $5.95 **E**

1. Kangaroos—Fiction 2. Animals—Fiction
ISBN 0-395-17104-0 (lib bdg); 0-395-13717-9 (pa)
LC 44-8099

Katy Kangaroo was most unfortunately unprovided with a pocket in which to carry her son Freddy. She asked other animals with no pockets how they carried their children but none of their answers seemed satisfactory. Finally a wise old owl advised her to try to find a pocket in the City, and so off she went and in the City she found just what she and Freddy needed

Pearson, Susan, 1946-

Happy birthday, Grampie; pictures by Ronald Himler. Dial Bks. for Young Readers 1987 unp il $10.95; lib bdg $10.89 **E**

1. Grandfathers—Fiction 2. Birthdays—Fiction 3. Old age—Fiction 4. Blind—Fiction
ISBN 0-8037-3457-3; 0-8037-3458-1 (lib bdg)
LC 85-31105

"Martha makes a very special card to bring when she and her parents drive to the home to celebrate Grampie's 89th birthday. Lately he has been speaking only in Swedish. A simple and moving book that conveys great family feeling." N Y Times Book Rev

Peet, Bill

Big bad Bruce. Houghton Mifflin 1977 38p il 13.95; pa $4.95 **E**

1. Bears—Fiction 2. Witches—Fiction
ISBN 0-395-25150-8; 0-395-32922-1 (pa)
LC 76-62502

Bruce, a bear bully, never picks on anyone his own size until he is diminished in more ways than one by a small but very independent witch

"The best elements of a Saturday-morning cartoon show are delivered in this picture-book story which will satisfy young readers and listeners as well as the adults who share it with them. The language of the text is almost musical, with lots of words used for the sheer pleasure or appropriateness of their sounds. The illustrations are colorful and amusing." Child Book Rev Serv

Cowardly Clyde. Houghton Mifflin 1979 38p il $13.95; pa $3.95 **E**

1. Horses—Fiction 2. Courage—Fiction
ISBN 0-395-27802-3; 0-395-36171-0 (pa)
LC 78-24343

"Brave Sir Galavant and his cowardly steed Clyde take up the challenge to rid the farmers of the terrible 'giant owl-eyed ox-footed ogre.' Clyde, who quivers at a scarecrow, is terrified, but finds that by acting brave, you become brave." Read Teach

"The tale is nonsensical, but the combination of swash-buckling knight and anti-hero Clyde, and the action that ends in victory, should appeal to the read-aloud

Peet, Bill—*Continued*
audience. The writing is brisk and casual; the illustrations are colorful and vigorous." Bull Cent Child Books

Eli; illustrated by the author. Houghton Mifflin 1978 38p il $13.95; pa $3.95 E

1. Lions—Fiction 2. Vultures—Fiction 3. Friendship—Fiction
ISBN 0-395-26454-5; 0-395-36611-9 (pa)
LC 77-17500

"The story of pathetic Eli, a 'king of the jungle' who's too old to fight. Feeding on leftovers one day, Eli is disgusted by hovering vultures, but 'noblesse oblige' compels him to rescue one bird, Vera, from a jackal who snatches her. Eli routs the jackal and earns the unwelcome friendship of the birds. Not even his most outrageous insults rid the lion of his faithful companions. And a good thing, too. Comes the day when the hunters are closing in on him; Vera and the flock persuade Eli to play dead, and swoop down on him. The hunters see no glory in hauling off a dead body, apparently the feast of vultures, and the old cat is saved." Publ Wkly

"A too-obvious ending is countered by the author-artist's flair for exaggerated expressions, plentiful action, and bold use of color." Booklist

Huge Harold; written and illustrated by Bill Peet. Houghton Mifflin 1961 unp il lib bdg $13.95; pa $4.95 E

1. Rabbits—Fiction 2. Stories in rhyme
ISBN 0-395-18449-5 (lib bdg); 0-395-32923-X (pa)
LC 61-5131

"Harold the rabbit grows and grows—to dimensions which deprive him of normal hiding places but help him, after a bizarre chase, to an astonishing and wonderful achievement." Horn Book

This story, "told in rhyming couplets and colored drawings, is action filled and laughable." Booklist

No such things. Houghton Mifflin 1983 32p il $13.95; pa $3.95 E

1. Animals, Mythical—Fiction 2. Stories in rhyme
ISBN 0-395-33888-3; 0-395-39594-1 (pa)
LC 82-23234

Describes in rhyme a variety of fantastical creatures such as the blue-snouted Twumps, the pie-faced Pazeeks, and the fancy Fandangos

"The concepts of the nonsensical beasts are more impressive than the text; the pictures should appeal because of their animation and their expressions." Bull Cent Child Books

The whingdingdilly; written and illustrated by Bill Peet. Houghton Mifflin 1970 60p il $13.95; pa $3.95 E

1. Dogs—Fiction 2. Witches—Fiction
ISBN 0-395-24729-2; 0-395-31381-3 (pa)
LC 71-98521

"Scamps, the dog, wants to be a horse, but a well-meaning witch turns him into a Whingdingdilly with the hump of a camel, zebra's tail, giraffe's neck, elephant's front legs and ears, rhinoceros' nose, and reindeer's horns." Adventuring With Books. 2d edition

Peppé, Rodney, 1934-

Circus numbers. New ed. Delacorte Press 1986 c1969 unp il lib bdg $11.95 E

1. Counting 2. Circus—Fiction
ISBN 0-385-29424-7
LC 85-7071

A reissue of the title first published 1969

In this book readers encounter 1 ringmaster, 2 horses etc. up to 10 clowns, 20 doves and then "100 elephants, divided according to units of 10 (9 to a cage drawn by the 10th). . . . Sets of bright blue stars are sprinkled through the book, providing a second chance to count each number. Minimum text in large, clear upper- and lower-case type together with the impact of the [author's] jolly, poster-like illustrations set a smart tempo." Libr J

The mice who lived in a shoe. Lothrop, Lee & Shepard Bks. 1982 c1981 unp il $12.95 E

1. Mice—Fiction
ISBN 0-688-00844-5
LC 81-82061

First published 1981 in the United Kingdom

"The old-woman-in-a-shoe story is given a new angle here when a family of mice takes refuge in a discarded, well-worn boot. Tired of being victims of the wind, rain, and a feisty cat, the mice decide to act. Some clever renovation (holes become windows, rips are turned into doors) and a new tower structure built out of the shoe's opening provide a safe, cozy, even spiffy home. Glowing colors spark the large pictures, in which the rehabbing efforts of the mice are humorously shown and topped off with funny conversation-balloon comments." Booklist

Petersham, Maud, 1889-1971

The box with red wheels; a picture book by Maud and Miska Petersham. Macmillan 1949 unp il $12.95; pa $4.95 E

1. Animals—Fiction
ISBN 0-02-771350-4; 0-02-044760-4 (pa)
LC 49-11325

The barnyard animals were curious to find out what was in the box with red wheels. Their surprising discovery was as much a revelation to them as it was to the occupant of the box with red wheels

The circus baby; a picture book by Maud and Miska Petersham. Macmillan 1950 unp il $13.95; pa $3.95 E

1. Elephants—Fiction 2. Clowns—Fiction 3. Circus—Fiction
ISBN 0-02-771670-8; 0-689-71295-2 (pa) LC 50-9295

A picture book all about the circus elephant and her baby, and the circus clown family. When the mother elephant tried to train her child to eat at table, like the clown baby, the results were disastrous

The authors "have combined talents again to make a delightful picture book. The four-color circus scenes are bright and simple. Mother and Baby are wonderfully expressive but still quite real elephants, rather than the stuffed-toy variety so familiar in the nursery books." NY Times Book Rev

Pfanner, Louise

Louise builds a house; story and pictures by Louise Pfanner. Orchard Bks. 1989 c1987 unp il $12.95; lib bdg $12.99 E

1. Houses—Fiction
ISBN 0-531-05796-8; 0-531-08396-9 (lib bdg) LC 88-23415

"As Louise describes the house she will build and the reason for each of its architectural features, the house grows on the left-hand pages while Louise is depicted on the right engaged in each activity. This whimsical tale of imagination and spunk has a nice twist at the end, and the art is singular and direct." Horn Book Guide

Phillips, Mildred

The sign in Mendel's window; illustrated by Margot Zemach. Macmillan 1985 unp il $12.95 E

1. Jews—Fiction
ISBN 0-02-774600-3 LC 85-5049

When a stranger comes to Kosnov and accuses Mendel the butcher of stealing his money, the whole town joins in to show the police who is really guilty

"The story, an original creation, has exactly the right blend of peasant humor and folkloric elements to suit Margot Zemach's distinctive style. Her robust, vivid images capture the fabulist overtones of the theme, effectively playing the naive Mendel against the slick Tinker. Each of the characters is a separate personality, suggested by a subtle shift in posture, a twitch of an eyelid, or downward turn of a mouth. In true picture book fashion, text and illustrations complement and extend one another, making the book a fine choice for story hours and for independent reading." Horn Book

Pinkwater, Daniel Manus, 1941-

Aunt Lulu; by Daniel Pinkwater. Macmillan 1988 unp il $12.95; pa $3.95 E

1. Aunts—Fiction 2. Librarians—Fiction 3. Dogs—Fiction
ISBN 0-02-774661-5; 0-689-71413-0 (pa) LC 88-1736

Tired of working as a librarian in Alaska, Aunt Lulu takes her sled and her fourteen Huskies and moves to Parsippany, New Jersey

"Skeletal but energetic drawings are accomplished with colored felt-tip pens. The seemingly tossed-off lines are filled in with flat color that gives a mottling effect. The story's language is simple and its exposition rhythmic in a way that is tailor-made for young children." Booklist

Bear's picture; story and pictures by Daniel Pinkwater. Dutton 1984 c1972 unp il lib bdg $11.95 E

1. Bears—Fiction 2. Painting—Fiction
ISBN 0-525-44102-6 LC 83-25369

A reissue of the title first published 1972 by Holt, Rinehart and Winston

"Bear sets out to paint a picture. Two 'fine proper gentlemen' come along and say, 'Bears can't paint pictures.' They ask what Bear's painting is a picture of, and then say it looks silly. But Bear is happy with it because it is his picture." Child Book Rev Serv

"Ingeniously contrasting the bold primary hues Bear uses with sharp black-and-white drawings of the characters, Pinkwater achieves eye-filling effects." Publ Wkly

Guys from space; [by] Daniel Pinkwater. Macmillan 1989 unp il $13.95 E

1. Science fiction
ISBN 0-02-774672-0 LC 88-13485

A boy accompanies some guys from space on a visit to another planet, where they discover such incredibly amazing things as talking rocks and root beer with ice cream

"Daniel Pinkwater has once again put his offbeat imagination to work to create a silly story that will have readers smiling, chuckling and laughing. . . . The full-colored, vivid pictures convey the absurd antics in this out-of-this-world story." Child Book Rev Serv

Piper, Watty

The little engine that could; retold by Watty Piper; illustrated by George & Doris Hauman. 60th anniversary edition. Platt & Munk Pubs. 1990 c1930 unp il $12.95 E

1. Railroads—Fiction
ISBN 0-448-40041-3 LC 89-81287

First published 1930

"When a train carrying good things to children breaks down, the little blue engine proves his courage and determination. The rhythmic, repetitive text encourages children to help tell the story." Hodges. Books for Elem Sch Libr

Platt, Kin, 1911-

Big Max; with pictures by Robert Lopshire. Harper & Row 1965 64p il lib bdg $10.89; pa $3.50 E

1. Elephants—Fiction 2. Mystery and detective stories
ISBN 0-06-024751-7 (lib bdg); 0-06-444006-0 (pa) LC 65-14488

"An I can read mystery"

"Big Max the world's greatest detective, travels by umbrella to help the king find Jumbo, his prize elephant, who has mysteriously disappeared." Libr J

"The answer to the riddle of Jumbo's escape over the wall of the castle courtyard comes step by step through the dead-pan deductions of Big Max's professionally conducted sleuthing. The spontaneous fun of the text . . . has a happy complement in the pictures." Horn Book

Another available title about Big Max is entered below

Big Max in the mystery of the missing moose; pictures by Robert Lopshire. Harper & Row 1977 64p il lib bdg $8.89 E

1. Mystery and detective stories
ISBN 0-06-024757-6 LC 76-58727

"An I can read mystery"

Big Max, the detective, helps the zoo keeper find a missing moose

"It's hard to resist Robert Lopshire's drawings of the little detective with the oversized feet and Sherlock Holmes costume and umbrella." SLJ

Polacco, Patricia

Babushka's doll. Simon & Schuster Bks. for Young Readers 1990 unp il $14.95 **E**

1. Dolls—Fiction
ISBN 0-671-68343-8 LC 89-6122

"When Natasha wants something, she wants it now—not after her grandmother, Babushka, has finished her chores. Babushka gets tired of this attitude, and finally goes off to the market, leaving Natasha to play with a special doll that she keeps on a high shelf. The doll comes to life and subjects Natasha to the same sort of insistent whining that Natasha used on Babushka." SLJ

"Polacco's distinctive artwork interprets the story with style and verve. Using pencil, marker, and paint, she creates a series of varied compositions, highlighting muted shades with an occasional flare of bright colors and strong patterns. The dramatic and humorous effects created are all the more striking for the essential homeliness of her vision. A good, original story, illustrated with panache." Booklist

Just plain Fancy. Bantam Bks. 1990 unp il $14.95; lib bdg $15.99 **E**

1. Amish—Fiction 2. Peacocks—Fiction
ISBN 0-553-05884-3; 0-553-07062-2 (lib bdg) LC 89-27856

"In Naomi's Amish community, plainness is a way of life; still, Naomi would like just once to have something fancy. So when a peacock is mysteriously hatched among her chickens, Naomi's feelings are mixed. Delighted with Fancy's plumage, she also worries that her colorful bird will be shunned." Booklist

"The author-illustrator offers a lively story in a non-traditional setting that is depicted faithfully in both text and illustration." Horn Book

Rechenka's eggs; written and illustrated by Patricia Polacco. Philomel Bks. 1988 unp il lib bdg $13.95 **E**

1. Geese—Fiction 2. Easter—Fiction 3. Eggs—Fiction 4. Soviet Union—Fiction
ISBN 0-399-21501-8 LC 87-16588

An injured goose rescued by Babushka, having broken the painted eggs intended for the Easter Festival in Moscva, lays thirteen marvelously colored eggs to replace them, then leaves behind one final miracle in egg form before returning to her own kind

"Polacco achieves optimal dramatic contrast by using bold shapes against uncluttered white space and by contrasting rich colors and design details with faces in black and white." Bull Cent Child Books

Thunder cake. Philomel Bks. 1990 unp il $14.95 **E**

1. Thunderstorms—Fiction 2. Fear—Fiction 3. Grandmothers—Fiction
ISBN 0-399-22231-6 LC 89-33405

"Polacco illustrates a first-person narrative about a little girl's experience on her grandmother's farm in Michigan. A Russian immigrant, Baboushka placates her granddaughter's fears by baking a 'Thunder Cake' that requires the two of them to gather ingredients to the count of the approaching booms." Bull Cent Child Books

"It is not always that a picture book artist can construct an exceptional story, but Polacco succeeds with both words and art. . . . Against crisp, white backgrounds that offer the promise of the storm clearing, Grandmother and the child (in intricately patterned clothing) work, wonder, and love. The carefully drawn faces, done in pencil, contrast with the rest of the colorful folk art." Booklist

Uncle Vova's tree. Philomel Bks. 1989 unp il $14.95 **E**

1. Christmas—Fiction 2. Russian Americans—Fiction
ISBN 0-399-21617-0 LC 88-25522

"An entire family gathers to celebrate Christmas in the Russian tradition. Many customs are continued, but the most remembered is decorating the tree Uncle Vova and his wife planted when they first arrived from Russia. The following year, Uncle Vova is no longer alive yet his memory lingers." Child Book Rev Serv

"Polacco's combination of softly delineated faces; subtle shading of colors; brilliant, overlapping patterns; and areas of white space has an eclectic look, but she pulls these elements of her distinctive style together into an expressive presentation. In composition, color, and detail, the artwork glows with originality and verve. A fine read-aloud book for the Christmas season." Booklist

Politi, Leo, 1908-

Song of the swallows. Scribner 1987 c1949 unp il music $12.95; pa $4.95 **E**

1. Swallows—Fiction 2. California—Fiction 3. Missions—Fiction
ISBN 0-684-18831-7; 0-689-71140-9 (pa) LC 49-8215

Awarded the Caldecott Medal, 1950

A reissue of title first published 1949

"The swallows always appeared at the old Mission of Capistrano on St. Joseph's Day and Juan who lived nearby wondered how they could tell that from all others. This tender poetic story of the coming of springtime is touched by the kindliness of the good Fathers of the Mission as a little boy knew it. Lovely pictures in soft colors bring out the charm of the southern California landscape and the melody of the swallow song adds to the feeling of Spring." Horn Book

Polushkin, Maria

Kitten in trouble; pictures by Betsy Lewin. Bradbury Press 1988 unp il $12.95 **E**

1. Cats—Fiction
ISBN 0-02-774740-9 LC 85-5753

"A popeyed kitten flings himself into one adventure after another. Who could resist pouncing on ten wiggling toes, an enticing butterfly, or a freshly set table? Lewin uses colorful washes and a spare line, yet her few strokes translate into playful eagerness, surprise, anger, and wild abandon." SLJ

Who said meow? illustrated by Ellen Weiss. Bradbury Press 1988 unp il $12.95 **E**

1. Dogs—Fiction 2. Animals—Fiction
ISBN 0-02-774770-0 LC 87-28073

Adaptation of a Russian story by V. Suteev

"A puppy is awakened from his nap by a teasing kitten, and in pursuit he encounters a mouse, a dog, a bee and other creatures. He finds the kitten back in the house, and sure enough, it does say meow." N Y Times Book Rev

"The pictures, while simple, colorful, and pleasant, lack polish. Still, little ones should like the hide-and-seek

Polushkin, Maria—*Continued*
aspect of the book, and the occasional glimpses of kitty hiding in the corners will keep them turning the pages." Booklist

Pomerantz, Charlotte

The chalk doll; pictures by Frané Lessac. Lippincott 1989 30p il $12.95; lib bdg $12.89 **E**

1. Dolls—Fiction 2. Mothers and daughters—Fiction 3. Jamaica—Fiction
ISBN 0-397-32318-2; 0-397-32319-0 (lib bdg) LC 88-872

"Rose has a cold and must stay in bed. Before she settles in for a nap, she coaxes her mother to tell stories of her Jamaican childhood. The scene shifts from Rose's colorful room filled with toys to a simple little house in the village where her mother grew up. The stories are touching for the contrast between the poverty and yearning of these childhood memories and the obvious comfort of their present lives." Horn Book

"The stylized illustrations by the West Indian artists Frané Lessac are primitive in bright, oscillating colors, evoking poverty in a tropical paradise as well as mother-daughter affection in a well-appointed home." N Y Times Book Rev

Flap your wings and try; illustrated by Nancy Tafuri. Greenwillow Bks. 1989 unp il $12.95; lib bdg $12.88 **E**

1. Birds—Fiction 2. Stories in rhyme
ISBN 0-688-08019-7; 0-688-08020-0 (lib bdg) LC 88-18766

Following the advice of family members, a young bird learns to fly and tells other birds that to fly, they need only to flap their wings and try

"Tafuri's large, clear watercolors bring the viewer's eye right up to the nest, looking into the tiny eyes of the black-and-white adult gull and the brown fledgling. The rhyming text, in large print, has enough simplicity and repetition to encourage beginning readers." Horn Book

One duck, another duck; pictures by Jose Aruego and Ariane Dewey. Greenwillow Bks. 1984 unp il $10.25; lib bdg $10.88 **E**

1. Counting
ISBN 0-688-03744-5; 0-688-03745-3 (lib bdg) LC 83-20767

"When Danny, a little owl, and his grandmother go to the pond, he sees a mother duck and her babies and starts to count them with his grandmother's help. This basic counting book combines the task of learning to count with a slight but delightful story. It is charmingly illustrated in full color." Child Book Rev Serv

The piggy in the puddle; pictures by James Marshall. Macmillan 1974 unp il $13.95; pa $3.95 **E**

1. Pigs—Fiction 2. Stories in rhyme
ISBN 0-02-774900-2; 0-689-71293-6 (pa) LC 73-6047

The "rhythmic tale of a small pig that scorns soap and refuses to leave her puddle. Her pleasure is infectious and finally mother, father, and brother join her in 'the very merry middle' of the 'muddy little puddle.'" Booklist

"The soft pastel drawings add just the right touch to the humorous bedtime story which demands to be read aloud." Child Book Rev Serv

Where's the bear? pictures by Byron Barton; words by Charlotte Pomerantz. Greenwillow Bks. 1984 unp il $10.25; lib bdg $10.88; Puffin Bks. pa $3.95 **E**

1. Bears—Fiction 2. Stories in rhyme
ISBN 0-688-01752-5; 0-688-01753-3 (lib bdg); 0-14-050514-8 (pa) LC 83-1697

"A woman runs back into her village and alerts the people to something lurking in the woods. 'Where's the bear?' they ask, and follow her armed with hoes, hammers, and brooms. Back in the forest, they ask again 'Where?' 'There's the bear, there's the bear.' At least that's what the villagers think, but it's only rabbits, racoons, and birds making the noise. Then the bear really does appear, and it's a mad scramble to get back to the safety of home." Booklist

"This is ideal for the youngest children: brilliantly colored pictures, clear expressions, simple activities, and repetitive words that can be chanted. Preschool and kindergarten teachers could easily turn this into a game or skit. Children just learning to read can enjoy this on their own." Child Book Rev Serv

Porte-Thomas, Barbara Ann

Harry in trouble; [by] Barbara Ann Porte; pictures by Yossi Abolafia. Greenwillow Bks. 1989 47p il $12.95; lib bdg $12.88; Dell pa $2.95 **E**

ISBN 0-688-07633-5; 0-688-07722-6 (lib bdg); 0-440-40370-7 (pa) LC 87-21253

Harry is upset about losing his library card three times in a row, but feels better when he learns that his father and his friend Dorcas sometimes lose things

"Porte's story has an easy-to-read format which nicely fits the present tense childlike first-person narration. Abolafia's expressive cartoon style illustrations ably convey characters' emotions." SLJ

Other available titles about Harry are:
Harry's dog (1984)
Harry's mom (1985)
Harry's visit (1983)

The take-along dog; [by] Barbara Ann Porte; pictures by Emily Arnold McCully. Greenwillow Bks. 1989 unp il $11.95; lib bdg $11.88 **E**

1. Dogs—Fiction
ISBN 0-688-08053-7; 0-688-08054-5 (lib bdg) LC 88-18775

Because Mother does not like dogs, Sam and Abigail must take Benton with them everywhere, including trying to sneak him into the movies, the library, and the swimming pool

"The bright watercolor illustrations outlined in black ink portray Benton and his family with an appropriate amount of detail for the story. Benton is not only the bravest but also one of the cutest dog characters to be drawn recently, and many a reader will wish for just such a pup to take along." Horn Book

Potter, Beatrix, 1866-1943

The pie and the patty-pan. Warne il o.p.; Dover Publs. paperback available $1.75 E

1. Cats—Fiction 2. Dogs—Fiction
ISBN 0-486-23383-9 (pa)

First published 1905 with title: A tale of the pie and the patty-pan

"Ribby, a pussy cat, invites a little dog named Duchess to tea." Toronto Public Libr. Books for Boys & Girls

The story of Miss Moppet. Warne il $4.95; pa $2.25 E

1. Cats—Fiction 2. Mice—Fiction
ISBN 0-7232-3480-9; 0-7232-3505-8 (pa)

First published 1906

Miss Moppet is a kitten who uses her wiles to capture a curious mouse. But her trickery amounts to naught when she herself is outwitted

Other available titles about Moppet's brother Tom and sister Mittens are:
The complete adventures of Tom Kitten and his friends (1984)
The roly-poly pudding (1908)
The tale of Tom Kitten (1935)

The tailor of Gloucester. Warne il $4.95; pa $2.25 E

1. Tailoring—Fiction 2. Mice—Fiction 3. Christmas—Fiction
ISBN 0-7232-3462-0; 0-7232-3487-6 (pa)

First published in 1903

"The cat Simpkin looked after his master when he was ill, but it was the nimble-fingered mice who used snippets of cherry-coloured twist and so finished the embroidered waist coat for the worried tailor. A Christmastime story set in old Gloucester." Four to Fourteen

"A read-aloud classic in polished style, perfectly complemented by the author's exquisite watercolor illustrations." Hodges. Books for Elem Sch Libr

The tale of Jemima Puddle-duck E

1. Ducks—Fiction

Some editions are:
Bantam Bks. pa $2.25 (ISBN 0-553-15251-3)
Simon & Schuster $3.95 (ISBN 0-671-63236-1)
Warne pa $4.95 (ISBN 0-7232-3468-X)

First published 1908 by Warne

"Jemima Puddle-duck's obstinate determination to hatch her own eggs, makes a story of suspense and sly humor." Toronto Public Libr. Books for Boys & Girls

The tale of Mr. Jeremy Fisher. Warne il $4.95; pa $2.25 E

1. Frogs—Fiction
ISBN 0-7232-3466-3; 0-7232-3491-4 (pa)

First published 1906

A frog fishing from his lilly pad boat doesn't catch any fish, but one catches him

The tale of Mrs. Tiggy-Winkle. Warne il $4.95; pa $2.25 E

1. Hedgehogs—Fiction
ISBN 0-7232-3465-5; 0-7232-3490-6 (pa)

First published 1905

Lucie visits the laundry of Mrs. Tiggy-Winkle, a hedgehog, and finds her lost handerchiefs

The tale of Mrs. Tittlemouse. Warne il $4.95; pa $2.25 E

1. Mice—Fiction
ISBN 0-7232-3470-1; 0-7232-3495-7 (pa)

First published 1910

The story of a little mouse's funny house, the visitors she has there, and how she finally rids herself of the untidy, messy ones

The tale of Peter Rabbit. Warne il $4.95; pa $2.25 E

1. Rabbits—Fiction
ISBN 0-7232-3460-4; 0-7232-3485-X (pa)

Also available in a French language edition $5 (ISBN 0-7232-0650-3) and a Spanish language edition $4.95 (ISBN 0-7232-3556-2)

First published 1903

All about the famous rabbit family consisting of Flopsy, Mopsy, Cotton-tail and especially Peter Rabbit who disobeys Mother Rabbit's admonishment not to go into Mr. McGregor's garden

"Distinctive writing and a strong appeal to a small child's sense of justice and his sympathies make this an outstanding story. The water color illustrations add charm to the narrative by their simplicity of detail and delicacy of color." Child Books Too Good to Miss

Other available titles about Peter Rabbit and his family are:
The tale of Benjamin Bunny (1904)
The tale of Mr. Tod (1912)
The tale of the flopsy bunnies (1909)

The tale of Pigling Bland. Warne il $4.95; pa $2.25 E

1. Pigs—Fiction
ISBN 0-7232-3474-4; 0-7232-3499-X (pa)

First published 1913

"Pigling's story ends happily with a perfectly lovely little black Berkshire pig called Pigwig." Toronto Public Libr. Books for Boys & Girls

The tale of Squirrel Nutkin. Warne il $4.95; pa $2.25 E

1. Squirrels—Fiction
ISBN 0-7232-0593-0; 0-7232-6226-8 (pa)

First published 1903

Each day the squirrels gather nuts, Nutkin propounds a riddle to Mr. Brown, the owl, until impertinent Nutkin, over-estimating Mr. Brown's patience, gets his due

The tale of Timmy Tiptoes. Warne il $4.95; pa $2.25 E

1. Squirrels—Fiction
ISBN 0-7232-3471-X; 0-7232-3496-5 (pa)

First published 1911

An innocent squirrel accused of stealing nuts is forced down a hole in a tree, where he meets a friendly chipmunk

The tale of two bad mice. Warne il $4.95; pa $2.25 E

1. Mice—Fiction
ISBN 0-7232-3464-7; 0-7232-3489-2 (pa)

First published 1904

Potter, Beatrix, 1866-1943—*Continued*

"Two mischievous little mice pilfer a doll's house to equip their own. They are caught and finally make amends for what they have done. Perfectly charming illustrations and a most enticing tale." Adventuring With Books. 2d edition

Yours affectionately, Peter Rabbit: miniature letters. Warne 1984 c1983 96p il $6.95 **E**

1. Letters—Fiction
ISBN 0-7232-3178-8 LC 84-133834

Originally written between the years 1907 and 1912, as an invented correspondence between Peter Rabbit and the author's other characters

"This small-format book . . . contains the correspondence of such favorite Potter characters as Squirrel Nutkin, Tom Thumb and Peter Rabbit, written for some of Potter's favorite child friends. The letters inform readers of the further adventures of these characters and are typical of Potter wit. Though they have previously appeared in books for adults on the art and writing of Beatrix Potter, this is their first presentation in a book of the size she espoused 'for little hands to hold.'" SLJ

"Delightful illustrations, most of them from Beatrix Potter's books, accompany each letter." Horn Book

Prelutsky, Jack

The mean old mean hyena; illustrated by Arnold Lobel. Greenwillow Bks. 1978 unp il lib bdg $11.88 **E**

1. Hyenas—Fiction 2. Stories in rhyme
ISBN 0-688-84163-5 (lib bdg) LC 78-2300

A zebra, ostrich, elephant, and lion become the hapless victims of an incorrigible hyena's mean tricks

"Prelutsky's trickster tale is witty and alive with wonderfully onomatopoetic words and lilting rhythm. It makes a fine read-aloud book, especially for anyone who likes to ham it up. Prelutsky reminds us how dynamic poetry can be. A tour de force." Child Book Rev Serv

Preston, Edna Mitchell

Squawk to the moon, Little Goose; illustrated by Barbara Cooney. Viking 1974 unp il o.p.; Puffin Bks. paperback available $3.95 **E**

1. Geese—Fiction 2. Moon—Fiction
ISBN 0-14-050546-6 (pa) LC 72-91394

This is the "story of a gosling that is both silly and resourceful. . . . Tucked in for the night, Little Goose steals out for a night ramble; she sees the moon covered by a cloud and wakes the farmer with her squawking; it happens again when she sees the moon reflected in the pond and decides it has fallen. When she's caught by a fox, Little Goose squawks, but the disgruntled farmer won't get up a third time. However, Little Goose uses her wits and outfoxes the fox, going home to a maternal spank and cuddle." Bull Cent Child Books

"Ms. Cooney has infused her watercolor illustrations with so much personality, drollery and beauty that fortunate owners of this book will find themselves gazing at the pictures again and again, finding new aspects at which to marvel each time." Publ Wkly

Prokofiev, Sergey, 1891-1953

Peter and the wolf; translated by Maria Carlson; illustrated by Charles Mikolaycak. Viking 1982 unp il hardcover o.p. paperback available $3.95 **E**

1. Wolves—Fiction 2. Fairy tales
ISBN 0-14-050633-0 (pa) LC 81-70402

Another picture book version entered above under Patricia Gampton; edition focusing on musical elements entered in 784.2

This book retells the orchestral fairy tale of the boy who, ignoring his grandfather's warnings, proceeds to capture a wolf

"Prokofiev's classic, designed to teach children the instruments of an orchestra, has been published in picture book form before, but never better illustrated. The translation is smooth. . . . The paintings are rich in color, dramatic in details of costume or architecture, strong in composition, with distinctive individuality in the faces of people and of the wolf." Bull Cent Child Books

Provensen, Alice, 1918-

A book of seasons; [by] Alice and Martin Provensen. Random House 1976 unp il hardcover o.p. paperback available $1.95 **E**

1. Seasons
ISBN 0-394-83242-6 (pa) LC 75-36470

"A Random House picturebook"

Color pictures of the year-round activities of children provide the focus for this book about the changing seasons

Shaker Lane; by Alice and Martin Provensen. Viking Kestrel 1987 unp il lib bdg $14.95 **E**

ISBN 0-670-81568-3 LC 87-6283

"As the Herkimer sisters, rural inhabitants, grew old, they sold off parts of their land to those with modest incomes and a laid-back lifestyle. Then land developers arrived, created a reservoir, and forced the poor to move out to be replaced by middle-class families." SLJ

"It's always autumn in the Provensens' paintings of this quiet rural drama, with the browns and russets of land and sky providing a comfortable background for the rickety houses and piled-up yards of Shaker Lane's inhabitants. There's plenty of wry humor here, and the whole has a tone of inevitability rather than tragedy." Bull Cent Child Books

The year at Maple Hill Farm; [by] Alice and Martin Provensen. Atheneum Pubs. 1978 unp il $15.95; pa $3.95 **E**

1. Seasons—Fiction 2. Farm life—Fiction 3. Animals—Fiction
ISBN 0-689-30642-3; 0-689-71270-7 (pa) LC 77-18518

"A Jonathan Cape book"

Describes the seasonal changes on a farm and surrounding countryside throughout the year

"Each of the twelve double-page spreads has a running line of general comment across the tops of the pages . . . and captions for the other pictures, of which there may be one or several. The text is direct, mildly

Provensen, Alice, 1918-—*Continued*
humorous, and informative; the illustrations are perky and amusing, with soft, bright colors and the appeal of animals, animals, animals." Bull Cent Child Books

Rabe, Berniece
The balancing girl; pictures by Lillian Hoban. Dutton 1981 unp il $12.95; pa $3.95 E

1. School stories 2. Physically handicapped children—Fiction
ISBN 0-525-26160-5; 0-525-44364-9 (pa) LC 80-22100

"In a wheelchair, Margaret is in what appears to be a kindergarten class. She has a running feud with Tommy, who's a bit jealous because Margaret wins praise for balancing such things as magic markers or blocks, and who often knocks her projects over. No shrinking violet, Margaret issues a stern warning. [Her] masterpiece is a structure of dominoes which wins kudos and cash at a school carnival and also ends the feud." Bull Cent Child Books

"Hoban's smudgy charcoal sketches of moon-cheeked little kids give a homey warmth to Rabe's characters and their grade-school setting." Booklist

Another available title about Margaret is entered in the Fiction Section

Radin, Ruth Yaffe, 1938-
High in the mountains; illustrated by Ed Young. Macmillan 1989 unp il $13.95 E

1. Mountains—Fiction 2. Grandfathers—Fiction
ISBN 0-02-775650-5 LC 88-13395

"A young child tells what it is like to spend time with her Grandpa high up in the Colorado Rockies, experiencing the closeness of the mist, flowers in a meadow, deer in the forest, the song of a brook, and, finally, the drive on the curving, ascending road that takes them out of the valleys, above the tree line, where they pitch a tent on the tundra with the sky all around and crickets to sing them to sleep. In his translucent pastel chalk drawings, Ed Young pours into the readers eyes the changing colors and light throughout a mountain day and he wraps readers in the varied and awesome scenery of high places." Child Book Rev Serv

Rand, Gloria
Salty dog; illustrated by Ted Rand. Holt & Co. 1989 unp il lib bdg $13.95 E

1. Dogs—Fiction 2. Boats and boating—Fiction
ISBN 0-8050-0837-3 LC 88-13453

Salty the dog helps his master build a sailboat

"This engaging and affectionate tale is illustrated in brilliant watercolor spreads that pay close attention to detail. The rich atmosphere of a seagoing community is nicely evoked, and Salty appears in every illustration, growing from adorable miniscule pup to well-behaved dog." SLJ

Rappaport, Doreen
The Boston coffee party; pictures by Emily Arnold McCully. Harper & Row 1988 63p il $10.95; lib bdg $11.89; pa $3.50 E

1. United States—History—1775-1783, Revolution—Fiction 2. Boston (Mass.)—Fiction
ISBN 0-06-024824-6; 0-06-024825-4 (lib bdg); 0-06-444141-5 (pa) LC 87-45301

"An I can read book"

During the Revolutionary War, two young sisters help a group of Boston women get coffee from a greedy merchant

The "narrative moves along briskly, with charm, brevity and humor. The illustrations, by Emily Arnold McCully, are ample and accurately capture the details of the Revolutionary era from cobblestones to mobcaps." N Y Times Book Rev

Raskin, Ellen, 1928-1984
Ghost in a four-room apartment. Atheneum Pubs. 1969 unp il hardcover o.p. paperback available $1.95 E

1. Ghosts—Fiction
ISBN 0-689-70446-1 (pa) LC 69-13521

This story is about a poltergeist who haunts a four-room apartment and creates havoc there. The narrative is divided between the ghost, who recounts his activities, and a narrator who describes in verse the members of the haunted family and their relatives

"Bright blocks of colorfully detailed line drawings exploit the hilarity of bewildered guests trying to dodge objects flying about everywhere." N Y Times Book Rev

Nothing ever happens on my block. Atheneum Pubs. 1966 unp il hardcover o.p. paperback available $3.95 E

ISBN 0-689-71335-5 (pa) LC 66-12853

"Chester Filbert, the personification of the 'grass is greener,' sits on the curb longing to see fierce lions, monsters, or other fantastic sights. Meanwhile he misses all the fantastic events, including robberies and fires transpiring around him. Much of the fun is in combing the illustrations for all the things Chester is missing." Minnesota. Dept of Educ. Libr Div

"In all fairness to Chester all those thefts and parachute jumps never happened on my block either. This in no way detracts from the inventive excellence of the book, which is a delight." N Y Times Book Rev

Spectacles. Atheneum Pubs. 1968 unp il hardcover o.p. paperback available $4.50 E

1. Eyeglasses—Fiction
ISBN 0-689-71271-5 (pa) LC 68-12234

Even though nearsighted "Iris swears that there's a firebreathing dragon at the door, a giant pygmy nuthatch on the lawn, a chestnut mare in the parlor, her readers will see, by flipping the page each time, that it's only Great-aunt Fanny, her friend Chester, and the baby sitter respectively. Iris detests specs but gets them, anyway." SLJ

"Laughable picture book, conceived and illustrated with imagination and humor. May be useful with children resisting needed glasses." Booklist

Rawlins, Donna

Digging to China. Orchard Bks. 1989 c1988 unp il $12.95; lib bdg $12.99 **E**

ISBN 0-531-05814-X; 0-531-08414-0 (lib bdg)
LC 89-42536

First published 1988 in Australia

Hearing her friend Marj, the elderly lady next door, speak wistfully of China, Alexis digs a hole all the way through the earth to that exotic country and brings back a postcard for Marj's birthday

"This charming play adventure exactly matches a child's belief in his ability to do the impossible. The illustrations are suffused with a golden glow that sets off to advantage Chinese pagodas as well as Marj's flourishing garden and Alexis's red hair. An eccentric, original picture book." Horn Book

Ray, Deborah Kogan, 1940-

My daddy was a soldier; a World War II story; written and illustrated by Deborah Kogan Ray. Holiday House 1990 unp il $12.95 **E**

1. World War, 1939-1945—Fiction 2. Fathers—Fiction

ISBN 0-8234-0795-0 LC 89-20056

While Daddy's away fighting in the Pacific, Jeannie plants a victory garden, collects scrap, and sends letters to her father as she anxiously awaits his return

"Few books on World War II for this age level are available, and this one presents an important page of history from a point of view easily understood by children. Ray's story projects a strong family image during a time of crisis in a detailed, realistic, and heartwarming fashion." Booklist

Rayner, Mary, 1933-

Mr. and Mrs. Pig's evening out. Atheneum Pubs. 1976 unp il $13.95 **E**

1. Pigs—Fiction

ISBN 0-689-30530-3 LC 76-4476

"Even though Mrs. Pig assures them she has hired a very nice lady from the babysitting agency, her 10 piglets moan and groan in protest. She goes to the door and ushers in a cloaked, sinister figure, the babysitter who answers to the name of Mrs. Wolf. Tension mounts as Mrs. Wolf turns on the oven and makes for the piglets' bedroom, where she grabs one brother and heads back to the preheated oven. The piglets rally round to rescue their brother for an exciting and victorious ending." N Y Times Book Rev

"If humour and terror (resolved) are the ingredients of treasured nursery-stories, Mary Rayner's [book] will be loved till its sturdy binding falls off. . . . [The] book has style, wit, excitement, high drama, and pathos." Times Lit Suppl

Other available titles about Mr. and Mrs. Pig and their piglets are:

Garth Pig and the ice cream lady (1977)
Mrs. Pig gets cross and other stories (1987)
Mrs. Pig's bulk buy (1981)

Reid, Margarette S.

The button box; illustrated by Sarah Chamberlain. Dutton Children's Bks. 1990 unp il $12.95 **E**

1. Grandmothers—Fiction

ISBN 0-525-44590-0 LC 89-38566

In this book "a boy describes playing with his grandmother's button box. Sorting through this round treasure chest, he imagines the bottons as belonging to elegant costumes, rough and ready clothes, uniforms, and assorted other garments that are depicted, paper-doll-fashion, in the full-color illustrations." Bull Cent Child Books

"Chamberlain's variety of colorful buttons will encourage readers to study their details, count and match them. An easy-to-read uncomplicated book that includes a brief history of buttons." Child Book Rev Serv

Reiss, John J.

Colors; a book. Bradbury Press 1969 unp il lib bdg $12.89; Macmillan pa $3.95 **E**

1. Color

ISBN 0-02-776130-4 (lib bdg); 0-689-71119-0 (pa)
LC 69-13653

Things to eat and wear and animals to chase appear in this introduction to the primary and secondary colors

"The simplest of formats and a sophisticated use of color and design combine to make a big and beautiful first book for the child learning to distinguish colors. The text consists entirely of the names of colors and the names of objects pictured. . . . The shades are vibrant, the layout stunning." Saturday Rev

Numbers; a book. Bradbury Press 1971 unp il lib bdg $12.95; Macmillan pa $3.95 **E**

1. Counting

ISBN 0-02-776150-9 (lib bdg); 0-689-71120-4 (pa)
LC 76-151313

"This is a big, brilliantly colored picture book which first counts from one to ten and then by tens to one hundred and ends with the number one thousand (raindrops). It enumerates such things as shoes, starfish arms, baseball players, kites, radishes, crayons, beads, gumballs, and centipede legs. The colorful pages and clear drawings invite viewer participation both in identifying objects and counting them." Booklist

Shapes; a book. Bradbury Press 1974 unp il lib bdg $12.95; Macmillan pa $3.95 **E**

1. Size and shape

ISBN 0-02-776190-8 (lib bdg); 0-689-71121-2 (pa)
LC 73-76545

This book presents "examples of such shapes as oval, circle, triangle, rectangle, and square. Reiss carries it a bit farther, showing how squares form a cube, or circles a sphere, and he tosses in a few more complex shapes at the close of the book to intrigue the audience: a hexagon, an octagon, a pentagon. Examples of each shape are included; for rectangles, for example, there are doors, wooden planks, and sticks of gum. Animals cavort among the shapes, adding intrest to the visual appeal and the clearly presented concepts." Bull Cent Child Books

Rey, H. A. (Hans Augusto), 1898-1977

Cecily G. and the 9 monkeys. Houghton Mifflin 1942 31p il lib bdg $12.95; pa $3.95 E

1. Giraffes—Fiction 2. Monkeys—Fiction
ISBN 0-395-18430-4 (lib bdg); 0-395-50651-4 (pa) LC 42-20276

A nonsense book describing in prose and picture the adventures of a lonely giraffe, and some homeless little monkeys

"Mr. Rey's big, colored pictures of Cecily Giraffe are unexpected and laughable, and it's remarkable to how many surprising uses his nine young monkeys can put one obliging giraffe." N Y Public Libr

Curious George. Houghton Mifflin 1941 unp il $12.95; pa $3.95 E

1. Monkeys—Fiction
ISBN 0-395-15993-8; 0-395-15023-X (pa) LC 41-16054

Also available Spanish language edition $13.95 (ISBN 0-395-17075-3)

Also available book form adaptations from the Curious George film series, edited by Margaret Rey and Alan J. Shalleck

Curious George goes to the hospital was written by Margaret Rey and H. A. Rey in collaboration with the Children's Hospital Medical Center; and Curious George flies a kite was written by Margaret Rey with pictures by H. A. Rey

Colored picture book, with simple text, describing the adventures of a curious small monkey, and the difficulties he had in getting used to city life, before he went to live in the zoo

"The bright lithographs in red, yellow, and blue, are gay and lighthearted, following the story closely with the same speed and animated humour." Ont Libr Rev

Other available titles about Curious George are:
Curious George flies a kite (1958)
Curious George gets a medal (1957)
Curious George goes to the hospital (1966)
Curious George learns the alphabet (1963)
Curious George rides a bike (1952)
Curious George takes a job (1947)

Rice, Eve, 1951-

At Grammy's house; illustrated by Nancy Winslow Parker. Greenwillow Bks. 1990 32p il $12.95; lib bdg $12.88 E

1. Grandmothers—Fiction 2. Farm life—Fiction
ISBN 0-688-08874-0; 0-688-08875-9 (lib bdg) LC 89-34617

"A sister and brother walk over the hill to spend Sunday afternoon with their French-speaking grandmother. Licking spoons, milking the cow, shaking cream into butter, and setting the table are all part of the fun." SLJ

"Eve Rice once again reveals the freshness of her vision of childhood. . . . The soft-colored, grainy-textured artwork, with its sturdy, slightly stylized figures, is joined in perfect union with the text. And the Gallic touches—the French phrases with English translations and the little tricolored flag in the kitchen—add a bit of unexpected flavor." Horn Book

Benny bakes a cake; story and pictures by Eve Rice. Greenwillow Bks. 1981 unp il hardcover o.p. paperback available $3.95 E

1. Birthdays—Fiction 2. Cake—Fiction
ISBN 0-688-07814-1 (pa) LC 80-17313

"It is little Benny's birthday and he helps Mama make the birthday cake while his father and sister go off to do errands. Unfortunately, the dog ruins the birthday cake; fortunately, Papa has called home, so that when he shows up he has a beautiful cake in addition to all the surprise packages for the birthday boy." Bull Cent Child Books

"A simple story, simply told, for young children who will find it even more enjoyable after the first reading, when they can anticipate the impending disaster and happy solution. The illustrations are highly stylized, with spherical heads, moon faces, thoughtfully restricted and focused scenes, and just about the most cheerful colors one can hope for. A lovable book." SLJ

City night; pictures by Peter Sis. Greenwillow Bks. 1987 unp il $11.75; lib bdg $11.88 E

1. City life—Fiction 2. Night—Fiction 3. Stories in rhyme
ISBN 0-688-06856-1; 0-688-06857-X (lib bdg) LC 86-12021

The rhyming text follows a family as they set out for a nighttime jaunt through city streets

"Urban life after dark shines and glows in this book, with a texture and depth to the rough-hewn illustrations that will charm city-dwellers and country kids alike." Publ Wkly

Goodnight, goodnight. Greenwillow Bks. 1980 unp il $13.95; lib bdg $13.88; Puffin Bks. pa $3.95 E

1. Night—Fiction
ISBN 0-688-80254-0; 0-688-84254-2 (lib bdg); 0-14-050386-2 (pa) LC 79-17253

Everyone in town, including the cats, prepare for sleep

"The text is as brief as possible, yet smooth. Large, double-page spreads fill the picture book with a city's night scenes. Rice uses black and white, tempered by grainy textures for shadow and depth, brightened and warmed by spots of primary yellow wherever light shines from room or sky. Once again, the author-artist succeeds uniquely in conveying a happy, self-contained world satisfying to the souls of young children." Booklist

Peter's pockets; pictures by Nancy Winslow Parker. Greenwillow Bks. 1989 unp il $12.95; lib bdg $12.88 E

ISBN 0-688-07241-0; 0-688-07242-9 (lib bdg) LC 87-15640

Peter's new pants don't have any pockets, so Uncle Nick lets Peter use his until Peter's mother solves the problem in a clever and colorful way

"Parker's sturdy, rounded shapes and colored-pencil shading conserve the simplicity of Rice's story, which characteristically—and successfully—portrays the world from a young child's viewpoint." Bull Cent Child Books

Rice, Eve, 1951-—*Continued*

Sam who never forgets. Greenwillow Bks. 1977 unp il hardcover o.p. paperback available $3.95 E

1. Zoos—Fiction 2. Animals—Fiction
ISBN 0-688-07335-2 (pa) LC 76-30370

Sam is "a zoo keeper who 'never, never forgets' to feed the animals promptly at three o'clock. The beasts have their doubts when it looks like Sam has neglected to feed poor Elephant who is both hungry and crestfallen. Happily, Sam returns with a whole wagon of hay." SLJ

"A simple, unpretentious story with child appeal that lies in the naive, straightforward telling and elemental emotional interactions of the characters. . . . Rice has forsaken her pen drawings for bright, unlined colored shapes. The figures are pleasantly stylized, the scenes evenly composed; it's all precisely tuned to the younger picture-book audience." Booklist

Riddell, Chris

When the walrus comes; written and illustrated by Chris Riddell. Delacorte Press 1990 c1989 unp il $13.95 E

ISBN 0-385-29858-7 LC 89-31718

First published 1989 in the United Kingdom

"A boy draws a picture of a walrus and thus begins an imaginary adventure. Accompanied by his newly created companion, he sets sail for a tropical island inhabited by playful monkeys. The boy and the walrus join the monkeys in their spirited antics until the moon rises and it is time to return home. The slight story concludes with the boy gazing at his drawing, lost in his reverie. . . . Riddell's watercolors have a bright and friendly charm." SLJ

Robbins, Ken

City/country; a car trip in photographs. Viking Kestrel 1985 unp il $12.95 E

1. Automobiles—Fiction
ISBN 0-670-80743-5 LC 85-40165

Photographs and simple text capture the universal images of a car trip, as seen from a child's backseat perspective

"Hand-tinted photographs, never strident but often dramatic, almost fill the page space; a few words of continuous text form a running foot beneath each large picture. . . . This is a good book to use for encouraging observation, for establishing urban-rural contrasts, and for discussion of life-style concepts. The text is not impressive; the photographs are." Bull Cent Child Books

Roberts, Bethany

Waiting-for-papa stories; illustrated by Sarah Stapler. Harper & Row 1990 31p il $12.95; lib bdg $12.89 E

1. Rabbits—Fiction
ISBN 0-06-025050-X; 0-06-025051-8 (lib bdg) LC 89-36589

As Papa Rabbit's family anxiously awaits his return home, Mama Rabbit eases their fears by telling funny stories about Papa

"Stapler's illustrations suit the stories well. . . . Little details such as the bunny slippers in the bedroom and the bunny dolls held by some of the children add interest. The overall feeling is a cozy one of family warmth. Children are sure to be captivated by the charm and gentle humor of the stories." SLJ

Waiting-for-spring stories; illustrations by William Joyce. Harper & Row 1984 31p il lib bdg $14.89 E

1. Rabbits—Fiction
ISBN 0-06-025062-3 LC 83-49486

As the family passes the winter in their cozy home, Papa Rabbit tells them stories about other rabbits

"These brief tales can be used when there's a need for a filler in story hour, and although they are not of equal caliber, the tales stand up well in general for reading aloud. They are about small episodes, only one to do with spring, and provide enough variety, humor, and coziness to appeal to the read-aloud audience. The illustrations are pastel paintings, old-fashioned and rather sedate." Bull Cent Child Books

Robins, Joan

Addie meets Max; pictures by Sue Truesdell. Harper & Row 1985 31p il $9.95; lib bdg $9.89; pa $3.50 E

1. Friendship—Fiction
ISBN 0-06-025063-1; 0-06-025064-X (lib bdg); 0-06-444116-4 (pa) LC 84-48329

"An Early I can read book"

Addie discovers that the new boy next door, Max, and his dog are not so terrible when she helps him bury his newly lost tooth

"A realistic, mildly funny story is pleasant for reading aloud as well as for the beginning independent reader. The illustrations, line and wash, have vigor and humor." Bull Cent Child Books

Rockwell, Anne F., 1934-

Albert B. Cub & Zebra; an alphabet storybook; [by] Anne Rockwell. Crowell 1977 unp il $13.95; lib bdg $12.89 E

1. Alphabet 2. Stories without words
ISBN 0-690-01350-7; 0-690-01351-5 (lib bdg) LC 76-54224

"The wordless story of Albert B. Cub's search for his missing friend, Zebra, combines with an alphabet-puzzle format and the result functions well on all levels. The alphabet is clearly and attractively represented in large upper and lower case letters. The picture puzzles are crammed with fascinating objects and actions from apes under arches and artists painting angels to zebras eating zinnias in zoos. A more complicated story in words at the back of the book (suitable for reading aloud) supplements and explicates Rockwell's clear, brights, and amusing watercolors. There is a lot here to muse over, laugh at, and come back to over and over again." SLJ

Apples and pumpkins; pictures by Lizzy Rockwell. Macmillan 1989 unp il $12.95 E

1. Halloween—Fiction
ISBN 0-02-777270-5 LC 88-22628

Rockwell, Anne F., 1934-—*Continued*

In preparation for Halloween night, a family visits Mr. Comstock's farm to pick apples and pumpkins

"Lizzy Rockwell illustrates her mother's story in bright, autumnal colors and uses the same unadorned shapes the senior Rockwell has become noted for. The book's clean, airy design has an immediate child appeal, while the figures (reminiscent of those seen in Lois Lenski's art) are extremely personable. Nice seasonal fare for the youngest." Booklist

At the beach; [by] Anne & Harlow Rockwell. Macmillan 1987 unp il $12.95; pa $3.95 **E**

1. Beaches
ISBN 0-02-777940-8; 0-689-71494-7 (pa) LC 86-2943

"A young preschooler accompanies her mother to the beach and in a first-person narrative describes familiar beach activities such as putting on sunscreen and chasing sandpipers." SLJ

"Harlow Rockwell is at his best with the deceptively naive arrangements of pleasing shapes and strong primary colors, but the more crowded beach scenes afford a welcome contrast in their busy, if controlled, activity." Horn Book

Can I help? [by] Anne & Harlow Rockwell. Macmillan 1982 unp il $8.95 **E**

ISBN 0-02-777720-0 LC 82-15375
"My world"

"A small child lists all the ways in which she is helpful: she does household chores, helps wash the family car, amuses the neighbors' baby, and helps shop for groceries. Some things she can't help with until she's older . . . and for some things her parents help her." Bull Cent Child Books

"An affectionate look at the willingness of a young child to help and be helped. . . . The gay watercolors are vintage Rockwell. Preschoolers will find a kindred spirit in this industrious child." Booklist

Come to town; [by] Anne Rockwell. Crowell 1987 unp il lib bdg $12.89 **E**

1. City life—Fiction 2. Bears—Fiction
ISBN 0-690-04646-4 LC 86-6217

"In the morning a bear family wakes up and prepares for the day. Children go to school, shoppers go to the supermarket, workers go to their offices, and some people go to the library. At night, everyone is home and getting ready for bed. . . . The text is pared down to a minimum and selected pages use labeled, freestanding drawings to show the activities found in the places that are highlighted in the book. The pen-and-wash drawings on busier pages are reminiscent of Richard Scarry. Shapes and colors are softer, however, and the story's gentle, elemental approach will definitely appeal to preschoolers." Booklist

First comes spring; [by] Anne Rockwell. Crowell 1985 unp il $14.95; lib bdg $12.89 **E**

1. Seasons—Fiction 2. Bears—Fiction
ISBN 0-694-00106-6; 0-690-04455-0 (lib bdg) LC 84-45331

Bear Child notices that the clothes he wears, the things everyone does at work and play, and other parts of his world all change with the seasons

"For each season, Rockwell devotes one double-page spread to Bear Child's clothing and his house and yard. In the next scene, she widens the view to include Bear Child, his house, and his neighborhood. . . . The third double-page spread for each season removes groups of figures from the previous landscape, enlarges them, isolates them on a white background, and labels their activities. Children will enjoy poring over these illustrations, relating them to the rest of the book, and talking about what's happening. . . . The pen-and-ink drawings, glowing with Rockwell's soft yet brilliant watercolors, create a world that young children will want to explore again and again." Booklist

The first snowfall; [by] Anne & Harlow Rockwell. Macmillan 1987 unp il $12.95 **E**

1. Snow—Fiction
ISBN 0-02-777770-7 LC 86-23712

A child enjoys the special sights and activities of a snow-covered world with her father

"Children will vicariously enjoy the fragrance and warmth of the steaming hot cocoa the young girl drinks upon her return home. Only the illustration of her mother in an incorrect and awkward skiing position mars this otherwise inviting and useful introduction to the joys of the season." Horn Book

Happy birthday to me; [by] Anne & Harlow Rockwell. Macmillan 1981 unp il $8.95 **E**

1. Birthdays—Fiction
ISBN 0-02-777680-8 LC 81-3738
"My world"

This book utilizes "the authors' characteristic soft lines, rounded shapes and spectrum of primary colors washed to make the world lively but not startlingly bright. The text appears to be hand lettered, but is distinct and sized correctly for the pages. . . . [It] shows mother, father and son making preparations for the boy's party, children enjoying the festivities and the final thank-yous and goodbyes. The book expresses a very positive experience, with the many aspects of a party." SLJ

How my garden grew; [by] Anne & Harlow Rockwell. Macmillan 1982 unp il $8.95 **E**

1. Gardening—Fiction
ISBN 0-02-777660-3 LC 81-17145
"My world"

This book "presents a small child showing the reader where his lettuce and marigolds and pumpkins and sunflowers have come from." Christ Sci Monit

The book is "alive with realism and color. . . . The simple vocabulary and format clearly relate the process of planting, growing and harvesting a garden. Preschoolers can easily understand the theories of ecology and nature as bugs eat the insects and natural fish fertilizer is used to make a garden grow." SLJ

My back yard; [by] Anne and Harlow Rockwell. Macmillan 1984 unp il $8.95 **E**

1. Gardens—Fiction
ISBN 0-02-777690-5 LC 83-18717
"My world"

Rockwell, Anne F., 1934-—*Continued*

"A small girl describes her back yard: what grows there, what creatures inhabit it, what sorts of play space it has—and how much she enjoys it." Bull Cent Child Books

"Illustrated with soft but distinct watercolors." SLJ

My spring robin; pictures by Harlow Rockwell & Lizzy Rockwell. Macmillan 1989 unp il $12.95 **E**

1. Spring—Fiction 2. Robins—Fiction
ISBN 0-02-777611-5 LC 88-13333

"The Rockwells present a simple and briefly told story of a young girl who goes out on the first day of spring to search for the robin whose song so impressed her the previous summer. . . . Cheery, bright pencil-and-watercolor illustrations offer a child's perspective of the outdoors." SLJ

The night we slept outside; [by] Anne and Harlow Rockwell. Macmillan 1983 47p il hardcover o.p. paperback available $3.95 **E**

1. Camping—Fiction 2. Brothers—Fiction
ISBN 0-689-71070-4 (pa) LC 82-17963
"Ready-to-read"

"A small boy describes the experience he and his younger brother have when they use their new sleeping bags for a night outdoors. They are on the deck of their home, but it is still scary to see a mean raccoon's eyes shining, to hear the screech of an owl, to know a skunk is nearby. In fact, it's a relief when there's a thunder shower and they can go in and stop pretending that they are not afraid." Bull Cent Child Books

"Children will relate to the narrator's bravado as well as the fear both boys experience. The bland blue and gray illustrations do not heighten the suspense; nor do they detract from the narration. A story of mild adventure, told in short, easy-to-read sentences." SLJ

Our garage sale; by Anne Rockwell; pictures by Harlow Rockwell. Greenwillow Bks. 1984 unp il $10.25; lib bdg $10.88 **E**

1. Garage sales—Fiction
ISBN 0-688-80278-8; 0-688-84278-X (lib bdg) LC 80-16704

"This gives a clear account of what a garage sale is and why people have them. . . . The speaker is the younger child in a family that clears unwanted objects from attic, cellar, and garage to hold a sale in their driveway." Bull Cent Child Books

"Rockwell's plain lines and open compositions make everything look fresh and inviting. This should have its share of takers, especially among children whose streets and alleys have boasted such events." Booklist

Sick in bed; [by] Anne & Harlow Rockwell. Macmillan 1982 unp il $8.95 **E**

1. Sick—Fiction 2. Medical care—Fiction
ISBN 0-02-777730-8 LC 81-15637
"My world"

This book documents a "small boy's bout with illness from initial crankiness to joyful recovery. Painful elements—sore throat, fever, medication—are not minimized, but the sympathetic attention and special privileges accorded to homebound young patients offer cozy reassurance." Horn Book

"The Rockwells show through description and colorful pen-and-wash art the details of thermometers, throat-culture tubes and a medical examination. The illustrations create opportunities for discussion." SLJ

Willy can count. Arcade Pub. 1989 unp il $13.95 **E**

1. Counting 2. Color
ISBN 1-55970-013-0 LC 89-83839

"A little boy's walk with his mother down a country lane gives Rockwell the framework for this simple counting book. At mother's behest, Willy counts the sights along the way; one cow, two red birds, three chicks, four ladybugs, etc. But there are other items to count as well, and Rockwell has structured her pictures so that viewers get a head start on Willy. . . . Simple, doll-like figures and uncomplicated compositions make this especially useful for pre-schoolers." Booklist

Rogers, Jacqueline

The Christmas pageant. Grosset & Dunlap 1989 unp il $12.95 **E**

1. Christmas—Fiction 2. Pageants—Fiction
ISBN 0-448-40151-7

This book follows a group of children as they prepare for their annual Christmas pageant

"Each double-page, full-color painting captures the detail of rehearsal as a barn turns into Bethlehem. The children's expressions are priceless. Simple, direct and accurate, the text, which includes music for carols, could easily be used to narrate a pageant." Child Book Rev Serv

Root, Phyllis, 1949-

Soup for supper; illustrated by Sue Truesdell. Harper & Row 1986 24p il $13.95; lib bdg $13.89 **E**

1. Giants—Fiction
ISBN 0-06-025070-4; 0-06-025071-2 (lib bdg) LC 85-45273

A wee small woman catches a giant taking the vegetables from her garden and finds that they can share both vegetable soup and friendship

"Brisk and breezy watercolors outlined with quick pen sketches depict the fury, then celebrate friendship and cooperation. Throughout the tale Rumbleton and the wee small woman sing a song about the glories of vegetable soup. Words and music are provided at the end of the book." Booklist

Rosen, Michael, 1946-

We're going on a bear hunt; retold by Michael Rosen; illustrated by Helen Oxenbury. Margaret K. McElderry Bks. 1989 unp il $14.95 **E**

1. Bears—Fiction 2. Hunting—Fiction
ISBN 0-689-50476-4 LC 88-13338

"Glorious puddles of watercolor alternate with impish charcoal sketches in this refreshing interpretation of an old hand rhyme in which a man, four children, and a dog stalk the furry beast through mud and muck, high

Rosen, Michael, 1946-—*Continued*
and low. A book with a genuine atmosphere of togetherness and boundless enthusiasm for the hunt." SLJ

Ross, Pat
Meet M and M; pictures by Marylin Hafner. Pantheon Bks. 1980 41p il o.p.; Puffin Bks. paperback available $2.95 **E**

1. Friendship—Fiction
ISBN 0-14-032651-0 (pa) LC 79-190

"An I am reading book"

"Because they look so much alike, Mandy and Mimi like to pretend they're twins; they share everything, including bubble baths and toys. . . . Total amity. Then, 'one crabby day,' they have a squabble, it takes several miserable days more before they make up, and there is a happy reunion as they meet on the stairs halfway between their apartments." Bull Cent Child Books

"The author is clearly a keen observer of the nuances of close friendships—their making and breaking. Beginning readers will have no difficulty with the humorously told, very real incidents, and the way in which the impasse is breached and friendship restored is particularly childlike. The many black-and-white pencil drawings capture the girls' facial expressions especially well." Horn Book

Other available titles about M and M (Mandy and Mimi) are:
M and M and the bad news babies (1983)
M and M and the big bag (1981)
M and M and the haunted house game (1980)
M and M and the mummy mess (1985)
M and M and the super child afternoon (1987)

Ross, Tony, 1938-
The treasure of Cozy Cove; or, The voyage of the "Kipper". Farrar, Straus & Giroux 1990 c1989 unp il $12.95 **E**

1. Cats—Fiction
ISBN 0-374-37744-8 LC 89-84881

First published 1989 in the United Kingdom

"Two abandoned kittens find a berth with a seagoing cat looking for the treasure of Cozy Cove. Passing through many gripping adventures, they are nearly dead when rescued by a cat-loving old lady. They settle down to a happy life in her little home called Cozy Cove." Horn Book Guide

"The writing bobs along with just enough ahoy-me-heartiness, and the crayoned cartoons have both humor and shadows, splashed with energy and sufficient sophistication to keep both ends of the picture book set afloat and amused." Bull Cent Child Books

Rounds, Glen, 1906-
The morning the sun refused to rise; an original Paul Bunyan tale. Holiday House 1984 unp il lib bdg $11.95 **E**

1. Bunyan, Paul (Legendary character)—Fiction 2. Tall tales
ISBN 0-8234-0514-1 LC 83-49033

When the sun doesn't rise one morning, the King of Sweden contacts Paul Bunyan and asks him to find the cause of the catastrophe

"Rounds contributes another hilarious tall tale to the Paul Bunyan legend, a yeasty performance enhanced by comical and economical line drawings." Bull Cent Child Books

Washday on Noah's ark; a story of Noah's ark. Holiday House 1985 unp il $14.95 **E**

1. Noah's ark—Fiction 2. Tall tales
ISBN 0-8234-0555-9 LC 84-22380

When the forty-first day on the ark dawns bright and clear, Mrs. Noah decides to do the wash, and having no rope long enough, devises an ingenious clothesline

"This goes far afield from the original; Noah gets his information on the impending storm from weather reports, not God. And, as in many tall tales, animals are not given the best of treatment . . . but the simple shapes and softly textured colors make a nice combination. The art radiates a sense of movement and fun that young children will find appealing." Booklist

Russo, Marisabina
Waiting for Hannah. Greenwillow Bks. 1989 unp il $12.95; lib bdg $12.88 **E**

1. Infants—Fiction 2. Mothers and daughters—Fiction
ISBN 0-688-08015-4; 0-688-08016-2 (lib bdg) LC 87-37201

Hannah's mother recounts events during the summer when she was expecting her daughter. A universal story and a beautiful vignette of daily life in a family." Horn Book Guide

Ryden, Hope
Wild animals of Africa ABC; photographs and text by Hope Ryden. Lodestar Bks. 1989 unp il $12.95 **E**

1. Animals 2. Alphabet
ISBN 0-525-67290-7 LC 89-2529

Presents photographs and information about wild animals found in different parts of Africa, arranged alphabetically from aardvark to zebra

"The value of Ryden's book lies in the uncompromising quality of her powerful pictures, offering a vision of a vast and varied continent." Horn Book

Wild animals of America ABC; photographs and text by Hope Ryden. Lodestar Bks. 1988 unp il $14.95 **E**

1. Animals 2. Alphabet
ISBN 0-525-67245-1 LC 87-31127

"The author, a naturalist and skilled photographer, has assembled an alphabet book of full-color pictures of creatures—B for beaver, O for otter, P for possum—in their natural habitats." N Y Times Book Rev

"This volume will appeal to animal lovers and delight browsers and nature photographers; the images captured are superbly composed and clearly reproduced." SLJ

Rylant, Cynthia

All I see; story by Cynthia Rylant; pictures by Peter Catalanotto. Orchard Bks. 1988 unp il $15.95; lib bdg $15.99 **E**

1. Artists—Fiction 2. Painting—Fiction
ISBN 0-531-05777-1; 0-531-08377-2 (lib bdg)
LC 88-42547

"A Richard Jackson book"

"The story of a shy boy, Charlie, who, while summering by a lake, becomes fascinated with the work of a painter named Gregory. Secretly watching Gregory paint and hum Beethoven's Fifth symphony to his white cat, Charlie eventually communicates by canvas, leaving first a picture and then messages before coming out into the open for lessons, a gift of paints, and friendship." Bull Cent Child Books

"Soft-focus, soft-color illustrations—double-page watercolors—are full of sun and shadow, leaves and water, and gentle peace punctuated by bursts of energy, as when Gregory's cat springs while geese take flight. The pictures carry a sense of the mystery of art. This is romantic, but not sentimental." Libr J

Henry and Mudge; the first book of their adventures; story by Cynthia Rylant; pictures by Suçie Stevenson. Bradbury Press 1987 39p il $10.95; Aladdin Bks. (NY) pa $3.95 **E**

1. Dogs—Fiction
ISBN 0-02-778001-5; 0-689-71399-1 (pa)
LC 86-13615

This book tells "about a boy named Henry and his dog, Mudge. . . . Henry yearns for a dog and convinces his parents to get one. Mudge is small at first, but soon grows 'out of seven collars in a row' to become enormous, and Henry's best friend. Then comes a day when Mudge is lost, and boy and dog realize what they mean to each other." N Y Times Book Rev

"The stories are lighthearted and affectionate. Backed by line-and-wash cartoon drawings, they celebrate the familiar in a down-to-earth way that will please young readers." Booklist

Other available titles about Henry and Mudge are:
Henry and Mudge and the forever sea (1989)
Henry and Mudge and the happy cat (1990)
Henry and Mudge and the sparkle days (1988)
Henry and Mudge get the cold shivers (1989)
Henry and Mudge in puddle trouble (1987)
Henry and Mudge in the green time (1987)
Henry and Mudge under the yellow moon (1987)

Mr. Griggs' work; illustrated by Julie Downing. Orchard Bks. 1989 unp il $12.95; lib bdg $12.99 **E**

1. Postal service—Fiction
ISBN 0-531-05769-0; 0-531-08369-1 (lib bdg)
LC 88-1484

Mr. Griggs so loves his work at the post office that he thinks of it all the time and everything reminds him of it

"Line drawings and the controlled brightness of restrained crayon work are the media for pictures that have clean composition and that are nicely synchronized with the text. . . . Nice to have a story about someone who enjoys a job that is not glamorous." Bull Cent Child Books

Night in the country; pictures by Mary Szilagyi. Bradbury Press 1986 unp il lib bdg $13.95; Macmillan pa $4.95 **E**

1. Night—Fiction 2. Country life—Fiction
ISBN 0-02-777210-1; 0-689-71473-4 (pa)
LC 85-70963

Text and illustrations describe the sights and sounds of nighttime in the country

"Rich with nuances, the images and sounds evoked by the text have brought forth deeply shadowed drawings by the artist; likewise, the text will conjure up vivid imaginings in the minds of young children. The journey through nighttime fittingly concludes that night animals 'will spend a day in the country listening to you.' Each page invites children to look, listen and explore." SLJ

The relatives came; story by Cynthia Rylant; illustrated by Stephen Gammell. Bradbury Press 1985 unp il lib bdg $12.95 **E**

1. Family life—Fiction
ISBN 0-02-777220-9 LC 85-10929

A Caldecott Medal honor book, 1986

"The relatives have come—in an old station wagon that smells 'like a real car'—bringing with them hugs and laughs, quiet talk, and, at night when all are asleep hither and yon, 'all that new breathing.'" Booklist

"If there's anything more charming than the tone of voice in this story, it's the drawings that go with it. Stephen Gammell . . . fills the pages with bright, crayony pictures teeming with details that children should enjoy poring over for hours." N Y Times Book Rev

This year's garden; pictures by Mary Szilagyi. Bradbury Press 1984 unp il $12.95; Macmillan pa $3.95 **E**

1. Gardens—Fiction 2. Seasons—Fiction
ISBN 0-02-777970-X; 0-689-71122-0 (pa)
LC 84-10974

This book tells "about a family's planning of its summer vegetable garden, the seeding and harvesting, and the enjoyment of the preserved crop through the summer and fall—and then the planning again, as the bare brown garden patch waits, like the family, for next year's garden." Bull Cent Child Books

"Rylant's words are set against Szilagyi's richly colored pictures. Deep hues from a multicolored palette make the visual landscape as fertile as the story. Even city-bred readers will come away with a sense of what it's all about." Booklist

When I was young in the mountains; illustrated by Diane Goode. Dutton 1982 unp il $12.95; pa $3.95 **E**

ISBN 0-525-42525-X; 0-525-44198-0 (pa) LC 81-5359

A Caldecott Medal honor book, 1983

"Based on the author's memories of an Appalachian childhood, this is a nostalgic piece. . . . There is no story line, but a series of memories, each beginning, 'When I was young in the mountains . . .' as the author reminisces about the busy, peaceful life of an extended family and their community." Bull Cent Child Books

"The people in the story are poor in material things, but rich in family pleasures. The title becomes a pleasing refrain that is used to herald a change in topic. Illustrations and text are placed on a bed of white space,

Rylant, Cynthia—*Continued*
without borders, which makes them look uncrowded and imparts a great feeling of freedom." SLJ

Sachs, Elizabeth-Ann, 1946-
The boy who ate dog biscuits; by Elizabeth Sachs; illustrated by Margot Apple. Random House 1989 62p il lib bdg $5.99; pa $1.95 **E**

1. Dogs—Fiction 2. Brothers and sisters—Fiction
ISBN 0-394-94778-9 (lib bdg); 0-394-84778-4 (pa)
LC 89-3905

"A Stepping Stone book"

"Billy Getten helps out at the vet's office and occasionally munches on dog biscuits. He prefers a dog, like the new stray at Dr. Mike's (a woman veterinarian) to his baby sister Sarah. . . . The arrival of Billy's grandparent's for his birthday provides Billy with opportunities. . . . He runs errands for his elderly grandfather, and in a small crisis that occurs when he and his grandfather are alone with Sarah, Billy handles everything well. As a reward, he gets a four-legged birthday surprise. . . . The soft, expressive, black-line drawings will help draw readers." Booklist

Samuels, Barbara
Duncan & Dolores. Bradbury Press 1986 unp il $13.95; Macmillan pa $3.95 **E**

1. Cats—Fiction
ISBN 0-02-778210-7; 0-689-71294-4 (pa)
LC 85-17119

This is "the story of a small girl's adjustment to a newly-acquired cat. And vice versa. Duncan avoids her noisy roughness; she feels rebuffed and is jealous because the cat clearly prefers her older sister. However, Dolores gets the point, and the longed-for rapport ensues." Bull Cent Child Books

"The cheerful, childlike illustrations are remarkably expressive, clearly showing the rapidly alternating feelings of Duncan and the pleasant, sisterly relationship of sensible Faye and bouncy Dolores. The whole book is a charming illustration of the old aphorism that in getting to know cats, less is more." Horn Book

Samuels, Vyanne
Carry, go, bring, come; illustrated by Jennifer Northway. Four Winds Press 1989 c1988 unp il $13.95 **E**

1. Weddings—Fiction 2. Jamaica—Fiction
ISBN 0-02-778121-6
LC 89-1528

First published 1988 in the United Kingdom

"Leon's sister is getting married in just a few hours, and the family is in a flurry. . . . Young Leon becomes chief errand boy, with instructions to carry this, go there, bring this, come here, etc.—until he is laden with the bridal veil, a pink silk flower, a pair of blue shoes, yellow gloves, and a green bottle of perfume." SLJ

"The rich, lilting phrasing of West Indian speech conveys the joy, excitement, and humor of the situation when Leon's mother and the others '"look 'pon his fingers and his hands [and] look 'pon his head."' Northway's colorful drawings add to the vitality of the text and the portrayal of a warm, loving Black family." Horn Book

Sandburg, Carl, 1878-1967
The wedding procession of the Rag Doll and the Broom Handle and who was in it; pictures by Harriet Pincus. Harcourt Brace Jovanovich 1967 unp il hardcover o.p. paperback available $3.95 **E**

1. Dolls—Fiction 2. Marriage customs and rites—Fiction
ISBN 0-15-695487-7 (pa)
LC 67-2763

A picture book version of a tale from: Rootabaga stories, entered in the Story Collections Section

"A splendid procession at the rag doll's wedding is led by the nuptial pair, who are followed by limp and lumpy fun babies. Dolled up in birthday-party colors and quaintly modern costumes, they parade in a line—laughing, licking, tickling, wiggling, chuzzling, snozzling, clear to the 'last of all,' the staggering Sleepy heads." Horn Book

"Droll double-spread pictures capture perfectly the unique humor and imaginativeness of Sandburg's story." Notable Child Books, 1967

Sanders, Scott R. (Scott Russell), 1945-
Aurora means dawn; illustrated by Jill Kastner. Bradbury Press 1989 unp il $12.95 **E**

1. Frontier and pioneer life—Fiction 2. Ohio—Fiction
ISBN 0-02-778270-0
LC 88-24127

"Mr. and Mrs. Sheldon, traveling from Connecticut by covered wagon, arrive in Aurora, Ohio in 1800; they have been told that Aurora is a village with homes, a mill, and a store. What they find, using the land-company's map, is a surveyor's post. Trapped by debris from a storm, the family is able to reach their site when settlers from a nearby village help clear the road." Bull Cent Child Books

"The use of detail is engaging, yet it never slows the pace. Sentences are placed so that the action corresponds to that depicted in the luminous, vital, and well-composed watercolor paintings, enhancing the book's value for use with early elementary groups in classrooms and libraries." Horn Book

Sandin, Joan, 1942-
The long way westward. Harper & Row 1989 63p il $10.95; lib bdg $10.89 **E**

1. United States—Immigration and emigration—Fiction 2. Swedish Americans—Fiction
ISBN 0-06-025206-5; 0-06-025207-3 (lib bdg)
LC 89-2024

Sequel to: The long way to a new land (1981)

"An I can read book"

Relates the experiences of two young brothers and their family, immigrants from Sweden, from their arrival in New York through the journey to their new home in Minnesota

"The text does a nice job of evoking the mix of excitement and apprehension that gripped newcomers to the U.S. Details of the long train ride from New York pace the book and inform readers unobtrusively as the nicely detailed pen-and-wash drawings bring the story to life. A fine bit of historical fiction for beginning readers." Booklist

Say, Allen, 1937-

The bicycle man. Parnassus Press 1982 unp il lib bdg $13.95; pa $4.95 **E**

1. Bicycles and bicycling—Fiction 2. Japan—Fiction
ISBN 0-395-32254-5 (lib bdg); 0-395-50652-2 (pa)
LC 82-2980

The amazing tricks two American soldiers do on a borrowed bicycle are a fitting finale for the school sports day festivities in a small village in occupied Japan

"The kindly, openhearted story is beautifully pictured in a profusion of delicate pen-and-ink drawings washed in gentle colors. Meticulously hatched and cross-hatched, they reflect the guileless joy and exuberance of adults and children alike in a book that celebrates human friendship." Horn Book

The lost lake. Houghton Mifflin 1989 32p il $14.95 **E**

1. Fathers and sons—Fiction 2. Camping—Fiction
ISBN 0-395-50933-5 LC 89-11026

"Luke is disappointed in his relationship with his taciturn, work-absorbed father, with whom he is spending the summer. Early one morning his father awakens him with exciting news of a camping trip: they are going to find the Lost Lake, a very special and secret place Luke's father used to visit with his own father. But their arduous hike brings them to a lake that has since been discovered by many people; they agree to blaze a new trail and find their own private place." Horn Book

"Obviously, it will take an older child to understand the story's subtleties, but younger children will respond to the pleasing artwork. Using colors as crisp and clean as the outdoors, Say effectively alternates between scenes where father and son are the focus and those where the landscape predominates. Both in story and art, a substantial piece." Booklist

Schecter, Ben

Grandma remembers; story and pictures by Ben Shecter. Harper & Row 1989 unp il $13.95; lib bdg $13.89 **E**

1. Grandmothers—Fiction
ISBN 0-06-025617-6; 0-06-025618-4 (lib bdg)
LC 88-31986

"A Charlotte Zolotow book"

A boy and his grandmother take a final tour of the house she is leaving and relive memories of the wonderful times experienced there

"The story's quiet lesson is valuable, and Shecter's subdued watercolors emphasize the close ties between the unnamed boy and his grandmother (though she looks more like a great-grandmother). Thoughtful and soothing." Booklist

Scheer, Julian

Rain makes applesauce; by Julian Scheer & Marvin Bileck. Holiday House 1964 unp il $14.95 **E**

ISBN 0-8234-0091-3 LC 64-56216

A Caldecott Medal honor book, 1965

"A book of original nonsense, illustrated with intricate drawings. Small children live the refrains, 'Rain makes applesauce' and 'You're just talking silly talk,' and enjoy the fantastic details in the pictures." Hodges. Books for Elem Sch Libr

Schlein, Miriam

Big talk; pictures by Joan Auclair. Bradbury Press 1990 unp il $12.95 **E**

1. Kangaroos—Fiction
ISBN 0-02-781231-6 LC 89-35343

A newly illustrated edition of the title first published 1955 by W.R Scott

"With the typical bravado of the young, a small kangaroo brags to his mother about all the wonderful feats he can do. Like all mothers, she agrees that he will be able to do each one." Child Book Rev Serv

Each "scene includes a framed inset that depicts mother and child in conversation and a larger picture that humorously illustrates the boast. . . . Warm colors and Australian animals provide a rich, slightly exotic atmosphere to a story that is a natural for toddler storytimes." SLJ

Schotter, Roni

Captain Snap and the children of Vinegar Lane; illustrations by Marcia Sewall. Orchard Bks. 1989 unp il $14.95; lib bdg $14.99 **E**

1. Friendship—Fiction
ISBN 0-531-05797-6; 0-531-08397-7 (lib bdg)
LC 88-22489

The children of Vinegar Lane discover that bad-tempered old Captain Snap has a wonderful secret

"The twitchy, wiggly children of Vinegar Lane scamper through Sewall's woodcutesque paintings in this crackling good story of pint-sized neighbors who melt the Captain's hard heart with a couple of good deeds and a whole lot of high spirits." SLJ

Schroeder, Alan

Ragtime Tumpie; paintings by Bernie Fuchs. Little, Brown 1989 unp il lib bdg $14.95 **E**

1. Baker, Josephine, 1906-1975—Fiction
2. Blacks—Fiction 3. Dancing—Fiction
ISBN 0-316-77497-9 LC 87-37221

"Joy Street books"

A fictionalized account of "the childhood of Josephine Baker, the St. Louis girl who became the toast of Paris and, for many, epitomized the Jazz Age." Bull Cent Child Books

"This book evokes the magic of ragtime St. Louis, its down-and-out places and its joys. Both the prose and paintings are bursts of color. In Mr. Schroeder's first book for children, Ragtime Tumpie takes her place beside the other young heroines who inspire children to dream and to hold on to stubborn hope." N Y Times Book Rev

Schulman, Janet

The big hello; illustrated by Lillian Hoban. Greenwillow Bks. 1976 32p il $12.95; pa $3.95 E

1. Moving, Household—Fiction 2. Dolls—Fiction
ISBN 0-688-80036-X; 0-688-08405-2 (pa)
LC 75-33672

"A Greenwillow read-alone book"

"In running chatter, a small girl narrates the story of her move to California and her initial adjustments. As trouble so often seems to come in batches, the little girl loses her doll-confidante the first day in her new home. Fortunately, she gets a shaggy dog and, in finding her doll, gains a friend her own age. The style of the book is informal, its effect comfortingly positive. Divided into six chapters, the text is quite manageable and may boost a reader's sense of accomplishment. Cozy, typically Hoban-style pictures in green and brown add character." Booklist

Schwartz, Amy, 1954-

Annabelle Swift, kindergartner; story and pictures by Amy Schwartz. Orchard Bks. 1988 unp il $13.95; lib bdg $13.99 E

1. School stories 2. Sisters—Fiction
ISBN 0-531-05737-2; 0-531-08337-3 (lib bdg)
LC 87-15403

"Annabelle is starting school and her older sister Lucy prepares Annabelle for kindergarten, but some of her training backfires. In spite of some embarrassment in the classroom, Annabelle makes a hit with her fellow classmates." Child Book Rev Serv

"In illustrations that carefully evoke the naive and awkward drawings of children, Schwartz captures the essence of childhood complete with pedal-pushers, pinafores, and 6¢ milk. Line and wash illustrations in crayon-bright colors reveal a classroom that is cheerful, warm, and inviting. The children pictured are universal yet individual, while the adults are solid and supportive." SLJ

Bea and Mr. Jones; story and pictures by Amy Schwartz. Bradbury Press 1982 unp il o.p.; Puffin Bks. paperback available $3.95 E

1. Fathers—Fiction 2. School stories 3. Business—Fiction
ISBN 0-14-050439-7 (pa) LC 81-18031

"Bea is tired of kindergarten, and Mr. Jones is fed up with being chained to a desk all day. So the two decide to change places, a pleasure for both." Booklist

"A nice treatment of role reversal, this junior tall tale is told with simplicity and humor, and is illustrated with soft pencil drawings that have pudgy people, nice textural quality, and some funny details, such as Mr. Jones, lying on the floor and using blocks to spell out 'antidisestablishmentarianism.'" Bull Cent Child Books

The lady who put salt in her coffee; from the Peterkin papers by Lucretia Hale; adapted and illustrated by Amy Schwartz. Harcourt Brace Jovanovich 1989 unp il $13.95 E

ISBN 0-15-243475-5 LC 88-15725

When Mrs. Peterkin accidentally puts salt in her coffee, the entire family embarks on an elaborate quest to find someone to make it drinkable again

"This story, from Lucretia Hale's *The Peterkin Papers*, was published in a magazine in 1867 and as part of a collection of stories in 1880. . . . Schwartz rescues this, the best-known episode from those droll tales, and provides a smooth revision respectful of Hale's language. She also presents a new generation with artwork that re-creates the Victorian setting while echoing the humor of the narrative." Booklist

Oma and Bobo; story and pictures by Amy Schwartz. Bradbury Press 1987 unp il $13.95; Harper & Row pa $4.95 E

1. Dogs—Fiction 2. Grandmothers—Fiction
ISBN 0-02-781500-5; 0-06-443225-4 (pa)
LC 86-10665

"When Alice is told she can have a dog for her birthday, she hurries down to the pound and picks out an old black-and-white mutt she names Bobo. Oma, Alice's grandmother, is not keen on the idea of a dog." Booklist

"This is a fresh portrait of an unlikely friendship that allows room for both humor and dignity. Schwartz's eccentric illustrations have a 50's mood colored by an 80's sensibility, and are filled with witty details and patterns . . . exactly suiting the dry tone of the text." Bull Cent Child Books

Schwartz, David M., 1951-

How much is a million? pictures by Steven Kellogg. Lothrop, Lee & Shepard Bks. 1985 unp il $14.95; lib bdg $14.88 E

1. Million (The number) 2. Billion (The number) 3. Trillion (The number)
ISBN 0-688-04049-7; 0-688-04050-0 (lib bdg)
LC 84-5736

"Marvelosissimo the Mathematical Magician leads the reader through Steven Kellogg's scenes of fantasy to express the concepts of a million, a billion and a trillion. The text is all printed in capital letters to point out the expanding scenes portrayed in the fabulous illustrations. The idea is to make possible to children the awesome concept of large numbers. It is a delightful fantasy as a picture book, but it is even more compelling as a first reader." Okla State Dept of Educ

If you made a million; pictures by Steven Kellogg. Lothrop, Lee & Shepard Bks. 1989 unp il $14.95 E

1. Finance, Personal
ISBN 0-688-07017-5 LC 88-12819

Companion volume to: How much is a million?, entered above

The author examines "how one earns money, how checks are used instead of cash, why banks pay interest on money deposited, [and] why interest is charged on loans." Booklist

"The concepts of banks and banking . . . are all explained with absurd and humorous examples involving Ferris wheels, ogres, and rhinoceroses. . . . The best advice of all is 'Enjoying your work is more important than money.' Steven Kellogg's splendidly funny illustrations contain a troupe of two cats, one dog, numerous

Schwartz, David M., 1951-—*Continued*
kids, a unicorn, and the wonderful magician Marvelosissimo." Horn Book

Scott, Ann Herbert, 1926-

One good horse; a cowpuncher's counting book; pictures by Lynn Sweat. Greenwillow Bks. 1990 unp il $12.95; lib bdg $12.88 **E**

1. Counting
ISBN 0-688-09146-6; 0-688-09147-4 (lib bdg) LC 89-1984

While a cowboy and his son check the cattle, they count the things that they see

"An especially clean design distinguishes this counting book and adds to its considerable attraction. . . . The objects are appropriately western and the scenery beautifully spare and richly hued, evoking the Great Plains and mountians with subtle detail." Horn Book

Sam; drawings by Symeon Shimin. McGraw-Hill 1967 unp il $14.95 **E**

1. Blacks—Fiction 2. Family life—Fiction
ISBN 0-07-055803-5 LC 67-22968

"Each member of this black family is too preoccupied to give any attention to Sam, unitl they notice his dejection and provide a satisfying job for him to do." Best Books for Child. 2d edition

Seed, Jenny

Ntombi's song; illustrated by Anno Berry. Beacon Press 1989 c1987 unp il (Beacon Press night lights) $14.95 **E**

1. Zulus—Fiction 2. South Africa—Fiction
ISBN 0-8070-8318-6 LC 88-39522

First published 1987 in South Africa

When a speeding bus causes her to spill the sugar she is carrying home, Ntombi, a six-year-old Zulu girl, is determined to overcome her fears and find a way to earn money to buy more sugar

"This spirited, engaging story will fascinate four to eight year olds. Of special note are the communal interactions of adults and children, and the nurturing bond between Ntombi and Zanele [her older cousin]. . . . Zulu phrases (with English translations) are integrated into the text and the refrains of Ntombi's 'special song,' and highly visual descriptions of the South African landscape, intensified by Berry's fine-art illustrations, stimulate the imagination." Small Press

Segal, Lore Groszmann

Tell me a Mitzi; [by] Lore Segal; pictures by Harriet Pincus. Farrar, Straus & Giroux 1970 unp il $13.95 **E**

1. Family life—Fiction
ISBN 0-374-37392-2 LC 69-14980

The author injects an element of fantasy into these three stories of family life, the first of which deals with Mitzi's safari to grandma's and grandpa's house, the second with a confrontation with the common cold, and the third with her brother Jacob's encounter with a Presidential motorcade

"The illustrations, while they do not boast attractive children, are full of vitality and humor, the busy urban neighborhood and homely people having a rueful charm." Sutherland. The Best in Child Books

Tell me a Trudy; [by] Lore Segal; pictures by Rosemary Wells. Farrar, Straus & Giroux 1977 unp il $12.95; pa $4.95 **E**

1. Family life—Fiction
ISBN 0-374-37395-7; 0-374-47504-0 (pa) LC 77-24123

"Following the same format as 'Tell Me a Mitzi,' [entered above] a little girl named Martha cajoles her mother and her father into telling stories. Each tale features Trudy, her younger brother Jacob, and her parents and gently satirizes a common family situation. In the first story Trudy's grandma lures stubborn children to bed; in the second, parents are found squabbling over toys; the third story deals with Trudy's fear of robbers in the bathroom. . . . Flamboyant color and caricatured figures heighten the humor of a straight-faced text." Horn Book

Sendak, Maurice

Alligators all around; an alphabet. Harper & Row 1962 unp il lib bdg $12.89; pa $2.95 **E**

1. Alphabet
ISBN 0-06-025530-7 (lib bdg); 0-06-443254-8 (pa)

Originally published in smaller format as volume one of the "Nutshell library"

An alphabet book of alligators doing dishes, juggling jelly beans, throwing tantrums and wearing wigs, all from A to Z

Chicken soup with rice; a book of months. Harper & Row 1962 30p il lib bdg $12.89; pa $2.95 **E**

1. Seasons—Fiction
ISBN 0-06-025535-8 (lib bdg); 0-06-443253-X (pa)

Originally published in smaller format as volume two of the "Nutshell library"

Pictures and verse illustrate the delight of eating chicken soup with rice in every season of the year

In the night kitchen. Harper & Row 1970 unp il $14.95; lib bdg $14.89; pa $4.95 **E**

1. Fantastic fiction
ISBN 0-06-025489-0; 0-06-025490-4 (lib bdg); 0-06-443086-3 (pa) LC 70-105483

A Caldecott Medal honor book, 1971

"A small boy falls through the dark, out of his clothes, and into the bright, night kitchen where he is stirred into the cake batter and almost baked, jumps into the bread dough, kneads and shapes it into an airplane, and flies up over the top of the Milky Way to get milk for the bakers." Booklist

"A perfect midnight fantasy. The feelings, smells, sights, and comforting emotions which young children experience are here in lovely dream colors." Brooklyn. Art Books for Child

Sendak, Maurice—*Continued*

Kenny's window. Harper & Row 1956 unp il $12.95; lib bdg $12.89; pa $4.95 E

1. Dreams—Fiction
ISBN 0-06-025494-7; 0-06-025495-5 (lib bdg); 0-06-443209-2 (pa) LC 56-5148

"One night Kenny wakes up, and remembers a garden he has been dreaming about. It was a lovely garden, half filled with daylight and half with night. A rooster there gave him seven questions and told him to answer them. . . . One by one the questions from the dream are answered by Kenny." Publisher's note

One was Johnny; a counting book. Harper & Row 1962 unp il lib bdg $12.89; pa $2.95 E

1. Counting
ISBN 0-06-025540-4 (lib bdg); 0-06-443251-3 (pa)

Originally published in smaller format as volume three of the "Nutshell library"

Counting from one to ten and back again to one, Johnny, who starts off alone, acquires too many numbered visitors for his own comfort, until they disappear one by one

Outside over there. Harper & Row 1981 unp il $19.95; lib bdg $19.89; pa $7.95 E

1. Fairy tales 2. Sisters—Fiction
ISBN 0-06-025523-4; 0-06-025524-2 (lib bdg); 0-06-443185-1 (pa) LC 79-2682

A Caldecott Medal honor book, 1982

"An Ursula Nordstrom book"

With Papa off to sea and Mama despondent, Ida must go outside over there to rescue her baby sister from goblins who steal her to be a goblin's bride

"A gentle yet powerful story in the romantic tradition. . . . Soft in tones, rich in the use of light and color . . . the pictures are particularly distinctive for the tenderness with which the children's faces are drawn, the classic handling of texture, the imaginative juxtaposition of infant faces and the baroque landscape details that might have come from Renaissance paintings." Bull Cent Child Books

Pierre; a cautionary tale in five chapters and a prologue. Harper & Row 1962 48p il lib bdg $12.89; pa $2.95 E

ISBN 0-06-025965-5 (lib bdg); 0-06-443252-1 (pa)

Originally published in smaller format as volume four of the "Nutshell library"

A story in verse about a little boy called Pierre who insisted upon saying 'I don't care' until he said it once too often and learned a well needed lesson

The sign on Rosie's door; story and pictures by Maurice Sendak. Harper & Row 1960 46p il $12.95; lib bdg $12.89 E

ISBN 0-06-025505-6; 0-06-025506-4 (lib bdg) LC 60-9451

The sign on imaginative Rosie's door read, 'If you want to know a secret, knock three times.' The secret was that Rosie was now Alinda. With her friends Kathy, Sol, Pudgy, Dolly, and Lenny, and with the help of the Music Man, Alinda has a Fourth of July celebration. Then Alinda the lady singer leaves as Rosie becomes someone else

Very far away. Harper & Row 1957 52p il $12.95; lib bdg $12.89 E

1. Animals—Fiction
ISBN 0-06-025514-5; 0-06-025515-3 (lib bdg) LC 57-5356

Story about a little boy whose mother was too busy to answer all his questions so he packed up and went away—to a far place where everything would be more satisfatory. With him went a dreamy horse, a refined sparrow and a cat which wanted to sing. However, after an hour and a half of that they all got tired of it and Martin went home

"In this captivating story-picture book, Maurice Sendak blends the sublime and the ridiculous into a child-like presentation. . . . Text and illustrations are just right." Saturday Rev

Where the wild things are; story and pictures by Maurice Sendak. Harper & Row 1963 unp il $13.95; lib bdg $13.89; pa $4.95 E

1. Fantastic fiction
ISBN 0-06-025492-0; 0-06-025493-9 (lib bdg); 0-06-443178-9 (pa) LC 63-21253

Awarded the Caldecott Medal, 1964

"A tale of very few words about Max, sent to his room for cavorting around in his wolf suit, who dreamed of going where the wild things are, to rule them and share their rumpus. Then a longing to be 'where someone loved him best of all' swept over him." Book Week

"This vibrant picture book in luminous, understated full color has proved utterly engrossing to children with whom it has been shared. . . . A sincere, preceptive contribution which bears repeated examination." Horn Book

Serfozo, Mary

Who said red? illustrated by Keiko Narahashi. Margaret K. McElderry Bks. 1988 unp il $12.95 E

1. Color
ISBN 0-689-50455-1 LC 88-9345

This "picture book about colors also has a storyline as an extra treat for its preschool audience. The jaunty, rhyming text is a conversation between two playmates, a little boy searching for his lost red kite and his older sister." Booklist

This book has "very little text, and the door is wide open to the imagination. For the smallest child, familiar objects can be labeled and identified. Keiko Narahashi's watercolors are misty and delicate, but so accurate when looked at closely that children can identify not only types of leaves but a woodpecker, a monarch butterfly and a tiger lily. In several cases, finding the creatures becomes a hide-and-seek game that playfully builds a child's powers of observation." N Y Times Book Rev

Seuss, Dr.

The 500 hats of Bartholomew Cubbins. Random House 1990 c1938 unp il $7.95; lib bdg $8.99 E

1. Hats—Fiction
ISBN 0-394-84484-X; 0-394-94484-4 (lib bdg) LC 88-38412

"A Vanguard Press book"

A reissue of the title first published 1938 by Vanguard Press

"A read-aloud story telling what happened to Bartholomew Cubbins when he couldn't take his hat off before the King." Hodges. Books for Elem Sch Libr

"It is a lovely bit of tomfoolery which keeps up the suspense and surprise until the last page, and of the same ingenious and humorous imagination are the author's black and white illustrations in which a red cap and then an infinite number of red caps titillate the eye." N Y Times Book Rev

Another available title about Bartholomew Cubbins is: Bartholomew and the oobleck, entered below

And to think that I saw it on Mulberry Street. Random House 1989 c1937 unp il $9.95; lib bdg $10.95 E

1. Nonsense verses 2. Stories in rhyme
ISBN 0-394-84494-7; 0-394-94494-1 (lib bdg) LC 88-38411

"A Vanguard Press book"

A reissue of the title first published 1937 by Vanguard Press

This book tells in rhyme accompanied by pictures how little Marco saw a horse and wagon on Mulberry Street. Then "how that horse became a zebra, then a reindeer, then an elephant, and how the cart turned into a band wagon with a retinue of police to guide it through the traffic on Mulberry Street, only the book can properly explain." Christ Sci Monit

"A fresh, inspiring picture-story book in bright colors. . . . As convincing to a child as to the psychologist in quest of a book with an appeal to the child's imaginations." Horn Book

Another available title about Marco is: McElligot's pool, entered below

Bartholomew and the oobleck; written and illustrated by Dr. Seuss. Random House 1949 unp il $8.95; lib bdg $8.99; pa $3.95 E

ISBN 0-394-80075-3; 0-394-90075-8 (lib bdg); 0-394-84539-0 (pa) LC 49-11423

A Caldecott Medal honor book, 1950

"King Derwin, dissatisfied with only rain, sunshine, fog and snow, orders the royal magicians to produce oobleck. The greenish, sticky stuff was alost disastrous and it is Bartholomew Cubbins who rescues the kingdom." Wis Libr Bull

The cat in the hat. Random House 1957 61p il $6.95; lib bdg $7.95 E

1. Cats—Fiction 2. Nonsense verses 3. Stories in rhyme
ISBN 0-394-80001-X; 0-394-90001-4 (lib bdg) LC 57-1811

Also available in a bilingual Spanish-English edition $6.95, lib bdg, $6.99 (ISBN 0-394-81626-9)

A nonsense story in verse illustrated by the author about an unusual cat and his tricks which he displayed for the children one rainy day

The cat in the hat comes back! Beginner Bks. 1958 61p il $6.95; lib bdg $7.99 E

1. Cats—Fiction 2. Nonsense verses 3. Stories in rhyme
ISBN 0-394-80002-8; 0-394-90002-2 (lib bdg) LC 58-9017

In this sequel to the title entered above, "the cat comes back and wreaks havoc in the house of Sally and the teller of the story. But, of course, all is eventually put right. " Libr J

Green eggs and ham. Beginner Bks. 1960 62p il $6.95; lib bdg $7.99 E

1. Food—Fiction 2. Nonsense verses 3. Stories in rhyme
ISBN 0-394-80016-8; 0-394-90016-2 (lib bdg) LC 60-13493

This book is about "Sam-I-Am who wins a determined campaign to make another Seuss character eat a plate of green eggs and ham." Libr J

"The happy theme of refusal-to-eat changing to relish will be doubly enjoyable to the child who finds many common edibles as nauseating as the title repast. The pacing throughout is magnificent, and the opening five pages, on which the focal character introduces himself with a placard: 'I am Sam,' are unsurpassed in the controlled-vocabulary literature." Saturday Rev

Horton hatches the egg. Random House 1940 unp il $10.95; lib bdg $10.99 E

1. Elephants—Fiction 2. Nonsense verses 3. Stories in rhyme
ISBN 0-394-80077-X; 0-394-90077-4 (lib bdg) LC 40-27753

"Horton, the elephant, is faithful one hundred percent as he carries out his promise to watch a bird's egg while she takes a rest. Hilarious illustrations and a surprise ending." Adventuring with Books. 2d edition

Horton hears a Who! Random House 1954 unp il $9.95; lib bdg $11.99 E

1. Elephants—Fiction 2. Nonsense verses 3. Stories in rhyme
ISBN 0-394-80078-8; 0-394-90078-2 (lib bdg) LC 54-7012

"Although considered the biggest blame fool in the Jungle of Nool, the faithful and kindhearted elephant of 'Horton hatches the egg' [entered above] believing that a person's a person no matter how small, stanchly defends the Whos, too-small-to-be-seen inhabitants of Whoville, a town which exists on a dust speck." Booklist

"The verses are full of the usual lively, informal language and amazing rhymes that have delighted such a world-wide audience in the good 'doctor's' other books. The story, with its moral, does not match the gayety of some of the older books. But the pictures are as wildly original and funny as ever." N Y Her Trib Books

Seuss, Dr.—*Continued*

How the Grinch stole Christmas. Random House 1957 unp il $6.95; lib bdg $7.99 E

1. Christmas—Fiction 2. Nonsense verses 3. Stories in rhyme
ISBN 0-394-80079-6; 0-394-90079-0 (lib bdg) LC 57-7526

"The Grinch lived on a mountain where it was able to ignore the people of the valley except at Christmas time when it had to endure the sound of their singing. One year it decided to steal all the presents so there would be no Christmas, but much to its amazement discovered that people did not need presents to enjoy Christmas. It there-upon reformed, returned the presents and joined in the festivities." Bull Cent Child Books

"The verse is as lively and the pages are as bright and colorful as anyone could wish. Reading the book aloud will be a fascinating exercise." Saturday Rev

If I ran the circus. Random House 1956 unp il $9.95; lib bdg $10.99 E

1. Circus—Fiction 2. Nonsense verses 3. Stories in rhyme
ISBN 0-394-80080-X; 0-394-90080-4 (lib bdg) LC 56-9469

The author-illustrator "presents the fabulous Circus McGurkus with its highly imaginative young owner, Morris McGurk and its intrepid performer, Sneelock, behind whose store the circus is to be housed. There are the expected number of strange creatures with nonsensical names, but the real humor lies in the situations, and especially those involving Mr. Sneelock. There is fun for the entire family here." Bull Cent Child Books

If I ran the zoo. Random House 1950 unp il $9.95; lib bdg $11.99 E

1. Zoos—Fiction 2. Nonsense verses 3. Stories in rhyme
ISBN 0-394-80081-8; 0-394-90081-2 (lib bdg) LC 50-10185

A Caldecott Medal honor book, 1951

"Assembled here are the rare and wonderful creatures which young Gerald McGrew collects from far and unusual places for the 'gol-darndest zoo on the face of the earth." Booklist

"As you turn the pages, the imaginings get wilder and funnier, the rhymes more hilarious. There will be no age limits for this book, because families will be forced to share rereading and quotation, for a long long time." N Y Her Trib Books

McElligot's pool; written and illustrated by Dr. Seuss. Random House 1947 unp il $8.95; lib bdg $9.99 E

1. Fishing—Fiction 2. Nonsense verses 3. Stories in rhyme
ISBN 0-394-80083-4; 0-394-90083-9 (lib bdg) LC 47-4895

A Caldecott Medal honor book, 1948

"In spite of warnings that there are no fish in McElligot's Pool, a boy continues to fish and to imagine the rare and wonderful denizens of the deep which he just 'might' catch." Hodges. Books for Elem Sch Libr

"Fine color surrounding a host of strange creatures enlivens this amazing fish story for all ages." Horn Book

Oh, the places you'll go! Random House 1990 unp il $12.95; lib bdg $13.99 E

1. Stories in rhyme
ISBN 0-679-80527-3; 0-679-90527-8 (lib bdg) LC 89-36892

Advice in rhyme for proceeding in life; weathering fear, loneliness, and confusion; and being in charge of your actions

"The combination of the lively text and wacky, offbeat pictures will delight both children and their parents." Child Book Rev Serv

Shachtman, Tom, 1942-

Parade! photographs by Chuck Saaf. Macmillan 1985 61p il $14.95 E

1. Parades 2. Thanksgiving Day
ISBN 0-02-782540-X LC 85-7308

"A behind-the-scenes view of Macy's Annual Thanksgiving Day Parade in New York City. Chuck Saaf's color photographs of the floats, balloons, bands, float builders, makeup artists and many other areas of the parade make the book especially interesting. The text is informative, well-written and includes information about the beginning of parades. An excellent book for any library, even if you already have a book on parades." Okla State Dept of Educ

Shannon, George, 1952-

Dance away! illustrated by Jose Aruego and Ariane Dewey. Greenwillow Bks. 1982 unp il $13.95; lib bdg $13.88 E

1. Rabbits—Fiction 2. Foxes—Fiction 3. Dancing—Fiction
ISBN 0-688-00838-0; 0-688-00839-9 (lib bdg) LC 81-6391

"One day Rabbit discovers his friends in the paws of a hungry fox but through his dance is able to outwit the rascal and save them all." Booklist

"The synthesis of well-defined, identifiable characters with the text is irresistible. The brevity of the plot, the perceivable conflict, and the humor of the illustrations suggest a special appeal to preschoolers." Horn Book

The Piney Woods peddler; pictures by Nancy Tafuri. Greenwillow Bks. 1981 32p il lib bdg $12.88 E

1. Peddlers and peddling—Fiction
ISBN 0-688-84304-2 LC 81-2219

"The Piney Woods peddler promises his 'dear darling daughter' a silver dollar for some pretty things but ends up bringing her a dime instead, this after trading downward from the family horse. She's happy, though—'it's . . . dear and darling like me!'—and the peddler strikes out anew for the promised silver dollar." Booklist

"Strong, humorously exaggerated paintings reflect the brash, folklike quality of the story; and from the imaginative title page to the finale showing the swaggering peddler singing on his way, the book is a fine example of integrated design." Horn Book

Sharmat, Marjorie Weinman, 1928-

Gila monsters meet you at the airport; pictures by Byron Barton. Macmillan 1980 unp il $13.95; pa $3.95 **E**

1. Moving, Household—Fiction 2. West (U.S.)—Fiction
ISBN 0-02-782450-0; 0-689-71383-5 (pa) LC 80-12264

A New York City boy's preconceived ideas of life in the West make him very apprehensive about the family's move there

"The exaggeration is amusing, the style yeasty, with a nice final touch; the illustrations are comic and awkward, but add little that's not inherent in the story." Bull Cent Child Books

Goodnight, Andrew: goodnight, Craig; pictures by Mary Chalmers. Harper & Row 1969 32p il lib bdg $11.89 **E**

1. Sleep—Fiction 2. Brothers—Fiction
ISBN 0-06-025548-X LC 69-10205

"Andrew refuses to settle down to sleep until he obtains from his older brother Craig a promise to play ball with him the next day." Booklist

"The pale, demure illustrations have a note of humor, and the young listener should relish the fun and the typical bedtime pranks." Saturday Rev

Griselda's new year; pictures by Normand Chartier. Macmillan 1979 63p il hardcover o.p. paperback available $3.95 **E**

1. Geese—Fiction 2. New Year—Fiction
ISBN 0-689-71341-X (pa) LC 79-11375

"Ready-to-read"

"Griselda, a silly goose blows her Happy New Year Horn and wishes herself the best year yet. She resolves to be good, brave and kind—to make someone happy. The way fair Griselda goes about keeping her vows is related in six chapters, the fun escalating in each." Publ Wkly

This text for beginning readers is "illustrated by humorous animal pictures, softly-tinted line drawings. . . . The read-aloud audience should enjoy the comic miscarriage of her good intentions; there are verve and wit in the style and in the development of Griselda's good deeds, unappreciated by the recipients but completely satisfying to the silly goose." Bull Cent Child Books

Mooch the messy; pictures by Ben Shecter. Harper & Row 1976 61p il lib bdg $10.89 **E**

1. Rats—Fiction
ISBN 0-06-025532-3 LC 76-3842

"An I can read book"

"Mooch the rat likes to live in a mess: shoes on the table, candy under the bed, clothing draped over every piece of furniture. He is delighted when his father comes to visit, and shows off the glories of his tunnels; his father, however, thinks Mooch's hole is in dreadful condition and does not approve, when they go on a picnic, of his son's practice of leaving jam jars open for the ants to get into. So Mooch tidies his hole and pleases Father; he is sorry to see Father leave but immediately, happily, scatters things about in comfortable chaos." Bull Cent Child Books

"Ben Shecter's brown-and-gold drawings are suitably homey, with just the right amount of expression and detail." Booklist

Nate the Great; illustrated by Marc Simont. Coward, McCann & Geoghegan 1972 60p il $10.95; lib bdg $6.99; Dell pa $2.95 **E**

1. Mystery and detective stories
ISBN 0-698-20627-4; 0-698-30444-6 (lib bdg); 0-440-46126-X (pa) LC 75-183552

"A Break-of-day book"

Nate the Great, a junior detective who has found missing balloons, books, slippers, chickens and even a goldfish, is now in search of a painting of a dog by Annie, the girl down the street

"The illustrations capture the exaggerated, tongue-in-cheek humor of the story." Booklist

Other available titles about Nate the Great are:
Nate the Great and the boring beach bag (1987)
Nate the Great and the fishy prize (1985)
Nate the Great and the Halloween hunt (1989)
Nate the Great and the lost list (1975)
Nate the Great and the missing key (1981)
Nate the Great and the musical note (1990)
Nate the Great and the phony clue (1977)
Nate the Great and the snowy trail (1982)
Nate the Great and the sticky case (1978)
Nate the Great goes down in the dumps (1989)
Nate the Great goes undercover (1974)
Nate the Great stalks stupidweed (1986)

Sharmat, Mitchell, 1927-

Gregory, the terrible eater; by Mitchell Sharmat; illustrated by Jose Aruego and Ariane Dewey. Four Winds Press 1980 unp il $13.95; Scholastic pa $2.95 **E**

1. Goats—Fiction 2. Diet—Fiction
ISBN 0-590-07586-1; 0-590-40250-1 (pa) LC 79-19172

"Gregory is not your average goat. In fact, he's the original goat gourmet, abandoning bottle caps in favor of bananas and trading last year's boots for bread and butter." SLJ

"Aruego and Dewey's illustrations are highly amusing, thanks to their goats' dot-eyed facial expressions. Colors are darker than usual, with the animals in gray, army green, and dark ochre. There is energy in the pictures; they are beguiling and help to carry the humor that sometimes falters in the story, which is truer to young humans than to goats." Booklist

Sharples, Joseph

The flyaway pantaloons; illustrated by Sue Scullard; verses by Joseph Sharples. Carolrhoda Bks. 1990 unp il lib bdg $12.95 **E**

1. Clothing and dress—Fiction 2. Stories in rhyme
ISBN 0-87614-408-3 LC 89-37454

A pair of pantaloons relates how, after being blown off its clothesline, it had an exciting adventure before returning where it belonged

"The twist to this modest storyline is the setting—a Renaissance city that looks like a blend of Florence and Venice. Vistas of red-tile roofs, bustling streets, and busy marketplaces and waterfronts are ambitiously rendered. Every corner of the page is packed with people, patterns,

Sharples, Joseph—*Continued*
and color, plus a plethora of detail that makes each picture a miniature lesson in social history." Booklist

Shaw, Charles, 1892-1974

It looked like spilt milk. Harper & Row 1947 unp il $12.95; lib bdg $12.89; pa $3.95 E

ISBN 0-06-025566-8; 0-06-025565-X (lib bdg); 0-06-443159-2 (pa) LC 47-30767

White silhouettes on a blue background with simple captions: "sometimes it looked like a tree," "Sometimes it looked like a bird," etc. lead to a surprise ending "sometimes it looked like split milk, but what it was was—"

"What one thing could look like all of these? On the last page you are told, and I could no more tell you now than I could spoil an adult mystery by a review that gives away its solution." N Y Her Trib Books

Shaw, Nancy (Nancy E.)

Sheep in a jeep; illustrated by Margot Apple. Houghton Mifflin 1986 32p il lib bdg $12.95; pa $3.95 E

1. Sheep—Fiction 2. Stories in rhyme
ISBN 0-395-41105-X (lib bdg); 0-395-47030-7 (pa) LC 86-3101

"When five sheep pile into one little jeep, there is trouble . . . [as] the poor woolly travelers push, shove, and attempt to drive their way from one calamity to another." Horn Book

"Shaw demonstrates a promising capacity for creating nonsense rhymes. . . . Veteran illustrator Apple's whimsical portraits of the sheep bring the story to life. Pleasing and lighthearted, this has much appeal for young readers." Publ Wkly

Shub, Elizabeth

The white stallion; illustrated by Rachel Isadora. Greenwillow Bks. 1982 56p il $11.95; lib bdg $11.88; Bantam Bks. pa $2.50 E

1. Horses—Fiction 2. West (U.S.)—Fiction
ISBN 0-688-01210-8; 0-688-01211-6 (lib bdg); 0-553-15244-0 (pa) LC 81-20308

"A Greenwillow read-alone book"

Retold from James Frank Dobie's Tales of the mustang

Carried away from her wagon train in Texas in 1845 by the old mare she is riding, a little girl is befriended by a white stallion

"The quietly compelling story, framed by the grandmother's opening and closing lines to her granddaughter, is riveting without ever sensationalizing or anthropomorphizing. Elizabeth Shub's straightforward, lean text is part of the book's quality and appeal, but even more credit goes to the superb ink drawings." SLJ

Shulevitz, Uri, 1935-

Dawn; words and pictures by Uri Shulevitz. Farrar, Straus & Giroux 1974 unp il $14.95; pa $4.95 E

ISBN 0-374-31707-0; 0-374-41689-3 (pa) LC 74-9761

"Drawn from a Chinese poem, the spare text tells of an old man and his grandson asleep by the shore of a mountain lake. With the approach of daylight, the watercolor illustrations, which start out small, dark, and blurred, slowly become more focused and detailed: the moon casts a soft glow; a breeze riffles the water; mists rise. As the old man and the boy push out on to the lake in their boat, a hint of color suffuses the scene; and finally, in a visual tour-de-force, the sun rises over the mountain and they are bathed in full color." SLJ

"The purity of the hues, well-produced on ample spreads, the subtle graphic development from scene to scene, and the sharply focused simplicity of the few words make this a true art experience." Horn Book

Hanukah money; by Sholem Aleichem; translated and adapted by Uri Shulevitz and Elizabeth Shub; illustrated by Uri Shulevitz. Greenwillow Bks. 1978 30p il lib bdg $11.88 E

1. Jews—Fiction 2. Hanukkah—Fiction
ISBN 0-688-84120-1 LC 77-26693

"A vignette of pre-World War I Eastern European Jewish life, in which the home ritual of lighting Hanukah candles and the traditional practice of frying potato pancakes becomes intertwined with the holiday custom of giving money to children as a gift for a joyous season." Horn Book

"Some passages seem to echo chanted prayer rhythms. Beginning, middle, and end, however, are a bit vague in direction, as are transitions, particularly into a last dream. . . . Still, such an atmospheric piece will evoke nostalgia in adults reading aloud and will further acculturate children involved in their own traditional celebrations." Booklist

One Monday morning. Scribner 1967 unp il lib bdg $13.95; pa $4.95 E

ISBN 0-684-13195-1 (lib bdg); 0-689-71062-3 (pa) LC 66-24483

"'One Monday morning, the king, the queen, and the little prince came to visit me. But I wasn't home. . . .' So goes the daydream of a small child in a drab tenement. As the week progresses, the royal entourage, in the panoply of playing card figures, increases. Their pageantry blots out the grey background while commonplace activities play counterpoint to the fantasy theme." Moorachian. What is a City?

"Humor, dignity, imagination, and a remarkable interplay between text and illustration make . . . [this] a beautiful book that is easy and fun to read. . . . Children will be able to identify, understand, and enjoy both worlds of [the book's] imaginative child." Wis Libr Bull

Rain, rain, rivers; words and pictures by Uri Shulevitz. Farrar, Straus & Giroux 1969 unp il $13.95; pa $3.95 E

1. Rain and rainfall
ISBN 0-374-36171-1; 0-374-46195-3 (pa) LC 73-85370

Shulevitz, Uri, 1935-—*Continued*

A child indoors watches the rain on the window and in the streets and tells how it falls on the fields, hills, and seas

"There is no story line but interest is captured and held by the beauty of the striking illustrations and the strong, pervasive mood they evoke." Booklist

"Gray, softly cartooned drawings accompany the poem; they are self-contained in their frame against a gray blue page, but seem spacious nonetheless, and quite effective in displaying the lighthearted abandon of the moving figures." Booklist

Siebert, Diane

Train song; paintings by Mike Wimmer. Crowell 1990 unp il $14.95; lib bdg $14.89 **E**

1. Railroads—Fiction 2. Stories in rhyme
ISBN 0-690-04726-6; 0-690-04728-2 (lib bdg) LC 88-389

Rhymed text and illustrations describe the journey of a transcontinental train

"Wimmer's luminous, nostalgic paintings will enable readers to grasp the beauty and power of the trains and the landscape across which they travel." Publ Wkly

Truck song; pictures by Byron Barton. Crowell 1984 unp il $12.95; lib bdg $12.89; pa $3.95 **E**

1. Trucks—Fiction 2. Stories in rhyme
ISBN 0-690-04410-0; 0-690-04411-9 (lib bdg); 0-06-443134-7 (pa) LC 83-46173

"Vivid illustrations and a rhythmic text describe the transcontinental journey of a truck driver. Readers/listeners get a sense of overland travel and the diverse American landscape it provides." Soc Educ

Skofield, James

All wet! All wet! illustrated by Diane Stanley. Harper & Row 1984 31p il lib bdg $12.89 **E**

1. Rain and rainfall—Fiction 2. Animals—Fiction
ISBN 0-06-025752-0 LC 82-47713

"A Charlotte Zolotow book"

"The sights, smells, and sounds of a rainy day in the woods, as experienced by a small boy and several animals, are the focus of this book." Sci Child

"The poetic text is balanced by carefully rendered illustrations accurately depicting the various occupants of the woods. Several cross-sectional drawings even show animals as they huddle in their homes beneath the ground." Horn Book

Nightdances; pictures by Karen Gundersheimer. Harper & Row 1981 unp il $12.95; lib bdg $11.89 **E**

1. Dancing—Fiction 2. Night—Fiction 3. Stories in rhyme
ISBN 0-06-025741-5; 0-06-025742-3 (lib bdg) LC 80-8943

"Autumn 'windmusic' wakes a small boy: he tiptoes outside, and gradually the spirit of the wild nightworld enters him until he dances, tumbles and sings in celebration, under the moon. Mama and Papa join him, and each dances an individual expression of joy, culminating in a wordless dance of the three together, before they 'slow dance, soft dance on inside' and back to bed." SLJ

Slobodkina, Esphyr, 1908-

Caps for sale; a tale of a peddler, some monkeys & their monkey business; told and illustrated by Esphyr Slobodkina. Addison-Wesley 1947 unp il $11.95; lib bdg $11.89; pa $3.95 **E**

1. Monkeys—Fiction 2. Peddlers and peddling—Fiction
ISBN 0-201-09147-X; 0-06-025778-4 (lib bdg); 0-06-443143-6 (pa) LC 47-29233

A picture book story which "provides hilarious confusion. A cap peddler takes a nap under a tree. When he wakes up, his caps have disappeared. He looks up in the tree and sees countless monkeys, each wearing a cap and grinning." Parent's Guide To Child Read

Small, David, 1945-

Imogene's antlers; written and illustrated by David Small. Crown 1985 unp il $10.95 **E**

ISBN 0-517-55564-6 LC 84-12085

One Thursday Imogene wakes up with a pair of antlers growing out of her head and causes a sensation wherever she goes

The author "maximizes the inherent humor of the absurd situation by allowing the imaginative possibilities of Imogene's predicament to run rampant. The brief text is supported by Small's expansive watercolors. They brim with humorous details. His jolly caricatures—whether fatter, more elongated, more egg-headed or more content than the norm—delight with their exaggerated comic reactions. Hilarious, with a subtle lesson in acceptance." SLJ

Smucker, Anna Egan

No star nights; paintings by Steve Johnson. Knopf 1989 unp il $12.95; lib bdg $13.99 **E**

1. Steel industry and trade—Fiction
ISBN 0-394-89925-3; 0-394-99925-8 (lib bdg) LC 88-2782

A young girl growing up in a steel mill town in the 1950s describes her childhood and how it was affected by the local industry

"The book is handsomely designed, from gray endpapers to full-page paintings alternating a dusky glow with scenes hazed by air pollution." Bull Cent Child Books

Spier, Peter, 1927-

Bored—nothing to do! Doubleday 1978 unp il $11.95; pa $5.95 **E**

1. Airplanes—Fiction
ISBN 0-385-13177-1; 0-385-24104-6 (pa) LC 77-20726

Spier, Peter, 1927-—*Continued*

"A mother orders her young sons to 'do' something: 'I was never bored at your age!' So they do. Guided by a handbook, the boys misappropriate the wheels from a baby carriage, bed sheets, wire from a fence and every essential requirement to construct an airplane—including the engine from the family car. Wheeling the impressive flyer out of the garage, the boys take off and soar over the countryside until their parents espy them and screech them down. The enterprising brothers then take their craft apart and return each borrowed bit." Publ Wkly

"The text is almost superfluous, but the colorful, detailed drawings offer great scope for discussion, poring over, and enjoying a fantasy to which young children will relate." Child Book Rev Serv

Dreams. Doubleday 1986 unp il $12.95; lib bdg $13.99 **E**

ISBN 0-385-19336-X; 0-385-19337-8 (lib bdg) LC 85-13130

Two children watch cloud formations and interpret them for themselves

"Alternating spreads show vague outlines of shapes in the clouds; on following pages they become concrete shapes: animals stampeding, two knights facing a fierce dragon, gigantic fish swimming by. Watercolors in pastoral shades carry the story; an admonishment to readers to 'dream' at the end of the book is the only text. It's a concept that's full of charm and potential. However, the most successful spreads, those that capture the everchanging fleetingness of clouds, are the ones in which the object is only hinted at, not explicitly spelled out." Publ Wkly

Fast-slow, high-low; a book of opposites. Doubleday 1972 unp il $10.95; lib bdg $11.95; pa $5.95 **E**

1. English language—Synonyms and antonyms
ISBN 0-385-06781-X; 0-385-02876-8 (lib bdg); 0-385-24093-7 (pa) LC 72-76207

"Pages filled with delightful drawings, in pairs, that illustrate objects or concepts like fast or slow, young or old, over or under, heavy or light, dark or light, and so on. There is no print on the pages save the headings. The book may require adult interpretation in many instances, since some of the pictures may need translations. . . . Useful for development of awareness of differences, yet limited by the subtlety of some examples, the book is not the best choice for learning opposites but it is probably the most attractive." Bull Cent Child Books

Gobble, growl, grunt. Doubleday 1971 unp il hardcover o.p. paperback available $6.95 **E**

1. Animals 2. Animal communication
ISBN 0-385-24094-5 (pa) LC 79-144300

"Over 600 animals parade across double-page spreads, identified by name and the sound each animal makes. There is no need for any other text; the illustrations speak for themselves in a humorous and lighthearted fashion." Publ Wkly

"Children who enjoy pictures of animals will have hours of fun poring over the lively illustrations while parents can use the book with young children to identify animals and their sounds." Booklist

Oh, were they ever happy! Doubleday 1978 unp il $12.95; pa $6.95 **E**

1. House painting—Fiction
ISBN 0-385-13175-5; 0-385-24477-0 (pa) LC 77-78144

One Saturday morning while their parents are away, the three Noonan children decide to paint the house

"While the text relates a straight-faced narrative of the escapade, Spier's colorful illustrations depict the comedy as many-hued dollops of paint haphazardly appear. . . . The final scene—a full view of the house-of-many-colors—is sure to induce giggles from children and sympathetic groans from adults reading the story aloud." Booklist

Peter Spier's Christmas! Doubleday 1983 unp il $12.95; lib bdg $13.99; pa $6.95 **E**

1. Christmas—Fiction 2. Stories without words
ISBN 0-385-13183-6; 0-385-13184-4 (lib bdg); 0-385-24580-7 (pa) LC 80-2875

Illustrations without text follow the activities of three young children and their parents as they prepare for, and finally celebrate, Christmas

"Spier's colorful, charming drawings aptly change tone as the activities portrayed become more or less hectic. Small, carefully conceived and executed details, such as a new evergreen beginning to grow on the hillside from which the Christmas trees have been cut, make this book visually pleasing." SLJ

Peter Spier's rain. Doubleday 1982 unp il $12.95; pa $6.95 **E**

1. Rain and rainfall—Fiction 2. Stories without words
ISBN 0-385-15484-4; 0-385-24105-4 (pa) LC 81-43056

"In the opening picture a girl and her younger brother, a dog and a cat play in a backyard garden, and a cloud appears as a gray smudge in the corner. On the next page raindrops fall, and the cat is the first to take cover. The youngsters, in rain gear, go on a watercolored adventure through their town. . . . When the rain becomes a downpour and the the wind pops their umbrella inside out, the children run home for games, dinner and bed, and a peek from the window. The storm ends in the night . . . dark clouds scud away, the sun rises, and in the morning the children are back in the golden fresh garden." N Y Times Book Rev

"At first glance the pages appear crowded; but the eye moves easily from one vibrant watercolor to the next, and the book's appeal lies in the abundant detail that invites repeated exploration." Horn Book

Tin Lizzie; written and illustrated by Peter Spier. Doubleday 1975 unp il hardcover o.p. paperback available $6.95 **E**

1. Automobiles—Fiction
ISBN 0-385-23401-5 (pa) LC 74-1510

Chronicles the experiences of a Model T Ford with a series of owners from 1909 to the present day

"Spier's drawings are invariably pleasing, detailed-filled panoramas that capture the changing face of changing times; the full-color paintings are suffused with the rumpled comfort of an unstarched cotton shirt. What might, in different hands, have made us carsick becomes, under Spier's direction, an enjoyable piece of Americana." NY Times Book Rev

Spurr, Elizabeth

Mrs. Minetta's car pool; illustrations by Blanche Sims. Atheneum Pubs. 1985 32p il lib bdg $11.95 **E**

1. Automobiles—Fiction
ISBN 0-689-31103-6 LC 84-20483

"Mrs. Minetta, the stereotyped little old lady in red sports car, offers to take the four children from the Cherry Tree Cul-de-Sac to school on Fridays. But when they all ride off in her red sports car, strange things happen. The car becomes airborne, and off they fly—and not to school. For the next four Fridays, they fly to the beach, the mountains, an amusement park and a dude ranch. . . . Spurr has taken the mundane reality of suburbia and crafted a well-written story sure to tickle and amuse. Sims' delightful pen-and-inks, many with full-color washes, reinforce the lighthearted adventure." SLJ

Stanley, Diane, 1943-

Captain Whiz-Bang. Morrow 1987 unp il $12.95; lib bdg $12.88 **E**

1. Cats—Fiction
ISBN 0-688-06226-1; 0-688-06227-X (lib bdg) LC 86-16432

Annie names her Christmas kitten for a favorite comic-strip character. "As 'winter turns to spring,' we see Annie and Whiz-Bang growing up together—playing, dreaming, winning the Elm Street Cat Olympics—until Annie gets married and leaves the cat to doze in the sun and dream 'of the old days.' Annie returns one Christmas with her own child, who finds it hard to believe that sleepy Whiz-Bang is the same rambunctious cat she's heard about from her mother." Publ Wkly

"Although adults may best appreciate the story's poignancy, children will certainly respond to its warmth and gentleness. The story begins in the 1930s, and Stanley carries out the Captain Whiz-Bang theme with cover art that depicts the comic strip. . . . This is obviously a very personal story, but one whose tender mood will have high appeal." Booklist

Fortune; written and illustrated by Diane Stanley. Morrow Junior Bks. 1989 30p il $12.95; lib bdg $12.88 **E**

1. Fairy tales
ISBN 0-688-07210-0; 0-688-07211-9 (lib bdg) LC 88-13204

"Omar, a poor and not very clever farmer, must seek his fortune before he and Sunny, his much more sensible betrothed, can marry. In a market town nearby, a strange woman sells him a dancing tiger he names Fortune, and in no time at all, Omar's fortune is made. Now, dazzled by his own success, Omar fancies himself too grand to marry a commoner. But there is enchantment at work here, and when Omar decides to seek a princess for a bride, he sets in motion a chain of events that leaves him humbled but happily wed to Sunny." SLJ

"The illustrations, echoing the delicacy and meticulous detail of Persian miniatures, are a sparkling accompaniment to the vibrant text." Horn Book

The good-luck pencil; pictures by Bruce Degen. Four Winds Press 1986 unp il $11.95 **E**

ISBN 0-02-786800-1 LC 85-13122

A magic pencil which Mary Ann discovers accidentally brings her fantasies to life

"Stanley's story feeds right into a child's make-believe world, and Degen's three-color art brings the whole thing to life. The pictures on every page and the uncomplicated text make this a good possibility for those at the reading-on-their-own stage." Booklist

Steig, William, 1907-

The amazing bone. Farrar, Straus & Giroux 1976 unp il $14.95; Puffin Bks. pa $3.95 **E**

1. Pigs—Fiction 2. Bones—Fiction
ISBN 0-374-30248-0; 0-14-050247-5 (pa) LC 76-26479

A Caldecott Medal honor book, 1977

On her way home from school, Pearl finds an unusual bone that has unexpected powers

"Steig's marvelously straightfaced telling comes with a panoply of ultra-spring landscapes for pink-dressed Pearl to tiptoe through. And there's no holding back the chortles at the wonderfully expressive faces the artist delights in. This is a tight mesh of witty storytelling and art bound to please any audience." Booklist

Amos & Boris. Farrar, Straus & Giroux 1971 unp il $14.95; Puffin Bks. pa $3.95 **E**

1. Mice—Fiction 2. Whales—Fiction
ISBN 0-374-30278-2; 0-14-050229-7 (pa) LC 72-165403

This story "has two heroes, Amos the mouse and Boris the whale, 'a devoted pair of friends with nothing at all in common, except good hearts and a willingness to help their fellow mammal.' And help each other they do indeed, in a most uncommon way." Publ Wkly

"The water-color paintings deftly convey changing qualities of light—day and night, sunshine and rain—and a realistic flowing and heaving of seawater. . . . [The] genuine story builds its atmosphere and mood with freshness, compassion, and child interest, and is enhanced by the illustrations." Horn Book

Brave Irene. Farrar, Straus & Giroux 1986 unp il $13.95; pa $3.95 **E**

ISBN 0-374-30947-7; 0-374-40927-7 (pa) LC 86-80957

"Hardworking Mrs. Bobbin has just finished a beautiful ballgown for the duchess, but she has a headache and can't deliver it. Brave and devoted daughter Irene takes charge, tucking her mother snugly into bed and determinedly marching out into a raging snowstorm with the dress. Howling 'GO HO-WO-WOME' at poor Irene, the fierce wind rips the box open and the gown sails out, 'waltzing through the powdered air with tissue-paper attendants.'" Publ Wkly

"With sure writing and well-composed, riveting art, Steig keeps readers with Irene every step of the long way. The pictures, which take up about two-thirds of each page, are done in winter blues, purples, and grays that gradually get darker as Irene trudges on. An overlay of swirling white snow adds appropriate atmosphere. A good choice for reading aloud—especially to primary-grade children, who will appreciate the story's vitality." Booklist

Steig, William, 1907-—*Continued*

Caleb & Kate. Farrar, Straus & Giroux 1977 unp il $13.95; pa $3.95 **E**

1. Dogs—Fiction 2. Witches—Fiction
ISBN 0-374-31016-5; 0-374-41038-0 (pa) LC 77-4947

"Though Caleb the carpenter loves Kate the weaver very much, he leaves her one day because of a quarrel. In the deep woods where he is resting Yedida the witch turns him into a dog. The tale of his faithfulness and love for his wife, even though he is a dog, is . . . told. Their love is shared to the end, when a remarkable turn of events enables him to return to his former self." Child Book Rev Serv

"The well-cadenced storytelling has a certain old-fashioned elegance of language, and the humor is emphasized by an atmosphere of mock-pathos. William Steig is a superb artist with the literary ingenuity to produce durable, energetic stories; the result is another unified picture book in which text and illustrations are fully worthy of each other." Horn Book

Doctor De Soto. Farrar, Straus & Giroux 1982 unp il $13.95 **E**

1. Dentists—Fiction 2. Mice—Fiction 3. Animals—Fiction
ISBN 0-374-31803-4 LC 82-15701

A Newbery Medal honor book, 1983

"Dr. De Soto is a mouse dentist who, with his assistant Mrs. De Soto, treats all creatures large and small but none that are injurious to mice. When Fox begs for help, the couple face a dilemma. He is in pain and professional ethics demand that they pull his aching tooth and replace it with a sound one." Publ Wkly

This "book goes beyond the usual tale of wit versus might; the story achieves comic heights partly through the delightful irony of the situation—how often is a dentist at the mercy of his patient?—as well as through the orchestration of text and illustration. Watercolor paintings, with the artist's firm line and luscious color, depict with aplomb the eminently dentistlike mouse as he goes about his business." Horn Book

Farmer Palmer's wagon ride; story and pictures by William Steig. Farrar, Straus & Giroux 1974 unp il $11.95 **E**

1. Pigs—Fiction 2. Donkeys—Fiction
ISBN 0-374-32288-0 LC 74-9949

"Farmer Palmer (a pig) and his hired hand (a donkey) have a catastrophe-ridden return from market." LC. Child Books, 1974

"The text, longer than that of most picture books, boasts some captivating and original onomatopoeia, lending itself to reading aloud. Full-color illustrations add action, expression, and countryside colors appropriate to the story." Booklist

Roland, the minstrel pig. Windmill Bks. 1968 32p il hardcover o.p. paperback available $5.95 **E**

1. Pigs—Fiction
ISBN 0-671-66841-2 (pa) LC 68-14923

Roland sets out to see the world, armed with his lute and his sweet voice, but a scheming fox almost roasts him before he is rescued by the king

"The story is somewhat traditional, but Mr. Steig . . . gives it a grand style and infuses it with special graces: the modest accomplishments of Roland's balladry . . . moments of peril and poignancy, gentle humor and illustrations that range from the hauntingly lovely to the regally resplendent." N Y Times Book Rev

Shrek! Farrar, Straus & Giroux 1990 unp il $10.95; lib bdg $10.95 **E**

1. Monsters—Fiction
ISBN 0-374-36877-5; 0-374-36878-3 (lib bdg) LC 89-61252

"Michael di Capua books"

"Shrek is the ugliest monster around and this is the tale of his encounters with a witch, dragon, knight, lightening and thunder on his quest to find the ugly princess. The text includes rhymes, aliteration and unusual words." Child Book Rev Serv

"The pictures are just as nutty as the story, blending with the text so thoroughly, sometimes echoing, sometimes expanding it, that it's hard to imagine one without the other. . . . The fast-forward movement of the story and the inventive challenging language, full of surprises, make this especially fun to read aloud." SLJ

Solomon the rusty nail. Farrar, Straus & Giroux 1985 unp il $13.95; pa $3.95 **E**

1. Rabbits—Fiction 2. Fantastic fiction
ISBN 0-374-37131-8; 0-374-46903-2 (pa) LC 85-81024

"If he scratches his nose and wiggles his toes at the same time, young Solomon rabbit turns into a rusty nail. He uses his trick lightly, but one day taunts a smart cat who catches and eventually nails him to the side of a clapboard house." N Y Times Book Rev

"The illustrations are inimitably Steig, although a trifle quieter in color than his work usually is." Horn Book

Spinky sulks. Farrar, Straus & Giroux 1988 unp il $13.95; pa $4.95 **E**

ISBN 0-374-38321-9; 0-374-46990-3 (pa) LC 88-81292

"Michael di Capua books"

"Storming out of his house, feeling angry and unappreciated, Spinky heads into the yard for a good sulk, and nothing can entice him out of it—not apologies from brother Hitch (with his 'slimy voice'), daisies from sister Willamina, visits from buddies Smudge and Iggie, a box of candy, a delicious tray of lunch, a circus parade, a prancing clown bearing ice cream. Finally, Spinky figures out how to stop sulking in a way that allows him to save face." Publ Wkly

Sylvester and the magic pebble. Simon & Schuster 1969 unp il $12.95; pa $5.95 **E**

1. Donkeys—Fiction
ISBN 0-671-66154-X; 0-671-66269-4 (pa) LC 80-12314

Awarded the Caldecott Medal, 1970

"Sylvester the young donkey was a pebble collector; one day he found a flaming red stone, shiny and round—and quite unaccountably able to grant wishes. Overjoyed, Sylvester was planning to share his magic with his family when 'a mean, hungry lion' appeared. Startled and panicky, Sylvester wished himself transformed into a rock. In vain his grieving parents searched for their beloved child; all worried animals took up the hunt. Then, after months of sorrow and mourning, poor Sylvester was fortuitously but logically restored. A remarkable atmosphere of childlike innocence pervades the book; beautiful pictures in full, natural color show daily

Steig, William, 1907-—*Continued*
and seasonal changes in the lush countryside and greatly extend the kindly humor and the warm, unselfconscious tenderness." Horn Book

Steptoe, John, 1950-1989

Baby says. Lothrop, Lee & Shepard Bks. 1988 unp il $11.95; lib bdg $11.88 **E**

1. Brothers—Fiction 2. Infants—Fiction
ISBN 0-688-07423-5; 0-688-07424-3 (lib bdg) LC 87-17296

"Little brother keeps throwing his Teddy bear until he finally topples the block city Big Brother is building. All ends well when understanding Big Brother realizes that Little Brother only wants to help. After hugs and kisses, the project is started over again—together." Child Book Rev Serv

"Once again John Steptoe expresses his individuality and skill as an artist. . . . With simplicity of style and soft, pastel colored pencil drawings the author-artist depicts the tender, caring relationship of an older brother for his baby brother." Horn Book

Stevie. Harper & Row 1969 unp il $12.95; lib bdg $12.88; pa $3.95 **E**

1. Blacks—Fiction
ISBN 0-06-025763-6; 0-06-025764-4 (lib bdg); 0-06-443122-3 (pa) LC 69-16700

A small black boy, Robert "tells the story of the intruder, Stevie, who comes to stay at his house because both parents are working. Stevie is a pest. He tags along after Robert, he messes up toys, he wants everything he sees. Worst of all, 'my momma never said nothin' to him.' But Robert is an only child, and after Stevie goes, the house is still. He remembers the games they played, the way Stevie looked up to him." Saturday Rev

"Warm and touching, the first-person story is effectively told in idiomatic language and is illustrated with expressive lifelike paintings in dark and brilliant colors." Booklist

Stevenson, James, 1929-

"Could be worse!". Greenwillow Bks. 1977 unp il $13.95; lib bdg $13.88 **E**

1. Grandfathers—Fiction 2. Dreams—Fiction
ISBN 0-688-80075-0; 0-688-84075-2 (lib bdg) LC 76-28534

"Two children comment on the fact that their grandfather, a quiet, harassed-looking gentleman, goes through the same routine every morning. Same food. Same reactions to any reports of trouble by the children: 'Could be worse.' But one day Grandpa fools them and tells a long, involved story of a dream-fantasy in which he went from one peril to another. 'What do you think of that?' And the children gleefully shout, 'Could be worse!'" Bull Cent Child Books

"Stevenson's sketchy watercolors, arranged in panels, trace Grandpa's adventures as he wanders precipitously through air, over land, and under sea, into and out of danger. A read-aloud picture story guaranteed to tickle young funny bones and, without prompting, to elicit a chorus of 'could be worse' before the last page is turned." Booklist

Other available titles about Grandpa, Mary Ann, and Louie are:
Grandpa's great city tour (1983)
Grandpa's too-good garden (1989)
The great big especially beautiful Easter egg (1983)
No friends (1986)
That dreadful day (1985)
That terrible Halloween night (1980)
There's nothing to do! (1986)
We can't sleep (1982)
We hate rain! (1988)
What's under my bed? (1983)
Will you please feed our cat? (1987)
Worse than Willy! (1984)

Emma. Greenwillow Bks. 1985 unp il $11.75; lib bdg $11.88; pa $3.95 **E**

1. Witches—Fiction
ISBN 0-688-04020-9; 0-688-04021-7 (lib bdg); 0-688-07336-0 (pa) LC 84-4141

"Stevenson tells the story of two green-faced broom-flying witches, Lavinia and Dolores, who are looking for something terrible to do, and a pint-sized amiable witch named Emma, who wants to fly." SLJ

"The exaggerated humor, obvious characterization, straightforward plotline, and 'right over might' theme are well suited to the comic-book format, balloon-encased dialogue, agile line, and no-nonsense colors: Emma's curls are electric red, the witches' faces pea green. Like the Saturday afternoon movies of the thirties and forties, this book should enthrall a restless audience. And while it is an obvious alternative to ghouls and ghosties for Halloween, it is not limited to one season." Horn Book

Other available titles about Emma, Lavinia, and Dolores are:
Emma at the beach(1990)
Fried feathers for Thanksgiving (1986)
Happy Valentine's Day, Emma! (1987)
Un-Happy New Year, Emma! (1989)
Yuck! (1984)

Fast friends; two stories. Greenwillow Bks. 1979 64p il lib bdg $10.88 **E**

1. Friendship—Fiction 2. Animals—Fiction
ISBN 0-688-84197-X LC 78-14828

"A Greenwillow read-alone book"

"'Fast friends' is an apt pun for [these] two stories. In the first, the better tale, a snail and a turtle discover the speedy joys of skateboarding. In the second, a mouse and a turtle learn about the reciprocity of friendship. James Stevenson's loose jointed illustrations keep things moving." SLJ

Monty. Greenwillow Bks. 1979 unp il lib bdg $12.88 **E**

1. Alligators—Fiction 2. Animals—Fiction
ISBN 0-688-84209-7 LC 78-11409

"Tom, Doris, and Arthur (a rabbit, a duck, and a frog) always call for their alligator friend Monty when it's time to cross the river to get to school. One day Monty decides he's had enough of being taken for granted, enough of listening to his three friends order him about with 'Don't wobble so much,' 'Let's see some more speed,' and 'More to the right!' He announces he's taking a vacation. The efforts the three students make to find another way to cross the river are hilarious." Bull Cent Child Books

Another available title about Monty is:
No need for Monty (1987)

Stevenson, James, 1929-—*Continued*

Mr. Hacker; pictures by Frank Modell. Greenwillow Bks. 1990 32p il $12.95; lib bdg $12.88 **E**

1. Cats—Fiction 2. Dogs—Fiction
ISBN 0-688-09216-0; 0-688-09217-9 (lib bdg)
LC 89-30479

Mr. Hacker begins to regret his move from the noisy city to the quiet country, until he is befriended by a stray cat and dog

"This never becomes sentimental, mainly because Mr. Hacker and the stray animals are cantankerous individuals. Angry, astonished, bewildered, he's distractedly trying to get the right food to the right animal at the right time, and it's not easy because—though the animals are never anthropomorphized—they're as odd and assertive as he is. A funny, gentle pet story that will have wide appeal." Booklist

"The expressive illustrations, in watercolor and black pen, capture the often rewarding, sometimes frustrating relationship between man and beast." Horn Book

National Worm Day. Greenwillow Bks. 1990 40p il $12.95; lib bdg $12.88 **E**

1. Animals—Fiction
ISBN 0-688-08771-X; 0-688-08772-8 (lib bdg)
LC 88-34915

This volume contains three stories about Herbie the worm, Daisy the mole, Amelia the snail, and Rupert the rhinoceros

"Stevenson's watercolor illustrations are as marvelous as ever, with his careful use of white space enhancing his cartoon style. His characters come alive with their own distinct personalities and types of humor. His use of ironic wit will make children chuckle and will bring them back again and again to the funny antics of these lovable animals." SLJ

The night after Christmas. Greenwillow Bks. 1981 unp il $13.95; lib bdg $13.88 **E**

1. Teddy bears—Fiction 2. Dolls—Fiction 3. Dogs—Fiction
ISBN 0-688-00547-0; 0-688-00548-9 (lib bdg)
LC 81-1022

"Replaced by new toys, an old teddy bear and a worn-out doll are thrown away the day after Christmas. They try to make a new life for themselves, but it is a stray dog who befriends them and finds a way for them to become beloved toys again." Child Book Rev Serv

"The author's style is casual but smooth, his structure tight, and his illustrations, especially the snow-swirled outdoor scenes, evocative." Bull Cent Child Books

Quick! turn the page! Greenwillow Bks. 1990 unp il $12.95; lib bdg $12.88 **E**

ISBN 0-688-09308-6; 0-688-09309-4 (lib bdg)
LC 89-34616

"To find out what happens when Eddie has nobody to play with, or how the mouse will get past the cat, readers are told to turn the page. In most cases, a problem or question is depicted on one page, and its solution or answer on the next." SLJ

"Preschoolers will love these happy, wry solutions to all sorts of zany predicaments and desires. Stevenson's scratchy, cartoon-style, color drawings, sharpened by his whimsical sense of humor, make this a delightful find for young children." Booklist

The stowaway. Greenwillow Bks. 1990 unp il $12.95; lib bdg $12.88 **E**

1. Mice—Fiction 2. Steamboats—Fiction
ISBN 0-688-08619-5; 0-688-08620-9 (lib bdg)
LC 89-25861

Companion volume to: The Sea View Hotel (1978)

Hubie, the mouse, goes on "vacation with his parents, aboard the ocean liner *Hedonia*, circa 1936. Seasick in the lap of luxury, Hubie wishes for the trip to end; but when he encounters a mysterious stowaway, he finds adventure and friendship. The cartoon-style format, with several illustrations per page and thought/speech balloons carrying the text, gives the pages a busy look, but Stevenson's informal style is part of his charm. His many fans will find this a pleasant excursion." Booklist

Which one is Whitney? Greenwillow Bks. 1990 40p il $12.95; lib bdg $12.88 **E**

ISBN 0-688-09061-3; 0-688-09062-1 (lib bdg)
LC 89-34614

Follows the amusing adventures of Whitney, a clever dugong, as he tries to find his place in the world

"Stevenson may be the first to feature a dugong as a protagonist; in his gifted hands this slow, fat, marine mammal has truly childlike qualities and great appeal. Three chapter-stories in an easy-to-read picture book introduce clever Whitney, a fast thinker and slow drifter. Stevenson's familiar watercolor and black pen illustrations are right on target, enhancing the humor of the vignettes." SLJ

The worst person in the world. Greenwillow Bks. 1978 unp il lib bdg $12.88 **E**

1. Friendship—Fiction
ISBN 0-688-84127-9 LC 77-22141

"A grumpy old man known as the worst person in the world lives alone in a neglected old house until a friendly creature named Ugly follows him home, tidies up, and invites the neighborhood children to a party." Publisher's note

"A blithe if predictable story illustrated by cartoon-style drawings. . . . Not the sturdiest of plots or the most original concept, but the style is jaunty and the pictures amusing." Bull Cent Child Books

Stock, Catherine

Armien's fishing trip. Morrow Junior Bks. 1990 unp il $13.95; lib bdg $13.88 **E**

1. Fishing—Fiction 2. South Africa—Fiction
ISBN 0-688-08395-1; 0-688-08396-X (lib bdg)
LC 89-3266

While visiting his aunt and uncle in the little South African village of Kalk Bay, Armien stows away in his uncle's fishing boat and becomes an unexpected hero

"This is universal adventure specifically set. The town and Armien's friends are an ethnic and cultural mix, a fishing community united by their bond with the sea. Double-page spreads of all the neighbors at the dock are likewise multi-colorful, a strong and sunny contrast to the stormy, blue-washed pages of Armien's heroic rescue of fisherman Sam." Bull Cent Child Books

Stolz, Mary, 1920-

Emmett's pig; pictures by Garth Williams. Harper & Row 1959 61p il lib bdg $10.89 **E**

1. Pigs—Fiction
ISBN 0-06-025856-X LC 58-7763

"An I can read book"

"Although Emmett lives in a city apartment and is surrounded by toy pigs, pictures and books about pigs, his great desire for a real live pig is finally granted as a birthday present—a pig to be his own, but to be boarded on a farm outside the city." Wis Libr Bull

This book is "far above the average in both interest and illustration." Bookmark

Storm in the night; illustrated by Pat Cummings. Harper & Row 1988 unp il $13.95; lib bdg $13.89; pa $4.95 **E**

1. Thunderstorms—Fiction 2. Grandfathers—Fiction 3. Fear—Fiction
ISBN 0-06-025912-4; 0-06-025913-2 (lib bdg); 0-06-443256-4 (pa) LC 85-45838

After a power failure during a thunderstorm, Thomas, his grandfather and Ringo the cat go out on the porch. Grandfather tells Thomas a story of his own childhood fear of storms and how concern for his equally frightened pet helped him to overcome it

"Presenting a glorified portrayal of a white cat, a beautiful black child, and a gentle old man, the dark, shadowy paintings are made luminous by 'the carrot-colored flames in the wood stove' or by lightning slashing across the navy-blue sky; every illustration is imbued with the boy's sensory awareness during a night of wonder and discovery." Horn Book

Swift, Hildegarde Hoyt, d. 1977

The little red lighthouse and the great gray bridge; by Hildegarde H. Swift and Lynd Ward. Harcourt Brace Jovanovich 1942 unp il $15.95; pa $4.95 **E**

1. George Washington Bridge (N.Y. and N.J.)—Fiction 2. Lighthouses—Fiction
ISBN 0-15-247040-9; 0-15-652840-1 (pa) LC 42-36286

"After the great beacon atop the . . . George Washington Bridge was installed, the little red lighthouse feared he would no longer be useful, but when an emergency arose, the little lighthouse proved that he was still important." Hodges. Books for Elem Sch Libr

"The story is written with imagination and a gift for bringing alive this little lighthouse and its troubles. . . . [Lynd Ward's] illustrations have some distinction and one in particular, the fog creeping over the river clutching at the river boats, has atmosphere, rhythm and good colour." Ont Libr Rev

Szilagyi, Mary

Thunderstorm. Bradbury Press 1985 unp il $12.95 **E**

1. Thunderstorms—Fiction 2. Fear—Fiction
ISBN 0-02-788580-1 LC 84-24570

A little girl is comforted by her mother during a thunderstorm and she in turn comforts the family dog

"The atmospheric conditions are vividly portrayed in strong, softly-colored drawings—particularly lovely is a double-page illustration of a brilliantly blue bird flying in the sudden hush that precedes the storm. The little girl and the dog are all the more special for being rather plain and ordinary. A common occurrence of immense interest to most children, well and carefully portrayed." Horn Book

Tafuri, Nancy

The ball bounced. Greenwillow Bks. 1989 unp il $11.95 **E**

ISBN 0-688-07871-0 LC 87-37582

"A baby, hitching a ride in his mother's laundry basket, throws a ball. Off it goes, scaring the cat, dog, and bird and bouncing into a table and door until it finally stops at the baby's basket. 'And the baby laughed.' Tafuri accompanies the simple story line with her distinctive large, full-colored pictures done in water-color paints and black pen outlines." SLJ

Do not disturb. Greenwillow Bks. 1987 unp il $11.75; lib bdg $11.88 **E**

1. Camping—Fiction 2. Animals—Fiction 3. Stories without words
ISBN 0-688-06541-4; 0-688-06542-2 (lib bdg) LC 86-357

"A few succinct words—'It was the first day of summer'—help to establish the fact that a family of one dog, two parents, and three children are setting up camp near a woodland lake. Now the narrative becomes purely pictorial, with definitive line drawing, enticing color, and interesting perspectives." Horn Book

Early morning in the barn. Greenwillow Bks. 1983 unp il $14.95; lib bdg $14.88; Puffin Bks. pa $3.95 **E**

1. Animals—Fiction 2. Stories without words
ISBN 0-688-02328-2; 0-688-02329-0 (lib bdg); 0-14-050511-3 (pa) LC 83-1436

"With sunup on the farm comes a cock crowing, a mother hen and chicks running outside, and an array of other familiar barnyard animals all greeting the morning with their respective vocalizations." Booklist

"This boldly colorful, wordless picture book (the only text is some animal sounds) is a perfect beginning book for the nursery set. The colors have the impact of poster paint but with some of the subtle gradations of watercolors. The young reader can watch the travels of new chicks past quacking ducks, baaing lambs, and slurping pigs as they go to their mother. A charmer." Child Book Rev Serv

Follow me! Greenwillow Bks. 1990 unp il $13.95; lib bdg $13.88 **E**

1. Seals (Animals)—Fiction 2. Crabs—Fiction 3. Stories without words
ISBN 0-688-08773-6; 0-688-08774-4 (lib bdg) LC 89-23259

"A baby sea lion exhibits the curiosity of a youngster as the baby explores a crab's world. Children will have no trouble following the wordless story told in Tafuri's usual direct, appealing style. Mama sea lion's careful observation of the journey is the ultimate reassurance." Horn Book Guide

Tafuri, Nancy—*Continued*

Have you seen my duckling? Greenwillow Bks. 1984 unp il $13.95; lib bdg $13.88; Puffin Bks. pa $3.95 E

1. Ducks—Fiction
ISBN 0-688-02797-0; 0-688-02798-9 (lib bdg); 0-14-050532-6 (pa) LC 83-17196

A Caldecott Medal honor book, 1985

"In a picture book virtually wordless except for the repeated question of the title, seven ducklings obediently cluster in their nest, while the eighth—more daring and more curious—scrambles after an errant butterfly. Succeeding pages depict the mother duck's anxious search for her offspring among the flora and fauna of a watery habitat. But, as anyone can see, the venturesome duckling has not strayed far, and it is thoroughly enjoying a small measure of freedom just beyond the range of the mother's vision." Horn Book

"Tafuri's artwork . . . features clean lines, generous figures, and clear, cool colors. She also adds nice detail—feathers, for instance, that you can almost feel under your hands." Booklist

Rabbit's morning. Greenwillow Bks. 1985 unp il $13.95; lib bdg $13.88 E

1. Rabbits—Fiction 2. Stories without words
ISBN 0-688-04063-2; 0-688-04064-0 (lib bdg) LC 84-10229

"In a nearly wordless picture book, a young rabbit explores the meadow, sighting neighboring beavers, deer, mice, pheasants and other animals in the course of its journey. Tafuri's watercolors contain the essence of a summer dawn's translucence, incorporating minimal text into borderless double-page spreads filled with animals and their babies that are certain to appeal to preschoolers and beginning readers." SLJ

Taylor, Mark

Henry the explorer; illustrations by Graham Booth. Atheneum Pubs. 1966 unp il o.p.; Little, Brown paperback available $5.95 E

ISBN 0-316-83384-3 (pa) LC 66-9534

"One morning after breakfast Henry packed his explorer's kit and, with his dog, set out to explore the world. By nightfall he had made several important discoveries—including the fact that he was far from home and unsure of the way. Henry's safe return ahead of the search party and his anticipation of his next exploring expedition climax . . . [a] mildly suspenseful picture-book story." Booklist

Tejima, Keizaburō

Fox's dream; by Tejima. Philomel Bks. 1987 unp il lib bdg $13.95; pa $5.95 E

1. Foxes—Fiction
ISBN 0-399-21455-0 (lib bdg); 0-399-22017-8 (pa) LC 86-30295

Wandering through a winter forest, a lonely fox has an enchanting vision and then finds the companionship for which he has been longing

"It is the compelling power of the colored woodcuts that will attract readers to this book; but on more careful consideration, readers will find that the text conveys the quiet sensitivity of haiku poetry which perfectly matches the Japanese woodcuts." SLJ

Owl lake; by Tejima. Philomel Bks. 1987 unp il lib bdg $13.95 E

1. Night—Fiction 2. Owls—Fiction
ISBN 0-399-21426-7 LC 86-25173

"In this translation of a prize winning Japanese picture book, the life of an owl family is presented through simple poetic language accompanied by large, striking woodcuts. Tejima's woodcuts, in four colors, fill the pages with bold artistic expression. . . . Tejima has successfully designed a simple, realistic presentation of the life of a nocturnal creature." SLJ

Testa, Fulvio, 1947-

If you take a paintbrush; a book of colors. Dial Bks. for Young Readers 1983 unp il hardcover o.p. paperback available $3.95 E

1. Color
ISBN 0-8037-0282-5 (pa) LC 82-45512

"The book begins with endpapers that have tubes of paint, rulers, compasses, and other art supplies scattered in delightful disarray. Following this are short but clear statements about a color—'yellow is the color of the sun.' This faces a bordered picture that features the sun beating down on the sands of the desert as two children atop a camel ride by. 'Brown is the color of chocolate' is illustrated by two young bakers watching as a third oozes frosting down the side of a cake." Booklist

"Simple, yet imaginative, the book deals with the concept of color in an attractive, appealing manner." Child Book Rev Serv

If you take a pencil. Dial Bks. for Young Readers 1982 unp il $10.95; pa $3.95 E

1. Drawing—Fiction 2. Counting
ISBN 0-8037-4023-9; 0-8037-0165-9 (pa) LC 82-1505

This story describes "the busy day of two friends who take a pencil and draw two cats. Three, four and more numbers follow, represented by bright scenes in a garden (six orange trees), until the playmates land on a desert island with 12 treasure chests, empty except for one with 'a small treasure—a pencil.'" Publ Wkly

"In the guise of a counting book, this is actually an exceedingly handsome and amusing gallery of pictures by Fulvio Testa. . . . Funny, mysterious, playful, hiding numerous puzzles within the pictures, anticipating later pictures in earlier ones, the book serves as much to elicit stories out of its perusers as to tell stories to them." SLJ

Thaler, Mike, 1936-

Owly; pictures by David Wiesner. Harper & Row 1982 unp il $12.95; lib bdg $12.89 E

1. Owls—Fiction
ISBN 0-06-026151-X; 0-06-026152-8 (lib bdg) LC 81-47727

When Owly asks his mother question after question about the world, she finds just the right ways to help him find the answers

"This is a charming bedtime story sure to inspire a cozy moment between parent and child. Soft washes lend

Thaler, Mike, 1936-—*Continued*
some feeling to the tale, but the slightly cartooned Owly and his mother don't engender as much response as the words do." Booklist

Thayer, Jane, 1904-

The popcorn dragon; written by Jane Thayer; illustrated by Lisa McCue. Morrow Junior Bks. 1989 unp il $12.95; lib bdg $12.88 E

1. Dragons—Fiction
ISBN 0-688-08340-4; 0-688-08876-7 (lib bdg) LC 88-39855

A newly illustrated edition of the title first published 1953

Though his hot breath is the envy of all the other animals, a young dragon learns that showing off does not make friends

"McCue's new full-color illustrations capture the whimsical mood of the fable. The animals, although too coy, have appealing humanlike expressions which convey their envy and contempt." SLJ

The puppy who wanted a boy; illustrated by Lisa McCue. Morrow 1986 unp il hardcover o.p. paperback available $4.95 E

1. Dogs—Fiction 2. Christmas—Fiction
ISBN 0-688-08293-9 (pa) LC 85-15465

A newly illustrated edition of the title first published 1958

"More than anything in the world, Petey, a puppy, wanted a boy for Christmas. Nothing else his mother suggested would do, and none of the other dogs would give him their boys. Dejected, Petey passes the Home for Boys where a lonely newcomer sits on the steps. Petey has found not one boy, but 50 boys full of love." SLJ

"It is the same, somewhat sentimental but certainly appealing tale that Thayer fashioned in 1958, when this was originally published; however, McCue's affectionately drawn, warmly colored illustrations go a long way toward perking up the story. What dog lover can resist a puppy who longs for and finally finds a home? Not many, and McCue's Petey will go straight to their hearts." Booklist

Thiele, Colin, 1920-

Farmer Schulz's ducks; illustrated by Mary Milton. Harper & Row 1988 c1986 32p il $12.95; lib bdg $12.89 E

1. Ducks—Fiction 2. Australia—Fiction
ISBN 0-06-026182-X; 0-06-026183-8 (lib bdg) LC 87-21713

First published 1986 in Australia

After the growing traffic from the nearby city turns the road next to their Australian farm into a dangerous highway, Farmer Schulz's youngest daughter Anna solves the problem of how to get her family's ducks safely across the road every day

"A charming story, related in descriptive prose which almost enables readers to smell the Australian countryside. The accompanying watercolor illustrations are strong in color and design, and each is set off by plenty of white space." SLJ

Thomas, Jane Resh, 1936-

Saying good-bye to Grandma; illustrated by Marcia Sewall. Clarion Bks. 1988 48p il lib bdg $13.95 E

1. Death—Fiction 2. Grandmothers—Fiction
ISBN 0-89919-645-4 LC 87-20826

"An anecdotal account of seven-year-old Suzie's trip to her grandparent's house to attend her grandmother's funeral. Activities with her cousins, her feelings about her grandmother, and relating to her grieving grandfather are all conveyed." Child Book Rev Serv

"Marcia Sewall's colorful, loose, almost faceless illustrations are just sketchy enough to contribute to the book's universality; a child could picture himself or herself in any of these scenes." N Y Times Book Rev

Thompson, Carol

Time. Delacorte Press 1989 unp il $12.95 E

1. Bears—Fiction 2. Time—Fiction
ISBN 0-385-29765-3 LC 88-18148

"A day in the life of Little Bear features each of his activities with a question, 'What time is it?' The page opposite displays the time on a colorful clock with the corresponding word under it. The simple minimal text along with the illustrations will help young children learn the concept of time." Child Book Rev Serv

Thornhill, Jan

The wildlife 1 2 3; a nature counting book. Simon & Schuster Bks. for Young Readers 1989 unp il $14.95 E

1. Counting 2. Animals
ISBN 0-671-67926-0 LC 89-5970

Illustrations of animals from around the world accompany the numbers one to twenty, twenty-five, fifty, 100, and 1000. Notes in the back of the book describe the animals

"Thornhill goes far beyond the realm of the traditional counting book and gives children a myraid of fascinating images to dream upon. From a picturesque panda to orange-eyed alligators, the author uses color and action to create a visual extravaganza." Sci Child

Titherington, Jeanne, 1951-

Pumpkin, pumpkin. Greenwillow Bks. 1986 23p il $13.95; lib bdg $13.88; pa $3.95 E

ISBN 0-688-05695-4; 0-688-05696-2 (lib bdg); 0-688-09930-0 (pa) LC 84-25334

"Softly colored pencil illustrations in a realistic style effectively communicate Jamie's pride as a very young gardener. He plants a seed, then grows and harvests a pumpkin from which he saves seeds for next year. The large, detailed drawings capture Jamie's anticipation and pleasure just right. The garden creatures appearing on every page and grandpa, whom we catch sight of now and then, are a delightful supporting cast. Nonreaders can easily follow the story in pictures alone. Very large, clear print on facing pages makes the simple narrative inviting for beginning readers, too." SLJ

Tompert, Ann, 1918-

Grandfather Tang's story; illustrated by Robert Andrew Parker. Crown 1990 unp il $12.95; lib bdg $13.99 **E**

1. Foxes—Fiction
ISBN 0-517-57487-X; 0-517-57272-9 (lib bdg)
LC 89-22205

"An old Chinese man sits beneath a tree with his granddaughter, telling her the tale of two foxes who change themselves into ever-fiercer animals as they compete for dominance. As he speaks, he rearranges two tangram puzzles to form the shapes of the animals. . . . Directions for making tangrams, described as ancient Chinese puzzles, appear on the book's last page." Booklist

"Parker's watercolor washes complement the text, adding energy and tension, as well as evoking oriental brushwork technique. However, the text is strong enough to stand on its own, and will be valued by storytellers and listeners alike." SLJ

Little fox goes to the end of the world; a story by Ann Tompert; with pictures by John Wallner. Crown 1976 unp il o.p.; Scholastic paperback available $3.95 **E**

1. Foxes—Fiction
ISBN 0-590-41467-4 (pa) LC 75-44381

"A wily little fox tells mother of her plans to travel to the end of the world. Mother is afraid for her, but Little Fox is prepared for all contingencies. With child-like bravado the young vixen describes how she would fend off bears, elephants and crocodiles on her voyage." N Y Times Book Rev

"The brief story is related in the style of a child's exuberant prattle, with the setting rapidly switching from forest to mountains to sea. Wallner's bold, colorful crayon illustrations are so full of action that they seem to leap off the oversized pages." SLJ

Nothing sticks like a shadow; illustrated by Lynn Munsinger. Houghton Mifflin 1984 32p il lib bdg $12.95; pa $4.95 **E**

1. Shades and shadows—Fiction 2. Animals—Fiction
ISBN 0-395-35391-2 (lib bdg); 0-395-47950-9 (pa)
LC 83-18554

"Woodchuck bets Rabbit a new hat he can't escape his shadow, whereupon the latter progresses from one trick to dozens more, trying to prove that he can." Publ Wkly

"There have been many books about shadows; this is one of the better ones. The soft pastel illustrations, combined with the large, easy-to-read print, will fascinate young readers so much that they will not want to put the book down until they discover whether rabbit can ever lose his shadow." Child Book Rev Serv

Tresselt, Alvin R.

Hide and seek fog; by Alvin Tresselt; illustrated by Roger Duvoisin. Lothrop, Lee & Shepard Bks. 1965 unp il lib bdg $14.88; pa $3.95 **E**

1. Fog
ISBN 0-688-51169-4 (lib bdg); 0-688-07813-3 (pa)
LC 65-14087

A Caldecott Medal honor book, 1966

"This is not a plotted story but rather a mood picture book . . . describing a fog which rolls in from the sea to veil an Atlantic seacoast village for three days. The beautiful paintings, most of them double-spreads, and the brief, poetic text sensitively and effectively evoke the atmosphere of the 'worst fog in twenty years' and depict the reactions of children and grown-ups to it." Booklist

Rain drop splash; by Alvin Tresselt; pictures by Leonard Weisgard. Lothrop, Lee & Shepard Bks. 1946 unp il lib bdg $13.88 **E**

1. Rain and rainfall
ISBN 0-688-51165-1 LC 46-11878

A Caldecott Medal honor book, 1947

"The brief, poetic text follows the falling raindrops as they form first a puddle and then a pond, spilling over into a brook, tumbling into a lake, overflowing into a river until, just before the sun comes out, the river flows into the sea." Bookmark

"Striking pictures in tones of yellow and brown . . . describe a rainstorm in terms a small child can understand." Booklist

Wake up, city! [by] Alvin Tresselt; pictures by Carolyn Ewing. Lothrop, Lee & Shepard Bks. 1990 unp il $12.95; lib bdg $12.88 **E**

1. City life—Fiction
ISBN 0-688-08652-7; 0-688-08653-5 (lib bdg)
LC 89-45901

A revised and newly illustrated edition of the title first published 1957

"Tresselt's description of some of the things that happen when the day starts in a large city are just as applicable now as then; Ewing's paintings add some touches that will please feminists (a policewoman, a woman bus driver—at least, a bus driver who could be a woman) and some that relect the architectural variety, the bustle of various activities, and the multiracial composition of the urban scene." Bull Cent Child Books

White snow, bright snow; by Alvin Tresselt; illustrated by Roger Duvoisin. Lothrop, Lee & Shepard Bks. 1988 c1947 unp il $11.95; lib bdg $11.88; pa $3.95 **E**

1. Snow—Fiction
ISBN 0-688-41161-4; 0-688-51161-9 (lib bdg); 0-688-08294-7 (pa) LC 88-10018

Awarded the Caldecott Medal, 1948

A reissue of the title first published 1947

When it begins to look, feel, and smell like snow, everyone prepares for a winter blizzard

Turkle, Brinton Cassaday, 1915-

Deep in the forest; by Brinton Turkle. Dutton 1976 unp il $12.95; pa $3.95 **E**

1. Bears—Fiction 2. Stories without words
ISBN 0-525-28617-9; 0-525-44322-3 (pa)
LC 76-21691

"An inquisitive bear cub wanders away from his mother and discovers an attractive, well-kept log cabin in the forest. Like Goldilocks in the fairy tale, he sam-

Turkle, Brinton Cassaday, 1915- — *Continued*

ples food, chairs, and beds, and the havoc he raises is discovered by the little girl and her parents upon their return from a walk. Except for the names on the porridge bowls, the book is wordless. The gray, yellow, and white illustrations not only give a rustic early American charm to the interior scenes but graphically portray the emotions of the bears and of the human beings." Horn Book

Do not open; by Brinton Turkle. Dutton 1981 unp il $13.95; pa $3.95 **E**

1. Seashore—Fiction 2. Cats—Fiction 3. Magic—Fiction
ISBN 0-525-28785-X; 0-525-44224-3 (pa)
LC 80-10289

"Elderly Miss Moody and her cat, Captain Kidde, find a bottle on the seashore. Miss Moody ignores the label warning 'DO NOT OPEN' and liberates a horror. But the spunky woman tells the thing only mice scare her so it becomes a mouse that Kidde takes care of 'tout de suite.'" Publ Wkly

"The strong, simple composition that is typical of Turkle is especially well suited to the still isolation of deserted beaches, and the combination of rich color used with restraint and the framed squares of clear print adds to the visual appeal of the pages. The story is a nice blend of realism and fantasy." Bull Cent Child Books

Obadiah the Bold; story and pictures by Brinton Turkle. Viking 1965 unp il $13.95; Puffin Bks. pa $3.95 **E**

1. Society of Friends—Fiction 2. Nantucket (Mass.)—Fiction
ISBN 0-670-52001-2; 0-14-050233-5 (pa)
LC 65-13350

"This story, with its setting in Nantucket about one hundred years ago, shows young Obadiah in the midst of a happy Quaker family. Brothers will tease, however, and when Obadiah wants to 'play pirate' (in hopes of someday being one), he is not spared a little fright. An understanding father helps his son think about following in the footsteps of another kind of seafarer, his grandfather, Captain Obadiah Starbuck." Read Ladders for Hum Relat. 6th edition

Other available titles about Obadiah are:
The adventures of Obadiah (1972)
Rachel and Obadiah (1978)
Thy friend, Obadiah (1969)

Turner, Ann Warren

Heron Street; paintings by Lisa Desimini. Harper & Row 1989 unp il $12.95; lib bdg $14.89 **E**

1. Man—Influence on nature—Fiction
ISBN 0-06-026184-6; 0-06-026185-4 (lib bdg)
LC 87-24948

"A Charlotte Zolotow book"

A story "about the development of and changes in a marsh from the time of its settlement before the American Revolution through the present." SLJ

"While the narrative is a comprehensible entity, it takes on added dimension when accompanied by the brilliantly colored paintings. The artist's rich, gemstone shades in conjunction with repeated, somewhat stylized shapes transform realistic detail into panoramic impressions—an ideal interpretation for the narrative perspective while setting it in a specific time and locale." Horn Book

Through moon and stars and night skies; by Ann Turner; pictures by James Graham Hale. Harper & Row 1989 unp il $12.95; lib bdg $12.89 **E**

1. Adoption—Fiction 2. Parent and child—Fiction
ISBN 0-06-026189-7; 0-06-026190-0 (lib bdg)
LC 87-35044

"A Charlotte Zolotow book"

A boy who came from Southeast Asia to be adopted by a couple in this country remembers how unfamiliar and frightening some of the things were in his new home, before he accepted the love to be found there

"This touching, memorable tale is illustrated in warm watercolor-and-ink pictures that gently contrast the narrator's Asian home with his new life in America. It will serve as a meaningful introduction to adoption as well as a starting point for a discussion on cultural transitions." SLJ

Udry, Janice May

The moon jumpers; pictures by Maurice Sendak. Harper & Row 1959 unp il $14.95 **E**

1. Night—Fiction
ISBN 0-06-026145-5
LC 58-7757

A Caldecott Medal honor book, 1960

"Here is a child's exhilaration and enchantment with the liveliness of summer nights, with the magic of moonlight and the downy warmth of the night wind. The goldfish play with the moonfish in the lily pond, the fireflies come from the woods, and a giant moth flies by on his search for moon flowers. At this time the call of 'Children, oh, children' from the house is meaningless, for there are no children present, only Moon Jumpers." Lutheran Educ

"There are black-and-white drawings and brief text in between double-page spreads in full luminous color. The pictures are the kind that children can enter directly 'into' and feel . . . the exhilaration of just being alive and full of motion." Horn Book

A tree is nice; pictures by Marc Simont. Harper & Row 1956 unp il $12.95; lib bdg $12.89; pa $4.95 **E**

1. Trees—Fiction
ISBN 0-06-026155-2; 0-06-026156-0 (lib bdg); 0-06-443147-9 (pa)
LC 56-5153

Awarded the Caldecott Medal, 1957

"In childlike terms and in enticing pictures, colored and black and white, author and artist set forth reasons why trees are nice to have around—trees fill up the sky, they make everything beautiful, cats get away from dogs in them, leaves come down and can be played in, and trees are nice to climb in, to hang a swing in, or to plant. A picture book sure to please young children." Booklist

Udry, Janice May—*Continued*

What Mary Jo shared; pictures: Eleanor Mill. Whitman, A. 1966 unp il lib bdg $12.95; Scholastic pa $2.25 **E**

1. Blacks—Fiction 2. School stories
ISBN 0-8075-8842-3 (lib bdg); 0-590-40731-7 (pa)
LC 66-16082

"Whenever Mary Jo selected something to 'show and tell', her classmates had already chosen it. Finally she brought a very special person to share with the class—her father." N Y Public Libr. Black Exper in Child Books

"The writing is smooth and natural, and the illustrations, done in soft colors and black and white, are charming." We Build Together

Ungerer, Tomi, 1931-

Crictor. Harper & Row 1958 32p il $12.95; lib bdg $12.89; pa $4.95 **E**

1. Snakes—Fiction
ISBN 0-06-026180-3; 0-06-026181-1 (lib bdg); 0-06-443044-8 (pa)
LC 58-5288

"An entertaining bit of nonsense about the boa constrictor that was sent to Madame Bodot, who lived and taught school in a little French town. She called the snake Crictor and he became a great pet, learned, debonair and brave. The boys used him for a slide and the girls for a jump-rope. When Crictor captured a burglar by coiling around him until the police came, he was awarded impressive tokens of esteem and affection of the townspeople. Engaging line drawings echo the restrained and elegant absurdities of the text." Bull Cent Child Books

Moon Man. Harper & Row 1967 40p il lib bdg $12.89; pa $4.95 **E**

1. Science fiction
ISBN 0-06-026235-4 (lib bdg); 0-06-443052-9 (pa)
LC 66-12135

First published 1966 in the United Kingdom

"Descending to Earth on the fiery tail of a comet Moon Man is captured and thrown into jail by panicky officials as a suspected invader. He escapes by means of unique lunar powers, has a gay time until the police begin pursuit and then, realizing that he can never live peacefully on this planet, returns to the moon via a spacecraft built by a long-forgotten scientist. The cleverly imaginative tale and the boldly drawn illustrations filled with strong colors, action, and humor make the oversize picture book a natural for small [children]." Booklist

The three robbers. Atheneum Pubs. 1987 c1962 unp il lib bdg $14.95; pa $4.95 **E**

1. Robbers and outlaws—Fiction
ISBN 0-689-31391-8 (lib bdg); 0-689-70418-6 (pa)
LC 87-11549

A reissue of the title first published 1962

Three robbers who roam the countryside are subdued by the charm of a little girl named Tiffany

"With vigorous, sweeping design and stained glass colors on black and midnight blue Tomi Ungerer presents three of the most charming fierce robbers." Christ Sci Monit

Van Allsburg, Chris

Ben's dream; story and pictures by Chris Van Allsburg. Houghton Mifflin 1982 31p il lib bdg $14.95 **E**

1. Dreams—Fiction
ISBN 0-395-32084-4
LC 81-20029

"When rain spoils Ben's ball game with Margaret, he returns to an empty house, falls asleep in his father's chair, and embarks on a dream. In a marvelous series of double-page black-and-white pictures meticulously textured with hatching, one shares Ben's voyage past such sights as the Statue of Liberty, the Sphinx, and the Mount Rushmore presidents, all with flood waters lapping about their respective chins and waists. Dramatic angles, closeups from above and below, and careful architectural details which recall the work of David Macaulay dazzle the eye and the imagination as Ben's little house floats upon the waters on its splendid excursion. . . . A visual tour de force." Horn Book

The garden of Abdul Gasazi; written and illustrated by Chris Van Allsburg. Houghton Mifflin 1979 unp il lib bdg $15.95 **E**

1. Magic—Fiction 2. Dogs—Fiction
ISBN 0-395-27804-X
LC 79-016844

A Caldecott Medal honor book, 1980

"When Fritz, the naughty dog, ran into the garden of Abdul Gasazi, a retired magician, Alan was terrified, for he knew that dogs were not allowed beyond the vine-covered wall. Fritz eluded Alan, who ultimately came to the magician's imposing house and politely requested the return of the dog. His request was granted, but Fritz, who had been turned into a duck, compounded his original naughtiness by flying away with Alan's cap." Horn Book

The full page "lithographlike drawings are astonishing—eerie, monumental, surreal and witty all at once—and the effect of the whole is original and unforgettable." Books of the Times

Jumanji; written and illustrated by Chris Van Allsburg. Houghton Mifflin 1981 unp il $14.95 **E**

1. Games—Fiction
ISBN 0-395-30448-2
LC 80-29632

Awarded the Caldecott Medal, 1982

"Two children, alone at home while their parents are gone for the afternoon, play a game they have found lying under a tree. Judy reads the rules for the game, 'Jumanji,' and realizes that it must be played to the end; not until they begin play do she and Peter know why that's true. With each roll of the dice, there's a new hazard: a menacing lion, a troop of destructive monkeys, a torrential monsoon, a herd of rhinos, etc." Bull Cent Child Books

"Through the masterly use of light and shadow, the interplay of design elements, and audacious changes in perspective and composition, the artist conveys an impression of color without losing the dramatic contrast of black and white." Horn Book

Just a dream. Houghton Mifflin 1990 unp il $17.95 **E**

1. Environmental protection—Fiction 2. Pollution—Fiction 3. Dreams—Fiction
ISBN 0-395-53308-2
LC 90-41343

Van Allsburg, Chris—*Continued*

"Walter, an environmental ignoramus of a 10-year-old, is careless or scornful of such elementary actions as recycling or tree planting. One nightmarish evening, however, he visits a future where his daydreams of technological paradise are demolished. Instead, there is merely a horrifically exacerbated continuation of today's eco-problems: landfills, expressways, smog, lifeless oceans, and vanished wilderness. Walter awakens reformed, and is rewarded with another dream: the future redeemed." SLJ

"Once again Van Allsburg demonstrates his unique artistic magic in combining foresight, wisdom and striking artwork to deliver an ecological message concerning conservation and renewal. . . . The full-color, striking paintings evoke the intense revelations of Walter's dreams." Child Book Rev Serv

The mysteries of Harris Burdick. Houghton Mifflin 1984 unp il lib bdg $14.95 E

ISBN 0-395-35393-9 LC 84-9006

Presents a series of loosely related drawings each accompanied by a title and a caption which the reader may use to make up his or her own story

Rendered in the author's "signature velvet black and white . . . the pictures are nothing short of spectacular. . . . While some may find this just an excuse for handsome artwork, others will see its great potential for stretching a child's imagination. Although the book could be used in countless ways, primarily it will make storytellers of children. They will need little prompting once they set their eyes on Van Allsburg's provocative scenes. An inventive, useful concoction." Booklist

The Polar Express; written and illustrated by Chris Van Allsburg. Houghton Mifflin 1985 unp il $16.95 E

1. North Pole—Fiction 2. Santa Claus—Fiction 3. Christmas—Fiction

ISBN 0-395-38949-6 LC 85-10907

Awarded the Caldecott Medal, 1986

A magical train ride on Christmas Eve takes a boy to the North Pole to receive a special gift from Santa Claus

"Whether the read-aloud audience gets the message or not, they will probably enjoy the several appeals of a story that has Santa Claus and a journey in it; along with older readers-aloud, they will surely appreciate the stunning paintings in which Van Allsburg uses dark, rich colors and misty shapes in contrast with touches of bright white-gold light to create scenes, interior and exterior, that have a quality of mystery that imbues the strong composition to achieve a soft, evocative mood." Bull Cent Child Books

The stranger. Houghton Mifflin 1986 unp il lib bdg $16.95 E

ISBN 0-395-42331-7 LC 86-15235

"A mysterious figure, accidentally struck down by a farmer's truck, stays with the farmer's family until he recovers his memory, participating in the life of the farm. The man—it seems—is Jack Frost, or the spirit of winter; the weather cannot continue its change without him, and when he recalls his function, he takes his leave of his human friends with tears in his eyes." N Y Times Book Rev

"The full-color illustrations, framed in white, evoke an old-fashioned New England landscape at the end of summer; some are remarkably peaceful in tone, others slightly spooky by virtue of brooding colors, unexpected perspectives, or the stranger's peculiar expressions." Bull Cent Child Books

Two bad ants. Houghton Mifflin 1988 31p il lib bdg $16.95 E

1. Ants—Fiction

ISBN 0-395-48668-8 LC 88-12988

"Accustomed to the orderly and uneventful life in the ant hole, all the ants enter the bizarre world of a kitchen in the search for sugar crystals for the queen. Two greedy ants stay behind in the sugar bowl, eating their fill and then falling asleep. Their slumbers end when a giant scoop drops them into a sea of boiling brown coffee. Further mishaps include a heated stay in the toaster, a hazardous swirl in the garbage disposal and a zap in an electrical outlet. When the ant troops return, the two bad ants gladly rejoin their friends and head for the safety of home." Publ Wkly

"The book is a visual tour-de-force. The highly linear, hard-edged drawings look like fine etchings which have been magnified—a technique which enhances the sense of being reduced to ant size." SLJ

The wreck of the Zephyr; written and illustrated by Chris Van Allsburg. Houghton Mifflin 1983 unp il lib bdg $15.95 E

ISBN 0-395-33075-0 LC 82-23371

"The story-within-a-story is a fantasy told by an old man, a tale of a boy who sees flying boats and is determined that he, too, will learn to make his boat, the Zephyr, fly. He succeeds, but the boat is wrecked, and he suffers a broken leg. The tale over, the old man limps away." Bull Cent Child Books

The "story depends heavily on the virtuoso illustrations. Although the book is illustrated in full color, it displays recognizable hallmarks of the artist's work: beauty of composition, striking contrasts of light and shadow, and especially the fascinating ambiguity of illusion and reality. The confident forms and the colors—clean and sharp yet constantly modulating—carry an unusual emotional impact, while the paintings themselves convey a sense of clarity, solidity, and force." Horn Book

The Z was zapped; a play in twenty-six acts; performed by the Caslon Players; written and directed by Chris Van Allsburg. Houghton Mifflin 1987 unp il $16.95 E

1. Alphabet

ISBN 0-395-44612-0 LC 87-14988

At head of title: The Alphabet Theatre proudly presents

This book presents a "series of beautifully executed full-page black-and-white illustrations showing letters undergoing varieties of existential *Angst* on a tasteful little stage, each with an explanatory line of copy printed on its backside." N Y Times Book Rev

"Children can try to guess what action has occured, thereby increasing their vocabulary and the fun, or they can turn the page and read the text, or better yet—do both. This clever romp resembles old vaudeville theater, with one curious act following the next." SLJ

Van Laan, Nancy

Possum come a-knockin'; illustrated by George Booth. Knopf 1990 unp il $11.95; lib bdg $12.99 E

1. Opossums—Fiction 2. Stories in rhyme
ISBN 0-394-82206-4; 0-394-92206-9 (lib bdg)
LC 88-12751

The narrator "sees a possum a-knockin' at the door. While Granny is a-rockin' and a-knittin', and Ma's a-cookin' and Pa's a-fixin', . . . [the boy] unsuccessfully tries to tell them about the possum." Booklist

The author has produced a wonderfully rhythmic and funny trickster tale told in a controlled dialect that is consistent throughout. Booth's critters—possum, cat, and dog—are priceless. Friend possum is the wiliest and slyest varmint one could imagine. The humans are pretty funny, too, while the stage set is appropriately countrified. The story is a raucous romp." Horn Book

Van Leeuwen, Jean

Tales of Oliver Pig; pictures by Arnold Lobel. Dial Bks. for Young Readers 1979 64p il lib bdg $9.89; pa $4.95 E

1. Pigs—Fiction 2. Family life—Fiction
ISBN 0-8037-8736-7 (lib bdg); 0-8037-8737-5 (pa)
LC 79-4276

"Dial easy-to-read"

"Oliver encounters many true-to-life situations and decides how to cope with them: what to do on a rainy day, how to make a bad day into a good one, what to do when Grandma comes, how to dress for the snow, and most confusing, what to do when Mother cries." Child Book Rev Serv

The book is "filled with the warmth of the commonplace, the jostling joys and sorrows of siblings and the love of a pig family. . . . Arnold Lobel's illustrations, often in miniature, carry on the tender, yet never sentimental tone." SLJ

Other available titles about the Pig family are:
Amanda Pig and her big brother Oliver (1982)
More tales of Amanda Pig (1985)
More tales of Oliver Pig (1981)
Oliver, Amanda, and Grandmother Pig (1987)
Oliver and Amanda's Christmas (1989)
Oliver Pig at school (1990)
Tales of Amanda Pig (1983)

Varley, Susan

Badger's parting gifts. Lothrop, Lee & Shepard Bks. 1984 unp il $13; lib bdg $12.88 E

1. Death—Fiction 2. Badgers—Fiction
3. Animals—Fiction
ISBN 0-688-02699-0; 0-688-02703-2 (lib bdg)
LC 83-17500

"Badger is an old animal who has been an inspiration to the other animals throughout his life. Knowing he will soon travel the 'Long Tunnel,' his great desire is to leave something for the others to remember. His legacy is revealed through the accomplishments of the others, all having learned their skills from him." Child Book Rev Serv

"The animal world Varley creates is a gentle place, her pen-and-ink drawings delicately etched, alive with grace and movement and washed with watercolors that register the moods and temperatures and textures of her pastoral setting in this tale of death and friendship." SLJ

Vigna, Judith

Boot weather; story and pictures by Judith Vigna. Whitman, A. 1989 unp il lib bdg $12.95 E

1. Snow—Fiction
ISBN 0-8075-0837-3
LC 88-20563

"When Kim puts on her boots to play in the snow, she can imagine all sorts of exciting adventures. Walking up a slide becomes a mountain climb. Slipping across the ice turns into a moment as a hockey player. In her boots, Kim can go anywhere, do anything, 'and still be home for lunch.'" Booklist

A "likable combination of prepositional instruction and make-believe play. . . . The concept is appealing and instructive, if slightly static in execution, and like Kim's slide, makes a great jumping-off point for adventures in both grammar and fantasy." Bull Cent Child Books

Vincent, Gabrielle

Ernest and Celestine. Greenwillow Bks. 1982 unp il hardcover o.p. paperback available $3.95 E

1. Bears—Fiction 2. Mice—Fiction 3. Toys—Fiction
ISBN 0-688-06525-2 (pa)
LC 81-6392

"Ernest, is a portly bear who lives with Celestine, a mouse child, in a humble but cozy house. . . . Celestine loses her beloved duck-doll named Gideon in the snow. Ernest finds it beyond repair and tries unsuccessfully to console Celestine with new stuffed animals. Finally with Celestine's help, he designs a new Gideon just in time for Christmas." Booklist

"The illustrations are watercolors full of whimsy and warmth, which, with the text, convey a great sense of mutual appreciation and pleasure shared. Because the text is entirely written in uncluttered dialogue, eyes are pulled to the detailed illustrations. The books are translated from the French, and their origin is apparent in the character's environment and dress." SLJ

Other available titles about Ernest and Celestine are:
Bravo, Ernest and Celestine! (1982)
Ernest and Celestine at the circus (1989)
Ernest and Celestine's patchwork quilt (1985)
Ernest and Celestine's picnic (1982)
Feel better, Ernest! (1988)
Merry Christmas, Ernest and Celestine (1984)
Smile, Ernest and Celestine (1982)
Where are you, Ernest and Celestine? (1986)

Viorst, Judith

Alexander and the terrible, horrible, no good, very bad day; illustrated by Ray Cruz. Atheneum Pubs. 1972 unp il $12.95; pa $3.95 E

ISBN 0-689-30072-7; 0-689-71350-9 (pa)
LC 72-75289

Also available in a Spanish language edition

The author "describes the plight of a boy for whom everything goes wrong from the moment he steps out of bed and discovers he has gum stuck in his hair to his return to bed that night when he has to wear his

Viorst, Judith—*Continued*
hated railroad-train pajamas and the cat decides to sleep with one of his brothers instead of with him. His mother consoles him by remarking that some days are like that." Booklist

"Small listeners can enjoy the litany of disaster, and perhaps be stimulated to discuss the possibility that one contributes by expectation. The illustrations capture the grumpy dolor of the story, ruefully funny." Sutherland. The Best In Child Books

Another available title about Alexander, also available in a Spanish language edition is:
Alexander, who used to be rich last Sunday (1978)

Earrings! illustrated by Nola Langner Malone. Atheneum Pubs. 1990 unp il $13.95 **E**

ISBN 0-689-31615-1 LC 89-17846

"The curly-haired protagonist pleads, cajoles and bargains to get pierced ears; she points out that she is the only girl in 'her class, the world or the solar system' without them. She promises to walk the dog, clean her room, read a book a week for a year and be nice to her little brother if she is only granted her wish." Publ Wkly

"Viorst homes in on minor childhood crises with the perfect blend of humor and insight, and Malone's expressive and comic figures are miniature character studies in themselves." Horn Book

The good-bye book; illustrated by Kay Chorao. Atheneum Pubs. 1988 unp il $12.95 **E**

1. Parent and child—Fiction
ISBN 0-689-31308-X LC 87-1778

"A small boy begs, wheedles and worries through his parents' preparations to leave for the night without him." Publ Wkly

"Viorst hits close to home in her maddeningly believable monologue. The story's inherent humor is highlighted by Chorao's imaginative, full-color pictures that show the parents going about the business of getting ready for an evening out as the boy throws a tantrum in the foreground. Using a male baby-sitter provides a nice touch." Booklist

My mama says there aren't any zombies, ghosts, vampires, creatures, demons, monsters, fiends, goblins, or things. Atheneum Pubs. 1973 unp il $12.95; pa $3.95 **E**

1. Monsters—Fiction 2. Mothers—Fiction
ISBN 0-689-30102-2; 0-689-71204-9 (pa)
LC 73-76331

This book deals humorously with the childhood sense of being threatened by "imaginary monsters and a mother's reassurances that they don't exist. While wanting to believe his mother, Nick is also aware that she often makes mistakes . . . like the time she made Nick wear his boots on a sunny day." SLJ

Rosie and Michael; illustrated by Lorna Tomei. Atheneum Pubs. 1974 unp il $13.95; pa $3.95 **E**

1. Friendship—Fiction
ISBN 0-689-30439-0; 0-689-71272-3 (pa)
LC 74-75571

"Rosie and Michael catalog the humorous, sometimes elaborate particulars of their eventful friendship: she likes him even when he's dopey and he likes her even when she's grouchy. . . . In the same vein further testimonials reflecting magnanimity and loyal support dispatch any chagrin that either buddy might harbor. Though repetition begins to weigh heavily, the serio-comic message is buoyed by Tomei's detailed, grotesquely interpretive pen-and-ink caricatures that lend a 'Mad' magazine touch to the whole panoply." Booklist

The tenth good thing about Barney; illustrated by Erik Blegvad. Atheneum Pubs. 1971 25p il $12.95; pa $3.95 **E**

1. Death—Fiction 2. Cats—Fiction
ISBN 0-689-20688-7; 0-689-71203-0 (pa)
LC 71-154764

"A little boy saddened by the death of his cat thinks of nine good things about Barney to say at his funeral. Later his father helps him discover a tenth good thing: Barney is in the ground helping grow flowers and trees and grass and 'that's a pretty nice job for a cat.'" Booklist

"The author succinctly and honestly handles both the emotions stemming from the loss of a beloved pet and the questions about the finality of death which naturally arise in such a situation. . . . An unusually good book that handles a difficult subject straightforwardly and with no trace of the macabre." Horn Book

Voigt, Cynthia

Stories about Rosie; illustrated by Dennis Kendrick. Atheneum Pubs. 1986 47p il $12.95 **E**

1. Dogs—Fiction
ISBN 0-689-31296-2 LC 86-3640

"Rosie is a half Springer, half Brittany Spaniel who lives with a family of four. The family's job is to take care of Rosie; her job, on the other hand, is to be happy, a task at which she succeeds with enthusiasm. Four episodes show Rosie's adventures both inside and outside of her home, including encounters with a bat and a deer." SLJ

"The cartoon-style art—alternating on double-page spreads between black-and-white and color-and-wash illustrations—is most expressive when depicting Rosie's many demeanors and renders the humans flat and indistinctive, a perspective probably in keeping with Rosie's and thus appropriate for this recreational enjoyment." Booklist

Waber, Bernard

An anteater named Arthur. Houghton Mifflin 1967 46p il lib bdg $13.95; pa $4.95 **E**

1. Aardvark—Fiction
ISBN 0-395-20336-8 (lib bdg); 0-395-25936-3 (pa)
LC 67-20374

Waber, Bernard—*Continued*

"Although Arthur is an anteater, he embodies the exasperating, if lovable, ways of all little boys from the moment he declines the red ants his mother offers him for breakfast, wanting brown ones instead, until he dashes back to the house to kiss his mother goodby before going off to school." Bruno. Books for Sch Libr, 1968

Bernard. Houghton Mifflin 1982 48p il lib bdg $10.95; pa $3.95 E

1. Dogs—Fiction
ISBN 0-395-31865-3 (lib bdg); 0-395-42648-0 (pa)
LC 81-13193

"Bernard is a fine black-and-white mutt with a happy home—or so he thinks. One day his owners have a huge quarrel and decide to separate, but both of them want Bernard. Such a quandry for a faithful dog! So Bernard runs away from the awful decision. He takes logical steps to find a new home; he tries to be friendly, good with children, well-behaved in public, a fine watchdog—but nothing works. Finally his owners find him, take him home, comfort him, and decide to share him in the future." Horn Book

"The line and wash drawings are bright and are replete with action and humor, and the story is told with a recurrent pattern that should appeal to the read-aloud audience, with a brisk pace and light style." Bull Cent Child Books

The house on East 88th Street. Houghton Mifflin 1962 48p il lib bdg $13.95 E

1. Crocodiles—Fiction 2. New York (N.Y.)—Fiction
ISBN 0-395-18157-7 LC 62-8144

"In an amusing fantasy, Mr. and Mrs. Joseph F. Primm and their young son Joshua move into a new home in New York City and discover a crocodile [named Lyle] in the bathtub. The illustrations detail the wrought iron railings, the graceful doorway with its fan-light, the sweeping staircase, elaborate fireplaces, and ornate chandeliers, characteristic of a comfortable old brownstone dwelling." Moorachian. What is a City?

Other available titles about Lyle are:
Funny, funny Lyle (1987)
Lovable Lyle (1969)
Lyle and the birthday party (1966)
Lyle finds his mother (1974)
Lyle, Lyle, crocodile (1965)

I was all thumbs. Houghton Mifflin 1975 48p il lib bdg $13.95; pa $4.95 E

1. Octopus—Fiction
ISBN 0-395-21404-1 (lib bdg); 0-395-53969-2 (pa)
LC 75-11689

An octopus who has known only the quiet world of the laboratory tells of his unceremonious introduction to the perils and pleasures of ocean life

"The illustrations have color, movement, and a merry quality; the story has a felicitous blend of bland treatment of a silly situation and a witty use of cliché phrases when they are delightfully inappropriate to the situation." Bull Cent Child Books

Ira sleeps over. Houghton Mifflin 1972 48p il lib bdg $13.95; pa $4.95 E

ISBN 0-395-13893-0 (lib bdg); 0-395-20503-4 (pa)
LC 72-75605

"A small boy's joy in being asked to spend the night with a friend who lives next door is unrestrained until his sister raises the question of whether or not he should take his teddy bear. Torn between fear of being considered babyish and fear of what it may be like to sleep without his bear, Ira has a hard time deciding what to do. His dilemma is resolved happily, however, when he discovers that his friend Reggie also has a nighttime bear companion. An appealing picture book which depicts common childhood qualms with empathy and humor in brief text and colorful illustrations." Booklist

Another available title about Ira is:
Ira says goodbye (1988)

Waddell, Martin

Amy said; written by Martin Waddell; illustrated by Charlotte Voake. Little, Brown 1990 c1989 unp il $12.95 E

1. Brothers and sisters—Fiction
ISBN 0-316-91636-6 LC 89-84974

"Joy Street books"

First published 1989 in the United Kingdom

A young boy and his older sister visit their grandmother and have a wonderful time getting into all sorts of mischief

"Half the fun in this book is wondering whether Gran will ever catch on to the children's mischief; the other half is in Voake's understated watercolors, which splendidly convey the exuberance with which young children unwittingly destroy the established sense of order in a household." Horn Book

Wade, Barrie

Little monster; story by Barrie Wade; pictures by Katinka Kew. Lothrop, Lee & Shepard Bks. 1990 unp il $12.95; lib bdg $12.88 E

1. Brothers and sisters—Fiction
ISBN 0-688-09596-8; 0-688-09597-6 (lib bdg)
LC 89-37277

Mandy, who is usually perfectly behaved, tries acting bad like her brother and reveals to her surprised mother that there is a little monster in everyone

"To children who worry about whether or not their parents will always love them—even when they're naughty—this reassuring book delivers a resounding 'yes.' . . . Wade's uncomplicated text and Kew's soft watercolors each do their part to convey this important message." Publ Wkly

Wahl, Jan, 1933-

Humphrey's bear; illustrated by William Joyce. Holt & Co. 1987 unp il $12.95 E

1. Bears—Fiction
ISBN 0-03-071542-3 LC 85-5541

"Humphrey's father thinks he may be too old to sleep with his toy bear. In Humphrey's dream he and that bear, who once belonged to his father, escape to sail in a night sky." N Y Times Book Rev

"The dream sequence, illustrated in dark seagoing vistas, and the island landscapes are effective. For characterization, this isn't as consistent and beguiling as other favorite storytime bears, but Humphrey's is better than the average." Publ Wkly

Wallace, Ian, 1950-

Chin Chiang and the dragon's dance; written and illustrated by Ian Wallace. Atheneum Pubs. 1984 unp il lib bdg $12.95 **E**

1. Grandfathers—Fiction 2. Chinese New Year—Fiction
ISBN 0-689-50299-0 LC 83-13442

"A Margaret K. McElderry book"

"Now that he is finally old enough to dance the New Year's good luck dragon dance with his grandfather, Chin Chiang fears he will disgrace the family with his clumsiness. Frightened, he races out of his grandfather's shop and down the street to the public library where he meets an old woman who gives him the courage to try. Vibrant, full-page, highly detailed watercolors follow the episodes. Sharp, definitive, static, somewhat like Oriental silkscreens, they establish the Chinese setting and occasionally experiment with perspective and form in a fresh and engaging way." Child Book Rev Serv

Walter, Mildred Pitts, 1922-

Brother to the wind; pictures by Diane and Leo Dillon. Lothrop, Lee & Shepard Bks. 1985 unp il $12.95; lib bdg $12.88 **E**

1. Flight—Fiction 2. Africa—Fiction
ISBN 0-688-03811-5; 0-688-03812-3 (lib bdg)
LC 83-26800

With the help of Good Snake, Emeke, a young African boy gets his dearest wish

"Elements of folk legend—such as the wise woman, the oracular snake and its magic talismans, talking animals—contribute a timeless power to Emeke's lessons of faith and self-reliance. The illustrations emphasize the coalition of dream and necessity, which fuels Emeke's ingenuity. Vibrantly colored scenes of Emeke's daily life in the village are superimposed against personifications of the surreal forces which inspire his imagination." Horn Book

My mama needs me; pictures by Pat Cummings. Lothrop, Lee & Shepard Bks. 1983 unp il $12.95; lib bdg $12.88 **E**

1. Infants—Fiction 2. Parent and child—Fiction 3. Blacks—Fiction
ISBN 0-688-01670-7; 0-688-01671-5 (lib bdg)
LC 82-12654

Coretta Scott King Award for illustration, 1984

"A warm portrayal of a young black child's reaction to the arrival of his baby sister. Jason is invited out to play with friends, go over to a neighbor's for cookies, and feed the ducks in the pond. And while he reluctantly participates in some of these activities, Jason's overriding concern is to be home in case his mama needs him." Booklist

"The decorative illustrations show a warm family situation, and at the end one sees a cheerful view of Jason in a multi-racial neighborhood. An encouraging book, especially for the child who is a trifle uncertain about the arrival of a new sibling." Horn Book

Two and too much; illustrated by Pat Cummings. Bradbury Press 1990 unp il lib bdg $12.95 **E**

1. Brothers and sisters—Fiction 2. Blacks—Fiction
ISBN 0-02-792290-1 LC 88-14888

"A seven-year-old learns more about taking care of his typically disaster-prone two-year-old sister than he really wants to know. Lively, vivid, realistic illustrations full of everyday detail tell a warm and recognizable family story." Horn Book Guide

Ward, Lynd Kendall, 1905-1985

The biggest bear; by Lynd Ward. Houghton Mifflin 1988 84p il lib bdg $13.95; pa $3.95 **E**

1. Bears—Fiction
ISBN 0-395-14806-5; 0-395-15024-8 (pa)
LC 88-176366

Awarded the Caldecott Medal, 1953

A reissue of the title first published 1952

"Johnny Orchard never did acquire the bearskin for which he boldly went hunting. Instead, he brought home a cuddly bear cub, which grew in size and appetite to mammoth proportions and worried his family and neighbors half to death." Child Books Too Good to Miss

Watanabe, Shigeo, 1928-

How do I put it on? getting dressed; story by Shigeo Watanabe; pictures by Yasuo Ohtomo. Philomel Bks. 1979 28p il lib bdg $8.95; pa $3.95 **E**

1. Bears—Fiction 2. Clothing and dress—Fiction
ISBN 0-399-20761-9 (lib bdg); 0-399-21040-7 (pa)
LC 79-12714

"An I can do it all by myself book"

Original Japanese edition, 1977

A young bear demonstrates the wrong and right way to put on a shirt, pants, a cap, and shoes

"The single-mindedness of this most elementary of how-to's, and its ingenuous protagonist, combine to appeal to the very youngest of book lovers. . . . [The text asks] 'Do I put it on like this?' Children will chime in with the bear's answers; soon second-guessing the bruin becomes a rewarding game during inevitably requested rereadings. Illustrations, large and in color, are uncluttered." Booklist

Other available titles about Bear are:
Daddy, play with me! (1985)
Get set! Go! (1981)
I can build a house! (1983)
I can ride it! (1982)
I can take a bath! (1987)
I can take a walk! (1984)
Ice cream is falling! (1989)
I'm the king of the castle! (1982)
It's my birthday! (1988)
What a good lunch! (1980)
Where's my daddy? (1982)

Watson, Clyde

Applebet: an ABC; pictures by Wendy Watson. Farrar, Straus & Giroux 1982 unp il $12.95 E

1. Alphabet 2. Stories in rhyme
ISBN 0-374-30384-3 LC 81-19399

"Alphabetical sequence becomes the organizing principle for an . . . original picture book recounting the adventures of a farmer and her daughter Bet as they journey one sunny day to the distant town where the marvels of a harvest exposition—from potables to puppets, magicians to malefactors—dazzle their senses." Horn Book

"The sing-song rhyme pattern is chant-worthy, but it's the pictures that make this a standout. The small-scale drawings are ablaze with autumnal colors. The use of light and shadow makes readers aware of the warm Indian summer sunshine casting its glow on the whole affair. All the pictures, whether framed or sprawling over the pages feature characters having a fine time. Readers will, too." Booklist

Valentine foxes; pictures by Wendy Watson. Orchard Bks. 1989 unp il $13.95; lib bdg $13.99 E

1. Foxes—Fiction 2. Valentine's Day—Fiction
ISBN 0-531-05800-X; 0-531-08400-0 (lib bdg) LC 88-22392

Four little foxes prepare a cake and a Valentine surprise for their parents

"Rosy, pleasant illustrations accompany the story, as does a recipe for pound cake." Publ Wkly

Weiss, Nicki, 1951-

Maude and Sally. Greenwillow Bks. 1983 unp il $10.25; lib bdg $10.88 E

1. Friendship—Fiction
ISBN 0-688-01635-9; 0-688-01638-3 (lib bdg) LC 82-12003

When her best friend Sally goes to summer camp, Maude finds she can become best friends with Emmylou also

"Bright, cheerful pictures of varying shapes and sizes are contained within a line border, and the straightforward text is creatively placed throughout. Filled with details but not cluttered, the pale-colored illustrations often include conversational asides which add extra interest to a book designed with taste and originality." Horn Book

Where does the brown bear go? Greenwillow Bks. 1989 unp il $12.95; lib bdg $13.88 E

1. Animals—Fiction 2. Night—Fiction
ISBN 0-688-07862-1; 0-688-07863-X (lib bdg) LC 87-36980

When the lights go down on the city street and the sun sinks far behind the seas, the animals of the world are on their way home for the night

"The rich, dark colors of a velvet night sky, polka dotted with stars, form the background for this enchanting lullaby. . . . Repetition and alliteration are skillfully employed in the verses; the rhythm and rhymes are so perfect that it takes only a reading or two before the poem is committed to memory. . . . Altogether, an exquisite book to end a young one's day." Horn Book

Wells, Rosemary, 1943-

Good night, Fred. Dial Bks. for Young Readers 1981 unp il lib bdg $8.44; pa $3.95 E

1. Telephone—Fiction 2. Brothers—Fiction
ISBN 0-8037-2992-8 (lib bdg); 0-8037-0059-8 (pa) LC 81-65849

"Fred, a toddler, bounces off the sofa and breaks the telephone. Big brother Arthur calmly dismantles the phone while Fred pesters him: 'Are you sure Grandma's not in there?' At last, Fred goes to bed, waking to a silent house. He traipses downstairs, in pajamas, to begin a fantasy romp with a tiny Grandma who has come out of the ringing phone. The only trace of the adventure when Arthur returns (from the garage) is a suddenly intact phone." SLJ

The "story and pictures are enchanting and the caring between Fred and Arthur is real and heart-warming. A good book for story-telling to preschoolers." Child Book Rev Serv

Hazel's amazing mother. Dial Bks. for Young Readers 1985 unp il $11.95; lib bdg $11.89; pa $3.95 E

1. Mothers—Fiction
ISBN 0-8037-0209-4; 0-8037-0210-8 (lib bdg); 0-8037-0703-7 (pa) LC 85-1447

When Hazel and her beloved doll Eleanor are set upon by bullies, Hazel's mother comes to the rescue in a surprising way

"The power of maternal love may be exaggerated here, but the lap audience will understand that mothers are their defenders and will do extraordinary things for their young. As is true of other books by Wells, the characters are small animals in appearance; in behavior they are people. . . . Breezy and funny, but also touching, this should appeal to children's sense of justice as well as their faith in parental omnipotence." Bull Cent Child Books

A lion for Lewis. Dial Bks. for Young Readers 1982 unp il $9.95; lib bdg $9.89; pa $3.95 E

1. Brothers and sisters—Fiction
ISBN 0-8037-4683-0; 0-8037-4686-5 (lib bdg); 0-8037-0096-2 (pa) LC 82-70197

"Playing in the attic one day, Sophie and George agree—when their little brother Lewis pleads for inclusion in their 'let's pretend' games—that he can take part, but Lewis gets tired of being assigned minor roles. He never gets to be the doctor or nurse, he's just the patient; he never gets to play mother or father, he's only the baby. But revenge comes (and it 'is' sweet) when Lewis spots a lion costume into which he zips himself." Bull Cent Child Books

"As in many of her picture books, the author-artist in words and images is uncannily sensitive to the feelings and predicaments of young children. Her soft watercolors are perfect storytelling tableaux first showing the hapless Lewis and the rather smug older children and later, the little boy triumphantly turning the tables with his outrageous antics." Horn Book

Wells, Rosemary, 1943-—*Continued*

The little lame prince; based on a story by Dinah Maria Mulock Craik. Dial Bks. for Young Readers 1990 unp il $12.95; lib bdg $12.89 E

1. Fairy tales 2. Pigs—Fiction
ISBN 0-8037-0788-6; 0-8037-0789-4 (lib bdg) LC 89-23482

"This adaptation of the Craik classic is presented in a picture book format. By the time Prince Francisco, a piglet, is three-years-old, he has been crippled in a careless accident, his parents are dead, his evil uncle is ruling the country having exiled Francisco. With the help of a flying cape, courtesy of his fairy grandmother, Francisco reclaims his kingdom. The watercolors add to the enchantment of a timeless tale that acquaints a whole new generation with the courageous, handicapped hero." Child Book Rev Serv

Max's first word. Dial Bks. for Young Readers 1979 unp il $3.50 E

1. Vocabulary—Fiction 2. Brothers and sisters—Fiction 3. Rabbits—Fiction
ISBN 0-8037-6066-3 LC 79-59745

"Very first books"

The book depicts "the trials of put-upon Ruby and her infant brother, Max. . . . Ruby puts a cup on Max's high-chair tray and orders him to say 'cup.' Slamming the cup firmly down, Max shouts 'Bang!' And 'Bang!' is what he responds to all Ruby's teaching as she points out things in the kitchen. . . . When she hands Max an apple, she says 'yum-yum,' whereupon the tricky baby hollers 'Delicious!'" Publ Wkly

Other available titles about Max are:
Max's bath (1985)
Max's bedtime (1985)
Max's birthday (1985)
Max's breakfast (1985)
Max's chocolate chicken (1989)
Max's Christmas (1986)
Max's new suit (1979)
Max's ride (1979)
Max's toys (1979)

Morris's disappearing bag; a Christmas story. Dial Bks. for Young Readers 1975 unp il $9.95; lib bdg $9.89; pa $3.95 E

1. Rabbits—Fiction 2. Christmas—Fiction
ISBN 0-8037-5441-8; 0-8037-5510-4 (lib bdg); 0-8037-5509-0 (pa) LC 75-9202

"Christmas day can be full of disappointments, especially if you only get a teddy bear, and your older brother and sisters get nifty gifts like a hockey stick, a beauty kit, and a chemistry set. . . . Morris is so frustrated with his gift that he invents a disappearing bag, one that becomes an instant hit with his brother and sisters. With new bargaining power due to his bag, Morris finally gets his chance to share the older children's gifts." Babbling Bookworm

"Christmas, magic, and getting the family temporarily to disappear add up to three irresistible themes, and Wells treats them imaginatively. The author-artist does, along with careful color and line work, some wonderful things with Morris' ears and eyes, expressing exactly the sentiments of a putout preschool rabbit." Booklist

Noisy Nora; story and pictures by Rosemary Wells. Dial Bks. for Young Readers 1973 unp il $9.95; lib bdg $9.89; pa $3.95 E

1. Mice—Fiction 2. Stories in rhyme
ISBN 0-8037-6638-6; 0-8037-6639-4 (lib bdg); 0-8037-6193-7 (pa) LC 72-6068

Little Nora, tired of being ignored, tries to gain her family's attention by being noisy. When this doesn't work Nora disappears but returns when she is sure she has been missed

"A small book with rhymed verses and anthropomorphic mice has been illustrated with buoyant pastel drawings that add humorous details to the story. . . . The universal emotion of a child's feeling slighted because of its siblings has been given life in a simple book." Horn Book

Peabody. Dial Bks. for Young Readers 1983 unp il $13.95; lib bdg $13.89; pa $3.95 E

1. Teddy bears—Fiction 2. Dolls—Fiction
ISBN 0-8037-0004-0; 0-8037-0005-9 (lib bdg); 0-8037-0211-6 (pa) LC 83-7207

Annie's affection for Peabody, her teddy bear, is temporarily overshadowed by the novelty of a new talking birthday doll

"The vibrantly colored, white-bordered pictures, with their seasonal cycle of familiar experiences, are a pleasure to look at—something readers will want to do again and again to catch the subtle reversal of toy and human expressions." Booklist

Shy Charles; written and illustrated by Rosemary Wells. Dial Bks. for Young Readers 1988 unp il $11.95; lib bdg $11.89 E

1. Mice—Fiction 2. Stories in rhyme
ISBN 0-8037-0511-5; 0-8037-0564-6 (lib bdg) LC 87-27247

"Charles, a young mouse, is perfectly happy playing by himself, and social contacts are an endless ordeal. He can't or won't say 'thank you' in public places, can't or won't cope with dancing lessons or football. But when the baby sitter falls down the stairs, Charles is able to comfort her and call for help, before resuming his shy silence." N Y Times Book Rev

"Wells' illustrations . . . show the plump, large-eared cast to be full of charm and cleverness. Facial expressions, posture, and background details substantially extend the humor of the story. The simple rhythm of the rhyming text is subtle and playful." SLJ

Timothy goes to school; story and pictures by Rosemary Wells. Dial Bks. for Young Readers 1981 unp il $11.95; lib bdg $11.89; pa $3.95 E

1. School stories 2. Raccoons—Fiction
ISBN 0-8037-8948-3; 0-8037-8949-1 (lib bdg); 0-8037-0021-0 (pa) LC 80-20785

"Timothy, a little raccoon, runs eagerly to school on his first day, only to suffer weeks of pure torture. Best-dressed, over-achieving Claude puts Timothy down at every turn and nothing the poor victim's loving mother can do or say is any comfort. Timothy prays in vain that Claude will disgrace himself somehow and is about

Wells, Rosemary, 1943-—*Continued*
to quit school at the time of a class entertainment. Claude suavely plays the saxophone; Grace toe dances. Timothy hears Violet, sitting beside him, say she can't stand it any more, with that smarmy Grace. Thus a morale-boosting friendship is born between the snubbed ones." Publ Wkly

"It is amazing that the illustrator can show so much emotion—Timothy's misery, his mother's anxiety, and Claude's scorn—in their beady little eyes. In a small gem of a book the outcome inspires the reader with a sense of jubilation." Horn Book

Westcott, Nadine Bernard, 1949-

The lady with the alligator purse; adapted and illustrated by Nadine Bernard Westcott. Little, Brown 1988 unp il $12.95; pa $4.95 **E**

1. Nonsense verses
ISBN 0-316-93135-7; 0-316-93136-5 (pa)
LC 87-21368

"Joy Street books"

"Westcott adapts a jump rope rhyme about the misadventures of Tiny Tim to create a zany book of nonsense that demands reading aloud. After the mischievous baby drinks his bathwater, eats the soap, and tries to stuff the bathtub down his throat, his mother calls the doctor, the nurse, and the lady with the alligator purse. When medical cures fail, the lady produces pizza. The colorful illustrations filled with frenzied activities sustain the silliness and the absurdity of the story." SLJ

Skip to my Lou; adapted and illustrated by Nadine Bernard Westcott. Little, Brown 1989 unp il music lib bdg $12.95 **E**

1. Farm life—Fiction 2. Stories in rhyme
ISBN 0-316-93137-3 LC 88-7306

"Joy Street books"

When his parents leave a young boy in charge of the farm for a day, chaos erupts as the animals take over the house

"Westcott's lively sense of fun pervades the whole book through jacket, endpapers, and title page, as she animates her own vision of the familiar song's good-natured nonsense. Organized souls will be relieved to see that all the animals join in the clean-up and leave the house restored to order before the grownups return. A musical score is included." Horn Book

Westman, Barbara

The day before Christmas; a story of Charlotte and Emilio. Harper & Row 1990 unp il $14.95; lib bdg $14.89 **E**

1. Christmas—Fiction 2. Dogs—Fiction
ISBN 0-06-026428-4; 0-06-026429-2 (lib bdg)
LC 89-29424

Young dogs Charlotte and Emilio spend Christmas Eve playing in the snow, wrapping presents, trimming the tree, and going for a sleigh ride

"Here's a quickly read, amusing Christmas story for the youngest. . . . The story is simple enough to hold little ones' attention, but the main attraction is the artwork. Boldly colored, looking as if a child might have drawn them, these pictures are smile producers." Booklist

Wiesner, David

Free fall. Lothrop, Lee & Shepard Bks. 1988 unp il $13.95; lib bdg $13.88 **E**

1. Dreams—Fiction 2. Stories without words
ISBN 0-688-05583-4; 0-688-05584-2 (lib bdg)
LC 87-22834

A Caldecott Medal honor book, 1989

A young boy dreams of daring adventures in the company of imaginary creatures inspired by the things surrounding his bed

"Technical virtuosity is the trademark of the double-page watercolor spreads. Especially notable is the solidity of forms and architectural details." SLJ

Hurricane. Clarion Bks. 1990 unp il $14.95 **E**

1. Hurricanes—Fiction 2. Brothers—Fiction
ISBN 0-395-54382-7 LC 90-30070

"A family weathers a hurricane; the next day, in the post-hurricane yard, the two boys in the family play on a great fallen elm, imagining it to be a jungle, a pirate ship, and a space ship. A handsome book, affording opportunities for sharing fears and dreams of adventure." Horn Book Guide

Wild, Margaret, 1948-

Mr. Nick's knitting; written by Margaret Wild; illustrated by Dee Huxley. Harcourt Brace Jovanovich 1989 unp il lib bdg $12.95 **E**

1. Knitting—Fiction 2. Friendship—Fiction
ISBN 0-15-200518-8 LC 88-35778

"Gulliver books"

"Mr. Nick and Mrs. Jolley, two portly commuters, pass the time on their daily train rides by knitting. When Mrs. Jolley is hospitalized, Mr. Nick knits her a remarkable get-well present." N Y Times Book Rev

"The warm, gentle illustrations reflect Mr. Nick's orderly life; every page is framed in a simple geometric border except for the one hectic week when Mr. Nick is creating his surprise. Then, he knits at work, in the bathtub, and even while cooking spaghetti. With the return of the bordered pages, one knows that the crisis is past and all will be well with these two unusual friends." Horn Book

The very best of friends; written by Margaret Wild; illustrated by Julie Vivas. Harcourt Brace Jovanovich 1990 unp il lib bdg $13.95 **E**

1. Cats—Fiction 2. Farm life—Fiction 3. Death—Fiction
ISBN 0-15-200625-7 LC 89-36464

"Gulliver books"

Since Jessie has never cared for her farmer husband's cat William, her difficult adjustment period after her husband's death makes William doubt if he is still welcome on the farm

"The cycle of death and reconciliation doesn't really comprise a plot, but young listeners will be held by the loss and recovery of a vulnerable pet. . . . Vivas' spare watercolor spreads are strong on expressive postures and unexpected perspectives. There may be a moment of confusion between the gray spotted dogs and the gray striped cat, all remarkably alike in shape, but the main

Wild, Margaret, 1948-—*Continued*
characters and creatures ultimately emerge with unmistakable individuality and homely appeal." Bull Cent Child Books

Wildsmith, Brian, 1930-

Bear's adventure. Pantheon Bks. 1982 c1981 unp il $9.95; lib bdg $16.99 **E**

1. Bears—Fiction
ISBN 0-394-85295-8; 0-394-95295-2 (lib bdg)
LC 81-18814

First published 1981 in the United Kingdom

"A bear climbs into a balloon while two balloonists are having a picnic lunch, then comes to earth (the balloon punctured by a bird's bill) to lead a parade, then he's interviewed on TV, then he wins a race at a sports stadium, then he rides in a helicopter, etc. etc. And nobody knows he's a bear, but thinks he's a man in costume." Bull Cent Child Books

"The absurdity of a shaggy bear being mistaken for a visiting celebrity is prolonged in dazzling colour and geometrical patterns elegantly deployed; angles and perspective are manipulated to give an air of fantasy to solid objects, and the whole book has an airy quality that adds a fairy-tale touch to the comedy of incongruity." Grow Point

Brian Wildsmith's birds. Watts 1967 unp il o.p.; Oxford Univ. Press paperback available $5.95 **E**

1. Birds—Pictorial works
ISBN 0-19-272117-8 (pa)

"Mr. Wildsmith has tied a series of pictures of birds . . . to their group names: a watch of nightingales, a nye of pheasants, a congregation of plover, et cetera. There is no other text." Saturday Rev

"Birds—how well the subject lends itself to this artist's exquisite use of color!. . . The child will have fun with the terms while absorbing truly beautiful illustrations." Horn Book

Brian Wildsmith's circus. Watts 1970 unp il o.p.; Oxford Univ. Press paperback available $5.95 **E**

1. Circus—Pictorial works
ISBN 0-19-272102-X (pa)

First published 1970 in the United kingdom. Paperback edition has title: The circus

"Enclosed between a notice that the circus is coming to town and an announcement of its move to the next place is a series of pictures with no text. In double-page spreads Brian Wildsmith has painted vibrant, beautiful illustrations of animals and acrobats, clowns and jugglers, birds on a seesaw, and the full panoply of a circus parade. The pictures have action and humor and . . . are remarkable for the quality of the colors." Saturday Rev

Brian Wildsmith's wild animals. Watts 1967 unp il o.p.; Oxford Univ. Press paperback available $5.95 **E**

1. Mammals—Pictorial works
ISBN 0-19-272103-8 (pa)

First published 1967 in the United Kingdom. Paperback edition has title: Wild animals

"A pride of lions, a lepe of leopards, a skulk of foxes, and a cete of badgers are among the cleverly captured groups of wild beasts that stalk the vivid, glowing pages of this fascinating picture book. A splendid, eyecatching . . . volume." Booklist

A Christmas story. Knopf 1989 unp il $12.95; lib bdg $15.99 **E**

1. Jesus Christ—Nativity—Fiction 2. Donkeys—Fiction
ISBN 0-679-80074-3; 0-679-90074-8 (lib bdg)
LC 89-7959

A young donkey reunites with her mother in a Bethlehem stable and witnesses a miracle

"Spectacular illustrations show the Nativity as backdrop for a story of a small donkey whose mother carries Mary to Bethlehem. A neighbor, Rebecca, offers to care for the donkey, but he pines so for his mother that she promises to take him to her. At each stop on the road, Rebecca asks if anyone has seen a donkey and two people, and is improbably but miraculously steered in the directions of the stable. . . . For children who already know the Christmas story, this is a chance to see it from another point of view." SLJ

Daisy. Pantheon Bks. 1984 unp il lib bdg $11.99 **E**

1. Dairy cattle—Fiction
ISBN 0-394-95975-2 LC 83-12150

"Daisy, a discontented cow who longs to see the world, attracts a television crew when she wanders away and walks onto the rooftops of a village nestled on a hillside. Shortly thereafter, she is starring in Hollywood Westerns, in bubble-bath ads, and on magazine covers and being feted at banquets with delicacies like caviar and smoked salmon. But the homesick cow longs for grass, buttercups, and her old field." Horn Book

"Wildsmith's message about happiness being found in your own backyard may seem didactic to adults but less obvious to little ones. Whether or not children catch the book's philosophical drift, they will enjoy the buoyant pictures that cascade with unusual shapes and carnival colors. The split pages work exceptionally well, with each cleverly revealing a new aspect of the story." Booklist

Fishes. Oxford Univ. Press 1985 c1968 unp $9.95; pa $4.95 **E**

1. Fishes—Pictorial works
ISBN 0-19-279639-9; 0-19-272151-8 (pa)

First United States edition published 1968 by Franklin Watts with title: Brian Wildsmith's fishes

The author "presents groups of fishes. A cluster of porcupine fish, a hover of trout, a spread of sticklebacks, and flocks, schools, and streams of other fish swim across the pages in a riot of color." Booklist

Pelican. Pantheon Bks. 1983 c1982 unp il lib bdg $10.99 **E**

1. Pelicans—Fiction
ISBN 0-394-95668-0 LC 82-12431

"Paul finds a pelican egg and when the egg hatches, he tries to teach the baby pelican to fish. The pelican already knows how to fish, but pretends he doesn't so he can stay longer with Paul." Child Book Rev Serv

"The text is adequate in structure, and the style is unexceptionable; it is, as is usually true of Wildsmith's books, the lavish and striking use of color in handsomely composed paintings that is impressive: the frozen food

Wildsmith, Brian, 1930-—*Continued*
counter glows with magenta and royal blue, the landscape is effulgently vernal, the farmer's clothes are dazzling: yellow shirt and boots, blue pants, red and green jacket." Bull Cent Child Books

Wilhelm, Hans, 1945-

A cool kid—like me! Crown 1990 unp il $12.95; lib bdg $13.99 **E**

1. Grandmothers—Fiction
ISBN 0-517-57821-2; 0-517-57822-0 (lib bdg) LC 89-49370

"The boy who tells this story is so cool that he doesn't like to be hugged, except by his Grandma. Only to her will he confess the awful truth: his coolness is merely a facade, and he's actually terrified without the night-light on. When Grandma goes on vacation, she gives the boy a teddy bear to keep him company. Although his parents think he's too old for a stuffed animal . . . in Grandma's absence the bear becomes a confidant, listening patiently as the boy tells of his inner fears." Publ Wkly

"With softly painted illustrations as sensitive as the message, this unusual story gives kids license to be kids, and it reminds everyone that cuddly toys still have their place, even in a high-tech world." Booklist

Willard, Nancy

Simple pictures are best; story by Nancy Willard; pictures by Tomie de Paola. Harcourt Brace Jovanovich 1977 unp il hardcover o.p. paperback available $3.95 **E**

1. Photography—Fiction
ISBN 0-15-682625-9 (pa) LC 76-4923

A shoemaker and his wife being photographed for their wedding anniversary keep adding items to the picture despite the photographer's admonition that "Simple pictures are best"

"De Paola's colorful, deadpan illustrations perfectly complement Willard's funny tale in the folk tradition. . . . The smooth flowing cumulative story, simple and direct but rich in pithy descriptions and similes, is certain to be a story time hit." SLJ

Williams, Barbara

Albert's toothache; illustrated by Kay Chorao. Dutton 1974 unp il $11.95; pa $3.95 **E**

1. Turtles—Fiction
ISBN 0-525-25368-8; 0-525-45037-8 (pa) LC 74-4040

This is the "story of a small turtle, toothless as are all of his kind, who takes to his bed with an announced toothache. His mother worries; his father thunders incredulous impatience; his siblings cast scorn. So it goes until grandmother investigates and discovers 'where' he has a toothache." Libr J

"The humor of the concise dialogue and of the stylized repetitions of the narrative is carefully reflected in the sepia-line and half-tone drawings that reveal the anthropomorphically domestic life of the turtles." Horn Book

Jeremy isn't hungry; pictures by Martha Alexander. Dutton 1978 unp il $10.95; pa $3.95 **E**

1. Infants—Fiction 2. Brothers—Fiction
ISBN 0-525-32760-6; 0-525-44536-6 (pa) LC 78-4924

"Mama's taking a shower and rushing to get dressed while preschooler Davey tries to help by caring for his younger brother, Jeremy. Jeremy is crying, probably from hunger, and Mama says feed him. Davey's problems (from getting Jeremy into his chair to deciphering contents of a baby food bottle when he can't read) are hilariously understated in a running conversation between him and his mother." Booklist

"Probably nobody but Alexander could have matched the harrowing goings on as perfectly as she does with her spirited scenes. . . . Each page is crazy fun and the story as a whole is as suspenseful as a novel." Publ Wkly

Kevin's grandma; illustrated by Kay Chorao. Dutton 1975 unp il $11.95; pa $3.95 **E**

1. Grandmothers—Fiction
ISBN 0-525-33115-8; 0-525-45039-4 (pa) LC 74-23713

"The small storyteller's much loved grandma does all the things a grandma is expected to do. But Kevin tells him how his grandmother is different. She's into Yoga and Judo and brings Kevin peanut butter soup on her Honda and sky dives." Child Book Rev Serv

"Whether or not readers identify with the gentle, loving grandma or the equally loving, madcap one, they will be delighted by the black-and-white line drawings by Kay Chorao and will sympathize with Kevin, who can't help making the truth a little more interesting." Babbling Bookworm

Williams, Jay, 1914-1978

Everyone knows what a dragon looks like; illustrated by Mercer Mayer. Four Winds Press 1976 unp il $14.95; pa $5.95; Scholastic pa $5.95 **E**

1. Dragons—Fiction 2. China—Fiction
ISBN 0-02-793090-4; 0-02-045600-X (pa); 0-590-07751-1 (pa) LC 74-13121

Because of the road sweeper's belief in him, a dragon saves the city of Wu from the Wild Horsemen of the north

"The theme of this story is that appearances can be deceiving. Mercer Mayer provides a series of emotionally expressive illustrations scaled down to a child's eye level. The humanized characters realistically portray fear, anger or joy. . . . Careful attention has been paid to the background detail, perspective and layout, drawing the eye into each superb illustration and creating a three-dimensional effect." N Y Times Book Rev

Williams, Karen Lynn

Galimoto; illustrated by Catherine Stock. Lothrop, Lee & Shepard Bks. 1990 unp il $12.95; lib bdg $12.88 **E**

1. Toys—Fiction 2. Malawi—Fiction
ISBN 0-688-08789-2; 0-688-08790-6 (lib bdg) LC 89-2258

Williams, Karen Lynn—*Continued*

"In Malawi, Africa, according to the author's note, *galimoto* are intricate and popular push toys crafted by children. Williams tells the story of seven-year-old Kondi's quest to find ample scrap material to fashion his own toy pickup truck. Visits to his uncle's shop, the miller, and the trash heap yield enough wire to allow him to create a plaything which he proudly uses to lead his friends in their evening game. Kondi's perseverance and the pleasure he takes in his accomplishment are just two of the delights of this appealing story. Stock's graceful watercolors portray life in a bustling village and include enough detail . . . to give readers the flavor of a day in this southern African nation." Horn Book

Williams, Linda (Linda D.)

The little old lady who was not afraid of anything; illustrated by Megan Lloyd. Crowell 1986 unp il $13.95; lib bdg $13.89; Harper & Row pa $4.95 E

ISBN 0-690-04584-0; 0-690-04586-7 (lib bdg); 0-06-443183-5 (pa) LC 85-48250

A little old lady who is not afraid of anything must deal with a pumpkin head, a tall black hat, and other spooky objects that follow her through the dark woods trying to scare her

"A delightful picture book, perfect for both independent reading pleasure and for telling aloud." SLJ

Williams, Suzanne

Mommy doesn't know my name; illustrated by Andrew Shachat. Houghton Mifflin 1990 unp il $13.95 E

1. Names, Personal—Fiction 2. Mothers and daughters—Fiction

ISBN 0-395-54228-6 LC 89-78205

"Mother calls her daughter a chickadee, a pumpkin, an alligator and other endearing names. The little girl pictures herself as each and begins to think that Mother does not know her name." Child Book Rev Serv

"Text and illustrations resonate with the strength of preschoolers' needs to understand and assert their own identities. . . . The pastel illustrations take Williams' idea, give it form, and then magnify it several decibels. . . . It's a fun, crazy book that works extremely well." SLJ

Williams, Vera B.

A chair for my mother. Greenwillow Bks. 1982 unp il $13.95; lib bdg $12.88; pa $4.95 E

1. Single parent family—Fiction 2. Saving and thrift—Fiction 3. Chairs—Fiction

ISBN 0-688-00914-X; 0-688-00915-8 (lib bdg); 0-688-04074-8 (pa) LC 81-7010

A Caldecott Medal honor book, 1983

A child, her waitress mother, and her grandmother save dimes to buy a comfortable armchair after all their furniture is lost in a fire

"The cheerful paintings take up the full left-hand page and face, in most cases, a small chunk of the text set against a modulated wash of a complementing color; a border containing a pertinent motif surrounds the two pages, further unifying the design. The result is a superbly conceived picture book expressing the joyful spirit of a loving family." Horn Book

Other available titles about Rosa and her family are:
Music, music for everyone (1984)
Something special for me (1983)

Cherries and cherry pits. Greenwillow Bks. 1986 unp il $13.95; lib bdg $13.88 E

1. Blacks—Fiction 2. Drawing—Fiction

ISBN 0-688-05145-6; 0-688-05146-4 (lib bdg) LC 85-17156

"Bidemmi, a young black child, draws splendid pictures. 'As she draws, she tells the story of what she is drawing,' always starting with the word 'this.' Bidemmi's brightly colored words and pictures introduce children to the man with the nice face that's dark brown; to the tiny, white, grandmotherly lady; and to the tall boy who is much like Bidemmi's own brother. Finally, Bidemmi tells her story, revealing her wish for her neighborhood and her world. Each story involves cherries—buying, sharing, and enjoying them." SLJ

"Williams' portraits of Bidemmi drawing are done in watercolor; the drawings Bidemmi makes are done with bright markers, some being simple sketches, others filling the page with color, looking like naive, but glorious icons. The interior stories are well integrated with each other, and the whole adds up to a study of child as artist that is fresh, vibrant, and exciting." Bull Cent Child Books

Stringbean's trip to the shining sea; greetings from Vera B. Williams, story and pictures; and Jennifer Williams, more pictures. Greenwillow Bks. 1987 unp il $11.95; lib bdg $11.88; Scholastic pa $3.95 E

1. West (U.S.)—Fiction

ISBN 0-688-07161-9; 0-688-07162-7 (lib bdg); 0-590-42906-X (pa) LC 86-29502

"Stringbean and big brother Fred (joined en route by Potato, Stringbean's dog) take a car trip from their home in Kansas to the Pacific Ocean, and their pilgrimage is recorded herein in the form of a mock photo and postcard album." Bull Cent Child Books

"The use of mixed media—watercolors, Magic Markers, and colored pencils—is as aesthetically pleasing as it is skillful. Nothing has been forgotten; nothing more needs to be added. Not for the usual picture-book set, this travelogue storybook will appeal to slightly older audiences." Horn Book

Three days on a river in a red canoe. Greenwillow Bks. 1984 unp il $13.95; lib bdg $13.88; pa $3.95 E

1. Canoes and canoeing—Fiction 2. Camping—Fiction

ISBN 0-688-80307-5; 0-688-84307-7 (lib bdg); 0-688-04072-1 (pa) LC 80-23893

In this book, a "canoe trip for two children and two adults is recorded with all its interesting detail in a spontaneous first-person account and engaging full-color drawings on carefully designed pages. Driving to a river site, making camp, paddling the craft, negotiating a waterfall, swimming, fishing, dealing with a sudden storm, and even rescuing one overboard child are all described as important incidents in a summertime adventure." Horn Book

Willis, Jeanne

Earthlets, as explained by Professor Xargle; illustrated by Tony Ross. Dutton 1989 unp il $12.95 **E**

1. Extraterrestrial beings—Fiction 2. Infants—Fiction
ISBN 0-525-44465-3 LC 88-23692

Professor Xargle's class of extraterrestrials learns about the physical characteristics and behavior of the human baby

"This funny view of babies is fraught with Professor Xargle's well-meaning, zany misinterpretations. Willis's clever and original text will particularly delight older siblings who may also find that babies are a separate species. Ross's inspired paintings bristle with out-of-this-world color and imagination." Publ Wkly

Wilson, Sarah, 1934-

The day that Henry cleaned his room; written and illustrated by Sarah Wilson. Simon & Schuster Bks. for Young Readers 1990 unp il $13.95 **E**

1. Cleanliness—Fiction
ISBN 0-671-69202-X LC 89-11571

When Henry cleans his room, he attracts the attention of reporters, scientists, the army, and something long and green and scaly that lives under Henry's bed

"Wilson's hilariously hyperbolic look at an all-too-familiar chore is sure to be a favorite with kids. They will find lots to look at—and chuckle over—in the illustrations of Henry's veritable disaster area." Publ Wkly

Winter, Jeanette

Follow the drinking gourd; story and pictures by Jeanette Winter. Knopf 1988 unp il music lib bdg $14.99 **E**

1. Slavery—Fiction 2. Underground railroad—Fiction 3. Blacks—Fiction
ISBN 0-394-99694-1 LC 88-9661

By following directions in a song, taught them by an old sailor, runaway slaves journey north along the Underground Railroad to freedom in Canada

"Complementing the few lines of text per page are dark-hued illustrations horizontally framed with a fine black line and plenty of white space. . . . The art carries the weight of introducing children to a riveting piece of U.S. history, and the music included at the end of the book will fix it in their minds." Bull Cent Child Books

Winthrop, Elizabeth

Katharine's doll; illustrated by Marylin Hafner. Dutton 1983 unp il $11.95 **E**

1. Friendship—Fiction 2. Dolls—Fiction
ISBN 0-525-44061-5 LC 83-1408

"A Unicorn book"

"Katharine and Molly are best friends who do everything together until a third party comes between them—in this case, a beautiful doll named Charlotte, a gift to Katharine from her grandmother." SLJ

"Illustrated with neat, attractive pencil drawings, the appealing story touches quietly on feelings of jealousy and possessiveness and on the value of friendship." Horn Book

Shoes; illustrated by William Joyce. Harper & Row 1986 19p il $13.95; lib bdg $11.89; pa $3.95 **E**

1. Shoes—Fiction 2. Stories in rhyme
ISBN 0-06-026591-4; 0-06-026592-2 (lib bdg); 0-06-443171-1 (pa) LC 85-45841

"A jaunty rhyme about shoes of all kinds—'shoes for fishing, shoes for wishing, shoes for muddy squishing.' The roly-poly figures are drawn from a child's perspective." N Y Times Book Rev

"This lilting rhyme about shoes and feet easily pleases. . . . Backing the verses are full-color drawings of children busily involved with one kind of shoe or another. Joyce's pictures are animated, energetic, and warmly colored. People and objects are somewhat stylized and slightly scruffy in appearance. Strictly speaking, the illustrations are not cartoons, but their figures and composition reflect a style reminiscent of comic strips of an earlier era." Booklist

Tough Eddie; illustrated by Lillian Hoban. Dutton 1985 unp il $10.95; pa $3.95 **E**

1. Sex role—Fiction
ISBN 0-525-44164-6; 0-525-44496-3 (pa) LC 84-13664

"Little Eddie loves building spaceships, wearing cowboy boots and feeling tough around his buddies, but he really loves his secret dollhouse. A showdown with sister Nellie blows his cover to his pals. It takes his courage to remain absolutely still when there is a bee on his nose, as well as the support of his friends, to make Eddie realize that there's nothing wrong with a boy who plays with dolls." SLJ

"Hogan's slightly raffish looking children are an appealing extension of the text, in which young children can enjoy familiar situations and relationships, a convincing demonstration of bravery, and a shift from the stereotypical sex role." Bull Cent Child Books

Wiseman, Bernard

Morris and Boris at the circus; by B. Wiseman. Harper & Row 1988 64p il $10.95; lib bdg $10.89; pa $3.50 **E**

1. Moose—Fiction 2. Bears—Fiction 3. Circus—Fiction
ISBN 0-06-026477-2; 0-06-026478-0 (lib bdg); 0-06-444143-1 (pa) LC 87-45682

"An I can read book"

"Morris the Moose and his friend Boris the Bear . . . take a trip to the circus. Morris has never gone before, so he doesn't quite have the big picture. He thinks the clown's nose is red because he has a cold, and when they join the performers in the ring, Morris rides 'bearback' on Boris, instead of on a horse." Booklist

"The cartoon illustrations with bold colors provide ample context clues for beginning readers. This delightful combination of text and illustrations will entice children to read and re-read this book." SLJ

Other available titles about Morris and Boris are:
Christmas with Morris and Boris (1983)
Halloween with Morris and Boris (1975)
Morris and Boris (1974)
Morris goes to school (1970)

Wiseman, Bernard—*Continued*
Morris has a cold (1978)
Morris tells Boris Mother Moose stories and rhymes (1979)
Morris the moose (1989)

Wishinsky, Frieda
Oonga boonga; pictures by Suçie Stevenson. Little, Brown 1990 unp il $13.95 **E**

1. Infants—Fiction 2. Brothers and sisters—Fiction
ISBN 0-316-94872-1 LC 88-37109

"Baby Louise is crying. She keeps crying no matter what anyone in the family tries—and they try everything from lullabies and cuddling to bottles. They play Mozart for her; they play rock and roll. Then, brother Daniel comes home from school and says, 'Oonga Boonga.' It works, so the family starts oonga boonga-ing like mad. But when Daniel leaves the house, it's cry-me-a-river time again. It's clear to everyone that the secret lies not in the oonga boonga, but with Daniel. He makes the baby smile even with a final 'Bonka Wonka, Louise.'" Booklist

"This is a warm, funny celebration of the one-of-a-kind, intuitive bond between baby and big brother or sister. The understated text provides a perfect jumping-off point for Stevenson's exuberant touch, which ranges from broad comedy . . . to more subtle humor." Publ Wkly

Wisniewski, David
Elfwyn's saga; story and pictures by David Wisniewski. Lothrop, Lee & Shepard Bks. 1990 unp il $13.95; lib bdg $13.88 **E**

1. Fairy tales 2. Vikings—Fiction
ISBN 0-688-09589-5; 0-688-09590-9 (lib bdg) LC 89-35308

"Elfwyn is born blind, but she grows up to destroy that original curse as well as a subsequent one threatening her clan. Loosely based on the legends and history of Iceland, the story is full of elements and motifs—magic, the battle between good and evil—which entrance young people. Cut-paper illustrations dazzle the eye and bring power and drama to an exciting folkloric tale." Horn Book Guide

The warrior and the wise man; story and pictures by David Wisniewski. Lothrop, Lee & Shepard Bks. 1989 unp il $13.95; lib bdg $13.88 **E**

1. Fairy tales 2. Japan—Fiction
ISBN 0-688-07889-3; 0-688-07890-7 (lib bdg) LC 88-21678

This original fairy tale "describes the quests of the twin sons of the emperor of Japan for five magical elements of the world: earth, water, fire, wind, and cloud. The brother who returns first will inherit the throne." Booklist

"The striking cut-paper illustrations, executed and reproduced with virtuosity, make use of black silhouettes against emotionally charged colors that modulate and change from page to page and create a dynamic, almost cinematographic effect. In a detailed end note Wisniewski explicates the visual references to be seen in the costumes, decorations, and artifacts and thus establishes the historical, religious, and artistic authenticity of his work." Horn Book

Wittman, Sally, 1941-
A special trade; pictures by Karen Gundersheimer. Harper & Row 1978 unp il lib bdg $10.89; pa $3.95 **E**

1. Friendship—Fiction 2. Old age—Fiction
ISBN 0-06-026554-X (lib bdg); 0-06-443071-5 (pa) LC 77-25673

"Old Bartholomew used to take Nelly, a little girl, for walks in her stroller. Now she takes him for walks in his wheelchair." Babbling Bookworm

"A heartwarming story. . . . Small, detailed illustrations in color perfectly convey the special feeling of friendship and love." Horn Book

Wolf, Janet, 1957-
The rosy fat magenta radish. Little, Brown 1990 unp il lib bdg $14.95 **E**

1. Gardening—Fiction
ISBN 0-316-95045-9 LC 89-15463

"Joy Street books"

"Nora has been eagerly awaiting Saturday, when neighbor Jim will help her plant seeds for radishes 'the color of Nora's favorite paint at school: magenta.'" Publ Wkly

"Labelled tools of the trade appear in the endpapers; here and throughout the book simple, childlike lines are filled in with crayon-bright color. The art, framed in white borders, takes up most of the space in this large-format book and adds much to the joyful story about the rewards of gardening's labors." SLJ

Wolff, Ashley, 1956-
Come with me. Dutton 1990 unp il lib bdg $12.95 **E**

1. Dogs—Fiction
ISBN 0-525-44555-2 LC 89-34482

A little boy tells a newborn puppy all the things they'll do in the meadow and by the sea when the puppy is old enough to come to live with him

"Double-page watercolors in a wide but misted palette, with soft contours and no harsh lines, perfectly suit the quietly joyful mood of innocent love. . . . Words and pictures present the California coastal setting and the boy's rehearsal of this important childhood relationship with a romantic affection that stops short of cloying. A book that's well-suited for both read-aloud and one-on-one sharing." SLJ

Only the cat saw. Dodd, Mead 1985 unp il $13.95; Puffin Bks. pa $3.95 **E**

1. Night—Fiction 2. Cats—Fiction 3. Family life—Fiction
ISBN 0-399-21698-7; 0-14-050853-8 (pa) LC 85-7031

As Amy and her family get ready to settle down for the night, the cat gets ready to explore and sees many things

"This not only portrays a warm family but also gives a sense of the nocturnal cycle picking up after most children consider everything to have wound down. The oil paintings are rich in texture with surprising blends of color, dramatic shapes, and satisfying compositions. A clever invitation for young listeners to participate in

Wolff, Ashley, 1956-—*Continued*
sharing a book aloud, as each can name the pictured answer that alternates with pages of text." Bull Cent Child Books

A year of beasts. Dutton 1986 unp il $11.95; pa $3.95 **E**

1. Animals—Pictorial works 2. Seasons
ISBN 0-525-44240-5; 0-525-44541-2 (pa) LC 85-27419

"Again focusing on the family from the author's earlier *A Year of Birds* [entered below] the linoleum block prints with clear black lines and bright but translucent washes record the changing seasons of a New England landscape and its nonhuman as well as human inhabitants." SLJ

"Warm but never cute, handsome without becoming pretentious, commanding attention without overwhelming the subject, this is a child's calendar, a celebration of family, and an evocation of nature's wonders—all scaled to the preschooler's perception. A satisfying and handsome production." Horn Book

A year of birds. Dodd, Mead 1984 unp il $13.95; Penguin Bks. pa $3.95 **E**

1. Birds—Pictorial works 2. Seasons
ISBN 0-399-21697-9; 0-14-050854-6 (pa) LC 83-27470

"Handsome, vividly colored linoleum block prints are the artistic centerpieces of this month-by-month catalog of birds that 'visit Ellie's house' in the course of a year. The succinct text simply states names of birds and the month they are likely to be seen ('Grosbeaks, purple finches, and black-capped chickadees in January . . .'), while charming two-page spreads evoke seasonal characteristics of each month. . . . The pictures of Ellie and her parents have a cozy warmth and tell a wordless story besides, showing Ellie's mother's advancing pregnancy until, in July, a new baby appears. . . . A quietly appealing, well-conceived introduction to the months of the year and changing seasons." Booklist

Wood, Audrey

Elbert's bad word; illustrated by Audrey and Don Wood. Harcourt Brace Jovanovich 1988 unp il $13.95 **E**

1. Parties—Fiction
ISBN 0-15-225320-3 LC 86-7557

"A bad word, spoken by a small boy at a fashionable garden party, creates havoc, and the child, Elbert, gets his mouth scrubbed out with soap. The bad word, in the shape of a long-tailed furry monster, will not go away until a wizard-gardener cooks up some really delicious, super-long words that everyone at the party applauds. This single-idea cautionary tale has lively, absurdist pictures of tiara-crowned, formally dressed adults recoiling in horror or cavorting with glee when Elbert, the only child at the party, speaks a word." SLJ

Heckedy Peg; illustrated by Don Wood. Harcourt Brace Jovanovich 1987 unp il lib bdg $14.95 **E**

1. Fairy tales 2. Witches—Fiction
ISBN 0-15-233678-8 LC 86-33639

"This original story reads like a pure folktale. The poor mother of seven children, each named for a day of the week, goes off to market promising to return with individual gifts that each child has requested and admonishing them to lock the door to strangers and not to touch the fire. The gullible children are tricked into disobeying their mother by the witch, Heckedy Peg, who turns them all into various kinds of food. The mother can rescue her children only by guessing which child is the fish, the roast rib, the bread. . . . This story, deep and rich with folk wisdom, is stunningly illustrated with Don Wood's luminous paintings. . . . With variety of color and line he enhances every nuance of the text, from the individuality of the children and the stalwart mother to the unrelenting evil of the witch. A tour de force in every way." SLJ

King Bidgood's in the bathtub; written by Audrey Wood; illustrated by Don Wood. Harcourt Brace Jovanovich 1985 unp il lib bdg $14.95 **E**

1. Kings, queens, rulers, etc.—Fiction 2. Baths—Fiction
ISBN 0-15-242730-9 LC 85-5472

A Caldecott Medal honor book, 1986

Despite pleas from his court, a fun-loving king refuses to get out of his bathtub to rule his kingdom

"The few simple words of text per large, well-designed page invite story-telling—but keep the group very small, so the children can be close enough to pore over the brilliant, robust illustrations." SLJ

The napping house; illustrated by Don Wood. Harcourt Brace Jovanovich 1984 unp il lib bdg $13.95 **E**

1. Sleep—Fiction
ISBN 0-15-256708-9 LC 83-13035

"In this sleepytime cumulative tale, all are pleasantly napping until a pesky flea starts the clamor that wakes up the whole family—mouse, cat, dog, child, and granny." Child Book Rev Serv

"The cool blues and greens are superseded by warm colors and bursts of action as each sleeper wakes, ending in an eruption of color and energy as naptime ends. A deft matching of text and pictures adds to the appeal of cumulation, and to the silliness of the mound of sleepers—just the right kind of humor for the lap audience." Bull Cent Child Books

Oh my baby bear! Harcourt Brace Jovanovich 1990 unp il $12.95 **E**

1. Bears—Fiction
ISBN 0-15-257698-3 LC 89-7564

Baby Bear discovers that he is now old enough to dress himself, eat breakfast by himself, and give himself a bath, but perhaps most wonderful of all he will never be too big for a goodnight kiss

"Wood's distinctive watercolor illustrations are warm and reassuring; she manages to convey the humor of Baby Bear's early solo efforts without ever making fun of him. Children are sure to identify with his growing independence, making this a perfect choice for the story hour or bedtime." Booklist

Woodruff, Elvira

Tubtime; illustrated by Suçie Stevenson. Holiday House 1990 unp il $14.95 E

1. Baths—Fiction 2. Sisters—Fiction
ISBN 0-8234-0777-2 LC 89-36609

"The three dirty O'Mally sisters are taking a bubble bath after a mud fight. Mom, who is on the phone, keeps calling upstairs to see if they are all right. . . . Encased in the bubbles the sisters blow are chickens, frogs, and finally a big alligator. As long as the alligator is in his bubble, the girls are safe, but he seems perilously close to breaking out. The fantastic happenings in the bathroom, which escalate with impunity, are neatly juxtaposed against Mom's mundane conversation downstairs. Illustrating the goings-on is Stevenson's rambunctious, cartoon-style art, colored in pastels. Bubbling over with good cheer." Booklist

Wright, Jill, 1942-

The old woman and the jar of uums; pictures by Glen Rounds. Putnam 1990 unp il $14.95 E

1. Magic—Fiction
ISBN 0-399-21736-3 LC 88-29708

A little old woman and a naughty boy named Jackie McPhee fall under the spell of a magic jar, making them say "Uumm," and must go to the hideous Willy Nilly Man to get the charm lifted

"Rich characterizations, spicy details, and a plot steeped in the folklore tradition form a tasty morsel indeed. Rounds' scratchy, angular ink-and-color drawings provide mouth-watering country flavor and briskly illustrate the grumpy, the sassy, the timid, and the determined of the story." Booklist

Another available title about the old lady and the Willy Nilly Man is entered below

The old woman and the Willy Nilly Man; pictures by Glen Rounds. Putnam 1987 unp il $13.95 (k-3) E

1. Shoes—Fiction
ISBN 0-399-21355-4 LC 86-9377

"The old woman has a problem: every night when she tries to sleep, her shoes go dancing all over the house, keeping her awake with the racket they make. At wit's end, she consults the Willy Nilly Man, a scary hermit and conjure man who lives back in the woods. When the Willy Nilly Man tricks her, the old woman retaliates and finally breaks down his gruff exterior so that he cures her shoes of their annoying habit, and the two of them become friends. . . . The characterizations . . . are based on stories the author heard in the Oklahoma countryside and the hills of Arkansas." SLJ

"Glen Rounds' full-color, down-home drawings—clean-lined, spacious, and wickedly funny—complete an effective story-hour selection for anyone comfortable with the dialect, which occasionally seems stagy in a printed text." Bull Cent Child Books

Yarbrough, Camille, 1948-

Cornrows; illustrated by Carole Byard. Coward, McCann & Geoghegan 1979 unp il $7.95; pa $5.95 E

1. Blacks—Fiction 2. Hair and hairdressing—Fiction
ISBN 0-698-20462-X; 0-698-20529-4 (pa)
LC 78-24010

Coretta Scott King Award for illustration, 1980

This story illustrates how the hair style of cornrows, a symbol in Africa since ancient times, can today in this country symbolize the courage of Afro-Americans

"Dialect is used but not overused. Byard's black-and-white drawings . . . are attractive and welcome." SLJ

Yeoman, John

Old Mother Hubbard's dog dresses up; [by] John Yeoman & Quentin Blake. Houghton Mifflin 1990 unp il $6.95 E

1. Dogs—Fiction 2. Stories in rhyme
ISBN 0-395-53358-9 LC 89-27026

First published 1989 in the United Kingdom

When Old Mother Hubbard complains to her dog about the ragged condition of his coat, he resorts to wearing a variety of disguises and drives her to distraction

"The books' appeal lies in the dog's irreverent behavior, which will intrigue children. Blake's familiar, energetic, blackline and watercolor illustrations are perfectly paired with these brief rhymes, reinforcing the silly unpredictability of each." SLJ

Other available titles about Old Mother Hubbard's dog are:
Old Mother Hubbard's dog learns to play (1990)
Old Mother Hubbard's dog needs a doctor (1990)
Old Mother Hubbard's dog takes up sport (1990)

Yolen, Jane

Commander Toad in space; pictures by Bruce Degen. Coward, McCann & Geoghegan 1980 63p il lib bdg $8.99; pa $5.95 E

1. Toads—Fiction
ISBN 0-698-30724-0 (lib bdg); 0-698-20522-7 (pa)
LC 79-10467

A "beginning-to-read book with brave space explorers, a ship named the 'Star Warts,' and a monster who calls himself Deep Wader. . . . The adventure of Commander Toad and his colleagues is a clever spoof and really funny reading. . . . Degen picks up on [the spoof] by drawing mock-serious amphibious characters and a horrible, yet somehow foolish, Wader. This hits the nail on the countdown button for primary as well as some older problem readers." Booklist

Other available titles about Commander Toad are:
Commander Toad and the big black hole (1983)
Commander Toad and the dis-asteroid (1985)
Commander Toad and the intergalactic spy (1986)
Commander Toad and the Planet of the Grapes (1982)
Commander Toad and the space pirates (1987)

The girl who loved the wind; pictures by Ed Young. Crowell 1972 unp il o.p.; Harper & Row paperback available $4.50 E

1. Winds—Fiction
ISBN 0-06-443088-X (pa) LC 71-171012

Yolen, Jane—*Continued*

"The bittersweet tale of a wealthy merchant's daughter, Danina, protected from the world so carefully that her exquisite palace becomes a prison, and she finally flies away with the wind. The striking illustrations, combining watercolor and collage, are stylized and oriental. The story unfolds at a measured pace, with a subtly implied message that life must be a mixture of happiness and sadness." Booklist

Mice on ice; pictures by Lawrence Di Fiori. Dutton 1980 71p il $7.95 **E**

1. Ice skating—Fiction 2. Kidnapping—Fiction 3. Mice—Fiction
ISBN 0-525-34872-7 LC 79-19342

"A Smart cat book"

Horace Hopper, the famous inventor of a magic ice-making formula, must rescue Rosa Burrow-Minder, star of the Mice Capades, from Gomer, the Rat King and his henchmen, who kidnap her and hold her for ransom

"This variant of a classic story line has all the right hokey elements of fun it needs: a show, an ingenue, a hero, a villain, and a bit of magic. . . . Di Fiori's drawings borrow heavily from old-time cartoon forms, a colorful interpretation and most appropriate." Booklist

No bath tonight; pictures by Nancy Winslow Parker. Crowell 1978 unp il $12.89; lib bdg $12.89 **E**

1. Baths—Fiction 2. Grandmothers—Fiction
ISBN 0-690-03881-X; 0-690-03882-8 (lib bdg) LC 77-26605

"Little Jeremy is a past master at collecting wounds that rule out bathtime. He gets dirtier each day. . . . Then wily Grandma visits. Having drunk her tea, she tells the boy what the leaves reveal and offers to make child tea. That, she says, will disclose days in the life of Jeremy. Grandma makes child tea of the boy in the bathtub and predicts a pleasant future from her divinations. As she always does, Yolen delivers a sprightly tale, matched in *brio* by Parker's inimitable scenes, in crayony hues. A treat." Publ Wkly

Owl moon; illustrated by John Schoenherr. Philomel Bks. 1987 unp il lib bdg $13.95 **E**

1. Owls—Fiction 2. Fathers and daughters—Fiction
ISBN 0-399-21457-7 LC 87-2300

Awarded the Caldecott Medal, 1988

"The poetic narrative is told from the point of view of a child who 'has been waiting to go owling with Pa for a long, long time.' The father and child venture forth on a cold winter night not to capture, but to commune with, the great horned owl." SLJ

This book "conveys the scary majesty of winter woods at night in language that seldom overreaches either character or subject. . . . Jane Yolen and John Schoenherr, who are both prolific, have done excellent work in the past, but this book has a magic that is extremely rare in books for any age." N Y Times Book Rev

Piggins and the royal wedding; illustrated by Jane Dyer. Harcourt Brace Jovanovich 1989 c1988 unp il $13.95 **E**

1. Mystery and detective stories 2. Pigs—Fiction
ISBN 0-15-261687-X LC 88-5399

"Piggins, the imperturbable butler, is summoned to solve the mystery of a missing wedding ring. The royal family, the well-dressed Reynard family, and their cozy Edwardian period home are all amusingly depicted in the busy and colorful illustrations." Horn Book

Other available titles about Piggins are:
Piggins (1987)
Picnic with Piggins (1988)

Sky dogs; illustrated by Barry Moser. Harcourt Brace Jovanovich 1990 unp il $15.95 **E**

1. Siksika Indians—Fiction 2. Indians of North America—Fiction 3. Horses—Fiction
ISBN 0-15-275480-6 LC 89-26960

"In this lyrical tale drawn from Blackfoot legend, an old man recounts the origin of his name, He-who-loves-horses. He describes the coming of horses, 'Sky Dogs,' from across the plains, and the wonder and awe he and his people felt when they first saw these 'big . . . elk, with tails of straw." Publ Wkly

"The text is smooth, poetic, and nicely suited to reading aloud or telling. Moser's paintings—all red, gold, and brown—are starkly effective." Bull Cent Child Books

Yorinks, Arthur, 1953-

Company's coming; illustrated by David Small. Crown 1988 unp il $12.95 **E**

1. Extraterrestrial beings—Fiction
ISBN 0-517-56751-2 LC 87-13579

"Shirley has invited her relatives to dinner and Moe is tinkering in the backyard when a flying saucer lands. The hilarious dialogue in this storybook 'is as well timed as the best comedy act,' and pen-and-ink illustrations capture the mayhem perfectly." N Y Times Book Rev

Hey, Al; story by Arthur Yorinks; pictures by Richard Egielski. Farrar, Straus & Giroux 1986 unp il $13.95; pa $4.95 **E**

1. Fantastic fiction
ISBN 0-374-33060-3; 0-374-42985-5 (pa) LC 86-80955

Awarded the Caldecott Medal, 1987

"Al, a janitor, and his faithful dog, Eddie, live in a single room on the West Side. . . . Their tiny home is crowded and cramped; their life is an endless struggle. Al and Eddie are totally miserable until a large and mysterious bird offers them a change of fortune." Publisher's note

"Egielski's solid naturalism provides just the visual foil needed to establish the surreal character of this fantasy. The muted earth tones of the one-room flat contrast symbolically with the bright hues of the birds' plumage and the foliage of the floating paradise. The anatomical appropriateness of Al and Eddie plays neatly against the flamboyant depiction of the plants. Text and pictures work together to challenge readers' concept of reality." SLJ

It happened in Pinsk; story by Arthur Yorinks; pictures by Richard Egielski. Farrar, Straus & Giroux 1983 unp il $12.95; pa $3.95 **E**

1. Head—Fiction
ISBN 0-374-34658-5; 0-374-43649-5 (pa) LC 83-1727

Yorinks, Arthur, 1953-—*Continued*

"Shoe salesman Irv Irving and his wife have all of life's comforts—nice clothes, good food, a telephone—but Irv, jealous of nearly everyone else, simply is not satisfied. When he awakes one morning and finds he is missing his head, his pragmatic wife outfits him with a new one, made of old socks and a pillowcase; Irv then has the chance to find out what it is like to be someone else." SLJ

"Carefully rendered detail in the city's architecture and in its inhabitants' dress conveys the flavor of Pinsk. And the artist's distinctive almost caricatured treatment of human figures is perfectly suited to the offbeat nature of the tale. With enthusiasm and wit the lavish illustrations match the rhythm and humor of the text." Horn Book

Oh, Brother; story by Arthur Yorinks; pictures by Richard Egielski. Farrar, Straus & Giroux 1989 unp il $15.95 **E**

1. Brothers—Fiction 2. Twins—Fiction
ISBN 0-374-35599-1 LC 89-61251

"Michael Di Capua books"

The "misadventures of quarrelsome twins as they make their way from Rotten's Home for Lost Boys to the Queen of England's court, squabbling all the while." SLJ

"The early-twentieth-century setting is a perfect showcase for Egielski's satirical combination of softly rounded shapes and absurdly deadpan characters. Even the literal colors project an earnestness that never betrays the tongue-in-cheek tone of the text." Bull Cent Child Books

Young, Ed

The other bone. Harper & Row 1984 unp il lib bdg $14.89 **E**

1. Dogs—Fiction 2. Stories without words
ISBN 0-06-026871-9 LC 83-47706

"This canine companion volume to the adventures of a cat in 'Up a Tree' [entered below] is based on a fable. A dog discovers a bone in a garbage can and races off with it—only to lose it in a pool of water when he growls at his reflection." SLJ

"With restrained humor the artist captures the dog's anticipation, pride, bewilderment, and disappointment." Horn Book

Up a tree. Harper & Row 1983 unp il lib bdg $14.89 **E**

1. Cats—Fiction 2. Stories without words
ISBN 0-06-026814-X LC 82-47733

"The story of a cat that—chasing a butterfly—climbs a tree, is treed by a dog, fears the descent, repels a robed and turbaned rescuer on a ladder, and finally comes down when a fishmonger walks by." Bull Cent Child Books

"Fine red lines frame most of the drawings, setting off the soft gray-and-white illustrations of the cat and of the helpful bystanders. Elegantly designed book, superb in its depiction of feline expressions, both fierce and wistful." Horn Book

Young, James, 1956-

A million chameleons. Little, Brown 1990 unp il $11.95 **E**

1. Chameleons—Fiction 2. Color—Fiction 3. Stories in rhyme
ISBN 0-316-97129-4 LC 90-52567

A million chameleons visit the zoo, climb a tree, and ride a merry-go-round, changing color as they go

"The vivid colors, appealing illustrations and rhyming text which deftly captures the joyous mood make this book as much fun as a day at the carnival." Publ Wkly

Zalben, Jane Breskin

Happy Passover, Rosie; story and pictures by Jane Breskin Zalben. Holt & Co. 1990 unp il $13.95 **E**

1. Passover—Fiction 2. Bears—Fiction
ISBN 0-8050-1221-4 LC 89-19979

Companion volume to: Beni's first Chanukah (1988)

A young bear named Rosie celebrates her first Passover with her family. The book includes an explanation of the seder plate and a list of the Four Questions, in English and Hebrew

"Soft, decorative illustrations, similar in style to the illustrations in some Haggadot and depicting a warm, loving bear family highlight this narration of a family Seder. . . . This simple, pleasant story is a welcome addition to the growing collection of picture books with Jewish themes." Publ Wkly

Zemach, Harve

The judge; an untrue tale; with pictures by Margot Zemach. Farrar, Straus & Giroux 1969 unp il $14.95; pa $4.95 **E**

1. Judges—Fiction 2. Stories in rhyme
ISBN 0-374-33960-0; 0-374-43962-1 (pa) LC 79-87209

A Caldecott Medal honor book, 1970

"Enthroned on his bench, a curmudgeon of a judge hears a prisoner plead that he didn't know that what he did was against the law, but that he had seen a horrible beast. 'This man has told an untrue tale. Throw him in jail!' Each additional prisoner adds to the story; each infuriates the judge." Sutherland. The Best in Child Books

Mommy, buy me a china doll; pictures by Margot Zemach. Farrar, Straus & Giroux 1975 c1966 unp il $10.95; pa $4.95 **E**

1. Folk songs—United States
ISBN 0-374-35005-1; 0-374-45286-5 (pa) LC 66-16943

A reprint of the title first published 1966 by Follett

A "picture book version of the cumulative folk song that has the appeals of repetition, of a chain of mildly nonsensical actions, and of a warmly satisfying ending. Eliza Lou's request for a china doll leads to proposals that it be bought with Daddy's feather bed, so Daddy would have to sleep in the horsey's bed, and the horsey would have to sleep in Sister's bed, and so on, and so on. Each page of print is faced by a full-page illustration in color, humorous in mood." Bull Cent Child Books

Zemach, Harve—*Continued*

The princess and Froggie; stories by Harve and Kaethe Zemach; pictures by Margot Zemach. Farrar, Straus & Giroux 1975 unp il $9.95 **E**

1. Frogs—Fiction 2. Friendship—Fiction
ISBN 0-374-36116-9 LC 75-697

"Three disarming vignettes starring 'the princess' and her friend Froggie, who is adept at easing crisis situations. . . . Coupled with Margot Zemach's unconventional graphic interpretation, the stories become droll farce. The frumpy princess in a shapeless Sunday dress with a be-draggled ribbon in her hair is a merry departure from the usual type; and Mama doesn't recall any royal matrons on the scene lately. Blithe tongue-in-cheek comedy for the very young." Booklist

Ziebel, Peter

Look closer! Clarion Bks. 1989 unp il lib bdg $13.95 **E**

ISBN 0-89919-815-5 LC 88-29186

Close-up photographs present unusual views of common items, such as a toothbrush, orange, or umbrella, accompanied by brief questions providing a clue to each object's identity

"The concept is clear, relevant, and naturally organized with attention to association of words and/or graphic images. . . . Ziebel's photography, set off by striking book design, makes this a stand-out in the concept-book genre." Bull Cent Child Books

Ziefert, Harriet

A new coat for Anna; pictures by Anita Lobel. Knopf 1986 unp il lib bdg $10.99; pa $3.95 **E**

1. Coats—Fiction
ISBN 0-394-97426-3 (lib bdg); 0-394-89861-3 (pa) LC 86-2722

Set in a war-torn town in post-World War II Eastern Europe. Even though there is no money, Anna's mother finds a way to make Anna a badly needed winter coat

"Ziefert's writing is clear and succinct, but it is in Lobel's brightly colored paintings that the story truly unfolds. From crumbling rooms cluttered with mementos of a better life to the charm of the tiny sheep farm, the illustrations bring to life another time, another place, and a little girl whose delight in her new coat is just as great as that of many a young reader of this book. The expressiveness of the faces in Lobel's paintings brings life to the story. Ziefert's tale, based on a true story, carries a simple lesson that will be understood and cherished by all ages." SLJ

Zion, Gene

Harry the dirty dog; pictures by Margaret Bloy Graham. Harper & Row 1956 unp il $12.95; lib bdg $12.89; pa $3.95 **E**

1. Dogs—Fiction
ISBN 0-06-026865-4; 0-06-026866-2 (lib bdg); 0-06-443009-X (pa) LC 56-8137

"A runaway dog becomes so dirty his family almost doesn't recognize him. Harry's flight from scrubbing brush and bath water takes him on a tour of the city. Road repairs, railroad yards, construction sites, and coal deliveries contribute to his grimy appearance and show aspects of city life that contrast with the tidy suburb that is 'home.'" Moorachian. What is a City?

"Harry's fun and troubles are told simply, and the drawings are full of action and humor. The combination will have great appeal for the very young." Horn Book

Other available titles about Harry are:
Harry and the lady next door (1960)
Harry by the sea (1965)
No roses for Harry! (1958)

Zolotow, Charlotte, 1915-

The hating book; pictures by Ben Shecter. Harper & Row 1969 32p il $12.95; lib bdg $12.89; pa $3.95 **E**

1. Friendship—Fiction
ISBN 0-06-026923-5; 0-06-026924-3 (lib bdg); 0-06-443197-5 (pa) LC 69-14444

"A little girl tells of several instances of being rebuffed by her friend, ending with the comment, 'I hated my friend.' Finally, at the urging of her mother, she goes to see the friend and asks her why she's been so 'rotten.' The answer is that 'Sue said Jane said you said I looked like a freak.' The actual remark had been that she looked 'neat.' The point of the book is clear as the two friends make plans to play together the following day." Read Ladders for Hum Relat. 6th edition

I know a lady; pictures by James Stevenson. Greenwillow Bks. 1984 unp il $11.75; lib bdg $11.88; Penguin Bks. pa $3.95 **E**

1. Old age—Fiction
ISBN 0-688-03837-9; 0-688-03838-7 (lib bdg); 0-14-050550-4 (pa) LC 83-25361

Sally describes a loving and lovable old lady in her neighborhood who grows flowers, waves to children when they pass her house, and bakes cookies for them at Christmas

"With virtuoso skill the artist uses scratchy lines to catch just the right tilt of a dog's tail and the bulge of a cookie-filled cheek. The amiable old lady is brought to life, complete with her slight stoop, sensible shoes, and shapeless but still spry body. Her house is a perfectly conceived setting as the illustrator lovingly pictures her stove and comfortable rocking chairs. A feeling of warmth and affection suffuses the pictures." Horn Book

Mr. Rabbit and the lovely present; pictures by Maurice Sendak. Harper & Row 1962 unp il $13.95; lib bdg $13.89; pa $3.50 **E**

1. Birthdays—Fiction 2. Color—Fiction 3. Rabbits—Fiction
ISBN 0-06-026945-6; 0-06-026946-4 (lib bdg); 0-06-443020-0 (pa) LC 62-7590

A Caldecott Medal honor book, 1963

"A serious little girl and a tall, other-worldly white rabbit converse about a present for her mother. "But what?' said the little girl. 'Yes, what?' said Mr. Rabbit.' It requires a day of searching—for red, yellow, green, and blue, all things the mother likes, to make a basket

Zolotow, Charlotte, 1915—*Continued*
of fruit for the present." Horn Book

"The quiet story, told in dialogue, is illustrated in richly colored pictures which exactly fit the fanciful mood." Hodges. Books for Elem Sch Libr

My friend John; pictures by Ben Shecter. Harper & Row 1968 32p il $12.95; lib bdg $12.89 **E**

1. Friendship—Fiction
ISBN 0-06-026947-2; 0-06-026948-0 (lib bdg) LC 68-10209

A picture book about "two small boys who are best friends, carrying on their routine activities. Particulary interesting is the author's implication that the minor differences which exist between the two are not a deterrent to the formation of a valid friendship." SLJ

"The drawings in this warm and engaging picture book are uncluttered, expressive, and altogether likable." Booklist

My grandson Lew; pictures by William Pène Du Bois. Harper & Row 1974 30p il $12.95; lib bdg $12.95; pa $3.95 **E**

1. Death—Fiction 2. Grandfathers—Fiction
ISBN 0-06-026961-8; 0-06-026962-6 (lib bdg); 0-06-443066-9 (pa) LC 73-166336

"An Ursula Nordstrom book"

"Warm, rich, and beautiful, a comforting consideration of death. Lew, now six, awakes and remembers back to when he was two and his grandfather came to him in the night when he called. . . . Lew recounts the images he has retained and then his mother tells of her remembrances, concluding, 'We will remember him together and neither of us will be so lonely as we would be if we had to remember him alone.' Pène du Bois' finely washed illustrations exude a serenity and understanding perfectly in tune with the story." Booklist

One step, two—; pictures by Cindy Wheeler. [rev ed]. Lothrop, Lee & Shepard Bks. 1981 unp il $12.95 **E**

1. Spring—Fiction 2. Mothers and daughters—Fiction
ISBN 0-688-41971-2 LC 80-11749

First published 1955

In this "discovery story, a mother and her preschool-age daughter go walking on a spring morning. En route to the corner and back, they count their steps, the flowers in a window box and clothes on a line. They notice the colors of animals and objects, hear the sound of bells and a garbage truck and smell some flowers. Returning home, the little girl falls asleep in her mother's arms." SLJ

"Black sketchy lines provide background for warm, deep-toned colors that give focus to main happenings. While some of the picture remains outlined, the girl and her mother, the flowers, clothesline, or bird are colorfully depicted depending on the story's emphasis." Booklist

Over and over; pictures by Garth Williams. Harper & Row 1987 c1957 unp il $7.95; lib bdg $14.89 **E**

1. Holidays—Fiction 2. Seasons—Fiction
ISBN 0-694-00195-3; 0-06-026956-1 (lib bdg) LC 86-29487

A reissue of the title first published 1957

A little girl and her mother observe the passage of the seasons as they celebrate the year's holidays, beginning with Christmas and ending after Thanksgiving with a birthday wish that the cycle begin all over again

The quarreling book; pictures by Arnold Lobel. Harper & Row 1963 unp il $12.95; lib bdg $12.89; pa $3.95 **E**

ISBN 0-06-026975-8; 0-06-026976-6 (lib bdg); 0-06-443034-0 (pa) LC 63-14445

"Father forgets to kiss Mother goodbye when starting to work one morning, so Mother is unhappy and becomes cross with Jonathan James who takes out his feelings on his sister, and the chain continues until reversed by the dog who thinks being shoved off the bed is just a game and lots of fun. The sequence, then starts in happy reverse until at five, with the rain ending, Mr. James comes home and kisses Mrs. James." SLJ

It is "a worthwhile book which clearly demonstrates the far-reaching effects one's actions have on others. Even the youngest child will grasp its lesson easily. The illustrations are whimsical, detailed and expressive." NY Times Book Rev

The quiet mother and the noisy little boy; illustrations by Marc Simont. Harper & Row 1989 30p il $12.95; lib bdg $12.89 **E**

1. Mothers and sons—Fiction
ISBN 0-06-026978-2; 0-06-026979-0 (lib bdg) LC 88-936

A newly illustrated edition of the title first published 1953 in a different version by Lothrop, Lee & Shepard

A noisy little boy discovers the pleasure of a quiet moment with his mother after his very noisy cousin pays a visit to their house

Sleepy book; illustrations by Ilse Plume. newly il ed. Harper & Row 1988 unp il $13.95; lib bdg $13.89 **E**

1. Sleep 2. Animals
ISBN 0-06-026967-7; 0-06-026968-5 (lib bdg) LC 87-45861

A newly illustrated edition of the title first published 1958 by Lothrop

Describes how each animal sleeps in its own special place, in its own special way

"Plume's full-page drawings on the right are windows into a great green room of childhood from which human sleepy-heads can look outward onto an enchanting world of nature. Her top and bottom borders on the left pages frame the spare, poetic narrative." SLJ

Something is going to happen; pictures by Catherine Stock. Harper & Row 1988 unp il $12.95; lib bdg $12.89 **E**

1. Snow—Fiction 2. Family life—Fiction
ISBN 0-06-027028-4; 0-06-027029-2 (lib bdg) LC 87-26661

"One by one, as the members of a family awaken on a cold November Monday, they are all stirred by the feeling that 'something is going to happen.' When they open the front door together, they discover, to their surprise and delight, the first snow of winter. . . . Rhythm and repetition empower short, simple sentences, skillfully paced to build anticipation. The rounded shapes and muted hues of Stock's watercolor paintings enhance the story's sense of homey security, and contrast success-

Zolotow, Charlotte, 1915-—*Continued*
fully with the snowy white double-page spread which serves as its climax." SLJ

A tiger called Thomas; pictures by Catherine Stock. Lothrop, Lee & Shepard Bks. 1988 c1963 unp il $12.95; lib bdg $12.88 **E**

1. Halloween—Fiction

ISBN 0-688-06696-8; 0-688-06697-6 (lib bdg) LC 86-20878

A newly illustrated edition of the title first published 1963

"Shy Thomas thinks that no one in his new neighborhood will like him, so he just sits on his new porch and watches, instead of trying to make friends—until Halloween night. Dressed in his tiger outfit, Thomas makes his first foray into the new neighborhood . . . and returns—surprised—with a whole passel of new friends." SLJ

"The story has a simple but satisfying plot, light writing style, and a gentle message." Bull Cent Child Books

"Stock's new full-color illustrations [replace] the original two-tone artwork by Kurt Werth. . . . Brightening the sensitive pencil drawings with washes of rich, harmonious colors, she creates a convincing time and place for the story's setting." Booklist

William's doll; pictures by William Pène Du Bois. Harper & Row 1972 30p il $13.95; lib bdg $12.89; pa $3.95 **E**

1. Dolls—Fiction 2. Sex role—Fiction

ISBN 0-06-027047-0; 0-06-027048-9 (lib bdg); 0-06-443067-7 (pa) LC 70-183173

When little William asks for a doll, the other boys scorn him and his father tries to interest him in conventional boys' playthings such as a basketball and a train. His sympathetic grandmother buys him the doll, explaining his need to have it to love and care for so that he can practice being a father

"Very, very special. The strong, yet delicate pictures . . . convey a gentleness of spirit and longing most effectively, as William pantomimes his craving." N Y Times Book Rev

PART 2
AUTHOR, TITLE, SUBJECT, AND ANALYTICAL INDEX

AUTHOR, TITLE, SUBJECT AND ANALYTICAL INDEX

This index to the books in the Classified Catalog includes author, title, subject and analytical entries, added entries for illustrators and joint authors, and name and subject cross-references, all arranged in one alphabet. The number in bold face type at the end of each entry refers to the Dewey Decimal Classification where the main entry for the book will be found.

For further directions for use of this index, see page ix.

1 2 3, play with me. Gundersheimer, K. **E**

The **2nd** Raffi songbook. Raffi. **782.42**

3-2-1 Contact **505**

4B goes wild. Gilson, J. **Fic**

4th of July *See* Fourth of July

6th grade can really kill you. DeClements, B. **Fic**

7 x 7 tales of a sevensleeper. Johansen, H. **Fic**

17 kings and 42 elephants. Mahy, M. **E**

The **18th** emergency. Byars, B. C. **Fic**

24 hours in a forest. Watts, B. **574.5**

The **25¢** miracle. Nelson, T. **Fic**

The **26** letters. Ogg, O. **411**

26 letters and 99 cents. Hoban, T. **E**

101 costumes for all ages, all occasions. Cummings, R. **391**

101 things to do with a baby. Ormerod, J. **E**

263 brain busters. Phillips, L. **793.73**

The **500** hats of Bartholomew Cubbins. Seuss, Dr. **E**

1492 blues. Priore, F. V.
In Holiday plays round the year p229-38 **812.008**

The **1940s**. Wood, T. **909.82**

The **1950s**. Tames, R. **909.82**

12,000 words **423**

A

The **A** B C bunny. Gág, W. **E**

A.B.C.'s *See* Alphabet

A B C, say with me. Gundersheimer, K. **E**

A B Cedar. Lyon, G. E. **E**

A, B, see! Hoban, T. **E**

A-hunting we will go. See Langstaff, J. M. Oh, a-hunting we will go **781.62**

A.I.D.S. (Disease) *See* AIDS (Disease)

A my name is Alice. Bayer, J. **E**

A to zoo: subject access to children's picture books. Lima, C. W. **011.6**

A was an archer and shot at a frog
In A Nursery companion p10-15 **820.8**

AAAS *See* American Association for the Advancement of Science

AACR *See* Anglo-American cataloguing rules

Aamodt, Alice
(jt. auth) Johnson, S. A. Wolf pack **599.74**

Aardema, Verna
Bimwili & the Zimwi (k-2) **398.2**
Bringing the rain to Kapiti Plain (k-2) **398.2**
Oh, Kojo! How could you! (k-3) **398.2**
Princess Gorilla and a new kind of water (k-2) **398.2**
Rabbit makes a monkey of lion (k-2) **398.2**
The Sloogeh Dog and the stolen aroma
In The Scott, Foresman anthology of children's literature p317-19 **808.8**
The Vingananee and the tree toad (k-3) **398.2**
What's so funny, Ketu? (k-2) **398.2**
Who's in Rabbit's house? (k-3) **398.2**
Why mosquitoes buzz in people's ears (k-3) **398.2**

Aardvark

Fiction

Brown, M. T. Arthur's nose **E**
Mwalimu. Awful aardvark (k-2) **398.2**
Waber, B. An anteater named Arthur **E**

Aaron, Jane
(il) Wachter, O. No more secrets for me **362.7**

Aaron's gift. Levoy, M.
In Levoy, M. The witch of Fourth Street, and other stories **S C**

Aaron's shirt. Gould, D. **E**

Aaseng, Nathan, 1956-
From rags to riches (5 and up) **920**

Aaseng, Nathan, 1956-—*Continued*
The inventors: Nobel prizes in chemistry, physics, and medicine (5 and up) **609**
Midstream changes (5 and up) **331.7**
The problem solvers (5 and up) **920**
The unsung heroes (5 and up) **920**
AASL *See* American Association of School Librarians
Abacus
Dilson, J. The abacus: a pocket computer (5 and up) **513.028**
Abandoned children
Fiction
Townsend, J. R. Dan alone (6 and up) **Fic**
Voigt, C. Homecoming (6 and up) **Fic**
Abandoned towns *See* Ghost towns
Abbott, Jacob, 1803-1879
See/See also pages in the following book(s):
Jordan, A. M. From Rollo to Tom Sawyer, and other papers p72-81 **028.5**
Abbott, R. Tucker (Robert Tucker), 1919-
Seashells of the world (5 and up) **594**
Abbott, Robert Tucker *See* Abbott, R. Tucker (Robert Tucker), 1919-
Abby. Caines, J. F. **E**
ABC, Ed Emberley's. Emberley, E. **E**
ABC of things, Helen Oxenbury's. Oxenbury, H. **E**
ABC, Quentin Blake's. Blake, Q. **E**
A,B,C,D, tummy, toes, hands, knees. Hennessy, B. G. **E**
ABCs *See* Alphabet
The **ABC's** of origami. Sarasas, C. **736**
Abe and the runaways. Watson, W. J. *In* Holiday plays round the year p247-54 **812.008**
Abe Lincoln grows up. Sandburg, C. **92**
also in Sandburg, C. The Sandburg treasury p383-477 **818**
Abe Lincoln: log cabin to White House. North, S. **92**
Abebe, Daniel
Ethiopia—in pictures. See Ethiopia—in pictures **963**
Abells, Chana Byers
The children we remember (3-6) **940.54**
Abel's island. Steig, W. **Fic**
Abiyoyo. Seeger, P. **398.2**
Aboard a steam locomotive. Scarry, H. **625.2**
Abolafia, Yossi, 1944-
(il) Porte-Thomas, B. A. Harry in trouble **E**
(il) Prelutsky, J. It's Valentine's Day **811**
(il) Prelutsky, J. My parents think I'm sleeping: poems **811**
Abolitionists
Ferris, J. Walking the road to freedom: a story about Sojourner Truth (3-5) **92**
McKissack, P. C. Frederick Douglass: the black lion (4 and up) **92**
Miller, D. T. Frederick Douglass and the fight for freedom (6 and up) **92**
Ortiz, V. Sojourner Truth, a self-made woman (6 and up) **92**
About a fisherman and his wife. Grimm, J. *In* Grimm, J. About wise men and simpletons p5-14 **398.2**
About dying. Stein, S. B. **155.9**
About the B'nai Bagels. Konigsburg, E. L. **Fic**
About wise men and simpletons. Grimm, J. **398.2**
Abraham Lincoln. D'Aulaire, I. **92**
Abrams, Kathie
(il) Schwartz, A. Busy buzzing bumblebees and other tongue twisters **808.88**
Abridged Dewey decimal classification and relative index. Dewey, M. **025.4**
Abridged Readers' guide to periodical literature **051**
Absolute zero. Cresswell, H. See note under Cresswell, H. Ordinary Jack **Fic**
Abuse of children *See* Child abuse
Abuse of wives *See* Wife abuse
Accardo, Anthony
(il) Cooper, K. Where did you get those eyes? **929**
Accept me as I am: best books of juvenile nonfiction on impairments and disabilities. Friedberg, J. B. **016**
Accidents
See also Wounds and injuries
Fiction
Bauer, M. D. On my honor (4 and up) **Fic**
Prevention
See also Safety education
Brown, M. T. Dinosaurs, beware! (k-2) **613.6**
Acid rain
Baines, J. D. Acid rain (5 and up) **363.7**
Hare, T. Acid rain (5 and up) **363.7**
See/See also pages in the following book(s):
Pringle, L. P. Living in a risky world (6 and up) **363**
Ackerman, Karen, 1951-
Song and dance man **E**

AUTHOR, TITLE, SUBJECT, AND ANALYTICAL INDEX
SIXTEENTH EDITION

Acoustics *See* Sound

Acquaye, Alfred Allotey
Ethiopia—in pictures. See Ethiopia—in pictures 963

Acquired immune deficiency syndrome *See* AIDS (Disease)

Acrobats and acrobatics
Schmidt, D. I am a Jesse White tumbler 796.47

Across five Aprils. Hunt, I. **Fic**

Acting
See/See also pages in the following book(s):
Bauer, C. F. Handbook for storytellers p351-67 372.6

Costume

See Costume

Action alphabet. Neumeier, M. **E**

Action contraptions. Blocksma, M. **745.592**

Activities for anyone, anytime, anywhere. Robinson, J. **790.1**

Actors and actresses
Gish, L. An actor's life for me (3-5) **92**
Haskins, J. Shirley Temple Black (4 and up) **92**
Kamen, G. Charlie Chaplin (4 and up) **92**

Fiction

Greenfield, E. Grandpa's face **E**
Konigsburg, E. L. Up from Jericho Tel (5 and up) **Fic**
McCully, E. A. Zaza's big break **E**

An **actor's** life for me. Gish, L. **92**

Actresses *See* Actors and actresses

Adam (Biblical figure)

About

Hutton, W. Adam and Eve (k-3) **222**

Adam and Eve. Hutton, W. **222**

Adam of the road. Vining, E. G. **Fic**

Adams, Adrienne
The Easter egg artists **E**

Adams, John Quincy, 1767-1848

About

Kent, Z. John Quincy Adams, sixth president of the United States (4 and up) **92**

Adams, Michael
(il) Alcott, L. M. Little women **Fic**

Adams, Richard, 1920-
Watership Down (6 and up) **Fic**
See/See also pages in the following book(s):
Crosscurrents of criticism p308-14 **028.5**

Adams, Richard Craig
Science with computers (6 and up) **507**

Adams, Samuel, 1722-1803

About

Fritz, J. Why don't you get a horse, Sam Adams? (3-5) **92**

Adamson, Lynda G.
A reference guide to historical fiction for children and young adults **016.8**

Addams, Jane, 1860-1935
See/See also pages in the following book(s):
Jacobs, W. J. Great lives: human rights p173-81 (5 and up) **920**

Addie meets Max. Robins, J. **E**

The **Adélie** penguin. Dewey, J. **598**

Adetunji, Ezekiel Aderogba
Musa and Kojere
In The Crest and the hide, and other African stories of heroes, chiefs, bards, hunters, sorcerers, and common people p89-93 **398.2**

Adhesives
See/See also pages in the following book(s):
Cobb, V. Gobs of goo p13-17 (2-4) **547**

Adkins, Jan
The art and industry of sandcastles (4 and up) **728.8**
Letterbox: the art & history of letters (4 and up) **745.6**
Moving heavy things (5 and up) **621.8**
Symbols, a silent language (4-6) **302.2**
Toolchest (5 and up) **684**

Adler, David A., 1947-
Banks: where the money is (2-4) **332.1**
The carsick zebra and other animal riddles (1-3) **793.73**
Jackie Robinson: he was the first (3-5) **92**
Martin Luther King, Jr.: free at last (2-4) **92**
Our Golda: the story of Golda Meir (3-5) **92**
A picture book of Abraham Lincoln (1-3) **92**
A picture book of Benjamin Franklin (1-3) **92**
A picture book of George Washington (1-3) **92**
A picture book of Hanukkah (1-3) **296.4**
A picture book of Martin Luther King, Jr. (1-3) **92**
A picture book of Passover (1-3) **296.4**
A picture book of Thomas Jefferson (1-3) **92**
Redwoods are the tallest trees in the world (k-3) **585**
Roman numerals (2-4) **513**
A teacher on roller skates and other school riddles (k-3) **793.73**
The twisted witch, and other spooky riddles (1-3) **793.73**

Adler, Irving
Mathematics (4 and up) **510**

Adoff, Arnold, 1935-
All the colors of the race: poems (4-6) **811**
Black is brown is tan **E**
Eats: poems (3-5) **811**
Malcolm X (2-5) **92**
Sports pages (4 and up) **811**
(ed) I am the darker brother. See I am the darker brother **811.008**
(ed) My black me: a beginning book of black poetry. See My black me: a beginning book of black poetry **811.008**

Adolescence
Johnson, E. W. People, love, sex, and families (5 and up) **613.9**
Madaras, L. The what's happening to my body? book for boys: a growing up guide for parents and sons (6 and up) **613.9**
Madaras, L. The what's happening to my body? book for girls: a growing up guide for parents and daughters (6 and up) **613.9**
Shaw, D. Make the most of a good thing: you! (5 and up) **613**

Fiction

Blume, J. Are you there God? it's me, Margaret (5 and up) **Fic**
Blume, J. Then again, maybe I won't (5 and up) **Fic**
Hall, L. Dagmar Schultz and the angel Edna (6 and up) **Fic**
Terris, S. Author! Author! (6 and up) **Fic**

Adolescents *See* Youth

Adoption
Krementz, J. How it feels to be adopted (4 and up) **362.7**

Fiction

Caines, J. F. Abby **E**
Howard, E. Her own song (4 and up) **Fic**
Jones, R. C. The Believers (5 and up) **Fic**
Magorian, M. Good night, Mr. Tom (6 and up) **Fic**
Myers, W. D. Me, Mop, and the Moondance Kid (4-6) **Fic**
Neufeld, J. Edgar Allan (5 and up) **Fic**
Turner, A. W. Through moon and stars and night skies **E**

Adoption, Interracial *See* Interracial adoption

Adventure along the white river in the sky. Mayo, G.
In Mayo, G. Star tales p19-22 **398.2**

Adventure and adventurers

Fiction

Aiken, J. Bridle the wind (6 and up) **Fic**
Alexander, L. The Illyrian adventure (5 and up) **Fic**
Alexander, L. The marvelous misadventures of Sebastian (4 and up) **Fic**
Alexander, L. Westmark (5 and up) **Fic**
Fleischman, S. The whipping boy (5 and up) **Fic**
Garfield, L. The December Rose (5 and up) **Fic**
Kendall, S. The Bell Reef (5 and up) **Fic**
Kennedy, R. Amy's eyes (5 and up) **Fic**

The **adventure** of Countess Jeanne. Uden, G.
In The Scott, Foresman anthology of children's literature p474-78 **808.8**

The **adventure** of the German student. San Souci, R.
In San Souci, R. Short & shivery p96-102 **398.2**

Adventure stories *See* Adventure and adventurers—Fiction

Adventures in your national parks (4 and up) **917.3**

The **adventures** of a fisher lad. Quayle, E.
In Quayle, E. The shining princess, and other Japanese legends p57-68 **398.2**

The **adventures** of Ali Baba Bernstein. Hurwitz, J. **Fic**

Adventures of Caliph Haroun-al-Raschid
The Adventures of Haroun-al-Raschid, Caliph of Bagdad
In The Arabian nights entertainments p316-19 **398.2**

The **Adventures** of Haroun-al-Raschid, Caliph of Bagdad
In The Arabian nights entertainments p316-19 **398.2**

The **adventures** of High John the Conqueror. Sanfield, S. **398.2**

The **adventures** of Huckleberry Finn. Twain, M. **Fic**

The **Adventures** of Jack and Jill and Old Dame Gill
In A Nursery companion p38-39 **820.8**

The **adventures** of Johnny May. Branscum, R. **Fic**

The **adventures** of Obadiah. Turkle, B. C. See note under Turkle, B. C. Obadiah the Bold **E**

The **adventures** of Odysseus and The tale of Troy. See Colum, P. The children's Homer: The adventures of Odysseus and The tale of Troy **883**

The **adventures** of Pinocchio. Collodi, C. **Fic**

The **Adventures** of Prince Camaralzaman and the Princess Badoura
In The Arabian nights entertainments p216-66 **398.2**

The **adventures** of Rama. Beach, M. C. **891**

The **adventures** of Taxi Dog. Barracca, D. **E**

The **adventures** of Tom Sawyer. Twain, M. **Fic**

The **adventures** of Tom Sawyer [excerpt]. Twain, M.
In The Random House book of humor for children p293-300 **817.008**

The **adventures** of Treehorn. Heide, F. P. See note under Heide, F. P. The shrinking of Treehorn **Fic**

Adventuring with books. National Council of Teachers of English. Committee on the Elementary School Booklist **011.6**

Advertising
See/See also pages in the following book(s):
Schmitt, L. Smart spending p1-13 (5 and up) **640.73**

AECT *See* Association for Educational Communications and Technology

Aeneas (Legendary character)
See/See also pages in the following book(s):
Hamilton, E. Mythology p319-42 (6 and up) **292**

Aeronautics
See also Airplanes; Airships; Flight; Rockets (Aeronautics)

History

Berliner, D. Before the Wright brothers (5 and up) **629.13**
Boyne, W. J. The Smithsonian book of flight for young people (4 and up) **629.13**
Gibbons, G. Flying (k-2) **629.13**
Maurer, R. Airborne (5 and up) **629.13**
Taylor, R. L. The first flight (4 and up) **629.13**
Tessendorf, K. C. Barnstormers & daredevils (4 and up) **629.13**

Aeronautics, Military
See also World War, 1914-1918—Aerial operations; World War, 1939-1945—Aerial operations
Sullivan, G. The Thunderbirds (4 and up) **797.5**

Aesop
Aesop's fables [illus. by Heidi Holder] **398.2**
Aesop's fables [illus. by Lisbeth Zwerger] (1-3) **398.2**
Anno, M. Anno's Aesop **398.2**
Bolliger, M. Tales of a long afternoon **398.2**
Cauley, L. B. The town mouse and the country mouse **398.2**
Galdone, P. Three Aesop fox fables **398.2**
The Hare and the tortoise. See The Hare and the tortoise **398.2**
Jacobs, J. The fables of Aesop **398.2**
McFarland, J. B. The exploding frog and other fables from Aesop **398.2**
Stevens, J. The town mouse and the country mouse **398.2**

Aesop's fables [illus. by Heidi Holder]. Aesop. **398.2**

Aesop's fables [illus. by Lisbeth Zwerger]. Aesop. **398.2**

Afanas'ev, A. N. (Aleksandr Nikolaevich), 1826-1871
Russian fairy tales (4 and up) **398.2**
Contents: The wondrous wonder, the marvelous marvel; The fox physician; The death of the cock; Misery; The castle of the fly; The turnip; Riddles; The enchanted ring; The just reward; Salt; The golden slipper; Emelya the simpleton; The three kingdoms; The pike with the long teeth; The bad wife; The miser; The nobleman and the peasant; Ivanushka the Little Fool; The crane and the heron; Aliosha Popovich; The fox confessor; The bear; The spider; Baba Yaga and the brave youth; Prince Ivan and Princess Martha; The cat, the cock, and the fox; Baldak Borisievich; Know Not; The magic shirt; The three pennies; The princess who wanted to solve riddles; A soldier's riddle; The dead body; The frog princess; The speedy messenger; Vasilisa, the priest's daughter; The wise maiden and the seven robbers; The mayoress; Ivan the Simpleton; Father Nicholas and the thief; Burenshka, the little red cow; The jester; The precious hide; The cross is pledged as security; The daydreamer; The taming of the shrew; Quarrelsome Demyan; The magic box; Bukhtan Bukhtanovich; The fox and the woodcock; The fox and the crane; The two rivers; Nodey, the priest's grandson; The poor wretch; The fiddler in hell; The old woman who ran away; The singing tree and the talking bird; The ram who lost half his skin; The fox as midwife; The fox, the hare, and the cock; Baba Yaga; The ram, the cat, and the twelve wolves; The fox and the woodpecker; The snotty goat; Right and wrong; The potter; The self-playing gusla; Marco the Rich and Vasily the Luckless; Ivanko the bear's son; The secret ball; The indiscreet wife; The cheater cheated; The Maiden Tsar; Ivan the Cow's Son; The wolf and the goat; The wise little girl; Danilo the Luckless; Ivan the peasant's son and thumb-sized man; Death of a miser; The footless champion and the handless champion; Old favors are soon forgotten; The sheep, the fox, and the wolf; The brave laborer; Daughter and stepdaughter; The stubborn wife; Snow White and the fox; Foma Berennikov; The peasant, the bear, and the fox; Good advice; Horns; The armless maiden; Frolka Stay-at-Home; The milk of wild beasts; How a husband weaned his wife from fairy tales; The cock and the hen; The fox and the lobster; Nikita the Tanner; The wolf; The goat shedding on one side; The bold knight, the apples of youth, and the water of life; Two out of the sack; The man who did not know

Afanas'ev, A. N. (Aleksandr Nikolaevich), 1826-1871—*Continued*
fear; The merchant's daughter and the maidservant; The priest's laborer; The peasant and the corpse; The arrant fool; Lutoniushka; Barter; The grumbling old woman; The white duck; If you don't like it don't listen; The magic swan geese; Prince Danila Govorila; The wicked sisters; The princess who never smiled; Baba Yaga; Jack Frost; Husband and wife; Little Sister Fox and the wolf; The three kingdoms, copper, silver, and golden; The cock and the hand mill; Tereschichka; King Bear; Magic; The one-eyed evil; Sister Alionushka, brother Ivanushka; The seven Semyons; The merchant's daughter and the slanderer; The robbers; The lazy maiden; The miraculous pipe; The Sea King and Vasilisa the Wise; The fox as mourner; Vasilisa the Beautiful; The bun; The foolish wolf; The bear, the dog, and the cat; The bear and the cock; Dawn, Evening, and Midnight; Two Ivans, soldier's sons; Prince Ivan and Byely Polyanin; The crystal mountain; Koshchey the Deathless; The Firebird and Princess Vasilisa; Beasts in a pit; The dog and the woodpecker; Two kinds of luck; Go I know not whither—fetch I know not what; The wise wife; The goldfish; The golden-bristled pig, the golden-feathered duck, and the golden-maned mare; The duck with golden eggs; Elena the Wise; Treasure-trove; Maria Morevna; The soldier and the king; The sorceress; Ilya Muromets and the dragon; The devil who was a potter; Clever answers; Dividing the goose; The feather of Finist, the Bright Falcon; The Sun, the Moon, and the Raven; The bladder, the straw, and the shoe; The thief; The vampire; The beggar's plan; Woman's way; The foolish German; The enchanted princess; The raven and the lobster; Prince Ivan, the firebird, and the gray wolf; Shemiaka the judge

Russian folk tales (4 and up) **398.2**
Contents: Ivan Tsarevich, the grey wolf and the firebird; Sister Alyonushka and Brother Ivanushka; Finist the falcon; Marya Morevna; The white duck; Vasilisa the Beautiful; The frog princess

Afanas'ev, Aleksandr Nikolaevich *See* Afanas'ev, A. N. (Aleksandr Nikolaevich), 1826-1871

Afghanistan
Afghanistan—in pictures (5 and up) **958.1**
Clifford, M. L. The land and people of Afghanistan (5 and up) **958.1**

Afghanistan—in pictures (5 and up) **958.1**

Africa

Fiction

Graham, L. B. Song of the boat E
Greenfield, E. Africa dream E
Grifalconi, A. Darkness and the butterfly E
Grifalconi, A. Osa's pride E
Walter, M. P. Brother to the wind E

Folklore

See Folklore—Africa

Social life and customs

Chiasson, J. C. African journey (4 and up) **960**
Musgrove, M. Ashanti to Zulu: African traditions (3-6) **960**

Africa, East
Feelings, M. Jambo means hello E
Feelings, M. Moja means one E

Africa, South *See* South Africa

Africa, Southern

Folklore

See Folklore—Africa, Southern

Africa, West

Folklore

See Folklore—Africa, West

Africa dream. Greenfield, E. **E**

African cookery *See* Cookery, African

African crafts. Kerina, J. **745.5**

African journey. Chiasson, J. C. **960**

Afro-Americans *See* Blacks

After the Goat Man. Byars, B. C. **Fic**

After the wedding. Sebestyen, O.
In Connections: short stories by outstanding writers for young adults p206-16 **S C**

Afternoon of the elves. Lisle, J. T. **Fic**

Agard, John, 1949-
The calypso alphabet **E**

Agave blooms just once. Jernigan, G. **E**

Age *See* Old age

The **age** of chivalry. Bulfinch, T.
In Bulfinch, T. Bulfinch's Mythology **291**

The **age** of fable. Bulfinch, T.
In Bulfinch, T. Bulfinch's Mythology **291**

The **aged** mother. Grimm, J.
In Grimm, J. The complete Grimm's fairy tales p826-27 **398.2**

Agee, Jon
The incredible painting of Felix Clousseau **E**

Agnes de Mille: dancing off the earth. Gherman, B. **92**

The **agony** of Alice. Naylor, P. R. **Fic**

Agosín, Marjorie, 1955-
A huge black umbrella
In Where angels glide at dawn p99-104 **S C**

Agre, Patricia
(il) DeSantis, K. A dentist's tools **617.6**
(il) DeSantis, K. A doctor's tools **610.69**
(il) Sobol, H. L. A book of vegetables **635**
(il) Sobol, H. L. We don't look like our Mom and Dad **362.7**

Agricultural laborers
See also Migrant labor

Agriculture
Ancona, G. The American family farm (5 and up) **630.1**
Ashabranner, B. K. Born to the land: an American portrait (5 and up) **978.9**
Gibbons, G. Farming (k-2) **630.1**

Agriculture—*Continued*
See/See also pages in the following book(s):
Harris, J. L. Science in ancient Rome p35-41 (5 and up) **509**
Aher, Jackie
(il) Madaras, L. The what's happening to my body? book for boys: a growing up guide for parents and sons **613.9**
(il) Madaras, L. The what's happening to my body? book for girls: a growing up guide for parents and daughters **613.9**
Ahlberg, Allan
Ten in a bed (3-5) **Fic**
(jt. auth) Ahlberg, J. The baby's catalogue **E**
(jt. auth) Ahlberg, J. Each peach pear plum **E**
(jt. auth) Ahlberg, J. Funnybones **E**
(jt. auth) Ahlberg, J. Jeremiah in the dark woods **Fic**
(jt. auth) Ahlberg, J. Peek-a-boo! **E**
(jt. auth) Ahlberg, J. Starting school **E**
Ahlberg, Janet
The baby's catalogue **E**
Each peach pear plum **E**
Funnybones **E**
Jeremiah in the dark woods (1-3) **Fic**
Peek-a-boo! **E**
Starting school **E**
Ai-po-hua *See* Eberhard, Wolfram, 1909-1989
Aïda. Price, L. **792.5**
AIDS (Disease)
Hausherr, R. Children and the AIDS virus (1-3) **616.97**
Silverstein, A. Learning about AIDS (4-6) **616.97**
See/See also pages in the following book(s):
Ashabranner, B. K. People who make a difference p41-46 (5 and up) **920**
Fiction
Jordan, M. Losing Uncle Tim (2-4) **Fic**
Aiiieeeeeeeeee!. Rockwell, T.
In Rockwell, T. How to eat fried worms, and other plays p79-107 **812**
Aiken, Joan, 1924-
Arabel and Mortimer (4-6) **Fic**
Black hearts in Battersea. See note under Aiken, J. The wolves of Willoughby Chase **Fic**
Bridle the wind (6 and up) **Fic**
Dido and Pa. See note under Aiken, J. The wolves of Willoughby Chase **Fic**
Give yourself a fright: thirteen tales of the supernatural (6 and up) **S C**
Contents: Wing Quack Flap; The old poet; Do not alight here; The lame king; The jealous apprentice; A rhyme for silver; The ill-natured muse; The Erl King's daughter; The end of silence; The King of Nowhere; Aunt Susan; Find me; Give yourself a fright
Midnight is a place (5 and up) **Fic**
Mortimer says nothing. See note under Aiken, J. Arabel and Mortimer **Fic**
Mortimer's cross. See note under Aiken, J. Arabel and Mortimer **Fic**
Nightbirds on Nantucket. See note under Aiken, J. The wolves of Willoughby Chase **Fic**
Past eight o'clock (3-6) **S C**
Contents: Past eight o'clock; Your cradle is green; Pappa's going to buy you a mocking bird; Bye, Baby Bunting; Oh, can ye sew cushions; Lullay, lulla; Hushabye baby on the tree top; Four angels to my bed
The shadow guests (5 and up) **Fic**
Up the chimney down, and other stories (5 and up) **S C**
Contents: The last chimney cuckoo; Miss Hooting's legacy; The gift giving; The dog on the roof; The missing heir; Up the chimney down; Christmas at Troy; The midnight rose; The happiest sheep in London; The fire dogs; Potter's gray
The wolves of Willoughby Chase (5 and up) **Fic**
See/See also pages in the following book(s):
Townsend, J. R. A sense of story p17-23 **028.5**
Aikido
See/See also pages in the following book(s):
Ribner, S. The martial arts p121-24, 139-52 (5 and up) **796.8**
Ailisli, Akram
You have to trust your heart
In Face to face: a collection of stories by celebrated Soviet and American writers p203-21 **S C**
Aina-kizz and the black-bearded Bai. Riordan, J.
In Riordan, J. The woman in the moon, and other tales of forgotten heroines p42-46 **398.2**
Air
Branley, F. M. Air is all around you (k-3) **551.5**
Pollution
See also Greenhouse effect
See/See also pages in the following book(s):
Woods, G. Pollution p11-19 (6 and up) **363.7**
Air is all around you. Branley, F. M. **551.5**
Air pilots
See also Women air pilots
Levinson, N. S. Chuck Yeager: the man who broke the sound barrier (5 and up) **92**
Provensen, A. The glorious flight: across the Channel with Louis Blériot, July 25, 1909 (1-4) **92**
Tessendorf, K. C. Barnstormers & daredevils (4 and up) **629.13**

Air raid—Pearl Harbor! Taylor, T. **940.54**
Air warfare *See* Aeronautics, Military; World War, 1914-1918—Aerial operations; World War, 1939-1945—Aerial operations
Airborne. Maurer, R. **629.13**
Aircraft carriers
See/See also pages in the following book(s):
Marrin, A. Victory in the Pacific p30-42 (6 and up) **940.54**
Airmail to the moon. Birdseye, T. **E**
Airplanes
Barton, B. Airplanes (k-1) **387.7**
Barton, B. Airport (k-1) **387.7**
Rockwell, A. F. Planes (k-1) **629.133**
Rogers, F. Going on an airplane (k-2) **387.7**
Wyler, R. Science fun with toy boats and planes (2-4) **507**
Design and construction
Provensen, A. The glorious flight: across the Channel with Louis Blériot, July 25, 1909 (1-4) **92**
Engines
Moxon, J. How jet engines are made (4 and up) **629.1**
Fiction
Mark, J. Thunder and Lightnings (5 and up) **Fic**
Spier, P. Bored—nothing to do! **E**
Models
Churchill, E. R. Instant paper airplanes (3-5) **745.592**
Churchill, E. R. Paper toys that fly, soar, zoom, & whistle (4 and up) **745.592**
Simon, S. The paper airplane book (3-5) **745.592**
Airplanes, Military
Graham, I. Combat aircraft (4 and up) **623.7**
Airports
Barton, B. Airport (k-1) **387.7**
Rogers, F. Going on an airplane (k-2) **387.7**
Airships
Munro, R. Blimps (2-4) **629.133**
Stoff, J. Dirigible (3-6) **629.133**
Akaba, Suekichi, 1910-
(il) Ishii, M. The tongue-cut sparrow **398.2**
(il) Yagawa, S. The crane wife **398.2**
AKC *See* American Kennel Club
Al Hoad, Abdul Latif
We live in Saudi Arabia (4-6) **953.8**
ALA filing rules **025.3**
Alabama
McNair, S. Alabama
In America the beautiful **973**
Aladdin
Aladdin and the wonderful lamp
In The Arabian nights entertainments p295-315 **398.2**
In Best-loved folktales of the world p467-77 **398.2**
In The Blue fairy book p72-85 **398.2**
Carrick, C. Aladdin and the wonderful lamp **398.2**
Hunt, V. Aladdin and the wonderful lamp
In The Scott, Foresman anthology of children's literature p295-302 **808.8**
Lang, A. Aladdin and the wonderful lamp **398.2**
Thane, A. Aladdin and his wonderful lamp
In Thane, A. Plays from famous stories and fairy tales p38-57 **812**
Aladdin and his wonderful lamp. Thane, A.
In Thane, A. Plays from famous stories and fairy tales p38-57 **812**
Aladdin and the wonderful lamp
In The Arabian nights entertainments p295-315 **398.2**
In Best-loved folktales of the world p467-77 **398.2**
In The Blue fairy book p72-85 **398.2**
Aladdin and the wonderful lamp. Carrick, C. **398.2**
Aladdin and the wonderful lamp. Hunt, V.
In The Scott, Foresman anthology of children's literature p295-302 **808.8**
Aladdin and the wonderful lamp. Lang, A. **398.2**
Alamo (San Antonio, Tex.)
Fisher, L. E. The Alamo (4 and up) **976.4**
Alan and Naomi. Levoy, M. **Fic**
Alan Mendelsohn, the boy from Mars. Pinkwater, D. M. **Fic**
Alaska
Heinrichs, A. Alaska
In America the beautiful **973**
Fiction
George, J. C. Water sky (5 and up) **Fic**
London, J. The call of the wild (5 and up) **Fic**
London, J. White Fang (5 and up) **Fic**
Morey, W. Gentle Ben (5 and up) **Fic**
Albert B. Cub & Zebra. Rockwell, A. F. **E**
Albert's toothache. Williams, B. **E**
Alborough, Jez
(il) King-Smith, D. Martin's mice **Fic**

Album of birds. McGowen, T. **598**
Album of dinosaurs. McGowen, T. **567.9**
Album of horses. Henry, M. **636.1**
Album of rocks and minerals. McGowen, T. **549**
Album of sharks. McGowen, T. **597**
An **album** of the Vietnam War. Lawson, D. **959.704**
Alcock, Vivien, 1924-
The cuckoo sister (6 and up) **Fic**
Ghostly companions (5 and up) **S C**
Contents: The Sea Bride; Patchwork; The strange companions; Siren song; A change of aunts; The good-looking boy; The whisperer; A fall of snow; QWERTYUIOP; The masquerade
The monster garden (4 and up) **Fic**
The stonewalkers (5 and up) **Fic**
Alcohol
Hyde, M. O. Alcohol: uses and abuses (6 and up) **616.86**
O'Neill, C. Focus on alcohol (3-6) **362.29**
See/See also pages in the following book(s):
Hyde, M. O. Drug wars p50-56 (6 and up) **363.4**
Alcohol and youth *See* Youth—Alcohol use
Alcohol: uses and abuses. Hyde, M. O. **616.86**
Alcoholics
Rosenberg, M. B. Not my family: sharing the truth about alcoholism (4 and up) **362.29**
Alcoholism
Hyde, M. O. Alcohol: uses and abuses (6 and up) **616.86**
O'Neill, C. Focus on alcohol (3-6) **362.29**
Alcorn, John, 1935-
(il) The Fireside book of children's songs. See The Fireside book of children's songs **782.42**
Alcott, Louisa May, 1832-1888
Eight cousins. See note under Alcott, L. M. Little women **Fic**
Jo's boys. See note under Alcott, L. M. Little women **Fic**
Little men. See note under Alcott, L. M. Little women **Fic**
Little women (5 and up) **Fic**
Little women; dramatization. See Hackett, W. A merry Christmas
An old-fashioned Thanksgiving (3-5) **Fic**
Rose in bloom. See note under Alcott, L. M. Little women **Fic**
See/See also pages in the following book(s):
Only connect: readings on children's literature p253-57 **028.5**
Alderman, Clifford Lindsey
The story of the thirteen colonies (5 and up) **973.2**
Alderson, Brian
(comp) The Helen Oxenbury nursery rhyme book. See The Helen Oxenbury nursery rhyme book **398.8**
Alderson, Sue Ann, 1940-
Ida and the wool smugglers **E**
Aldiborontiphoskyphorniostikos. Stennet, R. *In* A Nursery companion p108-12 **820.8**
Aldo Applesauce. Hurwitz, J. See note under Hurwitz, J. Much ado about Aldo **Fic**
Aldo Ice Cream. Hurwitz, J. See note under Hurwitz, J. Much ado about Aldo **Fic**
Aldo Peanut Butter. Hurwitz, J. See note under Hurwitz, J. Much ado about Aldo **Fic**
Aleichem, Sholem *See* Sholem Aleichem, 1859-1916
Aleksin, Anatolii, 1924-
None of my business
In Face to face: a collection of stories by celebrated Soviet and American writers p153-63 **S C**
(ed) Face to face: a collection of stories by celebrated Soviet and American writers. See Face to face: a collection of stories by celebrated Soviet and American writers **S C**
Alenoushka and her brother
Afanas'ev, A. N. Sister Alionushka, brother Ivanushka
In Afanas'ev, A. N. Russian fairy tales p406-10 **398.2**
Afanas'ev, A. N. Sister Alyonushka and Brother Ivanushka
In Afanas'ev, A. N. Russian folk tales p19-24 **398.2**
Alex and the cat. Griffith, H. V. **E**
Alexander, the Great, 356-323 B.C.
See/See also pages in the following book(s):
Coolidge, O. E. The golden days of Greece p178-95 (4-6) **938**
Alexander, Ellen
Llama and the great flood (1-3) **398.2**
Alexander, Lloyd
The beggar queen. See note under Alexander, L. Westmark **Fic**
The black cauldron. See note under Alexander, L. The book of three **Fic**
The book of three (5 and up) **Fic**
The castle of Llyr. See note under Alexander, L. The book of three **Fic**
The cat and the fiddler
In Alexander, L. The town cats, and other tales p95-111 **S C**
The cat who wished to be a man (4-6) **Fic**

Alexander, Lloyd—*Continued*
The Drackenberg adventure. See note under Alexander, L. The Illyrian adventure **Fic**
The El Dorado adventure. See note under Alexander, L. The Illyrian adventure **Fic**
The first two lives of Lukas-Kasha (4 and up) **Fic**
The High King (5 and up) **Fic**
The Illyrian adventure (5 and up) **Fic**
The Jedera adventure. See note under Alexander, L. The Illyrian adventure **Fic**
The Kestrel. See note under Alexander, L. Westmark **Fic**
The marvelous misadventures of Sebastian (4 and up) **Fic**
The painter's cat
In Alexander, L. The town cats, and other tales p79-93 **S C**
The Philadelphia adventure. See note under Alexander, L. The Illyrian adventure **Fic**
Taran Wanderer. See note under Alexander, L. The book of three **Fic**
The town cats, and other tales (3-5) **S C**
Contents: The town cats; The Cat-King's daughter; The cat who said no; The cat and the golden egg; The cobbler and his cat; The painter's cat; The cat and the fiddler; The apprentice cat
Westmark (5 and up) **Fic**
See/See also pages in the following book(s):
Newbery and Caldecott Medal books, 1966-1975 p48-55 **028.5**

Alexander, Martha G.
And my mean old mother will be sorry, Blackboard Bear. See note under Alexander, M. We're in big trouble, Blackboard Bear **E**
Blackboard Bear. See note under Alexander, M. We're in big trouble, Blackboard Bear **E**
Bobo's dream **E**
Even that moose won't listen to me **E**
How my library grew, by Dinah **E**
I sure am glad to see you, Blackboard Bear. See note under Alexander, M. We're in big trouble, Blackboard Bear **E**
Move over, Twerp **E**
Nobody asked me if I wanted a baby sister **E**
We're in big trouble, Blackboard Bear **E**
When the new baby comes, I'm moving out **E**
(il) Williams, B. Jeremy isn't hungry **E**

Alexander, Sally Hobart
Mom can't see me (3-5) **362.4**

Alexander, Sue, 1933-
Nadia the Willful **E**

Alexander and the terrible, horrible, no good, very bad day. Viorst, J. **E**

Alexander and the wind-up mouse. Lionni, L. **E**

Alexander, who used to be rich last Sunday. Viorst, J. See note under Viorst, J. Alexander and the terrible, horrible, no good, very bad day **E**

Al(exandra) the Great. Greene, C. C. See note under Greene, C. C. A girl called Al **Fic**

Alexeieff, Alexander, 1901-1982
(il) Afanas'ev, A. N. Russian fairy tales **398.2**

Alfie gets in first. Hughes, S. **E**

Alfie gives a hand. Hughes, S. See note under Hughes, S. Alfie gets in first **E**

Alfie's feet. Hughes, S. See note under Hughes, S. Alfie gets in first **E**

The **Alfred** summer. Slepian, J. **Fic**

Algae
Daegling, M. Monster seaweeds (4 and up) **589.4**
Kavaler, L. Green magic: algae rediscovered (5 and up) **589.3**

Alger, Leclaire *See* Leodhas, Sorche Nic, 1898-1968

Ali Baba and the forty thieves
Ali Baba and the forty thieves
In Best-loved folktales of the world p478-85 **398.2**
The Forty thieves
In The Blue fairy book p242-50 **398.2**
Lang, A. The forty thieves
In Womenfolk and fairy tales p51-64 **398.2**
McVitty, W. Ali Baba and the forty thieves **398.2**

Ali Cogia, a merchant of Bagdad
Story of Ali Cogia, merchant of Bagdad
In The Arabian nights entertainments p346-57 **398.2**

Alice in rapture, sort of. Naylor, P. R. **Fic**

Alice's adventures in Wonderland. Carroll, L. **Fic**
also in Carroll, L. The complete works of Lewis Carroll p9-120 **828**

Alice's adventures in Wonderland, and Through the looking glass. Carroll, L. **Fic**

Aliens, Illegal
See/See also pages in the following book(s):
Meltzer, M. The Hispanic Americans p117-26 (6 and up) **305.8**

Aliens from outer space *See* Extraterrestrial beings

Aliki
Corn is maize (k-3) **633.1**
Digging up dinosaurs (k-3) **567.9**
Dinosaur bones (k-3) **567.9**
Dinosaurs are different (k-3) **567.9**
Feelings (k-3) **152.4**
Fossils tell of long ago (k-3) **560**
How a book is made (2-5) **686**
The King's day: Louis XIV of France (3-5) **92**
The many lives of Benjamin Franklin (1-3) **92**
A medieval feast (2-5) **394.1**
My feet (k-3) **612**
My five senses (k-3) **612.8**
My hands (k-3) **612**
My visit to the dinosaurs (k-3) **567.9**
Overnight at Mary Bloom's **E**
The story of Johnny Appleseed (k-3) **92**
The two of them **E**
Use your head, dear **E**
We are best friends **E**
A weed is a flower: the life of George Washington Carver (k-3) **92**
Welcome, little baby **E**
Wild and woolly mammoths (k-3) **569**
(il) Brandenberg, F. Aunt Nina and her nephews and nieces **E**
(il) Brandenberg, F. Leo and Emily **E**
(il) Brandenberg, F. Nice new neighbors **E**
(il) Cole, J. Evolution **575**
(il) Heilbroner, J. This is the house where Jack lives **E**

Aliosha Popovich. Afanas'ev, A. N.
In Afanas'ev, A. N. Russian fairy tales p67-71 **398.2**

Alison's zinnia. Lobel, A. **E**

Alistair in outer space. Bollen, M. S. See note under Bollen, M. S. Alistair's elephant **E**

Alistair underwater. Bollen, M. S. See note under Bollen, M. S. Alistair's elephant **E**

Alistair's elephant. Bollen, M. S. **E**
See note under Bollen, M. S. Alistair underwater **E**

Alistair's time machine. Bollen, M. S. See note under Bollen, M. S. Alistair underwater **E**
See note under Bollen, M. S. Alistair's elephant **E**

All about football. Sullivan, G. **796.332**

All about Sam. Lowry, L. See note under Lowry, L. Anastasia Krupnik **Fic**

All about whales. Patent, D. H. **599.5**

The **all-around** pumpkin book. Cuyler, M. **641.3**

All asleep. Pomerantz, C. **811**

All day long: fifty rhymes of the never was and always is. McCord, D. T. W. **811**

All God's critters got a place in the choir. Staines, B. **782.42**

All Hallows' Eve *See* Halloween

All I see. Rylant, C. **E**

All in a day. Anno, M. **E**

All in a day's work. Johnson, N. **331.7**

All in one piece. Murphy, J. **E**

All kinds of feet. Goor, R. **591.4**

The **all** new Jonah Twist. Honeycutt, N. **Fic**

All-of-a-kind family. Taylor, S. **Fic**

All-of-a-kind family downtown. Taylor, S. See note under Taylor, S. All-of-a-kind family **Fic**

All-of-a-kind family uptown. Taylor, S. See note under Taylor, S. All-of-a-kind family **Fic**

All of our noses are here. Schwartz, A.
In Schwartz, A. All of our noses are here, and other noodle tales p22-37 **398.2**

All of our noses are here, and other noodle tales. Schwartz, A. **398.2**

All shapes and sizes. Hughes, S. **E**

All the colors of the race: poems. Adoff, A. **811**

All the money in the world. Brittain, B. **Fic**

All the stars in the sky. Rylant, C.
In Rylant, C. Children of Christmas p32-38 **S C**

All things are linked. Verwhilghen, L. A.
In The Crest and the hide, and other African stories of heroes, chiefs, bards, hunters, sorcerers, and common people p101-04 **398.2**

All times, all peoples: a world history of slavery. Meltzer, M. **326**

All together now. Bridgers, S. E. **Fic**

All us come cross the water. Clifton, L.
In Free to be—a family p133-37 **810.8**

All wet! All wet! Skofield, J. **E**

All women are alike
Asbjørnsen, P. C. Not a pin to choose between them
In Best-loved folktales of the world p340-44 **398.2**

Allard, Harry, 1928-
Bumps in the night E
It's so nice to have a wolf around the house
In The Laugh book p111-18 **808.8**
Miss Nelson has a field day. See note under Allard, H. Miss Nelson is missing! E
Miss Nelson is back. See note under Allard, H. Miss Nelson is missing! E
Miss Nelson is missing! E

Allegories
See also Fables
Adams, R. Watership Down (6 and up) **Fic**
Babbitt, N. Kneeknock Rise (4-6) **Fic**
Corbett, W. J. The song of Pentecost (5 and up) **Fic**

Allen, Anne
Sports for the handicapped (5 and up) **796**

Allen, Gary
(il) George, J. C. One day in the tropical rain forest **574.5**
(il) George, J. C. One day in the woods **574.5**

Allen, Jonathan, 1957-
(il) Mahy, M. The great white man-eating shark E

Allen, Pamela
Bertie and the bear E

Allen, Thomas B., 1928-
On Granddaddy's farm (1-3) **630.1**
(il) Bulla, C. R. The chalk box kid E
(il) Cameron, A. The most beautiful place in the world **Fic**
(il) Hendershot, J. In coal country E
(il) Jukes, M. Blackberries in the dark **Fic**

Allender, David
(il) Raffi. Shake my sillies out **782.42**

Allerleirauh. Grimm, J.
In The Green fairy book p276-81 **398.2**
In Grimm, J. The complete Grimm's fairy tales p326-31 **398.2**

Alligators
Bare, C. S. Never kiss an alligator! (k-2) **597.9**
Scott, J. D. Alligator (4 and up) **597.9**
Stone, L. M. Alligators and crocodiles (2-4) **597.9**

Fiction

Aliki. Use your head, dear E
Hurd, T. Mama don't allow E
Minarik, E. H. No fighting, no biting! E
Stevenson, J. Monty E

Alligators all around. Sendak, M. E
Alligators and crocodiles. Stone, L. M. **597.9**

Allison, Linda, 1948-
Gee, Wiz! (4 and up) **507**

Allosaurus
See/See also pages in the following book(s):
Thomson, P. Auks, rocks and the odd dinosaur p67-72 (5 and up) **508**

Allusions
Brewer's dictionary of phrase and fable **803**

Almanacs
Chase's annual events **394.2**
Information please almanac, atlas & yearbook **031.02**
The World almanac and book of facts **031.02**

Almedingen, E. M. (Edith Martha), 1898-1971
The crimson oak (5 and up) **Fic**

Almedingen, Edith Martha *See* Almedingen, E. M. (Edith Martha), 1898-1971

Almost starring Skinnybones. Park, B. **Fic**

Aloise, Frank E.
(il) Phelan, M. K. The story of the Louisiana Purchase **973.4**
(il) Siegel, B. George and Martha Washington at home in New York **973.4**

Alotaibi, Muhammad
Bedouin: the nomads of the desert (5 and up) **956**

Alphabatics. Macdonald, S. E

Alphabet
Agard, J. The calypso alphabet E
Anno, M. Anno's alphabet E
Azarian, M. A farmer's alphabet E
Bayer, J. A my name is Alice E
Blake, Q. Quentin Blake's ABC E
Boynton, S. A is for angry E
Cassedy, S. Roomrimes: poems (3-6) **811**
Crews, D. We read: A to Z E
Demi. Demi's Find-the-animal A.B.C. E
Duke, K. The guinea pig ABC E
Ehlert, L. Eating the alphabet E
Eichenberg, F. Ape in a cape E
Emberley, E. Ed Emberley's ABC E
Feelings, M. Jambo means hello E
Folsom, M. Easy as pie E
Gág, W. The A B C bunny E
Gardner, B. Have you ever seen—? E
Geisert, A. Pigs from A to Z E
Gundersheimer, K. A B C, say with me E
Hoban, T. 26 letters and 99 cents E
Hoban, T. A, B, see! E
Hoguet, S. R. I unpacked my grandmother's trunk E

Alphabet—*Continued*
Hughes, S. Lucy & Tom's a.b.c E
Hunt, J. Illuminations (2-4) 909.07
If there were dreams to sell (k-3) 821.008
Isadora, R. City seen from A to Z E
Jernigan, G. Agave blooms just once E
Kellogg, S. Aster Aardvark's alphabet adventures E
Kitchen, B. Animal alphabet E
Lear, E. An Edward Lear alphabet (k-2) 821
Lobel, A. Alison's zinnia E
Lobel, A. On Market Street E
Lyon, G. E. A B Cedar E
Macdonald, S. Alphabatics E
Martin, B. Chicka chicka boom boom E
Merriam, E. Halloween A B C (k-2) 811
Miller, J. The farm alphabet book E
Neumeier, M. Action alphabet E
Ogg, O. The 26 letters 411
Owens, M. B. A caribou alphabet E
Oxenbury, H. Helen Oxenbury's ABC of things E
A Peaceable kingdom (k-3) 811
Rockwell, A. F. Albert B. Cub & Zebra E
Ryden, H. Wild animals of Africa ABC E
Ryden, H. Wild animals of America ABC E
Sarasas, C. The ABC's of origami (4-6) 736
Sendak, M. Alligators all around E
Van Allsburg, C. The Z was zapped E
Watson, C. Applebet: an ABC E
Wells, C. A Christmas alphabet (k-3) 811

Alphabet art: thirteen ABCs from around the world. Fisher, L. E. 745.6

Alphabet books *See* Alphabet

Alphabet soup. Banks, K. E

Alphabets
See also Lettering
Fisher, L. E. Alphabet art: thirteen ABCs from around the world (4 and up) 745.6

Alpine animals
Hirschi, R. Who lives in—the mountains? (k-2) 591.5

Alps

Fiction

Spyri, J. Heidi (4 and up) Fic

Alred, Jean Lynn
(il) MacFarlane, R. B. A. Making your own nature museum 508

Al's blind date. Greene, C. C. See note under Greene, C. C. A girl called Al Fic

ALSC *See* Association for Library Service to Children (U.S.)

ALSC International Relations Committee *See* Association for Library Service to Children (U.S.). International Relations Committee

Alsop, Mary O'Hara *See* O'Hara, Mary, 1885-1980

Altman, Susan R.
Extraordinary black Americans (5 and up) 920

Altogether, one at a time. Konigsburg, E. L. S C

Always room for one more. Leodhas, S. N. 781.62

Always to remember. Ashabranner, B. K. 959.704

Alyasha Popovich
Afanas'ev, A. N. Aliosha Popovich
In Afanas'ev, A. N. Russian fairy tales p67-71 398.2

Alzheimer's disease
Beckelman, L. Alzheimer's disease (4-6) 616.8
Frank, J. Alzheimer's disease (6 and up) 616.8
Landau, E. Alzheimer's disease (5 and up) 616.8
See/See also pages in the following book(s):
Dinner, S. H. Nothing to be ashamed of: growing up with mental illness in your family p109-25 (5 and up) 362.2

Amahl and the night visitors. Menotti, G. C. Fic

Amanda Pig and her big brother Oliver. Van Leeuwen, J. See note under Van Leeuwen, J. Tales of Oliver Pig E

Amari, Suad
Cooking the Lebanese way (5 and up) 641.5

Amazing animal groups. Venino, S. 591.5

Amazing animals of Australia (4 and up) 591.9

Amazing animals of the sea (5 and up) 599.5

The **amazing** bone. Steig, W. E
The **amazing** egg. McClung, R. M. 591.1
Amazing otters. Brownell, M. B. 599.74
Amazing spiders. Schnieper, C. 595.4
The **amazing,** the incredible super dog. Bonsall, C. N. E
The **amazing** things animals do. McGrath, S. 591.5
Amazon River valley
Cobb, V. This place is wet (2-4) 574.5
Ambassadors *See* Diplomats
Amelia Bedelia. Parish, P. E
Amelia Bedelia and the baby. Parish, P. See note under Parish, P. Amelia Bedelia E
Amelia Bedelia and the surprise shower. Parish, P. See note under Parish, P. Amelia Bedelia E
Amelia Bedelia goes camping. Parish, P. See note under Parish, P. Amelia Bedelia E
Amelia Bedelia helps out. Parish, P. See note under Parish, P. Amelia Bedelia E
Amelia Bedelia's family album. Parish, P. See note under Parish, P. Amelia Bedelia E
America
See also Central America; Latin America
Exploration
D'Aulaire, I. Columbus (1-4) 92
Fritz, J. Brendan the Navigator (3-5) 398.2
Fritz, J. Where do you think you're going, Christopher Columbus? (3-5) 92
Krensky, S. Who really discovered America? (4-6) 970.01
Levinson, N. S. Christopher Columbus: voyager to the unknown (4 and up) 92
Sandak, C. R. Columbus Day (4-6) 394.2
Exploration—Fiction
Baker, B. Walk the world's rim (5 and up) Fic
America, I hear you: a story about George Gershwin. Mitchell, B. 92
America the beautiful (4 and up) 973
American Association for the Advancement of Science
The Best science books & A-V materials for children. See The Best science books & A-V materials for children 016.5
Science Books & Films. See Science Books & Films 016.5
American Association of School Librarians
Information power 027.8
American bison *See* Bison
The **American** book of days 394.2
American Christmas, Diane Goode's 810.8
American colonies *See* United States—History—1600-1775, Colonial period
American composers *See* Composers, American
The **American** family farm. Ancona, G. 630.1
American folk songs for children in home, school and nursery school. Seeger, R. C. 781.62
The **American** Heritage children's dictionary (3-6) 423
The **American** Heritage first dictionary (1-3) 423
The **American** Heritage picture dictionary. Hillerich, R. L. 423
American history for children and young adults: an annotated bibliographic index. VanMeter, V. 016.973
The **American** Indian in America. Jones, J. C.
In The In America series 305.8
American Indian music and musical instruments. Fichter, G. S. 780.89
American Indian mythology. Marriott, A. L. 398.2
American Indians *See* Indians; Indians of North America
American Kennel Club
The complete dog book 636.7
American Library Association
See also American Association of School Librarians; Association for Library Service to Children (U.S.)
American Library Association. Children's Services Division *See* Association for Library Service to Children (U.S.)
American Library Association. Office for Intellectual Freedom
Intellectual freedom manual. See Intellectual freedom manual 323.44
Newsletter on Intellectual Freedom. See Newsletter on Intellectual Freedom 323.44
American Library Association publications
ALA filing rules 025.3
American Association of School Librarians. Information power 027.8
The Arbuthnot lectures, 1970-1979/1980-1989 028.5
Association for Library Service to Children (U.S.). International Relations Committee. Children's books of international interest 011.6
Association for Library Service to Chil-

American Library Association publications— *Continued*
dren (U.S.). Notable Children's Books, 1976-1980, Reevaluation Committee. Notable children's books, 1976-1980 **011.6**
Bauer, C. F. Handbook for storytellers **372.6**
Booklist **028.1**
Carroll, F. L. Exciting, funny, scary, short, different, and sad books kids like about animals, science, sports, families, songs, and other things **011.6**
Cataloging correctly for kids **025.3**
Champlin, C. Storytelling with puppets **372.6**
Cianciolo, P. J. Picture books for children **011.6**
Cuddigan, M. Growing pains **011.6**
DeWit, D. Children's faces looking up **372.6**
Egoff, S. A. Worlds within **028.5**
Gorman, M. The concise AACR2, 1988 revision **025.3**
Gregory, R. W. Anniversaries and holidays **394.2**
Intellectual freedom manual **323.44**
Journal of Youth Services in Libraries **027.6205**
Lacy, L. E. Art and design in children's picture books **741.6**
Newsletter on Intellectual Freedom **323.44**
Nichols, J. Storytimes for two-year-olds **027.62**
Notable children's films and videos, filmstrips, and recordings, 1973-1986 **016.3713**
Olexer, M. E. Poetry anthologies for children and young people **011.6**
Richardson, S. K. Magazines for children **011.6**
Rochman, H. Tales of love and terror **028**
School Library Media Quarterly **027.805**
Smith, J. B. Library media center programs for middle schools: a curriculum-based approach **027.8**
Subject index to poetry for children and young people, 1957-1975 **808.81**

American literature
See also Latin American literature
Black authors—History and criticism

See/See also pages in the following book(s):
Crosscurrents of criticism p159-67 **028.5**

Collected works
Diane Goode's American Christmas **810.8**
Free to be—a family **810.8**
Free to be—you and me **810.8**

American loyalists

Fiction
O'Dell, S. Sarah Bishop (6 and up) **Fic**

American newspapers
Fleming, T. J. Behind the headlines (5 and up) **071**

American nicknames. Shankle, G. E. **929.4**

American poetry

Black authors—Collected works
I am the darker brother (5 and up) **811.008**
My black me: a beginning book of black poetry (5 and up) **811.008**

Collected works
Click, rumble, roar (2-5) **811.008**
Creatures (3-5) **821.008**
Dilly dilly piccalilli (2-4) **808.81**
Dinosaurs: poems (3-5) **811.008**
Ghost poems (1-4) **821.008**
Good books, good times! (1-3) **811.008**
A Great big ugly man came up and tied his horse to me (k-3) **821.008**
If there were dreams to sell (k-3) **821.008**
In the witch's kitchen (3-6) **811.008**
Knock at a star (3-6) **821.008**
Laughable limericks (4 and up) **821.008**
The Merry-go-round poetry book (k-2) **811.008**
Monster poems (1-4) **821.008**
More surprises (1-3) **811.008**
My tang's tungled and other ridiculous situations (3-6) **821.008**
A New treasury of children's poetry **821.008**
Of quarks, quasars, and other quirks (5 and up) **821.008**
Oh, such foolishness! (3-6) **821.008**
Oh, that's ridiculous! (3-6) **821.008**
On city streets (5 and up) **811.008**
The Oxford book of children's verse **821.008**
The Oxford book of children's verse in America **811.008**
A Paper zoo (1-4) **811.008**
The Place my words are looking for (4 and up) **811.008**
Poem stew (3-6) **811.008**
Poems for Jewish holidays (k-3) **811.008**
Poems for mothers (3-5) **811.008**
Poems to read to the very young (k-2) **821.008**
Poetry for holidays (1-4) **811.008**
The Poetry troupe **821.008**
Rainbow in the sky (k-4) **821.008**
The Random House book of poetry for children **821.008**
Read-aloud rhymes for the very young (k-2) **821.008**

American poetry — Collected works — *Continued*
Reflections on a gift of watermelon pickle . . . and other modern verse (6 and up) **811.008**
Shrieks at midnight (4 and up) **821.008**
Surprises (1-3) **811.008**
This delicious day (5 and up) **811.008**
Tripp, W. Marguerite, go wash your feet (1-3) **821.008**
A Week of lullabies (k-2) **811.008**
Wider than the sky: poems to grow up with (5 and up) **821.008**
Witch poems (1-4) **821.008**
American poets *See* Poets, American
American Revolution *See* United States—History—1775-1783, Revolution
The **American** Revolution. Morris, R. B. **973.3**
The **American** Revolution, 1760-1783. Bliven, B. **973.3**
The **American** revolutionaries: a history in their own words, 1750-1800 (6 and up) **973.3**
American wit and humor
Phillips, L. How do you get a horse out of the bathtub? (5 and up) **793.73**
Schwartz, A. Flapdoodle: pure nonsense from American folklore (4 and up) **398**
Schwartz, A. Tomfoolery: trickery and foolery with words (4 and up) **398**
Schwartz, A. Unriddling: all sorts of riddles to puzzle your guessery (4 and up) **398.6**
Schwartz, A. Witcracks: jokes and jests from American folklore (4 and up) **398**
Americans at home. Huntington, L. P. **728**
America's bald eagle. Ryden, H. **598**
Amerindians *See* Indians; Indians of North America
Ames, Gerald
(jt. auth) Wyler, R. Magic secrets **793.8**
(jt. auth) Wyler, R. Spooky tricks **793.8**
Ames, Lee J., 1921-
Draw 50 beasties and yugglies and turnover uglies and things that go bump in the night (4 and up) **743**
Draw 50 boats, ships, trucks & trains (4 and up) **743**
Draw 50 buildings and other structures (4 and up) **743**
Draw 50 cars, trucks, and motorcycles (4 and up) **743**
Draw 50 cats (4 and up) **743**
Draw 50 dinosaurs and other prehistoric animals (4 and up) **743**
Draw 50 dogs (4 and up) **743**
Draw 50 famous cartoons (4 and up) **741.5**
Draw 50 holiday decorations (4 and up) **743**
Draw 50 horses (4 and up) **743**
Draw 50 sharks, whales, and other sea creatures (4 and up) **743**
The **amethyst** ring. O'Dell, S. See note under O'Dell, S. The captive **Fic**
Amish
Ammon, R. Growing up Amish (5 and up) **289.7**
Fiction
Polacco, P. Just plain Fancy **E**
Ammon, Richard
Growing up Amish (5 and up) **289.7**
Among the dolls. Sleator, W. **Fic**
Amos, William Hopkins
Life in ponds and streams (k-3) **591.92**
Amos & Boris. Steig, W. **E**
Amos Fortune, free man. Yates, E. **92**
Amphibians
See also Frogs; Salamanders
Stebbins, R. C. A field guide to western reptiles and amphibians **597.6**
See/See also pages in the following book(s):
McClung, R. M. The amazing egg p67-74 (4 and up) **591.1**
Weber, W. J. Care of uncommon pets p123-40 (5 and up) **636.088**
Amstutz, Andre
(il) Ahlberg, A. Ten in a bed **Fic**
Amusement parks
Fiction
Slepian, J. The night of the Bozos (6 and up) **Fic**
Amusements
See also Games
Caney, S. Steven Caney's kids' America (4 and up) **790.1**
Cole, A. I saw a purple cow, and 100 other recipes for learning **372.1**
Cole, A. Purple cow to the rescue **372.1**
Robinson, J. Activities for anyone, anytime, anywhere (5 and up) **790.1**
Rockwell, A. F. Things to play with (k-1) **793**
Amy goes fishing. Marzollo, J. **E**
Amy said. Waddell, M. **E**
Amy's eyes. Kennedy, R. **Fic**
Anancy and bad news to Cow-Mother. Berry, J.
In Berry, J. Spiderman Anancy p94-100 **398.2**

Anancy and Dog and Puss and friendship. Berry, J.
In Berry, J. Spiderman Anancy p87-93 **398.2**

Anancy and friend. Berry, J.
In Berry, J. Spiderman Anancy p36-38 **398.2**

Anancy and looking for a wife. Berry, J.
In Berry, J. Spiderman Anancy p1-5 **398.2**

Anancy and storm and the Reverend Man-Cow. Berry, J.
In Berry, J. Spiderman Anancy p78-86 **398.2**

Anancy and the Hide-Away-Garden. Berry, J.
In Berry, J. Spiderman Anancy p39-44 **398.2**

Anancy and the making of the Bro title. Berry, J.
In Berry, J. Spiderman Anancy p11-21 **398.2**

Anancy, Dog and Old Higue Dry-Skull. Berry, J.
In Berry, J. Spiderman Anancy p22-26 **398.2**

Anancy, Lion and Tiger's last day. Berry, J.
In Berry, J. Spiderman Anancy p116-19 **398.2**

Anancy, Old Witch and King-Daughter. Berry, J.
In Berry, J. Spiderman Anancy p6-10 **398.2**

Anancy runs into Tiger's trouble. Berry, J.
In Berry, J. Spiderman Anancy p69-71 **398.2**

Anancy, Tiger and the Shine-Dancer-Shine. Berry, J.
In Berry, J. Spiderman Anancy p107-15 **398.2**

Anansi and Candlefly. Sherlock, Sir P. M.
In Sherlock, Sir P. M. West Indian folk-tales p97-104 **398.2**

Anansi and his visitor, Turtle. Kaula, E. M.
In Best-loved folktales of the world p618-19 **398.2**
In The Laugh book p201-03 **808.8**

Anansi and Nothing go hunting for wives. Courlander, H.
In Courlander, H. The cow-tail switch, and other West African stories p95-102 **398.2**

Anansi and Snake the postman. Sherlock, Sir P. M.
In Sherlock, Sir P. M. West Indian folk-tales p71-76 **398.2**

Anansi and the alligator eggs. Sherlock, Sir P. M.
In Sherlock, Sir P. M. Anansi, the spider man p84-93 **398.2**

Anansi and the crabs. Sherlock, Sir P. M.
In Sherlock, Sir P. M. Anansi, the spider man p95-103 **398.2**

Anansi and the Fish Country. Sherlock, Sir P. M.
In Sherlock, Sir P. M. Anansi, the spider man p70-75 **398.2**

Anansi and the Old Hag. Sherlock, Sir P. M.
In Sherlock, Sir P. M. Anansi, the spider man p20-29 **398.2**

Anansi and the plantains. Sherlock, Sir P. M.
In Sherlock, Sir P. M. Anansi, the spider man p64-69 **398.2**

Anansi and Turtle and Pigeon. Sherlock, Sir P. M.
In Sherlock, Sir P. M. Anansi, the spider man p31-34 **398.2**

Anansi hunts with Tiger. Sherlock, Sir P. M.
In Sherlock, Sir P. M. West Indian Folk-tales p118-24 **398.2**

Anansi play with fire, Anansi get burned. Jagendorf, M. A.
In Best-loved folktales of the world p741-44 **398.2**

Anansi the spider. McDermott, G. **398.2**

Anansi the spider-man
Aardema, V. Oh, Kojo! How could you! **398.2**
Berry, J. Spiderman Anancy **398.2**
Bryan, A. The dancing granny **398.2**
Courlander, H. Anansi and Nothing go hunting for wives
In Courlander, H. The cow-tail switch, and other West African stories p95-102 **398.2**
Courlander, H. Anansi's fishing expedition
In Courlander, H. The cow-tail switch, and other West African stories p47-58 **398.2**
Courlander, H. Anansi's hat-shaking dance
In Best-loved folktales of the world p615-17 **398.2**
In The Scott, Foresman anthology of children's literature p313-14 **808.8**
Haley, G. E. A story, a story **398.2**
How Spider obtained the Sky-God's stories
In Best-loved folktales of the world p620-23 **398.2**
Jagendorf, M. A. Anansi play with fire, Anansi get burned
In Best-loved folktales of the world p741-44 **398.2**

Anansi the spider-man—*Continued*
Kaula, E. M. Anansi and his visitor, Turtle
In Best-loved folktales of the world p618-19 398.2
In The Laugh book p201-03 808.8
McDermott, G. Anansi the spider 398.2
Rohmer, H. Brother Anansi and the cattle ranch 398.2
Sherlock, Sir P. M. Anansi and Candlefly
In Sherlock, Sir P. M. West Indian folk-tales p97-104 398.2
Sherlock, Sir P. M. Anansi and Snake the postman
In Sherlock, Sir P. M. West Indian folk-tales p71-76 398.2
Sherlock, Sir P. M. Anansi hunts with Tiger
In Sherlock, Sir P. M. West Indian Folk-tales p118-24 398.2
Sherlock, Sir P. M. Anansi, the spider man 398.2
Sherlock, Sir P. M. Anansi's old riding-horse
In Sherlock, Sir P. M. West Indian folk-tales p105-11 398.2
Sherlock, Sir P. M. Born a monkey, live a monkey
In Sherlock, Sir P. M. West Indian folk-tales p135-43 398.2
Sherlock, Sir P. M. Dry-Bone and Anansi
In Sherlock, Sir P. M. West Indian folk-tales p77-85 398.2
Sherlock, Sir P. M. Mancrow, bird of darkness
In Sherlock, Sir P. M. West Indian folk-tales p65-70 398.2
Sherlock, Sir P. M. Mr. Wheeler
In Sherlock, Sir P. M. West Indian folk-tales p144-51 398.2
Sherlock, Sir P. M. The Sea-Mammy
In Sherlock, Sir P. M. West Indian folk-tales p130-34 398.2
Sherlock, Sir P. M. Tiger in the forest, Anansi in the web
In The Scott, Foresman anthology of children's literature p392-93 808.8
In Sherlock, Sir P. M. West Indian folk-tales p59-64 398.2
Sherlock, Sir P. M. Tiger story, Anansi story
In Sherlock, Sir P. M. West Indian folk-tales p45-58 398.2
Sherlock, Sir P. M. Why women won't listen
In Sherlock, Sir P. M. West Indian folk-tales p112-17 398.2
Sherlock, Sir P. M. Work-let-me-see
In Sherlock, Sir P. M. West Indian folk-tales p125-29 398.2

Anansi's fishing expedition. Courlander, H.
In Courlander, H. The cow-tail switch, and other West African stories p47-58 398.2

Anansi's hat-shaking dance. Courlander, H.
In Best-loved folktales of the world p615-17 398.2
In The Scott, Foresman anthology of children's literature p313-14 808.8

Anansi's old riding-horse. Sherlock, Sir P. M.
In Sherlock, Sir P. M. West Indian folk-tales p105-11 398.2

Anastasia again! Lowry, L. See note under Lowry, L. Anastasia Krupnik Fic

Anastasia, ask your analyst. Lowry, L. See note under Lowry, L. Anastasia Krupnik Fic

Anastasia at your service. Lowry, L. See note under Lowry, L. Anastasia Krupnik Fic

Anastasia has the answers. Lowry, L. See note under Lowry, L. Anastasia Krupnik Fic

Anastasia Krupnik. Lowry, L. Fic

Anastasia on her own. Lowry, L. See note under Lowry, L. Anastasia Krupnik Fic

Anastasia's chosen career. Lowry, L. See note under Lowry, L. Anastasia Krupnik Fic

Anatomy
See also Physiology

Anatomy, Human
Brenner, B. Bodies (k-2) 612
Bruun, R. D. The human body (4 and up) 612
Cole, J. The magic school bus inside the human body (2-4) 612
Elting, M. The Macmillan book of the human body (4 and up) 612
Miller, J. The human body (4 and up) 612
Settel, J. Why does my nose run? (4 and up) 612
Seuling, B. You can't sneeze with your eyes open & other freaky facts about the human body (4 and up) 612
Whitfield, P. J. Why do our bodies stop growing? (5 and up) 612

Ancient Egypt. Cohen, D. 932

Ancient Egypt. Hart, G. 932

Ancient Egypt. See Hart, G. Exploring the past: ancient Egypt 932

Ancient history *See* History, Ancient
The **ancient** Maya. Beck, B. L. **972**
Ancient Rome. Corbishley, M. **937**
Ancient Rome. James, S. **937**
The **ancient** world. Briquebec, J. **930**
Ancona, George, 1929-
The American family farm (5 and up) **630.1**
Bananas (3-5) **641.3**
Dancing is (3-5) **793.3**
Handtalk zoo (k-3) **419**
Monster movers (3-5) **621.8**
Riverkeeper (3-6) **333.91**
Sheep dog (4 and up) **636.7**
Turtle watch (2-4) **597.9**
(il) Alexander, S. H. Mom can't see me **362.4**
(il) Anderson, J. The first Thanksgiving feast **974.4**
(il) Anderson, J. From map to museum **930.1**
(il) Anderson, J. Pioneer settlers of New France **971.01**
(il) Brenner, B. Bodies **612**
(il) Brenner, B. Faces **612.8**
(jt. auth) Charlip, R. Handtalk: an ABC of finger spelling & sign language **419**
(il) Charlip, R. Handtalk birthday **419**
(il) Climo, S. City! San Francisco **979.4**
(il) Rosenberg, M. B. Artists of handcrafted furniture at work **749**
(il) Rosenberg, M. B. Being a twin, having a twin **155.4**
(il) Rosenberg, M. B. Being adopted **362.7**
(il) Rosenberg, M. B. Finding a way **362.4**
(il) Rosenberg, M. B. Living in two worlds **306.8**
(il) Rosenberg, M. B. Making a new home in America **325.73**
(il) Rosenberg, M. B. My friend Leslie **362.4**
Ancona, Mary Beth
(jt. auth) Charlip, R. Handtalk: an ABC of finger spelling & sign language **419**
And a nightmare. Gorog, J.
In Gorog, J. Three dreams and a nightmare, and other tales of the dark **S C**
And all between. Snyder, Z. K. See note under Snyder, Z. K. Below the root **Fic**
And condors danced. Snyder, Z. K. **Fic**
And my mean old mother will be sorry, Blackboard Bear. Alexander, M. G. See note under Alexander, M. We're in big trouble, Blackboard Bear **E**
—and now Miguel. Krumgold, J. **Fic**
And one for all. Nelson, T. **Fic**
And seven! Calvino, I.
In The Scott, Foresman anthology of children's literature p260-62 **808.8**
And then there was one. Facklam, M. **591.5**
And then what happened, Paul Revere? Fritz, J. **92**
And this is Laura. Conford, E. **Fic**
And to think that I saw it on Mulberry Street. Seuss, Dr. **E**
And you give me a pain, Elaine. Pevsner, S. **Fic**
Andersen, Hans Christian, 1805-1875
Blockhead Hans
In The Yellow fairy book p313-18 **398.2**
The emperor's new clothes (2-5) **Fic**
also in The Scott, Foresman anthology of children's literature p537-40 **808.8**
also in Tomie dePaola's favorite nursery tales p87-95 **398.2**
also in The Yellow fairy book p21-25 **398.2**
The emperor's new clothes; adaptation. See Rockwell, A. F. The emperor's new clothes **Fic**
Hans Andersen: his classic fairy tales (3-6) **S C**
Contents: The tinderbox; The nightingale; The princess and the pea; The swineherd; The ugly duckling; The dung beetle; The snowman; The snow queen; The darning needle; The steadfast soldier; The little match girl; Little Claus and Big Claus; The emperor's new clothes; The wild swans; The old house; The little mermaid; The red shoes; Inchelina
Hans Christian Andersen's The fir tree (2-5) **Fic**
How to tell a true princess
In The Yellow fairy book p254-55 **398.2**
The little match girl (2-5) **Fic**
The nightingale (2-5) **Fic**
also in Shedlock, M. L. The art of the story-teller p243-58 **372.6**
also in The Yellow fairy book p291-300 **398.2**
The nightingale; dramatization. See Thane, A. The Emperor's nightingale
The princess and the pea (1-4) **Fic**
also in Tomie dePaola's favorite nursery tales p64-67 **398.2**
The princess and the peas
In The Classic fairy tales p217 **398.2**
The princess on the pea
In Shedlock, M. L. The art of the story-teller p259-60 **372.6**
The real princess
In The Scott, Foresman anthology of children's literature p502-03 **808.8**

Andersen, Hans Christian, 1805-1875—*Continued*
The Snow Queen (4-6) **Fic**
The Snow Queen; adaptation. See Ehrlich, A. The Snow Queen **Fic**
The steadfast tin soldier (1-4) **Fic**
also in The Yellow fairy book p308-12 **398.2**
A story about a darning needle
In The Yellow fairy book p319-21 **398.2**
The story of Big Klaus and Little Klaus
In The Yellow fairy book p225-36 **398.2**
The swineherd (1-4) **Fic**
also in The Classic fairy tales p232-35 **398.2**
also in Shedlock, M. L. The art of the story-teller p235-42 **372.6**
also in The Yellow fairy book p249-53 **398.2**
Thumbelina
In The Yellow fairy book p279-90 **398.2**
Thumbeline (1-4) **Fic**
The tinder box
In Best-loved folktales of the world p358-64 **398.2**
In The Classic fairy tales p207-15 **398.2**
In The Yellow fairy book p265-73 **398.2**
The tinder box; adaptation. See Moser, B. The tinderbox **Fic**
Tommelise
In The Classic fairy tales p221-29 **398.2**
The ugly duckling (1-4) **Fic**
The wild swans (2-5) **Fic**
The wild swans; adaptation. See Ehrlich, A. The wild swans **E**
See/See also pages in the following book(s):
Crosscurrents of criticism p277-82 **028.5**
Only connect: readings on children's literature p233-37 **028.5**
Sendak, M. Caldecott & Co.: notes on books and pictures p27-37 **028.5**

Andersen, Karen Born
What's the matter, Sylvie, can't you ride? **E**

Anderson, Celia Catlett, 1936-
Nonsense literature for children **028.5**

Anderson, Dave
The story of basketball (5 and up) **796.323**
The story of football (5 and up) **796.332**

Anderson, Joan
The first Thanksgiving feast (3-5) **974.4**
From map to museum (5 and up) **930.1**
Pioneer settlers of New France (3-5) **971.01**
(jt. auth) Ancona, G. The American family farm **630.1**

Anderson, Lena
(il) Björk, C. Linnea in Monet's garden **Fic**
(il) Björk, C. Linnea's almanac **508**
(il) Björk, C. Linnea's windowsill garden **635**

Anderson, Madelyn Klein
Arthritis (5 and up) **616.7**
Siberia (5 and up) **957**

Anderson, Pauline, 1918-
Planning school library media facilities **027.8**

Anderson, Vicki, 1928-
Fiction sequels for readers age 10-16 **016.8**

Andreas and the magic bells. Levoy, M.
In Levoy, M. The witch of Fourth Street, and other stories **S C**

Andrews, Benny, 1930-
(il) I am the darker brother. See I am the darker brother **811.008**

Andrews, Charles J.
Hughes, R. P. Fell's United States coin book **737.4**

Andrews, Eva L.
(comp) Subject index to poetry for children and young people, 1957-1975. See Subject index to poetry for children and young people, 1957-1975 **808.81**

Andrews, Jan, 1942-
Very last first time **E**

Andrews, William George, 1930-
The land and the people of the Soviet Union (5 and up) **947**

Andrew's bath. McPhail, D. M. **E**

Andry, Andrew C.
How babies are made (k-3) **612.6**

Andy and the lion. Daugherty, J. H. **E**

Anecdotes and adventures of fifteen gentlemen. Sharpe, R. S.
In A Nursery companion p70-74 **820.8**

The **angel** and the soldier boy. Collington, P. **E**

Angel in charge. Delton, J. See note under Delton, J. Angel's mother's wedding **Fic**

Angel Mae: a tale of Trotter Street. Hughes, S. **E**

Angela, private citizen. Robinson, N. K. **Fic**

Angelina and Alice. Holabird, K. See note under Holabird, K. Angelina ballerina **E**

Angelina and the princess. Holabird, K. See note under Holabird, K. Angelina ballerina E
Angelina at the fair. Holabird, K. See note under Holabird, K. Angelina ballerina E
Angelina ballerina. Holabird, K. E
Angelina on stage. Holabird, K. See note under Holabird, K. Angelina ballerina E
Angelina's birthday surprise. Holabird, K. See note under Holabird, K. Angelina ballerina E
Angelina's Christmas. Holabird, K. See note under Holabird, K. Angelina ballerina E
Angell, Judie, 1937-
Dear Lola (4-6) Fic
Dear Marsha
In Connections: short stories by outstanding writers for young adults p2-13 S C
A home is to share—and share—and share— (4-6) Fic
Tina Gogo (6 and up) Fic
Angelo, Valenti, 1897-
(il) Bulla, C. R. St. Valentine's Day 394.2
Angels & other strangers: family Christmas stories. Paterson, K. S C
Angels and other strangers. Paterson, K.
In Paterson, K. Angels & other strangers: family Christmas stories p1-16 S C
Angel's mother's baby. Delton, J. See note under Delton, J. Angel's mother's wedding Fic
Angel's mother's boyfriend. Delton, J. See note under Delton, J. Angel's mother's wedding Fic
Angel's mother's wedding. Delton, J. Fic
Angles are easy as pie. Froman, R. 516
Anglo-American cataloguing rules
Gorman, M. The concise AACR2, 1988 revision 025.3
Anglo-American cataloguing rules, 2nd edition, 1988 revision. See Gorman, M. The concise AACR2, 1988 revision 025.3
Anglo-Argentine War, 1982 *See* Falkland Islands War, 1982
Anglo-Saxons
See/See also pages in the following book(s):
Lyttle, R. B. Land beyond the river p62-76 (6 and up) 940.1
Angus and the cat. Flack, M. See note under Flack, M. Angus and the ducks E
also in The Read-aloud treasury p156-78 808.8
Angus and the ducks. Flack, M. E
Angus lost. Flack, M. See note under Flack, M. Angus and the ducks E
Anholt, Catherine
Tom's rainbow walk E
Animal abuse
Arnold, C. Pets without homes (k-3) 636.088
Curtis, P. The animal shelter (5 and up) 636.08
Pringle, L. P. The animal rights controversy (6 and up) 179
Animal alphabet. Kitchen, B. E
Animal architects (4 and up) 591.5
Animal camouflage. Powzyk, J. A. 591.5
Animal communication
Johnson, R. L. The secret language: pheromones in the animal world (5 and up) 591.5
McGrath, S. How animals talk (k-3) 591.5
McNulty, F. With love from Koko (1-3) 599.88
Patent, D. H. Singing birds and flashing fireflies (k-2) 591.5
Patterson, F. Koko's kitten (1-4) 599.88
Patterson, F. Koko's story (1-4) 599.88
Spier, P. Gobble, growl, grunt E
Van Woerkom, D. Hidden messages (2-4) 595.7
Animal fact/animal fable. Simon, S. 591
Animal families of the wild (5 and up) 591
The **animal** family. Jarrell, R. Fic
Animal-foot hitter
In The Naked bear p24-30 398.2
Animal homes. Podendorf, I. 591.5
Animal intelligence
Harrar, G. Signs of the apes, songs of the whales (4 and up) 591.5
Sattler, H. R. Fish facts & bird brains: animal intelligence (5 and up) 591.5
Animal numbers. Kitchen, B. E
Animal painting and illustration
Ames, L. J. Draw 50 cats (4 and up) 743
Ames, L. J. Draw 50 dinosaurs and other prehistoric animals (4 and up) 743
Ames, L. J. Draw 50 dogs (4 and up) 743
Ames, L. J. Draw 50 horses (4 and up) 743
Ames, L. J. Draw 50 sharks, whales, and other sea creatures (4 and up) 743
Arnosky, J. Drawing from nature (5 and up) 743

Animal painting and illustration—*Continued*
Arnosky, J. Drawing life in motion (4 and up) **743**
Arnosky, J. Sketching outdoors in autumn (5 and up) **743**
Arnosky, J. Sketching outdoors in spring (5 and up) **743**
Arnosky, J. Sketching outdoors in summer (5 and up) **743**
Arnosky, J. Sketching outdoors in winter (5 and up) **743**
Frame, P. Drawing cats and kittens (4 and up) **743**
Animal rhymes. See A Peaceable kingdom **811**
The **animal** rights controversy. Pringle, L. P. **179**
The **animal** shelter. Curtis, P. **636.08**
Animal stories *See* Animals—Fiction
The **animal,** the vegetable, and John D Jones. Byars, B. C. **Fic**
Animal tracks
Arnosky, J. Crinkleroot's book of animal tracking (3-5) **591.5**
Animals
See also Alpine animals; Desert animals; Forest animals; Freshwater animals; Mammals; Marine animals; Pets; Prairie animals; Prehistoric animals; Primates; Rare animals; Vertebrates; names of individual animals
Ancona, G. Handtalk zoo (k-3) **419**
Animal families of the wild (5 and up) **591**
Cole, J. Large as life daytime animals (k-3) **591**
Cole, J. Large as life nighttime animals (k-3) **591**
Dunrea, O. Deep down underground **E**
Gardner, B. Can you imagine—? **E**
Heberman, E. The city kid's field guide (4 and up) **591**
Hoban, T. A children's zoo (k-2) **591**
Kitchen, B. Animal alphabet **E**
Kitchen, B. Animal numbers **E**
Kitchen, B. Gorilla/Chinchilla and other animal rhymes **E**
Lavies, B. Tree trunk traffic (k-2) **591.5**
Lilly, K. Kenneth Lilly's animals (3 and up) **599**
Machotka, H. What do you do at a petting zoo? (k-2) **590.74**
Miller, J. Farm counting book **E**
Parnall, P. Feet! **E**
Pope, J. Do animals dream? (4 and up) **591**
Rinard, J. E. Helping our animal friends (k-3) **636.088**
Rinard, J. E. The world beneath your feet (k-3) **591.9**
Ryden, H. Wild animals of Africa ABC **E**
Ryden, H. Wild animals of America ABC **E**
Selsam, M. E. Keep looking! (k-2) **599**
Simon, S. Animal fact/animal fable (1-4) **591**
Spier, P. Gobble, growl, grunt **E**
Staines, B. All God's critters got a place in the choir (k-2) **782.42**
Thornhill, J. The wildlife 1 2 3 **E**
Zolotow, C. Sleepy book **E**

Camouflage

See Camouflage (Biology)

Fiction

Aardema, V. Rabbit makes a monkey of lion (k-2) **398.2**
Aardema, V. The Vingananee and the tree toad (k-3) **398.2**
Aardema, V. Who's in Rabbit's house? (k-3) **398.2**
Aardema, V. Why mosquitoes buzz in people's ears (k-3) **398.2**
Allard, H. Bumps in the night **E**
Aylesworth, J. One crow **E**
Banks, M. Animals of the night **E**
Base, G. The eleventh hour (4-6) **Fic**
Bonsall, C. N. Piggle **E**
Brett, J. Annie and the wild animals **E**
Brett, J. The mitten (k-2) **398.2**
Brown, M. W. Baby animals **E**
Burningham, J. Mr. Gumpy's outing **E**
Burningham, J. The shopping basket **E**
Carle, E. Rooster's off to see the world **E**
Carris, J. D. Pets, vets, and Marty Howard (5 and up) **Fic**
Cherry, L. Who's sick today? **E**
Coatsworth, E. J. Under the green willow **E**
Cole, B. No more baths **E**
Corbett, W. J. The song of Pentecost (5 and up) **Fic**
Cushman, D. Possum stew **E**
De Regniers, B. S. May I bring a friend? **E**
Demi. Demi's Count the animals 1 2 3 **E**
Demi. Demi's Find-the-animal A.B.C. **E**
Downing, J. White snow, blue feather **E**
Ets, M. H. In the forest **E**
Ets, M. H. Play with me **E**
Flack, M. Ask Mr. Bear **E**
Galdone, P. Henny Penny (k-2) **398.2**
Galdone, P. The monkey and the crocodile (k-2) **398.2**
Gannett, R. S. My father's dragon (1-4) **Fic**
Ginsburg, M. Where does the sun go at night? **E**
Grahame, K. The open road (2-5) **Fic**

Animals—Fiction—*Continued*
Grahame, K. The wind in the willows (4-6) **Fic**
Guarino, D. Is your mama a llama? **E**
Heine, H. Friends **E**
Howe, D. Bunnicula (4-6) **Fic**
Howe, J. The celery stalks at midnight (4-6) **Fic**
Howe, J. Scared silly: a Halloween treat **E**
Hutchins, P. 1 hunter **E**
Hutchins, P. What game shall we play? **E**
Jacques, B. Mattimeo (6 and up) **Fic**
Jacques, B. Redwall (6 and up) **Fic**
Jarrell, R. The animal family (4 and up) **Fic**
Jukes, M. Lights around the palm **E**
Kasza, K. When the elephant walks **E**
Kellogg, S. Aster Aardvark's alphabet adventures **E**
Kellogg, S. Chicken Little (k-3) **398.2**
Kessler, L. P. Old Turtle's winter games **E**
Kherdian, D. The cat's midsummer jamboree **E**
Kipling, R. The jungle books (4 and up) **S C**
Kipling, R. Just so stories (3-6) **S C**
Lawson, R. Rabbit Hill (3-6) **Fic**
Lawson, R. The tough winter (3-6) **Fic**
Lester, J. Further tales of Uncle Remus (4-6) **398.2**
Lester, J. The knee-high man, and other tales (k-3) **398.2**
Lester, J. More tales of Uncle Remus (4-6) **398.2**
Lester, J. The tales of Uncle Remus (4-6) **398.2**
Lewin, H. Jafta **E**
Lexau, J. M. Who took the farmer's [hat]? **E**
Lobel, A. Fables (3-5) **Fic**
Lobel, A. Grasshopper on the road **E**
Low, J. Mice twice **E**
Lyon, G. E. A regular rolling Noah **E**
Mahy, M. 17 kings and 42 elephants **E**
Marzollo, J. Pretend you're a cat **E**
Maxner, J. Nicholas Cricket **E**
McKissack, P. C. Nettie Jo's friends **E**
Milne, A. A. The house at Pooh Corner (1-4) **Fic**
Milne, A. A. The Pooh story book (1-4) **Fic**
Milne, A. A. Winnie-the-Pooh (1-4) **Fic**
Milne, A. A. The world of Pooh (1-4) **Fic**
Parks, V. D. Jump! the adventures of Brer Rabbit (1-4) **398.2**
Parks, V. D. Jump again! more adventures of Brer Rabbit (1-4) **398.2**
Parnall, P. Winter barn **E**
Payne, E. Katy No-Pocket **E**
Petersham, M. The box with red wheels **E**
Plume, I. The Bremen town musicians (k-3) **398.2**
Polushkin, M. Who said meow? **E**
Provensen, A. The year at Maple Hill Farm **E**
Rice, E. Sam who never forgets **E**
Rylant, C. Every living thing (5 and up) **S C**
Sendak, M. Very far away **E**
Siberell, A. Whale in the sky (k-3) **398.2**
Skofield, J. All wet! All wet! **E**
Steig, W. Doctor De Soto **E**
Steig, W. The real thief (2-5) **Fic**
Stevenson, J. Fast friends **E**
Stevenson, J. Monty **E**
Stevenson, J. National Worm Day **E**
Tafuri, N. Do not disturb **E**
Tafuri, N. Early morning in the barn **E**
Tompert, A. Nothing sticks like a shadow **E**
Tresselt, A. R. The mitten (k-2) **398.2**
Varley, S. Badger's parting gifts **E**
Weiss, N. Where does the brown bear go? **E**
Zimmerman, H. W. Henny Penny (k-2) **398.2**

Folklore

Parks, V. D. Jump on over! the adventures of Brer Rabbit and his family (1-4) **398.2**

Food

See also Herbivores
Epstein, S. Bugs for dinner? (4-6) **591.5**

Habitations

Animal architects (4 and up) **591.5**
McCauley, J. R. Animals and their hiding places (k-3) **591.5**
McCauley, J. R. Animals that live in trees (k-3) **591.5**
McClung, R. M. Animals that build their homes (k-3) **591.5**
Podendorf, I. Animal homes (2-4) **591.5**
Pringle, L. P. Home (4 and up) **591.5**
The Secret world of animals (4 and up) **591.5**

Habits and behavior

See also Animals—Food
Arnosky, J. Secrets of a wildlife watcher (4 and up) **591.5**
Facklam, M. Partners for life (3-6) **591.5**
Freedman, R. When winter comes (k-3) **591.5**
Hess, L. Secrets in the meadow (4 and up) **591.5**
Hirschland, R. B. How animals care for their babies (k-3) **591.5**

Animals—Habits and behavior—*Continued*
Hornblow, L. Animals do the strangest things (1-3) **591.5**
How animals behave: a new look at wildlife (5 and up) **591.5**
Hughey, P. Scavengers and decomposers: the cleanup crew (5 and up) **591.5**
Kohl, J. Pack, band, and colony (5 and up) **591.5**
Kohl, J. The view from the oak (6 and up) **591.5**
Kostyal, K. M. Animals at play (k-3) **591.5**
McCauley, J. R. Animals in summer (k-3) **591.5**
McCauley, J. R. Ways animals sleep (k-3) **591.5**
McGrath, S. The amazing things animals do (4 and up) **591.5**
Neuman, P. When winter comes (1-3) **591.5**
Parnall, P. Woodpile (1-4) **591.5**
Pringle, L. P. Animals at play (5 and up) **591.5**
Pringle, L. P. Feral: tame animals gone wild (5 and up) **591.5**
Rinard, J. E. Creatures of the night (k-3) **591.5**
San Souci, D. North country night (2-4) **591.5**
Venino, S. Amazing animal groups (k-3) **591.5**

Hibernation

Facklam, M. Do not disturb (3-6) **591.5**

Infancy

Grosvenor, D. K. Zoo babies (k-3) **590.74**
Heller, R. Chickens aren't the only ones (k-1) **591.1**
Hirschland, R. B. How animals care for their babies (k-3) **591.5**
Lauber, P. What's hatching out of that egg? (k-3) **591.1**

Mistreatment

See Animal abuse

Photography

See Photography of animals

Pictorial works

Eichenberg, F. Ape in a cape **E**
Eichenberg, F. Dancing in the moon **E**
Hader, B. The big snow **E**
Wolff, A. A year of beasts **E**

Poetry

Belloc, H. The bad child's book of beasts, and More beasts for worse children, and A moral alphabet (1-4) **821**
Carle, E. Eric Carle's animals, animals (1-3) **808.81**
De Regniers, B. S. It does not say meow, and other animal riddle rhymes (k-1) **793.73**
Esbensen, B. J. Words with wrinkled knees: animal poems (2-5) **811**
Hooper, P. A bundle of beasts (3-6) **811**
Lear, E. Edward Lear's The Scroobious Pip **821**
Lewis, J. P. A hippopotamusn't and other animal verses (k-3) **811**
Mizumura, K. If I were a cricket . . . (k-2) **811**
A Paper zoo (1-4) **811.008**
A Peaceable kingdom (k-3) **811**
Singer, M. Turtle in July (2-4) **811**
Yolen, J. Ring of earth: a child's book of seasons (3-6) **811**

See/See also pages in the following book(s):
Favorite poems, old and new p153-79 (4-6) **808.81**
Piping down the valleys wild p105-60 **808.81**
Rainbow in the sky p229-60 (k-4) **821.008**
The Scott, Foresman anthology of children's literature p49-75 **808.8**

Australia

Amazing animals of Australia (4 and up) **591.9**
Powzyk, J. A. Wallaby Creek (3-6) **591.9**

Animals, Domestic *See* Domestic animals
Animals, Extinct *See* Extinct animals
Animals, Fossil *See* Fossils
Animals, Mythical
See also Dragons; Mermaids and mermen
Lurie, A. Fabulous beasts (4 and up) **398**
McHargue, G. The beasts of never (4 and up) **398**
McHargue, G. Meet the werewolf (4 and up) **398**
Schwartz, A. Kickle snifters and other fearsome critters (2-5) **398**
Stockton, F. The Griffin and the Minor Canon (3-5) **Fic**

Fiction

Hunter, M. A stranger came ashore (6 and up) **Fic**
Peet, B. No such things **E**

Animals, Working *See* Working animals
Animals and the handicapped
Smith, E. S. A service dog goes to school (3-5) **636.7**
See/See also pages in the following book(s):
Ashabranner, B. K. People who make a difference p31-40 (5 and up) **920**

Animals and their hiding places. McCauley, J. R. 591.5
Animals, animals, Eric Carle's. Carle, E. 808.81
Animals at play. Kostyal, K. M. 591.5
Animals at play. Pringle, L. P. 591.5
Animals do the strangest things. Hornblow, L. 591.5
Animals helping people. Venino, S. 636.088
Animals in art
See also Marine animals in art
Animals in summer. McCauley, J. R. 591.5
Animals in the pit
Afanas'ev, A. N. Beasts in a pit
In Afanas'ev, A. N. Russian fairy tales p498 398.2
Animals of the Bible. Bible. Selections 220.8
Animals of the night. Banks, M. E
Animals that build their homes. McClung, R. M. 591.5
Animals that live in trees. McCauley, J. R. 591.5
Anna Banana: 101 jump-rope rhymes (2-4) 398.8
Anna Banana and me. Blegvad, L. E
Annabelle Swift, kindergartner. Schwartz, A. E
Anna's silent world. Wolf, B. 362.4
Anne Boleyn. Leach, M.
In Leach, M. Whistle in the graveyard p22-23 398.2
Anne Frank: life in hiding. Hurwitz, J. 92
Anne of Avonlea. Montgomery, L. M. See note under Montgomery, L. M. Anne of Green Gables Fic
Anne of Green Gables. Montgomery, L. M. Fic
Anne of Ingleside. Montgomery, L. M. See note under Montgomery, L. M. Anne of Green Gables Fic
Anne of the island. Montgomery, L. M. See note under Montgomery, L. M. Anne of Green Gables Fic
Anne of Windy Poplars. Montgomery, L. M. See note under Montgomery, L. M. Anne of Green Gables Fic
Anne's house of dreams. Montgomery, L. M. See note under Montgomery, L. M. Anne of Green Gables Fic
Annie and the Old One. Miles, M. Fic
Annie and the wild animals. Brett, J. E
Annie's monster. Corcoran, B. Fic
Anniversaries and holidays. Gregory, R. W. 394.2
Anno, Masaichiro
Anno's mysterious multiplying jar (2-5) 512
Anno, Mitsumasa, 1926-
All in a day E
Anno's Aesop (2-4) 398.2
Contents: The fox and the grapes; The bear and the travelers; The dog and his reflection; The rabbit and the turtle; The donkey in the lion's skin; The old lion; The fox and the goat; The donkey and his burdens; The goat and the donkey; The bald man and the fly; The ants; The farmer and the fox; The fox and the crow; The grasshopper and the ants; The wolf and the crane; The fox and the stork; The boy who cried wolf; The farmer and his sons; The goose that laid the golden eggs; The miser; The two dogs; The farmer and his animals; The shipwrecked man and the sea; The north wind and the sun; The hurricane; The enemies; The blacksmith and his dog; The musician; The fortune teller; The astronomer; The hunter and the woodcutter; The fox and the shepherd; The bandit and the mulberry tree; The walnut tree; The woodcutter and the noble trees; The oak tree and Jupiter; Jupiter and the woodcutters; The mistress and her servants; The fat hens; The cat and the mice; The house mouse and the field mouse
Anno's alphabet E
Anno's Britain E
Anno's counting book E
Anno's counting house E
Anno's flea market E
Anno's journey E
Anno's math games (k-3) 513
Anno's math games II (k-3) 513
Anno's medieval world (3-6) 909.07
Anno's sundial (4 and up) 529
Anno's U.S.A E
Socrates and the three little pigs (4-6) 511
Topsy-turvies E
Upside-downers E
(jt. auth) Anno, M. Anno's mysterious multiplying jar 512
(il) Nozaki, A. Anno's hat tricks 153.4
Anno's Aesop. Anno, M. 398.2
Anno's alphabet. Anno, M. E
Anno's Britain. Anno, M. E
Anno's counting book. Anno, M. E
Anno's counting house. Anno, M. E
Anno's flea market. Anno, M. E
Anno's hat tricks. Nozaki, A. 153.4
Anno's journey. Anno, M. E
Anno's math games. Anno, M. 513
Anno's math games II. Anno, M. 513
Anno's medieval world. Anno, M. 909.07
Anno's mysterious multiplying jar. Anno, M. 512

Anno's sundial. Anno, M. **529**
Anno's U.S.A. Anno, M. **E**
The **Annotated** Mother Goose **398.8**
Annual events, Chase's **394.2**
Another Cinderella. Stiles, N.
In Free to be—a family p25-32 **810.8**
Another story about the little rabs. Parks, V. D.
In Parks, V. D. Jump on over! the adventures of Brer Rabbit and his family **398.2**
Ansige Karamba, the glutton. Courlander, H.
In Courlander, H. The cow-tail switch, and other West African stories p119-28 **398.2**
Ant cities. Dorros, A. **595.7**
An **ant** colony. Fischer-Nagel, H. **595.7**
Antarctic regions
Cowcher, H. Antarctica (1-3) **998**
Swan, R. Destination: Antarctica (4-6) **998**
Antarctica. Cowcher, H. **998**
An **anteater** named Arthur. Waber, B. **E**
The **antelope** chase. Mayo, G.
In Mayo, G. Star tales p29-32 **398.2**
Anthony, Susan Brownell, 1820-1906
See/See also pages in the following book(s):
Jacobs, W. J. Great lives: human rights p147-54 (5 and up) **920**
Anthony Burns: the defeat and triumph of a fugitive slave. Hamilton, V. **92**
Anthropology
Periodicals
Faces **306.05**
Antiquities
See also Archeology
Antiquity of man *See* Man—Origin
Antisemitism
See also Jews—Persecutions
Fiction
Levitin, S. The return (6 and up) **Fic**
Antlers
See also Horns
Antonacci, Robert Joseph, 1916-
Basketball for young champions (5 and up) **796.323**
Antrodemus *See* Allosaurus
Ants
Dorros, A. Ant cities (k-3) **595.7**
Fischer-Nagel, H. An ant colony (3-6) **595.7**
Overbeck, C. Ants (4 and up) **595.7**
Patent, D. H. Looking at ants (3-5) **595.7**
Van Woerkom, D. Hidden messages (2-4) **595.7**
See/See also pages in the following book(s):
Simon, S. Pets in a jar (4 and up) **639**
Fiction
Van Allsburg, C. Two bad ants **E**
Any me I want to be: poems. Kuskin, K. **811**
Any number can play. Sullivan, G. **796**
The **Apache**. McKissack, P. C. **970.004**
Apache Indians
McKissack, P. C. The Apache (2-4) **970.004**
Shorto, R. Geronimo and the struggle for Apache freedom (5 and up) **92**
See/See also pages in the following book(s):
Ehrlich, A. Wounded Knee: an Indian history of the American West (6 and up) **970.004**
Hofsinde, R. Indian costumes p13-20 (3-6) **391**
Apartheid *See* South Africa—Race relations
Apartment houses
Fiction
Berends, P. B. The case of the elevator duck (3-5) **Fic**
Hurwitz, J. Busybody Nora (2-4) **Fic**
Ape in a cape. Eichenberg, F. **E**
Apes
See also Chimpanzees; Gorillas
Selsam, M. E. A first look at monkeys and apes (1-3) **599.8**
Apfel, Necia H., 1930-
It's all relative (6 and up) **530.1**
Nebulae (4 and up) **523.1**
Aphrodite (Greek deity)
Gates, D. Two queens of heaven: Aphrodite [and] Demeter (4 and up) **292**
Hodges, M. The arrow and the lamp **292**
Apiculture *See* Bees
Apollo (Greek deity)
Gates, D. The golden god: Apollo (4 and up) **292**
Appalachian Mountains
Fiction
Caudill, R. A certain small shepherd (4 and up) **Fic**
Caudill, R. Did you carry the flag today, Charley? (2-4) **Fic**
Cleaver, V. Trial Valley (5 and up) **Fic**
Cleaver, V. Where the lillies bloom (5 and up) **Fic**
Hamilton, V. M. C. Higgins the great (6 and up) **Fic**
Houston, G. The year of the perfect Christmas tree **E**
Smith, D. B. Return to Bitter Creek (5 and up) **Fic**

Appaloosa horses. Patent, D. H. 636.1
Appel, Martin, 1948-
The first book of baseball (4-6) 796.357
Appelard and Liverwurst. Mayer, M. E
Appetite disorders *See* Eating disorders
Apple, Margot
(il) Delton, J. Angel's mother's wedding Fic
(il) O'Connor, J. Yours till Niagara Falls, Abby Fic
(il) Sachs, E.-A. The boy who ate dog biscuits E
(il) Shaw, N. Sheep in a jeep E
Apple
Johnson, S. A. Apple trees (4 and up) 634
Parnall, P. Apple tree (k-3) 634
Patent, D. H. An apple a day (3-6) 634
Schnieper, C. An apple tree through the year (3-6) 634
An **apple** a day. Patent, D. H. 634
Apple Computer Inc.
See/See also pages in the following book(s):
Aaseng, N. From rags to riches p64-75 (5 and up) 920
Apple is my sign. Riskind, M. Fic
Apple of contentment
Thane, A. The apple of contentment
In Thane, A. Plays from famous stories and fairy tales p153-68 812
Apple tree. Parnall, P. 634
Apple tree Christmas. Noble, T. H. E
An **apple** tree through the year. Schnieper, C. 634
Apple trees. Johnson, S. A. 634
Applebet: an ABC. Watson, C. E
Apples and pumpkins. Rockwell, A. F. E
Appleseed, Johnny, 1774-1845
About
Aliki. The story of Johnny Appleseed (k-3) 92
Kellogg, S. Johnny Appleseed (2-4) 92
Applied arts *See* Decorative arts
Appraisal 016.5
The **apprentice** cat. Alexander, L.
In Alexander, L. The town cats, and other tales p113-26 S C
Apprentices
Fiction
Fleischman, P. Saturnalia (5 and up) Fic
Garfield, L. The apprentices (6 and up) S C
The **apprentices**. Garfield, L. S C
Apseloff, Marilyn F.
(jt. auth) Anderson, C. C. Nonsense literature for children 028.5
Apt. 3. Keats, E. J. E
Apuleius
Hodges, M. The arrow and the lamp 292
Aquariums
See also Marine aquariums
Johnston, G. Windows on wildlife (3-6) 590.74
Pope, J. Taking care of your fish (3-5) 639.3
Aquatic animals *See* Marine animals
Aquatic plants *See* Marine plants
Arab countries
See also Bahrain
Haskins, J. Count your way through the Arab world (2-4) 909
Social life and customs
Alotaibi, M. Bedouin: the nomads of the desert (5 and up) 956
An **Arab** family. Dutton, R. 953
An **Arab** village. See Dutton, R. An Arab family 953
Arabel and Mortimer. Aiken, J. Fic
Arabian nights
Aladdin and the wonderful lamp
In The Blue fairy book p72-85 398.2
The Arabian nights entertainments 398.2
The Forty thieves
In The Blue fairy book p242-50 398.2
Lang, A. The forty thieves
In Womenfolk and fairy tales p51-64 398.2
The Story of Prince Ahmed and the Fairy Paribanou
In The Blue fairy book p342-73 398.2
The **Arabian** nights entertainments (5 and up) 398.2
Arabian Peninsula
See also Oman
Arabic folklore *See* Arabs—Folklore
Arabs
See also Bedouins
See/See also pages in the following book(s):
Lyttle, R. B. Land beyond the river p71-91 (6 and up) 940.1
Folklore
The Arabian nights entertainments (5 and up) 398.2
Carrick, C. Aladdin and the wonderful lamp (2-4) 398.2
Lang, A. Aladdin and the wonderful lamp (2-4) 398.2
McVitty, W. Ali Baba and the forty thieves (1-3) 398.2

Arachne (Greek mythology)
See/See also pages in the following book(s):
Climo, S. Someone saw a spider p5-12 (4 and up) **398.2**

Arachne's gift. Climo, S.
In Climo, S. Someone saw a spider p5-12 **398.2**

Araki, Chiyo
Origami in the classroom (4 and up) **736**

Arapaho Indians
See/See also pages in the following book(s):
Ehrlich, A. Wounded Knee: an Indian history of the American West (6 and up) **970.004**

Arbuthnot, May Hill, 1884-1969
(jt. auth) Sutherland, Z. Children and books **028.5**

The **Arbuthnot** lectures, 1970-1979/1980-1989 **028.5**

Archaeology *See* Archeology

Archambault, Ariane
(jt. auth) Corbeil, J.-C. The Facts on File junior visual dictionary **423**

Archambault, John
Counting sheep **E**
(jt. auth) Martin, B. Barn dance! **E**
(jt. auth) Martin, B. Chicka chicka boom boom **E**
(jt. auth) Martin, B. The ghost-eye tree **E**
(jt. auth) Martin, B. Knots on a counting rope **E**
(jt. auth) Martin, B. Listen to the rain **E**
(jt. auth) Martin, B. Up and down on the merry-go-round **E**

Archbold, Rick, 1950-
(jt. auth) Ballard, R. D. The lost wreck of the Isis **910.4**

Archeology
See also Excavations (Archeology); Man, Prehistoric; names of groups of people and names of regions, countries, cities, etc. with the subdivision Antiquities
Anderson, J. From map to museum (5 and up) **930.1**
Gallant, R. A. Lost cities (4 and up) **930**
Hackwell, W. J. Digging to the past: excavations in ancient lands (4 and up) **930.1**
Hackwell, W. J. Diving to the past: recovering ancient wrecks (4 and up) **910.4**
Lauber, P. Tales mummies tell (5 and up) **930.1**
Weiss, M. E. Sky watchers of ages past (5 and up) **523**

Archer's goon. Jones, D. W. **Fic**

Architectural engineering *See* Building

Architecture
Isaacson, P. M. Round buildings, square buildings, & buildings that wiggle like a fish (4 and up) **720**

Details

See also Woodwork

Architecture, Domestic
See also Houses
Huntington, L. P. Americans at home (6 and up) **728**
Weiss, H. Shelters: from tepee to igloo (4 and up) **728**

Architecture, Gothic
Macaulay, D. Cathedral: the story of its construction (4 and up) **726**

Architecture, Roman
Macaulay, D. City: a story of Roman planning and construction (4 and up) **711**

The **Arctic** and Antarctica. Gilbreath, A. **998**

Arctic explorer: the story of Matthew Henson. Ferris, J. **92**

The **arctic** fox. LaBonte, G. **599.74**

Arctic memories. Ekoomiak, N. **998**

Arctic regions
See also North Pole
Ekoomiak, N. Arctic memories (3-5) **998**

Fiction

George, J. C. Julie of the wolves (6 and up) **Fic**
Houston, J. A. Frozen fire (6 and up) **Fic**
Paulsen, G. Dogsong (6 and up) **Fic**

Ardizzone, Edward, 1900-1979
(il) Estes, E. Pinky Pye **Fic**
(il) Estes, E. The witch family **Fic**
(il) Fox, P. A likely place **Fic**
(il) Nesbit, E. Long ago when I was young **92**
(il) Thomas, D. A child's Christmas in Wales **828**
See/See also pages in the following book(s):
Sendak, M. Caldecott & Co.: notes on books and pictures p119-21, 133-37 **028.5**

Ardley, Neil, 1937-
Music (4 and up) **784.19**
Working with water (4 and up) **507**

Are you my mother? Eastman, P. D. E
Are you there God? it's me, Margaret. Blume, J. Fic
Arenas, Reinaldo, 1943-1990
With my eyes closed
In Where angels glide at dawn p35-41 S C
Argentina
Fox, G. The land and people of Argentina (5 and up) 982
Argonauts (Greek mythology)
Colum, P. The Golden Fleece and the heroes who lived before Achilles (5 and up) 292
Evslin, B. Jason and the Argonauts (6 and up) 292
Fisher, L. E. Jason and the golden fleece (3-6) 292
See/See also pages in the following book(s):
Hamilton, E. Mythology p159-79 (6 and up) 292
Arid regions
See also Deserts
Arithmetic
Froman, R. The greatest guessing game (2-4) 513
Study and teaching—Periodicals
Arithmetic Teacher 510.7
Arithmetic Teacher 510.7
Arizona
Heinrichs, A. Arizona
In America the beautiful 973
The **ark**. Geisert, A. 222
Arkansas
Heinrichs, A. Arkansas
In America the beautiful 973
Fiction
Branscum, R. The adventures of Johnny May (4-6) Fic
Greene, B. Get on out of here, Philip Hall (4-6) Fic
Greene, B. Philip Hall likes me, I reckon maybe (4-6) Fic
Greene, B. Summer of my German soldier (6 and up) Fic
Arkin, Alan, 1934-
The lemming condition (5 and up) Fic
Arly. Peck, R. N. Fic
Armadillos
Blassingame, W. The strange armadillo (4 and up) 599.3
Lavies, B. It's an armadillo (1-3) 599.3
Fiction
Kipling, R. The beginning of the armadilloes (1-4) Fic
Armaments
See also Arms control
Armbruster, Ann
Tornadoes (4-6) 551.55
Armenia
Folklore
See Folklore—Armenia
Armenian Americans
Fiction
Kherdian, D. A song for Uncle Harry (4-6) Fic
Armenian massacres, 1915-1923
Kherdian, D. The road from home [biography of Veron Kherdian] (6 and up) 92
Armenians
Turkey
Kherdian, D. The road from home [biography of Veron Kherdian] (6 and up) 92
Armer, Laura Adams, 1874-1963
See/See also pages in the following book(s):
Newbery Medal books, 1922-1955 p101-06 028.5
Armien's fishing trip. Stock, C. E
The **armless** maiden. Afanas'ev, A. N.
In Afanas'ev, A. N. Russian fairy tales p294-99 398.2
Arms and armor
Byam, M. Arms & armor (4 and up) 355.8
Wilkinson, F. Arms and armor (3-5) 623.4
Arms control
Fiction
Langton, J. The fragile flag (5 and up) Fic
Armstrong, Louis, 1900-1971
About
Collier, J. L. Louis Armstrong: an American success story (5 and up) 92
Armstrong, William Howard
Sounder (5 and up) Fic
See/See also pages in the following book(s):
Newbery and Caldecott Medal books, 1966-1975 p58-65 028.5
Army Engineer Corps *See* United States. Army. Corps of Engineers
Army life *See* Soldiers
Arndt, Ursula
(il) Barth, E. Hearts, cupids, and red roses 394.2
(il) Barth, E. Holly, reindeer, and colored lights 394.2
(il) Barth, E. Lilies, rabbits, and painted eggs 394.2
(il) Barth, E. Shamrocks, harps, and shil-

Arndt, Ursula—*Continued*
lelaghs **394.2**
(il) Barth, E. Turkeys, Pilgrims, and Indian corn **394.2**
(il) Barth, E. Witches, pumpkins, and grinning ghosts **394.2**
(il) A Christmas feast: poems, sayings, greetings, and wishes. See A Christmas feast: poems, sayings, greetings, and wishes **808.81**
(il) Giblin, J. Fireworks, picnics, and flags **394.2**

Arno, Enrico, 1913-1981
(il) Coolidge, O. E. The golden days of Greece **938**
(il) Fritz, J. Brendan the Navigator **398.2**

Arnold, Arthur
(il) Arnold, C. A walk on the Great Barrier Reef **574.92**

Arnold, Caroline, 1944-
Cheetah (3-5) **599.74**
Dinosaur mountain (4 and up) **567.9**
Dinosaurs down under and other fossils from Australia (4 and up) **567.9**
Giraffe (3-5) **599.73**
Hippo (3-5) **599.73**
Kangaroo (3-5) **599.2**
Koala (3-5) **599.2**
Llama (3-5) **599.73**
Ostriches and other flightless birds (3-6) **598**
Pain: what is it? how do we deal with it? (6 and up) **616**
Penguin (3-6) **598**
Pets without homes (k-3) **636.088**
Saving the peregrine falcon (3-6) **598**
Too fat? Too thin? Do you have a choice? (6 and up) **613.2**
Trapped in tar (3-5) **560**
Tule elk (3-6) **599.73**
A walk on the Great Barrier Reef (3-6) **574.92**
Zebra (3-5) **599.72**

Arnold, Guy
Datelines of world history (5 and up) **909**

Arnold of the Ducks. Gerstein, M. **E**

Arnosky, Jim
Come out, muskrats (k-2) **599.32**
Crinkleroot's book of animal tracking (3-5) **591.5**
Deer at the brook **E**
Drawing from nature (5 and up) **743**
Drawing life in motion (4 and up) **743**
Flies in the water, fish in the air: a personal introduction to fly fishing (5 and up) **799.1**
Freshwater fish & fishing (4 and up) **799.1**
In the forest (4 and up) **758**
Near the sea (4 and up) **758**
Raccoons and ripe corn **E**
Secrets of a wildlife watcher (4 and up) **591.5**
Sketching outdoors in autumn (5 and up) **743**
Sketching outdoors in spring (5 and up) **743**
Sketching outdoors in summer (5 and up) **743**
Sketching outdoors in winter (5 and up) **743**
Watching foxes (k-2) **599.74**

Arnott, Kathleen
The rubber man
In Best-loved folktales of the world p627-30 **398.2**
Unanana and the elephant
In The Scott, Foresman anthology of children's literature p314-17 **808.8**
In Womenfolk and fairy tales p127-34 **398.2**

Arnow, Jan, 1947-
Louisville Slugger (4 and up) **796.357**

Around the world in 80 dishes. Linde, P. van der. **641.5**

Arrant fool
Afanas'ev, A. N. The arrant fool
In Afanas'ev, A. N. Russian fairy tales p334-36 **398.2**

The **arrow** and the lamp. Hodges, M. **292**

Arrow to the sun. McDermott, G. **398.2**

Arrowood, Clinton
(il) Elliott, D. Frogs and the ballet **792.8**

Arroz con leche (k-3) **782.42**

Art
See also Caribbean region in art; Decoration and ornament; Folk art; Graphic arts; subjects and themes in art
See/See also pages in the following book(s):
Bauer, C. F. Celebrations p1-24 **808.8**

Museums

Brown, L. K. Visiting the art museum (k-3) **708**

Art, American
See/See also pages in the following book(s):
Caney, S. Steven Caney's kids' America p202-35 (4 and up) **790.1**

Art, Graphic *See* Graphic arts

Art, Indian *See* Indians of North America—Art

Art, Jewish *See* Jewish art and symbolism
Art and design in children's picture books. Lacy, L. E. **741.6**
The **art** and industry of sandcastles. Adkins, J. **728.8**
Art appreciation
Brown, L. K. Visiting the art museum (k-3) **708**
Chermayeff, I. First words (k-3) **410**
Woolf, F. Picture this (4 and up) **759**
Art galleries *See* Art—Museums
Art industries and trade *See* Decorative arts
The **art** lesson. De Paola, T. **E**
The **art** of base-stealing. Sullivan, G. **796.357**
The **art** of Beatrix Potter. Potter, B. **741.6**
Art of Maurice Sendak. Lanes, S. G. **741.6**
The **art** of the story-teller. Shedlock, M. L. **372.6**
Arthritis
Anderson, M. K. Arthritis (5 and up) **616.7**
Arthur, King
About
Lister, R. The legend of King Arthur (4 and up) **398.2**
Pyle, H. The story of King Arthur and his knights (6 and up) **398.2**
Pyle, H. The story of the Grail and the passing of Arthur (6 and up) **398.2**
Sutcliff, R. The light beyond the forest (4 and up) **398.2**
Sutcliff, R. The road to Camlann (4 and up) **398.2**
Sutcliff, R. The sword and the circle (4 and up) **398.2**
See/See also pages in the following book(s):
Shedlock, M. L. The art of the story-teller p173-78 **372.6**
Fiction
Bulla, C. R. The sword in the tree (2-5) **Fic**
Yolen, J. The dragon's boy (5 and up) **Fic**
Arthur, Alex
Shell (4 and up) **594**
Arthur, Chester Alan, 1830-1886
About
Simon, C. Chester A. Arthur: twenty-first president of the United States (4 and up) **92**
Arthur, Kay, 1933-
Mother goes modern
In Holiday plays round the year p267-84 **812.008**
Arthur, for the very first time. MacLachlan, P. **Fic**
Arthur goes to camp. Brown, M. T. See note under Brown, M. Arthur's nose **E**
Arthur in the cave. Thomas, W. J.
In Shedlock, M. L. The art of the story-teller p173-78 **372.6**
Arthur Mitchell. Tobias, T. **92**
Arthur the Kid. Coren, A. **Fic**
Arthurian romances
See also Grail
Hastings, S. Sir Gawain and the Green Knight (3 and up) **398.2**
Hastings, S. Sir Gawain and the loathly lady (3 and up) **398.2**
Lister, R. The legend of King Arthur (4 and up) **398.2**
Pyle, H. The story of King Arthur and his knights (6 and up) **398.2**
Pyle, H. The story of Sir Launcelot and his companions (6 and up) **398.2**
Pyle, H. The story of the champions of the Round Table (6 and up) **398.2**
Pyle, H. The story of the Grail and the passing of Arthur (6 and up) **398.2**
Sutcliff, R. The light beyond the forest (4 and up) **398.2**
Sutcliff, R. The road to Camlann (4 and up) **398.2**
Sutcliff, R. The sword and the circle (4 and up) **398.2**
Arthur's adventure in the abandoned house. Krahn, F. **E**
Arthur's April Fool. Brown, M. T. See note under Brown, M. Arthur's nose **E**
Arthur's baby. Brown, M. T. See note under Brown, M. Arthur's nose **E**
Arthur's birthday. Brown, M. T. See note under Brown, M. Arthur's nose **E**
Arthur's Christmas. Brown, M. T. See note under Brown, M. Arthur's nose **E**
Arthur's Christmas cookies. Hoban, L. **E**
Arthur's eyes. Brown, M. T. See note under Brown, M. Arthur's nose **E**
Arthur's funny money. Hoban, L. See note under Hoban, L. Arthur's Christmas cookies **E**
Arthur's great big valentine. Hoban, L. See note under Hoban, L. Arthur's Christmas cookies **E**
Arthur's Halloween. Brown, M. T. See note under Brown, M. Arthur's nose **E**
Arthur's Halloween costume. Hoban, L. See note under Hoban, L. Arthur's Christmas cookies **E**

Arthur's Honey Bear. Hoban, L. See note under Hoban, L. Arthur's Christmas cookies E

Arthur's loose tooth. Hoban, L. See note under Hoban, L. Arthur's Christmas cookies E

Arthur's new power. Hoban, R. See note under Hoban, R. Dinner at Alberta's E

Arthur's nose. Brown, M. T. E

Arthur's pen pal. Hoban, L. See note under Hoban, L. Arthur's Christmas cookies E

Arthur's pet business. Brown, M. T. See note under Brown, M. Arthur's nose E

Arthur's prize reader. Hoban, L. See note under Hoban, L. Arthur's Christmas cookies E

Arthur's teacher trouble. Brown, M. T. See note under Brown, M. Arthur's nose E

Arthur's Thanksgiving. Brown, M. T. See note under Brown, M. Arthur's nose E

Arthur's tooth. Brown, M. T. See note under Brown, M. Arthur's nose E

Arthur's valentine. Brown, M. T. See note under Brown, M. Arthur's nose E

Artificial satellites

Branley, F. M. From Sputnik to space shuttles (3-6) **629.44**

Branley, F. M. Rockets and satellites (k-3) **629.4**

Artists

See also Child artists; Illustrators; Painters; Women artists

Goffstein, M. B. Lives of the artists (5 and up) **920**

Fiction

Cooney, B. Hattie and the wild waves E

Leaf, M. The eyes of the dragon E

Rylant, C. All I see E

Artists, American

Oneal, Z. Grandma Moses: painter of rural America (4 and up) **92**

Sills, L. Inspirations (5 and up) **920**

Artists, French

Degas, E. Meet Edgar Degas (3-5) **759.4**

Artists, Italian

Provensen, A. Leonardo da Vinci: the artist, inventor, scientist (3 and up) **92**

Ventura, P. Michelangelo's world (5 and up) **92**

Artists' materials

Sattler, H. R. Recipes for art and craft materials (4 and up) **745.5**

Artists of handcrafted furniture at work. Rosenberg, M. B. **749**

Arts, American

See/See also pages in the following book(s):

Tunis, E. The young United States, 1783 to 1830 p123-28 (5 and up) **973**

Arts, Applied *See* Decorative arts

Arts, Decorative *See* Decoration and ornament; Decorative arts

Arts and crafts *See* Handicraft

Aruego, Ariane *See* Dewey, Ariane

Aruego, Jose

Look what I can do E

We hide, you seek E

(il) Ginsburg, M. The chick and the duckling E

(il) Ginsburg, M. Where does the sun go at night? E

(il) Kraus, R. Owliver E

(il) Kraus, R. Whose mouse are you? E

(il) Pomerantz, C. One duck, another duck E

(il) Raffi. Five little ducks **782.42**

(il) Sharmat, M. Gregory, the terrible eater E

Arwin, Melanie Gaines

(il) Ribner, S. The martial arts **796.8**

As: a surfeit of similes. Juster, N. **427**

As I went over the water. See Sendak, M. Hector Protector, and As I went over the water **398.8**

As it is with strangers. Pfeffer, S. B.

In Connections: short stories by outstanding writers for young adults p74-82 **S C**

Asbjørnsen, Peter Christen, 1812-1885

Boots and the troll

In Best-loved folktales of the world p296-300 **398.2**

Chicken Licken

In Tomie dePaola's favorite nursery tales p105-11 **398.2**

East o' the sun and west o' the moon

In The Scott, Foresman anthology of children's literature p236-41 **808.8**

East of the sun and west of the moon

In Best-loved folktales of the world p287-95 **398.2**

In The Blue fairy book p19-29 **398.2**

In Womenfolk and fairy tales p111-26 **398.2**

East of the sun and west of the moon: old tales from the North (3-6) **398.2**

Contents: East of the sun and west of the moon; The blue belt; The lassie and her godmother; The three princesses of Whiteland; The widow's son; The three princesses in the blue mountain

Farmer Weatherbeard

In The Red fairy book p294-302 **398.2**

Asbjørnsen, Peter Christen, 1812-1885 — *Continued*
The giant who had no heart in his body
In Best-loved folktales of the world p304-10 **398.2**
Gudbrand on the hillside
In Best-loved folktales of the world p300-04 **398.2**
The house on the hill
In Tomie dePaola's favorite nursery tales p122-26 **398.2**
The husband who was to mind the house
In The Scott, Foresman anthology of children's literature p235-36 **808.8**
In Womenfolk and fairy tales p106-110 **398.2**
Kari Woodengown
In The Red fairy book p189-201 **398.2**
The lad who went to the North Wind
In Best-loved folktales of the world p310-13 **398.2**
The master-maid
In The Blue fairy book p120-35 **398.2**
The master thief
In Best-loved folktales of the world p313-25 **398.2**
In The Red fairy book p67-81 **398.2**
The mastermaid
In Best-loved folktales of the world p327-39 **398.2**
Not a pin to choose between them
In Best-loved folktales of the world p340-44 **398.2**
The pancake
In The Scott, Foresman anthology of children's literature p228-29 **808.8**
Princess on the glass hill
In Best-loved folktales of the world p345-52 **398.2**
In The Blue fairy book p332-41 **398.2**
Soria Moria Castle
In The Red fairy book p30-41 **398.2**
In The Scott, Foresman anthology of children's literature p230-35 **808.8**
The three billy goats gruff
In Best-loved folktales of the world p326-27 **398.2**
In The Scott, Foresman anthology of children's literature p227-28 **808.8**
In Tomie dePaola's favorite nursery tales p42-45 **398.2**
The three sisters who were entrapped into a mountain
In Womenfolk and fairy tales p156-63 **398.2**
Why the bear is stumpy-tailed
In Best-loved folktales of the world p353 **398.2**
Why the sea is salt
In Best-loved folktales of the world p354-57 **398.2**
In The Blue fairy book p136-40 **398.2**
Hague, K. East of the sun and west of the moon **398.2**

Asch, Frank
Bear shadow. See note under Asch, F. Sand cake **E**
Bear's bargain. See note under Asch, F. Sand cake **E**
Bread and honey. See note under Asch, F. Sand cake **E**
Goodbye house. See note under Asch, F. Sand cake **E**
Happy birthday, Moon. See note under Asch, F. Sand cake **E**
Here comes the cat! **E**
Just like Daddy. See note under Asch, F. Sand cake **E**
Milk and cookies. See note under Asch, F. Sand cake **E**
Moongame. See note under Asch, F. Sand cake **E**
Sand cake **E**
Skyfire. See note under Asch, F. Sand cake **E**

Ash, Maureen
The story of the women's movement (3-6) **305.4**

Ashabranner, Brent K., 1921-
Always to remember (5 and up) **959.704**
Born to the land: an American portrait (5 and up) **978.9**
Into a strange land: unaccompanied refugee youth in America (5 and up) **362.84**
People who make a difference (5 and up) **920**
(jt. auth) Ashabranner, M. Counting America **304.6**

Ashabranner, Jennifer
(il) Ashabranner, B. K. Always to remember **959.704**

Ashabranner, Melissa
Counting America (5 and up) **304.6**
(jt. auth) Ashabranner, B. K. Into a strange land: unaccompanied refugee youth in America **362.84**

Ashanti (African people)

Folklore

Aardema, V. Oh, Kojo! How could you! (k-3) **398.2**
Courlander, H. The cow-tail switch, and other West African stories (4-6) **398.2**
McDermott, G. Anansi the spider (k-3) **398.2**

Ashanti to Zulu: African traditions. Musgrove, M. **960**

Ashby, Ruth
Sea otters (4-6) **599.74**
Tigers (4-6) **599.74**

Ashe, Rosalind
Children's literary houses (3-5) **028.5**
Asher, Sandy, 1942-
Princess Bee and the royal good-night story **E**
Where do you get your ideas? (5 and up) **808**
Wild words! (5 and up) **808**
Ashes. Babbitt, N.
In Babbitt, N. The Devil's storybook p63-71 **S C**
Ashley, L. F.
(ed) Only connect: readings on children's literature. See Only connect: readings on children's literature **028.5**
Ashpet
Ashpet
In Grandfather tales p115-23 **398.2**
Ashtenputtel. Grimm, J.
In Best-loved folktales of the world p68-75 **398.2**
Asia
Description and travel
Ceserani, G. P. Marco Polo (3-6) **92**
Asimov, Isaac, 1920-
Comets and meteors (3-5) **523.6**
How did we find out about blood? (5 and up) **612.1**
How did we find out about DNA? (5 and up) **574.87**
How did we find out about microwaves? (5 and up) **621.381**
How did we find out about Neptune? (5 and up) **523.4**
How did we find out about nuclear power? (5 and up) **539.7**
How did we find out about photosynthesis? (5 and up) **581.1**
How did we find out about sunshine? (5 and up) **523.7**
How did we find out about superconductivity? (5 and up) **537.6**
How did we find out the Earth is round? (5 and up) **525**
Mythology and the universe (3-5) **523.1**
Pluto: a double planet? (3-5) **523.4**
Words from the myths (6 and up) **292**
Ask another question. Chaikin, M. **296.4**
Ask anybody. Greene, C. C. **Fic**
Ask Mr. Bear. Flack, M. **E**
Asking about sex and growing up. Cole, J. **613.9**
Asleep-by-the-Stream. Curtis, E. S.
In Curtis, E. S. The girl who married a ghost, and other tales from the North American Indian p35-41 **398.2**
The **ass,** the table, and the stick. Jacobs, J.
In Jacobs, J. English fairy tales p206-10 **398.2**
Assateague Island National Seashore (Md. and Va.)
Fiction
Henry, M. Misty of Chincoteague (4 and up) **Fic**
Association for Educational Communications and Technology
American Association of School Librarians. Information power **027.8**
Association for Library Service to Children (U.S.)
The Arbuthnot lectures, 1970-1979/1980-1989. See The Arbuthnot lectures, 1970-1979/1980-1989 **028.5**
Association for Library Service to Children (U.S.). International Relations Committee
Children's books of international interest **011.6**
Association for Library Service to Children (U.S.). Notable Children's Books, 1976-1980, Reevaluation Committee
Notable children's books, 1976-1980 **011.6**
Association for Library Service to Children (U.S.). Notable Films, Filmstrips, and Recordings, 1973-1986 Retrospective Task Force
Notable children's films and videos, filmstrips, and recordings, 1973-1986. See Notable children's films and videos, filmstrips, and recordings, 1973-1986 **016.3713**
Associations
See also Clubs
Aster Aardvark's alphabet adventures. Kellogg, S. **E**
Asteroids
Lauber, P. Voyagers from space (4 and up) **523.5**
Astrid Lindgren: storyteller to the world. Hurwitz, J. **92**
Astrology
Schwartz, A. Telling fortunes (4-6) **133.3**
See/See also pages in the following book(s):
Jobb, J. The night sky book p55-59 (4 and up) **523**
The **astronaut** training book for kids. Long, K. **629.45**
Astronautics
See also Space flight
Barton, B. I want to be an astronaut (k-1) **629.45**
History
Smith, H. E. Daring the unknown: a history of NASA (5 and up) **629.4**

Astronautics—*Continued*
Vocational guidance
Long, K. The astronaut training book for kids (5 and up) **629.45**
Astronomers
Ferris, J. What are you figuring now? a story about Benjamin Banneker (3-5) **92**
Heckart, B. H. Edmond Halley, the man and his comet (4 and up) **92**
Astronomy
See also Black holes (Astronomy); Satellites
Asimov, I. Mythology and the universe (3-5) **523.1**
Atkinson, S. Journey into space (4-6) **523**
Berger, M. Star gazing, comet tracking, and sky mapping (5 and up) **523**
Branley, F. M. Mysteries of planet earth (6 and up) **525**
Branley, F. M. Sun dogs and shooting stars (5 and up) **523**
Cole, J. The magic school bus, lost in the solar system (2-4) **523**
Dickinson, T. Exploring the night sky (5 and up) **523**
Hirst, R. My place in space (2-4) **520**
Jobb, J. The night sky book (4 and up) **523**
Lampton, C. The space telescope (5 and up) **522**
Lampton, C. Stars & planets (3-6) **523**
Simon, S. Look to the night sky: an introduction to star watching (4 and up) **523**
Weiss, M. E. Sky watchers of ages past (5 and up) **523**
Wyler, R. The starry sky (k-4) **520**
Periodicals
Odyssey: space exploration and astronomy for young people **520.5**
Astrop, John
(il) Coren, A. Arthur the Kid **Fic**
Astrophysics
See also Black holes (Astronomy)
At Grammy's house. Rice, E. **E**
At the back of the North Wind. MacDonald, G. **Fic**
At the beach. Rockwell, A. F. **E**
At the behest of the pike
Afanas'ev, A. N. Emelya the simpleton
In Afanas'ev, A. N. Russian fairy tales p46-48 **398.2**
At the home. Konigsburg, E. L.
In Konigsburg, E. L. Throwing shadows **S C**
At the sign of the beckoning finger. Gorog, J.
In Gorog, J. Three dreams and a nightmare, and other tales of the dark **S C**
At the sound of the beep. Sachs, M. **Fic**
Ata, Te
Moroney, L. Baby rattlesnake **398.2**
Atalanta [short story]. Miles, B.
In Free to be—you and me p128-35 **810.8**
Atatürk, Kemal, 1881-1938
See/See also pages in the following book(s):
Spencer, W. The land and people of Turkey p105-26, 135-39 (5 and up) **956.1**
Atene, Ann
(il) Cooper, L. P. More fun with Spanish **468**
Athena (Greek deity)
Gates, D. The warrior goddess: Athena (4 and up) **292**
Athletes
See also Black athletes; Women athletes
Dictionaries
Berger, M. Sports (5 and up) **796.03**
Athletics
See also Sports; Track athletics
Atkinson, Allen, d. 1987
(il) Bianco, M. W. The velveteen rabbit **Fic**
Atkinson, Stuart
Journey into space (4-6) **523**
Atlases
Goode's world atlas **912**
Hammond ambassador world atlas **912**
Hammond citation world atlas **912**
National Geographic atlas of the world **912**
National Geographic picture atlas of our world **912**
Rand McNally children's atlas of the United States (4-6) **912**
Rand McNally children's world atlas (4-6) **912**
Rand McNally cosmopolitan world atlas **912**
See/See also pages in the following book(s):
Mango, K. N. Mapmaking p40-49 (4 and up) **526**
Atmosphere
See also Air
Atocha (Ship) *See* Nuestra Señora de Atocha (Ship)

Atomic bomb
Physiological effect
Coerr, E. Sadako and the thousand paper cranes [biography of Sadako Sasaki] (3-6) **92**
Atomic energy *See* Nuclear energy
Atomic submarines *See* Nuclear submarines
Atoms
Berger, M. Atoms, molecules, and quarks (6 and up) **539**
Berger, M. Our atomic world (4 and up) **539.7**
Bronowski, J. Biography of an atom (4 and up) **539**
Atoms, molecules, and quarks. Berger, M. **539**
Atonement, Day of *See* Yom Kippur
Atwater, Florence Carroll
(jt. auth) Atwater, R. T. Mr. Popper's penguins **Fic**
Atwater, Richard Tupper, 1892-1948
Mr. Popper's penguins (3-5) **Fic**
Auch, Mary Jane
Kidnapping Kevin Kowalski (4-6) **Fic**
Auclair, Joan
(il) Schlein, M. Big talk **E**
Audette, Anna Held
(il) Click, rumble, roar. See Click, rumble, roar **811.008**
Audio video market place **371.3025**
Audiovisual materials
See/See also pages in the following book(s):
England, C. ChildView: evaluating and reviewing materials for children p182-93 **028.5**
Bibliography
The Best science books & A-V materials for children **016.5**
Notable children's films and videos, filmstrips, and recordings, 1973-1986 **016.3713**
Cataloging
See Cataloging—Audiovisual materials
Catalogs
The Elementary school library collection **011.6**
Directories
Audio video market place **371.3025**
Children's media market place **070.5025**
Reviews
Parents' Choice: a review of children's media **028.1**
Science Books & Films **016.5**
Audubon, John James, 1785-1851
Fiction
Brenner, B. On the frontier with Mr. Audubon (4 and up) **Fic**
Audubon Society *See* National Audubon Society
The **Audubon** Society field guide to North American fishes, whales, and dolphins (5 and up) **597**
Auks, rocks and the odd dinosaur. Thomson, P. **508**
Aulnoy, Madame d', 1650 or 51-1705
The Blue Bird
In The Green fairy book p1-26 **398.2**
Felicia and the pot of pinks
In The Blue fairy book p148-56 **398.2**
The golden branch
In The Red fairy book p220-37 **398.2**
Graciosa and Percinet
In The Red fairy book p158-74 **398.2**
The little good mouse
In The Red fairy book p146-57 **398.2**
Princess Mayblossom
In The Red fairy book p13-29 **398.2**
Princess Rosette
In The Red fairy book p89-103 **398.2**
The story of Pretty Goldilocks
In The Blue fairy book p193-205 **398.2**
The white cat
In Best-loved folktales of the world p32-45 **398.2**
In The Blue fairy book p157-73 **398.2**
The wonderful sheep
In The Blue fairy book p214-30 **398.2**
The yellow dwarf
In The Blue fairy book p30-50 **398.2**
In The Classic fairy tales p68-80 **398.2**
San Souci, R. The white cat **398.2**
Aunt Lulu. Pinkwater, D. M. **E**
Aunt Nina and her nephews and nieces. Brandenberg, F. **E**
Aunt Nina, goodnight. Brandenberg, F. See note under Brandenberg, F. Aunt Nina and her nephews, and nieces **E**
Aunt Nina's visit. Brandenberg, F. See note under Brandenberg, F. Aunt Nina and her nephews, and nieces **E**
Aunt Susan. Aiken, J.
In Aiken, J. Give yourself a fright: thirteen tales of the supernatural p147-56 **S C**
Aunts
Fiction
Brandenberg, F. Aunt Nina and her nephews and nieces **E**
Byers, R. M. Mycca's baby **E**
Caines, J. F. Just us women **E**
Denslow, S. P. Night owls **E**
Fox, P. The village by the sea (5 and up) **Fic**
Hest, A. Fancy Aunt Jess **E**

Aunts—Fiction—*Continued*
MacLachlan, P. Seven kisses in a row (2-4) **Fic**
Pinkwater, D. M. Aunt Lulu **E**
Rodowsky, C. F. The gathering room (5 and up) **Fic**
Aurora means dawn. Sanders, S. R. **E**
Auroras
See/See also pages in the following book(s):
Gallant, R. A. Rainbows, mirages and sundogs p39-45 (4 and up) **551.5**
Australia
See also Great Barrier Reef (Australia)
Australia—in pictures (5 and up) **994**
Animals
See Animals—Australia
Fiction
Baker, J. Where the forest meets the sea **E**
Gleeson, L. Eleanor, Elizabeth (5 and up) **Fic**
Klein, R. Enemies (3-5) **Fic**
Park, R. Playing Beatie Bow (5 and up) **Fic**
Thiele, C. Farmer Schulz's ducks **E**
Thiele, C. Shadow shark (5 and up) **Fic**
Wrightson, P. Balyet (5 and up) **Fic**
Wrightson, P. A little fear (5 and up) **Fic**
Wrightson, P. The Nargun and the stars (5 and up) **Fic**
Australia—in pictures (5 and up) **994**
Australian aborigines
Fiction
Wrightson, P. Balyet (5 and up) **Fic**
Folklore
Nunes, S. Tiddalick the frog (k-2) **398.2**
Austria
Fiction
Härtling, P. Crutches (5 and up) **Fic**
Orgel, D. The devil in Vienna (6 and up) **Fic**
Ausubel, Nathan, 1899-1986
It could always be worse
In Best-loved folktales of the world p459-60 **398.2**
When Hershel eats
In Best-loved folktales of the world p462-64 **398.2**
Author! Author! Terris, S. **Fic**
Authors
See also Child authors; Women authors
Newbery and Caldecott Medal books, 1966-1975 **028.5**
Newbery and Caldecott Medal books, 1976-1985 **028.5**
Newbery Medal books, 1922-1955 **028.5**
Dictionaries
Authors of books for young people **920.003**
Fifth book of junior authors & illustrators **920.003**
Fourth book of junior authors and illustrators **920.003**
The Junior book of authors **920.003**
More junior authors **920.003**
Sixth book of junior authors & illustrators **920.003**
Something about the author **920.003**
Something about the author: autobiography series **920.003**
Third book of junior authors **920.003**
Twentieth-century children's writers **920.003**
Dictionaries—Indexes
Children's authors and illustrators: an index to biographical dictionaries **920.003**
Fiction
Greenwald, S. Mariah Delany's Author-of-the-Month Club (4-6) **Fic**
Sachs, M. A summer's lease (5 and up) **Fic**
Terris, S. Author! Author! (6 and up) **Fic**
Authors, American
Bulla, C. R. A grain of wheat: a writer begins (3-5) **92**
Burleigh, R. A man named Thoreau (3-5) **92**
Kresh, P. Isaac Bashevis Singer: the story of a storyteller (6 and up) **92**
Mitchell, B. Between two worlds: a story about Pearl Buck (3-5) **92**
Once upon a time—: celebrating the magic of children's books in honor of the twentieth anniversary of Reading is Fundamental **028.5**
Peet, B. Bill Peet: an autobiography (4 and up) **92**
Stern, P. V. D. Henry David Thoreau: writer and rebel (5 and up) **92**
Stevenson, J. Higher on the door (k-2) **92**
Stevenson, J. July (k-2) **92**
Stevenson, J. When I was nine (k-2) **92**
Wilder, L. I. West from home (6 and up) **92**
Authors, Black *See* Black authors
Authors, Canadian
Little, J. Little by Little (5 and up) **92**
Authors, English
Collins, D. R. The country artist: a story about Beatrix Potter (3-5) **92**
Foreman, M. War boy: a country childhood (5 and up) **92**
Kamen, G. Kipling, storyteller of East and West (3-5) **92**

Authors, English—*Continued*
Nesbit, E. Long ago when I was young (5 and up) **92**
Taylor, J. Beatrix Potter: artist, storyteller and countrywoman **92**
Authors, French
Quackenbush, R. M. Who said there's no man on the moon? a story of Jules Verne (2-4) **92**
Authors, Swedish
Hurwitz, J. Astrid Lindgren: storyteller to the world (4 and up) **92**
Authors of books for young people **920.003**
Authorship
See also Journalism
Asher, S. Where do you get your ideas? (5 and up) **808**
Asher, S. Wild words! (5 and up) **808**
Benjamin, C. L. Writing for kids (4 and up) **808**
Cassedy, S. In your own words (6 and up) **808**
Hunter, M. Talent is not enough **808.06**
Fiction
Hahn, M. D. Daphne's book (5 and up) **Fic**
Hunter, M. A sound of chariots (5 and up) **Fic**
Snyder, Z. K. Libby on Wednesdays (5 and up) **Fic**
Automata *See* Robots
Automobile drivers
Fiction
Bate, L. How Georgina drove the car very carefully from Boston to New York **E**
Burningham, J. Mr. Gumpy's motor car **E**
Automobile industry
Mitchell, B. We'll race you, Henry: a story about Henry Ford (3-5) **92**
Automobile racing
Graham, I. Racing cars (4 and up) **629.228**
Automobiles
Cole, J. Cars and how they go (2-4) **629.222**
Graham, I. Racing cars (4 and up) **629.228**
Rockwell, A. F. Cars (k-1) **629.222**
Sutton, R. Car (4 and up) **629.222**
Fiction
Fleming, I. Chitty-Chitty-Bang-Bang (4-6) **Fic**
Oxenbury, H. The car trip **E**
Robbins, K. City/country **E**
Spier, P. Tin Lizzie **E**
Spurr, E. Mrs. Minetta's car pool **E**
Models
Weiss, H. Model cars and trucks and how to build them (4 and up) **629.22**
Service stations
Gibbons, G. Fill it up! (k-3) **629.28**
Autumn Street. Lowry, L. **Fic**
Avi, 1937-
The fighting ground (5 and up) **Fic**
S.O.R. losers (5 and up) **Fic**
The true confessions of Charlotte Doyle (6 and up) **Fic**
Aviation *See* Aeronautics
Aviators *See* Air pilots
Avishai, Susan
(il) Herman, C. The house on Walenska Street **Fic**
The **awakening** water. Crosher, G. R. **Fic**
Awards, Literary *See* Literary prizes
Away is a strange place to be. Hoover, H. M. **Fic**
Awful aardvark. Mwalimu. **398.2**
Awkward aardvark. See Mwalimu. Awful aardvark **398.2**
Axle the freeway cat. Hurd, T. **E**
Aylesworth, Jim, 1943-
The completed hickory dickory dock (k-2) **398.8**
Hanna's hog **E**
One crow **E**
Aylesworth, Thomas G.
Moving continents (6 and up) **551.1**
Azarian, Mary
A farmer's alphabet **E**
(il) Hall, D. The man who lived alone **Fic**
The **Aztec** sun goddess. Riordan, J.
In Riordan, J. The woman in the moon, and other tales of forgotten heroines p80-83 **398.2**
Aztecs
See also Toltecs
Beck, B. L. The Aztecs (4 and up) **972**
Fisher, L. E. Pyramid of the sun, pyramid of the moon (4 and up) **972**
Legends
Bierhorst, J. Doctor Coyote (1-4) **398.2**
The **Aztecs**. Beck, B. L. **972**

B

"B" is for Betsy. Haywood, C. **Fic**
Bà-Năm. Lee, J. M. **E**
Baba Yaga
Afanas'ev, A. N. Baba Yaga
In Afanas'ev, A. N. Russian fairy tales p194-95 **398.2**

Baba Yaga—*Continued*
Afanas'ev, A. N. Baba Yaga [another story]
In Afanas'ev, A. N. Russian fairy tales p363-65 **398.2**
The Baba Yaga
In Best-loved folktales of the world p411-14 **398.2**
Cole, J. Bony-Legs **398.2**
Leach, M. Baba Yaga
In Leach, M. Whistle in the graveyard p86 **398.2**
Lent, B. Baba Yaga **398.2**
Williams-Ellis, A. Baba Yaga
In Williams-Ellis, A. Tales from the enchanted world p113-24 **398.2**

Baba Yaga and the brave youth
Afanas'ev, A. N. Baba Yaga and the brave youth
In Afanas'ev, A. N. Russian fairy tales p76-79 **398.2**

Babar and Father Christmas. Brunhoff, J. de. See note under Brunhoff, J. de. The story of Babar, the little elephant **E**

Babar and his children. Brunhoff, J. de. See note under Brunhoff, J. de. The story of Babar, the little elephant **E**

Babar and the ghost. Brunhoff, L. de. See note under Brunhoff, J. de. The story of Babar, the little elephant **E**

Babar and Zephir. Brunhoff, J. de. See note under Brunhoff, J. de. The story of Babar, the little elephant **E**

Babar learns to cook. Brunhoff, L. de. See note under Brunhoff, J. de. The story of Babar, the little elephant **E**

Babar loses his crown. Brunhoff, L. de. See note under Brunhoff, J. de. The story of Babar, the little elephant **E**

Babar saves the day. Brunhoff, L. de. See note under Brunhoff, J. de. The story of Babar, the little elephant **E**

Babar the king. Brunhoff, J. de. See note under Brunhoff, J. de. The story of Babar, the little elephant **E**

Babar visits another planet. Brunhoff, L. de. See note under Brunhoff, J. de. The story of Babar, the little elephant **E**

Babar's ABC. Brunhoff, L. de. See note under Brunhoff, J. de. The story of Babar, the little elephant **E**

Babar's anniversary album. Brunhoff, L. de. See note under Brunhoff, J. de. The story of Babar, the little elephant **E**

Babar's birthday surprise. Brunhoff, L. de. See note under Brunhoff, J. de. The story of Babar, the little elephant **E**

Babar's book of color. Brunhoff, L. de. See note under Brunhoff, J. de. The story of Babar, the little elephant **E**

Babar's bookmobile. Brunhoff, L. de. See note under Brunhoff, J. de. The story of Babar, the little elephant **E**

Babar's busy year. Brunhoff, L. de. See note under Brunhoff, J. de. The story of Babar, the little elephant **E**

Babar's counting book. Brunhoff, L. de. See note under Brunhoff, J. de. The story of Babar, the little elephant **E**

Babar's French lessons. Brunhoff, L. de. See note under Brunhoff, J. de. The story of Babar, the little elephant **E**

Babar's little circus star. Brunhoff, L. de. See note under Brunhoff, J. de. The story of Babar, the little elephant **E**

Babar's little girl. Brunhoff, L. de. See note under Brunhoff, J. de. The story of Babar, the little elephant **E**

Babar's mystery. Brunhoff, L. de. See note under Brunhoff, J. de. The story of Babar, the little elephant **E**

Babar's trunk. Brunhoff, L. de. See note under Brunhoff, J. de. The story of Babar, the little elephant **E**

Babbitt, Ellen
The monkey and the crocodile
In Best-loved folktales of the world p593-94 **398.2**

Babbitt, Natalie
The Devil's other storybook (4-6) **S C**
Contents: The fortunes of Madame Organza; Justice; The soldier; Boating; How Akbar went to Bethlehem; The signpost; Lessons; The fall and rise of Bathbone; Simple sentences; The ear
The Devil's storybook (4-6) **S C**
Contents: Wishes; The very pretty lady; The harps of Heaven; The imp in the basket; Nuts; A palindrome; Ashes; Perfection; The rose and the minor demon; The power of speech
The eyes of the Amaryllis (5 and up) **Fic**
Goody Hall (4-6) **Fic**
The harps of Heaven
In The Random House book of humor for children p134-43 **817.008**
Kneeknock Rise (4-6) **Fic**
Nellie: a cat on her own **E**
The search for delicious (5 and up) **Fic**
The something **E**
Tuck everlasting (5 and up) **Fic**
(il) Worth, V. More small poems **811**
(il) Worth, V. Small poems **811**
(il) Worth, V. Small poems again **811**
(il) Worth, V. Still more small poems **811**

Babe. King-Smith, D. Fic
Babe Didrikson: athlete of the century. Knudson, R. R. 92
Babies *See* Infants
Babies. Isadora, R. E
Baboon-skins
Berger, T. Baboon-skins
In Berger, T. Black fairy tales p124-34 398.2

Babouschka
Baboushka
In The Family read-aloud Christmas treasury p32-33 808.8
Mikolaycak, C. Babushka 398.2
Robbins, R. Baboushka and the three kings 398.2
Baboushka *See* Babouschka
Baboushka and the three kings. Robbins, R. 398.2

Babushka *See* Babouschka
Babushka. Mikolaycak, C. 398.2
Babushka's doll. Polacco, P. E
Baby animals. Brown, M. W. E
Baby bears and how they grow. Buxton, J. H. 599.74
Baby Beluga. Raffi. 782.42
Baby birds and how they grow. McCauley, J. R. 598
Baby dinosaurs. Sattler, H. R. 567.9
Baby Dot: a dinosaur story. Cuyler, M. E
A **baby** for Max. Lasky, K. E
Baby rattlesnake. Moroney, L. 398.2
Baby says. Steptoe, J. E
A **baby** sister for Frances. Hoban, R. See note under Hoban, R. Bedtime for Frances E
The **baby-sitter**. Porte-Thomas, B. A.
In Porte-Thomas, B. A. Jesse's ghost, and other stories p15-21 S C
The **baby-sitter**. Yolen, J.
In Things that go bump in the night p15-24 S C
Baby sitters
Fiction
Fox, P. A likely place (3-5) Fic
Keller, H. What Alvin wanted E
Lowry, L. Taking care of Terrific (5 and up) Fic
The **baby** Uggs are hatching. Prelutsky, J. 811

The **Baby's** bedtime book (k-1) 808.81
The **baby's** catalogue. Ahlberg, J. E
The **Baby's** good morning book (k-1) 808.81
The **Baby's** lap book (k-1) 398.8
The **Baby's** story book (k-1) 398.2
Bacchus *See* Dionysus (Greek deity)
Bach, Alice
Moses' ark: stories from the Bible (4-6) 222

Bachaus, Ken
(il) Thayer, E. L. Casey at the bat 811
Bachelis, Faren Maree
El Salvador (4 and up) 972.84
Back in the beforetime. Curry, J. L. 398.2

Back to school with Betsy. Haywood, C. See note under Haywood, C. "B" is for Betsy Fic
Back yard Angel. Delton, J. See note under Delton, J. Angel's mother's wedding Fic
Backbone of the king. Brown, M. 398.2
Backyard hunter: the praying mantis. Lavies, B. 595.7
Backyard insects. Selsam, M. E. 595.7
Bacon, Joan Chase *See* Bowden, Joan Chase, 1925-
Bacon, Josephine, 1942-
Cooking the Israeli way (5 and up) 641.5

Bacon, Paul, 1923-
(il) Golenbock, P. Teammates [biography of Jackie Robinson] 92
(il) Sandburg, C. The Sandburg treasury 818

Bacteriology
Berger, M. Germs make me sick! (k-3) 616.9

The **bad** child's book of beasts. Belloc, H.
In Belloc, H. The bad child's book of beasts, and More beasts for worse children, and A moral alphabet 821

The **bad** child's book of beasts, and More beasts for worse children, and A moral alphabet. Belloc, H. 821
The **Bad** compadre
In The Monkey's haircut, and other stories told by the Maya p94-106 398.2

A **bad** road for cats. Rylant, C.
In Rylant, C. Every living thing p56-65 S C

The **bad** times of Irma Baumlein. Brink, C. R. Fic

The **bad** wife. Afanas'ev, A. N.
In Afanas'ev, A. N. Russian fairy tales p56-57 398.2

The **badger** and the magic fan. Johnston, T. 398.2
Badgers
Lavine, S. A. Wonders of badgers (4 and up) 599.74
Fiction
Eckert, A. W. Incident at Hawk's Hill (6 and up) Fic
Hoban, R. Bedtime for Frances E
Varley, S. Badger's parting gifts E
Badger's parting gifts. Varley, S. E
Bagged wolf. Kendall, C.
In Kendall, C. Sweet and sour p49-59 398.2
Baggett, Nancy, 1943-
(jt. auth) Settel, J. Why does my nose run? 612
Bagnold, Enid
National Velvet (5 and up) Fic
Bags are big! Renfro, N. 745.54
Bagthorpes abroad. Cresswell, H. See note under Cresswell, H. Ordinary Jack Fic
Bagthorpes haunted. Cresswell, H. See note under Cresswell, H. Ordinary Jack Fic
Bagthorpes liberated. Cresswell, H. See note under Cresswell, H. Ordinary Jack Fic
Bagthorpes unlimited. Cresswell, H. See note under Cresswell, H. Ordinary Jack Fic
Bagthorpes v. the world. Cresswell, H. See note under Cresswell, H. Ordinary Jack Fic
Bahamas
Poetry
Greenfield, E. Under the Sunday tree (2-4) 811
Bahrain
Social life and customs
Jacobsen, P. O. A family in the Persian Gulf (2-4) 953
Bahti, Tom, 1926-1972
(il) Baylor, B. Before you came this way 709.01
(il) Baylor, B. When clay sings 970.004
Bailey, Bernadine, 1901-
Zimbabwe—in pictures. See Zimbabwe—in pictures 968.91
Bailey, Carolyn Sherwin, 1875-1961
Miss Hickory (3-5) Fic
See/See also pages in the following book(s):
Newbery Medal books, 1922-1955 p290-99 028.5
Bailey, Joseph H.
(il) Giants from the past: the age of mammals. See Giants from the past: the age of mammals 569
(il) McCauley, J. R. Let's explore a river 574.92
Baines, John D. (John David), 1943-
Acid rain (5 and up) 363.7
Baja California (Mexico: Peninsula)
Fiction
O'Dell, S. The black pearl (6 and up) Fic
Treviño, E. B. de. El Güero (5 and up) Fic
Baker, Alan, 1951-
(il) Kipling, R. The butterfly that stamped Fic
(il) Lister, R. The legend of King Arthur 398.2
(il) Pearce, P. The battle of Bubble and Squeak Fic
Baker, Augusta, 1911-
Storytelling: art and technique 372.6
Baker, Barbara, 1947-
Digby and Kate again E
Baker, Betty, 1928-1987
The Pig War (k-2) 973.6
Walk the world's rim (5 and up) Fic
Baker, Charles
The Christmas doubters
In The Big book of Christmas plays p265-74 808.82
Baker, Jeannie
Home in the sky E
Where the forest meets the sea E
Baker, Josephine, 1906-1975
Fiction
Schroeder, A. Ragtime Tumpie E
Baker, Keith, 1953-
The magic fan E
Baker, Leslie A.
Morning beach E
Baker, Olaf
Where the buffaloes begin (2-4) Fic
Baker, Pamela J., 1947-
My first book of sign (k-3) 419
The **Baker** Street Irregulars in the case of the blackmail boys. Dicks, T. See note under Dicks, T. The Baker Street Irregulars in the case of the missing masterpiece Fic
The **Baker** Street Irregulars in the case of the cinema swindle. Dicks, T. See note under Dicks, T. The Baker Street Irregulars in the case of the missing masterpiece Fic
The **Baker** Street Irregulars in the case of the cop catchers. Dicks, T. See note under Dicks, T. The Baker Street Irregulars in the case of the missing masterpiece Fic

The **Baker** Street Irregulars in the case of the crooked kids. Dicks, T. See note under Dicks, T. The Baker Street Irregulars in the case of the missing masterpiece **Fic**
The **Baker** Street Irregulars in the case of the ghost grabbers. Dicks, T. See note under Dicks, T. The Baker Street Irregulars in the case of the missing masterpiece **Fic**
The **Baker** Street Irregulars in the case of the missing masterpiece. Dicks, T. **Fic**
The **baker's** daughter. Crossley-Holland, K.
In Crossley-Holland, K. British folk tales p331-33 **398.2**
A **Baker's** dozen
In Diane Goode's American Christmas p43-45 **810.8**
The **baker's** dozen. Forest, H. **398.2**
Baking
See also Bread; Cake
Zubrowski, B. Messing around with baking chemistry (5 and up) **540.7**
Fiction
Hoban, L. Arthur's Christmas cookies **E**
The **balancing** girl. Rabe, B. **E**
Bald eagle
Patent, D. H. Where the bald eagles gather (4 and up) **598**
Ryden, H. America's bald eagle (4 and up) **598**
Baldak Borisievich
Afanas'ev, A. N. Baldak Borisievich
In Afanas'ev, A. N. Russian fairy tales p90-96 **398.2**
Balder (Norse deity)
Barth, E. Balder and the mistletoe (3-5) **293**
Balder and the mistletoe. Barth, E. **293**
Balestrino, Philip
The skeleton inside you (k-3) **611**
Balian, Lorna
Humbug witch **E**
The **ball** bounced. Tafuri, N. **E**
The **ballad** of Belle Dorcas. Hooks, W. H. **Fic**
The **ballad** of Biddy Early. Willard, N. **811**
Ballard, Robert D.
Exploring the Titanic (4 and up) **910.4**
The lost wreck of the Isis (4 and up) **910.4**
Ballerinas and bears. Rylant, C.
In Rylant, C. Children of Christmas p20-25 **S C**
Ballet
Elliott, D. Frogs and the ballet (4 and up) **792.8**
Isadora, R. My ballet class (1-3) **792.8**
Krementz, J. A very young dancer (3-6) **792.8**
Kuklin, S. Going to my ballet class (4-6) **792.8**
Fiction
Gauch, P. L. Dance, Tanya **E**
Holabird, K. Angelina ballerina **E**
Isadora, R. Max **E**
Ballet dancers
Tobias, T. Arthur Mitchell (2-5) **92**
Ballets
Stories, plots, etc.
Fonteyn, Dame M. Swan lake (3-5) **Fic**
Klein, N. Baryshnikov's Nutcracker (3 and up) **792.8**
Balloon trip. Scarry, H. **629.13**
Balloons
Scarry, H. Balloon trip (3-6) **629.13**
Zubrowski, B. Balloons (3-6) **507**
Fiction
Calhoun, M. Hot-air Henry **E**
Coerr, E. The big balloon race **E**
Du Bois, W. P. The twenty-one balloons (5 and up) **Fic**
Inkpen, M. The blue balloon **E**
Lamorisse, A. The red balloon (1-4) **Fic**
Balloons, Dirigible *See* Airships
Balyet. Wrightson, P. **Fic**
La **Bamba**. Soto, G.
In Soto, G. Baseball in April, and other stories p81-89 **S C**
Bambi. Salten, F. **Fic**
Bamboo-cutter and the moon-child
Quayle, E. The shining princess
In Quayle, E. The shining princess, and other Japanese legends p13-23 **398.2**
Banana
Ancona, G. Bananas (3-5) **641.3**
Bandalee. Sherlock, Sir P. M.
In Sherlock, Sir P. M. Anansi, the spider man p47-57 **398.2**
Bandit Ben rides again. Gotwalt, H. L. M.
In Gotwalt, H. L. M. Everyday plays for boys and girls p17-28 **812**
Bands (Music)
Fiction
Hurd, T. Mama don't allow **E**
Maxner, J. Nicholas Cricket **E**
Bang, Molly
Delphine **E**
The Grey Lady and the Strawberry Snatcher **E**
The paper crane **E**
Ten, nine, eight **E**
Wiley and the Hairy Man (1-4) **398.2**

Bangs, Edward, 1756-1818
Steven Kellogg's Yankee Doodle (k-3) **782.42**

Bank Street College of Education
Merrill, J. The toothpaste millionaire **Fic**

Banks, Kate, 1960-
Alphabet soup **E**

Banks, Lynne Reid *See* Reid Banks, Lynne, 1929-

Banks, Merry
Animals of the night **E**

Banks and banking
Adler, D. A. Banks: where the money is (2-4) **332.1**

Banks: where the money is. Adler, D. A. **332.1**

Bannan, Jan Gumprecht
Sand dunes (3-6) **551.3**

Banneker, Benjamin, 1731-1806
About
Ferris, J. What are you figuring now? a story about Benjamin Banneker (3-5) **92**

The **banza**. Wolkstein, D. **398.2**

Baobab
Bash, B. Tree of life: the world of the African baobab (3-5) **583**

Baptists
See also Mennonites

Bar mitzvah
Greenfeld, H. Bar mitzvah (5 and up) **296.4**
Metter, B. Bar mitzvah, bat mitzvah (4 and up) **296.4**

Bar mitzvah, bat mitzvah. Metter, B. **296.4**

The **barbecue**. Lester, J.
In Lester, J. More tales of Uncle Remus p79-81 **398.2**

Barber, Antonia, 1932-
The Mousehole cat **E**

Barberis, Juan Carlos
(il) Cole, J. The human body: how we evolved **573.2**

Barber's fifth brother
The Story of the barber's fifth brother
In The Arabian nights entertainments p196-208 **398.2**

Barbie. Soto, G.
In Soto, G. Baseball in April, and other stories p33-42 **S C**

Bare, Colleen Stanley
Elephants on the beach (1-3) **599.74**
Guinea pigs don't read books (k-2) **636.088**
Never kiss an alligator! (k-2) **597.9**
Sea lions (3-5) **599.74**

A **bargain** for Frances. Hoban, R. See note under Hoban, R. Bedtime for Frances **E**

Baring, Maurice, 1874-1945
The blue rose
In Shedlock, M. L. The art of the story-teller p204-12 **372.6**

Baring-Gould, Ceil
(ed) The Annotated Mother Goose. See The Annotated Mother Goose **398.8**

Baring-Gould, William Stuart, 1913-
(ed) The Annotated Mother Goose. See The Annotated Mother Goose **398.8**

Barker, William H.
Younde goes to town
In Best-loved folktales of the world p623-25 **398.2**

Barkin, Carol, 1944-
Happy Thanksgiving! (4-6) **394.2**
Happy Valentine's Day! (4-6) **394.2**
Jobs for kids (5 and up) **650.1**
The scary Halloween costume book (3-6) **391**
(jt. auth) James, E. How to be school smart **371.3**

Barkley, James
(il) Armstrong, W. H. Sounder **Fic**

Barlow, Genevieve
The search for the magic lake
In Best-loved folktales of the world p767-73 **398.2**

Barlow, Gillian, 1944-
(il) Wise, W. The black falcon **Fic**

Barlowe, Dorothea *See* Barlowe, Dot, 1926-

Barlowe, Dot, 1926-
(il) Zim, H. S. Seashores **574.92**
(il) Zim, H. S. Trees **582.16**

Barlowe, Sy
(il) Zim, H. S. Seashores **574.92**
(il) Zim, H. S. Trees **582.16**

Barmecide feast
The Story of the barber's sixth brother
In The Arabian nights entertainments p209-15 **398.2**

Barn dance! Martin, B. **E**

Barn gravity. Springer, N.
In Herds of thunder, manes of gold p83-93 **808.8**

Barnes, Harold
The proud cock
In Shedlock, M. L. The art of the story-teller p191-94 **372.6**

Barnett, Moneta, 1922-1976
(il) Greenfield, E. Me and Neesie **E**
(il) Greenfield, E. Sister **Fic**

Barnhart, Clarence Lewis, 1900-
Scott, Foresman intermediate dictionary. See Scott, Foresman intermediate dictionary **423**
Thorndike-Barnhart children's dictionary. See Thorndike-Barnhart children's dictionary **423**
(ed) The World Book dictionary. See The World Book dictionary **423**

Barnhart, Robert K.
(ed) The World Book dictionary. See The World Book dictionary **423**

Barns

Fiction

Lindbergh, R. Benjamin's barn **E**

Barnstormers & daredevils. Tessendorf, K. C. **629.13**

Baron, Nancy
Getting started in calligraphy (5 and up) **745.6**

Barr, Jene, 1900-1985
(jt. auth) Antonacci, R. J. Basketball for young champions **796.323**

Barracca, Debra
The adventures of Taxi Dog **E**

Barracca, Sal
(jt. auth) Barracca, D. The adventures of Taxi Dog **E**

Barrett, Angela
(il) Andersen, H. C. The Snow Queen **Fic**
(il) Andersen, H. C. The wild swans **Fic**
(il) Riordan, J. The woman in the moon, and other tales of forgotten heroines **398.2**

Barrett, Judi, 1941-
Benjamin's 365 birthdays **E**
Cloudy with a chance of meatballs
In Rainy day: stories and poems p3-11 **808.8**

Barrett, Peter
(il) Herriot, J. Moses the kitten **Fic**

Barrett, Ron, 1937-
(il) Barrett, J. Benjamin's 365 birthdays **E**
(il) Kennedy, X. J. Ghastlies, goops & pincushions: nonsense verse **811**

Barrie, J. M. (James Matthew), 1860-1937
Peter Pan (3-5) **Fic**

Barrie, James Matthew *See* Barrie, J. M. (James Matthew), 1860-1937

Bars and restaurants *See* Restaurants, bars, etc.

Barss, William
(il) Asimov, I. Words from the myths **292**

Barstow, Barbara
Beyond picture books **011.6**

Barter
Afanas'ev, A. N. Barter
In Afanas'ev, A. N. Russian fairy tales p338-40 **398.2**

Barth, Edna
Balder and the mistletoe (3-5) **293**
Hearts, cupids, and red roses (3-6) **394.2**
Holly, reindeer, and colored lights (3-6) **394.2**
Jack-o'-lantern (2-4) **398.2**
Lilies, rabbits, and painted eggs (3-6) **394.2**
Shamrocks, harps, and shillelaghs (3-6) **394.2**
Turkeys, Pilgrims, and Indian corn (3-6) **394.2**
Witches, pumpkins, and grinning ghosts (3-6) **394.2**
(comp) A Christmas feast: poems, sayings, greetings, and wishes. See A Christmas feast: poems, sayings, greetings, and wishes **808.81**

Bartholdi, Frédéric Auguste, 1834-1904

About

Maestro, B. The story of the Statue of Liberty (k-3) **974.7**
See/See also pages in the following book(s):
Burchard, S. The Statue of Liberty p14-33 (5 and up) **974.7**
Fisher, L. E. The Statue of Liberty p38-43 (4 and up) **974.7**
Shapiro, M. J. How they built the Statue of Liberty (4 and up) **974.7**

Bartholomew and the oobleck. Seuss, Dr. **E**

Bartlett, John, 1820-1905
Familiar quotations **808.88**

Bartlett, Robert Merrill, 1898-
Thanksgiving Day (1-3) **394.2**

Barton, Byron
Airplanes (k-1) **387.7**
Airport (k-1) **387.7**
Boats (k-1) **387.2**
Bones, bones, dinosaur bones **E**
Building a house (k-1) **690**
Dinosaurs, dinosaurs (k-2) **567.9**
I want to be an astronaut (k-1) **629.45**
Machines at work (k-1) **690**
Trains (k-1) **625.1**
Trucks (k-1) **629.224**
(il) Adler, D. A. Roman numerals **513**
(il) Froman, R. Angles are easy as pie **516**
(il) Ginsburg, M. Good morning, chick **E**

Barton, Byron—*Continued*
(il) Greene, C. C. A girl called Al **Fic**
(il) Kalan, R. Jump, frog, jump! **E**
(il) Pomerantz, C. Where's the bear? **E**
(il) Prelutsky, J. The snopp on the sidewalk, and other poems **811**
(il) Sharmat, M. W. Gila monsters meet you at the airport **E**
(il) Siebert, D. Truck song **E**
(il) Simon, S. The paper airplane book **745.592**

Barton, Clara, 1821-1912
See/See also pages in the following book(s):
Jacobs, W. J. Great lives: human rights p138-46 (5 and up) **920**

Barton, Harriett
(il) Branley, F. M. Rain & hail **551.57**
(il) In the witch's kitchen. See In the witch's kitchen **811.008**
(il) Showers, P. No measles, no mumps for me **614.4**

Baryshnikov, Mikhail, 1948-
Klein, N. Baryshnikov's Nutcracker **792.8**

Baryshnikov's Nutcracker. Klein, N. **792.8**

Bas mitzvah *See* Bat mitzvah

Base, Graeme, 1958-
The eleventh hour (4-6) **Fic**

Baseball
Appel, M. The first book of baseball (4-6) **796.357**
Grosshandler, H. Everyone wins at tee ball (k-3) **796.357**
Kalb, J. The easy baseball book (3-5) **796.357**
Kreutzer, P. Little League's official how-to-play baseball book (4 and up) **796.357**
Ritter, L. S. The story of baseball (5 and up) **796.357**
Sullivan, G. The art of base-stealing (5 and up) **796.357**
Sullivan, G. Baseball kids (4 and up) **796.357**
Sullivan, G. Better baseball for boys (4 and up) **796.357**
Sullivan, G. Pitcher (3-6) **796.357**
See/See also pages in the following book(s):
Bauer, C. F. Celebrations p25-42 **808.8**

Biography

Adler, D. A. Jackie Robinson: he was the first (3-5) **92**
Golenbock, P. Teammates [biography of Jackie Robinson] (1-4) **92**
Scott, R. Jackie Robinson (5 and up) **92**

Equipment and supplies

Arnow, J. Louisville Slugger (4 and up) **796.357**
Jaspersohn, W. Bat, ball, glove (3-5) **796.357**

Fiction

Christopher, M. The hit-away kid (2-4) **Fic**
Cohen, B. Thank you, Jackie Robinson (4-6) **Fic**
Day, A. Frank and Ernest play ball **E**
Hurwitz, J. Baseball fever **Fic**
Isadora, R. Max **E**
Kessler, L. P. Here comes the strikeout **E**
Konigsburg, E. L. About the B'nai Bagels (4-6) **Fic**
Myers, W. D. Me, Mop, and the Moondance Kid (4-6) **Fic**
Park, B. Skinnybones (4-6) **Fic**
Slote, A. Matt Gargan's boy (4-6) **Fic**
Smith, R. K. Bobby Baseball (4-6) **Fic**
Tunis, J. R. The kid from Tomkinsville (5 and up) **Fic**
Williams, K. L. Baseball and butterflies (2-4) **Fic**

Poetry

Thayer, E. L. Casey at the bat **811**

Baseball and butterflies. Williams, K. L. **Fic**

Baseball cards

Fiction

Slote, A. The trading games (4-6) **Fic**

Baseball fever. Hurwitz, J. **Fic**

Baseball in April. Soto, G.
In Soto, G. Baseball in April, and other stories p13-22 **S C**

Baseball in April, and other stories. Soto, G. **S C**

Baseball kids. Sullivan, G. **796.357**

Bash, Barbara
Desert giant (3-5) **583**
Tree of life: the world of the African baobab (3-5) **583**
Urban roosts: where birds nest in the city (1-4) **598**

BASIC (Computer program language)
Simon, S. How to talk to your computer (k-3) **005**

Basic collection of children's books in Spanish. Schon, I. **011.6**

Basil and the lost colony. Titus, E. See note under Titus, E. Basil of Baker Street **Fic**

Basil and the pygmy cats. Titus, E. See note under Titus, E. Basil of Baker Street **Fic**

Basil in Mexico. Titus, E. See note under Titus, E. Basil of Baker Street **Fic**

Basil in the Wild West. Titus, E. See note under Titus, E. Basil of Baker Street **Fic**

Basil of Baker Street. Titus, E. Fic
A **basket** full of white eggs. Swann, B. 398.6
Basketball
Anderson, D. The story of basketball (5 and up) 796.323
Antonacci, R. J. Basketball for young champions (5 and up) 796.323
Boyd, B. C. Hoops: behind the scenes with the Boston Celtics (5 and up) 796.323
Sullivan, G. Better basketball for boys (4 and up) 796.323
Sullivan, G. Better basketball for girls (4 and up) 796.323
Biography
Deegan, P. J. Michael Jordan: basketball's soaring star (4 and up) 92
Basketball for young champions. Antonacci, R. J. 796.323
Baskin, Barbara Holland, 1929-
Books for the gifted child 011.6
More notes from a different drummer 016.8
Notes from a different drummer 016.8
Baskin, Leonard, 1922-
(il) Segal, L. G. The book of Adam to Moses 222
Bassett, Jeni
(il) Kroll, S. The biggest pumpkin ever E
Bastianele
In Best-loved folktales of the world p154-56 398.2
Bat, ball, glove. Jaspersohn, W. 796.357
Bat mitzvah
Metter, B. Bar mitzvah, bat mitzvah (4 and up) 296.4
The **bat-poet**. Jarrell, R. Fic
Bate, Lucy
How Georgina drove the car very carefully from Boston to New York E
Baths
Fiction
Burningham, J. Time to get out of the bath, Shirley E
Cole, B. No more baths E
McPhail, D. M. Andrew's bath E
Wood, A. King Bidgood's in the bathtub E
Woodruff, E. Tubtime E
Yolen, J. No bath tonight E
Bathwater's hot. Hughes, S. E
Bats
Hopf, A. L. Bats (3-6) 599.4
Schlein, M. The billions of bats (3-5) 599.4
Shebar, S. S. Bats (5 and up) 599.4
Fiction
Jarrell, R. The bat-poet Fic
Bats, butterflies, and bugs. Sullivan, S. C. A. 745.592
Batten, John Dickson, 1860-1932
(il) Jacobs, J. English fairy tales 398.2
Battered children *See* Child abuse
Battered wives *See* Wife abuse
Battle in the Arctic seas. Taylor, T. 940.54
The **battle** of Bubble and Squeak. Pearce, P. Fic
The **Battle** of Gettysburg. Carter, A. R. 973.7
The **Battle** of Gettysburg. Johnson, N. 973.7
Bauer, Caroline Feller, 1935-
Celebrations 808.8
Handbook for storytellers 372.6
Marika the snowmaiden
In Snowy day: stories and poems p45-49 808.8
Presenting reader's theater 808.82
This way to books 028.5
(ed) Halloween: stories and poems. See Halloween: stories and poems 808.8
(ed) Rainy day: stories and poems. See Rainy day: stories and poems 808.8
(ed) Snowy day: stories and poems. See Snowy day: stories and poems 808.8
(ed) Windy day: stories and poems. See Windy day: stories and poems 808.8
Bauer, Marion Dane
On my honor (4 and up) Fic
Rain of fire (5 and up) Fic
Shelter from the wind (5 and up) Fic
Baum, L. Frank (Lyman Frank), 1856-1919
Dorothy and the Wizard in Oz. See note under Baum, L. F. The Wizard of Oz Fic
The land of Oz. See note under Baum, L. F. The Wizard of Oz Fic
Little Wizard stories of Oz. See note under Baum, L. F. The Wizard of Oz Fic
The magic of Oz. See note under Baum, L. F. The Wizard of Oz Fic
The marvelous land of Oz. See note under Baum, L. F. The Wizard of Oz Fic
Ozma of Oz. See note under Baum, L. F. The Wizard of Oz Fic
The patchwork girl of Oz. See note under Baum, L. F. The Wizard of Oz Fic
The tin woodsman of Oz. See note under Baum, L. F. The Wizard of Oz Fic
The Wizard of Oz (3-6) Fic

Baum, L. Frank (Lyman Frank), 1856-1919—*Continued*
See/See also pages in the following book(s):
Only connect: readings on children's literature p156-69 **028.5**
Baum, Lyman Frank *See* Baum, L. Frank (Lyman Frank), 1856-1919
Baumfree, Isabella *See* Truth, Sojourner, d. 1883
Baumli, Othmar, 1936-
(il) Schnieper, C. An apple tree through the year **634**
Bawden, Nina, 1925-
Carrie's war (4 and up) **Fic**
The finding (4 and up) **Fic**
Henry (5 and up) **Fic**
The outside child (5 and up) **Fic**
The peppermint pig (5 and up) **Fic**
The robbers (5 and up) **Fic**
Squib (5 and up) **Fic**
The witch's daughter (4 and up) **Fic**
See/See also pages in the following book(s):
Townsend, J. R. A sounding of storytellers p18-29 **028.5**
Bayer, Jane, d. 1985
A my name is Alice **E**
Bayless, Roger
(il) Kohl, J. The view from the oak **591.5**
Bayley, Nicola, 1949-
(il) Barber, A. The Mousehole cat **E**
(il) Nicola Bayley's book of nursery rhymes. See Nicola Bayley's book of nursery rhymes **398.8**
Baylor, Byrd
Before you came this way (1-4) **709.01**
The best town in the world **E**
The desert is theirs (1-4) **574.5**
Desert voices (1-4) **811**
Guess who my favorite person is **E**
Hawk, I'm your brother **E**
If you are a hunter of fossils (3-5) **560**
I'm in charge of celebrations (3-6) **Fic**
Moon song (1-3) **398.2**
The other way to listen **E**
The way to start a day (1-3) **291.4**
When clay sings (1-4) **970.004**
Baynes, Pauline, 1922-
(il) Godden, R. Four dolls **S C**
(il) Lewis, C. S. The lion, the witch and the wardrobe **Fic**
(il) Noah and the ark. See Noah and the ark **222**
(comp) Thanks be to God. See Thanks be to God **242**

Bazaars *See* Fairs
Bea and Mr. Jones. Schwartz, A. **E**
Beach, Milo Cleveland
The adventures of Rama (4 and up) **891**
Beach day. Oxenbury, H. **E**
The **beachcomber's** book. Kohn, B. **745.5**
Beaches
Rockwell, A. F. At the beach **E**
Fiction
Asch, F. Sand cake **E**
Brown, M. T. D.W. all wet **E**
Burningham, J. Come away from the water, Shirley **E**
Cooney, B. Hattie and the wild waves **E**
Oxenbury, H. Beach day **E**
Poetry
McMillan, B. One sun: a book of terse verse (k-3) **811**
Beacons of light: lighthouses. Gibbons, G. **387.1**
Beady Bear. Freeman, D. **E**
Beagle Expedition (1831-1836)
Hyndley, K. The voyage of the Beagle [biography of Charles Darwin] (4 and up) **92**
Bealer, Alex W.
Only the names remain (4-6) **970.004**
The **beam**. Grimm, J.
In Grimm, J. The complete Grimm's fairy tales p645 **398.2**
Beam of straw
Grimm, J. The beam
In Grimm, J. The complete Grimm's fairy tales p645 **398.2**
Beano *See* Bingo
Beanpole. Park, B. **Fic**
Beans on the roof. Byars, B. C. **Fic**
Bear, the dog, and the cat
Afanas'ev, A. N. The bear, the dog, and the cat
In Afanas'ev, A. N. Russian fairy tales p453-55 **398.2**
The **bear**. Afanas'ev, A. N.
In Afanas'ev, A. N. Russian fairy tales p74-75 **398.2**
Bear and skrattel
Rockwell, A. F. The cat on the Dovrefell
In Rockwell, A. F. Puss in boots, and other stories p75-79 **398.2**
Bear and the cock
Afanas'ev, A. N. The bear and the cock
In Afanas'ev, A. N. Russian fairy tales p455-56 **398.2**
The **bear** and the kingbird. Grimm, J. **398.2**

A **bear** called Paddington. Bond, M. Fic
Bear shadow. Asch, F. See note under Asch, F. Sand cake E
Beard, Charles Austin, 1874-1948
Charles A. Beard's The presidents in American history (5 and up) 920
Bearman: exploring the world of black bears. Pringle, L. P. 599.74
Bears
See also Grizzly bear; Polar bears
Brenner, B. Two orphan cubs (k-3) 599.74
Buxton, J. H. Baby bears and how they grow (k-3) 599.74
Pringle, L. P. Bearman: exploring the world of black bears (3-5) 599.74
Schwartz, A. Fat man in a fur coat, and other bear stories (4 and up) 599.74
Fiction
Alexander, M. G. We're in big trouble, Blackboard Bear E
Allen, P. Bertie and the bear E
Asch, F. Sand cake E
Banks, K. Alphabet soup E
Berenstain, S. Bears on wheels E
Bond, M. A bear called Paddington (2-5) Fic
Bond, M. Paddington's storybook (2-5) S C
Brett, J. Goldilocks and the three bears (k-2) 398.2
Carlstrom, N. W. Jesse Bear, what will you wear? E
Dalgliesh, A. The bears on Hemlock Mountain (1-4) Fic
Day, A. Frank and Ernest E
Day, A. Frank and Ernest play ball E
Gage, W. Cully Cully and the bear E
Galdone, P. The three bears (k-2) 398.2
Johnson, A. The grizzly (5 and up) Fic
Jonas, A. Two bear cubs E
Kimmel, E. A. The Chanukkah guest E
Marshall, J. Goldilocks and the three bears (k-2) 398.2
McCloskey, R. Blueberries for Sal E
McCully, E. A. Zaza's big break E
McLeod, E. The bear's bicycle E
McPhail, D. M. The bear's toothache E
McPhail, D. M. Fix-it E
McPhail, D. M. Lost! E
Milne, A. A. The house at Pooh Corner (1-4) Fic
Milne, A. A. The Pooh story book (1-4) Fic
Milne, A. A. Winnie-the-Pooh (1-4) Fic
Milne, A. A. The world of Pooh (1-4) Fic
Minarik, E. H. Little Bear E
Morey, W. Gentle Ben (5 and up) Fic
Murphy, J. Peace at last E
Murphy, J. What next, Baby Bear! E
Peet, B. Big bad Bruce E
Pinkwater, D. M. Bear's picture E
Pomerantz, C. Where's the bear? E
Rockwell, A. F. Come to town E
Rockwell, A. F. First comes spring E
Rosen, M. We're going on a bear hunt E
Thompson, C. Time E
Turkle, B. C. Deep in the forest E
Vincent, G. Ernest and Celestine E
Wahl, J. Humphrey's bear E
Ward, L. K. The biggest bear E
Watanabe, S. How do I put it on? E
Wildsmith, B. Bear's adventure E
Wiseman, B. Morris and Boris at the circus E
Wood, A. Oh my baby bear! E
Zalben, J. B. Happy Passover, Rosie E
Poetry
Yolen, J. The three bears rhyme book (k-2) 811
Bear's adventure. Wildsmith, B. E
Bear's bargain. Asch, F. See note under Asch, F. Sand cake E
The **bear's** bicycle. McLeod, E. E
The **bears'** house. Sachs, M. Fic
The **bears** on Hemlock Mountain. Dalgliesh, A. Fic
Bears on wheels. Berenstain, S. E
Bear's paw
Afanas'ev, A. N. The bear
In Afanas'ev, A. N. Russian fairy tales p74-75 398.2
Bear's picture. Pinkwater, D. M. E
The **bear's** speech. Cortázar, J.
In Where angels glide at dawn p3-5 S C
The **bear's** toothache. McPhail, D. M. E
Bearskin
Grimm, J. Bearskin
In Grimm, J. The complete Grimm's fairy tales p467-72 398.2
In Grimm, J. The juniper tree, and other tales from Grimm v2 p217-27 398.2
Pyle, H. Bearskin
In Pyle, H. The wonder clock p1-14 398.2
Beastly neighbors. Rights, M. 508
Beasts in a pit. Afanas'ev, A. N.
In Afanas'ev, A. N. Russian fairy tales p498 398.2
The **beasts** of never. McHargue, G. 398
Beat the story-drum, pum-pum. Bryan, A. 398.2
Beat the turtle drum. Greene, C. C. Fic
Beaton, Margaret
Syria (4 and up) 956.91

Beatrix Potter: artist, storyteller and countrywoman. Taylor, J. **92**
Beats me, Claude. Nixon, J. L. **E**
Beatty, Patricia
Charley Skedaddle (5 and up) **Fic**
Eight mules from Monterey (5 and up) **Fic**
Turn homeward, Hannalee (5 and up) **Fic**
Beaumont, William, 1785-1853
About
Epstein, S. Dr. Beaumont and the man with the hole in his stomach (4-6) **92**
The **beautiful** girl of the moon tower. Hamilton, V.
In Hamilton, V. The people could fly: American black folktales p53-59 **398.2**
Beauty, Personal *See* Grooming, Personal
Beauty: a retelling of the story of Beauty & the beast. McKinley, R. **Fic**
Beauty and the beast
Berger, T. The beauty & the beast
In Berger, T. Black fairy tales p55-67 **398.2**
Brett, J. Beauty and the beast **398.2**
Ehrlich, A. Beauty and the beast
In Ehrlich, A. The Random House book of fairy tales p82-93 **398.2**
Hutton, W. Beauty and the beast **398.2**
Le Prince de Beaumont, Madame. Beauty and the beast **398.2**
also in The Classic fairy tales p139-50 **398.2**
also in Sleeping beauty & other favourite fairy tales p45-62 **398.2**
Martin, E. Beauty and the beast
In Martin, E. Tales of the Far North p89-99 **398.2**
Mayer, M. Beauty and the beast **398.2**
McKinley, R. Beauty: a retelling of the story of Beauty & the beast **Fic**
Villeneuve, M. de. Beauty and the beast
In Best-loved folktales of the world p8-23 **398.2**
In The Blue fairy book p100-19 **398.2**
In The Scott, Foresman anthology of children's literature p206-16 **808.8**
Beavers
Lane, M. The beaver (1-3) **599.32**
Michener, J. A. Centennial
In Animal families of the wild: animal stories p49-64 **591**
Rue, L. L. Meet the beaver (4 and up) **599.32**
Ryden, H. The beaver (3-5) **599.32**
Because of a blintz. Simon, S.
In Simon, S. More wise men of Helm and their merry tales p69-79 **398.2**
Becca backward, Becca frontward. McMillan, B. **428**
Bechstein, Ludwig, 1801-1860
The three dogs
In The Green fairy book p360-66 **398.2**
The three musicians
In The Green fairy book p353-59 **398.2**
Beck, Barbara L.
The ancient Maya (4 and up) **972**
The Aztecs (4 and up) **972**
The Incas (4 and up) **985**
Beckelman, Laurie
Alzheimer's disease (4-6) **616.8**
Transplants (4-6) **617.9**
(ed) Hjelmeland, A. Drinking & driving **363.1**
(ed) Turck, M. Crack & cocaine **362.29**
Becket, Thomas à *See* Thomas, à Becket, Saint, Archbishop of Canterbury, 1118?-1170
Becuma of the white skin
Stephens, J. Becuma of the White Skin
In Stephens, J. Irish fairy tales p219-55 **398.2**
The **bed** book. Plath, S. **811**
The **bed** just so, a story. Hardendorff, J. B.
In Halloween: stories and poems p53-57 **808.8**
Bed-knob and broomstick. Norton, M. **Fic**
Beddows, Eric, 1951-
(il) Fleischman, P. Joyful noise: poems for two voices **811**
(il) Fleischman, P. Shadow play **E**
Bedore, Bernie, 1923-
The mufferaw catfish
In Bauer, C. F. Celebrations p85-86 **808.8**
Bedouins
Alotaibi, M. Bedouin: the nomads of the desert (5 and up) **956**
Fiction
Alexander, S. Nadia the Willful **E**
Bedrick, Jeffrey K.
(il) Smith, H. E. Weather **551.5**
The **bedspread**. Fair, S. **E**
Bedtime
Fiction
Bunting, E. No nap **E**
Cooney, N. E. Go away monsters, lickety split! **E**
Poetry
Plath, S. The bed book (k-2) **811**
Bedtime for Frances. Hoban, R. **E**
Bedtime snacks. Yep, L.
In Yep, L. The rainbow people p4-10 **398.2**

The **Bee-man** of Orn. Stockton, F. Fic
"**Bee** my valentine!". Cohen, M. See note under Cohen, M. See you in second grade! E
Beereeun the miragemaker. Parker, K. L.
In The Scott, Foresman anthology of children's literature p345-49 808.8
Bees
Fischer-Nagel, H. Life of the honeybee (3-6) 595.7
Harrison, V. The world of honeybees (k-2) 595.7
Lauber, P. From flower to flower (2-4) 582
Pringle, L. P. Killer bees (4 and up) 595.7
Watts, B. Honeybee (k-3) 595.7
Beetle who went on his travels
Andersen, H. C. The dung beetle
In Andersen, H. C. Hans Andersen: his classic fairy tales p48-56 S C
Beetles
See also Ladybirds
Johnson, S. A. Beetles (4 and up) 595.7
Milne, L. J. Nature's clean-up crew: the burying beetles (4 and up) 595.7
See/See also pages in the following book(s):
Zim, H. S. Insects (4 and up) 595.7
Beezus and Ramona. Cleary, B. See note under Cleary, B. Ramona the pest Fic
Beezus and Ramona [excerpt]. Cleary, B.
In The Random House book of humor for children p100-19 817.008
Befana (Legendary character)
De Paola, T. The legend of Old Befana (k-3) 398.2
Plume, I. The story of Befana (1-3) 398.2
Before the sun dies. Gallant, R. A. 575
Before the Wright brothers. Berliner, D. 629.13
Before you came this way. Baylor, B. 709.01
Before you were three. Harris, R. H. 155.4
The **beggar** queen. Alexander, L. See note under Alexander, L. Westmark Fic
Beggar's plan
Afanas'ev, A. N. The beggar's plan
In Afanas'ev, A. N. Russian fairy tales p599 398.2
The **beginning** of the armadilloes. Kipling, R. Fic
also in Kipling, R. Just so stories S C
Behavior *See* Human behavior
Behavior modification
Fiction
Sleator, W. House of stairs (5 and up) Fic
Behind barbed wire: the imprisonment of Japanese Americans during World War II. Davis, D. S. 940.54
Behind rebel lines: the incredible story of Emma Edmonds, Civil War spy. Reit, S. 92
Behind the attic wall. Cassedy, S. Fic
Behind the headlines. Fleming, T. J. 071
Behr, Joyce
(il) Nelson, E. L. The funny song-book 782.42
(il) Rosenbloom, J. Laughs, hoots & giggles 808.87
Behrens, June
Dolphins! (2-4) 599.5
Being a twin, having a twin. Rosenberg, M. B. 155.4
Being adopted. Rosenberg, M. B. 362.7
Being born. Kitzinger, S. 612.6
Being fashionable ain't always healthy. Lester, J.
In Lester, J. More tales of Uncle Remus p129-38 398.2
Beinush, the alert policeman. Simon, S.
In Simon, S. More wise men of Helm and their merry tales p102-10 398.2
Beisner, Monika
(il) Lurie, A. Fabulous beasts 398
(il) Lurie, A. The heavenly zoo 398.2
Belgium
Hargrove, J. Belgium (4 and up) 949.3
The **Believers**. Jones, R. C. Fic
Belinda's hurricane. Winthrop, E. Fic
Bell, Anthea
The nutcracker (2-4) Fic
Bell, Neill, 1946-
The book of where (5 and up) 910
The **Bell** Reef. Kendall, S. Fic
Bellairs, John
The chessmen of doom. See note under Bellairs, J. The curse of the blue figurine Fic
The curse of the blue figurine (5 and up) Fic
The dark secret of Weatherend. See note under Bellairs, J. The treasure of Alpheus Winterborn Fic
The eyes of the killer robot. See note under Bellairs, J. The curse of the blue figurine Fic

Bellairs, John—*Continued*
The figure in the shadows. See note under Bellairs, J. The house with a clock in its walls **Fic**
The house with a clock in its walls (5 and up) **Fic**
The lamp from the warlock's tomb. See note under Bellairs, J. The treasure of Alpheus Winterborn **Fic**
The letter, the witch, and the ring. See note under Bellairs, J. The house with a clock in its walls **Fic**
The mummy, the will and the crypt. See note under Bellairs, J. The curse of the blue figurine **Fic**
The revenge of the wizard's ghost. See note under Bellairs, J. The curse of the blue figurine **Fic**
The secret of the underground room. See note under Bellairs, J. The curse of the blue figurine **Fic**
The spell of the sorcerer's skull. See note under Bellairs, J. The curse of the blue figurine **Fic**
The treasure of Alpheus Winterborn (5 and up) **Fic**
The trolley to yesterday. See note under Bellairs, J. The curse of the blue figurine **Fic**

Bellamy, David J.
The rock pool (1-4) **574.92**

Bellamy, Francis
About
Swanson, J. I pledge allegiance (2-4) **323.6**

Bellamy, John, 1948-
The Doubleday children's thesaurus (4-6) **423**

Bellan-Gillen, Patricia
(il) Baker, P. J. My first book of sign **419**

Belloc, Hilaire, 1870-1953
The bad child's book of beasts
In Belloc, H. The bad child's book of beasts, and More beasts for worse children, and A moral alphabet **821**
The bad child's book of beasts, and More beasts for worse children, and A moral alphabet (1-4) **821**
A moral alphabet
In Belloc, H. The bad child's book of beasts, and More beasts for worse children, and A moral alphabet **821**
More beasts for worse children
In Belloc, H. The bad child's book of beasts, and More beasts for worse children, and A moral alphabet **821**

The **bells** of Christmas. Hamilton, V. **Fic**

Bellville, Cheryl Walsh, 1944-
Farming today yesterday's way (2-4) **630.1**

Beloved Benjamin is waiting. Karl, J. **Fic**

Below the root. Snyder, Z. K. **Fic**

Belpré, Pura
The Three Magi
In The Family read-aloud Christmas treasury p82-89 **808.8**

Beltrami, Giacomo Constantino, 1779-1855
See/See also pages in the following book(s):
McCall, E. S. Biography of a river: the living Mississippi p67-75 (6 and up) **977**

Bemelmans, Ludwig, 1898-1962
Madeline **E**
Madeline and the bad hat. See note under Bemelmans, L. Madeline **E**
Madeline and the gypsies. See note under Bemelmans, L. Madeline **E**
Madeline in London. See note under Bemelmans, L. Madeline **E**
Madeline's Christmas. See note under Bemelmans, L. Madeline **E**
Madeline's rescue **E**
See/See also pages in the following book(s):
Caldecott Medal books, 1938-1957 p255-65 **028.5**

Ben & Jerry's Homemade Inc.
Jaspersohn, W. Ice cream (3-5) **637**

Ben and me. Lawson, R. **Fic**

Ben and the porcupine. Carrick, C. **E**

Bencastro, Mario
A clown's story
In Where angels glide at dawn p57-65 **S C**

Benchley, Nathaniel, 1915-1981
Feldman Fieldmouse (3-5) **Fic**
A ghost named Fred **E**

Bend and stretch. Ormerod, J. **E**

Bender, Lionel
Desert (3-5) **574.5**

Bendick, Jeanne, 1919-
Egyptian tombs (4 and up) **932**
How much & how many? (5 and up) **530.8**

Bendis, Keith
(il) Thayer, E. L. Casey at the bat **811**

Beneath a blue umbrella: rhymes. Prelutsky, J. **811**

Benét, Rosemary
A book of Americans (4 and up) **811**

Benét, Stephen Vincent, 1898-1943
(jt. auth) Benét, R. A book of Americans **811**

Benjamin, Carol Lea
Cartooning for kids (4-6) **741.5**

Benjamin, Carol Lea—*Continued*
Writing for kids (4 and up) **808**
Benjamin Franklin. D'Aulaire, I. **92**
Benjamin West and his cat Grimalkin. Henry, M. **92**
Benjamin's 365 birthdays. Barrett, J. **E**
Benjamin's barn. Lindbergh, R. **E**
Bennett, Anna Elizabeth
Little witch (3-5) **Fic**
Bennett, Jill, 1934-
(il) King-Smith, D. Harry's Mad **Fic**
Bennett, Jill, 1947-
Teeny tiny (k-1) **398.2**
Bennett, Linda, 1942-
(il) Jobb, J. The night sky book **523**
Bennett, Olivia
A family in Egypt (3-5) **962**
Bennett Cerf's book of animal riddles. Cerf, B. **793.73**
Bennett Cerf's book of riddles. Cerf, B. **793.73**
Benny bakes a cake. Rice, E. **E**
Benny's luck. Sholem Aleichem.
In Sholem Aleichem. Holiday tales of Sholem Aleichem **S C**
Ben's dream. Van Allsburg, C. **E**
Ben's trumpet. Isadora, R. **E**
Benson, Islay
Long live Christmas
In The Big book of Christmas plays p213-27 **808.82**
Benson, Patrick
(il) Mayne, W. The green book of Hob stories **E**
Benson, Sally, 1900-1972
Stories of the gods and heroes (5 and up) **292**
Bensusen, Sally J.
(il) Branley, F. M. Mysteries of planet earth **525**
(il) Branley, F. M. Mysteries of the universe **523.1**
Bent, Jennifer
(il) Agard, J. The calypso alphabet **E**
Beowulf. Crossley-Holland, K. **829**
Beowulf against Grendel. Nye, R.
In Bauer, C. F. Celebrations p105-08 **808.8**
Bereavement
Bernstein, J. E. Loss and how to cope with it (5 and up) **155.9**
Hyde, M. O. Meeting death (5 and up) **155.9**
Krementz, J. How it feels when a parent dies (4 and up) **155.9**
LeShan, E. J. Learning to say good-by (4 and up) **155.9**
Rogers, F. When a pet dies (k-1) **155.9**
Bibliography
Bernstein, J. E. Books to help children cope with separation and loss v3 **016.3627**
Berends, Polly Berrien
The case of the elevator duck (3-5) **Fic**
Berenstain, Jan, 1923-
(jt. auth) Berenstain, S. Bears on wheels **E**
Berenstain, Stan, 1923-
Bears on wheels **E**
Berenzy, Alix
A Frog Prince (2-4) **E**
Berger, Barbara, 1945-
Grandfather Twilight **E**
Berger, Gilda
Sharks (2-4) **597**
Whales (2-4) **599.5**
Berger, Melvin, 1927-
Atoms, molecules, and quarks (6 and up) **539**
Bright stars, red giants, and white dwarfs (5 and up) **523.8**
Germs make me sick! (k-3) **616.9**
Our atomic world (4 and up) **539.7**
Sports (5 and up) **796.03**
Star gazing, comet tracking, and sky mapping (5 and up) **523**
Switch on, switch off (k-3) **537**
UFOs, ETs & visitors from space (5 and up) **001.9**
Why I cough, sneeze, shiver, hiccup, & yawn (k-3) **612.8**
Berger, Terry
Black fairy tales (4 and up) **398.2**
Contents: The moss-green princess; The serpent's bride; The fairy frog; The enchanted buck; The beauty & the beast; The story of the shining princess; The three little eggs; The rabbit prince; The fairy bird; Baboon-skins
Bergman, Thomas
Finding a common language (1-3) **362.4**
On our own terms (1-3) **362.4**
One day at a time (1-3) **616.99**
Seeing in special ways (1-3) **362.4**
We laugh, we love, we cry (1-3) **362.3**
Berliner, Don, 1930-
Before the Wright brothers (5 and up) **629.13**
Bernard. Waber, B. **E**
Bernie and the Bessledorf ghost. Naylor, P. R. **Fic**
Bernstein, Joanne E.
Books to help children cope with separation and loss v3 **016.3627**
Loss and how to cope with it (5 and up) **155.9**
Bernstein, Zena
(il) O'Brien, R. C. Mrs. Frisby and the rats of NIMH **Fic**

Berries
See also Strawberries
Fiction
Degen, B. Jamberry **E**
Berrill, Margaret
Mummies, masks, & mourners (4-6) **393**
Berry, Anno
(il) Seed, J. Ntombi's song **E**
Berry, Christine
Mama went walking **E**
Berry, James
Spiderman Anancy (5 and up) **398.2**
Contents: Anancy and looking for a wife; Anancy, Old Witch and King-Daughter; Anancy and the making of the Bro title; Anancy, Dog and Old Higue Dry-Skull; Monkey, Tiger and the Magic Trials; Tiger and Anancy meet for war; Anancy and friend; Anancy and the Hide-Away Garden; Tiger and the Stump-a-Foot Celebration Dance; Mrs Anancy, chicken soup and Anancy; Ratbat and Tacooma's tree; Bro Tiger goes dead; Anancy runs into Tiger's trouble; Mrs Dog first-child and Monkey-Mother; Anancy and storm and the Reverend Man-Cow; Anancy and Dog and Puss and friendship; Anancy and bad news to Cow-Mother; Mrs Puss, Dog and thieves; Anancy, Tiger and the Shine-Dancer-Shine; Anancy, Lion and Tiger's last day
Berry, Louise A.
(jt. auth) Miller, C. G. Coastal rescue: preserving our seashores **333.91**
Bert Breen's barn. Edmonds, W. D. **Fic**
Bertie and the bear. Allen, P. **E**
Beshore, George W.
Science in ancient China (5 and up) **509**
Beskow, Elsa, 1874-1953
Pelle's new suit **E**
The **best** bad thing. Uchida, Y. See note under Uchida, Y. A jar of dreams **Fic**
Best books *See* Books and reading—Best books
Best books for children, preschool through grade 6 **011.6**
The **best** boy in the world. Schwartz, A.
In Schwartz, A. All of our noses are here, and other noodle tales p38-57 **398.2**
The **best** Christmas pageant ever. Robinson, B. **Fic**
The **best** Christmas pageant ever [excerpt]. Robinson, B.
In The Random House book of humor for children p144-53 **817.008**
Best friends. Cohen, M. See note under Cohen, M. See you in second grade! **E**
Best friends. Kellogg, S. **E**
Best friends for Frances. Hoban, R. See note under Hoban, R. Bedtime for Frances **E**
The **best:** high/low books for reluctant readers. Pilla, M. L. **011.6**
The **Best** in children's books **028.1**
The **best-kept** secret. Rodda, E. **Fic**
The **best-laid** plans of Jonah Twist. Honeycutt, N. **Fic**
Best-loved folktales of the world **398.2**
The **best** present. Keller, H. **E**
The **Best** science books & A-V materials for children **016.5**
The **Best** science books for children. See The Best science books & A-V materials for children **016.5**
The **best** singing games for children of all ages. Bley, E. S. **796.1**
Best that life has to give
Pyle, H. Best that life has to give
In Pyle, H. The wonder clock p305-18 **398.2**
The **best** town in the world. Baylor, B. **E**
Best wishes, amen (5 and up) **808.88**
Best witches: poems for Halloween. Yolen, J. **811**
Bet you can! science possibilities to fool you. Cobb, V. **793.8**
Bet you can't! science impossibilities to fool you. Cobb, V. **793.8**
Betancourt, Jeanne, 1941-
Smile! how to cope with braces (4 and up) **617.6**
Bethancourt, T. Ernesto
User friendly
In Connections: short stories by outstanding writers for young adults p108-21 **S C**
Bethune, Mary Jane McLeod, 1875-1955
About
Greenfield, E. Mary McLeod Bethune (2-5) **92**
McKissack, P. C. Mary McLeod Bethune: a great American educator (4 and up) **92**
The **betrothal**. Kendall, C.
In Kendall, C. Sweet and sour p80-85 **398.2**
Betsy and Billy. Haywood, C. See note under Haywood, C. "B" is for Betsy **Fic**
Betsy and Joe. Lovelace, M. H. See note under Lovelace, M. H. Betsy-Tacy **Fic**
Betsy and Mr. Kilpatrick. Haywood, C. See note under Haywood, C. "B" is for Betsy **Fic**

Betsy and Tacy go downtown. Lovelace, M. H. See note under Lovelace, M. H. Betsy-Tacy **Fic**

Betsy and Tacy go over the big hill. Lovelace, M. H. See note under Lovelace, M. H. Betsy-Tacy **Fic**

Betsy and the boys. Haywood, C. See note under Haywood, C. "B" is for Betsy **Fic**

Betsy and the circus. Haywood, C. See note under Haywood, C. "B" is for Betsy **Fic**

Betsy and the great world. Lovelace, M. H. See note under Lovelace, M. H. Betsy-Tacy **Fic**

Betsy in spite of herself. Lovelace, M. H. See note under Lovelace, M. H. Betsy-Tacy **Fic**

Betsy-Tacy. Lovelace, M. H. **Fic**

Betsy-Tacy and Tib. Lovelace, M. H. See note under Lovelace, M. H. Betsy-Tacy **Fic**

Betsy was a junior. Lovelace, M. H. See note under Lovelace, M. H. Betsy-Tacy **Fic**

Betsy's busy summer. Haywood, C. See note under Haywood, C. "B" is for Betsy **Fic**

Betsy's little star. Haywood, C. See note under Haywood, C. "B" is for Betsy **Fic**

Betsy's play school. Haywood, C. See note under Haywood, C. "B" is for Betsy **Fic**

Betsy's wedding. Lovelace, M. H. See note under Lovelace, M. H. Betsy-Tacy **Fic**

Betsy's winterhouse. Haywood, C. See note under Haywood, C. "B" is for Betsy **Fic**

Better baseball for boys. Sullivan, G. **796.357**

Better basketball for boys. Sullivan, G. **796.323**

Better basketball for girls. Sullivan, G. **796.323**

Better bicycling for boys and girls. Sullivan, G. **796.6**

Better BMX riding and racing for boys and girls. Sullivan, G. **796.6**

Better football for boys. Sullivan, G. **796.332**

Better homes and gardens cookies for kids **641.8**

Better Homes and Gardens junior cook book. See New junior cook book **641.5**

Better Homes and Gardens step-by-step kids' cook book (4 and up) **641.5**

Better not get wet, Jesse Bear. Carlstrom, N. W. See note under Carlstrom, N. W. Jesse Bear, what will you wear? **E**

Better roller skating for boys and girls. Sullivan, G. **796.2**

Better soccer for boys and girls. Sullivan, G. **796.334**

Better swimming for boys and girls. Sullivan, G. **797.2**

Better tennis for boys and girls. Sullivan, G. **796.342**

Better wait till Martin comes. Hamilton, V.
In Hamilton, V. The people could fly: American black folktales p133-37 **398.2**

Better weight training for boys. Sullivan, G. **613.7**

Better wrestling for boys. Sullivan, G. **796.8**

Betty Booker and the skipper. Roach, M. K.
In Roach, M. K. Encounters with the invisible world **S C**

Betty Crocker's cookbook for boys and girls. Crocker, B. **641.5**

Betty Crocker's new boys and girls cookbook. See Crocker, B. Betty Crocker's cookbook for boys and girls **641.5**

Betty Friedan: a voice for women's rights. Meltzer, M. **92**

Between two worlds: a story about Pearl Buck. Mitchell, B. **92**

Beverages
Osborne, C. Middle Eastern food and drink (4-6) **641.5**
See/See also pages in the following book(s):
Penner, L. R. The colonial cookbook p111-15 (5 and up) **641.5**

Beware of redheads
Afanas'ev, A. N. The cheater cheated
In Afanas'ev, A. N. Russian fairy tales p228-29 **398.2**

Beyond picture books. Barstow, B. **011.6**

Beyond silence. Cameron, E. **Fic**

Beyond the ridge. Goble, P. **Fic**

Bhend, Käthi
(il) Johansen, H. 7 x 7 tales of a sevensleeper **Fic**

Bianchi, John
(il) Dickinson, T. Exploring the night sky **523**

Bianco, Margery Williams, 1880-1944
The velveteen rabbit (2-4) **Fic**

Bible
The Holy Bible [King James Bible. Oxford Univ. Press] **220.5**
The Holy Bible: revised standard version **220.5**
Biography
Hofman, Y. The world of the Bible for young readers (5 and up) **220.9**
Natural history
Bible. Selections. Animals of the Bible (1-4) **220.8**
Paterson, J. Consider the lilies (5 and up) **220.8**

Bible. N.T. Selections
The Christ child (k-3) **232.9**
The Christmas story (k-3) **232.9**
Christmas, the King James Version **232.9**
Easter, the King James Version (4 and up) **232.9**

Bible. Selections
Animals of the Bible (1-4) **220.8**
Tomie dePaola's book of Bible stories **220.9**

Bible stories
Bach, A. Moses' ark: stories from the Bible (4-6) **222**
Bible. Selections. Tomie dePaola's book of Bible stories **220.9**
Brown, M. W. Christmas in the barn (k-2) **232.9**
Chaikin, M. Exodus (2-4) **222**
Chaikin, M. Joshua in the Promised Land (4 and up) **222**
Chaikin, M. The seventh day: the story of the Jewish Sabbath (4 and up) **222**
De Paola, T. David and Goliath (k-3) **222**
De Paola, T. The miracles of Jesus (1-3) **232.9**
De Paola, T. Noah and the ark (k-2) **222**
Fisher, L. E. The seven days of creation (k-3) **222**
Fisher, L. E. The Wailing Wall (4 and up) **221.9**
Geisert, A. The ark (k-3) **222**
Gellman, M. Does God have a big toe? (4-6) **221.9**
Hofman, Y. The world of the Bible for young readers (5 and up) **220.9**
Hogrogian, N. Noah's ark (k-3) **222**
Hutton, W. Adam and Eve (k-3) **222**
Hutton, W. Jonah and the great fish (k-3) **224**
Laird, E. The road to Bethlehem (4-6) **232.9**
Noah and the ark (1-3) **222**
Segal, L. G. The book of Adam to Moses (4-6) **222**
Singer, I. B. The wicked city (3-6) **222**
Spier, P. The Book of Jonah (k-3) **224**
Stoddard, S. The Doubleday illustrated children's Bible (4-6) **220.9**
Winthrop, E. A child is born: the Christmas story (k-3) **232.9**
Winthrop, E. He is risen: the Easter story (2-5) **232.9**

Bibliography
See also Books
Best books
See Books and reading—Best books
Bibliography
Ettlinger, J. R. T. Choosing books for young people v2 **011.6**

The **bicycle** man. Say, A. **E**

Bicycle racing
Sullivan, G. Better BMX riding and racing for boys and girls (4 and up) **796.6**

Bicycle to treachery. Quackenbush, R. M. See note under Quackenbush, R. M. Express train to trouble **Fic**

Bicycles and bicycling
Rockwell, A. F. Bikes (k-2) **629.227**
Sullivan, G. Better bicycling for boys and girls (4 and up) **796.6**
Fiction
Andersen, K. B. What's the matter, Sylvie, can't you ride? **E**
McLeod, E. The bear's bicycle **E**
Say, A. The bicycle man **E**

Bierhorst, John
Doctor Coyote (1-4) **398.2**
(ed) In the trail of the wind: American Indian poems and ritual orations. See In the trail of the wind: American Indian poems and ritual orations **897**
(ed) The Monkey's haircut, and other stories told by the Maya. See The Monkey's haircut, and other stories told by the Maya **398.2**
(ed) The Naked bear. See The Naked bear **398.2**
(ed) The Sacred path. See The Sacred path **897**
(ed) The Whistling skeleton. See The Whistling skeleton **398.2**

Biesty, Stephen
(il) Hart, G. Exploring the past: ancient Egypt **932**

The **big** Alfie and Annie Rose storybook. Hughes, S. See note under Hughes, S. Alfie gets in first **E**

Big Apple Circus
Machotka, H. The magic ring (3-6) **791.3**

Big bad Bruce. Peet, B. **E**
The **big** balloon race. Coerr, E. **E**
Big bang theory *See* Universe
The **big** beast book. Booth, J. **567.9**
The **Big** book of Christmas plays **808.82**
The **big** concrete lorry. Hughes, S. See note under Hughes, S. Angel Mae: a tale of Trotter Street **E**
Big Dipper *See* Ursa Major
The **Big** Dipper. Branley, F. M. **523.8**
The **Big** Dipper and you. Krupp, E. C. **523**
Big feet of the Empress Tu Chin. Carpenter, F.
In Carpenter, F. Tales of a Chinese grandmother p81-88 **398.2**
Big game hunting *See* Hunting
Big green drawing book, Ed Emberley's. Emberley, E. **741.2**
The **big** hello. Schulman, J. **E**
Big Jack and Little Jack
Big Jack and Little Jack
In The Jack tales p67-75 **398.2**
Big like me. Hines, A. G. **E**
Big Max. Platt, K. **E**
Big Max in the mystery of the missing moose. Platt, K. **E**
Big old bones. Carrick, C. **E**
Big Red. Kjelgaard, J. **Fic**
Big red barn. Brown, M. W. **E**
Big red drawing book, Ed Emberley's. Emberley, E. **741.2**
Big Shoe, Little Shoe. Cazet, D. **E**
The **big** sneeze. Brown, R. **E**
The **big** snow. Hader, B. **E**
The **big** stretch: the complete book of the amazing rubber band. Graham, A. **678**
Big talk. Schlein, M. **E**
Big wheels. Rockwell, A. F. **629.225**
The **biggest** bear. Ward, L. K. **E**
The **biggest** house in the world. Lionni, L. **E**
The **biggest** pumpkin ever. Kroll, S. **E**
The **biggest** tongue twister book in the world. Brandreth, G. D. **808.88**
The **biggest** truck. Lyon, D. **E**
Bikes. Rockwell, A. F. **629.227**
Bileck, Marvin, 1920-
(jt. auth) Scheer, J. Rain makes applesauce **E**
Bilibin, Ivan ÎAkovlevich, 1876-1942
(il) Afanas'ev, A. N. Russian folk tales **398.2**
Bilingual books
Spanish-English
Arroz con leche (k-3) **782.42**
Emberley, R. My house/mi casa: a book in two languages (k-3) **463**
Emberley, R. Taking a walk/caminando: a book in two languages (k-3) **463**
Lomas Garza, C. Family pictures **E**
Perl, L. Piñatas and paper flowers (4 and up) **394.2**
Rohmer, H. Brother Anansi and the cattle ranch (3-6) **398.2**
Tortillitas para mamá and other nursery rhymes (k-2) **398.8**
Bilingual education *See* Education, Bilingual
Bill and Pete. De Paola, T. **E**
Bill and Pete go down the Nile. De Paola, T. **E**
Bill Cosby: America's most famous father. Haskins, J. **92**
Bill is with me now. Leach, M.
In Leach, M. Whistle in the graveyard p66-67 **398.2**
Bill Peet: an autobiography. Peet, B. **92**
Billion (The number)
Schwartz, D. M. How much is a million? **E**
A **billion** for Boris. Rodgers, M. See note under Rodgers, M. Freaky Friday **Fic**
The **billions** of bats. Schlein, M. **599.4**
Billy. Crossley-Holland, K.
In Crossley-Holland, K. British folk tales p244-46 **398.2**
Billy Mosby's nightride. San Souci, R.
In San Souci, R. Short & shivery p103-11 **398.2**
Bimwili & the Zimwi. Aardema, V. **398.2**
Binary numbers. Watson, C. **513**
Binary system (Mathematics)
Watson, C. Binary numbers (2-4) **513**
Binch, Caroline
(il) Nichols, G. Come on into my tropical garden **821**
Bingo
See/See also pages in the following book(s):
Aaseng, N. The unsung heroes p44-51 (5 and up) **920**
Bingo Brown and the language of love. Byars, B. C. See note under Byars, B. C. The burning questions of Bingo Brown **Fic**
Bingo Brown, gypsy lover. Byars, B. C. See note under Byars, B. C. The burning questions of Bingo Brown **Fic**
Binky brothers, detectives. Lawrence, J. **E**
The **binnacle** boy. Fleischman, P.
In Fleischman, P. Graven images p1-23 **S C**

Binnorie
Jacobs, J. Binnorie
In Jacobs, J. English fairy tales p44-47 **398.2**

Biography
See/See also pages in the following book(s):
The Scott, Foresman anthology of children's literature p725-62 **808.8**

Bibliography
Breen, K. Index to collective biographies for young readers **920**

Dictionaries
Webster's new biographical dictionary **920.003**

Indexes
Breen, K. Index to collective biographies for young readers **920**

Biography of a river: the living Mississippi. McCall, E. S. **977**

Biography of an atom. Bronowski, J. **539**

Biology
See also Marine biology

Bioluminescence
Silverstein, A. Nature's living lights (5 and up) **574.1**

Birch, Reginald Bathurst, 1856-1943
(il) Rainbow in the sky. See Rainbow in the sky **821.008**

Birches. Frost, R. **811**

The **Bird** bride
In The Monkey's haircut, and other stories told by the Maya p25-31 **398.2**

The **bird** of fortune. Walker, B. K.
In Walker, B. K. A treasury of Turkish folktales for children p108-13 **398.2**

Bird of power. Marriott, A. L.
In Marriott, A. L. American Indian mythology **398.2**

The **bird** that made milk. Lester, J.
In Lester, J. How many spots does a leopard have? and other tales p5-11 **398.2**

Bird watch: a book of poetry. Yolen, J. **811**

Bird who spoke three times
Sawyer, R. The bird who spoke three times
In Sawyer, R. The way of the storyteller p297-304 **372.6**

Bird Woman *See* Sacagawea, 1786-1884

Birds

See also Birds of prey; Cage birds; Canaries; Crows; Eagles; Herons; Loons; Ostriches; Owls; Parrots; Peacocks; Pelicans; Pigeons; Robins; Storks; Swallows; Vultures

Arnold, C. Ostriches and other flightless birds (3-6) **598**
Burnie, D. Bird (4 and up) **598**
Burton, M. Birds (5 and up) **598**
Cole, J. A bird's body **598**
George, J. C. One day in the woods (4-6) **574.5**
McCauley, J. R. Baby birds and how they grow (k-3) **598**
McGowen, T. Album of birds (4 and up) **598**
Selsam, M. E. A first look at birds (1-3) **598**
Zim, H. S. Birds (4 and up) **598**
See/See also pages in the following book(s):
Chrystie, F. N. Pets p126-38 (4 and up) **636.088**
McClung, R. M. The amazing egg p85-95 (4 and up) **591.1**
Pringle, L. P. Feral: tame animals gone wild p15-23 (5 and up) **591.5**
Weber, W. J. Care of uncommon pets p180-205 (5 and up) **636.088**

Eggs and nests
Bash, B. Urban roosts: where birds nest in the city (1-4) **598**
Selsam, M. E. A first look at bird nests (1-3) **598**

Fiction
De Paola, T. Bill and Pete **E**
De Paola, T. Bill and Pete go down the Nile **E**
Eastman, P. D. Are you my mother? **E**
Ehlert, L. Feathers for lunch **E**
Lionni, L. Inch by inch **E**
Lionni, L. Nicolas, where have you been? **E**
Pomerantz, C. Flap your wings and try **E**

Flight
Kaufmann, J. Birds are flying (k-3) **598**

Pictorial works
Wildsmith, B. Brian Wildsmith's birds **E**
Wolff, A. A year of birds **E**

Poetry
Fleischman, P. I am phoenix: poems for two voices (4 and up) **811**
Yolen, J. Bird watch: a book of poetry (3-6) **811**

See/See also pages in the following book(s):
Favorite poems, old and new p279-97 (4-6) **808.81**
Piping down the valleys wild p127-38 **808.81**
Rainbow in the sky p217-29 (k-4) **821.008**

Protection
Arnold, C. Saving the peregrine falcon (3-6) **598**

Birds—Protection—*Continued*
McNulty, F. Peeping in the shell (2-5) **639.9**
Patent, D. H. The whooping crane (5 and up) **639.9**
Scott, J. D. Orphans from the sea (4 and up) **639.9**
North America
Peterson, R. T. A field guide to the birds **598**
Robbins, C. S. Birds of North America (4 and up) **598**
West (U.S.)
Peterson, R. T. A field guide to western birds **598**
Birds are flying. Kaufmann, J. **598**
Birds, beasts, and the third thing. Lawrence, D. H. **821**
A **bird's** body. Cole, J. **598**
Birds, Brian Wildsmith's. Wildsmith, B. **E**
The **Bird's** Christmas Carol. Wiggin, K. D. S. **Fic**
Birds of North America. Robbins, C. S. **598**
Birds of prey
See also names of birds of prey
DeWitt, L. Eagles, hawks, and other birds of prey (4 and up) **598**
Selsam, M. E. A first look at owls, eagles, and other hunters of the sky (1-3) **598**
The **birds** of summer. Mayo, G.
In Mayo, G. Star tales p47-54 **398.2**
Birdseye, Tom
Airmail to the moon **E**
A song of stars (3-5) **398.2**
Birkhead, Mike
(il) Harrison, V. The world of a falcon **598**
Birmingham, Lucy, 1956-
Japan (3-5) **952**
Biro, Val, 1921-
(il) Grahame, K. The open road **Fic**
Birth *See* Childbirth
Birth of a foal. Isenbart, H.-H. **636.1**
The **birth** of Bran. Stephens, J.
In Stephens, J. Irish fairy tales p91-108 **398.2**
The **Birth** of Fin MacCoul
In Best-loved folktales of the world p256-64 **398.2**
The **birth** of Maui. Te Kanawa, K.
In Te Kanawa, K. Land of the long white cloud p11-16 **398.2**
A **birthday** for Frances. Hoban, R. See note under Hoban, R. Bedtime for Frances **E**
The **birthday** of the Infanta. Wilde, O.
In Wilde, O. The Happy Prince, and other stories p70-92 **S C**
The **birthday** party. Oxenbury, H. **E**
The **birthday** pie. Gotwalt, H. L. M.
In Gotwalt, H. L. M. Special plays for holidays p135-43 **812**
Birthday poems. Livingston, M. C. **811**
The **birthday** tree. Fleischman, P. **Fic**
Birthdays
Charlip, R. Handtalk birthday (k-3) **419**
Gibbons, G. Happy birthday! (k-2) **394.2**
Gregory, R. W. Anniversaries and holidays **394.2**
Laird, E. Happy birthday! (1-3) **394.2**
Perl, L. Candles, cakes, and donkey tails (3-6) **392**
Fiction
Barrett, J. Benjamin's 365 birthdays **E**
Base, G. The eleventh hour (4-6) **Fic**
Brandenberg, F. Aunt Nina and her nephews and nieces **E**
Carrick, C. Paul's Christmas birthday **E**
Conrad, P. Staying nine (3-5) **Fic**
Flack, M. Ask Mr. Bear **E**
Hutchins, P. Happy birthday, Sam **E**
Little, L. J. I can do it by myself **E**
Oppenheim, S. L. Waiting for Noah **E**
Oxenbury, H. The birthday party **E**
Pearson, S. Happy birthday, Grampie **E**
Rice, E. Benny bakes a cake **E**
Rockwell, A. F. Happy birthday to me **E**
Walter, M. P. Have a happy— (4-6) **Fic**
Willard, N. The high rise glorious skittle skat roarious sky pie angel food cake (2-4) **Fic**
Zolotow, C. Mr. Rabbit and the lovely present **E**
Poetry
Livingston, M. C. Birthday poems (k-3) **811**
Bishop, Claire Huchet
The ferryman
In With a deep sea smile p42-55 **372.6**
The five Chinese brothers (1-3) **398.2**
Bisignano, Alphonse
Cooking the Italian way (5 and up) **641.5**
Bison
Freedman, R. Buffalo hunt (4 and up) **970.004**
Lepthien, E. U. Buffalo (2-4) **599.73**
Patent, D. H. Buffalo (4 and up) **599.73**
Fiction
Baker, O. Where the buffaloes begin (2-4) **Fic**

Bison—Fiction—*Continued*
Goble, P. Buffalo woman (1-3) **398.2**
Biter bit
The Biter bit
In The Green fairy book p194-201 **398.2**
Bits and bytes: a computer dictionary for beginners. Simon, S. **004**
Bittern and the hoopoe
Grimm, J. The bittern and the hoopoe
In Grimm, J. The complete Grimm's fairy tales p710-11 **398.2**
Björk, Christina
Linnea in Monet's garden (3-5) **Fic**
Linnea's almanac (2-5) **508**
Linnea's windowsill garden (3-6) **635**
Björkman, Steve
(il) Levine, E. I hate English! **E**
Black, David
Plants (5 and up) **581**
Black, Shirley Temple, 1928-
About
Haskins, J. Shirley Temple Black (4 and up) **92**
Black, Brown and Gray
Black, Brown and Gray
In Best-loved folktales of the world p270-75 **398.2**
The **Black** Americans: a history in their own words, 1619-1983 (6 and up) **305.8**
Black and white. Macaulay, D. **E**
Black art (Magic) *See* Witchcraft
Black athletes
Adler, D. A. Jackie Robinson: he was the first (3-5) **92**
Deegan, P. J. Michael Jordan: basketball's soaring star (4 and up) **92**
Golenbock, P. Teammates [biography of Jackie Robinson] (1-4) **92**
Scott, R. Jackie Robinson (5 and up) **92**
Black authors
McKissack, P. C. Paul Laurence Dunbar, a poet to remember (4 and up) **92**
Walker, A. Langston Hughes, American poet (2-5) **92**
Bio-bibliography
Rollock, B. T. Black authors and illustrators of children's books **920.003**
Black authors and illustrators of children's books. Rollock, B. T. **920.003**
Black Beauty. Sewell, A. **Fic**
Black Bull of Norroway
The Black Bull of Norroway
In The Blue fairy book p380-84 **398.2**
Crossley-Holland, K. The Black Bull of Norway
In Crossley-Holland, K. British folk tales p59-70 **398.2**
Jacobs, J. Black Bull of Norroway
In The Scott, Foresman anthology of children's literature p157-59 **808.8**
The **black** cat's eyes. Leach, M.
In Leach, M. Whistle in the graveyard p95-97 **398.2**
The **black** cauldron. Alexander, L. See note under Alexander, L. The book of three **Fic**
Black dancers
Haskins, J. Katherine Dunham (5 and up) **92**
Tobias, T. Arthur Mitchell (2-5) **92**
Black death *See* Plague
Black educators
Greenfield, E. Mary McLeod Bethune (2-5) **92**
McKissack, P. C. Mary McLeod Bethune: a great American educator (4 and up) **92**
Black entertainers
Haskins, J. Bill Cosby: America's most famous father (5 and up) **92**
The **Black** experience in children's books **016.3058**
Black fairy tales. Berger, T. **398.2**
The **black** falcon. Wise, W. **Fic**
Black folklore *See* Blacks—Folklore
Black Gold (Race horse)
Fiction
Henry, M. Black Gold (4-6) **Fic**
Black hearts in Battersea. Aiken, J. See note under Aiken, J. The wolves of Willoughby Chase **Fic**
Black heroes of the American Revolution. Davis, B. **973.3**
Black holes (Astronomy)
Branley, F. M. Journey into a black hole (k-3) **523.8**
The **black** horse. Hodges, M.
In Hodges, M. If you had a horse **398.2**
Black is brown is tan. Adoff, A. **E**
Black literature (American) *See* American literature—Black authors
Black musicians
Mitchell, B. Raggin': a story about Scott Joplin (3-5) **92**
The **black** pearl. O'Dell, S. **Fic**
Black poetry (American) *See* American poetry—Black authors

Black singers
Jackson, J. Make a joyful noise unto the Lord! The life of Mahalia Jackson, queen of gospel singers (5 and up) **92**
The **black** snowman. Mendez, P. **E**
Black soldiers
Davis, B. Black heroes of the American Revolution (5 and up) **973.3**
Black spirituals *See* Spirituals (Songs)
The **Black** Stallion. Farley, W. **Fic**
The **Black** Stallion and Flame. Farley, W. See note under Farley, W. The Black Stallion **Fic**
The **Black** Stallion and Satan. Farley, W. See note under Farley, W. The Black Stallion **Fic**
The **Black** Stallion and the girl. Farley, W. See note under Farley, W. The Black Stallion **Fic**
The **Black** Stallion challenged! Farley, W. See note under Farley, W. The Black Stallion **Fic**
The **Black** Stallion legend. Farley, W. See note under Farley, W. The Black Stallion **Fic**
The **Black** Stallion mystery. Farley, W. See note under Farley, W. The Black Stallion **Fic**
The **Black** Stallion picture book. Farley, W. See note under Farley, W. The Black Stallion **Fic**
The **Black** Stallion returns. Farley, W. See note under Farley, W. The Black Stallion **Fic**
The **Black** Stallion revolts. Farley, W. See note under Farley, W. The Black Stallion **Fic**
The **Black** Stallion's courage. Farley, W. See note under Farley, W. The Black Stallion **Fic**
The **Black** Stallion's filly. Farley, W. See note under Farley, W. The Black Stallion **Fic**
The **Black** Stallion's ghost. Farley, W. See note under Farley, W. The Black Stallion **Fic**
The **Black** Stallion's sulky colt. Farley, W. See note under Farley, W. The Black Stallion **Fic**
Black Thief and Knight of the Glen
The Black Thief and Knight of the Glen *In* The Red fairy book p54-66 **398.2**
Black women
Ferris, J. Go free or die: a story about Harriet Tubman (3-5) **92**
Ferris, J. Walking the road to freedom: a story about Sojourner Truth (3-5) **92**
Greenfield, E. Childtimes: a three-generation memoir (4 and up) **920**
Greenfield, E. Mary McLeod Bethune (2-5) **92**
Haskins, J. Katherine Dunham (5 and up) **92**
McKissack, P. C. Mary McLeod Bethune: a great American educator (4 and up) **92**
Ortiz, V. Sojourner Truth, a self-made woman (6 and up) **92**
Blackbeard's treasure. Leach, M.
In Leach, M. Whistle in the graveyard p45-46 **398.2**
Blackberries in the dark. Jukes, M. **Fic**
Blackberry ink. Merriam, E. **811**
Blackboard Bear. Alexander, M. G. See note under Alexander, M. We're in big trouble, Blackboard Bear **E**
Blackburn, G. Meredith
(comp) In the witch's kitchen. See In the witch's kitchen **811.008**
(comp) Index to poetry for children and young people. See Index to poetry for children and young people **808.81**
(comp) My tang's tungled and other ridiculous situations. See My tang's tungled and other ridiculous situations **821.008**
Blackburn, John Brewton
(comp) Of quarks, quasars, and other quirks. See Of quarks, quasars, and other quirks **821.008**
Blackburn, Lorraine A.
(comp) In the witch's kitchen. See In the witch's kitchen **811.008**
(comp) Index to poetry for children and young people. See Index to poetry for children and young people **808.81**
(comp) They've discovered a head in the box for the bread, and other laughable limericks. See They've discovered a head in the box for the bread, and other laughable limericks **821.008**
Blackfoot Indians *See* Siksika Indians
Blacklock, Craig
(il) Nicholson, D. Wild boars **599.73**
Blacks
Spangler, E. The Blacks in America *In* The In America series **305.8**
Bibliography
The Black experience in children's books **016.3058**
Biography
Adler, D. A. Martin Luther King, Jr.: free at last (2-4) **92**
Adler, D. A. A picture book of Martin Luther King, Jr. (1-3) **92**
Adoff, A. Malcolm X (2-5) **92**

Blacks—Biography—*Continued*
Aliki. A weed is a flower: the life of George Washington Carver (k-3) **92**
Altman, S. R. Extraordinary black Americans (5 and up) **920**
Darby, J. Martin Luther King, Jr (5 and up) **92**
Ferris, J. Arctic explorer: the story of Matthew Henson (3-6) **92**
Ferris, J. What are you figuring now? a story about Benjamin Banneker (3-5) **92**
Greenfield, E. Paul Robeson (2-5) **92**
Hamilton, V. Anthony Burns: the defeat and triumph of a fugitive slave (5 and up) **92**
Haskins, J. The life and death of Martin Luther King, Jr (5 and up) **92**
McKissack, P. C. Frederick Douglass: the black lion (4 and up) **92**
McKissack, P. C. Jesse Jackson: a biography (4 and up) **92**
McKissack, P. C. Martin Luther King, Jr., a man to remember (4 and up) **92**
Miller, D. T. Frederick Douglass and the fight for freedom (6 and up) **92**
Mitchell, B. A pocketful of goobers: a story about George Washington Carver (3-5) **92**
Mitchell, B. Shoes for everyone: a story about Jan Matzeliger (3-5) **92**
Patrick, D. Martin Luther King, Jr (4 and up) **92**
Patterson, L. Martin Luther King, Jr., and the freedom movement (6 and up) **92**
Patterson, L. Sure hands, strong heart: the life of Daniel Hale Williams (4 and up) **92**
Yates, E. Amos Fortune, free man (4 and up) **92**

Civil rights

Adler, D. A. Martin Luther King, Jr.: free at last (2-4) **92**
Adler, D. A. A picture book of Martin Luther King, Jr. (1-3) **92**
Darby, J. Martin Luther King, Jr (5 and up) **92**
Haskins, J. The life and death of Martin Luther King, Jr (5 and up) **92**
McKissack, P. C. The Civil Rights Movement in America from 1865 to the present (5 and up) **323.4**
McKissack, P. C. Martin Luther King, Jr., a man to remember (4 and up) **92**
Patrick, D. Martin Luther King, Jr (4 and up) **92**
Patterson, L. Martin Luther King, Jr., and the freedom movement (6 and up) **92**

Fiction

Alexander, M. G. Bobo's dream **E**
Armstrong, W. H. Sounder (5 and up) **Fic**
Bogart, J. E. Daniel's dog **E**
Boyd, C. D. Charlie Pippin (4-6) **Fic**
Brenner, B. Wagon wheels **E**
Caines, J. F. Abby **E**
Caines, J. F. I need a lunch box **E**
Caines, J. F. Just us women **E**
Cameron, A. The stories Julian tells (2-4) **Fic**
Childress, A. A hero ain't nothin' but a sandwich (6 and up) **Fic**
Clifton, L. The lucky stone (3-5) **Fic**
Cohen, B. Thank you, Jackie Robinson (4-6) **Fic**
Collier, J. L. Jump ship to freedom (6 and up) **Fic**
Collier, J. L. War comes to Willy Freeman (6 and up) **Fic**
Collier, J. L. Who is Carrie? (6 and up) **Fic**
Daly, N. Not so fast, Songololo **E**
Fitzhugh, L. Nobody's family is going to change (5 and up) **Fic**
Flournoy, V. The patchwork quilt **E**
Fox, P. How many miles to Babylon? (4-6) **Fic**
Greene, B. Get on out of here, Philip Hall (4-6) **Fic**
Greene, B. Philip Hall likes me, I reckon maybe (4-6) **Fic**
Greenfield, E. Grandmama's joy **E**
Greenfield, E. Me and Neesie **E**
Greenfield, E. She come bringing me that little baby girl **E**
Greenfield, E. Sister (4 and up) **Fic**
Hamilton, V. The bells of Christmas (4-6) **Fic**
Hamilton, V. Cousins (5 and up) **Fic**
Hamilton, V. The house of Dies Drear (5 and up) **Fic**
Hamilton, V. M. C. Higgins the great (6 and up) **Fic**
Hamilton, V. The magical adventures of Pretty Pearl (6 and up) **Fic**
Hamilton, V. The mystery of Drear House (5 and up) **Fic**
Hamilton, V. The planet of Junior Brown (6 and up) **Fic**
Hamilton, V. Willie Bea and the time the Martians landed (5 and up) **Fic**
Hamilton, V. Zeely (4 and up) **Fic**
Hansen, J. The gift-giver (4-6) **Fic**
Hayes, S. Eat up, Gemma **E**
Hayes, S. Happy Christmas, Gemma **E**
Hooks, W. H. The ballad of Belle Dorcas (3-5) **Fic**
Howard, E. F. Chita's Christmas tree **E**
Howard, E. F. The train to Lulu's **E**
Isadora, R. Ben's trumpet **E**
Johnson, A. Do like Kyla **E**
Johnson, A. Tell me a story, Mama **E**
Jordan, J. Kimako's story (2-4) **Fic**

Blacks—Fiction—*Continued*
Konigsburg, E. L. Jennifer, Hecate, Macbeth, William McKinley, and me, Elizabeth (4-6) **Fic**
Lexau, J. M. I should have stayed in bed **E**
Lexau, J. M. The rooftop mystery **E**
Little, L. J. I can do it by myself **E**
Mathis, S. B. Sidewalk story (3-5) **Fic**
McKissack, P. C. Flossie & the fox **E**
McKissack, P. C. Mirandy and Brother Wind **E**
Mendez, P. The black snowman **E**
Myers, W. D. Fast Sam, Cool Clyde, and Stuff (6 and up) **Fic**
Myers, W. D. The Mouse rap (6 and up) **Fic**
Myers, W. D. Scorpions (6 and up) **Fic**
Myers, W. D. The young landlords (6 and up) **Fic**
Petry, A. L. Tituba of Salem Village (6 and up) **Fic**
Schroeder, A. Ragtime Tumpie **E**
Scott, A. H. Sam **E**
Sebestyen, O. Words by heart (5 and up) **Fic**
Steptoe, J. Stevie **E**
Tate, E. E. Just an overnight guest (4-6) **Fic**
Taylor, M. D. The gold Cadillac (3-5) **Fic**
Taylor, M. D. Roll of thunder, hear my cry (4 and up) **Fic**
Taylor, M. D. Song of the trees (4 and up) **Fic**
Udry, J. M. What Mary Jo shared **E**
Voigt, C. Come a stranger (6 and up) **Fic**
Wagner, J. J. T. (3-6) **Fic**
Walter, M. P. Have a happy— (4-6) **Fic**
Walter, M. P. Justin and the best biscuits in the world (3-6) **Fic**
Walter, M. P. Mariah keeps cool (3-5) **Fic**
Walter, M. P. My mama needs me **E**
Walter, M. P. Two and too much **E**
Wilkinson, B. S. Ludell (6 and up) **Fic**
Williams, V. B. Cherries and cherry pits **E**
Winter, J. Follow the drinking gourd **E**
Yarbrough, C. Cornrows **E**
Yarbrough, C. The shimmershine queens (4-6) **Fic**

Folklore

Bang, M. Wiley and the Hairy Man (1-4) **398.2**
Hamilton, V. The people could fly: American black folktales (4 and up) **398.2**
Lester, J. Further tales of Uncle Remus (4-6) **398.2**
Lester, J. The knee-high man, and other tales (k-3) **398.2**
Lester, J. More tales of Uncle Remus (4-6) **398.2**
Lester, J. The tales of Uncle Remus (4-6) **398.2**
Parks, V. D. Jump! the adventures of Brer Rabbit (1-4) **398.2**
Parks, V. D. Jump again! more adventures of Brer Rabbit (1-4) **398.2**
Parks, V. D. Jump on over! the adventures of Brer Rabbit and his family (1-4) **398.2**
San Souci, R. The boy and the ghost (k-3) **398.2**
Sanfield, S. The adventures of High John the Conqueror (4 and up) **398.2**

History

McKissack, P. C. The Civil Rights Movement in America from 1865 to the present (5 and up) **323.4**

History—Sources

The Black Americans: a history in their own words, 1619-1983 (6 and up) **305.8**

Poetry

Brooks, G. Bronzeville boys and girls (2-5) **811**
Clifton, L. Everett Anderson's goodbye (k-3) **811**
Fields, J. The green lion of Zion Street (k-3) **811**
Giovanni, N. Spin a soft black song: poems for children (3-6) **811**
Greenfield, E. Daydreamers (3-6) **811**
Greenfield, E. Honey, I love, and other love poems (2-4) **811**
Greenfield, E. Nathaniel talking (2-4) **811**
Grimes, N. Something on my mind **811**
Hughes, L. The dream keeper, and other poems (5 and up) **811**

The **Blacks** in America. Spangler, E.
In The In America series **305.8**

Blackwell, Elizabeth, 1821-1910

About

Wilson, D. C. I will be a doctor! (5 and up) **92**

Blackwood, Basil Temple, 1870-1917
(il) Belloc, H. The bad child's book of beasts, and More beasts for worse children, and A moral alphabet **821**

The **bladder,** the straw, and the shoe. Afanas'ev, A. N.
In Afanas'ev, A. N. Russian fairy tales p590 **398.2**

Blades, Ann
Mary of Mile 18 (2-4) **Fic**
(il) Alderson, S. A. Ida and the wool smugglers **E**

Blaine, Marge
The terrible thing that happened at our house E
Blair, David Nelson
The land and people of Bolivia (5 and up) **984**
Blair's nightmare. Snyder, Z. K. See note under Snyder, Z. K. The headless cupid **Fic**
Blaisdell, Elinore
(il) De la Mare, W. Rhymes and verses **821**
Blaisdell, Elizabeth
(il) Lamb, C. Tales from Shakespeare **822.3**
Blake, Quentin, 1932-
Quentin Blake's ABC **E**
(il) Aiken, J. Arabel and Mortimer **Fic**
(il) Dahl, R. Matilda **Fic**
(il) Kipling, R. How the camel got his hump **Fic**
(il) Mahy, M. The great piratical rumbustification & The librarian and the robbers **Fic**
(il) Mahy, M. Nonstop nonsense **828**
(il) Nash, O. Custard and company: poems **811**
(il) Of quarks, quasars, and other quirks. See Of quarks, quasars, and other quirks **821.008**
(jt. auth) Yeoman, J. Old Mother Hubbard's dog dresses up **E**
Blankets
Fiction
Keller, H. Geraldine's blanket **E**
Blassingame, Wyatt
The look-it-up book of presidents (5 and up) **920**
The strange armadillo (4 and up) **599.3**
Wonders of crows (5 and up) **598**
Wonders of egrets, bitterns, and herons (5 and up) **598**
Wonders of sharks (4 and up) **597**
Blaustein, Hank
(il) Bawden, N. Squib **Fic**
Blegvad, Erik
Self-portrait: Erik Blegvad (4 and up) **92**
(il) Blegvad, L. Anna Banana and me **E**
(il) Craft, R. The winter bear **E**
(il) Kendall, C. The Gammage cup **Fic**
(il) Langton, J. The fragile flag **Fic**
(il) Norton, M. Bed-knob and broomstick **Fic**
(il) Stolz, M. Cat walk **Fic**
(il) This little pig-a-wig, and other rhymes about pigs. See This little pig-a-wig, and other rhymes about pigs **398.8**
(il) Viorst, J. The tenth good thing about Barney **E**
See/See also pages in the following book(s):
Sendak, M. Caldecott & Co.: notes on books and pictures p129-30 **028.5**
Blegvad, Lenore
Anna Banana and me **E**
(comp) This little pig-a-wig, and other rhymes about pigs. See This little pig-a-wig, and other rhymes about pigs **398.8**
Bleifeld, Maurice
Experimenting with a microscope (5 and up) **502.8**
Blériot, Louis, 1872-1936
About
Provensen, A. The glorious flight: across the Channel with Louis Blériot, July 25, 1909 (1-4) **92**
Bley, Edgar S.
The best singing games for children of all ages **796.1**
Blia Xiong
Spagnoli, C. Nine-in-one, Grr! Grr! **398.2**
Blimps *See* Airships
Blimps. Munro, R. **629.133**
Blind
Alexander, S. H. Mom can't see me (3-5) **362.4**
Bergman, T. Seeing in special ways (1-3) **362.4**
Butler, B. Maggie by my side (4 and up) **362.4**
Hunter, E. F. Child of the silent night [biography of Laura Dewey Bridgman] (3-5) **92**
Peare, C. O. The Helen Keller story (5 and up) **92**
Books and reading
See also Talking books
Jensen, V. A. Catching **E**
Jensen, V. A. Red thread riddles **793.73**
Books and reading—Bibliography
For younger readers: braille and talking books **011.6**
Fiction
Bawden, N. The witch's daughter (4 and up) **Fic**
Coutant, H. The gift (2-5) **Fic**
Keats, E. J. Apt. 3 **E**
Martin, B. Knots on a counting rope **E**
Pearson, S. Happy birthday, Grampie **E**
Taylor, T. The cay (5 and up) **Fic**
Yolen, J. The seeing stick (2-4) **Fic**

Blind, Dogs for the *See* Guide dogs
Bliven, Bruce, 1916-
The American Revolution, 1760-1783 (5 and up) **973.3**
The story of D-Day: June 6, 1944 (5 and up) **940.54**
Blizzards
Fiction
Clifford, E. Help! I'm a prisoner in the library (3-5) **Fic**
Noble, T. H. Apple tree Christmas **E**
Bloch, Lucienne S., 1909-
(il) Hurd, E. T. Starfish **593.9**
The **block** book. Couture, S. A. **E**
Block city. Stevenson, R. L. **821**
Blockhead Hans. Andersen, H. C.
In The Yellow fairy book p313-18 **398.2**
Blocksma, Dewey, 1943-
(jt. auth) Blocksma, M. Action contraptions **745.592**
Blocksma, Mary
Action contraptions (2-5) **745.592**
Blood, Charles L., 1929-
The goat in the rug **E**
Blood
Asimov, I. How did we find out about blood? (5 and up) **612.1**
Cole, J. Cuts, breaks, bruises, and burns (3-5) **612**
Showers, P. A drop of blood (k-3) **612.1**
Circulation
Parker, S. The heart and blood (4 and up) **612.1**
Diseases
See also Leukemia
The **blood-and-thunder** adventure on Hurricane Peak. Mahy, M. **Fic**
Bloom, Lloyd
(il) Alexander, S. Nadia the Willful **E**
(il) Burleigh, R. A man named Thoreau **92**
(il) Johnston, T. Yonder **E**
(il) Jukes, M. Like Jake and me **Fic**
(il) MacLachlan, P. Arthur, for the very first time **Fic**
(il) Poems for Jewish holidays. See Poems for Jewish holidays **811.008**
Bloom, Mary
(il) Curtis, P. Greff, the story of a guide dog **636.7**
Blos, Joan W.
A gathering of days: a New England girl's journal, 1830-32 (6 and up) **Fic**
The grandpa days **E**
Old Henry **E**
See/See also pages in the following book(s):
Newbery and Caldecott Medal books, 1976-1985 p65-73 **028.5**
Blossom Culp and the sleep of death. Peck, R. See note under Peck, R. The ghost belonged to me **Fic**
The **blossom** on the bough. Dowden, A. O. T. **582.16**
A **Blossom** promise. Byars, B. C. See note under Byars, B. C. The not-just-anybody family **Fic**
The **Blossoms** and the Green Phantom. Byars, B. C. See note under Byars, B. C. The not-just-anybody family **Fic**
The **Blossoms** meet the Vulture Lady. Byars, B. C. See note under Byars, B. C. The not-just-anybody family **Fic**
Blow me a kiss, Miss Lilly. Carlstrom, N. W. **E**
The **blue** balloon. Inkpen, M. **E**
Blue Beard. Perrault, C.
In Best-loved folktales of the world p28-32 **398.2**
In The Blue fairy book p290-95 **398.2**
In The Classic fairy tales p106-09 **398.2**
Blue bird
Aulnoy, Madame d'. The Blue Bird
In The Green fairy book p1-26 **398.2**
The **blue** book of Hob stories. Mayne, W. See note under Mayne, W. The green book of Hob stories **E**
A **blue-eyed** daisy. Rylant, C. **Fic**
A **blue-eyed** daisy [excerpt]. Rylant, C.
In Face to face: a collection of stories by celebrated Soviet and American writers p223-28 **S C**
The **Blue** fairy book (4-6) **398.2**
Blue light
Grimm, J. The blue light
In Grimm, J. The complete Grimm's fairy tales p530-34 **398.2**
Blue Monday and Friday the Thirteenth. Perl, L. **398**
Blue moose. Pinkwater, D. M. **Fic**
Blue Mountains
The Blue Mountains
In The Yellow fairy book p256-64 **398.2**
Blue rose
Baring, M. The blue rose
In Shedlock, M. L. The art of the story-teller p204-12 **372.6**
Blue sea. Kalan, R. **E**
Blue silver. Sandburg, C.
In Sandburg, C. Rootabaga stories pt 2 p175-79 **S C**
In Sandburg, C. The Sandburg treasury p159-60 **818**

The **blue** stone. Kennedy, R.
In Kennedy, R. Collected stories p37-96 S C

Blue Sun
In The Monkey's haircut, and other stories told by the Maya p107-12 398.2

The **blue** whale. Grosvenor, D. K. 599.5

Blue willow. Gates, D. Fic

Bluebeard (Folk tale)
Perrault, C. Blue Beard
In Best-loved folktales of the world p28-32 398.2
In The Blue fairy book p290-95 398.2
In The Classic fairy tales p106-09 398.2
Perrault, C. Bluebeard
In Sleeping beauty & other favourite fairy tales p33-40 398.2

Blueberries for Sal. McCloskey, R. E

Blumberg, Rhoda, 1917-
Commodore Perry in the land of the Shogun (5 and up) 952
The great American gold rush (5 and up) 979.4
The incredible journey of Lewis and Clark (5 and up) 978
Sharks (4 and up) 597

Blume, Judy
Are you there God? it's me, Margaret (5 and up) Fic
Freckle juice (2-4) Fic
Fudge-a-mania. See note under Blume, J. Tales of a fourth grade nothing Fic
It's not the end of the world (4-6) Fic
Just as long as we're together (5 and up) Fic
Otherwise known as Sheila the Great (4-6) Fic
The Pain and the Great One E
Superfudge. See note under Blume, J. Tales of a fourth grade nothing Fic
Tales of a fourth grade nothing (3-6) Fic
Tales of a fourth grade nothing [excerpt]
In The Random House book of humor for children p3-14 817.008
Then again, maybe I won't (5 and up) Fic

Blumpoe the Grumpoe meets Arnold the cat. Okimoto, J. D. E

Boar out there. Rylant, C.
In Rylant, C. Every living thing p15-18 S C

Boars
Nicholson, D. Wild boars (3-6) 599.73

The **boasting** contest. Yep, L.
In Yep, L. The rainbow people p106-15 398.2

Boat book. Gibbons, G. 387.2

Boating. Babbitt, N.
In Babbitt, N. The Devil's other storybook p25-32 S C

Boats, Submarine *See* Submarines; Submersibles

Boats. Barton, B. 387.2

Boats. Rockwell, A. F. 387.2

Boats and boating
See also Sailing; Ships
Barton, B. Boats (k-1) 387.2
Gibbons, G. Boat book (k-2) 387.2
Rockwell, A. F. Boats (k-1) 387.2
Scarry, H. Life on a barge (3-6) 386
Scarry, H. Life on a fishing boat (3-6) 639.2
Wyler, R. Science fun with toy boats and planes (2-4) 507
Fiction
Maestro, B. Ferryboat E
Rand, G. Salty dog E

Bob and Ray
Prodigy Street
In The Random House book of humor for children p176-80 817.008

Bobby Baseball. Smith, R. K. Fic

Bobcat
Ryden, H. Bobcat (5 and up) 599.74

Bobo's dream. Alexander, M. G. E

Boccaccio, Giovanni, 1313-1375
Decameron; adaptation. See Wise, W. The black falcon Fic

Bock, William Sauts, 1939-
(il) Bealer, A. W. Only the names remain 970.004
(il) Wolfson, E. From Abenaki to Zuni 970.004

Bodart, Joni *See* Bodart-Talbot, Joni

Bodart-Talbot, Joni
Booktalk! 2-3 028

Bodecker, N. M., d. 1988
It's raining, said John Twaining (k-2) 398.8
Snowman sniffles, and other verse (3-5) 811
(il) Eager, E. Half magic Fic
(il) Eager, E. Seven-day magic Fic

Bodies. Brenner, B. 612

The **bodies** in the Bessledorf Hotel. Naylor, P. R. See note under Naylor, P. R. Bernie and the Bessledorf ghost Fic

Body, Human *See* Anatomy, Human; Physiology

Bodybuilding (Weight lifting) *See* Weight lifting

Boehm, David A. (David Alfred), 1914-
Japan—in pictures. See Japan—in pictures 952

Bogart, Jo Ellen
Daniel's dog E

Boggart
Briggs, K. M. The boggart
In Best-loved folktales of the world p211-12 398.2

Boggs, Ralph Steele, 1901-
Don Demonio's mother-in-law
In Best-loved folktales of the world p160-65 398.2
Tonino and the fairies
In Best-loved folktales of the world p166-69 398.2

Bogs *See* Marshes

Bohemia (Czechoslovakia)
Folklore
See Folklore—Bohemia (Czechoslovakia)

Boiko, Claire
We interrupt this program—
In The Big book of Christmas plays p200-12 808.82

Bold knight, the apples of youth, and the water of life
Afanas'ev, A. N. The bold knight, the apples of youth, and the water of life
In Afanas'ev, A. N. Russian fairy tales p314-20 398.2

Bolivia
Blair, D. N. The land and people of Bolivia (5 and up) 984
Morrison, M. Bolivia (4 and up) 984

Bollen, Marilyn Sadler
Alistair in outer space. See note under Bollen, M. S. Alistair's elephant E
Alistair underwater. See note under Bollen, M. S. Alistair's elephant E
Alistair's elephant. See note under Bollen, M. S. Alistair underwater E
Alistair's elephant E
Alistair's time machine. See note under Bollen, M. S. Alistair underwater E

Bollen, Roger
(il) Bollen, M. S. Alistair's elephant E

Bolliger, Max
Tales of a long afternoon (k-3) 398.2

Bolognese, Don
Pen & ink (4 and up) 741.2
(il) Brenner, B. Wagon wheels E
(il) Gates, D. The warrior goddess: Athena 292
(jt. auth) Raphael, E. Drawing history: Ancient Egypt 741

Bonaparte, Napoleon *See* Napoleon I, Emperor of the French, 1769-1821

Bond, Felicia, 1954-
Poinsettia & her family E
Poinsettia and the firefighters E
(il) Branley, F. M. The sky is full of stars 523.8
(il) Brown, M. W. Big red barn E
(il) Kramer, S. How to think like a scientist 507
(il) Numeroff, L. J. If you give a mouse a cookie E

Bond, Michael, 1926-
A bear called Paddington (2-5) Fic
The complete adventures of Olga da Polga (2-5) Fic
More about Paddington. See note under Bond, M. A bear called Paddington Fic
Olga carries on
In Bond, M. The complete adventures of Olga da Polga p253-387 Fic
Olga meets her match
In Bond, M. The complete adventures of Olga da Polga p129-252 Fic
Olga takes charge
In Bond, M. The complete adventures of Olga da Polga p389-[512] Fic
Paddington abroad. See note under Bond, M. A bear called Paddington Fic
Paddington at large. See note under Bond, M. A bear called Paddington Fic
Paddington at the fair. See note under Bond, M. A bear called Paddington Fic
Paddington at the seaside. See note under Bond, M. A bear called Paddington Fic
Paddington at the tower. See note under Bond, M. A bear called Paddington Fic
Paddington at the zoo. See note under Bond, M. A bear called Paddington Fic
Paddington at work. See note under Bond, M. A bear called Paddington Fic
Paddington Bear. See note under Bond, M. A bear called Paddington Fic
Paddington goes to town. See note under Bond, M. A bear called Paddington Fic
Paddington helps out. See note under Bond, M. A bear called Paddington Fic
Paddington marches on. See note under Bond, M. A bear called Paddington Fic
Paddington on screen. See note under Bond, M. A bear called Paddington Fic
Paddington on top. See note under Bond, M. A bear called Paddington Fic

Bond, Michael, 1926-—*Continued*
Paddington takes the air. See note under Bond, M. A bear called Paddington Fic
Paddington takes the test. See note under Bond, M. A bear called Paddington Fic
Paddington takes to TV. See note under Bond, M. A bear called Paddington Fic
Paddington's art exhibition. See note under Bond, M. A bear called Paddington Fic
Paddington's lucky day. See note under Bond, M. A bear called Paddington Fic
Paddington's storybook (2-5) S C
Contents: A spot of decorating; Paddington cleans up; Paddington dines out; A visit to the bank; A day by the sea; Something nasty in the kitchen; Paddington and the "finishing touch"; Paddington steps out; Paddington and the "cold snap"; Paddington and the Christmas pantomime
The tales of Olga da Polga (2-5) Fic
also in Bond, M. The complete adventures of Olga da Polga p5-128 Fic
Bond, Nancy
A place to come back to (6 and up) Fic
A string in the harp (6 and up) Fic
Bonds of affection. DuBois, G.
In Holiday plays round the year p151-60 812.008
Boneless. San Souci, R.
In San Souci, R. Short & shivery p127-32 398.2
Bones
See also Skeleton
Balestrino, P. The skeleton inside you (k-3) 611
Parker, S. Skeleton (4 and up) 596
Fiction
Steig, W. The amazing bone E
Bones, bones, dinosaur bones. Barton, B. E
Bonfires and broomsticks. Norton, M.
In Norton, M. Bed-knob and broomstick p97-189 Fic
Bonforte, Lisa
(il) Berger, G. Whales 599.5
Bong Way Wong *See* El Chino
Bonnard, Pierre, 1867-1947
See/See also pages in the following book(s):
Goffstein, M. B. Lives of the artists (5 and up) 920
Bonners, Susan, 1947-
A penguin year (k-3) 598
(il) Esbensen, B. J. Cold stars and fireflies 811
(il) Newton, J. R. A forest is reborn 574.5
(il) Newton, J. R. Rain shadow 574.5
Bonnett, Leslie
Simple Wang
In Best-loved folktales of the world p528-31 398.2
Bonsall, Crosby Newell, 1921-
The amazing, the incredible super dog E
The day I had to play with my sister E
Piggle E
Tell me some more E
Who's a pest? E
Who's afraid of the dark? E
Bony-Legs. Cole, J. 398.2
Boo!. Crossley-Holland, K.
In Crossley-Holland, K. British folk tales p338 398.2
A **book** about names. Meltzer, M. 929.4
Book awards *See* Literary prizes
The **book** finder. See Dreyer, S. S. The bookfinder 011.6
Book illustration *See* Illustration of books
Book industries and trade
See also Publishers and publishing
Aliki. How a book is made (2-5) 686
Greenfeld, H. Books: from writer to reader (6 and up) 070.5
Book of a thousand and one nights *See* Arabian nights
The **book** of Adam to Moses. Segal, L. G. 222
A **book** of Americans. Benét, R. 811
Book of animal riddles, Bennett Cerf's. Cerf, B. 793.73
Book of Bible stories, Tomie dePaola's. Bible. Selections 220.9
Book of children's verse in America, The Oxford 811.008
Book of children's verse, The Oxford 821.008
Book of Christmas carols, Tomie dePaola's 782.28
The **book** of eagles. Sattler, H. R. 598
Book of flight for young people, The Smithsonian. Boyne, W. J. 629.13
Book of Greek gods and heroes, The Macmillan. Low, A. 292
The **book** of holidays around the world. Van Straalen, A. 394.2
Book of humor for children, The Random House 817.008

The **Book** of Jonah. Spier, P. 224
The **Book** of knowledge. See The New book of knowledge 031
Book of nursery and Mother Goose rhymes, Marguerite de Angeli's 398.8
Book of nursery rhymes, Nicola Bayley's 398.8
The **book** of pigericks: pig limericks. Lobel, A. 811
Book of poems, Tomie dePaola's 808.81
Book of poetry for children, The Random House 821.008
Book of popular science, The New 503
Book of riddles, Bennett Cerf's. Cerf, B. 793.73
A **book** of seasons. Provensen, A. E
The **book** of think. Burns, M. 153.4
The **book** of three. Alexander, L. Fic
A **book** of vegetables. Sobol, H. L. 635
The **book** of where. Bell, N. 910
Bookbird 028.505
The **bookfinder**. Dreyer, S. S. 011.6
Booklist 028.1
Books
See also Printing
Aliki. How a book is made (2-5) 686
Greenfeld, H. Books: from writer to reader (6 and up) 070.5
Conservation and restoration
Greenfield, J. Books: their care and repair 025.7
Reviews
Appraisal 016.5
The Best in children's books 028.1
Bookbird 028.505
Booklist 028.1
Bulletin of the Center for Children's Books 028.1
Children's literature review 028.5
Emergency Librarian 027.6205
England, C. ChildView: evaluating and reviewing materials for children 028.5
Five Owls 028.505
Gillespie, J. T. Juniorplots 3: a book talk guide for use with readers ages 12-16 028.1
Gillespie, J. T. Juniorplots: a book talk manual for teachers and librarians 028.1
Gillespie, J. T. More juniorplots: a guide for teachers and librarians 028.1
The Horn Book Guide to Children's and Young Adult Books 028.505
The Horn Book Magazine 028.505
Journal of Youth Services in Libraries 027.6205
Kimmel, M. M. For reading out loud! 028.5
The Kobrin Letter 028.505
Publisher's Weekly 070.505
School Library Journal 027.805
Science Books & Films 016.5
Spirt, D. L. Introducing bookplots 3 028.1
The Web 028.1
Reviews—Bibliography
Ettlinger, J. R. T. Choosing books for young people v2 011.6
Reviews—Indexes
Children's book review index 028.1
Books, Talking *See* Talking books
Books & basics. See Matthews, J. G. ClipArt & dynamic designs for libraries & media centers 021.7
Books about Negro life for children. See The Black experience in children's books 016.3058
Books and reading
Bauer, C. F. Celebrations 808.8
Bauer, C. F. This way to books 028.5
Bodart-Talbot, J. Booktalk! 2-3 028
Butler, D. Cushla and her books 362.4
Chambers, A. Introducing books to children 028.5
Cook, E. The ordinary and the fabulous 028.5
England, C. ChildView: evaluating and reviewing materials for children 028.5
Gillespie, J. T. Juniorplots 3: a book talk guide for use with readers ages 12-16 028.1
Gillespie, J. T. Juniorplots: a book talk manual for teachers and librarians 028.1
Gillespie, J. T. More juniorplots: a guide for teachers and librarians 028.1
Greene, E. Storytelling: a selected annotated bibliography 016.3726
Hazard, P. Books, children, and men 028.5
Hearne, B. G. Choosing books for children 028.5
Kimmel, M. M. For reading out loud! 028.5
Kobrin, B. Eyeopeners! 028.5
MacDonald, M. R. Booksharing: 101 programs to use with preschoolers 027.62
National Council of Teachers of English. Committee on Literature in the Elementary Language Arts. Raising readers 028.5
Once upon a time—: celebrating the magic of children's books in honor of the twentieth anniversary of Reading is Fundamental 028.5
Rochman, H. Tales of love and terror 028
Spirt, D. L. Introducing bookplots 3 028.1
Thomas, R. L. Primaryplots 028

Books and reading—*Continued*
Trelease, J. The new read-aloud handbook **028.5**
Best books
Adamson, L. G. A reference guide to historical fiction for children and young adults **016.8**
Association for Library Service to Children (U.S.). Notable Children's Books, 1976-1980, Reevaluation Committee. Notable children's books, 1976-1980 **011.6**
Barstow, B. Beyond picture books **011.6**
Baskin, B. H. Books for the gifted child **011.6**
Best books for children, preschool through grade 6 **011.6**
The Best in children's books **028.1**
The Best science books & A-V materials for children **016.5**
Bookbird **028.505**
Booklist **028.1**
Books for children **011.6**
Carroll, F. L. Exciting, funny, scary, short, different, and sad books kids like about animals, science, sports, families, songs, and other things **011.6**
Cianciolo, P. J. Picture books for children **011.6**
Freeman, J. Books kids will sit still for **011.6**
The Horn Book Magazine **028.505**
Kennedy, D. M. Science & technology in fact and fiction: a guide to children's books **016.5**
National Council of Teachers of English. Committee on the Elementary School Booklist. Adventuring with books **011.6**
National Council of Teachers of English. Committee on the Junior High and Middle School Booklist. Your reading: a booklist for junior high and middle school students **011.6**
Notable children's trade books in the field of social studies **016.3**
Olexer, M. E. Poetry anthologies for children and young people **011.6**
Outstanding science trade books for children **016.5**
Wilson, G. Books for children to read alone **011.6**
Fiction
Browne, A. I like books **E**
Greenwald, S. It all began with Jane Eyre (6 and up) **Fic**
Periodicals
Wilson Library Bulletin **020.5**
Poetry
Good books, good times! (1-3) **811.008**
Books, children, and men. Hazard, P. **028.5**
Books for children *See* Children's literature
Books for children **011.6**
Books for children to read alone. Wilson, G. **011.6**
Books for the gifted child. Baskin, B. H. **011.6**
Books: from writer to reader. Greenfeld, H. **070.5**
Books in Spanish for children and young adults: an annotated guide [series I-V]. Schon, I. **011.6**
Books kids will sit still for. Freeman, J. **011.6**
Books: their care and repair. Greenfield, J. **025.7**
Books to help children cope with separation and loss v3. Bernstein, J. E. **016.3627**
Booksharing: 101 programs to use with preschoolers. MacDonald, M. R. **027.62**
Booktalk! 2-3. Bodart-Talbot, J. **028**
Booktalk: occasional writing on literature and children. Chambers, A. **028.5**
The **bookworm**. Chaloner, G.
In Holiday plays round the year p212-19 **812.008**
The **Boomer** fireman's fast Sooner hound. Conroy, J.
In The Scott, Foresman anthology of children's literature p368-70 **808.8**
Boot weather. Vigna, J. **E**
Booth, George, 1926-
(il) Van Laan, N. Possum come a-knockin' **E**
Booth, Graham, 1935-
(il) Branley, F. M. Weight and weightlessness **531**
(il) My tang's tungled and other ridiculous situations. See My tang's tungled and other ridiculous situations **821.008**
(il) Taylor, M. Henry the explorer **E**
Booth, Jerry
The big beast book (3-6) **567.9**
Boots *See* Shoes
Boots and the troll
Asbjørnsen, P. C. Boots and the troll
In Best-loved folktales of the world p296-300 **398.2**
Boots made of buffalo leather
Grimm, J. The boots of buffalo-leather
In Grimm, J. The complete Grimm's fairy tales p808-11 **398.2**
The **boots** of buffalo-leather. Grimm, J.
In Grimm, J. The complete Grimm's fairy tales p808-11 **398.2**

Bored—nothing to do! Spier, P. E

Borglum, Gutzon, 1867-1941

About

St. George, J. The Mount Rushmore story (6 and up) 92

Borland, Hal, 1900-1978

Plants of Christmas (5 and up) 398

Born a monkey, live a monkey. Sherlock, Sir P. M.

In Sherlock, Sir P. M. West Indian folk-tales p135-43 398.2

Born different. Drimmer, F. 920

Born into light. Jacobs, P. S. Fic

Born to the land: an American portrait. Ashabranner, B. K. 978.9

Bornstein, Ruth Lercher, 1927-

(il) MacLachlan, P. Mama One, Mama Two E

Bornstein, Sandy

What makes you what you are (5 and up) 575.1

Borrowed children. Lyon, G. E. Fic

The **Borrowers**. Norton, M. Fic

The **Borrowers** afield. Norton, M. See note under Norton, M. The Borrowers Fic

The **Borrowers** afloat. Norton, M. See note under Norton, M. The Borrowers Fic

The **Borrowers** aloft. Norton, M. See note under Norton, M. The Borrowers Fic

The **Borrowers** avenged. Norton, M. See note under Norton, M. The Borrowers Fic

Borski, Lucia Merecka

The jolly tailor

In Rainy day: stories and poems p23-33 808.8

Borten, Helen

Halloween (1-3) 394.2

Borton, Elizabeth *See* Treviño, Elizabeth Borton de, 1904-

Boschung, Herbert T., Jr.

The Audubon Society field guide to North American fishes, whales, and dolphins. See The Audubon Society field guide to North American fishes, whales, and dolphins 597

Boston, L. M. (Lucy Maria), 1892-1990

The children of Green Knowe (4-6) Fic

An enemy at Green Knowe. See note under Boston, L. M. The children of Green Knowe Fic

The river at Green Knowe. See note under Boston, L. M. The children of Green Knowe Fic

The sea egg (3-5) Fic

A stranger at Green Knowe. See note under Boston, L. M. The children of Green Knowe Fic

Treasure of Green Knowe. See note under Boston, L. M. The children of Green Knowe Fic

See/See also pages in the following book(s):

Townsend, J. R. A sense of story p23-34 028.5

Boston, Lucy Maria *See* Boston, L. M. (Lucy Maria), 1892-1990

Boston, Peter, 1918-

(il) Boston, L. M. The children of Green Knowe Fic

(il) Boston, L. M. The sea egg Fic

Boston (Mass.)

Fiction

Fleischman, P. Saturnalia (5 and up) Fic

Forbes, E. Johnny Tremain (5 and up) Fic

Lowry, L. Taking care of Terrific (5 and up) Fic

McCloskey, R. Make way for ducklings E

Rappaport, D. The Boston coffee party E

Wibberley, L. John Treegate's musket (6 and up) Fic

Boston Celtics (Basketball team)

Boyd, B. C. Hoops: behind the scenes with the Boston Celtics (5 and up) 796.323

The **Boston** coffee party. Rappaport, D. E

Boston Massacre, 1770

Phelan, M. K. The story of the Boston Massacre (5 and up) 973.3

See/See also pages in the following book(s):

Davis, B. Black heroes of the American Revolution p33-40 (5 and up) 973.3

Boston Post Road. See Gibbons, G. From path to highway: the story of the Boston Post Road 388.1

Botany

See also Plants

Lerner, C. Plant families (4 and up) 582

Ecology

Cole, J. Plants in winter (k-3) 581.5

Terminology

See also Plant names, Popular

Botany, Economic

See also Plant conservation

Rahn, J. E. More plants that changed history (5 and up) 909

Botswana

Botswana—in pictures (5 and up) 968.83

Botswana—in pictures (5 and up) **968.83**

Bouki dances the kokioko
In The Magic orange tree, and other Haitian folktales p79-86 **398.2**

Bouki rents a horse. Courlander, H.
In Best-loved folktales of the world p738-40 **398.2**

Bouncing and bending light. Taylor, B. **535**

Bourhill, E. J.
Fairy tales from South Africa; adaptation. See Berger, T. Black fairy tales **398.2**

Bourns, Phillips
(il) Casagrande, L. B. Focus on Mexico **972**

Bowden, Joan Chase, 1925-
Why the tides ebb and flow (k-2) **398.2**

Bowman, James Cloyd, 1880-1961
The pig-headed wife
In Best-loved folktales of the world p384-86 **398.2**
In The Scott, Foresman anthology of children's literature p248-49 **808.8**
Timo and the Princess Vendla
In The Scott, Foresman anthology of children's literature p249-51 **808.8**

Bowman, Leslie W.
(il) Kinsey-Warnock, N. The Canada geese quilt **Fic**
(il) Patterson, N. R. The Christmas cup **Fic**
(il) Treviño, E. B. de. El Güero **Fic**

Box and Cox. Chetwin, G. **E**

The **box** of delights; or, When the wolves were running. Masefield, J. **Fic**

Box Turtle at Long Pond. George, W. T. **E**

The **box** with red wheels. Petersham, M. **E**

A **boy,** a dog, and a friend. Mayer, M. See note under Mayer, M. A boy, a dog, and a frog **E**

A **boy,** a dog, and a frog. Mayer, M. **E**

The **boy,** Abe. Smith, B.
In Holiday plays round the year p161-68 **812.008**

The **boy** and the ghost. San Souci, R. **398.2**

The **Boy** and the wolves
In The Yellow fairy book p138-40 **398.2**

The **boy,** his sisters, and the magic horse. Timpanelli, G.
In Timpanelli, G. Tales from the roof of the world p1-13 **398.2**

Boy meets girl [play]. Stone, P.
In Free to be—you and me p24-31 **810.8**

The **boy** of the three-year nap. Snyder, D. **398.2**

Boy Pu-nia and the king of the sharks
MacDonald, M. R. Punia and the king of the sharks
In MacDonald, M. R. Twenty tellable tales p163-73 **372.6**

The **boy** who ate dog biscuits. Sachs, E.-A. **E**

Boy who could keep a secret
The boy who could keep a secret
In The Scott, Foresman anthology of children's literature p265-71 **808.8**

Boy who cried "Wolf"
Rockwell, A. F. The boy who cried wolf
In Rockwell, A. F. Puss in boots, and other stories p40-41 **398.2**
Wolf! Wolf!
In The Tall book of nursery tales p74-76 **398.2**

The **boy** who drew unicorns. Yolen, J.
In Face to face: a collection of stories by celebrated Soviet and American writers p141-51 **S C**
In Yolen, J. The faery flag p48-57 **S C**

The **Boy** who learned the songs of birds
In The Naked bear p60-66 **398.2**

The **boy** who owned the school. Paulsen, G. **Fic**

The **boy** who reversed himself. Sleator, W. **Fic**

The **boy** who shot the star to find his friend. Mayo, G.
In Mayo, G. Star tales p65-68 **398.2**

The **boy** who took care of the pigs. Brenner, A.
In Bauer, C. F. Celebrations p152-54 **808.8**

The **Boy** who turned himself into a peanut
In The Baby's story book p26-29 **398.2**

The **boy** who was followed home. Mahy, M. **E**

The **boy** who was never afraid. Smedberg, A.
In The Scott, Foresman anthology of children's literature p244-47 **808.8**

The **Boy** who was sacrificed
In The Whistling skeleton p73-83 **398.2**

Boyd, Brendan C.
Hoops: behind the scenes with the Boston Celtics (5 and up) **796.323**

Boyd, Candy Dawson, 1946-
Charlie Pippin (4-6) **Fic**

Boyd, Patti
(il) Antonacci, R. J. Basketball for young champions 796.323

The **boyhood** of Fionn. Stephens, J.
In Stephens, J. Irish fairy tales p35-89 398.2

Boyne, Walter J., 1929-
The Smithsonian book of flight for young people (4 and up) 629.13

Boynton, Sandra
A is for angry E

Boys

Employment

See Children—Employment

A **boy's** Thanksgiving Day. See Child, L. M. F. Over the river and through the wood 811

Bozzo, Frank
(il) McHargue, G. The beasts of never 398

Brady, Irene, 1943-
(il) McClung, R. M. Gorilla 599.88
(il) McClung, R. M. Lili: a giant panda of Sichuan 599.74
(il) McNulty, F. Peeping in the shell 639.9

Bragdon, Lillian J.
(jt. auth) Harris, J. The land and people of France 944

Brahman, the tiger and the jackal
Steel, F. A. W. The tiger, the Brahman, and the jackal
In The Scott, Foresman anthology of children's literature p341-43 808.8
The Tiger, the Brahman, and the jackal
In Best-loved folktales of the world p580-83 398.2

Braille books *See* Blind—Books and reading

Brain
Bruun, R. D. The brain—what it is, what it does (1-3) 612.8
Facklam, M. The brain (6 and up) 612.8
Martin, P. D. Messengers to the brain: our fantastic five senses (5 and up) 612.8
Parker, S. The brain and nervous system (4 and up) 612.8
Sharp, P. Brain power! (4 and up) 612.8
Silverstein, A. World of the brain (6 and up) 612.8
Stafford, P. Your two brains (5 and up) 612.8
Yepsen, R. B. Smarten up! how to increase your brain power (5 and up) 153

See/See also pages in the following book(s):
Arnold, C. Pain: what is it? how do we deal with it? p30-39 (6 and up) 616

The **brain**. Facklam, M. 612.8

The **brain** and nervous system. Parker, S. 612.8

Brain power! Sharp, P. 612.8

The **brain—what** it is, what it does. Bruun, R. D. 612.8

Bramwell, Martyn
Mammals: the small plant-eaters (4 and up) 599
The oceans (4-6) 551.46
Rivers and lakes (4-6) 551.48
Weather (4-6) 551.5

Brancato, Robin F.
White chocolate
In Connections: short stories by outstanding writers for young adults p84-93 S C

Brandenberg, Aliki *See* Aliki

Brandenberg, Franz, 1932-
Aunt Nina and her nephews and nieces E
Aunt Nina, goodnight. See note under Brandenberg, F. Aunt Nina and her nephews, and nieces E
Aunt Nina's visit. See note under Brandenberg, F. Aunt Nina and her nephews, and nieces E
Leo and Emily E
Leo and Emily and the dragon. See note under Brandenberg, F. Leo and Emily E
Leo and Emily's big ideas. See note under Brandenberg, F. Leo and Emily E
Leo and Emily's zoo. See note under Brandenberg, F. Leo and Emily E
Nice new neighbors E

Brandon *See* Brendan, Saint, the Voyager, ca. 483-577

Brandreth, Gyles Daubeney, 1948-
The biggest tongue twister book in the world (4 and up) 808.88

Brandt, Sue R., 1916-
Facts about the fifty states (4 and up) 973
How to write a report (4 and up) 808

Branley, Franklyn Mansfield, 1915-
Air is all around you (k-3) 551.5
The Big Dipper (k-3) 523.8
The Christmas sky (3-6) 232.9
Color, from rainbows to lasers (6 and up) 535.6
Earthquakes (k-3) 551.2
Eclipse: darkness in daytime (k-3) 523.7
Flash, crash, rumble, and roll (k-3) 551.5

Branley, Franklyn Mansfield, 1915-—*Continued*
From Sputnik to space shuttles (3-6) **629.44**
Gravity is a mystery (k-3) **531**
High sounds, low sounds (k-3) **534**
Hurricane watch (k-3) **551.55**
Is there life in outer space? (k-3) **574.999**
It's raining cats and dogs (3-6) **551.5**
Journey into a black hole (k-3) **523.8**
The moon seems to change (k-3) **523.3**
Mysteries of life on earth and beyond (6 and up) **574.999**
Mysteries of planet earth (6 and up) **525**
Mysteries of the universe (6 and up) **523.1**
Oxygen keeps you alive (k-3) **574.1**
Rain & hail (k-3) **551.57**
Rockets and satellites (k-3) **629.4**
Saturn (4 and up) **523.4**
Shooting stars (k-3) **523.6**
The sky is full of stars (k-3) **523.8**
Snow is falling (k-3) **551.57**
Star guide (3-6) **523.8**
The sun (k-3) **523.7**
Sun dogs and shooting stars (5 and up) **523**
Sunshine makes the seasons (k-3) **525**
Superstar (3-6) **523.8**
Uranus (3-6) **523.4**
Volcanoes (k-3) **551.2**
Weight and weightlessness (k-3) **531**
What happened to the dinosaurs? (k-3) **567.9**
What makes day and night (k-3) **525**
What the moon is like (k-3) **523.3**

Branscum, Robbie
The adventures of Johnny May (4-6) **Fic**

Bransom, Paul, 1885-1979
(il) Lippincott, J. W. Wilderness champion **Fic**

Brats. Kennedy, X. J. **811**

Brave Irene. Steig, W. **E**

Brave laborer
Afanas'ev, A. N. The brave laborer
In Afanas'ev, A. N. Russian fairy tales p276-77 **398.2**

Brave little tailor
Ehrlich, A. The valiant little tailor
In Ehrlich, A. The Random House book of fairy tales p102-17 **398.2**
Grimm, J. The brave little tailor
In Best-loved folktales of the world p61-68 **398.2**
In The Blue fairy book p304-12 **398.2**
Grimm, J. The valiant little tailor
In Grimm, J. The complete Grimm's fairy tales p112-20 **398.2**
Thane, A. The brave little tailor
In Thane, A. Plays from famous stories and fairy tales p397-413 **812**

Brave tin soldier
Andersen, H. C. The steadfast tin soldier **Fic**
also in Andersen, H. C. Hans Andersen: his classic fairy tales p98-102 **S C**
also in The Yellow fairy book p308-12 **398.2**
Ehrlich, A. The steadfast tin soldier
In Ehrlich, A. The Random House book of fairy tales p130-37 **398.2**

Bravo, Ernest and Celestine! Vincent, G. See note under Vincent, G. Ernest and Celestine **E**

Bray, Marian Flandrick, 1957-
Flight of the Swan
In Herds of thunder, manes of gold p6-18 **808.8**

Bread
Morris, A. Bread, bread, bread (k-3) **641.8**
See/See also pages in the following book(s):
Penner, L. R. The colonial cookbook p87-92 (5 and up) **641.5**
Rockwell, H. I did it p45-56 (1-3) **745.5**

Bread and honey. Asch, F. See note under Asch, F. Sand cake **E**

Bread and jam for Frances. Hoban, R. See note under Hoban, R. Bedtime for Frances **E**

Bread, bread, bread. Morris, A. **641.8**

Break a leg. Lawson, A.
In Things that go bump in the night p103-21 **S C**

Breaker's bridge. Yep, L.
In Yep, L. The rainbow people p124-34 **398.2**

Breakthrough. Jacobs, F. **615**

A **breath** of air. Leach, M.
In Leach, M. Whistle in the graveyard p105 **398.2**

Breathing *See* Respiration

Breda, Frederick
(il) Silverstein, A. Hamsters: all about them **636.088**

Bredeson, Lynn Gates
(il) Bauer, C. F. Celebrations **808.8**
(il) Bauer, C. F. Presenting reader's theater **808.82**

Breen, Karen, 1943-
Index to collective biographies for young readers **920**

Bremen town musicians
Grimm, J. The Bremen town musicians
In Best-loved folktales of the world p142-44 **398.2**
In Grimm, J. About wise men and simpletons p111-15 **398.2**
In Grimm, J. The complete Grimm's fairy tales p144-48 **398.2**
In The Scott, Foresman anthology of children's literature p188-90 **808.8**
Grimm, J. The musicians of Bremen
In Grimm, J. Tales from Grimm p87-100 **398.2**
Plume, I. The Bremen town musicians **398.2**

Brendan, Saint, the Voyager, ca. 483-577
About
Fritz, J. Brendan the Navigator (3-5) **398.2**

Brendan the Navigator. Fritz, J. **398.2**

Brennan, John, 1952-
Zoo day (k-3) **590.74**

Brenner, Anita, 1905-1974
The boy who took care of the pigs
In Bauer, C. F. Celebrations p152-54 **808.8**

Brenner, Barbara
Bodies (k-2) **612**
Faces (k-2) **612.8**
On the frontier with Mr. Audubon (4 and up) **Fic**
A snake-lover's diary (5 and up) **597.9**
Two orphan cubs (k-3) **599.74**
Wagon wheels **E**

Brenner, Fred, 1920-
(il) George, J. C. One day in the desert **574.5**
(il) Monjo, F. N. The drinking gourd **E**

Brenner, Martha
Fireworks tonight! (5 and up) **662**

Brent, Isabelle
(il) Bible. N.T. Selections. The Christmas story **232.9**

Brer Alligator learns about trouble. Lester, J.
In Lester, J. More tales of Uncle Remus p81-84 **398.2**

Brer Bear and Brer Rabbit take care of Brer Fox and Brer Wolf. Lester, J.
In Lester, J. Further tales of Uncle Remus p59-68 **398.2**

Brer Bear, Brer Turtle, and the rope-pulling contest. Lester, J.
In Lester, J. Further tales of Uncle Remus p19-22 **398.2**

Brer Bear gets tricked by Brer Frog. Lester, J.
In Lester, J. Further tales of Uncle Remus p16-19 **398.2**

Brer Billy Goat tricks Brer Wolf. Lester, J.
In Lester, J. Further tales of Uncle Remus p116-18 **398.2**

Brer Buzzard and Brer Hawk. Lester, J.
In Lester, J. Further tales of Uncle Remus p35-37 **398.2**

Brer Buzzard bites the dust—again. Lester, J.
In Lester, J. Further tales of Uncle Remus p38-41 **398.2**

Brer Deer and King Sun's daughter. Lester, J.
In Lester, J. Further tales of Uncle Remus p133-41 **398.2**

Brer Fox and Brer Rabbit go hunting. Lester, J.
In Lester, J. The tales of Uncle Remus p42-43 **398.2**

Brer Fox and Brer Turtle. Lester, J.
In Lester, J. Further tales of Uncle Remus p12-15 **398.2**

Brer Fox and Mr. Man. Lester, J.
In Lester, J. Further tales of Uncle Remus p3-7 **398.2**

Brer Fox and the grapes. Lester, J.
In Lester, J. More tales of Uncle Remus p10-14 **398.2**

Brer Fox and Uncle Mud Turtle. Lester, J.
In Lester, J. Further tales of Uncle Remus p49-53 **398.2**

Brer Fox, Brer Rabbit, and King Deer's daughter. Lester, J.
In Lester, J. The tales of Uncle Remus p131-34 **398.2**

Brer Fox gets away for once. Lester, J.
In Lester, J. Further tales of Uncle Remus p68-70 **398.2**

Brer Fox gets out-foxed. Parks, V. D.
In Parks, V. D. Jump on over! the adventures of Brer Rabbit and his family **398.2**

Brer Fox gets tricked again. Lester, J.
In Lester, J. More tales of Uncle Remus p84-87 **398.2**
In Lester, J. The tales of Uncle Remus p75-78 **398.2**

Brer Fox gets tricked by the frogs. Lester, J.
In Lester, J. Further tales of Uncle Remus p15-16 **398.2**

Brer Fox goes hunting but Brer Rabbit bags the game. Parks, V. D.
In Parks, V. D. Jump! the adventures of Brer Rabbit p11-16 **398.2**

Brer Fox sets a fire. Lester, J.
In Lester, J. More tales of Uncle Remus p106-08 **398.2**

Brer Fox takes Miz Cricket to dinner. Lester, J.
In Lester, J. Further tales of Uncle Remus p118-22 **398.2**

Brer Fox tries to get revenge. Lester, J.
In Lester, J. Further tales of Uncle Remus p86-94 **398.2**

Brer Fox wants to make music. Lester, J.
In Lester, J. Further tales of Uncle Remus p25-29 **398.2**

Brer Lion meets the creature. Lester, J.
In Lester, J. The tales of Uncle Remus p65-68 **398.2**

Brer Polecat finds a winter home. Lester, J.
In Lester, J. Further tales of Uncle Remus p56-58 **398.2**

Brer Possum hears the singing. Lester, J.
In Lester, J. The tales of Uncle Remus p87-91 **398.2**

Brer Rabbit advises Brer Lion. Lester, J.
In Lester, J. More tales of Uncle Remus p96-98 **398.2**

Brer Rabbit and Brer Bear. Parks, V. D.
In Parks, V. D. Jump on over! the adventures of Brer Rabbit and his family **398.2**

Brer Rabbit and Brer Bullfrog. Lester, J.
In Lester, J. More tales of Uncle Remus p87-92 **398.2**

Brer Rabbit and Brer Fox kill a cow. Lester, J.
In Lester, J. More tales of Uncle Remus p6-10 **398.2**

Brer Rabbit and Brer Lion. Lester, J.
In Lester, J. The tales of Uncle Remus p60-62 **398.2**

Brer Rabbit and Mr. Man's chickens. Lester, J.
In Lester, J. More tales of Uncle Remus p75-79 **398.2**

Brer Rabbit and Sister Cow. Lester, J.
In Lester J. The tales of Uncle Remus p23-26 **398.2**

Brer Rabbit and the gizzard eater. Lester, J.
In Lester, J. More tales of Uncle Remus p117-22 **398.2**

Brer Rabbit and the little girl. Lester, J.
In Lester, J. The tales of Uncle Remus p78-81 **398.2**

Brer Rabbit and the mosquitoes. Lester, J.
In Lester, J. The tales of Uncle Remus p124-27 **398.2**

Brer Rabbit and the mosquitoes. Parks, V. D.
In Parks, V. D. Jump again! more adventures of Brer Rabbit p23-29 **398.2**

Brer Rabbit and the Tar Baby. Lester, J.
In Lester, J. The tales of Uncle Remus p10-16 **398.2**

Brer Rabbit breaks up the party. Lester, J.
In Lester, J. The tales of Uncle Remus p134-37 **398.2**

Brer Rabbit, Brer Bear, and the honey. Lester, J.
In Lester, J. More tales of Uncle Remus p45-50 **398.2**

Brer Rabbit, Brer Coon, and the frogs. Lester, J.
In Lester, J. More tales of Uncle Remus p30-33 **398.2**

Brer Rabbit, Brer Fox, and the chickens. Lester, J.
In Lester, J. Further tales of Uncle Remus p77-86 **398.2**

Brer Rabbit builds a tower. Lester, J.
In Lester, J. More tales of Uncle Remus p108-11 **398.2**

Brer Rabbit, businessman. Lyra, C.
In Best-loved folktales of the world p763-67 **398.2**

Brer Rabbit catches Wattle Weasel. Lester, J.
In Lester, J. More tales of Uncle Remus p70-75 **398.2**

Brer Rabbit comes to dinner. Lester, J.
In Lester, J. The tales of Uncle Remus p8-10 **398.2**

Brer Rabbit doctors Brer Fox's burns. Lester, J.
In Lester, J. More tales of Uncle Remus p104-06 **398.2**

Brer Rabbit eats the butter. Lester, J.
In Lester, J. The tales of Uncle Remus p46-50 **398.2**

Brer Rabbit falls in love. Lester, J.
In Lester, J. More tales of Uncle Remus p14-22 **398.2**

Brer Rabbit finally gets beaten. Lester, J.
In Lester, J. The tales of Uncle Remus p31-34 **398.2**

Brer Rabbit finds his match. Parks, V. D.
In Parks, V. D. Jump! the adventures of Brer Rabbit p19-24 **398.2**

Brer Rabbit gets a little comeuppance. Lester, J.
In Lester, J. More tales of Uncle Remus p94-96 **398.2**

Brer Rabbit gets beaten again. Lester, J.
In Lester, J. The tales of Uncle Remus p69-71 **398.2**

Brer Rabbit gets Brer Fox's dinner. Lester, J.
In Lester, J. More tales of Uncle Remus p3-6 **398.2**

Brer Rabbit gets caught one more time. Lester, J.
In Lester, J. The tales of Uncle Remus p37-40 **398.2**

Brer Rabbit gets even. Lester, J.
In Lester, J. The tales of Uncle Remus p16-23 **398.2**

Brer Rabbit gets the house to himself. Lester, J.
In Lester, J. More tales of Uncle Remus p36-38 **398.2**

Brer Rabbit gets the meat. Lester, J.
In Lester, J. More tales of Uncle Remus p56-60 **398.2**

Brer Rabbit gets the meat again. Lester, J.
In Lester, J. The tales of Uncle Remus p115-17 **398.2**

Brer Rabbit gets the money. Lester, J.
In Lester, J. The tales of Uncle Remus p104-06 **398.2**

Brer Rabbit goes back to Mr. Man's garden. Lester, J.
In Lester, J. The tales of Uncle Remus p81-86 **398.2**

Brer Rabbit grossly deceives Brer Fox. Parks, V. D.
In Parks, V. D. Jump! the adventures of Brer Rabbit p27-32 **398.2**

Brer Rabbit, he's a good fisherman. Parks, V. D.
In Parks, V. D. Jump again! more adventures of Brer Rabbit p2-5 **398.2**

Brer Rabbit makes a deal with Mr. Man. Lester, J.
In Lester, J. More tales of Uncle Remus p100-04 **398.2**

Brer Rabbit meets up with Cousin Wildcat. Lester, J.
In Lester, J. More tales of Uncle Remus p92-94 **398.2**

Brer Rabbit outwits Mr. Man. Lester, J.
In Lester, J. The tales of Uncle Remus p137-41 **398.2**

Brer Rabbit saves Brer Wolf—maybe. Lester, J.
In Lester, J. More tales of Uncle Remus p111-14 **398.2**

Brer Rabbit saves his meat. Lester, J.
In Lester, J. The tales of Uncle Remus p51-53 **398.2**

Brer Rabbit scares everybody. Lester, J.
In Lester, J. More tales of Uncle Remus p60-64 **398.2**

Brer Rabbit takes care of Brer Tiger. Lester, J.
In Lester, J. The tales of Uncle Remus p62-65 **398.2**

Brer Rabbit tells on Brer Wolf. Lester, J.
In Lester, J. The tales of Uncle Remus p122-24 **398.2**

Brer Rabbit to the rescue. Lester, J.
In Lester, J. The tales of Uncle Remus p110-12 **398.2**

Brer Rabbit tricks Brer Bear. Lester, J.
In Lester, J. The tales of Uncle Remus p71-74 **398.2**

Brer Rabbit tricks Brer Fox again. Lester, J.
In Lester, J. The tales of Uncle Remus p44-46 **398.2**

Brer Rabbit's children. Lester, J.
In Lester, J. The tales of Uncle Remus p54-56 **398.2**

Brer Rabbit's Christmas
In Diane Goode's American Christmas p63-65 **810.8**

Brer Rabbit's courtship. Parks, V. D.
In Parks, V. D. Jump again! more adventures of Brer Rabbit p31-39 **398.2**

Brer Rabbit's laughing place. Lester, J.
In Lester, J. More tales of Uncle Remus p33-35 **398.2**

Brer Rabbit's luck. Lester, J.
In Lester, J. The tales of Uncle Remus p145-51 **398.2**

Brer Rabbit's money mint. Lester, J.
In Lester, J. More tales of Uncle Remus p98-100 **398.2**

Brer Rabbit's riddle. Lester, J.
In Lester, J. The tales of Uncle Remus p91-95 **398.2**

Brer Snake catches Brer Wolf. Lester, J.
In Lester, J. More tales of Uncle Remus p50-56 **398.2**

Brer Turtle and Brer Mink. Lester, J.
In Lester, J. Further tales of Uncle Remus p112-16 **398.2**

Brer Turtle, Brer Rabbit, and Brer Fox. Lester, J.
In Lester, J. The tales of Uncle Remus p26-29 **398.2**

Brer Turtle takes care of Brer Buzzard. Lester, J.
In Lester, J. Further tales of Uncle Remus p22-24 **398.2**

Brer Turtle takes flying lessons. Lester, J.
In Lester, J. Further tales of Uncle Remus p33-35 **398.2**
Brer Wolf and the pigs. Lester, J.
In Lester, J. Further tales of Uncle Remus p95-100 **398.2**
Brer Wolf, Brer Fox, and the little Rabbits. Lester, J.
In Lester, J. The tales of Uncle Remus p141-44 **398.2**
Brer Wolf gets in more trouble. Lester, J.
In Lester, J. The tales of Uncle Remus p117-22 **398.2**
Brer Wolf tries to catch Brer Rabbit. Lester, J.
In Lester, J. The tales of Uncle Remus p29-31 **398.2**
Brett, Jan, 1949-
Annie and the wild animals **E**
Beauty and the beast (1-3) **398.2**
Goldilocks and the three bears (k-2) **398.2**
The mitten (k-2) **398.2**
The wild Christmas reindeer **E**
(il) Bunting, E. The Mother's Day mice **E**
(il) Cross, D. H. Some plants have funny names **581**
(il) Lear, E. The owl and the pussycat **821**
(il) The Twelve days of Christmas. See The Twelve days of Christmas **782.42**
Brewer, Ebenezer Cobham, 1810-1897
Brewer's dictionary of phrase and fable. See Brewer's dictionary of phrase and fable **803**
Brewer's dictionary of phrase and fable **803**
Brewster, Patience, 1952-
(il) Valentine poems. See Valentine poems **808.81**
Brewton, John Edmund, 1898-
(comp) In the witch's kitchen. See In the witch's kitchen **811.008**
(comp) Index to children's poetry. See Index to children's poetry **808.81**
(comp) Index to poetry for children and young people. See Index to poetry for children and young people **808.81**
(comp) Laughable limericks. See Laughable limericks **821.008**
(comp) My tang's tungled and other ridiculous situations. See My tang's tungled and other ridiculous situations **821.008**
(comp) Of quarks, quasars, and other quirks. See Of quarks, quasars, and other quirks **821.008**
(comp) Shrieks at midnight. See Shrieks at midnight **821.008**
(comp) They've discovered a head in the box for the bread, and other laughable limericks. See They've discovered a head in the box for the bread, and other laughable limericks **821.008**
Brewton, Sara Westbrook
(comp) Index to children's poetry. See Index to children's poetry **808.81**
(comp) Index to poetry for children and young people. See Index to poetry for children and young people **808.81**
(comp) Laughable limericks. See Laughable limericks **821.008**
(comp) My tang's tungled and other ridiculous situations. See My tang's tungled and other ridiculous situations **821.008**
(comp) Of quarks, quasars, and other quirks. See Of quarks, quasars, and other quirks **821.008**
(comp) Shrieks at midnight. See Shrieks at midnight **821.008**
Brezhnev, Leonid Il'ich, 1906-1982
See/See also pages in the following book(s):
Andrews, W. G. The land and the people of the Soviet Union p135-40 (5 and up) **947**
Brian Wildsmith's birds. Wildsmith, B. **E**
Brian Wildsmith's circus. Wildsmith, B. **E**
Brian Wildsmith's fishes. See Wildsmith, B. Fishes **E**
Brian Wildsmith's Mother Goose. See Mother Goose [illus. by Brian Wildsmith] **398.8**
Brian Wildsmith's wild animals. Wildsmith, B. **E**
Briar Rose. Rockwell, A. F.
In Rockwell, A. F. Puss in boots, and other stories p53-59 **398.2**
Bridal customs *See* Marriage customs and rites
The **bride** who out talked the water kelpie. Leodhas, S. N.
In The Scott, Foresman anthology of children's literature p162-67 **808.8**
Bridge, Linda McCarter
The playful dolphins (k-3) **599.5**
Bridge to Terabithia. Paterson, K. **Fic**
Bridgers, Sue Ellen, 1942-
All together now (6 and up) **Fic**
Home before dark (6 and up) **Fic**
Life's a beach
In Connections: short stories by outstanding writers for young adults p27-43 **S C**

Bridges
See also names of bridges
History
Weitzman, D. L. Windmills, bridges & old machines (5 and up) **620**
Bridgman, Laura Dewey, 1829-1889
About
Hunter, E. F. Child of the silent night (3-5) **92**
Bridle the wind. Aiken, J. **Fic**
A **brief** moment in the life of Angus Bethune. Crutcher, C.
In Connections: short stories by outstanding writers for young adults p54-70 **S C**
Brier Rose. Grimm, J.
In Grimm, J. About wise men and simpletons p23-27 **398.2**
Brierley, Louise
(il) De la Mare, W. Peacock pie **821**
(il) Kipling, R. The elephant's child **Fic**
Briggs, Katharine Mary
The boggart
In Best-loved folktales of the world p211-12 **398.2**
An encyclopedia of fairies **398.03**
The hand of glory
In Best-loved folktales of the world p213-14 **398.2**
Kate Crackernuts (6 and up) **Fic**
Briggs, Raymond
Father Christmas **E**
The snowman **E**
(jt. auth) Anno, M. All in a day **E**
(il) Festivals. See Festivals **394.2**
(il) The Mother Goose treasury. See The Mother Goose treasury **398.8**
Bright, Robert, 1902-1988
Georgie **E**
Georgie and the robbers. See note under Bright, R. Georgie **E**
My red umbrella **E**
Bright-Hawk's feather
Afanas'ev, A. N. The feather of Finist, the Bright Falcon
In Afanas'ev, A. N. Russian fairy tales p580-88 **398.2**
Afanas'ev, A. N. Finist the falcon
In Afanas'ev, A. N. Russian folk tales p25-36 **398.2**
Bright stars, red giants, and white dwarfs. Berger, M. **523.8**
Bright sun brings it to light
Grimm, J. The bright sun brings it to light
In Grimm, J. The complete Grimm's fairy tales p528-29 **398.2**
Brighty of the Grand Canyon. Henry, M. **Fic**
Brill, Marlene Targ- *See* Targ-Brill, Marlene
Brimner, Larry Dane
Karate (5 and up) **796.8**
Brinckloe, Julie
Fireflies! **E**
(il) Lindgren, A. Lotta on Troublemaker Street **Fic**
Bringing the rain to Kapiti Plain. Aardema, V. **398.2**
Brink, Carol Ryrie, 1895-1981
The bad times of Irma Baumlein (4-6) **Fic**
Caddie Woodlawn (4-6) **Fic**
See/See also pages in the following book(s):
Newbery Medal books, 1922-1955 p139-44 **028.5**
Brinsmead, H. F. (Hesba Fay), 1922-
See/See also pages in the following book(s):
Townsend, J. R. A sense of story p39-44 **028.5**
Brinsmead, Hesba Fay *See* Brinsmead, H. F. (Hesba Fay), 1922-
Briquebec, John
The ancient world (4 and up) **930**
British cookery *See* Cookery, British
British folk tales. Crossley-Holland, K. **398.2**
British Museum (Natural History)
Burnie, D. Bird **598**
Byam, M. Arms & armor **355.8**
Parker, S. Skeleton **596**
Symes, R. F. Rocks & minerals **549**
Brittain, Bill
All the money in the world (4-6) **Fic**
Devil's donkey (3-6) **Fic**
Dr. Dredd's wagon of wonders. See note under Brittain, B. Devil's donkey **Fic**
The wish giver. See note under Brittain, B. Devil's donkey **Fic**
Bro Tiger goes dead. Berry, J.
In Berry, J. Spiderman Anancy p66-68 **398.2**
Broadcasting
See also Television broadcasting
The **brocaded** slipper. Vuong, L. D.
In Vuong, L. D. The brocaded slipper, and other Vietnamese tales **398.2**
The **brocaded** slipper, and other Vietnamese tales. Vuong, L. D. **398.2**
The **Broccoli** tapes. Slepian, J. **Fic**
Broderick. Ormondroyd, E. **E**
Broekel, Ray, 1923-
Hocus pocus: magic you can do (3-5) **793.8**
Now you see it: easy magic for beginners (3-5) **793.8**
Snakes (2-4) **597.9**
Sound experiments (2-4) **534**

Broekel, Ray, 1923-—*Continued*
(jt. auth) White, L. B. Math-a-magic: number tricks for magicians 793.8
Broken chain. Soto, G.
In Soto, G. Baseball in April, and other stories p1-12 S C
Broken windows. Paterson, K.
In Paterson, K. Angels & other strangers: family Christmas stories p105-18 S C
Bronowski, Jacob, 1908-1974
Biography of an atom (4 and up) 539
The **bronze** bow. Speare, E. G. Fic
Bronze ring
The Bronze ring
In The Blue fairy book p1-11 398.2
Bronzeville boys and girls. Brooks, G. 811
Brooke, Leonard Leslie, 1862-1940
See/See also pages in the following book(s):
A Horn Book sampler on children's books and reading p60-69, 224-27 028.5
Brooke, William J.
A telling of the tales: five stories (4-6) S C
Contents: The waking of the prince; The growin' of Paul Bunyan; The fitting of the slipper; The working of John Henry; The telling of a tale
Brooklyn (New York, N.Y.)
Fiction
Chaikin, M. Finders weepers (3-5) Fic
Fox, P. How many miles to Babylon? (4-6) Fic
Hest, A. Fancy Aunt Jess E
Slepian, J. The Alfred summer (5 and up) Fic
Brooklyn Dodgers (Baseball team)
Golenbock, P. Teammates [biography of Jackie Robinson] (1-4) 92
Brooks, Gwendolyn
Bronzeville boys and girls (2-5) 811
Brooks, Polly Schoyer
Queen Eleanor: independent spirit of the medieval world (6 and up) 92
Brooks, Walter R., 1886-1958
Freddy and the men from Mars. See note under Brooks, W. R. Freddy the detective Fic
Freddy and the perilous adventure. See note under Brooks, W. R. Freddy the detective Fic
Freddy goes camping. See note under Brooks, W. R. Freddy the detective Fic
Freddy goes to Florida. See note under Brooks, W. R. Freddy the detective Fic
Freddy the cowboy. See note under Brooks, W. R. Freddy the detective Fic
Freddy the detective (3-5) Fic
Freddy the politician. See note under Brooks, W. R. Freddy the detective Fic
The **broomstick** beauty. Miller, H. L.
In Holiday plays round the year p129-40 812.008
Brother Anansi and the cattle ranch. Rohmer, H. 398.2
Brother and sister
Grimm, J. Brother and sister
In Grimm, J. The complete Grimm's fairy tales p67-73 398.2
In Grimm, J. The juniper tree, and other tales from Grimm v1 p42-54 398.2
In The Red fairy book p82-88 398.2
Brother and sister. San Souci, R.
In San Souci, R. Short & shivery p117-22 398.2
Brother Breeze and the pear tree. Sherlock, Sir P. M.
In Sherlock, Sir P. M. Anansi, the spider man p13-19 398.2
A **brother** for the orphelines. Carlson, N. S. See note under Carlson, N. S. The happy orpheline Fic
Brother Gaily. Grimm, J.
In Grimm, J. The juniper tree, and other tales from Grimm v1 p129-49 398.2
Brother Lustig
Grimm, J. Brother Gaily
In Grimm, J. The juniper tree, and other tales from Grimm v1 p129-49 398.2
Grimm, J. Brother Lustig
In Grimm, J. The complete Grimm's fairy tales p367-77 398.2
Brother moose. Levin, B. Fic
Brother to the wind. Walter, M. P. E
Brotherhood of Sleeping Car Porters
McKissack, P. C. A long hard journey (5 and up) 331.8
Brothers
Fiction
Bauer, M. D. Rain of fire (5 and up) Fic
Blume, J. Tales of a fourth grade nothing (3-6) Fic
Bulla, C. R. The Christmas coat E
Carrick, C. Patrick's dinosaurs E
Carrick, C. What happened to Patrick's dinosaurs? E
Freedman, F. B. Brothers: a Hebrew legend (k-2) 398.2
Keats, E. J. Apt. 3 E
Kellogg, S. Much bigger than Martin E
Oppenheim, J. Left & right E

Brothers—Fiction—*Continued*
Rockwell, A. F. The night we slept outside E
Sharmat, M. W. Goodnight, Andrew: goodnight, Craig E
Steptoe, J. Baby says E
Wells, R. Good night, Fred E
Wiesner, D. Hurricane E
Williams, B. Jeremy isn't hungry E
Williams, K. L. Baseball and butterflies (2-4) Fic
Yorinks, A. Oh, Brother E

Poetry

Margolis, R. J. Secrets of a small brother (1-3) **811**

Brothers: a Hebrew legend. Freedman, F. B. **398.2**

Brothers and sisters
See also Twins
Bonsall, C. N. The day I had to play with my sister E
Cole, J. The new baby at your house (k-3) **306.8**
Lasky, K. A baby for Max E
Ormerod, J. 101 things to do with a baby E
Rosenberg, M. B. Finding a way (2-4) **362.4**

Fiction

Alexander, M. G. Nobody asked me if I wanted a baby sister E
Alexander, M. G. When the new baby comes, I'm moving out E
Alexander, S. Nadia the Willful E
Angell, J. A home is to share—and share—and share— (4-6) Fic
Bawden, N. The outside child (5 and up) Fic
Blume, J. The Pain and the Great One E
Bogart, J. E. Daniel's dog E
Brown, M. T. D.W. all wet E
Browne, A. The tunnel E
Byars, B. C. Go and hush the baby E
Byars, B. C. The night swimmers (5 and up) Fic
Byars, B. C. The not-just-anybody family (5 and up) Fic
Byars, B. C. The summer of the swans (5 and up) Fic
Caines, J. F. Abby E
Cassedy, S. M.E. and Morton (6 and up) Fic
Cleaver, V. The Kissimmee Kid (6 and up) Fic
Cleaver, V. Trial Valley (5 and up) Fic
Cleaver, V. Where the lillies bloom (5 and up) Fic
Conrad, P. My Daniel (5 and up) Fic
Cresswell, H. Dear Shrink (5 and up) Fic
Fox, P. The stone-faced boy (4-6) Fic
Garfield, L. Young Nick and Jubilee (5 and up) Fic
Greene, C. C. I and Sproggy (5 and up) Fic
Greenfield, E. She come bringing me that little baby girl E
Havill, J. Jamaica tag-along E
Hines, A. G. Big like me E
Hughes, S. Lucy & Tom's a.b.c E
Hughes, S. Lucy & Tom's 1.2.3. E
Hurwitz, J. Superduper Teddy (2-4) Fic
Hutchins, P. Titch E
Hutchins, P. You'll soon grow into them, Titch E
James, B. Natalie underneath E
Jukes, M. Lights around the palm E
Keller, H. What Alvin wanted E
Khalsa, D. K. My family vacation E
Kropp, P. Moonkid and Liberty (6 and up) Fic
Lively, P. Fanny's sister (3-5) Fic
Lowry, L. The one hundredth thing about Caroline (5 and up) Fic
Lowry, L. Switcharound (5 and up) Fic
Martin, B. The ghost-eye tree E
Moeri, L. Save Queen of Sheba (4 and up) Fic
Nelson, T. And one for all (6 and up) Fic
Nixon, J. L. A family apart (5 and up) Fic
O'Donnell, E. L. Maggie doesn't want to move E
Pearson, K. The sky is falling (6 and up) Fic
Pevsner, S. And you give me a pain, Elaine (4 and up) Fic
Rabe, B. Margaret's moves (3-6) Fic
Sachs, E.-A. The boy who ate dog biscuits E
Shyer, M. F. Welcome home, Jellybean (5 and up) Fic
Slepian, J. The Broccoli tapes (5 and up) Fic
Voigt, C. Dicey's song (6 and up) Fic
Voigt, C. Homecoming (6 and up) Fic
Waddell, M. Amy said E
Wade, B. Little monster E
Walter, M. P. Two and too much E
Wells, R. A lion for Lewis E
Wells, R. Max's first word E
Wishinsky, F. Oonga boonga E

Brothers Grimm
See also Grimm, Jacob, 1785-1863; Grimm, Wilhelm, 1786-1859

Brown, Dee Alexander
Bury my heart at Wounded Knee; adaptation. See Ehrlich, A. Wounded Knee: an Indian history of the American West **970.004**

Brown, Jacob
(il) McMane, F. Track & field basics **796.4**

Brown, Jeff, 1926-
Flat Stanley **E**

Brown, Judith Gwyn
(il) Bellairs, J. The treasure of Alpheus Winterborn **Fic**
(il) Naylor, P. R. Maudie in the middle **Fic**
(il) A New treasury of children's poetry. See A New treasury of children's poetry **821.008**
(il) Robinson, B. The best Christmas pageant ever **Fic**

Brown, Laurene Krasny
Dinosaurs alive and well!: a guide to good health (k-3) **613**
Dinosaurs divorce (k-4) **306.89**
Dinosaurs travel (k-3) **910**
Visiting the art museum (k-3) **708**

Brown, Marc Tolon
Arthur goes to camp. See note under Brown, M. Arthur's nose **E**
Arthur's April Fool. See note under Brown, M. Arthur's nose **E**
Arthur's baby. See note under Brown, M. Arthur's nose **E**
Arthur's birthday. See note under Brown, M. Arthur's nose **E**
Arthur's Christmas. See note under Brown, M. Arthur's nose **E**
Arthur's eyes. See note under Brown, M. Arthur's nose **E**
Arthur's Halloween. See note under Brown, M. Arthur's nose **E**
Arthur's nose **E**
Arthur's pet business. See note under Brown, M. Arthur's nose **E**
Arthur's teacher trouble. See note under Brown, M. Arthur's nose **E**
Arthur's Thanksgiving. See note under Brown, M. Arthur's nose **E**
Arthur's tooth. See note under Brown, M. Arthur's nose **E**
Arthur's valentine. See note under Brown, M. Arthur's nose **E**
D.W. all wet **E**
Dinosaurs, beware! (k-2) **613.6**
Finger rhymes (k-2) **796.1**
Hand rhymes (k-2) **796.1**
Play rhymes (k-2) **796.1**
Your first garden book (1-3) **635**
(il) Aardema, V. Oh, Kojo! How could you! **398.2**
(il) Aardema, V. What's so funny, Ketu? **398.2**
(il) Bowden, J. C. Why the tides ebb and flow **398.2**
(jt. auth) Brown, L. K. Dinosaurs alive and well!: a guide to good health **613**
(jt. auth) Brown, L. K. Dinosaurs divorce **306.89**
(jt. auth) Brown, L. K. Dinosaurs travel **910**
(jt. auth) Brown, L. K. Visiting the art museum **708**
(jt. auth) Krensky, S. Dinosaurs, beware! **613.6**
(jt. auth) Your first garden book **635**
(il) The Family read-aloud Christmas treasury. See The Family read-aloud Christmas treasury **808.8**
(il) Read-aloud rhymes for the very young. See Read-aloud rhymes for the very young **821.008**
(il) Wolkstein, D. The banza **398.2**

Brown, Marcia, 1918-
Backbone of the king (5 and up) **398.2**
Dick Whittington and his cat (k-3) **398.2**
Once upon a mouse (k-3) **398.2**
Stone soup (k-3) **398.2**
(il) Cendrars, B. Shadow **841**
(il) Perrault, C. Cinderella **398.2**
(il) Sherlock, Sir P. M. Anansi, the spider man **398.2**
(il) Sing a song of popcorn. See Sing a song of popcorn **808.81**
See/See also pages in the following book(s):
Caldecott Medal books, 1938-1957 p267-83 **028.5**
Newbery and Caldecott Medal books, 1976-1985 p239-53 **028.5**

Brown, Margaret Wise, 1910-1952
Baby animals **E**
Big red barn **E**
Christmas in the barn (k-2) **232.9**
The fish with the deep sea smile (1-3) **818**
Stories included are: The shy little horse; The good little bad little pig; The steam roller: a fantasy; The garden; Sneakers, that rapscallion cat; Sneakers comes to town; The sky follows Sneakers to town; Sneakers and the Easter flowers; The Easter surprise; Sneakers and the Easter bunnies; The country happens to Sneakers again; The dead bird; The fierce yellow pumpkin; Christmas Eve; How the little city boy changed places with the little country boy for a year; The rat that said boo to the cat; The children's clock; The little girl's medicine; The polite little polar bear; The wonderful kitten; The wild black crows—a circular song; The little black cat who went to Mattituck; The pale blue flower; The wonderful day
Goodnight moon **E**
Margaret Wise Brown's A child's good night book **E**
Nibble nibble: poems for children (k-3) **811**
The runaway bunny **E**
Wait till the moon is full **E**
Wheel on the chimney **E**
See/See also pages in the following book(s):
Sendak, M. Caldecott & Co.: notes on books and pictures p125-27 **028.5**

Brown, Marion Marsh
Singapore (4 and up) **959.57**
Brown, Mary Barrett
(il) Esbensen, B. J. Great northern diver: the loon **598**
Brown, Richard Eric, 1946-
(il) Kyte, K. S. The kids' complete guide to money **332.024**
Brown, Rick *See* Brown, Richard Eric, 1946-
Brown, Ruth
The big sneeze **E**
A dark, dark tale **E**
Brown, Tricia
Chinese New Year (2-4) **394.2**
Browne, Anthony
Gorilla **E**
I like books **E**
Things I like **E**
The tunnel **E**
Willy the champ **E**
(il) Carroll, L. Alice's adventures in Wonderland **Fic**
Brownell, M. Barbara
Amazing otters (k-3) **599.74**
The **brownie**. Hunter, M.
In Hunter, M. A furl of fairy wind: four stories p3-15 **S C**
Brownie of Blednock
The Brownie of Blednock
In Best-loved folktales of the world p275-79 **398.2**
Browning, Robert, 1812-1889
The Pied Piper of Hamelin
In The Scott, Foresman anthology of children's literature p107-11 **808.8**
The Pied Piper of Hamelin; dramatization. See Thane, A. The Pied Piper of Hamelin
The **Browns** take the day off. Schwartz, A.
In Schwartz, A. There is a carrot in my ear, and other noodle tales p9-14 **398.2**
Bruh Alligator and Bruh Deer. Hamilton, V.
In Hamilton, V. The people could fly: American black folktales p26-30 **398.2**
Bruh Alligator meets Trouble. Hamilton, V.
In Hamilton, V. The people could fly: American black folktales p35-42 **398.2**
Bruh Lizard and Bruh Rabbit. Hamilton, V.
In Hamilton, V. The people could fly: American black folktales p31-34 **398.2**
Bruner, Stephen
(il) Horvatic, A. Simple machines **531**
Brunhoff, Jean de, 1899-1937
Babar and Father Christmas. See note under Brunhoff, J. de. The story of Babar, the little elephant **E**
Babar and his children. See note under Brunhoff, J. de. The story of Babar, the little elephant **E**
Babar and Zephir. See note under Brunhoff, J. de. The story of Babar, the little elephant **E**
Babar the king. See note under Brunhoff, J. de. The story of Babar, the little elephant **E**
The story of Babar, the little elephant **E**
Travels of Babar. See note under Brunhoff, J. de. The story of Babar, the little elephant **E**
See/See also pages in the following book(s):
Only connect: readings on children's literature p176-82 **028.5**
Sendak, M. Caldecott & Co.: notes on books and pictures p95-105 **028.5**
Brunhoff, Laurent de, 1925-
Babar and the ghost. See note under Brunhoff, J. de. The story of Babar, the little elephant **E**
Babar learns to cook. See note under Brunhoff, J. de. The story of Babar, the little elephant **E**
Babar loses his crown. See note under Brunhoff, J. de. The story of Babar, the little elephant **E**
Babar saves the day. See note under Brunhoff, J. de. The story of Babar, the little elephant **E**
Babar visits another planet. See note under Brunhoff, J. de. The story of Babar, the little elephant **E**
Babar's ABC. See note under Brunhoff, J. de. The story of Babar, the little elephant **E**
Babar's anniversary album. See note under Brunhoff, J. de. The story of Babar, the little elephant **E**
Babar's birthday surprise. See note under Brunhoff, J. de. The story of Babar, the little elephant **E**
Babar's book of color. See note under Brunhoff, J. de. The story of Babar, the little elephant **E**
Babar's bookmobile. See note under Brunhoff, J. de. The story of Babar, the little elephant **E**
Babar's busy year. See note under Brunhoff, J. de. The story of Babar, the little elephant **E**
Babar's counting book. See note under Brunhoff, J. de. The story of Babar, the little elephant **E**

Brunhoff, Laurent de, 1925-—*Continued*
Babar's French lessons. See note under Brunhoff, J. de. The story of Babar, the little elephant **E**
Babar's little circus star. See note under Brunhoff, J. de. The story of Babar, the little elephant **E**
Babar's little girl. See note under Brunhoff, J. de. The story of Babar, the little elephant **E**
Babar's mystery. See note under Brunhoff, J. de. The story of Babar, the little elephant **E**
Babar's trunk. See note under Brunhoff, J. de. The story of Babar, the little elephant **E**
Meet Babar and his family. See note under Brunhoff, J. de. The story of Babar, the little elephant **E**
See/See also pages in the following book(s):
Only connect: readings on children's literature p176-82 **028.5**

Bruno, Barbara
(il) Robinson, J. Activities for anyone, anytime, anywhere **790.1**

Brusca, María Cristina
(il) Berry, C. Mama went walking **E**

Bruun, Bertel
(jt. auth) Bruun, R. D. The brain—what it is, what it does **612.8**
(jt. auth) Bruun, R. D. The human body **612**
(jt. auth) Robbins, C. S. Birds of North America **598**

Bruun, Peter
(il) Bruun, R. D. The brain—what it is, what it does **612.8**

Bruun, Ruth Dowling
The brain—what it is, what it does (1-3) **612.8**
The human body (4 and up) **612**

Bryan, Ashley, 1923-
Beat the story-drum, pum-pum (1-4) **398.2**
Contents: Hen and Frog; Why Bush Cow and Elephant are bad friends; The husband who counted the spoonfuls; Why Frog and Snake never play together; How animals got their tails
The cat's purr (k-2) **398.2**
The dancing granny (1-4) **398.2**
Lion and the ostrich chicks, and other African tales (4-6) **398.2**
Contents: Lion and the ostrich chicks; Son of the wind; Jackal's favorite game; The foolish boy
Tortoise, Hare, and the sweet potatoes
In Bauer, C. F. Celebrations p231-34 **808.8**
Turtle knows your name (1-3) **398.2**
Why Frog and Snake never play together
In The Scott, Foresman anthology of children's literature p310-13 **808.8**
(il) What a morning! See What a morning! **782.25**

Bryan, William Jennings, 1860-1925
See/See also pages in the following book(s):
Jacobs, W. J. Great lives: human rights p182-88 (5 and up) **920**

Bubble, the shoe and the straw
Afanas'ev, A. N. The bladder, the straw, and the shoe
In Afanas'ev, A. N. Russian fairy tales p590 **398.2**

Bubonic plague *See* Plague

Buchanan, George
(il) Nesbit, E. Long ago when I was young **92**

Buchanan, Yvonne
(il) Branley, F. M. Uranus **523.4**

Buck, Pearl S. (Pearl Sydenstricker), 1892-1973
About
Mitchell, B. Between two worlds: a story about Pearl Buck (3-5) **92**

The **buck** stops here: the presidents of the United States. Provensen, A. **920**

Budd, Warren
(jt. auth) Ames, L. J. Draw 50 sharks, whales, and other sea creatures **743**
(il) Silverstein, A. World of the brain **612.8**

Buddhism
See/See also pages in the following book(s):
Major, J. S. The land and people of Mongolia p131-37 (5 and up) **951.7**

Buddy Morris, Alias Fat Man. Hall, M. M.
In Things that go bump in the night p186-98 **S C**

Budgets, Personal *See* Finance, Personal

Budulinek
Fillmore, P. Budulinek
In The Scott, Foresman anthology of children's literature p271-74 **808.8**

Buehner, Mark
(il) Barracca, D. The adventures of Taxi Dog **E**

Buffalo, American *See* Bison
Buffalo. Lepthien, E. U. **599.73**
Buffalo. Patent, D. H. **599.73**
Buffalo Brenda. Pinkwater, J. **Fic**
Buffalo hunt. Freedman, R. **970.004**
Buffalo woman. Goble, P. **398.2**
Bugs. Parker, N. W. **595.7**
Bugs for dinner? Epstein, S. **591.5**

Buholzer, Theres
Life of the snail (3-6) **594**

Building
See also Carpentry
Barton, B. Building a house (k-1) **690**

Building—*Continued*
Barton, B. Machines at work (k-1) **690**
Gibbons, G. How a house is built (k-2) **690**
Gibbons, G. Up goes the skyscraper! (k-2) **690**
Macaulay, D. Unbuilding (4 and up) **690**
Macaulay, D. Underground (4 and up) **624.1**
Robbins, K. Building a house (3-6) **690**
Walker, L. Housebuilding for children (2 and up) **690**
Building a house. Barton, B. **690**
Building a house. Robbins, K. **690**
Buildings
Models
Weiss, H. Model buildings and how to make them (4 and up) **690**
Buildings in art
Ames, L. J. Draw 50 buildings and other structures (4 and up) **743**
Bukhtan Bukhtanovich
Afanas'ev, A. N. Bukhtan Bukhtanovich
In Afanas'ev, A. N. Russian fairy tales p168-70 **398.2**
The **Bul-Bul** Bird. Lerchis-Puskaitis, A.
In Best-loved folktales of the world p395-99 **398.2**
Bulfinch, Thomas, 1796-1867
Bulfinch's mythology (6 and up) **291**
Bulfinch's mythology. Bulfinch, T. **291**
Bull, Peter
(il) Hyndley, K. The voyage of the Beagle [biography of Charles Darwin] **92**
Bulla, Clyde Robert, 1914-
The cardboard crown (3-5) **Fic**
The chalk box kid **E**
The Christmas coat **E**
Daniel's duck **E**
A grain of wheat: a writer begins (3-5) **92**
A lion to guard us (3-5) **Fic**
Shoeshine girl (3-5) **Fic**
St. Valentine's Day (1-3) **394.2**
The sword in the tree (2-5) **Fic**
Bulletin of the Center for Children's Books **028.1**
Bullfights
Biography
Say, A. El Chino (2-5) **92**
Fiction
Leaf, M. The story of Ferdinand **E**
Wojciechowska, M. Shadow of a bull (6 and up) **Fic**
Bulls
Fiction
Leaf, M. The story of Ferdinand **E**
The **bully** of Barkham Street. Stolz, M. See note under Stolz, M. A dog on Barkham Street **Fic**
Bumps in the night. Allard, H. **E**
Bun
Afanas'ev, A. N. The bun
In Afanas'ev, A. N. Russian fairy tales p447-49 **398.2**
A **bundle** of beasts. Hooper, P. **811**
Bunker, Chang, 1811-1874
See/See also pages in the following book(s):
Drimmer, F. Born different p92-121 (6 and up) **920**
Bunker, Eng, 1811-1874
See/See also pages in the following book(s):
Drimmer, F. Born different p92-121 (6 and up) **920**
Bunnicula. Howe, D. **Fic**
Bunnies and bonnets. McGowan, J.
In Holiday plays round the year p255-66 **812.008**
Bunting, Anne Eve *See* Bunting, Eve, 1928-
Bunting, Eve, 1928-
Ghost's hour, spook's hour **E**
How many days to America? **E**
In the haunted house **E**
The man who could call down owls **E**
The Mother's Day mice **E**
No nap **E**
Our sixth-grade sugar babies (4-6) **Fic**
Scary, scary Halloween **E**
The Wall **E**
The Wednesday surprise **E**
Bunyan, Paul (Legendary character)
Kellogg, S. Paul Bunyan (k-3) **398.2**
Rounds, G. Ol' Paul, the mighty logger (3-6) **398.2**
Fiction
Rounds, G. The morning the sun refused to rise **E**
Bunyip
The Bunyip
In Best-loved folktales of the world p608-10 **398.2**
Buonarroti, Michel Angelo *See* Michelangelo Buonarroti, 1475-1564
Burch, Robert, 1925-
Christmas with Ida Early (4 and up) **Fic**
Ida Early comes over the mountain (4 and up) **Fic**
Queenie Peavy (5 and up) **Fic**
Burchard, Sue
The Statue of Liberty (5 and up) **974.7**
Burenushka, the little red cow. Afanas'ev, A. N.
In Afanas'ev, A. N. Russian fairy tales p146-50 **398.2**

Burford, Kay
(il) Jordan, J. Kimako's story **Fic**
Burger, Carl, 1888-1967
(il) Gipson, F. B. Old Yeller **Fic**
Buried treasure
Fine, J. C. Sunken ships & treasure (5 and up) **910.4**
Gibbons, G. Sunken treasure (2-4) **910.4**
Hidden treasures of the sea (4 and up) **910.4**
Schwartz, A. Gold & silver, silver & gold (5 and up) **910.4**
See/See also pages in the following book(s):
Cook, J. L. The mysterious undersea world p62-71 (4 and up) **551.46**
Fiction
Bellairs, J. The treasure of Alpheus Winterborn (5 and up) **Fic**
Cole, J. Don't tell the whole world! **E**
Hamilton, V. The mystery of Drear House (5 and up) **Fic**
Kendall, S. The Bell Reef (5 and up) **Fic**
Kennedy, R. Amy's eyes (5 and up) **Fic**
Myers, W. D. The Mouse rap (6 and up) **Fic**
Stevenson, R. L. Treasure Island (6 and up) **Fic**
Burkert, Nancy Ekholm
(il) Andersen, H. C. Hans Christian Andersen's The fir tree **Fic**
(il) Andersen, H. C. The nightingale **Fic**
(il) Dahl, R. James and the giant peach **Fic**
(il) Lear, E. Edward Lear's The Scroobious Pip **821**
Burks, John B., 1942-
Norway—in pictures. See Norway—in pictures **948.1**
Burleigh, Robert, 1936-
A man named Thoreau (3-5) **92**
Burleson, Joe
(il) Naylor, P. R. The witch's eye **Fic**
Burnett, Frances Hodgson, 1849-1924
A little princess (4-6) **Fic**
A little princess; dramatization. See Thane, A. The little princess
The secret garden (4-6) **Fic**
Burnford, Sheila, 1918-1984
The incredible journey (4 and up) **Fic**
Burnie, David
Bird (4 and up) **598**
Plant (4 and up) **581**
Tree (4 and up) **582.16**
The **burning** questions of Bingo Brown. Byars, B. C. **Fic**
Burningham, John, 1936-
Come away from the water, Shirley **E**
Granpa **E**
Hey! get off our train **E**
John Patrick Norman McHennessy—the boy who was always late **E**
Mr. Gumpy's motor car **E**
Mr. Gumpy's outing **E**
The shopping basket **E**
Slam bang **E**
Sniff shout. See note under Burningham, J. Slam bang **E**
Time to get out of the bath, Shirley **E**
Wobble pop. See note under Burningham, J. Slam bang **E**
(il) Fleming, I. Chitty-Chitty-Bang-Bang **Fic**
(il) Grahame, K. The wind in the willows **Fic**
Burns, Anthony, 1834-1862
About
Hamilton, V. Anthony Burns: the defeat and triumph of a fugitive slave (5 and up) **92**
Burns, Marilyn
The book of think (4 and up) **153.4**
The Hanukkah book (4 and up) **296.4**
I am not a short adult! (3-6) **305.23**
The I hate mathematics! book (5 and up) **513**
Math for smarty pants (5 and up) **513**
This book is about time (5 and up) **529**
Burrell, Galen
(il) Hirschi, R. City geese **598**
(il) Hirschi, R. Headgear **599.73**
(il) Hirschi, R. Who lives in—the forest? **591.5**
(il) Hirschi, R. Who lives in—the mountains? **591.5**
(il) Hirschi, R. Who lives on—the prairie? **591.5**
Burris, Burmah
(il) Carlson, B. W. Listen! and help tell the story **372.6**
Burros *See* Donkeys
Burroway, Janet, 1936-
(jt. auth) Lord, J. V. The giant jam sandwich **E**
Burstein, Chaya M.
A kid's catalog of Israel (4 and up) **956.94**
Burstein, Fred
Rebecca's nap **E**
Burt Dow, deep-water man. McCloskey, R. **E**
Burton, Maurice, 1898-
Birds (5 and up) **598**
Warm-blooded animals (5 and up) **599**
Burton, Virginia Lee, 1909-1968
Katy and the big snow **E**

Burton, Virginia Lee, 1909-1968 — *Continued*
The little house E
Mike Mulligan and his steam shovel E
(il) Andersen, H. C. The emperor's new clothes Fic
See/See also pages in the following book(s):
Caldecott Medal books, 1938-1957 p88-97 028.5
The Illustrator's notebook p45-49 741.6

Burundi
Description and travel
Powzyk, J. A. Tracking wild chimpanzees in Kibira National Park (3-6) 599.88

Burying grounds *See* Cemeteries

Buses
Crews, D. School bus E

Bush, George, 1924-
About
Kent, Z. George Bush: forty-first president of the United States (4 and up) 92
Sullivan, G. George Bush (5 and up) 92

Bushy bride
Moe, J. E. Bushy bride
In The Red fairy book p322-28 398.2

Business
See/See also pages in the following book(s):
Caney, S. Steven Caney's kids' America p386-401 (4 and up) 790.1
Fiction
Merrill, J. The toothpaste millionaire (4-6) Fic
Schwartz, A. Bea and Mr. Jones E

Business people
Aaseng, N. From rags to riches (5 and up) 920
Aaseng, N. The problem solvers (5 and up) 920
Aaseng, N. The unsung heroes (5 and up) 920

Buster's world. Reuter, B. Fic

Busy buzzing bumblebees and other tongue twisters. Schwartz, A. 808.88

The **Busy** farmer's wife
In Juba this and Juba that p60-61 372.6

Busybody Nora. Hurwitz, J. Fic

Butler, Beverly, 1932-
Maggie by my side (4 and up) 362.4

Butler, Dorothy, 1925-
Cushla and her books 362.4
My brown bear Barney E

Butler, John, 1952-
(il) Animal families of the wild. See Animal families of the wild 591
(il) Lane, M. The fish 597

Butterflies
See also Caterpillars
Fischer-Nagel, H. Life of the butterfly (3-6) 595.7
Gibbons, G. Monarch butterfly (1-3) 595.7
Herberman, E. The great butterfly hunt (4-6) 595.7
Mitchell, R. T. Butterflies and moths (4 and up) 595.7
Ryder, J. Where butterflies grow (k-2) 595.7
Saintsing, D. The world of butterflies (k-2) 595.7
Whalley, P. E. S. Butterfly & moth (4 and up) 595.7
See/See also pages in the following book(s):
Simon, S. Pets in a jar (4 and up) 639
Zim, H. S. Insects (4 and up) 595.7
Fiction
Kipling, R. The butterfly that stamped (1-4) Fic
Williams, K. L. Baseball and butterflies (2-4) Fic

Butterflies and moths. Mitchell, R. T. 595.7

Butterfly & moth. Whalley, P. E. S. 595.7

The **butterfly** man. Yep, L.
In Yep, L. The rainbow people p60-68 398.2

Butterfly soul. Crossley-Holland, K.
In Crossley-Holland, K. British folk tales p365-67 398.2

The **butterfly** that stamped. Kipling, R. Fic
also in Kipling, R. Just so stories S C

Butterworth, Oliver, 1915-1990
The enormous egg (4 and up) Fic

The **button** box. Reid, M. S. E

A **button** in her ear. Litchfield, A. B. 617.8

Butwin, Frances
The Jews in America
In The In America series 305.8

Buxton, Jane Heath, 1948-
Baby bears and how they grow (k-3) 599.74

Buzzard man
In The Monkey's haircut, and other stories told by the Maya p37-43 398.2

By command of Prince Daniel
Afanas'ev, A. N. Prince Danila Govorila
In Afanas'ev, A. N. Russian fairy tales p351-56 398.2

By the Great Horn Spoon! Fleischman, S. **Fic**
By the shores of Silver Lake. Wilder, L. I. See note under Wilder, L. I. Little house in the big woods **Fic**
Byam, Michèle
Arms & armor (4 and up) **355.8**
Byard, Carole, 1941-
(il) Greenfield, E. Africa dream **E**
(il) Greenfield, E. Grandmama's joy **E**
(il) Little, L. J. I can do it by myself **E**
(il) Mendez, P. The black snowman **E**
(il) Tobias, T. Arthur Mitchell **92**
(il) Walter, M. P. Have a happy— **Fic**
(il) Yarbrough, C. Cornrows **E**
Byars, Betsy Cromer, 1928-
The 18th emergency (4-6) **Fic**
After the Goat Man (5 and up) **Fic**
The animal, the vegetable, and John D Jones (5 and up) **Fic**
Beans on the roof (2-4) **Fic**
Bingo Brown and the language of love. See note under Byars, B. C. The burning questions of Bingo Brown **Fic**
Bingo Brown, gypsy lover. See note under Byars, B. C. The burning questions of Bingo Brown **Fic**
A Blossom promise. See note under Byars, B. C. The not-just-anybody family **Fic**
The Blossoms and the Green Phantom. See note under Byars, B. C. The not-just-anybody family **Fic**
The Blossoms meet the Vulture Lady. See note under Byars, B. C. The not-just-anybody family **Fic**
The burning questions of Bingo Brown (4 and up) **Fic**
The cartoonist (4 and up) **Fic**
Cracker Jackson (5 and up) **Fic**
The Cybil war (4-6) **Fic**
Go and hush the baby **E**
The Golly Sisters go West **E**
Hooray for the Golly sisters! **E**
The house of wings (4-6) **Fic**
The midnight fox (4-6) **Fic**
The midnight fox [excerpt]
In The Random House book of humor for children p51-65 **817.008**
The night swimmers (5 and up) **Fic**
The not-just-anybody family (5 and up) **Fic**
The pinballs (5 and up) **Fic**
The summer of the swans (5 and up) **Fic**
Trouble River (4-6) **Fic**
The TV kid (4-6) **Fic**
The two-thousand-pound goldfish (5 and up) **Fic**
See/See also pages in the following book(s):
Newbery and Caldecott Medal books, 1966-1975 p68-72, 75-78 **028.5**
Bye, Baby Bunting. Aiken, J.
In Aiken, J. Past eight o'clock p53-70 **S C**
"Bye-Bye"
In The Magic orange tree, and other Haitian folktales p189-93 **398.2**
Byers, Rinda M.
Mycca's baby **E**

C

C D C? Steig, W. **793.73**
The **cabbage** donkey. Grimm, J.
In The Yellow fairy book p42-49 **398.2**
Cabeza de Vaca, Alvar Nuñez *See* Nuñez Cabeza de Vaca, Alvar, 16th cent.
The **cabin** faced west. Fritz, J. **Fic**
Cabinet officers
Parker, N. W. The president's cabinet and how it grew (3-5) **353.04**
Cable car to catastrophe. Quackenbush, R. M. See note under Quackenbush, R. M. Express train to trouble **Fic**
A **cache** of jewels and other collective nouns. Heller, R. **428**
Cactus
Bash, B. Desert giant (3-5) **583**
Overbeck, C. Cactus (4 and up) **583**
Fiction
Keats, E. J. Clementina's cactus **E**
Caddie Woodlawn. Brink, C. R. **Fic**
Caffeine
Perry, R. L. Focus on nicotine and caffeine (3-6) **616.86**
Cage birds
See also Canaries
See/See also pages in the following book(s):
Chrystie, F. N. Pets p60-85 (4 and up) **636.088**
Caines, Jeannette Franklin, 1938-
Abby **E**
Daddy **E**
I need a lunch box **E**
Just us women **E**
Cairo (Egypt)
Fiction
Heide, F. P. The day of Ahmed's secret **E**
Cake
Fiction
Forest, H. The woman who flummoxed the fairies (k-2) **398.2**
Parker, N. W. Love from Aunt Betty **E**

Cake—Fiction—*Continued*
Rice, E. Benny bakes a cake **E**
Willard, N. The high rise glorious skittle skat roarious sky pie angel food cake (2-4) **Fic**

Calabro, Marian
Operation grizzly bear (5 and up) **599.74**

Calaprice, Alice
(jt. auth) Heinrich, B. An owl in the house **598**

Caldecott, Randolph, 1846-1886
See/See also pages in the following book(s):
Caldecott Medal books, 1938-1957 p1-5 **028.5**
The Illustrator's notebook p30-40 **741.6**
Illustrators of children's books p66-75 (v1) **741.6**
Only connect: readings on children's literature p317-25 **028.5**
Sendak, M. Caldecott & Co.: notes on books and pictures p21-25 **028.5**

Caldecott & Co.: notes on books and pictures. Sendak, M. **028.5**

Caldecott Medal books
Bemelmans, L. See Bemelmans, L. Madeline's rescue (1954) **E**
Brown, M. See Brown, M. Once upon a mouse (1962) **398.2**
Brown, M. See Cendrars, B. Shadow (1983) **841**
Brown, M. See Perrault, C. Cinderella (1955) **398.2**
Burton, V. L. See Burton, V. L. The little house (1943) **E**
Cooney, B. See Cooney, B. Chanticleer and the fox (1959) **E**
Cooney, B. See Hall, D. Ox-cart man (1980) **E**
D'Aulaire, I. and D'Aulaire, E. P. See D'Aulaire, I. Abraham Lincoln (1940) **92**
Dillon, L. and Dillon, D. See Aardema, V. Why mosquitoes buzz in people's ears (1976) **398.2**
Dillon, L. and Dillon, D. See Musgrove, M. Ashanti to Zulu: African traditions (1977) **960**
Duvoisin, R. See Tresselt, A. R. White snow, bright snow (1948) **E**
Egielski, R. See Yorinks, A. Hey, Al (1987) **E**
Emberley, E. See Emberley, B. Drummer Hoff (1968) **398.8**
Gammel, S. See Ackerman, K. Song and dance man (1989) **E**
Goble, P. See Goble, P. The girl who loved wild horses (1979) **E**
Hader, B. and Hader, E. See Hader, B. The big snow (1949) **E**
Haley, G. E. See Haley, G. E. A story, a story (1971) **398.2**
Handforth, T. See Handforth, T. Mei Li (1939) **E**
Hogrogian, N. See Hogrogian, N. One fine day (1972) **398.2**
Hogrogian, N. See Leodhas, S. N. Always room for one more (1966) **781.62**
Hyman, T. S. See Hodges, M. Saint George and the dragon (1985) **398.2**
Jones, E. O. See Field, R. Prayer for a child (1945) **242**
Keats, E. J. See Keats, E. J. The snowy day (1963) **E**
Lathrop, D. P. See Bible. Selections. Animals of the Bible (1938) **220.8**
Lent, B. See Mosel, A. The funny little woman (1973) **398.2**
Lobel, A. See Lobel, A. Fables (1981) **Fic**
Macauley, D. See Macaulay, D. Black and white (1990) **E**
McCloskey, R. See McCloskey, R. Make way for ducklings (1942) **E**
McCloskey, R. See McCloskey, R. Time of wonder (1958) **E**
McDermott, G. See McDermott, G. Arrow to the sun (1975) **398.2**
Milhous, K. See Milhous, K. The egg tree (1951) **E**
Montresor, B. See De Regniers, B. S. May I bring a friend? (1965) **E**
Ness, E. See Ness, E. Sam, Bangs & Moonshine (1967) **E**
Petersham, Maud and Petersham, Miska See The Rooster crows (1946) **398.8**
Politi, L. See Politi, L. Song of the swallows (1950) **E**
Provensen, A. and Provensen, M. See Provensen, A. The glorious flight: across the Channel with Louis Blériot, July 25, 1909 (1984) **92**
Rojankovsky, F. See Langstaff, J. M. Frog went a-courtin' (1956) **781.62**
Schoenherr, J. See Yolen, J. Owl moon (1988) **E**
Sendak, M. See Sendak, M. Where the wild things are (1964) **E**
Shulevitz, U. See Ransome, A. The Fool of the World and the flying ship (1969) **398.2**
Sidjakov, N. See Robbins, R. Baboushka and the three kings (1961) **398.2**
Simont, M. See Udry, J. M. A tree is nice (1957) **E**
Slobodkin, L. See Thurber, J. Many moons (1944) **Fic**
Steig, W. See Steig, W. Sylvester and the magic pebble (1970) **E**
Van Allsburg, C. See Van Allsburg, C. Jumanji (1982) **E**

Caldecott Medal books—*Continued*
Van Allsburg, C. See Van Allsburg, C. The Polar Express (1986) **E**
Ward, L. K. See Ward, L. K. The biggest bear (1953) **E**
Young, E. See Young, E. Lon Po Po (1990) **398.2**

Caldecott Medal books (as subject)
Caldecott Medal books, 1938-1957 **028.5**
Lacy, L. E. Art and design in children's picture books **741.6**
Newbery and Caldecott Medal books, 1966-1975 **028.5**
Newbery and Caldecott Medal books, 1976-1985 **028.5**

Caldecott Medal books, 1938-1957 **028.5**

Caldwell, John
(il) Sullivan, G. Any number can play **796**

Caleb & Kate. Steig, W. **E**

The **calendar**. Porte-Thomas, B. A.
In Porte-Thomas, B. A. Jesse's ghost, and other stories p65-71 **S C**

Calendar art. Fisher, L. E. **529**

Calendars
Chase's annual events **394.2**
Fisher, L. E. Calendar art (4 and up) **529**
Gregory, R. W. Anniversaries and holidays **394.2**
Perl, L. Blue Monday and Friday the Thirteenth (4-6) **398**
See/See also pages in the following book(s):
Bauer, C. F. Celebrations p43-62 **808.8**

A **calf** is born. Kaizuki, K. **636.2**

Calhoun, Mary, 1926-
Cross-country cat **E**
Depend on Katie John. See note under Calhoun, M. Katie John **Fic**
Honestly, Katie John. See note under Calhoun, M. Katie John **Fic**
Hot-air Henry **E**
Katie John (4-6) **Fic**
Katie John and Heathcliff. See note under Calhoun, M. Katie John **Fic**

Calico bush. Field, R. **Fic**

California
Stein, R. C. California
In America the beautiful **973**
Fiction
Beatty, P. Eight mules from Monterey (5 and up) **Fic**
Gates, D. Blue willow (4 and up) **Fic**
Politi, L. Song of the swallows **E**
Snyder, Z. K. And condors danced (5 and up) **Fic**
Snyder, Z. K. The velvet room (5 and up) **Fic**
Soto, G. Baseball in April, and other stories (5 and up) **S C**
Uchida, Y. A jar of dreams (5 and up) **Fic**
Gold discoveries
Blumberg, R. The great American gold rush (5 and up) **979.4**
See/See also pages in the following book(s):
Meltzer, M. The Chinese Americans p25-32 (6 and up) **305.8**
Gold discoveries—Fiction
Fleischman, S. By the Great Horn Spoon! (4-6) **Fic**

Caliph Stork
The Story of Caliph Stork
In The Green fairy book p32-42 **398.2**

Calisthenics *See* Gymnastics

Call it courage. Sperry, A. **Fic**

The **call** of the wild. London, J. **Fic**

Callanan, Cecelia C.
Cupid and Company
In Holiday plays round the year p189-91 **812.008**

Callaway, Henry, 1817-1890
Famine does not make a man clever
In The Crest and the hide, and other African stories of heroes, chiefs, bards, hunters, sorcerers, and common people p73-76 **398.2**

Callen, Larry
Fifteen minutes
In The Random House book of humor for children p283-92 **817.008**
Pinch (5 and up) **Fic**

Calligraphy
Adkins, J. Letterbox: the art & history of letters (4 and up) **745.6**
Baron, N. Getting started in calligraphy (5 and up) **745.6**

Calmenson, Stephanie
Dinner guests
In The Read-aloud treasury p100-11 **808.8**
The lion and the mouse
In The Read-aloud treasury p188-89 **808.8**
What am I? (k-2) **793.73**
(comp) The Laugh book. See The Laugh book **808.8**
(comp) Miss Mary Mack and other children's street rhymes. See Miss Mary Mack and other children's street rhymes **796.1**
(comp) The Read-aloud treasury. See The Read-aloud treasury **808.8**

Calsada, David
(il) Cummings, E. E. Hist whist and other poems for children **811**

Calvino, Italo
And seven!
In The Scott, Foresman anthology of children's literature p260-62 **808.8**
The **calypso** alphabet. Agard, J. **E**
Camaralzaman, and Badoura, Princess of China
The Adventures of Prince Camaralzaman and the Princess Badoura
In The Arabian nights entertainments p216-66 **398.2**
Cambodia
Chandler, D. P. The land and people of Cambodia (5 and up) **959.6**
Camel gets his own back. Crouch, M.
In The Scott, Foresman anthology of children's literature p344-45 **808.8**
Camels
Waters, J. F. Camels: ships of the desert (k-3) **599.73**
Fiction
Kipling, R. How the camel got his hump (1-4) **Fic**
Cameron, Ann, 1943-
Julian, dream doctor. See note under Cameron, A. The stories Julian tells **Fic**
Julian, secret agent. See note under Cameron, A. The stories Julian tells **Fic**
Julian's glorious summer. See note under Cameron, A. The stories Julian tells **Fic**
More stories Julian tells. See note under Cameron, A. The stories Julian tells **Fic**
The most beautiful place in the world (2-4) **Fic**
The night we started dancing
In Free to be—a family p96-104 **810.8**
The stories Julian tells (2-4) **Fic**
The stories Julian tells [excerpt]
In The Random House book of humor for children p44-50 **817.008**
Cameron, Eleanor, 1912-
Beyond silence (6 and up) **Fic**
The court of the stone children (5 and up) **Fic**
Julia and the hand of God. See note under Cameron, E. A room made of windows **Fic**
Julia's magic. See note under Cameron, E. A room made of windows **Fic**
Mr. Bass's planetoid. See note under Cameron, E. The wonderful flight to the Mushroom Planet **Fic**
The private worlds of Julia Redfern. See note under Cameron, E. A room made of windows **Fic**
A room made of windows (5 and up) **Fic**
Stowaway to the Mushroom Planet. See note under Cameron, E. The wonderful flight to the Mushroom Planet **Fic**
That Julia Redfern. See note under Cameron, E. A room made of windows **Fic**
Time and Mr. Bass. See note under Cameron, E. The wonderful flight to the Mushroom Planet **Fic**
To the green mountains (6 and up) **Fic**
The wonderful flight to the Mushroom Planet (4-6) **Fic**
Cameron, Fiona
(jt. auth) Kristensen, P. S. We live in Egypt **962**
Cameron, Tracey
(il) Schwartz, A. Telling fortunes **133.3**
Camouflage (Biology)
Dewey, J. Can you find me? (2-4) **591.5**
McCauley, J. R. Animals and their hiding places (k-3) **591.5**
Powzyk, J. A. Animal camouflage (3-6) **591.5**
Selsam, M. E. Backyard insects (k-3) **595.7**
Fiction
Aruego, J. We hide, you seek **E**
Camp Fat. Konigsburg, E. L.
In Konigsburg, E. L. Altogether, one at a time p29-59 **S C**
Camping
Fiction
Gilson, J. 4B goes wild (4-6) **Fic**
Johnson, A. The grizzly (5 and up) **Fic**
Locker, T. Where the river begins **E**
Rockwell, A. F. The night we slept outside **E**
Say, A. The lost lake **E**
Tafuri, N. Do not disturb **E**
Williams, V. B. Three days on a river in a red canoe **E**
Camps
Fiction
Cole, B. The goats (5 and up) **Fic**
Danziger, P. There's a bat in bunk five (5 and up) **Fic**
O'Connor, J. Yours till Niagara Falls, Abby **Fic**
Can I help? Rockwell, A. F. **E**
Can I keep him? Kellogg, S. **E**
Can the whales be saved? Whitfield, P. J. **574.5**
Can you find me? Dewey, J. **591.5**
Can you imagine—? Gardner, B. **E**
Canada
Shepherd, J. A. Canada (4 and up) **971**

Canada—*Continued*
Children
See Children—Canada
Fiction
Blades, A. Mary of Mile 18 (2-4) **Fic**
Burnford, S. The incredible journey (4 and up) **Fic**
Carlson, N. S. The talking cat, and other stories of French Canada (3-6) **S C**
Ellis, S. Next-door neighbors (4 and up) **Fic**
Lippincott, J. W. Wilderness champion (5 and up) **Fic**
Folklore
See Folklore—Canada
History—0-1763 (New France)
Anderson, J. Pioneer settlers of New France (3-5) **971.01**
Immigration and emigration
Kurelek, W. They sought a new world (4 and up) **325**
Social life and customs
Kurelek, W. A northern nativity (4 and up) **232.9**
Canada. National Gallery *See* National Gallery of Canada
The **Canada** geese quilt. Kinsey-Warnock, N. **Fic**
Canada goose *See* Geese
Canadian authors *See* Authors, Canadian
Canadian fairy tales. See Martin, E. Tales of the Far North **398.2**
Canals
Scarry, H. Life on a barge (3-6) **386**
Canaries
See/See also pages in the following book(s):
Chrystie, F. N. Pets p60-68 (4 and up) **636.088**
Cancer
See also Leukemia
Silverstein, A. Cancer: can it be stopped? (6 and up) **616.99**
Fiction
Little, J. Mama's going to buy you a mockingbird (5 and up) **Fic**
Candles
See/See also pages in the following book(s):
Burns, M. The Hanukkah book p27-39 (4 and up) **296.4**
Candles, cakes, and donkey tails. Perl, L. **392**
Candy Floss. Godden, R.
In Godden, R. Four dolls p108-37 **S C**
Caney, Steven
Steven Caney's kids' America (4 and up) **790.1**
Cannibal Island
In The Naked bear p44-51 **398.2**
Cannon, Annie
(il) McNulty, F. With love from Koko **599.88**
Canoe in the rapids. Carlson, N. S.
In Carlson, N. S. The talking cat, and other stories of French Canada p54-65 **S C**
In The Scott, Foresman anthology of children's literature p355-58 **808.8**
Canoeing is for me. Moran, T. **797.1**
Canoes and canoeing
Moran, T. Canoeing is for me (3-5) **797.1**
Fiction
Williams, V. B. Three days on a river in a red canoe **E**
Can't rest. Leach, M.
In Leach, M. Whistle in the graveyard p43-44 **398.2**
Can't you make them behave, King George? [biography of George III, King of Great Britain]. Fritz, J. **92**
Canterbury tales. Cohen, B. **Fic**
Cap o' Rushes
Jacobs, J. Cap o' Rushes
In Jacobs, J. English fairy tales p51-56 **398.2**
In Womenfolk and fairy tales p77-82 **398.2**
Williams-Ellis, A. Cap o' Rushes
In Williams-Ellis, A. Tales from the enchanted world p8-16 **398.2**
Cape Cod (Mass.)
Fiction
Fritz, J. The good giants and the bad pukwudgies (k-3) **398.2**
Čapek, Jindra
(il) Bolliger, M. Tales of a long afternoon **398.2**
Capote, Truman, 1924-1984
A Christmas memory (3-5) **Fic**
Caps for sale. Slobodkina, E. **E**
Captain Snap and the children of Vinegar Lane. Schotter, R. **E**
Captain Whiz-Bang. Stanley, D. **E**
The **captive**. O'Dell, S. **Fic**
Car. Sutton, R. **629.222**
The **car** trip. Oxenbury, H. **E**
Caras, Roger A.
Animal families of the wild. See Animal families of the wild **591**
The endless migration [excerpt]
In Animal families of the wild: animal stories p69-79 **591**

Carbon
Bronowski, J. Biography of an atom (4 and up) **539**
Carbon 14 dating *See* Radiocarbon dating
The **cardboard** crown. Bulla, C. R. **Fic**
Cardiovascular system
See also Blood—Circulation; Heart
Care of uncommon pets. Weber, W. J. **636.088**
Career changes
Aaseng, N. Midstream changes (5 and up) **331.7**
Careers *See* Occupations
Caribbean canvas. Lessac, F. **811**
Caribbean cookery *See* Cookery, Caribbean
Caribbean region
See also West Indies
Fiction
Taylor, T. The cay (5 and up) **Fic**
Poetry
Nichols, G. Come on into my tropical garden (3-5) **821**
Social life and customs
Agard, J. The calypso alphabet **E**
Caribbean region in art
Lessac, F. Caribbean canvas **811**
Caribou
Caras, R. A. The endless migration
In Animal families of the wild: animal stories p69-79 **591**
Owens, M. B. A caribou alphabet **E**
A **caribou** alphabet. Owens, M. B. **E**
Caricatures *See* Cartoons and caricatures
Carl goes shopping. Day, A. **E**
Carl of the drab coat
Stephens, J. The Carl of the Drab Coat
In Stephens, J. Irish fairy tales p173-200 **398.2**
Carle, Eric
Do you want to be my friend? **E**
Eric Carle's animals, animals (1-3) **808.81**
The grouchy ladybug **E**
A house for Hermit Crab **E**
The mixed-up chameleon **E**
Rooster's off to see the world **E**
The very busy spider **E**
The very hungry caterpillar **E**
(il) Green, N. The hole in the dike **E**
Carlota [excerpt]. O'Dell, S.
In Face to face: a collection of stories by celebrated Soviet and American writers p165-76 **S C**
Carlson, Bernice Wells
Listen! and help tell the story **372.6**
(jt. auth) Hunt, K. Masks and mask makers **391**
Carlson, Lori
(ed) Where angels glide at dawn. See Where angels glide at dawn **S C**
Carlson, Nancy L., 1953-
I like me! **E**
Carlson, Natalie Savage
A brother for the orphelines. See note under Carlson, N. S. The happy orpheline **Fic**
The canoe in the rapids
In The Scott, Foresman anthology of children's literature p355-58 **808.8**
The family under the bridge (3-5) **Fic**
A grandmother for the orphelines. See note under Carlson, N. S. The happy orpheline **Fic**
The happy orpheline (3-5) **Fic**
Little Nichet's baby sister
In The Scott, Foresman anthology of children's literature p352-54 **808.8**
The orphelines in the enchanted castle. See note under Carlson, N. S. The happy orpheline **Fic**
A pet for the orphelines. See note under Carlson, N. S. The happy orpheline **Fic**
Spooky night **E**
The talking cat
In Best-loved folktales of the world p688-94 **398.2**
The talking cat, and other stories of French Canada (3-6) **S C**
Contents: Skunk in Tante Odette's oven; The talking cat; Jean Labadie's big black dog; Speckled hen's egg; Canoe in the rapids; Ghostly fishermen; "Loup-garou" in the woods
Carlstrom, Nancy White, 1948-
Better not get wet, Jesse Bear. See note under Carlstrom, N. W. Jesse Bear, what will you wear? **E**
Blow me a kiss, Miss Lilly **E**
Grandpappy **E**
It's about time, Jesse Bear, and other rhymes. See note under Carlstrom, N. W. Jesse Bear, what will you wear? **E**
Jesse Bear, what will you wear? **E**
Carmi, Giora
(il) Barkin, C. Happy Thanksgiving! **394.2**
(il) Kimmel, E. A. The Chanukkah guest **E**
Carnegie, Andrew, 1835-1919
See/See also pages in the following book(s):
Jacobs, W. J. Great lives: human rights p155-64 (5 and up) **920**
Carnivorous plants *See* Insectivorous plants
Carnivorous plants. Overbeck, C. **583**
Carols
The Friendly beasts (k-3) **782.28**
Mohr, J. Silent night (k-2) **782.28**

Carols—*Continued*
Raffi. The Raffi Christmas treasury **782.42**
Tom Glazer's Christmas songbook **782.28**
Tomie dePaola's book of Christmas carols **782.28**
The Twelve days of Christmas **782.42**
We wish you a merry Christmas **782.28**
What a morning! **782.25**
See/See also pages in the following book(s):
Take joy! The Tasha Tudor Christmas book p66-125 **394.2**

The **Carosyn**. MacDonald, G.
In MacDonald, G. The complete fairy tales of George MacDonald **S C**

Carousel. Crews, D. **E**

The **carp** in the bathtub. Cohen, B. **Fic**

Carpenter, Frances
Tales of a Chinese grandmother (4 and up) **398.2**
Contents: Inside the bright red gate; How Pan Ku made the world; Sisters in the sun; Gentle Gwan Yin; God that lived in the kitchen; Guardians of the gate; Painted eyebrow; Ting Lan and the lamb; Daughter of the dragon king; Big feet of the Empress Tu Chin; Grateful fox fairy; Two dutiful sons; King of the monkeys; Lady with the horse's head; Poet and the peony princess; First emperor's magic whip; Wonderful pear tree; How the eight old ones crossed the sea; White snake; Prince Chi Ti's city; Ko-Ai's lost shoe; Spinning maid and the cowherd; Lost star princess; Mandarin and the butterflies; Heng O, the moon lady; Cheng's fighting cricket; Maid in the mirror; Miss Lin, the sea goddess; Simple Seng and the parrot; Old Old One's birthday

Carpenter, Humphrey
The Oxford companion to children's literature **028.5**

Carpentry
Walker, L. Carpentry for children (4 and up) **694**

Tools

Adkins, J. Toolchest (5 and up) **684**
Lasson, R. If I had a hammer: woodworking with seven basic tools (4 and up) **684**

Carpentry for children. Walker, L. **694**

Carpets
See also Rugs

Fiction

Parkin, R. The red carpet **E**

Carran, Betty
Romania (4 and up) **949.8**

Carriages and carts
Tunis, E. Wheels: a pictorial history (5 and up) **388.3**

Carrick, Carol
Aladdin and the wonderful lamp (2-4) **398.2**
Ben and the porcupine **E**
Big old bones **E**
The crocodiles still wait (1-3) **567.9**
Dark and full of secrets. See note under Carrick, C. Ben and the porcupine **E**
The foundling. See note under Carrick, C. Ben and the porcupine **E**
In the moonlight, waiting **E**
Left behind. See note under Carrick, C. Ben and the porcupine **E**
Octopus (2-4) **594**
Patrick's dinosaurs **E**
Paul's Christmas birthday **E**
Sleep out. See note under Carrick, C. Ben and the porcupine **E**
Stay away from Simon! (3-5) **Fic**
The washout. See note under Carrick, C. Ben and the porcupine **E**
What a wimp! (3-5) **Fic**
What happened to Patrick's dinosaurs? **E**

Carrick, Donald
Harald and the great stag **E**
Milk (k-1) **637**
(il) Bunting, E. Ghost's hour, spook's hour **E**
(il) Bunting, E. The Wednesday surprise **E**
(il) Carrick, C. Aladdin and the wonderful lamp **398.2**
(il) Carrick, C. Ben and the porcupine **E**
(il) Carrick, C. Big old bones **E**
(il) Carrick, C. The crocodiles still wait **567.9**
(il) Carrick, C. In the moonlight, waiting **E**
(il) Carrick, C. Octopus **594**
(il) Carrick, C. Patrick's dinosaurs **E**
(il) Carrick, C. Paul's Christmas birthday **E**
(il) Carrick, C. Stay away from Simon! **Fic**
(il) Carrick, C. What a wimp! **Fic**
(il) Carrick, C. What happened to Patrick's dinosaurs? **E**
(il) Caudill, R. Wind, sand and sky **811**
(il) Hooks, W. H. Moss gown **398.2**
(il) Margolis, R. J. Secrets of a small brother **811**
(il) Uchida, Y. Journey to Topaz **Fic**

Carriers, Aircraft *See* Aircraft carriers

Carrie's war. Bawden, N. **Fic**

Carris, Joan Davenport, 1938-
Pets, vets, and Marty Howard (5 and up) **Fic**

Carroll, Charles, 1946-
(il) Conford, E. Me and the terrible two **Fic**

Carroll, Frances Laverne
Exciting, funny, scary, short, different, and sad books kids like about animals, science, sports, families, songs, and other things **011.6**
Carroll, Lewis, 1832-1898
Alice's adventures in Wonderland (4 and up) **Fic**
Alice's adventures in Wonderland, and Through the looking glass (4 and up) **Fic**
The complete works of Lewis Carroll **828**
Lewis Carroll's Jabberwocky **821**
Through the looking glass, and what Alice found there (4 and up) **Fic**
The walrus and the carpenter **821**
See/See also pages in the following book(s):
Horn Book reflections on children's books and reading p286-90 **028.5**
Only connect: readings on children's literature p238-43 **028.5**
Carroll, Pamela
(il) Silverstein, A. Life in a tidal pool **574.92**
(il) Silverstein, A. Nature's living lights **574.1**
(il) Simon, S. The largest dinosaurs **567.9**
Carroll, Walter
(il) Silverstein, A. Life in a tidal pool **574.92**
(il) Silverstein, A. Nature's living lights **574.1**
The **carrot** seed. Krauss, R. **E**
Carry, go, bring, come. Samuels, V. **E**
Carrying the running-aways. Hamilton, V.
In Hamilton, V. The people could fly: American black folktales p141-46 **398.2**
Cars (Automobiles) *See* Automobiles
Cars. Rockwell, A. F. **629.222**
Cars and how they go. Cole, J. **629.222**
The **carsick** zebra and other animal riddles. Adler, D. A. **793.73**
Carson, Rachel, 1907-1964
About
Harlan, J. Sounding the alarm: a biography of Rachel Carson (5 and up) **92**
Kudlinski, K. V. Rachel Carson: pioneer of ecology (4 and up) **92**
Carson, Robert, 1932-
Mississippi
In America the beautiful **973**
Carter, Alden R.
The Battle of Gettysburg (4 and up) **973.7**
Tree house
In Connections: short stories by outstanding writers for young adults p192-204 **S C**
Carter, Angela, 1940-
(comp) Sleeping beauty & other favourite fairy tales. See Sleeping beauty & other favourite fairy tales **398.2**
Carter, David A.
(il) Simon, S. How to be an ocean scientist in your own home **551.46**
Carter, Dorothy Sharp
The first flute
In The Scott, Foresman anthology of children's literature p402-05 **808.8**
Greedy Mariani
In Best-loved folktales of the world p731-34 **398.2**
How El Bizarron fooled the Devil
In Best-loved folktales of the world p745-48 **398.2**
How the Devil constructed a church
In Best-loved folktales of the world p753-55 **398.2**
The three fairies
In The Scott, Foresman anthology of children's literature p398-99 **808.8**
Carter, James Earl *See* Carter, Jimmy, 1924-
Carter, Jimmy, 1924-
About
Wade, L. R. James Carter: thirty-ninth president of the United States (4 and up) **92**
Cartography *See* Map drawing; Maps
Cartooning for kids. Benjamin, C. L. **741.5**
The **cartoonist**. Byars, B. C. **Fic**
Cartoons and caricatures
Ames, L. J. Draw 50 famous cartoons (4 and up) **741.5**
Benjamin, C. L. Cartooning for kids (4-6) **741.5**
Hoff, S. The young cartoonist (4 and up) **741.5**
Weiss, H. Cartoons and cartooning (4 and up) **741.5**
See/See also pages in the following book(s):
Illustrators of children's books p197-214 (v1) **741.6**
Cartoons and cartooning. Weiss, H. **741.5**
Carts *See* Carriages and carts
Carty, Leo, 1931-
(il) Mathis, S. B. Sidewalk story **Fic**
Carver, George Washington, 1864?-1943
About
Aliki. A weed is a flower: the life of George Washington Carver (k-3) **92**

Carver, George Washington, 1864?-1943—
About—*Continued*
Mitchell, B. A pocketful of goobers: a story about George Washington Carver (3-5) **92**
Carving, Wood *See* Wood carving
Casagrande, Louis B.
Focus on Mexico (4 and up) **972**
A **case** for Jenny Archer. Conford, E. **Fic**
The **case** of the Baker Street Irregular. Newman, R. **Fic**
The **case** of the borrowed baby. See Meyers, S. P.J. Clover, private eye: the case of the borrowed baby
The **case** of the elevator duck. Berends, P. B. **Fic**
The **case** of the Halloween hoot. See Meyers, S. P.J. Clover, private eye: the case of the Halloween hoot **Fic**
The **case** of the Indian curse. Newman, R. See note under Newman, R. The case of the Baker Street Irregular **Fic**
The **case** of the missing masterpiece. See Dicks, T. The Baker Street Irregulars in the case of the missing masterpiece **Fic**
The **case** of the missing mouse. See Meyers, S. P.J. Clover, private eye: the case of the missing mouse
The **case** of the murdered players. Newman, R. See note under Newman, R. The case of the Baker Street Irregular **Fic**
The **case** of the muttering mummy. Hildick, E. W. See note under Hildick, E. W. The case of the purloined parrot **Fic**
The **case** of the phantom frog. Hildick, E. W. See note under Hildick, E. W. The case of the purloined parrot **Fic**
The **case** of the purloined parrot. Hildick, E. W. **Fic**
The **case** of the stolen laundry. See Meyers, S. P.J. Clover, private eye: the case of the stolen laundry
The **case** of the threatened king. Newman, R. See note under Newman, R. The case of the Baker Street Irregular **Fic**
The **Case** of the uncooked eggs
In The Magic orange tree, and other Haitian folktales p49-55 **398.2**
The **case** of the vanishing corpse. Newman, R. See note under Newman, R. The case of the Baker Street Irregular **Fic**
The **case** of the wandering weathervanes. Hildick, E. W. See note under Hildick, E. W. The case of the purloined parrot **Fic**
The **case** of the watching boy. Newman, R. See note under Newman, R. The case of the Baker Street Irregular **Fic**
Caseley, Judith, 1951-
The cousins **E**
When Grandpa came to stay **E**
Casey, Brigid
(jt. auth) Lavine, S. A. Wonders of draft horses **636.1**
Casey, Denise
The friendly prairie dog (k-3) **599.32**
Casey at the bat. Thayer, E. L. **811**
Casilla, Robert
(il) Adler, D. A. Jackie Robinson: he was the first **92**
(il) Adler, D. A. Martin Luther King, Jr.: free at last **92**
(il) Adler, D. A. A picture book of Martin Luther King, Jr. **92**
(il) Howard, E. F. The train to Lulu's **E**
Cassedy, Sylvia, 1930-1989
Behind the attic wall (5 and up) **Fic**
In your own words (6 and up) **808**
Lucie Babbidge's house (4-6) **Fic**
M.E. and Morton (6 and up) **Fic**
Roomrimes: poems (3-6) **811**
Cassette tape recordings, Video *See* Videotapes
Cassie Binegar. MacLachlan, P. **Fic**
Cassie's journey. Harvey, B. **Fic**
The **castle** in the attic. Winthrop, E. **Fic**
The **castle** of Llyr. Alexander, L. See note under Alexander, L. The book of three **Fic**
The **castle** of the fly. Afanas'ev, A. N.
In Afanas'ev, A. N. Russian fairy tales p25-26 **398.2**
Castles
Adkins, J. The art and industry of sandcastles (4 and up) **728.8**
Macaulay, D. Castle (4 and up) **728.8**
Unstead, R. J. See inside a castle (5 and up) **728.8**
Fiction
Goodall, J. S. Creepy castle **E**
Models
Cummings, R. Make your own model forts & castles (5 and up) **623**
Pictorial works
Goodall, J. S. The story of a castle (3-6) **942**
Cat, the cock and the fox
Afanas'ev, A. N. The cat, the cock, and the fox
In Afanas'ev, A. N. Russian fairy tales p86-88 **398.2**
CAT (Computerized axial tomography) *See* Tomography, Computerized axial
Cat and Dog. Sherlock, Sir P. M.
In Sherlock, Sir P. M. West Indian folktales p93-96 **398.2**

Cat and Dog and the return of the dead
In The Magic orange tree, and other Haitian folktales p65-68 **398.2**
Cat and mouse in partnership. Grimm, J.
In Grimm, J. The complete Grimm's fairy tales p21-23 **398.2**
In The Yellow fairy book p1-3 **398.2**
Cat and mouse keep house. Grimm, J.
In Grimm, J. Tales from Grimm p27-38 **398.2**
The **cat** and the fiddler. Alexander, L.
In Alexander, L. The town cats, and other tales p95-111 **S C**
The **cat** and the fox. Grimm, J.
In Grimm, J. More tales from Grimm p61-62 **398.2**
The **cat** and the golden egg. Alexander, L.
In Alexander, L. The town cats, and other tales p49-61 **S C**
Cat and the mouse
Jacobs, J. Cat and the mouse
In Jacobs, J. English fairy tales p188-89 **398.2**
In Tomie dePaola's favorite nursery tales p114-16 **398.2**
Cat and the mouse in partnership
Grimm, J. Cat and mouse in partnership
In Grimm, J. The complete Grimm's fairy tales p21-23 **398.2**
In The Yellow fairy book p1-3 **398.2**
Grimm, J. Cat and mouse keep house
In Grimm, J. Tales from Grimm p27-38 **398.2**
The **cat** ate my gymsuit. Danziger, P. **Fic**
The **cat** goes fiddle-i-fee. Galdone, P. **398.8**
The **cat** in the hat. Seuss, Dr. **E**
The **Cat** in the Hat beginner book dictionary (k-3) **423**
The **cat** in the hat comes back! Seuss, Dr. **E**
The **Cat-King's** daughter. Alexander, L.
In Alexander, L. The town cats, and other tales p19-33 **S C**
Cat 'n mouse
Cat 'n mouse
In The Jack tales p127-34 **398.2**
The **cat** on the Dovrefell. Rockwell, A. F.
In Rockwell, A. F. Puss in boots, and other stories p75-79 **398.2**
Cat poems (1-3) **808.81**
Cat stories. Porte-Thomas, B. A.
In Porte-Thomas, B. A. Jesse's ghost, and other stories p23-28 **S C**
The **cat** that walked by himself. Kipling, R. **Fic**
also in Kipling, R. Just so stories **S C**
Cat walk. Stolz, M. **Fic**
The **cat** who became a poet. Mahy, M.
In Mahy, M. Nonstop nonsense p14-19 **828**
The **cat** who loved to sing. Hogrogian, N. **E**
The **cat** who said no. Alexander, L.
In Alexander, L. The town cats, and other tales p35-48 **S C**
The **cat** who thought she was a dog & the dog who thought he was a cat. Singer, I. B.
In Singer, I. B. Stories for children p308-12 **S C**
The **cat** who thought she was a dog and the dog who thought he was a cat. Singer, I. B.
In Singer, I. B. Naftali the storyteller and his horse, Sus, and other stories p103-08 **S C**
The **cat** who went to heaven. Coatsworth, E. J. **Fic**
The **cat** who wished to be a man. Alexander, L. **Fic**
The **cat** with the beckoning paw. MacDonald, M. R.
In MacDonald, M. R. When the lights go out p115-17 **372.6**
Catalanotto, Peter
Dylan's day out **E**
(il) Rylant, C. All I see **E**
Cataloging
Cataloging correctly for kids **025.3**
Gorman, M. The concise AACR2, 1988 revision **025.3**
Miller, R. E. Commonsense cataloging **025.3**
Audiovisual materials
Frost, C. O. Media access and organization **025.3**
Cataloging correctly for kids **025.3**
Catalogs, Classified
The Elementary school library collection **011.6**
Junior high school library catalog **011.6**
Catalogs, Library *See* Library catalogs
Catalogs, Subject
Subject guide to Children's books in print **015.73**

Catalogue of the world's most popular coins. Reinfeld, F. **737.4**
Catch me & kiss me & say it again: rhymes. Watson, C. **811**
Catch the wind! Gibbons, G. **796.1**
The **catchee**. Konigsburg, E. L.
In Konigsburg, E. L. Throwing shadows **S C**
Catching. Jensen, V. A. **E**
Catchpole, Clive
Deserts (2-4) **574.5**
Grasslands (2-4) **574.5**
Jungles (2-4) **574.5**
Mountains (2-4) **574.5**
Caterina the wise. Riordan, J.
In Riordan, J. The woman in the moon, and other tales of forgotten heroines p27-34 **398.2**
Caterpillars
Selsam, M. E. A first look at caterpillars (1-3) **595.7**
Selsam, M. E. Terry and the caterpillars (k-3) **595.7**
Fiction
Carle, E. The very hungry caterpillar **E**
Cathedral mouse. Chorao, K. **E**
Cathedral: the story of its construction. Macaulay, D. **726**
Cathedrals
Macaulay, D. Cathedral: the story of its construction (4 and up) **726**
Fiction
Chorao, K. Cathedral mouse **E**
Catholics
United States—Fiction
Delton, J. Kitty from the start (2-4) **Fic**
Catlin, George, 1796-1872
(il) Fronval, G. Indian signs and signals **419**
Cats
Cole, J. A cat's body **636.8**
De Paola, T. The kids' cat book (2-4) **636.8**
Hausherr, R. My first kitten (1-3) **636.8**
Henry, M. Benjamin West and his cat Grimalkin (4 and up) **92**
Hess, L. A cat's nine lives (2-5) **636.8**
Kuklin, S. Taking my cat to the vet (k-2) **636.8**
Overbeck, C. Cats (4 and up) **636.8**
Patterson, F. Koko's kitten (1-4) **599.88**
Seuss, Dr. The cat in the hat comes back! **E**
Simon, N. Cats do, dogs don't (k-2) **636.088**
See/See also pages in the following book(s):
Chrystie, F. N. Pets p26-39 (4 and up) **636.088**
Pringle, L. P. Feral: tame animals gone wild p55-65 (5 and up) **591.5**
Fiction
Alexander, L. The cat who wished to be a man (4-6) **Fic**
Alexander, L. The town cats, and other tales (3-5) **S C**
Asch, F. Here comes the cat! **E**
Babbitt, N. Nellie: a cat on her own **E**
Baker, B. Digby and Kate again **E**
Barber, A. The Mousehole cat **E**
Bonsall, C. N. The amazing, the incredible super dog **E**
Brandenberg, F. Aunt Nina and her nephews and nieces **E**
Brett, J. Annie and the wild animals **E**
Brown, R. A dark, dark tale **E**
Bryan, A. The cat's purr (k-2) **398.2**
Bunting, E. Scary, scary Halloween **E**
Burnford, S. The incredible journey (4 and up) **Fic**
Calhoun, M. Cross-country cat **E**
Calhoun, M. Hot-air Henry **E**
Carlson, N. S. Spooky night **E**
Chalmers, M. Throw a kiss, Harry **E**
Cleary, B. Socks (3-5) **Fic**
Coatsworth, E. J. The cat who went to heaven (4 and up) **Fic**
De Regniers, B. S. So many cats! **E**
Ehlert, L. Feathers for lunch **E**
Emberley, M. Ruby **E**
Estes, E. Pinky Pye (4-6) **Fic**
Fox, P. One-eyed cat (5 and up) **Fic**
Gág, W. Millions of cats **E**
Galdone, P. King of the Cats (k-2) **398.2**
Gantos, J. Rotten Ralph **E**
Griffith, H. V. Alex and the cat **E**
Herriot, J. Moses the kitten (2-4) **Fic**
Hoban, T. One little kitten **E**
Hogrogian, N. The cat who loved to sing **E**
Hurd, T. Axle the freeway cat **E**
Iwamatsu, T. Momo's kitten **E**
King-Smith, D. Martin's mice (3-5) **Fic**
Kipling, R. The cat that walked by himself (1-4) **Fic**
Le Guin, U. K. Catwings (2-4) **Fic**
Le Guin, U. K. Catwings return (2-4) **Fic**
Neville, E. C. It's like this, Cat (5 and up) **Fic**
Newberry, C. T. Marshmallow **E**
Oakley, G. The church mouse **E**
Okimoto, J. D. Blumpoe the Grumpoe meets Arnold the cat **E**
Ormerod, J. Kitten day **E**
Ormerod, J. The saucepan game **E**
Polushkin, M. Kitten in trouble **E**
Potter, B. The pie and the patty-pan **E**
Potter, B. The story of Miss Moppet **E**
Ross, T. The treasure of Cozy Cove **E**

Cats—Fiction—*Continued*
Samuels, B. Duncan & Dolores E
Selden, G. The cricket in Times Square (3-6) Fic
Seuss, Dr. The cat in the hat E
Slepian, J. The Broccoli tapes (5 and up) Fic
Snyder, Z. K. The witches of Worm (5 and up) Fic
Stanley, D. Captain Whiz-Bang E
Stevens, J. How the Manx cat lost its tail (k-2) 398.2
Stevenson, J. Mr. Hacker E
Stolz, M. Cat walk (3-6) Fic
Turkle, B. C. Do not open E
Uchida, Y. The two foolish cats (k-3) 398.2
Viorst, J. The tenth good thing about Barney E
Wagner, J. J. T. (3-6) Fic
Wild, M. The very best of friends E
Wolff, A. Only the cat saw E
Young, E. Up a tree E
Poetry
Cat poems (1-3) 808.81
Cats are cats 808.81
Galdone, P. Three little kittens (k-1) 398.8

Cats are cats 808.81
Cat's baptism
In The Magic orange tree, and other Haitian folktales p123-26 398.2
A **cat's** body. Cole, J. 636.8
Cat's cradle *See* String figures
Cat's cradle, owl's eyes. Gryski, C. 793.9
Cats do, dogs don't. Simon, N. 636.088
The **cat's** elbow, and other secret languages. Schwartz, A. 652
Cats in art
Ames, L. J. Draw 50 cats (4 and up) 743
Frame, P. Drawing cats and kittens (4 and up) 743
The **cat's** midsummer jamboree. Kherdian, D. E
A **cat's** nine lives. Hess, L. 636.8
The **cat's** purr. Bryan, A. 398.2
Catskill Mountains (N.Y.)
Fiction
George, J. C. My side of the mountain (5 and up) Fic
George, J. C. On the far side of the mountain (5 and up) Fic
Catskin. Reeves, J.
In Reeves, J. English fables and fairy stories p81-96 398.2
Catskins
In Grandfather tales p106-14 398.2
Cattle
See also Bulls; Dairy cattle
Kaizuki, K. A calf is born (k-2) 636.2
Fiction
Cooper, S. The silver cow: a Welsh tale (1-3) 398.2
Dennis, W. Flip and the cows E
Ernst, L. C. When Bluebell sang E
Krasilovsky, P. The cow who fell in the canal E
Catwings. Le Guin, U. K. Fic
Catwings return. Le Guin, U. K. Fic
Caudill, Rebecca, 1899-1985
A certain small shepherd (4 and up) Fic
Did you carry the flag today, Charley? (2-4) Fic
A pocketful of cricket E
Wind, sand and sky (1-4) 811
Cauld, cauld, forever cauld. Leach, M.
In Leach, M. Whistle in the graveyard p53 398.2
Cauld lad of Hilton
Jacobs, J. Cauld lad of Hilton
In Jacobs, J. English fairy tales p203-05 398.2
Cauley, Lorinda Bryan, 1951-
The town mouse and the country mouse (k-3) 398.2
(il) Kipling, R. The beginning of the armadilloes Fic
(il) Kipling, R. The elephant's child Fic
(il) Lear, E. The owl and the pussycat 821
(il) Old MacDonald had a farm. See Old MacDonald had a farm 781.62
Caulkins, Janet (Janet Hillier)
The picture life of Mikhail Gorbachev (4 and up) 92
The **cave**. Jaramillo Levi, E.
In Where angels glide at dawn p43-48 S C
Cave drawings
Baylor, B. Before you came this way (1-4) 709.01
See/See also pages in the following book(s):
Ogg, O. The 26 letters p15-41 411
Cave dwellers
Fiction
Gerrard, R. Mik's mammoth E
Caves
Gans, R. Caves (k-3) 551.4
The **cay**. Taylor, T. Fic
Cayard, Bruce
(il) Espy, W. R. A children's almanac of words at play 808.87

Caylus, Anne Claude Philippe de Tubières, comte de, 1692-1765
Fairy gifts
In The Green fairy book p64-67 **398.2**
Heart of ice
In The Green fairy book p106-36 **398.2**
Rosanella
In The Green fairy book p48-55 **398.2**
Sylvain and Jocosa
In The Green fairy book p56-63 **398.2**
Cazet, Denys, 1938-
Big Shoe, Little Shoe **E**
"Never spit on your shoes" **E**
CBC *See* Children's Book Council (New York, N.Y.)
Cecily G. and the 9 monkeys. Rey, H. A. **E**
Cecily Parsley's nursery rhymes. Potter, B. **398.8**
The **cedar** box. Porte-Thomas, B. A.
In Porte-Thomas, B. A. Jesse's ghost, and other stories p33-39 **S C**
The **Cegua**. San Souci, R.
In San Souci, R. Short & shivery p41-47 **398.2**
Celebrating life: Jewish rites of passage. Drucker, M. **296.4**
Celebrations. Bauer, C. F. **808.8**
Celebrations. Livingston, M. C. **811**
The **celery** stalks at midnight. Howe, J. **Fic**
The **celestial** bear: stories of the Big Dipper. Monroe, J. G.
In Monroe, J. G. They dance in the sky p15-27 **398.2**
Cellini, Joseph
(il) Hunter, M. The kelpie's pearls **Fic**
Celtics (Basketball team) *See* Boston Celtics (Basketball team)
Cemeteries
Fiction
Lee, J. M. Bà-Năm **E**
Rodowsky, C. F. The gathering room (5 and up) **Fic**
Cendrars, Blaise, 1887-1961
Shadow (1-3) **841**
Censorship
Periodicals
Newsletter on Intellectual Freedom **323.44**
Census
See also United States—Census
Centennial [excerpt]. Michener, J. A.
In Animal families of the wild: animal stories p49-64 **591**
Centerburg tales. McCloskey, R. **Fic**
Central America
Fiction
Moeri, L. The forty-third war **Fic**
Central Pacific Railroad
See/See also pages in the following book(s):
Meltzer, M. The Chinese Americans p4-23 (6 and up) **305.8**
Ceramics
See also Pottery
Cerebral palsy
Emmert, M. I'm the big sister now (3-5) **362.4**
Fiction
Howard, E. Circle of giving (4-6) **Fic**
Little, J. Mine for keeps (4-6) **Fic**
Southall, I. Let the balloon go (4 and up) **Fic**
Ceres (Roman deity) *See* Demeter (Greek deity)
Cerf, Bennett, 1898-1971
Bennett Cerf's book of animal riddles (k-3) **793.73**
Bennett Cerf's book of riddles (k-3) **793.73**
A **certain** small shepherd. Caudill, R. **Fic**
Ceserani, Gian Paolo, 1939-
Marco Polo (3-6) **92**
Chac
In The Monkey's haircut, and other stories told by the Maya p66-69 **398.2**
Chaco Culture National Historical Park (N.M.)
Trimble, S. The village of blue stone (4-6) **970.004**
See/See also pages in the following book(s):
Weiss, M. E. Sky watchers of ages past p26-33 (5 and up) **523**
Chagall, Marc, 1887-1985
About
Raboff, E. Marc Chagall (4 and up) **759.7**
Chaikin, Miriam, 1928-
Ask another question (4 and up) **296.4**
Esther (1-3) **296.4**
Exodus (2-4) **222**
Feathers in the wind. See note under Chaikin, M. Yossi asks the angels for help **Fic**
Finders weepers (3-5) **Fic**
Friends forever. See note under Chaikin, M. Finders weepers **Fic**

Chaikin, Miriam, 1928-—*Continued*
Getting even. See note under Chaikin, M. Finders weepers **Fic**
Hanukkah (k-2) **296.4**
Joshua in the Promised Land (4 and up) **222**
Light another candle (3-6) **296.4**
Lower! Higher! You're a liar! See note under Chaikin, M. Finders weepers **Fic**
Make noise, make merry (3-6) **296.4**
Menorahs, mezuzas, and other Jewish symbols (5 and up) **296.4**
A nightmare in history (5 and up) **940.54**
The seventh day: the story of the Jewish Sabbath (4 and up) **222**
Shake a palm branch (3-6) **296.4**
Sound the shofar (3-6) **296.4**
Yossi asks the angels for help (3-5) **Fic**
Yossi tries to help God. See note under Chaikin, M. Yossi asks the angels for help **Fic**

Chaikovsky, P. I. *See* Tchaikovsky, Peter Ilich, 1840-1893

Chain of fire. Naidoo, B. **Fic**

A **chair** for my mother. Williams, V. B. **E**

Chair Person. Jones, D. W.
In Things that go bump in the night p122-63 **S C**

Chairs
Fiction
Williams, V. B. A chair for my mother **E**

Chaka, Zulu Chief, 1787?-1828
About
Stanley, D. Shaka, king of the Zulus (2-4) **92**

Chalk, Gary
(il) Jacques, B. Mattimeo **Fic**
(il) Jacques, B. Redwall **Fic**

The **chalk** box kid. Bulla, C. R. **E**

The **chalk** doll. Pomerantz, C. **E**

Chalmers, Mary, 1927-
Come to the doctor, Harry. See note under Chalmers, M. Throw a kiss, Harry **E**
Merry Christmas, Harry. See note under Chalmers, M. Throw a kiss, Harry **E**
Take a nap, Harry. See note under Chalmers, M. Throw a kiss, Harry **E**
Throw a kiss, Harry **E**
(il) Nordstrom, U. The secret language **Fic**
(il) Sharmat, M. W. Goodnight, Andrew: goodnight, Craig **E**

Chaloner, Gwen
The bookworm
In Holiday plays round the year p212-19 **812.008**

Chamberlain, Sarah
(il) Reid, M. S. The button box **E**

Chambers, Aidan, 1934-
Booktalk: occasional writing on literature and children **028.5**
Introducing books to children **028.5**

Chambliss, Maxie
(il) Cooney, N. E. Go away monsters, lickety split! **E**

Chameleons
Schnieper, C. Chameleons (3-6) **597.9**
Fiction
Carle, E. The mixed-up chameleon **E**
Mwenye Hadithi. Crafty Chameleon **E**
Young, J. A million chameleons **E**

Champlin, Connie (Constance J.)
Storytelling with puppets **372.6**

Chancy and the grand rascal. Fleischman, S. **Fic**

Chandler, David P.
The land and people of Cambodia (5 and up) **959.6**

Chang, Isabelle Chin, 1924-
The Chinese Red Riding Hoods
In The Scott, Foresman anthology of children's literature p322-23 **808.8**
In Womenfolk and fairy tales p14-19 **398.2**

Chang, Margaret Scrogin
In the eye of war (4 and up) **Fic**

Chang, Raymond
(jt. auth) Chang, M. S. In the eye of war **Fic**

Chang, Shih-nan
A clever judge
In Best-loved folktales of the world p547-48 **398.2**

A **change** of aunts. Alcock, V.
In Alcock, V. Ghostly companions **S C**

Changeling
Crossley-Holland, K. The changeling
In Crossley-Holland, K. British folk tales p212-14 **398.2**
Grimm, J. The elves: third story
In Grimm, J. The complete Grimm's fairy tales p200 **398.2**
Grimm, J. The goblins
In Grimm, J. The juniper tree, and other tales from Grimm v1 p150-51 **398.2**
Grimm, J. The woman and the changeling elf
In Grimm, J. About wise men and simpletons p34 **398.2**

The **changeling**. Snyder, Z. K. **Fic**
The **changeling**. Yep, L.
In Yep, L. The rainbow people p170-77 **398.2**
Changes, changes. Hutchins, P. **E**
Changing careers *See* Career changes
Chang's paper pony. Coerr, E. **E**
Chanticleer and Partlett
Grimm, J. The death of the little hen
In Grimm, J. The complete Grimm's fairy tales p365-67 **398.2**
Chanticleer and the fox. Cooney, B. **E**
Chanukah *See* Hanukkah
The **Chanukkah** guest. Kimmel, E. A. **E**
Chaplin, Charlie, 1889-1977
About
Kamen, G. Charlie Chaplin (4 and up) **92**
Chapman, John *See* Appleseed, Johnny, 1774-1845
The **chapter** of kings. Collins, J.
In A Nursery companion p80-89 **820.8**
Charbonneau, Claudette, 1936-
(jt. auth) Lander, P. S. The land and people of Finland **948.97**
Charbonneau, Eileen
The ghosts of Stony Clove (5 and up) **Fic**
The **Charcoal** cruncher
In The Monkey's haircut, and other stories told by the Maya p113-17 **398.2**
Charger. Crossley-Holland, K.
In Crossley-Holland, K. British folk tales p307-08 **398.2**
Charlemagne, Emperor, 742-814
See/See also pages in the following book(s):
Bulfinch, T. Bulfinch's mythology (6 and up) **291**
Charles A. Beard's The presidents in American history. Beard, C. A. **920**
Charles the Great *See* Charlemagne, Emperor, 742-814
Charley Skedaddle. Beatty, P. **Fic**
Charlie Chaplin. Kamen, G. **92**
Charlie Pippin. Boyd, C. D. **Fic**
Charlip, Remy
Handtalk: an ABC of finger spelling & sign language (k-3) **419**
Handtalk birthday (k-3) **419**
Thirteen **E**
(il) Yolen, J. The seeing stick **Fic**
Charlot, Jean, 1898-1979
(jt. auth) Brown, M. W. Margaret Wise Brown's A child's good night book **E**
(il) Clark, A. N. Secret of the Andes **Fic**
(il) Krumgold, J. —and now Miguel **Fic**
See/See also pages in the following book(s):
Sendak, M. Caldecott & Co.: notes on books and pictures p125-27 **028.5**
Charlotte's web. White, E. B. **Fic**
Charmed. Singer, M. **Fic**
Charms
Clifton, L. The lucky stone (3-5) **Fic**
Chartier, Normand, 1945-
(il) Selsam, M. E. Keep looking! **599**
(il) Sharmat, M. W. Griselda's new year **E**
Chase, Helen M.
(ed) Chase's annual events. See Chase's annual events **394.2**
Chase, Richard, 1904-1988
(ed) Grandfather tales. See Grandfather tales **398.2**
(ed) The Jack tales. See The Jack tales **398.2**
Chase, William DeRoy, 1922-
(ed) Chase's annual events. See Chase's annual events **394.2**
Chase's annual events **394.2**
Chase's calendar of annual events. See Chase's annual events **394.2**
Chastain, Madye Lee
(il) Courlander, H. The cow-tail switch, and other West African stories **398.2**
Chatelain, Héli
Ngunza, who outwitted death
In The Crest and the hide, and other African stories of heroes, chiefs, bards, hunters, sorcerers, and common people p63-68 **398.2**
Chaucer, Geoffrey, d. 1400
Canterbury tales; adaptation. See Cohen, B. Canterbury tales **Fic**
Nun's priest's tale; adaptation. See Cooney, B. Chanticleer and the fox **E**
Chavez, Cesar, 1927-
See/See also pages in the following book(s):
Jacobs, W. J. Great lives: human rights p238-44 (5 and up) **920**
Morey, J. Famous Mexican Americans p1-13 (5 and up) **920**
Ché! [biography of Ernesto Guevara]. Neimark, A. E. **92**
Cheaper by the dozen [excerpt]. Gilbreth, F. B.
In The Random House book of humor for children p242-47 **817.008**

The **cheater** cheated. Afanas'ev, A. N.
In Afanas'ev, A. N. Russian fairy tales p228-29 **398.2**

Check it out! the book about libraries. Gibbons, G. **027**

Cheetahs
Arnold, C. Cheetah (3-5) **599.74**

Chelm and their history, The fools of. Singer, I. B. **Fic**

Chemically active!: experiments you can do at home. Cobb, V. **540.7**

The **chemist** who lost his head: the story of Antoine Laurent Lavoisier. Grey, V. **92**

Chemistry
Cobb, V. Gobs of goo (2-4) **547**

Experiments

Cobb, V. Chemically active!: experiments you can do at home (5 and up) **540.7**

Gardner, R. Kitchen chemistry: science experiments to do at home (4 and up) **540.7**

Kramer, A. How to make a chemical volcano and other mysterious experiments (4-6) **540.7**

Zubrowski, B. Messing around with baking chemistry (5 and up) **540.7**

Chemists
Grey, V. The chemist who lost his head: the story of Antoine Laurent Lavoisier (5 and up) **92**

Chen, Ju-hong
(il) Birdseye, T. A song of stars **398.2**
(il) Nunes, S. Tiddalick the frog **398.2**

Chen, Tony
(il) Sewell, A. Black Beauty **Fic**

Cheney, Patricia
The land and people of Zimbabwe (5 and up) **968.91**

Cheng, Judith, 1955-
(il) Alcott, L. M. Little women **Fic**
(il) Spyri, J. Heidi **Fic**

Cheng's fighting cricket
Carpenter, F. Cheng's fighting cricket
In Carpenter, F. Tales of a Chinese grandmother p217-25 **398.2**

Chermayeff, Ivan, 1932-
First words (k-3) **410**

Chermayeff, Jane Clark
(jt. auth) Chermayeff, I. First words **410**

Chernobyl Nuclear Accident, Chernobyl, Ukraine, 1986
See/See also pages in the following book(s):
Pringle, L. P. Nuclear energy: troubled past, uncertain future p62-76 (5 and up) **621.48**

Chernoff, Goldie Taub
Easy costumes you don't have to sew (3-5) **391**

Cherokee Indians
Bealer, A. W. Only the names remain (4-6) **970.004**
Cwiklik, R. Sequoyah and the Cherokee alphabet (5 and up) **92**

Fiction

Jones, W. Edge of two worlds (5 and up) **Fic**

Cherries and cherry pits. Williams, V. B. **E**

Cherry, Lynne, 1952-
The great kapok tree **E**
Who's sick today? **E**
(il) Ryder, J. Where butterflies grow **595.7**
(il) Van Woerkom, D. Hidden messages **595.7**

Chess, Victoria, 1939-
(il) Aardema, V. Princess Gorilla and a new kind of water **398.2**
(il) Adler, D. A. The twisted witch, and other spooky riddles **793.73**
(il) Lewis, J. P. A hippopotamusn't and other animal verses **811**
(il) Prelutsky, J. The queen of Eene **811**

Chessare, Michele
(il) Bulla, C. R. The cardboard crown **Fic**
(il) Bulla, C. R. A lion to guard us **Fic**
(il) Cassedy, S. Roomrimes: poems **811**
(il) Kennedy, X. J. The Owlstone crown **Fic**
(il) Rainy day: stories and poems. See Rainy day: stories and poems **808.8**

The **chessmen** of doom. Bellairs, J. See note under Bellairs, J. The curse of the blue figurine **Fic**

Chester A. Arthur: twenty-first president of the United States. Simon, C. **92**

Chester Cricket's new home. Selden, G. See note under Selden, G. The cricket in Times Square **Fic**

Chester Cricket's pigeon ride. Selden, G. See note under Selden, G. The cricket in Times Square **Fic**

Chester's way. Henkes, K. **E**

Chestnut pudding
In The Naked bear p3-10 **398.2**

Chetwin, Grace
Box and Cox **E**
Gom on Windy Mountain (5 and up) **Fic**
The riddle and the rune (5 and up) **Fic**

Chevalier, Tracy, 1962-
(ed) Twentieth-century children's writers. See Twentieth-century children's writers **920.003**
The **Cheyenne**. Fradin, D. B. **970.004**
Cheyenne Indians
Fradin, D. B. The Cheyenne (2-4) **970.004**
See/See also pages in the following book(s):
Ehrlich, A. Wounded Knee: an Indian history of the American West (6 and up) **970.004**
Fiction
Goble, P. Death of the iron horse **E**
Legends
Goble, P. Her seven brothers (k-3) **398.2**
Chiasson, John C.
African journey (4 and up) **960**
Chicanos *See* Mexican Americans
Chichen Itza Site (Mexico)
See/See also pages in the following book(s):
Gallant, R. A. Lost cities (4 and up) **930**
The **chick** and the duckling. Ginsburg, M. **E**
A **chick** hatches. Cole, J. **636.5**
Chicka chicka boom boom. Martin, B. **E**
Chickadee (Periodical)
Outdoor fun. **796.1**
Chickadee: the Canadian magazine for young children **505**
Chickasaw Indians
Legends
Moroney, L. Baby rattlesnake (k-2) **398.2**
Chicken Licken
In The Tall book of nursery tales p55-61 **398.2**
Chicken Licken. Asbjørnsen, P. C.
In Tomie dePaola's favorite nursery tales p105-11 **398.2**
Chicken-Little
Asbjørnsen, P. C. Chicken Licken
In Tomie dePaola's favorite nursery tales p105-11 **398.2**
Chicken Licken
In The Tall book of nursery tales p55-61 **398.2**
Galdone, P. Henny Penny **398.2**
Henny-Penny
In The Baby's story book p42-44 **398.2**
Jacobs, J. Henny-Penny
In Jacobs, J. English fairy tales p113-16 **398.2**
In The Scott, Foresman anthology of children's literature p151-52 **808.8**
Kellogg, S. Chicken Little **398.2**
Ormerod, J. The story of Chicken Licken **398.2**
Oxenbury, H. Henny-Penny
In Oxenbury, H. The Helen Oxenbury nursery story book p40-46 **398.2**
Rockwell, A. F. Henny-Penny
In Rockwell, A. F. The three bears & 15 other stories p63-70 **398.2**
Zimmerman, H. W. Henny Penny **398.2**
Chicken soup with rice. Sendak, M. **E**
Chickens
See also Roosters
Cole, J. A chick hatches (k-3) **636.5**
Johnson, S. A. Inside an egg (4 and up) **598**
Selsam, M. E. Egg to chick (k-3) **636.5**
See/See also pages in the following book(s):
McClung, R. M. The amazing egg p1-8 (4 and up) **591.1**
Weber, W. J. Care of uncommon pets p93-109 (5 and up) **636.088**
Fiction
Fox, M. Hattie and the fox **E**
Galdone, P. The little red hen (k-2) **398.2**
Ginsburg, M. The chick and the duckling **E**
Ginsburg, M. Good morning, chick **E**
Heine, H. The most wonderful egg in the world **E**
Hutchins, P. Rosie's walk **E**
Kasza, K. The wolf's chicken stew **E**
King-Smith, D. The fox busters (3-5) **Fic**
Lane, M. H. Something to crow about **E**
Manes, S. Some of the adventures of Rhode Island Red (3-6) **Fic**
Marshall, J. Wings **E**
Oakley, G. Hetty and Harriet **E**
Pinkwater, D. M. The Hoboken chicken emergency (3-6) **Fic**
Zemach, M. The little red hen (k-2) **398.2**
Chickens aren't the only ones. Heller, R. **591.1**
Chief Kama and the duiker. Marolen, D.
In The Crest and the hide, and other African stories of heroes, chiefs, bards, hunters, sorcerers, and common people p123-28 **398.2**
A **chief** names his heirs. Kwarteng, K.
In The Crest and the hide, and other African stories of heroes, chiefs, bards, hunters, sorcerers, and common people p7-11 **398.2**

The **chief** of Agogo and the chief of Mampo. Prempeh, A. K.
In The Crest and the hide, and other African stories of heroes, chiefs, bards, hunters, sorcerers, and common people p19-24 398.2

Child, Charles, 1902-
(il) Benét, R. A book of Americans 811

Child, Lydia Maria Francis, 1802-1880
Over the river and through the wood (k-2) 811

Child abuse
See also Child molesting

Fiction

Bawden, N. Squib (5 and up) Fic
Byars, B. C. Cracker Jackson (5 and up) Fic
Magorian, M. Good night, Mr. Tom (6 and up) Fic

Child and parent *See* Parent and child

Child artists
I never saw another butterfly 741.9

Periodicals

Stone Soup 810.8

Child authors
I never saw another butterfly 741.9
MacDonald, M. R. The skit book (4 and up) 812.008
Miracles: poems by children of the English-speaking world 821.008

Periodicals

Stone Soup 810.8

Child care centers
See also Nursery schools

Child development
Harris, R. H. Before you were three 155.4

A **child** is born: the Christmas story. Winthrop, E. 232.9

Child molesting
Terkel, S. N. Feeling safe, feeling strong (4 and up) 362.7
Wachter, O. No more secrets for me (2-5) 362.7

The **child** of calamity. Yep, L.
In Yep, L. The rainbow people p46-52 398.2

Child of the owl. Yep, L. Fic

Child of the silent night [biography of Laura Dewey Bridgman]. Hunter, E. F. 92

Child rearing
See also Toilet training

Childbirth
Cole, J. How you were born (k-2) 612.6
Kitzinger, S. Being born (3-5) 612.6

Childcraft dictionary. See The World Book student dictionary 423

Childe Rowland
Jacobs, J. Childe Rowland
In Jacobs, J. English fairy tales p117-24 398.2

Childhood Education 372.05

Children
See also Abandoned children; Handicapped children; Infants; Runaway children; Youth
Anno, M. All in a day E
Burns, M. I am not a short adult! (3-6) 305.23

Abuse

See Child abuse

Adoption

See Adoption

Books and reading

Paterson, K. The spying heart 028.5
Rollock, B. T. Public library services for children 027.62

Development

See Child development

Employment

See also Moneymaking projects for children
Barkin, C. Jobs for kids (5 and up) 650.1

Employment—Fiction

Beatty, P. Turn homeward, Hannalee (5 and up) Fic

Canada

Kurelek, W. A prairie boy's summer (3-5) 971.27
Kurelek, W. A prairie boy's winter (3-5) 971.27

Italy

Italy (3-5) 945

Japan

Birmingham, L. Japan (3-5) 952

Nepal

Pitkänen, M. A. The children of Nepal (2-4) 954.96

Spain

Spain (3-5) 946

Turkey

Turkey (3-5) 956.1

West (U.S.)

Freedman, R. Children of the wild West (4 and up) 978

Children, Retarded *See* Mentally handicapped children; Slow learning children

Children and adults
See also Conflict of generations; Parent and child

Children and books. Sutherland, Z. 028.5

Children and television *See* Television and children

Children and the AIDS virus. Hausherr, R. 616.97

The **children** and the Zimwi. See Aardema, V. Bimwili & the Zimwi 398.2

Children of Christmas. Rylant, C. S C

The **children** of Green Knowe. Boston, L. M. Fic

Children of immigrants

Freedman, R. Immigrant kids (4 and up) 325.73

Children of intermarriage

Godden, R. Fu-dog (1-3) Fic

Rosenberg, M. B. Living in two worlds (2-4) 306.8

The **children** of Nepal. Pitkänen, M. A. 954.96

The **children** of Odin. Colum, P. 293

Children of the wild West. Freedman, R. 978

Children of working parents

Fiction

Blaine, M. The terrible thing that happened at our house E

The **children** we remember. Abells, C. B. 940.54

A **children's** almanac of words at play. Espy, W. R. 808.87

Children's authors and illustrators: an index to biographical dictionaries 920.003

Children's Book Council (New York, N.Y.)

Notable children's trade books in the field of social studies. See Notable children's trade books in the field of social studies 016.3

Outstanding science trade books for children. See Outstanding science trade books for children 016.5

Children's book review index 028.1

Children's books. See Books for children 011.6

Children's books in print 015.73

Children's books of international interest. Association for Library Service to Children (U.S.). International Relations Committee 011.6

The **children's** clock. Brown, M. W.

In Brown, M. W. The fish with the deep sea smile p87-89 818

Children's faces looking up. DeWit, D. 372.6

Children's games in street and playground. Opie, I. A. 796.1

The **children's** Homer: The adventures of Odysseus and The tale of Troy. Colum, P. 883

Children's libraries

See also Libraries and schools; Young adults' library services

Bauer, C. F. Celebrations 808.8

MacDonald, M. R. Booksharing: 101 programs to use with preschoolers 027.62

Nichols, J. Storytimes for two-year-olds 027.62

Rollock, B. T. Public library services for children 027.62

Periodicals

Emergency Librarian 027.6205

Journal of Youth Services in Libraries 027.6205

Children's literary houses. Ashe, R. 028.5

Children's literature

See also Caldecott Medal books; Fairy tales; Newbery Medal books; Picture books for children

Bauer, C. F. This way to books 028.5

Once upon a time—: celebrating the magic of children's books in honor of the twentieth anniversary of Reading is Fundamental 028.5

Paterson, K. The spying heart 028.5

Bibliography

Anderson, V. Fiction sequels for readers age 10-16 016.8

Association for Library Service to Children (U.S.). International Relations Committee. Children's books of international interest 011.6

Association for Library Service to Children (U.S.). Notable Children's Books, 1976-1980, Reevaluation Committee. Notable children's books, 1976-1980 011.6

Barstow, B. Beyond picture books 011.6

Baskin, B. H. Books for the gifted child 011.6

Baskin, B. H. More notes from a different drummer 016.8

Baskin, B. H. Notes from a different drummer 016.8

Bernstein, J. E. Books to help children cope with separation and loss v3 016.3627

Best books for children, preschool through grade 6 011.6

The Best in children's books 028.1

Books for children 011.6

Carroll, F. L. Exciting, funny, scary, short, different, and sad books kids like about animals, science, sports, families, songs, and other things 011.6

Children's literature — Bibliography — *Continued*
Children's books in print **015.73**
Cuddigan, M. Growing pains **011.6**
Dreyer, S. S. The bookfinder **011.6**
The Elementary school library collection **011.6**
Ettlinger, J. R. T. Choosing books for young people v2 **011.6**
Fiction, folklore, fantasy & poetry for children, 1876-1985 **011.6**
For younger readers: braille and talking books **011.6**
Freeman, J. Books kids will sit still for **011.6**
Friedberg, J. B. Accept me as I am: best books of juvenile nonfiction on impairments and disabilities **016**
A Guide to non-sexist children's books v2 **011.6**
Hall, S. Using picture storybooks to teach literary devices **016.8**
Hearne, B. G. Choosing books for children **028.5**
Kennedy, D. M. Science & technology in fact and fiction: a guide to children's books **016.5**
Kimmel, M. M. For reading out loud! **028.5**
National Council of Teachers of English. Committee on the Elementary School Booklist. Adventuring with books **011.6**
National Council of Teachers of English. Committee on the Junior High and Middle School Booklist. Your reading: a booklist for junior high and middle school students **011.6**
Schon, I. Basic collection of children's books in Spanish **011.6**
Schon, I. Books in Spanish for children and young adults: an annotated guide [series I-V] **011.6**
Subject guide to Children's books in print **015.73**
Thomas, R. L. Primaryplots **028**
Trelease, J. The new read-aloud handbook **028.5**
Wilson, G. Books for children to read alone **011.6**

See/See also pages in the following book(s):
Bauer, C. F. Handbook for storytellers p101-80, 285-98 **372.6**
The Scott, Foresman anthology of children's literature p877-962 **808.8**

Bio-bibliography

Authors of books for young people **920.003**
Fifth book of junior authors & illustrators **920.003**
Fourth book of junior authors and illustrators **920.003**
The Junior book of authors **920.003**
More junior authors **920.003**
Rollock, B. T. Black authors and illustrators of children's books **920.003**
Sixth book of junior authors & illustrators **920.003**
Something about the author **920.003**
Something about the author: autobiography series **920.003**
Third book of junior authors **920.003**
Twentieth-century children's writers **920.003**

Dictionaries

Carpenter, H. The Oxford companion to children's literature **028.5**

History and criticism

Anderson, C. C. Nonsense literature for children **028.5**
The Arbuthnot lectures, 1970-1979/1980-1989 **028.5**
Ashe, R. Children's literary houses (3-5) **028.5**
Caldecott Medal books, 1938-1957 **028.5**
Chambers, A. Booktalk: occasional writing on literature and children **028.5**
Chambers, A. Introducing books to children **028.5**
Children's literature review **028.5**
Cook, E. The ordinary and the fabulous **028.5**
Crosscurrents of criticism **028.5**
Egoff, S. A. Worlds within **028.5**
England, C. ChildView: evaluating and reviewing materials for children **028.5**
Field, C. W. Values in selected children's books of fiction and fantasy **028.5**
Hazard, P. Books, children, and men **028.5**
Hearne, B. G. Choosing books for children **028.5**
Horn Book reflections on children's books and reading **028.5**
A Horn Book sampler on children's books and reading **028.5**
Huck, C. S. Children's literature in the elementary school **028.5**
The Illustrator's notebook **741.6**
Illustrators of children's books **741.6**
Jordan, A. M. From Rollo to Tom Sawyer, and other papers **028.5**
Kobrin, B. Eyeopeners! **028.5**
Newbery and Caldecott Medal books, 1966-1975 **028.5**
Newbery and Caldecott Medal books, 1976-1985 **028.5**
Newbery Medal books, 1922-1955 **028.5**
Only connect: readings on children's literature **028.5**

Children's literature—History and criticism —*Continued*
Ross, E. S. The spirited life: Bertha Mahony Miller and children's books 92
Sendak, M. Caldecott & Co.: notes on books and pictures 028.5
Sutherland, Z. Children and books 028.5
Townsend, J. R. A sense of story 028.5
Townsend, J. R. A sounding of storytellers 028.5
Townsend, J. R. Written for children 028.5
Twentieth-century children's writers 920.003
Yolen, J. Touch magic 028.5

See/See also pages in the following book(s):
The Scott, Foresman anthology of children's literature p802-25, 846-77 808.8

Periodicals
Bookbird 028.505
Cricket 051
Five Owls 028.505
Highlights for Children 051
The Horn Book Guide to Children's and Young Adult Books 028.505
The Horn Book Magazine 028.505
The Kobrin Letter 028.505

Reviews—Indexes
Children's book review index 028.1

Reviews—Periodicals
Bulletin of the Center for Children's Books 028.1
Parents' Choice: a review of children's media 028.1
The Web 028.1

Study and teaching
See/See also pages in the following book(s):
The Scott, Foresman anthology of children's literature p826-46 808.8

Technique
Hunter, M. Talent is not enough 808.06

Children's Literature Center
Books for children. See Books for children 011.6
Children's literature in the elementary school. Huck, C. S. 028.5
Children's literature review 028.5
Children's Magazine Guide 051
Children's media market place 070.5025
Children's moneymaking projects *See* Moneymaking projects for children
The **children's** own Longfellow. Longfellow, H. W. 811
Children's poetry
See also Lullabies; Nonsense verses; Nursery rhymes; Tongue twisters

Children's songs
See also Lullabies
Children's songs, The Fireside book of 782.42
Children's thesaurus, Roget's. Schiller, A. 423
A **children's** zoo. Hoban, T. 591
Childress, Alice, 1920-
A hero ain't nothin' but a sandwich (6 and up) Fic
A **child's** Christmas in Wales. Thomas, D. 828
A **child's** garden of verses. Stevenson, R. L. 821
Child's grave
Grimm, J. The shroud
In Grimm, J. The complete Grimm's fairy tales p502-03 398.2
A **Child's** treasury of poems (3-5) 821.008
Childtimes: a three-generation memoir. Greenfield, E. 920
ChildView: evaluating and reviewing materials for children. England, C. 028.5
Chile
Hintz, M. Chile (4 and up) 983
Chimney sweeps: yesterday and today. Giblin, J. 697
Chimneys
Giblin, J. Chimney sweeps: yesterday and today (4-6) 697
The **chimpanzee** family book. Goodall, J. 599.88
Chimpanzees
Goodall, J. The chimpanzee family book (3-5) 599.88
Goodall, J. Chimps (4-6) 599.88
Goodall, J. My life with the chimpanzees (3-6) 92
Klingsheim, T. B. Julius (1-4) 599.88
Powzyk, J. A. Tracking wild chimpanzees in Kibira National Park (3-6) 599.88

Fiction
Browne, A. I like books E
Browne, A. Things I like E
Browne, A. Willy the champ E
Hoban, L. Arthur's Christmas cookies E
Chimps. Goodall, J. 599.88
Chin, Alex
(il) Brandreth, G. D. The biggest tongue twister book in the world 808.88
Chin, Richard, 1946-
(jt. auth) Ribner, S. The martial arts 796.8
Chin Chiang and the dragon's dance. Wallace, I. E
China
Fritz, J. China homecoming (6 and up) 951.05

China—*Continued*
Fritz, J. Homesick: my own story (5 and up) **92**
Haskins, J. Count your way through China (2-4) **951**
Major, J. S. The land and people of China (5 and up) **951**
See/See also pages in the following book(s):
Meltzer, M. The Chinese Americans p53-64 (6 and up) **305.8**
Description and travel
Humble, R. The travels of Marco Polo (4-6) **910.4**
Fiction
DeJong, M. The house of sixty fathers (4-6) **Fic**
Flack, M. The story about Ping **E**
Handforth, T. Mei Li **E**
Lattimore, D. N. The dragon's robe (3-5) **Fic**
Leaf, M. The eyes of the dragon **E**
Schlein, M. The year of the panda (3-5) **Fic**
Williams, J. Everyone knows what a dragon looks like **E**
Yep, L. The serpent's children (6 and up) **Fic**
Yolen, J. The seeing stick (2-4) **Fic**
Folklore
See Folklore—China
History
Fisher, L. E. The Great Wall of China (4 and up) **951**
McLenighan, V. China, a history to 1949 (4 and up) **951**
History—1912-1949
Fritz, J. China's Long March (6 and up) **951.04**
Science
See Science—China
China, a history to 1949. McLenighan, V. **951**
China homecoming. Fritz, J. **951.05**
China's Long March. Fritz, J. **951.04**
Chincoteague Island (Va.)
Fiction
Henry, M. Misty of Chincoteague (4 and up) **Fic**
Chinese
Great Britain
Godden, R. Fu-dog (1-3) **Fic**
North America—Fiction
Yee, P. Tales from Gold Mountain (4 and up) **S C**
United States—Fiction
Levine, E. I hate English! **E**
Chinese Americans
See also Chinese—United States
Meltzer, M. The Chinese Americans (6 and up) **305.8**
Waters, K. Lion dancer: Ernie Wan's Chinese New Year (k-3) **394.2**
Fiction
Coerr, E. Chang's paper pony **E**
Howard, E. Her own song (4 and up) **Fic**
Lord, B. B. In the Year of the Boar and Jackie Robinson (4-6) **Fic**
Yep, L. Child of the owl (5 and up) **Fic**
Yep, L. Dragonwings (5 and up) **Fic**
Social life and customs
Brown, T. Chinese New Year (2-4) **394.2**
A **Chinese** fairy tale. Housman, L.
In Bauer, C. F. Celebrations p4-11 **808.8**
The **Chinese** mirror. Ginsburg, M. **398.2**
Chinese New Year
Brown, T. Chinese New Year (2-4) **394.2**
Waters, K. Lion dancer: Ernie Wan's Chinese New Year (k-3) **394.2**
Fiction
Wallace, I. Chin Chiang and the dragon's dance **E**
The **Chinese** Red Riding Hoods. Chang, I. C.
In The Scott, Foresman anthology of children's literature p322-23 **808.8**
In Womenfolk and fairy tales p14-19 **398.2**
Chinese science *See* Science—China
A **Chinese** zoo: fables and proverbs. Demi. **398.2**
Chinook wind: stories from the Northwest Coast. Monroe, J. G.
In Monroe, J. G. They dance in the sky p95-106 **398.2**
Chippewa Indians
Osinski, A. The Chippewa (2-4) **970.004**
See/See also pages in the following book(s):
Hofsinde, R. Indian costumes p61-71 (3-6) **391**
Legends
Esbensen, B. J. Ladder to the sky (k-3) **398.2**
Esbensen, B. J. The star maiden: an Ojibway tale (k-3) **398.2**

Chirping insects. Johnson, S. A. 595.7
Chita's Christmas tree. Howard, E. F. E
Chitty-Chitty-Bang-Bang. Fleming, I. Fic
Chivalry
See also Civilization, Medieval
Bulfinch, T. Bulfinch's mythology (6 and up) 291
Chocolate fever. Smith, R. K. Fic
The **chocolate** war [excerpt]. Cormier, R.
In Face to face: a collection of stories by celebrated Soviet and American writers p2-8 S C
Choctaw Indians
Lepthien, E. U. The Choctaw (2-4) 970.004
Choosing books for children. Hearne, B. G. 028.5
Choosing books for young people v2. Ettlinger, J. R. T. 011.6
Chorao, Kay
Cathedral mouse E
George told Kate. See note under Chorao, K. Kate's box E
Kate's box E
Kate's car. See note under Chorao, K. Kate's box E
Kate's quilt. See note under Chorao, K. Kate's box E
Kate's snowman. See note under Chorao, K. Kate's box E
Ups and downs with Oink and Pearl E
(comp) The Baby's bedtime book. See The Baby's bedtime book 808.81
(comp) The Baby's good morning book. See The Baby's good morning book 808.81
(comp) The Baby's lap book. See The Baby's lap book 398.8
(comp) The Baby's story book. See The Baby's story book 398.2
(il) Crowe, R. L. Clyde monster E
(il) Monster poems. See Monster poems 821.008
(il) Viorst, J. The good-bye book E
(il) Viorst, J. My mama says there aren't any zombies, ghosts, vampires, creatures, demons, monsters, fiends, goblins, or things E
(il) Williams, B. Albert's toothache E
(il) Williams, B. Kevin's grandma E
Chortles: new and selected wordplay poems. Merriam, E. 811
Chrisman, Arthur Bowie, 1889-1953
See/See also pages in the following book(s):
Newbery Medal books, 1922-1955 p40-43 028.5
Christ *See* Jesus Christ
The **Christ** child. Bible. N.T. Selections 232.9
Christelow, Eileen, 1943-
Five little monkeys jumping on the bed E
(il) Aylesworth, J. The completed hickory dickory dock 398.8
(il) Dilly dilly piccalilli. See Dilly dilly piccalilli 808.81
Christian, Rebecca
Cooking the Spanish way (5 and up) 641.5
Christian missions *See* Missions, Christian
Christian saints
Cole, J. A gift from Saint Francis (2-4) 92
De Paola, T. Francis, the poor man of Assisi (3-5) 92
Fritz, J. The man who loved books [biography of Saint Columba] (3-5) 92
Christiana, David
(il) Schwartz, A. Fat man in a fur coat, and other bear stories 599.74
(il) Schwartz, A. Gold & silver, silver & gold 910.4
Christianity
Fiction
Speare, E. G. The bronze bow (6 and up) Fic
Christiansen, C. B.
My mother's house, my father's house E
Christina Katerina & the box. Gauch, P. L. See note under Gauch, P. L. Christina Katerina and the time she quit the family E
Christina Katerina and the great bear train. Gauch, P. L. See note under Gauch, P. L. Christina Katerina and the time she quit the family E
Christina Katerina and the time she quit the family. Gauch, P. L. E
Christmas
See also Jesus Christ—Nativity
Barth, E. Holly, reindeer, and colored lights (3-6) 394.2
Borland, H. Plants of Christmas (5 and up) 398
Cooney, B. Christmas (1-3) 394.2
De Paola, T. The family Christmas tree book (k-3) 394.2
Diane Goode's American Christmas 810.8
The Family read-aloud Christmas treasury 808.8
Giblin, J. The truth about Santa Claus (4 and up) 394.2
Henderson, K. Christmas trees (2-4) 394.2
Lubin, L. B. Christmas gift-bringers 394.2

Christmas—*Continued*
Take joy! The Tasha Tudor Christmas book **394.2**
See/See also pages in the following book(s):
Bauer, C. F. Celebrations p257-78 **808.8**

Drama

The Big book of Christmas plays **808.82**

Fiction

Andersen, H. C. Hans Christian Andersen's The fir tree (2-5) **Fic**
Bell, A. The nutcracker (2-4) **Fic**
Brett, J. The wild Christmas reindeer **E**
Briggs, R. Father Christmas **E**
Bulla, C. R. The Christmas coat **E**
Burch, R. Christmas with Ida Early (4 and up) **Fic**
Capote, T. A Christmas memory (3-5) **Fic**
Carlson, N. S. The family under the bridge (3-5) **Fic**
Carrick, C. Paul's Christmas birthday **E**
Caudill, R. A certain small shepherd (4 and up) **Fic**
Climo, S. The cobweb Christmas **E**
Cooney, B. The little juggler (3-6) **398.2**
Croll, C. The little snowgirl: an old Russian tale (k-2) **398.2**
De Paola, T. The clown of God (k-3) **398.2**
De Paola, T. An early American Christmas **E**
De Paola, T. The legend of Old Befana (k-3) **398.2**
Dickens, C. A Christmas carol in prose (4 and up) **Fic**
Godden, R. The story of Holly and Ivy **E**
Greene, E. The legend of the Christmas rose (2-4) **398.2**
Hamilton, V. The bells of Christmas (4-6) **Fic**
Hayes, S. Happy Christmas, Gemma **E**
Henry, O. The gift of the Magi (5 and up) **Fic**
Hoban, L. Arthur's Christmas cookies **E**
Hoban, L. It's really Christmas **E**
Hoffmann, E. T. A. Nutcracker (3 and up) **Fic**
Houston, G. The year of the perfect Christmas tree **E**
Howard, E. F. Chita's Christmas tree **E**
Hughes, S. Angel Mae: a tale of Trotter Street **E**
Jennings, L. M. The Christmas Tomten **E**
Jukes, M. Lights around the palm **E**
Klein, N. Baryshnikov's Nutcracker (3 and up) **792.8**
Koralek, J. The cobweb curtain **E**
Kroll, S. Santa's crash-bang Christmas **E**
Mendez, P. The black snowman **E**
Merriam, E. The Christmas box **E**
Moeri, L. Star Mother's youngest child **E**
Noble, T. H. Apple tree Christmas **E**
Paterson, K. Angels & other strangers: family Christmas stories (5 and up) **S C**
Patterson, N. R. The Christmas cup (3-5) **Fic**
Plume, I. The story of Befana (1-3) **398.2**
Polacco, P. Uncle Vova's tree **E**
Potter, B. The tailor of Gloucester **E**
Robbins, R. Baboushka and the three kings (1-4) **398.2**
Robinson, B. The best Christmas pageant ever (4-6) **Fic**
Rogers, J. The Christmas pageant **E**
Rylant, C. Children of Christmas (4 and up) **S C**
Seuss, Dr. How the Grinch stole Christmas **E**
Spier, P. Peter Spier's Christmas! **E**
Thayer, J. The puppy who wanted a boy **E**
Van Allsburg, C. The Polar Express **E**
Van Leeuwen, J. The great Christmas kidnapping caper (3-5) **Fic**
Walter, M. P. Have a happy— (4-6) **Fic**
Wells, R. Morris's disappearing bag **E**
Westman, B. The day before Christmas **E**
Wiggin, K. D. S. The Bird's Christmas Carol (3-5) **Fic**

See/See also pages in the following book(s):
Take joy! The Tasha Tudor Christmas book p14-55 **394.2**

Pictorial works

Munro, R. Christmastime in New York City (2-4) **394.2**

Poetry

A Christmas feast: poems, sayings, greetings, and wishes (4 and up) **808.81**
Christmas in the stable (2-4) **811.008**
Christmas poems (k-3) **808.81**
McGinley, P. The year without a Santa Claus (k-3) **811**
Moore, C. C. The night before Christmas (k-3) **811**
The Oxford book of Christmas poems (4 and up) **808.81**
Prelutsky, J. It's Christmas (1-3) **811**
Wells, C. A Christmas alphabet (k-3) **811**

See/See also pages in the following book(s):
Take joy! The Tasha Tudor Christmas book p56-64 **394.2**

Christmas—*Continued*
Wales
Thomas, D. A child's Christmas in Wales (5 and up) **828**
A **Christmas** alphabet. Wells, C. **811**
The **Christmas** apple. Sawyer, R.
In Bauer, C. F. Celebrations p259-64 **808.8**
Christmas at the Cratchits. Newman, D.
In The Big book of Christmas plays p240-49 **808.82**
Christmas at the O.K. Corral. Miller, P.
In Holiday plays round the year p14-22 **812.008**
Christmas at Troy. Aiken, J.
In Aiken, J. Up the chimney down, and other stories p149-70 **S C**
The **Christmas** box. Merriam, E. **E**
A **Christmas** carol. Thane, A.
In The Big book of Christmas plays p277-97 **808.82**
A **Christmas** carol in prose. Dickens, C. **Fic**
Christmas carols *See* Carols
Christmas coast to coast. Olfson, L.
In The Big book of Christmas plays p80-98 **808.82**
The **Christmas** coat. Bulla, C. R. **E**
Christmas crafts. Meyer, C. **745.59**
The **Christmas** cup. Patterson, N. R. **Fic**
Christmas decorations
Meyer, C. Christmas crafts (5 and up) **745.59**
Parish, P. December decorations (1-3) **745.59**
See/See also pages in the following book(s):
Araki, C. Origami in the classroom p33-40 (Book I) (4 and up) **736**
A Pumpkin in a pear tree p97-106 (1-4) **745.59**
The **Christmas** doubters. Baker, C.
In The Big book of Christmas plays p265-74 **808.82**
Christmas dreams of a prairie boy. See Kurelek, W. A northern nativity **232.9**
Christmas Eve. Brown, M. W.
In Brown, M. W. The fish with the deep sea smile p71-73 **818**
Christmas Eve letter. Hark, M.
In The Big book of Christmas plays p41-58 **808.82**
Christmas every day
Thane, A. Christmas every day
In Thane, A. Plays from famous stories and fairy tales p216-30 **812**
Christmas every day. Howells, W. D.
In The Family read-aloud Christmas treasury p114-19 **808.8**
A **Christmas** feast: poems, sayings, greetings, and wishes (4 and up) **808.81**
Christmas gift-bringers. Lubin, L. B. **394.2**
Christmas in old New England. Clapp, P.
In Holiday plays round the year p28-36 **812.008**
Christmas in the barn. Brown, M. W. **232.9**
Christmas in the stable (2-4) **811.008**
Christmas in the stable. Lindgren, A. **232.9**
A **Christmas** memory. Capote, T. **Fic**
The **Christmas** pageant. Rogers, J. **E**
Christmas poems (k-3) **808.81**
A **Christmas** promise. Miller, H. L.
In The Big book of Christmas plays p99-117 **808.82**
The **Christmas** question. Newman, D.
In Holiday plays round the year p23-27 **812.008**
The **Christmas** roast. Rettich, M.
In Bauer, C. F. Celebrations p265-67 **808.8**
Christmas shopping early. Hark, M.
In Holiday plays round the year p3-13 **812.008**
The **Christmas** sky. Branley, F. M. **232.9**
The **Christmas** story. Bible. N.T. Selections **232.9**
A **Christmas** story. Wildsmith, B. **E**
Christmas, the King James Version. Bible. N.T. Selections **232.9**
The **Christmas** thief. Williams, J.
In The Family read-aloud Christmas treasury p44-49 **808.8**
The **Christmas** Tomten. Jennings, L. M. **E**
Christmas treasury, The Raffi. Raffi **782.42**
The **Christmas** tree man. Rylant, C.
In Rylant, C. Children of Christmas p1-5 **S C**
Christmas trees. Henderson, K. **394.2**
The **Christmas** turkey. Sanfield, S.
In Sanfield, S. The adventures of High John the Conqueror **398.2**
The **Christmas** umbrella. Gotwalt, H. L. M.
In Gotwalt, H. L. M. Special plays for holidays p75-87 **812**
The **Christmas** whale. Duvoisin, R.
In The Family read-aloud Christmas treasury p72-79 **808.8**
Christmas with Ida Early. Burch, R. **Fic**
Christmas with Morris and Boris. Wiseman, B. See note under Wiseman, B. Morris and Boris at the circus **E**

Christmastime in New York City. Munro, R. **394.2**
Christopher, Saint, 3rd cent.?
See/See also pages in the following book(s):
Shedlock, M. L. The art of the story-teller p168-72 **372.6**
Christopher, John, 1922-
The city of gold and lead. See note under Christopher, J. The White Mountains **Fic**
Empty world (5 and up) **Fic**
Fireball (5 and up) **Fic**
The pool of fire. See note under Christopher, J. The White Mountains **Fic**
When the Tripods came. See note under Christopher, J. The White Mountains **Fic**
The White Mountains (5 and up) **Fic**
See/See also pages in the following book(s):
Townsend, J. R. A sense of story p48-53 **028.5**
Christopher, Matt, 1917-
The hit-away kid (2-4) **Fic**
Tackle without a team (5 and up) **Fic**
Takedown (6 and up) **Fic**
Christopher Columbus: voyager to the unknown. Levinson, N. S. **92**
The **Christopher** Robin story book. Milne, A. A. **828**
Chronicles of Narnia. See Lewis, C. S. The lion, the witch and the wardrobe **Fic**
Chronology, Historical
Arnold, G. Datelines of world history (5 and up) **909**
Chrystie, Francis N., 1904-1986
Pets (4 and up) **636.088**
Chuck Yeager: the man who broke the sound barrier. Levinson, N. S. **92**
Chukovskiĭ, Korneĭ, 1882-1969
Ginsburg, M. Good morning, chick **E**
See/See also pages in the following book(s):
Crosscurrents of criticism p261-74 **028.5**
Chung, Okwha
Cooking the Korean way (5 and up) **641.5**
Chunk o' meat
Chunk o' meat
In Grandfather tales p222-25 **398.2**
Church
See also Christianity
The **church** cat abroad. Oakley, G. See note under Oakley, G. The church mouse **E**
The **church** mice adrift. Oakley, G. See note under Oakley, G. The church mouse **E**
The **church** mice and the moon. Oakley, G. See note under Oakley, G. The church mouse **E**
The **church** mice at bay. Oakley, G. See note under Oakley, G. The church mouse **E**
The **church** mice at Christmas. Oakley, G. See note under Oakley, G. The church mouse **E**
The **church** mice in action. Oakley, G. See note under Oakley, G. The church mouse **E**
The **church** mice spread their wings. Oakley, G. See note under Oakley, G. The church mouse **E**
The **church** mouse. Oakley, G. **E**
Churchill, E. Richard (Elmer Richard)
Fast & funny paper toys you can make (3 and up) **745.592**
Instant paper airplanes (3-5) **745.592**
Paper toys that fly, soar, zoom, & whistle (4 and up) **745.592**
Churchill, Elmer Richard *See* Churchill, E. Richard (Elmer Richard)
Chwast, Seymour
(il) Goldin, B. D. Just enough is plenty: a Hanukkah tale **E**
Cianciolo, Patricia J.
Picture books for children **011.6**
Ciardi, John, 1916-1986
The hopeful trout and other limericks (2-4) **811**
I met a man (1-3) **811**
You read to me, I'll read to you (1-4) **811**
Cicadas
See/See also pages in the following book(s):
Johnson, S. A. Chirping insects (4 and up) **595.7**
Cimino, Stephanie
About
Krementz, J. A very young skier (3-6) **796.93**
Cinderella
Climo, S. The Egyptian Cinderella **398.2**
Ehrlich, A. Cinderella
In Ehrlich, A. The Random House book of fairy tales p138-49 **398.2**
Farjeon, E. The glass slipper **Fic**
Galdone, P. Cinderella **398.2**
Grimm, J. Ashtenputtel
In Best-loved folktales of the world p68-75 **398.2**
Grimm, J. Cinderella
In Grimm, J. The complete Grimm's fairy tales p121-28 **398.2**
In Grimm, J. Tales from Grimm p101-22 **398.2**

Cinderella—*Continued*
Huck, C. S. Princess Furball **398.2**
Karlin, B. Cinderella **398.2**
Louie, A.-L. Yeh-Shen **398.2**
Perrault, C. Cinderella **398.2**
also in Best-loved folktales of the world p3-8 **398.2**
also in The Blue fairy book p64-71 **398.2**
also in The Scott, Foresman anthology of children's literature p200-04 **808.8**
also in Sleeping beauty & other favourite fairy tales p103-12 **398.2**
Perrault, C. Cinderilla
In The Classic fairy tales p123-27 **398.2**
Thane, A. Cinderella
In Thane, A. Plays from famous stories and fairy tales p430-49 **812**
Cinderella. Porte-Thomas, B. A.
In Porte-Thomas, B. A. Jesse's ghost, and other stories p55-63 **S C**
Cinderilla. Perrault, C.
In The Classic fairy tales p123-27 **398.2**
Cindy, a hearing ear dog. Curtis, P. **636.7**
Ciphers
Janeczko, P. B. Loads of codes and secret ciphers (5 and up) **652**
Mango, K. N. Codes, ciphers, and other secrets (4 and up) **652**
Schwartz, A. The cat's elbow, and other secret languages (4 and up) **652**
Fiction
Myrick, M. The Secret Three **E**
Circle of fire. Hooks, W. H. **Fic**
Circle of giving. Howard, E. **Fic**
A **circle** of seasons. Livingston, M. C. **811**
Circles, triangles and squares. Hoban, T. **E**
Circus
Machotka, H. The magic ring (3-6) **791.3**
See/See also pages in the following book(s):
Caney, S. Steven Caney's kids' America p292-313 (4 and up) **790.1**
Fiction
Peppé, R. Circus numbers **E**
Petersham, M. The circus baby **E**
Seuss, Dr. If I ran the circus **E**
Wiseman, B. Morris and Boris at the circus **E**
Pictorial works
Wildsmith, B. Brian Wildsmith's circus **E**
Poetry
Prelutsky, J. Circus (k-3) **811**
Circus. Prelutsky, J. **811**
The **circus** baby. Petersham, M. **E**
Circus, Brian Wildsmith's. Wildsmith, B. **E**
Circus daze. Gotwalt, H. L. M.
In Gotwalt, H. L. M. Everyday plays for boys and girls p3-16 **812**
Circus numbers. Peppé, R. **E**
Cirulis, Gunars, 1923-
Fortune's favorite
In Face to face: a collection of stories by celebrated Soviet and American writers p115-29 **S C**
Cisneros, Henry
See/See also pages in the following book(s):
Morey, J. Famous Mexican Americans p14-26 (5 and up) **920**
Cities and towns
Fiction
Burton, V. L. The little house **E**
Jonas, A. Round trip **E**
Pictorial works
Von Tscharner, R. New Providence (3-6) **307.7**
England—Pictorial works
Goodall, J. S. The story of a main street (3-6) **942**
Goodall, J. S. The story of an English village (3-6) **942**
Cities and towns, Ruined, extinct, etc.
See also Excavations (Archeology); Ghost towns
Gallant, R. A. Lost cities (4 and up) **930**
Citizenship
Swanson, J. I pledge allegiance (2-4) **323.6**
City: a story of Roman planning and construction. Macaulay, D. **711**
City/country. Robbins, K. **E**
City geese. Hirschi, R. **598**
The **city** kid's field guide. Heberman, E. **591**
City life
Freedman, R. Immigrant kids (4 and up) **325.73**
Maestro, B. Taxi **E**
Provensen, A. Town & country (k-2) **307.7**
Fiction
Florian, D. City street **E**
Isadora, R. City seen from A to Z **E**
Keats, E. J. Apt. 3 **E**
Mohr, N. Felita (3-5) **Fic**
Rice, E. City night **E**
Rockwell, A. F. Come to town **E**
Tresselt, A. R. Wake up, city! **E**
Poetry
On city streets (5 and up) **811.008**

City mouse and the country mouse
In The Tall book of nursery tales p12-15 **398.2**
City night. Rice, E. **E**
The **city** of gold and lead. Christopher, J. See note under Christopher, J. The White Mountains **Fic**
City planning
Rome
Macaulay, D. City: a story of Roman planning and construction (4 and up) **711**
City! San Francisco. Climo, S. **979.4**
City seen from A to Z. Isadora, R. **E**
City street. Florian, D. **E**
Civil engineering
Macaulay, D. City: a story of Roman planning and construction (4 and up) **711**
Macaulay, D. Underground (4 and up) **624.1**
See/See also pages in the following book(s):
Harris, J. L. Science in ancient Rome p15-22 (5 and up) **509**
Civil rights
See also Blacks—Civil rights
Jacobs, W. J. Great lives: human rights (5 and up) **920**
Rocha, R. The Universal Declaration of Human Rights (k-2) **341**
The **Civil** Rights Movement in America from 1865 to the present. McKissack, P. C. **323.4**
Civil War
United States
See United States—History—1861-1865, Civil War
The **Civil** War. Jordan, R. P. **973.7**
Civilization
See also Japan—Civilization
Lauber, P. Tales mummies tell (5 and up) **930.1**
Rahn, J. E. More plants that changed history (5 and up) **909**
Dictionaries
Lands and peoples **910.3**
Civilization, Ancient
Early humans (4 and up) **930.1**
Gallant, R. A. Lost cities (4 and up) **930**
Hackwell, W. J. Digging to the past: excavations in ancient lands (4 and up) **930.1**
Civilization, Greek
Coolidge, O. E. The golden days of Greece (4-6) **938**
Glubok, S. Olympic games in ancient Greece (5 and up) **796.48**
Odijk, P. The Greeks (5 and up) **938**
Civilization, Medieval
Aliki. A medieval feast (2-5) **394.1**
Anno, M. Anno's medieval world (3-6) **909.07**
Hunt, J. Illuminations (2-4) **909.07**
Lasker, J. Merry ever after (3-5) **392**
Lasker, J. A tournament of knights (1-3) **394**
Sancha, S. The Luttrell village (6 and up) **942.03**
Sancha, S. Walter Dragun's town (6 and up) **942.03**
Civilization, Modern
Poetry
Of quarks, quasars, and other quirks (5 and up) **821.008**
Civilization and science *See* Science and civilization
Clairvoyance
See also Extrasensory perception
Clap your hands (k-2) **796.1**
Clapp, Patricia, 1912-
Christmas in old New England
In Holiday plays round the year p28-36 **812.008**
Constance: a story of early Plymouth (5 and up) **Fic**
Jane-Emily (5 and up) **Fic**
Witches' children (6 and up) **Fic**
Clare, of Assisi, Saint, 1194-1253
About
De Paola, T. Francis, the poor man of Assisi (3-5) **92**
Clark, Ann Nolan, 1896-
Secret of the Andes (4 and up) **Fic**
See/See also pages in the following book(s):
Newbery Medal books, 1922-1955 p390-404 **028.5**
Clark, Christopher Stuart- *See* Stuart-Clark, Christopher
Clark, Margaret Goff
The vanishing manatee (4 and up) **599.5**
Clark, Tim W.
(il) Casey, D. The friendly prairie dog **599.32**
Clark, William, 1770-1838
About
Blumberg, R. The incredible journey of Lewis and Clark (5 and up) **978**
Clarke, Rebecca Sophia, 1833-1906
Jeffers, S. Wild Robin **E**
Class clown. Hurwitz, J. **Fic**
Class president. Hurwitz, J. See note under Hurwitz, J. Class clown **Fic**

The **Classic** fairy tales 398.2
Classification, Dewey Decimal
Dewey, M. Abridged Dewey decimal classification and relative index 025.4
Cleaning
See also Laundry
Cleanliness
See also Hygiene
Fiction
Hutchins, P. Where's the baby? E
Wilson, S. The day that Henry cleaned his room E
Clear the cow pasture, I'm coming in for a landing!: a story of Amelia Earhart. Quackenbush, R. M. 92
Cleary, Beverly
Beezus and Ramona. See note under Cleary, B. Ramona the pest Fic
Beezus and Ramona [excerpt]
In The Random House book of humor for children p100-19 817.008
Dear Mr. Henshaw (4-6) Fic
Ellen Tebbits (3-5) Fic
Henry and Beezus. See note under Cleary, B. Henry Huggins Fic
Henry and Ribsy. See note under Cleary, B. Henry Huggins Fic
Henry and the clubhouse. See note under Cleary, B. Henry Huggins Fic
Henry and the paper route. See note under Cleary, B. Henry Huggins Fic
Henry Huggins (3-5) Fic
Mitch and Amy (3-5) Fic
The mouse and the motorcycle (3-5) Fic
Muggie Maggie (2-4) Fic
Otis Spofford (3-5) Fic
Ralph S. Mouse. See note under Cleary, B. The mouse and the motorcycle Fic
Ramona and her father. See note under Cleary, B. Ramona the pest Fic
Ramona and her mother. See note under Cleary, B. Ramona the pest Fic
Ramona and the Three Wise Persons
In The Family read-aloud Christmas treasury p6-15 808.8
Ramona, forever. See note under Cleary, B. Ramona the pest Fic
Ramona Quimby, age 8. See note under Cleary, B. Ramona the pest Fic
Ramona the brave. See note under Cleary, B. Ramona the pest Fic
Ramona the pest (3-5) Fic
The real hole E
Ribsy. See note under Cleary, B. Henry Huggins Fic
Runaway Ralph. See note under Cleary, B. The mouse and the motorcycle Fic
Socks (3-5) Fic
See/See also pages in the following book(s):
Newbery and Caldecott Medal books, 1976-1985 p122-35 028.5
Cleaver, Bill
(jt. auth) Cleaver, V. Ellen Grae Fic
(jt. auth) Cleaver, V. Grover Fic
(jt. auth) Cleaver, V. Hazel Rye Fic
(jt. auth) Cleaver, V. The Kissimmee Kid Fic
(jt. auth) Cleaver, V. Lady Ellen Grae Fic
(jt. auth) Cleaver, V. Queen of hearts Fic
(jt. auth) Cleaver, V. Trial Valley Fic
(jt. auth) Cleaver, V. Where the lillies bloom Fic
See/See also pages in the following book(s):
Townsend, J. R. A sounding of storytellers p30-40 028.5
Cleaver, Elizabeth, 1939-1985
The enchanted caribou (2-4) 398.2
Cleaver, Vera
Ellen Grae (4-6) Fic
Grover (4-6) Fic
Hazel Rye (5 and up) Fic
The Kissimmee Kid (6 and up) Fic
Lady Ellen Grae (4-6) Fic
Queen of hearts (6 and up) Fic
Trial Valley (5 and up) Fic
Where the lillies bloom (5 and up) Fic
See/See also pages in the following book(s):
Townsend, J. R. A sounding of storytellers p30-40 028.5
Clemens, Samuel Langhorne *See* Twain, Mark, 1835-1910
Clementina's cactus. Keats, E. J. E
Clements, Bruce
I tell a lie every so often (6 and up) Fic
Clergy
Fiction
Corcoran, B. Annie's monster (5 and up) Fic
Clever Alice
Grimm, J. Clever Elsie
In Grimm, J. Tales from Grimm p123-34 398.2
In Grimm, J. The complete Grimm's fairy tales p171-74 398.2
Clever answers
Afanas'ev, A. N. Clever answers
In Afanas'ev, A. N. Russian fairy tales p578-79 398.2
Clever Elsie. Grimm, J.
In Grimm, J. Tales from Grimm p123-34 398.2
In Grimm, J. The complete Grimm's fairy tales p171-74 398.2

Clever folk
Grimm, J. Wise folks
In Grimm, J. The complete Grimm's fairy tales p476-80 **398.2**
Clever Frog. Curry, J. L.
In Curry, J. L. Back in the beforetime p57-59 **398.2**
Clever Grethel
De la Mare, W. Clever Grethel
In Womenfolk and fairy tales p71-76 **398.2**

Grimm, J. Clever Gretel
In Grimm, J. The complete Grimm's fairy tales p360-63 **398.2**
Clever Hans. Grimm, J.
In Grimm, J. The complete Grimm's fairy tales p166-68 **398.2**
A **clever** judge. Chang, S.-N.
In Best-loved folktales of the world p547-48 **398.2**
Clever Kate. Shub, E. **398.2**
Clever Manka
Fillmore, P. Clever Manka
In Best-loved folktales of the world p447-51 **398.2**
In The Scott, Foresman anthology of children's literature p274-77 **808.8**
In Womenfolk and fairy tales p146-55 **398.2**

Clever student and the master of black arts
Pyle, H. Clever student and the master of black arts
In Pyle, H. The wonder clock p49-61 **398.2**

Clever tailor
Grimm, J. The cunning little tailor
In Grimm, J. The complete Grimm's fairy tales p525-28 **398.2**
Grimm, J. The story of a clever tailor
In The Green fairy book p324-27 **398.2**

The **clever** thief. Protter, E.
In Best-loved folktales of the world p555-57 **398.2**
The **clever** thieves. Tashjian, V. A.
In The Scott, Foresman anthology of children's literature p279 **808.8**
The **clever** wife. Kendall, C.
In Kendall, C. Sweet and sour p14-17 **398.2**
CLICK!: a story about George Eastman. Mitchell, B. **92**
Click, rumble, roar (2-5) **811.008**
Cliff dwellers and cliff dwellings
Trimble, S. The village of blue stone (4-6) **970.004**
Clifford, Eth, 1915-
The dastardly murder of Dirty Pete (3-5) **Fic**
Harvey's horrible snake disaster (3-5) **Fic**
Harvey's marvelous monkey mystery. See note under Clifford, E. Harvey's horrible snake disaster **Fic**
Harvey's wacky parrot adventure. See note under Clifford, E. Harvey's horrible snake disaster **Fic**
Help! I'm a prisoner in the library (3-5) **Fic**
The remembering box (3-5) **Fic**
The rocking chair rebellion (6 and up) **Fic**

Clifford, Mary Louise
The land and people of Afghanistan (5 and up) **958.1**
Clifton, Lucille, 1936-
All us come cross the water
In Free to be—a family p133-37 **810.8**
Everett Anderson's goodbye (k-3) **811**
Everett Anderson's nine month long. See note under Clifton, L. Everett Anderson's goodbye **811**
The lucky stone (3-5) **Fic**
Some of the days of Everett Anderson. See note under Clifton, L. Everett Anderson's goodbye **811**
Three wishes [short story]
In Free to be—you and me p114-18 **810.8**

Climate
See also Greenhouse effect; Meteorology; Weather
Lambert, D. Weather and its work (5 and up) **551.6**
Climbing plants
Petrides, G. A. A field guide to trees and shrubs **582.1**
Climo, Shirley, 1928-
City! San Francisco (4 and up) **979.4**
The cobweb Christmas **E**
Cobweb Christmas [excerpt]
In The Family read-aloud Christmas treasury p122-31 **808.8**
The Egyptian Cinderella (k-2) **398.2**
Someone saw a spider (4 and up) **398.2**
Contents: Arachne's gift; The cloud spinner; The spider brothers make the rainbow; How spider got his waistline; The prophet and the spider; The spider and the king; Father spider comes to dinner; The spellbound spider; Sally-Maud, Zachary Dee, and the dream spinner
ClipArt & dynamic designs for libraries & media centers. Matthews, J. G. **021.7**
The **cloak**. Garfield, L.
In Garfield, L. The apprentices **S C**
Clocks. Zubrowski, B. **681.1**
Clocks and how they go. Gibbons, G. **681.1**

Clocks and watches
Gibbons, G. Clocks and how they go (2-4) **681.1**
McMillan, B. Time to— (k-2) **529**
Zubrowski, B. Clocks (4 and up) **681.1**
Fiction
Stolz, M. The cuckoo clock (4-6) **Fic**
Clod's comb. Kendall, C.
In Kendall, C. Sweet and sour p86-88 **398.2**
Close your eyes. Marzollo, J. **E**
Clothing and dress
See also Coats; Costume
Cobb, V. Getting dressed (1-3) **646**
Kuskin, K. The Philharmonic gets dressed **E**
Fiction
Fox, M. Shoes from Grandpa **E**
Gould, D. Aaron's shirt **E**
Hughes, S. Two shoes, new shoes **E**
Hutchins, P. You'll soon grow into them, Titch **E**
Neitzel, S. The jacket I wear in the snow **E**
Sharples, J. The flyaway pantaloons **E**
Watanabe, S. How do I put it on? **E**
Clothing trade
Henry, S. Everyone wears his name: a biography of Levi Strauss (5 and up) **92**
The **cloud** book. De Paola, T. **551.57**
The **cloud** spinner. Climo, S.
In Climo, S. Someone saw a spider p17-24 **398.2**
Clouds
De Paola, T. The cloud book (k-3) **551.57**
See/See also pages in the following book(s):
Tannenbaum, B. Making and using your own weather station p55-74 (5 and up) **551.6**
Cloudy with a chance of meatballs. Barrett, J.
In Rainy day: stories and poems p3-11 **808.8**
The **clover** and the bee. Dowden, A. O. T. **582**
The **clown** of God. De Paola, T. **398.2**
Clowns
See/See also pages in the following book(s):
Araki, C. Origami in the classroom p26-30 (Book II) (4 and up) **736**
Fiction
Petersham, M. The circus baby **E**
A **clown's** story. Bencastro, M.
In Where angels glide at dawn p57-65 **S C**
Clubs
Fiction
Greenwald, S. Mariah Delany's Author-of-the-Month Club (4-6) **Fic**
Honeycutt, N. Invisible Lissa (3-5) **Fic**
Myrick, M. The Secret Three **E**
Clyde monster. Crowe, R. L. **E**
Clymer, Eleanor Lowenton, 1906-
The horse in the attic (4 and up) **Fic**
Coal mines and mining
Fiction
Hendershot, J. In coal country **E**
Coastal rescue: preserving our seashores. Miller, C. G. **333.91**
Coats
Fiction
Hest, A. The purple coat **E**
Ziefert, H. A new coat for Anna **E**
Coatsworth, Elizabeth Jane, 1893-1986
The cat who went to heaven (4 and up) **Fic**
Under the green willow **E**
See/See also pages in the following book(s):
Newbery Medal books, 1922-1955 p94-98 **028.5**
Cobb, Theo
(il) Cobb, V. Chemically active!: experiments you can do at home **540.7**
(il) Cobb, V. The secret life of cosmetics: a science experiment book **668**
(il) Cobb, V. Sneakers meet your feet **685**
Cobb, Vicki
Bet you can! science possibilities to fool you (4 and up) **793.8**
Bet you can't! science impossibilities to fool you (4 and up) **793.8**
Chemically active!: experiments you can do at home (5 and up) **540.7**
Feeding yourself (1-3) **394.1**
Getting dressed (1-3) **646**
Gobs of goo (2-4) **547**
How to really fool yourself (5 and up) **152.1**
Keeping clean (1-3) **646.7**
Magic—naturally! science entertainment & amusements (4 and up) **793.8**
The monsters who died (3-5) **567.9**
More power to you (4-6) **621.31**
More science experiments you can eat (5 and up) **507**
Science experiments you can eat (5 and up) **507**
The scoop on ice cream (4-6) **637**
The secret life of cosmetics: a science experiment book (5 and up) **668**
The secret life of hardware: a science experiment book (5 and up) **670**
Skyscraper going up! (1-3) **690**
Sneakers meet your feet (4-6) **685**

Cobb, Vicki—*Continued*
This place is wet (2-4) **574.5**
The trip of a drip (4-6) **628.1**
Why can't you unscramble an egg? and other not such dumb questions about matter (3-5) **530**
Why doesn't the earth fall up? (3-5) **531**
Writing it down (1-3) **681**

The **cobbler** and his cat. Alexander, L.
In Alexander, L. The town cats, and other tales p63-77 **S C**

Cobblestone **973.05**

The **cobweb** Christmas. Climo, S. **E**

Cobweb Christmas [excerpt]. Climo, S.
In The Family read-aloud Christmas treasury p122-31 **808.8**

The **cobweb** curtain. Koralek, J. **E**

Coca-Cola Company
See/See also pages in the following book(s):
Aaseng, N. The unsung heroes p10-18 (5 and up) **920**

Cocaine
See also Crack (Drug)
Shulman, J. Focus on cocaine and crack (3-6) **362.29**
Turck, M. Crack & cocaine (4-6) **362.29**
See/See also pages in the following book(s):
Hyde, M. O. Drug wars p11-20 (6 and up) **363.4**

Cochise, Apache Chief, d. 1874
See/See also pages in the following book(s):
Ehrlich, A. Wounded Knee: an Indian history of the American West (6 and up) **970.004**

Cochrane, Josephine Garis, d. 1913
See/See also pages in the following book(s):
Aaseng, N. The problem solvers p25-30 (5 and up) **920**

Cock and the bean
Afanas'ev, A. N. The death of the cock
In Afanas'ev, A. N. Russian fairy tales p17-19 **398.2**

Cock and the hand mill
Afanas'ev, A. N. The cock and the hand mill
In Afanas'ev, A. N. Russian fairy tales p387-89 **398.2**

The **cock** and the hen. Afanas'ev, A. N.
In Afanas'ev, A. N. Russian fairy tales p309 **398.2**

Cock and the mouse
The Cock and the mouse
In Best-loved folktales of the world p157-58 **398.2**

The **cock** and the mouse and the little red hen. Rockwell, A. F.
In Rockwell, A. F. The three bears & 15 other stories p17-32 **398.2**

Cock, the mouse and the little red hen
Rockwell, A. F. The cock and the mouse and the little red hen
In Rockwell, A. F. The three bears & 15 other stories p17-32 **398.2**

Cockroaches
Kerby, M. Cockroaches (4-6) **595.7**
Fiction
James, M. Shoebag (5 and up) **Fic**

CoConis, Constantinos *See* CoConis, Ted

CoConis, Ted
(il) Byars, B. C. The summer of the swans **Fic**
(il) Gates, D. The golden god: Apollo **292**

Codes, ciphers, and other secrets. Mango, K. N. **652**

Coerr, Eleanor, 1922-
The big balloon race **E**
Chang's paper pony **E**
The Josefina story quilt **E**
Sadako and the thousand paper cranes [biography of Sadako Sasaki] (3-6) **92**

Coffin cash. Kendall, C.
In Kendall, C. Sweet and sour p108-12 **398.2**

Coffin lid
Afanas'ev, A. N. The peasant and the corpse
In Afanas'ev, A. N. Russian fairy tales p333-34 **398.2**

Cogancherry, Helen
(il) Burstein, F. Rebecca's nap **E**
(il) Herman, C. Millie Cooper, 3B **Fic**
(il) Herman, C. Millie Cooper, take a chance **Fic**

Cohen, Barbara, 1932-
Canterbury tales (4 and up) **Fic**
Contents: The nun's priest's tale; The pardoner's tale; The wife of Bath's tale; The franklin's tale
The carp in the bathtub (2-4) **Fic**
Molly's Pilgrim (2-4) **Fic**
Thank you, Jackie Robinson (4-6) **Fic**
Yussel's prayer (3-5) **398.2**

Cohen, Daniel, 1936-
Ancient Egypt (3-6) **932**
Dinosaurs (1-3) **567.9**
Monster dinosaur (5 and up) **567.9**
Phone call from a ghost (4-6) **133.1**
Prehistoric animals (4-6) **560**
The world of UFOs (6 and up) **001.9**
(jt. auth) Cohen, S. What kind of dog is that? **636.7**

Cohen, Jene Barr *See* Barr, Jene, 1900-1985

Cohen, Miriam
"Bee my valentine!". See note under Cohen, M. See you in second grade! **E**
Best friends. See note under Cohen, M. See you in second grade! **E**

Cohen, Miriam—*Continued*
Don't eat too much turkey! See note under Cohen, M. See you in second grade! E
First grade takes a test. See note under Cohen, M. See you in second grade! E
It's George! See note under Cohen, M. See you in second grade! E
Jim meets The Thing. See note under Cohen, M. See you in second grade! E
Jim's dog Muffins. See note under Cohen, M. See you in second grade! E
Liar, liar, pants on fire! See note under Cohen, M. See you in second grade! E
Lost in the museum. See note under Cohen, M. See you in second grade! E
The new teacher. See note under Cohen, M. See you in second grade! E
No good in art. See note under Cohen, M. See you in second grade! E
The real skin rubber monster mask. See note under Cohen, M. See you in second grade! E
See you in second grade! E
See you tomorrow, Charles. See note under Cohen, M. See you in second grade! E
So what? See note under Cohen, M. See you in second grade! E
Starring first grade. See note under Cohen, M. See you in second grade! E
When will I read? See note under Cohen, M. See you in second grade! E
Will I have a friend? See note under Cohen, M. See you in second grade! E

Cohen, Susan, 1938-
What kind of dog is that? (4 and up) **636.7**

Cohen, Vivien
(il) Johnson, E. W. Love and sex and growing up **613.9**

Cohn, Janice
I had a friend named Peter E

Cohn, Ronald H.
(il) Patterson, F. Koko's kitten **599.88**
(il) Patterson, F. Koko's story **599.88**

Coins
Hoban, T. 26 letters and 99 cents E
Hughes, R. P. Fell's United States coin book **737.4**
Reinfeld, F. Catalogue of the world's most popular coins **737.4**
See/See also pages in the following book(s):
Caney, S. Steven Caney's kids' America p376-82 (4 and up) **790.1**

The **cold** & hot winter. Hurwitz, J. See note under Hurwitz, J. The hot & cold summer **Fic**

Cold stars and fireflies. Esbensen, B. J. **811**

Coldrey, Jennifer
The world of a jellyfish (k-2) **593.7**

Cole, Ann
I saw a purple cow, and 100 other recipes for learning **372.1**
A Pumpkin in a pear tree. See A Pumpkin in a pear tree **745.59**
Purple cow to the rescue **372.1**

Cole, Babette
The silly book **E**

Cole, Brock, 1938-
The goats (5 and up) **Fic**
No more baths **E**
The winter wren **E**
(il) Paton Walsh, J. Gaffer Samson's luck **Fic**
(il) Reid Banks, L. The Indian in the cupboard **Fic**

Cole, Davis *See* Elting, Mary, 1909-

Cole, Joanna
Asking about sex and growing up (4-6) **613.9**
A bird's body **598**
Bony-Legs (k-3) **398.2**
Cars and how they go (2-4) **629.222**
A cat's body **636.8**
A chick hatches (k-3) **636.5**
Cuts, breaks, bruises, and burns (3-5) **612**
A dog's body **636.7**
Don't tell the whole world! **E**
Evolution (k-3) **575**
A frog's body **597.8**
A gift from Saint Francis (2-4) **92**
A horse's body **636.1**
How you were born (k-2) **612.6**
The human body: how we evolved (4 and up) **573.2**
An insect's body **595.7**
Large as life daytime animals (k-3) **591**
Large as life nighttime animals (k-3) **591**
The magic school bus at the waterworks (2-4) **551.48**
The magic school bus inside the Earth (2-4) **551.1**
The magic school bus inside the human body (2-4) **612**
The magic school bus, lost in the solar system (2-4) **523**
My puppy is born (k-3) **636.7**
The new baby at your house (k-3) **306.8**
Plants in winter (k-3) **581.5**
A snake's body **597.9**

Cole, Joanna—*Continued*
Your new potty 649
(comp) Anna Banana: 101 jump-rope rhymes. See Anna Banana: 101 jump-rope rhymes 398.8
(comp) Best-loved folktales of the world. See Best-loved folktales of the world 398.2
(comp) The Laugh book. See The Laugh book 808.8
(comp) A New treasury of children's poetry. See A New treasury of children's poetry 821.008
(comp) The Read-aloud treasury. See The Read-aloud treasury 808.8

Cole, William, 1919-
(comp) Oh, such foolishness! See Oh, such foolishness! 821.008
(comp) Oh, that's ridiculous! See Oh, that's ridiculous! 821.008
(comp) Poem stew. See Poem stew 811.008

Coleridge, Sara, 1802-1852
January brings the snow (k-2) 821

Collado, Alfredo Villanueva *See* Villanueva Collado, Alfredo

Collage
See/See also pages in the following book(s):
The Illustrator's notebook p90-92 741.6

The **collection** program in schools. Van Orden, P. J. 027.8

Collective settlements
Israel
Taylor, A. A kibbutz in Israel (3-5) 956.94

College and school drama
Periodicals
Plays 808.82

College and school journalism
Fiction
Conford, E. Dear Lovey Hart: I am desperate (6 and up) Fic

Collier, Christopher, 1930-
(jt. auth) Collier, J. L. Jump ship to freedom Fic
(jt. auth) Collier, J. L. My brother Sam is dead Fic
(jt. auth) Collier, J. L. War comes to Willy Freeman Fic
(jt. auth) Collier, J. L. Who is Carrie? Fic

Collier, James Lincoln, 1928-
Jump ship to freedom (6 and up) Fic
Louis Armstrong: an American success story (5 and up) 92
My brother Sam is dead (6 and up) Fic
War comes to Willy Freeman (6 and up) Fic
Who is Carrie? (6 and up) Fic

Collington, Peter
The angel and the soldier boy E

Collins, David R.
The country artist: a story about Beatrix Potter (3-5) 92

Collins, John, 1738-1808
The chapter of kings
In A Nursery companion p80-89 820.8

Collodi, Carlo, 1826-1890
The adventures of Pinocchio (3-6) Fic
The adventures of Pinocchio; dramatization. See Thane, A. Pinocchio goes to school

Colombia
Fiction
Kendall, S. The Bell Reef (5 and up) Fic

Colombo, Cristoforo *See* Columbus, Christopher

The **colonial** cookbook. Penner, L. R. 641.5

Colonial craftsmen and the beginnings of American industry. Tunis, E. 670

Colonial living. Tunis, E. 973.2

Color
Branley, F. M. Color, from rainbows to lasers (6 and up) 535.6
Crews, D. Freight train E
Ehlert, L. Color farm E
Ehlert, L. Color zoo E
Emberley, E. Green says go (k-3) 535.6
Hoban, T. Is it red? Is it yellow? Is it blue? E
Hoban, T. Of colors and things (k-2) 535.6
Jonas, A. Color dance E
McMillan, B. Growing colors E
My first look at colors E
Reiss, J. J. Colors E
Rockwell, A. F. Willy can count E
Serfozo, M. Who said red? E
Taylor, B. Color and light (3-5) 535
Testa, F. If you take a paintbrush E
Fiction
Anholt, C. Tom's rainbow walk E
Lionni, L. Little blue and little yellow E
Young, J. A million chameleons E
Zolotow, C. Mr. Rabbit and the lovely present E
Poetry
O'Neill, M. L. D. Hailstones and halibut bones (k-3) 811

Color and light. Taylor, B. **535**
Color dance. Jonas, A. **E**
Color farm. Ehlert, L. **E**
Color, from rainbows to lasers. Branley, F. M. **535.6**
Color printing
See/See also pages in the following book(s):
The Illustrator's notebook p97-106 **741.6**
Color zoo. Ehlert, L. **E**
Colorado
Kent, D. Colorado
In America the beautiful **973**
Colors. Reiss, J. J. **E**
Colours. See My first look at colors **E**
Coltman, Paul, 1917-
Tog the Ribber; or, Granny's tale (3-5) **821**
Colum, Padraic, 1881-1972
The children of Odin (5 and up) **293**
The children's Homer: The adventures of Odysseus and The tale of Troy (4 and up) **883**
The Golden Fleece and the heroes who lived before Achilles (5 and up) **292**
How Ma-ui fished up the great island
In Best-loved folktales of the world p599-601 **398.2**
See/See also pages in the following book(s):
A Horn Book sampler on children's books and reading p120-24 **028.5**
Columba, Saint, 521-597
About
Fritz, J. The man who loved books (3-5) **92**
The **Columbia** Granger's index to poetry **808.81**
Columbus, Christopher
About
D'Aulaire, I. Columbus (1-4) **92**
Fritz, J. Where do you think you're going, Christopher Columbus? (3-5) **92**
Levinson, N. S. Christopher Columbus: voyager to the unknown (4 and up) **92**
Sandak, C. R. Columbus Day (4-6) **394.2**
Columbus. D'Aulaire, I. **92**
Columbus Day
Sandak, C. R. Columbus Day (4-6) **394.2**
See/See also pages in the following book(s):
Araki, C. Origami in the classroom p10-16 (Book I) (4 and up) **736**
Comanche Indians
See/See also pages in the following book(s):
Freedman, R. Indian chiefs p53-71 (6 and up) **920**
Comaroni, John Philip, 1937-
(ed) Dewey, M. Abridged Dewey decimal classification and relative index **025.4**
Combat aircraft. Graham, I. **623.7**
Come a stranger. Voigt, C. **Fic**
Come a tide. Lyon, G. E. **E**
Come again in the spring. Kennedy, R.
In Kennedy, R. Collected stories p9-20 **S C**
Come away from the water, Shirley. Burningham, J. **E**
Come back, Amelia Bedelia. Parish, P. See note under Parish, P. Amelia Bedelia **E**
Come on into my tropical garden. Nichols, G. **821**
Come out, muskrats. Arnosky, J. **599.32**
Come sing, Jimmy Jo. Paterson, K. **Fic**
Come to the doctor, Harry. Chalmers, M. See note under Chalmers, M. Throw a kiss, Harry **E**
Come to town. Rockwell, A. F. **E**
Come with me. Wolff, A. **E**
The **comeback** dog. Thomas, J. R. **Fic**
Comedians
Kamen, G. Charlie Chaplin (4 and up) **92**
The **comely** lady and the clay nose. MacLachlan, P.
In MacLachlan, P. Tomorrow's wizard p42-55 **S C**
Comets
See also Halley's comet
Asimov, I. Comets and meteors (3-5) **523.6**
Lauber, P. Voyagers from space (4 and up) **523.5**
See/See also pages in the following book(s):
Berger, M. Star gazing, comet tracking, and sky mapping p47-61 (5 and up) **523**
Simon, S. Look to the night sky: an introduction to star watching (4 and up) **523**
Comets and meteors. Asimov, I. **523.6**
The **comeuppance** of Brer Wolf. Parks, V. D.
In Parks, V. D. Jump! the adventures of Brer Rabbit p3-9 **398.2**
The **Comic** adventures of Old Dame Trot and her cat
In A Nursery companion p40-43 **820.8**

The **Comic** adventures of Old Mother Hubbard and her dog (k-3) **398.8**
The **comic** adventures of Old Mother Hubbard and her dog. Martin, S. C.
In A Nursery companion p28-31 **820.8**
Comic books, strips, etc.
See also Cartoons and caricatures
Coming-and-going men. Fleischman, P. **S C**
The **coming** of buffalo. Marriott, A. L.
In Marriott, A. L. American Indian mythology **398.2**
The **coming** of corn (Cheyenne). Marriott, A. L.
In Marriott, A. L. American Indian mythology **398.2**
The **coming** of corn (Mikasuki). Marriott, A. L.
In Marriott, A. L. American Indian mythology **398.2**
The **coming** of corn (Zuni). Marriott, A. L.
In Marriott, A. L. American Indian mythology **398.2**
Commager, Henry Steele, 1902-
The great Constitution (5 and up) **342**
Commander Toad and the big black hole. Yolen, J. See note under Yolen, T. Commander Toad in space **E**
Commander Toad and the dis-asteroid. Yolen, J. See note under Yolen, T. Commander Toad in space **E**
Commander Toad and the intergalactic spy. Yolen, J. See note under Yolen, T. Commander Toad in space **E**
Commander Toad and the Planet of the Grapes. Yolen, J. See note under Yolen, T. Commander Toad in space **E**
Commander Toad and the space pirates. Yolen, J. See note under Yolen, T. Commander Toad in space **E**
Commander Toad in space. Yolen, J. **E**
Commire, Anne
(ed) Something about the author. See Something about the author **920.003**
Commodore Perry in the land of the Shogun. Blumberg, R. **952**
Commonsense cataloging. Miller, R. E. **025.3**
Communes *See* Collective settlements
Communicable diseases
Patent, D. H. Germs! (4 and up) **616.9**
Communication
Silverstein, A. Wonders of speech (6 and up) **302.2**
See/See also pages in the following book(s):
Burns, M. I am not a short adult! p109-24 (3-6) **305.23**
Communication among animals *See* Animal communication
Communication arts *See* Language arts
Community development
See also City planning
Community life
Huff, B. A. Greening the city streets **635**
Companies *See* Corporations
Companion to music, The Oxford first. McLeish, K. **780**
Company's coming. Yorinks, A. **E**
Comparative religion *See* Religions
The **complete** adventures of Olga da Polga. Bond, M. **Fic**
The **complete** adventures of Tom Kitten and his friends. Potter, B. See note under Potter, B. The story of Miss Moppet **E**
The **complete** dog book. American Kennel Club **636.7**
The **complete** fairy tales of George Macdonald. MacDonald, G. **S C**
The **complete** frog. Lacey, E. A. **597.8**
The **complete** Grimm's fairy tales. Grimm, J. **398.2**
The **complete** nonsense of Edward Lear. Lear, E. **821**
The **complete** story of the three blind mice. Ivimey, J. W. **E**
Complete version of ye three blind mice. See Ivimey, J. W. The complete story of the three blind mice **E**
The **complete** works of Lewis Carroll. Carroll, L. **828**
The **completed** hickory dickory dock. Aylesworth, J. **398.8**
Composers
Ventura, P. Great composers (5 and up) **780.9**
See/See also pages in the following book(s):
McLeish, K. The Oxford first companion to music (5 and up) **780**
Composers, American
Mitchell, B. America, I hear you: a story about George Gershwin (3-5) **92**
Mitchell, B. Raggin': a story about Scott Joplin (3-5) **92**
Composition (Music)
See/See also pages in the following book(s):
McLeish, K. The Oxford first companion to music (5 and up) **780**
Compton yearbook. See Compton's encyclopedia and fact-index **031**

Compton's encyclopedia and fact-index **031**
Compton's MultiMedia encyclopedia. See Compton's encyclopedia and fact-index **031**
Compulsory labor *See* Slavery
Computer programming *See* Programming (Computers)
Computerized axial tomography *See* Tomography, Computerized axial
Computers
See also Electronic data processing
Adams, R. C. Science with computers (6 and up) **507**
Simon, S. Meet the computer (k-3) **004**
Dictionaries
Simon, S. Bits and bytes: a computer dictionary for beginners (k-3) **004**
Computers and audiovisuals. See Matthews, J. G. ClipArt & dynamic designs for libraries & media centers **021.7**
Concentration camps
See also Japanese Americans—Evacuation and relocation, 1942-1945
Fiction
Innocenti, R. Rose Blanche (5 and up) **Fic**
The **concise** AACR2, 1988 revision. Gorman, M. **025.3**
Conduct of life *See* Human behavior
Cone, Molly
Mishmash (3-5) **Fic**
Mishmash and the big fat problem. See note under Cone, M. Mishmash **Fic**
Mishmash and the robot. See note under Cone, M. Mishmash **Fic**
Mishmash and the sauerkraut mystery. See note under Cone, M. Mishmash **Fic**
Mishmash and the substitute teacher. See note under Cone, M. Mishmash **Fic**
Cone, Patricia Clapp *See* Clapp, Patricia, 1912-
Conflict of generations
LeShan, E. J. Grandparents: a special kind of love (4 and up) **306.8**
LeShan, E. J. When grownups drive you crazy (4 and up) **306.8**
Conford, Ellen
And this is Laura (4-6) **Fic**
A case for Jenny Archer (2-4) **Fic**
Dear Lovey Hart: I am desperate (6 and up) **Fic**
Dreams of victory (4-6) **Fic**
Felicia the critic (4-6) **Fic**
Genie with the light blue hair (5 and up) **Fic**
Jenny Archer, author. See note under Conford, E. A case for Jenny Archer **Fic**
Jenny Archer to the rescue. See note under Conford, E. A case for Jenny Archer **Fic**
A job for Jenny Archer. See note under Conford, E. A case for Jenny Archer **Fic**
Lenny Kandell, smart aleck (4 and up) **Fic**
The luck of Pokey Bloom (3-6) **Fic**
Me and the terrible two (3-6) **Fic**
A royal pain (6 and up) **Fic**
Seven days to a brand-new me (6 and up) **Fic**
What's cooking, Jenny Archer? See note under Conford, E. A case for Jenny Archer **Fic**
Why me? (5 and up) **Fic**
The **conjure** wives. MacDonald, M. R. *In* MacDonald, M. R. When the lights go out p79-85 **372.6**
Conklin, Paul
(il) Ashabranner, B. K. Born to the land: an American portrait **978.9**
(il) Ashabranner, B. K. People who make a difference **920**
(il) Thomson, P. Keepers and creatures at the National Zoo **590.74**
Conley, Andrea
(jt. auth) Mallory, K. Rescue of the stranded whales **639.9**
Conly, Jane Leslie
R-T, Margaret, and the rats of NIMH (4 and up) **Fic**
Racso and the rats of NIMH (4 and up) **Fic**
Connecticut
Kent, D. Connecticut
In America the beautiful **973**
Fiction
Dalgliesh, A. The courage of Sarah Noble (2-4) **Fic**
History—1600-1775, Colonial period—Fiction
Speare, E. G. The witch of Blackbird Pond (6 and up) **Fic**
Connections: short stories by outstanding writers for young adults (6 and up) **S C**
Conner, Kenyon
About
Schmidt, D. I am a Jesse White tumbler **796.47**
Conover, Chris, 1950-
Mother Goose and the sly fox (k-2) **398.2**
Six little ducks (k-2) **782.42**
(il) Grimm, J. The bear and the kingbird **398.2**
Conrad, Pam, 1947-
My Daniel (5 and up) **Fic**

Conrad, Pam, 1947-—*Continued*
Prairie songs (5 and up) **Fic**
Staying nine (3-5) **Fic**
Stonewords (5 and up) **Fic**
The Tub People **E**

Conroy, Jack, 1899-1990
The Boomer fireman's fast Sooner hound
In The Scott, Foresman anthology of children's literature p368-70 **808.8**

Conservation of energy *See* Energy conservation

Conservation of forests *See* Forests and forestry

Conservation of natural resources
See also Nature conservation

Fiction

Cherry, L. The great kapok tree **E**

Conservation of plants *See* Plant conservation

Conservation of wildlife *See* Wildlife conservation

Consider the lilies. Paterson, J. **220.8**

Constance: a story of early Plymouth. Clapp, P. **Fic**

The **Constitution**. Mabie, M. C. J. **342**

Constitutional history
See also United States—Constitutional history

Constitutional law
Stein, R. C. The story of the powers of the Supreme Court (4-6) **347**

Construction *See* Building

Consuls *See* Diplomats

Consumer education
Kyte, K. S. The kids' complete guide to money (4 and up) **332.024**
Schmitt, L. Smart spending (5 and up) **640.73**

Periodicals

Zillions **640.73**

Consumer Reports Books (Firm)
Parent's choice guide to videocassettes for children. See Parent's choice guide to videocassettes for children **016.79143**

Contact lenses
Silverstein, A. Glasses and contact lenses (6 and up) **617.7**

The **contest**. Hogrogian, N. **398.2**

The **contests** at Cowlick. Kennedy, R.
In Kennedy, R. Collected stories p107-16 **S C**

Continental drift
Aylesworth, T. G. Moving continents (6 and up) **551.1**
See/See also pages in the following book(s):
Gallant, R. A. Our restless earth p48-55 (4 and up) **550**

Conundrums *See* Riddles

"A **convention** of delegates". Hauptly, D. J. **342**

Conveying machinery
Ancona, G. Monster movers (3-5) **621.8**

Conveyors *See* Conveying machinery

Cook, Elizabeth
The ordinary and the fabulous **028.5**

Cook, Jan Leslie
The mysterious undersea world (4 and up) **551.46**

Cook, Scott
(il) McKissack, P. C. Nettie Jo's friends **E**

Cookbook for boys and girls, Betty Crocker's. Crocker, B. **641.5**

Cooke, Edna
(il) Dodge, M. M. Hans Brinker; or, The silver skates **Fic**

Cookery
See also Baking; Food

Barkin, C. Happy Valentine's Day! (4-6) **394.2**
Better Homes and Gardens step-by-step kids' cook book (4 and up) **641.5**
Cobb, V. More science experiments you can eat (5 and up) **507**
Cobb, V. Science experiments you can eat (5 and up) **507**
Crocker, B. Betty Crocker's cookbook for boys and girls (3-6) **641.5**
Cuyler, M. The all-around pumpkin book (4-6) **641.3**
Hautzig, E. R. Holiday treats (3 and up) **641.5**
Linde, P. van der. Around the world in 80 dishes (3-6) **641.5**
Meyer, C. Christmas crafts (5 and up) **745.59**
New junior cook book (3-6) **641.5**
Penner, L. R. The colonial cookbook (5 and up) **641.5**
Perl, L. Hunter's stew and hangtown fry: what pioneer America ate and why (4 and up) **641.5**
Perl, L. Slumps, grunts, and snickerdoodles: what Colonial America ate and why (4 and up) **641.5**
A Pumpkin in a pear tree (1-4) **745.59**
Walker, B. M. The Little House cookbook (5 and up) **641.5**
See/See also pages in the following book(s):
Caney, S. Steven Caney's kids' America p148-79 (4 and up) **790.1**
Kohn, B. The beachcomber's book p68-76 (3-6) **745.5**

Fiction

Joosse, B. M. Jam day **E**

Cookery, African
Nabwire, C. R. Cooking the African way (5 and up) **641.5**
Cookery, British
Hill, B. W. Cooking the English way (5 and up) **641.5**
Cookery, Caribbean
Kaufman, C. D. Cooking the Caribbean way (5 and up) **641.5**
Cookery, Chinese
Yu, L. Cooking the Chinese way (5 and up) **641.5**
Cookery, French
Waldee, L. M. Cooking the French way (5 and up) **641.5**
Cookery, German
Parnell, H. Cooking the German way (5 and up) **641.5**
Cookery, Greek
Villios, L. W. Cooking the Greek way (5 and up) **641.5**
Cookery, Hungarian
Hargittai, M. Cooking the Hungarian way (5 and up) **641.5**
Cookery, Indic
Madavan, V. Cooking the Indian way (5 and up) **641.5**
Cookery, Israeli
Bacon, J. Cooking the Israeli way (5 and up) **641.5**
Cookery, Italian
Bisignano, A. Cooking the Italian way (5 and up) **641.5**
Cookery, Japanese
Weston, R. Cooking the Japanese way (5 and up) **641.5**
Cookery, Jewish
Bacon, J. Cooking the Israeli way (5 and up) **641.5**
See/See also pages in the following book(s):
Burns, M. The Hanukkah book p57-69 (4 and up) **296.4**
Cookery, Korean
Chung, O. Cooking the Korean way (5 and up) **641.5**
Cookery, Lebanese
Amari, S. Cooking the Lebanese way (5 and up) **641.5**
Cookery, Middle Eastern
Osborne, C. Middle Eastern food and drink (4-6) **641.5**
Cookery, Norwegian
Munsen, S. Cooking the Norwegian way (5 and up) **641.5**
Cookery, Polish
Zamojska-Hutchins, D. Cooking the Polish way (5 and up) **641.5**
Cookery, Russian
Plotkin, G. Cooking the Russian way (5 and up) **641.5**
Cookery, Spanish
Christian, R. Cooking the Spanish way (5 and up) **641.5**
Cookery, Vietnamese
Nguyen, C. T. Cooking the Vietnamese way (5 and up) **641.5**
Cookies
Better homes and gardens cookies for kids **641.8**

Cooking the African way. Nabwire, C. R. **641.5**
Cooking the Caribbean way. Kaufman, C. D. **641.5**
Cooking the Chinese way. Yu, L. **641.5**
Cooking the English way. Hill, B. W. **641.5**
Cooking the French way. Waldee, L. M. **641.5**
Cooking the German way. Parnell, H. **641.5**
Cooking the Greek way. Villios, L. W. **641.5**
Cooking the Hungarian way. Hargittai, M. **641.5**
Cooking the Indian way. Madavan, V. **641.5**
Cooking the Israeli way. Bacon, J. **641.5**
Cooking the Italian way. Bisignano, A. **641.5**
Cooking the Japanese way. Weston, R. **641.5**
Cooking the Korean way. Chung, O. **641.5**
Cooking the Lebanese way. Amari, S. **641.5**
Cooking the Norwegian way. Munsen, S. **641.5**
Cooking the Polish way. Zamojska-Hutchins, D. **641.5**
Cooking the Russian way. Plotkin, G. **641.5**
Cooking the Spanish way. Christian, R. **641.5**
Cooking the Vietnamese way. Nguyen, C. T. **641.5**

A **cool** kid—like me! Wilhelm, H. **E**
Coolidge, Olivia Ensor, 1908-
The golden days of Greece (4-6) **938**
The **Coomacka-Tree**. Sherlock, Sir P. M.
In Sherlock, Sir P. M. West Indian folk-tales p7-12 **398.2**
Cooney, Barbara, 1917-
Chanticleer and the fox **E**

Cooney, Barbara, 1917-—*Continued*
Christmas (1-3) **394.2**
Hattie and the wild waves **E**
Island boy **E**
The little juggler (3-6) **398.2**
Miss Rumphius **E**
(il) Brown, M. W. Christmas in the barn **232.9**
(il) Godden, R. The story of Holly and Ivy **E**
(il) Hall, D. Ox-cart man **E**
(il) Houston, G. The year of the perfect Christmas tree **E**
(il) Kesselman, W. A. Emma **E**
(il) Preston, E. M. Squawk to the moon, Little Goose **E**
(il) Salten, F. Bambi **Fic**
(il) Seeger, R. C. American folk songs for children in home, school and nursery school **781.62**
(il) Tortillitas para mamá and other nursery rhymes. See Tortillitas para mamá and other nursery rhymes **398.8**
See/See also pages in the following book(s):
Newbery and Caldecott Medal books, 1976-1985 p211-19 **028.5**

Cooney, Nancy Evans, 1932-
Go away monsters, lickety split! **E**

Cooper, Chris
How everyday things work (5 and up) **600**

Cooper, Floyd
(il) Galbraith, K. O. Laura Charlotte **E**
(il) Greenfield, E. Grandpa's face **E**
(il) Howard, E. F. Chita's Christmas tree **E**

Cooper, Ilene
(ed) A Guide to non-sexist children's books. See A Guide to non-sexist children's books v2 **011.6**

Cooper, Kay
Where did you get those eyes? (5 and up) **929**

Cooper, Lee Pelham
Fun with German (4 and up) **438**
More fun with Spanish (4 and up) **468**

Cooper, Martha
(il) Waters, K. Lion dancer: Ernie Wan's Chinese New Year **394.2**

Cooper, Michael, 1950-
Klondike fever (5 and up) **971.9**

Cooper, Susan, 1935-
The dark is rising. See note under Cooper, S. Over sea, under stone **Fic**
Dawn of fear (5 and up) **Fic**
Greenwitch. See note under Cooper, S. Over sea, under stone **Fic**
The grey king (5 and up) **Fic**
Over sea, under stone (5 and up) **Fic**
Seaward (6 and up) **Fic**
The selkie girl (2-4) **398.2**
The silver cow: a Welsh tale (1-3) **398.2**
Silver on the tree. See note under Cooper, S. Over sea, under stone **Fic**
See/See also pages in the following book(s):
Newbery and Caldecott Medal books, 1976-1985 p6-17 **028.5**

Copway, George, Chippewa Chief, ca. 1818-ca. 1863
Esbensen, B. J. Ladder to the sky **398.2**

Coral reefs. Johnson, S. A. **574.92**

Coral reefs and islands
Arnold, C. A walk on the Great Barrier Reef (3-6) **574.92**
Johnson, S. A. Coral reefs (4 and up) **574.92**
See/See also pages in the following book(s):
Cook, J. L. The mysterious undersea world p33-45 (4 and up) **551.46**

Corbeil, Jean-Claude
The Facts on File junior visual dictionary (3-6) **423**

Corbett, Scott, 1913-
The deadly hoax (5 and up) **Fic**
The disappearing dog trick. See note under Corbett, S. The lemonade trick **Fic**
The discontented ghost (6 and up) **Fic**
Grave doubts (4 and up) **Fic**
The hairy horror trick. See note under Corbett, S. The lemonade trick **Fic**
The hangman's ghost trick. See note under Corbett, S. The lemonade trick **Fic**
The lemonade trick (3-5) **Fic**
The mailbox trick. See note under Corbett, S. The lemonade trick **Fic**

Corbett, W. J.
The song of Pentecost (5 and up) **Fic**

Corbishley, Mike
Ancient Rome (5 and up) **937**

Corcoran, Barbara, 1911-
Annie's monster (5 and up) **Fic**

Corduroy. Freeman, D. **E**
In The Read-aloud treasury p190-206 **808.8**

Coren, Alan, 1938-
Arthur the Kid (3-5) **Fic**

Cormier, Robert
The chocolate war [excerpt]
In Face to face: a collection of stories by celebrated Soviet and American writers p2-8 **S C**

Corn
Aliki. Corn is maize (k-3) **633.1**
See/See also pages in the following book(s):
Barth, E. Turkeys, Pilgrims, and Indian corn p79-83 (3-6) **394.2**

The **Corn** in the rock
In The Monkey's haircut, and other stories told by the Maya p52-55 **398.2**
Corn is maize. Aliki. **633.1**
Cornelius. Lionni, L. **E**
Cornrows. Yarbrough, C. **E**
Cornwall (England)
Fiction
Paton Walsh, J. Unleaving (6 and up) **Fic**
Corporations
Aaseng, N. From rags to riches (5 and up) **920**
Corps of Engineers *See* United States. Army. Corps of Engineers
Corrigan, Barbara, 1922-
(il) Tom Glazer's Christmas songbook. See Tom Glazer's Christmas songbook **782.28**
Cortázar, Julio, 1914-1984
The bear's speech
In Where angels glide at dawn p3-5 **S C**
Corwin, Judith Hoffman
Papercrafts (3 and up) **745.54**
(il) Mango, K. N. Mapmaking **526**
Cosby, Bill, 1937-
About
Haskins, J. Bill Cosby: America's most famous father (5 and up) **92**
Cosmetics
Cobb, V. The secret life of cosmetics: a science experiment book (5 and up) **668**
Cosmic quest. Poynter, M. **574.999**
Cosmology *See* Universe
Cosner, Shaaron, 1940-
War nurses (6 and up) **355.3**
Costa Rica
Natural history
See Natural history—Costa Rica
Costabel, Eva Deutsch, 1924-
The Jews of New Amsterdam (2-4) **974.7**
Costume
See also Clothing and dress
Barkin, C. The scary Halloween costume book (3-6) **391**
Chernoff, G. T. Easy costumes you don't have to sew (3-5) **391**
Cummings, R. 101 costumes for all ages, all occasions **391**
Parish, P. Let's be early settlers with Daniel Boone (2-5) **745.5**
See/See also pages in the following book(s):
Caney, S. Steven Caney's kids' America p130-45 (4 and up) **790.1**
Cote d'Ivoire (Ivory Coast)—in pictures (5 and up) **966.68**
Cothran, Jean
With a wig, with a wag
In With a deep sea smile p86-92 **372.6**
Cottam, Clarence
(jt. auth) Zim, H. S. Insects **595.7**
Cotton
Selsam, M. E. Cotton (3-5) **633.5**
Coughlan, Margaret N., 1925-
(comp) Books for children. See Books for children **011.6**
Could anything be worse? Hirsh, M. **398.2**
"Could be worse!". Stevenson, J. **E**
Counseling
See also Vocational guidance
Count the animals 1 2 3, Demi's. Demi **E**
Count your way through China. Haskins, J. **951**
Count your way through Japan. Haskins, J. **952**
Count your way through the Arab world. Haskins, J. **909**
Counting
See also Numeration
Anno, M. Anno's counting book **E**
Anno, M. Anno's counting house **E**
Archambault, J. Counting sheep **E**
Aylesworth, J. One crow **E**
Bang, M. Ten, nine, eight **E**
Berenstain, S. Bears on wheels **E**
Carle, E. Rooster's off to see the world **E**
Christelow, E. Five little monkeys jumping on the bed **E**
Crews, D. Ten black dots **E**
De Regniers, B. S. So many cats! **E**
Demi. Demi's Count the animals 1 2 3 **E**
Dunrea, O. Deep down underground **E**
Eichenberg, F. Dancing in the moon **E**
Feelings, M. Moja means one **E**
Gardner, B. Can you imagine—? **E**
Gerstein, M. Roll over! **E**
Giganti, P., Jr. How many snails? **E**
Gundersheimer, K. 1 2 3, play with me **E**
Hoban, T. 26 letters and 99 cents **E**
Hughes, S. Lucy & Tom's 1.2.3. **E**
Hutchins, P. 1 hunter **E**
Kitchen, B. Animal numbers **E**
Langstaff, J. M. Over in the meadow (k-2) **781.62**
Macdonald, S. Numblers **E**
Magee, D. Trucks you can count on (k-2) **629.224**
McMillan, B. Counting wildflowers **E**

Counting—*Continued*
Miller, J. Farm counting book E
Oakes, B. Puzzlers E
Peppé, R. Circus numbers E
Pomerantz, C. One duck, another duck E
Reiss, J. J. Numbers E
Rockwell, A. F. Willy can count E
Scott, A. H. One good horse E
Sendak, M. One was Johnny E
Ten potatoes in a pot, and other counting rhymes (k-2) 398.8
Testa, F. If you take a pencil E
Thornhill, J. The wildlife 1 2 3 E
Bibliography
Roberts, P. Counting books are more than numbers: an annotated action bibliography 016.510
Counting America. Ashabranner, M. 304.6
Counting book, Anno's. Anno, M. E
Counting books *See* Counting
Counting books are more than numbers: an annotated action bibliography. Roberts, P. 016.510
Counting house, Anno's. Anno, M. E
Counting sheep. Archambault, J. E
Counting wildflowers. McMillan, B. E
Country and western music *See* Country music
The **country** artist: a story about Beatrix Potter. Collins, D. R. 92
The **country** bunny and the little gold shoes. Heyward, D. E
The **country** happens to Sneakers again. Brown, M. W.
In Brown, M. W. The fish with the deep sea smile p60-61 818
Country life
Fiction
Burch, R. Christmas with Ida Early (4 and up) Fic
Burch, R. Ida Early comes over the mountain (4 and up) Fic
Callen, L. Pinch (5 and up) Fic
Hall, D. The man who lived alone (2-4) Fic
Johnston, T. Yonder E
Lyon, G. E. Come a tide E
Martin, B. Barn dance! E
Rylant, C. Night in the country E
Poetry
Fatchen, M. The country mail is coming (3-5) 821
England
Sancha, S. The Luttrell village (6 and up) 942.03
The **country** mail is coming. Fatchen, M. 821
Country music
Fiction
Paterson, K. Come sing, Jimmy Jo (5 and up) Fic
Country pay. Fleischman, P.
In Fleischman, P. Coming-and-going men p123-47 S C
Coupe, Robert
(jt. auth) Coupe, S. Sharks 597
Coupe, Sheena
Sharks (5 and up) 597
Couper, Heather
The moon (4 and up) 523.3
Courage
Fiction
Giff, P. R. The gift of the pirate queen (4-6) Fic
Peet, B. Cowardly Clyde E
The **courage** of Kazan. Walker, B. K.
In Walker, B. K. A treasury of Turkish folktales for children p67-74 398.2
The **courage** of Sarah Noble. Dalgliesh, A. Fic
Courlander, Harold, 1908-
Anansi's hat-shaking dance
In Best-loved folktales of the world p615-17 398.2
In The Scott, Foresman anthology of children's literature p313-14 808.8
Bouki rents a horse
In Best-loved folktales of the world p738-40 398.2
The cow-tail switch, and other West African stories (4-6) 398.2
Contents: The cow-tail switch; Kaddo's wall; Talk; The one you don't see coming; Kassa, the strong one; Anansi's fishing expedition; Younde goes to town; The singing tortoise; Time; The messenger to Maftam; Guinea Fowl and Rabbit get justice; Anansi and Nothing go hunting for wives; How Soko brought debt to Ashanti; Hungry Spider and the Turtle; Throw Mountains; Ansige Karamba, the glutton; Don't shake hands with everybody
The deer and the jaguar share a house
In Best-loved folktales of the world p774-76 398.2
The departure of the giants
In The Crest and the hide, and other African stories of heroes, chiefs, bards, hunters, sorcerers, and common people p95-99 398.2
The fire on the mountain
In Best-loved folktales of the world p653-56 398.2
In The Scott, Foresman anthology of children's literature p303-04 808.8
The leopard's daughter
In With a deep sea smile p56-60 372.6

Courlander, Harold, 1908-—*Continued*
Moses and Ojje Ben Onogh
In The Crest and the hide, and other African stories of heroes, chiefs, bards, hunters, sorcerers, and common people p111-13 **398.2**
Paul Bunyan's cornstalk
In Best-loved folktales of the world p668-71 **398.2**
The search: who gets the chief's daughter
In With a deep sea smile p70-74 **372.6**
Talk
In Best-loved folktales of the world p613-15 **398.2**
The tiger's whisker
In Best-loved folktales of the world p558-60 **398.2**
Uncle Bouqui and Godfather Malice
In The Scott, Foresman anthology of children's literature p394-96 **808.8**
(comp) The Crest and the hide, and other African stories of heroes, chiefs, bards, hunters, sorcerers, and common people. See The Crest and the hide, and other African stories of heroes, chiefs, bards, hunters, sorcerers, and common people **398.2**

The **court** of the stone children. Cameron, E. **Fic**

The **courting** contest. Lester, J.
In Lester, J. More tales of Uncle Remus p26-29 **398.2**

Courts and courtiers
Aliki. A medieval feast (2-5) **394.1**

Cousin Greylegs, the great red fox and Grandfather Mole
Pyle, H. Cousin Greylegs, the great red fox and Grandfather Mole
In Pyle, H. The wonder clock p77-88 **398.2**

Cousins, Lucy
(il) The Little dog laughed. See The Little dog laughed **398.8**

Cousins
Fiction
Caseley, J. The cousins **E**
Clifford, E. Harvey's horrible snake disaster (3-5) **Fic**
Greenwald, S. Will the real Gertrude Hollings please stand up? (5 and up) **Fic**
Hamilton, V. Cousins (5 and up) **Fic**

Coutant, Helen
First snow (2-4) **Fic**
The gift (2-5) **Fic**

Couture, Susan Arkin
The block book **E**

Coverlets *See* Quilts

Coville, Bruce
Dapplegrim
In Herds of thunder, manes of gold p149-56 **808.8**
Duffy's jacket
In Things that go bump in the night p52-60 **S C**
The taming of Bucephalus
In Herds of thunder, manes of gold p65-70 **808.8**
(ed) Herds of thunder, manes of gold. See Herds of thunder, manes of gold **808.8**

Coville, Katherine
(il) Barkin, C. The scary Halloween costume book **391**
(il) San Souci, R. Short & shivery **398.2**

The **cow** on the roof. Jones, T. G.
In Best-loved folktales of the world p283-84 **398.2**

The **cow-tail** switch. Courlander, H.
In Courlander, H. The cow-tail switch, and other West African stories p5-12 **398.2**

The **cow-tail** switch, and other West African stories. Courlander, H. **398.2**

The **cow** that ate the piper. Crossley-Holland, K.
In Crossley-Holland, K. British folk tales p283-86 **398.2**

The **cow** that went oink. Most, B. **E**

The **cow** who fell in the canal. Krasilovsky, P. **E**

Cowardly Clyde. Peet, B. **E**

Cowboy dreams. Khalsa, D. K. **E**

Cowboys of the wild West. Freedman, R. **978**

Cowcher, Helen
Antarctica (1-3) **998**

Cowhands
Freedman, R. Cowboys of the wild West (4 and up) **978**
Fiction
James, W. Smoky, the cow horse (6 and up) **Fic**
Khalsa, D. K. Cowboy dreams **E**

Cows *See* Cattle

Cows in the parlor. McFarland, C. **636.2**

Coxe, Molly
(il) Branley, F. M. The Big Dipper **523.8**

Coyote (Legendary character)
Baylor, B. Moon song (1-3) **398.2**
Bierhorst, J. Doctor Coyote (1-4) **398.2**
Curry, J. L. Back in the beforetime (4-6) **398.2**

Coyote and Badger. Curry, J. L.
In Curry, J. L. Back in the beforetime p78-88 **398.2**

The **Coyote** and the bear
In The Diane Goode book of American folk tales and songs p25-31 **398.2**

Coyote and the salmon. Curry, J. L.
In Curry, J. L. Back in the beforetime p42-47 **398.2**

Coyote dreams. Nunes, S. **E**

Coyote makes the constellations. Mayo, G.
In Mayo, G. Star tales p15-16 **398.2**

Coyote rides a star. Curry, J. L.
In Curry, J. L. Back in the beforetime p48-51 **398.2**

Coyote rides the Sun. Curry, J. L.
In Curry, J. L. Back to the beforetime p100-106 **398.2**

Coyote scatters the stars: myths from the Southwest. Monroe, J. G.
In Monroe, J. G. They dance in the sky p28-43 **398.2**

Coyotes
Fiction
Nunes, S. Coyote dreams **E**

Coyote's crying song. MacDonald, M. R.
In MacDonald, M. R. Twenty tellable tales p10-19 **372.6**

Coyote's rain song. MacDonald, M. R.
In MacDonald, M. R. Twenty tellable tales p20-23 **372.6**

Coyote's squirrel hunt. Curry, J. L.
In Curry, J. L. Back in the beforetime p74-77 **398.2**

Crab
In Best-loved folktales of the world p152-54 **398.2**

The **crab** that played with the sea. Kipling, R. **Fic**
also in Kipling, R. Just so stories **S C**

Crabs
Holling, H. C. Pagoo (4 and up) **595.3**
Johnson, S. A. Hermit crabs (4 and up) **595.3**
McDonald, M. Is this a house for Hermit Crab? (k-2) **595.3**
Fiction
Carle, E. A house for Hermit Crab **E**
Kipling, R. The crab that played with the sea (1-4) **Fic**
Tafuri, N. Follow me! **E**

Crack (Drug)
Shulman, J. Focus on cocaine and crack (3-6) **362.29**
Turck, M. Crack & cocaine (4-6) **362.29**
See/See also pages in the following book(s):
Hyde, M. O. Drug wars p21-28 (6 and up) **363.4**

Crack & cocaine. Turck, M. **362.29**

The **crack-of-dawn** walkers. Hest, A. **E**

Cracker Jackson. Byars, B. C. **Fic**

The **cradle** didn't rock. Lester, J.
In Lester, J. The tales of Uncle Remus p106-09 **398.2**

Craft, Ruth
The winter bear **E**

Crafts (Arts) *See* Handicraft

Crafty Chameleon. Mwenye Hadithi. **E**

Craig, Helen
(il) Holabird, K. Angelina ballerina **E**

Craik, Dinah Maria Mulock, 1826-1887
The little lame prince; adaptation. See Wells, R. The little lame prince **E**

Crampton, Patricia
Peter and the wolf **E**

Crampton, W. G. (William G.)
Flag (4 and up) **929.9**

Crampton, William G. *See* Crampton, W. G. (William G.)

Crane and the heron
Afanas'ev, A. N. The crane and the heron
In Afanas'ev, A. N. Russian fairy tales p66 **398.2**

The **crane** wife. Yagawa, S. **398.2**

Cranes, derricks, etc.
Marston, H. I. Load lifters: derricks, cranes, and helicopters (3-6) **621.8**
Stephen, R. J. Cranes (2-4) **621.8**

Cranes (Birds)
McNulty, F. Peeping in the shell (2-5) **639.9**
Patent, D. H. The whooping crane (5 and up) **639.9**
Fiction
Byars, B. C. The house of wings (4-6) **Fic**

Cranes. Stephen, R. J. **621.8**

Crawford, Elizabeth D.
(ed) Fourth book of junior authors and illustrators. See Fourth book of junior authors and illustrators **920.003**

Crawford, Marc
(jt. auth) Katz, W. L. The Lincoln Brigade **946.081**

Crawford, Ruth *See* Seeger, Ruth Crawford, 1901-1953

Crazy in love. Kennedy, R.
In Kennedy, R. Collected stories p161-90 **S C**

Creation
Fisher, L. E. The seven days of creation (k-3) **222**
Hamilton, V. In the beginning; creation stories from around the world (5 and up) **291**

Creation—*Continued*
Hutton, W. Adam and Eve (k-3) **222**
Poetry
Lewis, R. In the night, still dark (1-3) **811**
Creative thinking
See/See also pages in the following book(s):
Yepsen, R. B. Smarten up! how to increase your brain power p75-90 (5 and up) **153**
The **creature** with no claws. Lester, J.
In Lester, J. Further tales of Uncle Remus p53-56 **398.2**
Creatures (3-5) **821.008**
Creatures of the night. Rinard, J. E. **591.5**
Creatures small and furry. Crump, D. J. **599**
Creepy castle. Goodall, J. S. **E**
The **cremation** of Sam McGee. Service, R. W. **811**
Cresswell, Helen
Absolute zero. See note under Cresswell, H. Ordinary Jack **Fic**
Bagthorpes abroad. See note under Cresswell, H. Ordinary Jack **Fic**
Bagthorpes haunted. See note under Cresswell, H. Ordinary Jack **Fic**
Bagthorpes liberated. See note under Cresswell, H. Ordinary Jack **Fic**
Bagthorpes unlimited. See note under Cresswell, H. Ordinary Jack **Fic**
Bagthorpes v. the world. See note under Cresswell, H. Ordinary Jack **Fic**
Dear Shrink (5 and up) **Fic**
Ordinary Jack (5 and up) **Fic**
The secret world of Polly Flint (4-6) **Fic**
Zero and the commercial
In Bauer, C. F. Celebrations p213-18 **808.8**
See/See also pages in the following book(s):
Townsend, J. R. A sense of story p57-63 **028.5**
The **crest** and the hide. Verwhilghen, L. A.
In The Crest and the hide, and other African stories of heroes, chiefs, bards, hunters, sorcerers, and common people p13-18 **398.2**
The **Crest** and the hide, and other African stories of heroes, chiefs, bards, hunters, sorcerers, and common people (5 and up) **398.2**
The **crested** curassow. Sherlock, Sir P. M.
In Sherlock, Sir P. M. West Indian folk-tales p13-20 **398.2**
Creswick, Paul, 1866-1947
Robin Hood (5 and up) **398.2**

Crete (Greece)
Antiquities
See/See also pages in the following book(s):
Gallant, R. A. Lost cities (4 and up) **930**
Crews, Donald
Carousel **E**
Freight train **E**
Harbor **E**
Parade **E**
School bus **E**
Ten black dots **E**
Truck **E**
We read: A to Z **E**
(il) Branley, F. M. Eclipse: darkness in daytime **523.7**
(il) Giganti, P., Jr. How many snails? **E**
(il) Kalan, R. Blue sea **E**
Cribb, Joe
Money (4 and up) **332.4**
Cricket (Periodical)
Cricket's jokes, riddles and other stuff. See Cricket's jokes, riddles and other stuff **793.73**
Cricket (Periodical) **051**
Cricket and Mountain Lion. Curry, J. L.
In Curry, J. L. Back in the beforetime p70-73 **398.2**
Cricket and the crackerbox kid. Ferguson, A. **Fic**
The **cricket** in Times Square. Selden, G. **Fic**
Crickets
Cole, J. An insect's body **595.7**
See/See also pages in the following book(s):
Johnson, S. A. Chirping insects (4 and up) **595.7**
Fiction
Caudill, R. A pocketful of cricket **E**
Maxner, J. Nicholas Cricket **E**
Selden, G. The cricket in Times Square (3-6) **Fic**
Cricket's jokes, riddles and other stuff (1-4) **793.73**
Crictor. Ungerer, T. **E**
Criminals
See also Robbers and outlaws
The **crimson** oak. Almedingen, E. M. **Fic**
Crinkleroot's book of animal tracking. Arnosky, J. **591.5**
Crinkleroot's book of animal tracks and wildlife signs. See Arnosky, J. Crinkleroot's book of animal tracking **591.5**
Crisman, Ruth
The Mississippi (4 and up) **977**

Criticism
See also Books—Reviews

Crocker, Betty
Betty Crocker's cookbook for boys and girls (3-6) **641.5**

Crockett, Davy, 1786-1836
About
Dewey, A. The narrow escapes of Davy Crockett **E**
Quackenbush, R. M. Quit pulling my leg! a story of Davy Crockett (2-4) **92**

Crocodile beat. Jorgensen, G. **E**

Crocodiles
See also Alligators
Carrick, C. The crocodiles still wait (1-3) **567.9**
Stone, L. M. Alligators and crocodiles (2-4) **597.9**
Fiction
De Paola, T. Bill and Pete **E**
De Paola, T. Bill and Pete go down the Nile **E**
Guy, R. Mother Crocodile (k-3) **398.2**
Hoban, R. Dinner at Alberta's **E**
Jorgensen, G. Crocodile beat **E**
Lionni, L. Cornelius **E**
Waber, B. The house on East 88th Street **E**

The **crocodiles** still wait. Carrick, C. **567.9**

Crofford, Emily
Healing warrior: a story about Sister Elizabeth Kenny (3-5) **92**

Croll, Carolyn, 1945-
The little snowgirl: an old Russian tale (k-2) **398.2**
(il) Berger, M. Switch on, switch off **537**
(il) Coerr, E. The big balloon race **E**

Crompton, Anne E.
Night crawler
In Things that go bump in the night p91-102 **S C**
White horses
In Herds of thunder, manes of gold p55-64 **808.8**

Cronin, John
About
Ancona, G. Riverkeeper (3-6) **333.91**

Crook, George, 1828-1890
See/See also pages in the following book(s):
Ehrlich, A. Wounded Knee: an Indian history of the American West (6 and up) **970.004**

Crosher, G. R.
The awakening water (5 and up) **Fic**

Cross, Diana Harding
Some plants have funny names (k-3) **581**

Cross, Wilbur, 1918-
Egypt (4 and up) **962**

Cross-country cat. Calhoun, M. **E**

The **cross** is pledged as security. Afanas'ev, A. N.
In Afanas'ev, A. N. Russian fairy tales p159-60 **398.2**

Cross purposes. MacDonald, G.
In MacDonald, G. The complete fairy tales of George MacDonald **S C**

Cross-surety
Afanas'ev, A. N. The cross is pledged as security
In Afanas'ev, A. N. Russian fairy tales p159-60 **398.2**

Cross your fingers. Jukes, M.
In Free to be—a family p113-21 **810.8**

Cross your fingers, spit in your hat: superstitions and other beliefs. Schwartz, A. **398**

Crosscurrents of criticism **028.5**

Crossing the bridge. Leach, M.
In Leach, M. Whistle in the graveyard p75 **398.2**

Crossley-Holland, Kevin
Beowulf (5 and up) **829**
British folk tales (4 and up) **398.2**
Short stories included are: Sea-woman; The piper and the pooka; The frog prince; Three heads of the well; A village of fools; The slumber king; Dathera dad; Tom Tit Tot; King of the cats; Her; The black bull of Norway; Samuel's ghost; The dark horseman; Mossycoat; The green children; The small-tooth dog; Jack and the beanstalk; Goldilocks and the three bears; Slam and the ghosts; The last of the Picts; Monday, Tuesday; Mare's eggs; The history of Tom Thumb; Fear and fly; The oldest of them all; The dauntless girl; Dick Whittington; The changeling; The fine field of flax; The farmer and the boggart; Fair Gruagach; Billy; Magpies in the crabtree; The shepherd's tale; The pedlar of Swaffham; Hughbo; The cow that ate the piper; Fairy ointment; Poll; The mule; Charger; Yellow Lily; The baker's daughter; The wildman; Boo; The lambton worm; The wise men of Gotham; The three blows; Butterfly soul

Crouch, Marcus
Camel gets his own back
In The Scott, Foresman anthology of children's literature p344-45 **808.8**
Lambikin
In The Scott, Foresman anthology of children's literature p343-45 **808.8**

The **Crow**
In The Yellow fairy book p92-94 **398.2**

The **crow** and Mrs. Gaddy. Gage, W. See note under Gage, W. Mrs. Gaddy and the ghost **E**

Crow and the lobster
Afanas'ev, A. N. The raven and the lobster
In Afanas'ev, A. N. Russian fairy tales p612 **398.2**

The **crow** and the snake. Walker, B. K.
In Walker, B. K. A treasury of Turkish folktales for children p17-19 **398.2**
Crow Boy. Iwamatsu, A. J. **E**
Crow Indians
See/See also pages in the following book(s):
Hofsinde, R. Indian costumes p33-39 (3-6) **391**
Crowe, Robert L.
Clyde monster **E**
Crows
Blassingame, W. Wonders of crows (5 and up) **598**
Crozat, François
(il) Andersen, H. C. The nightingale **Fic**
Cruelty to animals *See* Animal abuse
Crumbs on the table
Grimm, J. The crumbs on the table
In Grimm, J. The complete Grimm's fairy tales p768-69 **398.2**
Crump, Donald J.
Creatures small and furry (k-3) **599**
Crusades
See/See also pages in the following book(s):
Brooks, P. S. Queen Eleanor: independent spirit of the medieval world p31-50 (6 and up) **92**
Crutcher, Chris, 1946-
A brief moment in the life of Angus Bethune
In Connections: short stories by outstanding writers for young adults p54-70 **S C**
Crutches. Härtling, P. **Fic**
Cruz, Ray
(il) Hazen, B. S. The gorilla did it **E**
(il) Hurwitz, J. Baseball fever **Fic**
(il) Mohr, N. Felita **Fic**
(il) Viorst, J. Alexander and the terrible, horrible, no good, very bad day **E**
Cryptography
Janeczko, P. B. Loads of codes and secret ciphers (5 and up) **652**
Mango, K. N. Codes, ciphers, and other secrets (4 and up) **652**
Schwartz, A. The cat's elbow, and other secret languages (4 and up) **652**
Crystal ball
Grimm, J. The crystal ball
In Grimm, J. The complete Grimm's fairy tales p798-801 **398.2**
Crystal coffin
Grimm, J. The crystal coffin
In The Green fairy book p290-95 **398.2**
Grimm, J. The glass coffin
In Grimm, J. The complete Grimm's fairy tales p672-78 **398.2**
Crystal mountain
Afanas'ev, A. N. The crystal mountain
In Afanas'ev, A. N. Russian fairy tales p482-84 **398.2**
Crystallography
Stangl, J. Crystals and crystal gardens you can grow (4 and up) **548**
Crystals and crystal gardens you can grow. Stangl, J. **548**
CT (Computerized tomography) *See* Tomography, Computerized axial
Cuban Americans
See/See also pages in the following book(s):
Meltzer, M. The Hispanic Americans p44-60 (6 and up) **305.8**
The **cuckoo** clock. Stolz, M. **Fic**
The **cuckoo** sister. Alcock, V. **Fic**
Cuddigan, Maureen
Growing pains **011.6**
Cuffari, Richard, 1925-
(il) Barth, E. Balder and the mistletoe **293**
(il) Byars, B. C. The cartoonist **Fic**
(il) Byars, B. C. The TV kid **Fic**
(il) Cohen, B. Thank you, Jackie Robinson **Fic**
(il) Gates, D. Mightiest of the mortals: Heracles **292**
(il) Perl, L. Hunter's stew and hangtown fry: what pioneer America ate and why **641.5**
(il) Perl, L. Slumps, grunts, and snickerdoodles: what Colonial America ate and why **641.5**
(il) Pope, E. M. The Perilous Gard **Fic**
(il) Roche, P. K. Dollhouse magic **745.592**
(il) Sitomer, M. How did numbers begin? **513**
Cully Cully and the bear. Gage, W. **E**
Cultural anthropology *See* Ethnology
Cummings, E. E. (Edward Estlin), 1894-1962
Hist whist (k-2) **811**
Hist whist and other poems for children (3-6) **811**
Cummings, Edward Estlin *See* Cummings, E. E. (Edward Estlin), 1894-1962
Cummings, Pat, 1950-
(il) Caines, J. F. I need a lunch box **E**
(il) Caines, J. F. Just us women **E**
(il) Stolz, M. Storm in the night **E**
(il) Walter, M. P. My mama needs me **E**
(il) Walter, M. P. Two and too much **E**
Cummings, Rhoda Woods
(jt. auth) Fisher, G. L. The survival guide for kids with LD (learning differences) **371.9**

Cummings, Richard, 1931-
101 costumes for all ages, all occasions **391**
Make your own model forts & castles (5 and up) **623**

Cundiff, L. L.
(il) Shorto, R. Geronimo and the struggle for Apache freedom **92**

The **cunning** little tailor. Grimm, J.
In Grimm, J. The complete Grimm's fairy tales p525-28 **398.2**

Cupid (Roman deity) *See* Eros (Greek deity)

Cupid and Company. Callanan, C. C.
In Holiday plays round the year p189-91 **812.008**

Cupp, David
(il) Curtis, P. The animal shelter **636.08**
(il) Curtis, P. Cindy, a hearing ear dog **636.7**

Cupples, Pat
(il) Sportworks. See Sportworks **796**

Cure for story-telling
Afanas'ev, A. N. How a husband weaned his wife from fairy tales
In Afanas'ev, A. N. Russian fairy tales p308 **398.2**

Curie, Marie, 1867-1934
About
McGowen, T. Radioactivity: from the Curies to the atomic age (6 and up) **539.7**

Curie, Pierre, 1859-1906
About
McGowen, T. Radioactivity: from the Curies to the atomic age (6 and up) **539.7**

Curiosities and wonders
See also Monsters
Guinness book of records **032.02**

Curious George. Rey, H. A. **E**

Curious George flies a kite. Rey, M. See note under Rey, H. A. Curious George **E**

Curious George gets a medal. Rey, H. A. See note under Rey, H. A. Curious George **E**

Curious George goes to the hospital. Rey, H. A. See note under Rey, H. A. Curious George **E**

Curious George goes to the hospital. Rey, M. See note under Rey, H. A. Curious George **E**

Curious George learns the alphabet. Rey, H. A. See note under Rey, H. A. Curious George **E**

Curious George rides a bike. Rey, H. A. See note under Rey, H. A. Curious George **E**

Curious George takes a job. Rey, H. A. See note under Rey, H. A. Curious George **E**

Curran, Emily
(jt. auth) Willow, D. Science sensations **507**

Curriculum materials centers *See* Instructional materials centers

Curry, Jane Louise, 1932-
Back in the beforetime (4-6) **398.2**
Contents: How Old Man Above created the World; Roadrunner's pack; How Coyote stole the Sun; Mountain-making; Measuring Worm's great climb; The theft of fire; Coyote and the salmon; Coyote rides a star; Gopher's revenge; Clever Frog; The lost brother; The war between beasts and birds; Cricket and Mountain Lion; Coyote's squirrel hunt; Coyote and Badger; Mole and the Sun; The making of First Man; The waking of Men; The last council; Dog's choice

The **curse** of the blue figurine. Bellairs, J. **Fic**

Curtis, Edward S., 1868-1952
The deserted children
In Best-loved folktales of the world p697-99 **398.2**
The girl who married a ghost
In Best-loved folktales of the world p699-704 **398.2**
The girl who married a ghost, and other tales from The North American Indian (4 and up) **398.2**
Contents: The girl who married a ghost; The dance of the spirit monster; Asleep-by-the-Stream; The deserted children; Fox and the bears; The woman dressed like a man; The dirty bride; How the world was saved; The lost boys

Curtis, Patricia, 1923-
The animal shelter (5 and up) **636.08**
Cindy, a hearing ear dog (3-5) **636.7**
Greff, the story of a guide dog (5 and up) **636.7**

Cushla and her books. Butler, D. **362.4**

Cushman, Doug
Possum stew **E**

Custard and company: poems. Nash, O. **811**

The **cut-ups**. Marshall, J. **E**

The **cut-ups** at Camp Custer. Marshall, J. See note under Marshall, J. The cut-ups **E**

The **cut-ups** carry on. Marshall, J. See note under Marshall, J. The cut-ups **E**

The **cut-ups** cut loose. Marshall, J. See note under Marshall, J. The cut-ups **E**

Cutchins, Judy
Scoots, the bog turtle (1-3) **597.9**
(jt. auth) Johnston, G. Scaly babies **597.9**
(jt. auth) Johnston, G. Windows on wildlife **590.74**

Cuts, breaks, bruises, and burns. Cole, J. **612**

Cuyler, Margery
The all-around pumpkin book (4-6) **641.3**
Baby Dot: a dinosaur story **E**
Cwiklik, Robert
King Philip and the war with the colonists (5 and up) **92**
Sequoyah and the Cherokee alphabet (5 and up) **92**
The **Cybil** war. Byars, B. C. **Fic**
Cycling *See* Bicycles and bicycling
Czar Trojan's ears. Kaufman, W. I.
In Best-loved folktales of the world p455-57 **398.2**
Czechoslovakia
Fiction
Procházková, I. The season of secret wishes (4-6) **Fic**

D

D Day *See* Normandy (France), Attack on, 1944
D.N.A. *See* DNA
D.W. all wet. Brown, M. T. **E**
The **Da** Trang crab. Terada, A. M.
In Terada, A. M. Under the starfruit tree p37-41 **398.2**
Da Vinci, Leonardo *See* Leonardo, da Vinci, 1452-1519
Daddy. Caines, J. F. **E**
Daddy makes the best spaghetti. Hines, A. G. **E**
Daddy, play with me! Watanabe, S. See note under Watanabe, S. How do I put it on? **E**
Daegling, Mary
Monster seaweeds (4 and up) **589.4**
Daggie Dogfoot. See King-Smith, D. Pigs might fly **Fic**
Dagmar Schultz and the angel Edna. Hall, L. **Fic**
Dagmar Schultz and the powers of darkness. Hall, L. See note under Hall, L. Dagmar Schultz and the angel Edna **Fic**
Dahl, Roald
James and the giant peach (4-6) **Fic**
James and the giant peach; dramatization. See George, R. R. Roald Dahl's James and the giant peach **822**
Matilda (4-6) **Fic**
The witches [excerpt]
In The Random House book of humor for children p120-29 **817.008**
(jt. auth) George, R. R. Roald Dahl's James and the giant peach **822**
Dairy cattle
Gibbons, G. The milk makers (k-2) **637**
Fiction
Wildsmith, B. Daisy **E**
Dairying
See also Dairy cattle
Bellville, C. W. Farming today yesterday's way (2-4) **630.1**
Carrick, D. Milk (k-1) **637**
Gibbons, G. The milk makers (k-2) **637**
Giblin, J. Milk: the fight for purity (5 and up) **637**
McFarland, C. Cows in the parlor (1-3) **636.2**
Daisy. Wildsmith, B. **E**
Daisy Rothschild. Leslie-Melville, B. **599.73**
Dakota Indians
See also Oglala Indians
Osinski, A. The Sioux (2-4) **970.004**
See/See also pages in the following book(s):
Ehrlich, A. Wounded Knee: an Indian history of the American West (6 and up) **970.004**
Freedman, R. Indian chiefs p115-39 (6 and up) **920**
Hofsinde, R. Indian costumes p86-91 (3-6) **391**
Legends
Goble, P. Iktomi and the berries (k-3) **398.2**
Goble, P. Iktomi and the boulder (k-3) **398.2**
Goble, P. Iktomi and the ducks (k-3) **398.2**
Dalfunka, where the rich live forever. Singer, I. B.
In Singer, I. B. Naftali the storyteller and his horse, Sus, and other stories p29-35 **S C**
In Singer, I. B. Stories for children p254-59 **S C**
Dalgliesh, Alice, 1893-1979
The bears on Hemlock Mountain (1-4) **Fic**
The courage of Sarah Noble (2-4) **Fic**
The Fourth of July story (2-4) **973.3**
The Thanksgiving story (k-2) **974.4**
Dalkey, Kara, 1953-
The ghost of Wan Li Road
In Things that go bump in the night p82-90 **S C**
The **Dallas** Titans get ready for bed. Kuskin, K. **E**
Daly, Niki, 1946-
Not so fast, Songololo **E**
Dame Dearlove's ditties for the nursery
In A Nursery companion p62-65 **820.8**

Dame Gudbrand
Asbjørnsen, P. C. Gudbrand on the hill-side
In Best-loved folktales of the world p300-04 **398.2**
Dame Wiggins of Lee—and her seven wonderful cats. Sharpe, R. S.
In A Nursery companion p58-61 **820.8**
Dan alone. Townsend, J. R. **Fic**
Dance away! Shannon, G. **E**
The **dance** of the spirit monster. Curtis, E. S.
In Curtis, E. S. The girl who married a ghost, and other tales from the North American Indian p21-30 **398.2**
Dance, Tanya. Gauch, P. L. **E**
Dance Theatre of Harlem
Tobias, T. Arthur Mitchell (2-5) **92**
Dancers
See also Ballet dancers; Black dancers
Gherman, B. Agnes de Mille: dancing off the earth (5 and up) **92**
Dancing
See also Ballet; Folk dancing
Ancona, G. Dancing is (3-5) **793.3**
See/See also pages in the following book(s):
Caney, S. Steven Caney's kids' America p324-31 (4 and up) **790.1**
McLeish, K. The Oxford first companion to music (5 and up) **780**
Fiction
Martin, B. Barn dance! **E**
McKissack, P. C. Mirandy and Brother Wind **E**
Paxton, T. Engelbert the elephant **E**
Schroeder, A. Ragtime Tumpie **E**
Shannon, G. Dance away! **E**
Skofield, J. Nightdances **E**
The **dancing** braves. Mayo, G.
In Mayo, G. Star tales p71-72 **398.2**
The **dancing** feather. Marriott, A. L.
In Marriott, A. L. American Indian mythology **398.2**
The **dancing** granny. Bryan, A. **398.2**
Dancing in the moon. Eichenberg, F. **E**
Dancing is. Ancona, G. **793.3**
The **dancing** skeleton. DeFelice, C. C. **398.2**
Dancing teepees: poems of American Indian youth (3-5) **897**
Dandelion. Freeman, D. **E**
The **dandies'** rout. Sheridan, C.
In A Nursery companion p113-17 **820.8**
The **Danes** in America. Petersen, P. L.
In The In America series **305.8**
Danger—icebergs!. Gans, R. **551.3**
Danger in Tibet. Quackenbush, R. M. See note under Quackenbush, R. M. Express train to trouble **Fic**
Daniel, Alan, 1939-
(il) Howe, D. Bunnicula **Fic**
Daniel, Mark, 1954-
(ed) A Child's treasury of poems. See A Child's treasury of poems **821.008**
Daniel's dog. Bogart, J. E. **E**
Daniel's duck. Bulla, C. R. **E**
Danilo the Luckless. Afanas'ev, A. N.
In Afanas'ev, A. N. Russian fairy tales p255-61 **398.2**
Danilo the unfortunate
Afanas'ev, A. N. Danilo the Luckless
In Afanas'ev, A. N. Russian fairy tales p255-61 **398.2**
Danish Americans
Petersen, P. L. The Danes in America
In The In America series **305.8**
Danny and the dinosaur. Hoff, S. **E**
Danziger, Paula, 1944-
The cat ate my gymsuit (5 and up) **Fic**
Everyone else's parents said yes (4-6) **Fic**
Make like a tree and leave (4-6) **Fic**
There's a bat in bunk five (5 and up) **Fic**
Daphne's book. Hahn, M. D. **Fic**
Dapplegrim
Coville, B. Dapplegrim
In Herds of thunder, manes of gold p149-56 **808.8**
Hodges, M. Dapplegrim
In Hodges, M. If you had a horse **398.2**
Moe, J. E. Dapplegrim
In The Red fairy book p246-56 **398.2**
Darby, Jean
Martin Luther King, Jr (5 and up) **92**
Daring the unknown: a history of NASA. Smith, H. E. **629.4**
Dark Ages *See* Middle Ages
Dark and full of secrets. Carrick, C. See note under Carrick, C. Ben and the porcupine **E**
A **dark,** dark tale. Brown, R. **E**
The **dark** horseman. Crossley-Holland, K.
In Crossley-Holland, K. British folk tales p77-85 **398.2**
The **dark** is rising. Cooper, S. See note under Cooper, S. Over sea, under stone **Fic**
The **dark** princess. Kennedy, R.
In Kennedy, R. Collected stories p141-54 **S C**

The **dark** secret of Weatherend. Bellairs, J. See note under Bellairs, J. The treasure of Alpheus Winterborn **Fic**

Darke, Alison Claire
(il) Andersen, H. C. The nightingale **Fic**

Darkness and the butterfly. Grifalconi, A. **E**

Darling, Kathy
(jt. auth) Cobb, V. Bet you can! science possibilities to fool you **793.8**
(jt. auth) Cobb, V. Bet you can't! science impossibilities to fool you **793.8**

Darling, Louis
(il) Butterworth, O. The enormous egg **Fic**
(il) Cleary, B. Ellen Tebbits **Fic**
(il) Cleary, B. Henry Huggins **Fic**
(il) Cleary, B. The mouse and the motorcycle **Fic**
(il) Cleary, B. Otis Spofford **Fic**
(il) Cleary, B. Ramona the pest **Fic**

Darling Roland. Grimm, J.
In Best-loved folktales of the world p84-87 **398.2**

Darning needle
Andersen, H. C. The darning needle
In Andersen, H. C. Hans Andersen: his classic fairy tales p94-97 **S C**
Andersen, H. C. A story about a darning needle
In The Yellow fairy book p319-21 **398.2**

Darrow, Clarence, 1857-1938
See/See also pages in the following book(s):
Jacobs, W. J. Great lives: human rights p207-16 (5 and up) **920**

Darrow, Whitney, 1909-
(il) The Fireside book of fun and game songs. See The Fireside book of fun and game songs **782.42**

Dart, Raymond A. (Raymond Arthur), 1893-1988
See/See also pages in the following book(s):
Lasky, K. Traces of life p64-72 (5 and up) **573.2**

Darwin, Beatrice
(il) Cleary, B. Socks **Fic**

Darwin, Charles, 1809-1882
About
Hyndley, K. The voyage of the Beagle (4 and up) **92**
See/See also pages in the following book(s):
Gallant, R. A. Before the sun dies p52-57 (6 and up) **575**
Horn Book reflections on children's books and reading p276-81 **028.5**
Lasky, K. Traces of life p32-42 (5 and up) **573.2**

Darwinism *See* Evolution

The **dastardly** murder of Dirty Pete. Clifford, E. **Fic**

Data processing *See* Electronic data processing

Datelines of world history. Arnold, G. **909**

Dathera dad. Crossley-Holland, K.
In Crossley-Holland, K. British folk tales p45-46 **398.2**

Daugherty, James Henry, 1887-1974
Andy and the lion **E**
(il) Sandburg, C. Abe Lincoln grows up **92**
See/See also pages in the following book(s):
Newbery Medal books, 1922-1955 p178-91 **028.5**

Daughter and stepdaughter
Afanas'ev, A. N. Daughter and stepdaughter
In Afanas'ev, A. N. Russian fairy tales p278-79 **398.2**

The **daughter** and the helper. Timpanelli, G.
In Timpanelli, G. Tales from the roof of the world p15-27 **398.2**

Daughter of Earth. McDermott, G. **292**

Daughter of the dragon king
Carpenter, F. Daughter of the dragon king
In Carpenter, F. Tales of a Chinese grandmother p72-80 **398.2**

Daughters and fathers *See* Fathers and daughters

Daughters and mothers *See* Mothers and daughters

D'Aulaire, Edgar Parin, 1898-1986
(jt. auth) D'Aulaire, I. Abraham Lincoln **92**
(jt. auth) D'Aulaire, I. Benjamin Franklin **92**
(jt. auth) D'Aulaire, I. Columbus **92**
(jt. auth) D'Aulaire, I. George Washington **92**
(jt. auth) D'Aulaire, I. Pocahontas **92**
See/See also pages in the following book(s):
Caldecott Medal books, 1938-1957 p49-62 **028.5**

D'Aulaire, Ingri, 1904-1980
Abraham Lincoln (2-4) **92**
Benjamin Franklin (2-4) **92**
Columbus (1-4) **92**
George Washington (2-4) **92**
Persephone
In Bauer, C. F. Celebrations p199-202 **808.8**
Pocahontas (2-4) **92**
See/See also pages in the following book(s):
Caldecott Medal books, 1938-1957 p45-49, 55-62 **028.5**

D'Aulnoy, Madame *See* Aulnoy, Madame d', 1650 or 51-1705
The **dauntless** girl. Crossley-Holland, K.
In Crossley-Holland, K. British folk tales p182-89 **398.2**
David, King of Israel
About
De Paola, T. David and Goliath (k-3) **222**
David, Thomas
(il) Isenbart, H.-H. Birth of a foal **636.1**
David and Goliath. De Paola, T. **222**
Davie, Helen
(il) Esbensen, B. J. Ladder to the sky **398.2**
(il) Esbensen, B. J. The star maiden: an Ojibway tale **398.2**
Davis, Burke, 1913-
Black heroes of the American Revolution (5 and up) **973.3**
Davis, Daniel S.
Behind barbed wire: the imprisonment of Japanese Americans during World War II (5 and up) **940.54**
Davis, Don
The moon (4-6) **523.3**
Davis, Lambert
(il) Hamilton, V. The bells of Christmas **Fic**
Davis, Nelle
(il) Silverstein, A. The mystery of sleep **154.6**
Davis, Robert, 1881-1949
The jokes of Single-Toe
In The Scott, Foresman anthology of children's literature p254-56 **808.8**
Davy Crockett meets his match
In The Diane Goode book of American folk tales and songs p9-11 **398.2**
Dawn. Shulevitz, U. **E**
Dawn, Evening, and Midnight. Afanas'ev, A. N.
In Afanas'ev, A. N. Russian fairy tales p457-63 **398.2**
Dawn of fear. Cooper, S. **Fic**
Dawn, twilight and midnight
Afanas'ev, A. N. Dawn, Evening, and Midnight
In Afanas'ev, A. N. Russian fairy tales p457-63 **398.2**
Day, Alexandra
Carl goes shopping **E**
Frank and Ernest **E**
Frank and Ernest play ball **E**
Day, Dorothy, 1897-1980
See/See also pages in the following book(s):
Jacobs, W. J. Great lives: human rights p217-28 (5 and up) **920**
Day, Edward C.
John Tabor's ride **E**
Day
See also Night
Branley, F. M. What makes day and night (k-3) **525**
The **day** before Christmas. Westman, B. **E**
The **day** boy and the night girl. MacDonald, G.
In MacDonald, G. The complete fairy tales of George MacDonald **S C**
A **day** by the sea. Bond, M.
In Bond, M. Paddington's storybook p66-82 **S C**
The **day** Dad made toast. Durkee, S.
In Free to be—a family p83-89 **810.8**
The **day** I got lost. Singer, I. B.
In Singer, I. B. Stories for children p115-21 **S C**
The **day** I had to play with my sister. Bonsall, C. N. **E**
The **day** Jimmy's boa ate the wash. Noble, T. H. **E**
A **day** no pigs would die. Peck, R. N. **Fic**
The **day** of Ahmed's secret. Heide, F. P. **E**
Day of Atonement *See* Yom Kippur
The **day** that Henry cleaned his room. Wilson, S. **E**
The **day** the goose got loose. Lindbergh, R. **E**
The **day** the teacher went bananas. Howe, J. **E**
The **day** we walked on the moon. Sullivan, G. **629.45**
The **day** we went to see snow. Villanueva Collado, A.
In Where angels glide at dawn p27-33 **S C**
A **day** with Wilbur Robinson. Joyce, W. **E**
The **daydreamer**. Afanas'ev, A. N.
In Afanas'ev, A. N. Russian fairy tales p161 **398.2**
Daydreamers. Greenfield, E. **811**
Days with Frog and Toad. Lobel, A. See note under Lobel, A. Frog and Toad are friends **E**
De Angeli, Marguerite Lofft, 1889-1987
The door in the wall (4-6) **Fic**

De Angeli, Marguerite Lofft, 1889-1987— *Continued*
(il) Marguerite de Angeli's book of nursery and Mother Goose rhymes. See Marguerite de Angeli's book of nursery and Mother Goose rhymes **398.8**
See/See also pages in the following book(s):
Newbery Medal books, 1922-1955 p337-52 **028.5**

De Brunhoff, Jean *See* Brunhoff, Jean de, 1899-1937

De Brunhoff, Laurent *See* Brunhoff, Laurent de, 1925-

De Groat, Diane
(il) Hurwitz, J. DeDe takes charge **Fic**
(il) Hurwitz, J. Hurricane Elaine **Fic**
(il) McDonnell, C. Don't be mad, Ivy **Fic**
(il) McDonnell, C. Lucky charms & birthday wishes **Fic**
(il) McDonnell, C. Toad food & measle soup **Fic**
(il) Shreve, S. R. The flunking of Joshua T. Bates **Fic**
(il) Simon, S. Animal fact/animal fable **591**

De La Fontaine, Jean *See* La Fontaine, Jean de, 1621-1695

De la Mare, Walter, 1873-1956
Clever Grethel
In Womenfolk and fairy tales p71-76 **398.2**
Molly Whuppie (k-3) **398.2**
also in The Scott, Foresman anthology of children's literature p159-62 **808.8**
also in Womenfolk and fairy tales p20-29 **398.2**
Peacock pie (4 and up) **821**
Rhymes and verses (4 and up) **821**
See/See also pages in the following book(s):
Horn Book reflections on children's books and reading p265-70 **028.5**

De Larrea, Victoria
(il) De Regniers, B. S. Waiting for Mama **E**
(il) Juba this and Juba that. See Juba this and Juba that **372.6**
(il) Perl, L. Candles, cakes, and donkey tails **392**
(il) Perl, L. Piñatas and paper flowers **394.2**

De Leeuw, Adèle, 1899-1988
A legend of Saint Nicholas
In Best-loved folktales of the world p174-76 **398.2**
Why there are no tigers in Borneo
In Best-loved folktales of the world p602-05 **398.2**

De Lint, Charles, 1951-
Wooden bones
In Things that go bump in the night p64-81 **S C**

De Mejo, Oscar, 1911-
(il) Gellman, M. Does God have a big toe? **221.9**

De Mille, Agnes
About
Gherman, B. Agnes de Mille: dancing off the earth (5 and up) **92**

De Montreville, Doris
(ed) Fourth book of junior authors and illustrators. See Fourth book of junior authors and illustrators **920.003**
(ed) Third book of junior authors. See Third book of junior authors **920.003**

De Osma, Lupe *See* Osma, Lupe de

De Paola, Thomas Anthony *See* De Paola, Tomie, 1934-

De Paola, Tomie, 1934-
The art lesson **E**
Bill and Pete **E**
Bill and Pete go down the Nile **E**
The cloud book (k-3) **551.57**
The clown of God (k-3) **398.2**
David and Goliath (k-3) **222**
An early American Christmas **E**
The family Christmas tree book (k-3) **394.2**
Francis, the poor man of Assisi (3-5) **92**
Helga's dowry **E**
The kids' cat book (2-4) **636.8**
The knight and the dragon **E**
The legend of Old Befana (k-3) **398.2**
The legend of the Indian paintbrush (k-3) **398.2**
The miracles of Jesus (1-3) **232.9**
The mysterious giant of Barletta **E**
Nana Upstairs & Nana Downstairs **E**
Noah and the ark (k-2) **222**
Now one foot, now the other **E**
The popcorn book (k-3) **641.3**
The quicksand book (k-3) **552**
Sing, Pierrot, sing **E**
Tomie dePaola's book of Christmas carols. See Tomie dePaola's book of Christmas carols **782.28**
Tomie dePaola's book of poems. See Tomie dePaola's book of poems **808.81**
Tomie dePaola's Favorite nursery tales. See Tomie dePaola's Favorite nursery tales **398.2**
Tony's bread: an Italian folktale (k-2) **398.2**
(il) Adler, D. A. The carsick zebra and other animal riddles **793.73**
(il) Bennett, J. Teeny tiny **398.2**

De Paola, Tomie, 1934-—*Continued*
(il) The Comic adventures of Old Mother Hubbard and her dog. See The Comic adventures of Old Mother Hubbard and her dog **398.8**
(il) The Friendly beasts. See The Friendly beasts **782.28**
(il) Fritz, J. Can't you make them behave, King George? [biography of George III, King of Great Britain] **92**
(il) Fritz, J. The good giants and the bad pukwudgies **398.2**
(il) Fritz, J. Shhh! we're writing the Constitution **342**
(il) Ghost poems. See Ghost poems **821.008**
(il) Hale, S. J. Mary had a little lamb **811**
(il) Johnston, T. The badger and the magic fan **398.2**
(il) Johnston, T. The quilt story **E**
(il) Johnston, T. The vanishing pumpkin **E**
(il) Kroll, S. Santa's crash-bang Christmas **E**
(il) Moore, C. C. The night before Christmas **811**
(il) Murphy, S. R. Tattie's river journey **E**
(il) Oh, such foolishness! See Oh, such foolishness! **821.008**
(il) Tomie dePaola's Mother Goose. See Tomie dePaola's Mother Goose **398.8**
(il) Willard, N. Simple pictures are best **E**

De Regniers, Beatrice Schenk
Everyone is good for something (k-3) **398.2**
It does not say meow, and other animal riddle rhymes (k-1) **793.73**
Jack the giant killer (k-3) **398.2**
A little house of your own **E**
Little Sister and the Month Brothers (k-3) **398.2**
May I bring a friend? **E**
So many cats! **E**
Waiting for Mama **E**
The way I feel—sometimes (1-3) **811**
(comp) Sing a song of popcorn. See Sing a song of popcorn **808.81**

De Rosas, Juan Manuel José Domingo Ortiz *See* Rosas, Juan Manuel José Domingo Ortiz de, 1793-1877

De Saint-Exupéry, Antoine *See* Saint-Exupéry, Antoine de, 1900-1944

De Sauza, James
Rohmer, H. Brother Anansi and the cattle ranch **398.2**

De Soto, Hernando *See* Soto, Hernando de, ca. 1500-1542

De Treviño, Elizabeth Borton *See* Treviño, Elizabeth Borton de, 1904-

De Villeneuve, Madame *See* Villeneuve, Madame de

The **deacon's** ghost. San Souci, R.
In San Souci, R. Short & shivery p88-91 **398.2**

The **dead** bird. Brown, M. W.
In Brown, M. W. The fish with the deep sea smile p62-63 **818**

Dead body
Afanas'ev, A. N. The dead body
In Afanas'ev, A. N. Russian fairy tales p118-19 **398.2**

Dead man. Leach, M.
In Leach, M. Whistle in the graveyard p111-12 **398.2**

The **dead** man in Indian Creek. Hahn, M. D. **Fic**

A **dead** man who talks. Simon, S.
In Simon, S. More wise men of Helm and their merry tales p24-30 **398.2**

The **Dead** wife
In The Yellow fairy book p149-51 **398.2**

Deadline!. Gibbons, G. **070**

The **deadly** hoax. Corbett, S. **Fic**

Deaf
Bergman, T. Finding a common language (1-3) **362.4**
Hunter, E. F. Child of the silent night [biography of Laura Dewey Bridgman] (3-5) **92**
Levine, E. S. Lisa and her soundless world (1-3) **617.8**
Peare, C. O. The Helen Keller story (5 and up) **92**
Peterson, J. W. I have a sister—my sister is deaf (k-3) **362.4**
Wolf, B. Anna's silent world (2-4) **362.4**

Education

Neimark, A. E. A deaf child listened: Thomas Gallaudet, pioneer in American education (6 and up) **92**

Fiction

Riskind, M. Apple is my sign (5 and up) **Fic**

Means of communication

See also Sign language

Deaf, Dogs for *See* Hearing ear dogs

A **deaf** child listened: Thomas Gallaudet, pioneer in American education. Neimark, A. E. **92**

Deafness
Levine, E. S. Lisa and her soundless world (1-3) **617.8**

Deafness—*Continued*
Litchfield, A. B. A button in her ear (1-3) **617.8**
Dealing with dragons. Wrede, P. C. **Fic**
Dean, Pamela
Juniper, Gentian, and Rosemary
In Things that go bump in the night p255-76 **S C**
Dear Lola. Angell, J. **Fic**
Dear Lovey Hart: I am desperate. Conford, E. **Fic**
Dear Marsha. Angell, J.
In Connections: short stories by outstanding writers for young adults p2-13 **S C**
Dear Mr. Henshaw. Cleary, B. **Fic**
Dear Shrink. Cresswell, H. **Fic**
Death
See also Bereavement
Bernstein, J. E. Loss and how to cope with it (5 and up) **155.9**
Hyde, M. O. Meeting death (5 and up) **155.9**
The Kids' book about death and dying (5 and up) **155.9**
Krementz, J. How it feels when a parent dies (4 and up) **155.9**
LeShan, E. J. Learning to say good-by (4 and up) **155.9**
Rogers, F. When a pet dies (k-1) **155.9**
Stein, S. B. About dying (k-3) **155.9**
See/See also pages in the following book(s):
LeShan, E. J. When a parent is very sick p105-20 (4 and up) **155.9**
Fiction
Alexander, S. Nadia the Willful **E**
Aliki. The two of them **E**
Bond, N. A place to come back to (6 and up) **Fic**
Cameron, E. Beyond silence (6 and up) **Fic**
Carlstrom, N. W. Blow me a kiss, Miss Lilly **E**
Caseley, J. When Grandpa came to stay **E**
Cleaver, V. Grover (4-6) **Fic**
Clifford, E. The remembering box (3-5) **Fic**
Cohn, J. I had a friend named Peter **E**
Coutant, H. First snow (2-4) **Fic**
De Paola, T. Nana Upstairs & Nana Downstairs **E**
Dragonwagon, C. Winter holding spring (2-4) **Fic**
Foley, P. John and the fiddler (3-5) **Fic**
Greene, C. C. Beat the turtle drum (5 and up) **Fic**
Hamilton, V. Cousins (5 and up) **Fic**
Härtling, P. Old John (4 and up) **Fic**
Hermes, P. You shouldn't have to say good-bye (5 and up) **Fic**
Hunter, M. A sound of chariots (5 and up) **Fic**
Jordan, M. Losing Uncle Tim (2-4) **Fic**
Jukes, M. Blackberries in the dark (2-4) **Fic**
L'Engle, M. A ring of endless light (5 and up) **Fic**
Little, J. Mama's going to buy you a mockingbird (5 and up) **Fic**
Lowry, L. A summer to die (3-6) **Fic**
Miles, M. Annie and the Old One (1-4) **Fic**
Paterson, K. Bridge to Terabithia (4 and up) **Fic**
Slepian, J. The Broccoli tapes (5 and up) **Fic**
Smith, D. B. A taste of blackberries (4-6) **Fic**
Thomas, J. R. Saying good-bye to Grandma **E**
Varley, S. Badger's parting gifts **E**
Viorst, J. The tenth good thing about Barney **E**
Wild, M. The very best of friends **E**
Zolotow, C. My grandson Lew **E**
Poetry
Clifton, L. Everett Anderson's goodbye (k-3) **811**
Death masks *See* Masks (Sculpture)
Death of a miser. Afanas'ev, A. N.
In Afanas'ev, A. N. Russian fairy tales p268 **398.2**
The **death** of Brer Fox. Lester, J.
In Lester, J. The tales of Uncle Remus p57-60 **398.2**
The **death** of Brer Wolf. Lester, J.
In Lester, J. The tales of Uncle Remus p40-42 **398.2**
The **death** of Koschei the Deathless. Ralston, W.
In The Red fairy book p42-53 **398.2**
The **Death** of Low Horn
In The Whistling skeleton p45-61 **398.2**
The **death** of the cock. Afanas'ev, A. N.
In Afanas'ev, A. N. Russian fairy tales p17-19 **398.2**
Death of the iron horse. Goble, P. **E**
The **death** of the little hen. Grimm, J.
In Grimm, J. The complete Grimm's fairy tales p365-67 **398.2**
Death of the Sun-Hero
The Death of the Sun-Hero
In The Yellow fairy book p213-15 **398.2**

The **death** waltz. San Souci, R.
In San Souci, R. Short & shivery p133-38 **398.2**
Death's messengers. Grimm, J.
In Grimm, J. The complete Grimm's fairy tales p718-20 **398.2**
December decorations. Parish, P. **745.59**
The **December** Rose. Garfield, L. **Fic**
December stillness. Hahn, M. D. **Fic**
Decision making
See also Problem solving
Declaration of Independence *See* United States. Declaration of Independence
DeClements, Barthe, 1920-
6th grade can really kill you (5 and up) **Fic**
Decoration and ornament
Haldane, S. Painting faces (4-6) **745.5**
Decorative arts
See also Decoration and ornament; Folk art
Tunis, E. Colonial craftsmen and the beginnings of American industry (5 and up) **670**
DeDe takes charge. Hurwitz, J. **Fic**
The **dedication** of the cemetery. Simon, S.
In Simon, S. More wise men of Helm and their merry tales p50-53 **398.2**
Deegan, Paul Joseph, 1937-
Michael Jordan: basketball's soaring star (4 and up) **92**
Deep diving vehicles *See* Submersibles
Deep down underground. Dunrea, O. **E**
Deep in the forest. Turkle, B. C. **E**
Deer
See also Elk; Reindeer
Arnosky, J. Deer at the brook **E**
Fiction
Carrick, D. Harald and the great stag **E**
Rawlings, M. K. The yearling (6 and up) **Fic**
Salten, F. Bambi (4-6) **Fic**
The **deer** and the jaguar share a house. Courlander, H.
In Best-loved folktales of the world p774-76 **398.2**
Deer at the brook. Arnosky, J. **E**
Deer boy
In The Whistling skeleton p27-37 **398.2**
Deer hunting. Sanfield, S.
In Sanfield, S. The adventures of High John the Conqueror **398.2**
Deer of the five colors
Uchida, Y. Deer of five colors
In Uchida, Y. The magic listening cap **398.2**
The **Deer** Woman. Marriott, A. L.
In Marriott, A. L. American Indian mythology **398.2**
Deere, John, 1804-1886
See/See also pages in the following book(s):
Aaseng, N. The problem solvers p13-18 (5 and up) **920**
DeFelice, Cynthia C.
The dancing skeleton (k-3) **398.2**
Weasel (4 and up) **Fic**
Defoe, Daniel, 1661?-1731
Robinson Crusoe (5 and up) **Fic**
Degas, Edgar, 1834-1917
Meet Edgar Degas (3-5) **759.4**
Degas, Hilaire Germain Edgar *See* Degas, Edgar, 1834-1917
Degen, Bruce, 1945-
Jamberry **E**
(il) Carlstrom, N. W. Jesse Bear, what will you wear? **E**
(il) Coerr, E. The Josefina story quilt **E**
(il) Cole, J. The magic school bus at the waterworks **551.48**
(il) Cole, J. The magic school bus inside the Earth **551.1**
(il) Cole, J. The magic school bus inside the human body **612**
(il) Cole, J. The magic school bus, lost in the solar system **523**
(il) Stanley, D. The good-luck pencil **E**
(il) Yolen, J. Commander Toad in space **E**
(il) Yolen, J. Dinosaur dances **811**
Dégh, Linda
A stroke of luck
In Best-loved folktales of the world p457-59 **398.2**
Deities *See* Gods and goddesses
DeJong, Meindert, 1906-
The house of sixty fathers (4-6) **Fic**
The wheel on the school (4-6) **Fic**
See/See also pages in the following book(s):
Newbery Medal books, 1922-1955 p427-39 **028.5**
Townsend, J. R. A sense of story p68-74 **028.5**
Del Monte, Jacques
Hughes, R. P. Fell's United States coin book **737.4**
Delaware
Kent, D. Delaware
In America the beautiful **973**
DeLeeuw, Adèle *See* De Leeuw, Adèle, 1899-1988

Delphine. Bang, M. E

Delton, Judy
Angel in charge. See note under Delton, J. Angel's mother's wedding Fic
Angel's mother's baby. See note under Delton, J. Angel's mother's wedding Fic
Angel's mother's boyfriend. See note under Delton, J. Angel's mother's wedding Fic
Angel's mother's wedding (3-5) Fic
Back yard Angel. See note under Delton, J. Angel's mother's wedding Fic
I'm telling you now E
Kitty from the start (2-4) Fic
Kitty in high school. See note under Delton, J. Kitty from the start Fic
Kitty in the middle. See note under Delton, J. Kitty from the start Fic
Kitty in the summer. See note under Delton, J. Kitty from the start Fic
The new girl at school E

Dementia praecox *See* Schizophrenia

Demeter (Greek deity)
Gates, D. Two queens of heaven: Aphrodite [and] Demeter (4 and up) 292
McDermott, G. Daughter of Earth (2-4) 292

Demi, 1942-
A Chinese zoo: fables and proverbs (3-5) 398.2
Demi's Count the animals 1 2 3 E
Demi's Find-the-animal A.B.C. E
Dragon kites and dragonflies (k-2) 398.8
The empty pot (k-3) 398.2
The magic boat (k-3) 398.2
(il) Andersen, H. C. The nightingale Fic
(il) Chaikin, M. Light another candle 296.4
(il) Chaikin, M. Make noise, make merry 296.4

Demi's Count the animals 1 2 3. Demi. E

Demi's Find-the-animal A.B.C. Demi. E

Demon's mother-in-law
Boggs, R. S. Don Demonio's mother-in-law
In Best-loved folktales of the world p160-65 398.2

Demonstrations (Protest) *See* Protests, demonstrations, etc.

Demuth, Jack
(il) Demuth, P. Joel, growing up a farm man 630.1

Demuth, Patricia, 1948-
Joel, growing up a farm man (5 and up) 630.1

Denmark
Fiction
Lowry, L. Number the stars (4 and up) Fic
Matas, C. Lisa's war (5 and up) Fic
Reuter, B. Buster's world (4 and up) Fic

Dennis, Wesley
Flip and the cows E
(il) Henry, M. Album of horses 636.1
(jt. auth) Henry, M. Benjamin West and his cat Grimalkin 92
(il) Henry, M. Black Gold Fic
(il) Henry, M. Brighty of the Grand Canyon Fic
(il) Henry, M. Justin Morgan had a horse Fic
(il) Henry, M. King of the wind Fic
(il) Henry, M. Misty of Chincoteague Fic

Denslow, Sharon Phillips
Night owls E

Denslow, William Wallace, 1856-1915
(il) Baum, L. F. The Wizard of Oz Fic

Dental care. Ward, B. R. 617.6

Dentistry
See also Orthodontics
DeSantis, K. A dentist's tools (k-2) 617.6
Kuklin, S. When I see my dentist (k-2) 617.6
Rockwell, H. My dentist (k-1) 617.6
Rogers, F. Going to the dentist (k-2) 617.6

Dentists
Fiction
Steig, W. Doctor De Soto E

A **dentist's** tools. DeSantis, K. 617.6

Denton, Terry
(il) Fox, M. Night noises E

Deoxyribonucleic acid *See* DNA

DePaola, Tomie *See* De Paola, Tomie, 1934-

Department stores
Gibbons, G. Department store (k-3) 381
Fiction
Day, A. Carl goes shopping E

The **departure** of the giants. Courlander, H.
In The Crest and the hide, and other African stories of heroes, chiefs, bards, hunters, sorcerers, and common people p95-99 398.2

Depend on Katie John. Calhoun, M. See note under Calhoun, M. Katie John Fic

Depressions, Economic
Fiction
Burch, R. Ida Early comes over the mountain (4 and up) Fic

Depressions, Economic—Fiction—*Continued*
Lyon, G. E. Borrowed children (5 and up) **Fic**
Snyder, Z. K. The velvet room (5 and up) **Fic**
Taylor, M. D. Roll of thunder, hear my cry (4 and up) **Fic**
Taylor, M. D. Song of the trees (4 and up) **Fic**

Deraney, Michael J.
(il) Cohen, B. Molly's Pilgrim **Fic**
(il) Cohen, B. Yussel's prayer **398.2**

Derricks *See* Cranes, derricks, etc.

DeSantis, Kenny
A dentist's tools (k-2) **617.6**
A doctor's tools (k-2) **610.69**

Description *See* names of cities with the subdivision Description

Desert. Bender, L. **574.5**

Desert animals
See also Camels
Poetry
Baylor, B. Desert voices (1-4) **811**

Desert ecology
Baylor, B. The desert is theirs (1-4) **574.5**
Bender, L. Desert (3-5) **574.5**
Catchpole, C. Deserts (2-4) **574.5**
George, J. C. One day in the desert (4-6) **574.5**
Simon, S. Deserts (3-5) **574.5**
Weiwandt, T. The hidden life of the desert (3-5) **574.5**

Desert giant. Bash, B. **583**

The **desert** is theirs. Baylor, B. **574.5**

Desert plants
See also Cactus

Desert voices. Baylor, B. **811**

The **deserted** children. Curtis, E. S.
In Best-loved folktales of the world p697-99 **398.2**
In Curtis, E. S. The girl who married a ghost, and other tales from the North American Indian p45-51 **398.2**

Deserted mine
Sawyer, R. The deserted mine
In Sawyer, R. The way of the storyteller p285-94 **372.6**

Deserts
Fiction
Baylor, B. I'm in charge of celebrations (3-6) **Fic**
Nunes, S. Coyote dreams **E**
Poetry
Caudill, R. Wind, sand and sky (1-4) **811**
Siebert, D. Mojave (1-3) **811**

Deserts. Catchpole, C. **574.5**

Deserts. Simon, S. **574.5**

Design, Decorative *See* Decoration and ornament

Desimini, Lisa, 1965-
(il) Turner, A. W. Heron Street **E**

Desoxyribonucleic acid *See* DNA

Desserts
See/See also pages in the following book(s):
Penner, L. R. The colonial cookbook p97-110 (5 and up) **641.5**

Destination: Antarctica. Swan, R. **998**

Detectives
Wormser, R. Pinkerton: America's first private eye (5 and up) **92**

Deuchar, Ian
The prince and the mermaid (2-5) **398.2**

Deulin, Charles
The enchanted canary
In The Red fairy book p257-73 **398.2**
The enchanted watch
In The Green fairy book p43-47 **398.2**
The little soldier
In The Green fairy book p157-74 **398.2**
The nettle spinner
In The Red fairy book p286-93 **398.2**

Deutsch, Babette, 1895-1982
Master and man
In The Scott, Foresman anthology of children's literature p279-82 **808.8**

Developing library-museum partnerships to serve young people. Jay, H. L. **027.8**

Devil
Fiction
Babbitt, N. The Devil's other storybook (4-6) **S C**
Babbitt, N. The Devil's storybook (4-6) **S C**
Brittain, B. Devil's donkey (3-6) **Fic**

The **Devil** and his grandmother. Grimm, J.
In Grimm, J. The complete Grimm's fairy tales p563-66 **398.2**
In The Yellow fairy book p38-41 **398.2**

The **devil** and his three golden hairs. Grimm, J.
In Grimm, J. The juniper tree, and other tales from Grimm v1 p80-93 **398.2**

The **devil** in Vienna. Orgel, D. **Fic**

Devil who was a potter
Afanas'ev, A. N. The devil who was a potter
In Afanas'ev, A. N. Russian fairy tales p576-77 **398.2**

The **Devil** with the three golden hairs. Grimm, J.
In Grimm, J. The complete Grimm's fairy tales p151-58 **398.2**
The **devil** with the three golden hairs. Hogrogian, N. **398.2**
The **devil's** arithmetic. Yolen, J. **Fic**
Devil's donkey. Brittain, B. **Fic**
The **Devil's** other storybook. Babbitt, N. **S C**
Devil's sooty brother
Grimm, J. The Devil's sooty brother
In Grimm, J. The complete Grimm's fairy tales p463-66 **398.2**
The **Devil's** storybook. Babbitt, N. **S C**
The **devil's** three gold hairs. Grimm, J.
In Best-loved folktales of the world p78-84 **398.2**
The **Devil's** trick. Singer, I. B.
In Singer, I. B. Zlateh the goat, and other stories p71-73 **398.2**
Devonshire, Hilary
Drawing (4 and up) **741.2**
The **devoted** friend. Wilde, O.
In Wilde, O. The Happy Prince, and other stories p27-39 **S C**
Devotional exercises
See also Meditation
Dew drop dead. Howe, J. **Fic**
Dewey, Ariane
The narrow escapes of Davy Crockett **E**
(jt. auth) Aruego, J. We hide, you seek **E**
(il) Ginsburg, M. The chick and the duckling **E**
(il) Ginsburg, M. Where does the sun go at night? **E**
(il) Kraus, R. Owliver **E**
(il) Pomerantz, C. One duck, another duck **E**
(il) Raffi. Five little ducks **782.42**
(il) Sharmat, M. Gregory, the terrible eater **E**
Dewey, Jennifer
The Adélie penguin (2-4) **598**
Can you find me? (2-4) **591.5**
(il) Hurd, E. T. Song of the sea otter **599.74**
(il) Simon, S. New questions and answers about dinosaurs **567.9**
(il) Sugarman, J. Snowflakes **551.57**
(il) Trimble, S. The village of blue stone **970.004**
Dewey, Melvil, 1851-1931
Abridged Dewey decimal classification and relative index **025.4**
Dewey Decimal Classification *See* Classification, Dewey Decimal
DeWit, Dorothy, 1916-1980
Children's faces looking up **372.6**
Small Star and the mud pony
In The Scott, Foresman anthology of children's literature p383-87 **808.8**
DeWitt, Lynda
Eagles, hawks, and other birds of prey (4 and up) **598**
Di Fiori, Lawrence
(il) Erickson, R. E. A toad for Tuesday **Fic**
(il) Yolen, J. Mice on ice **E**
Di Grazia, Thomas, d. 1983
(il) Andersen, H. C. The steadfast tin soldier **Fic**
(il) Sholem Aleichem. Holiday tales of Sholom Aleichem **S C**
Diabetes
Tiger, S. Diabetes (5 and up) **616.4**
Fiction
Giff, P. R. The gift of the pirate queen (4-6) **Fic**
Dialectics *See* Logic
Diamond, Donna, 1950-
(il) Clifford, E. The remembering box **Fic**
(il) Greene, C. C. Beat the turtle drum **Fic**
(il) Hautzig, E. R. A gift for Mama **Fic**
(il) Hodges, M. The arrow and the lamp **292**
(il) Meltzer, M. Dorothea Lange: life through the camera **92**
(il) Paterson, K. Bridge to Terabithia **Fic**
Diamond, Judith
Laos (4 and up) **959.4**
Diamonds and toads
Perrault, C. The fairies
In Sleeping beauty & other favourite fairy tales p63-68 **398.2**
Perrault, C. The fairy
In The Classic fairy tales p100-02 **398.2**
Perrault, C. Toads and diamonds
In The Blue fairy book p274-77 **398.2**
In The Scott, Foresman anthology of children's literature p199-200 **808.8**
The **Diane** Goode book of American folk tales and songs (2-5) **398.2**
Diane Goode's American Christmas **810.8**
The **diary** of a church mouse. Oakley, G. See note under Oakley, G. The church mouse **E**

The **diary** of a young girl. Frank, A. 92
Dias, Earl Joseph, 1916-
Video Christmas
In The Big book of Christmas plays p26-40 808.82
DiCerto, J. J.
The pony express (4 and up) 383
Dicey's song. Voigt, C. Fic
Dick Whittington. Crossley-Holland, K.
In Crossley-Holland, K. British folk tales p190-211 398.2
Dick Whittington and his cat
Brown, M. Dick Whittington and his cat 398.2
Crossley-Holland, K. Dick Whittington
In Crossley-Holland, K. British folk tales p190-211 398.2
The History of Whittington
In The Blue fairy book p206-13 398.2
Jacobs, J. Dick Whittington and his cat
In Best-loved folktales of the world p221-28 398.2
Jacobs, J. Whittington and his cat
In Jacobs, J. English fairy tales p167-78 398.2
Reeves, J. Dick Whittington and his cat
In Reeves, J. English fables and fairy stories p221-34 398.2
Thane, A. Dick Whittington and his cat
In Thane, A. Plays from famous stories and fairy tales p414-29 812
Dickens, Charles, 1812-1870
A Christmas carol in prose (4 and up) Fic
A Christmas carol in prose; dramatization. See Thane, A. A Christmas carol
Dicker, Eva Barash
(jt. auth) Greene, L. Sign language talk 419
Dickinson, Emily, 1830-1886
I'm nobody! who are you? (3-6) 811
Poems for youth (5 and up) 811
Dickinson, Peter, 1927-
Merlin dreams (5 and up) Fic
See/See also pages in the following book(s):
Townsend, J. R. A sounding of storytellers p41-54 028.5
Dickinson, Terence
Exploring the night sky (5 and up) 523
Dicks, Terrance
The Baker Street Irregulars in the case of the blackmail boys. See note under Dicks, T. The Baker Street Irregulars in the case of the missing masterpiece Fic
The Baker Street Irregulars in the case of the cinema swindle. See note under Dicks, T. The Baker Street Irregulars in the case of the missing masterpiece Fic
The Baker Street Irregulars in the case of the cop catchers. See note under Dicks, T. The Baker Street Irregulars in the case of the missing masterpiece Fic
The Baker Street Irregulars in the case of the crooked kids. See note under Dicks, T. The Baker Street Irregulars in the case of the missing masterpiece Fic
The Baker Street Irregulars in the case of the ghost grabbers. See note under Dicks, T. The Baker Street Irregulars in the case of the missing masterpiece Fic
The Baker Street Irregulars in the case of the missing masterpiece (5 and up) Fic
Dictionaries *See* Encyclopedias and dictionaries
Dictionaries, Biographical *See* Biography—Dictionaries
Dictionaries, Multilingual *See* Polyglot dictionaries
Dictionaries, Picture *See* Picture dictionaries
A **dictionary** of days. Dunkling, L. 394.2
A **dictionary** of fairies. See Briggs, K. M. An encyclopedia of fairies 398.03
Dictionary of phrase and fable, Brewer's 803
Did you carry the flag today, Charley? Caudill, R. Fic
Dido and Pa. Aiken, J. See note under Aiken, J. The wolves of Willoughby Chase Fic
Didrikson, Babe *See* Zaharias, Babe Didrikson, 1911-1956
Diet
Ward, B. R. Diet and nutrition (4 and up) 641.1

Fiction

Sharmat, M. Gregory, the terrible eater E
Diet and nutrition. Ward, B. R. 641.1
Diets, Reducing *See* Reducing
Different dragons. Little, J. Fic
Dig, drill, dump, fill. Hoban, T. 621.8
Dig to disaster. Quackenbush, R. M. See note under Quackenbush, R. M. Express train to trouble Fic
Digby and Kate again. Baker, B. E
Digestion
Epstein, S. Dr. Beaumont and the man with the hole in his stomach (4-6) 92

Digestion—*Continued*
Parker, S. Food and digestion (4 and up) **612.3**
Showers, P. What happens to a hamburger (k-3) **612.3**
Digging to China. Rawlins, D. **E**
Digging to the past: excavations in ancient lands. Hackwell, W. J. **930.1**
Digging up dinosaurs. Aliki. **567.9**
Dillon, Diane
(il) Aardema, V. Who's in Rabbit's house? **398.2**
(il) Aardema, V. Why mosquitoes buzz in people's ears **398.2**
(il) Bach, A. Moses' ark: stories from the Bible **222**
(il) Graham, L. B. Song of the boat **E**
(il) Greenfield, E. Honey, I love, and other love poems **811**
(il) Hamilton, V. The people could fly: American black folktales **398.2**
(il) Musgrove, M. Ashanti to Zulu: African traditions **960**
(il) Paterson, K. The tale of the mandarin ducks **398.2**
(il) Price, L. Aïda **792.5**
(il) Walter, M. P. Brother to the wind **E**
See/See also pages in the following book(s):
Newbery and Caldecott Medal books, 1976-1985 p170-92 **028.5**
Dillon, Eilís, 1920-
Saint Patrick and the snakes
In Bauer, C. F. Celebrations p170-71 **808.8**
Dillon, Leo, 1933-
(il) Aardema, V. Who's in Rabbit's house? **398.2**
(il) Aardema, V. Why mosquitoes buzz in people's ears **398.2**
(il) Bach, A. Moses' ark: stories from the Bible **222**
(il) Graham, L. B. Song of the boat **E**
(il) Greenfield, E. Honey, I love, and other love poems **811**
(il) Hamilton, V. The people could fly: American black folktales **398.2**
(il) Musgrove, M. Ashanti to Zulu: African traditions **960**
(il) Paterson, K. The tale of the mandarin ducks **398.2**
(il) Price, L. Aïda **792.5**
(il) Walter, M. P. Brother to the wind **E**
See/See also pages in the following book(s):
Newbery and Caldecott Medal books, 1976-1985 p170-92 **028.5**
Dilly dilly piccalilli (2-4) **808.81**
Dilson, Jesse
The abacus: a pocket computer (5 and up) **513.028**
Dinner, Sherry H.
Nothing to be ashamed of: growing up with mental illness in your family (5 and up) **362.2**
Dinner at Alberta's. Hoban, R. **E**
Dinner guests. Calmenson, S.
In The Read-aloud treasury p100-11 **808.8**
Dinners and dining
Fiction
Friedman, I. R. How my parents learned to eat **E**
History
Aliki. A medieval feast (2-5) **394.1**
Poetry
Poem stew (3-6) **811.008**
Dinosaur. Norman, D. **567.9**
Dinosaur Bob and his adventures with the family Lazardo. Joyce, W. **E**
Dinosaur bones. Aliki. **567.9**
Dinosaur dances. Yolen, J. **811**
Dinosaur dig. Lasky, K. **567.9**
Dinosaur discoveries. West, R. **745.54**
The **dinosaur** is the biggest animal that ever lived, and other wrong ideas you thought were true. Simon, S. **500**
Dinosaur mountain. Arnold, C. **567.9**
Dinosaur National Monument (Colo. and Utah)
Arnold, C. Dinosaur mountain (4 and up) **567.9**
Dinosaurs
Aliki. Digging up dinosaurs (k-3) **567.9**
Aliki. Dinosaur bones (k-3) **567.9**
Aliki. Dinosaurs are different (k-3) **567.9**
Aliki. My visit to the dinosaurs (k-3) **567.9**
Arnold, C. Dinosaur mountain (4 and up) **567.9**
Arnold, C. Dinosaurs down under and other fossils from Australia (4 and up) **567.9**
Barton, B. Dinosaurs, dinosaurs (k-2) **567.9**
Booth, J. The big beast book (3-6) **567.9**
Branley, F. M. What happened to the dinosaurs? (k-3) **567.9**
Carrick, C. The crocodiles still wait (1-3) **567.9**
Cobb, V. The monsters who died (3-5) **567.9**
Cohen, D. Dinosaurs (1-3) **567.9**
Cohen, D. Monster dinosaur (5 and up) **567.9**

Dinosaurs—*Continued*
Eldredge, N. The fossil factory (4-6) **560**
Elting, M. The Macmillan book of dinosaurs and other prehistoric creatures (4 and up) **560**
Gibbons, G. Dinosaurs (k-2) **567.9**
Jacobs, F. Supersaurus (1-3) **567.9**
Lasky, K. Dinosaur dig (3 and up) **567.9**
Lauber, P. Dinosaurs walked here, and other stories fossils tell (3-5) **560**
Lauber, P. The news about dinosaurs (4-6) **567.9**
McGowen, T. Album of dinosaurs (4 and up) **567.9**
Most, B. The littlest dinosaurs (k-2) **567.9**
Norman, D. Dinosaur (4 and up) **567.9**
Peters, D. A gallery of dinosaurs & other early reptiles (4-6) **567.9**
Sattler, H. R. Baby dinosaurs (1-4) **567.9**
Sattler, H. R. Dinosaurs of North America (5 and up) **567.9**
Sattler, H. R. Tyrannosaurus rex and its kin: the Mesozoic monsters (4-6) **567.9**
Simon, S. The largest dinosaurs (1-3) **567.9**
Simon, S. New questions and answers about dinosaurs (3-6) **567.9**
Simon, S. The smallest dinosaurs (1-3) **567.9**
West, R. Dinosaur discoveries (3-5) **745.54**

Dictionaries

Sattler, H. R. The new illustrated dinosaur dictionary (5 and up) **567.9**

Fiction

Barton, B. Bones, bones, dinosaur bones **E**
Butterworth, O. The enormous egg (4 and up) **Fic**
Carrick, C. Patrick's dinosaurs **E**
Carrick, C. What happened to Patrick's dinosaurs? **E**
Cuyler, M. Baby Dot: a dinosaur story **E**
Hoff, S. Danny and the dinosaur **E**
Joyce, W. Dinosaur Bob and his adventures with the family Lazardo **E**
Most, B. Whatever happened to the dinosaurs? **E**

Poetry

Dinosaurs: poems (3-5) **811.008**
Yolen, J. Dinosaur dances (3-5) **811**

Dinosaurs alive and well!: a guide to good health. Brown, L. K. **613**
Dinosaurs are different. Aliki. **567.9**
Dinosaurs, beware! Brown, M. T. **613.6**
Dinosaurs divorce. Brown, L. K. **306.89**
Dinosaurs down under and other fossils from Australia. Arnold, C. **567.9**
Dinosaurs in art
Ames, L. J. Draw 50 dinosaurs and other prehistoric animals (4 and up) **743**
Dinosaurs of North America. Sattler, H. R. **567.9**
Dinosaurs: poems (3-5) **811.008**
Dinosaurs travel. Brown, L. K. **910**
Dinosaurs walked here, and other stories fossils tell. Lauber, P. **560**
Dionysus (Greek deity)
See/See also pages in the following book(s):
Coolidge, O. E. The golden days of Greece p98-112 (4-6) **938**
Diop, Birago, 1906-1989
Guy, R. Mother Crocodile **398.2**
Diplomats
Haskins, J. Shirley Temple Black (4 and up) **92**
Direction (Motion pictures) *See* Motion pictures—Production and direction
Direction sense
See/See also pages in the following book(s):
Mango, K. N. Mapmaking p9-21 (4 and up) **526**
Dirigible. Stoff, J. **629.133**
Dirigible balloons *See* Airships
The **dirty** bride. Curtis, E. S.
In Curtis, E. S. The girl who married a ghost, and other tales from the North American Indian p73-80 **398.2**
Dirty shepherdess
Sébillot, P. The dirty shepherdess
In The Green fairy book p180-85 **398.2**
Disabled *See* Handicapped
DiSalvo-Ryan, DyAnne, 1954-
(il) Cleary, B. The real hole **E**
(il) Siegel, B. Sam Ellis's island **325.73**
The **disappearance** of Peter Rugg. Roach, M. K.
In Roach, M. K. Encounters with the invisible world **S C**
The **disappearing** dog trick. Corbett, S. See note under Corbett, S. The lemonade trick **Fic**

Disarmament *See* Arms control
Disasters
See also Accidents; Natural disasters
The **disastrous** dog. Lively, P.
In Lively, P. Uninvited ghosts, and other stories p29-39 **S C**
The **discontented** ghost. Corbett, S. **Fic**
Discoveries (in geography)
See/See also pages in the following book(s):
Mango, K. N. Mapmaking p58-70 (4 and up) **526**
Discovering flies. O'Toole, C. **595.7**
Discovering frogs. Florian, D. **597.8**
Discovering seashells. Florian, D. **594**
Diseases
See also Sick; names of diseases and groups of diseases; and subjects with the subdivision *Diseases*
Krementz, J. How it feels to fight for your life (4 and up) **362.1**
See/See also pages in the following book(s):
Giblin, J. Milk: the fight for purity p35-41 (5 and up) **637**
Disney, Walt, 1901-1966
See/See also pages in the following book(s):
Sendak, M. Caldecott & Co.: notes on books and pictures p107-17 **028.5**
Disney (Walt) Productions *See* Walt Disney Productions
Displaced persons *See* Refugees
The **distant** planets. Yeomans, D. K. **523.4**
The **Ditmars** tale of wonders. Grimm, J.
In Grimm, J. The complete Grimm's fairy tales p662 **398.2**
Ditmarsch tale of wonders
Grimm, J. The Ditmars tale of wonders
In Grimm, J. The complete Grimm's fairy tales p662 **398.2**
Dividing the goose
Afanas'ev, A. N. Dividing the goose
In Afanas'ev, A. N. Russian fairy tales p579-80 **398.2**
Divination
Schwartz, A. Telling fortunes (4-6) **133.3**
Diving, Scuba *See* Scuba diving
Diving into darkness: a submersible explores the sea. Johnson, R. L. **551.46**
Diving to the past: recovering ancient wrecks. Hackwell, W. J. **910.4**
Divorce
Brown, L. K. Dinosaurs divorce (k-4) **306.89**
Krementz, J. How it feels when parents divorce (4 and up) **306.89**
Stein, S. B. On divorce (k-3) **306.89**

Fiction
Blume, J. It's not the end of the world (4-6) **Fic**
Caines, J. F. Daddy **E**
Carrick, C. What a wimp! (3-5) **Fic**
Christiansen, C. B. My mother's house, my father's house **E**
Cleary, B. Dear Mr. Henshaw (4-6) **Fic**
Greene, C. C. Ask anybody (5 and up) **Fic**
Hurwitz, J. DeDe takes charge (3-5) **Fic**
Kropp, P. Moonkid and Liberty (6 and up) **Fic**
Slote, A. Matt Gargan's boy (4-6) **Fic**
Dix, Dorothea Lynde, 1802-1887
See/See also pages in the following book(s):
Jacobs, W. J. Great lives: human rights p56-63 (5 and up) **920**
DNA
Asimov, I. How did we find out about DNA? (5 and up) **574.87**
Do animals dream? Pope, J. **591**
Do bananas chew gum? Gilson, J. **Fic**
Do like Kyla. Johnson, A. **E**
Do not alight here. Aiken, J.
In Aiken, J. Give yourself a fright: thirteen tales of the supernatural p31-43 **S C**
Do not disturb. Facklam, M. **591.5**
Do not disturb. Tafuri, N. **E**
Do-not-know
Afanas'ev, A. N. Know Not
In Afanas'ev, A. N. Russian fairy tales p97-109 **398.2**
Do not open. Turkle, B. C. **E**
Do you want to be my friend? Carle, E. **E**
Do your ears hang low?: 50 more musical fingerplays. Glazer, T. **796.1**
Doc Rabbit, Bruh Fox, and Tar Baby. Hamilton, V.
In Hamilton, V. The people could fly: American Black folktales p13-19 **398.2**
The **Doctor** and his pupil
In Best-loved folktales of the world p50-53 **398.2**
Doctor Coyote. Bierhorst, J. **398.2**
Doctor De Soto. Steig, W. **E**
Doctor Know-all
Crab
In Best-loved folktales of the world p152-54 **398.2**
Grimm, J. Doctor Know-It-All
In Grimm, J. Tales from Grimm p77-86 **398.2**

Doctor Know-all—*Continued*
Grimm, J. Doctor Knowall
In Grimm, J. The complete Grimm's fairy tales p456-58 **398.2**
Doctor Know-It-All. Grimm, J.
In Grimm, J. Tales from Grimm p77-86 **398.2**
Doctors *See* Physicians
A **doctor's** tools. DeSantis, K. **610.69**
Dodds, Dayle Ann
Wheel away! **E**
Dodge, Mary Mapes, 1830-1905
Hans Brinker; or, The silver skates (4 and up) **Fic**
Dodgers (Baseball team) *See* Brooklyn Dodgers (Baseball team)
Dodgson, Charles Lutwidge *See* Carroll, Lewis, 1832-1898
Dodson, Bert
(il) Evslin, B. Jason and the Argonauts **292**
(il) Smith, E. S. A guide dog goes to school **362.4**
Does God have a big toe? Gellman, M. **221.9**
The **Dog** and the bone
In The Baby's story book p12-13 **398.2**
The **dog** and the bone. Rockwell, A. F.
In Rockwell, A. F. The three bears & 15 other stories p100-01 **398.2**
Dog and the sparrow
Grimm, J. The dog and the sparrow
In Grimm, J. The complete Grimm's fairy tales p280-82 **398.2**
Dog and the woodpecker
Afanas'ev, A. N. The dog and the woodpecker
In Afanas'ev, A. N. Russian fairy tales p499-500 **398.2**
A **dog** on Barkham Street. Stolz, M. **Fic**
The **dog** on the roof. Aiken, J.
In Aiken, J. Up the chimney down, and other stories p66-95 **S C**
Dog poems (1-3) **808.81**
Dog racing
See also Sled dog racing
Dogs
See also Sheep dogs
American Kennel Club. The complete dog book **636.7**
Cohen, S. What kind of dog is that? (4 and up) **636.7**
Cole, J. A dog's body **636.7**
Cole, J. My puppy is born (k-3) **636.7**
Fischer-Nagel, H. A puppy is born (1-4) **636.7**
Hausherr, R. My first puppy (1-3) **636.7**
Kuklin, S. Taking my dog to the vet (k-2) **636.7**
Pinkwater, J. Superpuppy: how to choose, raise, and train the best possible dog for you (5 and up) **636.7**
Pope, J. Taking care of your dog (3-5) **636.7**
Siegel, M.-E. More than a friend: dogs with a purpose (5 and up) **636.7**
Silverstein, A. Dogs: all about them (5 and up) **636.7**
Simon, N. Cats do, dogs don't (k-2) **636.088**
See/See also pages in the following book(s):
Chrystie, F. N. Pets p3-25 (4 and up) **636.088**
Pringle, L. P. Feral: tame animals gone wild p37-53 (5 and up) **591.5**
Fiction
Alexander, M. G. Bobo's dream **E**
Armstrong, W. H. Sounder (5 and up) **Fic**
Baker, B. Digby and Kate again **E**
Barracca, D. The adventures of Taxi Dog **E**
Bemelmans, L. Madeline's rescue **E**
Bonsall, C. N. The amazing, the incredible super dog **E**
Burnford, S. The incredible journey (4 and up) **Fic**
Carrick, C. Ben and the porcupine **E**
Catalanotto, P. Dylan's day out **E**
Cone, M. Mishmash (3-5) **Fic**
Corcoran, B. Annie's monster (5 and up) **Fic**
Day, A. Carl goes shopping **E**
Estes, E. Ginger Pye (4-6) **Fic**
Ferguson, A. Cricket and the crackerbox kid (4-6) **Fic**
Flack, M. Angus and the ducks **E**
Gackenbach, D. What's Claude doing? **E**
Gág, W. Nothing At All **E**
Gardiner, J. R. Stone Fox (2-5) **Fic**
Gipson, F. B. Old Yeller (6 and up) **Fic**
Griffith, H. V. Alex and the cat **E**
Griffith, H. V. Plunk's dreams **E**
Jones, D. W. Dogsbody (6 and up) **Fic**
Jordan, J. Kimako's story (2-4) **Fic**
Kellogg, S. Pinkerton, behave! **E**
Khalsa, D. K. I want a dog **E**
Khalsa, D. K. Julian **E**
Kjelgaard, J. Big Red (4 and up) **Fic**
Lippincott, J. W. Wilderness champion (5 and up) **Fic**
Little, J. Different dragons (3-5) **Fic**
London, J. The call of the wild (5 and up) **Fic**
London, J. White Fang (5 and up) **Fic**
Mahy, M. Making friends **E**
Oxenbury, H. Our dog **E**
Peet, B. The whingdingdilly **E**

Dogs—Fiction—*Continued*
Pinkwater, D. M. Aunt Lulu E
Polushkin, M. Who said meow? E
Porte-Thomas, B. A. The take-along dog E
Potter, B. The pie and the patty-pan E
Rand, G. Salty dog E
Rawls, W. Where the red fern grows Fic
Rylant, C. Henry and Mudge E
Sachs, E.-A. The boy who ate dog biscuits E
Schwartz, A. Oma and Bobo E
Sendak, M. Higglety pigglety pop! (2-4) Fic
Steig, W. Caleb & Kate E
Steig, W. Dominic (4 and up) Fic
Stevenson, J. Mr. Hacker E
Stevenson, J. The night after Christmas E
Stolz, M. A dog on Barkham Street (4-6) Fic
Thayer, J. The puppy who wanted a boy E
Thomas, J. R. The comeback dog (3-5) Fic
Van Allsburg, C. The garden of Abdul Gasazi E
Voigt, C. Stories about Rosie E
Waber, B. Bernard E
Westman, B. The day before Christmas E
Wolff, A. Come with me E
Yeoman, J. Old Mother Hubbard's dog dresses up E
Young, E. The other bone E
Zion, G. Harry the dirty dog E

Poetry

Dog poems (1-3) **808.81**

Training

Curtis, P. Cindy, a hearing ear dog (3-5) **636.7**
Smith, E. S. A service dog goes to school (3-5) **636.7**

See/See also pages in the following book(s):
Pinkwater, J. Superpuppy: how to choose, raise, and train the best possible dog for you p144-87 (5 and up) **636.7**

Dogs & dragons, trees & dreams: a collection of poems. Kuskin, K. **811**
Dogs: all about them. Silverstein, A. **636.7**
A **dog's** body. Cole, J. **636.7**
Dog's choice. Curry, J. L.
In Curry, J. L. Back in the beforetime p128-31 **398.2**
Dogs for the blind *See* Guide dogs
Dogs for the deaf *See* Hearing ear dogs
Dogs in art
Ames, L. J. Draw 50 dogs (4 and up) **743**
The **dog's** nose is cold. Sherlock, Sir P. M.
In Sherlock, Sir P. M. West Indian folk-tales p34-38 **398.2**
Dogsbody. Jones, D. W. **Fic**
Dogsled to dread. Quackenbush, R. M. See note under Quackenbush, R. M. Express train to trouble **Fic**
Dogsong. Paulsen, G. **Fic**
Doherty, Berlie
White Peak Farm (5 and up) **Fic**
Dolan, Edward F., 1924-
Starting soccer (5 and up) **796.334**
The **doll** in the garden. Hahn, M. D. **Fic**
The **dollar** watch and the five jack rabbits. Sandburg, C.
In Sandburg, C. Rootabaga stories pt 1 p117-24 **S C**
In Sandburg, C. The Sandburg treasury p57-61 **818**
Dollhouse magic. Roche, P. K. **745.592**
The **dollhouse** murders. Wright, B. R. **Fic**
Dollhouse people. Pearson, T. C. **745.592**
Dollhouses
Roche, P. K. Dollhouse magic (2-4) **745.592**

Fiction

Godden, R. The doll's house (2-4) **Fic**
Sachs, M. The bears' house (4-6) **Fic**
Sachs, M. Fran Ellen's house (4-6) **Fic**
Sleator, W. Among the dolls (4 and up) **Fic**

Dolls
Pearson, T. C. Dollhouse people (3-5) **745.592**

See/See also pages in the following book(s):
Pellowski, A. The story vine p77-91 **372.6**

Fiction

Bailey, C. S. Miss Hickory (3-5) **Fic**
Brink, C. R. The bad times of Irma Baumlein (4-6) **Fic**
Cassedy, S. Lucie Babbidge's house (4-6) **Fic**
Field, R. Hitty: her first hundred years (4 and up) **Fic**
Godden, R. The doll's house (2-4) **Fic**
Godden, R. Four dolls (3-5) **S C**
Godden, R. The story of Holly and Ivy **E**
Goffstein, M. B. Goldie the dollmaker (3-5) **Fic**
Hutchins, P. Changes, changes **E**
McKissack, P. C. Nettie Jo's friends **E**
Polacco, P. Babushka's doll **E**

Dolls—Fiction—*Continued*
Pomerantz, C. The chalk doll E
Sandburg, C. The wedding procession of the Rag Doll and the Broom Handle and who was in it E
Schulman, J. The big hello E
Sleator, W. Among the dolls (4 and up) Fic
Stevenson, J. The night after Christmas E
Wells, R. Peabody E
Winthrop, E. Katharine's doll E
Zolotow, C. William's doll E

The **doll's** house. Godden, R. Fic

Dolphin adventure. Grover, W. 599.5

Dolphins
The Audubon Society field guide to North American fishes, whales, and dolphins (5 and up) 597
Behrens, J. Dolphins! (2-4) 599.5
Bridge, L. M. The playful dolphins (k-3) 599.5
Grover, W. Dolphin adventure (3-5) 599.5
Morris, R. A. Dolphin (k-3) 599.5
Patent, D. H. Dolphins and porpoises (5 and up) 599.5
Patent, D. H. Looking at dolphins and porpoises (3-5) 599.5
Reeves, R. R. The Sea World book of dolphins (4 and up) 599.5
Rinard, J. E. Dolphins: our friends in the sea (4 and up) 599.5
Sattler, H. R. Whales, the nomads of the sea (4 and up) 599.5

Fiction

Kendall, S. The Bell Reef (5 and up) Fic
L'Engle, M. A ring of endless light (5 and up) Fic

Dolphins and porpoises. Patent, D. H. 599.5

Dolphins: our friends in the sea. Rinard, J. E. 599.5

Domanska, Janina
(il) Coatsworth, E. J. Under the green willow E
(il) If all the seas were one sea. See If all the seas were one sea 398.8
(il) Kelly, E. P. The trumpeter of Krakow Fic

Domestic animals
See also Pets; Working animals
Tafuri, N. Spots, feathers, and curly tails (k-2) 636
See/See also pages in the following book(s):
Chrystie, F. N. Pets p159-88 (4 and up) 636.088

Fiction

Brown, M. W. Big red barn E
Lindbergh, R. The day the goose got loose E
Most, B. The cow that went oink E

Domestic relations
See also Family

Dominic. Steig, W. Fic

Don Demonio's mother-in-law. Boggs, R. S.
In Best-loved folktales of the world p160-65 398.2

Donagh and the giants. McCarty, T.
In The Scott, Foresman anthology of children's literature p456-58 808.8

Donkey
Grimm, J. The donkey
In Grimm, J. The complete Grimm's fairy tales p632-35 398.2

Donkey cabbage
Grimm, J. The cabbage donkey
In The Yellow fairy book p42-49 398.2
Grimm, J. Donkey cabbages
In Grimm, J. The complete Grimm's fairy tales p551-58 398.2

The **donkey** driver and the thief. Protter, E.
In Best-loved folktales of the world p488-89 398.2

Donkey-skin
Perrault, C. Donkey-skin
In Sleeping beauty & other favourite fairy tales p81-92 398.2

The **donkey,** the table, and the stick. Reeves, J.
In Reeves, J. English fables and fairy stories p195-210 398.2

Donkeys
See/See also pages in the following book(s):
Henry, M. Album of horses p98-101 (4 and up) 636.1
Pringle, L. P. Feral: tame animals gone wild p67-85 (5 and up) 591.5

Fiction

Henry, M. Brighty of the Grand Canyon (4 and up) Fic
Steig, W. Farmer Palmer's wagon ride E
Steig, W. Sylvester and the magic pebble E
Wildsmith, B. A Christmas story E

Donor banks: saving lives with organ and tissue transplants. Lee, S. 362.1

Don't be greedy story. Marriott, A. L.
In Marriott, A. L. American Indian mythology 398.2

Don't be mad, Ivy. McDonnell, C. Fic

Don't eat too much turkey! Cohen, M. See note under Cohen, M. See you in second grade! E

Don't feel sorry for Paul. Wolf, B. **362.4**
Don't forget the bacon! Hutchins, P. **E**
Don't shake hands with everybody. Courlander, H.
In Courlander, H. The cow-tail switch, and other West African stories p129-32 **398.2**
Don't sing before breakfast, don't sleep in the moonlight. Perl, L. **398**
Don't tell the whole world! Cole, J. **E**
Don't throw stones from not-yours to yours
In Best-loved folktales of the world p495-96 **398.2**
Dooling, Michael
(il) Hurwitz, J. Astrid Lindgren: storyteller to the world **92**
(il) Oneal, Z. A long way to go **Fic**
The **door**. Hussey, L. A.
In Things that go bump in the night p38-51 **S C**
The **door** in the wall. De Angeli, M. L. **Fic**
The **doorbell** rang. Hutchins, P. **E**
Dorfman, Ariel
The rebellion of the magical rabbits
In Where angels glide at dawn p7-25 **S C**
Doris knows everything. Goldberg, W.
In Free to be—a family p124-25 **810.8**
Dorothea Lange: life through the camera. Meltzer, M. **92**
Dorothy and the Wizard in Oz. Baum, L. F. See note under Baum, L. F. The Wizard of Oz **Fic**
Dorros, Arthur
Ant cities (k-3) **595.7**
Feel the wind (k-3) **551.5**
Me and my shadow (k-3) **535**
(il) Branley, F. M. What makes day and night **525**
(il) Wyler, R. Magic secrets **793.8**
Dots, spots, speckles, and stripes. Hoban, T. **E**
Doty, Roy, 1922-
(il) Blume, J. Tales of a fourth grade nothing **Fic**
(il) James, E. How to be school smart **371.3**
(il) Zubrowski, B. Balloons **507**
(il) Zubrowski, B. Clocks **681.1**
(il) Zubrowski, B. Tops **745.592**
(il) Zubrowski, B. Wheels at work **621.8**
Double-dare O'Toole. Greene, C. C. **Fic**
Double dog dare. Gilson, J. See note under Gilson, J. 4B goes wild **Fic**
The **double** life of Pocahontas. Fritz, J. **92**
The **Doubleday** children's dictionary. Grisewood, J. **423**
The **Doubleday** children's thesaurus. Bellamy, J. **423**
The **Doubleday** illustrated children's Bible. Stoddard, S. **220.9**
Douglass, Frederick, 1817?-1895
About
McKissack, P. C. Frederick Douglass: the black lion (4 and up) **92**
Miller, D. T. Frederick Douglass and the fight for freedom (6 and up) **92**
See/See also pages in the following book(s):
Jacobs, W. J. Great lives: human rights p64-72 (5 and up) **920**
The **dove** dove. Terban, M. **793.73**
Doves *See* Pigeons
Dow, Charles Henry, 1851-1902
See/See also pages in the following book(s):
Aaseng, N. From rags to riches p19-23 (5 and up) **920**
Dow, Jill
(il) Bellamy, D. J. The rock pool **574.92**
Dow, Lesley
Whales (5 and up) **599.5**
Dow Jones & Co., Inc.
See/See also pages in the following book(s):
Aaseng, N. From rags to riches p19-23 (5 and up) **920**
Dowden, Anne Ophelia Todd, 1907-
The blossom on the bough (5 and up) **582.16**
The clover and the bee (5 and up) **582**
From flower to fruit (5 and up) **582**
State flowers (5 and up) **582.13**
(il) Borland, H. Plants of Christmas **398**
(il) Paterson, J. Consider the lilies **220.8**
Down by the bay. Raffi. **782.42**
Down under, down under. McGovern, A. **574.92**
Downey, William R., 1954-
(il) Simon, S. Poisonous snakes **597.9**
Downing, Julie
White snow, blue feather **E**
(il) Rabe, B. Margaret's moves **Fic**
(il) Rylant, C. Mr. Griggs' work **E**
Doyle, Sir Arthur Conan, 1859-1930
Sherlock Holmes' Christmas Goose; dramatization. See Nolan, P. T. Sherlock Holmes' Christmas goose
Parodies, travesties, etc.
Titus, E. Basil of Baker Street (3-5) **Fic**
Doyle, Conan *See* Doyle, Sir Arthur Conan, 1859-1930

Dr. Beaumont and the man with the hole in his stomach. Epstein, S. **92**

Dr. Dredd's wagon of wonders. Brittain, B. See note under Brittain, B. Devil's donkey **Fic**

The **Drackenberg** adventure. Alexander, L. See note under Alexander, L. The Illyrian adventure **Fic**

Draft horses. Patent, D. H. **636.1**

Dragon and his grandmother
Grimm, J. The Devil and his grandmother
In Grimm, J. The complete Grimm's fairy tales p563-66 **398.2**
In The Yellow fairy book p38-41 **398.2**
Grimm, J. The dragon and his grandmother
In Grimm, J. Tales from Grimm p225-34 **398.2**

Dragon kites and dragonflies. Demi. **398.8**

Dragon of the north
The Dragon of the north
In The Yellow fairy book p9-20 **398.2**

The **dragon** tunnel. Lively, P.
In Lively, P. Uninvited ghosts, and other stories p50-63 **S C**

Dragondrums. McCaffrey, A. See note under McCaffrey, A. Dragonsong **Fic**

Dragonflies
McLaughlin, M. Dragonflies (3-5) **595.7**
Overbeck, C. Dragonflies (4 and up) **595.7**

Dragons

Fiction

De Paola, T. The knight and the dragon **E**
Gannett, R. S. My father's dragon (1-4) **Fic**
Grahame, K. The reluctant dragon (3-5) **Fic**
Hodges, M. Saint George and the dragon (2-5) **398.2**
Kimmel, M. M. Magic in the mist (1-4) **Fic**
Leaf, M. The eyes of the dragon **E**
Sargent, S. Weird Henry Berg (4-6) **Fic**
Thayer, J. The popcorn dragon **E**
Williams, J. Everyone knows what a dragon looks like **E**
Wrede, P. C. Dealing with dragons (6 and up) **Fic**

The **dragon's** boy. Yolen, J. **Fic**

The **dragon's** robe. Lattimore, D. N. **Fic**

Dragonsinger. McCaffrey, A. See note under McCaffrey, A. Dragonsong **Fic**

Dragonsong. McCaffrey, A. **Fic**

Dragonwagon, Crescent
Half a moon and one whole star **E**
Winter holding spring (2-4) **Fic**

Dragonwings. Yep, L. **Fic**

Dragunsky, Victor
Traffic on Sadovoi Road
In Face to face: a collection of stories by celebrated Soviet and American writers p131-40 **S C**

Drakesbill and his friends
Drakestail
In Best-loved folktales of the world p45-50 **398.2**
Marelle, C. Drakestail
In The Red fairy book p202-07 **398.2**

Drakestail
In Best-loved folktales of the world p45-50 **398.2**

Drakestail. Marelle, C.
In The Red fairy book p202-07 **398.2**

Drama
See also College and school drama; Folk drama; One act plays
See/See also pages in the following book(s):
Kaye, C. B. Word works p63-76 (4 and up) **410**

Collected works

Bauer, C. F. Presenting reader's theater **808.82**

Indexes

Play index **808.82**

Periodicals

Plays **808.82**

Drama in education
Bauer, C. F. Presenting reader's theater **808.82**

Draw 50 beasties and yugglies and turnover uglies and things that go bump in the night. Ames, L. J. **743**

Draw 50 boats, ships, trucks & trains. Ames, L. J. **743**

Draw 50 buildings and other structures. Ames, L. J. **743**

Draw 50 cars, trucks, and motorcycles. Ames, L. J. **743**

Draw 50 cats. Ames, L. J. **743**

Draw 50 dinosaurs and other prehistoric animals. Ames, L. J. **743**

Draw 50 dogs. Ames, L. J. **743**

Draw 50 famous cartoons. Ames, L. J. **741.5**

Draw 50 holiday decorations. Ames, L. J. **743**

Draw 50 horses. Ames, L. J. 743
Draw 50 sharks, whales, and other sea creatures. Ames, L. J. 743
Drawing
See also Pen drawing
Ames, L. J. Draw 50 beasties and yugglies and turnover uglies and things that go bump in the night (4 and up) 743
Ames, L. J. Draw 50 boats, ships, trucks & trains (4 and up) 743
Ames, L. J. Draw 50 buildings and other structures (4 and up) 743
Ames, L. J. Draw 50 cars, trucks, and motorcycles (4 and up) 743
Ames, L. J. Draw 50 cats (4 and up) 743
Ames, L. J. Draw 50 dinosaurs and other prehistoric animals (4 and up) 743
Ames, L. J. Draw 50 dogs (4 and up) 743
Ames, L. J. Draw 50 famous cartoons (4 and up) 741.5
Ames, L. J. Draw 50 holiday decorations (4 and up) 743
Ames, L. J. Draw 50 horses (4 and up) 743
Ames, L. J. Draw 50 sharks, whales, and other sea creatures (4 and up) 743
Arnosky, J. Drawing from nature (5 and up) 743
Arnosky, J. Drawing life in motion (4 and up) 743
Arnosky, J. Sketching outdoors in autumn (5 and up) 743
Arnosky, J. Sketching outdoors in spring (5 and up) 743
Arnosky, J. Sketching outdoors in summer (5 and up) 743
Arnosky, J. Sketching outdoors in winter (5 and up) 743
Benjamin, C. L. Cartooning for kids (4-6) 741.5
Devonshire, H. Drawing (4 and up) 741.2
Emberley, E. Ed Emberley's big green drawing book (2-5) 741.2
Emberley, E. Ed Emberley's big red drawing book (2-5) 741.2
Emberley, E. Ed Emberley's drawing book: make a world (2-5) 741.2
Emberley, E. Ed Emberley's drawing book of faces (2-5) 743
Emberley, E. Ed Emberley's great thumbprint drawing book (2-5) 743
Emberley, E. Ed Emberley's picture pie: a circle drawing book (2-5) 741.2
Frame, P. Drawing cats and kittens (4 and up) 743
Raphael, E. Drawing history: Ancient Egypt (4 and up) 741

Fiction
Drescher, H. Simon's book E
Testa, F. If you take a pencil E
Williams, V. B. Cherries and cherry pits E
Drawing book: make a world, Ed Emberley's. Emberley, E. 741.2
Drawing book of faces, Ed Emberley's. Emberley, E. 743
Drawing cats and kittens. Frame, P. 743
Drawing from nature. Arnosky, J. 743
Drawing history: Ancient Egypt. Raphael, E. 741
Drawing life in motion. Arnosky, J. 743
The **dreadful** future of Blossom Culp. Peck, R. See note under Peck, R. The ghost belonged to me Fic
Dream flier. Yep, L.
In Yep, L. The rainbow people p154-60 398.2
The **dream** keeper, and other poems. Hughes, L. 811
Dream wolf. Goble, P. E
Dreamers & doers: inventors who changed our world. Richards, N. 920
Dreams
Silverstein, A. The mystery of sleep (4-6) 154.6
See/See also pages in the following book(s):
Stafford, P. Your two brains p49-57 (5 and up) 612.8
Fiction
Briggs, R. The snowman E
Burningham, J. Hey! get off our train E
Collington, P. The angel and the soldier boy E
Griffith, H. V. Plunk's dreams E
Sendak, M. Kenny's window E
Stevenson, J. "Could be worse!" E
Van Allsburg, C. Ben's dream E
Van Allsburg, C. Just a dream E
Wiesner, D. Free fall E
Poetry
Greenfield, E. Daydreamers (3-6) 811
Dreams. Spier, P. E
Dreams of victory. Conford, E. Fic
Drescher, Henrik, 1955-
Simon's book E
(il) Poems of A. Nonny Mouse. See Poems of A. Nonny Mouse 808.81
Dress *See* Clothing and dress
Dreyer, Sharon Spredemann
The bookfinder 011.6
Drighi, Laura
(il) Italy. See Italy 945
Drimmer, Frederick
Born different (6 and up) 920

Drinking & driving. Hjelmeland, A. **363.1**

Drinking companions. Pu, S.-L.
In Best-loved folktales of the world p550-54 **398.2**

The **drinking** gourd. Monjo, F. N. **E**

Drinking of alcoholic beverages
See also Alcoholism; Drunk driving; Youth—Alcohol use

Drinking problem *See* Alcoholism

Drivers, Automobile *See* Automobile drivers

Driving under the influence of alcohol *See* Drunk driving

A **drop** of blood. Showers, P. **612.1**

Droughts

Fiction

Aardema, V. Bringing the rain to Kapiti Plain (k-2) **398.2**

Drucker, Malka, 1945-
Celebrating life: Jewish rites of passage (4 and up) **296.4**
Hanukkah (4 and up) **296.4**

Drug abuse
See also Alcoholism
Friedman, D. P. Focus on drugs and the brain (3-6) **616.86**
Hyde, M. O. Drug wars (6 and up) **363.4**
Hyde, M. O. Know about drugs (4 and up) **616.86**
Seixas, J. S. Drugs—what they are, what they do (1-3) **616.86**
Shulman, J. Focus on cocaine and crack (3-6) **362.29**
Woods, G. Drug use and drug abuse (4 and up) **616.86**

Fiction

Childress, A. A hero ain't nothin' but a sandwich (6 and up) **Fic**

Drug traffic
See/See also pages in the following book(s):
Hyde, M. O. Drug wars p67-91 (6 and up) **363.4**

Drug use and drug abuse. Woods, G. **616.86**

Drug wars. Hyde, M. O. **363.4**

Drugs
See also Psychotropic drugs
Friedman, D. P. Focus on drugs and the brain (3-6) **616.86**
Hyde, M. O. Know about drugs (4 and up) **616.86**
Seixas, J. S. Drugs—what they are, what they do (1-3) **616.86**
Woods, G. Drug use and drug abuse (4 and up) **616.86**

Fiction

Christopher, M. Tackle without a team (5 and up) **Fic**

Drugs, Psychotropic *See* Psychotropic drugs

Druids and Druidism

Fiction

Pope, E. M. The Perilous Gard (6 and up) **Fic**

Drummer
Grimm, J. The drummer
In Grimm, J. The complete Grimm's fairy tales p781-91 **398.2**

Drummer Hoff. Emberley, B. **398.8**

Drunk driving
Hjelmeland, A. Drinking & driving (4-6) **363.1**

Dry-Bone and Anansi. Sherlock, Sir P. M.
In Sherlock, Sir P. M. West Indian folk-tales p77-85 **398.2**

Dryden, John Fairfield, 1839-1911
See/See also pages in the following book(s):
Aaseng, N. The problem solvers p19-24 (5 and up) **920**

Drying out. Rylant, C.
In Rylant, C. Every living thing p34-41 **S C**

Du Bois, William Pène, 1916-
The twenty-one balloons (5 and up) **Fic**
(il) Caudill, R. A certain small shepherd **Fic**
(il) Zolotow, C. My grandson Lew **E**
(il) Zolotow, C. William's doll **E**
See/See also pages in the following book(s):
Newbery Medal books, 1922-1955 p302-17 **028.5**

Dubanevich, Arlene, 1950-
Pigs in hiding **E**

DuBois, Daniel
(jt. auth) Fronval, G. Indian signs and signals **419**

DuBois, Graham
Bonds of affection
In Holiday plays round the year p151-60 **812.008**
The end of the road
In Holiday plays round the year p179-88 **812.008**
Every day is Thanksgiving
In Holiday plays round the year p47-58 **812.008**

Duck with golden eggs
Afanas'ev, A. N. The duck with golden eggs
In Afanas'ev, A. N. Russian fairy tales p541-44 **398.2**

Ducks
Goldin, A. R. Ducks don't get wet (k-3) **598**
See/See also pages in the following book(s):
Weber, W. J. Care of uncommon pets p110-22 (5 and up) **636.088**

Ducks—*Continued*

Fiction

Berends, P. B. The case of the elevator duck (3-5) **Fic**
Flack, M. Angus and the ducks **E**
Flack, M. The story about Ping **E**
Gerstein, M. Arnold of the Ducks **E**
Ginsburg, M. The chick and the duckling **E**
Hurd, E. T. Last one home is a green pig **E**
McCloskey, R. Make way for ducklings **E**
Paterson, K. The tale of the mandarin ducks (1-3) **398.2**
Potter, B. The tale of Jemima Puddle-duck **E**
Quackenbush, R. M. Express train to trouble (2-4) **Fic**
Tafuri, N. Have you seen my duckling? **E**
Thiele, C. Farmer Schulz's ducks **E**

Ducks don't get wet. Goldin, A. R. **598**

Duder, Tessa
Jellybean (5 and up) **Fic**

Dudley Pippin and the principal [short story]. Ressner, P.
In Free to be—you and me p88-89 **810.8**

Duffy's jacket. Coville, B.
In Things that go bump in the night p52-60 **S C**

Duke, Kate
The guinea pig ABC **E**
Guinea pigs far and near **E**
(il) Cole, J. Don't tell the whole world! **E**

Dull Knife, Cheyenne Chief
See/See also pages in the following book(s):
Ehrlich, A. Wounded Knee: an Indian history of the American West (6 and up) **970.004**

The **dumb** cake. Garfield, L.
In Garfield, L. The apprentices **S C**

Dumb cane and daffodils. Lerner, C. **581.6**

Dummling and the golden goose. Thane, A.
In Thane, A. Plays from famous stories and fairy tales p105-19 **812**

Dun cow
Afanas'ev, A. N. Burenushka, the little red cow
In Afanas'ev, A. N. Russian fairy tales p146-50 **398.2**

Dunbar, Paul Laurence, 1872-1906

About

McKissack, P. C. Paul Laurence Dunbar, a poet to remember (4 and up) **92**

Duncan, Beverly K.
(comp) Christmas in the stable. See Christmas in the stable **811.008**

Duncan & Dolores. Samuels, B. **E**

Dunes *See* Sand dunes

The **dung** beetle. Andersen, H. C.
In Andersen, H. C. Hans Andersen: his classic fairy tales p48-56 **S C**

Dunham, Katherine

About

Haskins, J. Katherine Dunham (5 and up) **92**

Dunkling, Leslie, 1935-
A dictionary of days **394.2**

Dunlop, John Boyd, 1840-1921
See/See also pages in the following book(s):
Aaseng, N. The unsung heroes p19-23 (5 and up) **920**

Dunn, Wendy (Wendy Rader)
(jt. auth) Morey, J. Famous Mexican Americans **920**

Dunning, Stephen
(comp) Reflections on a gift of watermelon pickle . . . and other modern verse. See Reflections on a gift of watermelon pickle . . . and other modern verse **811.008**

Dunrea, Olivier, 1953-
Deep down underground **E**

Dunton, Mary Jane
(il) Moore, L. Something new begins: new and selected poems **811**

Duntze, Dorothée
(il) Andersen, H. C. The princess and the pea **Fic**
(il) Andersen, H. C. The swineherd **Fic**

The **duplicate**. Sleator, W. **Fic**

Durán, Cheli
Hildilid's night **E**

Durant, William Crapo, 1861-1947
See/See also pages in the following book(s):
Aaseng, N. The unsung heroes p29-37 (5 and up) **920**

Duration of life
Grimm, J. The duration of life
In Grimm, J. The complete Grimm's fairy tales p716-18 **398.2**

Durell, Ann, 1930-
(comp) The Diane Goode book of American folk tales and songs. See The Diane Goode book of American folk tales and songs **398.2**

Durenceau, Andre
(il) Mitchell, R. T. Butterflies and moths **595.7**

Dürer, Albrecht, 1471-1528
About
Raboff, E. Albrecht Dürer (4 and up) **759.3**
Durkee, Sarah
The day Dad made toast
In Free to be—a family p83-89 **810.8**
The right family
In Free to be—a family p44-48 **810.8**
Durrell, Gerald Malcolm, 1925-
The whispering land [excerpt]
In Animal families of the wild: animal stories p5-16 **591**
Dutton, Roderic
An Arab family (3-5) **953**
Duval, Jonathan
(il) Atkinson, S. Journey into space **523**
Duvoisin, Roger, 1904-1980
The Christmas whale
In The Family read-aloud Christmas treasury p72-79 **808.8**
Our Veronica goes to Petunia's farm. See note under Duvoisin, R. Veronica **E**
Petunia **E**
Petunia, beware! See note under Duvoisin, R. Petunia **E**
Petunia, I love you. See note under Duvoisin, R. Petunia **E**
Petunia takes a trip. See note under Duvoisin, R. Petunia **E**
Petunia the silly goose stories. See note under Duvoisin, R. Petunia **E**
Petunia's Christmas. See note under Duvoisin, R. Petunia **E**
Veronica **E**
(il) Carlson, N. S. The talking cat, and other stories of French Canada **S C**
(il) Fatio, L. The happy lion **E**
(il) Tresselt, A. R. Hide and seek fog **E**
(il) Tresselt, A. R. White snow, bright snow **E**
See/See also pages in the following book(s):
Caldecott Medal books, 1938-1957 p166-83 **028.5**
The **dwarf-wizard** of Uxmal. Shetterly, S. H. **398.2**
Dwarfs
Kuklin, S. Thinking big (2-5) **362.4**
Dwellings *See* Architecture, Domestic
Dyer, Jane
(il) Yolen, J. Piggins and the royal wedding **E**
(il) Yolen, J. The three bears rhyme book **811**
Dylan's day out. Catalanotto, P. **E**
Dynamite Dinah. Mills, C. **Fic**
Dyslexia
Fiction
Greenwald, S. Will the real Gertrude Hollings please stand up? (5 and up) **Fic**

E

E.S.P. *See* Extrasensory perception
Each peach pear plum. Ahlberg, J. **E**
Eads, James Buchanan, 1820-1887
See/See also pages in the following book(s):
McCall, E. S. Biography of a river: the living Mississippi p101-05, 117-21 (6 and up) **977**
Eager, Edward, 1911-1964
Half magic (4-6) **Fic**
Half magic [excerpt]
In The Random House book of humor for children p154-72 **817.008**
Knight's castle. See note under Eager, E. Half magic **Fic**
Magic by the lake. See note under Eager, E. Half magic **Fic**
Seven-day magic (4-6) **Fic**
The time garden. See note under Eager, E. Half magic **Fic**
Eagle, Ellen, 1953-
(il) Branley, F. M. Star guide **523.8**
Eagle, Michael
(il) Lauber, P. Voyagers from space **523.5**
Eagles
See also Bald eagle
Lang, A. Eagles (3-6) **598**
Mannix, D. P. The last eagle
In Animal families of the wild: animal stories p35-43 **591**
Sattler, H. R. The book of eagles (4 and up) **598**
Van Wormer, J. Eagles (4 and up) **598**
Eagles, hawks, and other birds of prey. DeWitt, L. **598**
Ear
Parker, S. The ear and hearing (4 and up) **612.8**
Showers, P. Ears are for hearing (k-3) **612.8**
The **ear**. Babbitt, N.
In Babbitt, N. The Devil's other storybook p73-81 **S C**
The **ear** and hearing. Parker, S. **612.8**
Ear of corn
Grimm, J. The ear of corn
In Grimm, J. The complete Grimm's fairy tales p791-92 **398.2**

Earhart, Amelia, 1898-1937
About
Lauber, P. Lost star: the story of Amelia Earhart (5 and up) **92**
Quackenbush, R. M. Clear the cow pasture, I'm coming in for a landing!: a story of Amelia Earhart (2-4) **92**
Earl Gerald. Leach, M.
In Leach, M. Whistle in the graveyard p20-21 **398.2**
Earl Mar's daughter
Jacobs, J. Earl Mar's daughter
In Jacobs, J. English fairy tales p159-63 **398.2**
Early, Biddy, 1798-1874
Poetry
Willard, N. The ballad of Biddy Early (4 and up) **811**
Early, Margaret
(il) McVitty, W. Ali Baba and the forty thieves **398.2**
An **early** American Christmas. De Paola, T. **E**
Early humans (4 and up) **930.1**
Early moon. Sandburg, C.
In Sandburg, C. The Sandburg treasury p161-207 **818**
Early morning in the barn. Tafuri, N. **E**
Early thunder. Fritz, J. **Fic**
Earrings!. Viorst, J. **E**
Ears are for hearing. Showers, P. **612.8**
Earth
Asimov, I. How did we find out the Earth is round? (5 and up) **525**
Branley, F. M. Mysteries of planet earth (6 and up) **525**
Branley, F. M. What makes day and night (k-3) **525**
Fradin, D. B. Earth (2-4) **525**
Lauber, P. Seeing Earth from space (4 and up) **525**
Simon, S. Earth, our planet in space (1-4) **525**
See/See also pages in the following book(s):
Gallant, R. A. Our restless earth p11-21 (4 and up) **550**
Internal structure
Cole, J. The magic school bus inside the Earth (2-4) **551.1**
McNulty, F. How to dig a hole to the other side of the world (2-4) **551.1**
Poetry
Livingston, M. C. Earth songs **811**
Earth gnome
Grimm, J. The earth gnome
In Grimm, J. More tales from Grimm p171-187 **398.2**
Grimm, J. The gnome
In Grimm, J. The complete Grimm's fairy tales p420-24 **398.2**
Grimm, J. Wanda Gág's The earth gnome **398.2**
Earth, our planet in space. Simon, S. **525**
Earth sciences
Lauber, P. Seeing Earth from space (4 and up) **525**
Earth songs. Livingston, M. C. **811**
Earthenware *See* Pottery
Earthlets, as explained by Professor Xargle. Willis, J. **E**
Earthquakes
Branley, F. M. Earthquakes (k-3) **551.2**
See/See also pages in the following book(s):
Gallant, R. A. Our restless earth p56-62 (4 and up) **550**
Our violent earth p8-21 (4 and up) **363.3**
Earthworks (Archeology) *See* Excavations (Archeology)
East *See* Asia
East (Near East) *See* Middle East
East Africa *See* Africa, East
East o' the sun and west o' the moon
Asbjørnsen, P. C. East o' the sun and west o' the moon
In The Scott, Foresman anthology of children's literature p236-41 **808.8**
Asbjørnsen, P. C. East of the sun and west of the moon
In Best-loved folktales of the world p287-95 **398.2**
In The Blue fairy book p19-29 **398.2**
In Womenfolk and fairy tales p111-26 **398.2**
Hague, K. East of the sun and west of the moon **398.2**
East of the sun and west of the moon: old tales from the North. Asbjørnsen, P. C. **398.2**
Easter
Barth, E. Lilies, rabbits, and painted eggs (3-6) **394.2**
Fisher, A. L. Easter (1-3) **394.2**
Gibbons, G. Easter (k-2) **394.2**
Winthrop, E. He is risen: the Easter story (2-5) **232.9**
See/See also pages in the following book(s):
Araki, C. Origami in the classroom p21-25 (Book II) (4 and up) **736**
Fiction
Adams, A. The Easter egg artists **E**
Heyward, D. The country bunny and the little gold shoes **E**
Hoban, T. Where is it? **E**
Milhous, K. The egg tree **E**
Polacco, P. Rechenka's eggs **E**

Easter—*Continued*

Poetry

Easter poems (3-5) **808.81**

The **Easter** egg artists. Adams, A. **E**

Easter egg decoration *See* Egg decoration

Easter poems (3-5) **808.81**

The **Easter** surprise. Brown, M. W.
In Brown, M. W. The fish with the deep sea smile p53 **818**

Eastman, George, 1854-1932

About

Mitchell, B. CLICK!: a story about George Eastman (3-5) **92**

See/See also pages in the following book(s):
Richards, N. Dreamers & doers: inventors who changed our world p121-53 (6 and up) **920**

Eastman, Mary Huse, 1870-1963
Index to fairy tales, 1949-1972. See Index to fairy tales, 1949-1972 **398.2**
Index to fairy tales, 1973-1977. See Index to fairy tales, 1973-1977 **398.2**

Eastman, P. D. (Philip D.), 1909-1986
Are you my mother? **E**
The Cat in the Hat beginner book dictionary. See The Cat in the Hat beginner book dictionary **423**

Eastman, Philip D. *See* Eastman, P. D. (Philip D.), 1909-1986

Easy as pie. Folsom, M. **E**

The **easy** baseball book. Kalb, J. **796.357**

Easy costumes you don't have to sew. Chernoff, G. T. **391**

The **easy** hockey book. Kalb, J. **796.962**

Eat up, Gemma. Hayes, S. **E**

Eat your poison, dear. Howe, J. See note under Howe, J. Dew drop dead **Fic**

Eating *See* Dinners and dining

Eating customs
See also Table etiquette

Eating disorders

See/See also pages in the following book(s):
Dinner, S. H. Nothing to be ashamed of: growing up with mental illness in your family p126-40 (5 and up) **362.2**

Eating the alphabet. Ehlert, L. **E**

Eats: poems. Adoff, A. **811**

Ebeneezer Never-Could-Sneezer. Patillo, G. S.
In With a deep sea smile p75-81 **372.6**

Eberhard, Wolfram, 1909-1989
Faithful even in death
In Best-loved folktales of the world p531-34 **398.2**
Money makes cares
In Best-loved folktales of the world p548-50 **398.2**

The **ebony** horse. Hodges, M.
In Hodges, M. If you had a horse **398.2**

Eckart, Chuck
(il) Jaspersohn, W. How the forest grew **574.5**

Eckert, Allan W.
Incident at Hawk's Hill (6 and up) **Fic**

Eclipse: darkness in daytime. Branley, F. M. **523.7**

Eclipses, Lunar

See/See also pages in the following book(s):
Gallant, R. A. Rainbows, mirages and sundogs p65-72 (4 and up) **551.5**

Eclipses, Solar
Branley, F. M. Eclipse: darkness in daytime (k-3) **523.7**

See/See also pages in the following book(s):
Gallant, R. A. Rainbows, mirages and sundogs p72-81 (4 and up) **551.5**

Ecology
See also Desert ecology; Environmental protection; Forest ecology; Grassland ecology; Marine ecology; Pond ecology; Prairie ecology; Rain forest ecology; Tundra ecology

Daegling, M. Monster seaweeds (4 and up) **589.4**
Facklam, M. Partners for life (3-6) **591.5**
Hess, L. Secrets in the meadow (4 and up) **591.5**
Hughey, P. Scavengers and decomposers: the cleanup crew (5 and up) **591.5**
Kuhn, D. More than just a flower garden (2-4) **635.9**
Kuhn, D. More than just a vegetable garden (2-4) **635**
Lavies, B. Tree trunk traffic (k-2) **591.5**
Newton, J. R. Rain shadow (2-5) **574.5**
Norsgaard, E. J. Nature's great balancing act (4-6) **574.5**
Parnall, P. Apple tree (k-3) **634**

Fiction

George, J. C. Who really killed Cock Robin? (3-7) **Fic**

Ecuador
Lephien, E. U. Ecuador (4 and up) **986.6**

Ed Emberley's ABC. Emberley, E. **E**

Ed Emberley's big green drawing book. Emberley, E. **741.2**

Ed Emberley's big red drawing book. Emberley, E. **741.2**

Ed Emberley's drawing book: make a world. Emberley, E. **741.2**

Ed Emberley's drawing book of faces. Emberley, E. **743**

Ed Emberley's great thumbprint drawing book. Emberley, E. **743**

Ed Emberley's picture pie: a circle drawing book. Emberley, E. **741.2**

Eddie and his big deals. Haywood, C. See note under Haywood, C. Little Eddie **Fic**

Eddie and the fire engine. Haywood, C. See note under Haywood, C. Little Eddie **Fic**

Eddie's menagerie. Haywood, C. See note under Haywood, C. Little Eddie **Fic**

Eddie's valuable property. Haywood, C. See note under Haywood, C. Little Eddie **Fic**

Eden, Maxwell
Kiteworks: explorations in kite building & flying (5 and up) **796.1**

Edens, Cooper, 1945-
(comp) The Glorious Mother Goose. See The Glorious Mother Goose **398.8**

Edgar Allan. Neufeld, J. **Fic**

Edge of two worlds. Jones, W. **Fic**

Edison, Thomas A. (Thomas Alva), 1847-1931
See/See also pages in the following book(s):
Richards, N. Dreamers & doers: inventors who changed our world p77-119 (6 and up) **920**

Edith herself. Howard, E. **Fic**

Edman, Polly
(jt. auth) Jensen, V. A. Red thread riddles **793.73**

Edmond Halley, the man and his comet. Heckart, B. H. **92**

Edmonds, S. Emma E. (Sarah Emma Evelyn), 1841-1898
About
Reit, S. Behind rebel lines: the incredible story of Emma Edmonds, Civil War spy (4 and up) **92**

Edmonds, Sarah Emma Evelyn *See* Edmonds, S. Emma E. (Sarah Emma Evelyn), 1841-1898

Edmonds, Walter Dumaux, 1903-
Bert Breen's barn (6 and up) **Fic**
The matchlock gun (4-6) **Fic**

See/See also pages in the following book(s):
Newbery Medal books, 1922-1955 p210-24 **028.5**

Edna St. Vincent Millay's poems selected for young people. Millay, E. S. **811**

Education
See also Schools
United States—History
Loeper, J. J. Going to school in 1776 (4 and up) **370.9**
Loeper, J. J. Going to school in 1876 (4 and up) **370.9**

See/See also pages in the following book(s):
Freedman, R. Children of the wild West p59-69 (4 and up) **978**

Education, Bilingual
See/See also pages in the following book(s):
Meltzer, M. The Hispanic Americans p105-11 (6 and up) **305.8**

Education, Elementary
Cole, A. Purple cow to the rescue **372.1**
Periodicals
Childhood Education **372.05**
Instructor **372.05**

Education, Preschool
See also Nursery schools
Cole, A. I saw a purple cow, and 100 other recipes for learning **372.1**
Cole, A. Purple cow to the rescue **372.1**

Educational counseling
See also Vocational guidance

Educators
See also Black educators; Teachers

An **Edward** Lear alphabet. Lear, E. **821**

Edward Lear's The Scroobious Pip. Lear, E. **821**

Edwards, Linda
(il) Gilson, J. 4B goes wild **Fic**

Edwards, Roberta
Five silly fishermen (k-2) **398.2**

Edžiņš. Lacis, V.
In Face to face: a collection of stories by celebrated Soviet and American writers p185-92 **S C**

The **eel's** disguise. Yep, L.
In Yep, L. The rainbow people p38-44 **398.2**

Egan, E. W. (Edward Welstead), 1922-
Sri Lanka—in pictures. See Sri Lanka—in pictures **954.93**

Egan, Edward Welstead *See* Egan, E. W. (Edward Welstead), 1922-

Egg decoration
Fiction
Adams, A. The Easter egg artists **E**

Egg decoration—Fiction—*Continued*
Milhous, K. The egg tree **E**
Egg thoughts, and other Frances songs. Hoban, R. **811**
Egg to chick. Selsam, M. E. **636.5**
The **egg** tree. Milhous, K. **E**
Eggs
Cole, J. A chick hatches (k-3) **636.5**
Johnson, S. A. Inside an egg (4 and up) **598**
McClung, R. M. The amazing egg (4 and up) **591.1**
McNulty, F. Peeping in the shell (2-5) **639.9**
Selsam, M. E. Egg to chick (k-3) **636.5**
See/See also pages in the following book(s):
Markle, S. Exploring spring p43-51 (4 and up) **508**
Fiction
Polacco, P. Rechenka's eggs **E**
Egielski, Richard
(il) Brooke, W. J. A telling of the tales: five stories **S C**
(il) Chaikin, M. Finders weepers **Fic**
(il) Conrad, P. The Tub People **E**
(il) Kennedy, R. Amy's eyes **Fic**
(il) Yorinks, A. Hey, Al **E**
(il) Yorinks, A. It happened in Pinsk **E**
(il) Yorinks, A. Oh, Brother **E**
See/See also pages in the following book(s):
Sendak, M. Caldecott & Co.: notes on books and pictures p139-41 **028.5**
Egoff, Sheila A.
Worlds within **028.5**
(ed) Only connect: readings on children's literature. See Only connect: readings on children's literature **028.5**
Egypt
Cross, W. Egypt (4 and up) **962**
Egypt—in pictures (5 and up) **962**
Antiquities
Bendick, J. Egyptian tombs (4 and up) **932**
Hart, G. Ancient Egypt (4 and up) **932**
Perl, L. Mummies, tombs, and treasure (4 and up) **393**
Civilization
Cohen, D. Ancient Egypt (3-6) **932**
Hart, G. Ancient Egypt (4 and up) **932**
Hart, G. Exploring the past: ancient Egypt (4 and up) **932**
Macaulay, D. Pyramid (4 and up) **726**
Raphael, E. Drawing history: Ancient Egypt (4 and up) **741**
See/See also pages in the following book(s):
The Prince who knew his fate (1-3) **398.2**
Fiction
De Paola, T. Bill and Pete go down the Nile **E**
Stolz, M. Zekmet, the stone carver (2-4) **Fic**
Folklore
See Folklore—Egypt
History
Cohen, D. Ancient Egypt (3-6) **932**
Hart, G. Exploring the past: ancient Egypt (4 and up) **932**
Social life and customs
Bennett, O. A family in Egypt (3-5) **962**
Kristensen, P. S. We live in Egypt (4-6) **962**
The **Egypt** game. Snyder, Z. K. **Fic**
Egypt—in pictures (5 and up) **962**
The **Egyptian** Cinderella. Climo, S. **398.2**
Egyptian language
Katan, N. J. Hieroglyphs, the writing of ancient Egypt **493**
Egyptian tombs. Bendick, J. **932**
Ehlert, Lois, 1934-
Color farm **E**
Color zoo **E**
Eating the alphabet **E**
Feathers for lunch **E**
Growing vegetable soup **E**
Planting a rainbow **E**
(il) Martin, B. Chicka chicka boom boom **E**
Ehrlich, Amy, 1942-
Leo, Zack, and Emmie **E**
Leo, Zack, and Emmie together again **E**
The Random House book of fairy tales (k-3) **398.2**
Contents: The emperor's new clothes; The sleeping beauty in the wood; The elves and the shoemaker; Rapunzel; The twelve dancing princesses; Jack and the beanstalk; Snow White; Puss in boots; Beauty and the beast; The frog prince; The valiant little tailor; Red Riding Hood; The real princess; The steadfast tin soldier; Cinderella; Hansel and Gretel; Rumpelstiltskin; The Snow Queen; Thumbelina
Rapunzel (1-3) **398.2**
The Snow Queen (2-4) **Fic**
The story of Hanukkah (1-3) **296.4**
The wild swans **E**
Wounded Knee: an Indian history of the American West (6 and up) **970.004**
Eichenberg, Fritz, 1901-1990
Ape in a cape **E**
Dancing in the moon **E**
(il) Sandburg, C. Rainbows are made: poems **811**
(il) Sewell, A. Black Beauty **Fic**
(il) Thomas, D. A child's Christmas in Wales **828**
Eight cousins. Alcott, L. M. See note under Alcott, L. M. Little women **Fic**

Eight days of Luke. Jones, D. W. Fic
Eight immortals
Carpenter, F. How the eight old ones crossed the sea
In Carpenter, F. Tales of a Chinese grandmother p150-58 398.2
Eight mules from Monterey. Beatty, P. Fic
Eighty-one brothers
Quayle, E. The white hare and the crocodiles
In Quayle, E. The shining princess, and other Japanese legends p24-32 398.2
Einzig, Susan, 1922-
(il) Pearce, P. Tom's midnight garden Fic
Eisenberg, Lisa, 1949-
(jt. auth) McMullan, K. Snakey riddles 793.73
Eitzen, Allan
(il) Phelan, M. K. The story of the Boston Massacre 973.3
Ekey, Robert
Fire! in Yellowstone (2-4) 574.5
Ekoomiak, Normee
Arctic memories (3-5) 998
El Chino
About
Say, A. El Chino (2-5) 92
The **El Dorado** adventure. Alexander, L. See note under Alexander, L. The Illyrian adventure Fic
El Salvador
Bachelis, F. M. El Salvador (4 and up) 972.84
Elbert, Virginie
Folk toys around the world and how to make them (5 and up) 745.592
Elbert's bad word. Wood, A. E
The **elders** of Chelm & Genendel's key. Singer, I. B.
In Singer, I. B. Stories for children p3-7 S C
In Singer, I. B. When Shlemiel went to Warsaw & other stories p45-51 398.2
Eldredge, Douglas
(jt. auth) Eldredge, N. The fossil factory 560
Eldredge, Gregory
(jt. auth) Eldredge, N. The fossil factory 560
Eldredge, Niles
The fossil factory (4-6) 560
Eleanor, of Aquitaine *See* Eleanor, Queen, consort of Henry II, King of England, 1122?-1204
Eleanor, Queen, consort of Henry II, King of England, 1122?-1204
About
Brooks, P. S. Queen Eleanor: independent spirit of the medieval world (6 and up) 92
Fiction
Konigsburg, E. L. A proud taste for scarlet and miniver (5 and up) Fic
Eleanor, Elizabeth. Gleeson, L. Fic
Eleanor Roosevelt: first lady of the world. Faber, D. 92
Elections
Hewett, J. Getting elected (4 and up) 324
Electric conductors
See also Superconductors and superconductivity
Electric lines
See/See also pages in the following book(s):
Macaulay, D. Underground p67-77 (4 and up) 624.1
Electric power
Cobb, V. More power to you (4-6) 621.31
Electricity
Asimov, I. How did we find out about superconductivity? (5 and up) 537.6
Berger, M. Switch on, switch off (k-3) 537
See/See also pages in the following book(s):
Cobb, V. The secret life of hardware: a science experiment book p66-84 (5 and up) 670
Experiments
Markle, S. Power up (3-5) 537
Math, I. More wires and watts: understanding and using electricity (6 and up) 537
Electrocardiography
See/See also pages in the following book(s):
Aaseng, N. The inventors: Nobel prizes in chemistry, physics, and medicine p27-33 (5 and up) 609
Electromagnetic waves
See also Infrared radiation
Electron microscope and microscopy
Grillone, L. Small worlds close up (5 and up) 500
Electronic data processing
Dictionaries
Simon, S. Bits and bytes: a computer dictionary for beginners (k-3) 004
Elementary education *See* Education, Elementary
Elementary English Review. See Language Arts 372.605
The **Elementary** school library collection 011.6

Elena the Wise
Afanas'ev, A. N. Elena the Wise
In Afanas'ev, A. N. Russian fairy tales p545-49 **398.2**

Elephant crossing. Yoshida, T. **599.6**

Elephant Man *See* Merrick, Joseph Carey, 1862 or 3-1890

The **elephant** man [biography of Joseph Carey Merrick]. Howell, M. **92**

Elephant school. Stewart, J. **636.088**

Elephant seals. Johnson, S. A. **599.74**

Elephants
Schlein, M. Elephants (4-6) **599.6**
Yoshida, T. Elephant crossing (1-3) **599.6**

Fiction

Bollen, M. S. Alistair's elephant **E**
Brunhoff, J. de. The story of Babar, the little elephant **E**
Chorao, K. Kate's box **E**
Day, A. Frank and Ernest **E**
Day, A. Frank and Ernest play ball **E**
Kipling, R. The elephant's child (1-4) **Fic**
Lobel, A. Uncle Elephant **E**
Murphy, J. All in one piece **E**
Murphy, J. Five minutes' peace **E**
Paxton, T. Engelbert the elephant **E**
Petersham, M. The circus baby **E**
Platt, K. Big Max **E**
Seuss, Dr. Horton hatches the egg **E**
Seuss, Dr. Horton hears a Who! **E**

Training

Stewart, J. Elephant school (4-6) **636.088**

The **elephant's** child. Kipling, R. **Fic**
also in Kipling, R. Just so stories **S C**
also in The Random House book of humor for children p83-92 **817.008**
also in The Scott, Foresman anthology of children's literature p487-91 **808.8**

Elephants on the beach. Bare, C. S. **599.74**

The **elevator**. Sleator, W.
In Things that go bump in the night p6-14 **S C**

The **eleventh** hour. Base, G. **Fic**

Elfwyn's saga. Wisniewski, D. **E**

Eli. Peet, B. **E**

Elijah the slave. Singer, I. B.
In Singer, I. B. Stories for children p206-09 **S C**

Eliot, T. S. (Thomas Stearns), 1888-1965
Growltiger's last stand (2-5) **811**

Eliot, Thomas Stearns *See* Eliot, T. S. (Thomas Stearns), 1888-1965

Elizabeth I, Queen of England, 1533-1603

About

Stanley, D. Good Queen Bess: the story of Elizabeth I of England (3-5) **92**

Elizabeth, Empress of Russia, 1709-1762

Fiction

Almedingen, E. M. The crimson oak (5 and up) **Fic**

Elizabeth Petrovna *See* Elizabeth, Empress of Russia, 1709-1762

Elk
Arnold, C. Tule elk (3-6) **599.73**

Ella of all of a kind family. Taylor, S. See note under Taylor, S. All-of-a-kind family **Fic**

Elledge, Scott
(ed) Wider than the sky: poems to grow up with. See Wider than the sky: poems to grow up with **821.008**

Elleman, Barbara
(ed) Association for Library Service to Children (U.S.). International Relations Committee. Children's books of international interest **011.6**

Ellen Grae. Cleaver, V. **Fic**

Ellen Tebbits. Cleary, B. **Fic**

Elliott, Bob
See also Bob and Ray

Elliott, Donald
Frogs and the ballet (4 and up) **792.8**

Elliott, Elizabeth Shippen Green *See* Green, Elizabeth Shippen, 1871-1954

Ellis, Amabel Williams- *See* Williams-Ellis, Amabel, 1894-1984

Ellis, Sarah
Next-door neighbors (4 and up) **Fic**

Ellis Island. Fisher, L. E. **325.73**

Ellis Island Immigration Station
Fisher, L. E. Ellis Island (4 and up) **325.73**
Jacobs, W. J. Ellis Island (3-5) **325.73**
Siegel, B. Sam Ellis's island (3-6) **325.73**

Elting, Mary, 1909-
The Macmillan book of dinosaurs and other prehistoric creatures (4 and up) **560**
The Macmillan book of the human body (4 and up) **612**

Elves and the shoemaker
Ehrlich, A. The elves and the shoemaker
In Ehrlich, A. The Random House book of fairy tales p22-25 **398.2**
Galdone, P. The elves and the shoemaker **398.2**
Grimm, J. The elves and the shoemaker
In The Family read-aloud Christmas treasury p18-21 **808.8**

Elves and the shoemaker—*Continued*
In The Scott, Foresman anthology of children's literature p187-88 **808.8**
In Tomie dePaola's favorite nursery tales p100-04 **398.2**
Grimm, J. The elves and the shoemaker whose work they did
In Grimm, J. About wise men and simpletons p31-32 **398.2**
Grimm, J. The elves: first story
In Grimm, J. The complete Grimm's fairy tales p197-98 **398.2**
Grimm, J. The shoemaker and the elves
In Grimm, J. More tales from Grimm p251-57 **398.2**
Littledale, F. The elves and the shoemaker **398.2**
Oxenbury, H. The elves and the shoemaker
In Oxenbury, H. The Helen Oxenbury nursery story book p47-53 **398.2**
Rockwell, A. F. The shoemaker and the elves
In Rockwell, A. F. The three bears & 15 other stories p71-77 **398.2**
Thane, A. The elves and the shoemaker
In Thane, A. Plays from famous stories and fairy tales p90-104 **812**
The **elves** ask a servant girl to be godmother. Grimm, J.
In Grimm, J. About wise men and simpletons p33 **398.2**
The **elves**: first story. Grimm, J.
In Grimm, J. The complete Grimm's fairy tales p197-98 **398.2**
The **elves**: second story. Grimm, J.
In Grimm, J. The complete Grimm's fairy tales p199 **398.2**
The **elves**: third story. Grimm, J.
In Grimm, J. The complete Grimm's fairy tales p200 **398.2**
Emberley, Barbara
Drummer Hoff (k-3) **398.8**
(il) Branley, F. M. Flash, crash, rumble, and roll **551.5**
(il) Branley, F. M. The moon seems to change **523.3**
(il) Simon, S. Bits and bytes: a computer dictionary for beginners **004**
(il) Simon, S. How to talk to your computer **005**
(il) Simon, S. Meet the computer **004**
Emberley, Ed
Ed Emberley's ABC **E**
Ed Emberley's big green drawing book (2-5) **741.2**
Ed Emberley's big red drawing book (2-5) **741.2**
Ed Emberley's drawing book: make a world (2-5) **741.2**
Ed Emberley's drawing book of faces (2-5) **743**
Ed Emberley's great thumbprint drawing book (2-5) **743**
Ed Emberley's picture pie: a circle drawing book (2-5) **741.2**
Green says go (k-3) **535.6**
The wing on a flea **E**
(il) Branley, F. M. Flash, crash, rumble, and roll **551.5**
(il) Branley, F. M. The moon seems to change **523.3**
(il) Emberley, B. Drummer Hoff **398.8**
(il) Simon, S. Bits and bytes: a computer dictionary for beginners **004**
(il) Simon, S. How to talk to your computer **005**
(il) Simon, S. Meet the computer **004**
See/See also pages in the following book(s):
Newbery and Caldecott Medal books, 1966-1975 p199-207 **028.5**
Emberley, Michael, 1960-
Ruby **E**
Emberley, Rebecca
My house/mi casa: a book in two languages (k-3) **463**
Taking a walk/caminando: a book in two languages (k-3) **463**
Embroidery
Fiction
Fair, S. The bedspread **E**
Embryology
See also Fetus; Reproduction
Selsam, M. E. Egg to chick (k-3) **636.5**
Emelya the simpleton. Afanas'ev, A. N.
In Afanas'ev, A. N. Russian fairy tales p46-48 **398.2**
Emergency Librarian **027.6205**
The **emergency** room. Rockwell, A. F. **362.1**
Emigration *See* Immigration and emigration
Emma. Kesselman, W. A. **E**
Emma. Stevenson, J. **E**
Emma at the beach. Stevenson, J. See note under Stevenson, J. Emma **E**
Emma's pet. McPhail, D. M. See note under McPhail, D. M. Fix-it **E**
Emma's vacation. McPhail, D. M. See note under McPhail, D. M. Fix-it **E**
Emmert, Amy
About
Emmert, M. I'm the big sister now (3-5) **362.4**
Emmert, Michelle
I'm the big sister now (3-5) **362.4**

Emmet Otter's Jug-Band Christmas. Hoban, R.
In The Family read-aloud Christmas treasury p92-101 **808.8**

Emmett's pig. Stolz, M. **E**

Emotions
Aliki. Feelings (k-3) **152.4**

Emperors *See* Kings, queens, rulers, etc.

Emperor's new clothes
Andersen, H. C. The emperor's new clothes **Fic**
also in Andersen, H. C. Hans Andersen: his classic fairy tales p119-24 **S C**
also in The Scott, Foresman anthology of children's literature p537-40 **808.8**
also in Tomie dePaola's favorite nursery tales p87-95 **398.2**
also in The Yellow fairy book p21-25 **398.2**
Ehrlich, A. The emperor's new clothes
In Ehrlich, A. The Random House book of fairy tales p3-9 **398.2**
Rockwell, A. F. The emperor's new clothes **Fic**

The **Emperor's** nightingale. Thane, A.
In Thane, A. Plays from famous stories and fairy tales p3-19 **812**

Empire State Building (New York, N.Y.)
Macaulay, D. Unbuilding (4 and up) **690**

Employees

Training

See also Apprentices

Employment guidance *See* Vocational guidance

Employment of children *See* Children—Employment

Employment of women *See* Women—Employment

The **empty** pot. Demi. **398.2**

Empty world. Christopher, J. **Fic**

The **enchanted** boy. Hunter, M.
In Hunter, M. A furl of fairy wind: four stories p17-29 **S C**

Enchanted buck
Berger, T. The enchanted buck
In Berger, T. Black fairy tales p43-54 **398.2**

Enchanted canary
Deulin, C. The enchanted canary
In The Red fairy book p257-73 **398.2**

The **enchanted** caribou. Cleaver, E. **398.2**

Enchanted cave of Cesh Corran
Stephens, J. The enchanted cave of Cesh Corran
In Stephens, J. Irish fairy tales p201-18 **398.2**

The **enchanted** goat. Simon, S.
In Simon, S. More wise men of Helm and their merry tales p80-101 **398.2**

Enchanted horse
The Enchanted horse
In The Arabian nights entertainments p358-89 **398.2**

Enchanted pig
The Enchanted pig
In The Red fairy book p104-15 **398.2**

The **enchanted** princess. Afanas'ev, A. N.
In Afanas'ev, A. N. Russian fairy tales p600-11 **398.2**

The **enchanted** ring. Afanas'ev, A. N.
In Afanas'ev, A. N. Russian fairy tales p31-37 **398.2**

The **enchanted** ring. Fénelon, F. de S. de L. M.
In The Green fairy book p137-44 **398.2**

Enchanted snake
The Enchanted snake
In The Green fairy book p186-93 **398.2**

The **enchanted** tapestry. San Souci, R. **398.2**

Enchanted watch
Deulin, C. The enchanted watch
In The Green fairy book p43-47 **398.2**

The **enchanted** world. See Williams-Ellis, A. Tales from the enchanted world **398.2**

Encounters with the invisible world. Roach, M. K. **S C**

Encyclopedia Brown and the case of the dead eagles. Sobol, D. J. See note under Sobol, D. J. Encyclopedia Brown, boy detective **Fic**

Encyclopedia Brown and the case of the disgusting sneakers. Sobol, D. J. See note under Sobol, D. J. Encyclopedia Brown, boy detective **Fic**

Encyclopedia Brown and the case of the exploding plumbing. Sobol, D. J. See note under Sobol, D. J. Encyclopedia Brown, boy detective **Fic**

Encyclopedia Brown and the case of the midnight visitor. Sobol, D. J. See note under Sobol, D. J. Encyclopedia Brown, boy detective **Fic**

Encyclopedia Brown and the case of the mysterious handprints. Sobol, D. J. See note under Sobol, D. J. Encyclopedia Brown, boy detective **Fic**

Encyclopedia Brown and the case of the secret pitch. Sobol, D. J. See note under Sobol, D. J. Encyclopedia Brown, boy detective **Fic**

Encyclopedia Brown and the case of the treasure hunt. Sobol, D. J. See note under Sobol, D. J. Encyclopedia Brown, boy detective **Fic**

Encyclopedia Brown, boy detective. Sobol, D. J. **Fic**

Encyclopedia Brown carries on. Sobol, D. J. See note under Sobol, D. J. Encyclopedia Brown, boy detective **Fic**

Encyclopedia Brown finds the clues. Sobol, D. J. See note under Sobol, D. J. Encyclopedia Brown, boy detective **Fic**

Encyclopedia Brown gets his man. Sobol, D. J. See note under Sobol, D. J. Encyclopedia Brown, boy detective **Fic**

Encyclopedia Brown keeps the peace. Sobol, D. J. See note under Sobol, D. J. Encyclopedia Brown, boy detective **Fic**

Encyclopedia Brown lends a hand. Sobol, D. J. See note under Sobol, D. J. Encyclopedia Brown, boy detective **Fic**

Encyclopedia Brown saves the day. Sobol, D. J. See note under Sobol, D. J. Encyclopedia Brown, boy detective **Fic**

Encyclopedia Brown sets the pace. Sobol, D. J. See note under Sobol, D. J. Encyclopedia Brown, boy detective **Fic**

Encyclopedia Brown shows the way. Sobol, D. J. See note under Sobol, D. J. Encyclopedia Brown, boy detective **Fic**

Encyclopedia Brown solves them all. Sobol, D. J. See note under Sobol, D. J. Encyclopedia Brown, boy detective **Fic**

Encyclopedia Brown takes the cake! Sobol, D. J. See note under Sobol, D. J. Encyclopedia Brown, boy detective **Fic**

Encyclopedia Brown takes the case. Sobol, D. J. See note under Sobol, D. J. Encyclopedia Brown, boy detective **Fic**

Encyclopedia Brown tracks them down. Sobol, D. J. See note under Sobol, D. J. Encyclopedia Brown, boy detective **Fic**

Encyclopedia buying guide. See Kister, K. F. Best encyclopedias: a guide to general and specialized encyclopedias **016**

An **encyclopedia** of fairies. Briggs, K. M. **398.03**

Encyclopedia of the nations, Worldmark **910.3**

Encyclopedias and dictionaries

See also Picture dictionaries; Polyglot dictionaries; names of languages and subjects with the subdivision Dictionaries

Compton's encyclopedia and fact-index **031**

The Guinness book of answers **032.02**

Kane, J. N. Famous first facts: a record of first happenings, discoveries, and inventions in American history **031.02**

Merit students encyclopedia **031**

The New book of knowledge **031**

The World Book encyclopedia **031**

Bibliography

Kister, K. F. Best encyclopedias: a guide to general and specialized encyclopedias **016**

The **end** of Brer Bear. Lester, J.

In Lester, J. The tales of Uncle Remus p74-75 **398.2**

The **end** of silence. Aiken, J.

In Aiken, J. Give yourself a fright: thirteen tales of the supernatural p123-35 **S C**

The **end** of the road. DuBois, G.

In Holiday plays round the year p179-88 **812.008**

The **end** of the world: the buffalo go. Marriott, A. L.

In Marriott, A. L. American Indian mythology **398.2**

Endangered species

See also Rare animals; Wildlife conservation

Ancona, G. Turtle watch (2-4) **597.9**

Pringle, L. P. Saving our wildlife (5 and up) **639.9**

Fiction

Schlein, M. The year of the panda (3-5) **Fic**

Endicott, James R., 1946-

(il) Martin, B. Listen to the rain **E**

The **endless** migration [excerpt]. Caras, R. A.

In Animal families of the wild: animal stories p69-79 **591**

Enemies. Klein, R. **Fic**

Enemies of the eye. Fleischman, P.

In Fleischman, P. Coming-and-going men p51-80 **S C**

The **enemy**. Garfield, L.

In Garfield, L. The apprentices **S C**

An **enemy** at Green Knowe. Boston, L. M. See note under Boston, L. M. The children of Green Knowe **Fic**

Energy *See* Force and energy
Energy conservation
Gardiner, B. Energy demands (5 and up) **333.79**
Energy demands. Gardiner, B. **333.79**
Engelbert the elephant. Paxton, T. **E**
Engelhart, Margaret, 1924-
(jt. auth) Kurelek, W. They sought a new world **325**
Engineers Corps *See* United States. Army. Corps of Engineers
England, Claire
ChildView: evaluating and reviewing materials for children **028.5**
England
England—in pictures (5 and up) **942**
Farm life
See Farm life—England
Fiction
Doherty, B. White Peak Farm (5 and up) **Fic**
History
See Great Britain—History
Social life and customs
Sancha, S. The Luttrell village (6 and up) **942.03**
Sancha, S. Walter Dragun's town (6 and up) **942.03**
Social life and customs—Pictorial works
Goodall, J. S. The story of a castle (3-6) **942**
Goodall, J. S. The story of a farm (3-6) **942**
Goodall, J. S. The story of a main street (3-6) **942**
Goodall, J. S. The story of an English village (3-6) **942**
England—in pictures (5 and up) **942**
Engle, Eloise Katherine *See* Paananen, Eloise
English fables and fairy stories. Reeves, J. **398.2**
English fairy tales. Jacobs, J. **398.2**
English folk and fairy tales. See Jacobs, J. English fairy tales **398.2**
English language
Comparison
McMillan, B. Super, super, superwords (k-2) **422**
Composition and exercises
Benjamin, C. L. Writing for kids (4 and up) **808**
Cassedy, S. In your own words (6 and up) **808**
Dictionaries
12,000 words **423**
The American Heritage children's dictionary (3-6) **423**
The American Heritage first dictionary (1-3) **423**
The Cat in the Hat beginner book dictionary (k-3) **423**
Grisewood, J. The Doubleday children's dictionary (4 and up) **423**
Hillerich, R. L. The American Heritage picture dictionary (k-1) **423**
The Lincoln writing dictionary for children (4 and up) **423**
Macmillan dictionary for children (3 and up) **423**
Macmillan dictionary for students (4 and up) **423**
Macmillan very first dictionary (1-3) **423**
Scott, Foresman intermediate dictionary (5 and up) **423**
Thorndike-Barnhart children's dictionary (3-5) **423**
Webster's elementary dictionary (4-6) **423**
Webster's intermediate dictionary (5 and up) **423**
Webster's school dictionary (6 and up) **423**
Webster's third new international dictionary of the English language **423**
Webster's II Riverside children's dictionary (3-6) **423**
Words for new readers (k-1) **423**
The World Book dictionary (5 and up) **423**
The World Book student dictionary (3-5) **423**
Etymology
Asimov, I. Words from the myths (6 and up) **292**
Sarnoff, J. Words: a book about the origins of everyday words and phrases (4 and up) **422**
Terban, M. Guppies in tuxedos: funny eponyms (3-5) **422**
Terban, M. Superdupers! really funny real words (3-5) **427**
Grammar
Heller, R. Kites sail high: a book about verbs (k-2) **428**
Heller, R. Many luscious lollipops: a book about adjectives (k-2) **428**
Idioms
Terban, M. Mad as a wet hen! and other funny idioms (3-5) **427**
Terban, M. Punching the clock: funny action idioms (3-6) **427**
Study and teaching—Periodicals
Language Arts **372.605**
Synonyms and antonyms
Bellamy, J. The Doubleday children's thesaurus (4-6) **423**
Hoban, T. Exactly the opposite **E**
Hoban, T. Push pull, empty full **E**
McMillan, B. Becca backward, Becca frontward (k-2) **428**

English language—Synonyms and antonyms —*Continued*
McMillan, B. Here a chick, there a chick (k-2) **428**
The Random House thesaurus **423**
Schiller, A. Roget's children's thesaurus (3-5) **423**
Schiller, A. Roget's student thesaurus (5 and up) **423**
Spier, P. Fast-slow, high-low **E**

Terms and phrases

Heller, R. A cache of jewels and other collective nouns (k-2) **428**
Hooper, P. A bundle of beasts (3-6) **811**
Juster, N. As: a surfeit of similes (3-5) **427**
Terban, M. Mad as a wet hen! and other funny idioms (3-5) **427**

English literature

Collected works

A Nursery companion **398.8**

English poetry

Collected works

A Child's treasury of poems (3-5) **821.008**
Creatures (3-5) **821.008**
Dilly dilly piccalilli (2-4) **808.81**
Ghost poems (1-4) **821.008**
A Great big ugly man came up and tied his horse to me (k-3) **821.008**
If there were dreams to sell (k-3) **821.008**
Knock at a star (3-6) **821.008**
Laughable limericks (4 and up) **821.008**
Miracles: poems by children of the English-speaking world **821.008**
Monster poems (1-4) **821.008**
My tang's tungled and other ridiculous situations (3-6) **821.008**
A New treasury of children's poetry **821.008**
Of quarks, quasars, and other quirks (5 and up) **821.008**
Oh, such foolishness! (3-6) **821.008**
Oh, that's ridiculous! (3-6) **821.008**
The Oxford book of children's verse **821.008**
Poems to read to the very young (k-2) **821.008**
The Poetry troupe **821.008**
Rainbow in the sky (k-4) **821.008**
The Random House book of poetry for children **821.008**
Read-aloud rhymes for the very young (k-2) **821.008**
Shrieks at midnight (4 and up) **821.008**
Tripp, W. Marguerite, go wash your feet (1-3) **821.008**
Wider than the sky: poems to grow up with (5 and up) **821.008**
Witch poems (1-4) **821.008**

Engvick, William
(ed) Lullabies and night songs. See Lullabies and night songs **782.42**

Enigmas *See* Curiosities and wonders

Enik, Ted
(il) Cobb, V. Why can't you unscramble an egg? and other not such dumb questions about matter **530**
(il) Cobb, V. Why doesn't the earth fall up? **531**

Enk, Scott
(ed) Turkey. See Turkey **956.1**

The **enormous** egg. Butterworth, O. **Fic**

Enright, Elizabeth, 1909-1968
Gone-Away Lake (4-6) **Fic**
Thimble summer (4-6) **Fic**
See/See also pages in the following book(s):
Newbery Medal books, 1922-1955 p168-75 **028.5**

Enright, Maginel Wright
(il) Dodge, M. M. Hans Brinker; or, The silver skates **Fic**

Entertainers
See also Black entertainers

Fiction

Ackerman, K. Song and dance man **E**
Byars, B. C. The Golly Sisters go West **E**
Byars, B. C. Hooray for the Golly sisters! **E**

Envious man and him who was envied
The Story of the envious man and of him who was envied
In The Arabian nights entertainments p86-101 **398.2**

Environment
See also Environmental protection

Environment, Space *See* Space environment

Environmental health
Pringle, L. P. Living in a risky world (6 and up) **363**

Environmental pollution *See* Pollution

Environmental protection

Fiction

Van Allsburg, C. Just a dream **E**

Ephron, Delia
How to hang up the telephone
In The Random House book of humor for children p268-69 **817.008**

An **epidemic** of ducks. Sanfield, S.
In Sanfield, S. The adventures of High John the Conqueror **398.2**

Epigrams
See also Proverbs; Quotations
Best wishes, amen (5 and up) **808.88**

Epilepsy
Fiction
Girion, B. A handful of stars (6 and up) Fic
Howard, E. Edith herself (4-6) Fic
Epstein, Beryl Williams, 1910-
(jt. auth) Epstein, S. Bugs for dinner? 591.5
(jt. auth) Epstein, S. Dr. Beaumont and the man with the hole in his stomach 92
Epstein, Sam, 1909-
Bugs for dinner? (4-6) 591.5
Dr. Beaumont and the man with the hole in his stomach (4-6) 92
Equestrianism *See* Horseback riding
Eric Carle's animals, animals. Carle, E. 808.81
Erickson, Russell E.
A toad for Tuesday (2-4) Fic
Warton and the contest. See note under Erickson, R. E. A toad for Tuesday Fic
The **Erie** Canal (k-4) 781.62
Eriksson, Eva
(il) Lindgren, B. Sam's car E
(il) Lindgren, B. The wild baby E
(il) Nilsson, U. If you didn't have me Fic
The **Erl** King's daughter. Aiken, J.
In Aiken, J. Give yourself a fright: thirteen tales of the supernatural p109-22 S C
Ernest and Celestine. Vincent, G. E
Ernest and Celestine at the circus. Vincent, G. See note under Vincent, G. Ernest and Celestine E
Ernest and Celestine's patchwork quilt. Vincent, G. See note under Vincent, G. Ernest and Celestine E
Ernest and Celestine's picnic. Vincent, G. See note under Vincent, G. Ernest and Celestine E
Ernst, Lisa Campbell, 1957-
Sam Johnson and the blue ribbon quilt E
When Bluebell sang E
Eros (Greek deity)
Hodges, M. The arrow and the lamp 292
Eros and Psyche
In Best-loved folktales of the world p180-86 398.2
Esbensen, Barbara Juster
Cold stars and fireflies (4 and up) 811
Great northern diver: the loon (1-4) 598
Ladder to the sky (k-3) 398.2
The star maiden: an Ojibway tale (k-3) 398.2
Words with wrinkled knees: animal poems (2-5) 811
Escape to Witch Mountain. Key, A. Fic
Eskimos *See* Inuit
ESP *See* Extrasensory perception
Espenshade, Edward Bowman, 1910-
(ed) Goode's world atlas. See Goode's world atlas 912
Espionage
See also Spies
Espy, Willard R.
A children's almanac of words at play (3-6) 808.87
The **esrog**. Sholem Aleichem.
In Sholem Aleichem. Holiday tales of Sholem Aleichem S C
Esteban and the ghost. Hancock, S. 398.2
Estes, Eleanor, 1906-1988
Ginger Pye (4-6) Fic
The hundred dresses (4-6) Fic
The middle Moffat. See note under Estes, E. The Moffats Fic
The Moffat Museum. See note under Estes, E. The Moffats Fic
The Moffats (4-6) Fic
Pinky Pye (4-6) Fic
Rufus M. See note under Estes, E. The Moffats Fic
The witch family (2-5) Fic
See/See also pages in the following book(s):
Newbery Medal books, 1922-1955 p374-87 028.5
Townsend, J. R. A sense of story p79-85 028.5
Estevan, d. 1539
Fiction
Baker, B. Walk the world's rim (5 and up) Fic
O'Dell, S. The King's fifth (5 and up) Fic
Esther, Queen of Persia
About
Chaikin, M. Esther (1-3) 296.4
Ethiopia
Ethiopia—in pictures (5 and up) 963
Fradin, D. B. Ethiopia (4 and up) 963
Ethiopia—in pictures (5 and up) 963
Ethnic groups
See also Minorities
The In America series (5 and up) 305.8

Ethnic relations
See also Race relations
Ethnology
See also Costume
Africa
Chiasson, J. C. African journey (4 and up) **960**
Musgrove, M. Ashanti to Zulu: African traditions (3-6) **960**
Kenya
See also Masai (African people)
Etiquette
See also Table etiquette
Joslin, S. What do you do, dear? (k-2) **395**
Joslin, S. What do you say, dear? (k-2) **395**
Fiction
Hoban, R. Dinner at Alberta's **E**
Ets, Marie Hall, 1893-
Gilberto and the Wind **E**
In the forest **E**
Just me **E**
Play with me **E**
Ettlinger, John R. T.
Choosing books for young people v2 **011.6**
Eugenie
(il) Merriam, E. Mommies at work **331.4**
(il) Raffi. One light, one sun **782.42**
Eulenspiegel
Williams, J. The Christmas thief
In The Family read-aloud Christmas treasury p44-49 **808.8**
Europe
Folklore
See Folklore—Europe
History
Lyttle, R. B. Land beyond the river (6 and up) **940.1**
Pictorial works
Anno, M. Anno's journey **E**
European War, 1914-1918 *See* World War, 1914-1918
Eutemey, Loring
(il) Kettelkamp, L. Magic made easy **793.8**
Evacuation and relocation of Japanese Americans, 1942-1945 *See* Japanese Americans—Evacuation and relocation, 1942-1945
Evans, C. S. (Charles Seddon), 1883-1944
The sleeping beauty (3-5) **398.2**
Evans, Charles Seddon *See* Evans, C. S. (Charles Seddon), 1883-1944
Evans, Ivor H.
(ed) Brewer's dictionary of phrase and fable. See Brewer's dictionary of phrase and fable **803**
Evans, J. Edward
Freedom of the press (5 and up) **323.44**
Eve (Biblical figure)
About
Hutton, W. Adam and Eve (k-3) **222**
Even that moose won't listen to me. Alexander, M. G. **E**
An **evening** at Alfie's. Hughes, S. See note under Hughes, S. Alfie gets in first **E**
Everett Anderson's goodbye. Clifton, L. **811**
Everett Anderson's nine month long. Clifton, L. See note under Clifton, L. Everett Anderson's goodbye **811**
Every day is Thanksgiving. DuBois, G.
In Holiday plays round the year p47-58 **812.008**
Every living thing. Rylant, C. **S C**
Everyday plays for boys and girls. Gotwalt, H. L. M. **812**
Everyone asked about you. Gross, T. F. **E**
Everyone else's parents said yes. Danziger, P. **Fic**
Everyone is good for something. De Regniers, B. S. **398.2**
Everyone knows what a dragon looks like. Williams, J. **E**
Everyone wears his name: a biography of Levi Strauss. Henry, S. **92**
Everyone wins at tee ball. Grosshandler, H. **796.357**
Eve's various children
Grimm, J. Eve's various children
In Grimm, J. The complete Grimm's fairy tales p734-36 **398.2**
Evil *See* Good and evil
The **evil** spell. McCully, E. A. See note under McCully, E. A. Zaza's big break **E**
Evinrude, Ole, 1877-1934
See/See also pages in the following book(s):
Aaseng, N. The problem solvers p39-45 (5 and up) **920**
Evolution
Cole, J. Evolution (k-3) **575**
Gallant, R. A. Before the sun dies (6 and up) **575**
Evslin, Bernard, 1922-
Hercules (5 and up) **292**
Jason and the Argonauts (6 and up) **292**

Ewing, C. S.
(il) Silverman, M. Festival of freedom **296.4**
(il) Tresselt, A. R. Wake up, city! **E**
Ewing, Juliana Horatia, 1841-1885
Murdoch's rath
In Bauer, C. F. Celebrations p183-88 **808.8**
Ex-service men *See* Veterans
Exactly the opposite. Hoban, T. **E**
Excavations (Archeology)
Goor, R. Pompeii: exploring a Roman ghost town (5 and up) **937**
Humphrey, K. L. Pompeii (4 and up) **937**
Exceptional children
See also Handicapped children
Exciting, funny, scary, short, different, and sad books kids like about animals, science, sports, families, songs, and other things. Carroll, F. L. **011.6**
Exercise
See also T'ai chi ch'üan
Fiction
Ormerod, J. Bend and stretch **E**
Exercises, Reducing *See* Reducing
Exiles *See* Refugees
Exodus. Chaikin, M. **222**
Expanding universe *See* Universe
Experimenting with a microscope. Bleifeld, M. **502.8**
Experimenting with air and flight. Walker, O. H. **507**
The **exploding** frog and other fables from Aesop. McFarland, J. B. **398.2**
Explorations *See* Discoveries (in geography)
The **explorer** of Barkham Street. Stolz, M. See note under Stolz, M. A dog on Barkham Street **Fic**
Explorers
Ceserani, G. P. Marco Polo (3-6) **92**
D'Aulaire, I. Columbus (1-4) **92**
Ferris, J. Arctic explorer: the story of Matthew Henson (3-6) **92**
Fritz, J. Where do you think you're going, Christopher Columbus? (3-5) **92**
Humble, R. The travels of Marco Polo (4-6) **910.4**
Levinson, N. S. Christopher Columbus: voyager to the unknown (4 and up) **92**
Swan, R. Destination: Antarctica (4-6) **998**
Exploring spring. Markle, S. **508**
Exploring summer. Markle, S. **508**
Exploring the night sky. Dickinson, T. **523**
Exploring the past: ancient Egypt. Hart, G. **932**
Exploring the Titanic. Ballard, R. D. **910.4**
Exploring winter. Markle, S. **508**
Exploring your solar system. Rathbun, E. **523.2**
Exploring your world: the adventure of geography **910.3**
Express highways
Fiction
Hurd, T. Axle the freeway cat **E**
Express train to trouble. Quackenbush, R. M. **Fic**
Extinct animals
See also Prehistoric animals; Rare animals
Facklam, M. And then there was one (4-6) **591.5**
Giants from the past: the age of mammals (5 and up) **569**
The **extinguished** lights. Singer, I. B.
In Singer, I. B. The power of light p13-20 **S C**
In Singer, I. B. Stories for children p15-21 **S C**
Extraordinary black Americans. Altman, S. R. **920**
Extrasensory perception
Fiction
Conford, E. And this is Laura (4-6) **Fic**
Mahy, M. The haunting (5 and up) **Fic**
Sleator, W. Into the dream (5 and up) **Fic**
Extraterrestrial beings
See/See also pages in the following book(s):
Berger, M. UFOs, ETs & visitors from space (5 and up) **001.9**
Fiction
Willis, J. Earthlets, as explained by Professor Xargle **E**
Yorinks, A. Company's coming **E**
Extraterrestrial communication *See* Interstellar communication
Exupéry, Antoine de Saint- *See* Saint-Exupéry, Antoine de, 1900-1944
Eye
Parker, S. The eye and seeing (4 and up) **612.8**
The **eye** and seeing. Parker, S. **612.8**
Eye winker, Tom Tinker, chin chopper. Glazer, T. **796.1**
Eyeglasses
Silverstein, A. Glasses and contact lenses (6 and up) **617.7**
Fiction
Giff, P. R. Watch out, Ronald Morgan! **E**

Eyeglasses—Fiction—*Continued*
Raskin, E. Spectacles **E**

Eyeopeners!. Kobrin, B. **028.5**

Eyes of marriage. Terada, A. M.
In Terada, A. M. Under the starfruit tree p64-68 **398.2**

The **eyes** of the Amaryllis. Babbitt, N. **Fic**

The **eyes** of the dragon. Leaf, M. **E**

The **eyes** of the killer robot. Bellairs, J. See note under Bellairs, J. The curse of the blue figurine **Fic**

F

Faber, Doris, 1924-
Eleanor Roosevelt: first lady of the world (4 and up) **92**

Fables
Aesop. Aesop's fables **398.2**
Aesop. Aesop's fables (1-3) **398.2**
Anno, M. Anno's Aesop (2-4) **398.2**
The Baby's story book (k-1) **398.2**
Bierhorst, J. Doctor Coyote (1-4) **398.2**
Bolliger, M. Tales of a long afternoon (k-3) **398.2**
Brown, M. Once upon a mouse (k-3) **398.2**
Cauley, L. B. The town mouse and the country mouse (k-3) **398.2**
Cooney, B. Chanticleer and the fox **E**
Demi. A Chinese zoo: fables and proverbs (3-5) **398.2**
Galdone, P. The monkey and the crocodile (k-2) **398.2**
Galdone, P. Three Aesop fox fables (k-3) **398.2**
The Hare and the tortoise (k-3) **398.2**
Jacobs, J. The fables of Aesop (4 and up) **398.2**
McFarland, J. B. The exploding frog and other fables from Aesop (k-3) **398.2**
Stevens, J. The town mouse and the country mouse (k-2) **398.2**
Tomie dePaola's Favorite nursery tales (k-3) **398.2**
Wildsmith, B. The hare and the tortoise (k-2) **398.2**
Wildsmith, B. The miller, the boy and the donkey (k-2) **398.2**
Wildsmith, B. The rich man and the shoe-maker (k-2) **398.2**
See/See also pages in the following book(s):
The Scott, Foresman anthology of children's literature p408-17 **808.8**

Bibliography
See/See also pages in the following book(s):
Bauer, C. F. Handbook for storytellers p121-24 **372.6**

Fables. Lobel, A. **Fic**

The **fables** of Aesop. Jacobs, J. **398.2**

Fabulous beasts. Lurie, A. **398**

Face
Haldane, S. Painting faces (4-6) **745.5**

Face in art
Emberley, E. Ed Emberley's drawing book of faces (2-5) **743**

The **face** in the cloth. Yolen, J.
In Yolen, J. The faery flag p87-100 **S C**

Face to face: a collection of stories by celebrated Soviet and American writers (5 and up) **S C**

Faces. Brenner, B. **612.8**
306.05

Facklam, Howard
Plants: extinction or survival? (6 and up) **581**
(jt. auth) Facklam, M. The brain **612.8**

Facklam, Margery
And then there was one (4-6) **591.5**
The brain (6 and up) **612.8**
Do not disturb (3-6) **591.5**
Partners for life (3-6) **591.5**
(jt. auth) Facklam, H. Plants: extinction or survival? **581**

Facklam, Paul
(il) Facklam, M. The brain **612.8**

Factorials
Anno, M. Anno's mysterious multiplying jar (2-5) **512**

Facts, Miscellaneous *See* Curiosities and wonders

Facts about the fifty states. Brandt, S. R. **973**

The **facts** and fictions of Minna Pratt. MacLachlan, P. **Fic**

The **Facts** on File junior visual dictionary. Corbeil, J.-C. **423**

The **faery** flag. Yolen, J. **S C**

The **faery** flag [story]. Yolen, J.
In Yolen, J. The faery flag p3-11 **S C**

Fair, Sylvia
The bedspread **E**

Fair Catherine and the Pif-paf Poltrie
Grimm, J. Fair Katrinelje and Pif-paf-Poltrie
In Grimm, J. The complete Grimm's fairy tales p593-94 **398.2**

Fair exchange. Mahy, M.
In Mahy, M. Nonstop nonsense p31-36 **828**
Fair Gruagach. Crossley-Holland, K.
In Crossley-Holland, K. British folk tales p228-43 **398.2**
Fair Katrinelje and Pif-paf-Poltrie. Grimm, J.
In Grimm, J. The complete Grimm's fairy tales p593-94 **398.2**
Fair one with golden locks
Aulnoy, Madame d'. The story of Pretty Goldilocks
In The Blue fairy book p193-205 **398.2**
A **fair** wind for Troy. Gates, D. **292**
Fairclough, Chris
(il) Devonshire, H. Drawing **741.2**
(il) James, I. Italy **945**
(il) Lancaster, J. Paper sculpture **745.54**
(il) Wright, L. Masks **745.59**
Fairer-than-a-fairy
Fairer-than-a-fairy
In The Yellow fairy book p126-33 **398.2**
Fairies
Dictionaries
Briggs, K. M. An encyclopedia of fairies **398.03**
Fiction
Kimmel, E. A. Hershel and the Hanukkah goblins **E**
Mayne, W. The green book of Hob stories **E**
Poetry
See/See also pages in the following book(s):
Favorite poems, old and new p369-97 (4-6) **808.81**
The **fairies**. Perrault, C.
In Sleeping beauty & other favourite fairy tales p63-68 **398.2**
Fairs
Fiction
Handforth, T. Mei Li **E**
The **fairy**. Perrault, C.
In The Classic fairy tales p100-02 **398.2**
Fairy bird
Berger, T. The fairy bird
In Berger, T. Black fairy tales p106-23 **398.2**
The **fairy** child. Martin, E.
In Martin, E. Tales of the Far North p55-59 **398.2**
The **fairy** doll. Godden, R.
In Godden, R. Four dolls p32-65 **S C**
Fairy frog
Berger, T. The fairy frog
In Berger, T. Black fairy tales p33-42 **398.2**
Fairy gifts. Caylus, A. C. P. de T., comte de.
In The Green fairy book p64-67 **398.2**
The **fairy** grotto. Vuong, L. D.
In Vuong, L. D. The brocaded slipper, and other Vietnamese tales **398.2**
Fairy ointment. Crossley-Holland, K.
In Crossley-Holland, K. British folk tales p287-92 **398.2**
Fairy ointment. Jacobs, J.
In Jacobs, J. English fairy tales p211-14 **398.2**
Fairy tale. Mujica, B. L.
In Where angels glide at dawn p77-97 **S C**
Fairy tale. Strasser, T.
In Connections: short stories by outstanding writers for young adults p123-36 **S C**
Fairy tales
Afanas'ev, A. N. Russian fairy tales (4 and up) **398.2**
Afanas'ev, A. N. Russian folk tales (4 and up) **398.2**
Ahlberg, A. Ten in a bed (3-5) **Fic**
Ahlberg, J. Jeremiah in the dark woods (1-3) **Fic**
Alexander, L. The first two lives of Lukas-Kasha (4 and up) **Fic**
Alexander, L. The town cats, and other tales (3-5) **S C**
Andersen, H. C. The emperor's new clothes (2-5) **Fic**
Andersen, H. C. Hans Andersen: his classic fairy tales (3-6) **S C**
Andersen, H. C. The nightingale (2-5) **Fic**
Andersen, H. C. The princess and the pea (1-4) **Fic**
Andersen, H. C. The Snow Queen (4-6) **Fic**
Andersen, H. C. The steadfast tin soldier (1-4) **Fic**
Andersen, H. C. The swineherd (1-4) **Fic**
Andersen, H. C. Thumbeline (1-4) **Fic**
Andersen, H. C. The wild swans (2-5) **Fic**
The Arabian nights entertainments (5 and up) **398.2**
Asbjørnsen, P. C. East of the sun and west of the moon: old tales from the North (3-6) **398.2**
Barrie, J. M. Peter Pan (3-5) **Fic**
Bell, A. The nutcracker (2-4) **Fic**

Fairy tales—*Continued*
Berenzy, A. A Frog Prince (2-4) **E**
Berger, T. Black fairy tales (4 and up) **398.2**
Best-loved folktales of the world **398.2**
Bianco, M. W. The velveteen rabbit (2-4) **Fic**
The Blue fairy book (4-6) **398.2**
Brett, J. Beauty and the beast (1-3) **398.2**
Carpenter, F. Tales of a Chinese grandmother (4 and up) **398.2**
Carrick, C. Aladdin and the wonderful lamp (2-4) **398.2**
The Classic fairy tales **398.2**
Climo, S. The Egyptian Cinderella (k-2) **398.2**
Cole, J. Bony-Legs (k-3) **398.2**
Collodi, C. The adventures of Pinocchio (3-6) **Fic**
Crampton, P. Peter and the wolf **E**
Croll, C. The little snowgirl: an old Russian tale (k-2) **398.2**
De la Mare, W. Molly Whuppie (k-3) **398.2**
De Paola, T. Helga's dowry **E**
De Regniers, B. S. Jack the giant killer (k-3) **398.2**
De Regniers, B. S. Little Sister and the Month Brothers (k-3) **398.2**
Deuchar, I. The prince and the mermaid (2-5) **398.2**
Ehrlich, A. The Random House book of fairy tales (k-3) **398.2**
Ehrlich, A. Rapunzel (1-3) **398.2**
Ehrlich, A. The Snow Queen (2-4) **Fic**
Ehrlich, A. The wild swans **E**
Evans, C. S. The sleeping beauty (3-5) **398.2**
Farjeon, E. The glass slipper (3-6) **Fic**
Fleischman, P. Shadow play **E**
Fonteyn, Dame M. Swan lake (3-5) **Fic**
Gág, W. Wanda Gág's The sorcerer's apprentice (k-3) **398.2**
Galdone, P. Cinderella (k-2) **398.2**
Galdone, P. The elves and the shoemaker (k-2) **398.2**
Galdone, P. The gingerbread boy (k-2) **398.2**
Galdone, P. King of the Cats (k-2) **398.2**
Galdone, P. Puss in boots (k-2) **398.2**
Goodall, J. S. Puss in boots (k-3) **398.2**
Grahame, K. The reluctant dragon (3-5) **Fic**
The Green fairy book (4-6) **398.2**
Grimm, J. About wise men and simpletons (3-6) **398.2**
Grimm, J. The bear and the kingbird (k-3) **398.2**
Grimm, J. The complete Grimm's fairy tales (4 and up) **398.2**
Grimm, J. The fisherman and his wife (k-3) **398.2**
Grimm, J. Hansel and Gretel (k-3) **398.2**
Grimm, J. The juniper tree, and other tales from Grimm (4 and up) **398.2**
Grimm, J. More tales from Grimm (4-6) **398.2**
Grimm, J. The seven ravens (k-3) **398.2**
Grimm, J. Tales from Grimm (4-6) **398.2**
Grimm, J. The twelve dancing princesses (k-3) **398.2**
Grimm, J. Wanda Gág's Jorinda and Joringel (k-3) **398.2**
Grimm, J. Wanda Gág's The earth gnome (k-2) **398.2**
Grimm, J. Wanda Gag's The six swans (1-3) **398.2**
Hague, K. East of the sun and west of the moon (4-6) **398.2**
Hoffmann, E. T. A. Nutcracker (3 and up) **Fic**
Hogrogian, N. The devil with the three golden hairs (k-3) **398.2**
Hogrogian, N. The Glass Mountain (k-3) **398.2**
Hooks, W. H. Moss gown (k-3) **398.2**
Huck, C. S. Princess Furball (1-3) **398.2**
Hunter, M. A furl of fairy wind: four stories (2-5) **S C**
Hunter, M. The kelpie's pearls (4-6) **Fic**
Hunter, M. The wicked one (4 and up) **Fic**
Hutton, W. Beauty and the beast (1-4) **398.2**
Irwin, P. K. P. A flask of sea water (2-4) **Fic**
Isadora, R. The princess and the frog (k-2) **398.2**
Jacobs, J. English fairy tales (4-6) **398.2**
Jacobs, J. Tattercoats (k-2) **398.2**
Jeffers, S. Wild Robin **E**
Jennings, L. M. The Christmas Tomten **E**
Karlin, B. Cinderella (k-2) **398.2**
Kismaric, C. The rumor of Pavel and Paali (1-3) **398.2**
Klein, N. Baryshnikov's Nutcracker (3 and up) **792.8**
Lang, A. Aladdin and the wonderful lamp (2-4) **398.2**
Lattimore, D. N. The dragon's robe (3-5) **Fic**
Le Prince de Beaumont, Madame. Beauty and the beast (1-4) **398.2**
Lesser, R. Hansel and Gretel (1-3) **398.2**
Lewis, J. P. The tsar & the amazing cow **E**
Lindgren, A. The Tomten **E**

Fairy tales—*Continued*
Lindgren, A. The Tomten and the fox **E**
Littledale, F. The elves and the shoemaker (k-3) **398.2**
Louie, A.-L. Yeh-Shen (2-4) **398.2**
MacDonald, G. At the back of the North Wind (4-6) **Fic**
MacDonald, G. The complete fairy tales of George Macdonald (4 and up) **S C**
MacDonald, G. The light princess (3-6) **Fic**
MacDonald, G. The princess and the goblin (3-6) **Fic**
MacDonald, M. R. Twenty tellable tales **372.6**
Mahy, M. The seven Chinese brothers (1-3) **398.2**
Marshak, S. The Month-Brothers (1-3) **398.2**
Marshall, E. Troll country **E**
Martin, E. Tales of the Far North (2-5) **398.2**
Mayer, M. Beauty and the beast (1-4) **398.2**
McDermott, G. Tim O'Toole and the wee folk **E**
McKinley, R. Beauty: a retelling of the story of Beauty & the beast (5 and up) **Fic**
McVitty, W. Ali Baba and the forty thieves (1-3) **398.2**
Montresor, B. The witches of Venice **E**
Moser, B. The tinderbox **Fic**
Nesbit, E. Melisande (k-2) **398.2**
Norton, M. The Borrowers (3-6) **Fic**
Ormerod, J. The frog prince (k-3) **398.2**
Oxenbury, H. The Helen Oxenbury nursery story book (k-1) **398.2**
Perrault, C. Cinderella (k-3) **398.2**
Perrault, C. Puss in boots (k-3) **398.2**
The Prince who knew his fate (1-3) **398.2**
Prokofiev, S. Peter and the wolf **E**
Pyle, H. King Stork (k-3) **398.2**
Pyle, H. The wonder clock (4-6) **398.2**
Rayevsky, I. The talking tree (k-3) **398.2**
The Red fairy book (4-6) **398.2**
Reeves, J. English fables and fairy stories (4-6) **398.2**
Riordan, J. The woman in the moon, and other tales of forgotten heroines (4 and up) **398.2**
Rockwell, A. F. The emperor's new clothes (1-4) **Fic**
Rockwell, A. F. Puss in boots, and other stories (2-4) **398.2**
Rockwell, A. F. The three bears & 15 other stories (k-3) **398.2**
Rogasky, B. Rapunzel (1-3) **398.2**
Rogasky, B. The water of life (1-3) **398.2**
Ross, T. Hansel and Gretel (k-3) **398.2**
Ross, T. Mrs. Goat and her seven little kids (k-2) **398.2**
San Souci, R. Robert D. San Souci's The six swans (2-4) **398.2**
San Souci, R. The white cat (2-4) **398.2**
Sandburg, C. Rootabaga stories **S C**
Sanderson, R. The twelve dancing princesses (k-3) **398.2**
Sendak, M. Outside over there **E**
Sleeping beauty & other favourite fairy tales (3 and up) **398.2**
Stanley, D. Fortune **E**
Stephens, J. Irish fairy tales (6 and up) **398.2**
Stockton, F. The Bee-man of Orn (4-6) **Fic**
The Tall book of nursery tales (k-2) **398.2**
Thurber, J. Many moons (1-4) **Fic**
Uchida, Y. The magic listening cap (3-6) **398.2**
Vuong, L. D. The brocaded slipper, and other Vietnamese tales (3-6) **398.2**
Watson, R. J. Tom Thumb (k-3) **398.2**
Wells, R. The little lame prince **E**
Wilde, O. The Happy Prince, and other stories (3-6) **S C**
Wilde, O. The selfish giant (2-5) **Fic**
Williams-Ellis, A. Tales from the enchanted world (4 and up) **398.2**
Wisniewski, D. Elfwyn's saga **E**
Wisniewski, D. The warrior and the wise man **E**
Womenfolk and fairy tales (3-6) **398.2**
Wood, A. Heckedy Peg **E**
Wrede, P. C. Dealing with dragons (6 and up) **Fic**
The Yellow fairy book (4-6) **398.2**
Yolen, J. The sleeping beauty (k-2) **398.2**
Yolen, J. Sleeping ugly (2-4) **Fic**
Yolen, J. Tam Lin (3-6) **398.2**
Zelinsky, P. O. Rumpelstiltskin (k-4) **398.2**

See/See also pages in the following book(s):
The Scott, Foresman anthology of children's literature p147-408 **808.8**

Bibliography

Lynn, R. N. Fantasy literature for children and young adults **016.8**

History and criticism

See/See also pages in the following book(s):
Cook, E. The ordinary and the fabulous **028.5**
A Horn Book sampler on children's books and reading p143-54 **028.5**
Only connect: readings on children's literature p111-20 **028.5**

Fairy tales—*Continued*

Indexes

Index to fairy tales, 1949-1972 **398.2**
Index to fairy tales, 1973-1977 **398.2**
Index to fairy tales, 1978-1986 **398.2**

Fairy Tell-True
Grimm, J. Our Lady's child
In Grimm, J. The complete Grimm's fairy tales p23-39 **398.2**

Faithful even in death. Eberhard, W.
In Best-loved folktales of the world p531-34 **398.2**

Faithful John
Grimm, J. Faithful John
In Grimm, J. The complete Grimm's fairy tales p43-51 **398.2**
Grimm, J. Trusty John
In The Blue fairy book p296-303 **398.2**

Falada and the goosegirl. Hodges, M.
In Hodges, M. If you had a horse **398.2**

Falcons
Arnold, C. Saving the peregrine falcon (3-6) **598**
Harrison, V. The world of a falcon (k-2) **598**

Fiction

Wise, W. The black falcon (3-6) **Fic**

Falkland Islands War, 1982
See/See also pages in the following book(s):
Fox, G. The land and people of Argentina p175-82 (5 and up) **982**

The **fall** and rise of Bathbone. Babbitt, N.
In Babbitt, N. The Devil's other storybook p53-61 **S C**

A **fall** of snow. Alcock, V.
In Alcock, V. Ghostly companion **S C**

Falling stars *See* Meteors

Falsehood *See* Truthfulness and falsehood

Familiar quotations. Bartlett, J. **808.88**

Families. Jenness, A. **306.8**

Family
See also Brothers and sisters; Cousins; Grandfathers; Grandmothers; Parent and child; Single parent family; Stepfamilies
Jenness, A. Families (4 and up) **306.8**

Poetry

Adoff, A. All the colors of the race: poems (4-6) **811**

See/See also pages in the following book(s):
Favorite poems, old and new p29-57 (4-6) **808.81**

A **family** apart. Nixon, J. L. **Fic**

The **family** Christmas tree book. De Paola, T. **394.2**

Family histories *See* Genealogy

A **family** in Egypt. Bennett, O. **962**

A **family** in Italy. Hubley, P. **945**

A **family** in Mexico. Moran, T. **972**

A **family** in Morocco. Stewart, J. **964**

A **family** in the Persian Gulf. Jacobsen, P. O. **953**

Family life
Bennett, O. A family in Egypt (3-5) **962**
Dutton, R. An Arab family (3-5) **953**
Free to be—a family **810.8**
Hubley, P. A family in Italy (3-5) **945**
Moran, T. A family in Mexico (3-5) **972**
Stewart, J. A family in Morocco (3-5) **964**

Fiction

Adoff, A. Black is brown is tan **E**
Ahlberg, J. Peek-a-boo! **E**
Alcott, L. M. Little women (5 and up) **Fic**
Alcott, L. M. An old-fashioned Thanksgiving (3-5) **Fic**
Armstrong, W. H. Sounder (5 and up) **Fic**
Bawden, N. The peppermint pig (5 and up) **Fic**
Bawden, N. The robbers (5 and up) **Fic**
Blaine, M. The terrible thing that happened at our house **E**
Blume, J. Just as long as we're together (5 and up) **Fic**
Blume, J. Tales of a fourth grade nothing (3-6) **Fic**
Bond, F. Poinsettia & her family **E**
Branscum, R. The adventures of Johnny May (4-6) **Fic**
Bridgers, S. E. Home before dark (6 and up) **Fic**
Byars, B. C. The animal, the vegetable, and John D Jones (5 and up) **Fic**
Byars, B. C. Beans on the roof (2-4) **Fic**
Byars, B. C. The cartoonist (4 and up) **Fic**
Byars, B. C. The not-just-anybody family (5 and up) **Fic**
Byars, B. C. The two-thousand-pound goldfish (5 and up) **Fic**
Byers, R. M. Mycca's baby **E**
Cameron, A. The stories Julian tells (2-4) **Fic**
Chaikin, M. Finders weepers (3-5) **Fic**
Chang, M. S. In the eye of war (4 and up) **Fic**

Family life—Fiction—*Continued*
Cleaver, V. Queen of hearts (6 and up) Fic
Conford, E. And this is Laura (4-6) Fic
Conford, E. The luck of Pokey Bloom (3-6) Fic
Conrad, P. Staying nine (3-5) Fic
Cooney, B. Island boy E
Coutant, H. First snow (2-4) Fic
Cresswell, H. Ordinary Jack (5 and up) Fic
Danziger, P. Everyone else's parents said yes (4-6) Fic
Danziger, P. Make like a tree and leave (4-6) Fic
Delton, J. Angel's mother's wedding (3-5) Fic
Ellis, S. Next-door neighbors (4 and up) Fic
Estes, E. The Moffats (4-6) Fic
Fitzhugh, L. Nobody's family is going to change (5 and up) Fic
Flournoy, V. The patchwork quilt E
Fox, P. The stone-faced boy (4-6) Fic
Gauch, P. L. Christina Katerina and the time she quit the family E
Grove, V. Good-bye, my wishing star (5 and up) Fic
Hahn, M. D. Daphne's book (5 and up) Fic
Hamilton, V. The bells of Christmas (4-6) Fic
Hamilton, V. M. C. Higgins the great (6 and up) Fic
Hamilton, V. Willie Bea and the time the Martians landed (5 and up) Fic
Hoban, R. The sorely trying day E
Honeycutt, N. The best-laid plans of Jonah Twist (3-5) Fic
Howard, E. F. Chita's Christmas tree E
Hurwitz, J. Hurricane Elaine (4-6) Fic
Hurwitz, J. Rip-roaring Russell (2-4) Fic
Hutchins, P. Rats! (2-4) Fic
Johansen, H. 7 x 7 tales of a sevensleeper (2-4) Fic
Johnston, T. Yonder E
Joosse, B. M. Jam day E
Karl, J. Beloved Benjamin is waiting (4-6) Fic
Kinsey-Warnock, N. The Canada geese quilt (3-5) Fic
Krensky, S. Lionel at large E
L'Engle, M. Meet the Austins (5 and up) Fic
Levinson, R. I go with my family to Grandma's E
Lindgren, A. Lotta on Troublemaker Street (1-3) Fic
Little, J. From Anna (4-6) Fic
Little, J. Look through my window (4-6) Fic
Lowry, L. Anastasia Krupnik (4-6) Fic
Lowry, L. Switcharound (5 and up) Fic
Lyon, G. E. Borrowed children (5 and up) Fic
MacLachlan, P. Cassie Binegar (4-6) Fic
MacLachlan, P. Seven kisses in a row (2-4) Fic
McDonnell, C. Toad food & measle soup (2-4) Fic
Naylor, P. R. Maudie in the middle (3-5) Fic
Neufeld, J. Edgar Allan (5 and up) Fic
Park, R. Playing Beatie Bow (5 and up) Fic
Paterson, K. Come sing, Jimmy Jo (5 and up) Fic
Pearce, P. The battle of Bubble and Squeak (3-6) Fic
Pevsner, S. And you give me a pain, Elaine (4 and up) Fic
Pevsner, S. Keep stompin' till the music stops (4 and up) Fic
Porte-Thomas, B. A. Ruthann and her pig (3-5) Fic
Raskin, E. Figgs & phantoms (5 and up) Fic
Robinson, N. K. Angela, private citizen (3-5) Fic
Rodowsky, C. F. The gathering room (5 and up) Fic
Rylant, C. A blue-eyed daisy (5 and up) Fic
Rylant, C. A fine white dust (5 and up) Fic
Rylant, C. The relatives came E
Sachs, M. The bears' house (4-6) Fic
Sachs, M. Fran Ellen's house (4-6) Fic
Scott, A. H. Sam E
Sebestyen, O. Words by heart (5 and up) Fic
Segal, L. G. Tell me a Mitzi E
Segal, L. G. Tell me a Trudy E
Shreve, S. R. The flunking of Joshua T. Bates (3-5) Fic
Smith, D. B. The first hard times (4-6) Fic
Smith, D. B. Return to Bitter Creek (5 and up) Fic
Smith, R. K. The war with Grandpa (4-6) Fic
Sorensen, V. E. Miracles on Maple Hill (4 and up) Fic
Tate, E. E. Just an overnight guest (4-6) Fic
Townsend, J. R. Dan alone (6 and up) Fic
Uchida, Y. A jar of dreams (5 and up) Fic
Uchida, Y. Journey home (5 and up) Fic
Van Leeuwen, J. Tales of Oliver Pig E
Walter, M. P. Have a happy— (4-6) Fic

Family life—Fiction—*Continued*
Walter, M. P. Justin and the best biscuits in the world (3-6) Fic
Walter, M. P. Mariah keeps cool (3-5) Fic
Wolff, A. Only the cat saw E
Yep, L. The serpent's children (6 and up) Fic
Zolotow, C. Something is going to happen E
Family pictures. Lomas Garza, C. E
Family pose. Hughes, D. Fic
The **Family** read-aloud Christmas treasury 808.8
The **family** storytelling handbook. Pellowski, A. 372.6
The **family** under the bridge. Carlson, N. S. Fic
Family violence
See also Child abuse; Wife abuse
The **famine**. Lester, J.
In Lester, J. More tales of Uncle Remus p40-44 398.2
Famine does not make a man clever. Callaway, H.
In The Crest and the hide, and other African stories of heroes, chiefs, bards, hunters, sorcerers, and common people p73-76 398.2
Famines
Fine, J. C. The hunger road (5 and up) 338.1
Famous first facts: a record of first happenings, discoveries, and inventions in American history. Kane, J. N. 031.02
Famous Mexican Americans. Morey, J. 920
The **famous** Stanley kidnapping case. Snyder, Z. K. See note under Snyder, Z. K. The headless cupid Fic
Fanaticism
Fiction
Jones, R. C. The Believers (5 and up) Fic
Fancy Aunt Jess. Hest, A. E
Fancy dress *See* Costume
Fanny's sister. Lively, P. Fic
Fantastic fiction
See also Science fiction
Alexander, L. The book of three (5 and up) Fic
Alexander, L. The High King (5 and up) Fic
Babbitt, N. Tuck everlasting (5 and up) Fic
Baum, L. F. The Wizard of Oz (3-6) Fic
Bond, N. A string in the harp (6 and up) Fic
Boston, L. M. The children of Green Knowe (4-6) Fic
Boston, L. M. The sea egg (3-5) Fic
Carroll, L. Alice's adventures in Wonderland (4 and up) Fic
Carroll, L. Alice's adventures in Wonderland, and Through the looking glass (4 and up) Fic
Carroll, L. Through the looking glass, and what Alice found there (4 and up) Fic
Chetwin, G. Gom on Windy Mountain (5 and up) Fic
Chetwin, G. The riddle and the rune (5 and up) Fic
Christopher, J. Fireball (5 and up) Fic
Cooper, S. The grey king (5 and up) Fic
Cooper, S. Over sea, under stone (5 and up) Fic
Cooper, S. Seaward (6 and up) Fic
Corbett, S. The lemonade trick (3-5) Fic
Cresswell, H. The secret world of Polly Flint (4-6) Fic
Dahl, R. James and the giant peach (4-6) Fic
Dickinson, P. Merlin dreams (5 and up) Fic
Eager, E. Half magic (4-6) Fic
Eager, E. Seven-day magic (4-6) Fic
Gannett, R. S. My father's dragon (1-4) Fic
Gorog, J. Three dreams and a nightmare, and other tales of the dark (5 and up) S C
Hamilton, V. The magical adventures of Pretty Pearl (6 and up) Fic
Hoban, R. The mouse and his child (4-6) Fic
Hunter, M. The haunted mountain (5 and up) Fic
Jacques, B. Mattimeo (6 and up) Fic
Jacques, B. Redwall (6 and up) Fic
James, M. Shoebag (5 and up) Fic
Jones, D. W. Dogsbody (6 and up) Fic
Jones, D. W. Eight days of Luke (5 and up) Fic
Jones, D. W. Howl's moving castle (6 and up) Fic
Joyce, W. George shrinks E
Juster, N. The phantom tollbooth (5 and up) Fic
Karl, J. Beloved Benjamin is waiting (4-6) Fic
Kelleher, V. The red king (6 and up) Fic
Kendall, C. The Gammage cup (5 and up) Fic
Kennedy, R. Amy's eyes (5 and up) Fic

Fantastic fiction—*Continued*
Kennedy, X. J. The Owlstone crown (5 and up) **Fic**
Key, A. Escape to Witch Mountain (5 and up) **Fic**
Key, A. The forgotten door (5 and up) **Fic**
Langton, J. The fledgling (5 and up) **Fic**
Le Guin, U. K. A wizard of Earthsea (6 and up) **Fic**
L'Engle, M. A wrinkle in time (5 and up) **Fic**
Lewis, C. S. The lion, the witch and the wardrobe (4 and up) **Fic**
Masefield, J. The box of delights; or, When the wolves were running (5 and up) **Fic**
McCaffrey, A. Dragonsong (6 and up) **Fic**
McKillip, P. A. The riddle-master of Hed (5 and up) **Fic**
McKinley, R. The hero and the crown (6 and up) **Fic**
Norton, M. Bed-knob and broomstick (3-5) **Fic**
Pearce, P. Tom's midnight garden (4 and up) **Fic**
Pope, E. M. The Perilous Gard (6 and up) **Fic**
Reid Banks, L. The Indian in the cupboard (5 and up) **Fic**
Rodda, E. The best-kept secret (3-5) **Fic**
Sargent, S. Weird Henry Berg (4-6) **Fic**
Sendak, M. In the night kitchen **E**
Sendak, M. Where the wild things are **E**
Singer, M. Charmed (5 and up) **Fic**
Sleator, W. Among the dolls (4 and up) **Fic**
Snyder, Z. K. Below the root (5 and up) **Fic**
Steig, W. Solomon the rusty nail **E**
Things that go bump in the night (5 and up) **S C**
Tolkien, J. R. R. The hobbit (4 and up) **Fic**
Travers, P. L. Mary Poppins (4-6) **Fic**
Wells, R. Through the hidden door (5 and up) **Fic**
Winthrop, E. The castle in the attic (4-6) **Fic**
Wrightson, P. A little fear (5 and up) **Fic**
Wrightson, P. The Nargun and the stars (5 and up) **Fic**
Yorinks, A. Hey, Al **E**
See/See also pages in the following book(s):
The Scott, Foresman anthology of children's literature p479-571 **808.8**

Bibliography
Lynn, R. N. Fantasy literature for children and young adults **016.8**

History and criticism
Egoff, S. A. Worlds within **028.5**

See/See also pages in the following book(s):
Crosscurrents of criticism p169-96 **028.5**
Only connect: readings on children's literature p106-75 **028.5**

Fantasy for children. See Lynn, R. N. Fantasy literature for children and young adults **016.8**
Fantasy literature for children and young adults. Lynn, R. N. **016.8**

Farber, Norma
How does it feel to be old? (2-4) **811**
(comp) These small stones. See These small stones **808.81**

Farjeon, Eleanor, 1881-1965
The glass slipper (3-6) **Fic**
The lady's room
In With a deep sea smile p82-85 **372.6**
See/See also pages in the following book(s):
A Horn Book sampler on children's books and reading p255-58 **028.5**

Farley, Walter, 1915-1989
The Black Stallion (4 and up) **Fic**
The Black Stallion and Flame. See note under Farley, W. The Black Stallion **Fic**
The Black Stallion and Satan. See note under Farley, W. The Black Stallion **Fic**
The Black Stallion and the girl. See note under Farley, W. The Black Stallion **Fic**
The Black Stallion challenged! See note under Farley, W. The Black Stallion **Fic**
The Black Stallion legend. See note under Farley, W. The Black Stallion **Fic**
The Black Stallion mystery. See note under Farley, W. The Black Stallion **Fic**
The Black Stallion picture book. See note under Farley, W. The Black Stallion **Fic**
The Black Stallion returns. See note under Farley, W. The Black Stallion **Fic**
The Black Stallion revolts. See note under Farley, W. The Black Stallion **Fic**
The Black Stallion's courage. See note under Farley, W. The Black Stallion **Fic**
The Black Stallion's filly. See note under Farley, W. The Black Stallion **Fic**
The Black Stallion's ghost. See note under Farley, W. The Black Stallion **Fic**

Farley, Walter, 1915-1989—*Continued*
The Black Stallion's sulky colt. See note under Farley, W. The Black Stallion **Fic**
Son of the Black Stallion. See note under Farley, W. The Black Stallion **Fic**
The young Black Stallion. See note under Farley, W. The Black Stallion **Fic**
The **farm** alphabet book. Miller, J. **E**
Farm animals *See* Domestic animals
Farm counting book. Miller, J. **E**
Farm life
Allen, T. B. On Granddaddy's farm (1-3) **630.1**
Ancona, G. The American family farm (5 and up) **630.1**
Bellville, C. W. Farming today yesterday's way (2-4) **630.1**
Demuth, P. Joel, growing up a farm man (5 and up) **630.1**
Gibbons, G. Farming (k-2) **630.1**
Graff, N. P. The strength of the hills (4 and up) **630.1**
Kunhardt, E. I want to be a farmer **E**
Provensen, A. Town & country (k-2) **307.7**
See/See also pages in the following book(s):
Tunis, E. The young United States, 1783 to 1830 p15-27 (5 and up) **973**
Fiction
Aylesworth, J. Hanna's hog **E**
Azarian, M. A farmer's alphabet **E**
Beatty, P. Charley Skedaddle (5 and up) **Fic**
Blades, A. Mary of Mile 18 (2-4) **Fic**
Brown, M. W. Big red barn **E**
Brown, R. The big sneeze **E**
Carrick, C. In the moonlight, waiting **E**
Caudill, R. A pocketful of cricket **E**
Doherty, B. White Peak Farm (5 and up) **Fic**
Edmonds, W. D. Bert Breen's barn (6 and up) **Fic**
Enright, E. Thimble summer (4-6) **Fic**
Fleischman, S. McBroom tells the truth (3-5) **Fic**
Fleischman, S. The scarebird **E**
Gardam, J. The hollow land (5 and up) **Fic**
Griffith, H. V. Grandaddy's place **E**
Grove, V. Good-bye, my wishing star (5 and up) **Fic**
Herriot, J. Moses the kitten (2-4) **Fic**
Howard, E. Edith herself (4-6) **Fic**
Hunt, I. Across five Aprils (5 and up) **Fic**
Khalsa, D. K. Julian **E**
King-Smith, D. Pigs might fly (4-6) **Fic**
Lindbergh, R. Benjamin's barn **E**
Lionni, L. Six crows **E**
Lobel, A. A treeful of pigs **E**
Lunn, J. L. S. The root cellar (5 and up) **Fic**
Nilsson, U. If you didn't have me (3-5) **Fic**
Noble, T. H. Apple tree Christmas **E**
Noble, T. H. The day Jimmy's boa ate the wash **E**
Paterson, K. Park's quest (5 and up) **Fic**
Paulsen, G. The winter room (5 and up) **Fic**
Peck, R. N. A day no pigs would die (6 and up) **Fic**
Provensen, A. The year at Maple Hill Farm **E**
Rice, E. At Grammy's house **E**
Seredy, K. The Good Master (4-6) **Fic**
Thomas, J. R. The comeback dog (3-5) **Fic**
Westcott, N. B. Skip to my Lou **E**
Wild, M. The very best of friends **E**
Pictorial works
Florian, D. A year in the country **E**
Canada
Kurelek, W. A prairie boy's summer (3-5) **971.27**
Kurelek, W. A prairie boy's winter (3-5) **971.27**
England—Pictorial works
Goodall, J. S. The story of a farm (3-6) **942**
Missouri
Bulla, C. R. A grain of wheat: a writer begins (3-5) **92**
The **farmer** and his hired help. Protter, E. *In* Best-loved folktales of the world p490-95 **398.2**
The **farmer** and the boggart. Crossley-Holland, K.
In Crossley-Holland, K. British folk tales p224-27 **398.2**
The **farmer** and the snake. Lester, J.
In Lester, J. The knee-high man, and other tales p24-26 **398.2**
Farmer boy. Wilder, L. I. See note under Wilder, L. I. Little house in the big woods **Fic**
The **Farmer** in the dell **782.42**
Farmer Palmer's wagon ride. Steig, W. **E**
Farmer Schulz's ducks. Thiele, C. **E**
Farmer Weatherbeard
Asbjørnsen, P. C. Farmer Weatherbeard
In The Red fairy book p294-302 **398.2**
A **farmer's** alphabet. Azarian, M. **E**
Farming *See* Agriculture
Farming. Gibbons, G. **630.1**
Farming on shares
How Bobtail beat the Devil
In Grandfather tales p88-98 **398.2**

Farming today yesterday's way. Bellville, C. W. **630.1**

Farrell, Kate
(comp) Talking to the sun: an illustrated anthology of poems for young people. See Talking to the sun: an illustrated anthology of poems for young people **808.81**

The **farthest** shore. Le Guin, U. K. See note under Le Guin, U. K. A wizard of Earthsea

Fascism

Germany

See also National socialism

Fashion

See also Clothing and dress; Costume

Fasick, Adele M., 1930-
(jt. auth) England, C. ChildView: evaluating and reviewing materials for children **028.5**

Fast & funny paper toys you can make. Churchill, E. R. **745.592**

Fast friends. Stevenson, J. **E**

Fast Sam, Cool Clyde, and Stuff. Myers, W. D. **Fic**

Fast-slow, high-low. Spier, P. **E**

Fasts and feasts

See also Holidays

The American book of days **394.2**

Judaism

See also Hanukkah; Passover; Rosh ha-Shanah; Sukkoth; Yom Kippur

Judaism—Fiction

Sholem Aleichem. Holiday tales of Sholom Aleichem (5 and up) **S C**

Judaism—Poetry

Poems for Jewish holidays (k-3) **811.008**

Fat man in a fur coat, and other bear stories. Schwartz, A. **599.74**

Fat men from space. Pinkwater, D. M. **Fic**

Fatchen, Max
The country mail is coming (3-5) **821**

Father Bear comes home. Minarik, E. H. See note under Minarik, E. H. Little Bear **E**

Father Christmas. Briggs, R. **E**

Father Fox's feast of songs. Watson, C. **782.42**

Father Fox's pennyrhymes. Watson, C. **811**

Father Nicholas and the thief. Afanas'ev, A. N.
In Afanas'ev, A. N. Russian fairy tales p145-46 **398.2**

Father spider comes to dinner. Climo, S.
In Climo, S. Someone saw a spider p77-86 **398.2**

Fathers

Fiction

Hines, A. G. Daddy makes the best spaghetti **E**
James, B. Natalie underneath **E**
Konigsburg, E. L. Journey to an 800 number (4 and up) **Fic**
Ray, D. K. My daddy was a soldier **E**
Schwartz, A. Bea and Mr. Jones **E**
Slote, A. Moving in (4-6) **Fic**

Poetry

Clifton, L. Everett Anderson's goodbye (k-3) **811**

Fathers and daughters

Fiction

Alcock, V. The monster garden (4 and up) **Fic**
Boyd, C. D. Charlie Pippin (4-6) **Fic**
Browne, A. Gorilla **E**
Caines, J. F. Daddy **E**
Marzollo, J. Amy goes fishing **E**
Nelson, T. The 25¢ miracle (5 and up) **Fic**
Yolen, J. Owl moon **E**

Fathers and sons

Fiction

Asch, F. Sand cake **E**
Bunting, E. The Wall **E**
Hermes, P. Kevin Corbett eats flies (4 and up) **Fic**
Horenstein, H. Sam goes trucking **E**
Howker, J. Isaac Campion (5 and up) **Fic**
Hurwitz, J. Baseball fever **Fic**
Say, A. The lost lake **E**
Slote, A. The trading games (4-6) **Fic**
Smith, R. K. Bobby Baseball (4-6) **Fic**
Yep, L. Dragonwings (5 and up) **Fic**

Fatio, Louise
The happy lion **E**

Favorite Greek myths. Osborne, M. P. **292**

Favorite nursery tales, Tomie dePaola's **398.2**

Favorite poems, old and new (4-6) **808.81**

Fayerweather Street School. Unit
The Kids' book about death and dying. See The Kids' book about death and dying **155.9**

Fear

Fiction

Babbitt, N. The something **E**
Blegvad, L. Anna Banana and me **E**
Blume, J. Otherwise known as Sheila the Great (4-6) **Fic**
Bond, F. Poinsettia and the firefighters **E**

Fear—Fiction—*Continued*
Bonsall, C. N. Who's afraid of the dark? E
Browne, A. The tunnel E
Bunting, E. Ghost's hour, spook's hour E
Byars, B. C. The 18th emergency (4-6) Fic
Cooney, N. E. Go away monsters, lickety split! E
Crowe, R. L. Clyde monster E
Grifalconi, A. Darkness and the butterfly E
Little, J. Different dragons (3-5) Fic
Martin, B. The ghost-eye tree E
Mayer, M. There's a nightmare in my closet E
Polacco, P. Thunder cake E
Stolz, M. Storm in the night E
Szilagyi, M. Thunderstorm E

Fear and fly. Crossley-Holland, K.
In Crossley-Holland, K. British folk tales p175-77 **398.2**

The **fearsome** inn. Singer, I. B.
In Singer, I. B. Stories for children p290-307 **S C**

Feast of Lights *See* Hanukkah

Feast of Tabernacles *See* Sukkoth

The **feather** of Finist, the Bright Falcon. Afanas'ev, A. N.
In Afanas'ev, A. N. Russian fairy tales p580-88 **398.2**

The **feathered** serpent. O'Dell, S. See note under O'Dell, S. The captive **Fic**

Featherly, Jay
Mustangs: wild horses of the American West (3-6) **636.1**

Feathers for lunch. Ehlert, L. **E**

Feathers in the wind. Chaikin, M. See note under Chaikin, M. Yossi asks the angels for help **Fic**

A **February** failure. Gotwalt, H. L. M.
In Gotwalt, H. L. M. Special plays for holidays p99-106 **812**

Feeding behavior in animals *See* Animals—Food

Feeding yourself. Cobb, V. **394.1**

Feel better, Ernest! Vincent, G. See note under Vincent, G. Ernest and Celestine **E**

Feel the wind. Dorros, A. **551.5**

Feeling safe, feeling strong. Terkel, S. N. **362.7**

Feelings, Muriel, 1938-
Jambo means hello E
Moja means one E

Feelings, Tom, 1933-
(il) Feelings, M. Jambo means hello **E**
(il) Feelings, M. Moja means one **E**
(il) Greenfield, E. Daydreamers **811**
(il) Grimes, N. Something on my mind **811**
(il) Kerina, J. African crafts **745.5**
(il) Lester, J. To be a slave **326**

Feelings. Aliki. **152.4**

Feet *See* Foot

Feet!. Parnall, P. **E**

Feiffer, Jules
(il) Juster, N. The phantom tollbooth **Fic**

Feinstein, Steve
Egypt—in pictures. See Egypt—in pictures **962**
Israel—in pictures. See Israel—in pictures **956.94**
Turkey—in pictures (5 and up) **956.1**

Feldman Fieldmouse. Benchley, N. **Fic**

Felicia and the pot of pinks. Aulnoy, Madame d'
In The Blue fairy book p148-56 **398.2**

Felicia the critic. Conford, E. **Fic**

Felita. Mohr, N. **Fic**

Fell's United States coin book. Hughes, R. P. **737.4**

Felts, Shirley, 1934-
(il) Cresswell, H. The secret world of Polly Flint **Fic**
(il) Kendall, C. Sweet and sour **398.2**

Female role *See* Sex role

Feminism
See also Women's movement
Ash, M. The story of the women's movement (3-6) **305.4**
Ferris, J. Walking the road to freedom: a story about Sojourner Truth (3-5) **92**
Meltzer, M. Betty Friedan: a voice for women's rights (4 and up) **92**
Ortiz, V. Sojourner Truth, a self-made woman (6 and up) **92**

Fencing
See also Kendo

Fénelon, François de Salignac de La Mothe-, 1651-1715
The enchanted ring
In The Green fairy book p137-44 **398.2**

Fenton, Ann D.
(comp) Peterson, C. S. Index to children's songs **782.42**

Feral: tame animals gone wild. Pringle, L. P. 591.5

Ferdinand Faithful and Ferdinand Unfaithful
Grimm, J. Ferdinand Faithful and Ferdinand Unfaithful
In Grimm, J. The juniper tree, and other tales from Grimm v2 p298-309 398.2
Grimm, J. Ferdinand the Faithful and Ferdinand the Unfaithful
In Grimm, J. The complete Grimm's fairy tales p566-71 398.2

Ferguson, Alane
Cricket and the crackerbox kid (4-6) Fic

Ferguson, Amos, 1920-
(il) Greenfield, E. Under the Sunday tree 811

Fernandez, Laura
(il) Little, J. Different dragons Fic

Ferrari, Deborah A. Glockner- *See* Glockner-Ferrari, Deborah A.

Ferrari, Mark J.
(il) Patent, D. H. Humpback whales 599.5

Ferrets
Hess, L. Time for ferrets (3-5) 636.08

Ferris, Helen Josephine, 1890-1969
(comp) Favorite poems, old and new. See Favorite poems, old and new 808.81

Ferris, Jeri
Arctic explorer: the story of Matthew Henson (3-6) 92
Go free or die: a story about Harriet Tubman (3-5) 92
Walking the road to freedom: a story about Sojourner Truth (3-5) 92
What are you figuring now? a story about Benjamin Banneker (3-5) 92

Ferryboat. Maestro, B. E

The **ferryman**. Bishop, C. H.
In With a deep sea smile p42-55 372.6

Fertilization of plants
Dowden, A. O. T. The clover and the bee (5 and up) 582
Dowden, A. O. T. From flower to fruit (5 and up) 582
Lauber, P. From flower to flower (2-4) 582

Festival of freedom. Silverman, M. 296.4

Festivals
Dunkling, L. A dictionary of days 394.2
Festivals (3-6) 394.2

History
Aliki. A medieval feast (2-5) 394.1

Jews
See Fasts and feasts—Judaism

United States
The American book of days 394.2

Festivals (3-6) 394.2

Fetus
Kitzinger, S. Being born (3-5) 612.6

Fetz, Ingrid, 1915-
(il) Laughable limericks. See Laughable limericks 821.008

Fiammenghi, Gioia
(il) Froman, R. The greatest guessing game 513
(il) Meyers, S. P.J. Clover, private eye: the case of the Halloween hoot Fic
(il) Smith, R. K. Chocolate fever Fic

Fichter, George S.
American Indian music and musical instruments (5 and up) 780.89
The space shuttle (4 and up) 629.44

Fiction
See also Fantastic fiction; Historical fiction; Mystery and detective stories; Science fiction; subjects with the subdivision Fiction

Fiction, folklore, fantasy & poetry for children, 1876-1985 011.6

Fiction sequels for readers age 10-16. Anderson, V. 016.8

Fiddler in hell
Afanas'ev, A. N. The fiddler in hell
In Afanas'ev, A. N. Russian fairy tales p180-82 398.2

Field, Carolyn W., 1916-
Values in selected children's books of fiction and fantasy 028.5

Field, Elinor Whitney *See* Whitney, Elinor, 1889-

Field, Eugene, 1850-1895
Poems of childhood 811

Field, Rachel, 1894-1942
Calico bush (4 and up) Fic
Hitty: her first hundred years (4 and up) Fic
Prayer for a child (k-3) 242
See/See also pages in the following book(s):
Newbery Medal books, 1922-1955 p76-88 028.5

The **field** [short story]. Roiphe, A. R.
In Free to be—you and me p96-99 810.8

Field athletics *See* Track athletics

A **field** guide to the birds. Peterson, R. T. 598

A **field** guide to trees and shrubs. Petrides, G. A. **582.1**
A **field** guide to western birds. Peterson, R. T. **598**
A **field** guide to western reptiles and amphibians. Stebbins, R. C. **597.6**
Field of boliauns
The Field of boliauns
In Best-loved folktales of the world p235-37 **398.2**
Fields, Julia
The green lion of Zion Street (k-3) **811**
Fiend
Afanas'ev, A. N. The vampire
In Afanas'ev, A. N. Russian fairy tales p593-98 **398.2**
The **fierce** yellow pumpkin. Brown, M. W.
In Brown, M. W. The fish with the deep sea smile p65-69 **818**
Fieser, Stephen
(il) Branley, F. M. The Christmas sky **232.9**
Fifteen minutes. Callen, L.
In The Random House book of humor for children p283-92 **817.008**
Fifth book of junior authors & illustrators **920.003**
Fifty young men and a turtle. Marriott, A. L.
In Marriott, A. L. American Indian mythology **398.2**
Figgs & phantoms. Raskin, E. **Fic**
The **fighting** ground. Avi. **Fic**
The **figure** in the shadows. Bellairs, J. See note under Bellairs, J. The house with a clock in its walls **Fic**
A **figure** of speech. Mazer, N. F. **Fic**
Files and filing
ALA filing rules **025.3**
Filial piety. Shedlock, M. L.
In Shedlock, M. L. The art of the story-teller p229-32 **372.6**
Filipino Americans
Winter, F. H. The Filipinos in America
In The In America series **305.8**
The **Filipinos** in America. Winter, F. H.
In The In America series **305.8**
Filisky, Michael, 1947-
(jt. auth) White, S. V. Sterling **639.9**
Fill, bowl, fill
Fill, bowl! Fill!
In The Jack tales p89-95 **398.2**
Fill it up! Gibbons, G. **629.28**
Fillmore, Parker
Budulinek
In The Scott, Foresman anthology of children's literature p271-74 **808.8**
Clever Manka
In Best-loved folktales of the world p447-51 **398.2**
In The Scott, Foresman anthology of children's literature p274-77 **808.8**
In Womenfolk and fairy tales p146-55 **398.2**
The forest bride
In Best-loved folktales of the world p387-94 **398.2**
Films *See* Motion pictures
Filmstrips
See/See also pages in the following book(s):
Bauer, C. F. Handbook for storytellers p202-08 **372.6**
Crosscurrents of criticism p88-95 **028.5**
The **filthy** beast. Garfield, L.
In Garfield, L. The apprentices **S C**
Fin MacCoul and the Fenians of Erin in the Castle of Fear Dubb
In Best-loved folktales of the world p264-70 **398.2**
Finance, Personal
Barkin, C. Jobs for kids (5 and up) **650.1**
Kyte, K. S. The kids' complete guide to money (4 and up) **332.024**
Schwartz, D. M. If you made a million **E**
Wilkinson, E. Making cents (4 and up) **332.024**
See/See also pages in the following book(s):
Burns, M. I am not a short adult! p53-64 (3-6) **305.23**
Finch, C.
The gamut and time-table in verse
In A Nursery companion p90-93 **820.8**
Find me. Aiken, J.
In Aiken, J. Give yourself a fright: thirteen tales of the supernatural p157-59 **S C**
Find-the-animal A.B.C, Demi's. Demi **E**
Find the constellations. Rey, H. A. **523.8**
Finders weepers. Chaikin, M. **Fic**
The **finding**. Bawden, N. **Fic**
Finding a common language. Bergman, T. **362.4**
Finding a way. Rosenberg, M. B. **362.4**
Fine, Anne
My war with Goggle-eyes (5 and up) **Fic**
Fine, John Christopher
The hunger road (5 and up) **338.1**
Sunken ships & treasure (5 and up) **910.4**
The **fine** field of flax. Crossley-Holland, K.
In Crossley-Holland, K. British folk tales p218-23 **398.2**

A **fine** white dust. Rylant, C. Fic
Finger, Charles Joseph, 1869-1941
See/See also pages in the following book(s):
Newbery Medal books, 1922-1955 p37-38 **028.5**
Finger play
Brown, M. T. Finger rhymes (k-2) **796.1**
Brown, M. T. Hand rhymes (k-2) **796.1**
Brown, M. T. Play rhymes (k-2) **796.1**
Clap your hands (k-2) **796.1**
Glazer, T. Do your ears hang low?: 50 more musical fingerplays (k-3) **796.1**
Glazer, T. Eye winker, Tom Tinker, chin chopper (k-3) **796.1**
Grayson, M. F. Let's do fingerplays (k-2) **796.1**
The Lap-time song and play book (k-2) **782.42**
Trot, trot to Boston: play rhymes for baby (k-1) **398.8**
See/See also pages in the following book(s):
Carlson, B. W. Listen! and help tell the story p15-40 **372.6**
Pellowski, A. The story vine p92-98 **372.6**
With a deep sea smile p93-100 **372.6**
Finist the falcon. Afanas'ev, A. N.
In Afanas'ev, A. N. Russian folk tales p25-36 **398.2**
Finkelstein, Norman H.
Remember not to forget (3-5) **940.54**
Finland
Lander, P. S. The land and people of Finland (5 and up) **948.97**
Finn MacCool *See* Finn MacCumhaill, 3rd cent.
Finn MacCumhaill, 3rd cent.
See/See also pages in the following book(s):
Best-loved folktales of the world p256-75 **398.2**
Riordan, J. The woman in the moon, and other tales of forgotten heroines p35-41 (4 and up) **398.2**
Stephens, J. Irish fairy tales p35-108 (6 and up) **398.2**
Finney, Denise
(il) Catchpole, C. Jungles **574.5**
Finnish Americans
Paananen, E. The Finns in America
In The In America series **305.8**
The **Finns** in America. Paananen, E.
In The In America series **305.8**
Finn's men and the mean mare. Hodges, M.
In Hodges, M. If you had a horse **398.2**
Finzel the farsighted. Fleischman, P. **Fic**
Fir tree
Andersen, H. C. Hans Christian Andersen's The fir tree **Fic**
The fir tree
In Take joy! p14-22 **394.2**
Fire-bird, the horse of power, and the Princess Vasilissa
Afanas'ev, A. N. The Firebird and Princess Vasilisa
In Afanas'ev, A. N. Russian fairy tales p494-97 **398.2**
Ransome, A. The firebird, the horse of power and the Princess Vasilissa
In Best-loved folktales of the world p414-22 **398.2**
Fire departments
Wolf, B. Firehouse (3-6) **363.3**
The **fire** dogs. Aiken, J.
In Aiken, J. Up the chimney down, and other stories p212-27 **S C**
Fire engines
Marston, H. I. Fire trucks (2-4) **628.9**
Rockwell, A. F. Fire engines (k-1) **628.9**
Fire fighters
Kunhardt, E. I want to be a fire-fighter **E**
Maass, R. Fire fighters (2-3) **628.9**
Wolf, B. Firehouse (3-6) **363.3**
Fiction
Bond, F. Poinsettia and the firefighters **E**
Fire fighting
Gibbons, G. Fire! Fire! (1-3) **363.3**
Fire! Fire! Gibbons, G. **363.3**
Fire! in Yellowstone. Ekey, R. **574.5**
The **fire** on the mountain. Courlander, H.
In Best-loved folktales of the world p653-56 **398.2**
In The Scott, Foresman anthology of children's literature p303-04 **808.8**
Fire prevention
See also types of institutions, buildings, industries, and vehicles with the subdivision Fires and fire prevention
Wolf, B. Firehouse (3-6) **363.3**
The **fire** test. Lester, J.
In Lester, J. More tales of Uncle Remus p66-70 **398.2**
Fire trucks. Marston, H. I. **628.9**
Firearms
Wilkinson, F. Arms and armor (3-5) **623.4**
Fiction
Fox, P. One-eyed cat (5 and up) **Fic**

Fireball. Christopher, J. Fic
The **Firebird** and Princess Vasilisa. Afanas′ev, A. N.
In Afanas′ev, A. N. Russian fairy tales p494-97 398.2
Fireflies
Johnson, S. A. Fireflies (4 and up) 595.7
Fiction
Brinckloe, J. Fireflies! E
Fireflies!. Brinckloe, J. E
Fireflies. Johnson, S. A. 595.7
Firehouse. Wolf, B. 363.3
Fires
See also subjects with the subdivision Fires and fire prevention
See/See also pages in the following book(s):
Our violent earth p72-79 (4 and up) 363.3
The **Fireside** book of children's songs 782.42
The **Fireside** book of fun and game songs 782.42
Fireweed. Paton Walsh, J. Fic
Fireworks
Brenner, M. Fireworks tonight! (5 and up) 662
Fireworks, picnics, and flags. Giblin, J. 394.2
Fireworks tonight! Brenner, M. 662
The **first** bard among the Soninke. Sako, O.
In The Crest and the hide, and other African stories of heroes, chiefs, bards, hunters, sorcerers, and common people p1-5 398.2
The **first** book of baseball. Appel, M. 796.357
The **first** book of football. Madden, J. 796.332
The **first** book of how to run a meeting. See Powers, D. G. How to run a meeting 060.4
The **first** book of letter writing. See Mischel, F. How to write a letter 808
The **first** book of the American Revolution. See Morris, R. B. The American Revolution 973.3
The **first** book of the ancient Maya. See Beck, B. L. The ancient Maya 972
The **first** book of the Aztecs. See Beck, B. L. The Aztecs 972
The **first** book of the Incas. See Beck, B. L. The Incas 985
The **first** book of World War II. See Snyder, L. L. World War II 940.53
First Calender
The Story of the first calender, son of a king
In The Arabian nights entertainments p68-74 398.2
First came the Indians. Wheeler, M. J. 970.004
First comes spring. Rockwell, A. F. E
The **first** commune. Sholem Aleichem.
In Sholem Aleichem. Holiday tales of Sholem Aleichem S C
First companion to music, The Oxford. McLeish, K. 780
First day of school. Oxenbury, H. E
First dream: the ugly mug. Gorog, J.
In Gorog, J. Three dreams and a nightmare, and other tales of the dark S C
First emperor's magic whip
Carpenter, F. First emperor's magic whip
In Carpenter, F. Tales of a Chinese grandmother p134-41 398.2
The **first** flight. Taylor, R. L. 629.13
The **first** flute. Carter, D. S.
In The Scott, Foresman anthology of children's literature p402-05 808.8
The **first** four years. Wilder, L. I. See note under Wilder, L. I. Little house in the big woods Fic
First generation children *See* Children of immigrants
First grade takes a test. Cohen, M. See note under Cohen, M. See you in second grade! E
The **first** hard times. Smith, D. B. Fic
The **first** important wish. MacLachlan, P.
In MacLachlan, P. Tomorrow's wizard p13-31 S C
A **first** look at animals with backbones. Selsam, M. E. 596
A **first** look at bird nests. Selsam, M. E. 598
A **first** look at birds. Selsam, M. E. 598
A **first** look at caterpillars. Selsam, M. E. 595.7
A **first** look at flowers. Selsam, M. E. 582.13
A **first** look at insects. Selsam, M. E. 595.7
A **first** look at kangaroos, koalas, and other animals with pouches. Selsam, M. E. 599.2

A **first** look at monkeys and apes. Selsam, M. E. **599.8**
A **first** look at owls, eagles, and other hunters of the sky. Selsam, M. E. **598**
A **first** look at poisonous snakes. Selsam, M. E. **597.9**
A **first** look at rocks. Selsam, M. E. **552**
A **first** look at seals, sea lions, and walruses. Selsam, M. E. **599.74**
A **first** look at seashells. Selsam, M. E. **594**
A **first** look at sharks. Selsam, M. E. **597**
A **first** look at the world of plants. Selsam, M. E. **581**
First old man and the hind
The Story of the first old man and of the hind
In The Arabian nights entertainments p13-18 **398.2**
First prayers (k-3) **242**
The **first** Shlemiel. Singer, I. B.
In The Laugh book p132-40 **808.8**
In Singer, I. B. Zlateh the goat, and other stories p55-65 **398.2**
First snow. Coutant, H. **Fic**
The **first** snowfall. Rockwell, A. F. **E**
The **first** Thanksgiving feast. Anderson, J. **974.4**
First things first. Fraser, B. **398.9**
The **first** two lives of Lukas-Kasha. Alexander, L. **Fic**
First words. Chermayeff, I. **410**
Fischer-Nagel, Andreas, 1951-
(jt. auth) Fischer-Nagel, H. An ant colony **595.7**
(jt. auth) Fischer-Nagel, H. The housefly **595.7**
(jt. auth) Fischer-Nagel, H. Inside the burrow: the life of the golden hamster **636.08**
(jt. auth) Fischer-Nagel, H. Life of the butterfly **595.7**
(jt. auth) Fischer-Nagel, H. Life of the honeybee **595.7**
(jt. auth) Fischer-Nagel, H. Life of the ladybug **595.7**
(jt. auth) Fischer-Nagel, H. A look through the mouse hole **599.32**
(jt. auth) Fischer-Nagel, H. A puppy is born **636.7**
(jt. auth) Fischer-Nagel, H. Season of the white stork **598**
Fischer-Nagel, Heiderose, 1956-
An ant colony (3-6) **595.7**
The housefly (3-6) **595.7**
Inside the burrow: the life of the golden hamster (3-6) **636.08**
Life of the butterfly (3-6) **595.7**
Life of the honeybee (3-6) **595.7**
Life of the ladybug (3-6) **595.7**
A look through the mouse hole (3-6) **599.32**
A puppy is born (1-4) **636.7**
Season of the white stork (3-6) **598**
Fish, Helen Dean
(ed) Bible. Selections. Animals of the Bible **220.8**
The **fish**. Lane, M. **597**
Fish. Parker, S. **597**
Fish and the ring
Jacobs, J. Fish and the ring
In Jacobs, J. English fairy tales p190-94 **398.2**
Reeves, J. The fish and the ring
In Reeves, J. English fables and fairy stories p35-48 **398.2**
The **fish** angel. Levoy, M.
In Levoy, M. The witch of Fourth Street, and other stories **S C**
Fish facts & bird brains: animal intelligence. Sattler, H. R. **591.5**
Fish for supper. Goffstein, M. B. **E**
Fish is fish. Lionni, L. **E**
The **fish** with the deep sea smile. Brown, M. W. **818**
Fisher, Aileen Lucia, 1906-
Easter (1-3) **394.2**
Listen, rabbit **E**
Sing the songs of Thanksgiving
In Holiday plays round the year p101-11 **812.008**
A tree to trim
In The Big book of Christmas plays p59-79 **808.82**
Fisher, Dorothy Canfield, 1879-1958
Thanksgiving Day
In Bauer, C. F. Celebrations p243-48 **808.8**
Understood Betsy [excerpt]
In The Random House book of humor for children p31-35 **817.008**
Fisher, Gary L.
The survival guide for kids with LD (learning differences) (5 and up) **371.9**
Fisher, Leonard Everett, 1924-
The Alamo (4 and up) **976.4**
Alphabet art: thirteen ABCs from around the world (4 and up) **745.6**
Calendar art (4 and up) **529**
Ellis Island (4 and up) **325.73**
The Great Wall of China (4 and up) **951**
Jason and the golden fleece (3-6) **292**
Look around **E**
Monticello (4 and up) **973.4**
Number art: thirteen 1 2 3s from around the world (4 and up) **513**

Fisher, Leonard Everett, 1924-—*Continued*
The Olympians **292**
Pyramid of the sun, pyramid of the moon (4 and up) **972**
The seven days of creation (k-3) **222**
The sports (4 and up) **796**
The Statue of Liberty (4 and up) **974.7**
Symbol art (4 and up) **302.2**
Theseus and the Minotaur (1-3) **292**
The Tower of London (4 and up) **942.1**
The Wailing Wall (4 and up) **221.9**
The White House (4 and up) **975.3**
(il) Alderman, C. L. The story of the thirteen colonies **973.2**
(il) Livingston, M. C. Celebrations **811**
(il) Livingston, M. C. A circle of seasons **811**
(il) Livingston, M. C. Earth songs **811**
(il) Livingston, M. C. Sea songs **811**
(il) Livingston, M. C. Sky songs **811**
(il) Morris, R. B. The American Revolution **973.3**
(il) Singer, I. B. The wicked city **222**

Fisheries
Scarry, H. Life on a fishing boat (3-6) **639.2**

The **fisherman** and his soul. Wilde, O.
In Wilde, O. The Happy Prince, and other stories p93-134 **S C**

Fisherman and his wife
Grimm, J. About a fisherman and his wife
In Grimm, J. About wise men and simpletons p5-14 **398.2**
Grimm, J. The fisherman and his wife **398.2**
also in Best-loved folktales of the world p88-94 **398.2**
also in Grimm, J. The complete Grimm's fairy tales p103-12 **398.2**
also in Grimm, J. The juniper tree, and other tales from Grimm v1 p94-112 **398.2**
also in Grimm, J. Tales from Grimm p149-70 **398.2**
Grimm, J. The story of the fisherman and his wife
In The Green fairy book p343-52 **398.2**
Rockwell, A. F. The fisherman and his wife
In Rockwell, A. F. Puss in boots, and other stories p42-52 **398.2**

The **fisherman** and the gatekeeper. Junne, I. K.
In Best-loved folktales of the world p567-68 **398.2**

Fisherman and the genie
The Fisherman and the genie
In Best-loved folktales of the world p485-88 **398.2**
The Story of the fisherman
In The Arabian nights entertainments p23-28 **398.2**

Fisherman's son and the Gruagach of tricks
The Fisherman's son and the Gruagach of tricks
In Best-loved folktales of the world p237-46 **398.2**

Fishes
See also Aquariums; Jellyfish; Sticklebacks
Arnosky, J. Freshwater fish & fishing (4 and up) **799.1**
Freedman, R. Killer fish (3-5) **597**
Parker, S. Fish (4 and up) **597**
Pope, J. Taking care of your fish (3-5) **639.3**
Zim, H. S. Fishes (4 and up) **597**
See/See also pages in the following book(s):
Chrystie, F. N. Pets p86-102 (4 and up) **636.088**
McClung, R. M. The amazing egg p55-65 (4 and up) **591.1**

Fiction
Cohen, B. The carp in the bathtub (2-4) **Fic**
Kalan, R. Blue sea **E**
Lionni, L. Fish is fish **E**
Lionni, L. Swimmy **E**

Pictorial works
Wildsmith, B. Fishes **E**

North America
The Audubon Society field guide to North American fishes, whales, and dolphins (5 and up) **597**

Fishes. Wildsmith, B. **E**

Fishing
See also Fly casting
Arnosky, J. Freshwater fish & fishing (4 and up) **799.1**
Scarry, H. Life on a fishing boat (3-6) **639.2**
See/See also pages in the following book(s):
Bauer, C. F. Celebrations p81-102 **808.8**

Fiction
Goffstein, M. B. Fish for supper **E**
Marzollo, J. Amy goes fishing **E**
Seuss, Dr. McElligot's pool **E**
Stock, C. Armien's fishing trip **E**

Fishing boat, Life on a. Scarry, H. **639.2**

Fitcher's bird. Grimm, J.
In Grimm, J. The complete Grimm's fairy tales p216-20 **398.2**

Fitcher's feathered bird. Grimm, J.
In Grimm, J. The juniper tree, and other tales from Grimm v1 p71-79 **398.2**

The **fitting** of the slipper. Brooke, W. J.
In Brooke, W. J. A telling of the tales: five stories p51-74 **S C**

Fitzgerald, John D., 1907-1988
The Great Brain (4 and up) **Fic**
The Great Brain at the academy. See note under Fitzgerald, J. D. The Great Brain **Fic**
The Great Brain does it again. See note under Fitzgerald, J. D. The Great Brain **Fic**
The Great Brain reforms. See note under Fitzgerald, J. D. The Great Brain **Fic**
Me and my little brain. See note under Fitzgerald, J. D. The Great Brain **Fic**
More adventures of the Great Brain. See note under Fitzgerald, J. D. The Great Brain **Fic**
The return of the Great Brain. See note under Fitzgerald, J. D. The Great Brain **Fic**

Fitzhugh, Louise, 1928-1974
Harriet the spy (4 and up) **Fic**
Harriet the spy [excerpt]
In The Random House book of humor for children p248-58 **817.008**
The long secret (4 and up) **Fic**
Nobody's family is going to change (5 and up) **Fic**

The **five** brothers. Pino Saavedra, Y.
In Best-loved folktales of the world p776-80 **398.2**

The **five** Chinese brothers. Bishop, C. H. **398.2**

The **five** hundred hats of Batholomew Cubbins. See Seuss, Dr. The 500 hats of Bartholomew Cubbins **E**

Five little ducks. Raffi. **782.42**

Five little monkeys jumping on the bed. Christelow, E. **E**

Five minutes' peace. Murphy, J. **E**

Five Owls **028.505**

Five queer brothers
Bishop, C. H. The five Chinese brothers **398.2**
Mahy, M. The seven Chinese brothers **398.2**

Five servants
Grimm, J. The six servants
In Grimm, J. The complete Grimm's fairy tales p600-07 **398.2**
In Grimm, J. Tales from Grimm p39-64 **398.2**

Five silly fishermen. Edwards, R. **398.2**

Fix-it. McPhail, D. M. **E**

Flack, Marjorie, 1897-1958
Angus and the cat. See note under Flack, M. Angus and the ducks **E**
also in The Read-aloud treasury p156-78 **808.8**
Angus and the ducks **E**
Angus lost. See note under Flack, M. Angus and the ducks **E**
Ask Mr. Bear **E**
The story about Ping **E**
(il) Heyward, D. The country bunny and the little gold shoes **E**

Flag. Crampton, W. G. **929.9**

Flagler, John J.
The labor movement in the United States (5 and up) **331.8**

Flags
Crampton, W. G. Flag (4 and up) **929.9**

United States

Haban, R. D. How proudly they wave (4 and up) **929.9**

The **flail** from heaven. Grimm, J.
In Grimm, J. The complete Grimm's fairy tales p514-15 **398.2**

Flail which came from the clouds
Grimm, J. The flail from heaven
In Grimm, J. The complete Grimm's fairy tales p514-15 **398.2**

Flame-colored taffeta. Sutcliff, R. **Fic**

Flap your wings and try. Pomerantz, C. **E**

Flapdoodle: pure nonsense from American folklore. Schwartz, A. **398**

Flash, crash, rumble, and roll. Branley, F. M. **551.5**

A **flask** of sea water. Irwin, P. K. P. **Fic**

Flat Stanley. Brown, J. **E**

Flax leavings
Grimm, J. The hurds
In Grimm, J. The complete Grimm's fairy tales p656-57 **398.2**
Grimm, J. Lucky scraps
In Grimm, J. More tales from Grimm p59-60 **398.2**

Flea market, Anno's. Anno, M. **E**

The **fledgling.** Langton, J. **Fic**

Fleischman, Albert Sidney *See* Fleischman, Sid, 1920-

Fleischman, Paul
The birthday tree (2-4) **Fic**
Coming-and-going men (6 and up) **S C**
Contents: The shade cutter; Enemies of the eye; Slaves of sham; Country pay
Finzel the farsighted (2-4) **Fic**
Graven images (6 and up) **S C**
Contents: The binnacle boy; Saint Crispin's follower; The man of influence
The Half-a-Moon Inn (4-6) **Fic**
I am phoenix: poems for two voices (4 and up) **811**

Fleischman, Paul—*Continued*
Joyful noise: poems for two voices (4 and up) **811**
Saturnalia (5 and up) **Fic**
Shadow play **E**
Fleischman, Sid, 1920-
By the Great Horn Spoon! (4-6) **Fic**
Chancy and the grand rascal (4-6) **Fic**
The ghost on Saturday night (3-5) **Fic**
Humbug Mountain (4-6) **Fic**
McBroom and the big wind. See note under Fleischman, S. McBroom tells the truth **Fic**
McBroom tells a lie. See note under Fleischman, S. McBroom tells the truth **Fic**
McBroom tells the truth (3-5) **Fic**
McBroom's almanac. See note under Fleischman, S. McBroom tells the truth **Fic**
McBroom's almanac [excerpt]
In The Random House book of humor for children p173-75 **817.008**
The midnight horse (3-6) **Fic**
Mr. Mysterious & Company (4-6) **Fic**
The scarebird **E**
The whipping boy (5 and up) **Fic**
Fleming, Ian, 1908-1964
Chitty-Chitty-Bang-Bang (4-6) **Fic**
Fleming, Ronald Lee
(jt. auth) Von Tscharner, R. New Providence **307.7**
Fleming, Thomas J., 1927-
Behind the headlines (5 and up) **071**
Fletcher, Sarah *See* Greene, Carol
Flexner, Stuart Berg
(ed) The Random House school dictionary. See The Random House school dictionary **423**
(ed) The Random House thesaurus. See The Random House thesaurus **423**
Flies
Fischer-Nagel, H. The housefly (3-6) **595.7**
O'Toole, C. Discovering flies (3-6) **595.7**
Flies in the water, fish in the air: a personal introduction to fly fishing. Arnosky, J. **799.1**
Flight
Experiments
Walker, O. H. Experimenting with air and flight (6 and up) **507**
Fiction
Walter, M. P. Brother to the wind **E**
History
Berliner, D. Before the Wright brothers (5 and up) **629.13**
Boyne, W. J. The Smithsonian book of flight for young people (4 and up) **629.13**
Gibbons, G. Flying (k-2) **629.13**
Maurer, R. Airborne (5 and up) **629.13**
Flight of the Swan. Bray, M. F.
In Herds of thunder, manes of gold p6-18 **808.8**
Flip and the cows. Dennis, W. **E**
A **flock** of gryphons. Lively, P.
In Lively, P. Uninvited ghosts, and other stories p90-107 **S C**
Floethe, Richard, 1901-
(il) Streatfeild, N. Theatre shoes, or other people's shoes **Fic**
Floods
See/See also pages in the following book(s):
Our violent earth p80-91 (4 and up) **363.3**
Fiction
Lyon, G. E. Come a tide **E**
Murphy, S. R. Tattie's river journey **E**
Flora, James, 1914-
The great green Turkey Creek monster **E**
Flores, Patrick Fernández, 1929-
See/See also pages in the following book(s):
Morey, J. Famous Mexican Americans p27-38 (5 and up) **920**
Florian, Douglas, 1950-
City street **E**
Discovering frogs (1-3) **597.8**
Discovering seashells (1-3) **594**
Nature walk **E**
Turtle day **E**
A year in the country **E**
Florida
Stone, L. M. Florida
In America the beautiful **973**
Fiction
Cleaver, V. The Kissimmee Kid (6 and up) **Fic**
Khalsa, D. K. My family vacation **E**
Lenski, L. Strawberry girl (4-6) **Fic**
Peck, R. N. Arly (5 and up) **Fic**
Rawlings, M. K. The yearling (6 and up) **Fic**
Flossie & the fox. McKissack, P. C. **E**
Flournoy, Valerie, 1952-
The patchwork quilt **E**
Flower gardening
Kuhn, D. More than just a flower garden (2-4) **635.9**
A **flower** grows. Robbins, K. **582.13**
Flower queen's daughter
The Flower queen's daughter
In The Yellow fairy book p192-97 **398.2**

Flowers
See also State flowers; Wild flowers
Dowden, A. O. T. The clover and the bee (5 and up) 582
Dowden, A. O. T. From flower to fruit (5 and up) 582
Laird, E. Rosy's garden: a child's keepsake of flowers (3-5) 635.9
Lauber, P. From flower to flower (2-4) 582
Patent, D. H. Flowers for everyone (4 and up) 635.9
Robbins, K. A flower grows (2-4) 582.13
Selsam, M. E. A first look at flowers (1-3) 582.13
Wexler, J. Flowers, fruits, seeds (k-2) 582

Fiction
Ehlert, L. Planting a rainbow E
Lobel, A. Alison's zinnia E
Lobel, A. The rose in my garden E

Flowers. Zim, H. S. 582.13
Flowers for everyone. Patent, D. H. 635.9
Flowers, fruits, seeds. Wexler, J. 582
The **flunking** of Joshua T. Bates. Shreve, S. R. Fic
The **fly**. Vo, D. M.
In Best-loved folktales of the world p572-75 398.2
Fly casting
Arnosky, J. Flies in the water, fish in the air: a personal introduction to fly fishing (5 and up) 799.1
The **flyaway** pantaloons. Sharples, J. E
Flying *See* Flight
Flying. Gibbons, G. 629.13
Flying saucers *See* Unidentified flying objects
Flying ship
The Flying ship
In The Yellow fairy book p198-205 398.2
Ransome, A. The Fool of the World and the flying ship 398.2
also in Best-loved folktales of the world p403-11 398.2
Focus on alcohol. O'Neill, C. 362.29
Focus on cocaine and crack. Shulman, J. 362.29
Focus on drugs and the brain. Friedman, D. P. 616.86
Focus on marijuana. Zeller, P. K. 362.29
Focus on Mexico. Casagrande, L. B. 972
Focus on nicotine and caffeine. Perry, R. L. 616.86
Fog
Tresselt, A. R. Hide and seek fog E
Foley, Patricia
John and the fiddler (3-5) Fic
Folk art
See also Decorative arts; Handicraft
Elbert, V. Folk toys around the world and how to make them (5 and up) 745.592
Folk dancing
Ancona, G. Dancing is (3-5) 793.3
Folk drama
Thane, A. Plays from famous stories and fairy tales (4-6) 812
Folk lore *See* Folklore
Folk music

United States
See also Country music

Folk songs
Arroz con leche (k-3) 782.42
The Fireside book of children's songs 782.42
Hush little baby (k-1) 781.62
I know an old lady who swallowed a fly 782.42
Langstaff, J. M. Frog went a-courtin' (k-3) 781.62
Langstaff, J. M. Oh, a-hunting we will go (k-2) 781.62
Langstaff, J. M. Over in the meadow (k-2) 781.62
There's a hole in the bucket (k-2) 781.62
Wendy Watson's Frog went a-courting (k-2) 781.62

United States
The Diane Goode book of American folk tales and songs (2-5) 398.2
The Erie Canal (k-4) 781.62
The Farmer in the dell 782.42
The Fox went out on a chilly night (k-3) 781.62
Old MacDonald had a farm (k-2) 781.62
Quackenbush, R. M. She'll be comin' round the mountain (k-3) 781.62
Seeger, R. C. American folk songs for children in home, school and nursery school 781.62
Zemach, H. Mommy, buy me a china doll E

Folk songs, English
London Bridge is falling down! (k-2) 781.62

Folk songs, Scottish
Leodhas, S. N. Always room for one more (k-3) 781.62

Folk toys around the world and how to make them. Elbert, V. **745.592**

Folklore

See also Blacks—Folklore; Legends; Tongue twisters; topics as themes in folklore and names of ethnic, national or occupational groups with the subdivision *Folklore*

The Baby's story book (k-1) **398.2**
Barth, E. Jack-o'-lantern (2-4) **398.2**
Best-loved folktales of the world **398.2**
The Blue fairy book (4-6) **398.2**
Bowden, J. C. Why the tides ebb and flow (k-2) **398.2**
Brett, J. Goldilocks and the three bears (k-2) **398.2**
Climo, S. Someone saw a spider (4 and up) **398.2**
Conover, C. Mother Goose and the sly fox (k-2) **398.2**
Edwards, R. Five silly fishermen (k-2) **398.2**
Ehrlich, A. The Random House book of fairy tales (k-3) **398.2**
Galdone, P. The gingerbread boy (k-2) **398.2**
Galdone, P. Henny Penny (k-2) **398.2**
Galdone, P. The little red hen (k-2) **398.2**
Galdone, P. The three bears (k-2) **398.2**
The Green fairy book (4-6) **398.2**
Hodges, M. If you had a horse (4 and up) **398.2**
Kellogg, S. Chicken Little (k-3) **398.2**
Leach, M. Whistle in the graveyard (4-6) **398.2**
MacDonald, M. R. Twenty tellable tales **372.6**
MacDonald, M. R. When the lights go out **372.6**
Marshall, J. Goldilocks and the three bears (k-2) **398.2**
McGovern, A. Too much noise (k-3) **398.2**
Opie, I. A. Children's games in street and playground **796.1**
Ormerod, J. The story of Chicken Licken (k-2) **398.2**
Oxenbury, H. The Helen Oxenbury nursery story book (k-1) **398.2**
Pellowski, A. The story vine **372.6**
Perl, L. Blue Monday and Friday the Thirteenth (4-6) **398**
Pyle, H. The wonder clock (4-6) **398.2**
The Red fairy book (4-6) **398.2**
Riordan, J. The woman in the moon, and other tales of forgotten heroines (4 and up) **398.2**
Rockwell, A. F. Puss in boots, and other stories (2-4) **398.2**
Rockwell, A. F. The three bears & 15 other stories (k-3) **398.2**
Rohmer, H. Brother Anansi and the cattle ranch (3-6) **398.2**
San Souci, R. Short & shivery (4 and up) **398.2**
Sawyer, R. Journey cake, ho! (k-2) **398.2**
Schwartz, A. All of our noses are here, and other noodle tales (1-3) **398.2**
Schwartz, A. I saw you in the bathtub, and other folk rhymes (1-3) **398.2**
Schwartz, A. In a dark, dark room, and other scary stories (k-3) **398.2**
Schwartz, A. Ten copycats in a boat, and other riddles (1-3) **398.6**
Schwartz, A. There is a carrot in my ear, and other noodle tales (1-3) **398.2**
Shannon, G. Stories to solve (3 and up) **398.2**
Shulevitz, U. The treasure (k-3) **398.2**
Stevens, J. How the Manx cat lost its tail (k-2) **398.2**
Swann, B. A basket full of white eggs (k-3) **398.6**
The Tall book of nursery tales (k-2) **398.2**
Tomie dePaola's Favorite nursery tales (k-3) **398.2**
Watson, R. J. Tom Thumb (k-3) **398.2**
Williams-Ellis, A. Tales from the enchanted world (4 and up) **398.2**
Womenfolk and fairy tales (3-6) **398.2**
The Yellow fairy book (4-6) **398.2**
Yolen, J. Touch magic **028.5**
Zemach, H. A penny a look (k-3) **398.2**
Zemach, M. The little red hen (k-2) **398.2**
Zemach, M. The three wishes (k-2) **398.2**
Zimmerman, H. W. Henny Penny (k-2) **398.2**

See/See also pages in the following book(s):
Crosscurrents of criticism p205-16 **028.5**
The Scott, Foresman anthology of children's literature p147-408 **808.8**
With a deep sea smile p41-92 **372.6**

Bibliography

See/See also pages in the following book(s):
Bauer, C. F. Handbook for storytellers p104-15, 157-80 **372.6**

Indexes

Index to fairy tales, 1949-1972 **398.2**
Index to fairy tales, 1973-1977 **398.2**
Index to fairy tales, 1978-1986 **398.2**
MacDonald, M. R. The storyteller's sourcebook **398**

Africa

Aardema, V. Bringing the rain to Kapiti Plain (k-2) **398.2**

Folklore—Africa—*Continued*
Bryan, A. Lion and the ostrich chicks, and other African tales (4-6) **398.2**
The Crest and the hide, and other African stories of heroes, chiefs, bards, hunters, sorcerers, and common people (5 and up) **398.2**
Grifalconi, A. The village of round and square houses (k-3) **398.2**
Haley, G. E. A story, a story (k-3) **398.2**
Knutson, B. How the guinea fowl got her spots (k-3) **398.2**
Lester, J. How many spots does a leopard have? and other tales (2-5) **398.2**
Lottridge, C. B. The name of the tree (k-3) **398.2**
Mwalimu. Awful aardvark (k-2) **398.2**
Steptoe, J. Mufaro's beautiful daughters (k-3) **398.2**

Africa, East

Aardema, V. Who's in Rabbit's house? (k-3) **398.2**

Africa, Southern

Berger, T. Black fairy tales (4 and up) **398.2**

Africa, West

Aardema, V. Princess Gorilla and a new kind of water (k-2) **398.2**
Aardema, V. Why mosquitoes buzz in people's ears (k-3) **398.2**
Courlander, H. The cow-tail switch, and other West African stories (4-6) **398.2**

Armenia

Hogrogian, N. The contest (1-3) **398.2**
Hogrogian, N. One fine day (k-3) **398.2**

Bohemia (Czechoslovakia)

Gág, W. Gone is gone (k-3) **398.2**

Canada

Martin, E. Tales of the Far North (2-5) **398.2**

China

Birdseye, T. A song of stars (3-5) **398.2**
Bishop, C. H. The five Chinese brothers (1-3) **398.2**
Carpenter, F. Tales of a Chinese grandmother (4 and up) **398.2**
Demi. A Chinese zoo: fables and proverbs (3-5) **398.2**
Demi. The empty pot (k-3) **398.2**
Demi. The magic boat (k-3) **398.2**
Hodges, M. The voice of the great bell (k-3) **398.2**
Kendall, C. Sweet and sour (4-6) **398.2**
Lee, J. M. Legend of the Li River (k-3) **398.2**
Lee, J. M. Legend of the Milky Way (k-3) **398.2**
Louie, A.-L. Yeh-Shen (2-4) **398.2**
Mahy, M. The seven Chinese brothers (1-3) **398.2**
Mosel, A. Tikki Tikki Tembo (k-2) **398.2**
San Souci, R. The enchanted tapestry (k-3) **398.2**
Torre, B. L. The luminous pearl (k-3) **398.2**
Wolkstein, D. The magic wings (2-4) **398.2**
Yep, L. The rainbow people (4 and up) **398.2**
Young, E. Lon Po Po (1-3) **398.2**
Zhang Xiu Shi. Monkey and the White Bone Demon (3-6) **398.2**

Czechoslovakia

See also Folklore—Bohemia (Czechoslovakia)

Egypt

Climo, S. The Egyptian Cinderella (k-2) **398.2**
The Prince who knew his fate (1-3) **398.2**

England

See Folklore—Great Britain

Europe

Bulfinch, T. Bulfinch's mythology (6 and up) **291**

France

Brett, J. Beauty and the beast (1-3) **398.2**
Brown, M. Stone soup (k-3) **398.2**
Deuchar, I. The prince and the mermaid (2-5) **398.2**
Galdone, P. Cinderella (k-2) **398.2**
Galdone, P. Puss in boots (k-2) **398.2**
Goodall, J. S. Puss in boots (k-3) **398.2**
Hutton, W. Beauty and the beast (1-4) **398.2**
Le Prince de Beaumont, Madame. Beauty and the beast (1-4) **398.2**
Mayer, M. Beauty and the beast (1-4) **398.2**
Perrault, C. Cinderella (k-3) **398.2**
Perrault, C. Puss in boots (k-3) **398.2**
San Souci, R. The white cat (2-4) **398.2**
Sleeping beauty & other favourite fairy tales (3 and up) **398.2**

Germany

Ehrlich, A. Rapunzel (1-3) **398.2**
Gág, W. Wanda Gág's The sorcerer's apprentice (k-3) **398.2**
Galdone, P. The elves and the shoemaker (k-2) **398.2**
Galdone, P. Little Red Riding Hood (k-2) **398.2**
Goodall, J. S. Little Red Riding Hood (k-2) **398.2**
Grimm, J. About wise men and simpletons (3-6) **398.2**
Grimm, J. The bear and the kingbird (k-3) **398.2**

Folklore—Germany—*Continued*
Grimm, J. The complete Grimm's fairy tales (4 and up) **398.2**
Grimm, J. The fisherman and his wife (k-3) **398.2**
Grimm, J. Hansel and Gretel (k-3) **398.2**
Grimm, J. The juniper tree, and other tales from Grimm (4 and up) **398.2**
Grimm, J. Little Red Cap (k-2) **398.2**
Grimm, J. More tales from Grimm (4-6) **398.2**
Grimm, J. The seven ravens (k-3) **398.2**
Grimm, J. Tales from Grimm (4-6) **398.2**
Grimm, J. The twelve dancing princesses (k-3) **398.2**
Grimm, J. Wanda Gág's Jorinda and Joringel (k-3) **398.2**
Grimm, J. Wanda Gág's The earth gnome (k-2) **398.2**
Grimm, J. Wanda Gag's The six swans (1-3) **398.2**
Hogrogian, N. The devil with the three golden hairs (k-3) **398.2**
Hogrogian, N. The Glass Mountain (k-3) **398.2**
Hyman, T. S. Little Red Riding Hood (k-2) **398.2**
Isadora, R. The princess and the frog (k-2) **398.2**
Lesser, R. Hansel and Gretel (1-3) **398.2**
Littledale, F. The elves and the shoemaker (k-3) **398.2**
Marshall, J. Little Red Riding Hood (k-2) **398.2**
Ormerod, J. The frog prince (k-3) **398.2**
Plume, I. The Bremen town musicians (k-3) **398.2**
Rogasky, B. Rapunzel (1-3) **398.2**
Rogasky, B. The water of life (1-3) **398.2**
Ross, T. Hansel and Gretel (k-3) **398.2**
Ross, T. Mrs. Goat and her seven little kids (k-2) **398.2**
San Souci, R. Robert D. San Souci's The six swans (2-4) **398.2**
Sanderson, R. The twelve dancing princesses (k-3) **398.2**
Shub, E. Clever Kate (1-3) **398.2**
Zelinsky, P. O. Rumpelstiltskin (k-4) **398.2**

Ghana
McDermott, G. Anansi the spider (k-3) **398.2**

Great Britain
Bennett, J. Teeny tiny (k-1) **398.2**
Cooper, S. The selkie girl (2-4) **398.2**
Crossley-Holland, K. British folk tales (4 and up) **398.2**
De la Mare, W. Molly Whuppie (k-3) **398.2**
De Regniers, B. S. Jack the giant killer (k-3) **398.2**
Galdone, P. King of the Cats (k-2) **398.2**
Galdone, P. The teeny-tiny woman (k-2) **398.2**
Galdone, P. The three little pigs (k-2) **398.2**
Galdone, P. The three sillies (k-3) **398.2**
Galdone, P. What's in fox's sack? (k-2) **398.2**
Jacobs, J. English fairy tales (4-6) **398.2**
Jacobs, J. Tattercoats (k-2) **398.2**
Marshall, J. The three little pigs (k-2) **398.2**
Opie, I. A. The lore and language of schoolchildren **398**
Reeves, J. English fables and fairy stories (4-6) **398.2**
San Souci, R. Young Merlin (2-5) **398.2**
Scieszka, J. The true story of the three little pigs (k-3) **398.2**
Seuling, B. The teeny tiny woman (k-2) **398.2**
Zemach, M. The three little pigs (k-2) **398.2**

Great Britain—Dictionaries
Briggs, K. M. An encyclopedia of fairies **398.03**

Haiti
The Magic orange tree, and other Haitian folktales (5 and up) **398.2**
Wolkstein, D. The banza (k-3) **398.2**

India
Brown, M. Once upon a mouse (k-3) **398.2**
Galdone, P. The monkey and the crocodile (k-2) **398.2**
Godden, R. The valiant chatti-maker (3-6) **398.2**

Iran
Wolkstein, D. The Red Lion (3-5) **398.2**

Ireland
Stephens, J. Irish fairy tales (6 and up) **398.2**

Italy
De Paola, T. The legend of Old Befana (k-3) **398.2**
De Paola, T. The mysterious giant of Barletta **E**
De Paola, T. Tony's bread: an Italian folktale (k-2) **398.2**
Plume, I. The story of Befana (1-3) **398.2**
Rayevsky, I. The talking tree (k-3) **398.2**

Ivory Coast
Tadjo, V. Lord of the dance (1-3) **398.2**

Folklore—*Continued*

Jamaica

Sherlock, Sir P. M. Anansi, the spider man (4-6) **398.2**

Japan

Ishii, M. The tongue-cut sparrow (k-3) **398.2**
Johnston, T. The badger and the magic fan (k-3) **398.2**
McDermott, G. The stonecutter (k-3) **398.2**
Morimoto, J. The inch boy (k-3) **398.2**
Mosel, A. The funny little woman (k-2) **398.2**
Paterson, K. The tale of the mandarin ducks (1-3) **398.2**
Quayle, E. The shining princess, and other Japanese legends (5 and up) **398.2**
Snyder, D. The boy of the three-year nap (1-3) **398.2**
Stamm, C. Three strong women (k-3) **398.2**
Uchida, Y. The magic listening cap (3-6) **398.2**
Uchida, Y. The two foolish cats (k-3) **398.2**
Yagawa, S. The crane wife (1-3) **398.2**

Korea

Ginsburg, M. The Chinese mirror (k-3) **398.2**

Laos

Spagnoli, C. Nine-in-one, Grr! Grr! (k-2) **398.2**

Latin America

Arroz con leche (k-3) **782.42**
Perl, L. Piñatas and paper flowers (4 and up) **394.2**
Tortillitas para mamá and other nursery rhymes (k-2) **398.8**

Latvia

Langton, J. The hedgehog boy (k-3) **398.2**

Liberia

Aardema, V. The Vingananee and the tree toad (k-3) **398.2**

Mexico

Shetterly, S. H. The dwarf-wizard of Uxmal (3-5) **398.2**

Nigeria

Bryan, A. Beat the story-drum, pum-pum (1-4) **398.2**

Norway

Asbjørnsen, P. C. East of the sun and west of the moon: old tales from the North (3-6) **398.2**
Galdone, P. The three Billy Goats Gruff (k-2) **398.2**
Hague, K. East of the sun and west of the moon (4-6) **398.2**
Hague, K. The man who kept house (k-3) **398.2**

Persia

See Folklore—Iran

Peru

Alexander, E. Llama and the great flood (1-3) **398.2**

Philippines

Galdone, P. The turtle and the monkey (k-2) **398.2**

Poland

Simon, S. More wise men of Helm and their merry tales (4 and up) **398.2**

Scotland

Forest, H. The woman who flummoxed the fairies (k-2) **398.2**
Yolen, J. Tam Lin (3-6) **398.2**

Senegal

Guy, R. Mother Crocodile (k-3) **398.2**

South Africa

Seeger, P. Abiyoyo (k-2) **398.2**

Southern States

Bang, M. Wiley and the Hairy Man (1-4) **398.2**
Grandfather tales (4 and up) **398.2**
Harper, W. The Gunniwolf (k-1) **398.2**
The Jack tales (4-6) **398.2**
San Souci, R. The talking eggs (k-3) **398.2**

Soviet Union

See also Folklore—Ukraine

Afanas'ev, A. N. Russian fairy tales (4 and up) **398.2**
Afanas'ev, A. N. Russian folk tales (4 and up) **398.2**
Cole, J. Bony-Legs (k-3) **398.2**
Croll, C. The little snowgirl: an old Russian tale (k-2) **398.2**
De Regniers, B. S. Everyone is good for something (k-3) **398.2**
Ginsburg, M. The magic stove (k-2) **398.2**
Lent, B. Baba Yaga (k-3) **398.2**
Mikolaycak, C. Babushka (k-3) **398.2**
Morgan, P. The turnip (k-2) **398.2**
Ransome, A. The Fool of the World and the flying ship (k-3) **398.2**
Reyher, R. H. My mother is the most beautiful woman in the world (1-4) **398.2**
Robbins, R. Baboushka and the three kings (1-4) **398.2**
Sherman, J. Vassilisa the wise (2-4) **398.2**

Spain

Hancock, S. Esteban and the ghost (k-3) **398.2**

Sudan

Aardema, V. What's so funny, Ketu? (k-2) **398.2**

Sweden

Greene, E. The legend of the Christmas rose (2-4) **398.2**

Folklore—*Continued*

Tibet (China)

Timpanelli, G. Tales from the roof of the world (4-6) **398.2**

Turkey

Walker, B. K. A treasury of Turkish folktales for children (4 and up) **398.2**

Ukraine

Brett, J. The mitten (k-2) **398.2**
Kismaric, C. The rumor of Pavel and Paali (1-3) **398.2**
Tresselt, A. R. The mitten (k-2) **398.2**

United States

DeFelice, C. C. The dancing skeleton (k-3) **398.2**
The Diane Goode book of American folk tales and songs (2-5) **398.2**
Forest, H. The baker's dozen (k-3) **398.2**
Galdone, J. The tailypo (k-3) **398.2**
Hooks, W. H. The three little pigs and the fox (k-3) **398.2**
Lester, J. The knee-high man, and other tales (k-3) **398.2**
The Rooster crows (k-2) **398.8**
Schwartz, A. Flapdoodle: pure nonsense from American folklore (4 and up) **398**
Schwartz, A. Kickle snifters and other fearsome critters (2-5) **398**
Schwartz, A. More scary stories to tell in the dark (4 and up) **398.2**
Schwartz, A. Scary stories to tell in the dark (4 and up) **398.2**
Schwartz, A. Tomfoolery: trickery and foolery with words (4 and up) **398**
Schwartz, A. Whoppers (4 and up) **398.2**
Schwartz, A. Witcracks: jokes and jests from American folklore (4 and up) **398**

Vietnam

Lee, J. M. Toad is the uncle of heaven (k-3) **398.2**
Terada, A. M. Under the starfruit tree (4-6) **398.2**
Vuong, L. D. The brocaded slipper, and other Vietnamese tales (3-6) **398.2**

Wales

Cooper, S. The silver cow: a Welsh tale (1-3) **398.2**

West Indies

Berry, J. Spiderman Anancy (5 and up) **398.2**
Bryan, A. The cat's purr (k-2) **398.2**
Bryan, A. The dancing granny (1-4) **398.2**
Bryan, A. Turtle knows your name (1-3) **398.2**
Sherlock, Sir P. M. West Indian folk-tales (4-6) **398.2**

Zanzibar

Aardema, V. Bimwili & the Zimwi (k-2) **398.2**
Aardema, V. Rabbit makes a monkey of lion (k-2) **398.2**

Follow me! Tafuri, N. **E**
Follow the drinking gourd. Winter, J. **E**
The **folly** of panic. Shedlock, M. L.
In Shedlock, M. L. The art of the story-teller p222-24 **372.6**
Folsom, Marcia McClintock
(jt. auth) Folsom, M. Easy as pie **E**
(jt. auth) Folsom, M. The Macmillan book of how things work **600**
Folsom, Mary Elting *See* Elting, Mary, 1909-
Folsom, Michael
Easy as pie **E**
The Macmillan book of how things work (4 and up) **600**
Foma Berennikov. Afanas'ev, A. N.
In Afanas'ev, A. N. Russian fairy tales p284-87 **398.2**
Fonteyn, Dame Margot, 1919-1991
Swan lake (3-5) **Fic**
Food
See also Animals—Food
Foodworks (4-6) **641.3**
Seixas, J. S. Junk food—what it is, what it does (1-3) **641.3**
See/See also pages in the following book(s):
Schmitt, L. Smart spending p74-84 (5 and up) **640.73**

Fiction

Pinkwater, D. M. Fat men from space (3-6) **Fic**
Seuss, Dr. Green eggs and ham **E**

Poetry

Adoff, A. Eats: poems (3-5) **811**
Poem stew (3-6) **811.008**

Food and digestion. Parker, S. **612.3**
Food service
See also Restaurants, bars, etc.
Food supply
Fine, J. C. The hunger road (5 and up) **338.1**
Horwitz, J. Night markets (3-6) **381**
Foodworks (4-6) **641.3**
The **fool**. Garfield, L.
In Garfield, L. The apprentices **S C**
The **Fool** of the World and the flying ship. Ransome, A. **398.2**
also in Best-loved folktales of the world p403-11 **398.2**
The **foolish** boy. Bryan, A.
In Bryan, A. Lion and the ostrich chicks, and other African folk tales p60-86 **398.2**

Foolish German
Afanas'ev, A. N. The foolish German
In Afanas'ev, A. N. Russian fairy tales p600 **398.2**
The **foolish** man. Tashjian, V. A.
In The Scott, Foresman anthology of children's literature p277-79 **808.8**
Foolish milkmaid
In The Tall book of nursery tales p23-24 **398.2**
The **foolish** wishes. Perrault, C.
In Sleeping beauty & other favourite fairy tales p41-44 **398.2**
Foolish wolf
Afanas'ev, A. N. The foolish wolf
In Afanas'ev, A. N. Russian fairy tales p450-52 **398.2**
The **fools** of Chelm and the stupid carp. Singer, I. B.
In Singer, I. B. Naftali the storyteller and his horse, Sus, and other stories p75-81 **S C**
In Singer, I. B. Stories for children p71-76 **S C**
The **fools** of Chelm and the stupid carp [excerpt]. Singer, I. B.
In The Random House book of humor for children p205-11 **817.008**
The **fools** of Chelm and their history. Singer, I. B. **Fic**
Fool's paradise. Singer, I. B.
In Singer, I. B. Zlateh the goat, and other stories p5-16 **398.2**
Foot
Aliki. My feet (k-3) **612**
Goor, R. All kinds of feet (k-3) **591.4**
Parnall, P. Feet! **E**
Silverstein, A. The story of your foot (5 and up) **612**
Football
See also Soccer
Anderson, D. The story of football (5 and up) **796.332**
Kuskin, K. The Dallas Titans get ready for bed **E**
Madden, J. The first book of football (5 and up) **796.332**
Sullivan, G. All about football (4 and up) **796.332**
Sullivan, G. Better football for boys (4 and up) **796.332**
Sullivan, G. Quarterback (4 and up) **796.332**
Fiction
Christopher, M. Tackle without a team (5 and up) **Fic**
Kessler, L. P. Kick, pass, and run **E**
Footless and blind champions
Afanas'ev, A. N. The footless champion and the handless champion
In Afanas'ev, A. N. Russian fairy tales p269-73 **398.2**
The **footless** champion and the handless champion. Afanas'ev, A. N.
In Afanas'ev, A. N. Russian fairy tales p269-73 **398.2**
Footwear *See* Shoes
For being good. Rylant, C.
In Rylant, C. Children of Christmas p13-19 **S C**
For reading out loud! Kimmel, M. M. **028.5**
For rent. Martin, C. E. See note under Martin, C. E. Island winter **E**
For younger readers: braille and talking books **011.6**
Forberg, Ati
(il) Fisher, A. L. Easter **394.2**
Forbes, Esther, 1891-1967
Johnny Tremain (5 and up) **Fic**
See/See also pages in the following book(s):
Newbery Medal books, 1922-1955 p245-54 **028.5**
The **Forbidden** apple
In The Magic orange tree, and other Haitian folktales p171-75 **398.2**
Forbidden fruit. Yee, P.
In Yee, P. Tales from Gold Mountain p45-50 **S C**
Forbidden room
Grimm, J. Fitcher's bird
In Grimm, J. The complete Grimm's fairy tales p216-20 **398.2**
Grimm, J. Fitcher's feathered bird
In Grimm, J. The juniper tree, and other tales from Grimm v1 p71-79 **398.2**
Force, Eden
John Muir (5 and up) **92**
Force and energy
Asimov, I. How did we find out about sunshine? (5 and up) **523.7**
White, J. R. The hidden world of forces (5 and up) **531**
Forced labor *See* Slavery
Ford, George
(il) Greenfield, E. Paul Robeson **92**
Ford, Gerald R., 1913-
About
Sipiera, P. P. Gerald Ford: thirty-eighth president of the United States (4 and up) **92**

Ford, H. J. (Henry Justice), 1860-1941
(il) The Arabian nights entertainments. See The Arabian nights entertainments **398.2**
(il) The Blue fairy book. See The Blue fairy book **398.2**
(il) The Green fairy book. See The Green fairy book **398.2**
(il) The Red fairy book. See The Red fairy book **398.2**
(il) The Yellow fairy book. See The Yellow fairy book **398.2**

Ford, Henry, 1863-1947

About

Mitchell, B. We'll race you, Henry: a story about Henry Ford (3-5) **92**

Ford, Henry Justice *See* Ford, H. J. (Henry Justice), 1860-1941

Ford, Peter, 1936-
(jt. auth) Howell, M. The elephant man [biography of Joseph Carey Merrick] **92**

Foreman, Michael, 1938-
War boy: a country childhood (5 and up) **92**
(il) Andersen, H. C. Hans Andersen: his classic fairy tales **S C**
(il) Barrie, J. M. Peter Pan **Fic**
(il) Dickens, C. A Christmas carol in prose **Fic**
(il) Kipling, R. The crab that played with the sea **Fic**
(il) Kipling, R. Just so stories **S C**
(il) Quayle, E. The shining princess, and other Japanese legends **398.2**
(il) Sleeping beauty & other favourite fairy tales. See Sleeping beauty & other favourite fairy tales **398.2**
(il) Stevenson, R. L. A child's garden of verses **821**
(il) Te Kanawa, K. Land of the long white cloud **398.2**

Forest, Heather
The baker's dozen (k-3) **398.2**
The woman who flummoxed the fairies (k-2) **398.2**

Forest animals
Hirschi, R. Who lives in—the forest? (k-2) **591.5**

Forest bride
Fillmore, P. The forest bride
In Best-loved folktales of the world p387-94 **398.2**

Forest ecology
See also Rain forest ecology
Ekey, R. Fire! in Yellowstone (2-4) **574.5**
George, J. C. One day in the woods (4-6) **574.5**
Jaspersohn, W. How the forest grew (2-4) **574.5**
Lerner, C. A forest year (3-5) **574.5**
Newton, J. R. A forest is reborn (2-4) **574.5**
Patent, D. H. Yellowstone fires (2-4) **574.5**
Romanova, N. Once there was a tree (2-4) **582.16**
Schwartz, D. M. The hidden life of the forest (3-5) **574.5**
Vogel, C. G. The great Yellowstone fire (3-6) **574.5**
Watts, B. 24 hours in a forest (5 and up) **574.5**

Pictorial works

Arnosky, J. In the forest (4 and up) **758**

Forest fires
Ekey, R. Fire! in Yellowstone (2-4) **574.5**
Newton, J. R. A forest is reborn (2-4) **574.5**
Patent, D. H. Yellowstone fires (2-4) **574.5**
Vogel, C. G. The great Yellowstone fire (3-6) **574.5**

A **forest** is reborn. Newton, J. R. **574.5**

Forest reserves
See also National parks and reserves

A **forest** year. Lerner, C. **574.5**

Forests and forestry
See also Trees
Dowden, A. O. T. The blossom on the bough (5 and up) **582.16**

The **forgetful** wishing well: poems for young people. Kennedy, X. J. **811**

The **forgotten** door. Key, A. **Fic**

Forshay-Lunsford, Cin
Love potion
In Connections: short stories by outstanding writers for young adults p159-68 **S C**

Forsslund, Karl-Erik, 1872-1941
Lindgren, A. The Tomten and the fox **E**

Forsyth, Adrian
Journey through a tropical jungle (4 and up) **574.5**

Fort, Mar'ia Rosa
Tarma
In Where angels glide at dawn p67-75 **S C**

Fortification
Macaulay, D. Castle (4 and up) **728.8**
Mulvihill, M. Roman forts (5 and up) **937**

History

Giblin, J. Walls (5 and up) **623**

Fortification—*Continued*
Models
Cummings, R. Make your own model forts & castles (5 and up) **623**
Fortnum, Margaret Emily Noel *See* Fortnum, Peggy, 1919-
Fortnum, Peggy, 1919-
(il) Bond, M. A bear called Paddington **Fic**
(il) Bond, M. Paddington's storybook **S C**
(il) Streatfeild, N. Thursday's child **Fic**
(il) Wilde, O. The Happy Prince, and other stories **S C**
Fortune, Amos, 1709 or 10-1801
About
Yates, E. Amos Fortune, free man (4 and up) **92**
Fortune. Stanley, D. **E**
Fortune seekers
Grimm, J. The three lucky ones
In Grimm, J. More tales from Grimm p189-96 **398.2**
Grimm, J. The three sons of fortune
In Grimm, J. The complete Grimm's fairy tales p342-44 **398.2**
Fortune telling
Schwartz, A. Telling fortunes (4-6) **133.3**
See/See also pages in the following book(s):
Caney, S. Steven Caney's kids' America p301-06 (4 and up) **790.1**
Fiction
Fleischman, P. Finzel the farsighted (2-4) **Fic**
Fortunée
Aulnoy, Madame d'. Felicia and the pot of pinks
In The Blue fairy book p148-56 **398.2**
Fortune's favorite. Cirulis, G.
In Face to face: a collection of stories by celebrated Soviet and American writers p115-29 **S C**
The **fortunes** of Madame Organza. Babbitt, N.
In Babbitt, N. The Devil's other storybook p3-9 **S C**
The **Forty** thieves
In The Blue fairy book p242-50 **398.2**
The **forty** thieves. Lang, A.
In Womenfolk and fairy tales p51-64 **398.2**
The **forty-third** war. Moeri, L. **Fic**
The **fossil** factory. Eldredge, N. **560**
Fossils
See also Mammals, Fossil; Prehistoric animals; Reptiles, Fossil
Aliki. Dinosaur bones (k-3) **567.9**
Aliki. Fossils tell of long ago (k-3) **560**
Arnold, C. Dinosaurs down under and other fossils from Australia (4 and up) **567.9**
Arnold, C. Trapped in tar (3-5) **560**
Baylor, B. If you are a hunter of fossils (3-5) **560**
Cobb, V. The monsters who died (3-5) **567.9**
Cohen, D. Prehistoric animals (4-6) **560**
Cole, J. Evolution (k-3) **575**
Eldredge, N. The fossil factory (4-6) **560**
Elting, M. The Macmillan book of dinosaurs and other prehistoric creatures (4 and up) **560**
Gibbons, G. Prehistoric animals (k-2) **560**
Lauber, P. Dinosaurs walked here, and other stories fossils tell (3-5) **560**
Taylor, P. D. Fossil (4 and up) **560**
See/See also pages in the following book(s):
Gallant, R. A. Before the sun dies p61-71 (6 and up) **575**
Fiction
Carrick, C. Big old bones **E**
Fossils tell of long ago. Aliki. **560**
Foster, Larry, 1909-
(il) Grosvenor, D. K. The blue whale **599.5**
Foster, Lawrence J. *See* Foster, Larry, 1909-
Foster home care
Fiction
Angell, J. Tina Gogo (6 and up) **Fic**
Byars, B. C. The pinballs (5 and up) **Fic**
Cresswell, H. Dear Shrink (5 and up) **Fic**
MacLachlan, P. Mama One, Mama Two **E**
Nixon, J. L. A family apart (5 and up) **Fic**
Paterson, K. The great Gilly Hopkins (5 and up) **Fic**
The **foundling**. Carrick, C. See note under Carrick, C. Ben and the porcupine **E**
Four angels to my bed. Aiken, J.
In Aiken, J. Past eight o'clock p117-28 **S C**
Four clever brothers
Grimm, J. The four skillful brothers
In Grimm, J. The complete Grimm's fairy tales p580-84 **398.2**
Four dolls. Godden, R. **S C**
Four hairs from the beard of the Devil
In The Magic orange tree, and other Haitian folktales p43-48 **398.2**
Four on the shore. Marshall, E. See note under Marshall, E. Three by the sea **E**

The **four** questions. Schwartz, L. S. **296.4**
The **four** skillful brothers. Grimm, J.
In Grimm, J. The complete Grimm's fairy tales p580-84 **398.2**
Fourth book of junior authors and illustrators **920.003**
Fourth of July
Dalgliesh, A. The Fourth of July story (2-4) **973.3**
Giblin, J. Fireworks, picnics, and flags (3-6) **394.2**
Phelan, M. K. The Fourth of July (1-3) **394.2**
Fiction
Hines, A. G. Mean old Uncle Jack **E**
The **Fourth** of July story. Dalgliesh, A. **973.3**
Fowler, Jim
(il) Grover, W. Dolphin adventure **599.5**
Fowler, Virginie *See* Elbert, Virginie
Fox, Dan
Go in and out the window. See Go in and out the window **782.42**
Fox, Geoffrey
The land and people of Argentina (5 and up) **982**
Fox, Mem, 1946-
Hattie and the fox **E**
Koala Lou **E**
Night noises **E**
Shoes from Grandpa **E**
Fox, Paula
How many miles to Babylon? (4-6) **Fic**
A likely place (3-5) **Fic**
One-eyed cat (5 and up) **Fic**
The slave dancer (5 and up) **Fic**
The stone-faced boy (4-6) **Fic**
The village by the sea (5 and up) **Fic**
See/See also pages in the following book(s):
Newbery and Caldecott Medal books, 1966-1975 p116-25 **028.5**
Townsend, J. R. A sense of story p89-94 **028.5**
Townsend, J. R. A sounding of storytellers p55-65 **028.5**
Fox all week. Marshall, E. See note under Marshall, E. Fox and his friends **E**
Fox and his friends. Marshall, E. **E**
Fox and the bear. Uchida, Y.
In Uchida, Y. The magic listening cap **398.2**
Fox and the bears. Curtis, E. S.
In Curtis, E. S. The girl who married a ghost, and other tales from the North American Indian p54-57 **398.2**
Fox and the cat
Grimm, J. The cat and the fox
In Grimm, J. More tales from Grimm p61-62 **398.2**
Grimm, J. The fox and the cat
In Grimm, J. The complete Grimm's fairy tales p354-55 **398.2**
Fox and the crane
Afanas'ev, A. N. The fox and the crane
In Afanas'ev, A. N. Russian fairy tales p171-72 **398.2**
Fox and the crow
Fox and the crow
In The Tall book of nursery tales p77-78 **398.2**
Fox and the geese
Grimm, J. The fox and the geese
In Grimm, J. The complete Grimm's fairy tales p393-94 **398.2**
Fox and the hare
Afanas'ev, A. N. The fox, the hare, and the cock
In Afanas'ev, A. N. Russian fairy tales p192-94 **398.2**
Fox and the horse
Grimm, J. The fox and the horse
In Grimm, J. The complete Grimm's fairy tales p595-96 **398.2**
Fox and the lobster
Afanas'ev, A. N. The fox and the lobster
In Afanas'ev, A. N. Russian fairy tales p310 **398.2**
Fox and the woodcock
Afanas'ev, A. N. The fox and the woodcock
In Afanas'ev, A. N. Russian fairy tales p171 **398.2**
Fox and the woodpecker
Afanas'ev, A. N. The fox and the woodpecker
In Afanas'ev, A. N. Russian fairy tales p199 **398.2**
Fox as chief mourner
Afanas'ev, A. N. The fox as mourner
In Afanas'ev, A. N. Russian fairy tales p437-38 **398.2**
The **fox** as midwife. Afanas'ev, A. N.
In Afanas'ev, A. N. Russian fairy tales p191-92 **398.2**
The **fox** as mourner. Afanas'ev, A. N.
In Afanas'ev, A. N. Russian fairy tales p437-38 **398.2**
Fox at school. Marshall, E. See note under Marshall, E. Fox and his friends **E**
Fox be nimble. Marshall, J. See note under Marshall, E. Fox and his friends **E**

The **fox** busters. King-Smith, D. Fic
Fox confessor
Afanas′ev, A. N. The fox confessor
In Afanas′ev, A. N. Russian fairy tales p72-74 **398.2**
Fox in love. Marshall, E. See note under Marshall, E. Fox and his friends E
Fox on the job. Marshall, J. See note under Marshall, E. Fox and his friends E
Fox on wheels. Marshall, E. See note under Marshall, E. Fox and his friends E
Fox physician
Afanas′ev, A. N. The fox physician
In Afanas′ev, A. N. Russian fairy tales p15-17 **398.2**
The **fox,** the hare, and the cock. Afanas′ev, A. N.
In Afanas′ev, A. N. Russian fairy tales p192-94 **398.2**
The **Fox** went out on a chilly night (k-3) **781.62**
Fox without a tail
Hogrogian, N. One fine day **398.2**
Foxes
Arnosky, J. Watching foxes (k-2) **599.74**
LaBonte, G. The arctic fox (3-5) **599.74**
Lane, M. The fox (1-3) **599.74**
Lavine, S. A. Wonders of foxes (4 and up) **599.74**
Leighner, A. M. Reynard (2-4) **599.74**
Schnieper, C. On the trail of the fox (3-6) **599.74**

Fiction

Byars, B. C. The midnight fox (4-6) **Fic**
Cooney, B. Chanticleer and the fox E
Fox, M. Hattie and the fox E
Galdone, P. Three Aesop fox fables (k-3) **398.2**
Galdone, P. What's in fox's sack? (k-2) **398.2**
Hogrogian, N. One fine day (k-3) **398.2**
Hutchins, P. Rosie's walk E
King-Smith, D. The fox busters (3-5) **Fic**
Lindgren, A. The Tomten and the fox E
Marshall, E. Fox and his friends E
Marshall, J. Wings E
McKissack, P. C. Flossie & the fox E
Shannon, G. Dance away! E
Tejima, K. Fox's dream E
Tompert, A. Grandfather Tang's story E
Tompert, A. Little fox goes to the end of the world E
Watson, C. Valentine foxes E
Fox's dream. Tejima, K. E
The **Foxwife**. Yolen, J.
In Yolen, J. The faery flag p12-20 S C

Fradin, Dennis B.
The Cheyenne (2-4) **970.004**
Earth (2-4) **525**
Ethiopia (4 and up) **963**
The Georgia colony (4 and up) **975.8**
Medicine (6 and up) **610**
The New York Colony (4 and up) **974.7**
The Pawnee (2-4) **970.004**
The Pennsylvania colony (4 and up) **974.8**
The Republic of Ireland (4 and up) **941.5**
The Shoshoni (2-4) **970.004**
The **fragile** flag. Langton, J. **Fic**
Frame, Paul, 1913-
Drawing cats and kittens (4 and up) **743**
(il) Calhoun, M. Katie John **Fic**
Frampton, David
(il) Chaikin, M. Joshua in the Promised Land **222**
(il) Chaikin, M. The seventh day: the story of the Jewish Sabbath **222**
(il) Kuskin, K. Jerusalem, shining still **956.94**
(il) Merriam, E. Fresh paint **811**
Fran Ellen's house. Sachs, M. **Fic**
France
Harris, J. The land and people of France (5 and up) **944**

Fiction

Aiken, J. Bridle the wind (6 and up) **Fic**
Carlson, N. S. The happy orpheline (3-5) **Fic**
Fatio, L. The happy lion **E**

Folklore

See Folklore—France

History—1789-1799, Revolution

See/See also pages in the following book(s):
Grey, V. The chemist who lost his head: the story of Antoine Laurent Lavoisier (5 and up) **92**

History—1940-1945, German occupation—Fiction

Roth-Hano, R. Touch wood (6 and up) **Fic**

Kings, queens, rulers, etc.

Aliki. The King's day: Louis XIV of France (3-5) **92**
Brooks, P. S. Queen Eleanor: independent spirit of the medieval world (6 and up) **92**

France—*Continued*
Legends
See Legends—France
Francis, of Assisi, Saint, 1182-1226
About
Cole, J. A gift from Saint Francis (2-4) **92**
De Paola, T. Francis, the poor man of Assisi (3-5) **92**
Francis, the poor man of Assisi. De Paola, T. **92**
Frank, Anne, 1929-1945
The diary of a young girl (6 and up) **92**
About
Hurwitz, J. Anne Frank: life in hiding (3-5) **92**
Frank, Dick, 1932-
(il) Stein, S. B. About dying **155.9**
Frank, Josette, 1893-1989
(comp) Poems to read to the very young. See Poems to read to the very young **821.008**
Frank, Julia
Alzheimer's disease (6 and up) **616.8**
Frank and Ernest. Day, A. **E**
Frank and Ernest play ball. Day, A. **E**
Frankenberg, Robert
(il) Mowat, F. Owls in the family **636.6**
Franklin, Benjamin, 1706-1790
About
Adler, D. A. A picture book of Benjamin Franklin (1-3) **92**
Aliki. The many lives of Benjamin Franklin (1-3) **92**
D'Aulaire, I. Benjamin Franklin (2-4) **92**
Fritz, J. What's the big idea, Ben Franklin? (3-5) **92**
See/See also pages in the following book(s):
Jacobs, W. J. Great lives: human rights p36-44 (5 and up) **920**
Fiction
Lawson, R. Ben and me (5 and up) **Fic**
The **franklin's** tale. Cohen, B.
In Cohen, B. Canterbury tales **Fic**
Frannie's fruits. Kimmelman, L. **E**
Frascino, Edward
(il) Kipling, R. The elephant's child **Fic**
(il) White, E. B. The trumpet of the swan **Fic**
Fraser, Betty, 1928-
First things first (k-2) **398.9**
(il) Simon, S. Pets in a jar **639**
Fraser, Claud Lovat, 1890-1921
See/See also pages in the following book(s):
Sendak, M. Caldecott & Co.: notes on books and pictures p93-94 **028.5**
Frau Trude
Grimm, J. Frau Trude
In Grimm, J. The complete Grimm's fairy tales p208-09 **398.2**
Grimm, J. Mrs. Gertrude
In Grimm, J. The juniper tree, and other tales from Grimm v2 p310-13 **398.2**
Freaks *See* Monsters
Freaky Friday. Rodgers, M. **Fic**
Freaky Friday [excerpt]. Rodgers, M.
In The Random House book of humor for children p262-67 **817.008**
Freckle juice. Blume, J. **Fic**
Freddy and the men from Mars. Brooks, W. R. See note under Brooks, W. R. Freddy the detective **Fic**
Freddy and the perilous adventure. Brooks, W. R. See note under Brooks, W. R. Freddy the detective **Fic**
Freddy goes camping. Brooks, W. R. See note under Brooks, W. R. Freddy the detective **Fic**
Freddy goes to Florida. Brooks, W. R. See note under Brooks, W. R. Freddy the detective **Fic**
Freddy the cowboy. Brooks, W. R. See note under Brooks, W. R. Freddy the detective **Fic**
Freddy the detective. Brooks, W. R. **Fic**
Freddy the politician. Brooks, W. R. See note under Brooks, W. R. Freddy the detective **Fic**
Frederick. Lionni, L. **E**
Frederick and Catherine
Grimm, J. Frederick and Catherine
In Grimm, J. The complete Grimm's fairy tales p283-89 **398.2**
Grimm, J. Frederick and Katelizabeth
In Grimm, J. The juniper tree, and other tales from Grimm v2 p187-200 **398.2**
Shub, E. Clever Kate **398.2**
Frederick and Katelizabeth. Grimm, J.
In Grimm, J. The juniper tree, and other tales from Grimm v2 p187-200 **398.2**
Frederick Douglass and the fight for freedom. Miller, D. T. **92**
Frederick Douglass: the black lion. McKissack, P. C. **92**
Free, John Brand
(il) Dutton, R. An Arab family **953**

Free fall. Wiesner, D. **E**
Free to be—a family **810.8**
Free to be—you and me **810.8**
Freedman, Florence B. (Florence Bernstein)
Brothers: a Hebrew legend (k-2) **398.2**
Freedman, Russell
Buffalo hunt (4 and up) **970.004**
Children of the wild West (4 and up) **978**
Cowboys of the wild West (4 and up) **978**
Immigrant kids (4 and up) **325.73**
Indian chiefs (6 and up) **920**
Killer fish (3-5) **597**
Killer snakes (2-5) **597.9**
Lincoln: a photobiography (4 and up) **92**
Rattlesnakes (3-5) **597.9**
Sharks (3-5) **597**
When winter comes (k-3) **591.5**
Freedom. Sanfield, S.
In Sanfield, S. The adventures of High John the Conqueror **398.2**
Freedom of information
See also Censorship
Weiss, A. E. Who's to know? (5 and up) **323.44**
Freedom of the press
Evans, J. E. Freedom of the press (5 and up) **323.44**
Weiss, A. E. Who's to know? (5 and up) **323.44**
Freeman, Don, 1908-1978
Beady Bear **E**
Corduroy **E**
In The Read-aloud treasury p190-206 **808.8**
Dandelion **E**
Norman the doorman **E**
A pocket for Corduroy **E**
Freeman, Judy
Books kids will sit still for **011.6**
Freeman, Tony
Photography (2-4) **770**
Freight train. Crews, D. **E**
French Americans
Kunz, V. B. The French in America
In The In America series **305.8**
French and Indian War *See* United States—History—1755-1763, French and Indian War
French artists *See* Artists, French
French authors *See* Authors, French
French Canadians
Fiction
Carlson, N. S. The talking cat, and other stories of French Canada (3-6) **S C**
The **French** in America. Kunz, V. B.
In The In America series **305.8**
French language editions
Lionni, L. Inch by inch **E**
Potter, B. The tale of Peter Rabbit **E**
Fresh brats. Kennedy, X. J. **811**
Fresh paint. Merriam, E. **811**
Freshman, Shelley
(il) Henry, O. The gift of the Magi **Fic**
Freshwater animals
Amos, W. H. Life in ponds and streams (k-3) **591.92**
McCauley, J. R. Let's explore a river (k-3) **574.92**
Freshwater fish & fishing. Arnosky, J. **799.1**
Freshwater plants
McCauley, J. R. Let's explore a river (k-3) **574.92**
Freund, Rudolf, 1915-
(il) Zim, H. S. Flowers **582.13**
Fried feathers for Thanksgiving. Stevenson, J. See note under Stevenson, J. Emma **E**
Friedan, Betty
About
Meltzer, M. Betty Friedan: a voice for women's rights (4 and up) **92**
Friedberg, Joan Brest, 1927-
Accept me as I am: best books of juvenile nonfiction on impairments and disabilities **016**
Friedhoffer, Robert
Magic tricks, science facts (5 and up) **793.8**
Friedman, David P.
Focus on drugs and the brain (3-6) **616.86**
Friedman, Ina R.
How my parents learned to eat **E**
Friedman, Judith, 1945-
(il) Jordan, M. Losing Uncle Tim **Fic**
Friedman, Marvin, 1930-
(il) Callen, L. Pinch **Fic**
(il) Chaikin, M. Ask another question **296.4**
(il) Chaikin, M. Shake a palm branch **296.4**
(il) Metter, B. Bar mitzvah, bat mitzvah **296.4**
The **Friendly** beasts (k-3) **782.28**
The **friendly** prairie dog. Casey, D. **599.32**
The **friendly** wolf. See Goble, P. Dream wolf **E**

Friends, Society of *See* Society of Friends
Friends. Heine, H. E
Friends. Isadora, R. E
Friends are like that. Hermes, P. Fic
Friends first. McDonnell, C. Fic
Friends forever. Chaikin, M. See note under Chaikin, M. Finders weepers Fic
The **friends** of Kwan Ming. Yee, P.
In Yee, P. Tales from Gold Mountain p25-31 S C
Friendship
See also Imaginary playmates
Rogers, F. Making friends (k-1) **155.4**
Fiction
Aiken, J. Bridle the wind (6 and up) Fic
Aliki. Overnight at Mary Bloom's E
Aliki. We are best friends E
Angell, J. Tina Gogo (6 and up) Fic
Auch, M. J. Kidnapping Kevin Kowalski (4-6) Fic
Bawden, N. The robbers (5 and up) Fic
Blume, J. Just as long as we're together (5 and up) Fic
Bond, N. A place to come back to (6 and up) Fic
Brandenberg, F. Leo and Emily E
Brandenberg, F. Nice new neighbors E
Bridgers, S. E. All together now (6 and up) Fic
Bulla, C. R. The cardboard crown (3-5) Fic
Byars, B. C. The Cybil war (4-6) Fic
Byars, B. C. The pinballs (5 and up) Fic
Carlstrom, N. W. Blow me a kiss, Miss Lilly E
Cassedy, S. M.E. and Morton (6 and up) Fic
Cohen, B. Thank you, Jackie Robinson (4-6) Fic
Cole, B. The goats (5 and up) Fic
Conford, E. Me and the terrible two (3-6) Fic
Coutant, H. The gift (2-5) Fic
Ehrlich, A. Leo, Zack, and Emmie E
Ehrlich, A. Leo, Zack, and Emmie together again E
Ellis, S. Next-door neighbors (4 and up) Fic
Erickson, R. E. A toad for Tuesday (2-4) Fic
Ferguson, A. Cricket and the crackerbox kid (4-6) Fic
Fleischman, S. The scarebird E
Foley, P. John and the fiddler (3-5) Fic
Gardam, J. The hollow land (5 and up) Fic
Giff, P. R. Love, from the fifth-grade celebrity (4-6) Fic
Greene, B. Get on out of here, Philip Hall (4-6) Fic
Greene, B. Philip Hall likes me, I reckon maybe (4-6) Fic
Greene, C. C. Ask anybody (5 and up) Fic
Greene, C. C. A girl called Al (5 and up) Fic
Hahn, M. D. Daphne's book (5 and up) Fic
Hamilton, V. The planet of Junior Brown (6 and up) Fic
Härtling, P. Crutches (5 and up) Fic
Havill, J. Jamaica tag-along E
Heine, H. Friends E
Hermes, P. Friends are like that (5 and up) Fic
Hermes, P. I hate being gifted (5 and up) Fic
Hermes, P. Kevin Corbett eats flies (4 and up) Fic
Honeycutt, N. The all new Jonah Twist (3-5) Fic
Howard, E. Circle of giving (4-6) Fic
Howe, J. A night without stars (5 and up) Fic
Howe, J. Pinky and Rex E
Hurwitz, J. The hot & cold summer (3-5) Fic
Isadora, R. Friends E
Jones, J. B. Secrets of a summer spy (5 and up) Fic
Kellogg, S. Best friends E
Klein, R. Enemies (3-5) Fic
Konigsburg, E. L. Jennifer, Hecate, Macbeth, William McKinley, and me, Elizabeth (4-6) Fic
Krumgold, J. Onion John (5 and up) Fic
Levoy, M. Alan and Naomi (6 and up) Fic
Lisle, J. T. Afternoon of the elves (4-6) Fic
Little, J. Kate (4-6) Fic
Little, J. Look through my window (4-6) Fic
Lovelace, M. H. Betsy-Tacy (2-4) Fic
Lowry, L. Autumn Street (4 and up) Fic
Lowry, L. Number the stars (4 and up) Fic
Lowry, L. Rabble Starkey (5 and up) Fic
Luttrell, I. Ottie Slockett E
Mahy, M. Making friends E
Mark, J. Thunder and Lightnings (5 and up) Fic
Marshall, J. George and Martha E
Mathis, S. B. Sidewalk story (3-5) Fic

Friendship—Fiction—*Continued*
McDonnell, C. Don't be mad, Ivy (2-4) **Fic**
McDonnell, C. Lucky charms & birthday wishes (2-4) **Fic**
Miles, B. The trouble with thirteen (5 and up) **Fic**
Mills, C. Dynamite Dinah (3-5) **Fic**
Myers, W. D. Fast Sam, Cool Clyde, and Stuff (6 and up) **Fic**
Myers, W. D. Me, Mop, and the Moondance Kid (4-6) **Fic**
O'Connor, J. Yours till Niagara Falls, Abby **Fic**
Orgel, D. The devil in Vienna (6 and up) **Fic**
Paterson, K. Bridge to Terabithia (4 and up) **Fic**
Peck, R. N. Soup (5 and up) **Fic**
Peet, B. Eli **E**
Robins, J. Addie meets Max **E**
Ross, P. Meet M and M **E**
Rylant, C. A fine white dust (5 and up) **Fic**
Schotter, R. Captain Snap and the children of Vinegar Lane **E**
Slepian, J. The Alfred summer (5 and up) **Fic**
Slepian, J. The night of the Bozos (6 and up) **Fic**
Slepian, J. Risk 'n' roses (5 and up) **Fic**
Smith, D. B. Last was Lloyd (4-6) **Fic**
Smith, D. B. A taste of blackberries (4-6) **Fic**
Smith, J. L. The kid next door and other headaches (2-4) **Fic**
Snyder, Z. K. The changeling (5 and up) **Fic**
Snyder, Z. K. Libby on Wednesdays (5 and up) **Fic**
Speare, E. G. The sign of the beaver (5 and up) **Fic**
Stevenson, J. Fast friends **E**
Stevenson, J. The worst person in the world **E**
Viorst, J. Rosie and Michael **E**
Weiss, N. Maude and Sally **E**
Wells, R. Through the hidden door (5 and up) **Fic**
Wild, M. Mr. Nick's knitting **E**
Winthrop, E. Katharine's doll **E**
Wittman, S. A special trade **E**
Zemach, H. The princess and Froggie **E**
Zolotow, C. The hating book **E**
Zolotow, C. My friend John **E**

Poetry

Lyon, G. E. Together **E**
Prelutsky, J. Rolling Harvey down the hill (1-3) **811**

The **friendship**. Taylor, M. D. See note under Taylor, M. D. Song of the trees **Fic**

The **fright** before Christmas. Howe, J. See note under Howe, J. Scared silly: a Halloween treat **E**

Frightening the monster in Wizard's Hole. Mahy, M.
In Mahy, M. Nonstop nonsense p103-11 **828**

Fritz, Jean
And then what happened, Paul Revere? (2-4) **92**
Brendan the Navigator (3-5) **398.2**
The cabin faced west (3-6) **Fic**
Can't you make them behave, King George? [biography of George III, King of Great Britain] (3-5) **92**
China homecoming (6 and up) **951.05**
China's Long March (6 and up) **951.04**
The double life of Pocahontas (4 and up) **92**
Early thunder (6 and up) **Fic**
George Washington's breakfast (2-4) **Fic**
The good giants and the bad pukwudgies (k-3) **398.2**
The great little Madison (5 and up) **92**
Homesick: my own story (5 and up) **92**
Homesick: my own story [excerpt]
In Face to face: a collection of stories by celebrated Soviet and American writers p57-75 **S C**
Make way for Sam Houston (4 and up) **92**
The man who loved books [biography of Saint Columba] (3-5) **92**
Shhh! we're writing the Constitution (3-5) **342**
Stonewall [biography of Stonewall Jackson] (4 and up) **92**
What's the big idea, Ben Franklin? (3-5) **92**
Where do you think you're going, Christopher Columbus? (3-5) **92**
Where was Patrick Henry on the 29th of May? (3-5) **92**
Who's that stepping on Plymouth Rock? (3-5) **974.4**
Why don't you get a horse, Sam Adams? (3-5) **92**
Will you sign here, John Hancock? (3-5) **92**

Fritz, Michael
(il) Fritz, J. China homecoming **951.05**

Fritz, Ronald
(il) Keller, C. Tongue twisters **808.88**

Frog and Toad all year. Lobel, A. See note under Lobel, A. Frog and Toad are friends **E**

Frog and Toad are friends. Lobel, A. E
Frog and Toad together. Lobel, A. See note under Lobel, A. Frog and Toad are friends E
Frog goes to dinner. Mayer, M. See note under Mayer, M. A boy, a dog, and a frog E
A **Frog** he would a-wooing go. See Langstaff, J. M. Frog went a-courtin' **781.62**
The **frog-king**. Grimm, J.
In Grimm, J. The complete Grimm's fairy tales p17-20 **398.2**
In Grimm, J. The juniper tree, and other tales from Grimm v2 p169-77 **398.2**
Frog on his own. Mayer, M. See note under Mayer, M. A boy, a dog, and a frog E
Frog prince
Crossley-Holland, K. The frog prince
In Crossley-Holland, K. British folk tales p24-27 **398.2**
Ehrlich, A. The frog prince
In Ehrlich, A. The Random House book of fairy tales p94-101 **398.2**
Grimm, J. The frog-king
In Grimm, J. The complete Grimm's fairy tales p17-20 **398.2**
In Grimm, J. The juniper tree, and other tales from Grimm v2 p169-77 **398.2**
Grimm, J. The frog prince
In Best-loved folktales of the world p95-98 **398.2**
In The Classic fairy tales p185-87 **398.2**
In Grimm, J. Tales from Grimm p179-90 **398.2**
In Tomie dePaola's favorite nursery tales p21-30 **398.2**
Isadora, R. The princess and the frog **398.2**
Ormerod, J. The frog prince **398.2**
Rockwell, A. F. The frog prince
In Rockwell, A. F. Puss in boots, and other stories p66-74 **398.2**
A **Frog** Prince. Berenzy, A. E
The **frog** princess. Afanas'ev, A. N.
In Afanas'ev, A. N. Russian fairy tales p119-23 **398.2**
In Afanas'ev, A. N. Russian folk tales p69-77 **398.2**
Frog queen
Afanas'ev, A. N. The frog princess
In Afanas'ev, A. N. Russian fairy tales p119-23 **398.2**
In Afanas'ev, A. N. Russian folk tales p69-77 **398.2**
Frog travelers
The two frogs
In Shedlock, M. L. The art of the story-teller p213-15 **372.6**
Frog went a-courtin'. Langstaff, J. M. **781.62**
Frog went a-courting, Wendy Watson's **781.62**
Frog, where are you? Mayer, M. See note under Mayer, M. A boy, a dog, and a frog E
Frogs
See also Toads
Cole, J. A frog's body **597.8**
Florian, D. Discovering frogs (1-3) **597.8**
Lacey, E. A. The complete frog (4-6) **597.8**
Parker, N. W. Frogs, toads, lizards, and salamanders (k-3) **597.6**
See/See also pages in the following book(s):
Simon, S. Pets in a jar (4 and up) **639**

Fiction

Berenzy, A. A Frog Prince (2-4) E
Kalan, R. Jump, frog, jump! E
Lionni, L. Fish is fish E
Lionni, L. It's mine! E
Lobel, A. Frog and Toad are friends E
Mayer, M. A boy, a dog, and a frog E
Nunes, S. Tiddalick the frog (k-2) **398.2**
Potter, B. The tale of Mr. Jeremy Fisher E
Zemach, H. The princess and Froggie E
Frogs and the ballet. Elliott, D. **792.8**
A **frog's** body. Cole, J. **597.8**
Frogs, toads, lizards, and salamanders. Parker, N. W. **597.6**
Frolka Stay-at-Home
Afanas'ev, A. N. Frolka Stay-at-Home
In Afanas'ev, A. N. Russian fairy tales p299-302 **398.2**
From Abenaki to Zuni. Wolfson, E. **970.004**
From Anna. Little, J. **Fic**
From bad to good to bad to good. Kendall, C.
In Kendall, C. Sweet and sour p39-41 **398.2**
From flower to flower. Lauber, P. **582**
From flower to fruit. Dowden, A. O. T. **582**
From hand to mouth. Giblin, J. **394.1**
From map to museum. Anderson, J. **930.1**

From path to highway: the story of the Boston Post Road. Gibbons, G. **388.1**
From rags to riches. Aaseng, N. **920**
From Rollo to Tom Sawyer, and other papers. Jordan, A. M. **028.5**
From Sputnik to space shuttles. Branley, F. M. **629.44**
From the hills of Georgia: an autobiography in paintings. O'Kelley, M. L. **92**
From the mixed-up files of Mrs. Basil E. Frankweiler. Konigsburg, E. L. **Fic**
From Tiger to Anansi. Sherlock, Sir P. M. *In* Sherlock, Sir P. M. Anansi, the spider man p3-12 **398.2**
Froman, Robert
Angles are easy as pie (2-4) **516**
The greatest guessing game (2-4) **513**
Mushrooms and molds (1-3) **589.2**
Frontier and pioneer life
Aliki. The story of Johnny Appleseed (k-3) **92**
Kellogg, S. Johnny Appleseed (2-4) **92**
Parish, P. Let's be early settlers with Daniel Boone (2-5) **745.5**
Quackenbush, R. M. Quit pulling my leg! a story of Davy Crockett (2-4) **92**
Walker, B. M. The Little House cookbook (5 and up) **641.5**
Fiction
Brenner, B. Wagon wheels **E**
Brink, C. R. Caddie Woodlawn (4-6) **Fic**
Byars, B. C. The Golly Sisters go West **E**
Byars, B. C. Hooray for the Golly sisters! **E**
Byars, B. C. Trouble River (4-6) **Fic**
Clements, B. I tell a lie every so often (6 and up) **Fic**
Conrad, P. Prairie songs (5 and up) **Fic**
Dalgliesh, A. The courage of Sarah Noble (2-4) **Fic**
DeFelice, C. C. Weasel (4 and up) **Fic**
Field, R. Calico bush (4 and up) **Fic**
Fleischman, S. Chancy and the grand rascal (4-6) **Fic**
Fleischman, S. Humbug Mountain (4-6) **Fic**
Fleischman, S. Mr. Mysterious & Company (4-6) **Fic**
Fritz, J. The cabin faced west (3-6) **Fic**
Gipson, F. B. Old Yeller (6 and up) **Fic**
Harvey, B. Cassie's journey (2-4) **Fic**
Henry, M. San Domingo: the medicine hat stallion (4-6) **Fic**
Jones, W. Edge of two worlds (5 and up) **Fic**
Levin, B. Brother moose (5 and up) **Fic**
MacLachlan, P. Sarah, plain and tall (3-5) **Fic**
Nixon, J. L. Beats me, Claude **E**
Sanders, S. R. Aurora means dawn **E**
Speare, E. G. The sign of the beaver (5 and up) **Fic**
Turner, A. W. Grasshopper summer (4-6) **Fic**
Wilder, L. I. Little house in the big woods (4-6) **Fic**
California
Blumberg, R. The great American gold rush (5 and up) **979.4**
Canada
Anderson, J. Pioneer settlers of New France (3-5) **971.01**
West (U.S.)
Freedman, R. Children of the wild West (4 and up) **978**
Freedman, R. Cowboys of the wild West (4 and up) **978**
Tunis, E. Frontier living (5 and up) **978**
Frontier living. Tunis, E. **978**
Frontier Wolf. Sutcliff, R. **Fic**
Fronval, George
Indian signs and signals (4 and up) **419**
Frost, Carolyn O., 1940-
Media access and organization **025.3**
Frost, Robert, 1874-1963
Birches (1-3) **811**
Stopping by woods on a snowy evening (k-3) **811**
Frozen fire. Houston, J. A. **Fic**
Frozen stars *See* Black holes (Astronomy)
Fruit
See also Apple; Berries
Dowden, A. O. T. From flower to fruit (5 and up) **582**
Ehlert, L. Eating the alphabet **E**
McMillan, B. Growing colors **E**
Wexler, J. Flowers, fruits, seeds (k-2) **582**
Fryatt, Norma R.
(ed) A Horn Book sampler on children's books and reading. See A Horn Book sampler on children's books and reading **028.5**
Fryer, Deborah J.
(ed) The Columbia Granger's index to poetry. See The Columbia Granger's index to poetry **808.81**
Ftera, Constance
(il) Simon, S. The optical illusion book **152.14**
Fu-dog. Godden, R. **Fic**
Fuchs, Bernie
(il) Schroeder, A. Ragtime Tumpie **E**

Fudge-a-mania. Blume, J. See note under Blume, J. Tales of a fourth grade nothing **Fic**
Fuja, Abayomi
The funeral of the hyena's mother
In Best-loved folktales of the world p642-44 **398.2**
The hunter and his magic flute
In Best-loved folktales of the world p638-42 **398.2**
Oni and the great bird
In Best-loved folktales of the world p644-49 **398.2**
The wise dog
In Best-loved folktales of the world p634-38 **398.2**
The wooden spoon and the whip
In Best-loved folktales of the world p649-51 **398.2**
Fujikawa, Gyo, 1908-
(il) Stevenson, R. L. A child's garden of verses **821**
Fuller, Elizabeth
(il) Butler, D. My brown bear Barney **E**
Fuller, Muriel
(ed) More junior authors. See More junior authors **920.003**
Fun and game songs, The Fireside book of **782.42**
Fun with German. Cooper, L. P. **438**
Fun with Spanish. See Cooper, L. P. More fun with Spanish **468**
Funai, Mamoru, 1932-
(il) Morris, R. A. Dolphin **599.5**
Fundevogel
Grimm, J. Fundevogel
In Grimm, J. The complete Grimm's fairy tales p241-44 **398.2**
The **funeral** of the hyena's mother. Fuja, A.
In Best-loved folktales of the world p642-44 **398.2**
Funeral rites and ceremonies
Berrill, M. Mummies, masks, & mourners (4-6) **393**
Perl, L. Mummies, tombs, and treasure (4 and up) **393**
See/See also pages in the following book(s):
The Kids' book about death and dying p31-46 (5 and up) **155.9**
Fungi
See also Mushrooms
Funny, funny Lyle. Waber, B. See note under Waber, B. The house on East 88th Street **E**
The **funny** little woman. Mosel, A. **398.2**
The **funny** song-book. Nelson, E. L. **782.42**
Funnybones. Ahlberg, J. **E**
A **furl** of fairy wind. Hunter, M.
In Hunter, M. A furl of fairy wind: four stories p49-54 **S C**
A **furl** of fairy wind: four stories. Hunter, M. **S C**
Furniture
Rosenberg, M. B. Artists of handcrafted furniture at work (4 and up) **749**
The **furry** news. Leedy, L. **070**
Further tales of Uncle Remus. Lester, J. **398.2**

G

G.I.'s *See* Soldiers—United States
Gaber, Susan
(il) Forest, H. The baker's dozen **398.2**
(il) Forest, H. The woman who flummoxed the fairies **398.2**
Gabrielson, Ira Noel, 1889-1977
(jt. auth) Zim, H. S. Birds **598**
Gackenbach, Dick, 1927-
What's Claude doing? **E**
(il) Smith, J. L. The kid next door and other headaches **Fic**
Gaffer Samson's luck. Paton Walsh, J. **Fic**
Gaffney-Kessell, Walter
(il) Cole, J. The human body: how we evolved **573.2**
(il) Conford, E. Lenny Kandell, smart aleck **Fic**
(il) Epstein, S. Bugs for dinner? **591.5**
(il) George, J. C. One day in the alpine tundra **574.5**
(il) Schlein, M. The billions of bats **599.4**
Gág, Wanda, 1893-1946
The A B C bunny **E**
Gone is gone (k-3) **398.2**
Millions of cats **E**
Nothing At All **E**
Wanda Gág's The sorcerer's apprentice (k-3) **398.2**
(il) Grimm, J. More tales from Grimm **398.2**
(il) Grimm, J. Tales from Grimm **398.2**
Grimm, J. Wanda Gág's Jorinda and Joringel **398.2**
Grimm, J. Wanda Gág's The earth gnome **398.2**
Grimm, J. Wanda Gag's The six swans **398.2**
See/See also pages in the following book(s):
A Horn Book sampler on children's books and reading p34-38 **028.5**

Gage, Wilson, 1922-
The crow and Mrs. Gaddy. See note under Gage, W. Mrs. Gaddy and the ghost **E**
Cully Cully and the bear **E**
Mike's toads **Fic**
Mrs. Gaddy and the fast-growing vine. See note under Gage, W. Mrs. Gaddy and the ghost **E**
Mrs. Gaddy and the ghost **E**
Gál, László, 1933-
(il) Irwin, P. K. P. A flask of sea water **Fic**
(il) Martin, E. Tales of the Far North **398.2**
(il) San Souci, R. The enchanted tapestry **398.2**
Galaxies
Apfel, N. H. Nebulae (4 and up) **523.1**
Simon, S. Galaxies (2-5) **523.1**
Galaxy (Milky Way) *See* Milky Way
Galbraith, Kathryn Osebold
Laura Charlotte **E**
Galdone, Joanna
The tailypo (k-3) **398.2**
Galdone, Paul, 1914-1986
The cat goes fiddle-i-fee (k-1) **398.8**
Cinderella (k-2) **398.2**
The elves and the shoemaker (k-2) **398.2**
The gingerbread boy (k-2) **398.2**
Henny Penny (k-2) **398.2**
King of the Cats (k-2) **398.2**
also in Halloween: stories and poems p3-7 **808.8**
The little red hen (k-2) **398.2**
Little Red Riding Hood (k-2) **398.2**
The monkey and the crocodile (k-2) **398.2**
Puss in boots (k-2) **398.2**
The teeny-tiny woman (k-2) **398.2**
Three Aesop fox fables (k-3) **398.2**
The three bears (k-2) **398.2**
The three Billy Goats Gruff (k-2) **398.2**
Three little kittens (k-1) **398.8**
The three little pigs (k-2) **398.2**
The three sillies (k-3) **398.2**
The turtle and the monkey (k-2) **398.2**
What's in fox's sack? (k-2) **398.2**
(il) Andersen, H. C. The princess and the pea **Fic**
(il) Andersen, H. C. The steadfast tin soldier **Fic**
(il) Barth, E. Jack-o'-lantern **398.2**
(il) Branley, F. M. High sounds, low sounds **534**
(il) Bulla, C. R. The sword in the tree **Fic**
(il) Corbett, S. The lemonade trick **Fic**
(il) De Regniers, B. S. It does not say meow, and other animal riddle rhymes **793.73**
(il) Galdone, J. The tailypo **398.2**
(il) The Hare and the tortoise. See The Hare and the tortoise **398.2**
(il) Ivimey, J. W. The complete story of the three blind mice **E**
(il) Lear, E. The owl and the pussycat **821**
(il) Titus, E. Basil of Baker Street **Fic**
Galimoto. Williams, K. L. **E**
Gallagher, Susan
(il) Stolz, M. Night of ghosts and hermits **574.92**
Gallant, Roy A.
Before the sun dies (6 and up) **575**
Lost cities (4 and up) **930**
Our restless earth (4 and up) **550**
Rainbows, mirages and sundogs (4 and up) **551.5**
Gallaudet, T. H. (Thomas Hopkins), 1787-1851
About
Neimark, A. E. A deaf child listened: Thomas Gallaudet, pioneer in American education (6 and up) **92**
Gallaudet, Thomas Hopkins *See* Gallaudet, T. H. (Thomas Hopkins), 1787-1851
Gallaz, Christophe
(jt. auth) Innocenti, R. Rose Blanche **Fic**
Galleries, Art *See* Art—Museums
A **gallery** of dinosaurs & other early reptiles. Peters, D. **567.9**
Gallo, Donald R.
(ed) Connections: short stories by outstanding writers for young adults. See Connections: short stories by outstanding writers for young adults **S C**
Gallymanders! Gallymanders!
In Grandfather tales p18-28 **398.2**
Gamble, James, b. 1803?
See/See also pages in the following book(s):
Aaseng, N. From rags to riches p10-18 (5 and up) **920**
Gambler's eyes. Yee, P.
In Yee, P. Tales from Gold Mountain p39-44 **S C**
Gambling Hans
Grimm, J. Gambling Hansel
In Grimm, J. The complete Grimm's fairy tales p378-80 **398.2**
Gambling Hansel. Grimm, J.
In Grimm, J. The complete Grimm's fairy tales p378-80 **398.2**

Game protection
See also Birds—Protection
Game songs, The Fireside book of fun and 782.42
Games
See also Indoor games; Singing games; Sports; Word games; names of types of games and of individual games
Anna Banana: 101 jump-rope rhymes (2-4) 398.8
Hoguet, S. R. I unpacked my grandmother's trunk E
Kaye, P. Games for reading 372.4
Miss Mary Mack and other children's street rhymes (1-4) 796.1
Opie, I. A. Children's games in street and playground 796.1
A Pumpkin in a pear tree (1-4) 745.59
The RIF guide to encouraging young readers 372.4
Robinson, J. Activities for anyone, anytime, anywhere (5 and up) 790.1
Rockwell, A. F. Games (and how to play them) (k-4) 796.1
Sportworks (4 and up) 796
Stamp your feet (k-2) 796.1
Zaslavsky, C. Tic tac toe, and other three-in-a row games from ancient Egypt to the modern computer (4 and up) 794
Fiction
Bonsall, C. N. Piggle E
Van Allsburg, C. Jumanji E
Games (and how to play them). Rockwell, A. F. 796.1
Games for reading. Kaye, P. 372.4
The **Gammage** cup. Kendall, C. Fic
Gammell, Stephen, 1943-
(il) Ackerman, K. Song and dance man E
(il) Baker, O. Where the buffaloes begin Fic
(il) Birdseye, T. Airmail to the moon E
(il) Blos, J. W. Old Henry E
(il) Dancing teepees: poems of American Indian youth. See Dancing teepees: poems of American Indian youth 897
(il) Fritz, J. Stonewall [biography of Stonewall Jackson] 92
(il) Halloween poems. See Halloween poems 808.81
(il) Hunter, M. A furl of fairy wind: four stories S C
(il) Lyon, G. E. Come a tide E
(il) Lyon, G. E. A regular rolling Noah E
(il) Martin, R. Will's mammoth E
(il) McHargue, G. Meet the werewolf 398
(il) Rylant, C. The relatives came E
(il) Schwartz, A. More scary stories to tell in the dark 398.2
(il) Schwartz, A. Scary stories to tell in the dark 398.2
(il) Thanksgiving poems. See Thanksgiving poems 808.81
The **gamut** and time-table in verse. Finch, C.
In A Nursery companion p90-93 820.8
Gannett, Deborah Sampson, 1760-1827
About
McGovern, A. The secret soldier: the story of Deborah Sampson (3-5) 92
Gannett, Ruth Chrisman, 1896-1979
(il) Bailey, C. S. Miss Hickory Fic
(il) Gannett, R. S. My father's dragon Fic
(il) Reyher, R. H. My mother is the most beautiful woman in the world 398.2
Gannett, Ruth Stiles, 1923-
My father's dragon (1-4) Fic
Gans, Roma, 1894-
Caves (k-3) 551.4
Danger—icebergs! (k-3) 551.3
Rock collecting (k-3) 552
Gantos, Jack
Happy birthday Rotten Ralph. See note under Gantos, J. Rotten Ralph E
Rotten Ralph E
Rotten Ralph's rotten Christmas. See note under Gantos, J. Rotten Ralph E
Rotten Ralph's show and tell. See note under Gantos, J. Rotten Ralph E
Rotten Ralph's trick or treat! See note under Gantos, J. Rotten Ralph E
Worse than rotten, Ralph. See note under Gantos, J. Rotten Ralph E
The **Gaping,** wide-mouthed waddling frog
In A Nursery companion p54-57 820.8
Garage sales
Fiction
Rockwell, A. F. Our garage sale E
Garbage *See* Refuse and refuse disposal
Garbage!. Hadingham, E. 363.7
Gardam, Jane
The hollow land (5 and up) Fic
A long way from Verona (6 and up) Fic
The **garden**. Brown, M. W.
In Brown, M. W. The fish with the deep sea smile p33-38 818
The **garden** of Abdul Gasazi. Van Allsburg, C. E
Gardening
See also Flower gardening; Vegetable gardening

Gardening—*Continued*
Björk, C. Linnea's windowsill garden (3-6) **635**
Brown, M. T. Your first garden book (1-3) **635**
Huff, B. A. Greening the city streets **635**
See/See also pages in the following book(s):
Caney, S. Steven Caney's kids' America p96-106 (4 and up) **790.1**
Fiction
Ehlert, L. Planting a rainbow **E**
Rockwell, A. F. How my garden grew **E**
Wolf, J. The rosy fat magenta radish **E**

Gardens
Fiction
Hurd, T. The pea patch jig **E**
Rockwell, A. F. My back yard **E**
Rylant, C. This year's garden **E**

Gardiner, Brian
Energy demands (5 and up) **333.79**

Gardiner, John Reynolds, 1944-
Stone Fox (2-5) **Fic**

Gardner, Beau, 1941-
Can you imagine—? **E**
Have you ever seen—? **E**
(il) The Upside down riddle book. See The Upside down riddle book **793.73**

Gardner, Herb, 1934-
How I crossed the street for the first time all by myself [short story]
In Free to be—you and me p100-11 **810.8**

Gardner, Richard M. *See* Cummings, Richard, 1931-

Gardner, Robert, 1929-
Kitchen chemistry: science experiments to do at home (4 and up) **540.7**

Garelick, May, 1910-1989
(jt. auth) Brenner, B. Two orphan cubs **599.74**

Garfield, Leon
The apprentices (6 and up) **S C**
Contents: The lamplighter's funeral; Mirror, mirror; Moss and blister; The cloak; The valentine; Labour-in-vain; The fool; Rosy starling; The dumb cake; Tom Titmarsh's devil; The filthy beast; The enemy
The December Rose (5 and up) **Fic**
Young Nick and Jubilee (5 and up) **Fic**
See/See also pages in the following book(s):
Townsend, J. R. A sense of story p97-104 **028.5**
Townsend, J. R. A sounding of storytellers p66-80 **028.5**

Garis, Howard R., 1873-1962
Uncle Wiggily's Christmas
In The Family read-aloud Christmas treasury p58-63 **808.8**

Garland, Sherry
Vietnam, rebuilding a nation (4 and up) **959.704**

Garments *See* Clothing and dress

Garner, Alan, 1934-
See/See also pages in the following book(s):
Townsend, J. R. A sense of story p108-16 **028.5**
Townsend, J. R. A sounding of storytellers p81-96 **028.5**

Garr, David J.
(il) Nardi, T. J. Karate basics **796.8**

Garrison, Christian
Little pieces of the West Wind
In Windy day: stories and poems p22-31 **808.8**

Garrison, William Lloyd, 1805-1879
See/See also pages in the following book(s):
Jacobs, W. J. Great lives: human rights p80-90 (5 and up) **920**

Garson, Eugenia
(ed) The Laura Ingalls Wilder songbook. See The Laura Ingalls Wilder songbook **782.42**

Garth Pig and the ice cream lady. Rayner, M. See note under Rayner, M. Mr. and Mrs. Pig's evening out **E**

Garza, Carmen Lomas *See* Lomas Garza, Carmen

Gases
See/See also pages in the following book(s):
Asimov, I. How did we find out about superconductivity? p25-36 (5 and up) **537.6**

Gates, Doris, 1901-
Blue willow (4 and up) **Fic**
A fair wind for Troy (4 and up) **292**
The golden god: Apollo (4 and up) **292**
Lord of the sky: Zeus (4 and up) **292**
Mightiest of the mortals: Heracles (4 and up) **292**
Two queens of heaven: Aphrodite [and] Demeter (4 and up) **292**
The warrior goddess: Athena (4 and up) **292**

A **gathering** of days: a New England girl's journal, 1830-32. Blos, J. W. **Fic**

The **gathering** room. Rodowsky, C. F. **Fic**

Gauch, Patricia Lee
Christina Katerina & the box. See note under Gauch, P. L. Christina Katerina and the time she quit the family **E**
Christina Katerina and the great bear train. See note under Gauch, P. L. Christina Katerina and the time she quit the family **E**
Christina Katerina and the time she quit the family **E**
Dance, Tanya **E**
This time, Tempe Wick? (3-5) **Fic**

Gauguin, Paul, 1848-1903
About
Raboff, E. Paul Gauguin (4 and up) 759.4

Gaul, Randy, 1959-
(il) Fleischman, P. Coming-and-going men S C

Gawain (Legendary character)
Hastings, S. Sir Gawain and the Green Knight (3 and up) 398.2
Hastings, S. Sir Gawain and the loathly lady (3 and up) 398.2

Gawain and the Grene Knight
Hastings, S. Sir Gawain and the Green Knight 398.2

Gay, Kathlyn
Science in ancient Greece (5 and up) 509

Gazetteers
See also Names, Geographical
Webster's new geographical dictionary 910.3

Geary, Robert
(il) Howell, M. The elephant man [biography of Joseph Carey Merrick] 92

Gee, Wiz! Allison, L. 507

Geese
Hirschi, R. City geese (3-5) 598
Fiction
Duvoisin, R. Petunia E
Langton, J. The fledgling (5 and up) Fic
Polacco, P. Rechenka's eggs E
Preston, E. M. Squawk to the moon, Little Goose E
Sharmat, M. W. Griselda's new year E

Gehm, Charles
(il) Peck, R. N. Soup Fic

Geisel, Theodor Seuss *See* Seuss, Dr.

Geisert, Arthur
The ark (k-3) 222
Pigs from A to Z E

Gellman, Marc
Does God have a big toe? (4-6) 221.9

Gender identity *See* Sex role

Genealogy
Cooper, K. Where did you get those eyes? (5 and up) 929
Perl, L. The great ancestor hunt (5 and up) 929
See/See also pages in the following book(s):
Caney, S. Steven Caney's kids' America p26-37 (4 and up) 790.1

The **general.** Terada, A. M.
In Terada, A. M. Under the starfruit tree p78-82 398.2

General Motors Corp.
See/See also pages in the following book(s):
Aaseng, N. The unsung heroes p24-38 (5 and up) 920

General Moulton strikes a bargain. Roach, M. K.
In Roach, M. K. Encounters with the invisible world S C

Generals
Fritz, J. Stonewall [biography of Stonewall Jackson] (4 and up) 92
Weidhorn, M. Robert E. Lee (5 and up) 92

Generation gap *See* Conflict of generations

Genetics
Bornstein, S. What makes you what you are (5 and up) 575.1
Patent, D. H. Grandfather's nose (k-2) 575.1

Genghis Khan, 1162-1227
See/See also pages in the following book(s):
Lyttle, R. B. Land beyond the river p125-34 (6 and up) 940.1
Major, J. S. The land and people of Mongolia p61-76 (5 and up) 951.7

The **genie** of Sutton Place. Selden, G. Fic

Genie with the light blue hair. Conford, E. Fic

Gennaro, Joseph, 1924-
(jt. auth) Grillone, L. Small worlds close up 500

Gentle Ben. Morey, W. Fic

The **gentle** giant-killer. Gotwalt, H. L. M.
In Gotwalt, H. L. M. Everyday plays for boys and girls p101-15 812

Gentle Gwan Yin. Carpenter, F.
In Carpenter, F. Tales of a Chinese grandmother p29-38 398.2

Geography
See also Atlases; Discoveries (in geography); Maps; Voyages and travels; names of countries, states, etc. with the subdivisions *Description and travel* and *Geography,* e.g. *United States—Description and travel; United States—Geography;* etc.
Bell, N. The book of where (5 and up) 910
Dictionaries
Exploring your world: the adventure of geography 910.3
Lands and peoples 910.3
Webster's new geographical dictionary 910.3
Worldmark encyclopedia of the nations 910.3
Periodicals
National Geographic World (3-6) 910.5

Geology
Aylesworth, T. G. Moving continents (6 and up) **551.1**
Cole, J. The magic school bus inside the Earth (2-4) **551.1**
Gallant, R. A. Our restless earth (4 and up) **550**
Lauber, P. Dinosaurs walked here, and other stories fossils tell (3-5) **560**
McNulty, F. How to dig a hole to the other side of the world (2-4) **551.1**
North America
O'Neill, C. Natural wonders of North America (5 and up) **557**

Geometry
Froman, R. Angles are easy as pie (2-4) **516**
Hoban, T. Shapes, shapes, shapes (k-2) **516**
Rogers, P. The shapes game (k-2) **516**
Testa, F. If you look around you (k-3) **516**

George III, King of Great Britain, 1738-1820
About
Fritz, J. Can't you make them behave, King George? (3-5) **92**

George, Jean Craighead, 1919-
Julie of the wolves (6 and up) **Fic**
My side of the mountain (5 and up) **Fic**
On the far side of the mountain (5 and up) **Fic**
One day in the alpine tundra (4-6) **574.5**
One day in the desert (4-6) **574.5**
One day in the prairie (4-6) **574.5**
One day in the tropical rain forest (4-6) **574.5**
One day in the woods (4-6) **574.5**
Water sky (5 and up) **Fic**
Who really killed Cock Robin? (3-7) **Fic**
See/See also pages in the following book(s):
Newbery and Caldecott Medal books, 1966-1975 p96-106, 109-12 **028.5**

George, Lindsay Barrett
(il) George, W. T. Box Turtle at Long Pond **E**

George, Richard R.
Roald Dahl's James and the giant peach (3-5) **822**

George, William T.
Box Turtle at Long Pond **E**

George and Martha. Marshall, J. **E**
George and Martha back in town. Marshall, J. See note under Marshall, J. George and Martha **E**
George and Martha encore. Marshall, J. See note under Marshall, J. George and Martha **E**
George and Martha, one fine day. Marshall, J. See note under Marshall, J. George and Martha **E**
George and Martha rise and shine. Marshall, J. See note under Marshall, J. George and Martha **E**
George and Martha, round and round. Marshall, J. See note under Marshall, J. George and Martha **E**
George and Martha, tons of fun. Marshall, J. See note under Marshall, J. George and Martha **E**
George and Martha Washington at home in New York. Siegel, B. **973.4**
George Bush. Sullivan, G. **92**
George Bush: forty-first president of the United States. Kent, Z. **92**

George, Saint, d. 303
About
Hodges, M. Saint George and the dragon (2-5) **398.2**

George shrinks. Joyce, W. **E**
George told Kate. Chorao, K. See note under Chorao, K. Kate's box **E**
George Washington. D'Aulaire, I. **92**
George Washington and the birth of our nation. Meltzer, M. **92**

George Washington Bridge (N.Y. and N.J.)
Swift, H. H. The little red lighthouse and the great gray bridge **E**

George Washington's breakfast. Fritz, J. **Fic**
George's dream. Sanfield, S.
In Sanfield, S. The adventures of High John the Conqueror **398.2**

Georgia, Lowell
(il) Bridge, L. M. The playful dolphins **599.5**

Georgia
Fradin, D. B. The Georgia colony (4 and up) **975.8**
Kent, Z. Georgia
In America the beautiful **973**
Fiction
Beatty, P. Turn homeward, Hannalee (5 and up) **Fic**
Burch, R. Christmas with Ida Early (4 and up) **Fic**
Burch, R. Ida Early comes over the mountain (4 and up) **Fic**
Burch, R. Queenie Peavy (5 and up) **Fic**
Wilkinson, B. S. Ludell (6 and up) **Fic**

The **Georgia** colony. Fradin, D. B. **975.8**
Georgia music. Griffith, H. V. **E**
Georgie. Bright, R. **E**
Georgie and the robbers. Bright, R. See note under Bright, R. Georgie **E**

Geothermal resources
Jacobs, L. Letting off steam (3-6) **621.44**
Geraldine's big snow. Keller, H. **E**
Geraldine's blanket. Keller, H. **E**
Gerber, Daniel F., 1898-1974
See/See also pages in the following book(s):
Aaseng, N. The problem solvers p47-52 (5 and up) **920**
Gerber, Dorothy Scott, d. 1988
See/See also pages in the following book(s):
Aaseng, N. The problem solvers p47-52 (5 and up) **920**
Gerbils
Pope, J. Taking care of your gerbils (3-5) **636.088**
See/See also pages in the following book(s):
Weber, W. J. Care of uncommon pets p82-92 (5 and up) **636.088**
Fiction
Pearce, P. The battle of Bubble and Squeak (3-6) **Fic**
Gergely, Tibor, 1900-1978
(il) Brown, M. W. Wheel on the chimney **E**
Geringer, Laura
A three hat day **E**
German Americans
De Paola, T. An early American Christmas **E**
German cookery *See* Cookery, German
German language
Cooper, L. P. Fun with German (4 and up) **438**
Germans
Canada—Fiction
Little, J. From Anna (4-6) **Fic**
Germany
Folklore
See Folklore—Germany
History
Stewart, G. Germany (4 and up) **943.087**
History—1933-1945
Koehn, I. Mischling, second degree: my childhood in Nazi Germany (6 and up) **92**
Shirer, W. L. The rise and fall of Adolf Hitler (6 and up) **943.086**
Politics and government—1933-1945
Shirer, W. L. The rise and fall of Adolf Hitler (6 and up) **943.086**
Germs!. Patent, D. H. **616.9**
Germs make me sick! Berger, M. **616.9**
Germy Blew it. Jones, R. C. See note under Jones, R. C. Germy blew the Bugle **Fic**
Germy blew it—again! Jones, R. C. See note under Jones, R. C. Germy blew the Bugle **Fic**
Germy blew the Bugle. Jones, R. C. **Fic**
Geronimo, Apache Chief, 1829-1909
About
Shorto, R. Geronimo and the struggle for Apache freedom (5 and up) **92**
See/See also pages in the following book(s):
Ehrlich, A. Wounded Knee: an Indian history of the American West (6 and up) **970.004**
Geronimo and the struggle for Apache freedom. Shorto, R. **92**
Gerontology
See also Old age
Gerrard, Roy, 1935-
Mik's mammoth **E**
Gershwin, George, 1898-1937
About
Mitchell, B. America, I hear you: a story about George Gershwin (3-5) **92**
Gerst, Tom
Indonesia—in pictures. See Indonesia—in pictures **959.8**
Gerstein, Mordicai, 1935-
Arnold of the Ducks **E**
The mountains of Tibet **E**
Roll over! **E**
(il) Levy, E. Something queer is going on (a mystery) **E**
Get on out of here, Philip Hall. Greene, B. **Fic**
Get ready for robots! Lauber, P. **629.8**
Get set! Go! Watanabe, S. See note under Watanabe, S. How do I put it on? **E**
Getting dressed. Cobb, V. **646**
Getting elected. Hewett, J. **324**
Getting even. Chaikin, M. See note under Chaikin, M. Finders weepers **Fic**
Getting ready for bed *See* Bedtime
Getting something on Maggie Marmelstein. Sharmat, M. W. See note under Sharmat, M. W. Mysteriously yours, Maggie Marmelstein **Fic**
Getting started in calligraphy. Baron, N. **745.6**
Getting your period. Marzollo, J. **612.6**
Gettysburg (Pa.), Battle of, 1863
Carter, A. R. The Battle of Gettysburg (4 and up) **973.7**
Johnson, N. The Battle of Gettysburg (5 and up) **973.7**
See/See also pages in the following book(s):
Voices from the Civil War p94-103 (6 and up) **973.7**

Ghana
Ghana—in pictures (5 and up) **966.7**
Hintz, M. Ghana (4 and up) **966.7**
Folklore
See Folklore—Ghana
Ghana—in pictures (5 and up) **966.7**
Ghastlies, goops & pincushions: nonsense verse. Kennedy, X. J. **811**
Gherman, Beverly
Agnes de Mille: dancing off the earth (5 and up) **92**
Georgia O'Keeffe (5 and up) **92**
Ghost abbey. Westall, R. **Fic**
The **ghost** belonged to me. Peck, R. **Fic**
Ghost dance
See/See also pages in the following book(s):
Ehrlich, A. Wounded Knee: an Indian history of the American West (6 and up) **970.004**
Ghost dancers. Smith, S.
In Things that go bump in the night p61-63 **S C**
The **ghost** drum. Price, S. **Fic**
The **ghost-eye** tree. Martin, B. **E**
Ghost in a four-room apartment. Raskin, E. **E**
The **ghost** in the shed. Roach, M. K.
In Roach, M. K. Encounters with the invisible world **S C**
A **ghost** named Fred. Benchley, N. **E**
The **ghost** of Misery Hill. San Souci, R.
In San Souci, R. Short & shivery p139-43 **398.2**
Ghost of the spring and the shrew
Afanas'ev, A. N. The bad wife
In Afanas'ev, A. N. Russian fairy tales p56-57 **398.2**
The **ghost** of Thomas Kempe. Lively, P. **Fic**
The **ghost** of Wan Li Road. Dalkey, K.
In Things that go bump in the night p82-90 **S C**
The **ghost** on Brass's Hill. Leach, M.
In Leach, M. Whistle in the graveyard p106-07 **398.2**
The **ghost** on Saturday night. Fleischman, S. **Fic**
Ghost poems (1-4) **821.008**
The **Ghost** Squad and the Ghoul of Grunberg. Hildick, E. W. See note under Hildick, E. W. The Ghost Squad breaks through **Fic**
The **Ghost** Squad and the Halloween conspiracy. Hildick, E. W. See note under Hildick, E. W. The Ghost Squad breaks through **Fic**
The **Ghost** Squad and the menace of the Malevs. Hildick, E. W. See note under Hildick, E. W. The Ghost Squad breaks through **Fic**
The **Ghost** Squad and the prowling hermits. Hildick, E. W. See note under Hildick, E. W. The Ghost Squad breaks through **Fic**
The **Ghost** Squad breaks through. Hildick, E. W. **Fic**
The **Ghost** Squad flies Concorde. Hildick, E. W. See note under Hildick, E. W. The Ghost Squad breaks through **Fic**
Ghost story
In The Whistling skeleton p62-72 **398.2**
Ghost story. Porte-Thomas, B. A.
In Porte-Thomas, B. A. Jesse's ghost, and other stories p41-43 **S C**
Ghost towns
See also Cities and towns, Ruined, extinct, etc.
Fiction
Clifford, E. The dastardly murder of Dirty Pete (3-5) **Fic**
Ghost vision. Kortum, J. **Fic**
The **ghost** who came out of the book. Mahy, M.
In Mahy, M. Nonstop nonsense p86-92 **828**
Ghostly companions. Alcock, V. **S C**
Ghostly fishermen. Carlson, N. S.
In Carlson, N. S. The talking cat, and other stories of French Canada p66-76 **S C**
The **ghostly** little girl. San Souci, R.
In San Souci, R. Short & shivery p48-52 **398.2**
The **ghostly** spools. Leach, M.
In Leach, M. Whistle in the graveyard p76-77 **398.2**
Ghosts
Cohen, D. Phone call from a ghost (4-6) **133.1**
Fiction
Aiken, J. The shadow guests (5 and up) **Fic**
Alcock, V. Ghostly companions (5 and up) **S C**
Allard, H. Bumps in the night **E**
Benchley, N. A ghost named Fred **E**
Bennett, J. Teeny tiny (k-1) **398.2**
Bright, R. Georgie **E**
Cassedy, S. Behind the attic wall (5 and up) **Fic**
Charbonneau, E. The ghosts of Stony Clove (5 and up) **Fic**
Clapp, P. Jane-Emily (5 and up) **Fic**
Conrad, P. Stonewords (5 and up) **Fic**

Ghosts—Fiction—*Continued*
Corbett, S. The discontented ghost (6 and up) **Fic**
Dickens, C. A Christmas carol in prose (4 and up) **Fic**
Fleischman, S. The midnight horse (3-6) **Fic**
Gage, W. Mrs. Gaddy and the ghost **E**
Galdone, P. The teeny-tiny woman (k-2) **398.2**
Hahn, M. D. The doll in the garden (4-6) **Fic**
Hahn, M. D. Wait till Helen comes (4-6) **Fic**
Hancock, S. Esteban and the ghost (k-3) **398.2**
Hildick, E. W. The Ghost Squad breaks through (5 and up) **Fic**
Klaveness, J. O. The Griffin legacy (6 and up) **Fic**
Leach, M. Whistle in the graveyard (4-6) **398.2**
Lively, P. The ghost of Thomas Kempe (4-6) **Fic**
Martin, B. The ghost-eye tree **E**
Naylor, P. R. Bernie and the Bessledorf ghost (4-6) **Fic**
Peck, R. The ghost belonged to me (5 and up) **Fic**
Raskin, E. Ghost in a four-room apartment **E**
Roach, M. K. Encounters with the invisible world (5 and up) **S C**
San Souci, R. The boy and the ghost (k-3) **398.2**
San Souci, R. Short & shivery (4 and up) **398.2**
Schwartz, A. In a dark, dark room, and other scary stories (k-3) **398.2**
Schwartz, A. More scary stories to tell in the dark (4 and up) **398.2**
Schwartz, A. Scary stories to tell in the dark (4 and up) **398.2**
Seuling, B. The teeny tiny woman (k-2) **398.2**
Westall, R. Ghost abbey (5 and up) **Fic**

See/See also pages in the following book(s):
Caney, S. Steven Caney's kids' America p342-47 (4 and up) **790.1**

Poetry

Ghost poems (1-4) **821.008**

The **ghost's** bride. Yep, L.
In Yep, L. The rainbow people p54-59 **398.2**

The **ghost's** cap. San Souci, R.
In San Souci, R. Short & shivery p22-27 **398.2**

Ghost's hour, spook's hour. Bunting, E. **E**

Ghosts I have been. Peck, R. See note under Peck, R. The ghost belonged to me **Fic**

Ghosts I have been [excerpt]. Peck, R.
In The Random House book of humor for children p36-43 **817.008**

The **ghosts** of Stony Clove. Charbonneau, E. **Fic**

Giant and the herdboy
The Giants and the herd-boy
In The Yellow fairy book p75-77 **398.2**

Giant and the tailor
Grimm, J. The giant and the tailor
In Grimm, J. The complete Grimm's fairy tales p745-47 **398.2**

The **giant** elk skin. Mayo, G.
In Mayo, G. Star tales p43-44 **398.2**

The **giant** jam sandwich. Lord, J. V. **E**

Giant panda
Jin Xuqi. The giant panda (5 and up) **599.74**
McClung, R. M. Lili: a giant panda of Sichuan (3-6) **599.74**
Schlein, M. Pandas (4-6) **599.74**
Schlein, M. Project panda watch (4 and up) **599.74**

Fiction

Schlein, M. The year of the panda (3-5) **Fic**

Giant who had no heart
Asbjørnsen, P. C. The giant who had no heart in his body
In Best-loved folktales of the world p304-10 **398.2**

The **giant** who had no heart in his body. Asbjørnsen, P. C.
In Best-loved folktales of the world p304-10 **398.2**

Giant with the golden hair
Grimm, J. The devil and his three golden hairs
In Grimm, J. The juniper tree, and other tales from Grimm v1 p80-93 **398.2**
Grimm, J. The Devil with the three golden hairs
In Grimm, J. The complete Grimm's fairy tales p151-58 **398.2**
Grimm, J. The devil's three gold hairs
In Best-loved folktales of the world p78-84 **398.2**
Hogrogian, N. The devil with the three golden hairs **398.2**
Martin, E. The three golden hairs
In Martin, E. Tales of the Far North p29-38 **398.2**

Giants

Fiction

De la Mare, W. Molly Whuppie (k-3) 398.2
De Paola, T. The mysterious giant of Barletta E
De Regniers, B. S. Jack the giant killer (k-3) 398.2
Root, P. Soup for supper E
Seeger, P. Abiyoyo (k-2) 398.2
Wilde, O. The selfish giant (2-5) Fic

The **Giants** and the herd-boy
In The Yellow fairy book p75-77 398.2

Giants from the past: the age of mammals (5 and up) 569

The **giant's** heart. MacDonald, G.
In MacDonald, G. The complete fairy tales of George MacDonald S C

Gibbons, Gail
Beacons of light: lighthouses (1-3) 387.1
Boat book (k-2) 387.2
Catch the wind! (1-3) 796.1
Check it out! the book about libraries (k-3) 027
Clocks and how they go (2-4) 681.1
Deadline! (1-3) 070
Department store (k-3) 381
Dinosaurs (k-2) 567.9
Easter (k-2) 394.2
Farming (k-2) 630.1
Fill it up! (k-3) 629.28
Fire! Fire! (1-3) 363.3
Flying (k-2) 629.13
From path to highway: the story of the Boston Post Road (1-3) 388.1
Halloween (k-2) 394.2
Happy birthday! (k-2) 394.2
How a house is built (k-2) 690
Lights! Camera! Action! (1-3) 791.43
The milk makers (k-2) 637
Monarch butterfly (1-3) 595.7
New road! (k-3) 625.7
Playgrounds (k-1) 796
The post office book (k-3) 383
The pottery place (1-3) 666
Prehistoric animals (k-2) 560
The seasons of Arnold's apple tree E
Sun up, sun down (1-3) 523.7
Sunken treasure (2-4) 910.4
Thanksgiving Day (k-2) 394.2
Tool book (k-2) 621.9
Trains (k-2) 625.1
Tunnels (k-3) 624.1
Up goes the skyscraper! (k-2) 690
Valentine's Day (k-2) 394.2
Weather forecasting (1-3) 551.6
Weather words and what they mean (1-3) 551.6
Zoo (k-2) 590.74
(il) Cole, J. Cars and how they go 629.222

Giblin, James, 1933-
Chimney sweeps: yesterday and today (4-6) 697
Fireworks, picnics, and flags (3-6) 394.2
From hand to mouth (4 and up) 394.1
Let there be light: a book about windows (5 and up) 690
Milk: the fight for purity (5 and up) 637
The truth about Santa Claus (4 and up) 394.2
Walls (5 and up) 623

Giff, Patricia Reilly
The gift of the pirate queen (4-6) Fic
Happy birthday, Ronald Morgan! See note under Giff, P. R. Watch out, Ronald Morgan! E
Loretta P. Sweeny, where are you? (4-6) Fic
Love, from the fifth-grade celebrity (4-6) Fic
Ronald Morgan goes to bat. See note under Giff, P. R. Watch out, Ronald Morgan! E
Watch out, Ronald Morgan! E

The **gift**. Coutant, H. Fic
A **gift** for Mama. Hautzig, E. R. Fic
A **gift** from Saint Francis. Cole, J. 92
The **gift-giver**. Hansen, J. Fic
The **gift** giving. Aiken, J.
In Aiken, J. Up the chimney down, and other stories p50-65 S C
The **gift** of the Magi. Henry, O. Fic
The **gift** of the pirate queen. Giff, P. R. Fic
The **gift** of the sacred dog. Goble, P. 398.2

Gifted children
Baskin, B. H. Books for the gifted child 011.6

Fiction

Hermes, P. I hate being gifted (5 and up) Fic

Gifts
Hautzig, E. R. Make it special (4-6) 745.59

Fiction

Bang, M. Delphine E
Bunting, E. The Mother's Day mice E
Hautzig, E. R. A gift for Mama (3-6) Fic
Patterson, N. R. The Christmas cup (3-5) Fic

Giganti, Paul, Jr.
How many snails? E

Gila monsters meet you at the airport. Sharmat, M. W. E
Gilberto and the Wind. Ets, M. H. E
Gilbreath, Alice (Alice Thompson)
The Arctic and Antarctica (4 and up) 998
Gilbreth, Frank B. (Frank Bunker), 1911-
Cheaper by the dozen [excerpt]
In The Random House book of humor for children p242-47 817.008
Gilchrist, Jan Spivey
(il) Greenfield, E. Nathaniel talking 811
Gill, Margery, 1925-
(il) Cooper, S. Dawn of fear Fic
(il) Cooper, S. Over sea, under stone Fic
Gillen, Patricia Bellan- *See* Bellan-Gillen, Patricia
Gillespie, Jessie
(il) Wiggin, K. D. S. The Bird's Christmas Carol Fic
Gillespie, John Thomas, 1928-
Juniorplots 3: a book talk guide for use with readers ages 12-16 028.1
Juniorplots: a book talk manual for teachers and librarians 028.1
More juniorplots: a guide for teachers and librarians 028.1
(ed) Best books for children, preschool through grade 6. See Best books for children, preschool through grade 6 011.6
Gillham, Charles E.
How the little owl's name was changed
In The Scott, Foresman anthology of children's literature p390-91 808.8
Gilliland, Judith Heide
(jt. auth) Heide, F. P. The day of Ahmed's secret E
Gilson, Jamie, 1933-
4B goes wild (4-6) Fic
Do bananas chew gum? (4-6) Fic
Double dog dare. See note under Gilson, J. 4B goes wild Fic
Harvey, the beer can king. See note under Gilson, J. Hello, my name is Scrambled Eggs Fic
Hello, my name is Scrambled Eggs (4 and up) Fic
Hobie Hanson, greatest hero of the mall. See note under Gilson, J. 4B goes wild Fic
Hobie Hanson, you're weird. See note under Gilson, J. 4B goes wild Fic
Thirteen ways to sink a sub. See note under Gilson, J. 4B goes wild Fic
Ginger for the heart. Yee, P.
In Yee, P. Tales from Gold Mountain p33-38 S C
Ginger Pye. Estes, E. Fic
Gingerbread boy
Galdone, P. The gingerbread boy 398.2
The Gingerbread boy
In The Baby's story book p14-19 398.2
In The Tall book of nursery tales p16-22 398.2
The Gingerbread man
In The Read-aloud treasury p135-43 808.8
Oxenbury, H. The gingerbread boy
In Oxenbury, H. The Helen Oxenbury nursery story book p32-39 398.2
Rockwell, A. F. The gingerbread man
In Rockwell, A. F. The three bears & 15 other stories p33-44 398.2
The **Gingerbread** man
In The Read-aloud treasury p135-43 808.8
The **gingerbread** man. Rockwell, A. F.
In Rockwell, A. F. The three bears & 15 other stories p33-44 398.2
Ginsburg, Mirra
The chick and the duckling E
The Chinese mirror (k-3) 398.2
Good morning, chick E
The magic stove (k-2) 398.2
The sun's asleep behind the hill E
Where does the sun go at night? E
Giovanni, Nikki
Spin a soft black song: poems for children (3-6) 811
Giovanopoulos, Paul
(il) Fox, P. How many miles to Babylon? Fic
(il) LeShan, E. J. Learning to say good-by 155.9
Gipsies *See* Gypsies
Gipson, Frederick Benjamin, 1903-1973
Old Yeller (6 and up) Fic
Giraffes
Arnold, C. Giraffe (3-5) 599.73
Leslie-Melville, B. Daisy Rothschild (1-3) 599.73
Sattler, H. R. Giraffes (5 and up) 599.73
See/See also pages in the following book(s):
Thomson, P. Auks, rocks and the odd dinosaur p27-31 (5 and up) 508
Fiction
Rey, H. A. Cecily G. and the 9 monkeys E
Girion, Barbara, 1937-
A handful of stars (6 and up) Fic

A **girl** called Al. Greene, C. C. **Fic**
Girl Scouts
World Association of Girl Guides and Girl Scouts. Trefoil round the world **369.463**
Girl Scouts of the United States of America
Kudlinski, K. V. Juliette Gordon Low: America's first Girl Scout (4 and up) **92**
The **Girl** who could think
In Windy day: stories and poems p2-9 **808.8**
The **girl** who loved the wind. Yolen, J. **E**
The **girl** who loved wild horses. Goble, P. **E**
The **girl** who married a ghost. Curtis, E. S.
In Best-loved folktales of the world p699-704 **398.2**
In Curtis, E. S. The girl who married a ghost, and other tales from the North American Indian p5-20 **398.2**
The **girl** who married a ghost, and other tales from The North American Indian. Curtis, E. S. **398.2**
The **Girl** who used her wits
In With a deep sea smile p64-69 **372.6**
The **girl** who was already queen. Timpanelli, G.
In Timpanelli, G. Tales from the roof of the world p43-51 **398.2**
Girl with the horse's head
Carpenter, F. Lady with the horse's head
In Carpenter, F. Tales of a Chinese grandmother p98-106 **398.2**
The **girl** with the silver eyes. Roberts, W. D. **Fic**
The **girl** without hands. Grimm, J.
In Grimm, J. The complete Grimm's fairy tales p160-66 **398.2**
Girls
Employment
See Children—Employment
Girls' clubs
See also Girl Scouts
GIs *See* Soldiers—United States
Gish, Lillian, 1896?-
An actor's life for me (3-5) **92**
Githens, Elizabeth M.
(il) Cooper, L. P. Fun with German **438**
Give us a great big smile, Rosy Cole. Greenwald, S. **Fic**
Give yourself a fright. Aiken, J.
In Aiken, J. Give yourself a fright: thirteen tales of the supernatural p160-80 **S C**
Give yourself a fright: thirteen tales of the supernatural. Aiken, J. **S C**
The **Gizzard**
In The Magic orange tree, and other Haitian folktales p99-112 **398.2**
Glacier National Park (Mont.)
Patent, D. H. Where the bald eagles gather (4 and up) **598**
Glaciers
Simon, S. Icebergs and glaciers (3-5) **551.3**
Walker, S. M. Glaciers (4-6) **551.3**
Glanzman, Louis S., 1922-
(il) Lindgren, A. Pippi Longstocking **Fic**
Glaser, Byron
(jt. auth) Neumeier, M. Action alphabet **E**
Glass, Andrew
(il) Brittain, B. Devil's donkey **Fic**
(il) Carlson, N. S. Spooky night **E**
(il) Fleischman, P. Graven images **S C**
The **glass** coffin. Grimm, J.
In Grimm, J. The complete Grimm's fairy tales p672-78 **398.2**
Glass mountain
The Glass mountain
In The Yellow fairy book p114-18 **398.2**
The **Glass** Mountain. Hogrogian, N. **398.2**
A **glass** of water, please. Marriott, A. L.
In Marriott, A. L. American Indian mythology **398.2**
The **glass** slipper. Farjeon, E. **Fic**
The **glass** slippers. Gotwalt, H. L. M.
In Gotwalt, H. L. M. Everyday plays for boys and girls p170-81 **812**
Glasses and contact lenses. Silverstein, A. **617.7**
Glazer, Tom
Do your ears hang low?: 50 more musical fingerplays (k-3) **796.1**
Eye winker, Tom Tinker, chin chopper (k-3) **796.1**
Music for ones and twos **782.42**
Tom Glazer's Christmas songbook. See Tom Glazer's Christmas songbook **782.28**
Tom Glazer's Treasury of songs for children (3-5) **782.42**
The Mother Goose songbook. See The Mother Goose songbook **782.42**

Gleeson, Libby
Eleanor, Elizabeth (5 and up) **Fic**
Global warming *See* Greenhouse effect
Global warming. Pringle, L. P. **363.7**
Globes
Lambert, D. Maps and globes (3-5) **912**
See/See also pages in the following book(s):
Mango, K. N. Mapmaking p27-35 (4 and up) **526**
Glockner-Ferrari, Deborah A.
(il) Patent, D. H. Humpback whales **599.5**
Glooskap gets two surprises. Norman, H.
In Norman, H. How Glooskap outwits the Ice Giants, and other tales of the Maritime Indians p29-37 **398.2**
The **glorious** flight: across the Channel with Louis Blériot, July 25, 1909. Provensen, A. **92**
The **Glorious** Mother Goose (k-2) **398.8**
Glossaries *See* Encyclopedias and dictionaries
Glubok, Shirley
Olympic games in ancient Greece (5 and up) **796.48**
GM *See* General Motors Corp.
The **gnome**. Grimm, J.
In Grimm, J. The complete Grimm's fairy tales p420-24 **398.2**
Go and hush the baby. Byars, B. C. **E**
Go away monsters, lickety split! Cooney, N. E. **E**
Go, close the door. Simon, S.
In Simon, S. More wise men of Helm and their merry tales p16-23 **398.2**
Go free or die: a story about Harriet Tubman. Ferris, J. **92**
Go I know not whither, fetch I know not what
Afanas'ev, A. N. Go I know not whither, bring back I know not what
In Afanas'ev, A. N. Russian fairy tales p504-20 **398.2**
Go I know not whither, bring back I know not what. Afanas'ev, A. N.
In Afanas'ev, A. N. Russian fairy tales p504-20 **398.2**
Go in and out the window **782.42**
The **goat** in the rug. Blood, C. L. **E**
The **goat** shedding on one side. Afanas'ev, A. N.
In Afanas'ev, A. N. Russian fairy tales p312-13 **398.2**
Goats
Fiction
Blood, C. L. The goat in the rug **E**
Galdone, P. The three Billy Goats Gruff (k-2) **398.2**
Sharmat, M. Gregory, the terrible eater **E**
The **goats**. Cole, B. **Fic**
Goats in the turnip field
Johnny and the three goats
In Tomie dePaola's favorite nursery tales p70-74 **398.2**
Gobble, growl, grunt. Spier, P. **E**
The **gobble-uns'll** git you ef you don't watch out! Riley, J. W. **811**
Goble, Paul
Beyond the ridge (2-4) **Fic**
Buffalo woman (1-3) **398.2**
Death of the iron horse **E**
Dream wolf **E**
The gift of the sacred dog (2-4) **398.2**
The girl who loved wild horses **E**
The great race of the birds and animals (1-3) **398.2**
Her seven brothers (k-3) **398.2**
Iktomi and the berries (k-3) **398.2**
Iktomi and the boulder (k-3) **398.2**
Iktomi and the ducks (k-3) **398.2**
Star Boy (2-4) **398.2**
See/See also pages in the following book(s):
Newbery and Caldecott Medal books, 1976-1985 p205-09 **028.5**
The **goblin** spider. San Souci, R.
In San Souci, R. Short & shivery p160-65 **398.2**
Gobs of goo. Cobb, V. **547**
God and the Devil share the harvest. Lerchis-Puskaitis, A.
In Best-loved folktales of the world p394-95 **398.2**
God that lived in the kitchen. Carpenter, F.
In Carpenter, F. Tales of a Chinese grandmother p39-46 **398.2**
Goddard, Robert Hutchings, 1882-1945
See/See also pages in the following book(s):
Richards, N. Dreamers & doers: inventors who changed our world p1-37 (6 and up) **920**
Godden, Rumer, 1907-
Candy Floss
In Godden, R. Four dolls p108-37 **S C**
The doll's house (2-4) **Fic**
The fairy doll
In Godden, R. Four dolls p32-65 **S C**
Four dolls (3-5) **S C**
Fu-dog (1-3) **Fic**
Impunity Jane
In Godden, R. Four dolls p6-28 **S C**
The story of Holly and Ivy **E**
also in Godden, R. Four dolls p68-106 **S C**
The valiant chatti-maker (3-6) **398.2**

Goddesses *See* Gods and goddesses

The **godfather**. Grimm, J.
In Grimm, J. The complete Grimm's fairy tales p206-08 **398.2**

Godfather Death. Grimm, J.
In Grimm, J. The complete Grimm's fairy tales p209-12 **398.2**
In Grimm, J. The juniper tree, and other tales from Grimm v2 p228-35 **398.2**

Gods and goddesses
See also Religions; names of individual gods and goddesses
See/See also pages in the following book(s):
Hamilton, E. Mythology [21-76] (6 and up) **292**

God's food. Grimm, J.
In Grimm, J. The complete Grimm's fairy tales p822 **398.2**

Goembel, Ponder
(il) Swann, B. A basket full of white eggs **398.6**

Goffe, Toni
(il) Clap your hands. See Clap your hands **796.1**
(il) Stamp your feet. See Stamp your feet **796.1**

Goffstein, M. B.
Fish for supper **E**
Goldie the dollmaker (3-5) **Fic**
Lives of the artists (5 and up) **920**
My Noah's ark **E**
Two piano tuners (3-5) **Fic**

Goggles. Keats, E. J. See note under Keats. E. J. The snowy day **E**

Gogh, Vincent van, 1853-1890
About
Raboff, E. Vincent van Gogh (4 and up) **759.9492**
See/See also pages in the following book(s):
Goffstein, M. B. Lives of the artists (5 and up) **920**

Going a-traveling
Grimm, J. Going a traveling
In Grimm, J. The complete Grimm's fairy tales p630-31 **398.2**

Going ape. Phillips, L. **793.73**

Going on an airplane. Rogers, F. **387.7**

Going to my ballet class. Kuklin, S. **792.8**

Going to school in 1776. Loeper, J. J. **370.9**

Going to school in 1876. Loeper, J. J. **370.9**

Going to the dentist. Rogers, F. **617.6**

Going to the hospital. Rogers, F. **362.1**

Gold & silver, silver & gold. Schwartz, A. **910.4**

The **gold** Cadillac. Taylor, M. D. **Fic**

The **gold-children**. Grimm, J.
In Grimm, J. The complete Grimm's fairy tales p388-93 **398.2**

Gold mines and mining
See also Klondike River Valley (Yukon)—Gold discoveries
See/See also pages in the following book(s):
Meltzer, M. The Chinese Americans p25-32 (6 and up) **305.8**
Fiction
Coerr, E. Chang's paper pony **E**

Gold rush *See* California—Gold discoveries

Gold-spinners
The Water-lily
In The Blue fairy book p174-81 **398.2**

Gold! the Klondike adventure. Ray, D. **971.9**

Goldberg, Whoopi
Doris knows everything
In Free to be—a family p124-25 **810.8**

Golden arm
Jacobs, J. Golden arm
In Jacobs, J. English fairy tales p138-39 **398.2**

The **golden** axe. Uchida, Y.
In Uchida, Y. The magic listening cap **398.2**

Golden bird
Grimm, J. The golden bird
In Grimm, J. The complete Grimm's fairy tales p272-79 **398.2**
In Grimm, J. The juniper tree, and other tales from Grimm v2 p201-16 **398.2**

Golden blackbird
Sébillot, P. The Golden Blackbird
In The Green fairy book p151-56 **398.2**

The **golden** branch. Aulnoy, Madame d'.
In The Red fairy book p220-37 **398.2**

The **golden-bristled** pig, the golden-feathered duck, and the golden-maned mare. Afanas'ev, A. N.
In Afanas'ev, A. N. Russian fairy tales p533-41 **398.2**

Golden crab
The Golden crab
In The Yellow fairy book p26-31 **398.2**

The **golden** days of Greece. Coolidge, O. E. **938**

Golden fish
Afanas'ev, A. N. The goldfish
In Afanas'ev, A. N. Russian fairy tales p528-32 **398.2**
Golden Fleece (Greek mythology) *See* Argonauts (Greek mythology)
The **Golden** Fleece and the heroes who lived before Achilles. Colum, P. **292**
The **golden** god: Apollo. Gates, D. **292**
Golden goose
Grimm, J. The golden goose
In Best-loved folktales of the world p122-26 **398.2**
In Grimm, J. About wise men and simpletons p47-51 **398.2**
In Grimm, J. The complete Grimm's fairy tales p322-26 **398.2**
In The Red fairy book p340-45 **398.2**
Rockwell, A. F. The golden goose
In Rockwell, A. F. Puss in boots, and other stories p30-39 **398.2**
Thane, A. Dummling and the golden goose
In Thane, A. Plays from famous stories and fairy tales p105-19 **812**
Golden key
Grimm, J. The golden key
In Grimm, J. The complete Grimm's fairy tales p812 **398.2**
In Grimm, J. More tales from Grimm **398.2**
The **golden** key. MacDonald, G.
In MacDonald, G. The complete fairy tales of George MacDonald **S C**
Golden lads
Grimm, J. The gold-children
In Grimm, J. The complete Grimm's fairy tales p388-93 **398.2**
Grimm, J. The golden lads
In The Green fairy book p311-18 **398.2**
Golden life. Kendall, C.
In Kendall, C. Sweet and sour p89-91 **398.2**
Golden mermaid
Grimm, J. The golden mermaid
In The Green fairy book p328-38 **398.2**
Golden slipper
Afanas'ev, A. N. The golden slipper
In Afanas'ev, A. N. Russian fairy tales p44-46 **398.2**
The **golden** snuff-box. Reeves, J.
In Reeves, J. English fables and fairy stories p157-76 **398.2**
The **golden** touch. Hawthorne, N.
In The Scott, Foresman anthology of children's literature p430-37 **808.8**
Goldenhair. Martin, E.
In Martin, E. Tales of the Far North p71-80 **398.2**
The **goldfish**. Afanas'ev, A. N.
In Afanas'ev, A. N. Russian fairy tales p528-32 **398.2**
Goldie the dollmaker. Goffstein, M. B. **Fic**
Goldilocks and the three bears
In The Read-aloud treasury p214-24 **808.8**
Goldilocks and the three bears. Brett, J. **398.2**
Goldilocks and the three bears. Crossley-Holland, K.
In Crossley-Holland, K. British folk tales p135-39 **398.2**
Goldilocks and the three bears. Marshall, J. **398.2**
Goldilocks and the three bears. Oxenbury, H.
In Oxenbury, H. The Helen Oxenbury nursery story book p6-12 **398.2**
Goldin, Augusta R.
Ducks don't get wet (k-3) **598**
Goldin, Barbara Diamond
Just enough is plenty: a Hanukkah tale **E**
Goldman, Emma, 1869-1940
See/See also pages in the following book(s):
Jacobs, W. J. Great lives: human rights p191-98 (5 and up) **920**
Goldner, Jameson C.
(il) Dolan, E. F. Starting soccer **796.334**
Goldner, Kathryn Allen
(jt. auth) Vogel, C. G. The great Yellowstone fire **574.5**
Goldsmith, Diane Hoyt- *See* Hoyt-Goldsmith, Diane
The **goldspinners**. Sholem Aleichem.
In Sholem Aleichem. Holiday tales of Sholem Aleichem **S C**
Golem
San Souci, R. The golem
In San Souci, R. Short & shivery p149-54 **398.2**
Singer, I. B. The golem **398.2**
Golenbock, Peter, 1946-
Teammates [biography of Jackie Robinson] (1-4) **92**
Goliath (Biblical figure)
About
De Paola, T. David and Goliath (k-3) **222**
The **Golly** Sisters go West. Byars, B. C. **E**

Golovikka
Afanas'ev, A. N. The mayoress
In Afanas'ev, A. N. Russian fairy tales p141 398.2
Gom on Windy Mountain. Chetwin, G. Fic
Gompers, Samuel, 1850-1924
See/See also pages in the following book(s):
Jacobs, W. J. Great lives: human rights p165-72 (5 and up) 920
Gondola to danger. Quackenbush, R. M. See note under Quackenbush, R. M. Express train to trouble Fic
Gone-Away Lake. Enright, E. Fic
Gone is gone. Gág, W. 398.2
Good advice
Afanas'ev, A. N. Good advice
In Afanas'ev, A. N. Russian fairy tales p289-91 398.2
Good and evil
Fiction
Briggs, K. M. Kate Crackernuts (6 and up) Fic
Cooper, S. The grey king (5 and up) Fic
Cooper, S. Over sea, under stone (5 and up) Fic
Sleator, W. The green futures of Tycho (5 and up) Fic
Good bargain
Grimm, J. The good bargain
In Grimm, J. The complete Grimm's fairy tales p51-55 398.2
Good books, good times! (1-3) 811.008
The **good-bye** book. Viorst, J. E
Good-bye, my wishing star. Grove, V. Fic
The **good-for-nothings**. Grimm, J.
In Grimm, J. More tales from Grimm p77-83 398.2
The **good** giants and the bad pukwudgies. Fritz, J. 398.2
The **good** little bad little pig. Brown, M. W.
In Brown, M. W. The fish with the deep sea smile p18-22 818
Good little mouse
Aulnoy, Madame d'. The little good mouse
In The Red fairy book p146-57 398.2
The **good-looking** boy. Alcock, V.
In Alcock, V. Ghostly companions S C
The **good-luck** pencil. Stanley, D. E
The **Good** Master. Seredy, K. Fic
Good morning, chick. Ginsburg, M. E
Good morning, world! See Words for new readers 423
Good night, Fred. Wells, R. E
Good night, Mr. Tom. Magorian, M. Fic
Good-night, Owl! Hutchins, P. E
Good Queen Bess: the story of Elizabeth I of England. Stanley, D. 92
Good work, Amelia Bedelia. Parish, P. See note under Parish, P. Amelia Bedelia E
Goodall, Jane
The chimpanzee family book (3-5) 599.88
Chimps (4-6) 599.88
My life with the chimpanzees (3-6) 92
Goodall, John S., 1908-
Creepy castle E
Little Red Riding Hood (k-2) 398.2
Naughty Nancy goes to school E
Paddy goes traveling. See note under Goodall, J. S. Paddy to the rescue E
Paddy to the rescue E
Paddy under water. See note under Goodall, J. S. Paddy to the rescue E
Puss in boots (k-3) 398.2
The story of a castle (3-6) 942
The story of a farm (3-6) 942
The story of a main street (3-6) 942
The story of an English village (3-6) 942
Goodbye house. Asch, F. See note under Asch, F. Sand cake E
Goodbye old year, hello new year. Modell, F. E
Goode, Diane
(il) Barrie, J. M. Peter Pan Fic
(il) The Diane Goode book of American folk tales and songs. See The Diane Goode book of American folk tales and songs 398.2
Diane Goode's American Christmas. See Diane Goode's American Christmas 810.8
(il) Ehrlich, A. The Random House book of fairy tales 398.2
(il) Levinson, R. I go with my family to Grandma's E
(il) Levinson, R. Watch the stars come out E
(il) Rylant, C. When I was young in the mountains E
Goode, J. Paul, 1862-1932
Goode's world atlas. See Goode's world atlas 912
Goode's school atlas. See Goode's world atlas 912
Goode's world atlas 912
Gooding, Beverley
(il) Grahame, K. The open road Fic

Goodnight, Andrew: goodnight, Craig. Sharmat, M. W. **E**
Goodnight, goodnight. Rice, E. **E**
Goodnight moon. Brown, M. W. **E**
Goodrich, Samuel Griswold, 1793-1860
See/See also pages in the following book(s):
Jordan, A. M. From Rollo to Tom Sawyer, and other papers p61-71 **028.5**
Goody Hall. Babbitt, N. **Fic**
Goodyear, Charles, 1800-1860
See/See also pages in the following book(s):
Richards, N. Dreamers & doers: inventors who changed our world p39-75 (6 and up) **920**
Goor, Nancy, 1944-
(jt. auth) Goor, R. All kinds of feet **591.4**
(jt. auth) Goor, R. Heads **591.4**
(jt. auth) Goor, R. In the driver's seat **629.04**
(jt. auth) Goor, R. Insect metamorphosis **595.7**
(jt. auth) Goor, R. Pompeii: exploring a Roman ghost town **937**
(jt. auth) Goor, R. Shadows **535**
(jt. auth) Goor, R. Signs **659.13**
Goor, Ron, 1940-
All kinds of feet (k-3) **591.4**
Heads (2-4) **591.4**
In the driver's seat (2-4) **629.04**
Insect metamorphosis (2-6) **595.7**
Pompeii: exploring a Roman ghost town (5 and up) **937**
Shadows (k-3) **535**
Signs (k-2) **659.13**
(il) Selsam, M. E. Backyard insects **595.7**
Goose girl
Grimm, J. The goose girl
In Best-loved folktales of the world p98-103 **398.2**
In The Blue fairy book p266-73 **398.2**
In Grimm, J. The complete Grimm's fairy tales p404-11 **398.2**
Goose girl at the well
Grimm, J. The goose-girl at the well
In Grimm, J. The complete Grimm's fairy tales p725-34 **398.2**
Gopher's revenge. Curry, J. L.
In Curry, J. L. Back in the beforetime p52-56 **398.2**
Gorbachev, Mikhail
About
Caulkins, J. The picture life of Mikhail Gorbachev (4 and up) **92**
See/See also pages in the following book(s):
Andrews, W. G. The land and the people of the Soviet Union (5 and up) **947**
Gordillo, Henry E. F.
(il) Harris, R. H. Before you were three **155.4**
Gordon, Eugene, 1923-
Nepal—in pictures. See Nepal—in pictures **954.96**
Saudi Arabia—in pictures. See Saudi Arabia—in pictures **953.8**
Senegal—in pictures. See Senegal—in pictures **966.3**
Gore, Sheila
My shadow (k-2) **535**
Gore Gorinskoe
Afanas'ev, A. N. Misery
In Afanas'ev, A. N. Russian fairy tales p20-24 **398.2**
Woe
In Best-loved folklore tales of the world p441-46 **398.2**
Gorey, Edward, 1925-
(il) Bellairs, J. The house with a clock in its walls **Fic**
(il) Ciardi, J. You read to me, I'll read to you **811**
(il) Heide, F. P. The shrinking of Treehorn **Fic**
(il) Lear, E. The Jumblies **821**
Gorilla. Browne, A. **E**
Gorilla/Chinchilla and other animal rhymes. Kitchen, B. **E**
The **gorilla** did it. Hazen, B. S. **E**
Gorillas
McClung, R. M. Gorilla (4 and up) **599.88**
McNulty, F. With love from Koko (1-3) **599.88**
Patterson, F. Koko's kitten (1-4) **599.88**
Patterson, F. Koko's story (1-4) **599.88**
Schlein, M. Gorillas (4-6) **599.88**
Fiction
Browne, A. Gorilla **E**
Hazen, B. S. The gorilla did it **E**
Howe, J. The day the teacher went bananas **E**
Gorman, Michael, 1941-
The concise AACR2, 1988 revision **025.3**
Gorog, Judith, 1938-
Three dreams and a nightmare, and other tales of the dark (5 and up) **S C**
Contents: Mall rat; First dream: the ugly mug; The perfect solution; The mirror; Three grains of rice: from the bones of an Arab folktale; Prosperity; Second dream: Carlo the silent; Hedwig the wise; Sad eyes; At the sign of the beckoning finger; Third dream: the price of magic; In her belfry; Overture; And a nightmare
Gossip wolf and the fox. Grimm, J.
In Grimm, J. The complete Grimm's fairy tales p353-54 **398.2**

Gothic architecture *See* Architecture, Gothic
Gotwalt, Helen Louise Miller
Everyday plays for boys and girls (4 and up) **812**
Contents: Circus daze; Bandit Ben rides again; So long at the fair; Sourdough Sally; The paper bag mystery; The trial of Mother Goose; The return of Bobby Shafto; The mouse that soared; The gentle giant-killer; Simple Simon's reward; Shirley Holmes and the FBI; Vicky gets the vote; The little nut tree; The glass slippers; The miraculous tea party
Special plays for holidays **812**
Contents: The greedy goblin; The softhearted ghost; The runaway unicorn; Thanks to butter-fingers; Pilgrim parting; Squeaknibble's Christmas; The Christmas umbrella; Softy the Snowman; A February failure; The missing Linc; The tree of hearts; The birthday pie; THe Mount Vernon cricket; The White House rabbit; The magic carpet sweeper
Gould, Ceil Baring- *See* Baring-Gould, Ceil
Gould, Deborah
Aaron's shirt **E**
Gould, William Baring- *See* Baring-Gould, William Stuart, 1913-
Goulding, Ray, 1922-1990
See also Bob and Ray
Gounaud, Karen Jo
A very mice joke book **793.73**
Gow, Bill
(il) MacLean, N. Hockey basics **796.962**
(il) MacLean, N. Ice skating basics **796.91**
Graciosa and Percinet
Aulnoy, Madame d'. Graciosa and Percinet
In The Red fairy book p158-74 **398.2**
Graff, Nancy Price, 1953-
The strength of the hills (4 and up) **630.1**
Graff, Stewart
The story of World War II (4-6) **940.54**
Graham, Ada
The big stretch: the complete book of the amazing rubber band (3-6) **678**
Graham, Frank, 1913-
(jt. auth) Graham, A. The big stretch: the complete book of the amazing rubber band **678**
Graham, Ian, 1953-
Combat aircraft (4 and up) **623.7**
Racing cars (4 and up) **629.228**
Graham, Lorenz B., 1902-1989
Song of the boat **E**
Graham, Margaret Bloy, 1920-
(il) Zion, G. Harry the dirty dog **E**
Graham Oakley's magical changes. Oakley, G. **E**
Grahame, Kenneth, 1859-1932
The open road (2-5) **Fic**
The reluctant dragon (3-5) **Fic**
The reluctant dragon; dramatization. See Thane, A. The reluctant dragon
The wind in the willows (4-6) **Fic**
See/See also pages in the following book(s):
A Horn Book sampler on children's books and reading p50-54 **028.5**
Grail
See also Arthurian romances
Fiction
Pyle, H. The story of the Grail and the passing of Arthur (6 and up) **398.2**
Sutcliff, R. The light beyond the forest (4 and up) **398.2**
A **grain** of wheat: a writer begins. Bulla, C. R. **92**
Gramatky, Hardie, 1907-1979
Little Toot **E**
Grammar
See also English language—Grammar
Grand Canyon (Ariz.)
Fiction
Henry, M. Brighty of the Grand Canyon (4 and up) **Fic**
Grandaddy's place. Griffith, H. V. **E**
Grandfather tales (4 and up) **398.2**
Grandfather Tang's story. Tompert, A. **E**
Grandfather Twilight. Berger, B. **E**
Grandfathers
Fiction
Ackerman, K. Song and dance man **E**
Aliki. The two of them **E**
Blos, J. W. The grandpa days **E**
Burningham, J. Granpa **E**
Byars, B. C. The house of wings (4-6) **Fic**
Carlstrom, N. W. Grandpappy **E**
Caseley, J. When Grandpa came to stay **E**
Cazet, D. Big Shoe, Little Shoe **E**
De Paola, T. Now one foot, now the other **E**
Goffstein, M. B. Two piano tuners (3-5) **Fic**
Greenfield, E. Grandpa's face **E**
Griffith, H. V. Georgia music **E**
Griffith, H. V. Grandaddy's place **E**
Härtling, P. Old John (4 and up) **Fic**
Hest, A. The crack-of-dawn walkers **E**
Hest, A. The purple coat **E**
Hunter, M. The mermaid summer (4 and up) **Fic**
Locker, T. Where the river begins **E**
Martin, B. Knots on a counting rope **E**
Mazer, N. F. A figure of speech (6 and up) **Fic**
Pearson, S. Happy birthday, Grampie **E**
Radin, R. Y. High in the mountains **E**
Slote, A. The trading games (4-6) **Fic**

Grandfathers—Fiction—*Continued*
Smith, R. K. The war with Grandpa (4-6) **Fic**
Stevenson, J. "Could be worse!" **E**
Stolz, M. Storm in the night **E**
Wallace, I. Chin Chiang and the dragon's dance **E**
Walter, M. P. Justin and the best biscuits in the world (3-6) **Fic**
Zolotow, C. My grandson Lew **E**
Grandfather's nose. Patent, D. H. **575.1**
Grandma and Grandpa. Oxenbury, H. **E**
Grandma Moses *See* Moses, Grandma, 1860-1961
Grandma remembers. Schecter, B. **E**
Grandmama's joy. Greenfield, E. **E**
Grandmas at the lake. McCully, E. A. **E**
A **grandmother** for the orphelines. Carlson, N. S. See note under Carlson, N. S. The happy orpheline **Fic**
Grandmothers
Fiction
Babbitt, N. The eyes of the Amaryllis (5 and up) **Fic**
Bawden, N. The robbers (5 and up) **Fic**
Bunting, E. The Wednesday surprise **E**
Cameron, A. The most beautiful place in the world (2-4) **Fic**
Cleaver, V. Queen of hearts (6 and up) **Fic**
Clifford, E. The remembering box (3-5) **Fic**
Daly, N. Not so fast, Songololo **E**
De Paola, T. Nana Upstairs & Nana Downstairs **E**
Gleeson, L. Eleanor, Elizabeth (5 and up) **Fic**
Goffstein, M. B. Fish for supper **E**
Greenfield, E. Grandmama's joy **E**
Grifalconi, A. Osa's pride **E**
Hamilton, V. Cousins (5 and up) **Fic**
Hest, A. The midnight eaters **E**
Jukes, M. Blackberries in the dark (2-4) **Fic**
Keller, H. The best present **E**
Kinsey-Warnock, N. The Canada geese quilt (3-5) **Fic**
Lasky, K. Sea swan **E**
Levinson, R. I go with my family to Grandma's **E**
Luenn, N. Nessa's fish **E**
McCully, E. A. Grandmas at the lake **E**
Oppenheim, S. L. Waiting for Noah **E**
Patterson, N. R. The Christmas cup (3-5) **Fic**
Polacco, P. Thunder cake **E**
Reid, M. S. The button box **E**
Rice, E. At Grammy's house **E**
Schecter, B. Grandma remembers **E**
Schwartz, A. Oma and Bobo **E**
Thomas, J. R. Saying good-bye to Grandma **E**
Voigt, C. Dicey's song (6 and up) **Fic**
Wilhelm, H. A cool kid—like me! **E**
Williams, B. Kevin's grandma **E**
Winthrop, E. Belinda's hurricane (2-4) **Fic**
Yep, L. Child of the owl (5 and up) **Fic**
Yolen, J. No bath tonight **E**
Grandmother's tale. Singer, I. B.
In Singer, I. B. Zlateh the goat, and other stories p21-23 **398.2**
Grandpa buys a pumpkin egg. Schwartz, A.
In Schwartz, A. There is a carrot in my ear, and other noodle tales p44-57 **398.2**
The **grandpa** days. Blos, J. W. **E**
Grandpa Joe's brother. Leach, M.
In Leach, M. Whistle in the graveyard p64-65 **398.2**
Grandpa misses the boat. Schwartz, A.
In Schwartz, A. All of our noses are here, and other noodle tales p18-21 **398.2**
Grandpappy. Carlstrom, N. W. **E**
Grandparents
Allen, T. B. On Granddaddy's farm (1-3) **630.1**
LeShan, E. J. Grandparents: a special kind of love (4 and up) **306.8**
See/See also pages in the following book(s):
Bauer, C. F. Celebrations p63-80 **808.8**
Fiction
Branscum, R. The adventures of Johnny May (4-6) **Fic**
Bridgers, S. E. All together now (6 and up) **Fic**
Hurd, E. T. I dance in my red pajamas **E**
Oxenbury, H. Grandma and Grandpa **E**
Grandpa's face. Greenfield, E. **E**
Grandpa's great city tour. Stevenson, J. See note under Stevenson, J. "Could be worse!" **E**
Grandpa's too-good garden. Stevenson, J. See note under Stevenson, J. "Could be worse!" **E**
Granfa' Grig had a pig, and other rhymes without reason from Mother Goose (k-3) **398.8**
Granger, Edith
(ed) The Columbia Granger's index to poetry. See The Columbia Granger's index to poetry **808.81**
Granger's index to poetry. See The Columbia Granger's index to poetry **808.81**

Granpa. Burningham, J. **E**

Grant, Leigh
(il) Bulla, C. R. Shoeshine girl **Fic**

Graphic arts
Handbooks, manuals, etc.
Matthews, J. G. ClipArt & dynamic designs for libraries & media centers **021.7**

Graphology
See/See also pages in the following book(s):
Caney, S. Steven Caney's kids' America p307-10 (4 and up) **790.1**

Grasshopper on the road. Lobel, A. **E**

Grasshopper summer. Turner, A. W. **Fic**

Grassland ecology
Catchpole, C. Grasslands (2-4) **574.5**
Schwartz, D. M. The hidden life of the meadow (3-5) **574.5**

Grasslands. Catchpole, C. **574.5**

Grateful beasts
The Grateful beasts
In The Yellow fairy book p64-74 **398.2**

Grateful crane
Uchida, Y. Grateful stork
In Uchida, Y. The magic listening cap **398.2**

Grateful fox fairy
Carpenter, F. Grateful fox fairy
In Carpenter, F. Tales of a Chinese grandmother p89-97 **398.2**

Grateful stork. Uchida, Y.
In Uchida, Y. The magic listening cap **398.2**

The **grateful** tombstone. Terada, A. M.
In Terada, A. M. Under the starfruit tree p130-31 **398.2**

Grave doubts. Corbett, S. **Fic**

Grave mound
Grimm, J. The grave-mound
In Grimm, J. The complete Grimm's fairy tales p792-96 **398.2**

Graven images. Fleischman, P. **S C**

Graves, Ruth
(ed) The RIF guide to encouraging young readers. See The RIF guide to encouraging young readers **372.4**

Graves *See* Tombs

Graveyards *See* Cemeteries

Gravitation
Branley, F. M. Gravity is a mystery (k-3) **531**
Branley, F. M. Weight and weightlessness (k-3) **531**

Gravity is a mystery. Branley, F. M. **531**

Gray, Elizabeth Janet *See* Vining, Elizabeth Gray, 1902-

Gray moss on green trees. Jagendorf, M. A.
In The Scott, Foresman anthology of children's literature p387-88 **808.8**

Graylegs. Hatch, M. C.
In The Scott, Foresman anthology of children's literature p220-25 **808.8**

Grayson, Marion F., 1906-1976
Let's do fingerplays (k-2) **796.1**

The **great** American gold rush. Blumberg, R. **979.4**

The **great** ancestor hunt. Perl, L. **929**

Great Barrier Reef (Australia)
Arnold, C. A walk on the Great Barrier Reef (3-6) **574.92**
McGovern, A. Down under, down under (3-6) **574.92**

Great bell
Carpenter, F. Ko-Ai's lost shoe
In Carpenter, F. Tales of a Chinese grandmother p175-81 **398.2**

The **great** big especially beautiful Easter egg. Stevenson, J. See note under Stevenson, J. "Could be worse!" **E**

A **Great** big ugly man came up and tied his horse to me (k-3) **821.008**

The **Great** Brain. Fitzgerald, J. D. **Fic**

The **Great** Brain at the academy. Fitzgerald, J. D. See note under Fitzgerald, J. D. The Great Brain **Fic**

The **Great** Brain does it again. Fitzgerald, J. D. See note under Fitzgerald, J. D. The Great Brain **Fic**

The **Great** Brain reforms. Fitzgerald, J. D. See note under Fitzgerald, J. D. The Great Brain **Fic**

Great Britain
See also England
Fiction
Aiken, J. Midnight is a place (5 and up) **Fic**
Aiken, J. The shadow guests (5 and up) **Fic**
Aiken, J. The wolves of Willoughby Chase (5 and up) **Fic**
Alcock, V. The stonewalkers (5 and up) **Fic**
Bagnold, E. National Velvet (5 and up) **Fic**
Bawden, N. The finding (4 and up) **Fic**
Bawden, N. The peppermint pig (5 and up) **Fic**
Bond, M. A bear called Paddington (2-5) **Fic**
Bond, M. Paddington's storybook (2-5) **S C**
Boston, L. M. The children of Green Knowe (4-6) **Fic**
Burnett, F. H. A little princess (4-6) **Fic**

Great Britain—Fiction—*Continued*
Cooper, S. Dawn of fear (5 and up) **Fic**
Cooper, S. Over sea, under stone (5 and up) **Fic**
Corbett, S. The discontented ghost (6 and up) **Fic**
Dickens, C. A Christmas carol in prose (4 and up) **Fic**
Gardam, J. The hollow land (5 and up) **Fic**
Gardam, J. A long way from Verona (6 and up) **Fic**
Howker, J. Isaac Campion (5 and up) **Fic**
King-Smith, D. Pigs might fly (4-6) **Fic**
King-Smith, D. Sophie's snail (3-5) **Fic**
Lively, P. Fanny's sister (3-5) **Fic**
Lively, P. The ghost of Thomas Kempe (4-6) **Fic**
Magorian, M. Good night, Mr. Tom (6 and up) **Fic**
Mark, J. Thunder and Lightnings (5 and up) **Fic**
Masefield, J. The box of delights; or, When the wolves were running (5 and up) **Fic**
Paton Walsh, J. Gaffer Samson's luck (4-6) **Fic**
Paton Walsh, J. Lost and found (2-4) **Fic**
Pope, E. M. The Perilous Gard (6 and up) **Fic**
Sewell, A. Black Beauty (4-6) **Fic**
Streatfeild, N. Theatre shoes, or other people's shoes (5 and up) **Fic**
Streatfeild, N. Thursday's child (4 and up) **Fic**
Townsend, J. R. Dan alone (6 and up) **Fic**
Townsend, J. R. The visitors (6 and up) **Fic**
Vining, E. G. Adam of the road (5 and up) **Fic**
Westall, R. Ghost abbey (5 and up) **Fic**
Westall, R. The machine gunners (6 and up) **Fic**
Wiseman, D. Jeremy Visick (5 and up) **Fic**

Folklore
See Folklore—Great Britain

History—0-1066—Fiction
Sutcliff, R. Flame-colored taffeta (5 and up) **Fic**
Sutcliff, R. Frontier Wolf (6 and up) **Fic**
Sutcliff, R. Sun horse, moon horse (5 and up) **Fic**

History—1154-1399, Plantagenets—Fiction
De Angeli, M. L. The door in the wall (4-6) **Fic**

Kings, queens, rulers, etc.
Brooks, P. S. Queen Eleanor: independent spirit of the medieval world (6 and up) **92**
Fritz, J. Can't you make them behave, King George? [biography of George III, King of Great Britain] (3-5) **92**
Stanley, D. Good Queen Bess: the story of Elizabeth I of England (3-5) **92**

Legends
See Legends—Great Britain

Pictorial works
Anno, M. Anno's Britain **E**

The **great** butterfly hunt. Herberman, E. **595.7**
The **great** calamity and if. Simon, S.
In Simon, S. More wise men of Helm and their merry tales p54-62 **398.2**
The **great** Christmas kidnapping caper. Van Leeuwen, J. **Fic**
Great composers. Ventura, P. **780.9**
The **great** Constitution. Commager, H. S. **342**
The **great** Gilly Hopkins. Paterson, K. **Fic**
The **great** green Turkey Creek monster. Flora, J. **E**
The **great** kapok tree. Cherry, L. **E**
Great Lakes
Henderson, K. The Great Lakes (2-4) **551.4**
Great Lakes region

Fiction
Holling, H. C. Paddle-to-the-sea (4-6) **Fic**

The **great** little Madison. Fritz, J. **92**
Great lives: human rights. Jacobs, W. J. **920**
The **great** mushroom mistake. Lively, P.
In Lively, P. Uninvited ghosts, and other stories p108-19 **S C**
Great northern diver: the loon. Esbensen, B. J. **598**
Great painters. Ventura, P. **759**
The **great** piratical rumbustification & The librarian and the robbers. Mahy, M. **Fic**
The **great** race of the birds and animals. Goble, P. **398.2**
The **Great** Red Cat. MacDonald, M. R.
In MacDonald, M. R. When the lights go out p47-60 **372.6**
The **great** rescue operation. Van Leeuwen, J. **Fic**
The **great** river monster. Marriott, A. L.
In Marriott, A. L. American Indian mythology **398.2**

The **great** snake of Wagadou. Sako, O.
In The Crest and the hide, and other African stories of heroes, chiefs, bards, hunters, sorcerers, and common people p105-09 **398.2**

Great thumbprint drawing book, Ed Emberley's. Emberley, E. **743**

The **great** tug-of-war. Johnston, H. A. S.
In The Scott, Foresman anthology of children's literature p306-10 **808.8**

The **great** Voyager adventure. Harris, A. **523.4**

Great Wall of China
Fiction
Lee, J. M. Legend of the Li River (k-3) **398.2**

The **Great** Wall of China. Fisher, L. E. **951**

The **great** white cat. Williams-Ellis, A.
In Williams-Ellis, A. Tales from the enchanted world p17-23 **398.2**

The **great** white man-eating shark. Mahy, M. **E**

The **great** Yellowstone fire. Vogel, C. G. **574.5**

The **greatest** guessing game. Froman, R. **513**

Grecian king and the physician Douban
The Greek king and the physician Douban
In The Arabian nights entertainments p29-31 **398.2**

Greece
Stein, R. C. Greece (4 and up) **949.5**
History
Coolidge, O. E. The golden days of Greece (4-6) **938**
Odijk, P. The Greeks (5 and up) **938**
Science
See Science—Greece

The **greedy** goblin. Gotwalt, H. L. M.
In Gotwalt, H. L. M. Special plays for holidays p3-16 **812**

Greedy Mariani. Carter, D. S.
In Best-loved folktales of the world p731-34 **398.2**

The **Greedy** wife
In The Diane Goode book of American folk tales and songs p55-57 **398.2**

Greek Americans
Jones, J. C. The Greeks in America
In The In America series **305.8**

Greek civilization *See* Civilization, Greek

The **Greek** king and the physician Douban
In The Arabian nights entertainments p29-31 **398.2**

Greek mythology *See* Mythology, Classical

Greek science *See* Science—Greece

The **Greeks**. Odijk, P. **938**

The **Greeks** in America. Jones, J. C.
In The In America series **305.8**

Green, Anne Canevari
(il) Berger, M. Sports **796.03**
(il) Bleifeld, M. Experimenting with a microscope **502.8**
(il) Brandt, S. R. How to write a report **808**
(il) Gallant, R. A. Our restless earth **550**
(il) Kerby, M. Cockroaches **595.7**
(il) Mischel, F. How to write a letter **808**
(il) Powers, D. G. How to run a meeting **060.4**
(il) Tannenbaum, B. Making and using your own weather station **551.6**
(il) Walker, O. H. Experimenting with air and flight **507**

Green, Diana Huss
(ed) Parent's choice guide to videocassettes for children. See Parent's choice guide to videocassettes for children **016.79143**

Green, Elizabeth Shippen, 1871-1954
(il) Lamb, C. Tales from Shakespeare **822.3**

Green, Michael, 1943-
(il) Bianco, M. W. The velveteen rabbit **Fic**

Green, Norma
The hole in the dike **E**

The **green** book of Hob stories. Mayne, W. **E**

The **green** children. Crossley-Holland, K.
In Crossley-Holland, K. British folk tales p100-11 **398.2**

Green eggs and ham. Seuss, Dr. **E**

The **Green** fairy book (4-6) **398.2**

The **green** futures of Tycho. Sleator, W. **Fic**

Green gourd
Green gourd
In Grandfather tales p213-21 **398.2**

The **green** lion of Zion Street. Fields, J. **811**

Green magic: algae rediscovered. Kavaler, L. **589.3**

Green marmalade to you. Mahy, M.
In Mahy, M. Nonstop nonsense p95-98 **828**

The **green** mist. San Souci, R.
In San Souci, R. Short & shivery p35-40 **398.2**

The **green** ribbon. Schwartz, A.
In Schwartz, A. In a dark, dark room, and other scary stories p24-33 **398.2**
Green says go. Emberley, E. **535.6**
Greenaway, Kate, 1846-1901
See/See also pages in the following book(s):
A Horn Book sampler on children's books and reading p41-49 **028.5**
Illustrators of children's books p75-86 (v1) **741.6**
Greenberg, Lorna
(ed) Beck, B. L. The ancient Maya **972**
(ed) Beck, B. L. The Aztecs **972**
(ed) Beck, B. L. The Incas **985**
Greenberg, Martin Harry
(ed) Things that go bump in the night. See Things that go bump in the night **S C**
Greene, Bette, 1934-
Get on out of here, Philip Hall (4-6) **Fic**
Philip Hall likes me, I reckon maybe (4-6) **Fic**
Summer of my German soldier (6 and up) **Fic**
Greene, Carol
Presidents (2-4) **920**
The Supreme Court (1-3) **347**
Greene, Constance C.
Al(exandra) the Great. See note under Greene, C. C. A girl called Al **Fic**
Al's blind date. See note under Greene, C. C. A girl called Al **Fic**
Ask anybody (5 and up) **Fic**
Beat the turtle drum (5 and up) **Fic**
Double-dare O'Toole (4 and up) **Fic**
A girl called Al (5 and up) **Fic**
I and Sproggy (5 and up) **Fic**
I know you, Al. See note under Greene, C. C. A girl called Al **Fic**
Isabelle and little orphan Frannie. See note under Greene, C. C. Isabelle the itch **Fic**
Isabelle shows her stuff. See note under Greene, C. C. Isabelle the itch **Fic**
Isabelle the itch (4-6) **Fic**
Just plain Al. See note under Greene, C. C. A girl called Al **Fic**
Your old pal, Al. See note under Greene, C. C. A girl called Al **Fic**
Greene, Ellin, 1927-
The legend of the Christmas rose (2-4) **398.2**
Storytelling: a selected annotated bibliography **016.3726**
(jt. auth) Baker, A. Storytelling: art and technique **372.6**
Greene, Laura, 1935-
Sign language talk (5 and up) **419**
Greenfeld, Howard
Bar mitzvah (5 and up) **296.4**
Books: from writer to reader (6 and up) **070.5**
Greenfield, Eloise, 1929-
Africa dream **E**
Childtimes: a three-generation memoir (4 and up) **920**
Daydreamers (3-6) **811**
Grandmama's joy **E**
Grandpa's face **E**
Honey, I love, and other love poems (2-4) **811**
Mary McLeod Bethune (2-5) **92**
Me and Neesie **E**
Nathaniel talking (2-4) **811**
Paul Robeson (2-5) **92**
She come bringing me that little baby girl **E**
Sister (4 and up) **Fic**
Under the Sunday tree (2-4) **811**
(jt. auth) Little, L. J. I can do it by myself **E**
Greenfield, Jane
Books: their care and repair **025.7**
Greenhouse effect
Johnson, R. L. The greenhouse effect (5 and up) **363.7**
Pringle, L. P. Global warming (3-5) **363.7**
Greening the city streets. Huff, B. A. **635**
Greenland

Fiction

Haugaard, E. C. Leif the unlucky (6 and up) **Fic**
Kortum, J. Ghost vision (5 and up) **Fic**
Greenstein, Susan
(il) Hyde, M. O. Know about drugs **616.86**
Greenwald, Sheila
Give us a great big smile, Rosy Cole (3-5) **Fic**
It all began with Jane Eyre (6 and up) **Fic**
Mariah Delany's Author-of-the-Month Club (4-6) **Fic**
Rosy Cole's great American guilt club. See note under Greenwald, S. Give us a great big smile, Rosy Cole **Fic**
Rosy's romance. See note under Greenwald, S. Give us a great big smile, Rosy Cole **Fic**
Valentine Rosy. See note under Greenwald, S. Give us a great big smile, Rosy Cole **Fic**
Will the real Gertrude Hollings please stand up? (5 and up) **Fic**

Greenwald, Sheila—*Continued*
Write on, Rosy! See note under Greenwald, S. Give us a great big smile, Rosy Cole **Fic**
Greenwitch. Cooper, S. See note under Cooper, S. Over sea, under stone **Fic**
Greer, Gery
Max and me and the time machine (5 and up) **Fic**
Greff, the story of a guide dog. Curtis, P. **636.7**
Gregory, Ruth W. (Ruth Wilhelme), 1910-
Anniversaries and holidays **394.2**
Gregory, the terrible eater. Sharmat, M. **E**
Greg's microscope. Selsam, M. E. **502.8**
Greinke, Geri
(il) Tambourines! Tambourines to glory! See Tambourines! Tambourines to glory! **242**
Gretz, Susanna
Teddy bears 1 to 10. See note under Gretz, S. Teddy bears go shopping **E**
Teddy bears ABC. See note under Gretz, S. Teddy bears go shopping **E**
Teddy bears at the seaside. See note under Gretz, S. Teddy bears go shopping **E**
Teddy bears cure a cold. See note under Gretz, S. Teddy bears go shopping **E**
Teddy bears go shopping **E**
Teddy bears' moving day. See note under Gretz, S. Teddy bears go shopping **E**
Teddy bears stay indoors. See note under Gretz, S. Teddy bears go shopping **E**
Teddy bears take the train. See note under Gretz, S. Teddy bears go shopping **E**
Grey, Vivian
The chemist who lost his head: the story of Antoine Laurent Lavoisier (5 and up) **92**
The **grey** king. Cooper, S. **Fic**
The **Grey** Lady and the Strawberry Snatcher. Bang, M. **E**
Grey Owl, 1888-1938
How we made Christmas
In The Family read-aloud Christmas treasury p104-07 **808.8**
Greyfoot
Hatch, M. C. Graylegs
In The Scott, Foresman anthology of children's literature p220-25 **808.8**
Griego, Margot C.
(comp) Tortillitas para mamá and other nursery rhymes. See Tortillitas para mamá and other nursery rhymes **398.8**
Grifalconi, Ann
Darkness and the butterfly **E**
Osa's pride **E**
The village of round and square houses (k-3) **398.2**
(il) Byars, B. C. The midnight fox **Fic**
(il) Clifton, L. Everett Anderson's goodbye **811**
(il) McGovern, A. The secret soldier: the story of Deborah Sampson [Gannett] **92**
Griffin, Gillett G. (Gillett Good), 1928-
(il) Chrystie, F. N. Pets **636.088**
Griffin
Grimm, J. The griffin
In Grimm, J. The complete Grimm's fairy tales p681-88 **398.2**
The **Griffin** and the Minor Canon. Stockton, F. **Fic**
The **Griffin** legacy. Klaveness, J. O. **Fic**
Griffith, Helen V.
Alex and the cat **E**
Georgia music **E**
Grandaddy's place **E**
Plunk's dreams **E**
Griffiths, Ann Hagen
(il) Sullivan, G. Better swimming for boys and girls **797.2**
(il) Sullivan, G. Better weight training for boys **613.7**
Grigoli, Valorie
Patriotic holidays and celebrations (4 and up) **394.2**
Grillone, Lisa
Small worlds close up (5 and up) **500**
Grimes, Nikki
Something on my mind **811**
Grimké, Angelina Emily, 1805-1879
See/See also pages in the following book(s):
Jacobs, W. J. Great lives: human rights p47-55 (5 and up) **920**
Grimké, Sarah Moore, 1792-1873
See/See also pages in the following book(s):
Jacobs, W. J. Great lives: human rights p47-55 (5 and up) **920**
Grimm, Jacob, 1785-1863
About wise men and simpletons (3-6) **398.2**
Contents: About a fisherman and his wife; The wolf and the seven kids; Brier Rose; The elves and the shoemaker whose work they did; The elves ask a servant girl to be godmother; The woman and the changeling elf; Rapunzel; The golden goose; The white dove; The queen bee; The three feathers; The water of life; Rumpelstiltskin; The six swans; King Thrushbeard; Hansel and Gretel; The Bremen town musicians
Allerleirauh
In The Green fairy book p276-81 **398.2**
Ashtenputtel
In Best-loved folktales of the world p68-75 **398.2**
The bear and the kingbird (k-3) **398.2**

Grimm, Jacob, 1785-1863—*Continued*
The brave little tailor
In Best-loved folktales of the world p61-68 **398.2**
In The Blue fairy book p304-12 **398.2**
The brave little tailor; dramatization. See Thane, A. The brave little tailor
The Bremen town musicians
In Best-loved folktales of the world p142-44 **398.2**
In The Scott, Foresman anthology of children's literature p188-90 **808.8**
The Bremen town musicians; adaptation. See Plume, I. The Bremen town musicians **398.2**
Brother and sister
In The Red fairy book p82-88 **398.2**
The cabbage donkey
In The Yellow fairy book p42-49 **398.2**
Cat and mouse in partnership
In The Yellow fairy book p1-3 **398.2**
The complete Grimm's fairy tales (4 and up) **398.2**
Contents: The frog-king, or Iron Henry; Cat and mouse in partnership; Our Lady's child; The story of the youth who went forth to learn what fear was; The wolf and the seven little kids; Faithful John; The good bargain; The strange musician; The twelve brothers; The pack of ragamuffins; Brother and sister; Rapunzel; The three little men in the wood; The three spinners; Hänsel and Gretel; The three snake-leaves; The white snake; The straw, the coal, and the bean; The fisherman and his wife; The valiant little tailor; Cinderella; The riddle; The mouse, the bird, and the sausage; Mother Holle; The seven ravens; Little Red-Cap; The Bremen town-musicians; The singing bone; The Devil with the three golden hairs; The louse and the flea; The girl without hands; Clever Hans; The three languages; Clever Elsie; The tailor in heaven; The wishing-table, the gold-ass, and the cudgel in the sack; Thumbling; The wedding of Mrs. Fox; The elves; The robber bridegroom; Herr Korbes; The godfather; Frau Trude; Godfather Death; Thumbling's travels; Fitcher's bird; The juniper tree; Old Sultan; The six swans; Little Briar-Rose; Fundevogel; King Thrushbeard; Little Snow-White; The knapsack, the hat, and the horn; Rumpelstiltskin; Sweetheart Roland; The golden bird; The dog and the sparrow; Frederick and Catherine; The two brothers; The little peasant; The queen bee; The three feathers; The golden goose; Allerleirauh; The hare's bride; The twelve huntsmen; The thief and his master; Jorinda and Joringel; The three sons of fortune; How six men got on in the world; The wolf and the man; The wolf and the fox; Gossip Wolf and the fox; The fox and the cat; The pink; Clever Gretel; The old man and his grandson; The water-nixie; The death of the little hen; Brother Lustig; Gambling Hansel; Hans in luck; Hans married; The gold-children; The fox and the geese; The poor man and the rich man; The singing, soaring lark; The goose-girl; The young giant; The gnome; The King of the Golden Mountain; The raven; The peasant's wise daughter; Old Hildebrand; The three little birds; The water of life; Doctor Knowall; The spirit in the bottle; The Devil's sooty brother; Bearskin; The willow-wren and the bear; Sweet porridge; Wise folks; Tales of the paddock; The poor miller's boy and the cat; The two travelers; Hans the Hedgehog; The shroud; The Jew among thorns; The skillful huntsman; The flail from heaven; The two king's children; The cunning little tailor; The bright sun brings it to light; The blue light; The willful child; The three-army surgeons; The seven Swabians; The three apprentices; The king's son who feared nothing; Donkey cabbages; The old woman in the wood; The three brothers; The Devil and his grandmother; Ferdinand the Faithful and Ferdinand the Unfaithful; The iron stove; The lazy spinner; The four skillful brothers; One-eye, Two-eyes, and Three-eyes; Fair Katrinelje and Pif-paf-Poltrie; The fox and the horse; The shoes that were danced to pieces; The six servants; The white bride and the black bride; Iron Hans; The three black princesses; Knoist and his three sons; The maid of Brakel; My household; The lambkin and the little fish; Simeli Mountain; Going a traveling; The donkey; The ungrateful son; The turnip; The old man made young again; The Lord's animals and the Devil's; The beam; The old beggar-woman; The three sluggards; The twelve idle servants; The shepherd boy; The star-money; The stolen farthings; Looking for a bride; The hurds; The sparrow and his four children; The story of Schlauraffen Land; The Ditmars tale of wonders; A riddling tale; Snow-White and Rose-Red; The wise servant; The glass coffin; Lazy Harry; The griffin; Strong Hans; The peasant in heaven; Lean Lisa; The hut in the forest; Sharing joy and sorrow; The willow-wren; The sole; The bittern and the hoopoe; The owl; The moon; The duration of life; Death's messengers; Master Pfriem; The goose-girl at the well; Eve's various children; The nixie of the mill-pond; The little folks' presents; The giant and the tailor; The nail; The poor boy in the grave; The true bride; The hare and the hedgehog; The spindle, the shuttle, and the needle; The peasant and the Devil; The crumbs on the table; The sea-hare; The master-thief; The drummer; The ear of corn; The grave-mound; Old Rinkrank; The crystal ball; Maid Maleen; The boots of buffalo-leather; The golden key; St. Joseph in the forest; The twelve apostles; The rose; Poverty and humility lead to heaven; God's food; The three green twigs; Our Lady's little glass; The aged mother; The heavenly wedding; The hazel-branch
The crystal coffin
In The Green fairy book p290-95 **398.2**
Darling Roland
In Best-loved folktales of the world p84-87 **398.2**
The devil and his grandmother
In The Yellow fairy book p38-41 **398.2**
The devil with the three golden hairs; adaptation. See Hogrogian, N. The devil with the three golden hairs **398.2**
The devil's three gold hairs
In Best-loved folktales of the world p78-84 **398.2**
The elves and the shoemaker
In The Family read-aloud Christmas treasury p18-21 **808.8**
In The Scott, Foresman anthology of children's literature p187-88 **808.8**
In Tomie dePaola's favorite nursery tales p100-04 **398.2**
The elves and the shoemaker; adaptation. See Galdone, P. The elves and the shoemaker **398.2**
The elves and the shoemaker; adaptation. See Littledale, F. The elves and the shoemaker **398.2**
The elves and the shoemaker; dramatization. See Thane, A. The elves and the shoemaker
The fisherman and his wife (k-3) **398.2**
also in Best-loved folktales of the world p88-94 **398.2**

Grimm, Jacob, 1785-1863—*Continued*

Frederick and Catherine; adaptation. See Shub, E. Clever Kate 398.2

Frog King; adaptation. See Isadora, R. The princess and the frog 398.2

Frog King; adaptation. See Ormerod, J. The frog prince 398.2

The frog prince

In Best-loved folktales of the world p95-98 398.2

In The Classic fairy tales p185-87 398.2

In Tomie dePaola's favorite nursery tales p21-30 398.2

The golden goose

In Best-loved folktales of the world p122-26 398.2

In The Red fairy book p340-45 398.2

The golden goose; dramatization. See Thane, A. Dummling and the golden goose

The golden lads

In The Green fairy book p311-18 398.2

The golden mermaid

In The Green fairy book p328-38 398.2

The goose girl

In Best-loved folktales of the world p98-103 398.2

In The Blue fairy book p266-73 398.2

Hansel and Gretel (k-3) 398.2

also in Best-loved folktales of the world p145-51 398.2

also in The Classic fairy tales p238-44 398.2

Hansel and Gretel; adaptation. See Lesser, R. Hansel and Gretel 398.2

Hansel and Gretel; adaptation. See Ross, T. Hansel and Gretel 398.2

Hansel and Gretel; dramatization. See Thane, A. Hansel and Gretel

Hansel and Grettel

In The Blue fairy book p251-58 398.2

In The Scott, Foresman anthology of children's literature p178-82 808.8

How six men travelled through the wide world

In The Yellow fairy book p95-99 398.2

The iron stove

In The Yellow fairy book p32-37 398.2

Jack my Hedgehog

In The Green fairy book p304-10 398.2

Jorinde and Joringel

In The Green fairy book p271-75 398.2

The juniper tree

In Best-loved folktales of the world p115-22 398.2

The juniper tree, and other tales from Grimm (4 and up) 398.2

Contents: v 1 The three feathers; Hans my hedgehog; The story of one who set out to study fear; Brother and sister; Spindle, shuttle, and needle; The twelve huntsmen; Fitcher's feathered bird; The devil and his three golden hairs; The fisherman and his wife; The master thief; Brother Gaily; The goblins; Hansel and Gretel v2 The frog king; or, Iron Henry; The poor miller's boy and the little cat; Frederick and Katelizabeth; The golden bird; Bearskin; Godfather Death; Many-Fur; Rapunzel; Snow-White and the seven dwarfs; Rabbit's bride; The two journeymen; Ferdinand Faithful and Ferdinand Unfaithful; Mrs. Gertrude; The juniper tree

Lazy Heinz

In Bauer, C. F. Celebrations p140-43 808.8

Little One-eye, Little Two-eyes, and Little Three-eyes

In The Green fairy book p262-70 398.2

Little Red Cap (k-2) 398.2

Little Red Riding Hood

In Best-loved folktales of the world p112-14 398.2

Little Red Riding Hood; adaptation. See Galdone, P. Little Red Riding Hood 398.2

Little Red Riding Hood; adaptation. See Hyman, T. S. Little Red Riding Hood 398.2

Little Red Riding Hood; adaptation. See Marshall, J. Little Red Riding Hood 398.2

The marvellous musician

In The Red fairy book p354-56 398.2

The merman and the farmer

In Best-loved folktales of the world p151-52 398.2

More tales from Grimm (4-6) 398.2

Contents: The golden key; The seven Swabians; The wolf and the fox; Mother Holle; The water nixie; The mouse, the bird, and the sausage; Thorn Rose, the sleeping beauty; The sweet porridge; The little shepherd boy; The twelve lazy servants; Lucky scraps; The cat and the fox; The soldier and his magic helpers; The gook-for-nothings; The star dollars; A trip to Schlaraffenland; The three languages; The straw, the coal, and the bean; The wishing table, the gold donkey, and the cudgel-in-the-sack; The tailor who went to Heaven; Presents of the little folk; The three spinners; The six swans; The queen bee; The hedgehog and the rabbit; The earth gnome; The three lucky ones; The sorcerer's apprentice; Iron Hans; Jorinda and Joringel; The wolf and the seven little kids; The shoemaker and the elves

Mother Holle

In Best-loved folktales of the world p134-36 398.2

In The Red fairy book p303-06 398.2

The queen bee

In Best-loved folktales of the world p140-41 398.2

Rapunzel

In Best-loved folktales of the world p75-78 398.2

In The Red fairy book p282-85 398.2

Rapunzel; adaptation. See Ehrlich, A. Rapunzel 398.2

Grimm, Jacob, 1785-1863—*Continued*
Rapunzel; adaptation. See Rogasky, B. Rapunzel **398.2**
Rapunzel; dramatization. See Thane, A. Rapunzel
The raven; adaptation. See Hogrogian, N. The Glass Mountain **398.2**
The riddle
In The Green fairy book p300-03 **398.2**
Rumpelstiltskin
In Best-loved folktales of the world p131-33 **398.2**
In The Classic fairy tales p197-98 **398.2**
In Tomie dePaola's favorite nursery tales p46-52 **398.2**
Rumpelstiltskin; adaptation. See Zelinsky, P. O. Rumpelstiltskin **398.2**
Rumpelstiltskin; dramatization. See Thane, A. Rumpelstiltskin
Rumpelstiltzkin
In The Blue fairy book p96-99 **398.2**
In The Scott, Foresman anthology of children's literature p185-87 **808.8**
The seven ravens (k-3) **398.2**
The six swans
In The Yellow fairy book p4-8 **398.2**
The six swans; adaptation. See San Souci, R. Robert D. San Souci's The six swans **398.2**
Sleeping beauty
In Best-loved folktales of the world p137-39 **398.2**
Snow-White
In Best-loved folktales of the world p53-61 **398.2**
Snow-White and Rose-Red
In The Blue fairy book p259-65 **398.2**
Snow-White and the seven dwarfs
In The Scott, Foresman anthology of children's literature p182-85 **808.8**
Snowdrop
In The Classic Fairy tales p177-82 **398.2**
In The Red fairy book p329-39 **398.2**
The sorcerer's apprentice; adaptation. See Gág, W. Wanda Gág's The sorcerer's apprentice **398.2**
Spindle, shuttle, and needle
In The Green fairy book p286-89 **398.2**
The spirit in the bottle
In The Scott, Foresman anthology of children's literature p190-92 **808.8**
The story of a clever tailor
In The Green fairy book p324-27 **398.2**
The story of the fisherman and his wife
In The Green fairy book p343-52 **398.2**
The tale of a youth who set out to learn what fear was
In The Blue fairy book p86-95 **398.2**
Tales from Grimm (4-6) **398.2**
Contents: Hansel and Gretel; Cat and mouse keep house; Six servants; Spindle, shuttle, and needle; Doctor Know-It-All; The musicians of Bremen; Cinderella; Clever Elsie; Rapunzel; The fisherman and his wife; The three brothers; Lazy Heinz; The frog prince; Lean Liesl and Lanky Lenz; The dragon and his grandmother; Snow White and Rose Red
Thousand-Furs
In Best-loved folktales of the world p126-31 **398.2**
The three dwarfs
In The Red fairy book p238-45 **398.2**
The three snake-leaves
In The Green fairy book p296-99 **398.2**
Tom Thumb
In Best-loved folktales of the world p104-09 **398.2**
Trusty John
In The Blue fairy book p296-303 **398.2**
The turnip
In The Scott, Foresman anthology of children's literature p192-94 **808.8**
The twelve brothers
In The Red fairy book p274-81 **398.2**
In Womenfolk and fairy tales p36-43 **398.2**
The twelve dancing princesses (k-3) **398.2**
also in The Classic fairy tales p191-94 **398.2**
The twelve dancing princesses; adaptation. See Sanderson, R. The twelve dancing princesses **398.2**
The twelve dancing princesses; dramatization. See Thane, A. The twelve dancing princesses
The twelve huntsmen
In The Green fairy book p282-85 **398.2**
Wanda Gág's Jorinda and Joringel (k-3) **398.2**
Wanda Gág's The earth gnome (k-2) **398.2**
Wanda Gag's The six swans (1-3) **398.2**
The war of the wolf and the fox
In The Green fairy book p339-42 **398.2**
The water of life; adaptation. See Rogasky, B. The water of life **398.2**
The white snake
In The Green fairy book p319-23 **398.2**
The wolf and the seven little kids
In Best-loved folktales of the world p109-11 **398.2**

Grimm, Jacob, 1785-1863—*Continued*
The wolf and the seven little kids; adaptation. See Ross, T. Mrs. Goat and her seven little kids 398.2

Grimm, Wilhelm, 1786-1859
Fairy tales by the Brothers Grimm are listed under Jacob Grimm

Grindley, Sally
I don't want to! E

Grinnell, George Bird, 1849-1938
The lost woman
In Best-loved folktales of the world p704-11 398.2
(comp) The Whistling skeleton. See The Whistling skeleton 398.2

Grinny Granny Wolf. Lester, J.
In Lester, J. More tales of Uncle Remus p64-66 398.2

Griselda's new year. Sharmat, M. W. E

Grisewood, John
The Doubleday children's dictionary (4 and up) 423

The **grizzly**. Johnson, A. Fic

Grizzly bear
Calabro, M. Operation grizzly bear (5 and up) 599.74
Patent, D. H. The way of the grizzly (4 and up) 599.74

Grooming, Personal
Cobb, V. Keeping clean (1-3) 646.7

The **groom's** crimes. Yen, T. C. C.
In Best-loved folktales of the world p546-47 398.2

Gross, Ruth Belov, 1929-
Snakes (3-5) 597.9
True stories about Abraham Lincoln (2-4) 92

Gross, Theodore Faro
Everyone asked about you E

Grosshandler, Henry
Everyone wins at tee ball (k-3) 796.357

Grosshandler, Janet
(jt. auth) Grosshandler, H. Everyone wins at tee ball 796.357

Grossman, Nancy, 1940-
(il) Caudill, R. Did you carry the flag today, Charley? Fic

Grossman, Robert, 1940-
(il) Byars, B. C. The 18th emergency Fic

Grosvenor, Donna K.
The blue whale (k-3) 599.5
Zoo babies (k-3) 590.74

The **grouchy** ladybug. Carle, E. E

Ground-hogs *See* Marmots

The **ground** parrot and the albatross. Te Kanawa, K.
In Te Kanawa, K. Land of the long white cloud p113-14 398.2

Groundhog dance. MacDonald, M. R.
In MacDonald, M. R. Twenty tellable tales p35-42 372.6

Grove, Vicki
Good-bye, my wishing star (5 and up) Fic

Grover, Wayne
Dolphin adventure (3-5) 599.5

Grover. Cleaver, V. Fic

The **growin'** of Paul Bunyan. Brooke, W. J.
In Brooke, W. J. A telling of the tales: five stories p37-48 S C

Growing colors. McMillan, B. E

Growing pains. Cuddigan, M. 011.6

The **growing** story. Krauss, R. E

Growing up. Singer, I. B.
In Singer, I. B. Naftali the storyteller and his horse, Sus, and other stories p113-29 S C
In Singer, I. B. Stories for children p217-30 S C

Growing up. Soto, G.
In Soto, G. Baseball in April, and other stories p97-107 S C

Growing up Amish. Ammon, R. 289.7

Growing vegetable soup. Ehlert, L. E

Growltiger's last stand. Eliot, T. S. 811

Growth

Fiction

Cooney, B. Island boy E
Krauss, R. The growing story E
McMillan, B. Step by step E

Grumbling old woman
Afanas'ev, A. N. The grumbling old woman
In Afanas'ev, A. N. Russian fairy tales p340-41 398.2

Grundtvig, Sven, 1824-1883
The most obedient wife
In The Scott, Foresman anthology of children's literature p217-20 808.8

Gryski, Camilla, 1948-
Cat's cradle, owl's eyes (4-6) 793.9
Many stars & more string games (4-6) 793.9
Super string games (4-6) 793.9

Guardi, Francesco, 1712-1793
See/See also pages in the following book(s):
Goffstein, M. B. Lives of the artists (5 and up) 920

Guardians of the gate
Carpenter, F. Guardians of the gate
In Carpenter, F. Tales of a Chinese grandmother p47-55 **398.2**
Guarino, Deborah
Is your mama a llama? **E**
Guatemala
Fiction
Cameron, A. The most beautiful place in the world (2-4) **Fic**
Gudbrand on the hillside. Asbjørnsen, P. C.
In Best-loved folktales of the world p300-04 **398.2**
El **Guëro**. Treviño, E. B. de. **Fic**
Guerrillas
Neimark, A. E. Ché! [biography of Ernesto Guevara] (6 and up) **92**
Guess, George *See* Sequoyah, 1770?-1843
Guess again: more weird & wacky inventions. Murphy, J. **609**
Guess who my favorite person is. Baylor, B. **E**
Guests. Paterson, K.
In Paterson, K. Angels & other strangers: family Christmas stories p17-25 **S C**
Guevara, Che *See* Guevara, Ernesto, 1928-1967
Guevara, Ernesto, 1928-1967
About
Neimark, A. E. Ché! (6 and up) **92**
Guidance, Vocational *See* Vocational guidance
A **guide** dog goes to school. Smith, E. S. **362.4**
Guide dogs
Butler, B. Maggie by my side (4 and up) **362.4**
Curtis, P. Greff, the story of a guide dog (5 and up) **636.7**
Smith, E. S. A guide dog goes to school (3-5) **362.4**
See/See also pages in the following book(s):
Silverstein, A. Dogs: all about them p188-96 (5 and up) **636.7**
Guide to encouraging young readers, The RIF **372.4**
A **Guide** to non-sexist children's books v2 **011.6**
Guide to reference books for school media centers. Wynar, C. G. **011.6**
Guide to videocassettes for children. See Parent's choice guide to videocassettes for children **016.79143**
Guinea fowl
Fiction
Knutson, B. How the guinea fowl got her spots (k-3) **398.2**
Guinea Fowl and Rabbit get justice. Courlander, H.
In Courlander, H. The cow-tail switch, and other West African stories p87-94 **398.2**
The **guinea** pig ABC. Duke, K. **E**
Guinea pigs
Bare, C. S. Guinea pigs don't read books (k-2) **636.088**
Duke, K. The guinea pig ABC **E**
Duke, K. Guinea pigs far and near **E**
Hess, L. Making friends with guinea pigs (4-6) **636.088**
Sproule, A. Guinea pigs (4 and up) **636.088**
See/See also pages in the following book(s):
Weber, W. J. Care of uncommon pets p32-43 (5 and up) **636.088**
Fiction
Bond, M. The complete adventures of Olga da Polga (2-5) **Fic**
Bond, M. The tales of Olga da Polga (2-5) **Fic**
Guinea pigs don't read books. Bare, C. S. **636.088**
Guinea pigs far and near. Duke, K. **E**
The **Guinness** book of answers **032.02**
Guinness book of records **032.02**
Guinness book of sports records **796.03**
Guinness book of sports records, winners & champions. See Guinness book of sports records **796.03**
Guinness book of world records. See Guinness book of records **032.02**
Guinness sports record book. See Guinness book of sports records **796.03**
Gulnara the Tartar warrior. Riordan, J.
In Riordan, J. The woman in the moon, and other tales of forgotten heroines p20-26 **398.2**
Gunawolf
Harper, W. The Gunniwolf **398.2**
MacDonald, M. R. The gunny wolf
In MacDonald, M. R. Twenty tellable tales p68-74 **372.6**
Gundersheimer, Karen, 1939-
1 2 3, play with me **E**
A B C, say with me **E**
(il) Calmenson, S. What am I? **793.73**
(il) Hest, A. The midnight eaters **E**
(il) The Merry-go-round poetry book. See The Merry-go-round poetry book **811.008**
(il) Wittman, S. A special trade **E**
The **Gunniwolf**. Harper, W. **398.2**
The **gunny** wolf. MacDonald, M. R.
In MacDonald, M. R. Twenty tellable tales p68-74 **372.6**

Guppies in tuxedos: funny eponyms. Terban, M. **422**

Guravich, Dan
(il) Matthews, D. Polar bear cubs **599.74**

Gustafson, Dana
(il) Haskins, J. Count your way through the Arab world **909**

Gustafson, Scott, 1956-
(il) Moore, C. C. The night before Christmas **811**

Gutmann, Bessie Pease
(il) Carroll, L. Alice's adventures in Wonderland **Fic**

Guy, Rosa
Mother Crocodile (k-3) **398.2**

Guys from space. Pinkwater, D. M. **E**

Gymnastics
See also Acrobats and acrobatics
Krementz, J. A very young gymnast (3-6) **796.44**
Murdock, T. Gymnastics (4 and up) **796.44**

Gypsies
See/See also pages in the following book(s):
Lyttle, R. B. Land beyond the river p92-105 (6 and up) **940.1**

H

Haas, Carolyn, 1926-
(jt. auth) Cole, A. Purple cow to the rescue **372.1**

Haas, Irene
(il) De Regniers, B. S. A little house of your own **E**

Haban, Rita D.
How proudly they wave (4 and up) **929.9**

Habitat for Humanity Inc.
Shachtman, T. The president builds a house (3-5) **363.5**

Hackett, Walter
A merry Christmas
In The Big book of Christmas plays p332-48 **808.82**

Hackwell, W. John
Digging to the past: excavations in ancient lands (4 and up) **930.1**
Diving to the past: recovering ancient wrecks (4 and up) **910.4**

Haddad, Helen R.
Potato printing (4-6) **761**

Hader, Berta, 1891-1976
The big snow **E**
See/See also pages in the following book(s):
Caldecott Medal books, 1938-1957 p185-99 **028.5**

Hader, Elmer Stanley, 1889-1973
(jt. auth) Hader, B. The big snow **E**
See/See also pages in the following book(s):
Caldecott Medal books, 1938-1957 p185-99 **028.5**

Hadingham, Evan
Garbage! (5 and up) **363.7**

Hadingham, Janet
(jt. auth) Hadingham, E. Garbage! **363.7**

Hadithi, Mwenye *See* Mwenye Hadithi

Hadler, Terry
(il) Jefferis, D. Helicopters **629.133**
(il) Jefferis, D. Supersonic flight **629.133**

Hafiz, the stone-cutter. Shedlock, M. L.
In Shedlock, M. L. The art of the story-teller p179-82 **372.6**

Hafner, Marylin, 1925-
(il) Berger, M. Germs make me sick! **616.9**
(il) Cobb, V. Feeding yourself **394.1**
(il) Cobb, V. Getting dressed **646**
(il) Cobb, V. Keeping clean **646.7**
(il) Cobb, V. Writing it down **681**
(il) Gage, W. Mrs. Gaddy and the ghost **E**
(il) The Laugh book. See The Laugh book **808.8**
(il) Prelutsky, J. It's Christmas **811**
(il) Prelutsky, J. It's Halloween **811**
(il) Prelutsky, J. It's Thanksgiving **811**
(il) Ross, P. Meet M and M **E**
(il) Winthrop, E. Katharine's doll **E**

Hague, Kathleen, 1949-
East of the sun and west of the moon (4-6) **398.2**
The man who kept house (k-3) **398.2**

Hague, Michael, 1948-
(il) Barrie, J. M. Peter Pan **Fic**
(il) Baum, L. F. The Wizard of Oz **Fic**
(il) Bianco, M. W. The velveteen rabbit **Fic**
(il) Burnett, F. H. The secret garden **Fic**
(il) Carroll, L. Alice's adventures in Wonderland **Fic**
(il) Grahame, K. The reluctant dragon **Fic**
(il) Grahame, K. The wind in the willows **Fic**
(jt. auth) Hague, K. East of the sun and west of the moon **398.2**

Hague, Michael, 1948-—*Continued*
(jt. auth) Hague, K. The man who kept house 398.2
(il) Lewis, C. S. The lion, the witch and the wardrobe Fic
(il) Mayer, M. The unicorn and the lake E
(il) Moore, C. C. The night before Christmas 811
(il) Sandburg, C. Rootabaga stories S C
Hahn, Mary Downing, 1937-
Daphne's book (5 and up) Fic
The dead man in Indian Creek (5 and up) Fic
December stillness (6 and up) Fic
The doll in the garden (4-6) Fic
Wait till Helen comes (4-6) Fic
Haiku
In a spring garden (k-3) 895.6
Hail
Branley, F. M. Rain & hail (k-3) 551.57
Hailstones and halibut bones. O'Neill, M. L. D. 811
Hair and hairdressing
Fiction
Yarbrough, C. Cornrows E
Hairston, Martha
(il) Burns, M. The I hate mathematics! book 513
The **hairy** horror trick. Corbett, S. See note under Corbett, S. The lemonade trick Fic
The **Hairy** toe, a story
In Halloween: stories and poems p20-21 808.8
Haiti
Folklore
See Folklore—Haiti
Haldane, Suzanne
Painting faces (4-6) 745.5
Hale, James
(il) Turner, A. W. Through moon and stars and night skies E
Hale, Lucretia Peabody, 1820-1900
The Peterkins' Christmas tree
In Diane Goode's American Christmas p11-15 810.8
Schwartz, A. The lady who put salt in her coffee E
Hale, Sarah Josepha
Mary had a little lamb (k-2) 811
Haley, Gail E.
A story, a story (k-3) 398.2
(il) Konigsburg, E. L. Altogether, one at a time S C
See/See also pages in the following book(s):
Newbery and Caldecott Medal books, 1966-1975 p223-29, 232-35 028.5
Half a moon and one whole star. Dragonwagon, C. E
The **Half-a-Moon** Inn. Fleischman, P. Fic
Half-chick
The Half-chick
In Best-loved folktales of the world p171-74 398.2
In The Green fairy book p27-31 398.2
In The Scott, Foresman anthology of children's literature p252-54 808.8
Half-chick. See Barnes, H. The proud cock
Half magic. Eager, E. Fic
Half magic [excerpt]. Eager, E.
In The Random House book of humor for children p154-72 817.008
Halfway home. Rylant, C.
In Rylant, C. Children of Christmas p6-12 S C
Hall, Donald, 1928-
The man who lived alone (2-4) Fic
Ox-cart man E
(ed) The Oxford book of children's verse in America. See The Oxford book of children's verse in America 811.008
Hall, Katy *See* McMullan, Kate, 1947-
Hall, Lynn, 1937-
Dagmar Schultz and the angel Edna (6 and up) Fic
Dagmar Schultz and the powers of darkness. See note under Hall, L. Dagmar Schultz and the angel Edna Fic
The secret of life of Dagmar Schultz. See note under Hall, L. Dagmar Schultz and the angel Edna Fic
Hall, Melissa Mia
Buddy Morris, Alias Fat Man
In Things that go bump in the night p186-98 S C
Hall, Susan, 1940-
Using picture storybooks to teach literary devices 016.8
Halley, Edmond, 1656-1742
About
Heckart, B. H. Edmond Halley, the man and his comet (4 and up) 92
Halley's comet
Heckart, B. H. Edmond Halley, the man and his comet (4 and up) 92
Halliday, Ian
Saturn (4-6) 523.4
Halloween
Barkin, C. The scary Halloween costume book (3-6) 391
Barth, E. Witches, pumpkins, and grinning ghosts (3-6) 394.2

Halloween—*Continued*
Borten, H. Halloween (1-3) **394.2**
Gibbons, G. Halloween (k-2) **394.2**
Halloween: stories and poems (2-4) **808.8**

See/See also pages in the following book(s):
Araki, C. Origami in the classroom p18-27 (Book I) (4 and up) **736**
Bauer, C. F. Celebrations p103-18 **808.8**

Fiction

Barth, E. Jack-o'-lantern (2-4) **398.2**
Bunting, E. In the haunted house **E**
Bunting, E. Scary, scary Halloween **E**
Carlson, N. S. Spooky night **E**
Estes, E. The witch family (2-5) **Fic**
Hamilton, V. Willie Bea and the time the Martians landed (5 and up) **Fic**
Hancock, S. Esteban and the ghost (k-3) **398.2**
Howe, J. Scared silly: a Halloween treat **E**
Johnston, T. The vanishing pumpkin **E**
Kroll, S. The biggest pumpkin ever **E**
Marshall, E. Space case **E**
Meyers, S. P.J. Clover, private eye: the case of the Halloween hoot (4-6) **Fic**
Miller, E. Mousekin's golden house **E**
Rockwell, A. F. Apples and pumpkins **E**
Zolotow, C. A tiger called Thomas **E**

Poetry

Cummings, E. E. Hist whist (k-2) **811**
Halloween poems (k-3) **808.81**
In the witch's kitchen (3-6) **811.008**
Merriam, E. Halloween A B C (k-2) **811**
Prelutsky, J. It's Halloween (1-3) **811**
Yolen, J. Best witches: poems for Halloween (3-5) **811**

Halloween A B C. Merriam, E. **811**
Halloween howls. Maestro, G. **793.73**
Halloween poems (k-3) **808.81**
The **Halloween** pony. San Souci, R.
In San Souci, R. Short & shivery p166-70 **398.2**
Halloween: stories and poems (2-4) **808.8**
Halloween with Morris and Boris. Wiseman, B. See note under Wiseman, B. Morris and Boris at the circus **E**
Halos (Meteorology)
See/See also pages in the following book(s):
Gallant, R. A. Rainbows, mirages and sundogs p46-57 (4 and up) **551.5**
Halpern, Joan
(il) Cohen, B. The carp in the bathtub **Fic**
Halsey, William Darrach, 1918-
(ed) Macmillan dictionary for students. See Macmillan dictionary for students **423**

Hamal Hasan and the baby day. Walker, B. K.
In Walker, B. K. A treasury of Turkish folktales for children p123-26 **398.2**
Hamanaka, Sheila
The journey (5 and up) **305.8**
(il) Hurwitz, J. Class clown **Fic**
(il) Kudlinski, K. V. Juliette Gordon Low: America's first Girl Scout **92**
(il) Merriam, E. Chortles: new and selected wordplay poems **811**
(il) Merriam, E. A poem for a pickle: funnybone verses **811**
Hamann, Brad
(il) Folsom, M. The Macmillan book of how things work **600**
Hamberger, John
(il) Elting, M. The Macmillan book of dinosaurs and other prehistoric creatures **560**
Hamilton, Edith, 1867-1963
Mythology (6 and up) **292**
Hamilton, Virginia, 1936-
Anthony Burns: the defeat and triumph of a fugitive slave (5 and up) **92**
The bells of Christmas (4-6) **Fic**
Cousins (5 and up) **Fic**
The house of Dies Drear (5 and up) **Fic**
In the beginning; creation stories from around the world (5 and up) **291**
M. C. Higgins the great (6 and up) **Fic**
The magical adventures of Pretty Pearl (6 and up) **Fic**
The mystery of Drear House (5 and up) **Fic**
The people could fly [story]
In Face to face: a collection of stories by celebrated Soviet and American writers p177-83 **S C**
The people could fly: American black folktales (4 and up) **398.2**
Contents: He Lion, Bruh Bear and Bruh Rabbit; Doc Rabbit, Bruh Fox, and Tar Baby; Tappin, the land turtle; Bruh Alligator and Bruh Deer; Bruh Lizard and Bruh Rabbit; Bruh Alligator meets Trouble; Wolf and birds and the Fish-Horse; The beautiful girl of the moon tower; A wolf and Little Daughter; Manuel had a riddle; Papa John's tall tale; The two Johns; Wiley, his mama, and the Hairy Man; John and the Devil's daughter; The peculiar such thing; Little Eight John; Jack and the Devil; Better wait till Martin comes; Carrying the running-aways; How Nehemiah got free; The talking cooter; The riddle tale of freedom; The most useful slave; The people could fly
The planet of Junior Brown (6 and up) **Fic**
Willie Bea and the time the Martians landed (5 and up) **Fic**
Zeely (4 and up) **Fic**

Hamilton, Virginia, 1936-—*Continued*
See/See also pages in the following book(s):
Newbery and Caldecott Medal books, 1966-1975 p129-40 **028.5**
Townsend, J. R. A sounding of storytellers p97-110 **028.5**
Hammer & saw. Weiss, H. **684**
Hammid, Hella, 1921-
(il) Cole, J. The new baby at your house **306.8**
Hammond, Tim
Sports (4 and up) **796**
Hammond ambassador world atlas **912**
Hammond citation world atlas **912**
Hampton, Blake
(il) Andry, A. C. How babies are made **612.6**
Hamsters
Fischer-Nagel, H. Inside the burrow: the life of the golden hamster (3-6) **636.08**
Silverstein, A. Hamsters: all about them (5 and up) **636.088**
See/See also pages in the following book(s):
Weber, W. J. Care of uncommon pets p44-57 (5 and up) **636.088**
Hancock, John, 1737-1793
About
Fritz, J. Will you sign here, John Hancock? (3-5) **92**
Hancock, Sibyl
Esteban and the ghost (k-3) **398.2**
Hand
Aliki. My hands (k-3) **612**
Silverstein, A. The story of your hand (5 and up) **612**
Hand of glory
Briggs, K. M. The hand of glory
In Best-loved folktales of the world p213-14 **398.2**
Hand rhymes. Brown, M. T. **796.1**
Handbook for storytellers. Bauer, C. F. **372.6**
Handedness *See* Left- and right-handedness
Handelsman, J. B.
(il) Fritz, J. Who's that stepping on Plymouth Rock? **974.4**
Handforth, Thomas, 1897-1948
Mei Li **E**
See/See also pages in the following book(s):
Caldecott Medal books, 1938-1957 p23-43 **028.5**
A **handful** of stars. Girion, B. **Fic**
Handicapped
See also Mentally handicapped; Physically handicapped
Fiction—Bibliography
Baskin, B. H. More notes from a different drummer **016.8**
Baskin, B. H. Notes from a different drummer **016.8**
Handicapped and animals *See* Animals and the handicapped
Handicapped children
See also Mentally handicapped children; Physically handicapped children
Butler, D. Cushla and her books **362.4**
Fiction
Slepian, J. The Alfred summer (5 and up) **Fic**
Handicraft
See also Egg decoration; Folk art
Barkin, C. Happy Valentine's Day! (4-6) **394.2**
Blocksma, M. Action contraptions (2-5) **745.592**
Caney, S. Steven Caney's kids' America (4 and up) **790.1**
Churchill, E. R. Fast & funny paper toys you can make (3 and up) **745.592**
Cuyler, M. The all-around pumpkin book (4-6) **641.3**
Elbert, V. Folk toys around the world and how to make them (5 and up) **745.592**
Haddad, H. R. Potato printing (4-6) **761**
Irvine, J. How to make pop-ups (3-6) **736**
Kerina, J. African crafts (4 and up) **745.5**
Kohn, B. The beachcomber's book (3-6) **745.5**
Meyer, C. Christmas crafts (5 and up) **745.59**
Parish, P. December decorations (1-3) **745.59**
Parish, P. Let's be early settlers with Daniel Boone (2-5) **745.5**
Pearson, T. C. Dollhouse people (3-5) **745.592**
Pellowski, A. Hidden stories in plants (4 and up) **398**
Pettit, F. H. The stamp-pad printing book (5 and up) **761**
A Pumpkin in a pear tree (1-4) **745.59**
Renfro, N. Bags are big! **745.54**
Roche, P. K. Dollhouse magic (2-4) **745.592**
Rockwell, H. I did it (1-3) **745.5**
Sancha, S. Walter Dragun's town (6 and up) **942.03**
Sullivan, S. C. A. Bats, butterflies, and bugs (3-5) **745.592**
Tunis, E. Colonial craftsmen and the beginnings of American industry (5 and up) **670**

Handicraft—*Continued*
Walker, L. Carpentry for children (4 and up) **694**
Walther, T. Make mine music! (5 and up) **784.19**
Wilkes, A. My first activity book (1-5) **745.5**
Wiseman, A. S. Making musical things (3-6) **784.19**
Wright, L. Masks (4 and up) **745.59**
See/See also pages in the following book(s):
Bauer, C. F. This way to books p303-28 **028.5**
Burns, M. The Hanukkah book p87-101 (4 and up) **296.4**
Equipment and supplies
Sattler, H. R. Recipes for art and craft materials (4 and up) **745.5**
Handtalk: an ABC of finger spelling & sign language. Charlip, R. **419**
Handtalk birthday. Charlip, R. **419**
Handtalk zoo. Ancona, G. **419**
Handville, Robert, 1924-
(il) Gates, D. Lord of the sky: Zeus **292**
Handwriting
See also Calligraphy; Graphology
Fiction
Cleary, B. Muggie Maggie (2-4) **Fic**
Hangin' out with Cici. Pascal, F. **Fic**
The **hangman's** ghost trick. Corbett, S. See note under Corbett, S. The lemonade trick **Fic**
Hani, Shabō
(il) Overbeck, C. Cactus **583**
(il) Overbeck, C. How seeds travel **582**
Hanna's hog. Aylesworth, J. **E**
Hano, Renée Roth- *See* Roth-Hano, Renée, 1931-
Hans Andersen: his classic fairy tales. Andersen, H. C. **S C**
Hans Brinker; or, The silver skates. Dodge, M. M. **Fic**
Hans Christian Andersen's The fir tree. Andersen, H. C. **Fic**
Hans Clodhopper
Andersen, H. C. Blockhead Hans
In The Yellow fairy book p313-18 **398.2**
Hans in luck
Grimm, J. Hans in luck
In Grimm, J. The complete Grimm's fairy tales p381-86 **398.2**
Hans married
Grimm, J. Hans married
In Grimm, J. The complete Grimm's fairy tales p387-88 **398.2**
Hans my hedgehog
Grimm, J. Hans my hedgehog
In Grimm, J. The juniper tree, and other tales from Grimm v1 p11-22 **398.2**
Grimm, J. Hans the Hedgehog
In Grimm, J. The complete Grimm's fairy tales p497-502 **398.2**
Grimm, J. Jack my Hedgehog
In The Green fairy book p304-10 **398.2**
Hans the Hedgehog. Grimm, J.
In Grimm, J. The complete Grimm's fairy tales p497-502 **398.2**
Hansel and Gretel *See* Hansel and Grethel
Hansel and Grethel
Ehrlich, A. Hansel and Gretel
In Ehrlich, A. The Random House book of fairy tales p150-65 **398.2**
Grimm, J. Hansel and Gretel **398.2**
also in Best-loved folktales of the world p145-51 **398.2**
also in The Classic fairy tales p238-44 **398.2**
also in Grimm, J. About wise men and simpletons p99-107 **398.2**
also in Grimm, J. The complete Grimm's fairy tales p86-94 **398.2**
also in Grimm, J. The juniper tree, and other tales from Grimm v1 p152-68 **398.2**
also in Grimm, J. Tales from Grimm p3-26 **398.2**
Grimm, J. Hansel and Grettel
In The Blue fairy book p251-58 **398.2**
In The Scott, Foresman anthology of children's literature p178-82 **808.8**
Lesser, R. Hansel and Gretel **398.2**
Ross, T. Hansel and Gretel **398.2**
Thane, A. Hansel and Gretel
In Thane, A. Plays from famous stories and fairy tales p335-51 **812**
Hansen, Joyce
The gift-giver (4-6) **Fic**
Hanson, Mary Beth
(jt. auth) Cuddigan, M. Growing pains **011.6**
Hanson, Peter E.
(il) Ferris, J. Walking the road to freedom: a story about Sojourner Truth **92**
(il) Mitchell, B. A pocketful of goobers: a story about George Washington Carver **92**
Hanson, Rick
(il) Swanson, J. I pledge allegiance **323.6**

Hanukah money. Shulevitz, U. E
Hanukkah
Adler, D. A. A picture book of Hanukkah (1-3) **296.4**
Burns, M. The Hanukkah book (4 and up) **296.4**
Chaikin, M. Hanukkah (k-2) **296.4**
Chaikin, M. Light another candle (3-6) **296.4**
Drucker, M. Hanukkah (4 and up) **296.4**
Ehrlich, A. The story of Hanukkah (1-3) **296.4**
Hirsh, M. I love Hanukkah (k-3) **296.4**
Koralek, J. Hanukkah, the festival of lights (k-3) **296.4**
Fiction
Chaikin, M. Yossi asks the angels for help (3-5) **Fic**
Goldin, B. D. Just enough is plenty: a Hanukkah tale **E**
Kimmel, E. A. The Chanukkah guest **E**
Kimmel, E. A. Hershel and the Hanukkah goblins **E**
Manushkin, F. Latkes and applesauce **E**
Shulevitz, U. Hanukah money **E**
Singer, I. B. The power of light (4 and up) **S C**
Hanukkah. Drucker, M. **296.4**
The **Hanukkah** book. Burns, M. **296.4**
A **Hanukkah** Eve in Warsaw. Singer, I. B.
In Singer, I. B. Naftali the storyteller and his horse, Sus, and other stories p51-71 **S C**
In Singer, I. B. Stories for children p53-70 **S C**
A **Hanukkah** evening in my parents' house. Singer, I. B.
In Singer, I. B. The power of light p3-9 **S C**
In Singer, I. B. Stories for children p155-59 **S C**
Hanukkah in the poorhouse. Singer, I. B.
In Singer, I. B. The power of light p75-87 **S C**
In Singer, I. B. Stories for children p271-82 **S C**
The **Hanukkah** Santa Claus. Levoy, M.
In Levoy, M. The witch of Fourth Street, and other stories **S C**
Hanukkah, the festival of lights. Koralek, J. **296.4**
The **happiest** ending. Uchida, Y. See note under Uchida, Y. A jar of dreams **Fic**
The **happiest** sheep in London. Aiken, J.
In Aiken, J. Up the chimney down, and other stories p191-211 **S C**
Happily after all. Stevenson, L. C. **Fic**
Happy birthday! Gibbons, G. **394.2**
Happy birthday! Laird, E. **394.2**
Happy birthday, Grampie. Pearson, S. **E**
Happy birthday, Moon. Asch, F. See note under Asch, F. Sand cake **E**
Happy birthday, Ronald Morgan! Giff, P. R. See note under Giff, P. R. Watch out, Ronald Morgan! **E**
Happy birthday Rotten Ralph. Gantos, J. See note under Gantos, J. Rotten Ralph **E**
Happy birthday, Sam. Hutchins, P. **E**
Happy birthday to me. Rockwell, A. F. **E**
Happy Christmas, Gemma. Hayes, S. **E**
Happy Christmas to all. Nolan, J. C.
In The Big book of Christmas plays p137-50 **808.82**
Happy Dens. Yolen, J.
In Yolen, J. The faery flag p103-19 **S C**
The **happy** lion. Fatio, L. **E**
The **happy** orpheline. Carlson, N. S. **Fic**
Happy Passover, Rosie. Zalben, J. B. **E**
The **happy** prince. Wilde, O.
In Wilde, O. The Happy Prince, and other stories p1-12 **S C**
The **Happy** Prince, and other stories. Wilde, O. **S C**
Happy Thanksgiving! Barkin, C. **394.2**
Happy Valentine's Day! Barkin, C. **394.2**
Happy Valentine's Day, Emma! Stevenson, J. See note under Stevenson, J. Emma **E**
Harald and the great stag. Carrick, D. **E**
Harbors
Crews, D. Harbor **E**
Hardendorff, Jeanne B.
The bed just so, a story
In Halloween: stories and poems p53-57 **808.8**
Hardy, Ralph
(jt. auth) Lambert, D. Weather and its work **551.6**
Hardy Hardhead
Hardy Hardhead
In The Jack tales p96-105 **398.2**
Hare, Tony
Acid rain (5 and up) **363.7**
Hare and the hedgehog
Grimm, J. The hare and the hedgehog
In Grimm, J. The complete Grimm's fairy tales p760-64 **398.2**
Grimm, J. The hedgehog and the rabbit
In Grimm, J. More tales from Grimm p163-70 **398.2**

The **hare** and the lion. See Aardema, V. Rabbit makes a monkey of lion 398.2

Hare and the tortoise
The Hare and the tortoise 398.2
The Hare and the turtle
In The Baby's story book p35 398.2
Wildsmith, B. The hare and the tortoise 398.2

The **Hare** and the tortoise (k-3) 398.2

Hare in the moon
Shedlock, M. L. The true spirit of a festival day
In Shedlock, M. L. The art of the story-teller p225-28 372.6

The **hare** that ran away. Shedlock, M. L.
In The Scott, Foresman anthology of children's literature p341 808.8

The **hare's** bride. Grimm, J.
In Grimm, J. The complete Grimm's fairy tales p332-33 398.2

Hargittai, Magdolna
Cooking the Hungarian way (5 and up) 641.5

Hargrove, Jim, 1947-
Belgium (4 and up) 949.3
Nebraska
In America the beautiful 973

Harik, Elsa M.
The Lebanese in America
In The In America series 305.8

Hark, Mildred
Christmas Eve letter
In The Big book of Christmas plays p41-58 808.82
Christmas shopping early
In Holiday plays round the year p3-13 812.008
A star in the window
In The Big book of Christmas plays p118-33 808.82

Härkönen, Reijo
(jt. auth) Pitkänen, M. A. The children of Nepal 954.96

Harlan, Judith
Sounding the alarm: a biography of Rachel Carson (5 and up) 92

Harlem (New York, N.Y.)
Fiction
Childress, A. A hero ain't nothin' but a sandwich (6 and up) Fic
Myers, W. D. Fast Sam, Cool Clyde, and Stuff (6 and up) Fic
Myers, W. D. The Mouse rap (6 and up) Fic
Myers, W. D. Scorpions (6 and up) Fic
Myers, W. D. The young landlords (6 and up) Fic
Wagner, J. J. T. (3-6) Fic

Harlem Dance Theatre *See* Dance Theatre of Harlem

Harley-Davidson motorcycle
Jaspersohn, W. Motorcycle: the making of a Harley-Davidson (5 and up) 629.227

Harmon, Mary K.
(ed) Powers, D. G. How to run a meeting 060.4

Harmonica
Fiction
McCloskey, R. Lentil E

Harness, Cheryl
(il) Gould, D. Aaron's shirt E
(il) Moore, C. C. The night before Christmas 811

Harold & Chester in Scared silly. See Howe, J. Scared silly: a Halloween treat E

Harold and the purple crayon. Johnson, C. E

Harold's ABC. Johnson, C. See note under Johnson, C. Harold and the purple crayon E

Harold's circus. Johnson, C. See note under Johnson, C. Harold and the purple crayon E

Harold's trip to the sky. Johnson, C. See note under Johnson, C. Harold and the purple crayon E

Harper, Wilhelmina
The Gunniwolf (k-1) 398.2

Harpist in the wind. McKillip, P. A. See note under McKillip, P. A. The riddle-master of Hed Fic

The **harps** of Heaven. Babbitt, N.
In Babbitt, N. The Devil's storybook p21-35 S C
In The Random House book of humor for children p134-43 817.008

Harrar, George
Radical robots (5 and up) 629.8
Signs of the apes, songs of the whales (4 and up) 591.5

Harrar, Linda
(jt. auth) Harrar, G. Signs of the apes, songs of the whales 591.5

Harriet the spy. Fitzhugh, L. Fic

Harriet the spy [excerpt]. Fitzhugh, L.
In The Random House book of humor for children p248-58 817.008

Harrington, Ty
Maine
In America the beautiful 973

Harris, Alan, 1944-
The great Voyager adventure (5 and up) 523.4

Harris, Jacqueline L., 1929-
Science in ancient Rome (5 and up) 509

Harris, Joel Chandler, 1848-1908
The wonderful tar-baby story
In Best-loved folktales of the world p666-68 **398.2**
In The Scott, Foresman anthology of children's literature p377-78 **808.8**
Lester, J. Further tales of Uncle Remus **398.2**
Lester, J. More tales of Uncle Remus **398.2**
Lester, J. The tales of Uncle Remus **398.2**
Parks, V. D. Jump! the adventures of Brer Rabbit **398.2**
Parks, V. D. Jump again! more adventures of Brer Rabbit **398.2**
Parks, V. D. Jump on over! the adventures of Brer Rabbit and his family **398.2**

Harris, Jonathan, 1921-
The land and people of France (5 and up) **944**

Harris, Karen H., 1934-
(jt. auth) Baskin, B. H. Books for the gifted child **011.6**
(jt. auth) Baskin, B. H. More notes from a different drummer **016.8**
(jt. auth) Baskin, B. H. Notes from a different drummer **016.8**

Harris, Robie H.
Before you were three **155.4**

Harrison, Michael, 1939-
(ed) The Oxford book of Christmas poems. See The Oxford book of Christmas poems **808.81**

Harrison, Mimi
(il) Betancourt, J. Smile! how to cope with braces **617.6**

Harrison, Ted, 1926-
(il) Service, R. W. The cremation of Sam McGee **811**
(il) Service, R. W. The shooting of Dan McGrew **811**

Harrison, Virginia, 1966-
The world of a falcon (k-2) **598**
The world of honeybees (k-2) **595.7**
The world of snakes (k-2) **597.9**

Harry and the lady next door. Zion, G. See note under Zion, G. Harry the dirty dog **E**

Harry by the sea. Zion, G. See note under Zion, G. Harry the dirty dog **E**

Harry Cat's pet puppy. Selden, G. See note under Selden, G. The cricket in Times Square **Fic**

Harry in trouble. Porte-Thomas, B. A. **E**

Harry Kitten and Tucker Mouse. Selden, G. See note under Selden, G. The cricket in Times Square **Fic**

Harry the dirty dog. Zion, G. **E**

Harry's dog. Porte-Thomas, B. A. See note under Porte-Thomas, B. A. Harry in trouble **E**

Harry's Mad. King-Smith, D. **Fic**

Harry's mom. Porte-Thomas, B. A. See note under Porte-Thomas, B. A. Harry in trouble **E**

Harry's visit. Porte-Thomas, B. A. See note under Porte-Thomas, B. A. Harry in trouble **E**

Hart, Carole, 1943-
(ed) Free to be—you and me. See Free to be—you and me **810.8**

Hart, George, 1945-
Ancient Egypt (4 and up) **932**
Exploring the past: ancient Egypt (4 and up) **932**

Hart, Jane
(comp) Singing bee! See Singing bee! **782.42**

Hartelius, Margaret A.
(il) Chernoff, G. T. Easy costumes you don't have to sew **391**

Härtling, Peter, 1933-
Crutches (5 and up) **Fic**
Old John (4 and up) **Fic**

A **Harvest** of Russian children's literature **891.7**

Harvey, Brett
Cassie's journey (2-4) **Fic**

Harvey, Roland, 1945-
(il) Hirst, R. My place in space **520**

Harvey, the beer can king. Gilson, J. See note under Gilson, J. Hello, my name is Scrambled Eggs **Fic**

Harvey's horrible snake disaster. Clifford, E. **Fic**

Harvey's marvelous monkey mystery. Clifford, E. See note under Clifford, E. Harvey's horrible snake disaster **Fic**

Harvey's wacky parrot adventure. Clifford, E. See note under Clifford, E. Harvey's horrible snake disaster **Fic**

Hasan and Allah's greatness. Walker, B. K.
In Walker, B. K. A treasury of Turkish folktales for children p139-47 **398.2**

Hasan, the heroic mouse-child. Walker, B. K.
In Walker, B. K. A treasury of Turkish folktales for children p8-10 **398.2**

Haskins, James, 1941-
Bill Cosby: America's most famous father (5 and up) **92**
Count your way through China (2-4) **951**

Haskins, James, 1941-—*Continued*
Count your way through Japan (2-4) **952**
Count your way through the Arab world (2-4) **909**
Katherine Dunham (5 and up) **92**
The life and death of Martin Luther King, Jr (5 and up) **92**
Shirley Temple Black (4 and up) **92**
The Statue of Liberty: America's proud lady (4 and up) **974.7**

Hassall, Joan, 1906-
(il) The Oxford Nursery rhyme book. See The Oxford Nursery rhyme book **398.8**

Hasselriis, Malthé
(il) Carpenter, F. Tales of a Chinese grandmother **398.2**

Hastings, Selina
Sir Gawain and the Green Knight (3 and up) **398.2**
Sir Gawain and the loathly lady (3 and up) **398.2**

Hatch, Jane M.
(ed) The American book of days. See The American book of days **394.2**

Hatch, Mary Cottam, 1912-1970
Graylegs
In The Scott, Foresman anthology of children's literature p220-25 **808.8**
The talking pot
In The Scott, Foresman anthology of children's literature p225-27 **808.8**

The **hating** book. Zolotow, C. **E**

Hats
Morris, A. Hats, hats, hats (k-3) **391**
Fiction
Geringer, L. A three hat day **E**
Johnston, T. The witch's hat **E**
Keats, E. J. Jennie's hat **E**
Seuss, Dr. The 500 hats of Bartholomew Cubbins **E**

Hats, hats, hats. Morris, A. **391**

Hats to disappear with. Junne, I. K.
In Best-loved folktales of the world p561-62 **398.2**

Hatsuno's great-grandmother. Means, F. C.
In The Scott, Foresman anthology of children's literature p639-44 **808.8**

Hattie and the fox. Fox, M. **E**

Hattie and the wild waves. Cooney, B. **E**

Haubrich, Kathy
(il) Mitchell, B. We'll race you, Henry: a story about Henry Ford **92**

Haufrecht, Herbert, 1909-
The Laura Ingalls Wilder songbook. See The Laura Ingalls Wilder songbook **782.42**

Haugaard, Erik Christian
Leif the unlucky (6 and up) **Fic**

Hauman, Doris, 1898-
(il) Dickinson, E. Poems for youth **811**
(il) Piper, W. The little engine that could **E**

Hauman, George, 1890-1961
(il) Dickinson, E. Poems for youth **811**
(il) Piper, W. The little engine that could **E**

Haunted house jokes. Phillips, L. **793.73**

The **haunted** mountain. Hunter, M. **Fic**

The **haunting**. Mahy, M. **Fic**

Hauptly, Denis J., 1945-
"A convention of delegates" (5 and up) **342**

Hauser, Paula
Baskin, B. H. Books for the gifted child **011.6**

Hausherr, Rosmarie
Children and the AIDS virus (1-3) **616.97**
My first kitten (1-3) **636.8**
My first puppy (1-3) **636.7**
(il) Roy, R. Move over, wheelchairs coming through! **362.4**
(il) Roy, R. Whose shoes are these? **391**

Hautzig, Esther Rudomin
A gift for Mama (3-6) **Fic**
Holiday treats (3 and up) **641.5**
Make it special (4-6) **745.59**

Have a happy—. Walter, M. P. **Fic**

Have you ever seen—? Gardner, B. **E**

Have you seen my duckling? Tafuri, N. **E**

Havill, Juanita
Jamaica tag-along **E**

Hawaii
McNair, S. Hawaii
In America the beautiful **973**
Fiction
Slepian, J. The Broccoli tapes (5 and up) **Fic**
Legends
See Legends—Hawaii

Hawes, Charles Boardman, 1889-1923
See/See also pages in the following book(s):
Newbery Medal books, 1922-1955 p30-32 **028.5**

Hawes, Judy
My daddy longlegs (k-3) **595.4**

Hawk, I'm your brother. Baylor, B. E
Hawks
Fiction
Baylor, B. Hawk, I'm your brother E
Hawthorne, Nathaniel, 1804-1864
The golden touch
In The Scott, Foresman anthology of children's literature p430-37 **808.8**
Lady Eleanore's mantle; adaptation. See San Souci, R. Lady Eleanore's mantle
The winged horse
In Herds of thunder, manes of gold p96-110 **808.8**
A wonder-book, and Tanglewood tales (5 and up) **292**
Haycraft, Howard, 1905-
(ed) The Junior book of authors. See The Junior book of authors **920.003**
Hayes, Sarah
Eat up, Gemma E
Happy Christmas, Gemma E
(comp) Clap your hands. See Clap your hands **796.1**
(comp) Stamp your feet. See Stamp your feet **796.1**
Hays, Michael, 1956-
(il) Seeger, P. Abiyoyo **398.2**
(il) Taylor, M. D. The gold Cadillac **Fic**
The **haystack** cricket and how things are different up in the moon towns. Sandburg, C.
In Sandburg, C. Rootabaga stories pt 2 p123-29 **S C**
In Sandburg, C. The Sandburg treasury p139-42 **818**
Haywood, Carolyn, 1898-1990
"B" is for Betsy (2-4) **Fic**
Back to school with Betsy. See note under Haywood, C. "B" is for Betsy **Fic**
Betsy and Billy. See note under Haywood, C. "B" is for Betsy **Fic**
Betsy and Mr. Kilpatrick. See note under Haywood, C. "B" is for Betsy **Fic**
Betsy and the boys. See note under Haywood, C. "B" is for Betsy **Fic**
Betsy and the circus. See note under Haywood, C. "B" is for Betsy **Fic**
Betsy's busy summer. See note under Haywood, C. "B" is for Betsy **Fic**
Betsy's little star. See note under Haywood, C. "B" is for Betsy **Fic**
Betsy's play school. See note under Haywood, C. "B" is for Betsy **Fic**
Betsy's winterhouse. See note under Haywood, C. "B" is for Betsy **Fic**
Eddie and his big deals. See note under Haywood, C. Little Eddie **Fic**
Eddie and the fire engine. See note under Haywood, C. Little Eddie **Fic**
Eddie's menagerie. See note under Haywood, C. Little Eddie **Fic**
Eddie's valuable property. See note under Haywood, C. Little Eddie **Fic**
Little Eddie (2-4) **Fic**
Merry Christmas from Betsy. See note under Haywood, C. "B" is for Betsy **Fic**
Merry Christmas from Eddie. See note under Haywood, C. Little Eddie **Fic**
A present for Santa Claus
In The Family read-aloud Christmas treasury p36-41 **808.8**
Snowbound with Betsy. See note under Haywood, C. "B" is for Betsy **Fic**
Haywood, Mary Carolyn *See* Haywood, Carolyn, 1898-1990
Hazard, Paul, 1878-1944
Books, children, and men **028.5**
The **hazel-branch**. Grimm, J.
In Grimm, J. The complete Grimm's fairy tales p830 **398.2**
Hazel-nut child
The Hazel-nut child
In The Yellow fairy book p222-24 **398.2**
Hazel Rye. Cleaver, V. **Fic**
Hazel's amazing mother. Wells, R. **E**
Hazen, Barbara Shook, 1930-
The gorilla did it **E**
Hazen, Edith P.
(ed) The Columbia Granger's index to poetry. See The Columbia Granger's index to poetry **808.81**
He came down. Paterson, K.
In Paterson, K. Angels & other strangers: family Christmas stories p81-89 **S C**
He is risen: the Easter story. Winthrop, E. **232.9**
He Lion, Bruh Bear and Bruh Rabbit. Hamilton, V.
In Hamilton, V. The people could fly: American black folktales p5-12 **398.2**
Head
Goor, R. Heads (2-4) **591.4**
Fiction
Yorinks, A. It happened in Pinsk **E**
Headgear. Hirschi, R. **599.73**
The **headless** cupid. Snyder, Z. K. **Fic**
The **Headless** Horseman rides tonight. Prelutsky, J. **811**
Heads of state
See also Kings, queens, rulers, etc. Presidents; names of individual heads of state

Heady, Eleanor B.
Men of different colors
In The Scott, Foresman anthology of children's literature p305-06 **808.8**
The **healing** spring. Martin, E.
In Martin, E. Tales of the Far North p9-15 **398.2**
Healing warrior: a story about Sister Elizabeth Kenny. Crofford, E. **92**
Health
See also Hygiene
Brown, L. K. Dinosaurs alive and well!: a guide to good health (k-3) **613**
Shaw, D. Make the most of a good thing: you! (5 and up) **613**
Environmental aspects
See Environmental health
Health care *See* Medical care
Healy, Katherine
About
Krementz, J. A very young skater (3-6) **796.91**
Hearing
Parker, S. The ear and hearing (4 and up) **612.8**
Showers, P. Ears are for hearing (k-3) **612.8**
Hearing aids
Litchfield, A. B. A button in her ear (1-3) **617.8**
Hearing ear dogs
Curtis, P. Cindy, a hearing ear dog (3-5) **636.7**
Hearn, Lafcadio, 1850-1904
Momotaro
In Best-loved folktales of the world p503-05 **398.2**
The old woman and her dumpling
In Womenfolk and fairy tales p44-50 **398.2**
The old woman and her dumpling; adaptation. See Mosel, A. The funny little woman **398.2**
The old woman who lost her dumplings
In Best-loved folktales of the world p506-09 **398.2**
The soul of the great bell; adaptation. See Hodges, M. The voice of the great bell **398.2**
Hearne, Betsy Gould
Choosing books for children **028.5**
Hearne, Elizabeth G. *See* Hearne, Betsy Gould
Heart
See also Blood—Circulation
Parker, S. The heart and blood (4 and up) **612.1**
Diseases
Silverstein, A. Heart disease: America's #1 killer (6 and up) **616.1**
The **heart** and blood. Parker, S. **612.1**
Heart disease: America's #1 killer. Silverstein, A. **616.1**
Heart of ice
Caylus, A. C. P. de T., comte de. Heart of ice
In The Green fairy book p106-36 **398.2**
Hearts, cupids, and red roses. Barth, E. **394.2**
Heaven to Betsy. Lovelace, M. H. See note under Lovelace, M. H. Betsy-Tacy **Fic**
The **heavenly** wedding. Grimm, J.
In Grimm, J. The complete Grimm's fairy tales p828-29 **398.2**
The **heavenly** zoo. Lurie, A. **398.2**
Heberman, Ethan
The city kid's field guide (4 and up) **591**
Heckart, Barbara Hooper
Edmond Halley, the man and his comet (4 and up) **92**
Heckedy Peg. Wood, A. **E**
Hector lives in the United States now. Hewett, J. **305.8**
Hector Protector, and As I went over the water. Sendak, M. **398.8**
The **hedgehog** and the rabbit. Grimm, J.
In Grimm, J. More tales from Grimm p163-70 **398.2**
The **hedgehog** boy. Langton, J. **398.2**
Hedgehogs
Fiction
Potter, B. The tale of Mrs. Tiggy-Winkle **E**
Hedwig the wise. Gorog, J.
In Gorog, J. Three dreams and a nightmare, and other tales of the dark **S C**
Heide, Dirk van der *See* Young, Stanley, 1906-1975
Heide, Florence Parry, 1919-
The adventures of Treehorn. See note under Heide, F. P. The shrinking of Treehorn **Fic**
The day of Ahmed's secret **E**
The shrinking of Treehorn (2-5) **Fic**
Treehorn's treasure. See note under Heide, F. P. The shrinking of Treehorn **Fic**
Treehorn's wish. See note under Heide, F. P. The shrinking of Treehorn **Fic**
Heidi. Spyri, J. **Fic**
Heidi. Thane, A.
In Thane, A. Plays from famous stories and fairy tales p315-34 **812**

Heifer hide
The heifer hide
In The Jack tales p161-71 **398.2**
Heighway, Richard
(il) Jacobs, J. The fables of Aesop **398.2**
Heilbroner, Joan
This is the house where Jack lives **E**
Heine, Helme
Friends **E**
The most wonderful egg in the world **E**
Heinrich, Bernd, 1940-
An owl in the house (4 and up) **598**
Heinrichs, Ann
Alaska
In America the beautiful **973**
Arizona
In America the beautiful **973**
Arkansas
In America the beautiful **973**
Montana
In America the beautiful **973**
Oklahoma
In America the beautiful **973**
Rhode Island
In America the beautiful **973**
Heinrichs, Susan
The Pacific Ocean (2-4) **910**
Heins, Paul
(ed) Crosscurrents of criticism. See Crosscurrents of criticism **028.5**
Heir of sea & fire. McKillip, P. A. See note under McKillip, P. A. The riddle-master of Hed **Fic**
The **heiress,** or the croak of doom. Rockwell, T.
In Rockwell, T. How to eat fried worms, and other plays p109-42 **812**
The **Helen** Keller story. Peare, C. O. **92**
The **Helen** Oxenbury nursery rhyme book (k-2) **398.8**
The **Helen** Oxenbury nursery story book. Oxenbury, H. **398.2**
Helen Oxenbury's ABC of things. Oxenbury, H. **E**
Helga's dowry. De Paola, T. **E**
Helicopters
Jefferis, D. Helicopters (4 and up) **629.133**
Helium
See/See also pages in the following book(s):
Asimov, I. How did we find out about superconductivity? p37-48 (5 and up) **537.6**
Hellard, Susan
(il) Asher, S. Where do you get your ideas? **808**
Heller, Linda
(il) Adler, D. A. A picture book of Hanukkah **296.4**
(il) Adler, D. A. A picture book of Passover **296.4**
(il) Ginsburg, M. The magic stove **398.2**
Heller, Ruth
A cache of jewels and other collective nouns (k-2) **428**
Chickens aren't the only ones (k-1) **591.1**
Kites sail high: a book about verbs (k-2) **428**
Many luscious lollipops: a book about adjectives (k-2) **428**
(il) Climo, S. The Egyptian Cinderella **398.2**
Hello, Mrs. Piggle-Wiggle. MacDonald, B. See note under MacDonald, B. Mrs. Piggle-Wiggle **Fic**
Hello, my name is Scrambled Eggs. Gilson, J. **Fic**
Helmer, Jean Cassels
(il) Kavaler, L. Green magic: algae rediscovered **589.3**
Help! I'm a prisoner in the library. Clifford, E. **Fic**
Helping our animal friends. Rinard, J. E. **636.088**
Helweg, Hans H., 1917-
(il) Bond, M. The complete adventures of Olga da Polga **Fic**
(il) Bond, M. The tales of Olga da Polga **Fic**
Hen and Frog. Bryan, A.
In Bryan, A. Beat the story-drum, pum-pum p3-13 **398.2**
Henbest, Nigel
(jt. auth) Couper, H. The moon **523.3**
Hendershot, Judith, 1940-
In coal country **E**
Henderson, Kathy
Christmas trees (2-4) **394.2**
The Great Lakes (2-4) **551.4**
Hendry, Linda
(il) Foodworks. See Foodworks **641.3**
Heng O, the moon lady. Carpenter, F.
In Carpenter, F. Tales of a Chinese grandmother p206-16 **398.2**
Henkes, Kevin, 1960-
Chester's way **E**
Jessica **E**
Julius, the baby of the world **E**
Sheila Rae, the brave **E**

Henneberger, Robert, 1921-
(il) Cameron, E. The wonderful flight to the Mushroom Planet **Fic**
Hennessy, B. G. (Barbara G.)
A,B,C,D, tummy, toes, hands, knees **E**
The missing tarts **E**
Hennessy, Barbara G. *See* Hennessy, B. G. (Barbara G.)
Henny-Penny
In The Baby's story book p42-44 **398.2**
Henny Penny. Galdone, P. **398.2**
Henny-Penny. Jacobs, J.
In Jacobs, J. English fairy tales p113-16 **398.2**
In The Scott, Foresman anthology of children's literature p151-52 **808.8**
Henny-Penny. Oxenbury, H.
In Oxenbury, H. The Helen Oxenbury nursery story book p40-46 **398.2**
Henny-Penny. Rockwell, A. F.
In Rockwell, A. F. The three bears & 15 other stories p63-70 **398.2**
Henny Penny. Zimmerman, H. W. **398.2**
Henriquez, Elsa
(il) The Magic orange tree, and other Haitian folktales. See The Magic orange tree, and other Haitian folktales **398.2**
Henry, Marguerite, 1902-
Album of horses (4 and up) **636.1**
Benjamin West and his cat Grimalkin (4 and up) **92**
Black Gold (4-6) **Fic**
Brighty of the Grand Canyon (4 and up) **Fic**
Justin Morgan had a horse (4 and up) **Fic**
King of the wind (4 and up) **Fic**
Misty of Chincoteague (4 and up) **Fic**
Mustang, wild spirit of the West (5 and up) **Fic**
San Domingo: the medicine hat stallion (4-6) **Fic**
Sea Star, orphan of Chincoteague. See note under Henry, M. Misty of Chincoteague **Fic**
Stormy, Misty's foal. See note under Henry, M. Misty of Chincoteague **Fic**
See/See also pages in the following book(s):
Newbery Medal books, 1922-1955 p320-24, 327-34 **028.5**
Henry, O., 1862-1910
The gift of the Magi (5 and up) **Fic**
Henry, Patrick, 1736-1799
About
Fritz, J. Where was Patrick Henry on the 29th of May? (3-5) **92**
Henry, Sondra
Everyone wears his name: a biography of Levi Strauss (5 and up) **92**
(jt. auth) Taitz, E. Israel **956.94**
Henry. Bawden, N. **Fic**
Henry and Beezus. Cleary, B. See note under Cleary, B. Henry Huggins **Fic**
Henry and Mudge. Rylant, C. **E**
Henry and Mudge and the forever sea. Rylant, C. See note under Rylant, C. Henry and Mudge **E**
Henry and Mudge and the happy cat. Rylant, C. See note under Rylant, C. Henry and Mudge **E**
Henry and Mudge and the sparkle days. Rylant, C. See note under Rylant, C. Henry and Mudge **E**
Henry and Mudge get the cold shivers. Rylant, C. See note under Rylant, C. Henry and Mudge **E**
Henry and Mudge in puddle trouble. Rylant, C. See note under Rylant, C. Henry and Mudge **E**
Henry and Mudge in the green time. Rylant, C. See note under Rylant, C. Henry and Mudge **E**
Henry and Mudge under the yellow moon. Rylant, C. See note under Rylant, C. Henry and Mudge **E**
Henry and Ribsy. Cleary, B. See note under Cleary, B. Henry Huggins **Fic**
Henry and the clubhouse. Cleary, B. See note under Cleary, B. Henry Huggins **Fic**
Henry and the paper route. Cleary, B. See note under Cleary, B. Henry Huggins **Fic**
Henry Huggins. Cleary, B. **Fic**
Henry Reed, Inc. Robertson, K. **Fic**
Henry Reed's babysitting service. Robertson, K. See note under Robertson, K. Henry Reed, Inc. **Fic**
Henry Reed's big show. Robertson, K. See note under Robertson, K. Henry Reed, Inc. **Fic**
Henry Reed's journey. Robertson, K. See note under Robertson, K. Henry Reed, Inc. **Fic**
Henry Reed's think tank. Robertson, K. See note under Robertson, K. Henry Reed, Inc. **Fic**
Henry the explorer. Taylor, M. **E**
Henson, Matthew Alexander, 1866-1955
About
Ferris, J. Arctic explorer: the story of Matthew Henson (3-6) **92**

Henstra, Friso
(il) Lewis, J. P. The tsar & the amazing cow **E**
Hepler, Susan Ingrid
(jt. auth) Huck, C. S. Children's literature in the elementary school **028.5**
Her. Crossley-Holland, K.
In Crossley-Holland, K. British folk tales p58 **398.2**
Her Majesty's servants. Kipling, R.
In Kipling, R. The jungle books **S C**
Her own song. Howard, E. **Fic**
Her seven brothers. Goble, P. **398.2**
Heracles (Legendary character) *See* Hercules (Legendary character)
Herberman, Ethan
The great butterfly hunt (4-6) **595.7**
Herbert, Don
Mr. Wizard's supermarket science (4 and up) **507**
Herbie Jones. Kline, S. **Fic**
Herbie Jones and Hamburger Head. Kline, S. See note under Kline, S. Herbie Jones **Fic**
Herbie Jones and the class gift. Kline, S. See note under Kline, S. Herbie Jones **Fic**
Herbie Jones and the monster ball. Kline, S. See note under Kline, S. Herbie Jones **Fic**
Herbivores
Bramwell, M. Mammals: the small plant-eaters (4 and up) **599**
Stidworthy, J. Mammals: the large plant-eaters (4 and up) **599**
Hercules (Legendary character)
Evslin, B. Hercules (5 and up) **292**
Gates, D. Mightiest of the mortals: Heracles (4 and up) **292**
See/See also pages in the following book(s):
Colum, P. The Golden Fleece and the heroes who lived before Achilles p244-94 (5 and up) **292**
Hamilton, E. Mythology p224-43 (6 and up) **292**
Herd boy and the weaving maiden
Carpenter, F. Spinning maid and the cowherd
In Carpenter, F. Tales of a Chinese grandmother p182-89 **398.2**
Herds of thunder, manes of gold (4 and up) **808.8**
Here a chick, there a chick. McMillan, B. **428**
Here come the killer bees. See Pringle, L. P. Killer bees **595.7**
Here come the monster trucks. Sullivan, G. **629.223**
Here comes the cat! Asch, F. **E**
Here comes the strikeout. Kessler, L. P. **E**
Hereditary succession *See* Inheritance and succession
Heredity
Showers, P. Me and my family tree (k-3) **575.1**
See/See also pages in the following book(s):
Gallant, R. A. Before the sun dies p72-81 (6 and up) **575**
Herguth, Margaret S.
North Dakota
In America the beautiful **973**
Herman, Charlotte
The house on Walenska Street (3-5) **Fic**
Millie Cooper, 3B (3-5) **Fic**
Millie Cooper, take a chance (3-5) **Fic**
Hermes, Patricia, 1936-
Friends are like that (5 and up) **Fic**
I hate being gifted (5 and up) **Fic**
Kevin Corbett eats flies (4 and up) **Fic**
You shouldn't have to say good-bye (5 and up) **Fic**
Hermit crabs *See* Crabs
Hermit crabs. Johnson, S. A. **595.3**
Hermod and Hadvor
Hermod and Hadvor
In The Yellow fairy book p301-07 **398.2**
A **hero** ain't nothin' but a sandwich. Childress, A. **Fic**
The **hero** and the crown. McKinley, R. **Fic**
Heroes, gods & emperors from Roman mythology. Usher, K. **292**
Heroin
See/See also pages in the following book(s):
Hyde, M. O. Drug wars p29-40 (6 and up) **363.4**
Heroism *See* Courage
Heron Street. Turner, A. W. **E**
Herons
Blassingame, W. Wonders of egrets, bitterns, and herons (5 and up) **598**
Herr Korbes
Grimm, J. Herr Korbes
In Grimm, J. The complete Grimm's fairy tales p205-06 **398.2**
Herriot, James
Moses the kitten (2-4) **Fic**
Hershel and the Hanukkah goblins. Kimmel, E. A. **E**
Hershele and Hanukkah. Singer, I. B.
In Singer, I. B. The power of light p63-72 **S C**
In Singer, I. B. Stories for children p184-93 **S C**

Hershey, Milton Snavely, 1857-1945
See/See also pages in the following book(s):
Aaseng, N. From rags to riches p33-38 (5 and up) **920**
Hershey Foods Corp.
See/See also pages in the following book(s):
Aaseng, N. From rags to riches p33-38 (5 and up) **920**
Herzog, George, 1901-1984
(jt. auth) Courlander, H. The cow-tail switch, and other West African stories **398.2**
Heslop, Michael
(il) Cooper, S. The grey king **Fic**
Hess, Lilo
A cat's nine lives (2-5) **636.8**
Making friends with guinea pigs (4-6) **636.088**
Secrets in the meadow (4 and up) **591.5**
That snake in the grass (3-5) **597.9**
Time for ferrets (3-5) **636.08**
Hest, Amy
The crack-of-dawn walkers **E**
Fancy Aunt Jess **E**
The midnight eaters **E**
The purple coat **E**
Hetty and Harriet. Oakley, G. **E**
Hewett, Joan
Getting elected (4 and up) **324**
Hector lives in the United States now (3-5) **305.8**
Hewett, Richard
(il) Arnold, C. Cheetah **599.74**
(il) Arnold, C. Dinosaur mountain **567.9**
(il) Arnold, C. Dinosaurs down under and other fossils from Australia **567.9**
(il) Arnold, C. Giraffe **599.73**
(il) Arnold, C. Hippo **599.73**
(il) Arnold, C. Kangaroo **599.2**
(il) Arnold, C. Koala **599.2**
(il) Arnold, C. Llama **599.73**
(il) Arnold, C. Ostriches and other flightless birds **598**
(il) Arnold, C. Penguin **598**
(il) Arnold, C. Pets without homes **636.088**
(il) Arnold, C. Saving the peregrine falcon **598**
(il) Arnold, C. Trapped in tar **560**
(il) Arnold, C. Tule elk **599.73**
(il) Arnold, C. Zebra **599.72**
(il) Hewett, J. Getting elected **324**
(il) Hewett, J. Hector lives in the United States now **305.8**
Hewlett, William R.
See/See also pages in the following book(s):
Aaseng, N. From rags to riches p58-63 (5 and up) **920**
Hewlett-Packard Co.
See/See also pages in the following book(s):
Aaseng, N. From rags to riches p58-63 (5 and up) **920**
Hey, Al. Yorinks, A. **E**
Hey! get off our train. Burningham, J. **E**
Hey world, here I am! Little, J. **811**
Heyman, Ken, 1930-
(il) Morris, A. Bread, bread, bread **641.8**
(il) Morris, A. Hats, hats, hats **391**
Heyward, DuBose, 1885-1940
The country bunny and the little gold shoes **E**
Hi, cat! Keats, E. J. See note under Keats. E. J. The snowy day **E**
Hi Johnny. Hunter, M.
In Hunter, M. A furl of fairy wind: four stories p31-47 **S C**
Hiawatha, 15th cent.
About
McClard, M. Hiawatha and the Iroquois league (5 and up) **92**
Hiawatha. Longfellow, H. W. **811**
Hiawatha and the Iroquois league. McClard, M. **92**
Hiawatha's childhood. Longfellow, H. W. **811**
Hic! Hic! Hic! MacDonald, M. R.
In MacDonald, M. R. Twenty tellable tales p142-53 **372.6**
Hickman, Janet
(jt. auth) Huck, C. S. Children's literature in the elementary school **028.5**
The **hidden** life of the desert. Weiwandt, T. **574.5**
The **hidden** life of the forest. Schwartz, D. M. **574.5**
The **hidden** life of the meadow. Schwartz, D. M. **574.5**
The **hidden** life of the pond. Schwartz, D. M. **574.92**
Hidden messages. Van Woerkom, D. **595.7**
Hidden stories in plants. Pellowski, A. **398**
Hidden treasures of the sea (4 and up) **910.4**
The **hidden** world of forces. White, J. R. **531**
Hidden worlds (5 and up) **500**
Hidden worlds. Simon, S. **500**
Hide and seek fog. Tresselt, A. R. **E**
Hieroglyphics
Katan, N. J. Hieroglyphs, the writing of ancient Egypt **493**
See/See also pages in the following book(s):
Ogg, O. The 26 letters p42-68 **411**

Hieroglyphs, the writing of ancient Egypt. Katan, N. J. **493**
Higglety pigglety pop! Sendak, M. **Fic**
High in the mountains. Radin, R. Y. **E**
High interest-low vocabulary books
Bibliography
Pilla, M. L. The best: high/low books for reluctant readers **011.6**
High John the Conqueror, The adventures of. Sanfield, S. **398.2**
The **High** King. Alexander, L. **Fic**
The **high** rise glorious skittle skat roarious sky pie angel food cake. Willard, N. **Fic**
High school libraries *See* School libraries (High school)
High sounds, low sounds. Branley, F. M. **534**
Higham, Charles
The Maoris (5 and up) **993**
Higher on the door. Stevenson, J. **92**
Highlights for Children **051**
Highwater, Jamake
Moonsong lullaby (k-2) **811**
The **highwayman**. Noyes, A. **821**
Highways *See* Roads
Hiking
See also Walking
Hildebrandt, Greg, 1939-
(il) Dickens, C. A Christmas carol in prose **Fic**
Hildick, E. W. (Edmund Wallace), 1925-
The case of the muttering mummy. See note under Hildick, E. W. The case of the purloined parrot **Fic**
The case of the phantom frog. See note under Hildick, E. W. The case of the purloined parrot **Fic**
The case of the purloined parrot (3-6) **Fic**
The case of the wandering weathervanes. See note under Hildick, E. W. The case of the purloined parrot **Fic**
The Ghost Squad and the Ghoul of Grunberg. See note under Hildick, E. W. The Ghost Squad breaks through **Fic**
The Ghost Squad and the Halloween conspiracy. See note under Hildick, E. W. The Ghost Squad breaks through **Fic**
The Ghost Squad and the menace of the Malevs. See note under Hildick, E. W. The Ghost Squad breaks through **Fic**
The Ghost Squad and the prowling hermits. See note under Hildick, E. W. The Ghost Squad breaks through **Fic**
The Ghost Squad breaks through (5 and up) **Fic**
The Ghost Squad flies Concorde. See note under Hildick, E. W. The Ghost Squad breaks through **Fic**
Hildick, Edmund Wallace *See* Hildick, E. W. (Edmund Wallace), 1925-
Hildilid's night. Durán, C. **E**
Hill, Barbara W., 1941-
Cooking the English way (5 and up) **641.5**
Hill, Donna, 1921-
(ed) Third book of junior authors. See Third book of junior authors **920.003**
Hillerich, Robert L., 1927-
The American Heritage picture dictionary (k-1) **423**
Himler, Ronald
(il) Banks, M. Animals of the night **E**
(il) Baylor, B. The best town in the world **E**
(il) Baylor, B. Moon song **398.2**
(il) Bunting, E. The Wall **E**
(il) Byars, B. C. After the Goat Man **Fic**
(il) Caines, J. F. Daddy **E**
(il) Coerr, E. Sadako and the thousand paper cranes [biography of Sadako Sasaki] **92**
(il) Dragonwagon, C. Winter holding spring **Fic**
(il) Glazer, T. Eye winker, Tom Tinker, chin chopper **796.1**
(il) Howard, E. Edith herself **Fic**
(il) Nunes, S. Coyote dreams **E**
(il) Pearson, S. Happy birthday, Grampie **E**
(il) Turner, A. W. Nettie's trip South **Fic**
Hindley, Judy
The tree (3-5) **582.16**
Hinemoa and Tutanekai. Te Kanawa, K. *In* Te Kanawa, K. Land of the long white cloud p35-44 **398.2**
Hines, Anna Grossnickle, 1946-
Big like me **E**
Daddy makes the best spaghetti **E**
It's just me, Emily **E**
Mean old Uncle Jack **E**
Hintz, Martin, 1945-
Chile (4 and up) **983**
Ghana (4 and up) **966.7**
Hungary (4 and up) **943.9**
Morocco (4 and up) **964**
Hippo. Arnold, C. **599.73**
Hippopotamus
Arnold, C. Hippo (3-5) **599.73**
Duvoisin, R. Veronica **E**
Schlein, M. Hippos (4-6) **599.73**

Hippopotamus—*Continued*
Fiction
Mahy, M. The boy who was followed home E
Marshall, J. George and Martha E
Mwenye Hadithi. Hot Hippo E
A **hippopotamusn't** and other animal verses. Lewis, J. P. 811
Hippos. Schlein, M. 599.73
Hiroshima (Japan)
Bombardment, 1945
Coerr, E. Sadako and the thousand paper cranes [biography of Sadako Sasaki] (3-6) 92
Maruki, T. Hiroshima no pika 940.54
Morimoto, J. My Hiroshima (2-4) 940.54
Hiroshima no pika. Maruki, T. 940.54
Hirschi, Ron
City geese (3-5) 598
Headgear (4 and up) 599.73
Spring (k-2) 508
Who lives in—the forest? (k-2) 591.5
Who lives in—the mountains? (k-2) 591.5
Who lives on—the prairie? (k-2) 591.5
Winter (k-2) 508
Hirschland, Roger B.
How animals care for their babies (k-3) 591.5
Hirsh, Marilyn, 1944-1988
Could anything be worse? (k-3) 398.2
I love Hanukkah (k-3) 296.4
Hirst, Robin
My place in space (2-4) 520
Hirst, Sally
(jt. auth) Hirst, R. My place in space 520
Hiscock, Bruce, 1940-
(il) Hughey, P. Scavengers and decomposers: the cleanup crew 591.5
Hispanic Americans
Meltzer, M. The Hispanic Americans (6 and up) 305.8
Fiction
Lomas Garza, C. Family pictures E
Hist whist. Cummings, E. E. 811
Hist whist and other poems for children. Cummings, E. E. 811
Historical chronology *See* Chronology, Historical
Historical fiction
See/See also pages in the following book(s):
Horn Book reflections on children's books and reading p137-50 028.5
The Scott, Foresman anthology of children's literature p688-724 808.8
Bibliography
Adamson, L. G. A reference guide to historical fiction for children and young adults 016.8
History and criticism
See/See also pages in the following book(s):
Crosscurrents of criticism p219-25, 234-40 028.5
Only connect: readings on children's literature p17-27 028.5
History
See also World history
History, Ancient
Briquebec, J. The ancient world (4 and up) 930
History, Modern
1900-1999 (20th century)
Tames, R. The 1950s (6 and up) 909.82
Wood, T. The 1940s (6 and up) 909.82
The **History** of an apple pie
In The Baby's story book p25 398.2
In A Nursery companion p20-22 820.8
The **History** of Jack and the bean-stalk
In The Classic Fairy tales p164-74 398.2
The **History** of Jack and the giants
In The Classic fairy tales p51-65 398.2
The **History** of Jack the giant killer
In The Blue fairy book p374-79 398.2
The **History** of sixteen wonderful old women
In A Nursery companion p66-69 820.8
The **History** of the house that Jack built
In A Nursery companion p23-27 820.8
History of the young king of the Black Isles
The Story of the young king of the Black Isles
In The Arabian nights entertainments p48-53 398.2
The **History** of Tom Thumb
In The Classic fairy tales p33-46 398.2
The **history** of Tom Thumb. Crossley-Holland, K.
In Crossley-Holland, K. British folk tales p155-74 398.2
History of Tom Thumb. Jacobs, J.
In Jacobs, J. English fairy tales p140-47 398.2

The **History** of Whittington
In The Blue fairy book p206-13 **398.2**
The **hit-away** kid. Christopher, M. **Fic**
Hitler, Adolf, 1889-1945
About
Shirer, W. L. The rise and fall of Adolf Hitler (6 and up) **943.086**
Hitty: her first hundred years. Field, R. **Fic**
Hitz, Demi *See* Demi, 1942-
Hjelmeland, Andy
Drinking & driving (4-6) **363.1**
Hoad, Abdul Latif Al *See* Al Hoad, Abdul Latif
Hoban, Abrom *See* Hoban, Brom
Hoban, Brom
(il) Drucker, M. Hanukkah **296.4**
Hoban, Lillian
Arthur's Christmas cookies **E**
Arthur's funny money. See note under Hoban, L. Arthur's Christmas cookies **E**
Arthur's great big valentine. See note under Hoban, L. Arthur's Christmas cookies **E**
Arthur's Halloween costume. See note under Hoban, L. Arthur's Christmas cookies **E**
Arthur's Honey Bear. See note under Hoban, L. Arthur's Christmas cookies **E**
Arthur's loose tooth. See note under Hoban, L. Arthur's Christmas cookies **E**
Arthur's pen pal. See note under Hoban, L. Arthur's Christmas cookies **E**
Arthur's prize reader. See note under Hoban, L. Arthur's Christmas cookies **E**
It's really Christmas **E**
(il) Cohen, M. See you in second grade! **E**
(il) Delton, J. I'm telling you now **E**
(il) Delton, J. The new girl at school **E**
(il) Hoban, R. Egg thoughts, and other Frances songs **811**
(il) Hoban, R. The mouse and his child **Fic**
(il) Hoban, R. The sorely trying day **E**
(il) Howe, J. The day the teacher went bananas **E**
(il) Hurwitz, J. Busybody Nora **Fic**
(il) Hurwitz, J. Rip-roaring Russell **Fic**
(il) Hurwitz, J. Superduper Teddy **Fic**
(il) Oppenheim, S. L. Waiting for Noah **E**
(il) Rabe, B. The balancing girl **E**
(il) Schulman, J. The big hello **E**
(il) Winthrop, E. Tough Eddie **E**
Hoban, Russell
Arthur's new power. See note under Hoban, R. Dinner at Alberta's **E**
A baby sister for Frances. See note under Hoban, R. Bedtime for Frances **E**
A bargain for Frances. See note under Hoban, R. Bedtime for Frances **E**
Bedtime for Frances **E**
Best friends for Frances. See note under Hoban, R. Bedtime for Frances **E**
A birthday for Frances. See note under Hoban, R. Bedtime for Frances **E**
Bread and jam for Frances. See note under Hoban, R. Bedtime for Frances **E**
Dinner at Alberta's **E**
Egg thoughts, and other Frances songs (k-2) **811**
Emmet Otter's Jug-Band Christmas
In The Family read-aloud Christmas treasury p92-101 **808.8**
The mouse and his child (4-6) **Fic**
The sorely trying day **E**
Hoban, Tana
26 letters and 99 cents **E**
A, B, see! **E**
A children's zoo (k-2) **591**
Circles, triangles and squares **E**
Dig, drill, dump, fill (k-2) **621.8**
Dots, spots, speckles, and stripes **E**
Exactly the opposite **E**
I read signs (k-2) **659.13**
I read symbols (k-2) **659.13**
I walk and read (k-2) **659.13**
Is it larger? Is it smaller? **E**
Is it red? Is it yellow? Is it blue? **E**
Is it rough? Is it smooth? Is it shiny? **E**
Look again! **E**
Look! look! look! **E**
Of colors and things (k-2) **535.6**
One little kitten **E**
Over, under & through, and other spatial concepts **E**
Push pull, empty full **E**
Round & round & round **E**
Shadows and reflections **779**
Shapes, shapes, shapes (k-2) **516**
Take another look **E**
Where is it? **E**
The **hobbit**. Tolkien, J. R. R. **Fic**
The **hobby** horse; or, The high road to learning. See A was an archer and shot at a frog
Hobie Hanson, greatest hero of the mall. Gilson, J. See note under Gilson, J. 4B goes wild **Fic**
Hobie Hanson, you're weird. Gilson, J. See note under Gilson, J. 4B goes wild **Fic**

Hoboes *See* Tramps

The **Hoboken** chicken emergency. Pinkwater, D. M. **Fic**

Hobson, Burton
(jt. auth) Reinfeld, F. Catalogue of the world's most popular coins **737.4**

Hobyahs
The Hobyahs
In Juba this and Juba that p51-54 **372.6**
MacDonald, M. R. The Hobyahs
In MacDonald, M. R. When the lights go out p96-103 **372.6**

The **Hoca** and the candle. Walker, B. K.
In Walker, B. K. A treasury of Turkish folktales for children p47-48 **398.2**

The **Hoca** as Tamerlane's tax collector. Walker, B. K.
In Walker, B. K. A treasury of Turkish folktales for children p45-46 **398.2**

Hockerman, Dennis
(il) Haskins, J. Count your way through China **951**

Hockey *See* Ice hockey

Hockey basics. MacLean, N. **796.962**

Hocus pocus: magic you can do. Broekel, R. **793.8**

Hodder, Elizabeth
Stepfamilies (5 and up) **306.8**

Hodges, C. Walter (Cyril Walter), 1909-
(il) Serraillier, I. The silver sword **Fic**

Hodges, Cyril Walter *See* Hodges, C. Walter (Cyril Walter), 1909-

Hodges, Margaret
The arrow and the lamp **292**
If you had a horse (4 and up) **398.2**
Contents: The ebony horse; Horses of the sun; Finn's men and the mean mare; The horse who built the wall; Pecos Bill's widow-maker; Falada and the goosegirl; Dapplegrim; The black horse; The Raksh of Rustem
Saint George and the dragon (2-5) **398.2**
The voice of the great bell (k-3) **398.2**

Hodges, Sarah Margaret *See* Hodges, Margaret

Hoff, Syd, 1912-
Danny and the dinosaur **E**
The young cartoonist (4 and up) **741.5**
(il) Lexau, J. M. I should have stayed in bed **E**
(il) Lexau, J. M. The rooftop mystery **E**
(il) Schwartz, A. I saw you in the bathtub, and other folk rhymes **398.2**

Hoffman, Sanford
(il) Rosenbloom, J. Knock-knock! who's there **808.87**
(il) Rosenbloom, J. Laughs, hoots & giggles **808.87**

Hoffman, Yair *See* Hofman, Ya'ir

Hoffmann, E. T. A. (Ernst Theodor Amadeus), 1776-1822
Nutcracker (3 and up) **Fic**
The nutcracker; adaptation. See Bell, A. The nutcracker **Fic**

Hoffmann, Ernst Theodor Amadeus *See* Hoffmann, E. T. A. (Ernst Theodor Amadeus), 1776-1822

Hoffmeister, Donald Frederick, 1916-
(jt. auth) Zim, H. S. Mammals **599**

Hofman, Ya'ir
The world of the Bible for young readers (5 and up) **220.9**

Hofsinde, Robert, 1902-1973
Indian costumes (3-6) **391**
Indian sign language (3-6) **419**

Hogrogian, Nonny
The cat who loved to sing **E**
The contest (1-3) **398.2**
The devil with the three golden hairs (k-3) **398.2**
The Glass Mountain (k-3) **398.2**
Noah's ark (k-3) **222**
One fine day (k-3) **398.2**
(il) Grimm, J. About wise men and simpletons **398.2**
(jt. auth) Kherdian, D. The cat's midsummer jamboree **E**
(il) Kherdian, D. A song for Uncle Harry **Fic**
(il) Leodhas, S. N. Always room for one more **781.62**
See/See also pages in the following book(s):
Newbery and Caldecott Medal books, 1966-1975 p179-85, 237-42 **028.5**

Hoguet, Susan Ramsay
I unpacked my grandmother's trunk **E**
Solomon Grundy **E**

Hoisting machinery
Marston, H. I. Load lifters: derricks, cranes, and helicopters (3-6) **621.8**

Hok Lee and the dwarfs
The Story of Hok Lee and the dwarfs
In The Green fairy book p229-33 **398.2**

Hokanson, Lars
(il) Finkelstein, N. H. Remember not to forget **940.54**

Hokanson, Lois
(il) Finkelstein, N. H. Remember not to forget **940.54**

Holabird, Katharine
Angelina and Alice. See note under Holabird, K. Angelina ballerina **E**
Angelina and the princess. See note under Holabird, K. Angelina ballerina **E**
Angelina at the fair. See note under Holabird, K. Angelina ballerina **E**

Holabird, Katharine—*Continued*
Angelina ballerina E
Angelina on stage. See note under Holabird, K. Angelina ballerina E
Angelina's birthday surprise. See note under Holabird, K. Angelina ballerina E
Angelina's Christmas. See note under Holabird, K. Angelina ballerina E

Holder, Heidi
(il) Aesop. Aesop's fables [illus. by Heidi Holder] **398.2**

"Hold'im down, Brer Fox". Lester, J.
In Lester, J. The tales of Uncle Remus p6-8 **398.2**

Holding, James, 1907-
The prisoner
In The Scott, Foresman anthology of children's literature p349-51 **808.8**

The **hole** in the dike. Green, N. **E**

A **hole** is to dig. Krauss, R. **E**

Holes and peeks. Jonas, A. **E**

The **holes** in the bagels. Simon, S.
In Simon, S. More wise men of Helm and their merry tales p36-43 **398.2**

Holiday decorations
Ames, L. J. Draw 50 holiday decorations (4 and up) **743**
Hautzig, E. R. Make it special (4-6) **745.59**
Parish, P. December decorations (1-3) **745.59**
A Pumpkin in a pear tree (1-4) **745.59**

Holiday plays round the year (4 and up) **812.008**

Holiday tales of Sholom Aleichem. Sholem Aleichem. **S C**

Holiday treats. Hautzig, E. R. **641.5**

Holidays
See also Christmas; Fasts and feasts
The American book of days **394.2**
Bauer, C. F. Celebrations **808.8**
Chase's annual events **394.2**
Dunkling, L. A dictionary of days **394.2**
Festivals (3-6) **394.2**
Gregory, R. W. Anniversaries and holidays **394.2**
Grigoli, V. Patriotic holidays and celebrations (4 and up) **394.2**
Perl, L. Blue Monday and Friday the Thirteenth (4-6) **398**
Perl, L. Piñatas and paper flowers (4 and up) **394.2**
Tudor, T. A time to keep: the Tasha Tudor book of holidays (k-3) **394.2**
Van Straalen, A. The book of holidays around the world (4 and up) **394.2**

Drama
Gotwalt, H. L. M. Special plays for holidays **812**
Holiday plays round the year (4 and up) **812.008**

Fiction
Zolotow, C. Over and over **E**

Poetry
Livingston, M. C. Celebrations (1-3) **811**
Poetry for holidays (1-4) **811.008**

Holidays, Jewish *See* Fasts and feasts—Judaism

Holland, Isabelle
The journey home (4 and up) **Fic**
See/See also pages in the following book(s):
Crosscurrents of criticism p137-43 **028.5**

Holland, Kevin Crossley- *See* Crossley-Holland, Kevin

Holland *See* Netherlands

Holling, Holling C., 1900-1973
Minn of the Mississippi (4-6) **Fic**
Paddle-to-the-sea (4-6) **Fic**
Pagoo (4 and up) **595.3**
Seabird (4-6) **Fic**
Tree in the trail (4 and up) **Fic**

Holling, Lucille Webster
(il) Holling, H. C. Pagoo **595.3**

The **hollow** land. Gardam, J. **Fic**

Holly, reindeer, and colored lights. Barth, E. **394.2**

Holm, Anne, 1922-
North to freedom (6 and up) **Fic**

Holman, Felice
Secret City, U.S.A (6 and up) **Fic**
Slake's limbo (6 and up) **Fic**

Holmes, Bea
(il) Hunter, E. F. Child of the silent night [biography of Laura Dewey Bridgman] **92**

Holmes, Sally
(il) Andersen, H. C. The Snow Queen **Fic**

Holocaust, Jewish (1933-1945)
See also World War, 1939-1945—Jews
Chaikin, M. A nightmare in history (5 and up) **940.54**
Finkelstein, N. H. Remember not to forget (3-5) **940.54**
Hurwitz, J. Anne Frank: life in hiding (3-5) **92**
Meltzer, M. Never to forget: the Jews of the Holocaust (6 and up) **940.54**
Meltzer, M. Rescue: the story of how Gentiles saved Jews in the Holocaust (6 and up) **940.54**
Rossel, S. The Holocaust (5 and up) **940.54**

Holocaust, Jewish (1933-1945)—*Continued*
Fiction
Orgel, D. The devil in Vienna (6 and up) Fic
Orlev, U. The island on Bird Street (5 and up) Fic
Roth-Hano, R. Touch wood (6 and up) Fic
Yolen, J. The devil's arithmetic (4 and up) Fic
Pictorial works
Abells, C. B. The children we remember (3-6) 940.54
Holtze, Sally Holmes
(ed) Fifth book of junior authors & illustrators. See Fifth book of junior authors & illustrators 920.003
(ed) Sixth book of junior authors & illustrators. See Sixth book of junior authors & illustrators 920.003
The **Holy** Bible [King James Bible. Oxford Univ. Press]. Bible 220.5
The **Holy** Bible: revised standard version. Bible 220.5
Holy days *See* Fasts and feasts
Holy Grail *See* Grail
Hom, Nancy
(il) Spagnoli, C. Nine-in-one, Grr! Grr! 398.2
Home. Pringle, L. P. 591.5
Home before dark. Bridgers, S. E. Fic
Home economics
See also House cleaning
Home in the sky. Baker, J. E
Home instruction
See also Child development
A **home** is to share—and share—and share—. Angell, J. Fic
Home life *See* Family life
Homecoming. Voigt, C. Fic
The **homecoming**. Yep, L.
In Yep, L. The rainbow people p144-51 398.2
Homeless people
See also Refugees; Runaway children; Tramps
See/See also pages in the following book(s):
Ashabranner, B. K. People who make a difference p101-06 (5 and up) 920
Fiction
Corcoran, B. Annie's monster (5 and up) Fic
Hahn, M. D. December stillness (6 and up) Fic
Holman, F. Secret City, U.S.A (6 and up) Fic
Howe, J. Dew drop dead (4-6) Fic
Spinelli, J. Maniac Magee (5 and up) Fic
Homer
Adaptations
Colum, P. The children's Homer: The adventures of Odysseus and The tale of Troy (4 and up) 883
Picard, B. L. The Iliad of Homer (6 and up) 883
Homer Price. McCloskey, R. Fic
Homer Price [excerpt]. McCloskey, R.
In The Random House book of humor for children p181-94 817.008
Homesick: my own story. Fritz, J. 92
Homesick: my own story [excerpt]. Fritz, J.
In Face to face: a collection of stories by celebrated Soviet and American writers p57-75 S C
Hominids: a look back at our ancestors. Sattler, H. R. 573.3
Honestly, Katie John. Calhoun, M. See note under Calhoun, M. Katie John Fic
Honesty
See also Truthfulness and falsehood
Honey, I love, and other love poems. Greenfield, E. 811
Honeybee. Watts, B. 595.7
Honeycutt, Natalie
The all new Jonah Twist (3-5) Fic
The best-laid plans of Jonah Twist (3-5) Fic
Invisible Lissa (3-5) Fic
Hong Kong
Fiction
Levinson, R. Our home is the sea E
Honorable Minu
Barker, W. H. Younde goes to town
In Best-loved folktales of the world p623-25 398.2
Hood, George Percy Jacomb- *See* Jacomb-Hood, George Percy, 1857-1929
Hood, Robin (Legendary character) *See* Robin Hood (Legendary character)
Hook, Richard
(il) Humble, R. The travels of Marco Polo 910.4
Hooks, William H.
The ballad of Belle Dorcas (3-5) Fic
Circle of fire (5 and up) Fic
Moss gown (k-3) 398.2
The three little pigs and the fox (k-3) 398.2
The **hooks** of heaven. Roach, M. K.
In Roach, M. K. Encounters with the invisible world S C
Hooper, Patricia, 1941-
A bundle of beasts (3-6) 811

Hoops: behind the scenes with the Boston Celtics. Boyd, B. C. **796.323**

Hooray for the Golly sisters! Byars, B. C. **E**

Hoover, H. M., 1935-
Away is a strange place to be (4-6) **Fic**
Orvis (5 and up) **Fic**
The shepherd moon (6 and up) **Fic**

Hoover, William H.
See/See also pages in the following book(s):
Aaseng, N. The unsung heroes p41-44 (5 and up) **920**

Hop-o'-my-Thumb
Perrault, C. Hop o' my Thumb
In Sleeping beauty & other favourite fairy tales p69-80 **398.2**
Perrault, C. Little Poucet
In The Classic fairy tales p130-36 **398.2**
Perrault, C. Little Thumb
In The Blue fairy book p231-41 **398.2**

The **hopeful** trout and other limericks. Ciardi, J. **811**

Hopf, Alice Lightner, 1904-1988
Bats (3-6) **599.4**
Spiders (4 and up) **595.4**

Hopi Indians
Tomchek, A. H. The Hopi (2-4) **970.004**

Hopkins, Lee Bennett, 1938-
Pass the poetry, please! **372.6**
(comp) Click, rumble, roar. See Click, rumble, roar **811.008**
(comp) Creatures. See Creatures **821.008**
(comp) Dinosaurs: poems. See Dinosaurs: poems **811.008**
(comp) Good books, good times! See Good books, good times! **811.008**
(comp) More surprises. See More surprises **811.008**
(comp) Side by side. See Side by side **808.81**
(comp) Surprises. See Surprises **811.008**
(comp) Whitman, W. Voyages **811**

Horenstein, Henry
Sam goes trucking **E**
(il) Boyd, B. C. Hoops: behind the scenes with the Boston Celtics **796.323**

The **Horn** Book Guide to Children's and Young Adult Books **028.505**

Horn book magazine
Crosscurrents of criticism **028.5**
Horn Book reflections on children's books and reading **028.5**
A Horn Book sampler on children's books and reading **028.5**

The **Horn** Book Magazine **028.505**

Horn Book reflections on children's books and reading **028.5**

A **Horn** Book sampler on children's books and reading **028.5**

Hornblow, Arthur, 1893-1976
(jt. auth) Hornblow, L. Animals do the strangest things **591.5**

Hornblow, Leonora, 1920-
Animals do the strangest things (1-3) **591.5**

Horne, Daniel
(il) San Souci, R. Young Merlin **398.2**

Horns
Hirschi, R. Headgear (4 and up) **599.73**

Horns
Afanas'ev, A. N. Horns
In Afanas'ev, A. N. Russian fairy tales p292-94 **398.2**

Horrible Harry and the green slime. Kline, S. See note under Kline, S. Horrible Harry in room 2B **Fic**

Horrible Harry in room 2B. Kline, S. **Fic**

Horrible Harry's secret. Kline, S. See note under Kline, S. Horrible Harry in room 2B **Fic**

Horror

Fiction

Aiken, J. Give yourself a fright: thirteen tales of the supernatural (6 and up) **S C**
Alcock, V. The stonewalkers (5 and up) **Fic**
Corbett, S. The deadly hoax (5 and up) **Fic**
MacDonald, M. R. When the lights go out **372.6**
Schwartz, A. In a dark, dark room, and other scary stories (k-3) **398.2**
Schwartz, A. More scary stories to tell in the dark (4 and up) **398.2**
Things that go bump in the night (5 and up) **S C**

Horror films

Fiction

Byars, B. C. The two-thousand-pound goldfish (5 and up) **Fic**

Horror stories *See* Horror—Fiction
The **horse** and his boy. Lewis, C. S. See note under Lewis, C. S. The lion, the witch and the wardrobe **Fic**
Horse and toad
In The Magic orange tree, and other Haitian folktales p143-50 **398.2**
The **horse** in the attic. Clymer, E. L. **Fic**
A **horse** of a different color. Patent, D. H. **636.1**

Horse racing

Fiction

Henry, M. Black Gold (4-6) **Fic**

The **horse** who built the wall. Hodges, M.
In Hodges, M. If you had a horse **398.2**

Horseback riding

Krementz, J. A very young rider (3-6) **798.2**
Sayer, A. The young rider's handbook (5 and up) **636.1**

Horses

See also Ponies

Bellville, C. W. Farming today yesterday's way (2-4) **630.1**
Cole, J. A horse's body **636.1**
Featherly, J. Mustangs: wild horses of the American West (3-6) **636.1**
Henry, M. Album of horses (4 and up) **636.1**
Isenbart, H.-H. Birth of a foal (3-6) **636.1**
Jurmain, S. Once upon a horse (6 and up) **636.1**
LaBonte, G. The miniature horse (3-5) **636.1**
Lavine, S. A. Wonders of draft horses (4 and up) **636.1**
Patent, D. H. Appaloosa horses (4 and up) **636.1**
Patent, D. H. Draft horses (4 and up) **636.1**
Patent, D. H. A horse of a different color (4 and up) **636.1**
Patent, D. H. Horses of America (4 and up) **636.1**
Patent, D. H. Quarter horses (4 and up) **636.1**
Patent, D. H. Where the wild horses roam (4 and up) **639.9**

See/See also pages in the following book(s):

Chrystie, F. N. Pets p189-212 (4 and up) **636.088**
Pringle, L. P. Feral: tame animals gone wild p87-101 (5 and up) **591.5**

Fiction

Bagnold, E. National Velvet (5 and up) **Fic**
Clymer, E. L. The horse in the attic (4 and up) **Fic**
Dennis, W. Flip and the cows **E**
Farley, W. The Black Stallion (4 and up) **Fic**
Goble, P. The gift of the sacred dog (2-4) **398.2**
Goble, P. The girl who loved wild horses **E**
Henry, M. Justin Morgan had a horse (4 and up) **Fic**
Henry, M. King of the wind (4 and up) **Fic**
Henry, M. Mustang, wild spirit of the West (5 and up) **Fic**
Herds of thunder, manes of gold (4 and up) **808.8**
Hodges, M. If you had a horse (4 and up) **398.2**
James, W. Smoky, the cow horse (6 and up) **Fic**
Lawson, R. Mr. Revere and I (5 and up) **Fic**
Locker, T. The mare on the hill **E**
Peet, B. Cowardly Clyde **E**
Sewell, A. Black Beauty (4-6) **Fic**
Shub, E. The white stallion **E**
Ward, L. K. The silver pony (2-4) **Fic**
Yolen, J. Sky dogs **E**

A **horse's** body. Cole, J. **636.1**

Horses in art

Ames, L. J. Draw 50 horses (4 and up) **743**

Horses of America. Patent, D. H. **636.1**
Horses of the sun. Hodges, M.
In Hodges, M. If you had a horse **398.2**
Horton hatches the egg. Seuss, Dr. **E**
Horton hears a Who! Seuss, Dr. **E**

Horvatic, Anne

Simple machines (1-3) **531**

Horwitz, Joshua

Night markets (3-6) **381**

Hosking Smith, Jan

(il) Mitchell, B. America, I hear you: a story about George Gershwin **92**
(il) Mitchell, B. CLICK!: a story about George Eastman **92**

Hospitals

Rockwell, A. F. The emergency room (k-2) **362.1**
Rogers, F. Going to the hospital (k-2) **362.1**

Fiction

Howe, J. A night without stars (5 and up) **Fic**
Keller, H. The best present **E**

Hospitals, Military

Cosner, S. War nurses (6 and up) **355.3**

The **hot** & cold summer. Hurwitz, J. **Fic**
Hot-air Henry. Calhoun, M. **E**
Hot fudge. Howe, J. See note under Howe, J. Scared silly: a Halloween treat **E**
Hot Hippo. Mwenye Hadithi **E**
Hotels, motels, etc.
Okimoto, J. D. Blumpoe the Grumpoe meets Arnold the cat **E**
Fiction
Fleischman, P. The Half-a-Moon Inn (4-6) **Fic**
Naylor, P. R. Bernie and the Bessledorf ghost (4-6) **Fic**
Hotu-puku. Te Kanawa, K.
In Te Kanawa, K. Land of the long white cloud p87-90 **398.2**
Hough, Charlotte Woodyatt, 1924-
The magic pencil
In Bauer, C. F. Celebrations p12-14 **808.8**
The **house** at Pooh Corner. Milne, A. A. **Fic**
also in Milne, A. A. The world of Pooh p153-314 **Fic**
House cleaning
Rockwell, A. F. Nice and clean (k-2) **648**
House construction
See also Houses
A **house** for Hermit Crab. Carle, E. **E**
House in the wood
Grimm, J. The hut in the forest
In Grimm, J. The complete Grimm's fairy tales p698-704 **398.2**
The **house** of Dies Drear. Hamilton, V. **Fic**
A **house** of pomegranates. See Wilde, O. The Happy Prince, and other stories **S C**
The **house** of sixty fathers. DeJong, M. **Fic**
House of stairs. Sleator, W. **Fic**
The **house** of wings. Byars, B. C. **Fic**
The **house** on East 88th Street. Waber, B. **E**
The **house** on the hill. Asbjørnsen, P. C.
In Tomie dePaola's favorite nursery tales p122-26 **398.2**
The **house** on Walenska Street. Herman, C. **Fic**
House painting
Fiction
Spier, P. Oh, were they ever happy! **E**
House that Jack built
The House that Jack built
In The Baby's story book p30-32 **398.2**
Rockwell, A. F. The house that Jack built
In Rockwell, A. F. The three bears & 15 other stories p45-52 **398.2**
The **house** with a clock in its walls. Bellairs, J. **Fic**
Housebuilding for children. Walker, L. **690**
The **housefly**. Fischer-Nagel, H. **595.7**
Household pests
See also Cockroaches
Houses
Barton, B. Building a house (k-1) **690**
Gibbons, G. How a house is built (k-2) **690**
Huntington, L. P. Americans at home (6 and up) **728**
Robbins, K. Building a house (3-6) **690**
Walker, L. Housebuilding for children (2 and up) **690**
Weiss, H. Shelters: from tepee to igloo (4 and up) **728**
See/See also pages in the following book(s):
Caney, S. Steven Caney's kids' America p66-93 (4 and up) **790.1**
Fiction
Burton, V. L. The little house **E**
Calhoun, M. Katie John (4-6) **Fic**
Lobel, A. Ming Lo moves the mountain **E**
Pfanner, L. Louise builds a house **E**
Houses in literature
Ashe, R. Children's literary houses (3-5) **028.5**
Housing
Shachtman, T. The president builds a house (3-5) **363.5**
Housman, Laurence, 1865-1959
A Chinese fairy tale
In Bauer, C. F. Celebrations p4-11 **808.8**
Houston, Gloria
The year of the perfect Christmas tree **E**
Houston, James A., 1921-
Frozen fire (6 and up) **Fic**
(il) Wheeler, M. J. First came the Indians **970.004**
Houston, Samuel, 1793-1863
About
Fritz, J. Make way for Sam Houston (4 and up) **92**
How a book is made. Aliki. **686**
How a fish swam in the air and a hare in water
Afanas'ev, A. N. The indiscreet wife
In Afanas'ev, A. N. Russian fairy tales p226-27 **398.2**

How a house is built. Gibbons, G. **690**

How a husband weaned his wife from fairy tales. Afanas'ev, A. N.
In Afanas'ev, A. N. Russian fairy tales p308 **398.2**

How a seed grows. Jordan, H. J. **582**

How a skyscraper and a railroad train got picked up and carried away from Pig's Eye Valley far in the Pickax Mountains. Sandburg, C.
In Sandburg, C. Rootabaga stories pt 2 p155-61 **S C**
In Sandburg, C. The Sandburg treasury p152-54 **818**

How a witch escaped
In The Monkey's haircut, and other stories told by the Maya p118-20 **398.2**

How Akbar went to Bethlehem. Babbitt, N.
In Babbitt, N. The Devil's other storybook p33-39 **S C**

How animals behave: a new look at wildlife (5 and up) **591.5**

How animals care for their babies. Hirschland, R. B. **591.5**

How animals got their tails. Bryan, A.
In Bryan, A. Beat the story-drum, pum-pum p53-[70] **398.2**

How animals talk. McGrath, S. **591.5**

How babies are made. Andry, A. C. **612.6**

How Bimbo the Snip's thumb stuck to his nose when the wind changed. Sandburg, C.
In Sandburg, C. Rootabaga stories pt 1 p102-07 **S C**
In Sandburg, C. The Sandburg treasury p51-54 **818**

How Bobtail beat the Devil
In Grandfather tales p88-98 **398.2**

How Boots befooled the king
Pyle, H. How Boots befooled the king
In Pyle, H. The wonder clock p135-47 **398.2**

How Bozo the Button Buster busted all his buttons when a mouse came. Sandburg, C.
In Sandburg, C. Rootabaga stories pt 2 p55-59 **S C**
In Sandburg, C. The Sandburg treasury p110-12 **818**

How Brer Fox and Brer Dog became enemies. Lester, J.
In Lester, J. The tales of Uncle Remus p4-6 **398.2**

How Brer Rabbit became a scary monster. Lester, J.
In Lester, J. The tales of Uncle Remus p127-31 **398.2**

How Brer Rabbit frightened his neighbors. Parks, V. D.
In Parks, V. D. Jump on over! the adventures of Brer Rabbit and his family **398.2**

How Brer Weasel was caught. Parks, V. D.
In Parks, V. D. Jump again! more adventures of Brer Rabbit p15-21 **398.2**

How Christ was chased
In The Monkey's haircut, and other stories told by the Maya p133-35 **398.2**

How Coyote stole the sun. Curry, J. L.
In Curry, J. L. Back in the beforetime p10-21 **398.2**

How crab got a hard back. Sherlock, Sir P. M.
In Sherlock, Sir P. M. West Indian folk-tales p86-92 **398.2**

How death came to the world (Kiowa). Marriott, A. L.
In Marriott, A. L. American Indian mythology **398.2**

How death came to the world (Modoc). Marriott, A. L.
In Marriott, A. L. American Indian mythology **398.2**

How Deep Red Roses goes back and forth between the clock and the looking glass. Sandburg, C.
In Sandburg, C. Rootabaga stories pt 2 p79-85 **S C**
In Sandburg, C. The Sandburg treasury p121-23 **818**

How Deli kept his part of the bargain. Walker, B. K.
In Walker, B. K. A treasury of Turkish folktales for children p80-84 **398.2**

How did numbers begin? Sitomer, M. **513**

How did we find out about blood? Asimov, I. **612.1**

How did we find out about DNA? Asimov, I. **574.87**

How did we find out about microwaves? Asimov, I. **621.381**

How did we find out about Neptune? Asimov, I. **523.4**

How did we find out about nuclear power? Asimov, I. **539.7**

How did we find out about photosynthesis? Asimov, I. **581.1**

How did we find out about sunshine? Asimov, I. **523.7**

How did we find out about superconductivity? Asimov, I. **537.6**

How did we find out the Earth is round? Asimov, I. **525**

How Dippy the Wisp and Slip Me Liz came in the moonshine where the Potato Face Blind Man sat with his accordion. Sandburg, C.
In Sandburg, C. Rootabaga stories pt 2 p95-102 **S C**
In Sandburg, C. The Sandburg treasury p127-31 **818**

How do I put it on? Watanabe, S. **E**

How do you get a horse out of the bathtub? Phillips, L. **793.73**

How does it feel to be old? Farber, N. **811**

How El Bizarron fooled the Devil. Carter, D. S.
In Best-loved folktales of the world p745-48 **398.2**

How everyday things work. Cooper, C. **600**

How fear came. Kipling, R.
In Kipling, R. The jungle books **S C**

How footbinding started
Carpenter, F. Big feet of the Empress Tu Chin
In Carpenter, F. Tales of a Chinese grandmother p81-88 **398.2**

How Frog lost his tail. Kaula, E. M.
In Best-loved folktales of the world p626-27 **398.2**

How Georgina drove the car very carefully from Boston to New York. Bate, L. **E**

How Gimme the Ax found out about the zigzag railroad and who made it zigzag. Sandburg, C.
In Sandburg, C. Rootabaga stories pt 1 p51-56 **S C**
In Sandburg, C. The Sandburg treasury p31-32 **818**

How Glooskap made human beings. Norman, H.
In Norman, H. How Glooskap outwits the Ice Giants, and other tales of the Maritime Indians p1-10 **398.2**

How Glooskap outwits the Ice Giants. Norman, H.
In Norman, H. How Glooskap outwits the Ice Giants, and other tales of the Maritime Indians p11-19 **398.2**

How Glooskap outwits the Ice Giants, and other tales of the Maritime Indians. Norman, H. **398.2**

How Glooskap sang through the rapids and found a new home. Norman, H.
In Norman, H. How Glooskap outwits the Ice Giants, and other tales of the Maritime Indians p51-60 **398.2**

How Googler and Gaggler, the two Christmas babies, came home with monkey wrenches. Sandburg, C.
In Sandburg, C. Rootabaga stories pt 2 p63-69 **S C**
In Sandburg, C. The Sandburg treasury p113-17 **818**

How Henry Hagglyhoagly played the guitar with his mittens on. Sandburg, C.
In Sandburg, C. Rootabaga stories pt 1 p145-50 **S C**
In Sandburg, C. The Sandburg treasury p69-71 **818**

How horses came to the Navaho. Marriott, A. L.
In Marriott, A. L. American Indian mythology **398.2**

How Hot Balloons and his pigeon daughters crossed over into the Rootabaga Country. Sandburg, C.
In Sandburg, C. Rootabaga stories pt 2 p103-10 **S C**
In Sandburg, C. The Sandburg treasury p131-34 **818**

How I crossed the street for the first time all by myself [short story]. Gardner, H.
In Free to be—you and me p100-11 **810.8**

How I hunted the little fellows. Zhitkov, B. **Fic**

How it feels to be adopted. Krementz, J. **362.7**

How it feels to fight for your life. Krementz, J. **362.1**

How it feels when a parent dies. Krementz, J. **155.9**

How it feels when parents divorce. Krementz, J. **306.89**

How Jack went to seek his fortune
Jacobs, J. How Jack went to seek his fortune
In Jacobs, J. English fairy tales p24-27 **398.2**
In Tomie dePaola's favorite nursery tales p118-21 **398.2**

How jet engines are made. Moxon, J. **629.1**

How Johnny the Wham sleeps in money all the time and Joe the Wimp shines and sees things. Sandburg, C.
In Sandburg, C. Rootabaga stories pt 2 p70-75 **S C**
In Sandburg, C. The Sandburg treasury p117-20 **818**

How Ma-ui fished up the great island
Colum, P. How Ma-ui fished up the great island
In Best-loved folktales of the world p599-601 **398.2**

How magic friend fox helped Glooskap against the panther-witch. Norman, H.
In Norman, H. How Glooskap outwits the Ice Giants, and other tales of the Maritime Indians p39-49 **398.2**

How many days to America? Bunting, E. **E**

How many miles to Babylon? Fox, P. **Fic**

How many snails? Giganti, P., Jr. **E**

How many spots does a leopard have? Lester, J.
In Lester, J. How many spots does a leopard have? and other tales p53-57 **398.2**

How many spots does a leopard have? and other tales. Lester, J. **398.2**

How much & how many? Bendick, J. **530.8**

How much is a million? Schwartz, D. M. **E**

How my garden grew. Rockwell, A. F. **E**

How my library grew, by Dinah. Alexander, M. G. **E**

How my parents learned to eat. Friedman, I. R. **E**

How Nehemiah got free. Hamilton, V.
In Hamilton, V. The people could fly: American black folktales p147-50 **398.2**

How Old Man Above created the World. Curry, J. L.
In Curry, J. L. Back in the beforetime p1-4 **398.2**

How one turned his troubles to some account
Pyle, H. How one turned his troubles to some account
In Pyle, H. The wonder clock p27-38 **398.2**

How Pan Ku made the world
Carpenter, F. How Pan Ku made the world
In Carpenter, F. Tales of a Chinese grandmother p14-21 **398.2**

How paper is made. Perrins, L. **676**

How Pink Peony sent Spuds, the ballplayer, up to pick four moons. Sandburg, C.
In Sandburg, C. Rootabaga stories pt 2 p86-92 **S C**
In Sandburg, C. The Sandburg treasury p124-26 **818**

How pizza came to Queens. Khalsa, D. K. **E**

How platypuses came to Australia. Parker, K. L.
In Best-loved folktales of the world p605-07 **398.2**

How pleasant to know Mr. Lear! Lear, E. **821**

How proudly they wave. Haban, R. D. **929.9**

How Rag Bag Mammy kept her secret while the wind blew away the Village of Hat Pins. Sandburg, C.
In Sandburg, C. Rootabaga stories pt 2 p29-35 **S C**
In Sandburg, C. The Sandburg treasury p100-02 **818**

How seeds travel. Overbeck, C. **582**

How six men got on in the world. Grimm, J.
In Grimm, J. The complete Grimm's fairy tales p344-49 **398.2**

How six men travelled through the wide world
Grimm, J. How six men got on in the world
In Grimm, J. The complete Grimm's fairy tales p344-49 **398.2**
Grimm, J. How six men travelled through the wide world
In The Yellow fairy book p95-99 **398.2**

How six men travelled through the wide world—*Continued*
Grimm, J. The soldier and his magic helpers
In Grimm, J. More tales from Grimm p63-75 **398.2**

How six pigeons came back to Hatrack the Horse after many accidents and six telegrams. Sandburg, C.
In Sandburg, C. Rootabaga stories pt 2 p36-41 **S C**
In Sandburg, C. The Sandburg treasury p103-06 **818**

How six umbrellas took off their straw hats to show respect to the one big umbrella. Sandburg, C.
In Sandburg, C. Rootabaga stories pt 2 p48-54 **S C**
In Sandburg, C. The Sandburg treasury p107-10 **818**

How Soko brought debt to Ashanti. Courlander, H.
In Courlander, H. The cow-tail switch, and other West African stories p103-06 **398.2**

How spider got his waistline. Climo, S.
In Climo, S. Someone saw a spider p43-52 **398.2**

How Spider obtained the Sky-God's stories
In Best-loved folktales of the world p620-23 **398.2**

How summer came to Canada. Macmillan, C.
In The Scott, Foresman anthology of children's literature p469-72 **808.8**

How Sun, Moon and Wind went out to dinner
In Best-loved folktales of the world p592-93 **398.2**

How the alphabet was made. Kipling, R.
In Kipling, R. Just so stories **S C**

How the animals came to Earth. Lester, J.
In Lester, J. The tales of Uncle Remus p1-3 **398.2**

How the animals lost their tails and got them back traveling from Philadelphia to Medicine Hat. Sandburg, C.
In Sandburg, C. Rootabaga stories pt 1 p177-88 **S C**
In Sandburg, C. The Sandburg treasury p81-86 **818**

How the Bear nursed the Alligators. Lester, J.
In Lester, J. Further tales of Uncle Remus p108-12 **398.2**

How the camel got his hump. Kipling, R. **Fic**
In Kipling, R. Just so stories **S C**

How the Christ Child was warmed
In The Monkey's haircut, and other stories told by the Maya p131-32 **398.2**

How the Dao people came to be. Terada, A. M.
In Terada, A. M. Under the starfruit tree p54-58 **398.2**

How the Devil constructed a church. Carter, D. S.
In Best-loved folktales of the world p753-55 **398.2**

How the eight old ones crossed the sea. Carpenter, F.
In Carpenter, F. Tales of a Chinese grandmother p150-58 **398.2**

How the first letter was written. Kipling, R.
In Kipling, R. Just so stories **S C**

How the five rusty rats helped find a new village. Sandburg, C.
In Sandburg, C. Rootabaga stories pt 1 p20-26 **S C**
In Sandburg, C. The Sandburg treasury p19-23 **818**

How the forest grew. Jaspersohn, W. **574.5**

How the gecko came to be. Terada, A. M.
In Terada, A. M. Under the starfruit tree p69-71 **398.2**

How the good gifts were used by two
Pyle, H. How the good gifts were used by two
In Pyle, H. The wonder clock p121-33 **398.2**

How the Grinch stole Christmas. Seuss, Dr. **E**

How the guinea fowl got her spots. Knutson, B. **398.2**

How the half boys came to be. Marriott, A. L.
In Marriott, A. L. American Indian mythology **398.2**

How the hat ashes shovel helped Snoo Foo. Sandburg, C.
In Sandburg, C. Rootabaga stories pt 1 p87-91 **S C**

How the hot ashes shovel helped Snoo Foo. Sandburg, C.
In Sandburg, C. The Sandburg treasury p45-46 **818**

How the leopard got his spots. Kipling, R.
In Kipling, R. Just so stories **S C**

How the little city boy changed places with the little country boy for a year. Brown, M. W.
In Brown, M. W. The fish with the deep sea smile p76-81 **818**

How the little owl's name was changed. Gillham, C. E.
In The Scott, Foresman anthology of children's literature p390-91 **808.8**

How the Manx cat lost its tail. Stevens, J. **398.2**

How the people came to the middle place. Marriott, A. L.
In Marriott, A. L. American Indian mythology **398.2**

How the Potato Face Blind Man enjoyed himself on a fine spring morning. Sandburg, C.
In Sandburg, C. Rootabaga stories pt 1 p34-39 **S C**
In Sandburg, C. The Sandburg treasury p25-26 **818**

How the princess' pride was broken
Pyle, H. How the princess' pride was broken
In Pyle, H. The wonder clock p267-78 **398.2**

How the Raja's son won the Princess Labam
How the Raja's son won the Princess Labam
In Best-loved folktales of the world p583-91 **398.2**

How the rhinoceros got his skin. Kipling, R.
In Kipling, R. Just so stories **S C**

How the three wild Babylonian Baboons went away in the rain eating bread and butter. Sandburg, C.
In Sandburg, C. Rootabaga stories pt 2 p43-47 **S C**
In Sandburg, C. The Sandburg treasury p106-07 **818**

How the tiger got its stripes. Terada, A. M.
In Terada, A. M. Under the starfruit tree p7-9 **398.2**

How the whale got his throat. Kipling, R.
In Kipling, R. Just so stories **S C**

How the White House really works. Sullivan, G. **975.3**

How the world was made (Cheyenne). Marriott, A. L.
In Marriott, A. L. American Indian mythology **398.2**

How the world was made (Modoc). Marriott, A. L.
In Marriott, A. L. American Indian mythology **398.2**

How the world was saved. Curtis, E. S.
In Curtis, E. S. The girl who married a ghost, and other tales from the North American Indian p81-95 **398.2**

How they bring back the Village of Cream Puffs when the wind blows it away. Sandburg, C.
In Sandburg, C. Rootabaga stories pt 1 p13-19 **S C**
In Sandburg, C. The Sandburg treasury p17-19 **818**
In The Scott, Foresman anthology of children's literature p542-44 **808.8**

How they broke away to go to the Rootabaga Country. Sandburg, C.
In Sandburg, C. Rootabaga stories pt 1 p3-12 **S C**
In Sandburg, C. The Sandburg treasury p10-16 **818**

How they built the Statue of Liberty. Shapiro, M. J. **974.7**

How things work, The Macmillan book of. Folsom, M. **600**

How three went out into the wide world
Pyle, H. How three went out into the wide world
In Pyle, H. The wonder clock p39-48 **398.2**

How to be a wildlife photographer. Van Wormer, J. **778.9**

How to be an ocean scientist in your own home. Simon, S. **551.46**

How to be naturally geographic. See Bell, N. The book of where **910**

How to be school smart. James, E. **371.3**

How to become a witch. Leach, M.
In Leach, M. Whistle in the graveyard p98-99 **398.2**

How to break a bad habit. MacDonald, M. R.
In MacDonald, M. R. Twenty tellable tales p75-78 **372.6**

How to dig a hole to the other side of the world. McNulty, F. **551.1**

How to eat fried worms. Rockwell, T. **Fic**

How to eat fried worms; dramatization. Rockwell, T.
In Rockwell, T. How to eat fried worms, and other plays p21-78 **812**

How to eat fried worms [excerpt]. Rockwell, T.
In The Random House book of humor for children p301-05 **817.008**

How to eat fried worms, and other plays. Rockwell, T. **812**

How to hang up the telephone. Ephron, D.
In The Random House book of humor for children p268-69 **817.008**

How to make a chemical volcano and other mysterious experiments. Kramer, A. **540.7**

How to make pop-ups. Irvine, J. **736**
How to play better soccer. Jackson, C. P. **796.334**
How to really fool yourself. Cobb, V. **152.1**
How to run a meeting. Powers, D. G. **060.4**
How to talk to your computer. Simon, S. **005**
How to tell a true princess. Andersen, H. C.
In The Yellow fairy book p254-55 **398.2**
How to tell corn fairies if you see 'em. Sandburg, C.
In Sandburg, C. Rootabaga stories pt 1 p169-76 **S C**
In Sandburg, C. The Sandburg treasury p81-86 **818**
How to think like a scientist. Kramer, S. **507**
How to write a letter. Mischel, F. **808**
How to write a report. Brandt, S. R. **808**
How two sweetheart dippies sat in the moonlight on a lumberyard fence and heard about the sooners and the boomers. Sandburg, C.
In Sandburg, C. Rootabaga stories pt 2 p111-20 **S C**
In Sandburg, C. The Sandburg treasury p134-39 **818**
How two went into partnership
Pyle, H. How two went into partnership
In Pyle, H. The wonder clock p279-90 **398.2**
How we made Christmas. Grey Owl.
In The Family read-aloud Christmas treasury p104-07 **808.8**
How you were born. Cole, J. **612.6**
Howard, Elizabeth Fitzgerald
Chita's Christmas tree **E**
The train to Lulu's **E**
Howard, Ellen
Circle of giving (4-6) **Fic**
Edith herself (4-6) **Fic**
Her own song (4 and up) **Fic**
Howard, Richard
(il) Graff, N. P. The strength of the hills **630.1**
Howe, Deborah, 1946-1978
Bunnicula (4-6) **Fic**
Howe, James, 1946-
The celery stalks at midnight (4-6) **Fic**
The day the teacher went bananas **E**
Dew drop dead (4-6) **Fic**
Eat your poison, dear. See note under Howe, J. Dew drop dead **Fic**
The fright before Christmas. See note under Howe, J. Scared silly: a Halloween treat **E**
Hot fudge. See note under Howe, J. Scared silly: a Halloween treat **E**
Howliday Inn. See note under Howe, J. The celery stalks at midnight **Fic**
A night without stars (5 and up) **Fic**
Nighty-nightmare. See note under Howe, J. The celery stalks at midnight **Fic**
Pinky and Rex **E**
Pinky and Rex get married. See note under Howe, J. Pinky and Rex **E**
Scared silly: a Halloween treat **E**
Stage fright. See note under Howe, J. Dew drop dead **Fic**
What Eric knew. See note under Howe, J. Dew drop dead **Fic**
(jt. auth) Howe, D. Bunnicula **Fic**
Howell, Michael
The elephant man [biography of Joseph Carey Merrick] (4 and up) **92**
Howell, Troy
(il) Byars, B. C. The night swimmers **Fic**
(il) Montgomery, L. M. Anne of Green Gables **Fic**
(il) Osborne, M. P. Favorite Greek myths **292**
(il) Spyri, J. Heidi **Fic**
(il) Thomas, J. R. The comeback dog **Fic**
Howells, William Dean, 1837-1920
Christmas every day
In The Family read-aloud Christmas treasury p114-19 **808.8**
Howker, Janni
Isaac Campion (5 and up) **Fic**
Howland, Deborah
(il) Branscum, R. The adventures of Johnny May **Fic**
Howliday Inn. Howe, J. See note under Howe, J. The celery stalks at midnight **Fic**
Howl's moving castle. Jones, D. W. **Fic**
Hoyt-Goldsmith, Diane
Totem pole (3-5) **970.004**
Hubble Space Telescope
Lampton, C. The space telescope (5 and up) **522**
Hubley, John, 1948-
(jt. auth) Hubley, P. A family in Italy **945**
Hubley, Penny
A family in Italy (3-5) **945**
Huck, Charlotte S.
Children's literature in the elementary school **028.5**
Princess Furball (1-3) **398.2**

The **Huckabuck** family and how they raised popcorn in Nebraska and quit and came back. Sandburg, C.
In Sandburg, C. Rootabaga stories pt 2 p137-44 **S C**
In Sandburg, C. The Sandburg treasury p145-49 **818**

Hudden and Dudden and Donald O'Neary
Jacobs, J. Hudden and Dudden and Donald O'Neary
In The Scott, Foresman anthology of children's literature p168-71 **808.8**

Hudson, Mark, 1961-
(il) Kendall, S. The Bell Reef **Fic**

Hudson River (N.Y. and N.J.)
Ancona, G. Riverkeeper (3-6) **333.91**

Huerta, Dolores, 1930-
See/See also pages in the following book(s):
Morey, J. Famous Mexican Americans p39-49 (5 and up) **920**

Huff, Barbara A.
Greening the city streets **635**

Huffman, Tom
(il) Adler, D. A. Banks: where the money is **332.1**
(il) Seixas, J. S. Drugs—what they are, what they do **616.86**
(il) Seixas, J. S. Junk food—what it is, what it does **641.3**
(il) Seixas, J. S. Tobacco **616.86**
(il) Seixas, J. S. Water: what it is, what it does **553.7**
(il) Terban, M. The dove dove **793.73**
(il) Terban, M. Punching the clock: funny action idioms **427**

A **huge** black umbrella. Agosín, M.
In Where angels glide at dawn p99-104 **S C**

Huge Harold. Peet, B. **E**

Huggins, Edward
The magic mill
In The Scott, Foresman anthology of children's literature p284-87 **808.8**

Hughbo. Crossley-Holland, K.
In Crossley-Holland, K. British folk tales p265-69 **398.2**

Hughes, Arthur, 1832-1915
(il) MacDonald, G. The complete fairy tales of George Macdonald **S C**
(il) MacDonald, G. The princess and the goblin **Fic**

Hughes, Dean, 1943-
Family pose (5 and up) **Fic**

Hughes, E. Thomas, 1945-
(jt. auth) Hughes, M. S. The great potato book **641.3**

Hughes, Edward James *See* Hughes, Ted, 1930-

Hughes, George
(il) Clifford, E. The dastardly murder of Dirty Pete **Fic**
(il) Clifford, E. Help! I'm a prisoner in the library **Fic**

Hughes, Langston, 1902-1967
The dream keeper, and other poems (5 and up) **811**

About

Walker, A. Langston Hughes, American poet (2-5) **92**

Hughes, Meredith Sayles
The great potato book (3-5) **641.3**

Hughes, Richard, 1941-
Nothing
In Bauer, C. F. Celebrations p144-45 **808.8**

Hughes, Roderick P.
Fell's United States coin book **737.4**

Hughes, Shirley
Alfie gets in first **E**
Alfie gives a hand. See note under Hughes, S. Alfie gets in first **E**
Alfie's feet. See note under Hughes, S. Alfie gets in first **E**
All shapes and sizes **E**
Angel Mae: a tale of Trotter Street **E**
Bathwater's hot **E**
The big Alfie and Annie Rose storybook. See note under Hughes, S. Alfie gets in first **E**
The big concrete lorry. See note under Hughes, S. Angel Mae: a tale of Trotter Street **E**
An evening at Alfie's. See note under Hughes, S. Alfie gets in first **E**
Lucy & Tom's a.b.c **E**
Lucy & Tom's 1.2.3. **E**
Moving Molly **E**
Noisy. See note under Hughes, S. Bathwater's hot **E**
Out and about **E**
The snow lady. See note under Hughes, S. Angel Mae: a tale of Trotter Street **E**
Two shoes, new shoes **E**
When we went to the park. See note under Hughes, S. Bathwater's hot **E**
(il) Burnett, F. H. The secret garden **Fic**

Hughes, Ted, 1930-
Season songs (6 and up) **821**

Hughey, Patricia
Scavengers and decomposers: the cleanup crew (5 and up) **591.5**

Hugo, Victor, 1802-1885
Les Misérables; dramatization. See Thane, A. Little Cosette and Father Christmas

Hull, Jim
(il) Thayer, E. L. Casey at the bat **811**
Hulst, Sandra
(il) Blocksma, M. Action contraptions **745.592**
Human anatomy *See* Anatomy, Human
Human behavior
Burns, M. I am not a short adult! (3-6) **305.23**
Human body *See* Physiology
The **human** body. Bruun, R. D. **612**
The **human** body. Miller, J. **612**
The **human** body: how we evolved. Cole, J. **573.2**
Human race *See* Man
Human relations
See also Parent and child
Humble, Richard, 1945-
The travels of Marco Polo (4-6) **910.4**
U-boat (4 and up) **940.54**
Humbug Mountain. Fleischman, S. **Fic**
Humbug witch. Balian, L. **E**
Hummel, Berta, 1909-1946
See/See also pages in the following book(s):
Aaseng, N. The unsung heroes p60-65 (5 and up) **920**
Hummel, Mary Innocentia *See* Hummel, Berta, 1909-1946
Humor *See* Wit and humor
Humorous poetry
Bodecker, N. M. Snowman sniffles, and other verse (3-5) **811**
Ciardi, J. You read to me, I'll read to you (1-4) **811**
Lewis, J. P. A hippopotamusn't and other animal verses (k-3) **811**
Lobel, A. Whiskers & rhymes (1-3) **811**
Merriam, E. Blackberry ink (k-2) **811**
My tang's tungled and other ridiculous situations (3-6) **821.008**
Nash, O. Custard and company: poems (3 and up) **811**
Prelutsky, J. The new kid on the block: poems (3-6) **811**
Prelutsky, J. Rolling Harvey down the hill (1-3) **811**
Prelutsky, J. Something big has been here (3-5) **811**
Silverstein, S. A light in the attic (3 and up) **811**
Silverstein, S. Where the sidewalk ends (3 and up) **811**
Tripp, W. Marguerite, go wash your feet (1-3) **821.008**
Yolen, J. Dinosaur dances (3-5) **811**
Humorous stories
Ahlberg, J. Jeremiah in the dark woods (1-3) **Fic**
Chetwin, G. Box and Cox **E**
Cole, B. The silly book **E**
Conford, E. A case for Jenny Archer (2-4) **Fic**
Hall, L. Dagmar Schultz and the angel Edna (6 and up) **Fic**
Hurwitz, J. The adventures of Ali Baba Bernstein (2-4) **Fic**
Noble, T. H. Meanwhile back at the ranch **E**
The Random House book of humor for children (4-6) **817.008**
Humpback whales. Patent, D. H. **599.5**
Humphrey, Kathryn Long
Pompeii (4 and up) **937**
Humphrey's bear. Wahl, J. **E**
The **hundred** dresses. Estes, E. **Fic**
Hungarian cookery *See* Cookery, Hungarian
Hungary
Hintz, M. Hungary (4 and up) **943.9**
Fiction
Seredy, K. The Good Master (4-6) **Fic**
Seredy, K. The white stag (4-6) **Fic**
The **hunger** road. Fine, J. C. **338.1**
Hungerford, Hesba Brinsmead *See* Brinsmead, H. F. (Hesba Fay), 1922-
Hungry spider and the turtle
Courlander, H. Hungry Spider and the Turtle
In Courlander, H. The cow-tail switch, and other West African stories p107-12 **398.2**
Kaula, E. M. Anansi and his visitor, Turtle
In Best-loved folktales of the world p618-19 **398.2**
The **hungry** stranger. Stotter, R.
In Pellowski, A. The family storytelling handbook p126-29 **372.6**
Hunt, Bernice Kohn *See* Kohn, Bernice
Hunt, Irene, 1907-
Across five Aprils (5 and up) **Fic**
Up a road slowly **Fic**
See/See also pages in the following book(s):
Newbery and Caldecott Medal books, 1966-1975 p22-33 **028.5**
Hunt, Isobel Violet *See* Hunt, Violet, 1866-1942
Hunt, Jonathan
Illuminations (2-4) **909.07**
Hunt, Joyce
(jt. auth) Selsam, M. E. A first look at animals with backbones **596**
(jt. auth) Selsam, M. E. A first look at bird nests **598**
(jt. auth) Selsam, M. E. A first look at birds **598**
(jt. auth) Selsam, M. E. A first look at caterpillars **595.7**

Hunt, Joyce—*Continued*
(jt. auth) Selsam, M. E. A first look at insects **595.7**
(jt. auth) Selsam, M. E. A first look at kangaroos, koalas, and other animals with pouches **599.2**
(jt. auth) Selsam, M. E. A first look at monkeys and apes **599.8**
(jt. auth) Selsam, M. E. A first look at owls, eagles, and other hunters of the sky **598**
(jt. auth) Selsam, M. E. A first look at poisonous snakes **597.9**
(jt. auth) Selsam, M. E. A first look at rocks **552**
(jt. auth) Selsam, M. E. A first look at seals, sea lions, and walruses **599.74**
(jt. auth) Selsam, M. E. A first look at seashells **594**
(jt. auth) Selsam, M. E. A first look at sharks **597**
(jt. auth) Selsam, M. E. A first look at the world of plants **581**
(jt. auth) Selsam, M. E. Keep looking! **599**

Hunt, Kari
Masks and mask makers (5 and up) **391**

Hunt, Patricia, 1929-
Snowy owls (3-5) **598**

Hunt, Violet, 1866-1942
Aladdin and the wonderful lamp
In The Scott, Foresman anthology of children's literature p295-302 **808.8**

Hunter, Edith Fisher, 1919-
Child of the silent night [biography of Laura Dewey Bridgman] (3-5) **92**

Hunter, Kristin, 1931-
Two's enough of a crowd
In The Scott, Foresman anthology of children's literature p654-58 **808.8**

Hunter, Mollie, 1922-
A furl of fairy wind: four stories (2-5) **S C**
Contents: The brownie; The enchanted boy; Hi Johnny; A furl of fairy wind
The haunted mountain (5 and up) **Fic**
The kelpie's pearls (4-6) **Fic**
The mermaid summer (4 and up) **Fic**
A sound of chariots (5 and up) **Fic**
A stranger came ashore (6 and up) **Fic**
Talent is not enough **808.06**
The wicked one (4 and up) **Fic**

Hunter, Norman, 1899-
The unexpected banquet
In Bauer, C. F. Celebrations p45-51 **808.8**

The **hunter** and his magic flute. Fuja, A.
In Best-loved folktales of the world p638-42 **398.2**

The **hunter** and his medicine spear. Kabungo, O.
In The Crest and the hide, and other African stories of heroes, chiefs, bards, hunters, sorcerers, and common people p47-51 **398.2**

The **hunter** in the haunted forest. San Souci, R.
In San Souci, R. Short & shivery p112-16 **398.2**

Hunter's stew and hangtown fry: what pioneer America ate and why. Perl, L. **641.5**

Hunting

Fiction

Carrick, D. Harald and the great stag **E**
Gage, W. Cully Cully and the bear **E**
Rosen, M. We're going on a bear hunt **E**

The **hunting** of the snark. Carroll, L.
In Carroll, L. The complete works of Lewis Carroll p677-99 **828**

Huntingdon, Margaret Lane Hastings, Countess of *See* Lane, Margaret, 1907-

Huntington, Lee Pennock
Americans at home (6 and up) **728**

Hurd, Clement, 1908-1988
(il) Brown, M. W. Goodnight moon **E**
(il) Brown, M. W. The runaway bunny **E**
(il) Hurd, E. T. Johnny Lion's book **E**
(il) Hurd, E. T. Last one home is a green pig **E**

Hurd, Edith Thacher, 1910-
I dance in my red pajamas **E**
Johnny Lion's bad day. See note under Hurd, E. T. Johnny Lion's book **E**
Johnny Lion's book **E**
Johnny Lion's rubber boots. See note under Hurd, E. T. Johnny Lion's book **E**
Last one home is a green pig **E**
Song of the sea otter (2-4) **599.74**
Starfish (k-3) **593.9**

Hurd, Michael
The Oxford junior companion to music (5 and up) **780.3**

Hurd, Thacher
Axle the freeway cat **E**
Little Mouse's big valentine **E**
Mama don't allow **E**
Mystery on the docks **E**
The pea patch jig **E**
(il) Dodds, D. A. Wheel away! **E**

The **hurds**. Grimm, J.
In Grimm, J. The complete Grimm's fairy tales p656-57 **398.2**

Hurray for Ali Baba Bernstein. Hurwitz, J. See note under Hurwitz, J. The adventures of Ali Baba Bernstein **Fic**
Hurricane. Wiesner, D. **E**
Hurricane Elaine. Hurwitz, J. **Fic**
Hurricane watch. Branley, F. M. **551.55**
Hurricanes
See also Storms
Branley, F. M. Hurricane watch (k-3) **551.55**
See/See also pages in the following book(s):
Our violent earth p42-51 (4 and up) **363.3**
Fiction
Wiesner, D. Hurricane **E**
Winthrop, E. Belinda's hurricane (2-4) **Fic**
Hurwitz, Johanna
The adventures of Ali Baba Bernstein (2-4) **Fic**
Aldo Applesauce. See note under Hurwitz, J. Much ado about Aldo **Fic**
Aldo Ice Cream. See note under Hurwitz, J. Much ado about Aldo **Fic**
Aldo Peanut Butter. See note under Hurwitz, J. Much ado about Aldo **Fic**
Anne Frank: life in hiding (3-5) **92**
Astrid Lindgren: storyteller to the world (4 and up) **92**
Baseball fever **Fic**
Busybody Nora (2-4) **Fic**
Class clown (2-4) **Fic**
Class president. See note under Hurwitz, J. Class clown **Fic**
The cold & hot winter. See note under Hurwitz, J. The hot & cold summer **Fic**
DeDe takes charge (3-5) **Fic**
The hot & cold summer (3-5) **Fic**
Hurray for Ali Baba Bernstein. See note under Hurwitz, J. The adventures of Ali Baba Bernstein **Fic**
Hurricane Elaine (4-6) **Fic**
Much ado about Aldo (3-5) **Fic**
New neighbors for Nora. See note under Hurwitz, J. Busybody Nora **Fic**
Nora and Mrs. Mind-Your-Own-Business. See note under Hurwitz, J. Busybody Nora **Fic**
Rip-roaring Russell (2-4) **Fic**
Russell and Elisa. See note under Hurwitz, J. Rip-roaring Russell **Fic**
Russell rides again. See note under Hurwitz, J. Rip-roaring Russell **Fic**
Russell sprouts. See note under Hurwitz, J. Rip-roaring Russell **Fic**
String beans
In Bauer, C. F. Celebrations p65-67 **808.8**
Superduper Teddy (2-4) **Fic**
Teacher's pet. See note under Hurwitz, J Class clown **Fic**
Husband and the parrot
The Story of the husband and the parrot
In The Arabian nights entertainments p32-33 **398.2**
Husband and wife
Afanas'ev, A. N. Husband and wife
In Afanas'ev, A. N. Russian fairy tales p369-70 **398.2**
The **husband** who counted the spoonfuls. Bryan, A.
In Bryan, A. Beat the story-drum, pum-pum p30-40 **398.2**
The **husband** who was to mind the house. Asbjørnsen, P. C.
In The Scott, Foresman anthology of children's literature p235-36 **808.8**
In Womenfolk and fairy tales p106-110 **398.2**
Hush little baby (k-1) **781.62**
Hushabye baby on the tree top. Aiken, J.
In Aiken, J. Past eight o'clock p99-116 **S C**
Hussey, Leigh Ann
The door
In Things that go bump in the night p38-51 **S C**
The **hut** in the forest. Grimm, J.
In Grimm, J. The complete Grimm's fairy tales p698-704 **398.2**
Hutchins, Danuta Zamojska- *See* Zamojska-Hutchins, Danuta
Hutchins, Laurence
(il) Hutchins, P. Rats! **Fic**
Hutchins, Pat, 1942-
1 hunter **E**
Changes, changes **E**
Don't forget the bacon! **E**
The doorbell rang **E**
Good-night, Owl! **E**
Happy birthday, Sam **E**
Rats! (2-4) **Fic**
Rosie's walk **E**
The tale of Thomas Mead **E**
Titch **E**
What game shall we play? **E**
Where's the baby? **E**
The wind blew **E**
You'll soon grow into them, Titch **E**
Hutchinson, Anne Marbury, 1591-1643
See/See also pages in the following book(s):
Jacobs, W. J. Great lives: human rights p3-8 (5 and up) **920**
Hutton, Warwick
Adam and Eve (k-3) **222**
Beauty and the beast (1-4) **398.2**
Jonah and the great fish (k-3) **224**

Hutton, Warwick—*Continued*
Theseus and the Minotaur (3-5) **292**
(il) Cooper, S. The selkie girl **398.2**
(il) Cooper, S. The silver cow: a Welsh tale **398.2**
Hutu and Pare. Te Kanawa, K.
In Te Kanawa, K. Land of the long white cloud p105-10 **398.2**
Huxley, Anthony Julian, 1920-
(jt. auth) Black, D. Plants **581**
Huxley, Dee
(il) Wild, M. Mr. Nick's knitting **E**
Huynh, Quang Nhuong
The land I lost: adventures of a boy in Vietnam (4 and up) **92**
Hyde, Lawrence E.
(jt. auth) Hyde, M. O. Meeting death **155.9**
Hyde, Margaret Oldroyd, 1917-
Alcohol: uses and abuses (6 and up) **616.86**
Drug wars (6 and up) **363.4**
Know about drugs (4 and up) **616.86**
Know about smoking (4 and up) **616.86**
Meeting death (5 and up) **155.9**
Hyenas
Fiction
Prelutsky, J. The mean old mean hyena **E**
Hygiene
See also Health
Cobb, V. Keeping clean (1-3) **646.7**
Madaras, L. The what's happening to my body? book for boys: a growing up guide for parents and sons (6 and up) **613.9**
Madaras, L. The what's happening to my body? book for girls: a growing up guide for parents and daughters (6 and up) **613.9**
Shaw, D. Make the most of a good thing: you! (5 and up) **613**
Hyman, Trina Schart, 1939-
Little Red Riding Hood (k-2) **398.2**
Self-portrait: Trina Schart Hyman (4 and up) **92**
(il) Barrie, J. M. Peter Pan **Fic**
(il) Brink, C. R. The bad times of Irma Baumlein **Fic**
(il) Brink, C. R. Caddie Woodlawn **Fic**
(il) Cameron, E. A room made of windows **Fic**
(il) Cat poems. See Cat poems **808.81**
(il) Christmas poems. See Christmas poems **808.81**
(il) Cohen, B. Canterbury tales **Fic**
(il) Dickens, C. A Christmas carol in prose **Fic**
(il) Farber, N. How does it feel to be old? **811**
(il) Fonteyn, Dame M. Swan lake **Fic**
(il) Fritz, J. The man who loved books [biography of Saint Columba] **92**
(il) Fritz, J. Why don't you get a horse, Sam Adams? **92**
(il) Fritz, J. Will you sign here, John Hancock? **92**
(il) Gates, D. Two queens of heaven: Aphrodite [and] Demeter **292**
(il) Hodges, M. Saint George and the dragon **398.2**
(il) Kimmel, E. A. Hershel and the Hanukkah goblins **E**
(il) Kimmel, M. M. Magic in the mist **Fic**
(il) Moeri, L. Star Mother's youngest child **E**
(il) Pyle, H. King Stork **398.2**
(il) Rogasky, B. Rapunzel **398.2**
(il) Rogasky, B. The water of life **398.2**
(il) Sleator, W. Among the dolls **Fic**
(il) Thomas, D. A child's Christmas in Wales **828**
(il) Winthrop, E. The castle in the attic **Fic**
(il) Witch poems. See Witch poems **821.008**
See/See also pages in the following book(s):
Newbery and Caldecott Medal books, 1976-1985 p264-78 **028.5**
Hyndley, Kate
The voyage of the Beagle [biography of Charles Darwin] (4 and up) **92**

I

I am a Jesse White tumbler. Schmidt, D. **796.47**
I am not a short adult! Burns, M. **305.23**
I am phoenix: poems for two voices. Fleischman, P. **811**
I am the darker brother (5 and up) **811.008**
I and Sproggy. Greene, C. C. **Fic**
I ate the loaf
In Best-loved folktales of the world p170 **398.2**
I can build a house! Watanabe, S. See note under Watanabe, S. How do I put it on? **E**
I can do it by myself. Little, L. J. **E**
I can ride it! Watanabe, S. See note under Watanabe, S. How do I put it on? **E**
I can take a bath! Watanabe, S. See note under Watanabe, S. How do I put it on? **E**

I can take a walk! Watanabe, S. See note under Watanabe, S. How do I put it on? E
I dance in my red pajamas. Hurd, E. T. E
I did it. Rockwell, H. 745.5
I don't want to! Grindley, S. E
I go along. Peck, R.
In Connections: short stories by outstanding writers for young adults p184-90 S C
I go with my family to Grandma's. Levinson, R. E
I had a friend named Peter. Cohn, J. E
I hate being gifted. Hermes, P. Fic
I hate English! Levine, E. E
The I hate mathematics! book. Burns, M. 513
I have a sister—my sister is deaf. Peterson, J. W. 362.4
I, Juan de Pareja. Treviño, E. B. de. Fic
I know a lady. Zolotow, C. E
I know an old lady who swallowed a fly 782.42
I know what I'll do. Walker, B. K.
In Walker, B. K. A treasury of Turkish folktales for children p36 398.2
I know you, Al. Greene, C. C. See note under Greene, C. C. A girl called Al Fic
I like books. Browne, A. E
I like me! Carlson, N. L. E
I like the library. Rockwell, A. F. 027.4
I love Hanukkah. Hirsh, M. 296.4
I met a man. Ciardi, J. 811
I need a lunch box. Caines, J. F. E
I never saw another butterfly 741.9
I pledge allegiance. Swanson, J. 323.6
I read signs. Hoban, T. 659.13
I read symbols. Hoban, T. 659.13
I saw a purple cow, and 100 other recipes for learning. Cole, A. 372.1
I saw you in the bathtub, and other folk rhymes. Schwartz, A. 398.2
I should have stayed in bed. Lexau, J. M. E
I sure am glad to see you, Blackboard Bear. Alexander, M. G. See note under Alexander, M. We're in big trouble, Blackboard Bear E
I tell a lie every so often. Clements, B. Fic
I took my frog to the library. Kimmel, E. A. E
I unpacked my grandmother's trunk. Hoguet, S. R. E
I walk and read. Hoban, T. 659.13
I want a dog. Khalsa, D. K. E
I want to be a farmer. Kunhardt, E. E
I want to be a fire-fighter. Kunhardt, E. E
I want to be an astronaut. Barton, B. 629.45
I was a 98-pound duckling. Van Leeuwen, J. Fic
I was a second grade werewolf. Pinkwater, D. M. Fic
I was all thumbs. Waber, B. E
I went to the library
In Juba this and Juba that p73 372.6
I will be a doctor! [biography of Elizabeth Blackwell]. Wilson, D. C. 92
Ibargüengoitia, Jorge, 1928-1983
Paletón and the musical elephant
In Where angels glide at dawn p51-55 S C
IBBY *See* International Board on Books for Young People
Ice cream, ices, etc.
Cobb, V. The scoop on ice cream (4-6) 637
Jaspersohn, W. Ice cream (3-5) 637
Ice cream is falling! Watanabe, S. See note under Watanabe, S. How do I put it on? E
Ice hockey
Kalb, J. The easy hockey book (3-5) 796.962
MacLean, N. Hockey basics (4 and up) 796.962
Solomon, C. Playing hockey (2-4) 796.962
Ice skating
Krementz, J. A very young skater (3-6) 796.91
MacLean, N. Ice skating basics (4 and up) 796.91
Biography
Trenary, J. Time of my life: Jill Trenary (4 and up) 92
Fiction
Dodge, M. M. Hans Brinker; or, The silver skates (4 and up) Fic
Yolen, J. Mice on ice E
Ice skating basics. MacLean, N. 796.91
Icebergs
Gans, R. Danger—icebergs! (k-3) 551.3
Simon, S. Icebergs and glaciers (3-5) 551.3

Icebergs and glaciers. Simon, S. 551.3
Iceland
Lepthien, E. U. Iceland (4 and up) 949.12
Ichikawa, Satomi, 1949-
(il) Gauch, P. L. Dance, Tanya E
(il) Laird, E. Happy birthday! 394.2
(il) Laird, E. Rosy's garden: a child's keepsake of flowers 635.9
Ida and the wool smugglers. Alderson, S. A. E
Ida Early comes over the mountain. Burch, R. Fic
Idaho
Kent, Z. Idaho
In America the beautiful 973
Identity *See* Individuality
If all the seas were one sea (k-2) 398.8
If I had a hammer: woodworking with seven basic tools. Lasson, R. 684
If I had a paka: poems in eleven languages. Pomerantz, C. 811
If I ran the circus. Seuss, Dr. E
If I ran the zoo. Seuss, Dr. E
If I were a cricket . . . Mizumura, K. 811
If I were in charge of the world and other worries. Viorst, J. 811
If there were dreams to sell (k-3) 821.008
If you are a hunter of fossils. Baylor, B. 560
If you didn't have me. Nilsson, U. Fic
If you don't like it don't listen
Afanas'ev, A. N. If you don't like it don't listen
In Afanas'ev, A. N. Russian fairy tales p345-48 398.2
If you give a mouse a cookie. Numeroff, L. J. E
If you had a horse. Hodges, M. 398.2
If you look around you. Testa, F. 516
If you made a million. Schwartz, D. M. E
If you take a paintbrush. Testa, F. E
If you take a pencil. Testa, F. E
If you're happy and you know it. Weiss, N. 782.42
Igloos
Yue, C. The igloo 728
Iktomi and the berries. Goble, P. 398.2
Iktomi and the boulder. Goble, P. 398.2
Iktomi and the ducks. Goble, P. 398.2
The **Iliad** of Homer. Picard, B. L. 883
The **ill-natured** muse. Aiken, J.
In Aiken, J. Give yourself a fright: thirteen tales of the supernatural p89-108 S C
Illegal aliens *See* Aliens, Illegal
Illinois
Stein, R. C. Illinois
In America the beautiful 973
Fiction
Hunt, I. Across five Aprils (5 and up) Fic
Illness *See* Diseases
Illumination of books and manuscripts
Beach, M. C. The adventures of Rama (4 and up) 891
Hunt, J. Illuminations (2-4) 909.07
Illuminations. Hunt, J. 909.07
Illusions *See* Optical illusions
The **illustrated** dinosaur dictionary. See Sattler, H. R. The new illustrated dinosaur dictionary 567.9
Illustration of books
The Illustrator's notebook 741.6
Illustrators of children's books 741.6
Lacy, L. E. Art and design in children's picture books 741.6
See/See also pages in the following book(s):
Horn Book reflections on children's books and reading p73-93 028.5
A Horn Book sampler on children's books and reading p41-91 028.5
Newbery and Caldecott Medal books, 1966-1975 p276-89 028.5
Only connect: readings on children's literature p289-336 028.5
The Scott, Foresman anthology of children's literature p846-77 808.8
Illustrators
Blegvad, E. Self-portrait: Erik Blegvad (4 and up) 92
Caldecott Medal books, 1938-1957 028.5
Collins, D. R. The country artist: a story about Beatrix Potter (3-5) 92
Foreman, M. War boy: a country childhood (5 and up) 92
Hyman, T. S. Self-portrait: Trina Schart Hyman (4 and up) 92
The Illustrator's notebook 741.6
Illustrators of children's books 741.6
Newbery and Caldecott Medal books, 1966-1975 028.5
Newbery and Caldecott Medal books, 1976-1985 028.5

Illustrators—*Continued*
Once upon a time—: celebrating the magic of children's books in honor of the twentieth anniversary of Reading is Fundamental **028.5**
Peet, B. Bill Peet: an autobiography (4 and up) **92**
Rollock, B. T. Black authors and illustrators of children's books **920.003**
Sendak, M. Caldecott & Co.: notes on books and pictures **028.5**
Stevenson, J. Higher on the door (k-2) **92**
Stevenson, J. July (k-2) **92**
Stevenson, J. When I was nine (k-2) **92**
Taylor, J. Beatrix Potter: artist, storyteller and countrywoman **92**

Dictionaries

Fifth book of junior authors & illustrators **920.003**
Fourth book of junior authors and illustrators **920.003**
The Junior book of authors **920.003**
More junior authors **920.003**
Sixth book of junior authors & illustrators **920.003**
Something about the author **920.003**
Something about the author: autobiography series **920.003**
Third book of junior authors **920.003**

Dictionaries—Indexes

Children's authors and illustrators: an index to biographical dictionaries **920.003**

The **Illustrator's** notebook **741.6**

Illustrators of children's books **741.6**

The **Illyrian** adventure. Alexander, L. **Fic**

Ilya Muromets and the dragon. Afanas'ev, A. N.
In Afanas'ev, A. N. Russian fairy tales p569-75 **398.2**

Ilyá Múromets and the nightingale robber
Afanas'ev, A. N. Ilya Muromets and the dragon
In Afanas'ev, A. N. Russian fairy tales p569-75 **398.2**

I'm coming up the stairs. Leach, M.
In Leach, M. Whistle in the graveyard p57-58 **398.2**

I'm in charge of celebrations. Baylor, B. **Fic**

I'm nobody! who are you? Dickinson, E. **811**

I'm not Oscar's friend anymore. Sharmat, M. W.
In Bauer, C. F. Celebrations p282-85 **808.8**

I'm telling you now. Delton, J. **E**

I'm the big sister now. Emmert, M. **362.4**

I'm the king of the castle! Watanabe, S. See note under Watanabe, S. How do I put it on? **E**

"I'm Tipingee, she's Tipingee, we're Tipingee, too"
In The Magic orange tree, and other Haitian folktales p129-34 **398.2**

Imaginary playmates

Fiction

Bogart, J. E. Daniel's dog **E**
Greenfield, E. Me and Neesie **E**
Henkes, K. Jessica **E**

Immigrant kids. Freedman, R. **325.73**

Immigration and emigration
See also Canada—Immigration and emigration; Children of immigrants; Refugees; names of countries with the subdivision Immigration and emigration; names of countries, cities, etc. with the subdivision Foreign population; and names of nationality groups
See/See also pages in the following book(s):
Bauer, C. F. Celebrations p241-56 **808.8**

Fiction

Cohen, B. Molly's Pilgrim (2-4) **Fic**

Immunity
Patent, D. H. Germs! (4 and up) **616.9**
Showers, P. No measles, no mumps for me (k-3) **614.4**

Immunization *See* Vaccination

Imogene's antlers. Small, D. **E**

The **imp** in the basket. Babbitt, N.
In Babbitt, N. The Devil's storybook p37-46 **S C**

The **important** visitor. Oxenbury, H. **E**

Impunity Jane. Godden, R.
In Godden, R. Four dolls p6-28 **S C**

In a box. Sanfield, S.
In Sanfield, S. The adventures of High John the Conqueror **398.2**

In a dark, dark room. Schwartz, A.
In Schwartz, A. In a dark, dark room, and other scary stories p34-41 **398.2**

In a dark, dark room, and other scary stories. Schwartz, A. **398.2**

In a spring garden (k-3) **895.6**

The **In** America series (5 and up) **305.8**

In Arkansas stick to bears: don't mess with swampland skeeters. Jagendorf, M. A.
In The Scott, Foresman anthology of children's literature p372-73 **808.8**

In coal country. Hendershot, J. E
In her belfry. Gorog, J.
In Gorog, J. Three dreams and a nightmare, and other tales of the dark S C
In my garden. Oechsli, H. 635
In one era and out the other [excerpt]. Levenson, S.
In The Random House book of humor for children p95-99 817.008
In other words. See Schiller, A. Roget's children's thesaurus 423
In the beginning; creation stories from around the world. Hamilton, V. 291
In the driver's seat. Goor, R. 629.04
In the eye of war. Chang, M. S. Fic
In the forest. Arnosky, J. 758
In the forest. Ets, M. H. E
In the graveyard. Schwartz, A.
In Schwartz, A. In a dark, dark room, and other scary stories p18-23 398.2
In the haunted house. Bunting, E. E
In the Land of Souls
In The Yellow fairy book p152-54 398.2
In the moonlight, waiting. Carrick, C. E
In the night kitchen. Sendak, M. E
In the night, still dark. Lewis, R. 811
In the trail of the wind: American Indian poems and ritual orations (5 and up) 897
In the village of the weavers. Konigsburg, E. L.
In Konigsburg, E. L. Throwing shadows S C
In the witch's kitchen (3-6) 811.008
In the Year of the Boar and Jackie Robinson. Lord, B. B. Fic
In their own words: a history of the American Negro. See The Black Americans: a history in their own words, 1619-1983 305.8
In this proud land. Wolf, B. 305.8
In two worlds: a Yup'ik Eskimo family. Jenness, A. 970.004
In your own words. Cassedy, S. 808
Incas
Beck, B. L. The Incas (4 and up) 985
See/See also pages in the following book(s):
Blair, D. N. The land and people of Bolivia p33-44 (5 and up) 984
Fiction
Clark, A. N. Secret of the Andes (4 and up) Fic
Incest
See/See also pages in the following book(s):
Terkel, S. N. Feeling safe, feeling strong p32-43 (4 and up) 362.7
The **inch** boy. Morimoto, J. 398.2
Inch by inch. Lionni, L. E
Inchelina. Andersen, H. C.
In Andersen, H. C. Hans Andersen: his classic fairy tales p178-[88] S C
Incident at Hawk's Hill. Eckert, A. W. Fic
Incisa, Monica
(il) Kennedy, X. J. The forgetful wishing well: poems for young people 811
The **incredible** journey. Burnford, S. Fic
The **incredible** journey of Lewis and Clark. Blumberg, R. 978
The **incredible** painting of Felix Clousseau. Agee, J. E
Independence Day (United States) *See* Fourth of July
Index to children's poetry 808.81
Index to children's songs. Peterson, C. S. 782.42
Index to collective biographies for young readers. Breen, K. 920
Index to fairy tales, 1949-1972 398.2
Index to fairy tales, 1973-1977 398.2
Index to fairy tales, 1978-1986 398.2
Index to poetry for children and young people 808.81
Index to poetry, The Columbia Granger's 808.81
An **index** to young readers' collective biographies. See Breen, K. Index to collective biographies for young readers 920
Indexes
See also Periodicals—Indexes
India
India—in pictures (5 and up) 954
Fiction
Kipling, R. The jungle books (4 and up) S C
Kipling, R. Just so stories (3-6) S C
Folklore
See Folklore—India
India—in pictures (5 and up) 954
Indian chiefs. Freedman, R. 920
The **Indian** Cinderella. Macmillan, C.
In Best-loved folktales of the world p694-96 398.2

Indian costumes. Hofsinde, R. **391**
The **Indian** in the cupboard. Reid Banks, L. **Fic**
Indian sign language. Hofsinde, R. **419**
Indian signs and signals. Fronval, G. **419**
Indiana
Stein, R. C. Indiana
In America the beautiful **973**
Indians
Poetry
In the trail of the wind: American Indian poems and ritual orations (5 and up) **897**
The Sacred path (5 and up) **897**
Indians of Central America
See also Mayas
Indians of Mexico
See also Aztecs; Mayas; Papago Indians; Toltecs
Indians of North America
See also names of peoples and linguistic families
Jones, J. C. The American Indian in America
In The In America series **305.8**
Wheeler, M. J. First came the Indians (2-4) **970.004**
See/See also pages in the following book(s):
Barth, E. Turkeys, Pilgrims, and Indian corn p60-69 (3-6) **394.2**
Freedman, R. Children of the wild West p38-57 (4 and up) **978**
McCall, E. S. Biography of a river: the living Mississippi (6 and up) **977**
Antiquities
Anderson, J. From map to museum (5 and up) **930.1**
Art
Baylor, B. Before you came this way (1-4) **709.01**
Baylor, B. When clay sings (1-4) **970.004**
Biography
Freedman, R. Indian chiefs (6 and up) **920**
Costume and adornment
Hofsinde, R. Indian costumes (3-6) **391**
Dictionaries
Wolfson, E. From Abenaki to Zuni (4 and up) **970.004**
Fiction
Baker, O. Where the buffaloes begin (2-4) **Fic**
Dalgliesh, A. The courage of Sarah Noble (2-4) **Fic**
Goble, P. Beyond the ridge (2-4) **Fic**
Goble, P. Dream wolf **E**
Goble, P. The girl who loved wild horses **E**
Lampman, E. S. White captives (5 and up) **Fic**
Levin, B. Brother moose (5 and up) **Fic**
Martin, B. Knots on a counting rope **E**
O'Dell, S. Island of the Blue Dolphins (5 and up) **Fic**
O'Dell, S. Streams to the river, river to the sea (5 and up) **Fic**
O'Dell, S. Zia (5 and up) **Fic**
Reid Banks, L. The Indian in the cupboard (5 and up) **Fic**
Speare, E. G. The sign of the beaver (5 and up) **Fic**
Yolen, J. Sky dogs **E**
Folklore
See also Indians of North America—Legends
Housing
Yue, D. The tipi: a center of native American life (4 and up) **728**
Languages
See also Indians of North America—Sign language
Legends
Cleaver, E. The enchanted caribou (2-4) **398.2**
Curry, J. L. Back in the beforetime (4-6) **398.2**
Curtis, E. S. The girl who married a ghost, and other tales from The North American Indian (4 and up) **398.2**
De Paola, T. The legend of the Indian paintbrush (k-3) **398.2**
Goble, P. Buffalo woman (1-3) **398.2**
Goble, P. The gift of the sacred dog (2-4) **398.2**
Goble, P. The great race of the birds and animals (1-3) **398.2**
Longfellow, H. W. Hiawatha (k-3) **811**
Longfellow, H. W. Hiawatha's childhood (k-3) **811**
Marriott, A. L. American Indian mythology **398.2**
Mayo, G. Star tales (4 and up) **398.2**
Monroe, J. G. They dance in the sky: native American star myths (4 and up) **398.2**
The Naked bear (4 and up) **398.2**
Norman, H. How Glooskap outwits the Ice Giants, and other tales of the Maritime Indians (3-6) **398.2**
Siberell, A. Whale in the sky (k-3) **398.2**
Steptoe, J. The story of Jumping Mouse (1-3) **398.2**
The Whistling skeleton (3-6) **398.2**
Music
See Indians of North America—Songs and music

Indians of North America—*Continued*
Mythology
See Indians of North America—Legends
Poetry
Dancing teepees: poems of American Indian youth (3-5) **897**
Highwater, J. Moonsong lullaby (k-2) **811**
Longfellow, H. W. Hiawatha (k-3) **811**
Longfellow, H. W. Hiawatha's childhood (k-3) **811**
Sign language
Fronval, G. Indian signs and signals (4 and up) **419**
Hofsinde, R. Indian sign language (3-6) **419**
Songs and music
Fichter, G. S. American Indian music and musical instruments (5 and up) **780.89**
Wars
See also United States—History—1755-1763, French and Indian War
Ehrlich, A. Wounded Knee: an Indian history of the American West (6 and up) **970.004**
Great Plains
Freedman, R. Buffalo hunt (4 and up) **970.004**
Northwest coast of North America
Hoyt-Goldsmith, D. Totem pole (3-5) **970.004**
Southwestern States
Baylor, B. When clay sings (1-4) **970.004**
West (U.S.)
Ehrlich, A. Wounded Knee: an Indian history of the American West (6 and up) **970.004**

Indians of South America
See also Incas

Indic cookery *See* Cookery, Indic

The **indiscreet** wife. Afanas'ev, A. N.
In Afanas'ev, A. N. Russian fairy tales p226-27 **398.2**

Individuality
Free to be—you and me **810.8**

Indonesia
Indonesia—in pictures (5 and up) **959.8**

Indonesia—in pictures (5 and up) **959.8**

Indoor games
See/See also pages in the following book(s):
Bauer, C. F. This way to books p267-302 **028.5**

Infants
Cole, J. How you were born (k-2) **612.6**
Cole, J. The new baby at your house (k-3) **306.8**
Jonas, A. When you were a baby **E**
Lasky, K. A baby for Max **E**
Ormerod, J. 101 things to do with a baby **E**
Fiction
Ahlberg, J. The baby's catalogue **E**
Ahlberg, J. Peek-a-boo! **E**
Alexander, M. G. Nobody asked me if I wanted a baby sister **E**
Alexander, M. G. When the new baby comes, I'm moving out **E**
Aliki. Welcome, little baby **E**
Byars, B. C. Go and hush the baby **E**
Byers, R. M. Mycca's baby **E**
Cleary, B. Socks (3-5) **Fic**
Greenfield, E. She come bringing me that little baby girl **E**
Hayes, S. Eat up, Gemma **E**
Hennessy, B. G. A,B,C,D, tummy, toes, hands, knees **E**
Hines, A. G. Big like me **E**
Hughes, S. Angel Mae: a tale of Trotter Street **E**
Hutchins, P. Where's the baby? **E**
Isadora, R. Babies **E**
Keller, H. What Alvin wanted **E**
Lively, P. Fanny's sister (3-5) **Fic**
McMillan, B. Step by step **E**
Mills, C. Dynamite Dinah (3-5) **Fic**
Ormerod, J. Bend and stretch **E**
Ormerod, J. The saucepan game **E**
Russo, M. Waiting for Hannah **E**
Steptoe, J. Baby says **E**
Walter, M. P. My mama needs me **E**
Williams, B. Jeremy isn't hungry **E**
Willis, J. Earthlets, as explained by Professor Xargle **E**
Wishinsky, F. Oonga boonga **E**

Information please almanac, atlas & yearbook **031.02**

Information power. American Association of School Librarians **027.8**

Infrared radiation
White, J. R. The invisible world of the infrared (5 and up) **535**

Ingestion disorders *See* Eating disorders

Ingle, Lester
(jt. auth) Zim, H. S. Seashores **574.92**

Ingraham, Erick
(il) Calhoun, M. Cross-country cat **E**
(il) Calhoun, M. Hot-air Henry **E**

Inheritance and succession
Fiction
King-Smith, D. Harry's Mad (3-5) **Fic**

Injuries *See* Accidents; Wounds and injuries

Inkpen, Mick
The blue balloon **E**

The **inn** of lost time. Namioka, L.
In Connections: short stories by outstanding writers for young adults p138-57 **S C**
Innocenti, Roberto
Rose Blanche (5 and up) **Fic**
(il) Collodi, C. The adventures of Pinocchio **Fic**
(il) Dickens, C. A Christmas carol in prose **Fic**
Inns *See* Hotels, motels, etc.
Innuit *See* Inuit
Inoculation *See* Vaccination
Inouye, Carol
(il) Torre, B. L. The luminous pearl **398.2**
Insane *See* Mentally ill
The **insect** kingdom that didn't get started. Mahy, M.
In Mahy, M. Nonstop nonsense p55-59 **828**
Insect metamorphosis. Goor, R. **595.7**
Insectivorous plants
Overbeck, C. Carnivorous plants (4 and up) **583**
Insects
See also Ants; Butterflies; Dragonflies; Moths; Wasps
Goor, R. Insect metamorphosis (2-6) **595.7**
Johnson, S. A. Chirping insects (4 and up) **595.7**
Johnson, S. A. Water insects (4 and up) **595.7**
Mound, L. A. Insect (4 and up) **595.7**
Parker, N. W. Bugs (1-3) **595.7**
Selsam, M. E. Backyard insects (k-3) **595.7**
Selsam, M. E. A first look at insects (1-3) **595.7**
Zim, H. S. Insects (4 and up) **595.7**
See/See also pages in the following book(s):
McClung, R. M. The amazing egg p41-54 (4 and up) **591.1**
Norsgaard, E. J. Nature's great balancing act p21-41 (4-6) **574.5**
Poetry
Fleischman, P. Joyful noise: poems for two voices (4 and up) **811**
See/See also pages in the following book(s):
Favorite poems, old and new p121-49 (4-6) **808.81**
Insects as carriers of disease
See also Lyme disease
An **insect's** body. Cole, J. **595.7**
Inside an egg. Johnson, S. A. **598**
Inside my feet. Kennedy, R.
In Kennedy, R. Collected stories p223-70 **S C**
The **inside-outside** book of London. Munro, R. **942.1**
The **inside-outside** book of New York City. Munro, R. **974.7**
The **inside-outside** book of Washington, D.C. Munro, R. **975.3**
Inside the bright red gate. Carpenter, F.
In Carpenter, F. Tales of a Chinese grandmother p1-13 **398.2**
Inside the burrow: the life of the golden hamster. Fischer-Nagel, H. **636.08**
Inspirations. Sills, L. **920**
Instant paper airplanes. Churchill, E. R. **745.592**
Instructional materials centers
See also School libraries
American Association of School Librarians. Information power **027.8**
Anderson, P. Planning school library media facilities **027.8**
Smith, J. B. Library media center programs for middle schools: a curriculum-based approach **027.8**
Handbooks, manuals, etc.
Matthews, J. G. ClipArt & dynamic designs for libraries & media centers **021.7**
Periodicals
School Library Media Quarterly **027.805**
Yearbooks
School Library Media Annual **027.805**
Instructor **372.05**
Intellect
Yepsen, R. B. Smarten up! how to increase your brain power (5 and up) **153**
Intellectual freedom
See also Freedom of information
Intellectual freedom manual **323.44**
Periodicals
Newsletter on Intellectual Freedom **323.44**
Intellectual freedom manual **323.44**
Intelligence *See* Intellect
Intelligence and luck
In Best-loved folktales of the world p452-54 **398.2**
Intermarriage, Children of *See* Children of intermarriage

International Board on Books for Young People
Bookbird. See Bookbird 028.505
International dictionary of the English language, Webster's third new 423
International Institute for Children's Literature and Reading Research
Bookbird. See Bookbird 028.505
International politics *See* World politics
International relations
See also World politics
International Wildlife 591.05
Internment camps *See* Concentration camps
Interpreting and translating *See* Translating and interpreting
Interracial adoption
Rosenberg, M. B. Being adopted (2-4) 362.7
Sobol, H. L. We don't look like our Mom and Dad (2-5) 362.7
Interracial relations *See* Race relations
Interstellar communication
Poynter, M. Cosmic quest (5 and up) 574.999
Interstellar pig. Sleator, W. Fic
Into a strange land: unaccompanied refugee youth in America. Ashabranner, B. K. 362.84
Into the dream. Sleator, W. Fic
Introducing bookplots 3. Spirt, D. L. 028.1
Introducing books to children. Chambers, A. 028.5
Inuit
Ekoomiak, N. Arctic memories (3-5) 998
Jenness, A. In two worlds: a Yup'ik Eskimo family (4 and up) 970.004
Yue, C. The igloo 728
See/See also pages in the following book(s):
Thomson, P. Auks, rocks and the odd dinosaur p33-37 (5 and up) 508
Fiction
Andrews, J. Very last first time E
George, J. C. Julie of the wolves (6 and up) Fic
George, J. C. Water sky (5 and up) Fic
Houston, J. A. Frozen fire (6 and up) Fic
Kortum, J. Ghost vision (5 and up) Fic
Luenn, N. Nessa's fish E
Paulsen, G. Dogsong (6 and up) Fic
Folklore
San Souci, R. Song of Sedna (2-4) 398.2
Invalids *See* Sick
Invasion of privacy *See* Privacy, Right of
Inventions
Aaseng, N. The inventors: Nobel prizes in chemistry, physics, and medicine (5 and up) 609
Macaulay, D. The way things work (5 and up) 600
Murphy, J. Guess again: more weird & wacky inventions (4 and up) 609
Inventors
Aaseng, N. The inventors: Nobel prizes in chemistry, physics, and medicine (5 and up) 609
Mitchell, B. CLICK!: a story about George Eastman (3-5) 92
Mitchell, B. Shoes for everyone: a story about Jan Matzeliger (3-5) 92
Mitchell, B. We'll race you, Henry: a story about Henry Ford (3-5) 92
Provensen, A. Leonardo da Vinci: the artist, inventor, scientist (3 and up) 92
Richards, N. Dreamers & doers: inventors who changed our world (6 and up) 920
Invertebrates
Simon, S. Pets in a jar (4 and up) 639
Invisible Lissa. Honeycutt, N. Fic
Invisible playmates *See* Imaginary playmates
The **invisible** world of the infrared. White, J. R. 535
Inviting Jason. Konigsburg, E. L.
In Konigsburg, E. L. Altogether, one at a time p1-12 S C
IOU's. Sebestyen, O. Fic
Iowa
Kent, D. Iowa
In America the beautiful 973
Fiction
Naylor, P. R. Maudie in the middle (3-5) Fic
Ira says goodbye. Waber, B. See note under Waber, B. Ira sleeps over E
Ira sleeps over. Waber, B. E
Iran
Iran—in pictures (5 and up) 955
Tames, R. Take a trip to Iran (1-3) 955
Folklore
See Folklore—Iran
Iran—in pictures (5 and up) 955
Iraq
Iraq—in pictures (5 and up) 956.7
Tames, R. Take a trip to Iraq (1-3) 956.7

Iraq—in pictures (5 and up) **956.7**

Ireland, Norma Olin, 1907-
(comp) Index to fairy tales, 1949-1972. See Index to fairy tales, 1949-1972 **398.2**
(comp) Index to fairy tales, 1973-1977. See Index to fairy tales, 1973-1977 **398.2**
(comp) Index to fairy tales, 1978-1986. See Index to fairy tales, 1978-1986 **398.2**

Ireland
Fradin, D. B. The Republic of Ireland (4 and up) **941.5**

Fiction

McDermott, G. Tim O'Toole and the wee folk **E**

Folklore

See Folklore—Ireland

Legends

See Legends—Ireland

Irish Americans
Johnson, J. E. The Irish in America
In The In America series **305.8**

Fiction

Giff, P. R. The gift of the pirate queen (4-6) **Fic**

Irish fairy tales. Stephens, J. **398.2**

The **Irish** in America. Johnson, J. E.
In The In America series **305.8**

Irish Red. Kjelgaard, J. See note under Kjelgaard, J. Big Red **Fic**

Iron Hans
Grimm, J. Iron Hans
In Grimm, J. The complete Grimm's fairy tales p612-20 **398.2**
In Grimm, J. More tales from Grimm p207-28 **398.2**

Iron stove
Grimm, J. The iron stove
In Grimm, J. The complete Grimm's fairy tales p571-77 **398.2**
In The Yellow fairy book p32-37 **398.2**

Iroquois Indians
McClard, M. Hiawatha and the Iroquois league (5 and up) **92**
See/See also pages in the following book(s):
Hofsinde, R. Indian costumes p40-48 (3-6) **391**

Legends

The Naked bear (4 and up) **398.2**

Irraweka, mischief-maker. Sherlock, Sir P. M.
In Sherlock, Sir P. M. West Indian folk-tales p21-26 **398.2**

Irvine, Joan, 1951-
How to make pop-ups (3-6) **736**

Irving, James Gordon
(il) Zim, H. S. Birds **598**
(il) Zim, H. S. Fishes **597**
(il) Zim, H. S. Insects **595.7**
(il) Zim, H. S. Mammals **599**

Irving, Washington, 1783-1859
The adventure of the German student; adaptation. See San Souci, R. The adventure of the German student
Rip Van Winkle (5 and up) **Fic**
Rip Van Winkle; dramatization. See Thane, A. Rip Van Winkle

Irwin, Patricia Kathleen Page, 1916-
A flask of sea water (2-4) **Fic**

Is anybody up? Kandoian, E. **E**

Is anyone home? Maris, R. **E**

A **is** for angry. Boynton, S. **E**

Is it larger? Is it smaller? Hoban, T. **E**

Is it red? Is it yellow? Is it blue? Hoban, T. **E**

Is it rough? Is it smooth? Is it shiny? Hoban, T. **E**

Is there life in outer space? Branley, F. M. **574.999**

Is this a house for Hermit Crab? McDonald, M. **595.3**

Is your mama a llama? Guarino, D. **E**

Isaac Bashevis Singer: the story of a story-teller. Kresh, P. **92**

Isaac Campion. Howker, J. **Fic**

Isaacson, Philip M., 1924-
Round buildings, square buildings, & buildings that wiggle like a fish (4 and up) **720**

Isabelle and little orphan Frannie. Greene, C. C. See note under Greene, C. C. Isabelle the itch **Fic**

Isabelle shows her stuff. Greene, C. C. See note under Greene, C. C. Isabelle the itch **Fic**

Isabelle the itch. Greene, C. C. **Fic**

Isadora, Rachel
Babies **E**
Ben's trumpet **E**
City seen from A to Z **E**
Friends **E**
Max **E**
My ballet class (1-3) **792.8**
The princess and the frog (k-2) **398.2**
(il) McKissack, P. C. Flossie & the fox **E**
(il) Shub, E. The white stallion **E**

Isenbart, Hans-Heinrich, 1923-
Birth of a foal (3-6) **636.1**

Ishi

About

Kroeber, T. Ishi, last of his tribe (5 and up) **92**

Ishi, last of his tribe. Kroeber, T. 92
Ishii, Momoko, 1907-
The tongue-cut sparrow (k-3) 398.2
Islamic countries
See also Arab countries
Island boy. Cooney, B. E
Island of the Blue Dolphins. O'Dell, S. Fic
The **island** on Bird Street. Orlev, U. Fic
Island rescue. Martin, C. E. See note under Martin, C. E. Island winter E
Island winter. Martin, C. E. E
Islands
Fiction
Cooney, B. Island boy E
Jones, J. B. Secrets of a summer spy (5 and up) Fic
Martin, C. E. Island winter E
Israel
Burstein, C. M. A kid's catalog of Israel (4 and up) 956.94
Israel—in pictures (5 and up) 956.94
Jones, H. H. Israel (4 and up) 956.94
Lawton, C. Passport to Israel (5 and up) 956.94
Rutland, J. Take a trip to Israel (1-3) 956.94
Taitz, E. Israel (4 and up) 956.94
Collective settlements
See Collective settlements—Israel
Politics and government
Adler, D. A. Our Golda: the story of Golda Meir (3-5) 92
Social life and customs
Taylor, A. A kibbutz in Israel (3-5) 956.94
Israel—in pictures (5 and up) 956.94
Israeli cookery *See* Cookery, Israeli
It all began with Jane Eyre. Greenwald, S. Fic
It could always be worse. Ausubel, N.
In Best-loved folktales of the world p459-60 398.2
It does not say meow, and other animal riddle rhymes. De Regniers, B. S. 793.73
It happened in Pinsk. Yorinks, A. E
It is time to go to sleep. Schwartz, A.
In Schwartz, A. There is a carrot in my ear, and other noodle tales p58-63 398.2
It looked like spilt milk. Shaw, C. E
Italian family. See Hubley, P. A family in Italy 945
Italy
Hubley, P. A family in Italy (3-5) 945
James, I. Italy (4-6) 945
Children
See Children—Italy
Folklore
See Folklore—Italy
Social life and customs
Italy (3-5) 945
Italy (3-5) 945
It's about time, Jesse Bear, and other rhymes. Carlstrom, N. W. See note under Carlstrom, N. W. Jesse Bear, what will you wear? E
It's all relative. Apfel, N. H. 530.1
It's an armadillo. Lavies, B. 599.3
It's Christmas. Prelutsky, J. 811
It's George! Cohen, M. See note under Cohen, M. See you in second grade! E
It's Halloween. Prelutsky, J. 811
It's just me, Emily. Hines, A. G. E
It's like this, Cat. Neville, E. C. Fic
It's mine! Lionni, L. E
It's my birthday! Watanabe, S. See note under Watanabe, S. How do I put it on? E
It's not easy being George. Smith, J. L. See note under Smith, J. L. The kid next door and other headaches Fic
It's not the end of the world. Blume, J. Fic
It's raining cats and dogs. Branley, F. M. 551.5
It's raining cats and dogs. Keller, C. 793.73
It's raining, said John Twaining. Bodecker, N. M. 398.8
It's really Christmas. Hoban, L. E
It's snowing! It's snowing! Prelutsky, J. 811
It's so nice to have a wolf around the house. Allard, H.
In The Laugh book p111-18 808.8
It's Thanksgiving. Prelutsky, J. 811
It's Valentine's Day. Prelutsky, J. 811
Ivan and the gray wolf
Afanas'ev, A. N. Ivan Tsarevich, the grey wolf and the firebird
In Afanas'ev, A. N. Russian folk tales p7-18 398.2
Afanas'ev, A. N. Prince Ivan, the firebird, and the gray wolf
In Afanas'ev, A. N. Russian fairy tales p612-24 398.2
Ivan the Cow's Son
Afanas'ev, A. N. Ivan the Cow's Son
In Afanas'ev, A. N. Russian fairy tales p234-49 398.2

Ivan the peasant's son and the little man, himself one finger tall, his mustache seven versts in length
Afanas'ev, A. N. Ivan the peasant's son and the thumb-sized man
In Afanas'ev, A. N. Russian fairy tales p262-68 **398.2**
Ivan the peasant's son and the thumb-sized man. Afanas'ev, A. N.
In Afanas'ev, A. N. Russian fairy tales p262-68 **398.2**
Ivan the Simpleton
Afanas'ev, A. N. Ivan the Simpleton
In Afanas'ev, A. N. Russian fairy tales p142-45 **398.2**
Ivan Tsarevich and Bailoi Polyanyin
Afanas'ev, A. N. Prince Ivan and Byely Polyanin
In Afanas'ev, A. N. Russian fairy tales p475-82 **398.2**
Ivan Tsarevich, the grey wolf and the firebird. Afanas'ev, A. N.
In Afanas'ev, A. N. Russian folk tales p7-18 **398.2**
Ivanko the bear's son. Afanas'ev, A. N.
In Afanas'ev, A. N. Russian fairy tales p221-23 **398.2**
Ivanushka the Little Fool
Afanas'ev, A. N. Ivanushka the Little Fool
In Afanas'ev, A. N. Russian fairy tales p62-65 **398.2**
Ivashko and the wise woman
Afanas'ev, A. N. Tereshichka
In Afanas'ev, A. N. Russian fairy tales p389-93 **398.2**
Ivimey, John W. (John William), b. 1868
The complete story of the three blind mice **E**
Ivory Coast
Cote d'Ivoire (Ivory Coast)—in pictures (5 and up) **966.68**
Folklore
See Folklore—Ivory Coast
The **Ivory** Coast in pictures. See Cote d'Ivoire (Ivory Coast)—in pictures **966.68**
Iwamatsu, Atushi Jun, 1908-
Crow Boy **E**
Umbrella **E**
(jt. auth) Iwamatsu, T. Momo's kitten **E**
Iwamatsu, Tomoe, 1908-
Momo's kitten **E**
Izawa, Masana
(il) Johnson, S. A. Mosses **588**
(il) Johnson, S. A. Mushrooms **589.2**
Izzy, willy-nilly. Voigt, C. **Fic**

J

J. C. Penney Company, Inc.
See/See also pages in the following book(s):
Aaseng, N. From rags to riches p39-47 (5 and up) **920**
J. T. Wagner, J. **Fic**
Jabberwocky, Lewis Carroll's. Carroll, L. **821**
Jablow, Alta
A tug-of-war
In Best-loved folktales of the world p658-60 **398.2**
Jack and his golden snuff-box
Jacobs, J. Jack and his golden snuff-box
In Jacobs, J. English fairy tales p81-92 **398.2**
Reeves, J. The golden snuff-box
In Reeves, J. English fables and fairy stories p157-76 **398.2**
Jack and King Marock
Jack and King Marock
In The Jack tales p135-50 **398.2**
Jack and the bean-stalk
Crossley-Holland, K. Jack and the beanstalk
In Crossley-Holland, K. British folk tales p118-31 **398.2**
Ehrlich, A. Jack and the beanstalk
In Ehrlich, A. The Random House book of fairy tales p46-57 **398.2**
The History of Jack and the bean-stalk
In The Classic Fairy tales p164-74 **398.2**
Jack and the beanstalk
In The Red fairy book p133-45 **398.2**
Jacobs, J. Jack and the beanstalk
In Best-loved folktales of the world p193-98 **398.2**
In Jacobs, J. English fairy tales p59-67 **398.2**
Reeves, J. Jack and the beanstalk
In Reeves, J. English fables and fairy stories p127-46 **398.2**
Rockwell, A. F. Jack and the beanstalk
In Rockwell, A. F. Puss in boots, and other stories p1-11 **398.2**
Thane, A. Jack and the magic beanstalk
In Thane, A. Plays from famous stories and fairy tales p366-80 **812**
Jack and the bean tree
Jack and the bean tree
In The Jack tales p31-39 **398.2**
Jack and the bull
Jack and the bull
In The Jack tales p21-30 **398.2**

Jack and the Devil. Hamilton, V.
In Hamilton, V. The people could fly: American black folktales p126-32 **398.2**

Jack and the doctor's girl
Jack and the doctor's girl
In The Jack tales p114-26 **398.2**

Jack and the king's girl
Jack and the king's girl
In The Jack tales p83-88 **398.2**

Jack and the magic beanstalk. Thane, A.
In Thane, A. Plays from famous stories and fairy tales p366-80 **812**

Jack and the northwest wind
Jack and the North West Wind
In The Jack tales p47-57 **398.2**

Jack and the robbers
Jack and the robbers
In The Jack tales p40-46 **398.2**
In The Scott, Foresman anthology of children's literature p358-61 **808.8**
MacDonald, M. R. Jack and the robbers
In MacDonald, M. R. Twenty tellable tales p95-103 **372.6**

Jack and the varmints
Jack and the varmints
In The Jack tales p58-66 **398.2**

Jack Frost. Afanas'ev, A. N.
In Afanas'ev, A. N. Russian fairy tales p366-69 **398.2**

Jack Frost. San Souci, R.
In San Souci, R. Short & shivery p9-14 **398.2**

Jack Hannaford
Jacobs, J. Jack Hannaford
In Jacobs, J. English fairy tales p40-43 **398.2**
Reeves, J. Jack Hannaford
In Reeves, J. English fables and fairy stories p1-9 **398.2**

Jack in the giants' new ground
Jack in the giants' newground
In Best-loved folktales of the world p674-85 **398.2**
In The Jack tales p3-20 **398.2**

Jack my Hedgehog. Grimm, J.
In The Green fairy book p304-10 **398.2**

Jack-o'-lantern. Barth, E. **398.2**

Jack Straw. Snyder, M.
In Things that go bump in the night p243-54 **S C**

The **Jack** tales (4-6) **398.2**

Jack the giant-killer
De Regniers, B. S. Jack the giant killer **398.2**
The History of Jack and the giants
In The Classic fairy tales p51-65 **398.2**
The History of Jack the giant killer
In The Blue fairy book p374-79 **398.2**
Jacobs, J. Jack the giant-killer
In Best-loved folktales of the world p198-206 **398.2**
In Jacobs, J. English fairy tales p99-112 **398.2**

Jackal's favorite game. Bryan, A.
In Bryan, A. Lion and the ostrich chicks, and other African folk tales p40-59 **398.2**

The **jacket** I wear in the snow. Neitzel, S. **E**

Jackie Robinson: he was the first. Adler, D. A. **92**

Jack's hunting trips
Jack's hunting trips
In The Jack tales p161-71 **398.2**

Jackson, Andrew, 1767-1845
See/See also pages in the following book(s):
Bealer, A. W. Only the names remain p57-71 (4-6) **970.004**

Jackson, C. Paul (Caary Paul), 1902-
How to play better soccer (4 and up) **796.334**

Jackson, Caary Paul *See* Jackson, C. Paul (Caary Paul), 1902-

Jackson, Jesse
Make a joyful noise unto the Lord! The life of Mahalia Jackson, queen of gospel singers (5 and up) **92**

Jackson, Jesse L., 1941-
About
McKissack, P. C. Jesse Jackson: a biography (4 and up) **92**

Jackson, Mahalia, 1911-1972
About
Jackson, J. Make a joyful noise unto the Lord! The life of Mahalia Jackson, queen of gospel singers (5 and up) **92**

Jackson, Shirley, 1919-1965
Life among the savages [excerpt]
In The Random House book of humor for children p66-73 **817.008**
The witchcraft of Salem Village (4 and up) **133.4**

Jackson, Stonewall, 1824-1863
About
Fritz, J. Stonewall (4 and up) **92**

Jackson, Thomas Jonathan *See* Jackson, Stonewall, 1824-1863

Jacobi, Kathy
(il) Fleischman, P. The Half-a-Moon Inn **Fic**
(il) MacLachlan, P. Tomorrow's wizard **S C**

Jacobs, Francine, 1935-
Breakthrough (5 and up) **615**
Supersaurus (1-3) **567.9**

Jacobs, Joseph, 1854-1916
Black Bull of Norroway
In The Scott, Foresman anthology of children's literature p157-59 **808.8**
Cap o' Rushes
In Womenfolk and fairy tales p77-82 **398.2**
The cat and the mouse
In Tomie dePaola's favorite nursery tales p114-16 **398.2**
Dick Whittington and his cat
In Best-loved folktales of the world p221-28 **398.2**
English fairy tales (4-6) **398.2**
Contents: Tom Tit Tot; Three sillies; Rose-tree; Old woman and her pig; How Jack went to seek his fortune; Mr. Vinegar; Nix Nought Nothing; Jack Hannaford; Binnorie; Cap o' Rushes; Teeny-Tiny; Jack and the beanstalk; Story of the three little pigs; Master and his pupil; Titty Mouse and Tatty Mouse; Jack and his golden snuff-box; Story of the three bears; Jack the giant-killer; Henny-Penny; Childe Rowland; Molly Whuppie; Red Ettin; Golden arm; History of Tom Thumb; Mr. Fox; Lazy Jack; Johnny-cake; Earl Mar's daughter; Mr. Miacca; Whittington and his cat; Laidly Worm of Spindleston Heugh; Cat and mouse; Fish and the ring; Magpie's nest; Kate Crackernuts; Cauld lad of Hilton; The ass, the table, and the stick; Fairy ointment; Well of the World's End; Master of all masters; Three heads of the well; Mouse and mouser; The strange visitor
The fables of Aesop (4 and up) **398.2**
Henny Penny
In The Scott, Foresman anthology of children's literature p151-52 **808.8**
How Jack went to seek his fortune
In Tomie dePaola's favorite nursery tales p118-21 **398.2**
Hudden and Dudden and Donald O'Neary
In The Scott, Foresman anthology of children's literature p168-71 **808.8**
Jack and the beanstalk
In Best-loved folktales of the world p193-98 **398.2**
Jack the giant-killer
In Best-loved folktales of the world p198-206 **398.2**
Johnny Cake
In Tomie dePaola's favorite nursery tales p11-15 **398.2**
Kate Crackernuts
In Womenfolk and fairy tales p65-70 **398.2**
King O'Toole and his goose
In The Scott, Foresman anthology of children's literature p176-78 **808.8**
Lazy Jack
In Best-loved folktales of the world p214-15 **398.2**
The little red hen
In Tomie dePaola's favorite nursery tales p16-19 **398.2**
Master of all masters
In Best-loved folktales of the world p231-32 **398.2**
In Tomie dePaola's favorite nursery tales p84-85 **398.2**
Molly Whuppie
In Best-loved folktales of the world p216-18 **398.2**
Mr. Fox
In Womenfolk and fairy tales p30-35 **398.2**
Munachar and Manachar
In The Scott, Foresman anthology of children's literature p171-73 **808.8**
Tattercoats (k-2) **398.2**
also in The Scott, Foresman anthology of children's literature p155-57 **808.8**
Teeny-Tiny
In Best-loved folktales of the world p219-20 **398.2**
The three bears
In Tomie dePaola's favorite nursery tales p55-61 **398.2**
The three little pigs
In Tomie dePaola's favorite nursery tales p34-38 **398.2**
Tom Tit Tot
In Best-loved folktales of the world p207-11 **398.2**
In The Scott, Foresman anthology of children's literature p153-55 **808.8**
Galdone, P. King of the Cats **398.2**
Galdone, P. The three little pigs **398.2**
Galdone, P. The three sillies **398.2**
The Hare and the tortoise. See The Hare and the tortoise **398.2**

Jacobs, Linda
Letting off steam (3-6) **621.44**

Jacobs, Paul Samuel
Born into light (6 and up) **Fic**

Jacobs, William Jay
Ellis Island (3-5) **325.73**
Great lives: human rights (5 and up) **920**

Jacobsen, Karen
Korea (2-4) **951.9**
South Africa (2-4) **968**
Thailand (2-4) **959.3**

Jacobsen, Peter Otto
A family in the Persian Gulf (2-4) **953**

Jacobson, Helen
Mischel, F. How to write a letter **808**

Jacomb-Hood, George Percy, 1857-1929
(il) The Blue fairy book. See The Blue fairy book **398.2**

Jacques, Brian
Mattimeo (6 and up) **Fic**
Redwall (6 and up) **Fic**

Jacuzzi, Candido, 1903-1986
See/See also pages in the following book(s):
Aaseng, N. The problem solvers p61-68 (5 and up) **920**

Jafta. Lewin, H. E
Jafta and the wedding. Lewin, H. See note under Lewin, H. Jafta E
Jafta's father. Lewin, H. See note under Lewin, H. Jafta E
Jafta's mother. Lewin, H. See note under Lewin, H. Jafta E
Jafta—the journey. Lewin, H. See note under Lewin, H. Jafta E
Jafta—the town. Lewin, H. See note under Lewin, H. Jafta E
Jagendorf, M. A. (Moritz Adolph), b. 1888
Anansi play with fire, Anansi get burned
In Best-loved folktales of the world p741-44 **398.2**
Gray moss on green trees
In The Scott, Foresman anthology of children's literature p387-88 **808.8**
In Arkansas stick to bears: don't mess with swampland skeeters
In The Scott, Foresman anthology of children's literature p372-73 **808.8**
King clothes
In The Scott, Foresman anthology of children's literature p259-60 **808.8**
The king of the mountains
In The Scott, Foresman anthology of children's literature p400-01 **808.8**
Mike Hooter and the smart bears in Mississippi
In The Scott, Foresman anthology of children's literature p370-72 **808.8**
Oversmart is bad luck
In The Scott, Foresman anthology of children's literature p401-02 **808.8**
Pancho Villa and the Devil
In The Scott, Foresman anthology of children's literature p406-07 **808.8**
The sacred drum of Tepozteco
In The Scott, Foresman anthology of children's literature p405-06 **808.8**
The story of the smart parrot
In Best-loved folktales of the world p748-49 **398.2**
The tale of the golden vase and the bright monkeys
In The Scott, Foresman anthology of children's literature p326-27 **808.8**
Uncle Bouqui and little Malice
In Best-loved folktales of the world p734-38 **398.2**
Who rules the roost?
In The Scott, Foresman anthology of children's literature p396-98 **808.8**
Jagendorf, Moritz Adolph *See* Jagendorf, M. A. (Moritz Adolph), b. 1888
The **jaguar** and the crested curassow. Sherlock, Sir P. M.
In Sherlock, Sir P. M. West Indian folktales p27-33 **398.2**
Jakobsen, Arild
(il) Klingsheim, T. B. Julius **599.88**
Jam day. Joosse, B. M. **E**
Jamaica

Fiction

Pomerantz, C. The chalk doll **E**
Samuels, V. Carry, go, bring, come **E**

Folklore

See Folklore—Jamaica
Jamaica tag-along. Havill, J. **E**
Jamberry. Degen, B. **E**
Jambo means hello. Feelings, M. **E**
James, Betsy
Natalie underneath **E**
What's that room for? See note under James, B. Natalie underneath **E**
James, Derek
(il) Alcott, L. M. Little women **Fic**
James, Elizabeth
How to be school smart (5 and up) **371.3**
(jt. auth) Barkin, C. Happy Valentine's Day! **394.2**
(jt. auth) Barkin, C. Jobs for kids **650.1**
(jt. auth) Barkin, C. The scary Halloween costume book **391**
James, Ian
Italy (4-6) **945**
James, Mary, 1927-
Shoebag (5 and up) **Fic**
James, Simon
Ancient Rome (4 and up) **937**
James, Will, 1892-1942
Smoky, the cow horse (6 and up) **Fic**
See/See also pages in the following book(s):
Newbery Medal books, 1922-1955 p47-48 **028.5**
James and the giant peach. Dahl, R. **Fic**
James and the giant peach, Roald Dahl's. George, R. R. **822**
James Marshall's Mother Goose (k-3) **398.8**
Jamestown (Va.)

History

Fritz, J. The double life of Pocahontas (4 and up) **92**
Jane-Emily. Clapp, P. **Fic**
Jane gets a donkey. Schwartz, A.
In Schwartz, A. All of our noses are here, and other noodle tales p8-17 **398.2**
Jane grows a carrot. Schwartz, A.
In Schwartz, A. There is a carrot in my ear, and other noodle tales p40-43 **398.2**

Janeczko, Paul B., 1945-
Loads of codes and secret ciphers (5 and up) **652**
(comp) The Place my words are looking for. See The Place my words are looking for **811.008**
(comp) This delicious day. See This delicious day **811.008**
Janie's private eyes. Snyder, Z. K. See note under Snyder, Z. K. The headless cupid **Fic**
January brings the snow. Coleridge, S. **821**
Japan
Haskins, J. Count your way through Japan (2-4) **952**
Japan—in pictures (5 and up) **952**
Children
See Children—Japan
Civilization
See/See also pages in the following book(s):
Blumberg, R. Commodore Perry in the land of the Shogun p44-53 (5 and up) **952**
Fiction
Baker, K. The magic fan **E**
Coatsworth, E. J. The cat who went to heaven (4 and up) **Fic**
Friedman, I. R. How my parents learned to eat **E**
Iwamatsu, A. J. Crow Boy **E**
Kalman, M. Sayonora, Mrs. Kackleman **E**
Paterson, K. The master puppeteer (6 and up) **Fic**
Paterson, K. Of nightingales that weep (6 and up) **Fic**
Say, A. The bicycle man **E**
Watkins, Y. K. So far from the bamboo grove (6 and up) **Fic**
Wisniewski, D. The warrior and the wise man **E**
Folklore
See Folklore—Japan
Foreign relations—United States
Blumberg, R. Commodore Perry in the land of the Shogun (5 and up) **952**
Social life and customs
Birmingham, L. Japan (3-5) **952**
Japan—in pictures (5 and up) **952**
Japanese Americans
Hamanaka, S. The journey (5 and up) **305.8**
Leathers, N. L. The Japanese in America *In* The In America series **305.8**
Evacuation and relocation, 1942-1945
Davis, D. S. Behind barbed wire: the imprisonment of Japanese Americans during World War II (5 and up) **940.54**
Hamanaka, S. The journey (5 and up) **305.8**
Evacuation and relocation, 1942-1945—Fiction
Uchida, Y. Journey to Topaz **Fic**
Fiction
Uchida, Y. A jar of dreams (5 and up) **Fic**
Uchida, Y. Journey home (5 and up) **Fic**
Japanese civilization *See* Japan—Civilization
Japanese fencing *See* Kendo
The **Japanese** in America. Leathers, N. L. *In* The In America series **305.8**
Japanese poetry
Collected works
In a spring garden (k-3) **895.6**
Jaques, Faith, 1923-
(il) Masefield, J. The box of delights; or, When the wolves were running **Fic**
A **jar** of dreams. Uchida, Y. **Fic**
Jaramillo Levi, Enrique, 1944-
The cave
In Where angels glide at dawn p43-48 **S C**
Jarrell, Randall, 1914-1965
The animal family (4 and up) **Fic**
The bat-poet **Fic**
Jason (Greek mythology)
Evslin, B. Jason and the Argonauts (6 and up) **292**
Fisher, L. E. Jason and the golden fleece (3-6) **292**
Jason and the Argonauts. Evslin, B. **292**
Jason and the golden fleece. Fisher, L. E. **292**
Jaspersohn, William
Bat, ball, glove (3-5) **796.357**
How the forest grew (2-4) **574.5**
Ice cream (3-5) **637**
Motorcycle: the making of a Harley-Davidson (5 and up) **629.227**
Jataka stories
Galdone, P. The monkey and the crocodile (k-2) **398.2**
Jay, Hilda L., 1921-
Developing library-museum partnerships to serve young people **027.8**
Jay, John, 1745-1829
See/See also pages in the following book(s):
Hauptly, D. J. "A convention of delegates" p89-104 (5 and up) **342**

Jay, M. Ellen
(jt. auth) Jay, H. L. Developing library-museum partnerships to serve young people 027.8
Jazz musicians
Collier, J. L. Louis Armstrong: an American success story (5 and up) 92
The **jealous** apprentice. Aiken, J.
In Aiken, J. Give yourself a fright: thirteen tales of the supernatural p56-69 S C
The **jealous** husband. Terada, A. M.
In Terada, A. M. Under the starfruit tree p10-13 398.2
Jean Labadie's big black dog. Carlson, N. S.
In Carlson, N. S. The talking cat, and other stories of French Canada p30-42 S C
Jean-Pierre and the old witch. Martin, E.
In Martin, E. Tales of the Far North p61-69 398.2
The **Jedera** adventure. Alexander, L. See note under Alexander, L. The Illyrian adventure Fic
Jefferis, David
Helicopters (1-3) 629.133
Supersonic flight (4 and up) 629.133
Jeffers, Susan
Three jovial huntsmen (k-2) 398.8
Wild Robin E
(il) Brown, M. W. Baby animals E
(il) Ehrlich, A. The Snow Queen Fic
(il) Ehrlich, A. The wild swans E
(il) Frost, R. Stopping by woods on a snowy evening 811
(il) Grimm, J. Hansel and Gretel 398.2
(il) Lindbergh, R. Benjamin's barn E
(il) Longfellow, H. W. Hiawatha 811
(il) Marzollo, J. Close your eyes E
(il) Mohr, J. Silent night 782.28
Jefferson, Thomas, 1743-1826
About
Adler, D. A. A picture book of Thomas Jefferson (1-3) 92
Quackenbush, R. M. Pass the quill, I'll write a draft: a story of Thomas Jefferson (2-4) 92
See/See also pages in the following book(s):
Phelan, M. K. The story of the Louisiana Purchase p15-26, 53-63 (5 and up) 973.4
Homes and haunts
Fisher, L. E. Monticello (4 and up) 973.4
Jellybean. Duder, T. Fic
Jellyfish
Coldrey, J. The world of a jellyfish (k-2) 593.7
Jenkins, William Atwell, 1922-
(jt. auth) Schiller, A. Roget's children's thesaurus 423
(jt. auth) Schiller, A. Roget's student thesaurus 423
Jenness, Aylette
Families (4 and up) 306.8
In two worlds: a Yup'ik Eskimo family (4 and up) 970.004
Jennie's hat. Keats, E. J. E
Jennifer, Hecate, Macbeth, William McKinley, and me, Elizabeth. Konigsburg, E. L. Fic
Jennings, Linda M.
The Christmas Tomten E
Jenny Archer, author. Conford, E. See note under Conford, E. A case for Jenny Archer Fic
Jenny Archer to the rescue. Conford, E. See note under Conford, E. A case for Jenny Archer Fic
Jenny Green Teeth. Leach, M.
In Leach, M. Whistle in the graveyard p85 398.2
Jensen, Virginia Allen
Catching E
Red thread riddles 793.73
Jeremiah in the dark woods. Ahlberg, J. Fic
Jeremy isn't hungry. Williams, B. E
Jeremy Visick. Wiseman, D. Fic
Jernigan, E. W.
(il) Jernigan, G. Agave blooms just once E
Jernigan, Gisela, 1948-
Agave blooms just once E
Jerusalem
Kuskin, K. Jerusalem, shining still (2-4) 956.94
Jerusalem, shining still. Kuskin, K. 956.94
Jesse Bear, what will you wear? Carlstrom, N. W. E
Jesse Jackson: a biography. McKissack, P. C. 92
Jesse White Tumbling Team
Schmidt, D. I am a Jesse White tumbler 796.47
Jesse's ghost. Porte-Thomas, B. A.
In Porte-Thomas, B. A. Jesse's ghost, and other stories p45-53 S C
Jesse's ghost, and other stories. Porte-Thomas, B. A. S C
Jessica. Henkes, K. E
Jester
Afanas'ev, A. N. The jester
In Afanas'ev, A. N. Russian fairy tales p151-55 398.2

Jesus Christ

About

Bible. N.T. Selections. Easter, the King James Version (4 and up) **232.9**
De Paola, T. The miracles of Jesus (1-3) **232.9**
Fisher, A. L. Easter (1-3) **394.2**
Winthrop, E. He is risen: the Easter story (2-5) **232.9**
Branley, F. M. The Christmas sky (3-6) **232.9**

Fiction

Speare, E. G. The bronze bow (6 and up) **Fic**

Nativity

Bible. N.T. Selections. The Christ child (k-3) **232.9**
Bible. N.T. Selections. The Christmas story (k-3) **232.9**
Bible. N.T. Selections. Christmas, the King James Version **232.9**
Brown, M. W. Christmas in the barn (k-2) **232.9**
Koralek, J. The cobweb curtain **E**
Kurelek, W. A northern nativity (4 and up) **232.9**
Laird, E. The road to Bethlehem (4-6) **232.9**
Lindgren, A. Christmas in the stable (k-2) **232.9**
Winthrop, E. A child is born: the Christmas story (k-3) **232.9**

Nativity—Fiction

Menotti, G. C. Amahl and the night visitors (2-4) **Fic**
Wildsmith, B. A Christmas story **E**

Jett-Simpson, Mary, 1938-
(ed) National Council of Teachers of English. Committee on the Elementary School Booklist. Adventuring with books **011.6**

Jew among the thorns
Grimm, J. The Jew among thorns
In Grimm, J. The complete Grimm's fairy tales p503-08 **398.2**

The **Jew** among thorns. Grimm, J.
In Grimm, J. The complete Grimm's fairy tales p503-08 **398.2**

Jewett, Eleanore Myers, 1890-1967
Which was witch?
In The Scott, Foresman anthology of children's literature p336-38 **808.8**

The **Jewish** Americans: a history in their own words, 1650-1950 (6 and up) **305.8**

Jewish art and symbolism
Chaikin, M. Menorahs, mezuzas, and other Jewish symbols (5 and up) **296.4**

Jewish cookery *See* Cookery, Jewish

Jewish holidays *See* Fasts and feasts—Judaism

Jewish legends *See* Legends, Jewish

Jewish literature
See also Yiddish literature

History and criticism

See/See also pages in the following book(s):
Meltzer, M. World of our fathers: the Jews of Eastern Europe p155-75 (6 and up) **305.8**

Jewish New Year *See* Rosh ha-Shanah

Jewish refugees *See* Refugees, Jewish

Jewish wit and humor
See/See also pages in the following book(s):
Bauer, C. F. Celebrations p119-34 **808.8**

Jews

Education

See/See also pages in the following book(s):
Meltzer, M. World of our fathers: the Jews of Eastern Europe p112-29 (6 and up) **305.8**

Festivals

See Fasts and feasts—Judaism

Fiction

Caseley, J. When Grandpa came to stay **E**
Chaikin, M. Yossi asks the angels for help (3-5) **Fic**
Clifford, E. The remembering box (3-5) **Fic**
Cohen, B. Molly's Pilgrim (2-4) **Fic**
Goldin, B. D. Just enough is plenty: a Hanukkah tale **E**
Hest, A. Fancy Aunt Jess **E**
Kimmel, E. A. Hershel and the Hanukkah goblins **E**
Little, J. Kate (4-6) **Fic**
Phillips, M. The sign in Mendel's window **E**
Sholem Aleichem. Holiday tales of Sholom Aleichem (5 and up) **S C**
Shulevitz, U. Hanukah money **E**
Singer, I. B. The fools of Chelm and their history (3-6) **Fic**
Singer, I. B. The power of light (4 and up) **S C**
Singer, I. B. Stories for children (4 and up) **S C**
Yolen, J. The devil's arithmetic (4 and up) **Fic**

Folklore

Cohen, B. Yussel's prayer (3-5) **398.2**
Freedman, F. B. Brothers: a Hebrew legend (k-2) **398.2**
Hirsh, M. Could anything be worse? (k-3) **398.2**

Jews—Folklore—*Continued*
Simon, S. More wise men of Helm and their merry tales (4 and up) **398.2**
Singer, I. B. Mazel and Shlimazel (2-5) **398.2**
Singer, I. B. When Shlemiel went to Warsaw & other stories (4 and up) **398.2**
Singer, I. B. Zlateh the goat, and other stories (4 and up) **398.2**

History
Fisher, L. E. The Wailing Wall (4 and up) **221.9**

Persecutions
See also Holocaust, Jewish (1933-1945)

See/See also pages in the following book(s):
Meltzer, M. World of our fathers: the Jews of Eastern Europe p36-62, 196-218, 232-52 (6 and up) **305.8**

Restoration
See also Zionism

Rites and ceremonies
See Judaism—Customs and practices

Austria—Fiction
Orgel, D. The devil in Vienna (6 and up) **Fic**

Eastern Europe
Meltzer, M. World of our fathers: the Jews of Eastern Europe (6 and up) **305.8**

Ethiopia—Fiction
Levitin, S. The return (6 and up) **Fic**

France—Fiction
Roth-Hano, R. Touch wood (6 and up) **Fic**

Germany
Koehn, I. Mischling, second degree: my childhood in Nazi Germany (6 and up) **92**

Netherlands
Frank, A. The diary of a young girl (6 and up) **92**
Hurwitz, J. Anne Frank: life in hiding (3-5) **92**
Reiss, J. The upstairs room (4 and up) **92**

New York (N.Y.)
Costabel, E. D. The Jews of New Amsterdam (2-4) **974.7**

New York (N.Y.)—Fiction
Chaikin, M. Finders weepers (3-5) **Fic**
Cohen, B. The carp in the bathtub (2-4) **Fic**
Levoy, M. Alan and Naomi (6 and up) **Fic**
Taylor, S. All-of-a-kind family (4-6) **Fic**

Poland—Fiction
Hautzig, E. R. A gift for Mama (3-6) **Fic**
Orlev, U. The island on Bird Street (5 and up) **Fic**
Singer, I. B. Naftali the storyteller and his horse, Sus, and other stories (4 and up) **S C**

Soviet Union—Fiction
Herman, C. The house on Walenska Street (3-5) **Fic**

United States
Butwin, F. The Jews in America
In The In America series **305.8**

United States—Fiction
Konigsburg, E. L. About the B'nai Bagels (4-6) **Fic**
Levitin, S. Silver days (5 and up) **Fic**

United States—History—Sources
The Jewish Americans: a history in their own words, 1650-1950 (6 and up) **305.8**

Jews and Gentiles
See also Antisemitism

The **Jews** in America. Butwin, F.
In The In America series **305.8**

Jews in literature
See/See also pages in the following book(s):
Crosscurrents of criticism p150-58 **028.5**

The **Jews** of New Amsterdam. Costabel, E. D. **974.7**

The **jigsaw** puzzle, a story. Stamper, J. B.
In Halloween: stories and poems p25-35 **808.8**

Jim meets The Thing. Cohen, M. See note under Cohen, M. See you in second grade! **E**

Jimmy's boa and the big splash birthday bash. Noble, T. H. See note under Noble, T. H. The day Jimmy's boa ate the wash **E**

Jimmy's boa bounces back. Noble, T. H. See note under Noble, T. H. The day Jimmy's boa ate the wash **E**

Jim's dog Muffins. Cohen, M. See note under Cohen, M. See you in second grade! **E**

Jin Xuqi
The giant panda (5 and up) **599.74**

A **job** for Jenny Archer. Conford, E. See note under Conford, E. A case for Jenny Archer **Fic**

Job placement guidance *See* Vocational guidance

Jobb, Jamie
The night sky book (4 and up) **523**

Jobs, Steven
See/See also pages in the following book(s):
Aaseng, N. From rags to riches p64-75 (5 and up) **920**

Jobs *See* Occupations
Jobs for kids. Barkin, C. **650.1**
Jobson, Ron
(il) Jefferis, D. Helicopters **629.133**
(il) Jefferis, D. Supersonic flight **629.133**
Joel, growing up a farm man. Demuth, P. **630.1**
Johansen, Hanna, 1939-
7 x 7 tales of a sevensleeper (2-4) **Fic**
Johanson, Donald C.
See/See also pages in the following book(s):
Lasky, K. Traces of life p12-20 (5 and up) **573.2**
John, Helen
(il) Taylor, S. All-of-a-kind family **Fic**
John and the Devil's daughter. Hamilton, V.
In Hamilton, V. The people could fly: American black folktales p107-15 **398.2**
John and the fiddler. Foley, P. **Fic**
John Henry (Legendary character)
Keats, E. J. John Henry (k-3) **398.2**
John Henry. Winter, B.
In Holiday plays round the year p239-46 **812.008**
John in court. Sanfield, S.
In Sanfield, S. The adventures of High John the Conqueror **398.2**
John Muir. Force, E. **92**
John Patrick Norman McHennessy—the boy who was always late. Burningham, J. **E**
John Tabor's ride. Day, E. C. **E**
John Treegate's musket. Wibberley, L. **Fic**
John wins a bet. Sanfield, S.
In Sanfield, S. The adventures of High John the Conqueror **398.2**
Johnny and the three goats
In Tomie dePaola's favorite nursery tales p70-74 **398.2**
Johnny Appleseed. Kellogg, S. **92**
Johnny-cake
Jacobs, J. Johnny-cake
In Jacobs, J. English fairy tales p155-58 **398.2**
In Tomie dePaola's favorite nursery tales p11-15 **398.2**
Sawyer, R. Journey cake, ho! **398.2**
Williams-Ellis, A. Johnny-cake
In Williams-Ellis, A. Tales from the enchanted world p96-101 **398.2**
Johnny Gloke
Reeves, J. Johnny Gloke
In Reeves, J. English fables and fairy stories p23-34 **398.2**
Johnny Lion's bad day. Hurd, E. T. See note under Hurd, E. T. Johnny Lion's book **E**
Johnny Lion's book. Hurd, E. T. **E**
Johnny Lion's rubber boots. Hurd, E. T. See note under Hurd, E. T. Johnny Lion's book **E**
Johnny Tremain. Forbes, E. **Fic**
John's memory. Sanfield, S.
In Sanfield, S. The adventures of High John the Conqueror **398.2**
Johnson, Amy
(il) Ferris, J. What are you figuring now? a story about Benjamin Banneker **92**
Johnson, Angela
Do like Kyla **E**
Tell me a story, Mama **E**
Johnson, Annabel, 1921-
The grizzly (5 and up) **Fic**
Johnson, Crockett, 1906-1975
Harold and the purple crayon **E**
Harold's ABC. See note under Johnson, C. Harold and the purple crayon **E**
Harold's circus. See note under Johnson, C. Harold and the purple crayon **E**
Harold's trip to the sky. See note under Johnson, C. Harold and the purple crayon **E**
A picture for Harold's room. See note under Johnson, C. Harold and the purple crayon **E**
(il) Krauss, R. The carrot seed **E**
Johnson, Edgar, 1912-
(jt. auth) Johnson, A. The grizzly **Fic**
Johnson, Eric W.
Love and sex and growing up (4 and up) **613.9**
People, love, sex, and families (5 and up) **613.9**
Johnson, Holly
(il) Alcott, L. M. An old-fashioned Thanksgiving **Fic**
Johnson, James E.
The Irish in America
In The In America series **305.8**
The Scots and Scotch-Irish in America
In The In America series **305.8**
Johnson, Milton, 1932-
(il) O'Dell, S. The black pearl **Fic**
Johnson, Neil
All in a day's work (4 and up) **331.7**
The Battle of Gettysburg (5 and up) **973.7**

Johnson, Pamela
(il) Facklam, M. Do not disturb **591.5**
(il) Facklam, M. Partners for life **591.5**
(il) Freedman, R. When winter comes **591.5**
(il) Stolz, M. The cuckoo clock **Fic**
(il) Stolz, M. Quentin Corn **Fic**

Johnson, Pamela Ford
(il) Cohen, D. Prehistoric animals **560**

Johnson, Rebecca L.
Diving into darkness: a submersible explores the sea (4 and up) **551.46**
The greenhouse effect (5 and up) **363.7**
The secret language: pheromones in the animal world (5 and up) **591.5**

Johnson, Steve
(il) Smucker, A. E. No star nights **E**

Johnson, Sylvia A.
Apple trees (4 and up) **634**
Beetles (4 and up) **595.7**
Chirping insects (4 and up) **595.7**
Coral reefs (4 and up) **574.92**
Elephant seals (4 and up) **599.74**
Fireflies (4 and up) **595.7**
Hermit crabs (4 and up) **595.3**
Inside an egg (4 and up) **598**
Ladybugs (4 and up) **595.7**
Mosses (4 and up) **588**
Mushrooms (4 and up) **589.2**
Potatoes (4 and up) **635**
Rice (4 and up) **633.1**
Wasps (4 and up) **595.7**
Water insects (4 and up) **595.7**
Wheat (4 and up) **633.1**
Wolf pack (4 and up) **599.74**
(jt. auth) Casagrande, L. B. Focus on Mexico **972**

Johnston, Annie Bronn
Fiction
Henry, M. Mustang, wild spirit of the West (5 and up) **Fic**

Johnston, Ginny, 1946-
Scaly babies (3-5) **597.9**
Windows on wildlife (3-6) **590.74**
(jt. auth) Cutchins, J. Scoots, the bog turtle **597.9**

Johnston, Hugh Anthony Stephen, 1913-1967
The great tug-of-war
In The Scott, Foresman anthology of children's literature p306-10 **808.8**

Johnston, Tony
The badger and the magic fan (k-3) **398.2**
The quilt story **E**
The vanishing pumpkin **E**
The witch's hat **E**
Yonder **E**

The **joke**. Pogodin, R. P.
In Face to face: a collection of stories by celebrated Soviet and American writers p91-99 **S C**

Jokes
Cricket's jokes, riddles and other stuff (1-4) **793.73**
Keller, C. It's raining cats and dogs (2-4) **793.73**
Phillips, L. Going ape (3-5) **793.73**
Phillips, L. Haunted house jokes (3-5) **793.73**
Phillips, L. How do you get a horse out of the bathtub? (5 and up) **793.73**
Rosenbloom, J. Knock-knock! who's there (4 and up) **808.87**
Schwartz, A. Witcracks: jokes and jests from American folklore (4 and up) **398**

Jokes of Single-Toe
Davis, R. The jokes of Single-Toe
In The Scott, Foresman anthology of children's literature p254-56 **808.8**

Jokes, riddles and other stuff, Cricket's **793.73**

The **jolly** tailor. Borski, L. M.
In Rainy day: stories and poems p23-33 **808.8**

Jonah (Biblical figure)
About
Hutton, W. Jonah and the great fish (k-3) **224**
Spier, P. The Book of Jonah (k-3) **224**

Jonah and the great fish. Hutton, W. **224**

Jonas, Ann
Color dance **E**
Holes and peeks **E**
Now we can go **E**
The quilt **E**
Reflections **E**
Round trip **E**
The trek **E**
Two bear cubs **E**
When you were a baby **E**

Jones, Corbett
(il) Cuyler, M. The all-around pumpkin book **641.3**

Jones, Diana Wynne
Archer's goon (6 and up) **Fic**
Chair Person
In Things that go bump in the night p122-63 **S C**
Dogsbody (6 and up) **Fic**
Eight days of Luke (5 and up) **Fic**
Howl's moving castle (6 and up) **Fic**

Jones, Dolores Blythe
(ed) Children's media market place. See Children's media market place **070.5025**

Jones, Elizabeth Orton, 1910-
(il) Field, R. Prayer for a child **242**
See/See also pages in the following book(s):
Caldecott Medal books, 1938-1957 p118-30 **028.5**
Jones, Helen Hinckley, 1903-
Israel (4 and up) **956.94**
Jones, Janice Beare
Secrets of a summer spy (5 and up) **Fic**
Jones, Jayne Clark
The American Indian in America
In The In America series **305.8**
The Greeks in America
In The In America series **305.8**
Jones, Malcolm, 1952-
(jt. auth) Parks, V. D. Jump! the adventures of Brer Rabbit **398.2**
Jones, Pattie Ridley
(jt. auth) Greenfield, E. Childtimes: a three-generation memoir **920**
Jones, Rebecca C., 1947-
The Believers (5 and up) **Fic**
Germy Blew it. See note under Jones, R. C. Germy blew the Bugle **Fic**
Germy blew it—again! See note under Jones, R. C. Germy blew the Bugle **Fic**
Germy blew the Bugle (4-6) **Fic**
Jones, T. Gwynn (Thomas Gwynn), 1871-1949
The cow on the roof
In Best-loved folktales of the world p283-84 **398.2**
Jones, Thomas Gwynn *See* Jones, T. Gwynn (Thomas Gwynn), 1871-1949
Jones, Weyman
Edge of two worlds (5 and up) **Fic**
Joosse, Barbara M., 1949-
Jam day **E**
Joplin, Scott, 1868-1917
About
Mitchell, B. Raggin': a story about Scott Joplin (3-5) **92**
Jordan, Alice Mabel
From Rollo to Tom Sawyer, and other papers **028.5**
Jordan, Helene J.
How a seed grows (k-3) **582**
Jordan, June, 1936-
Kimako's story (2-4) **Fic**
Jordan, MaryKate
Losing Uncle Tim (2-4) **Fic**
Jordan, Michael
About
Deegan, P. J. Michael Jordan: basketball's soaring star (4 and up) **92**
Jordan, Robert Paul
The Civil War (6 and up) **973.7**
Jordan
Jordan—in pictures (5 and up) **956.95**
Jordan—in pictures (5 and up) **956.95**
Jorgensen, Gail
Crocodile beat **E**
Jorinda and Joringel. Grimm, J.
In Grimm, J. The complete Grimm's fairy tales p339-42 **398.2**
In Grimm, J. More tales from Grimm p229-39 **398.2**
Jorinde and Joringel
Grimm, J. Jorinda and Joringel
In Grimm, J. The complete Grimm's fairy tales p339-42 **398.2**
In Grimm, J. More tales from Grimm p229-39 **398.2**
Grimm, J. Jorinde and Joringel
In The Green fairy book p271-75 **398.2**
Grimm, J. Wanda Gág's Jorinda and Joringel **398.2**
Jo's boys. Alcott, L. M. See note under Alcott, L. M. Little women **Fic**
The **Josefina** story quilt. Coerr, E. **E**
Joseph, Nez Percé Chief, 1840-1904
See/See also pages in the following book(s):
Freedman, R. Indian chiefs p90-113 (6 and up) **920**
Jacobs, W. J. Great lives: human rights p131-37 (5 and up) **920**
Joseph & Koza. Singer, I. B.
In Singer, I. B. Stories for children p139-54 **S C**
Joshua (Biblical figure)
About
Chaikin, M. Joshua in the Promised Land (4 and up) **222**
Joshua. Porte-Thomas, B. A.
In Porte-Thomas, B. A. Jesse's ghost, and other stories p89-100 **S C**
Joshua in the Promised Land. Chaikin, M. **222**
Joslin, Sesyle
What do you do, dear? (k-2) **395**
What do you say, dear? (k-2) **395**
Journal of Youth Services in Libraries **027.6205**
Journalism
See also College and school journalism
See/See also pages in the following book(s):
Kaye, C. B. Word works p77-90 (4 and up) **410**
Fiction
Sharmat, M. W. Mysteriously yours, Maggie Marmelstein (3-6) **Fic**

Journals *See* Periodicals
The **journey**. Hamanaka, S. 305.8
Journey cake, ho! Sawyer, R. 398.2
The **journey** home. Holland, I. Fic
Journey home. Uchida, Y. Fic
Journey into a black hole. Branley, F. M. 523.8
Journey into space. Atkinson, S. 523
Journey through a tropical jungle. Forsyth, A. 574.5
Journey to an 800 number. Konigsburg, E. L. Fic
Journey to Asamando. Kwarteng, K.
In The Crest and the hide, and other African stories of heroes, chiefs, bards, hunters, sorcerers, and common people p115-21 398.2
Journey to Jo'burg. Naidoo, B. Fic
Journey to the planets. Lauber, P. 523.4
Journey to Topaz. Uchida, Y. Fic
Journeys *See* Voyages and travels
Joyce, William
A day with Wilbur Robinson E
Dinosaur Bob and his adventures with the family Lazardo E
George shrinks E
(il) Manes, S. Some of the adventures of Rhode Island Red Fic
(il) Maxner, J. Nicholas Cricket E
(il) Wahl, J. Humphrey's bear E
(il) Winthrop, E. Shoes E
Joyful noise: poems for two voices. Fleischman, P. 811
Joyner, Jerry, 1938-
(jt. auth) Charlip, R. Thirteen E
Juan, de Pareja
Treviño, E. B. de. I, Juan de Pareja (6 and up) Fic
Juba this and Juba that 372.6
Stories included are: The yellow ribbon; The Snooks family; The Hobyahs; Sody saleratus; The busy farmer's wife; The lion hunt; The shopping trip; I went to the library
Judaism
See also Fasts and feasts—Judaism
Customs and practices
See also Bar mitzvah; Bat mitzvah
Chaikin, M. Menorahs, mezuzas, and other Jewish symbols (5 and up) 296.4
Drucker, M. Celebrating life: Jewish rites of passage (4 and up) 296.4
The **judge**. Zemach, H. E
Judges
Fiction
Zemach, H. The judge E
Judkis, Jim
(il) Rogers, F. Going on an airplane 387.7
(il) Rogers, F. Going to the dentist 617.6
(il) Rogers, F. Going to the hospital 362.1
(il) Rogers, F. Making friends 155.4
(il) Rogers, F. Moving 155.4
(il) Rogers, F. When a pet dies 155.9
Judo
See/See also pages in the following book(s):
Ribner, S. The martial arts p42-82 (5 and up) 796.8
The **juggler** of Notre Dame. Sawyer, R.
In Sawyer, R. The way of the storyteller p273-81 372.6
Jukes, Mavis
Blackberries in the dark (2-4) Fic
Cross your fingers
In Free to be—a family p113-21 810.8
Lights around the palm E
Like Jake and me (2-4) Fic
Two can play the same game
In Free to be—a family p74-77 810.8
Julia and the hand of God. Cameron, E. See note under Cameron, E. A room made of windows Fic
Julian. Khalsa, D. K. E
Julian, dream doctor. Cameron, A. See note under Cameron, A. The stories Julian tells Fic
Julian, secret agent. Cameron, A. See note under Cameron, A. The stories Julian tells Fic
Julian's glorious summer. Cameron, A. See note under Cameron, A. The stories Julian tells Fic
Julia's magic. Cameron, E. See note under Cameron, E. A room made of windows Fic
Julie of the wolves. George, J. C. Fic
Julius. Klingsheim, T. B. 599.88
Julius, the baby of the world. Henkes, K. E
July. Stevenson, J. 92
Jumanji. Van Allsburg, C. E
The **Jumblies**. Lear, E. 821
Jump!. Kalbfleisch, S. 796.2
Jump! the adventures of Brer Rabbit. Parks, V. D. 398.2
Jump again! more adventures of Brer Rabbit. Parks, V. D. 398.2
Jump on over! the adventures of Brer Rabbit and his family. Parks, V. D. 398.2

Jump, frog, jump! Kalan, R. **E**
Jump rope *See* Rope skipping
Jump rope rhymes
Anna Banana: 101 jump-rope rhymes (2-4) **398.8**
Jump ship to freedom. Collier, J. L. **Fic**
The **jungle** books. Kipling, R. **S C**
Jungle ecology
Catchpole, C. Jungles (2-4) **574.5**
Podendorf, I. Jungles (2-4) **574.5**
Jungles. Catchpole, C. **574.5**
Jungles. Podendorf, I. **574.5**
The **Junior** book of authors **920.003**
Junior companion to music, The Oxford. Hurd, M. **780.3**
Junior cook book, Better Homes and Gardens. See New junior cook book **641.5**
Junior high school libraries *See* School libraries (High school)
Junior high school library catalog **011.6**
Junior karate. Kozuki, R. **796.8**
Junior thesaurus: In other words II. See Schiller, A. Roget's student thesaurus **423**
Juniorplots 3: a book talk guide for use with readers ages 12-16. Gillespie, J. T. **028.1**
Juniorplots: a book talk manual for teachers and librarians. Gillespie, J. T. **028.1**
Juniper, Gentian, and Rosemary. Dean, P.
In Things that go bump in the night p255-76 **S C**
Juniper tree
Grimm, J. The juniper tree
In Best-loved folktales of the world p115-22 **398.2**
In Grimm, J. The complete Grimm's fairy tales p220-29 **398.2**
In Grimm, J. The juniper tree, and other tales from Grimm v2 p314-32 **398.2**
The **juniper** tree, and other tales from Grimm. Grimm, J. **398.2**
Junk food—what it is, what it does. Seixas, J. S. **641.3**
Junk in space. Maurer, R. **363.7**
Junne, I. K.
The fisherman and the gatekeeper
In Best-loved folktales of the world p567-68 **398.2**
Hats to disappear with
In Best-loved folktales of the world p561-62 **398.2**
Mister Lazybones
In Best-loved folktales of the world p565-67 **398.2**
Jupiter (Planet)
Simon, S. Jupiter (1-4) **523.4**
See/See also pages in the following book(s):
Harris, A. The great Voyager adventure p21-32 (5 and up) **523.4**
Kelch, J. W. Small worlds: exploring the 60 moons of our solar system p51-65 (6 and up) **523.9**
Jupiter (Roman deity) *See* Zeus (Greek deity)
Jurmain, Suzanne
Once upon a horse (6 and up) **636.1**
Just a dream. Van Allsburg, C. **E**
Just an overnight guest. Tate, E. E. **Fic**
Just as long as we're together. Blume, J. **Fic**
Just enough is plenty: a Hanukkah tale. Goldin, B. D. **E**
Just like Daddy. Asch, F. See note under Asch, F. Sand cake **E**
Just me. Ets, M. H. **E**
Just one ghost. Terada, A. M.
In Terada, A. M. Under the starfruit tree p128-29 **398.2**
Just plain Al. Greene, C. C. See note under Greene, C. C. A girl called Al **Fic**
Just plain Fancy. Polacco, P. **E**
Just reward
Afanas'ev, A. N. The just reward
In Afanas'ev, A. N. Russian fairy tales p39-40 **398.2**
Just say hiç! Walker, B. K.
In Walker, B. K. A treasury of Turkish folktales for children p76-79 **398.2**
Just so stories. Kipling, R. **S C**
Just us women. Caines, J. F. **E**
Juster, Norton, 1929-
As: a surfeit of similes (3-5) **427**
The phantom tollbooth (5 and up) **Fic**
The phantom tollbooth [excerpt]
In The Random House book of humor for children p130-33 **817.008**
Justice. Babbitt, N.
In Babbitt, N. The Devil's other storybook p11-17 **S C**
Justin and the best biscuits in the world. Walter, M. P. **Fic**
Justin Morgan had a horse. Henry, M. **Fic**
Juvenile delinquency
Fiction
Myers, W. D. Scorpions (6 and up) **Fic**
Juvenile miscellany (Periodical)
See/See also pages in the following book(s):
Jordan, A. M. From Rollo to Tom Sawyer, and other papers p46-60 **028.5**

The **Juvenile** numerator
In A Nursery companion p36-37 **820.8**

K

Kaa's hunting. Kipling, R.
In Kipling, R. The jungle books **S C**
Kabungo, Oliver
The hunter and his medicine spear
In The Crest and the hide, and other African stories of heroes, chiefs, bards, hunters, sorcerers, and common people p47-51 **398.2**
The wonderful thing
In The Crest and the hide, and other African stories of heroes, chiefs, bards, hunters, sorcerers, and common people p25-29 **398.2**
Kaddo's wall. Courlander, H.
In Courlander, H. The cow-tail switch, and other West African stories p13-24 **398.2**
Kahlo, Frida, 1907-1954
See/See also pages in the following book(s):
Sills, L. Inspirations p18-27 (5 and up) **920**
Kahukura and the fairies. Te Kanawa, K.
In Te Kanawa, K. Land of the long white cloud p45-50 **398.2**
Kaizuki, Kiyonori
A calf is born (k-2) **636.2**
Kalan, Robert
Blue sea **E**
Jump, frog, jump! **E**
Kalb, Jonah
The easy baseball book (3-5) **796.357**
The easy hockey book (3-5) **796.962**
Kalbfleisch, Susan
Jump! (3-6) **796.2**
Kalman, Maira
Sayonora, Mrs. Kackleman **E**
Kalmenoff, Matthew
(il) Asimov, I. How did we find out the Earth is round? **525**
Kamen, Gloria
Charlie Chaplin (4 and up) **92**
Kipling, storyteller of East and West (3-5) **92**
(il) Levine, E. S. Lisa and her soundless world **617.8**
Kamerman, Sylvia E.
(ed) The Big book of Christmas plays. See The Big book of Christmas plays **808.82**
(ed) Holiday plays round the year. See Holiday plays round the year **812.008**
Kamikaze airplanes
See/See also pages in the following book(s):
Marrin, A. Victory in the Pacific p198-207 (6 and up) **940.54**
Kampuchea *See* Cambodia
Kandoian, Ellen
Is anybody up? **E**
Kane, Henry Bugbee
(il) McCord, D. T. W. All day long: fifty rhymes of the never was and always is **811**
(il) McCord, D. T. W. One at a time **811**
(il) McCord, D. T. W. Take sky: more rhymes of the never was and always is **811**
Kane, Joseph Nathan, 1899-
Famous first facts: a record of first happenings, discoveries, and inventions in American history **031.02**
Kangaroos
Arnold, C. Kangaroo (3-5) **599.2**
Fiction
Payne, E. Katy No-Pocket **E**
Schlein, M. Big talk **E**
Kansas
Kent, Z. Kansas
In America the beautiful **973**
Kappeler, Markus, 1953-
(jt. auth) Jin Xuqi The giant panda **599.74**
Karaçor and the giants. Walker, B. K.
In Walker, B. K. A treasury of Turkish folktales for children p52-61 **398.2**
Karas, G. Brian
(il) Cobb, V. The scoop on ice cream **637**
(il) Hughes, M. S. The great potato book **641.3**
Karate
Brimner, L. D. Karate (5 and up) **796.8**
Kozuki, R. Junior karate (5 and up) **796.8**
Nardi, T. J. Karate basics (4 and up) **796.8**
See/See also pages in the following book(s):
Ribner, S. The martial arts p10-41, 83-120 (5 and up) **796.8**
Karate basics. Nardi, T. J. **796.8**
The **Karate** Kid. Soto, G.
In Soto, G. Baseball in April, and other stories p69-80 **S C**
Kari Woodengown
Asbjørnsen, P. C. Kari Woodengown
In The Red fairy book p189-201 **398.2**
Karl, Jean, 1927-
Beloved Benjamin is waiting (4-6) **Fic**

Karlin, Barbara
Cinderella (k-2) **398.2**
Karmi, Giyora *See* Carmi, Giora
Kassa, the strong one. Courlander, H.
In Courlander, H. The cow-tail switch, and other West African stories p41-46 **398.2**
Kastner, Jill
(il) Denslow, S. P. Night owls **E**
(il) Gross, R. B. True stories about Abraham Lincoln **92**
(il) Sanders, S. R. Aurora means dawn **E**
Kasza, Keiko
When the elephant walks **E**
The wolf's chicken stew **E**
Katan, Norma Jean
Hieroglyphs, the writing of ancient Egypt **493**
Kate. Little, J. **Fic**
Kate Crackernuts. Briggs, K. M. **Fic**
Kate Crackernuts. Jacobs, J.
In Jacobs, J. English fairy tales p198-202 **398.2**
In Womenfolk and fairy tales p65-70 **398.2**
Kate Crackernuts. Rockwell, A. F.
In Rockwell, A. F. Puss in boots, and other stories p19-26 **398.2**
Kate's box. Chorao, K. **E**
Kate's car. Chorao, K. See note under Chorao, K. Kate's box **E**
Kate's quilt. Chorao, K. See note under Chorao, K. Kate's box **E**
Kate's snowman. Chorao, K. See note under Chorao, K. Kate's box **E**
Katharine's doll. Winthrop, E. **E**
Katherine Crackernuts
Jacobs, J. Kate Crackernuts
In Jacobs, J. English fairy tales p198-202 **398.2**
In Womenfolk and fairy tales p65-70 **398.2**
Rockwell, A. F. Kate Crackernuts
In Rockwell, A. F. Puss in boots, and other stories p19-26 **398.2**
Katie John. Calhoun, M. **Fic**
Katie John and Heathcliff. Calhoun, M. See note under Calhoun, M. Katie John **Fic**
Katy and the big snow. Burton, V. L. **E**
Katy No-Pocket. Payne, E. **E**
Katz, Bill *See* Katz, William A., 1924-
Katz, David, 1928-
(jt. auth) Allison, L. Gee, Wiz! **507**
Katz, Elizabeth, 1933-
India—in pictures. See India—in pictures **954**
Katz, Michael Jay, 1950-
(comp) Ten potatoes in a pot, and other counting rhymes. See Ten potatoes in a pot, and other counting rhymes **398.8**
Katz, William A., 1924-
(ed) Magazines for school libraries. See Magazines for school libraries **011.6**
Katz, William Loren
The Lincoln Brigade (5 and up) **946.081**
Katzman, Marylyn
(il) Kerina, J. African crafts **745.5**
Kaufman, Cheryl Davidson
Cooking the Caribbean way (5 and up) **641.5**
Kaufman, Richard
(il) Friedhoffer, R. Magic tricks, science facts **793.8**
Kaufman, William I.
Czar Trojan's ears
In Best-loved folktales of the world p455-57 **398.2**
Kaufmann, John
Birds are flying (k-3) **598**
Kaula, Edna Mason
Anansi and his visitor, Turtle
In Best-loved folktales of the world p618-19 **398.2**
In The Laugh book p201-03 **808.8**
How Frog lost his tail
In Best-loved folktales of the world p626-27 **398.2**
Kavaler, Lucy
Green magic: algae rediscovered (5 and up) **589.3**
Kawashima, Kazunari
(il) Johnson, S. A. Hermit crabs **595.3**
Kaye, Cathryn Berger
Word works (4 and up) **410**
Kaye, Peggy, 1948-
Games for reading **372.4**
Kazakov, Yuri Pavlovich, 1927-
Quiet morning
In Face to face: a collection of stories by celebrated Soviet and American writers p39-55 **S C**
Keaney, Leonie
(jt. auth) Brennan, J. Zoo day **590.74**
Keates, Colin
(il) Norman, D. Dinosaur **567.9**
Keats, Ezra Jack, 1916-1983
Apt. 3 **E**
Clementina's cactus **E**
Goggles. See note under Keats. E. J. The snowy day **E**

Keats, Ezra Jack, 1916-1983—*Continued*
Hi, cat! See note under Keats. E. J. The snowy day E
Jennie's hat E
John Henry (k-3) **398.2**
A letter to Amy. See note under Keats. E. J. The snowy day E
Louie E
Louie's search. See note under Keats, E. J. Louie E
Pet show! See note under Keats. E. J. The snowy day E
Peter's chair. See note under Keats. E. J. The snowy day E
Regards to the man in the moon. See note under Keats, E. J. Louie E
The snowy day E
The trip. See note under Keats, E. J. Louie E
Whistle for Willie. See note under Keats. E. J. The snowy day E
(il) In a spring garden. See In a spring garden **895.6**
Keegan, Marcia
(il) Highwater, J. Moonsong lullaby **811**
Keep looking! Selsam, M. E. **599**
Keep stompin' till the music stops. Pevsner, S. **Fic**
Keepers and creatures at the National Zoo. Thomson, P. **590.74**
Keeping, Charles, 1924-
(il) Crossley-Holland, K. Beowulf **829**
(il) Kipling, R. The beginning of the armadilloes **Fic**
(il) Sewell, A. Black Beauty **Fic**
Keeping clean. Cobb, V. **646.7**
Kehret, Peg
Sisters, long ago (5 and up) **Fic**
Keillor, Garrison
Lake Wobegon days [excerpt]
In The Random House book of humor for children p259-61 **817.008**
Keith, Eros, 1942-
(il) Fox, P. The slave dancer **Fic**
(il) Hamilton, V. The house of Dies Drear **Fic**
Keith, Hal, 1934-
(il) Math, I. More wires and watts: understanding and using electricity **537**
Keith, Harold, 1903-
Rifles for Watie (6 and up) **Fic**
Kelch, Joseph W., 1958-
Small worlds: exploring the 60 moons of our solar system (6 and up) **523.9**
Kelleher, Victor, 1939-
The red king (6 and up) **Fic**
Keller, Beverly
No beasts! no children! [excerpt]
In The Random House book of humor for children p270-75 **817.008**
Keller, Charles, 1942-
It's raining cats and dogs (2-4) **793.73**
Tongue twisters (3-6) **808.88**
Keller, Helen, 1880-1968
About
Peare, C. O. The Helen Keller story (5 and up) **92**
Keller, Holly
The best present E
Geraldine's big snow E
Geraldine's blanket E
What Alvin wanted E
(il) Berger, M. Why I cough, sneeze, shiver, hiccup, & yawn **612.8**
(il) Branley, F. M. Air is all around you **551.5**
(il) Branley, F. M. Shooting stars **523.6**
(il) Branley, F. M. Snow is falling **551.57**
(il) Gans, R. Rock collecting **552**
(il) Lauber, P. Snakes are hunters **597.9**
(il) Showers, P. Ears are for hearing **612.8**
Keller, Ronald
(il) Millay, E. S. Edna St. Vincent Millay's poems selected for young people **811**
Kelley, True, 1946-
(il) Balestrino, P. The skeleton inside you **611**
(il) Branley, F. M. It's raining cats and dogs **551.5**
(il) Branley, F. M. Sun dogs and shooting stars **523**
(il) Branley, F. M. Superstar **523.8**
(il) Branley, F. M. What the moon is like **523.3**
(il) Cole, A. I saw a purple cow, and 100 other recipes for learning **372.1**
(il) Cole, A. Purple cow to the rescue **372.1**
(il) Cole, J. Cuts, breaks, bruises, and burns **612**
(il) Eldredge, N. The fossil factory **560**
(il) Lauber, P. Get ready for robots! **629.8**
Kellogg, Elijah, 1813-1901
See/See also pages in the following book(s):
Jordan, A. M. From Rollo to Tom Sawyer, and other papers p102-12 **028.5**
Kellogg, Steven, 1941-
Aster Aardvark's alphabet adventures E
Best friends E
Can I keep him? E
Chicken Little (k-3) **398.2**
Johnny Appleseed (2-4) **92**
Much bigger than Martin E

Kellogg, Steven, 1941-—*Continued*
The mysterious tadpole E
The mystery of the missing red mitten E
Paul Bunyan (k-3) 398.2
Pecos Bill (k-3) 398.2
Pinkerton, behave! E
Prehistoric Pinkerton. See note under Kellogg, S. Pinkerton, behave! E
Ralph's secret weapon E
A Rose for Pinkerton. See note under Kellogg, S. Pinkerton, behave! E
Tallyho, Pinkerton! See note under Kellogg, S. Pinkerton, behave! E
(il) Bayer, J. A my name is Alice E
(il) Caines, J. F. Abby E
(il) Ehrlich, A. Leo, Zack, and Emmie E
(il) Ehrlich, A. Leo, Zack, and Emmie together again E
(il) Guarino, D. Is your mama a llama? E
(il) Lindbergh, R. The day the goose got loose E
(il) Mahy, M. The boy who was followed home E
(il) Mayer, M. Appelard and Liverwurst E
(il) Mayer, M. Liverwurst is missing E
(il) Noble, T. H. The day Jimmy's boa ate the wash E
(il) Paxton, T. Engelbert the elephant E
(il) Schwartz, D. M. How much is a million? E
(il) Schwartz, D. M. If you made a million E
(il) Van Leeuwen, J. The great Christmas kidnapping caper Fic

Kelly, Eric Philbrook, 1884-1960
The trumpeter of Krakow (5 and up) Fic
See/See also pages in the following book(s):
Newbery Medal books, 1922-1955 p67-73 028.5

Kelly's creek. Smith, D. B. Fic

Keloğlan and the twelve dancing princesses. Walker, B. K.
In Walker, B. K. A treasury of Turkish folktales for children p29-34 398.2

The **kelpie's** pearls. Hunter, M. Fic

Kelsey, Alice Geer
Three Fridays
In The Scott, Foresman anthology of children's literature p293-94 808.8

Kemp, Claire Minter- *See* Minter-Kemp, Claire

Kemp, Moira
(il) Williams-Ellis, A. Tales from the enchanted world 398.2

Kemp-Welch, Lucy Elizabeth, 1869-1958
(il) Sewell, A. Black Beauty Fic

Kendall, Carol
The Gammage cup (5 and up) Fic
Sweet and sour (4-6) 398.2

Kendall, Jane F.
Miranda and the movies (6 and up) Fic

Kendall, Sarita
The Bell Reef (5 and up) Fic

Kendo
See/See also pages in the following book(s):
Ribner, S. The martial arts p153-65 (5 and up) 796.8

Kendrick, Dennis
(il) Asher, S. Wild words! 808
(il) Hyde, M. O. Know about smoking 616.86
(il) Voigt, C. Stories about Rosie E

Kene Bourama, a Manding hero. Sako, O.
In The Crest and the hide, and other African stories of heroes, chiefs, bards, hunters, sorcerers, and common people p43-46 398.2

Kennaway, Adrienne, 1945-
(il) Mwalimu. Awful aardvark 398.2
(il) Mwenye Hadithi. Crafty Chameleon E
(il) Mwenye Hadithi. Hot Hippo E

Kennedy, DayAnn M.
Science & technology in fact and fiction: a guide to children's books 016.5

Kennedy, Dorothy M. (Dorothy Mintzlaff), 1931-
(comp) Knock at a star. See Knock at a star 821.008

Kennedy, Richard, 1932-
Amy's eyes (5 and up) Fic
Richard Kennedy: collected stories (3-5) S C

Contents: The porcelain man; Come again in the spring; The parrot and the thief; The blue stone; The leprechaun's story; The contests at Cowlick; Song of the horse; The rise and fall of Ben Gizzard; The dark princess; Crazy in love; The lost Kingdom of Karnica; Oliver Hyde's dishcloth concert; The Mouse God; Inside my feet

Kennedy, X. J.
Brats (3-6) 811
The forgetful wishing well: poems for young people (4 and up) 811
Fresh brats (3-6) 811
Ghastlies, goops & pincushions: nonsense verse (3-6) 811
The Owlstone crown (5 and up) Fic
(comp) Knock at a star. See Knock at a star 821.008

Kenneth Lilly's animals. Lilly, K. 599

Kenny, Elizabeth, 1886-1952

About

Crofford, E. Healing warrior: a story about Sister Elizabeth Kenny (3-5) 92

Kenny's window. Sendak, M. E

Kent, Deborah, 1948-

Colorado
In America the beautiful 973

Connecticut
In America the beautiful 973

Delaware
In America the beautiful 973

Iowa
In America the beautiful 973

Louisiana
In America the beautiful 973

Maryland
In America the beautiful 973

Massachusetts
In America the beautiful 973

New Jersey
In America the beautiful 973

Ohio
In America the beautiful 973

Pennsylvania
In America the beautiful 973

South Carolina
In America the beautiful 973

Washington, D. C.
In America the beautiful 973

Kent, Jack, 1920-1985

(il) Folsom, M. Easy as pie E

Kent, Zachary

George Bush: forty-first president of the United States (4 and up) 92

Georgia
In America the beautiful 973

Idaho
In America the beautiful 973

John Quincy Adams, sixth president of the United States (4 and up) 92

Kansas
In America the beautiful 973

Ronald Reagan, fortieth president of the United States (4 and up) 92

Kentucky

McNair, S. Kentucky
In America the beautiful 973

Fiction

Lyon, G. E. Borrowed children (5 and up) Fic

Kenya

Kenya—in pictures (5 and up) 967.62

Maren, M. The land and people of Kenya (5 and up) 967.62

Kenya—in pictures (5 and up) 967.62

Keplik, the match man. Levoy, M.
In Levoy, M. The witch of Fourth Street, and other stories S C

Kerby, Mona

Cockroaches (4-6) 595.7

Kerina, Jane

African crafts (4 and up) 745.5

Kerley, Ted

(jt. auth) Kreutzer, P. Little League's official how-to-play baseball book 796.357

Kerr, Judith

When Hitler stole Pink Rabbit (4 and up) Fic

Kerr, M. E.

Sunny days and sunny nights
In Connections: short stories by outstanding writers for young adults p218-26 S C

Kerrod, Robin, 1938-

Mammals: primates, insect eaters, and baleen whales (4 and up) 599

See inside a space station (4-6) 629.44

Kertong. Kendall, C.
In Kendall, C. Sweet and sour p66-72 398.2

Kessell, Walter Gaffney- *See* Gaffney-Kessell, Walter

Kesselman, Wendy Ann

Emma E

Kessler, Ethel

Stan the hot dog man E

Kessler, Leonard P., 1920-

Here comes the strikeout E

Kick, pass, and run E

Last one in is a rotten egg E

Old Turtle's riddle and joke book (1-3) 793.73

Old Turtle's winter games E

(il) Branley, F. M. Saturn 523.4

(il) Goldin, A. R. Ducks don't get wet 598

(jt. auth) Kessler, E. Stan the hot dog man E

(il) Lawrence, J. Binky brothers, detectives E

Kesteven, G. R. *See* Crosher, G. R.

The **Kestrel**. Alexander, L. See note under Alexander, L. Westmark Fic

Kettelkamp, Larry, 1933-

Magic made easy (4 and up) 793.8

The magic of sound (4-6) 534

Kevin Corbett eats flies. Hermes, P. Fic

Kevin's grandma. Williams, B. E

Kew, Katinka

(il) Wade, B. Little monster E

Key, Alexander, 1904-1979

Escape to Witch Mountain (5 and up) Fic

The forgotten door (5 and up) Fic

Key, Francis Scott, 1779-1843

The Star-Spangled Banner 782.42

Keys *See* Locks and keys
Keystone kids. Tunis, J. R. See note under Tunis, J. R. The kid from Tomkinsville Fic
Khalsa, Dayal Kaur
Cowboy dreams E
How pizza came to Queens E
I want a dog E
Julian E
My family vacation E
Kherdian, David, 1931-
The cat's midsummer jamboree E
The road from home [biography of Veron Kherdian] (6 and up) 92
A song for Uncle Harry (4-6) Fic
Kherdian, Nonny Hogrogian *See* Hogrogian, Nonny
Kherdian, Veron, 1907-
About
Kherdian, D. The road from home (6 and up) 92
Khruschev, Nikita *See* Khrushchev, Nikita Sergeevich, 1894-1971
Khrushchev, Nikita Sergeevich, 1894-1971
See/See also pages in the following book(s):
Andrews, W. G. The land and the people of the Soviet Union p124-34 (5 and up) 947
Kibbutz *See* Collective settlements—Israel
A **kibbutz** in Israel. Taylor, A. 956.94
Kick, pass, and run. Kessler, L. P. E
Kickle snifters and other fearsome critters. Schwartz, A. 398
The **kid** from Tomkinsville. Tunis, J. R. Fic
The **kid** in the red jacket. Park, B. Fic
The **kid** next door and other headaches. Smith, J. L. Fic
Kiddell-Monroe, Joan, 1908-1972
(il) Picard, B. L. The Iliad of Homer 883
(il) Reeves, J. English fables and fairy stories 398.2
(il) Sherlock, Sir P. M. West Indian folk-tales 398.2
Kidnapping
Fiction
Auch, M. J. Kidnapping Kevin Kowalski (4-6) Fic
Fleischman, P. The Half-a-Moon Inn (4-6) Fic
Mayer, M. Liverwurst is missing E
Yolen, J. Mice on ice E
Kidnapping Kevin Kowalski. Auch, M. J. Fic
Kids' America, Steven Caney's. Caney, S. 790.1
The **Kids'** book about death and dying (5 and up) 155.9
The **kids'** cat book. De Paola, T. 636.8
A **kid's** catalog of Israel. Burstein, C. M. 956.94
The **kids'** complete guide to money. Kyte, K. S. 332.024
Kilcup, Rick
Randy the red-horned rainmoose
In The Big book of Christmas plays p228-39 808.82
Killer bees. Pringle, L. P. 595.7
Killer fish. Freedman, R. 597
Killer snakes. Freedman, R. 597.9
Kimako's story. Jordan, J. Fic
Kimmel, Eric A.
The Chanukkah guest E
Hershel and the Hanukkah goblins E
I took my frog to the library E
Kimmel, Margaret Mary
For reading out loud! 028.5
Magic in the mist (1-4) Fic
Kimmelman, Leslie
Frannie's fruits E
Kindergarten
Fiction
Cleary, B. Ramona the pest (3-5) Fic
King, Dave
(il) Early humans. See Early humans 930.1
(il) Hammond, T. Sports 796
(il) Wilkes, A. My first activity book 745.5
King, Kevin
(il) Henry, O. The gift of the Magi Fic
King, Martin Luther, 1929-1968
About
Adler, D. A. Martin Luther King, Jr.: free at last (2-4) 92
Adler, D. A. A picture book of Martin Luther King, Jr. (1-3) 92
Darby, J. Martin Luther King, Jr (5 and up) 92
Haskins, J. The life and death of Martin Luther King, Jr (5 and up) 92
McKissack, P. C. Martin Luther King, Jr., a man to remember (4 and up) 92
Patrick, D. Martin Luther King, Jr (4 and up) 92
Patterson, L. Martin Luther King, Jr., and the freedom movement (6 and up) 92
See/See also pages in the following book(s):
Jacobs, W. J. Great lives: human rights p257-66 (5 and up) 920
King Alfred
Thane, A. King Alfred and the cakes
In Thane, A. Plays from famous stories and fairy tales p143-52 812

King Bartek
King Bartek
In The Scott, Foresman anthology of children's literature p262-65 **808.8**

King Bear
Afanas'ev, A. N. King Bear
In Afanas'ev, A. N. Russian fairy tales p393-98 **398.2**

King Bidgood's in the bathtub. Wood, A. **E**

King clothes. Jagendorf, M. A.
In The Scott, Foresman anthology of children's literature p259-60 **808.8**

King Frost
Afanas'ev, A. N. Jack Frost
In Afanas'ev, A. N. Russian fairy tales p366-69 **398.2**
San Souci, R. Jack Frost
In San Souci, R. Short & shivery p9-14 **398.2**
The Story of King Frost
In Best-loved folktales of the world p422-25 **398.2**
In The Yellow fairy book p209-12 **398.2**

King Kojata
King Kojata
In The Green fairy book p202-15 **398.2**

King Lion and Mr. Man. Lester, J.
In Lester, J. Further tales of Uncle Remus p8-12 **398.2**

The **King** of Colchester's daughter
In The Classic Fairy tales p159-61 **398.2**

The **King** of Nowhere. Aiken, J.
In Aiken, J. Give yourself a fright: thirteen tales of the supernatural p136-46 **S C**

King of the cats. Crossley-Holland, K.
In Crossley-Holland, K. British folk tales p55-57 **398.2**

King of the Cats. Galdone, P. **398.2**
also in Halloween: stories and poems p3-7 **808.8**

King of the Golden Mountain
Grimm, J. The King of the Golden Mountain
In Grimm, J. The complete Grimm's fairy tales p425-30 **398.2**

King of the monkeys. Carpenter, F.
In Carpenter, F. Tales of a Chinese grandmother p107-16 **398.2**

The **king** of the mountains. Jagendorf, M. A.
In The Scott, Foresman anthology of children's literature p400-01 **808.8**

King of the wind. Henry, M. **Fic**

King O'Toole and his goose
Jacobs, J. King O'Toole and his goose
In The Scott, Foresman anthology of children's literature p176-78 **808.8**

King Philip and the war with the colonists. Cwiklik, R. **92**

King Philip's War, 1675-1676
Cwiklik, R. King Philip and the war with the colonists (5 and up) **92**

King-Smith, Dick, 1922-
Babe (3-5) **Fic**
The fox busters (3-5) **Fic**
Harry's Mad (3-5) **Fic**
Magnus Powermouse (4-6) **Fic**
Martin's mice (3-5) **Fic**
Pigs might fly (4-6) **Fic**
Sophie's snail (3-5) **Fic**

King Stork
Pyle, H. King Stork **398.2**
also in Pyle, H. The wonder clock p291-304 **398.2**

King Thrushbeard
Grimm, J. King Thrushbeard
In Grimm, J. About wise men and simpletons p91-95 **398.2**
In Grimm, J. The complete Grimm's fairy tales p244-48 **398.2**

The **King** with a terrible temper
In With a deep sea smile p61-63 **372.6**

King Wren
Grimm, J. The willow-wren
In Grimm, J. The complete Grimm's fairy tales p705-08 **398.2**

The **kingdom** with no rules, no laws, and no king. Stiles, N.
In Free to be—a family p142-47 **810.8**

Kingman, Lee, 1919-
(ed) The Illustrator's notebook. See The Illustrator's notebook **741.6**
(comp) Illustrators of children's books. See Illustrators of children's books **741.6**
(ed) Newbery and Caldecott Medal books, 1966-1975. See Newbery and Caldecott Medal books, 1966-1975 **028.5**
(ed) Newbery and Caldecott Medal books, 1976-1985. See Newbery and Caldecott Medal books, 1976-1985 **028.5**

Kings, queens, rulers, etc.
See also Presidents; names of countries with the subdivision Kings, queens, rulers, etc.; also names of individual kings, queens, and rulers

Fiction

Wood, A. King Bidgood's in the bathtub **E**

The **King's** ankus. Kipling, R.
In Kipling, R. The jungle books **S C**
The **King's** day: Louis XIV of France. Aliki. **92**
The **King's** fifth. O'Dell, S. **Fic**
The **king's** son who feared nothing. Grimm, J.
In Grimm, J. The complete Grimm's fairy tales p545-50 **398.2**
Kinsey-Warnock, Natalie
The Canada geese quilt (3-5) **Fic**
Kiowa Indians
See/See also pages in the following book(s):
Freedman, R. Indian chiefs p29-51 (6 and up) **920**
Kipling, Rudyard, 1865-1936
The beginning of the armadilloes (1-4) **Fic**
The butterfly that stamped (1-4) **Fic**
The cat that walked by himself (1-4) **Fic**
The crab that played with the sea (1-4) **Fic**
The elephant's child (1-4) **Fic**
also in The Random House book of humor for children p83-92 **817.008**
also in The Scott, Foresman anthology of children's literature p487-91 **808.8**
How the camel got his hump (1-4) **Fic**
The jungle books (4 and up) **S C**
Contents: Mowgli's brothers; Kaa's hunting; How fear came; "Tiger! Tiger!"; The King's ankus; Letting in the jungle; Red Dog; The spring running; "Rikki-tikki-tavi"; The white seal; The miracle of Purun Bhagat; The undertakers; Quiquern; Toomai of the elephants; Her Majesty's servants
Just so stories (3-6) **S C**
Contents: How the whale got his throat; How the camel got his hump; How the rhinoceros got his skin; How the leopard got his spots; The elephant's child; The sing-song of Old Man Kangaroo; The beginning of the armadilloes; How the first letter was written; How the alphabet was made; The crab that played with the sea; The cat that walked by himself; The butterfly that stamped
About
Kamen, G. Kipling, storyteller of East and West (3-5) **92**
Kipling, storyteller of East and West. Kamen, G. **92**
Kirama and Kankejan. Sako, O.
In The Crest and the hide, and other African stories of heroes, chiefs, bards, hunters, sorcerers, and common people p31-41 **398.2**
Kisander. Sherlock, Sir P. M.
In Sherlock, Sir P. M. Anansi, the spider man p35-40 **398.2**
Kishida, Isao
(il) Johnson, S. A. Beetles **595.7**
Kismaric, Carole, 1942-
The rumor of Pavel and Paali (1-3) **398.2**
A **kiss** for Little Bear. Minarik, E. H. See note under Minarik, E. H. Little Bear **E**
Kiss Me. Sandburg, C.
In Sandburg, C. Rootabaga stories pt 2 p170-73 **S C**
In Sandburg, C. The Sandburg treasury p158-59 **818**
The **Kissimmee** Kid. Cleaver, V. **Fic**
Kister, Kenneth F., 1935-
Best encyclopedias: a guide to general and specialized encyclopedias **016**
Kister's Concise guide to best encyclopedias. See Kister, K. F. Best encyclopedias: a guide to general and specialized encyclopedias **016**
Kistler, Irene Brady *See* Brady, Irene, 1943-
Kitchen, Bert
Animal alphabet **E**
Animal numbers **E**
Gorilla/Chinchilla and other animal rhymes **E**
Kitchen chemistry: science experiments to do at home. Gardner, R. **540.7**
Kitchen god
Carpenter, F. God that lived in the kitchen
In Carpenter, F. Tales of a Chinese grandmother p39-46 **398.2**
Kites
Eden, M. Kiteworks: explorations in kite building & flying (5 and up) **796.1**
Gibbons, G. Catch the wind! (1-3) **796.1**
Kites sail high: a book about verbs. Heller, R. **428**
Kiteworks: explorations in kite building & flying. Eden, M. **796.1**
Kitten day. Ormerod, J. **E**
Kitten in trouble. Polushkin, M. **E**
Kitty from the start. Delton, J. **Fic**
Kitty in high school. Delton, J. See note under Delton, J. Kitty from the start **Fic**
Kitty in the middle. Delton, J. See note under Delton, J. Kitty from the start **Fic**
Kitty in the summer. Delton, J. See note under Delton, J. Kitty from the start **Fic**
Kitzinger, Sheila, 1929-
Being born (3-5) **612.6**
Kjelgaard, Jim, 1910-1959
Big Red (4 and up) **Fic**

Kjelgaard, Jim, 1910-1959—*Continued*
Irish Red. See note under Kjelgaard, J. Big Red **Fic**
Outlaw Red. See note under Kjelgaard, J. Big Red **Fic**

KKK *See* Ku Klux Klan

Klagsbrun, Francine
(ed) Free to be—you and me. See Free to be—you and me **810.8**

Klaveness, Jan O'Donnell
The Griffin legacy (6 and up) **Fic**

Klee, Paul, 1879-1940
About
Raboff, E. Paul Klee (4 and up) **759.3**

Klein, Michael J., 1940-
(jt. auth) Poynter, M. Cosmic quest **574.999**

Klein, Norma, 1938-1989
Baryshnikov's Nutcracker (3 and up) **792.8**

Klein, Robin, 1936-
Enemies (3-5) **Fic**

Klein, Suzanna
(il) Womenfolk and fairy tales. See Womenfolk and fairy tales **398.2**

Kliman, Gilbert
(jt. auth) Stein, S. B. About dying **155.9**

Kline, Suzy, 1943-
Herbie Jones (3-5) **Fic**
Herbie Jones and Hamburger Head. See note under Kline, S. Herbie Jones **Fic**
Herbie Jones and the class gift. See note under Kline, S. Herbie Jones **Fic**
Herbie Jones and the monster ball. See note under Kline, S. Herbie Jones **Fic**
Horrible Harry and the green slime. See note under Kline, S. Horrible Harry in room 2B **Fic**
Horrible Harry in room 2B (2-4) **Fic**
Horrible Harry's secret. See note under Kline, S. Horrible Harry in room 2B **Fic**
What's the matter with Herbie Jones? See note under Kline, S. Herbie Jones **Fic**

Kling Kling bird. Sherlock, Sir P. M.
In Sherlock, Sir P. M. Anansi, the spider man p41-46 **398.2**

Klingsheim, Trygve Bj
Julius (1-4) **599.88**

Klondike fever. Cooper, M. **971.9**

Klondike River Valley (Yukon)
Gold discoveries
Cooper, M. Klondike fever (5 and up) **971.9**
Ray, D. Gold! the Klondike adventure (5 and up) **971.9**

Klotzbeacher, Donovan
(il) Kettelkamp, L. Magic made easy **793.8**

Knapsack, the hat, and the horn
Grimm, J. The knapsack, the hat, and the horn
In Grimm, J. The complete Grimm's fairy tales p258-64 **398.2**

The **Knee-high** man
In The Diane Goode book of American folk tales and songs p19-21 **398.2**

The **knee-high** man. Lester, J.
In Lester, J. The knee-high man, and other tales p27-29 **398.2**
In The Scott, Foresman anthology of children's literature p375-76 **808.8**

The **knee-high** man, and other tales. Lester, J. **398.2**

Kneeknock Rise. Babbitt, N. **Fic**

Knight, Christopher G.
(il) Lasky, K. A baby for Max **E**
(il) Lasky, K. Dinosaur dig **567.9**
(il) Lasky, K. Sugaring time **633.6**

Knight, Hilary
(il) Benchley, N. Feldman Fieldmouse **Fic**
(il) Le Prince de Beaumont, Madame. Beauty and the beast **398.2**
(il) MacDonald, B. Mrs. Piggle-Wiggle **Fic**
(il) Side by side. See Side by side **808.81**

Knight, Maxwell B.
(jt. auth) Lasky, K. A baby for Max **E**

The **knight** and the dragon. De Paola, T. **E**

Knights and knighthood
Fiction
Bulla, C. R. The sword in the tree (2-5) **Fic**
De Paola, T. The knight and the dragon **E**
Greer, G. Max and me and the time machine (5 and up) **Fic**
Hodges, M. Saint George and the dragon (2-5) **398.2**
Lasker, J. A tournament of knights (1-3) **394**

Knight's castle. Eager, E. See note under Eager, E. Half magic **Fic**

Knights of the Round Table *See* Arthurian romances

Knitting
Fiction
Wild, M. Mr. Nick's knitting **E**

Knock at a star (3-6) **821.008**

Knock-knock! who's there. Rosenbloom, J. **808.87**

Knoist and his three sons
Grimm, J. Knoist and his three sons
In Grimm, J. The complete Grimm's fairy tales p622 **398.2**
Knots on a counting rope. Martin, B. **E**
Knott, John
(il) Roche, P. K. Dollhouse magic **745.592**
Know about drugs. Hyde, M. O. **616.86**
Know about smoking. Hyde, M. O. **616.86**
Know Not. Afanas'ev, A. N.
In Afanas'ev, A. N. Russian fairy tales p97-109 **398.2**
Knowlton, MaryLee, 1946-
(ed) Spain. See Spain **946**
Knudsen, Arvid
(jt. auth) Owens-Knudsen, V. Photography basics **770**
Knudsen, Vick Owens- *See* Owens-Knudsen, Vick
Knudson, R. Rozanne, 1932-
Babe Didrikson: athlete of the century (4 and up) **92**
Knutson, Barbara
How the guinea fowl got her spots (k-3) **398.2**
Ko-Ai's lost shoe. Carpenter, F.
In Carpenter, F. Tales of a Chinese grandmother p175-81 **398.2**
Koala Lou. Fox, M. **E**
Koalas
Arnold, C. Koala (3-5) **599.2**
Fiction
Fox, M. Koala Lou **E**
Kobrin, Beverly
Eyeopeners! **028.5**
The **Kobrin** Letter **028.505**
Koch, Kenneth, 1925-
(comp) Talking to the sun: an illustrated anthology of poems for young people. See Talking to the sun: an illustrated anthology of poems for young people **808.81**
Kocsis, J. C.
(il) Jones, W. Edge of two worlds **Fic**
Koehn, Ilse, 1929-1991
Mischling, second degree: my childhood in Nazi Germany (6 and up) **92**
Kogan, Deborah *See* Ray, Deborah Kogan, 1940-
Kohl, Herbert R.
(jt. auth) Kohl, J. Pack, band, and colony **591.5**
(jt. auth) Kohl, J. The view from the oak **591.5**
Kohl, Judith
Pack, band, and colony (5 and up) **591.5**
The view from the oak (6 and up) **591.5**
Kohler, Keith
(il) Hornblow, L. Animals do the strangest things **591.5**
Kohn, Bernice
The beachcomber's book (3-6) **745.5**
Koike, Hiroo
(il) Johnson, S. A. Apple trees **634**
Koizumi, Yakumo *See* Hearn, Lafcadio, 1850-1904
Koko's kitten. Patterson, F. **599.88**
Koko's story. Patterson, F. **599.88**
Kondo, Yukio
(il) Apfel, N. H. It's all relative **530.1**
Konigsburg, E. L.
About the B'nai Bagels (4-6) **Fic**
Altogether, one at a time (4-6) **S C**
Contents: Inviting Jason; The Night of the Leonids; Camp Fat; Momma at the Pearly Gates
From the mixed-up files of Mrs. Basil E. Frankweiler (4 and up) **Fic**
Jennifer, Hecate, Macbeth, William McKinley, and me, Elizabeth (4-6) **Fic**
Journey to an 800 number (4 and up) **Fic**
A proud taste for scarlet and miniver (5 and up) **Fic**
Throwing shadows (5 and up) **S C**
Contents: On Shark's Tooth Beach; The catchee; In the village of the weavers; At the home; With Bert & Ray
Up from Jericho Tel (5 and up) **Fic**
See/See also pages in the following book(s):
Newbery and Caldecott Medal books, 1966-1975 p36-44 **028.5**
Townsend, J. R. A sounding of storytellers p111-24 **028.5**
Koplin, Hermine M.
(jt. auth) Siegel, M.-E. More than a friend: dogs with a purpose **636.7**
Koplin, Stephanie Bee
(il) Siegel, M.-E. More than a friend: dogs with a purpose **636.7**
Kopper, Lisa, 1950-
(il) Lewin, H. Jafta **E**
Koralek, Jenny
The cobweb curtain **E**
Hanukkah, the festival of lights (k-3) **296.4**
Korea
Jacobsen, K. Korea (2-4) **951.9**
Solberg, S. E. The land and people of Korea (5 and up) **951.9**
South Korea—in pictures (5 and up) **951.9**

Korea—*Continued*
Fiction
Watkins, Y. K. So far from the bamboo grove (6 and up) **Fic**
Folklore
See Folklore—Korea
Korea in pictures. See South Korea—in pictures **951.9**
Korean Americans
Patterson, W. The Koreans in America *In* The In America series **305.8**
Sobol, H. L. We don't look like our Mom and Dad (2-5) **362.7**
Korean cookery *See* Cookery, Korean
The **Koreans** in America. Patterson, W. *In* The In America series **305.8**
Korman, Gordon, 1963-
A reasonable sum
In Connections: short stories by outstanding writers for young adults p45-52 **S C**
Kors, Erika W.
(il) Asimov, I. How did we find out about microwaves? **621.381**
(il) Asimov, I. How did we find out about Neptune? **523.4**
(il) Asimov, I. How did we find out about photosynthesis? **581.1**
(il) Asimov, I. How did we find out about superconductivity? **537.6**
(il) Brenner, B. Two orphan cubs **599.74**
Kortum, Jeanie
Ghost vision (5 and up) **Fic**
Koschei without death
Afanas'ev, A. N. Koshchey the Deathless *In* Afanas'ev, A. N. Russian fairy tales p485-94 **398.2**
Koshchey the Deathless. Afanas'ev, A. N. *In* Afanas'ev, A. N. Russian fairy tales p485-94 **398.2**
Kossin, Sandy
(il) Kalb, J. The easy baseball book **796.357**
Kostyal, K. M., 1951-
Animals at play (k-3) **591.5**
Kovalski, Maryann, 1951-
The wheels on the bus (k-2) **782.42**
Kozuki, Russell
Junior karate (5 and up) **796.8**
Kraft, Stephen
(il) Simon, S. More wise men of Helm and their merry tales **398.2**
Krahn, Fernando, 1935-
Arthur's adventure in the abandoned house **E**
(il) They've discovered a head in the box for the bread, and other laughable limericks. See They've discovered a head in the box for the bread, and other laughable limericks **821.008**
Kramer, Alan
How to make a chemical volcano and other mysterious experiments (4-6) **540.7**
Kramer, Anthony
(il) Giff, P. R. Loretta P. Sweeny, where are you? **Fic**
(il) Kettelkamp, L. The magic of sound **534**
(il) Zaslavsky, C. Tic tac toe, and other three-in-a row games from ancient Egypt to the modern computer **794**
Kramer, Stephen
How to think like a scientist (3-5) **507**
Krasilovsky, Phyllis, 1926-
The cow who fell in the canal **E**
The man who didn't wash his dishes *In* The Read-aloud treasury p179-87 **808.8**
Kraus, Fred
(il) Severn, B. Magic fun for everyone **793.8**
Kraus, Robert, 1925-
Owliver **E**
Where are you going, little mouse? See note under Kraus, R. Whose mouse are you? **E**
Whose mouse are you? **E**
Krause, Ute
Pig surprise **E**
(il) Luttrell, I. Ottie Slockett **E**
Krauss, Ruth
The carrot seed **E**
The growing story **E**
A hole is to dig **E**
A very special house **E**
Kreloff, Elliot
(il) Cobb, V. The trip of a drip **628.1**
Krementz, Jill
How it feels to be adopted (4 and up) **362.7**
How it feels to fight for your life (4 and up) **362.1**
How it feels when a parent dies (4 and up) **155.9**
How it feels when parents divorce (4 and up) **306.89**
A very young dancer (3-6) **792.8**
A very young gymnast (3-6) **796.44**
A very young musician (3-6) **788**
A very young rider (3-6) **798.2**
A very young skater (3-6) **796.91**
A very young skier (3-6) **796.93**
A visit to Washington, D.C (k-2) **975.3**

Krensky, Stephen, 1953-
The American Heritage first dictionary. See The American Heritage first dictionary 423
Lionel at large E
Lionel in the fall. See note under Krensky, S. Lionel at large E
Lionel in the spring. See note under Krensky, S. Lionel at large E
Who really discovered America? (4-6) 970.01
Witch hunt (2-4) 133.4
(jt. auth) Brown, M. T. Dinosaurs, beware! 613.6

Kresh, Paul
Isaac Bashevis Singer: the story of a storyteller (6 and up) 92

Kreutzer, Peter
Little League's official how-to-play baseball book (4 and up) 796.357

Kristensen, Preben Sejer
We live in Egypt (4-6) 962
(jt. auth) Jacobsen, P. O. A family in the Persian Gulf 953

Kroc, Ray
See/See also pages in the following book(s):
Aaseng, N. The unsung heroes p70-75 (5 and up) 920

Kroeber, Theodora, 1897-1979
Ishi, last of his tribe (5 and up) 92

Kroll, Steven
The biggest pumpkin ever E
One tough turkey E
Santa's crash-bang Christmas E

Kropp, Paul, 1948-
Moonkid and Liberty (6 and up) Fic

Krumgold, Joseph, 1908-1980
—and now Miguel (6 and up) Fic
Onion John (5 and up) Fic
See/See also pages in the following book(s):
Newbery Medal books, 1922-1955 p407-23 028.5

Krupp, E. C. (Edwin C.)
The Big Dipper and you (3-5) 523

Krupp, Edwin C. *See* Krupp, E. C. (Edwin C.)

Krupp, Robin Rector, 1946-
(il) Krupp, E. C. The Big Dipper and you 523

Krush, Beth
(il) Enright, E. Gone-Away Lake Fic
(il) Norton, M. The Borrowers Fic
(il) Sorensen, V. E. Miracles on Maple Hill Fic

Krush, Joe
(il) Enright, E. Gone-Away Lake Fic
(il) Norton, M. The Borrowers Fic
(il) Sorensen, V. E. Miracles on Maple Hill Fic

Krushchev, Nikita *See* Khrushchev, Nikita Sergeevich, 1894-1971

Ku Klux Klan
Meltzer, M. The truth about the Ku Klux Klan (6 and up) 322.4
Fiction
Hooks, W. H. Circle of fire (5 and up) Fic

Kubinyi, Laszlo, 1937-
(il) Alexander, L. The town cats, and other tales S C
(il) Hunter, M. The haunted mountain Fic

Kublai Khan, 1216-1294
See/See also pages in the following book(s):
Humble, R. The travels of Marco Polo (4-6) 910.4
Major, J. S. The land and people of Mongolia p88-97 (5 and up) 951.7

Kudlinski, Kathleen V.
Juliette Gordon Low: America's first Girl Scout (4 and up) 92
Rachel Carson: pioneer of ecology (4 and up) 92

Kuhn, Bob
(il) Kjelgaard, J. Big Red Fic

Kuhn, Dwight
More than just a flower garden (2-4) 635.9
More than just a vegetable garden (2-4) 635
(il) Schwartz, D. M. The hidden life of the forest 574.5
(il) Schwartz, D. M. The hidden life of the meadow 574.5
(il) Schwartz, D. M. The hidden life of the pond 574.92

Kuklin, Susan
Going to my ballet class (4-6) 792.8
Taking my cat to the vet (k-2) 636.8
Taking my dog to the vet (k-2) 636.7
Thinking big (2-5) 362.4
When I see my dentist (k-2) 617.6
When I see my doctor (k-2) 610.69

Kulkin, Mary-Ellen *See* Siegel, Mary-Ellen

Kumin, Maxine, 1925-
The microscope [biography of Antoni van Leeuwenhoek] (k-3) 92

Kunhardt, Edith
I want to be a farmer E
I want to be a fire-fighter E

Kunitz, Stanley, 1905-
(ed) The Junior book of authors. See The Junior book of authors 920.003

Kunz, Virginia Brainard
The French in America
In The In America series 305.8

Kupe's discovery of Aotearoa. Te Kanawa, K.
In Te Kanawa, K. Land of the long white cloud p27-34 **398.2**

Kurelek, William, 1927-1977
Lumberjack (3-5) **634.9**
A northern nativity (4 and up) **232.9**
A prairie boy's summer (3-5) **971.27**
A prairie boy's winter (3-5) **971.27**
They sought a new world (4 and up) **325**

Kuribayashi, Satoshi, 1939-
(il) Johnson, S. A. Fireflies **595.7**
(il) Overbeck, C. Ants **595.7**

Kuskin, Karla
Any me I want to be: poems (1-4) **811**
The Dallas Titans get ready for bed **E**
Dogs & dragons, trees & dreams: a collection of poems (2-4) **811**
Jerusalem, shining still (2-4) **956.94**
Near the window tree: poems and notes (2-5) **811**
The Philharmonic gets dressed **E**
(il) What shall we do and Alee galloo! play songs and singing games for young children. See What shall we do and Alee galloo! play songs and singing games for young children **796.1**

Kustanowitz, Shulamit E.
Henrietta Szold: Israel's helping hand (4 and up) **92**

Kuwait
Kuwait—in pictures (5 and up) **953**

Kuwait—in pictures (5 and up) **953**

Kuzma, Stephen
(il) Adoff, A. Sports pages **811**

Kwarteng, Kingsley
A chief names his heirs
In The Crest and the hide, and other African stories of heroes, chiefs, bards, hunters, sorcerers, and common people p7-11 **398.2**
Journey to Asamando
In The Crest and the hide, and other African stories of heroes, chiefs, bards, hunters, sorcerers, and common people p115-21 **398.2**

Kyte, Kathleen Sharar, 1946-
The kids' complete guide to money (4 and up) **332.024**

L

La Fontaine, Jean de, 1621-1695
Wildsmith, B. The hare and the tortoise **398.2**
Wildsmith, B. The miller, the boy and the donkey **398.2**
Wildsmith, B. The rich man and the shoe-maker **398.2**

La Salle, Réné Robert Cavelier *See* La Salle, Robert Cavelier, sieur de, 1643-1687

La Salle, Robert Cavelier, sieur de, 1643-1687
See/See also pages in the following book(s):
McCall, E. S. Biography of a river: the living Mississippi p25-30 (6 and up) **977**

Labhardt, Felix, 1950-
(il) Schnieper, C. On the trail of the fox **599.74**

LaBonte, Gail
The arctic fox (3-5) **599.74**
The miniature horse (3-5) **636.1**

Labor
See also Migrant labor

The **labor** movement in the United States. Flagler, J. J. **331.8**

Labor unions
Flagler, J. J. The labor movement in the United States (5 and up) **331.8**

Labour-in-vain. Garfield, L.
In Garfield, L. The apprentices **S C**

Lacey, Elizabeth A.
The complete frog (4-6) **597.8**

Lacis, Vilis, 1904-1966
Edžiņš
In Face to face: a collection of stories by celebrated Soviet and American writers p185-92 **S C**

Lacoe, Addie
The scarlet batling
In Things that go bump in the night p199-216 **S C**

Lacy, Lyn Ellen
Art and design in children's picture books **741.6**

Lad who went to the north wind
Asbjørnsen, P. C. The lad who went to the North Wind
In Best-loved folktales of the world p310-13 **398.2**

Ladder to the sky. Esbensen, B. J. **398.2**

Ladies first [short story]. Rodgers, M.
In Free to be—you and me p39-45 **810.8**

Lady Eleanore's mantle. San Souci, R.
In San Souci, R. Short & shivery p62-67 **398.2**
Lady Ellen Grae. Cleaver, V. **Fic**
The **lady** of stone. Terada, A. M.
In Terada, A. M. Under the starfruit tree p115-19 **398.2**
Lady of the moon
Carpenter, F. Heng O, the moon lady
In Carpenter, F. Tales of a Chinese grandmother p206-16 **398.2**
The **lady** who put salt in her coffee. Schwartz, A. **E**
The **lady** with the alligator purse. Westcott, N. B. **E**
Lady with the horse's head. Carpenter, F.
In Carpenter, F. Tales of a Chinese grandmother p98-106 **398.2**
Ladybirds
Fischer-Nagel, H. Life of the ladybug (3-6) **595.7**
Johnson, S. A. Ladybugs (4 and up) **595.7**
Fiction
Carle, E. The grouchy ladybug **E**
Ladybugs *See* Ladybirds
Ladybugs. Johnson, S. A. **595.7**
The **lady's** room. Farjeon, E.
In With a deep sea smile p82-85 **372.6**
Lagerlöf, Selma, 1858-1940
Greene, E. The legend of the Christmas rose **398.2**
Laidly worm of Spindleston
Jacobs, J. Laidly Worm of Spindleston Heugh
In Jacobs, J. English fairy tales p182-87 **398.2**
Williams-Ellis, A. The Laidly Worm of Spindlestone Heugh
In Williams-Ellis, A. Tales from the enchanted world p134-41 **398.2**
Laidly Worm of Spindleston Heugh. Jacobs, J.
In Jacobs, J. English fairy tales p182-87 **398.2**
Laird, Elizabeth
Happy birthday! (1-3) **394.2**
The road to Bethlehem (4-6) **232.9**
Rosy's garden: a child's keepsake of flowers (3-5) **635.9**
Lake Te Anau. Te Kanawa, K.
In Te Kanawa, K. Land of the long white cloud p85-86 **398.2**
Lake Wobegon days [excerpt]. Keillor, G.
In The Random House book of humor for children p259-61 **817.008**
Lakes
Bramwell, M. Rivers and lakes (4-6) **551.48**
Fiction
McCully, E. A. Grandmas at the lake **E**
Lalicki, Barbara
(comp) If there were dreams to sell. See If there were dreams to sell **821.008**
Lamb, Charles, 1775-1834
Tales from Shakespeare **822.3**
Lamb, Mary, 1764-1847
(jt. auth) Lamb, C. Tales from Shakespeare **822.3**
Lamb, Susan Condie
(il) Griffith, H. V. Plunk's dreams **E**
Lamb and the fish
Grimm, J. The lambkin and the little fish
In Grimm, J. The complete Grimm's fairy tales p625-27 **398.2**
Lambert, David, 1932-
Maps and globes (3-5) **912**
Weather and its work (5 and up) **551.6**
Lambert, Shirley
(jt. auth) Matthews, J. G. ClipArt & dynamic designs for libraries & media centers **021.7**
Lambikin
Crouch, M. Lambikin
In The Scott, Foresman anthology of children's literature p343-45 **808.8**
The **lambkin** and the little fish. Grimm, J.
In Grimm, J. The complete Grimm's fairy tales p625-27 **398.2**
The **lambton** worm. Crossley-Holland, K.
In Crossley-Holland, K. British folk tales p339-46 **398.2**
The **lame** king. Aiken, J.
In Aiken, J. Give yourself a fright: thirteen tales of the supernatural p44-55 **S C**
Lamme, Linda Leonard
National Council of Teachers of English. Committee on Literature in the Elementary Language Arts. Raising readers **028.5**
Lamorisse, Albert, 1922-1970
The red balloon (1-4) **Fic**
The **lamp** from the warlock's tomb. Bellairs, J. See note under Bellairs, J. The treasure of Alpheus Winterborn **Fic**
The **lamplighter's** funeral. Garfield, L.
In Garfield, L. The apprentices **S C**
Lampman, Evelyn Sibley
White captives (5 and up) **Fic**

Lamps
Fiction
Goffstein, M. B. Goldie the dollmaker (3-5) **Fic**
The **lampstand** princess. Vuong, L. D.
In Vuong, L. D. The brocaded slipper, and other Vietnamese tales **398.2**
Lampton, Christopher
The space telescope (5 and up) **522**
Stars & planets (3-6) **523**
The sun (4 and up) **523.7**
Lancaster, John, 1930-
Paper sculpture (4 and up) **745.54**
Lancelot (Legendary character)
Pyle, H. The story of Sir Launcelot and his companions (6 and up) **398.2**
Land, Edwin H.
See/See also pages in the following book(s):
Aaseng, N. The problem solvers p53-59 (5 and up) **920**
The **land** and people of Afghanistan. Clifford, M. L. **958.1**
The **land** and people of Argentina. Fox, G. **982**
The **land** and people of Bolivia. Blair, D. N. **984**
The **land** and people of Cambodia. Chandler, D. P. **959.6**
The **land** and people of China. Major, J. S. **951**
The **land** and people of Finland. Lander, P. S. **948.97**
The **land** and people of France. Harris, J. **944**
The **land** and people of Kenya. Maren, M. **967.62**
The **land** and people of Korea. Solberg, S. E. **951.9**
The **land** and people of Mongolia. Major, J. S. **951.7**
The **land** and people of Scotland. Meek, J. **941.1**
The **land** and people of South Africa. Paton, J. **968**
The **land** and people of Turkey. Spencer, W. **956.1**
The **land** and people of Zimbabwe. Cheney, P. **968.91**
The **land** and the people of the Soviet Union. Andrews, W. G. **947**
Land beyond the river. Lyttle, R. B. **940.1**
The **land** I lost: adventures of a boy in Vietnam. Huynh, Q. N. **92**
The **land** of Oz. Baum, L. F. See note under Baum, L. F. The Wizard of Oz **Fic**
Land of the long white cloud. Te Kanawa, K. **398.2**
Land surveying *See* Surveying
Landau, Elaine
Alzheimer's disease (5 and up) **616.8**
Lyme disease (4 and up) **616.9**
Tropical rain forests around the world (4 and up) **574.5**
Lander, Patricia Slade
The land and people of Finland (5 and up) **948.97**
Landlord and tenant
Fiction
Myers, W. D. The young landlords (6 and up) **Fic**
Lands and peoples **910.3**
The **landscape** of memory. Meltzer, M. **153.1**
Lane, Margaret, 1907-
The beaver (1-3) **599.32**
The fish (1-3) **597**
The fox (1-3) **599.74**
The spider (1-3) **595.4**
Lane, Megan Halsey
Something to crow about **E**
Lanes, Selma G.
Art of Maurice Sendak **741.6**
(jt. auth) Gish, L. An actor's life for me **92**
Lang, Andrew, 1844-1912
Aladdin and the wonderful lamp (2-4) **398.2**
The forty thieves
In Womenfolk and fairy tales p51-64 **398.2**
The Terrible Head
In The Blue fairy book p182-92 **398.2**
(ed) The Arabian nights entertainments. See The Arabian nights entertainments **398.2**
(ed) The Blue fairy book. See The Blue fairy book **398.2**
(ed) The Green fairy book. See The Green fairy book **398.2**
(ed) The Red fairy book. See The Red fairy book **398.2**
(ed) The Yellow fairy book. See The Yellow fairy book **398.2**
See/See also pages in the following book(s):
Only connect: readings on children's literature p244-52 **028.5**
Lang, Aubrey
Eagles (3-6) **598**
Lang, Glenna
(il) Stevenson, R. L. My shadow **821**
Lange, Dorothea, 1895-1965
About
Meltzer, M. Dorothea Lange: life through the camera (4 and up) **92**

Langford, Alton
(il) Milton, J. Whales **599.5**
Langley, Jonathan
(il) Kipling, R. How the camel got his hump **Fic**
Langstaff, John M.
Frog went a-courtin' (k-3) **781.62**
Oh, a-hunting we will go (k-2) **781.62**
Over in the meadow (k-2) **781.62**
(ed) What a morning! See What a morning! **782.25**
Langston Hughes, American poet. Walker, A. **92**
Langton, Jane
The fledgling (5 and up) **Fic**
The fragile flag (5 and up) **Fic**
The hedgehog boy (k-3) **398.2**
Language and languages
See also Sign language; names of languages or groups of cognate languages; also classes of people with the subdivision Language
Chermayeff, I. First words (k-3) **410**
Language arts
Kaye, C. B. Word works (4 and up) **410**
Language Arts **372.605**
Language games *See* Literary recreations
Lanting, Frans
(il) Johnson, S. A. Elephant seals **599.74**
The **Lantuch**. Singer, I. B.
In Singer, I. B. Naftali the storyteller and his horse, Sus, and other stories p39-46 **S C**
In Singer, I. B. Stories for children p231-36 **S C**
Lantz, Paul, 1908-
(il) Edmonds, W. D. The matchlock gun **Fic**
(il) Gates, D. Blue willow **Fic**
Laos
Diamond, J. Laos (4 and up) **959.4**
Folklore
See Folklore—Laos
The **Lap-time** song and play book (k-2) **782.42**
Large as life daytime animals. Cole, J. **591**
Large as life nighttime animals. Cole, J. **591**
Large print books
Aiken, J. Arabel and Mortimer **Fic**
Alcock, V. The cuckoo sister **Fic**
Armstrong, W. H. Sounder **Fic**
Babbitt, N. Tuck everlasting **Fic**
Bagnold, E. National Velvet **Fic**
Barrie, J. M. Peter Pan **Fic**
Bauer, M. D. On my honor **Fic**
Baum, L. F. The Wizard of Oz **Fic**
Bawden, N. The peppermint pig **Fic**
Bawden, N. The witch's daughter **Fic**
Blume, J. Tales of a fourth grade nothing **Fic**
Blume, J. Then again, maybe I won't **Fic**
Brink, C. R. Caddie Woodlawn **Fic**
Burnett, F. H. The secret garden **Fic**
Byars, B. C. The burning questions of Bingo Brown **Fic**
Byars, B. C. Cracker Jackson **Fic**
Byars, B. C. The night swimmers **Fic**
Byars, B. C. The pinballs **Fic**
Byars, B. C. The summer of the swans **Fic**
Childress, A. A hero ain't nothin' but a sandwich **Fic**
Cleary, B. Dear Mr. Henshaw **Fic**
Cleary, B. Henry Huggins **Fic**
Cleary, B. The mouse and the motorcycle **Fic**
Cleary, B. Ramona the pest **Fic**
Cole, B. The goats **Fic**
Collier, J. L. My brother Sam is dead **Fic**
Cooper, S. The grey king **Fic**
Cooper, S. Over sea, under stone **Fic**
Cresswell, H. Ordinary Jack **Fic**
Dahl, R. James and the giant peach **Fic**
Dahl, R. Matilda **Fic**
Danziger, P. There's a bat in bunk five **Fic**
DeClements, B. 6th grade can really kill you **Fic**
Estes, E. Ginger Pye **Fic**
Fitzgerald, J. D. The Great Brain **Fic**
Fitzhugh, L. Harriet the spy **Fic**
Fleischman, S. The whipping boy **Fic**
Fritz, J. Homesick: my own story **92**
Garfield, L. The December Rose **Fic**
Greene, B. Philip Hall likes me, I reckon maybe **Fic**
Greene, B. Summer of my German soldier **Fic**
Greene, C. C. Beat the turtle drum **Fic**
Greene, C. C. A girl called Al **Fic**
Hamilton, V. M. C. Higgins the great **Fic**
Hamilton, V. The planet of Junior Brown **Fic**
Howker, J. Isaac Campion **Fic**
Hunter, M. The kelpie's pearls **Fic**
Juster, N. The phantom tollbooth **Fic**
King-Smith, D. Harry's Mad **Fic**
King-Smith, D. Martin's mice **Fic**
Konigsburg, E. L. From the mixed-up files of Mrs. Basil E. Frankweiler **Fic**

Large print books—*Continued*
Konigsburg, E. L. Jennifer, Hecate, Macbeth, William McKinley, and me, Elizabeth **Fic**
L'Engle, M. A wrinkle in time **Fic**
Lindgren, A. Pippi Longstocking **Fic**
London, J. The call of the wild **Fic**
Lowry, L. Anastasia Krupnik **Fic**
Lowry, L. Rabble Starkey **Fic**
Lowry, L. Taking care of Terrific **Fic**
MacDonald, G. The princess and the goblin **Fic**
MacLachlan, P. Arthur, for the very first time **Fic**
MacLachlan, P. Sarah, plain and tall **Fic**
McKinley, R. The hero and the crown **Fic**
Norton, M. Bed-knob and broomstick **Fic**
O'Dell, S. Island of the Blue Dolphins **Fic**
O'Dell, S. Sing down the moon **Fic**
O'Dell, S. Streams to the river, river to the sea **Fic**
Paterson, K. Bridge to Terabithia **Fic**
Paterson, K. The great Gilly Hopkins **Fic**
Pearce, P. Tom's midnight garden **Fic**
Peck, R. The ghost belonged to me **Fic**
Peck, R. N. A day no pigs would die **Fic**
Raskin, E. The Westing game **Fic**
Rawls, W. Where the red fern grows **Fic**
Reid Banks, L. The Indian in the cupboard **Fic**
Rockwell, T. How to eat fried worms **Fic**
Rodgers, M. Freaky Friday **Fic**
Selden, G. The cricket in Times Square **Fic**
Speare, E. G. The sign of the beaver **Fic**
Speare, E. G. The witch of Blackbird Pond **Fic**
Sperry, A. Call it courage **Fic**
Stevenson, R. L. A child's garden of verses **821**
Taylor, M. D. Roll of thunder, hear my cry **Fic**
Taylor, T. The cay **Fic**
Voigt, C. Dicey's song **Fic**
White, E. B. Stuart Little **Fic**
Wilder, L. I. Little house in the big woods **Fic**
Yep, L. Dragonwings **Fic**

The **largest** dinosaurs. Simon, S. **567.9**

Larrecq, John M., 1926-1980
(il) Ormondroyd, E. Broderick **E**
(il) Ormondroyd, E. Theodore **E**
(il) Ormondroyd, E. Theodore's rival **E**

Larrick, Nancy
(comp) Cats are cats. See Cats are cats **808.81**
(comp) The Merry-go-round poetry book. See The Merry-go-round poetry book **811.008**
(comp) Mice are nice. See Mice are nice **808.81**
(comp) On city streets. See On city streets **811.008**
(ed) Piping down the valleys wild. See Piping down the valleys wild **808.81**
(comp) Poetry for holidays. See Poetry for holidays **811.008**
(comp) Room for me and a mountain lion. See Room for me and a mountain lion **808.81**
(comp) Songs from Mother Goose. See Songs from Mother Goose **782.42**
(comp) Tambourines! Tambourines to glory! See Tambourines! Tambourines to glory! **242**
(comp) When the dark comes dancing. See When the dark comes dancing **808.81**

Larsen, Janet
(il) Terada, A. M. Under the starfruit tree **398.2**

Larsen, Ronald J., 1948-
The Puerto Ricans in America
In The In America series **305.8**

Lasers
See/See also pages in the following book(s):
Aaseng, N. The inventors: Nobel prizes in chemistry, physics, and medicine p59-67 (5 and up) **609**

Lasker, Joe
Merry ever after (3-5) **392**
A tournament of knights (1-3) **394**
(il) Climo, S. The cobweb Christmas **E**

Lasky, Kathryn
A baby for Max **E**
Dinosaur dig (3 and up) **567.9**
Sea swan **E**
Sugaring time (5 and up) **633.6**
Traces of life (5 and up) **573.2**

The **lass** who went out at the cry of dawn. Leodhas, S. N.
In Womenfolk and fairy tales p83-92 **398.2**

Lasson, Robert, 1922-
If I had a hammer: woodworking with seven basic tools (4 and up) **684**

The **last** battle. Lewis, C. S. See note under Lewis, C. S. The lion, the witch and the wardrobe **Fic**

The **last** chimney cuckoo. Aiken, J.
In Aiken, J. Up the chimney down, and other stories p1-26 **S C**
The **last** council. Curry, J. L.
In Curry, J. L. Back in the beforetime p121-27 **398.2**
The **last** eagle [excerpt]. Mannix, D. P.
In Animal families of the wild: animal stories p35-43 **591**
The **last** important wish. MacLachlan, P.
In MacLachlan, P. Tomorrow's wizard p68-80 **S C**
Last names first. Lee, M. P. **929.4**
Last of the Feni
Stephens, J. Oisin's mother
In Stephens, J. Irish fairy tales p109-32 **398.2**
The **last** of the Picts. Crossley-Holland, K.
In Crossley-Holland, K. British folk tales p142-44 **398.2**
Last one home is a green pig. Hurd, E. T. **E**
Last one in is a rotten egg. Kessler, L. P. **E**
Last Remaining
In The Naked bear p87-92 **398.2**
The **Last** tiger in Haiti
In The Magic orange tree, and other Haitian folktales p183-87 **398.2**
Last was Lloyd. Smith, D. B. **Fic**
Lathrop, Dorothy P., 1891-1980
(il) Bible. Selections. Animals of the Bible **220.8**
(il) Field, R. Hitty: her first hundred years **Fic**
See/See also pages in the following book(s):
Caldecott Medal books, 1938-1957 p7-21 **028.5**
Latin America
Fiction
Where angels glide at dawn (5 and up) **S C**
Folklore
See Folklore—Latin America
Latin American literature
Bibliography
Schon, I. Basic collection of children's books in Spanish **011.6**
Schon, I. Books in Spanish for children and young adults: an annotated guide [series I-V] **011.6**
Latinos (U.S.) *See* Hispanic Americans
Latkes and applesauce. Manushkin, F. **E**
Latsis, Vilas *See* Lacis, Vilis, 1904-1966
Lattimore, Deborah Nourse
The dragon's robe (3-5) **Fic**
Why there is no arguing in heaven (3-6) **398.2**
(il) Stolz, M. Zekmet, the stone carver **Fic**
Latvia
Folklore
See Folklore—Latvia
Lauber, Patricia, 1924-
Dinosaurs walked here, and other stories fossils tell (3-5) **560**
From flower to flower (2-4) **582**
Get ready for robots! (k-3) **629.8**
Journey to the planets (4 and up) **523.4**
Lost star: the story of Amelia Earhart (5 and up) **92**
The news about dinosaurs (4-6) **567.9**
Seeds pop, stick, glide (2-4) **582**
Seeing Earth from space (4 and up) **525**
Snakes are hunters (k-3) **597.9**
Tales mummies tell (5 and up) **930.1**
Volcano: the eruption and healing of Mount St. Helens (4 and up) **551.2**
Voyagers from space (4 and up) **523.5**
What's hatching out of that egg? (k-3) **591.1**
The **Laugh** book (4-6) **808.8**
Laughable limericks (4 and up) **821.008**
Laughing dumpling
Hearn, L. The old woman and her dumpling
In Womenfolk and fairy tales p44-50 **398.2**
Hearn, L. The old woman who lost her dumplings
In Best-loved folktales of the world p506-09 **398.2**
Laughs, hoots & giggles. Rosenbloom, J. **808.87**
Laundry
Fiction
Freeman, D. A pocket for Corduroy **E**
Laura Charlotte. Galbraith, K. O. **E**
The **Laura** Ingalls Wilder songbook (3 and up) **782.42**
Lauré, Jason, 1940-
Zambia (4 and up) **968.94**
Zimbabwe (4 and up) **968.91**
Lauter, Richard
(il) Smith, R. K. The war with Grandpa **Fic**
Lautrec, Henri de Toulouse- *See* Toulouse-Lautrec, Henri de, 1864-1901
Lavallee, Barbara
(il) Cobb, V. This place is wet **574.5**
Lavender. San Souci, R.
In San souci, R. Short & shivery p155-59 **398.2**

Lavies, Bianca
Backyard hunter: the praying mantis (2-4) **595.7**
It's an armadillo (1-3) **599.3**
Lily pad pond (k-2) **574.92**
The secretive timber rattlesnake (3-6) **597.9**
Tree trunk traffic (k-2) **591.5**

Lavine, Sigmund A.
Wonders of badgers (4 and up) **599.74**
Wonders of draft horses (4 and up) **636.1**
Wonders of foxes (4 and up) **599.74**
Wonders of tigers (4 and up) **599.74**
Wonders of turkeys (5 and up) **598**

Lavoisier, Antoine Laurent, 1743-1794

About

Grey, V. The chemist who lost his head: the story of Antoine Laurent Lavoisier (5 and up) **92**

Law
See also Constitutional law

Lawrence, D. H. (David Herbert), 1885-1930
Birds, beasts, and the third thing (3-6) **821**

Lawrence, David Herbert *See* Lawrence, D. H. (David Herbert), 1885-1930

Lawrence, James
Binky brothers, detectives **E**

Lawrence, John, 1933-
(il) Lively, P. Uninvited ghosts, and other stories **S C**

Lawrence, R. D., 1921-
Wolves (3-6) **599.74**

Lawson, Amy
Break a leg
In Things that go bump in the night p103-21 **S C**

Lawson, Don
An album of the Vietnam War (5 and up) **959.704**

Lawson, Robert, 1892-1957
Ben and me (5 and up) **Fic**
Mr. Revere and I (5 and up) **Fic**
Rabbit Hill (3-6) **Fic**
The tough winter (3-6) **Fic**
(il) Atwater, R. T. Mr. Popper's penguins **Fic**
(il) Leaf, M. The story of Ferdinand **E**
(il) Vining, E. G. Adam of the road **Fic**
See/See also pages in the following book(s):
Caldecott Medal books, 1938-1957 p64-78 **028.5**
Newbery Medal books, 1922-1955 p258-60, 263-67 **028.5**

Lawton, Clive
Passport to Israel (5 and up) **956.94**

Lazare, Jerry, 1927-
(il) Burch, R. Queenie Peavy **Fic**

Lazarevich, Mila
(il) Glazer, T. Do your ears hang low?: 50 more musical fingerplays **796.1**

Lazy Harry. Grimm, J.
In Grimm, J. The complete Grimm's fairy tales p678-81 **398.2**

Lazy Heinz
Grimm, J. Lazy Harry
In Grimm, J. The complete Grimm's fairy tales p678-81 **398.2**
Grimm, J. Lazy Heinz
In Bauer, C. F. Celebrations p140-43 **808.8**
In Grimm, J. Tales from Grimm p191-200 **398.2**

Lazy Jack
Jacobs, J. Lazy Jack
In Best-loved folktales of the world p214-15 **398.2**
In Jacobs, J. English fairy tales p152-54 **398.2**
Lazy Jack
In The Tall book of nursery tales p71-73 **398.2**
Rockwell, A. F. Lazy Jack
In Rockwell, A. F. The three bears & 15 other stories p92-99 **398.2**

Lazy Keloğlan and the sultan's daughter. Walker, B. K.
In Walker, B. K. A treasury of Turkish folktales for children p20-22 **398.2**

The **lazy** maiden. Afanas'ev, A. N.
In Afanas'ev, A. N. Russian fairy tales p423-25 **398.2**

Lazy spinner
Grimm, J. The lazy spinner
In Grimm, J. The complete Grimm's fairy tales p577-79 **398.2**

Lazy Tok. Skipper, M.
In Bauer, C. F. Celebrations p137-40 **808.8**

Le Cain, Errol, 1941-1989
(il) De la Mare, W. Molly Whuppie **398.2**
(il) Eliot, T. S. Growltiger's last stand **811**
(il) Grimm, J. The twelve dancing princesses **398.2**
(il) Lang, A. Aladdin and the wonderful lamp **398.2**
(il) Longfellow, H. W. Hiawatha's childhood **811**

Le Guin, Ursula K., 1929-
Catwings (2-4) **Fic**
Catwings return (2-4) **Fic**
The farthest shore. See note under Le Guin, U. K. A wizard of Earthsea **Fic**

Le Guin, Ursula K., 1929-—*Continued*
Tehanu. See note under Le Guin, U. K. A wizard of Earthsea **Fic**
The Tombs of Atuan. See note under Le Guin, U. K. A wizard of Earthsea **Fic**
A wizard of Earthsea (6 and up) **Fic**
See/See also pages in the following book(s):
Crosscurrents of criticism p333-41 **028.5**

Le Prince de Beaumont, Madame, 1711-1780
Beauty and the beast (1-4) **398.2**
also in The Classic fairy tales p139-50 **398.2**
also in Sleeping beauty & other favourite fairy tales p45-62 **398.2**
Prince Hyacinth and the dear little princess
In The Blue fairy book p12-18 **398.2**
Sweetheart
In Sleeping beauty & other favourite fairy tales p113-24 **398.2**
The tale of the three wishes
In The Classic fairy tales p153-55 **398.2**

Le Sieg, Theo *See* Seuss, Dr.

Leach, Maria, 1892-1977
Bill is with me now
In Leach, M. Whistle in the graveyard p66-67 **398.2**
Whistle in the graveyard (4-6) **398.2**
Contents: White House ghosts; Earl Gerald; Anne Boleyn; White ghosts; Skull race; Nobody here but you and me; What's the matter; Old Tom comes home; 'Tain't so; One handful; Can't rest; Blackbeard's treasure; The tired ghost; Cauld, cauld, forever cauld; The outside man; I'm coming up the stairs; The man on Morvan's Road; Staring at you; The sea captain at the door; Grandpa Joe's brother; Bill is with me now; Tony and his harp; Crossing the bridge; The ghostly spools; Tick, tick, tick; Pumpkin; Jenny Green Teeth; Baba Yaga; Nuinumma-Kwiten; Pot-Tilter; Willie Winkie; Raw Head and Bloody Bones; The black cat's eyes; How to become a witch; Next turn to the right; A breath of air; The ghost on Brass's Hill; Sunrise; Dead man

Leaf, Margaret
The eyes of the dragon **E**

Leaf, Munro, 1905-
The story of Ferdinand **E**

Leakey, Louis Seymour Bazett, 1903-1972
See/See also pages in the following book(s):
Lasky, K. Traces of life p88-93 (5 and up) **573.2**

Leakey, Mary D. (Mary Douglas), 1913-
See/See also pages in the following book(s):
Lasky, K. Traces of life p52-60 (5 and up) **573.2**

Lean Liesl and Lanky Lenz
Grimm, J. Lean Liesl and Lanky Lenz
In Grimm, J. Tales from Grimm p201-03 **398.2**
Grimm, J. Lean Lisa
In Grimm, J. The complete Grimm's fairy tales p696-98 **398.2**

Lean Lisa. Grimm, J.
In Grimm, J. The complete Grimm's fairy tales p696-98 **398.2**

Lear, Edward, 1812-1888
The complete nonsense of Edward Lear **821**
An Edward Lear alphabet (k-2) **821**
Edward Lear's The Scroobious Pip **821**
How pleasant to know Mr. Lear! **821**
The Jumblies (2-6) **821**
The nonsense verse of Edward Lear **821**
The owl and the pussycat (k-2) **821**

Learning, Art of *See* Study, Method of

Learning about AIDS. Silverstein, A. **616.97**

Learning and scholarship
See also Education

Learning disabilities
Fisher, G. L. The survival guide for kids with LD (learning differences) (5 and up) **371.9**

Fiction

Cassedy, S. M.E. and Morton (6 and up) **Fic**
DeClements, B. 6th grade can really kill you (5 and up) **Fic**
Gilson, J. Do bananas chew gum? (4-6) **Fic**
Pevsner, S. Keep stompin' till the music stops (4 and up) **Fic**
Smith, D. B. Kelly's creek (4-6) **Fic**

Learning resource centers *See* Instructional materials centers

Learning to say good-by. LeShan, E. J. **155.9**

Leathers, Noel L.
The Japanese in America
In The In America series **305.8**

Leatherwood, Stephen
(jt. auth) Reeves, R. R. The Sea World book of dolphins **599.5**

Leaves. Whittington, M. K.
In Things that go bump in the night p232-42 **S C**

Lebanese Americans
Harik, E. M. The Lebanese in America
In The In America series **305.8**

Lebanese cookery *See* Cookery, Lebanese

The **Lebanese** in America. Harik, E. M.
In The In America series **305.8**

Lebanon
Lebanon—in pictures (5 and up) **956.92**
Tames, R. Take a trip to Lebanon (1-3) **956.92**

Lebanon—in pictures (5 and up) **956.92**

Leckie, Robert
The story of World War II (5 and up) **940.53**

Leder, Dora
(il) Simon, N. Cats do, dogs don't **636.088**

Lee, Alan
(il) Dickinson, P. Merlin dreams **Fic**

Lee, Jeanne M.
Bà-Năm **E**
Legend of the Li River (k-3) **398.2**
Legend of the Milky Way (k-3) **398.2**
Toad is the uncle of heaven (k-3) **398.2**

Lee, Jody A.
(il) Montgomery, L. M. Anne of Green Gables **Fic**

Lee, Martin
Paul Revere (5 and up) **92**

Lee, Mary Price
Last names first (5 and up) **929.4**

Lee, Richard S. (Richard Sandoval), 1927-
(jt. auth) Lee, M. P. Last names first **929.4**

Lee, Robert E. (Robert Edward), 1807-1870
About
Weidhorn, M. Robert E. Lee (5 and up) **92**

Lee, Sally
Donor banks: saving lives with organ and tissue transplants (5 and up) **362.1**

Leech, John, 1817-1864
(il) Dickens, C. A Christmas carol in prose **Fic**

Leedy, Loreen, 1959-
The furry news (k-3) **070**

Leekley, Thomas
The theft of fire
In Best-loved folktales of the world p712-18 **398.2**

Leeuwenhoek, Antoni van, 1632-1723

About
Kumin, M. The microscope (k-3) **92**

Left & right. Oppenheim, J. **E**

Left- and right-handedness
Silverstein, A. The story of your hand (5 and up) **612**
See/See also pages in the following book(s):
Stafford, P. Your two brains p33-40 (5 and up) **612.8**

Left behind. Carrick, C. See note under Carrick, C. Ben and the porcupine **E**

The **legend** of King Arthur. Lister, R. **398.2**

The **legend** of Old Befana. De Paola, T. **398.2**

The **legend** of Saint Elizabeth. Sawyer, R.
In Sawyer, R. The way of the storyteller p307-15 **372.6**

A **legend** of Saint Nicholas. De Leeuw, A.
In Best-loved folktales of the world p174-76 **398.2**

The **legend** of Scarface. San Souci, R. **398.2**

The **legend** of Scotland. Carroll, L.
In Carroll, L. The complete works of Lewis Carroll p999-1005 **828**

The **Legend** of St. Christopher
In Shedlock, M. L. The art of the story-teller p168-72 **372.6**

The **legend** of the Christmas rose. Greene, E. **398.2**

The **legend** of the Indian paintbrush. De Paola, T. **398.2**

Legend of the Li River. Lee, J. M. **398.2**

Legend of the Milky Way. Lee, J. M. **398.2**

Legends
See also Folklore; Mythology
De Paola, T. The clown of God (k-3) **398.2**
Lurie, A. The heavenly zoo (4 and up) **398.2**
See/See also pages in the following book(s):
The Scott, Foresman anthology of children's literature p456-78 **808.8**
Indexes
Index to fairy tales, 1949-1972 **398.2**
Index to fairy tales, 1973-1977 **398.2**
Index to fairy tales, 1978-1986 **398.2**
France
Cooney, B. The little juggler (3-6) **398.2**
Great Britain
Brown, M. Dick Whittington and his cat (k-3) **398.2**
Hawaii
Brown, M. Backbone of the king (5 and up) **398.2**
Ireland
Stephens, J. Irish fairy tales (6 and up) **398.2**

Legends, Chickasaw *See* Chickasaw Indians—Legends

Legends, Indian *See* Indians of North America—Legends

Legends, Jewish
Singer, I. B. The golem (5 and up) **398.2**

Legends of Charlemagne. Bulfinch, T.
In Bulfinch, T. Bulfinch's Mythology **291**

Legerdemain *See* Magic

LeGuin, Ursula *See* Le Guin, Ursula K., 1929-

Leif the unlucky. Haugaard, E. C. **Fic**

Leighner, Alice Mills
Reynard (2-4) **599.74**

Lembo, Diana
(jt. auth) Gillespie, J. T. Juniorplots: a book talk manual for teachers and librarians 028.1
Lemel and Tzipa. Singer, I. B.
In Singer, I. B. Naftali the storyteller and his horse, Sus, and other stories p85-98 S C
In Singer, I. B. Stories for children p103-14 S C
Lemieux, Michèle
(il) Cole, J. A gift from Saint Francis 92
(il) Menotti, G. C. Amahl and the night visitors Fic
Lemke, Horst, 1922-
(il) Linde, P. van der. Around the world in 80 dishes 641.5
The **lemming** condition. Arkin, A. Fic
Lemmings
Fiction
Arkin, A. The lemming condition (5 and up) Fic
The **lemonade** trick. Corbett, S. Fic
Lemurs
See/See also pages in the following book(s):
Kohl, J. Pack, band, and colony (5 and up) 591.5
L'Engle, Madeleine, 1918-
Many waters. See note under L'Engle, M. A wrinkle in time Fic
Meet the Austins (5 and up) Fic
A ring of endless light (5 and up) Fic
A swiftly tilting planet. See note under L'Engle, M. A wrinkle in time Fic
A wind in the door. See note under L'Engle, M. A wrinkle in time Fic
A wrinkle in time (5 and up) Fic
See/See also pages in the following book(s):
Townsend, J. R. A sense of story p120-26 028.5
Lenin, Vladimir Il'ich, 1870-1924
See/See also pages in the following book(s):
Andrews, W. G. The land and the people of the Soviet Union (5 and up) 947
Lenny Kandell, smart aleck. Conford, E. Fic
Lenses
Taylor, B. Bouncing and bending light (3-5) 535
Lenski, Lois, 1893-1974
Strawberry girl (4-6) Fic
(il) Lovelace, M. H. Betsy-Tacy Fic
See/See also pages in the following book(s):
Newbery Medal books, 1922-1955 p270-87 028.5
Lent, Blair, 1930-
Baba Yaga (k-3) 398.2
(il) Andersen, H. C. The little match girl Fic
(il) Mosel, A. The funny little woman 398.2
(il) Mosel, A. Tikki Tikki Tembo 398.2
See/See also pages in the following book(s):
Newbery and Caldecott Medal books, 1966-1975 p244-55 028.5
Lentil. McCloskey, R. E
Leo and Emily. Brandenberg, F. E
Leo and Emily and the dragon. Brandenberg, F. See note under Brandenberg, F. Leo and Emily E
Leo and Emily's big ideas. Brandenberg, F. See note under Brandenberg, F. Leo and Emily E
Leo and Emily's zoo. Brandenberg, F. See note under Brandenberg, F. Leo and Emily E
Leo, Zack, and Emmie. Ehrlich, A. E
Leo, Zack, and Emmie together again. Ehrlich, A. E
Leodhas, Sorche Nic, 1898-1968
Always room for one more (k-3) 781.62
The bride who out talked the water kelpie
In The Scott, Foresman anthology of children's literature p162-67 808.8
The lass who went out at the cry of dawn
In Womenfolk and fairy tales p83-92 398.2
The stolen bairn and the Sidh
In Womenfolk and fairy tales p1-13 398.2
The woman who flummoxed the fairies
In Womenfolk and fairy tales p135-45 398.2
Leonard, Marcia
(comp) Cricket's jokes, riddles and other stuff. See Cricket's jokes, riddles and other stuff 793.73
Leonardo, da Vinci, 1452-1519
About
Provensen, A. Leonardo da Vinci: the artist, inventor, scientist (3 and up) 92
Raboff, E. Leonardo da Vinci (4 and up) 759.5
The **leopard's** daughter. Courlander, H.
In With a deep sea smile p56-60 372.6
Lephien, Emilie U. (Emilia Utteg)
Ecuador (4 and up) 986.6
The **leprechaun** shoemakers. Watts, F. B.
In Holiday plays round the year p220-28 812.008
The **leprechaun's** story. Kennedy, R.
In Kennedy, R. Collected stories p97-106 S C

Leprince de Beaumont, Madame *See* Le Prince de Beaumont, Madame, 1711-1780

Lepthien, Emilie U. (Emilie Utteg)
Buffalo (2-4) **599.73**
The Choctaw (2-4) **970.004**
Iceland (4 and up) **949.12**
Luxembourg (4 and up) **949.35**
The Mandans (2-4) **970.004**
South Dakota
In America the beautiful **973**

Lerchis-Puskaitis, A.
The Bul-Bul Bird
In Best-loved folktales of the world p395-99 **398.2**
God and the Devil share the harvest
In Best-loved folktales of the world p394-95 **398.2**

Lerner, Carol, 1927-
Dumb cane and daffodils (4-6) **581.6**
A forest year (3-5) **574.5**
Moonseed and mistletoe (4-6) **581.6**
Plant families (4 and up) **582**
(il) Selsam, M. E. Tree flowers **582.16**

LeShan, Eda J.
Grandparents: a special kind of love (4 and up) **306.8**
Learning to say good-by (4 and up) **155.9**
When a parent is very sick (4 and up) **155.9**
When grownups drive you crazy (4 and up) **306.8**

Leslie-Melville, Betty
Daisy Rothschild (1-3) **599.73**

Lessac, Frané
Caribbean canvas **811**
(il) Pomerantz, C. The chalk doll **E**

Lesser, Rika
Hansel and Gretel (1-3) **398.2**

Lessons. Babbitt, N.
In Babbitt, N. The Devil's other storybook p47-52 **S C**

Lester, Helen
The revenge of the Magic Chicken **E**

Lester, Julius
Further tales of Uncle Remus (4-6) **398.2**

Contents: Brer Fox and Mr. Man; King Lion and Mr. Man; Brer Fox and Brer Turtle; Brer Fox gets tricked by the frogs; Brer Bear gets tricked by Brer Frog; Brer Bear, Brer Turtle, and the rope-pulling contest; Brer Turtle takes care of Brer Buzzard; Brer Fox wants to make music; The Pimmerly Plum; Brer Turtle takes flying lessons; Brer Buzzard and Brer Hawk; Brer Buzzard bites the dust—again; The Wise Bird and the Foolish Bird; The most-beautiful-bird in-the-world contest; Brer Fox and Uncle Mud Turtle; The creature with no claws; Brer Polecat finds a winter home; Brer Bear and Brer Rabbit take care of Brer Fox and Brer Wolf; Brer Fox gets away for once; Taily-po; Brer Rabbit, Brer Fox, and the chickens; Brer Fox tries to get revenge; Brer Wolf and the pigs; Mr. Benjamin Ram and his wonderful fiddle; Mr. Benjamin Ram triumphs again; How the Bear nursed the Alligators; Brer Turtle and Brer Mink; Brer Billy Goat tricks Brer Wolf; Brer Fox takes Miz Cricket to dinner; Miz Cricket makes the creatures run; The story of the Doodang; Brer Deer and King Sun's daughter; Teenchy-Tiny Duck's magical satchel

How many spots does a leopard have? and other tales (2-5) **398.2**

Contents: Why the Sun and the Moon live in the sky; The bird that made milk; The monster who swallowed everything; Tug-of-war; Why dogs chase cats; The town where snoring was not allowed; The town where sleeping was not allowed; The woman and the tree children; Why monkeys live in trees; What is the most important part of the body?; How many spots does a leopard have?; The wonderful healing leaves

The knee-high man
In The Scott, Foresman anthology of children's literature p375-76 **808.8**

The knee-high man, and other tales (k-3) **398.2**

Contents: What is trouble?; Why dogs hate cats; Mr. Rabbit and Mr. Bear; Why the waves have whitecaps; The farmer and the snake; The knee-high man

More tales of Uncle Remus (4-6) **398.2**

Contents: Brer Rabbit gets Brer Fox's dinner; Brer Rabbit and Brer Fox kill a cow; Brer Fox and the grapes; Brer Rabbit falls in love; The Ol' African helps out; The courting contest; Brer Rabbit, Brer Coon, and the frogs; Brer Rabbit's laughing place; Brer Rabbit gets the house to himself; Miz Partridge tricks Brer Rabbit; The famine; Brer Rabbit, Brer Bear, and the honey; Brer Snake catches Brer Wolf; Brer Rabbit gets the meat; Brer Rabbit scares everybody; Grinny Granny Wolf; The fire test; Brer Rabbit catches Wattle Weasel; Brer Rabbit and Mr. Man's chickens; The barbecue; Brer Alligator learns about trouble; Brer Fox gets tricked again; Brer Rabbit and Brer Bullfrog; Brer Rabbit meets up with Cousin Wildcat; Brer Rabbit gets a little comeuppance; Brer Rabbit advises Brer Lion; Brer Rabbit's money mint; Brer Rabbit makes a deal with Mr. Man; Brer Rabbit doctors Brer Fox's burns; Brer Fox sets a fire; Brer Rabbit builds a tower; Brer Rabbit saves Brer Wolf—maybe; Mammy-Bammy Big-Money takes care of Brer Wolf; Brer Rabbit and the gizzard eater; Why dogs are always sniffing; Being fashionable ain't always healthy; The race

People who could fly
In Best-loved folktales of the world p663-65 **398.2**

The tales of Uncle Remus (4-6) **398.2**

Contents: How the animals came to Earth; How Brer Fox and Brer Dog became enemies; "Hold'im down, Brer Fox"; Brer Rabbit comes to dinner; Brer Rabbit and the Tar Baby; Brer Rabbit gets even; Brer Rabbit and Sister Cow; Brer Turtle, Brer Rabbit, and Brer Fox; Brer Wolf tries to catch Brer Rabbit; Brer Rabbit finally gets beaten; Mr. Jack Sparrow meets his end; Brer Rabbit gets caught one more time; The death of Brer Wolf; Brer Fox and Brer Rabbit go hunting; Brer Rabbit tricks Brer Fox again; Brer Rabbit eats the butter; Brer Rabbit saves his meat; Brer Rabbit's children; The death of Brer Fox; Brer Rabbit and Brer Lion; Brer Rabbit takes care of Brer Tiger; Brer Lion meets the creature; The talking house; Brer Rabbit gets beaten again; Brer Rabbit tricks Brer Bear; The end of Brer Bear; Brer Fox gets tricked again; Brer Rabbit and the little girl; Brer Rabbit goes back to Mr. Man's garden; Brer Possum hears the singing; Brer Rabbit's riddle; The Moon in the pond; Why Brer Bear has no tail; Wiley Wolf and Riley Rabbit; Brer Rabbit gets the money; The cradle didn't rock; Brer Rabbit to the rescue; The noise in the woods; Brer Rabbit gets the meat again; Brer Wolf gets in more trouble; Brer Rabbit tells on Brer Wolf; Brer Rabbit and the mosquitoes; How Brer Rabbit became a scary monster; Brer Fox, Brer Rabbit, and King Deer's

Lester, Julius—*Continued*
daughter; Brer Rabbit breaks up the party; Brer Rabbit outwits Mr. Man; Brer Wolf, Brer Fox, and the little Rabbits; Brer Rabbit's luck
To be a slave (6 and up) **326**
Why the waves have whitecaps
In The Scott, Foresman anthology of children's literature p376 **808.8**

Let George do it. Pendleton, E.
In Holiday plays round the year p169-78 **812.008**

Let the balloon go. Southall, I. **Fic**

Let the circle be unbroken. Taylor, M. D. See note under Taylor, M. D. Song of the trees **Fic**

Let there be light: a book about windows. Giblin, J. **690**

Let's be early settlers with Daniel Boone. Parish, P. **745.5**

Let's do fingerplays. Grayson, M. F. **796.1**

Let's explore a river. McCauley, J. R. **574.92**

Let's go to Iran. See Tames, R. Take a trip to Iran **955**

Let's go to Iraq. See Tames, R. Take a trip to Iraq **956.7**

Let's go to Israel. See Rutland, J. Take a trip to Israel **956.94**

Let's go to Lebanon. See Tames, R. Take a trip to Lebanon **956.92**

Let's go to Morocco. See Lye, K. Take a trip to Morocco **964**

Let's go to Saudi Arabia. See Lye, K. Take a trip to Saudi Arabia **953.8**

Let's go to Syria. See Lye, K. Take a trip to Syria **956.91**

Let's go to Turkey. See Lye, K. Take a trip to Turkey **956.1**

The **letter,** the witch, and the ring. Bellairs, J. See note under Bellairs, J. The house with a clock in its walls **Fic**

A **letter** to Amy. Keats, E. J. See note under Keats. E. J. The snowy day **E**

Letter writing
Mischel, F. How to write a letter (5 and up) **808**

Letterbox: the art & history of letters. Adkins, J. **745.6**

Lettering
See also Alphabets
Adkins, J. Letterbox: the art & history of letters (4 and up) **745.6**
Fisher, L. E. Alphabet art: thirteen ABCs from around the world (4 and up) **745.6**

Letters

Fiction
Potter, B. Yours affectionately, Peter Rabbit: miniature letters **E**

Letting in the jungle. Kipling, R.
In Kipling, R. The jungle books **S C**

Letting off steam. Jacobs, L. **621.44**

Leukemia
Bergman, T. One day at a time (1-3) **616.99**
Coerr, E. Sadako and the thousand paper cranes [biography of Sadako Sasaki] (3-6) **92**
Monroe, J. Leukemia (4-6) **616.99**

Fiction
Kehret, P. Sisters, long ago (5 and up) **Fic**

Levasseur-Regourd, Anny-Chantal
Our sun and the inner planets (4-6) **523.7**

Levenson, Sam, 1911-1980
In one era and out the other [excerpt]
In The Random House book of humor for children p95-99 **817.008**

Levey, Judith S., 1936-
(ed) Macmillan dictionary for children. See Macmillan dictionary for children **423**

Levi, Enrique Jaramillo *See* Jaramillo Levi, Enrique, 1944-

Levi Strauss & Co.
Henry, S. Everyone wears his name: a biography of Levi Strauss (5 and up) **92**

Levin, Betty, 1927-
Brother moose (5 and up) **Fic**

Levine, Edna Simon, 1910-
Lisa and her soundless world (1-3) **617.8**

Levine, Ellen
I hate English! **E**

Levine, Joe
(il) Hirst, R. My place in space **520**

Levinson, Nancy Smiler, 1938-
Christopher Columbus: voyager to the unknown (4 and up) **92**
Chuck Yeager: the man who broke the sound barrier (5 and up) **92**

Levinson, Riki
I go with my family to Grandma's **E**
Our home is the sea **E**
Watch the stars come out **E**

Levitin, Sonia, 1934-
The return (6 and up) **Fic**
Silver days (5 and up) **Fic**

Levoy, Myron
Alan and Naomi (6 and up) **Fic**
The witch of Fourth Street, and other stories (4-6) **S C**
Contents: The witch of Fourth Street; Vincent-the-Good and the electric train; Andreas and the magic bells; Mrs. Dunn's lovely, lovely farm; Keplik, the match man; The fish angel; Aaron's gift; The Hanukkah Santa Claus

Levy, Elizabeth, 1942-
Something queer at the ball park. See note under Levy, E. Something queer is going on (a mystery) **E**
Something queer at the birthday party. See note under Levy, E. Something queer is going on (a mystery) **E**
Something queer at the haunted school. See note under Levy, E. Something queer is going on (a mystery) **E**
Something queer at the lemonade stand. See note under Levy, E. Something queer is going on (a mystery) **E**
Something queer at the library. See note under Levy, E. Something queer is going on (a mystery) **E**
Something queer in rock 'n' roll. See note under Levy, E. Something queer is going on (a mystery) **E**
Something queer is going on (a mystery) **E**
Something queer on vacation. See note under Levy, E. Something queer is going on (a mystery) **E**
(jt. auth) Harris, R. H. Before you were three **155.4**

Lewin, Betsy, 1937-
(il) Polushkin, M. Kitten in trouble **E**

Lewin, Hugh, 1939-
Jafta **E**
Jafta and the wedding. See note under Lewin, H. Jafta **E**
Jafta's father. See note under Lewin, H. Jafta **E**
Jafta's mother. See note under Lewin, H. Jafta **E**
Jafta—the journey. See note under Lewin, H. Jafta **E**
Jafta—the town. See note under Lewin, H. Jafta **E**

Lewin, Ted
Tiger trek (2-4) **599.74**
(il) Bagnold, E. National Velvet **Fic**
(il) Clymer, E. L. The horse in the attic **Fic**
(il) Garfield, L. Young Nick and Jubilee **Fic**
(il) Heide, F. P. The day of Ahmed's secret **E**
(il) Herds of thunder, manes of gold. See Herds of thunder, manes of gold **808.8**
(il) Knudson, R. R. Babe Didrikson: athlete of the century **92**
(il) Kudlinski, K. V. Rachel Carson: pioneer of ecology **92**
(il) O'Dell, S. Island of the Blue Dolphins **Fic**
(il) Yolen, J. Bird watch: a book of poetry **811**

Lewis, Allen
(il) Field, R. Calico bush **Fic**

Lewis, C. S. (Clive Staples), 1898-1963
The horse and his boy. See note under Lewis, C. S. The lion, the witch and the wardrobe **Fic**
The last battle. See note under Lewis, C. S. The lion, the witch and the wardrobe **Fic**
The lion, the witch and the wardrobe (4 and up) **Fic**
The magician's nephew. See note under Lewis, C. S. The lion, the witch and the wardrobe **Fic**
Prince Caspian. See note under Lewis, C. S. The lion, the witch and the wardrobe **Fic**
The silver chair. See note under Lewis, C. S. The lion, the witch and the wardrobe **Fic**
The voyage of the Dawn Treader. See note under Lewis, C. S. The lion, the witch and the wardrobe **Fic**
See/See also pages in the following book(s):
Horn Book reflections on children's books and reading p225-37 **028.5**
Only connect: readings on children's literature p170-75 **028.5**

Lewis, Clive Staples *See* Lewis, C. S. (Clive Staples), 1898-1963

Lewis, Elizabeth Foreman, 1892-1958
See/See also pages in the following book(s):
Newbery Medal books, 1922-1955 p109-13 **028.5**

Lewis, J. Patrick
A hippopotamusn't and other animal verses (k-3) **811**
The tsar & the amazing cow **E**

Lewis, Meriwether, 1774-1809
About
Blumberg, R. The incredible journey of Lewis and Clark (5 and up) **978**

Lewis, Richard
In the night, still dark (1-3) **811**
(ed) In a spring garden. See In a spring garden **895.6**
(comp) Miracles: poems by children of the English-speaking world. See Miracles: poems by children of the English-speaking world **821.008**

Lewis, T. (Thomas)
(il) Carroll, L. Alice's adventures in Wonderland, and Through the looking glass **Fic**
(il) Cwiklik, R. Sequoyah and the Cherokee alphabet **92**
(il) Stevenson, R. L. A child's garden of verses **821**

Lewis, Thomas *See* Lewis, T. (Thomas)
Lewis and Clark Expedition (1804-1806)
Blumberg, R. The incredible journey of Lewis and Clark (5 and up) **978**
Fiction
O'Dell, S. Streams to the river, river to the sea (5 and up) **Fic**
Lewis Carroll's Jabberwocky. Carroll, L. **821**
Lexau, Joan M.
I should have stayed in bed **E**
The rooftop mystery **E**
Who took the farmer's [hat]? **E**
Lexington, Battle of, 1775
Poetry
Longfellow, H. W. Paul Revere's ride (k-3) **811**
Li, Yao-wen
(jt. auth) Kendall, C. Sweet and sour **398.2**
Liar, liar, pants on fire! Cohen, M. See note under Cohen, M. See you in second grade! **E**
Libby on Wednesdays. Snyder, Z. K. **Fic**
Liberia
Liberia—in pictures (5 and up) **966.62**
Folklore
See Folklore—Liberia
Liberia—in pictures (5 and up) **966.62**
The **librarian** and the robbers. Mahy, M.
In Mahy, M. The great piratical rumbustification & The librarian and the robbers p44-63 **Fic**
Librarians
Fiction
Pinkwater, D. M. Aunt Lulu **E**
Libraries
See also Instructional materials centers; Public libraries
Gibbons, G. Check it out! the book about libraries (k-3) **027**
Censorship
Intellectual freedom manual **323.44**
Fiction
Alexander, M. G. How my library grew, by Dinah **E**
Beatty, P. Eight mules from Monterey (5 and up) **Fic**
Bonsall, C. N. Tell me some more **E**
Clifford, E. Help! I'm a prisoner in the library (3-5) **Fic**
Kimmel, E. A. I took my frog to the library **E**
Handbooks, manuals, etc.
Matthews, J. G. ClipArt & dynamic designs for libraries & media centers **021.7**
Periodicals
Wilson Library Bulletin **020.5**
Libraries, Children's *See* Children's libraries
Libraries, School *See* School libraries
Libraries and schools
Jay, H. L. Developing library-museum partnerships to serve young people **027.8**
Library catalogs
ALA filing rules **025.3**
Library media center programs for middle schools: a curriculum-based approach. Smith, J. B. **027.8**
Library of Congress. Children's Literature Center *See* Children's Literature Center
Library of Congress. National Library Service for the Blind and Physically Handicapped
For younger readers: braille and talking books. See For younger readers: braille and talking books **011.6**
Library science
See also Library services
Periodicals
Wilson Library Bulletin **020.5**
Library services
MacDonald, M. R. Booksharing: 101 programs to use with preschoolers **027.62**
Library services to young adults *See* Young adults' library services
Library Talk **027.805**
Libya
Targ-Brill, M. Libya (4 and up) **961.2**
Life, Kay
(il) Cleary, B. Muggie Maggie **Fic**
Life
Origin
See/See also pages in the following book(s):
Gallant, R. A. Before the sun dies p25-35 (6 and up) **575**
Life (Biology)
See also Reproduction
Life among the savages [excerpt]. Jackson, S.
In The Random House book of humor for children p66-73 **817.008**
The **life** and death of Martin Luther King, Jr. Haskins, J. **92**
Life in a tidal pool. Silverstein, A. **574.92**
Life in ponds and streams. Amos, W. H. **591.92**
Life of the butterfly. Fischer-Nagel, H. **595.7**
Life of the honeybee. Fischer-Nagel, H. **595.7**
Life of the ladybug. Fischer-Nagel, H. **595.7**

Life of the snail. Buholzer, T. **594**
Life on a barge. Scarry, H. **386**
Life on a fishing boat. Scarry, H. **639.2**
Life on other planets
Branley, F. M. Is there life in outer space? (k-3) **574.999**
Branley, F. M. Mysteries of life on earth and beyond (6 and up) **574.999**
Poynter, M. Cosmic quest (5 and up) **574.999**
See/See also pages in the following book(s):
Berger, M. UFOs, ETs & visitors from space (5 and up) **001.9**
Gallant, R. A. Before the sun dies p152-59 (6 and up) **575**
Life's a beach. Bridgers, S. E.
In Connections: short stories by outstanding writers for young adults p27-43 **S C**
Light
Taylor, B. Bouncing and bending light (3-5) **535**
Taylor, B. Color and light (3-5) **535**
Light and shade *See* Shades and shadows
Light another candle. Chaikin, M. **296.4**
The **light** beyond the forest. Sutcliff, R. **398.2**
A **light** in the attic. Silverstein, S. **811**
The **light** princess. MacDonald, G. **Fic**
In MacDonald, G. The complete fairy tales of George MacDonald **S C**
The **light** princess, and other tales. See MacDonald, G. The complete fairy tales of George Macdonald **S C**
Lighthouses
Gibbons, G. Beacons of light: lighthouses (1-3) **387.1**
Fiction
Swift, H. H. The little red lighthouse and the great gray bridge **E**
Lightning
Branley, F. M. Flash, crash, rumble, and roll (k-3) **551.5**
Lights, Feast of *See* Hanukkah
Lights around the palm. Jukes, M. **E**
Lights! Camera! Action! Gibbons, G. **791.43**
Like Jake and me. Jukes, M. **Fic**
Like meat loves salt
Like meat loves salt
In Grandfather tales p124-29 **398.2**
A **likely** place. Fox, P. **Fic**
Lili: a giant panda of Sichuan. McClung, R. M. **599.74**
Lilies, rabbits, and painted eggs. Barth, E. **394.2**
Lillegard, Dee
Nevada
In America the beautiful **973**
Lilly, Charles
(il) Greene, B. Philip Hall likes me, I reckon maybe **Fic**
Lilly, Kenneth
Kenneth Lilly's animals (3 and up) **599**
(il) Cole, J. Large as life daytime animals **591**
(il) Cole, J. Large as life nighttime animals **591**
(il) Lane, M. The fox **599.74**
Lily pad pond. Lavies, B. **574.92**
Lima, Carolyn W.
A to zoo: subject access to children's picture books **011.6**
Lima, John A.
(jt. auth) Lima, C. W. A to zoo: subject access to children's picture books **011.6**
Limericks
Ciardi, J. The hopeful trout and other limericks (2-4) **811**
Laughable limericks (4 and up) **821.008**
Lobel, A. The book of pigericks: pig limericks (1-3) **811**
They've discovered a head in the box for the bread, and other laughable limericks (4 and up) **821.008**
Lin Zheng
(il) Zhang Xiu Shi. Monkey and the White Bone Demon **398.2**
Lincoln, Abraham, 1809-1865
About
Adler, D. A. A picture book of Abraham Lincoln (1-3) **92**
D'Aulaire, I. Abraham Lincoln (2-4) **92**
Freedman, R. Lincoln: a photobiography (4 and up) **92**
Gross, R. B. True stories about Abraham Lincoln (2-4) **92**
North, S. Abe Lincoln: log cabin to White House (5 and up) **92**
Sandburg, C. Abe Lincoln grows up (5 and up) **92**
Lincoln, Patricia Henderson
(il) Gish, L. An actor's life for me **92**
The **Lincoln** Brigade. Katz, W. L. **946.081**
The **Lincoln** writing dictionary for children (4 and up) **423**
Linda-Gold and the old king. Wahlenberg, A.
In The Scott, Foresman anthology of children's literature p242-44 **808.8**
Lindbergh, Charles, 1902-1974
See/See also pages in the following book(s):
Tessendorf, K. C. Barnstormers & daredevils p42-50 (4 and up) **629.13**

Lindbergh, Reeve
Benjamin's barn E
The day the goose got loose E
Lindblom, Steven, 1946-
(il) Eldredge, N. The fossil factory **560**
Linde, Polly van der
Around the world in 80 dishes (3-6) **641.5**
Linde, Tasha van der
(jt. auth) Linde, P. van der Around the world in 80 dishes **641.5**
Lindgren, Astrid, 1907-
Christmas in the stable (k-2) **232.9**
Lotta on Troublemaker Street (1-3) **Fic**
Pippi goes on board. See note under Lindgren, A. Pippi Longstocking **Fic**
Pippi in the South Seas. See note under Lindgren, A. Pippi Longstocking **Fic**
Pippi Longstocking (3-6) **Fic**
Ronia, the robber's daughter (4-6) **Fic**
The Tomten **E**
The Tomten and the fox **E**

About

Hurwitz, J. Astrid Lindgren: storyteller to the world (4 and up) **92**
Lindgren, Barbro, 1937-
Sam's ball. See note under Lindgren, B. Sam's car **E**
Sam's bath. See note under Lindgren, B. Sam's car **E**
Sam's car **E**
Sam's cookie. See note under Lindgren, B. Sam's car **E**
Sam's potty. See note under Lindgren, B. Sam's car **E**
Sam's teddy bear. See note under Lindgren, B. Sam's car **E**
Sam's wagon. See note under Lindgren, B. Sam's car **E**
The wild baby **E**
The wild baby gets a puppy. See note under Lindgren, B. The wild baby **E**
The wild baby goes to sea. See note under Lindgren, B. The wild baby **E**
Linguistics *See* Language and languages
Link, Martin A.
(jt. auth) Blood, C. L. The goat in the rug **E**
Linley, Mike
The snake in the grass (3-6) **597.9**
(jt. auth) Harrison, V. The world of snakes **597.9**
Linn, David
(il) Cohen, D. Phone call from a ghost **133.1**

Linnea in Monet's garden. Björk, C. **Fic**
Linnea's almanac. Björk, C. **508**
Linnea's windowsill garden. Björk, C. **635**
The **Lion** and the mouse
In The Baby's story book p62-63 **398.2**
In The Tall book of nursery tales p108-09 **398.2**
The **lion** and the mouse. Calmenson, S.
In The Read-aloud treasury p188-89 **808.8**
The **lion** and the mouse. Rockwell, A. F.
In Rockwell, A. F. The three bears & 15 other stories p14-16 **398.2**
Lion and the ostrich chicks. Bryan, A.
In Bryan, A. Lion and the ostrich chicks, and other African folk tales p3-23 **398.2**
Lion and the ostrich chicks, and other African tales. Bryan, A. **398.2**
Lion dancer: Ernie Wan's Chinese New Year. Waters, K. **394.2**
A **lion** for Lewis. Wells, R. **E**
The **Lion** hunt
In Juba this and Juba that p62-70 **372.6**
The **lion,** the witch and the wardrobe. Lewis, C. S. **Fic**
A **lion** to guard us. Bulla, C. R. **Fic**
Lionel at large. Krensky, S. **E**
Lionel in the fall. Krensky, S. See note under Krensky, S. Lionel at large **E**
Lionel in the spring. Krensky, S. See note under Krensky, S. Lionel at large **E**
Liongo, a hero of Shanga. Steere, E.
In The Crest and the hide, and other African stories of heroes, chiefs, bards, hunters, sorcerers, and common people p77-87 **398.2**
Lionni, Leo, 1910-
Alexander and the wind-up mouse **E**
The biggest house in the world **E**
Cornelius **E**
Fish is fish **E**
Frederick **E**
Inch by inch **E**
It's mine! **E**
Little blue and little yellow **E**
Nicolas, where have you been? **E**
Six crows **E**
Swimmy **E**
Lions
Jorgensen, G. Crocodile beat **E**
McGuire, L. Lions (4-6) **599.74**
Yoshida, T. Young lions (1-3) **599.74**

Fiction

Daugherty, J. H. Andy and the lion **E**
Fatio, L. The happy lion **E**

Lions—Fiction—*Continued*
Freeman, D. Dandelion E
Hurd, E. T. Johnny Lion's book E
Peet, B. Eli E

The **lion's** den. Walker, B. K.
In Walker, B. K. A treasury of Turkish folktales for children p16 398.2

Lippincott, Gary
(il) Cohen, D. Ancient Egypt 932

Lippincott, Joseph Wharton, 1887-1976
Wilderness champion (5 and up) Fic

Lippman, Peter J., 1936-
(il) Cobb, V. Science experiments you can eat 507

Liquor problem *See* Alcoholism

Lisa and her soundless world. Levine, E. S. 617.8

Lisa's war. Matas, C. Fic

Lisker, Sonia O., 1933-
(il) Blume, J. Freckle juice Fic

Lisle, Janet Taylor, 1947-
Afternoon of the elves (4-6) Fic

Lisowski, Gabriel, 1946-
(il) Levoy, M. The witch of Fourth Street, and other stories S C

Listen! and help tell the story. Carlson, B. W. 372.6

Listen, rabbit. Fisher, A. L. E

Listen to the rain. Martin, B. E

Lister, Robin
The legend of King Arthur (4 and up) 398.2

Litchfield, Ada Bassett
A button in her ear (1-3) 617.8
Making room for Uncle Joe (2-5) Fic

Literary prizes
See also Caldecott Medal books; Newbery Medal books
See/See also pages in the following book(s):
Crosscurrents of criticism p51-57 028.5
The Scott, Foresman anthology of children's literature p962-71 808.8

Literary recreations
See also Word games
Phillips, L. 263 brain busters (4-6) 793.73

Literature
See also Children's literature; English literature; Jews in literature

Collected works

Bauer, C. F. Celebrations 808.8
Carlson, B. W. Listen! and help tell the story 372.6
The Family read-aloud Christmas treasury 808.8
Halloween: stories and poems (2-4) 808.8
Herds of thunder, manes of gold (4 and up) 808.8
Juba this and Juba that 372.6
The Laugh book (4-6) 808.8
Rainy day: stories and poems (2-4) 808.8
The Read-aloud treasury (k-2) 808.8
Sawyer, R. The way of the storyteller 372.6
The Scott, Foresman anthology of children's literature 808.8
Shedlock, M. L. The art of the story-teller 372.6
Snowy day: stories and poems (2-4) 808.8
Windy day: stories and poems (2-4) 808.8
With a deep sea smile 372.6

Dictionaries

Brewer's dictionary of phrase and fable 803

History and criticism

See also Authors

Stories, plots, etc.

Gillespie, J. T. Juniorplots 3: a book talk guide for use with readers ages 12-16 028.1
Gillespie, J. T. Juniorplots: a book talk manual for teachers and librarians 028.1
Gillespie, J. T. More juniorplots: a guide for teachers and librarians 028.1
Rochman, H. Tales of love and terror 028
Spirt, D. L. Introducing bookplots 3 028.1
Thomas, R. L. Primaryplots 028

Study and teaching

Hall, S. Using picture storybooks to teach literary devices 016.8

Lithography
See/See also pages in the following book(s):
The Illustrator's notebook p109-14 741.6

Little, Jean, 1932-
Different dragons (3-5) Fic
From Anna (4-6) Fic
Hey world, here I am! (4-6) 811
Kate (4-6) Fic
Little by Little (5 and up) 92
Look through my window (4-6) Fic
Mama's going to buy you a mockingbird (5 and up) Fic
Mine for keeps (4-6) Fic

Little, Lessie Jones, 1906-1986
I can do it by myself E
(jt. auth) Greenfield, E. Childtimes: a three-generation memoir 920

Little, Malcolm *See* Malcolm X, 1925-1965
Little Bear. Minarik, E. H. **E**
Little Bear goes to the moon. Minarik, E. H.
In The Read-aloud treasury p70-83 **808.8**
Little Bear's friend. Minarik, E. H. See note under Minarik, E. H. Little Bear **E**
Little Bear's son
Afanas'ev, A. N. Ivanko the bear's son
In Afanas'ev, A. N. Russian fairy tales p221-23 **398.2**
Little Bear's visit. Minarik, E. H. See note under Minarik, E. H. Little Bear **E**
The **little** black cat who went to Mattituck. Brown, M. W.
In Brown, M. W. The fish with the deep sea smile p115-20 **818**
Little blue and little yellow. Lionni, L. **E**
The **Little** blue dishes
In The Family read-aloud Christmas treasury p52-53 **808.8**
Little brawl at Allen
Stephens, J. The little brawl at Allen
In Stephens, J. Irish fairy tales p157-72 **398.2**
Little Briar-Rose. Grimm, J.
In Grimm, J. The complete Grimm's fairy tales p237-41 **398.2**
Little Burnt-Face. Olcott, F. J.
In The Scott, Foresman anthology of children's literature p388-90 **808.8**
Little Buttercup. MacDonald, M. R.
In MacDonald, M. R. When the lights go out p7-20 **372.6**
Little by Little. Little, J. **92**
Little Claus and Big Claus
Andersen, H. C. Little Claus and Big Claus
In Andersen, H. C. Hans Andersen: his classic fairy tales p107-18 **S C**
Andersen, H. C. The story of Big Klaus and Little Klaus
In The Yellow fairy book p225-36 **398.2**
Little cock and little hen
Afanas'ev, A. N. The cock and the hen
In Afanas'ev, A. N. Russian fairy tales p309 **398.2**
Little Cosette and Father Christmas. Thane, A.
In The Big book of Christmas plays p313-31 **808.82**
Little crab and his magic eyes. MacDonald, M. R.
In MacDonald, M. R. Twenty tellable tales p24-34 **372.6**
Little Czar Novishny, the false sister, and the faithful beasts
Afanas'ev, A. N. The milk of wild beasts
In Afanas'ev, A. N. Russian fairy tales p304-07 **398.2**
Little daylight. MacDonald, G.
In MacDonald, G. The complete fairy tales of George MacDonald **S C**
The **Little** dog laughed (k-2) **398.8**
Little Eddie. Haywood, C. **Fic**
Little Eight John. Hamilton, V.
In Hamilton, V. The people could fly: American black folktales p121-25 **398.2**
The **little** engine that could. Piper, W. **E**
Little farmer
Grimm, J. The little peasant
In Grimm, J. The complete Grimm's fairy tales p311-16 **398.2**
A **little** fear. Wrightson, P. **Fic**
Little Finger of the watermelon patch. Vuong, L. D.
In Vuong, L. D. The brocaded slipper, and other Vietnamese tales **398.2**
The **little** folks' presents. Grimm, J.
In Grimm, J. The complete Grimm's fairy tales p742-45 **398.2**
Little fool Ivan
Afanas'ev, A. N. The golden-bristled pig, the golden-feathered duck, and the golden-maned mare
In Afanas'ev, A. N. Russian fairy tales p533-41 **398.2**
Little fox goes to the end of the world. Tompert, A. **E**
The **little** girl's medicine. Brown, M. W.
In Brown, M. W. The fish with the deep sea smile p91-96 **818**
Little Golden Sun and Little Golden Star. Martin, E.
In Martin, E. Tales of the Far North p39-53 **398.2**
Little Goldenhood
Marelle, C. The true history of Little Golden-hood
In The Red fairy book p215-19 **398.2**
The **little** good mouse. Aulnoy, Madame d'.
In The Red fairy book p146-57 **398.2**
Little green frog
The Little green frog
In The Yellow fairy book p50-59 **398.2**
The **little** house. Burton, V. L. **E**
The **Little** House cookbook. Walker, B. M. **641.5**

Little house in the big woods. Wilder, L. I. **Fic**
A **little** house of your own. De Regniers, B. S. **E**
Little house on the prairie. Wilder, L. I. See note under Wilder, L. I. Little house in the big woods **Fic**
The **Little** hunchback
In The Arabian nights entertainments p187-95 **398.2**
The **little** juggler. Cooney, B. **398.2**
The **little** lame prince. Wells, R. **E**
Little League Baseball, Inc.
Kreutzer, P. Little League's official how-to-play baseball book (4 and up) **796.357**
Little League's official how-to-play baseball book. Kreutzer, P. **796.357**
The **little** lizard's sorrow. Vo, D. M.
In Best-loved folktales of the world p569-72 **398.2**
The **Little** man & the little maid
In A Nursery companion p101-03 **820.8**
Little man and big cow
The Wee, wee mannie
In Best-loved folktales of the world p281-82 **398.2**
Little match girl
Andersen, H. C. The little match girl **Fic**
also in Andersen, H. C. Hans Andersen: his classic fairy tales p103-06 **S C**
Little men. Alcott, L. M. See note under Alcott, L. M. Little women **Fic**
Little mermaid
Andersen, H. C. The little mermaid
In Andersen, H. C. Hans Andersen: his classic fairy tales p149-70 **S C**
Little monster. Wade, B. **E**
Little Mouse's big valentine. Hurd, T. **E**
Little Nichet's baby sister. Carlson, N. S.
In The Scott, Foresman anthology of children's literature p352-54 **808.8**
The **little** nut tree. Gotwalt, H. L. M.
In Gotwalt, H. L. M. Everyday plays for boys and girls p159-69 **812**
The **little** old lady who was not afraid of anything. Williams, L. **E**
Little old woman and her pig
In The Tall book of nursery tales p92-97 **398.2**
Little One-eye, Little Two-eyes, and Little Three-eyes. Grimm, J.
In The Green fairy book p262-70 **398.2**
Little Orphant Annie. See Riley, J. W. The gobble-uns'll git you ef you don't watch out! **811**
The **little** peasant. Grimm, J.
In Grimm, J. The complete Grimm's fairy tales p311-16 **398.2**
Little pieces of the West Wind. Garrison, C.
In Windy day: stories and poems p22-31 **808.8**
The **little** porridge pot. Oxenbury, H.
In Oxenbury, H. The Helen Oxenbury nursery story book p19-24 **398.2**
The **little** pot. Rockwell, A. F.
In Rockwell, A. F. The Three bears & 15 other stories p110-12 **398.2**
Little Poucet. Perrault, C.
In The Classic fairy tales p130-36 **398.2**
The **little** prince. Saint-Exupéry, A. de. **Fic**
A **little** princess. Burnett, F. H. **Fic**
The **little** princess. Thane, A.
In Thane, A. Plays from famous stories and fairy tales p283-302 **812**
Little Red Cap. Grimm, J. **398.2**
also in Grimm, J. The complete Grimm's fairy tales p139-43 **398.2**
Little red hen
Galdone, P. The little red hen **398.2**
Jacobs, J. The little red hen
In Tomie dePaola's favorite nursery tales p16-19 **398.2**
The Little red hen
In The Baby's story book p52-55 **398.2**
In The Tall book of nursery tales p79-83 **398.2**
Oxenbury, H. The little red hen
In Oxenbury, H. The Helen Oxenbury nursery story book p65-72 **398.2**
Zemach, M. The little red hen **398.2**
Little red hen and the fox
In The Tall book of nursery tales p51-53 **398.2**
The **little** red lighthouse and the great gray bridge. Swift, H. H. **E**
Little Red Riding Hood
Ehrlich, A. Red Riding Hood
In Ehrlich, A. The Random House book of fairy tales p118-25 **398.2**
Emberley, M. Ruby **E**
Galdone, P. Little Red Riding Hood **398.2**
Goodall, J. S. Little Red Riding Hood **398.2**
Grimm, J. Little Red Cap **398.2**
also in Grimm, J. The complete Grimm's fairy tales p139-43 **398.2**

Little Red Riding Hood—*Continued*
Grimm, J. Little Red Riding Hood
In Best-loved folktales of the world p112-14 **398.2**
Hyman, T. S. Little Red Riding Hood **398.2**
Little Red Riding Hood
In The Baby's story book p36-41 **398.2**
In The Blue fairy book p51-53 **398.2**
In The Read-aloud treasury p89-99 **808.8**
In The Tall book of nursery tales p7-11 **398.2**
Marshall, J. Little Red Riding Hood **398.2**
Oxenbury, H. Little Red Riding Hood
In Oxenbury, H. The Helen Oxenbury nursery story book p58-64 **398.2**
Perrault, C. The little red Riding-Hood
In The Classic fairy tales p95-97 **398.2**
In Sleeping beauty & other favourite fairy tales p21-25 **398.2**
Rockwell, A. F. Little Red Riding Hood
In Rockwell, A. F. The Three bears & 15 other stories p102-09 **398.2**
Young, E. Lon Po Po **398.2**
Little rhymes for little folks
In A Nursery companion p44-45 **820.8**
Little rooster and the Turkish sultan
MacDonald, M. R. The little rooster and the Turkish Sultan
In MacDonald, M. R. Twenty tellable tales p57-67 **372.6**
Little Scar Face
Olcott, F. J. Little Burnt-Face
In The Scott, Foresman anthology of children's literature p388-90 **808.8**
The **little** shepherd boy. Grimm, J.
In Grimm, J. More tales from Grimm p47-49 **398.2**
Little Sister and the Month Brothers. De Regniers, B. S. **398.2**
Little sister and the Zimwi. See Aardema, V. Bimwili & the Zimwi **398.2**
Little Sister Fox and the wolf
Afanas'ev, A. N. Little Sister Fox and the wolf
In Afanas'ev, A. N. Russian fairy tales p371-75 **398.2**
Little Snow-White. Grimm, J.
In Grimm, J. The complete Grimm's fairy tales p249-58 **398.2**
The **little** snowgirl: an old Russian tale. Croll, C. **398.2**
Little soldier
Deulin, C. The little soldier
In The Green fairy book p157-74 **398.2**
Little Thumb. Perrault, C.
In The Blue fairy book p231-41 **398.2**
Little Toot. Gramatky, H. **E**
Little town on the prairie. Wilder, L. I. See note under Wilder, L. I. Little house in the big woods **Fic**
Little witch. Bennett, A. E. **Fic**
Little Wizard stories of Oz. Baum, L. F. See note under Baum, L. F. The Wizard of Oz **Fic**
Little women. Alcott, L. M. **Fic**
Littledale, Freya, 1929-
The elves and the shoemaker (k-3) **398.2**
The **littlest** dinosaurs. Most, B. **567.9**
Littlewood, Valerie
(il) Godden, R. Fu-dog **Fic**
Litzinger, Rosanne
(il) Oppenheim, J. Left & right **E**
Lively, Penelope, 1933-
Fanny's sister (3-5) **Fic**
The ghost of Thomas Kempe (4-6) **Fic**
Uninvited ghosts, and other stories (4 and up) **S C**
Contents: A Martian comes to stay; The disastrous dog; Uninvited ghosts; The dragon tunnel; Time trouble; Princess by mistake; A flock of gryphons; The great mushroom mistake
See/See also pages in the following book(s):
Crosscurrents of criticism p342-48 **028.5**
Townsend, J. R. A sounding of storytellers p125-38 **028.5**
Liverwurst is missing. Mayer, M. **E**
The **lives** of spiders. Patent, D. H. **595.4**
Lives of the artists. Goffstein, M. B. **920**
Livestock
See also Cattle
The **living** Constitution: landmark Supreme Court decisions. Sgroi, P. P. **342**
Living in a risky world. Pringle, L. P. **363**
Living in two worlds. Rosenberg, M. B. **306.8**
The **Living** Kuan-yin. Kendall, C.
In Kendall, C. Sweet and sour p23-29 **398.2**
Livingston, Myra Cohn
Birthday poems (k-3) **811**
Celebrations (1-3) **811**
A circle of seasons (1-3) **811**
Earth songs **811**

Livingston, Myra Cohn—*Continued*
My head is red and other riddle rhymes (k-2) **793.73**
Sea songs **811**
Sky songs **811**
A song I sang to you: a selection of poems (k-3) **811**
(comp) Cat poems. See Cat poems **808.81**
(comp) Dilly dilly piccalilli. See Dilly dilly piccalilli **808.81**
(comp) Dog poems. See Dog poems **808.81**
(comp) Easter poems. See Easter poems **808.81**
(comp) Halloween poems. See Halloween poems **808.81**
(comp) Lear, E. How pleasant to know Mr. Lear! **821**
(comp) New Year's poems. See New Year's poems **808.81**
(comp) Poems for Jewish holidays. See Poems for Jewish holidays **811.008**
(comp) Poems for mothers. See Poems for mothers **811.008**
(il) The Scott, Foresman anthology of children's literature. See The Scott, Foresman anthology of children's literature **808.8**
(comp) Thanksgiving poems. See Thanksgiving poems **808.81**
(comp) These small stones. See These small stones **808.81**
(comp) Valentine poems. See Valentine poems **808.81**
(ed) Why am I grown so cold? See Why am I grown so cold? **808.81**

Lizard in the sun. Ryder, J. **597.9**

Lizard music. Pinkwater, D. M. **Fic**

Lizards
Parker, N. W. Frogs, toads, lizards, and salamanders (k-3) **597.6**
Ryder, J. Lizard in the sun (k-2) **597.9**
Schnieper, C. Lizards (3-6) **597.9**
See/See also pages in the following book(s):
Weber, W. J. Care of uncommon pets p157-79 (5 and up) **636.088**

Llama and the great flood. Alexander, E. **398.2**

Llamas
Arnold, C. Llama (3-5) **599.73**
Fiction
Guarino, D. Is your mama a llama? **E**

Lloyd, David
(jt. auth) Ormerod, J. The frog prince **398.2**

Lloyd, Megan
(il) More surprises. See More surprises **811.008**
(il) Surprises. See Surprises **811.008**
(il) Williams, L. The little old lady who was not afraid of anything **E**

Load lifters: derricks, cranes, and helicopters. Marston, H. I. **621.8**

Loads of codes and secret ciphers. Janeczko, P. B. **652**

Lobel, Anita, 1934-
Alison's zinnia **E**
(il) Huck, C. S. Princess Furball **398.2**
(il) Lively, P. Fanny's sister **Fic**
(il) Lobel, A. On Market Street **E**
(il) Lobel, A. The rose in my garden **E**
(il) Lobel, A. A treeful of pigs **E**
(il) Meyer, C. Christmas crafts **745.59**
(il) Moore, C. C. The night before Christmas **811**
(il) Shub, E. Clever Kate **398.2**
(il) Singing bee! See Singing bee! **782.42**
(il) Ziefert, H. A new coat for Anna **E**

Lobel, Arnold
The book of pigericks: pig limericks (1-3) **811**
Days with Frog and Toad. See note under Lobel, A. Frog and Toad are friends **E**
Fables (3-5) **Fic**
Frog and Toad all year. See note under Lobel, A. Frog and Toad are friends **E**
Frog and Toad are friends **E**
Frog and Toad together. See note under Lobel, A. Frog and Toad are friends **E**
Grasshopper on the road **E**
Ming Lo moves the mountain **E**
Mouse soup **E**
Mouse tales **E**
On Market Street **E**
On the day Peter Stuyvesant sailed into town **E**
Owl at home **E**
The rose in my garden **E**
Small pig **E**
A treeful of pigs **E**
Uncle Elephant **E**
Very Tall Mouse and Very Short Mouse *In* The Read-aloud treasury p207-13 **808.8**
Whiskers & rhymes (1-3) **811**
(il) Durán, C. Hildilid's night **E**
(il) Geringer, L. A three hat day **E**
(il) Kumin, M. The microscope [biography of Antoni van Leeuwenhoek] **92**
(il) Myrick, M. The Secret Three **E**
(il) Parish, P. Let's be early settlers with Daniel Boone **745.5**
(il) Prelutsky, J. Circus **811**
(il) Prelutsky, J. The Headless Horseman rides tonight **811**

Lobel, Arnold—*Continued*
(il) Prelutsky, J. The mean old mean hyena E
(il) Prelutsky, J. Nightmares: poems to trouble your sleep **811**
(il) Prelutsky, J. Tyrannosaurus was a beast **811**
(il) The Random House book of Mother Goose. See The Random House book of Mother Goose **398.8**
(il) The Random House book of poetry for children. See The Random House book of poetry for children **821.008**
(il) Selsam, M. E. Greg's microscope **502.8**
(il) Selsam, M. E. Terry and the caterpillars **595.7**
(il) Van Leeuwen, J. Tales of Oliver Pig **E**
(il) Zolotow, C. The quarreling book **E**
See/See also pages in the following book(s):
Newbery and Caldecott Medal books, 1976-1985 p220-28 **028.5**

Locker, Thomas, 1937-
The mare on the hill **E**
Sailing with the wind **E**
Where the river begins **E**

Locks and keys

Fiction

Hughes, S. Alfie gets in first **E**

Lockwood, Elizabeth
(il) Timpanelli, G. Tales from the roof of the world **398.2**

Locomotives
Sattler, H. R. Train whistles (k-2) **385**
Scarry, H. Aboard a steam locomotive (4 and up) **625.2**

Locusts
See/See also pages in the following book(s):
Johnson, S. A. Chirping insects (4 and up) **595.7**

Fiction

Lobel, A. Grasshopper on the road **E**

Locusts, Seventeen-year *See* Cicadas

Lodge boy and thrown away
In The Naked bear p79-86 **398.2**

Loeper, John J.
Going to school in 1776 (4 and up) **370.9**
Going to school in 1876 (4 and up) **370.9**

Lofting, Hugh, 1886-1947
See/See also pages in the following book(s):
Horn Book reflections on children's books and reading p218-24 **028.5**
Newbery Medal books, 1922-1955 p21-27 **028.5**

Lofts, Pamela
(il) Fox, M. Koala Lou **E**

Logging *See* Lumber and lumbering

Logic
Nozaki, A. Anno's hat tricks (1-4) **153.4**

Logic. Kendall, C.
In Kendall, C. Sweet and sour p21-22 **398.2**

LOGO (Computer program language)
Simon, S. How to talk to your computer (k-3) **005**

Loh, Morag Jeanette, 1935-
Tucking Mommy in **E**

Loki (Norse deity)
Barth, E. Balder and the mistletoe (3-5) **293**

Lollar, Coleman
Tunisia—in pictures. See Tunisia—in pictures **961.1**

Lomas Garza, Carmen
Family pictures **E**

Lon Po Po. Young, E. **398.2**

London, Jack, 1876-1916
The call of the wild (5 and up) **Fic**
White Fang (5 and up) **Fic**

London (England)

Description

Munro, R. The inside-outside book of London (2-4) **942.1**

Fiction

Alcock, V. The cuckoo sister (6 and up) **Fic**
Bawden, N. The robbers (5 and up) **Fic**
Bulla, C. R. A lion to guard us (3-5) **Fic**
Garfield, L. The apprentices (6 and up) **S C**
Garfield, L. The December Rose (5 and up) **Fic**
Garfield, L. Young Nick and Jubilee (5 and up) **Fic**
Newman, R. The case of the Baker Street Irregular (5 and up) **Fic**
Paton Walsh, J. Fireweed (5 and up) **Fic**

History

Fisher, L. E. The Tower of London (4 and up) **942.1**

London (England). Tower *See* Tower of London (England)

London Bridge is falling down! (k-2) **781.62**

Long, Kim
The astronaut training book for kids (5 and up) **629.45**

Long ago when I was young. Nesbit, E. **92**

A **long** hard journey. McKissack, P. C. **331.8**

Long-life name
Mosel, A. Tikki Tikki Tembo 398.2
Long live Christmas. Benson, I.
In The Big book of Christmas plays p213-27 808.82
Long Sash and his people. Marriott, A. L.
In Marriott, A. L. American Indian mythology 398.2
The **long** secret. Fitzhugh, L. Fic
A **long** way from Verona. Gardam, J. Fic
A **long** way to go. Oneal, Z. Fic
The **long** way westward. Sandin, J. E
The **long** winter. Wilder, L. I. See note under Wilder, L. I. Little house in the big woods Fic
Longevity
See also Old age
Longfellow, Henry Wadsworth, 1807-1882
The children's own Longfellow (5 and up) 811
Hiawatha (k-3) 811
Hiawatha's childhood (k-3) 811
Paul Revere's ride (k-3) 811
also in Longfellow, H. W. The children's own Longfellow 811
Look again! Hoban, T. E
Look around. Fisher, L. E. E
Look closer! Ziebel, P. E
The **look-it-up** book of presidents. Blassingame, W. 920
Look! look! look! Hoban, T. E
Look through my window. Little, J. Fic
A **look** through the mouse hole. Fischer-Nagel, H. 599.32
Look to the night sky: an introduction to star watching. Simon, S. 523
Look what I can do. Aruego, J. E
Looking at ants. Patent, D. H. 595.7
Looking at dolphins and porpoises. Patent, D. H. 599.5
Looking for a bride. Grimm, J.
In Grimm, J. The complete Grimm's fairy tales p655-56 398.2
Looking for home. MacDonald, M. R.
In MacDonald, M. R. When the lights go out p29-32 372.6
Loons
Esbensen, B. J. Great northern diver: the loon (1-4) 598
Lopez, Nancy, 1957-
See/See also pages in the following book(s):
Morey, J. Famous Mexican Americans p51-62 (5 and up) 920
LoPrete, Tere
(il) Livingston, M. C. My head is red and other riddle rhymes 793.73
Lopshire, Robert
(il) Baker, B. The Pig War 973.6
(il) Platt, K. Big Max E
(il) Platt, K. Big Max in the mystery of the missing moose E
Lord, Bette Bao
In the Year of the Boar and Jackie Robinson (4-6) Fic
Lord, John Vernon, 1939-
The giant jam sandwich E
(il) Lear, E. The nonsense verse of Edward Lear 821
Lord Bag of Rice
Quayle, E. My Lord Bag-o'-Rice
In Quayle, E. The shining princess, and other Japanese legends p33-43 398.2
The **Lord** of the clouds
In The Monkey's haircut, and other stories told by the Maya p70-71 398.2
Lord of the dance. Tadjo, V. 398.2
Lord of the sky: Zeus. Gates, D. 292
Lord Sun's bride
In The Monkeys haircut, and other stories told by the Maya p84-91 398.2
Lord's animals
Grimm, J. The Lord's animals and the Devil's
In Grimm, J. The complete Grimm's fairy tales p642-44 398.2
The **Lord's** animals and the Devil's. Grimm, J.
In Grimm, J. The complete Grimm's fairy tales p642-44 398.2
Lord's Day *See* Sabbath
The **lore** and language of schoolchildren. Opie, I. A. 398
Lorenzini, Carlo *See* Collodi, Carlo, 1826-1890
Loretta P. Sweeny, where are you? Giff, P. R. Fic
Lorraine, Walter H.
(il) Fleischman, S. McBroom tells the truth Fic
(il) Hawes, J. My daddy longlegs 595.4
Losing Uncle Tim. Jordan, M. Fic
Loss and how to cope with it. Bernstein, J. E. 155.9
Lost!. McPhail, D. M. E
Lost and found. Paton Walsh, J. Fic
The **lost** boys. Curtis, E. S.
In Curtis, E. S. The girl who married a ghost, and other tales from the North American Indian p99-100 398.2

The **lost** brother. Curry, J. L.
In Curry, J. L. Back in the beforetime p60-67 **398.2**
The **Lost** children
In The Monkey's haircut, and other stories told by the Maya p92-93 **398.2**
Lost cities. Gallant, R. A. **930**
Lost in the Amazon. Quackenbush, R. M. See note under Quackenbush, R. M. Express train to trouble **Fic**
Lost in the museum. Cohen, M. See note under Cohen, M. See you in second grade! **E**
The **lost** Kingdom of Karnica. Kennedy, R.
In Kennedy, R. Collected stories p191-200 **S C**
The **lost** lake. Say, A. **E**
Lost star princess
Carpenter, F. Lost star princess
In Carpenter, F. Tales of a Chinese grandmother p190-97 **398.2**
Lost star: the story of Amelia Earhart. Lauber, P. **92**
The **lost** woman. Grinnell, G. B.
In Best-loved folktales of the world p704-11 **398.2**
The **lost** wreck of the Isis. Ballard, R. D. **910.4**
Lot (Biblical figure)
About
Singer, I. B. The wicked city (3-6) **222**
Lotta on Troublemaker Street. Lindgren, A. **Fic**
Lottridge, Celia B. (Celia Barker)
The name of the tree (k-3) **398.2**
Lougheed, Robert
(il) Henry, M. Mustang, wild spirit of the West **Fic**
(il) Henry, M. San Domingo: the medicine hat stallion **Fic**
Louie, Ai-Ling, 1949-
Yeh-Shen (2-4) **398.2**
Louie. Keats, E. J. **E**
Louie's search. Keats, E. J. See note under Keats, E. J. Louie **E**
Louis XIV, King of France, 1638-1715
About
Aliki. The King's day: Louis XIV of France (3-5) **92**
Louis Armstrong: an American success story. Collier, J. L. **92**
Louise builds a house. Pfanner, L. **E**
Louisiana
Kent, D. Louisiana
In America the beautiful **973**
Louisiana Purchase
Phelan, M. K. The story of the Louisiana Purchase (5 and up) **973.4**
Louisville Slugger. Arnow, J. **796.357**
The **loup-garou.** San Souci, R.
In San Souci, R. Short & shivery p144-48 **398.2**
"Loup-garou" in the woods. Carlson, N. S.
In Carlson, N. S. The talking cat, and other stories of French Canada p77-87 **S C**
The **louse** and the flea. Grimm, J.
In Grimm, J. The complete Grimm's fairy tales p158-60 **398.2**
Lovable Lyle. Waber, B. See note under Waber, B. The house on East 88th Street **E**
Love and sex and growing up. Johnson, E. W. **613.9**
The **love** crystal. Taylor, M.
In The Scott, Foresman anthology of children's literature p338-40 **808.8**
Love from Aunt Betty. Parker, N. W. **E**
Love, from the fifth-grade celebrity. Giff, P. R. **Fic**
Love poetry
Greenfield, E. Honey, I love, and other love poems (2-4) **811**
Mizumura, K. If I were a cricket . . . (k-2) **811**
Love potion. Forshay-Lunsford, C.
In Connections: short stories by outstanding writers for young adults p159-68 **S C**
Lovelace, Maud Hart, 1892-
Betsy and Joe. See note under Lovelace, M. H. Betsy-Tacy **Fic**
Betsy and Tacy go downtown. See note under Lovelace, M. H. Betsy-Tacy **Fic**
Betsy and Tacy go over the big hill. See note under Lovelace, M. H. Betsy-Tacy **Fic**
Betsy and the great world. See note under Lovelace, M. H. Betsy-Tacy **Fic**
Betsy in spite of herself. See note under Lovelace, M. H. Betsy-Tacy **Fic**
Betsy-Tacy (2-4) **Fic**
Betsy-Tacy and Tib. See note under Lovelace, M. H. Betsy-Tacy **Fic**
Betsy was a junior. See note under Lovelace, M. H. Betsy-Tacy **Fic**
Betsy's wedding. See note under Lovelace, M. H. Betsy-Tacy **Fic**
Heaven to Betsy. See note under Lovelace, M. H. Betsy-Tacy **Fic**
The **lovers** of Dismal Swamp. San Souci, R.
In San Souci, R. Short & shivery p123-26 **398.2**

Low, Alice, 1926-
The Macmillan book of Greek gods and heroes (3-6) **292**
(comp) The Family read-aloud Christmas treasury. See The Family read-aloud Christmas treasury **808.8**

Low, Joseph, 1911-
Mice twice **E**
(il) Griffith, H. V. Alex and the cat **E**
(il) Jordan, H. J. How a seed grows **582**

Low, Juliette Gordon, 1860-1927
About
Kudlinski, K. V. Juliette Gordon Low: America's first Girl Scout (4 and up) **92**

Low, Madeline Slovenz- *See* Slovenz-Low, Madeline

Low vocabulary-high interest books *See* High interest-low vocabulary books

Lowe, Edwin S., 1910-1986
See/See also pages in the following book(s):
Aaseng, N. The unsung heroes p45-51 (5 and up) **920**

Lowenstein, Bernice
(il) Conford, E. The luck of Pokey Bloom **Fic**

Lower! Higher! You're a liar! Chaikin, M. See note under Chaikin, M. Finders weepers **Fic**

Lowry, Lois
All about Sam. See note under Lowry, L. Anastasia Krupnik **Fic**
Anastasia again! See note under Lowry, L. Anastasia Krupnik **Fic**
Anastasia, ask your analyst. See note under Lowry, L. Anastasia Krupnik **Fic**
Anastasia at your service. See note under Lowry, L. Anastasia Krupnik **Fic**
Anastasia has the answers. See note under Lowry, L. Anastasia Krupnik **Fic**
Anastasia Krupnik (4-6) **Fic**
Anastasia on her own. See note under Lowry, L. Anastasia Krupnik **Fic**
Anastasia's chosen career. See note under Lowry, L. Anastasia Krupnik **Fic**
Autumn Street (4 and up) **Fic**
Number the stars (4 and up) **Fic**
The one hundredth thing about Caroline (5 and up) **Fic**
Rabble Starkey (5 and up) **Fic**
A summer to die (3-6) **Fic**
Switcharound (5 and up) **Fic**
Taking care of Terrific (5 and up) **Fic**
Us and Uncle Fraud (4 and up) **Fic**
Your move, J.P.! (5 and up) **Fic**

Loyalists, American *See* American Loyalists

Lubin, Leonard B., 1943-
Christmas gift-bringers **394.2**
(il) Conly, J. L. R-T, Margaret, and the rats of NIMH **Fic**
(il) Conly, J. L. Racso and the rats of NIMH **Fic**

Lucie Babbidge's house. Cassedy, S. **Fic**

Luck and intelligence
Intelligence and luck
In Best-loved folktales of the world p452-54 **398.2**

The **luck** of Pokey Bloom. Conford, E. **Fic**

Lucky charms & birthday wishes. McDonnell, C. **Fic**

Lucky scraps. Grimm, J.
In Grimm, J. More tales from Grimm p59-60 **398.2**

The **lucky** stone. Clifton, L. **Fic**

The **lucky** table. Osma, L. de.
In Best-loved folktales of the world p760-63 **398.2**

Lucy & Tom's a.b.c. Hughes, S. **E**

Lucy & Tom's 1.2.3. Hughes, S. **E**

Ludell. Wilkinson, B. S. **Fic**

Ludell and Willie. Wilkinson, B. S. See note under Wilkinson, B. S. Ludell **Fic**

Lueders, Edward
(comp) Reflections on a gift of watermelon pickle . . . and other modern verse. See Reflections on a gift of watermelon pickle . . . and other modern verse **811.008**

Luenn, Nancy, 1954-
Nessa's fish **E**

Lullabies
The Baby's bedtime book (k-1) **808.81**
Bang, M. Ten, nine, eight **E**
Hush little baby (k-1) **781.62**
Lullabies and night songs (k-3) **782.42**
The Lullaby songbook (1-3) **782.42**
Marzollo, J. Close your eyes **E**
Pomerantz, C. All asleep (k-2) **811**
A Week of lullabies (k-2) **811.008**
When the dark comes dancing (k-3) **808.81**
See/See also pages in the following book(s):
Rainbow in the sky p421-33 (k-4) **821.008**

Lullabies and night songs (k-3) **782.42**

The **Lullaby** songbook (1-3) **782.42**

Lullay, lulla. Aiken, J.
In Aiken, J. Past eight o'clock p87-98 **S C**

Lulu and the witch baby. O'Connor, J. See note under O'Connor, J. Lulu goes to witch school
In E

Lulu goes to witch school. O'Connor, J. E

Lumber and lumbering
Kurelek, W. Lumberjack (3-5) 634.9

The **lumber-room**. Saki.
In The Random House book of humor for children p74-82 817.008

Lumberjack. Kurelek, W. 634.9

The **luminous** pearl. Torre, B. L. 398.2

Lunar eclipses *See* Eclipses, Lunar

Lunar expeditions *See* Space flight to the moon

Lunn, Janet Louise Swoboda, 1928-
The root cellar (5 and up) Fic

Lunsford, Cin Forshay- *See* Forshay-Lunsford, Cin

Lurie, Alison
Fabulous beasts (4 and up) 398
The heavenly zoo (4 and up) 398.2

Lustig, Loretta, 1944-
(il) Best wishes, amen. See Best wishes, amen 808.88

Lutoniushka
Afanas'ev, A. N. Lutoniushka
In Afanas'ev, A. N. Russian fairy tales p336-37 398.2

Luttrell, Ida, 1934-
Ottie Slockett E

The **Luttrell** village. Sancha, S. 942.03

Luxembourg
Lepthien, E. U. Luxembourg (4 and up) 949.35

Luzak, Dennis
(il) Levinson, R. Our home is the sea E

Lye, Keith
Passport to Spain (5 and up) 946
Take a trip to Morocco (1-3) 964
Take a trip to Saudi Arabia (1-3) 953.8
Take a trip to Syria (1-3) 956.91
Take a trip to Turkey (1-3) 956.1

Lying *See* Truthfulness and falsehood

Lyle and the birthday party. Waber, B. See note under Waber, B. The house on East 88th Street E

Lyle finds his mother. Waber, B. See note under Waber, B. The house on East 88th Street E

Lyle, Lyle, crocodile. Waber, B. See note under Waber, B. The house on East 88th Street E

Lyme disease
Landau, E. Lyme disease (4 and up) 616.9
Silverstein, A. Lyme disease, the great imitator (6 and up) 616.9

Lynch, Patrick, 1962-
(il) Nesbit, E. Melisande 398.2

Lynch, Wayne
(il) Lang, A. Eagles 598

Lynn, Ruth Nadelman, 1948-
Fantasy literature for children and young adults 016.8

Lyon, David
The biggest truck E

Lyon, George Ella, 1949-
A B Cedar E
Borrowed children (5 and up) Fic
Come a tide E
A regular rolling Noah E
Together E

Lyra, Carmen
Brer Rabbit, businessman
In Best-loved folktales of the world p763-67 398.2

Lyttle, Richard B.
Land beyond the river (6 and up) 940.1

M

M and M and the bad news babies. Ross, P. See note under Ross, P. Meet M and M E

M and M and the big bag. Ross, P. See note under Ross, P. Meet M and M E

M and M and the haunted house game. Ross, P. See note under Ross, P. Meet M and M E

M and M and the mummy mess. Ross, P. See note under Ross, P. Meet M and M E

M and M and the super child afternoon. Ross, P. See note under Ross, P. Meet M and M E

M. C. Higgins the great. Hamilton, V. Fic

M.E. and Morton. Cassedy, S. Fic

M.I.A.'s *See* Missing in action

Maas, Selve
The old traveler
In The Scott, Foresman anthology of children's literature p282-84 808.8

Maass, Robert
Fire fighters (2-3) 628.9

Mabie, Margot C. J.
The Constitution (6 and up) 342

Mabinogion
See/See also pages in the following book(s):
Bulfinch, T. Bulfinch's mythology (6 and up) **291**

Macaulay, David, 1946-
Black and white **E**
Castle (4 and up) **728.8**
Cathedral: the story of its construction (4 and up) **726**
City: a story of Roman planning and construction (4 and up) **711**
Mill (4 and up) **690**
Pyramid (4 and up) **726**
Unbuilding (4 and up) **690**
Underground (4 and up) **624.1**
The way things work (5 and up) **600**
Why the chicken crossed the road **E**

Maccabbees, Feast of the *See* Hanukkah

MacCarthy, Patricia
(il) Mahy, M. 17 kings and 42 elephants **E**

MacDonald, Betty, d. 1958
Hello, Mrs. Piggle-Wiggle. See note under MacDonald, B. Mrs. Piggle-Wiggle **Fic**
Mrs. Piggle-Wiggle (2-4) **Fic**
Mrs. Piggle-Wiggle's farm. See note under MacDonald, B. Mrs. Piggle-Wiggle **Fic**
Mrs. Piggle-Wiggle's magic. See note under MacDonald, B. Mrs. Piggle-Wiggle **Fic**
Mrs. Piggle-Wiggle's magic [excerpt]
In The Random House book of humor for children p15-30 **817.008**

MacDonald, George, 1824-1905
At the back of the North Wind (4-6) **Fic**
The complete fairy tales of George Macdonald (4 and up) **S C**
Contents: The light princess; The giant's heart; The shadows; The Carosyn; Little daylight; Cross purposes; The golden key; The day boy and the night girl
The light princess (3-6) **Fic**
The princess and the goblin (3-6) **Fic**
See/See also pages in the following book(s):
Horn Book reflections on children's books and reading p203-10 **028.5**
Sendak, M. Caldecott & Co.: notes on books and pictures p45-49 **028.5**

MacDonald, Margaret Read
Booksharing: 101 programs to use with preschoolers **027.62**
The skit book (4 and up) **812.008**
The storyteller's sourcebook **398**
Twenty tellable tales **372.6**
Stories included are: A whale of a tale; Coyote's crying song; Coyote's rain song; Little crab and his magic eyes; Groundhog dance; Old one-eye; Parley Garfield and the frogs; The little rooster and the Turkish Sultan; The gunny wolf; How to break a bad habit; Sody sallyrytus; Turkey tale; Jack and the robbers; Roly poly rice ball; Udala tree; The rabbit and the well; Hic! Hic! Hic!; Mr. Fox; Punia and the king of the sharks; The magic fox
When the lights go out **372.6**
Stories included are: Little Buttercup; The Wee Little Tyke; Looking for home; Wicked John and the Devil; The Great Red Cat; The wizard clip; The tinker and the ghost; The conjure wives; Sop doll; The Hobyahs; Old Ben; Sam'l; The cat with the beckoning paw; Totanguak; The red silk handkerchief; The strange visitor; Who lives in the skull?

Macdonald, Suse, 1940-
Alphabatics **E**
Numblers **E**
(jt. auth) Oakes, B. Puzzlers **E**

MacFarlane, Ruth B. Alford
Making your own nature museum (5 and up) **508**

The **machine** gunners. Westall, R. **Fic**

Machinery
See also Conveying machinery; Hoisting machinery
Adkins, J. Moving heavy things (5 and up) **621.8**
Ancona, G. Monster movers (3-5) **621.8**
Cooper, C. How everyday things work (5 and up) **600**
Horvatic, A. Simple machines (1-3) **531**
Macaulay, D. The way things work (5 and up) **600**
Rockwell, A. F. Big wheels (k-1) **629.225**
Rockwell, A. F. Machines (k-1) **621.8**
Weiss, H. Machines and how they work (4 and up) **621.8**
Zubrowski, B. Wheels at work (4-6) **621.8**

History
Weitzman, D. L. Windmills, bridges & old machines (5 and up) **620**

Pictorial works
Hoban, T. Dig, drill, dump, fill (k-2) **621.8**

Poetry
Click, rumble, roar (2-5) **811.008**

Machines. Rockwell, A. F. **621.8**

Machines and how they work. Weiss, H. **621.8**

Machines at work. Barton, B. **690**

Machotka, Hana
The magic ring (3-6) **791.3**
What do you do at a petting zoo? (k-2) **590.74**

Mackay, Donald A.
(il) Fox, P. The stone-faced boy **Fic**

MacLachlan, Patricia
Arthur, for the very first time (4-6) **Fic**
Cassie Binegar (4-6) **Fic**
The facts and fictions of Minna Pratt (4 and up) **Fic**
Mama One, Mama Two **E**
Sarah, plain and tall (3-5) **Fic**
Seven kisses in a row (2-4) **Fic**

MacLachlan, Patricia—*Continued*
Tomorrow's wizard (3-6) **S C**
Contents: The wizard; The first important wish; Three-0; The comely lady and the clay nose; The perfect fiddle; The last important wish
Unclaimed treasures (5 and up) **Fic**
MacLean, Norman
Hockey basics (4 and up) **796.962**
Ice skating basics (4 and up) **796.91**
MacLeish, Archibald, 1892-1982
See/See also pages in the following book(s):
A Horn Book sampler on children's books and reading p243-47 **028.5**
Macmillan, Cyrus
How summer came to Canada
In The Scott, Foresman anthology of children's literature p469-72 **808.8**
The Indian Cinderella
In Best-loved folktales of the world p694-96 **398.2**
The **Macmillan** book of dinosaurs and other prehistoric creatures. Elting, M. **560**
The **Macmillan** book of Greek gods and heroes. Low, A. **292**
The **Macmillan** book of how things work. Folsom, M. **600**
The **Macmillan** book of the human body. Elting, M. **612**
Macmillan contemporary dictionary. See Macmillan dictionary for students **423**
Macmillan dictionary. See Macmillan dictionary for students **423**
Macmillan dictionary for children (3 and up) **423**
Macmillan dictionary for students (4 and up) **423**
Macmillan very first dictionary (1-3) **423**
Mad as a wet hen! and other funny idioms. Terban, M. **427**
Madaras, Area
(jt. auth) Madaras, L. The what's happening to my body? book for girls: a growing up guide for parents and daughters **613.9**
Madaras, Lynda
The what's happening to my body? book for boys: a growing up guide for parents and sons (6 and up) **613.9**
The what's happening to my body? book for girls: a growing up guide for parents and daughters (6 and up) **613.9**
Madavan, Vijay
Cooking the Indian way (5 and up) **641.5**
Madden, Andrea Clarke
(il) Hoffmann, E. T. A. Nutcracker **Fic**
Madden, Don, 1927-
(il) Branley, F. M. Gravity is a mystery **531**
(il) Branley, F. M. Is there life in outer space? **574.999**
(il) Branley, F. M. Oxygen keeps you alive **574.1**
(il) Branley, F. M. The sun **523.7**
(il) Showers, P. A drop of blood **612.1**
(il) Showers, P. Me and my family tree **575.1**
(il) Sullivan, G. Pitcher **796.357**
(il) Sullivan, G. Quarterback **796.332**
Madden, John
The first book of football (5 and up) **796.332**
Madeline. Bemelmans, L. **E**
Madeline and the bad hat. Bemelmans, L. See note under Bemelmans, L. Madeline **E**
Madeline and the gypsies. Bemelmans, L. See note under Bemelmans, L. Madeline **E**
Madeline in London. Bemelmans, L. See note under Bemelmans, L. Madeline **E**
Madeline's Christmas. Bemelmans, L. See note under Bemelmans, L. Madeline **E**
Madeline's rescue. Bemelmans, L. **E**
Madison, James, 1751-1836
About
Fritz, J. The great little Madison (5 and up) **92**
See/See also pages in the following book(s):
Hauptly, D. J. "A convention of delegates" p23-40 (5 and up) **342**
Maestro, Betsy, 1944-
Ferryboat **E**
A more perfect union (2-4) **342**
Snow day **E**
The story of the Statue of Liberty (k-3) **974.7**
Taxi **E**
Temperature and you (1-3) **536**
Maestro, Giulio, 1942-
Halloween howls (2-4) **793.73**
A raft of riddles (2-4) **793.73**
Riddle romp (2-4) **793.73**
Riddle roundup (2-4) **793.73**
What's a frank frank? (2-4) **793.73**
(il) Branley, F. M. Hurricane watch **551.55**
(il) Branley, F. M. Rockets and satellites **629.4**
(il) Branley, F. M. Sunshine makes the seasons **525**
(il) Cobb, V. More science experiments you can eat **507**

Maestro, Giulio, 1942-—*Continued*
(il) Gans, R. Caves **551.4**
(il) Maestro, B. Ferryboat **E**
(il) Maestro, B. A more perfect union **342**
(il) Maestro, B. Snow day **E**
(il) Maestro, B. The story of the Statue of Liberty **974.7**
(il) Maestro, B. Taxi **E**
(jt. auth) Maestro, B. Temperature and you **536**
(il) Sattler, H. R. Train whistles **385**
(il) Simon, S. The dinosaur is the biggest animal that ever lived, and other wrong ideas you thought were true **500**
(il) Terban, M. Guppies in tuxedos: funny eponyms **422**
(il) Terban, M. Mad as a wet hen! and other funny idioms **427**
(il) Terban, M. Superdupers! really funny real words **427**
Magazines *See* Periodicals
Magazines for children. Richardson, S. K. **011.6**
Magazines for school libraries **011.6**
Magee, Doug, 1947-
Trucks you can count on (k-2) **629.224**
Maggie by my side. Butler, B. **362.4**
Maggie doesn't want to move. O'Donnell, E. L. **E**
Maggie Marmelstein for president. Sharmat, M. W. See note under Sharmat, M. W. Mysteriously yours, Maggie Marmelstein **Fic**
Maggie's gift. Paterson, K.
In Paterson, K. Angels & other strangers: family Christmas stories p49-63 **S C**
Magi
Branley, F. M. The Christmas sky (3-6) **232.9**
Menotti, G. C. Amahl and the night visitors (2-4) **Fic**
Magic
Broekel, R. Hocus pocus: magic you can do (3-5) **793.8**
Broekel, R. Now you see it: easy magic for beginners (3-5) **793.8**
Cobb, V. Magic—naturally! science entertainment & amusements (4 and up) **793.8**
Friedhoffer, R. Magic tricks, science facts (5 and up) **793.8**
Kettelkamp, L. Magic made easy (4 and up) **793.8**
Severn, B. Magic fun for everyone (6 and up) **793.8**
Sheridan, J. Nothing's impossible! stunts to entertain and amaze (5 and up) **793.8**
White, L. B. Math-a-magic: number tricks for magicians (3-6) **793.8**
Wyler, R. Magic secrets (1-3) **793.8**
Wyler, R. Spooky tricks (1-3) **793.8**
Fiction
Fleischman, S. Mr. Mysterious & Company (4-6) **Fic**
Hooks, W. H. The ballad of Belle Dorcas (3-5) **Fic**
Kimmel, M. M. Magic in the mist (1-4) **Fic**
Lester, H. The revenge of the Magic Chicken **E**
Mahy, M. The blood-and-thunder adventure on Hurricane Peak (4-6) **Fic**
Stolz, M. The cuckoo clock (4-6) **Fic**
Turkle, B. C. Do not open **E**
Van Allsburg, C. The garden of Abdul Gasazi **E**
Wright, J. The old woman and the jar of uums **E**
Magic. Afanas'ev, A. N.
In Afanas'ev, A. N. Russian fairy tales p399-404 **398.2**
The **magic** bed-knob. Norton, M.
In Norton, M. Bed-knob and broomstick p11-94 **Fic**
The **magic** boat. Demi. **398.2**
Magic box
Afanas'ev, A. N. The magic box
In Afanas'ev, A. N. Russian fairy tales p164-68 **398.2**
Sawyer, R. The magic box
In Sawyer, R. The way of the storyteller p219-25 **372.6**
In The Scott, Foresman anthology of children's literature p256-59 **808.8**
The **magic** brocade. Protter, E.
In Best-loved folktales of the world p539-44 **398.2**
Magic by the lake. Eager, E. See note under Eager, E. Half magic **Fic**
The **magic** carpet sweeper. Gotwalt, H. L. M.
In Gotwalt, H. L. M. Special plays for holidays p170-81 **812**
The **magic** crossbow. Terada, A. M.
In Terada, A. M. Under the starfruit tree p120-25 **398.2**
The **magic** fan. Baker, K. **E**
The **magic** fox. MacDonald, M. R.
In MacDonald, M. R. Twenty tellable tales p174-80 **372.6**
Magic fun for everyone. Severn, B. **793.8**
Magic in the mist. Kimmel, M. M. **Fic**
The **Magic** kettle
In Best-loved folktales of the world p523-25 **398.2**
In The Scott, Foresman anthology of children's literature p328-29 **808.8**

The **magic** listening cap. Uchida, Y. **398.2**
The **magic** listening cap [story]. Uchida, Y.
  In Uchida, Y. The magic listening cap **398.2**
Magic made easy. Kettelkamp, L. **793.8**
The **magic** mill. Huggins, E.
  In The Scott, Foresman anthology of children's literature p284-87 **808.8**
Magic mortar. Uchida, Y.
  In Uchida, Y. The magic listening cap **398.2**
The **Magic** Moscow. Pinkwater, D. M. See note under Pinkwater, D. M. Fat men from space **Fic**
The **magic** nutmeg-grater. Thane, A.
  In Thane, A. Plays from famous stories and fairy tales p198-215 **812**
The **magic** of Oz. Baum, L. F. See note under Baum, L. F. The Wizard of Oz **Fic**
The **magic** of sound. Kettelkamp, L. **534**
The **Magic** orange tree
  In Best-loved folktales of the world p727-30 **398.2**
  In The Magic orange tree, and other Haitian folktales p13-21 **398.2**
The **Magic** orange tree, and other Haitian folktales (5 and up) **398.2**
The **magic** pencil. Hough, C. W.
  In Bauer, C. F. Celebrations p12-14 **808.8**
Magic ring
 The Magic ring
  In The Yellow fairy book p178-91 **398.2**
The **magic** ring. Machotka, H. **791.3**
The **magic** school bus at the waterworks. Cole, J. **551.48**
The **magic** school bus inside the Earth. Cole, J. **551.1**
The **magic** school bus inside the human body. Cole, J. **612**
The **magic** school bus, lost in the solar system. Cole, J. **523**
Magic secrets. Wyler, R. **793.8**
Magic shirt
 Afanas'ev, A. N. The magic shirt
  In Afanas'ev, A. N. Russian fairy tales p110-13 **398.2**
The **magic** stove. Ginsburg, M. **398.2**
Magic swan
 The Magic swan
  In The Green fairy book p175-79 **398.2**
Magic swan geese
 Afanas'ev, A. N. The magic swan geese
  In Afanas'ev, A. N. Russian fairy tales p349-51 **398.2**
Magic tricks, science facts. Friedhoffer, R. **793.8**
The **magic** wings. Wolkstein, D. **398.2**
The **Magic** world of words. See Macmillan very first dictionary **423**
The **magical** adventures of Pretty Pearl. Hamilton, V. **Fic**
Magical changes, Graham Oakley's. Oakley, G. **E**
Magicians
Fiction
 Fleischman, S. The midnight horse (3-6) **Fic**
 Seeger, P. Abiyoyo (k-2) **398.2**
The **magician's** nephew. Lewis, C. S. See note under Lewis, C. S. The lion, the witch and the wardrobe **Fic**
Magician's pupil
 Afanas'ev, A. N. Magic
  In Afanas'ev, A. N. Russian fairy tales p399-404 **398.2**
Magic—naturally! science entertainment & amusements. Cobb, V. **793.8**
Magnus Powermouse. King-Smith, D. **Fic**
Magon, Jymn
 We'll do lunch
  In Things that go bump in the night p164-85 **S C**
Magorian, Michelle, 1947-
 Good night, Mr. Tom (6 and up) **Fic**
The **magpie** and the milk. Walker, B. K.
  In Walker, B. K. A treasury of Turkish folktales for children p11-13 **398.2**
Magpies in the crabtree. Crossley-Holland, K.
  In Crossley-Holland, K. British folk tales p247 **398.2**
Magpie's nest
 Jacobs, J. Magpie's nest
  In Jacobs, J. English fairy tales p195-97 **398.2**
Mahy, Margaret
 17 kings and 42 elephants **E**
 The blood-and-thunder adventure on Hurricane Peak (4-6) **Fic**
 The boy who was followed home **E**
 The great piratical rumbustification & The librarian and the robbers (3-6) **Fic**
 The great white man-eating shark **E**
 The haunting (5 and up) **Fic**
 The librarian and the robbers
  In Mahy, M. The great piratical rumbustification & The librarian and the robbers p44-63 **Fic**
 Making friends **E**

Mahy, Margaret—*Continued*
Nonstop nonsense (4-6) **828**
Includes the following stories: Strange events in the life of the Delmonico family: the birthday present; The cat who became a poet; Why Ann hung upside down; Fair exchange; Strange events in the life of the Delmonico family: trouble in the supermarket; The insect kingdom that didn't get started; Strange events in the life of the Delmonico family: phone talk; The ghost who came out of the book; Green marmalade to you; Frightening the monster in Wizard's Hole
The seven Chinese brothers (1-3) **398.2**

Maid in the mirror
Carpenter, F. Maid in the mirror
In Carpenter, F. Tales of a Chinese grandmother p226-34 **398.2**

Maid Lena
Maid Lena
In Best-loved folktales of the world p368-76 **398.2**

Maid Maleen
Grimm, J. Maid Maleen
In Grimm, J. The complete Grimm's fairy tales p801-07 **398.2**

Maid of Brakel
Grimm, J. The Maid of Brakel
In Grimm, J. The complete Grimm's fairy tales p623 **398.2**

The **maid** who chose a husband. Riordan, J.
In Riordan, J. The woman in the moon, and other tales of forgotten heroines p53-58 **398.2**

Maiden Tsar
Afanas'ev, A. N. The Maiden Tsar
In Afanas'ev, A. N. Russian fairy tales p229-34 **398.2**

Maiden with the wooden helmet
Quayle, E. The wooden bowl
In Quayle, E. The shining princess, and other Japanese legends p97-102 **398.2**

Maiden without hands
Grimm, J. The girl without hands
In Grimm, J. The complete Grimm's fairy tales p160-66 **398.2**

The **maidens** of the northern crown. Mayo, G.
In Mayo, G. Star tales p75-78 **398.2**

Maiden's visit
Grimm, J. The elves ask a servant girl to be godmother
In Grimm, J. About wise men and simpletons p33 **398.2**
Grimm, J. The elves: second story
In Grimm, J. The complete Grimm's fairy tales p199 **398.2**

The **mailbox** trick. Corbett, S. See note under Corbett, S. The lemonade trick **Fic**

Maine
Harrington, T. Maine
In America the beautiful **973**
Fiction
Carlstrom, N. W. Grandpappy **E**
Martin, C. E. Island winter **E**
McCloskey, R. Blueberries for Sal **E**
McCloskey, R. One morning in Maine **E**
McCloskey, R. Time of wonder **E**

Maitland, Antony, 1935-
(il) Lively, P. The ghost of Thomas Kempe **Fic**

Majeski, Bill
Whatever happened to good old Ebenezer Scrooge?
In The Big book of Christmas plays p151-68 **808.82**

Major, John S.
The land and people of China (5 and up) **951**
The land and people of Mongolia (5 and up) **951.7**

Mak, Kam
(il) Schlein, M. The year of the panda **Fic**

Make a joyful noise unto the Lord! The life of Mahalia Jackson, queen of gospel singers. Jackson, J. **92**

Make a world. See Emberley, E. Ed Emberley's drawing book: make a world **741.2**

Make-believe playmates *See* Imaginary playmates

Make it special. Hautzig, E. R. **745.59**

Make like a tree and leave. Danziger, P. **Fic**

Make mine music! Walther, T. **784.19**

Make noise, make merry. Chaikin, M. **296.4**

Make the most of a good thing: you! Shaw, D. **613**

Make way for ducklings. McCloskey, R. **E**

Make way for Sam Houston. Fritz, J. **92**

Make your own model forts & castles. Cummings, R. **623**

Makeup (Cosmetics) *See* Cosmetics

Making a new home in America. Rosenberg, M. B. **325.73**

Making and using your own weather station. Tannenbaum, B. **551.6**

Making cents. Wilkinson, E. **332.024**

Making friends. Mahy, M. **E**

Making friends. Ormerod, J. See note under Ormerod, J. Bend and stretch **E**

Making friends. Rogers, F. **155.4**
Making friends with guinea pigs. Hess, L. **636.088**
Making musical things. Wiseman, A. S. **784.19**
The **making** of First Man. Curry, J. L.
In Curry, J. L. Back in the beforetime p107-15 **398.2**
Making room for Uncle Joe. Litchfield, A. B. **Fic**
Making your own nature museum. MacFarlane, R. B. A. **508**
Malawi
Fiction
Williams, K. L. Galimoto **E**
Malaysia
Wright, D. K. Malaysia (4 and up) **959.5**
Malcolm X, 1925-1965
About
Adoff, A. Malcolm X (2-5) **92**
Malcolmson, Anne, 1910-
Pecos Bill and his bouncing bride
In The Scott, Foresman anthology of children's literature p365-68 **808.8**
Male role *See* Sex role
Mali
Mali—in pictures (5 and up) **966.23**
Mali—in pictures (5 and up) **966.23**
Mall rat. Gorog, J.
In Gorog, J. Three dreams and a nightmare, and other tales of the dark **S C**
Mallory, Ken
Rescue of the stranded whales (5 and up) **639.9**
Malloy, Vivi
About
Krementz, J. A very young rider (3-6) **798.2**
Malone, Nola Langner
(il) Viorst, J. Earrings! **E**
Mama don't allow. Hurd, T. **E**
Mama One, Mama Two. MacLachlan, P. **E**
Mama went walking. Berry, C. **E**
Mama's going to buy you a mockingbird. Little, J. **Fic**
Mammals
See also groups of mammals; and names of mammals
Burton, M. Warm-blooded animals (5 and up) **599**
Crump, D. J. Creatures small and furry (k-3) **599**
Hirschi, R. Headgear (4 and up) **599.73**
Kerrod, R. Mammals: primates, insect eaters, and baleen whales (4 and up) **599**
O'Toole, C. Mammals: the hunters (4 and up) **599**
Parker, S. Mammal (4 and up) **599**
Zim, H. S. Mammals (4 and up) **599**
See/See also pages in the following book(s):
McClung, R. M. The amazing egg p97-107 (4 and up) **591.1**
Pictorial works
Wildsmith, B. Brian Wildsmith's wild animals **E**
Mammals, Fossil
Arnold, C. Trapped in tar (3-5) **560**
Giants from the past: the age of mammals (5 and up) **569**
Mammals, Marine
See also Seals (Animals); Whales
Amazing animals of the sea (5 and up) **599.5**
Mammals: primates, insect eaters, and baleen whales. Kerrod, R. **599**
Mammals: the large plant-eaters. Stidworthy, J. **599**
Mammals: the small plant-eaters. Bramwell, M. **599**
Mammoths
Aliki. Wild and woolly mammoths (k-3) **569**
Fiction
Gerrard, R. Mik's mammoth **E**
Martin, R. Will's mammoth **E**
Mammy-Bammy Big-Money takes care of Brer Wolf. Lester, J.
In Lester, J. More tales of Uncle Remus p114-17 **398.2**
Man
Influence of environment
See also Environmental health
Influence on nature—Fiction
Turner, A. W. Heron Street **E**
Origin
See also Evolution
Cole, J. The human body: how we evolved (4 and up) **573.2**
Lasky, K. Traces of life (5 and up) **573.2**
Man, Prehistoric
See also Cave dwellers
Cole, J. The human body: how we evolved (4 and up) **573.2**
Early humans (4 and up) **930.1**
Lasky, K. Traces of life (5 and up) **573.2**
Sattler, H. R. Hominids: a look back at our ancestors (5 and up) **573.3**

Man, the boy and the donkey
Rockwell, A. F. The miller, his son, and the donkey
In Rockwell, A. F. Puss in boots, and other stories p27-29 **398.2**

Man chooses death
In Best-loved folktales of the world p632 **398.2**

Man in the red suit. Moessinger, W.
In Holiday plays round the year p37-46 **812.008**

A **man** named Thoreau. Burleigh, R. **92**

The **man** of influence. Fleischman, P.
In Fleischman, P. Graven images p61-85 **S C**

The **man** on Morvan's Road. Leach, M.
In Leach, M. Whistle in the graveyard p59-60 **398.2**

The **man** who bought a dream. Uchida, Y.
In Uchida, Y. The magic listening cap **398.2**

The **man** who could call down owls. Bunting, E. **E**

Man who did not know fear
Afanas'ev, A. N. The man who did not know fear
In Afanas'ev, A. N. Russian fairy tales p325-27 **398.2**

The **man** who didn't wash his dishes. Krasilovsky, P.
In The Read-aloud treasury p179-87 **808.8**

The **man** who kept house. Hague, K. **398.2**

The **man** who lived alone. Hall, D. **Fic**

The **man** who loved books [biography of Saint Columba]. Fritz, J. **92**

Man who was going to mind the house
Asbjørnsen, P. C. The husband who was to mind the house
In The Scott, Foresman anthology of children's literature p235-36 **808.8**
In Womenfolk and fairy tales p106-110 **398.2**
Gág, W. Gone is gone **398.2**
Hague, K. The man who kept house **398.2**
Riordan, J. The nagging husband
In Riordan, J. The woman in the moon, and other tales of forgotten heroines p15-19 **398.2**

Manabozho (Legendary character) *See* Nanabozho (Legendary character)

Manabozho and his toe
In Best-loved folktales of the world p718-19 **398.2**

Manatees
Clark, M. G. The vanishing manatee (4 and up) **599.5**
Sibbald, J. H. The manatee (3-5) **599.5**

Mancarella, Michael
(jt. auth) Matthews, J. G. ClipArt & dynamic designs for libraries & media centers **021.7**

Mancrow, bird of darkness. Sherlock, Sir P. M.
In Sherlock, Sir P. M. West Indian folk-tales p65-70 **398.2**

Mandan Indians
Lepthien, E. U. The Mandans (2-4) **970.004**

Mandarin and the butterflies
Carpenter, F. Mandarin and the butterflies
In Carpenter, F. Tales of a Chinese grandmother p198-205 **398.2**

Manes, Stephen, 1949-
Some of the adventures of Rhode Island Red (3-6) **Fic**

Mangelsen, Thomas D.
(il) Hirschi, R. Spring **508**
(il) Hirschi, R. Winter **508**

Mango, Karin N., 1936-
Codes, ciphers, and other secrets (4 and up) **652**
Mapmaking (4 and up) **526**

Maniac Magee. Spinelli, J. **Fic**

Mann, Peggy
Israel—in pictures. See Israel—in pictures **956.94**

Manners *See* Etiquette

Manning-Sanders, Ruth, 1895-1988
(comp) Festivals. See Festivals **394.2**

Mannix, Daniel P. (Daniel Pratt), 1878-1957
The last eagle [excerpt]
In Animal families of the wild: animal stories p35-43 **591**

Manuel had a riddle. Hamilton, V.
In Hamilton, V. The people could fly: American black folktales p65-75 **398.2**

Manufactures
Cobb, V. The secret life of hardware: a science experiment book (5 and up) **670**

Manushkin, Fran
Latkes and applesauce **E**

Many-fur. Grimm, J.
In Grimm, J. The juniper tree, and other tales from Grimm v2 p236-44 **398.2**

Many-furred creature
Grimm, J. Allerleirauh
In The Green fairy book p276-81 **398.2**
In Grimm, J. The complete Grimm's fairy tales p326-31 **398.2**

Many-furred creature—*Continued*
Grimm, J. Many-fur
In Grimm, J. The juniper tree, and other tales from Grimm v2 p236-44 **398.2**
Grimm, J. Thousand-Furs
In Best-loved folktales of the world p126-31 **398.2**
Many happy reruns. Paterson, K.
In Paterson, K. Angels & other strangers: family Christmas stories p26-39 **S C**
The **many** lives of Benjamin Franklin. Aliki. **92**
Many luscious lollipops: a book about adjectives. Heller, R. **428**
Many, many weddings in one corner house. Sandburg, C.
In Sandburg, C. Rootabaga stories pt 2 p17-21 **S C**
In Sandburg, C. The Sandburg treasury p95-97 **818**
Many moons. Thurber, J. **Fic**
Many stars & more string games. Gryski, C. **793.9**
Many waters. L'Engle, M. See note under L'Engle, M. A wrinkle in time **Fic**
Maoris
Higham, C. The Maoris (5 and up) **993**
See/See also pages in the following book(s):
New Zealand—in pictures (5 and up) **993**
Folklore
Te Kanawa, K. Land of the long white cloud (3-6) **398.2**
Map drawing
Mango, K. N. Mapmaking (4 and up) **526**
Maple sugar
Lasky, K. Sugaring time (5 and up) **633.6**
Mapmaking. Mango, K. N. **526**
Maps
Lambert, D. Maps and globes (3-5) **912**
Maps and globes. Lambert, D. **912**
Maraslis, Demetra
(il) Yolen, J. The seeing stick **Fic**
The **marble** champ. Soto, G.
In Soto, G. Baseball in April, and other stories p90-96 **S C**
Marbury v. Madison
See/See also pages in the following book(s):
Sgroi, P. P. The living Constitution: landmark Supreme Court decisions p1-38 (5 and up) **342**
Marcellino, Fred
(il) Perrault, C. Puss in boots **398.2**
Marches (Demonstrations) *See* Protests, demonstrations, etc.
Marchesi, Stephen
(il) Meltzer, M. Betty Friedan: a voice for women's rights **92**
Marco Polo. Ceserani, G. P. **92**
Marco the Rich and Vasily the Luckless. Afanas'ev, A. N.
In Afanas'ev, A. N. Russian fairy tales p213-20 **398.2**
The **mare** on the hill. Locker, T. **E**
Marelle, Charles
Drakestail
In The Red fairy book p202-07 **398.2**
The ratcatcher
In The Red fairy book p208-14 **398.2**
The true history of Little Golden-hood
In The Red fairy book p215-19 **398.2**
Maren, Michael
The land and people of Kenya (5 and up) **967.62**
Mare's eggs. Crossley-Holland, K.
In Crossley-Holland, K. British folk tales p153-54 **398.2**
Mare's nest
Schwartz, A. Grandpa buys a pumpkin egg
In Schwartz, A. There is a carrot in my ear, and other noodle tales p44-57 **398.2**
Margaret Wise Brown's A child's good night book. Brown, M. W. **E**
Margaret's moves. Rabe, B. **Fic**
Margolis, Richard J.
Secrets of a small brother (1-3) **811**
Marguerite de Angeli's book of nursery and Mother Goose rhymes (k-2) **398.8**
Marguerite, go wash your feet. Tripp, W. **821.008**
Maria Morevna. Afanas'ev, A. N.
In Afanas'ev, A. N. Russian fairy tales p553-62 **398.2**
Mariah Delany's Author-of-the-Month Club. Greenwald, S. **Fic**
Mariah keeps cool. Walter, M. P. **Fic**
Marietta's choice. McCarty, T.
In The Scott, Foresman anthology of children's literature p291-92 **808.8**
Marihuana *See* Marijuana
Marijuana
Stwertka, E. Marijuana (5 and up) **616.86**
Zeller, P. K. Focus on marijuana (3-6) **362.29**
See/See also pages in the following book(s):
Hyde, M. O. Drug wars p41-49 (6 and up) **363.4**

Marika the snowmaiden. Bauer, C. F.
In Snowy day: stories and poems p45-49 **808.8**

Marine animals
See also Mammals, Marine
Arnold, C. A walk on the Great Barrier Reef (3-6) **574.92**
Freedman, R. Killer fish (3-5) **597**
Holling, H. C. Pagoo (4 and up) **595.3**
Johnson, S. A. Coral reefs (4 and up) **574.92**
Parker, S. Seashore (4 and up) **574.92**
Stolz, M. Night of ghosts and hermits (3-5) **574.92**

Marine animals in art
Ames, L. J. Draw 50 sharks, whales, and other sea creatures (4 and up) **743**

Marine aquariums
See/See also pages in the following book(s):
Cook, J. L. The mysterious undersea world p90-99 (4 and up) **551.46**

Marine biology
Cook, J. L. The mysterious undersea world (4 and up) **551.46**
Kohn, B. The beachcomber's book (3-6) **745.5**
McGovern, A. Down under, down under (3-6) **574.92**
McGovern, A. Night dive (3-5) **797.2**
Zim, H. S. Seashores (4 and up) **574.92**

Marine ecology
Bellamy, D. J. The rock pool (1-4) **574.92**
Silverstein, A. Life in a tidal pool (4-6) **574.92**

Marine plants
See also Freshwater plants
Parker, S. Seashore (4 and up) **574.92**

Marine pollution
See also Oil spills
Miller, C. G. Coastal rescue: preserving our seashores (5 and up) **333.91**

Maris, Ron
Is anyone home? **E**

Mark, Jan
Thunder and Lightnings (5 and up) **Fic**

Markets
Horwitz, J. Night markets (3-6) **381**

Markle, Sandra, 1946-
Exploring spring (4 and up) **508**
Exploring summer (4 and up) **508**
Exploring winter (4 and up) **508**
Power up (3-5) **537**
The young scientist's guide to successful science projects (5 and up) **507.8**

Marks, Alan
(il) Andersen, H. C. The ugly duckling **Fic**

Marks, Claude, 1915-1991
Go in and out the window. See Go in and out the window **782.42**

Marks, J. *See* Highwater, Jamake

Marmots
McNulty, F. Woodchuck (k-3) **599.32**

Marolen, Daniel
Chief Kama and the duiker
In The Crest and the hide, and other African stories of heroes, chiefs, bards, hunters, sorcerers, and common people p123-28 **398.2**

Marrella, Maria Pia
(il) MacLachlan, P. Seven kisses in a row **Fic**

Marriage
See also Divorce; Family; Weddings

Marriage customs and rites
Lasker, J. Merry ever after (3-5) **392**

Fiction

Sandburg, C. The wedding procession of the Rag Doll and the Broom Handle and who was in it **E**

Marrin, Albert, 1936-
Victory in the Pacific (6 and up) **940.54**

Marriott, Alice Lee, 1910-
American Indian mythology **398.2**
Includes the following tales: Bird of power; The coming of buffalo; The of corn (Cheyenne); The coming of corn (Mikasuki); The coming of corn (Zuni); The dancing feather; The Deer Woman; Don't be greedy story; The end of the world: the buffalo go; Fifty young men and a turtle; A glass of water, please; The great river monster; How death came to the world (Kiowa); How death came to the world (Modoc); How horses came to the Navaho; How the half boys came to be; How the people came to the middle place; How the world was made (Modoc); Long Sash and his people; Over the hill; The painted turtle; The peyote religion; Pursuit of the bear; The race between buffalo and man; The River of Separation; The sacred bluff; Saynday and Smallpox: the white man's gift; Thunder and his helpers; Tsali of the Cherokees; The under water village; Why the bear waddles when he walks; The womb of the earth; The world beyond; Yellow Hair: George Armstrong Custer

Marriott, J. Willard, 1900-1985
See/See also pages in the following book(s):
Aaseng, N. From rags to riches p48-57 (5 and up) **920**

Marriott, Pat, 1920-
(il) Aiken, J. The wolves of Willoughby Chase **Fic**

Marriott Corporation
See/See also pages in the following book(s):
Aaseng, N. From rags to riches p48-57 (5 and up) **920**

Mars, W. T. (Witold T.)
(il) Bartlett, R. M. Thanksgiving Day **394.2**
(il) Taylor, T. Air raid—Pearl Harbor! **940.54**

Mars, Witold T. *See* Mars, W. T. (Witold T.)

Mars (Planet)
Simon, S. Mars (1-4) **523.4**
See/See also pages in the following book(s):
Kelch, J. W. Small worlds: exploring the 60 moons of our solar system p38-48 (6 and up) **523.9**

Marschall, Ken
(il) Ballard, R. D. Exploring the Titanic **910.4**

Marshak, S. (Samuil), 1887-1964
The Month-Brothers (1-3) **398.2**

Marshak, Samuil *See* Marshak, S. (Samuil), 1887-1964

Marshall, Edward, 1942-
See also Marshall, James, 1942-
Four on the shore. See note under Marshall, E. Three by the sea **E**
Fox all week. See note under Marshall, E. Fox and his friends **E**
Fox and his friends **E**
Fox at school. See note under Marshall, E. Fox and his friends **E**
Fox in love. See note under Marshall, E. Fox and his friends **E**
Fox on wheels. See note under Marshall, E. Fox and his friends **E**
Space case **E**
Three by the sea **E**
Troll country **E**

Marshall, James, 1942-
See also Marshall, Edward, 1942-
The cut-ups **E**
The cut-ups at Camp Custer. See note under Marshall, J. The cut-ups **E**
The cut-ups carry on. See note under Marshall, J. The cut-ups **E**
The cut-ups cut loose. See note under Marshall, J. The cut-ups **E**
Fox be nimble. See note under Marshall, E. Fox and his friends **E**
Fox on the job. See note under Marshall, E. Fox and his friends **E**
George and Martha **E**
George and Martha back in town. See note under Marshall, J. George and Martha **E**
George and Martha encore. See note under Marshall, J. George and Martha **E**
George and Martha, one fine day. See note under Marshall, J. George and Martha **E**
George and Martha rise and shine. See note under Marshall, J. George and Martha **E**
George and Martha, round and round. See note under Marshall, J. George and Martha **E**
George and Martha, tons of fun. See note under Marshall, J. George and Martha **E**
Goldilocks and the three bears (k-2) **398.2**
Little Red Riding Hood (k-2) **398.2**
Merry Christmas, space case. See note under Marshall, E. Space case **E**
Taking care of Carruthers. See note under Marshall, J. Yummers! **E**
The three little pigs (k-2) **398.2**
Three up a tree. See note under Marshall, E. Three by the sea **E**
What's the matter with Carruthers? See note under Marshall, J. Yummers! **E**
Wings **E**
Yummers! **E**
Yummers too: the second course. See note under Marshall, J. Yummers! **E**
(il) Allard, H. Bumps in the night **E**
(jt. auth) Allard, H. Miss Nelson is missing! **E**
(il) Hoban, R. Dinner at Alberta's **E**
(il) James Marshall's Mother Goose. See James Marshall's Mother Goose **398.8**
(il) Karlin, B. Cinderella **398.2**
(il) Marshall, E. Fox and his friends **E**
(il) Marshall, E. Space case **E**
(il) Marshall, E. Three by the sea **E**
(il) Marshall, E. Troll country **E**
(il) McFarland, J. B. The exploding frog and other fables from Aesop **398.2**
(il) Phillips, L. Haunted house jokes **793.73**
(il) Pomerantz, C. The piggy in the puddle **E**

Marshes

Fiction

Smith, D. B. Kelly's creek (4-6) **Fic**

Marshmallow. Newberry, C. T. **E**

Marstall, Bob
(il) George, J. C. One day in the prairie **574.5**

Marston, Hope Irvin, 1935-
Fire trucks (2-4) **628.9**
Load lifters: derricks, cranes, and helicopters (3-6) **621.8**

Marsupials
Selsam, M. E. A first look at kangaroos, koalas, and other animals with pouches (1-3) **599.2**

Martens, Anne Coulter
Santa Claus is twins
In The Big book of Christmas plays p169-85 **808.82**

Martial arts
Ribner, S. The martial arts (5 and up) **796.8**

The **martial** arts. Ribner, S. **796.8**
A **Martian** comes to stay. Lively, P.
In Lively, P. Uninvited ghosts, and other stories p9-28 **S C**
Martin, Alexander C.
(jt. auth) Zim, H. S. Flowers **582.13**
(jt. auth) Zim, H. S. Trees **582.16**
Martin, Bill, 1916-
Barn dance! **E**
Chicka chicka boom boom **E**
The ghost-eye tree **E**
Knots on a counting rope **E**
Listen to the rain **E**
Up and down on the merry-go-round **E**
Martin, Charles E.
For rent. See note under Martin, C. E. Island winter **E**
Island rescue. See note under Martin, C. E. Island winter **E**
Island winter **E**
Sam saves the day. See note under Martin, C. E. Island winter **E**
Summer business. See note under Martin, C. E. Island winter **E**
Martin, Eva
Tales of the Far North (2-5) **398.2**
Contents: The healing spring; The princess of Tomboso; The three golden hairs; Little Golden Sun and Little Golden Star; The fairy child; Jean-Pierre and the old witch; Goldenhair; St. Nicholas and the children; Beauty and the beast; Ti-Jean and the unicorn; Ti-Jean brings home the moon; Ti-Jean and the white cat
Martin, Paul D., 1946-
Messengers to the brain: our fantastic five senses (5 and up) **612.8**
Martin, Rafe, 1946-
Will's mammoth **E**
Martin, Sarah Catherine, 1768-1826
The comic adventures of Old Mother Hubbard and her dog
In A Nursery companion p28-31 **820.8**
Martin, William Ivan *See* Martin, Bill, 1916-
Martin Luther King, Jr., a man to remember. McKissack, P. C. **92**
Martin Luther King, Jr., and the freedom movement. Patterson, L. **92**
Martinez, Vilma
See/See also pages in the following book(s):
Morey, J. Famous Mexican Americans p63-74 (5 and up) **920**
Martins, George
(il) Giovanni, N. Spin a soft black song: poems for children **811**
Martin's mice. King-Smith, D. **Fic**
Maruki, Toshi, 1912-
Hiroshima no pika **940.54**
The **marvellous** musician. Grimm, J.
In The Red fairy book p354-56 **398.2**
The **marvelous** land of Oz. Baum, L. F. See note under Baum, L. F. The Wizard of Oz **Fic**
The **marvelous** misadventures of Sebastian. Alexander, L. **Fic**
Marvin, Frederic
(il) Cleaver, V. Grover **Fic**
Mary Beth
(jt. auth) Ancona, G. Handtalk zoo **419**
(jt. auth) Charlip, R. Handtalk birthday **419**
Mary had a little lamb. Hale, S. J. **811**
Mary of Mile 18. Blades, A. **Fic**
Mary Poppins. Travers, P. L. **Fic**
Mary Poppins and the house next door. Travers, P. L. See note under Travers, P. L. Mary Poppins **Fic**
Mary Poppins comes back. Travers, P. L. See note under Travers, P. L. Mary Poppins **Fic**
Mary Poppins from A to Z. Travers, P. L. See note under Travers, P. L. Mary Poppins **Fic**
Mary Poppins in Cherry Tree Lane. Travers, P. L. See note under Travers, P. L. Mary Poppins **Fic**
Mary Poppins opens the door. Travers, P. L. See note under Travers, P. L. Mary Poppins **Fic**
Marya Morevna
Afanas'ev, A. N. Maria Morevna
In Afanas'ev, A. N. Russian fairy tales p553-62 **398.2**
Afanas'ev, A. N. Marya Morevna
In Afanas'ev, A. N. Russian folk tales p37-50 **398.2**
Ralston, W. The death of Koschei the Deathless
In The Red fairy book p42-53 **398.2**
Maryland
Kent, D. Maryland
In America the beautiful **973**
Marzollo, Jean
Amy goes fishing **E**
Close your eyes **E**
Getting your period (5 and up) **612.6**
Pretend you're a cat **E**
The teddy bear book (k-2) **811**
Masai (African people)
Folklore
Aardema, V. Who's in Rabbit's house? (k-3) **398.2**
Masefield, John, 1878-1967
The box of delights; or, When the wolves were running (5 and up) **Fic**
Masheris, Robert
(il) Kustanowitz, S. E. Henrietta Szold: Israel's helping hand **92**

Masks (Facial)
Hunt, K. Masks and mask makers (5 and up) **391**
Wright, L. Masks (4 and up) **745.59**
Masks (Sculpture)
Hunt, K. Masks and mask makers (5 and up) **391**
Masks and mask makers. Hunt, K. **391**
Mason, Joseph, 1807-1883
Fiction
Brenner, B. On the frontier with Mr. Audubon (4 and up) **Fic**
The **masquerade**. Alcock, V.
In Alcock, V. Ghostly companions **S C**
Mass communication *See* Communication
Massachusetts
Kent, D. Massachusetts
In America the beautiful **973**
History—1600-1775, Colonial period
See also Plymouth Rock
Anderson, J. The first Thanksgiving feast (3-5) **974.4**
Dalgliesh, A. The Thanksgiving story (k-2) **974.4**
Sewall, M. The pilgrims of Plimoth (3-6) **974.4**
History—1600-1775, Colonial period—Fiction
Clapp, P. Constance: a story of early Plymouth (5 and up) **Fic**
Clapp, P. Witches' children (6 and up) **Fic**
Master and his pupil
Gág, W. Wanda Gág's The sorcerer's apprentice **398.2**
Grimm, J. The sorcerer's apprentice
In Grimm, J. More tales from Grimm p197-205 **398.2**
Jacobs, J. Master and his pupil
In Jacobs, J. English fairy tales p73-76 **398.2**
Master and man. Deutsch, B.
In The Scott, Foresman anthology of children's literature p279-82 **808.8**
The **master** cat. Perrault, C.
In The Blue fairy book p141-47 **398.2**
In The Classic fairy tales p113-16 **398.2**
In The Scott, Foresman anthology of children's literature p204-06 **808.8**
Master Frog. Vuong, L. D.
In Vuong, L. D. The brocaded slipper, and other Vietnamese tales **398.2**
Master Jacob
Pyle, H. Master Jacob
In Pyle, H. The wonder clock p161-74 **398.2**
Master James' nightmare. Sutherland, Z.
In The Scott, Foresman anthology of children's literature p378-83 **808.8**
Master-maid
Asbjørnsen, P. C. The master-maid
In The Blue fairy book p120-35 **398.2**
Master of all masters
Jacobs, J. Master of all masters
In Best-loved folktales of the world p231-32 **398.2**
In Jacobs, J. English fairy tales p220-21 **398.2**
In Tomie dePaola's favorite nursery tales p84-85 **398.2**
Master Pfriem
Grimm, J. Master Pfriem
In Grimm, J. The complete Grimm's fairy tales p720-24 **398.2**
The **master** puppeteer. Paterson, K. **Fic**
Master thief
Afanas'ev, A. N. The thief
In Afanas'ev, A. N. Russian fairy tales p590-93 **398.2**
Asbjørnsen, P. C. The master thief
In Best-loved folktales of the world p313-25 **398.2**
In The Red fairy book p67-81 **398.2**
Grimm, J. The master-thief
In Grimm, J. The complete Grimm's fairy tales p773-80 **398.2**
In Grimm, J. The juniper tree, and other tales from Grimm v1 p113-28 **398.2**
Williams-Ellis, A. The Master-Thief
In Williams-Ellis, A. Tales from the enchanted world p77-95 **398.2**
The **Master** thief [another story]
In The Magic orange tree, and other Haitian folktales p135-41 **398.2**
The **mastermaid**. Asbjørnsen, P. C.
In Best-loved folktales of the world p327-39 **398.2**
Masters, Robert V. *See* Boehm, David A. (David Alfred), 1914-
Master's walking stick. Sanfield, S.
In Sanfield, S. The adventures of High John the Conqueror **398.2**
Masuda, Modoki
(il) Johnson, S. A. Water insects **595.7**
Mataora and Niwareka in the Underworld. Te Kanawa, K.
In Te Kanawa, K. Land of the long white cloud p67-80 **398.2**
Matas, Carol, 1949-
Lisa's war (5 and up) **Fic**

The **matchlock** gun. Edmonds, W. D. **Fic**
Materia medica
See also Drugs
Math, Irwin, 1940-
More wires and watts: understanding and using electricity (6 and up) **537**
Math-a-magic: number tricks for magicians. White, L. B. **793.8**
Math for smarty pants. Burns, M. **513**
Math games, Anno's. Anno, M. **513**
Math games II, Anno's. Anno, M. **513**
Mathematical recreations
Phillips, L. 263 brain busters (4-6) **793.73**
White, L. B. Math-a-magic: number tricks for magicians (3-6) **793.8**
Mathematics
See also Arithmetic; Binary system (Mathematics)
Adler, I. Mathematics (4 and up) **510**
Anno, M. Anno's mysterious multiplying jar (2-5) **512**
Anno, M. Anno's math games (k-3) **513**
Anno, M. Anno's math games II (k-3) **513**
Anno, M. Socrates and the three little pigs (4-6) **511**
Burns, M. The I hate mathematics! book (5 and up) **513**
Burns, M. Math for smarty pants (5 and up) **513**
Nozaki, A. Anno's hat tricks (1-4) **153.4**
Mathers, Petra
(il) Chaikin, M. Yossi asks the angels for help **Fic**
(il) Couture, S. A. The block book **E**
(il) Kimmelman, L. Frannie's fruits **E**
Mathews, William H.
South Korea—in pictures. See South Korea—in pictures **951.9**
Mathis, Sharon Bell, 1937-
Sidewalk story (3-5) **Fic**
Matilda. Dahl, R. **Fic**
Matisse, Henri
About
Munthe, N. Meet Matisse (4 and up) **759.4**
Raboff, E. Henri Matisse (4 and up) **759.4**
The **Matsuyama** mirror. Quayle, E.
In Quayle, E. The shining princess, and other Japanese legends p90-96 **398.2**
Matt Gargan's boy. Slote, A. **Fic**
Matter
Cobb, V. Why can't you unscramble an egg? and other not such dumb questions about matter (3-5) **530**
Matter of brogues
Sawyer, R. A matter of brogues
In Sawyer, R. The way of the storyteller p259-70 **372.6**
Matthews, Downs
Polar bear cubs (2-4) **599.74**
Matthews, Jenny
(il) Stewart, J. A family in Morocco **964**
Matthews, Judy Gay
ClipArt & dynamic designs for libraries & media centers **021.7**
Mattimeo. Jacques, B. **Fic**
Matzeliger, Jan
About
Mitchell, B. Shoes for everyone: a story about Jan Matzeliger (3-5) **92**
Maude and Sally. Weiss, N. **E**
Maudie in the middle. Naylor, P. R. **Fic**
Maui and the birds. Te Kanawa, K.
In Te Kanawa, K. Land of the long white cloud p117-18 **398.2**
Maui and the Great Fish. Te Kanawa, K.
In Te Kanawa, K. Land of the long white cloud p17-22 **398.2**
Maui tames the Sun. Te Kanawa, K.
In Te Kanawa, K. Land of the long white cloud p23-26 **398.2**
Maurer, R. (Richard)
Airborne (5 and up) **629.13**
Junk in space (4-6) **363.7**
Maurer, Richard *See* Maurer, R. (Richard)
Mausoleums *See* Tombs
Max. Isadora, R. **E**
Max and me and the time machine. Greer, G. **Fic**
Maxie, Rosie, and Earl—partners in grime. Park, B. **Fic**
Maxims *See* Proverbs
Maxner, Joyce
Nicholas Cricket **E**
Max's bath. Wells, R. See note under Wells, R. Max's first word **E**
Max's bedtime. Wells, R. See note under Wells, R. Max's first word **E**
Max's birthday. Wells, R. See note under Wells, R. Max's first word **E**
Max's breakfast. Wells, R. See note under Wells, R. Max's first word **E**
Max's chocolate chicken. Wells, R. See note under Wells, R. Max's first word **E**
Max's Christmas. Wells, R. See note under Wells, R. Max's first word **E**
Max's first word. Wells, R. **E**
Max's new suit. Wells, R. See note under Wells, R. Max's first word **E**

Max's ride. Wells, R. See note under Wells, R. Max's first word E
Max's toys. Wells, R. See note under Wells, R. Max's first word E
May, Sophia *See* Clarke, Rebecca Sophia, 1833-1906
May I bring a friend? De Regniers, B. S. E
Mayas
Beck, B. L. The ancient Maya (4 and up) **972**
See/See also pages in the following book(s):
Weiss, M. E. Sky watchers of ages past p35-49 (5 and up) **523**
Fiction
O'Dell, S. The captive (6 and up) **Fic**
Legends
Lattimore, D. N. Why there is no arguing in heaven (3-6) **398.2**
The Monkey's haircut, and other stories told by the Maya (5 and up) **398.2**
Shetterly, S. H. The dwarf-wizard of Uxmal (3-5) **398.2**
Mayer, Marianna, 1945-
Beauty and the beast (1-4) **398.2**
The unicorn and the lake E
Mayer, Mercer, 1943-
Appelard and Liverwurst E
A boy, a dog, and a friend. See note under Mayer, M. A boy, a dog, and a frog E
A boy, a dog, and a frog E
Frog goes to dinner. See note under Mayer, M. A boy, a dog, and a frog E
Frog on his own. See note under Mayer, M. A boy, a dog, and a frog E
Frog, where are you? See note under Mayer, M. A boy, a dog, and a frog E
Liverwurst is missing E
One frog too many. See note under Mayer, M. A boy, a dog, and a frog E
There's a nightmare in my closet E
There's an alligator under my bed E
(il) Fitzgerald, J. D. The Great Brain **Fic**
(il) Mayer, M. Beauty and the beast **398.2**
(il) Williams, J. Everyone knows what a dragon looks like E
Mayne, William, 1928-
The blue book of Hob stories. See note under Mayne, W. The green book of Hob stories E
The green book of Hob stories E
The red book of Hob stories. See note under Mayne, W. The green book of Hob stories E
See/See also pages in the following book(s):
Townsend, J. R. A sense of story p130-38 **028.5**
Townsend, J. R. A sounding of storytellers p139-52 **028.5**
Mayo, Gretchen
Star tales (4 and up) **398.2**
Contents: Coyote makes the constellations; Adventure along the white river in the sky; The race for the prize fish; The antelope chase; The spirit of the snow goose; The tale of the hungry skunk; The giant elk skin; The birds of summer; The never ending bear hunt; Moon and his sister; The boy who shot the star to find his friend; The dancing braves; The maidens of the northern crown; Morning Star takes a wife
Mayor Gimpel's golden shoes. Simon, S.
In Simon, S. More wise men of Helm and their merry tales p44-49 **398.2**
The **mayoress**. Afanas'ev, A. N.
In Afanas'ev, A. N. Russian fairy tales p141 **398.2**
Mazel & Shlimazel. Singer, I. B.
In Singer, I. B. Stories for children p22-40 **S C**
Mazel and Shlimazel. Singer, I. B. **398.2**
Mazer, Norma Fox, 1931-
A figure of speech (6 and up) **Fic**
McBroom and the big wind. Fleischman, S. See note under Fleischman, S. McBroom tells the truth **Fic**
See note under Fleischman, S. McBroom tells the truth **Fic**
McBroom tells a lie. Fleischman, S. See note under Fleischman, S. McBroom tells the truth **Fic**
McBroom tells the truth. Fleischman, S. **Fic**
McBroom's almanac. Fleischman, S. See note under Fleischman, S. McBroom tells the truth **Fic**
McBroom's almanac [excerpt]. Fleischman, S.
In The Random House book of humor for children p173-75 **817.008**
McCaffrey, Anne
Dragondrums. See note under McCaffrey, A. Dragonsong **Fic**
Dragonsinger. See note under McCaffrey, A. Dragonsong **Fic**
Dragonsong (6 and up) **Fic**
McCall, Edith S.
Biography of a river: the living Mississippi (6 and up) **977**
McCarthy, Betty
Utah
In America the beautiful **973**
McCarty, Toni
Donagh and the giants
In The Scott, Foresman anthology of children's literature p456-58 **808.8**

McCarty, Toni—*Continued*
Marietta's choice
In The Scott, Foresman anthology of children's literature p291-92 **808.8**
Vassilissa the valiant
In The Scott, Foresman anthology of children's literature p289-91 **808.8**

McCauley, Jane R., 1947-
Animals and their hiding places (k-3) **591.5**
Animals in summer (k-3) **591.5**
Animals that live in trees (k-3) **591.5**
Baby birds and how they grow (k-3) **598**
Let's explore a river (k-3) **574.92**
Ways animals sleep (k-3) **591.5**

McCay, Winsor, 1871-1934
See/See also pages in the following book(s):
Sendak, M. Caldecott & Co.: notes on books and pictures p77-85 **028.5**

McClard, Megan
Hiawatha and the Iroquois league (5 and up) **92**

McCloskey, Robert, 1914-
Blueberries for Sal **E**
Burt Dow, deep-water man **E**
Centerburg tales (4-6) **Fic**
Homer Price (4-6) **Fic**
Homer Price [excerpt]
In The Random House book of humor for children p181-94 **817.008**
Lentil **E**
Make way for ducklings **E**
One morning in Maine **E**
Time of wonder **E**
(il) Robertson, K. Henry Reed, Inc. **Fic**
See/See also pages in the following book(s):
Caldecott Medal books, 1938-1957 p80-86 **028.5**
A Horn Book sampler on children's books and reading p125-27 **028.5**

McClung, Robert M.
The amazing egg (4 and up) **591.1**
Animals that build their homes (k-3) **591.5**
Gorilla (4 and up) **599.88**
Lili: a giant panda of Sichuan (3-6) **599.74**

McClure, Gillian, 1948-
(il) Coltman, P. Tog the Ribber; or, Granny's tale **821**

McCord, David Thompson Watson, 1897-
All day long: fifty rhymes of the never was and always is (4-6) **811**
One at a time (4-6) **811**
Speak up: more rhymes of the never was and always is (4-6) **811**
Take sky: more rhymes of the never was and always is (4-6) **811**

McCormick, Dell J.
When the rain came up from China
In Rainy day: stories and poems p47-53 **808.8**

McCrady, Lady, 1951-
(il) Willow, D. Science sensations **507**

McCue, Lisa
(il) Thayer, J. The popcorn dragon **E**
(il) Thayer, J. The puppy who wanted a boy **E**

McCully, Emily Arnold
The evil spell. See note under McCully, E. A. Zaza's big break **E**
Grandmas at the lake **E**
The show must go on. See note under McCully, E. A. Zaza's big break **E**
You lucky duck! See note under McCully, E. A. Zaza's big break **E**
Zaza's big break **E**
(il) Adoff, A. Black is brown is tan **E**
(il) Blos, J. W. The grandpa days **E**
(il) Byars, B. C. Go and hush the baby **E**
(il) Greene, C. C. I and Sproggy **Fic**
(il) Greene, C. C. Isabelle the itch **Fic**
(il) Hurd, E. T. I dance in my red pajamas **E**
(il) Joosse, B. M. Jam day **E**
(il) O'Connor, J. Lulu goes to witch school **E**
(il) Plath, S. The bed book **811**
(il) Porte-Thomas, B. A. The take-along dog **E**
(il) Rappaport, D. The Boston coffee party **E**
(il) Rockwell, T. How to eat fried worms **Fic**

McCurdy, Michael
(il) Alcott, L. M. An old-fashioned Thanksgiving **Fic**
(il) Norman, H. How Glooskap outwits the Ice Giants, and other tales of the Maritime Indians **398.2**

McDermott, Gerald
Anansi the spider (k-3) **398.2**
Arrow to the sun (k-3) **398.2**
Daughter of Earth (2-4) **292**
The stonecutter (k-3) **398.2**
Tim O'Toole and the wee folk **E**
See/See also pages in the following book(s):
Newbery and Caldecott Medal books, 1966-1975 p266-75 **028.5**

McDonald, Jo
Australia—in pictures. See Australia—in pictures **994**

McDonald, Maurice
See/See also pages in the following book(s):
Aaseng, N. The unsung heroes p68-75 (5 and up) **920**

McDonald, Megan
Is this a house for Hermit Crab? (k-2) **595.3**
McDonald, Richard
See/See also pages in the following book(s):
Aaseng, N. The unsung heroes p68-75 (5 and up) **920**
McDonald's Corp.
See/See also pages in the following book(s):
Aaseng, N. The unsung heroes p66-75 (5 and up) **920**
McDonnell, Christine, 1949-
Don't be mad, Ivy (2-4) **Fic**
Friends first (6 and up) **Fic**
Lucky charms & birthday wishes (2-4) **Fic**
Toad food & measle soup (2-4) **Fic**
McElhinney, Susan
(il) Rinard, J. E. Helping our animal friends **636.088**
McElligot's pool. Seuss, Dr. **E**
McFadden, Eliza
(il) Weiss, M. E. Sky watchers of ages past **523**
McFarland, Cynthia
Cows in the parlor (1-3) **636.2**
McFarland, John B., 1943-
The exploding frog and other fables from Aesop (k-3) **398.2**
McGinley, Phyllis, 1905-1978
The year without a Santa Claus (k-3) **811**
McGovern, Ann
Down under, down under (3-6) **574.92**
Night dive (3-5) **797.2**
The secret soldier: the story of Deborah Sampson [Gannett] (3-5) **92**
Too much noise (k-3) **398.2**
McGowan, Jane
Bunnies and bonnets
In Holiday plays round the year p255-66 **812.008**
Miss Lonelyheart
In Holiday plays round the year p198-211 **812.008**
McGowen, Tom
Album of birds (4 and up) **598**
Album of dinosaurs (4 and up) **567.9**
Album of rocks and minerals (4 and up) **549**
Album of sharks (4 and up) **597**
Radioactivity: from the Curies to the atomic age (6 and up) **539.7**
McGrath, Susan, 1955-
The amazing things animals do (4 and up) **591.5**
How animals talk (k-3) **591.5**
Saving our animal friends (k-3) **591**
McGreal, Elizabeth Yates *See* Yates, Elizabeth, 1905-
McGugan, Laurie
(il) Kalbfleisch, S. Jump! **796.2**
McGuire, Leslie, 1945-
Lions (4-6) **599.74**
McHargue, Georgess
The beasts of never (4 and up) **398**
Meet the werewolf (4 and up) **398**
Meet the witches (4 and up) **133.4**
McIlwraith, Maureen *See* Hunter, Mollie, 1922-
McIntyre, Brian
(il) Catchpole, C. Deserts **574.5**
(il) Catchpole, C. Mountains **574.5**
McKenna, Nancy Durrell
(il) Taylor, A. A kibbutz in Israel **956.94**
McKie, Roy
(il) Cerf, B. Bennett Cerf's book of animal riddles **793.73**
(il) Cerf, B. Bennett Cerf's book of riddles **793.73**
(il) Herbert, D. Mr. Wizard's supermarket science **507**
McKillip, Patricia A., 1948-
Harpist in the wind. See note under McKillip, P. A. The riddle-master of Hed **Fic**
Heir of sea & fire. See note under McKillip, P. A. The riddle-master of Hed **Fic**
The riddle-master of Hed (5 and up) **Fic**
McKinley, Robin
Beauty: a retelling of the story of Beauty & the beast (5 and up) **Fic**
The hero and the crown (6 and up) **Fic**
The outlaws of Sherwood (6 and up) **398.2**
See/See also pages in the following book(s):
Newbery and Caldecott Medal books, 1976-1985 p138-52 **028.5**
McKissack, Fredrick, 1939-
(jt. auth) McKissack, P. C. The Civil Rights Movement in America from 1865 to the present **323.4**
(jt. auth) McKissack, P. C. Frederick Douglass: the black lion **92**
(jt. auth) McKissack, P. C. A long hard journey **331.8**
McKissack, Pat *See* McKissack, Patricia C., 1944-
McKissack, Patricia C., 1944-
The Apache (2-4) **970.004**
The Civil Rights Movement in America from 1865 to the present (5 and up) **323.4**

McKissack, Patricia C., 1944-—*Continued*
Flossie & the fox E
Frederick Douglass: the black lion (4 and up) 92
Jesse Jackson: a biography (4 and up) 92
A long hard journey (5 and up) 331.8
Martin Luther King, Jr., a man to remember (4 and up) 92
Mary McLeod Bethune: a great American educator (4 and up) 92
Mirandy and Brother Wind E
Nettie Jo's friends E
Paul Laurence Dunbar, a poet to remember (4 and up) 92

McLaughlin, Molly
Dragonflies (3-5) 595.7

McLeish, Kenneth, 1940-
The Oxford first companion to music (5 and up) 780

McLeish, Valerie
(jt. auth) McLeish, K. The Oxford first companion to music 780

McLenighan, Valjean, 1947-
China, a history to 1949 (4 and up) 951

McLeod, Emilie, 1926-1982
The bear's bicycle E

McLuhan, Marshall, 1911-1980
See/See also pages in the following book(s):
Crosscurrents of criticism p98-120 028.5

McMane, Fred
Track & field basics (4 and up) 796.4

McManus, Patrick F.
The skunk ladder
In The Random House book of humor for children p276-82 817.008

McMillan, Bruce
Becca backward, Becca frontward (k-2) 428
Counting wildflowers E
Growing colors E
Here a chick, there a chick (k-2) 428
One sun: a book of terse verse (k-3) 811
Step by step E
Super, super, superwords (k-2) 422
Time to— (k-2) 529
(il) Hale, S. J. Mary had a little lamb 811

McMullan, Kate, 1947-
Snakey riddles (k-2) 793.73

McNair, Sylvia
Alabama
In America the beautiful 973
Hawaii
In America the beautiful 973
Kentucky
In America the beautiful 973
Tennessee
In America the beautiful 973
Thailand (4 and up) 959.3
Vermont
In America the beautiful 973
Virginia
In America the beautiful 973

McNulty, Faith
How to dig a hole to the other side of the world (2-4) 551.1
Peeping in the shell (2-5) 639.9
Whales: their life in the sea (5 and up) 599.5
With love from Koko (1-3) 599.88
Woodchuck (k-3) 599.32

McPhail, David M.
Andrew's bath E
The bear's toothache E
Emma's pet. See note under McPhail, D. M. Fix-it E
Emma's vacation. See note under McPhail, D. M. Fix-it E
Fix-it E
Lost! E
Pig Pig and the magic photo album. See note under McPhail, D. M. Pig Pig grows up E
Pig Pig gets a job. See note under McPhail, D. M. Pig Pig grows up E
Pig Pig goes to camp. See note under McPhail, D. M. Pig Pig grows up E
Pig Pig grows up E
Pig Pig rides. See note under McPhail, D. M. Pig Pig grows up E
(il) McLeod, E. The bear's bicycle E
(il) The Mother Goose songbook. See The Mother Goose songbook 782.42

McVitty, Walter
Ali Baba and the forty thieves (1-3) 398.2

Me and my family tree. Showers, P. 575.1

Me and my little brain. Fitzgerald, J. D. See note under Fitzgerald, J. D. The Great Brain Fic

Me and my shadow. Dorros, A. 535

Me and Neesie. Greenfield, E. E

Me and the terrible two. Conford, E. Fic

Me, Mop, and the Moondance Kid. Myers, W. D. Fic

Meacham, Mary, 1946-
(jt. auth) Carroll, F. L. Exciting, funny, scary, short, different, and sad books kids like about animals, science, sports, families, songs, and other things 011.6

Meadow, Secrets in the. Hess, L. 591.5

Meadway, Wendy
(il) O'Toole, C. Discovering flies 595.7

Meaker, Marijane *See* Kerr, M. E.
Meal planning *See* Nutrition
The **mean** old mean hyena. Prelutsky, J. E
Mean old Uncle Jack. Hines, A. G. E
Means, Florence Crannell, 1891-1980
Hatsuno's great-grandmother
In The Scott, Foresman anthology of children's literature p639-44 **808.8**
Meanwhile back at the ranch. Noble, T. H. E
Mear, Roger
(il) Swan, R. Destination: Antarctica **998**
Measures *See* Weights and measures
Measuring Worm's great climb. Curry, J. L.
In Curry, J. L. Back in the beforetime p26-32 **398.2**
Mechanics
Adkins, J. Moving heavy things (5 and up) **621.8**
Horvatic, A. Simple machines (1-3) **531**
Meddaugh, Susan
(il) Aardema, V. Bimwili & the Zimwi **398.2**
(il) Bunting, E. In the haunted house **E**
(il) Bunting, E. No nap **E**
(il) Ciardi, J. The hopeful trout and other limericks **811**
(il) De Regniers, B. S. The way I feel—sometimes **811**
Media access and organization. Frost, C. O. **025.3**
Media programs: district and school. See American Association of School Librarians. Information power **027.8**
Medical care
DeSantis, K. A doctor's tools (k-2) **610.69**
Kuklin, S. When I see my doctor (k-2) **610.69**
Rockwell, A. F. The emergency room (k-2) **362.1**
Rogers, F. Going to the hospital (k-2) **362.1**
Fiction
Rockwell, A. F. Sick in bed **E**
Medicine
See also Health; Hygiene; names of diseases and groups of diseases
Fradin, D. B. Medicine (6 and up) **610**
Rockwell, H. My doctor (k-1) **610.69**
See/See also pages in the following book(s):
Harris, J. L. Science in ancient Rome p42-49 (5 and up) **509**
Medicine, Military
See also Hospitals, Military
Medicine, Veterinary *See* Veterinary medicine
Medieval civilization *See* Civilization, Medieval
A **medieval** feast. Aliki. **394.1**
Medieval world, Anno's. Anno, M. **909.07**
Meditation
See/See also pages in the following book(s):
Yepsen, R. B. Smarten up! how to increase your brain power p97-106 (5 and up) **153**
Meek, James
The land and people of Scotland (5 and up) **941.1**
Meet Babar and his family. Brunhoff, L. de. See note under Brunhoff, J. de. The story of Babar, the little elephant **E**
Meet Edgar Degas. Degas, E. **759.4**
Meet M and M. Ross, P. **E**
Meet Matisse. Munthe, N. **759.4**
Meet the Austins. L'Engle, M. **Fic**
Meet the beaver. Rue, L. L. **599.32**
Meet the computer. Simon, S. **004**
Meet the moose. Rue, L. L. **599.73**
Meet the opossum. Rue, L. L. **599.2**
Meet the werewolf. McHargue, G. **398**
Meet the witches. McHargue, G. **133.4**
Meeting death. Hyde, M. O. **155.9**
Megan's island. Roberts, W. D. **Fic**
Megas, Georgios A.
The twelve months
In Best-loved folktales of the world p186-90 **398.2**
Meggendorfer, Lothar
See/See also pages in the following book(s):
Sendak, M. Caldecott & Co.: notes on books and pictures p51-60 **028.5**
Mei Li. Handforth, T. **E**
Meier, Max
(il) Schnieper, C. Amazing spiders **595.4**
(il) Schnieper, C. Chameleons **597.9**
(il) Schnieper, C. Lizards **597.9**
Meigs, Cornelia Lynde, 1884-1972
See/See also pages in the following book(s):
Newbery Medal books, 1922-1955 p117-24 **028.5**
Meir, Golda, 1898-1978
About
Adler, D. A. Our Golda: the story of Golda Meir (3-5) **92**
Melcher, Frederic Gershom, 1879-1963
See/See also pages in the following book(s):
Newbery Medal books, 1922-1955 p1-5 **028.5**
Melisande. Nesbit, E. **398.2**
Meltzer, Milton, 1915-
All times, all peoples: a world history of slavery (4 and up) **326**

Meltzer, Milton, 1915-—*Continued*
Betty Friedan: a voice for women's rights (4 and up) **92**
A book about names (5 and up) **929.4**
The Chinese Americans (6 and up) **305.8**
Dorothea Lange: life through the camera (4 and up) **92**
George Washington and the birth of our nation (5 and up) **92**
The Hispanic Americans (6 and up) **305.8**
The landscape of memory (6 and up) **153.1**
Never to forget: the Jews of the Holocaust (6 and up) **940.54**
Rescue: the story of how Gentiles saved Jews in the Holocaust (6 and up) **940.54**
The truth about the Ku Klux Klan (6 and up) **322.4**
World of our fathers: the Jews of Eastern Europe (6 and up) **305.8**
(ed) The American revolutionaries: a history in their own words, 1750-1800. See The American revolutionaries: a history in their own words, 1750-1800 **973.3**
(ed) The Black Americans: a history in their own words, 1619-1983. See The Black Americans: a history in their own words, 1619-1983 **305.8**
(ed) The Jewish Americans: a history in their own words, 1650-1950. See The Jewish Americans: a history in their own words, 1650-1950 **305.8**
(ed) Voices from the Civil War. See Voices from the Civil War **973.7**

Melville, Betty Leslie- *See* Leslie-Melville, Betty

Melzack, Ronald
The Sedna legend
In Best-loved folktales of the world p721-23 **398.2**

Memoirs of the little man and the little maid. See The Little man & the little maid

Memory
Meltzer, M. The landscape of memory (6 and up) **153.1**
See/See also pages in the following book(s):
Yepsen, R. B. Smarten up! how to increase your brain power p65-74 (5 and up) **153**

Men of different colors. Heady, E. B.
In The Scott, Foresman anthology of children's literature p305-06 **808.8**

Menaseh's dream. Singer, I. B.
In Singer, I. B. Stories for children p313-21 **S C**
In Singer, I. B. When Shlemiel went to Warshaw & other stories p83-96 **398.2**

Menashe and Rachel. Singer, I. B.
In The Scott, Foresman anthology of children's literature p678-81 **808.8**
In Singer, I. B. The power of light p31-39 **S C**
In Singer, I. B. Stories for children p122-29 **S C**

Mendez, Phil
The black snowman **E**

Mendez, Raymond A.
(il) Cole, J. An insect's body **595.7**

Mennonites
See also Amish

Fiction

Blades, A. Mary of Mile 18 (2-4) **Fic**

Menorahs, mezuzas, and other Jewish symbols. Chaikin, M. **296.4**

Menotti, Gian Carlo, 1911-
Amahl and the night visitors (2-4) **Fic**

Menstruation
Marzollo, J. Getting your period (5 and up) **612.6**
Nourse, A. E. Menstruation (6 and up) **612.6**

Mental illness
Dinner, S. H. Nothing to be ashamed of: growing up with mental illness in your family (5 and up) **362.2**

Fiction

MacLachlan, P. Mama One, Mama Two **E**

Mentally handicapped

Bibliography

Friedberg, J. B. Accept me as I am: best books of juvenile nonfiction on impairments and disabilities **016**

Fiction

Bridgers, S. E. All together now (6 and up) **Fic**
Carrick, C. Stay away from Simon! (3-5) **Fic**
Litchfield, A. B. Making room for Uncle Joe (2-5) **Fic**

Mentally handicapped children
See also Slow learning children
Bergman, T. We laugh, we love, we cry (1-3) **362.3**

Fiction

Cleaver, V. Ellen Grae (4-6) **Fic**
Shyer, M. F. Welcome home, Jellybean (5 and up) **Fic**
Slepian, J. Risk 'n' roses (5 and up) **Fic**

Mentally ill
Fiction
Corcoran, B. Annie's monster (5 and up) Fic
Levoy, M. Alan and Naomi (6 and up) Fic
Lisle, J. T. Afternoon of the elves (4-6) Fic
Merchant and the genie
The Story of the merchant and the genius
In The Arabian nights entertainments p6-12 **398.2**
Merchant's daughter and the maidservant
Afanas'ev, A. N. The merchant's daughter and the maidservant
In Afanas'ev, A. N. Russian fairy tales p327-31 **398.2**
Merchant's daughter and the slanderer
Afanas'ev, A. N. The merchant's daughter and the slanderer
In Afanas'ev, A. N. Russian fairy tales p415-18 **398.2**
Merit students encyclopedia **031**
Merlin (Legendary character)
San Souci, R. Young Merlin (2-5) **398.2**
Fiction
Dickinson, P. Merlin dreams (5 and up) Fic
Yolen, J. The dragon's boy (5 and up) Fic
Merlin dreams. Dickinson, P. Fic
The **mermaid** summer. Hunter, M. Fic
Mermaids and mermen
Fiction
Hunter, M. The mermaid summer (4 and up) Fic
The **merman** and the farmer. Grimm, J.
In Best-loved folktales of the world p151-52 **398.2**
Merriam, Eve, 1916-
Blackberry ink (k-2) **811**
Chortles: new and selected wordplay poems (3-6) **811**
The Christmas box **E**
Fresh paint (4 and up) **811**
Halloween A B C (k-2) **811**
Mommies at work (k-3) **331.4**
A poem for a pickle: funnybone verses (k-2) **811**
You be good and I'll be night: jump-on-the-bed poems (k-2) **811**
Merrick, Joseph Carey, 1862 or 3-1890
About
Howell, M. The elephant man (4 and up) **92**
See/See also pages in the following book(s):
Drimmer, F. Born different p122-49 (6 and up) **920**
Merrill, Jean, d. 1985
The pushcart war (5 and up) **Fic**
The toothpaste millionaire (4-6) **Fic**
The **merry** adventures of Robin Hood of great renown in Nottinghamshire. Pyle, H. **398.2**
A **merry** Christmas. Hackett, W.
In The Big book of Christmas plays p332-48 **808.82**
Merry Christmas, Amelia Bedelia. Parish, P. See note under Parish, P. Amelia Bedelia **E**
Merry Christmas, Ernest and Celestine. Vincent, G. See note under Vincent, G. Ernest and Celestine **E**
Merry Christmas from Betsy. Haywood, C. See note under Haywood, C. "B" is for Betsy **Fic**
Merry Christmas from Eddie. Haywood, C. See note under Haywood, C. Little Eddie **Fic**
Merry Christmas, Harry. Chalmers, M. See note under Chalmers, M. Throw a kiss, Harry **E**
Merry Christmas, space case. Marshall, J. See note under Marshall, E. Space case **E**
Merry ever after. Lasker, J. **392**
The **Merry-go-round** poetry book (k-2) **811.008**
Mesopotamia *See* Iraq
The **messenger** to Maftam. Courlander, H.
In Courlander, H. The cow-tail switch, and other West African stories p79-86 **398.2**
Messengers
Afanas'ev, A. N. The speedy messenger
In Afanas'ev, A. N. Russian fairy tales p124-30 **398.2**
Grimm, J. Death's messengers
In Grimm, J. The complete Grimm's fairy tales p718-20 **398.2**
Messengers to the brain: our fantastic five senses. Martin, P. D. **612.8**
Messiness *See* Cleanliness
Messing around with baking chemistry. Zubrowski, B. **540.7**
Metallurgy
See/See also pages in the following book(s):
Harris, J. L. Science in ancient Rome p28-34 (5 and up) **509**
Meteorology
See also Climate; Weather
Branley, F. M. Sun dogs and shooting stars (5 and up) **523**
Gallant, R. A. Rainbows, mirages and sundogs (4 and up) **551.5**

Meteorology—*Continued*

Experiments

Tannenbaum, B. Making and using your own weather station (5 and up) **551.6**

Meteors

Asimov, I. Comets and meteors (3-5) **523.6**

Branley, F. M. Shooting stars (k-3) **523.6**

Lauber, P. Voyagers from space (4 and up) **523.5**

See/See also pages in the following book(s):

Simon, S. Look to the night sky: an introduction to star watching (4 and up) **523**

Metric system

See/See also pages in the following book(s):

Bendick, J. How much & how many? p23-28 (5 and up) **530.8**

Metropolitan Museum of Art (New York, N.Y.)

Go in and out the window **782.42**

Talking to the sun: an illustrated anthology of poems for young people. See Talking to the sun: an illustrated anthology of poems for young people **808.81**

Fiction

Konigsburg, E. L. From the mixed-up files of Mrs. Basil E. Frankweiler (4 and up) **Fic**

Metter, Bert

Bar mitzvah, bat mitzvah (4 and up) **296.4**

Mexican Americans

Hewett, J. Hector lives in the United States now (3-5) **305.8**

Pinchot, J. The Mexicans in America *In* The In America series **305.8**

Wolf, B. In this proud land (4 and up) **305.8**

See/See also pages in the following book(s):

Meltzer, M. The Hispanic Americans p61-71, 79-88, 127-32 (6 and up) **305.8**

Biography

Morey, J. Famous Mexican Americans (5 and up) **920**

Fiction

Soto, G. Baseball in April, and other stories (5 and up) **S C**

The **Mexicans** in America. Pinchot, J. *In* The In America series **305.8**

Mexico

Casagrande, L. B. Focus on Mexico (4 and up) **972**

Fiction

O'Dell, S. The captive (6 and up) **Fic**

O'Dell, S. The King's fifth (5 and up) **Fic**

Social life and customs

Moran, T. A family in Mexico (3-5) **972**

Meyer, Carolyn

Christmas crafts (5 and up) **745.59**

Meyers, Susan

P.J. Clover, private eye: the case of the borrowed baby. See note under Meyers, S. P.J. Clover, private eye: the case of the Halloween hoot **Fic**

P.J. Clover, private eye: the case of the Halloween hoot (4-6) **Fic**

P.J. Clover, private eye: the case of the missing mouse. See note under Meyers, S. P.J. Clover, private eye: the case of the Halloween hoot **Fic**

P.J. Clover, private eye: the case of the stolen laundry. See note under Meyers, S. P.J. Clover, private eye: the case of the Halloween hoot **Fic**

MIA's *See* Missing in action

Mice

Fischer-Nagel, H. A look through the mouse hole (3-6) **599.32**

Pope, J. Taking care of your mice and rats (3-5) **636.088**

Silverstein, A. Mice: all about them (5 and up) **599.32**

Sproule, A. Mice and rats (4 and up) **636.088**

Wexler, J. Pet mice (3-6) **636.088**

See/See also pages in the following book(s):

Thomson, P. Auks, rocks and the odd dinosaur p73-77 (5 and up) **508**

Weber, W. J. Care of uncommon pets p58-70 (5 and up) **636.088**

Fiction

Asch, F. Here comes the cat! **E**

Benchley, N. Feldman Fieldmouse (3-5) **Fic**

Brandenberg, F. Nice new neighbors **E**

Bunting, E. The Mother's Day mice **E**

Carle, E. Do you want to be my friend? **E**

Cauley, L. B. The town mouse and the country mouse (k-3) **398.2**

Chorao, K. Cathedral mouse **E**

Cleary, B. The mouse and the motorcycle (3-5) **Fic**

Conly, J. L. R-T, Margaret, and the rats of NIMH (4 and up) **Fic**

Conly, J. L. Racso and the rats of NIMH (4 and up) **Fic**

Corbett, W. J. The song of Pentecost (5 and up) **Fic**

Emberley, M. Ruby **E**

Erickson, R. E. A toad for Tuesday (2-4) **Fic**

Freeman, D. Norman the doorman **E**

Goodall, J. S. Creepy castle **E**

Mice—Fiction—*Continued*
Goodall, J. S. Naughty Nancy goes to school E
Gundersheimer, K. 1 2 3, play with me E
Henkes, K. Chester's way E
Henkes, K. Julius, the baby of the world E
Henkes, K. Sheila Rae, the brave E
Hoban, L. It's really Christmas E
Holabird, K. Angelina ballerina E
Hurd, T. Little Mouse's big valentine E
Hurd, T. The pea patch jig E
Ivimey, J. W. The complete story of the three blind mice E
Jacques, B. Mattimeo (6 and up) Fic
Jacques, B. Redwall (6 and up) Fic
King-Smith, D. Magnus Powermouse (4-6) Fic
King-Smith, D. Martin's mice (3-5) Fic
Kraus, R. Whose mouse are you? E
Kroll, S. The biggest pumpkin ever E
Lawson, R. Ben and me (5 and up) Fic
Lionni, L. Alexander and the wind-up mouse E
Lionni, L. Frederick E
Lionni, L. Nicolas, where have you been? E
Lobel, A. Mouse soup E
Lobel, A. Mouse tales E
Miller, E. Mousekin's golden house E
Noll, S. Watch where you go E
Numeroff, L. J. If you give a mouse a cookie E
Oakley, G. The church mouse E
O'Brien, R. C. Mrs. Frisby and the rats of NIMH (4 and up) Fic
Ormondroyd, E. Broderick E
Peppé, R. The mice who lived in a shoe E
Potter, B. The story of Miss Moppet E
Potter, B. The tailor of Gloucester E
Potter, B. The tale of Mrs. Tittlemouse E
Potter, B. The tale of two bad mice E
Selden, G. The cricket in Times Square (3-6) Fic
Sharp, M. The rescuers (3-6) Fic
Steig, W. Abel's island (3-6) Fic
Steig, W. Amos & Boris E
Steig, W. Doctor De Soto E
Stevens, J. The town mouse and the country mouse (k-2) 398.2
Stevenson, J. The stowaway E
Titus, E. Basil of Baker Street (3-5) Fic
Van Leeuwen, J. The great Christmas kidnapping caper (3-5) Fic
Van Leeuwen, J. The great rescue operation (3-5) Fic
Vincent, G. Ernest and Celestine E
Wells, R. Noisy Nora E
Wells, R. Shy Charles E
White, E. B. Stuart Little (3-6) Fic
Yolen, J. Mice on ice E

Poetry

Mice are nice 808.81
Mice and rats. Sproule, A. 636.088
Mice are nice 808.81
Mice on ice. Yolen, J. E
Mice twice. Low, J. E
The **mice** who lived in a shoe. Peppé, R. E
Michaels, James
(il) Churchill, E. R. Fast & funny paper toys you can make 745.592
(il) Churchill, E. R. Instant paper airplanes 745.592
(il) Churchill, E. R. Paper toys that fly, soar, zoom, & whistle 745.592
Michaels, Steve
(il) Crofford, E. Healing warrior: a story about Sister Elizabeth Kenny 92
Michelangelo Buonarroti, 1475-1564

About

Raboff, E. Michelangelo Buonarroti (4 and up) 759.5
Ventura, P. Michelangelo's world (5 and up) 92
Michelangelo's world. Ventura, P. 92
Michener, James A. (James Albert), 1907-
Centennial [excerpt]
In Animal families of the wild: animal stories p49-64 591
Michigan
Stein, R. C. Michigan
In America the beautiful 973
The **microscope** [biography of Antoni van Leeuwenhoek]. Kumin, M. 92
Microscope and microscopy
See also Electron microscope and microscopy
Bleifeld, M. Experimenting with a microscope (5 and up) 502.8
Hidden worlds (5 and up) 500
Kumin, M. The microscope [biography of Antoni van Leeuwenhoek] (k-3) 92
Selsam, M. E. Greg's microscope (1-3) 502.8
Simon, S. Hidden worlds (5 and up) 500
See/See also pages in the following book(s):
Aaseng, N. The inventors: Nobel prizes in chemistry, physics, and medicine p35-41 (5 and up) 609
Microwaves
Asimov, I. How did we find out about microwaves? (5 and up) 621.381

Mid-career changes *See* Career changes
Middle Ages
See also Civilization, Medieval
Fiction
Carrick, D. Harald and the great stag E
Greer, G. Max and me and the time machine (5 and up) Fic
Lindgren, A. Ronia, the robber's daughter (4-6) Fic
Vining, E. G. Adam of the road (5 and up) Fic
Middle East
See also Arab countries; Bahrain; Oman
Social life and customs
Osborne, C. Middle Eastern food and drink (4-6) **641.5**
Middle Eastern cookery *See* Cookery, Middle Eastern
Middle Eastern food and drink. Osborne, C. **641.5**
The **middle** Moffat. Estes, E. See note under Estes, E. The Moffats **Fic**
Midgets *See* Dwarfs
Midnight dance
Afanas'ev, A. N. The secret ball
In Afanas'ev, A. N. Russian fairy tales p224-26 **398.2**
The **midnight** eaters. Hest, A. **E**
The **midnight** fox. Byars, B. C. **Fic**
The **midnight** fox [excerpt]. Byars, B. C.
In The Random House book of humor for children p51-65 **817.008**
The **midnight** horse. Fleischman, S. **Fic**
Midnight is a place. Aiken, J. **Fic**
The **midnight** mass of the Dead. San Souci, R.
In San Souci, R. Short & shivery p53-57 **398.2**
The **midnight** rose. Aiken, J.
In Aiken, J. Up the chimney down, and other stories p171-90 **S C**
Midstream changes. Aaseng, N. **331.7**
Midway, Battle of, 1942
See/See also pages in the following book(s):
Marrin, A. Victory in the Pacific p56-65 (6 and up) **940.54**
Migdale, Lawrence
(il) Hoyt-Goldsmith, D. Totem pole **970.004**
Mightiest of the mortals: Heracles. Gates, D. **292**
Migrant labor
Wolf, B. In this proud land (4 and up) **305.8**
Fiction
Bridgers, S. E. Home before dark (6 and up) **Fic**
Gates, D. Blue willow (4 and up) **Fic**
Snyder, Z. K. The velvet room (5 and up) **Fic**
Migration *See* Immigration and emigration
Mike Fink. York, C. B.
In The Scott, Foresman anthology of children's literature p364-65 **808.8**
Mike Hooter and the smart bears in Mississippi. Jagendorf, M. A.
In The Scott, Foresman anthology of children's literature p370-72 **808.8**
Mike Mulligan and his steam shovel. Burton, V. L. **E**
Mike's toads. Gage, W. **Fic**
Mikolaycak, Charles, 1937-
Babushka (k-3) **398.2**
(il) Bunting, E. The man who could call down owls **E**
(il) Chaikin, M. Exodus **222**
(il) Gates, D. A fair wind for Troy **292**
(il) Greene, E. The legend of the Christmas rose **398.2**
(il) Kismaric, C. The rumor of Pavel and Paali **398.2**
(il) The Lullaby songbook. See The Lullaby songbook **782.42**
(il) Noyes, A. The highwayman **821**
(il) Prokofiev, S. Peter and the wolf **E**
(il) Whitman, W. Voyages **811**
(il) Winthrop, E. A child is born: the Christmas story **232.9**
(il) Winthrop, E. He is risen: the Easter story **232.9**
(il) Yolen, J. Tam Lin **398.2**
Mik's mammoth. Gerrard, R. **E**
Mildred. Rodowsky, C. F.
In Connections: short stories by outstanding writers for young adults p95-104 **S C**
Miles, Betty
Atalanta [short story]
In Free to be—you and me p128-35 **810.8**
The trouble with thirteen (5 and up) **Fic**
Miles, Miska, 1899-1986
Annie and the Old One (1-4) **Fic**
Milhous, Katherine, 1894-1977
The egg tree **E**
See/See also pages in the following book(s):
Caldecott Medal books, 1938-1957 p213-28 **028.5**

Military art and science
See also Aeronautics, Military
Military hospitals *See* Hospitals, Military
Military personnel
See also Soldiers
Military personnel missing in action *See* Missing in action
Milk
Carrick, D. Milk (k-1) **637**
Giblin, J. Milk: the fight for purity (5 and up) **637**
Milk and cookies. Asch, F. See note under Asch, F. Sand cake **E**
The **milk** makers. Gibbons, G. **637**
The **milk** of wild beasts. Afanas'ev, A. N.
In Afanas'ev, A. N. Russian fairy tales p304-07 **398.2**
Milk: the fight for purity. Giblin, J. **637**
Milky Way
Fiction
Birdseye, T. A song of stars (3-5) **398.2**
Lee, J. M. Legend of the Milky Way (k-3) **398.2**
Mill, Eleanor
(il) Litchfield, A. B. A button in her ear **617.8**
(il) Udry, J. M. What Mary Jo shared **E**
Mill. Macaulay, D. **690**
Millard, Peter
(il) Taylor, B. Bouncing and bending light **535**
(il) Taylor, B. Color and light **535**
Millay, Edna St. Vincent, 1892-1950
Edna St. Vincent Millay's poems selected for young people (4 and up) **811**
Miller, Bertha E. Mahony
(ed) Caldecott Medal books, 1938-1957. See Caldecott Medal books, 1938-1957 **028.5**
(comp) Illustrators of children's books. See Illustrators of children's books **741.6**
(ed) Newbery Medal books, 1922-1955. See Newbery Medal books, 1922-1955 **028.5**
About
Ross, E. S. The spirited life: Bertha Mahony Miller and children's books **92**
Miller, Christina G.
Coastal rescue: preserving our seashores (5 and up) **333.91**
Miller, Don, 1923-
(il) Walker, A. Langston Hughes, American poet **92**
Miller, Douglas T.
Frederick Douglass and the fight for freedom (6 and up) **92**
Miller, Edna
Mousekin finds a friend. See note under Miller, E. Mousekin's golden house **E**
Mousekin takes a trip. See note under Miller, E. Mousekin's golden house **E**
Mousekin's ABC. See note under Miller, E. Mousekin's golden house **E**
Mousekin's birth. See note under Miller, E. Mousekin's golden house **E**
Mousekin's Christmas Eve. See note under Miller, E. Mousekin's golden house **E**
Mousekin's close call. See note under Miller, E. Mousekin's golden house **E**
Mousekin's Easter basket. See note under Miller, E. Mousekin's golden house **E**
Mousekin's fables. See note under Miller, E. Mousekin's golden house **E**
Mousekin's family. See note under Miller, E. Mousekin's golden house **E**
Mousekin's frosty friend. See note under Miller, E. Mousekin's golden house **E**
Mousekin's golden house **E**
Mousekin's mystery. See note under Miller, E. Mousekin's golden house **E**
Mousekin's Thanksgiving. See note under Miller, E. Mousekin's golden house **E**
Mousekin's woodland sleepers. See note under Miller, E. Mousekin's golden house **E**
Miller, Grambs
(il) Froman, R. Mushrooms and molds **589.2**
Miller, Helen L.
The broomstick beauty
In Holiday plays round the year p129-40 **812.008**
A Christmas promise
In The Big book of Christmas plays p99-117 **808.82**
Mister Snow White's Thanksgiving
In Holiday plays round the year p71-82 **812.008**
Red carpet Christmas
In The Big book of Christmas plays p3-25 **808.82**
Strictly Puritan
In Holiday plays round the year p83-90 **812.008**
Miller, Helen Louise *See* Gotwalt, Helen Louise Miller
Miller, Jane, 1925-1989
The farm alphabet book **E**
Farm counting book **E**
Miller, Jon, 1947-
(il) King-Smith, D. The fox busters **Fic**
Miller, Jonathan, 1934-
The human body (4 and up) **612**

Miller, Margaret, 1945-
Who uses this? **E**
(il) Cole, J. My puppy is born **636.7**
(il) Cole, J. Your new potty **649**
(il) Schlein, M. Pigeons **598**
(il) Scott, E. Ramona: behind the scenes of a television show **791.45**
(il) Shachtman, T. The president builds a house **363.5**

Miller, Patsy
Christmas at the O.K. Corral
In Holiday plays round the year p14-22 **812.008**

Miller, Ron, 1947-
(il) Adler, I. Mathematics **510**
(il) Lampton, C. Stars & planets **523**

Miller, Rosalind E.
Commonsense cataloging **025.3**

The **miller,** his son, and the donkey. Rockwell, A. F.
In Rockwell, A. F. Puss in boots, and other stories p27-29 **398.2**

The **miller,** the boy and the donkey. Wildsmith, B. **398.2**

Miller's boy and his cat
Grimm, J. The poor miller's boy and the cat
In Grimm, J. The complete Grimm's fairy tales p482-85 **398.2**
Grimm, J. The poor miller's boy and the little cat
In Grimm, J. The juniper tree, and other tales from Grimm v2 p178-86 **398.2**

Millie Cooper, 3B. Herman, C. **Fic**

Millie Cooper, take a chance. Herman, C. **Fic**

Millinery
See also Hats

Million (The number)
Schwartz, D. M. How much is a million? **E**

A **million** chameleons. Young, J. **E**

Millions of cats. Gág, W. **E**

Mills, Claudia, 1954-
Dynamite Dinah (3-5) **Fic**

Mills, Lauren A.
(il) MacDonald, G. At the back of the North Wind **Fic**
(il) Montgomery, L. M. Anne of Green Gables **Fic**

Mills, Yaroslava Surmach *See* Yaroslava, 1925-

Mills and millwork
Macaulay, D. Mill (4 and up) **690**

Milne, A. A. (Alan Alexander), 1882-1956
The Christopher Robin story book (k-3) **828**
The house at Pooh Corner (1-4) **Fic**
also in Milne, A. A. The world of Pooh p153-314 **Fic**
Now we are six (k-3) **821**
also in Milne, A. A. The world of Christopher Robin p119-234 **821**
The Pooh story book (1-4) **Fic**
Pooh's bedtime book (1-3) **828**
When we were very young (k-3) **821**
also in Milne, A. A. The world of Christopher Robin p1-118 **821**
Winnie-the-Pooh (1-4) **Fic**
also in Milne, A. A. The world of Pooh p7-149 **Fic**
The world of Christopher Robin (k-3) **821**
The world of Pooh (1-4) **Fic**

Milne, Alan Alexander *See* Milne, A. A. (Alan Alexander), 1882-1956

Milne, Lorus Johnson, 1912-
Nature's clean-up crew: the burying beetles (4 and up) **595.7**

Milne, Margery Joan Greene, 1914-
(jt. auth) Milne, L. J. Nature's clean-up crew: the burying beetles **595.7**

Milner, Angela
(jt. auth) Norman, D. Dinosaur **567.9**

Milton, Joyce
Whales (1-3) **599.5**

Milton, Mary
(il) Thiele, C. Farmer Schulz's ducks **E**

Mime
Straub, C. Mime: basics for beginners (6 and up) **792.3**

Minard, Rosemary, 1939-
(ed) Womenfolk and fairy tales. See Womenfolk and fairy tales **398.2**

Minarik, Else Holmelund
Father Bear comes home. See note under Minarik, E. H. Little Bear **E**
A kiss for Little Bear. See note under Minarik, E. H. Little Bear **E**
Little Bear **E**
Little Bear goes to the moon
In The Read-aloud treasury p70-83 **808.8**
Little Bear's friend. See note under Minarik, E. H. Little Bear **E**
Little Bear's visit. See note under Minarik, E. H. Little Bear **E**
No fighting, no biting! **E**

Mind *See* Intellect

Mine for keeps. Little, J. **Fic**

Mineralogy
McGowen, T. Album of rocks and minerals (4 and up) **549**
Podendorf, I. Rocks and minerals (1-4) **549**

Mineralogy—*Continued*
Symes, R. F. Rocks & minerals (4 and up) **549**
Zim, H. S. Rocks and minerals (4 and up) **549**
Miners
Fiction
Wiseman, D. Jeremy Visick (5 and up) **Fic**
Mines and mineral resources
See also Coal mines and mining
Ming Lo moves the mountain. Lobel, A. **E**
The **miniature** horse. LaBonte, G. **636.1**
Minkowitz, Miriam
A tale of three Ralphs
In Free to be—a family p20-22 **810.8**
Minn of the Mississippi. Holling, H. C. **Fic**
Minnesota
Stein, R. C. Minnesota
In America the beautiful **973**
Fiction
Lovelace, M. H. Betsy-Tacy (2-4) **Fic**
Paulsen, G. The winter room (5 and up) **Fic**
Minnikin. Moe, J. E.
In The Red fairy book p307-21 **398.2**
Minor, Wendell
(il) Siebert, D. Mojave **811**
Minorities
The In America series (5 and up) **305.8**
Minotaur (Greek mythology)
Fisher, L. E. Theseus and the Minotaur (1-3) **292**
Hutton, W. Theseus and the Minotaur (3-5) **292**
Minstrels
Fiction
Vining, E. G. Adam of the road (5 and up) **Fic**
Minter-Kemp, Claire
(il) King-Smith, D. Sophie's snail **Fic**
Mintz, Barbara
(jt. auth) Katan, N. J. Hieroglyphs, the writing of ancient Egypt **493**
The **miracle** of Purun Bhagat. Kipling, R.
In Kipling, R. The jungle books **S C**
Miracles
Fiction
Cooney, B. The little juggler (3-6) **398.2**
De Paola, T. The clown of God (k-3) **398.2**
The **miracles** of Jesus. De Paola, T. **232.9**
Miracles on Maple Hill. Sorensen, V. E. **Fic**
Miracles: poems by children of the English-speaking world **821.008**
Miraculous pipe
Afanas'ev, A. N. The miraculous pipe
In Afanas'ev, A. N. Russian fairy tales p425-27 **398.2**
The **miraculous** tea party. Gotwalt, H. L. M.
In Gotwalt, H. L. M. Everyday plays for boys and girls p182-92 **812**
Mirages
See/See also pages in the following book(s):
Gallant, R. A. Rainbows, mirages and sundogs p14-22 (4 and up) **551.5**
Miranda and the movies. Kendall, J. F. **Fic**
Mirandy and Brother Wind. McKissack, P. C. **E**
Mirepoix, Camille
Afghanistan—in pictures. See Afghanistan—in pictures **958.1**
Egypt—in pictures. See Egypt—in pictures **962**
Jordan—in pictures. See Jordan—in pictures **956.95**
Kuwait—in pictures. See Kuwait—in pictures **953**
Lebanon—in pictures. See Lebanon—in pictures **956.92**
Liberia—in pictures. See Liberia—in pictures **966.62**
The **mirror**. Gorog, J.
In Gorog, J. Three dreams and a nightmare, and other tales of the dark **S C**
A **mirror,** a carpet, and a lemon. Walker, B. K.
In Walker, B. K. A treasury of Turkish folktales for children p132-34 **398.2**
Mirror, mirror. Garfield, L.
In Garfield, L. The apprentices **S C**
Mirror of Matsuyama
Quayle, E. The Matsuyama mirror
In Quayle, E. The shining princess, and other Japanese legends p90-96 **398.2**
Mirrors
Taylor, B. Bouncing and bending light (3-5) **535**
Miscellaneous facts *See* Curiosities and wonders
Mischel, Florence
How to write a letter (5 and up) **808**
Mischling, second degree: my childhood in Nazi Germany. Koehn, I. **92**
Miser
Afanas'ev, A. N. The miser
In Afanas'ev, A. N. Russian fairy tales p58-59 **398.2**

Miserly farmer
Carpenter, F. Wonderful pear tree
In Carpenter, F. Tales of a Chinese grandmother p142-49 **398.2**

The **Miser's** jar
In The Monkey's haircut, and other stories told by the Maya p32-36 **398.2**

Misery. Afanas'ev, A. N.
In Afanas'ev, A. N. Russian fairy tales p20-24 **398.2**

Mishmash. Cone, M. **Fic**

Mishmash and the big fat problem. Cone, M. See note under Cone, M. Mishmash **Fic**

Mishmash and the robot. Cone, M. See note under Cone, M. Mishmash **Fic**

Mishmash and the sauerkraut mystery. Cone, M. See note under Cone, M. Mishmash **Fic**

Mishmash and the substitute teacher. Cone, M. See note under Cone, M. Mishmash **Fic**

Miss Bianca. Sharp, M. See note under Sharp, M. The rescuers **Fic**

Miss Bianca in the salt mines. Sharp, M. See note under Sharp, M. The rescuers **Fic**

Miss Hickory. Bailey, C. S. **Fic**

Miss Hooting's legacy. Aiken, J.
In Aiken, J. Up the chimney down, and other stories p27-49 **S C**

Miss Lin, the sea goddess. Carpenter, F.
In Carpenter, F. Tales of a Chinese grandmother p235-41 **398.2**

Miss Lonelyheart. McGowan, J.
In Holiday plays round the year p198-211 **812.008**

Miss Mary Mack and other children's street rhymes (1-4) **796.1**

Miss Nelson has a field day. Allard, H. See note under Allard, H. Miss Nelson is missing! **E**

Miss Nelson is back. Allard, H. See note under Allard, H. Miss Nelson is missing! **E**

Miss Nelson is missing! Allard, H. **E**

Miss Rumphius. Cooney, B. **E**

Missing children
See also Runaway children

The **missing** heir. Aiken, J.
In Aiken, J. Up the chimney down, and other stories p96-117 **S C**

Missing in action

Fiction

Smith, D. B. The first hard times (4-6) **Fic**

The **missing** Linc. Gotwalt, H. L. M.
In Gotwalt, H. L. M. Special plays for holidays p107-20 **812**

The **missing** tarts. Hennessy, B. G. **E**

Missions

Fiction

Politi, L. Song of the swallows **E**

Missions, Christian

Fiction

O'Dell, S. Zia (5 and up) **Fic**

Mississippi
Carson, R. Mississippi
In America the beautiful **973**

Fiction

Taylor, M. D. Roll of thunder, hear my cry (4 and up) **Fic**
Taylor, M. D. Song of the trees (4 and up) **Fic**

Mississippi bridge. Taylor, M. D. See note under Taylor, M. D. Song of the trees **Fic**

Mississippi River
Crisman, R. The Mississippi (4 and up) **977**
McCall, E. S. Biography of a river: the living Mississippi (6 and up) **977**

Fiction

Holling, H. C. Minn of the Mississippi (4-6) **Fic**
Twain, M. The adventures of Huckleberry Finn (5 and up) **Fic**
Twain, M. The adventures of Tom Sawyer (5 and up) **Fic**

Mississippi River valley
Crisman, R. The Mississippi (4 and up) **977**

Mississippi valley *See* Mississippi River valley

Missouri
See also Saint Louis (Mo.)
Sanford, W. R. Missouri
In America the beautiful **973**

Fiction

Twain, M. The adventures of Huckleberry Finn (5 and up) **Fic**
Twain, M. The adventures of Tom Sawyer (5 and up) **Fic**

Mister Jack sparrow meets his end. See Lester, J. Mr. Jack Sparrow meets his end

Mister Lazybones. Junne, I. K.
In Best-loved folktales of the world p565-67 **398.2**

Mister Snow White's Thanksgiving. Miller, H. L.
In Holiday plays round the year p71-82 **812.008**

Mister Thirty. Terada, A. M.
In Terada, A. M. Under the starfruit tree p18-21 **398.2**
Misty of Chincoteague. Henry, M. **Fic**
Mitch, Dale
(jt. auth) Trenary, J. Time of my life: Jill Trenary **92**
Mitch and Amy. Cleary, B. **Fic**
Mitchell, Arthur, 1934-
About
Tobias, T. Arthur Mitchell (2-5) **92**
Mitchell, Barbara, 1941-
America, I hear you: a story about George Gershwin (3-5) **92**
Between two worlds: a story about Pearl Buck (3-5) **92**
CLICK!: a story about George Eastman (3-5) **92**
A pocketful of goobers: a story about George Washington Carver (3-5) **92**
Raggin': a story about Scott Joplin (3-5) **92**
Shoes for everyone: a story about Jan Matzeliger (3-5) **92**
We'll race you, Henry: a story about Henry Ford (3-5) **92**
Mitchell, Hetty
(il) Mitchell, B. Raggin': a story about Scott Joplin **92**
(il) Mitchell, B. Shoes for everyone: a story about Jan Matzeliger **92**
Mitchell, Kathy, 1948-
(il) Baum, L. F. The Wizard of Oz **Fic**
(il) Carroll, L. Alice's adventures in Wonderland, and Through the looking glass **Fic**
Mitchell, Robert T.
Butterflies and moths (4 and up) **595.7**
The **mitten**. Brett, J. **398.2**
The **mitten**. Tresselt, A. R. **398.2**
The **mixed-up** chameleon. Carle, E. **E**
The **mixed-up** feet and the silly bridegroom. Singer, I. B.
In Singer, I. B. Zlateh the goat, and other stories p39-50 **398.2**
Miyamoto, Lance R.
(il) Cobb, V. Magic—naturally! science entertainment & amusements **793.8**
Miz Cricket makes the creatures run. Lester, J.
In Lester, J. Further tales of Uncle Remus p122-27 **398.2**
Miz Partridge tricks Brer Rabbit. Lester, J.
In Lester, J. More tales of Uncle Remus p39-40 **398.2**
Mizgir
Afanas'ev, A. N. The spider
In Afanas'ev, A. N. Russian fairy tales p75-76 **398.2**
Mizumura, Kazue
If I were a cricket . . . (k-2) **811**
(il) Adler, D. A. Redwoods are the tallest trees in the world **585**
(il) Cole, J. Plants in winter **581.5**
Model airplanes *See* Airplanes—Models
Model buildings and how to make them. Weiss, H. **690**
Model cars *See* Automobiles—Models
Model cars and trucks and how to build them. Weiss, H. **629.22**
Modell, Frank
Goodbye old year, hello new year **E**
One zillion valentines **E**
(il) Stevenson, J. Mr. Hacker **E**
Modern history *See* History, Modern
Modesitt, Jeanne
Vegetable soup **E**
Modest sisters
Carpenter, F. Sisters in the sun
In Carpenter, F. Tales of a Chinese grandmother p22-28 **398.2**
Moe, Jørgen Engebretsen, 1813-1882
Bushy bride
In The Red fairy book p322-28 **398.2**
Dapplegrim
In The Red fairy book p246-56 **398.2**
Minnikin
In The Red fairy book p307-21 **398.2**
The seven foals
In The Red fairy book p346-53 **398.2**
The three princesses of Whiteland
In The Red fairy book p175-81 **398.2**
Moeri, Louise
The forty-third war (6 and up) **Fic**
Save Queen of Sheba (4 and up) **Fic**
Star Mother's youngest child **E**
Moessinger, William
Man in the red suit
In Holiday plays round the year p37-46 **812.008**
The **Moffat** Museum. Estes, E. See note under Estes, E. The Moffats **Fic**
The **Moffats**. Estes, E. **Fic**
Mohr, Joseph, 1792-1848
Silent night (k-2) **782.28**
Mohr, Nicholasa, 1935-
Felita (3-5) **Fic**
Moja means one. Feelings, M. **E**
Mojave. Siebert, D. **811**
Molan, Chris
(il) Berrill, M. Mummies, masks, & mourners **393**

Moldoff, Kirk
(il) Elting, M. The Macmillan book of the human body 612

Molds (Botany)
Froman, R. Mushrooms and molds (1-3) 589.2

Mole and the Sun. Curry, J. L.
In Curry, J. L. Back in the beforetime p89 398.2

The **Mole** catcher
In The Monkey's haircut, and other stories told by the Maya p121-30 398.2

Molecules
Berger, M. Atoms, molecules, and quarks (6 and up) 539

Molina, Gloria
About
Hewett, J. Getting elected (4 and up) 324

Molk, Laurel
(il) Carlstrom, N. W. Grandpappy E

Mollusks
See also Snails
Selsam, M. E. A first look at seashells (1-3) 594

Molly Whipple. Reeves, J.
In Reeves, J. English fables and fairy stories p183-94 398.2

Molly Whuppie
De la Mare, W. Molly Whuppie 398.2
also in The Scott, Foresman anthology of children's literature p159-62 808.8
also in Womenfolk and fairy tales p20-29 398.2
Jacobs, J. Molly Whuppie
In Best-loved folktales of the world p216-18 398.2
In Jacobs, J. English fairy tales p125-30 398.2
Reeves, J. Molly Whipple
In Reeves, J. English fables and fairy stories p183-94 398.2

Molly's Pilgrim. Cohen, B. Fic

Mom can't see me. Alexander, S. H. 362.4

Momma at the Pearly Gates. Konigsburg, E. L.
In Konigsburg, E. L. Altogether, one at a time p61-79 S C

Mommies at work. Merriam, E. 331.4

Mommy, buy me a china doll. Zemach, H. E

Mommy doesn't know my name. Williams, S. E

Momo's kitten. Iwamatsu, T. E

Momotaro
Hearn, L. Momotaro
In Best-loved folktales of the world p503-05 398.2
Quayle, E. Momotaro—The peach warrior
In Quayle, E. The shining princess, and other Japanese legends p77-89 398.2
Uchida, Y. Momotaro: boy-of-the-peach
In The Scott, Foresman anthology of children's literature p330-32 808.8

Mom's home. Ormerod, J. See note under Ormerod, J. Bend and stretch E

Monarch butterfly. Gibbons, G. 595.7

Monarchs *See* Kings, queens, rulers, etc.

Monday, Tuesday. Crossley-Holland, K.
In Crossley-Holland, K. British folk tales p145-52 398.2

Monet, Claude, 1840-1926
Björk, C. Linnea in Monet's garden (3-5) Fic

Money
Brittain, B. All the money in the world (4-6) Fic
Cribb, J. Money (4 and up) 332.4
See/See also pages in the following book(s):
Caney, S. Steven Caney's kids' America p376-85 (4 and up) 790.1

Money makes cares. Eberhard, W.
In Best-loved folktales of the world p548-50 398.2

Moneymaking projects for children
Barkin, C. Jobs for kids (5 and up) 650.1
Wilkinson, E. Making cents (4 and up) 332.024

Mongan's frenzy
Stephens, J. Mongan's frenzy
In Stephens, J. Irish fairy tales p257-318 398.2

Mongolia
Major, J. S. The land and people of Mongolia (5 and up) 951.7

Mongolians *See* Mongols

Mongols
See/See also pages in the following book(s):
Lyttle, R. B. Land beyond the river p135-46 (6 and up) 940.1

Monjo, F. N.
The drinking gourd E

The **monk** and the drunk. Kendall, C.
In Kendall, C. Sweet and sour p106-07 398.2

Monkey and the crocodile
Babbitt, E. The monkey and the crocodile
In Best-loved folktales of the world p593-94 **398.2**
Galdone, P. The monkey and the crocodile **398.2**
Monkey and the White Bone Demon. Zhang Xiu Shi. **398.2**
Monkey, Tiger and the Magic Trials. Berry, J.
In Berry, J. Spiderman Anancy p27-33 **398.2**
The **Monkey** who asked for Misery
In The Magic orange tree, and other Haitian folktales p113-16 **398.2**
Monkeys
Selsam, M. E. A first look at monkeys and apes (1-3) **599.8**
Fiction
Riddell, C. When the walrus comes **E**
Christelow, E. Five little monkeys jumping on the bed **E**
Galdone, P. The turtle and the monkey (k-2) **398.2**
Hurd, E. T. Last one home is a green pig **E**
Rey, H. A. Cecily G. and the 9 monkeys **E**
Rey, H. A. Curious George **E**
Slobodkina, E. Caps for sale **E**
The **Monkey's** haircut
In The Monkey's haircut, and other stories told by the Maya p138-43 **398.2**
The **Monkey's** haircut, and other stories told by the Maya (5 and up) **398.2**
Monroe, Jean Guard
They dance in the sky: native American star myths (4 and up) **398.2**
Contents: Seven dancing stars: legends of the Pleiades; The celestial bear: stories of the Big Dipper; Coyote scatters the stars: myths from the Southwest; When stars fell to earth: legends of the Pawnee; Morning star: legends of the Plains Indians; They live in the sky: stories of the California Indians; Chinook wind: stories from the Northwest Coast; Star beings: tales from the Southeast
Monroe, Joan Kiddell- *See* Kiddell-Monroe, Joan, 1908-1972
Monroe, Judy
Leukemia (4-6) **616.99**
(jt. auth) Chung, O. Cooking the Korean way **641.5**
(jt. auth) Nguyen, C. T. Cooking the Vietnamese way **641.5**
Monsanto Company
See/See also pages in the following book(s):
Aaseng, N. The problem solvers p69-75 (5 and up) **920**
Monson, Dianne L.
(jt. auth) Sutherland, Z. Children and books **028.5**
Monster dinosaur. Cohen, D. **567.9**
The **monster** garden. Alcock, V. **Fic**
The **monster** in the third dresser drawer and other stories about Adam Joshua. Smith, J. L. See note under Smith, J. L. The kid next door and other headaches **Fic**
Monster movers. Ancona, G. **621.8**
Monster poems (1-4) **821.008**
Monster seaweeds. Daegling, M. **589.4**
The **monster** who swallowed everything. Lester, J.
In Lester, J. How many spots does a leopard have? and other tales p13-15 **398.2**
Monsters
See also Dragons; Giants
Fiction
Alcock, V. The monster garden (4 and up) **Fic**
Crowe, R. L. Clyde monster **E**
Drescher, H. Simon's book **E**
Hutchins, P. Where's the baby? **E**
Steig, W. Shrek! **E**
Viorst, J. My mama says there aren't any zombies, ghosts, vampires, creatures, demons, monsters, fiends, goblins, or things **E**
Poetry
Creatures (3-5) **821.008**
Monster poems (1-4) **821.008**
Prelutsky, J. The Headless Horseman rides tonight (2-5) **811**
Prelutsky, J. Nightmares: poems to trouble your sleep (2-5) **811**
Riley, J. W. The gobble-uns'll git you ef you don't watch out! (1-4) **811**
Monsters in art
Ames, L. J. Draw 50 beasties and yugglies and turnover uglies and things that go bump in the night (4 and up) **743**
Montana
Heinrichs, A. Montana
In America the beautiful **973**
Monteith, Ann
(il) Cole, J. A dog's body **636.7**
Monteith, Jim
(il) Cole, J. A dog's body **636.7**
Montenegro, Valerie J.
(ed) The Best science books & A-V materials for children. See The Best science books & A-V materials for children **016.5**
Montgomery, Bertha Vining
(jt. auth) Nabwire, C. R. Cooking the African way **641.5**

Montgomery, L. M. (Lucy Maud), 1874-1942
Anne of Avonlea. See note under Montgomery, L. M. Anne of Green Gables **Fic**
Anne of Green Gables (5 and up) **Fic**
Anne of Ingleside. See note under Montgomery, L. M. Anne of Green Gables **Fic**
Anne of the island. See note under Montgomery, L. M. Anne of Green Gables **Fic**
Anne of Windy Poplars. See note under Montgomery, L. M. Anne of Green Gables **Fic**
Anne's house of dreams. See note under Montgomery, L. M. Anne of Green Gables **Fic**
Montgomery, Lucy Maud *See* Montgomery, L. M. (Lucy Maud), 1874-1942
The **Month-Brothers**. Marshak, S. **398.2**
Months
Poetry
Coleridge, S. January brings the snow (k-2) **821**
Monticello. Fisher, L. E. **973.4**
Montresor, Beni, 1926-
The witches of Venice **E**
(il) De Regniers, B. S. May I bring a friend? **E**
Monty. Stevenson, J. **E**
Monuments
Fiction
Alcock, V. The stonewalkers (5 and up) **Fic**
Mooch the messy. Sharmat, M. W. **E**
Moon
Branley, F. M. The moon seems to change (k-3) **523.3**
Branley, F. M. What the moon is like (k-3) **523.3**
Couper, H. The moon (4 and up) **523.3**
Davis, D. The moon (4-6) **523.3**
Simon, S. The moon (1-4) **523.3**
See/See also pages in the following book(s):
Kelch, J. W. Small worlds: exploring the 60 moons of our solar system p24-37 (6 and up) **523.9**
Simon, S. Look to the night sky: an introduction to star watching (4 and up) **523**
Eclipses
See Eclipses, Lunar
Fiction
Baylor, B. Moon song (1-3) **398.2**
Preston, E. M. Squawk to the moon, Little Goose **E**
Moon, Voyages to *See* Space flight to the moon
The **moon**. Grimm, J.
In Grimm, J. The complete Grimm's fairy tales p713-15 **398.2**
Moon and his sister. Mayo, G.
In Mayo, G. Star tales p61-62 **398.2**
The **Moon** in the pond. Lester, J.
In Lester, J. The tales of Uncle Remus p96-99 **398.2**
The **moon** jumpers. Udry, J. M. **E**
Moon Man. Ungerer, T. **E**
The **moon** seems to change. Branley, F. M. **523.3**
Moon song. Baylor, B. **398.2**
Moonbeam Dawson and the Killer bear. Okimoto, J. D.
In Connections: short stories by outstanding writers for young adults p15-25 **S C**
Mooney, Martha T.
(ed) Sears list of subject headings. See Sears list of subject headings **025.4**
Moongame. Asch, F. See note under Asch, F. Sand cake **E**
Moonkid and Liberty. Kropp, P. **Fic**
Moonlight. Ormerod, J. **E**
Moonseed and mistletoe. Lerner, C. **581.6**
Moonsong lullaby. Highwater, J. **811**
Moore, Adrienne *See* Kennaway, Adrienne, 1945-
Moore, Clement Clarke, 1779-1863
The night before Christmas (k-3) **811**
A visit from St. Nicholas
In Diane Goode's American Christmas p74-78 **810.8**
In The Scott, Foresman anthology of children's literature p144-45 **808.8**
Moore, Jim, 1946-
(il) Sheridan, J. Nothing's impossible! stunts to entertain and amaze **793.8**
Moore, Lilian, 1909-
Something new begins: new and selected poems (4 and up) **811**
Moose
Rue, L. L. Meet the moose (4 and up) **599.73**
Fiction
Alexander, M. G. Even that moose won't listen to me **E**
Pinkwater, D. M. Blue moose (1-3) **Fic**
Wiseman, B. Morris and Boris at the circus **E**
The **Moose** wife
In The Naked bear p52-59 **398.2**
A **moral** alphabet. Belloc, H.
In Belloc, H. The bad child's book of beasts, and More beasts for worse children, and A moral alphabet **821**

Moran, Tom, 1943-
Canoeing is for me (3-5) **797.1**
A family in Mexico (3-5) **972**
Mordvinoff, Nicolas, 1911-1973
See/See also pages in the following book(s):
Caldecott Medal books, 1938-1957 p230-41 **028.5**
More about Paddington. Bond, M. See note under Bond, M. A bear called Paddington **Fic**
More adventures of the Great Brain. Fitzgerald, J. D. See note under Fitzgerald, J. D. The Great Brain **Fic**
More all-of-a-kind family. Taylor, S. See note under Taylor, S. All-of-a-kind family **Fic**
More beasts for worse children. Belloc, H.
In Belloc, H. The bad child's book of beasts, and More beasts for worse children, and A moral alphabet **821**
More fun with Spanish. Cooper, L. P. **468**
More junior authors **920.003**
More juniorplots: a guide for teachers and librarians. Gillespie, J. T. **028.1**
More notes from a different drummer. Baskin, B. H. **016.8**
A **more** perfect union. Maestro, B. **342**
More plants that changed history. Rahn, J. E. **909**
More power to you. Cobb, V. **621.31**
More scary stories to tell in the dark. Schwartz, A. **398.2**
More science experiments you can eat. Cobb, V. **507**
More small poems. Worth, V. **811**
More stories Julian tells. Cameron, A. See note under Cameron, A. The stories Julian tells **Fic**
More surprises (1-3) **811.008**
More tales from Grimm. Grimm, J. **398.2**
More tales of Amanda Pig. Van Leeuwen, J. See note under Van Leeuwen, J. Tales of Oliver Pig **E**
More tales of Oliver Pig. Van Leeuwen, J. See note under Van Leeuwen, J. Tales of Oliver Pig **E**
More tales of Uncle Remus. Lester, J. **398.2**
More than a friend: dogs with a purpose. Siegel, M.-E. **636.7**
More than just a flower garden. Kuhn, D. **635.9**
More than just a vegetable garden. Kuhn, D. **635**
More wires and watts: understanding and using electricity. Math, I. **537**
More wise men of Helm and their merry tales. Simon, S. **398.2**
Moreton, Ann
(il) Hopf, A. L. Spiders **595.4**
Morey, Janet (Janet Nomura)
Famous Mexican Americans (5 and up) **920**
Morey, Walt, 1907-
Gentle Ben (5 and up) **Fic**
Morgan, Mary
(il) Patent, D. H. Singing birds and flashing fireflies **591.5**
Morgan, Pierr
The turnip (k-2) **398.2**
Morgan horse
Fiction
Henry, M. Justin Morgan had a horse (4 and up) **Fic**
Mori, Tsuyoshi, 1928-
(jt. auth) Anno, M. Socrates and the three little pigs **511**
Morimoto, Junko
The inch boy (k-3) **398.2**
My Hiroshima (2-4) **940.54**
Moriya, Noboru
(il) Johnson, S. A. Rice **633.1**
Morning beach. Baker, L. A. **E**
Morning star: legends of the Plains Indians. Monroe, J. G.
In Monroe, J. G. They dance in the sky p63-78 **398.2**
Morning Star takes a wife. Mayo, G.
In Mayo, G. Star tales p81-86 **398.2**
The **morning** the sun refused to rise. Rounds, G. **E**
Moroccan family. See Stewart, J. A family in Morocco **964**
Morocco
Hintz, M. Morocco (4 and up) **964**
Lye, K. Take a trip to Morocco (1-3) **964**
Morocco—in pictures (5 and up) **964**
Social life and customs
Stewart, J. A family in Morocco (3-5) **964**
Morocco—in pictures (5 and up) **964**
Moroney, Lynn
Baby rattlesnake (k-2) **398.2**
Morrill, Leslie H.
(il) Cobb, V. How to really fool yourself **152.1**

Morrill, Leslie H.—*Continued*
(il) Dog poems. See Dog poems **808.81**
(il) Giff, P. R. Love, from the fifth-grade celebrity **Fic**
(il) Howe, J. The celery stalks at midnight **Fic**
(il) Howe, J. Scared silly: a Halloween treat **E**

Morris, Ann
Bread, bread, bread (k-3) **641.8**
Hats, hats, hats (k-3) **391**

Morris, Christopher G.
(ed) Macmillan very first dictionary. See Macmillan very first dictionary **423**

Morris, Douglas
(il) Siegel, B. A new look at the Pilgrims **973.2**

Morris, Richard Brandon, 1904-1989
The American Revolution (4-6) **973.3**

Morris, Robert A.
Dolphin (k-3) **599.5**

Morris and Boris. Wiseman, B. See note under Wiseman, B. Morris and Boris at the circus **E**

Morris and Boris at the circus. Wiseman, B. **E**

Morris goes to school. Wiseman, B. See note under Wiseman, B. Morris and Boris at the circus **E**

Morris has a cold. Wiseman, B. See note under Wiseman, B. Morris and Boris at the circus **E**

Morris tells Boris Mother Moose stories and rhymes. Wiseman, B. See note under Wiseman, B. Morris and Boris at the circus **E**

Morris the moose. Wiseman, B. See note under Wiseman, B. Morris and Boris at the circus **E**

Morrison, Bill, 1935-
Squeeze a sneeze (k-3) **811**
(il) Broekel, R. Now you see it: easy magic for beginners **793.8**
(il) Cobb, V. The secret life of hardware: a science experiment book **670**
(il) Kalb, J. The easy hockey book **796.962**

Morrison, Lillian, 1917-
(comp) Best wishes, amen. See Best wishes, amen **808.88**
(comp) Sprints and distances. See Sprints and distances **808.81**

Morrison, Marion
Bolivia (4 and up) **984**

Morris's disappearing bag. Wells, R. **E**

Mortimer says nothing. Aiken, J. See note under Aiken, J. Arabel and Mortimer **Fic**

Mortimer's cross. Aiken, J. See note under Aiken, J. Arabel and Mortimer **Fic**

Morton, Miriam, d. 1985
(ed) A Harvest of Russian children's literature. See A Harvest of Russian children's literature **891.7**

Mosaics
See/See also pages in the following book(s):
Rockwell, H. I did it p9-17 (1-3) **745.5**

Mosel, Arlene
The funny little woman (k-2) **398.2**
Tikki Tikki Tembo (k-2) **398.2**

Moser, Barry
The tinderbox **Fic**
(il) Hamilton, V. In the beginning; creation stories from around the world **291**
(il) Parks, V. D. Jump! the adventures of Brer Rabbit **398.2**
(il) Parks, V. D. Jump again! more adventures of Brer Rabbit **398.2**
(il) Parks, V. D. Jump on over! the adventures of Brer Rabbit and his family **398.2**
(il) Thayer, E. L. Casey at the bat **811**
(il) Willard, N. The ballad of Biddy Early **811**
(il) Yolen, J. Sky dogs **E**

Moses (Biblical figure)

About

Chaikin, M. Exodus (2-4) **222**

Moses, Anna Mary Robertson *See* Moses, Grandma, 1860-1961

Moses, Grandma, 1860-1961
(il) Moore, C. C. The night before Christmas **811**

About

Oneal, Z. Grandma Moses: painter of rural America (4 and up) **92**

Moses and Ojje Ben Onogh. Courlander, H.
In The Crest and the hide, and other African stories of heroes, chiefs, bards, hunters, sorcerers, and common people p111-13 **398.2**

Moses' ark: stories from the Bible. Bach, A. **222**

Moses supposes his toeses are roses and 7 other silly old rhymes. Patz, N. **398.8**

Moses the kitten. Herriot, J. **Fic**

The **mosquito** and the water buffalo. Walker, B. K.
In Walker, B. K. A treasury of Turkish folktales for children p14 **398.2**

Mosquitoes
Patent, D. H. Mosquitoes (4 and up) **595.7**

Mosquitoes—*Continued*

Fiction

Aardema, V. Why mosquitoes buzz in people's ears (k-3) **398.2**

Moss, Joyce, 1951-
(jt. auth) Wilson, G. Books for children to read alone **011.6**

Moss and blister. Garfield, L.
In Garfield, L. The apprentices **S C**

Moss gown. Hooks, W. H. **398.2**

Moss-green princess
Berger, T. The moss-green princess
In Berger, T. Black fairy tales p3-14 **398.2**

Mosses
Johnson, S. A. Mosses (4 and up) **588**

Mossycoat. Crossley-Holland, K.
In Crossley-Holland, K. British folk tales p86-99 **398.2**

Most, Bernard, 1937-
The cow that went oink **E**
The littlest dinosaurs (k-2) **567.9**
Whatever happened to the dinosaurs? **E**

The **most-beautiful-bird** in-the-world contest. Lester, J.
In Lester, J. Further tales of Uncle Remus p44-49 **398.2**

The **most** beautiful place in the world. Cameron, A. **Fic**

Most frugal of men
The Most frugal of men
In Best-loved folktales of the world p537-38 **398.2**

Most obedient wife
Grundtvig, S. The most obedient wife
In The Scott, Foresman anthology of children's literature p217-20 **808.8**

The **most** useful slave. Hamilton, V.
In Hamilton, V. The people could fly: American black folktales p160-65 **398.2**

The **most** wonderful egg in the world. Heine, H. **E**

Motels *See* Hotels, motels, etc.

The **moth** and the star. Thurber, J.
In The Random House book of humor for children p93-94 **817.008**

Mother and daughter. Soto, G.
In Soto, G. Baseball in April, and other stories p60-68 **S C**

Mother Crocodile. Guy, R. **398.2**

Mother goes modern. Arthur, K.
In Holiday plays round the year p267-84 **812.008**

Mother Goose
The Annotated Mother Goose **398.8**
The Comic adventures of Old Mother Hubbard and her dog **398.8**
The Glorious Mother Goose **398.8**
Granfa' Grig had a pig, and other rhymes without reason from Mother Goose **398.8**
James Marshall's Mother Goose **398.8**
Jeffers, S. Three jovial huntsmen **398.8**
The Little dog laughed **398.8**
Marguerite de Angeli's book of nursery and Mother Goose rhymes **398.8**
Martin, S. C. The comic adventures of Old Mother Hubbard and her dog
In A Nursery companion p28-31 **820.8**
Mother Goose [illus. by Michael Hague] **398.8**
Mother Goose [illus. by Tasha Tudor] **398.8**
Mother Goose [illus. by Brian Wildsmith] **398.8**
The Mother Goose songbook **782.42**
The Mother Goose treasury **398.8**
Nicola Bayley's book of nursery rhymes **398.8**
The Random House book of Mother Goose **398.8**
The Real Mother Goose **398.8**
Songs from Mother Goose **782.42**
Tail feathers from Mother Goose **398.8**
Tomie dePaola's Mother Goose **398.8**
Wendy Watson's Mother Goose **398.8**
See/See also pages in the following book(s):
Sendak, M. Caldecott & Co.: notes on books and pictures p11-20 **028.5**

Mother Goose [illus. by Michael Hague] (k-2) **398.8**

Mother Goose [illus. by Tasha Tudor] (k-2) **398.8**

Mother Goose [illus. by Brian Wildsmith] (k-2) **398.8**

Mother Goose and the sly fox. Conover, C. **398.2**

The **Mother** Goose songbook (k-2) **782.42**

The **Mother** Goose treasury (k-3) **398.8**

Mother Hildegarde
Pyle, H. Mother Hildegarde
In Pyle, H. The wonder clock p189-202 **398.2**

Mother Holle
Grimm, J. Mother Holle
In Best-loved folktales of the world p134-36 **398.2**
In Grimm, J. The complete Grimm's fairy tales p133-36 **398.2**
In Grimm, J. More tales from Grimm p15-22 **398.2**
In The Red fairy book p303-06 **398.2**

The **Mother** of Ghosts
In The Naked bear p37-43 **398.2**

Mother of the waters
In The Magic orange tree, and other Haitian folktales p151-56 **398.2**

Mother Swan's daughters
In The Naked bear p72-78 **398.2**

Mothers

Fiction

Aliki. Welcome, little baby **E**
Hennessy, B. G. A,B,C,D, tummy, toes, hands, knees **E**
Hermes, P. You shouldn't have to say good-bye (5 and up) **Fic**
Sebestyen, O. IOU's (6 and up) **Fic**
Viorst, J. My mama says there aren't any zombies, ghosts, vampires, creatures, demons, monsters, fiends, goblins, or things **E**
Wells, R. Hazel's amazing mother **E**

Poetry

Poems for mothers (3-5) **811.008**

Mothers and daughters
Alexander, S. H. Mom can't see me (3-5) **362.4**

Fiction

Berry, C. Mama went walking **E**
Duder, T. Jellybean (5 and up) **Fic**
Galbraith, K. O. Laura Charlotte **E**
Hines, A. G. It's just me, Emily **E**
Johnson, A. Tell me a story, Mama **E**
Johnston, T. The quilt story **E**
Loh, M. J. Tucking Mommy in **E**
Lowry, L. Rabble Starkey (5 and up) **Fic**
MacLachlan, P. Mama One, Mama Two **E**
Pascal, F. Hangin' out with Cici (5 and up) **Fic**
Pomerantz, C. The chalk doll **E**
Rodgers, M. Freaky Friday (4 and up) **Fic**
Russo, M. Waiting for Hannah **E**
Stevenson, L. C. Happily after all (4 and up) **Fic**
Willard, N. The high rise glorious skittle skat roarious sky pie angel food cake (2-4) **Fic**
Williams, S. Mommy doesn't know my name **E**
Zolotow, C. One step, two— **E**

Mothers and sons

Fiction

Auch, M. J. Kidnapping Kevin Kowalski (4-6) **Fic**
Lindgren, B. The wild baby **E**
Zolotow, C. The quiet mother and the noisy little boy **E**

Mother's Day
See/See also pages in the following book(s):
Araki, C. Origami in the classroom p32-36 (Book II) (4 and up) **736**

The **Mother's** Day mice. Bunting, E. **E**

A **mother's** yarn. Riordan, J.
In Riordan, J. The woman in the moon, and other tales of forgotten heroines p7-14 **398.2**

Moths
See also Caterpillars
Mitchell, R. T. Butterflies and moths (4 and up) **595.7**
Whalley, P. E. S. Butterfly & moth (4 and up) **595.7**
See/See also pages in the following book(s):
Zim, H. S. Insects (4 and up) **595.7**

Motion
Cobb, V. Why doesn't the earth fall up? (3-5) **531**

Motion picture actors and actresses *See* Actors and actresses

Motion picture direction *See* Motion pictures—Production and direction

Motion picture production *See* Motion pictures—Production and direction

Motion pictures
See also Videotapes
See/See also pages in the following book(s):
Bauer, C. F. Handbook for storytellers p211-18 **372.6**

Catalogs

Parent's choice guide to videocassettes for children **016.79143**

Fiction

Kendall, J. F. Miranda and the movies (6 and up) **Fic**

Production and direction

Gibbons, G. Lights! Camera! Action! (1-3) **791.43**

Motivation (Psychology)
See also Wishes

Motorcycle: the making of a Harley-Davidson. Jaspersohn, W. **629.227**

Motorcycles
See also Harley-Davidson motorcycle

Mound, L. A. (Laurence Alfred), 1934-
Insect (4 and up) **595.7**

Mound, Laurence Alfred *See* Mound, L. A. (Laurence Alfred), 1934-

Mounseer Nongtongpaw. Shelley, M. W.
In A Nursery companion p118-22 **820.8**

Mount Rushmore National Memorial (S.D.)
St. George, J. The Mount Rushmore story [biography of Gutzon Borglum] (6 and up) **92**

The **Mount** Rushmore story [biography of Gutzon Borglum]. St. George, J. **92**

Mount Saint Helens (Wash.)

Lauber, P. Volcano: the eruption and healing of Mount St. Helens (4 and up) **551.2**

Place, M. T. Mount St. Helens (5 and up) **551.2**

See/See also pages in the following book(s):

Our violent earth p24-33 (4 and up) **363.3**

The **Mount** Vernon cricket. Gotwalt, H. L. M.

In Gotwalt, H. L. M. Special plays for holidays p144-57 **812**

Mountain animals *See* Alpine animals

Mountain ecology

Catchpole, C. Mountains (2-4) **574.5**

George, J. C. One day in the alpine tundra (4-6) **574.5**

Mountain-making. Curry, J. L.

In Curry, J. L. Back in the beforetime p22-25 **398.2**

Mountain witch and the peddler. Uchida, Y.

In Uchida, Y. The magic listening cap **398.2**

Mountains

See also Appalachian Mountains; Catskill Mountains (N.Y.); Ozark Mountains

Peters, L. W. The sun, the wind and the rain (k-2) **551.4**

Fiction

Lobel, A. Ming Lo moves the mountain **E**

Radin, R. Y. High in the mountains **E**

Mountains. Catchpole, C. **574.5**

The **mountains** of Tibet. Gerstein, M. **E**

Mouse *See* Mice

Mouse, the bird, and the sausage

Grimm, J. The mouse, the bird, and the sausage

In Grimm, J. The complete Grimm's fairy tales p131-33 **398.2**

In Grimm, J. More tales from Grimm p27-30 **398.2**

The **mouse** and his child. Hoban, R. **Fic**

Mouse and mouser

Jacobs, J. Mouse and mouser

In Jacobs, J. English fairy tales p48-50 **398.2**

The **mouse** and the elephant. Walker, B. K.

In Walker, B. K. A treasury of Turkish folktales for children p1-3 **398.2**

The **mouse** and the motorcycle. Cleary, B. **Fic**

The **Mouse** God. Kennedy, R.

In Kennedy, R. Collected stories p213-22 **S C**

The **Mouse** rap. Myers, W. D. **Fic**

Mouse soup. Lobel, A. **E**

Mouse tales. Lobel, A. **E**

The **mouse** that soared. Gotwalt, H. L. M.

In Gotwalt, H. L. M. Everyday plays for boys and girls p90-100 **812**

The **Mousehole** cat. Barber, A. **E**

Mousekin finds a friend. Miller, E. See note under Miller, E. Mousekin's golden house **E**

Mousekin takes a trip. Miller, E. See note under Miller, E. Mousekin's golden house **E**

Mousekin's ABC. Miller, E. See note under Miller, E. Mousekin's golden house **E**

Mousekin's birth. Miller, E. See note under Miller, E. Mousekin's golden house **E**

Mousekin's Christmas Eve. Miller, E. See note under Miller, E. Mousekin's golden house **E**

Mousekin's close call. Miller, E. See note under Miller, E. Mousekin's golden house **E**

Mousekin's Easter basket. Miller, E. See note under Miller, E. Mousekin's golden house **E**

Mousekin's fables. Miller, E. See note under Miller, E. Mousekin's golden house **E**

Mousekin's family. Miller, E. See note under Miller, E. Mousekin's golden house **E**

Mousekin's frosty friend. Miller, E. See note under Miller, E. Mousekin's golden house **E**

Mousekin's golden house. Miller, E. **E**

Mousekin's mystery. Miller, E. See note under Miller, E. Mousekin's golden house **E**

Mousekin's Thanksgiving. Miller, E. See note under Miller, E. Mousekin's golden house **E**

Mousekin's woodland sleepers. Miller, E. See note under Miller, E. Mousekin's golden house **E**

Mouth organ *See* Harmonica

Move over, Twerp. Alexander, M. G. **E**

Move over, wheelchairs coming through! Roy, R. **362.4**

Moving, Household

Rogers, F. Moving (k-1) **155.4**

Fiction

Anno, M. Anno's counting house **E**

Delton, J. Kitty from the start (2-4) **Fic**

Grove, V. Good-bye, my wishing star (5 and up) **Fic**

Hermes, P. Kevin Corbett eats flies (4 and up) **Fic**

Hughes, S. Moving Molly **E**

Moving, Household—Fiction—*Continued*
Kropp, P. Moonkid and Liberty (6 and up) **Fic**
O'Donnell, E. L. Maggie doesn't want to move **E**
Park, B. The kid in the red jacket (4-6) **Fic**
Schulman, J. The big hello **E**
Sharmat, M. W. Gila monsters meet you at the airport **E**
Slote, A. Moving in (4-6) **Fic**

Moving continents. Aylesworth, T. G. **551.1**

Moving heavy things. Adkins, J. **621.8**

Moving in. Slote, A. **Fic**

Moving Molly. Hughes, S. **E**

Moving pictures *See* Motion pictures

Mowat, Farley
Never cry wolf [excerpt]
In Animal families of the wild: animal stories p21-29 **591**
Owls in the family (4 and up) **636.6**

Mowgli's brothers. Kipling, R.
In Kipling, R. The jungle books **S C**

Moxon, Julian
How jet engines are made (4 and up) **629.1**

Mozley, Charles, 1915-
(il) MacDonald, G. At the back of the North Wind **Fic**

Mr. and Mrs. Pig's evening out. Rayner, M. **E**

Mr. Bass's planetoid. Cameron, E. See note under Cameron, E. The wonderful flight to the Mushroom Planet **Fic**

Mr. Benjamin Ram and his wonderful fiddle. Lester, J.
In Lester, J. Further tales of Uncle Remus p101-06 **398.2**

Mr. Benjamin Ram triumphs again. Lester, J.
In Lester, J. Further tales of Uncle Remus p106-08 **398.2**

Mr. Brown washes his underwear. Schwartz, A.
In Schwartz, A. There is a carrot in my ear, and other noodle tales p28-38 **398.2**

Mr. Fox
Jacobs, J. Mr. Fox
In Jacobs, J. English fairy tales p148-51 **398.2**
In Womenfolk and fairy tales p30-35 **398.2**
MacDonald, M. R. Mr. Fox
In MacDonald, M. R. Twenty tellable tales p154-62 **372.6**

Mr. Griggs' work. Rylant, C. **E**

Mr. Gumpy's motor car. Burningham, J. **E**

Mr. Gumpy's outing. Burningham, J. **E**

Mr. Hacker. Stevenson, J. **E**

Mr. Jack Sparrow meets his end. Lester, J.
In Lester, J. The tales of Uncle Remus p35-37 **398.2**

Mr. Miacca
Jacobs, J. Mr. Miacca
In Jacobs, J. English fairy tales p164-66 **398.2**

Mr. Mysterious & Company. Fleischman, S. **Fic**

Mr. Nick's knitting. Wild, M. **E**

Mr. Popper's penguins. Atwater, R. T. **Fic**

Mr. Rabbit and Mr. Bear. Lester, J.
In Lester, J. The knee-high man, and other tales p12-20 **398.2**

Mr. Rabbit and the lovely present. Zolotow, C. **E**

Mr. Revere and I. Lawson, R. **Fic**

Mr. Vinegar
Jacobs, J. Mr. Vinegar
In Jacobs, J. English fairy tales p28-32 **398.2**
Rockwell, A. F. Mr. Vinegar
In Rockwell, A. F. Puss in boots, and other stories p60-65 **398.2**

Mr. Wheeler. Sherlock, Sir P. M.
In Sherlock, Sir P. M. West Indian folk-tales p144-51 **398.2**

Mr. Wizard's supermarket science. Herbert, D. **507**

Mrs. Anancy, chicken soup and Anancy. Berry, J.
In Berry, J. Spiderman Anancy p54-59 **398.2**

Mrs. Dog first-child and Monkey-Mother. Berry, J.
In Berry, J. Spiderman Anancy p72-77 **398.2**

Mrs. Dunn's lovely, lovely farm. Levoy, M.
In Levoy, M. The witch of Fourth Street, and other stories **S C**

Mrs. Frisby and the rats of NIMH. O'Brien, R. C. **Fic**

Mrs. Gaddy and the fast-growing vine. Gage, W. See note under Gage, W. Mrs. Gaddy and the ghost **E**

Mrs. Gaddy and the ghost. Gage, W. **E**

Mrs. Gertrude. Grimm, J.
In Grimm, J. The juniper tree, and other tales from Grimm v2 p310-13 **398.2**

Mrs. Goat and her seven little kids. Ross, T. **398.2**
Mrs. Minetta's car pool. Spurr, E. **E**
Mrs. Pig gets cross and other stories. Rayner, M. See note under Rayner, M. Mr. and Mrs. Pig's evening out **E**
Mrs. Piggle-Wiggle. MacDonald, B. **Fic**
Mrs. Piggle-Wiggle's farm. MacDonald, B. See note under MacDonald, B. Mrs. Piggle-Wiggle **Fic**
Mrs. Piggle-Wiggle's magic. MacDonald, B. See note under MacDonald, B. Mrs. Piggle-Wiggle **Fic**
Mrs. Piggle-Wiggle's magic [excerpt]. MacDonald, B.
In The Random House book of humor for children p15-30 **817.008**
Mrs. Pig's bulk buy. Rayner, M. See note under Rayner, M. Mr. and Mrs. Pig's evening out **E**
Mrs. Puss, Dog and thieves. Berry, J.
In Berry, J. Spiderman Anancy p101-06 **398.2**
Much ado about Aldo. Hurwitz, J. **Fic**
Much bigger than Martin. Kellogg, S. **E**
Mufaro's beautiful daughters. Steptoe, J. **398.2**
The **mufferaw** catfish. Bedore, B.
In Bauer, C. F. Celebrations p85-86 **808.8**
Muggie Maggie. Cleary, B. **Fic**
Muir, John, 1838-1914
About
Force, E. John Muir (5 and up) **92**
Mujica, Barbara Louise
Fairy tale
In Where angels glide at dawn p77-97 **S C**
Mukerji, Dhan Gopal, 1890-1936
See/See also pages in the following book(s):
Newbery Medal books, 1922-1955 p53-58 **028.5**
The **mule.** Crossley-Holland, K.
In Crossley-Holland, K. British folk tales p295-303 **398.2**
The **mule** story. Porte-Thomas, B. A.
In Porte-Thomas, B. A. Jesse's ghost, and other stories p29-31 **S C**
Mules
See/See also pages in the following book(s):
Henry, M. Album of horses p102-05 (4 and up) **636.1**
Mullins, June B., 1927-
(jt. auth) Friedberg, J. B. Accept me as I am: best books of juvenile nonfiction on impairments and disabilities **016**
Mullins, Patricia
(il) Fox, M. Hattie and the fox **E**
(il) Fox, M. Shoes from Grandpa **E**
(il) Jorgensen, G. Crocodile beat **E**
Multilingual dictionaries *See* Polyglot dictionaries
Multimedia materials *See* Audiovisual materials
Mulvihill, Margaret
Roman forts (5 and up) **937**
Mummies
Berrill, M. Mummies, masks, & mourners (4-6) **393**
Lauber, P. Tales mummies tell (5 and up) **930.1**
Perl, L. Mummies, tombs, and treasure (4 and up) **393**
Mummies, masks, & mourners. Berrill, M. **393**
Mummies, tombs, and treasure. Perl, L. **393**
The **mummy,** the will and the crypt. Bellairs, J. See note under Bellairs, J. The curse of the blue figurine **Fic**
Munachar and Manachar
Jacobs, J. Munachar and Manachar
In The Scott, Foresman anthology of children's literature p171-73 **808.8**
Munachar and Manachar
In Best-loved folktales of the world p232-34 **398.2**
Municipal planning *See* City planning
Muñoz, William, 1949-
(il) Patent, D. H. Appaloosa horses **636.1**
(il) Patent, D. H. An apple a day **634**
(il) Patent, D. H. Buffalo **599.73**
(il) Patent, D. H. Draft horses **636.1**
(il) Patent, D. H. Flowers for everyone **635.9**
(il) Patent, D. H. A horse of a different color **636.1**
(il) Patent, D. H. Quarter horses **636.1**
(il) Patent, D. H. The way of the grizzly **599.74**
(il) Patent, D. H. Wheat, the golden harvest **633.1**
(il) Patent, D. H. Where the bald eagles gather **598**
(il) Patent, D. H. Where the wild horses roam **639.9**
(il) Patent, D. H. The whooping crane **639.9**
(il) Patent, D. H. Wild turkey, tame turkey **598**
(il) Patent, D. H. Yellowstone fires **574.5**
Munro, H. H. (Hector Hugh) *See* Saki, 1870-1916

Munro, Roxie, 1945-
Blimps (2-4) **629.133**
Christmastime in New York City (2-4) **394.2**
The inside-outside book of London (2-4) **942.1**
The inside-outside book of New York City (2-4) **974.7**
The inside-outside book of Washington, D.C. (2-4) **975.3**
Munsen, Sylvia
Cooking the Norwegian way (5 and up) **641.5**
Munsinger, Lynn, 1951-
(il) Gounaud, K. J. A very mice joke book **793.73**
(il) Lester, H. The revenge of the Magic Chicken **E**
(il) Tompert, A. Nothing sticks like a shadow **E**
Munthe, Nelly, 1947-
Meet Matisse (4 and up) **759.4**
Mural painting and decoration
See also Mosaics
Murcko, Denise *See* Wilms, Denise
Murdoch's rath. Ewing, J. H.
In Bauer, C. F. Celebrations p183-88 **808.8**
Murdock, Tony
Gymnastics (4 and up) **796.44**
Murphy, Jeff
(il) Lasson, R. If I had a hammer: woodworking with seven basic tools **684**
Murphy, Jill, 1949-
All in one piece **E**
Five minutes' peace **E**
Peace at last **E**
What next, Baby Bear! **E**
Murphy, Jim, 1947-
Guess again: more weird & wacky inventions (4 and up) **609**
Murphy, Roxane
(il) MacDonald, M. R. Twenty tellable tales **372.6**
(il) MacDonald, M. R. When the lights go out **372.6**
Murphy, Shirley Rousseau, 1928-
Tattie's river journey **E**
Murray, John, 1923-
Old ghosts at home
In Holiday plays round the year p112-28 **812.008**
Murray and Fred. Stevenson, J.
In Stevenson, J. Fast friends p5-37 **E**
Musa and Kojere. Adetunji, E. A.
In The Crest and the hide, and other African stories of heroes, chiefs, bards, hunters, sorcerers, and common people p89-93 **398.2**
Muscles
Parker, S. The skeleton and movement (4 and up) **612.7**
Musculoskeletal system
See also Bones; Muscles
Museums
See also Art—Museums
Fiction
Cameron, E. The court of the stone children (5 and up) **Fic**
Freeman, D. Norman the doorman **E**
Howe, J. Pinky and Rex **E**
Technique
Arnold, C. Dinosaurs down under and other fossils from Australia (4 and up) **567.9**
Museums and schools
Jay, H. L. Developing library-museum partnerships to serve young people **027.8**
Musgrove, Margaret, 1943-
Ashanti to Zulu: African traditions (3-6) **960**
Mushrooms
Froman, R. Mushrooms and molds (1-3) **589.2**
Johnson, S. A. Mushrooms (4 and up) **589.2**
Selsam, M. E. Mushrooms (2-4) **589.2**
Mushrooms and molds. Froman, R. **589.2**
Music
See also Composition (Music); Operas—Stories, plots, etc.; Songs
McLeish, K. The Oxford first companion to music (5 and up) **780**
Ventura, P. Great composers (5 and up) **780.9**
Dictionaries
Hurd, M. The Oxford junior companion to music (5 and up) **780.3**
Fiction
Kherdian, D. The cat's midsummer jamboree **E**
Study and teaching
Krementz, J. A very young musician (3-6) **788**
Music, American
See also Spirituals (Songs)
See/See also pages in the following book(s):
Caney, S. Steven Caney's kids' America p314-24 (4 and up) **790.1**
Music, Indian *See* Indians of North America—Songs and music

Music, Popular (Songs, etc.)
See also Country music
Music. Ardley, N. **784.19**
Music for ones and twos. Glazer, T. **782.42**
Music, music for everyone. Williams, V. B. See note under Williams, V. B. A chair for my mother **E**
Musical instruments
Ardley, N. Music (4 and up) **784.19**
Fichter, G. S. American Indian music and musical instruments (5 and up) **780.89**
Walther, T. Make mine music! (5 and up) **784.19**
Wiseman, A. S. Making musical things (3-6) **784.19**
See/See also pages in the following book(s):
McLeish, K. The Oxford first companion to music (5 and up) **780**
The **musician**. Terada, A. M.
In Terada, A. M. Under the starfruit tree p132-34 **398.2**
Musicians
See also Composers
Fiction
Alexander, L. The marvelous misadventures of Sebastian (4 and up) **Fic**
Duder, T. Jellybean (5 and up) **Fic**
Isadora, R. Ben's trumpet **E**
MacLachlan, P. The facts and fictions of Minna Pratt (4 and up) **Fic**
Musicians, Black *See* Black musicians
The **musicians** of Bremen. Grimm, J.
In Grimm, J. Tales from Grimm p87-100 **398.2**
Muskrats
Arnosky, J. Come out, muskrats (k-2) **599.32**
Mussino, Attilio
(il) Collodi, C. The adventures of Pinocchio **Fic**
Mustafa Kemal *See* Atatürk, Kemal, 1881-1938
Mustang, wild spirit of the West. Henry, M. **Fic**
Mustangs: wild horses of the American West. Featherly, J. **636.1**
Mutsmag
Mutsmag
In Grandfather tales p40-51 **398.2**
Mwalimu
Awful aardvark (k-2) **398.2**
Mwenye Hadithi
Crafty Chameleon **E**
Hot Hippo **E**

My back yard. Rockwell, A. F. **E**
My backyard history book. Weitzman, D. L. **973**
My ballet class. Isadora, R. **792.8**
My black me: a beginning book of black poetry (5 and up) **811.008**
My brother Sam is dead. Collier, J. L. **Fic**
My brown bear Barney. Butler, D. **E**
My daddy longlegs. Hawes, J. **595.4**
My daddy was a soldier. Ray, D. K. **E**
My Daniel. Conrad, P. **Fic**
My dentist. Rockwell, H. **617.6**
My doctor. Rockwell, H. **610.69**
My family vacation. Khalsa, D. K. **E**
My father's dragon. Gannett, R. S. **Fic**
My feet. Aliki. **612**
My first activity book. Wilkes, A. **745.5**
My first book of sign. Baker, P. J. **419**
My first dictionary. See The American Heritage first dictionary **423**
My first kitten. Hausherr, R. **636.8**
My first look at colors **E**
My first look at home See note under My first look at colors **E**
My first look at numbers See note under My first look at colors **E**
My first look at opposites See note under My first look at colors **E**
My first look at seasons See note under My first look at colors **E**
My first look at shapes See note under My first look at colors **E**
My first look at sizes See note under My first look at colors **E**
My first look at touch See note under My first look at colors **E**
My first nature book. Wilkes, A. **508**
My first picture dictionary. See Words for new readers **423**
My first puppy. Hausherr, R. **636.7**
My five senses. Aliki. **612.8**
My friend Flicka. O'Hara, M.
In Herds of thunder, manes of gold p111-35 **808.8**
My friend John. Zolotow, C. **E**
My friend Leslie. Rosenberg, M. B. **362.4**
My Grandma. Pogrebin, L. C.
In Free to be—a family p52-56 **810.8**

My grandson Lew. Zolotow, C. **E**
My hands. Aliki **612**
My head is red and other riddle rhymes. Livingston, M. C. **793.73**
My Hiroshima. Morimoto, J. **940.54**
My house/mi casa: a book in two languages. Emberley, R. **463**
My household
Grimm, J. My household
In Grimm, J. The complete Grimm's fairy tales p624 **398.2**
My life with the chimpanzees. Goodall, J. **92**
My Lord Bag-o'-Rice. Quayle, E.
In Quayle, E. The shining princess, and other Japanese legends p33-43 **398.2**
My mama needs me. Walter, M. P. **E**
My mama says there aren't any zombies, ghosts, vampires, creatures, demons, monsters, fiends, goblins, or things. Viorst, J. **E**
My mother got married (and other disasters). Park, B. **Fic**
My mother is the most beautiful woman in the world. Reyher, R. H. **398.2**
My mother's house, my father's house. Christiansen, C. B. **E**
My name is not Angelica. O'Dell, S. **Fic**
My Noah's ark. Goffstein, M. B. **E**
My parents think I'm sleeping: poems. Prelutsky, J. **811**
My place in space. Hirst, R. **520**
My puppy is born. Cole, J. **636.7**
My red umbrella. Bright, R. **E**
My shadow. Gore, S. **535**
My shadow. Stevenson, R. L. **821**
My side of the mountain. George, J. C. **Fic**
My spring robin. Rockwell, A. F. **E**
My tang's tungled and other ridiculous situations (3-6) **821.008**
My visit to the dinosaurs. Aliki **567.9**
My war with Goggle-eyes. Fine, A. **Fic**
Mycca's baby. Byers, R. M. **E**
Mycenae (Ancient city)
See/See also pages in the following book(s):
Gallant, R. A. Lost cities (4 and up) **930**
Myers, Lou
See/See also pages in the following book(s):
Sendak, M. Caldecott & Co.: notes on books and pictures p131-32 **028.5**
Myers, Walter Dean, 1937-
Fast Sam, Cool Clyde, and Stuff (6 and up) **Fic**
Me, Mop, and the Moondance Kid (4-6) **Fic**
The Mouse rap (6 and up) **Fic**
Scorpions (6 and up) **Fic**
The treasure of Lemon Brown
In Face to face: a collection of stories by celebrated Soviet and American writers p101-13 **S C**
The young landlords (6 and up) **Fic**
Myrick, Mildred
The Secret Three **E**
Myron Mere. Rockwell, T.
In Rockwell, T. How to eat fried worms, and other plays p1-20 **812**
The **mysteries** of Harris Burdick. Van Allsburg, C. **E**
Mysteries of life on earth and beyond. Branley, F. M. **574.999**
Mysteries of planet earth. Branley, F. M. **525**
Mysteries of the universe. Branley, F. M. **523.1**
The **mysterious** disappearance of Leon (I mean Noel). Raskin, E. **Fic**
The **mysterious** giant of Barletta. De Paola, T. **E**
Mysterious multiplying jar, Anno's. Anno, M. **512**
The **mysterious** tadpole. Kellogg, S. **E**
The **mysterious** undersea world. Cook, J. L. **551.46**
Mysteriously yours, Maggie Marmelstein. Sharmat, M. W. **Fic**
Mystery and detective stories
Babbitt, N. Goody Hall (4-6) **Fic**
Base, G. The eleventh hour (4-6) **Fic**
Bellairs, J. The curse of the blue figurine (5 and up) **Fic**
Berends, P. B. The case of the elevator duck (3-5) **Fic**
Brooks, W. R. Freddy the detective (3-5) **Fic**
Cameron, E. The court of the stone children (5 and up) **Fic**
Christopher, M. Tackle without a team (5 and up) **Fic**
Clifford, E. The dastardly murder of Dirty Pete (3-5) **Fic**
Clymer, E. L. The horse in the attic (4 and up) **Fic**
Corbett, S. Grave doubts (4 and up) **Fic**
Dicks, T. The Baker Street Irregulars in the case of the missing masterpiece (5 and up) **Fic**
Giff, P. R. Loretta P. Sweeny, where are you? (4-6) **Fic**
Hahn, M. D. The dead man in Indian Creek (5 and up) **Fic**

Mystery and detective stories—*Continued*
Hamilton, V. The house of Dies Drear (5 and up) **Fic**
Hamilton, V. The mystery of Drear House (5 and up) **Fic**
Hildick, E. W. The case of the purloined parrot (3-6) **Fic**
Hildick, E. W. The Ghost Squad breaks through (5 and up) **Fic**
Howe, D. Bunnicula (4-6) **Fic**
Howe, J. The celery stalks at midnight (4-6) **Fic**
Howe, J. Dew drop dead (4-6) **Fic**
Hurd, T. Mystery on the docks **E**
Klaveness, J. O. The Griffin legacy (6 and up) **Fic**
Konigsburg, E. L. Up from Jericho Tel (5 and up) **Fic**
Lawrence, J. Binky brothers, detectives **E**
Levy, E. Something queer is going on (a mystery) **E**
Lexau, J. M. The rooftop mystery **E**
Meyers, S. P.J. Clover, private eye: the case of the Halloween hoot (4-6) **Fic**
Naylor, P. R. Bernie and the Bessledorf ghost (4-6) **Fic**
Newman, R. The case of the Baker Street Irregular (5 and up) **Fic**
Pearce, P. The way to Sattin Shore (5 and up) **Fic**
Platt, K. Big Max **E**
Platt, K. Big Max in the mystery of the missing moose **E**
Quackenbush, R. M. Express train to trouble (2-4) **Fic**
Raskin, E. The mysterious disappearance of Leon (I mean Noel) (4 and up) **Fic**
Raskin, E. The tattooed potato and other clues (5 and up) **Fic**
Raskin, E. The Westing game (5 and up) **Fic**
Roberts, W. D. Megan's island (5 and up) **Fic**
Roberts, W. D. To Grandmother's house we go (4-6) **Fic**
Roberts, W. D. The view from the cherry tree (5 and up) **Fic**
Sachs, M. At the sound of the beep (4-6) **Fic**
Sharmat, M. W. Nate the Great **E**
Sobol, D. J. Encyclopedia Brown, boy detective (3-5) **Fic**
Titus, E. Basil of Baker Street (3-5) **Fic**
Wright, B. R. The dollhouse murders (4-6) **Fic**
Yolen, J. Piggins and the royal wedding **E**

The **mystery** of Drear House. Hamilton, V. **Fic**
The **mystery** of sleep. Silverstein, A. **154.6**
The **mystery** of the missing red mitten. Kellogg, S. **E**
Mystery on the docks. Hurd, T. **E**
Mythical animals *See* Animals, Mythical

Mythology
See also Animals, Mythical; Gods and goddesses
Bulfinch, T. Bulfinch's mythology (6 and up) **291**
Hamilton, V. In the beginning; creation stories from around the world (5 and up) **291**
Lurie, A. The heavenly zoo (4 and up) **398.2**
See/See also pages in the following book(s):
Cook, E. The ordinary and the fabulous **028.5**

Indexes
Index to fairy tales, 1949-1972 **398.2**
Index to fairy tales, 1973-1977 **398.2**
Index to fairy tales, 1978-1986 **398.2**

Mythology, Classical
See also Aphrodite (Greek deity); Apollo (Greek deity); Athena (Greek deity); Demeter (Greek deity); Dionysus (Greek deity); Eros (Greek deity); Persephone (Greek deity); Psyche (Greek deity); Zeus (Greek deity)
Asimov, I. Words from the myths (6 and up) **292**
Benson, S. Stories of the gods and heroes (5 and up) **292**
Colum, P. The Golden Fleece and the heroes who lived before Achilles (5 and up) **292**
Fisher, L. E. The Olympians **292**
Gates, D. A fair wind for Troy (4 and up) **292**
Hamilton, E. Mythology (6 and up) **292**
Hawthorne, N. A wonder-book, and Tanglewood tales (5 and up) **292**
Hodges, M. The arrow and the lamp **292**
Low, A. The Macmillan book of Greek gods and heroes (3-6) **292**
McDermott, G. Daughter of Earth (2-4) **292**
Osborne, M. P. Favorite Greek myths (3-6) **292**
Usher, K. Heroes, gods & emperors from Roman mythology (5 and up) **292**
See/See also pages in the following book(s):
The Scott, Foresman anthology of children's literature p419-37 **808.8**

Mythology, Norse
Barth, E. Balder and the mistletoe (3-5) **293**

Mythology, Norse—*Continued*
Colum, P. The children of Odin (5 and up) **293**
Hamilton, E. Mythology (6 and up) **292**
See/See also pages in the following book(s):
The Scott, Foresman anthology of children's literature p437-50 **808.8**
Mythology. Hamilton, E. **292**
Mythology and the universe. Asimov, I. **523.1**

N

Nabwire, Constance R.
Cooking the African way (5 and up) **641.5**
Nach, James
England—in pictures. See England—in pictures **942**
(jt. auth) Feinstein, S. Turkey—in pictures **956.1**
Naden, Corinne J.
(ed) Best books for children, preschool through grade 6. See Best books for children, preschool through grade 6 **011.6**
(jt. auth) Gillespie, J. T. Juniorplots 3: a book talk guide for use with readers ages 12-16 **028.1**
Nadia the Willful. Alexander, S. **E**
Naftali the storyteller and his horse, Sus. Singer, I. B.
In Singer, I. B. Naftali the storyteller and his horse, Sus, and other stories p3-23 **S C**
In Singer, I. B. Stories for children p167-83 **S C**
Naftali the storyteller and his horse, Sus, and other stories. Singer, I. B. **S C**
Nagel, Andreas Fischer- *See* Fischer-Nagel, Andreas, 1951-
Nagel, Heiderose Fischer- *See* Fischer-Nagel, Heiderose, 1956-
The **nagging** husband. Riordan, J.
In Riordan, J. The woman in the moon, and other tales of forgotten heroines p15-19 **398.2**
Naidoo, Beverley
Chain of fire (5 and up) **Fic**
Journey to Jo'burg (5 and up) **Fic**
Nail
Grimm, J. The nail
In Grimm, J. The complete Grimm's fairy tales p748-49 **398.2**
Nail soup. Rockwell, A. F.
In Rockwell, A. F. Puss in boots, and other stories p12-18 **398.2**
The **Naked** bear (4 and up) **398.2**
The **Name**
In The Magic orange tree, and other Haitian folktales p117-22 **398.2**
The **name** of the tree. Lottridge, C. B. **398.2**
Names, Geographical
See also Gazetteers
United States
Shankle, G. E. American nicknames **929.4**
Names, Personal
Lee, M. P. Last names first (5 and up) **929.4**
Meltzer, M. A book about names (5 and up) **929.4**
Fiction
Hurwitz, J. The adventures of Ali Baba Bernstein (2-4) **Fic**
Mosel, A. Tikki Tikki Tembo (k-2) **398.2**
Williams, S. Mommy doesn't know my name **E**
United States
Shankle, G. E. American nicknames **929.4**
Namioka, Lensey
The inn of lost time
In Connections: short stories by outstanding writers for young adults p138-57 **S C**
Nana Upstairs & Nana Downstairs. De Paola, T. **E**
Nanabozho (Legendary character)
See/See also pages in the following book(s):
Best-loved folktales of the world p712-19 **398.2**
Nanabush (Legendary character) *See* Nanabozho (Legendary character)
Nantucket (Mass.)
Fiction
Turkle, B. C. Obadiah the Bold **E**
Napoleon I, Emperor of the French, 1769-1821
See/See also pages in the following book(s):
Phelan, M. K. The story of the Louisiana Purchase p27-34, 78-88 (5 and up) **973.4**
The **napping** house. Wood, A. **E**
Narahashi, Keiko
(il) Serfozo, M. Who said red? **E**
Narcotic traffic *See* Drug traffic
Narcotics
See also Opium
Nardi, Thomas J.
Karate basics (4 and up) **796.8**
The **Nargun** and the stars. Wrightson, P. **Fic**

Narraganset Indians
Fiction
Fleischman, P. Saturnalia (5 and up) **Fic**
The **narrow** escapes of Davy Crockett. Dewey, A. **E**
NASA *See* United States. National Aeronautics and Space Administration
Nash, Ogden, 1902-1971
Custard and company: poems (3 and up) **811**
Lear, E. Edward Lear's The Scroobious Pip **821**
Nasreddin Hoca and the third shot. Walker, B. K.
In Walker, B. K. A treasury of Turkish folktales for children p43-44 **398.2**
Nasreddin Hoca, seller of wisdom. Walker, B. K.
In Walker, B. K. A treasury of Turkish folktales for children p37-42 **398.2**
Natalie underneath. James, B. **E**
Nate the Great. Sharmat, M. W. **E**
Nate the Great and the boring beach bag. Sharmat, M. W. See note under Sharmat, M. W. Nate the Great **E**
Nate the Great and the fishy prize. Sharmat, M. W. See note under Sharmat, M. W. Nate the Great **E**
Nate the Great and the Halloween hunt. Sharmat, M. W. See note under Sharmat, M. W. Nate the Great **E**
Nate the Great and the lost list. Sharmat, M. W. See note under Sharmat, M. W. Nate the Great **E**
Nate the Great and the missing key. Sharmat, M. W. See note under Sharmat, M. W. Nate the Great **E**
Nate the Great and the musical note. Sharmat, M. W. See note under Sharmat, M. W. Nate the Great **E**
Nate the Great and the phony clue. Sharmat, M. W. See note under Sharmat, M. W. Nate the Great **E**
Nate the Great and the snowy trail. Sharmat, M. W. See note under Sharmat, M. W. Nate the Great **E**
Nate the Great and the sticky case. Sharmat, M. W. See note under Sharmat, M. W. Nate the Great **E**
Nate the Great goes down in the dumps. Sharmat, M. W. See note under Sharmat, M. W. Nate the Great **E**
Nate the Great goes undercover. Sharmat, M. W. See note under Sharmat, M. W. Nate the Great **E**
Nate the Great stalks stupidweed. Sharmat, M. W. See note under Sharmat, M. W. Nate the Great **E**
Nathaniel talking. Greenfield, E. **811**
National Aeronautics and Space Administration (U.S.) *See* United States. National Aeronautics and Space Administration
National Audubon Society
The Audubon Society field guide to North American fishes, whales, and dolphins. See The Audubon Society field guide to North American fishes, whales, and dolphins **597**
National Council for the Social Studies
Notable children's trade books in the field of social studies. See Notable children's trade books in the field of social studies **016.3**
National Council of Teachers of English. Committee on Literature in the Elementary Language Arts
Raising readers **028.5**
National Council of Teachers of English. Committee on the Elementary School Booklist
Adventuring with books **011.6**
National Council of Teachers of English. Committee on the Junior High and Middle School Booklist
Your reading: a booklist for junior high and middle school students **011.6**
National Gallery of Canada
Degas, E. Meet Edgar Degas **759.4**
National Geographic atlas of the world **912**
National Geographic picture atlas of our world **912**
National Geographic Society (U.S.)
Adventures in your national parks. See Adventures in your national parks **917.3**
Amazing animals of Australia. See Amazing animals of Australia **591.9**
Amazing animals of the sea. See Amazing animals of the sea **599.5**
Amos, W. H. Life in ponds and streams **591.92**
Animal architects. See Animal architects **591.5**
Bridge, L. M. The playful dolphins **599.5**
Brownell, M. B. Amazing otters **599.74**
Buxton, J. H. Baby bears and how they grow **599.74**
Cook, J. L. The mysterious undersea world **551.46**
Crump, D. J. Creatures small and furry **599**

National Geographic Society (U.S.)—*Continued*
Exploring your world: the adventure of geography. See Exploring your world: the adventure of geography **910.3**
Giants from the past: the age of mammals. See Giants from the past: the age of mammals **569**
Grosvenor, D. K. The blue whale **599.5**
Grosvenor, D. K. Zoo babies **590.74**
Hidden treasures of the sea. See Hidden treasures of the sea **910.4**
Hidden worlds. See Hidden worlds **500**
Hirschland, R. B. How animals care for their babies **591.5**
How animals behave: a new look at wildlife. See How animals behave: a new look at wildlife **591.5**
Jordan, R. P. The Civil War **973.7**
Kostyal, K. M. Animals at play **591.5**
Martin, P. D. Messengers to the brain: our fantastic five senses **612.8**
McCauley, J. R. Animals and their hiding places **591.5**
McCauley, J. R. Animals in summer **591.5**
McCauley, J. R. Animals that live in trees **591.5**
McCauley, J. R. Baby birds and how they grow **598**
McCauley, J. R. Let's explore a river **574.92**
McCauley, J. R. Ways animals sleep **591.5**
McClung, R. M. Animals that build their homes **591.5**
McGrath, S. The amazing things animals do **591.5**
McGrath, S. How animals talk **591.5**
McGrath, S. Saving our animal friends **591**
National Geographic atlas of the world. See National Geographic atlas of the world **912**
National Geographic picture atlas of our world. See National Geographic picture atlas of our world **912**
National Geographic World. See National Geographic World **910.5**
O'Neill, C. Natural wonders of North America **557**
O'Neill, C. You won't believe your eyes! **152.14**
Our violent earth. See Our violent earth **363.3**
Rathbun, E. Exploring your solar system **523.2**
Rinard, J. E. Creatures of the night **591.5**
Rinard, J. E. Dolphins: our friends in the sea **599.5**
Rinard, J. E. Helping our animal friends **636.088**
Rinard, J. E. Wildlife, making a comeback **591**
Rinard, J. E. The world beneath your feet **591.9**
Rinard, J. E. Zoos without cages **590.74**
Scott, J. A. The story of America: a National Geographic picture atlas **973**
The Secret world of animals. See The Secret world of animals **591.5**
Venino, S. Amazing animal groups **591.5**
Venino, S. Animals helping people **636.088**
Why in the world? See Why in the world? **500**
Why on earth? See Why on earth? **500**

National Geographic World (3-6) **910.5**

National Library Service for the Blind and Physically Handicapped *See* Library of Congress. National Library Service for the Blind and Physically Handicapped

National monuments *See* National parks and reserves

National Museum of Natural History (U.S.)
Thomson, P. Auks, rocks and the odd dinosaur (5 and up) **508**

National parks and reserves
Adventures in your national parks (4 and up) **917.3**
Young, D. The Sierra Club book of our national parks (4 and up) **917.3**

National Science Teachers Association
Outstanding science trade books for children. See Outstanding science trade books for children **016.5**

National socialism
Shirer, W. L. The rise and fall of Adolf Hitler (6 and up) **943.086**

National songs, American
Bangs, E. Steven Kellogg's Yankee Doodle (k-3) **782.42**
Key, F. S. The Star-Spangled Banner **782.42**

National Velvet. Bagnold, E. **Fic**

National Worm Day. Stevenson, J. **E**

National Zoological Park (U.S.)
Thomson, P. Keepers and creatures at the National Zoo (5 and up) **590.74**

Native Americans *See* Indians of North America

Natti, Susanna, 1948-
(il) Giff, P. R. Watch out, Ronald Morgan! **E**
(il) Krensky, S. Lionel at large **E**

Natural disasters
Our violent earth (4 and up) **363.3**

Natural enemies. Yep, L.
In Yep, L. The rainbow people p12-18 **398.2**

Natural history
Whitfield, P. J. Can the whales be saved? (4 and up) **574.5**
Whitfield, P. J. Why do the seasons change? (4 and up) **508**

Dictionaries
The New book of popular science **503**

Periodicals
Chickadee: the Canadian magazine for young children **505**
Owl **505**
Ranger Rick **505**
Your Big Backyard **505**

Costa Rica
Forsyth, A. Journey through a tropical jungle (4 and up) **574.5**

Venezuela
George, J. C. One day in the tropical rain forest (4-6) **574.5**

Natural resources
See also Conservation of natural resources; Forests and forestry

Natural selection
See also Evolution

Natural steam energy *See* Geothermal resources

Natural wonders of North America. O'Neill, C. **557**

Naturalists
Force, E. John Muir (5 and up) **92**

Nature
Peters, L. W. The sun, the wind and the rain (k-2) **551.4**

Pictorial works
Florian, D. Nature walk **E**

Poetry
Ryder, J. Under your feet (k-3) **811**

Nature, Effect of man on *See* Man—Influence on nature

Nature conservation
See also Plant conservation; Wildlife conservation
Ancona, G. Riverkeeper (3-6) **333.91**
Force, E. John Muir (5 and up) **92**
Whitfield, P. J. Can the whales be saved? (4 and up) **574.5**

Nature in poetry
Brown, M. W. Nibble nibble: poems for children (k-3) **811**
Esbensen, B. J. Cold stars and fireflies (4 and up) **811**
Hughes, T. Season songs (6 and up) **821**
In a spring garden (k-3) **895.6**
Room for me and a mountain lion (5 and up) **808.81**
See/See also pages in the following book(s):
Piping down the valleys wild p161-74 **808.81**

Nature photography
See also Photography of animals

Nature study
Arnosky, J. Secrets of a wildlife watcher (4 and up) **591.5**
Björk, C. Linnea's almanac (2-5) **508**
Hidden worlds (5 and up) **500**
MacFarlane, R. B. A. Making your own nature museum (5 and up) **508**
Rights, M. Beastly neighbors (4 and up) **508**
Wilkes, A. My first nature book (1-4) **508**

Nature walk. Florian, D. **E**

Nature's clean-up crew: the burying beetles. Milne, L. J. **595.7**

Nature's great balancing act. Norsgaard, E. J. **574.5**

Nature's living lights. Silverstein, A. **574.1**

Naughty Nancy goes to school. Goodall, J. S. **E**

Navaho Indians *See* Navajo Indians

Navajo Indians
Osinski, A. The Navajo (2-4) **970.004**
See/See also pages in the following book(s):
Ehrlich, A. Wounded Knee: an Indian history of the American West (6 and up) **970.004**

Fiction
Blood, C. L. The goat in the rug **E**
Miles, M. Annie and the Old One (1-4) **Fic**
O'Dell, S. Sing down the moon (5 and up) **Fic**

Naylor, Phyllis Reynolds, 1933-
The agony of Alice (5 and up) **Fic**
Alice in rapture, sort of (5 and up) **Fic**
Bernie and the Bessledorf ghost (4-6) **Fic**
The bodies in the Bessledorf Hotel. See note under Naylor, P. R. Bernie and the Bessledorf ghost **Fic**
Maudie in the middle (3-5) **Fic**
The witch herself. See note under Naylor, P. R. The witch's eye **Fic**
Witch water. See note under Naylor, P. R. The witch's eye **Fic**
The witch's eye (5 and up) **Fic**
Witch's sister. See note under Naylor, P. R. The witch's eye **Fic**

Nazism *See* National socialism

NCSS *See* National Council for the Social Studies

Near East *See* Middle East
Near the sea. Arnosky, J. **758**
Near the window tree: poems and notes. Kuskin, K. **811**
Neatness *See* Cleanliness
Nebraska
Hargrove, J. Nebraska
In America the beautiful **973**
Fiction
Conrad, P. My Daniel (5 and up) **Fic**
Conrad, P. Prairie songs (5 and up) **Fic**
Ruckman, I. Night of the twisters (3-6) **Fic**
Nebulae, Extragalactic *See* Galaxies
Nebulae. Apfel, N. H. **523.1**
Neel, Alice, 1900-1984
See/See also pages in the following book(s):
Sills, L. Inspirations p28-39 (5 and up) **920**
Negri, Rocco
(il) Byars, B. C. Trouble River **Fic**
Negroes *See* Blacks
Negron, William
(il) Berger, M. Star gazing, comet tracking, and sky mapping **523**
Neighborhood *See* Community life
Neimark, Anne E.
Ché! [biography of Ernesto Guevara] (6 and up) **92**
A deaf child listened: Thomas Gallaudet, pioneer in American education (6 and up) **92**
Neitzel, Shirley
The jacket I wear in the snow **E**
Nellie: a cat on her own. Babbitt, N. **E**
Nelson, Esther L.
The funny song-book **782.42**
Nelson, Gail A.
Baskin, B. H. Books for the gifted child **011.6**
Nelson, Theresa, 1948-
The 25¢ miracle (5 and up) **Fic**
And one for all (6 and up) **Fic**
Nepal
Nepal—in pictures (5 and up) **954.96**
Pitkänen, M. A. The children of Nepal (2-4) **954.96**
Children
See Children—Nepal
Nepal, Sikkim and Bhutan (Himalayan kingdoms) in pictures. See Nepal—in pictures **954.96**
Nepal—in pictures (5 and up) **954.96**
Neptune (Planet)
Asimov, I. How did we find out about Neptune? (5 and up) **523.4**
Yeomans, D. K. The distant planets (4-6) **523.4**
See/See also pages in the following book(s):
Harris, A. The great Voyager adventure p53-60 (5 and up) **523.4**
Kelch, J. W. Small worlds: exploring the 60 moons of our solar system p97-108 (6 and up) **523.9**
Nervous system
Berger, M. Why I cough, sneeze, shiver, hiccup, & yawn (k-3) **612.8**
Parker, S. The brain and nervous system (4 and up) **612.8**
Silverstein, A. World of the brain (6 and up) **612.8**
Diseases
See also Epilepsy
Nesbit, E. (Edith), 1858-1924
Long ago when I was young (5 and up) **92**
Melisande (k-2) **398.2**
The story of the treasure seekers [excerpt]
In The Random House book of humor for children p195-204 **817.008**
See/See also pages in the following book(s):
Horn Book reflections on children's books and reading p211-17 **028.5**
Nesbit, Edith *See* Nesbit, E. (Edith), 1858-1924
Ness, Evaline, 1911-1986
Sam, Bangs & Moonshine **E**
(il) Caudill, R. A pocketful of cricket **E**
See/See also pages in the following book(s):
Newbery and Caldecott Medal books, 1966-1975 p186-98 **028.5**
Nessa's fish. Luenn, N. **E**
Netherlands
Fiction
DeJong, M. The wheel on the school (4-6) **Fic**
Dodge, M. M. Hans Brinker; or, The silver skates (4 and up) **Fic**
Green, N. The hole in the dike **E**
Krasilovsky, P. The cow who fell in the canal **E**
History—1940-1945, German occupation
Frank, A. The diary of a young girl (6 and up) **92**
Reiss, J. The upstairs room (4 and up) **92**
Nettie Jo's friends. McKissack, P. C. **E**
Nettie's trip South. Turner, A. W. **Fic**
Nettle spinner
Deulin, C. The nettle spinner
In The Red fairy book p286-93 **398.2**
Neufeld, John, 1938-
Edgar Allan (5 and up) **Fic**

Neugebauer, Michael
(il) Goodall, J. The chimpanzee family book **599.88**
Neuhaus, David
(il) Friedman, D. P. Focus on drugs and the brain **616.86**
(il) O'Neill, C. Focus on alcohol **362.29**
(il) Perry, R. L. Focus on nicotine and caffeine **616.86**
(il) Shulman, J. Focus on cocaine and crack **362.29**
(il) Zeller, P. K. Focus on marijuana **362.29**
Neuman, Pearl
When winter comes (1-3) **591.5**
Neumeier, Marty
Action alphabet **E**
Neurology *See* Nervous system
Nevada
Lillegard, D. Nevada
In America the beautiful **973**
Nevelson, Louise, 1900-1988
See/See also pages in the following book(s):
Goffstein, M. B. Lives of the artists (5 and up) **920**
Never cry wolf [excerpt]. Mowat, F.
In Animal families of the wild: animal stories p21-29 **591**
The **never-ending** bear hunt. Mayo, G.
In Mayo, G. Star tales p57-58 **398.2**
Never kick a slipper at the moon. Sandburg, C.
In Sandburg, C. Rootabaga stories pt 1 p151-55 **S C**
In Sandburg, C. The Sandburg treasury p71-72 **818**
Never kiss an alligator! Bare, C. S. **597.9**
"Never spit on your shoes". Cazet, D. **E**
Never to forget: the Jews of the Holocaust. Meltzer, M. **940.54**
Neville, Emily Cheney, 1919-
It's like this, Cat (5 and up) **Fic**
The **new** baby at your house. Cole, J. **306.8**
New biographical dictionary, Webster's **920.003**
The **New** book of knowledge **031**
The **New** book of popular science **503**
A **new** coat for Anna. Ziefert, H. **E**
New England
Description and travel
Gibbons, G. From path to highway: the story of the Boston Post Road (1-3) **388.1**
Fiction
Alcott, L. M. Little women (5 and up) **Fic**
Alcott, L. M. An old-fashioned Thanksgiving (3-5) **Fic**
Brittain, B. Devil's donkey (3-6) **Fic**
Fleischman, P. Coming-and-going men (6 and up) **S C**
Hall, D. The man who lived alone (2-4) **Fic**
Hall, D. Ox-cart man **E**
Jacobs, P. S. Born into light (6 and up) **Fic**
Roach, M. K. Encounters with the invisible world (5 and up) **S C**
New England Aquarium Corporation
Mallory, K. Rescue of the stranded whales (5 and up) **639.9**
White, S. V. Sterling (2-4) **639.9**
New geographical dictionary, Webster's **910.3**
The **new** girl at school. Delton, J. **E**
New Hampshire
Fiction
Bailey, C. S. Miss Hickory (3-5) **Fic**
Blos, J. W. A gathering of days: a New England girl's journal, 1830-32 (6 and up) **Fic**
The **new** illustrated dinosaur dictionary. Sattler, H. R. **567.9**
New international dictionary of the English language, Webster's third **423**
New Jersey
Kent, D. New Jersey
In America the beautiful **973**
Fiction
Kendall, J. F. Miranda and the movies (6 and up) **Fic**
New junior cook book (3-6) **641.5**
The **new** kid on the block: poems. Prelutsky, J. **811**
A **new** look at the Pilgrims. Siegel, B. **973.2**
New Mexico
Ashabranner, B. K. Born to the land: an American portrait (5 and up) **978.9**
Stein, R. C. New Mexico
In America the beautiful **973**
Fiction
Krumgold, J. —and now Miguel (6 and up) **Fic**
New Mexico. Stein, R. C.
In America the beautiful **973**
New neighbors for Nora. Hurwitz, J. See note under Hurwitz, J. Busybody Nora **Fic**
New Orleans (La.)
See/See also pages in the following book(s):
McCall, E. S. Biography of a river: the living Mississippi (6 and up) **977**

New patches for old. Walker, B. K.
In Walker, B. K. A treasury of Turkish folktales for children p135-38 **398.2**

New Providence. Von Tscharner, R. **307.7**

New questions and answers about dinosaurs. Simon, S. **567.9**

The **new** read-aloud handbook. Trelease, J. **028.5**

New road! Gibbons, G. **625.7**

The **new** teacher. Cohen, M. See note under Cohen, M. See you in second grade! **E**

A **New** treasury of children's poetry **821.008**

New Year

Fiction

Modell, F. Goodbye old year, hello new year **E**
Sharmat, M. W. Griselda's new year **E**

Poetry

New Year's poems (1-3) **808.81**

New Year, Chinese *See* Chinese New Year

New Year's hats for the statues. Uchida, Y.
In Snowy day: stories and poems p3-11 **808.8**

New Year's poems (1-3) **808.81**

New York (N.Y.)

Commerce

Horwitz, J. Night markets (3-6) **381**

Description

Huff, B. A. Greening the city streets **635**
Munro, R. The inside-outside book of New York City (2-4) **974.7**

Fiction

Baker, J. Home in the sky **E**
Greene, C. C. I and Sproggy (5 and up) **Fic**
Hansen, J. The gift-giver (4-6) **Fic**
Holman, F. Slake's limbo (6 and up) **Fic**
Hurwitz, J. Busybody Nora (2-4) **Fic**
Hurwitz, J. Superduper Teddy (2-4) **Fic**
Jordan, J. Kimako's story (2-4) **Fic**
Khalsa, D. K. How pizza came to Queens **E**
Levinson, R. I go with my family to Grandma's **E**
Levoy, M. The witch of Fourth Street, and other stories (4-6) **S C**
Merrill, J. The pushcart war (5 and up) **Fic**
Neville, E. C. It's like this, Cat (5 and up) **Fic**
Raskin, E. The mysterious disappearance of Leon (I mean Noel) (4 and up) **Fic**
Selden, G. The cricket in Times Square (3-6) **Fic**
Taylor, S. All-of-a-kind family (4-6) **Fic**
Van Leeuwen, J. The great Christmas kidnapping caper (3-5) **Fic**
Van Leeuwen, J. The great rescue operation (3-5) **Fic**
Waber, B. The house on East 88th Street **E**

History

Costabel, E. D. The Jews of New Amsterdam (2-4) **974.7**
Siegel, B. George and Martha Washington at home in New York (4-6) **973.4**

See/See also pages in the following book(s):
Tunis, E. The young United States, 1783 to 1830 p113-21 (5 and up) **973**

History—Fiction

Lobel, A. On the day Peter Stuyvesant sailed into town **E**

Social life and customs—Pictorial works

Munro, R. Christmastime in New York City (2-4) **394.2**

New York (N.Y.). Statue of Liberty *See* Statue of Liberty (New York, N.Y.)

New York (State)

Stein, R. C. New York
In America the beautiful **973**

Fiction

Edmonds, W. D. Bert Breen's barn (6 and up) **Fic**
Edmonds, W. D. The matchlock gun (4-6) **Fic**
Irving, W. Rip Van Winkle (5 and up) **Fic**
O'Dell, S. Sarah Bishop (6 and up) **Fic**

History

Fradin, D. B. The New York Colony (4 and up) **974.7**

The **New York** Colony. Fradin, D. B. **974.7**

New York Public Library
The Black experience in children's books. See The Black experience in children's books **016.3058**

New Zealand
See also Maoris
New Zealand—in pictures (5 and up) **993**

New Zealand—in pictures (5 and up) **993**

Newberry, Clare Turlay, 1903-1970
Marshmallow **E**

Newbery, John
See/See also pages in the following book(s):
Newbery Medal books, 1922-1955 p6-9 **028.5**
Only connect: readings on children's literature p28-38 **028.5**

Newbery and Caldecott Medal books, 1966-1975 **028.5**
Newbery and Caldecott Medal books, 1976-1985 **028.5**
Newbery Medal books
Alexander, L. The High King (1969) **Fic**
Bailey, C. S. Miss Hickory (1947) **Fic**
Blos, J. W. A gathering of days: a New England girl's journal, 1830-32 (1980) **Fic**
Brink, C. R. Caddie Woodlawn (1936) **Fic**
Byars, B. C. The summer of the swans (1971) **Fic**
Clark, A. N. Secret of the Andes (1953) **Fic**
Cleary, B. Dear Mr. Henshaw (1984) **Fic**
Coatsworth, E. J. The cat who went to heaven (1931) **Fic**
Cooper, S. The grey king (1976) **Fic**
De Angeli, M. L. The door in the wall (1950) **Fic**
DeJong, M. The wheel on the school (1955) **Fic**
Du Bois, W. P. The twenty-one balloons (1948) **Fic**
Edmonds, W. D. The matchlock gun (1942) **Fic**
Enright, E. Thimble summer (1939) **Fic**
Estes, E. Ginger Pye (1952) **Fic**
Field, R. Hitty: her first hundred years (1930) **Fic**
Fleischman, P. Joyful noise: poems for two voices (1989) **811**
Fleischman, S. The whipping boy (1987) **Fic**
Forbes, E. Johnny Tremain (1944) **Fic**
Fox, P. The slave dancer (1974) **Fic**
Freedman, R. Lincoln: a photobiography (1988) **92**
George, J. C. Julie of the wolves (1973) **Fic**
Hamilton, V. M. C. Higgins the great (1975) **Fic**
Henry, M. King of the wind (1949) **Fic**
Hunt, I. Up a road slowly (1967) **Fic**
James, W. Smoky, the cow horse (1927) **Fic**
Keith, H. Rifles for Watie (1958) **Fic**
Kelly, E. P. The trumpeter of Krakow (1929) **Fic**
Konigsburg, E. L. From the mixed-up files of Mrs. Basil E. Frankweiler (1968) **Fic**
Krumgold, J. —and now Miguel (1954) **Fic**
Krumgold, J. Onion John (1960) **Fic**
Lawson, R. Rabbit Hill (1945) **Fic**
L'Engle, M. A wrinkle in time (1963) **Fic**
Lenski, L. Strawberry girl (1946) **Fic**
Lowry, L. Number the stars (1990) **Fic**
MacLachlan, P. Sarah, plain and tall (1986) **Fic**
McKinley, R. The hero and the crown (1985) **Fic**
Neville, E. C. It's like this, Cat (1964) **Fic**
O'Brien, R. C. Mrs. Frisby and the rats of NIMH (1972) **Fic**
O'Dell, S. Island of the Blue Dolphins (1961) **Fic**
Paterson, K. Bridge to Terabithia (1978) **Fic**
Raskin, E. The Westing game (1979) **Fic**
Seredy, K. The white stag (1938) **Fic**
Sorensen, V. E. Miracles on Maple Hill (1957) **Fic**
Speare, E. G. The bronze bow (1962) **Fic**
Speare, E. G. The witch of Blackbird Pond (1959) **Fic**
Sperry, A. Call it courage (1941) **Fic**
Spinelli, J. Maniac Magee (1991) **Fic**
Taylor, M. D. Roll of thunder, hear my cry (1977) **Fic**
Treviño, E. B. de. I, Juan de Pareja (1966) **Fic**
Vining, E. G. Adam of the road (1943) **Fic**
Voigt, C. Dicey's song (1983) **Fic**
Willard, N. A visit to William Blake's inn (1982) **811**
Wojciechowska, M. Shadow of a bull (1965) **Fic**
Yates, E. Amos Fortune, free man (1951) **92**
Newbery Medal books (as subject)
Newbery and Caldecott Medal books, 1966-1975 **028.5**
Newbery and Caldecott Medal books, 1976-1985 **028.5**
Newbery Medal books, 1922-1955 **028.5**
Newbery Medal books, 1922-1955 **028.5**
Newlands, Anne
(comp) Degas, E. Meet Edgar Degas **759.4**
Newman, Alan R.
(jt. auth) Saul, W. Science fare: an illustrated guide and catalog of toys, books, and activities for kids **507**
Newman, Deborah
Christmas at the Cratchits
In The Big book of Christmas plays p240-49 **808.82**

Newman, Deborah—*Continued*
The Christmas question
In Holiday plays round the year p23-27 **812.008**

Newman, Robert, 1909-1988
The case of the Baker Street Irregular (5 and up) **Fic**
The case of the Indian curse. See note under Newman, R. The case of the Baker Street Irregular **Fic**
The case of the murdered players. See note under Newman, R. The case of the Baker Street Irregular **Fic**
The case of the threatened king. See note under Newman, R. The case of the Baker Street Irregular **Fic**
The case of the vanishing corpse. See note under Newman, R. The case of the Baker Street Irregular **Fic**
The case of the watching boy. See note under Newman, R. The case of the Baker Street Irregular **Fic**

The **news** about dinosaurs. Lauber, P. **567.9**

Newsletter on Intellectual Freedom **323.44**

Newsom, Carol, 1948-
(il) Carris, J. D. Pets, vets, and Marty Howard **Fic**
(il) Hermes, P. Kevin Corbett eats flies **Fic**
(il) Lear, E. An Edward Lear alphabet **821**

Newspapers
See also American newspapers; Periodicals
Gibbons, G. Deadline! (1-3) **070**
Leedy, L. The furry news (k-3) **070**
Fiction
Jones, R. C. Germy blew the Bugle (4-6) **Fic**

Newton, James R.
A forest is reborn (2-4) **574.5**
Rain shadow (2-5) **574.5**

Next-door neighbors. Ellis, S. **Fic**

Next turn to the right. Leach, M.
In Leach, M. Whistle in the graveyard p103-04 **398.2**

Nez Percé Indians
Osinski, A. The Nez Perce (2-4) **970.004**
See/See also pages in the following book(s):
Freedman, R. Indian chiefs p91-113 (6 and up) **920**

Ng, Simon
(il) Yee, P. Tales from Gold Mountain **S C**

Ngunza, who outwitted death. Chatelain, H.
In The Crest and the hide, and other African stories of heroes, chiefs, bards, hunters, sorcerers, and common people p63-68 **398.2**

Nguyen, Chi Thien, 1933-
Cooking the Vietnamese way (5 and up) **641.5**

Nibble nibble: poems for children. Brown, M. W. **811**

Nice and clean. Rockwell, A. F. **648**

Nice new neighbors. Brandenberg, F. **E**

Nicholas I, Emperor of Russia, 1796-1855
See/See also pages in the following book(s):
Andrews, W. G. The land and the people of the Soviet Union p70-74 (5 and up) **947**

Nicholas Cricket. Maxner, J. **E**

Nichols, Grace
Come on into my tropical garden (3-5) **821**

Nichols, Judy
Storytimes for two-year-olds **027.62**

Nicholson, Darrel
Wild boars (3-6) **599.73**

Nicholson, Sir William, 1872-1949
(il) Bianco, M. W. The velveteen rabbit **Fic**

Nicknames
Meltzer, M. A book about names (5 and up) **929.4**
Shankle, G. E. American nicknames **929.4**

Nicola Bayley's book of nursery rhymes (k-1) **398.8**

Nicolas, where have you been? Lionni, L. **E**

Nielsen, Kay Rasmus, 1886-1957
(il) Asbjørnsen, P. C. East of the sun and west of the moon: old tales from the North **398.2**

Nielsen, Nancy J.
(ed) Fisher, G. L. The survival guide for kids with LD (learning differences) **371.9**

Nigeria
Nigeria—in pictures (5 and up) **966.9**
Folklore
See Folklore—Nigeria

Nigeria—in pictures (5 and up) **966.9**

Night
See also Bedtime; Day
Banks, M. Animals of the night **E**
Branley, F. M. What makes day and night (k-3) **525**
Fiction
Aliki. Overnight at Mary Bloom's **E**

Night—Fiction—*Continued*
Babbitt, N. The something E
Berger, B. Grandfather Twilight E
Bond, F. Poinsettia and the firefighters E
Bonsall, C. N. Who's afraid of the dark? E
Brown, M. W. Goodnight moon E
Brown, M. W. Margaret Wise Brown's A child's good night book E
Brown, M. W. Wait till the moon is full E
Bunting, E. Ghost's hour, spook's hour E
Cooney, N. E. Go away monsters, lickety split! E
Crowe, R. L. Clyde monster E
Denslow, S. P. Night owls E
Dragonwagon, C. Half a moon and one whole star E
Durán, C. Hildilid's night E
Fox, M. Night noises E
Ginsburg, M. The sun's asleep behind the hill E
Grifalconi, A. Darkness and the butterfly E
Murphy, J. Peace at last E
Rice, E. City night E
Rice, E. Goodnight, goodnight E
Rylant, C. Night in the country E
Skofield, J. Nightdances E
Tejima, K. Owl lake E
Udry, J. M. The moon jumpers E
Weiss, N. Where does the brown bear go? E
Wolff, A. Only the cat saw E

Poetry

Highwater, J. Moonsong lullaby (k-2) **811**

The **night** after Christmas. Stevenson, J. E
The **night** before Christmas. Moore, C. C. **811**
Night crawler. Crompton, A. E.
In Things that go bump in the night p91-102 **S C**
Night dive. McGovern, A. **797.2**
Night in the country. Rylant, C. E
The **night** it rained. Schwartz, A.
In Schwartz, A. In a dark, dark room, and other scary stories p42-49 **398.2**
Night markets. Horwitz, J. **381**
Night noises. Fox, M. E
Night of ghosts and hermits. Stolz, M. **574.92**
The **night** of the Bozos. Slepian, J. **Fic**
The **Night** of the Leonids. Konigsburg, E. L.
In Konigsburg, E. L. Altogether, one at a time p13-28 **S C**
Night of the twisters. Ruckman, I. **Fic**
Night owls. Denslow, S. P. E
The **night** sky book. Jobb, J. **523**
The **night** swimmers. Byars, B. C. **Fic**
The **night** we slept outside. Rockwell, A. F. E
The **night** we started dancing. Cameron, A.
In Free to be—a family p96-104 **810.8**
A **night** without stars. Howe, J. **Fic**
Nightbirds on Nantucket. Aiken, J. See note under Aiken, J. The wolves of Willoughby Chase **Fic**
Nightdances. Skofield, J. E
Nightingale
Andersen, H. C. The nightingale **Fic**
also in Andersen, H. C. Hans Andersen: his classic fairy tales p19-28 **S C**
also in Shedlock, M. L. The art of the story-teller p243-58 **372.6**
also in The Yellow fairy book p291-300 **398.2**
Thane, A. The Emperor's nightingale
In Thane, A. Plays from famous stories and fairy tales p3-19 **812**
The **nightingale** and the rose. Wilde, O.
In Wilde, O. The Happy Prince, and other stories p13-20 **S C**
Nightingales

Fiction

Andersen, H. C. The nightingale (2-5) **Fic**

A **nightmare** in history. Chaikin, M. **940.54**
Nightmares: poems to trouble your sleep. Prelutsky, J. **811**
Nighty-nightmare. Howe, J. See note under Howe, J. The celery stalks at midnight **Fic**
Nikita the Tanner
Afanas'ev, A. N. Nikita the Tanner
In Afanas'ev, A. N. Russian fairy tales p310-11 **398.2**
Nilsson, Lennart, 1922-
(il) Kitzinger, S. Being born **612.6**
Nilsson, Ulf, 1948-
If you didn't have me (3-5) **Fic**
Nine-in-one, Grr! Grr! Spagnoli, C. **398.2**
The **nineteen** fifties. See Tames, R. The 1950s **909.82**
The **nineteen** forties. See Wood, T. The 1940s **909.82**

Ninjitsu *See* Ninjutsu
Ninjutsu
See/See also pages in the following book(s):
Ribner, S. The martial arts p174-80 (5 and up) **796.8**
Nix in the pond
Grimm, J. The nixie of the mill-pond
In Grimm, J. The complete Grimm's fairy tales p736-42 **398.2**
The Nixy
In The Yellow fairy book p108-13 **398.2**
Nix Nought Nothing
Jacobs, J. Nix Nought Nothing
In Jacobs, J. English fairy tales p33-39 **398.2**
The **nixie** of the mill-pond. Grimm, J.
In Grimm, J. The complete Grimm's fairy tales p736-42 **398.2**
Nixon, Joan Lowery, 1927-
Beats me, Claude **E**
A family apart (5 and up) **Fic**
NLS/BPH *See* Library of Congress. National Library Service for the Blind and Physically Handicapped
No bath tonight. Yolen, J. **E**
No beasts! no children! [excerpt]. Keller, B.
In The Random House book of humor for children p270-75 **817.008**
No fighting, no biting! Minarik, E. H. **E**
No friends. Stevenson, J. See note under Stevenson, J. "Could be worse!" **E**
No good in art. Cohen, M. See note under Cohen, M. See you in second grade! **E**
The **no-guitar** blues. Soto, G.
In Soto, G. Baseball in April, and other stories p43-51 **S C**
No measles, no mumps for me. Showers, P. **614.4**
No more baths. Cole, B. **E**
No more secrets for me. Wachter, O. **362.7**
No nap. Bunting, E. **E**
No need for Monty. Stevenson, J. See note under Stevenson, J. Monty **E**
No roses for Harry! Zion, G. See note under Zion, G. Harry the dirty dog **E**
No star nights. Smucker, A. E. **E**
No such things. Peet, B. **E**
Noah and the ark (1-3) **222**
Noah and the ark. De Paola, T. **222**
Noah's ark
De Paola, T. Noah and the ark (k-2) **222**
Geisert, A. The ark (k-3) **222**
Hogrogian, N. Noah's ark (k-3) **222**
Noah and the ark (1-3) **222**
Fiction
Rounds, G. Washday on Noah's ark **E**
Nobel prizes
Aaseng, N. The inventors: Nobel prizes in chemistry, physics, and medicine (5 and up) **609**
Noble, Trinka Hakes
Apple tree Christmas **E**
The day Jimmy's boa ate the wash **E**
Jimmy's boa and the big splash birthday bash. See note under Noble, T. H. The day Jimmy's boa ate the wash **E**
Jimmy's boa bounces back. See note under Noble, T. H. The day Jimmy's boa ate the wash **E**
Meanwhile back at the ranch **E**
Nobleman and the peasant
Afanas'ev, A. N. The nobleman and the peasant
In Afanas'ev, A. N. Russian fairy tales p59-61 **398.2**
Nobody asked me if I wanted a baby sister. Alexander, M. G. **E**
Nobody believes in witches. Watkins, M. S.
In Holiday plays round the year p141-50 **812.008**
Nobody here but you and me. Leach, M.
In Leach, M. Whistle in the graveyard p28-29 **398.2**
Nobody's family is going to change. Fitzhugh, L. **Fic**
Nockels, David
(il) Lane, M. The beaver **599.32**
Nodey, the priest's grandson
Afanas'ev, A. N. Nodey, the priest's grandson
In Afanas'ev, A. N. Russian fairy tales p173-77 **398.2**
Nodset, Joan L. *See* Lexau, Joan M.
Nogales, Luis
See/See also pages in the following book(s):
Morey, J. Famous Mexican Americans p75-87 (5 and up) **920**
The **noise** in the woods. Lester, J.
In Lester, J. The tales of Uncle Remus p113-15 **398.2**
Noisy. Hughes, S. See note under Hughes, S. Bathwater's hot **E**
Noisy Nora. Wells, R. **E**
Nolan, Dennis, 1945-
(il) Ryder, J. Under your feet **811**
Nolan, Jeannette Covert
Happy Christmas to all
In The Big book of Christmas plays p137-50 **808.82**

Nolan, Paul T., 1919-
Sherlock Holmes' Christmas goose
In The Big book of Christmas plays p298-312 **808.82**
Noll, Sally
Watch where you go **E**
Non-proliferation of nuclear weapons *See* Arms control
Nonbook materials *See* Audiovisual materials
None of my business. Aleksin, A.
In Face to face: a collection of stories by celebrated Soviet and American writers p153-63 **S C**
Nonnast, Marie
(il) Dalgliesh, A. The Fourth of July story **973.3**
Nonsense literature for children. Anderson, C. C. **028.5**
The **nonsense** verse of Edward Lear. Lear, E. **821**
Nonsense verses
See also Limericks; Tongue twisters
Belloc, H. The bad child's book of beasts, and More beasts for worse children, and A moral alphabet (1-4) **821**
Carroll, L. Lewis Carroll's Jabberwocky **821**
Carroll, L. The walrus and the carpenter **821**
Ciardi, J. I met a man (1-3) **811**
Cummings, E. E. Hist whist and other poems for children (3-6) **811**
A Great big ugly man came up and tied his horse to me (k-3) **821.008**
Heilbroner, J. This is the house where Jack lives **E**
Kennedy, X. J. Brats (3-6) **811**
Kennedy, X. J. Fresh brats (3-6) **811**
Kennedy, X. J. Ghastlies, goops & pincushions: nonsense verse (3-6) **811**
Lear, E. The complete nonsense of Edward Lear **821**
Lear, E. An Edward Lear alphabet (k-2) **821**
Lear, E. Edward Lear's The Scroobious Pip **821**
Lear, E. How pleasant to know Mr. Lear! **821**
Lear, E. The Jumblies (2-6) **821**
Lear, E. The nonsense verse of Edward Lear **821**
Lear, E. The owl and the pussycat (k-2) **821**
Merriam, E. Blackberry ink (k-2) **811**
Morrison, B. Squeeze a sneeze (k-3) **811**
Oh, such foolishness! (3-6) **821.008**
Oh, that's ridiculous! (3-6) **821.008**
Prelutsky, J. The baby Uggs are hatching (k-3) **811**
Prelutsky, J. Beneath a blue umbrella: rhymes (k-3) **811**
Prelutsky, J. The queen of Eene (k-3) **811**
Prelutsky, J. Ride a purple pelican (k-3) **811**
Prelutsky, J. The sheriff of Rottenshot: poems (2-5) **811**
Prelutsky, J. The snopp on the sidewalk, and other poems (k-4) **811**
Seuss, Dr. And to think that I saw it on Mulberry Street **E**
Seuss, Dr. The cat in the hat **E**
Seuss, Dr. The cat in the hat comes back! **E**
Seuss, Dr. Green eggs and ham **E**
Seuss, Dr. Horton hatches the egg **E**
Seuss, Dr. Horton hears a Who! **E**
Seuss, Dr. How the Grinch stole Christmas **E**
Seuss, Dr. If I ran the circus **E**
Seuss, Dr. If I ran the zoo **E**
Seuss, Dr. McElligot's pool **E**
Silverstein, S. A light in the attic (3 and up) **811**
Silverstein, S. Where the sidewalk ends (3 and up) **811**
Watson, C. Father Fox's pennyrhymes (k-3) **811**
Westcott, N. B. The lady with the alligator purse **E**
Willard, N. A visit to William Blake's inn (2-5) **811**
See/See also pages in the following book(s):
Piping down the valleys wild p21-36 **808.81**
Rainbow in the sky p351-82 (k-4) **821.008**
Nonstop nonsense. Mahy, M. **828**
The **noodle**. Kendall, C.
In Kendall, C. Sweet and sour p100-05 **398.2**
Noonan, Julia
(il) Yep, L. Sweetwater **Fic**
Nora and Mrs. Mind-Your-Own-Business. Hurwitz, J. See note under Hurwitz, J. Busybody Nora **Fic**
Nordstrom, Ursula, 1910-1988
The secret language (3-5) **Fic**
The **Norka**
In The Red fairy book p116-22 **398.2**
Norman, David
Dinosaur (4 and up) **567.9**
Norman, Howard
How Glooskap outwits the Ice Giants, and other tales of the Maritime Indians (3-6) **398.2**
Contents: How Glooskap made human beings; How Glooskap outwits the Ice Giants; Why the sea winds are the strength they are today; Glooskap gets two surprises;

Norman, Howard—*Continued*
How magic friend fox helped Glooskap against the panther-witch; How Glooskap sang through the rapids and found a new home

Norman the doorman. Freeman, D. **E**

Normandy (France), Attack on, 1944
Bliven, B. The story of D-Day: June 6, 1944 (5 and up) **940.54**

Norodom Sihanouk, Prince, 1922-
See/See also pages in the following book(s):
Chandler, D. P. The land and people of Cambodia p110-31 (5 and up) **959.6**

A **Norse** lullaby. Van Vorst, M. L. **811**

Norse mythology *See* Mythology, Norse

Norsemen *See* Vikings

Norsgaard, Campbell
(il) Norsgaard, E. J. Nature's great balancing act **574.5**

Norsgaard, E. Jaediker (Ernestine Jaediker)
Nature's great balancing act (4-6) **574.5**

Norsgaard, Ernestine Jaediker *See* Norsgaard, E. Jaediker (Ernestine Jaediker)

North, Sterling, 1906-1974
Abe Lincoln: log cabin to White House (5 and up) **92**
Rascal (5 and up) **599.74**

North American Indians *See* Indians of North America

North Carolina
Stein, R. C. North Carolina
In America the beautiful **973**
Fiction
Hooks, W. H. Circle of fire (5 and up) **Fic**

North country night. San Souci, D. **591.5**

North Dakota
Herguth, M. S. North Dakota
In America the beautiful **973**

North Pole
See also Arctic regions
Ferris, J. Arctic explorer: the story of Matthew Henson (3-6) **92**
Fiction
Van Allsburg, C. The Polar Express **E**

The **North** Pole computer caper. Priore, F. V.
In The Big book of Christmas plays p189-99 **808.82**

North to freedom. Holm, A. **Fic**

Northern lights *See* Auroras

A **northern** nativity. Kurelek, W. **232.9**

Northern Rhodesia *See* Zambia

Northmen *See* Vikings

Northway, Jennifer
(il) Samuels, V. Carry, go, bring, come **E**

Northwest, Pacific *See* Pacific Northwest

Norton, Alice Mary *See* Norton, Andre, 1912-

Norton, Andre, 1912-
See/See also pages in the following book(s):
Townsend, J. R. A sense of story p143-49 **028.5**

Norton, Mary, 1903-
Bed-knob and broomstick (3-5) **Fic**
Bonfires and broomsticks
In Norton, M. Bed-knob and broomstick p97-189 **Fic**
The Borrowers (3-6) **Fic**
The Borrowers afield. See note under Norton, M. The Borrowers **Fic**
The Borrowers afloat. See note under Norton, M. The Borrowers **Fic**
The Borrowers aloft. See note under Norton, M. The Borrowers **Fic**
The Borrowers avenged. See note under Norton, M. The Borrowers **Fic**
The magic bed-knob
In Norton, M. Bed-knob and broomstick p11-94 **Fic**
Poor Stainless. See note under Norton, M. The Borrowers **Fic**

Norway
Norway—in pictures (5 and up) **948.1**
Folklore
See Folklore—Norway

Norway—in pictures (5 and up) **948.1**

Nose
Fiction
Brown, M. T. Arthur's nose **E**

Not a pin to choose between them. Asbjørnsen, P. C.
In Best-loved folktales of the world p340-44 **398.2**

The **not-just-anybody** family. Byars, B. C. **Fic**

Not my family: sharing the truth about alcoholism. Rosenberg, M. B. **362.29**

Not so fast, Songololo. Daly, N. **E**

Notable children's books, 1976-1980. Association for Library Service to Children (U.S.). Notable Children's Books, 1976-1980, Reevaluation Committee **011.6**

Notable children's films and videos, filmstrips, and recordings, 1973-1986 **016.3713**

Notable children's trade books in the field of social studies **016.3**

Notes from a different drummer. Baskin, B. H. **016.8**

Nothing. Hughes, R.
In Bauer, C. F. Celebrations p144-45 **808.8**

Nothing At All. Gág, W. E
Nothing ever happens on my block. Raskin, E. E
Nothing sticks like a shadow. Tompert, A. E
Nothing to be ashamed of: growing up with mental illness in your family. Dinner, S. H. 362.2
Nothing's impossible! stunts to entertain and amaze. Sheridan, J. 793.8
Noureddin and the beautiful Persian
Noureddin and the fair Persian
In The Arabian nights entertainments p267-94 398.2
Nourse, Alan Edward, 1928-
Menstruation (6 and up) 612.6
Nova (Television program)
Hadingham, E. Garbage! 363.7
Harrar, G. Radical robots 629.8
Heberman, E. The city kid's field guide 591
Herberman, E. The great butterfly hunt 595.7
Maurer, R. Airborne 629.13
Maurer, R. Junk in space 363.7
Novelty and romancement. Carroll, L.
In Carroll, L. The complete works of Lewis Carroll p970-78 828
Now one foot, now the other. De Paola, T. E
Now we are six. Milne, A. A. 821
also in Milne, A. A. The world of Christopher Robin p119-234 821
Now we can go. Jonas, A. E
Now you see it: easy magic for beginners. Broekel, R. 793.8
Noyes, Alfred, 1880-1958
The highwayman (5 and up) 821
Nozaki, Akihiro
Anno's hat tricks (1-4) 153.4
Ntombi's song. Seed, J. E
Nuckelavee. San Souci, R.
In San Souci, R. Short & shivery p92-95 398.2
Nuclear energy
Asimov, I. How did we find out about nuclear power? (5 and up) 539.7
Pringle, L. P. Nuclear energy: troubled past, uncertain future (5 and up) 621.48
Nuclear physics
Berger, M. Our atomic world (4 and up) 539.7
Nuclear power. See Pringle, L. P. Nuclear energy: troubled past, uncertain future 621.48
Nuclear submarines
Rutland, J. See inside a submarine (4-6) 623.8
Nuclear weapons
See also Atomic bomb
Nuclear weapons and disarmament *See* Arms control
Nuestra Señora de Atocha (Ship)
Gibbons, G. Sunken treasure (2-4) 910.4
Nuinumma-Kwiten. Leach, M.
In Leach, M. Whistle in the graveyard p88 398.2
Number art: thirteen 1 2 3s from around the world. Fisher, L. E. 513
Number systems *See* Numeration
Number the stars. Lowry, L. Fic
Number theory
See also Factorials; Numeration
Numbers. Reiss, J. J. E
Numblers. Macdonald, S. E
Numerals
Adler, D. A. Roman numerals (2-4) 513
Fisher, L. E. Number art: thirteen 1 2 3s from around the world (4 and up) 513
Numeration
See also Counting
Sitomer, M. How did numbers begin? (2-4) 513
Numeroff, Laura Joffe
If you give a mouse a cookie E
Numismatics
See also Coins
Nunes, Susan, 1937-
Coyote dreams E
Tiddalick the frog (k-2) 398.2
Nuñez Cabeza de Vaca, Alvar, 16th cent. Fiction
Baker, B. Walk the world's rim (5 and up) Fic
The **nun's** priest's tale. Cohen, B.
In Cohen, B. Canterbury tales Fic
A **Nursery** companion 398.8
Nursery novelties
In A Nursery companion p16-19 820.8
Nursery rhyme book, The Helen Oxenbury 398.8
Nursery rhymes
See also Jump rope rhymes
The Annotated Mother Goose 398.8
Aylesworth, J. The completed hickory dickory dock (k-2) 398.8
The Baby's bedtime book (k-1) 808.81
The Baby's good morning book (k-1) 808.81
The Baby's lap book (k-1) 398.8

Nursery rhymes—*Continued*
Bodecker, N. M. It's raining, said John Twaining (k-2) **398.8**
Brown, M. T. Finger rhymes (k-2) **796.1**
Brown, M. T. Hand rhymes (k-2) **796.1**
Brown, M. T. Play rhymes (k-2) **796.1**
A Child's treasury of poems (3-5) **821.008**
Clap your hands (k-2) **796.1**
The Comic adventures of Old Mother Hubbard and her dog (k-3) **398.8**
Demi. Dragon kites and dragonflies (k-2) **398.8**
Emberley, B. Drummer Hoff (k-3) **398.8**
Galdone, P. The cat goes fiddle-i-fee (k-1) **398.8**
Galdone, P. Three little kittens (k-1) **398.8**
Gerstein, M. Roll over! **E**
The Glorious Mother Goose (k-2) **398.8**
Granfa' Grig had a pig, and other rhymes without reason from Mother Goose (k-3) **398.8**
Hale, S. J. Mary had a little lamb (k-2) **811**
The Helen Oxenbury nursery rhyme book (k-2) **398.8**
Hoguet, S. R. Solomon Grundy **E**
If all the seas were one sea (k-2) **398.8**
James Marshall's Mother Goose (k-3) **398.8**
The Lap-time song and play book (k-2) **782.42**
The Little dog laughed (k-2) **398.8**
Lobel, A. Whiskers & rhymes (1-3) **811**
London Bridge is falling down! (k-2) **781.62**
Marguerite de Angeli's book of nursery and Mother Goose rhymes (k-2) **398.8**
Miss Mary Mack and other children's street rhymes (1-4) **796.1**
Mother Goose [illus. by Michael Hague] (k-2) **398.8**
Mother Goose [illus. by Tasha Tudor] (k-2) **398.8**
Mother Goose [illus. by Brian Wildsmith] (k-2) **398.8**
The Mother Goose songbook (k-2) **782.42**
The Mother Goose treasury (k-3) **398.8**
Nicola Bayley's book of nursery rhymes (k-1) **398.8**
A Nursery companion **398.8**
The Oxford Nursery rhyme book **398.8**
Patz, N. Moses supposes his toeses are roses and 7 other silly old rhymes (k-2) **398.8**
Potter, B. Cecily Parsley's nursery rhymes (k-3) **398.8**
Prelutsky, J. Beneath a blue umbrella: rhymes (k-3) **811**
Prelutsky, J. Ride a purple pelican (k-3) **811**
Rainbow in the sky (k-4) **821.008**
The Random House book of Mother Goose (k-2) **398.8**
Read-aloud rhymes for the very young (k-2) **821.008**
The Real Mother Goose (k-2) **398.8**
The Rooster crows (k-2) **398.8**
Sendak, M. Hector Protector, and As I went over the water (k-1) **398.8**
Sing a song of sixpence (k-2) **398.8**
Songs from Mother Goose (k-3) **782.42**
Stamp your feet (k-2) **796.1**
Tail feathers from Mother Goose (k-2) **398.8**
Ten potatoes in a pot, and other counting rhymes (k-2) **398.8**
This little pig-a-wig, and other rhymes about pigs (k-2) **398.8**
To market! To market! (k-2) **398.8**
Tomie dePaola's Mother Goose (k-2) **398.8**
Tortillitas para mamá and other nursery rhymes (k-2) **398.8**
Trot, trot to Boston: play rhymes for baby (k-1) **398.8**
Watson, C. Catch me & kiss me & say it again: rhymes (k-1) **811**
Watson, C. Father Fox's pennyrhymes (k-3) **811**
Wendy Watson's Mother Goose (k-2) **398.8**

Dictionaries

The Oxford dictionary of nursery rhymes **398.8**

Nursery schools

See also Education, Preschool

Fiction

Grindley, S. I don't want to! **E**
Hurwitz, J. Rip-roaring Russell (2-4) **Fic**
Oxenbury, H. First day of school **E**

Nursery story book, The Helen Oxenbury. Oxenbury, H. **398.2**

Nurses

Cosner, S. War nurses (6 and up) **355.3**
Crofford, E. Healing warrior: a story about Sister Elizabeth Kenny (3-5) **92**

The **nutcracker**. Bell, A. **Fic**

Nutcracker. Hoffmann, E. T. A. **Fic**

Nutrition

See also Diet

Foodworks (4-6) **641.3**
Seixas, J. S. Junk food—what it is, what it does (1-3) **641.3**
Ward, B. R. Diet and nutrition (4 and up) **641.1**

Nutrition—*Continued*
See/See also pages in the following book(s):
Yepsen, R. B. Smarten up! how to increase your brain power p23-32 (5 and up) **153**

Nuts. Babbitt, N.
In Babbitt, N. The Devil's storybook p47-51 **S C**

Nutt, Ken, 1951-
(il) Fleischman, P. I am phoenix: poems for two voices **811**

Nye, Robert, 1939-
Beowulf against Grendel
In Bauer, C. F. Celebrations p105-08 **808.8**

NYPL *See* New York Public Library

O

Oakes, Bill
Puzzlers **E**
(jt. auth) Macdonald, S. Numblers **E**

Oakley, Annie, 1860-1926
About
Quackenbush, R. M. Who's that girl with the gun? a story of Annie Oakley (2-4) **92**

Oakley, Graham
The church cat abroad. See note under Oakley, G. The church mouse **E**
The church mice adrift. See note under Oakley, G. The church mouse **E**
The church mice and the moon. See note under Oakley, G. The church mouse **E**
The church mice at bay. See note under Oakley, G. The church mouse **E**
The church mice at Christmas. See note under Oakley, G. The church mouse **E**
The church mice in action. See note under Oakley, G. The church mouse **E**
The church mice spread their wings. See note under Oakley, G. The church mouse **E**
The church mouse **E**
The diary of a church mouse. See note under Oakley, G. The church mouse **E**
Graham Oakley's magical changes **E**
Hetty and Harriet **E**

Oatman, Olive Ann
Fiction
Lampman, E. S. White captives (5 and up) **Fic**

Obadiah the Bold. Turkle, B. C. **E**

Obesity
Control
See Reducing

Obojski, Robert
(ed) Reinfeld, F. Catalogue of the world's most popular coins **737.4**

O'Brien, Anne Sibley, 1952-
(il) Havill, J. Jamaica tag-along **E**

O'Brien, John, 1953-
(il) Glazer, T. Tom Glazer's Treasury of songs for children **782.42**
(il) Schwartz, A. Flapdoodle: pure nonsense from American folklore **398**

O'Brien, Robert C.
Mrs. Frisby and the rats of NIMH (4 and up) **Fic**
See/See also pages in the following book(s):
Newbery and Caldecott Medal books, 1966-1975 p83-92 **028.5**

Occult sciences
See also Astrology; Divination; Fortune telling; Magic; Witchcraft
Fiction
Snyder, Z. K. The headless cupid (5 and up) **Fic**

Occupational guidance *See* Vocational guidance

Occupations
Johnson, N. All in a day's work (4 and up) **331.7**
Merriam, E. Mommies at work (k-3) **331.4**
Miller, M. Who uses this? **E**
Rosenberg, M. B. Artists of handcrafted furniture at work (4 and up) **749**

Ocean
See also Pacific Ocean; Seashore
Bramwell, M. The oceans (4-6) **551.46**
Cook, J. L. The mysterious undersea world (4 and up) **551.46**
Simon, S. Oceans (3-5) **551.46**
See/See also pages in the following book(s):
Gallant, R. A. Our restless earth p70-79 (4 and up) **550**

Ocean bottom
See/See also pages in the following book(s):
Mango, K. N. Mapmaking p78-85 (4 and up) **526**

Oceanographic submersibles *See* Submersibles

Oceanography
Experiments
Simon, S. How to be an ocean scientist in your own home (4 and up) **551.46**

The **oceans.** Bramwell, M. **551.46**
O'Connell, Susan M.
(ed) The Best science books & A-V materials for children. See The Best science books & A-V materials for children **016.5**
O'Connor, Jane, 1947-
Lulu and the witch baby. See note under O'Connor, J. Lulu goes to witch school **E**
Lulu goes to witch school **E**
Yours till Niagara Falls, Abby **Fic**
Octopus
Carrick, C. Octopus (2-4) **594**
Fiction
Waber, B. I was all thumbs **E**
O'Cuilleanáin, Eilís Dillon *See* Dillon, Eilís, 1920-
Oddities *See* Curiosities and wonders
O'Dell, Scott, 1903-1989
The amethyst ring. See note under O'Dell, S. The captive **Fic**
The black pearl (6 and up) **Fic**
The captive (6 and up) **Fic**
Carlota [excerpt]
In Face to face: a collection of stories by celebrated Soviet and American writers p165-76 **S C**
The feathered serpent. See note under O'Dell, S. The captive **Fic**
Island of the Blue Dolphins (5 and up) **Fic**
The King's fifth (5 and up) **Fic**
My name is not Angelica (5 and up) **Fic**
Sarah Bishop (6 and up) **Fic**
Sing down the moon (5 and up) **Fic**
Streams to the river, river to the sea (5 and up) **Fic**
Zia (5 and up) **Fic**
See/See also pages in the following book(s):
Townsend, J. R. A sense of story p154-59 **028.5**
Odijk, Pamela, 1942-
The Greeks (5 and up) **938**
O'Donnell, Elizabeth Lee
Maggie doesn't want to move **E**
Odysseus (Greek mythology)
Colum, P. The children's Homer: The adventures of Odysseus and The tale of Troy (4 and up) **883**
See/See also pages in the following book(s):
Asimov, I. Words from the myths p201-11 (6 and up) **292**
Hamilton, E. Mythology p291-318 (6 and up) **292**
Odyssey: space exploration and astronomy for young people **520.5**
Oechsli, Helen
In my garden (1-3) **635**
Oechsli, Kelly
(jt. auth) Oechsli, H. In my garden **635**
(il) Poetry for holidays. See Poetry for holidays **811.008**
Of colors and things. Hoban, T. **535.6**
Of nightingales that weep. Paterson, K. **Fic**
Of quarks, quasars, and other quirks (5 and up) **821.008**
Off limits. Sanfield, S.
In Sanfield, S. The adventures of High John the Conqueror **398.2**
Office management
See also Files and filing
Offshore oil well drilling *See* Oil well drilling, Submarine
Ogawa, Hiroshi
(il) Johnson, S. A. Wasps **595.7**
Ogden, Bill
(il) Cobb, V. More power to you **621.31**
Ogg, Oscar
The 26 letters **411**
Oglala Indians
See/See also pages in the following book(s):
Freedman, R. Indian chiefs p11-27 (6 and up) **920**
Ogre of Rashomon
Quayle, E. The ogre of Rashomon
In Quayle, E. The shining princess, and other Japanese legends p103-11 **398.2**
Ogunleye, Kunle
Peki, the musician
In The Crest and the hide, and other African stories of heroes, chiefs, bards, hunters, sorcerers, and common people p53-62 **398.2**
Oh, a-hunting we will go. Langstaff, J. M. **781.62**
Oh, Brother. Yorinks, A. **E**
Oh, can ye sew cushions? Aiken, J.
In Aiken, J. Past eight o'clock p71-86 **S C**
Oh, Kojo! How could you! Aardema, V. **398.2**

Oh my baby bear! Wood, A. **E**
Oh, such foolishness! (3-6) **821.008**
Oh, that's ridiculous! (3-6) **821.008**
Oh, the places you'll go! Seuss, Dr. **E**
Oh, were they ever happy! Spier, P. **E**
O'Hara, Mary, 1885-1980
My friend Flicka
In Herds of thunder, manes of gold p111-35 **808.8**
Ohio
Kent, D. Ohio
In America the beautiful **973**
Fiction
Cameron, E. To the green mountains (6 and up) **Fic**
DeFelice, C. C. Weasel (4 and up) **Fic**
Hamilton, V. The bells of Christmas (4-6) **Fic**
Hamilton, V. The house of Dies Drear (5 and up) **Fic**
McCloskey, R. Lentil **E**
Sanders, S. R. Aurora means dawn **E**
Ohtomo, Yasuo, 1946-
(il) Watanabe, S. How do I put it on? **E**
Oi! get off our train. See Burningham, J. Hey! get off our train **E**
Oil painting *See* Painting
Oil spills
Smith, R. Sea otter rescue (5 and up) **639.9**
Oil well drilling, Submarine
Rutland, J. See inside an oil rig and tanker (4-6) **665.5**
Oils and fats
See/See also pages in the following book(s):
Cobb, V. Gobs of goo p5-12 (2-4) **547**
Oisin's mother. Stephens, J.
In Stephens, J. Irish fairy tales p109-32 **398.2**
O'Keeffe, Georgia, 1887-1986
About
Gherman, B. Georgia O'Keeffe (5 and up) **92**
See/See also pages in the following book(s):
Sills, L. Inspirations p6-17 (5 and up) **920**
O'Kelley, Mattie Lou
From the hills of Georgia: an autobiography in paintings (2-4) **92**
Okie, Susan
(jt. auth) Ride, S. K. To space & back **629.45**
Okimoto, Jean Davies, 1942-
Blumpoe the Grumpoe meets Arnold the cat **E**
Moonbeam Dawson and the Killer bear
In Connections: short stories by outstanding writers for young adults p15-25 **S C**
Oklahoma
Heinrichs, A. Oklahoma
In America the beautiful **973**
Fiction
Bauer, M. D. Shelter from the wind (5 and up) **Fic**
The **Ol'** African helps out. Lester, J.
In Lester, J. More tales of Uncle Remus p22-26 **398.2**
Ol' Paul, the mighty logger. Rounds, G. **398.2**
Olcott, Frances Jenkins, 1872?-1963
Little Burnt-Face
In The Scott, Foresman anthology of children's literature p388-90 **808.8**
Old acquaintance is soon forgot
Afanas'ev, A. N. Old favors are soon forgotten
In Afanas'ev, A. N. Russian fairy tales p273-75 **398.2**
Old age
Fiction
Carlstrom, N. W. Blow me a kiss, Miss Lilly **E**
Cleaver, V. Queen of hearts (6 and up) **Fic**
Clifford, E. The rocking chair rebellion (6 and up) **Fic**
Coutant, H. The gift (2-5) **Fic**
Härtling, P. Old John (4 and up) **Fic**
Hest, A. The midnight eaters **E**
Jones, J. B. Secrets of a summer spy (5 and up) **Fic**
Kesselman, W. A. Emma **E**
Kessler, E. Stan the hot dog man **E**
Lasky, K. Sea swan **E**
Lee, J. M. Bà-Năm **E**
Mazer, N. F. A figure of speech (6 and up) **Fic**
Pearson, S. Happy birthday, Grampie **E**
Wittman, S. A special trade **E**
Zolotow, C. I know a lady **E**
Poetry
Farber, N. How does it feel to be old? (2-4) **811**
Old beggar woman
Grimm, J. The old beggar-woman
In Grimm, J. The complete Grimm's fairy tales p646 **398.2**
Old Ben. MacDonald, M. R.
In MacDonald, M. R. When the lights go out p104-08 **372.6**
Old Dry Frye
Old Dry Frye
In Grandfather tales p100-05 **398.2**

An **old-fashioned** Thanksgiving. Alcott, L. M. Fic

Old favors are soon forgotten. Afanas'ev, A. N.
In Afanas'ev, A. N. Russian fairy tales p273-75 398.2

Old Fire Dragaman
Old Fire Dragaman
In The Jack tales p106-13 398.2

Old Fuddlement. Kendall, C.
In Kendall, C. Sweet and sour p45-48 398.2

Old Gally Mander
Gallymanders! Gallymanders!
In Grandfather tales p18-28 398.2

Old ghosts at home. Murray, J.
In Holiday plays round the year p112-28 812.008

Old Henry. Blos, J. W. E

Old Hildebrand
Grimm, J. Old Hildebrand
In Grimm, J. The complete Grimm's fairy tales p440-44 398.2

Old house
Andersen, H. C. The old house
In Andersen, H. C. Hans Andersen: his classic fairy tales p140-48 S C

The **old** jar. Yep, L.
In Yep, L. The rainbow people p96-105 398.2

Old John. Härtling, P. Fic

Old MacDonald had a farm (k-2) 781.62

Old man and his grandson
Grimm, J. The old man and his grandson
In Grimm, J. The complete Grimm's fairy tales p363-64 398.2

Old man made young again
Grimm, J. The old man made young again
In Grimm, J. The complete Grimm's fairy tales p640-42 398.2

The **old** man who made dead trees bloom. Quayle, E.
In Quayle, E. The shining princess, and other Japanese legends p69-76 398.2

Old man who made withered trees to flower
Quayle, E. The old man who made dead trees bloom
In Quayle, E. The shining princess, and other Japanese legends p69-76 398.2

The **old** meadow. Selden, G. See note under Selden, G. The cricket in Times Square Fic

Old Mother Hubbard and her dog, The comic adventures of 398.8

Old Mother Hubbard's dog dresses up. Yeoman, J. E

Old Mother Hubbard's dog learns to play. Yeoman, J. See note under Yeoman, J. Old Mother Hubbard's dog dresses up E

Old Mother Hubbard's dog needs a doctor. Yeoman, J. See note under Yeoman, J. Old Mother Hubbard's dog dresses up E

Old Mother Hubbard's dog takes up sport. Yeoman, J. See note under Yeoman, J. Old Mother Hubbard's dog dresses up E

Old Old One's birthday. Carpenter, F.
In Carpenter, F. Tales of a Chinese grandmother p252-61 398.2

Old One-Eye
MacDonald, M. R. Old one-eye
In MacDonald, M. R. Twenty tellable tales p43-51 372.6
Old One-Eye
In Grandfather tales p205-07 398.2

Old Rinkrank
Grimm, J. Old Rinkrank
In Grimm, J. The complete Grimm's fairy tales p796-98 398.2

Old Roaney
Old Roaney
In Grandfather tales p195-204 398.2

Old sow and the three shoats
In Grandfather tales p81-87 398.2

Old Sultan
Grimm, J. Old Sultan
In Grimm, J. The complete Grimm's fairy tales p230-32 398.2

Old Tom comes home. Leach, M.
In Leach, M. Whistle in the graveyard p33 398.2

The **old** traveler. Maas, S.
In The Scott, Foresman anthology of children's literature p282-84 808.8

Old Turtle's riddle and joke book. Kessler, L. P. 793.73

Old Turtle's winter games. Kessler, L. P. E

The **old** woman and her dumpling. Hearn, L.
In Womenfolk and fairy tales p44-50 398.2

Old woman and her pig
Jacobs, J. Old woman and her pig
In Jacobs, J. English fairy tales p120-23 398.2
Little old woman and her pig
In The Tall book of nursery tales p92-97 398.2

The **old** woman and the jar of uums. Wright, J. **E**
Old woman and the tramp
The Old woman and the tramp
In Best-loved folktales of the world p377-81 **398.2**
Rockwell, A. F. Nail soup
In Rockwell, A. F. Puss in boots, and other stories p12-18 **398.2**
The **old** woman and the Willy Nilly Man. Wright, J. **E**
Old woman in the wood
Grimm, J. The old woman in the wood
In Grimm, J. The complete Grimm's fairy tales p558-60 **398.2**
The **old** woman who lost her dumplings. Hearn, L.
In Best-loved folktales of the world p506-09 **398.2**
Old woman who met the months
Megas, G. A. The twelve months
In Best-loved folktales of the world p186-90 **398.2**
Old woman who ran away
Afanas'ev, A. N. The old woman who ran away
In Afanas'ev, A. N. Russian fairy tales p182-83 **398.2**
Old Yeller. Gipson, F. B. **Fic**
The **oldest** of them all. Crossley-Holland, K.
In Crossley-Holland, K. British folk tales p178-81 **398.2**
Ole & Trufa. Singer, I. B.
In Singer, I. B. Stories for children p249-53 **S C**
Olexer, Marycile E., 1941-
Poetry anthologies for children and young people **011.6**
Olfson, Lewy
Christmas coast to coast
In The Big book of Christmas plays p80-98 **808.82**
Olga carries on. Bond, M.
In Bond, M. The complete adventures of Olga da Polga p253-387 **Fic**
Olga meets her match. Bond, M.
In Bond, M. The complete adventures of Olga da Polga p129-252 **Fic**
Olga takes charge. Bond, M.
In Bond, M. The complete adventures of Olga da Polga p389-[512] **Fic**
Oliver, Jenni
(il) Coleridge, S. January brings the snow **821**
(il) Lowry, L. A summer to die **Fic**
Oliver, Amanda, and Grandmother Pig. Van Leeuwen, J. See note under Van Leeuwen, J. Tales of Oliver Pig **E**
Oliver and Amanda's Christmas. Van Leeuwen, J. See note under Van Leeuwen, J. Tales of Oliver Pig **E**
Oliver Hyde's dishcloth concert. Kennedy, R.
In Kennedy, R. Collected stories p201-12 **S C**
Oliver Pig at school. Van Leeuwen, J. See note under Van Leeuwen, J. Tales of Oliver Pig **E**
Olmos, Edward James
See/See also pages in the following book(s):
Morey, J. Famous Mexican Americans p88-97 (5 and up) **920**
Olubo, Joseph
(il) Berry, J. Spiderman Anancy **398.2**
The **Olympians.** Fisher, L. E. **292**
Olympic games
Glubok, S. Olympic games in ancient Greece (5 and up) **796.48**
Trenary, J. Time of my life: Jill Trenary (4 and up) **92**
Olympic games in ancient Greece. Glubok, S. **796.48**
Oma and Bobo. Schwartz, A. **E**
Oman
Social life and customs
Dutton, R. An Arab family (3-5) **953**
On city streets (5 and up) **811.008**
On divorce. Stein, S. B. **306.89**
On Granddaddy's farm. Allen, T. B. **630.1**
On Market Street. Lobel, A. **E**
On my honor. Bauer, M. D. **Fic**
On our own terms. Bergman, T. **362.4**
On Shark's Tooth Beach. Konigsburg, E. L.
In Konigsburg, E. L. Throwing shadows **S C**
On the banks of Plum Creek. Wilder, L. I. See note under Wilder, L. I. Little house in the big woods **Fic**
On the day Peter Stuyvesant sailed into town. Lobel, A. **E**
On the far side of the mountain. George, J. C. **Fic**
On the frontier with Mr. Audubon. Brenner, B. **Fic**
On the trail of the fox. Schnieper, C. **599.74**
Once there was a tree. Romanova, N. **582.16**

Once upon a horse. Jurmain, S. **636.1**
Once upon a mouse. Brown, M. **398.2**
Once upon a time—: celebrating the magic of children's books in honor of the twentieth anniversary of Reading is Fundamental **028.5**
One act plays
The Big book of Christmas plays **808.82**
Gotwalt, H. L. M. Everyday plays for boys and girls (4 and up) **812**
Gotwalt, H. L. M. Special plays for holidays **812**
Holiday plays round the year (4 and up) **812.008**
Thane, A. Plays from famous stories and fairy tales (4-6) **812**
One at a time. McCord, D. T. W. **811**
One crow. Aylesworth, J. **E**
One day at a time. Bergman, T. **616.99**
One day in the alpine tundra. George, J. C. **574.5**
One day in the desert. George, J. C. **574.5**
One day in the prairie. George, J. C. **574.5**
One day in the tropical rain forest. George, J. C. **574.5**
One day in the woods. George, J. C. **574.5**
One duck, another duck. Pomerantz, C. **E**
One-eye, Two-eyes, Three-eyes
Grimm, J. Little One-eye, Little Two-eyes, and Little Three-eyes
In The Green fairy book p262-70 **398.2**
Grimm, J. One-eye, Two-eyes, and Three-eyes
In Grimm, J. The complete Grimm's fairy tales p585-92 **398.2**
One-eyed cat. Fox, P. **Fic**
The **one-eyed** evil. Afanas'ev, A. N.
In Afanas'ev, A. N. Russian fairy tales p404-06 **398.2**
One-eyed Likho
Afanas'ev, A. N. The one-eyed evil
In Afanas'ev, A. N. Russian fairy tales p404-06 **398.2**
One fine day. Hogrogian, N. **398.2**
One frog too many. Mayer, M. See note under Mayer, M. A boy, a dog, and a frog **E**
One good horse. Scott, A. H. **E**
One good turn deserves another
Pyle, H. One good turn deserves another
In Pyle, H. The wonder clock p89-104 **398.2**
One hairball. Kendall, C.
In Kendall, C. Sweet and sour p73-77 **398.2**
One-handed girl
Afanas'ev, A. N. The armless maiden
In Afanas'ev, A. N. Russian fairy tales p294-99 **398.2**
One handful. Leach, M.
In Leach, M. Whistle in the graveyard p41-42 **398.2**
One hundred and one costumes for all ages, all occasions. See Cummings, R. 101 costumes for all ages, all occasions **391**
One hundred and one things to do with a baby. Ormerod, J. **E**
The **one** hundredth thing about Caroline. Lowry, L. **Fic**
One hunter. See Hutchins, P. 1 hunter **E**
One inch fellow
Morimoto, J. The inch boy **398.2**
One light, one sun. Raffi. **782.42**
One little kitten. Hoban, T. **E**
One Monday morning. Shulevitz, U. **E**
One morning in Maine. McCloskey, R. **E**
"One, my darling, come to Mama"
In The Magic orange tree, and other Haitian folktales p165-70 **398.2**
One parent family *See* Single parent family
One step, two—. Zolotow, C. **E**
One sun: a book of terse verse. McMillan, B. **811**
One tough turkey. Kroll, S. **E**
One two three, play with me. See Gundersheimer, K. 1 2 3, play with me **E**
One was Johnny. Sendak, M. **E**
The **One** who would not listen to his own dream
In The Magic orange tree, and other Haitian folktales p71-74 **398.2**
The **one** you don't see coming. Courlander, H.
In Courlander, H. The cow-tail switch, and other West African stories p31-40 **398.2**
One zillion valentines. Modell, F. **E**
Oneal, Elizabeth *See* Oneal, Zibby, 1934-
Oneal, Zibby, 1934-
Grandma Moses: painter of rural America (4 and up) **92**
A long way to go (3-5) **Fic**
O'Neill, Catharine
(il) Fatchen, M. The country mail is coming **821**
O'Neill, Catherine, 1950-
Focus on alcohol (3-6) **362.29**

O'Neill, Catherine, 1950-—*Continued*
Natural wonders of North America (5 and up) 557
You won't believe your eyes! (4 and up) 152.14
O'Neill, Mary Le Duc, 1908-1990
Hailstones and halibut bones (k-3) 811
Oni and the great bird. Fuja, A.
In Best-loved folktales of the world p644-49 398.2
Onion John. Krumgold, J. Fic
Only a fair day's huntin'
Only a fair day's huntin'
In Grandfather tales p180-85 398.2
Only connect: readings on children's literature 028.5
Only the cat saw. Wolff, A. E
Only the names remain. Bealer, A. W. 970.004
Ontario Science Centre
Foodworks. See Foodworks 641.3
Oona and the giant Cuchulain. Riordan, J.
In Riordan, J. The woman in the moon, and other tales of forgotten heroines p35-41 398.2
Oonga boonga. Wishinsky, F. E
The **open** road. Grahame, K. Fic
Operas
Stories, plots, etc.
Price, L. Aïda (4 and up) 792.5
Rosenberg, J. Sing me a story (4-6) 792.5
Operation grizzly bear. Calabro, M. 599.74
Opie, Iona Archibald
Children's games in street and playground 796.1
The lore and language of schoolchildren 398
(ed) The Classic fairy tales. See The Classic fairy tales 398.2
(ed) A Nursery companion. See A Nursery companion 398.8
(ed) The Oxford book of children's verse. See The Oxford book of children's verse 821.008
(ed) The Oxford dictionary of nursery rhymes. See The Oxford dictionary of nursery rhymes 398.8
(comp) The Oxford Nursery rhyme book. See The Oxford Nursery rhyme book 398.8
(ed) Tail feathers from Mother Goose. See Tail feathers from Mother Goose 398.8
Opie, Peter, d. 1982
(ed) The Classic fairy tales. See The Classic fairy tales 398.2
(ed) A Nursery companion. See A Nursery companion 398.8
(jt. auth) Opie, I. A. Children's games in street and playground 796.1
(ed) The Oxford book of children's verse. See The Oxford book of children's verse 821.008
(ed) The Oxford dictionary of nursery rhymes. See The Oxford dictionary of nursery rhymes 398.8
(comp) The Oxford Nursery rhyme book. See The Oxford Nursery rhyme book 398.8
Opium
See/See also pages in the following book(s):
Rahn, J. E. More plants that changed history p101-18 (5 and up) 909
Opossums
Rue, L. L. Meet the opossum (4 and up) 599.2
Fiction
Van Laan, N. Possum come a-knockin' E
Oppenheim, Joanne
Left & right E
Oppenheim, Shulamith Levey
Waiting for Noah E
The **optical** illusion book. Simon, S. 152.14
Optical illusions
Anno, M. Topsy-turvies E
Anno, M. Upside-downers E
Cobb, V. How to really fool yourself (5 and up) 152.1
O'Neill, C. You won't believe your eyes! (4 and up) 152.14
Simon, S. The optical illusion book (4 and up) 152.14
Optics
Gallant, R. A. Rainbows, mirages and sundogs (4 and up) 551.5
Orbaan, Albert
(il) Bliven, B. The American Revolution, 1760-1783 973.3
(il) Bliven, B. The story of D-Day: June 6, 1944 940.54
The **orchard** murder. Roach, M. K.
In Roach, M. K. Encounters with the invisible world S C
Orchestra
Kuskin, K. The Philharmonic gets dressed E
See/See also pages in the following book(s):
McLeish, K. The Oxford first companion to music (5 and up) 780
The **ordinary** and the fabulous. Cook, E. 028.5
Ordinary Jack. Cresswell, H. Fic
Oregon
Stein, R. C. Oregon
In America the beautiful 973

Oregon country *See* Pacific Northwest
Organ preservation (Anatomy) *See* Preservation of organs, tissues, etc.
Organ transplantation *See* Transplantation of organs, tissues, etc.
Organized labor *See* Labor unions
Orgel, Doris
The devil in Vienna (6 and up) **Fic**
Orient *See* Asia
Orienteering *See* Direction sense
Origami
Araki, C. Origami in the classroom (4 and up) **736**
Sarasas, C. The ABC's of origami (4-6) **736**
See/See also pages in the following book(s):
Pellowski, A. The family storytelling handbook p74-84 **372.6**
Origami in the classroom. Araki, C. **736**
The **Origin** of death
In Best-loved folktales of the world p631-32 **398.2**
Origin of life *See* Life—Origin
Origin of man *See* Man—Origin
Origin of species *See* Evolution
Orlev, Uri, 1931-
The island on Bird Street (5 and up) **Fic**
Orloff, Denis
(il) Von Tscharner, R. New Providence **307.7**
Ormai, Stella
(il) Cobb, V. Bet you can! science possibilities to fool you **793.8**
(il) Creatures. See Creatures **821.008**
(il) Simon, S. Shadow magic **535**
(il) Simon, S. Soap bubble magic **793.8**
Ormerod, Jan
101 things to do with a baby **E**
Bend and stretch **E**
The frog prince (k-3) **398.2**
Kitten day **E**
Making friends. See note under Ormerod, J. Bend and stretch **E**
Mom's home. See note under Ormerod, J. Bend and stretch **E**
Moonlight **E**
The saucepan game **E**
The story of Chicken Licken (k-2) **398.2**
Sunshine **E**
This little nose. See note under Ormerod, J. Bend and stretch **E**
(il) Hayes, S. Eat up, Gemma **E**
(il) Hayes, S. Happy Christmas, Gemma **E**
Ormondroyd, Edward
Broderick **E**
Theodore **E**
Theodore's rival **E**
Ornament *See* Decoration and ornament
Orphans

Fiction

Aiken, J. Midnight is a place (5 and up) **Fic**
Angell, J. Dear Lola (4-6) **Fic**
Bawden, N. The finding (4 and up) **Fic**
Carlson, N. S. The happy orpheline (3-5) **Fic**
Cassedy, S. Behind the attic wall (5 and up) **Fic**
Cassedy, S. Lucie Babbidge's house (4-6) **Fic**
Cleaver, V. Trial Valley (5 and up) **Fic**
Cleaver, V. Where the lillies bloom (5 and up) **Fic**
Fleischman, S. The midnight horse (3-6) **Fic**
Garfield, L. Young Nick and Jubilee (5 and up) **Fic**
Godden, R. The story of Holly and Ivy **E**
Holland, I. The journey home (4 and up) **Fic**
Howard, E. Edith herself (4-6) **Fic**
Hughes, D. Family pose (5 and up) **Fic**
L'Engle, M. Meet the Austins (5 and up) **Fic**
Levin, B. Brother moose (5 and up) **Fic**
Lunn, J. L. S. The root cellar (5 and up) **Fic**
Reeder, C. Shades of gray (4 and up) **Fic**
Spinelli, J. Maniac Magee (5 and up) **Fic**
Stolz, M. The cuckoo clock (4-6) **Fic**
Streatfeild, N. Thursday's child (4 and up) **Fic**
Orphans from the sea. Scott, J. D. **639.9**
The **orphelines** in the enchanted castle. Carlson, N. S. See note under Carlson, N. S. The happy orpheline **Fic**
Ortega, Jose
(il) Where angels glide at dawn. See Where angels glide at dawn **S C**
Ortega, Kay
See/See also pages in the following book(s):
Morey, J. Famous Mexican Americans p98-105 (5 and up) **920**
Orthodontics
Betancourt, J. Smile! how to cope with braces (4 and up) **617.6**
Ortiz, Fran
(il) Brown, T. Chinese New Year **394.2**
Ortiz, Victoria
Sojourner Truth, a self-made woman (6 and up) **92**

Orvis. Hoover, H. M. **Fic**
Osa's pride. Grifalconi, A. **E**
Osborn, Jaime
About
Kuklin, S. Thinking big (2-5) **362.4**
Osborn, Robert
(il) Ciardi, J. I met a man **811**
Osborne, Christine
Middle Eastern food and drink (4-6) **641.5**
Osborne, Mary Pope, 1949-
Favorite Greek myths (3-6) **292**
Osinski, Alice
The Chippewa (2-4) **970.004**
The Navajo (2-4) **970.004**
The Nez Perce (2-4) **970.004**
The Sioux (2-4) **970.004**
Osma, Lupe de
The lucky table
In Best-loved folktales of the world p760-63 **398.2**
Three magic oranges
In Best-loved folktales of the world p756-60 **398.2**
Osman, Tony
(jt. auth) Cooper, C. How everyday things work **600**
Ostriches
Arnold, C. Ostriches and other flightless birds (3-6) **598**
Ostriches and other flightless birds. Arnold, C. **598**
Otani, June
(il) Ten potatoes in a pot, and other counting rhymes. See Ten potatoes in a pot, and other counting rhymes **398.8**
The **other** bone. Young, E. **E**
The **other** way to listen. Baylor, B. **E**
Otherwise known as Sheila the Great. Blume, J. **Fic**
Otis Spofford. Cleary, B. **Fic**
O'Toole, Christopher
Discovering flies (3-6) **595.7**
Mammals: the hunters (4 and up) **599**
Harrison, V. The world of honeybees **595.7**
O'Toole, Thomas, 1941-
Botswana—in pictures. See Botswana—in pictures **968.83**
Mali—in pictures. See Mali—in pictures **966.23**
Zimbabwe—in pictures. See Zimbabwe—in pictures **968.91**
Otters
Ashby, R. Sea otters (4-6) **599.74**
Brownell, M. B. Amazing otters (k-3) **599.74**
Hurd, E. T. Song of the sea otter (2-4) **599.74**
Smith, R. Sea otter rescue (5 and up) **639.9**
Ottie Slockett. Luttrell, I. **E**
Otwe. See Aardema, V. What's so funny, Ketu? **398.2**
Our atomic world. Berger, M. **539.7**
Our dog. Oxenbury, H. **E**
Our garage sale. Rockwell, A. F. **E**
Our Golda: the story of Golda Meir. Adler, D. A. **92**
Our home is the sea. Levinson, R. **E**
Our Lady's child. Grimm, J.
In Grimm, J. The complete Grimm's fairy tales p23-39 **398.2**
Our Lady's juggler
Cooney, B. The little juggler **398.2**
De Paola, T. The clown of God **398.2**
Sawyer, R. The juggler of Notre Dame
In Sawyer, R. The way of the storyteller p273-81 **372.6**
Our Lady's little glass. Grimm, J.
In Grimm, J. The complete Grimm's fairy tales p825-26 **398.2**
Our restless earth. Gallant, R. A. **550**
Our sixth-grade sugar babies. Bunting, E. **Fic**
Our sun and the inner planets. Levasseur-Regourd, A.-C. **523.7**
Our Veronica goes to Petunia's farm. Duvoisin, R. See note under Duvoisin, R. Veronica **E**
Our violent earth (4 and up) **363.3**
Our young folks (Periodical)
See/See also pages in the following book(s):
Jordan, A. M. From Rollo to Tom Sawyer, and other papers p123-30 **028.5**
Out and about. Hughes, S. **E**
Outdoor fun (1-4) **796.1**
Outdoor life
See also Camping
Fiction
George, J. C. My side of the mountain (5 and up) **Fic**
George, J. C. On the far side of the mountain (5 and up) **Fic**
Outdoor recreation
Adventures in your national parks (4 and up) **917.3**
Outdoor fun (1-4) **796.1**
Outdoor survival *See* Wilderness survival
Outer space
Exploration
Branley, F. M. Is there life in outer space? (k-3) **574.999**

Outer space—Exploration—*Continued*
Branley, F. M. Mysteries of life on earth and beyond (6 and up) **574.999**
Cole, J. The magic school bus, lost in the solar system (2-4) **523**
Harris, A. The great Voyager adventure (5 and up) **523.4**
Lampton, C. Stars & planets (3-6) **523**
Rathbun, E. Exploring your solar system (4 and up) **523.2**
Sullivan, G. The day we walked on the moon (4 and up) **629.45**

Outlaw boy
Outlaw boy
In Grandfather tales p65-74 **398.2**

Outlaw Red. Kjelgaard, J. See note under Kjelgaard, J. Big Red **Fic**

The **outlaws** of Sherwood. McKinley, R. **398.2**

The **outside** child. Bawden, N. **Fic**

The **outside** man. Leach, M.
In Leach, M. Whistle in the graveyard p54-56 **398.2**

Outside over there. Sendak, M. **E**

Outstanding science trade books for children **016.5**

Over and over. Zolotow, C. **E**

Over in the meadow. Langstaff, J. M. **781.62**

Over sea, under stone. Cooper, S. **Fic**

Over the hill. Marriott, A. L.
In Marriott, A. L. American Indian mythology **398.2**

Over the river and through the wood. Child, L. M. F. **811**

Over, under & through, and other spatial concepts. Hoban, T. **E**

Overbeck, Cynthia
Ants (4 and up) **595.7**
Cactus (4 and up) **583**
Carnivorous plants (4 and up) **583**
Cats (4 and up) **636.8**
Dragonflies (4 and up) **595.7**
How seeds travel (4 and up) **582**
(jt. auth) Young, D. The Sierra Club book of our national parks **917.3**

Overland journeys to the Pacific (U.S.)
Blumberg, R. The great American gold rush (5 and up) **979.4**
See/See also pages in the following book(s):
Freedman, R. Children of the wild West p13-23 (4 and up) **978**

Fiction

Coerr, E. The Josefina story quilt **E**
Harvey, B. Cassie's journey (2-4) **Fic**

Overnight at Mary Bloom's. Aliki **E**

Oversmart is bad luck. Jagendorf, M. A.
In The Scott, Foresman anthology of children's literature p401-02 **808.8**

Overture. Gorog, J.
In Gorog, J. Three dreams and a nightmare, and other tales of the dark **S C**

Overweight

Control

See Reducing

Owen, William, 1942-
(jt. auth) Rue, L. L. Meet the beaver **599.32**
(jt. auth) Rue, L. L. Meet the moose **599.73**

Owens, Gail, 1939-
(il) Byars, B. C. The Cybil war **Fic**
(il) Cohn, J. I had a friend named Peter **E**
(il) Emmert, M. I'm the big sister now **362.4**
(il) Hurwitz, J. The adventures of Ali Baba Bernstein **Fic**
(il) Hurwitz, J. The hot & cold summer **Fic**
(il) Litchfield, A. B. Making room for Uncle Joe **Fic**
(il) Milne, A. A. Pooh's bedtime book **828**

Owens, Mary Beth
A caribou alphabet **E**

Owens-Knudsen, Vick
Photography basics (5 and up) **770**

OWL (Periodical)
Outdoor fun **796.1**

Owl
In The Magic orange tree, and other Haitian folktales p29-36 **398.2**

The **owl**. Grimm, J.
In Grimm, J. The complete Grimm's fairy tales p711-13 **398.2**
505

The **owl** and the pussycat. Lear, E. **821**

Owl at home. Lobel, A. **E**

An **owl** in the house. Heinrich, B. **598**

Owl lake. Tejima, K. **E**

Owl moon. Yolen, J. **E**

Owliver. Kraus, R. **E**

Owls
Heinrich, B. An owl in the house (4 and up) **598**
Hunt, P. Snowy owls (3-5) **598**
Mowat, F. Owls in the family (4 and up) **636.6**

Fiction

Bunting, E. The man who could call down owls **E**

Owls—Fiction—*Continued*
Erickson, R. E. A toad for Tuesday (2-4) **Fic**
Hutchins, P. Good-night, Owl! **E**
Kraus, R. Owliver **E**
Lobel, A. Owl at home **E**
Tejima, K. Owl lake **E**
Thaler, M. Owly **E**
Yolen, J. Owl moon **E**
Owls in the family. Mowat, F. **636.6**
The **Owlstone** crown. Kennedy, X. J. **Fic**
Owly. Thaler, M. **E**
Ox-cart man. Hall, D. **E**
Oxenbury, Helen, 1938-
Beach day **E**
The birthday party **E**
The car trip **E**
First day of school **E**
Grandma and Grandpa **E**
The Helen Oxenbury nursery story book (k-1) **398.2**
Contents: Goldilocks and the three bears; The turnip; The little porridge pot; The three little pigs; The gingerbread boy; Henny-Penny; The elves and the shoemaker; The three billy goats gruff; Little Red Riding Hood; The little red hen
Helen Oxenbury's ABC of things **E**
The important visitor **E**
Our dog **E**
Pippo gets lost **E**
Playing **E**
Shopping trip **E**
Tom and Pippo and the dog. See note under Oxenbury, H. Pippo gets lost **E**
Tom and Pippo and the washing machine. See note under Oxenbury, H. Pippo gets lost **E**
Tom and Pippo go for a walk. See note under Oxenbury, H. Pippo gets lost **E**
Tom and Pippo go shopping. See note under Oxenbury, H. Pippo gets lost **E**
Tom and Pippo in the garden. See note under Oxenbury, H. Pippo gets lost **E**
Tom and Pippo in the snow. See note under Oxenbury, H. Pippo gets lost **E**
Tom and Pippo make a friend. See note under Oxenbury, H. Pippo gets lost **E**
Tom and Pippo make a mess. See note under Oxenbury, H. Pippo gets lost **E**
Tom and Pippo read a story. See note under Oxenbury, H. Pippo gets lost **E**
Tom and Pippo see the moon. See note under Oxenbury, H. Pippo gets lost **E**
Tom and Pippo's day. See note under Oxenbury, H. Pippo gets lost **E**
(il) The Helen Oxenbury nursery rhyme book. See The Helen Oxenbury nursery rhyme book **398.8**
(il) Rosen, M. We're going on a bear hunt **E**
The **Oxford** book of children's verse **821.008**
The **Oxford** book of children's verse in America **811.008**
The **Oxford** book of Christmas poems (4 and up) **808.81**
The **Oxford** companion to children's literature. Carpenter, H. **028.5**
The **Oxford** dictionary of nursery rhymes **398.8**
The **Oxford** first companion to music. McLeish, K. **780**
The **Oxford** junior companion to music. Hurd, M. **780.3**
The **Oxford** Nursery rhyme book **398.8**
Oxford Scientific Films
Coldrey, J. The world of a jellyfish **593.7**
Harrison, V. The world of a falcon **598**
Harrison, V. The world of honeybees **595.7**
Harrison, V. The world of snakes **597.9**
Linley, M. The snake in the grass **597.9**
Saintsing, D. The world of butterflies **595.7**
Oxygen
Branley, F. M. Oxygen keeps you alive (k-3) **574.1**
Oxygen keeps you alive. Branley, F. M. **574.1**
Ozark Mountains
Fiction
Rawls, W. Where the red fern grows **Fic**
Ozma of Oz. Baum, L. F. See note under Baum, L. F. The Wizard of Oz **Fic**

P

P.J. Clover, private eye: the case of the borrowed baby. Meyers, S. See note under Meyers, S. P.J. Clover, private eye: the case of the Halloween hoot **Fic**
P.J. Clover, private eye: the case of the Halloween hoot. Meyers, S. **Fic**
P.J. Clover, private eye: the case of the missing mouse. Meyers, S. See note under Meyers, S. P.J. Clover, private eye: the case of the Halloween hoot **Fic**
P.J. Clover, private eye: the case of the stolen laundry. Meyers, S. See note under Meyers, S. P.J. Clover, private eye: the case of the Halloween hoot **Fic**

Paananen, Eloise
The Finns in America
In The In America series **305.8**

Pacific Northwest
Baker, B. The Pig War (k-2) **973.6**

Pacific Ocean
Heinrichs, S. The Pacific Ocean (2-4) **910**

Pack, band, and colony. Kohl, J. **591.5**

The **pack** of ragamuffins. Grimm, J.
In Grimm, J. The complete Grimm's fairy tales p65-66 **398.2**

Packard, David
See/See also pages in the following book(s):
Aaseng, N. From rags to riches p58-63 (5 and up) **920**

Packer, Vin *See* Kerr, M. E.

Paddington abroad. Bond, M. See note under Bond, M. A bear called Paddington **Fic**

Paddington and the Christmas pantomime. Bond, M.
In Bond, M. Paddington's storybook p146-[60] **S C**

Paddington and the "cold snap". Bond, M.
In Bond, M. Paddington's storybook p131-45 **S C**

Paddington and the "finishing touch". Bond, M.
In Bond, M. Paddington's storybook p97-111 **S C**

Paddington at large. Bond, M. See note under Bond, M. A bear called Paddington **Fic**

Paddington at the fair. Bond, M. See note under Bond, M. A bear called Paddington **Fic**

Paddington at the seaside. Bond, M. See note under Bond, M. A bear called Paddington **Fic**

Paddington at the tower. Bond, M. See note under Bond, M. A bear called Paddington **Fic**

Paddington at the zoo. Bond, M. See note under Bond, M. A bear called Paddington **Fic**

Paddington at work. Bond, M. See note under Bond, M. A bear called Paddington **Fic**

Paddington Bear. Bond, M. See note under Bond, M. A bear called Paddington **Fic**

Paddington cleans up. Bond, M.
In Bond, M. Paddington's storybook p21-36 **S C**

Paddington dines out. Bond, M.
In Bond, M. Paddington's storybook p37-51 **S C**

Paddington goes to town. Bond, M. See note under Bond, M. A bear called Paddington **Fic**

Paddington helps out. Bond, M. See note under Bond, M. A bear called Paddington **Fic**

Paddington marches on. Bond, M. See note under Bond, M. A bear called Paddington **Fic**

Paddington on screen. Bond, M. See note under Bond, M. A bear called Paddington **Fic**

Paddington on top. Bond, M. See note under Bond, M. A bear called Paddington **Fic**

Paddington steps out. Bond, M.
In Bond, M. Paddington's storybook p112-30 **S C**

Paddington takes the air. Bond, M. See note under Bond, M. A bear called Paddington **Fic**

Paddington takes the test. Bond, M. See note under Bond, M. A bear called Paddington **Fic**

Paddington takes to TV. Bond, M. See note under Bond, M. A bear called Paddington **Fic**

Paddington's art exhibition. Bond, M. See note under Bond, M. A bear called Paddington **Fic**

Paddington's lucky day. Bond, M. See note under Bond, M. A bear called Paddington **Fic**

Paddington's storybook. Bond, M. **S C**

Paddle-to-the-sea. Holling, H. C. **Fic**

Paddy goes traveling. Goodall, J. S. See note under Goodall, J. S. Paddy to the rescue **E**

Paddy to the rescue. Goodall, J. S. **E**

Paddy under water. Goodall, J. S. See note under Goodall, J. S. Paddy to the rescue **E**

Page, P. K. *See* Irwin, Patricia Kathleen Page, 1916-

Page, Patricia Kathleen *See* Irwin, Patricia Kathleen Page, 1916-

Pageants

Fiction

Robinson, B. The best Christmas pageant ever (4-6) **Fic**

Rogers, J. The Christmas pageant **E**

Pagoo. Holling, H. C. **595.3**

Pain
Arnold, C. Pain: what is it? how do we deal with it? (6 and up) **616**

The **Pain** and the Great One. Blume, J. **E**

Pain: what is it? how do we deal with it? Arnold, C. **616**

Paine, Thomas, 1737-1809
See/See also pages in the following book(s):
Jacobs, W. J. Great lives: human rights p24-35 (5 and up) **920**

Paint
See/See also pages in the following book(s):
Cobb, V. The secret life of hardware: a science experiment book p21-30 (5 and up) **670**

Painted eyebrow
Carpenter, F. Painted eyebrow
In Carpenter, F. Tales of a Chinese grandmother p56-65 **398.2**

The **painted** turtle. Marriott, A. L.
In Marriott, A. L. American Indian mythology **398.2**

Painters
See also Artists
Ventura, P. Great painters (5 and up) **759**

Painters, American
Gherman, B. Georgia O'Keeffe (5 and up) **92**
Henry, M. Benjamin West and his cat Grimalkin (4 and up) **92**
O'Kelley, M. L. From the hills of Georgia: an autobiography in paintings (2-4) **92**

The **painter's** cat. Alexander, L.
In Alexander, L. The town cats, and other tales p79-93 **S C**

Painting
Fiction
Kesselman, W. A. Emma **E**
Pinkwater, D. M. Bear's picture **E**
Rylant, C. All I see **E**
History
Ventura, P. Great painters (5 and up) **759**
Woolf, F. Picture this (4 and up) **759**

Painting, Decorative *See* Decoration and ornament

Painting, Industrial
See also House painting

Painting, Modern
1900-1999 (20th century)
See/See also pages in the following book(s):
Simon, S. The optical illusion book p56-66 (4 and up) **152.14**

Painting faces. Haldane, S. **745.5**

Paisley, Tom *See* Bethancourt, T. Ernesto

Pakistan
Pakistan—in pictures (5 and up) **954.91**

Pakistan—in pictures (5 and up) **954.91**

Paladino, Catherine
Spring fleece (3-6) **636.3**

The **pale** blue flower. Brown, M. W.
In Brown, M. W. The fish with the deep sea smile p122-23 **818**

Paleček, Josef, 1932-
(il) Crampton, P. Peter and the wolf **E**

Paleontology *See* Fossils

Palestine
Fiction
Speare, E. G. The bronze bow (6 and up) **Fic**

Paletón and the musical elephant. Ibargüengoitia, J.
In Where angels glide at dawn p51-55 **S C**

A **palindrome.** Babbitt, N.
In Babbitt, N. The Devil's storybook p53-61 **S C**

Palmisciano, Diane
(il) Conford, E. A case for Jenny Archer **Fic**
(il) Patent, D. H. Grandfather's nose **575.1**

Panama Canal
St. George, J. Panama Canal (5 and up) **972.87**

Pancake
Asbjørnsen, P. C. The pancake
In The Scott, Foresman anthology of children's literature p228-29 **808.8**

Pancho Villa and the Devil. Jagendorf, M. A.
In The Scott, Foresman anthology of children's literature p406-07 **808.8**

Panda *See* Giant panda

Pandas. Schlein, M. **599.74**

Papa God and General Death
In The Magic orange tree, and other Haitian folktales p75-78 **398.2**

"Papa God first, Man next, Tiger last"
In The Magic orange tree, and other Haitian folktales p177-81 **398.2**

Papa God sends turtle doves
In The Magic orange tree, and other Haitian folktales p87-90 **398.2**

Papa John's tall tale. Hamilton, V.
In Hamilton, V. The people could fly: American black folktales p76-80 **398.2**

Papago Indians
Baylor, B. The desert is theirs (1-4) **574.5**
George, J. C. One day in the desert (4-6) **574.5**

Papa's parrot. Rylant, C.
In Rylant, C. Every living thing p19-25 **S C**

Paper
Perrins, L. How paper is made (4 and up) **676**
See/See also pages in the following book(s):
Rahn, J. E. More plants that changed history p1-52 (5 and up) **909**

The **paper** airplane book. Simon, S. **745.592**

The **paper** bag mystery. Gotwalt, H. L. M.
In Gotwalt, H. L. M. Everyday plays for boys and girls p51-63 **812**

Paper crafts
See also Origami
Araki, C. Origami in the classroom (4 and up) **736**
Chernoff, G. T. Easy costumes you don't have to sew (3-5) **391**
Churchill, E. R. Instant paper airplanes (3-5) **745.592**
Churchill, E. R. Paper toys that fly, soar, zoom, & whistle (4 and up) **745.592**
Corwin, J. H. Papercrafts (3 and up) **745.54**
Emberley, E. Ed Emberley's picture pie: a circle drawing book (2-5) **741.2**
Irvine, J. How to make pop-ups (3-6) **736**
Lancaster, J. Paper sculpture (4 and up) **745.54**
Renfro, N. Bags are big! **745.54**
Simon, S. The paper airplane book (3-5) **745.592**
West, R. Dinosaur discoveries (3-5) **745.54**
See/See also pages in the following book(s):
Pellowski, A. The family storytelling handbook p74-101 **372.6**
Rockwell, H. I did it p1-7, 19-35 (1-3) **745.5**

The **paper** crane. Bang, M. **E**
Paper folding, Japanese *See* Origami
Paper sculpture. Lancaster, J. **745.54**
Paper toys that fly, soar, zoom, & whistle. Churchill, E. R. **745.592**
A **Paper** zoo (1-4) **811.008**
Papercrafts. Corwin, J. H. **745.54**
Pappa's going to buy you a mocking bird. Aiken, J.
In Aiken, J. Past eight o'clock p43-52 **S C**

Parables
See also Fables

Parades
Crews, D. Parade **E**
Shachtman, T. Parade! **E**

The **parakeet** named Dreidel. Singer, I. B.
In Singer, I. B. The power of light p23-28 **S C**
In Singer, I. B. Stories for children p98-102 **S C**

The **pardoner's** tale. Cohen, B.
In Cohen, B. Canterbury tales **Fic**

Pareja, Juan de *See* Juan, de Pareja

Parent and child
See also Children of working parents; Conflict of generations; Fathers and daughters; Fathers and sons; Mothers and daughters; Mothers and sons
LeShan, E. J. When a parent is very sick (4 and up) **155.9**
LeShan, E. J. When grownups drive you crazy (4 and up) **306.8**
Rosenberg, M. B. Living in two worlds (2-4) **306.8**
Rosenberg, M. B. Not my family: sharing the truth about alcoholism (4 and up) **362.29**

Fiction

Blume, J. It's not the end of the world (4-6) **Fic**
Bulla, C. R. The cardboard crown (3-5) **Fic**
Burch, R. Queenie Peavy (5 and up) **Fic**
Byars, B. C. The animal, the vegetable, and John D Jones (5 and up) **Fic**
Christiansen, C. B. My mother's house, my father's house **E**
Cleary, B. Dear Mr. Henshaw (4-6) **Fic**
Coerr, E. The big balloon race **E**
Delton, J. I'm telling you now **E**
Dragonwagon, C. Winter holding spring (2-4) **Fic**
Hermes, P. You shouldn't have to say good-bye (5 and up) **Fic**
Johnson, A. The grizzly (5 and up) **Fic**
Konigsburg, E. L. Journey to an 800 number (4 and up) **Fic**
Sebestyen, O. IOU's (6 and up) **Fic**
Smith, D. B. Last was Lloyd (4-6) **Fic**
Terris, S. Author! Author! (6 and up) **Fic**
Turner, A. W. Through moon and stars and night skies **E**
Viorst, J. The good-bye book **E**
Walter, M. P. My mama needs me **E**

Parents' Choice: a review of children's media **028.1**
Parent's choice guide to videocassettes for children **016.79143**
Parents without partners *See* Single parent family

Paris (France)

Fiction

Bemelmans, L. Madeline **E**

Paris (France)—Fiction—*Continued*
Bemelmans, L. Madeline's rescue E
Björk, C. Linnea in Monet's garden (3-5) Fic
Carlson, N. S. The family under the bridge (3-5) Fic
Lamorisse, A. The red balloon (1-4) Fic

Parish, Peggy, 1927-1988
Amelia Bedelia E
Amelia Bedelia and the baby. See note under Parish, P. Amelia Bedelia E
Amelia Bedelia and the surprise shower. See note under Parish, P. Amelia Bedelia E
Amelia Bedelia goes camping. See note under Parish, P. Amelia Bedelia E
Amelia Bedelia helps out. See note under Parish, P. Amelia Bedelia E
Amelia Bedelia's family album. See note under Parish, P. Amelia Bedelia E
Come back, Amelia Bedelia. See note under Parish, P. Amelia Bedelia E
December decorations (1-3) 745.59
Good work, Amelia Bedelia. See note under Parish, P. Amelia Bedelia E
Let's be early settlers with Daniel Boone (2-5) 745.5
Merry Christmas, Amelia Bedelia. See note under Parish, P. Amelia Bedelia E
Play ball, Amelia Bedelia. See note under Parish, P. Amelia Bedelia E
Teach us, Amelia Bedelia. See note under Parish, P. Amelia Bedelia E
Thank you, Amelia Bedelia. See note under Parish, P. Amelia Bedelia E

Park, Barbara, 1947-
Almost starring Skinnybones (4-6) Fic
Beanpole (5 and up) Fic
The kid in the red jacket (4-6) Fic
Maxie, Rosie, and Earl—partners in grime (3-5) Fic
My mother got married (and other disasters) (4-6) Fic
Skinnybones (4-6) Fic

Park, Ruth
Playing Beatie Bow (5 and up) Fic
When the wind changed
In Windy day: stories and poems p46-53 808.8

Parker, Ely Samuel, 1828-1895
See/See also pages in the following book(s):
Ehrlich, A. Wounded Knee: an Indian history of the American West (6 and up) 970.004

Parker, K. Langloh (Katie Langloh), 1856-1940
Beereeun the miragemaker
In The Scott, Foresman anthology of children's literature p345-49 808.8
How platypuses came to Australia
In Best-loved folktales of the world p605-07 398.2

Parker, Katie Langloh *See* Parker, K. Langloh (Katie Langloh), 1856-1940

Parker, Lewis
(il) Little, J. Mine for keeps Fic

Parker, Nancy Winslow
Bugs (1-3) 595.7
Frogs, toads, lizards, and salamanders (k-3) 597.6
Love from Aunt Betty E
The president's cabinet and how it grew (3-5) 353.04
(il) Blood, C. L. The goat in the rug E
(il) Langstaff, J. M. Oh, a-hunting we will go 781.62
(il) Longfellow, H. W. Paul Revere's ride 811
(il) Neitzel, S. The jacket I wear in the snow E
(il) Rice, E. At Grammy's house E
(il) Rice, E. Peter's pockets E
(il) Yolen, J. No bath tonight E

Parker, Quanah, Comanche Chief, 1854?-1911
See/See also pages in the following book(s):
Freedman, R. Indian chiefs p52-71 (6 and up) 920

Parker, Robert Andrew, 1927-
(il) Baylor, B. Guess who my favorite person is E
(il) DeFelice, C. C. The dancing skeleton 398.2
(il) Freedman, F. B. Brothers: a Hebrew legend 398.2
(il) The Monkey's haircut, and other stories told by the Maya. See The Monkey's haircut, and other stories told by the Maya 398.2
(il) Taylor, T. Battle in the Arctic seas 940.54
(il) Tompert, A. Grandfather Tang's story E
(il) The Whistling skeleton. See The Whistling skeleton 398.2
(il) Wolkstein, D. The magic wings 398.2

Parker, Steve
The brain and nervous system (4 and up) 612.8
The ear and hearing (4 and up) 612.8
The eye and seeing (4 and up) 612.8
Fish (4 and up) 597
Food and digestion (4 and up) 612.3
The heart and blood (4 and up) 612.1
Mammal (4 and up) 599
Pond & river (4 and up) 574.92
Seashore (4 and up) 574.92

Parker, Steve—*Continued*
Skeleton (4 and up) **596**
The skeleton and movement (4 and up) **612.7**
Touch, taste and smell (4 and up) **612.8**
(jt. auth) Bramwell, M. Mammals: the small plant-eaters **599**

Parker, Tom, 1950-
(il) Lyon, G. E. A B Cedar **E**

Parkin, Rex
The red carpet **E**

Parkinson, Kathy
(il) The Farmer in the dell. See The Farmer in the dell **782.42**

Parks, Gordon
(il) Wagner, J. J. T. **Fic**

Parks, Van Dyke
Jump! the adventures of Brer Rabbit (1-4) **398.2**
Contents: The comeuppance of Brer Wolf; Brer Fox goes hunting but Brer Rabbit bags the game; Brer Rabbit finds his match; Brer Rabbit grossly deceives Brer Fox; The moon in the millpond
Jump again! more adventures of Brer Rabbit (1-4) **398.2**
Contents: Brer Rabbit, he's a good fisherman; The wonderful Tar-Baby story; How Brer Weasel was caught; Brer Rabbit and the mosquitoes; Brer Rabbit's courtship
Jump on over! the adventures of Brer Rabbit and his family (1-4) **398.2**
Contents: How Brer Rabbit frightened his neighbors; Brer Rabbit and Brer Bear; Why Brer Wolf didn't eat the little rabs; Another story about the little rabs; Brer Fox gets out-foxed

Parks
See also National parks and reserves

Park's quest. Paterson, K. **Fic**

Park's quest [excerpt]. Paterson, K.
In Face to face: a collection of stories by celebrated Soviet and American writers p195-202 **S C**

Parley, Peter *See* Goodrich, Samuel Griswold, 1793-1860

Parley Garfield and the frogs. MacDonald, M. R.
In MacDonald, M. R. Twenty tellable tales p52-56 **372.6**

Parliamentary practice
Powers, D. G. How to run a meeting (4 and up) **060.4**
Robert, H. M. The Scott, Foresman Robert's Rules of order newly revised **060.4**

Parnall, Peter
Apple tree (k-3) **634**
Feet! **E**
Winter barn **E**
Woodpile (1-4) **591.5**
(il) Baylor, B. The desert is theirs **574.5**
(il) Baylor, B. Desert voices **811**
(il) Baylor, B. Hawk, I'm your brother **E**
(il) Baylor, B. If you are a hunter of fossils **560**
(il) Baylor, B. I'm in charge of celebrations **Fic**
(il) Baylor, B. The other way to listen **E**
(il) Baylor, B. The way to start a day **291.4**
(il) Miles, M. Annie and the Old One **Fic**

Parnell, Helga
Cooking the German way (5 and up) **641.5**

Parrish, Maxfield, 1870-1966
(il) Field, E. Poems of childhood **811**
See/See also pages in the following book(s):
Sendak, M. Caldecott & Co.: notes on books and pictures p87-91 **028.5**

The **parrot** and the thief. Kennedy, R.
In Kennedy, R. Collected stories p21-28 **S C**

Parrot that fed his parents
Shedlock, M. L. Filial piety
In Shedlock, M. L. The art of the story-teller p229-32 **372.6**

Parrots

Fiction

King-Smith, D. Harry's Mad (3-5) **Fic**

Parsons, Ellen *See* Dragonwagon, Crescent

Particles (Nuclear physics)
See also Quarks

Parties

Fiction

Brandenberg, F. Aunt Nina and her nephews and nieces **E**
Oxenbury, H. The birthday party **E**
Wood, A. Elbert's bad word **E**

Partners for life. Facklam, M. **591.5**

Pascal, Francine, 1938-
Hangin' out with Cici (5 and up) **Fic**

Pass the poetry, please! Hopkins, L. B. **372.6**

Pass the quill, I'll write a draft: a story of Thomas Jefferson. Quackenbush, R. M. **92**

Passover
Adler, D. A. A picture book of Passover (1-3) **296.4**
Chaikin, M. Ask another question (4 and up) **296.4**
Schwartz, L. S. The four questions (k-3) **296.4**

Passover—*Continued*
Silverman, M. Festival of freedom (1-3) **296.4**

Fiction

Zalben, J. B. Happy Passover, Rosie **E**

The **Passover** exiles. Sholem Aleichem
In Sholem Aleichem. Holiday tales of Sholem Aleichem **S C**

Passport to Israel. Lawton, C. **956.94**

Passport to Spain. Lye, K. **946**

Past eight o'clock. Aiken, J. **S C**

Past eight o'clock [story]. Aiken, J.
In Aiken, J. Past eight o'clock p7-26 **S C**

Pastrana, Julia
See/See also pages in the following book(s):
Drimmer, F. Born different p72-91 (6 and up) **920**

Patchwork. Alcock, V.
In Alcock, V. Ghostly companions **S C**

The **patchwork** girl of Oz. Baum, L. F. See note under Baum, L. F. The Wizard of Oz **Fic**

The **patchwork** quilt. Flournoy, V. **E**

Patchwork quilts *See* Quilts

Pate, Rodney
(il) Myers, W. D. Me, Mop, and the Moondance Kid **Fic**

Patent, Dorothy Hinshaw
All about whales (2-4) **599.5**
Appaloosa horses (4 and up) **636.1**
An apple a day (3-6) **634**
Buffalo (4 and up) **599.73**
Dolphins and porpoises (5 and up) **599.5**
Draft horses (4 and up) **636.1**
Flowers for everyone (4 and up) **635.9**
Germs! (4 and up) **616.9**
Grandfather's nose (k-2) **575.1**
A horse of a different color (4 and up) **636.1**
Horses of America (4 and up) **636.1**
Humpback whales (1-3) **599.5**
The lives of spiders (5 and up) **595.4**
Looking at ants (3-5) **595.7**
Looking at dolphins and porpoises (3-5) **599.5**
Mosquitoes (4 and up) **595.7**
Quarter horses (4 and up) **636.1**
Seals, sea lions, and walruses (5 and up) **599.74**
Singing birds and flashing fireflies (k-2) **591.5**
Spider magic (2-4) **595.4**
The way of the grizzly (4 and up) **599.74**
Whales, giants of the deep (5 and up) **599.5**
Wheat, the golden harvest (4-6) **633.1**
Where the bald eagles gather (4 and up) **598**
Where the wild horses roam (4 and up) **639.9**
The whooping crane (5 and up) **639.9**
Wild turkey, tame turkey (3-6) **598**
Yellowstone fires (2-4) **574.5**

Paterson, John (John Barstow)
Consider the lilies (5 and up) **220.8**

Paterson, Katherine
Angels & other strangers: family Christmas stories (5 and up) **S C**
Contents: Angels and other strangers; Guests; Many happy reruns; Tidings of joy; Maggie's gift; Star of night; He came down; Woodrow Kennington works practically a miracle; Broken windows
Bridge to Terabithia (4 and up) **Fic**
Come sing, Jimmy Jo (5 and up) **Fic**
The great Gilly Hopkins (5 and up) **Fic**
The master puppeteer (6 and up) **Fic**
Of nightingales that weep (6 and up) **Fic**
Park's quest (5 and up) **Fic**
Park's quest [excerpt]
In Face to face: a collection of stories by celebrated Soviet and American writers p195-202 **S C**
The spying heart **028.5**
The tale of the mandarin ducks (1-3) **398.2**
(jt. auth) Paterson, J. Consider the lilies **220.8**
See/See also pages in the following book(s):
Newbery and Caldecott Medal books, 1976-1985 p38-49, 76-92 **028.5**

Paterson, William, 1745-1806
See/See also pages in the following book(s):
Hauptly, D. J. "A convention of delegates" p54-67 (5 and up) **342**

The **Paths** of learning strewed with flowers
In A Nursery companion p46-49 **820.8**

Patients *See* Sick

Patillo, Gilbert S.
Ebeneezer Never-Could-Sneezer
In With a deep sea smile p75-81 **372.6**

Paton, Jonathan
The land and people of South Africa (5 and up) **968**

Paton Walsh, Jill, 1937-
Fireweed (5 and up) **Fic**
Gaffer Samson's luck (4-6) **Fic**
Lost and found (2-4) **Fic**
Unleaving (6 and up) **Fic**
See/See also pages in the following book(s):
Townsend, J. R. A sounding of storytellers p153-65 **028.5**

Patrick, Diane
Martin Luther King, Jr (4 and up) **92**

Patrick's dinosaurs. Carrick, C. E
Patriotic holidays and celebrations. Grigoli, V. 394.2
Patriotism
Grigoli, V. Patriotic holidays and celebrations (4 and up) 394.2
Patterson, Francine
Koko's kitten (1-4) 599.88
Koko's story (1-4) 599.88
Patterson, Geoffrey, 1943-
A pig's tale E
Patterson, Lillie
Martin Luther King, Jr., and the freedom movement (6 and up) 92
Sure hands, strong heart: the life of Daniel Hale Williams (4 and up) 92
Patterson, Nancy Ruth
The Christmas cup (3-5) Fic
Patterson, Wayne
The Koreans in America
In The In America series 305.8
Patz, Nancy
Moses supposes his toeses are roses and 7 other silly old rhymes (k-2) 398.8
Paul Bunyan. Kellogg, S. 398.2
Paul Bunyan's cornstalk. Courlander, H.
In Best-loved folktales of the world p668-71 398.2
Paul Laurence Dunbar, a poet to remember. McKissack, P. C. 92
Paul Revere's ride. Longfellow, H. W. 811
also in Longfellow, H. W. The children's own Longfellow 811
Paul's Christmas birthday. Carrick, C. E
Paulsen, Gary
The boy who owned the school (6 and up) Fic
Dogsong (6 and up) Fic
The winter room (5 and up) Fic
Pawnee Indians
Fradin, D. B. The Pawnee (2-4) 970.004
Paxton, Tom, 1937-
Engelbert the elephant E
Payne, Emmy, 1919-
Katy No-Pocket E
Payson, Dale
(il) Clifton, L. The lucky stone Fic
The **pea** patch jig. Hurd, T. E
Peabody. Wells, R. E
Peace at last. Murphy, J. E
A **Peaceable** kingdom (k-3) 811
Peacock pie. De la Mare, W. 821
Peacocks
Fiction
Polacco, P. Just plain Fancy E

Peake, Mervyn Laurence, 1911-1968
(il) Stevenson, R. L. Treasure Island Fic
Pearce, Philippa, 1920-
The battle of Bubble and Squeak (3-6) Fic
Tom's midnight garden (4 and up) Fic
The way to Sattin Shore (5 and up) Fic
See/See also pages in the following book(s):
Townsend, J. R. A sense of story p163-68 028.5
Peare, Catherine Owens
The Helen Keller story (5 and up) 92
Pearl Harbor (Oahu, Hawaii), Attack on, 1941
Skipper, G. C. Pearl Harbor (4 and up) 940.54
Taylor, T. Air raid—Pearl Harbor! (5 and up) 940.54
See/See also pages in the following book(s):
Marrin, A. Victory in the Pacific p3-22 (6 and up) 940.54
Pearlfisheries
Fiction
O'Dell, S. The black pearl (6 and up) Fic
Pearson, Kit
The sky is falling (6 and up) Fic
Pearson, Susan, 1946-
Happy birthday, Grampie E
Pearson, Tracey Campbell
Dollhouse people (3-5) 745.592
(il) Hennessy, B. G. The missing tarts E
(il) Nixon, J. L. Beats me, Claude E
(il) Old MacDonald had a farm. See Old MacDonald had a farm 781.62
(il) Sing a song of sixpence. See Sing a song of sixpence 398.8
(il) We wish you a merry Christmas. See We wish you a merry Christmas 782.28
Peasant, the bear, and the fox
Afanas'ev, A. N. The peasant, the bear, and the fox
In Afanas'ev, A. N. Russian fairy tales p288-89 398.2
The **peasant** and the corpse. Afanas'ev, A. N.
In Afanas'ev, A. N. Russian fairy tales p333-34 398.2
Peasant and the devil
Grimm, J. The peasant and the Devil
In Grimm, J. The complete Grimm's fairy tales p767-68 398.2
Peasant and the hare
Afanas'ev, A. N. The daydreamer
In Afanas'ev, A. N. Russian fairy tales p161 398.2

Peasant Demyan
Afanas'ev, A. N. Quarrelsome Demyan
In Afanas'ev, A. N. Russian fairy tales p163-64 **398.2**
Peasant in heaven
Grimm, J. The peasant in heaven
In Grimm, J. The complete Grimm's fairy tales p695-96 **398.2**
Peasant's clever daughter
Grimm, J. The peasant's wise daughter
In Grimm, J. The complete Grimm's fairy tales p437-40 **398.2**
Peasant's riddle
Afanas'ev, A. N. Riddles
In Afanas'ev, A. N. Russian fairy tales p29-30 **398.2**
The **peasant's** wise daughter. Grimm, J.
In Grimm, J. The complete Grimm's fairy tales p437-40 **398.2**
Peck, Beth
(il) Bunting, E. How many days to America? **E**
(il) Capote, T. A Christmas memory **Fic**
Peck, Richard
Blossom Culp and the sleep of death. See note under Peck, R. The ghost belonged to me **Fic**
The dreadful future of Blossom Culp. See note under Peck, R. The ghost belonged to me **Fic**
The ghost belonged to me (5 and up) **Fic**
Ghosts I have been. See note under Peck, R. The ghost belonged to me **Fic**
Ghosts I have been [excerpt]
In The Random House book of humor for children p36-43 **817.008**
I go along
In Connections: short stories by outstanding writers for young adults p184-90 **S C**
Peck, Robert Newton, 1928-
Arly (5 and up) **Fic**
A day no pigs would die (6 and up) **Fic**
Soup (5 and up) **Fic**
Soup [excerpt]
In The Random House book of humor for children p235-41 **817.008**
Soup & me. See note under Peck, R. N. Soup **Fic**
Soup for president. See note under Peck, R. N. Soup **Fic**
Soup in the saddle. See note under Peck, R. N. Soup **Fic**
Soup on fire. See note under Peck, R. N. Soup **Fic**
Soup on ice. See note under Peck, R. N. Soup **Fic**
Soup on wheels. See note under Peck, R. N. Soup **Fic**
Soup's drum. See note under Peck, R. N. Soup **Fic**
Soup's goat. See note under Peck, R. N. Soup **Fic**
Soup's hoop. See note under Peck, R. N. Soup **Fic**
Soup's uncle. See note under Peck, R. N. Soup **Fic**
Pecos Bill (Legendary character)
Kellogg, S. Pecos Bill (k-3) **398.2**
Pecos Bill and his bouncing bride. Malcolmson, A.
In The Scott, Foresman anthology of children's literature p365-68 **808.8**
Pecos Bill's widow-maker. Hodges, M.
In Hodges, M. If you had a horse **398.2**
The **peculiar** such thing. Hamilton, V.
In Hamilton, V. The people could fly: American black folktales p116-20 **398.2**
Peddler of Ballaghadereen
Sawyer, R. The peddler of Ballaghadereen
In Sawyer, R. The way of the storyteller p239-47 **372.6**
In The Scott, Foresman anthology of children's literature p173-76 **808.8**
Peddlers and peddling
Fiction
Shannon, G. The Piney Woods peddler **E**
Slobodkina, E. Caps for sale **E**
The **pedlar** of Swaffham. Crossley-Holland, K.
In Crossley-Holland, K. British folk tales p251-64 **398.2**
The **pedlar's** dream. Reeves, J.
In Reeves, J. English fables and fairy stories p71-80 **398.2**
Peek-a-boo!. Ahlberg, J. **E**
Peeping in the shell. McNulty, F. **639.9**
Peepo!. See Ahlberg, J. Peek-a-boo! **E**
Peet, Bill
Big bad Bruce **E**
Bill Peet: an autobiography (4 and up) **92**
Cowardly Clyde **E**
Eli **E**
Huge Harold **E**
No such things **E**
The whingdingdilly **E**
Peigan Indians *See* Piegan Indians
Peki, the musician. Ogunleye, K.
In The Crest and the hide, and other African stories of heroes, chiefs, bards, hunters, sorcerers, and common people p53-62 **398.2**

Pelham, David
(il) Miller, J. The human body 612
Pelicans
Fiction
Wildsmith, B. Pelican E
Pelle's new suit. Beskow, E. E
Pellowski, Anne
The family storytelling handbook 372.6
Hidden stories in plants (4 and up) 398
The story vine 372.6
The world of storytelling 372.6
Pemberton, John Styth
See/See also pages in the following book(s):
Aaseng, N. The unsung heroes p10-18 (5 and up) 920
Pen & ink. Bolognese, D. 741.2
Pen drawing
Bolognese, D. Pen & ink (4 and up) 741.2
Pendleton, Edrie
Let George do it
In Holiday plays round the year p169-78 812.008
Pène du Bois, William *See* Du Bois, William Pène, 1916-
A **penguin** year. Bonners, S. 598
Penguins
Arnold, C. Penguin (3-6) 598
Bonners, S. A penguin year (k-3) 598
Cowcher, H. Antarctica (1-3) 998
Dewey, J. The Adélie penguin (2-4) 598
Durrell, G. M. The whispering land
In Animal families of the wild: animal stories p5-16 591
Fiction
Atwater, R. T. Mr. Popper's penguins (3-5) Fic
Penicillin
Jacobs, F. Breakthrough (5 and up) 615
Penmanship *See* Handwriting
Penner, Lucille Recht
The colonial cookbook (5 and up) 641.5
The Thanksgiving book (5 and up) 394.2
Penney, James Cash, 1875-1971
See/See also pages in the following book(s):
Aaseng, N. From rags to riches p39-47 (5 and up) 920
Penney (J. C.) Company, Inc. *See* J. C. Penney Company, Inc.
Pennsylvania
Kent, D. Pennsylvania
In America the beautiful 973
Fiction
Fritz, J. The cabin faced west (3-6) Fic
History
Fradin, D. B. The Pennsylvania colony (4 and up) 974.8
The **Pennsylvania** colony. Fradin, D. B. 974.8
Pennsylvania Dutch
Ammon, R. Growing up Amish (5 and up) 289.7
Fiction
Milhous, K. The egg tree E
A **penny** a look. Zemach, H. 398.2
Penny Power. See Zillions 640.73
Penny whistles. See Stevenson, R. L. A child's garden of verses 821
The **people** could fly [story]. Hamilton, V.
In Face to face: a collection of stories by celebrated Soviet and American writers p177-83 S C
In Hamilton, V. The people could fly: American black folktales p166-73 398.2
The **people** could fly: American black folktales. Hamilton, V. 398.2
People, love, sex, and families. Johnson, E. W. 613.9
People who could fly. Lester, J.
In Best-loved folktales of the world p663-65 398.2
People who make a difference. Ashabranner, B. K. 920
People's Republic of China *See* China
Peppé, Rodney, 1934-
Circus numbers E
The mice who lived in a shoe E
The **peppermint** pig. Bawden, N. Fic
Perception
Cobb, V. How to really fool yourself (5 and up) 152.1
O'Neill, C. You won't believe your eyes! (4 and up) 152.14
The **perfect** fiddle. MacLachlan, P.
In MacLachlan, P. Tomorrow's wizard p56-67 S C
The **perfect** solution. Gorog, J.
In Gorog, J. Three dreams and a nightmare, and other tales of the dark S C
Perfection. Babbitt, N.
In Babbitt, N. The Devil's storybook p73-77 S C
Pericles, 499-429 B.C.
See/See also pages in the following book(s):
Coolidge, O. E. The golden days of Greece p70-80 (4-6) 938

The **Perilous** Gard. Pope, E. M. **Fic**
Periodicals
The following magazines are entered in this catalog:
3-2-1 Contact **505**
Appraisal **016.5**
Arithmetic Teacher **510.7**
Bookbird **028.505**
Booklist **028.1**
Bulletin of the Center for Children's Books **028.1**
Chickadee: the Canadian magazine for young children **505**
Childhood Education **372.05**
Children's Magazine Guide **051**
Cobblestone **973.05**
Cricket **051**
Emergency Librarian **027.6205**
Faces **306.05**
Five Owls **028.505**
Highlights for Children **051**
The Horn Book Guide to Children's and Young Adult Books **028.505**
The Horn Book Magazine **028.505**
Instructor **372.05**
International Wildlife **591.05**
Journal of Youth Services in Libraries **027.6205**
The Kobrin Letter **028.505**
Library Talk **027.805**
National Geographic World (3-6) **910.5**
Newsletter on Intellectual Freedom **323.44**
Odyssey: space exploration and astronomy for young people **520.5**
Owl **505**
Parents' Choice: a review of children's media **028.1**
Plays **808.82**
Publisher's Weekly **070.505**
Ranger Rick **505**
The Reading Teacher **372.405**
School Library Journal **027.805**
School Library Media Quarterly **027.805**
Science and Children **507.05**
Science Books & Films **016.5**
The Science Teacher **507.05**
Sports Illustrated for Kids **796**
Stone Soup **810.8**
The Web **028.1**
Wilson Library Bulletin **020.5**
Your Big Backyard **505**
Zillions **640.73**
Zoonooz **591.05**

Bibliography

Magazines for school libraries **011.6**
Richardson, S. K. Magazines for children **011.6**

Indexes

Abridged Readers' guide to periodical literature **051**
Children's Magazine Guide **051**

Perl, Lila
Blue Monday and Friday the Thirteenth (4-6) **398**
Candles, cakes, and donkey tails (3-6) **392**
Don't sing before breakfast, don't sleep in the moonlight (4-6) **398**
The great ancestor hunt (5 and up) **929**
Hunter's stew and hangtown fry: what pioneer America ate and why (4 and up) **641.5**
Mummies, tombs, and treasure (4 and up) **393**
Piñatas and paper flowers (4 and up) **394.2**
Slumps, grunts, and snickerdoodles: what Colonial America ate and why (4 and up) **641.5**
Perlman, Raymond
(il) Zim, H. S. Rocks and minerals **549**
Perón, Juan Domingo, 1895-1974
See/See also pages in the following book(s):
Fox, G. The land and people of Argentina p111-25 (5 and up) **982**
Perrault, Charles, 1628-1703
Blue Beard
In Best-loved folktales of the world p28-32 **398.2**
In The Blue fairy book p290-95 **398.2**
In The Classic fairy tales p106-09 **398.2**
Bluebeard
In Sleeping beauty & other favourite fairy tales p33-40 **398.2**
Cinderella (k-3) **398.2**
also in Best-loved folktales of the world p3-8 **398.2**
also in The Blue fairy book p64-71 **398.2**
also in The Scott, Foresman anthology of children's literature p200-04 **808.8**
also in Sleeping beauty & other favourite fairy tales p103-12 **398.2**
Cinderella; dramatization. See Thane, A. Cinderella
Cinderilla
In The Classic fairy tales p123-27 **398.2**
Donkey-skin
In Sleeping beauty & other favourite fairy tales p81-92 **398.2**
The fairies
In Sleeping beauty & other favourite fairy tales p63-68 **398.2**
The fairy
In The Classic fairy tales p100-02 **398.2**
The foolish wishes
In Sleeping beauty & other favourite fairy tales p41-44 **398.2**

Perrault, Charles, 1628-1703—*Continued*
Hop o' my Thumb
In Sleeping beauty & other favourite fairy tales p69-80 **398.2**
Little Poucet
In The Classic fairy tales p130-36 **398.2**
The little red Riding-Hood
In The Classic fairy tales p95-97 **398.2**
In Sleeping beauty & other favourite fairy tales p21-25 **398.2**
Little Thumb
In The Blue fairy book p231-41 **398.2**
The master cat
In The Blue fairy book p141-47 **398.2**
In The Classic fairy tales p113-16 **398.2**
In The Scott, Foresman anthology of children's literature p204-06 **808.8**
Puss in boots (k-3) **398.2**
also in Best-loved folktales of the world p23-27 **398.2**
also in Sleeping beauty & other favourite fairy tales p26-32 **398.2**
Puss in boots; dramatization. See Thane, A. Puss in boots
Ricky with the tuft
In Sleeping beauty & other favourite fairy tales p93-102 **398.2**
The sleeping beauty; dramatization. See Thane, A. The sleeping beauty
The sleeping beauty in the wood
In The Blue fairy book p54-63 **398.2**
In The Classic fairy tales p85-92 **398.2**
In The Scott, Foresman anthology of children's literature p195-99 **808.8**
In Sleeping beauty & other favourite fairy tales p9-20 **398.2**
Toads and diamonds
In The Blue fairy book p274-77 **398.2**
In The Scott, Foresman anthology of children's literature p199-200 **808.8**
Galdone, P. Cinderella **398.2**
Galdone, P. Puss in boots **398.2**
Goodall, J. S. Puss in boots **398.2**

Perrins, Lesley, 1953-
How paper is made (4 and up) **676**

Perry, Matthew Calbraith, 1794-1858

About

Blumberg, R. Commodore Perry in the land of the Shogun (5 and up) **952**

Perry, Robert Louis, 1950-
Focus on nicotine and caffeine (3-6) **616.86**

Persephone (Greek deity)
McDermott, G. Daughter of Earth (2-4) **292**

Persephone. D'Aulaire, I.
In Bauer, C. F. Celebrations p199-202 **808.8**

Perseus (Greek mythology)
See/See also pages in the following book(s):
The Blue fairy book p182-92 (4-6) **398.2**
Hamilton, E. Mythology p197-208 (6 and up) **292**

Persia *See* Iran

Persian Gulf region
See also Bahrain

Personal conduct *See* Human behavior

Personal finance *See* Finance, Personal

Personal grooming *See* Grooming, Personal

Personal hygiene *See* Hygiene

Personal names *See* Names, Personal

Peru

Fiction

Clark, A. N. Secret of the Andes (4 and up) **Fic**

Folklore

See Folklore—Peru

Pesach *See* Passover

A **pet**. Rylant, C.
In Rylant, C. Every living thing p26-30 **S C**

A **pet** for the orphelines. Carlson, N. S. See note under Carlson, N. S. The happy orpheline **Fic**

Pet mice. Wexler, J. **636.088**

Pet show! Keats, E. J. See note under Keats. E. J. The snowy day **E**

Pet therapy
See/See also pages in the following book(s):
Curtis, P. The animal shelter p87-95 (5 and up) **636.08**

Peter I, the Great, Emperor of Russia, 1672-1725

About

Stanley, D. Peter the Great (3-5) **92**

Peter, Adeline
Raboff, E. Paul Gauguin **759.4**
Raboff, E. Vincent van Gogh **759.9492**

Peter and the wolf. Crampton, P. **E**

Peter and the wolf. Prokofiev, S. **784.2**

Peter and the wolf. Prokofiev, S. **E**

Peter and Wendy. See Barrie, J. M. Peter Pan **Fic**

Peter Bull
Peter Bull
In Best-loved folktales of the world p364-68 **398.2**

Peter Pan. Barrie, J. M. **Fic**
Peter Piper's practical principles of plain and perfect pronunciation
In A Nursery companion p75-79 **820.8**
Peter Prim's pride; or, Proverbs that will suit the young or the old
In A Nursery companion p94-95 **820.8**
Peter Spier's Christmas! Spier, P. **E**
Peter Spier's rain. Spier, P. **E**
Peter the Great. Stanley, D. **92**
Peterkin and the little grey hare
Pyle, H. Peterkin and the little grey hare
In Pyle, H. The wonder clock p175-88 **398.2**
The **Peterkins'** Christmas tree. Hale, L. P.
In Diane Goode's American Christmas p11-15 **810.8**
Peters, David, 1954-
A gallery of dinosaurs & other early reptiles (4-6) **567.9**
Peters, Lisa Westberg
The sun, the wind and the rain (k-2) **551.4**
Peter's chair. Keats, E. J. See note under Keats. E. J. The snowy day **E**
Peter's pockets. Rice, E. **E**
Petersen, Peter L., 1935-
The Danes in America
In The In America series **305.8**
Petersham, Maud, 1889-1971
The box with red wheels **E**
The circus baby **E**
(il) Bible. N.T. Selections. The Christ child **232.9**
(comp) The Rooster crows. See The Rooster crows **398.8**
See/See also pages in the following book(s):
Caldecott Medal books, 1938-1957 p132-49 **028.5**
Petersham, Miska, 1888-1960
(il) Bible. N.T. Selections. The Christ child **232.9**
(jt. auth) Petersham, M. The box with red wheels **E**
(jt. auth) Petersham, M. The circus baby **E**
(comp) The Rooster crows. See The Rooster crows **398.8**
See/See also pages in the following book(s):
Caldecott Medal books, 1938-1957 p132-49 **028.5**
Peterson, Carolyn Sue, 1938-
Index to children's songs **782.42**
Peterson, Jeanne Whitehouse
I have a sister—my sister is deaf (k-3) **362.4**
Peterson, Roger Tory, 1908-
A field guide to the birds **598**
A field guide to western birds **598**
Peterson first guide to birds of North America. See Peterson, R. T. A field guide to the birds **598**
Petrides, George A.
A field guide to trees and shrubs **582.1**
Petroleum industry and trade
Rutland, J. See inside an oil rig and tanker (4-6) **665.5**
Petrology
Selsam, M. E. A first look at rocks (1-3) **552**
Petronella, Michael, 1952-
(il) Nardi, T. J. Karate basics **796.8**
(il) Owens-Knudsen, V. Photography basics **770**
Petruccio, Steven J.
(il) Smith, E. S. A service dog goes to school **636.7**
(il) Wyler, R. The starry sky **520**
Petry, Ann Lane, 1911-
Tituba of Salem Village (6 and up) **Fic**
Pets
See also Domestic animals; names of animals, e.g. *Cats; Dogs*; etc.
Arnold, C. Pets without homes (k-3) **636.088**
Chrystie, F. N. Pets (4 and up) **636.088**
Rinard, J. E. Helping our animal friends (k-3) **636.088**
Rogers, F. When a pet dies (k-1) **155.9**
Simon, S. Pets in a jar (4 and up) **639**
Weber, W. J. Care of uncommon pets (5 and up) **636.088**
See/See also pages in the following book(s):
Caney, S. Steven Caney's kids' America p110-18 (4 and up) **790.1**
The Kids' book about death and dying p47-63 (5 and up) **155.9**
Sattler, H. R. Fish facts & bird brains: animal intelligence p93-109 (5 and up) **591.5**
Fiction
Angell, J. A home is to share—and share—and share— (4-6) **Fic**
Hutchins, P. Rats! (2-4) **Fic**
Kellogg, S. Can I keep him? **E**
Kellogg, S. The mysterious tadpole **E**
Kimmel, E. A. I took my frog to the library **E**
Pets in a jar. Simon, S. **639**
Pets, vets, and Marty Howard. Carris, J. D. **Fic**

Pets without homes. Arnold, C. **636.088**
Pettepiece, Thomas
(ed) Face to face: a collection of stories by celebrated Soviet and American writers. See Face to face: a collection of stories by celebrated Soviet and American writers **S C**
Pettit, Florence Harvey
The stamp-pad printing book (5 and up) **761**
Pettit, Robert M.
(il) Pettit, F. H. The stamp-pad printing book **761**
Petunia. Duvoisin, R. **E**
Petunia, beware! Duvoisin, R. See note under Duvoisin, R. Petunia **E**
Petunia, I love you. Duvoisin, R. See note under Duvoisin, R. Petunia **E**
Petunia takes a trip. Duvoisin, R. See note under Duvoisin, R. Petunia **E**
Petunia the silly goose stories. Duvoisin, R. See note under Duvoisin, R. Petunia **E**
Petunia's Christmas. Duvoisin, R. See note under Duvoisin, R. Petunia **E**
Pevsner, Stella
And you give me a pain, Elaine (4 and up) **Fic**
Keep stompin' till the music stops (4 and up) **Fic**
The **peyote** religion. Marriott, A. L.
In Marriott, A. L. American Indian mythology **398.2**
Peyton, K. M., 1929-
See/See also pages in the following book(s):
Townsend, J. R. A sense of story p172-78 **028.5**
Townsend, J. R. A sounding of storytellers p166-78 **028.5**
Pfanner, Louise
Louise builds a house **E**
Pfeffer, Susan Beth, 1948-
As it is with strangers
In Connections: short stories by outstanding writers for young adults p74-82 **S C**
Phantasmagoria and other poems. Carroll, L.
In Carroll, L. The complete works of Lewis Carroll p741-808 **828**
The **phantom** tollbooth. Juster, N. **Fic**
The **phantom** tollbooth [excerpt]. Juster, N.
In The Random House book of humor for children p130-33 **817.008**
Pharmacology
See also Drugs
Phelan, Mary Kay
The Fourth of July (1-3) **394.2**
The story of the Boston Massacre (5 and up) **973.3**
The story of the Louisiana Purchase (5 and up) **973.4**
The **Philadelphia** adventure. Alexander, L. See note under Alexander, L. The Illyrian adventure **Fic**
The **Philharmonic** gets dressed. Kuskin, K. **E**
Philip II, King of Macedonia, 382-336 B.C.
See/See also pages in the following book(s):
Coolidge, O. E. The golden days of Greece p160-77 (4-6) **938**
Philip, Sachem of the Wampanoags, d. 1676

About

Cwiklik, R. King Philip and the war with the colonists (5 and up) **92**
Philip Hall likes me, I reckon maybe. Greene, B. **Fic**
Philippines

Folklore

See Folklore—Philippines
Phillips, Louis
263 brain busters (4-6) **793.73**
Going ape (3-5) **793.73**
Haunted house jokes (3-5) **793.73**
How do you get a horse out of the bathtub? (5 and up) **793.73**
(comp) The Upside down riddle book. See The Upside down riddle book **793.73**
Phillips, Mildred
The sign in Mendel's window **E**
Philology *See* Language and languages
Phone call from a ghost. Cohen, D. **133.1**
Photographers
See also Women photographers

Fiction

Greenwald, S. Give us a great big smile, Rosy Cole (3-5) **Fic**
A **photographer's** day out. Carroll, L.
In Carroll, L. The complete works of Lewis Carroll p979-85 **828**
Photography
See also Space photography
Freeman, T. Photography (2-4) **770**
Owens-Knudsen, V. Photography basics (5 and up) **770**

Fiction

Willard, N. Simple pictures are best **E**

History

Mitchell, B. CLICK!: a story about George Eastman (3-5) **92**

Scientific applications

Grillone, L. Small worlds close up (5 and up) **500**
Simon, S. Hidden worlds (5 and up) **500**

Photography, Artistic
Hoban, T. Shadows and reflections 779
Photography basics. Owens-Knudsen, V. 770
Photography of animals
Van Wormer, J. How to be a wildlife photographer (6 and up) 778.9
Photosynthesis
Asimov, I. How did we find out about photosynthesis? (5 and up) 581.1
Physical education
See also T'ai chi ch'üan
Physically handicapped
See also Blind; Deaf
Howell, M. The elephant man [biography of Joseph Carey Merrick] (4 and up) 92
Bibliography
Friedberg, J. B. Accept me as I am: best books of juvenile nonfiction on impairments and disabilities 016
Biography
Drimmer, F. Born different (6 and up) 920
Fiction
King-Smith, D. Pigs might fly (4-6) Fic
Voigt, C. Izzy, willy-nilly (6 and up) Fic
Physically handicapped children
Bergman, T. On our own terms (1-3) 362.4
Rosenberg, M. B. Finding a way (2-4) 362.4
Rosenberg, M. B. My friend Leslie (1-3) 362.4
Roy, R. Move over, wheelchairs coming through! (3 and up) 362.4
Wolf, B. Don't feel sorry for Paul (3-6) 362.4
Fiction
Caudill, R. A certain small shepherd (4 and up) Fic
De Angeli, M. L. The door in the wall (4-6) Fic
Fleischman, P. The Half-a-Moon Inn (4-6) Fic
Howe, J. A night without stars (5 and up) Fic
Little, J. Mine for keeps (4-6) Fic
Rabe, B. The balancing girl E
Rabe, B. Margaret's moves (3-6) Fic
Southall, I. Let the balloon go (4 and up) Fic
Physicians
See also Women physicians
DeSantis, K. A doctor's tools (k-2) 610.69
Epstein, S. Dr. Beaumont and the man with the hole in his stomach (4-6) 92
Patterson, L. Sure hands, strong heart: the life of Daniel Hale Williams (4 and up) 92
Rockwell, H. My doctor (k-1) 610.69
Physics
See also Nuclear physics; Relativity (Physics)
Physiology
Brenner, B. Bodies (k-2) 612
Bruun, R. D. The human body (4 and up) 612
Cole, J. Cuts, breaks, bruises, and burns (3-5) 612
Cole, J. The magic school bus inside the human body (2-4) 612
Elting, M. The Macmillan book of the human body (4 and up) 612
Miller, J. The human body (4 and up) 612
Settel, J. Why does my nose run? (4 and up) 612
Seuling, B. You can't sneeze with your eyes open & other freaky facts about the human body (4 and up) 612
Whitfield, P. J. Why do our bodies stop growing? (5 and up) 612
Piano
Fiction
Goffstein, M. B. Two piano tuners (3-5) Fic
Picard, Barbara Leonie
The Iliad of Homer (6 and up) 883
Roland and Oliver
In The Scott, Foresman anthology of children's literature p458-61 808.8
Walther of Aquitaine
In The Scott, Foresman anthology of children's literature p472-74 808.8
Picasso, Pablo, 1881-1973
About
Raboff, E. Pablo Picasso (4 and up) 759.6
Picnic with Piggins. Yolen, J. See note under Yolen, J. Piggins and the royal wedding E
A **picture** book of Abraham Lincoln. Adler, D. A. 92
A **picture** book of Benjamin Franklin. Adler, D. A. 92
A **picture** book of George Washington. Adler, D. A. 92
A **picture** book of Hanukkah. Adler, D. A. 296.4
A **picture** book of Martin Luther King, Jr. Adler, D. A. 92
A **picture** book of Passover. Adler, D. A. 296.4

A **picture** book of Thomas Jefferson. Adler, D. A. **92**

Picture books for children
Lacy, L. E. Art and design in children's picture books **741.6**
A Nursery companion **398.8**
See/See also pages in the following book(s):
Caldecott Medal books, 1938-1957 p307-14 **028.5**
A Horn Book sampler on children's books and reading p219-33 **028.5**
The Illustrator's notebook p125-42 **741.6**
Illustrators of children's books p2-12, 36-57 (v2) **741.6**
Newbery and Caldecott Medal books, 1966-1975 p276-89 **028.5**

Bibliography
Cianciolo, P. J. Picture books for children **011.6**
Hall, S. Using picture storybooks to teach literary devices **016.8**
Lima, C. W. A to zoo: subject access to children's picture books **011.6**
Roberts, P. Counting books are more than numbers: an annotated action bibliography **016.510**

See/See also pages in the following book(s):
Bauer, C. F. Handbook for storytellers p285-98 **372.6**

Picture dictionaries
Corbeil, J.-C. The Facts on File junior visual dictionary (3-6) **423**
Emberley, R. My house/mi casa: a book in two languages (k-3) **463**
Emberley, R. Taking a walk/caminando: a book in two languages (k-3) **463**
Hillerich, R. L. The American Heritage picture dictionary (k-1) **423**
Words for new readers (k-1) **423**

A **picture** for Harold's room. Johnson, C. See note under Johnson, C. Harold and the purple crayon **E**

The **picture** life of Mikhail Gorbachev. Caulkins, J. **92**

Picture pie: a circle drawing book, Ed Emberley's. Emberley, E. **741.2**

Picture this. Woolf, F. **759**

Picture writing
See also Hieroglyphics

The **pie** and the patty-pan. Potter, B. **E**

The **piebald** calf. Kendall, C.
In Kendall, C. Sweet and sour p92-97 **398.2**

The **Pied** Piper
In Best-loved folktales of the world p228-31 **398.2**

Pied Piper of Hamelin
Browning, R. The Pied Piper of Hamelin
In The Scott, Foresman anthology of children's literature p107-11 **808.8**
Marelle, C. The ratcatcher
In The Red fairy book p208-14 **398.2**
The Pied Piper
In Best-loved folktales of the world p228-31 **398.2**
Thane, A. The Pied Piper of Hamelin
In Thane, A. Plays from famous stories and fairy tales p20-37 **812**

Piegan Indians
See/See also pages in the following book(s):
Hofsinde, R. Indian costumes p21-32 (3-6) **391**

Pieńkowski, Jan, 1936-
(il) Aiken, J. Past eight o'clock **S C**
(il) Bible. N.T. Selections. Christmas, the King James Version **232.9**
(il) Bible. N.T. Selections. Easter, the King James Version **232.9**

Piercy, Esther J., 1905-1967
Miller, R. E. Commonsense cataloging **025.3**

Pierre. Sendak, M. **E**

The **pig-headed** wife. Bowman, J. C.
In Best-loved folktales of the world p384-86 **398.2**
In The Scott, Foresman anthology of children's literature p248-49 **808.8**

Pig Pig and the magic photo album. McPhail, D. M. See note under McPhail, D. M. Pig Pig grows up **E**

Pig Pig gets a job. McPhail, D. M. See note under McPhail, D. M. Pig Pig grows up **E**

Pig Pig goes to camp. McPhail, D. M. See note under McPhail, D. M. Pig Pig grows up **E**

Pig Pig grows up. McPhail, D. M. **E**

Pig Pig rides. McPhail, D. M. See note under McPhail, D. M. Pig Pig grows up **E**

Pig surprise. Krause, U. **E**

The **Pig** War. Baker, B. **973.6**

Pig Wisps. Sandburg, C.
In Sandburg, C. Rootabaga stories pt 2 p165-69 **S C**
In Sandburg, C. The Sandburg treasury p155-57 **818**

Pigeons
Schlein, M. Pigeons (4-6) **598**
See/See also pages in the following book(s):
Chrystie, F. N. Pets p165-72 (4 and up) **636.088**

Fiction
Baker, J. Home in the sky **E**

Piggins. Yolen, J. See note under Yolen, J. Piggins and the royal wedding E
Piggins and the royal wedding. Yolen, J. E
Piggle. Bonsall, C. N. E
The **piggy** in the puddle. Pomerantz, C. E

Pigs
See/See also pages in the following book(s):
Bauer, C. F. Celebrations p149-66 **808.8**
Pringle, L. P. Feral: tame animals gone wild p25-35 (5 and up) **591.5**

Fiction
Aylesworth, J. Hanna's hog E
Bawden, N. The peppermint pig (5 and up) Fic
Bond, F. Poinsettia & her family E
Bond, F. Poinsettia and the firefighters E
Brooks, W. R. Freddy the detective (3-5) Fic
Callen, L. Pinch (5 and up) Fic
Carlson, N. L. I like me! E
Chorao, K. Ups and downs with Oink and Pearl E
Dubanevich, A. Pigs in hiding E
Galdone, P. The three little pigs (k-2) **398.2**
Geisert, A. Pigs from A to Z E
Goodall, J. S. Paddy to the rescue E
Keller, H. Geraldine's big snow E
King-Smith, D. Babe (3-5) Fic
King-Smith, D. Pigs might fly (4-6) Fic
Krause, U. Pig surprise E
Lobel, A. Small pig E
Lobel, A. A treeful of pigs E
Marshall, J. The three little pigs (k-2) **398.2**
Marshall, J. Yummers! E
McPhail, D. M. Pig Pig grows up E
Patterson, G. A pig's tale E
Pomerantz, C. The piggy in the puddle E
Porte-Thomas, B. A. Ruthann and her pig (3-5) Fic
Potter, B. The tale of Pigling Bland E
Rayner, M. Mr. and Mrs. Pig's evening out E
Scieszka, J. The true story of the three little pigs (k-3) **398.2**
Steig, W. The amazing bone E
Steig, W. Farmer Palmer's wagon ride E
Steig, W. Roland, the minstrel pig E
Stolz, M. Emmett's pig E
Stolz, M. Quentin Corn (4-6) Fic
Van Leeuwen, J. Tales of Oliver Pig E
Wells, R. The little lame prince E
White, E. B. Charlotte's web (3-6) Fic
Yolen, J. Piggins and the royal wedding E
Zemach, M. The three little pigs (k-2) **398.2**

Folklore
Hooks, W. H. The three little pigs and the fox (k-3) **398.2**

Poetry
Lobel, A. The book of pigericks: pig limericks (1-3) **811**
This little pig-a-wig, and other rhymes about pigs (k-2) **398.8**

Pigs from A to Z. Geisert, A. E
Pigs in hiding. Dubanevich, A. E
Pigs might fly. King-Smith, D. Fic
A **pig's** tale. Patterson, G. E

Pike, Zebulon Montgomery, 1779-1813
See/See also pages in the following book(s):
McCall, E. S. Biography of a river: the living Mississippi p39-45 (6 and up) **977**

Pike and other fish
Afanas'ev, A. N. The pike with the long teeth
In Afanas'ev, A. N. Russian fairy tales p54-55 **398.2**

The **pike** with the long teeth. Afanas'ev, A. N.
In Afanas'ev, A. N. Russian fairy tales p54-55 **398.2**

The **Pilgrim** painting. Rawls, J.
In Holiday plays round the year p91-100 **812.008**

Pilgrim parting. Gotwalt, H. L. M.
In Gotwalt, H. L. M. Special plays for holidays p54-66 **812**

Pilgrims (New England colonists)
Anderson, J. The first Thanksgiving feast (3-5) **974.4**
Barth, E. Turkeys, Pilgrims, and Indian corn (3-6) **394.2**
Bartlett, R. M. Thanksgiving Day (1-3) **394.2**
Dalgliesh, A. The Thanksgiving story (k-2) **974.4**
Sewall, M. The pilgrims of Plimoth (3-6) **974.4**
Siegel, B. A new look at the Pilgrims (4-6) **973.2**

Fiction
Clapp, P. Constance: a story of early Plymouth (5 and up) Fic

The **pilgrims** of Plimoth. Sewall, M. **974.4**

Pilla, Marianne Laino, 1955-
The best: high/low books for reluctant readers **011.6**

Pillar, Marjorie
Pizza man (k-2) **641.8**

Pilots, Airplane *See* Air pilots

Pima Indians
Baylor, B. Moon song (1-3) **398.2**

The **Pimmerly** Plum. Lester, J.
In Lester, J. Further tales of Uncle Remus p29-32 **398.2**

Piñatas and paper flowers. Perl, L. **394.2**

The **pinballs**. Byars, B. C. **Fic**

Pinch. Callen, L. **Fic**

Pinchot, Jane
The Mexicans in America
In The In America series **305.8**

Pincus, Harriet, 1938-
(il) Sandburg, C. The wedding procession of the Rag Doll and the Broom Handle and who was in it **E**
(il) Segal, L. G. Tell me a Mitzi **E**
See/See also pages in the following book(s):
Sendak, M. Caldecott & Co.: notes on books and pictures p133-37 **028.5**

The **pine-nut** thieves. Curry, J. L.
In Curry, J. L. Back in the beforetime p90-99 **398.2**

The **Piney** Woods peddler. Shannon, G. **E**

Pink
Grimm, J. The pink
In Grimm, J. The complete Grimm's fairy tales p355-60 **398.2**

The **Pink** fairy book. See The Blue fairy book **398.2**

Pinkerton, Allan, 1819-1884

About

Wormser, R. Pinkerton: America's first private eye (5 and up) **92**

Pinkerton, behave! Kellogg, S. **E**

Pinkney, J. Brian
(il) Hooks, W. H. The ballad of Belle Dorcas **Fic**
(il) San Souci, R. The boy and the ghost **398.2**

Pinkney, Jerry, 1939-
(il) Aardema, V. Rabbit makes a monkey of lion **398.2**
(il) Dragonwagon, C. Half a moon and one whole star **E**
(il) Fields, J. The green lion of Zion Street **811**
(il) Flournoy, V. The patchwork quilt **E**
(il) Greenfield, E. Childtimes: a three-generation memoir **920**
(il) Greenfield, E. Mary McLeod Bethune **92**
(il) Lester, J. Further tales of Uncle Remus **398.2**
(il) Lester, J. More tales of Uncle Remus **398.2**
(il) Lester, J. The tales of Uncle Remus **398.2**
(il) Marzollo, J. Pretend you're a cat **E**
(il) McKissack, P. C. Mirandy and Brother Wind **E**
(il) San Souci, R. The talking eggs **398.2**
(il) Singer, M. Turtle in July **811**
(il) Taylor, M. D. Song of the trees **Fic**

Pinkwater, Daniel Manus, 1941-
Alan Mendelsohn, the boy from Mars (5 and up) **Fic**
Aunt Lulu **E**
Bear's picture **E**
Blue moose (1-3) **Fic**
Fat men from space (3-6) **Fic**
Guys from space **E**
The Hoboken chicken emergency (3-6) **Fic**
I was a second grade werewolf (1-3) **Fic**
Lizard music (4 and up) **Fic**
The Magic Moscow. See note under Pinkwater, D. M. Fat men from space **Fic**
(jt. auth) Pinkwater, J. Superpuppy: how to choose, raise, and train the best possible dog for you **636.7**

Pinkwater, Jill
Buffalo Brenda (5 and up) **Fic**
Superpuppy: how to choose, raise, and train the best possible dog for you (5 and up) **636.7**

Pinkwater, Manus *See* Pinkwater, Daniel Manus, 1941-

Pinky and Rex. Howe, J. **E**

Pinky and Rex get married. Howe, J. See note under Howe, J. Pinky and Rex **E**

Pinky Pye. Estes, E. **Fic**

Pino Saavedra, Yolando, 1901-
The five brothers
In Best-loved folktales of the world p776-80 **398.2**

Pinocchio goes to school. Thane, A.
In Thane, A. Plays from famous stories and fairy tales p352-65 **812**

Pinto, Ralph
(il) Lester, J. The knee-high man, and other tales **398.2**

Pioneer life *See* Frontier and pioneer life

Pioneer settlers of New France. Anderson, J. **971.01**

Piper, Watty
The little engine that could **E**

The **piper** and the pooka. Crossley-Holland, K.
In Crossley-Holland, K. British folk tales p17-23 **398.2**

Piping down the valleys wild **808.81**
Pippi goes on board. Lindgren, A. See note under Lindgren, A. Pippi Longstocking **Fic**
Pippi in the South Seas. Lindgren, A. See note under Lindgren, A. Pippi Longstocking **Fic**
Pippi Longstocking. Lindgren, A. **Fic**
Pippo gets lost. Oxenbury, H. **E**
The **pirate**. Schwartz, A.
In Schwartz, A. In a dark, dark room, and other scary stories p50-59 **398.2**
Pirates
Stevenson, R. L. Treasure Island (6 and up) **Fic**
Fiction
Burningham, J. Come away from the water, Shirley **E**
Kennedy, R. Amy's eyes (5 and up) **Fic**
Pitcher. Sullivan, G. **796.357**
Pitkänen, Matti A.
The children of Nepal (2-4) **954.96**
Pizza
Pillar, M. Pizza man (k-2) **641.8**
Pizza man. Pillar, M. **641.8**
Place, Marian T. (Marian Templeton), 1910-
Mount St. Helens (5 and up) **551.2**
The **Place** my words are looking for (4 and up) **811.008**
A **place** to come back to. Bond, N. **Fic**
Plague
Fiction
Christopher, J. Empty world (5 and up) **Fic**
Planes. Rockwell, A. F. **629.133**
The **planet** of Junior Brown. Hamilton, V. **Fic**
Planets
See also Satellites; names of planets
Cole, J. The magic school bus, lost in the solar system (2-4) **523**
Harris, A. The great Voyager adventure (5 and up) **523.4**
Lampton, C. Stars & planets (3-6) **523**
Lauber, P. Journey to the planets (4 and up) **523.4**
See/See also pages in the following book(s):
Jobb, J. The night sky book p81-103 (4 and up) **523**
Simon, S. Look to the night sky: an introduction to star watching (4 and up) **523**
Planning school library media facilities. Anderson, P. **027.8**
Plant. Burnie, D. **581**
Plant conservation
Facklam, H. Plants: extinction or survival? (6 and up) **581**
Plant-eating animals *See* Herbivores
Plant families. Lerner, C. **582**
Plant lore *See* Plants—Folklore
Plant names, Popular
Cross, D. H. Some plants have funny names (k-3) **581**
Planting a pear tree
In Best-loved folktales of the world p545-46 **398.2**
Planting a rainbow. Ehlert, L. **E**
Planting things. Rylant, C.
In Rylant, C. Every living thing p48-55 **S C**
Plants
See also Climbing plants; Flowers; Freshwater plants; Insectivorous plants; Mosses
Björk, C. Linnea's windowsill garden (3-6) **635**
Black, D. Plants (5 and up) **581**
Burnie, D. Plant (4 and up) **581**
Cole, J. Plants in winter (k-3) **581.5**
Cross, D. H. Some plants have funny names (k-3) **581**
Lerner, C. Plant families (4 and up) **582**
Paterson, J. Consider the lilies (5 and up) **220.8**
Selsam, M. E. A first look at the world of plants (1-3) **581**
Wyler, R. Science fun with peanuts and popcorn (2-4) **507**
See/See also pages in the following book(s):
Barth, E. Holly, reindeer, and colored lights p24-32 (3-6) **394.2**
Fertilization
See Fertilization of plants
Folklore
Borland, H. Plants of Christmas (5 and up) **398**
Pellowski, A. Hidden stories in plants (4 and up) **398**
Plants, Poisonous *See* Poisonous plants
Plants. Black, D. **581**
Plants: extinction or survival? Facklam, H. **581**
Plants in winter. Cole, J. **581.5**
Plants of Christmas. Borland, H. **398**
Plate tectonics
Aylesworth, T. G. Moving continents (6 and up) **551.1**

Plath, Sylvia
The bed book (k-2) **811**

Plato
See/See also pages in the following book(s):
Coolidge, O. E. The golden days of Greece p128-41 (4-6) **938**

Platt, Kin, 1911-
Big Max **E**
Big Max in the mystery of the missing moose **E**

Play
Rockwell, A. F. Things to play with (k-1) **793**

Poetry

See/See also pages in the following book(s):
Favorite poems, old and new p99-117 (4-6) **808.81**

Play ball, Amelia Bedelia. Parish, P. See note under Parish, P. Amelia Bedelia **E**

Play index **808.82**

Play rhymes. Brown, M. T. **796.1**

Play with me. Ets, M. H. **E**

The **playful** dolphins. Bridge, L. M. **599.5**

Playgrounds
Gibbons, G. Playgrounds (k-1) **796**

Playing. Oxenbury, H. **E**

Playing Beatie Bow. Park, R. **Fic**

Playing hockey. Solomon, C. **796.962**

Playmates, Imaginary *See* Imaginary playmates

Plays *See* Drama—Collected works; One act plays

Plays **808.82**

Plays from famous stories and fairy tales. Thane, A. **812**

Pledge of Allegiance
Swanson, J. I pledge allegiance (2-4) **323.6**

Plotkin, Gregory
Cooking the Russian way (5 and up) **641.5**

Plotkin, Rita
(jt. auth) Plotkin, G. Cooking the Russian way **641.5**

Plots (Drama, fiction, etc.)
See also Ballets—Stories, plots, etc.

Plotz, Helen, 1913-
(ed) A Week of lullabies. See A Week of lullabies **811.008**

Plume, Ilse
The Bremen town musicians (k-3) **398.2**
The story of Befana (1-3) **398.2**
(il) Bianco, M. W. The velveteen rabbit **Fic**
(il) Langton, J. The hedgehog boy **398.2**
(il) The Twelve days of Christmas. See The Twelve days of Christmas **782.42**
(il) Zolotow, C. Sleepy book **E**

Plunk's dreams. Griffith, H. V. **E**

Pluto (Planet)
Asimov, I. Pluto: a double planet? (3-5) **523.4**
Yeomans, D. K. The distant planets (4-6) **523.4**
See/See also pages in the following book(s):
Kelch, J. W. Small worlds: exploring the 60 moons of our solar system p109-14 (6 and up) **523.9**

Plymouth Rock
Fritz, J. Who's that stepping on Plymouth Rock? (3-5) **974.4**

Pocahontas, d. 1617

About
D'Aulaire, I. Pocahontas (2-4) **92**
Fritz, J. The double life of Pocahontas (4 and up) **92**

A **pocket** for Corduroy. Freeman, D. **E**

A **pocketful** of cricket. Caudill, R. **E**

A **pocketful** of goobers: a story about George Washington Carver. Mitchell, B. **92**

Podendorf, Illa, 1903-1983
Animal homes (2-4) **591.5**
Jungles (2-4) **574.5**
Rocks and minerals (1-4) **549**

A **poem** for a pickle: funnybone verses. Merriam, E. **811**

Poem stew (3-6) **811.008**

Poems for Jewish holidays (k-3) **811.008**

Poems for mothers (3-5) **811.008**

Poems for youth. Dickinson, E. **811**

Poems of A. Nonny Mouse (1-3) **808.81**

Poems of childhood. Field, E. **811**

Poems selected for young poeple, Edna St. Vincent Millay's. Millay, E. S. **811**

Poems to read to the very young (k-2) **821.008**

Poet and the peony princess
Carpenter, F. Poet and the peony princess *In* Carpenter, F. Tales of a Chinese grandmother p124-33 **398.2**

Poetics
Cassedy, S. In your own words (6 and up) **808**
The Place my words are looking for (4 and up) **811.008**

Poetry
See also American poetry; English poetry; Humorous poetry; Indians of North America—Poetry; Love poetry; Sea poetry; subjects with the subdivision Poetry

Poetry—*Continued*
See/See also pages in the following book(s):
Bauer, C. F. This way to books p193-266 **028.5**
Horn Book reflections on children's books and reading p151-200 **028.5**
A Horn Book sampler on children's books and reading p237-61 **028.5**
Bibliography
Olexer, M. E. Poetry anthologies for children and young people **011.6**

See/See also pages in the following book(s):
Bauer, C. F. Handbook for storytellers p137-57 **372.6**
Collected works
The Baby's bedtime book (k-1) **808.81**
The Baby's good morning book (k-1) **808.81**
Carle, E. Eric Carle's animals, animals (1-3) **808.81**
Cat poems (1-3) **808.81**
Cats are cats **808.81**
A Christmas feast: poems, sayings, greetings, and wishes (4 and up) **808.81**
Christmas in the stable (2-4) **811.008**
Christmas poems (k-3) **808.81**
Dog poems (1-3) **808.81**
Easter poems (3-5) **808.81**
Favorite poems, old and new (4-6) **808.81**
Halloween poems (k-3) **808.81**
The Helen Oxenbury nursery rhyme book (k-2) **398.8**
Lessac, F. Caribbean canvas **811**
Mice are nice **808.81**
New Year's poems (1-3) **808.81**
The Oxford book of Christmas poems (4 and up) **808.81**
Piping down the valleys wild **808.81**
Poems of A. Nonny Mouse (1-3) **808.81**
Room for me and a mountain lion (5 and up) **808.81**
Side by side (1-3) **808.81**
Sing a song of popcorn **808.81**
Sprints and distances (5 and up) **808.81**
Talking to the sun: an illustrated anthology of poems for young people **808.81**
Thanksgiving poems (k-3) **808.81**
These small stones (3-5) **808.81**
Tomie dePaola's book of poems (2-4) **808.81**
Valentine poems (k-3) **808.81**
When the dark comes dancing (k-3) **808.81**
Why am I grown so cold? (5 and up) **808.81**

See/See also pages in the following book(s):
Carlson, B. W. Listen! and help tell the story p41-62, 79-98, 125-72 **372.6**
The Scott, Foresman anthology of children's literature p2-146 **808.8**
With a deep sea smile p15-40 **372.6**
Indexes
The Columbia Granger's index to poetry **808.81**
Index to children's poetry **808.81**
Index to poetry for children and young people **808.81**
Subject index to poetry for children and young people, 1957-1975 **808.81**
Study and teaching
Hopkins, L. B. Pass the poetry, please! **372.6**

Poetry anthologies for children and young people. Olexer, M. E. **011.6**
Poetry for holidays (1-4) **811.008**
The **Poetry** troupe **821.008**
Poets, American
McKissack, P. C. Paul Laurence Dunbar, a poet to remember (4 and up) **92**
Walker, A. Langston Hughes, American poet (2-5) **92**
Pogány, Willy, 1882-1955
(il) Colum, P. The children of Odin **293**
(il) Colum, P. The children's Homer: The adventures of Odysseus and The tale of Troy **883**
(il) Colum, P. The Golden Fleece and the heroes who lived before Achilles **292**
Pogodin, Radii Petrovich
The joke
In Face to face: a collection of stories by celebrated Soviet and American writers p91-99 **S C**
Pogrebin, Letty Cottin
My Grandma
In Free to be—a family p52-56 **810.8**
Poinsettia & her family. Bond, F. **E**
Poinsettia and the firefighters. Bond, F. **E**
The **pointing** finger. Kendall, C.
In Kendall, C. Sweet and sour p60-62 **398.2**
Poisonous animals
See also Rattlesnakes
Poisonous plants
Lerner, C. Dumb cane and daffodils (4-6) **581.6**
Lerner, C. Moonseed and mistletoe (4-6) **581.6**
Poisonous snakes. Simon, S. **597.9**
Poker Face the Baboon and Hot Dog the Tiger. Sandburg, C.
In Sandburg, C. Rootabaga stories pt 1 p40-45 **S C**

Poker Face the Baboon and Hot Dog the Tiger—*Continued*
In Sandburg, C. The Sandburg treasury p27-29 **818**

Pol Pot
See/See also pages in the following book(s):
Chandler, D. P. The land and people of Cambodia (5 and up) **959.6**

Polacco, Patricia
Babushka's doll **E**
Just plain Fancy **E**
Rechenka's eggs **E**
Thunder cake **E**
Uncle Vova's tree **E**
(il) Thayer, E. L. Casey at the bat **811**

Poland
Fiction
Hautzig, E. R. A gift for Mama (3-6) **Fic**
Kelly, E. P. The trumpeter of Krakow (5 and up) **Fic**
Orlev, U. The island on Bird Street (5 and up) **Fic**
Singer, I. B. Naftali the storyteller and his horse, Sus, and other stories (4 and up) **S C**
Folklore
See Folklore—Poland

Polar bear cubs. Matthews, D. **599.74**

Polar bears
Matthews, D. Polar bear cubs (2-4) **599.74**
Ryder, J. White bear, ice bear (k-2) **599.74**

The **Polar** Express. Van Allsburg, C. **E**

Polar regions
See also Antarctic regions; Arctic regions; North Pole
Gilbreath, A. The Arctic and Antarctica (4 and up) **998**

Polish refugees *See* Refugees, Polish

The **polite** little polar bear. Brown, M. W.
In Brown, M. W. The fish with the deep sea smile p101-04 **818**

Politi, Leo, 1908-
Song of the swallows **E**
See/See also pages in the following book(s):
Caldecott Medal books, 1938-1957 p201-11 **028.5**

Politicians
See also Women politicians

Poll. Crossley-Holland, K.
In Crossley-Holland, K. British folk tales p293-94 **398.2**

Pollack, Pam
(comp) The Random House book of humor for children. See The Random House book of humor for children **817.008**

Pollination *See* Fertilization of plants

Pollution
See also Air—Pollution; Environmental protection; Marine pollution; Water—Pollution
Hare, T. Acid rain (5 and up) **363.7**
Woods, G. Pollution (6 and up) **363.7**
Fiction
Van Allsburg, C. Just a dream **E**

Polo, Marco, 1254-1323?
About
Ceserani, G. P. Marco Polo (3-6) **92**
Humble, R. The travels of Marco Polo (4-6) **910.4**

Polushkin, Maria
Kitten in trouble **E**
Who said meow? **E**

Polyglot dictionaries
Chermayeff, I. First words (k-3) **410**

Polyglot glossaries, phrase books, etc. *See* Polyglot dictionaries

Polynesia
Fiction
Sperry, A. Call it courage (5 and up) **Fic**

Polynesians
See also Maoris

Pomerantz, Charlotte
All asleep (k-2) **811**
The chalk doll **E**
Flap your wings and try **E**
If I had a paka: poems in eleven languages (1-3) **811**
One duck, another duck **E**
The piggy in the puddle **E**
Where's the bear? **E**

Pompeii (Ancient city)
Goor, R. Pompeii: exploring a Roman ghost town (5 and up) **937**
Humphrey, K. L. Pompeii (4 and up) **937**
See/See also pages in the following book(s):
Gallant, R. A. Lost cities (4 and up) **930**

Pond & river. Parker, S. **574.92**

Pond ecology
Amos, W. H. Life in ponds and streams (k-3) **591.92**
Lavies, B. Lily pad pond (k-2) **574.92**
Parker, S. Pond & river (4 and up) **574.92**
Reid, G. K. Pond life (4 and up) **574.92**

Pond ecology—*Continued*
Schwartz, D. M. The hidden life of the pond (3-5) **574.92**
Pond life. Reid, G. K. **574.92**
Ponies
Sayer, A. The young rider's handbook (5 and up) **636.1**
See/See also pages in the following book(s):
Henry, M. Album of horses p86-97 (4 and up) **636.1**
Fiction
Coerr, E. Chang's paper pony **E**
Henry, M. Misty of Chincoteague (4 and up) **Fic**
Henry, M. San Domingo: the medicine hat stallion (4-6) **Fic**
Pony express
DiCerto, J. J. The pony express (4 and up) **383**
The **Pooh** story book. Milne, A. A. **Fic**
Pooh's bedtime book. Milne, A. A. **828**
The **pool** of fire. Christopher, J. See note under Christopher, J. The White Mountains **Fic**
Poor
Fiction
Holman, F. Secret City, U.S.A (6 and up) **Fic**
Poor boy in the grave
Grimm, J. The poor boy in the grave
In Grimm, J. The complete Grimm's fairy tales p749-52 **398.2**
Poor man and the rich man
Grimm, J. The poor man and the rich man
In Grimm, J. The complete Grimm's fairy tales p394-98 **398.2**
The **poor** miller's boy and the cat. Grimm, J.
In Grimm, J. The complete Grimm's fairy tales p482-85 **398.2**
The **poor** miller's boy and the little cat. Grimm, J.
In Grimm, J. The juniper tree, and other tales from Grimm v2 p178-86 **398.2**
Poor Stainless. Norton, M. See note under Norton, M. The Borrowers **Fic**
Poor wretch
Afanas'ev, A. N. The poor wretch
In Afanas'ev, A. N. Russian fairy tales p177-79 **398.2**
Popcorn
De Paola, T. The popcorn book (k-3) **641.3**
Wyler, R. Science fun with peanuts and popcorn (2-4) **507**
The **popcorn** book. De Paola, T. **641.3**
The **popcorn** dragon. Thayer, J. **E**
Pope, Elizabeth Marie, 1917-
The Perilous Gard (6 and up) **Fic**
Pope, Joyce
Do animals dream? (4 and up) **591**
Taking care of your dog (3-5) **636.7**
Taking care of your fish (3-5) **639.3**
Taking care of your gerbils (3-5) **636.088**
Taking care of your mice and rats (3-5) **636.088**
Taking care of your rabbit (3-5) **636.088**
(jt. auth) Lilly, K. Kenneth Lilly's animals **599**
(jt. auth) Whitfield, P. J. Why do the seasons change? **508**
The **porcelain** man. Kennedy, R.
In Kennedy, R. Collected stories p1-8 **S C**
Porcupines
Fiction
Carrick, C. Ben and the porcupine **E**
Porcupine's grandson
In The Naked bear p93-100 **398.2**
Porpoises
Patent, D. H. Dolphins and porpoises (5 and up) **599.5**
Patent, D. H. Looking at dolphins and porpoises (3-5) **599.5**
Porte, Barbara Ann *See* Porte-Thomas, Barbara Ann
Porte-Thomas, Barbara Ann
Harry in trouble **E**
Harry's dog. See note under Porte-Thomas, B. A. Harry in trouble **E**
Harry's mom. See note under Porte-Thomas, B. A. Harry in trouble **E**
Harry's visit. See note under Porte-Thomas, B. A. Harry in trouble **E**
Jesse's ghost, and other stories (5 and up) **S C**
Contents: The storyteller; The baby-sitter; Cat stories; The mule story; The cedar box; Ghost story; Jesse's ghost; Cinderella; The calender; Talk; Joshua
Ruthann and her pig (3-5) **Fic**
The take-along dog **E**
Porter, George
(il) Cleary, B. Mitch and Amy **Fic**
Porter, William Sydney *See* Henry, O., 1862-1910
Ports *See* Harbors
Possum come a-knockin'. Van Laan, N. **E**
Possum stew. Cushman, D. **E**
The **post** office book. Gibbons, G. **383**
Postal service
Gibbons, G. The post office book (k-3) **383**

Postal service—*Continued*
Fiction
Rylant, C. Mr. Griggs' work E
Pot, Pol *See* Pol Pot
Pot that would not stop boiling
In The Tall book of nursery tales p117-19 398.2
Pot-Tilter. Leach, M.
In Leach, M. Whistle in the graveyard p88 398.2
The **Potato** Face Blind Man who lost the diamond rabbit on his gold accordion. Sandburg, C.
In Sandburg, C. Rootabaga stories pt 1 p29-33 S C
In Sandburg, C. The Sandburg treasury p23-24 818
Potato printing. Haddad, H. R. 761
Potatoes
Hughes, M. S. The great potato book (3-5) 641.3
Johnson, S. A. Potatoes (4 and up) 635
Turner, D. Potatoes (1-3) 635
Potter, Beatrix, 1866-1943
The art of Beatrix Potter 741.6
Cecily Parsley's nursery rhymes (k-3) 398.8
The complete adventures of Tom Kitten and his friends. See note under Potter, B. The story of Miss Moppet E
The pie and the patty-pan E
The roly-poly pudding. See note under Potter, B. The story of Miss Moppet E
The story of Miss Moppet E
The tailor of Gloucester E
The tale of Benjamin Bunny. See note under Potter, B. The tale of Peter Rabbit E
The tale of Jemima Puddle-duck E
The tale of Mr. Jeremy Fisher E
The tale of Mr. Tod. See note under Potter, B. The tale of Peter Rabbit E
The tale of Mrs. Tiggy-Winkle E
The tale of Mrs. Tittlemouse E
The tale of Peter Rabbit E
The tale of Pigling Bland E
The tale of Squirrel Nutkin E
The tale of the flopsy bunnies. See note under Potter, B. The tale of Peter Rabbit E
The tale of Timmy Tiptoes E
The tale of Tom Kitten. See note under Potter, B. The story of Miss Moppet E
The tale of two bad mice E
Yours affectionately, Peter Rabbit: miniature letters E
About
Collins, D. R. The country artist: a story about Beatrix Potter (3-5) 92
Taylor, J. Beatrix Potter: artist, storyteller and countrywoman 92
See/See also pages in the following book(s):
Horn Book reflections on children's books and reading p253-59 028.5
A Horn Book sampler on children's books and reading p228-33 028.5
Illustrators of children's books p55-64 (v3) 741.6
Only connect: readings on children's literature p258-65 028.5
Sendak, M. Caldecott & Co.: notes on books and pictures p61-76 028.5
Potter
Afanas'ev, A. N. The potter
In Afanas'ev, A. N. Russian fairy tales p208-10 398.2
Potter's gray. Aiken, J.
In Aiken, J. Up the chimney down, and other stories p228-48 S C
Pottery
Baylor, B. When clay sings (1-4) 970.004
Gibbons, G. The pottery place (1-3) 666
The **pottery** place. Gibbons, G. 666
Pottle o' brains
Riordan, J. A pottle o' brains
In Riordan, J. The woman in the moon, and other tales of forgotten heroines p47-52 398.2
Poultry
See also Ducks; Geese; Turkeys
Poverty
See also Poor
Fiction
Grove, V. Good-bye, my wishing star (5 and up) Fic
Poverty and humility lead to heaven. Grimm, J.
In Grimm, J. The complete Grimm's fairy tales p820-21 398.2
Powell, Whitney
(il) Lasky, K. Traces of life 573.2
Power (Mechanics)
See also Electric power
The **power** of light. Singer, I. B. S C
The **power** of light [story]. Singer, I. B.
In Singer, I. B. The power of light p53-60 S C
In Singer, I. B. Stories for children p210-16 S C
The **power** of speech. Babbitt, N.
In Babbitt, N. The Devil's storybook p91-101 S C

Power up. Markle, S. **537**
Powers, David Guy
How to run a meeting (4 and up) **060.4**
Powhatan Indians
D'Aulaire, I. Pocahontas (2-4) **92**
Fritz, J. The double life of Pocahontas (4 and up) **92**
Powzyk, Joyce Ann
Animal camouflage (3-6) **591.5**
Tracking wild chimpanzees in Kibira National Park (3-6) **599.88**
Wallaby Creek (3-6) **591.9**
(il) Bawden, N. Henry **Fic**
(il) Sattler, H. R. The new illustrated dinosaur dictionary **567.9**
(il) Sattler, H. R. Tyrannosaurus rex and its kin: the Mesozoic monsters **567.9**
Poynter, Margaret
Cosmic quest (5 and up) **574.999**
Pozzi, Angela
(il) Dilson, J. The abacus: a pocket computer **513.028**
Pragoff, Fiona
(il) Gore, S. My shadow **535**
Prairie animals
Hirschi, R. Who lives on—the prairie? (k-2) **591.5**
A **prairie** boy's summer. Kurelek, W. **971.27**
A **prairie** boy's winter. Kurelek, W. **971.27**
Prairie dogs
Casey, D. The friendly prairie dog (k-3) **599.32**
Prairie ecology
George, J. C. One day in the prairie (4-6) **574.5**
Prairie lightning. Roop, P.
In Herds of thunder, manes of gold p35-53 **808.8**
Prairie songs. Conrad, P. **Fic**
Prairie-town boy. Sandburg, C.
In Sandburg, C. The Sandburg treasury p263-382 **818**
Prayer for a child. Field, R. **242**
Prayers
Field, R. Prayer for a child (k-3) **242**
First prayers (k-3) **242**
Tambourines! Tambourines to glory! (3-6) **242**
Thanks be to God **242**
Fiction
Cohen, B. Yussel's prayer (3-5) **398.2**
Praying mantis
Lavies, B. Backyard hunter: the praying mantis (2-4) **595.7**
Precious hide
Afanas'ev, A. N. The precious hide
In Afanas'ev, A. N. Russian fairy tales p156-58 **398.2**
Pregnancy
Cole, J. How you were born (k-2) **612.6**
Kitzinger, S. Being born (3-5) **612.6**
Prehistoric animals
See also Dinosaurs; Extinct animals
Cohen, D. Prehistoric animals (4-6) **560**
Gibbons, G. Prehistoric animals (k-2) **560**
Sattler, H. R. Pterosaurs, the flying reptiles (1-4) **567.9**
Prehistoric man *See* Man, Prehistoric
Prehistoric Pinkerton. Kellogg, S. See note under Kellogg, S. Pinkerton, behave! **E**
Prejudices
See also Antisemitism
Fiction
Fleischman, P. Saturnalia (5 and up) **Fic**
Hooks, W. H. Circle of fire (5 and up) **Fic**
Taylor, M. D. The gold Cadillac (3-5) **Fic**
Uchida, Y. A jar of dreams (5 and up) **Fic**
Uchida, Y. Journey home (5 and up) **Fic**
Yarbrough, C. The shimmershine queens (4-6) **Fic**
Prelutsky, Jack
The baby Uggs are hatching (k-3) **811**
Beneath a blue umbrella: rhymes (k-3) **811**
Circus (k-3) **811**
The Headless Horseman rides tonight (2-5) **811**
It's Christmas (1-3) **811**
It's Halloween (1-3) **811**
It's snowing! It's snowing! (1-3) **811**
It's Thanksgiving (1-3) **811**
It's Valentine's Day (1-3) **811**
The mean old mean hyena **E**
My parents think I'm sleeping: poems (2-4) **811**
The new kid on the block: poems (3-6) **811**
Nightmares: poems to trouble your sleep (2-5) **811**
The queen of Eene (k-3) **811**
Ride a purple pelican (k-3) **811**
Rolling Harvey down the hill (1-3) **811**
The sheriff of Rottenshot: poems (2-5) **811**
The snopp on the sidewalk, and other poems (k-4) **811**

Prelutsky, Jack—*Continued*
Something big has been here (3-5) **811**
Tyrannosaurus was a beast (2-5) **811**
Lindgren, B. The wild baby **E**
(comp) Poems of A. Nonny Mouse. See Poems of A. Nonny Mouse **808.81**
(ed) The Random House book of poetry for children. See The Random House book of poetry for children **821.008**
(comp) Read-aloud rhymes for the very young. See Read-aloud rhymes for the very young **821.008**

Prempeh, Alfred Kofi
The chief of Agogo and the chief of Mampo
In The Crest and the hide, and other African stories of heroes, chiefs, bards, hunters, sorcerers, and common people p19-24 **398.2**

Preschool education *See* Education, Preschool

A **present** for Santa Claus. Haywood, C.
In The Family read-aloud Christmas treasury p36-41 **808.8**

Presenting reader's theater. Bauer, C. F. **808.82**

Presentneed, Bymeby, and Hereafter
Presentneed, Bymeby, and Hereafter
In Grandfather tales p140-49 **398.2**

Presents of the little folk
Grimm, J. The little folks' presents
In Grimm, J. The complete Grimm's fairy tales p742-45 **398.2**
Grimm, J. Presents of the little folk
In Grimm, J. More tales from Grimm p123-30 **398.2**

Preservation of organs, tissues, etc.
Lee, S. Donor banks: saving lives with organ and tissue transplants (5 and up) **362.1**

Preservation of wildlife *See* Wildlife conservation

The **president** builds a house. Shachtman, T. **363.5**

Presidents

United States

Adler, D. A. A picture book of Abraham Lincoln (1-3) **92**
Adler, D. A. A picture book of George Washington (1-3) **92**
Adler, D. A. A picture book of Thomas Jefferson (1-3) **92**
Beard, C. A. Charles A. Beard's The presidents in American history (5 and up) **920**
Blassingame, W. The look-it-up book of presidents (5 and up) **920**
D'Aulaire, I. Abraham Lincoln (2-4) **92**
D'Aulaire, I. George Washington (2-4) **92**
Freedman, R. Lincoln: a photobiography (4 and up) **92**
Fritz, J. The great little Madison (5 and up) **92**
Greene, C. Presidents (2-4) **920**
Gross, R. B. True stories about Abraham Lincoln (2-4) **92**
Kent, Z. George Bush: forty-first president of the United States (4 and up) **92**
Kent, Z. John Quincy Adams, sixth president of the United States (4 and up) **92**
Kent, Z. Ronald Reagan, fortieth president of the United States (4 and up) **92**
Meltzer, M. George Washington and the birth of our nation (5 and up) **92**
North, S. Abe Lincoln: log cabin to White House (5 and up) **92**
Quackenbush, R. M. Pass the quill, I'll write a draft: a story of Thomas Jefferson (2-4) **92**
Simon, C. Chester A. Arthur: twenty-first president of the United States (4 and up) **92**
Sipiera, P. P. Gerald Ford: thirty-eighth president of the United States (4 and up) **92**
Sullivan, G. George Bush (5 and up) **92**
Sullivan, G. How the White House really works (5 and up) **975.3**
Wade, L. R. James Carter: thirty-ninth president of the United States (4 and up) **92**

United States—Impeachment

See/See also pages in the following book(s):
Sgroi, P. P. The living Constitution: landmark Supreme Court decisions p88-123 (5 and up) **342**

United States—Pictorial works

Provensen, A. The buck stops here: the presidents of the United States (3-6) **920**

United States—Spouses

Faber, D. Eleanor Roosevelt: first lady of the world (4 and up) **92**

Presidents. Greene, C. **920**

The **president's** cabinet and how it grew. Parker, N. W. **353.04**

The **presidents** in American history, Charles A. Beard's. Beard, C. A. **920**

Press
See also Freedom of the press; Newspapers

Preston, Edna Mitchell
Squawk to the moon, Little Goose **E**

Pretend you're a cat. Marzollo, J. **E**

Price, Leontyne
Aïda (4 and up) **792.5**

Price, Norman, 1877-1951
(il) Stevenson, R. L. Treasure Island **Fic**
Price, Susan, 1955-
The ghost drum (4 and up) **Fic**
Prichard, Mari
(jt. auth) Carpenter, H. The Oxford companion to children's literature **028.5**
Priest's laborer
Afanas'ev, A. N. The priest's laborer
In Afanas'ev, A. N. Russian fairy tales p332 **398.2**
Primaryplots. Thomas, R. L. **028**
Primates
See/See also pages in the following book(s):
Sattler, H. R. Fish facts & bird brains: animal intelligence p51-75 (5 and up) **591.5**
Primates, insect-eaters, and baleen whales. Kerrod, R. **599**
Primavera, Elise, 1954-
(il) Fritz, J. Make way for Sam Houston **92**
(il) Gauch, P. L. Christina Katerina and the time she quit the family **E**
(il) Yolen, J. Best witches: poems for Halloween **811**
The **prince** and the mermaid. Deuchar, I. **398.2**
Prince Caspian. Lewis, C. S. See note under Lewis, C. S. The lion, the witch and the wardrobe **Fic**
Prince Chu Ti's city
Carpenter, F. Prince Chu Ti's city
In Carpenter, F. Tales of a Chinese grandmother p166-74 **398.2**
Prince Danila Govorila. Afanas'ev, A. N.
In Afanas'ev, A. N. Russian fairy tales p351-56 **398.2**
Prince Darling
In The Blue fairy book p278-89 **398.2**
Prince Desire and Princess Mignonetta
Le Prince de Beaumont, Madame. Prince Hyacinth and the dear little princess
In The Blue fairy book p12-18 **398.2**
Prince Featherhead and the Princess Celandine
Prince Featherhead and the Princess Celandine
In The Green fairy book p85-99 **398.2**
Prince Fickle and Fair Helena
Prince Fickle and Fair Helena
In The Green fairy book p216-21 **398.2**
Prince Hedgehog
Prince Hedgehog
In Best-loved folktales of the world p425-27 **398.2**
Prince Hyacinth and the dear little princess. Le Prince de Beaumont, Madame.
In The Blue fairy book p12-18 **398.2**
Prince Ivan and Byely Polyanin. Afanas'ev, A. N.
In Afanas'ev, A. N. Russian fairy tales p475-82 **398.2**
Prince Ivan and Princess Martha
Afanas'ev, A. N. Prince Ivan and Princess Martha
In Afanas'ev, A. N. Russian fairy tales p79-86 **398.2**
Prince Ivan, the firebird, and the gray wolf. Afanas'ev, A. N.
In Afanas'ev, A. N. Russian fairy tales p612-24 **398.2**
Prince Narcissus and the Princess Potentilla
Prince Narcissus and the Princess Potentilla
In The Green fairy book p68-84 **398.2**
Prince Ring
Prince Ring
In The Yellow fairy book p237-48 **398.2**
Prince Vivien and Princess Placida
Prince Vivien and Princess Placida
In The Green fairy book p238-61 **398.2**
The **Prince** who knew his fate (1-3) **398.2**
Prince who was afraid of nothing
Grimm, J. The king's son who feared nothing
In Grimm, J. The complete Grimm's fairy tales p545-50 **398.2**
The **princess** and Froggie. Zemach, H. **E**
The **princess** and the frog. Isadora, R. **398.2**
The **princess** and the goatherd. Walker, B. K.
In Walker, B. K. A treasury of Turkish folktales for children p118-22 **398.2**
The **princess** and the goblin. MacDonald, G. **Fic**
The **Princess** and the pea
In The Baby's story book p20-23 **398.2**
The **princess** and the pea. Andersen, H. C. **Fic**
also in Andersen, H. C. Hans Andersen: his classic fairy tales p29-31 **S C**
also in Tomie dePaola's favorite nursery tales p64-67 **398.2**
The **princess** and the peas. Andersen, H. C.
In The Classic fairy tales p217 **398.2**

The **princess** and the pig. Walker, B. K.
In Walker, B. K. A treasury of Turkish folktales for children p114-17 **398.2**

Princess and the vagabone
Sawyer, R. The princess and the vagabone
In Sawyer, R. The way of the storyteller p319-33 **372.6**

Princess Bee and the royal good-night story. Asher, S. **E**

Princess by mistake. Lively, P.
In Lively, P. Uninvited ghosts, and other stories p75-89 **S C**

Princess Furball. Huck, C. S. **398.2**

Princess Golden-Hair and the great black raven
Pyle, H. Princess Golden-Hair and the great black raven
In Pyle, H. The wonder clock p63-76 **398.2**

Princess Gorilla and a new kind of water. Aardema, V. **398.2**

Princess in the chest
Afanas'ev, A. N. The sorceress
In Afanas'ev, A. N. Russian fairy tales p567-68 **398.2**

Princess Kwan Yin
Carpenter, F. Gentle Gwan Yin
In Carpenter, F. Tales of a Chinese grandmother p29-38 **398.2**

Princess Mayblossom. Aulnoy, Madame d'.
In The Red fairy book p13-29 **398.2**

The **princess** of Tomboso. Martin, E.
In Martin, E. Tales of the Far North p17-27 **398.2**

Princess on the glass hill
Asbjørnsen, P. C. Princess on the glass hill
In Best-loved folktales of the world p345-52 **398.2**
In The Blue fairy book p332-41 **398.2**

Princess on the pea
Andersen, H. C. How to tell a true princess
In The Yellow fairy book p254-55 **398.2**
Andersen, H. C. The princess and the pea **Fic**
also in Andersen, H. C. Hans Andersen: his classic fairy tales p29-31 **S C**
also in Tomie dePaola's favorite nursery tales p64-67 **398.2**
Andersen, H. C. The princess and the peas
In The Classic fairy tales p217 **398.2**
Andersen, H. C. The princess on the pea
In Shedlock, M. L. The art of the story-teller p259-60 **372.6**
Andersen, H. C. The real princess
In The Scott, Foresman anthology of children's literature p502-03 **808.8**
Ehrlich, A. The real princess
In Ehrlich, A. The Random House book of fairy tales p126-29 **398.2**
The Princess and the pea
In The Baby's story book p20-23 **398.2**

Princess Printaniere
Aulnoy, Madame d'. Princess Mayblossom
In The Red fairy book p13-29 **398.2**

Princess Rosette
Aulnoy, Madame d'. Princess Rosette
In The Red fairy book p89-103 **398.2**

The **princess** who never smiled. Afanas'ev, A. N.
In Afanas'ev, A. N. Russian fairy tales p360-63 **398.2**

Princess who wanted to solve riddles
Afanas'ev, A. N. The princess who wanted to solve riddles
In Afanas'ev, A. N. Russian fairy tales p115-17 **398.2**

Princess who would not smile
Afanas'ev, A. N. The princess who never smiled
In Afanas'ev, A. N. Russian fairy tales p360-63 **398.2**

Pringle, Laurence P.
The animal rights controversy (6 and up) **179**
Animals at play (5 and up) **591.5**
Bearman: exploring the world of black bears (3-5) **599.74**
Feral: tame animals gone wild (5 and up) **591.5**
Global warming (3-5) **363.7**
Home (4 and up) **591.5**
Killer bees (4 and up) **595.7**
Living in a risky world (6 and up) **363**
Nuclear energy: troubled past, uncertain future (5 and up) **621.48**
Saving our wildlife (5 and up) **639.9**
Throwing things away (6 and up) **363.7**

Printing
See also Color printing
Aliki. How a book is made (2-5) **686**
Greenfeld, H. Books: from writer to reader (6 and up) **070.5**
Haddad, H. R. Potato printing (4-6) **761**
Pettit, F. H. The stamp-pad printing book (5 and up) **761**

History

Ogg, O. The 26 letters **411**

Priore, Frank V.
1492 blues
In Holiday plays round the year p229-38 **812.008**

Priore, Frank V.—*Continued*
The North Pole computer caper
In The Big book of Christmas plays p189-99 **808.82**
The **prisoner**. Holding, J.
In The Scott, Foresman anthology of children's literature p349-51 **808.8**
Prisoners of war
See also Missing in action
Prisoners of war, German
Fiction
Greene, B. Summer of my German soldier (6 and up) **Fic**
Privacy, Right of
Weiss, A. E. Who's to know? (5 and up) **323.44**
The **private** worlds of Julia Redfern. Cameron, E. See note under Cameron, E. A room made of windows **Fic**
Prizes, Literary *See* Literary prizes
Probabilities
Anno, M. Socrates and the three little pigs (4-6) **511**
The **problem** solvers. Aaseng, N. **920**
Problem solving
Burns, M. The book of think (4 and up) **153.4**
Nozaki, A. Anno's hat tricks (1-4) **153.4**
Procházková, Iva
The season of secret wishes (4-6) **Fic**
Procter, William, b. 1801?
See/See also pages in the following book(s):
Aaseng, N. From rags to riches p10-18 (5 and up) **920**
Procter & Gamble Co.
See/See also pages in the following book(s):
Aaseng, N. From rags to riches p10-18 (5 and up) **920**
Prodigy Street. Bob and Ray.
In The Random House book of humor for children p176-80 **817.008**
Professions
See also Occupations
The **professor** of smells. Yep, L.
In Yep, L. The rainbow people p20-35 **398.2**
Programming (Computers)
Simon, S. How to talk to your computer (k-3) **005**
Project panda watch. Schlein, M. **599.74**
Project Voyager
Branley, F. M. Uranus (3-6) **523.4**
Harris, A. The great Voyager adventure (5 and up) **523.4**
Projectors
See/See also pages in the following book(s):
Bauer, C. F. Handbook for storytellers p208-11 **372.6**
Prokofiev, Sergey, 1891-1953
Peter and the wolf (1-4) **784.2**
Peter and the wolf **E**
Crampton, P. Peter and the wolf **E**
The **prophet** and the spider. Climo, S.
In Climo, S. Someone saw a spider p57-62 **398.2**
Proserpina (Roman deity) *See* Persephone (Greek deity)
Prosperity. Gorog, J.
In Gorog, J. Three dreams and a nightmare, and other tales of the dark **S C**
Protection of birds *See* Birds—Protection
Protection of environment *See* Environmental protection
Protection of wildlife *See* Wildlife conservation
Protests, demonstrations, etc.
Fiction
Langton, J. The fragile flag (5 and up) **Fic**
Protter, Eric
The clever thief
In Best-loved folktales of the world p555-57 **398.2**
The donkey driver and the thief
In Best-loved folktales of the world p488-89 **398.2**
The farmer and his hired help
In Best-loved folktales of the world p490-95 **398.2**
The magic brocade
In Best-loved folktales of the world p539-44 **398.2**
The tale of the Oki Islands
In Best-loved folktales of the world p512-16 **398.2**
Proud cock
Barnes, H. The proud cock
In Shedlock, M. L. The art of the story-teller p191-94 **372.6**
A **proud** taste for scarlet and miniver. Konigsburg, E. L. **Fic**
Provensen, Alice, 1918-
A book of seasons **E**
The buck stops here: the presidents of the United States (3-6) **920**
The glorious flight: across the Channel with Louis Blériot, July 25, 1909 (1-4) **92**
Leonardo da Vinci: the artist, inventor, scientist (3 and up) **92**
Shaker Lane **E**
Town & country (k-2) **307.7**

Provensen, Alice, 1918-—*Continued*
The year at Maple Hill Farm E
(il) Lawrence, D. H. Birds, beasts, and the third thing **821**
(il) A Peaceable kingdom. See A Peaceable kingdom **811**
(il) Willard, N. A visit to William Blake's inn **811**
(il) Willard, N. The voyage of the Ludgate Hill **811**
See/See also pages in the following book(s):
Newbery and Caldecott Medal books, 1976-1985 p255-62 **028.5**

Provensen, Martin, 1916-1987
(il) Lawrence, D. H. Birds, beasts, and the third thing **821**
(il) A Peaceable kingdom. See A Peaceable kingdom **811**
(jt. auth) Provensen, A. A book of seasons E
(jt. auth) Provensen, A. The glorious flight: across the Channel with Louis Blériot, July 25, 1909 **92**
(jt. auth) Provensen, A. Leonardo da Vinci: the artist, inventor, scientist **92**
(jt. auth) Provensen, A. Town & country **307.7**
(jt. auth) Provensen, A. The year at Maple Hill Farm E
(il) Willard, N. A visit to William Blake's inn **811**
(il) Willard, N. The voyage of the Ludgate Hill **811**
See/See also pages in the following book(s):
Newbery and Caldecott Medal books, 1976-1985 p255-62 **028.5**

Proverbs
Fraser, B. First things first (k-2) **398.9**

Prudent Hans
Grimm, J. Clever Hans
In Grimm, J. The complete Grimm's fairy tales p166-68 **398.2**

Psyche (Greek deity)
Hodges, M. The arrow and the lamp **292**

Psychoactive drugs *See* Psychotropic drugs

Psychokinesis

Fiction

Roberts, W. D. The girl with the silver eyes (4-6) **Fic**
Sleator, W. Into the dream (5 and up) **Fic**

Psychology, Applied
See also Behavior modification

Psychology, Pathological
See also Mental illness

Psychotropic drugs
Friedman, D. P. Focus on drugs and the brain (3-6) **616.86**
See/See also pages in the following book(s):
Yepsen, R. B. Smarten up! how to increase your brain power p33-43 (5 and up) **153**

Pterosaurs, the flying reptiles. Sattler, H. R. **567.9**

Pu, Sung-ling, 1640-1715
Drinking companions
In Best-loved folktales of the world p550-54 **398.2**

Public libraries
Rockwell, A. F. I like the library (k-1) **027.4**

Public library services for children. Rollock, B. T. **027.62**

Public utilities
Macaulay, D. Underground (4 and up) **624.1**

Publishers and publishing
See also Book industries and trade
Aliki. How a book is made (2-5) **686**

Directories

Children's media market place **070.5025**

Periodicals

Publisher's Weekly **070.505**

Publisher's Weekly **070.505**

Puddocky
Puddocky
In The Green fairy book p222-28 **398.2**

Pueblo Indians
Yue, C. The Pueblo (4 and up) **970.004**
See/See also pages in the following book(s):
Hofsinde, R. Indian costumes p72-78 (3-6) **391**

Legends

McDermott, G. Arrow to the sun (k-3) **398.2**

Social life and customs

Trimble, S. The village of blue stone (4-6) **970.004**

Puerto Ricans

New York (N.Y.)—Fiction

Mohr, N. Felita (3-5) **Fic**

United States

Larsen, R. J. The Puerto Ricans in America
In The In America series **305.8**
See/See also pages in the following book(s):
Meltzer, M. The Hispanic Americans p18-25, 32-36 (6 and up) **305.8**

The **Puerto** Ricans in America. Larsen, R. J.
In The In America series 305.8
Puerto Rico
See/See also pages in the following book(s):
Meltzer, M. The Hispanic Americans p26-32 (6 and up) 305.8
Pumping iron *See* Weight lifting
Pumpkin
Cuyler, M. The all-around pumpkin book (4-6) 641.3
Fiction
Kroll, S. The biggest pumpkin ever E
Pumpkin. Leach, M.
In Leach, M. Whistle in the graveyard p80-81 398.2
A **Pumpkin** in a pear tree (1-4) 745.59
Pumpkin, pumpkin. Titherington, J. E
Punching the clock: funny action idioms. Terban, M. 427
Punctuation personified
In A Nursery companion p54-57 820.8
Punia and the king of the sharks. MacDonald, M. R.
In MacDonald, M. R. Twenty tellable tales p163-73 372.6
Puppet show made easy! Renfro, N. 791.5
Puppets and puppet plays
Champlin, C. Storytelling with puppets 372.6
Renfro, N. Puppet show made easy! (3-6) 791.5
Fiction
Collodi, C. The adventures of Pinocchio (3-6) Fic
Fleischman, P. Shadow play E
Keats, E. J. Louie E
Paterson, K. The master puppeteer (6 and up) Fic
A **puppy** is born. Fischer-Nagel, H. 636.7
The **puppy** who wanted a boy. Thayer, J. E
also in Diane Goode's American Christmas p31-37 810.8
also in The Family read-aloud Christmas treasury p22-25 808.8
Purim
Chaikin, M. Esther (1-3) 296.4
Chaikin, M. Make noise, make merry (3-6) 296.4
Puritans
Fiction
Speare, E. G. The witch of Blackbird Pond (6 and up) Fic
The **purple** coat. Hest, A. E
Purple cow to the rescue. Cole, A. 372.1
Pursell, Weimer
(il) Bronowski, J. Biography of an atom 539
Pursuit of the bear. Marriott, A. L.
In Marriott, A. L. American Indian mythology 398.2
Push pull, empty full. Hoban, T. E
The **pushcart** war. Merrill, J. Fic
Puskaitis, A. Lerchis- *See* Lerchis-Puskaitis, A.
Puss in boots
Ehrlich, A. Puss in boots
In Ehrlich, A. The Random House book of fairy tales p74-81 398.2
Galdone, P. Puss in boots 398.2
Goodall, J. S. Puss in boots 398.2
Perrault, C. The master cat
In The Blue fairy book p141-47 398.2
In The Classic fairy tales p113-16 398.2
In The Scott, Foresman anthology of children's literature p204-06 808.8
Perrault, C. Puss in boots 398.2
also in Best-loved folktales of the world p23-27 398.2
also in Sleeping beauty & other favourite fairy tales p26-32 398.2
Rockwell, A. F. Puss in boots
In Rockwell, A. F. Puss in boots, and other stories p80-88 398.2
Thane, A. Puss in boots
In Thane, A. Plays from famous stories and fairy tales p249-66 812
Puss in boots, and other stories. Rockwell, A. F. 398.2
Put that man to bed
In The Magic orange tree, and other Haitian folktales p37-42 398.2
Putawai. Te Kanawa, K.
In Te Kanawa, K. Land of the long white cloud p91-100 398.2
Puzzlers. Oakes, B. E
Puzzles
See also Riddles
Anno, M. Topsy-turvies E
Anno, M. Upside-downers E
Phillips, L. 263 brain busters (4-6) 793.73
Pyle, Howard, 1853-1911
The apple of contentment; dramatization. See Thane, A. The apple of contentment
King Stork (k-3) 398.2
The merry adventures of Robin Hood of great renown in Nottinghamshire (5 and up) 398.2
The story of King Arthur and his knights (6 and up) 398.2

Pyle, Howard, 1853-1911—*Continued*
The story of Sir Launcelot and his companions (6 and up) **398.2**
The story of the champions of the Round Table (6 and up) **398.2**
The story of the Grail and the passing of Arthur (6 and up) **398.2**
The wonder clock (4-6) **398.2**
Contents: Bearskin; Water of life; How one turned his troubles to some account; How three went out into the wide world; Clever student and the master of black arts; Princess Golden-Hair and the great black raven; Cousin Greylegs, the great red fox and Grandfather Mole; One good turn deserves another; White bird; How the good gifts were used by two; How Boots befooled the king; The step-mother; Master Jacob; Peterkin and the little grey hare; Mother Hildegarde; Which is best; Simpleton and his little black hen; Swan maiden; Three little pigs and the ogre; The staff and the fiddle; How the princess' pride was broken; How two went into partnership; King Stork; Best that life has to give
See/See also pages in the following book(s):
Illustrators of children's books p105-22 (v1) **741.6**

Pyramid of the sun, pyramid of the moon. Fisher, L. E. **972**

Pyramids
Bendick, J. Egyptian tombs (4 and up) **932**
Macaulay, D. Pyramid (4 and up) **726**

Pythons
Cole, J. A snake's body **597.9**

Q

Quackenbush, Robert M., 1929-
Bicycle to treachery. See note under Quackenbush, R. M. Express train to trouble **Fic**
Cable car to catastrophe. See note under Quackenbush, R. M. Express train to trouble **Fic**
Clear the cow pasture, I'm coming in for a landing!: a story of Amelia Earhart (2-4) **92**
Danger in Tibet. See note under Quackenbush, R. M. Express train to trouble **Fic**
Dig to disaster. See note under Quackenbush, R. M. Express train to trouble **Fic**
Dogsled to dread. See note under Quackenbush, R. M. Express train to trouble **Fic**
Express train to trouble (2-4) **Fic**
Gondola to danger. See note under Quackenbush, R. M. Express train to trouble **Fic**
Lost in the Amazon. See note under Quackenbush, R. M. Express train to trouble **Fic**
Pass the quill, I'll write a draft: a story of Thomas Jefferson (2-4) **92**
Quit pulling my leg! a story of Davy Crockett (2-4) **92**
Rickshaw to horror. See note under Quackenbush, R. M. Express train to trouble **Fic**
She'll be comin' round the mountain (k-3) **781.62**
Stage door to terror. See note under Quackenbush, R. M. Express train to trouble **Fic**
Stairway to doom. See note under Quackenbush, R. M. Express train to trouble **Fic**
Surfboard to peril. See note under Quackenbush, R. M. Express train to trouble **Fic**
Taxi to intrigue. See note under Quackenbush, R. M. Express train to trouble **Fic**
Texas trail to calamity. See note under Quackenbush, R. M. Express train to trouble **Fic**
Who said there's no man on the moon? a story of Jules Verne (2-4) **92**
Who's that girl with the gun? a story of Annie Oakley (2-4) **92**
(il) Keller, C. It's raining cats and dogs **793.73**

Quakers *See* Society of Friends

Quarks
Berger, M. Atoms, molecules, and quarks (6 and up) **539**

The **quarrel**. Sherlock, Sir P. M.
In Sherlock, Sir P. M. Anansi, the spider man p105-12 **398.2**

The **quarreling** book. Zolotow, C. **E**

Quarrelsome Demyan. Afanas'ev, A. N.
In Afanas'ev, A. N. Russian fairy tales p163-64 **398.2**

Quarrelsome goat
Afanas'ev, A. N. The goat shedding on one side
In Afanas'ev, A. N. Russian fairy tales p312-13 **398.2**

Quarter horses. Patent, D. H. **636.1**

Quarterback. Sullivan, G. **796.332**

Quayle, Eric
The shining princess, and other Japanese legends (5 and up) **398.2**
Contents: The shining princess; The white hare and the crocodiles; My Lord Bag-o-Rice; The tongue-cut sparrow; The adventures of a fisher lad; The old man who made dead trees bloom; Momotaro—The peach warrior; The Matsuyama mirror; The wooden bowl; The ogre of Rashomon

Québec (Province)
Ekoomiak, N. Arctic memories (3-5) **998**

Queen bee
Grimm, J. The queen bee
In Best-loved folktales of the world p140-41 **398.2**

Queen bee—*Continued*
In Grimm, J. About wise men and simpletons p55-57 **398.2**
In Grimm, J. The complete Grimm's fairy tales p317-19 **398.2**
In Grimm, J. More tales from Grimm p155-62 **398.2**
Queen Eleanor: independent spirit of the medieval world. Brooks, P. S. **92**
The **queen** of Eene. Prelutsky, J. **811**
Queen of hearts. Cleaver, V. **Fic**
Queen of heaven
Carpenter, F. Miss Lin, the sea goddess
In Carpenter, F. Tales of a Chinese grandmother p235-41 **398.2**
Queenie Peavy. Burch, R. **Fic**
Queens *See* Kings, queens, rulers, etc.
Quentin Blake's ABC. Blake, Q. **E**
Quentin Corn. Stolz, M. **Fic**
Questions and answers
Phillips, L. How do you get a horse out of the bathtub? (5 and up) **793.73**
Quick! turn the page! Stevenson, J. **E**
Quicksand
De Paola, T. The quicksand book (k-3) **552**
The **quicksand** book. De Paola, T. **552**
Quiet morning. Kazakov, Y. P.
In Face to face: a collection of stories by celebrated Soviet and American writers p39-55 **S C**
The **quiet** mother and the noisy little boy. Zolotow, C. **E**
The **quilt**. Jonas, A. **E**
The **Quilt** of men's eyes
In The Naked bear p101-09 **398.2**
The **quilt** story. Johnston, T. **E**
Quilting
Fiction
Ernst, L. C. Sam Johnson and the blue ribbon quilt **E**
Flournoy, V. The patchwork quilt **E**
Quilts
Fiction
Coerr, E. The Josefina story quilt **E**
Johnston, T. The quilt story **E**
Jonas, A. The quilt **E**
Kinsey-Warnock, N. The Canada geese quilt (3-5) **Fic**
Quiquern. Kipling, R.
In Kipling, R. The jungle books **S C**
Quit pulling my leg! a story of Davy Crockett. Quackenbush, R. M. **92**
Quotations
See also Proverbs
Bartlett, J. Familiar quotations **808.88**
QWERTYUIOP. Alcock, V.
In Alcock, V. Ghostly companions **S C**

R

R-T, Margaret, and the rats of NIMH. Conly, J. L. **Fic**
Ra, Carol F.
(comp) Trot, trot to Boston: play rhymes for baby. See Trot, trot to Boston: play rhymes for baby **398.8**
Rabbi Leib & the witch Cunegunde. Singer, I. B.
In Singer, I. B. Stories for children p89-97 **S C**
In Singer, I. B. When Shlemiel went to Warsaw & other stories p29-42 **398.2**
Rabbit and Coyote
In The Monkey's haircut, and other stories told by the Maya p72-76 **398.2**
Rabbit and Puma
In The Monkey's haircut, and other stories told by the Maja p77-80 **398.2**
The **rabbit** and the well. MacDonald, M. R.
In MacDonald, M. R. Twenty tellable tales p126-41 **372.6**
The **rabbit** and the wolf. Walker, B. K.
In Walker, B. K. A treasury of Turkish folktales for children p15 **398.2**
Rabbit gets married
In The Monkey's haircut, and other stories told by the Maya p81-83 **398.2**
Rabbit Hill. Lawson, R. **Fic**
Rabbit makes a monkey of lion. Aardema, V. **398.2**
Rabbit prince
Berger, T. The rabbit prince
In Berger, T. Black fairy tales p91-105 **398.2**
Rabbits
Pope, J. Taking care of your rabbit (3-5) **636.088**
See/See also pages in the following book(s):
Weber, W. J. Care of uncommon pets p14-31 (5 and up) **636.088**
Fiction
Adams, A. The Easter egg artists **E**
Adams, R. Watership Down (6 and up) **Fic**
Bianco, M. W. The velveteen rabbit (2-4) **Fic**
Brown, M. W. Goodnight moon **E**
Brown, M. W. The runaway bunny **E**

Rabbits—Fiction—*Continued*
Cazet, D. Big Shoe, Little Shoe E
Fisher, A. L. Listen, rabbit E
Gág, W. The A B C bunny E
The Hare and the tortoise (k-3) **398.2**
Heyward, D. The country bunny and the little gold shoes E
Hoban, T. Where is it? E
Lawson, R. Rabbit Hill (3-6) **Fic**
Lawson, R. The tough winter (3-6) **Fic**
Modesitt, J. Vegetable soup E
Newberry, C. T. Marshmallow E
Peet, B. Huge Harold E
Potter, B. The tale of Peter Rabbit E
Roberts, B. Waiting-for-papa stories E
Roberts, B. Waiting-for-spring stories E
Shannon, G. Dance away! E
Steig, W. Solomon the rusty nail E
Tafuri, N. Rabbit's morning E
Wells, R. Max's first word E
Wells, R. Morris's disappearing bag E
Wildsmith, B. The hare and the tortoise (k-2) **398.2**
Zolotow, C. Mr. Rabbit and the lovely present E

Rabbit's bride
Grimm, J. The hare's bride
In Grimm, J. The complete Grimm's fairy tales p332-33 **398.2**
Grimm, J. Rabbit's bride
In Grimm, J. The juniper tree, and other tales from Grimm v2 p275-77 **398.2**

Rabbit's morning. Tafuri, N. E

Rabble Starkey. Lowry, L. **Fic**

Rabe, Berniece
The balancing girl E
Margaret's moves (3-6) **Fic**

Rabin, Mindy
(il) West, R. Dinosaur discoveries **745.54**

Rabinowitz, Sholem Yakov *See* Sholem Aleichem, 1859-1916

Raboff, Ernest
Albrecht Dürer (4 and up) **759.3**
Diego Rodriguez de Silva y Velasquez (4 and up) **759.6**
Frederic Remington (4 and up) **759.13**
Henri de Toulouse-Lautrec (4 and up) **759.4**
Henri Matisse (4 and up) **759.4**
Henri Rousseau (4 and up) **759.4**
Leonardo da Vinci (4 and up) **759.5**
Marc Chagall (4 and up) **759.7**
Michelangelo Buonarroti (4 and up) **759.5**
Pablo Picasso (4 and up) **759.6**
Paul Gauguin (4 and up) **759.4**
Paul Klee (4 and up) **759.3**
Pierre-Auguste Renoir (4 and up) **759.4**
Raphael Sanzio (4 and up) **759.5**
Rembrandt (4 and up) **759.9492**
Vincent van Gogh (4 and up) **759.9492**

Raccoons
Arnosky, J. Raccoons and ripe corn E
North, S. Rascal (5 and up) **599.74**

Fiction

Brown, M. W. Wait till the moon is full E
Wells, R. Timothy goes to school E

Raccoons and ripe corn. Arnosky, J. E

The **race**. Lester, J.
In Lester, J. More tales of Uncle Remus p139-41 **398.2**

Race awareness

Poetry

Adoff, A. All the colors of the race: poems (4-6) **811**

The **race** between the buffalo and man. Marriott, A. L.
In Marriott, A. L. American Indian mythology **398.2**

The **race** for the prize fish. Mayo, G.
In Mayo, G. Star tales p25-26 **398.2**

Race relations

Fiction

Adoff, A. Black is brown is tan E
Neufeld, J. Edgar Allan (5 and up) **Fic**
Sebestyen, O. Words by heart (5 and up) **Fic**
Spinelli, J. Maniac Magee (5 and up) **Fic**
Taylor, M. D. The gold Cadillac (3-5) **Fic**
Taylor, T. The cay (5 and up) **Fic**
Voigt, C. Come a stranger (6 and up) **Fic**

Races of people *See* Ethnology

Rachel and Obadiah. Turkle, B. C. See note under Turkle, B. C. Obadiah the Bold E

Rachlin, Carol K.
(jt. auth) Marriott, A. L. American Indian mythology **398.2**

Racing cars. Graham, I. **629.228**

Rackham, Arthur, 1867-1939
(il) Evans, C. S. The sleeping beauty **398.2**
(il) Stephens, J. Irish fairy tales **398.2**
See/See also pages in the following book(s):
A Horn Book sampler on children's books and reading p50-59 **028.5**

Racso and the rats of NIMH. Conly, J. L. **Fic**

Radiation
See also Infrared radiation
Radical robots. Harrar, G. 629.8
Radin, Ruth Yaffe, 1938-
High in the mountains E
Radio
See/See also pages in the following book(s):
Aaseng, N. The inventors: Nobel prizes in chemistry, physics, and medicine p19-25 (5 and up) 609
Radioactive fallout
See/See also pages in the following book(s):
Giblin, J. Milk: the fight for purity p68-77 (5 and up) 637
Radioactivity
McGowen, T. Radioactivity: from the Curies to the atomic age (6 and up) 539.7
Radiocarbon dating
See/See also pages in the following book(s):
Aaseng, N. The inventors: Nobel prizes in chemistry, physics, and medicine p53-57 (5 and up) 609
Rae, Mary Maki
(il) The Farmer in the dell. See The Farmer in the dell 782.42
Raffi
The 2nd Raffi songbook (k-2) 782.42
Baby Beluga (k-2) 782.42
Down by the bay (k-2) 782.42
Five little ducks (k-2) 782.42
One light, one sun (k-2) 782.42
The Raffi Christmas treasury 782.42
The Raffi singable songbook (k-2) 782.42
Shake my sillies out (k-2) 782.42
Wheels on the bus (k-2) 782.42
The **Raffi** Christmas treasury. Raffi. 782.42
The **Raffi** singable songbook. Raffi. 782.42
A **raft** of riddles. Maestro, G. 793.73
Raggin': a story about Scott Joplin. Mitchell, B. 92
Raglin, Tim
(il) Kipling, R. The elephant's child Fic
(il) Kipling, R. How the camel got his hump Fic
Ragtime Tumpie. Schroeder, A. E
Rahn, Joan Elma, 1929-
More plants that changed history (5 and up) 909
Raible, Alton, 1918-
(il) Snyder, Z. K. Below the root Fic
(il) Snyder, Z. K. The changeling Fic
(il) Snyder, Z. K. The Egypt game Fic
(il) Snyder, Z. K. The headless cupid Fic
(il) Snyder, Z. K. The velvet room Fic
(il) Snyder, Z. K. The witches of Worm Fic
A **railroad** comes to Helm. Simon, S.
In Simon, S. More wise men of Helm and their merry tales p31-35 398.2
Railroads
Barton, B. Trains (k-1) 625.1
Crews, D. Freight train E
Gibbons, G. Trains (k-2) 625.1
Rockwell, A. F. Trains (k-2) 625.1
Employees
McKissack, P. C. A long hard journey (5 and up) 331.8
Fiction
Burningham, J. Hey! get off our train E
Goble, P. Death of the iron horse E
Howard, E. F. The train to Lulu's E
Lyon, G. E. A regular rolling Noah E
Piper, W. The little engine that could E
Siebert, D. Train song E
History
Scarry, H. Aboard a steam locomotive (4 and up) 625.2
Poetry
See/See also pages in the following book(s):
Piping down the valleys wild p175-80 808.81
Signaling
Sattler, H. R. Train whistles (k-2) 385
Rain & hail. Branley, F. M. 551.57
Rain and rainfall
See also Acid rain
Branley, F. M. Flash, crash, rumble, and roll (k-3) 551.5
Branley, F. M. It's raining cats and dogs (3-6) 551.5
Branley, F. M. Rain & hail (k-3) 551.57
Newton, J. R. Rain shadow (2-5) 574.5
Shulevitz, U. Rain, rain, rivers E
Tresselt, A. R. Rain drop splash E
Fiction
Martin, B. Listen to the rain E
Skofield, J. All wet! All wet! E
Spier, P. Peter Spier's rain E
Rain drop splash. Tresselt, A. R. E
Rain forest ecology
Cobb, V. This place is wet (2-4) 574.5
Forsyth, A. Journey through a tropical jungle (4 and up) 574.5
George, J. C. One day in the tropical rain forest (4-6) 574.5
Landau, E. Tropical rain forests around the world (4 and up) 574.5

Rain forests
Fiction
Baker, J. Where the forest meets the sea E
Cherry, L. The great kapok tree E
Rain makes applesauce. Scheer, J. E
Rain of fire. Bauer, M. D. Fic
Rain, rain, rivers. Shulevitz, U. E
Rain shadow. Newton, J. R. **574.5**
Rainbow in the sky (k-4) **821.008**
The **rainbow** people. Yep, L. **398.2**
The **rainbow** people [story]. Yep, L.
In Yep, L. The rainbow people p178-90 **398.2**
Rainbows are made: poems. Sandburg, C. **811**
Rainbows, mirages and sundogs. Gallant, R. A. **551.5**
Rainy day: stories and poems (2-4) **808.8**
The **Raksh** of Rustem. Hodges, M.
In Hodges, M. If you had a horse **398.2**
Ralph S. Mouse. Cleary, B. See note under Cleary, B. The mouse and the motorcycle **Fic**
Ralph's secret weapon. Kellogg, S. E
Ralston, William, 1848-1911
The death of Koschei the Deathless
In The Red fairy book p42-53 **398.2**
Ram
Aulnoy, Madame d'. The wonderful sheep
In The Blue fairy book p214-30 **398.2**
Ram, the cat, and the twelve wolves
Afanas'ev, A. N. The ram, the cat, and the twelve wolves
In Afanas'ev, A. N. Russian fairy tales p196-98 **398.2**
Ram who lost half his skin
Afanas'ev, A. N. The ram who lost half his skin
In Afanas'ev, A. N. Russian fairy tales p188-91 **398.2**
Rāma (Hindu deity)
Beach, M. C. The adventures of Rama (4 and up) **891**
Ramírez, Blandina Cárdenas, 1944-
See/See also pages in the following book(s):
Morey, J. Famous Mexican Americans p106-18 (5 and up) **920**
Ramona (Television program)
Scott, E. Ramona: behind the scenes of a television show (4 and up) **791.45**
Ramona and her father. Cleary, B. See note under Cleary, B. Ramona the pest **Fic**
Ramona and her mother. Cleary, B. See note under Cleary, B. Ramona the pest **Fic**
Ramona and the Three Wise Persons. Cleary, B.
In The Family read-aloud Christmas treasury p6-15 **808.8**
Ramona: behind the scenes of a television show. Scott, E. **791.45**
Ramona, forever. Cleary, B. See note under Cleary, B. Ramona the pest **Fic**
Ramona Quimby, age 8. Cleary, B. See note under Cleary, B. Ramona the pest **Fic**
Ramona the brave. Cleary, B. See note under Cleary, B. Ramona the pest **Fic**
Ramona the pest. Cleary, B. **Fic**
Ranch life
Ashabranner, B. K. Born to the land: an American portrait (5 and up) **978.9**
Fiction
Noble, T. H. Meanwhile back at the ranch E
Snyder, Z. K. And condors danced (5 and up) **Fic**
Rand, Gloria
Salty dog E
Rand, Ted
(il) Lear, E. The Jumblies **821**
(il) Longfellow, H. W. Paul Revere's ride **811**
(il) Martin, B. Barn dance! E
(il) Martin, B. The ghost-eye tree E
(il) Martin, B. Knots on a counting rope E
(il) Martin, B. Up and down on the merry-go-round E
(il) Peters, L. W. The sun, the wind and the rain **551.4**
(il) Rand, G. Salty dog E
(il) Stevenson, R. L. My shadow **821**
Rand McNally children's atlas of the United States (4-6) **912**
Rand McNally children's world atlas (4-6) **912**
Rand McNally cosmopolitan world atlas **912**
Rand McNally Goode's world atlas. See Goode's world atlas **912**
Randolph, Edmund Jennings, 1753-1813
See/See also pages in the following book(s):
Hauptly, D. J. "A convention of delegates" p41-53 (5 and up) **342**
The **Random** House book of fairy tales. Ehrlich, A. **398.2**
The **Random** House book of humor for children (4-6) **817.008**
The **Random** House book of Mother Goose (k-2) **398.8**

The **Random** House book of poetry for children 821.008
The **Random** House school dictionary (4 and up) 423
The **Random** House thesaurus 423
Randy the red-horned rainmoose. Kilcup, R.
In The Big book of Christmas plays p228-39 808.82
Ranger Rick 505
Ransome, Arthur, 1884-1967
The firebird, the horse of power and the Princess Vasilissa
In Best-loved folktales of the world p414-22 398.2
The Fool of the World and the flying ship (k-3) 398.2
also in Best-loved folktales of the world p403-11 398.2
Salt
In Best-loved folktales of the world p428-38 398.2
Ransome, James
(il) Johnson, A. Do like Kyla E
Rao, Anthony
(il) Sattler, H. R. Dinosaurs of North America 567.9
(il) Simon, S. The smallest dinosaurs 567.9
Rape
See/See also pages in the following book(s):
Terkel, S. N. Feeling safe, feeling strong p54-65 (4 and up) 362.7
Raphael, 1483-1520
About
Raboff, E. Raphael Sanzio (4 and up) 759.5
Raphael, Elaine
Drawing history: Ancient Egypt (4 and up) 741
(jt. auth) Bolognese, D. Pen & ink 741.2
Rappaport, Doreen
The Boston coffee party E
Rapunzel
Ehrlich, A. Rapunzel 398.2
also in Ehrlich, A. The Random House book of fairy tales p26-33 398.2
Grimm, J. Rapunzel
In Best-loved folktales of the world p75-78 398.2
In Grimm, J. About wise men and simpletons p39-42 398.2
In Grimm, J. The complete Grimm's fairy tales p73-77 398.2
In Grimm, J. The juniper tree, and other tales from Grimm v2 p247-55 398.2
In Grimm, J. Tales from Grimm p135-48 398.2
In The Red fairy book p282-85 398.2
Rogasky, B. Rapunzel 398.2
Thane, A. Rapunzel
In Thane, A. Plays from famous stories and fairy tales p180-97 812
Rare animals
See also Endangered species; Extinct animals
Facklam, M. And then there was one (4-6) 591.5
Fiction
Burningham, J. Hey! get off our train E
Rare plants
See also Endangered species
Rascal. North, S. 599.74
Raskin, Ellen, 1928-1984
Figgs & phantoms (5 and up) Fic
Ghost in a four-room apartment E
The mysterious disappearance of Leon (I mean Noel) (4 and up) Fic
Nothing ever happens on my block E
Spectacles E
The tattooed potato and other clues (5 and up) Fic
The Westing game (5 and up) Fic
(il) Cleaver, V. Ellen Grae Fic
(il) Cleaver, V. Lady Ellen Grae Fic
(il) A Paper zoo. See A Paper zoo 811.008
(il) Piping down the valleys wild. See Piping down the valleys wild 808.81
(il) Shrieks at midnight. See Shrieks at midnight 821.008
See/See also pages in the following book(s):
Newbery and Caldecott Medal books, 1976-1985 p51-61 028.5
The **rat** that said boo to the cat. Brown, M. W.
In Brown, M. W. The fish with the deep sea smile p84-86 818
Ratbat and Tacooma's tree. Berry, J.
In Berry, J. Spiderman Anancy p60-65 398.2
The **ratcatcher**. Marelle, C.
In The Red fairy book p208-14 398.2
Rathbun, Elizabeth
Exploring your solar system (4 and up) 523.2
Rats
Pope, J. Taking care of your mice and rats (3-5) 636.088
Sproule, A. Mice and rats (4 and up) 636.088
See/See also pages in the following book(s):
Weber, W. J. Care of uncommon pets p71-81 (5 and up) 636.088

Rats—*Continued*

Fiction

Conly, J. L. R-T, Margaret, and the rats of NIMH (4 and up) **Fic**
Conly, J. L. Racso and the rats of NIMH (4 and up) **Fic**
Hurd, T. Mystery on the docks **E**
Hutchins, P. Rats! (2-4) **Fic**
O'Brien, R. C. Mrs. Frisby and the rats of NIMH (4 and up) **Fic**
Sharmat, M. W. Mooch the messy **E**

Rats!. Hutchins, P. **Fic**

Rattlesnakes
Freedman, R. Rattlesnakes (3-5) **597.9**
Lavies, B. The secretive timber rattlesnake (3-6) **597.9**

Fiction

Moroney, L. Baby rattlesnake (k-2) **398.2**

Rauch, Roberta
(il) Brown, M. W. The fish with the deep sea smile **818**

Raven
Grimm, J. The raven
In Grimm, J. The complete Grimm's fairy tales p431-36 **398.2**
Hogrogian, N. The Glass Mountain **398.2**

The **raven** and the lobster. Afanas'ev, A. N.
In Afanas'ev, A. N. Russian fairy tales p612 **398.2**

The **Raven** brings light
In Best-loved folktales of the world p719-21 **398.2**

Ravens

Fiction

Aiken, J. Arabel and Mortimer (4-6) **Fic**

Raw Head and Bloody Bones. Leach, M.
In Leach, M. Whistle in the graveyard p91 **398.2**

Rawlings, Marjorie Kinnan, 1896-1953
The yearling (6 and up) **Fic**

Rawlins, Donna
Digging to China **E**
(il) Loh, M. J. Tucking Mommy in **E**

Rawlins, Janet
(il) Gardam, J. The hollow land **Fic**

Rawls, James
The Pilgrim painting
In Holiday plays round the year p91-100 **812.008**

Rawls, Wilson, 1913-
Where the red fern grows **Fic**

Ray, Deborah Kogan, 1940-
My daddy was a soldier **E**
(il) Coerr, E. Chang's paper pony **E**
(il) Cummings, E. E. Hist whist **811**
(il) Harvey, B. Cassie's journey **Fic**
(il) Peterson, J. W. I have a sister—my sister is deaf **362.4**
(il) Poems for mothers. See Poems for mothers **811.008**

Ray, Delia
Gold! the Klondike adventure (5 and up) **971.9**

Ray, James Earl, 1928-
See/See also pages in the following book(s):
Haskins, J. The life and death of Martin Luther King, Jr (5 and up) **92**

Rayevsky, Inna
The talking tree (k-3) **398.2**

Rayevsky, Robert
(il) Rayevsky, I. The talking tree **398.2**

Rayner, Mary, 1933-
Garth Pig and the ice cream lady. See note under Rayner, M. Mr. and Mrs. Pig's evening out **E**
Mr. and Mrs. Pig's evening out **E**
Mrs. Pig gets cross and other stories. See note under Rayner, M. Mr. and Mrs. Pig's evening out **E**
Mrs. Pig's bulk buy. See note under Rayner, M. Mr. and Mrs. Pig's evening out **E**
(il) King-Smith, D. Babe **Fic**
(il) King-Smith, D. Magnus Powermouse **Fic**
(il) King-Smith, D. Pigs might fly **Fic**
(il) Paton Walsh, J. Lost and found **Fic**

The **read-aloud** handbook. See Trelease, J. The new read-aloud handbook **028.5**

Read-aloud rhymes for the very young (k-2) **821.008**

The **Read-aloud** treasury (k-2) **808.8**

Reade, Deborah
(il) Trimble, S. The village of blue stone **970.004**

Reading
Chambers, A. Introducing books to children **028.5**
Kaye, P. Games for reading **372.4**
The RIF guide to encouraging young readers **372.4**

Fiction

Bunting, E. The Wednesday surprise **E**
Gilson, J. Do bananas chew gum? (4-6) **Fic**
Hutchins, P. The tale of Thomas Mead **E**

Periodicals

The Reading Teacher **372.405**

Reading Is Fundamental, Inc.
Once upon a time—: celebrating the magic of children's books in honor of the twentieth anniversary of Reading is Fundamental. See Once upon a time—: celebrating the magic of children's books in honor of the twentieth anniversary of Reading is Fundamental **028.5**
The RIF guide to encouraging young readers. See The RIF guide to encouraging young readers **372.4**
The **Reading** Teacher **372.405**
Reagan, Ronald, 1911-
About
Kent, Z. Ronald Reagan, fortieth president of the United States (4 and up) **92**
The **real** hole. Cleary, B. **E**
The **Real** Mother Goose (k-2) **398.8**
The **real** princess. Andersen, H. C.
In The Scott, Foresman anthology of children's literature p502-03 **808.8**
The **real** princess. Ehrlich, A.
In Ehrlich, A. The Random House book of fairy tales p126-29 **398.2**
The **real** skin rubber monster mask. Cohen, M. See note under Cohen, M. See you in second grade! **E**
The **real** thief. Steig, W. **Fic**
Really a sukkah. Sholem Aleichem
In Sholem Aleichem. Holiday tales of Sholem Aleichem **S C**
Realms of copper, silver, and gold
Afanas'ev, A. N. The three kingdoms
In Afanas'ev, A. N. Russian fairy tales p49-53 **398.2**
A **reasonable** sum. Korman, G.
In Connections: short stories by outstanding writers for young adults p45-52 **S C**
Reasoning
See also Logic
Rebecca's nap. Burstein, F. **E**
The **rebellion** of the magical rabbits. Dorfman, A.
In Where angels glide at dawn p7-25 **S C**
Rechenka's eggs. Polacco, P. **E**
Recipes for art and craft materials. Sattler, H. R. **745.5**
Recreation
See also Amusements
Recreations, Literary *See* Literary recreations
The **red** balloon. Lamorisse, A. **Fic**
The **red** book of Hob stories. Mayne, W. See note under Mayne, W. The green book of Hob stories **E**
The **red** carpet. Parkin, R. **E**
Red carpet Christmas. Miller, H. L.
In The Big book of Christmas plays p3-25 **808.82**
Red Cloud, Sioux Chief, 1822-1909
See/See also pages in the following book(s):
Ehrlich, A. Wounded Knee: an Indian history of the American West (6 and up) **970.004**
Freedman, R. Indian chiefs p10-27 (6 and up) **920**
Red Dog. Kipling, R.
In Kipling, R. The jungle books **S C**
Red-Ettin
Jacobs, J. Red Ettin
In Jacobs, J. English fairy tales p131-37 **398.2**
The Red Etin
In The Blue fairy book p385-90 **398.2**
The **Red** fairy book (4-6) **398.2**
The **red** king. Kelleher, V. **Fic**
The **Red** Lion. Wolkstein, D. **398.2**
Red Riding Hood. Ehrlich, A.
In Ehrlich, A. The Random House book of fairy tales p118-25 **398.2**
Red Robe's dream
In The Whistling skeleton p91-103 **398.2**
Red shoes
Andersen, H. C. The red shoes
In Andersen, H. C. Hans Andersen: his classic fairy tales p171-77 **S C**
The **red** silk handerchief. MacDonald, M. R.
In MacDonald, M. R. When the lights go out p129-32 **372.6**
Red thread riddles. Jensen, V. A. **793.73**
Reducing
Arnold, C. Too fat? Too thin? Do you have a choice? (6 and up) **613.2**
Fiction
Marshall, J. Yummers! **E**
Redwall. Jacques, B. **Fic**
Redwood
Adler, D. A. Redwoods are the tallest trees in the world (k-3) **585**
Redwoods are the tallest trees in the world. Adler, D. A. **585**
Reeder, Carolyn
Shades of gray (4 and up) **Fic**
Reese, Pee Wee, 1919-
About
Golenbock, P. Teammates [biography of Jackie Robinson] (1-4) **92**

Reeves, James, 1909-1978
English fables and fairy stories (4-6) 398.2

Contents: Jack Hannaford; Tattercoats; Johnny Gloke; The fish and the ring; The two princesses; The story of Tom Thumb; The pedlar's dream; Catskin; The tulip bed; Simpleton Peter; The well of the three heads; Jack and the beanstalk; Tom Tit Tot; The golden snuffbox; The stars in the sky; Molly Whipple; The donkey, the table, and the stick; The Well of the World's End; Dick Whittington and his cat

Reeves, Randall R.
The Sea World book of dolphins (4 and up) 599.5

Reference books
Bibliography
Reference books for young readers 011.6
Wynar, C. G. Guide to reference books for school media centers 011.6

Reference Books Bulletin. See Booklist 028.1

Reference books for young readers 011.6

A **reference** guide to historical fiction for children and young adults. Adamson, L. G. 016.8

Reflections. Jonas, A. E

Reflections on a gift of watermelon pickle . . . and other modern verse (6 and up) 811.008

Reflexes
Berger, M. Why I cough, sneeze, shiver, hiccup, & yawn (k-3) 612.8

Reformers
Jacobs, W. J. Great lives: human rights (5 and up) 920

Refugees
Ashabranner, B. K. Into a strange land: unaccompanied refugee youth in America (5 and up) 362.84
Fiction
Bunting, E. How many days to America? E
Holm, A. North to freedom (6 and up) Fic

Refugees, Jewish
Fiction
Kerr, J. When Hitler stole Pink Rabbit (4 and up) Fic

Refugees, Polish
Fiction
Serraillier, I. The silver sword (5 and up) Fic

Refuse and refuse disposal
Hadingham, E. Garbage! (5 and up) 363.7
Maurer, R. Junk in space (4-6) 363.7
Pringle, L. P. Throwing things away (6 and up) 363.7

Regan, Ken
(il) Klein, N. Baryshnikov's Nutcracker 792.8

Regards to the man in the moon. Keats, E. J. See note under Keats, E. J. Louie E

Regourd, Anny-Chantal Levasseur- *See* Levasseur-Regourd, Anny-Chantal

A **regular** rolling Noah. Lyon, G. E. E

Reid, Barbara
(il) Irvine, J. How to make pop-ups 736

Reid, George K.
Pond life (4 and up) 574.92

Reid, Margarette S.
The button box E

Reid Banks, Lynne, 1929-
The Indian in the cupboard (5 and up) Fic
The return of the Indian. See note under Reid Banks, L. The Indian in the cupboard Fic
The secret of the Indian. See note under Reid Banks, L. The Indian in the cupboard Fic

Reincarnation
Fiction
Gerstein, M. The mountains of Tibet E
Kehret, P. Sisters, long ago (5 and up) Fic

Reindeer
Fiction
Brett, J. The wild Christmas reindeer E

Reinfeld, Fred, 1910-1964
Catalogue of the world's most popular coins 737.4

Reingold, Michael
(il) Tiger, S. Diabetes 616.4

Reisberg, Veg
(il) Moroney, L. Baby rattlesnake 398.2

Reiss, Johanna
The upstairs room (4 and up) 92

Reiss, John J.
Colors E
Numbers E
Shapes E

Reit, Seymour
Behind rebel lines: the incredible story of Emma Edmonds, Civil War spy (4 and up) 92

The **relatives** came. Rylant, C. E

Relativity (Physics)
Apfel, N. H. It's all relative (6 and up) 530.1
Fiction
Stannard, R. The time and space of Uncle Albert (5 and up) Fic

Religion
Fiction
Jones, R. C. The Believers (5 and up) Fic
Rylant, C. A fine white dust (5 and up) Fic

Religions
See also Gods and goddesses
Fiction
Blume, J. Are you there God? it's me, Margaret (5 and up) **Fic**
Religious art and symbolism
See also Jewish art and symbolism
Religious poetry
Tambourines! Tambourines to glory! (3-6) **242**
Relocation of Japanese Americans, 1942-1945
See Japanese Americans—Evacuation and relocation, 1942-1945
The **reluctant** dragon. Grahame, K. **Fic**
The **reluctant** dragon. Thane, A.
In Thane, A. Plays from famous stories and fairy tales p267-82 **812**
The **Remarkable** adventures of an old woman and her pig
In A Nursery companion p96-100 **820.8**
The **remarkable** rocket. Wilde, O.
In Wilde, O. The Happy Prince, and other stories p40-51 **S C**
Rembrandt Harmenszoon van Rijn, 1606-1669
About
Raboff, E. Rembrandt (4 and up) **759.9492**
See/See also pages in the following book(s):
Goffstein, M. B. Lives of the artists (5 and up) **920**
Remember not to forget. Finkelstein, N. H. **940.54**
The **remembering** box. Clifford, E. **Fic**
Remington, Frederic, 1861-1909
About
Raboff, E. Frederic Remington (4 and up) **759.13**
Remkiewicz, Frank
(il) Kline, S. Horrible Harry in room 2B **Fic**
Rench, Janice E.
(jt. auth) Terkel, S. N. Feeling safe, feeling strong **362.7**
Renfro, Nancy
Bags are big! **745.54**
Puppet show made easy! (3-6) **791.5**
(jt. auth) Champlin, C. Storytelling with puppets **372.6**
Renoir, Auguste, 1841-1919
About
Raboff, E. Pierre-Auguste Renoir (4 and up) **759.4**
Report writing
Brandt, S. R. How to write a report (4 and up) **808**
Reporters and reporting
See also Journalism
Fleming, T. J. Behind the headlines (5 and up) **071**
Reproduction
See also Genetics
Andry, A. C. How babies are made (k-3) **612.6**
Cole, J. A chick hatches (k-3) **636.5**
Cole, J. My puppy is born (k-3) **636.7**
Fischer-Nagel, H. A puppy is born (1-4) **636.7**
Heller, R. Chickens aren't the only ones (k-1) **591.1**
Kaizuki, K. A calf is born (k-2) **636.2**
Lauber, P. What's hatching out of that egg? (k-3) **591.1**
McClung, R. M. The amazing egg (4 and up) **591.1**
Reproductive system
See also Reproduction
Reptiles
See also Lizards; Snakes
Johnston, G. Scaly babies (3-5) **597.9**
Stebbins, R. C. A field guide to western reptiles and amphibians **597.6**
See/See also pages in the following book(s):
McClung, R. M. The amazing egg p75-84 (4 and up) **591.1**
Weber, W. J. Care of uncommon pets p141-79 (5 and up) **636.088**
Reptiles, Fossil
See also Dinosaurs
Carrick, C. The crocodiles still wait (1-3) **567.9**
Lasky, K. Dinosaur dig (3 and up) **567.9**
Peters, D. A gallery of dinosaurs & other early reptiles (4-6) **567.9**
Sattler, H. R. Pterosaurs, the flying reptiles (1-4) **567.9**
The **Republic** of Ireland. Fradin, D. B. **941.5**
Rescue of the stranded whales. Mallory, K. **639.9**
Rescue: the story of how Gentiles saved Jews in the Holocaust. Meltzer, M. **940.54**
The **rescuers**. Sharp, M. **Fic**
Research
See/See also pages in the following book(s):
Brandt, S. R. How to write a report p30-51 (4 and up) **808**

Respiration
Branley, F. M. Oxygen keeps you alive (k-3) **574.1**
Ressner, Phil
Dudley Pippin and the principal [short story]
In Free to be—you and me p88-89 **810.8**
Restaurants, bars, etc.
Fiction
Day, A. Frank and Ernest **E**
Pinkwater, D. M. Blue moose (1-3) **Fic**
History
See/See also pages in the following book(s):
Tunis, E. The tavern at the ferry p49-58 (5 and up) **973.2**
Retarded children *See* Mentally handicapped children; Slow learning children
Retired. Rylant, C.
In Rylant, C. Every living thing p8-14 **S C**
Rettich, Margret
The Christmas roast
In Bauer, C. F. Celebrations p265-67 **808.8**
Television in the snow
In Bauer, C. F. Celebrations p218-20 **808.8**
The **return**. Levitin, S. **Fic**
The **return** of Bobby Shafto. Gotwalt, H. L. M.
In Gotwalt, H. L. M. Everyday plays for boys and girls p78-89 **812**
The **return** of the Great Brain. Fitzgerald, J. D. See note under Fitzgerald, J. D. The Great Brain **Fic**
The **return** of the Indian. Reid Banks, L. See note under Reid Banks, L. The Indian in the cupboard **Fic**
Return to Bitter Creek. Smith, D. B. **Fic**
Reuben, Joel
Kenya—in pictures. See Kenya—in pictures **967.62**
Reusable space vehicles *See* Space shuttles
Reuter, Bjarne
Buster's world (4 and up) **Fic**
The **revenge** of the Iron Chink. Yee, P.
In Yee, P. Tales from Gold Mountain p57-62 **S C**
The **revenge** of the Magic Chicken. Lester, H. **E**
The **revenge** of the wizard's ghost. Bellairs, J. See note under Bellairs, J. The curse of the blue figurine **Fic**
Revere, Paul, 1735-1818
About
Fritz, J. And then what happened, Paul Revere? (2-4) **92**
Lee, M. Paul Revere (5 and up) **92**
Fiction
Lawson, R. Mr. Revere and I (5 and up) **Fic**
Poetry
Longfellow, H. W. Paul Revere's ride (k-3) **811**
Rey, H. A. (Hans Augusto), 1898-1977
Cecily G. and the 9 monkeys **E**
Curious George **E**
Curious George gets a medal. See note under Rey, H. A. Curious George **E**
Curious George goes to the hospital. See note under Rey, H. A. Curious George **E**
Curious George learns the alphabet. See note under Rey, H. A. Curious George **E**
Curious George rides a bike. See note under Rey, H. A. Curious George **E**
Curious George takes a job. See note under Rey, H. A. Curious George **E**
Find the constellations **523.8**
(il) Payne, E. Katy No-Pocket **E**
Rey, Hans Augusto *See* Rey, H. A. (Hans Augusto), 1898-1977
Rey, Margaret
Curious George flies a kite. See note under Rey, H. A. Curious George **E**
Curious George goes to the hospital. See note under Rey, H. A. Curious George **E**
Reyher, Rebecca Hourwich, 1897-1987
My mother is the most beautiful woman in the world (1-4) **398.2**
Reynard. Leighner, A. M. **599.74**
Reynolds, Lura Schield
(jt. auth) Naylor, P. R. Maudie in the middle **Fic**
Rhinoceros
Fiction
Mayer, M. Appelard and Liverwurst **E**
Mayer, M. Liverwurst is missing **E**
Rhode Island
Heinrichs, A. Rhode Island
In America the beautiful **973**
Fiction
Manes, S. Some of the adventures of Rhode Island Red (3-6) **Fic**
Rhodesia, Northern *See* Zambia
Rhodesia, Southern *See* Zimbabwe
Rhodesia in pictures. See Zimbabwe—in pictures **968.91**

Rhyme
See also Stories in rhyme
A **rhyme** for silver. Aiken, J.
In Aiken, J. Give yourself a fright: thirteen tales of the supernatural p70-88 **S C**
Rhymes and verses. De la Mare, W. **821**
Ribner, Susan
The martial arts (5 and up) **796.8**
Ribsy. Cleary, B. See note under Cleary, B. Henry Huggins **Fic**
Ricci, Dino
(il) Trenary, J. Time of my life: Jill Trenary **92**
Riccio, Frank
(il) McClard, M. Hiawatha and the Iroquois league **92**
Rice, Eve, 1951-
At Grammy's house **E**
Benny bakes a cake **E**
City night **E**
Goodnight, goodnight **E**
Peter's pockets **E**
Sam who never forgets **E**
Rice
Johnson, S. A. Rice (4 and up) **633.1**
Rice cake that rolled away. Uchida, Y.
In Uchida, Y. The magic listening cap **398.2**
Rice cakes for the new year. Terada, A. M.
In Terada, A. M. Under the starfruit tree p105-08 **398.2**
The **rich** man and the shoe-maker. Wildsmith, B. **398.2**
Richard Kennedy: collected stories. Kennedy, R. **S C**
Richards, Norman, 1932-
Dreamers & doers: inventors who changed our world (6 and up) **920**
Richardson, Selma K.
Magazines for children **011.6**
Richter, Mischa, 1910-
(il) Meltzer, M. A book about names **929.4**
Rickshaw to horror. Quackenbush, R. M. See note under Quackenbush, R. M. Express train to trouble **Fic**
Ricky with the tuft. Perrault, C.
In Sleeping beauty & other favourite fairy tales p93-102 **398.2**
Riddell, Chris
When the walrus comes **E**
Riddle
Grimm, J. The riddle
In The Green fairy book p300-03 **398.2**
In Grimm, J. The complete Grimm's fairy tales p128-31 **398.2**
The **riddle** and the rune. Chetwin, G. **Fic**
The **riddle-master** of Hed. McKillip, P. A. **Fic**
Riddle romp. Maestro, G. **793.73**
Riddle roundup. Maestro, G. **793.73**
The **riddle** tale of freedom. Hamilton, V.
In Hamilton, V. The people could fly: American black folktales p156-59 **398.2**
Riddles
Adler, D. A. The carsick zebra and other animal riddles (1-3) **793.73**
Adler, D. A. A teacher on roller skates and other school riddles (k-3) **793.73**
Adler, D. A. The twisted witch, and other spooky riddles (1-3) **793.73**
Calmenson, S. What am I? (k-2) **793.73**
Cerf, B. Bennett Cerf's book of animal riddles (k-3) **793.73**
Cerf, B. Bennett Cerf's book of riddles (k-3) **793.73**
Cricket's jokes, riddles and other stuff (1-4) **793.73**
De Regniers, B. S. It does not say meow, and other animal riddle rhymes (k-1) **793.73**
Gounaud, K. J. A very mice joke book **793.73**
Jensen, V. A. Red thread riddles **793.73**
Kessler, L. P. Old Turtle's riddle and joke book (1-3) **793.73**
Livingston, M. C. My head is red and other riddle rhymes (k-2) **793.73**
Maestro, G. Halloween howls (2-4) **793.73**
Maestro, G. A raft of riddles (2-4) **793.73**
Maestro, G. Riddle romp (2-4) **793.73**
Maestro, G. Riddle roundup (2-4) **793.73**
Maestro, G. What's a frank frank? (2-4) **793.73**
McMullan, K. Snakey riddles (k-2) **793.73**
Phillips, L. Going ape (3-5) **793.73**
Phillips, L. Haunted house jokes (3-5) **793.73**
Schwartz, A. Ten copycats in a boat, and other riddles (1-3) **398.6**
Schwartz, A. Tomfoolery: trickery and foolery with words (4 and up) **398**
Schwartz, A. Unriddling: all sorts of riddles to puzzle your guessery (4 and up) **398.6**
Shannon, G. Stories to solve (3 and up) **398.2**
Swann, B. A basket full of white eggs (k-3) **398.6**
Terban, M. The dove dove (3-6) **793.73**
The Upside down riddle book (k-2) **793.73**

Riddles—*Continued*
See/See also pages in the following book(s):
With a deep sea smile p101-06 **372.6**

Riddles. Afanas'ev, A. N.
In Afanas'ev, A. N. Russian fairy tales p29-30 **398.2**

Riddling tale
Grimm, J. A riddling tale
In Grimm, J. The complete Grimm's fairy tales p663 **398.2**

Ride, Sally K.
To space & back (4 and up) **629.45**

Ride a purple pelican. Prelutsky, J. **811**

Rider Chan and the night river. Yee, P.
In Yee, P. Tales from Gold Mountain p51-56 **S C**

Riding *See* Horseback riding

RIF *See* Reading Is Fundamental, Inc.

The **RIF** guide to encouraging young readers **372.4**

Rifles for Watie. Keith, H. **Fic**

Riggle, Judith
(jt. auth) Barstow, B. Beyond picture books **011.6**

Right- and left-handedness *See* Left- and right-handedness

Right and wrong
Afanas'ev, A. N. Right and wrong
In Afanas'ev, A. N. Russian fairy tales p202-08 **398.2**

The **right** family. Durkee, S.
In Free to be—a family p44-48 **810.8**

Right to know *See* Freedom of information

Rights, Mollie
Beastly neighbors (4 and up) **508**

Riis, Jacob A. (Jacob August), 1849-1914
See/See also pages in the following book(s):
Jacobs, W. J. Great lives: human rights p199-206 (5 and up) **920**

"Rikki-tikki-tavi". Kipling, R.
In Kipling, R. The jungle books **S C**

Riley, James Whitcomb, 1849-1916
The gobble-uns'll git you ef you don't watch out! (1-4) **811**

Rinard, Judith E., 1947-
Creatures of the night (k-3) **591.5**
Dolphins: our friends in the sea (4 and up) **599.5**
Helping our animal friends (k-3) **636.088**
Wildlife, making a comeback (4 and up) **591**
The world beneath your feet (k-3) **591.9**
Zoos without cages (5 and up) **590.74**

Rinciari, Ken
(il) Leach, M. Whistle in the graveyard **398.2**

Ring of earth: a child's book of seasons. Yolen, J. **811**

A **ring** of endless light. L'Engle, M. **Fic**

Ringgold, Faith
See/See also pages in the following book(s):
Sills, L. Inspirations p40-51 (5 and up) **920**

Riordan, James, 1936-
The woman in the moon, and other tales of forgotten heroines (4 and up) **398.2**
Contents: The woman in the moon; A mother's yarn; The nagging husband; Gulnara the Tartar warrior; Caterina the wise; Oona and the giant Cuchulain; Aina-kizz and the black-bearded Bai; A pottle o' brains; The maid who chose a husband; Three strong women; The wonderful pearl; The squire's bride; The Aztec sun goddess

Rip-roaring Russell. Hurwitz, J. **Fic**

Rip Van Winkle. Irving, W. **Fic**

Rip Van Winkle. Thane, A.
In Thane, A. Plays from famous stories and fairy tales p381-96 **812**

Ripley, Catherine
(ed) Outdoor fun. See Outdoor fun **796.1**

Riquet with the tuft
Perrault, C. Ricky with the tuft
In Sleeping beauty & other favourite fairy tales p93-102 **398.2**

The **rise** and fall of Adolf Hitler. Shirer, W. L. **943.086**

The **rise** and fall of Ben Gizzard. Kennedy, R.
In Kennedy, R. Collected stories p125-40 **S C**

Risk 'n' roses. Slepian, J. **Fic**

Riskind, Mary, 1944-
Apple is my sign (5 and up) **Fic**

Riswold, Gilbert
(il) Johnson, A. The grizzly **Fic**

Ritchie, Alice
Two of everything
In The Scott, Foresman anthology of children's literature p323-26 **808.8**

Ritter, Lawrence S.
The story of baseball (5 and up) **796.357**

Ritz, Karen
(il) Collins, D. R. The country artist: a story about Beatrix Potter **92**
(il) Ferris, J. Go free or die: a story about Harriet Tubman **92**
(il) Mitchell, B. Between two worlds: a story about Pearl Buck **92**

The **river** at Green Knowe. Boston, L. M. See note under Boston, L. M. The children of Green Knowe **Fic**

River ecology
Parker, S. Pond & river (4 and up) **574.92**

The **River** of Separation. Marriott, A. L.
In Marriott, A. L. American Indian mythology **398.2**
The **River** Shore Club. Simon, S.
In Simon, S. More wise men of Helm and their merry tales p111-19 **398.2**
Rivera, Frida Kahlo *See* Kahlo, Frida, 1907-1954
Riverkeeper. Ancona, G. **333.91**
Rivers, Alice
(jt. auth) Jenness, A. In two worlds: a Yup'ik Eskimo family **970.004**
Rivers
Bramwell, M. Rivers and lakes (4-6) **551.48**
McCauley, J. R. Let's explore a river (k-3) **574.92**
Fiction
Byars, B. C. Trouble River (4-6) **Fic**
Locker, T. Where the river begins **E**
Rivers and lakes. Bramwell, M. **551.48**
Roach, Con
(il) MacLean, N. Hockey basics **796.962**
Roach, Marilynne K.
Encounters with the invisible world (5 and up) **S C**
Contents: The ghost in the shed; Betty Booker and the skipper; The rock on Hopkins Hill; The orchard murder; The witch of Wellfleet; The hooks of heaven; General Moulton strikes a bargain; Sam Hart accepts a wager; The temporary death of Molly Swett; The disappearance of Peter Rugg
Roach (Insect) *See* Cockroaches
The **road** from home [biography of Veron Kherdian]. Kherdian, D. **92**
The **road** to Bethlehem. Laird, E. **232.9**
The **road** to Camlann. Sutcliff, R. **398.2**
The **road** to Memphis. Taylor, M. D. See note under Taylor, M. D. Song of the trees **Fic**
Roadrunner's pack. Curry, J. L.
In Curry, J. L. Back in the beforetime p5-9 **398.2**
Roads
See also Express highways
Gibbons, G. New road! (k-3) **625.7**
History
Gibbons, G. From path to highway: the story of the Boston Post Road (1-3) **388.1**
Roald Dahl's James and the giant peach. George, R. R. **822**
Robber bridegroom
Grimm, J. The robber bridegroom
In Grimm, J. The complete Grimm's fairy tales p200-04 **398.2**
San Souci, R. The robber bridegroom
In San Souci R. Short & shivery p1-8 **398.2**
Robbers
Afanas'ev, A. N. The robbers
In Afanas'ev, A. N. Russian fairy tales p419-23 **398.2**
The **robbers**. Bawden, N. **Fic**
Robbers and outlaws
Fiction
Coren, A. Arthur the Kid (3-5) **Fic**
Fleischman, S. The ghost on Saturday night (3-5) **Fic**
Fleischman, S. The whipping boy (5 and up) **Fic**
Garfield, L. Young Nick and Jubilee (5 and up) **Fic**
Lindgren, A. Ronia, the robber's daughter (4-6) **Fic**
Steig, W. The real thief (2-5) **Fic**
Ungerer, T. The three robbers **E**
Poetry
Noyes, A. The highwayman (5 and up) **821**
Robbins, Chandler S.
Birds of North America (4 and up) **598**
(jt. auth) Zim, H. S. Birds **598**
Robbins, Ken
Building a house (3-6) **690**
City/country **E**
A flower grows (2-4) **582.13**
Robbins, Maria Polushkin *See* Polushkin, Maria
Robbins, Ruth
Baboushka and the three kings (1-4) **398.2**
(il) Kroeber, T. Ishi, last of his tribe **92**
(il) Le Guin, U. K. A wizard of Earthsea **Fic**
Roberson, Jennifer
To ride the sea of grass
In Herds of thunder, manes of gold p157-76 **808.8**
Robert, Henry Martyn, 1837-1923
The Scott, Foresman Robert's Rules of order newly revised **060.4**
Robert, Sarah Corbin
(ed) Robert, H. M. The Scott, Foresman Robert's Rules of order newly revised **060.4**
Robert D. San Souci's The six swans. San Souci, R. **398.2**
Robert E. Lee. Weidhorn, M. **92**
Roberts, Bethany
Waiting-for-papa stories **E**
Waiting-for-spring stories **E**

Roberts, Patricia, 1936-
Counting books are more than numbers: an annotated action bibliography **016.510**

Roberts, Willo Davis
The girl with the silver eyes (4-6) **Fic**
Megan's island (5 and up) **Fic**
To Grandmother's house we go (4-6) **Fic**
The view from the cherry tree (5 and up) **Fic**

Robert's Rules of order. Robert, H. M. **060.4**

Robertson, James, 1935-
(il) Weitzman, D. L. My backyard history book **973**

Robertson, Keith, 1914-
Henry Reed, Inc. (4-6) **Fic**
Henry Reed's babysitting service. See note under Robertson, K. Henry Reed, Inc. **Fic**
Henry Reed's big show. See note under Robertson, K. Henry Reed, Inc. **Fic**
Henry Reed's journey. See note under Robertson, K. Henry Reed, Inc. **Fic**
Henry Reed's think tank. See note under Robertson, K. Henry Reed, Inc. **Fic**

Robeson, Paul, 1898-1976
About
Greenfield, E. Paul Robeson (2-5) **92**

Robin Hood (Legendary character)
Creswick, P. Robin Hood (5 and up) **398.2**
McKinley, R. The outlaws of Sherwood (6 and up) **398.2**
Pyle, H. The merry adventures of Robin Hood of great renown in Nottinghamshire (5 and up) **398.2**

Robins, Joan
Addie meets Max **E**

Robins
Fiction
Rockwell, A. F. My spring robin **E**

Robinson, Adjai, 1932-
The stepchild and the fruit trees
In The Scott, Foresman anthology of children's literature p319-21 **808.8**

Robinson, Barbara
The best Christmas pageant ever (4-6) **Fic**
The best Christmas pageant ever [excerpt]
In The Random House book of humor for children p144-53 **817.008**

Robinson, Charles, 1931-
(il) Brittain, B. All the money in the world **Fic**
(il) Smith, D. B. A taste of blackberries **Fic**

Robinson, Jackie, 1919-1972
About
Adler, D. A. Jackie Robinson: he was the first (3-5) **92**
Golenbock, P. Teammates (1-4) **92**
Scott, R. Jackie Robinson (5 and up) **92**

Robinson, Jeri
Activities for anyone, anytime, anywhere (5 and up) **790.1**

Robinson, Nancy K., 1942-
Angela, private citizen (3-5) **Fic**

Robinson Crusoe. Defoe, D. **Fic**

Robotics
Harrar, G. Radical robots (5 and up) **629.8**
Skurzynski, G. Robots: your high-tech world (5 and up) **629.8**

Robots
Harrar, G. Radical robots (5 and up) **629.8**
Lauber, P. Get ready for robots! (k-3) **629.8**
Skurzynski, G. Robots: your high-tech world (5 and up) **629.8**
Fiction
Hoover, H. M. Orvis (5 and up) **Fic**

Robson, Michael
New Zealand—in pictures. See New Zealand—in pictures **993**

Rocha, Ruth
The Universal Declaration of Human Rights (k-2) **341**

Roche, P. K. (Patricia K.), 1935-
Dollhouse magic (2-4) **745.592**

Roche, Patricia K. *See* Roche, P. K. (Patricia K.), 1935-

Rochman, Hazel
Tales of love and terror **028**

Rock collecting. Gans, R. **552**

Rock drawings, paintings, and engravings
See also Cave drawings

The **rock** on Hopkins Hill. Roach, M. K.
In Roach, M. K. Encounters with the invisible world **S C**

The **rock** pool. Bellamy, D. J. **574.92**

Rockets (Aeronautics)
Branley, F. M. Rockets and satellites (k-3) **629.4**

Rockets and satellites. Branley, F. M. **629.4**

The **rocking** chair rebellion. Clifford, E. **Fic**

Rocks
McGowen, T. Album of rocks and minerals (4 and up) **549**
Podendorf, I. Rocks and minerals (1-4) **549**

Rocks—*Continued*
Selsam, M. E. A first look at rocks (1-3) 552
Symes, R. F. Rocks & minerals (4 and up) 549
Zim, H. S. Rocks and minerals (4 and up) 549
Collectors and collecting
Gans, R. Rock collecting (k-3) 552
Rocks & minerals. Symes, R. F. 549
Rocks and minerals. Podendorf, I. 549
Rocks and minerals. Zim, H. S. 549
Rockwell, Anne F., 1934-
Albert B. Cub & Zebra E
Apples and pumpkins E
At the beach E
Big wheels (k-1) 629.225
Bikes (k-2) 629.227
Boats (k-1) 387.2
Can I help? E
Cars (k-1) 629.222
Come to town E
The emergency room (k-2) 362.1
The emperor's new clothes (1-4) Fic
Fire engines (k-1) 628.9
First comes spring E
The first snowfall E
Games (and how to play them) (k-4) 796.1
Happy birthday to me E
How my garden grew E
I like the library (k-1) 027.4
Machines (k-1) 621.8
My back yard E
My spring robin E
Nice and clean (k-2) 648
The night we slept outside E
Our garage sale E
Planes (k-1) 629.133
Puss in boots, and other stories (2-4) 398.2
Contents: Jack and the beanstalk; Nail soup; Kate Crackernuts; The miller, his son, and the donkey; The golden goose; The boy who cried wolf; The fisherman and his wife; Briar Rose; Mr. Vinegar; The frog prince; The cat on the Dovrefell; Puss in boots
Sick in bed E
Things that go (k-1) 629.04
Things to play with (k-1) 793
The three bears & 15 other stories (k-3) 398.2
Contents: The three bears; The lion and the mouse; The cock and the mouse and the little red hen; The gingerbread man; The house that Jack built; The water-nixie; The three billy goats Gruff; Henny-Penny; The shoemaker and the elves; Teeny-tiny; The three little pigs; Lazy Jack; The dog and the bone; Little Red Riding Hood; The little pot; The star money
The toolbox (k-1) 621.9
Trains (k-2) 625.1
Trucks (k-1) 629.224
Willy can count E
(il) Showers, P. What happens to a hamburger 612.3
Rockwell, Gail
(il) Conford, E. Dreams of victory Fic
Rockwell, Harlow, 1910-1988
I did it (1-3) 745.5
My dentist (k-1) 617.6
My doctor (k-1) 610.69
(jt. auth) Rockwell, A. F. At the beach E
(jt. auth) Rockwell, A. F. Can I help? E
(jt. auth) Rockwell, A. F. The emergency room 362.1
(jt. auth) Rockwell, A. F. The first snowfall E
(jt. auth) Rockwell, A. F. Happy birthday to me E
(jt. auth) Rockwell, A. F. How my garden grew E
(jt. auth) Rockwell, A. F. Machines 621.8
(jt. auth) Rockwell, A. F. My back yard E
(il) Rockwell, A. F. My spring robin E
(jt. auth) Rockwell, A. F. Nice and clean 648
(jt. auth) Rockwell, A. F. The night we slept outside E
(il) Rockwell, A. F. Our garage sale E
(jt. auth) Rockwell, A. F. Sick in bed E
(jt. auth) Rockwell, A. F. The toolbox 621.9
Rockwell, Lizzy
(il) Rockwell, A. F. Apples and pumpkins E
(il) Rockwell, A. F. My spring robin E
Rockwell, Thomas, 1933-
How to eat fried worms (3-6) Fic
How to eat fried worms [excerpt]
In The Random House book of humor for children p301-05 817.008
How to eat fried worms, and other plays (4-6) 812
Contents: Myron Mere; How to eat fried worms; Aiiieeeeeeeeee!; The heiress, or the croak of doom
Rodda, Emily, 1948-
The best-kept secret (3-5) Fic
Rodents
See/See also pages in the following book(s):
Weber, W. J. Care of uncommon pets p32-92 (5 and up) 636.088
Rodgers, Mary
A billion for Boris. See note under Rodgers, M. Freaky Friday Fic
Freaky Friday (4 and up) Fic
Freaky Friday [excerpt]
In The Random House book of humor for children p262-67 817.008
Ladies first [short story]
In Free to be—you and me p39-45 810.8

Rodgers, Mary—*Continued*
Summer switch. See note under Rodgers, M. Freaky Friday **Fic**
Rodman, Maia *See* Wojciechowska, Maia, 1927-
Rodowsky, Colby F., 1932-
The gathering room (5 and up) **Fic**
Mildred
In Connections: short stories by outstanding writers for young adults p95-104 **S C**
Roe, Richard, 1959-
(il) Neuman, P. When winter comes **591.5**
Roebuck, Alvah Curtis
See/See also pages in the following book(s):
Aaseng, N. From rags to riches p24-32 (5 and up) **920**
Roentgen, Wilhelm Conrad *See* Röntgen, Wilhelm Conrad, 1845-1923
Rofes, Eric E., 1954-
(ed) The Kids' book about death and dying. See The Kids' book about death and dying **155.9**
Roffe, Michael, 1928-
(il) Jefferis, D. Helicopters **629.133**
(il) Jefferis, D. Supersonic flight **629.133**
Rogasky, Barbara
Rapunzel (1-3) **398.2**
The water of life (1-3) **398.2**
Rogers, Fred
Going on an airplane (k-2) **387.7**
Going to the dentist (k-2) **617.6**
Going to the hospital (k-2) **362.1**
Making friends (k-1) **155.4**
Moving (k-1) **155.4**
When a pet dies (k-1) **155.9**
Rogers, Jacqueline
The Christmas pageant **E**
(il) Byars, B. C. The not-just-anybody family **Fic**
(il) LeShan, E. J. When a parent is very sick **155.9**
Rogers, Lynn L.
(il) Pringle, L. P. Bearman: exploring the world of black bears **599.74**
Rogers, Paul, 1950-
The shapes game (k-2) **516**
Roget's children's thesaurus. Schiller, A. **423**
Roget's student thesaurus. Schiller, A. **423**
Rohmer, Harriet
Brother Anansi and the cattle ranch (3-6) **398.2**
Roiphe, Anne Richardson, 1935-
The field [short story]
In Free to be—you and me p96-99 **810.8**
Rojankovsky, Feodor Stepanovich, 1891-1970
(il) Fritz, J. The cabin faced west **Fic**
(il) Langstaff, J. M. Frog went a-courtin' **781.62**
(il) Langstaff, J. M. Over in the meadow **781.62**
(il) The Tall book of nursery tales. See The Tall book of nursery tales **398.2**
See/See also pages in the following book(s):
Caldecott Medal books, 1938-1957 p285-95 **028.5**
A Horn Book sampler on children's books and reading p71-85 **028.5**
Roland
Grimm, J. Darling Roland
In Best-loved folktales of the world p84-87 **398.2**
Grimm, J. Sweetheart Roland
In Grimm, J. The complete Grimm's fairy tales p268-71 **398.2**
Roland and Oliver. Picard, B. L.
In The Scott, Foresman anthology of children's literature p458-61 **808.8**
Roland, the minstrel pig. Steig, W. **E**
Role conflict
See also Sex role
Roll of thunder, hear my cry. Taylor, M. D. **Fic**
Roll over! Gerstein, M. **E**
Roller skating
Sullivan, G. Better roller skating for boys and girls (4 and up) **796.2**
Rolling Harvey down the hill. Prelutsky, J. **811**
Rollock, Barbara T.
Public library services for children **027.62**
Rollock, Barbara T., 1924-
Black authors and illustrators of children's books **920.003**
The **roly-poly** pudding. Potter, B. See note under Potter, B. The story of Miss Moppet **E**
Roly poly rice ball. MacDonald, M. R.
In MacDonald, M. R. Twenty tellable tales p104-14 **372.6**
Roman architecture *See* Architecture, Roman
Roman Empire *See* Rome
Roman forts. Mulvihill, M. **937**
Roman mythology *See* Mythology, Classical
Roman numerals. Adler, D. A. **513**
Roman science *See* Science—Rome
Romances
See also Arthurian romances
Romania
Carran, B. Romania (4 and up) **949.8**

Romanova, N. (Natal'īā)
Once there was a tree (2-4) **582.16**
Romanova, Natal'īā *See* Romanova, N. (Natal'īā)
Romans
Ballard, R. D. The lost wreck of the Isis (4 and up) **910.4**
Rombola, John
(il) Archambault, J. Counting sheep **E**
Rome
Antiquities
Corbishley, M. Ancient Rome (5 and up) **937**
James, S. Ancient Rome (4 and up) **937**
Civilization
Corbishley, M. Ancient Rome (5 and up) **937**
James, S. Ancient Rome (4 and up) **937**
History, Military
Mulvihill, M. Roman forts (5 and up) **937**
Science
See Science—Rome
Rona and the legend of the moon. Te Kanawa, K.
In Te Kanawa, K. Land of the long white cloud p101-04 **398.2**
Ronald Morgan goes to bat. Giff, P. R. See note under Giff, P. R. Watch out, Ronald Morgan! **E**
Ronia, the robber's daughter. Lindgren, A. **Fic**
Röntgen, Wilhelm Conrad, 1845-1923
See/See also pages in the following book(s):
McGowen, T. Radioactivity: from the Curies to the atomic age p2-6, 38-39 (6 and up) **539.7**
The **rooftop** mystery. Lexau, J. M. **E**
Rookie of the year. Tunis, J. R. See note under Tunis, J. R. The kid from Tomkinsville **Fic**
Room for me and a mountain lion (5 and up) **808.81**
A **room** made of windows. Cameron, E. **Fic**
Roomrimes: poems. Cassedy, S. **811**
Roop, Peter, 1951-
Prairie lightning
In Herds of thunder, manes of gold p35-53 **808.8**
Roosevelt, Eleanor, 1884-1962
About
Faber, D. Eleanor Roosevelt: first lady of the world (4 and up) **92**
See/See also pages in the following book(s):
Jacobs, W. J. Great lives: human rights p245-56 (5 and up) **920**
The **Rooster** crows (k-2) **398.8**
The **rooster** who set out to see the world. See Carle, E. Rooster's off to see the world **E**
Roosters
Fiction
Cooney, B. Chanticleer and the fox **E**
Rooster's off to see the world. Carle, E. **E**
Root, Phyllis, 1949-
Soup for supper **E**
The **root** cellar. Lunn, J. L. S. **Fic**
Rootabaga stories. Sandburg, C. **S C**
also in Sandburg, C. The Sandburg treasury p9-160 **818**
Rope skipping
Kalbfleisch, S. Jump! (3-6) **796.2**
Rope skipping rhymes *See* Jump rope rhymes
Rosales, Melodye
(il) Byars, B. C. Beans on the roof **Fic**
Rosalie
In The Monkey's haircut, and other stories told by the Maya p56-65 **398.2**
Rosanella. Caylus, A. C. P. de T., comte de.
In The Green fairy book p48-55 **398.2**
Rosas, Juan Manuel José Domingo Ortiz de, 1793-1877
See/See also pages in the following book(s):
Fox, G. The land and people of Argentina p75-85 (5 and up) **982**
The **rose**. Grimm, J.
In Grimm, J. The complete Grimm's fairy tales p819-20 **398.2**
The **rose** and the minor demon. Babbitt, N.
In Babbitt, N. The Devil's storybook p79-89 **S C**
Rose Blanche. Innocenti, R. **Fic**
A **Rose** for Pinkerton. Kellogg, S. See note under Kellogg, S. Pinkerton, behave! **E**
Rose in bloom. Alcott, L. M. See note under Alcott, L. M. Little women **Fic**
The **rose** in my garden. Lobel, A. **E**
Rose-tree
Jacobs, J. Rose-tree
In Jacobs, J. English fairy tales p15-19 **398.2**
Rosen, Michael, 1946-
We're going on a bear hunt **E**

Rosenberg, Ethel Clifford *See* Clifford, Eth, 1915-
Rosenberg, Jane, 1949-
Sing me a story (4-6) **792.5**
Rosenberg, Maxine B., 1939-
Artists of handcrafted furniture at work (4 and up) **749**
Being a twin, having a twin (2-4) **155.4**
Being adopted (2-4) **362.7**
Finding a way (2-4) **362.4**
Living in two worlds (2-4) **306.8**
Making a new home in America (4-6) **325.73**
My friend Leslie (1-3) **362.4**
Not my family: sharing the truth about alcoholism (4 and up) **362.29**
Rosenberry, Vera
(il) Chaikin, M. Esther **296.4**
(il) Hurwitz, J. Anne Frank: life in hiding **92**
(il) Lyon, G. E. Together **E**
Rosenbloom, Joseph
Knock-knock! who's there (4 and up) **808.87**
Laughs, hoots & giggles (4 and up) **808.87**
Rosenblum, Richard, 1928-
(il) Branley, F. M. Earthquakes **551.2**
(il) Gans, R. Danger—icebergs! **551.3**
(il) Graham, A. The big stretch: the complete book of the amazing rubber band **678**
Rosh ha-Shanah
Chaikin, M. Sound the shofar (3-6) **296.4**
Rosie and Michael. Viorst, J. **E**
Rosie's walk. Hutchins, P. **E**
Ross, Clare Romano, 1922-
(il) Sprints and distances. See Sprints and distances **808.81**
Ross, Eulalie Steinmetz
The spirited life: Bertha Mahony Miller and children's books **92**
Ross, John, 1921-
(il) Sprints and distances. See Sprints and distances **808.81**
Ross, Pat
M and M and the bad news babies. See note under Ross, P. Meet M and M **E**
M and M and the big bag. See note under Ross, P. Meet M and M **E**
M and M and the haunted house game. See note under Ross, P. Meet M and M **E**
M and M and the mummy mess. See note under Ross, P. Meet M and M **E**
M and M and the super child afternoon. See note under Ross, P. Meet M and M **E**
Meet M and M **E**
Ross, Tony, 1938-
Hansel and Gretel (k-3) **398.2**
Mrs. Goat and her seven little kids (k-2) **398.2**
The treasure of Cozy Cove **E**
(il) Noble, T. H. Meanwhile back at the ranch **E**
(il) Willis, J. Earthlets, as explained by Professor Xargle **E**
Rossel, Seymour
The Holocaust (5 and up) **940.54**
Rossellini, Albert
Cote d'Ivoire (Ivory Coast)—in pictures. See Cote d'Ivoire (Ivory Coast)—in pictures **966.68**
Rosy Cole's great American guilt club. Greenwald, S. See note under Greenwald, S. Give us a great big smile, Rosy Cole **Fic**
The **rosy** fat magenta radish. Wolf, J. **E**
Rosy starling. Garfield, L.
In Garfield, L. The apprentices **S C**
Rosy's garden: a child's keepsake of flowers. Laird, E. **635.9**
Rosy's romance. Greenwald, S. See note under Greenwald, S. Give us a great big smile, Rosy Cole **Fic**
Roth, Henry, 1933-
(il) Branley, F. M. Color, from rainbows to lasers **535.6**
Roth, Otavio, 1952-
(il) Rocha, R. The Universal Declaration of Human Rights **341**
Roth-Hano, Renée, 1931-
Touch wood (6 and up) **Fic**
Rothman, Michael
(il) Ryder, J. Lizard in the sun **597.9**
(il) Ryder, J. White bear, ice bear **599.74**
Rotten Ralph. Gantos, J. **E**
Rotten Ralph's rotten Christmas. Gantos, J. See note under Gantos, J. Rotten Ralph **E**
Rotten Ralph's show and tell. Gantos, J. See note under Gantos, J. Rotten Ralph **E**
Rotten Ralph's trick or treat! Gantos, J. See note under Gantos, J. Rotten Ralph **E**

Round & round & round. Hoban, T. E
Round buildings, square buildings, & buildings that wiggle like a fish. Isaacson, P. M. 720
The **round** sultan and the straight answer. Walker, B. K.
In Walker, B. K. A treasury of Turkish folktales for children p127-31 398.2
Round trip. Jonas, A. E
Rounds, Glen, 1906-
The morning the sun refused to rise E
Ol' Paul, the mighty logger (3-6) 398.2
Washday on Noah's ark E
(il) Aylesworth, J. Hanna's hog E
(il) Gage, W. Mike's toads Fic
(il) I know an old lady who swallowed a fly. See I know an old lady who swallowed a fly 782.42
(il) Old MacDonald had a farm. See Old MacDonald had a farm 781.62
(il) Schwartz, A. Cross your fingers, spit in your hat: superstitions and other beliefs 398
(il) Schwartz, A. Kickle snifters and other fearsome critters 398
(il) Schwartz, A. Tomfoolery: trickery and foolery with words 398
(il) Schwartz, A. A twister of twists, a tangler of tongues 808.88
(il) Schwartz, A. Whoppers 398.2
(il) Schwartz, A. Witcracks: jokes and jests from American folklore 398
(il) Wright, J. The old woman and the jar of uums E
(il) Wright, J. The old woman and the Willy Nilly Man E
Rouse, W. H. D. (William Henry Denham), 1863-1950
The wise old shepherd
In Shedlock, M. L. The art of the storyteller p216-21 372.6
Rouse, William Henry Denham *See* Rouse, W. H. D. (William Henry Denham), 1863-1950
Rousseau, Henri Julien Félix, 1844-1910
About
Raboff, E. Henri Rousseau (4 and up) 759.4
Rowand, Phyllis
(il) Krauss, R. The growing story E
Roy, Jeroo
(il) Godden, R. The valiant chatti-maker 398.2
Roy, Ron, 1940-
Move over, wheelchairs coming through! (3 and up) 362.4
Whose shoes are these? (k-2) 391
Roy, Ronald *See* Roy, Ron, 1940-
A **royal** pain. Conford, E. Fic
Royalty *See* Kings, queens, rulers, etc.
Roybal, Edward R., 1916-
See/See also pages in the following book(s):
Morey, J. Famous Mexican Americans p119-29 (5 and up) 920
Royt, Kevin
(il) Bauer, C. F. Handbook for storytellers 372.6
Rubber
Graham, A. The big stretch: the complete book of the amazing rubber band (3-6) 678
See/See also pages in the following book(s):
Rahn, J. E. More plants that changed history p53-91 (5 and up) 909
The **rubber** man. Arnott, K.
In Best-loved folktales of the world p627-30 398.2
Rubel, Nicole
(il) Gantos, J. Rotten Ralph E
Ruby. Emberley, M. E
Ruckman, Ivy, 1931-
Night of the twisters (3-6) Fic
Ruddick, Bob
(jt. auth) Greer, G. Max and me and the time machine Fic
Rudman, Masha Kabakow
(jt. auth) Bernstein, J. E. Books to help children cope with separation and loss v3 016.3627
Rue, Len
(il) McGuire, L. Lions 599.74
(il) Schlein, M. Elephants 599.6
(il) Schlein, M. Hippos 599.73
Rue, Leonard Lee
Meet the beaver (4 and up) 599.32
Meet the moose (4 and up) 599.73
Meet the opossum (4 and up) 599.2
(il) McGuire, L. Lions 599.74
(il) Schlein, M. Elephants 599.6
(il) Schlein, M. Hippos 599.73
Ruff, Donna
(il) Adler, D. A. Our Golda: the story of Golda Meir 92
(il) Faber, D. Eleanor Roosevelt: first lady of the world 92
(il) Haskins, J. Shirley Temple Black 92
(il) Oneal, Z. Grandma Moses: painter of rural America 92
Ruffins, Reynold, 1930-
(jt. auth) Sarnoff, J. Words: a book about the origins of everyday words and phrases 422
(il) Waters, J. F. Camels: ships of the desert 599.73

Rufus M. Estes, E. See note under Estes, E. The Moffats Fic

Rugs
See also Carpets
Fiction
Blood, C. L. The goat in the rug E

A **ruined** Passover. Sholem Aleichem.
In Sholem Aleichem. Holiday tales of Sholem Aleichem S C

Ruins *See* Excavations (Archeology)

Rulers *See* Kings, queens, rulers, etc.

Rules of order *See* Parliamentary practice

Rumania *See* Romania

The **rumor** of Pavel and Paali. Kismaric, C. 398.2

Rumpelstiltskin
Ehrlich, A. Rumpelstiltskin
In Ehrlich, A. The Random House book of fairy tales p166-73 398.2
Grimm, J. Rumpelstiltskin
In Best-loved folktales of the world p131-33 398.2
In The Classic fairy tales p197-98 398.2
In Grimm, J. About wise men and simpletons p77-79 398.2
In Grimm, J. The complete Grimm's fairy tales p264-68 398.2
In Tomie dePaola's favorite nursery tales p46-52 398.2
Grimm, J. Rumpelstiltzkin
In The Blue fairy book p96-99 398.2
In The Scott, Foresman anthology of children's literature p185-87 808.8
Thane, A. Rumpelstiltskin
In Thane, A. Plays from famous stories and fairy tales p58-76 812
Zelinsky, P. O. Rumpelstiltskin 398.2

The **runaway** bunny. Brown, M. W. E

Runaway children
Fiction
Angell, J. Dear Lola (4-6) Fic
Bauer, M. D. Shelter from the wind (5 and up) Fic
Bawden, N. The finding (4 and up) Fic
Holman, F. Slake's limbo (6 and up) Fic
Hughes, D. Family pose (5 and up) Fic

Runaway Ralph. Cleary, B. See note under Cleary, B. The mouse and the motorcycle Fic

Runaway teenagers *See* Runaway children

The **runaway** unicorn. Gotwalt, H. L. M.
In Gotwalt, H. L. M. Special plays for holidays p28-38 812

The **runner** [excerpt]. Voigt, C.
In Face to face: a collection of stories by celebrated Soviet and American writers p23-38 S C

Rural life *See* Country life

Russell, Jim, 1933-
(il) Mark, J. Thunder and Lightnings Fic

Russell, John
A saga
In Shedlock, M. L. The art of the story-teller p165-67 372.6

Russell, William F., 1945-
(ed) Animal families of the wild. See Animal families of the wild 591

Russell and Elisa. Hurwitz, J. See note under Hurwitz, J. Rip-roaring Russell Fic

Russell rides again. Hurwitz, J. See note under Hurwitz, J. Rip-roaring Russell Fic

Russell sprouts. Hurwitz, J. See note under Hurwitz, J. Rip-roaring Russell Fic

Russia *See* Soviet Union

Russian Americans
Fiction
Polacco, P. Uncle Vova's tree E

Russian cookery *See* Cookery, Russian

Russian fairy tales. Afanas'ev, A. N. 398.2

Russian folk tales. Afanas'ev, A. N. 398.2

Russian literature
Collected works
A Harvest of Russian children's literature 891.7

Russo, Marisabina
Waiting for Hannah E
(il) A Week of lullabies. See A Week of lullabies 811.008

Russo, Susan, 1947-
(il) Adoff, A. Eats: poems 811

Rust, Graham
(il) Burnett, F. H. The secret garden Fic

Rustin, Bayard, 1910-1987
See/See also pages in the following book(s):
Jacobs, W. J. Great lives: human rights p229-37 (5 and up) 920

Ruth, Rod
(il) McGowen, T. Album of birds 598
(il) McGowen, T. Album of dinosaurs 567.9
(il) McGowen, T. Album of rocks and minerals 549
(il) McGowen, T. Album of sharks 597

Ruthann and her pig. Porte-Thomas, B. A. Fic

Rutherford, Ernest, 1871-1937
See/See also pages in the following book(s):
McGowen, T. Radioactivity: from the Curies to the atomic age p43-50 (6 and up) 539.7

Rutherford, Jenny
(il) Giff, P. R. The gift of the pirate queen **Fic**
Rutland, Jonathan
See inside a submarine (4-6) **623.8**
See inside an oil rig and tanker (4-6) **665.5**
Take a trip to Israel (1-3) **956.94**
Rutledge, Paul, 1945-
The Vietnamese in America
In The In America series **305.8**
Ryan, Cheli Durán *See* Durán, Cheli
Ryan, DyAnne DiSalvo- *See* DiSalvo-Ryan, DyAnne, 1954-
Rydberg, Abraham Viktor *See* Rydberg, Viktor, 1828-1895
Rydberg, Viktor, 1828-1895
Jennings, L. M. The Christmas Tomten **E**
Lindgren, A. The Tomten **E**
Ryden, Hope
America's bald eagle (4 and up) **598**
The beaver (3-5) **599.32**
Bobcat (5 and up) **599.74**
Wild animals of Africa ABC **E**
Wild animals of America ABC **E**
Ryder, Joanne
Lizard in the sun (k-2) **597.9**
Under your feet (k-3) **811**
Where butterflies grow (k-2) **595.7**
White bear, ice bear (k-2) **599.74**
Rylant, Cynthia
All I see **E**
A blue-eyed daisy (5 and up) **Fic**
A blue-eyed daisy [excerpt]
In Face to face: a collection of stories by celebrated Soviet and American writers p223-28 **S C**
Children of Christmas (4 and up) **S C**
Contents: The Christmas tree man; Halfway home; For being good; Ballerinas and bears; Silver packages; All the stars in the sky
Every living thing (5 and up) **S C**
Contents: Slower than the rest; Retired; Boar out there; Papa's parrot; A pet; Spaghetti; Drying out; Stray; Planting things; A bad road for cats; Safe; Shells
A fine white dust (5 and up) **Fic**
Henry and Mudge **E**
Henry and Mudge and the forever sea. See note under Rylant, C. Henry and Mudge **E**
Henry and Mudge and the happy cat. See note under Rylant, C. Henry and Mudge **E**
Henry and Mudge and the sparkle days. See note under Rylant, C. Henry and Mudge **E**
Henry and Mudge get the cold shivers. See note under Rylant, C. Henry and Mudge **E**
Henry and Mudge in puddle trouble. See note under Rylant, C. Henry and Mudge **E**
Henry and Mudge in the green time. See note under Rylant, C. Henry and Mudge **E**
Henry and Mudge under the yellow moon. See note under Rylant, C. Henry and Mudge **E**
Mr. Griggs' work **E**
Night in the country **E**
The relatives came **E**
This year's garden **E**
When I was young in the mountains **E**

S

S.O.R. losers. Avi. **Fic**
S.S.T.'s *See* Supersonic transport planes
Saaf, Chuck
(il) Shachtman, T. Parade! **E**
Saavedra, Dane
(jt. auth) Madaras, L. The what's happening to my body? book for boys: a growing up guide for parents and sons **613.9**
Saavedra, Yolando Pino *See* Pino Saavedra, Yolando, 1901-
Sabbath
Chaikin, M. The seventh day: the story of the Jewish Sabbath (4 and up) **222**
Sacagawea, 1786-1884
Fiction
O'Dell, S. Streams to the river, river to the sea (5 and up) **Fic**
Sachner, Mark, 1948-
(ed) Spain. See Spain **946**
Sachs, Betsy *See* Sachs, Elizabeth-Ann, 1946-
Sachs, Elizabeth-Ann, 1946-
The boy who ate dog biscuits **E**
Sachs, Marilyn, 1927-
At the sound of the beep (4-6) **Fic**
The bears' house (4-6) **Fic**
Fran Ellen's house (4-6) **Fic**
A summer's lease (5 and up) **Fic**
The **sacred** bluff. Marriott, A. L.
In Marriott, A. L. American Indian mythology **398.2**
The **sacred** drum of Tepozteco. Jagendorf, M. A.
In The Scott, Foresman anthology of children's literature p405-06 **808.8**

The **Sacred** path (5 and up) **897**

Sad eyes. Gorog, J.
In Gorog, J. Three dreams and a nightmare, and other tales of the dark **S C**

Sadako and the thousand paper cranes [biography of Sadako Sasaki]. Coerr, E. **92**

Sader, Marion
(ed) Reference books for young readers. See Reference books for young readers **011.6**

Sadler, Marilyn *See* Bollen, Marilyn Sadler

Safe. Rylant, C.
In Rylant, C. Every living thing p66-72 **S C**

Safety appliances
See also Accidents—Prevention

Safety education
See also Accidents—Prevention
Pringle, L. P. Living in a risky world (6 and up) **363**

Safety measures *See* Accidents—Prevention

A **saga**. Russell, J.
In Shedlock, M. L. The art of the story-teller p165-67 **372.6**

Sagarin, David
(il) On city streets. See On city streets **811.008**

The **sages** of Helm. Simon, S.
In Simon, S. More wise men of Helm and their merry tales p1-10 **398.2**

Sailing

Fiction

Locker, T. Sailing with the wind **E**

Sailing with the wind. Locker, T. **E**

Sailors' life *See* Seafaring life

Saint Crispin's follower. Fleischman, P.
In Fleischman, P. Graven images p25-59 **S C**

Saint Elizabeth and the roses
Sawyer, R. The legend of Saint Elizabeth
In Sawyer, R. The way of the storyteller p307-15 **372.6**

Saint-Exupéry, Antoine de, 1900-1944
The little prince (4 and up) **Fic**

Saint George and the dragon. Hodges, M. **398.2**

Saint Helens, Mount (Wash.) *See* Mount Saint Helens (Wash.)

Saint Louis (Mo.)
See/See also pages in the following book(s):
McCall, E. S. Biography of a river: the living Mississippi (6 and up) **977**

Saint Patrick and the snakes. Dillon, E.
In Bauer, C. F. Celebrations p170-71 **808.8**

Saint Patrick's Day
Barth, E. Shamrocks, harps, and shillelaghs (3-6) **394.2**
See/See also pages in the following book(s):
Bauer, C. F. Celebrations p167-94 **808.8**

Saint Valentine's Day *See* Valentine's Day

Saints
See also Christian saints

Saintsing, David
The world of butterflies (k-2) **595.7**

Saki, 1870-1916
The lumber-room
In The Random House book of humor for children p74-82 **817.008**

Sako, Ousmane
The first bard among the Soninke
In The Crest and the hide, and other African stories of heroes, chiefs, bards, hunters, sorcerers, and common people p1-5 **398.2**
The great snake of Wagadou
In The Crest and the hide, and other African stories of heroes, chiefs, bards, hunters, sorcerers, and common people p105-09 **398.2**
Kene Bourama, a Manding hero
In The Crest and the hide, and other African stories of heroes, chiefs, bards, hunters, sorcerers, and common people p43-46 **398.2**
Kirama and Kankejan
In The Crest and the hide, and other African stories of heroes, chiefs, bards, hunters, sorcerers, and common people p31-41 **398.2**

Salamanders
Parker, N. W. Frogs, toads, lizards, and salamanders (k-3) **597.6**

Salem (Mass.)

Fiction

Fritz, J. Early thunder (6 and up) **Fic**
Petry, A. L. Tituba of Salem Village (6 and up) **Fic**

History

Jackson, S. The witchcraft of Salem Village (4 and up) **133.4**
Krensky, S. Witch hunt (2-4) **133.4**

Sally-Maud, Zachary Dee, and the dream spinner. Climo, S.
In Climo, S. Someone saw a spider p107-16 **398.2**

Salt
Afanas'ev, A. N. Salt
In Afanas'ev, A. N. Russian fairy tales p40-44 **398.2**
Ransome, A. Salt
In Best-loved folktales of the world p428-38 **398.2**

Salt and bread
In Best-loved folktales of the world p381-83 **398.2**
Salten, Felix, 1869-1945
Bambi (4-6) **Fic**
Salter, Safaya
(il) Kipling, R. Just so stories **S C**
Salty dog. Rand, G. **E**
Sam. Scott, A. H. **E**
Sam and Jane go camping. Schwartz, A.
In Schwartz, A. There is a carrot in my ear, and other noodle tales p16-26 **398.2**
Sam and Sooky
Sam and Sooky
In Grandfather tales p150-55 **398.2**
Sam, Bangs & Moonshine. Ness, E. **E**
Sam Ellis's island. Siegel, B. **325.73**
Sam goes trucking. Horenstein, H. **E**
Sam Hart accepts a wager. Roach, M. K.
In Roach, M. K. Encounters with the invisible world **S C**
Sam Johnson and the blue ribbon quilt. Ernst, L. C. **E**
Sam saves the day. Martin, C. E. See note under Martin, C. E. Island winter **E**
Sam Syntax's cries of London
In A Nursery companion p104-07 **820.8**
Sam who never forgets. Rice, E. **E**
Sam'l. MacDonald, M. R.
In MacDonald, M. R. When the lights go out p109-14 **372.6**
Sam's ball. Lindgren, B. See note under Lindgren, B. Sam's car **E**
Sam's bath. Lindgren, B. See note under Lindgren, B. Sam's car **E**
Sam's car. Lindgren, B. **E**
Sam's cookie. Lindgren, B. See note under Lindgren, B. Sam's car **E**
Sam's girl friend. Schwartz, A.
In Schwartz, A. All of our noses are here, and other noodle tales p58-63 **398.2**
Sam's potty. Lindgren, B. See note under Lindgren, B. Sam's car **E**
Sam's teddy bear. Lindgren, B. See note under Lindgren, B. Sam's car **E**
Sam's wagon. Lindgren, B. See note under Lindgren, B. Sam's car **E**
Samton, Sheila White
(il) Gross, T. F. Everyone asked about you **E**
Samuels, Barbara
Duncan & Dolores **E**
Samuels, Vyanne
Carry, go, bring, come **E**
Samuel's ghost. Crossley-Holland, K.
In Crossley-Holland, K. British folk tales p73-76 **398.2**
San Diego (Calif.). Sea World *See* Sea World (San Diego, Calif.)
San Domingo: the medicine hat stallion. Henry, M. **Fic**
San Francisco (Calif.)
Climo, S. City! San Francisco (4 and up) **979.4**
Description
Wilder, L. I. West from home (6 and up) **92**
Fiction
Yep, L. Child of the owl (5 and up) **Fic**
Yep, L. Dragonwings (5 and up) **Fic**
San Nicolas Island (Calif.)
Fiction
O'Dell, S. Island of the Blue Dolphins (5 and up) **Fic**
San Souci, Daniel
North country night (2-4) **591.5**
(il) San Souci, R. The legend of Scarface **398.2**
(il) San Souci, R. Robert D. San Souci's The six swans **398.2**
(il) San Souci, R. Song of Sedna **398.2**
(il) Sherman, J. Vassilisa the wise **398.2**
San Souci, Robert, 1946-
The boy and the ghost (k-3) **398.2**
The enchanted tapestry (k-3) **398.2**
The legend of Scarface (2-4) **398.2**
Robert D. San Souci's The six swans (2-4) **398.2**
Short & shivery (4 and up) **398.2**
Contents: The robber bridegroom; Jack Frost; The waterfall of ghosts; The ghost's cap; The witch cat; The green mist; The Cegua; The ghostly little girl; The midnight mass of the Dead; Tailypo; Lady Eleanore's mantle; The soldier and the vampire; The skeleton's dance; Scared to death; Swallowed alive; The deacon's ghost; Nuckelavee; The adventure of the German student; Billy Mosby's night ride; The hunter in the haunted forest; Brother and sister; The lovers of Dismal Swamp; Boneless; The death waltz; The ghost of Misery Hill; The loup-garou; The golem; Lavender; The goblin spider; The Halloween pony
Song of Sedna (2-4) **398.2**
The talking eggs (k-3) **398.2**
The white cat (2-4) **398.2**
Young Merlin (2-5) **398.2**
Sancha, Sheila, 1924-
The Luttrell village (6 and up) **942.03**
Walter Dragun's town (6 and up) **942.03**

Sand
See also Quicksand
Sand cake. Asch, F. E
Sand Creek, Battle of, 1864
See/See also pages in the following book(s):
Ehrlich, A. Wounded Knee: an Indian history of the American West (6 and up) **970.004**
Sand dunes
Bannan, J. G. Sand dunes (3-6) **551.3**
Sand flat shadows. Sandburg, C.
In Sandburg, C. Rootabaga stories pt 1 p159-66 **S C**
Sandak, Cass R., 1950-
Columbus Day (4-6) **394.2**
Sandburg, Carl, 1878-1967
Abe Lincoln grows up (5 and up) **92**
also in Sandburg, C. The Sandburg treasury p383-477 **818**
Early moon
In Sandburg, C. The Sandburg treasury p161-207 **818**
The haystack cricket and how things are different up in the moon towns
In Sandburg, C. The Sandburg treasury p139-42 **818**
How Rag Bag Mammy kept her secret while the wind blew away the Village of Hat Pins
In Sandburg, C. The Sandburg treasury p100-02 **818**
How they bring back the Village of Cream Puffs when the wind blows it away
In The Scott, Foresman anthology of children's literature p542-44 **808.8**
Prairie-town boy
In Sandburg, C. The Sandburg treasury p263-382 **818**
Rainbows are made: poems (5 and up) **811**
Rootabaga stories **S C**
Contents pt 1: How they broke away to go to the Rootabaga Country; How they bring back the Village of Cream Puffs when the wind blows it away; How the five rusty rats helped find a new village; The Potato Face Blind Man who lost the diamond rabbit on his gold accordion; How the Potato Face Blind Man enjoyed himself on a fine spring morning; Poker Face the Baboon and Hot Dog the Tiger; The Toboggan-to-the-moon dream of the Potato Face Blind Man; How Gimme the Ax found out about the zigzag railroad and who made it zigzag; The story of Blixie Bimber and the power of the gold buckskin whincher; The story of Jason Squiff and why he had a popcorn hat, popcorn mittens, and popcorn shoes; The story of Rags Habakuk, the two blue rats, and the circus man who came with spot cash money; The wedding procession of the Rag Doll and the Broom Handle and who was in it; How the hat ashes shovel helped Snoo Foo; Three boys with jugs of molasses and secret ambitions; How Bimbo the Snip's thumb stuck to his nose when the wind changed; The two skyscrapers who decided to have a child; The dollar watch and the five jack-rabbits; The Wooden Indian and the Shaghorn Buffalo; The White Horse Girl and the Blue Wind Boy; What six girls with balloons told the Gray Man on Horseback; How Henry Hagglyhoagly played the guitar with his mittens on; Never kick a slipper at the moon; Sand flat shadows; How to tell corn fairies if you see 'em; How the animals lost their tails and got them back traveling from Philadelphia to Medicine Hat pt 2: The skyscraper to the moon and how the green rat with the rheumatism ran a thousand miles twice; Slipfoot and how he nearly always never gets what he goes after; Many, many weddings in one corner house; Shush, Shush, the big buff banty hen who laid an egg in the postmaster's hat; How Rag Bag Mammy kept her secret while the wind blew away the Village of Hat Pins; How six pigeons came back to Hatrack the Horse after many accidents and six telegrams; How the three wild Babylonian Baboons went away in the rain eating bread and butter; How six umbrellas took off their straw hats to show respect to the one big umbrella; How Bozo the Button Buster busted all his buttons when a mouse came; How Googler and Gaggler, the two Christmas babies, came home with monkey wrenches; How Johnny the Wham sleeps in money all the time and Joe the Wimp shines and sees things; How Deep Red Roses goes back and forth between the clock and the looking glass; How Pink Peony sent Spuds, the ballplayer up to pick four moons; How Dippy the Wisp and Slip Me Liz came in the moonshine where the Potato Face Blind Man sat with his accordion; How Hot Balloons and his pigeon daughters crossed over into the Rootabaga Country; How two sweetheart dippies sat in the moonlight on a lumberyard fence and heard about the sooners and the boomers; The haystack cricket and how things are different up in the moon towns; Why the big ball game between Hot Grounders and the Grand Standers was a hot game; The Huckabuck family and how they raised popcorn in Nebraska and quit and came back; Yang Yang and Hoo Hoo, or the song of the left foot of the shadow of the goose in Oklahoma; How a skyscraper and a railroad train got picked up and carried away from Pig's Eye Valley far in the Pickax Mountains; Pig Wisps; Kiss Me; Blue silver
also in Sandburg, C. The Sandburg treasury p9-160 **818**
The Sandburg treasury (5 and up) **818**
The wedding procession of the Rag Doll and the Broom Handle and who was in it **E**
The White Horse Girl and the Blue Wind Boy
In Herds of thunder, manes of gold p29-34 **808.8**
Wind song
In Sandburg, C. The Sandburg treasury p209-61 **818**
The **Sandburg** treasury. Sandburg, C. **818**
Sandcastles, The art and industry of. Adkins, J. **728.8**
Sanders, Ruth Manning- *See* Manning-Sanders, Ruth, 1895-1988
Sanders, Scott R. (Scott Russell), 1945-
Aurora means dawn **E**
Sanderson, Ruth, 1951-
The twelve dancing princesses (k-3) **398.2**
(il) Burnett, F. H. The secret garden **Fic**
(il) Byars, B. C. The animal, the vegetable, and John D Jones **Fic**
(il) Sleator, W. Into the dream **Fic**
(il) Spyri, J. Heidi **Fic**
(il) Yolen, J. The sleeping beauty **398.2**

Sandflat shadows. Sandburg, C.
In Sandburg, C. The Sandburg treasury p73-77 **818**
Sandin, Joan, 1942-
The long way westward **E**
(il) Arkin, A. The lemming condition **Fic**
(il) Bulla, C. R. Daniel's duck **E**
(il) Little, J. From Anna **Fic**
(il) Little, J. Look through my window **Fic**
(il) McNulty, F. Woodchuck **599.32**
Sandström, George F.
(il) Abbott, R. T. Seashells of the world **594**
Sandström, Marita
(il) Abbott, R. T. Seashells of the world **594**
Sanfield, Steve
The adventures of High John the Conqueror (4 and up) **398.2**
Contents: Master's walking stick; Just possum; "You better not do it"; In a box; Off limits; John wins a bet; This one and that one; Who's the fool now; George's dream; Deer hunting; John's memory; Freedom; An epidemic of ducks; John in court; Tops and bottoms; The Christmas turkey
Sanfilippo, Margaret
(il) Christopher, M. Tackle without a team **Fic**
(il) Christopher, M. Takedown **Fic**
Sanford, William R.
Missouri
In America the beautiful **973**
Sankey, Tom
(il) Gryski, C. Cat's cradle, owl's eyes **793.9**
(il) Gryski, C. Many stars & more string games **793.9**
(il) Gryski, C. Super string games **793.9**
Santa Claus
Giblin, J. The truth about Santa Claus (4 and up) **394.2**
Lubin, L. B. Christmas gift-bringers **394.2**
See/See also pages in the following book(s):
Barth, E. Holly, reindeer, and colored lights p43-54 (3-6) **394.2**
Fiction
Briggs, R. Father Christmas **E**
Kroll, S. Santa's crash-bang Christmas **E**
Van Allsburg, C. The Polar Express **E**
Poetry
Moore, C. C. The night before Christmas (k-3) **811**
Santa Claus is twins. Martens, A. C.
In The Big book of Christmas plays p169-85 **808.82**
Santa Fe Trail
Fiction
Holling, H. C. Tree in the trail (4 and up) **Fic**
Santa's crash-bang Christmas. Kroll, S. **E**
Santa's magic hat. Thornton, J. F.
In The Big book of Christmas plays p253-62 **808.82**
Santoro, Christopher
(il) Berger, G. Sharks **597**
(il) Lacey, E. A. The complete frog **597.8**
(il) Sattler, H. R. Giraffes **599.73**
(il) Sattler, H. R. Hominids: a look back at our ancestors **573.3**
(il) Sattler, H. R. Pterosaurs, the flying reptiles **567.9**
Sanzio, Raffaello *See* Raphael, 1483-1520
Sara Crewe. See Burnett, F. H. A little princess **Fic**
Sarah Bishop. O'Dell, S. **Fic**
Sarah, plain and tall. MacLachlan, P. **Fic**
Sarasas, Claude
The ABC's of origami (4-6) **736**
Sargent, Sarah, 1937-
Weird Henry Berg (4-6) **Fic**
Sarnoff, Jane
Words: a book about the origins of everyday words and phrases (4 and up) **422**
Sasaki, Sadako, 1943-1955
About
Coerr, E. Sadako and the thousand paper cranes (3-6) **92**
Saskatchewan
Fiction
Eckert, A. W. Incident at Hawk's Hill (6 and up) **Fic**
Satan *See* Devil
Satanta, Kiowa Chief, d. 1878
See/See also pages in the following book(s):
Freedman, R. Indian chiefs p28-51 (6 and up) **920**
Satellites
Kelch, J. W. Small worlds: exploring the 60 moons of our solar system (6 and up) **523.9**
Satellites, Artificial *See* Artificial satellites
Satō, Yūkō, 1928-
(il) Johnson, S. A. Chirping insects **595.7**
(il) Johnson, S. A. Ladybugs **595.7**
(il) Overbeck, C. Dragonflies **595.7**
Sattler, Helen Roney
Baby dinosaurs (1-4) **567.9**
The book of eagles (4 and up) **598**
Dinosaurs of North America (5 and up) **567.9**

Sattler, Helen Roney—*Continued*
Fish facts & bird brains: animal intelligence (5 and up) **591.5**
Giraffes (5 and up) **599.73**
Hominids: a look back at our ancestors (5 and up) **573.3**
The new illustrated dinosaur dictionary (5 and up) **567.9**
Pterosaurs, the flying reptiles (1-4) **567.9**
Recipes for art and craft materials (4 and up) **745.5**
Sharks, the super fish (4 and up) **597**
Train whistles (k-2) **385**
Tyrannosaurus rex and its kin: the Mesozoic monsters (4-6) **567.9**
Whales, the nomads of the sea (4 and up) **599.5**

Saturn (Planet)
Branley, F. M. Saturn (4 and up) **523.4**
Halliday, I. Saturn (4-6) **523.4**
Simon, S. Saturn (1-4) **523.4**
See/See also pages in the following book(s):
Harris, A. The great Voyager adventure p33-44 (5 and up) **523.4**
Kelch, J. W. Small worlds: exploring the 60 moons of our solar system p67-83 (6 and up) **523.9**

Saturnalia. Fleischman, P. **Fic**
The **saucepan** game. Ormerod, J. **E**
The **saucy** scarecrow. Thane, A.
In Thane, A. Plays from famous stories and fairy tales p130-42 **812**

Saudi Arabia
Lye, K. Take a trip to Saudi Arabia (1-3) **953.8**
Saudi Arabia—in pictures (5 and up) **953.8**
Social life and customs
Al Hoad, A. L. We live in Saudi Arabia (4-6) **953.8**

Saudi Arabia—in pictures (5 and up) **953.8**

Saul, Wendy, 1946-
Science fare: an illustrated guide and catalog of toys, books, and activities for kids **507**

Savage, Steele
(il) Benson, S. Stories of the gods and heroes **292**
(il) Hamilton, E. Mythology **292**

Save Queen of Sheba. Moeri, L. **Fic**

Saving and thrift
Fiction
Williams, V. B. A chair for my mother **E**

Saving our animal friends. McGrath, S. **591**
Saving our wildlife. Pringle, L. P. **639.9**
Saving the peregrine falcon. Arnold, C. **598**

Sawyer, Ruth, 1880-1970
The Christmas apple
In Bauer, C. F. Celebrations p259-64 **808.8**
Journey cake, ho! (k-2) **398.2**
The magic box
In The Scott, Foresman anthology of children's literature p256-59 **808.8**
The peddler of Ballaghadereen
In The Scott, Foresman anthology of children's literature p173-76 **808.8**
The way of the storyteller **372.6**
Stories included are: Wee Meg Barnileg and the fairies; The magic box; Señora, will you snip? Señora will you sew?; The peddler of Ballaghadereen; Where one is fed a hundred can dine; A matter of brogues; The juggler of Notre Dame; The deserted mine; The legend of Saint Elizabeth; The princess and the vagabone; The bird who spoke three times
See/See also pages in the following book(s):
Newbery Medal books, 1922-1955 p149-56 **028.5**

Saxons *See* Anglo-Saxons

Say, Allen, 1937-
The bicycle man **E**
El Chino (2-5) **92**
The lost lake **E**
(il) Snyder, D. The boy of the three-year nap **398.2**

Sayer, Angela
The young rider's handbook (5 and up) **636.1**

Saying good-bye to Grandma. Thomas, J. R. **E**
Saynday and Smallpox: the white man's gift. Marriott, A. L.
In Marriott, A. L. American Indian mythology **398.2**
Sayonora, Mrs. Kackleman. Kalman, M. **E**
Scaly babies. Johnston, G. **597.9**

Scandinavian literature
See also Swedish literature

Scandinavians
See also Vikings

Scanlan, Nancy
(il) Renfro, N. Bags are big! **745.54**
(il) Renfro, N. Puppet show made easy! **791.5**

The **scarebird**. Fleischman, S. **E**
Scared silly: a Halloween treat. Howe, J. **E**
Scared to death. San Souci, R.
In San Souci, R. Short & shivery p78-83 **398.2**
The **scarlet** batling. Lacoe, A.
In Things that go bump in the night p199-216 **S C**

Scarry, Huck, 1953-
Aboard a steam locomotive (4 and up) **625.2**
Balloon trip (3-6) **629.13**
Life on a barge (3-6) **386**
Life on a fishing boat (3-6) **639.2**
(il) Shapiro, M. J. How they built the Statue of Liberty **974.7**

The **scary** Halloween costume book. Barkin, C. **391**

Scary, scary Halloween. Bunting, E. **E**

Scary stories to tell in the dark. Schwartz, A. **398.2**

Scavengers and decomposers: the cleanup crew. Hughey, P. **591.5**

Schaaf, M. B. Goffstein *See* Goffstein, M. B.

Scharl, Josef, 1896-1954
(il) Grimm, J. The complete Grimm's fairy tales **398.2**

Schatell, Brian
(il) Cobb, V. Gobs of goo **547**

Schecter, Ben
Grandma remembers **E**

Scheer, Julian
Rain makes applesauce **E**

Scheiner, Jim
(il) McGovern, A. Down under, down under **574.92**
(il) McGovern, A. Night dive **797.2**

Scheiner, Martin
(il) McGovern, A. Down under, down under **574.92**
(il) McGovern, A. Night dive **797.2**

Schepp, Steven
(jt. auth) Andry, A. C. How babies are made **612.6**

Schick, Joel, 1945-
(il) Riley, J. W. The gobble-uns'll git you ef you don't watch out! **811**
(il) Rockwell, T. How to eat fried worms, and other plays **812**

Schiller, Andrew, 1919-
Roget's children's thesaurus (3-5) **423**
Roget's student thesaurus (5 and up) **423**

Schindler, S. D.
(il) Hooks, W. H. The three little pigs and the fox **398.2**
(il) Le Guin, U. K. Catwings **Fic**
(il) Le Guin, U. K. Catwings return **Fic**
(il) McDonald, M. Is this a house for Hermit Crab? **595.3**
(il) Rylant, C. Children of Christmas **S C**
(il) Rylant, C. Every living thing **S C**

Schizophrenia
See/See also pages in the following book(s):
Dinner, S. H. Nothing to be ashamed of: growing up with mental illness in your family p28-52 (5 and up) **362.2**

Schlein, Miriam
Big talk **E**
The billions of bats (3-5) **599.4**
Elephants (4-6) **599.6**
Gorillas (4-6) **599.88**
Hippos (4-6) **599.73**
Pandas (4-6) **599.74**
Pigeons (4-6) **598**
Project panda watch (4 and up) **599.74**
The year of the panda (3-5) **Fic**

Schmidt, Diane
I am a Jesse White tumbler **796.47**

Schmidt, Karen
(il) Merriam, E. You be good and I'll be night: jump-on-the-bed poems **811**

Schmitt, Lois
Smart spending (5 and up) **640.73**

Schneider, Howie
(il) Okimoto, J. D. Blumpoe the Grumpoe meets Arnold the cat **E**

Schneider, Rex, 1937-
(il) Dickinson, E. I'm nobody! who are you? **811**

Schnieper, Claudia
Amazing spiders (3-6) **595.4**
An apple tree through the year (3-6) **634**
Chameleons (3-6) **597.9**
Lizards (3-6) **597.9**
On the trail of the fox (3-6) **599.74**

Schoenherr, John, 1935-
(il) Eckert, A. W. Incident at Hawk's Hill **Fic**
(il) George, J. C. Julie of the wolves **Fic**
(il) McNulty, F. Whales: their life in the sea **599.5**
(il) North, S. Rascal **599.74**
(il) Yolen, J. Owl moon **E**

The **scholar** Be. Terada, A. M.
In Terada, A. M. Under the starfruit tree p42-49 **398.2**

Scholes, Percy Alfred, 1877-1958
Hurd, M. The Oxford junior companion to music **780.3**

Schon, Isabel
Basic collection of children's books in Spanish **011.6**
Books in Spanish for children and young adults: an annotated guide [series I-V] **011.6**

School bus. Crews, D. **E**
School drama *See* College and school drama
School libraries
American Association of School Librarians. Information power **027.8**
Anderson, P. Planning school library media facilities **027.8**
Smith, J. B. Library media center programs for middle schools: a curriculum-based approach **027.8**
Van Orden, P. J. The collection program in schools **027.8**
Catalogs
The Elementary school library collection **011.6**
Periodicals
Emergency Librarian **027.6205**
Library Talk **027.805**
School Library Journal **027.805**
School Library Media Quarterly **027.805**
Yearbooks
School Library Media Annual **027.805**
School libraries (Elementary school)
See also Children's libraries
School libraries (High school)
See also Young adults' library services
Catalogs
Junior high school library catalog **011.6**
School Library Journal **027.805**
School Library Media Annual **027.805**
School Library Media Quarterly **027.805**
School media centers *See* Instructional materials centers
School spirit. Spinelli, J.
In Connections: short stories by outstanding writers for young adults p170-80 **S C**
School stories
Ahlberg, J. Starting school **E**
Alexander, M. G. Move over, Twerp **E**
Allard, H. Miss Nelson is missing! **E**
Avi. S.O.R. losers (5 and up) **Fic**
Bunting, E. Our sixth-grade sugar babies (4-6) **Fic**
Burnett, F. H. A little princess (4-6) **Fic**
Burningham, J. John Patrick Norman McHennessy—the boy who was always late **E**
Byars, B. C. The burning questions of Bingo Brown (4 and up) **Fic**
Carrick, C. What a wimp! (3-5) **Fic**
Caudill, R. Did you carry the flag today, Charley? (2-4) **Fic**
Cazet, D. "Never spit on your shoes" **E**
Cleary, B. Dear Mr. Henshaw (4-6) **Fic**
Cleary, B. Ellen Tebbits (3-5) **Fic**
Cleary, B. Mitch and Amy (3-5) **Fic**
Cleary, B. Muggie Maggie (2-4) **Fic**
Cleary, B. Otis Spofford (3-5) **Fic**
Cleary, B. Ramona the pest (3-5) **Fic**
Cohen, B. Molly's Pilgrim (2-4) **Fic**
Cohen, M. See you in second grade! **E**
Conford, E. Dear Lovey Hart: I am desperate (6 and up) **Fic**
Conford, E. Seven days to a brand-new me (6 and up) **Fic**
Crews, D. School bus **E**
Cuyler, M. Baby Dot: a dinosaur story **E**
Dahl, R. Matilda (4-6) **Fic**
Danziger, P. The cat ate my gymsuit (5 and up) **Fic**
Danziger, P. Everyone else's parents said yes (4-6) **Fic**
Danziger, P. Make like a tree and leave (4-6) **Fic**
DeClements, B. 6th grade can really kill you (5 and up) **Fic**
DeJong, M. The wheel on the school (4-6) **Fic**
Delton, J. Kitty from the start (2-4) **Fic**
Delton, J. The new girl at school **E**
Ehrlich, A. Leo, Zack, and Emmie **E**
Ferguson, A. Cricket and the crackerbox kid (4-6) **Fic**
Fitzhugh, L. Harriet the spy (4 and up) **Fic**
Giff, P. R. Love, from the fifth-grade celebrity (4-6) **Fic**
Giff, P. R. Watch out, Ronald Morgan! **E**
Gilson, J. 4B goes wild (4-6) **Fic**
Hahn, M. D. Daphne's book (5 and up) **Fic**
Hansen, J. The gift-giver (4-6) **Fic**
Haywood, C. "B" is for Betsy (2-4) **Fic**
Herman, C. Millie Cooper, 3B (3-5) **Fic**
Hermes, P. Friends are like that (5 and up) **Fic**
Hermes, P. I hate being gifted (5 and up) **Fic**
Honeycutt, N. The all new Jonah Twist (3-5) **Fic**
Honeycutt, N. The best-laid plans of Jonah Twist (3-5) **Fic**
Honeycutt, N. Invisible Lissa (3-5) **Fic**
Howe, J. The day the teacher went bananas **E**
Hurwitz, J. Class clown (2-4) **Fic**
Hurwitz, J. Rip-roaring Russell (2-4) **Fic**
Iwamatsu, A. J. Crow Boy **E**
Jones, R. C. Germy blew the Bugle (4-6) **Fic**
Kline, S. Herbie Jones (3-5) **Fic**
Kline, S. Horrible Harry in room 2B (2-4) **Fic**
Kropp, P. Moonkid and Liberty (6 and up) **Fic**

School stories—*Continued*
Lord, B. B. In the Year of the Boar and Jackie Robinson (4-6) **Fic**
Lowry, L. Your move, J.P.! (5 and up) **Fic**
Mahy, M. The blood-and-thunder adventure on Hurricane Peak (4-6) **Fic**
McDonnell, C. Lucky charms & birthday wishes (2-4) **Fic**
Meyers, S. P.J. Clover, private eye: the case of the Halloween hoot (4-6) **Fic**
Mills, C. Dynamite Dinah (3-5) **Fic**
Naylor, P. R. The agony of Alice (5 and up) **Fic**
Noble, T. H. The day Jimmy's boa ate the wash **E**
Nordstrom, U. The secret language (3-5) **Fic**
O'Connor, J. Lulu goes to witch school **E**
Park, B. Almost starring Skinnybones (4-6) **Fic**
Park, B. Maxie, Rosie, and Earl—partners in grime (3-5) **Fic**
Park, B. Skinnybones (4-6) **Fic**
Paulsen, G. The boy who owned the school (6 and up) **Fic**
Pinkwater, J. Buffalo Brenda (5 and up) **Fic**
Rabe, B. The balancing girl **E**
Schwartz, A. Annabelle Swift, kindergartner **E**
Schwartz, A. Bea and Mr. Jones **E**
Sharmat, M. W. Mysteriously yours, Maggie Marmelstein (3-6) **Fic**
Shreve, S. R. The flunking of Joshua T. Bates (3-5) **Fic**
Snyder, Z. K. Libby on Wednesdays (5 and up) **Fic**
Udry, J. M. What Mary Jo shared **E**
Wells, R. Timothy goes to school **E**
Yarbrough, C. The shimmershine queens (4-6) **Fic**

Schools
See also Education
Law and legislation

See/See also pages in the following book(s):
Burns, M. I am not a short adult! p41-52 (3-6) **305.23**
United States—History
Loeper, J. J. Going to school in 1776 (4 and up) **370.9**
Loeper, J. J. Going to school in 1876 (4 and up) **370.9**

See/See also pages in the following book(s):
Freedman, R. Children of the wild West p59-69 (4 and up) **978**
Tunis, E. The young United States, 1783 to 1830 p129-33 (5 and up) **973**

Schools and libraries *See* Libraries and schools

Schotter, Roni
Captain Snap and the children of Vinegar Lane **E**

Schroeder, Alan
Ragtime Tumpie **E**

Schuett, Stacey
(il) Jukes, M. Lights around the palm **E**

Schulman, Janet
The big hello **E**

Schultz, John Frederick, 1944-
Nigeria—in pictures. See Nigeria—in pictures **966.9**

Schwartz, Alvin, 1927-
All of our noses are here, and other noodle tales (1-3) **398.2**
Contents: Jane gets a donkey; Grandpa misses the boat; All of our noses are here; The best boy in the world; Sam's girl friend
Busy buzzing bumblebees and other tongue twisters (k-3) **808.88**
The cat's elbow, and other secret languages (4 and up) **652**
Cross your fingers, spit in your hat: superstitions and other beliefs (4 and up) **398**
Fat man in a fur coat, and other bear stories (4 and up) **599.74**
Flapdoodle: pure nonsense from American folklore (4 and up) **398**
Gold & silver, silver & gold (5 and up) **910.4**
I saw you in the bathtub, and other folk rhymes (1-3) **398.2**
In a dark, dark room, and other scary stories (k-3) **398.2**
Contents: The teeth; In the graveyard; The green ribbon; In a dark, dark room; The night it rained; The pirate
Kickle snifters and other fearsome critters (2-5) **398**
More scary stories to tell in the dark (4 and up) **398.2**
Scary stories to tell in the dark (4 and up) **398.2**
Telling fortunes (4-6) **133.3**
Ten copycats in a boat, and other riddles (1-3) **398.6**
There is a carrot in my ear, and other noodle tales (1-3) **398.2**
Contents: The Browns take the day off; Sam and Jane go camping; Mr. Brown washes his underwear; Jane grows a carrot; Grandpa buys a pumpkin egg; It is time to go to sleep
Tomfoolery: trickery and foolery with words (4 and up) **398**
A twister of twists, a tangler of tongues (4 and up) **808.88**
Unriddling: all sorts of riddles to puzzle your guessery (4 and up) **398.6**

Schwartz, Alvin, 1927-—*Continued*
The wendigo
In Schwartz, A. Scary stories to tell in the dark p49-53 **398.2**
Whoppers (4 and up) **398.2**
Witcracks: jokes and jests from American folklore (4 and up) **398**

Schwartz, Amy, 1954-
Annabelle Swift, kindergartner **E**
Bea and Mr. Jones **E**
The lady who put salt in her coffee **E**
Oma and Bobo **E**
(il) Carlstrom, N. W. Blow me a kiss, Miss Lilly **E**
(il) Hest, A. The crack-of-dawn walkers **E**
(il) Hest, A. Fancy Aunt Jess **E**
(il) Hest, A. The purple coat **E**
(il) O'Donnell, E. L. Maggie doesn't want to move **E**

Schwartz, Daniel Bennett, 1929-
(il) Byars, B. C. The house of wings **Fic**

Schwartz, David M., 1951-
The hidden life of the forest (3-5) **574.5**
The hidden life of the meadow (3-5) **574.5**
The hidden life of the pond (3-5) **574.92**
How much is a million? **E**
If you made a million **E**

Schwartz, Lynne Sharon
The four questions (k-3) **296.4**

Schwarz, Frank
(il) Arnold, C. Pain: what is it? how do we deal with it? **616**

Schwarz, Jill Karla
(il) Best-loved folktales of the world. See Best-loved folktales of the world **398.2**

Schweninger, Ann
(il) Marzollo, J. Amy goes fishing **E**
(il) Marzollo, J. The teddy bear book **811**
(il) The Read-aloud treasury. See The Read-aloud treasury **808.8**

Science
Stangl, J. Crystals and crystal gardens you can grow (4 and up) **548**
Why in the world? (4 and up) **500**
Why on earth? (4 and up) **500**

Bibliography
The Best science books & A-V materials for children **016.5**
Kennedy, D. M. Science & technology in fact and fiction: a guide to children's books **016.5**
Outstanding science trade books for children **016.5**

Bibliography—Periodicals
Appraisal **016.5**
Science Books & Films **016.5**

Dictionaries
The New book of popular science **503**

Experiments
Adams, R. C. Science with computers (6 and up) **507**
Allison, L. Gee, Wiz! (4 and up) **507**
Ardley, N. Working with water (4 and up) **507**
Cobb, V. Gobs of goo (2-4) **547**
Cobb, V. More science experiments you can eat (5 and up) **507**
Cobb, V. Science experiments you can eat (5 and up) **507**
Cobb, V. The secret life of cosmetics: a science experiment book (5 and up) **668**
Cobb, V. The secret life of hardware: a science experiment book (5 and up) **670**
Foodworks (4-6) **641.3**
Herbert, D. Mr. Wizard's supermarket science (4 and up) **507**
Markle, S. The young scientist's guide to successful science projects (5 and up) **507.8**
Science experiments on file: experiments, demonstrations, and projects for school and home (6 and up) **507.8**
Taylor, B. Bouncing and bending light (3-5) **535**
Taylor, B. Color and light (3-5) **535**
Walker, O. H. Experimenting with air and flight (6 and up) **507**
Willow, D. Science sensations (3-5) **507**
Wyler, R. Science fun with mud and dirt (2-4) **507**
Wyler, R. Science fun with peanuts and popcorn (2-4) **507**
Wyler, R. Science fun with toy boats and planes (2-4) **507**
Wyler, R. Science fun with toy cars and trucks (2-4) **507**
Zubrowski, B. Balloons (3-6) **507**
Zubrowski, B. Wheels at work (4-6) **621.8**

Methodology
Kramer, S. How to think like a scientist (3-5) **507**

Miscellanea
Markle, S. Exploring spring (4 and up) **508**
Markle, S. Exploring summer (4 and up) **508**
Markle, S. Exploring winter (4 and up) **508**
Simon, S. The dinosaur is the biggest animal that ever lived, and other wrong ideas you thought were true (3-6) **500**

Science—*Continued*
Periodicals
3-2-1 Contact **505**
Pictorial works
Grillone, L. Small worlds close up (5 and up) **500**
Simon, S. Hidden worlds (5 and up) **500**
Study and teaching
Saul, W. Science fare: an illustrated guide and catalog of toys, books, and activities for kids **507**
Study and teaching—Periodicals
Science and Children **507.05**
The Science Teacher **507.05**
China—History
Beshore, G. W. Science in ancient China (5 and up) **509**
Greece—History
Gay, K. Science in ancient Greece (5 and up) **509**
Rome—History
Harris, J. L. Science in ancient Rome (5 and up) **509**
Science & technology in fact and fiction: a guide to children's books. Kennedy, D. M. **016.5**
Science and Children **507.05**
Science and civilization
Anno, M. Anno's medieval world (3-6) **909.07**
Beshore, G. W. Science in ancient China (5 and up) **509**
Gay, K. Science in ancient Greece (5 and up) **509**
Harris, J. L. Science in ancient Rome (5 and up) **509**
Science Books & Films **016.5**
Science Books, a quarterly review. See Science Books & Films **016.5**
Science experiments on file: experiments, demonstrations, and projects for school and home (6 and up) **507.8**
Science experiments you can eat. Cobb, V. **507**
Science fare: an illustrated guide and catalog of toys, books, and activities for kids. Saul, W. **507**
Science fiction
Alcock, V. The monster garden (4 and up) **Fic**
Cameron, E. The wonderful flight to the Mushroom Planet (4-6) **Fic**
Christopher, J. Empty world (5 and up) **Fic**
Christopher, J. The White Mountains (5 and up) **Fic**
Corbett, S. The deadly hoax (5 and up) **Fic**
Crosher, G. R. The awakening water (5 and up) **Fic**
Hoover, H. M. Away is a strange place to be (4-6) **Fic**
Hoover, H. M. Orvis (5 and up) **Fic**
Hoover, H. M. The shepherd moon (6 and up) **Fic**
Jacobs, P. S. Born into light (6 and up) **Fic**
Jones, D. W. Archer's goon (6 and up) **Fic**
Marshall, E. Space case **E**
Pinkwater, D. M. Alan Mendelsohn, the boy from Mars (5 and up) **Fic**
Pinkwater, D. M. Fat men from space (3-6) **Fic**
Pinkwater, D. M. Guys from space **E**
Pinkwater, D. M. Lizard music (4 and up) **Fic**
Service, P. F. Stinker from space (4-6) **Fic**
Sleator, W. The boy who reversed himself (5 and up) **Fic**
Sleator, W. The duplicate (6 and up) **Fic**
Sleator, W. The green futures of Tycho (5 and up) **Fic**
Sleator, W. House of stairs (5 and up) **Fic**
Sleator, W. Interstellar pig (5 and up) **Fic**
Sleator, W. Strange attractors (5 and up) **Fic**
Stannard, R. The time and space of Uncle Albert (5 and up) **Fic**
Townsend, J. R. The visitors (6 and up) **Fic**
Ungerer, T. Moon Man **E**
Verne, J. Twenty thousand leagues under the sea (5 and up) **Fic**
Yep, L. Sweetwater (6 and up) **Fic**
See/See also pages in the following book(s):
The Scott, Foresman anthology of children's literature p552-71 **808.8**
Science fun with mud and dirt. Wyler, R. **507**
Science fun with peanuts and popcorn. Wyler, R. **507**
Science fun with toy boats and planes. Wyler, R. **507**
Science fun with toy cars and trucks. Wyler, R. **507**
Science in ancient China. Beshore, G. W. **509**
Science in ancient Greece. Gay, K. **509**
Science in ancient Rome. Harris, J. L. **509**

Science sensations. Willow, D. 507
The **Science** Teacher 507.05
Science with computers. Adams, R. C. 507

Scientific recreations
Cobb, V. Bet you can! science possibilities to fool you (4 and up) 793.8
Cobb, V. Bet you can't! science impossibilities to fool you (4 and up) 793.8
Cobb, V. Magic—naturally! science entertainment & amusements (4 and up) 793.8
Friedhoffer, R. Magic tricks, science facts (5 and up) 793.8
Simon, S. Soap bubble magic (1-3) 793.8

Scientists
See also Women scientists
Aliki. A weed is a flower: the life of George Washington Carver (k-3) 92
Hyndley, K. The voyage of the Beagle [biography of Charles Darwin] (4 and up) 92
Kumin, M. The microscope [biography of Antoni van Leeuwenhoek] (k-3) 92
Mitchell, B. A pocketful of goobers: a story about George Washington Carver (3-5) 92
Provensen, A. Leonardo da Vinci: the artist, inventor, scientist (3 and up) 92

Scieszka, Jon
The true story of the three little pigs (k-3) 398.2

Scissors
Afanas'ev, A. N. The stubborn wife
In Afanas'ev, A. N. Russian fairy tales p280 398.2

Scofield, Penrod, 1933-
(il) Kresh, P. Isaac Bashevis Singer: the story of a storyteller 92

The **scoop** on ice cream. Cobb, V. 637
Scoots, the bog turtle. Cutchins, J. 597.9
Scorpions. Myers, W. D. Fic

Scotland
Meek, J. The land and people of Scotland (5 and up) 941.1

Fiction
Bawden, N. The witch's daughter (4 and up) Fic
Briggs, K. M. Kate Crackernuts (6 and up) Fic
Cameron, E. Beyond silence (6 and up) Fic
Hunter, M. The haunted mountain (5 and up) Fic
Hunter, M. The kelpie's pearls (4-6) Fic
Hunter, M. A sound of chariots (5 and up) Fic
Hunter, M. The wicked one (4 and up) Fic

Folklore
See Folklore—Scotland

The **Scots** and Scotch-Irish in America. Johnson, J. E.
In The In America series 305.8

Scots-Irish

United States
Johnson, J. E. The Scots and Scotch-Irish in America
In The In America series 305.8

Scott, Ann Hamilton
Fritz, J. The cabin faced west (3-6) Fic

Scott, Ann Herbert, 1926-
One good horse E
Sam E

Scott, Dred
See/See also pages in the following book(s):
Sgroi, P. P. The living Constitution: landmark Supreme Court decisions p39-87 (5 and up) 342

Scott, Elaine, 1940-
Ramona: behind the scenes of a television show (4 and up) 791.45

Scott, Jack Denton, 1915-
Alligator (4 and up) 597.9
Orphans from the sea (4 and up) 639.9
Swans (4 and up) 598

Scott, John Anthony, 1916-
The story of America: a National Geographic picture atlas (5 and up) 973

Scott, Richard, 1956-
Jackie Robinson (5 and up) 92

Scott, Robert Falcon, 1868-1912

About
Swan, R. Destination: Antarctica (4-6) 998

The **Scott,** Foresman anthology of children's literature 808.8
Scott, Foresman beginning dictionary. See Thorndike-Barnhart children's dictionary 423
Scott, Foresman intermediate dictionary (5 and up) 423
The **Scott,** Foresman Robert's Rules of order newly revised. Robert, H. M. 060.4

Scottish Americans
Johnson, J. E. The Scots and Scotch-Irish in America
In The In America series 305.8

Scouts and scouting
See also Girl Scouts

Scrofani, Joseph
(il) Epstein, S. Dr. Beaumont and the man with the hole in his stomach 92

The **Scroobious** Pip, Edward Lear's. Lear, E. **821**
Scuba diving
McGovern, A. Down under, down under (3-6) **574.92**
McGovern, A. Night dive (3-5) **797.2**
Scudder, Horace Elisha, 1838-1902
See/See also pages in the following book(s):
Jordan, A. M. From Rollo to Tom Sawyer, and other papers p113-22 **028.5**
Scull, Marie-Louise, 1943-
(il) MacDonald, M. R. The skit book **812.008**
Scullard, Sue
(il) Sharples, J. The flyaway pantaloons **E**
Sculptors, American
St. George, J. The Mount Rushmore story [biography of Gutzon Borglum] (6 and up) **92**
Sculpture
See also Masks (Sculpture)
Scuro, Vincent
(jt. auth) Lavine, S. A. Wonders of turkeys **598**
Sea animals *See* Marine animals
The **Sea** Bride. Alcock, V.
In Alcock, V. Ghostly companions **S C**
The **sea** captain at the door. Leach, M.
In Leach, M. Whistle in the graveyard p63 **398.2**
The **sea** egg. Boston, L. M. **Fic**
The **sea-hare**. Grimm, J.
In Grimm, J. The complete Grimm's fairy tales p769-72 **398.2**
The **Sea** King and Vasilisa the Wise. Afanas'ev, A. N.
In Afanas'ev, A. N. Russian fairy tales p427-37 **398.2**
Sea life *See* Seafaring life
Sea lions *See* Seals (Animals)
Sea lions. Bare, C. S. **599.74**
The **Sea-Mammy**. Sherlock, Sir P. M.
In Sherlock, Sir P. M. West Indian folk-tales p130-34 **398.2**
Sea monsters

Fiction

Kellogg, S. Ralph's secret weapon **E**
Sea mosses *See* Algae
Sea otter *See* Otters
Sea otter rescue. Smith, R. **639.9**
Sea otters. Ashby, R. **599.74**
Sea poetry
Livingston, M. C. Sea songs **811**
Sea shells *See* Shells
Sea songs. Livingston, M. C. **811**
Sea Star, orphan of Chincoteague. Henry, M. See note under Henry, M. Misty of Chincoteague **Fic**
Sea-stars *See* Starfishes
Sea stories
Avi. The true confessions of Charlotte Doyle (6 and up) **Fic**
Babbitt, N. The eyes of the Amaryllis (5 and up) **Fic**
Barber, A. The Mousehole cat **E**
Fox, P. The slave dancer (5 and up) **Fic**
Holling, H. C. Seabird (4-6) **Fic**
McCloskey, R. Burt Dow, deep-water man **E**
Thiele, C. Shadow shark (5 and up) **Fic**
Verne, J. Twenty thousand leagues under the sea (5 and up) **Fic**
Sea swan. Lasky, K. **E**
Sea turtles
Ancona, G. Turtle watch (2-4) **597.9**
Sea-woman. Crossley-Holland, K.
In Crossley-Holland, K. British folk tales p11-16 **398.2**
Sea World (San Diego, Calif.)
Reeves, R. R. The Sea World book of dolphins **599.5**
The **Sea** World book of dolphins. Reeves, R. R. **599.5**
Seabird. Holling, H. C. **Fic**
Seafaring life
See/See also pages in the following book(s):
Tunis, E. The young United States, 1783 to 1830 p81-95 (5 and up) **973**
Seals (Animals)
Bare, C. S. Elephants on the beach (1-3) **599.74**
Bare, C. S. Sea lions (3-5) **599.74**
Cowcher, H. Antarctica (1-3) **998**
Johnson, S. A. Elephant seals (4 and up) **599.74**
Patent, D. H. Seals, sea lions, and walruses (5 and up) **599.74**
Selsam, M. E. A first look at seals, sea lions, and walruses (1-3) **599.74**
White, S. V. Sterling (2-4) **639.9**

Fiction

Cooper, S. The selkie girl (2-4) **398.2**
Tafuri, N. Follow me! **E**
Seals, sea lions, and walruses. Patent, D. H. **599.74**
The **seal's** skin. Simpson, J.
In Best-loved folktales of the world p383-84 **398.2**

The **search** for delicious. Babbitt, N. **Fic**
The **search** for the magic lake. Barlow, G.
In Best-loved folktales of the world p767-73 **398.2**
The **search**: who gets the chief's daughter. Courlander, H.
In With a deep sea smile p70-74 **372.6**

Sears, Lora
(il) Nichols, J. Storytimes for two-year-olds **027.62**

Sears, Minnie Earl, 1873-1933
Sears list of subject headings. See Sears list of subject headings **025.4**

Sears, Richard Warren
See/See also pages in the following book(s):
Aaseng, N. From rags to riches p24-32 (5 and up) **920**

Sears list of subject headings **025.4**

Sears, Roebuck and Co.
See/See also pages in the following book(s):
Aaseng, N. From rags to riches p24-32 (5 and up) **920**

Seashells of the world. Abbott, R. T. **594**

Seashore
Kohn, B. The beachcomber's book (3-6) **745.5**
Parker, S. Seashore (4 and up) **574.92**
Stolz, M. Night of ghosts and hermits (3-5) **574.92**

Fiction
Baker, L. A. Morning beach **E**
Boston, L. M. The sea egg (3-5) **Fic**
Jonas, A. Reflections **E**
Myrick, M. The Secret Three **E**
Turkle, B. C. Do not open **E**

Seashore ecology
Miller, C. G. Coastal rescue: preserving our seashores (5 and up) **333.91**

Seashore in art
Arnosky, J. Near the sea (4 and up) **758**

Seashores. Zim, H. S. **574.92**
Seashores and shadows. See Thiele, C. Shadow shark **Fic**
The **season** of secret wishes. Procházková, I. **Fic**
Season of the white stork. Fischer-Nagel, H. **598**
Season songs. Hughes, T. **821**

Seasons
See also Spring; Summer; Winter
Branley, F. M. Sunshine makes the seasons (k-3) **525**
Lerner, C. A forest year (3-5) **574.5**
Provensen, A. A book of seasons **E**
Sendak, M. Chicken soup with rice **E**
Wolff, A. A year of beasts **E**
Wolff, A. A year of birds **E**
See/See also pages in the following book(s):
Simon, S. Look to the night sky: an introduction to star watching (4 and up) **523**

Fiction
Anno, M. Anno's counting book **E**
Dragonwagon, C. Winter holding spring (2-4) **Fic**
Gibbons, G. The seasons of Arnold's apple tree **E**
Hughes, S. Out and about **E**
Johnston, T. Yonder **E**
Provensen, A. The year at Maple Hill Farm **E**
Rockwell, A. F. First comes spring **E**
Rylant, C. This year's garden **E**
Zolotow, C. Over and over **E**

Pictorial works
Florian, D. A year in the country **E**

Poetry
Esbensen, B. J. Cold stars and fireflies (4 and up) **811**
Hughes, T. Season songs (6 and up) **821**
Livingston, M. C. A circle of seasons (1-3) **811**
Ryder, J. Under your feet (k-3) **811**
Yolen, J. Ring of earth: a child's book of seasons (3-6) **811**
See/See also pages in the following book(s):
Piping down the valleys wild p79-90 **808.81**
Rainbow in the sky p170-82 (k-4) **821.008**

The **seasons** of Arnold's apple tree. Gibbons, G. **E**
Seaward. Cooper, S. **Fic**
Seaweeds *See* Algae

Sebestyen, Ouida, 1924-
After the wedding
In Connections: short stories by outstanding writers for young adults p206-16 **S C**
IOU's (6 and up) **Fic**
Words by heart (5 and up) **Fic**

Sébillot, Paul, 1846-1918
The dirty shepherdess
In The Green fairy book p180-85 **398.2**
The Golden Blackbird
In The Green fairy book p151-56 **398.2**
The snuff-box
In The Green fairy book p145-50 **398.2**

Second Calender
The Story of the second calender, son of a king
In The Arabian nights entertainments p75-85 **398.2**

Second dream: Carlo the silent. Gorog, J.
In Gorog, J. Three dreams and a nightmare, and other tales of the dark **S C**

The **second** jungle book. See Kipling, R. The jungle books **S C**

Second old man and two black dogs
The Story of the second old man and of the two black dogs
In The Arabian nights entertainments p19-22 **398.2**

The **second** Raffi songbook. See Raffi. The 2nd Raffi songbook **782.42**

Secondary school libraries *See* School libraries (High school)

The **secret** ball. Afanas'ev, A. N.
In Afanas'ev, A. N. Russian fairy tales p224-26 **398.2**

Secret City, U.S.A. Holman, F. **Fic**

The **secret** garden. Burnett, F. H. **Fic**

The **secret** language. Nordstrom, U. **Fic**

The **secret** language: pheromones in the animal world. Johnson, R. L. **591.5**

The **secret** life of cosmetics: a science experiment book. Cobb, V. **668**

The **secret** life of hardware: a science experiment book. Cobb, V. **670**

The **secret** of life of Dagmar Schultz. Hall, L. See note under Hall, L. Dagmar Schultz and the angel Edna **Fic**

Secret of the Andes. Clark, A. N. **Fic**

The **secret** of the Indian. Reid Banks, L. See note under Reid Banks, L. The Indian in the cupboard **Fic**

The **secret** of the underground room. Bellairs, J. See note under Bellairs, J. The curse of the blue figurine **Fic**

Secret service
See also Spies

The **secret** soldier: the story of Deborah Sampson [Gannett]. McGovern, A. **92**

The **Secret** Three. Myrick, M. **E**

The **Secret** world of animals (4 and up) **591.5**

The **secret** world of Polly Flint. Cresswell, H. **Fic**

The **secretive** timber rattlesnake. Lavies, B. **597.9**

Secrets in the meadow. Hess, L. **591.5**

Secrets of a small brother. Margolis, R. J. **811**

Secrets of a summer spy. Jones, J. B. **Fic**

Secrets of a wildlife watcher. Arnosky, J. **591.5**

The **Sedna** legend. Melzack, R.
In Best-loved folktales of the world p721-23 **398.2**

See inside a castle. Unstead, R. J. **728.8**

See inside a space station. Kerrod, R. **629.44**

See inside a submarine. Rutland, J. **623.8**

See inside an oil rig and tanker. Rutland, J. **665.5**

See you in second grade! Cohen, M. **E**

See you tomorrow, Charles. Cohen, M. See note under Cohen, M. See you in second grade! **E**

Seed, Jenny
Ntombi's song **E**

Seeds
Dowden, A. O. T. From flower to fruit (5 and up) **582**
Facklam, H. Plants: extinction or survival? (6 and up) **581**
Jordan, H. J. How a seed grows (k-3) **582**
Lauber, P. Seeds pop, stick, glide (2-4) **582**
Overbeck, C. How seeds travel (4 and up) **582**
Wexler, J. Flowers, fruits, seeds (k-2) **582**

Seeds pop, stick, glide. Lauber, P. **582**

Seeger, Pete
Abiyoyo (k-2) **398.2**

Seeger, Ruth Crawford, 1901-1953
American folk songs for children in home, school and nursery school **781.62**

Seeing Earth from space. Lauber, P. **525**

Seeing eye dogs *See* Guide dogs

Seeing in special ways. Bergman, T. **362.4**

The **seeing** stick. Yolen, J. **Fic**

Sees in the night
In The Whistling skeleton p19-26 **398.2**

Segal, Lore Groszmann
The book of Adam to Moses (4-6) **222**
Tell me a Mitzi **E**
Tell me a Trudy **E**
(ed) Grimm, J. The juniper tree, and other tales from Grimm **398.2**

Segel, Elizabeth
(jt. auth) Kimmel, M. M. For reading out loud! **028.5**

Seiden, Art
(il) McMane, F. Track & field basics **796.4**

Seismology *See* Earthquakes
Seixas, Judith S.
Drugs—what they are, what they do (1-3) **616.86**
Junk food—what it is, what it does (1-3) **641.3**
Tobacco (1-3) **616.86**
Water: what it is, what it does (1-3) **553.7**

Seki, Keigo
The wife's portrait
In Best-loved folktales of the world p519-21 **398.2**
Selden, George, 1929-1989
Chester Cricket's new home. See note under Selden, G. The cricket in Times Square **Fic**
Chester Cricket's pigeon ride. See note under Selden, G. The cricket in Times Square **Fic**
The cricket in Times Square (3-6) **Fic**
The genie of Sutton Place (4 and up) **Fic**
Harry Cat's pet puppy. See note under Selden, G. The cricket in Times Square **Fic**
Harry Kitten and Tucker Mouse. See note under Selden, G. The cricket in Times Square **Fic**
The old meadow. See note under Selden, G. The cricket in Times Square **Fic**
Tucker's countryside. See note under Selden, G. The cricket in Times Square **Fic**

Self-defense
See also Aikido; Martial arts
Self-playing gusla
Afanas'ev, A. N. The self-playing gusla
In Afanas'ev, A. N. Russian fairy tales p211-13 **398.2**
Self-portrait: Erik Blegvad. Blegvad, E. **92**
Self-portrait: Trina Schart Hyman. Hyman, T. S. **92**
The **selfish** giant. Wilde, O. **Fic**
In Wilde, O. The Happy Prince, and other stories p21-26 **S C**
The **selkie** girl. Cooper, S. **398.2**
Selsam, Millicent Ellis, 1912-
Backyard insects (k-3) **595.7**
Cotton (3-5) **633.5**
Egg to chick (k-3) **636.5**
A first look at animals with backbones (1-3) **596**
A first look at bird nests (1-3) **598**
A first look at birds (1-3) **598**
A first look at caterpillars (1-3) **595.7**
A first look at flowers (1-3) **582.13**
A first look at insects (1-3) **595.7**
A first look at kangaroos, koalas, and other animals with pouches (1-3) **599.2**
A first look at monkeys and apes (1-3) **599.8**
A first look at owls, eagles, and other hunters of the sky (1-3) **598**
A first look at poisonous snakes (1-3) **597.9**
A first look at rocks (1-3) **552**
A first look at seals, sea lions, and walruses (1-3) **599.74**
A first look at seashells (1-3) **594**
A first look at sharks (1-3) **597**
A first look at the world of plants (1-3) **581**
Greg's microscope (1-3) **502.8**
Keep looking! (k-2) **599**
Mushrooms (2-4) **589.2**
Terry and the caterpillars (k-3) **595.7**
Tree flowers (4 and up) **582.16**
(jt. auth) Bronowski, J. Biography of an atom **539**
Seltzer, Meyer
(il) White, L. B. Math-a-magic: number tricks for magicians **793.8**
Seminole Indians
See/See also pages in the following book(s):
Hofsinde, R. Indian costumes p79-85 (3-6) **391**

Sendak, Maurice
Alligators all around **E**
Caldecott & Co.: notes on books and pictures **028.5**
Chicken soup with rice **E**
Hector Protector, and As I went over the water (k-1) **398.8**
Higglety pigglety pop! (2-4) **Fic**
In the night kitchen **E**
Kenny's window **E**
One was Johnny **E**
Outside over there **E**
Pierre **E**
The sign on Rosie's door **E**
Very far away **E**
Where the wild things are **E**
(il) DeJong, M. The house of sixty fathers **Fic**
(il) DeJong, M. The wheel on the school **Fic**
(il) Grimm, J. The juniper tree, and other tales from Grimm **398.2**
(il) Hoffmann, E. T. A. Nutcracker **Fic**
(il) Jarrell, R. The animal family **Fic**
(il) Jarrell, R. The bat-poet **Fic**
(il) Joslin, S. What do you do, dear? **395**
(il) Joslin, S. What do you say, dear? **395**
(il) Krauss, R. A hole is to dig **E**
(il) Krauss, R. A very special house **E**

Sendak, Maurice—*Continued*
(il) Lullabies and night songs. See Lullabies and night songs 782.42
(il) MacDonald, G. The light princess Fic
(il) Minarik, E. H. Little Bear E
(il) Minarik, E. H. No fighting, no biting! E
(il) Singer, I. B. Zlateh the goat, and other stories 398.2
(il) Stockton, F. The Bee-man of Orn Fic
(il) Stockton, F. The Griffin and the Minor Canon Fic
(il) Udry, J. M. The moon jumpers E
(il) Zolotow, C. Mr. Rabbit and the lovely present E

About

Lanes, S. G. Art of Maurice Sendak 741.6

Senegal
Senegal—in pictures (5 and up) 966.3

Folklore

See Folklore—Senegal

Senegal—in pictures (5 and up) 966.3

Señor Coyote and the dogs. Storm, D.
In Best-loved folktales of the world p686-88 398.2

Señora, will you snip? Señora, will you sew?
Sawyer, R. Señora, will you snip? Señora, will you sew?
In Sawyer, R. The way of the storyteller p229-36 372.6

Sense of direction *See* Direction sense

A **sense** of story. Townsend, J. R. 028.5

Senses and sensation
Aliki. My five senses (k-3) 612.8
Brenner, B. Faces (k-2) 612.8
Cobb, V. How to really fool yourself (5 and up) 152.1
Goor, R. Heads (2-4) 591.4
Kohl, J. The view from the oak (6 and up) 591.5
Martin, P. D. Messengers to the brain: our fantastic five senses (5 and up) 612.8

Sequoia *See* Redwood

Sequoyah, 1770?-1843

About

Cwiklik, R. Sequoyah and the Cherokee alphabet (5 and up) 92

Fiction

Jones, W. Edge of two worlds (5 and up) Fic

Sequoyah and the Cherokee alphabet. Cwiklik, R. 92

Seredy, Kate, 1899-1975
The Good Master (4-6) Fic
The white stag (4-6) Fic
See/See also pages in the following book(s):
Newbery Medal books, 1922-1955 p161-65 028.5

Serfozo, Mary
Who said red? E

Serial publications
See also Newspapers; Periodicals

The **serpent-slayer.** Kendall, C.
In Kendall, C. Sweet and sour p33-38 398.2

Serpent's bride
Berger, T. The serpent's bride
In Berger, T. Black fairy tales p15-32 398.2

The **serpent's** children. Yep, L. Fic

Serraillier, Ian, 1912-
The silver sword (5 and up) Fic

Service, Pamela F.
Stinker from space (4-6) Fic

Service, Robert W. (Robert William), 1874-1958
The cremation of Sam McGee (4 and up) 811
The shooting of Dan McGrew (4 and up) 811

A **service** dog goes to school. Smith, E. S. 636.7

Servitude *See* Slavery

Settel, Joanne
Why does my nose run? (4 and up) 612

Seuling, Barbara
The teeny tiny woman (k-2) 398.2
You can't sneeze with your eyes open & other freaky facts about the human body (4 and up) 612

Seuss, Dr.
The 500 hats of Bartholomew Cubbins E
And to think that I saw it on Mulberry Street E
Bartholomew and the oobleck E
The cat in the hat E
The cat in the hat comes back! E
Green eggs and ham E
Horton hatches the egg E
Horton hears a Who! E
How the Grinch stole Christmas E
If I ran the circus E
If I ran the zoo E
McElligot's pool E
Oh, the places you'll go! E

The **seven** Chinese brothers. Mahy, M. 398.2

Seven dancing stars: legends of the Pleiades. Monroe, J. G.
In Monroe, J. G. They dance in the sky p1-14 **398.2**

Seven-day magic. Eager, E. **Fic**

The **seven** days of creation. Fisher, L. E. **222**

Seven days to a brand-new me. Conford, E. **Fic**

Seven foals
Moe, J. E. The seven foals
In The Red fairy book p346-53 **398.2**

The **Seven-headed** serpent
In The Yellow fairy book p60-63 **398.2**

Seven kisses in a row. MacLachlan, P. **Fic**

Seven ravens
Grimm, J. The seven ravens **398.2**
In Grimm, J. The complete Grimm's fairy tales p137-39 **398.2**

Seven Simons
Afanas'ev, A. N. The seven Semyons
In Afanas'ev, A. N. Russian fairy tales p410-14 **398.2**

Seven Swabians
Grimm, J. The seven Swabians
In Grimm, J. The complete Grimm's fairy tales p538-42 **398.2**

The **Seven** voyages of Sindbad the sailor
In The Arabian nights entertainments p122-86 **398.2**

Seven x seven tales of a sevensleeper. See Johansen, H. 7 x 7 tales of a seven-sleeper **Fic**

Seventeen kings and forty-two elephants. Mahy, M. **E**

The **seventh** day: the story of the Jewish Sabbath. Chaikin, M. **222**

Seventh grade. Soto, G.
In Soto, G. Baseball in April, and other stories p52-59 **S C**

Severn, Bill
Magic fun for everyone (6 and up) **793.8**

Sewall, Marcia, 1935-
The pilgrims of Plimoth (3-6) **974.4**
(il) Fleischman, P. The birthday tree **Fic**
(il) Fleischman, P. Finzel the farsighted **Fic**
(il) Foley, P. John and the fiddler **Fic**
(il) Gardiner, J. R. Stone Fox **Fic**
(il) Kennedy, R. Richard Kennedy: collected stories **S C**
(il) Schotter, R. Captain Snap and the children of Vinegar Lane **E**
(il) Thomas, J. R. Saying good-bye to Grandma **E**

Sewell, Anna, 1820-1878
Black Beauty (4-6) **Fic**

Sewell, Helen Moore, 1896-1957
(il) Dalgliesh, A. The bears on Hemlock Mountain **Fic**
(il) Dalgliesh, A. The Thanksgiving story **974.4**
(il) Hughes, L. The dream keeper, and other poems **811**

Sewerage
See/See also pages in the following book(s):
Macaulay, D. Underground p57-65 (4 and up) **624.1**

The **sewing** machine. Siegel, B. **646.2**

Sewing machines
Siegel, B. The sewing machine (4 and up) **646.2**

Sex (Biology)
See also Reproduction

Sex crimes
See also Child molesting

Sex differences (Psychology)
See also Sex role

Sex education
Andry, A. C. How babies are made (k-3) **612.6**
Cole, J. Asking about sex and growing up (4-6) **613.9**
Johnson, E. W. Love and sex and growing up (4 and up) **613.9**
Johnson, E. W. People, love, sex, and families (5 and up) **613.9**
Madaras, L. The what's happening to my body? book for boys: a growing up guide for parents and sons (6 and up) **613.9**
Madaras, L. The what's happening to my body? book for girls: a growing up guide for parents and daughters (6 and up) **613.9**
Waxman, S. What is a girl? what is a boy? (k-1) **612.6**

Sex instruction *See* Sex education

Sex role

Bibliography

A Guide to non-sexist children's books v2 **011.6**

Fiction

Oneal, Z. A long way to go (3-5) **Fic**
Walter, M. P. Justin and the best biscuits in the world (3-6) **Fic**
Winthrop, E. Tough Eddie **E**
Zolotow, C. William's doll **E**

Sgroi, Peter P.
The living Constitution: landmark Supreme Court decisions (5 and up) **342**

Shachat, Andrew
(il) Williams, S. Mommy doesn't know my name E
Shachtman, Tom, 1942-
Parade! E
The president builds a house (3-5) 363.5
The **shade** cutter. Fleischman, P.
In Fleischman, P. Coming-and-going men p3-48 S C
Shades and shadows
Dorros, A. Me and my shadow (k-3) 535
Goor, R. Shadows (k-3) 535
Gore, S. My shadow (k-2) 535
Simon, S. Shadow magic (k-3) 535
Fiction
Fleischman, P. Shadow play E
Tompert, A. Nothing sticks like a shadow E
Pictorial works
Hoban, T. Shadows and reflections 779
Poetry
Stevenson, R. L. My shadow (k-3) 821
Shades of gray. Reeder, C. Fic
Shadow. Cendrars, B. 841
The **shadow** guests. Aiken, J. Fic
Shadow magic. Simon, S. 535
Shadow of a bull. Wojciechowska, M. Fic
Shadow play. Fleischman, P. E
Shadow shark. Thiele, C. Fic
Shadows. Goor, R. 535
The **shadows**. MacDonald, G.
In MacDonald, G. The complete fairy tales of George MacDonald S C
Shadows and reflections. Hoban, T. 779
Shaffer, Paul R.
(jt. auth) Zim, H. S. Rocks and minerals 549
Shaka *See* Chaka, Zulu Chief, 1787?-1828
Shaka, king of the Zulus. Stanley, D. 92
Shake a palm branch. Chaikin, M. 296.4
Shake my sillies out. Raffi. 782.42
Shaker Lane. Provensen, A. E
Shakers
Fiction
Peck, R. N. A day no pigs would die (6 and up) Fic
Shakespeare, William, 1564-1616
Adaptations
Lamb, C. Tales from Shakespeare 822.3
Shamrocks, harps, and shillelaghs. Barth, E. 394.2
Shanghai (China)
Fiction
Chang, M. S. In the eye of war (4 and up) Fic

Shankle, George Earlie
American nicknames 929.4
Shannon, David
(il) Lester, J. How many spots does a leopard have? and other tales 398.2
Shannon, George, 1952-
Dance away! E
The Piney Woods peddler E
Stories to solve (3 and up) 398.2
(jt. auth) Greene, E. Storytelling: a selected annotated bibliography 016.3726
Shannon, Monica, d. 1965
See/See also pages in the following book(s):
Newbery Medal books, 1922-1955 p127-34 028.5
Shape *See* Size and shape
Shapes. Reiss, J. J. E
The **shapes** game. Rogers, P. 516
Shapes, shapes, shapes. Hoban, T. 516
Shapiro, Mary J.
How they built the Statue of Liberty (4 and up) 974.7
Sharing joy and sorrow. Grimm, J.
In Grimm, J. The complete Grimm's fairy tales p704-05 398.2
Sharing love and sorrow
Grimm, J. Sharing joy and sorrow
In Grimm, J. The complete Grimm's fairy tales p704-05 398.2
Sharks
Berger, G. Sharks (2-4) 597
Blassingame, W. Wonders of sharks (4 and up) 597
Blumberg, R. Sharks (4 and up) 597
Coupe, S. Sharks (5 and up) 597
Freedman, R. Sharks (3-5) 597
Mahy, M. The great white man-eating shark E
McGowen, T. Album of sharks (4 and up) 597
Sattler, H. R. Sharks, the super fish (4 and up) 597
Selsam, M. E. A first look at sharks (1-3) 597
See/See also pages in the following book(s):
Freedman, R. Killer fish p7-13 (3-5) 597
Fiction
Thiele, C. Shadow shark (5 and up) Fic
Sharks, the super fish. Sattler, H. R. 597
Sharmat, Marjorie Weinman, 1928-
Getting something on Maggie Marmelstein. See note under Sharmat, M. W. Mysteriously yours, Maggie Marmelstein Fic
Gila monsters meet you at the airport E

Sharmat, Marjorie Weinman, 1928-—*Continued*
Goodnight, Andrew: goodnight, Craig E
Griselda's new year E
I'm not Oscar's friend anymore
In Bauer, C. F. Celebrations p282-85 **808.8**
Maggie Marmelstein for president. See note under Sharmat, M. W. Mysteriously yours, Maggie Marmelstein **Fic**
Mooch the messy E
Mysteriously yours, Maggie Marmelstein (3-6) **Fic**
Nate the Great E
Nate the Great and the boring beach bag. See note under Sharmat, M. W. Nate the Great E
Nate the Great and the fishy prize. See note under Sharmat, M. W. Nate the Great E
Nate the Great and the Halloween hunt. See note under Sharmat, M. W. Nate the Great E
Nate the Great and the lost list. See note under Sharmat, M. W. Nate the Great E
Nate the Great and the missing key. See note under Sharmat, M. W. Nate the Great E
Nate the Great and the musical note. See note under Sharmat, M. W. Nate the Great E
Nate the Great and the phony clue. See note under Sharmat, M. W. Nate the Great E
Nate the Great and the snowy trail. See note under Sharmat, M. W. Nate the Great E
Nate the Great and the sticky case. See note under Sharmat, M. W. Nate the Great E
Nate the Great goes down in the dumps. See note under Sharmat, M. W. Nate the Great E
Nate the Great goes undercover. See note under Sharmat, M. W. Nate the Great E
Nate the Great stalks stupidweed. See note under Sharmat, M. W. Nate the Great E

Sharmat, Mitchell, 1927-
Gregory, the terrible eater E

Sharp, Margery, 1905-
Miss Bianca. See note under Sharp, M. The rescuers **Fic**
Miss Bianca in the salt mines. See note under Sharp, M. The rescuers **Fic**
The rescuers (3-6) **Fic**
The turret. See note under Sharp, M. The rescuers **Fic**

Sharp, Pat
Brain power! (4 and up) **612.8**

Sharpe, Richard Scrafton, d. 1852
Anecdotes and adventures of fifteen gentlemen
In A Nursery companion p70-74 **820.8**
Dame Wiggins of Lee—and her seven wonderful cats
In A Nursery companion p58-61 **820.8**

Sharples, Joseph
The flyaway pantaloons E

Shaw, Charles, 1892-1974
It looked like spilt milk E

Shaw, Diana
Make the most of a good thing: you! (5 and up) **613**

Shaw, Nancy (Nancy E.)
Sheep in a jeep E

Shawnee Indians
Shorto, R. Tecumseh and the dream of an American Indian nation (5 and up) **92**

She come bringing me that little baby girl. Greenfield, E. E

Shebar, Sharon Sigmond, 1945-
Bats (5 and up) **599.4**

Shebar, Susan E.
(jt. auth) Shebar, S. S. Bats **599.4**

Shecter, Ben
(il) Benchley, N. A ghost named Fred E
(il) Sharmat, M. W. Mooch the messy E
(il) Sharmat, M. W. Mysteriously yours, Maggie Marmelstein **Fic**
(il) Zolotow, C. The hating book E
(il) Zolotow, C. My friend John E

Shedlock, Marie L., 1854-1935
The art of the story-teller **372.6**
Filial piety
In Shedlock, M. L. The art of the story-teller p229-32 **372.6**
The folly of panic
In Shedlock, M. L. The art of the story-teller p222-24 **372.6**
Hafiz, the stone-cutter
In Shedlock, M. L. The art of the story-teller p179-82 **372.6**
The hare that ran away
In The Scott, Foresman anthology of children's literature p341 **808.8**
Snegourka
In Shedlock, M. L. The art of the story-teller p195-97 **372.6**
The true spirit of a festival day
In Shedlock, M. L. The art of the story-teller p225-28 **372.6**

Sheep
Paladino, C. Spring fleece (3-6) **636.3**
Fiction
Alderson, S. A. Ida and the wool smugglers **E**
Carrick, C. In the moonlight, waiting **E**
Krumgold, J. —and now Miguel (6 and up) **Fic**
Shaw, N. Sheep in a jeep **E**
Poetry
Hale, S. J. Mary had a little lamb (k-2) **811**

Sheep, the fox, and the wolf
Afanas'ev, A. N. The sheep, the fox, and the wolf
In Afanas'ev, A. N. Russian fairy tales p275-76 **398.2**

Sheep dogs
Ancona, G. Sheep dog (4 and up) **636.7**

Sheep herders *See* Shepherds

Sheep in a jeep. Shaw, N. **E**

Sheila Rae, the brave. Henkes, K. **E**

Shein, Bob
(il) Phillips, L. Going ape **793.73**

Shell. Arthur, A. **594**

She'll be comin' round the mountain. Quackenbush, R. M. **781.62**

Shelley, Mary Wollstonecraft, 1797-1851
Mounseer Nongtongpaw
In A Nursery companion p118-22 **820.8**

Shellfish
See also Crabs; Mollusks

Shells
Abbott, R. T. Seashells of the world (5 and up) **594**
Arthur, A. Shell (4 and up) **594**
Florian, D. Discovering seashells (1-3) **594**
Selsam, M. E. A first look at seashells (1-3) **594**

Shells. Rylant, C.
In Rylant, C. Every living thing p73-81 **S C**

Shelter from the wind. Bauer, M. D. **Fic**

Shelters: from tepee to igloo. Weiss, H. **728**

Shemiaka the judge. Afanas'ev, A. N.
In Afanas'ev, A. N. Russian fairy tales p625-27 **398.2**

Shemyak the judge
Afanas'ev, A. N. Shemiaka the judge
In Afanas'ev, A. N. Russian fairy tales p625-27 **398.2**

Shepard, Ernest H. (Ernest Howard), 1879-1976
(il) Grahame, K. The reluctant dragon **Fic**
(il) Grahame, K. The wind in the willows **Fic**
(il) Milne, A. A. The Christopher Robin story book **828**
(il) Milne, A. A. The house at Pooh Corner **Fic**
(il) Milne, A. A. Now we are six **821**
(il) Milne, A. A. The Pooh story book **Fic**
(il) Milne, A. A. Pooh's bedtime book **828**
(il) Milne, A. A. When we were very young **821**
(il) Milne, A. A. Winnie-the-Pooh **Fic**
(il) Milne, A. A. The world of Christopher Robin **821**
(il) Milne, A. A. The world of Pooh **Fic**

Shepard, Mary Eleanor, 1909-
(il) Travers, P. L. Mary Poppins **Fic**

Shepherd, Jenifer A.
Canada (4 and up) **971**

The **shepherd** boy. Grimm, J.
In Grimm, J. The complete Grimm's fairy tales p651-52 **398.2**

Shepherd boy and the king
Grimm, J. The little shepherd boy
In Grimm, J. More tales from Grimm p47-49 **398.2**
Grimm, J. The shepherd boy
In Grimm, J. The complete Grimm's fairy tales p651-52 **398.2**

The **shepherd** moon. Hoover, H. M. **Fic**

Shepherds
Fiction
Krumgold, J. —and now Miguel (6 and up) **Fic**

The **shepherd's** tale. Crossley-Holland, K.
In Crossley-Holland, K. British folk tales p248-50 **398.2**

Sheridan, Caroline
The dandies' rout
In A Nursery companion p113-17 **820.8**

Sheridan, Jeff
Nothing's impossible! stunts to entertain and amaze (5 and up) **793.8**

Sheridan, Noel
Morocco—in pictures. See Morocco—in pictures **964**

The **sheriff** of Rottenshot: poems. Prelutsky, J. 811

Sherlock, Sir Philip Manderson, 1902-
Anansi, the spider man (4-6) 398.2
Contents: Who was Anansi; From Tiger to Anansi; Brother Breeze and the pear tree; Anansi and the Old Hag; Anansi and Turtle and Pigeon; Kisander; Kling Kling bird; Bandalee; Yung-Kyung-Pyung; Anansi and the plantains; Ticky-Picky Boom-Boom; Anansi and the alligator eggs; Anansi and the crabs; The quarrel; Anansi and the Fish Country
Tiger in the forest, Anansi in the web
In The Scott, Foresman anthology of children's literature p392-93 808.8
West Indian folk-tales (4-6) 398.2
Contents: The Coomacka-Tree; The crested curassow; Irraweka, mischief-maker; The jaguar and the crested curassow; The dog's nose is cold; The Warau people discover the earth; Tiger story, Anansi story; Tiger in the forest, Anansi in the web; Mancrow, bird of darkness; Anansi and Snake the postman; Dry-Bone and Anansi; How crab got a hard back; Cat and Dog; Anansi and Candlefly; Anansi's old riding-horse; Why women won't listen; Anansi hunts with Tiger; Work-let-me-see; The Sea-mammy; Born a monkey, live a monkey; Mr. Wheeler

Sherlock Holmes' Christmas goose. Nolan, P. T.
In The Big book of Christmas plays p298-312 808.82

Sherman, Josepha
Vassilisa the wise (2-4) 398.2

Sherman, Ori
(il) Ehrlich, A. The story of Hanukkah 296.4
(il) Schwartz, L. S. The four questions 296.4

Shetland (Scotland)
Fiction
Hunter, M. A stranger came ashore (6 and up) Fic

Shetland Islands *See* Shetland (Scotland)

Shetterly, Robert
(il) Schlein, M. Project panda watch 599.74
(il) Shetterly, S. H. The dwarf-wizard of Uxmal 398.2

Shetterly, Susan Hand, 1942-
The dwarf-wizard of Uxmal (3-5) 398.2

Shhh! we're writing the Constitution. Fritz, J. 342

Shimin, Symeon
(il) Fisher, A. L. Listen, rabbit E
(il) Hamilton, V. Zeely Fic
(il) Krumgold, J. Onion John Fic
(il) Phelan, M. K. The Fourth of July 394.2
(il) Scott, A. H. Sam E

Shimizu, Kiyoshi, 1924-
(il) Johnson, S. A. Inside an egg 598
(il) Overbeck, C. Carnivorous plants 583

The **shimmershine** queens. Yarbrough, C. Fic

The **shining** princess. Quayle, E.
In Quayle, E. The shining princess, and other Japanese legends p13-23 398.2

The **shining** princess, and other Japanese legends. Quayle, E. 398.2

Ship forever sailing. Young, S.
In Holiday plays round the year p59-70 812.008

Ships
See also Steamboats
Barton, B. Boats (k-1) 387.2
Crews, D. Harbor E
Gibbons, G. Boat book (k-2) 387.2
Rockwell, A. F. Boats (k-1) 387.2
Models—Fiction
Zhitkov, B. How I hunted the little fellows (2-4) Fic

Shipwrecks
Ballard, R. D. Exploring the Titanic (4 and up) 910.4
Ballard, R. D. The lost wreck of the Isis (4 and up) 910.4
Fine, J. C. Sunken ships & treasure (5 and up) 910.4
Gibbons, G. Sunken treasure (2-4) 910.4
Hackwell, W. J. Diving to the past: recovering ancient wrecks (4 and up) 910.4
Hidden treasures of the sea (4 and up) 910.4

Shirai, Shōhei, 1933-
(il) Johnson, S. A. Coral reefs 574.92

Shirer, William L. (William Lawrence)
The rise and fall of Adolf Hitler (6 and up) 943.086

Shirley Holmes and the FBI. Gotwalt, H. L. M.
In Gotwalt, H. L. M. Everyday plays for boys and girls p132-46 812

Shlemiel the businessman. Singer, I. B.
In Singer, I. B. Stories for children p130-38 S C
In Singer, I. B. When Shlemiel went to Warsaw & other stories p55-69 398.2

Shloime the mathematician. Simon, S.
In Simon, S. More wise men of Helm and their merry tales p11-15 398.2

Shoe industry
Cobb, V. Sneakers meet your feet (4-6) 685
Mitchell, B. Shoes for everyone: a story about Jan Matzeliger (3-5) 92

Shoebag. James, M. Fic

Shoemaker, Hurst H.
(jt. auth) Zim, H. S. Fishes 597

The **shoemaker** and the elves. Grimm, J.
In Grimm, J. More tales from Grimm p251-57 **398.2**
The **shoemaker** and the elves. Rockwell, A. F.
In Rockwell, A. F. The three bears & 15 other stories p71-77 **398.2**
Shoes
Roy, R. Whose shoes are these? (k-2) **391**
Fiction
Oppenheim, J. Left & right **E**
Winthrop, E. Shoes **E**
Wright, J. The old woman and the Willy Nilly Man (k-3) **E**
Shoes for everyone: a story about Jan Matzeliger. Mitchell, B. **92**
Shoes from Grandpa. Fox, M. **E**
The **shoes** that were danced to pieces. Grimm, J.
In Grimm, J. The complete Grimm's fairy tales p596-600 **398.2**
Shoeshine girl. Bulla, C. R. **Fic**
Shohet, Marti
(il) Markle, S. The young scientist's guide to successful science projects **507.8**
(il) Sattler, H. R. Recipes for art and craft materials **745.5**
Sholem Aleichem, 1859-1916
Holiday tales of Sholom Aleichem (5 and up) **S C**
Contents: Really a sukkah; Benny's luck; A ruined Passover; The esrog; The goldspinners; The Passover exiles; The first commune
Shulevitz, U. Hanukah money **E**
The **shooting** of Dan McGrew. Service, R. W. **811**
Shooting stars *See* Meteors
Shooting stars. Branley, F. M. **523.6**
Shopping
Fiction
Gretz, S. Teddy bears go shopping **E**
Lobel, A. On Market Street **E**
Oxenbury, H. Shopping trip **E**
The **shopping** basket. Burningham, J. **E**
The **Shopping** trip
In Juba this and Juba that p71-72 **372.6**
Shopping trip. Oxenbury, H. **E**
Short & shivery. San Souci, R. **398.2**
Short stories
Aiken, J. Give yourself a fright: thirteen tales of the supernatural (6 and up) **S C**
Aiken, J. Past eight o'clock (3-6) **S C**
Aiken, J. Up the chimney down, and other stories (5 and up) **S C**
Alcock, V. Ghostly companions (5 and up) **S C**
Alexander, L. The town cats, and other tales (3-5) **S C**
Andersen, H. C. Hans Andersen: his classic fairy tales (3-6) **S C**
Babbitt, N. The Devil's other storybook (4-6) **S C**
Babbitt, N. The Devil's storybook (4-6) **S C**
Bond, M. Paddington's storybook (2-5) **S C**
Brooke, W. J. A telling of the tales: five stories (4-6) **S C**
Carlson, N. S. The talking cat, and other stories of French Canada (3-6) **S C**
Connections: short stories by outstanding writers for young adults (6 and up) **S C**
Face to face: a collection of stories by celebrated Soviet and American writers (5 and up) **S C**
Fleischman, P. Coming-and-going men (6 and up) **S C**
Fleischman, P. Graven images (6 and up) **S C**
Garfield, L. The apprentices (6 and up) **S C**
Godden, R. Four dolls (3-5) **S C**
Gorog, J. Three dreams and a nightmare, and other tales of the dark (5 and up) **S C**
Hunter, M. A furl of fairy wind: four stories (2-5) **S C**
Kennedy, R. Richard Kennedy: collected stories (3-5) **S C**
Kipling, R. The jungle books (4 and up) **S C**
Kipling, R. Just so stories (3-6) **S C**
Konigsburg, E. L. Altogether, one at a time (4-6) **S C**
Konigsburg, E. L. Throwing shadows (5 and up) **S C**
Levoy, M. The witch of Fourth Street, and other stories (4-6) **S C**
Lively, P. Uninvited ghosts, and other stories (4 and up) **S C**
MacDonald, G. The complete fairy tales of George Macdonald (4 and up) **S C**
MacLachlan, P. Tomorrow's wizard (3-6) **S C**
Paterson, K. Angels & other strangers: family Christmas stories (5 and up) **S C**
Porte-Thomas, B. A. Jesse's ghost, and other stories (5 and up) **S C**
Roach, M. K. Encounters with the invisible world (5 and up) **S C**
Rylant, C. Children of Christmas (4 and up) **S C**
Rylant, C. Every living thing (5 and up) **S C**
Sandburg, C. Rootabaga stories **S C**

Short stories—*Continued*
Sholem Aleichem. Holiday tales of Sholom Aleichem (5 and up) **S C**
Singer, I. B. Naftali the storyteller and his horse, Sus, and other stories (4 and up) **S C**
Singer, I. B. The power of light (4 and up) **S C**
Singer, I. B. Stories for children (4 and up) **S C**
Soto, G. Baseball in April, and other stories (5 and up) **S C**
Things that go bump in the night (5 and up) **S C**
Where angels glide at dawn (5 and up) **S C**
Wilde, O. The Happy Prince, and other stories (3-6) **S C**
Yee, P. Tales from Gold Mountain (4 and up) **S C**
Yolen, J. The faery flag (5 and up) **S C**
See/See also pages in the following book(s):
With a deep sea smile p41-92 **372.6**

Shortall, Leonard W.
(il) Cone, M. Mishmash **Fic**
(il) Sobol, D. J. Encyclopedia Brown, boy detective **Fic**
(il) Stolz, M. A dog on Barkham Street **Fic**

Shorto, Russell
Geronimo and the struggle for Apache freedom (5 and up) **92**
Tecumseh and the dream of an American Indian nation (5 and up) **92**

Shortshanks
Moe, J. E. Minnikin
In The Red fairy book p307-21 **398.2**

Shoshoni Indians
Fradin, D. B. The Shoshoni (2-4) **970.004**
See/See also pages in the following book(s):
Freedman, R. Indian chiefs p73-89 (6 and up) **920**

The **show-and-tell** war and other stories about Adam Joshua. Smith, J. L. See note under Smith, J. L. The kid next door and other headaches **Fic**

The **show** must go on. McCully, E. A. See note under McCully, E. A. Zaza's big break **E**

Showers, Paul
A drop of blood (k-3) **612.1**
Ears are for hearing (k-3) **612.8**
Me and my family tree (k-3) **575.1**
No measles, no mumps for me (k-3) **614.4**
What happens to a hamburger (k-3) **612.3**

Shrek!. Steig, W. **E**

Shreve, Henry Miller, 1785-1851
See/See also pages in the following book(s):
McCall, E. S. Biography of a river: the living Mississippi p48-51, 57-64, 77-80, 82-84 (6 and up) **977**

Shreve, Susan Richards
The flunking of Joshua T. Bates (3-5) **Fic**

Shrewd Todie and Lyzer the miser. Singer, I. B.
In Bauer, C. F. Celebrations p121-25 **808.8**
In Singer, I. B. Stories for children p283-89 **S C**
In Singer, I. B. When Shlemiel went to Warsaw & other stories p3-13 **398.2**

Shrieks at midnight (4 and up) **821.008**

The **shrinking** of Treehorn. Heide, F. P. **Fic**

Shroud
Afanas'ev, A. N. The lazy maiden
In Afanas'ev, A. N. Russian fairy tales p423-25 **398.2**

The **shroud**. Grimm, J.
In Grimm, J. The complete Grimm's fairy tales p502-03 **398.2**

Shrubs
Petrides, G. A. A field guide to trees and shrubs **582.1**

Shub, Elizabeth
Clever Kate (1-3) **398.2**
The white stallion **E**
(jt. auth) Shulevitz, U. Hanukah money **E**

Shulevitz, Uri, 1935-
Dawn **E**
Hanukah money **E**
One Monday morning **E**
Rain, rain, rivers **E**
The treasure (k-3) **398.2**
(il) Ransome, A. The Fool of the World and the flying ship **398.2**
(il) Singer, I. B. The fools of Chelm and their history **Fic**
(il) Singer, I. B. The golem **398.2**
See/See also pages in the following book(s):
Newbery and Caldecott Medal books, 1966-1975 p209-16 **028.5**

Shulman, Jeffrey, 1951-
Focus on cocaine and crack (3-6) **362.29**

Shush, Shush, the big buff banty hen who laid an egg in the postmaster's hat. Sandburg, C.
In Sandburg, C. Rootabaga stories pt 2 p22-26 **S C**
In Sandburg, C. The Sandburg treasury p97-98 **818**

Shuster, Joe
See/See also pages in the following book(s):
Aaseng, N. The unsung heroes p53-59 (5 and up) **920**

Shuttles, Space *See* Space shuttles

Shy Charles. Wells, R. **E**

The **shy** little horse. Brown, M. W.
In Brown, M. W. The fish with the deep sea smile p11-15 **818**

Shyer, Marlene Fanta
Welcome home, Jellybean (5 and up) **Fic**

Sibbald, Jean H.
The manatee (3-5) **599.5**

Sibbick, John
(il) Usher, K. Heroes, gods & emperors from Roman mythology **292**

Siberell, Anne
Whale in the sky (k-3) **398.2**

Siberia (Soviet Union)
Anderson, M. K. Siberia (5 and up) **957**

Siblings *See* Brothers and sisters

Sick
LeShan, E. J. When a parent is very sick (4 and up) **155.9**

Fiction
Cherry, L. Who's sick today? **E**
Rockwell, A. F. Sick in bed **E**

Sick in bed. Rockwell, A. F. **E**

Sickness *See* Diseases

Side by side (1-3) **808.81**

Sidewalk story. Mathis, S. B. **Fic**

Sidi-Nouman
The Story of Sidi-Nouman
In The Arabian nights entertainments p331-45 **398.2**

Sidjakov, Nicolas, 1924-
(il) Robbins, R. Baboushka and the three kings **398.2**

Siebel, Fritz, 1913-
(il) Bonsall, C. N. Tell me some more **E**
(il) Lexau, J. M. Who took the farmer's [hat]? **E**
(il) Parish, P. Amelia Bedelia **E**

Siebert, Diane
Mojave (1-3) **811**
Train song **E**
Truck song **E**

Siegel, Beatrice
George and Martha Washington at home in New York (4-6) **973.4**
A new look at the Pilgrims (4-6) **973.2**
Sam Ellis's island (3-6) **325.73**
The sewing machine (4 and up) **646.2**

Siegel, Jerry
See/See also pages in the following book(s):
Aaseng, N. The unsung heroes p53-59 (5 and up) **920**

Siegel, Mary-Ellen
More than a friend: dogs with a purpose (5 and up) **636.7**

The **Sierra** Club book of our national parks. Young, D. **917.3**

Sight *See* Vision

The **sign** in Mendel's window. Phillips, M. **E**

Sign language
Ancona, G. Handtalk zoo (k-3) **419**
Baker, P. J. My first book of sign (k-3) **419**
Charlip, R. Handtalk: an ABC of finger spelling & sign language (k-3) **419**
Charlip, R. Handtalk birthday (k-3) **419**
Greene, L. Sign language talk (5 and up) **419**

Sign language talk. Greene, L. **419**

The **sign** of the beaver. Speare, E. G. **Fic**

The **sign** on Rosie's door. Sendak, M. **E**

The **signpost**. Babbitt, N.
In Babbitt, N. The Devil's other storybook p41-44 **S C**

Signs. Goor, R. **659.13**

Signs and signboards
Goor, R. Signs (k-2) **659.13**
Hoban, T. I read signs (k-2) **659.13**
Hoban, T. I read symbols (k-2) **659.13**
Hoban, T. I walk and read (k-2) **659.13**

Signs and symbols
Adkins, J. Symbols, a silent language (4-6) **302.2**
Barth, E. Hearts, cupids, and red roses (3-6) **394.2**
Barth, E. Holly, reindeer, and colored lights (3-6) **394.2**
Barth, E. Lilies, rabbits, and painted eggs (3-6) **394.2**
Barth, E. Shamrocks, harps, and shillelaghs (3-6) **394.2**
Barth, E. Turkeys, Pilgrims, and Indian corn (3-6) **394.2**
Barth, E. Witches, pumpkins, and grinning ghosts (3-6) **394.2**
Fisher, L. E. Symbol art (4 and up) **302.2**
Hoban, T. I read symbols (k-2) **659.13**
See/See also pages in the following book(s):
Caney, S. Steven Caney's kids' America p366-75 (4 and up) **790.1**

Signs of the apes, songs of the whales. Harrar, G. **591.5**

Sihanouk *See* Norodom Sihanouk, Prince, 1922-

Siksika Indians
See also Piegan Indians
See/See also pages in the following book(s):
Hofsinde, R. Indian costumes p21-32 (3-6) **391**

Fiction

Yolen, J. Sky dogs **E**

Legends

Goble, P. Star Boy (2-4) **398.2**
San Souci, R. The legend of Scarface (2-4) **398.2**

Silent night. Mohr, J. **782.28**

Sills, Leslie
Inspirations (5 and up) **920**

The **silly** book. Cole, B. **E**

Silly men and cunning wives
The Two old women's bet
In Best-loved folktales of the world p671-73 **398.2**
In Grandfather tales p160-61 **398.2**

The **silver** chair. Lewis, C. S. See note under Lewis, C. S. The lion, the witch and the wardrobe **Fic**

The **silver** cow: a Welsh tale. Cooper, S. **398.2**

Silver days. Levitin, S. **Fic**

Silver on the tree. Cooper, S. See note under Cooper, S. Over sea, under stone **Fic**

Silver packages. Rylant, C.
In Rylant, C. Children of Christmas p26-31 **S C**

The **silver** pony. Ward, L. K. **Fic**

The **silver** sword. Serraillier, I. **Fic**

Silverman, Judith, 1933-
Breen, K. Index to collective biographies for young readers **920**

Silverman, Maida
Festival of freedom (1-3) **296.4**

Silverstein, Alvin
Cancer: can it be stopped? (6 and up) **616.99**
Dogs: all about them (5 and up) **636.7**
Glasses and contact lenses (6 and up) **617.7**
Hamsters: all about them (5 and up) **636.088**
Heart disease: America's #1 killer (6 and up) **616.1**
Learning about AIDS (4-6) **616.97**
Life in a tidal pool (4-6) **574.92**
Lyme disease, the great imitator (6 and up) **616.9**
Mice: all about them (5 and up) **599.32**
The mystery of sleep (4-6) **154.6**
Nature's living lights (5 and up) **574.1**
The story of your foot (5 and up) **612**
The story of your hand (5 and up) **612**
Wonders of speech (6 and up) **302.2**
World of the brain (6 and up) **612.8**

Silverstein, Robert A.
(jt. auth) Silverstein, A. Lyme disease, the great imitator **616.9**
(il) Silverstein, A. Mice: all about them **599.32**

Silverstein, Shel
Ladies first; adaptation. See Rodgers, M. Ladies first
A light in the attic (3 and up) **811**
Where the sidewalk ends (3 and up) **811**

Silverstein, Virginia B.
(jt. auth) Silverstein, A. Cancer: can it be stopped? **616.99**
(jt. auth) Silverstein, A. Dogs: all about them **636.7**
(jt. auth) Silverstein, A. Glasses and contact lenses **617.7**
(jt. auth) Silverstein, A. Hamsters: all about them **636.088**
(jt. auth) Silverstein, A. Heart disease: America's #1 killer **616.1**
(jt. auth) Silverstein, A. Learning about AIDS **616.97**
(jt. auth) Silverstein, A. Life in a tidal pool **574.92**
(jt. auth) Silverstein, A. Lyme disease, the great imitator **616.9**
(jt. auth) Silverstein, A. Mice: all about them **599.32**
(jt. auth) Silverstein, A. The mystery of sleep **154.6**
(jt. auth) Silverstein, A. Nature's living lights **574.1**
(jt. auth) Silverstein, A. The story of your foot **612**
(jt. auth) Silverstein, A. The story of your hand **612**
(jt. auth) Silverstein, A. Wonders of speech **302.2**
(jt. auth) Silverstein, A. World of the brain **612.8**

Simeli Mountain
Grimm, J. Simeli Mountain
In Grimm, J. The complete Grimm's fairy tales p627-30 **398.2**

Simon, Charnan
Chester A. Arthur: twenty-first president of the United States (4 and up) **92**

Simon, Norma
Cats do, dogs don't (k-2) **636.088**

Simon, Seymour, 1931-
Animal fact/animal fable (1-4) **591**

Simon, Seymour, 1931-—*Continued*
Bits and bytes: a computer dictionary for beginners (k-3) **004**
Deserts (3-5) **574.5**
The dinosaur is the biggest animal that ever lived, and other wrong ideas you thought were true (3-6) **500**
Earth, our planet in space (1-4) **525**
Galaxies (2-5) **523.1**
Hidden worlds (5 and up) **500**
How to be an ocean scientist in your own home (4 and up) **551.46**
How to talk to your computer (k-3) **005**
Icebergs and glaciers (3-5) **551.3**
Jupiter (1-4) **523.4**
The largest dinosaurs (1-3) **567.9**
Look to the night sky: an introduction to star watching (4 and up) **523**
Mars (1-4) **523.4**
Meet the computer (k-3) **004**
The moon (1-4) **523.3**
New questions and answers about dinosaurs (3-6) **567.9**
Oceans (3-5) **551.46**
The optical illusion book (4 and up) **152.14**
The paper airplane book (3-5) **745.592**
Pets in a jar (4 and up) **639**
Poisonous snakes (4 and up) **597.9**
Saturn (1-4) **523.4**
Shadow magic (k-3) **535**
The smallest dinosaurs (1-3) **567.9**
Soap bubble magic (1-3) **793.8**
Stars (1-4) **523.8**
Storms (2-4) **551.5**
The sun (1-4) **523.7**
Uranus (1-4) **523.4**
Volcanoes (2-5) **551.2**
Whales (3-5) **599.5**

Simon, Solomon, 1895-1970
More wise men of Helm and their merry tales (4 and up) **398.2**
Contents: The sages of Helm; Shloime the mathematician; Go, close the door; A dead man who talks; A railroad comes to Helm; The holes in the bagels; Mayor Gimpel's golden shoes; The dedication of the cemetery; The great calamity and if; Yossel-Zissel the melamed; Because of a blintz; The enchanted goat; Beinush, the alert policeman; The River Shore Club

Simon's book. Drescher, H. **E**

Simont, Marc
(il) Branley, F. M. Journey into a black hole **523.8**
(il) Branley, F. M. Volcanoes **551.2**
(il) Branley, F. M. What happened to the dinosaurs? **567.9**
(il) Kuskin, K. The Dallas Titans get ready for bed **E**
(il) Kuskin, K. The Philharmonic gets dressed **E**
(il) Lord, B. B. In the Year of the Boar and Jackie Robinson **Fic**
(il) McCord, D. T. W. Speak up: more rhymes of the never was and always is **811**
(il) McNulty, F. How to dig a hole to the other side of the world **551.1**
(il) Schwartz, A. Ten copycats in a boat, and other riddles **398.6**
(il) Sharmat, M. W. Nate the Great **E**
(il) Udry, J. M. A tree is nice **E**
(il) Zolotow, C. The quiet mother and the noisy little boy **E**
See/See also pages in the following book(s):
Caldecott Medal books, 1938-1957 p297-306 **028.5**

Simple machines. Horvatic, A. **531**

Simple pictures are best. Willard, N. **E**

Simple Seng and the parrot
Carpenter, F. Simple Seng and the parrot
In Carpenter, F. Tales of a Chinese grandmother p242-51 **398.2**

Simple sentences. Babbitt, N.
In Babbitt, N. The Devil's other storybook p63-71 **S C**

Simple Simon's reward. Gotwalt, H. L. M.
In Gotwalt, H. L. M. Everyday plays for boys and girls p116-31 **812**

Simple Wang. Bonnett, L.
In Best-loved folktales of the world p528-31 **398.2**

Simpleton and his little black hen
Pyle, H. Simpleton and his little black hen
In Pyle, H. The wonder clock p217-28 **398.2**

Simpleton Peter. Reeves, J.
In Reeves, J. English fables and fairy stories p103-14 **398.2**

Simpson, Jacqueline
The seal's skin
In Best-loved folktales of the world p383-84 **398.2**

Simpson, Mary Jett- *See* Jett-Simpson, Mary, 1938-

Sims, Blanche
(il) Kimmel, E. A. I took my frog to the library **E**
(il) Spurr, E. Mrs. Minetta's car pool **E**

Sing a song of popcorn **808.81**

Sing a song of sixpence (k-2) **398.8**

Sing down the moon. O'Dell, S. **Fic**

Sing me a story. Rosenberg, J. **792.5**

Sing, Pierrot, sing. De Paola, T. **E**

The **sing-song** of Old Man Kangaroo. Kipling, R.
In Kipling, R. Just so stories **S C**

Sing the songs of Thanksgiving. Fisher, A. L.
In Holiday plays round the year p101-11 **812.008**
Singable songbook, The Raffi. Raffi **782.42**

Singapore
Brown, M. M. Singapore (4 and up) **959.57**

Singer, Arthur, 1917-1990
(il) Robbins, C. S. Birds of North America **598**

Singer, Isaac Bashevis, 1904-1991
The first Shlemiel
In The Laugh book p132-40 **808.8**
The fools of Chelm and the stupid carp [excerpt]
In The Random House book of humor for children p205-11 **817.008**
The fools of Chelm and their history (3-6) **Fic**
The golem (5 and up) **398.2**
Mazel and Shlimazel (2-5) **398.2**
Menashe and Rachel
In The Scott, Foresman anthology of children's literature p678-81 **808.8**
Naftali the storyteller and his horse, Sus, and other stories (4 and up) **S C**
Contents: Naftali the storyteller and his horse, Sus; Dalfunka, where the rich live forever; The Lantuch; A Hanukkah Eve in Warsaw; The fools of Chelm and the stupid carp; Lemel and Tzipa; The cat who thought she was a dog and the dog who thought he was a cat; Growing up
The power of light (4 and up) **S C**
Contents: A Hanukkah evening in my parents' house; The extinguished lights; The parakeet named Dreidel; Menashe and Rachel; The squire; The power of light; Hershele and Hanukkah; Hanukkah in the poorhouse
Shrewd Todie and Lyzer the miser
In Bauer, C. F. Celebrations p121-25 **808.8**
The snow in Chelm
In Snowy day: stories and poems p25-29 **808.8**
Stories for children (4 and up) **S C**
Contents: The elders of Chelm & Genendel's key; A tale of three wishes; The extinguished lights; Mazel & Shlimazel; Why Noah chose the dove; Zlateh the goat; A Hanukkah Eve in Warsaw; The fools of Chelm & the stupid carp; The wicked city; Rabbi Leib & the witch Cunegunde; The parakeet named Dreidel; Lemel & Tzipa; The day I got lost; Menashe & Rachel; Shlemiel the businessman; Joseph & Koza; A Hanukkah evening in my parents' house; Tsirtsur & Peziza; Naftali the storyteller & his horse, Sus; Hershele & Hanukkah; When Shlemiel went to Warsaw; Elijah the slave; The power of light; Growing up; The Lantuch; Utzel & his daughter, Poverty; The squire; Ole & Trufa; Dalfunka, where the rich live forever; Topiel & Tekla; Hanukkah in the poorhouse; Shrewd Todie & Lyzer the miser; The fearsome inn; The cat who thought she was a dog & the dog who thought he was a cat; Menaseh's dream; Tashlik
When Shlemiel went to Warsaw & other stories (4 and up) **398.2**
Contents: Shrewd Todie & Lyzer the miser; Tsirtsur & Peziza; Rabbi Leib & the witch Cunegunde; The elders of Chelm & Genendel's key; Shlemiel, the businessman; Utzel & his daughter Poverty; Menaseh's dream; When Shlemiel went to Warsaw
The wicked city (3-6) **222**
Zlateh the goat, and other stories (4 and up) **398.2**
Contents: Fool's paradise; Grandmother's tale; The snow in Chelm; The mixed-up feet and the silly bridegroom; The first shlemiel; The Devil's trick; Zlateh the goat

About
Kresh, P. Isaac Bashevis Singer: the story of a storyteller (6 and up) **92**

Singer, Marilyn, 1948-
Charmed (5 and up) **Fic**
Turtle in July (2-4) **811**
The **singer** of seeds. Yolen, J.
In Yolen, J. The faery flag p40-46 **S C**

Singers
See also Black singers
Jackson, J. Make a joyful noise unto the Lord! The life of Mahalia Jackson, queen of gospel singers (5 and up) **92**

Singing
See/See also pages in the following book(s):
McLeish, K. The Oxford first companion to music (5 and up) **780**
Singing bee! (k-3) **782.42**
Singing birds and flashing fireflies. Patent, D. H. **591.5**
The **Singing** bone
In The Magic orange tree, and other Haitian folktales p91-97 **398.2**
The **singing** bone. Grimm, J.
In Grimm, J. The complete Grimm's fairy tales p148-50 **398.2**

Singing games
Bley, E. S. The best singing games for children of all ages **796.1**
The Farmer in the dell **782.42**
The Fireside book of fun and game songs **782.42**
Glazer, T. Do your ears hang low?: 50 more musical fingerplays (k-3) **796.1**
Glazer, T. Eye winker, Tom Tinker, chin chopper (k-3) **796.1**
Glazer, T. Music for ones and twos **782.42**
The Lap-time song and play book (k-2) **782.42**
Seeger, R. C. American folk songs for children in home, school and nursery school **781.62**
What shall we do and Alee galloo! play songs and singing games for young children (k-2) **796.1**

The **singing,** soaring lark. Grimm, J.
In Grimm, J. The complete Grimm's fairy tales p399-404 **398.2**

The **singing** tortoise. Courlander, H.
In Courlander, H. The cow-tail switch, and other West African stories p65-72 **398.2**

Singing tree and the speaking bird
Afanas'ev, A. N. The singing tree and the talking bird
In Afanas'ev, A. N. Russian fairy tales p184-88 **398.2**

The **singing** tree and the talking bird. Afanas'ev, A. N.
In Afanas'ev, A. N. Russian fairy tales p184-88 **398.2**

Single parent family

Fiction

Byars, B. C. The night swimmers (5 and up) **Fic**
Duder, T. Jellybean (5 and up) **Fic**
Fine, A. My war with Goggle-eyes (5 and up) **Fic**
Greenfield, E. Sister (4 and up) **Fic**
Herman, C. The house on Walenska Street (3-5) **Fic**
Hurwitz, J. DeDe takes charge (3-5) **Fic**
Lowry, L. The one hundredth thing about Caroline (5 and up) **Fic**
Williams, V. B. A chair for my mother **E**

Sino-Japanese Conflict, 1937-1945

Fiction

Chang, M. S. In the eye of war (4 and up) **Fic**
DeJong, M. The house of sixty fathers (4-6) **Fic**

Siouan Indians
See also Dakota Indians; Mandan Indians; Oglala Indians

The **Sioux**. Osinski, A. **970.004**

Sioux Indians *See* Dakota Indians

Sipiera, Paul P.
Gerald Ford: thirty-eighth president of the United States (4 and up) **92**

Sir Gawain and the Green Knight *See* Gawain and the Grene Knight

Sir Gawain and the Green Knight. Hastings, S. **398.2**

Sir Gawain and the loathly lady. Hastings, S. **398.2**

Siren song. Alcock, V.
In Alcock, V. Ghostly companions **S C**

Sis, Peter
(il) Banks, K. Alphabet soup **E**
(il) Fleischman, S. The midnight horse **Fic**
(il) Fleischman, S. The scarebird **E**
(il) Fleischman, S. The whipping boy **Fic**
(il) Halloween: stories and poems. See Halloween: stories and poems **808.8**
(il) Rice, E. City night **E**
(il) Shannon, G. Stories to solve **398.2**

Sisco, Tim
(il) Shorto, R. Tecumseh and the dream of an American Indian nation **92**

Sister. Greenfield, E. **Fic**

Sister Alionushka, brother Ivanushka. Afanas'ev, A. N.
In Afanas'ev, A. N. Russian fairy tales p406-10 **398.2**

Sister Alyonushka and Brother Ivanushka. Afanas'ev, A. N.
In Afanas'ev, A. N. Russian folk tales p19-24 **398.2**

Sisters
Emmert, M. I'm the big sister now (3-5) **362.4**
Peterson, J. W. I have a sister—my sister is deaf (k-3) **362.4**

Fiction

Alcock, V. The cuckoo sister (6 and up) **Fic**
Byars, B. C. Hooray for the Golly sisters! **E**
Fair, S. The bedspread **E**
Greene, C. C. Beat the turtle drum (5 and up) **Fic**
Greenfield, E. Sister (4 and up) **Fic**
Holland, I. The journey home (4 and up) **Fic**
Howard, E. F. The train to Lulu's **E**
Johnson, A. Do like Kyla **E**
Kehret, P. Sisters, long ago (5 and up) **Fic**
Loh, M. J. Tucking Mommy in **E**
Lowry, L. A summer to die (3-6) **Fic**
Schwartz, A. Annabelle Swift, kindergartner **E**
Sendak, M. Outside over there **E**
Slepian, J. Risk 'n' roses (5 and up) **Fic**
Walter, M. P. Mariah keeps cool (3-5) **Fic**
Woodruff, E. Tubtime **E**

Sisters and brothers *See* Brothers and sisters

Sisters in the sun. Carpenter, F.
In Carpenter, F. Tales of a Chinese grandmother p22-28 **398.2**

Sisters, long ago. Kehret, P. Fic
Sitea, Linda
Zachary's divorce [short story]
In Free to be—you and me p124-27 810.8
Sitomer, Harry, 1903-
(jt. auth) Sitomer, M. How did numbers begin? 513
Sitomer, Mindel, 1903-
How did numbers begin? (2-4) 513
Sitting Bull, Dakota Chief, 1831-1890
See/See also pages in the following book(s):
Ehrlich, A. Wounded Knee: an Indian history of the American West (6 and up) 970.004
Freedman, R. Indian chiefs p114-39 (6 and up) 920
Six crows. Lionni, L. E
Six little ducks. Conover, C. 782.42
The **six** servants. Grimm, J.
In Grimm, J. The complete Grimm's fairy tales p600-07 398.2
In Grimm, J. Tales from Grimm p39-64 398.2
The **Six** sillies
In The Red fairy book p186-88 398.2
Six swans
Grimm, J. The six swans
In Grimm, J. About wise men and simpletons p83-87 398.2
In Grimm, J. The complete Grimm's fairy tales p232-37 398.2
In Grimm, J. More tales from Grimm p139-54 398.2
In The Yellow fairy book p4-8 398.2
Grimm, J. Wanda Gag's The six swans 398.2
San Souci, R. Robert D. San Souci's The six swans 398.2
Sixth book of junior authors & illustrators 920.003
Sixth grade can really kill you. See DeClements, B. 6th grade can really kill you Fic
Size and shape
Ehlert, L. Color farm E
Ehlert, L. Color zoo E
Emberley, E. The wing on a flea E
Fisher, L. E. Look around E
Hoban, T. Circles, triangles and squares E
Hoban, T. Is it larger? Is it smaller? E
Hoban, T. Is it red? Is it yellow? Is it blue? E
Hoban, T. Round & round & round E
Hughes, S. All shapes and sizes E
Reiss, J. J. Shapes E
Fiction
Jensen, V. A. Catching E
Jonas, A. Holes and peeks E
Joyce, W. George shrinks E
Kalan, R. Blue sea E
Skating *See* Ice skating; Roller skating
Skeleton
See also Bones
Balestrino, P. The skeleton inside you (k-3) 611
Parker, S. Skeleton (4 and up) 596
Parker, S. The skeleton and movement (4 and up) 612.7
Fiction
Ahlberg, J. Funnybones E
The **skeleton** and movement. Parker, S. 612.7
The **skeleton** inside you. Balestrino, P. 611
The **skeleton's** dance. San Souci, R.
In San Souci, R. Short & shivery p73-77 398.2
Sketching outdoors in autumn. Arnosky, J. 743
Sketching outdoors in spring. Arnosky, J. 743
Sketching outdoors in summer. Arnosky, J. 743
Sketching outdoors in winter. Arnosky, J. 743
Skillful hunter
Grimm, J. The skillful huntsman
In Grimm, J. The complete Grimm's fairy tales p508-14 398.2
The **skillful** huntsman. Grimm, J.
In Grimm, J. The complete Grimm's fairy tales p508-14 398.2
Skin diving
See/See also pages in the following book(s):
Cook, J. L. The mysterious undersea world p26-31 (4 and up) 551.46
Skinning a wizard. Zambreno, M. F.
In Things that go bump in the night p217-31 S C
Skinnybones. Park, B. Fic
Skip to it! See Kalbfleisch, S. Jump! 796.2
Skip to my Lou. Westcott, N. B. E
Skipper, G. C., 1939-
Pearl Harbor (4 and up) 940.54
Skipper, Mervyn
Lazy Tok
In Bauer, C. F. Celebrations p137-40 808.8
Skis and skiing
Krementz, J. A very young skier (3-6) 796.93
The **skit** book. MacDonald, M. R. 812.008

Skits
MacDonald, M. R. The skit book (4 and up) **812.008**
Skofield, James
All wet! All wet! **E**
Nightdances **E**
Skoonkin huntin'
Skoonkin huntin'
In Grandfather tales p137-39 **398.2**
Skoro, Martin
(il) Haskins, J. Count your way through Japan **952**
Skull race. Leach, M.
In Leach, M. Whistle in the graveyard p27 **398.2**
Skunk in Tante Odette's oven. Carlson, N. S.
In Carlson, N. S. The talking cat, and other stories of French Canada p3-16 **S C**
The **skunk** ladder. McManus, P. F.
In The Random House book of humor for children p276-82 **817.008**
Skurzynski, Gloria
Robots: your high-tech world (5 and up) **629.8**
Sky
See/See also pages in the following book(s):
Gallant, R. A. Rainbows, mirages and sundogs p27-38 (4 and up) **551.5**
Poetry
Livingston, M. C. Sky songs **811**
Sky dogs. Yolen, J. **E**
The **sky** follows Sneakers to town. Brown, M. W.
In Brown, M. W. The fish with the deep sea smile p47-50 **818**
The **sky** is falling. Pearson, K. **Fic**
The **sky** is full of stars. Branley, F. M. **523.8**
Sky songs. Livingston, M. C. **811**
Sky watchers of ages past. Weiss, M. E. **523**
Skyfire. Asch, F. See note under Asch, F. Sand cake **E**
Skyscraper going up! Cobb, V. **690**
The **skyscraper** to the moon and how the green rat with the rheumatism ran a thousand miles twice. Sandburg, C.
In Sandburg, C. Rootabaga stories pt 2 p3-8 **S C**
In Sandburg, C. The Sandburg treasury p91-93 **818**
Skyscrapers
Cobb, V. Skyscraper going up! (1-3) **690**
Gibbons, G. Up goes the skyscraper! (k-2) **690**
Macaulay, D. Unbuilding (4 and up) **690**
Slake's limbo. Holman, F. **Fic**
Slam and the ghosts. Crossley-Holland, K.
In Crossley-Holland, K. British folk tales p140-41 **398.2**
Slam bang. Burningham, J. **E**
The **slave** dancer. Fox, P. **Fic**
Slave trade
Fiction
Fox, P. The slave dancer (5 and up) **Fic**
Slavery
Fiction
Collier, J. L. Jump ship to freedom (6 and up) **Fic**
Collier, J. L. War comes to Willy Freeman (6 and up) **Fic**
Collier, J. L. Who is Carrie? (6 and up) **Fic**
Hooks, W. H. The ballad of Belle Dorcas (3-5) **Fic**
O'Dell, S. My name is not Angelica (5 and up) **Fic**
Turner, A. W. Nettie's trip South (3-5) **Fic**
Winter, J. Follow the drinking gourd **E**
History
Meltzer, M. All times, all peoples: a world history of slavery (4 and up) **326**
United States
See also Abolitionists
Hamilton, V. Anthony Burns: the defeat and triumph of a fugitive slave (5 and up) **92**
Lester, J. To be a slave (6 and up) **326**
Yates, E. Amos Fortune, free man (4 and up) **92**
Slaves of sham. Fleischman, P.
In Fleischman, P. Coming-and-going men p83-119 **S C**
Slavs
Folklore
De Regniers, B. S. Little Sister and the Month Brothers (k-3) **398.2**
Marshak, S. The Month-Brothers (1-3) **398.2**
Sleator, William
Among the dolls (4 and up) **Fic**
The boy who reversed himself (5 and up) **Fic**
The duplicate (6 and up) **Fic**
The elevator
In Things that go bump in the night p6-14 **S C**
The green futures of Tycho (5 and up) **Fic**
House of stairs (5 and up) **Fic**

Sleator, William—*Continued*
Interstellar pig (5 and up) Fic
Into the dream (5 and up) Fic
Strange attractors (5 and up) Fic
Sled dog racing
Fiction
Gardiner, J. R. Stone Fox (2-5) Fic
Sleep
See also Bedtime
Facklam, M. Do not disturb (3-6) **591.5**
McCauley, J. R. Ways animals sleep (k-3) **591.5**
Silverstein, A. The mystery of sleep (4-6) **154.6**
Zolotow, C. Sleepy book **E**
Fiction
Archambault, J. Counting sheep **E**
Asher, S. Princess Bee and the royal good-night story **E**
Bunting, E. No nap **E**
Burstein, F. Rebecca's nap **E**
Dragonwagon, C. Half a moon and one whole star **E**
Fox, M. Night noises **E**
Loh, M. J. Tucking Mommy in **E**
Sharmat, M. W. Goodnight, Andrew: goodnight, Craig **E**
Wood, A. The napping house **E**
Poetry
Pomerantz, C. All asleep (k-2) **811**
Prelutsky, J. My parents think I'm sleeping: poems (2-4) **811**
A Week of lullabies (k-2) **811.008**
Sleep out. Carrick, C. See note under Carrick, C. Ben and the porcupine **E**
Sleeping beauty
Ehrlich, A. The sleeping beauty in the wood
In Ehrlich, A. The Random House book of fairy tales p10-21 **398.2**
Evans, C. S. The sleeping beauty **398.2**
Grimm, J. Brier Rose
In Grimm, J. About wise men and simpletons p23-27 **398.2**
Grimm, J. Little Briar-Rose
In Grimm, J. The complete Grimm's fairy tales p237-41 **398.2**
Grimm, J. Sleeping beauty
In Best-loved folktales of the world p137-39 **398.2**
Grimm, J. Thorn Rose, the sleeping beauty
In Grimm, J. More tales from Grimm p31-41 **398.2**
Perrault, C. The sleeping beauty in the wood
In The Blue fairy book p54-63 **398.2**
In The Classic fairy tales p85-92 **398.2**
In The Scott, Foresman anthology of children's literature p195-99 **808.8**
In Sleeping beauty & other favourite fairy tales p9-20 **398.2**
Rockwell, A. F. Briar Rose
In Rockwell, A. F. Puss in boots, and other stories p53-59 **398.2**
Thane, A. The sleeping beauty
In Thane, A. Plays from famous stories and fairy tales p303-14 **812**
Yolen, J. The sleeping beauty **398.2**
Sleeping beauty & other favourite fairy tales (3 and up) **398.2**
The **sleeping** beauty in the wood. Ehrlich, A.
In Ehrlich, A. The Random House book of fairy tales p10-21 **398.2**
The **sleeping** beauty in the wood. Perrault, C.
In The Blue fairy book p54-63 **398.2**
In The Classic fairy tales p85-92 **398.2**
In The Scott, Foresman anthology of children's literature p195-99 **808.8**
In Sleeping beauty & other favourite fairy tales p9-20 **398.2**
Sleeping ugly. Yolen, J. **Fic**
Sleepy book. Zolotow, C. **E**
Sleight of hand *See* Magic
Slepian, Jan, 1921-
The Alfred summer (5 and up) **Fic**
The Broccoli tapes (5 and up) **Fic**
The night of the Bozos (6 and up) **Fic**
Risk 'n' roses (5 and up) **Fic**
Slides (Photography)
See/See also pages in the following book(s):
Bauer, C. F. Handbook for storytellers p202-08 **372.6**
Slipfoot and how he nearly always never gets what he goes after. Sandburg, C.
In Sandburg, C. Rootabaga stories pt 2 p9-13 **S C**
In Sandburg, C. The Sandburg treasury p93-95 **818**
Slippers. Yep, L.
In Yep, L. The rainbow people p162-68 **398.2**
SLJ/School Library Journal. See School Library Journal **027.805**
Slobodkin, Louis, 1903-1975
(il) Estes, E. The hundred dresses **Fic**
(il) Estes, E. The Moffats **Fic**
(il) Thurber, J. Many moons **Fic**
See/See also pages in the following book(s):
Caldecott Medal books, 1938-1957 p99-116 **028.5**
Slobodkina, Esphyr, 1908-
Caps for sale **E**

Sloggett, Nellie, 1851-1923
See/See also pages in the following book(s):
A Horn Book sampler on children's books and reading p23-27 **028.5**
The **Sloogeh** Dog and the stolen aroma. Aardema, V.
In The Scott, Foresman anthology of children's literature p317-19 **808.8**
Slote, Alfred
Matt Gargan's boy (4-6) **Fic**
Moving in (4-6) **Fic**
The trading games (4-6) **Fic**
Slovenz-Low, Madeline
(jt. auth) Waters, K. Lion dancer: Ernie Wan's Chinese New Year **394.2**
Slow learning children
See also Mentally handicapped children
Books and reading
Pilla, M. L. The best: high/low books for reluctant readers **011.6**
Fiction
Byars, B. C. The summer of the swans (5 and up) **Fic**
Slower than the rest. Rylant, C.
In Rylant, C. Every living thing p1-7 **S C**
The **slumber** king. Crossley-Holland, K.
In Crossley-Holland, K. British folk tales p38-44 **398.2**
Slumps, grunts, and snickerdoodles: what Colonial America ate and why. Perl, L. **641.5**
Small, David, 1945-
Imogene's antlers **E**
(il) Chetwin, G. Box and Cox **E**
(il) Juster, N. As: a surfeit of similes **427**
(il) Merriam, E. The Christmas box **E**
(il) Yorinks, A. Company's coming **E**
Small, Ernest *See* Lent, Blair, 1930-
Small pig. Lobel, A. **E**
Small poems. Worth, V. **811**
Small poems again. Worth, V. **811**
Small Star and the mud pony. DeWit, D.
In The Scott, Foresman anthology of children's literature p383-87 **808.8**
The **small-tooth** dog. Crossley-Holland, K.
In Crossley-Holland, K. British folk tales p112-17 **398.2**
Small worlds close up. Grillone, L. **500**
Small worlds: exploring the 60 moons of our solar system. Kelch, J. W. **523.9**
The **smallest** dinosaurs. Simon, S. **567.9**
Smart spending. Schmitt, L. **640.73**
Smarten up! how to increase your brain power. Yepsen, R. B. **153**
Smedberg, Alfred
The boy who was never afraid
In The Scott, Foresman anthology of children's literature p244-47 **808.8**
Smell
Parker, S. Touch, taste and smell (4 and up) **612.8**
Smile, Ernest and Celestine. Vincent, G. See note under Vincent, G. Ernest and Celestine **E**
Smile! how to cope with braces. Betancourt, J. **617.6**
Smith, Alvin
(il) Wojciechowska, M. Shadow of a bull **Fic**
Smith, Betty, 1896-1972
The boy, Abe
In Holiday plays round the year p161-68 **812.008**
Smith, Cat Bowman
(il) Asher, S. Princess Bee and the royal good-night story **E**
Smith, Dick King- *See* King-Smith, Dick, 1922-
Smith, Doris Buchanan
The first hard times (4-6) **Fic**
Kelly's creek (4-6) **Fic**
Last was Lloyd (4-6) **Fic**
Return to Bitter Creek (5 and up) **Fic**
A taste of blackberries (4-6) **Fic**
Smith, Dorothy B. Frizzell
(comp) Subject index to poetry for children and young people, 1957-1975. See Subject index to poetry for children and young people, 1957-1975 **808.81**
Smith, Edwin W.
Why there are cracks in Tortoise's shell
In Best-loved folktales of the world p652-53 **398.2**
Smith, Elizabeth Simpson
A guide dog goes to school (3-5) **362.4**
A service dog goes to school (3-5) **636.7**
Smith, Frances, 1954-
(il) Cutchins, J. Scoots, the bog turtle **597.9**
Smith, Howard Everett, 1927-
Daring the unknown: a history of NASA (5 and up) **629.4**
Weather (4-6) **551.5**

Smith, Hugh L., 1921-1968
(comp) Reflections on a gift of watermelon pickle . . . and other modern verse. See Reflections on a gift of watermelon pickle . . . and other modern verse **811.008**

Smith, Jan Hosking *See* Hosking Smith, Jan

Smith, Jane Bandy
Library media center programs for middle schools: a curriculum-based approach **027.8**

Smith, Janice Lee, 1949-
It's not easy being George. See note under Smith, J. L. The kid next door and other headaches **Fic**
The kid next door and other headaches (2-4) **Fic**
The monster in the third dresser drawer and other stories about Adam Joshua. See note under Smith, J. L. The kid next door and other headaches **Fic**
The show-and-tell war and other stories about Adam Joshua. See note under Smith, J. L. The kid next door and other headaches **Fic**
The turkeys' side of it. See note under Smith, J. L. The kid next door and other headaches **Fic**

Smith, Jessie Willcox, 1863-1935
(il) Alcott, L. M. Little women **Fic**
(il) MacDonald, G. At the back of the North Wind **Fic**
(il) MacDonald, G. The princess and the goblin **Fic**
(il) Moore, C. C. The night before Christmas **811**
(il) Spyri, J. Heidi **Fic**
(il) Stevenson, R. L. A child's garden of verses **821**

Smith, Joseph A., 1936-
(il) Evslin, B. Hercules **292**
(il) MacDonald, G. The princess and the goblin **Fic**

Smith, Lane
(il) Merriam, E. Halloween A B C **811**
(il) Scieszka, J. The true story of the three little pigs **398.2**

Smith, Robert Kimmel, 1930-
Bobby Baseball (4-6) **Fic**
Chocolate fever (4-6) **Fic**
The war with Grandpa (4-6) **Fic**

Smith, Robert L. (Robert Logan), 1944-
(il) Cwiklik, R. King Philip and the war with the colonists **92**

Smith, Roland, 1951-
Sea otter rescue (5 and up) **639.9**

Smith, Sherwood
Ghost dancers
In Things that go bump in the night p61-63 **S C**

Smith, Wendy
(il) Mahy, M. The blood-and-thunder adventure on Hurricane Peak **Fic**
(il) Mahy, M. Making friends **E**

Smith and the Devil
MacDonald, M. R. Wicked John and the Devil
In MacDonald, M. R. When the lights go out p33-46 **372.6**
Wicked John and the Devil
In Grandfather tales p29-39 **398.2**

The **Smithsonian** book of flight for young people. Boyne, W. J. **629.13**

Smithsonian Institution
Boyne, W. J. The Smithsonian book of flight for young people **629.13**

Smithsonian Institution. National Museum of Natural History *See* National Museum of Natural History (U.S.)

Smoking
Hyde, M. O. Know about smoking (4 and up) **616.86**
Perry, R. L. Focus on nicotine and caffeine (3-6) **616.86**
Seixas, J. S. Tobacco (1-3) **616.86**
Ward, B. R. Smoking and health (4 and up) **616.86**
See/See also pages in the following book(s):
Hyde, M. O. Drug wars p57-66 (6 and up) **363.4**

Smoking and health. Ward, B. R. **616.86**

Smoky, the cow horse. James, W. **Fic**

Smucker, Anna Egan
No star nights **E**

Smuggling

Fiction

Alderson, S. A. Ida and the wool smugglers **E**
Sutcliff, R. Flame-colored taffeta (5 and up) **Fic**

Snails
Buholzer, T. Life of the snail (3-6) **594**

Fiction

Lionni, L. The biggest house in the world **E**

The **snake** in the grass. Linley, M. **597.9**

A **snake-lover's** diary. Brenner, B. **597.9**

The **snake** princess. Terada, A. M.
In Terada, A. M. Under the starfruit tree p14-17 **398.2**

Snake-spoke. Yep, L.
In Yep, L. The rainbow people p86-95 **398.2**

Snakes
See also Pythons; Rattlesnakes
Brenner, B. A snake-lover's diary (5 and up) **597.9**
Broekel, R. Snakes (2-4) **597.9**

Snakes—*Continued*
Cole, J. A snake's body **597.9**
Freedman, R. Killer snakes (2-5) **597.9**
Gross, R. B. Snakes (3-5) **597.9**
Harrison, V. The world of snakes (k-2) **597.9**
Hess, L. That snake in the grass (3-5) **597.9**
Lauber, P. Snakes are hunters (k-3) **597.9**
Linley, M. The snake in the grass (3-6) **597.9**
Selsam, M. E. A first look at poisonous snakes (1-3) **597.9**
Simon, S. Poisonous snakes (4 and up) **597.9**
See/See also pages in the following book(s):
Chrystie, F. N. Pets p116-24 (4 and up) **636.088**
Weber, W. J. Care of uncommon pets p157-79 (5 and up) **636.088**
Fiction
Clifford, E. Harvey's horrible snake disaster (3-5) **Fic**
Mayer, M. The unicorn and the lake **E**
Noble, T. H. The day Jimmy's boa ate the wash **E**
Ungerer, T. Crictor **E**
Snakes are hunters. Lauber, P. **597.9**
A **snake's** body. Cole, J. **597.9**
Snakey riddles. McMullan, K. **793.73**
Sneakers and the Easter bunnies. Brown, M. W.
In Brown, M. W. The fish with the deep sea smile p54-59 **818**
Sneakers and the Easter flowers. Brown, M. W.
In Brown, M. W. The fish with the deep sea smile p51-52 **818**
Sneakers comes to town. Brown, M. W.
In Brown, M. W. The fish with the deep sea smile p44-46 **818**
Sneakers meet your feet. Cobb, V. **685**
Sneakers, that rapscallion cat. Brown, M. W.
In Brown, M. W. The fish with the deep sea smile p40-43 **818**
Snegourka. Shedlock, M. L.
In Shedlock, M. L. The art of the story-teller p195-97 **372.6**
Sneve, Virginia Driving Hawk
(comp) Dancing teepees: poems of American Indian youth. See Dancing teepees: poems of American Indian youth **897**
Sniff shout. Burningham, J. See note under Burningham, J. Slam bang **E**
The **Snooks** family
In Juba this and Juba that p47-50 **372.6**
The **snopp** on the sidewalk, and other poems. Prelutsky, J. **811**
Snorkeling *See* Skin diving
Snotty goat
Afanas'ev, A. N. The snotty goat
In Afanas'ev, A. N. Russian fairy tales p200-02 **398.2**
Snow
Branley, F. M. Snow is falling (k-3) **551.57**
Sugarman, J. Snowflakes (4-6) **551.57**
Fiction
Briggs, R. The snowman **E**
Burton, V. L. Katy and the big snow **E**
Downing, J. White snow, blue feather **E**
Keats, E. J. The snowy day **E**
Keller, H. Geraldine's big snow **E**
Kessler, E. Stan the hot dog man **E**
Maestro, B. Snow day **E**
Neitzel, S. The jacket I wear in the snow **E**
Rockwell, A. F. The first snowfall **E**
Tresselt, A. R. White snow, bright snow **E**
Vigna, J. Boot weather **E**
Zolotow, C. Something is going to happen **E**
Poetry
Prelutsky, J. It's snowing! It's snowing! (1-3) **811**
The **Snow-daughter** and the Fire-son
In The Yellow fairy book p206-08 **398.2**
Snow day. Maestro, B. **E**
The **snow** in Chelm. Singer, I. B.
In Singer, I. B. Zlateh the goat, and other stories p29-34 **398.2**
In Snowy day: stories and poems p25-29 **808.8**
Snow is falling. Branley, F. M. **551.57**
The **snow** lady. Hughes, S. See note under Hughes, S. Angel Mae: a tale of Trotter Street **E**
Snow man
Andersen, H. C. The snowman
In Andersen, H. C. Hans Andersen: his classic fairy tales p57-62 **S C**
Snow Queen
Andersen, H. C. The Snow Queen **Fic**
also in Andersen, H. C. Hans Andersen: his classic fairy tales p63-93 **S C**
Ehrlich, A. The Snow Queen **Fic**
also in Ehrlich, A. The Random House book of fairy tales p174-93 **398.2**
Snow White. Ehrlich, A.
In Ehrlich, A. The Random House book of fairy tales p58-73 **398.2**

Snow-White. Grimm, J.
In Best-loved folktales of the world p53-61 **398.2**

Snow-White and Rose-Red
Grimm, J. Snow-White and Rose-Red
In The Blue fairy book p259-65 **398.2**
In Grimm, J. The complete Grimm's fairy tales p664-71 **398.2**
In Grimm, J. Tales from Grimm p207-21 **398.2**

Snow White and the fox
Afanas'ev, A. N. Snow White and the fox
In Afanas'ev, A. N. Russian fairy tales p283-84 **398.2**

Snow White and the seven dwarfs
Ehrlich, A. Snow White
In Ehrlich, A. The Random House book of fairy tales p58-73 **398.2**
Grimm, J. Little Snow-White
In Grimm, J. The complete Grimm's fairy tales p249-58 **398.2**
Grimm, J. Snow-White
In Best-loved folktales of the world p53-61 **398.2**
Grimm, J. Snow-White and the seven dwarfs
In Grimm, J. The juniper tree, and other tales from Grimm v2 p256-74 **398.2**
In The Scott, Foresman anthology of children's literature p182-85 **808.8**
Grimm, J. Snowdrop
In The Classic Fairy tales p177-82 **398.2**
In The Red fairy book p329-39 **398.2**

Snowball, Peter
(il) Catchpole, C. Grasslands **574.5**

Snowbound with Betsy. Haywood, C. See note under Haywood, C. "B" is for Betsy **Fic**

Snowdrop. Grimm, J.
In The Classic Fairy tales p177-82 **398.2**
In The Red fairy book p329-39 **398.2**

Snowflake
Croll, C. The little snowgirl: an old Russian tale **398.2**
Shedlock, M. L. Snegourka
In Shedlock, M. L. The art of the story-teller p195-97 **372.6**

Snowflakes. Sugarman, J. **551.57**

The **snowman**. Andersen, H. C.
In Andersen, H. C. Hans Andersen: his classic fairy tales p57-62 **S C**

The **snowman**. Briggs, R. **E**

Snowman sniffles, and other verse. Bodecker, N. M. **811**

The **snowy** day. Keats, E. J. **E**

Snowy day: stories and poems (2-4) **808.8**

Snowy owls. Hunt, P. **598**

Snuff-box
Sébillot, P. The snuff-box
In The Green fairy book p145-50 **398.2**

Snyder, Dianne
The boy of the three-year nap (1-3) **398.2**

Snyder, Louis Leo, 1907-
World War II (4 and up) **940.53**

Snyder, Midori
Jack Straw
In Things that go bump in the night p243-54 **S C**

Snyder, Zilpha Keatley
And all between. See note under Snyder, Z. K. Below the root **Fic**
And condors danced (5 and up) **Fic**
Below the root (5 and up) **Fic**
Blair's nightmare. See note under Snyder, Z. K. The headless cupid **Fic**
The changeling (5 and up) **Fic**
The Egypt game (5 and up) **Fic**
The famous Stanley kidnapping case. See note under Snyder, Z. K. The headless cupid **Fic**
The headless cupid (5 and up) **Fic**
Janie's private eyes. See note under Snyder, Z. K. The headless cupid **Fic**
Libby on Wednesdays (5 and up) **Fic**
Until the celebration. See note under Snyder, Z. K. Below the root **Fic**
The velvet room (5 and up) **Fic**
The witches of Worm (5 and up) **Fic**

So far from the bamboo grove. Watkins, Y. K. **Fic**

So long at the fair. Gotwalt, H. L. M.
In Gotwalt, H. L. M. Everyday plays for boys and girls p29-38 **812**

So many cats! De Regniers, B. S. **E**

So what? Cohen, M. See note under Cohen, M. See you in second grade! **E**

Soap, soap, soap
Soap, soap, soap
In Grandfather tales p130-36 **398.2**

Soap bubble magic. Simon, S. **793.8**

Soaring lark
Grimm, J. The singing, soaring lark
In Grimm, J. The complete Grimm's fairy tales p399-404 **398.2**

Sobol, Donald J., 1924-
Encyclopedia Brown and the case of the dead eagles. See note under Sobol, D. J. Encyclopedia Brown, boy detective **Fic**
Encyclopedia Brown and the case of the disgusting sneakers. See note under Sobol, D. J. Encyclopedia Brown, boy detective **Fic**
Encyclopedia Brown and the case of the exploding plumbing. See note under Sobol, D. J. Encyclopedia Brown, boy detective **Fic**
Encyclopedia Brown and the case of the midnight visitor. See note under Sobol, D. J. Encyclopedia Brown, boy detective **Fic**
Encyclopedia Brown and the case of the mysterious handprints. See note under Sobol, D. J. Encyclopedia Brown, boy detective **Fic**
Encyclopedia Brown and the case of the secret pitch. See note under Sobol, D. J. Encyclopedia Brown, boy detective **Fic**
Encyclopedia Brown and the case of the treasure hunt. See note under Sobol, D. J. Encyclopedia Brown, boy detective **Fic**
Encyclopedia Brown, boy detective (3-5) **Fic**
Encyclopedia Brown carries on. See note under Sobol, D. J. Encyclopedia Brown, boy detective **Fic**
Encyclopedia Brown finds the clues. See note under Sobol, D. J. Encyclopedia Brown, boy detective **Fic**
Encyclopedia Brown gets his man. See note under Sobol, D. J. Encyclopedia Brown, boy detective **Fic**
Encyclopedia Brown keeps the peace. See note under Sobol, D. J. Encyclopedia Brown, boy detective **Fic**
Encyclopedia Brown lends a hand. See note under Sobol, D. J. Encyclopedia Brown, boy detective **Fic**
Encyclopedia Brown saves the day. See note under Sobol, D. J. Encyclopedia Brown, boy detective **Fic**
Encyclopedia Brown sets the pace. See note under Sobol, D. J. Encyclopedia Brown, boy detective **Fic**
Encyclopedia Brown shows the way. See note under Sobol, D. J. Encyclopedia Brown, boy detective **Fic**
Encyclopedia Brown solves them all. See note under Sobol, D. J. Encyclopedia Brown, boy detective **Fic**
Encyclopedia Brown takes the cake! See note under Sobol, D. J. Encyclopedia Brown, boy detective **Fic**
Encyclopedia Brown takes the case. See note under Sobol, D. J. Encyclopedia Brown, boy detective **Fic**
Encyclopedia Brown tracks them down. See note under Sobol, D. J. Encyclopedia Brown, boy detective **Fic**

Sobol, Harriet Langsam, 1936-
A book of vegetables (1-3) **635**
We don't look like our Mom and Dad (2-5) **362.7**

Soccer
Jackson, C. P. How to play better soccer (4 and up) **796.334**
Sullivan, G. Better soccer for boys and girls (4 and up) **796.334**
Fiction
Avi. S.O.R. losers (5 and up) **Fic**

Social anthropology *See* Ethnology

Social behavior *See* Human behavior

Social classes
Fiction
Konigsburg, E. L. Journey to an 800 number (4 and up) **Fic**

Social role
See also Sex role
Free to be—you and me **810.8**

Social sciences
Bibliography
Notable children's trade books in the field of social studies **016.3**

Societies
See also Clubs

Society of Friends
Henry, M. Benjamin West and his cat Grimalkin (4 and up) **92**
See/See also pages in the following book(s):
Tunis, E. The tavern at the ferry p1-10 (5 and up) **973.2**
Fiction
Turkle, B. C. Obadiah the Bold **E**

Socks. Cleary, B. **Fic**

Socrates
See/See also pages in the following book(s):
Coolidge, O. E. The golden days of Greece p113-27 (4-6) **938**

Socrates and the three little pigs. Anno, M. **511**

Sodom (Ancient city)
Singer, I. B. The wicked city (3-6) **222**

Sody sallyraytus
MacDonald, M. R. Sody sallyrytus
In MacDonald, M. R. Twenty tellable tales p79-89 **372.6**
Sody saleratus
In Juba this and Juba that p55-59 **372.6**
Sody Sallyraytus
In Grandfather tales p75-80 **398.2**

Soekarno, 1901-1970
See/See also pages in the following book(s):
Indonesia—in pictures p30-34 (5 and up) **959.8**
The **softhearted** ghost. Gotwalt, H. L. M.
In Gotwalt, H. L. M. Special plays for holidays p17-27 **812**
Softy the Snowman. Gotwalt, H. L. M.
In Gotwalt, H. L. M. Special plays for holidays p88-98 **812**
Soils
Wyler, R. Science fun with mud and dirt (2-4) **507**
Sojourner Truth *See* Truth, Sojourner, d. 1883
Sojourner Truth, a self-made woman. Ortiz, V. **92**
Solar eclipses *See* Eclipses, Solar
Solar radiation
See also Greenhouse effect
Solar system
See also Satellites
Kelch, J. W. Small worlds: exploring the 60 moons of our solar system (6 and up) **523.9**
Levasseur-Regourd, A.-C. Our sun and the inner planets (4-6) **523.7**
Rathbun, E. Exploring your solar system (4 and up) **523.2**
Solberg, S. E. (Sammy Edward), 1930-
The land and people of Korea (5 and up) **951.9**
Solberg, Sammy Edward *See* Solberg, S. E. (Sammy Edward), 1930-
Solbert, Ronni
(il) Brooks, G. Bronzeville boys and girls **811**
(il) Merrill, J. The pushcart war **Fic**
The **soldier**. Babbitt, N.
In Babbitt, N. The Devil's other storybook p19-23 **S C**
The **soldier** and his magic helpers. Grimm, J.
In Grimm, J. More tales from Grimm p63-75 **398.2**
The **soldier** and the king. Afanas'ev, A. N.
In Afanas'ev, A. N. Russian fairy tales p563-67 **398.2**
Soldier and the Tsar in the forest
Afanas'ev, A. N. The soldier and the king
In Afanas'ev, A. N. Russian fairy tales p563-67 **398.2**
The **soldier** and the vampire. San Souci, R.
In San Souci, R. Short & shivery p68-72 **398.2**
Soldier Jack
Soldier Jack
In The Jack tales p172-79 **398.2**
Soldiers
See also Women soldiers
United States
See also Black soldiers
McGovern, A. The secret soldier: the story of Deborah Sampson [Gannett] (3-5) **92**
Soldiers, Black *See* Black soldiers
Soldiers' life *See* Soldiers
Soldier's riddle
Afanas'ev, A. N. A soldier's riddle
In Afanas'ev, A. N. Russian fairy tales p117-18 **398.2**
Soldier's soup
Brown, M. Stone soup **398.2**
Sole
Grimm, J. The sole
In Grimm, J. The complete Grimm's fairy tales p709 **398.2**
Solga, Kim
(il) Rights, M. Beastly neighbors **508**
Solomon, Chuck
Playing hockey (2-4) **796.962**
Solomon Grundy. Hoguet, S. R. **E**
Solomon the rusty nail. Steig, W. **E**
Soman, David
(il) Johnson, A. Tell me a story, Mama **E**
Some of the adventures of Rhode Island Red. Manes, S. **Fic**
Some of the days of Everett Anderson. Clifton, L. See note under Clifton, L. Everett Anderson's goodbye **811**
Some plants have funny names. Cross, D. H. **581**
Someone saw a spider. Climo, S. **398.2**
The **something**. Babbitt, N. **E**
Something about the author **920.003**
Something about the author: autobiography series **920.003**
Something big has been here. Prelutsky, J. **811**
Something is going to happen. Zolotow, C. **E**
Something nasty in the kitchen. Bond, M.
In Bond, M. Paddington's storybook p83-96 **S C**
Something new begins: new and selected poems. Moore, L. **811**
Something on my mind. Grimes, N. **811**
Something queer at the ball park. Levy, E. See note under Levy, E. Something queer is going on (a mystery) **E**
Something queer at the birthday party. Levy, E. See note under Levy, E. Something queer is going on (a mystery) **E**

Something queer at the haunted school. Levy, E. See note under Levy, E. Something queer is going on (a mystery) **E**

Something queer at the lemonade stand. Levy, E. See note under Levy, E. Something queer is going on (a mystery) **E**

Something queer at the library. Levy, E. See note under Levy, E. Something queer is going on (a mystery) **E**

Something queer in rock 'n' roll. Levy, E. See note under Levy, E. Something queer is going on (a mystery) **E**

Something queer is going on (a mystery). Levy, E. **E**

Something queer on vacation. Levy, E. See note under Levy, E. Something queer is going on (a mystery) **E**

Something special for me. Williams, V. B. See note under Williams, V. B. A chair for my mother **E**

Something to crow about. Lane, M. H. **E**

Son of the Black Stallion. Farley, W. See note under Farley, W. The Black Stallion **Fic**

Son of the wind. Bryan, A.
In Bryan, A. Lion and the ostrich chicks, and other African folk tales p24-39 **398.2**

Song and dance man. Ackerman, K. **E**

A **song** for Uncle Harry. Kherdian, D. **Fic**

A **song** I sang to you: a selection of poems. Livingston, M. C. **811**

The **song** of Pentecost. Corbett, W. J. **Fic**

Song of Sedna. San Souci, R. **398.2**

A **song** of stars. Birdseye, T. **398.2**

Song of the boat. Graham, L. B. **E**

Song of the horse. Kennedy, R.
In Kennedy, R. Collected stories p117-24 **S C**

Song of the sea otter. Hurd, E. T. **599.74**

Song of the swallows. Politi, L. **E**

Song of the trees. Taylor, M. D. **Fic**

Songs
See also Carols; Folk songs
Bley, E. S. The best singing games for children of all ages **796.1**
Child, L. M. F. Over the river and through the wood (k-2) **811**
Conover, C. Six little ducks (k-2) **782.42**
The Fireside book of children's songs **782.42**
The Fireside book of fun and game songs **782.42**
Glazer, T. Do your ears hang low?: 50 more musical fingerplays (k-3) **796.1**
Glazer, T. Eye winker, Tom Tinker, chin chopper (k-3) **796.1**
Glazer, T. Music for ones and twos **782.42**
Glazer, T. Tom Glazer's Treasury of songs for children (3-5) **782.42**
Go in and out the window **782.42**
Kovalski, M. The wheels on the bus (k-2) **782.42**
The Lap-time song and play book (k-2) **782.42**
Lullabies and night songs (k-3) **782.42**
The Lullaby songbook (1-3) **782.42**
The Mother Goose songbook (k-2) **782.42**
Nelson, E. L. The funny song-book **782.42**
Raffi. The 2nd Raffi songbook (k-2) **782.42**
Raffi. Baby Beluga (k-2) **782.42**
Raffi. Down by the bay (k-2) **782.42**
Raffi. Five little ducks (k-2) **782.42**
Raffi. One light, one sun (k-2) **782.42**
Raffi. The Raffi Christmas treasury **782.42**
Raffi. The Raffi singable songbook (k-2) **782.42**
Raffi. Shake my sillies out (k-2) **782.42**
Raffi. Wheels on the bus (k-2) **782.42**
Singing bee! (k-3) **782.42**
Songs from Mother Goose (k-3) **782.42**
Staines, B. All God's critters got a place in the choir (k-2) **782.42**
Watson, C. Father Fox's feast of songs (k-3) **782.42**
Weiss, N. If you're happy and you know it (k-2) **782.42**
What shall we do and Alee galloo! play songs and singing games for young children (k-2) **796.1**
See/See also pages in the following book(s):
With a deep sea smile p107-22 **372.6**
Indexes
Peterson, C. S. Index to children's songs **782.42**

Songs, American
See also Folk songs—United States; National songs, American
The Laura Ingalls Wilder songbook (3 and up) **782.42**

Songs from Mother Goose (k-3) **782.42**

Songwriters *See* Composers

Sonoran Desert
George, J. C. One day in the desert (4-6) **574.5**

Sons and daughters. Yee, P.
In Yee, P. Tales from Gold Mountain p17-23 **S C**

Sons and fathers *See* Fathers and sons

Sons and mothers *See* Mothers and sons

Sop doll
MacDonald, M. R. Sop doll
In MacDonald, M. R. When the lights go out p86-95 **372.6**
Sop doll!
In The Jack tales p76-82 **398.2**

Sophie's snail. King-Smith, D. **Fic**

The **sorcerer's** apprentice. Grimm, J.
In Grimm, J. More tales from Grimm p197-205 **398.2**

The **sorcerer's** apprentice, Wanda Gág's. Gág, W. **398.2**

The **sorceress**. Afanas'ev, A. N.
In Afanas'ev, A. N. Russian fairy tales p567-68 **398.2**

The **sorely** trying day. Hoban, R. **E**

Sorensen, Virginia Eggertsen, 1912-
Miracles on Maple Hill (4 and up) **Fic**

Soria Moria Castle
Asbjørnsen, P. C. Soria Moria Castle
In The Red fairy book p30-41 **398.2**
In The Scott, Foresman anthology of children's literature p230-35 **808.8**

Sosa, Dan, 1923-
See/See also pages in the following book(s):
Morey, J. Famous Mexican Americans p130-39 (5 and up) **920**

Soto, Gary
Baseball in April, and other stories (5 and up) **S C**
Contents: Broken chain; Baseball in April; Two dreamers; Barbie; The no-guitar blues; Seventh grade; Mother and daughter; The Karate Kid; La Bamba; The marble champ; Growing up

Soto, Hernando de, ca. 1500-1542
See/See also pages in the following book(s):
McCall, E. S. Biography of a river: the living Mississippi p14-19 (6 and up) **977**

Souci, Daniel San *See* San Souci, Daniel

Sound
Branley, F. M. High sounds, low sounds (k-3) **534**
Kettelkamp, L. The magic of sound (4-6) **534**

Experiments

Broekel, R. Sound experiments (2-4) **534**

Sound experiments. Broekel, R. **534**

A **sound** of chariots. Hunter, M. **Fic**

Sound the shofar. Chaikin, M. **296.4**

Sounder. Armstrong, W. H. **Fic**

A **sounding** of storytellers. Townsend, J. R. **028.5**

Sounding the alarm: a biography of Rachel Carson. Harlan, J. **92**

Soup. Peck, R. N. **Fic**

Soup [excerpt]. Peck, R. N.
In The Random House book of humor for children p235-41 **817.008**

Soup & me. Peck, R. N. See note under Peck, R. N. Soup **Fic**

Soup for president. Peck, R. N. See note under Peck, R. N. Soup **Fic**

Soup for supper. Root, P. **E**

Soup in the saddle. Peck, R. N. See note under Peck, R. N. Soup **Fic**

Soup on fire. Peck, R. N. See note under Peck, R. N. Soup **Fic**

Soup on ice. Peck, R. N. See note under Peck, R. N. Soup **Fic**

Soup on wheels. Peck, R. N. See note under Peck, R. N. Soup **Fic**

Soup's drum. Peck, R. N. See note under Peck, R. N. Soup **Fic**

Soup's goat. Peck, R. N. See note under Peck, R. N. Soup **Fic**

Soup's hoop. Peck, R. N. See note under Peck, R. N. Soup **Fic**

Soup's uncle. Peck, R. N. See note under Peck, R. N. Soup **Fic**

Sourdough Sally. Gotwalt, H. L. M.
In Gotwalt, H. L. M. Everyday plays for boys and girls p39-50 **812**

South Africa
Jacobsen, K. South Africa (2-4) **968**
Paton, J. The land and people of South Africa (5 and up) **968**

Fiction

Daly, N. Not so fast, Songololo **E**
Lewin, H. Jafta **E**
Seed, J. Ntombi's song **E**
Stock, C. Armien's fishing trip **E**

Folklore

See Folklore—South Africa

Race relations—Fiction

Naidoo, B. Chain of fire (5 and up) **Fic**
Naidoo, B. Journey to Jo'burg (5 and up) **Fic**

South Carolina
Kent, D. South Carolina
In America the beautiful **973**

South Dakota
Lepthien, E. U. South Dakota
In America the beautiful **973**

Fiction

Turner, A. W. Grasshopper summer (4-6) **Fic**

South Korea—in pictures (5 and up) **951.9**

South Pole
See also Antarctic regions
Southall, Ivan, 1921-
Let the balloon go (4 and up) **Fic**
See/See also pages in the following book(s):
Townsend, J. R. A sense of story p182-89 **028.5**
Townsend, J. R. A sounding of storytellers p179-93 **028.5**
Southern Rhodesia *See* Zimbabwe
Southern States
Folklore
See Folklore—Southern States
Southey, Robert, 1774-1843
The story of the three bears
In The Classic fairy tales p201-05 **398.2**
In The Green fairy book p234-37 **398.2**
The **southpaw** [short story]. Viorst, J.
In Free to be—you and me p71-75 **810.8**
Sovereigns *See* Kings, queens, rulers, etc.
Soviet Union
Andrews, W. G. The land and the people of the Soviet Union (5 and up) **947**
Fiction
Almedingen, E. M. The crimson oak (5 and up) **Fic**
Face to face: a collection of stories by celebrated Soviet and American writers (5 and up) **S C**
Lewis, J. P. The tsar & the amazing cow **E**
Polacco, P. Rechenka's eggs **E**
Zhitkov, B. How I hunted the little fellows (2-4) **Fic**
Folklore
See Folklore—Soviet Union
Kings, queens, rulers, etc.
Stanley, D. Peter the Great (3-5) **92**
Politics and government
Caulkins, J. The picture life of Mikhail Gorbachev (4 and up) **92**
Space, Outer *See* Outer space
Space and time
Fiction
Cameron, E. Beyond silence (6 and up) **Fic**
Christopher, J. Fireball (5 and up) **Fic**
Conrad, P. Stonewords (5 and up) **Fic**
Cresswell, H. The secret world of Polly Flint (4-6) **Fic**
Greer, G. Max and me and the time machine (5 and up) **Fic**
Hahn, M. D. The doll in the garden (4-6) **Fic**
Lunn, J. L. S. The root cellar (5 and up) **Fic**
Park, R. Playing Beatie Bow (5 and up) **Fic**
Pascal, F. Hangin' out with Cici (5 and up) **Fic**
Pearce, P. Tom's midnight garden (4 and up) **Fic**
Sleator, W. The boy who reversed himself (5 and up) **Fic**
Sleator, W. The green futures of Tycho (5 and up) **Fic**
Sleator, W. Strange attractors (5 and up) **Fic**
Wiseman, D. Jeremy Visick (5 and up) **Fic**
Space case. Marshall, E. **E**
Space environment
Maurer, R. Junk in space (4-6) **363.7**
Space flight
Ride, S. K. To space & back (4 and up) **629.45**
Space flight to the moon
Fiction
Murphy, J. What next, Baby Bear! **E**
Space photography
See/See also pages in the following book(s):
Mango, K. N. Mapmaking p86-92 (4 and up) **526**
Space shuttles
Fichter, G. S. The space shuttle (4 and up) **629.44**
Ride, S. K. To space & back (4 and up) **629.45**
Space stations
Kerrod, R. See inside a space station (4-6) **629.44**
Vogt, G. Space stations (4 and up) **629.44**
Space Telescope *See* Hubble Space Telescope
The **space** telescope. Lampton, C. **522**
Space vehicles
See also Artificial satellites; Space shuttles
Space vehicles, Reusable *See* Space shuttles
Spaghetti. Rylant, C.
In Rylant, C. Every living thing p31-33 **S C**
Spagnoli, Cathy
Nine-in-one, Grr! Grr! (k-2) **398.2**
Spain
Lye, K. Passport to Spain (5 and up) **946**
Children
See Children—Spain
Fiction
Aiken, J. Bridle the wind (6 and up) **Fic**
Leaf, M. The story of Ferdinand **E**

Spain—Fiction—*Continued*
Wojciechowska, M. Shadow of a bull (6 and up) **Fic**
Folklore
See Folklore—Spain
History—1936-1939, Civil War
Katz, W. L. The Lincoln Brigade (5 and up) **946.081**
Social life and customs
Spain (3-5) **946**
Spain (3-5) **946**
Spanfeller, Jim (James J.), 1930-
(il) Cleaver, V. Where the lillies bloom **Fic**
Spangler, Earl
The Blacks in America
In The In America series **305.8**
Spangler, James Murray
See/See also pages in the following book(s):
Aaseng, N. The unsung heroes p39-44 (5 and up) **920**
Spangler, Stella S.
(jt. auth) Kennedy, D. M. Science & technology in fact and fiction: a guide to children's books **016.5**
Spanish America *See* Latin America
Spanish language
Cooper, L. P. More fun with Spanish (4 and up) **468**
Emberley, R. My house/mi casa: a book in two languages (k-3) **463**
Emberley, R. Taking a walk/caminando: a book in two languages (k-3) **463**
Spanish language editions
Cleary, B. Henry Huggins **Fic**
Cleary, B. Ramona the pest **Fic**
Eastman, P. D. Are you my mother? **E**
Kessler, L. P. Here comes the strikeout **E**
Lionni, L. Inch by inch **E**
Minarik, E. H. Little Bear **E**
Potter, B. The tale of Peter Rabbit **E**
Rey, H. A. Curious George **E**
Seuss, Dr. The cat in the hat **E**
Viorst, J. Alexander and the terrible, horrible, no good, very bad day **E**
Spanish literature
Bibliography
Schon, I. Basic collection of children's books in Spanish **011.6**
Schon, I. Books in Spanish for children and young adults: an annotated guide [series I-V] **011.6**
Sparrow and his four children
Grimm, J. The sparrow and his four children
In Grimm, J. The complete Grimm's fairy tales p657-60 **398.2**
The **Sparrow** with the slit tongue
In Best-loved folktales of the world p509-12 **398.2**
Spastic paralysis *See* Cerebral palsy
Speak up: more rhymes of the never was and always is. McCord, D. T. W. **811**
Speare, Elizabeth George, 1908-
The bronze bow (6 and up) **Fic**
The sign of the beaver (5 and up) **Fic**
The witch of Blackbird Pond (6 and up) **Fic**
Special plays for holidays. Gotwalt, H. L. M. **812**
A **special** trade. Wittman, S. **E**
Speckled hen's egg. Carlson, N. S.
In Carlson, N. S. The talking cat, and other stories of French Canada p43-53 **S C**
Spectacles. Raskin, E. **E**
Speech
Silverstein, A. Wonders of speech (6 and up) **302.2**
Speed, Lancelot, 1860-1931
(il) The Red fairy book. See The Red fairy book **398.2**
The **speedy** messenger. Afanas'ev, A. N.
In Afanas'ev, A. N. Russian fairy tales p124-30 **398.2**
Speirs, John
(il) Carroll, L. Alice's adventures in Wonderland, and Through the looking glass **Fic**
(il) Sewell, A. Black Beauty **Fic**
Speleology *See* Caves
The **spell** of the sorcerer's skull. Bellairs, J. See note under Bellairs, J. The curse of the blue figurine **Fic**
The **spellbound** spider. Climo, S.
In Climo, S. Someone saw a spider p91-100 **398.2**
Spells *See* Charms
Spencer, William
The land and people of Turkey (5 and up) **956.1**
Spenser, Edmund, 1552?-1599
Faerie Queene; adaptation. See Hodges, M. Saint George and the dragon **398.2**
Sperry, Armstrong, 1897-
Call it courage (5 and up) **Fic**
Sperry, Armstrong, 1897-1976
See/See also pages in the following book(s):
Newbery Medal books, 1922-1955 p194-207 **028.5**
The **spider**. Afanas'ev, A. N.
In Afanas'ev, A. N. Russian fairy tales p75-76 **398.2**

Spider and the flea
Grimm, J. The louse and the flea
In Grimm, J. The complete Grimm's fairy tales p158-60 **398.2**
The **spider** and the king. Climo, S.
In Climo, S. Someone saw a spider p67-72 **398.2**
The **spider** brothers make the rainbow. Climo, S.
In Climo, S. Someone saw a spider p29-38 **398.2**
Spider magic. Patent, D. H. **595.4**
Spiderman Anancy. Berry, J. **398.2**
Spiders
See also Tarantulas
Hawes, J. My daddy longlegs (k-3) **595.4**
Hopf, A. L. Spiders (4 and up) **595.4**
Lane, M. The spider (1-3) **595.4**
Patent, D. H. The lives of spiders (5 and up) **595.4**
Patent, D. H. Spider magic (2-4) **595.4**
Schnieper, C. Amazing spiders (3-6) **595.4**

Fiction

Carle, E. The very busy spider **E**
Climo, S. The cobweb Christmas **E**
Climo, S. Someone saw a spider (4 and up) **398.2**
Haley, G. E. A story, a story (k-3) **398.2**
Jukes, M. Like Jake and me (2-4) **Fic**
Koralek, J. The cobweb curtain **E**
McDermott, G. Anansi the spider (k-3) **398.2**
White, E. B. Charlotte's web (3-6) **Fic**
Spier, Peter, 1927-
The Book of Jonah (k-3) **224**
Bored—nothing to do! **E**
Dreams **E**
Fast-slow, high-low **E**
Gobble, growl, grunt **E**
Oh, were they ever happy! **E**
Peter Spier's Christmas! **E**
Peter Spier's rain **E**
Tin Lizzie **E**
We the people (2-4) **342**
(il) The Erie Canal. See The Erie Canal **781.62**
(il) The Fox went out on a chilly night. See The Fox went out on a chilly night **781.62**
(il) Key, F. S. The Star-Spangled Banner **782.42**
(il) Krasilovsky, P. The cow who fell in the canal **E**
(il) London Bridge is falling down! See London Bridge is falling down! **781.62**
(il) To market! To market! See To market! To market! **398.8**
See/See also pages in the following book(s):
Newbery and Caldecott Medal books, 1976-1985 p193-203 **028.5**
Spies
Reit, S. Behind rebel lines: the incredible story of Emma Edmonds, Civil War spy (4 and up) **92**
Spin a soft black song: poems for children. Giovanni, N. **811**
Spindle, shuttle and needle
Grimm, J. Spindle, shuttle, and needle
In The Green fairy book p286-89 **398.2**
In Grimm, J. The juniper tree, and other tales from Grimm v1 p55-62 **398.2**
In Grimm, J. Tales from Grimm p65-76 **398.2**
Grimm, J. The spindle, the shuttle, and the needle
In Grimm, J. The complete Grimm's fairy tales p764-67 **398.2**
Spinelli, Jerry, 1941-
Maniac Magee (5 and up) **Fic**
School spirit
In Connections: short stories by outstanding writers for young adults p170-80 **S C**
Spinky sulks. Steig, W. **E**
Spinning maid and the cowherd. Carpenter, F.
In Carpenter, F. Tales of a Chinese grandmother p182-89 **398.2**
Spirin, Gennadiĭ
(il) Romanova, N. Once there was a tree **582.16**
(il) San Souci, R. The white cat **398.2**
Spirit in the bottle
Grimm, J. The spirit in the bottle
In Grimm, J. The complete Grimm's fairy tales p458-62 **398.2**
In The Scott, Foresman anthology of children's literature p190-92 **808.8**
The **spirit** of the snow goose. Mayo, G.
In Mayo, G. Star tales p35-36 **398.2**
The **spirited** life: Bertha Mahony Miller and children's books. Ross, E. S. **92**
Spirits *See* Ghosts
Spirits of the railway. Yee, P.
In Yee, P. Tales from Gold Mountain p9-15 **S C**
Spirituals (Songs)
What a morning! **782.25**
Spirt, Diana L.
Introducing bookplots 3 **028.1**
(jt. auth) Ettlinger, J. R. T. Choosing books for young people v2 **011.6**

Spooky night. Carlson, N. S. **E**
Spooky tricks. Wyler, R. **793.8**
Sports
See also Games; Winter sports
Guinness book of sports records **796.03**
Hammond, T. Sports (4 and up) **796**
Sportworks (4 and up) **796**
Dictionaries
Berger, M. Sports (5 and up) **796.03**
History
Fisher, L. E. The sports (4 and up) **796**
Sullivan, G. Any number can play (3-6) **796**
Periodicals
Sports Illustrated for Kids **796**
Poetry
Adoff, A. Sports pages (4 and up) **811**
Sprints and distances (5 and up) **808.81**
The **sports.** Fisher, L. E. **796**
Sports for the handicapped
Allen, A. Sports for the handicapped (5 and up) **796**
Sports Illustrated for Kids **796**
Sports pages. Adoff, A. **811**
Sportworks (4 and up) **796**
A **spot** of decorating. Bond, M.
In Bond, M. Paddington's storybook p7-20 **S C**
Spots, feathers, and curly tails. Tafuri, N. **636**
Spowart, Robin
(il) Manushkin, F. Latkes and applesauce **E**
(il) Modesitt, J. Vegetable soup **E**
(il) Songs from Mother Goose. See Songs from Mother Goose **782.42**
Spring
Hirschi, R. Spring (k-2) **508**
Markle, S. Exploring spring (4 and up) **508**
See/See also pages in the following book(s):
Bauer, C. F. Celebrations p195-210 **808.8**
Fiction
Cole, B. The winter wren **E**
Rockwell, A. F. My spring robin **E**
Zolotow, C. One step, two— **E**
Spring fleece. Paladino, C. **636.3**
The **spring** running. Kipling, R.
In Kipling, R. The jungle books **S C**
Springer, Harriett
(il) Selsam, M. E. A first look at animals with backbones **596**
(il) Selsam, M. E. A first look at bird nests **598**
(il) Selsam, M. E. A first look at birds **598**
(il) Selsam, M. E. A first look at caterpillars **595.7**
(il) Selsam, M. E. A first look at flowers **582.13**
(il) Selsam, M. E. A first look at insects **595.7**
(il) Selsam, M. E. A first look at kangaroos, koalas, and other animals with pouches **599.2**
(il) Selsam, M. E. A first look at monkeys and apes **599.8**
(il) Selsam, M. E. A first look at owls, eagles, and other hunters of the sky **598**
(il) Selsam, M. E. A first look at poisonous snakes **597.9**
(il) Selsam, M. E. A first look at rocks **552**
(il) Selsam, M. E. A first look at seals, sea lions, and walruses **599.74**
(il) Selsam, M. E. A first look at seashells **594**
(il) Selsam, M. E. A first look at sharks **597**
(il) Selsam, M. E. A first look at the world of plants **581**
Springer, Nancy
Barn gravity
In Herds of thunder, manes of gold p83-93 **808.8**
Sprints and distances (5 and up) **808.81**
Sproule, Anna
Guinea pigs (4 and up) **636.088**
Mice and rats (4 and up) **636.088**
Sproule, Michael
(jt. auth) Sproule, A. Guinea pigs **636.088**
(jt. auth) Sproule, A. Mice and rats **636.088**
Sprug, Joseph W., 1922-
(comp) Index to fairy tales, 1978-1986. See Index to fairy tales, 1978-1986 **398.2**
Spurr, Elizabeth
Mrs. Minetta's car pool **E**
The **spying** heart. Paterson, K. **028.5**
Spyri, Johanna, 1827-1901
Heidi (4 and up) **Fic**
Heidi; dramatization. See Thane, A. Heidi
Squanto, d. 1622
See/See also pages in the following book(s):
Barth, E. Turkeys, Pilgrims, and Indian corn p63-68 (3-6) **394.2**
Squawk to the moon, Little Goose. Preston, E. M. **E**
Squeaknibble's Christmas. Gotwalt, H. L. M.
In Gotwalt, H. L. M. Special plays for holidays p67-74 **812**

Squeeze a sneeze. Morrison, B. **811**
Squib. Bawden, N. **Fic**
The **squire**. Singer, I. B.
In Singer, I. B. The power of light p43-50 **S C**
In Singer, I. B. Stories for children p242-48 **S C**
Squire's bride
Riordan, J. The squire's bride
In Riordan, J. The woman in the moon, and other tales of forgotten heroines p75-79 **398.2**
Squirrels
Fiction
Bawden, N. Henry (5 and up) **Fic**
Potter, B. The tale of Squirrel Nutkin **E**
Potter, B. The tale of Timmy Tiptoes **E**
Sri Lanka
Sri Lanka—in pictures (5 and up) **954.93**
Sri Lanka—in pictures (5 and up) **954.93**
SSTs *See* Supersonic transport planes
St. George, Judith, 1931-
The Mount Rushmore story [biography of Gutzon Borglum] (6 and up) **92**
Panama Canal (5 and up) **972.87**
The White House (5 and up) **975.3**
St. Joseph in the forest. Grimm, J.
In Grimm, J. The complete Grimm's fairy tales p815-18 **398.2**
St. Louis (Mo.) *See* Saint Louis (Mo.)
St. Martin, Alexis
About
Epstein, S. Dr. Beaumont and the man with the hole in his stomach (4-6) **92**
St. Nicholas
Afanas'ev, A. N. Father Nicholas and the thief
In Afanas'ev, A. N. Russian fairy tales p145-46 **398.2**
St. Nicholas (Periodical)
See/See also pages in the following book(s):
Jordan, A. M. From Rollo to Tom Sawyer, and other papers p131-43 **028.5**
St. Nicholas and the children
Martin, E. St. Nicholas and the children
In Martin, E. Tales of the Far North p81-88 **398.2**
St. Patrick's Day *See* Saint Patrick's Day
St. Valentine's Day *See* Valentine's Day
St. Valentine's Day. Bulla, C. R. **394.2**
Stadler, John
(il) Esbensen, B. J. Words with wrinkled knees: animal poems **811**
The **staff** and the fiddle. Pyle, H.
In Pyle, H. The wonder clock p253-66 **398.2**
Stafford, Patricia
Your two brains (5 and up) **612.8**
Stage door to terror. Quackenbush, R. M. See note under Quackenbush, R. M. Express train to trouble **Fic**
Stage fright. Howe, J. See note under Howe, J. Dew drop dead **Fic**
Staines, Bill
All God's critters got a place in the choir (k-2) **782.42**
Stairway to doom. Quackenbush, R. M. See note under Quackenbush, R. M. Express train to trouble **Fic**
Stalin, Joseph, 1879-1953
See/See also pages in the following book(s):
Andrews, W. G. The land and the people of the Soviet Union (5 and up) **947**
Stamm, Claus
Three strong women (k-3) **398.2**
also in Womenfolk and fairy tales p93-105 **398.2**
The **stamp-pad** printing book. Pettit, F. H. **761**
Stamp your feet (k-2) **796.1**
Stamper, J. B.
The jigsaw puzzle, a story
In Halloween: stories and poems p25-35 **808.8**
Stan the hot dog man. Kessler, E. **E**
Stangl, Jean
Crystals and crystal gardens you can grow (4 and up) **548**
Stanley, Diana, 1900-
(il) Carroll, L. Alice's adventures in Wonderland, and Through the looking glass **Fic**
Stanley, Diane, 1943-
Captain Whiz-Bang **E**
Fortune **E**
The good-luck pencil **E**
Good Queen Bess: the story of Elizabeth I of England (3-5) **92**
Peter the Great (3-5) **92**
Shaka, king of the Zulus (2-4) **92**
(il) Marshak, S. The Month-Brothers **398.2**
(il) Skofield, J. All wet! All wet! **E**
(il) Yolen, J. Sleeping ugly **Fic**
Stannard, Russell
The time and space of Uncle Albert (5 and up) **Fic**
Stanton, Elizabeth Cady, 1815-1902
See/See also pages in the following book(s):
Jacobs, W. J. Great lives: human rights p91-98 (5 and up) **920**

Stanton, Mary
Sunrise
In Herds of thunder, manes of gold p138-48 808.8

Stapler, Sarah
(il) Roberts, B. Waiting-for-papa stories E

Star beings: tales from the Southeast. Monroe, J. G.
In Monroe, J. G. They dance in the sky p107-18 398.2

Star Boy. Goble, P. 398.2

The **Star-child**. Wilde, O.
In Wilde, O. The Happy Prince, and other stories p135-54 S C

Star dollars
Grimm, J. The star dollars
In Grimm, J. More tales from Grimm p85-86 398.2
Grimm, J. The star-money
In Grimm, J. The complete Grimm's fairy tales p652-54 398.2
Rockwell, A. F. The star money
In Rockwell, A. F. The Three bears & 15 other stories p113-17 398.2

Star gazing, comet tracking, and sky mapping. Berger, M. 523

Star guide. Branley, F. M. 523.8

A **star** in the window. Hark, M.
In The Big book of Christmas plays p118-33 808.82

The **star** maiden: an Ojibway tale. Esbensen, B. J. 398.2

The **star-money**. Grimm, J.
In Grimm, J. The complete Grimm's fairy tales p652-54 398.2

The **star** money. Rockwell, A. F.
In Rockwell, A. F. The Three bears & 15 other stories p113-17 398.2

Star Mother's youngest child. Moeri, L. E

Star of night. Paterson, K.
In Paterson, K. Angels & other strangers: family Christmas stories p64-80 S C

The **Star-Spangled** Banner. Key, F. S. 782.42

Star tales. Mayo, G. 398.2

Starfishes
Hurd, E. T. Starfish (k-3) 593.9

Stargazer to the sultan. Walker, B. K.
In Walker, B. K. A treasury of Turkish folktales for children p98-107 398.2

Staring at you. Leach, M.
In Leach, M. Whistle in the graveyard p61-62 398.2

Starring first grade. Cohen, M. See note under Cohen, M. See you in second grade! E

The **starry** sky. Wyler, R. 520

Stars
See also Black holes (Astronomy); Supernovae
Apfel, N. H. Nebulae (4 and up) 523.1
Berger, M. Bright stars, red giants, and white dwarfs (5 and up) 523.8
Berger, M. Star gazing, comet tracking, and sky mapping (5 and up) 523
Branley, F. M. The Christmas sky (3-6) 232.9
Branley, F. M. The sky is full of stars (k-3) 523.8
Branley, F. M. Star guide (3-6) 523.8
Krupp, E. C. The Big Dipper and you (3-5) 523
Lampton, C. Stars & planets (3-6) 523
Rey, H. A. Find the constellations 523.8
Simon, S. Stars (1-4) 523.8
See/See also pages in the following book(s):
Simon, S. Look to the night sky: an introduction to star watching (4 and up) 523

Fiction
Goble, P. Her seven brothers (k-3) 398.2
Lurie, A. The heavenly zoo (4 and up) 398.2
Mayo, G. Star tales (4 and up) 398.2
Monroe, J. G. They dance in the sky: native American star myths (4 and up) 398.2

Stars & planets. Lampton, C. 523

Stars in the sky
Reeves, J. The stars in the sky
In Reeves, J. English fables and fairy stories p177-82 398.2

Starting school. Ahlberg, J. E

Starting soccer. Dolan, E. F. 796.334

Starvation
See also Famines

State flowers
Dowden, A. O. T. State flowers (5 and up) 582.13

Statesmen
See also Diplomats

Statistics

Yearbooks
Information please almanac, atlas & yearbook 031.02
The World almanac and book of facts 031.02

Statue of Liberty (New York, N.Y.)
Burchard, S. The Statue of Liberty (5 and up) 974.7

Statue of Liberty (New York, N.Y.)—*Continued*
Fisher, L. E. The Statue of Liberty (4 and up) **974.7**
Haskins, J. The Statue of Liberty: America's proud lady (4 and up) **974.7**
Maestro, B. The story of the Statue of Liberty (k-3) **974.7**
Shapiro, M. J. How they built the Statue of Liberty (4 and up) **974.7**
Stay away from Simon! Carrick, C. **Fic**
Staying nine. Conrad, P. **Fic**
The **steadfast** tin soldier. Andersen, H. C. **Fic**
also in Andersen, H. C. Hans Andersen: his classic fairy tales p98-102 **S C**
also in The Yellow fairy book p308-12 **398.2**
The **steadfast** tin soldier. Ehrlich, A.
In Ehrlich, A. The Random House book of fairy tales p130-37 **398.2**
Steam
Jacobs, L. Letting off steam (3-6) **621.44**
The **steam** roller: a fantasy. Brown, M. W.
In Brown, M. W. The fish with the deep sea smile p25-31 **818**
Steam-shovels
Fiction
Burton, V. L. Mike Mulligan and his steam shovel **E**
Steamboats
See/See also pages in the following book(s):
McCall, E. S. Biography of a river: the living Mississippi (6 and up) **977**
Fiction
Stevenson, J. The stowaway **E**
Stebbins, Robert C. (Robert Cyril), 1915-
A field guide to western reptiles and amphibians **597.6**
Steel, Flora Annie Webster, 1847-1929
The story of the three bears
In The Scott, Foresman anthology of children's literature p149-51 **808.8**
The tiger, the Brahman, and the jackal
In The Scott, Foresman anthology of children's literature p341-43 **808.8**
Steel industry and trade
Fiction
Smucker, A. E. No star nights **E**
Steele, Mark
(il) Hooper, P. A bundle of beasts **811**
Steere, Edward
Liongo, a hero of Shanga
In The Crest and the hide, and other African stories of heroes, chiefs, bards, hunters, sorcerers, and common people p77-87 **398.2**
Steig, William, 1907-
Abel's island (3-6) **Fic**
The amazing bone **E**
Amos & Boris **E**
Brave Irene **E**
C D C? (3-6) **793.73**
Caleb & Kate **E**
Doctor De Soto **E**
Dominic (4 and up) **Fic**
Farmer Palmer's wagon ride **E**
The real thief (2-5) **Fic**
Roland, the minstrel pig **E**
Shrek! **E**
Solomon the rusty nail **E**
Spinky sulks **E**
Sylvester and the magic pebble **E**
also in The Read-aloud treasury p112-34 **808.8**
See/See also pages in the following book(s):
Newbery and Caldecott Medal books, 1966-1975 p218-22 **028.5**
Stein, Gertrude, 1874-1946
See/See also pages in the following book(s):
A Horn Book sampler on children's books and reading p128-32 **028.5**
Stein, Jess M., 1914-1984
(ed) The Random House thesaurus. See The Random House thesaurus **423**
Stein, R. Conrad, 1937-
California
In America the beautiful **973**
Greece (4 and up) **949.5**
Illinois
In America the beautiful **973**
Indiana
In America the beautiful **973**
Michigan
In America the beautiful **973**
Minnesota
In America the beautiful **973**
New Mexico
In America the beautiful **973**
New York
In America the beautiful **973**
North Carolina
In America the beautiful **973**
Oregon
In America the beautiful **973**
The story of the powers of the Supreme Court (4-6) **347**
Texas
In America the beautiful **973**
West Virginia
In America the beautiful **973**

Stein, R. Conrad, 1937-—*Continued*
Wisconsin
In America the beautiful **973**
Stein, Sara Bonnett
About dying (k-3) **155.9**
On divorce (k-3) **306.89**
Stemple, Adam
The Lullaby songbook. See The Lullaby songbook **782.42**
Stemple, Jane H. Yolen *See* Yolen, Jane
Stennet, R.
Aldiborontiphoskyphorniostikos
In A Nursery companion p108-12 **820.8**
Step by step. McMillan, B. **E**
Step-by-step kids' cook book, Better Homes and Gardens **641.5**
Step-mother
Pyle, H. The step-mother
In Pyle, H. The wonder clock p149-60 **398.2**
The **stepchild** and the fruit trees. Robinson, A.
In The Scott, Foresman anthology of children's literature p319-21 **808.8**
Stepchildren
Fiction
Christopher, M. Takedown (6 and up) **Fic**
Hahn, M. D. Wait till Helen comes (4-6) **Fic**
Stepfamilies
Hodder, E. Stepfamilies (5 and up) **306.8**
Fiction
Park, B. My mother got married (and other disasters) (4-6) **Fic**
Stepfathers
Fiction
Jukes, M. Like Jake and me (2-4) **Fic**
Smith, D. B. The first hard times (4-6) **Fic**
Stephen, R. J.
Cranes (2-4) **621.8**
Stephens, James, 1882-1950
Irish fairy tales (6 and up) **398.2**
Contents: The story of Tuan Mac Cairill; The boyhood of Fionn; The birth of Bran; Oisin's mother; The wooing of Becfola; The little brawl at Allen; The Carl of the Drab Coat; The enchanted cave of Cesh Corran; Becuma of the White Skin; Mongan's frenzy
Stepmothers
Fiction
MacLachlan, P. Sarah, plain and tall (3-5) **Fic**
Steptoe, John, 1950-1989
Baby says **E**
Mufaro's beautiful daughters (k-3) **398.2**
Stevie **E**
In Free to be—a family p35-37 **810.8**
The story of Jumping Mouse (1-3) **398.2**
(il) Adoff, A. All the colors of the race: poems **811**
(il) Greenfield, E. She come bringing me that little baby girl **E**
(il) Guy, R. Mother Crocodile **398.2**
Sterling. White, S. V. **639.9**
Stermer, Dugald, 1936-
(il) Kortum, J. Ghost vision **Fic**
Stern, Philip Van Doren, 1900-1984
Henry David Thoreau: writer and rebel (5 and up) **92**
Steven Caney's kids' America. Caney, S. **790.1**
Steven Kellogg's Yankee Doodle. Bangs, E. **782.42**
Stevens, Janet
How the Manx cat lost its tail (k-2) **398.2**
The town mouse and the country mouse (k-2) **398.2**
(il) Lear, E. The owl and the pussycat **821**
Stevens, Thaddeus, 1792-1868
See/See also pages in the following book(s):
Jacobs, W. J. Great lives: human rights p99-106 (5 and up) **920**
Stevenson, Harvey
(il) Good books, good times! See Good books, good times! **811.008**
Stevenson, James, 1929-
"Could be worse!" **E**
Emma **E**
Emma at the beach. See note under Stevenson, J. Emma **E**
Fast friends **E**
Fried feathers for Thanksgiving. See note under Stevenson, J. Emma **E**
Grandpa's great city tour. See note under Stevenson, J. "Could be worse!" **E**
Grandpa's too-good garden. See note under Stevenson, J. "Could be worse!" **E**
The great big especially beautiful Easter egg. See note under Stevenson, J. "Could be worse!" **E**
Happy Valentine's Day, Emma! See note under Stevenson, J. Emma **E**
Higher on the door (k-2) **92**
July (k-2) **92**
Monty **E**
Mr. Hacker **E**
Murray and Fred
In Stevenson, J. Fast friends p5-37 **E**
National Worm Day **E**
The night after Christmas **E**
No friends. See note under Stevenson, J. "Could be worse!" **E**

Stevenson, James, 1929-—*Continued*
No need for Monty. See note under Stevenson, J. Monty **E**
Quick! turn the page! **E**
The stowaway **E**
That dreadful day. See note under Stevenson, J. "Could be worse!" **E**
That terrible Halloween night. See note under Stevenson, J. "Could be worse!" **E**
There's nothing to do! See note under Stevenson, J. "Could be worse!" **E**
Thomas and Clem
In Stevenson, J. Fast friends p38-64 **E**
Un-Happy New Year, Emma! See note under Stevenson, J. Emma **E**
We can't sleep. See note under Stevenson, J. "Could be worse!" **E**
We hate rain! See note under Stevenson, J. "Could be worse!" **E**
What's under my bed? See note under Stevenson, J. "Could be worse!" **E**
When I was nine (k-2) **92**
Which one is Whitney? **E**
Will you please feed our cat? See note under Stevenson, J. "Could be worse!" **E**
Worse than Willy! See note under Stevenson, J. "Could be worse!" **E**
The worst person in the world **E**
Yuck! See note under Stevenson, J. Emma **E**
(il) Gage, W. Cully Cully and the bear **E**
(il) Griffith, H. V. Georgia music **E**
(il) Griffith, H. V. Grandaddy's place **E**
(il) Phillips, L. How do you get a horse out of the bathtub? **793.73**
(il) Prelutsky, J. The baby Uggs are hatching **811**
(il) Prelutsky, J. The new kid on the block: poems **811**
(il) Prelutsky, J. Something big has been here **811**
(il) Zolotow, C. I know a lady **E**

Stevenson, Laura Caroline, 1946-
Happily after all (4 and up) **Fic**

Stevenson, Peter, 1953-
(il) Bellamy, J. The Doubleday children's thesaurus **423**

Stevenson, Robert Louis, 1850-1894
Block city (k-2) **821**
A child's garden of verses (k-4) **821**
My shadow (k-3) **821**
Treasure Island (6 and up) **Fic**
Poetry
Willard, N. The voyage of the Ludgate Hill (2-5) **811**

Stevenson, Suçie
(il) Porte-Thomas, B. A. Ruthann and her pig **Fic**
(il) Rylant, C. Henry and Mudge **E**
(il) Wishinsky, F. Oonga boonga **E**
(il) Woodruff, E. Tubtime **E**

Stevie. Steptoe, J. **E**
In Free to be—a family p35-37 **810.8**

Stewart, Arvis
(il) Conford, E. Felicia the critic **Fic**
(il) Low, A. The Macmillan book of Greek gods and heroes **292**

Stewart, Edgar
(il) Monroe, J. G. They dance in the sky: native American star myths **398.2**

Stewart, Gail, 1949-
Germany (4 and up) **943.087**

Stewart, John, 1920-
Elephant school (4-6) **636.088**

Stewart, Judy, 1948-
A family in Morocco (3-5) **964**

Stewart, Pat Ronson
(il) Wyler, R. Science fun with mud and dirt **507**
(il) Wyler, R. Science fun with peanuts and popcorn **507**
(il) Wyler, R. Science fun with toy boats and planes **507**
(il) Wyler, R. Science fun with toy cars and trucks **507**

Stewed, roasted, or live? Kendall, C.
In Kendall, C. Sweet and sour p98-99 **398.2**

The **stickleback**. See Lane, M. The fish **597**

Sticklebacks
Lane, M. The fish (1-3) **597**

Stidworthy, John
Mammals: the large plant-eaters (4 and up) **599**
(jt. auth) O'Toole, C. Mammals: the hunters **599**

Stifter, Adalbert, 1805-1868
See/See also pages in the following book(s):
Sendak, M. Caldecott & Co.: notes on books and pictures p39-43 **028.5**

Stiles, Norman, 1942-
Another Cinderella
In Free to be—a family p25-32 **810.8**
The kingdom with no rules, no laws, and no king
In Free to be—a family p142-47 **810.8**

Still more small poems. Worth, V. **811**

Stinker from space. Service, P. F. **Fic**

Stobbs, William
(il) Kipling, R. The cat that walked by himself **Fic**

Stock, Catherine
Armien's fishing trip E
(il) Lasky, K. Sea swan E
(il) Trot, trot to Boston: play rhymes for baby. See Trot, trot to Boston: play rhymes for baby **398.8**
(il) Walter, M. P. Justin and the best biscuits in the world **Fic**
(il) Williams, K. L. Galimoto E
(il) Zolotow, C. Something is going to happen E
(il) Zolotow, C. A tiger called Thomas E

Stockton, Frank, 1834-1902
The Bee-man of Orn (4-6) **Fic**
The Griffin and the Minor Canon (3-5) **Fic**

Stoddard, Sandol, 1927-
The Doubleday illustrated children's Bible (4-6) **220.9**

Stoff, Joshua
Dirigible (3-6) **629.133**

The **stolen** bairn and the Sidh. Leodhas, S. N.
In Womenfolk and fairy tales p1-13 **398.2**

Stolen farthings
Grimm, J. The stolen farthings
In Grimm, J. The complete Grimm's fairy tales p654-55 **398.2**

The **Stolen** girl
In The Whistling skeleton p38-44 **398.2**

Stolz, Mary, 1920-
The bully of Barkham Street. See note under Stolz, M. A dog on Barkham Street **Fic**
Cat walk (3-6) **Fic**
The cuckoo clock (4-6) **Fic**
A dog on Barkham Street (4-6) **Fic**
Emmett's pig E
The explorer of Barkham Street. See note under Stolz, M. A dog on Barkham Street **Fic**
Night of ghosts and hermits (3-5) **574.92**
Quentin Corn (4-6) **Fic**
Storm in the night E
Zekmet, the stone carver (2-4) **Fic**

Stone, Erika
(il) Stein, S. B. On divorce **306.89**

Stone, Helen, 1904-
(il) Bennett, A. E. Little witch **Fic**

Stone, Lynn M.
Alligators and crocodiles (2-4) **597.9**
Florida
In America the beautiful **973**

Stone, Peter, 1930-
Boy meets girl [play]
In Free to be—you and me p24-31 **810.8**

Stone
See also Rocks

Stone cutter
McDermott, G. The stonecutter **398.2**
Shedlock, M. L. Hafiz, the stone-cutter
In Shedlock, M. L. The art of the story-teller p179-82 **372.6**
The Stonecutter
In Best-loved folktales of the world p516-18 **398.2**

The **stone-faced** boy. Fox, P. **Fic**

Stone Fox. Gardiner, J. R. **Fic**

Stone monkey
Carpenter, F. King of the monkeys
In Carpenter, F. Tales of a Chinese grandmother p107-16 **398.2**

Stone soup. Brown, M. **398.2** **810.8**

The **Stonecutter**
In Best-loved folktales of the world p516-18 **398.2**

The **stonecutter**. McDermott, G. **398.2**

The **stonewalkers**. Alcock, V. **Fic**

Stonewall [biography of Stonewall Jackson]. Fritz, J. **92**

Stoneware *See* Pottery

Stonewords. Conrad, P. **Fic**

Stopping by woods on a snowy evening. Frost, R. **811**

Stories about Rosie. Voigt, C. E

Stories for children. Singer, I. B. **S C**

Stories in rhyme
Aardema, V. Bringing the rain to Kapiti Plain (k-2) **398.2**
Adoff, A. Black is brown is tan E
Ahlberg, J. Each peach pear plum E
Ahlberg, J. Peek-a-boo! E
Archambault, J. Counting sheep E
Aylesworth, J. One crow E
Barracca, D. The adventures of Taxi Dog E
Base, G. The eleventh hour (4-6) **Fic**
Bayer, J. A my name is Alice E
Bemelmans, L. Madeline E
Bemelmans, L. Madeline's rescue E
Blos, J. W. Old Henry E
Brown, M. W. Big red barn E
Brown, M. W. Goodnight moon E
Bunting, E. Scary, scary Halloween E
Carlstrom, N. W. Jesse Bear, what will you wear? E
Cherry, L. Who's sick today? E
Cole, B. The silly book E
Couture, S. A. The block book E

Stories in rhyme—*Continued*
Craft, R. The winter bear E
Crews, D. Ten black dots E
De Regniers, B. S. So many cats! E
Degen, B. Jamberry E
Dodds, D. A. Wheel away! E
Dragonwagon, C. Half a moon and one whole star E
Ehlert, L. Feathers for lunch E
Fisher, A. L. Listen, rabbit E
Fox, M. Shoes from Grandpa E
Gág, W. The A B C bunny E
Gerrard, R. Mik's mammoth E
Ginsburg, M. The sun's asleep behind the hill E
Gross, T. F. Everyone asked about you E
Guarino, D. Is your mama a llama? E
Hennessy, B. G. A,B,C,D, tummy, toes, hands, knees E
Hennessy, B. G. The missing tarts E
Hines, A. G. It's just me, Emily E
Hoban, T. One little kitten E
Hoban, T. Where is it? E
Hughes, S. All shapes and sizes E
Hughes, S. Bathwater's hot E
Hughes, S. Out and about E
Hughes, S. Two shoes, new shoes E
Hutchins, P. The tale of Thomas Mead E
Hutchins, P. The wind blew E
Ivimey, J. W. The complete story of the three blind mice E
Jorgensen, G. Crocodile beat E
Kalan, R. Jump, frog, jump! E
Kitchen, B. Gorilla/Chinchilla and other animal rhymes E
Kraus, R. Whose mouse are you? E
Lindbergh, R. Benjamin's barn E
Lindbergh, R. The day the goose got loose E
Lindgren, B. The wild baby E
Lobel, A. On Market Street E
Lobel, A. On the day Peter Stuyvesant sailed into town E
Lobel, A. The rose in my garden E
Lord, J. V. The giant jam sandwich E
Lyon, G. E. Together E
Mahy, M. 17 kings and 42 elephants E
Martin, B. Barn dance! E
Martin, B. Chicka chicka boom boom E
Martin, B. Listen to the rain E
Martin, B. Up and down on the merry-go-round E
Marzollo, J. Pretend you're a cat E
Maxner, J. Nicholas Cricket E
Neitzel, S. The jacket I wear in the snow E
Oppenheim, J. Left & right E
Parkin, R. The red carpet E
Paxton, T. Engelbert the elephant E
Peet, B. Huge Harold E
Peet, B. No such things E
Pomerantz, C. Flap your wings and try E
Pomerantz, C. The piggy in the puddle E
Pomerantz, C. Where's the bear? E
Prelutsky, J. The mean old mean hyena E
Rice, E. City night E
Seuss, Dr. And to think that I saw it on Mulberry Street E
Seuss, Dr. The cat in the hat E
Seuss, Dr. The cat in the hat comes back! E
Seuss, Dr. Green eggs and ham E
Seuss, Dr. Horton hatches the egg E
Seuss, Dr. Horton hears a Who! E
Seuss, Dr. How the Grinch stole Christmas E
Seuss, Dr. If I ran the circus E
Seuss, Dr. If I ran the zoo E
Seuss, Dr. McElligot's pool E
Seuss, Dr. Oh, the places you'll go! E
Sharples, J. The flyaway pantaloons E
Shaw, N. Sheep in a jeep E
Siebert, D. Train song E
Siebert, D. Truck song E
Skofield, J. Nightdances E
Van Laan, N. Possum come a-knockin' E
Watson, C. Applebet: an ABC E
Wells, R. Noisy Nora E
Wells, R. Shy Charles E
Westcott, N. B. Skip to my Lou E
Winthrop, E. Shoes E
Yeoman, J. Old Mother Hubbard's dog dresses up E
Young, J. A million chameleons E
Zemach, H. The judge E

The **stories** Julian tells. Cameron, A. **Fic**

The **stories** Julian tells [excerpt]. Cameron, A.
In The Random House book of humor for children p44-50 **817.008**

Stories of the gods and heroes. Benson, S. **292**

Stories to solve. Shannon, G. **398.2**

Stories without words
Alexander, M. G. Bobo's dream E
Anno, M. Anno's Britain E
Anno, M. Anno's counting book E
Anno, M. Anno's counting house E
Anno, M. Anno's flea market E
Anno, M. Anno's journey E
Anno, M. Anno's U.S.A E
Anno, M. Topsy-turvies E
Anno, M. Upside-downers E
Bang, M. The Grey Lady and the Strawberry Snatcher E
Briggs, R. The snowman E

Stories without words—*Continued*
Carle, E. Do you want to be my friend? **E**
Charlip, R. Thirteen **E**
Collington, P. The angel and the soldier boy **E**
Day, A. Carl goes shopping **E**
De Paola, T. Sing, Pierrot, sing **E**
Goodall, J. S. Creepy castle **E**
Goodall, J. S. Little Red Riding Hood (k-2) **398.2**
Goodall, J. S. Naughty Nancy goes to school **E**
Goodall, J. S. Paddy to the rescue **E**
Goodall, J. S. Puss in boots (k-3) **398.2**
Hutchins, P. Changes, changes **E**
Keats, E. J. Clementina's cactus **E**
Krahn, F. Arthur's adventure in the abandoned house **E**
Mayer, M. A boy, a dog, and a frog **E**
Ormerod, J. Moonlight **E**
Ormerod, J. Sunshine **E**
Oxenbury, H. Shopping trip **E**
Rockwell, A. F. Albert B. Cub & Zebra **E**
Spier, P. Peter Spier's Christmas! **E**
Spier, P. Peter Spier's rain **E**
Tafuri, N. Do not disturb **E**
Tafuri, N. Early morning in the barn **E**
Tafuri, N. Follow me! **E**
Tafuri, N. Rabbit's morning **E**
Turkle, B. C. Deep in the forest **E**
Ward, L. K. The silver pony (2-4) **Fic**
Wiesner, D. Free fall **E**
Young, E. The other bone **E**
Young, E. Up a tree **E**

Storks
Fischer-Nagel, H. Season of the white stork (3-6) **598**
Fiction
Brown, M. W. Wheel on the chimney **E**
DeJong, M. The wheel on the school (4-6) **Fic**

Storm, Dan
Señor Coyote and the dogs
In Best-loved folktales of the world p686-88 **398.2**

Storm, Linda W.
(il) Williams, K. L. Baseball and butterflies **Fic**

Storm in the night. Stolz, M. **E**

Storms
Simon, S. Storms (2-4) **551.5**
See/See also pages in the following book(s):
Our violent earth p40-65 (4 and up) **363.3**
Tannenbaum, B. Making and using your own weather station p75-89 (5 and up) **551.6**

Stormy, Misty's foal. Henry, M. See note under Henry, M. Misty of Chincoteague **Fic**

A **story,** a story. Haley, G. E. **398.2**

A **story** about a darning needle. Andersen, H. C.
In The Yellow fairy book p319-21 **398.2**

The **story** about Ping. Flack, M. **E**

The **story** of a castle. Goodall, J. S. **942**

The **story** of a clever tailor. Grimm, J.
In The Green fairy book p324-27 **398.2**

The **story** of a farm. Goodall, J. S. **942**

The **story** of a main street. Goodall, J. S. **942**

Story of Ali Cogia, merchant of Bagdad
In The Arabian nights entertainments p346-57 **398.2**

The **story** of America: a National Geographic picture atlas. Scott, J. A. **973**

The **story** of an English village. Goodall, J. S. **942**

Story of Baba Abdalla
Story of the blind Baba-Abdalla
In The Arabian nights entertainments p320-30 **398.2**

The **story** of Babar, the little elephant. Brunhoff, J. de. **E**

The **story** of baseball. Ritter, L. S. **796.357**

The **story** of basketball. Anderson, D. **796.323**

The **story** of Befana. Plume, I. **398.2**

The **story** of Big Klaus and Little Klaus. Andersen, H. C.
In The Yellow fairy book p225-36 **398.2**

The **story** of Blixie Bimber and the power of the gold buckskin whincher. Sandburg, C.
In Sandburg, C. Rootabaga stories pt 1 p59-64 **S C**
In Sandburg, C. The Sandburg treasury p33-36 **818**

The **story** of Chicken Licken. Ormerod, J. **398.2**

The **story** of D-Day: June 6, 1944. Bliven, B. **940.54**

The **story** of Ferdinand. Leaf, M. **E**

The **story** of football. Anderson, D. **796.332**

The **story** of Hanukkah. Ehrlich, A. **296.4**

The **Story** of Hok Lee and the dwarfs
In The Green fairy book p229-33 **398.2**

The **story** of Holly and Ivy. Godden, R. **E**
also in Godden, R. Four dolls p68-106 **S C**
The **story** of Jason Squiff and why he had a popcorn hat, popcorn mittens and popcorn shoes. Sandburg, C.
In Sandburg, C. Rootabaga stories pt 1 p65-71 **S C**
In Sandburg, C. The Sandburg treasury p36-39 **818**
The **story** of Johnny Appleseed. Aliki. **92**
The **story** of Jumping Mouse. Steptoe, J. **398.2**
The **story** of King Arthur and his knights. Pyle, H. **398.2**
The **Story** of King Frost
In Best-loved folktales of the world p422-25 **398.2**
In The Yellow fairy book p209-12 **398.2**
The **story** of Le Nuong. Terada, A. M.
In Terada, A. M. Under the starfruit tree p99-101 **398.2**
The **story** of Miss Moppet. Potter, B. **E**
The **story** of one who set out to study fear. Grimm, J.
In Grimm, J. The juniper tree, and other tales from Grimm v1 p23-41 **398.2**
The **story** of Pretty Goldilocks. Aulnoy, Madame d'.
In The Blue fairy book p193-205 **398.2**
The **Story** of Prince Ahmed and the Fairy Paribanou
In The Blue fairy book p342-73 **398.2**
The **story** of Rags Habakuk, the two blue rats, and the circus man who came with spot cash money. Sandburg, C.
In Sandburg, C. Rootabaga stories pt 1 p72-78 **S C**
In Sandburg, C. The Sandburg treasury p39-42 **818**
Story of Schlauraffen Land
Grimm, J. The story of Schlauraffen Land
In Grimm, J. The complete Grimm's fairy tales p660-61 **398.2**
Grimm, J. A trip to Schlaraffenland
In Grimm, J. More tales from Grimm p87-88 **398.2**
The **Story** of Sidi-Nouman
In The Arabian nights entertainments p331-45 **398.2**
The **Story** of Sigurd
In The Red fairy book p357-67 **398.2**
Story of Sinbad the Sailor
The Seven voyages of Sindbad the sailor
In The Arabian nights entertainments p122-86 **398.2**
The **story** of Sir Launcelot and his companions. Pyle, H. **398.2**
The **Story** of the barber's fifth brother
In The Arabian nights entertainments p196-208 **398.2**
The **Story** of the barber's sixth brother
In The Arabian nights entertainments p209-15 **398.2**
Story of the blind Baba-Abdalla
In The Arabian nights entertainments p320-30 **398.2**
The **story** of the Boston Massacre. Phelan, M. K. **973.3**
The **story** of the champions of the Round Table. Pyle, H. **398.2**
The **story** of the Doodang. Lester, J.
In Lester, J. Further tales of Uncle Remus p128-32 **398.2**
The **Story** of the envious man and of him who was envied
In The Arabian nights entertainments p86-101 **398.2**
The **Story** of the first calender, son of a king
In The Arabian nights entertainments p68-74 **398.2**
The **Story** of the first old man and of the hind
In The Arabian nights entertainments p13-18 **398.2**
The **Story** of the fisherman
In The Arabian nights entertainments p23-28 **398.2**
The **story** of the fisherman and his wife. Grimm, J.
In The Green fairy book p343-52 **398.2**
The **story** of the Grail and the passing of Arthur. Pyle, H. **398.2**
The **Story** of the husband and the parrot
In The Arabian nights entertainments p32-33 **398.2**
The **story** of the Louisiana Purchase. Phelan, M. K. **973.4**
The **Story** of the merchant and the genius
In The Arabian nights entertainments p6-12 **398.2**
The **story** of the powers of the Supreme Court. Stein, R. C. **347**
The **Story** of the second calender, son of a king
In The Arabian nights entertainments p75-85 **398.2**

The **Story** of the second old man and of the two black dogs
In The Arabian nights entertainments p19-22 **398.2**

Story of the shining princess
Berger, T. The story of the shining princess
In Berger, T. Black fairy tales p68-78 **398.2**

The **story** of the smart parrot. Jagendorf, M. A.
In Best-loved folktales of the world p748-49 **398.2**

The **story** of the Statue of Liberty. Maestro, B. **974.7**

The **Story** of the third calender, son of a king
In The Arabian nights entertainments p102-21 **398.2**

The **story** of the thirteen colonies. Alderman, C. L. **973.2**

Story of the three bears. Jacobs, J.
In Jacobs, J. English fairy tales p93-98 **398.2**

The **story** of the three bears. Southey, R.
In The Classic fairy tales p201-05 **398.2**
In The Green fairy book p234-37 **398.2**

The **story** of the three bears. Steel, F. A. W.
In The Scott, Foresman anthology of children's literature p149-51 **808.8**

The **Story** of the three calenders, sons of kings, and of five ladies of Bagdad
In The Arabian nights entertainments p54-67 **398.2**

Story of the three little pigs. Jacobs, J.
In Jacobs, J. English fairy tales p63-72 **398.2**

The **story** of the treasure seekers [excerpt]. Nesbit, E.
In The Random House book of humor for children p195-204 **817.008**

The **Story** of the vizier who was punished
In The Arabian nights entertainments p34-47 **398.2**

The **story** of the women's movement. Ash, M. **305.4**

The **Story** of the young king of the Black Isles
In The Arabian nights entertainments p48-53 **398.2**

The **story** of the youth who went forth to learn what fear was. Grimm, J.
In Grimm, J. The complete Grimm's fairy tales p29-39 **398.2**

The **story** of Tom Thumb. Reeves, J.
In Reeves, J. English fables and fairy stories p63-70 **398.2**

The **story** of Tuan Mac Cairill. Stephens, J.
In Stephens, J. Irish fairy tales p4-32 **398.2**

The **Story** of two sisters who were jealous of their young sister
In The Arabian nights entertainments p390-424 **398.2**

The **story** of World War II. Graff, S. **940.54**

The **story** of World War II. Leckie, R. **940.53**

The **story** of your foot. Silverstein, A. **612**

The **story** of your hand. Silverstein, A. **612**

The **story** vine. Pellowski, A. **372.6**

The **storyteller**. Porte-Thomas, B. A.
In Porte-Thomas, B. A. Jesse's ghost, and other stories p1-13 **S C**

The **storyteller's** sourcebook. MacDonald, M. R. **398**

Storytelling
Baker, A. Storytelling: art and technique **372.6**
Bauer, C. F. Handbook for storytellers **372.6**
Carlson, B. W. Listen! and help tell the story **372.6**
Champlin, C. Storytelling with puppets **372.6**
Cook, E. The ordinary and the fabulous **028.5**
DeWit, D. Children's faces looking up **372.6**
Juba this and Juba that **372.6**
MacDonald, M. R. Twenty tellable tales **372.6**
MacDonald, M. R. When the lights go out **372.6**
Nichols, J. Storytimes for two-year-olds **027.62**
Pellowski, A. The family storytelling handbook **372.6**
Pellowski, A. The story vine **372.6**
Pellowski, A. The world of storytelling **372.6**
Sawyer, R. The way of the storyteller **372.6**
Shedlock, M. L. The art of the story-teller **372.6**
With a deep sea smile **372.6**
Ziskind, S. Telling stories to children **372.6**

See/See also pages in the following book(s):
Bauer, C. F. This way to books p1-59 **028.5**

Storytelling—*Continued*
Horn Book reflections on children's books and reading p293-341 **028.5**
Bibliography
Greene, E. Storytelling: a selected annotated bibliography **016.3726**
Storytelling: a selected annotated bibliography. Greene, E. **016.3726**
Storytelling: art and technique. Baker, A. **372.6**
Storytelling with puppets. Champlin, C. **372.6**
Storytimes for two-year-olds. Nichols, J. **027.62**

Stotter, Ruth
The hungry stranger
In Pellowski, A. The family storytelling handbook p126-29 **372.6**
The **stowaway**. Stevenson, J. **E**
Stowaway to the Mushroom Planet. Cameron, E. See note under Cameron, E. The wonderful flight to the Mushroom Planet **Fic**
Stowe, Harriet Beecher, 1811-1896
See/See also pages in the following book(s):
Jacobs, W. J. Great lives: human rights p73-79 (5 and up) **920**
The **strange** armadillo. Blassingame, W. **599.3**
Strange attractors. Sleator, W. **Fic**
The **strange** companions. Alcock, V.
In Alcock, V. Ghostly companions **S C**
A **strange** encounter. Terada, A. M.
In Terada, A. M. Under the starfruit tree p95-98 **398.2**
Strange events in the life of the Delmonico family: phone talk. Mahy, M.
In Mahy, M. Nonstop nonsense p70-74 **828**
Strange events in the life of the Delmonico family: the birthday present. Mahy, M.
In Mahy, M. Nonstop nonsense p6-13 **828**
Strange events in the life of the Delmonico family: trouble in the supermarket. Mahy, M.
In Mahy, M. Nonstop nonsense p40-44 **828**
Strange godfather
Grimm, J. Godfather Death
In Grimm, J. The complete Grimm's fairy tales p209-12 **398.2**
In Grimm, J. The juniper tree, and other tales from Grimm v2 p228-35 **398.2**
The **strange** musician. Grimm, J.
In Grimm, J. The complete Grimm's fairy tales p56-58 **398.2**
Strange visitor
Jacobs, J. The strange visitor
In Jacobs, J. English fairy tales p179-82 **398.2**
MacDonald, M. R. The strange visitor
In MacDonald, M. R. When the lights go out p133-42 **372.6**
The **stranger**. Van Allsburg, C. **E**
A **stranger** at Green Knowe. Boston, L. M. See note under Boston, L. M. The children of Green Knowe **Fic**
A **stranger** came ashore. Hunter, M. **Fic**
Strasser, Todd, 1950-
Fairy tale
In Connections: short stories by outstanding writers for young adults p123-36 **S C**
Stratemeyer, Edward, 1862-1930
See/See also pages in the following book(s):
Only connect: readings on children's literature p63-73 **028.5**
Straub, Cindie
Mime: basics for beginners (6 and up) **792.3**
Straub, Matthew
(jt. auth) Straub, C. Mime: basics for beginners **792.3**
Straus, Nathan, 1848-1931
See/See also pages in the following book(s):
Giblin, J. Milk: the fight for purity p44-58 (5 and up) **637**
Strauss, Levi, 1829-1902
About
Henry, S. Everyone wears his name: a biography of Levi Strauss (5 and up) **92**
Strauss, Lindy *See* Edwards, Linda
Straw, the coal, and the bean
Grimm, J. The straw, the coal, and the bean
In Grimm, J. The complete Grimm's fairy tales p102-03 **398.2**
In Grimm, J. More tales from Grimm p95-98 **398.2**
The Straw, the coal, and the bean
In The Tall book of nursery tales p90-91 **398.2**
Straw ox
The straw ox
In Tomie dePaola's favorite nursery tales p75-82 **398.2**
Strawberries
Fiction
Bang, M. The Grey Lady and the Strawberry Snatcher **E**

Strawberry girl. Lenski, L. **Fic**
Stray. Rylant, C.
In Rylant, C. Every living thing p42-47 **S C**
Stray cow
Cooper, S. The silver cow: a Welsh tale **398.2**
Streams to the river, river to the sea. O'Dell, S. **Fic**
Streatfeild, Mary Noel *See* Streatfeild, Noel, 1895-1986
Streatfeild, Noel, 1895-1986
Theatre shoes, or other people's shoes (5 and up) **Fic**
Thursday's child (4 and up) **Fic**
The **strength** of the hills. Graff, N. P. **630.1**
Strictly Puritan. Miller, H. L.
In Holiday plays round the year p83-90 **812.008**
String beans. Hurwitz, J.
In Bauer, C. F. Celebrations p65-67 **808.8**
String figures
Gryski, C. Cat's cradle, owl's eyes (4-6) **793.9**
Gryski, C. Many stars & more string games (4-6) **793.9**
Gryski, C. Super string games (4-6) **793.9**
See/See also pages in the following book(s):
Pellowski, A. The story vine p3-46 **372.6**
A **string** in the harp. Bond, N. **Fic**
Stringbean's trip to the shining sea. Williams, V. B. **E**
Strogart, Alexander
(il) Park, B. Maxie, Rosie, and Earl—partners in grime **Fic**
A **stroke** of luck. Dégh, L.
In Best-loved folktales of the world p457-59 **398.2**
Strong Hans
Grimm, J. Strong Hans
In Grimm, J. The complete Grimm's fairy tales p688-95 **398.2**
Strugnell, Ann
(il) Cameron, A. The stories Julian tells **Fic**
Stuart, Nik
(jt. auth) Murdock, T. Gymnastics **796.44**
Stuart, Wray *See* Stuart, Nik
Stuart-Clark, Christopher
(ed) The Oxford book of Christmas poems. See The Oxford book of Christmas poems **808.81**
Stuart Little. White, E. B. **Fic**
The **stubborn** wife. Afanas'ev, A. N.
In Afanas'ev, A. N. Russian fairy tales p280 **398.2**
Stubbs, G. T. (Gordon Thomas), 1928-
(ed) Only connect: readings on children's literature. See Only connect: readings on children's literature **028.5**
Stubbs, Gordon Thomas *See* Stubbs, G. T. (Gordon Thomas), 1928-
Stubis, Talivaldis
(il) Wyler, R. Spooky tricks **793.8**
Student thesaurus, Roget's. Schiller, A. **423**
Study, Method of
James, E. How to be school smart (5 and up) **371.3**
Sturla, the historian
In Shedlock, M. L. The art of the story-teller p161-64 **372.6**
Sturton, Hugh *See* Johnston, Hugh Anthony Stephen, 1913-1967
Stuyvesant, Peter, 1592-1672
Lobel, A. On the day Peter Stuyvesant sailed into town **E**
Stwertka, Albert
(jt. auth) Stwertka, E. Marijuana **616.86**
Stwertka, Eve
Marijuana (5 and up) **616.86**
Subject guide to Children's books in print **015.73**
Subject headings
Sears list of subject headings **025.4**
Subject index to Children's Magazines. See Children's Magazine Guide **051**
Subject index to poetry for children and young people, 1957-1975 **808.81**
Submarine exploration *See* Underwater exploration
Submarines
See also Nuclear submarines
Humble, R. U-boat (4 and up) **940.54**
Weiss, H. Submarines and other underwater craft (4 and up) **623.8**
See/See also pages in the following book(s):
Marrin, A. Victory in the Pacific p142-67 (6 and up) **940.54**
Fiction
Verne, J. Twenty thousand leagues under the sea (5 and up) **Fic**
Submarines and other underwater craft. Weiss, H. **623.8**
Submersibles
Johnson, R. L. Diving into darkness: a submersible explores the sea (4 and up) **551.46**
Weiss, H. Submarines and other underwater craft (4 and up) **623.8**

Substance abuse
See also Alcoholism; Drug abuse
Subways
Holman, F. Slake's limbo (6 and up) Fic
See/See also pages in the following book(s):
Macaulay, D. Underground p93-107 (4 and up) 624.1
Successful science projects. See Markle, S. The young scientist's guide to successful science projects 507.8
Succoth (Feast of Tabernacles) *See* Sukkoth
Sudan
Folklore
See Folklore—Sudan
Suffrage
See also Women—Suffrage
Sugar
See also Maple sugar
Sugaring time. Lasky, K. 633.6
Sugarman, Joan, 1917-
Snowflakes (4-6) 551.57
Sukarno *See* Soekarno, 1901-1970
Sukiennik, Adelaide Weir, 1938-
(jt. auth) Friedberg, J. B. Accept me as I am: best books of juvenile nonfiction on impairments and disabilities 016
Sukkoth
Chaikin, M. Shake a palm branch (3-6) 296.4
Sullivan, George, 1927-
All about football (4 and up) 796.332
Any number can play (3-6) 796
The art of base-stealing (5 and up) 796.357
Baseball kids (4 and up) 796.357
Better baseball for boys (4 and up) 796.357
Better basketball for boys (4 and up) 796.323
Better basketball for girls (4 and up) 796.323
Better bicycling for boys and girls (4 and up) 796.6
Better BMX riding and racing for boys and girls (4 and up) 796.6
Better football for boys (4 and up) 796.332
Better roller skating for boys and girls (4 and up) 796.2
Better soccer for boys and girls (4 and up) 796.334
Better swimming for boys and girls (4 and up) 797.2
Better tennis for boys and girls (4 and up) 796.342
Better weight training for boys (4 and up) 613.7
Better wrestling for boys (4 and up) 796.8
The day we walked on the moon (4 and up) 629.45
George Bush (5 and up) 92
Here come the monster trucks (3-6) 629.223
How the White House really works (5 and up) 975.3
Pitcher (3-6) 796.357
Quarterback (4 and up) 796.332
The Thunderbirds (4 and up) 797.5
Sullivan, Jo Mary, 1946-
Liberia—in pictures. See Liberia—in pictures 966.62
Sullivan, St. Clair Adams
Bats, butterflies, and bugs (3-5) 745.592
Sullivan, Steve
(il) Krensky, S. Who really discovered America? 970.01
Sultanate of Oman *See* Oman
Summer
Kurelek, W. A prairie boy's summer (3-5) 971.27
Markle, S. Exploring summer (4 and up) 508
Summer business. Martin, C. E. See note under Martin, C. E. Island winter E
Summer camps *See* Camps
Summer of my German soldier. Greene, B. Fic
The **summer** of the swans. Byars, B. C. Fic
Summer switch. Rodgers, M. See note under Rodgers, M. Freaky Friday Fic
A **summer** to die. Lowry, L. Fic
A **summer's** lease. Sachs, M. Fic
Sun
Asimov, I. How did we find out about sunshine? (5 and up) 523.7
Branley, F. M. The sun (k-3) 523.7
Gibbons, G. Sun up, sun down (1-3) 523.7
Lampton, C. The sun (4 and up) 523.7
Levasseur-Regourd, A.-C. Our sun and the inner planets (4-6) 523.7
Simon, S. The sun (1-4) 523.7
Eclipses
See Eclipses, Solar
Fiction
Ginsburg, M. Where does the sun go at night? E
Sun, the moon, and Crow Crowson
Afanas'ev, A. N. The Sun, the Moon, and the Raven
In Afanas'ev, A. N. Russian fairy tales p588-89 398.2

Sun (in religion, folklore, etc.) *See* Sun worship

Sun dogs and shooting stars. Branley, F. M. **523**

Sun horse, moon horse. Sutcliff, R. **Fic**

The **Sun,** the Moon, and the Raven. Afanas'ev, A. N.
In Afanas'ev, A. N. Russian fairy tales p588-89 **398.2**

The **sun,** the wind and the rain. Peters, L. W. **551.4**

Sun up, sun down. Gibbons, G. **523.7**

Sun worship
Baylor, B. The way to start a day (1-3) **291.4**

Suncoast Seabird Sanctuary (Fla.)
Scott, J. D. Orphans from the sea (4 and up) **639.9**

Sundials
Anno, M. Anno's sundial (4 and up) **529**

Sunken ships & treasure. Fine, J. C. **910.4**

Sunken treasure. Gibbons, G. **910.4**

Sunny days and sunny nights. Kerr, M. E.
In Connections: short stories by outstanding writers for young adults p218-26 **S C**

Sunrise. Leach, M.
In Leach, M. Whistle in the graveyard p108 **398.2**

Sunrise. Stanton, M.
In Herds of thunder, manes of gold p138-48 **808.8**

The **sun's** asleep behind the hill. Ginsburg, M. **E**

Sunshine. Ormerod, J. **E**

Sunshine makes the seasons. Branley, F. M. **525**

Super string games. Gryski, C. **793.9**

Super, super, superwords. McMillan, B. **422**

Superconductors and superconductivity
Asimov, I. How did we find out about superconductivity? (5 and up) **537.6**

Superduper Teddy. Hurwitz, J. **Fic**

Superdupers! really funny real words. Terban, M. **427**

Superfudge. Blume, J. See note under Blume, J. Tales of a fourth grade nothing **Fic**

The **superior** pet. Yep, L.
In Yep, L. The rainbow people p80-85 **398.2**

Superman (Comic strip)
See/See also pages in the following book(s):
Aaseng, N. The unsung heroes p53-59 (5 and up) **920**

Supernatural

Fiction

Fleischman, P. Graven images (6 and up) **S C**
Lively, P. Uninvited ghosts, and other stories (4 and up) **S C**
Porte-Thomas, B. A. Jesse's ghost, and other stories (5 and up) **S C**
Wiseman, D. Jeremy Visick (5 and up) **Fic**
Wrightson, P. Balyet (5 and up) **Fic**
Yolen, J. The faery flag (5 and up) **S C**

Poetry

Why am I grown so cold? (5 and up) **808.81**
Yolen, J. The faery flag (5 and up) **S C**

Supernovae
Branley, F. M. Superstar (3-6) **523.8**

Superpuppy: how to choose, raise, and train the best possible dog for you. Pinkwater, J. **636.7**

Supersaurus. Jacobs, F. **567.9**

Supersonic flight. Jefferis, D. **629.133**

Supersonic transport planes
Jefferis, D. Supersonic flight (4 and up) **629.133**

Superstar. Branley, F. M. **523.8**

Superstition
Perl, L. Don't sing before breakfast, don't sleep in the moonlight (4-6) **398**
Schwartz, A. Cross your fingers, spit in your hat: superstitions and other beliefs (4 and up) **398**

Fiction

Babbitt, N. Kneeknock Rise (4-6) **Fic**

Supreme Court (U.S.) *See* United States. Supreme Court

The **Supreme** Court. Greene, C. **347**

Sure hands, strong heart: the life of Daniel Hale Williams. Patterson, L. **92**

Surfboard to peril. Quackenbush, R. M. See note under Quackenbush, R. M. Express train to trouble **Fic**

Surfing

Fiction

Ormondroyd, E. Broderick **E**

Surprises (1-3) **811.008**

Surveying
See/See also pages in the following book(s):
Mango, K. N. Mapmaking p64-71 (4 and up) **526**

Survival (after airplane accidents, shipwrecks, etc.)
Fiction
Defoe, D. Robinson Crusoe (5 and up) **Fic**
Moeri, L. Save Queen of Sheba (4 and up) **Fic**
Steig, W. Abel's island (3-6) **Fic**
Taylor, T. The cay (5 and up) **Fic**
Wyss, J. D. The Swiss family Robinson (5 and up) **Fic**
The **survival** guide for kids with LD (learning differences). Fisher, G. L. **371.9**
Sutcliff, Rosemary, 1920-
Flame-colored taffeta (5 and up) **Fic**
Frontier Wolf (6 and up) **Fic**
The light beyond the forest (4 and up) **398.2**
The road to Camlann (4 and up) **398.2**
Sun horse, moon horse (5 and up) **Fic**
The sword and the circle (4 and up) **398.2**
See/See also pages in the following book(s):
Horn Book reflections on children's books and reading p122-27 **028.5**
Townsend, J. R. A sense of story p193-99 **028.5**
Suteev, V. (Vladimir)
Polushkin, M. Who said meow? **E**
Suteev, Vladimir *See* Suteev, V. (Vladimir)
Suteyev, V.
Ginsburg, M. The chick and the duckling **E**
Sutherland, Dorothy B.
Wales (4 and up) **942.9**
Sutherland, Zena, 1915-
Children and books **028.5**
Master James' nightmare
In The Scott, Foresman anthology of children's literature p378-83 **808.8**
(ed) The Best in children's books. See The Best in children's books **028.1**
(comp) The Scott, Foresman anthology of children's literature. See The Scott, Foresman anthology of children's literature **808.8**
Sutton, Richard
Car (4 and up) **629.222**
Suzuki, Masaharu
(il) Johnson, S. A. Potatoes **635**
(il) Johnson, S. A. Wheat **633.1**
Swahili language
Feelings, M. Jambo means hello **E**
Feelings, M. Moja means one **E**
Swallowed alive. San Souci, R.
In San Souci, R. Short & shivery p84-87 **398.2**
Swallows
Fiction
Politi, L. Song of the swallows **E**
Swamps *See* Marshes
Swan, Robert
Destination: Antarctica (4-6) **998**
Swan lake. Fonteyn, Dame M. **Fic**
Swan maiden
Pyle, H. Swan maiden
In Pyle, H. The wonder clock p229-40 **398.2**
Swann, Brian
A basket full of white eggs (k-3) **398.6**
Swans
Scott, J. D. Swans (4 and up) **598**
Fiction
Andersen, H. C. The ugly duckling (1-4) **Fic**
White, E. B. The trumpet of the swan (3-6) **Fic**
Swanson, June
I pledge allegiance (2-4) **323.6**
Swanson, Maggie
(il) Hillerich, R. L. The American Heritage picture dictionary **423**
Sweat, Lynn, 1934-
(il) Pellowski, A. The family storytelling handbook **372.6**
(il) Pellowski, A. The story vine **372.6**
(il) Scott, A. H. One good horse **E**
Sweden
Fiction
Beskow, E. Pelle's new suit **E**
Lindgren, A. Pippi Longstocking (3-6) **Fic**
Nilsson, U. If you didn't have me (3-5) **Fic**
Folklore
See Folklore—Sweden
Swedish Americans
Fiction
Sandin, J. The long way westward **E**
Swedish authors *See* Authors, Swedish
Swedish literature
See/See also pages in the following book(s):
Crosscurrents of criticism p248-60 **028.5**
Sweet, Melissa
(il) Howe, J. Pinky and Rex **E**
Sweet, Ozzie, 1918-
(il) Scott, J. D. Alligator **597.9**
(il) Scott, J. D. Orphans from the sea **639.9**
(il) Scott, J. D. Swans **598**
Sweet and sour. Kendall, C. **398.2**
Sweet porridge. Grimm, J.
In Grimm, J. The complete Grimm's fairy tales p475-76 **398.2**
In Grimm, J. More tales from Grimm p43-46 **398.2**

Sweetheart. Le Prince de Beaumont, Madame.
In Sleeping beauty & other favourite fairy tales p113-24 **398.2**

Sweetheart Roland. Grimm, J.
In Grimm, J. The complete Grimm's fairy tales p268-71 **398.2**

Sweetwater. Yep, L. **Fic**

Swift, Hildegarde Hoyt, d. 1977
The little red lighthouse and the great gray bridge **E**

A **swiftly** tilting planet. L'Engle, M. See note under L'Engle, M. A wrinkle in time **Fic**

Swimming
Sullivan, G. Better swimming for boys and girls (4 and up) **797.2**
Fiction
Kessler, L. P. Last one in is a rotten egg **E**
Lasky, K. Sea swan **E**

Swimmy. Lionni, L. **E**

Swineherd
Andersen, H. C. The swineherd **Fic**
also in Andersen, H. C. Hans Andersen: his classic fairy tales p32-37 **S C**
also in The Classic fairy tales p232-35 **398.2**
also in Shedlock, M. L. The art of the story-teller p235-42 **372.6**
also in The Yellow fairy book p249-53 **398.2**
Thane, A. The swineherd
In Thane, A. Plays from famous stories and fairy tales p169-79 **812**

The **Swiss** family Robinson. Wyss, J. D. **Fic**

Switch on, switch off. Berger, M. **537**

Switcharound. Lowry, L. **Fic**

Switzerland
Fiction
Spyri, J. Heidi (4 and up) **Fic**

The **sword** and the circle. Sutcliff, R. **398.2**

The **sword** in the stone [excerpt]. White, T. H.
In The Random House book of humor for children p212-34 **817.008**

The **sword** in the tree. Bulla, C. R. **Fic**

Sylvain and Jocosa. Caylus, A. C. P. de T., comte de.
In The Green fairy book p56-63 **398.2**

Sylvester and the magic pebble. Steig, W. **E**
also in The Read-aloud treasury p112-34 **808.8**

Sylvie and Bruno. Carroll, L.
In Carroll, L. The complete works of Lewis Carroll p251-456 **828**

Sylvie and Bruno concluded. Carroll, L.
In Carroll, L. The complete works of Lewis Carroll p457-674 **828**

Symbol art. Fisher, L. E. **302.2**

Symbols *See* Signs and symbols

Symbols, a silent language. Adkins, J. **302.2**

Symes, R. F.
Rocks & minerals (4 and up) **549**

Syria
Beaton, M. Syria (4 and up) **956.91**
Lye, K. Take a trip to Syria (1-3) **956.91**
Syria—in pictures (5 and up) **956.91**
Syria—in pictures (5 and up) **956.91**

Szilagyi, Mary
Thunderstorm **E**
(il) Rylant, C. Night in the country **E**
(il) Rylant, C. This year's garden **E**

Szold, Henrietta, 1860-1945
About
Kustanowitz, S. E. Henrietta Szold: Israel's helping hand (4 and up) **92**

T

Taback, Simms, 1932-
(il) McGovern, A. Too much noise **398.2**
(il) McMullan, K. Snakey riddles **793.73**

Tabernacles, Feast of *See* Sukkoth

Table, the ass and the stick
Grimm, J. The wishing-table, the gold-ass, and the cudgel in the sack
In Grimm, J. The complete Grimm's fairy tales p177-87 **398.2**
Grimm, J. The wishing table, the gold donkey, and the cudgel-in-the sack
In Grimm, J. More tales from Grimm p99-115 **398.2**
Jacobs, J. The ass, the table, and the stick
In Jacobs, J. English fairy tales p206-10 **398.2**
Reeves, J. The donkey, the table, and the stick
In Reeves, J. English fables and fairy stories p195-210 **398.2**

Table etiquette
Giblin, J. From hand to mouth (4 and up) **394.1**

Tableware
Cobb, V. Feeding yourself (1-3) **394.1**

Tableware—*Continued*
Giblin, J. From hand to mouth (4 and up) **394.1**
Tackle without a team. Christopher, M. **Fic**
Tadjo, Véronique, 1955-
Lord of the dance (1-3) **398.2**
Tadpoles *See* Frogs
Tafuri, Nancy
The ball bounced **E**
Do not disturb **E**
Early morning in the barn **E**
Follow me! **E**
Have you seen my duckling? **E**
Rabbit's morning **E**
Spots, feathers, and curly tails (k-2) **636**
(il) Pomerantz, C. All asleep **811**
(il) Pomerantz, C. Flap your wings and try **E**
(il) Pomerantz, C. If I had a paka: poems in eleven languages **811**
(il) Shannon, G. The Piney Woods peddler **E**
T'ai chi ch'üan
See/See also pages in the following book(s):
Ribner, S. The martial arts p121-39 (5 and up) **796.8**
Tail feathers from Mother Goose (k-2) **398.8**
Tailor in heaven
Grimm, J. The tailor in heaven
In Grimm, J. The complete Grimm's fairy tales p175-77 **398.2**
Grimm, J. The tailor who went to Heaven
In Grimm, J. More tales from Grimm p117-22 **398.2**
The **tailor** of Gloucester. Potter, B. **E**
The **tailor** who went to Heaven. Grimm, J.
In Grimm, J. More tales from Grimm p117-22 **398.2**
Tailoring

Fiction

Potter, B. The tailor of Gloucester **E**
Taily-po
Galdone, J. The tailypo **398.2**
Lester, J. Taily-po
In Lester, J. Further tales of Uncle Remus p70-77 **398.2**
San Souci, R. Tailypo
In San Souci, R. Short & shivery p58-61 **398.2**
'Tain't so. Leach, M.
In Leach, M. Whistle in the graveyard p34-37 **398.2**
Taitz, Emily
Israel (4 and up) **956.94**
(jt. auth) Henry, S. Everyone wears his name: a biography of Levi Strauss **92**
Take a nap, Harry. Chalmers, M. See note under Chalmers, M. Throw a kiss, Harry **E**
Take a trip to Iran. Tames, R. **955**
Take a trip to Iraq. Tames, R. **956.7**
Take a trip to Israel. Rutland, J. **956.94**
Take a trip to Lebanon. Tames, R. **956.92**
Take a trip to Morocco. Lye, K. **964**
Take a trip to Saudi Arabia. Lye, K. **953.8**
Take a trip to Syria. Lye, K. **956.91**
Take a trip to Turkey. Lye, K. **956.1**
The **take-along** dog. Porte-Thomas, B. A. **E**
Take another look. Hoban, T. **E**
Take joy! The Tasha Tudor Christmas book **394.2**
Take sky: more rhymes of the never was and always is. McCord, D. T. W. **811**
Takedown. Christopher, M. **Fic**
Taking a walk/caminando: a book in two languages. Emberley, R. **463**
Taking care of Carruthers. Marshall, J. See note under Marshall, J. Yummers! **E**
Taking care of Terrific. Lowry, L. **Fic**
Taking care of your dog. Pope, J. **636.7**
Taking care of your fish. Pope, J. **639.3**
Taking care of your gerbils. Pope, J. **636.088**
Taking care of your mice and rats. Pope, J. **636.088**
Taking care of your rabbit. Pope, J. **636.088**
Taking my cat to the vet. Kuklin, S. **636.8**
Taking my dog to the vet. Kuklin, S. **636.7**
Tal Niv's kibbutz. See Taylor, A. A kibbutz in Israel **956.94**
The **tale** of a youth who set out to learn what fear was. Grimm, J.
In The Blue fairy book p86-95 **398.2**
The **tale** of Benjamin Bunny. Potter, B. See note under Potter, B. The tale of Peter Rabbit **E**
The **tale** of Jemima Puddle-duck. Potter, B. **E**
The **tale** of Mr. Jeremy Fisher. Potter, B. **E**
The **tale** of Mr. Tod. Potter, B. See note under Potter, B. The tale of Peter Rabbit **E**
The **tale** of Mrs. Tiggy-Winkle. Potter, B. **E**

The **tale** of Mrs. Tittlemouse. Potter, B. **E**

The **tale** of Peter Rabbit. Potter, B. **E**

The **tale** of Pigling Bland. Potter, B. **E**

The **tale** of Squirrel Nutkin. Potter, B. **E**

The **tale** of the flopsy bunnies. Potter, B. See note under Potter, B. The tale of Peter Rabbit **E**

The **tale** of the golden vase and the bright monkeys. Jagendorf, M. A.
In The Scott, Foresman anthology of children's literature p326-27 **808.8**

The **tale** of the hungry skunk. Mayo, G.
In Mayo, G. Star tales p39-40 **398.2**

The **tale** of the mandarin ducks. Paterson, K. **398.2**

The **tale** of the Oki Islands. Protter, E.
In Best-loved folktales of the world p512-16 **398.2**

A **tale** of the pie and the patty-pan. See Potter, B. The pie and the patty-pan **E**

The **tale** of the three wishes. Le Prince de Beaumont, Madame.
In The Classic fairy tales p153-55 **398.2**

The **tale** of Thomas Mead. Hutchins, P. **E**

A **tale** of three Ralphs. Minkowitz, M.
In Free to be—a family p20-22 **810.8**

A **tale** of three wishes. Singer, I. B.
In Singer, I. B. Stories for children p8-14 **S C**

The **tale** of Timmy Tiptoes. Potter, B. **E**

The **tale** of Tom Kitten. Potter, B. See note under Potter, B. The story of Miss Moppet **E**

The **tale** of two bad mice. Potter, B. **E**

Talent is not enough. Hunter, M. **808.06**

Tales from Gold Mountain. Yee, P. **S C**

Tales from Grimm. Grimm, J. **398.2**

Tales from Shakespeare. Lamb, C. **822.3**

Tales from the enchanted world. Williams-Ellis, A. **398.2**

Tales from the roof of the world. Timpanelli, G. **398.2**

Tales mummies tell. Lauber, P. **930.1**

Tales of a Chinese grandmother. Carpenter, F. **398.2**

Tales of a fourth grade nothing. Blume, J. **Fic**

Tales of a fourth grade nothing [excerpt]. Blume, J.
In The Random House book of humor for children p3-14 **817.008**

Tales of a long afternoon. Bolliger, M. **398.2**

Tales of Amanda Pig. Van Leeuwen, J. See note under Van Leeuwen, J. Tales of Oliver Pig **E**

Tales of love and terror. Rochman, H. **028**

The **tales** of Olga da Polga. Bond, M. **Fic**
also in Bond, M. The complete adventures of Olga da Polga p5-128 **Fic**

Tales of Oliver Pig. Van Leeuwen, J. **E**

Tales of the Far North. Martin, E. **398.2**

Tales of the paddock. Grimm, J.
In Grimm, J. The complete Grimm's fairy tales p480-82 **398.2**

The **tales** of Uncle Remus. Lester, J. **398.2**

Taliesin

Fiction

Bond, N. A string in the harp (6 and up) **Fic**

Talismans *See* Charms

Talk

Courlander, H. Talk
In Best-loved folktales of the world p613-15 **398.2**
In Courlander, H. The cow-tail switch, and other West African stories p25-30 **398.2**

Talk. Porte-Thomas, B. A.
In Porte-Thomas, B. A. Jesse's ghost, and other stories p73-88 **S C**

Talking books

Bibliography

For younger readers: braille and talking books **011.6**

The **talking** cat. Carlson, N. S.
In Best-loved folktales of the world p688-94 **398.2**
In Carlson, N. S. The talking cat, and other stories of French Canada p17-29 **S C**

The **talking** cat, and other stories of French Canada. Carlson, N. S. **S C**

The **talking** cooter. Hamilton, V.
In Hamilton, V. The people could fly: American black folktales p151-55 **398.2**

The **talking** eggs. San Souci, R. **398.2**

The **talking** house. Lester, J.
In Lester, J. The tales of Uncle Remus p68-69 **398.2**

The **Talking** mule
In The Diane Goode book of American folk tales and songs p13-15 **398.2**
The **talking** pot. Hatch, M. C.
In The Scott, Foresman anthology of children's literature p225-27 **808.8**
The **talking** taniwha of Rotorua. Te Kanawa, K.
In Te Kanawa, K. Land of the long white cloud p51-60 **398.2**
Talking to the sun: an illustrated anthology of poems for young people **808.81**
The **talking** tree. Rayevsky, I. **398.2**
The **Tall** book of nursery tales (k-2) **398.2**

Tall Cornstalk
Tall cornstalk
In Grandfather tales p186-94 **398.2**

Tall tales
Day, E. C. John Tabor's ride **E**
Dewey, A. The narrow escapes of Davy Crockett **E**
Kellogg, S. Paul Bunyan (k-3) **398.2**
Kellogg, S. Pecos Bill (k-3) **398.2**
Rounds, G. The morning the sun refused to rise **E**
Rounds, G. Washday on Noah's ark **E**
Schwartz, A. Whoppers (4 and up) **398.2**
Stamm, C. Three strong women (k-3) **398.2**

Tallyho, Pinkerton! Kellogg, S. See note under Kellogg, S. Pinkerton, behave! **E**
Tam and Cam. Terada, A. M.
In Terada, A. M. Under the starfruit tree p23-34 **398.2**
Tam Lin. Yolen, J. **398.2**

Tamarin, Alfred
(jt. auth) Glubok, S. Olympic games in ancient Greece **796.48**

Tambourines! Tambourines to glory! (3-6) **242**

Tames, Richard
The 1950s (6 and up) **909.82**
Take a trip to Iran (1-3) **955**
Take a trip to Iraq (1-3) **956.7**
Take a trip to Lebanon (1-3) **956.92**

The **taming** of Bucephalus. Coville, B.
In Herds of thunder, manes of gold p65-70 **808.8**

Taming of the shrew
Afanas'ev, A. N. The taming of the shrew
In Afanas'ev, A. N. Russian fairy tales p161-62 **398.2**

Tamlane
Jeffers, S. Wild Robin **E**
Williams-Ellis, A. Tamlane
In Williams-Ellis, A. Tales from the enchanted world p151-59 **398.2**
Yolen, J. Tam Lin **398.2**

Tamura, David
(il) Byers, R. M. Mycca's baby **E**

A **tangled** tale. Carroll, L.
In Carroll, L. The complete works of Lewis Carroll p882-969 **828**

Tannenbaum, Beulah
Making and using your own weather station (5 and up) **551.6**

Tannenbaum, Harold E.
(jt. auth) Tannenbaum, B. Making and using your own weather station **551.6**

A **Taoist** priest
In Best-loved folktales of the world p526-28 **398.2**

Tappin, the land turtle. Hamilton, V.
In Hamilton, V. The people could fly: American black folktales p20-25 **398.2**

Tar-baby
Harris, J. C. The wonderful tar-baby story
In Best-loved folktales of the world p666-68 **398.2**
In The Scott, Foresman anthology of children's literature p377-78 **808.8**
MacDonald, M. R. The rabbit and the well
In MacDonald, M. R. Twenty tellable tales p126-41 **372.6**

Taran Wanderer. Alexander, L. See note under Alexander, L. The book of three **Fic**

Tarantulas
See/See also pages in the following book(s):
Thomson, P. Auks, rocks and the odd dinosaur p89-93 (5 and up) **508**

Tarawa, Battle of, 1943
See/See also pages in the following book(s):
Marrin, A. Victory in the Pacific p121-37 (6 and up) **940.54**

Targ-Brill, Marlene
Libya (4 and up) **961.2**

Tarma. Fort, M. R.
In Where angels glide at dawn p67-75 **S C**

Tashjian, Virginia A.
The clever thieves
In The Scott, Foresman anthology of children's literature p279 **808.8**
The foolish man
In The Scott, Foresman anthology of children's literature p277-79 **808.8**
(comp) With a deep sea smile. See With a deep sea smile **372.6**

Tashlik. Singer, I. B.
In Singer, I. B. Stories for children p322-31 **S C**

Taste
Parker, S. Touch, taste and smell (4 and up) **612.8**

A **taste** of blackberries. Smith, D. B. **Fic**

Tate, Eleanora E., 1948-
Just an overnight guest (4-6) **Fic**

Tatham, Campbell *See* Elting, Mary, 1909-

Tattercoats
Jacobs, J. Tattercoats **398.2**
also in The Scott, Foresman anthology of children's literature p155-57 **808.8**
Reeves, J. Tattercoats
In Reeves, J. English fables and fairy stories p11-22 **398.2**

Tattie's river journey. Murphy, S. R. **E**

The **tattooed** potato and other clues. Raskin, E. **Fic**

The **tavern** at the ferry. Tunis, E. **973.2**

Taxi. Maestro, B. **E**

Taxi to intrigue. Quackenbush, R. M. See note under Quackenbush, R. M. Express train to trouble **Fic**

Taylor, Allegra
A kibbutz in Israel (3-5) **956.94**

Taylor, Barbara, 1954-
Bouncing and bending light (3-5) **535**
Color and light (3-5) **535**

Taylor, Elizabeth A.
(jt. auth) Armbruster, A. Tornadoes **551.55**

Taylor, Judy, 1932-
Beatrix Potter: artist, storyteller and countrywoman **92**

Taylor, Liba
(il) Bennett, O. A family in Egypt **962**

Taylor, Mark
Henry the explorer **E**
The love crystal
In The Scott, Foresman anthology of children's literature p338-40 **808.8**

Taylor, Mildred D.
The friendship. See note under Taylor, M. D. Song of the trees **Fic**
The gold Cadillac (3-5) **Fic**
Let the circle be unbroken. See note under Taylor, M. D. Song of the trees **Fic**
Mississippi bridge. See note under Taylor, M. D. Song of the trees **Fic**
The road to Memphis. See note under Taylor, M. D. Song of the trees **Fic**
Roll of thunder, hear my cry (4 and up) **Fic**
Song of the trees (4 and up) **Fic**
See/See also pages in the following book(s):
Newbery and Caldecott Medal books, 1976-1985 p21-34 **028.5**

Taylor, Paul D. (Paul Durnford), 1952-
Fossil (4 and up) **560**

Taylor, Richard L., d. 1982
The first flight (4 and up) **629.13**

Taylor, Sydney, 1904-
All-of-a-kind family (4-6) **Fic**
All-of-a-kind family downtown. See note under Taylor, S. All-of-a-kind family **Fic**
All-of-a-kind family uptown. See note under Taylor, S. All-of-a-kind family **Fic**
Ella of all of a kind family. See note under Taylor, S. All-of-a-kind family **Fic**
More all-of-a-kind family. See note under Taylor, S. All-of-a-kind family **Fic**

Taylor, Tamar
(il) Bate, L. How Georgina drove the car very carefully from Boston to New York **E**

Taylor, Theodore, 1921 or 2-
Air raid—Pearl Harbor! (5 and up) **940.54**
Battle in the Arctic seas (5 and up) **940.54**
The cay (5 and up) **Fic**

Tayzanne
In The Magic orange tree, and other Haitian folktales p57-63 **398.2**

Tchaikovsky, Peter Ilich, 1840-1893
Klein, N. Baryshnikov's Nutcracker **792.8**

Te Kanawa, Kiri
Land of the long white cloud (3-6) **398.2**

Contents: The birth of Maui; Maui and the Great Fish; Maui tames the Sun; Kupe's discovery of Aotearoa; Hinemoa and Tutanekai; Kahukura and the fairies; The talking taniwha of Rotorua; Te Kanawa and the visitors by firelight; Mataora and Niwareka in the Underworld; The enchanted hunting-ground; The trees of the forest; Lake Te Anau; Hotu-puku; Putawai; Rona and the legend of the moon; Hutu and Pare; The ground parrot and the albatross; Kakariki and kaka; Maui and the birds

Te Kanawa and the visitors by firelight. Te Kanawa, K.
In Te Kanawa, K. Land of the long white cloud p61-66 **398.2**

The **tea** server from heaven. Terada, A. M.
In Terada, A. M. Under the starfruit tree p83-87 **398.2**

Teach us, Amelia Bedelia. Parish, P. See note under Parish, P. Amelia Bedelia **E**

A **teacher** on roller skates and other school riddles. Adler, D. A. 793.73
Teachers
Shreve, S. R. The flunking of Joshua T. Bates (3-5) Fic
Fiction
Allard, H. Miss Nelson is missing! E
Danziger, P. The cat ate my gymsuit (5 and up) Fic
Howe, J. The day the teacher went bananas E
Naylor, P. R. The agony of Alice (5 and up) Fic
Peck, R. N. Arly (5 and up) Fic
Sachs, M. A summer's lease (5 and up) Fic
Teacher's pet. Hurwitz, J. See note under Hurwitz, J Class clown Fic
Teaching
See also Education
Teammates [biography of Jackie Robinson]. Golenbock, P. 92
Technology
Cooper, C. How everyday things work (5 and up) 600
Folsom, M. The Macmillan book of how things work (4 and up) 600
Macaulay, D. The way things work (5 and up) 600
Bibliography
Kennedy, D. M. Science & technology in fact and fiction: a guide to children's books 016.5
Dictionaries
The New book of popular science 503
Periodicals
3-2-1 Contact 505
Tecumseh, Shawnee Chief, 1768-1813
About
Shorto, R. Tecumseh and the dream of an American Indian nation (5 and up) 92
Tecumseh and the dream of an American Indian nation. Shorto, R. 92
The **teddy** bear book. Marzollo, J. 811
Teddy bears
Fiction
Butler, D. My brown bear Barney E
Freeman, D. Beady Bear E
Freeman, D. Corduroy E
Freeman, D. A pocket for Corduroy E
Gretz, S. Teddy bears go shopping E
Ormondroyd, E. Theodore E
Ormondroyd, E. Theodore's rival E
Stevenson, J. The night after Christmas E
Wells, R. Peabody E
Poetry
Marzollo, J. The teddy bear book (k-2) 811
Teddy bears 1 to 10. Gretz, S. See note under Gretz, S. Teddy bears go shopping E
Teddy bears ABC. Gretz, S. See note under Gretz, S. Teddy bears go shopping E
Teddy bears at the seaside. Gretz, S. See note under Gretz, S. Teddy bears go shopping E
Teddy bears cure a cold. Gretz, S. See note under Gretz, S. Teddy bears go shopping E
Teddy bears go shopping. Gretz, S. E
Teddy bears' moving day. Gretz, S. See note under Gretz, S. Teddy bears go shopping E
Teddy bears stay indoors. Gretz, S. See note under Gretz, S. Teddy bears go shopping E
Teddy bears take the train. Gretz, S. See note under Gretz, S. Teddy bears go shopping E
Teenagers *See* Youth
Teenagers, Runaway *See* Runaway children
Teenagers and alcohol *See* Youth—Alcohol use
Teenchy-Tiny Duck's magical satchel. Lester, J.
In Lester, J. Further tales of Uncle Remus p142-48 398.2
Teeny-Tiny
Jacobs, J. Teeny-Tiny
In Best-loved folktales of the world p219-20 398.2
In Jacobs, J. English fairy tales p57-58 398.2
Rockwell, A. F. Teeny-tiny
In Rockwell, A. F. The three bears & 15 other stories p78-80 398.2
Teeny tiny. Bennett, J. 398.2
Teeny-Tiny and the witch-woman. Walker, B. K.
In Walker, B. K. A treasury of Turkish folktales for children p49-51 398.2
The **teeny-tiny** woman. Galdone, P. 398.2
The **teeny** tiny woman. Seuling, B. 398.2
Teeth
Ward, B. R. Dental care (4 and up) 617.6
Fiction
Birdseye, T. Airmail to the moon E
McPhail, D. M. The bear's toothache E
The **teeth**. Schwartz, A.
In Schwartz, A. In a dark, dark room, and other scary stories p10-17 398.2

Tehanu. Le Guin, U. K. See note under Le Guin, U. K. A wizard of Earthsea **Fic**

Tejima, Keizaburō
Fox's dream **E**
Owl lake **E**

Telekinesis *See* Psychokinesis

Telephone
Fiction
Wells, R. Good night, Fred **E**

Telescope
See also Hubble Space Telescope
Hidden worlds (5 and up) **500**
See/See also pages in the following book(s):
Simon, S. Look to the night sky: an introduction to star watching (4 and up) **523**

Television
See/See also pages in the following book(s):
Bauer, C. F. Celebrations p211-26 **808.8**
Production and direction
Scott, E. Ramona: behind the scenes of a television show (4 and up) **791.45**

Television actors and actresses *See* Actors and actresses

Television and children
Fiction
Byars, B. C. The TV kid (4-6) **Fic**

Television broadcasting
See/See also pages in the following book(s):
Bauer, C. F. Handbook for storytellers p212-24 **372.6**
Burns, M. I am not a short adult! p75-92 (3-6) **305.23**

Television in the snow. Rettich, M.
In Bauer, C. F. Celebrations p218-20 **808.8**

Tell me a Mitzi. Segal, L. G. **E**

Tell me a story, Mama. Johnson, A. **E**

Tell me a Trudy. Segal, L. G. **E**

Tell me some more. Bonsall, C. N. **E**

Telling fortunes. Schwartz, A. **133.3**

The **telling** of a tale. Brooke, W. J.
In Brooke, W. J. A telling of the tales: five stories p111-32 **S C**

A **telling** of the tales: five stories. Brooke, W. J. **S C**

Telling stories to children. Ziskind, S. **372.6**

Temperature
Maestro, B. Temperature and you (1-3) **536**
See/See also pages in the following book(s):
Asimov, I. How did we find out about superconductivity? p7-24 (5 and up) **537.6**

Temperature and you. Maestro, B. **536**

Temple, Shirley *See* Black, Shirley Temple, 1928-

The **temporary** death of Molly Swett. Roach, M. K.
In Roach, M. K. Encounters with the invisible world **S C**

Ten black dots. Crews, D. **E**

Ten copycats in a boat, and other riddles. Schwartz, A. **398.6**

Ten in a bed. Ahlberg, A. **Fic**

Ten jugs of wine. Kendall, C.
In Kendall, C. Sweet and sour p18-20 **398.2**

Ten, nine, eight. Bang, M. **E**

Ten potatoes in a pot, and other counting rhymes (k-2) **398.8**

Tenant and landlord *See* Landlord and tenant

Tenggren, Gustaf, 1896-1970
(il) Hawthorne, N. A wonder-book, and Tanglewood tales **292**

Tennant, Pamela
The water nixie
In Shedlock, M. L. The art of the story-teller p198-203 **372.6**

Tennessee
McNair, S. Tennessee
In America the beautiful **973**
Description
Allen, T. B. On Granddaddy's farm (1-3) **630.1**
Fiction
Moser, B. The tinderbox **Fic**

Tenniel, Sir John, 1820-1914
(il) Carroll, L. Alice's adventures in Wonderland **Fic**
(il) Carroll, L. Alice's adventures in Wonderland, and Through the looking glass **Fic**
(il) Carroll, L. The complete works of Lewis Carroll **828**
(il) Carroll, L. Through the looking glass, and what Alice found there **Fic**

Tennis
Sullivan, G. Better tennis for boys and girls (4 and up) **796.342**

The **tenth** good thing about Barney. Viorst, J. **E**

Teotihuacán site (San Juan Teotihuacán, Mexico)
Fisher, L. E. Pyramid of the sun, pyramid of the moon (4 and up) **972**

Terada, Alice M.
They ran to me
In Terada, A. M. Under the starfruit tree p126 **398.2**

Terada, Alice M.—*Continued*
Under the starfruit tree (4-6) **398.2**
Stories included are: Under the starfruit tree; How the tiger got its stripes; The jealous husband; The snake princess; Mister Thirty; Tam and Cam; The Da Trang crab; The scholar Be; The war between gods; How the Dao people came to be; The worm and the snail; Eyes of marriage; How the gecko came to be; Truong Ba and the butcher's skin; The general; The tea server from heaven; Trial in the dragon's palace; A strange encounter; The story of Le Nuong; Rice cakes for the new year; Two brothers; The lady of stone; The magic crossbow; They ran to me; Just one ghost; The grateful tombstone; The musician

Terban, Marvin
The dove dove (3-6) **793.73**
Guppies in tuxedos: funny eponyms (3-5) **422**
Mad as a wet hen! and other funny idioms (3-5) **427**
Punching the clock: funny action idioms (3-6) **427**
Superdupers! really funny real words (3-5) **427**

Tereshichka. Afanas'ev, A. N.
In Afanas'ev, A. N. Russian fairy tales p389-93 **398.2**

Terezin (Czechoslovakia: Concentration camp)
I never saw another butterfly **741.9**

Terkel, Susan Neiburg, 1948-
Feeling safe, feeling strong (4 and up) **362.7**

Termites
See/See also pages in the following book(s):
Kohl, J. Pack, band, and colony (5 and up) **591.5**

The **terrible** black snake's revenge. Uchida, Y.
In Bauer, C. F. Celebrations p172-76 **808.8**

The **Terrible** Head. Lang, A.
In The Blue fairy book p182-92 **398.2**

Terrible leak. Uchida, Y.
In Uchida, Y. The magic listening cap **398.2**

The **terrible** thing that happened at our house. Blaine, M. **E**

Terris, Susan
Author! Author! (6 and up) **Fic**

Terry and the caterpillars. Selsam, M. E. **595.7**

Terwillegar, Jane C.
(jt. auth) Miller, R. E. Commonsense cataloging **025.3**

Tessendorf, K. C.
Barnstormers & daredevils (4 and up) **629.13**

Testa, Fulvio, 1947-
If you look around you (k-3) **516**
If you take a paintbrush **E**
If you take a pencil **E**

Teta, Jon A.
Iran—in pictures. See Iran—in pictures **955**
Iraq—in pictures. See Iraq—in pictures **956.7**
Pakistan—in pictures. See Pakistan—in pictures **954.91**

Teutonic peoples
See/See also pages in the following book(s):
Lyttle, R. B. Land beyond the river p36-50 (6 and up) **940.1**

Texas
Stein, R. C. Texas
In America the beautiful **973**

Fiction

Baylor, B. The best town in the world **E**
Gipson, F. B. Old Yeller (6 and up) **Fic**
Jones, W. Edge of two worlds (5 and up) **Fic**

History

Fisher, L. E. The Alamo (4 and up) **976.4**

Texas trail to calamity. Quackenbush, R. M. See note under Quackenbush, R. M. Express train to trouble **Fic**

Textile industry

History

Macaulay, D. Mill (4 and up) **690**

Thailand
Jacobsen, K. Thailand (2-4) **959.3**
McNair, S. Thailand (4 and up) **959.3**

Social life and customs

Stewart, J. Elephant school (4-6) **636.088**

Thaler, Mike, 1936-
Owly **E**

Thane, Adele
A Christmas carol
In The Big book of Christmas plays p277-97 **808.82**
Little Cosette and Father Christmas
In The Big book of Christmas plays p313-31 **808.82**
Plays from famous stories and fairy tales (4-6) **812**
Contents: The Emperor's nightingale; The Pied Piper of Hamelin; Aladdin and his wonderful lamp; Rumpelstiltskin; Tom Sawyer, pirate; The elves and the shoemaker; Dummling and the golden goose; The three wishes; The saucy scarecrow; King Alfred and the cakes; The apple of contentment; The swineherd; Rapunzel; The magic nutmeg-grater; Christmas every day; The twelve dancing princesses; Puss in boots; The reluctant dragon; The little princess; The sleeping beauty; Heidi; Hansel and Gretel; Pinocchio goes to school; Jack and the magic beanstalk; Rip Van Winkle; The brave little tailor; Dick Whittington and his cat; Cinderella

Thank you, Amelia Bedelia. Parish, P. See note under Parish, P. Amelia Bedelia **E**

Thank you, Jackie Robinson. Cohen, B. Fic

Thanks be to God 242

Thanks to butter-fingers. Gotwalt, H. L. M.
In Gotwalt, H. L. M. Special plays for holidays p39-53 812

The **Thanksgiving** book. Penner, L. R. 394.2

Thanksgiving Day
Anderson, J. The first Thanksgiving feast (3-5) 974.4
Barkin, C. Happy Thanksgiving! (4-6) 394.2
Barth, E. Turkeys, Pilgrims, and Indian corn (3-6) 394.2
Bartlett, R. M. Thanksgiving Day (1-3) 394.2
Dalgliesh, A. The Thanksgiving story (k-2) 974.4
Gibbons, G. Thanksgiving Day (k-2) 394.2
Penner, L. R. The Thanksgiving book (5 and up) 394.2
Shachtman, T. Parade! E
See/See also pages in the following book(s):
Bauer, C. F. Celebrations p241-48 808.8

Fiction

Alcott, L. M. An old-fashioned Thanksgiving (3-5) Fic
Bunting, E. How many days to America? E
Cohen, B. Molly's Pilgrim (2-4) Fic
Kroll, S. One tough turkey E

Poetry

Child, L. M. F. Over the river and through the wood (k-2) 811
Prelutsky, J. It's Thanksgiving (1-3) 811
Thanksgiving poems (k-3) 808.81

Thanksgiving Day. Fisher, D. C.
In Bauer, C. F. Celebrations p243-48 808.8

Thanksgiving poems (k-3) 808.81

The **Thanksgiving** story. Dalgliesh, A. 974.4

Tharlet, Eve
(il) Andersen, H. C. The princess and the pea Fic

That dreadful day. Stevenson, J. See note under Stevenson, J. "Could be worse!" E

That Julia Redfern. Cameron, E. See note under Cameron, E. A room made of windows Fic

That snake in the grass. Hess, L. 597.9

That terrible Halloween night. Stevenson, J. See note under Stevenson, J. "Could be worse!" E

Thayer, Ernest Lawrence, 1863-1940
Casey at the bat 811

Thayer, Jane, 1904-
The popcorn dragon E
The puppy who wanted a boy E
also in Diane Goode's American Christmas p31-37 810.8
also in The Family read-aloud Christmas treasury p22-25 808.8

Theater

Production and direction

See also Motion pictures—Production and direction

Theatre shoes, or other people's shoes. Streatfeild, N. Fic

Theatrical costume *See* Costume

The **theft** of fire. Curry, J. L.
In Curry, J. L. Back in the beforetime p33-41 398.2

The **theft** of fire. Leekley, T.
In Best-loved folktales of the world p712-18 398.2

Thelen, Mary
(il) Broekel, R. Hocus pocus: magic you can do 793.8

Then again, maybe I won't. Blume, J. Fic

Theodore. Ormondroyd, E. E

Theodore's rival. Ormondroyd, E. E

Therapeutics

See also Pet therapy

There is a carrot in my ear, and other noodle tales. Schwartz, A. 398.2

There once was a time. Ventura, P. 909

There's a bat in bunk five. Danziger, P. Fic

There's a hole in the bucket (k-2) 781.62

There's a nightmare in my closet. Mayer, M. E

There's an alligator under my bed. Mayer, M. E

There's nothing to do! Stevenson, J. See note under Stevenson, J. "Could be worse!" E

Thermal waters *See* Geothermal resources

Thermometers and thermometry
Maestro, B. Temperature and you (1-3) 536

These happy golden years. Wilder, L. I. See note under Wilder, L. I. Little house in the big woods Fic

These small stones (3-5) 808.81

Theseus (Greek mythology)
Fisher, L. E. Theseus and the Minotaur (1-3) 292
Hutton, W. Theseus and the Minotaur (3-5) 292

Theseus (Greek mythology)—*Continued*
See/See also pages in the following book(s):
Colum, P. The Golden Fleece and the heroes who lived before Achilles p219-44 (5 and up) **292**
Hamilton, E. Mythology p209-23 (6 and up) **292**
Theseus and the Minotaur. Fisher, L. E. **292**
Theseus and the Minotaur. Hutton, W. **292**
They dance in the sky: native American star myths. Monroe, J. G. **398.2**
They live in the sky: stories of the California Indians. Monroe, J. G.
In Monroe, J. G. They dance in the sky p79-94 **398.2**
They ran to me. Terada, A. M.
In Terada, A. M. Under the starfruit tree p126 **398.2**
They sought a new world. Kurelek, W. **325**
They've discovered a head in the box for the bread, and other laughable limericks (4 and up) **821.008**
The **thief**. Afanas'ev, A. N.
In Afanas'ev, A. N. Russian fairy tales p590-93 **398.2**
Thief and his master
Grimm, J. The thief and his master
In Grimm, J. The complete Grimm's fairy tales p337-38 **398.2**
The **thief** who kept his hands clean. Kendall, C.
In Kendall, C. Sweet and sour p30-32 **398.2**
Thiele, Colin, 1920-
Farmer Schulz's ducks **E**
Shadow shark (5 and up) **Fic**
Thievery. Kendall, C.
In Kendall, C. Sweet and sour p78-79 **398.2**
Thimble summer. Enright, E. **Fic**
Things I like. Browne, A. **E**
Things that go. Rockwell, A. F. **629.04**
Things that go bump in the night (5 and up) **S C**
Things that go grump in the night. Waters, E.
In Things that go bump in the night p25-37 **S C**
Things to play with. Rockwell, A. F. **793**
Thinking *See* Thought and thinking
Thinking big. Kuklin, S. **362.4**
Third book of junior authors **920.003**
Third Calender
The Story of the third calender, son of a king
In The Arabian nights entertainments p102-21 **398.2**
Third dream: the price of magic. Gorog, J.
In Gorog, J. Three dreams and a nightmare, and other tales of the dark **S C**
Thirteen. Charlip, R. **E**
Thirteen ways to sink a sub. Gilson, J. See note under Gilson, J. 4B goes wild **Fic**
Thirteenth son of the king of Erin
The Thirteenth son of the King of Erin
In Best-loved folktales of the world p247-55 **398.2**
This book is about time. Burns, M. **529**
This delicious day (5 and up) **811.008**
This is the house where Jack lives. Heilbroner, J. **E**
This little nose. Ormerod, J. See note under Ormerod, J. Bend and stretch **E**
This little pig-a-wig, and other rhymes about pigs (k-2) **398.8**
This one and that one. Sanfield, S.
In Sanfield, S. The adventures of High John the Conqueror **398.2**
This place is wet. Cobb, V. **574.5**
This time, Tempe Wick? Gauch, P. L. **Fic**
This way to books. Bauer, C. F. **028.5**
This year's garden. Rylant, C. **E**
Thomas, à Becket, Saint, Archbishop of Canterbury, 1118?-1170
See/See also pages in the following book(s):
Brooks, P. S. Queen Eleanor: independent spirit of the medieval world p82-86, 90-95 (6 and up) **92**
Thomas, Barbara Ann Porte- *See* Porte-Thomas, Barbara Ann
Thomas, Dylan, 1914-1953
A child's Christmas in Wales (5 and up) **828**
Thomas, Jane Resh, 1936-
The comeback dog (3-5) **Fic**
Saying good-bye to Grandma **E**
Thomas, Marlo
Free to be—a family. See Free to be—a family **810.8**
Free to be—you and me. See Free to be—you and me **810.8**

Thomas, Rebecca L.
Primaryplots 028

Thomas, W. Jenkyn (William Jenkyn)
Arthur in the cave
In Shedlock, M. L. The art of the story-teller p173-78 372.6

Thomas, William Jenkyn *See* Thomas, W. Jenkyn (William Jenkyn)

Thomas and Clem. Stevenson, J.
In Stevenson, J. Fast friends p38-64 E

Thomas Berennikov
Afanas'ev, A. N. Foma Berennikov
In Afanas'ev, A. N. Russian fairy tales p284-87 398.2

Thompson, Carol
Time E
(il) Grindley, S. I don't want to! E

Thompson, Sally Anne
(il) Pope, J. Taking care of your dog 636.7
(il) Pope, J. Taking care of your fish 639.3
(il) Pope, J. Taking care of your gerbils 636.088
(il) Pope, J. Taking care of your mice and rats 636.088
(il) Pope, J. Taking care of your rabbit 636.088

Thomson, Peggy, 1922-
Auks, rocks and the odd dinosaur (5 and up) 508
Keepers and creatures at the National Zoo (5 and up) 590.74

Thoreau, Henry David, 1817-1862
About
Burleigh, R. A man named Thoreau (3-5) 92
Stern, P. V. D. Henry David Thoreau: writer and rebel (5 and up) 92

Thorn Rose, the sleeping beauty. Grimm, J.
In Grimm, J. More tales from Grimm p31-41 398.2

Thorndike, Edward L. (Edward Lee), 1874-1949
Scott, Foresman intermediate dictionary. See Scott, Foresman intermediate dictionary 423
Thorndike-Barnhart children's dictionary. See Thorndike-Barnhart children's dictionary 423

Thorndike-Barnhart children's dictionary (3-5) 423

Thorndike-Barnhart intermediate dictionary. See Scott, Foresman intermediate dictionary 423

Thorndike century beginning dictionary. See Thorndike-Barnhart children's dictionary 423

Thornhill, Jan
The wildlife 1 2 3 E

Thornton, Jane Foster
Santa's magic hat
In The Big book of Christmas plays p253-62 808.82

Thought and thinking
See also Logic; Perception
Burns, M. The book of think (4 and up) 153.4

The **Thoughtless** abbot
In Best-loved folktales of the world p158-60 398.2

Thousand and one nights *See* Arabian nights

Thousand-Furs. Grimm, J.
In Best-loved folktales of the world p126-31 398.2

Thousand nights and a night *See* Arabian nights

Threatened species *See* Endangered species

Three-0. MacLachlan, P.
In MacLachlan, P. Tomorrow's wizard p32-41 S C

Three Aesop fox fables. Galdone, P. 398.2

The **three** apprentices. Grimm, J.
In Grimm, J. The complete Grimm's fairy tales p542-45 398.2

Three apprentices and the devil
Grimm, J. The three apprentices
In Grimm, J. The complete Grimm's fairy tales p542-45 398.2

Three army surgeons
Grimm, J. The three army-surgeons
In Grimm, J. The complete Grimm's fairy tales p535-38 398.2

Three bears
Brett, J. Goldilocks and the three bears 398.2
Crossley-Holland, K. Goldilocks and the three bears
In Crossley-Holland, K. British folk tales p135-39 398.2
Galdone, P. The three bears 398.2
Goldilocks and the three bears
In The Read-aloud treasury p214-24 808.8
Jacobs, J. Story of the three bears
In Jacobs, J. English fairy tales p93-98 398.2
Jacobs, J. The three bears
In Tomie dePaola's favorite nursery tales p55-61 398.2
Marshall, J. Goldilocks and the three bears 398.2
Oxenbury, H. Goldilocks and the three bears
In Oxenbury, H. The Helen Oxenbury nursery story book p6-12 398.2

Three bears—*Continued*
Rockwell, A. F. The three bears
In Rockwell, A. F. The three bears & 15 other stories p1-13 **398.2**
Southey, R. The story of the three bears
In The Classic fairy tales p201-05 **398.2**
In The Green fairy book p234-37 **398.2**
Steel, F. A. W. The story of the three bears
In The Scott, Foresman anthology of children's literature p149-51 **808.8**
The Three bears
In The Baby's story book p6-11 **398.2**
In The Tall book of nursery tales p37-45 **398.2**
The **three** bears & 15 other stories. Rockwell, A. F. **398.2**
The **three** bears rhyme book. Yolen, J. **811**
Three big sillies
In The Tall book of nursery tales p98-104 **398.2**
Three billy goats gruff
Asbjørnsen, P. C. The three billy goats gruff
In Best-loved folktales of the world p326-27 **398.2**
In The Scott, Foresman anthology of children's literature p227-28 **808.8**
In Tomie dePaola's favorite nursery tales p42-45 **398.2**
Galdone, P. The three Billy Goats Gruff **398.2**
Oxenbury, H. The three billy goats gruff
In Oxenbury, H. The Helen Oxenbury nursery story book p54-57 **398.2**
Rockwell, A. F. The three billy goats Gruff
In Rockwell, A. F. The three bears & 15 other stories p56-62 **398.2**
The Three Billy goats gruff
In The Baby's story book p48-51 **398.2**
In The Read-aloud treasury p84-88 **808.8**
In The Tall book of nursery tales p46-48 **398.2**
Three black princesses
Grimm, J. The three black princesses
In Grimm, J. The complete Grimm's fairy tales p620-21 **398.2**
Three blind mice, The complete story of the. Ivimey, J. W. **E**
The **three** blows. Crossley-Holland, K.
In Crossley-Holland, K. British folk tales p353-64 **398.2**
Three boys with jugs of molasses and secret ambitions. Sandburg, C.
In Sandburg, C. Rootabaga stories pt 1 p92-101 **S C**
In Sandburg, C. The Sandburg treasury p46-51 **818**
Three brothers
Grimm, J. The three brothers
In Grimm, J. The complete Grimm's fairy tales p561-62 **398.2**
In Grimm, J. Tales from Grimm p171-78 **398.2**
The Three brothers
In The Yellow fairy book p134-37 **398.2**
The **three** brothers and the hand of fate. Walker, B. K.
In Walker, B. K. A treasury of Turkish folktales for children p23-28 **398.2**
Three by the sea. Marshall, E. **E**
Three Calenders, sons of kings and five ladies of Bagdad
The Story of the three calenders, sons of kings, and of five ladies of Bagdad
In The Arabian nights entertainments p54-67 **398.2**
Three copecks
Afanas'ev, A. N. The three pennies
In Afanas'ev, A. N. Russian fairy tales p113-14 **398.2**
Three days on a river in a red canoe. Williams, V. B. **E**
Three dogs
Bechstein, L. The three dogs
In The Green fairy book p360-66 **398.2**
Three dreams and a nightmare, and other tales of the dark. Gorog, J. **S C**
The **three** dwarfs. Grimm, J.
In The Red fairy book p238-45 **398.2**
The **three** fairies. Carter, D. S.
In The Scott, Foresman anthology of children's literature p398-99 **808.8**
Three feathers
Grimm, J. The three feathers
In Grimm, J. About wise men and simpletons p58-61 **398.2**
In Grimm, J. The complete Grimm's fairy tales p319-22 **398.2**
In Grimm, J. The juniper tree, and other tales from Grimm v1 p3-10 **398.2**
Three Fridays
Kelsey, A. G. Three Fridays
In The Scott, Foresman anthology of children's literature p293-94 **808.8**

The **Three** girls with the journey-cakes
In The Diane Goode book of American folk tales and songs p43-51 **398.2**
The **three** golden hairs. Martin, E.
In Martin, E. Tales of the Far North p29-38 **398.2**
Three grains of rice: from the bones of an Arab folktale. Gorog, J.
In Gorog, J. Three dreams and a nightmare, and other tales of the dark **S C**
The **three** green twigs. Grimm, J.
In Grimm, J. The complete Grimm's fairy tales p823-25 **398.2**
The **Three** hares
In Best-loved folktales of the world p497-99 **398.2**
A **three** hat day. Geringer, L. **E**
Three heads of the well
Crossley-Holland, K. Three heads of the well
In Crossley-Holland, K. British folk tales p28-35 **398.2**
Jacobs, J. Three heads of the well
In Jacobs, J. English fairy tales p222-27 **398.2**
The King of Colchester's daughter
In The Classic Fairy tales p159-61 **398.2**
Reeves, J. The well of the three heads
In Reeves, J. English fables and fairy stories p115-26 **398.2**
Three jovial huntsmen. Jeffers, S. **398.8**
The **three** kingdoms. Afanas'ev, A. N.
In Afanas'ev, A. N. Russian fairy tales p49-53 **398.2**
Three kingdoms—the copper, the silver, and the golden
Afanas'ev, A. N. The three kingdoms, copper, silver, and golden
In Afanas'ev, A. N. Russian fairy tales p375-87 **398.2**
Three languages
Grimm, J. The three languages
In Grimm, J. The complete Grimm's fairy tales p169-71 **398.2**
In Grimm, J. More tales from Grimm p89-94 **398.2**
Three little birds
Grimm, J. The three little birds
In Grimm, J. The complete Grimm's fairy tales p445-49 **398.2**
Three little crones each with something big
Calvino, I. And seven!
In The Scott, Foresman anthology of children's literature p260-62 **808.8**
Three little eggs
Berger, T. The three little eggs
In Berger, T. Black fairy tales p79-90 **398.2**
Three little kittens. Galdone, P. **398.8**
Three little men in the wood
Grimm, J. The three dwarfs
In The Red fairy book p238-45 **398.2**
Grimm, J. The three little men in the wood
In Grimm, J. The complete Grimm's fairy tales p78-83 **398.2**
Three little pigs
Galdone, P. The three little pigs **398.2**
Hooks, W. H. The three little pigs and the fox **398.2**
Jacobs, J. Story of the three little pigs
In Jacobs, J. English fairy tales p63-72 **398.2**
Jacobs, J. The three little pigs
In Tomie dePaola's favorite nursery tales p34-38 **398.2**
Marshall, J. The three little pigs **398.2**
Oxenbury, H. The three little pigs
In Oxenbury, H. The Helen Oxenbury nursery story book p25-31 **398.2**
Rockwell, A. F. The three little pigs
In Rockwell, A. F. The three bears & 15 other stories p81-91 **398.2**
Scieszka, J. The true story of the three little pigs **398.2**
Three little pigs
In The Baby's story book p56-60 **398.2**
In The Green fairy book p100-05 **398.2**
In The Read-aloud treasury p144-55 **808.8**
In The Tall book of nursery tales p110-16 **398.2**
Zemach, M. The three little pigs **398.2**
The **three** little pigs and the fox. Hooks, W. H. **398.2**
Three little pigs and the ogre
Pyle, H. Three little pigs and the ogre
In Pyle, H. The wonder clock p241-51 **398.2**
Three little pigs and their mother
Old sow and the three shoats
In Grandfather tales p81-87 **398.2**
The **three** lucky ones. Grimm, J.
In Grimm, J. More tales from Grimm p189-96 **398.2**
The **Three** Magi. Belpré, P.
In The Family read-aloud Christmas treasury p82-89 **808.8**
Three magic oranges. Osma, L. de.
In Best-loved folktales of the world p756-60 **398.2**

Three Mile Island Nuclear Power Plant (Pa.)
See/See also pages in the following book(s):
Pringle, L. P. Nuclear energy: troubled past, uncertain future p30-44 (5 and up) **621.48**

Three musicians
Bechstein, L. The three musicians
In The Green fairy book p353-59 **398.2**

The **three** pennies. Afanas'ev, A. N.
In Afanas'ev, A. N. Russian fairy tales p113-14 **398.2**

Three princesses of Whiteland
Moe, J. E. The three princesses of Whiteland
In The Red fairy book p175-81 **398.2**

The **three** robbers. Ungerer, T. **E**

Three sillies
Galdone, P. The three sillies **398.2**
Jacobs, J. Three sillies
In Jacobs, J. English fairy tales p9-14 **398.2**
Three big sillies
In The Tall book of nursery tales p98-104 **398.2**

Three sisters
The Story of two sisters who were jealous of their young sister
In The Arabian nights entertainments p390-424 **398.2**
Williams-Ellis, A. The three sisters
In Williams-Ellis, A. Tales from the enchanted world p125-30 **398.2**

Three sisters trapped in a mountain
Asbjørnsen, P. C. The three sisters who were entrapped into a mountain
In Womenfolk and fairy tales p156-63 **398.2**

The **three** sisters who were entrapped into a mountain. Asbjørnsen, P. C.
In Womenfolk and fairy tales p156-63 **398.2**

Three sluggards
Grimm, J. The three sluggards
In Grimm, J. The complete Grimm's fairy tales p647 **398.2**

Three snake leaves
Grimm, J. The three snake-leaves
In The Green fairy book p296-99 **398.2**
In Grimm, J. The complete Grimm's fairy tales p94-97 **398.2**

The **three** sons of fortune. Grimm, J.
In Grimm, J. The complete Grimm's fairy tales p342-44 **398.2**

The **three** spinners. Grimm, J.
In Grimm, J. The complete Grimm's fairy tales p83-86 **398.2**
In Grimm, J. More tales from Grimm p131-37 **398.2**

Three spinning fairies
Grimm, J. The three spinners
In Grimm, J. The complete Grimm's fairy tales p83-86 **398.2**
In Grimm, J. More tales from Grimm p131-37 **398.2**

Three strong women. Riordan, J.
In Riordan, J. The woman in the moon, and other tales of forgotten heroines p59-68 **398.2**

Three strong women. Stamm, C. **398.2**
also in Womenfolk and fairy tales p93-105 **398.2**

Three sunsets and other poems. Carroll, L.
In Carroll, L. The complete works of Lewis Carroll p849-78 **828**

Three tests for the prince. Uchida, Y.
In Uchida, Y. The magic listening cap **398.2**

Three tricksters and the pot of butter. Walker, B. K.
In Walker, B. K. A treasury of Turkish folktales for children p88-90 **398.2**

Three two one. See 3-2-1 Contact **505**

Three up a tree. Marshall, J. See note under Marshall, E. Three by the sea **E**

Three wise men (Magi) *See* Magi

The **Three** wishes
In Best-loved folktales of the world p220-21 **398.2**
In The Tall book of nursery tales p85-89 **398.2**

The **three** wishes. Thane, A.
In Thane, A. Plays from famous stories and fairy tales p120-29 **812**

The **three** wishes. Zemach, M. **398.2**

Three wishes [short story]. Clifton, L.
In Free to be—you and me p114-18 **810.8**

Three wonderful beggars
Afanas'ev, A. N. Marco the Rich and Vasily the Luckless
In Afanas'ev, A. N. Russian fairy tales p213-20 **398.2**

Thrift *See* Saving and thrift

Through moon and stars and night skies. Turner, A. W. **E**

Through the hidden door. Wells, R. **Fic**

Through the looking glass, and what Alice found there. Carroll, L. **Fic**
also in Carroll, L. The complete works of Lewis Carroll p121-249 **828**

Throw a kiss, Harry. Chalmers, M. E
Throw Mountains. Courlander, H.
In Courlander, H. The cow-tail switch, and other West African stories p113-18 **398.2**
Throwing shadows. Konigsburg, E. L. **S C**
Throwing things away. Pringle, L. P. **363.7**
Thumb, Tom, 1838-1883
See/See also pages in the following book(s):
Drimmer, F. Born different p14-47 (6 and up) **920**
Thumbelina
Andersen, H. C. Inchelina
In Andersen, H. C. Hans Andersen: his classic fairy tales p178-[88] **S C**
Andersen, H. C. Thumbelina
In The Yellow fairy book p279-90 **398.2**
Andersen, H. C. Thumbeline **Fic**
Andersen, H. C. Tommelise
In The Classic fairy tales p221-29 **398.2**
Ehrlich, A. Thumbelina
In Ehrlich, A. The Random House book of fairy tales p194-205 **398.2**
Thumbling
Grimm, J. Thumbling
In Grimm, J. The complete Grimm's fairy tales p187-93 **398.2**
Grimm, J. Thumbling's travels
In Grimm, J. The complete Grimm's fairy tales p212-16 **398.2**
Grimm, J. Tom Thumb
In Best-loved folktales of the world p104-09 **398.2**
Thumbling's travels. Grimm, J.
In Grimm, J. The complete Grimm's fairy tales p212-16 **398.2**
Thunder and his helpers. Marriott, A. L.
In Marriott, A. L. American Indian mythology **398.2**
Thunder and Lightnings. Mark, J. **Fic**
Thunder cake. Polacco, P. **E**
Thunderbirds *See* United States. Air Force. Thunderbirds
The **Thunderbirds**. Sullivan, G. **797.5**
Thunderstorm. Szilagyi, M. **E**
Thunderstorms
Branley, F. M. Flash, crash, rumble, and roll (k-3) **551.5**
Fiction
Polacco, P. Thunder cake **E**
Stolz, M. Storm in the night **E**
Szilagyi, M. Thunderstorm **E**
Thurber, James, 1894-1961
Many moons (1-4) **Fic**
The moth and the star
In The Random House book of humor for children p93-94 **817.008**
Thursday's child. Streatfeild, N. **Fic**
Thy friend, Obadiah. Turkle, B. C. See note under Turkle, B. C. Obadiah the Bold **E**
Ti-Jean and the unicorn. Martin, E.
In Martin, E. Tales of the Far North p101-06 **398.2**
Ti-Jean and the white cat. Martin, E.
In Martin, E. Tales of the Far North p113-20 **398.2**
Ti-Jean brings home the moon. Martin, E.
In Martin, E. Tales of the Far North p107-12 **398.2**
Tibet (China)
Fiction
Gerstein, M. The mountains of Tibet **E**
Folklore
See Folklore—Tibet (China)
Tic tac toe, and other three-in-a row games from ancient Egypt to the modern computer. Zaslavsky, C. **794**
Tick, tick, tick. Leach, M.
In Leach, M. Whistle in the graveyard p79 **398.2**
Ticks
See also Lyme disease
Ticky-Picky Boom-Boom. Sherlock, Sir P. M.
In Sherlock, Sir P. M. Anansi, the spider man p76-83 **398.2**
Tiddalick the frog. Nunes, S. **398.2**
Tides
Fiction
Bowden, J. C. Why the tides ebb and flow (k-2) **398.2**
Tidings of joy. Paterson, K.
In Paterson, K. Angels & other strangers: family Christmas stories p40-48 **S C**
Tiegreen, Alan, 1935-
(il) Anna Banana: 101 jump-rope rhymes. See Anna Banana: 101 jump-rope rhymes **398.8**
(il) Cole, J. Asking about sex and growing up **613.9**
(il) Miss Mary Mack and other children's street rhymes. See Miss Mary Mack and other children's street rhymes **796.1**
(il) Smith, D. B. Kelly's creek **Fic**
(il) Smith, R. K. Bobby Baseball **Fic**
Tien
(il) Moore, C. C. The night before Christmas **811**
Tiger, Steven
Diabetes (5 and up) **616.4**

Tiger and Anancy meet for war. Berry, J.
In Berry, J. Spiderman Anancy p34-35 **398.2**

Tiger and the Stump-a-foot Celebration Dance. Berry, J.
In Berry, J. Spiderman Anancy p45-53 **398.2**

A **tiger** called Thomas. Zolotow, C. **E**

Tiger in the forest, Anansi in the web. Sherlock, Sir P. M.
In The Scott, Foresman anthology of children's literature p392-93 **808.8**
In Sherlock, Sir P. M. West Indian folktales p59-64 **398.2**

Tiger story, Anansi story. Sherlock, Sir P. M.
In Sherlock, Sir P. M. West Indian folktales p45-58 **398.2**

The **Tiger,** the Brahman, and the jackal
In Best-loved folktales of the world p580-83 **398.2**

"**Tiger!** Tiger!". Kipling, R.
In Kipling, R. The jungle books **S C**

Tiger trek. Lewin, T. **599.74**

Tigers
Ashby, R. Tigers (4-6) **599.74**
Lavine, S. A. Wonders of tigers (4 and up) **599.74**
Lewin, T. Tiger trek (2-4) **599.74**

Fiction

Spagnoli, C. Nine-in-one, Grr! Grr! (k-2) **398.2**

The **tiger's** whisker. Courlander, H.
In Best-loved folktales of the world p558-60 **398.2**

Tikki Tikki Tembo. Mosel, A. **398.2**

Till Eulenspiegel *See* Eulenspiegel

Tim O'Toole and the wee folk. McDermott, G. **E**

Time
See also Day; Night
Anno, M. Anno's sundial (4 and up) **529**
Burns, M. This book is about time (5 and up) **529**
McMillan, B. Time to— (k-2) **529**

Fiction

Thompson, C. Time **E**

Time. Courlander, H.
In Courlander, H. The cow-tail switch, and other West African stories p73-78 **398.2**

Time. Thompson, C. **E**

Time and Mr. Bass. Cameron, E. See note under Cameron, E. The wonderful flight to the Mushroom Planet **Fic**

Time and space *See* Space and time

The **time** and space of Uncle Albert. Stannard, R. **Fic**

Time for ferrets. Hess, L. **636.08**

The **time** garden. Eager, E. See note under Eager, E. Half magic **Fic**

Time-Life Books
Andry, A. C. How babies are made **612.6**

Time of my life: Jill Trenary. Trenary, J. **92**

Time of wonder. McCloskey, R. **E**

Time to—. McMillan, B. **529**

Time to get out of the bath, Shirley. Burningham, J. **E**

A **time** to keep: the Tasha Tudor book of holidays. Tudor, T. **394.2**

Time trouble. Lively, P.
In Lively, P. Uninvited ghosts, and other stories p64-74 **S C**

Timid hare
Shedlock, M. L. The folly of panic
In Shedlock, M. L. The art of the story-teller p222-24 **372.6**
Shedlock, M. L. The hare that ran away
In The Scott, Foresman anthology of children's literature p341 **808.8**

Timo and the Princess Vendla
Bowman, J. C. Timo and the Princess Vendla
In The Scott, Foresman anthology of children's literature p249-51 **808.8**

Timothy goes to school. Wells, R. **E**

Timpanelli, Gioia
Tales from the roof of the world (4-6) **398.2**
Contents: The boy, his sisters, and the magic horse; The daughter and the helper; The unwilling musician; The girl who was already queen

Tin Lizzie. Spier, P. **E**

The **tin** woodsman of Oz. Baum, L. F. See note under Baum, L. F. The Wizard of Oz **Fic**

Tina Gogo. Angell, J. **Fic**

Tinder box
Andersen, H. C. The tinder box
In Best-loved folktales of the world p358-64 **398.2**
In The Classic fairy tales p207-15 **398.2**
In The Yellow fairy book p265-73 **398.2**
Andersen, H. C. The tinderbox
In Andersen, H. C. Hans Andersen: his classic fairy tales p11-18 **S C**
Moser, B. The tinderbox **Fic**

The **tinder** box. Andersen, H. C.
In Andersen, H. C. Hans Andersen: his classic fairy tales p11-18 **S C**
In Best-loved folktales of the world p358-64 **398.2**
Ting Lan and the lamb
Carpenter, F. Ting Lan and the lamb
In Carpenter, F. Tales of a Chinese grandmother p66-71 **398.2**
Tinkelman, Murray, 1933-
(il) Dinosaurs: poems. See Dinosaurs: poems **811.008**
Tinker and the ghost
Hancock, S. Esteban and the ghost **398.2**
MacDonald, M. R. The tinker and the ghost
In MacDonald, M. R. When the lights go out p69-78 **372.6**
Tiny god. Uchida, Y.
In Uchida, Y. The magic listening cap **398.2**
The **tipi:** a center of native American life. Yue, D. **728**
The **tired** ghost. Leach, M.
In Leach, M. Whistle in the graveyard p48-49 **398.2**
Tisquantum *See* Squanto, d. 1622
Tit for tat
Tit for tat
In Best-loved folktales of the world p595-96 **398.2**
Titanic (Steamship)
Ballard, R. D. Exploring the Titanic (4 and up) **910.4**
Titch. Hutchins, P. **E**
Titherington, Jeanne, 1951-
Pumpkin, pumpkin **E**
(il) Prelutsky, J. It's snowing! It's snowing! **811**
Titty Mouse and Tatty Mouse
Jacobs, J. Titty Mouse and Tatty Mouse
In Jacobs, J. English fairy tales p77-80 **398.2**
Tituba
Fiction
Petry, A. L. Tituba of Salem Village (6 and up) **Fic**
Tituba of Salem Village. Petry, A. L. **Fic**
Titus, Eve
Basil and the lost colony. See note under Titus, E. Basil of Baker Street **Fic**
Basil and the pygmy cats. See note under Titus, E. Basil of Baker Street **Fic**
Basil in Mexico. See note under Titus, E. Basil of Baker Street **Fic**
Basil in the Wild West. See note under Titus, E. Basil of Baker Street **Fic**
Basil of Baker Street (3-5) **Fic**
TMI Nuclear Power Plant (Pa.) *See* Three Mile Island Nuclear Power Plant (Pa.)
To be a slave. Lester, J. **326**
To Grandmother's house we go. Roberts, W. D. **Fic**
To market! To market! (k-2) **398.8**
To ride the sea of grass. Roberson, J.
In Herds of thunder, manes of gold p157-76 **808.8**
To space & back. Ride, S. K. **629.45**
To the green mountains. Cameron, E. **Fic**
To your good health!
To your good health!
In The Scott, Foresman anthology of children's literature p287-89 **808.8**
In Shedlock, M. L. The art of the story-teller p183-90 **372.6**
Toad and Hawk
In The Monkey's haircut, and other stories told by the Maya p136-37 **398.2**
Toad food & measle soup. McDonnell, C. **Fic**
A **toad** for Tuesday. Erickson, R. E. **Fic**
Toad is the uncle of heaven. Lee, J. M. **398.2**
Toads
Parker, N. W. Frogs, toads, lizards, and salamanders (k-3) **597.6**
Fiction
Gage, W. Mike's toads **Fic**
Erickson, R. E. A toad for Tuesday (2-4) **Fic**
Lee, J. M. Toad is the uncle of heaven (k-3) **398.2**
Lobel, A. Frog and Toad are friends **E**
Yolen, J. Commander Toad in space **E**
Toads and diamonds. Perrault, C.
In The Blue fairy book p274-77 **398.2**
In The Scott, Foresman anthology of children's literature p199-200 **808.8**
Tobacco. Seixas, J. S. **616.86**
Tobias, Tobi
Arthur Mitchell (2-5) **92**
The **Toboggan-to-the-moon** dream of the Potato Face Blind Man. Sandburg, C.
In Sandburg, C. Rootabaga stories pt 1 p46-50 **S C**
In Sandburg, C. The Sandburg treasury p29-30 **818**
Todd, Justin, 1932-
(il) Carroll, L. Through the looking glass, and what Alice found there **Fic**

Tog the Ribber; or, Granny's tale. Coltman, P. 821
Together. Lyon, G. E. E
Toilet training
Cole, J. Your new potty 649
Tolkien, J. R. R. (John Ronald Reuel), 1892-1973
The hobbit (4 and up) Fic
Tolkien, John Ronald Reuel *See* Tolkien, J. R. R. (John Ronald Reuel), 1892-1973
Toltecs
See also Aztecs
Fisher, L. E. Pyramid of the sun, pyramid of the moon (4 and up) 972
Tom and Pippo and the dog. Oxenbury, H. See note under Oxenbury, H. Pippo gets lost E
Tom and Pippo and the washing machine. Oxenbury, H. See note under Oxenbury, H. Pippo gets lost E
Tom and Pippo go for a walk. Oxenbury, H. See note under Oxenbury, H. Pippo gets lost E
Tom and Pippo go shopping. Oxenbury, H. See note under Oxenbury, H. Pippo gets lost E
Tom and Pippo in the garden. Oxenbury, H. See note under Oxenbury, H. Pippo gets lost E
Tom and Pippo in the snow. Oxenbury, H. See note under Oxenbury, H. Pippo gets lost E
Tom and Pippo make a friend. Oxenbury, H. See note under Oxenbury, H. Pippo gets lost E
Tom and Pippo make a mess. Oxenbury, H. See note under Oxenbury, H. Pippo gets lost E
Tom and Pippo read a story. Oxenbury, H. See note under Oxenbury, H. Pippo gets lost E
Tom and Pippo see the moon. Oxenbury, H. See note under Oxenbury, H. Pippo gets lost E
Tom and Pippo's day. Oxenbury, H. See note under Oxenbury, H. Pippo gets lost E
Tom Glazer's Christmas songbook 782.28
Tom Glazer's Treasury of folk songs. See Glazer, T. Tom Glazer's Treasury of songs for children 782.42
Tom Glazer's Treasury of songs for children. Glazer, T. 782.42
Tom Sawyer, pirate. Thane, A.
In Thane, A. Plays from famous stories and fairy tales p77-89 812
Tom Thumb (Folk tale)
Crossley-Holland, K. The history of Tom Thumb
In Crossley-Holland, K. British folk tales p155-74 398.2
The History of Tom Thumb
In The Classic fairy tales p33-46 398.2
Jacobs, J. History of Tom Thumb
In Jacobs, J. English fairy tales p140-47 398.2
Reeves, J. The story of Tom Thumb
In Reeves, J. English fables and fairy stories p63-70 398.2
Watson, R. J. Tom Thumb 398.2
Tom Thumb. Grimm, J.
In Best-loved folktales of the world p104-09 398.2
Tom Tit Tot
Crossley-Holland, K. Tom Tit Tot
In Crossley-Holland, K. British folk tales p47-54 398.2
Jacobs, J. Tom Tit Tot
In Best-loved folktales of the world p207-11 398.2
In Jacobs, J. English fairy tales p1-8 398.2
In The Scott, Foresman anthology of children's literature p153-55 808.8
Reeves, J. Tom Tit Tot
In Reeves, J. English fables and fairy stories p147-56 398.2
Williams-Ellis, A. Tom-Tit-Tot
In Williams-Ellis, A. Tales from the enchanted world p185-95 398.2
Tom Titmarsh's devil. Garfield, L.
In Garfield, L. The apprentices S C
Tomatoes
Watts, B. Tomato (k-3) 635
Tombs
See also Cemeteries
Bendick, J. Egyptian tombs (4 and up) 932
The **Tombs** of Atuan. Le Guin, U. K. See note under Le Guin, U. K. A wizard of Earthsea Fic
Tomchek, Ann Heinrichs
The Hopi (2-4) 970.004
Tomei, Gordon
(il) Silverstein, A. Wonders of speech 302.2
Tomei, Lorna
(il) Viorst, J. Rosie and Michael E

Tomes, Margot, 1917-1991
(il) De Regniers, B. S. Everyone is good for something 398.2
(il) De Regniers, B. S. Little Sister and the Month Brothers 398.2
(il) Fritz, J. And then what happened, Paul Revere? 92
(il) Fritz, J. Homesick: my own story 92
(il) Fritz, J. What's the big idea, Ben Franklin? 92
(il) Fritz, J. Where do you think you're going, Christopher Columbus? 92
(il) Fritz, J. Where was Patrick Henry on the 29th of May? 92
(il) Gág, W. Wanda Gág's The sorcerer's apprentice 398.2
(il) Gauch, P. L. This time, Tempe Wick? Fic
(il) Giblin, J. Chimney sweeps: yesterday and today 697
(il) Grimm, J. Wanda Gág's Jorinda and Joringel 398.2
(il) Grimm, J. Wanda Gág's The earth gnome 398.2
(il) Grimm, J. Wanda Gag's The six swans 398.2
(il) If there were dreams to sell. See If there were dreams to sell 821.008
(il) Jacobs, J. Tattercoats 398.2
(il) Johnston, T. The witch's hat E
(il) The Lap-time song and play book. See The Lap-time song and play book 782.42
(il) Livingston, M. C. Birthday poems 811
(il) Livingston, M. C. A song I sang to you: a selection of poems 811
(il) New Year's poems. See New Year's poems 808.81
(il) Snowy day: stories and poems. See Snowy day: stories and poems 808.8
(il) Van Vorst, M. L. A Norse lullaby 811

Tomfoolery: trickery and foolery with words. Schwartz, A. 398

Tomie dePaola's book of Bible stories. Bible. Selections 220.9

Tomie dePaola's book of Christmas carols 782.28

Tomie dePaola's book of poems (2-4) 808.81

Tomie dePaola's Favorite nursery tales (k-3) 398.2

Tomie dePaola's Mother Goose (k-2) 398.8

Tommelise. Andersen, H. C.
In The Classic fairy tales p221-29 398.2

Tomography, Computerized axial
See/See also pages in the following book(s):
Aaseng, N. The inventors: Nobel prizes in chemistry, physics, and medicine p69-74 (5 and up) 609

Tomorrow's wizard. MacLachlan, P. S C

Tompert, Ann, 1918-
Grandfather Tang's story E
Little fox goes to the end of the world E
Nothing sticks like a shadow E

Tom's midnight garden. Pearce, P. Fic

Tom's rainbow walk. Anholt, C. E

The **Tomten**. Lindgren, A. E

The **Tomten** and the fox. Lindgren, A. E

Tongue-cut sparrow
Ishii, M. The tongue-cut sparrow 398.2
Quayle, E. The tongue-cut sparrow
In Quayle, E. The shining princess, and other Japanese legends p44-56 398.2
The Sparrow with the slit tongue
In Best-loved folktales of the world p509-12 398.2

The **tongue-twister**. Wiseman, B.
In The Laugh book p239-41 808.8

Tongue twisters
Brandreth, G. D. The biggest tongue twister book in the world (4 and up) 808.88
Keller, C. Tongue twisters (3-6) 808.88
Schwartz, A. Busy buzzing bumblebees and other tongue twisters (k-3) 808.88
Schwartz, A. A twister of twists, a tangler of tongues (4 and up) 808.88

Tonino and the fairies
Boggs, R. S. Tonino and the fairies
In Best-loved folktales of the world p166-69 398.2

Tony and his harp. Leach, M.
In Leach, M. Whistle in the graveyard p71-72 398.2

Tony's bread: an Italian folktale. De Paola, T. 398.2

Too fat? Too thin? Do you have a choice? Arnold, C. 613.2

Too much noise. McGovern, A. 398.2

Too much searching
In The Crest and the hide, and other African stories of heroes, chiefs, bards, hunters, sorcerers, and common people p69-72 398.2

Tool book. Gibbons, G. 621.9

The **toolbox**. Rockwell, A. F. 621.9

Toolchest. Adkins, J. 684

Tools
Gibbons, G. Tool book (k-2) 621.9
Miller, M. Who uses this? E

Tools—*Continued*
Rockwell, A. F. The toolbox (k-1) **621.9**
See/See also pages in the following book(s):
Cobb, V. The secret life of hardware: a science experiment book p46-65 (5 and up) **670**

Toomai of the elephants. Kipling, R.
In Kipling, R. The jungle books **S C**

The **toothpaste** millionaire. Merrill, J. **Fic**

Top of the News. See Journal of Youth Services in Libraries **027.6205**

Topiel & Tekla. Singer, I. B.
In Singer, I. B. Stories for children p260-70 **S C**

Tops. Zubrowski, B. **745.592**

Tops and bottoms. Sanfield, S.
In Sanfield, S. The adventures of High John the Conqueror **398.2**

Topsy-turvies. Anno, M. **E**

Tories, American *See* American Loyalists

Tornadoes
Armbruster, A. Tornadoes (4-6) **551.55**
George, J. C. One day in the prairie (4-6) **574.5**

Fiction

Ruckman, I. Night of the twisters (3-6) **Fic**

Torre, Betty L.
The luminous pearl (k-3) **398.2**

Tortillitas para mamá and other nursery rhymes (k-2) **398.8**

Tortoise and the hare
In The Tall book of nursery tales p105-07 **398.2**

Tortoise, Hare, and the sweet potatoes. Bryan, A.
In Bauer, C. F. Celebrations p231-34 **808.8**

Tortoises *See* Turtles

Totanguak. MacDonald, M. R.
In MacDonald, M. R. When the lights go out p118-28 **372.6**

Totem pole. Hoyt-Goldsmith, D. **970.004**

Totems and totemism
Hoyt-Goldsmith, D. Totem pole (3-5) **970.004**

Fiction

Siberell, A. Whale in the sky (k-3) **398.2**

Touch
Parker, S. Touch, taste and smell (4 and up) **612.8**

Touch magic. Yolen, J. **028.5**

Touch, taste and smell. Parker, S. **612.8**

Touch wood. Roth-Hano, R. **Fic**

Tough Eddie. Winthrop, E. **E**

The **tough** winter. Lawson, R. **Fic**

Toulouse-Lautrec, Henri de, 1864-1901

About

Raboff, E. Henri de Toulouse-Lautrec (4 and up) **759.4**

A **tournament** of knights. Lasker, J. **394**

The **tower** bird. Yolen, J.
In Yolen, J. The faery flag p82-84 **S C**

Tower of London (England)
Fisher, L. E. The Tower of London (4 and up) **942.1**

Town & country. Provensen, A. **307.7**

The **town** cats. Alexander, L.
In Alexander, L. The town cats, and other tales p3-17 **S C**

The **town** cats, and other tales. Alexander, L. **S C**

The **town** mouse and the country mouse. Cauley, L. B. **398.2**

The **town** mouse and the country mouse. Stevens, J. **398.2**

Town planning *See* City planning

The **town** where sleeping was not allowed. Lester, J.
In Lester, J. How many spots does a leopard have? and other tales p31-35 **398.2**

The **town** where snoring was not allowed. Lester, J.
In Lester, J. How many spots does a leopard have? and other tales p27-30 **398.2**

Townesend, Frances Eliza Hodgson Burnett
See Burnett, Frances Hodgson, 1849-1924

Towns *See* Cities and towns

Townsend, John Rowe
Dan alone (6 and up) **Fic**
A sense of story **028.5**
A sounding of storytellers **028.5**
The visitors (6 and up) **Fic**
Written for children **028.5**

Toys
Blocksma, M. Action contraptions (2-5) **745.592**
Churchill, E. R. Fast & funny paper toys you can make (3 and up) **745.592**
Elbert, V. Folk toys around the world and how to make them (5 and up) **745.592**
Sullivan, S. C. A. Bats, butterflies, and bugs (3-5) **745.592**

Toys—*Continued*
Zubrowski, B. Tops (4-6) **745.592**
See/See also pages in the following book(s):
Caney, S. Steven Caney's kids' America p238-89 (4 and up) **790.1**
Fiction
Andersen, H. C. The steadfast tin soldier (1-4) **Fic**
Bianco, M. W. The velveteen rabbit (2-4) **Fic**
Conrad, P. The Tub People **E**
Couture, S. A. The block book **E**
Craft, R. The winter bear **E**
Galbraith, K. O. Laura Charlotte **E**
Goffstein, M. B. My Noah's ark **E**
Howe, J. Pinky and Rex **E**
Hutchins, P. Changes, changes **E**
Jonas, A. Now we can go **E**
Lindgren, B. Sam's car **E**
Milne, A. A. The house at Pooh Corner (1-4) **Fic**
Milne, A. A. The Pooh story book (1-4) **Fic**
Milne, A. A. Winnie-the-Pooh (1-4) **Fic**
Milne, A. A. The world of Pooh (1-4) **Fic**
Oxenbury, H. Pippo gets lost **E**
Vincent, G. Ernest and Celestine **E**
Williams, K. L. Galimoto **E**

Tozuka, Takako
(il) Turkey. See Turkey **956.1**

Traces of life. Lasky, K. **573.2**

Track & field basics. McMane, F. **796.4**

Track athletics
McMane, F. Track & field basics (4 and up) **796.4**

Tracking wild chimpanzees in Kibira National Park. Powzyk, J. A. **599.88**

Tractors
Fiction
Burton, V. L. Katy and the big snow **E**

Trade fairs *See* Fairs

Trade unions *See* Labor unions

Trades *See* Occupations

The **trading** games. Slote, A. **Fic**

Traffic accidents
See also Drunk driving

Traffic on Sadovoi Road. Dragunsky, V.
In Face to face: a collection of stories by celebrated Soviet and American writers p131-40 **S C**

Train song. Siebert, D. **E**

The **train** to Lulu's. Howard, E. F. **E**

Train whistles. Sattler, H. R. **385**

Training, Toilet *See* Toilet training

Trains, Railroad *See* Railroads

Trains. Barton, B. **625.1**

Trains. Gibbons, G. **625.1**

Trains. Rockwell, A. F. **625.1**

Tramps
Fiction
Carlson, N. S. The family under the bridge (3-5) **Fic**

Transistors
See/See also pages in the following book(s):
Aaseng, N. The inventors: Nobel prizes in chemistry, physics, and medicine p42-51 (5 and up) **609**

Translating and interpreting
See/See also pages in the following book(s):
Crosscurrents of criticism p275-305 **028.5**

Transplantation of organs, tissues, etc.
Beckelman, L. Transplants (4-6) **617.9**
Lee, S. Donor banks: saving lives with organ and tissue transplants (5 and up) **362.1**

Transplants. Beckelman, L. **617.9**

Transportation
Rockwell, A. F. Things that go (k-1) **629.04**
See/See also pages in the following book(s):
Favorite poems, old and new p183-203 (4-6) **808.81**
Fiction
Levinson, R. I go with my family to Grandma's **E**
History
Tunis, E. Wheels: a pictorial history (5 and up) **388.3**

Trapped in tar. Arnold, C. **560**

Travel
Brown, L. K. Dinosaurs travel (k-3) **910**

Travelers
Fiction
Caines, J. F. Just us women **E**

Travels *See* Voyages and travels

Travels of Babar. Brunhoff, J. de. See note under Brunhoff, J. de. The story of Babar, the little elephant **E**

The **travels** of Marco Polo. Humble, R. **910.4**

Travers, P. L. (Pamela L.), 1906-
Mary Poppins (4-6) **Fic**
Mary Poppins and the house next door. See note under Travers, P. L. Mary Poppins **Fic**
Mary Poppins comes back. See note under Travers, P. L. Mary Poppins **Fic**

Travers, P. L. (Pamela L.), 1906- —*Continued*
Mary Poppins from A to Z. See note under Travers, P. L. Mary Poppins **Fic**
Mary Poppins in Cherry Tree Lane. See note under Travers, P. L. Mary Poppins **Fic**
Mary Poppins opens the door. See note under Travers, P. L. Mary Poppins **Fic**
Travers, Pamela L. *See* Travers, P. L. (Pamela L.), 1906-
Treasure
Afanas'ev, A. N. Treasure-trove
In Afanas'ev, A. N. Russian fairy tales p550-52 **398.2**
The Treasure
In Best-loved folktales of the world p438-41 **398.2**
The **treasure**. Shulevitz, U. **398.2**
Treasure Island. Stevenson, R. L. **Fic**
The **treasure** of Alpheus Winterborn. Bellairs, J. **Fic**
The **treasure** of Cozy Cove. Ross, T. **E**
Treasure of Green Knowe. Boston, L. M. See note under Boston, L. M. The children of Green Knowe **Fic**
The **treasure** of Lemon Brown. Myers, W. D.
In Face to face: a collection of stories by celebrated Soviet and American writers p101-13 **S C**
Treasure-trove. Afanas'ev, A. N.
In Afanas'ev, A. N. Russian fairy tales p550-52 **398.2**
Treasury of song's for children, Tom Glazer's. Glazer, T. **782.42**
A **treasury** of Turkish folktales for children. Walker, B. K. **398.2**
The **tree**. Hindley, J. **582.16**
Tree flowers. Selsam, M. E. **582.16**
Tree house. Carter, A. R.
In Connections: short stories by outstanding writers for young adults p192-204 **S C**
Tree in the trail. Holling, H. C. **Fic**
A **tree** is nice. Udry, J. M. **E**
The **tree** of hearts. Gotwalt, H. L. M.
In Gotwalt, H. L. M. Special plays for holidays p121-34 **812**
Tree of life: the world of the African baobab. Bash, B. **583**
A **tree** to trim. Fisher, A. L.
In The Big book of Christmas plays p59-79 **808.82**

Tree trunk traffic. Lavies, B. **591.5**
A **treeful** of pigs. Lobel, A. **E**
Treehorn's treasure. Heide, F. P. See note under Heide, F. P. The shrinking of Treehorn **Fic**
Treehorn's wish. Heide, F. P. See note under Heide, F. P. The shrinking of Treehorn **Fic**
Trees
See also Baobab; Redwood
Burnie, D. Tree (4 and up) **582.16**
Cole, J. Plants in winter (k-3) **581.5**
Dowden, A. O. T. The blossom on the bough (5 and up) **582.16**
Hindley, J. The tree (3-5) **582.16**
Lavies, B. Tree trunk traffic (k-2) **591.5**
Lyon, G. E. A B Cedar **E**
McCauley, J. R. Animals that live in trees (k-3) **591.5**
Romanova, N. Once there was a tree (2-4) **582.16**
Selsam, M. E. Tree flowers (4 and up) **582.16**
Fiction
Fleischman, P. The birthday tree (2-4) **Fic**
Gibbons, G. The seasons of Arnold's apple tree **E**
Holling, H. C. Tree in the trail (4 and up) **Fic**
Udry, J. M. A tree is nice **E**
Poetry
Frost, R. Birches (1-3) **811**
North America
Petrides, G. A. A field guide to trees and shrubs **582.1**
United States
Zim, H. S. Trees (4 and up) **582.16**
Trefoil round the world. World Association of Girl Guides and Girl Scouts **369.463**
The **trek**. Jonas, A. **E**
Trelease, Jim
The new read-aloud handbook **028.5**
Trenary, Jill
Time of my life: Jill Trenary (4 and up) **92**
Trenton (N.J.), Battle of, 1776
See/See also pages in the following book(s):
Tunis, E. The tavern at the ferry p94-99 (5 and up) **973.2**
Tresselt, Alvin R.
Hide and seek fog **E**
The mitten (k-2) **398.2**
Rain drop splash **E**
Wake up, city! **E**
White snow, bright snow **E**
Treviño, Elizabeth Borton de, 1904-
El Guëro (5 and up) **Fic**

Treviño, Elizabeth Borton de, 1904-—*Continued*
I, Juan de Pareja (6 and up) **Fic**
See/See also pages in the following book(s):
Newbery and Caldecott Medal books, 1966-1975 p5-19 **028.5**

Trial in the dragon's palace. Terada, A. M.
In Terada, A. M. Under the starfruit tree p88-94 **398.2**

Trial of brides
Grimm, J. Looking for a bride
In Grimm, J. The complete Grimm's fairy tales p655-56 **398.2**

The **trial** of Mother Goose. Gotwalt, H. L. M.
In Gotwalt, H. L. M. Everyday plays for boys and girls p64-77 **812**

Trial Valley. Cleaver, V. **Fic**

Tricks
See also Magic
Broekel, R. Hocus pocus: magic you can do (3-5) **793.8**
Broekel, R. Now you see it: easy magic for beginners (3-5) **793.8**
Cobb, V. Bet you can! science possibilities to fool you (4 and up) **793.8**
Cobb, V. Bet you can't! science impossibilities to fool you (4 and up) **793.8**
Cobb, V. Magic—naturally! science entertainment & amusements (4 and up) **793.8**
Friedhoffer, R. Magic tricks, science facts (5 and up) **793.8**
Kettelkamp, L. Magic made easy (4 and up) **793.8**
Severn, B. Magic fun for everyone (6 and up) **793.8**
Sheridan, J. Nothing's impossible! stunts to entertain and amaze (5 and up) **793.8**
White, L. B. Math-a-magic: number tricks for magicians (3-6) **793.8**
Wyler, R. Magic secrets (1-3) **793.8**
Wyler, R. Spooky tricks (1-3) **793.8**

Trillion (The number)
Schwartz, D. M. How much is a million? **E**

Trimble, Stephen, 1950-
The village of blue stone (4-6) **970.004**

Trimby, Elisa, 1948-
(il) Moore, C. C. The night before Christmas **811**

The **trip**. Keats, E. J. See note under Keats, E. J. Louie **E**

The **trip** of a drip. Cobb, V. **628.1**

A **trip** to Schlaraffenland. Grimm, J.
In Grimm, J. More tales from Grimm p87-88 **398.2**

Tripp, Wallace, 1940-
Marguerite, go wash your feet (1-3) **821.008**
(il) Granfa' Grig had a pig, and other rhymes without reason from Mother Goose. See Granfa' Grig had a pig, and other rhymes without reason from Mother Goose **398.8**
(comp) A Great big ugly man came up and tied his horse to me. See A Great big ugly man came up and tied his horse to me **821.008**

Trivas, Irene
(il) Blume, J. The Pain and the Great One **E**
(il) Christiansen, C. B. My mother's house, my father's house **E**

Trivia *See* Curiosities and wonders

Trojan War
Colum, P. The children's Homer: The adventures of Odysseus and The tale of Troy (4 and up) **883**
Picard, B. L. The Iliad of Homer (6 and up) **883**
See/See also pages in the following book(s):
Asimov, I. Words from the myths p177-201 (6 and up) **292**
Hamilton, E. Mythology p197-342 (6 and up) **292**

Troll country. Marshall, E. **E**

The **trolley** to yesterday. Bellairs, J. See note under Bellairs, J. The curse of the blue figurine **Fic**

Tropical rain forests *See* Rain forests

Tropical rain forests around the world. Landau, E. **574.5**

Trot, trot to Boston: play rhymes for baby (k-1) **398.8**

Trouble River. Byars, B. C. **Fic**

Trouble snake. Yep, L.
In Yep, L. The rainbow people p118-23 **398.2**

The **trouble** with thirteen. Miles, B. **Fic**

Trousers Mehmet and the sultan's daughter. Walker, B. K.
In Walker, B. K. A treasury of Turkish folktales for children p91-96 **398.2**

Troy (Ancient city)
See/See also pages in the following book(s):
Gallant, R. A. Lost cities (4 and up) **930**

Truck. Crews, D. **E**

Truck song. Siebert, D. **E**

Trucks
Barton, B. Trucks (k-1) **629.224**
Crews, D. Truck **E**
Magee, D. Trucks you can count on (k-2) **629.224**

Trucks—*Continued*
Rockwell, A. F. Trucks (k-1) **629.224**
Sullivan, G. Here come the monster trucks (3-6) **629.223**
Fiction
Horenstein, H. Sam goes trucking **E**
Lyon, D. The biggest truck **E**
Merrill, J. The pushcart war (5 and up) **Fic**
Siebert, D. Truck song **E**
Models
Weiss, H. Model cars and trucks and how to build them (4 and up) **629.22**
Trucks you can count on. Magee, D. **629.224**
The **true** book of animal homes. See Podendorf, I. Animal homes **591.5**
The **true** book of rocks and minerals. See Podendorf, I. Rocks and minerals **549**
True bride
Grimm, J. The true bride
In Grimm, J. The complete Grimm's fairy tales p752-60 **398.2**
The **true** confessions of Charlotte Doyle. Avi. **Fic**
The **true** history of Little Golden-hood. Marelle, C.
In The Red fairy book p215-19 **398.2**
The **true** spirit of a festival day. Shedlock, M. L.
In Shedlock, M. L. The art of the story-teller p225-28 **372.6**
True stories about Abraham Lincoln. Gross, R. B. **92**
The **true** story of the three little pigs. Scieszka, J. **398.2**
Truesdell, Sue
(il) Byars, B. C. The Golly Sisters go West **E**
(il) Byars, B. C. Hooray for the Golly sisters! **E**
(il) Little, J. Hey world, here I am! **811**
(il) Robins, J. Addie meets Max **E**
(il) Root, P. Soup for supper **E**
(il) Schwartz, A. Unriddling: all sorts of riddles to puzzle your guessery **398.6**
The **trumpet** of the swan. White, E. B. **Fic**
The **trumpeter** of Krakow. Kelly, E. P. **Fic**
Truong Ba and the butcher's skin. Terada, A. M.
In Terada, A. M. Under the starfruit tree p75-77 **398.2**
Trusty John. Grimm, J.
In The Blue fairy book p296-303 **398.2**
Truth, Sojourner, d. 1883
About
Ferris, J. Walking the road to freedom: a story about Sojourner Truth (3-5) **92**
Ortiz, V. Sojourner Truth, a self-made woman (6 and up) **92**
See/See also pages in the following book(s):
Jacobs, W. J. Great lives: human rights p107-16 (5 and up) **920**
The **truth** about Santa Claus. Giblin, J. **394.2**
The **truth** about the Ku Klux Klan. Meltzer, M. **322.4**
Truthfulness and falsehood
Fiction
Brink, C. R. The bad times of Irma Baumlein (4-6) **Fic**
Cleaver, V. Ellen Grae (4-6) **Fic**
Clements, B. I tell a lie every so often (6 and up) **Fic**
Tsali of the Cherokees. Marriott, A. L.
In Marriott, A. L. American Indian mythology **398.2**
The **tsar** & the amazing cow. Lewis, J. P. **E**
Tseng, Jean
(il) Mahy, M. The seven Chinese brothers **398.2**
(il) Stamm, C. Three strong women **398.2**
Tseng, Mou-sien
(il) Mahy, M. The seven Chinese brothers **398.2**
(il) Stamm, C. Three strong women **398.2**
Tsirtsur & Peziza. Singer, I. B.
In Singer, I. B. Stories for children p160-66 **S C**
In Singer, I. B. When Shlemiel went to Warsaw & other stories p17-26 **398.2**
Tuan Mac Cairill
Stephens, J. The story of Tuan Mac Cairill
In Stephens, J. Irish fairy tales p4-32 **398.2**
The **Tub** People. Conrad, P. **E**
The **tubeteika** affair. Zilinskaite, V.
In Face to face: a collection of stories by celebrated Soviet and American writers p77-89 **S C**
Tubières, Anne Claude Philippe de, comte de Caylus *See* Caylus, Anne Claude Philippe de Tubières, comte de, 1692-1765
Tubmaker who flew to the sky. Uchida, Y.
In Uchida, Y. The magic listening cap **398.2**

Tubman, Harriet, 1815?-1913
About
Ferris, J. Go free or die: a story about Harriet Tubman (3-5) **92**
Tubtime. Woodruff, E. **E**
Tuck everlasting. Babbitt, N. **Fic**
Tucker, Sian
(il) Rogers, P. The shapes game **516**
Tucker's countryside. Selden, G. See note under Selden, G. The cricket in Times Square **Fic**
Tucking Mommy in. Loh, M. J. **E**
Tudor, Tasha
Take joy! The Tasha Tudor Christmas book. See Take joy! The Tasha Tudor Christmas book **394.2**
A time to keep: the Tasha Tudor book of holidays (k-3) **394.2**
(il) Burnett, F. H. A little princess **Fic**
(il) Burnett, F. H. The secret garden **Fic**
(il) First prayers. See First prayers **242**
(il) Godden, R. The doll's house **Fic**
(il) Moore, C. C. The night before Christmas **811**
(il) Mother Goose. See Mother Goose [illus. by Tasha Tudor] **398.8**
A **tug-of-war**. Jablow, A.
In Best-loved folktales of the world p658-60 **398.2**
Tug-of-war. Lester, J.
In Lester, J. How many spots does a leopard have? and other tales p17-20 **398.2**
Tugboats
Fiction
Gramatky, H. Little Toot **E**
Tule elk. Arnold, C. **599.73**
Tulip bed
Reeves, J. The tulip bed
In Reeves, J. English fables and fairy stories p97-102 **398.2**
Tumors
See also Cancer
Tundra ecology
George, J. C. One day in the alpine tundra (4-6) **574.5**
Tunis, Edwin, 1897-1973
Colonial craftsmen and the beginnings of American industry (5 and up) **670**
Colonial living (5 and up) **973.2**
Frontier living (5 and up) **978**
The tavern at the ferry (5 and up) **973.2**
Wheels: a pictorial history (5 and up) **388.3**
The young United States, 1783 to 1830 (5 and up) **973**
Tunis, John R., 1889-1975
Keystone kids. See note under Tunis, J. R. The kid from Tomkinsville **Fic**
The kid from Tomkinsville (5 and up) **Fic**
Rookie of the year. See note under Tunis, J. R. The kid from Tomkinsville **Fic**
World Series. See note under Tunis, J. R. The kid from Tomkinsville **Fic**
Tunisia
Tunisia—in pictures (5 and up) **961.1**
Tunisia—in pictures (5 and up) **961.1**
The **tunnel**. Browne, A. **E**
Tunnels
Gibbons, G. Tunnels (k-3) **624.1**
Tunney, Linda
(il) Settel, J. Why does my nose run? **612**
(il) Stafford, P. Your two brains **612.8**
Tup and the ants
In The Monkey's haircut, and other stories told by the Maya p44-51 **398.2**
Turck, Mary
Crack & cocaine (4-6) **362.29**
Turkey
Feinstein, S. Turkey—in pictures (5 and up) **956.1**
Lye, K. Take a trip to Turkey (1-3) **956.1**
Spencer, W. The land and people of Turkey (5 and up) **956.1**
Children
See Children—Turkey
Folklore
See Folklore—Turkey
Social life and customs
Turkey (3-5) **956.1**
Turkey (3-5) **956.1**
Turkey tale. MacDonald, M. R.
In MacDonald, M. R. Twenty tellable tales p90-94 **372.6**
Turkeys
Lavine, S. A. Wonders of turkeys (5 and up) **598**
Patent, D. H. Wild turkey, tame turkey (3-6) **598**
Fiction
Kroll, S. One tough turkey **E**
Turkeys, Pilgrims, and Indian corn. Barth, E. **394.2**
The **turkeys'** side of it. Smith, J. L. See note under Smith, J. L. The kid next door and other headaches **Fic**
Turkle, Brinton Cassaday, 1915-
The adventures of Obadiah. See note under Turkle, B. C. Obadiah the Bold **E**

Turkle, Brinton Cassaday, 1915- — *Continued*
Deep in the forest **E**
Do not open **E**
Obadiah the Bold **E**
Rachel and Obadiah. See note under Turkle, B. C. Obadiah the Bold **E**
Thy friend, Obadiah. See note under Turkle, B. C. Obadiah the Bold **E**
(il) Child, L. M. F. Over the river and through the wood **811**
(il) Littledale, F. The elves and the shoemaker **398.2**

Turn homeward, Hannalee. Beatty, P. **Fic**

Turner, Ann Warren
Grasshopper summer (4-6) **Fic**
Heron Street **E**
Nettie's trip South (3-5) **Fic**
Through moon and stars and night skies **E**

Turner, Dorothy
Potatoes (1-3) **635**

Turner, Ellen Scott
(il) Renfro, N. Puppet show made easy! **791.5**

Turnip
Grimm, J. The turnip
In Grimm, J. The complete Grimm's fairy tales p637-40 **398.2**
In The Scott, Foresman anthology of children's literature p192-94 **808.8**
Morgan, P. The turnip **398.2**
Oxenbury, H. The turnip
In Oxenbury, H. The Helen Oxenbury nursery story book p13-18 **398.2**

The **turnip**. Afanas'ev, A. N.
In Afanas'ev, A. N. Russian fairy tales p26-27 **398.2**

The **turret**. Sharp, M. See note under Sharp, M. The rescuers **Fic**

Turska, Krystyna, 1933-
(il) Kipling, R. The elephant's child **Fic**
(il) Kipling, R. How the camel got his hump **Fic**

Turtle and his sister
In The Naked bear p110-15 **398.2**

The **turtle** and the monkey. Galdone, P. **398.2**

Turtle day. Florian, D. **E**

Turtle goes hunting
In The Naked bear p67-71 **398.2**

Turtle in July. Singer, M. **811**

Turtle knows your name. Bryan, A. **398.2**

Turtle watch. Ancona, G. **597.9**

Turtles
See also Sea turtles
Cutchins, J. Scoots, the bog turtle (1-3) **597.9**
George, W. T. Box Turtle at Long Pond **E**
See/See also pages in the following book(s):
Bauer, C. F. Celebrations p227-40 **808.8**
Weber, W. J. Care of uncommon pets p141-56 (5 and up) **636.088**
Fiction
Florian, D. Turtle day **E**
Galdone, P. The turtle and the monkey (k-2) **398.2**
The Hare and the tortoise (k-3) **398.2**
Holling, H. C. Minn of the Mississippi (4-6) **Fic**
Marshall, J. Yummers! **E**
Wildsmith, B. The hare and the tortoise (k-2) **398.2**
Williams, B. Albert's toothache **E**

Turtle's war party
In The Naked bear p31-36 **398.2**

Tuttle, Lisa, 1952-
(jt. auth) Ashe, R. Children's literary houses **028.5**

Tuttle, Merlin D.
(il) Hopf, A. L. Bats **599.4**

The **TV** kid. Byars, B. C. **Fic**

Twain, Mark, 1835-1910
The adventures of Huckleberry Finn (5 and up) **Fic**
The adventures of Tom Sawyer (5 and up) **Fic**
The adventures of Tom Sawyer [excerpt]
In The Random House book of humor for children p293-300 **817.008**
The adventures of Tom Sawyer; dramatization. See Thane, A. Tom Sawyer, pirate
See/See also pages in the following book(s):
Crosscurrents of criticism p320-29 **028.5**
Only connect: readings on children's literature p266-76 **028.5**

'Twas the night before Christmas. See Moore, C. C. The night before Christmas **811**

The **twelve** apostles. Grimm, J.
In Grimm, J. The complete Grimm's fairy tales p818-19 **398.2**

Twelve brothers
Grimm, J. The twelve brothers
In Grimm, J. The complete Grimm's fairy tales p59-64 398.2
In The Red fairy book p274-81 398.2
In Womenfolk and fairy tales p36-43 398.2

Twelve dancing princesses
Ehrlich, A. The twelve dancing princesses
In Ehrlich, A. The Random House book of fairy tales p34-45 398.2
Grimm, J. The shoes that were danced to pieces
In Grimm, J. The complete Grimm's fairy tales p596-600 398.2
Grimm, J. The twelve dancing princesses 398.2
also in The Classic fairy tales p191-94 398.2
Sanderson, R. The twelve dancing princesses 398.2
Thane, A. The twelve dancing princesses
In Thane, A. Plays from famous stories and fairy tales p231-48 812
The Twelve dancing princesses
In The Red fairy book p1-12 398.2

The **Twelve** days of Christmas 782.42

Twelve huntsmen
Grimm, J. The twelve huntsmen
In The Green fairy book p282-85 398.2
In Grimm, J. The complete Grimm's fairy tales p334-36 398.2
In Grimm, J. The juniper tree, and other tales from Grimm v1 p63-70 398.2

The **twelve** idle servants. Grimm, J.
In Grimm, J. The complete Grimm's fairy tales p648-50 398.2

Twelve idlers
Grimm, J. The twelve idle servants
In Grimm, J. The complete Grimm's fairy tales p648-50 398.2
Grimm, J. The twelve lazy servants
In Grimm, J. More tales from Grimm p51-58 398.2

The **twelve** lazy servants. Grimm, J.
In Grimm, J. More tales from Grimm p51-58 398.2

Twelve months
De Regniers, B. S. Little Sister and the Month Brothers 398.2
Marshak, S. The Month-Brothers 398.2

The **twelve** months. Megas, G. A.
In Best-loved folktales of the world p186-90 398.2

Twelve thousand words. See 12,000 words 423

Twelve windows
Grimm, J. The sea-hare
In Grimm, J. The complete Grimm's fairy tales p769-72 398.2

Twentieth-century children's writers 920.003

The **twenty-five** cent miracle. See Nelson, T. The 25¢ miracle Fic

Twenty-four hours in a forest. See Watts, B. 24 hours in a forest 574.5

The **twenty-one** balloons. Du Bois, W. P. Fic

Twenty-six letters and ninety-nine cents. See Hoban, T. 26 letters and 99 cents E

Twenty tellable tales. MacDonald, M. R. 372.6

Twenty thousand leagues under the sea. Verne, J. Fic

Twins
See also Brothers and sisters
Rosenberg, M. B. Being a twin, having a twin (2-4) 155.4

Fiction

Cleary, B. Mitch and Amy (3-5) Fic
Cleary, B. The real hole E
Conford, E. Me and the terrible two (3-6) Fic
Yorinks, A. Oh, Brother E

The **Twist-mouth** family
In The Diane Goode book of American folk tales and songs p61-63 398.2

The **twisted** witch, and other spooky riddles. Adler, D. A. 793.73

A **twister** of twists, a tangler of tongues. Schwartz, A. 808.88

Two and too much. Walter, M. P. E

Two bad ants. Van Allsburg, C. E

Two bear cubs. Jonas, A. E

The **two** brothers. Grimm, J.
In Grimm, J. The complete Grimm's fairy tales p290-311 398.2

Two brothers. Terada, A. M.
In Terada, A. M. Under the starfruit tree p109-14 398.2

Two can play the same game. Jukes, M.
In Free to be—a family p74-77 810.8

The **Two** donkeys
In The Magic orange tree, and other Haitian folktales p23-28 398.2

Two dreamers. Soto, G.
In Soto, G. Baseball in April, and other stories p23-32 S C

Two dutiful sons
Carpenter, F. Two dutiful sons
In Carpenter, F. Tales of a Chinese grandmother p117-23 398.2

Two Feathers
In The Naked bear p11-18 **398.2**
The **two** foolish cats. Uchida, Y. **398.2**
Two fools and the gifts for Mehmet. Walker, B. K.
In Walker, B. K. A treasury of Turkish folktales for children p85-87 **398.2**
The **Two** frogs
In Shedlock, M. L. The art of the story-teller p213-15 **372.6**
Two hundred and sixty-three brain busters. See Phillips, L. 263 brain busters **793.73**
Two Ivans, soldier's sons. Afanas'ev, A. N.
In Afanas'ev, A. N. Russian fairy tales p463-75 **398.2**
The **two** Johns. Hamilton, V.
In Hamilton, V. The people could fly: American black folktales p81-89 **398.2**
The **two** journeymen. Grimm, J.
In Grimm, J. The juniper tree, and other tales from Grimm v2 p278-97 **398.2**
Two kinds of luck
Afanas'ev, A. N. Two kinds of luck
In Afanas'ev, A. N. Russian fairy tales p501-04 **398.2**
Two king's children
Grimm, J. The two king's children
In Grimm, J. The complete Grimm's fairy tales p515-24 **398.2**
Two lost babes
Two lost babes
In Grandfather tales p162-69 **398.2**
Two of everything. Ritchie, A.
In The Scott, Foresman anthology of children's literature p323-26 **808.8**
The **two** of them. Aliki. **E**
The **Two** old women's bet
In Best-loved folktales of the world p671-73 **398.2**
In Grandfather tales p160-61 **398.2**
Two orphan cubs. Brenner, B. **599.74**
Two out of the knapsack
Afanas'ev, A. N. Two out of the sack
In Afanas'ev, A. N. Russian fairy tales p321-24 **398.2**
Two out of the sack. Afanas'ev, A. N.
In Afanas'ev, A. N. Russian fairy tales p321-24 **398.2**
Two piano tuners. Goffstein, M. B. **Fic**
Two princesses
Reeves, J. The two princesses
In Reeves, J. English fables and fairy stories p49-62 **398.2**
Two queens of heaven: Aphrodite [and] Demeter. Gates, D. **292**
The **two** rivers. Afanas'ev, A. N.
In Afanas'ev, A. N. Russian fairy tales p172 **398.2**
Two shoes, new shoes. Hughes, S. **E**
The **two** skyscrapers who decided to have a child. Sandburg, C.
In Sandburg, C. Rootabaga stories pt 1 p111-16 **S C**
In Sandburg, C. The Sandburg treasury p55-57 **818**
Two sons of Ivan, the soldier
Afanas'ev, A. N. Two Ivans, soldier's sons
In Afanas'ev, A. N. Russian fairy tales p463-75 **398.2**
The **two-thousand-pound** goldfish. Byars, B. C. **Fic**
Two travelers
Grimm, J. The two journeymen
In Grimm, J. The juniper tree, and other tales from Grimm v2 p278-97 **398.2**
Grimm, J. The two travelers
In Grimm, J. The complete Grimm's fairy tales p486-96 **398.2**
Two's enough of a crowd. Hunter, K.
In The Scott, Foresman anthology of children's literature p654-58 **808.8**
Tyler, D. D.
(il) Jacobs, F. Supersaurus **567.9**
Tyll Ulenspiegel *See* Eulenspiegel
Type and type founding
See/See also pages in the following book(s):
Ogg, O. The 26 letters p186-213 **411**
Typhoons
See also Hurricanes
Typography *See* Printing
Tyrannosaurus rex and its kin: the Mesozoic monsters. Sattler, H. R. **567.9**
Tyrannosaurus was a beast. Prelutsky, J. **811**

U

U-boat. Humble, R. **940.54**
U.F.O.'s *See* Unidentified flying objects
U.S.S.R. *See* Soviet Union
Uchida, Yoshiko
The best bad thing. See note under Uchida, Y. A jar of dreams **Fic**
The happiest ending. See note under Uchida, Y. A jar of dreams **Fic**
A jar of dreams (5 and up) **Fic**
Journey home (5 and up) **Fic**
Journey to Topaz **Fic**

Uchida, Yoshiko—*Continued*
The magic listening cap (3-6) **398.2**
Contents: The magic listening cap; Terrible leak; The wrestling match of the two Buddhas; Magic mortar; Tubmaker who flew to the sky; Three tests for the prince; Deer of five colors; The golden axe; Mountain witch and the peddler; The man who bought a dream; Fox and the bear; Tiny god; Rice cake that rolled away; Grateful stork
Momotaro: boy-of-the-peach
In The Scott, Foresman anthology of children's literature p330-32 **808.8**
New Year's hats for the statues
In Snowy day: stories and poems p3-11 **808.8**
The terrible black snake's revenge
In Bauer, C. F. Celebrations p172-76 **808.8**
The two foolish cats (k-3) **398.2**
Urashima Taro and the princess of the sea
In The Scott, Foresman anthology of children's literature p332-36 **808.8**

Udala tree. MacDonald, M. R.
In MacDonald, M. R. Twenty tellable tales p115-25 **372.6**

Uden, Grant, 1910-
The adventure of Countess Jeanne
In The Scott, Foresman anthology of children's literature p474-78 **808.8**

Udry, Janice May
The moon jumpers **E**
A tree is nice **E**
What Mary Jo shared **E**

UFOs *See* Unidentified flying objects

UFOs, ETs & visitors from space. Berger, M. **001.9**

Ugly duckling
Andersen, H. C. The ugly duckling **Fic**
In Andersen, H. C. Hans Andersen: his classic fairy tales p38-47 **S C**

Ukraine

Folklore

See Folklore—Ukraine

Ulrich, George
(il) Christopher, M. The hit-away kid **Fic**

Umbrella. Iwamatsu, A. J. **E**

Umbrellas and parasols

Fiction

Bright, R. My red umbrella **E**
Iwamatsu, A. J. Umbrella **E**

UN *See* United Nations

Un-Happy New Year, Emma! Stevenson, J. See note under Stevenson, J. Emma **E**

Unanana and the elephant
Arnott, K. Unanana and the elephant
In The Scott, Foresman anthology of children's literature p314-17 **808.8**
In Womenfolk and fairy tales p127-34 **398.2**

The **unanswerable.** Kendall, C.
In Kendall, C. Sweet and sour p63-65 **398.2**

Unborn child *See* Fetus

Unbuilding. Macaulay, D. **690**

Unclaimed treasures. MacLachlan, P. **Fic**

Uncle Boqui and Godfather Malice
Courlander, H. Uncle Bouqui and Godfather Malice
In The Scott, Foresman anthology of children's literature p394-96 **808.8**

Uncle Boqui and Tite Malice
Jagendorf, M. A. Uncle Bouqui and little Malice
In Best-loved folktales of the world p734-38 **398.2**

Uncle Boqui rents a horse
Courlander, H. Bouki rents a horse
In Best-loved folktales of the world p738-40 **398.2**

Uncle Bouqui and little Malice. Jagendorf, M. A.
In Best-loved folktales of the world p734-38 **398.2**

Uncle Elephant. Lobel, A. **E**

Uncle Vova's tree. Polacco, P. **E**

Uncle Wiggily's Christmas. Garis, H. R.
In The Family read-aloud Christmas treasury p58-63 **808.8**

Uncles

Fiction

Cassedy, S. Behind the attic wall (5 and up) **Fic**
Hines, A. G. Mean old Uncle Jack **E**
Jordan, M. Losing Uncle Tim (2-4) **Fic**
Kherdian, D. A song for Uncle Harry (4-6) **Fic**
Locker, T. Sailing with the wind **E**
Lowry, L. Us and Uncle Fraud (4 and up) **Fic**
MacLachlan, P. Seven kisses in a row (2-4) **Fic**
Reeder, C. Shades of gray (4 and up) **Fic**
Stannard, R. The time and space of Uncle Albert (5 and up) **Fic**

Under the green willow. Coatsworth, E. J. **E**

Under the starfruit tree. Terada, A. M. **398.2**
In Terada, A. M. Under the starfruit tree p3-6 **398.2**

Under the Sunday tree. Greenfield, E. **811**

The **under** water village. Marriott, A. L.
In Marriott, A. L. American Indian mythology **398.2**

Under your feet. Ryder, J. **811**
Underground. Macaulay, D. **624.1**
Underground railroad
Ferris, J. Go free or die: a story about Harriet Tubman (3-5) **92**
Fiction
Monjo, F. N. The drinking gourd **E**
Winter, J. Follow the drinking gourd **E**
Underground railroads *See* Subways
Understood Betsy [excerpt]. Fisher, D. C.
In The Random House book of humor for children p31-35 **817.008**
The **undertakers**. Kipling, R.
In Kipling, R. The jungle books **S C**
Underwater exploration
Ballard, R. D. Exploring the Titanic (4 and up) **910.4**
Ballard, R. D. The lost wreck of the Isis (4 and up) **910.4**
Cook, J. L. The mysterious undersea world (4 and up) **551.46**
Hackwell, W. J. Diving to the past: recovering ancient wrecks (4 and up) **910.4**
Johnson, R. L. Diving into darkness: a submersible explores the sea (4 and up) **551.46**
Underwater exploration devices *See* Submersibles
The **unexpected** banquet. Hunter, N.
In Bauer, C. F. Celebrations p45-51 **808.8**
Ungerer, Tomi, 1931-
Crictor **E**
Moon Man **E**
The three robbers **E**
(il) Brown, J. Flat Stanley **E**
(il) Oh, that's ridiculous! See Oh, that's ridiculous! **821.008**
(il) Spyri, J. Heidi **Fic**
See/See also pages in the following book(s):
Sendak, M. Caldecott & Co.: notes on books and pictures p133-37 **028.5**
Ungrateful son
Grimm, J. The ungrateful son
In Grimm, J. The complete Grimm's fairy tales p636 **398.2**
The **unicorn** and the lake. Mayer, M. **E**
Unicorns
Fiction
Mayer, M. The unicorn and the lake **E**
Unidentified flying objects
Berger, M. UFOs, ETs & visitors from space (5 and up) **001.9**
Cohen, D. The world of UFOs (6 and up) **001.9**
Fiction
Sleator, W. Into the dream (5 and up) **Fic**
Uninvited ghosts. Lively, P.
In Lively, P. Uninvited ghosts, and other stories p40-49 **S C**
Uninvited ghosts, and other stories. Lively, P. **S C**
Union of South Africa *See* South Africa
Union of Soviet Socialist Republics *See* Soviet Union
Unions, Labor *See* Labor unions
United Nations
See/See also pages in the following book(s):
Worldmark encyclopedia of the nations **910.3**
United States
Brandt, S. R. Facts about the fifty states (4 and up) **973**
Antiquities
See also Indians of North America—Antiquities
Biography
Ashabranner, B. K. People who make a difference (5 and up) **920**
Jacobs, W. J. Great lives: human rights (5 and up) **920**
Biography—Poetry
Benét, R. A book of Americans (4 and up) **811**
Census
Ashabranner, M. Counting America (5 and up) **304.6**
Constitutional history
Commager, H. S. The great Constitution (5 and up) **342**
Fritz, J. Shhh! we're writing the Constitution (3-5) **342**
Hauptly, D. J. "A convention of delegates" (5 and up) **342**
Mabie, M. C. J. The Constitution (6 and up) **342**
Maestro, B. A more perfect union (2-4) **342**
Sgroi, P. P. The living Constitution: landmark Supreme Court decisions (5 and up) **342**
Spier, P. We the people (2-4) **342**
Emigration
See United States—Immigration and emigration
Exploration
See West (U.S.)—Exploration
Foreign population
See also United States—Immigration and emigration
Foreign relations—Japan
Blumberg, R. Commodore Perry in the land of the Shogun (5 and up) **952**

United States—*Continued*

History

Scott, J. A. The story of America: a National Geographic picture atlas (5 and up) **973**

History—1600-1775, Colonial period

Alderman, C. L. The story of the thirteen colonies (5 and up) **973.2**

Fritz, J. Early thunder (6 and up) **Fic**

History—1600-1775, Colonial period—Biography

Fritz, J. Where was Patrick Henry on the 29th of May? (3-5) **92**

History—1600-1775, Colonial period—Fiction

Field, R. Calico bush (4 and up) **Fic**

History—1675-1676, King Philip's War

See King Philip's War, 1675-1676

History—1755-1763, French and Indian War

The American revolutionaries: a history in their own words, 1750-1800 (6 and up) **973.3**

History—1755-1763, French and Indian War—Fiction

Edmonds, W. D. The matchlock gun (4-6) **Fic**

History—1775-1783, Revolution

The American revolutionaries: a history in their own words, 1750-1800 (6 and up) **973.3**

Bliven, B. The American Revolution, 1760-1783 (5 and up) **973.3**

Davis, B. Black heroes of the American Revolution (5 and up) **973.3**

Morris, R. B. The American Revolution (4-6) **973.3**

See/See also pages in the following book(s):

Giblin, J. Fireworks, picnics, and flags p2-23 (3-6) **394.2**

Tunis, E. The tavern at the ferry p77-99 (5 and up) **973.2**

History—1775-1783, Revolution—Biography

Fritz, J. And then what happened, Paul Revere? (2-4) **92**

Fritz, J. Why don't you get a horse, Sam Adams? (3-5) **92**

Fritz, J. Will you sign here, John Hancock? (3-5) **92**

Lee, M. Paul Revere (5 and up) **92**

McGovern, A. The secret soldier: the story of Deborah Sampson [Gannett] (3-5) **92**

History—1775-1783, Revolution—Fiction

Avi. The fighting ground (5 and up) **Fic**

Collier, J. L. My brother Sam is dead (6 and up) **Fic**

Collier, J. L. War comes to Willy Freeman (6 and up) **Fic**

Forbes, E. Johnny Tremain (5 and up) **Fic**

Gauch, P. L. This time, Tempe Wick? (3-5) **Fic**

Klaveness, J. O. The Griffin legacy (6 and up) **Fic**

Lawson, R. Mr. Revere and I (5 and up) **Fic**

O'Dell, S. Sarah Bishop (6 and up) **Fic**

Rappaport, D. The Boston coffee party **E**

Wibberley, L. John Treegate's musket (6 and up) **Fic**

History—1783-1809

See also Louisiana Purchase

Phelan, M. K. The story of the Louisiana Purchase (5 and up) **973.4**

History—1783-1809—Fiction

Collier, J. L. Jump ship to freedom (6 and up) **Fic**

Collier, J. L. Who is Carrie? (6 and up) **Fic**

History—1783-1865

Tunis, E. The young United States, 1783 to 1830 (5 and up) **973**

History—1783-1865—Fiction

Nixon, J. L. A family apart (5 and up) **Fic**

History—1800-1899 (19th century)—Biography

Fritz, J. Make way for Sam Houston (4 and up) **92**

History—1812-1815, War of 1812

See/See also pages in the following book(s):

Key, F. S. The Star-Spangled Banner **782.42**

History—1815-1861

Baker, B. The Pig War (k-2) **973.6**

History—1861-1865, Civil War

Fritz, J. Stonewall [biography of Stonewall Jackson] (4 and up) **92**

Jordan, R. P. The Civil War (6 and up) **973.7**

See/See also pages in the following book(s):

Freedman, R. Lincoln: a photobiography p72-117 (4 and up) **92**

McCall, E. S. Biography of a river: the living Mississippi p103-10 (6 and up) **977**

History—1861-1865, Civil War—Biography

Reit, S. Behind rebel lines: the incredible story of Emma Edmonds, Civil War spy (4 and up) **92**

Weidhorn, M. Robert E. Lee (5 and up) **92**

United States—*Continued*
History—1861-1865, Civil War—Campaigns
See also Gettysburg (Pa.), Battle of, 1863
History—1861-1865, Civil War—Fiction
Beatty, P. Charley Skedaddle (5 and up) **Fic**
Beatty, P. Turn homeward, Hannalee (5 and up) **Fic**
Hunt, I. Across five Aprils (5 and up) **Fic**
Keith, H. Rifles for Watie (6 and up) **Fic**
Lunn, J. L. S. The root cellar (5 and up) **Fic**
Reeder, C. Shades of gray (4 and up) **Fic**
History—1861-1865, Civil War—Sources
Voices from the Civil War (6 and up) **973.7**
History—1914-1918, World War
See World War, 1914-1918—United States
History—Bibliography
VanMeter, V. American history for children and young adults: an annotated bibliographic index **016.973**
History—Dictionaries
Kane, J. N. Famous first facts: a record of first happenings, discoveries, and inventions in American history **031.02**
History—Miscellanea
Weitzman, D. L. My backyard history book (4 and up) **973**
History—Periodicals
Cobblestone **973.05**
History—Poetry
Benét, R. A book of Americans (4 and up) **811**

See/See also pages in the following book(s):
Favorite poems, old and new p401-55 (4-6) **808.81**
History, Local
Weitzman, D. L. My backyard history book (4 and up) **973**
Immigration and emigration
Fisher, L. E. Ellis Island (4 and up) **325.73**
Freedman, R. Immigrant kids (4 and up) **325.73**
Jacobs, W. J. Ellis Island (3-5) **325.73**
Kurelek, W. They sought a new world (4 and up) **325**
Rosenberg, M. B. Making a new home in America (4-6) **325.73**
Siegel, B. Sam Ellis's island (3-6) **325.73**
Immigration and emigration—Fiction
Levine, E. I hate English! **E**
Levinson, R. Watch the stars come out **E**
Levitin, S. Silver days (5 and up) **Fic**
Sandin, J. The long way westward **E**
Industries

See/See also pages in the following book(s):
Tunis, E. The young United States, 1783 to 1830 p60-71 (5 and up) **973**
Maps
Rand McNally children's atlas of the United States (4-6) **912**
Pictorial works
Anno, M. Anno's U.S.A **E**
Presidents
See Presidents—United States
Race relations

See/See also pages in the following book(s):
Meltzer, M. The Chinese Americans p102-54 (6 and up) **305.8**
Meltzer, M. The Hispanic Americans p89-99 (6 and up) **305.8**
Social life and customs
Caney, S. Steven Caney's kids' America (4 and up) **790.1**
Loeper, J. J. Going to school in 1876 (4 and up) **370.9**
Perl, L. Hunter's stew and hangtown fry: what pioneer America ate and why (4 and up) **641.5**
Tunis, E. The young United States, 1783 to 1830 (5 and up) **973**
Social life and customs—1600-1775, Colonial period
Loeper, J. J. Going to school in 1776 (4 and up) **370.9**
Penner, L. R. The colonial cookbook (5 and up) **641.5**
Perl, L. Slumps, grunts, and snickerdoodles: what Colonial America ate and why (4 and up) **641.5**
Tunis, E. Colonial craftsmen and the beginnings of American industry (5 and up) **670**
Tunis, E. Colonial living (5 and up) **973.2**
Tunis, E. The tavern at the ferry (5 and up) **973.2**
Soldiers
See Soldiers—United States
Statistics
Information please almanac, atlas & yearbook **031.02**
The World almanac and book of facts **031.02**
United States. Air Force. Thunderbirds
Sullivan, G. The Thunderbirds (4 and up) **797.5**

United States. Army. Corps of Engineers
See/See also pages in the following book(s):
McCall, E. S. Biography of a river: the living Mississippi (6 and up) **977**

United States. Declaration of Independence
Dalgliesh, A. The Fourth of July story (2-4) **973.3**
See/See also pages in the following book(s):
Giblin, J. Fireworks, picnics, and flags p2-20 (3-6) **394.2**

United States. National Aeronautics and Space Administration
Smith, H. E. Daring the unknown: a history of NASA (5 and up) **629.4**

United States. National Museum of Natural History *See* National Museum of Natural History (U.S.)

United States. Supreme Court
Greene, C. The Supreme Court (1-3) **347**
Sgroi, P. P. The living Constitution: landmark Supreme Court decisions (5 and up) **342**
Stein, R. C. The story of the powers of the Supreme Court (4-6) **347**

United States coin book, Fell's. Hughes, R. P. **737.4**

United States Naval Expedition to Japan (1852-1854)
Blumberg, R. Commodore Perry in the land of the Shogun (5 and up) **952**

The **Universal** Declaration of Human Rights. Rocha, R. **341**

Universe
Anno, M. Anno's medieval world (3-6) **909.07**
Asimov, I. Mythology and the universe (3-5) **523.1**
Atkinson, S. Journey into space (4-6) **523**
Branley, F. M. Mysteries of the universe (6 and up) **523.1**

University of Chicago. Center for Children's Books
The Best in children's books. See The Best in children's books **028.1**

Unleaving. Paton Walsh, J. **Fic**

Unriddling: all sorts of riddles to puzzle your guessery. Schwartz, A. **398.6**

Unstead, R. J. (Robert John)
See inside a castle (5 and up) **728.8**
(jt. auth) Wood, T. The 1940s **909.82**

Unstead, Robert John *See* Unstead, R. J. (Robert John)

The **unsung** heroes. Aaseng, N. **920**

Untermeyer, Louis, 1885-1977
(ed) Rainbow in the sky. See Rainbow in the sky **821.008**

Unthan, Carl Herman, 1848-1929
See/See also pages in the following book(s):
Drimmer, F. Born different p150-73 (6 and up) **920**

Until the celebration. Snyder, Z. K. See note under Snyder, Z. K. Below the root **Fic**

The **unwilling** musician. Timpanelli, G.
In Timpanelli, G. Tales from the roof of the world p29-41 **398.2**

Unwin, Nora Spicer, 1907-1982
(il) Yates, E. Amos Fortune, free man **92**

Up a road slowly. Hunt, I. **Fic**

Up a tree. Young, E. **E**

Up and down on the merry-go-round. Martin, B. **E**

Up from Jericho Tel. Konigsburg, E. L. **Fic**

Up goes the skyscraper! Gibbons, G. **690**

Up the chimney down. Aiken, J.
In Aiken, J. Up the chimney down, and other stories p118-48 **S C**

Up the chimney down, and other stories. Aiken, J. **S C**

Ups and downs with Oink and Pearl. Chorao, K. **E**

The **Upside** down riddle book (k-2) **793.73**

Upside-downers. Anno, M. **E**

The **upstairs** room. Reiss, J. **92**

Uranus (Planet)
Branley, F. M. Uranus (3-6) **523.4**
Simon, S. Uranus (1-4) **523.4**
Yeomans, D. K. The distant planets (4-6) **523.4**
See/See also pages in the following book(s):
Harris, A. The great Voyager adventure p45-52 (5 and up) **523.4**
Kelch, J. W. Small worlds: exploring the 60 moons of our solar system p84-94 (6 and up) **523.9**

Uraschimataro and the turtle
Quayle, E. The adventures of a fisher lad
In Quayle, E. The shining princess, and other Japanese legends p57-68 **398.2**
Uchida, Y. Urashima Taro and the princess of the sea
In The Scott, Foresman anthology of children's literature p332-36 **808.8**
Urashima
In Best-loved folktales of the world p521-23 **398.2**

Urashima Taro and the princess of the sea. Uchida, Y.
In The Scott, Foresman anthology of children's literature p332-36 **808.8**

Urban areas *See* Cities and towns
Urban life *See* City life
Urban planning *See* City planning
Urban renewal
See also City planning
Pictorial works
Von Tscharner, R. New Providence (3-6) **307.7**
Urban roosts: where birds nest in the city. Bash, B. **598**
Urbanovic, Jackie
(il) Fisher, G. L. The survival guide for kids with LD (learning differences) **371.9**
Ursa Major
Branley, F. M. The Big Dipper (k-3) **523.8**
Krupp, E. C. The Big Dipper and you (3-5) **523**
Ursell, Martin
(il) Corbett, W. J. The song of Pentecost **Fic**
Us and Uncle Fraud. Lowry, L. **Fic**
Use your head, dear. Aliki. **E**
User friendly. Bethancourt, T. E.
In Connections: short stories by outstanding writers for young adults p108-21 **S C**
Usher, Kerry
Heroes, gods & emperors from Roman mythology (5 and up) **292**
Using picture storybooks to teach literary devices. Hall, S. **016.8**
USSR *See* Soviet Union
Utah
McCarthy, B. Utah
In America the beautiful **973**
Fiction
Fitzgerald, J. D. The Great Brain (4 and up) **Fic**
Utzel & his daughter, Poverty. Singer, I. B.
In Singer, I. B. Stories for children p237-41 **S C**
In Singer, I. B. When Shlemiel went to Warsaw & other stories p73-80 **398.2**

V

Vaca, Alvar Nuñez Cabeza de *See* Nuñez Cabeza de Vaca, Alvar, 16th cent.
Vacations
Fiction
Baker, L. A. Morning beach **E**
Byars, B. C. The animal, the vegetable, and John D Jones (5 and up) **Fic**
Khalsa, D. K. My family vacation **E**

Vaccination
Showers, P. No measles, no mumps for me (k-3) **614.4**
Vachula, Monica
(il) The Crest and the hide, and other African stories of heroes, chiefs, bards, hunters, sorcerers, and common people. See The Crest and the hide, and other African stories of heroes, chiefs, bards, hunters, sorcerers, and common people **398.2**
Vagabonds *See* Tramps
Vagabonds (Folk tale)
Grimm, J. The good-for-nothings
In Grimm, J. More tales from Grimm p77-83 **398.2**
Grimm, J. The pack of ragamuffins
In Grimm, J. The complete Grimm's fairy tales p65-66 **398.2**
Vagin, Vladimir Vasil'evich, 1937-
(jt. auth) Asch, F. Here comes the cat! **E**
Vagrants *See* Tramps
Valdez, Luis
See/See also pages in the following book(s):
Morey, J. Famous Mexican Americans p140-52 (5 and up) **920**
The **valentine**. Garfield, L.
In Garfield, L. The apprentices **S C**
Valentine foxes. Watson, C. **E**
Valentine poems (k-3) **808.81**
Valentine Rosy. Greenwald, S. See note under Greenwald, S. Give us a great big smile, Rosy Cole **Fic**
Valentine's Day
Barkin, C. Happy Valentine's Day! (4-6) **394.2**
Barth, E. Hearts, cupids, and red roses (3-6) **394.2**
Bulla, C. R. St. Valentine's Day (1-3) **394.2**
Gibbons, G. Valentine's Day (k-2) **394.2**
See/See also pages in the following book(s):
Bauer, C. F. Celebrations p279-93 **808.8**
Fiction
Hurd, T. Little Mouse's big valentine **E**
Modell, F. One zillion valentines **E**
Watson, C. Valentine foxes **E**
Poetry
Prelutsky, J. It's Valentine's Day (1-3) **811**
Valentine poems (k-3) **808.81**
Valiant chattee-maker
Godden, R. The valiant chatti-maker **398.2**
The Valiant chattee-maker
In Best-loved folktales of the world p575-80 **398.2**

The **valiant** little tailor. Ehrlich, A.
In Ehrlich, A. The Random House book of fairy tales p102-17 **398.2**

The **valiant** little tailor. Grimm, J.
In Grimm, J. The complete Grimm's fairy tales p112-20 **398.2**

Vālmīki
Rāmāyaṇa; adaptation. See Beach, M. C. The adventures of Rama **891**

Values in selected children's books of fiction and fantasy. Field, C. W. **028.5**

The **vampire**. Afanas'ev, A. N.
In Afanas'ev, A. N. Russian fairy tales p593-98 **398.2**

Van Allsburg, Chris
Ben's dream **E**
The garden of Abdul Gasazi **E**
Jumanji **E**
Just a dream **E**
The mysteries of Harris Burdick **E**
The Polar Express **E**
The stranger **E**
Two bad ants **E**
The wreck of the Zephyr **E**
The Z was zapped **E**
See/See also pages in the following book(s):
Newbery and Caldecott Medal books, 1976-1985 p230-37 **028.5**

Van der Linde, Polly *See* Linde, Polly van der

Van der Linde, Tasha *See* Linde, Tasha van der

Van Gogh, Vincent *See* Gogh, Vincent van, 1853-1890

Van Laan, Nancy
Possum come a-knockin' **E**

Van Leeuwen, Jean
Amanda Pig and her big brother Oliver. See note under Van Leeuwen, J. Tales of Oliver Pig **E**
The great Christmas kidnapping caper (3-5) **Fic**
The great rescue operation (3-5) **Fic**
I was a 98-pound duckling (6 and up) **Fic**
More tales of Amanda Pig. See note under Van Leeuwen, J. Tales of Oliver Pig **E**
More tales of Oliver Pig. See note under Van Leeuwen, J. Tales of Oliver Pig **E**
Oliver, Amanda, and Grandmother Pig. See note under Van Leeuwen, J. Tales of Oliver Pig **E**
Oliver and Amanda's Christmas. See note under Van Leeuwen, J. Tales of Oliver Pig **E**
Oliver Pig at school. See note under Van Leeuwen, J. Tales of Oliver Pig **E**
Tales of Amanda Pig. See note under Van Leeuwen, J. Tales of Oliver Pig **E**
Tales of Oliver Pig **E**

Van Loon, Hendrik Willem, 1882-1944
See/See also pages in the following book(s):
Newbery Medal books, 1922-1955 p13-16 **028.5**

Van Orden, Phyllis J.
The collection program in schools **027.8**

Van Rynbach, Iris
(il) Child, L. M. F. Over the river and through the wood **811**

Van Steenburgh, D. Benjamin
(il) Hodges, M. If you had a horse **398.2**

Van Straalen, Alice
The book of holidays around the world (4 and up) **394.2**

Van Vorst, Marie Louise, 1867-1936
A Norse lullaby (k-1) **811**

Van Woerkom, Dorothy
Hidden messages (2-4) **595.7**

Van Wormer, Joe, 1913-
Eagles (4 and up) **598**
How to be a wildlife photographer (6 and up) **778.9**

Vanderwerf, Mary Ann
(jt. auth) Kennedy, D. M. Science & technology in fact and fiction: a guide to children's books **016.5**

The **vanishing** manatee. Clark, M. G. **599.5**

The **vanishing** pumpkin. Johnston, T. **E**

Vanishing species *See* Endangered species

VanMeter, Vandelia
American history for children and young adults: an annotated bibliographic index **016.973**

Varley, Susan
Badger's parting gifts **E**

Vasilisa the beauty
Afanas'ev, A. N. Vasilisa the Beautiful
In Afanas'ev, A. N. Russian fairy tales p439-47 **398.2**
In Afanas'ev, A. N. Russian folk tales p57-68 **398.2**
Sherman, J. Vassilisa the wise **398.2**

Vassilisa the wise. Sherman, J. **398.2**

Vassilissa the cunning and the tzar of the sea
Afanas'ev, A. N. The Sea King and Vasilisa the Wise
In Afanas'ev, A. N. Russian fairy tales p427-37 **398.2**

Vassilissa the valiant. McCarty, T.
In The Scott, Foresman anthology of children's literature p289-91 **808.8**

Vaults (Sepulchral) *See* Tombs
Vazuza and Volga
Afanas'ev, A. N. The two rivers
In Afanas'ev, A. N. Russian fairy tales p172 **398.2**
Vegetable gardening
Kuhn, D. More than just a vegetable garden (2-4) **635**
Oechsli, H. In my garden (1-3) **635**
Fiction
Ehlert, L. Growing vegetable soup **E**
Vegetable soup. Modesitt, J. **E**
Vegetables
See also Potatoes
Ehlert, L. Eating the alphabet **E**
McMillan, B. Growing colors **E**
Sobol, H. L. A book of vegetables (1-3) **635**
Vegetarianism
Fiction
Hurwitz, J. Much ado about Aldo (3-5) **Fic**
Vehicles
Goor, R. In the driver's seat (2-4) **629.04**
Rockwell, A. F. Big wheels (k-1) **629.225**
Rockwell, A. F. Things that go (k-1) **629.04**
Vehicles in art
Ames, L. J. Draw 50 boats, ships, trucks & trains (4 and up) **743**
Ames, L. J. Draw 50 cars, trucks, and motorcycles (4 and up) **743**
Velasquez, Eric
(il) Naidoo, B. Chain of fire **Fic**
(il) Naidoo, B. Journey to Jo'burg **Fic**
Velásquez, William C.
See/See also pages in the following book(s):
Morey, J. Famous Mexican Americans p153-66 (5 and up) **920**
Velázquez, Diego, 1599-1660
About
Raboff, E. Diego Rodriguez de Silva y Velasquez (4 and up) **759.6**
Treviño, E. B. de. I, Juan de Pareja (6 and up) **Fic**
The **velvet** room. Snyder, Z. K. **Fic**
The **velveteen** rabbit. Bianco, M. W. **Fic**
Venice (Italy)
Fiction
Montresor, B. The witches of Venice **E**
History
Ventura, P. Venice, birth of a city (4-6) **945**
Venice, birth of a city. Ventura, P. **945**
Venino, Suzanne
Amazing animal groups (k-3) **591.5**
Animals helping people (k-3) **636.088**
Vennema, Peter
(jt. auth) Stanley, D. Good Queen Bess: the story of Elizabeth I of England **92**
(jt. auth) Stanley, D. Shaka, king of the Zulus **92**
Ventura, Cynthia
(ed) Where angels glide at dawn. See Where angels glide at dawn **S C**
Ventura, Piero
Great composers (5 and up) **780.9**
Great painters (5 and up) **759**
Michelangelo's world (5 and up) **92**
There once was a time (5 and up) **909**
Venice, birth of a city (4-6) **945**
(il) Ceserani, G. P. Marco Polo **92**
Venus (Roman deity) *See* Aphrodite (Greek deity)
Verbitsky, Alexander
(il) Kreutzer, P. Little League's official how-to-play baseball book **796.357**
Verdi, Giuseppe, 1813-1901
Price, L. Aïda **792.5**
Vermont
McNair, S. Vermont
In America the beautiful **973**
Fiction
Henry, M. Justin Morgan had a horse (4 and up) **Fic**
Kinsey-Warnock, N. The Canada geese quilt (3-5) **Fic**
Peck, R. N. A day no pigs would die (6 and up) **Fic**
Peck, R. N. Soup (5 and up) **Fic**
Stevenson, L. C. Happily after all (4 and up) **Fic**
Verne, Jules, 1828-1905
Twenty thousand leagues under the sea (5 and up) **Fic**
About
Quackenbush, R. M. Who said there's no man on the moon? a story of Jules Verne (2-4) **92**
Veronica. Duvoisin, R. **E**
Vertebrates
Selsam, M. E. A first look at animals with backbones (1-3) **596**
Verwhilghen, Leo A.
All things are linked
In The Crest and the hide, and other African stories of heroes, chiefs, bards, hunters, sorcerers, and common people p101-04 **398.2**

Verwhilghen, Leo A.—*Continued*
The crest and the hide
In The Crest and the hide, and other African stories of heroes, chiefs, bards, hunters, sorcerers, and common people p13-18 **398.2**
The **very** best of friends. Wild, M. **E**
The **very** busy spider. Carle, E. **E**
Very far away. Sendak, M. **E**
A **Very** happy donkey
In The Magic orange tree, and other Haitian folktales p157-63 **398.2**
The **very** hungry caterpillar. Carle, E. **E**
Very last first time. Andrews, J. **E**
A **very** mice joke book. Gounaud, K. J. **793.73**
The **very** pretty lady. Babbitt, N.
In Babbitt, N. The Devil's storybook p13-20 **S C**
A **very** special house. Krauss, R. **E**
Very Tall Mouse and Very Short Mouse. Lobel, A.
In The Read-aloud treasury p207-13 **808.8**
A **very** young dancer. Krementz, J. **792.8**
A **very** young gymnast. Krementz, J. **796.44**
A **very** young musician. Krementz, J. **788**
A **very** young rider. Krementz, J. **798.2**
A **very** young skater. Krementz, J. **796.91**
A **very** young skier. Krementz, J. **796.93**
Veterans
Fiction
Bauer, M. D. Rain of fire (5 and up) **Fic**
Hahn, M. D. December stillness (6 and up) **Fic**
Veterinary medicine
Kuklin, S. Taking my cat to the vet (k-2) **636.8**
Kuklin, S. Taking my dog to the vet (k-2) **636.7**
See/See also pages in the following book(s):
Chrystie, F. N. Pets p213-54 (4 and up) **636.088**
Fiction
Carris, J. D. Pets, vets, and Marty Howard (5 and up) **Fic**
Vicky gets the vote. Gotwalt, H. L. M.
In Gotwalt, H. L. M. Everyday plays for boys and girls p147-58 **812**
Victory in the Pacific. Marrin, A. **940.54**
Video Christmas. Dias, E. J.
In The Big book of Christmas plays p26-40 **808.82**
Videotapes
Catalogs
Parent's choice guide to videocassettes for children **016.79143**
Vietnam
Garland, S. Vietnam, rebuilding a nation (4 and up) **959.704**
Fiction
Lee, J. M. Bà-Năm **E**
Folklore
See Folklore—Vietnam
Social life and customs
Huynh, Q. N. The land I lost: adventures of a boy in Vietnam (4 and up) **92**
Vietnam, rebuilding a nation. Garland, S. **959.704**
Vietnam Veterans Memorial (Washington, D.C.)
Ashabranner, B. K. Always to remember (5 and up) **959.704**
Fiction
Bunting, E. The Wall **E**
Hahn, M. D. December stillness (6 and up) **Fic**
Vietnam War, 1961-1975
Ashabranner, B. K. Always to remember (5 and up) **959.704**
Lawson, D. An album of the Vietnam War (5 and up) **959.704**
Fiction
Boyd, C. D. Charlie Pippin (4-6) **Fic**
Nelson, T. And one for all (6 and up) **Fic**
Vietnamese
United States
Coutant, H. First snow (2-4) **Fic**
United States—Fiction
Gilson, J. Hello, my name is Scrambled Eggs (4 and up) **Fic**
Vietnamese Americans
Rutledge, P. The Vietnamese in America
In The In America series **305.8**
Fiction
Paterson, K. Park's quest (5 and up) **Fic**
Vietnamese cookery *See* Cookery, Vietnamese
The **Vietnamese** in America. Rutledge, P.
In The In America series **305.8**
The **view** from the cherry tree. Roberts, W. D. **Fic**
The **view** from the oak. Kohl, J. **591.5**
Vigna, Judith
Boot weather **E**
Viguers, Ruth Hill
(comp) Illustrators of children's books. See Illustrators of children's books **741.6**

Vikings
See/See also pages in the following book(s):
Lyttle, R. B. Land beyond the river p106-24 (6 and up) **940.1**
Fiction
Haugaard, E. C. Leif the unlucky (6 and up) **Fic**
Wisniewski, D. Elfwyn's saga **E**
The **village** by the sea. Fox, P. **Fic**
Village in Egypt. See Bennett, O. A family in Egypt **962**
The **village** of blue stone. Trimble, S. **970.004**
A **village** of fools. Crossley-Holland, K.
In Crossley-Holland, K. British folk tales p36-37 **398.2**
The **village** of round and square houses. Grifalconi, A. **398.2**
Villages
Provensen, A. Town & country (k-2) **307.7**
Villanueva Collado, Alfredo
The day we went to see snow
In Where angels glide at dawn p27-33 **S C**
Villeneuve, Madame de
Beauty and the beast
In Best-loved folktales of the world p8-23 **398.2**
In The Blue fairy book p100-19 **398.2**
In The Scott, Foresman anthology of children's literature p206-16 **808.8**
Villios, Lynne W.
Cooking the Greek way (5 and up) **641.5**
Vincent, Gabrielle
Bravo, Ernest and Celestine! See note under Vincent, G. Ernest and Celestine **E**
Ernest and Celestine **E**
Ernest and Celestine at the circus. See note under Vincent, G. Ernest and Celestine **E**
Ernest and Celestine's patchwork quilt. See note under Vincent, G. Ernest and Celestine **E**
Ernest and Celestine's picnic. See note under Vincent, G. Ernest and Celestine **E**
Feel better, Ernest! See note under Vincent, G. Ernest and Celestine **E**
Merry Christmas, Ernest and Celestine. See note under Vincent, G. Ernest and Celestine **E**
Smile, Ernest and Celestine. See note under Vincent, G. Ernest and Celestine **E**
Where are you, Ernest and Celestine? See note under Vincent, G. Ernest and Celestine **E**
Vincent-the-Good and the electric train. Levoy, M.
In Levoy, M. The witch of Fourth Street, and other stories **S C**
Vinci, Leonardo da *See* Leonardo, da Vinci, 1452-1519
The **Vingananee** and the tree toad. Aardema, V. **398.2**
Vining, Elizabeth Gray, 1902-
Adam of the road (5 and up) **Fic**
See/See also pages in the following book(s):
Newbery Medal books, 1922-1955 p227-41 **028.5**
Violinists, violoncellists, etc.
Fiction
Foley, P. John and the fiddler (3-5) **Fic**
Greenwald, S. Give us a great big smile, Rosy Cole (3-5) **Fic**
Viorst, Judith
Alexander and the terrible, horrible, no good, very bad day **E**
Alexander, who used to be rich last Sunday. See note under Viorst, J. Alexander and the terrible, horrible, no good, very bad day **E**
Earrings! **E**
The good-bye book **E**
If I were in charge of the world and other worries (3-6) **811**
My mama says there aren't any zombies, ghosts, vampires, creatures, demons, monsters, fiends, goblins, or things **E**
Rosie and Michael **E**
The southpaw [short story]
In Free to be—you and me p71-75 **810.8**
The tenth good thing about Barney **E**
Virginia
McNair, S. Virginia
In America the beautiful **973**
Fiction
Beatty, P. Charley Skedaddle (5 and up) **Fic**
Paterson, K. Bridge to Terabithia (4 and up) **Fic**
Virtue goes to town. Yep, L.
In Yep, L. The rainbow people p136-42 **398.2**
Viruses
Berger, M. Germs make me sick! (k-3) **616.9**
Vision
See also Eye
Hidden worlds (5 and up) **500**
Parker, S. The eye and seeing (4 and up) **612.8**
See/See also pages in the following book(s):
Simon, S. The optical illusion book p12-16 (4 and up) **152.14**

Vision disorders
Fiction
Little, J. From Anna (4-6) **Fic**
A **visit** from St. Nicholas. Moore, C. C.
In Diane Goode's American Christmas p74-78 **810.8**
In The Scott, Foresman anthology of children's literature p144-45 **808.8**
See also Moore, C. C. The night before Christmas **811**
A **visit** to the bank. Bond, M.
In Bond, M. Paddington's storybook p52-65 **S C**
A **visit** to Washington, D.C. Krementz, J. **975.3**
A **visit** to William Blake's inn. Willard, N. **811**
Visiting the art museum. Brown, L. K. **708**
The **visitors**. Townsend, J. R. **Fic**
Vittorini, Domenico
The wooden bowl
In Bauer, C. F. Celebrations p68-70 **808.8**
Vivas, Julie, 1947-
(il) Wild, M. The very best of friends **E**
Vizier who was punished
The Story of the vizier who was punished
In The Arabian nights entertainments p34-47 **398.2**
Vo, Dinh Mai, 1933-
The fly
In Best-loved folktales of the world p572-75 **398.2**
The little lizard's sorrow
In Best-loved folktales of the world p569-72 **398.2**
(il) Coutant, H. First snow **Fic**
(il) Coutant, H. The gift **Fic**
(il) Huynh, Q. N. The land I lost: adventures of a boy in Vietnam **92**
(il) Vuong, L. D. The brocaded slipper, and other Vietnamese tales **398.2**
Voake, Charlotte
(il) Pearce, P. The way to Sattin Shore **Fic**
(il) Waddell, M. Amy said **E**
Vocabulary
Ahlberg, J. The baby's catalogue **E**
Burningham, J. Slam bang **E**
Hoban, T. Over, under & through, and other spatial concepts **E**
Kaye, C. B. Word works (4 and up) **410**
Maestro, B. Taxi **E**
McMillan, B. Super, super, superwords (k-2) **422**
Terban, M. Superdupers! really funny real words (3-5) **427**
Fiction
Wells, R. Max's first word **E**
Vocational guidance
Aaseng, N. Midstream changes (5 and up) **331.7**
Vocations *See* Occupations
Vogel, Carole Garbuny
The great Yellowstone fire (3-6) **574.5**
Vogt, Gregory
Space stations (4 and up) **629.44**
The **Voice** of death
In The Red fairy book p182-85 **398.2**
The **voice** of the great bell. Hodges, M. **398.2**
Voices from the Civil War (6 and up) **973.7**
Voight, Erna
(il) Prokofiev, S. Peter and the wolf **784.2**
Voigt, Cynthia
Come a stranger (6 and up) **Fic**
Dicey's song (6 and up) **Fic**
Homecoming (6 and up) **Fic**
Izzy, willy-nilly (6 and up) **Fic**
The runner [excerpt]
In Face to face: a collection of stories by celebrated Soviet and American writers p23-38 **S C**
Stories about Rosie **E**
See/See also pages in the following book(s):
Newbery and Caldecott Medal books, 1976-1985 p107-19 **028.5**
Volavková, Hana
(ed) I never saw another butterfly. See I never saw another butterfly **741.9**
Volcanoes
Branley, F. M. Volcanoes (k-3) **551.2**
Lauber, P. Volcano: the eruption and healing of Mount St. Helens (4 and up) **551.2**
Place, M. T. Mount St. Helens (5 and up) **551.2**
Simon, S. Volcanoes (2-5) **551.2**
See/See also pages in the following book(s):
Gallant, R. A. Our restless earth p56-62 (4 and up) **550**
Our violent earth p22-38 (4 and up) **363.3**
Volsunga saga
The Story of Sigurd
In The Red fairy book p357-67 **398.2**
Voluntarism
Fiction
Clifford, E. The rocking chair rebellion (6 and up) **Fic**

Von Mason, Stephen
(il) Rohmer, H. Brother Anansi and the cattle ranch **398.2**
Von Schmidt, Eric, 1931-
(il) Fleischman, S. By the Great Horn Spoon! **Fic**
(il) Fleischman, S. Chancy and the grand rascal **Fic**
(il) Fleischman, S. The ghost on Saturday night **Fic**
(il) Fleischman, S. Humbug Mountain **Fic**
(il) Fleischman, S. Mr. Mysterious & Company **Fic**
Von Tscharner, Renata
New Providence (3-6) **307.7**
Voting *See* Elections
The **voyage** of the Beagle [biography of Charles Darwin]. Hyndley, K. **92**
The **voyage** of the Dawn Treader. Lewis, C. S. See note under Lewis, C. S. The lion, the witch and the wardrobe **Fic**
The **voyage** of the Ludgate Hill. Willard, N. **811**
Voyagers from space. Lauber, P. **523.5**
Voyages. Whitman, W. **811**
Voyages and travels
See also Travel
Ceserani, G. P. Marco Polo (3-6) **92**
Humble, R. The travels of Marco Polo (4-6) **910.4**
Fiction
Bulla, C. R. A lion to guard us (3-5) **Fic**
Day, E. C. John Tabor's ride **E**
Lyon, G. E. A regular rolling Noah **E**
Vultures
Fiction
Peet, B. Eli **E**
Vuong, Lynette Dyer, 1938-
The brocaded slipper, and other Vietnamese tales (3-6) **398.2**
Contents: The brocaded slipper; Little Finger of the watermelon patch; The fairy grotto; Master Frog; The lampstand princess

W

Waber, Bernard
An anteater named Arthur **E**
Bernard **E**
Funny, funny Lyle. See note under Waber, B. The house on East 88th Street **E**
The house on East 88th Street **E**
I was all thumbs **E**
Ira says goodbye. See note under Waber, B. Ira sleeps over **E**
Ira sleeps over **E**
Lovable Lyle. See note under Waber, B. The house on East 88th Street **E**
Lyle and the birthday party. See note under Waber, B. The house on East 88th Street **E**
Lyle finds his mother. See note under Waber, B. The house on East 88th Street **E**
Lyle, Lyle, crocodile. See note under Waber, B. The house on East 88th Street **E**
Wachter, Oralee
No more secrets for me (2-5) **362.7**
Waddell, Martin
Amy said **E**
Wade, Barrie
Little monster **E**
Wade, Linda R.
James Carter: thirty-ninth president of the United States (4 and up) **92**
Wadlow, Robert Pershing, 1918-1940
See/See also pages in the following book(s):
Drimmer, F. Born different p48-71 (6 and up) **920**
Wagner, Jane
J. T. (3-6) **Fic**
Wagon wheels. Brenner, B. **E**
Wagons *See* Carriages and carts
Wahl, Jan, 1933-
Humphrey's bear **E**
Wahlenberg, Anna, 1858-1933
Linda-Gold and the old king
In The Scott, Foresman anthology of children's literature p242-44 **808.8**
Wailing Wall (Jerusalem) *See* Western Wall (Jerusalem)
The **Wailing** Wall. Fisher, L. E. **221.9**
Wainwright, Francis
(il) Collodi, C. The adventures of Pinocchio **Fic**
Wait till Helen comes. Hahn, M. D. **Fic**
Wait till Martin comes
In The Diane Goode book of American folk tales and songs p35-37 **398.2**
Wait till the moon is full. Brown, M. W. **E**
Waiting for Hannah. Russo, M. **E**
Waiting for Mama. De Regniers, B. S. **E**
Waiting for Noah. Oppenheim, S. L. **E**
Waiting-for-papa stories. Roberts, B. **E**
Waiting-for-spring stories. Roberts, B. **E**
Wake up, city! Tresselt, A. R. **E**
The **waking** of Men. Curry, J. L.
In Curry, J. L. Back in the beforetime p116 **398.2**

The **waking** of the prince. Brooke, W. J.
In Brooke, W. J. A telling of the tales: five stories p3-33 **S C**
Waldee, Lynne Marie
Cooking the French way (5 and up) **641.5**
Waldherr, Kris
(il) Ehrlich, A. Rapunzel **398.2**
Waldman, Neil, 1947-
(il) Luenn, N. Nessa's fish **E**
(il) Noyes, A. The highwayman **821**
Wales
Sutherland, D. B. Wales (4 and up) **942.9**
Fiction
Bawden, N. Carrie's war (4 and up) **Fic**
Bond, N. A string in the harp (6 and up) **Fic**
Cooper, S. The grey king (5 and up) **Fic**
Kimmel, M. M. Magic in the mist (1-4) **Fic**
Folklore
See Folklore—Wales
A **walk** on the Great Barrier Reef. Arnold, C. **574.92**
Walk the world's rim. Baker, B. **Fic**
Walker, Alice, 1944-
Langston Hughes, American poet (2-5) **92**
Walker, Barbara K.
A treasury of Turkish folktales for children (4 and up) **398.2**
Contents: The mouse and the elephant; Who's there? And what do you want?; Hasan, the heroic mouse-child; The magpie and the milk; The mosquito and the water buffalo; The rabbit and the wolf; The lion's den; The crow and the snake; Lazy Keloğlan and the sultan's daughter; The three brothers and the hand of fate; Keloğlan and the twelve dancing princesses; I know what I'll do; Nasreddin Hoca, seller of wisdom; Nasreddin Hoca and the third shot; The Hoca as Tamerlane's tax collector; The Hoca and the candle; Teeny-Tiny and the witch-woman; Karaçor and the giants; The wonderful pumpkin; The courage of Kazan; Just say hiç!; How Deli kept his part of the bargain; Two fools and the gifts for Mehmet; Three tricksters and the pot of butter; Trousers Mehmet and the sultan's daughter; Stargazer to the sultan; The bird of fortune; The princess and the pig; The princess and the goatherd; Hamal Hasan and the baby day; The round sultan and the straight answer; A mirror, a carpet, and a lemon; New patches for old; Hasan and Allah's greatness
Walker, Barbara Muhs, 1928-
The Little House cookbook (5 and up) **641.5**
Walker, Lester
Carpentry for children (4 and up) **694**
Housebuilding for children (2 and up) **690**
Walker, Ormiston H.
Experimenting with air and flight (6 and up) **507**
Walker, Sally M.
Glaciers (4-6) **551.3**
Walking
Fiction
Hest, A. The crack-of-dawn walkers **E**
Walking the road to freedom: a story about Sojourner Truth. Ferris, J. **92**
The **Wall**. Bunting, E. **E**
Wall Street Journal
See/See also pages in the following book(s):
Aaseng, N. From rags to riches p19-23 (5 and up) **920**
Wallaby Creek. Powzyk, J. A. **591.9**
Wallace, Daisy
(ed) Ghost poems. See Ghost poems **821.008**
(ed) Monster poems. See Monster poems **821.008**
(ed) Witch poems. See Witch poems **821.008**
Wallace, Ian, 1950-
Chin Chiang and the dragon's dance **E**
(il) Andrews, J. Very last first time **E**
(il) Lottridge, C. B. The name of the tree **398.2**
Wallner, Alexandra, 1946-
(il) Adler, D. A. A picture book of Abraham Lincoln **92**
(il) Adler, D. A. A picture book of Benjamin Franklin **92**
(il) Adler, D. A. A picture book of George Washington **92**
(il) Adler, D. A. A picture book of Thomas Jefferson **92**
Wallner, John C.
(il) Adler, D. A. A picture book of Abraham Lincoln **92**
(il) Adler, D. A. A picture book of Benjamin Franklin **92**
(il) Adler, D. A. A picture book of George Washington **92**
(il) Adler, D. A. A picture book of Thomas Jefferson **92**
(il) Adler, D. A. A teacher on roller skates and other school riddles **793.73**
(il) Blaine, M. The terrible thing that happened at our house **E**
(il) Easter poems. See Easter poems **808.81**
(il) Gilson, J. Hello, my name is Scrambled Eggs **Fic**
(il) Hurwitz, J. Much ado about Aldo **Fic**
(il) Kroll, S. One tough turkey **E**
(il) O'Neill, M. L. D. Hailstones and halibut bones **811**
(il) Tompert, A. Little fox goes to the end of the world **E**

Wallner, John C.—*Continued*
(il) When the dark comes dancing. See When the dark comes dancing **808.81**
(il) Yolen, J. Ring of earth: a child's book of seasons **811**

Walls
See also Western Wall (Jerusalem)
History
Giblin, J. Walls (5 and up) **623**

The **walrus** and the carpenter. Carroll, L. **821**

Walruses
Patent, D. H. Seals, sea lions, and walruses (5 and up) **599.74**
Selsam, M. E. A first look at seals, sea lions, and walruses (1-3) **599.74**
Fiction
Riddell, C. When the walrus comes **E**

Walsh, Jill Paton *See* Paton Walsh, Jill, 1937-

Walt Disney Productions
Peet, B. Bill Peet: an autobiography (4 and up) **92**

Walter, Mildred Pitts, 1922-
Brother to the wind **E**
Have a happy— (4-6) **Fic**
Justin and the best biscuits in the world (3-6) **Fic**
Mariah keeps cool (3-5) **Fic**
My mama needs me **E**
Two and too much **E**

Walter Dragun's town. Sancha, S. **942.03**

Walther, Tom, 1950-
Make mine music! (5 and up) **784.19**

Walther of Aquitaine. Picard, B. L.
In The Scott, Foresman anthology of children's literature p472-74 **808.8**

Wampanoag Indians
Cwiklik, R. King Philip and the war with the colonists (5 and up) **92**
Legends
Fritz, J. The good giants and the bad pukwudgies (k-3) **398.2**

Wanda Gág's Jorinda and Joringel. Grimm, J. **398.2**

Wanda Gág's The earth gnome. Grimm, J. **398.2**

Wanda Gag's The six swans. Grimm, J. **398.2**

Wanda Gág's The sorcerer's apprentice. Gág, W. **398.2**

War
Fiction
Moeri, L. The forty-third war **Fic**

The **war** between beasts and birds. Curry, J. L.
In Curry, J. L. Back in the beforetime p68-69 **398.2**

A **war** between gods. Terada, A. M.
In Terada, A. M. Under the starfruit tree p50-53 **398.2**

War boy: a country childhood. Foreman, M. **92**

War comes to Willy Freeman. Collier, J. L. **Fic**

War nurses. Cosner, S. **355.3**

War of 1812 *See* United States—History—1812-1815, War of 1812

War of the wolf and the fox
Grimm, J. The war of the wolf and the fox
In The Green fairy book p339-42 **398.2**

The **war** with Grandpa. Smith, R. K. **Fic**

The **Warau** people discover the earth. Sherlock, Sir P. M.
In Sherlock, Sir P. M. West Indian folktales p39-44 **398.2**

Ward, Brian R.
Dental care (4 and up) **617.6**
Diet and nutrition (4 and up) **641.1**
Smoking and health (4 and up) **616.86**
Parker, S. The ear and hearing **612.8**
Parker, S. The eye and seeing **612.8**
Parker, S. Food and digestion **612.3**
Parker, S. The heart and blood **612.1**
Parker, S. The skeleton and movement **612.7**
Parker, S. Touch, taste and smell **612.8**

Ward, John
(il) Sanfield, S. The adventures of High John the Conqueror **398.2**

Ward, Keith
(il) Farley, W. The Black Stallion **Fic**

Ward, Lynd Kendall, 1905-1985
The biggest bear **E**
The silver pony (2-4) **Fic**
(il) Coatsworth, E. J. The cat who went to heaven **Fic**
(il) Forbes, E. Johnny Tremain **Fic**
(il) Fritz, J. Early thunder **Fic**
(jt. auth) Swift, H. H. The little red lighthouse and the great gray bridge **E**

See/See also pages in the following book(s):
Caldecott Medal books, 1938-1957 p243-53 **028.5**

Ward, Martha E. (Martha Eads)
Authors of books for young people. See Authors of books for young people **920.003**

Ward, Rebecca
(il) Swan, R. Destination: Antarctica **998**

Warm-blooded animals. Burton, M. **599**
Warner, Susan, 1819-1885
See/See also pages in the following book(s):
Jordan, A. M. From Rollo to Tom Sawyer, and other papers p82-91 **028.5**
Warnock, Natalie Kinsey- *See* Kinsey-Warnock, Natalie
The **warrior** and the wise man. Wisniewski, D. **E**
The **warrior** goddess: Athena. Gates, D. **292**
Warton and the contest. Erickson, R. E. See note under Erickson, R. E. A toad for Tuesday **Fic**
Washakie, Shoshone Chief, 1797-1900
See/See also pages in the following book(s):
Freedman, R. Indian chiefs p72-89 (6 and up) **920**
Washburn, James K.
(il) Berends, P. B. The case of the elevator duck **Fic**
Washday on Noah's ark. Rounds, G. **E**
Washington, Booker T., 1856-1915
See/See also pages in the following book(s):
Jacobs, W. J. Great lives: human rights p119-30 (5 and up) **920**
Washington, George, 1732-1799
About
Adler, D. A. A picture book of George Washington (1-3) **92**
D'Aulaire, I. George Washington (2-4) **92**
Meltzer, M. George Washington and the birth of our nation (5 and up) **92**
Siegel, B. George and Martha Washington at home in New York (4-6) **973.4**
See/See also pages in the following book(s):
Hauptly, D. J. "A convention of delegates" p7-22 (5 and up) **342**
Fritz, J. George Washington's breakfast (2-4) **Fic**
Washington, Martha, 1731-1802
About
Siegel, B. George and Martha Washington at home in New York (4-6) **973.4**
Washington (D.C.)
Kent, D. Washington, D. C. *In* America the beautiful **973**
Krementz, J. A visit to Washington, D.C (k-2) **975.3**
Description
Munro, R. The inside-outside book of Washington, D.C. (2-4) **975.3**
Washington (George) Bridge (N.Y. and N.J.) *See* George Washington Bridge (N.Y. and N.J.)

Washington's Birthday
See/See also pages in the following book(s):
Araki, C. Origami in the classroom p14-16 (Book II) (4 and up) **736**
The **washout**. Carrick, C. See note under Carrick, C. Ben and the porcupine **E**
Wasps
Johnson, S. A. Wasps (4 and up) **595.7**
Fiction
Lord, J. V. The giant jam sandwich **E**
Watanabe, Shigeo, 1928-
Daddy, play with me! See note under Watanabe, S. How do I put it on? **E**
Get set! Go! See note under Watanabe, S. How do I put it on? **E**
How do I put it on? **E**
I can build a house! See note under Watanabe, S. How do I put it on? **E**
I can ride it! See note under Watanabe, S. How do I put it on? **E**
I can take a bath! See note under Watanabe, S. How do I put it on? **E**
I can take a walk! See note under Watanabe, S. How do I put it on? **E**
Ice cream is falling! See note under Watanabe, S. How do I put it on? **E**
I'm the king of the castle! See note under Watanabe, S. How do I put it on? **E**
It's my birthday! See note under Watanabe, S. How do I put it on? **E**
What a good lunch! See note under Watanabe, S. How do I put it on? **E**
Where's my daddy? See note under Watanabe, S. How do I put it on? **E**
Watch out, Ronald Morgan! Giff, P. R. **E**
Watch the stars come out. Levinson, R. **E**
Watch where you go. Noll, S. **E**
Watching foxes. Arnosky, J. **599.74**
Water
Cole, J. The magic school bus at the waterworks (2-4) **551.48**
Seixas, J. S. Water: what it is, what it does (1-3) **553.7**
Experiments
Ardley, N. Working with water (4 and up) **507**
Pollution
Ancona, G. Riverkeeper (3-6) **333.91**
See/See also pages in the following book(s):
Woods, G. Pollution p35-44 (6 and up) **363.7**
Purification
Cobb, V. The trip of a drip (4-6) **628.1**

Water animals *See* Marine animals
Water buffalo
Fiction
Aruego, J. Look what I can do E
Water insects. Johnson, S. A. 595.7
The **Water-lily**
In The Blue fairy book p174-81 398.2
The **water-nixie**. Grimm, J.
In Grimm, J. The complete Grimm's fairy tales p364-65 398.2
In Grimm, J. More tales from Grimm p23-25 398.2
The **water-nixie**. Rockwell, A. F.
In Rockwell, A. F. The three bears & 15 other stories p53-55 398.2
The **water** nixie. Tennant, P.
In Shedlock, M. L. The art of the story-teller p198-203 372.6
Water of life
Grimm, J. The water of life
In Grimm, J. About wise men and simpletons p65-73 398.2
In Grimm, J. The complete Grimm's fairy tales p449-55 398.2
Pyle, H. Water of life
In Pyle, H. The wonder clock p15-26 398.2
Rogasky, B. The water of life 398.2
Water sky. George, J. C. Fic
Water supply
Cobb, V. The trip of a drip (4-6) 628.1
Cole, J. The magic school bus at the waterworks (2-4) 551.48
Water: what it is, what it does. Seixas, J. S. 553.7
The **waterfall** of ghosts. San Souci, R.
In San Souci, R. Short & shivery p15-21 398.2
Waternick
Grimm, J. The water-nixie
In Grimm, J. The complete Grimm's fairy tales p364-65 398.2
In Grimm, J. More tales from Grimm p23-25 398.2
Rockwell, A. F. The water-nixie
In Rockwell, A. F. The three bears & 15 other stories p53-55 398.2
Tennant, P. The water nixie
In Shedlock, M. L. The art of the story-teller p198-203 372.6
Waters, Elisabeth
Things that go grump in the night
In Things that go bump in the night p25-37 S C
Waters, John F.
Camels: ships of the desert (k-3) 599.73
Waters, Kate
Lion dancer: Ernie Wan's Chinese New Year (k-3) 394.2
Watership Down. Adams, R. Fic
Watie, Stand, 1806-1871
Fiction
Keith, H. Rifles for Watie (6 and up) Fic
Watkins, Martha Swintz
Nobody believes in witches
In Holiday plays round the year p141-50 812.008
Watkins, Yoko Kawashima
So far from the bamboo grove (6 and up) Fic
Watling, James
(il) Krensky, S. Witch hunt 133.4
Watson, Clyde
Applebet: an ABC E
Binary numbers (2-4) 513
Catch me & kiss me & say it again: rhymes (k-1) 811
Father Fox's feast of songs (k-3) 782.42
Father Fox's pennyrhymes (k-3) 811
Valentine foxes E
Watson, Richard Jesse, 1951-
Tom Thumb (k-3) 398.2
(il) Willard, N. The high rise glorious skittle skat roarious sky pie angel food cake Fic
Watson, Wendy
(il) Bierhorst, J. Doctor Coyote 398.2
(il) Hennessy, B. G. A,B,C,D, tummy, toes, hands, knees E
(il) Moore, C. C. The night before Christmas 811
(il) Watson, C. Applebet: an ABC E
(il) Watson, C. Binary numbers 513
(il) Watson, C. Catch me & kiss me & say it again: rhymes 811
(il) Watson, C. Father Fox's feast of songs 782.42
(il) Watson, C. Father Fox's pennyrhymes 811
(il) Watson, C. Valentine foxes E
(il) Wendy Watson's Mother Goose. See Wendy Watson's Mother Goose 398.8
(il) Winthrop, E. Belinda's hurricane Fic
Watson, Wenta Jean
Abe and the runaways
In Holiday plays round the year p247-54 812.008
Watts, Barrie
24 hours in a forest (5 and up) 574.5
Honeybee (k-3) 595.7
Tomato (k-3) 635

Watts, Frances B.
The leprechaun shoemakers
In Holiday plays round the year p220-28 **812.008**
Watts, James, 1955-
(il) Curry, J. L. Back in the beforetime **398.2**
(il) Kennedy, X. J. Brats **811**
(il) Kennedy, X. J. Fresh brats **811**
Waxman, Stephanie, 1944-
What is a girl? what is a boy? (k-1) **612.6**
The **way** I feel—sometimes. De Regniers, B. S. **811**
The **way** of the grizzly. Patent, D. H. **599.74**
The **way** of the storyteller. Sawyer, R. **372.6**
The **way** things work. Macaulay, D. **600**
The **way** to Sattin Shore. Pearce, P. **Fic**
The **way** to start a day. Baylor, B. **291.4**
Ways animals sleep. McCauley, J. R. **591.5**
We are all one. Yep, L.
In Yep, L. The rainbow people p72-78 **398.2**
We are best friends. Aliki. **E**
We can't sleep. Stevenson, J. See note under Stevenson, J. "Could be worse!" **E**
We don't look like our Mom and Dad. Sobol, H. L. **362.7**
We hate rain! Stevenson, J. See note under Stevenson, J. "Could be worse!" **E**
We hide, you seek. Aruego, J. **E**
We interrupt this program—. Boiko, C.
In The Big book of Christmas plays p200-12 **808.82**
We laugh, we love, we cry. Bergman, T. **362.3**
We live in Egypt. Kristensen, P. S. **962**
We live in Saudi Arabia. Al Hoad, A. L. **953.8**
We read: A to Z. Crews, D. **E**
We the people. Spier, P. **342**
We wish you a merry Christmas **782.28**
Weapons and weaponry *See* Arms and armor
Weasel. DeFelice, C. C. **Fic**
Weather
See also Climate; Meteorology
Bramwell, M. Weather (4-6) **551.5**
Branley, F. M. It's raining cats and dogs (3-6) **551.5**
Gibbons, G. Weather words and what they mean (1-3) **551.6**
Lambert, D. Weather and its work (5 and up) **551.6**
Newton, J. R. Rain shadow (2-5) **574.5**
Smith, H. E. Weather (4-6) **551.5**
See/See also pages in the following book(s):
Piping down the valleys wild p37-50 **808.81**
Weather and its work. Lambert, D. **551.6**
Weather forecasting
Gibbons, G. Weather forecasting (1-3) **551.6**
Tannenbaum, B. Making and using your own weather station (5 and up) **551.6**
Weather words and what they mean. Gibbons, G. **551.6**
The **Web** **028.1**
Weber, Debora, 1955-
(il) Lee, M. P. Last names first **929.4**
Weber, William J.
Care of uncommon pets (5 and up) **636.088**
Webster's Beginning dictionary. See Webster's elementary dictionary **423**
Webster's elementary dictionary (4-6) **423**
Webster's geographical dictionary. See Webster's new geographical dictionary **910.3**
Webster's intermediate dictionary (5 and up) **423**
Webster's new biographical dictionary **920.003**
Webster's new geographical dictionary **910.3**
Webster's school dictionary (6 and up) **423**
Webster's third new international dictionary of the English language **423**
Webster's third new international dictionary of the English language; supplement. See 12,000 words **423**
Webster's II Riverside children's dictionary (3-6) **423**
Wedding of Mrs. Fox
Grimm, J. The wedding of Mrs. Fox
In Grimm, J. The complete Grimm's fairy tales p193-96 **398.2**
The **wedding** procession of the Rag Doll and the Broom Handle and who was in it. Sandburg, C. **E**
In Sandburg, C. Rootabaga stories pt 1 p81-86 **S C**
In Sandburg, C. The Sandburg treasury p43-45 **818**
Weddings
See also Marriage customs and rites
Lasker, J. Merry ever after (3-5) **392**
Fiction
Delton, J. Angel's mother's wedding (3-5) **Fic**
Samuels, V. Carry, go, bring, come **E**

The **Wednesday** surprise. Bunting, E. **E**
Wee, wee woman
Bennett, J. Teeny tiny **398.2**
Galdone, P. The teeny-tiny woman **398.2**
Seuling, B. The teeny tiny woman **398.2**
Wee little woman
In The Tall book of nursery tales p49-50 **398.2**
The **Wee** Little Tyke. MacDonald, M. R.
In MacDonald, M. R. When the lights go out p21-28 **372.6**
Wee Meg Barnileg and the fairies
Sawyer, R. Wee Meg Barnileg and the fairies
In Sawyer, R. The way of the storyteller p205-16 **372.6**
The **Wee,** wee mannie
In Best-loved folktales of the world p281-82 **398.2**
A **weed** is a flower: the life of George Washington Carver. Aliki. **92**
A **Week** of lullabies (k-2) **811.008**
Weevers, Peter
(il) Carroll, L. Alice's adventures in Wonderland **Fic**
Weidhorn, Manfred, 1931-
Robert E. Lee (5 and up) **92**
Weight and weightlessness. Branley, F. M. **531**
Weight control *See* Reducing
Weight lifting
Sullivan, G. Better weight training for boys (4 and up) **613.7**
Weightlessness
Branley, F. M. Weight and weightlessness (k-3) **531**
Weights and measures
See also Metric system
Bendick, J. How much & how many? (5 and up) **530.8**
Weihs, Erika
(il) Chaikin, M. Menorahs, mezuzas, and other Jewish symbols **296.4**
(il) Chaikin, M. Sound the shofar **296.4**
(il) Perl, L. Blue Monday and Friday the Thirteenth **398**
(il) Perl, L. Don't sing before breakfast, don't sleep in the moonlight **398**
(il) Perl, L. The great ancestor hunt **929**
(il) Perl, L. Mummies, tombs, and treasure **393**
Weinhaus, Karen Ann
(il) Glazer, T. Music for ones and twos **782.42**
(il) Knock at a star. See Knock at a star **821.008**
(il) Poem stew. See Poem stew **811.008**
(il) Schwartz, A. All of our noses are here, and other noodle tales **398.2**
(il) Schwartz, A. There is a carrot in my ear, and other noodle tales **398.2**
Weird Henry Berg. Sargent, S. **Fic**
Weisgard, Leonard, 1916-
(il) Brown, M. W. Nibble nibble: poems for children **811**
(il) Dalgliesh, A. The courage of Sarah Noble **Fic**
(il) Favorite poems, old and new. See Favorite poems, old and new **808.81**
(il) Kipling, R. The elephant's child **Fic**
(il) Tresselt, A. R. Rain drop splash **E**
See/See also pages in the following book(s):
Caldecott Medal books, 1938-1957 p151-64 **028.5**
Weisner, William
(il) Harper, W. The Gunniwolf **398.2**
Weiss, Ann E., 1943-
Who's to know? (5 and up) **323.44**
Weiss, Ellen, 1953-
(il) Aardema, V. The Vingananee and the tree toad **398.2**
(il) Chaikin, M. Hanukkah **296.4**
(il) Cuyler, M. Baby Dot: a dinosaur story **E**
(il) De Regniers, B. S. So many cats! **E**
(il) Polushkin, M. Who said meow? **E**
Weiss, Emil
(il) Neville, E. C. It's like this, Cat **Fic**
Weiss, Harvey
Cartoons and cartooning (4 and up) **741.5**
Hammer & saw (5 and up) **684**
Machines and how they work (4 and up) **621.8**
Model buildings and how to make them (4 and up) **690**
Model cars and trucks and how to build them (4 and up) **629.22**
Shelters: from tepee to igloo (4 and up) **728**
Submarines and other underwater craft (4 and up) **623.8**
Weiss, Jaqueline Shachter
(jt. auth) Field, C. W. Values in selected children's books of fiction and fantasy **028.5**
Weiss, Malcolm E.
Sky watchers of ages past (5 and up) **523**
Weiss, Nicki, 1951-
If you're happy and you know it (k-2) **782.42**
Maude and Sally **E**
Where does the brown bear go? **E**

Weiss, Renée Karol
(comp) A Paper zoo. See A Paper zoo 811.008

Weissman, Paul Robert, 1947-
(jt. auth) Harris, A. The great Voyager adventure 523.4

Weitzman, David L.
My backyard history book (4 and up) 973
Windmills, bridges & old machines (5 and up) 620

Weiwandt, Thomas
The hidden life of the desert (3-5) 574.5

Welch, Lucy Elizabeth Kemp- *See* Kemp-Welch, Lucy Elizabeth, 1869-1958

Welcome home, Jellybean. Shyer, M. F. Fic

Welcome, little baby. Aliki. E

We'll do lunch. Magon, J.
In Things that go bump in the night p164-85 S C

The **well** of the three heads. Reeves, J.
In Reeves, J. English fables and fairy stories p115-26 398.2

Well of the world's end
Jacobs, J. Well of the World's End
In Jacobs, J. English fairy tales p215-19 398.2
Reeves, J. The Well of the World's End
In Reeves, J. English fables and fairy stories p211-20 398.2
Williams-Ellis, A. The Well of the World's End
In Williams-Ellis, A. Tales from the enchanted world p55-61 398.2

We'll race you, Henry: a story about Henry Ford. Mitchell, B. 92

Wells, Carolyn, 1869-1942
A Christmas alphabet (k-3) 811

Wells, Haru
(il) Paterson, K. The master puppeteer Fic

Wells, Rosemary, 1943-
Good night, Fred E
Hazel's amazing mother E
A lion for Lewis E
The little lame prince E
Max's bath. See note under Wells, R. Max's first word E
Max's bedtime. See note under Wells, R. Max's first word E
Max's birthday. See note under Wells, R. Max's first word E
Max's breakfast. See note under Wells, R. Max's first word E
Max's chocolate chicken. See note under Wells, R. Max's first word E
Max's Christmas. See note under Wells, R. Max's first word E
Max's first word E
Max's new suit. See note under Wells, R. Max's first word E
Max's ride. See note under Wells, R. Max's first word E
Max's toys. See note under Wells, R. Max's first word E
Morris's disappearing bag E
Noisy Nora E
Peabody E
Shy Charles E
Through the hidden door (5 and up) Fic
Timothy goes to school E
(il) Segal, L. G. Tell me a Trudy E
(il) With a deep sea smile. See With a deep sea smile 372.6

The **wendigo.** Schwartz, A.
In Schwartz, A. Scary stories to tell in the dark p49-53 398.2

Wendy Watson's Frog went a-courting (k-2) 781.62

Wendy Watson's Mother Goose (k-2) 398.8

Wenzel, Gregory C.
(il) Berger, M. Atoms, molecules, and quarks 539
(il) Cobb, V. The monsters who died 567.9
(il) Silverstein, A. The story of your foot 612
(il) Silverstein, A. The story of your hand 612

We're going on a bear hunt. Rosen, M. E

We're in big trouble, Blackboard Bear. Alexander, M. G. E

Werewolves
McHargue, G. Meet the werewolf (4 and up) 398
Fiction
Pinkwater, D. M. I was a second grade werewolf (1-3) Fic

Werth, Kurt
(il) McGinley, P. The year without a Santa Claus 811

West, Benjamin, 1738-1820
About
Henry, M. Benjamin West and his cat Grimalkin (4 and up) 92

West, Emily G. *See* Payne, Emmy, 1919-

West, Robin
Dinosaur discoveries (3-5) 745.54

West (U.S.)

Children

See Children—West (U.S.)

Exploration

Blumberg, R. The incredible journey of Lewis and Clark (5 and up) **978**

Fiction

Byars, B. C. The Golly Sisters go West **E**
Byars, B. C. Hooray for the Golly sisters! **E**
Clifford, E. The dastardly murder of Dirty Pete (3-5) **Fic**
Coren, A. Arthur the Kid (3-5) **Fic**
Fleischman, S. Humbug Mountain (4-6) **Fic**
Harvey, B. Cassie's journey (2-4) **Fic**
Holland, I. The journey home (4 and up) **Fic**
Moeri, L. Save Queen of Sheba (4 and up) **Fic**
Sharmat, M. W. Gila monsters meet you at the airport **E**
Shub, E. The white stallion **E**
Williams, V. B. Stringbean's trip to the shining sea **E**

History

Ehrlich, A. Wounded Knee: an Indian history of the American West (6 and up) **970.004**
Freedman, R. Children of the wild West (4 and up) **978**
Freedman, R. Cowboys of the wild West (4 and up) **978**
Tunis, E. Frontier living (5 and up) **978**

West from home. Wilder, L. I. **92**

West Indian folk-tales. Sherlock, Sir P. M. **398.2**

West Indies

Fiction

O'Dell, S. My name is not Angelica (5 and up) **Fic**

Folklore

See Folklore—West Indies

West Virginia

Stein, R. C. West Virginia
In America the beautiful **973**

Fiction

Rylant, C. A blue-eyed daisy (5 and up) **Fic**

Westall, Robert, 1929-

Ghost abbey (5 and up) **Fic**
The machine gunners (6 and up) **Fic**

Westcott, Nadine Bernard, 1949-

The lady with the alligator purse **E**
Skip to my Lou **E**
(il) Raffi. Down by the bay **782.42**
(il) Raffi. The Raffi Christmas treasury **782.42**
(il) There's a hole in the bucket. See There's a hole in the bucket **781.62**

Western and country music *See* Country music

Western Europe *See* Europe

Western States *See* West (U.S.)

Western Wall (Jerusalem)

Fisher, L. E. The Wailing Wall (4 and up) **221.9**

The **Westing** game. Raskin, E. **Fic**

Westinghouse, George, 1846-1914

See/See also pages in the following book(s):
Aaseng, N. The problem solvers p31-37 (5 and up) **920**

Westman, Barbara

The day before Christmas **E**

Westmark. Alexander, L. **Fic**

Weston, Martha, 1947-

(il) Barkin, C. Happy Valentine's Day! **394.2**
(il) Booth, J. The big beast book **567.9**
(il) Burns, M. The book of think **153.4**
(il) Burns, M. The Hanukkah book **296.4**
(il) Burns, M. I am not a short adult! **305.23**
(il) Burns, M. Math for smarty pants **513**
(il) Burns, M. This book is about time **529**
(il) Cobb, V. Bet you can't! science impossibilities to fool you **793.8**
(il) Hautzig, E. R. Make it special **745.59**
(il) Kaye, C. B. Word works **410**
(il) Sharp, P. Brain power! **612.8**
(il) Wilkinson, E. Making cents **332.024**

Weston, Reiko

Cooking the Japanese way (5 and up) **641.5**

Wetherell, Elizabeth *See* Warner, Susan, 1819-1885

Wexler, Jerome

Flowers, fruits, seeds (k-2) **582**
Pet mice (3-6) **636.088**
(il) Cole, J. A bird's body **598**
(il) Cole, J. A cat's body **636.8**
(il) Cole, J. A chick hatches **636.5**
(il) Cole, J. A frog's body **597.8**
(il) Cole, J. A horse's body **636.1**
(il) Cole, J. An insect's body **595.7**
(il) Cole, J. A snake's body **597.9**
(il) Lauber, P. From flower to flower **582**
(il) Lauber, P. Seeds pop, stick, glide **582**
(il) Selsam, M. E. Cotton **633.5**
(il) Selsam, M. E. Mushrooms **589.2**

Weyl, Nancy
(il) Grayson, M. F. Let's do fingerplays **796.1**

Whale in the sky. Siberell, A. **398.2**

Whale of a tale. MacDonald, M. R.
In MacDonald, M. R. Twenty tellable tales p1-9 **372.6**

Whales
The Audubon Society field guide to North American fishes, whales, and dolphins (5 and up) **597**
Berger, G. Whales (2-4) **599.5**
Dow, L. Whales (5 and up) **599.5**
Grosvenor, D. K. The blue whale (k-3) **599.5**
Mallory, K. Rescue of the stranded whales (5 and up) **639.9**
McNulty, F. Whales: their life in the sea (5 and up) **599.5**
Milton, J. Whales (1-3) **599.5**
Patent, D. H. All about whales (2-4) **599.5**
Patent, D. H. Humpback whales (1-3) **599.5**
Patent, D. H. Whales, giants of the deep (5 and up) **599.5**
Sattler, H. R. Whales, the nomads of the sea (4 and up) **599.5**
Simon, S. Whales (3-5) **599.5**
See/See also pages in the following book(s):
Thomson, P. Auks, rocks and the odd dinosaur p83-87 (5 and up) **508**

Fiction

McCloskey, R. Burt Dow, deep-water man **E**
Steig, W. Amos & Boris **E**

Songs and music

Raffi. Baby Beluga (k-2) **782.42**

Whales, giants of the deep. Patent, D. H. **599.5**

Whales, the nomads of the sea. Sattler, H. R. **599.5**

Whales: their life in the sea. McNulty, F. **599.5**

Whaling

Fiction

Day, E. C. John Tabor's ride **E**
George, J. C. Water sky (5 and up) **Fic**
Holling, H. C. Seabird (4-6) **Fic**

Whalley, Paul Ernest Sutton
Butterfly & moth (4 and up) **595.7**

What a good lunch! Watanabe, S. See note under Watanabe, S. How do I put it on? **E**

What a morning! **782.25**

What a wimp! Carrick, C. **Fic**

What Alvin wanted. Keller, H. **E**

What am I? Calmenson, S. **793.73**

What are you figuring now? a story about Benjamin Banneker. Ferris, J. **92**

What do you do at a petting zoo? Machotka, H. **590.74**

What do you do, dear? Joslin, S. **395**

What do you say, dear? Joslin, S. **395**

What Eric knew. Howe, J. See note under Howe, J. Dew drop dead **Fic**

What game shall we play? Hutchins, P. **E**

What happened to Patrick's dinosaurs? Carrick, C. **E**

What happened to the dinosaurs? Branley, F. M. **567.9**

What happens to a hamburger. Showers, P. **612.3**

What is a girl? what is a boy? Waxman, S. **612.6**

What is the most important part of the body? Lester, J.
In Lester, J. How many spots does a leopard have? and other tales p45-51 **398.2**

What is trouble? Lester, J.
In Lester, J. The knee-high man, and other tales p5-8 **398.2**

What kind of dog is that? Cohen, S. **636.7**

What makes day and night. Branley, F. M. **525**

What makes you what you are. Bornstein, S. **575.1**

What Mary Jo shared. Udry, J. M. **E**

What next, Baby Bear! Murphy, J. **E**

What shall we do and Alee galloo! play songs and singing games for young children (k-2) **796.1**

What six girls with balloons told the Gray Man on Horseback. Sandburg, C.
In Sandburg, C. Rootabaga stories pt 1 p138-44 **S C**
In Sandburg, C. The Sandburg treasury p65-68 **818**

What the moon is like. Branley, F. M. **523.3**

Whatever happened to good old Ebenezer Scrooge? Majeski, B.
In The Big book of Christmas plays p151-68 **808.82**

Whatever happened to the dinosaurs? Most, B. E
What's a frank frank? Maestro, G. **793.73**
What's Claude doing? Gackenbach, D. **E**
What's cooking, Jenny Archer? Conford, E. See note under Conford, E. A case for Jenny Archer **Fic**
What's happening to my body? A growing up guide for mothers and daughters. See Madaras, L. The what's happening to my body? book for girls: a growing up guide for parents and daughters **613.9**
The **what's** happening to my body? book for boys: a growing up guide for parents and sons. Madaras, L. **613.9**
The **what's** happening to my body? book for girls: a growing up guide for parents and daughters. Madaras, L. **613.9**
What's hatching out of that egg? Lauber, P. **591.1**
What's in fox's sack? Galdone, P. **398.2**
What's so funny, Ketu? Aardema, V. **398.2**
What's that room for? James, B. See note under James, B. Natalie underneath **E**
What's the big idea, Ben Franklin? Fritz, J. **92**
What's the matter? Leach, M.
In Leach, M. Whistle in the graveyard p30 **398.2**
What's the matter, Sylvie, can't you ride? Andersen, K. B. **E**
What's the matter with Carruthers? Marshall, J. See note under Marshall, J. Yummers! **E**
What's the matter with Herbie Jones? Kline, S. See note under Kline, S. Herbie Jones **Fic**
What's under my bed? Stevenson, J. See note under Stevenson, J. "Could be worse!" **E**
Wheat
Johnson, S. A. Wheat (4 and up) **633.1**
Patent, D. H. Wheat, the golden harvest (4-6) **633.1**
Wheatley, Arabelle
(il) Kohn, B. The beachcomber's book **745.5**
Wheel away! Dodds, D. A. **E**
Wheel on the chimney. Brown, M. W. **E**
The **wheel** on the school. DeJong, M. **Fic**
Wheeler, Cindy, 1955-
(il) Zolotow, C. One step, two— **E**
Wheeler, Mary Jo
First came the Indians (2-4) **970.004**
Wheels
Zubrowski, B. Wheels at work (4-6) **621.8**
See/See also pages in the following book(s):
Weiss, H. Machines and how they work p40-49 (4 and up) **621.8**
Fiction
Dodds, D. A. Wheel away! **E**
Wheels: a pictorial history. Tunis, E. **388.3**
Wheels at work. Zubrowski, B. **621.8**
The **wheels** on the bus. Kovalski, M. **782.42**
Wheels on the bus. Raffi. **782.42**
When a parent is very sick. LeShan, E. J. **155.9**
When a pet dies. Rogers, F. **155.9**
When Bluebell sang. Ernst, L. C. **E**
When clay sings. Baylor, B. **970.004**
When Grandpa came to stay. Caseley, J. **E**
When grownups drive you crazy. LeShan, E. J. **306.8**
When Hershel eats. Ausubel, N.
In Best-loved folktales of the world p462-64 **398.2**
When Hitler stole Pink Rabbit. Kerr, J. **Fic**
When I see my dentist. Kuklin, S. **617.6**
When I see my doctor. Kuklin, S. **610.69**
When I was nine. Stevenson, J. **92**
When I was young in the mountains. Rylant, C. **E**
When Shlemiel went to Warsaw. Singer, I. B.
In Singer, I. B. Stories for children p194-205 **S C**
In Singer, I. B. When Shlemiel went to Warsaw & other stories p99-115 **398.2**
When Shlemiel went to Warsaw & other stories. Singer, I. B. **398.2**
When stars fell to earth: legends of the Pawnee. Monroe, J. G.
In Monroe, J. G. They dance in the sky p44-62 **398.2**
When the dark comes dancing (k-3) **808.81**
When the elephant walks. Kasza, K. **E**
When the lights go out. MacDonald, M. R. **372.6**
When the new baby comes, I'm moving out. Alexander, M. G. **E**
When the rain came up from China. McCormick, D. J.
In Rainy day: stories and poems p47-53 **808.8**

When the Tripods came. Christopher, J. See note under Christopher, J. The White Mountains **Fic**

When the walrus comes. Riddell, C. **E**

When the wind changed. Park, R.
In Windy day: stories and poems p46-53 **808.8**

When we went to the park. Hughes, S. See note under Hughes, S. Bathwater's hot **E**

When we were very young. Milne, A. A. **821**
also in Milne, A. A. The world of Christopher Robin p1-118 **821**

When will I read? Cohen, M. See note under Cohen, M. See you in second grade! **E**

When winter comes. Freedman, R. **591.5**

When winter comes. Neuman, P. **591.5**

When you were a baby. Jonas, A. **E**

Where angels glide at dawn (5 and up) **S C**

Where are you, Ernest and Celestine? Vincent, G. See note under Vincent, G. Ernest and Celestine **E**

Where are you going, little mouse? Kraus, R. See note under Kraus, R. Whose mouse are you? **E**

Where butterflies grow. Ryder, J. **595.7**

Where did you get those eyes? Cooper, K. **929**

Where do you get your ideas? Asher, S. **808**

Where do you think you're going, Christopher Columbus? Fritz, J. **92**

Where does the brown bear go? Weiss, N. **E**

Where does the sun go at night? Ginsburg, M. **E**

Where is it? Hoban, T. **E**

Where one is fed a hundred can dine
Sawyer, R. Where one is fed a hundred can dine
In Sawyer, R. The way of the storyteller p251-55 **372.6**

Where the bald eagles gather. Patent, D. H. **598**

Where the buffaloes begin. Baker, O. **Fic**

Where the forest meets the sea. Baker, J. **E**

Where the lillies bloom. Cleaver, V. **Fic**

Where the red fern grows. Rawls, W. **Fic**

Where the river begins. Locker, T. **E**

Where the sidewalk ends. Silverstein, S. **811**

Where the wild horses roam. Patent, D. H. **639.9**

Where the wild things are. Sendak, M. **E**

Where was Patrick Henry on the 29th of May? Fritz, J. **92**

Where's my daddy? Watanabe, S. See note under Watanabe, S. How do I put it on? **E**

Where's the baby? Hutchins, P. **E**

Where's the bear? Pomerantz, C. **E**

Which is best?
Pyle, H. Which is best?
In Pyle, H. The wonder clock p203-15 **398.2**

Which one is Whitney? Stevenson, J. **E**

Which was witch? Jewett, E. M.
In The Scott, Foresman anthology of children's literature p336-38 **808.8**

The **whingdingdilly**. Peet, B. **E**

The **whipping** boy. Fleischman, S. **Fic**

The **Whirlwinds** and the Stone Coats
In The Naked bear p19-23 **398.2**

Whiskers & rhymes. Lobel, A. **811**

The **whisperer**. Alcock, V.
In Alcock, V. Ghostly companions **S C**

The **whispering** land [excerpt]. Durrell, G. M.
In Animal families of the wild: animal stories p5-16 **591**

Whistle for Willie. Keats, E. J. See note under Keats. E. J. The snowy day **E**

Whistle in the graveyard. Leach, M. **398.2**

The **Whistling** skeleton (3-6) **398.2**

The **Whistling** skeleton [story]
In The Whistling skeleton p3-18 **398.2**

White, David Omar
(il) Berger, T. Black fairy tales **398.2**

White, E. B. (Elwyn Brooks), 1899-1985
Charlotte's web (3-6) **Fic**
Stuart Little (3-6) **Fic**
The trumpet of the swan (3-6) **Fic**

White, Elwyn Brooks *See* White, E. B. (Elwyn Brooks), 1899-1985

White, Jack R.
The hidden world of forces (5 and up) **531**
The invisible world of the infrared (5 and up) **535**

White, Laurence B.
Math-a-magic: number tricks for magicians (3-6) **793.8**
(jt. auth) Broekel, R. Hocus pocus: magic you can do **793.8**
(jt. auth) Broekel, R. Now you see it: easy magic for beginners **793.8**

White, Sandra Verrill
Sterling (2-4) **639.9**
White, T. H. (Terence Hanbury), 1906-1964
The sword in the stone [excerpt]
In The Random House book of humor for children p212-34 **817.008**
White, Terence Hanbury *See* White, T. H. (Terence Hanbury), 1906-1964
White, Timothy
(il) Friedhoffer, R. Magic tricks, science facts **793.8**
White (Jesse) Tumbling Team *See* Jesse White Tumbling Team
White and the black bride
Grimm, J. The white bride and the black bride
In Grimm, J. The complete Grimm's fairy tales p608-12 **398.2**
White bear, ice bear. Ryder, J. **599.74**
White bird (Fairy tale)
Pyle, H. White bird
In Pyle, H. The wonder clock p105-20 **398.2**
The **white** bride and the black bride. Grimm, J.
In Grimm, J. The complete Grimm's fairy tales p608-12 **398.2**
White captives. Lampman, E. S. **Fic**
White cat
Aulnoy, Madame d'. The white cat
In Best-loved folktales of the world p32-45 **398.2**
In The Blue fairy book p157-73 **398.2**
San Souci, R. The white cat **398.2**
White chocolate. Brancato, R. F.
In Connections: short stories by outstanding writers for young adults p84-93 **S C**
White dove
Grimm, J. The white dove
In Grimm, J. About wise men and simpletons p52-53 **398.2**
White duck
Afanas'ev, A. N. The white duck
In Afanas'ev, A. N. Russian fairy tales p342-45 **398.2**
In Afanas'ev, A. N. Russian folk tales p51-56 **398.2**
The White duck
In The Yellow fairy book p155-60 **398.2**
White Fang. London, J. **Fic**
White ghosts. Leach, M.
In Leach, M. Whistle in the graveyard p27 **398.2**
The **white** hare and the crocodiles. Quayle, E.
In Quayle, E. The shining princess, and other Japanese legends p24-32 **398.2**
The **White** Horse Girl and the Blue Wind Boy. Sandburg, C.
In Herds of thunder, manes of gold p29-34 **808.8**
In Sandburg, C. Rootabaga stories pt 1 p131-37 **S C**
In Sandburg, C. The Sandburg treasury p63-65 **818**
White horses. Crompton, A. E.
In Herds of thunder, manes of gold p55-64 **808.8**
White House (Washington, D.C.)
Fisher, L. E. The White House (4 and up) **975.3**
St. George, J. The White House (5 and up) **975.3**
Sullivan, G. How the White House really works (5 and up) **975.3**
White House ghosts. Leach, M.
In Leach, M. Whistle in the graveyard p17-19 **398.2**
The **White** House rabbit. Gotwalt, H. L. M.
In Gotwalt, H. L. M. Special plays for holidays p158-69 **812**
The **White** Mountains. Christopher, J. **Fic**
White Peak Farm. Doherty, B. **Fic**
The **white** seal. Kipling, R.
In Kipling, R. The jungle books **S C**
White snake. Carpenter, F.
In Carpenter, F. Tales of a Chinese grandmother p159-65 **398.2**
The **white** snake. Grimm, J.
In The Green fairy book p319-23 **398.2**
In Grimm, J. The complete Grimm's fairy tales p98-101 **398.2**
White snow, blue feather. Downing, J. **E**
White snow, bright snow. Tresselt, A. R. **E**
The **white** stag. Seredy, K. **Fic**
The **white** stallion. Shub, E. **E**
Whitebear Whittington
Whitebear Whittington
In Grandfather tales p52-64 **398.2**
Whitfield, Philip J.
Can the whales be saved? (4 and up) **574.5**
Why do our bodies stop growing? (5 and up) **612**
Why do the seasons change? (4 and up) **508**

Whitfield, Ruth
(jt. auth) Whitfield, P. J. Why do our bodies stop growing? **612**
Whitman, Walt, 1819-1892
Voyages (6 and up) **811**
Whitney, Elinor, 1889-
(ed) Caldecott Medal books, 1938-1957. See Caldecott Medal books, 1938-1957 **028.5**
(ed) Horn Book reflections on children's books and reading. See Horn Book reflections on children's books and reading **028.5**
(ed) Newbery Medal books, 1922-1955. See Newbery Medal books, 1922-1955 **028.5**
Whittington, Mary K.
Leaves
In Things that go bump in the night p232-42 **S C**
Whittington, Richard, d. 1423
Fiction
Brown, M. Dick Whittington and his cat (k-3) **398.2**
Whittington and his cat. Jacobs, J.
In Jacobs, J. English fairy tales p167-78 **398.2**
Whittling *See* Wood carving
Who is Carrie? Collier, J. L. **Fic**
Who killed Cock Robin
In A Nursery companion p32-35 **820.8**
Who lived in the skull
Afanas'ev, A. N. The castle of the fly
In Afanas'ev, A. N. Russian fairy tales p25-26 **398.2**
Who lives in—the forest? Hirschi, R. **591.5**
Who lives in—the mountains? Hirschi, R. **591.5**
Who lives in the skull? MacDonald, M. R.
In MacDonald, M. R. When the lights go out p143-47 **372.6**
Who lives on—the prairie? Hirschi, R. **591.5**
Who really discovered America? Krensky, S. **970.01**
Who really killed Cock Robin? George, J. C. **Fic**
Who rules the roost? Jagendorf, M. A.
In The Scott, Foresman anthology of children's literature p396-98 **808.8**
Who said meow? Polushkin, M. **E**
Who said red? Serfozo, M. **E**
Who said there's no man on the moon? a story of Jules Verne. Quackenbush, R. M. **92**
Who took the farmer's [hat]? Lexau, J. M. **E**
Who uses this? Miller, M. **E**
Who was Anansi? Sherlock, Sir P. M.
In Sherlock, Sir P. M. Anansi, the spider man p1-2 **398.2**
The **whooping** crane. Patent, D. H. **639.9**
Whooping cranes *See* Cranes (Birds)
Whoppers. Schwartz, A. **398.2**
Who's a pest? Bonsall, C. N. **E**
Who's afraid of the dark? Bonsall, C. N. **E**
Who's in Rabbit's house? Aardema, V. **398.2**
Who's sick today? Cherry, L. **E**
Who's that girl with the gun? a story of Annie Oakley. Quackenbush, R. M. **92**
Who's that stepping on Plymouth Rock? Fritz, J. **974.4**
Who's the fool now. Sanfield, S.
In Sanfield, S. The adventures of High John the Conqueror **398.2**
Who's there? and what do you want? Walker, B. K.
In Walker, B. K. A treasury of Turkish folktales for children p4-7 **398.2**
Who's to know? Weiss, A. E. **323.44**
Whose mouse are you? Kraus, R. **E**
Whose shoes are these? Roy, R. **391**
Why all men love the moon
How Sun, Moon and Wind went out to dinner
In Best-loved folktales of the world p592-93 **398.2**
Why am I grown so cold? (5 and up) **808.81**
Why Anna hung upside down. Mahy, M.
In Mahy, M. Nonstop nonsense p22-26 **828**
Why Brer Bear has no tail. Lester, J.
In Lester, J. The tales of Uncle Remus p99-101 **398.2**
Why Brer Wolf didn't eat the little rabs. Parks, V. D.
In Parks, V. D. Jump on over! the adventures of Brer Rabbit and his family **398.2**
Why Bush Cow and Elephant are bad friends. Bryan, A.
In Bryan, A. Beat the story-drum, pum-pum p14-29 **398.2**

Why can't you unscramble an egg? and other not such dumb questions about matter. Cobb, V. **530**

Why do our bodies stop growing? Whitfield, P. J. **612**

Why do the seasons change? Whitfield, P. J. **508**

Why does my nose run? Settel, J. **612**

Why doesn't the earth fall up? Cobb, V. **531**

Why dogs are always sniffing. Lester, J.
In Lester, J. More tales of Uncle Remus p123-28 **398.2**

Why dogs chase cats. Lester, J.
In Lester, J. How many spots does a leopard have? and other tales p21-26 **398.2**

Why dogs hate cats. Lester, J.
In Lester, J. The knee-high man, and other tales p9-11 **398.2**

Why don't you get a horse, Sam Adams? Fritz, J. **92**

Why Frog and Snake never play together. Bryan, A.
In Bryan, A. Beat the story-drum, pum-pum p41-52 **398.2**
In The Scott, Foresman anthology of children's literature p310-13 **808.8**

Why I cough, sneeze, shiver, hiccup, & yawn. Berger, M. **612.8**

Why in the world? (4 and up) **500**

Why me? Conford, E. **Fic**

Why monkeys live in trees. Lester, J.
In Lester, J. How many spots does a leopard have? and other tales p41-44 **398.2**

Why mosquitoes buzz in people's ears. Aardema, V. **398.2**

Why Noah chose the dove. Singer, I. B.
In Singer, I. B. Stories for children p41-44 **S C**

Why on earth? (4 and up) **500**

Why the bear has a stumpy tail
Asbjørnsen, P. C. Why the bear is stumpy-tailed
In Best-loved folktales of the world p353 **398.2**

Why the bear is stumpy-tailed. Asbjørnsen, P. C.
In Best-loved folktales of the world p353 **398.2**

Why the bear waddles when he walks. Marriott, A. L.
In Marriott, A. L. American Indian mythology **398.2**

Why the big ball game between Hot Grounders and the Grand Standers was a hot game. Sandburg, C.
In Sandburg, C. Rootabaga stories pt 2 p130-34 **S C**
In Sandburg, C. The Sandburg treasury p142-44 **818**

Why the chicken crossed the road. Macaulay, D. **E**

Why the dog and cat are enemies
Lester, J. Why dogs hate cats
In Lester, J. The knee-high man, and other tales p9-11 **398.2**

Why the parrot repeats man's words
In Best-loved folktales of the world p563-65 **398.2**

Why the sea is salt
Asbjørnsen, P. C. Why the sea is salt
In Best-loved folktales of the world p354-57 **398.2**
In The Blue fairy book p136-40 **398.2**

Why the sea winds are the strength they are today. Norman, H.
In Norman, H. How Glooskap outwits the Ice Giants, and other tales of the Maritime Indians p21-28 **398.2**

Why the sun and the moon live in the sky
In Best-loved folktales of the world p657-58 **398.2**

Why the Sun and the Moon live in the sky. Lester, J.
In Lester, J. How many spots does a leopard have? and other tales p1-4 **398.2**

Why the tides ebb and flow. Bowden, J. C. **398.2**

Why the waves have whitecaps. Lester, J.
In Lester, J. The knee-high man, and other tales p21-23 **398.2**
In The Scott, Foresman anthology of children's literature p376 **808.8**

Why there are cracks in Tortoise's shell. Smith, E. W.
In Best-loved folktales of the world p652-53 **398.2**

Why there are no tigers in Borneo. De Leeuw, A.
In Best-loved folktales of the world p602-05 **398.2**

Why there is no arguing in heaven. Lattimore, D. N. **398.2**

Why women won't listen. Sherlock, Sir P. M.
In Sherlock, Sir P. M. West Indian folk-tales p112-17 **398.2**

Wibberley, Leonard, 1915-1983
John Treegate's musket (6 and up) **Fic**

Wiberg, Harald, 1908-
(il) Jennings, L. M. The Christmas Tomten E
(il) Lindgren, A. Christmas in the stable 232.9
(il) Lindgren, A. The Tomten E
(il) Lindgren, A. The Tomten and the fox E

Wick, Tempe
Gauch, P. L. This time, Tempe Wick? (3-5) Fic

The **wicked** city. Singer, I. B. 222
In Singer, I. B. Stories for children p77-88 S C

Wicked John and the Devil
In Grandfather tales p29-39 398.2

Wicked John and the Devil. MacDonald, M. R.
In MacDonald, M. R. When the lights go out p33-46 372.6

The **wicked** one. Hunter, M. Fic

Wicked sisters
Afanas'ev, A. N. The wicked sisters
In Afanas'ev, A. N. Russian fairy tales p356-60 398.2

Wickstrom, Sylvie
(il) Bulla, C. R. The Christmas coat E
(il) Edwards, R. Five silly fishermen 398.2
(il) Raffi. Wheels on the bus 782.42

Wider than the sky: poems to grow up with (5 and up) 821.008

Wiese, Kurt, 1887-1974
(jt. auth) Bishop, C. H. The five Chinese brothers 398.2
(il) Brooks, W. R. Freddy the detective Fic
(jt. auth) Flack, M. The story about Ping E

Wiesner, David
Free fall E
Hurricane E
(il) Thaler, M. Owly E
(il) Yep, L. The rainbow people 398.2

Wife abuse

Fiction

Byars, B. C. Cracker Jackson (5 and up) Fic

The **wife** of Bath's tale. Cohen, B.
In Cohen, B. Canterbury tales Fic

The **wife's** portrait. Seki, K.
In Best-loved folktales of the world p519-21 398.2

Wiggin, Kate Douglas Smith, 1856-1923
The Bird's Christmas Carol (3-5) Fic

Wiggins, S. Michelle
(il) Carroll, L. Alice's adventures in Wonderland Fic
(il) Carroll, L. Through the looking glass, and what Alice found there Fic

Wight, James Alfred *See* Herriot, James

Wijngaard, Juan
(il) Hastings, S. Sir Gawain and the Green Knight 398.2
(il) Hastings, S. Sir Gawain and the loathly lady 398.2
(il) Koralek, J. Hanukkah, the festival of lights 296.4

Wild, Margaret, 1948-
Mr. Nick's knitting E
The very best of friends E

Wild and woolly mammoths. Aliki. 569

Wild animals. See Wildsmith, B. Brian Wildsmith's wild animals E

Wild animals, Brian Wildsmith's. Wildsmith, B. E

Wild animals of Africa ABC. Ryden, H. E

Wild animals of America ABC. Ryden, H. E

The **wild** baby. Lindgren, B. E

The **wild** baby gets a puppy. Lindgren, B. See note under Lindgren, B. The wild baby E

The **wild** baby goes to sea. Lindgren, B. See note under Lindgren, B. The wild baby E

The **wild** black crows—a circular song. Brown, M. W.
In Brown, M. W. The fish with the deep sea smile p114 818

Wild boars. Nicholson, D. 599.73

The **wild** Christmas reindeer. Brett, J. E

Wild flowers
McMillan, B. Counting wildflowers E
Zim, H. S. Flowers (4 and up) 582.13

Conservation

See Plant conservation

Wild Robin. Jeffers, S. E

Wild rosemary. Yakovlev, Y.
In Face to face: a collection of stories by celebrated Soviet and American writers p11-21 S C

Wild swans
Andersen, H. C. The wild swans Fic
In Andersen, H. C. Hans Andersen: his classic fairy tales p125-39 S C
Ehrlich, A. The wild swans E

The **wild** swans. Andersen, H. C.
In Andersen, H. C. Hans Andersen: his classic fairy tales p125-39 S C

Wild turkey, tame turkey. Patent, D. H. 598

Wild words! Asher, S. **808**
Wilde, Oscar, 1854-1900
The Happy Prince, and other stories (3-6) **S C**
Contents: The happy prince; The nightingale and the rose; The selfish giant; The devoted friend; The remarkable rocket; The young king; The birthday of the Infanta; The fisherman and his soul; The Star-child
The selfish giant (2-5) **Fic**
Wilder, Alec, 1907-1980
Lullabies and night songs. See Lullabies and night songs **782.42**
Wilder, Laura Ingalls, 1867-1957
By the shores of Silver Lake. See note under Wilder, L. I. Little house in the big woods **Fic**
Farmer boy. See note under Wilder, L. I. Little house in the big woods **Fic**
The first four years. See note under Wilder, L. I. Little house in the big woods **Fic**
Little house in the big woods (4-6) **Fic**
Little house on the prairie. See note under Wilder, L. I. Little house in the big woods **Fic**
Little town on the prairie. See note under Wilder, L. I. Little house in the big woods **Fic**
The long winter. See note under Wilder, L. I. Little house in the big woods **Fic**
On the banks of Plum Creek. See note under Wilder, L. I. Little house in the big woods **Fic**
These happy golden years. See note under Wilder, L. I. Little house in the big woods **Fic**
West from home (6 and up) **92**
The Laura Ingalls Wilder songbook. See The Laura Ingalls Wilder songbook **782.42**
About
Walker, B. M. The Little House cookbook (5 and up) **641.5**
Wilderness champion. Lippincott, J. W. **Fic**
Wilderness survival
Fiction
Eckert, A. W. Incident at Hawk's Hill (6 and up) **Fic**
George, J. C. Julie of the wolves (6 and up) **Fic**
Houston, J. A. Frozen fire (6 and up) **Fic**
O'Dell, S. Island of the Blue Dolphins (5 and up) **Fic**
The **wildlife** 1 2 3. Thornhill, J. **E**
Wildlife conservation
See also Birds—Protection
Ancona, G. Turtle watch (2-4) **597.9**
Cowcher, H. Antarctica (1-3) **998**
Facklam, M. And then there was one (4-6) **591.5**
Mallory, K. Rescue of the stranded whales (5 and up) **639.9**
McGrath, S. Saving our animal friends (k-3) **591**
Patent, D. H. Where the wild horses roam (4 and up) **639.9**
Patent, D. H. The whooping crane (5 and up) **639.9**
Pringle, L. P. Saving our wildlife (5 and up) **639.9**
Rinard, J. E. Wildlife, making a comeback (4 and up) **591**
Schlein, M. Project panda watch (4 and up) **599.74**
Smith, R. Sea otter rescue (5 and up) **639.9**
White, S. V. Sterling (2-4) **639.9**
Fiction
Schlein, M. The year of the panda (3-5) **Fic**
Periodicals
International Wildlife **591.05**
Wildlife, making a comeback. Rinard, J. E. **591**
The **wildman**. Crossley-Holland, K.
In Crossley-Holland, K. British folk tales p334-37 **398.2**
Wildsmith, Brian, 1930-
Bear's adventure **E**
Brian Wildsmith's birds **E**
Brian Wildsmith's circus **E**
Brian Wildsmith's wild animals **E**
A Christmas story **E**
Daisy **E**
Fishes **E**
The hare and the tortoise (k-2) **398.2**
The miller, the boy and the donkey (k-2) **398.2**
Pelican **E**
The rich man and the shoe-maker (k-2) **398.2**
(il) Mother Goose. See Mother Goose [illus. by Brian Wildsmith] **398.8**
(il) Stevenson, R. L. A child's garden of verses **821**
Wiley and the Hairy Man. Bang, M. **398.2**
Wiley, his mama, and the Hairy Man. Hamilton, V.
In Hamilton, V. The people could fly: American black folktales p90-103 **398.2**
Wiley Wolf and Riley Rabbit. Lester, J.
In Lester, J. The tales of Uncle Remus p101-04 **398.2**

Wilhelm, Hans, 1945-
A cool kid—like me! E
(il) Merriam, E. Blackberry ink 811

Wilhelm von Schmitz. Carroll, L.
In Carroll, L. The complete works of Lewis Carroll p986-98 828

Wilkes, Angela
My first activity book (1-5) 745.5
My first nature book (1-4) 508

Wilkin, Eloise Burns, 1904-1987
(il) Poems to read to the very young. See Poems to read to the very young 821.008

Wilkins, Mary Calhoun *See* Calhoun, Mary, 1926-

Wilkinson, Brenda Scott, 1946-
Ludell (6 and up) Fic
Ludell and Willie. See note under Wilkinson, B. S. Ludell Fic

Wilkinson, Elizabeth, 1926-
Making cents (4 and up) 332.024

Wilkinson, Frederick, 1922-
Arms and armor (3-5) 623.4

Wilkinson, Phil
(ed) Early humans. See Early humans 930.1

Will I have a friend? Cohen, M. See note under Cohen, M. See you in second grade! E

Will the real Gertrude Hollings please stand up? Greenwald, S. Fic

Will you please feed our cat? Stevenson, J. See note under Stevenson, J. "Could be worse!" E

Will you sign here, John Hancock? Fritz, J. 92

Willard, Nancy
The ballad of Biddy Early (4 and up) 811
The high rise glorious skittle skat roarious sky pie angel food cake (2-4) Fic
Simple pictures are best E
A visit to William Blake's inn (2-5) 811
The voyage of the Ludgate Hill (2-5) 811
See/See also pages in the following book(s):
Newbery and Caldecott Medal books, 1976-1985 p94-104 028.5

Willbie, R. T.
(il) Pope, J. Taking care of your dog 636.7
(il) Pope, J. Taking care of your fish 639.3
(il) Pope, J. Taking care of your gerbils 636.088
(il) Pope, J. Taking care of your mice and rats 636.088
(il) Pope, J. Taking care of your rabbit 636.088

Willful child
Grimm, J. The willful child
In Grimm, J. The complete Grimm's fairy tales p534-35 398.2

Williams, Barbara
Albert's toothache E
Jeremy isn't hungry E
Kevin's grandma E

Williams, Berkeley
(il) Grandfather tales. See Grandfather tales 398.2
(il) The Jack tales. See The Jack tales 398.2

Williams, Daniel Hale
About
Patterson, L. Sure hands, strong heart: the life of Daniel Hale Williams (4 and up) 92

Williams, Garth, 1912-
(il) Brown, M. W. Wait till the moon is full E
(il) Carlson, N. S. The family under the bridge Fic
(il) Carlson, N. S. The happy orpheline Fic
(il) Hoban, R. Bedtime for Frances E
(il) The Laura Ingalls Wilder songbook. See The Laura Ingalls Wilder songbook 782.42
(il) Prelutsky, J. Beneath a blue umbrella: rhymes 811
(il) Prelutsky, J. Ride a purple pelican 811
(il) Selden, G. The cricket in Times Square Fic
(il) Sharp, M. The rescuers Fic
(il) Stolz, M. Emmett's pig E
(il) Walker, B. M. The Little House cookbook 641.5
(il) White, E. B. Charlotte's web Fic
(il) White, E. B. Stuart Little Fic
(il) Wilder, L. I. Little house in the big woods Fic
(il) Zolotow, C. Over and over E

Williams, Jay, 1914-1978
The Christmas thief
In The Family read-aloud Christmas treasury p44-49 808.8
Everyone knows what a dragon looks like E

Williams, Jennifer
(il) Williams, V. B. Stringbean's trip to the shining sea E

Williams, Karen Lynn
Baseball and butterflies (2-4) Fic
Galimoto E

Williams, Kent
(il) Marzollo, J. Getting your period **612.6**
Williams, Linda (Linda D.)
The little old lady who was not afraid of anything **E**
Williams, Margery *See* Bianco, Margery Williams, 1880-1944
Williams, Richard, 1950-
(il) Kline, S. Herbie Jones **Fic**
Williams, Roger, 1604?-1683
See/See also pages in the following book(s):
Jacobs, W. J. Great lives: human rights p9-17 (5 and up) **920**
Williams, Suzanne
Mommy doesn't know my name **E**
Williams, Vera B.
A chair for my mother **E**
Cherries and cherry pits **E**
Music, music for everyone. See note under Williams, V. B. A chair for my mother **E**
Something special for me. See note under Williams, V. B. A chair for my mother **E**
Stringbean's trip to the shining sea **E**
Three days on a river in a red canoe **E**
William's doll. Zolotow, C. **E**
Williams-Ellis, Amabel, 1894-1984
Tales from the enchanted world (4 and up) **398.2**
Contents: Cap o' Rushes; The great white cat; Childe Rowland; The king, the saint and the goose; The country of the mice; The Well of the World's End; The magic bird; The Master-Thief; Johnny-Cake; My berries; Baba Yaga; The three sisters; Mr. Miacca; The Laidly Worm of Spindlestone Heugh; White-Faced Siminy; Anansi and Mrs. Dove; Tamlane; The waterfall; The fifty red night-caps; The bear in the coach; The Great Greedy Beast; Tom-Tit-Tot
Williamson, Ray A., 1938-
(jt. auth) Monroe, J. G. They dance in the sky: native American star myths **398.2**
Willie Bea and the time the Martians landed. Hamilton, V. **Fic**
Willie Winkie. Leach, M.
In Leach, M. Whistle in the graveyard p89-90 **398.2**
Willis, Jeanne
Earthlets, as explained by Professor Xargle **E**
Willow, Diane
Science sensations (3-5) **507**
The **willow-wren**. Grimm, J.
In Grimm, J. The complete Grimm's fairy tales p705-08 **398.2**
The **willow-wren** and the bear. Grimm, J.
In Grimm, J. The complete Grimm's fairy tales p472-74 **398.2**
Will's mammoth. Martin, R. **E**
Willy can count. Rockwell, A. F. **E**
Willy the champ. Browne, A. **E**
Wilms, Denise
(ed) A Guide to non-sexist children's books. See A Guide to non-sexist children's books v2 **011.6**
Wilner, Isabel
(comp) The Poetry troupe. See The Poetry troupe **821.008**
Wilsdorf, Anne
(il) De Regniers, B. S. Jack the giant killer **398.2**
Wilson, Dorothy Clarke
I will be a doctor! [biography of Elizabeth Blackwell] (5 and up) **92**
Wilson, George, 1920-
Books for children to read alone **011.6**
Wilson, Janet
(il) Bogart, J. E. Daniel's dog **E**
Wilson, John
(il) Adoff, A. Malcolm X **92**
Wilson, Richard, 1936-
(il) Bell, N. The book of where **910**
Wilson, Sarah, 1934-
The day that Henry cleaned his room **E**
Wilson Library Bulletin **020.5**
Wimmer, Mike
(il) Conrad, P. Staying nine **Fic**
(il) Siebert, D. Train song **E**
Winborn, Marsha
(il) Baker, B. Digby and Kate again **E**
The **Wind** and the sun
In The Baby's story book p46-47 **398.2**
The **wind** blew. Hutchins, P. **E**
A **wind** in the door. L'Engle, M. See note under L'Engle, M. A wrinkle in time **Fic**
The **wind** in the willows. Grahame, K. **Fic**
Wind, sand and sky. Caudill, R. **811**
Wind song. Sandburg, C.
In Sandburg, C. The Sandburg treasury p209-61 **818**
Windmills
History
Weitzman, D. L. Windmills, bridges & old machines (5 and up) **620**
Windmills, bridges & old machines. Weitzman, D. L. **620**
Windows
Giblin, J. Let there be light: a book about windows (5 and up) **690**

Windows on wildlife. Johnston, G. **590.74**
Winds
Dorros, A. Feel the wind (k-3) **551.5**
See/See also pages in the following book(s):
Tannenbaum, B. Making and using your own weather station p55-74 (5 and up) **551.6**
Fiction
Ets, M. H. Gilberto and the Wind **E**
Hutchins, P. The wind blew **E**
McKissack, P. C. Mirandy and Brother Wind **E**
Yolen, J. The girl who loved the wind **E**
Windy day: stories and poems (2-4) **808.8**
The **wine** bibber. Kendall, C.
In Kendall, C. Sweet and sour p42-44 **398.2**
The **wing** on a flea. Emberley, E. **E**
Wing Quack Flap. Aiken, J.
In Aiken, J. Give yourself a fright: thirteen tales of the supernatural p1-18 **S C**
The **winged** horse. Hawthorne, N.
In Herds of thunder, manes of gold p96-110 **808.8**
Wings. Marshall, J. **E**
Winkel, Lois, 1939-
(ed) The Elementary school library collection. See The Elementary school library collection **011.6**
Winn, Marie
(ed) The Fireside book of children's songs. See The Fireside book of children's songs **782.42**
(ed) The Fireside book of fun and game songs. See The Fireside book of fun and game songs **782.42**
(ed) What shall we do and Alee galloo! play songs and singing games for young children. See What shall we do and Alee galloo! play songs and singing games for young children **796.1**
Winnie-the-Pooh. Milne, A. A. **Fic**
also in Milne, A. A. The world of Pooh p7-149 **Fic**
Winter, Barbara
John Henry
In Holiday plays round the year p239-46 **812.008**
Winter, Frank H.
The Filipinos in America
In The In America series **305.8**
Winter, Jeanette
Follow the drinking gourd **E**
(il) Hush little baby. See Hush little baby **781.62**
Winter
Freedman, R. When winter comes (k-3) **591.5**
Hader, B. The big snow **E**
Hirschi, R. Winter (k-2) **508**
Kurelek, W. A prairie boy's winter (3-5) **971.27**
Markle, S. Exploring winter (4 and up) **508**
Neuman, P. When winter comes (1-3) **591.5**
Fiction
Craft, R. The winter bear **E**
Downing, J. White snow, blue feather **E**
Lindgren, A. The Tomten **E**
Lindgren, A. The Tomten and the fox **E**
Martin, C. E. Island winter **E**
Parnall, P. Winter barn **E**
Poetry
Frost, R. Stopping by woods on a snowy evening (k-3) **811**
Prelutsky, J. It's snowing! It's snowing! (1-3) **811**
Winter barn. Parnall, P. **E**
The **winter** bear. Craft, R. **E**
Winter holding spring. Dragonwagon, C. **Fic**
The **winter** room. Paulsen, G. **Fic**
Winter sports
See also Olympic games
Fiction
Kessler, L. P. Old Turtle's winter games **E**
The **winter** wren. Cole, B. **E**
Winthrop, Elizabeth
Belinda's hurricane (2-4) **Fic**
The castle in the attic (4-6) **Fic**
A child is born: the Christmas story (k-3) **232.9**
He is risen: the Easter story (2-5) **232.9**
Katharine's doll **E**
Shoes **E**
Tough Eddie **E**
Wisconsin
Stein, R. C. Wisconsin
In America the beautiful **973**
Fiction
Brink, C. R. Caddie Woodlawn (4-6) **Fic**
Enright, E. Thimble summer (4-6) **Fic**
Wilder, L. I. Little house in the big woods (4-6) **Fic**
Wisdom, Leon B.
(il) Key, A. Escape to Witch Mountain **Fic**
Wise, William, 1923-
The black falcon (3-6) **Fic**

The **Wise** Bird and the Foolish Bird. Lester, J.
In Lester, J. Further tales of Uncle Remus p41-44 **398.2**
The **wise** dog. Fuja, A.
In Best-loved folktales of the world p634-38 **398.2**
Wise folks. Grimm, J.
In Grimm, J. The complete Grimm's fairy tales p476-80 **398.2**
Wise little girl
Afanas'ev, A. N. The wise little girl
In Afanas'ev, A. N. Russian fairy tales p252-55 **398.2**
Wise maiden and the seven robbers
Afanas'ev, A. N. The wise maiden and the seven robbers
In Afanas'ev, A. N. Russian fairy tales p134-40 **398.2**
Wise men (Magi) *See* Magi
Wise men of Gotham
Crossley-Holland, K. The wise men of Gotham
In Crossley-Holland, K. British folk tales p347-52 **398.2**
Wise men of Helm
Singer, I. B. The snow in Chelm
In Singer, I. B. Zlateh the goat, and other stories p29-34 **398.2**
Wise old shepherd
Rouse, W. H. D. The wise old shepherd
In Shedlock, M. L. The art of the story-teller p216-21 **372.6**
Wise servant
Grimm, J. The wise servant
In Grimm, J. The complete Grimm's fairy tales p671-72 **398.2**
Wise wife
Afanas'ev, A. N. The wise wife
In Afanas'ev, A. N. Russian fairy tales p521-28 **398.2**
Wiseman, Ann Sayre, 1926-
Making musical things (3-6) **784.19**
Wiseman, Bernard
Christmas with Morris and Boris. See note under Wiseman, B. Morris and Boris at the circus **E**
Halloween with Morris and Boris. See note under Wiseman, B. Morris and Boris at the circus **E**
Morris and Boris. See note under Wiseman, B. Morris and Boris at the circus **E**
Morris and Boris at the circus **E**
Morris goes to school. See note under Wiseman, B. Morris and Boris at the circus **E**
Morris has a cold. See note under Wiseman, B. Morris and Boris at the circus **E**
Morris tells Boris Mother Moose stories and rhymes. See note under Wiseman, B. Morris and Boris at the circus **E**
Morris the moose. See note under Wiseman, B. Morris and Boris at the circus **E**
The tongue-twister
In The Laugh book p239-41 **808.8**
Wiseman, David, 1916-
Jeremy Visick (5 and up) **Fic**
Wisenfeld, Alison
(jt. auth) Hindley, J. The tree **582.16**
The **wish** giver. Brittain, B. See note under Brittain, B. Devil's donkey **Fic**
Wishes
Fiction
Zemach, M. The three wishes (k-2) **398.2**
Wishes. Babbitt, N.
In Babbitt, N. The Devil's storybook p3-11 **S C**
The **wishing-table,** the gold-ass, and the cudgel in the sack. Grimm, J.
In Grimm, J. The complete Grimm's fairy tales p177-87 **398.2**
The **wishing** table, the gold donkey, and the cudgel-in-the sack. Grimm, J.
In Grimm, J. More tales from Grimm p99-115 **398.2**
Wishinsky, Frieda
Oonga boonga **E**
Wisniewski, David
Elfwyn's saga **E**
The warrior and the wise man **E**
Wit and humor
See also American wit and humor; Humorous poetry; Humorous stories; Jewish wit and humor; Jokes
Cricket's jokes, riddles and other stuff (1-4) **793.73**
Espy, W. R. A children's almanac of words at play (3-6) **808.87**
The Laugh book (4-6) **808.8**
Rosenbloom, J. Laughs, hoots & giggles (4 and up) **808.87**
Schwartz, A. All of our noses are here, and other noodle tales (1-3) **398.2**
Schwartz, A. There is a carrot in my ear, and other noodle tales (1-3) **398.2**
History and criticism
See/See also pages in the following book(s):
Crosscurrents of criticism p197-216 **028.5**
Witch and her servants
The Witch and her servants
In The Yellow fairy book p161-77 **398.2**

The **witch** cat. San Souci, R.
In San Souci, R. Short & shivery p28-34 **398.2**
The **witch** family. Estes, E. **Fic**
The **witch** herself. Naylor, P. R. See note under Naylor, P. R. The witch's eye **Fic**
Witch hunt. Krensky, S. **133.4**
Witch in the stone boat
The Witch in the stone boat
In The Yellow fairy book p274-78 **398.2**
The **witch** of Blackbird Pond. Speare, E. G. **Fic**
The **witch** of Fourth Street. Levoy, M.
In Levoy, M. The witch of Fourth Street, and other stories **S C**
The **witch** of Fourth Street, and other stories. Levoy, M. **S C**
The **witch** of Wellfleet. Roach, M. K.
In Roach, M. K. Encounters with the invisible world **S C**
Witch poems (1-4) **821.008**
Witch water. Naylor, P. R. See note under Naylor, P. R. The witch's eye **Fic**
Witchcraft
Jackson, S. The witchcraft of Salem Village (4 and up) **133.4**
Krensky, S. Witch hunt (2-4) **133.4**
McHargue, G. Meet the witches (4 and up) **133.4**
Fiction
Bellairs, J. The house with a clock in its walls (5 and up) **Fic**
Bennett, A. E. Little witch (3-5) **Fic**
Briggs, K. M. Kate Crackernuts (6 and up) **Fic**
Clapp, P. Witches' children (6 and up) **Fic**
Konigsburg, E. L. Jennifer, Hecate, Macbeth, William McKinley, and me, Elizabeth (4-6) **Fic**
MacLachlan, P. Tomorrow's wizard (3-6) **S C**
Naylor, P. R. The witch's eye (5 and up) **Fic**
Petry, A. L. Tituba of Salem Village (6 and up) **Fic**
Snyder, Z. K. The witches of Worm (5 and up) **Fic**
Speare, E. G. The witch of Blackbird Pond (6 and up) **Fic**
The **witchcraft** of Salem Village. Jackson, S. **133.4**
Witches
Fiction
Balian, L. Humbug witch **E**
Brittain, B. Devil's donkey (3-6) **Fic**
Carlson, N. S. Spooky night **E**
Estes, E. The witch family (2-5) **Fic**
Johnston, T. The vanishing pumpkin **E**
Johnston, T. The witch's hat **E**
Mahy, M. The boy who was followed home **E**
Norton, M. Bed-knob and broomstick (3-5) **Fic**
O'Connor, J. Lulu goes to witch school **E**
Peet, B. Big bad Bruce **E**
Peet, B. The whingdingdilly **E**
Price, S. The ghost drum (4 and up) **Fic**
Steig, W. Caleb & Kate **E**
Stevenson, J. Emma **E**
Wood, A. Heckedy Peg **E**
Poetry
Witch poems (1-4) **821.008**
Yolen, J. Best witches: poems for Halloween (3-5) **811**
The **witches** [excerpt]. Dahl, R.
In The Random House book of humor for children p120-29 **817.008**
Witches' children. Clapp, P. **Fic**
The **witches** of Venice. Montresor, B. **E**
The **witches** of Worm. Snyder, Z. K. **Fic**
Witches, pumpkins, and grinning ghosts. Barth, E. **394.2**
The **witch's** daughter. Bawden, N. **Fic**
The **witch's** eye. Naylor, P. R. **Fic**
The **witch's** hat. Johnston, T. **E**
Witch's sister. Naylor, P. R. See note under Naylor, P. R. The witch's eye **Fic**
Witcracks: jokes and jests from American folklore. Schwartz, A. **398**
With a deep sea smile **372.6**
With a wig, with a wag. Cothran, J.
In With a deep sea smile p86-92 **372.6**
With Bert & Ray. Konigsburg, E. L.
In Konigsburg, E. L. Throwing shadows **S C**
With love from Koko. McNulty, F. **599.88**
With my eyes closed. Arenas, R.
In Where angels glide at dawn p35-41 **S C**
Wittman, Sally, 1941-
A special trade **E**
The **wizard**. MacLachlan, P.
In MacLachlan, P. Tomorrow's wizard p1-12 **S C**

The **wizard** clip. MacDonald, M. R.
In MacDonald, M. R. When the lights go out p61-68 **372.6**
A **wizard** of Earthsea. Le Guin, U. K. **Fic**
The **Wizard** of Oz. Baum, L. F. **Fic**
Wobble pop. Burningham, J. See note under Burningham, J. Slam bang **E**
Woe
In Best-loved folklore tales of the world p441-46 **398.2**
Wojciechowska, Maia, 1927-
Shadow of a bull (6 and up) **Fic**
Wolf/Child. Yolen, J.
In Yolen, J. The faery flag p61-78 **S C**
Wolf, Bernard, 1930-
Anna's silent world (2-4) **362.4**
Don't feel sorry for Paul (3-6) **362.4**
Firehouse (3-6) **363.3**
In this proud land (4 and up) **305.8**
Wolf, Janet, 1957-
The rosy fat magenta radish **E**
Wolf
Afanas'ev, A. N. The wolf
In Afanas'ev, A. N. Russian fairy tales p312 **398.2**
Wolf, the fox, and the jar of honey
Afanas'ev, A. N. The fox as midwife
In Afanas'ev, A. N. Russian fairy tales p191-92 **398.2**
Wolf, the she-goat and the kid
Afanas'ev, A. N. The wolf and the goat
In Afanas'ev, A. N. Russian fairy tales p249-51 **398.2**
Wolf and birds and the Fish-Horse. Hamilton, V.
In Hamilton, V. The people could fly: American black folktales p43-49 **398.2**
Wolf and Godfather Fox
Grimm, J. Gossip wolf and the fox
In Grimm, J. The complete Grimm's fairy tales p353-54 **398.2**
A **wolf** and Little Daughter. Hamilton, V.
In Hamilton, V. The people could fly: American black folktales p60-64 **398.2**
Wolf and the fox
Grimm, J. The wolf and the fox
In Grimm, J. The complete Grimm's fairy tales p351-53 **398.2**
In Grimm, J. More tales from Grimm p9-13 **398.2**
The **wolf** and the goat. Afanas'ev, A. N.
In Afanas'ev, A. N. Russian fairy tales p249-51 **398.2**
Wolf and the kids
In The Tall book of nursery tales p62-69 **398.2**
Wolf and the man
Grimm, J. The wolf and the man
In Grimm, J. The complete Grimm's fairy tales p350-51 **398.2**
Wolf and the seven little kids
Conover, C. Mother Goose and the sly fox **398.2**
Grimm, J. The wolf and the seven kids
In Grimm, J. About wise men and simpletons p17-19 **398.2**
Grimm, J. The wolf and the seven little kids
In Best-loved folktales of the world p109-11 **398.2**
In Grimm, J. The complete Grimm's fairy tales p39-42 **398.2**
In Grimm, J. More tales from Grimm p241-49 **398.2**
Ross, T. Mrs. Goat and her seven little kids **398.2**
Wolf and the kids
In The Tall book of nursery tales p62-69 **398.2**
Wolf man
In The Whistling skeleton p84-90 **398.2**
Wolf pack. Johnson, S. A. **599.74**
Wolf! Wolf!
In The Tall book of nursery tales p74-76 **398.2**
Wolfe, Diane
(il) Amari, S. Cooking the Lebanese way **641.5**
(il) Bacon, J. Cooking the Israeli way **641.5**
(il) Chung, O. Cooking the Korean way **641.5**
(il) Hargittai, M. Cooking the Hungarian way **641.5**
(il) Kaufman, C. D. Cooking the Caribbean way **641.5**
(il) Madavan, V. Cooking the Indian way **641.5**
(il) Nabwire, C. R. Cooking the African way **641.5**
(il) Nguyen, C. T. Cooking the Vietnamese way **641.5**
(il) Parnell, H. Cooking the German way **641.5**
(il) Plotkin, G. Cooking the Russian way **641.5**
(il) Villios, L. W. Cooking the Greek way **641.5**
(il) West, R. Dinosaur discoveries **745.54**
(il) Zamojska-Hutchins, D. Cooking the Polish way **641.5**

Wolfe, Robert L.
(il) Amari, S. Cooking the Lebanese way 641.5
(il) Bacon, J. Cooking the Israeli way 641.5
(il) Chung, O. Cooking the Korean way 641.5
(il) Hargittai, M. Cooking the Hungarian way 641.5
(il) Kaufman, C. D. Cooking the Caribbean way 641.5
(il) Madavan, V. Cooking the Indian way 641.5
(il) Moran, T. Canoeing is for me 797.1
(il) Nabwire, C. R. Cooking the African way 641.5
(il) Nguyen, C. T. Cooking the Vietnamese way 641.5
(il) Parnell, H. Cooking the German way 641.5
(il) Plotkin, G. Cooking the Russian way 641.5
(il) Villios, L. W. Cooking the Greek way 641.5
(il) West, R. Dinosaur discoveries 745.54
(il) Zamojska-Hutchins, D. Cooking the Polish way 641.5

Wolff, Ashley, 1956-
Come with me E
Only the cat saw E
A year of beasts E
A year of birds E
(il) Raffi. Baby Beluga 782.42
(il) Stevenson, R. L. Block city 821

Wolff, Barbara
(il) Parish, P. December decorations 745.59
(il) Selsam, M. E. Egg to chick 636.5

Wolff, Kathryn, 1926-
(ed) The Best science books & A-V materials for children. See The Best science books & A-V materials for children 016.5

The **wolf's** chicken stew. Kasza, K. E

Wolfson, Evelyn
From Abenaki to Zuni (4 and up) 970.004

Wolkstein, Diane
The banza (k-3) 398.2
The magic wings (2-4) 398.2
The Red Lion (3-5) 398.2
(comp) The Magic orange tree, and other Haitian folktales. See The Magic orange tree, and other Haitian folktales 398.2

Wolves
Johnson, S. A. Wolf pack (4 and up) 599.74
Lawrence, R. D. Wolves (3-6) 599.74
Mowat, F. Never cry wolf
In Animal families of the wild: animal stories p21-29 591
See/See also pages in the following book(s):
Kohl, J. Pack, band, and colony (5 and up) 591.5

Fiction

Blades, A. Mary of Mile 18 (2-4) Fic
Crampton, P. Peter and the wolf E
Galdone, P. Little Red Riding Hood (k-2) 398.2
Galdone, P. The three little pigs (k-2) 398.2
George, J. C. Julie of the wolves (6 and up) Fic
Goble, P. Dream wolf E
Goodall, J. S. Little Red Riding Hood (k-2) 398.2
Grimm, J. Little Red Cap (k-2) 398.2
Hyman, T. S. Little Red Riding Hood (k-2) 398.2
Kasza, K. The wolf's chicken stew E
Lippincott, J. W. Wilderness champion (5 and up) Fic
Marshall, J. Little Red Riding Hood (k-2) 398.2
Marshall, J. The three little pigs (k-2) 398.2
Prokofiev, S. Peter and the wolf E
Scieszka, J. The true story of the three little pigs (k-3) 398.2
Young, E. Lon Po Po (1-3) 398.2
Zemach, M. The three little pigs (k-2) 398.2

The **wolves** of Willoughby Chase. Aiken, J. Fic

The **woman** and the changeling elf. Grimm, J.
In Grimm, J. About wise men and simpletons p34 398.2

The **Woman** and the children of the sycamore tree
In Best-loved folktales of the world p633-34 398.2

The **woman** and the tree children. Lester, J.
In Lester, J. How many spots does a leopard have? and other tales p37-39 398.2

The **woman** dressed like a man. Curtis, E. S.
In Curtis, E. S. The girl who married a ghost, and other tales from the North American Indian p61-69 398.2

The **woman** in the moon. Riordan, J.
In Riordan, J. The woman in the moon, and other tales of forgotten heroines p2-6 398.2

The **woman** in the moon, and other tales of forgotten heroines. Riordan, J. 398.2
The **woman** who flummoxed the fairies. Forest, H. 398.2
The **woman** who flummoxed the fairies. Leodhas, S. N.
In Womenfolk and fairy tales p135-45 398.2
Woman's way
Afanas'ev, A. N. Woman's way
In Afanas'ev, A. N. Russian fairy tales p599 398.2
The **womb** of the earth. Marriott, A. L.
In Marriott, A. L. American Indian mythology 398.2
Women
See also Black women
Employment
Merriam, E. Mommies at work (k-3) 331.4
Fiction
Womenfolk and fairy tales (3-6) 398.2
Political activity
See also Women politicians
Suffrage—Fiction
Oneal, Z. A long way to go (3-5) Fic
Women air pilots
Lauber, P. Lost star: the story of Amelia Earhart (5 and up) 92
Quackenbush, R. M. Clear the cow pasture, I'm coming in for a landing!: a story of Amelia Earhart (2-4) 92
See/See also pages in the following book(s):
Tessendorf, K. C. Barnstormers & daredevils p63-74 (4 and up) 629.13
Women artists
Collins, D. R. The country artist: a story about Beatrix Potter (3-5) 92
Gherman, B. Georgia O'Keeffe (5 and up) 92
Hyman, T. S. Self-portrait: Trina Schart Hyman (4 and up) 92
O'Kelley, M. L. From the hills of Georgia: an autobiography in paintings (2-4) 92
Oneal, Z. Grandma Moses: painter of rural America (4 and up) 92
Sills, L. Inspirations (5 and up) 920
Taylor, J. Beatrix Potter: artist, storyteller and countrywoman 92
Women athletes
Knudson, R. R. Babe Didrikson: athlete of the century (4 and up) 92
Trenary, J. Time of my life: Jill Trenary (4 and up) 92
Women authors
Collins, D. R. The country artist: a story about Beatrix Potter (3-5) 92
Hurwitz, J. Astrid Lindgren: storyteller to the world (4 and up) 92
Little, J. Little by Little (5 and up) 92
Mitchell, B. Between two worlds: a story about Pearl Buck (3-5) 92
Nesbit, E. Long ago when I was young (5 and up) 92
Taylor, J. Beatrix Potter: artist, storyteller and countrywoman 92
Wilder, L. I. West from home (6 and up) 92
Women photographers
Meltzer, M. Dorothea Lange: life through the camera (4 and up) 92
Women physicians
Wilson, D. C. I will be a doctor! [biography of Elizabeth Blackwell] (5 and up) 92
Women politicians
Adler, D. A. Our Golda: the story of Golda Meir (3-5) 92
Women scientists
Harlan, J. Sounding the alarm: a biography of Rachel Carson (5 and up) 92
Kudlinski, K. V. Rachel Carson: pioneer of ecology (4 and up) 92
Women singers *See* Singers
Women soldiers
McGovern, A. The secret soldier: the story of Deborah Sampson [Gannett] (3-5) 92
Womenfolk and fairy tales (3-6) 398.2
Women's movement
See also Feminism
Ash, M. The story of the women's movement (3-6) 305.4
Women's rights *See* Feminism
A **wonder-book,** and Tanglewood tales. Hawthorne, N. 292
The **wonder** clock. Pyle, H. 398.2
The **Wonderful** birch
In The Red fairy book p123-32 398.2
The **wonderful** day. Brown, M. W.
In Brown, M. W. The fish with the deep sea smile p126-27 818
The **wonderful** flight to the Mushroom Planet. Cameron, E. Fic
Wonderful glass
Grimm, J. The godfather
In Grimm, J. The complete Grimm's fairy tales p206-08 398.2
The **wonderful** healing leaves. Lester, J.
In Lester, J. How many spots does a leopard have? and other tales p59-68 398.2
The **wonderful** kitten. Brown, M. W.
In Brown, M. W. The fish with the deep sea smile p106-10 818

Wonderful musician
Grimm, J. The marvellous musician
In The Red fairy book p354-56 **398.2**
Grimm, J. The strange musician
In Grimm, J. The complete Grimm's fairy tales p56-58 **398.2**
Wonderful pear tree. Carpenter, F.
In Carpenter, F. Tales of a Chinese grandmother p142-49 **398.2**
The **wonderful** pearl. Riordan, J.
In Riordan, J. The woman in the moon, and other tales of forgotten heroines p69-74 **398.2**
Wonderful porridge pot
Grimm, J. Sweet porridge
In Grimm, J. The complete Grimm's fairy tales p475-76 **398.2**
In Grimm, J. More tales from Grimm p43-46 **398.2**
Oxenbury, H. The little porridge pot
In Oxenbury, H. The Helen Oxenbury nursery story book p19-24 **398.2**
Wonderful pot
Hatch, M. C. The talking pot
In The Scott, Foresman anthology of children's literature p225-27 **808.8**
The **wonderful** pumpkin. Walker, B. K.
In Walker, B. K. A treasury of Turkish folktales for children p62-66 **398.2**
The **wonderful** sheep. Aulnoy, Madame d'.
In The Blue fairy book p214-30 **398.2**
The **wonderful** tar-baby story. Harris, J. C.
In Best-loved folktales of the world p666-68 **398.2**
In The Scott, Foresman anthology of children's literature p377-78 **808.8**
The **wonderful** Tar-Baby story. Parks, V. D.
In Parks, V. D. Jump again! more adventures of Brer Rabbit p7-13 **398.2**
The **wonderful** thing. Kabungo, O.
In The Crest and the hide, and other African stories of heroes, chiefs, bards, hunters, sorcerers, and common people p25-29 **398.2**
The **wonderful** Wizard of Oz. See Baum, L. F. The Wizard of Oz **Fic**
Wonders *See* Curiosities and wonders
Wonders of badgers. Lavine, S. A. **599.74**
Wonders of crows. Blassingame, W. **598**
Wonders of draft horses. Lavine, S. A. **636.1**
Wonders of egrets, bitterns, and herons. Blassingame, W. **598**
Wonders of foxes. Lavine, S. A. **599.74**
Wonders of sharks. Blassingame, W. **597**
Wonders of speech. Silverstein, A. **302.2**
Wonders of tigers. Lavine, S. A. **599.74**
Wonders of turkeys. Lavine, S. A. **598**
Wondrous wonder, the marvelous marvel
Afanas'ev, A. N. The wondrous wonder, the marvelous marvel
In Afanas'ev, A. N. Russian fairy tales p13-15 **398.2**
Wood, Audrey
Elbert's bad word **E**
Heckedy Peg **E**
King Bidgood's in the bathtub **E**
The napping house **E**
Oh my baby bear! **E**
Wood, Don, 1945-
(il) Wood, A. Elbert's bad word **E**
(il) Wood, A. Heckedy Peg **E**
(il) Wood, A. King Bidgood's in the bathtub **E**
(il) Wood, A. The napping house **E**
Wood, Tim
The 1940s (6 and up) **909.82**
Wood carving

Fiction

Bulla, C. R. Daniel's duck **E**
Woodchuck. McNulty, F. **599.32**
Woodchucks *See* Marmots
Woodcuts
See/See also pages in the following book(s):
The Illustrator's notebook p92-94 **741.6**
Wooden bones. De Lint, C.
In Things that go bump in the night p64-81 **S C**
The **wooden** bowl. Quayle, E.
In Quayle, E. The shining princess, and other Japanese legends p97-102 **398.2**
The **wooden** bowl. Vittorini, D.
In Bauer, C. F. Celebrations p68-70 **808.8**
The **Wooden** Indian and the Shaghorn Buffalo. Sandburg, C.
In Sandburg, C. Rootabaga stories pt 1 p125-27 **S C**
In Sandburg, C. The Sandburg treasury p61-62 **818**
The **wooden** spoon and the whip. Fuja, A.
In Best-loved folktales of the world p649-51 **398.2**

Woodpile. Parnall, P. **591.5**
Woodrow Kennington works practically a miracle. Paterson, K.
In Paterson, K. Angels & other strangers: family Christmas stories p90-104 **S C**
Woodruff, Elvira
Tubtime **E**
Woods, Geraldine, 1948-
Drug use and drug abuse (4 and up) **616.86**
Pollution (6 and up) **363.7**
Woods, Harold, 1945-
(jt. auth) Woods, G. Pollution **363.7**
Woods *See* Forests and forestry
Woodwork
See also Carpentry; Furniture
Adkins, J. Toolchest (5 and up) **684**
Lasson, R. If I had a hammer: woodworking with seven basic tools (4 and up) **684**
Weiss, H. Hammer & saw (5 and up) **684**
Wooing of Becfola
Stephens, J. The wooing of Becfola
In Stephens, J. Irish fairy tales p133-56 **398.2**
Wool, David
(il) Asimov, I. How did we find out about blood? **612.1**
(il) Asimov, I. How did we find out about DNA? **574.87**
(il) Asimov, I. How did we find out about nuclear power? **539.7**
(il) Asimov, I. How did we find out about sunshine? **523.7**
(il) Johnson, E. W. People, love, sex, and families **613.9**
Wool
Paladino, C. Spring fleece (3-6) **636.3**
Woolf, Felicity
Picture this (4 and up) **759**
Woolley, Catherine
See also Thayer, Jane, 1904-
Word books *See* Picture dictionaries
Word games
Espy, W. R. A children's almanac of words at play (3-6) **808.87**
Maestro, G. What's a frank frank? (2-4) **793.73**
Steig, W. C D C? (3-6) **793.73**
Terban, M. The dove dove (3-6) **793.73**
Word works. Kaye, C. B. **410**
Words *See* Vocabulary
Words, New
Dictionaries
12,000 words **423**
Words: a book about the origins of everyday words and phrases. Sarnoff, J. **422**
Words by heart. Sebestyen, O. **Fic**
Words for new readers (k-1) **423**
Words from the myths. Asimov, I. **292**
Words of power. Yolen, J.
In Yolen, J. The faery flag p21-39 **S C**
Words with wrinkled knees: animal poems. Esbensen, B. J. **811**
Work
Johnson, N. All in a day's work (4 and up) **331.7**
Work-let-me-see. Sherlock, Sir P. M.
In Sherlock, Sir P. M. West Indian folk-tales p125-29 **398.2**
Working animals
Ancona, G. Sheep dog (4 and up) **636.7**
Venino, S. Animals helping people (k-3) **636.088**
See/See also pages in the following book(s):
Silverstein, A. Dogs: all about them p86-90, 175-99 (5 and up) **636.7**
The **working** of John Henry. Brooke, W. J.
In Brooke, W. J. A telling of the tales: five stories p75-110 **S C**
Working parents, Children of *See* Children of working parents
Working with water. Ardley, N. **507**
Working women *See* Women—Employment
The **World** almanac and book of facts **031.02**
World Association of Girl Guides and Girl Scouts
Trefoil round the world **369.463**
World atlas, Goode's **912**
The **world** beneath your feet. Rinard, J. E. **591.9**
The **world** beyond. Marriott, A. L.
In Marriott, A. L. American Indian mythology **398.2**
The **World** Book dictionary (5 and up) **423**
The **World** Book encyclopedia **031**
The **World** Book student dictionary (3-5) **423**
The **World** Book year book. See The World Book encyclopedia **031**
World history
Arnold, G. Datelines of world history (5 and up) **909**
Ventura, P. There once was a time (5 and up) **909**
Dictionaries
Lands and peoples **910.3**
Worldmark encyclopedia of the nations **910.3**

The **world** of a falcon. Harrison, V. **598**
The **world** of a jellyfish. Coldrey, J. **593.7**
The **world** of butterflies. Saintsing, D. **595.7**
The **world** of Christopher Robin. Milne, A. A. **821**
The **world** of honeybees. Harrison, V. **595.7**
World of our fathers: the Jews of Eastern Europe. Meltzer, M. **305.8**
The **world** of Pooh. Milne, A. A. **Fic**
The **world** of snakes. Harrison, V. **597.9**
The **world** of storytelling. Pellowski, A. **372.6**
The **world** of the Bible for young readers. Hofman, Y. **220.9**
World of the brain. Silverstein, A. **612.8**
The **world** of UFOs. Cohen, D. **001.9**
World politics

Dictionaries

Worldmark encyclopedia of the nations **910.3**
World Series. Tunis, J. R. See note under Tunis, J. R. The kid from Tomkinsville **Fic**
World War, 1914-1918

Aerial operations

See/See also pages in the following book(s):
Boyne, W. J. The Smithsonian book of flight for young people p37-50 (4 and up) **629.13**

United States—Fiction

Oneal, Z. A long way to go (3-5) **Fic**
World War, 1939-1945
Graff, S. The story of World War II (4-6) **940.54**
Leckie, R. The story of World War II (5 and up) **940.53**
Snyder, L. L. World War II (4 and up) **940.53**
Wood, T. The 1940s (6 and up) **909.82**

Aerial operations

See/See also pages in the following book(s):
Boyne, W. J. The Smithsonian book of flight for young people p73-86 (4 and up) **629.13**

Battles, sieges, etc.

See World War, 1939-1945—Campaigns; World War, 1939-1945—Naval operations

Campaigns

See also Pearl Harbor (Oahu, Hawaii), Attack on, 1941

Campaigns—Philippines

See/See also pages in the following book(s):
Marrin, A. Victory in the Pacific p171-79 (6 and up) **940.54**

Causes

See also National socialism

Children

See/See also pages in the following book(s):
A Horn Book sampler on children's books and reading p195-216 **028.5**

Fiction

Bauer, M. D. Rain of fire (5 and up) **Fic**
Bawden, N. Henry (5 and up) **Fic**
Cooper, S. Dawn of fear (5 and up) **Fic**
Gardam, J. A long way from Verona (6 and up) **Fic**
Greene, B. Summer of my German soldier (6 and up) **Fic**
Innocenti, R. Rose Blanche (5 and up) **Fic**
Levitin, S. Silver days (5 and up) **Fic**
Levoy, M. Alan and Naomi (6 and up) **Fic**
Lowry, L. Autumn Street (4 and up) **Fic**
Lowry, L. Number the stars (4 and up) **Fic**
Matas, C. Lisa's war (5 and up) **Fic**
Orlev, U. The island on Bird Street (5 and up) **Fic**
Paton Walsh, J. Fireweed (5 and up) **Fic**
Pearson, K. The sky is falling (6 and up) **Fic**
Ray, D. K. My daddy was a soldier **E**
Serraillier, I. The silver sword (5 and up) **Fic**
Watkins, Y. K. So far from the bamboo grove (6 and up) **Fic**
Westall, R. The machine gunners (6 and up) **Fic**

Jews

See also Holocaust, Jewish (1933-1945)
Frank, A. The diary of a young girl (6 and up) **92**
Koehn, I. Mischling, second degree: my childhood in Nazi Germany (6 and up) **92**
Lowry, L. Number the stars (4 and up) **Fic**
Matas, C. Lisa's war (5 and up) **Fic**
Meltzer, M. Rescue: the story of how Gentiles saved Jews in the Holocaust (6 and up) **940.54**
Reiss, J. The upstairs room (4 and up) **92**

World War, 1939-1945—*Continued*
Naval operations
Humble, R. U-boat (4 and up) 940.54
Marrin, A. Victory in the Pacific (6 and up) 940.54
Taylor, T. Battle in the Arctic seas (5 and up) 940.54
Arctic Ocean
Taylor, T. Battle in the Arctic seas (5 and up) 940.54
Atlantic Ocean
Humble, R. U-boat (4 and up) 940.54
Great Britain—Personal narratives
Foreman, M. War boy: a country childhood (5 and up) 92
Japan
Maruki, T. Hiroshima no pika 940.54
Japan—Personal narratives
Morimoto, J. My Hiroshima (2-4) 940.54
Pacific Ocean
Marrin, A. Victory in the Pacific (6 and up) 940.54
United States
Davis, D. S. Behind barbed wire: the imprisonment of Japanese Americans during World War II (5 and up) 940.54
Hamanaka, S. The journey (5 and up) 305.8
World War II. Snyder, L. L. 940.53
Worldmark encyclopedia of the nations 910.3
Worlds within. Egoff, S. A. 028.5
The **worm** and the snail. Terada, A. M.
In Terada, A. M. Under the starfruit tree p59-63 398.2
Worms
Fiction
Lionni, L. Inch by inch E
Rockwell, T. How to eat fried worms (3-6) Fic
Wormser, Richard, 1933-
Pinkerton: America's first private eye (5 and up) 92
Worse than rotten, Ralph. Gantos, J. See note under Gantos, J. Rotten Ralph E
Worse than Willy! Stevenson, J. See note under Stevenson, J. "Could be worse!" E
Worship
Baylor, B. The way to start a day (1-3) 291.4
The **worst** person in the world. Stevenson, J. E
Worth, Valerie
More small poems (3-5) 811
Small poems (3-5) 811
Small poems again (3-5) 811
Still more small poems (3-5) 811
Wortis, Avi *See* Avi, 1937-
Wounded Knee: an Indian history of the American West. Ehrlich, A. 970.004
Wounds and injuries
Cole, J. Cuts, breaks, bruises, and burns (3-5) 612
Wozniak, Stephen
See/See also pages in the following book(s):
Aaseng, N. From rags to riches p64-75 (5 and up) 920
The **wreck** of the Zephyr. Van Allsburg, C. E
Wrede, Patricia C.
Dealing with dragons (6 and up) Fic
Wren and the bear
Grimm, J. The bear and the kingbird 398.2
Grimm, J. The willow-wren and the bear
In Grimm, J. The complete Grimm's fairy tales p472-74 398.2
Wrestling
Sullivan, G. Better wrestling for boys (4 and up) 796.8
Fiction
Christopher, M. Takedown (6 and up) Fic
The **wrestling** match of the two Buddhas. Uchida, Y.
In Uchida, Y. The magic listening cap 398.2
Wright, Betty Ren
The dollhouse murders (4-6) Fic
Wright, Blanche Fisher
(il) The Real Mother Goose. See The Real Mother Goose 398.8
Wright, David K.
Malaysia (4 and up) 959.5
Wright, Jill, 1942-
The old woman and the jar of uums E
The old woman and the Willy Nilly Man (k-3) E
Wright, Joan Richards
(jt. auth) Parker, N. W. Bugs 595.7
(jt. auth) Parker, N. W. Frogs, toads, lizards, and salamanders 597.6
Wright, Lyndie
Masks (4 and up) 745.59
Wright, Orville, 1871-1948
About
Taylor, R. L. The first flight (4 and up) 629.13

Wright, Wilbur, 1867-1912
About
Taylor, R. L. The first flight (4 and up) 629.13

Wright Brothers
See also Wright, Orville, 1871-1948; Wright, Wilbur, 1867-1912

Wrightson, Patricia, 1921-
Balyet (5 and up) Fic
A little fear (5 and up) Fic
The Nargun and the stars (5 and up) Fic
See/See also pages in the following book(s):
Townsend, J. R. A sense of story p204-11 028.5
Townsend, J. R. A sounding of storytellers p194-206 028.5

A **wrinkle** in time. L'Engle, M. Fic

Write on, Rosy! Greenwald, S. See note under Greenwald, S. Give us a great big smile, Rosy Cole Fic

Writers *See* Authors

Writing
See also Calligraphy
History
Ogg, O. The 26 letters 411
Materials and instruments
Cobb, V. Writing it down (1-3) 681

Writing (Authorship) *See* Authorship; Journalism

Writing for kids. Benjamin, C. L. 808

Writing it down. Cobb, V. 681

Written for children. Townsend, J. R. 028.5

Wu, Ch'êng-ên, ca. 1500-ca. 1582
Zhang Xiu Shi. Monkey and the White Bone Demon 398.2

Wyeth, N. C. (Newell Convers), 1882-1945
(il) Creswick, P. Robin Hood 398.2
(il) Defoe, D. Robinson Crusoe Fic
(il) Rawlings, M. K. The yearling Fic
(il) Stevenson, R. L. Treasure Island Fic

Wyeth, Newell Convers *See* Wyeth, N. C. (Newell Convers), 1882-1945

Wyler, Rose
Magic secrets (1-3) 793.8
Science fun with mud and dirt (2-4) 507
Science fun with peanuts and popcorn (2-4) 507
Science fun with toy boats and planes (2-4) 507
Science fun with toy cars and trucks (2-4) 507
Spooky tricks (1-3) 793.8
The starry sky (k-4) 520

Wynar, Christine Gehrt, 1933-
Guide to reference books for school media centers 011.6

Wynne, Patricia
(il) Bruun, R. D. The human body 612

Wyss, Johann David
The Swiss family Robinson (5 and up) Fic

X

X rays
See/See also pages in the following book(s):
Aaseng, N. The inventors: Nobel prizes in chemistry, physics, and medicine p10-17 (5 and up) 609

The **Xanadu** Manuscript. See Townsend, J. R. The visitors Fic

Y

Yaakov, Juliette
(ed) Junior high school library catalog. See Junior high school library catalog 011.6

Yachts and yachting
See also Sailing

Yagawa, Sumiko
The crane wife (1-3) 398.2

Yakovlev, Yuri
Wild rosemary
In Face to face: a collection of stories by celebrated Soviet and American writers p11-21 S C

Yamamoto, Joyce
(il) Raffi. The 2nd Raffi songbook 782.42
(il) Raffi. The Raffi singable songbook 782.42

Yana Indians
Kroeber, T. Ishi, last of his tribe (5 and up) 92

Yang Yang and Hoo Hoo. Sandburg, C.
In Sandburg, C. Rootabaga stories pt 2 p145-51 S C
In Sandburg, C. The Sandburg treasury p149-51 818

Yang Zhr Cheng
(il) Fritz, J. China's Long March 951.04

Yankee Doodle, Steven Kellogg's. Bangs, E. 782.42

Yarbrough, Camille, 1948-
Cornrows E
The shimmershine queens (4-6) Fic

Yard sales *See* Garage sales
Yarmolinsky, Babette Deutsch *See* Deutsch, Babette, 1895-1982
Yaroslava, 1925-
(il) Hautzig, E. R. Holiday treats **641.5**
(il) Tresselt, A. R. The mitten **398.2**
Yashima, Mitsu *See* Iwamatsu, Tomoe, 1908-
Yashima, Taro *See* Iwamatsu, Atushi Jun, 1908-
Yates, Elizabeth, 1905-
Amos Fortune, free man (4 and up) **92**
See/See also pages in the following book(s):
Newbery Medal books, 1922-1955 p355-71 **028.5**
Yates, John
(il) Turner, D. Potatoes **635**
Yeager, Chuck, 1923-
About
Levinson, N. S. Chuck Yeager: the man who broke the sound barrier (5 and up) **92**
The **year** at Maple Hill Farm. Provensen, A. **E**
A **year** in the country. Florian, D. **E**
A **year** of beasts. Wolff, A. **E**
A **year** of birds. Wolff, A. **E**
The **year** of the panda. Schlein, M. **Fic**
The **year** of the perfect Christmas tree. Houston, G. **E**
The **year** without a Santa Claus. McGinley, P. **811**
The **yearling**. Rawlings, M. K. **Fic**
Yee, Paul
Tales from Gold Mountain (4 and up) **S C**
Contents: Spirits of the railway; Sons and daughters; The friends of Kwan Ming; Ginger for the heart; Gambler's eyes; Forbidden fruit; Rider Chan and the night river; The revenge of the Iron Chink
Yeh-Shen. Louie, A.-L. **398.2**
Yellow dwarf
Aulnoy, Madame d'. The yellow dwarf
In The Blue fairy book p30-50 **398.2**
In The Classic fairy tales p68-80 **398.2**
The **Yellow** fairy book (4-6) **398.2**
Yellow Hair: George Armstrong Custer. Marriott, A. L.
In Marriott, A. L. American Indian mythology **398.2**
Yellow Lily. Crossley-Holland, K.
In Crossley-Holland, K. British folk tales p313-30 **398.2**
The **Yellow** ribbon
In Juba this and Juba that p44-46 **372.6**
Yellowstone fires. Patent, D. H. **574.5**
Yellowstone National Park
Calabro, M. Operation grizzly bear (5 and up) **599.74**
Ekey, R. Fire! in Yellowstone (2-4) **574.5**
Patent, D. H. Yellowstone fires (2-4) **574.5**
Vogel, C. G. The great Yellowstone fire (3-6) **574.5**
Yen, Tzu Chun Chiu
The groom's crimes
In Best-loved folktales of the world p546-47 **398.2**
Yeoman, Cushla, 1971-
About
Butler, D. Cushla and her books **362.4**
Yeoman, John
Old Mother Hubbard's dog dresses up **E**
Old Mother Hubbard's dog learns to play. See note under Yeoman, J. Old Mother Hubbard's dog dresses up **E**
Old Mother Hubbard's dog needs a doctor. See note under Yeoman, J. Old Mother Hubbard's dog dresses up **E**
Old Mother Hubbard's dog takes up sport. See note under Yeoman, J. Old Mother Hubbard's dog dresses up **E**
Yeomans, Donald K.
The distant planets (4-6) **523.4**
Yep, Laurence
Child of the owl (5 and up) **Fic**
Dragonwings (5 and up) **Fic**
The rainbow people (4 and up) **398.2**
Contents: Bedtime snacks; Natural enemies; The professor of smells; The eel's disguise; The child of calamity; The ghost's bride; The butterfly man; We are all one; The superior pet; Snake-spoke; The old jar; The boasting contest; Trouble snake; Breaker's bridge; Virtue goes to town; The homecoming; Dream flier; Slippers; The changeling; The rainbow people
The serpent's children (6 and up) **Fic**
Sweetwater (6 and up) **Fic**
Yepsen, Roger B.
Smarten up! how to increase your brain power (5 and up) **153**
Yiddish literature
History and criticism
See/See also pages in the following book(s):
Meltzer, M. World of our fathers: the Jews of Eastern Europe p155-75 (6 and up) **305.8**
Yokoyama, Masami
(il) Spain. See Spain **946**
Yolen, Jane
The baby-sitter
In Things that go bump in the night p15-24 **S C**

Yolen, Jane—*Continued*
Best witches: poems for Halloween (3-5) **811**
Bird watch: a book of poetry (3-6) **811**
The boy who drew unicorns
In Face to face: a collection of stories by celebrated Soviet and American writers p141-51 **S C**
Commander Toad and the big black hole. See note under Yolen, T. Commander Toad in space **E**
Commander Toad and the dis-asteroid. See note under Yolen, T. Commander Toad in space **E**
Commander Toad and the intergalactic spy. See note under Yolen, T. Commander Toad in space **E**
Commander Toad and the Planet of the Grapes. See note under Yolen, T. Commander Toad in space **E**
Commander Toad and the space pirates. See note under Yolen, T. Commander Toad in space **E**
Commander Toad in space **E**
The devil's arithmetic (4 and up) **Fic**
Dinosaur dances (3-5) **811**
The dragon's boy (5 and up) **Fic**
The faery flag (5 and up) **S C**
Stories included are: The faery flag; The foxwife; Words of power; The singer of seeds; The boy who drew unicorns; Wolf/Child; The tower bird; The face in the cloth; Happy Dens
The girl who loved the wind **E**
Mice on ice **E**
No bath tonight **E**
Owl moon **E**
Picnic with Piggins. See note under Yolen, J. Piggins and the royal wedding **E**
Piggins. See note under Yolen, J. Piggins and the royal wedding **E**
Piggins and the royal wedding **E**
Ring of earth: a child's book of seasons (3-6) **811**
The seeing stick (2-4) **Fic**
Sky dogs **E**
The sleeping beauty (k-2) **398.2**
Sleeping ugly (2-4) **Fic**
Tam Lin (3-6) **398.2**
The three bears rhyme book (k-2) **811**
Touch magic **028.5**
(ed) The Lap-time song and play book. See The Lap-time song and play book **782.42**
(ed) The Lullaby songbook. See The Lullaby songbook **782.42**
(ed) Things that go bump in the night. See Things that go bump in the night **S C**

Yom Kippur
Chaikin, M. Sound the shofar (3-6) **296.4**

Fiction
Cohen, B. Yussel's prayer (3-5) **398.2**

Yonder. Johnston, T. **E**

Yorinks, Arthur, 1953-
Company's coming **E**
Hey, Al **E**
It happened in Pinsk **E**
Oh, Brother **E**
See/See also pages in the following book(s):
Sendak, M. Caldecott & Co.: notes on books and pictures p139-41 **028.5**

York, Carol Beach
Mike Fink
In The Scott, Foresman anthology of children's literature p364-65 **808.8**

Yoshida, Toshi, 1911-
Elephant crossing (1-3) **599.6**
Young lions (1-3) **599.74**

Yoshino, Shin, 1943-
(il) Overbeck, C. Cats **636.8**

Yossel-Zissel the melamed. Simon, S.
In Simon, S. More wise men of Helm and their merry tales p63-68 **398.2**

Yossi asks the angels for help. Chaikin, M. **Fic**

Yossi tries to help God. Chaikin, M. See note under Chaikin, M. Yossi asks the angels for help **Fic**

You be good and I'll be night: jump-on-the-bed poems. Merriam, E. **811**

"You better not do it". Sanfield, S.
In Sanfield, S. The adventures of High John the Conqueror **398.2**

You can't sneeze with your eyes open & other freaky facts about the human body. Seuling, B. **612**

You have to trust your heart. Ailisli, A.
In Face to face: a collection of stories by celebrated Soviet and American writers p203-21 **S C**

You lucky duck! McCully, E. A. See note under McCully, E. A. Zaza's big break **E**

You read to me, I'll read to you. Ciardi, J. **811**

You shouldn't have to say good-bye. Hermes, P. **Fic**

You won't believe your eyes! O'Neill, C. **152.14**

You'll soon grow into them, Titch. Hutchins, P. **E**

Younde goes to town. Barker, W. H.
In Best-loved folktales of the world p623-25 **398.2**

Younde goes to town. Courlander, H.
In Courlander, H. The cow-tail switch, and other West African stories p59-64 **398.2**

Young, Debby
(il) A Pumpkin in a pear tree. See A Pumpkin in a pear tree **745.59**

Young, Donald
The Sierra Club book of our national parks (4 and up) **917.3**

Young, Ed
Lon Po Po (1-3) **398.2**
The other bone **E**
Up a tree **E**
(il) Cats are cats. See Cats are cats **808.81**
(il) Fritz, J. The double life of Pocahontas **92**
(il) Frost, R. Birches **811**
(il) Hodges, M. The voice of the great bell **398.2**
(il) Leaf, M. The eyes of the dragon **E**
(il) Lewis, R. In the night, still dark **811**
(il) Louie, A.-L. Yeh-Shen **398.2**
(il) Mice are nice. See Mice are nice **808.81**
(il) Radin, R. Y. High in the mountains **E**
(il) Wolkstein, D. The Red Lion **398.2**
(il) Yolen, J. The girl who loved the wind **E**

Young, Ella, 1867-1956
See/See also pages in the following book(s):
A Horn Book sampler on children's books and reading p237-42 **028.5**

Young, James, 1956-
A million chameleons **E**

Young, Noela
(il) Klein, R. Enemies **Fic**
(il) Rodda, E. The best-kept secret **Fic**

Young, Ruth
(il) Aylesworth, J. One crow **E**

Young, Stanley, 1906-1975
Ship forever sailing
In Holiday plays round the year p59-70 **812.008**

Young adults *See* Youth

Young adults' library services
See also Children's libraries; School libraries (High school)

Periodicals

Journal of Youth Services in Libraries **027.6205**

Young adults' literature

Bibliography

Anderson, V. Fiction sequels for readers age 10-16 **016.8**
National Council of Teachers of English. Committee on the Junior High and Middle School Booklist. Your reading: a booklist for junior high and middle school students **011.6**

History and criticism

See/See also pages in the following book(s):
Crosscurrents of criticism p98-120, 144-49 **028.5**

The **young** Black Stallion. Farley, W. See note under Farley, W. The Black Stallion **Fic**

The **young** cartoonist. Hoff, S. **741.5**

Young giant
Grimm, J. The young giant
In Grimm, J. The complete Grimm's fairy tales p412-20 **398.2**

Young head of the family
The Young head of the family
In Best-loved folktales of the world p534-37 **398.2**

The **young** king. Wilde, O.
In Wilde, O. The Happy Prince, and other stories p52-69 **S C**

The **young** landlords. Myers, W. D. **Fic**

Young lions. Yoshida, T. **599.74**

Young Melvin
In The Scott, Foresman anthology of children's literature p361-63 **808.8**

Young Merlin. San Souci, R. **398.2**

Young Nick and Jubilee. Garfield, L. **Fic**

The **young** rider's handbook. Sayer, A. **636.1**

The **young** scientist's guide to successful science projects. Markle, S. **507.8**

The **young** United States, 1783 to 1830. Tunis, E. **973**

Your Big Backyard **505**

Your cradle is green. Aiken, J.
In Aiken, J. Past eight o'clock p27-42 **S C**

Your first garden book. Brown, M. T. **635**

Your move, J.P.! Lowry, L. **Fic**

Your new potty. Cole, J. **649**

Your old pal, Al. Greene, C. C. See note under Greene, C. C. A girl called Al **Fic**

Your reading: a booklist for junior high and middle school students. National Council of Teachers of English. Committee on the Junior High and Middle School Booklist **011.6**

Your two brains. Stafford, P. **612.8**
Yours affectionately, Peter Rabbit: miniature letters. Potter, B. **E**
Yours till Niagara Falls, Abby. O'Connor, J. **Fic**
Youth
See also Adolescence; Runaway children
Alcohol use
Hjelmeland, A. Drinking & driving (4-6) **363.1**
Youth who could not shiver and shake
Grimm, J. The story of one who set out to study fear
In Grimm, J. The juniper tree, and other tales from Grimm v1 p23-41 **398.2**
Grimm, J. The story of the youth who went forth to learn what fear was
In Grimm, J. The complete Grimm's fairy tales p29-39 **398.2**
Grimm, J. The tale of a youth who set out to learn what fear was
In The Blue fairy book p86-95 **398.2**
Ypsilantis, George
(jt. auth) McClard, M. Hiawatha and the Iroquois league **92**
Yu, Ling
Cooking the Chinese way (5 and up) **641.5**
Yuck!. Stevenson, J. See note under Stevenson, J. Emma **E**
Yue, Charlotte
The igloo **728**
The Pueblo (4 and up) **970.004**
(jt. auth) Yue, D. The tipi: a center of native American life **728**
Yue, David
The tipi: a center of native American life (4 and up) **728**
(jt. auth) Yue, C. The igloo **728**
(jt. auth) Yue, C. The Pueblo **970.004**
Yukon Territory
History
See also Klondike River Valley (Yukon)—Gold discoveries
Poetry
Service, R. W. The cremation of Sam McGee (4 and up) **811**
Service, R. W. The shooting of Dan McGrew (4 and up) **811**
Yummers!. Marshall, J. **E**
Yummers too: the second course. Marshall, J. See note under Marshall, J. Yummers! **E**
Yung-Kyung-Pyung. Sherlock, Sir P. M.
In Sherlock, Sir P. M. Anansi, the spider man p59-63 **398.2**
Yussel's prayer. Cohen, B. **398.2**

Z

The Z was zapped. Van Allsburg, C. **E**
Zachary's divorce [short story]. Sitea, L.
In Free to be—you and me p124-27 **810.8**
Zaharias, Babe Didrikson, 1911-1956
About
Knudson, R. R. Babe Didrikson: athlete of the century (4 and up) **92**
Zalben, Jane Breskin
Happy Passover, Rosie **E**
(il) Carroll, L. Lewis Carroll's Jabberwocky **821**
(il) Carroll, L. The walrus and the carpenter **821**
Zallinger, Jean
(il) Cohen, D. Dinosaurs **567.9**
(il) Sattler, H. R. Baby dinosaurs **567.9**
(il) Sattler, H. R. The book of eagles **598**
(il) Sattler, H. R. Sharks, the super fish **597**
(il) Sattler, H. R. Whales, the nomads of the sea **599.5**
Zambia
Lauré, J. Zambia (4 and up) **968.94**
Zambreno, Mary Frances, 1954-
Skinning a wizard
In Things that go bump in the night p217-31 **S C**
Zamojska-Hutchins, Danuta
Cooking the Polish way (5 and up) **641.5**
Zanzibar
Folklore
See Folklore—Zanzibar
Zaslavsky, Claudia, 1917-
Tic tac toe, and other three-in-a row games from ancient Egypt to the modern computer (4 and up) **794**
Zaza's big break. McCully, E. A. **E**
Zebras
Arnold, C. Zebra (3-5) **599.72**
Zeely. Hamilton, V. **Fic**
Zekmet, the stone carver. Stolz, M. **Fic**
Zeldich, Arieh
(il) Andersen, H. C. The Snow Queen **Fic**

Zelinsky, Paul O.
Rumpelstiltskin (k-4) **398.2**
(il) Cleary, B. Dear Mr. Henshaw **Fic**
(il) Ginsburg, M. The sun's asleep behind the hill **E**
(il) Lesser, R. Hansel and Gretel **398.2**
(il) The Random House book of humor for children. See The Random House book of humor for children **817.008**
(il) Zhitkov, B. How I hunted the little fellows **Fic**

Zeller, Paula Klevan
Focus on marijuana (3-6) **362.29**

Zemach, Harve
The judge **E**
Mommy, buy me a china doll **E**
A penny a look (k-3) **398.2**
The princess and Froggie **E**
See/See also pages in the following book(s):
Sendak, M. Caldecott & Co.: notes on books and pictures p133-37 **028.5**

Zemach, Kaethe
(jt. auth) Zemach, H. The princess and Froggie **E**

Zemach, Margot
The little red hen (k-2) **398.2**
The three little pigs (k-2) **398.2**
The three wishes (k-2) **398.2**
(il) Ginsburg, M. The Chinese mirror **398.2**
(il) Grimm, J. The fisherman and his wife **398.2**
(il) Phillips, M. The sign in Mendel's window **E**
(il) Schwartz, A. The cat's elbow, and other secret languages **652**
(il) Singer, I. B. Mazel and Shlimazel **398.2**
(il) Singer, I. B. Naftali the storyteller and his horse, Sus, and other stories **S C**
(il) Singer, I. B. When Shlemiel went to Warsaw & other stories **398.2**
(il) Staines, B. All God's critters got a place in the choir **782.42**
(il) Uchida, Y. The two foolish cats **398.2**
(il) Zemach, H. The judge **E**
(il) Zemach, H. Mommy, buy me a china doll **E**
(il) Zemach, H. A penny a look **398.2**
(il) Zemach, H. The princess and Froggie **E**
See/See also pages in the following book(s):
Newbery and Caldecott Medal books, 1966-1975 p257-59, 272-75 **028.5**
Sendak, M. Caldecott & Co.: notes on books and pictures p133-37 **028.5**

Zemba, Lýdia Verona
Ghana—in pictures. See Ghana—in pictures **966.7**

Zenger, John Peter, 1697-1746
See/See also pages in the following book(s):
Jacobs, W. J. Great lives: human rights p18-23 (5 and up) **920**

Zeppelins *See* Airships

Zero and the commercial. Cresswell, H.
In Bauer, C. F. Celebrations p213-18 **808.8**

Zero gravity *See* Weightlessness

Zeus (Greek deity)
Gates, D. Lord of the sky: Zeus (4 and up) **292**

Zhang Xiu Shi
Monkey and the White Bone Demon (3-6) **398.2**

Zhitkov, Boris, 1882-1938
How I hunted the little fellows (2-4) **Fic**

Zia. O'Dell, S. **Fic**

Ziebel, Peter
Look closer! **E**
(il) Huff, B. A. Greening the city streets **635**

Ziefert, Harriet
A new coat for Anna **E**

Zilinskaite, Vytaute
The tubeteika affair
In Face to face: a collection of stories by celebrated Soviet and American writers p77-89 **S C**

Zillions **640.73**

Zim, Herbert S.
Birds (4 and up) **598**
Fishes (4 and up) **597**
Flowers (4 and up) **582.13**
Insects (4 and up) **595.7**
Mammals (4 and up) **599**
Rocks and minerals (4 and up) **549**
Seashores (4 and up) **574.92**
Trees (4 and up) **582.16**
(jt. auth) Mitchell, R. T. Butterflies and moths **595.7**
(jt. auth) Robbins, C. S. Birds of North America **598**

Zimbabwe
Cheney, P. The land and people of Zimbabwe (5 and up) **968.91**
Lauré, J. Zimbabwe (4 and up) **968.91**
Zimbabwe—in pictures (5 and up) **968.91**

Zimbabwe—in pictures (5 and up) **968.91**

Zimmer, Dirk
(il) Climo, S. Someone saw a spider **398.2**
(il) Cole, J. Bony-Legs **398.2**
(il) Day, E. C. John Tabor's ride **E**
(il) Hancock, S. Esteban and the ghost **398.2**

Zimmer, Dirk—*Continued*
(il) The Naked bear. See The Naked bear **398.2**
(il) Schwartz, A. In a dark, dark room, and other scary stories **398.2**
(il) Windy day: stories and poems. See Windy day: stories and poems **808.8**

Zimmerman, H. Werner
Henny Penny (k-2) **398.2**

Zion, Gene
Harry and the lady next door. See note under Zion, G. Harry the dirty dog **E**
Harry by the sea. See note under Zion, G. Harry the dirty dog **E**
Harry the dirty dog **E**
No roses for Harry! See note under Zion, G. Harry the dirty dog **E**

Zionism
Adler, D. A. Our Golda: the story of Golda Meir (3-5) **92**
Kustanowitz, S. E. Henrietta Szold: Israel's helping hand (4 and up) **92**

Ziroli, Claudia
(il) Madaras, L. The what's happening to my body? book for girls: a growing up guide for parents and daughters **613.9**

Ziskind, Sylvia, 1906-
Telling stories to children **372.6**

Zlateh the goat. Singer, I. B.
In Singer, I. B. Stories for children p45-52 **S C**
In Singer, I. B. Zlateh the goat, and other stories p79-90 **398.2**

Zlateh the goat, and other stories. Singer, I. B. **398.2**

Zodiacal light
See/See also pages in the following book(s):
Gallant, R. A. Rainbows, mirages and sundogs p58-64 (4 and up) **551.5**

Zolotow, Charlotte, 1915-
The hating book **E**
I know a lady **E**
Mr. Rabbit and the lovely present **E**
My friend John **E**
My grandson Lew **E**
One step, two— **E**
Over and over **E**
The quarreling book **E**
The quiet mother and the noisy little boy **E**
Sleepy book **E**
Something is going to happen **E**
A tiger called Thomas **E**
William's doll **E**

Zoo. Gibbons, G. **590.74**
Zoo babies. Grosvenor, D. K. **590.74**
Zoo day. Brennan, J. **590.74**

Zoologists
Goodall, J. My life with the chimpanzees (3-6) **92**

Zoology
See also Animals

Zoology, Economic
See also Wildlife conservation; Working animals

Zoonooz **591.05**

Zoos
See also National Zoological Park (U.S.)
Brennan, J. Zoo day (k-3) **590.74**
Gibbons, G. Zoo (k-2) **590.74**
Grosvenor, D. K. Zoo babies (k-3) **590.74**
Johnston, G. Windows on wildlife (3-6) **590.74**
Machotka, H. What do you do at a petting zoo? (k-2) **590.74**
Rinard, J. E. Zoos without cages (5 and up) **590.74**

Fiction
Rice, E. Sam who never forgets **E**
Seuss, Dr. If I ran the zoo **E**

Periodicals
Zoonooz **591.05**

Zoos without cages. Rinard, J. E. **590.74**

Zubrowski, Bernie, 1939-
Balloons (3-6) **507**
Clocks (4 and up) **681.1**
Messing around with baking chemistry (5 and up) **540.7**
Tops (4-6) **745.592**
Wheels at work (4-6) **621.8**

Zuiderveld, Sharon
(ed) Cataloging correctly for kids. See Cataloging correctly for kids **025.3**

Zulus
Stanley, D. Shaka, king of the Zulus (2-4) **92**

Fiction
Seed, J. Ntombi's song **E**

Zwerger, Lisbeth
(il) Aesop. Aesop's fables [illus. by Lisbeth Zwerger] **398.2**
(il) Andersen, H. C. The nightingale **Fic**
(il) Andersen, H. C. Thumbeline **Fic**
(il) Bell, A. The nutcracker **Fic**
(il) Dickens, C. A Christmas carol in prose **Fic**
(il) Grimm, J. Hansel and Gretel **398.2**
(il) Grimm, J. Little Red Cap **398.2**
(il) Grimm, J. The seven ravens **398.2**
(il) Henry, O. The gift of the Magi **Fic**
(il) Wilde, O. The selfish giant **Fic**

PART 3

DIRECTORY OF PUBLISHERS AND DISTRIBUTORS

DIRECTORY OF PUBLISHERS AND DISTRIBUTORS

21st Cent. Bks. (Frederick): 21st Cent. Bks., 38 S. Market St., Frederick, Md. 21701 Tel 301-698-0210

ABC-CLIO Inc., 130 Cremona Dr., Santa Barbara, Calif. 93116-1911 Tel 805-968-1911; refer orders to P.O. Box 1911, Santa Barbara, Calif. 93116-1911 Tel 800-422-2546

Abingdon Press, 201 8th Ave. S., P.O. Box 801, Nashville, Tenn. 37202 Tel 615-749-6347; 800-251-3320

Abrams: Harry N. Abrams Inc., 100 5th Ave., New York, N.Y. 10011 Tel 212-206-7715; 800-345-1359

Academy Chicago Pubs., 213 W. Institute Pl., Chicago, Ill. 60610 Tel 312-751-7302; 800-248-7323 (orders outside Ill.)

Ace Bks., 200 Madison Ave., New York, N.Y. 10016 Tel 212-951-8800; 800-223-0510

Adama Bks., 306 W. 38th St., New York, N.Y. 10018 Tel 212-594-5770; refer orders to Watts

Addison-Wesley Pub. Co., 1 Jacob Way, Reading, Mass. 01867 Tel 617-944-3700; 800-447-2226 (orders only)

Airmont Pub. Co. Inc., 401 Lafayette St., New York, N.Y. 10003 Tel 212-598-0222; 800-223-5251

Aladdin Bks. (NY): Aladdin Bks., c.o. Macmillan Pub. Co., 866 3rd Ave., New York, N.Y. 10022 Tel 212-702-2000; 800-257-5755; refer orders to 100 Front St., Box 500, Riverside, N.J. 08075-7500 Tel 609-461-6500
Imprint of Macmillan

Allison & Busby Ltd., 26 Grand Union Centre, 338 Ladbroke Grove, London W10 5BX, Eng. Tel (081) 968 7554; refer orders to Tiptree Bk. Services Ltd., St. Luke's Chase, Tiptree Colchester, Essex CO5 0SR, Eng. Tel Tiptree (0621) 816 362

Amereon Ltd., P.O. Box 1200, Mattituck, N.Y. 11952

American Assn. for the Advancement of Science, 1333 H St. N.W., Washington, D.C. 20005 Tel 202-326-6446

American Guidance Service Inc., Publishers' Bldg., Circle Pines, Minn. 55014-1796 Tel 612-786-4343; 800-328-2560

American Lib. Assn., 50 E. Huron St., Chicago, Ill. 60611 Tel 312-944-6780

Andersen Press Ltd., Random Century House, 20 Vauxhall Bridge Rd., London SW1V 2SA, Eng. Tel (071) 973 9720; refer orders to Tiptree Bk. Services Ltd., St. Luke's Chase, Tiptree Colchester, Essex CO5 0SR, Eng. Tel Tiptree (0621) 816 362

Arcade Pub., 141 5th Ave., New York, N.Y. 10010 Tel 212-475-2633; 800-343-9204; refer orders to Little, Brown

Arco Pub. Inc., 1 Gulf & Western Plaza, New York, N.Y. 10023 Tel 212-373-8931; refer orders to Prentice Hall Trade, Simon & Schuster Inc., 200 Old Tappan Rd., Old Tappan, N.J. 07675 Tel 800-223-2336 (orders only)

Artists & Writers Guild Inc., c.o. HarperCollins Pubs., 10 E. 53rd St., New York, N.Y. 10022-5299 Tel 212-207-7000

Association for Educ. Communications & Technology, 1126 16th St. N.W., Washington, D.C. 20036 Tel 202-466-4780

Astor-Honor Inc. Pubs., 48 E. 43rd St., New York, N.Y. 10017

Atheneum Pubs., c.o. Macmillan Pub. Co., 866 3rd Ave., New York, N.Y. 10022 Tel 212-702-2000; 800-257-5755; refer orders to 100 Front St., Box 500, Riverside, N.J. 08075-7500 Tel 609-461-6500
Margaret K. McElderry Bks. formerly an imprint of Atheneum Pubs.; now an imprint of Macmillan

Atlantic Monthly Press, 19 Union Sq. W., New York, N.Y. 10003 Tel 212-645-4462; refer orders to Publishers Resources Inc., P.O. Box 7018, La Vergne, Tenn. 37086-7018 Tel 800-937-5557

Avon Bks., 1350 Ave. of the Americas, New York, N.Y. 10019 Tel 212-261-6800; refer orders to P.O. Box 767, Dresden, Tenn. 38225 Tel 800-633-1670; 800-223-0690 (outside orders only)

AVSTAR Pub. Corp., 34C Burlinghoff Lane, Lebanon, N.J. 08833 Tel 908-236-6210; refer orders to P.O. Box 537, Lebanon, N.J. 08833

Ballantine Bks., 201 E. 50th St., New York, N.Y. 10022 Tel 212-751-2600; refer orders to 400 Hahn Rd., Westminster, Md. 21157 Tel 800-638-6460
Also uses imprints Fawcett Columbine; Fawcett Crest; and, Fawcett Girls Only

Bantam Bks. Inc., 666 5th Ave., New York, N.Y. 10103 Tel 212-765-6500; 800-223-6834
Also use imprint Loveswept

Barron's Educ. Ser. Inc., 250 Wireless Blvd., Hauppauge, N.Y. 11788 Tel 516-434-3311; 800-257-5729; 800-645-3476 (outside N.Y.)

Beacon Press, 25 Beacon St., Boston, Mass. 02108 Tel 617-742-2110; refer orders to HarperCollins Pubs., Keystone Ind. Park, Scranton, Pa. 18512 Tel 800-982-4377; 800-242-7737 (outside Pa.)

Bedrick Bks.: Peter Bedrick Bks. Inc., 2112 Broadway, Room 318, New York, N.Y. 10023 Tel 212-496-0751; refer orders, except individuals, to Publishers Group West, P.O. Box 8843, Emeryville, Calif. 94662 Tel 800-365-3453

Beech Tree Bks., 1350 Ave. of the Americas, New York, N.Y. 10019 Tel 212-261-6500; 800-843-9389; refer orders to 39 Plymouth St., Fairfield, N.J. 07007 Tel 201-227-7200
Imprint of Morrow

Beginner Bks., 201 E. 50th St., New York, N.Y. 10022 Tel 212-751-2600; 800-726-0600; refer orders to Random House, 400 Hahn Rd., Westminster, Md. 21157 Tel 800-492-0782

Behrman House Inc., 235 Watchung Ave., W. Orange, N.J. 07052 Tel 201-669-0447; 800-221-2755

Berkley Bks., 200 Madison Ave., New York, N.Y. 10016 Tel 212-951-8800; 800-223-0510

Black Butterfly Children's Bks., 625 Broadway, Suite 903, New York, N.Y. 10012 Tel 212-982-3158; refer orders to Consortium Bk. Sales & Distr., 287 E. 6th St., Suite 365, St. Paul, Minn. 55101 Tel 612-221-9035; 800-283-3572
Imprint of Writers & Readers Pub.

Bonanza Bks., 225 Park Ave. S., New York, N.Y. 10003 Tel 212-254-1600; 800-526-4264; refer orders to Random House
Imprint of Outlet

Bookwright Press (The), 387 Park Ave. S., New York, N.Y. 10016 Tel 212-686-7070; refer orders to Watts

Bowker: R. R. Bowker Co., 121 Chanlon Rd., New Providence, N.J. 07974 Tel 908-464-6800; 800-526-4902; refer orders to P.O. Box 31, New Providence, N.J. 07974

Bradbury Press Inc., 866 3rd Ave., New York, N.Y. 10022 Tel 212-702-9809; refer orders to Macmillan
Imprint of Macmillan Children's Bk. Group

Brodart Co., 500 Arch St., Williamsport, Pa. 17705 Tel 717-326-2461; 800-233-8467

Buccaneer Bks. Inc., P.O. Box 168, Cutchogue, N.Y. 11935 Tel 516-734-5650

Bullseye Bks., 201 E. 50th St., New York, N.Y. 10022 Tel 212-751-2600; 800-726-0600
Imprint of Knopf

Cambridge Univ. Press, Edinburgh Bldg., Shaftesbury Rd., Cambridge CB2 2RU, Eng. Tel Cambridge (0223) 312 393
Branch offices
U.S.: Cambridge Univ. Press, 40 W. 20th St., New York, N.Y. 10011-4211 Tel 212-924-3900; refer orders to 110 Midland Ave., Port Chester, N.Y. 10573 Tel 914-937-9600; 800-227-0247; 800-872-7423 (orders only)

Camden House (Charlotte): Camden House, Ferry Rd., Charlotte, Vt. 05445 Tel 802-425-3961; 800-334-3350

Carolrhoda Bks. Inc., 241 1st Ave. N., Minneapolis, Minn. 55401 Tel 612-332-3344; 800-328-4929

Checkerboard Press, c.o. Macmillan Pub. Co., 866 3rd Ave., New York, N.Y. 10022 Tel 212-702-2000; 800-257-5755

Chelsea House Pubs., 95 Madison Ave., New York, N.Y. 10016 Tel 212-683-4400

Children's Bk. Council Inc., 568 Broadway, New York, N.Y. 10012 Tel 212-966-1990

Children's Bk. Press, 1461 9th Ave., San Francisco, Calif. 94122 Tel 415-664-8500; refer orders to The Talman Co. Inc., 150 5th Ave., Room 514, New York, N.Y. 10011 Tel 212-620-3182; 800-537-8894

Childrens Press, 5440 N. Cumberland Ave., Chicago, Ill. 60656 Tel 312-693-0800; 800-621-1115

Chronicle Bks., 275 5th St., San Francisco, Calif. 94103 Tel 415-777-7240; 800-445-7577; 800-722-6657 (outside Calif.)

Clarion Bks., 215 Park Ave. S., New York, N.Y. 10003 Tel 212-420-5800; refer orders to Houghton Mifflin

Cobblehill Bks., 375 Hudson St., New York, N.Y. 10014 Tel 212-366-2000; refer orders to P.O. Box 120, Bergenfield, N.J. 07621-0120 Tel 201-387-0600; 800-526-0275

Collier Bks., c.o. Macmillan Pub. Co., 866 3rd Ave., New York, N.Y. 10022 Tel 212-702-2000; 800-257-5755; refer orders to 100 Front St., Box 500, Riverside, N.J. 08075-7500 Tel 609-461-6500

Columbia Univ. Press, 136 S. Broadway, Irvington, N.Y. 10533 Tel 914-591-9111

Compton's Learning Co., 310 S. Michigan Ave., 11th Floor, Chicago, Ill. 60604 Tel 312-347-7000
Formerly Compton

Consumers Union of U.S. Inc., 101 Truman Ave., Yonkers, N.Y. 10703 Tel 914-378-2000

Contemporary Bks. Inc., 180 N. Michigan Ave., Chicago, Ill. 60601 Tel 312-782-9181; 800-621-1918; refer orders to 3250 S. Western Ave., Chicago, Ill. 60608

Cornerstone Bks., 130 Cremona Dr., Santa Barbara, Calif. 93117; refer orders to P.O. Box 1911, Santa Barbara, Calif. 93116-1911 Tel 805-968-1911
Imprint of ABC-CLIO

Astor-Honor Inc. Pubs., 48 E. 43rd St., New York, N.Y. 10017

Coward-McCann Inc., 200 Madison Ave., New York, N.Y. 10016 Tel 212-951-8400; 800-631-8571; refer orders to 1 Grosset Dr., Kirkwood, N.Y. 13795 Tel 607-775-1740; 800-847-5515

Coward, McCann & Geoghegan See Coward-McCann

Creative Art Publs., 301 Riverland Rd., Fort Lauderdale, Fla. 33312 Tel 305-583-9207

Creative Arts Bk. Co., 833 Bancroft Way, Berkeley, Calif. 94710 Tel 415-848-4777

Creative Educ. Inc., 123 S. Broad St., Mankato, Minn. 56001 Tel 507-388-6273; refer orders to P.O. Box 227, Mankato, Minn. 56001
Formerly Creative Paperbacks

Crestwood House Inc., 866 3rd Ave., New York, N.Y. 10022 Tel 212-702-2000; 800-257-5755; refer orders to 100 Front St., Box 500, Riverside, N.J. 08075-7500 Tel 609-461-6500

Crowell: Thomas Y. Crowell Co., 10 E. 53rd St., New York, N.Y. 10022 Tel 212-207-7000; refer orders to HarperCollins Pubs., Keystone Ind. Park, Scranton, Pa. 18512 Tel 800-982-4377; 800-242-7737 (outside Pa.)
Formerly Lippincott & Crowell

Crown Pubs. Inc., 201 E. 50th St., New York, N.Y. 10022 Tel 212-572-2330; refer orders to Random House

Delacorte Press, 666 5th Ave., New York, N.Y. 10103 Tel 212-765-6500; 800-223-6834
Imprint of Dell

Dell Pub. Co. Inc., 666 5th Ave., New York, N.Y. 10103 Tel 212-765-6500; 800-223-6834

Dent: J. M. Dent & Sons Ltd., 91 Clapham High St., London SW4 9TA, Eng. Tel (071) 622 9933; refer orders to AA Distr. Services Ltd., Dunhams Lane, Letchworth, Hertfordshire SG6 1LF, Eng. Tel Letchworth (0462) 686 241
U.S. distributor: Biblio Distr. Centre, 4720 Boston Way, Lanham, Md. 20706

Deutsch: Andre Deutsch, 106 Great Russell St., London WC1B 3LJ, Eng. Tel (071) 580 2746; refer orders to Gollancz Services Ltd., 14 Eldon Way, Lineside Estate, Littlehampton, W. Sussex BN17 7HE, Eng. Tel Littlehampton (0903) 721 596
Childrens bks. distr. in the U.S. by Dutton

Dial Bks., 375 Hudson St., New York, N.Y. 10014 Tel 212-366-2000

Dial Bks. for Young Readers, 375 Hudson St., New York, N.Y. 10014 Tel 212-366-2000

Dillon Press Inc., 242 Portland Ave. S., Minneapolis, Minn. 55415 Tel 612-333-2691; 800-328-8322

Dodd, Mead & Co. Inc., 6 Ram Ridge Rd., Spring Valley, N.Y. 10977 Tel 914-352-3900; 800-237-3255
Out of business; childrens list acquired by Putnam & Grosset Group

Dog Ear Press (The), 132 Water St., Gardiner, Me. 04345 Tel 207-582-8227
Now Tilbury House

Doubleday, 666 5th Ave., New York, N.Y. 10103 Tel 212-765-6500; 800-223-6834

Dover Publs. Inc., 180 Varick St., New York, N.Y. 10014 Tel 212-255-3755; 800-223-3130; refer orders to 31 E. 2nd St., Mineola, N.Y. 11501 Tel 516-294-7000

Dutton: E. P. Dutton, 375 Hudson St., New York, N.Y. 10014 Tel 212-366-2000; refer orders to P.O. Box 120, Bergenfield, N.J. 07621-0120 Tel 201-387-0600; 800-526-0275

Dutton Children's Bks., 375 Hudson St., New York, N.Y. 10014 Tel 212-366-2000

Elsevier/Nelson Bks., 2 Park Ave., New York, N.Y. 10016
Now Lodestar Bks.

Elsevier-Dutton Pub. Co. Inc., 2 Park Ave., New York, N.Y. 10016 Tel 212-725-1818

Enslow Pubs., Bloy St. & Ramsey Ave., Hillside, N.J. 07205 Tel 908-964-4116; refer orders to P.O. Box 777, Hillside, N.J. 07205

Evans & Co.: M. Evans & Co. Inc., 216 E. 49th St., New York, N.Y. 10017 Tel 212-688-2810; refer orders to National Bk. Network, 4720 Boston Way, Lanham, Md. 20706 Tel 301-459-8696; 800-462-6420

Facts on File Inc., 460 Park Ave. S., New York, N.Y. 10016-7382 Tel 212-683-2244; 800-322-8755 (except N.Y., Hawaii, & Alaska)
Subsidiary of Commerce Clearing House

Farrar, Straus & Giroux Inc., 19 Union Sq. W., New York, N.Y. 10003 Tel 212-741-6900
Also uses imprint Noonday Press

Fawcett Bks., 201 E. 50th St., New York, N.Y. 10022 Tel 212-751-2600; refer orders to Ballantine Bks.

Fawcett Juniper, 201 E. 50th St., New York, N.Y. 10022 Tel 212-751-2600; refer orders to 400 Hahn Rd., Westminster, Md. 21157 Tel 800-638-6460
Imprint of Ballantine/Del Rey/Fawcett/Ivy Bks.

Faxon: F. W. Faxon Co. Inc., 15 Southwest Park, Westwood, Mass. 02090

Fell: Frederick Fell Pub. Inc., 2131 Hollywood Blvd., Suite 204, Hollywood, Fla. 33020 Tel 305-925-5242; 800-635-6366 (orders only)

Forest Press, 85 Watervliet Ave., Albany, N.Y. 12206 Tel 518-489-8549

Four Winds Press, 866 3rd Ave., New York, N.Y. 10003 Tel 212-505-3000; refer orders to Macmillan
Imprint of Macmillan Children's Bk. Group

Free Spirit Pub. Inc., 400 1st Ave. N., Suite 616, Minneapolis, Minn. 55401 Tel 612-338-2068; 800-735-7323

Freer Gallery of Art, Smithsonian Institution, 12th & Jefferson Dr. S.W., Washington, D.C. 20560

Funk & Wagnalls Inc., 53 E. 77th St., New York, N.Y. 10021 Tel 212-570-4500; refer orders to HarperCollins Pubs.

Gale Res. Co., 835 Penobscot Bldg., Detroit, Mich. 48226-4094 Tel 313-961-2242; 800-877-4253; refer orders to P.O. Box 33477, Detroit, Mich. 48232-5477

Gallaudet Univ. Press, 800 Florida Ave. N.E., Washington, D.C. 20002-3625 Tel 202-651-5488; 800-451-1073
Formerly Gallaudet College Press

Gambit Inc., 27 N. Main St., Meetinghouse Green, P.O. Box 306, Ipswich, Mass. 01938

Gareth Stevens Children's Bks., 1555 N. River Center Dr., River Center Bldg., Suite 201, Milwaukee, Wis. 53212 Tel 414-225-0333; 800-341-3569
Formerly Stevens, G.

Garland Pub. Inc., 136 Madison Ave., New York, N.Y. 10016 Tel 212-686-7492; 800-627-6273

Garrard Pub. Co., 1607 N. Market St., Champaign, Ill. 61820 Tel 217-352-7685

Gloucester Press, c.o. Franklin Watts Inc., 387 Park Ave. S., New York, N.Y. 10016 Tel 212-686-7070; 800-843-3749
Owned jointly by Watts; and, Aladdin Bks. (NY)

Godine: David R. Godine, Pub., Horticultural Hall, 300 Massachusetts Ave., Boston, Mass. 02115 Tel 617-536-0761; 800-445-6638

Golden Bks., 850 3rd Ave., New York, N.Y. 10022 Tel 212-753-8500
Imprint of Western

Golden Press Bks., 850 3rd Ave., New York, N.Y. 10022 Tel 212-753-8500
Goldencraft lib. bound bks. distr. by Childrens Press
Imprint of Western

Greenwillow Bks., 1350 Ave. of the Americas, New York, N.Y. 10019 Tel 212-261-6500; 800-843-9389; refer orders to 39 Plymouth St., Fairfield, N.J. 07007 Tel 201-227-7200
Imprint of Morrow

Greenwood Press, 88 Post Road W., Westport, Conn. 06881 Tel 203-226-3571; refer orders to P.O. Box 5007, Westport, Conn. 06881
Imprint of Greenwood Pub. Group

Grolier Inc., Sherman Turnpike, Danbury, Conn. 06816 Tel 203-797-3500

Grosset & Dunlap Inc., 200 Madison Ave., New York, N.Y. 10016 Tel 212-951-8400; 800-631-8571; refer orders to 1 Grosset Dr., Kirkwood, N.Y. 13795 Tel 607-775-1740; 800-847-5515

Guinness Bks., 33 London Rd., Enfield, Middlesex EN2 6DJ, Eng. Tel (081) 367 4567

Hammond Inc., 515 Valley St., Maplewood, N.J. 07040-1396 Tel 201-763-6000; 800-526-4953

Hancock House Pubs. Ltd., 19313 Zero Ave., Surrey, B.C., Can. V3S 5J9 Tel 604-538-1114

Harbinger House Inc., 2802 N. Alvernon Way, Tucson, Ariz. 85712 Tel 602-326-9595; 800-759-9945 (orders only)

Harcourt Brace Jovanovich Pubs., 1250 6th Ave., San Diego, Calif. 92101 Tel 619-231-6616; 800-543-1918

Harmony Bks., 201 E. 50th St., New York, N.Y. 10022 Tel 212-572-2330

Harmony Raine & Co., P.O. Box 133, Greenport, N.Y. 11944 Tel 516-734-5650

Harper & Row. See HarperCollins Pubs.

HarperCollins Pubs., 10 E. 53rd St., New York, N.Y. 10022-5299 Tel 212-207-7000; refer orders to Keystone Ind. Park, Scranton, Pa. 18512 Tel 800-982-4377; 800-242-7737 (outside Pa.)
Formed by merger of Harper & Row; and, William Collins & Sons

Hastings House Pubs., Inc., c.o. Kampmann & Co., 226 W. 26th St., New York, N.Y. 10001 Tel 212-727-0190

Heinemann, W.: William Heinemann, Ltd., Michelin House, 81 Fulham Rd., London SW3 6RB, Eng. Tel (071) 581 9393; refer orders to Reed Bk. Services Ltd., P.O. Box 5, Rushden, Northamptonshire NN10 9YX, Eng. Tel Rushden (0933) 58521
Branch offices
U.S.: William Heinemann, c.o. Trafalgar Sq., Howe Hill Rd., N. Pomfret, Vt. 05053 Tel 802-457-1911; 800-423-4525

Hill & Wang Inc., 19 Union Sq. W., New York, N.Y. 10003 Tel 212-741-6900

Holiday House Inc., 425 Madison Ave., New York, N.Y. 10017 Tel 212-688-0085

Holt & Co.: Henry Holt & Co., 115 W. 18th St., New York, N.Y. 10011 Tel 212-886-9200

Holt, Rinehart & Winston, 301 Commerce St., Suite 3700, Fort Worth, Tex. 76102 Tel 817-334-7500

Horn Bk. Inc., 14 Beacon St., Boston, Mass. 02108 Tel 617-227-1555; 800-325-1170

Houghton Mifflin Co., 2 Park St., Boston, Mass. 02108 Tel 617-725-5000; refer orders to Wayside Rd., Burlington, Mass. 01803 Tel 617-272-1500; 800-225-3362

Howell Bk. House Inc., c.o. Macmillan Pub. Co., 866 3rd Ave., New York, N.Y. 10022 Tel 212-702-2000; 800-257-5755
Imprint of Macmillan

Human Sciences Press Inc., 233 Spring St., New York, N.Y. 10013-1578 Tel 212-620-8000; 800-221-9369

Ivy Bks., 201 E. 50th St., New York, N.Y. 10022 Tel 212-572-2573

Jewish Publ. Soc., 1930 Chestnut St., Philadelphia, Pa. 19103-4599 Tel 215-564-5925; 800-234-3151 (orders)
Formerly Jewish Publ. Soc. of Am.

Kar-Ben Copies Inc., 6800 Tildenwood Lane, Rockville, Md. 20852 Tel 301-984-8733; 800-452-7236

Knopf: Alfred A. Knopf Inc., 225 Park Ave. S., New York, N.Y. 10003 Tel 212-254-1600; refer orders to Random House

Lerner Publs. Co., 241 1st Ave. N., Minneapolis, Minn. 55401 Tel 612-332-3344; 800-328-4929

Libraries Unlimited Inc., P.O. Box 3988, Englewood, Colo. 80155-3988 Tel 303-770-1200; 800-237-6124

Library of Congress, Washington, D.C. 20540 Tel 202-287-5093

Library of Congress. Natl. Lib. Service for the Blind & Physically Handicapped, Washington, D.C. 20542

Library Professional Publs., 925 Sherman Ave., Hamden, Conn. 06514 Tel 203-248-6307; refer orders to P.O. Box 4327, Hamden, Conn. 06514
Imprint of Shoe String Press

Linnet Bks., 925 Sherman Ave., Hamden, Conn. 06514 Tel 203-248-6307; refer orders to P.O. Box 4327, Hamden, Conn. 06514
Imprint of Shoe String Press

Lion Bks., 210 Nelson Rd., Suite B, Scarsdale, N.Y. 10583 Tel 914-725-2280

Lippincott. See HarperCollins Pubs.

Little, Brown & Co. Inc., 34 Beacon St., Boston, Mass. 02108 Tel 617-227-0730; refer orders to 200 West St., Waltham, Mass. 02254 Tel 617-890-0250; 800-343-9204

Liveright Pub. Corp., 500 5th Ave., New York, N.Y. 10110 Tel 212-354-5500

Lodestar Bks., 375 Hudson St., New York, N.Y. 10014 Tel 212-366-2000; refer orders to Penguin USA, P.O. Box 120, Bergenfield, N.Y. 07621-0120 Tel 201-387-0600; 800-526-0275

Lothrop, Lee & Shepard Bks., 1350 Ave. of the Americas, New York, N.Y. 10019 Tel 212-261-6500; 800-843-9389; refer orders to 39 Plymouth St., Fairfield, N.J. 07007 Tel 201-227-7200
Imprint of Morrow

Luce, R.B.: Robert B. Luce Inc., 540 Bornum Ave., Bridgeport, Conn. 06608

Macmillan Pub. Co., 866 3rd Ave., New York, N.Y. 10022 Tel 212-702-2000; 800-257-5755; refer orders to 100 Front St., Box 500, Riverside, N.J. 08075-7500 Tel 609-461-6500
Also uses imprints Howell Bk. House; and, Margaret K. McElderry Bks.

Macmillan Educ. Co., 866 3rd Ave., New York, N.Y. 10022 Tel 212-702-2000; 800-257-5755

Margaret K. McElderry Bks., c.o. Macmillan Pub. Co., 866 3rd Ave., New York, N.Y. 10022 Tel 212-702-2000; 800-257-5755; refer orders to 100 Front St., Box 500, Riverside, N.J. 08075-7500 Tel 609-461-6500
Imprint of Macmillan

McFarland & Co. Inc. Pubs., P.O. Box 611, Jefferson, N.C. 28640 Tel 919-246-4460

McGraw-Hill Int. Bk. Co., 1221 Ave. of the Americas, New York, N.Y. 10020 Tel 212-512-2000; refer orders to Princeton Rd., Hightstown, N.J. 08520-1450 Tel 800-338-3987

McKay, D.: David McKay Co. Inc., 201 E. 50th St., New York, N.Y. 10022 Tel 212-751-2600; 800-638-6460; refer orders to Random House Inc., 400 Hahn Rd., Westminster, Md. 21157 Tel 800-492-0782

Meredith Corp., 1716 Locust St., Des Moines, Iowa 50336 Tel 515-284-3000
Formerly Meredith Pub. Services

Merriam-Webster Inc., 47 Federal St., Springfield, Mass. 01102 Tel 413-734-3134; 800-828-1880; refer orders to P.O. Box 281, Springfield, Mass. 01102
Formerly G. & C. Merriam Co.

Messner: Julian Messner, Prentice-Hall Bldg., Route 9W, Englewood Cliffs, N.J. 07632 Tel 201-592-2950; refer orders to P.O. Box 1226, Westwood, N.J. 07675-1226 Tel 614-876-0371; 800-223-2336

Metropolitan Mus. of Art, 5th Ave. & 82nd St., New York, N.Y. 10028 Tel 212-879-5500

Modern Lib. (The), 201 E. 50th St., New York, N.Y. 10022 Tel 212-751-2600; 800-726-0600

Morrow: William Morrow & Co. Inc., 1350 Ave. of the Americas, New York, N.Y. 10019 Tel 212-261-6500; 800-843-9389; refer orders to 39 Plymouth St., Fairfield, N.J. 07007 Tel 201-227-7200

Morrow Junior Bks., 1350 Ave. of the Americas, New York, N.Y. 10019 Tel 212-261-6500; 800-843-9389; refer orders to 39 Plymouth St., Fairfield, N.J. 07007 Tel 201-227-7200

Mulberry Bks., 1350 Ave. of the Americas, New York, N.Y. 10019 Tel 212-261-6500; 800-843-9389; refer orders to 39 Plymouth St., Fairfield, N.J. 07007 Tel 201-227-7200
Imprint of Morrow

Nancy Renfro Studios, 1117 W. 9th St., Austin, Tex. 78703 Tel 512-472-2140

National Council of Teachers of English, 1111 Kenyon Rd., Urbana, Ill. 61801 Tel 217-328-3870

National Geographic Soc., 17th & M Sts. N.W., Washington, D.C. 20036 Tel 202-857-7000; 800-638-4077; refer orders to P.O. Box 1640, Washington, D.C. 20013-9861 Tel 301-921-1200

Neal-Schuman Pubs. Inc., 100 Varick St., New York, N.Y. 10013 Tel 212-925-8650

Nelson, T.: Thomas Nelson Pubs., Nelson Pl. at Elm Hill Pike, Nashville, Tenn. 37214-1000 Tel 615-889-9000; 800-251-4000; refer orders to P.O. Box 141000, Nashville, Tenn. 37214

New Am. Lib. Inc. (The), 375 Hudson St., New York, N.Y. 10014 Tel 212-366-2000; refer orders to Viking, P.O. Box 120, Bergenfield, N.J. 07621 Tel 201-387-0600; 800-526-0275
Also uses imprint NAL Bks.

New Directions Pub. Corp., 80 8th Ave., New York, N.Y. 10011 Tel 212-255-0230; refer orders to W. W. Norton & Co. Inc., 500 5th Ave., New York, N.Y. 10110 Tel 212-354-5500

New York Public Lib. Astor, Lenox & Tilden Foundations, 5th Ave. & 42nd St., New York, N.Y. 10018 Tel 212-930-0640; refer orders to NYPL Office of Branch Lib., 455 5th Ave., New York, N.Y. 10016 Tel 212-340-0897

Newmarket Press, 18 E. 48th St., New York, N.Y. 10017 Tel 212-832-3575; 800-669-3903; refer orders to MSI Assocs., 6 Ram Ridge Rd., Spring Valley, N.Y. 10977 Tel 914-352-3900

Newspaper Enterprise Assn. Inc., 200 Park Ave., New York, N.Y. 10166 Tel 212-557-9651

Nonesuch Press, 27 Wright's Lane, London W8 5TZ, Eng. Tel (071) 938 2200; refer orders to Penguin Group Distr., Bath Rd., Harmondsworth, W. Drayton, Middlesex UB7 0DA, Eng.

North-South Bks., c.o. Nord-Süd Verlag, CH-8617 Mönchaltorf, Switzerland
Imprint of Rada Matija AG

Ohio State Univ. Press, 1070 Carmack Rd., Room 180 Pressey Hall, Columbus, Ohio 43210-1002 Tel 614-292-6930

Orchard Bks., 387 Park Ave. S., New York, N.Y. 10016 Tel 212-686-7070; 800-843-3749

Oryx Press (The), 4041 N. Central at Indian School Rd., Phoenix, Ariz. 85012 Tel 602-265-6250
Some titles available in U.K. from Library Assn.

Overlook Press (The), 149 Wooster St., 4th Floor, New York, N.Y. 10012 Tel 212-477-7162

Oxford Univ. Press, Walton St., Oxford OX2 6DP, Eng. Tel (0865) 56767; refer orders to Oxford Univ. Press Distr. Services, Saxon Way West, Corby, Northamptonshire NM1 9ES, Eng. Tel Great Oakley (0536) 741 519
Branch offices
U.S.: Oxford Univ. Press, Inc., 200 Madison Ave., New York, N.Y. 10016 Tel 212-679-7300; 800-458-5833; refer orders to 2001 Evans Rd., Cary, N.C. 27513 Tel 800-451-7556

Pacer Bks., 200 Madison Ave., New York, N.Y. 10016 Tel 212-951-8800; 800-223-0510
Imprint of Berkley Pub. Group

Pantheon Bks. Inc., 201 E. 50th St., New York, N.Y. 10022 Tel 212-751-2600; 800-727-0600; refer orders to Random House Inc., 400 Hahn Rd., Westminster, Md. 21157 Tel 800-492-0782

Parents Mag. Press, 685 3rd Ave., New York, N.Y. 10017 Tel 212-878-8700

Parnassus Press, P.O. Box 8443, Emeryville, Calif. 94608
Wholly-owned unit of Houghton Mifflin

Penguin Bks. Ltd., 27 Wright's Lane, London W8 5TZ, Eng. Tel (071) 938 2200; refer orders to Bath Rd., Harmondsworth, Middlesex UB7 0DA, Eng. Tel (081) 759 1984
Branch offices
U.S.: Penguin Bks., 375 Hudson St., New York, N.Y. 10014 Tel 212-366-2000

Phillips: S. G. Phillips Inc., P.O. Box 83, Chatham, N.Y. 12037 Tel 518-392-3068

Philomel Bks., 200 Madison Ave., New York, N.Y. 10016 Tel 212-951-8400; 800-631-8571; refer orders to 1 Grosset Dr., Kirkwood, N.Y. 13795 Tel 607-775-1740; 800-847-5515

Picture Bk. Studio, 10 Central St., Saxonville, Mass. 01701 Tel 508-788-0911; 800-462-1252

Pippin Press, 229 E. 85th St., Gracie Station Box #92, New York, N.Y. 10028 Tel 212-288-4920

Platt & Munk Pubs., 200 Madison Ave., New York, N.Y. 10016 Tel 212-951-8400; 800-631-8571; refer orders to 1 Grosset Dr., Kirkwood, N.Y. 13795 Tel 607-775-1740; 800-847-5515

Plays Inc., 120 Boylston St., Boston, Mass. 02116 Tel 617-536-7420

Pocket Bks., Simon & Schuster Bldg., 1230 Ave. of the Americas, New York, N.Y. 10020 Tel 212-698-7000; 800-223-4022; refer orders to Prentice Hall Trade, Simon & Schuster Inc., 200 Old Tappan Rd., Old Tappan, N.J. 07675 Tel 201-767-5937; 800-223-2336 (orders only)

Potter: Clarkson N. Potter Inc. Pubs., 201 E. 50th St., New York, N.Y. 10022 Tel 212-572-2600
Imprint of Crown

Prentice-Hall Inc., Route 9W, Englewood Cliffs, N.J. 07632 Tel 201-592-2000; refer orders to Prentice Hall Trade, Simon & Schuster Inc., 200 Old Tappan Rd., Old Tappan, N.J. 07675 Tel 201-767-5937; 800-223-2336 (orders only)

Prentice-Hall Bks. for Young Readers, Simon & Schuster Bldg., 1230 Ave. of the Americas, New York, N.Y. 10020 Tel 212-698-7000

Prentice Hall Press, 15 Columbus Circle, New York, N.Y. 10023 Tel 212-373-8471; refer orders to Prentice Hall Trade, Simon & Schuster Inc., 200 Old Tappan Rd., Old Tappan, N.J. 07675 Tel 201-767-5937; 800-223-2336 (orders only)
Also uses imprint Prentice Hall/Parkside
Distributors

Puffin Bks. See Penguin Bks.

Putnam: G. P. Putnam's Sons, 200 Madison Ave., New York, N.Y. 10016 Tel 212-951-8400; 800-631-8571; refer orders to 1 Grosset Dr., Kirkwood, N.Y. 13795 Tel 607-775-1740; 800-847-5515

Putnam Pub. Group (The), 200 Madison Ave., New York, N.Y. 10016 Tel 212-951-8400; 800-631-8571; refer orders to 1 Grosset Dr., Kirkwood, N.Y. 13795 Tel 607-775-1740; 800-847-5515
Now Putnam & Grosset Group

R & S Bks., Tegnérgatan 28, Stockholm, Sweden Tel (08) 349960; refer orders to P.O. Box 45022, S-104 30 Stockholm, Sweden
Distributors
U.S.: Farrar, Straus & Giroux

Raintree Pubs. Inc., 310 W. Wisconsin Ave., Milwaukee, Wis. 53203 Tel 414-273-0873; 800-558-7264
Also uses imprints Raintree Childrens Bks.; and, Raintree Educ.

Rand McNally, 8255 Central Park Ave., Skokie, Ill. 60076-2970 Tel 312-673-9100; 800-323-4070; refer orders to P.O. Box 7600, Chicago, Ill. 60680-9915

Random House Inc., 201 E. 50th St., New York, N.Y. 10022 Tel 212-751-2600; 800-726-0600; refer orders to 400 Hahn Rd., Westminster, Md. 21157 Tel 800-733-3000

Riverside Pub. Co., 8420 W. Bryn Mawr Ave., Chicago, Ill. 60631 Tel 312-693-0040; 800-323-9540

Rourke Publs., P.O. Box 3328, Vero Beach, Fla. 32964 Tel 407-465-4575

Running Press Bk. Pubs., 125 S. 22nd St., Philadelphia, Pa. 19103 Tel 215-567-5080; 800-428-1111 (orders only)

Scarecrow Press Inc., 52 Liberty St., P.O. Box 4167, Metuchen, N.J. 08840 Tel 908-548-8600; 800-537-7107

Schocken Bks. Inc., 201 E. 50th St., New York, N.Y. 10022 Tel 212-751-2600; 800-726-0600

Scholastic Inc., 730 Broadway, New York, N.Y. 10003 Tel 212-505-3000

Scott, Foresman & Co., 1900 E. Lake Ave., Glenview, Ill. 60025 Tel 708-729-3000
Elhi & ESL titles distr. in Aust. & N.Z. by Ashton Scholastic; college texts by Jacaranda

Scribner: Charles Scribner's Sons, c.o. Macmillan Pub. Co., 866 3rd Ave., New York, N.Y. 10022 Tel 212-702-2000; 800-257-5755; refer orders to 100 Front St., Box 500, Riverside, N.J. 08075-7500 Tel 609-461-6500
Imprint of Macmillan

Scroll Press Inc., 2858 Valerie Ct., Merrick, N.Y. 11566

Seabury Press (The), HarperCollins Pubs., 10 E. 53rd St., New York, N.Y. 10022-5299 Tel 212-207-7000

Sierra Club Bks., 730 Polk St., San Francisco, Calif. 94109 Tel 415-776-2211; refer orders to Random House

Silver Burdett Press, 190 Sylvan Ave., Englewood Cliffs, N.J. 07632 Tel 201-592-2646; 800-624-4843; refer orders to P.O. Box 1226, Westwood, N.J. 07675-1226 Tel 800-223-2336

Silver Press, 190 Sylvan Ave., Englewood Cliffs, N.J. 07632 Tel 201-592-2646; 800-624-4843; refer orders to P.O. Box 1226, Westwood, N.J. 07675-1226 Tel 800-223-2336

Simon & Schuster Inc. Pubs., Simon & Schuster Bldg., 1230 Ave. of the Americas, New York, N.Y. 10020 Tel 212-698-7000

Simon & Schuster Bks. for Young Readers, 1230 Ave. of the Americas, New York, N.Y. 10020 Tel 212-698-7000; refer orders to 200 Old Tappan Rd., Old Tappan, N.J. 10023 Tel 800-223-2336 (orders only)

Smith, P.: Peter Smith Pub., Inc., 6 Lexington Ave., Magnolia, Mass. 01930 Tel 508-525-3562

St. James Press, 233 E. Ontario, Suite 600, Chicago, Ill. 60611 Tel 312-787-5800; 800-345-0392

St. Martin's Press Inc., 175 5th Ave., New York, N.Y. 10010 Tel 212-674-5151; 800-221-7945

Steck-Vaughn Co., 3520 Executive Center Dr., Travis Bldg., Suite 300, Austin, Tex. 78731 Tel 512-343-8227; refer orders to P.O. Box 26015, Austin, Tex. 78755 Tel 800-252-9317; 800-531-5015 (outside Tex.)

Stemmer House Pubs. Inc., 2627 Caves Rd., Owings Mills, Md. 21117 Tel 301-363-3690

Sterling Pub. Co. Inc., 387 Park Ave. S., New York, N.Y. 10016-8810 Tel 212-532-7160; 800-367-9692

Stevens, G.: Gareth Stevens Pubs., 1555 N. River Center Dr., River Center Bldg., Suite 201, Milwaukee, Wis. 53212 Tel 414-225-0333; 800-341-3569
Now Gareth Stevens Children's Bks.

Stewart, Tabori & Chang Inc., 575 Broadway, New York, N.Y. 10012 Tel 212-941-2800; refer orders to Workman Pub. Co. Inc., 708 Broadway, New York, N.Y. 10003 Tel 212-254-9000; 800-722-7202

Stravon Educ. Press, 845 3rd Ave., New York, N.Y. 10022 Tel 212-371-2880

Syracuse Univ. Press, 1600 Jamesville Ave., Syracuse, N.Y. 13244-5160 Tel 315-443-2597; 800-365-8929 (orders only)

Taylor Productions Ltd., 250 W. 24th St., New York, N.Y. 10011 Tel 212-425-3466; refer orders to Talman

Thames & Hudson Ltd., 30 Bloomsbury St., London WC1B 3QP, Eng. Tel (071) 636 5488; refer orders to 44 Clockhouse Rd., Farnborough, Hampshire GU14 7QZ, Eng. Tel Farnborough (0252) 541 602
Branch offices
U.S.: Thames & Hudson Inc., 500 5th Ave., New York, N.Y. 10110 Tel 212-354-3763; refer orders to Norton

Ticknor & Fields, 215 Park Ave. S., New York, N.Y. 10003 Tel 212-420-5800; 800-225-3362; refer orders to Houghton Mifflin

Time-Life Bks. Inc., 777 Duke St., Alexandria, Va. 22314 Tel 703-838-7000; refer trade orders to Little, Brown; school & lib. orders to Silver Burdett Co., 250 James St., CN1918, Morristown, N.J. 07960-1918 Tel 201-285-7700; 800-631-8081

TOR Bks., 49 W. 24th St., New York, N.Y. 10010 Tel 212-741-3100; refer orders to St. Martin's Press

Tundra Bks. Inc., 1434 St. Catherine St. W., Suite 308, Montreal, Que., Can. H3G 1R4 Tel 514-932-5434; refer orders to University of Toronto Press, 5201 Dufferin St., Downsview, Ont., Can. M3H 5T8 Tel 416-667-7791
Branch offices
U.S.: Tundra Bks. of Northern N.Y.

Tuttle: Charles E. Tuttle Co. Inc., 28 S. Main St., Rutland, Vt. 05701-0410 Tel 802-773-8930; refer orders to P.O. Box 410, Rutland, Vt. 05701-0410

Ultramarine Pub. Co. Inc., P.O. Box 303, Hastings-on-Hudson, N.Y. 10706 Tel 914-478-2522

United Nations, 2 United Nations Plaza, Sales Section, Pub. Div., Room DC2-853, New York, N.Y. 10017 Tel 212-963-8297

University of Calif. Press, 2120 Berkeley Way, Berkeley, Calif. 94720 Tel 415-642-4262; 800-822-6657

University of Chicago Press, 5801 S. Ellis Ave., Chicago, Ill. 60637 Tel 312-702-7700; refer orders to 11030 S. Langley Ave., Chicago, Ill. 60628 Tel 312-568-1550; 800-621-2736

University of Hawaii Press, 2840 Kolowalu St., Honolulu, Hawaii 96822 Tel 808-956-8830; 808-956-8697 (orders only)
Formerly University Press of Hawaii

Vanguard Press Inc., 424 Madison Ave., New York, N.Y. 10017 Tel 212-753-3906

Viking: Viking Penguin, 375 Hudson St., New York, N.Y. 10014 Tel 212-366-2000; refer orders to P.O. Box 120, Bergenfield, N.J. 07621-0120 Tel 201-387-0600; 800-526-0275
Now Viking Penguin
Also uses imprint Viking Kestrel

Viking Kestrel, 375 Hudson St., New York, N.Y. 10014 Tel 212-366-2000; refer orders to P.O. Box 120, Bergenfield, N.J. 07621-0120 Tel 201-387-0600
Imprint of Viking Penguin

Viking Penguin Inc., 375 Hudson St., New York, N.Y. 10014 Tel 212-366-2000; refer orders to P.O. Box 120, Bergenfield, N.J. 07621-0120 Tel 201-387-0600
Formerly Viking Press

Vintage Bks., 201 E. 50th St., New York, N.Y. 10022 Tel 212-751-2600; 800-726-0600; refer orders to Random House Inc., 400 Hahn Rd., Westminster, Md. 21157 Tel 800-492-0782

Walker & Co., 720 5th Ave., New York, N.Y. 10019 Tel 212-265-3632; 800-289-2553

Wanderer Bks., Simon & Schuster Bldg., 1230 Ave. of the Americas, New York, N.Y. 10020 Tel 212-245-6400; 800-223-2336

Warne: Frederick Warne & Co. Ltd., 27 Wright's Lane, London W8 5TZ, Eng. Tel (071) 938 2200; refer orders to Penguin Bks. Ltd., Bath Rd., Harmondsworth, Middlesex UB7 0DA, Eng. Tel (081) 759 1984
Branch offices
U.S.: Warne, 375 Hudson St., New York, N.Y. 10014 Tel 212-366-2000

Warwick Press, 387 Park Ave. S., New York, N.Y. 10016 Tel 212-686-7070; 800-672-6672
Imprint of Watts

Washington Sq. Press, Simon & Schuster Bldg., 1230 Ave. of the Americas, New York, N.Y. 10020 Tel 212-698-7000
Imprint of Pocket Bks.

Watts: Franklin Watts, Inc., 387 Park Ave. S., New York, N.Y. 10016 Tel 212-686-7070; 800-672-6672
Also uses imprint Warwick Press

Westminster Press (The), 100 Witherspoon St., Louisville, Ky. 40202-1396; refer orders to 925 Chestnut St., Philadelphia, Pa. 19107 Tel 215-928-2745; 800-462-0405; 800-523-1631 (orders only)
Also uses imprint Geneva Press
Merged with Knox Press to form Westminster/John Knox Press

Whitman, A.: Albert Whitman & Co., 5747 W. Howard St., Niles, Ill. 60648 Tel 312-647-1355

Wilshire Publs., 12021 Wilshire Blvd., Suite 208, Los Angeles, Calif. 90025 Tel 213-455-2706

Wilson, H.W.: The H. W. Wilson Co., 950 University Ave., Bronx, N.Y. 10452 Tel 212-588-8400; 800-367-6770

Windmill Bks. Inc., Simon & Schuster Bldg., 1230 Ave. of the Americas, New York, N.Y. 10020 Tel 212-245-6400
Imprint of Simon & Schuster

Winston Press, c.o. HarperCollins Pubs., 10 E. 53rd St., New York, N.Y. 10022-5299 Tel 212-207-7000; refer orders to Keystone Ind. Park, Scranton, Pa. 18512 Tel 800-982-4377; 800-242-7737 (outside Pa.)

Workman Pub. Co. Inc., 708 Broadway, New York, N.Y. 10003 Tel 212-254-5900; 800-722-7202

World Assn. of Girl Guides & Girl Scouts, 132 Ebury St., London SW1W 9QQ, Eng.

World Bk. Inc., Merchandise Mart Plaza, Room 510, Chicago, Ill. 60654 Tel 312-245-3456; 800-621-8202

Worldmark Press, 242 E. 50th St., New York, N.Y. 10022 Tel 212-355-3118